The Merriam-Webster Thesaurus

The Merriam-Webster Thesaurus

Merriam-Webster, Incorporated
Springfield, Massachusetts

A GENUINE MERRIAM-WEBSTER

The name *Webster* alone is no guarantee of excellence. It is used by a number of publishers and may serve mainly to mislead an unwary buyer.

Merriam-Webster™ is the name you should look for when you consider the purchase of dictionaries or other fine reference books. It carries the reputation of a company that has been publishing since 1831 and is your assurance of quality and authority.

Library of Congress Cataloging in Publication Data

The Merriam-Webster thesaurus.
p. cm.
ISBN-13: 978-0-87779-637-4 (pbk. : alk. paper)
ISBN-10: 0-87779-637-8 (pbk. : alk. paper)
1. English language—Synonyms and antonyms. I. Merriam-Webster, Inc.
PE1591.M477 2005
423′.12—dc22

2005001361

Made in the United States of America

89RRD0908

A powerful agent is the right word: it lights the reader's way and makes it plain; a close approximation to it will answer, and much traveling is done in a well-enough fashion by its help, but we do not welcome it and applaud it and rejoice in it as we do when the right one blazes out on us. Whenever we come upon one of those intensely right words in a book or a newspaper the resulting effect is physical as well as spiritual, and electrically prompt: it tingles exquisitely around through the walls of the mouth and tastes as tart and crisp and good as the autumn-butter that creams the sumac-berry.

—Mark Twain

PREFACE

This thesaurus is specially designed for those who want to enlarge their vocabularies and learn more about the rich variety of the English language. We hope and expect that users will readily turn to a dictionary whenever they need a better understanding of the meaning of any word used in the thesaurus.

In creating this thesaurus, the editors have drawn on years of experience with a thesaurus format that is at once easy to use, broad in its scope, and especially helpful to the user in the selection of the right word. We also believe that this thesaurus will prove to be highly useful as a vocabulary builder. We have parted ways with the more traditional approach of presenting long, undifferentiated lists of words that are tied to some topic or intellectual concept. Instead, we present a strictly alphabetical ordering of entries. These entries consist of lists of words that are centered on a specific—and specified—meaning. Main entries consist of lists of synonyms and related words, as well as antonyms and near antonyms whenever applicable. Phrases and idioms that function as synonyms are occasionally offered as well.

The purpose of the differentiated lists is to accommodate the various purposes for which a thesaurus is used. People use a thesaurus generally because they are dissatisfied with the word they already have in mind. They want a different word. The question is: how different?

If users of this thesaurus are trying to avoid a boring repetition of the same word, or are seeking to vary and enrich their vocabulary, then they will wish to select from the list of synonyms a word that shares the same basic meaning as the one they already have but differs from it in suggestion and tone. If they are seeking a word that is different from but still related to what they already have, then they will want to scan the lists of related words for a rewarding journey through the variety of possibilities that English offers.

If users are seeking a word that is to some degree opposite in meaning to what they have, then they will want to consult the lists of antonyms or near antonyms. By specifying the meaning under consideration, and by making distinctions between words that are truly synonymous and those that are only somewhat synonymous, we hope that we have given users the guidance they desire. We believe that this system minimizes the need to guess and to grope.

What makes this thesaurus unique is the content of the separate entries for each and every word appearing in the lists of synonyms. Since a user's search for the right word may start anywhere, the thesaurus is arranged so that any member of a synonym group can serve as the starting point. An entry for a listed synonym consists of a restatement of the meaning common to all the members of the group. A user who happens to use a particular synonym as a starting point should follow the cross-reference to the main entry for the complete listing of synonyms, related words, and any antonyms or near antonyms.

The thesaurus format is intended to encourage and facilitate users in finding the right word, which results in writing of greater precision and clarity. The word *thesaurus* literally means "treasury" in Latin, and we hope that the treasure trove of words contained in these pages will enhance the user's interest in and appreciation of the English language. We urge all users to read carefully the following sections entitled Introduction and Using Your Thesaurus in order to make the most of what the book has to offer. The Introduction contains an informative discussion of what distinguishes a synonym from a related word, an antonym from a near antonym. The section Using Your Thesaurus explains in detail the organization of the thesaurus and discusses the differences between the two basic types of entries. Study of this section is especially important.

The editor has been ably assisted in its composition by the editors Rose Martino Bigelow, Daniel B. Brandon, Adam Groff, Kory L. Stamper, and Deanna Stathis. The entire project was supervised by Madeline L. Novak, and Robert D. Copeland served as editor in charge of production. Stephen J. Perrault devised ways to facilitate the creation of the manuscript electronically. The difficult task of cross-referencing the text was accomplished by Christopher Chapin Connor and Allison S. Crawford. Credit for proofreading the text goes to Ilya A. Davidovich, Donna L. Rickerby, Maria Sansalone, Adrienne M. Scholz, Peter A. Sokolowski, Emily A. Vezina, and Judy Yeh. Michael D. Roundy acted as a consultant on miscellaneous scientific questions. Finally, John M. Morse, Merriam-Webster's President and Publisher, must be acknowledged and thanked for his unfailing support for this thesaurus.

Michael G. Belanger,
Editor

INTRODUCTION

Synonyms

The English language contains a wealth of words, and perhaps no other language has as many synonyms as English. Synonyms give color, precision, and variety to a person's writing, breaking up the dullness that can come from too many overused words.

So, just what are synonyms? Put simply, synonyms are words that mean the same thing. Words that are only somewhat similar in meaning—but do not mean the same thing—are not true synonyms. They are merely related words, and they belong in a different category. In this thesaurus a word is classified as a synonym if and only if it shares with another word at least one basic meaning.

Here's an example of how we arrived at a basic meaning shared by one group of words. The word *freight* can be defined as "goods or cargo carried by ship, train, truck, or airplane." We can break up the definition like this:

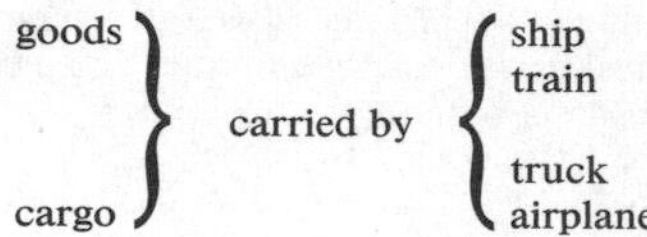

Since a person using *freight* as the starting point in his or her search for the right word is probably dissatisfied with that term, the word that he or she is seeking will most likely come under a broader or more basic meaning. We can phrase that more basic meaning as: "a mass or quantity of something taken up and carried, conveyed, or transported." The list of synonyms for *freight—burden, cargo, draft, haul, lading, load, loading, payload, weight*—can all be said to share this basic meaning.

If a word is more limited in scope than the basic meaning given at a main entry, then it cannot be regarded as a synonym. Hence, *truckload*, which refers specifically to the load carried by a truck, cannot be a synonym of *freight* and the other members of *freight's* synonym group. Likewise, the words *mass* and *quantity* cannot themselves be regarded as synonyms because the notion of being carried, conveyed, or transported is not an essential part of their meaning.

Related Words

Oftentimes thesaurus users are not looking for something that means exactly the same as the word they already have. To help in this situation, this thesaurus includes lists of related words, which are words whose meanings are close enough to the synonymy group to be of interest to the user. These related words do not qualify as synonyms because they have meanings that differ from the basic meaning shared by the synonymy group in some significant way.

For example, the word *funny* has the meaning of "causing or intended to cause laughter." A person who is making "funny faces" is causing, or at least trying to cause, others to laugh. *Witty*, which is certainly closely related to *funny*, has a slightly different meaning: "given to or marked by mature intelligent humor." A witty person is someone who has a habit of making clever remarks that display a grown-up sense of humor. Thus, *funny* and *witty* are related, but the words are not synonymous. Because of the close relationship between two words like *funny* and *witty*, all of the words listed as synonyms at *witty* are given as related words at *funny*.

The lists of related words at a main entry in the thesaurus may be likened to the hyperlinks that connect one Web site to another on the Internet. Following the links between Web sites often takes one to new and unexpected places. Thesaurus users are encouraged to go from one related entry to another in their search for just the right word.

Some words are not true synonyms of anything, but because they are so fundamentally useful, they have been included in this thesaurus among the lists of related words and in places where they are likely to be most helpful. For example, the word *ballast*, which refers to any type of "heavy material used to make a ship steady," is too narrow in meaning to have any synonyms of its own. It is related to the more general term *load*, however, and so, fittingly, it is included as a related word at the entry for *load*.

Antonyms

An antonym is a word whose meaning is directly opposite to another word's meaning. In this thesaurus, an antonym is a word that has a meaning that completely cancels out another word's meaning. *Short* and *tall* are complete opposites. Something cannot be both short and tall at the same time, and both words suggest about the same degree of difference from the norm or average in height. *Good* and *evil* are another pair of exact opposites. Logically, something cannot be both *good* and *evil* in the same way and at the same time.

Words that are only opposite in some aspect of their meaning cannot be said to be true antonyms. For example, *sad*, which means "causing unhappiness," is not a true antonym of *funny*, which means "causing or intended to cause laughter." The opposite of unhappiness is happiness, and so the opposite of sad is happy. There are things, like a frowning clown, that can be both funny and sad, so these words can't be antonyms. Pairs of words like *sad* and *funny* are better regarded as near antonyms.

Near Antonyms

Near antonyms are words that do not qualify as antonyms under the strict definition used for this thesaurus but that clearly have meanings in marked contrast with the members of a synonym group. For example, *afraid* is not so exactly opposite to *courageous* as *cowardly* is, but *afraid* and *courageous* certainly have markedly contrasting meanings and so are considered near antonyms. And just as a user may not be seeking a word that is exactly synonymous with another, he or she may likewise not be seeking a word that is exactly opposite. The user may simply want a word that lies somewhere on the opposite side of the range of meaning.

Phrases

This thesaurus also includes phrases that, taken as a whole, are synonymous with individual words. Within this category are some words that are commonly used in combination with one another but are not necessarily included as entry words in most dictionaries. Some of these fixed phrases represent virtually the only way in which the word is used in contemporary English. For example, *in jeopardy* appears as a synonymous phrase at *liable* because a person exposed to something dangerous or undesirable is a person in jeopardy. The word *jeopardy* is generally only used in the phrase *in jeopardy*.

Idioms constitute the other major class of word combinations that are entered under the heading of Phrases. Idioms are phrases that have a special meaning that is different from the literal meaning that a person would get if adding together the individual meanings of the components of the phrase. For example, the phrase *make good* is virtually meaningless if one attempts to piece together the literal meanings of *make* and *good*. As a fixed phrase, however, *make good* means "to reach a desired level of accomplishment" and is a synonym of *succeed*.

What this thesaurus does not enter are phrases that are simple restatements of the basic meaning shared by the members of the synonym group. The verb *remark*, for example, might be defined as "to express as an opinion." Such rewordings of a basic definition have no place in a thesaurus because they contribute nothing useful to the user's vocabulary.

Choosing the Right Word—Using Your Dictionary

Even after you have mastered all of these categories, deciding which word in a thesaurus entry is best for your purposes is not always easy. The basic meaning shared by the members of a synonym group cannot tell you everything you need to know in order to choose the word that best suits your needs.

Something that is "very pleasing to look at" can be described as *attractive, beauteous, beautiful, bonny, comely, cute, fair, gorgeous, handsome, knockout, lovely, pretty, ravishing, sightly, stunning,* or *taking*, but which word is best for describing a sunset? A city? Should you use *knockout* to describe a cathedral or *ravishing* for a sports car?

If after reviewing the synonyms, you decide that you still have not found the right word, then you have the list of related words to consider:

> ***related words*** alluring, appealing, charming, delightful, eye-catching, glamorous (*also* glamourous), prepossessing; elegant, exquisite, glorious, resplendent, splendid, statuesque, sublime, superb; flawless, perfect, radiant; dainty, delicate; personable, presentable

Now you have 38 words that mean the same thing or nearly the same thing as *beautiful*. Here's where you need a good dictionary. You can consult the dictionary to get a precise definition of any word in the lists, and perhaps an example of its use. You should always use this thesaurus along with a good dictionary.

EXPLANATORY NOTES

Every user of this thesaurus should read this section of the book carefully in order to use it effectively.

A thesaurus consists mostly of lists of words, and it is often difficult to know which word is best for a particular purpose. Because the English language has so many different ways of combining words with different shades of meaning, you should always use this thesaurus along with a reliable dictionary.

ENTRY ORDER

The first word of a thesaurus entry is called a **headword**. Headwords are printed in boldface type and are in alphabetical order. Alphabetization is by first letter, then second letter, and so on, regardless of any spaces or hyphens that may appear in them:

make *vb*
make–believe *adj*
make out *vb*

make over *vb*
Maker *n*
makeshift *adj*

When a headword contains a numeral, the numeral is alphabetized as though it were a spelled-out word:

anywise *adv*
A1 *adj*
apace *adv*

Homographs are words that are spelled the same, but each is a different part of speech or has a different etymology (word origin). Homographs that are different parts of speech are separate headwords:

hail *n* **1** a heavy fall of objects
hail *vb* **1** to declare enthusiastic approval of

Homographs that have a different etymology, even when they are the same part of speech, are entered as separate headwords. Those that are the same part of speech are grouped together and numbered in sequence:

¹list *n* a record of a series of items (as names or titles) usually arranged according to some system
²list *n* the act of positioning or an instance of being positioned at an angle
³list *n* a long narrow piece of material
¹list *vb* **1** to make a list of
²list *vb* to set or cause to be at an angle

Verbs that are used in combination with a preposition or an adverb are entered with the verb in boldface type followed by the preposition or adverb in parentheses in lightface type. Such combinations immediately follow the base verb in alphabetical order:

go *vb*
go (for) *vb*
go (on) *vb*
go (to) *vb*

When main entries are compound words, a closed form is entered before a hyphenated form and a hyphenated form is entered before a form that contains spaces:

nosedive *n*
nose–dive *vb*

open–air *adj*
open air *n*

PLURAL NOUNS

Some nouns are always pluralized when they are used a certain way. When there are no thesaurus entries which include the singular form of a such a noun, the plural form is given as the headword:

leavings *n pl* a remaining group or portion — see REMAINDER 1

When a noun is usually, but not always, used in plural form in a certain sense, the singular form is the headword, and the plural follows the label *usually*:

habiliment *n usually* **habiliments** *pl* covering for the human body — see CLOTHING

Such nouns are followed by *s* in parentheses in the synonym list:

clothing *n* covering for the human body

synonyms apparel, attire, clothes, dress, duds, habiliment(s), rags, raiment, togs, wear

When a noun is used in the singular form in one sense and in the plural form in another, the singular form is given as the headword. The plural form is indicated at the individual sense or senses:

provision *n* **1** something upon which the carrying out of an agreement or offer depends — see CONDITION 2 **2 provisions** *pl* substances intended to be eaten — see FOOD

VARIANTS

An alternate spelling or form of a headword is called a **variant**. Variants are shown in boldface after the headword and are preceded by *or* or *also*. The label *or* means that the variant is as common or nearly as common as the headword. The headword is usually the form that comes first alphabetically:

egotistic *or* **egotistical** *adj*
lighted *or* **lit** *adj*
OK *or* **okay** *vb*

However, if one of the spellings or forms is used slightly more frequently, the more common one is entered first even though it may not fall first alphabetically:

gizmo *or* **gismo** *n*

A variant that is preceded by the label *also* is not as common as the headword:

among *also* **amongst** *prep*
facade *also* **façade** *n*
naught *also* **nought** *n*

When two variants are separated from the headword by *also* but from each other by *or*, it means that they are both less common than the headword:

bogey *also* **bogy** *or* **bogie** *n*

Variants are also given in the word lists:

zero *n* the numerical symbol 0 or the absence of number or quantity represented by it ⟨anything multiplied by *zero* comes out to zero⟩
synonyms aught, cipher, goose egg, naught (*or* nought), nil, nothing, oh, zilch, zip

PARTS OF SPEECH

Every headword is followed by a part-of-speech label. The abbreviations for the parts of speech are *adj* (adjective), *adv* (adverb), *conj* (conjunction), *interj* (interjection), *n* (noun), *prep* (preposition), *pron* (pronoun), and *vb* (verb).

KINDS OF ENTRIES

There are two kinds of entries: main entries and secondary entries. Every headword with its part-of-speech label is followed by either one or more main entries, one or more secondary entries, or a combination of the two. If there is more than one entry, each one begins on a new line introduced by a boldface sense number. Main entries come first. A **main entry** consists of the meaning shared by the members of the synonym group, a verbal illustration, and lists of synonyms as well as any related words, phrases, near antonyms, and antonyms:

eagerness *n* urgent desire or interest
synonyms appetite, ardor, avidity, desirousness, enthusiasm, excitement, hunger, impatience, keenness, thirst
related words alacrity, quickness; ambition, gusto, zest
near antonyms unconcern; aloofness, detachment; impassivity, languor
antonyms apathy, indifference

A **secondary entry** has the same shared meaning that is shown at the main entry. The secondary entry does not contain lists of synonyms, antonyms, related words, phrases, or near antonyms. Instead, at the end of the entry, there is a direction to "see" the appropriate main entry at another headword. Secondary entries follow any main entries at a headword:

gain *vb* **1** to increase in
synonyms build (up), gather, grow (in), pick up
. . .
2 to receive as return for effort — see EARN 1
3 to become healthy and strong again after illness or weakness — see CONVALESCE

fade *vb* **1** to cease to be visible — see DISAPPEAR
2 to make white or whiter by removing color — see WHITEN

CROSS-REFERENCES

The direction at the end of every secondary entry to see another entry is called a **cross-reference**. The cross-reference tells you where the main entry for a word's synonym group is located. No matter which member of a synonym group you used to begin your search, you can always find your way to the entry that has the lists of all the synonyms and any related words, phrases, near antonyms, or antonyms. If there is more than one sense at the headword referred to in the cross-reference, the cross-reference will also include a sense number. If the headword has more than one numbered homograph, the cross-reference will send you to the right homograph number as well:

pain *vb* to feel or cause physical pain — see HURT 1

ranking *n* 1 a scheme of rank or order — see [3]SCALE 1

If a headword appears as more than one part of speech, the cross-reference is sending you to the same part of speech as the word you looked up. The cross-reference in the **ranking** example above tells you that the main entry where you will find *ranking* as a member of the synonym group with the shared meaning "a scheme of rank or order" is at sense 1 of the noun entry [3]**scale**:

[3]**scale** *n* 1 a scheme of rank or order ⟨how would you rate your experience on a *scale* of one to ten?⟩
synonyms graduation, ladder, ordering, ranking

SPECIAL USAGE LABELS

You will find special usage labels in italics after a headword whenever they apply. The labels are *chiefly British, British, chiefly Scottish, Scottish, Australian, chiefly dialect, chiefly Southern & Midland*, and *slang.*

These labels are placed directly after the part-of-speech label when the word has only one sense or when the label applies to all the senses:

afore *prep, chiefly dialect* 1
bairn *n, chiefly Scottish*
bobby *n, British*
dis *vb, slang* 1

The label comes after the sense number when the word has more than one sense and the label applies only to that sense:

jack *n* 1 *slang* something (as pieces of stamped metal or printed paper) customarily and legally used as a medium of exchange, a measure of value, or a means of payment — see MONEY

Special usage labels also appear in the word lists:

before *prep* 1 earlier than ⟨since I'm a faster runner, I got there *before* him⟩
synonyms afore [*chiefly dialect*], ahead of, ere, of, previous to, prior to, to

SHARED MEANING

The shared meaning follows the sense number when there is more than one sense and the part-of-speech label when there is only one sense. It is a meaning shared equally by the headword and the other members of the synonym group. This shared meaning is the "thing" that is referred to when we say that two or more words "mean the same thing" and thus are synonyms.

Sometimes there are words in parentheses within a shared meaning:

district *n* an area (as of a city) set apart for some purpose or having some special feature ⟨Independence Hall in Philadelphia's historic *district*⟩
synonyms neighborhood, quarter, section
related words belt, zone; department, . . .

In the shared meaning at **district**, the words in parentheses indicate that *district, neighborhood, quarter*, and *section* are synonyms when they refer to an area of a city or something like that, and that the words in the related words list also refer specifically to this type of area.

For information regarding the use and purpose of parentheses around certain words in entries for verbs, read below.

SOME NOTES ABOUT VERBS

A boldface verb headword followed by a lightface word in parentheses tells you to use the parenthetical word with the verb:

comply (with) *vb* 1 to act according to the commands of
hold off (on) *vb* to assign to a later time
knock (about) *vb* to move about from place to place aimlessly

If there are two words inside the parentheses and they are separated by *or*, then either word can be used with the verb:

fit (in *or* into) *vb* to put among or between others

These verbs appear in the synonym lists followed by their customary adverb or preposition in parentheses. These entries are treated this way in the thesaurus because such verb combinations are not the usual form of dictionary entries, but it is only when the verb is used with the adverb or preposition that it matches the shared meaning of its synonym group.

When the meaning of a verb requires a direct object, all of the words in the synonym list take a direct object. If a verb does not take an object, none of the synonyms will take an object.

VERBAL ILLUSTRATIONS

Every main entry in this thesaurus shows an example of typical use. The **verbal illustration**, as it is called, follows the shared meaning, is enclosed in angle brackets, and italicizes the synonym:

fight *vb* **1** to oppose (someone) in physical conflict ⟨a proud people who have fiercely *fought* all invaders of their homeland⟩
rich *adj* **1** having goods, property, or money in abundance ⟨Tanya's dad works as a chauffeur for the *richest* man in town, a big oil baron⟩

Words in parentheses after a boldface headword are italicized in the verbal illustration:

stick *vb* **1** to hold to something firmly as if by adhesion ⟨these magnets are strong enough to *stick* well to the refrigerator⟩

Some verbal illustrations in the thesaurus are complete sentences and others are only sentence fragments. Though it may look a little odd, for the sake of consistency, all verbal illustrations in this thesaurus begin with a lowercase letter unless the initial word is normally capitalized. Question marks and exclamation points are used when appropriate at the end of a verbal illustration, but otherwise no ending punctuation is used.

A WORD ABOUT SYNONYMS

If a word is used as the defining term in a shared meaning, it will not be listed as one of the synonyms. Since words can only be defined in terms of other words, the result of this restriction is that some terms that might be rightly regarded as synonyms do not appear in the synonym lists. Here is an example:

go *vb* . . . **2** to leave a place often for another
synonyms begone, clear out, depart, exit, get, get off, move, pull (out), quit, sally (forth), shove (off), take off, walk out

Leave, used as the defining term, could be considered another synonym, but it is not entered as such in this thesaurus because it has been used as a defining term.

RELATED WORDS

You will see that in most cases there are more related words than synonyms. That is because there is much more flexibility in choosing words for these lists. They do not have to match the shared meaning: they only need to relate to some aspect of it. Related words are often divided into subgroups separated by a semicolon. Words within each subgroup are generally closer in meaning to each other than to the members of the following subgroups. The subgroups tend to be presented in order of most relevant to least relevant.

object *n* **1** something material that can be perceived by the senses
synonyms thing
related words article, item, piece; being, entity, substance; commodity, good, ware; accessory, accompaniment; bauble, curio, knickknack, spangle, token, trinket

PHRASES

Listed in alphabetical order after the heading **phrases** at some of the main entries are expressions that are synonymous with the headword and the other members of the synonym group. Although they have essentially the same meaning as the synonyms, these phrases tend to be used only in certain ways, and you should be careful about substituting one of them for a word in the synonym list. Since phrases are not entered as headwords in the thesaurus, they do not come with verbal illustrations. It's a good idea to look them up in a dictionary before considering them.

NEAR ANTONYMS

Just as related words are not exact synonyms, near antonyms are not exact antonyms. Not every synonym group has near antonyms. As is the case with related words, when there are near antonyms, they are often divided into subgroups separated by a semicolon, with the members of each subgroup listed alphabetically.

have *vb* **1** to keep, control, or experience as one's own
synonyms command, enjoy, hold, occupy, own, possess, retain
related words keep, reserve, withhold; bear, carry; boast, show off, sport
near antonyms abandon, cede, disclaim, disown, hand over, relinquish, renounce, surrender, yield; discard, dump; decline, reject, repudiate, spurn; need, require
antonyms lack, want

ANTONYMS

The words in the antonym lists are the exact opposites of the headword and the words in the synonym lists. Not every synonym group has antonyms, and antonym lists tend to be shorter than near antonym lists. Antonyms are listed alphabetically, just as synonyms are. They appear as boldface headwords at their own alphabetical places in the thesaurus only if they are part of a synonym group elsewhere.

Ordinarily, all the words in an antonym list are synonyms of each other. Sometimes, however, a semicolon in an antonym list divides words which, while they are exact opposites of the words in the synonym group, are not synonyms of each other. Here is an example:

present *adj* **1** existing or in progress right now
synonyms current, extant, ongoing, present-day
antonyms ago, past; future

The opposite of "existing or in progress right now" is "*not* existing or in progress right now." All three of the words in the antonyms list fit that meaning. *Ago* and *past*, separated by a comma, are synonyms of each other; they both can mean "earlier than the present time." But *ago* and *past* are not synonyms of *future*, which means, of course, "occurring at a later time."

A NOTE ABOUT THE LISTS: WORD DUPLICATION

No word appears in more than one list at any single main entry. Some words have slight variations in meaning. If they are used one way, they are synonymous with a headword; if they are used another way, they are merely closely related. To avoid confusion, such words have been entered in a main entry's synonym list only. For example, *nice* is in the synonym list at *pleasant* where the shared meaning is "giving pleasure or contentment to the mind or senses." *Nice* is also in the synonym list at *amiable*, where the shared meaning is "having an easygoing and pleasing manner especially in social situations." If you go back to *pleasant*, you will find *amiable* among the related words. So it would stand to reason that *nice*, having the same meaning as *amiable*, would also be entered in the related word list at *pleasant*. Since it's already in the synonym list, however, it was left out of the related words.

Some words can have two meanings that are opposite of each other—or nearly so. *Nervy* can mean both "fearless" and "fearful, timid." Thus, at the thesaurus entry for *bold*, where the shared meaning is "inclined or willing to take risks," *nervy* might qualify as both a synonym and an antonym (or near antonym). And, indeed, *nervy* appears as a synonym, along with *adventuresome, adventurous, audacious, daring, dashing, emboldened, enterprising, gutsy, hardy, nerved, venturesome*, and *venturous*. Although the near antonym list contains *fearful* and *timid* as expected, *nervy* is left off the list. Again, this is to avoid confusion.

GUIDE WORDS

The two boldface words separated by a dot at the top of each page are **guide words**, and they show the alphabetical range of entries on the page. You can use them to find a word more quickly. The first guide word is the headword of the first entry beginning on that page, and the second guide is the headword of the last entry on the page.

The Merriam-Webster Thesaurus

aback *adv* without warning — see UNAWARES

abaft *adv* near, toward, or in the stern of a ship or the tail of an aircraft — see AFT

abaft *prep* at, to, or toward the rear of — see BEHIND 1

abandon *n* carefree freedom from constraint ⟨added spices to the stew with complete *abandon*⟩
synonyms abandonment, ease, lightheartedness, naturalness, spontaneity, unrestraint
related words ardor, enthusiasm, exuberance, fervor, spirit, warmth, zeal; carelessness, heedlessness, impulsiveness, indiscretion, insouciance, recklessness, thoughtlessness; excess, excessiveness, immoderacy, incontinence, indulgence, intemperance, licentiousness, permissiveness, wantonness, wildness
near antonyms embarrassment, reserve, reticence, self-consciousness, uneasiness; inhibition, repression, self-restraint, suppression; carefulness, discreetness, discretion, heedfulness; discipline, self-control, self-discipline, willpower
antonyms constraint, restraint

abandon *vb* to cause to remain behind — see LEAVE 1

abandoned *adj* left unoccupied or unused ⟨Marlene avoided walking past the *abandoned* house, with its broken windows and sagging porch⟩
synonyms derelict, deserted, disused, forgotten, forsaken, rejected, vacated
related words ignored, neglected, unattended, untended; castaway, cast-off, discarded, jettisoned, junked; desolate, godforsaken, miserable, shabby, wretched; empty, idle, vacant
near antonyms reclaimed, recovered, redeemed, rescued, retrieved, salvaged, saved; reconditioned, rehabilitated, restored; repeopled

abandonment *n* **1** carefree freedom from constraint — see ABANDON
2 the act of abandoning — see DERELICTION 1

abase *vb* **1** to lower in character or dignity — see DEBASE 1
2 to reduce to a lower standing in one's own eyes or in others' eyes — see HUMBLE

abash *vb* to throw into a state of self-conscious distress — see EMBARRASS 1

abashment *n* the emotional state of being made self-consciously uncomfortable — see EMBARRASSMENT 1

abate *vb* **1** to grow less in scope or intensity especially gradually — see DECREASE 2
2 to make smaller in amount, volume, or extent — see DECREASE 1

abatement *n* **1** something that is or may be subtracted — see DEDUCTION 1
2 the amount by which something is lessened — see DECREASE

abbey *n* a residence for men under religious vows — see MONASTERY

abbreviate *vb* to make less in extent or duration — see SHORTEN

abbreviation *n* a shortened version of a written work — see ABRIDGMENT

abdicate *vb* to give up (as a position of authority) formally ⟨the revolutionary government forced Nicholas II to *abdicate* the Russian throne⟩
synonyms abnegate, cede, relinquish, renounce, resign, step down (from), surrender
related words abjure, deny, disavow, disclaim, disown, waive; forsake, give up, hand over, yield; abandon, desert, quit, vacate
near antonyms appropriate, arrogate, assume, claim, confiscate; seize, take over, usurp, wrest; defend, guard, protect, safeguard, secure

abdomen *n* the part of the body between the chest and the pelvis — see STOMACH

abduct *vb* to carry a person away by unlawful force or against his or her will — see KIDNAP

aberrant *adj* **1** being out of the ordinary — see EXCEPTIONAL
2 departing from some accepted standard of what is normal — see DEVIANT

aberration *n* a serious mental disorder that prevents one from living a safe and normal life — see INSANITY 1

abet *vb* **1** to cause or encourage the development of — see INCITE 1
2 to provide (someone) with what is useful or necessary to achieve an end — see HELP 1

abettor *also* **abetter** *n* **1** one associated with another in wrongdoing — see ACCOMPLICE
2 someone associated with another to give assistance or moral support — see ALLY

abeyance *n* a state of temporary inactivity ⟨our weekend plans were held in *abeyance* until we could get a weather forecast⟩
synonyms doldrums, dormancy, latency, quiescence, suspense, suspension
related words inaction, inertia, inertness, motionlessness; impasse, standstill; coma, hibernation, hypnosis, repose, rest, sleep, slumber, torpor; recession, remission; idleness
near antonyms recommencement, renewal, resumption, resuscitation
antonyms continuance, continuation

abhor *vb* to dislike strongly — see HATE

abhorrence *n* something or someone that is hated — see HATE 2
2 a very strong dislike — see HATE 1

abhorrent *adj* causing intense displeasure, disgust, or resentment — see OFFENSIVE 1

abide *vb* **1** to continue to be in a place for a significant amount of time — see STAY 1
2 to have a home — see LIVE 1
3 to put up with (something painful or difficult) — see BEAR 2
4 to remain indefinitely in existence or in the same state — see CONTINUE 1

ability *n* the physical or mental power to do something ⟨as a result of the accident he lost the *ability* to walk⟩
synonyms capability, capacity, competence, competency, faculty
related words aptitude, aptness, endowment, facility, gift, knack, talent; adroitness, deftness, dexterity, prowess, skill; gray matter, instinct, intelligence, reason, understanding; potency, staying power, stuff; adequacy, effectiveness, effectualness, fitness, form, influence, resourcefulness, usefulness; means, resources, wherewithal
near antonyms helplessness, impotence, paralysis, powerlessness, weakness; defectiveness, deficien-

cy, inadequacy, ineffectiveness, ineffectualness, uselessness; debilitation, disablement, impairment, incapacitation
antonyms disability, inability, incapability, incapacity, incompetence, incompetency, ineptitude, ineptness

abjure *vb* to solemnly or formally reject or go back on (as something formerly adhered to) ⟨*abjured* some long-held beliefs when she converted to another religion⟩
synonyms recant, renounce, retract, take back, unsay, withdraw
related words contradict, deny, disavow, disclaim, disown, gainsay, negate, negative, repudiate; abandon, abnegate, forsake, give up, relinquish, spurn, surrender; controvert, disagree (with), disprove, dispute, rebut, refute; back down, back off, backtrack; disallow, recall, renege, revoke
near antonyms acknowledge, admit, affirm, assert, avow, claim, contend, declare, maintain, proclaim, profess, state; back, confirm, defend, endorse (*also* indorse), espouse, maintain, support, uphold; accept, adopt, embrace
antonyms adhere (to)

ablaze *adj* **1** being on fire ⟨the entire block was *ablaze* by the time fire fighters arrived⟩
synonyms afire, aflame, blazing, burning, combusting, fiery, flaming, ignited, inflamed, kindled, lighted (*or* lit)
related words aglow, alight, flaring, flickering, glowing, live, smoldering; broiling, hot, piping hot, red-hot, roasting, scalding, scorching, searing, sizzling; burnt, charred, incinerated, scorched, seared, singed
near antonyms choked, damped, dead, doused, extinguished, quenched, smothered, snuffed (out), stamped (out), suffocated
2 filled with much light — see BRIGHT 2

able *adj* having the required skills for an acceptable level of performance — see COMPETENT

able–bodied *adj* enjoying health and vigor — see HEALTHY 1

ably *adv* in a skillful or expert manner — see WELL 3

abnegate *vb* to give up (as a position of authority) formally — see ABDICATE

abnegation *n* the act or practice of giving up or rejecting something once enjoyed or desired — see RENUNCIATION

abnormal *adj* **1** being out of the ordinary — see EXCEPTIONAL
2 departing from some accepted standard of what is normal — see DEVIANT

abnormality *n* a person, thing, or event that is not normal — see FREAK 1

abode *n* the place where one lives — see HOME 1

abolish *vb* to put an end to by formal action ⟨the U.S. *abolished* slavery by constitutional amendment on December 6, 1865⟩
synonyms abrogate, annul, cancel, dissolve, invalidate, negate, nullify, quash, repeal, rescind, void
related words countermand, override, overrule, overturn, veto; retract, reverse, revoke, suspend, withdraw; ban, enjoin, forbid, outlaw, prohibit; disallow, dismiss, reject; eliminate, eradicate, erase, liquidate, remove, throw out, write off
phrases do away with
near antonyms establish, found, institute; formalize, legalize, legitimate, legitimize, validate; pass, ratify; allow, approve, authorize, clear, endorse (*also* indorse), permit, sanction, warrant; command, decree, mandate, prescribe, order

abominable *adj* causing intense displeasure, disgust, or resentment — see OFFENSIVE 1

abominate *vb* to dislike strongly — see HATE

abomination *n* something or someone that is hated — see HATE 2
2 a very strong dislike — see HATE 1

aboriginal *adj* belonging to a particular place by birth or origin — see NATIVE 1

abort *vb* to put an end to (something planned or previously agreed to) — see CANCEL 1

abortion *n* the act of putting an end to something planned or previously agreed to — see CANCELLATION

abortive *adj* producing no results — see FUTILE

abounding *adj* possessing or covered with great numbers or amounts of something specified — see RIFE

about *adv* **1** on all sides or in every direction — see AROUND 1
2 toward the opposite direction — see AROUND 2
3 very close to but not completely — see ALMOST

about *prep* **1** having to do with ⟨a story *about* a young man who goes off to war⟩
synonyms apropos of, concerning, of, on, regarding, respecting, toward (*or* towards)
related words as to, over
phrases as regards
2 close to — see AROUND 1
3 in random positions within the boundaries of — see AROUND 2

above *prep* higher than ⟨one minute our kite was *above* the telephone wires; the next minute it was tangled in them⟩
synonyms over
related words atop
near antonyms underneath
antonyms below, beneath, under

above *adv* to or in a higher place ⟨we eventually got used to the planes constantly flying *above*⟩
synonyms aloft, over, overhead, skyward
near antonyms underneath
antonyms below, beneath, under

abrade *vb* **1** to damage or diminish by continued friction ⟨ropes *abraded* by the rocks were a huge danger to the climbers⟩
synonyms chafe, erode, fray, fret, gall, rub, wear
related words file, gnaw, grate, graze, grind, nibble, rasp, sandblast, sandpaper, scour, scrape, scuff, shave; erase, reduce, rub out, wear out, wipe (away); bite, break down, break up, chew, corrode, decompose, disintegrate, dissolve, eat; hone, sharpen, whet
2 to make sore by continued rubbing — see CHAFE 1
3 to damage by rubbing against a sharp or rough surface — see SCRAPE 2

abreast *adj* having information especially as a result of study or experience — see FAMILIAR 2

abridge *vb* to make less in extent or duration — see SHORTEN

abridgment *or* **abridgement** *n* a shortened version of a written work ⟨this Italian-English pocket dictionary is an *abridgment* of the hardback edition⟩
synonyms abbreviation, condensation, digest
related words abstract, brief, outline, overview, précis, recap, recapitulation, résumé (*or* resume *also* resumé), review, sketch, sum, summariza-

tion, summary, summation, survey, syllabus, synopsis, wrap-up
near antonyms amplification, elaboration, enlargement, expansion

abrogate *vb* to put an end to by formal action — see ABOLISH

abrupt *adj* **1** being or characterized by direct, brief, and potentially rude speech or manner — see BLUNT 1
2 having an incline approaching the perpendicular — see STEEP 1

abruptly *adv* with great suddenness — see SHORT

abscond *vb* to get free from a dangerous or confining situation — see ESCAPE 1

absence *n* **1** a state of being without something necessary, desirable, or useful — see NEED 1
2 the fact or state of being absent — see LACK 1

absent *adj* **1** not at a certain place ⟨three students were *absent* because of the flu⟩
synonyms away, missing, out
related words AWOL, truant; departed, gone, retired; abroad, vacationing
near antonyms accompanying, attending, participating
antonyms here, present
2 not present or in evidence ⟨the usual stir of activity was *absent* in the city due to the report of an escaped lion from the zoo⟩
synonyms lacking, missing, nonexistent, wanting
related words dead, departed, extinct, lost, perished, vanished; defunct, done, expired, finished, lapsed, obsolete, over, passé; inadequate, insufficient, rare, scarce, sparse, uncommon
near antonyms active, alive, animate, living, thriving; current, going, prevailing, uncanceled; common, prevalent; apparent, conspicuous, evident, obvious, plain
antonyms existent, present
3 lost in thought and unaware of one's surroundings or actions — see ABSENTMINDED 1

absentminded *adj* **1** lost in thought and unaware of one's surroundings or actions ⟨the grieving woman was so *absentminded* that she left her key in the lock after opening the door⟩
synonyms absent, abstracted, preoccupied
related words absorbed, daydreaming, distracted, dreaming, dreamy, engrossed, faraway, intent, pensive, rapt; heedless, inattentive, insensible, oblivious, unaware, unconscious, unheeding, unknowing, unmindful, unobservant, unobserving, unperceiving, unperceptive, unseeing, unthinking, unwary, unwitting, vacant; befogged, befuddled, bemused, bewildered, confused, dazed, flighty, foggy, forgetful, forgetting, hazy, muddled, scatterbrained, unfocused
near antonyms alive, attentive, aware, conscious, heedful, mindful, observant, observing, open-eyed, sharp, vigilant, wary, watchful, wide-awake; clearheaded, unconfused
antonyms alert
2 inclined to forget what one has learned or to do what one should — see FORGETFUL

absolute *adj* **1** exercising power or authority without interference by others ⟨the *absolute* monarchy of Russia ended when Czar Nicholas II promised to share power with a legislative body⟩
synonyms autocratic, despotic, dictatorial, tyrannical (*also* tyrannic), tyrannous
related words authoritarian, totalitarian; arbitrary, high-handed, magisterial; domineering, imperious, masterful; all-powerful, almighty, omnipotent; autonomous, self-governing, sovereign; unconditional, unlimited
near antonyms circumscribed, restrained, restricted; constitutional, lawful
antonyms limited
2 having no exceptions or restrictions ⟨ironing is an *absolute* bore⟩ ⟨I want the *absolute* truth⟩
synonyms all-out, arrant, categorical (*also* categoric), complete, consummate, dead, downright, flat, out-and-out, outright, perfect, profound, pure, regular, sheer, simple, stark, thorough, thoroughgoing, total, unadulterated, unalloyed, unconditional, unequivocal, unmitigated, unqualified, utter
related words authentic, classic, genuine, real, veritable; constant, endless, eternal, perpetual, undying, unremitting; extreme, rank, unrestricted; confirmed, habitual, hopeless, inveterate; deadly, extraordinary, frightful, horrible, huge, main, superlative, supreme, surpassing, terrible, terrific
near antonyms doubtful, dubious, equivocal, qualified, questionable, restricted, uncertain
3 being entirely without fault or flaw — see PERFECT 1
4 free from added matter — see PURE 1
5 serving to put an end to all debate or questioning — see CONCLUSIVE 1

absolution *n* release from the guilt or penalty of an offense — see PARDON

absolve *vb* to free from a charge of wrongdoing — see EXCULPATE

absorb *vb* **1** to take in (something liquid) through small openings ⟨most of the spilled water was *absorbed* by the tablecloth⟩
synonyms drink, imbibe, soak (up), sponge, suck (up)
related words gulp, guzzle, quaff, sip, slurp, swallow, swig, swill
2 to hold the attention of — see ENGAGE 1

absorbed *adj* having the mind fixed on something — see ATTENTIVE

absorbing *adj* holding the attention or provoking interest — see INTERESTING

absorption *n* a focusing of the mind on something — see ATTENTION 1

abstain (from) *vb* to resist the temptation of — see FORBEAR

abstract *adj* **1** dealing with or expressing a quality or idea ⟨the book deals with *abstract* matters such as honesty and integrity on the job as well as practical subjects such as asking for a raise⟩
synonyms conceptual, theoretical (*also* theoretic)
related words conjectural, hypothetical, speculative; intellectual, mental, spiritual; ethereal, immaterial, incorporeal, insubstantial, metaphysical, nonmaterial, nonphysical, unsubstantial; impalpable, imperceptible, insensible, intangible, invisible; impractical, romantic, transcendent, transcendental, unreal, utopian, visionary
near antonyms material, physical; appreciable, detectable, discernable, noticeable, observable, palpable, perceptible, sensible, substantial, tangible, visible; defined, definite, distinct; actual, factual, real
antonyms concrete
2 using elements of form (as color, line, or texture) with little or no attempt at creating a realistic picture ⟨Cubism is a style of *abstract* art in

which natural forms are broken up into geometric shapes⟩
synonyms nonrealistic
related words impressionist, impressionistic; symbolist, symbolistic
near antonyms lifelike, natural
antonyms realistic, representational

abstract *n* a short statement of the main points — see SUMMARY

abstract *vb* to make into a short statement of the main points (as of a report) — see SUMMARIZE

abstracted *adj* lost in thought and unaware of one's surroundings or actions — see ABSENT-MINDED 1

abstruse *adj* difficult for one of ordinary knowledge or intelligence to understand — see PROFOUND 1

absurd *adj* **1** conceived or made without regard for reason or reality — see FANTASTIC 1
2 showing or marked by a lack of good sense or judgment — see FOOLISH 1
3 so foolish or pointless as to be worthy of scornful laughter — see RIDICULOUS 1

absurdity *n* **1** a foolish act or idea — see FOLLY 1
2 lack of good sense or judgment — see FOOLISHNESS 1

abundance *n* **1** a considerable amount — see LOT 2
2 an amount or supply more than sufficient to meet one's needs — see PLENTY 1

abundant *adj* being more than enough without being excessive — see PLENTIFUL

abuse *n* **1** harsh insulting language ⟨spectators hurled *abuse* at the visiting team⟩
synonyms fulmination, invective, vitriol, vituperation
related words blasphemy, curse, execration, imprecation, malediction, profanity; epithet, insult, put-down, slur; expletive, swearword; aspersion, bad-mouthing, belittlement, disparagement, revilement, vilification; castigation, chastisement, criticism, excoriation, opprobrium, rebuke, reprimand, reproof; broadside, diatribe, harangue, polemic, tirade
near antonyms acclaim, applause, commendation, praise; compliments, congratulations, endearments, felicitations; adulation, blarney, flattery, overpraise, soft soap
2 incorrect or improper use — see MISUSE

abuse *vb* **1** to inflict physical or emotional harm upon ⟨if you *abuse* your pet, he will always have an ugly disposition⟩
synonyms ill-treat, ill-use, maltreat, manhandle, mishandle, mistreat, misuse
related words molest, outrage, violate; harass, harm, hurt, injure, oppress, persecute, torment, torture, victimize, wrong
near antonyms care (for), cherish, foster, nurture; baby, cater (to), coddle, favor, gratify, humor, indulge, mollycoddle, pamper, spoil
2 to criticize harshly and usually publicly — see ATTACK 2
3 to put to a bad or improper use — see MISAPPLY
4 to take unfair advantage of — see EXPLOIT 1

abut *vb* to be adjacent to — see ADJOIN 1

abutting *adj* having a border in common — see ADJACENT

abysmal *adj* extending far downward or inward — see DEEP 1

abyss *n* an immeasurable depth or space ⟨looking down at the dark ocean from the ship's rail, Malcolm felt as though he was staring into an *abyss*⟩
synonyms chasm, gulf
related words cleft, crevasse, crevice, fissure; cavern, hole, hollow, pit; breadth, expanse, extent, reach, spread, stretch; emptiness, nothingness, vacuity, vacuum, void

academic *adj* of or relating to schooling or learning especially at an advanced level ⟨"If you spent more time in *academic* pursuits and less time in social ones, you could easily make good grades," the dean told Valerie⟩
synonyms educational, scholarly, scholastic
related words bookish, pedantic, professorial; curricular; educative, instructive; collegiate, graduate, postgraduate
near antonyms extracurricular; noncollegiate
antonyms nonacademic, unacademic

academy *n* a place or establishment for teaching and learning — see SCHOOL

accelerate *vb* to cause to move or proceed fast or faster — see HURRY 1

accent *n* a special notice or importance given to something — see EMPHASIS 1

accent *vb* to indicate the importance of by giving prominent display — see EMPHASIZE

accentuate *vb* to indicate the importance of by giving prominent display — see EMPHASIZE

accentuation *n* a special notice or importance given to something — see EMPHASIS 1

accept *vb* **1** to agree to receive whether willingly or reluctantly — see TAKE 2
2 to have a favorable opinion of — see APPROVE (OF)
3 to regard as right or true — see BELIEVE 1
4 to take to or upon oneself — see ASSUME 1

acceptability *n* the quality or state of meeting one's needs adequately — see SUFFICIENCY

acceptable *adj* of a level of quality that meets one's needs or standards — see ADEQUATE

acceptably *adv* in a satisfactory way — see WELL 1

accepting *adj* showing or expressing acceptance or approval — see POSITIVE

access *n* the means or right of entering or participating in — see ENTRANCE 1

access *vb* to go or come in or into — see ENTER 1

accessible *adj* **1** possible to get — see AVAILABLE 1
2 situated within easy reach — see CONVENIENT

accessory *adj* available to supply something extra when needed — see AUXILIARY

accessory *n* **1** something that is not necessary in itself but adds to the convenience or performance of the main piece of equipment ⟨bought a new car with lots of high-tech *accessories*⟩
synonyms accoutrement (*or* accouterment), adjunct, appendage, attachment
related words accompaniment, additive, complement, supplement; auxiliary, subsidiary; amenity, extra, filler, frill, incidental, luxury, nonessential, nonnecessity; equipment, furnishings, paraphernalia, trappings; adornment, decoration, embellishment, enhancement, garnish, ornament, trim
near antonyms essential, necessity, requirement, requisite
2 one associated with another in wrongdoing — see ACCOMPLICE

accident *n* **1** a chance and usually sudden event bringing loss or injury ⟨was involved in an *accident* on her way home from work⟩
synonyms casualty, mischance, mishap

related words calamity, cataclysm, catastrophe, cropper, deathblow, disaster, tragedy; bummer, knock, misadventure, misfortune; collision, crack-up, crash, smashup, wreck
near antonyms boon, break, fluke, godsend, miracle, strike, windfall; fortune, luck, serendipity
2 the uncertain course of events — see CHANCE 1

accidental *adj* happening by chance ⟨finding the gold was all the more remarkable because its discovery was entirely *accidental*⟩
synonyms casual, chance, fluky, fortuitous, inadvertent, incidental, unintended, unintentional, unplanned, unpremeditated, unwitting
related words coincidental; freak, odd; aimless, arbitrary, desultory, haphazard, random; uncertain, unexpected, unforeseeable, unforeseen; coerced, forced, involuntary; unconscious, unexpected, unprompted
near antonyms certain, destined, expected, fixed, foreordained, foreseeable, foreseen, inevitable, predestined, predetermined, predictable, preordained, prescribed, sure; conscious, freewill, knowing, unforced, voluntary, volunteer, willful (*or* wilful)
antonyms deliberate, intended, intentional, planned, premeditated

acclaim *n* public acknowledgment or admiration for an achievement — see GLORY 1

acclaim *vb* to declare enthusiastic approval of ⟨she was *acclaimed* by the critics for her realistic acting⟩
synonyms applaud, cheer, crack up, hail, laud, praise, salute, tout
related words ballyhoo; approve, commend, endorse (*also* indorse), favor, recommend, support; celebrate, emblazon, eulogize, extol (*also* extoll), glorify, sing; adulate, flatter, overpraise; deify, idolize
near antonyms belittle, disparage, put down; blame, censure, reprehend, reprobate; admonish, chide, criticize, rebuke, reprimand, reproach, reprove; castigate, excoriate, lambaste
antonyms knock, pan, slam

acclamation *n* enthusiastic and usually public expression of approval — see APPLAUSE

acclimate *vb* to change (something) so as to make it suitable for a new use or situation — see ADAPT

acclimatize *vb* to change (something) so as to make it suitable for a new use or situation — see ADAPT

accolade *n* **1** a formal expression of praise — see ENCOMIUM
2 public acknowledgment or admiration for an achievement — see GLORY 1

accommodate *vb* **1** to make or have room for ⟨the back seat *accommodates* three people comfortably⟩
synonyms fit, hold, take
related words carry, contain, seat; enclose (*also* inclose), encompass; harbor, house
2 to bring to a state free of conflicts, inconsistencies, or differences — see HARMONIZE 2
3 to change (something) so as to make it suitable for a new use or situation — see ADAPT
4 to do a service or favor for — see OBLIGE 1
5 to provide with living quarters or shelter — see HOUSE 1

accommodation *n* the act or practice of each side giving up something in order to reach an agreement — see CONCESSION 1

accompaniment *n* something that is found along with something else ⟨the sound of crickets was the perfect *accompaniment* to our summer evenings on the porch⟩
synonyms companion, concomitant
related words accessory, adjunct, appendage; complement, supplement; counterpart, fellow, mate; consequence, corollary, follow-up; fixings, trimmings

accompany *vb* to go along with in order to provide assistance, protection, or companionship ⟨children must be *accompanied* by a parent at all times⟩
synonyms attend, chaperone (*or* chaperon), convoy, escort, squire
related words associate, consort, pal (around), team (up); defend, guard, protect; bring, conduct, guide, lead, pilot, see, steer, usher; follow, shadow, tag, tag along, tail; hang (around), hover (over)
near antonyms abandon, desert, ditch, dump, forsake

accompanying *adj* present at the same time and place — see COINCIDENT

accomplice *n* one associated with another in wrongdoing ⟨the thief and his *accomplices* were eventually caught and brought to justice⟩
synonyms abettor (*also* abetter), accessory, cohort, confederate
related words collaborator, collaborationist, informant, informer; companion, comrade, crony, henchman, partner; conspirator, plotter, traitor; gangster, mobster, racketeer

accomplish *vb* to carry through (as a process) to completion — see PERFORM 1

accomplished *adj* having or showing exceptional knowledge, experience, or skill in a field of endeavor — see PROFICIENT

accomplishment *n* **1** a successful result brought about by hard work ⟨Jared's biggest *accomplishment* this week was finishing his art project⟩
synonyms achievement, attainment, coup, success, triumph
related words blockbuster, hit, jackpot, megahit, smash, winner; conquest, gain, victory, win; acquirement, skill; deed, feat, performance; completion, consummation, culmination, execution, fruition, fulfillment, implementation, realization
phrases a feather in one's cap
near antonyms botch, mess, muddle, shambles; bummer, bust, catastrophe, debacle (*also* débâcle), dud, failure, fiasco, fizzle, flop, washout; disappointment, letdown, loss, setback
2 the doing of an action — see COMMISSION 2
3 the state of being actual or complete — see FRUITION

accord *n* **1** a formal agreement between two or more nations or peoples — see TREATY
2 a state of consistency — see CONFORMITY 1
3 an arrangement about action to be taken — see AGREEMENT 2
4 the act or fact of being of one opinion about something — see AGREEMENT 1
5 the act or power of making one's own choices or decisions — see FREE WILL

accord *vb* **1** to be in agreement on every point — see CHECK 1
2 to give the ownership or benefit of (something) formally or publicly — see CONFER 1

accordance *n* a state of consistency — see CONFORMITY 1

accordingly *adv* for this or that reason — see THEREFORE
account *n* **1** a relating of events usually in the order in which they happened ⟨newspaper reporters must strive to provide an accurate *account* of what happened⟩
synonyms chronicle, history, narrative, record, report, story
related words version; deposition, documentation, testament, testimonial, testimony, witness; annals, diary, journal, log, logbook, memoir; anecdote, tale, yarn; epic, saga; recital, recitation
2 a record of goods sold or services performed together with the costs due — see [1]BILL 1
3 a sum of money set aside for a particular purpose — see FUND 1
4 the capacity for being useful for some purpose — see USE 2
5 the relative usefulness or importance of something as judged by specific qualities — see WORTH 1
account *vb* to think of in a particular way — see CONSIDER 1
account (for) *vb* to give the reason for or cause of — see EXPLAIN 2
accountable *adj* being the one who must meet an obligation or suffer the consequences for failing to do so — see RESPONSIBLE 1
accoutre *or* **accouter** *vb* to provide (someone) with what is needed for a task or activity — see FURNISH 1
accoutrement *or* **accouterment** *n* **1** something that is not necessary in itself but adds to the convenience or performance of the main piece of equipment — see ACCESSORY 1
2 accoutrements *or* **accouterments** *pl* items needed for the performance of a task or activity — see EQUIPMENT
accredit *vb* **1** to explain (something) as being the result of something else — see CREDIT 1
2 to give official or legal power to — see AUTHORIZE 1
accreditation *n* the granting of power to perform various acts or duties — see COMMISSION 1
accretion *n* something added (as by growth) — see INCREASE 1
accrual *n* something added (as by growth) — see INCREASE 1
accumulate *vb* **1** to become greater in extent, volume, amount, or number — see INCREASE 2
2 to bring together in one body or place — see GATHER 1
3 to gradually form into a layer, pile, or mass — see COLLECT 2
accumulating *n* the act or process of becoming greater in number — see MULTIPLICATION
accumulation *n* **1** a mass or quantity that has piled up or that has been gathered ⟨a vast *accumulation* of evidence about the dangers of smoking⟩
synonyms assemblage, collection, gathering
related words agglomerate, assortment, conglomerate, conglomeration, hodgepodge, hotchpotch, jumble, medley, mélange, mishmash, mix, mixture, motley, potpourri; agglomeration, clutter, hash, heap, litter, mass, pile; aggregate, aggregation, sum, totality; cache, fund, hoard, inventory, nest egg, reserve, stock, stockpile, store, supply
2 the act or process of becoming greater in number — see MULTIPLICATION
accuracy *n* the quality or state of being very accurate — see PRECISION
accurate *adj* **1** being in agreement with the truth or a fact or a standard — see CORRECT 1
2 following an original exactly — see FAITHFUL 2
3 meeting the highest standard of accuracy — see PRECISE 1
accuse *vb* to make a claim of wrongdoing against ⟨she was *accused* of cheating on the test⟩
synonyms charge, impeach, incriminate, indict
related words blame, castigate, censure, condemn, criticize, damn, denounce, fault, impugn, reproach, reprobate; chide, rebuke, reprove, tax; arraign, book, cite, summon; prosecute, sue, try; frame, implicate, inform (against), report; recriminate, retaliate
near antonyms advocate, champion, defend; excuse, forgive, justify, pardon, remit, shrive
antonyms absolve, acquit, clear, exculpate, exonerate, vindicate
accustomed *adj* being in the habit or custom ⟨Josh felt uncomfortably full, as he was not *accustomed* to eating so much⟩
synonyms given, habituated, used, wont
related words apt, inclined, liable, prone; hardened, inured; experienced, practiced (*or* practised), seasoned, veteran; addicted, hooked
near antonyms averse, disinclined, opposed; inexperienced, new, unseasoned
antonyms unaccustomed, unused
ace *adj* having or showing exceptional knowledge, experience, or skill in a field of endeavor — see PROFICIENT 1
ace *n* **1** a person with a high level of knowledge or skill in a field — see EXPERT
2 a very small amount — see PARTICLE 1
3 a very small distance or degree — see HAIR 1
ache *n* a sharp unpleasant sensation usually felt in some specific part of the body — see PAIN 1
ache *vb* to feel or cause physical pain — see HURT 1
ache (for) *vb* to have an earnest wish to own or enjoy — see DESIRE
achievable *adj* capable of being done or carried out — see POSSIBLE 1
achieve *vb* **1** to obtain (as a goal) through effort ⟨finally *achieved* stardom⟩
synonyms attain, hit, make, score, win
related words acquire, capture, carry, draw, garner, get, land, make, obtain, procure, realize, secure; amount (to), approach, equal, match, measure up (to), meet, rival, tie, touch; beat, excel, outdo, surpass, top
near antonyms fall short (of); fail (at); lose
2 to carry through (as a process) to completion — see PERFORM 1
achievement *n* **1** a successful result brought about by hard work — see ACCOMPLISHMENT 1
2 the doing of an action — see COMMISSION 2
3 the state of being actual or complete — see FRUITION
aching *adj* causing or feeling bodily pain — see PAINFUL 1
acid *adj* causing or characterized by the one of the four basic taste sensations that is produced chiefly by acids — see SOUR 1
acidic *adj* causing or characterized by the one of the four basic taste sensations that is produced chiefly by acids — see SOUR 1
acidity *n* **1** a harsh or sharp quality — see EDGE 1

2 biting sharpness of feeling or expression — see ACRIMONY 1

acidness *n* biting sharpness of feeling or expression — see ACRIMONY 1

acknowledge *vb* to accept the truth or existence of (something) usually reluctantly — see ADMIT

acknowledgment *also* **acknowledgement** *n* **1** a formal recognition of an achievement or praiseworthy deed — see COMMENDATION 1

2 an open declaration of something (as a fault or the commission of an offense) about oneself — see CONFESSION

acme *n* the highest part or point — see HEIGHT 1

acoustic *or* **acoustical** *adj* of, relating to, or experienced through the sense of hearing — see AUDITORY

acquaint *vb* **1** to impart knowledge of a new thing or situation to ⟨Mr. King spent the first week of class *acquainting* everyone with the new computers⟩

synonyms familiarize, initiate, introduce, orient, orientate

related words apprise, brief, clue (in), fill in, inform; educate, enlighten, ground, instruct, school, train; expose, present, subject; advise, tell, tip off, warn, wise up

2 to give information to — see ENLIGHTEN 1

3 to make (one person) known (to another) socially — see INTRODUCE 1

acquaintance *n* knowledge gained by personal experience ⟨Tiffany's *acquaintance* with cows is limited to a visit to a petting zoo when she was three⟩

synonyms cognizance, familiarity

related words association, experience, exposure, intimacy, involvement; initiation, introduction; awareness, comprehension, conception, inkling, notion, understanding; education, enlightenment, grounding, information, instruction, learning, schooling, training

near antonyms callowness, greenness, ignorance, inexperience

antonyms unfamiliarity

acquainted *adj* having information especially as a result of study or experience — see FAMILIAR 2

acquiescent *adj* receiving or enduring without offering resistance — see PASSIVE

acquirable *adj* possible to get — see AVAILABLE 1

acquire *vb* **1** to come to have gradually — see DEVELOP 2

2 to receive as return for effort — see EARN 1

acquisitive *adj* having or marked by an eager and often selfish desire especially for material possessions — see GREEDY 1

acquisitiveness *n* an intense selfish desire for wealth or possessions — see GREED

acquit *vb* **1** to free from a charge of wrongdoing — see EXCULPATE

2 to manage the actions of (oneself) in a particular way — see BEHAVE

acrid *adj* **1** having or showing deep-seated resentment — see BITTER 1

2 marked by the use of wit that is intended to cause hurt feelings — see SARCASTIC

acridness *n* **1** a harsh or sharp quality — see EDGE 1

2 biting sharpness of feeling or expression — see ACRIMONY 1

acrimonious *adj* having or showing deep-seated resentment — see BITTER 1

acrimoniousness *n* a harsh or sharp quality — see EDGE 1

acrimony *n* **1** biting sharpness of feeling or expression ⟨she responded with such *acrimony* that he never brought the subject up again⟩

synonyms acidity, acidness, acridness, asperity, bitterness, cattiness, tartness, virulence, vitriol

related words gruffness, harshness, hostility, relentlessness, severity, sternness, vehemence; coldness, crossness, discourteousness, iciness, impoliteness, incivility, nastiness, rudeness, sourness, surliness, ungraciousness; anger, animosity, bile, jaundice, malevolence, malice, rancor, scorn, spite, spleen, venom; jealousy, pique, resentment

near antonyms civility, cordiality, courtesy, diplomacy, geniality, graciousness, politeness, tactfulness; compassion, softness, sweetness, sympathy, tenderness, warmth; oiliness, smoothness, suaveness, unctuousness, urbanity

2 a harsh or sharp quality — see EDGE 1

across *adv* from one side to the other of an intervening space — see OVER 1

across *prep* to the opposite side of ⟨we swam *across* the lake and visited the other summer camp⟩

synonyms athwart, over, through

related words around, round; beyond, past

act *n* **1** a display of emotion or behavior that is insincere or intended to deceive — see MASQUERADE

2 a rule of conduct or action laid down by a governing authority and especially a legislator — see LAW 1

3 something done by someone — see ACTION 1

act *vb* **1** to present a portrayal or performance of ⟨a very talented student *acted* the part of Tiny Tim in our production of *A Christmas Carol*⟩

synonyms impersonate, perform, play, portray

related words depict, dramatize, enact, pantomime, render, represent, role-play, take on; overact, underplay; ape, clown, ham, imitate, masquerade, mime, mimic, pose (as); star (in)

2 to produce a desired effect ⟨the painkiller *acted* quickly⟩

synonyms operate, perform, take, work

related words behave, react, respond; affect, influence, sway; pan out, redound, result

phrases take effect

near antonyms backfire; fizzle

3 to give the impression of being — see SEEM

4 to have a certain purpose — see FUNCTION

act (toward) *vb* to behave toward in a stated way — see TREAT 1

action *n* **1** something done by someone ⟨judge people by their *actions*, not by their words⟩

synonyms act, deed, doing, exploit, feat, thing

related words accomplishment, achievement, attainment; adventure, experience; enterprise, initiative, undertaking; handiwork, performance, work; stunt, trick; activity, dealing; maneuver, measure, move, operation, procedure, proceeding, step, tactic

2 a court case for enforcing a right or claim — see LAWSUIT

3 active fighting during the course of a war — see COMBAT 1

4 actions *pl* the way or manner in which one conducts oneself — see BEHAVIOR

activate *vb* to cause to function ⟨the thermostat is

set to *activate* the heating system only when the temperature drops below 65 degrees⟩
synonyms actuate, crank (up), drive, move, propel, run, set off, spark, start, touch off, trigger, turn on
related words charge, electrify, energize, fire, fuel, generate, power, push; discharge, launch, release, switch, trip; reactivate, recharge; arouse, excite, stimulate, vitalize; incite, instigate, provoke, quicken, stir up; accelerate, catalyze, speed up, step up
near antonyms arrest, brake, chock, cut off, draw up, halt, jam, stall, stick, stop; decelerate, repress, slow, stunt, suppress
antonyms cut, deactivate, kill, shut off, turn off

active *adj* **1** being in effective operation ⟨the abandoned factory had not been *active* for years⟩
synonyms alive, functional, functioning, going, living, on, operating, operational, operative, running, working
related words effective, effectual; employable, operable, usable, viable, workable; performing, producing, productive, serving, useful, yielding; astir, bustling, busy, dynamic, flourishing, humming, roaring, thriving
phrases in commission
near antonyms deactivated, decommissioned; ineffective, ineffectual, useless; inoperable, unusable, unworkable; arrested, asleep, dormant, fallow, idle, inert, latent, lifeless, nonproductive, quiescent, sleepy, stagnating, unproductive, vegetating
antonyms broken, dead, inactive, inoperative, nonfunctional, nonfunctioning, nonoperating
2 having much high-spirited energy and movement — see LIVELY 1
3 involved in often constant activity — see BUSY 1

activity *n* energetic movement of the body for the sake of physical fitness — see EXERCISE 1

actor *n* one who acts professionally (as in a play, movie, or television show) ⟨my sister went to drama school to become an *actor*⟩
synonyms impersonator, mummer, player, trouper
related words barnstormer, entertainer, performer; actress, starlet; lead, leading lady, leading man, star; monologuist (*or* monologist); prima donna, scene-stealer, understudy; comedian, tragedian; ape, aper, ham, imitator, impressionist, masquerader, mime, mimic, pantomime, pantomimist, poser; buffoon, clown, harlequin, stooge, zany

actual *adj* existing in fact and not merely as a possibility ⟨the *actual* outcome of the election was quite different from what everybody expected⟩
synonyms concrete, existent, factual, real, true, very
related words attested, authenticated, confirmed, demonstrated, established, proven, substantiated, validated, verified; incontestable, incontrovertible, indisputable, indubitable, inescapable, irrefutable, undeniable, unquestionable; believable, convincing, literal, realistic, unmistakable, verifiable; authentic, bona fide, genuine, real-life; absolute, certain, final, hard, palpable, positive, substantial, tangible; authoritative, certifiable, certified
near antonyms alleged, assumed, reputed, supposed; conceived, envisaged, imagined, pictured, visualized; chimerical, fabled, fanciful, fictional, fictitious, legendary, illusory; fabricated, fake, imaginary, invented, made-up, make-believe, pretend, romantic; abstract, unreal
antonyms conjectural, hypothetical, ideal, nonexistent, possible, potential, theoretical (*also* theoretic)

actuality *n* **1** the fact of being or of being real — see EXISTENCE
2 the quality of being actual — see FACT 1
3 the state of being actual or complete — see FRUITION

actually *adv* **1** to tell the truth ⟨*actually*, I'd rather spend the evening at home⟩
synonyms forsooth, frankly, honestly, really, truly, truthfully, verily
related words absolutely, certainly, indisputably, indubitably, positively, realistically, undoubtedly, unquestionably, veritably
phrases in point of fact, in reality, in truth
2 in actual fact — see VERY 2

actuate *vb* **1** to cause to function — see ACTIVATE
2 to set or keep in motion — see MOVE 2

act up *vb* **1** to behave badly — see MISBEHAVE
2 to engage in attention-getting playful or boisterous behavior — see CUT UP

acute *adj* **1** able to sense slight impressions or differences ⟨dogs, with their *acute* sense of smell, are used for finding toxic substances undetectable by humans⟩
synonyms delicate, keen, perceptive, sensitive, sharp
related words accurate, clear, discerning, fine, good, piercing, precise, quick, receptive, sensible, subtle; hypersensitive, oversensitive, supersensitive
near antonyms bad, deadened, dimmed, dull, dulled, fading; dead, imperceptive, insensible, insensitive, numb; imprecise, inaccurate
2 needing immediate attention ⟨famine caused by an *acute* shortage of grain⟩
synonyms critical, crying, dire, imperative, imperious, instant, pressing, urgent
related words compelling, demanding, extreme, immediate, insistent, intense, overriding; crucial, desperate, grave, life-and-death, serious, severe, vital; dangerous, explosive, hazardous, perilous, precarious, unstable
near antonyms incidental, low-pressure, minor, negligible, trivial, unimportant; nonthreatening, safe, stable
antonyms noncritical, nonurgent
3 causing intense mental or physical distress — see SHARP 2
4 having a high musical pitch or range — see SHRILL

acuteness *n* a harsh or sharp quality — see EDGE 1

ad *n* a published statement informing the public of a matter of general interest — see ANNOUNCEMENT

adage *n* an often stated observation regarding something from common experience — see SAYING

adamant *adj* sticking to an opinion, purpose, or course of action in spite of reason, arguments, or persuasion — see OBSTINATE

adamantine *adj* sticking to an opinion, purpose, or course of action in spite of reason, arguments, or persuasion — see OBSTINATE

adapt *vb* to change (something) so as to make it

suitable for a new use or situation ⟨it always takes freshmen a little while to *adapt* themselves to high school⟩
synonyms acclimate, acclimatize, accommodate, adjust, condition, conform, fit, shape
related words readapt, readjust; customize, tailor; attune, harmonize, reconcile, suit, tune; establish, root, settle; acquaint, familiarize, orient, orientate; equip, prepare, prime, rehearse; harden, inure, season, toughen; alter, convert, make over, modify, redo, refashion, refit, remake, remodel, revamp, revise, rework, transform

adaptable *adj* **1** able to do many different kinds of things — see VERSATILE
2 capable of being readily changed — see FLEXIBLE 1

add *vb* **1** to join (something) to a mass, quantity, or number so as to bring about an overall increase ⟨the band recently *added* a saxophonist and a keyboard player to its ranks⟩ ⟨*add* another cup of flour to the mixture⟩
synonyms adjoin, annex, append, tack (on)
related words affix, attach, fasten, fix, graft, hitch, tie; infuse, inject, insert, introduce
near antonyms detach, disconnect, disjoin, separate, unfasten; amputate, cut, excise, lop off, sever
antonyms deduct, remove, subtract, take
2 to combine (numbers) into a single sum ⟨when she *added* all the phone charges she discovered an error in her bill⟩
synonyms foot (up), sum, total
related words calculate, cast, cipher, compute, figure, reckon, tally; count, enumerate, number

add (to) *vb* to make greater in size, amount, or number — see INCREASE 1

added *adj* resulting in an increase in amount or number — see ADDITIONAL

addendum *n* something added (as by growth) — see INCREASE 1

addict *n* **1** a person who regularly uses drugs especially illegally — see DOPER
2 a person with a strong and habitual liking for something — see FAN

addition *n* **1** a smaller structure added to a main building — see ANNEX
2 something added (as by growth) — see INCREASE 1
3 the act or process of becoming greater in number — see MULTIPLICATION

additional *adj* resulting in an increase in amount or number ⟨there turned out to be *additional* reasons for her absence besides those she had given⟩
synonyms added, another, else, farther, further, more, other
related words accessory, collateral, extraneous, side, supplemental, supplementary; fresh, new; extra, plus, spare, surplus
near antonyms fewer, less

additionally *adv* in addition to what has been said — see MORE 1

additive *adj* produced by a series of additions of identical or similar things — see CUMULATIVE

addle *vb* to throw into a state of mental uncertainty — see CONFUSE 1

addled *adj* having undergone organic breakdown — see ROTTEN 1

address *n* a usually formal discourse delivered to an audience — see SPEECH 1

address *vb* to occupy (oneself) diligently or with close attention — see APPLY 2

adduce *vb* to give as an example — see QUOTE 1

add up (to) *vb* **1** to be the same in meaning or effect — see AMOUNT (TO) 2
2 to have a total of — see AMOUNT (TO) 1

adept *adj* having or showing exceptional knowledge, experience, or skill in a field of endeavor — see PROFICIENT

adept *n* a person with a high level of knowledge or skill in a field — see EXPERT

adeptly *adv* in a skillful or expert manner — see WELL 3

adeptness *n* subtle or imaginative ability in inventing, devising, or executing something — see SKILL 1

adequacy *n* the quality or state of meeting one's needs adequately — see SUFFICIENCY

adequate *adj* of a level of quality that meets one's needs or standards ⟨this old computer is probably *adequate* if you just want to type a book report⟩
synonyms acceptable, all right, decent, fine, OK (*or* okay), passable, respectable, satisfactory, tolerable
related words agreeable, bearable, endurable, sufferable; average, fair, mediocre, middling, minimal, unexceptional; appropriate, correct, due, fitting, good, meet, proper, right, seemly, suitable, useful, worthy; gratifying, satisfying
near antonyms disreputable, improper, indecent, objectionable, unfit, unsuitable, unworthy, useless; bad, defective, faulty, imperfect, incomplete, lamentable, pitiful; dissatisfying, unsatisfying; insufficient, meager, mean, miserly, niggardly, poor, scanty, shabby, short, skimpy, spare, stingy; insufferable, intolerable, unbearable, unendurable; exceptional, exquisite, extreme, first-class, matchless, maximized, maximum, optimal, optimum, peerless, preeminent, superior, supreme, unmatched, unparalleled, unsurpassed
antonyms deficient, inadequate, lacking, unacceptable, unsatisfactory, wanting

adequately *adv* **1** in a satisfactory way — see WELL 1
2 in or to a degree or quantity that meets one's requirements or satisfaction — see ENOUGH 1

adhere *vb* to hold to something firmly as if by adhesion — see STICK 1

adhere (to) *vb* to give steadfast support to ⟨our coach *adheres to* the belief that we can win this game if we just have a positive attitude⟩
synonyms cling (to), hew (to), keep (to), stick (to *or* with)
related words cleave (to), hang on (to); back, confirm, defend, endorse (*also* indorse), espouse, support, uphold; accept, adopt, cherish, cultivate, embrace, follow, foster, heed
phrases abide by, live up to, stand by
near antonyms abandon, desert, forsake, give up, relinquish, spurn, surrender; abjure, disavow, disclaim, disown, recall, recant, reconsider, renege, renounce, retract, revoke, take back, unsay, withdraw
antonyms defect (from)

adherence *n* a physical sticking to as if by glue — see ADHESION

adherent *n* one who follows the opinions or teachings of another — see FOLLOWER

adhesion *n* a physical sticking to as if by glue

⟨mom prefers photo albums that keep the pictures in place by *adhesion* to the pages⟩

synonyms adherence, bonding

related words agglutination, clumping, cohesion; adhesiveness, attachment, cohesiveness, tenacity; cementing, glueing

adhesive *adj* being of such a thick consistency as to readily cling to objects upon contact — see STICKY 1

adhesive *n* a substance used to stick things together — see GLUE

adieu *n* an expression of good wishes at parting — see GOOD-BYE

adipose *adj* containing animal fat especially in unusual amounts — see FATTY

adiposity *n* the condition of having an excess of body fat — see CORPULENCE

adjacent *adj* having a border in common ⟨Crystal's house is *adjacent* to a wooded park⟩

synonyms abutting, adjoining, bordering, contiguous, flanking, fringing, joining, juxtaposed, skirting, touching, verging

related words close, closest, immediate, near, nearest, nearby, neighboring, next, next-door, nigh; attached, communicating, connecting, interconnecting, linked; bounding, embracing, encircling, enclosing, fencing, rimming, surrounding; marginal, peripheral, tangent, tangential

near antonyms apart, detached, free-standing, removed, separate, unattached, unconnected, unlinked; away, distant, far, far-off, farthest, remote; discontinuous, noncontinuous

antonyms nonadjacent

adjoin *vb* **1** to be adjacent to ⟨Colleen, whose bedroom *adjoins* her little brother's room, sometimes hears him talking in his sleep⟩

synonyms abut, border (on), flank, fringe, join, skirt, touch, verge (on)

related words attach (to), communicate (with), connect (with), link (with); bound, embrace, encircle, enclose (*also* inclose), fence, line, rim, surround; contact, converge, meet, neighbor

2 to join (something) to a mass, quantity, or number so as to bring about an overall increase — see ADD 1

adjoining *adj* having a border in common — see ADJACENT

adjourn *vb* to bring to a formal close for a period of time ⟨the meeting was *adjourned* by the chairperson until further notice⟩

synonyms recess, suspend

related words break off, discontinue, intermit, interrupt; defer, hold off, postpone, put off, reserve, shelve, table; abort, call off, cancel, dissolve, terminate; break up, close, conclude, wind up, wrap up

near antonyms inaugurate, launch, open; carry on, continue, draw out, extend, proceed, prolong; renew, reopen, resume; convene, convoke

adjudge *vb* to give an opinion about (something at issue or in dispute) — see JUDGE 1

adjudicate *vb* to give an opinion about (something at issue or in dispute) — see JUDGE 1

adjunct *n* something that is not necessary in itself but adds to the convenience or performance of the main piece of equipment — see ACCESSORY 1

adjure *vb* to issue orders to (someone) by right of authority — see COMMAND 1

adjust *vb* to change (something) so as to make it suitable for a new use or situation — see ADAPT

adjustable *adj* capable of being readily changed — see FLEXIBLE 1

adjutant *n* a person who helps a more skilled person — see HELPER

ad–lib *adj* made or done without previous thought or preparation — see EXTEMPORANEOUS

ad–lib *vb* to perform, make, or do without preparation — see IMPROVISE

administer *vb* **1** to give out (something) in appropriate amounts or to appropriate individuals ⟨the principal *administers* discipline fairly when students break the rules⟩

synonyms allocate, apportion, deal (out), dispense, distribute, dole (out), mete (out), parcel (out), portion, prorate

related words allot, allow, appropriate, assign, dish (out), divide, measure (out), ration, redistribute, split; bestow, disburse, furnish, issue, provide, share, supply; circulate, disperse, disseminate, scatter, spread; chip in, contribute, donate, pledge

near antonyms begrudge, deny, deprive (of), pinch, refuse, skimp, stint, withhold

2 to carry out effectively — see ENFORCE

3 to look after and make decisions about — see CONDUCT 1

administration *n* **1** lawful control over the affairs of a political unit (as a nation) — see RULE 2

2 the act or activity of looking after and making decisions about something — see CONDUCT 1

administrative *adj* suited for or relating to the directing of things — see EXECUTIVE

administrator *n* a person who manages or directs — see EXECUTIVE

admirable *adj* deserving of high regard or great approval ⟨it's *admirable* the way Kory helps her grandmother with chores and errands every Saturday⟩

synonyms commendable, creditable, laudable, meritorious, praiseworthy

related words awesome, distinctive, distinguished, excellent, honorable, noteworthy, noticeable, outstanding, reputable, worthy; invaluable, precious, priceless, valuable; delightful, enjoyable, pleasing, satisfying

near antonyms contemptible, deplorable, infamous, notorious, sorry, unlikable, unworthy, worthless; disgraceful, dishonorable, disreputable, low, mean, scandalous, seamy, shady, shameful, shocking, sordid, unsavory

antonyms censurable, discreditable, reprehensible

admiration *n* **1** a feeling of great approval and liking ⟨my *admiration* for Yoko increased when I discovered she had learned English only since coming to the U.S.⟩

synonyms appreciation, esteem, estimation, favor, regard, respect

related words acclamation, adoration, approbation, deference, homage, honor, praise, reverence, veneration, worship; delight, enjoyment, fancy; amazement, awe, wonder, wonderment

near antonyms condemnation, disapproval, disdain, opprobrium, scorn; disappointment, discontent, disenchantment, disgruntlement, disillusionment, displeasure, indignation, unhappiness; aversion, contempt, disgust, dislike, disregard, distaste

antonyms disfavor

2 the rapt attention and deep emotion caused by the sight of something extraordinary — see WONDER 2

admire *vb* to think very highly or favorably of ⟨I *admire* the way you handled such a touchy situation⟩
synonyms appreciate, esteem, regard, respect
related words acclaim, accredit, applaud, approve, commend, compliment, credit, praise; delight (in), drink (in), enjoy, relish, revel (in), savor; dig, fancy, favor, groove (on), like, love; adore, deify, idolize, revere, reverence, venerate, worship; cherish, prize, treasure, value
phrases set store by (*or* on)
near antonyms condemn, decry, deplore, disapprove, discount, discountenance, disdain, disfavor, dislike, dismiss, disregard, frown (on), scorn

admiring *adj* expressing approval — see FAVORABLE 1

admissible *adj* that may be permitted — see PERMISSIBLE

admission *n* **1** an open declaration of something (as a fault or the commission of an offense) about oneself — see CONFESSION
2 the means or right of entering or participating in — see ENTRANCE 1

admit *vb* to accept the truth or existence of (something) usually reluctantly ⟨Eliza readily *admitted* she hadn't read the assignment⟩ ⟨you can't bring yourself to *admit* your mistakes⟩
synonyms acknowledge, agree, allow, concede, confess, grant, own (up)
related words disburden, unburden, unload; affirm, avow, confirm, profess; accept, recognize, yield; announce, break, broadcast, communicate, declare, disclose, divulge, impart, publish, reveal, spill, tell, unveil; betray, blab, expose, give away, inform, leak, rat, squeal, talk, tattle, tip off, warn, wise up; breathe, whisper
near antonyms disallow, disavow, disclaim, disown; contradict, dispute, gainsay, negate, negative; rebut, refute, reject, repudiate; conceal, cover (up), hide, obscure, veil
antonyms deny

admittance *n* the means or right of entering or participating in — see ENTRANCE 1

admixture *n* a distinct entity formed by the combining of two or more different things — see BLEND

admonish *vb* to criticize (someone) usually gently so as to correct a fault — see REBUKE 1

admonishing *adj* serving as or offering a warning — see CAUTIONARY

admonition *n* the act or an instance of telling beforehand of danger or risk — see WARNING 1

admonitory *adj* serving as or offering a warning — see CAUTIONARY

adolescent *adj* **1** being in the early stage of life, growth, or development — see YOUNG
2 having or showing the annoying qualities (as silliness) associated with children — see CHILDISH
3 lacking in adult experience or maturity — see CALLOW

adopt *vb* to take for one's own use (something originated by another) ⟨the family *adopted* the American tradition of having turkey for Thanksgiving after they moved to the U.S.⟩
synonyms borrow, embrace, take up
related words domesticate, naturalize; appropriate, arrogate, take over, usurp; absorb, assimilate, incorporate; cherish, prize, treasure; cultivate, follow, heed, honor; use, utilize; bring up, foster, nurture, raise, rear; affect, assume, copy, imitate, pretend, put on, simulate
near antonyms abandon, forsake, give up, relinquish, surrender; abjure, abnegate, disown; reject, renounce, repudiate, spurn; discard, jettison, junk, throw away, throw out

adorable *adj* having qualities that tend to make one loved — see LOVABLE

adore *vb* **1** to feel passion, devotion, or tenderness for — see LOVE 2
2 to love or admire too much — see IDOLIZE
3 to offer honor or respect to (someone) as a divine power — see WORSHIP 1
4 to take pleasure in — see ENJOY 1

adoring *adj* **1** feeling or showing love — see LOVING
2 reflecting great admiration or devotion — see WORSHIPFUL

adorn *vb* to make more attractive by adding something that is beautiful or becoming — see DECORATE

adorning *adj* serving to add beauty — see DECORATIVE

adornment *n* something that decorates or beautifies — see DECORATION 1

adroit *adj* accomplished with trained ability — see SKILLFUL

adroitness *n* **1** mental skill or quickness — see DEXTERITY 1
2 subtle or imaginative ability in inventing, devising, or executing something — see SKILL 1

adulate *vb* **1** to love or admire too much — see IDOLIZE
2 to praise too much — see FLATTER 1

adulation *n* **1** excessive admiration of or devotion to a person — see WORSHIP
2 excessive praise — see FLATTERY

adulatory *adj* **1** overly or insincerely flattering — see FULSOME
2 reflecting great admiration or devotion — see WORSHIPFUL

adult *adj* fully grown or developed — see MATURE 1

adult *n* a fully grown person ⟨at the beach, the *adults* sat under broad umbrellas while the children splashed in the water⟩
synonyms grown-up
related words ancient, elder, graybeard, oldster, old-timer, senior, senior citizen
near antonyms kid, moppet, tad, toddler, tot, tyke; baby, infant; adolescent, juvenile, minor, youngster, youth; preteen, teenager, teenybopper
antonyms child

adulterant *n* something that is or that makes impure — see IMPURITY

adulterate *vb* to alter (something) for the worse with the addition of foreign or lower-grade substances ⟨the company was fined for *adulterating* its "all beef" frankfurters with cereal⟩
synonyms dilute, thin, water (down), weaken
related words befoul, contaminate, corrupt, defile, dirty, foul, infect, poison, pollute, soil, spoil, sully, taint; cheapen, debase, degrade; manipulate, misrepresent, tamper (with); counterfeit, fake, falsify, fudge; doctor, spike
near antonyms fertilize, lard; augment, supplement; clarify, clean, cleanse, distill, filter, flush, leach, pasteurize, purge, purify, refine; better, enhance, improve
antonyms enrich, fortify, richen, strengthen

adulterated *adj* containing foreign or lower-grade substances — see IMPURE
adulthood *n* the state of being fully grown or developed — see MATURITY
advance *n* **1** forward movement in time or place ⟨during her long convalescence, Penny was barely aware of the *advance* of the seasons⟩
synonyms advancement, furtherance, going, headway, march, onrush, passage, process, procession, progress, progression
related words current, drift, flow, flux, stream, way; advent, approach, arrival, coming, nearing; bound, jump, leap, step, stride; impetus, momentum
near antonyms backwash, ebb, reflux; retraction, retreat, return, reversal, reverse; about-face, turnabout, turnaround
antonyms recession, regression, retrogression
2 an instance of notable progress in the development of knowledge, technology, or skill ⟨with her new violin teacher, Nadia has made noticeable *advances* in her technique in just a few weeks⟩
synonyms advancement, breakthrough, enhancement, improvement, refinement
related words amelioration, boost, heightening, increase, melioration, strengthening, upgrade, uplift, upswing, uptrend, upturn; betterment, evolution, maturation, perfection, ripening; civilization, edification, education, enlightenment; renaissance, renascence, revival; discovery, find, windfall; innovation, invention
near antonyms breakdown, collapse, crash; hindrance, impediment, stumbling block; decline, decrease, deterioration, diminishment, failing, flagging, languishment, lapse, lessening, reduction, sinking, slowing, weakening, worsening; detriment, disablement, drawback, glitch, impairment, shortcoming
antonyms setback
advance *vb* **1** to give to another for temporary use with the understanding that it or a like thing will be returned — see LEND
2 to help the growth or development of — see FOSTER 1
3 to move forward along a course — see GO 1
4 to move higher in rank or position — see PROMOTE 1
5 to set before the mind for consideration — see PROPOSE 1
6 to move closer to — see COME 1
advanced *adj* **1** being far along in development ⟨an *advanced* civilization, among the first anywhere to use the plow, developed on the banks of the Nile River thousands of years ago⟩
synonyms developed, evolved, high, higher, improved, progressive, refined
related words full-blown, full-fledged, full-grown, full-scale; aged, grown, mature, matured, perfected, ripe, ripened; civilized, educated, enhanced, enlightened; contemporary, latest, modern, newest, newfangled, new-fashioned, novel, recent, up-to-date; early, precocious
near antonyms green, immature, underdeveloped, undersized, underweight, unripe, unripened; uncivilized, uneducated; early, primeval, primordial; antediluvian, antiquated, Neanderthal, oldfangled, old-fashioned
antonyms backward, low, lower, nonprogressive, primitive, retarded, rudimentary, undeveloped
2 being at a higher level than average — see HIGH 2
advancement *n* **1** a raising or a state of being raised to a higher rank or position ⟨Paul's rapid *advancement* in the company came as no surprise to those who knew he was the president's nephew⟩
synonyms ascent, elevation, preferment, promotion, rise, upgrade
related words aggrandizement, ennoblement, exaltation, glorification
near antonyms deposition, dethronement, dismissal, expulsion, impeachment, ouster, overthrow, removal, suspension, unmaking, unseating; downfall, fall
antonyms abasement, demotion, downgrade, reduction
2 an instance of notable progress in the development of knowledge, technology, or skill — see ADVANCE 2
3 forward movement in time or place — see ADVANCE 1
advantage *n* **1** the more favorable condition or position in a competition ⟨your experience volunteering at the hospital will put you at an *advantage* when you're applying for a job there⟩
synonyms better, drop, edge, jump, upper hand, vantage
related words allowance, head start, lead, margin, odds, start; ascendancy, command, dominance, mastery, predominance, superiority, supremacy, transcendence; favoritism, nepotism, precedence, preference, privilege, seniority; break, foothold, opportunity
near antonyms detriment, drawback, penalty, stranglehold; disparity, imbalance, inequality, unevenness; disability, impairment, shortcoming
antonyms disadvantage, handicap, liability
2 a thing that helps — see HELP 2
advantageous *adj* conferring benefits; promoting or contributing to personal or social well-being — see BENEFICIAL
advent *n* the act of coming upon a scene — see ARRIVAL
adventitious *adj* not being a vital part of or belonging to something — see EXTRINSIC
adventure *n* an exciting or noteworthy event that one experiences firsthand ⟨our quiet hike turned into quite an *adventure* when we encountered a bear and her cub⟩
synonyms experience, happening, time
related words escapade, lark; act, action, deed, doing, exploit; episode, occasion; baptism, ordeal, test, trial, tribulation; enterprise, risk, venture; expedition, exploration, feat, mission, performance, quest, stunt
near antonyms bore, bummer, bust, drag
adventure *vb* to place in danger — see ENDANGER
adventuresome *adj* inclined or willing to take risks — see BOLD 1
adventurous *adj* inclined or willing to take risks — see BOLD 1
adversary *n* **1** one that is hostile toward another — see ENEMY
2 one that takes a position opposite another in a competition or conflict — see OPPONENT 1
adverse *adj* **1** opposed to one's interests ⟨all the *adverse* publicity really caused the movie star's popularity to suffer⟩
synonyms counter, disadvantageous, hostile, in-

imical, negative, prejudicial, unfavorable, unfriendly, unsympathetic
related words bad, baleful, baneful, evil; damaging, deleterious, destructive, detrimental, fatal, harmful, hurtful, injurious, lethal, murderous, poisonous, ruinous, threatening, troublesome, unhealthy, wounding; dangerous, hazardous, imperiling, jeopardizing, parlous, perilous, risky, unsafe; defamatory, detractive, offensive, scathing, slanderous; antagonistic, antipathetic, inhospitable, intolerant, uncongenial, uncooperative; competing, conflicting, counteracting, countering, opposing, resistant, resisting
near antonyms beneficial, good, helpful, propitious, useful; harmless, innocent, innocuous, inoffensive, nondestructive, nonfatal, nonlethal, nonthreatening; unresisting, unresistant; tolerant, understanding; agreeable, affable, amiable, amicable, benign, benignant, congenial, cordial, complying, friendly, hospitable
antonyms advantageous, favorable, friendly, positive, supportive, sympathetic, well-disposed
2 causing or capable of causing harm — see HARMFUL

adversity *n* **1** bad luck or an example of this — see MISFORTUNE
2 something that is a cause for suffering or special effort especially in the attainment of a goal — see DIFFICULTY 1

advert (to) *vb* to make reference to or speak about briefly but specifically — see MENTION 1

advertise *vb* to make known openly or publicly — see ANNOUNCE

advertisement *n* a published statement informing the public of a matter of general interest — see ANNOUNCEMENT

advice *n* an opinion suggesting a wise or proper course of action <Stephanie got some good *advice* from the vet about dealing with her dog's habit of chasing cars>
synonyms counsel, guidance
related words recommendation, suggestion; hint, pointer, tip; data, feedback, information; answer, solution; advisement, consideration, thought; admonishment, admonition, caution, cautioning, expostulation, remonstration, urging, warning; judgment (*or* judgement), observation, verdict; assistance, briefing, coaching, direction, instruction, mentoring, priming, prompting, teaching, tutoring; interference, kibitzing, meddling; moralizing, pontificating, preaching; exhortation, lecture, lesson, sermon, speech

advisable *adj* suitable for bringing about a desired result under the circumstances — see EXPEDIENT

advise *vb* **1** to give advice to <a popular guidance counselor who has been *advising* students about their college plans for two decades>
synonyms counsel
related words admonish, caution, warn; brief, clue (in), fill in, inform, wise (up); coach, direct, lead, guide, instruct, mentor, teach, tutor; acquaint, apprise, familiarize; convince, encourage, induce, persuade, talk (into); beg, exhort, implore, prevail (upon), urge; propose, recommend, suggest
2 to put forward as one's choice for a wise or proper course of action <she *advised* calling ahead for a reservation at the new restaurant>
synonyms counsel, recommend, suggest
related words advocate, back, favor, support; exhort, urge; advance, propose, submit
3 to exchange viewpoints or seek advice for the purpose of finding a solution to a problem — see CONFER 2
4 to give information to — see ENLIGHTEN 1

advised *adj* decided on as a result of careful thought — see DELIBERATE 1

adviser *or* **advisor** *n* a person who gives advice especially professionally — see CONSULTANT

advocate *n* **1** a person who actively supports or favors a cause — see EXPONENT
2 a person whose profession is to conduct lawsuits for clients or to advise about legal rights and obligations — see LAWYER

advocate *vb* to promote the interests or cause of — see SUPPORT 1

aegis *n* means or method of defending — see DEFENSE 1

aeon *or* **eon** *n* a long or seemingly long period of time — see AGE 2

aerodrome *n, British* a place from which aircraft operate that usually has paved runways and a terminal — see AIRPORT

affability *n* the state or quality of having a pleasant or agreeable manner in socializing with others — see AMIABILITY 1

affable *adj* **1** having a relaxed, casual manner — see EASYGOING 1
2 having an easygoing and pleasing manner especially in social situations — see AMIABLE
3 showing a natural kindness and courtesy especially in social situations — see GRACIOUS 1

affair *n* **1** a brief romantic relationship <an *affair* between two teenagers spending the summer at the same beach resort>
synonyms love affair, romance
related words amour, intrigue; attachment, infatuation; entanglement, fling, flirtation; liaison, passion
2 a social gathering — see PARTY 1
3 something produced by physical or intellectual effort — see PRODUCT 1
4 something that happens — see EVENT 1
5 something to be dealt with — see MATTER 2

[1]**affect** *vb* **1** to act upon (a person or a person's feelings) so as to cause a response <Gary claims that scary movies don't *affect* him in the least>
synonyms impact, impress, influence, move, strike, sway, tell (on), touch
related words bias, color; inspire, stir; carry, engage, interest, involve, penetrate, pierce; afflict, agitate, bother, discomfort, discompose, disquiet, distress, disturb, fluster, harass, harry, perturb, pester, plague, smite, strain, stress, trouble, try, upset, worry, wring; allure, attract, bewitch, captivate, charm, dazzle, enchant
phrases get to
near antonyms bore, jade, pall, tire, weary
2 to be the business or affair of — see CONCERN 2

[2]**affect** *vb* to present a false appearance of — see FEIGN

affectation *n* the quality or state of appearing or trying to appear more important or more valuable than is the case — see PRETENSE 1

affected *adj* **1** lacking in natural or spontaneous quality — see ARTIFICIAL 1
2 self-consciously trying to present an appearance of grandeur or importance — see PRETENTIOUS 1

affectedness *n* the quality or state of appearing or trying to appear more important or more valuable than is the case — see PRETENSE 1

affecting *adj* having the power to affect the feelings or sympathies — see MOVING

[1]**affection** *n* a feeling of strong or constant regard for and dedication to someone — see LOVE 1

[2]**affection** *n* an abnormal state that disrupts a plant's or animal's normal bodily functioning — see DISEASE

affectionate *adj* feeling or showing love — see LOVING

affianced *adj* pledged in marriage — see ENGAGED

affiliate *n* a local unit of an organization — see CHAPTER

affiliated *adj* having a close connection like that between family members — see RELATED

affiliation *n* the state of having shared interests or efforts (as in social or business matters) — see ASSOCIATION 1

affirm *vb* **1** to state as a fact usually forcefully — see CLAIM 1
2 to state clearly and strongly — see ASSERT 1

affirmation *n* a solemn and often public declaration of the truth or existence of something — see PROTESTATION

affirmative *adj* showing or expressing acceptance or approval — see POSITIVE

affix *vb* to cause (something) to hold to another — see FASTEN 1

afflict *vb* to cause persistent suffering to ⟨the South was *afflicted* by a severe drought⟩ ⟨he's been *afflicted* by nightmares ever since the accident⟩
synonyms agonize, bedevil, curse, harrow, martyr, persecute, plague, rack, torment, torture
related words assail, attack, beset, set upon; badger, dog, hound, ride; agitate, annoy, bother, distress, disturb, harass, harry, irk, molest, pester; discomfort, discompose, disquiet, fluster, perturb, strain, stress, trouble, try, upset, vex, worry; crush, oppress, overpower, overwhelm, smite, strike, tyrannize; pain, prick, stab, sting, wring
near antonyms abet, aid, assist, help; deliver, release, relieve, reprieve; comfort, console, solace, soothe, succor

afflicting *adj* hard to accept or bear especially emotionally — see BITTER 2

affliction *n* **1** a state of great suffering of body or mind — see DISTRESS 1
2 deep sadness especially for the loss of someone or something loved — see SORROW

affluent *adj* having goods, property, or money in abundance — see RICH 1

affray *n* a rough and often noisy fight usually involving several people — see BRAWL 1

affright *vb* to strike with fear — see FRIGHTEN

affrighted *adj* filled with fear or dread — see AFRAID 1

affront *n* an act or expression showing scorn and usually intended to hurt another's feelings — see INSULT

affront *vb* to cause hurt feelings or deep resentment in — see INSULT

aficionado *n* a person with a strong and habitual liking for something — see FAN

afield *adv* off the desired or intended path or course — see WRONG 1

afire *adj* being on fire — see ABLAZE 1

aflame *adj* being on fire — see ABLAZE 1

aflutter *adj* feeling or showing uncomfortable feelings of uncertainty — see NERVOUS 1

afoot *adj* being in progress or development — see ONGOING 1

afore *adv, chiefly dialect* so as to precede something in order of time — see AHEAD 1

afore *prep, chiefly dialect* **1** earlier than — see BEFORE 1
2 preceding in space — see BEFORE 2

afraid *adj* **1** filled with fear or dread ⟨Melissa is *afraid* of flying, so she takes a train from Boston to visit her brother in Chicago⟩
synonyms affrighted, aghast, alarmed, fearful, frightened, horrified, scared, spooked, terrified, terrorized
related words fainthearted, fearsome, shrinking, shy, timid, timorous, tremulous; agitated, anxious, apprehensive, disconcerted, disquieted, disturbed, jittery, jumpy, nervous, panicky, perturbed, skittish, uneasy, upset, worried; appalled, dismayed, shocked, startled; cowed, daunted, intimidated, unnerved; coward, cowardly, craven, gutless, lily-livered, pusillanimous; careful, cautious, heedful, prudent, unadventurous, wary
near antonyms adventuresome, adventurous, audacious, bold, daredevil, daring, dashing, gutsy, plucky, spirited, spunky, venturesome, venturous; brave, courageous, gallant, hardy, heroic, intrepid, lionhearted, manful, stalwart, stout, stouthearted, valiant, valorous; assured, collected, composed, confident, cool, sanguine, sure, unperturbed; dauntless, resolute, undaunted
antonyms fearless, unafraid
2 having doubts about the wisdom of doing something — see HESITANT

afresh *adv* yet another time — see AGAIN 1

aft *adv* near, toward, or in the stern of a ship or the tail of an aircraft ⟨after transferring the controls to the copilot, the captain went *aft* to see what the disturbance was⟩
synonyms abaft, astern
related words after, back, backward, behind, posteriorly, rearward (*also* rearwards), rearwardly
near antonyms anteriorly; ahead, before
antonyms fore, forward

after *adj* being, occurring, or carried out at a time after something else — see SUBSEQUENT

after *adv* following in time or place ⟨upon seeing *The Nutcracker* for the first time, and for a long time *after*, Irma wanted to play the part of the Mouse King⟩
synonyms afterward (*or* afterwards), later, subsequently, thereafter
related words next; by and by, hereafter, presently, since, soon, then, thereupon
near antonyms antecedently, formerly; heretofore, theretofore
antonyms afore [*chiefly dialect*], before, beforehand, earlier, previously

after *prep* subsequent to in time or order ⟨the high school band came right *after* the mayor in the parade⟩
synonyms behind, following
related words next; since
near antonyms of, to, toward (*or* towards)
antonyms afore [*chiefly dialect*], ahead of, before, ere, previous to, prior to

aftereffect *n* a condition or occurrence traceable to a cause — see EFFECT 1

afterlife *n* unending existence after death — see ETERNITY 2

aftermath *n* a condition or occurrence traceable to a cause — see EFFECT 1

afterward *or* **afterwards** *adv* following in time or place — see AFTER

again *adv* **1** yet another time ⟨now I have to mop the floor *again* because you didn't wipe your feet⟩
synonyms afresh, anew, over
related words always, constantly, continuously, endlessly, ever, evermore, perpetually; frequently, often; recurrently, repeatedly; freshly, newly
near antonyms ne'er, never
antonyms nevermore
2 in addition to what has been said — see MORE 1
3 just the opposite being true — see CONTRARIWISE

against *prep* in or into contact with ⟨he leaned *against* the fence and it collapsed⟩ ⟨unwittingly rubbed his leg *against* some poison ivy⟩
synonyms on, upon
related words alongside, next, next to

agape *adj* having or showing signs of eagerly awaiting something — see EXPECTANT 1

age *n* **1** an extent of time associated with a particular person or thing ⟨the Bronze *Age* marks the beginning of the use of metal by ancient peoples⟩
synonyms day, epoch, era, period, time
related words cycle, generation, year; span, spell, stretch, while
2 a long or seemingly long period of time ⟨it took *ages* for the clerk to ring up three items⟩
synonyms aeon (*or* eon), cycle, eternity
related words infinity; lifetime
near antonyms flash, instant, jiffy, minute, moment, second, trice, twinkle, twinkling, wink; microsecond, nanosecond

age *vb* to become mature — see MATURE

aged *adj* **1** being of advanced years and especially past middle age — see ELDERLY
2 dating or surviving from the distant past — see ANCIENT 1

agency *n* something used to achieve an end — see AGENT 1

agenda *n* a listing of things to be presented or considered (as at a concert or play) — see PROGRAM 1

agent *n* **1** something used to achieve an end ⟨the whitening *agent* in the detergent is chlorine bleach⟩ ⟨the Church has been the traditional *agent* for social justice in impoverished countries⟩
synonyms agency, instrument, instrumentality, machinery, means, medium, organ, vehicle
related words determinant, expedient, factor, influence, ingredient, mechanism, tool; activator, catalyst, driver, energizer, executor, generator, instigator, launcher, mover, power, stimulus, trigger
2 a person who acts or does business for another ⟨the sports *agent* negotiated a record-breaking contract for the baseball player⟩
synonyms attorney, commissary, delegate, deputy, envoy, factor, procurator, proxy, representative
related words ambassador, emissary, foreign minister, legate, minister; alternate, backup, pinch hitter, relief, replacement, stand-in, sub, substitute, surrogate, understudy; informer, operative, spy; broker, distributor, manager; arbiter, arbitrator, go-between, intercessor, intermediary, interposer, liaison, mediator, middleman; mouthpiece, spokesperson

age–old *adj* dating or surviving from the distant past — see ANCIENT 1

agglomerate *vb* to form into a round compact mass — see WAD

aggrandize *vb* **1** to enhance the status of — see EXALT
2 to make greater in size, amount, or number — see INCREASE 1

aggravate *vb* to disturb the peace of mind of (someone) especially by repeated disagreeable acts — see IRRITATE 1

aggravating *adj* **1** causing annoyance — see ANNOYING

aggravation *n* **1** something that is a source of irritation — see ANNOYANCE 3
2 the act of making unwelcome intrusions upon another — see ANNOYANCE 1
3 the feeling of impatience or anger caused by another's repeated disagreeable acts — see ANNOYANCE 2

aggregate *n* a complete amount of something — see WHOLE

aggression *n* **1** an inclination to fight or quarrel — see BELLIGERENCE
2 the act or action of setting upon with force or violence — see ATTACK 1

aggressive *adj* **1** having or showing a bold forcefulness in the pursuit of a goal ⟨if you don't take a more *aggressive* approach to this yard pretty soon, the weeds are going to take over completely⟩
synonyms ambitious, assertive, enterprising, fierce, go-getting, high-pressure, in-your-face, militant, self-assertive
related words dynamic, energetic, gung ho, hustling, scrappy, strenuous, vigorous; emphatic, obtrusive; adventuresome, adventurous, venturesome, venturous; audacious, bold, brash, brassy, cheeky, cocksure, cocky, confident, determined, forward, impudent, insolent, overconfident, presumptuous, unapologetic, unsubdued, unyielding; dominating, domineering, imperious, lordly, magisterial, overbearing
near antonyms easygoing, laid-back, relaxed; acquiescent, compliant, deferential, resigned, submissive, yielding; cowering, cringing, groveling (*or* grovelling), shrinking; bashful, diffident, meek, mousy (*or* mousey), overmodest, passive, quiet, reserved, retiring, shy, subdued, timid, unobtrusive
antonyms low-pressure, unaggressive, unambitious, unassertive, unenterprising
2 feeling or displaying eagerness to fight — see BELLIGERENT
3 marked by or uttered with forcefulness — see EMPHATIC 1

aggressiveness *n* **1** readiness to engage in daring or difficult activity — see ENTERPRISE 2
2 the quality or state of being forceful (as in expression) — see VEHEMENCE 1
3 an inclination to fight or quarrel — see BELLIGERENCE

aggressor *n* one that starts armed conflict against another especially without reasonable cause ⟨the countries formed an alliance to deter potential *aggressors*⟩
synonyms invader, raider
related words initiator, instigator; ambuscader, assailant, attacker, pillager, plunderer; hawk, militarist, warmonger; belligerent, combatant
near antonyms defender; dove, pacifist, peacemaker; nonbelligerent

aggrieved *adj* having a feeling that one has been wronged or thwarted in one's ambitions — see DISCONTENTED
aghast *adj* filled with fear or dread — see AFRAID 1
agile *adj* moving easily — see GRACEFUL 1
agility *n* ease and grace in physical activity — see DEXTERITY 2
aging *adj* being of advanced years and especially past middle age — see ELDERLY
agitate *vb* **1** to cause (as a liquid) to move about in a circle especially repeatedly — see STIR 1
2 to trouble the mind of; to make uneasy — see DISTURB 1
3 to make a series of small irregular or violent movements — see SHAKE 1
agitated *adj* **1** being in a state of increased activity or agitation — see FEVERISH 1
2 feeling overwhelming fear or worry — see FRANTIC 1
agitating *adj* marked by or causing agitation or uncomfortable feelings — see NERVOUS 2
agitation *n* **1** a state of wildly excited activity or emotion — see FRENZY
2 an uneasy state of mind usually over the possibility of an anticipated misfortune or trouble — see ANXIETY 1
agitator *n* a person who stirs up public feelings especially of discontent ⟨a political *agitator* who led an unsuccessful revolt against the government⟩
synonyms demagogue (*also* demagog), exciter, firebrand, fomenter, incendiary, inciter, instigator, rabble-rouser
related words demonstrator, marcher, objector, picketer, protester (*or* protestor); advocate, champion, exponent, persuader, promoter, proponent, reformer, supporter; alarmist, extremist, insurgent, insurrectionist, radical, rebel, revolter, revolutionary, revolutionist, subversive, troublemaker
aglow *adj* having or being an outward sign of good feelings (as of love, confidence, or happiness) — see RADIANT 1
agog *adj* **1** having or showing signs of eagerly awaiting something — see EXPECTANT 1
2 showing urgent desire or interest — see EAGER
agonize *vb* **1** to cause persistent suffering to — see AFFLICT
2 to feel deep sadness or mental pain — see GRIEVE
agonizing *adj* **1** hard to accept or bear especially emotionally — see BITTER 2
2 intensely or unbearably painful — see EXCRUCIATING 1
3 causing intense mental or physical distress — see SHARP 2
agonizingly *adv* with feelings of bitterness or grief — see HARD 2
agony *n* **1** a situation or state that causes great suffering and unhappiness — see HELL 2
2 a state of great suffering of body or mind — see DISTRESS 1
3 a sudden intense expression of strong feeling — see OUTBURST 1
agrarian *adj* engaged in or concerned with agriculture — see AGRICULTURAL
agree *vb* **1** to have or come to the same opinion or point of view ⟨since we couldn't *agree*, we tossed a coin to decide the matter⟩
synonyms coincide, concur
related words accede (to), accept, acquiesce, assent (to), comply (with), consent (to), go (by), subscribe; affiliate, ally, associate, unite; collaborate, cooperate, get along
phrases see eye to eye
near antonyms clash, collide, conflict; bicker, counter, dispute, dissent, diverge, fall out, object, oppose, protest, quarrel, resist, rival; dissociate, separate, split
antonyms differ, disagree
2 to accept the truth or existence of (something) usually reluctantly — see ADMIT
3 to be in agreement on every point — see CHECK 1
4 to form a pleasing relationship — see HARMONIZE 1
agreeable *adj* **1** being to one's liking — see SATISFACTORY 1
2 giving pleasure or contentment to the mind or senses — see PLEASANT
3 having an easygoing and pleasing manner especially in social situations — see AMIABLE
4 having or marked by agreement in feeling or action — see HARMONIOUS 3
agreeableness *n* the state or quality of having a pleasant or agreeable manner in socializing with others — see AMIABILITY 1
agreeably *adv* in a pleasing way — see WELL 5
agreement *n* **1** the act or fact of being of one opinion about something ⟨I only had the energy to nod in *agreement* when Cheryl said we'd never worked so hard in all our lives⟩
synonyms accord, concurrence, consensus, unanimity, unison
related words accession, assent, consent; acceptance, acquiescence, compliance, concession, conformity; approbation, approval, favor; alliance, collaboration, collusion, complicity, conspiracy; concord, consonance, harmony, oneness, solidarity, understanding, union; empathy, rapport, sympathy
near antonyms conflict, discord, dissension; opposition, resistance; disapprobation, disapproval, disfavor
antonyms disagreement, dissent
2 an arrangement about action to be taken ⟨we finally reached an *agreement* regarding a fair division of the housework⟩
synonyms accord, bargain, compact, contract, convention, covenant, deal, pact, settlement, understanding
related words charter, treaty; pledge, promise; alliance, association, league, partnership; acceptance, approval, assent, concurrence, consent, OK (*or* okay)
3 a state of consistency — see CONFORMITY 1
agricultural *adj* engaged in or concerned with agriculture ⟨he grew up in an *agricultural* community⟩
synonyms agrarian, farming
related words pastoral, rural
near antonyms metropolitan, urban; industrial, industrialized
antonyms nonagricultural
agriculture *n* the science or occupation of cultivating the soil, producing crops, and raising livestock ⟨the forest was cut down, and the land given over to *agriculture*⟩
synonyms farming, husbandry
related words agronomy; animal husbandry
agriculturist *or* **agriculturalist** *n* a person who cul-

tivates the land and grows crops on it — see FARMER

agronomist *n* a person who cultivates the land and grows crops on it — see FARMER

aground *adj* resting on the shore or bottom of a body of water ⟨the villagers came to stare at the foreign ship that was *aground* on their beach and at the strangely dressed sailors on board⟩
synonyms beached, grounded, stranded
related words landed; alongshore
near antonyms offshore
antonyms afloat

ah *interj* how surprising, doubtful, or unbelievable — see NO

aha *interj* how surprising, doubtful, or unbelievable — see NO

ahead *adv* **1** so as to precede something in order of time ⟨we were cautioned not to fill out any of the test answers *ahead* of time⟩ ⟨call *ahead* for reservations⟩
synonyms afore [*chiefly dialect*], antecedently, anteriorly, before, beforehand, previously
related words formerly
phrases in advance
near antonyms behind, by and by, next, presently, subsequently
antonyms after, afterward (*or* afterwards), later
2 toward a point ahead in space or time — see ONWARD 1
3 toward or at a point lying in advance in space or time — see ALONG

ahead of *prep* **1** earlier than — see BEFORE 1
2 preceding in space — see BEFORE 2

aid *n* **1** a person who helps a more skilled person — see HELPER
2 a thing that helps — see HELP 2
3 an act or instance of helping — see HELP 1

aid *vb* to provide (someone) with what is useful or necessary to achieve an end — see HELP 1

aide *n* a person who helps a more skilled person — see HELPER

ailing *adj* **1** chronically or repeatedly suffering from poor health — see SICKLY 1
2 temporarily suffering from a disorder of the body — see SICK 1

ailment *n* an abnormal state that disrupts a plant's or animal's normal bodily functioning — see DISEASE

aim *n* something that one hopes or intends to accomplish — see GOAL

aim *vb* **1** to point or turn (something) toward a target or goal ⟨the anti-drug campaign was *aimed* primarily at preteens⟩
synonyms bend, cast, direct, head, level, set, train
related words bear, face; concentrate, focus; incline, orient, steer
near antonyms avert, curve, deflect, detour, divert, rechannel, shunt, sidetrack
2 to have in mind as a purpose or goal — see INTEND

aimless *adj* lacking a definite plan, purpose, or pattern — see RANDOM

aimlessly *adv* without definite aim, direction, rule, or method — see HIT OR MISS

air *n* **1** a rhythmic series of musical tones arranged to give a pleasing effect — see MELODY
2 a slight or gentle movement of air — see BREEZE 1
3 a special quality or impression associated with something — see AURA
4 ***airs*** *pl* a display of emotion or behavior that is insincere or intended to deceive — see MASQUERADE

air *vb* to make known (as an idea, emotion, or opinion) — see EXPRESS 1

airdrome *n* a place from which aircraft operate that usually has paved runways and a terminal — see AIRPORT

airfield *n* a place from which aircraft operate that usually has paved runways and a terminal — see AIRPORT

airman *n* one who flies or is qualified to fly an aircraft or spacecraft — see PILOT

airport *n* a place from which aircraft operate that usually has paved runways and a terminal ⟨the *airport* nearest us has plane service on only one major airline⟩
synonyms aerodrome [*British*], airdrome, airfield
related words air base, heliport; airstrip, landing field, landing strip, runway; launchpad, pad

airy *adj* **1** resembling air in lightness ⟨Aunt Helen's lemon pies are famous for their *airy* meringues⟩
synonyms ethereal, fluffy, gossamer, gossamery, light
related words dainty, delicate, downy, feathery, flimsy, insubstantial, tender, wispy; buoyant, lighter-than-air, lightweight, rarefied, unsubstantial, weightless
near antonyms firm, solid, substantial; bulky, burdensome, cumbersome, hefty, hulking, lumpish, ponderous, unwieldy, weighty
antonyms heavy, leaden
2 having little weight — see [1]LIGHT 1
3 located at a greater height than average or usual — see HIGH 3

akin *adj* **1** having a close connection like that between family members — see RELATED
2 having qualities in common — see ALIKE

alacritous *adj* having or showing the ability to respond without delay or hesitation — see QUICK 1

alacrity *n* cheerful readiness to do something ⟨having just acquired his driver's license that morning, Sam agreed with *alacrity* to drive his cousin to the airport⟩
synonyms amenability, gameness, goodwill, willingness
related words celebrity, quickness, rapidity, speed, speediness, swiftness; dispatch, promptitude, promptness; ardor, avidity, eagerness, enthusiasm, exuberance, fervor, gusto, keenness, relish, zeal, zest; agreeableness, geniality, good-naturedness, heartiness, warmth; open-mindedness, receptivity, responsiveness
near antonyms leisureliness, pokiness, slowness, sluggishness; apathy, disinterestedness, halfheartedness, indifference, lukewarmness, perfunctoriness; delay, dilatoriness, doubt, equivocation, hesitance, hesitancy, hesitation, reluctance, reservation, uncertainty, vacillation; disinclination, indisposition, recalcitrance, resistance, unwillingness; antipathy, averseness, aversion

à la mode *also* **a la mode** *adj* being in the latest or current fashion — see STYLISH

alarm *n* **1** suspicion or fear of future harm or misfortune — see APPREHENSION 1
2 the act or an instance of telling beforehand of danger or risk — see WARNING 1
3 the emotion experienced in the presence or threat of danger — see FEAR

alarm *vb* to strike with fear — see FRIGHTEN

alarmed *adj* filled with fear or dread — see AFRAID 1

alarming *adj* causing fear — see FEARFUL 1

albeit *conj* in spite of the fact that — see ALTHOUGH

album *n* a collection of writings — see ANTHOLOGY

alcohol *n* a fermented or distilled beverage that can make a person drunk ⟨once he joined the swim team, Sergei never again touched *alcohol*⟩
synonyms booze, drink, grog, intoxicant, liquor, moonshine, spirits
related words ale, beer, mead, sake (*or* saki), table wine, wine; brandy, gin, mescal, rum, tequila, vodka, whiskey (*or* whisky)

alcove *n* a hollowed-out space in a wall — see NICHE 1

alert *adj* **1** paying close attention usually for the purpose of anticipating approaching danger or opportunity ⟨Susan needed to stay *alert* throughout the train ride so as not to miss her stop⟩
synonyms attentive, awake, open-eyed, vigilant, watchful, wide-awake
related words alive, aware, conscious, sensitive; heedful, mindful, observant, observing, sharp, sharp-eyed; sleepless, wakeful; careful, cautious, chary, wary; prepared, ready
phrases on guard, on the alert
near antonyms absent, absentminded, absorbed, abstracted, daydreaming, dazed, distracted, dreaming, dreamy, engrossed, faraway, insensible, oblivious, preoccupied; asleep, sleeping, unaware, unconscious, unknowing, unperceiving, unseeing, unwitting; careless, heedless, inattentive, unheeding, unmindful, unobservant, unobserving, unthinking, unwary; unprepared, unready
2 having or showing a close attentiveness to avoiding danger or trouble — see CAREFUL 1
3 having or showing quickness of mind — see INTELLIGENT 1
4 having or showing the ability to respond without delay or hesitation — see QUICK 1

alert *n* the act or an instance of telling beforehand of danger or risk — see WARNING 1

alert *vb* to give notice to beforehand especially of danger or risk — see WARN

alertness *n* **1** a close attentiveness to avoiding danger — see CAUTION 1
2 the act or state of being constantly attentive and responsive to signs of opportunity, activity, or danger — see VIGILANCE

alias *n* **1** a descriptive or familiar name given instead of or in addition to the one belonging to an individual — see NICKNAME
2 a fictitious or assumed name — see PSEUDONYM

alibi *n* an explanation that frees one from fault or blame — see EXCUSE

alien *adj* **1** being, relating to, or characteristic of a country other than one's own — see FOREIGN 1
2 not being a vital part of or belonging to something — see EXTRINSIC

alienate *vb* **1** to cause to change from friendly or loving to unfriendly or uncaring — see ESTRANGE
2 to give over the legal possession or ownership of — see TRANSFER 1

alienation *n* the loss of friendship or affection — see ESTRANGEMENT

alight *adj* filled with much light — see BRIGHT 2

alight *vb* to come to rest after descending from the air ⟨a flock of eight swans circled above, then *alighted* on the pond⟩
synonyms land, light, perch, roost, settle, touch down
related words belly-land, crash-land
near antonyms arise, ascend, climb, rise; float, fly, glide, plane, soar, wing; hang, hover
antonyms take off

alike *adj* having qualities in common ⟨all the houses in the neighborhood are *alike* in that they all have a one-car garage and a fenced-in backyard⟩
synonyms akin, analogous, comparable, correspondent, corresponding, like, matching, parallel, resembling, similar, such, suchlike
related words commensurate, proportionate; tantamount, virtual; allied, kindred, related; approaching, approximating, close, coextensive, coincident, conformable, conforming, consistent, consonant, equal, equivalent, identical, indistinguishable, interchangeable, same, selfsame, synonymous, twin; homogeneous, unchanging, uniform, unvaried, unvarying
phrases on the order of
near antonyms disparate, distinct, distinguishable; variable, varied, varying; imprecise, inaccurate, inexact; unallied, unconnected, unrelated
antonyms different, dissimilar, diverse, unlike

alike *adv* in like manner — see ALSO 1

alikeness *n* the quality or state of having many qualities in common — see SIMILARITY 1

alive *adj* **1** having or showing life ⟨after crashing into the plate glass window the little bird was not only still *alive*, it seemed merely dazed⟩
synonyms animate, breathing, live, living
related words active, animated, dynamic, lively, thriving, vibrant, vital, vivacious; current, existent, existing, extant, going, prevailing, surviving
near antonyms dying, fading, moribund; stillborn; absent, extinct, fallen, finished, gone, lapsed, lost, nonexistent, perished, terminated, vanished, wiped out; barren, desert
antonyms breathless, dead, deceased, defunct, departed, expired, inanimate, lifeless, nonliving
2 marked by much life, movement, or activity ⟨the mall was *alive* with holiday shoppers⟩
synonyms animated, astir, bustling, busy, buzzing, flourishing, humming, lively, thriving, vibrant
related words abounding, crowded, overflowing, populous, swarming, teeming, thronging
antonyms asleep, dead, inactive, lifeless, sleepy
3 being in effective operation — see ACTIVE 1
4 having being at the present time — see EXTANT 1
5 having specified facts or feelings actively impressed on the mind — see CONSCIOUS

all *adj* not divided or scattered among several areas of interest or concern — see WHOLE 1

all *adv* **1** to a full extent or degree — see FULLY 1
2 for each one — see APIECE

all *pron* every person — see EVERYBODY

Allah *n* the being worshipped as the creator and ruler of the universe — see DEITY 2

all–around *also* **all-round** *adj* **1** not limited or specialized in application or purpose — see GENERAL 4
2 relating to the main elements and not to specific details — see GENERAL 2
3 able to do many different kinds of things — see VERSATILE

allay *vb* **1** to free from distress or disturbance — see CALM 1
2 to make more bearable or less severe — see HELP 2

allege *vb* to state as a fact usually forcefully — see CLAIM 1

allegiance *n* adherence to something to which one is bound by a pledge or duty — see FIDELITY

allegory *n* a story intended to teach a basic truth or moral about life ⟨Dr. Seuss's story "The Sneetches" is an *allegory* about tolerance for people's differences⟩
synonyms fable, parable
related words morality play; legend, myth, narrative, tale

allergic *adj* having a natural dislike for something — see ANTIPATHETIC

allergy *n* a strong feeling of not liking or approving — see DISLIKE 1

alleviate *vb* to make more bearable or less severe — see HELP 2

alleviation *n* reduction of or freedom from pain — see EASE 1

alliance *n* **1** a formal agreement between two or more nations or peoples — see TREATY
2 an association of persons, parties, or states for mutual assistance and protection — see CONFEDERACY
3 the state of having shared interests or efforts (as in social or business matters) — see ASSOCIATION 1

allied *adj* having a close connection like that between family members — see RELATED

all–important *adj* impossible to do without — see ESSENTIAL 1

allocate *vb* **1** to give as a share or portion — see ALLOT
2 to give out (something) in appropriate amounts or to appropriate individuals — see ADMINISTER 1
3 to keep or intend for a special purpose — see DEVOTE 1

allocation *n* **1** a sum of money allotted for a specific use by official or formal action — see APPROPRIATION
2 the act or process of giving out something to each member of a group — see DISTRIBUTION 1

allot *vb* to give as a share or portion ⟨each speaker was *allotted* five minutes to present his or her opinion in the debate⟩
synonyms allocate, allow, apportion, assign, ration
related words deal, dispense, distribute, divide, dole (out), measure, mete (out), parcel (out), portion, prorate, reserve; accord, award, grant; chip in, contribute, donate
near antonyms begrudge, deny, deprive (of); keep, retain, stint, withhold; appropriate, arrogate, confiscate

allotment *n* **1** a sum of money allotted for a specific use by official or formal action — see APPROPRIATION
2 something belonging to, due to, or contributed by an individual member of a group — see SHARE 1

all–out *adj* **1** having no exceptions or restrictions — see ABSOLUTE 2
2 trying all possibilities — see EXHAUSTIVE

all out *adv* with all power or resources being used — see FULL BLAST

all over *adv* in every place or in all places — see EVERYWHERE

allow *vb* **1** to give permission for or to approve of ⟨flash photography is not *allowed* inside the church⟩
synonyms have, permit, suffer
related words authorize, commission, license (*also* licence); accede (to), acquiesce, agree (to), assent (to), consent (to), OK (*or* okay), warrant; accord, concede, grant, sanction, vouchsafe; admit, brook, condone, countenance, endure, support, tolerate
near antonyms hinder, impede, obstruct; censure, disallow, disapprove, deny, interdict, refuse, reject, revoke, suppress, withhold; deplore, discountenance, dislike, disfavor, frown (at *or* on); check, curb, repress, restrain
antonyms ban, enjoin, forbid, prohibit, proscribe, veto
2 to give permission to ⟨Cindy's parents sometimes *allow* her to take the bus by herself downtown⟩
synonyms let, permit, suffer
related words authorize, commission, empower, license (*also* licence); approve, endorse (*also* indorse), sanction; free, liberate, release; cater (to), give in (to), humor, indulge
near antonyms deter, discourage; bar, block, constrain, curb, frustrate, hold back, impede, inhibit, obstruct, prevent
antonyms enjoin, forbid, prohibit
3 to accept the truth or existence of (something) usually reluctantly — see ADMIT
4 to give as a share or portion — see ALLOT
5 to make able or possible — see ENABLE 1

allowable *adj* that may be permitted — see PERMISSIBLE

allowance *n* **1** something belonging to, due to, or contributed by an individual member of a group — see SHARE 1
2 the approval by someone in authority for the doing of something — see PERMISSION

alloyed *adj* containing foreign or lower-grade substances — see IMPURE

all–powerful *adj* having unlimited power or authority — see OMNIPOTENT

all–purpose *adj* not limited or specialized in application or purpose — see GENERAL 4

all right *adj* **1** being to one's liking — see SATISFACTORY 1
2 not exposed to the threat of loss or injury — see SAFE 1
3 of a level of quality that meets one's needs or standards — see ADEQUATE

all right *adv* **1** in a satisfactory way — see WELL 1
2 used to express agreement — see YES

allude *vb* to convey an idea indirectly — see HINT

allure *n* the power of irresistible attraction — see CHARM 2

allure *vb* **1** to attract or delight as if by magic — see CHARM 1
2 to lead away from a usual or proper course by offering some pleasure or advantage — see LURE

allurement *n* **1** something that persuades one to perform an action for pleasure or gain — see LURE 1
2 the act or pressure of giving in to a desire especially when ill-advised — see TEMPTATION 1

alluring *adj* having an often mysterious or magical power to attract — see FASCINATING 1

ally *n* someone associated with another to give assistance or moral support ⟨in trying to convince his parents to send him to soccer camp, Toby had a real *ally* in his coach⟩
synonyms abettor (*also* abetter), backer, confederate, supporter, sympathizer
related words well-wisher; accessory, accomplice, collaborationist, collaborator; adjunct, assistant, coadjutor, helper; associate, cohort, colleague, fellow, partner; buddy, chum, companion, comrade, confidant, crony, familiar, friend, intimate, mate, pal
near antonyms belittler, detractor; adversary, enemy, foe, opponent

ally *vb* to form or enter into an association that furthers the interests of its members ⟨the area's small grape growers have *allied* and formed a cooperative that will help them get the best prices⟩
synonyms associate, band, club, confederate, conjoin, cooperate, federate, league, unite
related words collaborate, gang (up), team (up); incorporate, organize, unionize; affiliate; amalgamate, combine, conglomerate, consolidate, converge, group, join, merge; knot, link, tie, wed
near antonyms detach, disengage, dissolve, disunite, divorce, part, segregate, separate, sever, split, sunder; alienate, estrange, fall out
antonyms break up, disband

almighty *adj* having unlimited power or authority — see OMNIPOTENT

Almighty *n* the being worshipped as the creator and ruler of the universe — see DEITY 2

almost *adv* very close to but not completely ⟨we were *almost* finished with dinner when Uncle Richard showed up⟩ ⟨there were *almost* enough seats for everybody on the bus⟩
synonyms about, more or less, most, much, near, nearly, next to, nigh, practically, some, virtually, well-nigh
related words appreciably, by and large, chiefly, largely, mainly, mostly; partially, partly, somewhat
phrases as good as
near antonyms absolutely, altogether, completely, entirely, fully, plumb [*chiefly dialect*], quite, thoroughly; totally, utterly, wholly; barely, hardly, scarcely

alms *n* a gift of money or its equivalent to a charity, humanitarian cause, or public institution — see CONTRIBUTION

almsgiving *n* the giving of necessities and especially money to the needy — see CHARITY 1

aloft *adv* to or in a higher place — see ABOVE

alone *adj* **1** not being in the company of others ⟨no one realized Jeff was *alone* in his room so they all left for the movies without him⟩
synonyms lone, lonely, lonesome, solitary, solo, unaccompanied
related words unattended, unchaperoned; forlorn, friendless; cloistered, insulated, isolated, remote, retired, secluded, withdrawn; quarantined, segregated, separated, sequestered; separate, unattached, unconnected, unlinked; detached, disconnected, disjointed, dissociated, disunited, divided, fractionated; abandoned, adrift, deserted, desolate, forgotten, forsaken, lorn, neglected
near antonyms attended, chaperoned, escorted; adjacent, adjoining, communicating, contiguous, neighboring, next-door; attached, connected, coupled, linked
antonyms accompanied
2 being the one or ones of a class with no other members — see ONLY 2

alone *adv* **1** without aid or support ⟨Rebecca managed to find her way home *alone*⟩
synonyms independently, single-handedly, singly, solely, unaided, unassisted
related words individually, separately
phrases by oneself
near antonyms collectively, conjointly, cooperatively, jointly, mutually, together; en masse
2 for nothing other than — see SOLELY 1

along *adv* toward or at a point lying in advance in space or time ⟨traffic was inching *along* at a snail's pace⟩ ⟨work on the project is moving right *along*⟩
synonyms ahead, forth, forward, on, onward (*also* onwards)
related words before
near antonyms back, backward (*or* backwards), behind, rearward (*or* rearwards)

aloof *adj* having or showing a lack of friendliness or interest in others — see COOL 1

aloud *adv* with one's normal voice speaking the words ⟨Mr. Gripp likes to call on the sleepiest-looking students to read *aloud* from the textbook⟩
synonyms audibly, out, out loud
related words clearly, discernibly, distinctly, distinguishably, perceptibly, plainly; blatantly, boisterously, clamorously, loudly, lustily, mightily, noisily, resoundingly, stridently, thunderously, uproariously, vociferously
near antonyms faintly, feebly, low, noiselessly, quietly, softly
antonyms inaudibly, silently, soundlessly

alp *n* an elevation of land higher than a hill — see MOUNTAIN 1

alpha *n* the point at which something begins — see BEGINNING

alright *adj* **1** being to one's liking — see SATISFACTORY 1
2 not exposed to the threat of loss or injury — see SAFE 1

alright *adv* used to express agreement — see YES

also *adv* **1** in like manner ⟨we stayed at an historic London hotel, the same establishment that had *also* welcomed our grandparents many years ago⟩
synonyms alike, correspondingly, likewise, similarly, so
related words equally, equivalently, identically
near antonyms contrarily, conversely, inversely, oppositely, vice versa; diversely, unequally, variously
antonyms differently, dissimilarly, otherwise
2 in addition to what has been said — see MORE 1

alter *vb* **1** to make different in some way — see CHANGE 1
2 to remove the sex organs of — see NEUTER

alterable *adj* capable of being readily changed — see FLEXIBLE 1

alteration *n* the act, process, or result of making different — see CHANGE

altercation *n* an often noisy or angry expression of differing opinions — see ARGUMENT 1

alternative *n* the power, right, or opportunity to choose — see CHOICE 1

although *also* **altho** *conj* in spite of the fact that ⟨*although* I've been to his house several times, I still can't remember how to get there⟩
synonyms albeit, howbeit, though, when, while, whilst [*chiefly British*]
related words but, whereas

altitude *n* **1** the distance of something or someone from bottom to top — see HEIGHT 3
2 the most extreme or advanced point — see HEIGHT 2
3 *usually* **altitudes** *pl* an area of high ground — see HEIGHT 4

altogether *adv* **1** for the most part — see CHIEFLY
2 to a full extent or degree — see FULLY 1

altruistic *adj* having or showing a concern for the welfare of others — see CHARITABLE 1

always *adv* **1** on every relevant occasion ⟨Aunt Trina *always* insists we stay for dinner⟩
synonyms consistently, constantly, continually, ever, forever, incessantly, invariably, perpetually, unfailingly
related words commonly, frequently, oft, often, oftentimes (*or* ofttimes), recurrently, repeatedly; continuously, steadily, uninterruptedly; dependably, normally, ordinarily, regularly, routinely, typically, usually; inevitably; eternally, everlastingly
near antonyms intermittently, occasionally, periodically, sometimes, sporadically; infrequently, rarely, seldom, unusually
antonyms ne'er, never
2 for all time — see EVER 1

amalgam *n* a distinct entity formed by the combining of two or more different things — see BLEND

amalgamate *vb* **1** to mix thoroughly so that the things mixed cannot be recognized — see BLEND 1
2 to turn into a single mass that is more or less the same throughout — see BLEND 1

amalgamated *adj* made from the joining of two or more parts or elements — see COMPOSITE

amalgamation *n* a distinct entity formed by the combining of two or more different things — see BLEND

amass *vb* to bring together in one body or place — see GATHER 1

amateur *adj* lacking or showing a lack of expert skill — see AMATEURISH

amateur *n* a person who regularly or occasionally engages in an activity without being or becoming an expert at it ⟨a homemade doghouse that looked like it was built by an *amateur* who hadn't mastered basic carpentry⟩
synonyms dabbler, dilettante, potterer, putterer
related words apprentice, trainee; beginner, freshman, greenhorn, learner, neophyte, newcomer, novice, rookie, tenderfoot, tyro; hobbyist, tinkerer, trifler; layman, nonprofessional
near antonyms authority, pro, professional; maestro, virtuoso, whiz, wizard; artisan, artist, craftsman, workman; initiate, journeyman; specialist, technician; old hand, old-timer, vet, veteran
antonyms ace, adept, crackerjack, expert, master, past master

amateurish *adj* lacking or showing a lack of expert skill ⟨that's an *amateurish* wallpapering job—the pattern doesn't match at the seams⟩
synonyms amateur, dilettante, inexperienced, inexpert, nonprofessional, unprofessional, unskilled, unskillful
related words primitive, self-taught, uninitiated, unprepared, unqualified, unschooled, untaught, untrained, untutored; clumsy, crude, defective, faulty, flawed, unfinished, unpolished; beginning, green, new, raw, unpracticed, unseasoned, untested, untried; incapable, incompetent, unable, unfit, ungifted, untalented
near antonyms able, accomplished, capable, competent, dexterous (*also* dextrous), gifted, proficient, skilled, skillful, talented; experienced, practiced (*or* practised), seasoned, veteran; educated, fitted, initiated, knowledgeable, prepared, qualified, schooled, taught, trained, tutored, versed; all-around (*also* all-round), versatile, well-rounded; finished, polished
antonyms ace, adept, consummate, crackerjack, expert, master, masterful, masterly, professional, virtuoso

amatory *adj* of, relating to, or expressing sexual attraction — see EROTIC

amaze *vb* to make a strong impression on (someone) with something unexpected — see SURPRISE 1

amazed *adj* **1** affected with sudden and great wonder or surprise — see THUNDERSTRUCK
2 filled with amazement or wonder — see OPEN-MOUTHED

amazement *n* **1** the rapt attention and deep emotion caused by the sight of something extraordinary — see WONDER 2
2 the state of being strongly impressed by something unexpected or unusual — see SURPRISE 2

amazing *adj* **1** causing a strong emotional reaction because unexpected — see SURPRISING 1
2 causing wonder or astonishment — see MARVELOUS 1

ambassador *n* a person sent on a mission to represent another ⟨a beloved entertainer who has often been sent abroad by the president as his country's goodwill *ambassador*⟩
synonyms delegate, emissary, envoy, minister, legate, representative
related words agent, attaché, consul, deputy, diplomat, foreign minister, nuncio, procurator, proxy; apostle, evangelist, missionary; deputation, detachment, legation; courier, messenger; mouthpiece, spokesperson

ambiguity *n* the quality or state of having a veiled or uncertain meaning — see OBSCURITY 1

ambiguous *adj* having an often intentionally veiled or uncertain meaning — see OBSCURE 1

ambiguousness *n* the quality or state of having a veiled or uncertain meaning — see OBSCURITY 1

ambition *n* **1** eager desire for personal advancement ⟨"Talent without *ambition* will not make you a star," McKenzie's dance instructor liked to remind her⟩
synonyms aspiration, go-getting
related words determination, diligence, drive, energy, enterprise, go, hustle, industry, initiative, motivation, push; opportunism; aggression, assertiveness, daring, spirit; ardor, avidity, eagerness, keenness, passion; avarice, greed
near antonyms apathy, indifference, unconcern; idleness, indolence, inertia, laziness, lethargy, shiftlessness, sloth
2 readiness to engage in daring or difficult activity — see ENTERPRISE 2
3 something that one hopes or intends to accomplish — see GOAL

ambitious *adj* **1** having a strong desire for personal advancement ⟨an *ambitious* child actor and his even more ambitious mother, who will do anything to get him in commercials⟩
synonyms aspiring, go-getting, self-seeking

related words determined, diligent, driving, dynamic, enterprising, gung ho, hustling, industrious, motivated, scrappy, venturesome, venturous; animated, lively, spirited; ardent, avid, eager, energetic, impassioned, keen, raring, vigorous; aggressive, assertive, opportunistic, pushy, self-assertive
near antonyms apathetic, disinterested, indifferent, uneager, unenthusiastic, unexcited, uninterested; casual, easygoing, lackadaisical; halfhearted, lukewarm, tepid; lazy, lethargic, listless, shiftless, sluggish, spiritless; unaggressive, unassertive
2 having or showing a bold forcefulness in the pursuit of a goal — see AGGRESSIVE 1

ambrosial *adj* **1** having a pleasant smell — see FRAGRANT
2 very pleasing to the sense of taste — see DELICIOUS 1

ambuscade *n* a scheme in which hidden persons wait to attack by surprise — see AMBUSH 1

ambush *n* **1** a scheme in which hidden persons wait to attack by surprise ⟨revolutionaries laid an *ambush* for the king along the route his carriage would travel⟩
synonyms ambuscade, surprise, trap
related words assault, attack, charge, sally; capture, entrapment, snare; hunting, stalking
2 a device or scheme for capturing another by surprise — see TRAP 1

ambush *vb* to lie in wait for and attack by surprise ⟨the king's enemies planned to *ambush* the royal coach on the way to Paris and capture the king⟩
synonyms surprise, waylay
related words assail, assault, attack, storm, strike; jump, pounce (on), tackle; charge, sally; capture, ensnare, entrap, net, snare, trap; hunt, prey (on *or* upon), stalk
phrases lay for

ameliorate *vb* to make better — see IMPROVE

amenability *n* **1** a desire or disposition to please — see COMPLAISANCE
2 cheerful readiness to do something — see ALACRITY

amenable *adj* **1** having a desire or inclination (as for a specified course of action) — see WILLING 1
2 readily giving in to the command or authority of another — see OBEDIENT

amend *vb* **1** to make better — see IMPROVE
2 to remove errors, defects, deficiencies, or deviations from — see CORRECT 1

amendment *n* a change designed to correct or improve a written work — see CORRECTION 1

amenity *n* **1** an act or utterance that is a customary show of good manners — see CIVILITY 1
2 something adding to pleasure or comfort but not absolutely necessary — see LUXURY 1
3 something that adds to one's ease — see COMFORT 2
4 the state or quality of having a pleasant or agreeable manner in socializing with others — see AMIABILITY 1

American Indian *n* a member of any of the native peoples of the western hemisphere usually not including the Eskimos ⟨Jeremy's great-grandfather was an *American Indian*, a member of the Shoshones⟩
synonyms Amerindian (*also* Amerind), Indian, Native American
related words mestizo

Amerindian *also* **Amerind** *n* a member of any of the native peoples of the western hemisphere usually not including the Eskimos — see AMERICAN INDIAN

amiability *n* **1** the state or quality of having a pleasant or agreeable manner in socializing with others ⟨the waitress's *amiability* is what makes eating at the diner so much fun⟩
synonyms affability, agreeableness, amenity, amiableness, geniality, good-naturedness, good-temperedness, graciousness, niceness, pleasantness, sweetness
related words amenability, complaisance; amicability, amity, cordiality, friendliness; benignity, gentleness, kindness; cheerfulness, cheeriness, sunniness; civility, comity, considerateness, consideration, courteousness, courtesy, politeness, thoughtfulness; attractiveness, delightfulness, enjoyableness
near antonyms boorishness, discourtesy, impoliteness, incivility, rudeness, ungraciousness; biliousness, cantankerousness, churlishness, crankiness, fussiness, grouchiness, grumpiness, irascibility, irritability, peevishness, petulance, testiness; contentiousness, contrariness, orneriness, querulousness; hostility, unfriendliness
antonyms disagreeableness, unpleasantness
2 a desire or disposition to please — see COMPLAISANCE

amiable *adj* having an easygoing and pleasing manner especially in social situations ⟨the owner of the inn is an *amiable*, talkative widow who treats guests like family⟩
synonyms affable, agreeable, genial, good-natured, good-tempered, gracious, nice, sweet, well-disposed
related words amicable, cordial, friendly, neighborly; benign, gentle, kind; cheerful, cheery, sunny; companionable, sociable; civil, considerate, courteous, polite, thoughtful; accommodating, amenable, obliging; attractive, delightful, enjoyable
near antonyms boorish, discourteous, ill-mannered, impolite, inconsiderate, rude, surly, uncivil, unmannerly; bearish, bilious, cantankerous, choleric, churlish, crabby, cranky, dyspeptic, fussy, grouchy, grumpy, ill-humored, irascible, irritable, peevish, petulant, quick-tempered, snappish, testy, touchy; argumentative, contentious, contrary, ornery, querulous; unappealing, unattractive
antonyms disagreeable, ill-natured, ill-tempered, ungracious, unpleasant

amiableness *n* the state or quality of having a pleasant or agreeable manner in socializing with others — see AMIABILITY 1

amicable *adj* **1** having or marked by agreement in feeling or action — see HARMONIOUS 3
2 having or showing kindly feeling and sincere interest — see FRIENDLY 1

amid *or* **amidst** *prep* in or into the middle of — see AMONG

amiss *adv* **1** in a mistaken or inappropriate way — see WRONGLY
2 off the desired or intended path or course — see WRONG 1

amity *n* kindly concern, interest, or support — see GOODWILL 1

ammunition *n* means or method of defending — see DEFENSE 1

amnesty *n* release from the guilt or penalty of an offense — see PARDON

amok *or* **amuck** *adv* in a confused and reckless manner — see HELTER-SKELTER 1

among *also* **amongst** *prep* in or into the middle of ⟨a gull landed *among* the burgers-and-fries eaters at the outdoor snack bar, clearly looking for handouts⟩
synonyms amid (*or* amidst), mid, midst, through
related words between, betwixt
phrases in the thick of
near antonyms from, out of

amorous *adj* of, relating to, or expressing sexual attraction — see EROTIC

amorphous *adj* having no definite or recognizable form — see FORMLESS

amount *n* a given or particular mass or aggregate of matter ⟨is this small *amount* of food supposed to feed the whole hockey team?⟩
synonyms measure, quantity, volume
related words body, portion; many, number

amount (to) *vb* **1** to have a total of ⟨the expenses of the trip *amounted to* nearly double what we'd budgeted for⟩
synonyms add up (to), come (to), number, sum (to *or* into), total
related words average, equal, measure, reach; aggregate, comprise
2 to be the same in meaning or effect ⟨it makes no difference whether you're going to the game or to the movies, for it *amounts to* your unavailability for babysitting⟩
synonyms add up (to), come (to), correspond (to), equal
related words approach, match, measure (up), meet, rival, touch; connote, denote, express, import, mean, signify, smack (of), spell, suggest

ample *adj* **1** being more than enough without being excessive — see PLENTIFUL
2 more than adequate or average in capacity — see SPACIOUS

amplify *vb* **1** to express more fully and in greater detail — see EXPAND 1
2 to make greater in size, amount, or number — see INCREASE 1
3 to make markedly greater in measure or degree — see INTENSIFY

amplitude *n* an area over which activity, capacity, or influence extends — see RANGE 2

amulet *n* something worn or kept to bring good luck or keep away evil — see CHARM 1

amuse *vb* to cause (someone) to pass the time agreeably occupied ⟨Christie *amused* her four-year-old sister at the family reunion by showing her off to all the relatives⟩
synonyms disport, divert, entertain, regale
related words absorb, busy, distract, engage, engross, immerse, interest, involve, occupy; beguile, bewitch, captivate, charm, delight, enchant, enthrall (*or* enthral), fascinate; grip, hypnotize, intrigue, mesmerize; coddle, gratify, humor, indulge, mollycoddle, pamper, please, pleasure, spoil; appease, comfort, conciliate, console, content, mollify, oblige, pacify, placate, propitiate, soothe
near antonyms bore, jade; drain, enervate, exhaust, fatigue, tire, wear, wear out, weary; aggravate, annoy, bother, bug, chafe, disturb, exasperate, fret, gall, grate, harass, harry, irk, nettle, peeve, perturb, pester, pique, upset, vex

amusement *n* the act or activity of providing pleasure or amusement especially for the public — see ENTERTAINMENT 1

amusing *adj* providing amusement or enjoyment — see FUN

analgesic *n* something (as a drug) that relieves pain — see PAINKILLER

analogous *adj* having qualities in common — see ALIKE

analysis *n* **1** the separation and identification of the parts of a whole ⟨investigators took the mysterious powder to the lab for *analysis*⟩
synonyms anatomizing, assay, breakdown, dissection
related words assessment, evaluation, examination, inspection, investigation, scrutiny; arrangement, assortment, cataloging (*or* cataloguing), categorization, classification, codification, indexing; enumeration, inventory, itemization, tabulation; division, reduction, segmentation, separation, subdivision
near antonyms agglomeration, aggregation, amalgamation, assimilation, coalescence, conglomeration, consolidation, integration, synthesis, unification
2 a series of explanations or observations on something (as an event) — see COMMENTARY

analytic *or* **analytical** *adj* according to the rules of logic — see LOGICAL 1

analyze *vb* to identify and examine the basic elements or parts of (something) especially for discovering interrelationships ⟨*analyze* the park's ecosystem before deciding whether hunting should be allowed⟩
synonyms anatomize, assay, break down, dissect
related words assess, evaluate, examine, inspect, investigate, scrutinize; arrange, assort, catalog (*or* catalogue), categorize, classify, codify, diagram, index, order, schematize, sort, tabulate; divide, reduce, segment, separate, subdivide
near antonyms agglomerate, aggregate, amalgamate, assimilate, coalesce, conglomerate, consolidate, integrate, synthesize, unify

anarchic *adj* not restrained by or under the control of legal authority — see LAWLESS

anarchy *n* a state in which there is widespread wrongdoing and disregard for rules and authority ⟨the *anarchy* that the country experienced after the dictator drained the treasury and fled the country⟩
synonyms lawlessness, misrule
related words commotion, tumult, uproar; chaos, confusion, disarray, disorder, disorderliness, disorganization; disruption, disturbance, havoc, riot, strife, turbulence, turmoil, unrest, upheaval; mutiny, rebellion, revolution, uprising; criminality, outlawry
near antonyms law, lawfulness, legality, legitimacy, rule; calmness, harmony, order, orderliness, peace, peacefulness, quiet, tranquillity (*or* tranquility)

anathema *n* **1** a prayer that harm will come to someone — see CURSE 1
2 something or someone that is hated — see HATE 2

anatomize *vb* to identify and examine the basic elements or parts of (something) especially for discovering interrelationships — see ANALYZE

anatomizing *n* the separation and identification of the parts of a whole — see ANALYSIS 1

ancestor *n* **1** a person who is several generations earlier in an individual's line of descent ⟨Bridie's Irish *ancestors* immigrated to the United States in the 19th century during the Great Potato Famine⟩

synonyms father, forebear (*also* forbear), forefather, grandfather

related words grandmother, matriarch, patriarch; ancestry, antecedents

near antonyms children, issue, offspring, posterity, progeny, seed; heir, inheritor, son, successor

antonyms descendant (*or* descendent)

2 something belonging to an earlier time from which something else was later developed ⟨pinball machines—the *ancestors* of today's video games—go back to the 19th century⟩

synonyms antecedent, foregoer, forerunner, precursor, predecessor

related words archetype, model, original, prototype; father, mother

near antonyms by-product, derivative, offshoot, outgrowth, spin-off; daughter, son

antonyms descendant (*or* descendent)

ancestry *n* the line of ancestors from whom a person is descended ⟨a Cambodian immigrant who can trace her Khmer *ancestry* as far back as the 16th century⟩

synonyms birth, blood, bloodline, breeding, descent, extraction, family tree, genealogy, line, lineage, origin, parentage, pedigree, stock, strain

related words heredity, succession; family, house; kin, kindred, relations, relatives; race

near antonyms offspring; child, heir, inheritor, son, successor

antonyms issue, posterity, progeny, seed

anchor *n* one who reads and introduces news reports on a news program — see ANCHORPERSON

anchor *vb* **1** to put securely in place or in a desired position — see FASTEN 2

2 to stop at or near a place along the shore — see LAND 1

anchorage *n* a part of a body of water protected and deep enough to be a place of safety for ships — see HARBOR 1

anchorite *n* a person who lives away from others — see RECLUSE

anchorperson *n* one who reads and introduces news reports on a news program ⟨the new *anchorperson* did an admirable job of dealing with the late-breaking news story⟩

synonyms anchor

related words anchorman, anchorwoman; broadcaster, newscaster, telecaster; correspondent, interviewer, reporter; journalist, newsman

ancient *adj* **1** dating or surviving from the distant past ⟨Rome's *ancient* ruins are carefully preserved in the midst of the bustle of the modern city⟩

synonyms aged, age-old, antediluvian, antique, dateless, hoar, hoary, old, venerable

related words aging, mature; antiquated, obsolete, outmoded, out-of-date, passé; old-fashioned, old-time, old-world; durable, enduring, lasting, long-lived, permanent; ageless, hallowed, time-honored, timeless, time-tested, traditional, tried, tried-and-true; classic, classical; prehistoric, primeval, primordial

near antonyms fresh, young, youthful; contemporary, current, latest, mod, novel, present-day, ultramodern; untested, untried; brand-new, unused, unworn

antonyms modern, new, recent

2 being of advanced years and especially past middle age — see ELDERLY

3 relating to or occurring near the beginning of a process, series, or time period — see EARLY 1

ancient *n* a person of advanced years — see SENIOR CITIZEN

anecdote *n* a brief account of something interesting that happened especially to one personally — see STORY 2

anesthetic *n* something (as a drug) that relieves pain — see PAINKILLER

anew *adv* yet another time — see AGAIN 1

angel *n* **1** an innocent or gentle person — see LAMB

2 one that announces or indicates the later arrival of another — see FORERUNNER 1

anger *n* an intense emotional state of displeasure with someone or something ⟨Dave stifled his *anger* when the kids on the bus made fun of him⟩

synonyms angriness, furor, fury, indignation, irateness, ire, outrage, rage, spleen, wrath, wrathfulness

related words aggravation, annoyance, exasperation, irritation, vexation; animosity, antagonism, antipathy, bile, bitterness, contempt, enmity, grudge, hostility, rancor; envy, jaundice, jealousy, pique, resentment; malevolence, malice, spite, venom, virulence, vitriol; belligerence, contentiousness, contrariness, disputatiousness, orneriness, pugnacity, querulousness; blowup, flare-up, outburst; dander, dudgeon, huff, pet, rise, ruffle, temper; delirium, heat, passion, warmth

near antonyms calmness, forbearance, patience

antonyms delight, pleasure

anger *vb* to make angry ⟨it's virtually impossible to *anger* Mrs. Peterson—she's the most easygoing person I've ever known⟩

synonyms antagonize, enrage, incense, inflame, infuriate, madden, outrage, rankle, rile, roil

related words affront, aggravate, annoy, cross, exasperate, get, irritate, nettle, offend, peeve, pique, provoke, put out, ruffle, vex; embitter, envenom

phrases get one's goat, rub the wrong way

near antonyms allay, assuage, relieve; comfort, console, soothe; appease, conciliate, mollify, pacify, placate; calm, lull, quiet, settle; beguile, bewitch, captivate, charm, disarm, enchant

antonyms delight, gratify, please

angered *adj* feeling or showing anger — see ANGRY

angle *n* **1** a certain way in which something appears or may be regarded — see ASPECT 1

2 a way of looking at or thinking about something — see POINT OF VIEW

3 something that curves or is curved — see BEND 1

angle *vb* to set or cause to be at an angle — see LEAN 1

angling *n* the act of positioning or an instance of being positioned at an angle — see TILT

angriness *n* an intense emotional state of displeasure with someone or something — see ANGER

angry *adj* feeling or showing anger ⟨my sister gets really *angry* and practically throws a tantrum if her soccer team loses⟩

synonyms angered, apoplectic, enraged, foaming, fuming, furious, incensed, indignant, inflamed, infuriated, irate, ireful, mad, outraged, rabid, riled, roiled, shirty [*chiefly British*], sore, steaming, wrathful, wroth

related words ranting, raving, stormy; bristling, burning, cross, huffy, livid, seething, smoldering, worked up, wrought (up); acrid, acrimonious, antagonistic, antipathetic, bitter, embittered, inimical, malevolent, piqued, rancorous, resentful, spiteful, vindictive, virulent; antisocial, cold, cool, disagreeable, disapproving, distant, frigid, icy, ill-tempered, sulky, unfriendly, unpleasant; aggravated, annoyed, bearish, bilious, cantankerous, choleric, churlish, crabby, cranky, dyspeptic, exasperated, fretful, fussy, grouchy, grumpy, ill-humored, irascible, irritable, peevish, perturbed, petulant, put out, quick-tempered, snappish, testy, touchy; argumentative, belligerent, contentious, contrary, disputatious, ornery, pugnacious, quarrelsome, querulous

near antonyms accepting, accommodating, obliging; agreeable, amenable, complaisant; amicable, cordial, friendly; content, happy, satisfied; empathetic, sympathetic, tolerant, understanding; calm, pacific, peaceable, placid, serene, tranquil; affable, amiable, easygoing, genial, good-natured, good-tempered, kind, pleasant, sweet

antonyms delighted, pleased

anguish *n* **1** a state of great suffering of body or mind — see DISTRESS 1

2 deep sadness especially for the loss of someone or something loved — see SORROW

anguished *adj* expressing or suggesting mourning — see MOURNFUL 1

animal *adj* of or relating to the human body — see PHYSICAL 1

animal *n* one of the lower animals as distinguished from human beings ⟨we saw a lot of *animals* at the wildlife refuge—cranes, alligators, deer, a fox, even an armadillo⟩

synonyms beast, brute, creature, critter

related words varmint, vermin; biped, quadruped; carnivore, herbivore, insectivore; invertebrate, vertebrate

animate *adj* **1** having much high-spirited energy and movement — see LIVELY 1

2 having or showing life — see ALIVE 1

animate *vb* to give life, vigor, or spirit to ⟨Mr. Clark *animates* history for his sixth graders by frequently showing up for class dressed like some famous historical figure⟩

synonyms brace, energize, enliven, fire, invigorate, jazz (up), liven (up), pep (up), quicken, stimulate, vitalize, vivify

related words arouse, awake, awaken, raise, rouse, stir, wake (up); activate, actuate, drive, impel, motivate, move, propel; charge, electrify, galvanize; excite, ferment, foment, incite, inflame, instigate, kindle, provoke, set off, spark, trigger, turn on, whip (up); abet, boost, buoy, cheer, embolden, fortify, hearten, inspire, lift, rally, steel, strengthen; reactivate, reanimate, reawake, reawaken, recharge, recreate, reenergize, refresh, regenerate, rejuvenate, rekindle, renew, resurrect, resuscitate, revitalize, revive

near antonyms burn out, debilitate, do in, drain, enervate, enfeeble, exhaust, fag, fatigue, sap, tucker (out), undermine, weaken, wear, wear out; check, curb, inhibit, jade, quell, quench, repress, restrain, slow, still, stunt, suppress; daunt, demoralize, discourage, dishearten, dispirit

antonyms damp, dampen, deaden, dull

animated *adj* **1** having much high-spirited energy and movement — see LIVELY 1

2 marked by much life, movement, or activity — see ALIVE 2

animatedly *adv* in a quick and spirited manner — see GAILY 2

animately *adv* in a quick and spirited manner — see GAILY 2

animation *n* the quality or state of having abundant or intense activity — see VITALITY 1

animosity *n* a deep-seated ill will — see ENMITY

annalist *n* a student or writer of history — see HISTORIAN

annals *n pl* an account of important events in the order in which they happened — see HISTORY 1

annex *n* a smaller structure added to a main building ⟨a new *annex* that will serve as the permanent home for the school library⟩

synonyms addition, extension, penthouse

related words arm, ell, wing

annex *vb* to join (something) to a mass, quantity, or number so as to bring about an overall increase — see ADD 1

annihilate *vb* **1** to destroy all traces of ⟨the family's attempts to *annihilate* the roach population in their apartment had met with little success⟩

synonyms blot out, efface, eradicate, expunge, exterminate, extirpate, liquidate, obliterate, root (out), rub out, snuff (out), stamp (out), wipe out

related words decimate, demolish, destroy, devastate; dismantle, flatten, mow (down), raze, tear down; ruin, total, waste, wreck; blast, blow up, dash, dynamite, smash; atomize, consume, devour, dissolve, fragment, powder, pulverize, shatter, splinter; doom, finish, kill, terminate, zap; cancel, cut, discard, ditch, eject, excise, expel, jettison, oust, throw out

near antonyms conserve, preserve, protect, save; build, construct, create, fabricate, fashion, forge, form, frame, make, manufacture, shape; fix, mend, patch, rebuild, recondition, reconstruct, renew, renovate, repair, restore, revamp

2 to bring to a complete end the physical soundness, existence, or usefulness of — see DESTROY 1

annihilation *n* the state or fact of being rendered nonexistent, physically unsound, or useless — see DESTRUCTION

announce *vb* to make known openly or publicly ⟨Jeannie *announced* to everyone within hearing distance that she didn't care if she failed the test⟩

synonyms advertise, blaze, broadcast, declare, enunciate, placard, post, proclaim, promulgate, publicize, publish, sound

related words advise, apprise, inform, notify; communicate, impart, intimate; disclose, divulge, report, reveal; disseminate, spread

near antonyms conceal, hush (up), silence, suppress, withhold; recall, recant, retract, revoke

announcement *n* a published statement informing the public of a matter of general interest ⟨an *announcement* was in today's paper regarding the merger of the two banks⟩

synonyms ad, advertisement, bulletin, notice, notification, posting, release

related words broadside, circular, flier (*or* flyer), handbill, handout; bill, billboard, placard, poster, sign; broadcast, newscast, telecast; advertising, commercial, message, spot, word; communication, dispatch, report; ballyhoo, boost, buildup, campaign, plug, promotion, propaganda, publicity

annoy *vb* to disturb the peace of mind of (someone) especially by repeated disagreeable acts — see IRRITATE 1

annoyance *n* **1** the act of making unwelcome intrusions upon another ⟨they have an unlisted number in the hopes that it will reduce the constant *annoyance* by telephone salespeople⟩
synonyms aggravation, bedevilment, bothering, bugging, disturbance, harassment, harrying, pestering, teasing, vexation
related words molestation, offense (*or* offence), persecution, provocation, torment, torture
2 the feeling of impatience or anger caused by another's repeated disagreeable acts ⟨Carlene made known her *annoyance* at having to pick up her sister's dirty clothes⟩
synonyms aggravation, bother, exasperation, frustration, irritation, vexation
related words agitation, anger, angriness, discomfort, displeasure, distress, disturbance, indignation, irateness, ire, outrage, perturbation, resentment; dander, dudgeon, huff, peeve, pet, pique, umbrage, upset
near antonyms delight, pleasure
3 something that is a source of irritation ⟨flashing ads, visual clutter, and other *annoyances* that are the price for free information on the Internet⟩
synonyms aggravation, bother, exasperation, frustration, hassle, headache, inconvenience, irritant, nuisance, peeve, pest, problem, thorn
related words affront, insult, offense; upset, worry; affliction, cross, curse, menace, plague; plight, predicament, trial, tribulation; annoyer, disturber, offender
near antonyms delight, joy, pleasure
4 one who is obnoxiously annoying — see NUISANCE 1

annoyer *n* one who is obnoxiously annoying — see NUISANCE 1

annoying *adj* causing annoyance ⟨Sheldon has the *annoying* habit of eating all the pickles and leaving a jar full of pickle juice in the refrigerator⟩
synonyms aggravating, bothersome, disturbing, exasperating, frustrating, galling, irksome, irritating, maddening, nettling, peeving, pesty, rankling, riling, vexatious, vexing
related words burdensome, discomforting, displeasing, disquieting, distressing, importunate, inconveniencing; angering, enraging, infuriating; mischievous, offensive, pesky, troublesome, upsetting; stressful, tiresome, troubling, trying, worrisome
near antonyms delightful, pleasing

annuity *n* a sum of money allotted for a specific use by official or formal action — see APPROPRIATION

annul *vb* **1** to balance with an equal force so as to make ineffective — see OFFSET
2 to put an end to by formal action — see ABOLISH

anoint *vb* to rub an oily or sticky substance over — see SMEAR 1

anomalous *adj* departing from some accepted standard of what is normal — see DEVIANT

anomaly *n* a person, thing, or event that is not normal — see FREAK 1

anon *adv* at or within a short time — see SHORTLY 2

anonymity *n* the quality or state of being mostly or completely unknown — see OBSCURITY 2

anonymous *adj* **1** known but not named — see CERTAIN 1
2 not named or identified by a name — see NAMELESS 1
3 not widely known — see OBSCURE 2

another *adj* resulting in an increase in amount or number — see ADDITIONAL

answer *n* **1** something spoken or written in reaction especially to a question ⟨the standard *answer* of "Nothing" when asked, "What did you do in school today?"⟩
synonyms comeback, rejoinder, reply, response, retort, return
related words banter, persiflage, repartee; acknowledgment (*also* acknowledgement), comment, communication, correspondence, feedback, observation, reaction, remark; defense, explanation, justification, rebuttal, refutation
near antonyms challenge, cross-examination, grilling, interrogation, quiz; poll, questionnaire, survey
antonyms inquiry, query, question
2 something attained by mental effort and especially by computation ⟨the *answers* to the odd-numbered problems are at the back of the book⟩
synonyms result, solution
related words conclusion, determination, explanation, finding; clue, key

answer *vb* **1** to speak or write in reaction to a question or to another reaction ⟨Ryan didn't *answer* right away when Mrs. Jacobs asked him where he'd been for the last three hours⟩
synonyms rejoin, reply, respond, retort, return
related words acknowledge, comment, communicate, correspond, react, remark; explain, rebut, refute
near antonyms challenge, cross-examine, examine, grill, interrogate, pump, quiz; poll, query, survey
antonyms inquire, question
2 to be in agreement on every point — see CHECK 1
3 to do what is required by the terms of — see FULFILL 1
4 to find an answer for through reasoning — see SOLVE

answerable *adj* **1** being the one who must meet an obligation or suffer the consequences for failing to do so — see RESPONSIBLE 1
2 capable of having the reason for or cause of determined — see SOLVABLE

antagonism *n* a deep-seated ill will — see ENMITY

antagonist *n* **1** one that is hostile toward another — see ENEMY
2 one that takes a position opposite another in a competition or conflict — see OPPONENT 1

antagonistic *adj* marked by opposition or ill will — see HOSTILE 1

antagonize *vb* **1** to implant bitter feelings in — see EMBITTER
2 to make angry — see ANGER

antecedent *adj* going before another in time or order — see PREVIOUS

antecedent *n* **1** someone or something responsible for a result — see CAUSE 1
2 something belonging to an earlier time from which something else was later developed — see ANCESTOR 2

antecedently *adv* so as to precede something in order of time — see AHEAD 1

antedate *vb* to go or come before in time — see PRECEDE

antediluvian *adj* dating or surviving from the distant past — see ANCIENT 1
antediluvian *n* a person with old-fashioned ideas — see FOGY
anterior *adj* going before another in time or order — see PREVIOUS
anteriorly *adv* so as to precede something in order of time — see AHEAD 1
anthem *n* a religious song — see HYMN
anthology *n* a collection of writings <an *anthology* of American short stories>
synonyms album, compilation, miscellany
related words archives; digest
antic *adj* **1** causing or intended to cause laughter — see FUNNY 1
2 given to good-natured joking or teasing — see PLAYFUL
antic *n* a playful or mischievous act intended as a joke — see PRANK
anticipate *vb* **1** to believe in the future occurrence of (something) — see EXPECT
2 to realize or know about beforehand — see FORESEE
anticipated *adj* being in accordance with the prescribed, normal, or logical course of events — see DUE 2
anticipatory *adj* having or showing signs of eagerly awaiting something — see EXPECTANT 1
antipathetic *adj* having a natural dislike for something <a series of adventure books that turned boys who had been *antipathetic* to reading into avid readers>
synonyms allergic, averse
related words disinclined, loath (*or* loth), reluctant, unwilling; adverse, antagonistic, hostile, intolerant, negative, opposed, opposing, resistant, resisting, uncongenial, unfriendly, unsympathetic; disgusted, nauseated, repelled, repulsed, revolted, shocked, squeamish, turned off
near antonyms friendly, sympathetic, tolerant, understanding; admiring, appreciative, charmed, delighted, fond, pleased, tickled
antipathy *n* **1** a deep-seated ill will — see ENMITY
2 something or someone that is hated — see HATE 2
antipodal *adj* being as different as possible — see OPPOSITE
antipode *n* something that is as different as possible from something else — see OPPOSITE
antipodean *adj* being as different as possible — see OPPOSITE
antiquated *adj* having passed its time of use or usefulness — see OBSOLETE
antique *adj* **1** dating or surviving from the distant past — see ANCIENT 1
2 pleasantly reminiscent of an earlier time — see OLD-FASHIONED 1
antique *n* something belonging to or surviving from an earlier period <Shamika's house is filled with *antiques*, including a collection of 19th-century African masks>
synonyms relic
related words artifact, fossil; antiquities, ruins; remains, remnant, trace, vestige
antisocial *adj* having or showing a lack of friendliness or interest in others — see COOL 1
antithesis *n* something that is as different as possible from something else — see OPPOSITE
antithetical *adj* being as different as possible — see OPPOSITE
anxiety *n* **1** an uneasy state of mind usually over the possibility of an anticipated misfortune or trouble <Dorothy's *anxiety* about her brother's operation kept her awake all night>
synonyms agitation, anxiousness, apprehension, apprehensiveness, care, concern, disquiet, nervousness, perturbation, solicitude, uneasiness, worry
related words strain, stress, tension; alarm, anguish, consternation, desperation, desperateness, discomfort, discomposure, dismay, distraction, distress, disturbance, edginess, jitters, jumpiness; fear, fearfulness, torment, upset, vexation; doubt, dread, foreboding, incertitude, misgiving, presentiment, suspense, uncertainty
near antonyms calm, calmness, content, contentment, ease, peace, placidity, quiet, quietude, serenity, tranquillity (*or* tranquility); comfort, consolation, relief, solace
2 the emotion experienced in the presence or threat of danger — see FEAR
anxious *adj* **1** feeling or showing uncomfortable feelings of uncertainty — see NERVOUS 1
2 marked by or causing agitation or uncomfortable feelings — see NERVOUS 2
3 showing urgent desire or interest — see EAGER
anxiousness *n* an uneasy state of mind usually over the possibility of an anticipated misfortune or trouble — see ANXIETY 1
any *adj* being one of a group — see EACH
anyhow *adv* **1** in spite of everything — see REGARDLESS
2 without definite aim, direction, rule, or method — see HIT OR MISS
anymore *adv* at the present time — see NOW 1
anyway *adv* **1** in spite of everything — see REGARDLESS
2 without definite aim, direction, rule, or method — see HIT OR MISS
anywise *adv* **1** in any way or respect — see AT ALL
2 without definite aim, direction, rule, or method — see HIT OR MISS
A1 *adj* of the very best kind — see EXCELLENT
apace *adv* with great speed — see FAST 1
apart *adv* into parts or to pieces <the fancy new adjustable rake came *apart* the first time Chad tried to use it>
synonyms asunder, piecemeal
antonyms together
apartment *n* **1** a room or set of rooms in a private house or a block used as a separate dwelling place <a spacious six-room *apartment* that occupies the entire upper floor of a two-family house>
synonyms flat, lodgings, suite, tenement
related words condominium, duplex, penthouse, salon, studio, triplex; apartment house, tenement house, walk-up
2 an area within a building that has been set apart from surrounding space by a wall — see ROOM 2
apathetic *adj* **1** having or showing a lack of interest or concern — see INDIFFERENT 1
2 not feeling or showing emotion — see IMPASSIVE 1
apathy *n* **1** a lack of emotion or emotional expressiveness <the *apathy* of the people of that war-torn country comes from their having seen too many horrors>
synonyms impassivity, insensibility, numbness, phlegm
related words callousness, coldness, coolness,

hardheartedness, hardness, heartlessness, insensitivity, obduracy; blankness, deadness, emptiness, vacancy; aloofness, detachment, indifference, unconcern; stiffness, woodenness
near antonyms compassion, empathy, pity, sympathy; responsiveness, sensitivity; solicitude, tenderness, understanding, warmth; histrionics, hysteria, hysterics, melodrama
antonyms emotion, feeling, sensibility
2 lack of interest or concern — see INDIFFERENCE

ape *vb* to use (someone or something) as the model for one's speech, mannerisms, or behavior — see IMITATE 1

aper *n* a person who adopts the appearance or behavior of another especially in an obvious way — see COPYCAT

aperture *n* a place in a surface allowing passage into or through a thing — see HOLE 1

apex *n* **1** the highest part or point — see HEIGHT 1
2 the last and usually sharp or tapering part of something long and narrow — see POINT 2

aphorism *n* **1** an idea or statement about all of the members of a group or all the instances of a situation — see GENERALIZATION
2 an often stated observation regarding something from common experience — see SAYING

aphoristic *adj* marked by the use of few words to convey much information or meaning — see CONCISE

apiece *adv* for each one ⟨when you figure that it comes to six dollars *apiece*, it's too much to pay for used CDs⟩
synonyms all, each, per capita
related words apart, independently, individually, respectively, separately, singly
near antonyms altogether, collectively, together

apish *adj* using or marked by the use of something else as a basis or model — see IMITATIVE

aplomb *n* **1** evenness of emotions or temper — see EQUANIMITY
2 great faith in oneself or one's abilities — see CONFIDENCE 1

apologetic *adj* feeling sorrow for a wrong that one has done — see CONTRITE 1

apoplectic *adj* feeling or showing anger — see ANGRY

apostate *n* one who betrays a trust or an allegiance — see TRAITOR

apostle *n* a person who actively supports or favors a cause — see EXPONENT

apothecary *n* a person who prepares drugs according to a doctor's prescription — see DRUGGIST

appall *vb* to cause an often unpleasant surprise for — see SHOCK 1

appalling *adj* **1** causing intense displeasure, disgust, or resentment — see OFFENSIVE 1
2 extremely disturbing or repellent — see HORRIBLE 1

appanage *n* **1** something granted as a special favor — see PRIVILEGE
2 something to which one has a just claim — see RIGHT 1

apparatus *n* items needed for the performance of a task or activity — see EQUIPMENT

apparel *n* covering for the human body — see CLOTHING

apparel *vb* to outfit with clothes and especially fine or special clothes — see CLOTHE 1

apparent *adj* **1** appearing to be true on the basis of evidence that may or may not be confirmed ⟨at the start of the investigation, the *apparent* cause of the plane crash was mechanical failure⟩
synonyms assumed, evident, ostensible, presumed, reputed, seeming, supposed
related words external, outward, visible; conceivable, plausible; likely, probable; clear, distinct, manifest, obvious, plain; deceptive, delusive, delusory, illusive, illusory, imaginary; misleading, specious; fake, faked, feigned, phony (*also* phoney), pretended, pseudo, put-on; alleged, professed, purported, so-called
near antonyms authenticated, confirmed, corroborated, established, real, substantiated, valid, validated, verified
2 capable of being seen — see VISIBLE
3 not subject to misinterpretation or more than one interpretation — see CLEAR 2

apparently *adv* to all outward appearances ⟨*apparently*, Phil didn't know the cake was for the raffle, since he helped himself to a piece⟩
synonyms evidently, ostensibly, presumably, seemingly, supposedly
related words externally, outwardly, visibly; believably, credibly; maybe, mayhap, perchance, perhaps, possibly, professedly; allegedly, reputedly; clearly, distinctly, obviously, plainly; assuredly, positively, surely
near antonyms implausibly, impossibly, improbably, incredibly

apparition *n* the soul of a dead person thought of especially as appearing to living people — see GHOST

appeal *n* **1** an earnest request — see PLEA 1
2 the power of irresistible attraction — see CHARM 2

appeal (to) *vb* to make a request to (someone) in an earnest or urgent manner — see BEG

appealing *adj* having an often mysterious or magical power to attract — see FASCINATING 1

appear *vb* **1** to come into view ⟨a police car *appeared* just as Michael ran a red light⟩
synonyms come out, materialize, show up, turn up
related words reappear, resurface; bulk, loom; arrive, come; dawn, debut; arise, break, break out, emanate, erupt, issue, rise, spring (up), surface; happen, occur
near antonyms depart, leave, retire, withdraw
antonyms clear, disappear, dissolve, evanesce, evaporate, fade, go (away), melt (away), vanish
2 to give the impression of being — see SEEM

appearance *n* **1** the outward form of someone or something especially as indicative of a quality ⟨the dignified *appearance* of this church leader⟩ ⟨the country club's manicured lawns and well-groomed *appearance* in general⟩
synonyms aspect, look, mien, presence
related words air, attitude, bearing, behavior, comportment, demeanor, deportment, manner, poise, pose; carriage, posture, stance; color, complexion; countenance, face, features, physiognomy, visage
2 outward and often deceptive indication ⟨can't you at least give the *appearance* of listening to what I say?⟩
synonyms face, guise, name, semblance, show
related words affectation, display, fiction, imposture, make-believe, pose, pretense (*or* pretence),

simulation; cloak, disguise, exterior, facade (*also* façade), front, mask, masquerade, shell, surface
3 the act of coming upon a scene — see ARRIVAL
appease *vb* to lessen the anger or agitation of — see PACIFY
appeasing *adj* tending to lessen or avoid conflict or hostility — see PACIFIC 1
appellation *n* a word or combination of words by which a person or thing is regularly known — see NAME 1
append *vb* to join (something) to a mass, quantity, or number so as to bring about an overall increase — see ADD 1
appendage *n* something that is not necessary in itself but adds to the convenience or performance of the main piece of equipment — see ACCESSORY 1
appertain *vb* **1** to be the property of a person or group of persons — see BELONG 2
2 to have a relation or connection — see APPLY 1
appetite *n* **1** a need or desire for food — see HUNGER 1
2 a strong wish for something — see DESIRE
3 positive regard for something — see LIKING
4 urgent desire or interest — see EAGERNESS
appetizing *adj* very pleasing to the sense of taste — see DELICIOUS 1
applaud *vb* to declare enthusiastic approval of — see ACCLAIM
applauding *adj* expressing approval — see FAVORABLE 1
applause *n* enthusiastic and usually public expression of approval ⟨a design for a memorial for the victims of the attack that has received nothing but *applause* from officials, commentators, and the general public⟩
synonyms acclamation, cheering, cheers, ovation, plaudit(s), rave(s)
related words clapping; bravo, hallelujah, hosanna; acclaim, accolade, citation, commendation, compliment, encomium, eulogy, homage, paean, panegyric, salutation, tribute
near antonyms boo, hiss, hoot, jeer, raspberry, smirk, sneer, snicker, snigger, snort, whistle; gibe (*or* jibe), put-down, taunt
antonyms booing, hissing
appliance *n* an interesting and often novel device with a practical use — see GADGET
applicability *n* the fact or state of being pertinent — see PERTINENCE
applicable *adj* **1** capable of being put to use or account — see PRACTICAL 1
2 having to do with the matter at hand — see PERTINENT
3 meeting the requirements of a purpose or situation — see FIT 1
applicant *n* one who seeks an office, honor, position, or award — see CANDIDATE
application *n* the act or practice of employing something for a particular purpose — see USE 1
apply *vb* **1** to have a relation or connection ⟨does your rule about calling home *apply* to me as well?⟩
synonyms appertain, bear, pertain, refer, relate
related words affect, concern, interest, involve, touch; associate, connect, couple, interrelate, link, tie in; deal (with), treat
phrases have to do with
2 to occupy (oneself) diligently or with close attention ⟨Sam *applied* himself to writing thank-you letters to everyone who'd helped sponsor him for the jamboree⟩
synonyms address, bend, buckle, devote, give
related words readdress, reapply; knuckle down, set (to), settle (down); busy, commit, concern, engage, involve; exert, exhaust, put out, spend, strain, stress, tax, trouble, wear out; carry on, pitch in, plunge (in); grind, hump, hustle, peg (away), plod, plow, plug (away), work
near antonyms dally, dawdle, dillydally, fiddle, fool (around), idle, mess (around), monkey (around), play, potter, putter, trifle
3 to put a layer of on a surface — see SPREAD 2
4 to put into action or service — see USE 1
5 to bring to bear especially forcefully or effectively — see EXERT
6 to carry out effectively — see ENFORCE
appoint *vb* **1** to decide upon (the time or date for an event) usually from a position of authority ⟨at the *appointed* hour we were in our places⟩
synonyms designate, fix, name, set
related words adopt, assign, choose, determine, establish, opt (for), pick, pin down, prefer, select, settle, single (out), specify; arrange, coordinate, orchestrate; advertise, announce, declare, publish
2 to pick (someone) by one's authority for a specific position or duty ⟨Igor was *appointed* hall monitor for May⟩
synonyms assign, attach, commission, constitute, designate, detail, name
related words authorize, delegate, depute, deputize; inaugurate, induct, install, instate, ordain, invest; crown, enthrone, throne; choose, elect, handpick, nominate, select, single (out), vote (in)
near antonyms depose, dethrone, displace, eject, oust, overthrow, remove, throw out, uncrown, unmake
antonyms discharge, dismiss, expel, fire
appointment *n* **1** the state or fact of being chosen for a position or duty ⟨the *appointment* of the mayor's husband to the Board of Health came as a surprise⟩
synonyms assignment, commission, designation
related words billet, job, office, place, position, situation, spot, station; authorization, delegation, deputation, placement, ranking; induction, installation, installment (*or* instalment), instating, investiture, investment, ordination; choosing, election, nomination, picking, selection, singling out
near antonyms deposition, dethronement, ejection, ouster, overthrow, rejection, removal
antonyms discharge, dismissal, expulsion, firing
2 an agreement to be present at a specified time and place — see ENGAGEMENT 2
3 an assignment at which one regularly works for pay — see JOB 1
4 appointments *pl* the movable articles in a room — see FURNITURE
apportion *vb* **1** to give as a share or portion — see ALLOT
2 to give out (something) in appropriate amounts or to appropriate individuals — see ADMINISTER 1
apportionment *n* the act or process of giving out something to each member of a group — see DISTRIBUTION 1
apposite *adj* having to do with the matter at hand — see PERTINENT
appraisal *n* **1** an opinion on the nature, character, or quality of something — see ESTIMATION 1

2 the act of placing a value on the nature, character, or quality of something — see ESTIMATE 1

appraise *vb* to make an approximate or tentative judgment regarding — see ESTIMATE 1

appraisement *n* **1** an opinion on the nature, character, or quality of something — see ESTIMATION 1
2 the act of placing a value on the nature, character, or quality of something — see ESTIMATE 1

appreciable *adj* able to be perceived by a sense or by the mind — see PERCEPTIBLE

appreciate *vb* **1** to become greater in extent, volume, amount, or number — see INCREASE 2
2 to hold dear — see LOVE 1
3 to recognize the meaning of — see COMPREHEND 1
4 to think very highly or favorably of — see ADMIRE

appreciation *n* **1** a feeling of great approval and liking — see ADMIRATION 1
2 acknowledgment of having received something good from another — see THANKS
3 the knowledge gained from the process of coming to know or understand something — see COMPREHENSION

appreciative *adj* **1** expressing approval — see FAVORABLE 1
2 feeling or expressing gratitude — see GRATEFUL 1

appreciativeness *n* acknowledgment of having received something good from another — see THANKS

apprehend *vb* **1** to recognize the meaning of — see COMPREHEND 1
2 to take or keep under one's control by authority of law — see ARREST 1

apprehended *adj* taken and held prisoner — see CAPTIVE

apprehension *n* **1** suspicion or fear of future harm or misfortune ⟨Erica entered the dark cave with a great deal of *apprehension*⟩
synonyms alarm, apprehensiveness, dread, foreboding, misgiving
related words agitation, anxiousness, concern, disquiet, distress, disturbance, fearfulness, perturbation, solicitude, uneasiness; scruple, worry; doubt, incertitude, suspense, uncertainty, wariness; defeatism, pessimism; foreknowledge, premonition, presage, presentiment
near antonyms anticipation, excitement, hope, hopefulness; confidence, optimism, sanguinity
2 the act of taking or holding under one's control by authority of law — see ARREST
3 the emotion experienced in the presence or threat of danger — see FEAR
4 an uneasy state of mind usually over the possibility of an anticipated misfortune or trouble — see ANXIETY 1
5 the knowledge gained from the process of coming to know or understand something — see COMPREHENSION

apprehensiveness *n* **1** an uneasy state of mind usually over the possibility of an anticipated misfortune or trouble — see ANXIETY 1
2 suspicion or fear of future harm or misfortune — see APPREHENSION 1

apprentice *n* a person who helps a more skilled person — see HELPER

apprise *vb* to give information to — see ENLIGHTEN 1

approach *n* **1** an established course for traveling from one place to another — see PASSAGE 1
2 the means or procedure for doing something — see METHOD

approach *vb* **1** to come near or nearer ⟨The parade's *approaching* ! I can hear the band playing!⟩
synonyms close, draw on, near
related words arrive, attain, come, gain, hit, land, make, reach, show up, turn up; adjoin, border, touch, verge
near antonyms clear out, depart, exit, go, leave, light out, pull (out), quit, remove, run away, shove (off), take off, walk out
antonyms back (up *or* away), recede, retire, retreat, withdraw
2 to move closer to — see COME 1
3 to come near or nearer to in character or quality — see APPROXIMATE

approaching *adj* being soon to appear or take place — see FORTHCOMING

approbation *n* an acceptance of something as satisfactory — see APPROVAL 1

appropriate *adj* meeting the requirements of a purpose or situation — see FIT 1

appropriate *vb* **1** to take or make use of without authority or right ⟨archaeologists once *appropriated* artifacts excavated at ancient African sites for their museums in Europe⟩
synonyms arrogate, commandeer, preempt, usurp
related words annex, claim, confiscate, expropriate, preoccupy, sequester; grab, grasp, seize, snatch, steal, take over, wrench, wrest; encroach, infringe, invade, trespass
2 to take (something) without right and with an intent to keep — see STEAL 1

appropriately *adv* in a manner suitable for the occasion or purpose — see PROPERLY

appropriateness *n* the quality or state of being especially suitable or fitting ⟨Mrs. Bryce-Jones remarked on the *appropriateness* of window boxes on the cottage, noting they gave it a quaint, cheerful look⟩
synonyms aptness, felicitousness, fitness, fittingness, rightness, seemliness, suitability, suitableness
related words agreeableness, compatibility, congruity, harmoniousness; applicability, bearing, connection, materiality, pertinence, relevance; acceptability, adequacy, adequateness, satisfactoriness, serviceableness, usefulness
near antonyms inapplicability, irrelevance; meaninglessness, pointlessness; incompatibility, incongruity
antonyms inappropriateness, inaptness, infelicity, unfitness

appropriation *n* a sum of money allotted for a specific use by official or formal action ⟨the National Park Service received an increased *appropriation* for wildlife management⟩
synonyms allocation, allotment, annuity, grant, subsidy
related words advance, allowance, benefit, endowment, fund, stipend, trust

approval *n* an acceptance of something as satisfactory ⟨Does this dress I bought for the wedding meet with your *approval* ?⟩
synonyms approbation, blessing, favor, imprimatur, OK (*or* okay)
related words backing, endorsement, sanction,

support; benediction, goodwill; agreement, assent, concurrence, consent; countenance, liking, satisfaction
near antonyms refusal, rejection, repudiation; dislike, dissatisfaction; censure, condemnation, criticism, denunciation, deprecation, depreciation, disparagement, opprobrium, reprehension, reproach, reprobation
antonyms disapprobation, disapproval, disfavor

approve *vb* to give official acceptance of something as satisfactory ⟨as soon as the pond project was *approved*, the bulldozers were at the site⟩
synonyms authorize, clear, OK (*or* okay), ratify, sanction, warrant
related words accept, acknowledge, affirm, confirm; accredit, certify, endorse (*also* indorse), validate; initial, sign; allow, license (*or* licence), permit; reapprove
near antonyms ban, enjoin, forbid, interdict, prohibit; disregard, ignore, neglect, overlook; rebuff, rebut, refuse, spurn
antonyms decline, deny, disallow, disapprove, negative, reject, turn down

approve (of) *vb* to have a favorable opinion of ⟨Mrs. Pinkerton doesn't *approve of* people who stand in the "12 items or less" lane with 13 items⟩
synonyms accept, care (for), countenance, favor, OK (*or* okay), subscribe (to)
related words acclaim, applaud, laud, praise, salute; back (up), stand by, support, sustain, uphold; bear, endure, tolerate; assent (to), concur (with), consent (to); commend, recommend; enjoy, like
phrases go for, hold with
near antonyms censure, condemn, criticize, damn, denounce, deprecate, depreciate, disparage, reprehend, reprobate; detest, dislike, hate, loathe; object (to), oppose
antonyms disapprove (of), discountenance, disfavor, frown (on *or* upon)

approving *adj* **1** expressing approval — see FAVORABLE 1
2 showing or expressing acceptance or approval — see POSITIVE

approximate *adj* being such only when compared to something else — see COMPARATIVE

approximate *vb* to come near or nearer to in character or quality ⟨Rob's violin performance last night didn't even *approximate* what he's really capable of when he's not feeling sick⟩
synonyms approach, compare (with), measure up (to), stack up (against *or* with)
related words add up (to), amount (to), come (to); duplicate, equal, match; mirror, parallel, reflect; border (on), touch (on), verge (on)

apropos *adj* having to do with the matter at hand — see PERTINENT

apropos of *prep* having to do with — see ABOUT 1

apt *adj* **1** having a tendency to be or act in a certain way — see PRONE 1
2 meeting the requirements of a purpose or situation — see FIT 1

aptitude *n* a special and usually inborn ability — see TALENT

aptness *n* **1** an established pattern of behavior — see TENDENCY 1
2 the quality or state of being especially suitable or fitting — see APPROPRIATENESS

aquatic *adj* living, lying, or occurring below the surface of the water — see UNDERWATER

aqueduct *n* an open man-made passageway for water — see CHANNEL 1

arbiter *n* one who works with opposing sides in order to bring about an agreement — see MEDIATOR

arbitrary *adj* **1** having or showing a tendency to force one's will on others without any regard to fairness or necessity ⟨an *arbitrary* piano teacher who makes all her students do the same exercises over and over again⟩
synonyms dictatorial, high-handed, imperious, peremptory, willful (*or* wilful)
related words arrogant, commanding, demanding, dominant, domineering, haughty, imperative, lordly, masterful, overbearing, presumptuous; authoritarian, autocratic, despotic, totalitarian, tyrannical (*also* tyrannic), tyrannous; capricious, changeable, erratic, mercurial, whimsical; biased, inequitable, partisan, prejudiced, unequal, unfair, unjust, unreasonable; unconscionable, unethical, unprincipled, unscrupulous
near antonyms balanced, disinterested, dispassionate, equal, equitable, evenhanded, fair, impartial, just, nonpartisan, objective; rational, reasonable, understanding; unbiased, unprejudiced; ethical, honorable, irreproachable, law-abiding, moral, principled, unimpeachable
2 lacking a definite plan, purpose, or pattern — see RANDOM

arbitrate *vb* to give an opinion about (something at issue or in dispute) — see JUDGE 1

arbitrator *n* one who works with opposing sides in order to bring about an agreement — see MEDIATOR

arc *n* something that curves or is curved — see BEND 1

arc *vb* to turn away from a straight line or course — see CURVE 1

arch *adj* **1** coming before all others in importance — see FOREMOST 1
2 displaying or marked by rude boldness — see NERVY 1

arch *n* something that curves or is curved — see BEND 1

arch *vb* **1** to cause to turn away from a straight line — see BEND 1
2 to turn away from a straight line or course — see CURVE 1

archaic *adj* having passed its time of use or usefulness — see OBSOLETE

archetypal *adj* **1** constituting, serving as, or worthy of being a pattern to be imitated — see MODEL
2 having or showing the qualities associated with the members of a particular group or kind — see TYPICAL 1

archetype *n* something from which copies are made — see ORIGINAL

archive *n* a place where books, periodicals, and records are kept for use but not for sale — see LIBRARY

arctic *adj* having a low or subnormal temperature — see COLD 1

ardent *adj* **1** having or expressing great depth of feeling — see FERVENT
2 showing urgent desire or interest — see EAGER

ardor *n* **1** depth of feeling ⟨candidates for citizenship reciting the oath of allegiance to the United States with all the *ardor* that they could muster⟩
synonyms emotion, fervency, fervidness, fervor, heat, intensity, passion, vehemence, warmth

related words histrionics, mawkishness, melodrama, sappiness, sentimentality; eagerness, earnestness, enthusiasm, excitement, gusto, zest; fanaticism, fever, fire, hot-bloodedness, infatuation, mania, obsession, zeal; compassion, responsiveness, sympathy, tenderness
near antonyms aloofness, calmness, coldness, collectedness, composure, coolness, detachedness, dryness, phlegm, reserve, reservedness, reticence, taciturnity; apathy, indifference, unconcern; stiffness, woodenness
antonyms impassivity
2 urgent desire or interest — see EAGERNESS

arduous *adj* **1** requiring considerable physical or mental effort — see HARD 2
2 requiring much time, effort, or careful attention — see DEMANDING 1

arduously *adv* with great effort or determination — see HARD 1

area *n* **1** a part or portion having no fixed boundaries — see REGION 1
2 a region of activity, knowledge, or influence — see FIELD 2

arena *n* **1** a large room or building for enclosed public gatherings — see HALL 3
2 a region of activity, knowledge, or influence — see FIELD 2

argot *n* the special terms or expressions of a particular group or field — see TERMINOLOGY

argue *vb* **1** to state (something) as a reason in support of or against something under consideration ⟨Luis *argued* that a bake sale would make a lot less money than a car wash⟩
synonyms assert, contend, maintain, plead, reason
related words claim, insist; affirm, aver, avouch, avow; advance, offer, propose, submit; advise, counsel, recommend, suggest, urge; convince, persuade; advocate, champion, espouse, support; explain, justify, rationalize; consider, debate, discuss; counter, disprove, rebut, refute
2 to express different opinions about something often angrily ⟨Francesca didn't *argue* with her little brother the whole time they were at Walt Disney World⟩
synonyms bicker, brawl, dispute, fall out, fight, hassle, quarrel, row, scrap, spat, squabble, wrangle
related words challenge, dare, defy; clash, contend, contest; cavil, fuss, nitpick, quibble; consider, debate, discuss; kick, object, protest
phrases bandy words, fall foul
near antonyms coexist, get along; accept, agree, assent, concur, consent
3 to cause (someone) to agree with a belief or course of action by using arguments or earnest requests — see PERSUADE
4 to talk about (an issue) usually from various points of view and for the purpose of arriving at a decision or opinion — see DISCUSS

arguer *n* a person who takes part in a dispute — see DISPUTANT

argument *n* **1** an often noisy or angry expression of differing opinions ⟨the couple's *arguments* were often loud enough to be heard all over the neighborhood⟩
synonyms altercation, bicker, brawl, cross fire, disagreement, dispute, falling-out, fight, hassle, misunderstanding, quarrel, row, scrap, spat, squabble, tiff, wrangle
related words clash, run-in, skirmish, tussle; feud, vendetta; attack, contention, dissension; controversy, debate; fuss, objection, protest, protestation; affray, feud, fisticuffs, fracas, fray, free-for-all, melee
2 a statement given to explain a belief or act — see REASON 1
3 an exchange of views for the purpose of exploring a subject or deciding an issue — see DISCUSSION 1
4 an idea or opinion that is put forth in a discussion or debate — see CONTENTION

argumentative *adj* **1** given to arguing ⟨Ryan's *argumentative* nature is such that he's always insisting he didn't make the fouls that the referee calls⟩
synonyms contentious, disputatious, quarrelsome, scrappy
related words bellicose, belligerent, combative, pugnacious, truculent; balky, contrary, ornery, perverse, restive, wayward; disobedient, froward, insubordinate, intractable, recalcitrant, refractory; hardheaded, headstrong, mulish, obdurate, obstinate, pigheaded, resistant, self-willed, stubborn, unbending, uncompromising, uncooperative, unreasonable, unyielding, willful (*or* wilful)
near antonyms acquiescent, agreeable, amenable, complaisant, compliant, complying, conciliatory, cooperative, obliging; docile, obedient, submissive, tractable
2 feeling or displaying eagerness to fight — see BELLIGERENT

arid *adj* marked by little or no precipitation or humidity — see DRY 1

arise *vb* **1** to leave one's bed ⟨the travelers *arose* before dawn and were on their way as the sun came up⟩
synonyms get up, rise, uprise
related words arouse, awake, awaken, bestir, stir, wake
near antonyms doze, drop (off), nap, nod, sleep, slumber; bunk, perch, roost, settle; couch, lie (down), recline
antonyms bed (down), retire, turn in
2 to come to one's attention especially gradually or unexpectedly ⟨note in your report any problems that *arise* while you are conducting the experiment⟩
synonyms crop (up), emerge, materialize, spring (up), surface
related words appear, come out, show up, turn up; chance, come, come about, fall out, go (on), go off, hap, happen, occur, pass, transpire; interfere, interpose, intervene, intrude
3 to come into existence — see BEGIN 2
4 to move or extend upward — see ASCEND

aristocracy *n* the highest class in a society ⟨at one time in China only the *aristocracy* could own land⟩
synonyms gentry, upper class, upper crust
related words elect, elite, establishment, gentlefolk, jet set, nobility, quality, royalty, society
near antonyms commoners, (the) crowd, (the) masses, peasantry, peonage, (the) people, plebeians, (the) populace, (the) public, rank and file; bourgeoisie, middle class, working class; dregs, (the) herd, (the) mob, rabble, riffraff, scum, trash
antonyms proletarians, proletariat

aristocrat *n* a man of high birth or social position — see GENTLEMAN 1

aristocratic *adj* of high birth, rank, or station — see NOBLE 1

arithmetic *n* the act or process of performing mathematical operations to find a value — see CALCULATION

[1]**arm** *n* a portable weapon from which a shot is discharged by gunpowder — see GUN 1

[2]**arm** *n* **1** an area of land that juts out into a body of water — see [2]CAPE
2 the right or means to command or control others — see POWER 1

armada *n* a group of vehicles traveling together or under one management — see FLEET

armed forces *n pl* the combined army, air force, and navy of a nation ⟨our nation's *armed forces* are stationed throughout the world⟩
synonyms military, service, troops
related words GI's (*or* GIs), men-at-arms, rank and file, servicemen, servicewomen, soldiers, soldiery; militia, reserves; armor, defense
near antonyms civilians, noncombatants

armistice *n* a temporary stopping of fighting — see TRUCE

armor *n* **1** means or method of defending — see DEFENSE 1
2 something that encloses another thing especially to protect it — see [1]CASE

armory *n* a place where military arms are stored ⟨the soldier was sent to the *armory* to get a replacement weapon for the one that had been stolen⟩
synonyms arsenal, depot, dump, magazine
related words fort, fortress, stronghold; repository, storehouse, warehouse

army *n* **1** a large body of men and women organized for land warfare ⟨In 218 B.C., Hannibal marched into Italy with an *army* of 26,000, and even a few elephants, after crossing the Alps⟩
synonyms battalion, host, legion
related words infantry, ranks, regulars, soldiers, troops, troopers
2 a great number of persons or things gathered together — see CROWD 1

aroma *n* a sweet or pleasant smell — see FRAGRANCE

aromatic *adj* having a pleasant smell — see FRAGRANT

around *adv* **1** on all sides or in every direction ⟨he looked *around*⟩ ⟨butterflies were flying all *around*⟩
synonyms about, round
related words all over, everyplace, everywhere; abroad, afloat, hereabouts (*or* hereabout)
2 toward the opposite direction ⟨she turned *around* and saw him⟩
synonyms about, back, round
related words backward (*or* backwards), behind, down, downward, rearward (*or* rearwards); across, athwart, counter, counterclockwise
3 at, within, or to a short distance or time — see NEAR 1
4 from beginning to end — see THROUGH 1

around *prep* **1** close to ⟨I wouldn't stand *around* those rocks—there could be snakes under them⟩
synonyms about, by, near, next to
related words alongside, beside; across, along, at; circa
2 in random positions within the boundaries of ⟨huge, strangely shaped rocks were scattered *around* the canyon floor⟩
synonyms about, over, round, through, throughout
related words on

arouse *vb* **1** to cause to stop sleeping — see WAKE 1
2 to cease to be asleep — see WAKE 2
3 to rouse to strong feeling or action — see PROVOKE 1

arrange *vb* **1** to come to an agreement or decision concerning the details of ⟨*arrange* a time for the meeting⟩ ⟨*arrange* money matters for your trip⟩
synonyms decide, fix, set, settle
related words agree, contract, pledge, promise; draft, frame, hammer (out), intrigue, lay out, maneuver, map (out), plan, program, schematize, scheme, shape, square away, work out; affirm, approve, authorize, clear, confirm, OK (*or* okay), sanction, warrant; close, complete, conclude, end, finalize, finish, round (off *or* out), wind up, wrap up; bargain, chaffer, deal, dicker, haggle, horse-trade, negotiate
phrases dispose of
2 to put into a particular arrangement — see ORDER 1
3 to bring about through discussion and compromise — see NEGOTIATE 1
4 to work out the details of (something) in advance — see PLAN 1

arrangement *n* **1** a method worked out in advance for achieving some objective — see PLAN 1
2 the way in which something is sized, arranged, or organized — see FORMAT 1
3 the way in which the elements of something (as a work of art) are arranged — see COMPOSITION 3
4 the way objects in space or events in time are arranged or follow one another — see ORDER 1

arrant *adj* having no exceptions or restrictions — see ABSOLUTE 2

array *n* **1** a number of things considered as a unit — see GROUP 1
2 a usually small number of persons considered as a unit — see GROUP 2
3 dressy clothing — see FINERY
4 the way objects in space or events in time are arranged or follow one another — see ORDER 1

array *vb* **1** to make more attractive by adding something that is beautiful or becoming — see DECORATE
2 to outfit with clothes and especially fine or special clothes — see CLOTHE 1
3 to put into a particular arrangement — see ORDER 1

arrest *n* the act of taking or holding under one's control by authority of law ⟨there have been only two *arrests* for driving while intoxicated in the county in the last six months⟩
synonyms apprehension, pinch
related words bust [*slang*], raid; capture, entrapment, seizure; captivity, confinement, detention, enchainment, immurement, imprisonment, incarceration, restraint
near antonyms emancipation, liberation, release
antonyms discharge

arrest *vb* **1** to take or keep under one's control by authority of law ⟨the inept robber was promptly *arrested* by the off-duty policeman he had tried to hold up⟩
synonyms apprehend, bust [*slang*], nab, pick up, pinch, restrain, seize
related words bag, capture, catch, collar, get, grab, grapple, hook, land, nail, snare, snatch,

trap; confine, detain, hold, immure, imprison, incarcerate, intern, jail, lock (up); bind, enchain, fetter, handcuff, manacle, shackle, trammel
near antonyms emancipate, free, liberate, loose, loosen, release, spring; unbind, unchain
antonyms discharge
2 to bring (something) to a standstill — see [1]HALT 1
3 to hold the attention of as if by a spell — see ENTHRALL 1

arrested *adj* taken and held prisoner — see CAPTIVE

arresting *adj* **1** holding the attention or provoking interest — see INTERESTING
2 likely to attract attention — see NOTICEABLE

arrival *n* the act of coming upon a scene ⟨spring's late *arrival* meant we were still skiing in mid-April⟩ ⟨the groom blamed his belated *arrival* for the wedding on a huge traffic snarl⟩
synonyms advent, appearance
related words approach, entrance, ingress; beginning, birth, commencement, dawn, dawning, debut, genesis, inception, morning, onset, start
near antonyms dissipation, dissolution, evaporation, fading, melting, passing, vanishing; clearing out, egress, exit, exiting, leaving, retirement, withdrawal
antonyms departing, departure, disappearance, going

arrive *vb* to get to a destination — see COME 2

arrogance *n* an exaggerated sense of one's importance that shows itself in the making of excessive or unjustified claims ⟨in his *arrogance* the president of the club made all the arrangements for the annual banquet without consulting the members⟩
synonyms haughtiness, imperiousness, loftiness, lordliness, masterfulness, peremptoriness, pompousness, presumptuousness, pretense (*or* pretence), pretension, pretentiousness, self-importance, superciliousness, superiority
related words authoritativeness, bossiness, dominance, high-handedness; condescension, disdain, scorn; snobbery, snobbishness, snobbism, snootiness; cheek, cheekiness, impertinence, impudence, sauciness; boastfulness, bombast, braggadocio, swagger, vaingloriousness, vainglory; cockiness, complacence, conceit, egoism, egotism, pride, pridefulness, self-centeredness, self-conceit, self-satisfaction, smugness, vanity
near antonyms bashfulness, demureness, retiringness, shyness; diffidence, self-doubt, timidity; meekness, passiveness, passivity, submissiveness; quietness, reserve, reservedness
antonyms humility, modesty

arrogant *adj* having a feeling of superiority that shows itself in an overbearing attitude ⟨the *arrogant* young lawyer elbowed his way to the head of the line of customers, declaring that he was too busy to wait like everybody else⟩
synonyms cavalier, haughty, highfalutin, high-handed, high-hat, imperious, important, lofty, lordly, masterful, overweening, peremptory, pompous, presumptuous, pretentious, supercilious, superior, uppish, uppity
related words authoritarian, bossy, dominant, dominating, domineering, magisterial, pontificating; condescending, disdainful, patronizing; impertinent, impudent, saucy; snobbish, snobby, snooty; boastful, bombastic, braggart, bragging, cocky, swaggering, vain, vainglorious; complacent, conceited, egocentric, egoistic, egotistic (*or* egotistical), prideful, proud, self-centered, self-conceited, self-satisfied, smug, stuck-up
near antonyms bashful, cowering, cringing, demure, diffident, mousy (*or* mousey), overmodest, self-doubting, shrinking, shy, subdued, timid; acquiescent, compliant, deferential, meek, passive, submissive, unaggressive, unassertive, unassuming, unobtrusive, yielding; quiet, reserved, retiring
antonyms humble, modest

arrogate *vb* to take or make use of without authority or right — see APPROPRIATE 1

arsenal *n* a place where military arms are stored — see ARMORY

arsonist *n* a person who deliberately and unlawfully sets fire to a building or other property ⟨they finally caught the *arsonist*, but only after he'd set fire to four barns⟩
synonyms firebug, incendiary
related words igniter (*or* ignitor)

art *n* subtle or imaginative ability in inventing, devising, or executing something — see SKILL 1

artery *n* a passage cleared for public vehicular travel — see WAY 1

artful *adj* **1** clever at attaining one's ends by indirect and often deceptive means ⟨the lawyer, by her *artful* questioning, got the witness to admit he had been lying⟩
synonyms beguiling, cagey (*also* cagy), crafty, cunning, devious, foxy, guileful, slick, sly, subtle, wily
related words astute, cute, facile, glib, sharp, shrewd; crooked, deceitful, deceptive, dishonest, insidious, insinuating, Machiavellian, shady, shifty, slippery, sneaky, treacherous, tricky, underhand, underhanded, unscrupulous; backhanded, double-dealing, hypocritical, insincere, mealy-mouthed, smooth-tongued, two-faced; circuitous, circular, roundabout; clandestine, concealed, covert, furtive, hugger-mugger, secret, stealthy, surreptitious, undercover; calculating, designing, scheming, plotting
near antonyms obvious, open, patent, plain, public, unconcealed; aboveboard, candid, direct, forthright, frank, honest, natural, outspoken, plainspoken, real, simple, sincere, straightforward, unaffected, unpretending
antonyms artless, guileless, ingenuous
2 showing a use of the imagination and creativity especially in inventing — see CLEVER 1
3 accomplished with trained ability — see SKILLFUL

artfulness *n* **1** skill in achieving one's ends through indirect, subtle, or underhanded means — see CUNNING 1
2 subtle or imaginative ability in inventing, devising, or executing something — see SKILL 1

article *n* a short piece of writing typically expressing a point of view — see ESSAY 1

articulate *adj* able to express oneself clearly and well ⟨the television crew covering the science fair were looking for photogenic and *articulate* students to explain their projects on the air⟩
synonyms eloquent, fluent, well-spoken
related words facile, glib, smooth-tongued, voluble; expressive, outspoken, verbal, vocal; blabby, chatty, garrulous, loquacious, talkative, verbose; unfaltering, unhesitating
near antonyms faltering, halting, hesitant, maun-

dering, mumbling, muttering, sputtering, stammering, stumbling, stuttering; mute, speechless, tongue-tied, voiceless
antonyms inarticulate

articulate *vb* **1** to utter clearly and distinctly ⟨uses a very measured tone and *articulates* every syllable when issuing scoldings⟩
synonyms enunciate
related words express, pronounce, say, verbalize, vocalize, voice; speak out, speak up
near antonyms falter, grunt, halt, hesitate, maunder, sputter, stammer, stumble, stutter; mouth, mumble, murmur, mutter, whisper
2 to convey in appropriate or telling terms — see PHRASE
3 to express (a thought or emotion) in words — see SAY 1

articulateness *n* the art or power of speaking or writing in a forceful and convincing way — see ELOQUENCE

articulation *n* **1** an act, process, or means of putting something into words — see EXPRESSION 1
2 the clear and accurate pronunciation of words especially in public speaking — see DICTION 1

artifice *n* **1** a clever often underhanded means to achieve an end — see TRICK 1
2 skill in achieving one's ends through indirect, subtle, or underhanded means — see CUNNING 1
3 subtle or imaginative ability in inventing, devising, or executing something — see SKILL 1
4 the inclination or practice of misleading others through lies or trickery — see DECEIT
5 the use of clever underhanded actions to achieve an end — see TRICKERY

artificer *n* a person whose occupation requires skill with the hands — see ARTISAN

artificial *adj* **1** lacking in natural or spontaneous quality ⟨the beauty-pageant contestants' *artificial* smiles looked like they were glued on their faces⟩
synonyms affected, assumed, bogus, contrived, factitious, fake, false, feigned, forced, mechanical, mock, phony (*also* phoney), pretended, pseudo, put-on, sham, simulated, spurious, strained, unnatural
related words automatic, canned, concocted, fabricated, labored, manufactured, unauthentic, unreal, unrealistic; empty, facile, hollow, hypocritical, insincere, left-handed; exaggerated, histrionic, melodramatic, overacted, overdone, theatrical; cute, cutesy, goody-goody, mincing, overrefined, simpering; conventional, formal, impersonal, inflexible, rigid, stiff, stylized, wooden; artful, calculated, conscious, cultivated, deliberate, premeditated, studied
near antonyms authentic, bona fide, real, realistic, true; honest, ingenuous, sincere, unpretending; easy, effortless, smooth; extemporaneous, impromptu, impulsive, instinctive, unconscious, unprompted, unrehearsed
antonyms artless, genuine, natural, spontaneous, unaffected, unfeigned, unforced
2 not being or expressing what one appears to be or express — see INSINCERE
3 being such in appearance only and made with or manufactured from usually cheaper materials — see IMITATION

artillery *n* large firearms (as cannon or rockets) ⟨during the *artillery* attack families hid in their cellars⟩
synonyms guns, ordnance
related words ammunition, armament, arms, munitions, weaponry, weapons

artisan *n* a person whose occupation requires skill with the hands ⟨we visited a re-created 19th-century New England village that features an array of *artisans* —a cooper, a carpenter, a blacksmith, a potter, a glassblower⟩
synonyms artificer, craftsman, handicrafter, tradesman
related words artist, maker; journeyman, master; mechanic, smith, technician, wright; handyman

artist *n* a person with a high level of knowledge or skill in a field — see EXPERT

artistic *adj* of or relating to the fine arts — see CULTURAL

artistry *n* subtle or imaginative ability in inventing, devising, or executing something — see SKILL 1

artless *adj* **1** free from any intent to deceive or impress others — see GUILELESS
2 hastily or roughly constructed — see RUDE 1

artlessly *adv* without any attempt to impress by deception or exaggeration — see NATURALLY 3

artlessness *n* the quality or state of being simple and sincere — see NAÏVETÉ 1

as *conj* for the reason that — see SINCE

ascend *vb* to move or extend upward ⟨the path *ascended* so steeply at one point that we had to scramble up on our hands and knees⟩
synonyms arise, climb, lift, mount, rise, soar, up, uprise, upsweep, upturn
related words boost, elevate, raise, uplift, upraise; take off, zoom; crest, scale, surmount, top
near antonyms dive, nose-dive, plummet, plunge, sink, slide
antonyms decline, descend, dip, drop, fall (off)

ascendancy *n* controlling power or influence over others — see SUPREMACY 1

ascension *n* the act or an instance of rising or climbing up — see ASCENT 1

ascent *n* **1** the act or an instance of rising or climbing up ⟨our plane broke through some heavy low clouds during its *ascent* and leveled off once we were above them⟩
synonyms ascension, climb, rise, rising, soar
related words boost, hike, increase, raise; elevation, levitation, lift-off, raising, takeoff; heave, upheaval, uplifting, upraising, upsurge, upsweep, upswing, uptrend, upturn, upwelling
near antonyms dive, nosedive, plop, plummeting, plunge, sinking; decline, decrease
antonyms descent, dip, drop, fall
2 an upward slope ⟨we'd reached the final *ascent* of the trail to the summit⟩
synonyms rise, upgrade
related words grade, incline; climb, hump, mound, ridge, swell
near antonyms basin, depression, hollow
antonyms declension, decline, declivity, descent, downgrade
3 a raising or a state of being raised to a higher rank or position — see ADVANCEMENT 1

ascertain *vb* **1** to come to an awareness — see DISCOVER 1
2 to come upon after searching, study, or effort — see FIND 1

ascribe *vb* to explain (something) as being the result of something else — see CREDIT 1

aseptic *adj* free from filth, infection, or dangers to health — see SANITARY

ashamed *adj* suffering from or expressive of a feeling of responsibility for wrongdoing — see GUILTY 2

ashen *adj* lacking a healthy skin color — see PALE 2

ashes *n pl* the portion or bits of something left over or behind after it has been destroyed — see REMAINS 1

ashy *adj* lacking a healthy skin color — see PALE 2

aside from *prep* not including — see EXCEPT

as if *conj* the way it would be or one would do if ⟨she looked *as if* she wanted to ask one more question before we left⟩
synonyms as though, like

asinine *adj* showing or marked by a lack of good sense or judgment — see FOOLISH 1

asininity *n* **1** a foolish act or idea — see FOLLY 1
2 lack of good sense or judgment — see FOOLISHNESS 1

ask *vb* **1** to put a question or questions to ⟨my grandfather *asked* me all about my trip⟩
synonyms inquire (of), interrogate, query, question, quiz
related words cross-examine, examine, grill, pump; poll, survey
near antonyms rejoin, retort; comment, observe, remark
antonyms answer, reply, respond
2 to make a request of ⟨*ask* the sales clerk for assistance⟩
synonyms request, solicit
related words appeal (to), beg, beseech, entreat, implore, importune, invoke, petition, pray, supplicate; demand, enjoin, exact, press, require
phrases call on (*or* upon)
3 to set or receive as a price — see CHARGE 1

ask (for) *vb* **1** to make a request for ⟨don't be afraid to *ask for* help if you need it⟩
synonyms call (for), plead (for), quest, request, seek, solicit, sue (for)
related words apply (for), beg (for), clamor (for), urge; demand, enjoin, exact, insist (on), require, requisition
2 to act so as to make (something) more likely — see COURT 1
3 to give a request or demand for — see ORDER 2

askance *adv* with distrust ⟨we looked *askance* at the dealer's assertion that the car had never been in an accident⟩
synonyms distrustfully, doubtfully, doubtingly, dubiously, mistrustfully, skeptically, suspiciously
related words hesitantly, hesitatingly, incredulously, questioningly, quizzically, unbelievingly; charily, guardedly, warily; captiously, critically, cynically, deprecatingly, disapprovingly, disparagingly, negatively, reproachfully, unfavorably; anxiously, apprehensively, uncomfortably, uneasily
phrases with a grain of salt
near antonyms approvingly, favorably, positively; confidently, sanguinely; credulously, uncritically
antonyms trustfully, trustingly

askew *adj* inclined or twisted to one side — see AWRY

aslant *adj* inclined or twisted to one side — see AWRY

asleep *adj* **1** being in a state of suspended consciousness ⟨Paul was *asleep* when the earthquake struck⟩
synonyms dormant, dozing, napping, resting, sleeping, slumbering
related words drowsy, nodding, sleepy, slumberous (*or* slumbrous), somnolent; dreaming, reposing; hypnotized, mesmerized, semiconscious
near antonyms aware, conscious; sleepless; aroused, astir, up
antonyms awake, wakeful, wide-awake
2 lacking in sensation or feeling — see NUMB

aspect *n* **1** a certain way in which something appears or may be regarded ⟨depending on what *aspect* of college life you consider most important, there are several colleges which might be good for you⟩
synonyms angle, facet, hand, phase, side
related words air, appearance, character, color, complexion, condition, face, look, semblance, shape, state, visage; period, stage, step; point of view, position, posture, stance, standpoint, view, viewpoint; interpretation, reading, rendering, translation, version; article, case, component, count, detail, element, factor, instance, item, matter, part, particular, point, regard, respect
2 the outward form of someone or something especially as indicative of a quality — see APPEARANCE 1

asperity *n* **1** a harsh or sharp quality — see EDGE 1
2 biting sharpness of feeling or expression — see ACRIMONY 1
3 something that is a cause for suffering or special effort especially in the attainment of a goal — see DIFFICULTY 1

asperse *vb* to make untrue and harmful statements about — see SLANDER

aspersing *n* the making of false statements that damage another's reputation — see SLANDER

aspirant *n* one who seeks an office, honor, position, or award — see CANDIDATE

aspiration *n* **1** eager desire for personal advancement — see AMBITION 1
2 something that one hopes or intends to accomplish — see GOAL

aspire *vb* to have in mind as a purpose or goal — see INTEND

aspiring *adj* having a strong desire for personal advancement — see AMBITIOUS 1

ass *n* a sturdy and patient domestic mammal that is used especially to carry things — see DONKEY 1

assail *vb* **1** to criticize harshly and usually publicly — see ATTACK 2
2 to take sudden, violent action against — see ATTACK 1

assassin *n* a person who kills another person ⟨shot down by an unknown *assassin*⟩
synonyms killer, murderer
related words butcher, executioner, slaughterer, slayer

assault *n* the act or action of setting upon with force or violence — see ATTACK 1

assault *vb* to take sudden, violent action against — see ATTACK 1

assay *n* the separation and identification of the parts of a whole — see ANALYSIS 1

assay *vb* **1** to identify and examine the basic elements or parts of (something) especially for discovering interrelationships — see ANALYZE
2 to make an effort to do — see ATTEMPT

assemblage *n* **1** a body of people come together in one place — see GATHERING 1
2 a mass or quantity that has piled up or that has been gathered — see ACCUMULATION 1

3 a number of things considered as a unit — see GROUP 1
4 an organized group of objects acquired and maintained for study, exhibition, or personal pleasure — see COLLECTION 1

assemble *vb* **1** to come together into one body or place ⟨the graduates were told to *assemble* in the cafeteria an hour before the ceremony⟩
synonyms cluster, collect, concentrate, conglomerate, congregate, convene, converge, forgather (*or* foregather), gather, meet, rendezvous
related words affiliate, ally, associate, band (together), club, collaborate, confederate, conjoin, consolidate, consort, cooperate, couple, federate, gang (up), join, merge, unite
near antonyms depart, leave, take off; disjoin, dissociate, disunite
antonyms break up, disband, disperse, split up
2 to form by putting together parts or materials — see BUILD
3 to bring together in assembly by or as if by command — see CONVOKE
4 to bring together in one body or place — see GATHER 1

assembly *n* **1** a body of people come together in one place — see GATHERING 1
2 a body of persons gathered for religious worship — see CONGREGATION 1
3 a coming together of a number of persons for a specified purpose — see MEETING 1

assert *vb* **1** to state clearly and strongly ⟨Mrs. Cartwright is never afraid to *assert* her allegiance to flag and country⟩
synonyms affirm, aver, avouch, avow, declare, lay down, profess
related words advance, advertise, boost, plug, promote, publicize; announce, blaze, call, proclaim, pronounce, say; accent, accentuate, emphasize, stress, underline, underscore; advocate, champion, defend, espouse, support, uphold; assure, convince, persuade; explain, justify, rationalize
near antonyms minimize, understate; disregard, ignore, neglect, overlook
2 to state (something) as a reason in support of or against something under consideration — see ARGUE 1
3 to state as a fact usually forcefully — see CLAIM 1

assertion *n* **1** a solemn and often public declaration of the truth or existence of something — see PROTESTATION
2 an idea or opinion that is put forth in a discussion or debate — see CONTENTION

assertive *adj* **1** having or showing a bold forcefulness in the pursuit of a goal — see AGGRESSIVE 1
2 marked by or uttered with forcefulness — see EMPHATIC 1

assertiveness *n* the quality or state of being forceful (as in expression) — see VEHEMENCE 1

assess *vb* **1** to establish or apply as a charge or penalty — see IMPOSE
2 to make an approximate or tentative judgment regarding — see ESTIMATE 1

assessment *n* **1** a charge usually of money collected by the government from people or businesses for public use — see TAX
2 an opinion on the nature, character, or quality of something — see ESTIMATION 1
3 the act of placing a value on the nature, character, or quality of something — see ESTIMATE 1

assets *n pl* the total of one's money and property — see WEALTH 1

assiduity *n* attentive and persistent effort — see DILIGENCE

assiduous *adj* involved in often constant activity — see BUSY 1

assiduously *adv* with great effort or determination — see HARD 1

assiduousness *n* attentive and persistent effort — see DILIGENCE

assign *vb* **1** to give a task, duty, or responsibility to — see ENTRUST 1
2 to give as a share or portion — see ALLOT
3 to give over the legal possession or ownership of — see TRANSFER 1
4 to pick (someone) by one's authority for a specific position or duty — see APPOINT 2

assignment *n* **1** a piece of work that needs to be done regularly — see CHORE 1
2 a specific task with which a person or group is charged — see MISSION
3 something assigned to be read or studied — see LESSON
4 the state or fact of being chosen for a position or duty — see APPOINTMENT 1

assimilate *vb* to make a part of a body or system — see EMBODY 1

assist *n* an act or instance of helping — see HELP 1

assist *vb* to provide (someone) with what is useful or necessary to achieve an end — see HELP 1

assistance *n* an act or instance of helping — see HELP 1

assistant *n* a person who helps a more skilled person — see HELPER

associate *n* **1** a person frequently seen in the company of another ⟨after he took up skateboarding, Michael gained a whole new set of *associates*⟩
synonyms cohort, companion, comrade, crony, fellow, hobnobber, mate
related words colleague, coworker, equal, peer, workmate; accomplice, affiliate, ally, collaborator, confederate, partner; buddy, chum, confidant, familiar, friend, hearty, intimate, pal; compatriot, countryman; classmate, housemate, messmate, playmate, roommate, schoolmate, shipmate, teammate; attendant, escort; hanger-on, leech, parasite
2 a fellow worker — see COLLEAGUE

associate *vb* **1** to come or be together as friends ⟨a boy who would *associate* only with other hardcore basketball fans⟩
synonyms chum, consort, fraternize, hang around, hobnob, pal (around)
related words affiliate, ally, attach, band, bond, club, collaborate, collude, confederate, conjoin, connect, cooperate, couple, gang, get along, group, hook, interrelate, join, knot, league, link, mingle, mix, rally, relate, side, socialize, team, tie, wed
phrases rub elbows (with), rub shoulders (with), take up with
near antonyms avoid, cold-shoulder, shun, snub; alienate, estrange; break up, disband, disperse, split up; disjoin, dissociate, disunite, divorce, sever, split, sunder
2 to think of (something) in combination ⟨Kelly *associates* getting shots with ice cream cones, her treat every time she goes to the doctor⟩
synonyms connect, correlate, identify, link, relate

related words compare, equate, liken; group, join, lump (together), tie (together)
near antonyms contrast, differentiate, discriminate, distinguish, separate, set off
3 to come together to form a single unit — see UNITE 1
4 to form or enter into an association that furthers the interests of its members — see ALLY
5 to take part in social activities — see SOCIALIZE

association *n* **1** the state of having shared interests or efforts (as in social or business matters) ⟨Rita was honored for her long *association* with the Montgomery Benevolent Society⟩
synonyms affiliation, alliance, collaboration, confederation, connection, cooperation, hookup, liaison, linkup, partnership, relation, relationship, tie-up, union
related words business, dealings, interaction; exchange, interconnection, interrelation, mutualism, reciprocity, symbiosis; incorporation, integration, merger, unification; affinity, attachment, closeness, intimacy, rapport, sympathy; kinship, oneness, solidarity, togetherness, unity; companionship, company, fellowship
near antonyms breakup, dissolution, disunion; division, parting, separation, severance, split; alienation, divorce, estrangement
antonyms dissociation
2 a group of persons formally joined together for some common interest ⟨all *associations* meeting on school property must be registered with and approved by the principal's office⟩
synonyms brotherhood, club, college, congress, council, fellowship, fraternity, guild (*also* gild), institute, institution, junto, league, order, organization, society, sodality
related words collective, commune, community, cooperative; alliance, bloc, coalition, partnership; body, group; circle, clan, clique, coterie, lot, set; crew, outfit, party, squad, team; branch, chapter, local; faithful, fold, membership; sisterhood, sorority; cabal, confederacy, conspiracy; band, gang, ring; cartel, combine, syndicate
3 the fact or state of having something in common — see CONNECTION 1

assort *vb* to arrange or assign according to type — see CLASSIFY 1

assorted *adj* consisting of many things of different sorts — see MISCELLANEOUS

assortment *n* **1** an unorganized collection or mixture of various things — see MISCELLANY 1
2 the quality or state of being composed of many different elements or types — see VARIETY 1

assuage *vb* **1** to make more bearable or less severe — see HELP 2
2 to put a complete end to (a physical need or desire) — see SATISFY 1

assume *vb* **1** to take to or upon oneself ⟨Josh promised to *assume* responsibility for any damage to the flower beds caused by the volleyball game in the backyard⟩
synonyms accept, bear, shoulder, take over, undertake
related words adopt, embrace; back, endorse (*also* indorse), espouse, stand by, support, uphold; accede, acquiesce, agree, assent, consent
near antonyms abjure, recant, renounce, retract, take back; decline, refuse, reject, spurn, turn down; abstain, forbear, refrain; avoid, bypass, detour
antonyms disavow, disclaim, disown, repudiate
2 to take as true or as a fact without actual proof ⟨everyone *assumed*, wrongly, that someone else was bringing dessert⟩
synonyms postulate, premise, presume, presuppose, suppose
related words accept, believe, credit, swallow; conclude, deduce, gather, judge, infer, take; conjecture, figure, guess, reckon [*chiefly dialect*], surmise, suspect, think; conceive, dream, fancy, imagine, perceive, preconceive; hypothesize, speculate, theorize; affirm, allege, assert, aver, avouch, avow, claim, contend, declare, insist, maintain, profess
phrases take for granted
near antonyms challenge, disbelieve, discount, discredit, dispute, distrust, doubt, mistrust, question, suspect, wonder (about); deny, disavow, disclaim, disown, reject, repudiate; confute, disprove, rebut, refute
3 to form an opinion from little or no evidence — see GUESS 1
4 to present a false appearance of — see FEIGN

assumed *adj* **1** appearing to be true on the basis of evidence that may or may not be confirmed — see APPARENT 1
2 lacking in natural or spontaneous quality — see ARTIFICIAL 1

assumption *n* something taken as being true or factual and used as a starting point for a course of action or reasoning ⟨the widespread *assumption* that violent entertainment leads to violent behavior in children⟩ ⟨your argument is faulty because it's based on erroneous *assumptions*⟩
synonyms postulate, premise, presumption, presupposition, supposition
related words hypothesis, proposition, theory, thesis; axiom, truism, verity; belief, canon, doctrine, dogma, gospel, law; precept, principle, rule, standard, tenet; basis, foundation, ground; conclusion, deduction, inference; affirmation, assertion, avouchment, declaration

assurance *n* **1** a state of mind in which one is free from doubt — see CONFIDENCE 2
2 great faith in oneself or one's abilities — see CONFIDENCE 1

assure *vb* **1** to ease the grief or distress of — see COMFORT 1
2 to make sure, certain, or safe — see ENSURE

assured *adj* **1** having or showing a mind free from doubt — see CERTAIN 2
2 having or showing great faith in oneself or one's abilities — see CONFIDENT 1

assuredly *adv* without any question — see INDEED 1

assuredness *n* a state of mind in which one is free from doubt — see CONFIDENCE 2

astern *adv* near, toward, or in the stern of a ship or the tail of an aircraft — see AFT

as though *conj* the way it would be or one would do if — see AS IF

astir *adj* marked by much life, movement, or activity — see ALIVE 2

astonish *vb* to make a strong impression on (someone) with something unexpected — see SURPRISE 1

astonished *adj* **1** affected with sudden and great wonder or surprise — see THUNDERSTRUCK
2 filled with amazement or wonder — see OPEN-MOUTHED

astonishing *adj* **1** causing a strong emotional reaction because unexpected — see SURPRISING 1
2 causing wonder or astonishment — see MARVELOUS 1

astonishment *n* **1** the rapt attention and deep emotion caused by the sight of something extraordinary — see WONDER 2
2 the state of being strongly impressed by something unexpected or unusual — see SURPRISE 2

astound *vb* to make a strong impression on (someone) with something unexpected — see SURPRISE 1

astounded *adj* **1** affected with sudden and great wonder or surprise — see THUNDERSTRUCK
2 filled with amazement or wonder — see OPENMOUTHED

astounding *adj* **1** causing a strong emotional reaction because unexpected — see SURPRISING 1
2 causing wonder or astonishment — see MARVELOUS 1

astral *adj* of or relating to the stars — see STELLAR 1

astray *adv* off the desired or intended path or course — see WRONG 1

astronomical *also* **astronomic** *adj* unusually large — see HUGE

astronomically *adv* to a large extent or degree — see GREATLY 2

astute *adj* having or showing a practical cleverness or judgment — see SHREWD

asunder *adv* into parts or to pieces — see APART

as well as *prep* in addition to — see BESIDES 1

asylum *n* **1** a place where insane people are cared for — see MADHOUSE 1
2 something (as a building) that offers cover from the weather or protection from danger — see SHELTER

at all *adv* in any way or respect ⟨Ted wasn't *at all* pleased with the way his mother's birthday cake came out⟩
synonyms anywise, ever, half
related words somehow, someway; remotely
phrases by any means

athirst *adj* showing urgent desire or interest — see EAGER

athwart *adv* in a line or direction running from corner to corner — see CROSSWISE

athwart *prep* to the opposite side of — see ACROSS

atmosphere *n* **1** a special quality or impression associated with something — see AURA
2 the circumstances, conditions, or objects by which one is surrounded — see ENVIRONMENT

atom *n* a very small piece — see BIT 1

atomic *adj* very small in size — see TINY

atomize *vb* to reduce to fine particles — see POWDER

atone (for) *vb* to make up for (an offense) — see EXPIATE

atrocious *adj* **1** extremely disturbing or repellent — see HORRIBLE 1
2 extremely unsatisfactory — see WRETCHED 1

atrociousness *n* **1** the quality of inspiring intense dread or dismay — see HORROR 1
2 the state or quality of being utterly evil — see ENORMITY 1

atrocity *n* **1** the quality of inspiring intense dread or dismay — see HORROR 1
2 the state or quality of being utterly evil — see ENORMITY 1

attach *vb* **1** to cause (something) to hold to another — see FASTEN 1
2 to pick (someone) by one's authority for a specific position or duty — see APPOINT 2

attached *adj* having a liking or affection — see FOND 1

attachment *n* **1** a feeling of strong or constant regard for and dedication to someone — see LOVE 1
2 something that is not necessary in itself but adds to the convenience or performance of the main piece of equipment — see ACCESSORY 1

attack *n* **1** the act or action of setting upon with force or violence ⟨The USS Constitution was nicknamed "Old Ironsides" after its oaken hull successfully withstood a British *attack*⟩
synonyms aggression, assault, blitzkrieg, charge, descent, offense (*or* offence), offensive, onset, onslaught, raid, rush, strike
related words ambuscade, ambush; counterattack, counteroffensive, sally, sortie; foray, incursion, invasion; pillage, ravage, sack; air raid, blitz, bombardment; siege, storm
near antonyms defense, defensive, guard, shield; opposition, resistance; protection, security, shelter
2 a sudden experiencing of a physical or mental disorder ⟨malaria is characterized by periodic *attacks* of chills and fever⟩
synonyms bout, case, fit, seizure, siege, spell
related words recurrence, relapse; brainstorm, convulsion, pang, paroxysm, spasm, throe; breakdown, collapse, prostration
near antonyms arrest, relief, remission

attack *vb* **1** to take sudden, violent action against ⟨my dog unexpectedly *attacked* the mailman, sinking his teeth into the startled man's leg⟩
synonyms assail, assault, beset, charge, descend (on *or* upon), jump (on), pounce (on *or* upon), raid, rush, storm, strike
related words gang (up on), mob, swarm; mug, rob; ambuscade, ambush, surprise, waylay; blitz, bomb, bombard; beleaguer, besiege; harry, loot, pillage, plunder, ravage, sack; foray, invade, overrun
phrases fly at, give it to, go at, set upon
near antonyms cover, defend, guard, protect, secure, shield
2 to criticize harshly and usually publicly ⟨the mayor and all his aides were *attacked* mercilessly in the press when the scandal erupted⟩
synonyms abuse, assail, belabor, blast, castigate, excoriate, jump (on), lambaste (*or* lambast), scathe, slam, vituperate
related words berate, harangue, harass, harry, revile, scold; blaspheme, curse, execrate, imprecate, profane; affront, insult, slur; asperse, bad-mouth, belittle, disparage, put down; libel, slander, traduce; chastise, chide, criticize, rebuke, reprimand, reproof; fulminate, lash (out)
near antonyms acclaim, commend, compliment, laud, praise
3 to start work on energetically ⟨Courtney *attacked* the huge mess in her room with determination and enthusiasm⟩
synonyms tackle, wade (into)
related words address, approach, face; buckle (down to), concentrate (on), focus (on), knuckle down (to), zero in (on); fall (to), pitch in, plunge (in), settle (down); pursue, take up, undertake
phrases go at, have at, sail into

near antonyms avoid, evade, shun; dally, dawdle, dillydally, fiddle, fool, idle, lag, mess, monkey, play, poke, potter, putter, trifle

attain *vb* **1** to obtain (as a goal) through effort — see ACHIEVE 1
2 to receive as return for effort — see EARN 1

attainable *adj* **1** capable of being done or carried out — see POSSIBLE 1
2 possible to get — see AVAILABLE 1

attainment *n* **1** a successful result brought about by hard work — see ACCOMPLISHMENT 1
2 the state of being actual or complete — see FRUITION

attempt *n* an effort to do or accomplish something ⟨it took several *attempts* before we made good ice cream with an old-fashioned hand-cranked ice cream freezer⟩
synonyms crack, endeavor, essay, fling, go, pass, shot, stab, trial, try, whack
related words bid, striving, struggle, throes, undertaking; trial and error

attempt *vb* to make an effort to do ⟨after *attempting*— and failing—to start the lawn mower on my own, I finally succeeded with Dad's help⟩ ⟨don't even *attempt* walking on your broken foot⟩
synonyms assay, endeavor, essay, seek, strive, try
related words fight, strain, struggle, toil, trouble, work; aim, aspire, hope; assume, take up, undertake
phrases have a go at
near antonyms drop, give up, quit

attend *vb* **1** to go along with in order to provide assistance, protection, or companionship — see ACCOMPANY
2 to pay attention especially through the act of hearing — see LISTEN
3 to take charge of especially on behalf of another — see [2]TEND 1

attendant *adj* **1** coming as a result — see RESULTANT
2 present at the same time and place — see COINCIDENT

attendant *n* one that accompanies another for protection, guidance, or as a courtesy — see ESCORT

attending *adj* **1** being within the confines of a specified place — see PRESENT 2
2 present at the same time and place — see COINCIDENT

attention *n* **1** a focusing of the mind on something ⟨I need your full *attention* right now⟩
synonyms absorption, concentration, engrossment, enthrallment, immersion
related words fixation, obsession, preoccupation; alertness, application, awareness, consciousness, consideration, heedfulness, intentness, raptness
near antonyms absence, absentmindedness, abstractedness, abstraction, detachment, distraction, obliviousness, remoteness, unawareness, unconsciousness, withdrawal; disinterest, indifference, mindlessness, unconcern; befuddlement, bemusement, bewilderment, confusion
antonyms inattention
2 a state of being aware ⟨several mothers brought to the committee's *attention* the deplorable condition of the playground⟩
synonyms awareness, cognizance, ear, eye, heed, notice, observance, observation
related words advisement, care, concern, consideration, regard, watch; apprehension, discernment, grasp, mind, perception, recognition, thought, understanding
near antonyms disregard, neglect, obliviousness, unawareness

attentive *adj* **1** having the mind fixed on something ⟨Susan became particularly *attentive* when the sportscaster turned to field hockey, her favorite sport⟩
synonyms absorbed, engrossed, enthralled, focused (*also* focussed), immersed, intent, observant, rapt
related words interested, intrigued, involved; hypnotized, mesmerized; alert, alive, conscious, open-eyed, watchful, wide-awake
near antonyms daydreaming, dreamy, faraway, foggy, hazy, oblivious, preoccupied, remote; apathetic, disinterested, uninterested
antonyms absent, absentminded, abstracted, distracted, inattentive, unabsorbed, unfocused (*also* unfocussed), unobservant
2 given to or made with heedful anticipation of the needs and happiness of others — see THOUGHTFUL 1
3 paying close attention usually for the purpose of anticipating approaching danger or opportunity — see ALERT 1

attentiveness *n* the act or state of being constantly attentive and responsive to signs of opportunity, activity, or danger — see VIGILANCE

attest *vb* **1** to declare (something) to be true or genuine — see CERTIFY 1
2 to make a solemn declaration under oath for the purpose of establishing a fact — see TESTIFY

attestation *n* something presented in support of the truth or accuracy of a claim — see PROOF

attire *n* covering for the human body — see CLOTHING

attire *vb* to outfit with clothes and especially fine or special clothes — see CLOTHE 1

attorney *n* **1** a person who acts or does business for another — see AGENT 2
2 a person whose profession is to conduct lawsuits for clients or to advise about legal rights and obligations — see LAWYER

attraction *n* something that attracts interest — see MAGNET

attractive *adj* **1** having an often mysterious or magical power to attract — see FASCINATING 1
2 very pleasing to look at — see BEAUTIFUL

attractiveness *n* **1** the power of irresistible attraction — see CHARM 2
2 the qualities in a person or thing that as a whole give pleasure to the senses — see BEAUTY 1

attribute *n* something that sets apart an individual from others of the same kind — see CHARACTERISTIC

attribute *vb* to explain (something) as being the result of something else — see CREDIT 1

attrition *n* a gradual weakening, loss, or destruction — see CORROSION

atypical *adj* **1** being out of the ordinary — see EXCEPTIONAL
2 departing from some accepted standard of what is normal — see DEVIANT

audacious *adj* inclined or willing to take risks — see BOLD 1

audacity *n* shameless boldness — see EFFRONTERY

audibly *adv* with one's normal voice speaking the words — see ALOUD

audit *n* a close look at or over someone or something in order to judge condition — see INSPECTION

audit *vb* to look over closely (as for judging quality or condition) — see INSPECT

auditorium *n* a large room or building for enclosed public gatherings — see HALL 3

auditory *adj* of, relating to, or experienced through the sense of hearing <I have a bad *auditory* memory—unless I see a word in writing, and not just hear it, I forget it easily>
synonyms acoustic (*or* acoustical), aural, auricular
related words audible, clear, discernible, distinct, distinguishable, heard, perceptible
near antonyms faint, feeble, imperceptible, inaudible, indistinguishable, indistinct; low, noiseless, quiet, silent, soft, soundless

aught *n* the numerical symbol 0 or the absence of number or quantity represented by it — see ZERO 1

augment *vb* to make greater in size, amount, or number — see INCREASE 1

augmentation *n* something added (as by growth) — see INCREASE 1

augur *n* one who predicts future events or developments — see PROPHET

augur *vb* **1** to show signs of a favorable or successful outcome — see BODE
2 to tell of or describe beforehand — see FORETELL

auguring *n* a declaration that something will happen in the future — see PREDICTION

augury *n* something believed to be a sign or warning of a future event — see OMEN

august *adj* **1** having or showing a serious and reserved manner — see DIGNIFIED
2 large and impressive in size, grandeur, extent, or conception — see GRAND 1

augustness *n* **1** a dignified bearing or appearance befitting royalty — see MAJESTY 1
2 impressiveness of beauty on a large scale — see MAGNIFICENCE

auld lang syne *n* the events or experience of former times — see PAST

aura *n* a special quality or impression associated with something <the monastery perched high on a mountaintop had an *aura* of unreality and mystery about it>
synonyms air, atmosphere, climate, flavor, mood, note, temper
related words feel, feeling, sensation, sense, spirit; attribute, character, characteristic, image, mark, notion, peculiarity, picture, property, trait; color, illusion, overtone, semblance, suggestion, tone

aural *adj* of, relating to, or experienced through the sense of hearing — see AUDITORY

au revoir *n* an expression of good wishes at parting — see GOOD-BYE

auricular *adj* of, relating to, or experienced through the sense of hearing — see AUDITORY

aurora *n* the first appearance of light in the morning or the time of its appearance — see DAWN 1

auspice *n* something believed to be a sign or warning of a future event — see OMEN

auspicious *adj* **1** having qualities which inspire hope — see HOPEFUL 1
2 pointing toward a happy outcome — see FAVORABLE 2

austere *adj* **1** given to exacting standards of discipline and self-restraint — see SEVERE 1
2 harsh and threatening in manner or appearance — see GRIM 1

authentic *adj* **1** being exactly as appears or as claimed <found an *authentic* Native American arrowhead>
synonyms bona fide, genuine, real, right, true
related words actual, historical, original; lawful, legal, legitimate; identifiable, recognizable, verifiable; proven, substantiated, validated, verified; incontestable, incontrovertible, indisputable, indubitable, irrefutable, undeniable, undoubted, unmistakable, unquestionable; veritable, very; accurate, correct, proper; pure, unadulterated, unalloyed
near antonyms artificial, factitious, imitation, man-made, simulated, synthetic, unnatural; concocted, fabricated, manufactured; deceptive, delusive, delusory, misleading; unauthenticated, unverified
antonyms bogus, counterfeit, fake, false, mock, phony (*also* phoney), pseudo, sham, spurious, unauthentic, unreal
2 following an original exactly — see FAITHFUL 2

authentically *adv* in actual fact — see VERY 2

authenticate *vb* to declare (something) to be true or genuine — see CERTIFY 1

author *n* **1** a person who creates a written work <a brilliant novel by a first-time *author*>
synonyms penman, writer
related words coauthor, ghostwriter, hack, scribbler; autobiographer, biographer; novelist; essayist, pamphleteer; dramatist, playwright, scenarist, screenwriter, scriptwriter; bard, poet, rhymer (*or* rimer); columnist, journalist, newspaperman, reporter, sportswriter
2 a person who establishes a whole new field of endeavor — see FATHER 2

author *vb* to compose and set down on paper the words of — see WRITE 1

authoritarian *adj* **1** fond of ordering people around — see BOSSY
2 given to exacting standards of discipline and self-restraint — see SEVERE 1

authoritative *adj* **1** being the most accurate and apparently thorough — see DEFINITIVE 1
2 having power over the minds or behavior of others — see INFLUENTIAL 1

authority *n* **1** a person with a high level of knowledge or skill in a field — see EXPERT
2 lawful control over the affairs of a political unit (as a nation) — see RULE 2
3 the power to direct the thinking or behavior of others usually indirectly — see INFLUENCE 1
4 the right or means to command or control others — see POWER 1

authorization *n* **1** the approval by someone in authority for the doing of something — see PERMISSION
2 the granting of power to perform various acts or duties — see COMMISSION 1
3 the right to act or move freely — see FREEDOM 2

authorize *vb* **1** to give official or legal power to <only the school nurse is *authorized* to give any necessary shots>
synonyms accredit, certify, commission, empower, enable, invest, license (*or* licence), qualify
related words approve, clear, endorse (*also* indorse), OK (*or* okay), sanction; affirm, confirm, validate; inaugurate, induct, initiate, install, in-

state, swear in; allow, let, permit; enfranchise, entitle, privilege
near antonyms ban, bar, block, constrain, deny, disallow, disbar, discourage, disenfranchise, disfranchise, disqualify, exclude, hinder, hold back, impede, inhibit, obstruct, prevent, shut out, stop; enjoin, forbid, interdict, outlaw, prohibit, proscribe, veto
2 to give a right to — see ENTITLE 1
3 to give official acceptance of something as satisfactory — see APPROVE

authorized *adj* ordered or allowed by those in authority — see OFFICIAL

auto *n* a self-propelled passenger vehicle on wheels — see CAR

autocracy *n* a system of government in which the ruler has unlimited power — see DESPOTISM

autocrat *n* **1** a person who uses power or authority in a cruel, unjust, or harmful way — see DESPOT
2 one who rules over a people with a sole, supreme, and usually hereditary authority — see MONARCH

autocratic *adj* **1** exercising power or authority without interference by others — see ABSOLUTE 1
2 fond of ordering people around — see BOSSY

autograph *vb* to write one's name on (as a document) — see SIGN

automated *adj* designed to replace or decrease human labor and especially physical labor — see LABORSAVING

automatic *adj* **1** done instantly and without conscious thought or decision ⟨Carl's *automatic* use of the brakes prevented a serious accident⟩
synonyms instinctive, instinctual, involuntary, mechanical, spontaneous
related words conditioned, natural, reactive, reflex, simple, subliminal, unconscious, unforced; blind, inadvertent, unintended, unintentional, unwilling, unwitting; abrupt, quick, ready, sudden; ad-lib, extemporaneous, extempore, impromptu, improvised, offhand, offhanded, snap, spur-of-the-moment, unconsidered, unplanned, unpremeditated, unprepared, unprompted, unreasoned, unrehearsed, unstudied; casual, chance, chancy, haphazard, hasty, hit-or-miss, impetuous, impulsive, perfunctory, random, rash
near antonyms calculated, conscious, cultivated, deliberate, designed, intended, intentional, predetermined, prepared, projected, refined, rehearsed, volitional, voluntary, willed, willful (*or* wilful); advised, aforethought, careful, considered, foresighted, forethoughtful, measured, meticulous, reasoned, studied, thoughtful
2 designed to replace or decrease human labor and especially physical labor — see LABORSAVING

automobile *n* a self-propelled passenger vehicle on wheels — see CAR

automobile *vb* to travel by a motorized vehicle — see DRIVE 2

automobilist *n* a person who travels by automobile — see MOTORIST

autonomous *adj* not being under the rule or control of another — see FREE 1

autonomy *n* the state of being free from the control or power of another — see FREEDOM 1

autopsy *n* examination of a dead body especially to find out the cause of death ⟨the *autopsy* revealed an advanced stage of cancer⟩
synonyms postmortem, postmortem examination
related words dissection
near antonyms biopsy, vivisection

auxiliary *adj* available to supply something extra when needed ⟨the auditorium has an *auxiliary* cooling system used only on particularly sweltering days⟩
synonyms accessory, peripheral, supplemental, supplementary
related words backup, makeshift, substitute; added, additional, another, further; complementary, contributory; assistant, assisting, helping, supportive, tributary; secondary, subordinate, subservient, subsidiary; dispensable, excess, nonessential, superfluous, surplus, unessential
near antonyms basic, fundamental, primary, prime; all-important, essential, imperative, indispensable, integral, necessary, needed, needful, required, requisite, vital
antonyms chief, main, principal

avail *n* the capacity for being useful for some purpose — see USE 2

avail *vb* to provide with something useful or desirable — see BENEFIT

available *adj* **1** possible to get ⟨the nursery's orchids are *available* by mail order only⟩ ⟨fare information is readily *available* by using the toll-free number⟩
synonyms accessible, acquirable, attainable, obtainable, procurable
related words purchasable, rentable; furnished, provided, supplied; common, omnipresent, prevalent, ubiquitous, universal, widespread; free, free-for-all, open, public, unrestricted
phrases on hand
near antonyms limited, off-limits, restricted; deficient, lacking, missing, rare, scarce, uncommon
antonyms inaccessible, unattainable, unavailable, unobtainable
2 capable of or suitable for being used for a particular purpose — see USABLE 1

avarice *n* an intense selfish desire for wealth or possessions — see GREED

avaricious *adj* having or marked by an eager and often selfish desire especially for material possessions — see GREEDY 1

avariciousness *n* an intense selfish desire for wealth or possessions — see GREED

avenge *vb* to punish in kind the wrongdoer responsible for ⟨a play about a prince who struggles to *avenge* his father's death⟩
synonyms requite, retaliate, revenge
related words castigate, fix, get, penalize, punish, scourge; chasten, chastise, correct, discipline; redress, right; compensate, pay (back), recompense, repay
phrases get even (for)
near antonyms absolve, condone, excuse, forgive, pardon, remit

avenger *n* one who inflicts punishment in return for an injury or offense — see NEMESIS 1

avenue *n* **1** a passage cleared for public vehicular travel — see WAY 1
2 an established course for traveling from one place to another — see PASSAGE 1

aver *vb* **1** to state as a fact usually forcefully — see CLAIM 1
2 to state clearly and strongly — see ASSERT 1

average *adj* **1** being about midway between extremes of amount or size — see MIDDLE 2

2 being of the type that is encountered in the normal course of events — see ORDINARY 1
3 having or showing the qualities associated with the members of a particular group or kind — see TYPICAL 1

average *n* what is typical of a group, class, or series ⟨my cat's a cut above the *average* when it comes to being a finicky eater⟩
synonyms norm, normal, par, standard
related words golden mean, mean, median, middle; commonplace, ordinary, rule, run, status quo, usual; exemplar, representative
near antonyms abnormality, anomaly, deviation, exception, rarity

averse *adj* having a natural dislike for something — see ANTIPATHETIC

averseness *n* a strong feeling of not liking or approving — see DISLIKE 1

aversion *n* **1** a dislike so strong as to cause stomach upset or queasiness — see DISGUST
2 a strong feeling of not liking or approving — see DISLIKE 1
3 something or someone that is hated — see HATE 2

avert *vb* to keep from happening by taking action in advance — see PREVENT

averting *n* the act or practice of keeping something from happening — see PREVENTION

aviator *n* one who flies or is qualified to fly an aircraft or spacecraft — see PILOT

avid *adj* **1** having or marked by an eager and often selfish desire especially for material possessions — see GREEDY 1
2 showing urgent desire or interest — see EAGER

avidity *n* **1** an intense selfish desire for wealth or possessions — see GREED
2 urgent desire or interest — see EAGERNESS

avoid *vb* to get or keep away from (as a responsibility) through cleverness or trickery — see ESCAPE 2

avoidance *n* the act or a means of getting or keeping away from something undesirable — see ESCAPE 2

avoirdupois *n* the state or quality of being heavy — see WEIGHTINESS 1

avouch *vb* **1** to declare (something) to be true or genuine — see CERTIFY 1
2 to state as a fact usually forcefully — see CLAIM 1
3 to state clearly and strongly — see ASSERT 1

avouchment *n* a solemn and often public declaration of the truth or existence of something — see PROTESTATION

avow *vb* **1** to state as a fact usually forcefully — see CLAIM 1
2 to state clearly and strongly — see ASSERT 1

avowal *n* **1** a solemn and often public declaration of the truth or existence of something — see PROTESTATION
2 an open declaration of something (as a fault or the commission of an offense) about oneself — see CONFESSION

await *vb* **1** to believe in the future occurrence of (something) — see EXPECT
2 to remain in place in readiness or expectation of something — see WAIT

awaited *adj* being in accordance with the prescribed, normal, or logical course of events — see DUE 2

awake *adj* **1** not sleeping or able to sleep — see WAKEFUL
2 paying close attention usually for the purpose of anticipating approaching danger or opportunity — see ALERT 1

awake *vb* **1** to cause to stop sleeping — see WAKE 1
2 to cease to be asleep — see WAKE 2

awaken *vb* **1** to cause to stop sleeping — see WAKE 1
2 to cease to be asleep — see WAKE 2

award *n* something given in recognition of achievement ⟨Faye received the highest *award* in the 16 and under category for her poem⟩
synonyms decoration, distinction, honor, plume, premium, prize
related words badge, crown, cup, laurel, medal, order, ribbon, trophy; accolade, applause, bravo, encomium, eulogy, hallelujah, homage, paean, panegyric, plaudit, tribute; citation, commendation, compliment

award *vb* **1** to give something as a token of gratitude or admiration for a service or achievement — see REWARD
2 to give the ownership or benefit of (something) formally or publicly — see CONFER 1

aware *adj* having specified facts or feelings actively impressed on the mind — see CONSCIOUS

awareness *n* a state of being aware — see ATTENTION 2

awash *adj* containing, covered with, or thoroughly penetrated by water — see WET

away *adj* **1** not close in time or space — see DISTANT 1
2 not at a certain place — see ABSENT 1

away *adv* from this or that place ⟨don't walk *away* while I'm still talking to you⟩
synonyms hence, off
related words apart, aside, elsewhere; abroad, afar, afield, astray

awe *n* the rapt attention and deep emotion caused by the sight of something extraordinary — see WONDER 2

awed *adj* filled with amazement or wonder — see OPENMOUTHED

awesome *adj* causing wonder or astonishment — see MARVELOUS 1

awestruck *adj* **1** affected with sudden and great wonder or surprise — see THUNDERSTRUCK
2 filled with amazement or wonder — see OPENMOUTHED

awful *adj* **1** causing intense displeasure, disgust, or resentment — see OFFENSIVE 1
2 causing wonder or astonishment — see MARVELOUS 1
3 extremely disturbing or repellent — see HORRIBLE 1
4 extremely unsatisfactory — see WRETCHED 1

awful *adv* to a great degree — see VERY 1

awfully *adv* to a great degree — see VERY 1

awfulness *n* the quality of inspiring intense dread or dismay — see HORROR 1

awkward *adj* **1** lacking social grace and assurance ⟨preteens feeling *awkward* at their first formal dance⟩
synonyms clumsy, gauche, graceless, inelegant, roughhewn, stiff, stilted, uncomfortable, uneasy, ungraceful, wooden
related words gawky, lubberly, ungainly; boorish, clownish, uncouth; abashed, discomfited, discomforted, discomposed, disconcerted, discoun-

tenanced, embarrassed; agitated, bothered, chagrined, dismayed, disquieted, distressed, disturbed, fazed, flustered, jittery, jumpy, mortified, nervous, nonplussed (*also* nonplused), perturbed, rattled, unhinged, unsettled, upset; diffident, insecure, meek, modest, self-doubting, timid, unassertive, unassuming, unpretentious
near antonyms assured, calm, collected, composed, confident, cool, placid, poised, serene, secure, self-assured, self-confident, self-possessed, tranquil, undisturbed, unperturbed
antonyms graceful, suave, urbane
2 showing or marked by a lack of skill and tact (as in dealing with a situation) ⟨her *awkward* handling of the seating arrangements at the wedding reception resulted in many hurt feelings⟩
synonyms botched, bungling, clumsy, fumbled, inept, inexpert, maladroit
related words amateur, amateurish, crude, green, incompetent, ineffectual, inefficient, inexperienced, unpolished, unprofessional, unskilled, unskillful; careless, sloppy, tacky, tactless, undiplomatic; ill-advised, ineffective, ineffectual, misdirected, misguided
near antonyms able, accomplished, adept, capable, clever, competent, consummate, crackerjack, expert, masterful, masterly, polished, professional, proficient, skilled, skillful, talented; diplomatic, easy, effortless, gracious, smooth, tactful
antonyms adroit, deft, dexterous (*also* dextrous), facile
3 causing embarrassment ⟨the *awkward* situation of having to listen in as your teacher talks about you to your parents⟩
synonyms discomfiting, disconcerting, disturbing, embarrassing, flustering, uncomfortable
related words confusing, difficult, disagreeable, impossible, inconvenient, intolerable, troublesome, unpleasant, unwieldy; debasing, degrading, demeaning, humbling, humiliating, mortifying
near antonyms agreeable, comfortable, convenient, pleasing
4 causing difficulty, discomfort, or annoyance — see INCONVENIENT 1
5 difficult to use or operate especially because of size, weight, or design — see CUMBERSOME
6 lacking in physical ease and grace in movement or in the use of the hands — see CLUMSY 1

awning *n* a raised covering over something for decoration or protection — see CANOPY

awry *adj* inclined or twisted to one side ⟨the shutters that still remained on the run-down old house were all *awry*⟩
synonyms askew, aslant, cockeyed, crooked, listing, lopsided, oblique, skewed, slanted, slanting, slantwise, tilted, tipping, uneven
related words asymmetrical (*or* asymmetric), unbalanced, unsymmetrical; contorted, disordered, distorted, irregular
near antonyms ordered, orderly, regular, uniform; balanced, symmetrical (*or* symmetric)
antonyms even, level, straight

awry *adv* off the desired or intended path or course — see WRONG 1

[1]aye *also* **ay** *adv* for all time — see EVER 1

[2]aye *also* **ay** *adv* used to express agreement — see YES

babble *n* unintelligible or meaningless talk — see GIBBERISH

babble *vb* **1** to speak rapidly, inarticulately, and usually unintelligibly ⟨in such a rush to tell us the news that she just *babbled*⟩
synonyms chatter, drivel, gabble, gibber, jabber, prattle, sputter
related words gab, jaw, patter, prate, rattle, run on; maunder, mouth, mumble, murmur, mutter; stammer, stutter; chat, converse, palaver, rap, visit; discourse; screech, shout, shriek
near antonyms articulate, enunciate, pronounce
2 to engage in casual or rambling conversation — see CHAT

babbler *n* a person who talks constantly — see CHATTERBOX

babe *n* a recently born person — see BABY

babel *n* a place of uproar or confusion — see MADHOUSE 2

babushka *n* a scarf worn on the head — see BANDANNA

baby *n* a recently born person ⟨the *baby* is just learning to sit up, so be careful⟩
synonyms babe, child, infant, newborn
related words cherub; foundling, nursling, suckling; papoose; kid, moppet, toddler, tot, tyke; boy, nipper, tad; juvenile, minor, youngster, youth; brat, imp, squirt, urchin, whippersnapper; girl, hoyden, tomboy
phrases babe in arms
near antonyms adult, grown-up; elder, graybeard, oldster, old-timer, senior citizen

baby *vb* to treat with great or excessive care ⟨he *babied* his car, faithfully washing it every week⟩
synonyms coddle, dandle, mollycoddle, nurse, pamper, spoil
related words cater (to), humor, indulge; gratify, mother, oblige, please, satisfy
near antonyms control, discipline, restrain; oppress; neglect, overlook, slight
antonyms abuse, ill-treat, ill-use, maltreat, mishandle, mistreat, misuse

babyish *adj* having or showing the annoying qualities (as silliness) associated with children — see CHILDISH

babysitter *n* a girl or woman employed to care for a young child or children — see NURSE

back *adj* being at or in the part of something opposite the front part ⟨she carried all the presents in the *back* door, as the children were playing in the front yard⟩
synonyms hind, hindmost, posterior, rear, rearward
antonyms anterior, fore, forward, front

back *adv* toward the opposite direction — see AROUND 2

back *vb* **1** to promote the interests or cause of — see SUPPORT 1
2 to provide (someone) with what is useful or necessary to achieve an end — see HELP 1

back away *vb* to move back or away (as from something difficult, dangerous, or disagreeable) — see RETREAT 1

backbone *n* **1** a column of bones supporting the trunk of a vertebrate animal — see SPINE
2 the strength of mind that enables a person to endure pain or hardship — see FORTITUDE

back down *vb* to break a promise or agreement — see RENEGE

backdrop *n* the physical conditions or features that form the setting against which something is viewed — see BACKGROUND 1

backer *n* **1** a person who actively supports or favors a cause — see EXPONENT
2 a person who takes the responsibility for some other person or thing — see SPONSOR
3 someone associated with another to give assistance or moral support — see ALLY

background *n* **1** the physical conditions or features that form the setting against which something is viewed ⟨they got married on a mountain top with the sunset as *background*⟩
synonyms backdrop, ground
related words scene, scenery, set, stage; environment, milieu, setting, surroundings
near antonyms foreground; center, focal point, focus, heart
2 the place and time in which the action for a portion of a dramatic work (as a movie) is set — see SCENE 1

backhanded *adj* not being or expressing what one appears to be or express — see INSINCERE

backing *n* an act or instance of helping — see HELP 1

back of *prep* at, to, or toward the rear of — see BEHIND 1

back off *vb* to break a promise or agreement — see RENEGE

backpack *n* a soft-sided case designed for carrying belongings especially on the back — see PACK 1

backside *n* the part of the body upon which someone sits — see BUTTOCKS

backslider *n* a person who has sunk below the normal moral standard — see DEGENERATE

backstage *adj or adv* off or away from the part of the stage visible to the audience — see OFFSTAGE

back talk *n* disrespectful or argumentative talk given in response to a command or request ⟨his mother sent him to his room because of his constant *back talk*⟩
synonyms cheek, impertinence, impudence, insolence, sass, sauce
related words comeback, rejoinder, retort, riposte, wisecrack; discourtesy, disrespect, impoliteness, rudeness, tactlessness; audaciousness, audacity, boldness, brazenness; coarseness, crassness, crudity, vulgarity; abruptness, bluffness, bluntness, brusqueness, crossness, curtness, gruffness, surliness
near antonyms civility, cordiality, courtesy, diplomacy, politeness, tactfulness; consideration, gallantry, gentility, graciousness, smoothness, suaveness; deference, respect; affability

backup *adj* taking the place of one that came before — see NEW 1

backup *n* a person or thing that takes the place of another — see SUBSTITUTE

backward *adj* directed, turned, or done toward the back ⟨a *backward* turn on ice skates is hard to learn, because you can't see where you're going⟩
synonyms rearward, retrograde
related words reversed; hind, posterior, rear
near antonyms forward

backwater *n* a rural region that forms the edge of the settled or developed part of a country — see FRONTIER 2

backwoods *n* a rural region that forms the edge of the settled or developed part of a country — see FRONTIER 2

bad *adj* **1** falling short of a standard ⟨a *bad* first attempt at making meat loaf resulted in a soggy inedible mess⟩
synonyms deficient, inferior, lousy, off, poor, punk, rotten, substandard, unacceptable, ungodly, unsatisfactory, wanting, wretched, wrong
related words defective, faulty, flawed; execrable, lesser, low-grade, mediocre, reprehensible, second-rate, unspeakable; bum, useless, valueless, worthless; inadequate, insufficient, lacking; astray; scurrilous, villainous
phrases below (*or* under) par
near antonyms choice, excellent, exceptional, first-class, first-rate, premium, prime, superior; adequate, sufficient
antonyms acceptable, satisfactory
2 not conforming to a high moral standard; morally unacceptable ⟨stealing is just plain *bad*⟩
synonyms black, evil, immoral, iniquitous, nefarious, rotten, sinful, unethical, unrighteous, unsavory, vicious, vile, villainous, wicked, wrong
related words base, contemptible, despicable, dirty, disreputable, evil-minded, ignoble, ill, infernal, low, mean; atrocious, cruel, nasty; blamable, blameworthy, censurable, reprehensible; corrupt, debased, debauched, degenerate, depraved, dissolute, libertine, loose, perverted, reprobate; banned, barred, condemned, discouraged, forbidden, interdicted, outlawed, prohibited, proscribed, unauthorized, unclean; disallowed; execrable, lousy, miserable, wretched; erring, fallen, unprincipled, unscrupulous; improper, incorrect, indecent, indecorous, unbecoming
near antonyms high-minded, honest, honorable, law-abiding, legitimate, principled, reputable, right-minded, scrupulous, straight, upright; allowed, authorized, legal, licensed, permissible, permitted; approved, endorsed, sanctioned; abetted, encouraged, promoted, supported; clean, correct, decent, decorous, exemplary, proper, seemly; blameless, commendable, creditable, guiltless; chaste, immaculate, innocent, irreproachable, lily-white, perfect, pure, spotless
antonyms good, ethical, moral, right, righteous, virtuous
3 causing or capable of causing harm — see HARMFUL
4 engaging in or marked by childish misbehavior — see NAUGHTY
5 feeling unhappiness — see SAD 1
6 having a fault — see FAULTY
7 having undergone organic breakdown — see ROTTEN 1

8 not giving pleasure to the mind or senses — see UNPLEASANT
9 of low quality — see CHEAP 2
10 temporarily suffering from a disorder of the body — see SICK 1

bad *n* that which is morally unacceptable — see EVIL

badly *adv* in an unsatisfactory way ⟨I'm afraid you performed quite *badly* in our last rehearsal⟩
synonyms inadequately, poorly, unacceptably, unsatisfactorily
related words rottenly; intolerably, unbearably; inappropriately, incorrectly, indecently, rakishly, unsuitably; naughtily
near antonyms appropriately, congruously, correctly, decently, decorously, felicitously, fittingly, genteelly, rightly, seemly, suitably
antonyms acceptably, adequately, all right, fine, good, palatably, passably, so-so, tolerably

bad–mouth *vb* to express scornfully one's low opinion of — see DECRY 1

badness *n* the state or quality of being utterly evil — see ENORMITY 1

baffle *vb* **1** to prevent from achieving a goal — see FRUSTRATE
2 to throw into a state of mental uncertainty — see CONFUSE 1

bafflement *n* a state of mental uncertainty — see CONFUSION 1

bag *n* **1** a container made of a flexible material (as paper or plastic) ⟨she carries her towel and other supplies to the beach in a bright, colorful *bag* slung over her arm⟩
synonyms poke [*chiefly Southern & Midland*], pouch, sack
related words carryall, portmanteau, traveling bag; bundle, pack, package, packet, parcel; backpack, duffel bag, haversack, knapsack, rucksack; handbag, pocketbook, purse, tote bag
2 a container for carrying money and small personal items — see PURSE

bag *vb* **1** to extend outward beyond a usual point — see BULGE
2 to take physical control or possession of (something) suddenly or forcibly — see CATCH 1

bail out *vb* to remove from danger or harm — see SAVE 2

bairn *n, chiefly Scottish* a young person who is between infancy and adulthood — see CHILD 1

bait *n* **1** something used to attract animals to a hook or into a trap ⟨cheese is the traditional *bait* for trapping mice⟩
synonyms decoy, lure
related words ambush, trap; hook, snare, troll; appeal, attraction, call, draw, incentive, pull; enticement, seduction, temptation
near antonyms repellent
2 something that persuades one to perform an action for pleasure or gain — see LURE 1

bait *vb* to attack repeatedly with mean put-downs or insults — see TEASE 2

baiter *n* **1** a person who causes repeated emotional pain, distress, or annoyance to another — see TORMENTOR
2 one that tries to get a person to give in to a desire — see TEMPTER

balance *n* **1** a condition in which opposing forces are equal to one another ⟨in order to determine the weight of that beaker, you need to get the two pans of the scale in perfect *balance*⟩
synonyms equilibrium, equipoise, poise
related words counterbalance, counterpoise; firmness, fixedness, security, stability, steadiness
near antonyms changeability, fluctuation, inconstancy, insecurity, instability, mutability, precariousness, shakiness, unsteadiness, volatility
antonyms imbalance
2 a balanced, pleasing, or suitable arrangement of parts — see HARMONY 1
3 a device for measuring weight — see [1]SCALE
4 a force or influence that makes an opposing force ineffective or less effective — see COUNTERBALANCE
5 a remaining group or portion — see REMAINDER 1

balance *vb* to make equal in amount, degree, or status — see EQUALIZE

balanced *adj* **1** having full use of one's mind and control over one's actions — see SANE
2 having the parts agreeably related — see HARMONIOUS 2

bald *adj* **1** lacking a usual or natural covering — see NAKED 2
2 free from all additions or embellishment — see PLAIN 1

baleful *adj* **1** being or showing a sign of evil or calamity to come — see OMINOUS
2 causing or capable of causing harm — see HARMFUL
3 likely to cause or capable of causing death — see DEADLY

balk *vb* to prevent from achieving a goal — see FRUSTRATE

balky *adj* given to resisting authority or another's control — see DISOBEDIENT

[1]**ball** *n* **1** a more or less round body or mass ⟨the little rubber *ball* used in racquetball⟩ ⟨a *ball* of string⟩
synonyms globe, orb, sphere
related words egg, oval; circle, ring, round; chunk, clump, gob, hunk, lump, nugget, wad
near antonyms block, cube, rectangle, square
2 a usually round or cone-shaped little piece of lead made to be fired from a firearm — see BULLET

[2]**ball** *n* a social gathering for dancing — see DANCE

ball *vb* to form into a round compact mass — see WAD

ballad *n* a short musical composition for the human voice often with instrumental accompaniment — see SONG 1

balloon *vb* **1** to become greater in extent, volume, amount, or number — see INCREASE 2
2 to extend outward beyond a usual point — see BULGE

ballot *n* a piece of paper indicating a person's preferences in an election ⟨we collected all of the *ballots* from the students voting for class president⟩
synonyms vote
related words aye (*also* ay), nay, no, yea; blackball; referendum; ticket

ballyhoo *n* newsworthy information released to the media that is designed to gain public attention or support for a person, business, or cause — see PUBLICITY

ballyhoo *vb* **1** to praise or publicize lavishly and often excessively — see TOUT 1
2 to provide publicity for — see PUBLICIZE 1

balminess *n* lack of good sense or judgment — see FOOLISHNESS 1

balmy *adj* **1** having or showing a very abnormal or sick state of mind — see INSANE 1
2 marked by temperatures that are neither too high nor too low — see CLEMENT
3 not harsh or stern especially in manner, nature, or effect — see GENTLE 1
4 showing or marked by a lack of good sense or judgment — see FOOLISH 1
balustrade *n* a protective barrier consisting of a horizontal bar and its supports — see RAILING
ban *n* an order that something not be done or used — see PROHIBITION 2
ban *vb* **1** to order not to do or use or to be done or used — see FORBID
2 to prevent the participation or inclusion of — see EXCLUDE
banal *adj* **1** lacking in qualities that make for spirit and character — see WISHY-WASHY 1
2 used or heard so often as to be dull — see STALE
banality *n* an idea or expression that has been used by many people — see COMMONPLACE
bananas *adj* having or showing a very abnormal or sick state of mind — see INSANE 1
[1]**band** *n* **1** a circular strip — see RING 2
2 something that physically prevents free movement — see BOND 1
3 a line or long narrow section differing in color from the background — see STRIPE
[2]**band** *n* **1** a usually large group of musicians playing together <that traveling *band* needs to find a new singer>
synonyms orchestra, philharmonic, symphony, symphony orchestra
related words brass band; brasses, strings, woodwinds; combo, ensemble, group; company, troupe; duo, octet, quartet (*also* quartette), quintet, septet (*also* septette), sextet, trio
2 a group of people working together on a task — see GANG 1
band *vb* **1** to encircle or bind with or as if with a belt — see GIRD 1
2 to form or enter into an association that furthers the interests of its members — see ALLY
3 to gather into a tight mass by means of a line or cord — see TIE 1
4 to make stripes on — see STRIPE
bandage *vb* to cover with a bandage <her mother always *bandages* her scraped knees very carefully>
synonyms bind, dress
related words care (for), doctor, medicate, minister (to), nurse, treat; mend, heal
bandanna *or* **bandana** *n* a scarf worn on the head <she uses her colorful print *bandanna* to keep the hair out of her eyes>
synonyms babushka, handkerchief, kerchief, mantilla
related words shawl
bandwagon *n* a series of activities undertaken to achieve a goal — see CAMPAIGN
bandy *vb* to talk about (an issue) usually from various points of view and for the purpose of arriving at a decision or opinion — see DISCUSS
bane *n* a substance that by chemical action can kill or injure a living thing — see POISON
baneful *adj* causing or capable of causing harm — see HARMFUL
bang *n* **1** a hard strike with a part of the body or an instrument — see [1]BLOW
2 a loud explosive sound — see CLAP 1
3 a pleasurably intense stimulation of the feelings — see THRILL
bang *vb* **1** to come into usually forceful contact with something — see HIT 2
2 to deliver a blow to (someone or something) usually in a strong vigorous manner — see HIT 1
3 to shove into a closed position with force and noise — see SLAM 1
bangle *n* an ornament worn on a chain around the neck or wrist — see PENDANT
bang–up *adj* of the very best kind — see EXCELLENT
banish *vb* **1** to force to leave a country <in the old days, criminals were sometimes *banished*>
synonyms deport, displace, exile, expatriate, transport
related words dismiss, eject, eliminate, evict, exclude, expel, oust, throw out; excommunicate, ostracize, reject, repudiate, spurn; dispossess
near antonyms naturalize, repatriate; accept, admit, receive, take in; entertain, harbor, house, shelter
2 to drive or force out — see EJECT 1
banishment *n* the forced removal from a homeland — see EXILE 1
banister *n* a protective barrier consisting of a horizontal bar and its supports — see RAILING
[1]**bank** *n* **1** a number of things considered as a unit — see GROUP 1
2 a series of people or things arranged side by side — see ROW 1
[2]**bank** *n* a pile or ridge of granular matter (as sand or snow) <he likes to play on the *bank* of dirt the construction workers left>
synonyms bar, drift, mound
related words snowbank, snowdrift; embankment, sandbar; heap, hill, mass, mountain, stack
bank *vb* **1** to form into a pile or ridge of earth — see MOUND 1
2 to put in an account — see DEPOSIT 1
bank note *n* a piece of printed paper used as money — see [1]BILL 2
bankroll *n* available money — see FUND 2
bankrupt *vb* to cause to lose one's fortune and become unable to pay one's debts — see RUIN 1
banned *adj* that may not be permitted — see IMPERMISSIBLE
banner *adj* of the very best kind — see EXCELLENT
banner *n* a piece of cloth with a special design that is used as an emblem or for signaling — see FLAG 1
banning *n* the act of ordering that something not be done or used — see PROHIBITION 1
banquet *n* a large fancy meal often accompanied by ceremony or entertainment — see FEAST
banquet *vb* to entertain with a fancy meal — see FEAST
bantam *adj* of a size that is less than average — see SMALL 1
banter *n* good-natured teasing or exchanging of clever remarks <those particular students are known for their brilliant and witty *banter* at lunchtime>
synonyms chaff, give-and-take, jesting, joshing, persiflage, raillery, repartee
related words barb, crack, dig, gag, jest, joke, quip, sally, wisecrack, witticism; facetiousness, humorousness; fooling, kidding, mocking, razzing, ribbing, ridiculing; humor, wit, wordplay; chatter, chitchat, gossip, small talk

banter *vb* to make jokes — see JOKE
bantering *adj* marked by or expressive of mild or good-natured teasing — see QUIZZICAL
baptism *n* the process or an instance of being formally placed in an office or organization — see INSTALLATION 1
baptize *vb* **1** to give a name to — see NAME 1
2 to put into an office or welcome into an organization with special ceremonies — see INSTALL 1
bar *n* **1** a straight piece (as of wood or metal) that is longer than it is wide ⟨all of the prison's windows are partially covered with steel *bars*⟩
synonyms billet, rod
related words beam, board; band, strip; ingot, slab, stick
2 a line or long narrow section differing in color from the background — see STRIPE
3 a pile or ridge of granular matter (as sand or snow) — see [2]BANK
4 a place of business where alcoholic beverages are sold to be consumed on the premises — see BARROOM
5 an assembly of persons for the administration of justice — see COURT 3
6 something that makes movement or progress more difficult — see ENCUMBRANCE
bar *prep* not including — see EXCEPT
bar *vb* **1** to make stripes on — see STRIPE
2 to order not to do or use or to be done or used — see FORBID
3 to prevent the participation or inclusion of — see EXCLUDE
barb *n* an act or expression showing scorn and usually intended to hurt another's feelings — see INSULT
barbarian *n* an uncivilized person — see HEATHEN 2
barbaric *adj* having or showing the desire to inflict severe pain and suffering on others — see CRUEL 1
barbarity *n* the willful infliction of pain and suffering on others — see CRUELTY
barbarous *adj* **1** having or showing the desire to inflict severe pain and suffering on others — see CRUEL 1
2 not civilized — see SAVAGE 1
bard *n* a person who writes poetry — see POET
bare *adj* **1** being this and no more — see MERE
2 free from all additions or embellishment — see PLAIN 1
3 lacking a usual or natural covering — see NAKED 2
4 lacking or shed of clothing — see NAKED 1
5 lacking contents that could or should be present — see EMPTY 1
bare *vb* to make known (as information previously kept secret) — see REVEAL 1
barely *adv* by a very small margin — see JUST 2
bareness *n* the quality or state of being empty — see VACANCY 2
bargain *n* **1** something bought or offered for sale at a desirable price ⟨those shoes were a *bargain* because the store was going out of business⟩
synonyms buy, steal
related words markdown; bonus, freebie, gift, giveaway, premium, present; sale; boon, windfall
near antonyms overcharge, rip-off; markup; extravagance, luxury
2 an arrangement about action to be taken — see AGREEMENT 2
bargain *vb* to talk over or dispute the terms of a purchase ⟨they *bargained* with the car salesman for half an hour before settling on a price⟩
synonyms chaffer, deal, dicker, haggle, horse-trade, negotiate, palter
related words argue, bicker, clash, quibble, squabble, wrangle; comparison shop, shop (around); barter, exchange, trade; hawk, peddle; buy, purchase
barge *vb* to move heavily or clumsily — see LUMBER 1
bark *n* a boat equipped with one or more sails — see SAILBOAT
[1]**bark** *vb* to remove the natural covering of — see PEEL
[2]**bark** *vb* to speak sharply or irritably — see SNAP 1
baron *n* a person of rank, power, or influence in a particular field — see MAGNATE
baronial *adj* large and impressive in size, grandeur, extent, or conception — see GRAND 1
barrage *n* a rapid or overwhelming outpouring of many things at once ⟨the teacher's rapid-fire *barrage* of homework assignments went by too fast for me to write them all down⟩
synonyms bombardment, cannonade, fusillade, hail, salvo, shower, storm, volley
related words broadside, burst, deluge, flood, flood tide, flush, gush, inundation, outburst, outflow, outpouring, overflow, spate, surge, torrent; current, river, stream, tide; excess, glut, overabundance, overage, overkill, overmuch, oversupply, superabundance, superfluity, surfeit, surplus
near antonyms dribble, drip, trickle
barred *adj* **1** having stripes — see STRIPED
2 that may not be permitted — see IMPERMISSIBLE
barrel *n* **1** a considerable amount — see LOT 2
2 a metal container in the shape of a cylinder — see CAN
3 an enclosed wooden vessel for holding beverages — see CASK
barrel *vb* to proceed or move quickly — see HURRY 2
barren *adj* **1** producing inferior or only a small amount of vegetation ⟨if tobacco fields aren't allowed to lie idle once every few years, they will become *barren*⟩
synonyms impoverished, infertile, poor, stark, unproductive, waste
related words bleak, dead, desolate, inhospitable, lifeless; bankrupted, consumed, debilitated, depleted, diminished, drained, dried up, enfeebled, exhausted, expended, lessened, reduced, spent, used up; arid, desert, dry
near antonyms arable, tillable; green, verdant
antonyms fertile, fruitful, lush, luxuriant, productive, rich
2 not able to produce fruit or offspring — see STERILE 1
barren *n* land that is uninhabited or not fit for crops — see WASTELAND
barricade *n* a physical object that blocks the way — see BARRIER
barrier *n* a physical object that blocks the way ⟨there was a big *barrier* plastered with signs saying "Keep Out" around the trash compactor⟩
synonyms barricade, fence, hedge, wall
related words bar, encumbrance, handicap, hindrance, hurdle, impediment, obstacle, obstruc-

tion, roadblock, stop; fetter, hobble, manacle, shackle; constraint, curb, restraint, snag
near antonyms door, doorway, entrance, entry, entryway, gate, portal

barring *n* the act of ordering that something not be done or used — see PROHIBITION 1

barring *prep* not including — see EXCEPT

barroom *n* a place of business where alcoholic beverages are sold to be consumed on the premises ⟨her mother didn't like her even to walk past the *barroom* because she was worried that there might be drunk people inside⟩
synonyms bar, café (*also* cafe), groggery, grogshop, pub, public house [*chiefly British*], saloon, tavern
related words cabaret, dive, joint, nightclub, roadhouse, speakeasy; package store

barter *n* a giving or taking of one thing of value in return for another — see EXCHANGE 1

base *adj* not following or in accordance with standards of honor and decency — see IGNOBLE 2

base *n* **1** an immaterial thing upon which something else rests ⟨the firm belief that complete trust between husband and wife is the *base* of any successful marriage⟩
synonyms basis, bedrock, cornerstone, footing, foundation, ground, groundwork, keystone, underpinning
related words buttress, framework, prop, substructure, support; assumption, justification, premise, presumption, presupposition, theory, thesis, warrant; center, core, eye, focus, heart, hub, nucleus, seat; essence, quintessence, soul
2 a place from which an advance (as for military operations) is made ⟨the Army's *base* of attack was kept top secret until the battle began⟩
synonyms bridgehead, foothold
related words beachhead, center, front, headquarters; bastion, fastness, fortress, stronghold
3 a thing or place that is of greatest importance to an activity or interest — see CENTER 1
4 the lowest part, place, or point — see BOTTOM 3
5 the place from which a commander runs operations — see COMMAND 3

base *vb* to find a basis ⟨she *based* her argument against the death penalty on careful research⟩
synonyms ground, predicate, rest
related words establish, found; assume, postulate, premise, presume, presuppose, suppose

baseborn *adj* **1** belonging to the class of people of low social or economic rank — see IGNOBLE 1
2 born to a father and mother who are not married — see ILLEGITIMATE 1

basement *n* a room or set of rooms below the surface of the ground — see CELLAR

bash *vb* **1** to come into usually forceful contact with something — see HIT 2
2 to deliver a blow to (someone or something) usually in a strong vigorous manner — see HIT 1
3 to strike repeatedly — see BEAT 1

bashful *adj* not comfortable around people — see SHY 2

basic *adj* of or relating to the simplest facts or theories of a subject — see ELEMENTARY

basically *adv* for the most part — see CHIEFLY

basics *n pl* general or basic truths on which other truths or theories can be based — see PRINCIPLES 1

basis *n* an immaterial thing upon which something else rests — see BASE 1

bask *vb* to refrain from labor or exertion — see REST 1

bass *adj* having a low musical pitch or range — see DEEP 2

bastard *adj* born to a father and mother who are not married — see ILLEGITIMATE 1

bastion *n* a structure or place from which one can resist attack — see FORT

bat *n* **1** a hard strike with a part of the body or an instrument — see [1]BLOW
2 a heavy rigid stick used as a weapon or for punishment — see CLUB 1

bat *vb* **1** to deliver a blow to (someone or something) usually in a strong vigorous manner — see HIT 1
2 to strike repeatedly — see BEAT 1

batch *n* **1** a number of things considered as a unit — see GROUP 1
2 a usually small number of persons considered as a unit — see GROUP 2

bath *n* a room furnished with a fixture for flushing body waste — see TOILET

bathe *vb* to make wet — see WET

bathed *adj* containing, covered with, or thoroughly penetrated by water — see WET

bathroom *n* a room furnished with a fixture for flushing body waste — see TOILET

battalion *n* a large body of men and women organized for land warfare — see ARMY 1

batter *vb* to strike repeatedly — see BEAT 1

battery *n* **1** a number of things considered as a unit — see GROUP 1
2 a usually small number of persons considered as a unit — see GROUP 2

battle *n* **1** a forceful effort to reach a goal or objective — see STRUGGLE 1
2 a physical dispute between opposing individuals or groups — see FIGHT 1
3 active fighting during the course of a war — see COMBAT 1
4 an earnest effort for superiority or victory over another — see CONTEST 1

battle *vb* **1** to engage in a contest — see COMPETE
2 to enter into contest or conflict with — see ENGAGE 2
3 to oppose (someone) in physical conflict — see FIGHT 1
4 to strive to reduce or eliminate — see FIGHT 2

batty *adj* having or showing a very abnormal or sick state of mind — see INSANE 1

bauble *n* a small object displayed for its attractiveness or interest — see KNICKKNACK

bawdiness *n* the quality or state of being obscene — see OBSCENITY 1

bawdy *adj* **1** depicting or referring to sexual matters in a way that is unacceptable in polite society — see OBSCENE 1
2 hinting at or intended to call to mind matters regarded as indecent — see SUGGESTIVE 1

bawl *vb* **1** to shed tears often while making meaningless sounds as a sign of pain or distress — see CRY 1
2 to speak so as to be heard at a distance — see CALL 1

bay *n* **1** a part of a body of water that extends beyond the general shoreline — see GULF 1
2 one of the parts into which an enclosed space is divided — see COMPARTMENT

bay *vb* to make a long loud mournful sound — see HOWL 1

bazaar *n* an establishment where goods are sold to consumers — see SHOP 1

be *vb* **1** to have life ⟨stories that begin with the familiar line "once upon a time there *was* a beautiful maiden"⟩
synonyms breathe, exist, live, subsist
related words abide, continue, endure, last, lead, persist, survive; move; flourish, prosper, thrive
near antonyms disappear, evaporate, vanish; cease, end, stop
antonyms depart, die, expire, pass away, perish, succumb
2 to occupy a place or location — see STAND 1
3 to take or have a certain position within a group arranged in vertical classes — see RANK 1
4 to take place — see HAPPEN

be (to) *vb* to behave toward in a stated way — see TREAT 1

beach *n* the usually sandy or gravelly land bordering a body of water ⟨she loves walking along the *beach*, looking for shells that the waves cast up⟩
synonyms shore, strand
related words seaboard, seacoast, seashore, seaside; coast, coastline, shoreline; waterfront; bank, riverbank, riverside; esplanade; littoral

beached *adj* resting on the shore or bottom of a body of water — see AGROUND

beacon *n* something that provides illumination — see LIGHT 2

beak *n* the jaws of a bird together with their hornlike covering ⟨the bird cracked the walnut shell with its *beak* and ate its nut⟩
synonyms bill, nib
related words mouth; muzzle; mandible, maw, maxilla

beam *n* a narrow sharply defined line of light radiating from an object — see SHAFT 1

beam *vb* **1** to emit rays of light — see SHINE 1
2 to express an emotion (as amusement) by curving the lips upward — see SMILE 1

beaming *adj* **1** giving off or reflecting much light — see BRIGHT 1
2 having or being an outward sign of good feelings (as of love, confidence, or happiness) — see RADIANT 1

bear *n* an irritable and complaining person — see GROUCH

bear *vb* **1** to bring forth from the womb ⟨luckily, she turned out to be able to *bear* children after all⟩
synonyms drop, have, produce
related words deliver; create; breed, multiply, propagate, reproduce, spawn; beget, father, generate, get, mother, sire
phrases to give birth to
near antonyms abort, lose, miscarry
2 to put up with (something painful or difficult) ⟨I can't *bear* having to eat my vegetables in order to have ice cream⟩
synonyms abide, brook, countenance, endure, meet, stand, stick out, stomach, support, sustain, take, tolerate
related words accept, allow, permit, suffer, swallow; acquiesce, agree (with *or* to), assent (to), capitulate, consent (to), respect, submit (to), yield (to)
near antonyms decline, dismiss, refuse, reject, repudiate, spurn, turn down; combat, contest, fight, oppose, resist; avoid, bypass, circumvent, dodge, elude, escape, evade, miss; abstain, forbear, refrain
3 to have a relation or connection — see APPLY 1
4 to go on a specified course or in a certain direction — see HEAD 1
5 to hold up or serve as a foundation for — see SUPPORT 3
6 to keep in one's mind or heart — see HARBOR 1
7 to manage the actions of (oneself) in a particular way — see BEHAVE
8 to support and take from one place to another — see CARRY 1
9 to take to or upon oneself — see ASSUME 1
10 to wear or have on one's person — see CARRY 2

bearable *adj* capable of being endured ⟨the pain from a sprained ankle is annoying but *bearable*⟩
synonyms endurable, sufferable, supportable, sustainable, tolerable
related words livable (*also* liveable); acceptable, allowable, reasonable
near antonyms agonizing, appalling, awful, bad, cruel, dire, dreadful, excruciating, ghastly, harrowing, harsh, horrible, nasty, painful, rotten, terrible, tormenting, torturous, unfortunate, vicious, vile, wretched; unacceptable; acute, extreme, intense, piercing
antonyms insufferable, insupportable, intolerable, unbearable, unendurable, unsupportable

beard *vb* to oppose (something hostile or dangerous) with firmness or courage — see FACE 2

bear down on *vb* to push steadily against with some force — see PRESS 1

bearing *n* **1** the fact or state of being pertinent — see PERTINENCE
2 the fact or state of having something in common — see CONNECTION 1
3 the way or manner in which one conducts oneself — see BEHAVIOR

bearish *adj* having or showing a habitually bad temper — see ILL-TEMPERED

bear out *vb* to give evidence or testimony to the truth or factualness of — see CONFIRM

beast *n* **1** a mean, evil, or unprincipled person — see VILLAIN
2 a person whose behavior is offensive to others — see JERK 1
3 one of the lower animals as distinguished from human beings — see ANIMAL

beastly *adv* to a great degree — see VERY 1

beat *adj* depleted in strength, energy, or freshness — see WEARY 1

beat *n* **1** a hard strike with a part of the body or an instrument — see [1]BLOW
2 a rhythmic expanding and contracting — see PULSATION
3 the recurrent pattern formed by a series of sounds having a regular rise and fall in intensity — see RHYTHM

beat *vb* **1** to strike repeatedly ⟨they attacked and *beat* him, but fortunately he'll be fine⟩
synonyms bash, bat, batter, belt, bludgeon, buffet, bung (up), club, drub, flog, hammer, hide, lace, lambaste (*or* lambast), lick, maul, pelt, pommel, pound, pummel, thrash, thump, wallop, whale, whip
related words assail, attack, box, bust, cane, chop, clobber, clout, crack, cudgel, cuff, hit, horsewhip, knock, lam, lash, lay on, paste, punch, slap, smack, smash, sock, spank, swat, swipe, thwack, whack; gore, lacerate, wound; maim, mangle, mutilate

2 to achieve a victory over ⟨she always *beats* everyone at checkers, but she's not as good at chess⟩

synonyms best, clobber, conquer, crush, defeat, drub, lick, master, overbear, overcome, overmatch, prevail (over), rout, skunk, subdue, surmount, thrash, trim, triumph (over), trounce, wallop, whip, win (against), worst

related words nose out; excel, flourish, score, succeed; overpower, overthrow, subjugate, vanquish; exceed, outdo, surpass

phrases get around, get the better of

near antonyms fail

antonyms lose (to)

3 to be greater, better, or stronger than — see SURPASS 1

4 to expand and contract in a rhythmic manner — see PULSATE

5 to move or cause to move with a striking motion — see FLAP

6 to prevent from achieving a goal — see FRUSTRATE

7 to shape with a hammer — see HAMMER 1

8 to shine with a bright harsh light — see GLARE 1

9 to strike or cause to strike lightly and usually rhythmically — see [1]TAP

beater *n* one that defeats an enemy or opponent — see VICTOR 1

beating *n* failure to win a contest — see DEFEAT 1

beau *n* a male romantic companion — see BOYFRIEND

beau ideal *n* **1** someone of such unequaled perfection as to deserve imitation — see IDEAL 1

2 the most perfect type or example — see QUINTESSENCE 1

beauteous *adj* very pleasing to look at — see BEAUTIFUL

beauteousness *n* the qualities in a person or thing that as a whole give pleasure to the senses — see BEAUTY 1

beautiful *adj* very pleasing to look at ⟨a strikingly *beautiful* child who is being eagerly pursued by all the modeling agencies⟩

synonyms attractive, beauteous, bonny [*chiefly British*], comely, cute, fair, gorgeous, handsome, knockout, lovely, pretty, ravishing, sightly, stunning, taking

related words alluring, appealing, charming, delightful, eye-catching, glamorous (*also* glamourous), prepossessing; elegant, exquisite, glorious, resplendent, splendid, statuesque, sublime, superb; flawless, perfect, radiant; dainty, delicate; personable, presentable

near antonyms abhorrent, abominable, bad, disagreeable, disgusting, dreadful, foul, frightful, ghastly, hideous, horrible, loathsome, nasty, nauseating, objectionable, offensive, repellent, repugnant, repulsive, revolting, shocking, sickening, terrible; unappealing, unappetizing, unpleasant, unpleasing, unprepossessing

antonyms homely, ill-favored, plain, ugly, unattractive, unbeautiful, unhandsome, unlovely, unpretty, unsightly

beautify *vb* to make more attractive by adding something that is beautiful or becoming — see DECORATE

beautifying *adj* serving to add beauty — see DECORATIVE

beauty *n* **1** the qualities in a person or thing that as a whole give pleasure to the senses ⟨her *beauty* was enough to take your breath away⟩

synonyms attractiveness, beauteousness, comeliness, cuteness, fairness, gorgeousness, handsomeness, looks, loveliness, prettiness

related words allure, appeal, attraction, glamour (*also* glamor); charm, elegance, exquisiteness, flawlessness, gloriousness, perfection, radiance, resplendence; desirability, desirableness

near antonyms dreadfulness, foulness, ghastliness, grotesqueness, hideousness, loathsomeness, nastiness, offensiveness, repellency, repulsiveness, unattractiveness; blemish, flaw, imperfection

antonyms homeliness, plainness, ugliness, unsightliness

2 a lovely woman ⟨she was quite a *beauty* in her younger days⟩

synonyms eyeful, goddess, knockout, stunner

related words belle, charmer, honey

near antonyms hag, horror, witch

3 something very good of its kind — see JIM-DANDY

because *conj* for the reason that — see SINCE

because of *prep* as the result of ⟨I was late for school *because of* the snowstorm, which made driving very hazardous⟩

synonyms due to, owing to, through, with

beckon *vb* to direct or notify by a movement or gesture — see MOTION

becloud *vb* **1** to make (something) unclear to the understanding — see CONFUSE 2

2 to make dark, dim, or indistinct — see CLOUD 1

beclouded *adj* **1** covered over by clouds — see OVERCAST

2 filled with or dimmed by fine particles (as of dust or water) in suspension — see HAZY 1

become *vb* to eventually have as a state or quality ⟨many people *became* sick with the flu⟩ ⟨with autumn the days *become* crisper and breezier⟩

synonyms come, get, go, grow, run, turn, wax

related words alter, change, metamorphose, modify, mutate, transfigure, transform, transmute

near antonyms abide, be, continue, linger, remain, stay

becoming *adj* meeting the requirements of a purpose or situation — see FIT 1

bed *n* **1** a place set aside for sleeping ⟨the sofa in the living room will be your *bed* for the night⟩

synonyms bunk, pad, sack

related words bedstead, mattress, pallet; cot, couch, daybed, feather bed, four-poster, hammock, sofa, sofa bed, studio couch, trundle bed, water bed; bassinet, cradle, crib

2 the surface upon which a body of water lies — see BOTTOM 2

bed *vb* to go to one's bed in order to sleep ⟨the campers all *bedded* down for the night around 9 pm⟩

synonyms retire, turn in

related words bunk, perch, roost, settle; doze, drop (off), nap, nod, sleep, slumber, snooze; couch, lie (down), recline

near antonyms arouse, awake, awaken, rouse, wake, waken; bestir, stir, wake; reawake, reawaken; shift, stir

antonyms arise, get up, rise, uprise

bedaub *vb* to rub an oily or sticky substance over — see SMEAR 1

bedazzle *vb* to overpower with light — see DAZZLE

bedazzling *adj* giving off or reflecting much light — see BRIGHT 1
bedeck *vb* to make more attractive by adding something that is beautiful or becoming — see DECORATE
bedevil *vb* to cause persistent suffering to — see AFFLICT
bedevilment *n* the act of making unwelcome intrusions upon another — see ANNOYANCE 1
bedim *vb* to make dark, dim, or indistinct — see CLOUD 1
bedizen *vb* to make more attractive by adding something that is beautiful or becoming — see DECORATE
bedizened *adj* elaborately and often excessively decorated — see ORNATE
bedlam *n* a place of uproar or confusion — see MADHOUSE 2
bedrock *n* an immaterial thing upon which something else rests — see BASE 1
bedspread *n* a decorative cloth used as a top covering for a bed — see COUNTERPANE
beef *n* an expression of dissatisfaction, pain, or resentment — see COMPLAINT 1
beef *vb* to express dissatisfaction, pain, or resentment usually tiresomely — see COMPLAIN
beef (up) *vb* **1** to increase the ability of (as a muscle) to exert physical force — see STRENGTHEN 1
2 to make markedly greater in measure or degree — see INTENSIFY
beefy *adj* strongly and heavily built — see [1]HUSKY
beetle *vb* to extend outward beyond a usual point — see BULGE
befall *vb* to take place — see HAPPEN
befit *vb* to be fitting or proper — see DO 1
befitting *adj* meeting the requirements of a purpose or situation — see FIT 1
befog *vb* **1** to make (something) unclear to the understanding — see CONFUSE 2
2 to make dark, dim, or indistinct — see CLOUD 1
3 to throw into a state of mental uncertainty — see CONFUSE 1
befogged *adj* filled with or dimmed by fine particles (as of dust or water) in suspension — see HAZY 1
before *adv* so as to precede something in order of time — see AHEAD 1
before *prep* **1** earlier than <since I'm a faster runner, I got there *before* him>
synonyms afore [*chiefly dialect*], ahead of, ere, of, previous to, prior to, to
related words till, until, up to
phrases in advance of
near antonyms next, next to, since
antonyms after, following
2 preceding in space <the children always insisted on running *before* their parents>
synonyms afore [*chiefly dialect*], ahead of
related words against
phrases in advance of, in front of
antonyms after, following
beforehand *adv* **1** before the usual or expected time — see EARLY
2 so as to precede something in order of time — see AHEAD 1
befoul *vb* **1** to make dirty — see DIRTY
2 to make unfit for use by the addition of something harmful or undesirable — see CONTAMINATE
befuddle *vb* to throw into a state of mental uncertainty — see CONFUSE 1
befuddled *adj* suffering from mental confusion — see DIZZY 2
befuddlement *n* a state of mental uncertainty — see CONFUSION 1
beg *vb* to make a request to (someone) in an earnest or urgent manner <she *begged* her mother to let her go on the Girl Scout camporee>
synonyms appeal (to), beseech, conjure, entreat, implore, importune, petition, plead (to), pray, solicit, supplicate
related words mooch, sponge; ask, desire, invoke, request, sue; claim, coerce, command, compel, demand, force, insist, require
phrases call on (*or* call upon)
near antonyms hint, imply, intimate, suggest; appease, conciliate, gratify, mollify, oblige, pacify, placate, please, satisfy; comfort, console, content, quiet
beget *vb* to become the father of — see FATHER
begetter *n* a person who establishes a whole new field of endeavor — see FATHER 2
beggar *n* a person who lives by public begging <the poor *beggars* that are such a common sight in underdeveloped countries>
synonyms mendicant, panhandler
related words bum, drifter, hobo, tramp, vagabond, vagrant; pauper; hanger-on, leech, moocher, parasite, sponge, sponger; dependent; deadbeat, derelict, idler, ne'er-do-well
beggared *adj* lacking money or material possessions — see POOR 1
beggary *n* the state of lacking sufficient money or material possessions — see POVERTY 1
begin *vb* **1** to take the first step in (a process or course of action) <she *began* walking to school>
synonyms commence, embark (on *or* upon), enter (into *or* upon), get off, kick off, launch, open, start, strike (into)
related words create, generate, inaugurate, initiate, innovate, invent, originate; adopt, embrace, take on, take up; establish, father, found, institute, organize, pioneer, set up, spawn
phrases get to, set about
near antonyms cease, desist, discontinue, halt, lay off, quit, stop; close, complete; abandon, forsake, leave; abolish, demolish, destroy, exterminate, extinguish, phase out
antonyms conclude, end, finish, terminate
2 to come into existence <the storm *began* late in the day and lasted all night>
synonyms arise, commence, dawn, form, materialize, originate, set in, spring, start
related words be, breathe, exist, live, subsist; appear, arrive, emerge; continue, endure, last, persist, survive
near antonyms conclude, desist, discontinue, finish, halt, quit, terminate; disappear, dissolve, evaporate, vanish; depart, die, expire, pass away, perish
antonyms cease, end, stop
beginner *n* a person who is just starting out in a field of activity <although he is only a *beginner* at swimming, he is making excellent progress>
synonyms colt, fledgling, freshman, greenhorn, neophyte, newcomer, novice, recruit, rookie, tenderfoot, tyro
related words apprentice, cub; boot, novitiate;

amateur, dilettante; learner, student, trainee; candidate, entrant, probationer
near antonyms expert, master, pro, professional
antonyms old hand, old-timer, vet, veteran

beginning *n* the point at which something begins ⟨the actual *beginning* of the universe is still under debate, with some scientists believing in the big bang theory⟩
synonyms alpha, birth, commencement, dawn, genesis, inception, incipiency, launch, morning, onset, outset, start, threshold
related words creation, inauguration, initiation, institution, origination; cradle, fountainhead, origin, root, source, spring, well, wellspring; dawning, opening; appearance, arrival, emergence; infancy
near antonyms cessation, closing, closure, completion, finale, finish, period, stop, termination, windup
antonyms close, conclusion, end, ending

begone *vb* to leave a place often for another — see GO 2

begrime *vb* to make dirty — see DIRTY

beguile *vb* **1** to attract or delight as if by magic — see CHARM 1
2 to cause to believe what is untrue — see DECEIVE
3 to lead away from a usual or proper course by offering some pleasure or advantage — see LURE

beguiling *adj* **1** clever at attaining one's ends by indirect and often deceptive means — see ARTFUL 1
2 tending or having power to deceive — see DECEPTIVE 1

behave *vb* to manage the actions of (oneself) in a particular way ⟨if she *behaves* herself properly and sits quietly during church, she will get ice cream afterward⟩
synonyms acquit, bear, comport, conduct, demean, deport, quit
related words check, collect, compose, constrain, contain, control, curb, handle, inhibit, quiet, repress, restrain; moderate, modulate, temper; act, impersonate, play
near antonyms act up, carry on, cut up, misbehave, misconduct

behavior *n* the way or manner in which one conducts oneself ⟨he promised to be on his best *behavior* for the party⟩
synonyms actions, bearing, comportment, conduct, demeanor, deportment
related words etiquette, form, manners, mores, proprieties; amenity, civility, courtesy, decorum, politeness; air, attitude, carriage, poise, pose, posture, presence; aspect, look, mien; formality, protocol, rules; custom, habit, pattern, practice (*also* practise), trick, wont; convention, fashion, form, mode, style; affectation, attribute, characteristic, mark, trait; distinctiveness, oddity, peculiarity, singularity, strangeness, uniqueness, weirdness

behead *vb* to cut off the head of — see DECAPITATE

behemoth *n* something that is unusually large and powerful — see GIANT

behest *n* a statement of what to do that must be obeyed by those concerned — see COMMAND 1

behind *adj* not arriving, occurring, or settled at the due, usual, or proper time — see LATE 1

behind *prep* **1** at, to, or toward the rear of ⟨she preferred to be *behind* the lead hikers, who were always too much in a rush to enjoy the scenery⟩
synonyms abaft, back of
near antonyms ahead of
antonyms before, in front of
2 subsequent to in time or order — see AFTER

behindhand *adj* not arriving, occurring, or settled at the due, usual, or proper time — see LATE 1

behold *vb* to make note of (something) through the use of one's eyes — see SEE 1

being *n* **1** a member of the human race — see HUMAN
2 one that has a real and independent existence — see ENTITY

belabor *vb* to criticize harshly and usually publicly — see ATTACK 2

belated *adj* not arriving, occurring, or settled at the due, usual, or proper time — see LATE 1

belatedness *n* the quality or state of being late — see LATENESS

belch *vb* to throw out or off (something from within) often violently — see ERUPT 1

beldam *or* **beldame** *n* a mean or ugly old woman — see CRONE

beleaguer *vb* to surround (as a fortified place) with armed forces for the purpose of capturing or preventing commerce and communication — see BESIEGE

belie *vb* **1** to give a false idea of ⟨his bright smile *belied* his actual mood, which was really one of great sadness⟩
synonyms misrepresent
related words contradict; camouflage, cloak, conceal, counterfeit, disguise, hide, mask, obscure; color, deceive, distort, falsify, garble, mislead, twist; dissemble, feign, pretend
near antonyms bare, demonstrate, disclose, discover, exhibit, expose, evince, reveal; flaunt, parade, show off
antonyms betray, represent
2 to prove to be false — see DISPROVE

belief *n* **1** mental conviction of the truth of some statement or the reality of some being or phenomenon ⟨a *belief* in unicorns led him to look for them every time he walked through the woods⟩
synonyms credence, credit, faith
related words axiom, law, precept, principle, tenet; assurance, certainty, certitude, conviction, positiveness, sureness; confidence, dependance, reliance, trust; hope; doctrine, dogma, philosophy; dogmatism, fanaticism, insistence
near antonyms distrust, mistrust, skepticism, suspicion, uncertainty
antonyms disbelief, discredit, doubt, unbelief
2 an idea that is believed to be true or valid without positive knowledge — see OPINION 1

believable *adj* worthy of being accepted as true or reasonable ⟨she had a *believable* story for why her homework was late, so she didn't receive any punishment⟩
synonyms credible, likely, plausible, probable
related words acceptable, conceivable, imaginable, possible, practical, reasonable; dependable, reliable, trustworthy
near antonyms absurd, doubtful, dubious, fantastic, flimsy, outlandish, preposterous, questionable, ridiculous; impossible, inconceivable, unimaginable, unthinkable; skeptical, suspect, suspicious, uncertain, unsure; hopeless, unworkable, useless
antonyms far-fetched, implausible, improbable, incredible, unbelievable, unlikely

believe *vb* **1** to regard as right or true ⟨the teacher *believed* the student's explanation that the assignment was late because she was sick, even though she didn't bring in a note from the doctor⟩
synonyms accept, credit, swallow, trust
related words account, accredit, understand; assume, presume, suppose; conclude, deduce, infer
phrases set store by (*or* on)
near antonyms distrust, doubt, mistrust, question, suspect; challenge, dispute
antonyms disbelieve, discredit, reject
2 to have as an opinion ⟨he *believed* that his favorite tennis player was the best in the world⟩
synonyms consider, deem, feel, figure, guess, hold, imagine, reckon [*chiefly dialect*], suppose, think
related words esteem, regard, view; accept, conceive, perceive; depend, rely, trust; assume, presume, presuppose; conclude, deduce, infer
near antonyms distrust, doubt, mistrust, question, suspect; disbelieve, discredit, reject

belittle *vb* to express scornfully one's low opinion of — see DECRY 1

belittlement *n* the act of making a person or a thing seem little or unimportant — see DEPRECIATION

belittling *adj* intended to make a person or thing seem of little importance or value — see DEROGATORY

bellicose *adj* feeling or displaying eagerness to fight — see BELLIGERENT

bellicosity *n* an inclination to fight or quarrel — see BELLIGERENCE

belligerence *n* an inclination to fight or quarrel ⟨among the Native American tribes of the Colonial period, the Iroquois were known for their *belligerence*⟩
synonyms aggression, aggressiveness, bellicosity, combativeness, contentiousness, disputatiousness, fight, militancy, pugnacity, scrappiness, truculence
related words antagonism, fierceness, hostility, unfriendliness; acidity, biliousness, crabbiness, crankiness, crossness, disagreeableness, fretfulness, grouchiness, grumpiness, huffiness, irascibility, irritability, irritableness, orneriness, peevishness, pettishness, petulance, querulousness, rudeness, surliness, testiness, waspishness
phrases chip on one's shoulder
near antonyms affability, amiability, amicability, benevolence, complaisance, cordiality, friendliness, geniality, graciousness, pleasantness, sociability; gentleness, kindliness, mildness
antonyms pacifism

belligerent *adj* feeling or displaying eagerness to fight ⟨the coach became quite *belligerent* and spit on an umpire after being thrown out of the game⟩
synonyms aggressive, argumentative, bellicose, combative, contentious, discordant, disputatious, gladiatorial, militant, pugnacious, quarrelsome, scrappy, truculent, warlike
related words antagonistic, fierce, hostile, hot-tempered; acidic, bearish, bilious, choleric, crabby, cranky, cross, disagreeable, dyspeptic, fretful, grouchy, grumpy, huffy, ill-humored, ill-natured, ill-tempered, irascible, irritable, ornery, peevish, pettish, petulant, querulous, rude, snappish, snappy, surly, testy, touchy, ugly, waspish; battling, fighting, warring
phrases on the warpath
near antonyms affable, amiable, amicable, benevolent, complaisant, conciliatory, cordial, easygoing, friendly, genial, good-natured, good-tempered, gracious, ingratiating, obliging, pleasant, sociable; calm, quiet, relaxed, serene, tranquil; benign, gentle, kindly, mild
antonyms nonbelligerent, pacific, peaceable, peaceful

bellow *vb* to make a long loud deep noise or cry — see ROAR

belly *n* the part of the body between the chest and the pelvis — see STOMACH

belly *vb* to extend outward beyond a usual point — see BULGE

bellyache *n* abdominal pain especially when focused in the digestive organs — see STOMACHACHE

bellyache *vb* to express dissatisfaction, pain, or resentment usually tiresomely — see COMPLAIN

belong *vb* **1** to have or be in a usual or proper place ⟨your shoes *belong* in the closet, not out on the floor where people will trip on them⟩
synonyms go
related words place, stay; fit (in)
2 to be the property of a person or group of persons ⟨those textbooks *belong* to the school system, and you have to give them back at the end of the year⟩
synonyms appertain, pertain
related words have, hold, own, possess

belongings *n pl* transportable items that one owns — see POSSESSION 2

beloved *adj* granted special treatment or attention — see DARLING 1

beloved *n* a person with whom one is in love — see SWEETHEART

below *adv* **1** in or to a lower place ⟨he climbed *below* to fix the engine⟩
synonyms beneath, under, underneath
related words beside, near, nearby
near antonyms aloft, overhead
antonyms up
2 toward or in a lower position — see DOWN

below *prep* in a lower position than ⟨she sat *below* everyone else, on the floor⟩
synonyms beneath, under
related words underneath
antonyms above, over

[1]**belt** *n* a hard strike with a part of the body or an instrument — see [1]BLOW

[2]**belt** *n* a strip of flexible material (as leather) worn around the waist ⟨he loves his fancily decorated *belt*, but only gets to wear it on special occasions⟩
synonyms cincture, cummerbund, girdle, sash
related words band, waistband; circle, loop, ribbon, ring; baldric, bandolier (*or* bandoleer)
2 a broad geographical area — see REGION 2

belt *vb* **1** to deliver a blow to (someone or something) usually in a strong vigorous manner — see HIT 1
2 to encircle or bind with or as if with a belt — see GIRD 1
3 to strike repeatedly — see BEAT 1

bemoan *vb* **1** to feel or express sorrow for — see LAMENT 1
2 to feel sorry or dissatisfied about — see REGRET

bemoaning *adj* expressing or suggesting mourning — see MOURNFUL 1

bemuse *vb* to throw into a state of mental uncertainty — see CONFUSE 1

bench *n* a public official having authority to decide questions of law — see JUDGE 1
benchmark *n* something set up as an example against which others of the same type are compared — see STANDARD 1
bend *n* **1** something that curves or is curved <it's hard to see around that *bend* in the road, so be careful>
synonyms angle, arc, arch, bow, crook, curvature, curve, turn, wind
related words kink, warp; circle, ring, ringlet, round; coil, curl, curlicue (*also* curlycue), flexure, fold, loop, spiral, swirl, twist; decline, inclination, incline, slope; corner, turnoff
antonyms straight line
2 the act of positioning or an instance of being positioned at an angle — see TILT
bend *vb* **1** to cause to turn away from a straight line <she *bent* the knife when she got it stuck in the drawer>
synonyms arch, crook, curve, hook, swerve
related words arc, bow, round; deflect, divert; entwine, kink, swirl, turn, twine, twist, veer, warp; coil, curl, loop, spiral; dent, dimple; meander, weave, wind; decline, incline, slope
antonyms straighten, unbend, uncurl
2 to occupy (oneself) diligently or with close attention — see APPLY 2
3 to point or turn (something) toward a target or goal — see AIM 1
4 to turn away from a straight line or course — see CURVE 1
bending *adj* marked by a long series of irregular curves — see CROOKED 1
beneath *adv* in or to a lower place — see BELOW 1
beneath *prep* in a lower position than — see BELOW
benediction *n* a prayer calling for divine care, protection, or favor — see BLESSING 1
benefaction *n* a gift of money or its equivalent to a charity, humanitarian cause, or public institution — see CONTRIBUTION
benefactor *n* one that helps another with gifts or money <an anonymous *benefactor* gave our school a dozen new computers>
synonyms donator, donor, patron
related words almsgiver, philanthropist; contributor, giver; subscriber, supporter, helper
beneficence *n* a gift of money or its equivalent to a charity, humanitarian cause, or public institution — see CONTRIBUTION
beneficent *adj* **1** having or marked by sympathy and consideration for others — see HUMANE 1
2 having or showing a concern for the welfare of others — see CHARITABLE 1
beneficial *adj* conferring benefits; promoting or contributing to personal or social well-being <tutoring can often be as *beneficial* and rewarding for the tutor as for the student receiving the help>
synonyms advantageous, favorable, helpful, profitable, salutary
related words gratifying, rewarding, satisfying; promising, propitious; advisable, desirable, healthful, healthy, salubrious, wholesome
near antonyms bad, damaging, deleterious, harmful, injurious, unfavorable, unhelpful
antonyms disadvantageous, unfavorable, unhelpful
benefit *n* **1** a thing that helps — see HELP 2
2 something that provides happiness or does good for a person or thing — see BLESSING 2
benefit *vb* to provide with something useful or desirable <his summer job *benefited* him in two ways: by giving him spending money and by offering some work experience>
synonyms avail, profit, serve
related words succeed, work (for); aid, assist, help, improve; content, delight, gladden, gratify, please, satisfy; bless
near antonyms hinder, impede; damage, harm, hurt, impair, injure; afflict, distress, upset
benevolence *n* kindly concern, interest, or support — see GOODWILL 1
benevolent *adj* **1** having or marked by sympathy and consideration for others — see HUMANE 1
2 having or showing a concern for the welfare of others — see CHARITABLE 1
benighted *adj* lacking in education or the knowledge gained from books — see IGNORANT 1
benign *adj* not harsh or stern especially in manner, nature, or effect — see GENTLE 1
benignant *adj* having or marked by sympathy and consideration for others — see HUMANE 1
benison *n* a prayer calling for divine care, protection, or favor — see BLESSING 1
bent *n* a habitual attraction to some activity or thing — see INCLINATION 1
bent (on *or* upon) *adj* fully committed to achieving a goal — see DETERMINED
benumb *vb* to reduce or weaken in strength or feeling — see DULL 1
benumbed *adj* lacking in sensation or feeling — see NUMB
bequeath *vb* to give by means of a will — see LEAVE 2
bequest *n* something that is or may be inherited — see INHERITANCE
berate *vb* to criticize (someone) severely or angrily especially for personal failings — see SCOLD
bereaved *adj* suffering the death of a loved one <the *bereaved* parents cried often in the first year>
synonyms bereft
related words orphaned, widowed; distressed, grieving, melancholy, miserable, mournful, mourning, sad, sorrowing, suffering, unhappy, upset; bemoaning, crying, lamenting, wailing, weeping
bereft *adj* **1** suffering the death of a loved one — see BEREAVED
2 utterly lacking in something needed, wanted, or expected — see DEVOID 1
berserk *adv* in a confused and reckless manner — see HELTER-SKELTER 1
berth *n* an assignment at which one regularly works for pay — see JOB 1
beseech *vb* to make a request to (someone) in an earnest or urgent manner — see BEG
beseeching *adj* asking humbly — see SUPPLIANT
beset *vb* to take sudden, violent action against — see ATTACK 1
beside *prep* **1** in addition to — see BESIDES 1
2 not including — see EXCEPT
besides *adv* in addition to what has been said — see MORE 1
besides *prep* **1** in addition to <*besides* me, there are five people working on this project>
synonyms as well as, beside, over and above
related words plus; including
phrases along with, together with

near antonyms except (*also* excepting); less, minus
2 not including — see EXCEPT

besiege *vb* to surround (as a fortified place) with armed forces for the purpose of capturing or preventing commerce and communication ⟨the army *besieged* the fort for six months before it finally surrendered⟩
synonyms beleaguer, blockade, invest
related words barricade, block, cut off, dam, encircle; assail, assault, attack, beset; confine, insulate, isolate, quarantine
phrases lay siege to
near antonyms emancipate, free, liberate, release, rescue

besmear *vb* to rub an oily or sticky substance over — see SMEAR 1

besmirch *vb* to make dirty — see DIRTY

besmirched *adj* not clean — see DIRTY 1

bespatter *vb* to wet or soil by striking with something liquid or mushy — see SPLASH 2

bespeak *vb* **1** to arrange to have something (as a hotel room) held for one's future use — see RESERVE 1
2 to make known (something abstract) through outward signs — see SHOW 2

best *n* **1** dressy clothing — see FINERY
2 individuals carefully selected as being the best of a class — see ELITE

best *vb* to achieve a victory over — see BEAT 2

bestow *vb* to make a present of — see GIVE 1

bestowal *n* something given to someone without expectation of a return — see GIFT 1

bestrew *vb* to cover by or as if by scattering something over or on — see SCATTER 2

bet *n* the money or thing risked on the outcome of an uncertain event ⟨she offered the *bet* of a free lunch if her team won the World Series⟩
synonyms stake, wager
related words collateral; jackpot, kitty, pot

bet *vb* to risk (something) on the outcome of an uncertain event ⟨he *bet* a month's allowance on the World Series⟩
synonyms gamble, go, lay, stake, wager
related words bid, offer; adventure, chance, hazard, speculate, venture; endanger, imperil, jeopardize

bête noire *n* **1** something or someone that causes fear or dread especially without reason — see BOGEY 1
2 something or someone that is hated — see HATE 2

betide *vb* to take place — see HAPPEN

betray *vb* **1** to be unfaithful or disloyal to ⟨childhood friends of movie stars often *betray* them by telling their secrets to the supermarket tabloids⟩
synonyms cross, double-cross, sell (out)
related words give away; inform (on), rat (on), snitch (on), split (on) [*British*], tell (on)
phrases go back on
near antonyms defend, guard, protect, safeguard, save, shield
2 to make known (something abstract) through outward signs — see SHOW 2

betrayal *n* the act or fact of violating the trust or confidence of another ⟨the terrible *betrayal* of having her best friend reveal her confidences to others⟩
synonyms disloyalty, double cross, faithlessness, falseness, falsity, infidelity, perfidy, sellout, treachery, treason, unfaithfulness
related words abandonment, desertion; deceit, deception, double-dealing, duplicity, guile; fraud, informing, lying, snitching, talebearing, trickery
near antonyms dependability, reliability, trustworthiness; allegiance, devotion, faithfulness, fealty, fidelity, loyalty, staunchness, steadfastness; defense, protection, safeguard, shield

betrayer *n* **1** a person who provides secret information about another's wrongdoing — see INFORMER
2 one who betrays a trust or an allegiance — see TRAITOR

betrothal *n* the act or state of being engaged to be married — see ENGAGEMENT 1

betrothed *adj* pledged in marriage — see ENGAGED

betrothed *n* the person to whom one is engaged to be married ⟨he gazed lovingly at his *betrothed* throughout dinner⟩
synonyms fiancé, fiancée, intended
related words admirer, beau, beloved, boyfriend, darling, dear, favorite, fellow, flame, girlfriend, honey, love, lover, steady, swain, sweet, sweetheart, valentine; bride, groom

better *adv* to a greater or higher extent — see MORE 2

better *n* **1** one who is above another in rank, station, or office — see SUPERIOR
2 the more favorable condition or position in a competition — see ADVANTAGE 1

better *vb* **1** to be greater, better, or stronger than — see SURPASS 1
2 to make better — see IMPROVE

bettor *or* **better** *n* one that bets (as on the outcome of a contest or sports event) ⟨*bettors* on the horse race have to place their bets at least 20 minutes before the start of the race⟩
synonyms gambler, wagerer
related words dicer; speculator

beverage *n* a liquid suitable for drinking — see DRINK 1

bewail *vb* to feel or express sorrow for — see LAMENT 1

bewailing *adj* expressing or suggesting mourning — see MOURNFUL 1

beware (of) *vb* to be cautious of or on guard against ⟨*beware of* that parrot because it bites⟩
synonyms guard (against), mind, watch out (for)
related words attend, heed, mark, note, notice; behold, discern, observe, perceive, see, watch
phrases be on the lookout for, look out for
near antonyms discount, disregard, ignore, miss, overlook

bewilder *vb* to throw into a state of mental uncertainty — see CONFUSE 1

bewildered *adj* suffering from mental confusion — see DIZZY 2

bewilderment *n* a state of mental uncertainty — see CONFUSION 1

bewitch *vb* **1** to cast a spell on ⟨a wicked fairy *bewitched* Sleeping Beauty so that she would sleep for a hundred years⟩
synonyms charm, enchant, hex, spell
related words curse, jinx, possess; attract, beguile, captivate, fascinate, mesmerize, spellbind; entice, lure, seduce, tempt
near antonyms bless
2 to attract or delight as if by magic — see CHARM 1

bewitched *adj* being or appearing to be under a magic spell — see ENCHANTED

bewitching *adj* having an often mysterious or magical power to attract — see FASCINATING 1

bewitchment *n* **1** a spoken word or set of words believed to have magic power — see SPELL 1
2 the power to control natural forces through supernatural means — see MAGIC 1

beyond *adv* at or to a greater distance or more advanced point — see FARTHER

beyond *prep* **1** on or to the farther side of ⟨the arrow flew *beyond* the fence and in the woods⟩
synonyms over, past
related words outside
near antonyms inside
2 out of the reach or sphere of ⟨although the school can keep you from screaming during school hours, making someone be quiet after school is *beyond* their authority⟩
synonyms outside, outside of, without
related words except (*also* excepting)
near antonyms inside
antonyms within

bias *n* an attitude that always favors one way of feeling or acting especially without considering any other possibilities ⟨he had a powerful *bias* towards doing all math problems by the same method, regardless of the problem⟩
synonyms favor, one-sidedness, partiality, partisanship, prejudice
related words favoritism, nepotism; bent, inclination, leaning, penchant, predilection, predisposition, proclivity, propensity, tendency; preconception, prejudgment
near antonyms calm, detachment, dispassion, indifference; aversion, dislike, distaste
antonyms impartiality, neutrality, objectivity, open-mindedness

bias *vb* to cause to have often negative opinions formed without sufficient knowledge — see PREJUDICE

biased *adj* inclined to favor one side over another — see PARTIAL 1

Bible *n* a book made up of the writings accepted by Christians as coming from God ⟨she received a lovely *Bible* as a First Communion gift⟩
synonyms Book, Good Book, Holy Writ, Scripture

bicker *n* an often noisy or angry expression of differing opinions — see ARGUMENT 1

bicker *vb* to express different opinions about something often angrily — see ARGUE 2

bid *vb* to issue orders to (someone) by right of authority — see COMMAND 1

bide *vb* to remain in place in readiness or expectation of something — see WAIT

big *adj* **1** having great meaning or lasting effect — see IMPORTANT 1
2 of a size greater than average of its kind — see LARGE

bight *n* a part of a body of water that extends beyond the general shoreline — see GULF 1

bigness *n* the quality or state of being large in size — see LARGENESS

bigoted *adj* unwilling to grant other people social rights or to accept other viewpoints — see INTOLERANT 2

bilious *adj* having or showing a habitually bad temper — see ILL-TEMPERED

biliousness *n* readiness to show annoyance or impatience — see PETULANCE

[1]**bill** *n* **1** a record of goods sold or services performed together with the costs due ⟨luckily, the amount due on our electric *bill* wasn't too high this month, because we finally convinced everyone to stop wasting electricity⟩
synonyms account, check, invoice, statement, tab
related words receipt, reckoning; document, record; charge, cost, expense, fee, price, rate, toll; score, tally
2 a piece of printed paper used as money ⟨the United States twenty-dollar *bill* has a picture of Andrew Jackson on the front⟩
synonyms bank note, greenback, note
related words paper money, scrip; buck, dollar; cash, chips, currency, dough, legal tender, lucre, money, pelf; check, draft, money order
3 a sheet bearing an announcement for posting in a public place — see POSTER
4 the amount owed at a bar or restaurant or the slip of paper stating the amount — see CHECK 1

[2]**bill** *n* **1** the jaws of a bird together with their hornlike covering — see BEAK
2 the projecting front part of a hat or cap — see VISOR

[1]**billet** *n* a straight piece (as of wood or metal) that is longer than it is wide — see BAR 1

[2]**billet** *n* an assignment at which one regularly works for pay — see JOB 1

billet *vb* to provide with living quarters or shelter — see HOUSE 1

bill of fare *n* a list of foods served at or available for a meal — see MENU 1

billow *n* a moving ridge on the surface of water — see WAVE

billow *vb* to extend outward beyond a usual point — see BULGE

billy *n* a heavy rigid stick used as a weapon or for punishment — see CLUB 1

binary *adj* consisting of two members or parts that are usually joined — see DOUBLE 1

bind *vb* **1** to confine or restrain with or as if with chains ⟨prisons tend to *bind* convicted criminals for transport⟩ ⟨Angie feels *bound* to her boyfriend by love and loyalty⟩
synonyms chain, enchain, fetter, handcuff, manacle, shackle, trammel
related words lash, pinion, secure, tie, truss; attach, fasten, join, link; confine, constrain, curb, hamper, hinder, limit, restrict; entangle, tangle
near antonyms emancipate, free, liberate, loose, release, rescue; undo, unfasten, untangle, untie; detach, disengage
antonyms unbind, unfetter
2 to cover with a bandage — see BANDAGE
3 to gather into a tight mass by means of a line or cord — see TIE 1

binge *n* a time or instance of carefree fun — see FLING 1

biography *n* a history of a person's life ⟨an unauthorized *biography* of the actor made him very unhappy⟩
synonyms life, memoir
related words autobiography; chronicle, history, past, story; obituary; character sketch

bipartite *adj* consisting of two members or parts that are usually joined — see DOUBLE 1

birch *vb* to strike repeatedly with something long and thin or flexible — see WHIP 1

bird *n* a member of the human race — see HUMAN

birdman *n* one who flies or is qualified to fly an aircraft or spacecraft — see PILOT

bird's–eye *adj* relating to the main elements and not to specific details — see GENERAL 2

birth *n* **1** the act or instance of being born ⟨biology class will be showing a movie of the *birth* of kittens⟩
synonyms nativity
related words creation, genesis, origination, rise; bearing, childbearing, labor, parturition; begetting, breeding, fathering, generation, mothering, reproduction, siring, spawning; fatherhood, maternity, motherhood, parenthood, paternity
near antonyms abortion, miscarriage
2 the line of ancestors from whom a person is descended — see ANCESTRY
3 the point at which something begins — see BEGINNING

birthright *n* **1** something that is or may be inherited — see INHERITANCE
2 something to which one has a just claim — see RIGHT 1

bisect *vb* to divide by passing through or across — see INTERSECT

bit *n* **1** a very small piece ⟨she left only a *bit* of the broccoli on her plate, so she was allowed to have dessert⟩
synonyms atom, crumb, fleck, flyspeck, grain, granule, molecule, morsel, mote, nubbin, particle, patch, scrap, scruple, snippet, speck, tittle
related words ace, dab, glimmer, hint, hoot, iota, jot, lick, little, mite, modicum, ounce, peanuts, pinch, ray, shade, shred, smidgen (*also* smidgeon *or* smidgin), spot, strain, streak, suspicion, taste, touch, trace, whisper, whit; dash, driblet, drop; fragment, part, portion, section; bite, mouthful, nibble; handful, scattering, smattering, sprinkling; dose, shot; damn, darn; chip, flake, shard, shiver, sliver, splinter; clipping, paring, shaving; smithereens
near antonyms chunk, gob, lump, hunk, slab; abundance, barrel, bucket, bushel, deal, heaps, loads, mass, mountain, much, peck, pile, plenty, pot, profusion, quantity, raft, scads, stack, volume, wad, wealth
2 a broken or irregular part of something that often remains incomplete — see FRAGMENT
3 a very small amount — see PARTICLE 1
4 an indefinite but usually short period of time — see WHILE 1

bite *n* **1** a harsh or sharp quality — see EDGE 1
2 a small piece or quantity of food — see MORSEL 1
3 an uncomfortable degree of coolness — see CHILL

bite (at) *vb* to consume or wear away gradually — see EAT 2

bite (on) *vb* to crush or grind with the teeth ⟨she likes to *bite on* her pencils when she thinks hard⟩
synonyms champ, chew, chomp (on), crunch (on), gnaw (on), masticate, nibble
related words lap, lick, munch; consume, ingest, eat, swallow; bolt, devour, gobble (up *or* down), gorge, gulp, scarf, scoff, snack, wolf; peck (at), pick (at)

biting *adj* **1** causing intense discomfort to one's skin — see CUTTING 1
2 causing intense mental or physical distress — see SHARP 2
3 marked by the use of wit that is intended to cause hurt feelings — see SARCASTIC

bitter *adj* **1** having or showing deep-seated resentment ⟨a *bitter* attitude about always having to work on Saturday⟩ ⟨she's still *bitter* about the way her boyfriend broke up with her⟩
synonyms acrid, acrimonious, embittered, hard, rancorous, resentful, sore
related words disaffected, discontented, disgruntled, malcontent; contemptuous, cynical, disdainful, scornful; angry, cruel, harsh, irritated, mad, rough, savage, vicious; acid, caustic, cutting, mordant, sarcastic, trenchant
near antonyms caring, forgiving, gentle, kind, loving, sweet, sympathetic, tender, warm, warmhearted
2 hard to accept or bear especially emotionally ⟨discovering that he had been cut from the team was a *bitter* disappointment⟩
synonyms afflicting, agonizing, cruel, excruciating, galling, grievous, harrowing, harsh, heartrending, hurtful, painful, tormenting, tortuous
related words insufferable, insupportable, intolerable, unacceptable, unbearable, unendurable, unsupportable; appalling, awful, bad, dire, dreadful, ghastly, horrible, miserable, nasty, rotten, terrible, vile, wretched; acute, extreme, intense, piercing
near antonyms bearable, endurable, supportable, sustainable, tolerable; livable (*also* liveable), sufferable, survivable; acceptable, allowable, reasonable
antonyms gratifying, pleasing, sweet
3 causing intense discomfort to one's skin — see CUTTING 1
4 difficult to endure — see HARSH 1
5 having a low or subnormal temperature — see COLD 1
6 uncomfortably cool — see CHILLY 1

bitterly *adv* with feelings of bitterness or grief — see HARD 2

bitterness *n* **1** a deep-seated ill will — see ENMITY
2 a harsh or sharp quality — see EDGE 1
3 an uncomfortable degree of coolness — see CHILL
4 biting sharpness of feeling or expression — see ACRIMONY 1

bitty *adj* very small in size — see TINY

bivouac *n* a place where a group of people live for a short time in tents or cabins — see CAMP 1

bivouac *vb* to live in a camp or the outdoors — see CAMP

bizarre *adj* **1** conceived or made without regard for reason or reality — see FANTASTIC 1
2 different from the ordinary in a way that causes curiosity or suspicion — see ODD 2

blab *vb* **1** to engage in casual or rambling conversation — see CHAT
2 to relate sometimes questionable or secret information of a personal nature — see GOSSIP

blabber *n* **1** a person who talks constantly — see CHATTERBOX
2 unintelligible or meaningless talk — see GIBBERISH

black *adj* **1** having the color of soot or coal ⟨a little *black* dress blends into the night very well⟩
synonyms ebony, pitch-black, pitch-dark, pitchy, raven, sable
related words dark, dusky, inky; blackish, brunet (*or* brunette)
near antonyms bright, brilliant, light, pale
antonyms white
2 causing or marked by an atmosphere lacking in cheer — see GLOOMY 1

3 not conforming to a high moral standard; morally unacceptable — see BAD 2

black art *n* the power to control natural forces through supernatural means — see MAGIC 1

blackball *vb* to reject by or as if by a vote — see NEGATIVE 1

blacken *vb* **1** to make dirty — see DIRTY
2 to make untrue and harmful statements about — see SLANDER
3 to make dark, dim, or indistinct — see CLOUD 1

blackened *adj* not clean — see DIRTY 1

blackening *n* the making of false statements that damage another's reputation — see SLANDER

black magic *n* the power to control natural forces through supernatural means — see MAGIC 1

blackmailer *n* a person who gets money from another by using force or threats — see RACKETEER

blackness *n* a time or place of little or no light — see DARK 1

blackout *n* a temporary or permanent state of unconsciousness — see FAINT

black out *vb* to lose consciousness — see FAINT

blade *n* **1** a hand weapon with a length of metal sharpened on one or both sides and usually tapered to a sharp point — see SWORD
2 an instrument with a sharp edge for cutting — see KNIFE

blamable *adj* **1** deserving reproach or blame — see BLAMEWORTHY
2 responsible for a wrong — see GUILTY 1

blame *n* **1** responsibility for wrongdoing or failure ⟨willingly accepted the *blame* for not seeing that the kitchen was properly cleaned⟩
synonyms culpability, fault, guilt, rap
related words regret, remorse, self-reproach, shame; accountability, liability; complicity; blameworthiness, reprehensibleness, sinfulness; censure, condemnation, denunciation
near antonyms acclaim, plaudits, praise; achievement, success
antonyms blamelessness, faultlessness, guiltlessness, innocence
2 the state of being held as the cause of something that needs to be set right — see RESPONSIBILITY 1

blame *vb* to express one's unfavorable opinion of the worth or quality of — see CRITICIZE

blameless *adj* free from guilt or blame — see INNOCENT 2

blamelessness *n* the quality or state of being free from guilt or blame — see INNOCENCE 1

blameworthy *adj* deserving reproach or blame ⟨copying another student's work was certainly a *blameworthy* act⟩
synonyms blamable, censurable, culpable, reprehensible, reproachable
related words bad, guilty, sinful, wicked; foolish, irresponsible, reckless; chargeable, impeachable, indictable, punishable; criminal, illegal, illicit, unlawful; illegitimate, improper, wrongful
phrases at fault
near antonyms flawless, perfect, pure; guiltless, innocent
antonyms blameless, faultless, impeccable, irreproachable

blanch *vb* to make white or whiter by removing color — see WHITEN

blanched *adj* lacking a healthy skin color — see PALE 2

bland *adj* not harsh or stern especially in manner, nature, or effect — see GENTLE 1

blandish *vb* to get (someone) to do something by gentle urging, special attention, or flattery — see COAX

blank *adj* **1** not expressing any emotion ⟨the teacher knew no one was paying attention when she looked out and saw all those *blank* faces⟩
synonyms deadpan, expressionless, impassive, inexpressive, stolid, vacant
related words dull, empty, vacuous, vapid; enigmatic (*also* enigmatical), impenetrable, inscrutable, mysterious; dead, inactive, quiescent, sleepy, sluggish; indolent, languorous, lazy, lethargic, listless; motionless, static, still, wooden; reserved, restrained, reticent, taciturn; aloof, apathetic, detached, indifferent, phlegmatic; cold, cool
near antonyms active, alive, animated, bright, busy, dynamic, effervescent, energetic, expansive, exuberant, lively, vigorous, vital, vivacious; eloquent, revealing, revelatory, significant, vivid; emotional, melodramatic, theatrical, unreserved, unrestrained
antonyms demonstrative, expressive
2 lacking contents that could or should be present — see EMPTY 1

blank *n* **1** a piece of paper with information written or to be written on it — see FORM 2
2 empty space — see VACANCY 1

blanket *adj* belonging or relating to the whole — see GENERAL 1

blanket *vb* **1** to form a layer over — see COVER 2
2 to keep secret or shut off from view — see [1]HIDE 2

blankness *n* empty space — see VACANCY 1

blaring *adj* marked by a high volume of sound — see LOUD 1

blarney *n* excessive praise — see FLATTERY

blarney *vb* **1** to get (someone) to do something by gentle urging, special attention, or flattery — see COAX
2 to praise too much — see FLATTER 1

blaspheme *vb* to use offensive or indecent language — see SWEAR 1

blasphemous *adj* not showing proper reverence for the holy or sacred — see IRREVERENT

blasphemy *n* an act of great disrespect shown to God or to sacred ideas, people, or things ⟨in the 17th century the Quakers were persecuted for beliefs and practices that older churches regarded as *blasphemies*⟩
synonyms defilement, desecration, impiety, irreverence, sacrilege
related words cursing, profanity, swearing; affront, insult; violation; contamination, corruption, debasement, pollution; sin, trespass
near antonyms consecration, purification, sanctification; reverence, veneration
antonyms adoration, glorification, worship

blast *n* **1** a loud explosive sound — see CLAP 1
2 a sudden brief rush of wind — see GUST 1
3 the act or an instance of exploding — see EXPLOSION 1

blast *vb* **1** to cause to break open or into pieces by or as if by an explosive ⟨the highway engineers will have to *blast* that hill in order to put a road through it⟩
synonyms blow up, burst, demolish, explode, pop, shatter, smash
related words dynamite; annihilate, decimate, destroy; ruin, wreck; detonate, discharge; fragment, splinter

near antonyms collapse, implode
2 to cause (a projectile) to be driven forward with force — see SHOOT 1
3 to cause a weapon to release a missile with great force — see SHOOT 2
4 to criticize harshly and usually publicly — see ATTACK 2

blasting *adj* marked by a high volume of sound — see LOUD 1

blasting *n* a directed propelling of a missile by a firearm or artillery piece — see SHOT

blatant *adj* **1** engaging in or marked by loud and insistent cries especially of protest — see VOCIFEROUS
2 very noticeable especially for being incorrect or bad — see EGREGIOUS

blaze *n* the steady giving off of the form of radiation that makes vision possible — see LIGHT 1

blaze *vb* **1** to be on fire especially brightly — see BURN 1
2 to make known openly or publicly — see ANNOUNCE
3 to shine with a bright harsh light — see GLARE 1

blazing *adj* **1** being on fire — see ABLAZE 1
2 having or expressing great depth of feeling — see FERVENT

bleach *vb* to make white or whiter by removing color — see WHITEN

bleak *adj* **1** causing or marked by an atmosphere lacking in cheer — see GLOOMY 1
2 marked by wet and windy conditions — see FOUL 1
3 uncomfortably cool — see CHILLY 1

bleakness *n* an uncomfortable degree of coolness — see CHILL

bleary *adj* not seen or understood clearly — see FAINT 1

bleed *vb* **1** to feel deep sadness or mental pain — see GRIEVE
2 to flow forth slowly through small openings — see EXUDE
3 to remove (liquid) gradually or completely — see DRAIN 1
4 to rob by the use of trickery or threats — see FLEECE

bleed (for) *vb* to have sympathy for — see PITY

blemish *n* something that spoils the appearance or completeness of a thing ⟨a slight *blemish* on the mirror was the only break in the gleaming surface⟩
synonyms defect, deformity, disfigurement, fault, flaw, imperfection, mark, pockmark, scar
related words abnormality, distortion, irregularity, malformation; bug, glitch, kink; blot, blotch, spot, stain; failing, vice, weakness
near antonyms adornment, decoration, embellishment, enhancement, ornament

blemish *vb* **1** to affect slightly with something morally bad or undesirable — see TAINT 1
2 to reduce the soundness, effectiveness, or perfection of — see DAMAGE 1

[1]blench *vb* to draw back in fear, pain, or disgust — see FLINCH

[2]blench *vb* to make white or whiter by removing color — see WHITEN

blend *n* a distinct entity formed by the combining of two or more different things ⟨that fabric is a cotton and polyester *blend*, so it shouldn't shrink as much as pure cotton⟩
synonyms admixture, amalgam, amalgamation, combination, composite, compound, fusion, intermixture, mix, mixture
related words coalescence, concoction, incorporation, intermingling, mingling; assortment, hash, hodgepodge, hotchpotch, jumble, medley, mélange, mishmash, motley, patchwork, potpourri, variety; accumulation, aggregation, conglomeration
near antonyms component, constituent, element, ingredient

blend *vb* **1** to turn into a single mass that is more or less the same throughout ⟨she *blended* the ingredients for the brownies very thoroughly to eliminate lumps in the batter⟩
synonyms amalgamate, combine, commingle, fuse, incorporate, integrate, intermingle, intermix, merge, mingle, mix
related words fold, mix, stir, toss; coalesce, combine, compound, conjoin, join, link, unite
near antonyms cleave, disjoin, disunite, divide, divorce, part, rupture, sever, sunder; disperse, dissolve, scatter; detach, disengage, split
antonyms break down, break up, separate
2 to form a pleasing relationship — see HARMONIZE 1

bless *vb* **1** to make holy through prayers or ritual ⟨the priest *blessed* the water, thus allowing it to be used as holy water for various rites⟩
synonyms consecrate, hallow, sanctify
related words cleanse, purify; commit, dedicate, devote; reconsecrate
near antonyms defile, desecrate, profane; dirty, foul, pollute, soil, taint; curse, damn, execrate; cast out, condemn, damn, punish
2 to proclaim the glory of — see PRAISE 1

blessed *adj* **1** of, relating to, or being God — see HOLY 3
2 set apart or worthy of veneration by association with God — see HOLY 2

blessedness *n* **1** a feeling or state of well-being and contentment — see HAPPINESS 1
2 the quality or state of being spiritually pure or virtuous — see HOLINESS

blessing *n* **1** a prayer calling for divine care, protection, or favor ⟨that rabbi also always ends the service with a short *blessing*⟩
synonyms benediction, benison
related words Godspeed; appeal, entreaty, grace, invocation, orison, petition, plea, prayer, supplication; sanctification
antonyms anathema, curse, execration, imprecation, malediction
2 something that provides happiness or does good for a person or thing ⟨finding money on the sidewalk just when he needed to buy new sneakers was an unexpected *blessing*⟩
synonyms benefit, boon, felicity, godsend, good, manna, windfall
related words bonus, extra, lagniappe; advantage, aid, assistance, gift, help, relief, support; comfort, consolation, solace; delight, joy, pleasure
near antonyms hex, hoodoo, jinx; bother, irritant, nuisance, pest
antonyms affliction, bane, curse, evil, plague, scourge
3 an acceptance of something as satisfactory — see APPROVAL 1
4 the act of making something holy through religious ritual — see CONSECRATION

blind *adj* lacking the power of sight ⟨our old *blind* cat kept walking into walls and furniture⟩
synonyms eyeless, sightless, stone blind
related words unobservant, unobserving; blinded, purblind
near antonyms observant, observing
antonyms sighted

blind *vb* to overpower with light — see DAZZLE

blink *vb* **1** to shine with light at regular intervals ⟨she loves to sit in the dark and watch the lights on the Christmas tree *blink* in ever-changing patterns⟩
synonyms flash, twinkle, wink
related words flicker, glance, glimmer, glint, glisten, glister, glitter, scintillate, shimmer, sparkle; beam, gleam, irradiate, radiate
2 to rapidly open and close one's eyes — see WINK 1

bliss *n* a feeling or state of well-being and contentment — see HAPPINESS 1

blissful *adj* experiencing pleasure, satisfaction, or delight — see GLAD 1

blissfulness *n* a feeling or state of well-being and contentment — see HAPPINESS 1

blithe *adj* **1** having or showing a good mood or disposition — see CHEERFUL 1
2 indicative of or marked by high spirits or good humor — see MERRY

blithesome *adj* **1** having or showing a good mood or disposition — see CHEERFUL 1
2 indicative of or marked by high spirits or good humor — see MERRY

blitz *vb* to use bombs or artillery against — see BOMBARD

blitzkrieg *n* the act or action of setting upon with force or violence — see ATTACK 1

blob *n* **1** a small uneven mass — see LUMP 1
2 the quantity of fluid that falls naturally in one rounded mass — see DROP 1

bloc *n* **1** a group of people acting together within a larger group — see FACTION
2 an association of persons, parties, or states for mutual assistance and protection — see CONFEDERACY

block *n* **1** a number of things considered as a unit — see GROUP 1
2 something that makes movement or progress more difficult — see ENCUMBRANCE

block *vb* **1** to close up so that no empty spaces remain — see FILL 2
2 to prevent passage through — see CLOG 1

blockade *n* the cutting off of an area by military means to stop the flow of people or supplies ⟨it was the *blockade* of all the enemy's major ports that finally won the war⟩
synonyms investment, siege
related words encompassment, encirclement; confinement, insulation, isolation, quarantine, seclusion, segregation, sequestration; incarceration, internment
near antonyms emancipation, freedom, liberation, release, rescue

blockade *vb* to surround (as a fortified place) with armed forces for the purpose of capturing or preventing commerce and communication — see BESIEGE

blockbuster *n* **1** a person or thing that is successful — see HIT 1
2 something that is unusually large and powerful — see GIANT

blockhead *n* a stupid person — see IDIOT

bloke *n, chiefly British* an adult male human being — see MAN 1

blond *or* **blonde** *adj* of a pale yellow or yellowish brown color ⟨the little boy's *blond* hair darkened to brown as he grew older⟩
synonyms fair, flaxen, golden, sandy, straw, tawny
related words gold, light, white
near antonyms brunet (*or* brunette), dark, swarthy; black, ebony, raven
antonyms dark

blood *n* **1** a group of persons who come from the same ancestor — see FAMILY 1
2 the line of ancestors from whom a person is descended — see ANCESTRY

bloodline *n* the line of ancestors from whom a person is descended — see ANCESTRY

bloodstained *adj* containing, smeared, or stained with blood — see BLOODY 1

bloodthirsty *adj* eager for or marked by the shedding of blood, extreme violence, or killing ⟨the Goths were a wild and *bloodthirsty* people⟩
synonyms bloody, homicidal, murdering, murderous, sanguinary, sanguine
related words barbaric, barbarous, cruel, heartless, inhumane, sadistic, savage, vicious, wanton; antagonistic, fierce, gladiatorial, hostile; aggressive, assertive, bellicose, belligerent, combative, contentious, discordant, pugnacious, quarrelsome, scrappy, truculent, violent; merciless, pitiless, ruthless; fell, ferocious, grim; despiteful, hateful, malevolent, malicious, malign, malignant, mean, nasty, spiteful; destructive, devastating, ruinous
near antonyms appeasing, conciliatory, disarming, dovish, mollifying, pacific, pacifying, peaceable, peaceful, peacemaking, placating, propitiatory; unaggressive, unassertive; benign, benignant, compassionate, good-hearted, humane, kind, kindhearted, sympathetic, tenderhearted; tender, warm, warmhearted; clement, lenient, merciful; affable, amiable, amicable, benevolent, gentle, kindly; submissive, surrendering, yielding

bloody *adj* **1** containing, smeared, or stained with blood ⟨after the fight, her shirt was all *bloody*⟩
synonyms bloodstained, gory
related words carmine, crimson, red, ruby, sanguine; bloodthirsty, sanguinary
2 eager for or marked by the shedding of blood, extreme violence, or killing — see BLOODTHIRSTY

bloom *n* **1** a state or time of great activity, thriving, or achievement ⟨a handsome young man in the full *bloom* of youth⟩
synonyms blossom, flower, flush, heyday, prime
related words acme, apex, climax, meridian, peak, pinnacle, summit, zenith; glory, grandeur, splendor; haleness, heartiness; energy, force, potency, power, vigor
near antonyms decline; bottom, nadir; feebleness, fragility, frailty, weakness; illness, infirmity, sickness; shriveling, wilting, withering
2 a rosy appearance of the cheeks ⟨after a snowball fight, she came inside with a *bloom*⟩
synonyms blush, flush
related words brightness, brilliance, glow; pinkness, rosiness
3 the usually showy plant part that produces seeds — see FLOWER 1

bloom *vb* **1** to produce flowers ⟨forsythias only *bloom* at the beginning of spring⟩
synonyms blossom, blow, burgeon, flower, unfold
related words leaf, leave; bud; open
near antonyms dry (up), fade, shrivel, wilt, wither; die, drop, expire, perish
2 to develop a rosy facial color (as from excitement or embarrassment) — see BLUSH

blooming *adj* having a healthy reddish skin tone — see RUDDY

blossom *n* **1** a state or time of great activity, thriving, or achievement — see BLOOM 1
2 the usually showy plant part that produces seeds — see FLOWER 1

blossom *vb* to produce flowers — see BLOOM

blot *n* a mark of guilt or disgrace — see STAIN 1

blotch *n* a small area that is different (as in color) from the main part — see SPOT 1

blotch *vb* **1** to mark with blotches especially of different colors or shades — see MOTTLE 1
2 to mark with small spots especially unevenly — see SPOT

blotched *adj* having blotches of two or more colors — see PIED

blot out *vb* **1** to destroy all traces of — see ANNIHILATE 1
2 to keep secret or shut off from view — see [1]HIDE 2

[1]**blow** *n* a hard strike with a part of the body or an instrument ⟨he was dizzy for the rest of the day after the *blow* to his head⟩
synonyms bang, bat, beat, belt, bop, box, buffet, bust, chop, clap, clip, clout, crack, cuff, hit, hook, knock, lick, pound, punch, rap, slam, slap, slug, smack, smash, sock, spank, stroke, swat, swipe, thud, thump, thwack, wallop, whack
related words flick, jab, poke, roundhouse, stab; beating, battering, bludgeoning, clobbering, drubbing, hammering, lambasting, licking, pasting, pounding, pummeling, thrashing; flogging, walloping, whipping

[2]**blow** *n* a sudden brief rush of wind — see GUST 1

[1]**blow** *vb* **1** to breathe hard, quickly, or with difficulty — see GASP
2 to use up carelessly — see WASTE 1

[2]**blow** *vb* to produce flowers — see BLOOM

blow (out) *vb* to let or force out of the lungs — see EXHALE 1

blowout *n* a social gathering — see PARTY 1

blowup *n* an outburst or display of excited anger — see TANTRUM

blow up *vb* **1** to become very angry ⟨she *blew up* at everybody after a very long and very bad day⟩
synonyms flare (up), flip
related words fulminate, rant, vituperate; bristle, burn, foam, fume, rage, seethe; burst, explode; enrage, incense, inflame, infuriate, madden; aggravate, anger, annoy, bother, bug, displease, distress, exasperate, gall, get, irk, irritate, nettle, peeve, pique, provoke, put out, rile, vex; agitate, disturb, perturb, upset
phrases fly into a rage, fly off the handle, forget oneself, lose one's temper
near antonyms appease, conciliate, mollify, pacify, placate; comfort, console, quiet, soothe
antonyms calm (down)
2 to break open or into pieces usually because of internal pressure — see EXPLODE 1
3 to cause to break open or into pieces by or as if by an explosive — see BLAST 1

blowy *adj* marked by strong wind or more wind than usual — see WINDY 1

blubber *vb* to shed tears often while making meaningless sounds as a sign of pain or distress — see CRY 1

bludgeon *n* a heavy rigid stick used as a weapon or for punishment — see CLUB 1

bludgeon *vb* **1** to deliver a blow to (someone or something) usually in a strong vigorous manner — see HIT 1
2 to strike repeatedly — see BEAT 1

blue *adj* feeling unhappiness — see SAD 1

blue *n* **1** the expanse of air surrounding the earth — see SKY
2 the whole body of salt water that covers nearly three-fourths of the earth — see OCEAN

blueprint *n* a method worked out in advance for achieving some objective — see PLAN 1

blueprint *vb* to work out the details of (something) in advance — see PLAN 1

blues *n pl* a state or spell of low spirits — see SADNESS

bluff *adj* being or characterized by direct, brief, and potentially rude speech or manner — see BLUNT 1

bluff *n* a steep wall of rock, earth, or ice — see CLIFF

bluff *vb* to cause to believe what is untrue — see DECEIVE

blunder *n* an unintentional departure from truth or accuracy — see ERROR 1

blunt *adj* **1** being or characterized by direct, brief, and potentially rude speech or manner ⟨he values honesty and is quite *blunt* about telling people their flaws⟩
synonyms abrupt, bluff, brusque, crusty, curt, downright, snippy
related words gruff, rough, short; hearty, honest, sincere; candid, direct, forthright, foursquare, frank, free-spoken, open, outspoken, plain, plainspoken, straightforward; discourteous, disrespectful, impertinent, impolite, inconsiderate, rude, tactless, undiplomatic; closemouthed, laconic, reserved, reticent, terse, tight-lipped; artless, earnest, sincere; coarse, crass, crude, low, uncouth, vulgar
near antonyms civil, considerate, courteous, diplomatic, gracious, polite, politic, smooth, suave, tactful; loquacious, talkative, voluble; long-winded, prolix, verbose; courtly, cultivated, gallant, genteel, polished, refined
antonyms circuitous, mealymouthed
2 lacking sharpness of edge or point — see DULL 1

blunt *vb* to reduce or weaken in strength or feeling — see DULL 1

blunted *adj* lacking sharpness of edge or point — see DULL 1

blur *vb* **1** to make (something) unclear to the understanding — see CONFUSE 2
2 to make dark, dim, or indistinct — see CLOUD 1

blurt (out) *vb* to utter with a sudden burst of strong feeling — see EXCLAIM

blush *n* a rosy appearance of the cheeks — see BLOOM 2

blush *vb* to develop a rosy facial color (as from excitement or embarrassment) ⟨she *blushed* when she realized she had walked into the boys' bathroom by mistake⟩

synonyms bloom, color, crimson, flush, glow, redden
related words rouge; abash, chagrin, discomfit, disconcert, embarrass, faze, humiliate, mortify

bluster *n* **1** boastful speech or writing — see BOMBAST 1
2 loud, confused, and usually unharmonious sound — see NOISE 1

bluster *vb* to talk loudly and wildly — see RANT

blustery *adj* marked by strong wind or more wind than usual — see WINDY 1

board *n* a leg-mounted piece of furniture with a broad flat top designed for the serving of food — see TABLE 1

board *vb* **1** to provide food or meals for — see FEED 1
2 to provide with living quarters or shelter — see HOUSE 1

boarder *n* one who rents a room or apartment in another's house — see TENANT

boast *n* an asset that brings praise or renown — see GLORY 2

boast *vb* to praise or express pride in one's own possessions, qualities, or accomplishments often to excess ⟨he *boasted* that he was the best hockey goalie in the whole school⟩
synonyms brag, crow, swagger
related words puff (up); pride; gush; exult, glory, rejoice; brandish, display, exhibit, expose, flaunt, parade, show off; magnify, maximize
near antonyms bad-mouth, belittle, decry, deprecate, depreciate, diminish, discount, disparage, minimize; bemoan, lament, mourn, regret

boat *n* **1** a small buoyant structure for travel on water ⟨paddling the little *boat* across the lake is great exercise, but tiring⟩
synonyms bottom, craft, vessel, watercraft
related words canoe, catamaran, catboat, cockleshell, coracle, dinghy, dory, dugout, flatboat, float, gig, gondola, houseboat, ironclad, kayak, launch, life boat, longboat, motorboat, outrigger, pirogue, pontoon, punt, raft, rowboat, sail, sampan, scow, scull, shallop, shell, sloop, tender, umiak; bark, brig, brigantine, caravel, clipper, galleon, galley, junk, ketch, pinnace, sailboat, schooner, ship, square-rigger, windjammer, xebec, yacht; corvette, cutter, destroyer, fireship, flagship, gunboat, landing craft, privateer, torpedo boat, warship; argosy, barge, coaster, collier, containership, ferryboat, icebreaker, lighter, lightship, liner, merchantman, merchant ship, packet, revenuer, riverboat, showboat, steamboat, steamer, supertanker, taxi, towboat, trader, tugboat; sealer, shrimper, trawler, whaler; derelict, hulk, tub; air-cushion vehicle, hovercraft; hydrofoil, hydroplane
2 a large craft for travel by water — see SHIP

boat *vb* to travel on water in a vessel — see SAIL 1

[1]**bob** *vb* to make (as hair) shorter with or as if with the use of shears — see CLIP

[2]**bob** *vb* to make short up-and-down movements — see NOD

bobble *vb* **1** to make or do (something) in a clumsy or unskillful way — see BOTCH
2 to make short up-and-down movements — see NOD

bobby *n, British* a member of a force charged with law enforcement at the local level — see OFFICER 1

bobby–soxer *n* a young usually unmarried woman — see GIRL 1

bode *vb* to show signs of a favorable or successful outcome ⟨her natural gift for reading *boded* well for her future in school⟩
synonyms augur, forebode (*also* forbode), promise
related words forecast, foretell, predict, presage, prognosticate, prophesy; forewarn, warn; anticipate, divine, foreknow, foresee; foreshadow, portend, prefigure; allude, connote, hint, imply, insinuate, intimate, suggest
phrases bid fair, give promise of

bodiless *adj* not composed of matter — see IMMATERIAL 1

bodily *adj* of or relating to the human body — see PHYSICAL 1

boding *n* something believed to be a sign or warning of a future event — see OMEN

body *n* **1** the main or greater part of something as distinguished from its appendages ⟨the *body* of the novel was quite good, even if the beginning was a bit slow⟩
synonyms bulk, core, generality, main, mass, staple, weight
related words majority; aggregate, amount, entirety, sum, sum total, total, totality, whole; bottom, essence, essentiality, marrow, nature, quintessence, soul, stuff, substance; center, heart, hub, middle, nucleus, seat; affair, argument, burden, crux, focus, gist, kernel, nub, pitch, point, purport; matter, motif, subject, text, theme, topic
near antonyms accessory, adjunct, appendage, extension, offshoot; component, constituent, element, ingredient; division, part, piece, section, segment; angle, aspect, facet, feature, quality, side
2 a distinct and separate portion of matter ⟨the Atlantic is a gigantic *body* of water⟩
synonyms mass
related words aggregate, amount, bulk, quantity, volume; item, object, thing; material, stuff, substance; entirety, totality, whole
3 a group of people acting together within a larger group — see FACTION
4 a group of people sharing a common interest and relating together socially — see GANG 2
5 a member of the human race — see HUMAN
6 a usually small number of persons considered as a unit — see GROUP 2

bog *n* spongy land saturated or partially covered with water — see SWAMP

bog (down) *vb* to place in conflict or difficulties — see EMBROIL

bogey *also* **bogy** *or* **bogie** *n* **1** something or someone that causes fear or dread especially without reason ⟨math and math tests have long been *bogeys* for many students⟩
synonyms bête noire, bugaboo, bugbear, hobgoblin, ogre
related words apparition, ghost, phantasm, phantom, poltergeist, shade, specter (*or* spectre), spirit, spook, wraith; banshee, bogeyman, demon, devil, fiend, imp, incubus; fright, horror, monster, monstrosity, terror; bane, curse, plague, scourge, torment; abomination, anathema
2 the soul of a dead person thought of especially as appearing to living people — see GHOST

bogus *adj* **1** being such in appearance only and made with or manufactured from usually cheaper materials — see IMITATION

2 being such in appearance only and made or manufactured with the intention of committing fraud — see COUNTERFEIT
3 lacking in natural or spontaneous quality — see ARTIFICIAL 1

bohemian *n* a person who does not conform to generally accepted standards or customs — see NONCONFORMIST 1

boil *vb* **1** to be excited or emotionally stirred up with anger <she was *boiling* at the thought of her so-called best friend trying to steal her boyfriend>
synonyms burn, fume, rage, seethe, steam
related words fulminate, rant, rave; smolder; bristle, flare (up); chafe, fret, stew; agitate, convulse, shake; disturb, perturb, upset
2 to cook in a liquid heated to the point that it gives off steam <*boil* the potatoes very well before you try to mash them>
synonyms coddle, parboil, poach, simmer, stew
related words scald; braise, fricassee, pressure-cook, steam; reboil
3 to be in a state of violent rolling motion — see SEETHE 1

boisterous *adj* being rough or noisy in a high-spirited way <the fans at the baseball game became particularly *boisterous* after the home run>
synonyms knockabout, rambunctious, raucous, rowdy
related words rampageous, riotous, stormy, tempestuous, turbulent, violent; disorderly, raffish, ruffianly; headstrong, intractable, obstreperous, recalcitrant, uncontrollable, uncontrolled, undisciplined, ungovernable, uninhibited, unmanageable, unruly, wild, willful (*or* wilful); bubbly, buoyant, effervescent, exuberant, high-spirited, impassioned, lively, passionate, sprightly, vivacious; clamorous, loudmouthed, noisy, strident, vociferous; howling, screaming, yelling
near antonyms sedate, sober, solemn, somber (*or* sombre), staid; decorous, dignified, proper, seemly; calm, hushed, noiseless, peaceful, placid, quiet, restrained, serene, silent, soundless, tranquil; collected, composed, constrained, controlled, imperturbable, inhibited, repressed, self-controlled, unflappable, unruffled; moderate, reasonable, subdued, temperate; impassive, phlegmatic, stoic (*or* stoical), stolid; depressed; aloof, detached, indifferent
antonyms orderly

bold *adj* **1** inclined or willing to take risks <our youngest brother was the *boldest* one in the family, instantly taking to everything from skiing to skateboarding>
synonyms adventuresome, adventurous, audacious, daring, dashing, emboldened, enterprising, gutsy, hardy, nerved, nervy, venturesome, venturous
related words brash, daredevil, foolhardy, heedless, hotheaded, impetuous, imprudent, impulsive, incautious, madcap, overbold, overconfident, rash, reckless, spirited, thoughtless, wild; brave, courageous, dauntless, fearless, gallant, greathearted, heroic, intrepid, lionhearted, stalwart, stout, stouthearted, unafraid, undaunted, valiant, valorous; gritty, plucky, spirited, spunky; hasty, headlong, precipitate; absurd, asinine, balmy, brainless, crazy, foolish, half-witted, harebrained, insane, lunatic, mad, nutty, scatterbrained, silly, wacky, witless; unnecessary; dumb, idiotic, moronic, stupid; irrational, unreasonable
near antonyms chickenhearted, coward, cowardly, craven, lily-livered, pusillanimous, shy, timid, timorous; careful, cautious, heedful, prudent, wary; overcareful, overcautious; affrighted, afraid, alarmed, fainthearted, fearful, frightened, horrified, scared, shocked, spooked, startled, terrified, terrorized; unnerved; calm, cool, levelheaded, rational, reasonable, sage, sane, sensible, sound, wise; appalled, concerned, dismayed, upset, worried
antonyms unadventurous, unenterprising
2 displaying or marked by rude boldness — see NERVY 1
3 likely to attract attention — see NOTICEABLE
4 showing a lack of proper social reserve or modesty — see PRESUMPTUOUS 1
5 having an incline approaching the perpendicular — see STEEP 1

bold–faced *adj* displaying or marked by rude boldness — see NERVY 1

bolster *vb* to hold up or serve as a foundation for — see SUPPORT 3

bolt *n* something that makes a strong impression because it is so unexpected — see SURPRISE 1

bolt *vb* **1** to move suddenly and sharply (as in surprise) — see START 1
2 to proceed or move quickly — see HURRY 2
3 to hasten away from something dangerous or frightening — see RUN 2
4 to utter with a sudden burst of strong feeling — see EXCLAIM

bomb *vb* to use bombs or artillery against — see BOMBARD

bombard *vb* to use bombs or artillery against <the Allies *bombarded* Germany for a great many months during World War II>
synonyms blitz, bomb, shell
related words rake, strafe; assail, assault, attack, devastate, hit, pound, ravage, strike

bombardment *n* a rapid or overwhelming outpouring of many things at once — see BARRAGE

bombast *n* **1** boastful speech or writing <filling a speech with *bombast* about one's unique qualifications for student council is usually a bad idea>
synonyms bluster, brag, braggadocio, gas, grandiloquence, hot air, rant
related words rhapsody, rhetoric; babble, blab, chatter, drivel, gabble, gibber, jabber, prattle; jawing, patter, prating, yammering; egotism, self-conceit, self-importance
2 language that is impressive-sounding but not meaningful or sincere — see RHETORIC 1

bombastic *adj* marked by the use of impressive-sounding but mostly meaningless words and phrases — see RHETORICAL

bombshell *n* something that makes a strong impression because it is so unexpected — see SURPRISE 1

bona fide *adj* being exactly as appears or as claimed — see AUTHENTIC 1

bond *n* **1** something that physically prevents free movement <before they could release the captive, they had to undo a number of *bonds*>
synonyms band, bracelet, chain, fetter, handcuff(s), irons, ligature, manacle, shackle
related words confinement, constraint, curb, hamper, hindrance, restraint, restriction; entanglement, net, trammel, trap; collar, straitjacket (*also* straightjacket); hobble, tie
2 a uniting or binding force or influence <the

bond of love between them was so strong that even death could not break it⟩
synonyms cement, knot, ligature, link, tie
related words attachment, connection, entanglement, fastening, joint, linkage; affection, fondness, sympathy; fetter, handcuff, manacle, shackle, trammel; constraint, curb, hampering, limit, limitation, restraint, restriction
near antonyms detaching, disengaging, parting, separation; unbinding, unfastening, unfettering, untying; emancipation, freedom, liberation, release
3 a formal agreement to fulfill an obligation — see GUARANTEE 1

bondage *n* the state of being a slave — see SLAVERY 1

bonding *n* a physical sticking to as if by glue — see ADHESION

bondman *n* a person who is considered the property of another person — see SLAVE 1

bondsman *n* a person who is considered the property of another person — see SLAVE 1

bone *n, usually* **bones** *pl* a small cube marked on each side with one to six spots and usually played in pairs in various games — see DIE

bone (up) *vb* to use the mind to acquire knowledge — see STUDY 1

bonny *adj, chiefly British* very pleasing to look at — see BEAUTIFUL

bonus *n* something given in addition to what is ordinarily expected or owed ⟨this job offers a nice Christmas *bonus* in addition to the salary⟩
synonyms dividend, extra, gratuity, gravy, lagniappe, perquisite, tip
related words fillip; bestowal, presentation; benefaction, benevolence, bounty, charity, generosity, largess (*or* largesse), philanthropy; contribution, donation, gift, offering, present; grant, subsidy; boon, manna, windfall; favor, freebie (*or* freebee), giveaway, premium; award, prize, reward; fringe benefit

bon voyage *n* an expression of good wishes at parting — see GOOD-BYE

boo *n* a vocal sound made to express scorn or disapproval — see CATCALL

booby *n* a person who lacks good sense or judgment — see FOOL 1

boobytrap *vb* to place hidden explosive devices in or under — see MINE

booby trap *n* **1** a usually concealed explosive device designed to go off when disturbed ⟨luckily, the bomb squad didn't find any *booby traps*⟩
synonyms mine
related words bomb, explosive; pitfall, snare, trap; ambush
2 a danger or difficulty that is hidden or not easily recognized — see PITFALL 1

book *n* **1** a set of printed sheets of paper bound together between covers and forming a work of fiction or nonfiction ⟨I bought another new *book* yesterday, and I can't wait to read it⟩
synonyms tome, volume
related words hardback, paperback, pocket book; folio, quarto; guidebook, handbook, manual; catalog (*or* catalogue), dictionary, encyclopedia; booklet, brochure, circular, flier (*or* flyer), folder, leaflet, magazine, pamphlet, program; textbook, tract, treatise; novel, novelette, pulp
2 *cap* a book made up of the writings accepted by Christians as coming from God — see BIBLE

book *vb* to arrange to have something (as a hotel room) held for one's future use — see RESERVE 1

bookish *adj* suggestive of the vocabulary used in books ⟨*fealty* is a *bookish* synonym for *loyalty*⟩
synonyms erudite, learned, literary
related words academic, pedantic, scholastic; highbrow, intellectual; educated, schooled; formal
near antonyms chatty, conversational; familiar, informal; slangy
antonyms colloquial, nonliterary

booklet *n* a short printed publication with no cover or with a paper cover — see PAMPHLET

bookworm *n* a person slavishly devoted to intellectual or academic pursuits — see NERD

boom *n* a loud explosive sound — see CLAP 1

boom *vb* to make a long loud deep noise or cry — see ROAR

booming *adj* **1** marked by a high volume of sound — see LOUD 1
2 marked by vigorous growth and well-being especially economically — see PROSPEROUS 1

boon *adj* likely to seek or enjoy the company of others — see CONVIVIAL

boon *n* **1** a thing that helps — see HELP 2
2 an act of kind assistance — see FAVOR 1
3 something granted as a special favor — see PRIVILEGE
4 something that provides happiness or does good for a person or thing — see BLESSING 2

boor *n* a person whose behavior is offensive to others — see JERK 1

boorish *adj* having or showing crudely insensitive or impolite manners — see CLOWNISH

boost *n* **1** an act or instance of helping — see HELP 1
2 something added (as by growth) — see INCREASE 1
3 something that arouses action or activity — see IMPULSE

boost *vb* **1** to lift with effort — see HEAVE 1
2 to make greater in size, amount, or number — see INCREASE 1
3 to make markedly greater in measure or degree — see INTENSIFY
4 to move from a lower to a higher place or position — see RAISE 1
5 to provide publicity for — see PUBLICIZE 1

booster *n* a person who actively supports or favors a cause — see EXPONENT

boot (out) *vb* to drive or force out — see EJECT 1

bootleg *n* illegally produced liquor — see MOONSHINE 1

bootless *adj* producing no results — see FUTILE

booty *n* valuables stolen or taken by force — see LOOT

booze *n* a fermented or distilled beverage that can make a person drunk — see ALCOHOL

bop *n* a hard strike with a part of the body or an instrument — see [1]BLOW

bop *vb* to deliver a blow to (someone or something) usually in a strong vigorous manner — see HIT 1

border *n* **1** the line or relatively narrow space that marks the outer limit of something ⟨a rug with a fancily embroidered *border*⟩
synonyms bound, boundary, brim, circumference, compass, confines, edge, end, fringe, margin, perimeter, periphery, rim, skirt, verge
related words crest, hem, lip; ceiling, maximum;

demarcation, extent, limitation, measure, restriction, termination; borderland, frontier, march, pale
near antonyms center; inner, inside, interior
2 a region along the dividing line between two countries — see FRONTIER 1

border *vb* to serve as a border for ⟨that velvet *bordered* the sleeves on this shirt, until it fell off⟩
synonyms bound, fringe, margin, rim, skirt
related words edge, hem, trim; circumscribe, define, delineate, demarcate, frame, outline; circle, compass, encircle, girdle, girth, loop, ring, round, surround; check, confine, control, curb, limit, restrain, restrict

border (on) *vb* **1** to come very close to being ⟨that comment *borders on* insubordination, and you should be more careful in the future⟩
synonyms verge (on)
related words approach, near; appear, look, resemble, seem, suggest
2 to be adjacent to — see ADJOIN 1

bordering *adj* having a border in common — see ADJACENT

borderland *n* a region along the dividing line between two countries — see FRONTIER 1

bore *n* someone or something boring — see DRAG 1

1**bore** *vb* to make a hole or series of holes in — see PERFORATE

2**bore** *vb* to make weary and restless by being dull or monotonous ⟨the teacher's lifeless and unimaginative teaching style *bored* the students to death⟩
synonyms jade, tire, weary
related words pall; drain, enervate, exhaust, fatigue, wear, wear out; debilitate, disable, enfeeble; deject, demoralize, discourage, dishearten, dispirit
phrases put to sleep
near antonyms animate, energize, enliven, excite, galvanize, invigorate, stimulate, vitalize; amuse, entertain; allure, attract, beguile, bewitch, captivate, charm, enchant, enthrall (*or* enthral), fascinate, hypnotize, mesmerize; monopolize, preoccupy; busy, immerse, involve, occupy; rally, rouse, stir
antonyms absorb, engage, engross, grip, interest, intrigue

bored *adj* having one's patience, interest, or pleasure exhausted — see WEARY 2

boredom *n* the state of being bored ⟨she spends that whole class in a state of complete *boredom*, waiting for lunch⟩
synonyms doldrums, ennui, listlessness, restlessness, tedium, tiredness, weariness
related words cheerlessness, dispiritedness, joylessness, melancholy; languor, lassitude, lethargy, lifelessness, torpor; dullness (*also* dulness), monotonousness, monotony, sameness; apathy, indifference, unconcern
near antonyms beguilement, bewitchment, captivation, enchantment, fascination; absorption, engagement, engrossment, immersion, involvement; animation, enlivenment, excitement, invigoration, stimulation; amusement, entertainment

boring *adj* causing weariness, restlessness, or lack of interest ⟨I wish this book weren't so *boring;* I keep falling asleep whenever I try to read it⟩
synonyms drab, dreary, dry, dull, flat, heavy, humdrum, jading, leaden, monotonous, pedestrian, ponderous, stodgy, stuffy, stupid, tame, tedious, tiresome, tiring, unanimated, uninteresting, wearisome, weary, wearying
related words undramatic, unentertaining, uneventful, unexciting, uninspiring, unnewsworthy, unrewarding, unsatisfying, unsensational, unspectacular; annoying, bothersome, irksome, irritating; drudging, palling; draining, enervating, exhausting, fatiguing, wearing; debilitating, enfeebling; demoralizing, discouraging, disheartening, dispiriting; common, commonplace, ordinary, stale, unexceptional; lumbering, plodding, slow
near antonyms amazing, astonishing, astounding, awesome, eye-opening, fabulous, marvelous (*or* marvellous), sensational, spectacular, surprising, wonderful, wondrous; animating, energizing, enlivening, exciting, galvanizing, invigorating, stimulating; amusing, diverting, entertaining; alluring, attracting, attractive, beguiling, bewitching, captivating, charming, enchanting, enthralling, entrancing, fascinating; mesmerizing
antonyms absorbing, engaging, engrossing, gripping, interesting, intriguing, involving

born *adj* **1** being such from birth or by nature — see NATURAL 1
2 belonging to a particular place by birth or origin — see NATIVE 1

borrow *vb* to take for one's own use (something originated by another) — see ADOPT

bosom *adj* closely acquainted — see FAMILIAR 1

boss *adj, slang* of the very best kind — see EXCELLENT

boss *n* the person (as an employer or supervisor) who tells people and especially workers what to do ⟨every morning the *boss* hands out a list of top-priority tasks⟩
synonyms captain, chief, foreman, head, headman, helmsman, kingpin, leader, master, taskmaster
related words administrator, commander, director, executive, general, manager, overseer, principal, standard-bearer, straw boss, superintendent, superior, supervisor; dominator, lord, overlord, potentate, ruler; figurehead; slave driver; baron, czar (*also* tsar *or* tzar), king, magnate, mogul, president, prince
near antonyms dependent, inferior, secondary, subject, subordinate, underling

boss *vb* **1** to be in charge of ⟨she *bossed* that project for years, until she was promoted again⟩
synonyms captain, head, oversee, superintend, supervise
related words command, control, direct, guide, manage, order, run, shepherd, show, steer; quarterback; administer; monitor; govern, reign, rule
2 to exercise authority or power over — see GOVERN 1
3 to serve as leader of — see LEAD 2

boss (around) *vb* to issue orders to (someone) by right of authority — see COMMAND 1

bossy *adj* fond of ordering people around ⟨I don't want to work with him because he's so *bossy* and always runs roughshod over me⟩
synonyms authoritarian, autocratic, despotic, dictatorial, domineering, imperious, masterful, overbearing, peremptory, tyrannical (*also* tyrannic), tyrannous
related words arrogant, disdainful, haughty, lofty, lordly, proud, supercilious, superior; command-

ing, dictating; arbitrary, high-handed, imperial; authoritative, directorial, magisterial; aggressive, assertive, self-assertive; conceited, narcissistic, pompous, vain; all-powerful, almighty, omnipotent; firm, stern
near antonyms humble, meek, modest, unassuming; amenable, docile, obedient, tractable; indecisive, irresolute; acquiescent, compliant, passive, resigned, submissive, yielding

botch *vb* to make or do (something) in a clumsy or unskillful way ⟨the first time we tried to make a cake, we *botched* the job completely⟩
synonyms bobble, bungle, butcher, flub, foozle, foul up, fumble, louse up, mangle, mess (up), muff, murder
related words blunder, goof (up), gum (up); blemish, blight, damage, flaw, harm, hurt, impair, injure, mar, mutilate, ruin, spoil, vitiate; destroy, wreck; mishandle, mismanage
near antonyms ameliorate, better, enhance, help, improve, meliorate, rectify, refine, reform, remedy

botched *adj* showing or marked by a lack of skill and tact (as in dealing with a situation) — see AWKWARD 2

bother *n* **1** a state of noisy, confused activity — see COMMOTION
2 one who is obnoxiously annoying — see NUISANCE 1
3 something that is a source of irritation — see ANNOYANCE 3
4 the feeling of impatience or anger caused by another's repeated disagreeable acts — see ANNOYANCE 2

bother *vb* **1** to thrust oneself upon (another) without invitation ⟨I am never going to get this work done if people don't stop wandering into the room and *bothering* me⟩
synonyms bug, chivy, disturb, intrude (upon), pester
related words inconvenience, trouble; aggravate, anger, annoy, bedevil, devil, exasperate, fret, gall, get, gnaw, hassle, irritate, nettle, peeve, pique, put out, rile, torment, vex, worry; beleaguer, beset, besiege; distress, plague; afflict, harass, torment; grate, inflame, provoke; enrage, incense, inflame, infuriate, madden; agitate, perturb
near antonyms ignore, leave; appease, conciliate, mollify, oblige, placate; delight, gladden, gratify, please, satisfy; comfort, console, content
2 to disturb the peace of mind of (someone) especially by repeated disagreeable acts — see IRRITATE 1
3 to experience concern or anxiety — see WORRY 1
4 to trouble the mind of; to make uneasy — see DISTURB 1

bothering *n* the act of making unwelcome intrusions upon another — see ANNOYANCE 1

bothersome *adj* causing annoyance — see ANNOYING

bottom *n* **1** the side or part facing downward from something ⟨that side of the shelf is supposed to be the *bottom*, so turn it over before you assemble the bookcase⟩
synonyms underbelly, underbody, underside, undersurface
related words belly, sole; base, floor, foot, ground, seat, underpinning
near antonyms acme, apex, crest, crown, height, peak, pinnacle, roof, summit; cusp, head, point, tip
antonyms face, top
2 the surface upon which a body of water lies ⟨my missing fishing pole is probably lying on the *bottom* of the lake⟩
synonyms bed, floor
related words riverbed; base, basement, foundation, ground
near antonyms surface
3 the lowest part, place, or point ⟨sliding all the way to the *bottom* of the snow-covered slope⟩
synonyms base, foot, rock bottom
related words basis, bed, bedrock, foundation, ground, groundwork, keystone, seat, underpinning
near antonyms acme, apex, climax, crest, face, height, peak, pinnacle, summit, tip-top, zenith
antonyms head, top
4 the part of the body upon which someone sits — see BUTTOCKS
5 a small buoyant structure for travel on water — see BOAT 1

bottomless *adj* extending far downward or inward — see DEEP 1

bough *n* a major outgrowth from the main stem of a woody plant — see BRANCH 1

boulevard *n* a passage cleared for public vehicular travel — see WAY 1

bounce *n* active strength of body or mind — see VIGOR 1

bounce *vb* **1** to drive or force out — see EJECT 1
2 to strike and fly off at an angle — see GLANCE 1

bouncing *adj* **1** enjoying health and vigor — see HEALTHY 1
2 having much high-spirited energy and movement — see LIVELY 1

bound *adj* fully committed to achieving a goal — see DETERMINED 1

[1]**bound** *n* **1** a real or imaginary point beyond which a person or thing cannot go — see LIMIT
2 the line or relatively narrow space that marks the outer limit of something — see BORDER 1

[2]**bound** *n* an act of leaping into the air — see JUMP 1

[1]**bound** *vb* **1** to mark the limits of — see LIMIT 2
2 to serve as a border for — see BORDER

[2]**bound** *vb* **1** to move with a light bouncing step — see SKIP 1
2 to propel oneself upward or forward into the air — see JUMP 1

boundary *n* **1** a real or imaginary point beyond which a person or thing cannot go — see LIMIT
2 the line or relatively narrow space that marks the outer limit of something — see BORDER 1

bounded *adj* having distinct or certain limits — see LIMITED 1

boundless *adj* being or seeming to be without limits — see INFINITE

bounteous *adj* giving or sharing in abundance and without hesitation — see GENEROUS 1

bountiful *adj* **1** being more than enough without being excessive — see PLENTIFUL
2 giving or sharing in abundance and without hesitation — see GENEROUS 1

bountifully *adv* in a generous manner — see WELL 2

bountifulness *n* the quality or state of being generous — see LIBERALITY

bounty *n* **1** something offered or given in return for a service performed — see REWARD
2 the quality or state of being generous — see LIBERALITY

bouquet *n* **1** a bunch of flowers ⟨I bought my mother a nice *bouquet* for her birthday⟩
synonyms nosegay, posy
related words boutonniere, corsage; arrangement; garland, lei
2 a sweet or pleasant smell — see FRAGRANCE

bout *n* **1** a competitive encounter between individuals or groups carried on for amusement, exercise, or in pursuit of a prize — see GAME 1
2 a sudden experiencing of a physical or mental disorder — see ATTACK 2

bow *n* something that curves or is curved — see BEND 1

[1]**bow** *vb* **1** to cease resistance (as to another's arguments, demands, or control) — see YIELD 3
2 to give up and cease resistance (as to a liking, temptation, or habit) — see YIELD 1

[2]**bow** *vb* to turn away from a straight line or course — see CURVE 1

bowed *adj* bending downward or forward — see NODDING

bowing *adj* bending downward or forward — see NODDING

bowl *n* a large usually roofless building for sporting events with tiers of seats for spectators — see STADIUM

bowl *vb* **1** to move or proceed smoothly and readily — see FLOW 2
2 to proceed or move quickly — see HURRY 2

bowl (down *or* over) *vb* to strike (someone) so forcefully as to cause a fall — see FELL 1

bowl (over) *vb* **1** to cause an often unpleasant surprise for — see SHOCK 1
2 to make a strong impression on (someone) with something unexpected — see SURPRISE 1

bowled over *adj* affected with sudden and great wonder or surprise — see THUNDERSTRUCK

[1]**box** *n* a covered rectangular container for storing or transporting things — see CHEST

[2]**box** *n* a hard strike with a part of the body or an instrument — see [1]BLOW

boxer *n* one that engages in the sport of fighting with the fists ⟨that *boxer* is quite famous for being the youngest heavyweight champion ever⟩
synonyms fighter, prizefighter, pugilist
related words bantamweight, featherweight, flyweight, heavyweight, light heavyweight, lightweight, middleweight, welterweight

boy *n* a male person who has not yet reached adulthood ⟨a giggling little *boy* ran by⟩
synonyms lad, laddie, nipper, shaver, sonny, stripling, tad, youth
related words adolescent, juvenile, kid, minor, moppet, teenager, youngster; brat, gamin, hobbledehoy, imp, squirt, urchin, whippersnapper; schoolboy

boyfriend *n* a male romantic companion ⟨her *boyfriend* always brings her flowers for Valentine's Day⟩
synonyms beau, fellow, man, swain
related words admirer, crush, steady; gallant, suitor, wooer; beloved, darling, dear, favorite, flame, honey, love, lover, sweet, sweetheart, valentine; date, escort; groom, husband; fiancé, intended

brace *n* **1** something that holds up or serves as a foundation for something else — see SUPPORT 1
2 two things of the same or similar kind that match or are considered together — see PAIR

brace *vb* **1** to give life, vigor, or spirit to — see ANIMATE
2 to hold up or serve as a foundation for — see SUPPORT 3
3 to prepare (oneself) mentally or emotionally — see FORTIFY 1

bracelet *n* something that physically prevents free movement — see BOND 1

bracing *adj* having a renewing effect on the state of the body or mind — see TONIC

bracket *n* one of the units into which a whole is divided on the basis of a common characteristic — see CLASS 2

bracket *vb* to describe as similar — see COMPARE 1

brag *n* boastful speech or writing — see BOMBAST 1

brag *vb* to praise or express pride in one's own possessions, qualities, or accomplishments often to excess — see BOAST

braggadocio *n* boastful speech or writing — see BOMBAST 1

braid *n* a length of something formed of three or more strands woven together ⟨until she was fifteen, she had a *braid* that reached to her knees⟩
synonyms lace, lacing, plait
related words rickrack (*or* ricrac), stripe; pigtail

braid *vb* to form into a braid ⟨they taught each other how to *braid* yarn into bracelets⟩
synonyms plait, pleat
related words interlace, interweave, weave

brain *n* **1** a very smart person — see GENIUS 1
2 *often* **brains** *pl* the ability to learn and understand or to deal with problems — see INTELLIGENCE 1

brainless *adj* **1** not having or showing an ability to absorb ideas readily — see STUPID 1
2 showing or marked by a lack of good sense or judgment — see FOOLISH 1

brainlessness *n* **1** lack of good sense or judgment — see FOOLISHNESS 1
2 the quality or state of lacking intelligence or quickness of mind — see STUPIDITY 1

brainstorm *vb* to engage in an exchange of information or ideas — see COMMUNICATE 2

brainy *adj* having or showing quickness of mind — see INTELLIGENT 1

brake *n* a thick patch of shrubbery, small trees, or underbrush — see THICKET

brake *vb* to cause to move or proceed at a less rapid pace — see SLOW 1

braking *n* a usually gradual decrease in the pace or level of activity of something — see SLOWDOWN

brambly *adj* likely to cause a scratch — see SCRATCHY 1

branch *n* **1** a major outgrowth from the main stem of a woody plant ⟨I loved climbing among the *branches* of that old tree⟩
synonyms bough, limb
related words offshoot, outgrowth, shoot; spray, sprig, twig
2 a local unit of an organization — see CHAPTER

branch *vb* to extend outwards from or as if from a central point — see RADIATE 1

branch (out) *vb* to go or move in different directions from a central point — see SEPARATE 2

brand *n* **1** a device (as a word) identifying the maker of a piece of merchandise and legally reserved for the exclusive use of that person or company — see TRADEMARK 1

2 a mark of guilt or disgrace — see STAIN 1

brand–new *adj* **1** being in an original and unused or unspoiled state — see FRESH 1

2 recently made and never used before — see NEW 3

brash *adj* **1** displaying or marked by rude boldness — see NERVY 1

2 foolishly adventurous or bold — see FOOLHARDY 1

brashness *n* shameless boldness — see EFFRONTERY

brass *n* shameless boldness — see EFFRONTERY

brassiness *n* shameless boldness — see EFFRONTERY

brassy *adj* displaying or marked by rude boldness — see NERVY 1

brave *adj* feeling or displaying no fear by temperament ⟨the *brave* little boy sat still for the flu shot⟩

synonyms courageous, dauntless, doughty, fearless, gallant, greathearted, heroic, intrepid, lionhearted, manful, stalwart, stout, stouthearted, undaunted, valiant, valorous

related words determined, firm, game, plucky, resolute, undeterred, undismayed, unflinching, unswerving; mettlesome, spirited, spunky; adventuresome, adventurous, audacious, bold, daring, dashing, gutsy, hardy, venturesome, venturous; crazy, foolish, half-witted, insane, lunatic, mad, nutty; brash, brazen, daredevil, foolhardy, heedless, hotheaded, impetuous, imprudent, impulsive, incautious, madcap, overbold, overconfident, rash, reckless, thoughtless, wild; hasty, headlong, precipitate; comforted, emboldened, encouraged, heartened, reassured, unafraid

near antonyms mousy (*or* mousey), scary, shy, skittish, timid, timorous; anxious, apprehensive, nervous; careful, cautious, heedful, prudent, unadventurous; afraid, agitated, disconcerted, disquieted, disturbed, frightened, horrified, panicked, perturbed, scared, shocked, spooked, startled, terrified, terrorized, unnerved, upset; appalled, concerned, dismayed, worried

antonyms chicken, chickenhearted, coward, cowardly, craven, fainthearted, fearful, lily-livered, pusillanimous, timorous

brave *vb* to oppose (something hostile or dangerous) with firmness or courage — see FACE 2

bravery *n* **1** dressy clothing — see FINERY

2 strength of mind to carry on in spite of danger — see COURAGE

brawl *n* **1** a rough and often noisy fight usually involving several people ⟨they were thrown out of the party after starting a *brawl*⟩

synonyms affray, fracas, fray, free-for-all, melee, row, ruckus, ruction

related words battle, clash, combat, conflict, contest, fight, fisticuffs, scrap, scrimmage, scuffle, struggle, tussle; horseplay, roughhousing; altercation, argument, dispute, quarrel, spat, squabble, tiff, wrangle

2 an often noisy or angry expression of differing opinions — see ARGUMENT 1

brawl *vb* to express different opinions about something often angrily — see ARGUE 2

brawn *n* muscular strength — see MUSCLE 1

brawny *adj* **1** having muscles capable of exerting great physical force — see STRONG 1

2 marked by a well-developed musculature — see MUSCULAR 1

3 strongly and heavily built — see [1]HUSKY

brazen *adj* displaying or marked by rude boldness — see NERVY 1

brazen *vb* to oppose (something hostile or dangerous) with firmness or courage — see FACE 2

brazenness *n* shameless boldness — see EFFRONTERY

breach *n* **1** a failure to uphold the requirements of law, duty, or obligation ⟨the president's deliberate misstatements were widely seen as a *breach* of the public trust⟩

synonyms infraction, infringement, transgression, trespass, violation

related words offense, sin, wrong; disregard, forgetting, ignoring, nonobservance, overlooking; delinquency, dereliction, neglect; intrusion, invasion

near antonyms respecting, upholding

antonyms nonviolation, observance

2 a breaking of a moral or legal code — see OFFENSE 1

3 an open space in a barrier (as a wall or hedge) — see GAP 1

breach *vb* to fail to keep — see VIOLATE 1

bread *n* **1** *slang* something (as pieces of stamped metal or printed paper) customarily and legally used as a medium of exchange, a measure of value, or a means of payment — see MONEY

2 substances intended to be eaten — see FOOD

breadbasket *n, slang* the part of the body between the chest and the pelvis — see STOMACH

breadth *n* **1** a wide space or area — see EXPANSE

2 an area over which activity, capacity, or influence extends — see RANGE 2

break *n* **1** a momentary halt in an activity — see PAUSE

2 a period during which the usual routine of school or work is suspended — see VACATION

3 an open space in a barrier (as a wall or hedge) — see GAP 1

break *vb* **1** to cause to separate into pieces usually suddenly or forcibly ⟨I hated admitting to Mom that I had *broken* her favorite glass vase⟩

synonyms bust, fracture, fragment

related words blast, blow up, burst, detonate, explode; pop, shatter, shiver, smash; sliver, splinter, split; collapse, implode; demolish, destroy, ruin, wreck

near antonyms fix, heal, mend, patch, rebuild, reconstruct, repair

2 to bring (as an action or operation) to an immediate end — see STOP 1

3 to bring to a lower grade or rank — see DEMOTE

4 to change (as a secret message) from code into ordinary language — see DECODE

5 to come to a temporary halt in one's activity — see PAUSE

6 to cut into and turn over the sod of (a piece of land) using a bladed implement — see PLOW 1

7 to fail to keep — see VIOLATE 1

8 to find an answer for through reasoning — see SOLVE

9 to reduce the soundness, effectiveness, or perfection of — see DAMAGE 1

10 to stop functioning — see FAIL 1

11 to hasten away from something dangerous or frightening — see RUN 2

breakable *adj* easily broken — see FRAGILE 1

breakdown *n* **1** the process by which dead organic matter separates into simpler substances — see CORRUPTION 1
2 the separation and identification of the parts of a whole — see ANALYSIS 1

break down *vb* **1** to arrange or assign according to type — see CLASSIFY 1
2 to go through decomposition — see DECAY 1
3 to identify and examine the basic elements or parts of (something) especially for discovering interrelationships — see ANALYZE
4 to stop functioning — see FAIL 1
5 to yield to mental or emotional stress — see CRACK 2

break in *vb* **1** to enter a house or building by force usually with illegal intent ⟨the burglars *broke in* by smashing a window⟩
synonyms burglarize
related words invade, trespass; hold up, loot, plunder, rip off, rob, stick up; ransack, rifle; despoil, devastate, maraud, pillage, ravage, sack
2 to cause a disruption in a conversation or discussion — see INTERRUPT

breakneck *adj* moving, proceeding, or acting with great speed — see FAST 1

break off *vb* **1** to bring (as an action or operation) to an immediate end — see STOP 1
2 to come to an end — see CEASE 1

break out *vb* to develop suddenly and violently — see ERUPT 2

breakthrough *n* an instance of notable progress in the development of knowledge, technology, or skill — see ADVANCE 2

breakup *n* the act or process of a whole separating into two or more parts or pieces — see SEPARATION 1

break up *vb* **1** to cease to exist or cause to cease to exist as a group or organization — see DISBAND 1
2 to come to an end — see CEASE 1
3 to set or force apart — see SEPARATE 1

breast *n* the seat of one's deepest thoughts and emotions — see CORE 1

breast *vb* to oppose (something hostile or dangerous) with firmness or courage — see FACE 2

breath *n* **1** a momentary halt in an activity — see PAUSE
2 a slight or gentle movement of air — see BREEZE 1

breathe *vb* **1** to inhale and exhale air ⟨sometimes it gets so hot in here that it's hard to even *breathe*⟩
synonyms respire
related words expire, inspire; gasp, huff, pant, puff, wheeze; sniff, snore, snort, snuffle; yawn
near antonyms asphyxiate, choke, gag, smother, suffocate; garrotte (*or* garotte), stifle, strangle, throttle
2 to have life — see BE 1

breathe (out) *vb* to let or force out of the lungs — see EXHALE 1

breather *n* a momentary halt in an activity — see PAUSE

breathing *adj* having or showing life — see ALIVE 1

breathless *adj* **1** lacking fresh air — see STUFFY 1
2 moving, proceeding, or acting with great speed — see FAST 1
3 no longer living — see DEAD 1

breathtaking *adj* causing great emotional or mental stimulation — see EXCITING 1

breech *n* **1** the part of the body upon which someone sits — see BUTTOCKS
2 breeches *pl* an outer garment covering each leg separately from waist to ankle — see PANTS

breed *n* a number of persons or things that are grouped together because they have something in common — see SORT 1

breed *vb* **1** to bring forth offspring — see PROCREATE
2 to bring to maturity through care and education — see BRING UP 1

breeding *n* the line of ancestors from whom a person is descended — see ANCESTRY

breeze *n* **1** a slight or gentle movement of air ⟨a warm spring *breeze* ruffled our hair⟩
synonyms air, breath, puff, waft, zephyr
related words draft, whiff; land breeze, sea breeze; blast, blow, flurry, gale, northeaster, norther, northwester, southeaster, southwester, westerly, wind; squall, tempest, tornado, windstorm; airflow
near antonyms calm
2 something that is easy to do — see CINCH

breeze *vb* **1** to move or proceed smoothly and readily — see FLOW 2
2 to proceed or move quickly — see HURRY 2

breezy *adj* **1** having a relaxed, casual manner — see EASYGOING 1
2 marked by strong wind or more wind than usual — see WINDY 1

brevity *n* **1** the condition of being short ⟨the best quality a graduation speech can have is *brevity*⟩
synonyms briefness, conciseness, shortness
related words abbreviation, abridgment (*or* abridgement), compression, condensation, contraction, curtailment; decreasing, diminishing, lessening, reducing, shortening, shrinking; abruptness, brusqueness, curtness; pithiness, succinctness, terseness; littleness, minuteness, smallness, tininess
near antonyms extensiveness; elongating, elongation, extending, extension, prolongation, prolonging, protraction, stretching; expansion, growth, spread; diffuseness, prolixity, talkativeness, verboseness, volubility, wordiness; bigness, bulkiness, greatness, heftiness, largeness
antonyms lengthiness
2 the quality or state of being marked by or using only few words to convey much meaning — see SUCCINCTNESS

brew *vb* to be about to happen — see LOOM

bribable *adj* open to improper influence and especially bribery — see VENAL

bribe *n* something given or promised in order to improperly influence a person's conduct or decision ⟨that judge refused a huge *bribe* to dismiss the charges against the wealthy defendant⟩
synonyms fix, sop
related words incentive, incitement, motivation, spur, stimulation, stimulus; boost, goad, inducement; allurement, bait, enticement, lure, temptation; flattery, persuasion; decoy, snare, trap

bribe *vb* to influence someone with a bribe ⟨meat inspectors were *bribed*, and the contaminated beef was sold to the public⟩
synonyms have, square
related words fix, tamper (with); corrupt, debase, defile, dishonor, taint; allure, bait, entice, lure, tempt; motivate, provoke, spur, stimulate; goad, induce; flatter, persuade; snare, trap

bridal *n* a ceremony in which two people are united in matrimony — see WEDDING
bridgehead *n* a place from which an advance (as for military operations) is made — see BASE 2
bridle *vb* to keep from exceeding a desirable degree or level (as of expression) — see CONTROL 1
brief *adj* **1** marked by the use of few words to convey much information or meaning — see CONCISE
2 not lasting for a considerable time — see SHORT 2
brief *vb* to give information to — see ENLIGHTEN 1
briefly *adv* in a few words — see SHORTLY 1
briefness *n* **1** the condition of being short — see BREVITY 1
2 the quality or state of being marked by or using only few words to convey much meaning — see SUCCINCTNESS
brig *n* a place of confinement for persons held in lawful custody — see JAIL
bright *adj* **1** giving off or reflecting much light <in the desert the sun was so *bright* that it hurt my eyes> <the moon is *bright* tonight>
synonyms beaming, bedazzling, brilliant, dazzling, effulgent, glowing, incandescent, lambent, lucent, lucid, luminous, lustrous, radiant, refulgent, shining, shiny
related words blazing, burning, combusting, fiery, flaming; agleam, aglitter, blinding, flaring, flashing, flickering, glaring, gleaming, glimmering, glinting, glistening, glittering, scintillating, shimmering, sparkling, twinkling; burnished, polished; sunny
near antonyms blackened, dark, darkened, darkish, darkling, darksome, dimmed, dusky, gloomy, murky, obscure, obscured, pitch-black, pitch-dark, somber (*or* sombre), sunless; cloudy, shadowy, shady; gray (*also* grey), leaden, pale
antonyms dim, dull, lackluster
2 filled with much light <the display windows of department stores are especially *bright* at Christmastime>
synonyms ablaze, alight, brightened, illuminated, illumined, light, lighted (*or* lit)
related words floodlit (*or* floodlighted), highlighted, spotlighted (*or* spotlit); kindled, ignited
near antonyms gloomy, somber, sunless; cloudy, murky, obscured, shadowy; gray (*also* grey), leaden, pale
antonyms blackened, dark, darkened, darkish, darkling, dimmed, dusky, pitch-black, pitch-dark
3 having or showing a good mood or disposition — see CHEERFUL 1
4 having or showing quickness of mind — see INTELLIGENT 1
5 having qualities which inspire hope — see HOPEFUL 1
6 pointing toward a happy outcome — see FAVORABLE 2
7 serving to lift one's spirits — see CHEERFUL 2
brighten *vb* to become glad or hopeful — see CHEER (UP) 1
brightened *adj* filled with much light — see BRIGHT 2
brightness *n* the quality or state of having or giving off light — see BRILLIANCE 1
brilliance *n* **1** the quality or state of having or giving off light <the *brilliance* of the flash from the camera was so intense that I was blinded for a moment afterwards>
synonyms brightness, brilliancy, dazzle, effulgence, illumination, lightness, lucidity, luminosity, radiance, refulgence, splendor
related words blaze, flare, flicker, light; fluorescence, incandescence, luminescence; burnish, gloss, luster, polish, sheen, shine; fire, flame, glare, glow; flash, gleam, glimmer, glint, glisten, glitter, scintillation, shimmer, sparkle, twinkle
near antonyms dimness, dullness (*also* dulness), gloominess, somberness; cloudiness, haziness, murkiness, obscurity; colorlessness, grayness, paleness
antonyms blackness, dark, darkness, duskiness
2 impressiveness of beauty on a large scale — see MAGNIFICENCE
brilliancy *n* the quality or state of having or giving off light — see BRILLIANCE 1
brilliant *adj* **1** giving off or reflecting much light — see BRIGHT 1
2 having or showing quickness of mind — see INTELLIGENT 1
brilliant *n* a usually valuable stone cut and polished for ornament — see GEM 1
brim *n* **1** the line or relatively narrow space that marks the outer limit of something — see BORDER 1
2 the projecting front part of a hat or cap — see VISOR
brimful *adj* containing or seeming to contain the greatest quantity or number possible — see FULL 1
brimming *adj* containing or seeming to contain the greatest quantity or number possible — see FULL 1
brine *n* the whole body of salt water that covers nearly three-fourths of the earth — see OCEAN
bring *vb* to have a price of — see COST
bring about *vb* to be the cause of (a situation, action, or state of mind) — see EFFECT
bring up *vb* **1** to bring to maturity through care and education <it takes an immense commitment and a lot of love to *bring up* a child properly>
synonyms breed, foster, raise, rear
related words father, mother; attend, care (for), cultivate, mind, minister (to), nurse, nurture, watch; discipline, educate, instruct, mentor, school, teach, train, tutor; edify, enlighten, indoctrinate; feed, nourish, provide (for), supply; advance, forward, further, promote; prepare; direct, guide, lead, shepherd, show
near antonyms abuse, ill-treat, ill-use, maltreat, mishandle, mistreat; ignore, neglect; harm, hurt, injure
2 to present or bring forward for discussion — see INTRODUCE 2
brininess *n* the quality or state of being salty — see SALTINESS
briny *adj* of, relating to, or containing salt — see SALTY 1
brisk *adj* **1** having much high-spirited energy and movement — see LIVELY 1
2 moving, proceeding, or acting with great speed — see FAST 1
briskly *adv* with great speed — see FAST 1
briskness *n* the quality or state of having abundant or intense activity — see VITALITY 1
bristle *vb* to express one's anger usually violently — see RAGE 1
bristly *adj* covered with or as if with hair — see HAIRY 1

brittle *adj* having a texture that readily breaks into little pieces under pressure — see CRISP 1
broach *vb* **1** to penetrate the surface (as of water) from below <the immense whales *broaching* was a magnificent sight>
synonyms surface
related words break, emerge, rise
near antonyms dive, drop, founder, plunge, sink, submerge, submerse
2 to present or bring forward for discussion — see INTRODUCE 2
broad *adj* **1** having a greater than usual measure across — see WIDE 1
2 having considerable extent — see EXTENSIVE
3 not subject to misinterpretation or more than one interpretation — see CLEAR 2
4 relating to the main elements and not to specific details — see GENERAL 2
broadcast *vb* **1** to cause to be known over a considerable area or by many people — see SPREAD 1
2 to make known openly or publicly — see ANNOUNCE
broadly *adv* to a large extent or degree — see GREATLY 2
broad–minded *adj* **1** not bound by traditional ways or beliefs — see LIBERAL 1
2 willing to consider new or different ideas — see OPEN-MINDED 1
broadside *adv* with one side faced forward — see SIDEWAYS
brochure *n* a short printed publication with no cover or with a paper cover — see PAMPHLET
broiling *adj* having a notably high temperature — see HOT 1
broke *adj* lacking money or material possessions — see POOR 1
broken *adj* **1** having an uneven edge or outline — see RAGGED 1
2 not having a level or smooth surface — see UNEVEN 1
brokenhearted *adj* feeling unhappiness — see SAD 1
brood *vb* to cover and warm eggs to hatch them — see SET 1
brook *n* a natural body of running water smaller than a river — see CREEK 1
brook *vb* to put up with (something painful or difficult) — see BEAR 2
brooklet *n* a natural body of running water smaller than a river — see CREEK 1
brotherhood *n* **1** a group of persons formally joined together for some common interest — see ASSOCIATION 2
2 the body of people in a profession or field of activity — see CORPS
brotherly *adj* of, relating to, or befitting brothers — see FRATERNAL
browbeat *vb* to make timid or fearful by or as if by threats — see INTIMIDATE
brownie *n* an imaginary being usually having a small human form and magical powers — see FAIRY
browse *vb* **1** to feed on grass or herbs — see GRAZE
2 to take a quick or hasty look — see [1]GLANCE 2
bruise *n* a bodily injury in which small blood vessels are broken but the overlying skin is not — see CONTUSION
bruit (about) *vb* to make (as a piece of information) the subject of common talk without any authority or confirmation of accuracy — see RUMOR
brush *n* a brief clash between enemies or rivals — see ENCOUNTER
brush *vb* to pass lightly across or touch gently especially in passing <spiderwebs *brushed* her cheek as she walked through the basement>
synonyms graze, kiss, nudge, shave, skim
related words bump, contact, scrape, strike, sweep, swipe, touch; bounce, carom, glance, rebound, ricochet, sideswipe, skip; caress, cuddle, fondle, pet, stroke
near antonyms clash, collide, hit, knock, punch, slap, smack, smash, thwack, whack
brush (aside *or* off) *vb* to overlook or dismiss as of little importance — see EXCUSE 1
brush–off *n* treatment that is deliberately unfriendly — see COLD SHOULDER
brushwood *n* a thick patch of shrubbery, small trees, or underbrush — see THICKET
brusque *adj* being or characterized by direct, brief, and potentially rude speech or manner — see BLUNT 1
brutal *adj* **1** difficult to endure — see HARSH 1
2 having or showing the desire to inflict severe pain and suffering on others — see CRUEL 1
brutality *n* the willful infliction of pain and suffering on others — see CRUELTY
brute *n* **1** one of the lower animals as distinguished from human beings — see ANIMAL
2 a mean, evil, or unprincipled person — see VILLAIN
bubble *vb* to flow in a broken irregular stream — see GURGLE
bubbly *adj* joyously unrestrained — see EXUBERANT
buccaneer *n* someone who engages in robbery of ships at sea — see PIRATE
buck *n* **1** a man extremely interested in his clothing and personal appearance — see DANDY 1
2 an adult male human being — see MAN 1
buck *vb* **1** to move or cause to move with a sharp quick motion — see JERK 1
2 to refuse to give in to — see RESIST
buckaroo *n* a hired hand who tends cattle or horses at a ranch or on the range — see COWBOY
bucket *n* **1** a considerable amount — see LOT 2
2 a round container that is open at the top and outfitted with a handle — see PAIL
buckle *vb* to occupy (oneself) diligently or with close attention — see APPLY 2
bucolic *adj* of, relating to, associated with, or typical of open areas with few buildings or people — see RURAL
buddy *n* a person who has a strong liking for and trust in another — see FRIEND 1
budge *vb* **1** to cease resistance (as to another's arguments, demands, or control) — see YIELD 3
2 to change one's position — see MOVE 3
3 to change the place or position of — see MOVE 1
budget *n* **1** a sum of money set aside for a particular purpose — see FUND 1
2 the number of individuals or amount of something available at any given time — see SUPPLY
buff *n* a person with a strong and habitual liking for something — see FAN
buff *vb* **1** to make smooth by friction — see GRIND 1
2 to make smooth or glossy usually by repeatedly applying surface pressure — see POLISH
buffed *adj* having a shiny surface or finish — see GLOSSY

buffer *n* something that serves as a protective barrier — see CUSHION
buffer *vb* to lessen the shock of — see CUSHION
[1]**buffet** *n* a hard strike with a part of the body or an instrument — see [1]BLOW
[2]**buffet** *n* a storage case typically having doors and shelves — see CABINET
buffet *vb* to strike repeatedly — see BEAT 1
buffoon *n* a comically dressed performer (as at a circus) who entertains with playful tricks and ridiculous behavior — see CLOWN 1
bug *n* **1** a person with a strong and habitual liking for something — see FAN
2 an abnormal state that disrupts a plant's or animal's normal bodily functioning — see DISEASE
bug *vb* **1** to attack repeatedly with mean put-downs or insults — see TEASE 2
2 to disturb the peace of mind of (someone) especially by repeated disagreeable acts — see IRRITATE 1
3 to thrust oneself upon (another) without invitation — see BOTHER 1
bugaboo *n* something or someone that causes fear or dread especially without reason — see BOGEY 1
bugbear *n* something or someone that causes fear or dread especially without reason — see BOGEY 1
bugging *n* the act of making unwelcome intrusions upon another — see ANNOYANCE
build *n* the type of body that a person has — see PHYSIQUE
build *vb* to form by putting together parts or materials <he spent hours *building* a model airplane from a kit>
synonyms assemble, construct, erect, fabricate, make, make up, piece, put up, raise, rear, set up
related words fashion, forge, frame, manufacture, mold, produce, shape; prefabricate; begin, coin, create, generate, inaugurate, initiate, innovate, invent, originate; constitute, establish, father, found, institute, organize; conceive, concoct, contrive, cook up, design, devise, imagine, think (up); rebuild; rig up
phrases put together
near antonyms dismember; demolish, destroy, devastate, flatten, pulverize, raze, ruin, shatter, smash, wreck; blow up, explode
antonyms disassemble, dismantle, take down
build (up) *vb* **1** to become greater in extent, volume, amount, or number — see INCREASE 2
2 to increase in — see GAIN 1
3 to produce or bring about especially by long or repeated effort — see HAMMER (OUT)
building *n* something built as a dwelling, shelter, or place for human activity <English class will be in that big stone *building* over there>
synonyms edifice, structure
related words construction, erection; bungalow, cabin, chalet, cottage, house, lodge, summerhouse; hovel, hut, shack, shanty, shed; castle, château, estate, hall, manor, mansion, palace, villa; skyscraper, tower
bulge *n* a part that sticks out from the general mass of something <several *bulges* in the old vinyl flooring in the dingy bathroom>
synonyms jut, overhang, projection, protrusion, protuberance
related words dome; blob, bump, knob, lump, nub, swelling; block, piece, portion, section; enlargement, escalation, expansion, increase
near antonyms cavity, crater, hole; basin, dip, valley
antonyms concavity, dent, depression, hollow, indentation, pit
bulge *vb* to extend outward beyond a usual point <the sides of the returning camper's suitcase *bulged* with a month's worth of dirty laundry>
synonyms bag, balloon, beetle, belly, billow, jut, overhang, poke, project, protrude, stand out, start, stick out
related words dome; blow up, inflate; distend, expand, swell; mushroom, snowball; elongate, extend, lengthen, stretch
near antonyms compress, condense, constrict, contract, shrink
bulk *n* the main or greater part of something as distinguished from its appendages — see BODY 1
bulkiness *n* the quality or state of being large in size — see LARGENESS
bulky *adj* of a size greater than average of its kind — see LARGE
bull *n, slang* a member of a force charged with law enforcement at the local level — see OFFICER 1
bulldoze *vb* to force one's way — see PRESS 4
bullet *n* a usually round or cone-shaped little piece of lead made to be fired from a firearm <it is possible to make your own *bullets*, but it takes a lot of patience and some extra money>
synonyms ball, pellet
related words ammunition, cannonball, cap, cartridge, charge, gunshot, lead, load, missile, pop, projectile, round, shell, shot, slug; twenty-two
near antonyms blank
bulletin *n* a published statement informing the public of a matter of general interest — see ANNOUNCEMENT
bully *n* **1** a person who teases, threatens, or hurts smaller or weaker persons <the *bully* spent most of the afternoon in detention for pushing people down on the playground>
synonyms intimidator
related words antagonist, enemy; harrier, nuisance, persecutor, pest, tease, teaser; heckler; goon, hood, hoodlum, punk, rough, roughneck, rowdy, ruffian, thug, tough; cutthroat, felon, gangster, gunman, mobster, racketeer
2 a violent, brutal person who is often a member of an organized gang — see HOODLUM
bully *vb* to make timid or fearful by or as if by threats — see INTIMIDATE
bulwark *n* something that holds up or serves as a foundation for something else — see SUPPORT 1
bum *adj* of low quality — see CHEAP 2
bum *n* a homeless wanderer who may beg or steal for a living — see TRAMP
bummer *n* **1** something (as a situation or event) that is depressing — see DOWNER
2 something that disappoints — see DISAPPOINTMENT 2
3 something that has failed — see FAILURE 3
bump *n* **1** a small rounded mass of swollen tissue <that's a nasty *bump* on your arm where you hit the table>
synonyms knot, lump, node, nodule, swelling
related words growth, tumor, wart; hump, hunch; bruise, contusion; blob, chunk, clod, clump, gob, gobbet, hunk, knob, nub, nubble, nugget, wad
2 a forceful coming together of two things — see IMPACT 1

bump *vb* to come into usually forceful contact with something — see HIT 2

bumper *adj* unusually large — see HUGE

bumper *n* something that serves as a protective barrier — see CUSHION

bumpkin *n* an awkward or simple person especially from a small town or the country — see HICK

bumpy *adj* **1** marked by a series of sharp quick motions — see JERKY 1
2 not having a level or smooth surface — see UNEVEN 1

bunch *n* **1** a group of people sharing a common interest and relating together socially — see GANG 2
2 a number of things considered as a unit — see GROUP 1
3 a usually small number of persons considered as a unit — see GROUP 2

bunch *vb* to gather into a closely packed group — see PRESS 3

bundle *n* a wrapped or sealed case containing an item or set of items — see PACKAGE 1

bung *vb* to close up so that no empty spaces remain — see FILL 2

bungle *vb* to make or do (something) in a clumsy or unskillful way — see BOTCH

bungling *adj* showing or marked by a lack of skill and tact (as in dealing with a situation) — see AWKWARD 2

[1]**bunk** *n* a place set aside for sleeping — see BED 1

[2]**bunk** *n* **1** language, behavior, or ideas that are absurd and contrary to good sense — see NONSENSE 1
2 unintelligible or meaningless talk — see GIBBERISH

bunk *vb* to provide with living quarters or shelter — see HOUSE 1

buoy (up) *vb* to fill with courage or strength of purpose — see ENCOURAGE 1

buoyant *adj* **1** having or showing a good mood or disposition — see CHEERFUL 1
2 joyously unrestrained — see EXUBERANT

burden *n* **1** a mass or quantity of something taken up and carried, conveyed, or transported — see LOAD 1
2 a part of a song or hymn that is repeated every so often — see CHORUS 2
3 something one must do because of prior agreement — see OBLIGATION

burden *vb* **1** to place a weight or burden on — see LOAD 1
2 to make sad — see DEPRESS 1

burdensome *adj* **1** difficult to endure — see HARSH 1
2 requiring much time, effort, or careful attention — see DEMANDING 1

bureau *n* a large unit of a governmental, business, or educational organization — see DIVISION 2

bureaucrat *n* a worker in a government agency ⟨the *bureaucrats* at the town hall seem to think that we need a building permit to build a tree house⟩
synonyms functionary, public servant
related words clerk, officeholder, official; employee, underling, worker

burg *n* a thickly settled, highly populated area — see CITY

burgeon *vb* **1** to become greater in extent, volume, amount, or number — see INCREASE 2
2 to grow vigorously — see THRIVE 1
3 to produce flowers — see BLOOM

burgher *n* a person who lives in a town on a permanent basis ⟨many of the college students are regarded by the local *burghers* as obnoxious louts⟩
synonyms citizen, townie, villager
related words denizen, dweller, habitant, homeowner, inhabitant, national, native, occupant, resident, resider; town, townsfolk, townspeople; suburbanite, urbanite
near antonyms foreigner, guest, tourist, transient, visitor

burglarize *vb* **1** to enter a house or building by force usually with illegal intent — see BREAK IN 1
2 to remove valuables from (a place) unlawfully — see ROB

burial *n* the act or ceremony of putting a dead body in its final resting place ⟨the children wanted to give the dead bird a proper *burial* in the backyard⟩
synonyms burying, entombing, entombment, interment, interring, sepulture
related words embalmment, funeral
near antonyms cremation
antonyms disinterment, exhumation, unearthing

burlesque *n* a work that imitates and exaggerates another work for comic effect — see PARODY 1

burlesque *vb* to copy or exaggerate (someone or something) in order to make fun of — see MIMIC 1

burly *adj* strongly and heavily built — see [1]HUSKY

burn *vb* **1** to be on fire especially brightly ⟨all evening long we just sat there, contentedly watching the Yule log *burn*⟩
synonyms blaze, combust, flame, glow
related words fire, ignite, kindle; flare (up), light (up); flicker, gutter, waver; bake, broil, char, cook, melt, roast, scorch, swelter; smolder, spark, sputter; beam, brighten, radiate; beat (down), flash, glare, gleam, glimmer, glint, glisten, glitter, scintillate, shimmer, shine, sparkle, twinkle
2 to set (something) on fire ⟨it is not a good idea to try to *burn* old papers in the sink⟩
synonyms fire, ignite, inflame, kindle, light
related words char, scorch; bake, cremate, incinerate, kiln; brighten, illumine, illuminate, irradiate, lighten, radiate; scald, scathe, sear; rekindle, relight
near antonyms choke, smother, suffocate; stamp (out); blacken, darken, dim, dull, obscure
antonyms douse, extinguish, put out, quench, snuff (out)
3 to be excited or emotionally stirred up with anger — see BOIL 1
4 to shine with a bright harsh light — see GLARE 1

burnable *adj* capable of catching or being set on fire — see COMBUSTIBLE

burned–out *or* **burnt–out** *adj* depleted in strength, energy, or freshness — see WEARY 1

burning *adj* **1** being on fire — see ABLAZE 1
2 having a notably high temperature — see HOT 1
3 having or expressing great depth of feeling — see FERVENT

burnish *vb* to make smooth or glossy usually by repeatedly applying surface pressure — see POLISH

burnished *adj* having a shiny surface or finish — see GLOSSY

burnout *n* a complete depletion of energy or strength — see FATIGUE

burn out *vb* to use up all the physical energy of — see EXHAUST 1

burro *n* a sturdy and patient domestic mammal that is used especially to carry things — see DONKEY 1

burrow *n* the shelter or resting place of a wild animal — see DEN 1

burst *n* **1** a sudden and usually temporary growth of activity — see OUTBREAK
2 a sudden intense expression of strong feeling — see OUTBURST 1

burst *vb* **1** to break open or into pieces usually because of internal pressure — see EXPLODE 1
2 to cause to break open or into pieces by or as if by an explosive — see BLAST 1

burst (forth) *vb* to develop suddenly and violently — see ERUPT 2

bursting *adj* containing or seeming to contain the greatest quantity or number possible — see FULL 1

bursting *n* the act or an instance of exploding — see EXPLOSION 1

bury *vb* **1** to place (a dead body) in the earth, a tomb, or the sea ⟨he died on Tuesday and was *buried* on Friday⟩
synonyms entomb, inter
related words enshrine; conceal, cover, ensconce, hide; obscure, shade, shield; cloak, curtain, enshroud, shroud
near antonyms burn, cremate; bare, disclose, discover, display, exhibit, expose, reveal, show
antonyms disinter, exhume, unearth
2 to put into a hiding place — see [1]HIDE 1

burying *n* the act or ceremony of putting a dead body in its final resting place — see BURIAL

bush *n* a rural region that forms the edge of the settled or developed part of a country — see FRONTIER 2

bushed *adj* depleted in strength, energy, or freshness — see WEARY 1

bushel *n* a considerable amount — see LOT 2

business *n* **1** a commercial or industrial activity or organization — see ENTERPRISE 1
2 something to be dealt with — see MATTER 2
3 the buying and selling of goods especially on a large scale and between different places — see COMMERCE

bust *n* **1** a hard strike with a part of the body or an instrument — see [1]BLOW
2 something that has failed — see FAILURE 3

bust *vb* **1** to bring to a lower grade or rank — see DEMOTE
2 to cause to lose one's fortune and become unable to pay one's debts — see RUIN 1
3 to cause to separate into pieces usually suddenly or forcibly — see BREAK 1
4 to deliver a blow to (someone or something) usually in a strong vigorous manner — see HIT 1
5 *slang* to take or keep under one's control by authority of law — see ARREST 1

bustle *n* a state of noisy, confused activity — see COMMOTION

bustling *adj* marked by much life, movement, or activity — see ALIVE 2

busy *adj* **1** involved in often constant activity ⟨the deadline is in two days, so everyone at work has been extremely *busy*⟩
synonyms active, assiduous, diligent, employed, engaged, industrious, laborious, occupied, sedulous, working
related words absorbed, concentrating, engrossed, focused (*also* focussed), immersed, intent, preoccupied; alive, functional, functioning, going, living, operating, operational, operative, running; energetic, vigorous; indefatigable, tireless, untiring
near antonyms asleep, dormant, latent, quiescent, sleepy; inert, passive; dead, dull, slow; inoperative, nonoperating
antonyms idle, inactive, unemployed, unengaged, unoccupied
2 marked by much life, movement, or activity — see ALIVE 2

busy *vb* to hold the attention of — see ENGAGE 1

busybody *n* a person who meddles in the affairs of others ⟨that *busybody* across the street is always telling me how to tend to my own garden⟩
synonyms interferer, interloper, intruder, kibitzer, meddler
related words peeper, peeping Tom, snoop, snooper, spy; blabber, discloser, gossip, gossiper, prattler, revealer, teller; betrayer, talebearer, tattletale; snake, sneak; informer, snitcher, squealer, stool pigeon

but *adv* nothing more than — see JUST 3

but *conj* **1** if it were not for the fact that — see EXCEPT
2 in spite of that — see HOWEVER

but *prep* not including — see EXCEPT

butcher *vb* **1** to kill on a large scale — see MASSACRE
2 to make or do (something) in a clumsy or unskillful way — see BOTCH

butchery *n* the killing of a large number of people — see MASSACRE

[1]**butt** *n* the part of the body upon which someone sits — see BUTTOCKS

[2]**butt** *n* **1** a person or thing that is made fun of — see LAUGHINGSTOCK
2 a person or thing that is the object of abuse, criticism, or ridicule — see TARGET 1

butt in *vb* to interest oneself in what is not one's concern — see INTERFERE

buttocks *n pl* the part of the body upon which someone sits ⟨she slipped in the mud puddle and hit the ground square on her *buttocks*⟩
synonyms backside, bottom, breech, butt, fanny, hams, haunches, posterior, rear, rump, seat

buttress *n* **1** something or someone to which one looks for support — see DEPENDENCE 2
2 something that holds up or serves as a foundation for something else — see SUPPORT 1

buttress *vb* to hold up or serve as a foundation for — see SUPPORT 3

buy *n* something bought or offered for sale at a desirable price — see BARGAIN 1

buy *vb* to get possession of (something) by giving money in exchange for ⟨I really want to *buy* that new book, but I don't have enough money right now⟩
synonyms pick up, purchase, take
related words acquire, get, obtain, procure, secure; finance, pay (for), spring (for); barter (for), deal (for), exchange (for), trade (for); bargain (with), chaffer (with), dicker (over), horse-trade (with), negotiate (about), palter (with); bid, offer; rebuy, repurchase

buzz *n* **1** a communication by telephone — see CALL 3
2 a monotonous sound like that of an insect in motion — see HUM

buzz *vb* to fly, turn, or move rapidly with a fluttering or vibratory sound — see WHIRR

buzzing *adj* marked by much life, movement, or activity — see ALIVE 2

by *adv* at, within, or to a short distance or time — see NEAR 1

by *prep* **1** along the way of ⟨went *by* the woods to get to the summer cottage⟩
synonyms through, via
related words across, along, alongside, beyond, near, nearby, over; below, beneath, under, underneath; outside, past
phrases by way of
2 using the means or agency of ⟨try to convince them *by* reason alone, if possible⟩
synonyms per, through, with
phrases by means of, by (*or* in) virtue of, through the medium of
3 close to — see AROUND 1

by–and–by *n* time that is to come — see FUTURE 1

by and large *adv* for the most part — see CHIEFLY

bygone *adj* no longer existing — see EXTINCT

bylaw *n* a statement spelling out the proper procedure or conduct for an activity — see RULE 1

bypass *vb* to avoid by going around — see DETOUR 1

by–product *n* something that naturally develops or is developed from something else — see DERIVATIVE

byword *n* an often stated observation regarding something from common experience — see SAYING

cab *n* an automobile that carries passengers for a fare usually determined by the distance traveled — see TAXI

cabal *n* a group involved in secret or criminal activities — see RING 1

cabaret *n* a bar or restaurant offering special nighttime entertainment (as music, dancing, or comedy acts) — see NIGHTCLUB

cabin *n* **1** a small, simply constructed, and often temporary dwelling — see SHACK
2 an often small house for recreational or seasonal use — see COTTAGE
3 one of the parts into which an enclosed space is divided — see COMPARTMENT

cabinet *n* a storage case typically having doors and shelves ⟨the most precious knickknacks were kept in a *cabinet* with glass doors⟩
synonyms buffet, closet, cupboard, hutch, locker, sideboard
related words bookcase, secretary; shelving; console

cabinetwork *n* the movable articles in a room — see FURNITURE

cable *n* a length of braided, flexible material that is used for tying or connecting things — see CORD

cache *n* **1** a collection of things kept available for future use or need — see STORE 1
2 a supply stored up and often hidden away — see HOARD 1

cache *vb* **1** to put (something of future use or value) in a safe or secret place — see HOARD
2 to put into a hiding place — see [1]HIDE 1

caching *n* the placing of something out of sight — see CONCEALMENT 1

cackle *n* an explosive sound that is a sign of amusement — see LAUGH 1

cackle *vb* to engage in casual or rambling conversation — see CHAT

cackler *n* a person who talks constantly — see CHATTERBOX

cacophony *n* loud, confused, and usually unharmonious sound — see NOISE 1

cad *n* a person whose behavior is offensive to others — see JERK 1

cadaver *n* a dead body — see CORPSE

cadaverous *adj* **1** lacking a healthy skin color — see PALE 2
2 suffering extreme weight loss as a result of hunger or disease — see EMACIATED

caddy *n* a covered rectangular container for storing or transporting things — see CHEST

cadence *n* the recurrent pattern formed by a series of sounds having a regular rise and fall in intensity — see RHYTHM

cadenced *adj* marked by or occurring with a noticeable regularity in the rise and fall of sound — see RHYTHMIC

café *also* **cafe** *n* **1** a bar or restaurant offering special nighttime entertainment (as music, dancing, or comedy acts) — see NIGHTCLUB
2 a place of business where alcoholic beverages are sold to be consumed on the premises — see BARROOM
3 a public establishment where meals are served to paying customers for consumption on the premises — see RESTAURANT

cage *n* an enclosure with an open framework for keeping animals ⟨the dogs and cats at the animal shelter looked so sad in their *cages*⟩
synonyms coop, corral, pen, pound
related words fence; cote, dovecote, fold; aquarium, terrarium

cage *vb* to close or shut in by or as if by barriers — see ENCLOSE 1

cagey *also* **cagy** *adj* clever at attaining one's ends by indirect and often deceptive means — see ARTFUL 1

caginess *n* skill in achieving one's ends through indirect, subtle, or underhanded means — see CUNNING 1

cajole *vb* to get (someone) to do something by gentle urging, special attention, or flattery — see COAX

cake *n* a small usually rounded mass of minced food that has been fried ⟨the rich, tender *cakes* of crabmeat had been lightly fried⟩
synonyms croquette, cutlet, fritter, patty (*also* pattie)
related words finger, stick

cake *vb* to cover with a hardened layer — see ENCRUST

calamitous *adj* **1** bringing about ruin or misfortune — see FATAL 1
2 causing or tending to cause destruction — see DESTRUCTIVE 1

calamity *n* a sudden violent event that brings about great loss or destruction — see DISASTER

calculate *vb* **1** to determine (a value) by doing the necessary mathematical operations ⟨the family has been *calculating* what a week at the beach resort would end up costing⟩
synonyms compute, figure, reckon, work out
related words conjecture, estimate, guess, judge, suppose; add up, sum, tally, total; add, cipher, divide, multiply, subtract; calibrate, gauge (*also* gage), measure, scale; ascertain, discover, dope (out), figure out, find out; recompute, refigure
2 to decide the size, amount, number, or distance of (something) without actual measurement — see ESTIMATE 2
3 to work out the details of (something) in advance — see PLAN 1

calculated *adj* decided on as a result of careful thought — see DELIBERATE 1

calculation *n* the act or process of performing mathematical operations to find a value ⟨by my *calculation*, it should take me a month to save up for the sneakers⟩
synonyms arithmetic, ciphering, computation, figures, figuring, reckoning
related words mathematics; addition, division, multiplication, subtraction; appraisal, assessment, estimation, evaluation, judgment (*or* judgement)

calendar *n* a listing of things to be presented or considered (as at a concert or play) — see PROGRAM 1

caliber *or* **calibre** *n* degree of excellence — see QUALITY 1

call *n* **1** a natural vocal sound made by an animal ⟨a ranger who could immediately identify the *call* of every creature in the forest⟩
synonyms cry, note
related words bark, bay, bellow, bleat, bray, caterwaul, caw, cheep, chirp, grunt, hoot, howl, low, meow, moo, neigh, peep, roar, screech, squawk, squeak, squeal, twitter, whinny, yap, yelp, yip, yowl
2 a coming to see another briefly for social or business reasons ⟨we paid a *call* on the new neighbors the day after they moved in⟩
synonyms visit, visitation
related words meeting, rendezvous, tryst; stopover
3 a communication by telephone ⟨give me a *call* as soon as you arrive, so I'll know you got there safely⟩
synonyms buzz, ring
related words callback; toll call; message
4 an act or instance of asking for information — see QUESTION 2
5 an entitlement to something — see CLAIM 1

call *vb* **1** to speak so as to be heard at a distance ⟨we could hear someone *calling* for help from the other side of the wall⟩
synonyms bawl, cry, holler, shout, vociferate, yell
related words bellow, roar; whoop; scream, screech, shriek, shrill, squeak, squeal; caterwaul, howl, wail, yawp (*or* yaup), yowl
near antonyms breathe, mumble, murmur, mutter, whisper
2 to make a telephone call to ⟨use this cell phone to *call* me if there's an emergency⟩
synonyms dial, phone, ring (up) [*chiefly British*], telephone
related words beep, buzz
3 to make a brief visit ⟨the hospital posts the hours during which friends and relatives may *call*⟩
synonyms drop (by *or* in), pop (in), stop (by *or* in), visit
related words barge (in); look up, see; frequent, hang around (in), hang out (at), haunt, resort (to)
4 to put an end to (something planned or previously agreed to) — see CANCEL 1
5 to think of in a particular way — see CONSIDER 1
6 to utter one's distinctive animal sound — see CRY 2
7 to bring together in assembly by or as if by command — see CONVOKE
8 to decide the size, amount, number, or distance of (something) without actual measurement — see ESTIMATE 2
9 to demand or request the presence or service of — see SUMMON 1
10 to give a name to — see NAME 1

call (for) *vb* **1** to ask for (something) earnestly or with authority — see DEMAND 1
2 to make a request for — see ASK (FOR) 1

call (on *or* upon) *vb* to make a social call upon — see VISIT 1

caller *n* a person who visits another — see GUEST 1

calligraphy *n* writing done by hand — see HANDWRITING 2

calling *n* **1** the act of putting an end to something planned or previously agreed to — see CANCELLATION
2 the activity by which one regularly makes a living — see OCCUPATION

calling off *n* the act of putting an end to something planned or previously agreed to — see CANCELLATION

call off *vb* to put an end to (something planned or previously agreed to) — see CANCEL 1

callous *adj* having or showing a lack of sympathy or tender feelings — see HARD 1

callow *adj* lacking in adult experience or maturity ⟨a story about a *callow* youth who learns the value of hard work and self-reliance⟩
synonyms adolescent, green, immature, inexperienced, juvenile, puerile, raw, unfledged, unripe, unripened
related words babyish, childish, infantile; boyish, girlish, maidenly, virginal, youthful; ingenuous, innocent, naive (*or* naïve); unpracticed, unseasoned, untrained, untried
near antonyms advanced, precocious; knowing, sophisticated, worldly-wise
antonyms adult, experienced, grown-up, mature, ripe

calm *adj* **1** free from storms or physical disturbance ⟨after a stormy night of high winds and driving rains, the day dawned on a *calm* sea⟩
synonyms halcyon, hushed, peaceful, placid, quiet, serene, still, stilly, tranquil, untroubled
related words calming, pacific, restful, soothing; inactive, inert, quiescent, reposing, resting; smooth, unruffled; clear, cloudless, fair, rainless, sunny, sunshiny

near antonyms bleak, cloudy, dirty, foul, nasty, overcast, rainy, raw, rough, squally

antonyms agitated, angry, stormy, turbulent

2 free from emotional or mental agitation ⟨bystanders tried to help the injured person remain *calm* while they waited for the ambulance to arrive⟩

synonyms collected, composed, cool, coolheaded, placid, self-possessed, serene, tranquil, undisturbed, unperturbed, unshaken, untroubled, unworried

related words imperturbable, nerveless, unflappable, unshakable; disciplined, self-contained, self-controlled; affable, breezy, devil-may-care, easygoing, happy-go-lucky, laid-back, low-pressure; carefree, nonchalant, unconcerned; assured, confident, self-assured; aloof, detached, dispassionate, indifferent; impassive, phlegmatic, stolid

near antonyms anxious, bothered, distressed, worried; jittery, jumpy, nervous, skittish, tense; high-strung, uptight

antonyms agitated, discomposed, disturbed, flustered, perturbed, upset

3 free from disturbing noise or uproar — see QUIET 1

calm *n* a state of freedom from storm or disturbance ⟨vacationing city dwellers who are tired of the hustle and bustle enjoy the *calm* of the secluded mountain village⟩

synonyms calmness, hush, peace, peacefulness, placidity, quiet, quietness, quietude, repose, restfulness, sereneness, serenity, still, stillness, tranquillity (*or* tranquility)

related words lull, pause, respite; silence; comity, concord, harmony

near antonyms clamor, din, noise, racket

antonyms bustle, commotion, hubbub, hurly-burly, pandemonium, tumult, turmoil, uproar

calm *vb* **1** to free from distress or disturbance ⟨the president's reassuring words did much to *calm* the public during the national emergency⟩

synonyms allay, compose, quiet, settle, soothe, still, tranquilize (*also* tranquillize)

related words alleviate, assuage, ease, mitigate, relieve; appease, conciliate, mollify, pacify, placate; lull, relax, stupefy

near antonyms aggravate, heighten, intensify; arouse, excite, foment, incite, rouse, stir (up)

antonyms agitate, discompose, disquiet, disturb, perturb, upset

2 to gain emotional or mental control of — see COLLECT 1

calm (down) *vb* to become still and orderly — see QUIET 1

calming *adj* tending to calm the emotions and relieve stress — see SOOTHING 1

calmness *n* **1** a state of freedom from storm or disturbance — see CALM

2 evenness of emotions or temper — see EQUANIMITY

camaraderie *n* the feeling of closeness and friendship that exists between companions — see COMPANIONSHIP

camouflage *n* clothing put on to hide one's true identity or imitate someone or something else — see DISGUISE

camouflage *vb* to change the dress or looks of so as to conceal true identity — see DISGUISE

camp *n* **1** a place where a group of people live for a short time in tents or cabins ⟨the war forced people to flee their homes and to live in crowded *camps* along the border⟩

synonyms bivouac, campground, campsite, encampment

related words barracks; colony, plantation, settlement; shantytown; concentration camp, prison camp

2 a small, simply constructed, and often temporary dwelling — see SHACK

3 an often small house for recreational or seasonal use — see COTTAGE

camp *vb* to live in a camp or the outdoors ⟨rather than stay in motels, my family usually *camps* when we're on vacation⟩

synonyms bivouac, encamp

related words tent; backpack

phrases rough it

campaign *n* a series of activities undertaken to achieve a goal ⟨an all-out *campaign* to bring a minor league baseball team to the city⟩

synonyms bandwagon, cause, crusade, drive, movement

related words attack, march, offensive

campaigner *n* one who seeks an office, honor, position, or award — see CANDIDATE

camper *n* a motor vehicle that is specially equipped for living while traveling ⟨the family loaded up the *camper* and headed off for the tour of several national parks⟩

synonyms caravan, mobile home, motor home, trailer

related words van

campground *n* a place where a group of people live for a short time in tents or cabins — see CAMP 1

campsite *n* a place where a group of people live for a short time in tents or cabins — see CAMP 1

can *vb* **1** to bring (as an action or operation) to an immediate end — see STOP 1

2 to let go from office, service, or employment — see DISMISS 1

can *n* a metal container in the shape of a cylinder ⟨the shelter stores huge *cans* of water for an emergency⟩

synonyms barrel, drum

related words tube; tin

canal *n* an open man-made passageway for water — see CHANNEL 1

cancel *vb* **1** to put an end to (something planned or previously agreed to) ⟨please call to *cancel* your appointment with the dentist if you can't make it⟩

synonyms abort, call, call off, drop, recall, repeal, rescind, revoke

related words abrogate, annul, invalidate, nullify, void, write off; recant, retract, take back, withdraw; countermand, reverse; end, halt, stop, terminate; give up, relinquish, surrender

near antonyms engage, pledge, promise; begin, commence, initiate, start; take on, take up, undertake

antonyms continue, keep

2 to put an end to by formal action — see ABOLISH

3 to show (something written) to be no longer valid by drawing a cross over or a line through it — see X (OUT)

cancel (out) *vb* to balance with an equal force so as to make ineffective — see OFFSET

canceler *or* **canceller** *n* a force or influence that makes an opposing force ineffective or less effective — see COUNTERBALANCE

cancellation *n* the act of putting an end to something planned or previously agreed to ⟨the misbehavior of a few bad apples at the end of the football game resulted in the *cancellation* of the victory party⟩
synonyms abortion, calling, calling off, dropping, recall, repeal, rescission, revocation
related words annulment, invalidation, neutralization, nullification; abolishment, abolition, ending, halting, stopping, termination; giving up, relinquishment, surrender
near antonyms beginning, commencement, initiation; engagement, undertaking
antonyms continuation

candid *adj* free in expressing one's true feelings and opinions — see FRANK

candidate *n* one who seeks an office, honor, position, or award ⟨each *candidate* for student council was allowed to speak at the school assembly⟩
synonyms applicant, aspirant, campaigner, contender, hopeful, prospect, seeker
related words competitor, contestant, entrant; also-ran, dark horse, favorite, finisher, has-been, runner-up; nominee; claimant, pretender
near antonyms incumbent, officeholder; dropout

candor *n* the free expression of one's true feelings and opinions ⟨an interview in which the members of the rock band speak with *candor* about their recent squabbling⟩
synonyms directness, forthrightness, frankness, openheartedness, openness, plainness, straightforwardness
related words earnestness, sincerity, sobriety; artlessness, genuineness, naïveté (*also* naivete), simplicity, unsophistication; bluffness, bluntness, brusqueness; freedom, license (*or* licence), unrestraint
near antonyms inhibition, reserve, restraint; diplomacy, tact
antonyms dissembling, pretense (*or* pretence)

cane *n* a heavy rigid stick used as a weapon or for punishment — see CLUB 1

canine *n* a domestic mammal that is related to the wolves and foxes — see DOG

canniness *n* skill in achieving one's ends through indirect, subtle, or underhanded means — see CUNNING 1

cannonade *n* a rapid or overwhelming outpouring of many things at once — see BARRAGE

canny *adj* having or showing a practical cleverness or judgment — see SHREWD

canon *n* **1** a statement or body of statements concerning faith or morals proclaimed by a church — see DOCTRINE 1
2 a record of a series of items (as names or titles) usually arranged according to some system — see [1]LIST

canonize *vb* **1** to declare to be a saint and worthy of public respect — see SAINT
2 to love or admire too much — see IDOLIZE

canopy *n* a raised covering over something for decoration or protection ⟨trees line both sides of the garden path, with their foliage forming a leafy *canopy* for walkers⟩
synonyms awning, ceiling, roof, tent
related words screen, shade, shelter, shield, sunshade; canvas, fly

[1]cant *n* the degree to which something rises up from a position level with the horizon — see SLANT

[2]cant *n* **1** the pretending of having virtues, principles, or beliefs that one in fact does not have — see HYPOCRISY
2 the special terms or expressions of a particular group or field — see TERMINOLOGY

cant *vb* to set or cause to be at an angle — see LEAN 1

cantankerous *adj* having or showing a habitually bad temper — see ILL-TEMPERED

canted *adj* running in a slanting direction — see DIAGONAL

canticle *n* a religious song — see HYMN

canvas *n* a picture created with usually oil paint — see PAINTING

canvass *vb* to go around and approach (people) with a request for opinions or information ⟨we *canvassed* people all over town, asking if they would be interested in participating in a recycling program⟩
synonyms poll, solicit, survey
related words interrogate, interview, question; feel (out), sound (out)
near antonyms report

canyon *also* **cañon** *n* a narrow opening between hillsides or mountains that can be used for passage ⟨as the scouts made their way through the *canyon*, they marveled at the sheer walls of rock on both sides⟩
synonyms defile, flume, gap, gorge, gulch, gulf, notch, pass, ravine
related words abyss, chasm, cirque, cleft, crevasse, crevice, fissure; dale, glen, hollow, vale, valley; basin, floodplain, plain; arroyo, coulee, gully, gutter, wash [*Western*]

cap *n* **1** a covering for the head usually having a shaped crown — see HAT
2 a piece placed over an open container to hold in, protect, or conceal its contents — see COVER 1

capability *n* **1** a skill, an ability, or knowledge that makes a person able to do a particular job — see QUALIFICATION 1
2 the physical or mental power to do something — see ABILITY

capable *adj* having the required skills for an acceptable level of performance — see COMPETENT

capably *adv* in a skillful or expert manner — see WELL 3

capacious *adj* more than adequate or average in capacity — see SPACIOUS

capacity *n* **1** the largest number or amount that something can hold ⟨the seating *capacity* of the school auditorium is 800 people⟩
synonyms complement, content
related words area, room, space, volume; fill, load, measure
2 an assignment at which one regularly works for pay — see JOB 1
3 the action for which a person or thing is specially fitted or used or for which a thing exists — see ROLE
4 the physical or mental power to do something — see ABILITY

caparison *n* **1** dressy clothing — see FINERY
2 something that decorates or beautifies — see DECORATION 1

caparison *vb* to outfit with clothes and especially fine or special clothes — see CLOTHE 1

[1]cape *n* a sleeveless garment worn so as to hang over the shoulders, arms, and back ⟨the mysterious figure wrapped his *cape* tightly around his shoulders⟩

synonyms cloak, mantle, roquelaure

related words frock, gown, robe; shawl, stole, wrap; poncho, serape (*or* sarape)

[2]**cape** *n* an area of land that juts out into a body of water ⟨residents fled the *cape* as the hurricane roared up the coast⟩

synonyms arm, headland, peninsula, point, promontory, spit

related words breakwater, jetty

caper *n* a playful or mischievous act intended as a joke — see PRANK

caper *vb* to play and run about happily — see FROLIC 1

capital *adj* of the very best kind — see EXCELLENT

capital *n* **1** a thing or place that is of greatest importance to an activity or interest — see CENTER 1

2 the total of one's money and property — see WEALTH

capitalize *vb* to provide money for — see FINANCE 1

capitalize (on) *vb* to take unfair advantage of — see EXPLOIT 1

capitol *n* the building in which a state legislature meets ⟨the legislators were called to the *capitol* for an emergency session⟩

synonyms state house

related words meetinghouse; chamber, hall

capitulate *vb* **1** to cease resistance (as to another's arguments, demands, or control) — see YIELD 3

2 to yield to the control or power of enemy forces — see FALL 2

capitulating *n* the usually forced yielding of one's person or possessions to the control of another — see SURRENDER

capitulation *n* the usually forced yielding of one's person or possessions to the control of another — see SURRENDER

caprice *n* a sudden impulsive and apparently unmotivated idea or action — see WHIM

capricious *adj* **1** likely to change frequently, suddenly, or unexpectedly — see FICKLE 1

2 prone to sudden illogical changes of mind, ideas, or actions — see WHIMSICAL

capriciousness *n* an inclination to sudden illogical changes of mind, ideas, or actions — see WHIMSICALITY

capsize *vb* to turn on one's side or upside down ⟨a huge wave out of nowhere caused our little sailboat to *capsize*⟩

synonyms overturn, upset

related words invert, topple; keel over; heel, list, tilt; founder, sink, swamp

phrases turn turtle

antonyms right

capsule *n* **1** a small mass containing medicine to be taken orally — see PILL

2 something that encloses another thing especially to protect it — see [1]CASE 1

captain *n* **1** a person in overall command of a ship ⟨the *captain* is responsible for everything that happens to his ship in the course of a voyage⟩

synonyms commander, skipper

related words master; commanding officer; admiral, commodore, vice admiral

2 one in official command especially of a military force or base — see COMMANDER 1

3 the person (as an employer or supervisor) who tells people and especially workers what to do — see BOSS

captain *vb* **1** to be in charge of — see BOSS 1

2 to exercise authority or power over — see GOVERN 1

3 to serve as leader of — see LEAD 2

caption *n* **1** an explanation or description accompanying a pictorial illustration ⟨for the school yearbook, funny *captions* were written for snapshots showing a typical day at school⟩

synonyms legend

related words key; subtitle, translation; motto, tag line

2 a word or series of words often in larger letters placed at the beginning of a passage or at the top of a page in order to introduce or categorize — see HEADING

captious *adj* given to making or expressing unfavorable judgments about things — see CRITICAL 1

captivate *vb* to attract or delight as if by magic — see CHARM 1

captivating *adj* having an often mysterious or magical power to attract — see FASCINATING 1

captivation *n* the power of irresistible attraction — see CHARM 2

captive *adj* taken and held prisoner ⟨the *captive* soldiers were treated humanely by the guards⟩

synonyms apprehended, arrested, captured, caught, imprisoned, incarcerated, interned, jailed

related words bound, enslaved, indentured; subdued, subjugated

near antonyms emancipated, enfranchised, freed, liberated, released

antonyms free

captive *n* one that has been taken and held in confinement ⟨the *captives* in the concentration camp had devised a daring plan of escape⟩

synonyms capture, internee, prisoner

related words convict, jailbird; parolee

near antonyms custodian, guard, guardian, jailer (*or* jailor), keeper, warden

antonyms captor

captivity *n* the act of confining or the state of being confined — see INTERNMENT

capture *n* one that has been taken and held in confinement — see CAPTIVE

capture *vb* **1** to receive as return for effort — see EARN 1

2 to take physical control or possession of (something) suddenly or forcibly — see CATCH 1

captured *adj* taken and held prisoner — see CAPTIVE

car *n* a self-propelled passenger vehicle on wheels ⟨every teenager's dream of getting a driver's license and a first *car*⟩

synonyms auto, automobile, machine, motor, motorcar, motor vehicle

related words bus, coach, minibus; beach buggy, brougham, compact, convertible, coupe, dune buggy, fastback, gas-guzzler, hardtop, hatchback, hot rod, jeep, limousine, roadster, sedan, sports car, station wagon, stock car, subcompact, van; flivver, jalopy

caravan *n* **1** a group of vehicles traveling together or under one management — see FLEET

2 a motor vehicle that is specially equipped for living while traveling — see CAMPER

caravansary *or* **caravanserai** *n* a place that provides rooms and usually a public dining room for overnight guests — see HOTEL

carbon copy *n* **1** something or someone that strongly resembles another — see IMAGE 1

2 something that is made to look exactly like something else — see COPY

carcass *n* a dead body — see CORPSE

card *n* a person (as a writer) noted for or specializing in humor — see HUMORIST

cardinal *adj* coming before all others in importance — see FOREMOST 1

care *n* **1** strict attentiveness to what one is doing <that's an extremely valuable violin, so handle it with *care*>

synonyms carefulness, conscientiousness, heed, heedfulness, pains, scrupulousness

related words exactness, meticulousness, particularity, punctiliousness; dutifulness, responsibility; bother, effort, trouble; alertness, vigilance, watchfulness

antonyms carelessness, heedlessness

2 a close attentiveness to avoiding danger — see CAUTION 1

3 an uneasy state of mind usually over the possibility of an anticipated misfortune or trouble — see ANXIETY 1

4 responsibility for the safety and well-being of someone or something — see CUSTODY

5 the duty or function of watching or guarding for the sake of proper direction or control — see SUPERVISION 1

care *vb* to have an interest or concern for <a teacher who *cares* what happens to her students long after they leave her classroom>

synonyms mind, watch

related words attend, heed, regard; note, notice, observe; empathize (with), feel (for), sympathize (with)

phrases look out for

near antonyms disregard, ignore, overlook

care (for) *vb* **1** to take charge of especially on behalf of another — see [2]TEND 1

2 to attend to the needs and comforts of — see NURSE 1

3 to have a favorable opinion of — see APPROVE (OF)

4 to wish to have — see LIKE 1

careen *vb* **1** to make a series of unsteady side-to-side motions — see ROCK 1

2 to move forward while swaying from side to side — see STAGGER 1

career *vb* to proceed or move quickly — see HURRY 2

carefree *adj* having or showing a lack of concern or seriousness <passengers on a luxury cruise ship enjoying a *carefree* vacation> <*carefree* college students on spring break>

synonyms careless, cavalier, devil-may-care, easygoing, gay, happy-go-lucky, insouciant, lighthearted, unconcerned

related words breezy, nonchalant; casual, informal, laid-back, low-pressure, relaxed; heedless, irresponsible, lackadaisical, negligent, reckless

near antonyms earnest, grave, serious, somber (*or* sombre); careful, cautious, heedful, wary; concerned, upset, worried; long-suffering, overburdened, sorrowful

antonyms careworn

careful *adj* **1** having or showing a close attentiveness to avoiding danger or trouble <*careful* drivers slow down on slick or icy roadways>

synonyms alert, cautious, circumspect, considerate, gingerly, guarded, heedful, safe, wary

related words attentive, chary, observant, vigilant, watchful; foresighted, forethoughtful, provident; cagey (*also* cagy), noncommittal; calculating, scheming, shrewd; considerate, thoughtful; deliberate, slow

near antonyms bold, impetuous, rash, reckless; inattentive, unobservant; inconsiderate, thoughtless; lax, neglectful, negligent; imprudent, indiscreet, injudicious

antonyms careless, heedless, incautious, unguarded, unsafe, unwary

2 taking great care and effort — see PAINSTAKING

carefulness *n* **1** a close attentiveness to avoiding danger — see CAUTION 1

2 strict attentiveness to what one is doing — see CARE 1

careless *adj* **1** not paying or showing close attention especially for the purpose of avoiding trouble <a *careless* reporter who often doesn't get his facts straight> <a *careless* mistake that caused the plane to crash>

synonyms heedless, incautious, mindless, unguarded, unsafe, unwary

related words bold, impetuous, rash, reckless; inattentive, unobservant; blithe, inconsiderate, thoughtless; absentminded, forgetful, unmindful; lax, neglectful, negligent, remiss; imprudent, indiscreet, injudicious; inadvertent, unintentional, unplanned

near antonyms attentive, chary, observant, vigilant, watchful; foresighted, forethoughtful, provident; calculating, scheming, shrewd; considerate, thoughtful

antonyms alert, cautious, circumspect, gingerly, guarded, heedful, safe, wary

2 failing to give proper care and attention — see NEGLIGENT

3 having or showing a lack of concern or seriousness — see CAREFREE

carelessness *n* failure to take the care that a cautious person usually takes — see NEGLIGENCE 1

caress *vb* to touch or handle in a tender or loving manner — see FONDLE

caretaker *n* a person who takes care of a property sometimes for an absent owner — see CUSTODIAN 1

cargo *n* a mass or quantity of something taken up and carried, conveyed, or transported — see LOAD 1

caricature *n* **1** a poor, insincere, or insulting imitation of something — see MOCKERY 1

2 a work that imitates and exaggerates another work for comic effect — see PARODY 1

3 the representation of something in terms that go beyond the facts — see EXAGGERATION

caricature *vb* to copy or exaggerate (someone or something) in order to make fun of — see MIMIC 1

carnage *n* the killing of a large number of people — see MASSACRE

carnal *adj* **1** having to do with life on earth especially as opposed to that in heaven — see EARTHLY

2 of or relating to the human body — see PHYSICAL 1

3 pleasing to the physical senses — see SENSUAL

carnival *n* a time or program of special events and entertainment in honor of something — see FESTIVAL

carol *n* a religious song — see HYMN

carol *vb* to produce musical sounds with the voice — see SING 1

caroler *or* **caroller** *n* one who sings — see SINGER

carom *vb* to strike and fly off at an angle — see GLANCE 1

carousal *n* a bout of drinking — see CAROUSE

carouse *n* a bout of drinking ⟨the Old West custom of heading to the saloon at night for a *carouse* and some poker playing⟩
synonyms carousal, drunk, wassail
related words binge, jag, spree; blowout, orgy

carp *vb* **1** to express dissatisfaction, pain, or resentment usually tiresomely — see COMPLAIN
2 to make often peevish criticisms or objections about matters that are minor, unimportant, or irrelevant — see QUIBBLE

carper *n* a person given to harsh judgments and to finding faults — see CRITIC 1

carpet *vb* to form a layer over — see COVER 2

carping *adj* given to making or expressing unfavorable judgments about things — see CRITICAL 1

carriage *n* **1** a horse-drawn wheeled vehicle for carrying passengers ⟨a museum with a large collection of beautiful, old *carriages*⟩
synonyms equipage, rig
related words brougham, buckboard, cab, chaise, coach, hackney, hansom, surrey
2 a general way of holding the body — see POSTURE 1

carry *vb* **1** to support and take from one place to another ⟨each camper must be able to *carry* his or her own backpack⟩
synonyms bear, cart, convey, ferry, haul, lug, pack, tote, transport
related words deliver, hand over, transfer; forward, send, ship, transmit; bring, fetch, take; move, remove, shift
2 to wear or have on one's person ⟨I always *carry* a camera with me so as to never miss a great shot⟩
synonyms bear, pack
related words flaunt, show off, sport; display, exhibit, parade, show
3 to bring before the public in performance or exhibition — see PRESENT 1
4 to have as part of a whole — see INCLUDE
5 to hold up or serve as a foundation for — see SUPPORT 3
6 to receive as return for effort — see EARN 1

carryall *n* a bag carried by hand and designed to hold a traveler's clothing and personal articles — see TRAVELING BAG

carry away *vb* **1** to fill with overwhelming emotion (as wonder or delight) — see ENTRANCE
2 to subject to incapacitating emotional or mental stress — see OVERWHELM 1

carry on *vb* **1** to behave badly — see MISBEHAVE
2 to continue despite difficulties, opposition, or discouragement — see PERSEVERE
3 to look after and make decisions about — see CONDUCT 1

carry out *vb* to carry through (as a process) to completion — see PERFORM 1

cart *n* a wheeled usually horse-drawn vehicle used for hauling ⟨an old *cart* piled up with hay⟩
synonyms wagon, wain
related words barrow, pushcart, wheelbarrow; oxcart

cart *vb* to support and take from one place to another — see CARRY 1

cartel *n* a number of businesses or enterprises united for commercial advantage ⟨a *cartel* of oil-producing nations that controls production and influences prices⟩
synonyms combination, combine, syndicate, trust
related words chain, conglomerate, multinational; association, organization, pool

cartoon *n* **1** a picture using lines to represent the chief features of an object or scene — see DRAWING
2 a series of drawings that tell a story or part of a story — see COMIC STRIP

carve *vb* to create a three-dimensional representation of (something) using solid material — see SCULPT

carve (out) *vb* to produce or bring about especially by long or repeated effort — see HAMMER (OUT)

cascade *n* a fall of water usually from a great height — see WATERFALL

[1]**case** *n* **1** something that encloses another thing especially to protect it ⟨those binoculars come with their own *case*⟩
synonyms armor, capsule, casing, cocoon, cover, covering, housing, husk, jacket, pod, sheath, shell
related words bark, crust; mail, plate, plating, shield; hide, skin; envelope, wrapper; backing, coating, facing
2 a covered rectangular container for storing or transporting things — see CHEST

[2]**case** *n* **1** an individual awaiting or under medical care and treatment — see PATIENT
2 one of a group or collection that shows what the whole is like — see EXAMPLE
3 something that actually exists — see FACT 2
4 a statement given to explain a belief or act — see REASON 1
5 a sudden experiencing of a physical or mental disorder — see ATTACK 2
6 something that might happen — see EVENT 2
7 something that requires thought and skill for resolution — see PROBLEM 1

cash *n* something (as pieces of stamped metal or printed paper) customarily and legally used as a medium of exchange, a measure of value, or a means of payment — see MONEY

cashier *vb* to let go from office, service, or employment — see DISMISS 1

cash in (on) *vb* to take unfair advantage of — see EXPLOIT 1

casing *n* something that encloses another thing especially to protect it — see [1]CASE 1

cask *n* an enclosed wooden vessel for holding beverages ⟨*casks* of wine that had been in the castle for many years⟩
synonyms barrel, firkin, hogshead, keg, pipe, puncheon
related words tub, vat; can, drum

casket *n* **1** a box for holding a dead body — see COFFIN
2 a covered rectangular container for storing or transporting things — see CHEST

cast *n* **1** a declaration that something will happen in the future — see PREDICTION
2 a property that becomes apparent when light falls on an object and by which things that are identical in form can be distinguished — see COLOR 1
3 an instance of looking especially briefly — see LOOK 2

4 facial appearance regarded as an indication of mood or feeling — see LOOK 1
5 the outward appearance of something as distinguished from its substance — see FORM 1
cast *vb* **1** to get rid of as useless or unwanted — see DISCARD
2 to point or turn (something) toward a target or goal — see AIM 1
3 to put (something) into proper and usually carefully worked out written form — see COMPOSE 1
4 to send through the air especially with a quick forward motion of the arm — see THROW
cast (off) *vb* to throw or give off — see EMIT 1
cast (out) *vb* to drive or force out — see EJECT 1
cast about (for) *vb* to go in search of — see SEEK 1
cast around (for) *vb* to go in search of — see SEEK 1
castaway *n* one who is cast out or rejected by society — see OUTCAST
caste *n* one of the segments of society into which people are grouped — see CLASS 1
castigate *vb* **1** to criticize (someone) severely or angrily especially for personal failings — see SCOLD
2 to criticize harshly and usually publicly — see ATTACK 2
3 to inflict a penalty on for a fault or crime — see PUNISH
castigating *adj* inflicting, involving, or serving as punishment — see PUNITIVE
castigation *n* suffering, loss, or hardship imposed in response to a crime or offense — see PUNISHMENT
castigator *n* **1** a person given to harsh judgments and to finding faults — see CRITIC 1
2 one who inflicts punishment in return for an injury or offense — see NEMESIS 1
castle *n* a large impressive residence — see MANSION
castoff *n* one who is cast out or rejected by society — see OUTCAST
casual *adj* **1** not designed for special occasions <a restaurant where people in *casual* clothes are always welcome>
synonyms everyday, informal, workaday
related words sporty; shabby, sloppy, slovenly, unkempt
near antonyms best, Sunday; chic, elegant, fashionable, smart, stylish; neat, tidy, trim; semiformal
antonyms dressy, formal
2 happening by chance — see ACCIDENTAL
3 having or showing a lack of interest or concern — see INDIFFERENT 1
4 lacking in steadiness or regularity of occurrence — see FITFUL
casualness *n* lack of interest or concern — see INDIFFERENCE
casualty *n* **1** a person or thing harmed, lost, or destroyed <the real *casualties* in the war against drugs are millions of innocent children>
synonyms fatality, loss, victim
related words failure, loser
near antonyms gainer, victor, winner
2 a chance and usually sudden event bringing loss or injury — see ACCIDENT 1
cat *n* **1** a small domestic animal known for catching mice <the family's *cat* did a good job of keeping the house and yard free of all rodents>
synonyms feline, house cat, kitty, puss, pussy
related words mouser; kit, kitten; tabby, tomcat
2 *slang* an adult male human being — see MAN 1
cataclysm *n* **1** a great flow of water or of something that overwhelms — see FLOOD
2 a sudden violent event that brings about great loss or destruction — see DISASTER
3 a violent disturbance (as of the political or social order) — see CONVULSION
cataclysmal *or* **cataclysmic** *adj* **1** bringing about ruin or misfortune — see FATAL 1
2 causing or tending to cause destruction — see DESTRUCTIVE 1
3 marked by sudden or violent disturbance — see CONVULSIVE
catacomb *n, usually* **catacombs** *pl* an underground burial chamber — see CRYPT
catalog *or* **catalogue** *n* a record of a series of items (as names or titles) usually arranged according to some system — see [1]LIST
catalog *or* **catalogue** *vb* to put (someone or something) on a list — see [1]LIST 2
catamount *n* a large tawny cat of the wild — see COUGAR
catapult *vb* to send through the air especially with a quick forward motion of the arm — see THROW
cataract *n* **1** a fall of water usually from a great height — see WATERFALL
2 a great flow of water or of something that overwhelms — see FLOOD
catastrophe *n* **1** a sudden violent event that brings about great loss or destruction — see DISASTER
2 something that has failed — see FAILURE 3
catastrophic *adj* bringing about ruin or misfortune — see FATAL 1
catcall *n* a vocal sound made to express scorn or disapproval <the band's sloppy playing produced only *catcalls* from the crowd>
synonyms boo, hiss, hoot, jeer, raspberry, snort
related words smirk, sneer, snicker, snigger; gibe (*or* jibe), put-down, taunt; whistle
near antonyms applause, clapping
antonyms cheer
catch *n* **1** a danger or difficulty that is hidden or not easily recognized — see PITFALL 1
2 someone or something unusually desirable — see PRIZE 1
3 the total amount collected or obtained especially at one time — see HAUL 1
catch *vb* **1** to take physical control or possession of (something) suddenly or forcibly <we tried to *catch* the kitten before she could sneak out the door>
synonyms bag, capture, collar, corral, get, grab, grapple, hook, land, nab, nail, seize, snap (up), snare, snatch, trap
related words lasso, rope; apprehend, arrest, detain; clasp, clutch, grasp, grip, hold, secure; rend, wrest; ensnare, entangle, entrap; abduct, kidnap, spirit (away *or* off)
phrases lay hold of
near antonyms discharge, free, liberate, release; drop, loosen
antonyms miss
2 to become affected with (a disease or disorder) — see CONTRACT 1
3 to bring (something) to a standstill — see [1]HALT 1
4 to put securely in place or in a desired position — see FASTEN 2

5 to recognize the meaning of — see COMPREHEND 1

catching *adj* **1** capable of being passed by physical contact from one person to another — see CONTAGIOUS 1
2 exciting a similar feeling or reaction in others — see CONTAGIOUS 2

catch on *vb* to come to an awareness — see DISCOVER 1

catch on (to) *vb* to recognize the meaning of — see COMPREHEND 1

catch up (with) *vb* to move fast enough to get even with — see OVERTAKE

catchy *adj* **1** likely to attract attention — see NOTICEABLE
2 requiring exceptional skill or caution in performance or handling — see TRICKY

categorical *also* **categoric** *adj* having no exceptions or restrictions — see ABSOLUTE 2

categorize *vb* to arrange or assign according to type — see CLASSIFY 1

category *n* one of the units into which a whole is divided on the basis of a common characteristic — see CLASS 2

cater *vb* to provide food or meals for — see FEED 1

cater (to) *vb* to give in to (a desire) — see INDULGE

catnap *n* a short sleep — see [1]NAP

catnap *vb* **1** be in a state of sleep — see SLEEP 1
2 to sleep lightly or briefly — see NAP 1

catnapping *n* a natural periodic loss of consciousness during which the body restores itself — see SLEEP 1

cattily *adv* in a mean or spiteful manner — see NASTILY

cattiness *n* **1** biting sharpness of feeling or expression — see ACRIMONY 1
2 the desire to cause pain for the satisfaction of doing harm — see MALICE

catty *adj* having or showing a desire to cause someone pain or suffering for the sheer enjoyment of it — see HATEFUL

caught *adj* taken and held prisoner — see CAPTIVE

cause *n* **1** someone or something responsible for a result ⟨the much-debated *causes* of the American Civil War⟩
synonyms antecedent, occasion, reason
related words consideration, determinant, factor; impetus, incentive, inspiration, instigation, stimulus; mother, origin, root, source, spring
near antonyms ramification; denouement, repercussion; conclusion, end; by-product, side effect
antonyms aftereffect, aftermath, consequence, corollary, development, effect, fate, fruit, issue, outcome, outgrowth, product, result, resultant, sequel, sequence, upshot
2 a series of activities undertaken to achieve a goal — see CAMPAIGN

cause *vb* to be the cause of (a situation, action, or state of mind) — see EFFECT

caustic *adj* marked by the use of wit that is intended to cause hurt feelings — see SARCASTIC

caution *n* **1** a close attentiveness to avoiding danger ⟨the extreme *caution* with which the zookeeper handled the snake⟩
synonyms alertness, care, carefulness, cautiousness, circumspection, heedfulness, wariness
related words attentiveness, chariness, vigilance, watchfulness; foresight, foresightedness, providence; calculation, canniness, deliberateness, deliberation, shrewdness
near antonyms abruptness, hastiness, impetuousness, precipitousness, rashness, suddenness; inconsideration, thoughtlessness
antonyms brashness, carelessness, heedlessness, incautiousness, recklessness, unwariness
2 something extraordinary or surprising — see WONDER 1
3 something that tells of approaching danger or risk — see WARNING 2
4 the act or an instance of telling beforehand of danger or risk — see WARNING 1

caution *vb* to give notice to beforehand especially of danger or risk — see WARN

cautionary *adj* serving as or offering a warning ⟨the story of King Midas is a *cautionary* tale about the perils of wishing for something—you just might get it⟩
synonyms admonishing, admonitory, cautioning, warning
related words didactic, moralistic, moralizing; advisory, counseling (*or* counselling); punishing, punitive

cautioning *adj* serving as or offering a warning — see CAUTIONARY

cautious *adj* having or showing a close attentiveness to avoiding danger or trouble — see CAREFUL 1

cautiousness *n* a close attentiveness to avoiding danger — see CAUTION 1

cavalcade *n* **1** a group of vehicles traveling together or under one management — see FLEET
2 a staged presentation often with music that consists of a procession of narrated or enacted scenes — see PAGEANT

cavalier *adj* **1** having a feeling of superiority that shows itself in an overbearing attitude — see ARROGANT
2 having or showing a lack of concern or seriousness — see CAREFREE

cavalier *n* an honorable and courteous man ⟨a novel about the dashing *cavaliers* and gracious ladies of the South before the Civil War⟩
synonyms gentleman
related words knight, prince; blade, buck, dandy, fop, gallant; charmer, smoothy (*or* smoothie); aristocrat, patrician

cave *n* a naturally formed underground chamber with an opening to the surface ⟨Kentucky's Mammoth *Cave* is actually a series of large chambers on five levels⟩
synonyms cavern, grot, grotto
related words abyss, chasm, gulf, hollow; subway, tunnel; excavation, mine, pit, shaft, well; bunker, dugout, foxhole; burrow, covert, den, hole, lair, lodge, shelter

cave (in) *vb* to fall down or in as a result of physical pressure — see COLLAPSE 1

cavern *n* a naturally formed underground chamber with an opening to the surface — see CAVE

cavil *vb* to make often peevish criticisms or objections about matters that are minor, unimportant, or irrelevant — see QUIBBLE

caviler *or* **caviller** *n* a person given to harsh judgments and to finding faults — see CRITIC 1

caviling *or* **cavilling** *adj* given to making or expressing unfavorable judgments about things — see CRITICAL 1

cavity *n* a sunken area forming a separate space — see HOLE 2

cavort *vb* to play and run about happily — see FROLIC 1
cease *vb* **1** to come to an end <the rain finally *ceased*, and we were able to continue the baseball game>
synonyms break off, break up, close, conclude, die, discontinue, elapse, end, expire, finish, halt, lapse, leave off, let up, pass, quit, stop, terminate, wind up
related words desist (from), lay off (of), refrain (from); knock off; break down, conk (out), cut out, stall; pause, stay, suspend
near antonyms draw out, extend, prolong, protract
antonyms continue, hang on, persist
2 to bring (as an action or operation) to an immediate end — see STOP 1
cease–fire *n* a temporary stopping of fighting — see TRUCE
ceaseless *adj* **1** going on and on without any interruptions — see CONTINUOUS
2 lasting forever — see EVERLASTING
cede *vb* **1** to give (something) over to the control or possession of another usually under duress — see SURRENDER 1
2 to give over the legal possession or ownership of — see TRANSFER 1
3 to give up (as a position of authority) formally — see ABDICATE
ceiling *n* **1** a real or imaginary point beyond which a person or thing cannot go — see LIMIT
2 a raised covering over something for decoration or protection — see CANOPY
celebrant *n* one who engages in merrymaking especially in honor of a special occasion <all of the *celebrants* at the birthday party received a favor to take home>
synonyms celebrator, merrymaker, reveler (*or* reveller), roisterer
related words carouser, wassailer; cutup, skylarker
antonyms killjoy, party pooper
celebrate *vb* to act properly in relation to — see KEEP 1
celebrated *adj* widely known — see FAMOUS
celebration *n* a time or program of special events and entertainment in honor of something — see FESTIVAL
celebrator *n* one who engages in merrymaking especially in honor of a special occasion — see CELEBRANT
celebrity *n* **1** a person who is widely known and usually much talked about <*celebrities* from sports and entertainment attended the opening ceremonies of the Olympic Games>
synonyms figure, light, luminary, notable, personage, personality, somebody, standout, star, superstar, VIP
related words favorite, hero, idol; demigod, dignitary, eminence, immortal, pillar, worthy; baron, big shot, bigwig, magnate, mogul, nabob
near antonyms lightweight, mediocrity; has-been
antonyms nobody
2 the fact or state of being known to the public — see FAME
celerity *n* a high rate of movement or performance — see SPEED
celestial *adj* of, relating to, or suggesting heaven <movie scenes depicting life after death are usually accompanied by *celestial* music>
synonyms Elysian, empyreal, empyrean, heavenly, supernal
related words ethereal, supernatural, transcendent, transcendental, unearthly, unworldly; angelic, beatific, blissful; Olympian, utopian; cosmic, stellar
near antonyms earthly, mundane, terrestrial, worldly
antonyms hellish, infernal
cell *n* **1** an area within a building that has been set apart from surrounding space by a wall — see ROOM 2
2 one of the parts into which an enclosed space is divided — see COMPARTMENT
cellar *n* a room or set of rooms below the surface of the ground <an amazing variety of interesting things were found in the *cellar* of the old house>
synonyms basement
related words bunker, crawlway, foundation, hold
cement *n* **1** a substance used to stick things together — see GLUE
2 a uniting or binding force or influence — see BOND 2
cemetery *n* a piece of land used for burying the dead <many of the soldiers who died in the battle are buried in a *cemetery* nearby>
synonyms graveyard, potter's field
related words catacombs, churchyard; crypt, grave, mausoleum, sepulcher (*or* sepulchre), sepulture, tomb, vault
censor *vb* to remove objectionable parts from <the producers were told that they would have to *censor* their movie if they wanted a PG rating>
synonyms clean (up), expurgate
related words cleanse, purge, purify; abbreviate, edit, shorten; cut (out), delete, excise, expunge; repress, silence, suppress; censure, condemn, denounce; examine, review, screen, scrutinize
near antonyms approve, authorize, sanction
censurable *adj* **1** deserving reproach or blame — see BLAMEWORTHY
2 provoking or likely to provoke protest — see OBJECTIONABLE
censure *n* an often public or formal expression of disapproval <a rare *censure* of a senator by the full United States Senate for misconduct>
synonyms condemnation, denunciation, rebuke, reprimand, reproach, reproof, stricture
related words admonishment, admonition, castigation, chastisement, punishment; belittlement, criticism, deprecation, depreciation, disparagement
near antonyms acclamation, honor, tribute; encomium, eulogy, panegyric, plaudit(s), praise; approval, blessing, sanction
antonyms citation, commendation, endorsement
censure *vb* **1** to express public or formal disapproval of <a vote to *censure* the President for conduct that was unbecoming to his office>
synonyms condemn, denounce, rebuke, reprimand, reproach, reprove
related words admonish, castigate, chastise, punish; belittle, criticize, deprecate, depreciate, disparage
near antonyms acclaim, applause, honor; eulogize, laud, praise; approve, bless, sanction
antonyms cite, commend, endorse (*also* indorse)
2 to declare to be morally wrong or evil — see CONDEMN 1

3 to express one's unfavorable opinion of the worth or quality of — see CRITICIZE

censurer *n* a person given to harsh judgments and to finding faults — see CRITIC 1

center *n* **1** a thing or place that is of greatest importance to an activity or interest ⟨a stretch of coastline that has long been the area's *center* of tourism⟩
synonyms base, capital, core, cynosure, eye, focus, heart, hub, mecca, nucleus, seat
related words focus, headquarters; kernel, nub, pith; deep, thick; essence, quintessence, soul; attraction, lodestone, magnet
2 an area or point that is an equal distance from all points along an edge or outer surface ⟨the *center* of the earth⟩
synonyms core, middle, midpoint, midst
related words inside, interior
antonyms perimeter, periphery

center *vb* to bring (something) to a central point or under a single control — see CENTRALIZE

central *adj* coming before all others in importance — see FOREMOST 1

centralize *vb* to bring (something) to a central point or under a single control ⟨the company decided to *centralize* all of its operations at its Ohio plant⟩
synonyms center, compact, concentrate, consolidate, unify, unite
related words coordinate, harmonize, integrate, orchestrate; blend, coalesce, combine, fuse, incorporate, merge; conjoin, join, link; assemble, collect, gather; reunify, reunite
near antonyms segregate, separate
antonyms decentralize, spread (out)

cerebral *adj* **1** much given to learning and thinking — see INTELLECTUAL 1
2 of or relating to the mind — see MENTAL 1

cerebrum *n* the part of a person that feels, thinks, perceives, wills, and especially reasons — see MIND 1

ceremonial *adj* following or agreeing with established form, custom, or rules — see FORMAL 1

ceremonial *n* an oft-repeated action or series of actions performed in accordance with tradition or a set of rules — see RITE

ceremonious *adj* **1** marked by or showing careful attention to set forms and details ⟨a century ago everyday life was much more *ceremonious* than in our anything-goes era⟩
synonyms correct, decorous, formal, proper, starchy
related words sober, solemn, stately; chivalrous, courtly, gallant; genteel, polished, refined; civil, courteous, polite, red-carpet
near antonyms improper, indecorous, unmannerly; discourteous, impolite, rude
antonyms casual, easygoing, informal, laid-back
2 following or agreeing with established form, custom, or rules — see FORMAL 1

ceremony *n* an oft-repeated action or series of actions performed in accordance with tradition or a set of rules — see RITE

certain *adj* **1** known but not named ⟨a *certain* person told me that today is your birthday⟩
synonyms anonymous, one, some, unidentified, unnamed, unspecified
related words particular, specific
near antonyms known, named, specified
2 having or showing a mind free from doubt ⟨I'm *certain* that they'll arrive on time⟩
synonyms assured, clear, cocksure, confident, doubtless, positive, sanguine, sure
related words self-assured, self-conceited, self-confident; decisive, resolute, unfaltering, unhesitating, unwavering
near antonyms hesitant, indecisive, wavering; diffident, unassuming
antonyms doubtful, dubious, uncertain, unsure
3 having been established and usually not subject to change — see FIXED 1
4 impossible to avoid or evade — see INEVITABLE
5 not likely to fail — see INFALLIBLE 2

certainly *adv* without any question — see INDEED 1

certainty *n* a state of mind in which one is free from doubt — see CONFIDENCE 2

certificate *n* a written or printed paper giving information about or proof of something ⟨a *certificate* will be awarded to each person who completes the course in lifesaving⟩
synonyms document, instrument
related words credentials; diploma, parchment; warrant, writ; warranty; coupon, voucher

certify *vb* **1** to declare (something) to be true or genuine ⟨experts *certified* the letter as indeed having been written by Abraham Lincoln⟩
synonyms attest, authenticate, avouch, testify (to), vouch (for), witness
related words guarantee, warrant; affirm, assert, aver, avow, profess
2 to give official or legal power to — see AUTHORIZE 1

certitude *n* a state of mind in which one is free from doubt — see CONFIDENCE 2

cessation *n* the stopping of a process or activity — see END 1

chafe *vb* **1** to make sore by continued rubbing ⟨ill-fitting boots that had badly *chafed* my heels⟩
synonyms abrade, gall, irritate
related words graze, scrape, scratch; burn, inflame; flay, peel, skin
2 to damage or diminish by continued friction — see ABRADE 1
3 to disturb the peace of mind of (someone) especially by repeated disagreeable acts — see IRRITATE 1

chaff *n* **1** discarded or useless material — see GARBAGE
2 good-natured teasing or exchanging of clever remarks — see BANTER

chaff *vb* to make fun of in a good-natured way — see TEASE 1

chaffer *vb* to talk over or dispute the terms of a purchase — see BARGAIN

chaffing *adj* marked by or expressive of mild or good-natured teasing — see QUIZZICAL

chaffy *adj* having no usefulness — see WORTHLESS

chain *n* **1** a series of things linked together ⟨the *chain* of events that led the American colonies to seek independence from Great Britain⟩
synonyms concatenation, progression, sequence, string, train
related words chain reaction; belt, circle, cycle; continuum, gamut, scale, spectrum; flow, river, stream; file, line, queue, row, succession
2 something that makes movement or progress more difficult — see ENCUMBRANCE

3 something that physically prevents free movement — see BOND 1

chain *vb* **1** to confine or restrain with or as if with chains — see BIND 1
2 to put or bring together so as to form a new and longer whole — see CONNECT 1

chair *n* **1** a person in charge of a meeting ⟨all questions and comments should be directed to the *chair*⟩
synonyms chairman, chairperson, moderator, president, speaker
related words chairwoman
2 the place of leadership or command — see HEAD 2

chairman *n* a person in charge of a meeting — see CHAIR 1

chairperson *n* a person in charge of a meeting — see CHAIR 1

chalet *n* an often small house for recreational or seasonal use — see COTTAGE

challenge *n* a feeling or declaration of disapproval or dissent — see OBJECTION

challenge *vb* **1** to demand proof of the truth or rightness of ⟨don't hesitate to *challenge* any statement that generalizes about people⟩
synonyms contest, dispute, query, question
related words doubt, mistrust; kick (about), object (to), protest; combat, fight, oppose, resist
near antonyms back, defend, support; advocate, champion, promote; abide, endure, stomach, tolerate
antonyms accept, believe, embrace, swallow
2 to invite (someone) to take part in a contest or to perform a feat ⟨I *challenge* you to swim to the other side of the pond⟩
synonyms dare, defy, stump
related words beard, brave, brazen, breast, confront, face, outbrave

challenged *adj* deprived of the power to perform one or more natural bodily activities — see DISABLED

challenger *n* one who strives for the same thing as another — see COMPETITOR

challenging *adj* requiring much time, effort, or careful attention — see DEMANDING 1

chamber *n* **1** an area within a building that has been set apart from surrounding space by a wall — see ROOM 2
2 one of the parts into which an enclosed space is divided — see COMPARTMENT

chamber *vb* to provide with living quarters or shelter — see HOUSE 1

champ *n* the person who comes in first in a competition — see CHAMPION 1

champ *vb* to crush or grind with the teeth — see BITE (ON)

champion *n* **1** the person who comes in first in a competition ⟨the *champion* of the national spelling bee⟩
synonyms champ, victor, winner
related words finalist, semifinalist; medalist, prizewinner; star, superstar
near antonyms loser
2 a person who actively supports or favors a cause — see EXPONENT

champion *vb* to promote the interests or cause of — see SUPPORT 1

championship *n* the position occupied by the one who comes in first in a competition — see CROWN 2

chance *adj* happening by chance — see ACCIDENTAL

chance *n* **1** the uncertain course of events ⟨rather than leave everything to *chance*, let's plan how we're going to spend our time in New York City⟩
synonyms accident, circumstance, hap, hazard, luck
related words fortuitousness, randomness, uncertainty; fluke; destiny, doom, fate, fortune, lot; danger, peril, risk
near antonyms intent, intention, purpose; design, outline, plan, scheme
2 a favorable combination of circumstances, time, and place — see OPPORTUNITY
3 a measure of how often an event will occur instead of another — see PROBABILITY 2
4 a risky undertaking — see GAMBLE

chance *vb* **1** to take a chance on — see RISK 1
2 to take place — see HAPPEN

chance (upon) *vb* **1** to come upon face-to-face or as if face-to-face — see MEET
2 to come upon unexpectedly or by chance — see HAPPEN (ON *OR* UPON)

change *n* the act, process, or result of making different ⟨the positive *change* in our students' attitude toward people who are somehow different was a long and gradual process⟩
synonyms alteration, difference, modification, redoing, refashioning, remaking, remodeling, revamping, revise, revision, reworking, variation
related words amendment, correction, rectification; conversion, deformation, distortion, metamorphosis, mutation, transfiguration, transformation; fluctuation, oscillation, shift; displacement, replacement, substitution; adjustment, modulation, regulation
antonyms fixation, stabilization

change *vb* **1** to make different in some way ⟨Mother has *changed* the look of our living room more times than we care to remember⟩
synonyms alter, make over, modify, recast, redo, refashion, remake, remodel, revamp, revise, rework, vary
related words deform, metamorphose, mutate; revolutionize, transfigure, transform, transmute; commute, convert, exchange
antonyms fix, freeze, set, stabilize
2 to pass from one form, state, or level to another ⟨the weather in New England is constantly *changing*⟩
synonyms fluctuate, mutate, shift, vary
related words metamorphose, transmute; better, improve; deteriorate, worsen; seesaw, teeter, vacillate, waver
antonyms stabilize
3 to give up (something) and take something else in return ⟨would you mind *changing* your seat so my friends can sit together?⟩
synonyms commute, exchange, shift, substitute, swap, switch, trade
related words interchange; displace, replace, supersede; cede, surrender, yield

changeable *adj* **1** capable of being readily changed — see FLEXIBLE 1
2 likely to change frequently, suddenly, or unexpectedly — see FICKLE 1

changeful *adj* likely to change frequently, suddenly, or unexpectedly — see FICKLE 1

changeless *adj* not undergoing a change in condition — see CONSTANT 1

changelessness *n* the state of continuing without change — see CONSTANCY 1

changeover *n* a change in form, appearance, or use — see CONVERSION

changing *adj* not staying constant — see UNEVEN 2

channel *n* **1** an open man-made passageway for water ⟨water was drained from the swamp through a specially constructed *channel*⟩

synonyms aqueduct, canal, conduit, flume, raceway, watercourse, waterway

related words millrace, millstream; river, rivulet, stream

2 a narrow body of water between two land masses ⟨the world record for swimming the *channel* between France and Great Britain⟩

synonyms narrows, sound, strait

related words arm, bay, gulf, inlet; roads, roadstead; reach, stretch

3 a direct way of passing along information or supplies — see PIPELINE

4 a long hollow cylinder for carrying a substance (as a liquid or gas) — see PIPE 1

channel *vb* to cause to move to a central point or along a restricted pathway ⟨an athletic youth who *channeled* all of his energy into sports⟩

synonyms channelize, conduct, direct, funnel, pipe, siphon

related words carry, convey, transmit; concentrate, consolidate, focus

channelize *vb* to cause to move to a central point or along a restricted pathway — see CHANNEL

chant *vb* **1** to utter in musical or drawn out tones ⟨the frustrated crowd at the rock concert started to *chant*, "We want the show to start!"⟩

synonyms intone, sing

related words bellow, belt, roar; chime, chorus

2 to produce musical sounds with the voice — see SING 1

chaos *n* a state in which everything is out of order ⟨your room is in such *chaos* that it looks as though a tornado had struck⟩

synonyms confusion, disarrangement, disarray, disorder, disorganization, havoc, hell, jumble, mess, muddle, shambles

related words anarchy, lawlessness, misrule; knot, snarl, tangle; labyrinth, maze, web; maelstrom, storm; clutter, litter, mishmash, shuffle; hodgepodge, medley, miscellany, motley

near antonyms method, pattern, plan, system

antonyms order, orderliness

chaotic *adj* lacking in order, neatness, and often cleanliness — see MESSY

chap *n, chiefly British* an adult male human being — see MAN 1

chaparral *n* a thick patch of shrubbery, small trees, or underbrush — see THICKET

chaperone *or* **chaperon** *vb* to go along with in order to provide assistance, protection, or companionship — see ACCOMPANY

chapter *n* a local unit of an organization ⟨our *chapter* of the 4-H Club came in first in the competition⟩

synonyms affiliate, branch, local

related words arm, division, wing; offshoot; lodge, post

char *vb* to burn on the surface — see SCORCH

character *n* **1** a written or printed mark that is meant to convey information to the reader ⟨the pictorial *characters* of the ancient Egyptians were long a mystery⟩

synonyms sign, symbol

related words cipher, letter, numeral; hieroglyph, pictogram, pictograph; rune

2 a person of odd or whimsical habits — see ECCENTRIC

3 conduct that conforms to an accepted standard of right and wrong — see MORALITY 1

4 overall quality as seen or judged by people in general — see REPUTATION

5 something that sets apart an individual from others of the same kind — see CHARACTERISTIC

6 the set of qualities that make a person different from other people — see INDIVIDUALITY

7 the set of qualities that makes a person, a group of people, or a thing different from others — see NATURE 1

characteristic *adj* **1** serving to identify as belonging to an individual or group ⟨the *characteristic* taste of licorice⟩

synonyms classic, distinct, distinctive, distinguishing, identifying, individual, peculiar, proper, symptomatic, typical

related words idiosyncratic; identifiable, pronounced, unmistakable; general, generic; common, normal, regular, usual; particular, special, specific; archetypal, model, paradigmatic

antonyms atypical, nontypical

2 having or showing the qualities associated with the members of a particular group or kind — see TYPICAL 1

characteristic *n* something that sets apart an individual from others of the same kind ⟨the ability to fashion tools and other *characteristics* that distinguish human beings from other animals⟩

synonyms attribute, character, feature, mark, peculiarity, point, property, quality, trait

related words badge, indication, sign; emblem, symbol, token; excellence, merit, virtue; individuality, singularity, uniqueness

characterize *vb* **1** to point out the chief quality or qualities of an individual or group ⟨how would you *characterize* the mission of this environmental organization?⟩

synonyms define, depict, describe, portray, represent

related words categorize, classify, pigeonhole, type; identify, indicate, name, specify; distinguish, individualize, mark, particularize, stamp

2 to be an important feature of ⟨an unsightly rash *characterizes* chicken pox⟩

synonyms distinguish, mark

related words differentiate; customize, individualize, particularize

characterless *adj* lacking strength of will or character — see WEAK 2

charade *n* a display of emotion or behavior that is insincere or intended to deceive — see MASQUERADE

charge *n* **1** a formal claim of criminal wrongdoing against a person ⟨*charges* of burglary and armed robbery that have yet to be proved⟩

synonyms complaint, count, indictment, rap

related words accusation, allegation; arraignment, impeachment; implication, innuendo, insinuation; censure, condemnation, denunciation; incrimination

2 a specific task with which a person or group is charged — see MISSION

3 a statement of what to do that must be obeyed by those concerned — see COMMAND 1

4 something one must do because of prior agreement — see OBLIGATION
5 the act or action of setting upon with force or violence — see ATTACK 1
6 the amount of money that is demanded as payment for something — see PRICE 1
7 the duty or function of watching or guarding for the sake of proper direction or control — see SUPERVISION 1

charge *vb* **1** to set or receive as a price ⟨any shop would *charge* $100 to repair that thing⟩
synonyms ask, command, demand
related words overcharge, undercharge; bring, fetch, sell (for); discount, mark down, mark up; assess, price, value
2 to establish or apply as a charge or penalty — see IMPOSE
3 to give a task, duty, or responsibility to — see ENTRUST 1
4 to issue orders to (someone) by right of authority — see COMMAND 1
5 to make a claim of wrongdoing against — see ACCUSE
6 to put into (something) as much as can be held or contained — see FILL 1
7 to take sudden, violent action against — see ATTACK 1

charged *adj* having or expressing great depth of feeling — see FERVENT

charisma *n* the power of irresistible attraction — see CHARM 2

charitable *adj* **1** having or showing a concern for the welfare of others ⟨a *charitable* couple who have donated a sizable chunk of their fortune to the local university⟩
synonyms altruistic, beneficent, benevolent, humanitarian, philanthropic
related words selfless, self-sacrificing; bounteous, bountiful, free, freehanded, generous, greathearted, handsome, liberal, magnanimous, munificent, openhanded, openhearted, unselfish, unsparing; compassionate, humane, kind
near antonyms self-indulgent, self-seeking; cheap, closefisted, miserly, niggardly, parsimonious, stingy, tight, tightfisted; hardhearted, pitiless, unfeeling
antonyms self-centered, selfish
2 giving or sharing in abundance and without hesitation — see GENEROUS 1

charity *n* **1** the giving of necessities and especially money to the needy ⟨after amassing a fortune in the computer industry, they devoted themselves to *charity*⟩
synonyms almsgiving, philanthropy
related words altruism, humanitarianism; beneficence, benevolence, goodwill; alms, benefaction, contribution, donation; dole, relief, welfare; endowment, fund, grant, subsidy
2 a gift of money or its equivalent to a charity, humanitarian cause, or public institution — see CONTRIBUTION
3 kind, gentle, or compassionate treatment especially towards someone who is undeserving of it — see MERCY 1
4 the capacity for feeling for another's unhappiness or misfortune — see HEART 1

charlatan *n* one who makes false claims of identity or expertise — see IMPOSTOR

charley horse *n* a painful sudden tightening of a muscle — see CRAMP

charm *n* **1** something worn or kept to bring good luck or keep away evil ⟨an old cap that I use as a *charm* for whenever I play softball⟩
synonyms amulet, fetish (*also* fetich), mascot, mojo, phylactery, talisman
related words emblem, symbol, token, totem
near antonyms curse, hex, spell
antonyms hoodoo, jinx
2 the power of irresistible attraction ⟨a young singer with the kind of *charm* that turns a performer into a star⟩
synonyms allure, appeal, attractiveness, captivation, charisma, enchantment, fascination, glamour (*also* glamor), magic, magnetism, seductiveness, witchery
related words allurement, attraction, call, lure, seduction; agreeableness, delightfulness, desirableness, niceness, pleasantness, sweetness
near antonyms disagreeableness, distastefulness, obnoxiousness, offensiveness, unpleasantness
antonyms repulsion, repulsiveness
3 a spoken word or set of words believed to have magic power — see SPELL 1
4 an ornament worn on a chain around the neck or wrist — see PENDANT

charm *vb* **1** to attract or delight as if by magic ⟨a quaint seaside village that *charms* all who visit it⟩
synonyms allure, beguile, bewitch, captivate, enchant, fascinate, magnetize, wile
related words disarm, draw, entice, lure, pull, seduce, tempt; delight, gratify, please; arrest, enrapture, enthrall (*or* enthral), entrance; appeal (to), interest, intrigue; beckon, court, invite, solicit, woo
near antonyms disgust, offend, repel, revolt; annoy, displease, irk; bore, tire, weary
2 to cast a spell on — see BEWITCH 1

charmed *adj* being or appearing to be under a magic spell — see ENCHANTED

charmer *n* a person skilled in using supernatural forces — see MAGICIAN 1

charming *adj* having an often mysterious or magical power to attract — see FASCINATING 1

chart *n* an illustration of certain features of a geographical area — see MAP

chart *vb* to work out the details of (something) in advance — see PLAN 1

charter *vb* to take or get the temporary use of (something) for a set sum — see HIRE 1

charwoman *n* a female domestic servant — see MAID 1

chase *n* **1** an animal that is hunted or killed — see PREY
2 the act of going after or in the tracks of another — see PURSUIT

chase *vb* **1** to drive or force out — see EJECT 1
2 to go after or on the track of — see FOLLOW 2
3 to seek out (game) for food or sport — see HUNT 1

chasing *n* the act of going after or in the tracks of another — see PURSUIT

chasm *n* an immeasurable depth or space — see ABYSS

chaste *adj* free from any trace of the coarse or indecent ⟨as one would expect, the minister's small talk is always *chaste*, even though he likes a joke as much as the next person⟩
synonyms clean, decent, immaculate, modest, pure
related words spotless, stainless, unblemished, un-

defiled, unsoiled, unspotted, unstained, unsullied, untainted, untarnished; decorous, proper, seemly; cultivated, refined, tasteful; harmless, innocent, innocuous, inoffensive
near antonyms blemished, defiled, soiled, spotted, stained, sullied, tainted, tarnished; improper, indecorous, ribald, unseemly; crude, tacky, tasteless, unrefined
antonyms coarse, dirty, filthy, immodest, impure, indecent, obscene, smutty, unchaste, unclean, vulgar

chastely *adv* with purity of thought and deed — see PURELY

chasten *vb* to inflict a penalty on for a fault or crime — see PUNISH

chasteness *n* the quality or state of being morally pure — see CHASTITY

chastening *adj* inflicting, involving, or serving as punishment — see PUNITIVE

chastise *vb* to inflict a penalty on for a fault or crime — see PUNISH

chastisement *n* suffering, loss, or hardship imposed in response to a crime or offense — see PUNISHMENT

chastiser *n* one who inflicts punishment in return for an injury or offense — see NEMESIS 1

chastising *adj* inflicting, involving, or serving as punishment — see PUNITIVE

chastity *n* the quality or state of being morally pure ⟨a saint who is often held up as a model of *chastity*⟩
synonyms chasteness, modesty, purity
related words goodness, righteousness, virtuousness; morality, probity, rectitude; decency, decorum, propriety, seemliness
near antonyms badness, evil, sinfulness, unrighteousness, wickedness; impropriety, indecency
antonyms immodesty, impurity, unchastity

chat *n* friendly, informal conversation or an instance of this ⟨short *chats* between parents and teachers during the school's open house⟩
synonyms chatter, chitchat, gabfest, gossip, palaver, rap, small talk, table talk, talk, tête-à-tête
related words colloquy, conference, discourse, parley, powwow, symposium; debate, dialogue (*or* dialog), exchange, give-and-take

chat *vb* to engage in casual or rambling conversation ⟨the coffeehouse is a great place to meet friends and *chat* for hours⟩
synonyms babble, blab, cackle, chatter, converse, gab, gabble, gas, jabber, jaw, palaver, patter, prate, prattle, rap, rattle, run on, talk, twitter, visit
related words gossip, tattle; descant, discuss, expatiate
phrases shoot the breeze

chat (with) *vb* to communicate with by means of spoken words — see TALK 1

château *n* a large impressive residence — see MANSION

chattel *n* **1** a person who is considered the property of another person — see SLAVE 1
2 chattels *pl* transportable items that one owns — see POSSESSION 2

chatter *n* friendly, informal conversation or an instance of this — see CHAT

chatter *vb* **1** to engage in casual or rambling conversation — see CHAT
2 to speak rapidly, inarticulately, and usually unintelligibly — see BABBLE 1

chatterbox *n* a person who talks constantly ⟨my seat companion was a *chatterbox* who never once shut up during the whole trip⟩
synonyms babbler, blabber, cackler, chatterer, conversationalist, gabbler, jabberer, magpie, prattler, talker
related words blabbermouth, gossip, gossiper, talebearer, tattler, tattletale; converser

chatterer *n* a person who talks constantly — see CHATTERBOX

chatty *adj* **1** having the style and content of everyday conversation ⟨a time when campers were expected to write a *chatty* letter to their folks every week⟩
synonyms colloquial, conversational, gossipy, newsy
related words casual, familiar, informal, intimate; digressive, discursive, rambling; communicative, expansive, garrulous, talkative
near antonyms ceremonious, dignified, elevated, formal, solemn, stately
antonyms bookish, literary
2 fond of talking or conversation — see TALKATIVE

chauvinism *n* excessive favoritism towards one's own country ⟨their *chauvinism* blinded them to their country's faults⟩
synonyms jingoism, nationalism
related words loyalty, patriotism; xenophobia
near antonyms internationalism

chauvinist *n* one who shows excessive favoritism towards his or her country — see NATIONALIST

cheap *adj* **1** costing little ⟨e-mail is so popular because it's a *cheap* way to send messages⟩
synonyms cut-rate, inexpensive, low, reasonable
related words moderate, popular; discounted, lowered, reduced; wholesale
near antonyms precious, priceless, valuable; increased, inflated
antonyms costly, dear, expensive, high, premium
2 of low quality ⟨a *cheap* sweater that started to unravel almost as soon as I bought it⟩
synonyms bad, bum, cheesy, coarse, common, cut-rate, execrable, inferior, junky, lousy, low-grade, mediocre, miserable, poor, rotten, rubbishy, second-rate, shoddy, sleazy, terrible, trashy, trumpery, wretched
related words useless, valueless, worthless; flashy, garish, gaudy, meretricious, showy, tawdry; seedy, shabby, tacky; counterfeit, fake, phony (*also* phoney), sham
near antonyms elegant, handsome, tasteful; handcrafted, polished, refined
antonyms excellent, fine, first-class, first-rate, good, high-grade, superior, top-notch
3 giving or sharing as little as possible — see STINGY 1

cheapen *vb* to lower the price or value of — see DEPRECIATE 1

cheapness *n* the quality of being overly sparing with money — see PARSIMONY

cheapskate *n* a mean grasping person who is usually stingy with money — see MISER

cheat *n* a dishonest person who uses clever means to cheat others out of something of value — see TRICKSTER 1

cheat *vb* **1** to use dishonest methods to achieve a goal ⟨students who *cheat* on tests end up never knowing anything⟩
synonyms fudge

related words distort, falsify, misrepresent, twist; doctor, fake, tamper (with); color, elaborate, embellish, embroider, exaggerate, magnify, pad, stretch; dodge, evade, hedge
2 to fall short in satisfying the expectation or hope of — see DISAPPOINT
3 to rob by the use of trickery or threats — see FLEECE

cheater *n* a dishonest person who uses clever means to cheat others out of something of value — see TRICKSTER 1

check *n* **1** the amount owed at a bar or restaurant or the slip of paper stating the amount ⟨diners at the fancy restaurant often look shocked when they receive the *check*⟩
synonyms bill, tab
related words invoice, receipt; account, record, statement; charge, fee; score, tally
2 a close look at or over someone or something in order to judge condition — see INSPECTION
3 a record of goods sold or services performed together with the costs due — see [1]BILL 1
4 a small sheet of plastic, paper, or paperboard showing that the bearer has a claim to something (as admittance) — see TICKET 1
5 something that limits one's freedom of action or choice — see RESTRICTION 1

check *vb* **1** to be in agreement on every point ⟨their story of what happened *checks* with the report of the eyewitness⟩
synonyms accord, agree, answer, cohere, coincide, comport, conform, correspond, dovetail, fit, go, harmonize, jibe, square, tally
related words equal, match, parallel
near antonyms contradict, dispute, gainsay; negate, nullify; clash, conflict, jar
antonyms differ (from), disagree (with)
2 to bring (something) to a standstill — see [1]HALT 1
3 to keep from exceeding a desirable degree or level (as of expression) — see CONTROL 1

check (out) *vb* to look over closely (as for judging quality or condition) — see INSPECT

checklist *n* a record of a series of items (as names or titles) usually arranged according to some system — see [1]LIST

checkmate *vb* to prevent from achieving a goal — see FRUSTRATE

checkup *n* a close look at or over someone or something in order to judge condition — see INSPECTION

cheek *n* **1** disrespectful or argumentative talk given in response to a command or request — see BACK TALK
2 shameless boldness — see EFFRONTERY

cheekiness *n* shameless boldness — see EFFRONTERY

cheeky *adj* displaying or marked by rude boldness — see NERVY 1

cheep *vb* to make a short sharp sound like a small bird — see CHIRP

cheer *n* **1** a mood characterized by high spirits and amusement and often accompanied by laughter — see MIRTH
2 a feeling of ease from grief or trouble — see COMFORT 1
3 a state of mind dominated by a particular emotion — see MOOD 1
4 cheers *pl* enthusiastic and usually public expression of approval — see APPLAUSE

cheer *vb* **1** to declare enthusiastic approval of — see ACCLAIM
2 to ease the grief or distress of — see COMFORT 1

cheer (up) *vb* **1** to become glad or hopeful ⟨*cheer up* —things are bound to get better⟩
synonyms brighten, perk (up)
related words rejoice; liven (up), revive; beam, glow, radiate, sparkle; encourage, gladden, hearten
near antonyms despair, despond; brood, fret, mope
antonyms darken, sadden
2 to fill with courage or strength of purpose — see ENCOURAGE 1

cheerful *adj* **1** having or showing a good mood or disposition ⟨a *cheerful* person who is always fun to work with and a pleasure to be around⟩
synonyms blithe, blithesome, bright, buoyant, cheery, chipper, gay, gladsome, lightsome, sunny, upbeat
related words hopeful, optimistic, sanguine; jaunty, lively, perky, sprightly, vivacious; carefree, careless, cavalier, devil-may-care, easygoing, happy-go-lucky, insouciant, lighthearted, unconcerned; boon, jolly, jovial, merry, mirthful; glad, happy, pleased
near antonyms dull, lethargic, listless, sluggish, torpid; blue, dejected, depressed, heavyhearted, melancholy, sorrowful; discontented, disgruntled, unhappy
antonyms dour, gloomy, glum, morose, saturnine, sulky, sullen
2 serving to lift one's spirits ⟨a hospital with sunny, *cheerful* rooms that are designed to make a patient's stay as pleasant as possible⟩
synonyms bright, cheering, cheery, gay, glad
related words gladdening, heartening, heartwarming; gleaming, radiant, sparkling
near antonyms discouraging, disheartening; colorless, drab, dull, lackluster, lusterless
antonyms bleak, cheerless, dark, depressing, dismal, dreary, gloomy, gray (*also* grey)

cheerfully *adv* in a cheerful or happy manner — see GAILY 1

cheerfulness *n* a mood characterized by high spirits and amusement and often accompanied by laughter — see MIRTH

cheeriness *n* a mood characterized by high spirits and amusement and often accompanied by laughter — see MIRTH

cheering *adj* **1** making one feel good inside — see HEARTWARMING
2 serving to lift one's spirits — see CHEERFUL 2

cheering *n* enthusiastic and usually public expression of approval — see APPLAUSE

cheerless *adj* causing or marked by an atmosphere lacking in cheer — see GLOOMY 1

cheery *adj* **1** having or showing a good mood or disposition — see CHEERFUL 1
2 serving to lift one's spirits — see CHEERFUL 2

cheesy *adj* **1** marked by an obvious lack of style or good taste — see TACKY 1
2 of low quality — see CHEAP 2

chef *n* a person who prepares food by some manner of heating — see COOK

cherish *vb* **1** to feel passion, devotion, or tenderness for — see LOVE 2
2 to hold dear — see LOVE 1
3 to keep in one's mind or heart — see HARBOR 1

cherished *adj* granted special treatment or attention — see DARLING 1
chest *n* a covered rectangular container for storing or transporting things ‹a *chest* containing almost every tool that the home do-it-yourselfer is likely to need›
synonyms box, caddy, case, casket, locker, trunk
related words crate; footlocker; coffer, safe, safe-deposit box, strongbox; coffin; compartment, vault
chesterfield *n* a long upholstered piece of furniture designed for several sitters — see COUCH
chew *vb* to crush or grind with the teeth — see BITE (ON)
chew out *vb* to criticize (someone) severely or angrily especially for personal failings — see SCOLD
chew over *vb* **1** to give serious and careful thought to — see PONDER
2 to talk about (an issue) usually from various points of view and for the purpose of arriving at a decision or opinion — see DISCUSS
chewy *adj* not easily chewed — see TOUGH 1
chic *adj* being in the latest or current fashion — see STYLISH
chicanery *n* the use of clever underhanded actions to achieve an end — see TRICKERY
chick *n, slang* a young usually unmarried woman — see GIRL 1
chicken *adj* having or showing a shameful lack of courage — see COWARDLY
chicken *n* a person who shows a shameful lack of courage in the face of danger — see COWARD
chickenhearted *adj* having or showing a shameful lack of courage — see COWARDLY
chide *vb* to criticize (someone) usually gently so as to correct a fault — see REBUKE 1
chief *adj* **1** coming before all others in importance — see FOREMOST 1
2 highest in rank or authority — see HEAD
chief *n* the person (as an employer or supervisor) who tells people and especially workers what to do — see BOSS
chiefly *adv* for the most part ‹our video collection consists *chiefly* of comedies, but we have a few horror movies›
synonyms altogether, basically, by and large, generally, largely, mainly, mostly, overall, predominantly, primarily, principally, substantially
related words nearly, practically, virtually; approximately, broadly, roughly; commonly, frequently, normally, ordinarily, usually; incompletely, partially, partly
phrases in general, on the whole
near antonyms completely, entirely, fully, totally, wholly; barely, hardly, marginally, minimally, scarcely
child *n* **1** a young person who is between infancy and adulthood ‹an imaginative animated film that appeals to adults as well as to *children*›
synonyms bairn [*chiefly Scottish*], cub, juvenile, kid, youngster, youth
related words adolescent, minor; schoolboy, schoolchild, schoolgirl; moppet, nestling, toddler, tot, tyke; brat, imp, squirt, urchin, whippersnapper; cherub; preteen, subteen, teenager, teenybopper; lad, nipper, shaver, stripling, tad; bobby-soxer, hoyden, tomboy
near antonyms golden-ager, oldster, senior citizen
antonyms adult, grown-up
2 a recently born person — see BABY
childbearing *n* the act or process of giving birth to children — see CHILDBIRTH
childbirth *n* the act or process of giving birth to children ‹women who choose to undergo *childbirth* without the use of anesthetics and other drugs›
synonyms childbearing, delivery, labor, parturition
related words pains; pregnancy; abortion, miscarriage; cesarean section (*also* cesarian section)
childhood *n* the state or time of being a child ‹enjoy your *childhood* —it won't last forever›
synonyms youth
related words boyhood, girlhood; adolescence, minority; immaturity, juvenility; babyhood, infancy
near antonyms majority
antonyms adulthood
childish *adj* having or showing the annoying qualities (as silliness) associated with children ‹you almost spoiled the ceremony for everyone with your *childish* giggling›
synonyms adolescent, babyish, immature, infantile, juvenile, kiddish, puerile
related words boyish, girlish; childlike, innocent, naive (*or* naïve), simple, unsophisticated
near antonyms experienced, sophisticated, worldly-wise
antonyms adult, grown-up, mature
child's play *n* **1** something of little importance — see TRIFLE
2 something that is easy to do — see CINCH
chill *adj* **1** lacking in friendliness or warmth of feeling — see COLD 2
2 uncomfortably cool — see CHILLY 1
chill *n* an uncomfortable degree of coolness ‹there's a *chill* in the air, so you'd better wear a sweater›
synonyms bite, bitterness, bleakness, chilliness, nip, rawness, sharpness
related words briskness, crispness; coldness, frigidity, frigidness, frostiness, iciness; cold, freeze, snap
near antonyms balminess, warmth
chill *vb* to cause to lose heat — see COOL 1
chilliness *n* an uncomfortable degree of coolness — see CHILL
chilling *adj* uncomfortably cool — see CHILLY 1
chilly *adj* **1** uncomfortably cool ‹those *chilly* nights when a warm fire can be especially comforting›
synonyms bitter, bleak, chill, chilling, nippy, raw, sharp
related words brisk, crisp; arctic, cold, freezing, frigid, frosty, icy
near antonyms balmy, warm
2 lacking in friendliness or warmth of feeling — see COLD 2
chime *vb* to make the clear sound heard when metal vibrates — see RING 1
chime *n, usually* **chimes** *pl* a series of short high ringing sounds — see TINKLE
chime in *vb* to cause a disruption in a conversation or discussion — see INTERRUPT
chimera *n* a conception or image created by the imagination and having no objective reality — see FANTASY 1
chimerical *adj* not real and existing only in the imagination — see IMAGINARY
chine *n* a column of bones supporting the trunk of a vertebrate animal — see SPINE

chink *n* an irregular usually narrow break in a surface created by pressure — see CRACK 1
chink *vb* to make a repeated sharp light ringing sound — see JINGLE
chip *n* **1** a small flat piece separated from a whole ⟨wood *chips* were spread over the ground between the plants⟩
synonyms flake, sliver, splint, splinter
related words bit, disk (*or* disc), fragment, particle, scrap, shard; shiver, smithereens; shred, tatter; clipping, paring, shaving, snippet; leaf, sheet, slice; chunk, hunk, lump, slab
2 a V-shaped cut usually on an edge or a surface — see NOTCH 1
3 chips *pl* something (as pieces of stamped metal or printed paper) customarily and legally used as a medium of exchange, a measure of value, or a means of payment — see MONEY
chip in *vb* to make a donation as part of a group effort — see CONTRIBUTE 1
chipper *adj* **1** enjoying health and vigor — see HEALTHY 1
2 having or showing a good mood or disposition — see CHEERFUL 1
chirp *vb* to make a short sharp sound like a small bird ⟨the sparrows were *chirping* up a storm in the backyard⟩
synonyms cheep, chirrup, peep, pipe, tweet, twitter
related words cackle, chatter, jabber; sing, trill, warble
chirr *n* a monotonous sound like that of an insect in motion — see HUM
chirrup *vb* to make a short sharp sound like a small bird — see CHIRP
chisel *vb* to rob by the use of trickery or threats — see FLEECE
chitchat *n* friendly, informal conversation or an instance of this — see CHAT
chivalrous *adj* having, characterized by, or arising from a dignified and generous nature — see NOBLE 2
chivy *vb* to thrust oneself upon (another) without invitation — see BOTHER 1
chock–full *or* **chockful** *adj* containing or seeming to contain the greatest quantity or number possible — see FULL 1
choice *adj* having qualities that appeal to a refined taste ⟨*choice* chocolates for which chocolate lovers are willing to pay extra⟩
synonyms dainty, delicate, elegant, exquisite, rare, select
related words elite, exclusive; excellent, outstanding, premium, prime, superior
near antonyms coarse, gross, vulgar; commercial, mass-produced, popular; common, ordinary; average, mediocre, run-of-the-mill, second-rate
choice *n* **1** the power, right, or opportunity to choose ⟨you have no *choice* : you have to go to school⟩
synonyms alternative, discretion, option, pick, preference, way
related words say, voice, vote; inclination, liking, partiality, penchant, predilection, proclivity, propensity, tendency; discernment, judgment (*or* judgement), perspicacity
near antonyms coercion, duress, force; duty, obligation
2 a person or thing that is chosen ⟨my *choice* for best song of all time⟩
synonyms pick, selection
related words favorite, like, liking, preference; elective, option; appointment, designation, nomination; appointee, candidate, nominee
3 individuals carefully selected as being the best of a class — see ELITE
4 the act or power of making one's own choices or decisions — see FREE WILL
5 the act or process of selecting — see SELECTION 1
choir *n* an organized group of singers — see CHORUS 1
choke *vb* **1** to keep (someone) from breathing by exerting pressure on the windpipe ⟨let go of my throat—you're *choking* me!⟩
synonyms garrote (*or* garotte), strangle, throttle
related words asphyxiate, smother, suffocate
near antonyms restore, resuscitate, revive
2 to experience complete or partial blockage of the windpipe ⟨the recommended procedure for helping someone who is *choking*⟩
synonyms gag
related words heave, retch, throw up, vomit; asphyxiate, smother, suffocate
near antonyms breathe, respire
3 to be or cause to be killed by lack of breathable air — see SMOTHER 1
4 to prevent passage through — see CLOG 1
choke (back) *vb* to refrain from openly showing or uttering — see SUPPRESS 2
choker *n* an ornamental chain or string (as of beads) worn around the neck — see NECKLACE
choleric *adj* easily irritated or annoyed — see IRRITABLE
chomp (on) *vb* to crush or grind with the teeth — see BITE (ON)
choose *vb* **1** to decide to accept (someone or something) from a group of possibilities ⟨*choose* a computer that best suits your needs⟩
synonyms cull, elect, handpick, name, opt (for), pick, prefer, select, single (out), take
related words appoint, designate, nominate, tab; accept, adopt, embrace, espouse
near antonyms discard, jettison, throw away, throw out
antonyms decline, refuse, reject, turn down
2 to see fit ⟨you can wear whatever you *choose* to the party⟩
synonyms like, want, will, wish
related words crave, desire, fancy, hanker (for), hunger (for), long (for), yearn (for); decide, determine, resolve
3 to come to a judgment after discussion or consideration — see DECIDE 1
chooser *n* someone with the right or responsibility for making a selection — see SELECTOR
choosing *n* the act or process of selecting — see SELECTION 1
choosy *or* **choosey** *adj* **1** hard to please — see FINICKY
2 tending to select carefully — see SELECTIVE
chop *n* a hard strike with a part of the body or an instrument — see [1]BLOW
chop *vb* to cut into small pieces ⟨*chop* the onions before adding them to the pot⟩
synonyms dice, hash, mince
related words chip, grind, mash, puree, slice
chop (down) *vb* to bring down by cutting — see FELL 2

choppy *adj* lacking in steadiness or regularity of occurrence — see FITFUL
chorale *n* **1** a religious song — see HYMN
2 an organized group of singers — see CHORUS 1
chore *n* **1** a piece of work that needs to be done regularly ⟨everyone in this household is expected to do weekly *chores*⟩
synonyms assignment, duty, job, stint, task
related words endeavor, enterprise, project, undertaking; care, charge, commission, responsibility; function, mission, office; errand; circuit, round, route
2 a dull, unpleasant, or difficult piece of work ⟨cleaning everything out of the attic was a real *chore*⟩
synonyms headache, labor
related words drudgery, grind; effort, strain, sweat; burden, load, weight; bother, nuisance, trouble
near antonyms breeze, child's play, cinch, duck soup, snap
chortle *n* an explosive sound that is a sign of amusement — see LAUGH 1
chorus *n* **1** an organized group of singers ⟨the annual Christmas program presented by the school's *chorus*⟩
synonyms choir, chorale, glee club
related words ensemble; minstrelsy
2 a part of a song or hymn that is repeated every so often ⟨the whole congregation will join in for the *chorus*⟩
synonyms burden, refrain
related words repeat
chosen *adj* singled out from a number or group as more to one's liking — see SELECT 1
chow *n* **1** food eaten or prepared for eating at one time — see MEAL
2 substances intended to be eaten — see FOOD
christen *vb* to give a name to — see NAME 1
Christian name *n* a name that is placed before one's family name — see FORENAME
Christmastime *n* the season celebrating Christmas — see YULETIDE
chronic *adj* being such by habit and not likely to change — see HABITUAL 1
chronicle *n* **1** a relating of events usually in the order in which they happened — see ACCOUNT 1
2 an account of important events in the order in which they happened — see HISTORY 1
chronicler *n* a student or writer of history — see HISTORIAN
chronometer *n* a device to measure time — see TIMEPIECE
chubbiness *n* the condition of having an excess of body fat — see CORPULENCE
chubby *adj* having an excess of body fat — see FAT 1
chuck *vb* to send through the air especially with a quick forward motion of the arm — see THROW
chuckle *n* an explosive sound that is a sign of amusement — see LAUGH 1
chum *n* a person who has a strong liking for and trust in another — see FRIEND 1
chum *vb* to come or be together as friends — see ASSOCIATE 1
chumminess *n* the state of being in a very personal or private relationship — see FAMILIARITY 1
chummy *adj* closely acquainted — see FAMILIAR 1
chump *n* one who is easily deceived or cheated — see DUPE
chunk *n* a small uneven mass — see LUMP 1
chunky *adj* **1** having small pieces or lumps spread throughout ⟨*chunky* peanut butter adds an interesting layer of texture when paired with jelly⟩
synonyms clumpy, curdy, lumpy, nubbly, nubby
related words ropy, thick, viscous; clabbered [*dialect*], clotted, coagulated, congealed, curdled, gelled, thickened
antonyms smooth
2 being compact and broad in build and often short in stature — see STOCKY
3 having or being of relatively great depth or extent from one surface to its opposite — see THICK 1
church *n* **1** a building for public worship and especially Christian worship ⟨a city that is noted for its many historic *churches*⟩
synonyms kirk [*chiefly Scottish*], tabernacle, temple
related words abbey, bethel, cathedral, chapel, oratory, sanctuary, shrine; meetinghouse; mosque, pagoda, synagogue (*or* synagog)
2 a body of persons gathered for religious worship — see CONGREGATION 1
churchly *adj* of or relating to a church — see ECCLESIASTICAL
churl *n* a person whose behavior is offensive to others — see JERK 1
churlish *adj* having or showing crudely insensitive or impolite manners — see CLOWNISH
churn *vb* **1** to be in a state of violent rolling motion — see SEETHE 1
2 to cause (as a liquid) to move about in a circle especially repeatedly — see STIR 1
chutzpah *also* **chutzpa** *or* **hutzpah** *or* **hutzpa** *n* shameless boldness — see EFFRONTERY
cinch *n* something that is easy to do ⟨the clear instructions made setting up the audiovisual system a *cinch*⟩
synonyms breeze, child's play, duck soup, picnic, pushover, snap
related words nothing; sitting duck
phrases piece of cake
near antonyms bother, nuisance, trouble
antonyms chore, headache, labor
cinch *vb* to make sure, certain, or safe — see ENSURE
cincture *n* a strip of flexible material (as leather) worn around the waist — see [2]BELT
cinema *n* **1** the art or business of making a movie — see MOVIE 2
2 a building or part of a building where movies are shown — see THEATER 1
cipher *n* the numerical symbol 0 or the absence of number or quantity represented by it — see ZERO 1
ciphering *n* the act or process of performing mathematical operations to find a value — see CALCULATION
circle *n* **1** something with a perfectly round circumference ⟨a *circle* of columns surrounds the memorial to the fallen heroes⟩
synonyms ring, round
related words circlet; ellipse, loop, oval; ball, globe, orb, sphere
2 a circular strip — see RING 2
3 a group of people sharing a common interest and relating together socially — see GANG 2
4 a series of events or actions that repeat them-

selves regularly and in the same order — see CYCLE 1
circle *vb* **1** to form a circle around — see SURROUND
2 to pass completely around — see ENCIRCLE 1
circuitous *adj* **1** not straightforward or direct — see INDIRECT
2 using or containing more words than necessary to express an idea — see WORDY
circular *adj* not straightforward or direct — see INDIRECT
circular *n* a short printed publication with no cover or with a paper cover — see PAMPHLET
circulate *vb* **1** to cause to be known over a considerable area or by many people — see SPREAD 1
2 to make (as a piece of information) the subject of common talk without any authority or confirmation of accuracy — see RUMOR
circumference *n* **1** the distance around a round body <the *circumference* of the earth at the equator>
synonyms girth
related words waistline; equator; diameter, perimeter
2 the line or relatively narrow space that marks the outer limit of something — see BORDER 1
circumlocution *n* the use of too many words to express an idea — see VERBIAGE
circumlocutory *adj* using or containing more words than necessary to express an idea — see WORDY
circumnavigate *vb* to pass completely around — see ENCIRCLE 1
circumscribe *vb* **1** to set bounds or an upper limit for — see LIMIT 1
2 to mark the limits of — see LIMIT 2
circumscribed *adj* having distinct or certain limits — see LIMITED 1
circumspect *adj* having or showing a close attentiveness to avoiding danger or trouble — see CAREFUL 1
circumspection *n* a close attentiveness to avoiding danger — see CAUTION 1
circumstance *n* **1** a state or end that seemingly has been decided beforehand — see FATE 1
2 something that happens — see EVENT 1
3 the uncertain course of events — see CHANCE 1
circumstantial *adj* including many small descriptive features — see DETAILED 1
circumvent *vb* **1** to avoid having to comply with (something) especially through cleverness <students who try to *circumvent* the school's dress code>
synonyms dodge, sidestep, skirt
related words avoid, duck, elude, escape, eschew, evade, shake, shun; disobey, disregard, flout, ignore
phrases get around
near antonyms accede (to), acquiesce (to), assent (to)
antonyms comply (with), follow, keep, obey, observe
2 to avoid by going around — see DETOUR 1
circus *n* **1** a large usually roofless building for sporting events with tiers of seats for spectators — see STADIUM
2 a place of uproar or confusion — see MADHOUSE 2
citadel *n* a structure or place from which one can resist attack — see FORT
citation *n* **1** a formal expression of praise — see ENCOMIUM
2 a formal recognition of an achievement or praiseworthy deed — see COMMENDATION 1
3 a passage referred to, repeated, or offered as an example — see QUOTATION
cite *vb* **1** to give as an example — see QUOTE 1
2 to make reference to or speak about briefly but specifically — see MENTION 1
citify *vb* to accustom to the ways of the city <we've become so *citified* that many people have no idea where their food comes from>
synonyms urbanize
related words civilize, cultivate
citizen *n* **1** a person who owes allegiance to a government and is protected by it <conscientious *citizens* who regard voting as a duty as well as a right>
synonyms national, subject
related words compatriot, countryman; inhabitant, native, nonimmigrant, resident
near antonyms foreigner, stranger; immigrant, nonnative
antonyms alien, noncitizen
2 a person who lives in a town on a permanent basis — see BURGHER
city *n* a thickly settled, highly populated area <commuters who drive every day between their homes in the suburbs and their jobs in the *city*>
synonyms burg, megalopolis, metropolis, municipality, town
related words borough; conurbation; urban sprawl; suburbia
civil *adj* **1** of or relating to a nation — see NATIONAL
2 showing consideration, courtesy, and good manners — see POLITE 1
civility *n* **1** an act or utterance that is a customary show of good manners <after the usual *civilities,* the parents and the principal had a serious talk about the boy>
synonyms amenity, courtesy, formality, gesture
related words ceremony, observance, rite, ritual; etiquette, manners, proprieties; greetings, regards, respects; favor, grace, kindness
2 speech or behavior that is a sign of good breeding — see POLITENESS
civilization *n* **1** the way people live at a particular time and place <a study unit on the advanced *civilization* created by the Mayas over a thousand years ago>
synonyms culture, life, lifestyle, society
related words customs, manners, mores, values; folklore, heritage, tradition
2 a high level of taste and enlightenment as a result of extensive intellectual training and exposure to the arts — see CULTURE 1
civilized *adj* having or showing a taste for the fine arts and gracious living — see CULTIVATED
clack *vb* to make a series of short sharp noises — see RATTLE 1
claim *n* **1** an entitlement to something <I'm announcing my *claim* to that last slice of pizza>
synonyms call, pretense (*or* pretence), pretension, right
related words birthright, prerogative; favor, privilege; refusal
2 a legal right to participation in the advantages, profits, and responsibility of something — see INTEREST 1

3 a solemn and often public declaration of the truth or existence of something — see PROTESTATION

4 something that someone insists upon having — see DEMAND 1

claim *vb* **1** to state as a fact usually forcefully ⟨people who *claim* that they have been kidnapped by aliens from other worlds⟩
synonyms affirm, allege, assert, aver, avouch, avow, contend, declare, insist, maintain, profess, protest, warrant
related words announce, broadcast, proclaim; argue, rationalize, reason; confirm, justify, vindicate; defend, support, uphold
near antonyms disavow, disclaim, disown; challenge, dispute, question; confute, disprove, rebut, refute; contradict
antonyms deny, gainsay
2 to ask for (something) earnestly or with authority — see DEMAND 1

clairvoyance *n* the power of seeing or knowing about things that are not present to the senses ⟨people who claim to have *clairvoyance* are sometimes asked to help locate missing persons⟩
synonyms extrasensory perception, sixth sense
related words foreknowledge, foresight, prescience; telepathy

clamber *vb* to move (as up or over something) often with the help of the hands in holding or pulling — see CLIMB 1

clamor *n* **1** a violent shouting ⟨a *clamor* arose from the crowd as the prisoner was brought forward⟩
synonyms howl, hubbub, hue and cry, hullabaloo, noise, outcry, roar, tumult, uproar
related words clangor, din, jangle, racket
near antonyms mumble, mumbling, murmur, murmuring, rumble, rumbling
2 loud, confused, and usually unharmonious sound — see NOISE 1

clamor (for) *vb* to ask for (something) earnestly or with authority — see DEMAND 1

clamorous *adj* **1** engaging in or marked by loud and insistent cries especially of protest — see VOCIFEROUS
2 full of or characterized by the presence of noise — see NOISY 2
3 marked by a high volume of sound — see LOUD 1

clamp *vb* to put securely in place or in a desired position — see FASTEN 2

clamp down (on) *vb* to put a stop to (something) by the use of force — see QUELL 1

clam up *vb* to stop talking — see SHUT UP

clan *n* **1** a group of people sharing a common interest and relating together socially — see GANG 2
2 a group of persons who come from the same ancestor — see FAMILY 1

clandestine *adj* undertaken or done so as to escape being observed or known by others — see SECRET 1

clang *n* the loud sound made when metal strikes metal ⟨the horseshoe hit the stake with a satisfying *clang*⟩
synonyms clangor, clank, clash
related words chime, dingdong, peel, ring; clink, jangle, jingle, tinkle; clap, clop, crack, crash

clangor *n* **1** loud, confused, and usually unharmonious sound — see NOISE 1
2 the loud sound made when metal strikes metal — see CLANG

clangorous *adj* **1** full of or characterized by the presence of noise — see NOISY 2
2 making loud, confused, and usually unharmonious sounds — see NOISY 1
3 marked by a high volume of sound — see LOUD 1

clank *n* the loud sound made when metal strikes metal — see CLANG

clannish *adj* bound together by feelings of very close association — see CLOSE-KNIT

clap *n* **1** a loud explosive sound ⟨a *clap* of thunder that woke the whole house up⟩
synonyms bang, blast, boom, crack, crash, pop, report, slam, smash, snap, thwack, whack
related words clang, clangor, clank, clash; knock, rap, tap; clamor, howl, hubbub, hue and cry, hullabaloo, outcry, roar, tumult, uproar
2 a hard strike with a part of the body or an instrument — see [1]BLOW

clap *vb* to deliver a blow to (someone or something) usually in a strong vigorous manner — see HIT 1

claptrap *n* **1** language, behavior, or ideas that are absurd and contrary to good sense — see NONSENSE 1
2 unintelligible or meaningless talk — see GIBBERISH

clarification *n* a statement that makes something clear — see EXPLANATION 1

clarify *vb* **1** to remove usually visible impurities from ⟨*clarify* the melted butter by skimming off the milky bits⟩
synonyms clear, distill, filter, purify
related words process, refine; clean, cleanse, purge; extract, leach; screen, sieve, sift
near antonyms cloud, dull, muddy; contaminate, dirty, soil
2 to make plain or understandable — see EXPLAIN 1

clarity *n* **1** the state or quality of being easily seen through ⟨mountain streams with water of incredible *clarity*⟩
synonyms clearness, limpidity, limpidness, transparency
related words lucidity, lucidness, translucency; brightness, brilliance, effulgence, luminosity, luminousness; definition, resolution, sharpness
near antonyms fogginess, haziness, murkiness
antonyms cloudiness, opacity, opaqueness
2 clearness of expression — see SIMPLICITY 2

clash *n* **1** a physical dispute between opposing individuals or groups — see FIGHT 1
2 the loud sound made when metal strikes metal — see CLANG

clash *vb* to be out of harmony or agreement usually noticeably ⟨the colors of your shirt and pants *clash*⟩ ⟨Mom's idea of proper dress often *clashes* with mine⟩
synonyms collide, conflict, jar
related words mismatch; battle, combat, fight, war (against); chafe, gall, grate, jangle; differ, disagree
near antonyms agree, coincide, correspond
antonyms blend, harmonize, match

clash (with) *vb* to oppose (someone) in physical conflict — see FIGHT 1

clashing *adj* not being in agreement or harmony — see INCONSISTENT

clasp *n* the act or manner of holding — see HOLD 1

clasp *vb* **1** to put one's arms around and press tightly — see EMBRACE 1

2 to reach for and take hold of by embracing with the fingers or arms — see TAKE 1

class *n* **1** one of the segments of society into which people are grouped ⟨a politician who appeals to people of every *class*⟩
synonyms caste, estate, folk, order, stratum
related words bracket, echelon, grade, layer, level, tier; place, position, rank, standing, status; grouping, hierarchy, stratification; clan, family, people, race, tribe
2 one of the units into which a whole is divided on the basis of a common characteristic ⟨a new *class* of wireless devices that could be used for Internet access as well as personal communication⟩
synonyms bracket, category, division, family, grade, group, kind, order, rank(s), set, species, type
related words description, feather, ilk, nature, sort; branch, section, subdivision, subgroup, variety; breed, race; classification, heading, label, rubric, title
3 a number of persons or things that are grouped together because they have something in common — see SORT 1
4 a series of lectures on a subject — see COURSE 2
5 degree of excellence — see QUALITY 1
6 dignified or restrained beauty of form, appearance, or style — see ELEGANCE
7 high position within society — see RANK 2

class *vb* to arrange or assign according to type — see CLASSIFY 1

classic *adj* **1** constituting, serving as, or worthy of being a pattern to be imitated — see MODEL
2 of the very best kind — see EXCELLENT
3 serving to identify as belonging to an individual or group — see CHARACTERISTIC 1

classic *n* **1** someone of such unequaled perfection as to deserve imitation — see IDEAL 1
2 something (as a work of art) that is a great achievement and often its creator's greatest achievement — see MASTERPIECE
3 the most perfect type or example — see QUINTESSENCE 1

classical *adj* based on customs usually handed down from a previous generation — see TRADITIONAL 1

classify *vb* **1** to arrange or assign according to type ⟨*classify* the baseball cards in your collection on the basis of rarity⟩
synonyms assort, break down, categorize, class, grade, group, peg, place, range, rank, separate, sort
related words arrange, order, organize, systematize; alphabetize, catalog (*or* catalogue), codify, file, index, list; pigeonhole, shelve; distinguish, identify, recognize; cull, screen, sift, winnow
near antonyms confuse, disarrange, jumble, lump, mix (up), scramble
2 to put into a particular arrangement — see ORDER 1

clatter *n* a state of noisy, confused activity — see COMMOTION

clatter *vb* to make a series of short sharp noises — see RATTLE 1

clattering *adj* full of or characterized by the presence of noise — see NOISY 2

clattery *adj* full of or characterized by the presence of noise — see NOISY 2

clean *adj* **1** free from dirt or stain ⟨although the soccer team always starts out with *clean* uniforms, they don't stay that way for long⟩
synonyms immaculate, spick-and-span (*or* spic-and-span), spotless, stainless, unsoiled, unsullied
related words pure, taintless, undefiled, unpolluted, untainted, wholesome; cleanly, hygienic, sanitary; bleached, cleansed, purified, whitened; milky, snowy, white; flawless, unblemished; bright, shiny, sparkling
near antonyms dingy, greasy, grimy, mucky, muddy; defiled, polluted, tainted; blackened, discolored
antonyms besmirched, dirty, filthy, foul, grubby, soiled, spotted, stained, sullied, unclean
2 following or according to the rules — see FAIR 3
3 free from any trace of the coarse or indecent — see CHASTE
4 trying all possibilities — see EXHAUSTIVE

clean *adv* to a full extent or degree — see FULLY 1

clean *vb* **1** to make clean ⟨we *cleaned* the clothes before donating them to charity⟩
synonyms cleanse
related words decontaminate, purge, purify; disinfect, sanitize; brush, dry-clean, dust, launder, mop, rinse, scour, scrub, sweep, wash, wipe; brighten, deodorize, freshen, spruce (up), sweeten; pick up, straighten (up), tidy
near antonyms begrime, muddy; defile, pollute, taint; blacken, discolor
antonyms besmirch, dirty, foul, soil, spot, stain, sully
2 to take the internal organs out of — see GUT

clean (out) *vb* to make complete use of — see DEPLETE

clean (up) *vb* to remove objectionable parts from — see CENSOR

cleaner *n* a substance used for cleaning ⟨a kitchen shelf loaded with household *cleaners*⟩
synonyms cleanser, detergent, soap
related words disinfectant, purifier, solvent

cleanse *vb* **1** to free from moral guilt or blemish especially ceremonially — see PURIFY 1
2 to make clean — see CLEAN 1

cleanser *n* a substance used for cleaning — see CLEANER

cleansing *n* the act or fact of freeing from sin or moral guilt — see PURIFICATION

clear *adj* **1** easily seen through ⟨the *clear* glass walls of the aquarium's giant ocean tank⟩
synonyms limpid, liquid, lucent, pellucid, transparent
related words colorless, uncolored; lucid, translucent; crystal, crystalline, glassy, sparkling; bright, brilliant, effulgent, luminous
near antonyms foggy, hazy, misty, murky, smoky (*also* smokey)
antonyms cloudy, nontransparent, opaque
2 not subject to misinterpretation or more than one interpretation ⟨the meaning of her broad smile was *clear* to the whole class⟩
synonyms apparent, broad, clear-cut, decided, distinct, evident, lucid, manifest, obvious, open-and-shut, palpable, patent, perspicuous, plain, transparent, unambiguous, unequivocal, unmistakable
related words comprehendible, comprehensible, decipherable, fathomable, graspable, intelligible, knowable, understandable; self-evident, self-explanatory; simple, uncomplicated; overt, undisguised; appreciable, perceptible, recognizable,

sensible, tangible; discernible, noticeable, observable, visible
near antonyms incomprehensible, unfathomable, unintelligible, unknowable; imperceptible, inappreciable, insensible; delicate, subtle
antonyms dark, enigmatic, indistinct, mysterious, obscure, unclear; ambiguous, equivocal
3 having or showing a mind free from doubt — see CERTAIN 2
4 not stormy or cloudy — see FAIR 1
5 serving to put an end to all debate or questioning — see CONCLUSIVE 1
6 allowing passage without obstruction — see OPEN 1
7 free from guilt or blame — see INNOCENT 2

clear *vb* **1** to rid the surface of (as an area) from things in the way ⟨the early settlers worked hard to *clear* the land for crops⟩
synonyms free, open, unblock
related words ease, facilitate, loosen (up), smooth, unclog, unstop
near antonyms clog, dam, obstruct, plug, stop
antonyms block
2 to set (a person or thing) free of something that encumbers — see RID
3 to give what is owed for — see PAY 2
4 to remove the contents of — see EMPTY
5 to remove usually visible impurities from — see CLARIFY 1
6 to set free from entanglement or difficulty — see EXTRICATE
7 to arrange clear passage of (something) by removing obstructions — see OPEN 2
8 to free from a charge of wrongdoing — see EXCULPATE
9 to give official acceptance of something as satisfactory — see APPROVE
10 to take away from a place or position — see REMOVE 2

clear (up) *vb* to make plain or understandable — see EXPLAIN 1

clearance *n* the approval by someone in authority for the doing of something — see PERMISSION

clear–cut *adj* **1** not subject to misinterpretation or more than one interpretation — see CLEAR 2
2 so clearly expressed as to leave no doubt about the meaning — see EXPLICIT

cleared *adj* allowing passage without obstruction — see OPEN 1

clearheaded *adj* **1** having full use of one's mind and control over one's actions — see SANE
2 not having one's mind affected by alcohol — see SOBER 1

clearing *n* a small area of usually open land — see FIELD 1

clearness *n* the state or quality of being easily seen through — see CLARITY 1

clear out *vb* **1** to cause (members of a group) to move widely apart — see SCATTER 1
2 to get free from a dangerous or confining situation — see ESCAPE 1
3 to leave a place often for another — see GO 2

clear–sighted *adj* **1** having or showing a practical cleverness or judgment — see SHREWD
2 having unusually keen vision — see SHARP-EYED

cleave *vb* to hold to something firmly as if by adhesion — see STICK 1

cleft *n* an irregular usually narrow break in a surface created by pressure — see CRACK 1

clemency *n* kind, gentle, or compassionate treatment especially towards someone who is undeserving of it — see MERCY 1

clement *adj* marked by temperatures that are neither too high nor too low ⟨Hawaii is known for its delightfully *clement* climate⟩
synonyms balmy, equable, gentle, mild, moderate, temperate
related words clear, cloudless, fair, rainless, sunny, sunshiny; calm, halcyon, peaceful, placid, tranquil; delightful, fine, pleasant
near antonyms blustering, blustery, breezy, gusty; foggy, hazy, misty; bleak, cloudy, dirty, foul, nasty, overcast, rainy, raw, rough, squally, stormy, sunless
antonyms harsh, inclement, intemperate, severe

clench *vb* to have or keep in one's hands — see HOLD 1

clergyman *n* a person specially trained and authorized to conduct religious services in a Christian church ⟨a special memorial service that attracted *clergymen* from all over the city⟩
synonyms cleric, deacon, divine, dominie, ecclesiastic, father, minister, padre, parson, preacher, priest, reverend
related words evangelist, missionary; deaconess, priestess; dean, pastor, rector, vicar; chaplain, confessor; canon, curate; friar, mendicant, monastic, monk, religious
antonyms layman

cleric *n* a person specially trained and authorized to conduct religious services in a Christian church — see CLERGYMAN

clerical *adj* of, relating to, or characteristic of the clergy ⟨*clerical* duties such as providing spiritual counseling and leading classes in Bible study⟩
synonyms ministerial, pastoral, priestly, sacerdotal
related words evangelical, missionary; apostolic, canonical, episcopal, papal, patriarchal, pontifical; churchly, ecclesiastical (*or* ecclesiastic); divine, holy, religious, sacramental; rabbinic (*or* rabbinical)
antonyms lay, nonclerical

clerk *n* **1** a person whose job is to keep records ⟨you'll need to get a copy of your birth certificate from the office of the town *clerk*⟩
synonyms register, registrar, scribe
related words archivist, bookkeeper, recorder; annalist, chronicler
2 a person employed to sell goods or services especially in a store — see SALESPERSON

clever *adj* **1** showing a use of the imagination and creativity especially in inventing ⟨an inventor who was constantly coming up with *clever* devices for doing everyday chores⟩
synonyms artful, creative, imaginative, ingenious
related words innovative, novel, original; convenient, handy, practical, useful; complex, sophisticated; adroit, deft, dexterous (*also* dextrous); brainy, intelligent, sharp, smart
near antonyms dull, pedestrian, stodgy
antonyms uncreative, unimaginative
2 having or showing quickness of mind — see INTELLIGENT 1
3 skillful with the hands — see DEXTEROUS 1
4 given to or marked by mature intelligent humor — see WITTY

cleverness *n* **1** mental skill or quickness — see DEXTERITY 1

2 subtle or imaginative ability in inventing, devising, or executing something — see SKILL 1

cliché *n* an idea or expression that has been used by many people — see COMMONPLACE

click *vb* **1** to form a close personal relationship — see COMMUNE

2 to turn out as planned or desired — see SUCCEED 1

client *n* a person who buys a product or uses a service from a business — see CUSTOMER 1

cliff *n* a steep wall of rock, earth, or ice ⟨the *cliff* rises 200 feet from the island's south shore⟩
synonyms bluff, crag, escarpment, palisade, precipice, scarp
related words tor; bulwark, embankment

climate *n* **1** a special quality or impression associated with something — see AURA

2 the circumstances, conditions, or objects by which one is surrounded — see ENVIRONMENT

climax *n* **1** a point in a chain of events at which an important change (as in one's fortunes) occurs — see TURNING POINT

2 the highest part or point — see HEIGHT 1

climax *vb* to bring to a triumphant conclusion — see CROWN

climb *n* the act or an instance of rising or climbing up — see ASCENT 1

climb *vb* **1** to move (as up or over something) often with the help of the hands in holding or pulling ⟨visitors should use caution when *climbing* over the wet rocks along the shore⟩
synonyms clamber, scramble
related words shin, shinny; inch; mount, scale, surmount; claw, struggle

2 to move or extend upward — see ASCEND

clinch *vb* to make final, definite, or beyond dispute ⟨the rain *clinched* the matter: we would have the party indoors⟩
synonyms decide, settle
related words demonstrate, determine, establish, prove, show; clarify, clear (up), illuminate; conclude, end, finish
near antonyms confuse, muddle, muddy

clincher *n* something (as a fact or argument) that is decisive or overwhelming ⟨the fact that the resort had tennis courts was the *clincher* in our deciding to stay there⟩
synonyms crusher, topper
related words deathblow, knockout; coup

cling *vb* to hold to something firmly as if by adhesion — see STICK 1

cling (to) *vb* **1** to give steadfast support to — see ADHERE

2 to have or keep in one's hands — see HOLD 1

clink *vb* to make a repeated sharp light ringing sound — see JINGLE

clip *n* a hard strike with a part of the body or an instrument — see [1]BLOW

clip *vb* to make (as hair) shorter with or as if with the use of shears ⟨toddlers are often fearful the first time they get their hair *clipped*⟩
synonyms bob, crop, curtail, cut, cut back, dock, lop (off), nip, pare, prune, shave, shear, snip, trim
related words manicure, mow; abbreviate, abridge, shorten
near antonyms elongate, extend, lengthen

clique *n* a group of people sharing a common interest and relating together socially — see GANG 2

cloak *n* **1** something that covers or conceals like a piece of cloth ⟨the *cloak* of mystery that surrounds the royal family⟩
synonyms curtain, hood, mantle, mask, shroud, veil
related words cover, screen, shield; facade (*also* façade), face, veneer

2 a sleeveless garment worn so as to hang over the shoulders, arms, and back — see [1]CAPE

cloak *vb* **1** to change the dress or looks of so as to conceal true identity — see DISGUISE

2 to keep secret or shut off from view — see [1]HIDE 2

clobber *vb* **1** to deliver a blow to (someone or something) usually in a strong vigorous manner — see HIT 1

2 to defeat by a large margin — see WHIP 2

3 to achieve a victory over — see BEAT 2

clock *n* a device to measure time — see TIMEPIECE

clod *n* **1** a big clumsy often slow-witted person — see OAF

2 a small uneven mass — see LUMP 1

cloddish *adj* having or showing crudely insensitive or impolite manners — see CLOWNISH

clodhopper *n* an awkward or simple person especially from a small town or the country — see HICK

clog *n* something that makes movement or progress more difficult — see ENCUMBRANCE

clog *vb* **1** to prevent passage through ⟨the discovery that a ton of hair was *clogging* the drain in the tub⟩
synonyms block, choke, close (off), congest, dam, jam, obstruct, plug (up), stop (up), stuff
related words bung, fill, pack; flood, glut, inundate, overwhelm, swamp
near antonyms excavate, hollow (out), scoop (out); empty, lighten
antonyms clear, free, open (up), unclog

2 to create difficulty for the work or activity of — see HAMPER

cloister *n* a residence for men under religious vows — see MONASTERY

cloistered *adj* hidden from view — see SECLUDED

close *adj* **1** having little space between items or parts ⟨the soldiers marched in *close* formation against the enemy⟩
synonyms compact, crowded, dense, jam-packed, packed, serried, thick, tight
related words airtight, snug; compacted, compressed, condensed; firm, hard, solid; impenetrable, impermeable, impervious
near antonyms commodious, roomy, spacious
antonyms loose, uncrowded

2 not being distant in time, space, or significance ⟨my birthday is *close* to Christmas⟩ ⟨a shopping mall that is very *close* to the highway⟩ ⟨these words are *close* synonyms⟩
synonyms immediate, near, nearby, neighboring, next-door, nigh
related words abutting, adjacent, adjoining, bordering, contiguous; approaching, coming, forthcoming, oncoming, upcoming; accessible, convenient, handy
phrases at hand
near antonyms divorced, removed, separated
antonyms away, distant, far, faraway, far-off, remote

3 showing little difference in the standing of the competitors ⟨the election results were so *close* that the votes had to be recounted⟩

synonyms narrow, nip and tuck, tight
related words crowded
4 closely acquainted — see FAMILIAR 1
5 given to keeping one's activities hidden from public observation or knowledge — see SECRETIVE
6 giving or sharing as little as possible — see STINGY 1
7 lacking fresh air — see STUFFY 1
8 meeting the highest standard of accuracy — see PRECISE 1

close *adv* at, within, or to a short distance or time — see NEAR 1

[1]**close** *n* an open space wholly or partly enclosed (as by buildings or walls) — see COURT 2

[2]**close** *n* **1** the stopping of a process or activity — see END 1
2 the last part of a process or action — see FINALE

close *vb* **1** to position (something) so as to prevent passage through an opening ⟨be sure to *close* the gate when you leave⟩
synonyms shut
related words bar, batten (down), bolt, chain, fasten, latch, lock; plug, seal, stopper; secure; bang, clap, slam
near antonyms unbar, unbolt, unchain, unfasten, unlatch, unlock, unseal
antonyms open
2 to stop the operations of ⟨the merchant will *close* the store if business doesn't improve⟩
synonyms shut
related words phase out, turn off; extinguish, quell, suppress; gag, muzzle, silence; fail, fold
near antonyms build, expand
antonyms open, start
3 to bring (an event) to a natural or appropriate stopping point ⟨we'll *close* the assembly with the singing of our national anthem⟩
synonyms conclude, end, finish, round (off *or* out), terminate, wind up, wrap up
related words climax, crown; complete, consummate, perfect; halt, stop, suspend
antonyms begin, commence, inaugurate, open, start
4 to come to an end — see CEASE 1
5 to come near or nearer — see APPROACH 1

close (off) *vb* to prevent passage through — see CLOG 1

closefisted *adj* giving or sharing as little as possible — see STINGY 1

close–knit *adj* bound together by feelings of very close association ⟨a *close-knit* family that constantly keeps in touch⟩
synonyms clannish
related words bosom, chummy, close, familiar, friendly, intimate, thick; exclusive, snobbish, snobby; forbidding, inhospitable, unfriendly

closely *adv* to a close degree — see NEAR 2

closemouthed *adj* **1** given to keeping one's activities hidden from public observation or knowledge — see SECRETIVE
2 tending not to speak frequently (as by habit or inclination) — see SILENT 2

closeness *n* **1** the practice or habit of keeping secrets or keeping one's affairs secret — see SECRECY
2 the quality of being overly sparing with money — see PARSIMONY
3 the quality or state of being very accurate — see PRECISION
4 the state of being in a very personal or private relationship — see FAMILIARITY 1
5 the state or condition of being near — see PROXIMITY

closer *adj* being the less far of two — see NEAR 1

closet *n* **1** a storage case typically having doors and shelves — see CABINET
2 an area within a building that has been set apart from surrounding space by a wall — see ROOM 2

closet *vb* to close or shut in by or as if by barriers — see ENCLOSE 1

closing *adj* following all others of the same kind in order or time — see LAST

closing *n* the last part of a process or action — see FINALE

closure *n* the stopping of a process or activity — see END 1

clot *vb* to turn from a liquid into a substance resembling jelly — see COAGULATE

cloth *n* a woven or knitted material (as of cotton or nylon) ⟨cotton canvas was the *cloth* traditionally used for a ship's sails⟩
synonyms fabric, textile
related words fiber, thread, yarn

clothe *vb* **1** to outfit with clothes and especially fine or special clothes ⟨they liked to *clothe* the twins in identical outfits just to confuse people⟩
synonyms apparel, array, attire, caparison, costume, deck, dress, garb, garment, gown, invest, rig (out), robe, suit
related words cloak, mantle; drape, swaddle, swathe; accoutre (*or* accouter), equip, furnish, outfit
near antonyms divest, uncover, undrape, unveil
antonyms disrobe, strip, unclothe, undress
2 to convey in appropriate or telling terms — see PHRASE

clothes *n pl* covering for the human body — see CLOTHING

clothing *n* covering for the human body ⟨a store that sells both men's and women's *clothing*⟩
synonyms apparel, attire, clothes, dress, duds, habiliment(s), rags, raiment, togs, wear
related words garment, vestment; array, bravery, finery; tatters; costume, garb, getup, guise, outfit, rig, wardrobe; haberdashery

cloud *vb* **1** to make dark, dim, or indistinct ⟨unfortunately, smog *clouds* the view of the city from the hilltop⟩
synonyms becloud, bedim, befog, blacken, blur, darken, dim, fog, haze, mist, obscure, overcast, overcloud, overshadow, shadow, shroud
related words blot out, conceal, hide, screen, shade; camouflage, cloak, cover, curtain, disguise, mask, veil; distort, falsify, garble, misrepresent
near antonyms expose, reveal, uncover, unveil; clarify, clear, purify; highlight, spotlight
antonyms brighten, illuminate, illumine, light (up), lighten
2 to make (something) unclear to the understanding — see CONFUSE 2

cloudburst *n* a steady falling of water from the sky in significant quantity — see RAIN 1

clouded *adj* **1** covered over by clouds — see OVERCAST
2 filled with or dimmed by fine particles (as of dust or water) in suspension — see HAZY 1

cloudless *adj* not stormy or cloudy — see FAIR 1

cloudy *adj* **1** having visible particles in liquid sus-

pension ⟨the water coming out of the faucet was unusually *cloudy*⟩
synonyms muddy, roiled, turbid
related words dingy, filmy, hazy, unfiltered; inky, murky; nontransparent, opaque
near antonyms clarified, filtered, purified
antonyms clear
2 covered over by clouds — see OVERCAST
3 filled with or dimmed by fine particles (as of dust or water) in suspension — see HAZY 1

clout *n* **1** a hard strike with a part of the body or an instrument — see [1]BLOW
2 the power to direct the thinking or behavior of others usually indirectly — see INFLUENCE 1

clout *vb* to deliver a blow to (someone or something) usually in a strong vigorous manner — see HIT 1

clown *n* **1** a comically dressed performer (as at a circus) who entertains with playful tricks and ridiculous behavior ⟨a *clown* wearing big floppy shoes and a red wig⟩
synonyms buffoon, harlequin, zany
related words cutup, madcap; fool, jester, motley; mime, mummer; comedian, comedienne, comic, joker, jokester, wag
2 a person whose behavior is offensive to others — see JERK 1

clown (around) *vb* to engage in attention-getting playful or boisterous behavior — see CUT UP

clowning *n* wildly playful or mischievous behavior — see HORSEPLAY

clownish *adj* having or showing crudely insensitive or impolite manners ⟨the *clownish* antics of some of the teenagers at the wedding reception⟩
synonyms boorish, churlish, cloddish, loutish, uncouth
related words coarse, ill-bred, uncultivated, unpolished, unrefined; tasteless, vulgar; beastly, bestial; doltish, oafish, stupid; discourteous, impolite, rude, uncivil
antonyms cultivated, polished, refined, well-bred; courtly, genteel, gentlemanly, ladylike; civil, courteous, polite

club *n* **1** a heavy rigid stick used as a weapon or for punishment ⟨hit the prisoner with a *club* if he tries anything funny⟩
synonyms bat, billy, bludgeon, cane, cudgel, nightstick, rod, shillelagh, staff, truncheon
related words blackjack, mace; birch, switch; hammer, mallet, maul; walking stick
2 the meeting place of an organization ⟨the Scouts gather at their *club* every Monday evening⟩
synonyms clubhouse, lodge
related words den, hangout, haunt, hideaway, hideout, lair; camp, headquarters; meetinghouse
3 a group of persons formally joined together for some common interest — see ASSOCIATION 2

club *vb* **1** to form or enter into an association that furthers the interests of its members — see ALLY
2 to strike repeatedly — see BEAT 1

clubhouse *n* the meeting place of an organization — see CLUB 2

clue *n* a slight or indirect pointing to something (as a solution or explanation) — see HINT 1

clue *vb* to give information to — see ENLIGHTEN 1

clump *n* **1** a number of things considered as a unit — see GROUP 1
2 a small uneven mass — see LUMP 1

clump *vb* to move heavily or clumsily — see LUMBER 1

clumpy *adj* having small pieces or lumps spread throughout — see CHUNKY 1

clumsy *adj* **1** lacking in physical ease and grace in movement or in the use of the hands ⟨diamond cutting is no job for a *clumsy* person⟩
synonyms awkward, gawky, graceless, heavy-handed, lubberly, lumbering, lumpish, ungainly, unhandy
related words butterfingered, uncoordinated; oafish; bungling, gauche, inept, inexpert, maladroit, unskilled, unskillful; cumbersome, unwieldy
near antonyms expert, masterly, skilled, skillful; lissome (*also* lissom), lithe, nimble; light, light-footed, surefooted
antonyms deft, dexterous (*also* dextrous), graceful, handy
2 lacking social grace and assurance — see AWKWARD 1
3 showing or marked by a lack of skill and tact (as in dealing with a situation) — see AWKWARD 2
4 difficult to use or operate especially because of size, weight, or design — see CUMBERSOME
5 hastily or roughly constructed — see RUDE 1

cluster *n* **1** a number of things considered as a unit — see GROUP 1
2 a usually small number of persons considered as a unit — see GROUP 2

cluster *vb* **1** to come together into one body or place — see ASSEMBLE 1
2 to gather into a closely packed group — see PRESS 3

clutch *n* **1** a time or state of affairs requiring prompt or decisive action — see EMERGENCY
2 the right or means to command or control others — see POWER 1

clutch *vb* to have or keep in one's hands — see HOLD 1

clutter *n* an unorganized collection or mixture of various things — see MISCELLANY 1

cluttered *adj* lacking in order, neatness, and often cleanliness — see MESSY

coach *n* a person who trains performers or athletes ⟨a *coach* who is highly respected by all of the baseball players⟩
synonyms trainer
related words instructor, teacher; driller, drillmaster; adviser (*or* advisor), counselor (*or* counsellor), mentor

coach *vb* to give advice and instruction to (someone) regarding the course or process to be followed — see GUIDE 1

coadjutor *n* a person who helps a more skilled person — see HELPER

coagulate *vb* to turn from a liquid into a substance resembling jelly ⟨the blood *coagulated*, and a scab formed on the wound⟩
synonyms clot, congeal, gel, jell, jelly, set
related words concrete, firm (up), freeze, harden, solidify, stiffen; condense, thicken; curdle, lump (up)
near antonyms deliquesce, flux, fuse, liquefy, melt, thaw

coalesce *vb* to come together to form a single unit — see UNITE 1

coalition *n* **1** a group of people acting together within a larger group — see FACTION
2 an association of persons, parties, or states for mutual assistance and protection — see CONFEDERACY

coarse *adj* **1** made up of large particles ⟨*coarse* rock salt was sprinkled on the icy walkway⟩
synonyms grainy, granular, granulated
related words rough; unfiltered, unrefined; gravelly, gritty, sandy; pebbly, rocky, stony (*also* stoney); lumpy, mealy
near antonyms smooth; filtered, pulverized, refined
antonyms dusty, fine, floury, powdery
2 lacking in refinement or good taste ⟨the hockey player's *coarse* manners turned his date off completely⟩
synonyms common, crass, crude, gross, ill-bred, low, lowbred, lowbrow, raffish, rough, rough-hewn, rude, tasteless, uncouth, uncultivated, uncultured, unpolished, unrefined, vulgar
related words boorish, churlish, cloddish, clownish, loutish, ungentlemanly; clumsy, lubberly, lumpish, oafish; inconsiderate, insensitive, thoughtless; countrified (*also* countryfied), provincial, rustic; graceless, inelegant, tacky
near antonyms aristocratic, courtly, patrician; elegant, graceful, gracious; considerate, sensitive, thoughtful; citified, sophisticated, urbane
antonyms cultivated, cultured, genteel, polished, refined, smooth, tasteful, well-bred
3 depicting or referring to sexual matters in a way that is unacceptable in polite society — see OBSCENE 1
4 harsh and dry in sound — see HOARSE
5 not having a level or smooth surface — see UNEVEN 1
6 of low quality — see CHEAP 2

coarseness *n* **1** the quality or state of being obscene — see OBSCENITY 1
2 the quality or state of lacking refinement or good taste — see VULGARITY 1

coast *vb* to move or proceed smoothly and readily — see FLOW 2

coat *n* the hairy covering of a mammal especially when fine, soft, and thick — see FUR 1

coat *vb* to form a layer over — see COVER 2

coax *vb* to get (someone) to do something by gentle urging, special attention, or flattery ⟨trying to *coax* Dad into taking us on a ski trip, we mentioned what a great skier he is⟩
synonyms blandish, blarney, cajole, soft-soap, wheedle
related words adulate, flatter, overpraise; compliment, praise; beguile, charm, woo; beg, importune, urge; bug, nag, pester
near antonyms browbeat, bulldoze, bully, cow, intimidate; coerce, compel, constrain, force, oblige

cobble (together) *vb* to make or assemble roughly or hastily ⟨the stranded hikers *cobbled together* a rickety shelter for the night⟩
synonyms patch (together), throw up
related words dash (off)
phrases knock together
near antonyms craft, handcraft; fashion, forge, hammer (out), pound (out)

[1]**cock** *n* a fixture for controlling the flow of a liquid — see FAUCET

[2]**cock** *n* a quantity of things thrown or stacked on one another — see [1]PILE 1

[3]**cock** *n* the act of positioning or an instance of being positioned at an angle — see TILT

cock *vb* to set or cause to be at an angle — see LEAN 1

cockcrow *n* the first appearance of light in the morning or the time of its appearance — see DAWN 1

cockeyed *adj* **1** inclined or twisted to one side — see AWRY
2 showing or marked by a lack of good sense or judgment — see FOOLISH 1

cocksure *adj* having or showing a mind free from doubt — see CERTAIN 2

cocky *adj* displaying or marked by rude boldness — see NERVY 1

cocoon *n* something that encloses another thing especially to protect it — see [1]CASE 1

coddle *vb* **1** to cook in a liquid heated to the point that it gives off steam — see BOIL 2
2 to treat with great or excessive care — see BABY

code *n* a collection or system of rules of conduct ⟨Hammurabi was an ancient king of Babylon with a famous *code* of laws⟩
synonyms decalogue, law
related words constitution

codger *n* a person of odd or whimsical habits — see ECCENTRIC

codify *vb* to put into a particular arrangement — see ORDER 1

coequal *adj* resembling another in every respect — see SAME 1

coerce *vb* to cause (a person) to give in to pressure — see FORCE

coerced *adj* not made or done willingly or by choice — see INVOLUNTARY 1

coercion *n* the use of power to impose one's will on another — see FORCE 2

coeval *adj* existing or occurring at the same period of time — see CONTEMPORARY 1

coeval *n* a person who lives at the same time or is about the same age as another — see CONTEMPORARY

coexist *vb* to occur or exist at the same time — see COINCIDE 1

coexistence *n* the occurrence or existence of several things at once — see CONCURRENCE 1

coexistent *adj* **1** existing or occurring at the same period of time — see CONTEMPORARY 1
2 present at the same time and place — see COINCIDENT

coexisting *adj* **1** existing or occurring at the same period of time — see CONTEMPORARY 1
2 present at the same time and place — see COINCIDENT

coextensive *adj* existing or occurring at the same period of time — see CONTEMPORARY 1

coffer *n* a specially reinforced container to keep valuables safe — see SAFE

coffin *n* a box for holding a dead body ⟨*coffins* are said to be the preferred sleeping places of vampires⟩
synonyms casket
related words sarcophagus, vault; urn; sepulcher (*or* sepulchre), sepulture

cogency *n* **1** the capacity to persuade ⟨the *cogency* of Thomas Paine's case for American independence⟩
synonyms effectiveness, force, forcefulness, persuasiveness
related words impact, punch, strength; soundness, validity; pertinence, relevance
near antonyms invalidity, unsoundness; weakness
antonyms ineffectiveness
2 the quality of an utterance that provokes interest and produces an effect — see [1]PUNCH 1

cogent *adj* having the power to persuade ⟨the results of the DNA fingerprinting were the most *cogent* evidence for acquittal⟩
synonyms compelling, conclusive, convincing, decisive, effective, forceful, persuasive, satisfying, strong, telling
related words sound, valid, well-founded; important, significant, weighty; material, pertinent, relevant
near antonyms groundless, invalid, unfounded, unsound; inconsequential, insignificant, unimportant; immaterial, irrelevant
antonyms inconclusive, indecisive, ineffective, unconvincing
cogitate *vb* to give serious and careful thought to — see PONDER
cognizance *n* **1** a state of being aware — see ATTENTION 2
2 knowledge gained by personal experience — see ACQUAINTANCE
cognizant *adj* having specified facts or feelings actively impressed on the mind — see CONSCIOUS
cognomen *n* **1** a descriptive or familiar name given instead of or in addition to the one belonging to an individual — see NICKNAME
2 a word or combination of words by which a person or thing is regularly known — see NAME 1
cohere *vb* to be in agreement on every point — see CHECK 1
coherence *n* a balanced, pleasing, or suitable arrangement of parts — see HARMONY 1
coherent *adj* according to the rules of logic — see LOGICAL 1
cohort *n* **1** a person frequently seen in the company of another — see ASSOCIATE 1
2 one associated with another in wrongdoing — see ACCOMPLICE
coil *vb* to follow a circular or spiral course — see WIND
coiling *adj* turning around an axis like the thread of a screw — see SPIRAL
coinage *n* something (as a device) created for the first time through the use of the imagination — see INVENTION 1
coincide *vb* **1** to occur or exist at the same time ⟨the heaviest snowfall of the season *coincided* with the start of our week-long ski vacation⟩
synonyms coexist, concur
related words chance, happen, transpire
near antonyms antedate, precede, predate; follow, succeed
2 to be in agreement on every point — see CHECK 1
3 to have or come to the same opinion or point of view — see AGREE 1
coincidence *n* the occurrence or existence of several things at once — see CONCURRENCE 1
coincident *adj* present at the same time and place ⟨the hard economic times and the *coincident* increase in crime were a double strain on the city's social services⟩
synonyms accompanying, attendant, attending, coexistent, coexisting, coincidental, concomitant, concurrent
related words contemporaneous, contemporary, simultaneous, synchronous; associated, collateral, connected, linked, related; consequent, resultant, resulting; ensuing, following, subsequent; accidental, casual, chance, fluky, fortuitous, freak, incident, incidental
near antonyms unassociated, unconnected, unrelated
coincidental *adj* present at the same time and place — see COINCIDENT
coincidentally *adv* at one and the same time — see TOGETHER 1
coincidently *adv* at one and the same time — see TOGETHER 1
coitus *n* sexual union involving penetration of the vagina by the penis — see SEXUAL INTERCOURSE
cold *adj* **1** having a low or subnormal temperature ⟨the *cold* climate of the Yukon⟩ ⟨an unusually *cold* spring that was followed by a sweltering summer⟩
synonyms arctic, bitter, cool, coolish, freezing, frigid, frosty, glacial, ice-cold, icy, nipping, nippy, numbing, polar, shivery, snappy, wintry
related words subfreezing, subzero; cutting, keen, penetrating, piercing, sharp; bracing, brisk, crisp, invigorating, rigorous; chilled, cooled, frosted, frozen, iced, refrigerated, unheated
near antonyms lukewarm, tepid; heated, warmed
antonyms broiling, burning, fiery, hot, piping hot, red-hot, roasting, scalding, scorching, searing, sultry, summery, sweltering, torrid, tropical, warm, warming
2 lacking in friendliness or warmth of feeling ⟨the prisoners got only a *cold* stare when they tried to befriend the guard⟩
synonyms chill, chilly, cold-blooded, cool, frigid, frosty, glacial, icy, unfriendly, unsympathetic, wintry
related words hardhearted, heartless, pitiless, uncaring, unfeeling; reserved, soulless, undemonstrative, unemotional, unresponsive; apathetic, indifferent, unenthusiastic, uninterested; aloof, detached, impersonal
near antonyms compassionate, kind, kindhearted; demonstrative, emotional, expressive; eager, enthusiastic, passionate
antonyms cordial, friendly, genial, hearty, sympathetic, warm, warm-blooded, warmhearted
3 having or showing a lack of friendliness or interest in others — see COOL 1
4 having lost consciousness — see UNCONSCIOUS 1
cold *n* a weather condition marked by low temperatures ⟨the *cold* will stay with us for another day, then temperatures should rise⟩
synonyms freeze, snap
related words frost; glaciation, ice age; bite, chill, nip, wintriness
near antonyms heat wave; dog days
cold–blooded *adj* **1** having or showing a lack of sympathy or tender feelings — see HARD 1
2 lacking in friendliness or warmth of feeling — see COLD 2
3 not feeling or showing emotion — see IMPASSIVE 1
cold–shoulder *vb* to deliberately ignore or treat rudely — see SNUB 1
cold shoulder *n* treatment that is deliberately unfriendly ⟨at the party the two former friends gave each other the *cold shoulder*⟩
synonyms brush-off, rebuff, repulse, snub
related words dismissal, rejection; banishment, ostracism
near antonyms welcome
coliseum *n* a large usually roofless building for sporting events with tiers of seats for spectators — see STADIUM

collaborate *vb* to participate or assist in a joint effort to accomplish an end — see COOPERATE 1
collaboration *n* **1** the state of having shared interests or efforts (as in social or business matters) — see ASSOCIATION 1
2 the work and activity of a number of persons who individually contribute toward the efficiency of the whole — see TEAMWORK
collapse *n* **1** a complete depletion of energy or strength — see FATIGUE
2 a falling short of one's goals — see FAILURE 2
collapse *vb* **1** to fall down or in as a result of physical pressure ⟨the motel balcony *collapsed* under the weight of so many people⟩
synonyms cave (in), crumple, give, go, yield
related words deflate, flatten, melt; break, break down, conk (out), crash, die, fail, give out, stall; burst, shatter, smash; crack, pop, snap
phrases give way
near antonyms inflate, rise, swell
2 to be unsuccessful — see FAIL 2
collar *vb* to take physical control or possession of (something) suddenly or forcibly — see CATCH 1
colleague *n* a fellow worker ⟨on her first day at work her *colleagues* went out of their way to make her feel welcome⟩
synonyms associate, coworker
related words equal, fellow, peer; accomplice, ally, cohort, collaborator, confederate, partner; buddy, chum, companion, comrade, crony, pal; compatriot, countryman
collect *vb* **1** to gain emotional or mental control of ⟨applicants should *collect* their thoughts while waiting to be interviewed⟩
synonyms calm, compose, contain, control, recollect, settle
related words allay, lull, quiet, soothe, still, tranquilize (*also* tranquillize)
phrases pull oneself together
2 to gradually form into a layer, pile, or mass ⟨dust has been *collecting* under my bed for years⟩
synonyms accumulate, conglomerate, gather, heap, pile (up)
related words bank, drift, ridge
near antonyms disperse, dissipate, scatter
3 to bring together from several sources into a single volume or list — see COMPILE
4 to bring together in one body or place — see GATHER 1
5 to come together into one body or place — see ASSEMBLE 1
collected *adj* free from emotional or mental agitation — see CALM 2
collection *n* **1** an organized group of objects acquired and maintained for study, exhibition, or personal pleasure ⟨his stamp *collection* has become quite valuable⟩
synonyms assemblage, library
related words cache, hoard, repertory, reserve, stock, stockpile, store, supply; accumulation, gathering, heap, pile; clutter, jumble, litter
2 a mass or quantity that has piled up or that has been gathered — see ACCUMULATION 1
3 a number of things considered as a unit — see GROUP 1
collective *adj* used or done by a number of people as a group ⟨the cleanup of the neighborhood park was a *collective* effort for which many people should be thanked⟩
synonyms combined, common, communal, concerted, conjoint, joint, mutual, public, shared, united
related words cooperative, reciprocal, symbiotic; mass, popular; general, generic, universal
near antonyms personal, private; independent, separate; particular, special, specialized
antonyms individual, single, sole
college *n* a group of persons formally joined together for some common interest — see ASSOCIATION 2
collide *vb* **1** to be out of harmony or agreement usually noticeably — see CLASH
2 to come into usually forceful contact with something — see HIT 2
collision *n* **1** a forceful coming together of two things — see IMPACT 1
2 the violent coming together of two bodies into destructive contact — see CRASH 1
colloquial *adj* **1** used in or suitable for speech and not formal writing ⟨the new kid's rudeness soon began—to use a *colloquial* expression—to rub me the wrong way⟩
synonyms conversational, informal, nonliterary, unliterary, vernacular, vulgar
related words dialectal, dialectical, nonstandard, substandard, uneducated; slang, slangy
near antonyms educated, standard; correct, genteel, grammatical, proper
antonyms bookish, formal, learned, literary
2 having the style and content of everyday conversation — see CHATTY 1
colloquy *n* **1** a meeting featuring a group discussion — see FORUM
2 an exchange of views for the purpose of exploring a subject or deciding an issue — see DISCUSSION 1
3 talking or a talk between two or more people — see CONVERSATION
collusion *n* a secret agreement or cooperation between two parties for an illegal or dishonest purpose ⟨there was *collusion* between the two companies to fix prices⟩
synonyms complicity, connivance, conspiracy
related words chicanery, foul play, skulduggery (*or* skullduggery); double-dealing, duplicity; cover-up, frame-up; intrigue, plot, scheme
colonist *n* a person who settles in a new region — see FRONTIERSMAN
colonizer *n* a person who settles in a new region — see FRONTIERSMAN
colony *n* **1** a settlement in a new country or region ⟨the early history of New York City when it was a Dutch *colony*⟩
synonyms plantation
related words outpost; dependency, mandate, possession, protectorate, territory
2 a group of people with a common interest living in one place — see COMMUNITY 2
color *n* **1** a property that becomes apparent when light falls on an object and by which things that are identical in form can be distinguished ⟨a shirt that is available in every *color* of the rainbow⟩
synonyms cast, hue, shade, tinge, tint, tone
related words complementary color, primary color, secondary color; brightness, saturation, value; coloration, coloring
2 a substance used to color other materials — see PIGMENT
3 the hue or appearance of the skin and especially of the face — see COMPLEXION 1

4 **colors** *pl* a piece of cloth with a special design that is used as an emblem or for signaling — see FLAG 1
color *vb* **1** to give color or a different color to ⟨she's *colored* her hair for so long and so often that no one knows what her natural color is⟩
synonyms dye, paint, stain, tinge, tint
related words brighten, lighten; darken, tone (down); daub
near antonyms blanch, bleach, whiten
antonyms decolorize
2 to add to the interest of by including made-up details — see EMBROIDER
3 to change so much as to create a wrong impression or alter the meaning of — see GARBLE
4 to develop a rosy facial color (as from excitement or embarrassment) — see BLUSH
colorful *adj* marked by a variety of usually vivid colors ⟨the *colorful* robes and blankets of the Native Americans of the Southwest⟩
synonyms motley, multicolored, polychromatic, polychrome, varicolored, variegated
related words brave, bright, brilliant, gay; flashy, garish, gaudy, loud, showy, splashy; deep, rich, unbleached; checkered, dotted, plaid, striped; colored, pigmented; dappled, shaded; marbled, mottled, piebald, pied, pinto; flecked, spotted, streaked; specked, speckled; banded, barred, brindled (*or* brindle)
near antonyms achromatic; bleached, decolorized, faded, washed out; dull, faint, gray (*also* grey), neutral, pale, pallid
antonyms colorless; monochromatic, solid
coloring *n* **1** a substance used to color other materials — see PIGMENT
2 the hue or appearance of the skin and especially of the face — see COMPLEXION 1
3 the representation of something in terms that go beyond the facts — see EXAGGERATION
colorless *adj* lacking an addition of color ⟨since we can't decide what color to paint the doghouse, our latest home project remains *colorless* for the time being⟩
synonyms uncolored, undyed, unpainted, unstained, white
related words clear, limpid, liquid, lucent, pellucid, transparent; bleached, faded, washed; dull, faint, gray (*also* grey), neutral, pale, pallid
near antonyms colorful, multicolored, polychromatic, polychrome, varicolored, variegated
antonyms colored, dyed, painted, stained, tinged, tinted
colossal *adj* unusually large — see HUGE
colossally *adv* to a large extent or degree — see GREATLY 2
colosseum *n* a large usually roofless building for sporting events with tiers of seats for spectators — see STADIUM
colossus *n* something that is unusually large and powerful — see GIANT
colt *n* a person who is just starting out in a field of activity — see BEGINNER
coltish *adj* given to good-natured joking or teasing — see PLAYFUL
column *n* **1** a series of persons or things arranged one behind another — see LINE 1
2 an upright shaft that supports an overhead structure — see PILLAR 1
coma *n* a temporary or permanent state of unconsciousness — see FAINT
comb *vb* to look through (as a place) carefully or thoroughly in an effort to find or discover something — see SEARCH 1
combat *n* **1** active fighting during the course of a war ⟨a soldier who served through the war without actually seeing *combat*⟩
synonyms action, battle
related words attack, fire; hostilities, operations, warfare; duty, service
2 a physical dispute between opposing individuals or groups — see FIGHT 1
3 an earnest effort for superiority or victory over another — see CONTEST 1
combat *vb* **1** to oppose (someone) in physical conflict — see FIGHT 1
2 to strive to reduce or eliminate — see FIGHT 2
combative *adj* feeling or displaying eagerness to fight — see BELLIGERENT
combativeness *n* an inclination to fight or quarrel — see BELLIGERENCE
combination *n* **1** a distinct entity formed by the combining of two or more different things — see BLEND
2 the act or an instance of joining two or more things into one — see UNION 1
3 a number of businesses or enterprises united for commercial advantage — see CARTEL
4 an association of persons, parties, or states for mutual assistance and protection — see CONFEDERACY
combine *n* **1** a number of businesses or enterprises united for commercial advantage — see CARTEL
2 an association of persons, parties, or states for mutual assistance and protection — see CONFEDERACY
combine *vb* **1** to come together to form a single unit — see UNITE 1
2 to turn into a single mass that is more or less the same throughout — see BLEND 1
combined *adj* used or done by a number of people as a group — see COLLECTIVE
combining *n* the act or an instance of joining two or more things into one — see UNION 1
combust *vb* to be on fire especially brightly — see BURN 1
combustible *adj* capable of catching or being set on fire ⟨don't store oily rags and other *combustible* materials in a hot attic⟩
synonyms burnable, flammable, ignitable, inflammable
related words explosive, incendiary
near antonyms nonexplosive
antonyms fireproof, incombustible, noncombustible, nonflammable, noninflammable
combusting *adj* being on fire — see ABLAZE 1
come *vb* **1** to move closer to ⟨*come* here and sit by the fire⟩
synonyms advance, approach, near
related words drop (in), enter, pop (in)
near antonyms depart, exit, leave
antonyms go, retreat, withdraw
2 to get to a destination ⟨when do you think they'll *come* ?⟩
synonyms arrive, land, show up, turn up
related words hit, make, reach; pull (in), touch down; debark, disembark; barge (in), breeze (in), burst (in *or* into), waltz (in)
antonyms go

3 to eventually have as a state or quality — see BECOME
4 to take place — see HAPPEN
come (to) *vb* **1** to have a total of — see AMOUNT (TO) 1
2 to be the same in meaning or effect — see AMOUNT (TO) 2
come about *vb* to take place — see HAPPEN
come around *vb* to gain consciousness again — see COME TO
comeback *n* **1** a quick witty response — see RETORT 1
2 something spoken or written in reaction especially to a question — see ANSWER 1
3 the process or period of gradually regaining one's health and strength — see CONVALESCENCE
comedian *n* a person (as a writer) noted for or specializing in humor — see HUMORIST
comedown *n* a loss of status ⟨after a rapid rise to stardom, the rock band's *comedown* was just as quick⟩
synonyms decline, descent, down, downfall, fall
related words breakdown, collapse, crash, meltdown, ruin, undoing; defeat, disappointment, reversal, setback; bottom, nadir
near antonyms advance, headway, progress; flower, heyday, prime
antonyms aggrandizement, ascent, exaltation, rise, up
come down (with) *vb* to become affected with (a disease or disorder) — see CONTRACT 1
comedy *n* humorous entertainment ⟨presented a night of *comedy* as part of the week-long celebrations⟩
synonyms farce, humor, slapstick
related words burlesque, parody, satire; banter, persiflage, wit; foolery, fun, horseplay, monkeyshines, shenanigans
comeliness *n* the qualities in a person or thing that as a whole give pleasure to the senses — see BEAUTY 1
comely *adj* very pleasing to look at — see BEAUTIFUL
come out *vb* **1** to come to be ⟨in the end everything *came out* OK⟩
synonyms pan out, prove, turn out
related words develop, emerge, evolve, play out, unfold, work out
2 to come into view — see APPEAR 1
3 to become known — see GET OUT 1
come round *vb* to gain consciousness again — see COME TO
come to *vb* to gain consciousness again ⟨after being in a coma for months, the patient suddenly *came to*⟩
synonyms come around, come round, revive
related words pull through, rally, recover; awake, awaken, wake up
near antonyms black out, faint, pass out
comfort *n* **1** a feeling of ease from grief or trouble ⟨the mourners found *comfort* in their pastor's words⟩
synonyms cheer, consolation, relief, solace
related words encouragement, inspiration, uplift; assurance, reassurance; alleviation, assuagement, mitigation; contentment, gladness, happiness; commiseration, empathy, sympathy
near antonyms anguish, distress, heartache, heartbreak, torment, torture
2 something that adds to one's ease ⟨a family campground with all the *comforts* of home⟩
synonyms amenity, convenience, luxury
related words extra; benefit, help, service; delight, indulgence, joy, pleasure
antonyms burden, millstone, weight
3 reduction of or freedom from pain — see EASE 1
4 something adding to pleasure or comfort but not absolutely necessary — see LUXURY 1
comfort *vb* **1** to ease the grief or distress of ⟨the minister did his best to *comfort* the victims of the terrible tornado⟩
synonyms assure, cheer, console, reassure, solace, soothe
related words commiserate, condole, empathize, sympathize; boost, buoy (up), elevate, lift, uplift; allay, alleviate, assuage, relieve; calm, quiet, relax, tranquilize (*also* tranquillize)
near antonyms demoralize, discourage, dishearten; fret, upset, worry; aggravate, intensify, worsen; annoy, irk, irritate; harass, pester
antonyms distress, torment, torture, trouble
2 to fill with courage or strength of purpose — see ENCOURAGE 1
comfortable *adj* **1** providing physical comfort ⟨a large, overstuffed chair that is very *comfortable*⟩
synonyms cozy, cushy, easy, snug, soft
related words relaxing, reposeful, restful; genial, hospitable, inviting, pleasant; commodious, roomy, spacious; homelike, homely, homey
near antonyms hard, harsh, severe; inhospitable, uninviting, unpleasant
antonyms uncomfortable
2 enjoying physical comfort ⟨make yourself *comfortable* in the living room while I fix us some snacks⟩
synonyms cozy, relaxed, snug
related words content, contented, pleased, satisfied; peaceful, resting; easygoing, laid-back; undisturbed, unperturbed, untroubled
phrases at ease, at home
near antonyms discontented, displeased, dissatisfied; agitated, disturbed, perturbed, troubled
antonyms uncomfortable
3 being more than enough without being excessive — see PLENTIFUL
comforting *adj* **1** making one feel good inside — see HEARTWARMING
2 tending to calm the emotions and relieve stress — see SOOTHING 1
comforting *n* the giving of hope and strength in times of grief, distress, or suffering — see CONSOLATION 1
comfortless *adj* **1** causing discomfort — see UNCOMFORTABLE 1
2 causing or marked by an atmosphere lacking in cheer — see GLOOMY 1
comic *adj* causing or intended to cause laughter — see FUNNY 1
comic *n* **1** a person (as a writer) noted for or specializing in humor — see HUMORIST
2 a series of drawings that tell a story or part of a story — see COMIC STRIP
comical *adj* **1** causing or intended to cause laughter — see FUNNY 1
2 so foolish or pointless as to be worthy of scornful laughter — see RIDICULOUS 1
comic strip *n* a series of drawings that tell a story or part of a story ⟨a *comic strip* that is beloved by both children and adults⟩

synonyms cartoon, comic, funny
related words comic book, funny paper(s); animated cartoon, animation; caricature

coming *adj* **1** being soon to appear or take place — see FORTHCOMING
2 being the one that comes immediately after another — see NEXT
3 of a time after the present — see FUTURE

comity *n* peaceful coexistence — see HARMONY 2

command *n* **1** a statement of what to do that must be obeyed by those concerned ⟨the captain's *commands* were followed without question⟩
synonyms behest, charge, commandment, decree, dictate, direction, directive, edict, instruction, order, word
related words demand, requirement; injunction, mandate; law, precept, rule; ordinance, regulation, statute
near antonyms appeal, entreaty, petition, plea, urging; proposal, recommendation, suggestion
2 a highly developed skill in or knowledge of something ⟨a *command* of French that is the result of a year spent in France as an exchange student⟩
synonyms mastership, mastery, proficiency
related words virtuosity; fluency, literacy; experience, expertise, know-how, practice (*also* practise), skill(s); acquaintance, familiarity, intimacy
near antonyms incompetence, incompetency; ignorance, illiteracy, unfamiliarity
3 the place from which a commander runs operations ⟨the general set up his *command* in the old port city⟩
synonyms base, headquarters
related words home, seat
4 a place from which authority is exercised — see SEAT 1
5 the right or means to command or control others — see POWER 1

command *vb* **1** to issue orders to (someone) by right of authority ⟨the general *commanded* the troops to advance⟩
synonyms adjure, bid, boss (around), charge, direct, enjoin, instruct, order, tell
related words ask, petition, request; beg, beseech, entreat; advise, counsel, warn; appoint, assign, authorize, commission; oversee, superintend, supervise; conduct, control, lead, manage; coerce, compel, constrain, force, oblige, require
near antonyms comply (with), follow, keep, observe
antonyms mind, obey
2 to give an order ⟨the governor has *commanded* that all state flags be flown at half-mast⟩
synonyms decree, dictate, direct, ordain, order
related words ask, petition, request; demand, require
phrases call for
3 to ask for (something) earnestly or with authority — see DEMAND 1
4 to exercise authority or power over — see GOVERN 1
5 to keep, control, or experience as one's own — see HAVE 1
6 to look down on — see OVERLOOK 1
7 to serve as leader of — see LEAD 2
8 to set or receive as a price — see CHARGE 1

commandant *n* one in official command especially of a military force or base — see COMMANDER 1

commandeer *vb* **1** to take control of (a vehicle) by force ⟨an airliner *commandeered* by terrorists⟩
synonyms hijack (*also* highjack)
related words appropriate, confiscate, expropriate, seize
2 to take or make use of without authority or right — see APPROPRIATE 1

commander *n* **1** one in official command especially of a military force or base ⟨a surrender of the fort by the *commander* without a single shot having been fired⟩
synonyms captain, commandant, commanding officer
related words commissioned officer
phrases commander in chief
2 a person in overall command of a ship — see CAPTAIN 1

commanding *adj* highest in rank or authority — see HEAD

commanding officer *n* one in official command especially of a military force or base — see COMMANDER 1

commandment *n* a statement of what to do that must be obeyed by those concerned — see COMMAND 1

commemorate *vb* **1** to be a memorial of ⟨a stone obelisk *commemorates* the Battle of Bunker Hill⟩
synonyms memorialize
related words celebrate, keep, observe, remember; enshrine, exalt, glorify, honor; bless, consecrate, sanctify, solemnize
near antonyms disgrace, dishonor
2 to act properly in relation to — see KEEP 1

commemorating *adj* serving to preserve the memory of a person, thing, or an event — see COMMEMORATIVE

commemorative *adj* serving to preserve the memory of a person, thing, or an event ⟨*commemorative* stamps for the stars of American popular music⟩
synonyms commemorating, memorial, memorializing
related words dedicatory, testimonial; enshrining, glorifying, honorary

commemorative *n* something that serves to keep alive the memory of a person or event — see MEMORIAL

commence *vb* **1** to take the first step in (a process or course of action) — see BEGIN 1
2 to come into existence — see BEGIN 2

commencement *n* the point at which something begins — see BEGINNING

commend *vb* to put (something) into the possession or safekeeping of another — see GIVE 2

commendable *adj* deserving of high regard or great approval — see ADMIRABLE

commendation *n* **1** a formal recognition of an achievement or praiseworthy deed ⟨a firefighter who has been awarded several *commendations* for bravery⟩
synonyms acknowledgment (*also* acknowledgement), citation
related words decoration, medal, ribbon; accolade, award, prize, tribute; dedication
2 a formal expression of praise — see ENCOMIUM

commendatory *adj* expressing approval — see FAVORABLE 1

commensurate *adj* corresponding in size, amount, extent, or degree — see PROPORTIONAL

comment *n* **1** a briefly expressed opinion — see REMARK

2 comments *pl* a series of explanations or observations on something (as an event) — see COMMENTARY

comment *vb* to make a statement of one's opinion — see REMARK 1

commentary *n* a series of explanations or observations on something (as an event) ⟨the TV anchors provided a running *commentary* on the parade⟩
synonyms analysis, comment, exposition
related words annotation, explication; note, observation, remark; report, review, write-up

commerce *n* the buying and selling of goods especially on a large scale and between different places ⟨a government agency in charge of regulating interstate *commerce*⟩
synonyms business, marketplace, trade, traffic
related words free trade; dealings, horse-trading; merchandising, retailing, wholesaling; bartering

commercial *adj* fit or likely to be sold especially on a large scale ⟨the *commercial* fare produced by the Hollywood movie studios⟩
synonyms marketable, salable (*or* saleable)
related words mass-produced, wholesale
antonyms noncommercial, nonsalable, uncommercial, unmarketable, unsalable

commingle *vb* to turn into a single mass that is more or less the same throughout — see BLEND 1

commiserate (with) *vb* to have sympathy for — see PITY

commiseration *n* **1** sorrow or the capacity to feel sorrow for another's suffering or misfortune — see SYMPATHY 1
2 the capacity for feeling for another's unhappiness or misfortune — see HEART 1

commissary *n* a person who acts or does business for another — see AGENT 2

commission *n* **1** the granting of power to perform various acts or duties ⟨President Jefferson's *commission* to Lewis and Clark to explore the Louisiana Territory⟩
synonyms accreditation, authorization, delegation, license (*or* licence), mandate
related words commendation, consignment, entrustment; facilitation, fostering, promotion; commanding, directing, ordering
2 the doing of an action ⟨a single burglar was responsible for the *commission* of all the break-ins⟩
synonyms accomplishment, achievement, discharge, enactment, execution, fulfillment, implementation, performance, perpetration
related words dispatch, expedition; administration, direction, handling, management; application, operation, practice (*also* practise)
antonyms nonfulfillment, nonperformance
3 a select group of persons assigned to consider or take action on some matter — see COMMITTEE
4 the state or fact of being chosen for a position or duty — see APPOINTMENT 1

commission *vb* **1** to appoint as one's representative — see DELEGATE 1
2 to give official or legal power to — see AUTHORIZE 1
3 to give a task, duty, or responsibility to — see ENTRUST 1
4 to pick (someone) by one's authority for a specific position or duty — see APPOINT 2

commit *vb* **1** to carry through (as a process) to completion — see PERFORM 1
2 to obligate by prior agreement — see PLEDGE 1
3 to put (something) into the possession or safekeeping of another — see GIVE 2
4 to put in or as if in prison — see IMPRISON

commitment *n* something one must do because of prior agreement — see OBLIGATION

committee *n* a select group of persons assigned to consider or take action on some matter ⟨a *committee* in charge of planning the organization's annual Christmas party⟩
synonyms commission, panel
related words subcommittee; delegation, mission; assembly, body, congress, convocation, council, synod

commodious *adj* more than adequate or average in capacity — see SPACIOUS

commodities *n pl* products that are bought and sold in business — see MERCHANDISE

common *adj* **1** often observed or encountered ⟨horse ranches are a *common* sight in that part of the state⟩
synonyms commonplace, everyday, familiar, frequent, garden, household, ordinary, routine, ubiquitous, usual
related words normal, regular, standard; general, universal; ceaseless, constant, continual, continuous, incessant, unceasing; popular, prevailing, prevalent, rampant; perennial, recurrent, repeated
near antonyms aberrant, abnormal, irregular, unnatural; intermittent, occasional, sporadic
antonyms extraordinary, infrequent, rare, uncommon, unfamiliar, unusual
2 being of the type that is encountered in the normal course of events — see ORDINARY 1
3 belonging or relating to the whole — see GENERAL 1
4 belonging to the class of people of low social or economic rank — see IGNOBLE 1
5 held by or applicable to a majority of the people — see GENERAL 3
6 used or done by a number of people as a group — see COLLECTIVE
7 of average to below average quality — see MEDIOCRE 1
8 of low quality — see CHEAP 2
9 lacking in refinement or good taste — see COARSE 2

commoners *n pl* the body of the community as contrasted with the elite — see MASS 1

commonly *adv* according to the usual course of things — see NATURALLY 2

commonness *n* **1** the fact or state of happening often — see FREQUENCY
2 the quality or state of lacking refinement or good taste — see VULGARITY 1

commonplace *adj* **1** being of the type that is encountered in the normal course of events — see ORDINARY 1
2 often observed or encountered — see COMMON 1
3 used or heard so often as to be dull — see STALE

commonplace *n* an idea or expression that has been used by many people ⟨the familiar summertime *commonplace* that "it's not the heat, it's the humidity"⟩
synonyms banality, cliché, platitude, shibboleth, truism
related words inanity; generality, generalization,

simplification; adage, proverb, saw, saying; old wives' tale, stereotype
near antonyms profundity

commonsense *adj* based on sound reasoning or information — see GOOD 1

common sense *n* the ability to make intelligent decisions especially in everyday matters ⟨*common sense* should tell you not to meet face-to-face with someone who is just an online acquaintance⟩
synonyms discreetness, discretion, horse sense, levelheadedness, prudence, sense, sensibleness, wisdom, wit
related words street smarts; farsightedness, foresight, foresightedness, judgment (*or* judgement); brains, gray matter, intelligence; logicalness, practicality, rationality; discernment, discrimination, insight, sagacity, sapience; acumen, astuteness, keenness, penetration, perspicacity, shrewdness; care, caution, circumspection, precaution, premeditation
near antonyms shortsightedness; brainlessness, foolishness, idiocy, senselessness, stupidity; carelessness, heedlessness
antonyms imprudence, indiscretion

commonwealth *n* a body of people composed of one or more nationalities usually with its own territory and government — see NATION

commotion *n* a state of noisy, confused activity ⟨the *commotion* created when the nation's top rock band arrived in town⟩
synonyms bother, bustle, clatter, disturbance, furor, furore, fuss, hubbub, hullabaloo, hurly-burly, pandemonium, pother, row, ruckus, ruction, rumpus, shindy, squall, stew, stir, storm, to-do, tumult, turmoil, uproar, welter, whirl
related words cacophony, clamor, din, howl, hue and cry, outcry, noise, racket, roar; disorder, unrest, upheaval; eruption, flare-up, flurry, outbreak, outburst; brawl, fracas, fray, hassle, melee, scuffle; dither, fever, fret, lather, tizzy
near antonyms calm, hush, peace, quiet, quietude, rest, stillness, tranquillity (*or* tranquility); order, orderliness

communal *adj* used or done by a number of people as a group — see COLLECTIVE

commune *vb* to form a close personal relationship ⟨after a week in the wilderness, the scouts were really starting to *commune* with nature⟩
synonyms click, relate
related words bond; befriend

communicable *adj* capable of being passed by physical contact from one person to another — see CONTAGIOUS 1

communicate *vb* **1** to cause (something) to pass from one to another ⟨the infected cook unknowingly *communicated* the disease to hundreds of people⟩
synonyms convey, impart, spread, transfer, transfuse, transmit
related words deliver, hand over, surrender, turn over; broadcast, diffuse, disseminate, propagate; contaminate, infect, poison
near antonyms catch, come down (with), contract
2 to engage in an exchange of information or ideas ⟨for decades the two medical centers have been *communicating* about cancer research⟩
synonyms brainstorm, intercommunicate
related words correspond; converse, talk; bond, commune, relate; accost, approach, contact

communicate (with) *vb* to transmit information or requests to — see CONTACT

communication *n* a piece of conveyed information ⟨the latest *communication* from the crew of the space station⟩
synonyms dispatch, message
related words bulletin, communiqué, report; memo, memorandum, notice; epistle, letter, missive, note; electronic mail, e-mail; intelligence, news, tidings, word; command, directive, instruction, order

communion *n* a friendly relationship marked by ready communication and mutual understanding — see RAPPORT

community *n* **1** the people living in a particular area ⟨the whole *community* rallied to the aid of the family who had lost its home⟩
synonyms neighborhood
related words city, commune, town, village; denizens, dwellers, inhabitants, residents; citizenry, culture, people, populace, public, society
2 a group of people with a common interest living in one place ⟨a picturesque seacoast village that is known for its sizable *community* of artists⟩
synonyms colony
related words circle, clique, coterie, set, society; band, company, troop; clan, family
3 a group of people sharing a common interest and relating together socially — see GANG 2
4 the body of people in a profession or field of activity — see CORPS
5 the quality or state of having many qualities in common — see SIMILARITY 1

commutation *n* a giving or taking of one thing of value in return for another — see EXCHANGE 1

commute *vb* to give up (something) and take something else in return — see CHANGE 3

compact *adj* **1** having a consistency that does not easily yield to pressure — see FIRM 2
2 having little space between items or parts — see CLOSE 1
3 marked by the use of few words to convey much information or meaning — see CONCISE

compact *n* **1** a formal agreement between two or more nations or peoples — see TREATY
2 an arrangement about action to be taken — see AGREEMENT 2

compact *vb* **1** to bring (something) to a central point or under a single control — see CENTRALIZE
2 to reduce in size or volume by or as if by pressing parts or members together — see COMPRESS 1

compacting *n* the act or process of reducing the size or volume of something by or as if by pressing — see COMPRESSION

compactly *adv* in a few words — see SHORTLY 1

compactness *n* the quality or state of being marked by or using only few words to convey much meaning — see SUCCINCTNESS

companion *n* **1** a person frequently seen in the company of another — see ASSOCIATE 1
2 one that accompanies another for protection, guidance, or as a courtesy — see ESCORT
3 either of a pair matched in one or more qualities — see MATE 1
4 something that is found along with something else — see ACCOMPANIMENT

companionable *adj* **1** having or showing kindly feeling and sincere interest — see FRIENDLY 1
2 likely to seek or enjoy the company of others — see CONVIVIAL

companionship *n* the feeling of closeness and friendship that exists between companions ⟨the widow's pet cats provided her with her only *companionship*⟩
synonyms camaraderie, company, comradeship, fellowship, society
related words amity, benevolence, cordiality, friendliness, friendship, goodwill, kindliness; civility, comity, concord, harmony, rapport; charity, generosity; affinity, compassion, empathy, sympathy; chumminess, familiarity, inseparability, intimacy, nearness; affection, devotion, fondness, love
near antonyms forlornness, loneliness, lonesomeness

company *n* **1** an organized group of stage performers ⟨a city that is fortunate enough to have two thriving opera *companies*⟩
synonyms troop, troupe
related words stock company; cast, dramatis personae, ensemble
2 a group of people working together on a task — see GANG 1
3 a commercial or industrial activity or organization — see ENTERPRISE 1
4 the feeling of closeness and friendship that exists between companions — see COMPANIONSHIP

comparable *adj* having qualities in common — see ALIKE

comparative *adj* being such only when compared to something else ⟨if you consider the multimillionaire's yearly income, we're living in *comparative* poverty⟩
synonyms approximate, near, relative
related words alike, comparable, similar; equal, equivalent
near antonyms genuine, real, true
antonyms absolute, complete, downright, out-and-out, outright, perfect, pure, unqualified

compare *vb* **1** to describe as similar ⟨reviews that *compared* the adventure movie to a thrilling ride on a roller coaster⟩
synonyms bracket, equate, liken
related words associate, connect, couple, link; allude, refer, relate; equal, match, parallel
antonyms contrast
2 to regard or represent as equal or comparable — see EQUATE 1

compare (with) *vb* to come near or nearer to in character or quality — see APPROXIMATE

compartment *n* one of the parts into which an enclosed space is divided ⟨a backpack with many handy *compartments* for storing your camping gear⟩
synonyms bay, cabin, cell, chamber, cubicle
related words cubbyhole, pigeonhole, snuggery [*chiefly British*]; alcove, niche, nook, recess; cabinet, drawer; cavity, hole, hollow; booth, crib, stall; crypt, vault

compass *n* **1** an area over which activity, capacity, or influence extends — see RANGE 2
2 the line or relatively narrow space that marks the outer limit of something — see BORDER 1

compass *vb* **1** to carry through (as a process) to completion — see PERFORM 1
2 to pass completely around — see ENCIRCLE 1

compassion *n* **1** sorrow or the capacity to feel sorrow for another's suffering or misfortune — see SYMPATHY 1
2 the capacity for feeling for another's unhappiness or misfortune — see HEART 1

compassionate *adj* **1** having or marked by sympathy and consideration for others — see HUMANE 1
2 having or showing the capacity for sharing the feelings of another — see SYMPATHETIC 1

compatibility *n* peaceful coexistence — see HARMONY 2

compatible *adj* **1** having or marked by agreement in feeling or action — see HARMONIOUS 3
2 not having or showing any apparent conflict — see CONSISTENT

compatriot *n* a person living in or originally from the same country as another ⟨an appeal to all of his *compatriots* to come to their country's aid in its hour of need⟩
synonyms countryman
related words nationalist, patriot; citizen, national, subject; aborigine, native; homeboy, resident
near antonyms alien, foreigner, immigrant, outsider

compel *vb* to cause (a person) to give in to pressure — see FORCE

compelling *adj* having the power to persuade — see COGENT

compendious *adj* **1** covering everything or all important points — see ENCYCLOPEDIC
2 marked by the use of few words to convey much information or meaning — see CONCISE

compensate *vb* **1** to provide (someone) with a just payment for loss or injury ⟨you'll have to *compensate* the neighbors for cutting down their tree⟩
synonyms indemnify, recompense, recoup, remunerate, requite
related words refund, reimburse, repay; redress, remedy, repair; discharge, pay, quit
2 to give (someone) the sum of money owed for goods or services received — see PAY 1

compensate (for) *vb* to balance with an equal force so as to make ineffective — see OFFSET

compensation *n* **1** payment to another for a loss or injury ⟨a warehouse worker who received a large *compensation* for his crippling injury while on the job⟩
synonyms damages, indemnification, indemnity, quittance, recompense, recoupment, redress, remuneration, reparation, requital, restitution, satisfaction
related words amends, atonement, expiation; refund, reimbursement, repayment; adjustment, settlement; punishment, reprisal, retaliation
2 something (as money) that is given or received in return for goods or services — see PAYMENT 2
3 the act of offering money in exchange for goods or services — see PAYMENT 1

compete *vb* to engage in a contest ⟨prizefighters *competing* for the world heavyweight championship⟩
synonyms battle, contend, fight, race, vie
related words challenge, engage, play; jockey, maneuver; go out, try out; train, work

competence *n* the physical or mental power to do something — see ABILITY

competency *n* the physical or mental power to do something — see ABILITY

competent *adj* having the required skills for an acceptable level of performance ⟨any *competent* mechanic should be able to fix that⟩
synonyms able, capable, fit, good, qualified, suitable

related words accomplished, ace, adept, experienced, expert, master, masterful, masterly, practiced (*or* practised), proficient, seasoned, skilled, skillful, veteran; prepared, schooled, trained
near antonyms inexperienced, inexpert, unseasoned, unskilled, unskillful; unprepared, unschooled, untrained; beginning, green, new, raw, untested, untried
antonyms incompetent, inept, poor, unfit, unqualified

competently *adv* in a skillful or expert manner — see WELL 3

competition *n* **1** a competitive encounter between individuals or groups carried on for amusement, exercise, or in pursuit of a prize — see GAME 1
2 one who strives for the same thing as another — see COMPETITOR

competitor *n* one who strives for the same thing as another ⟨the *competitors* for the science award come from the best high schools in the country⟩
synonyms challenger, competition, contender, contestant, rival
related words finalist, semifinalist; entrant, player; adversary, antagonist, opponent

compilation *n* a collection of writings — see ANTHOLOGY

compile *vb* to bring together from several sources into a single volume or list ⟨*compiled* the best short stories ever written into one fat book⟩
synonyms collect
related words edit, redraft, revamp, revise, rework; accumulate, amass, assemble, gather, group

complacence *n* an often unjustified feeling of being pleased with oneself or with one's situation or achievements ⟨the *complacence* of some of the rich kids at the exclusive private school⟩
synonyms complacency, conceit, conceitedness, ego, egotism, pompousness, pride, pridefulness, self-admiration, self-conceit, self-esteem, self-importance, self-satisfaction, smugness, vaingloriousness, vainglory, vainness, vanity
related words assurance, confidence, self-assurance, self-confidence; self-righteousness; arrogance, disdainfulness, haughtiness, imperiousness, lordliness, self-assertion, snobbishness, superciliousness, superiority; overconfidence, presumption; pretense (*or* pretence), pretension, pretentiousness; egoism, self-centeredness, selfishness; self-respect
near antonyms diffidence, self-doubt; altruism, unselfishness; bashfulness, demureness, shyness, timidity, timidness; passiveness, passivity
antonyms humbleness, humility, modesty

complacency *n* an often unjustified feeling of being pleased with oneself or with one's situation or achievements — see COMPLACENCE

complacent *adj* having too high an opinion of oneself — see CONCEITED

complain *vb* to express dissatisfaction, pain, or resentment usually tiresomely ⟨the time-honored tradition of students *complaining* about the food in the cafeteria⟩
synonyms beef, bellyache, carp, crab, croak, fuss, gripe, grouse, growl, grumble, kick, moan, murmur, mutter, repine, squawk, wail, whine, yammer
related words object (to), protest, quarrel (with); cavil, quibble; fret, stew, worry; blubber, cry, sob; bemoan, bewail, deplore, lament
near antonyms accept, bear, countenance, endure, tolerate; applaud, cheer, commend
antonyms rejoice

complainant *n* the person in a legal proceeding who makes a charge of wrongdoing against another ⟨the *complainant* charged that the defendant had broken the ironclad contract that both had signed⟩
synonyms plaintiff, suer
related words accuser; litigant, party, suitor; appellant, petitioner, pleader
near antonyms accused
antonyms defendant

complainer *n* **1** a person who makes frequent complaints usually about little things — see CRYBABY
2 an irritable and complaining person — see GROUCH

complaint *n* **1** an expression of dissatisfaction, pain, or resentment ⟨a warning that if there were any more *complaints*, we were turning around and not going to the beach after all⟩
synonyms beef, fuss, grievance, gripe, grumble, murmur, plaint, squawk
related words challenge, demur, expostulation, kick, objection, protest, quibble, remonstrance
near antonyms commendation, compliment, plaudit; acclaim, applause, praise; approval, endorsement, sanction
2 a feeling or declaration of disapproval or dissent — see OBJECTION
3 a formal claim of criminal wrongdoing against a person — see CHARGE 1
4 an abnormal state that disrupts a plant's or animal's normal bodily functioning — see DISEASE

complaisance *n* a desire or disposition to please ⟨the *complaisance* of his girlfriend is such that she goes along with everything he says⟩
synonyms amenability, amiability, good-naturedness
related words affability, amicability, congeniality, cordiality, friendliness, geniality, sociability; agreeableness, graciousness, pleasantness; kindheartedness, kindliness, warmheartedness; compliance, docility, passivity, submissiveness
near antonyms disagreeableness, sullenness, surliness, ungraciousness; disobedience, intractability, recalcitrance

complement *n* **1** something that serves to complete or make up for a deficiency in something else ⟨with his practicality and her refreshing enthusiasm, they are perfect *complements* to each other⟩
synonyms supplement
related words addendum, addition, appendix; adjunct, annex, appendage, extension; accessory, appliance, attachment; additive, filler
2 the largest number or amount that something can hold — see CAPACITY 1

complement *vb* to serve as a completing element to ⟨this cap *complements* your Boy Scout uniform⟩
synonyms complete, round (off *or* out)
related words finish (off), flesh (out); adorn, beautify, decorate, embellish; better, enhance, improve; constitute, form, make up

complementary *adj* related to each other in such a way that one completes the other ⟨the *complementary* contributions of the cooking and cleanup committees were essential to the success of the church barbecue⟩
synonyms reciprocal, supplementary

related words cooperative, mutual, symbiotic; collective, combined, common, communal, conjoint, joint, shared, united
antonyms noncomplementary, nonreciprocal

complete *adj* **1** not lacking any part or member that properly belongs to it ⟨a *complete* deck of cards⟩
synonyms comprehensive, entire, full, grand, intact, integral, perfect, plenary, total, whole
related words unabridged, uncut, undiminished; all-out, exhaustive, extensive; full-blown, full-fledged, full-scale
near antonyms abbreviated, abridged, cut, diminished, reduced
antonyms imperfect, incomplete, partial
2 brought or having come to an end ⟨your education is never *complete* —there's always something more to learn⟩
synonyms completed, concluded, done, down, ended, finished, over, terminated, through, up
related words accomplished, achieved, attained, compassed, realized; dead, defunct, extinct, obsolete; expired
antonyms continuing, incomplete, ongoing, uncompleted, unfinished
3 covering everything or all important points — see ENCYCLOPEDIC
4 having no exceptions or restrictions — see ABSOLUTE 2
5 trying all possibilities — see EXHAUSTIVE

complete *vb* **1** to bring (something) to a state where nothing remains to be done — see FINISH 1
2 to serve as a completing element to — see COMPLEMENT

completed *adj* brought or having come to an end — see COMPLETE 2

completely *adv* **1** to a full extent or degree — see FULLY 1
2 with attention to all aspects or details — see THOROUGHLY 1

complex *adj* **1** having many parts or aspects that are usually interrelated ⟨this camera is a *complex* instrument that requires careful handling⟩ ⟨*complex* issues regarding free speech and school discipline⟩
synonyms complicated, convoluted, elaborate, intricate, involved, knotty, labyrinthine, sophisticated
related words composite, compound, heterogeneous, mixed, multifarious, varied; challenging, difficult, tough; impenetrable, incomprehensible, inexplicable, unfathomable, unintelligible
near antonyms oversimplified, simplified; homogeneous, uniform, unvaried
antonyms plain, simple, uncomplicated
2 made or done with great care or with much detail — see ELABORATE 1

complex *n* **1** a structure that is designed and built for a particular purpose — see FACILITY
2 something made up of many interdependent or related parts — see SYSTEM 1

complexion *n* **1** the hue or appearance of the skin and especially of the face ⟨a sunscreen for people with very light *complexions*⟩
synonyms color, coloring
related words shade, tint, tone; features, lineaments, looks; countenance, face, visage
2 the set of qualities that makes a person, a group of people, or a thing different from others — see NATURE 1

complexity *n* **1** the state or quality of having many interrelated parts or aspects ⟨the *complexity* of the company's computer system is such that a full-time repairman is needed⟩
synonyms complicatedness, elaborateness, intricacy, involution, sophistication
related words diversity, heterogeneousness; impenetrability, incomprehensibility, inexplicability
near antonyms simplification; homogeneity, uniformity
antonyms plainness, simpleness, simplicity
2 something that makes a situation more complicated or difficult — see COMPLICATION 1

compliance *n* **1** a readiness or willingness to yield to the wishes of others ⟨a strong-willed pop star who is not known for her *compliance*⟩
synonyms compliancy, deference, docility, obedience, submissiveness
related words amenability, amiability, complaisance, good-naturedness; servility, slavishness, subservience, subserviency; conformity; cooperativeness, receptiveness, receptivity; humoring, indulgence; acceptance, acquiescence, assent, consent; capitulation, submission, surrender; affability, amicability, congeniality, cordiality, friendliness, geniality, sociability
near antonyms animosity, antipathy, enmity, hostility, ill will
antonyms defiance, disobedience, intractability, recalcitrance
2 a bending to the authority or control of another — see OBEDIENCE 1

compliancy *n* a readiness or willingness to yield to the wishes of others — see COMPLIANCE 1

compliant *adj* readily giving in to the command or authority of another — see OBEDIENT

complicate *vb* to make complex or difficult ⟨the need to go to both a soccer game and band practice really *complicates* tonight's schedule⟩
synonyms perplex, sophisticate
related words develop, elaborate, expand; intensify, magnify; confound, confuse, mess (up), mix (up), muddle; entangle, snarl, tangle
near antonyms abbreviate, cut, shorten; ease, facilitate; disentangle, straighten (out), untangle; oversimplify
antonyms simplify, streamline

complicated *adj* **1** having many parts or aspects that are usually interrelated — see COMPLEX 1
2 made or done with great care or with much detail — see ELABORATE 1

complicatedness *n* the state or quality of having many interrelated parts or aspects — see COMPLEXITY 1

complication *n* **1** something that makes a situation more complicated or difficult ⟨the food allergies of the guests were just another *complication* for the couple trying to plan their wedding reception⟩
synonyms complexity, difficulty, intricacy
related words aftereffect, ramification, side effect; subtlety, technicality; annoyance, bother, headache, inconvenience, matter, trouble
phrases fly in the ointment
2 an abnormal state that disrupts a plant's or animal's normal bodily functioning — see DISEASE

complicity *n* a secret agreement or cooperation between two parties for an illegal or dishonest purpose — see COLLUSION

compliment *vb* to express to (someone) admiration

for his or her success or good fortune — see CONGRATULATE

complimentary *adj* **1** expressing approval — see FAVORABLE 1
2 not costing or charging anything — see FREE 4

compliments *n pl* best wishes <please extend our *compliments* to the chef for a great meal>
synonyms congratulations, felicitations, greetings, regards, respects
related words approval, blessing, endorsement; acknowledgment (*also* acknowledgement), citation, commendation; adulation, flattery, praise
near antonyms dig, gibe (*or* jibe), insult, putdown, taunt

comply (with) *vb* **1** to act according to the commands of — see OBEY
2 to do what is required by the terms of — see FULFILL 1

component *n* one of the parts that make up a whole — see ELEMENT 1

comport *vb* **1** to be in agreement on every point — see CHECK 1
2 to manage the actions of (oneself) in a particular way — see BEHAVE

comportment *n* the way or manner in which one conducts oneself — see BEHAVIOR

compose *vb* **1** to put (something) into proper and usually carefully worked out written form <the whole class *composed* a request to the governor asking that the endangered species be adopted as the official state animal>
synonyms cast, craft, draft, draw (up), formulate, frame, prepare
related words fabricate, fashion, form, mold, sculpture, shape; couch, express, phrase, state, verbalize, word; author, pen, write; conceive, concoct, devise; build, construct, make; assemble, compound, piece (together)
phrases put together
2 to be all the substance of — see CONSTITUTE 1
3 to free from distress or disturbance — see CALM 1
4 to gain emotional or mental control of — see COLLECT 1

composed *adj* free from emotional or mental agitation — see CALM 2

composer *n* a person who writes musical compositions <a versatile *composer* whose works include operas, symphonies, concertos, and sonatas>
synonyms musician, songwriter
related words arranger, scorer; librettist

composite *adj* made from the joining of two or more parts or elements <the movie's special effects included the use of many *composite* photographs>
synonyms amalgamated, compound
related words blended, combined, commingled, mingled, mixed; fused, integrated; interlaced, intermixed, intertwined, interwoven
near antonyms uncombined, unmixed
antonyms simple

composite *n* a distinct entity formed by the combining of two or more different things — see BLEND

composition *n* **1** a literary, musical, or artistic production <the *compositions* of Michelangelo include the dome of St. Peter's, the ceiling of the Sistine Chapel, and his monumental statue of David>
synonyms opus, piece, work
related words classic, magnum opus, masterpiece, pièce de résistance, showpiece; model, outline, sketch; étude
2 a short piece of writing done as a school exercise <a teacher who is fond of having her class write *compositions*>
synonyms paper, theme
related words article, essay, story
3 the way in which the elements of something (as a work of art) are arranged <student photographers learn the importance of *composition* in creating striking images>
synonyms arrangement, configuration, design, form, format, layout, makeup, pattern
related words motif, theme
4 a short piece of writing typically expressing a point of view — see ESSAY 1

composure *n* evenness of emotions or temper — see EQUANIMITY

compound *adj* made from the joining of two or more parts or elements — see COMPOSITE

compound *n* a distinct entity formed by the combining of two or more different things — see BLEND

compound *vb* **1** to make greater in size, amount, or number — see INCREASE 1
2 to put or bring together so as to form a new and longer whole — see CONNECT 1

comprehend *vb* **1** to recognize the meaning of <the age at which children can *comprehend* the difference between right and wrong>
synonyms appreciate, apprehend, catch, catch on (to), dig [*slang*], get, grasp, make, make out, perceive, see, seize, tumble (to), understand
related words absorb, assimilate, digest, take in; know, realize, sense; fathom, penetrate
near antonyms misapprehend, misconstrue, misinterpret, misunderstand
antonyms miss
2 to have a practical understanding of — see KNOW 1
3 to have as part of a whole — see INCLUDE

comprehension *n* the knowledge gained from the process of coming to know or understand something <the president's *comprehension* of the current situation in the Middle East>
synonyms appreciation, apprehension, grasp, grip, perception, understanding
related words absorption, assimilation, uptake; conception, visualization; awareness, consciousness, realization
near antonyms misapprehension, misinterpretation, misunderstanding

comprehensive *adj* **1** covering everything or all important points — see ENCYCLOPEDIC
2 not lacking any part or member that properly belongs to it — see COMPLETE 1
3 trying all possibilities — see EXHAUSTIVE

comprehensively *adv* with attention to all aspects or details — see THOROUGHLY 1

compress *vb* **1** to reduce in size or volume by or as if by pressing parts or members together <a science textbook that *compresses* a lot of information about human reproduction into a few short chapters>
synonyms compact, condense, constrict, contract, squeeze
related words cram, crowd, jam, jam-pack, pack; abbreviate, abridge, curtail, shorten; downsize, shrink; concentrate, consolidate; simplify, streamline; decrease, diminish, lessen

near antonyms disperse, dissipate, scatter; distend, inflate, swell
antonyms expand, open, outspread, outstretch
2 to become smaller in size or volume through the drawing together of particles of matter — see CONTRACT 2
compression *n* the act or process of reducing the size or volume of something by or as if by pressing ⟨the *compression* of a long, complicated story into a two-hour movie is never easy⟩
synonyms compacting, condensation, constriction, contraction, squeezing
related words abbreviation, abridgment (*or* abridgement), curtailment, shortening; concentration, consolidation; simplification, streamlining; decreasing, diminishment, lessening
near antonyms dispersion, dissipation, scattering; distension (*or* distention), inflation, swelling
antonyms expansion
comprise *vb* **1** to be made up of ⟨the mall *comprises* three department stores and eighty smaller shops selling specialized goods⟩
synonyms consist (of), contain
related words embrace, encompass, entail, include, involve, take in; assimilate, embody, incorporate
2 to be all the substance of — see CONSTITUTE 1
compromise *n* the act or practice of each side giving up something in order to reach an agreement — see CONCESSION 1
compromise *vb* to place in danger — see ENDANGER
compulsion *n* the use of power to impose one's will on another — see FORCE 2
compulsive *adj* caused by or suggestive of an irresistible urge ⟨his *compulsive* clowning around can sometimes be annoying⟩
synonyms impulsive, obsessive
related words uncontrollable, irrepressible; automatic, instinctive, involuntary, reflex, spontaneous; conditioned, mechanical; unconscious, unthinking, unwitting
near antonyms unforced, voluntary, willful (*or* wilful); controllable, manageable, resistible
compulsory *adj* forcing one's compliance or participation by or as if by law — see MANDATORY
compunction *n* an uneasy feeling about the rightness of what one is doing or going to do — see QUALM
computation *n* the act or process of performing mathematical operations to find a value — see CALCULATION
compute *vb* to determine (a value) by doing the necessary mathematical operations — see CALCULATE 1
comrade *n* **1** a person frequently seen in the company of another — see ASSOCIATE 1
2 a person who has a strong liking for and trust in another — see FRIEND 1
comradely *adj* having or showing kindly feeling and sincere interest — see FRIENDLY 1
comradeship *n* the feeling of closeness and friendship that exists between companions — see COMPANIONSHIP
con *vb* to commit to memory — see MEMORIZE
concatenate *vb* to put together into a series by means of or as if by means of a thread — see THREAD 2
concatenation *n* a series of things linked together — see CHAIN 1
concave *adj* curved inward — see HOLLOW
concavity *n* a sunken area forming a separate space — see HOLE 2
conceal *vb* **1** to put into a hiding place — see [1]HIDE 1
2 to keep secret or shut off from view — see [1]HIDE 2
concealment *n* **1** the placing of something out of sight ⟨your choice of the oven for the *concealment* of the money was unwise⟩
synonyms caching, hiding, secretion, stashing
related words burial, burying, entombment, interment, interring
near antonyms disinterment, unearthing
antonyms display, exhibition, exposure, parading, showing
2 a place where a person goes to hide — see HIDEOUT
concede *vb* **1** to accept the truth or existence of (something) usually reluctantly — see ADMIT
2 to cease resistance (as to another's arguments, demands, or control) — see YIELD 3
conceit *n* **1** an elaborate or fanciful way of expressing something ⟨the *conceit* that the crowd at the outdoor rock concert was a vast sea of people waving to the beat of the music⟩
synonyms metaphor
related words analogy, circumlocution, euphemism, simile
phrases figure of speech
2 a conception or image created by the imagination and having no objective reality — see FANTASY 1
3 an often unjustified feeling of being pleased with oneself or with one's situation or achievements — see COMPLACENCE
conceited *adj* having too high an opinion of oneself ⟨a *conceited* basketball player who was always too busy even to sign autographs⟩
synonyms complacent, egoistic, egotistic (*or* egotistical), important, overweening, pompous, prideful, proud, self-conceited, self-important, self-satisfied, smug, stuck-up, vain, vainglorious
related words boastful, braggart, bragging; arrogant, cavalier, disdainful, haughty, lordly, self-assertive, snobbish, supercilious, superior, uppity; domineering, high-handed, imperious; highfalutin, pretentious; overconfident, presumptuous; confident, self-assured, self-confident; self-centered, selfish
near antonyms diffident, self-doubting; meek, unassertive; down-to-earth, unassuming, unpretentious; bashful, retiring, shy
antonyms humble, modest
conceitedness *n* an often unjustified feeling of being pleased with oneself or with one's situation or achievements — see COMPLACENCE
conceivably *adv* it is possible — see PERHAPS
conceive *vb* to form a mental picture of — see IMAGINE 1
concentrate *vb* **1** to increase the amount of (a substance in a mixture) by removing other substances ⟨prolonged boiling is required to *concentrate* the sap when making maple syrup⟩
synonyms condense
related words distill (*or* distil), purify, refine; compact, harden, solidify; deepen, enhance, heighten, intensify; evaporate, extract, remove
near antonyms weaken
antonyms dilute, water (down)

2 to fix (as one's attention) steadily toward a central objective <a president who will try to *concentrate* public attention on the problems of inner cities>
synonyms fasten, focus, rivet, train
related words aim, direct, level, point, zero (in on); attend, heed, mind
3 to bring (something) to a central point or under a single control — see CENTRALIZE
4 to bring together in one body or place — see GATHER 1
5 to come together into one body or place — see ASSEMBLE 1

concentrated *adj* **1** having an abundance of some characteristic quality (as flavor) — see FULL-BODIED
2 not divided or scattered among several areas of interest or concern — see WHOLE 1

concentration *n* a focusing of the mind on something — see ATTENTION 1

concept *n* something imagined or pictured in the mind — see IDEA

conception *n* something imagined or pictured in the mind — see IDEA

conceptual *adj* dealing with or expressing a quality or idea — see ABSTRACT 1

concern *n* **1** a commercial or industrial activity or organization — see ENTERPRISE 1
2 an uneasy state of mind usually over the possibility of an anticipated misfortune or trouble — see ANXIETY 1

concern *vb* **1** to have (something) as a subject matter <the book *concerns* the challenges faced by children growing up in single-parent households>
synonyms cover, deal (with), pertain (to), treat (of)
related words appertain (to), bear (on *or* upon), refer (to), relate (to); allude (to), glance (upon), mention, touch (upon); offer, present; contain, embrace, encompass, entail, include, incorporate
phrases have to do with
near antonyms exclude, omit; disregard, ignore, neglect, overlook, pass over, slight
2 to be the business or affair of <the problems of air and water pollution that *concern* all of us>
synonyms affect, involve, touch
related words apply (to), relate (to); embroil, ensnare, entangle, implicate
3 to trouble the mind of; to make uneasy — see DISTURB 1

concerning *prep* having to do with — see ABOUT 1

concert *n* an entertainment featuring singing or the playing of musical instruments <during the summer various groups give *concerts* on the town green>
synonyms musicale
related words performance, presentation; recital; hootenanny, jam session, sing, songfest; festival

concert *vb* **1** to bring about through discussion and compromise — see NEGOTIATE 1
2 to participate or assist in a joint effort to accomplish an end — see COOPERATE 1

concerted *adj* used or done by a number of people as a group — see COLLECTIVE

concession *n* **1** the act or practice of each side giving up something in order to reach an agreement <when trying to get a raise in your allowance, it's good to know the art of *concession*>
synonyms accommodation, compromise, give-and-take, negotiation
related words arrangement, bargain, deal, understanding; agreement, settlement
2 an open declaration of something (as a fault or the commission of an offense) about oneself — see CONFESSION
3 something granted as a special favor — see PRIVILEGE

conciliate *vb* **1** to bring to a state free of conflicts, inconsistencies, or differences — see HARMONIZE 2
2 to lessen the anger or agitation of — see PACIFY

conciliating *adj* tending to lessen or avoid conflict or hostility — see PACIFIC 1

conciliator *n* one who works with opposing sides in order to bring about an agreement — see MEDIATOR

conciliatory *adj* tending to lessen or avoid conflict or hostility — see PACIFIC 1

concise *adj* marked by the use of few words to convey much information or meaning <a *concise* article on violence in the media that manages to say more than most books on the subject>
synonyms aphoristic, brief, compact, compendious, crisp, epigrammatic, laconic, pithy, succinct, summary, terse
related words abrupt, blunt, brusque, curt, short, snippy; abbreviated, abridged, condensed, shortened; meaty, substantial; meaningful, significant
near antonyms redundant, repetitious, tautological; enlarged, expanded, supplemented; embellished, embroidered, exaggerated
antonyms diffuse, long-winded, prolix, rambling, verbose, wordy

concisely *adv* in a few words — see SHORTLY 1

conciseness *n* **1** the condition of being short — see BREVITY 1
2 the quality or state of being marked by or using only few words to convey much meaning — see SUCCINCTNESS

conclude *vb* **1** to bring (an event) to a natural or appropriate stopping point — see CLOSE 3
2 to come to an end — see CEASE 1
3 to bring about through discussion and compromise — see NEGOTIATE 1
4 to come to a judgment after discussion or consideration — see DECIDE 1
5 to form an opinion through reasoning and information — see INFER 1

concluded *adj* brought or having come to an end — see COMPLETE 2

concluding *adj* following all others of the same kind in order or time — see LAST

conclusion *n* **1** an opinion arrived at through a process of reasoning <the detective's *conclusion* that the murderer had to be left-handed>
synonyms deduction, determination, inference
related words decision, judgment (*or* judgement), ruling, verdict; conjecture, guess, surmise; assumption, presumption, supposition
2 a position arrived at after consideration — see DECISION 1
3 a condition or occurrence traceable to a cause — see EFFECT 1
4 the last part of a process or action — see FINALE
5 the stopping of a process or activity — see END 1

conclusive *adj* **1** serving to put an end to all debate or questioning <the archeological discovery was *conclusive* proof that the Vikings had indeed settled in North America around 1000 A.D.>

synonyms absolute, clear, decisive, definitive
related words incontestable, incontrovertible, indisputable, indubitable, irrefutable, undeniable, unquestionable; unchallenged, uncontested, undisputed; unambiguous, unequivocal; certain, definite, positive, sure
near antonyms debatable, disputable, questionable, refutable; ambiguous, equivocal
antonyms inconclusive, indecisive, unclear
2 having the power to persuade — see COGENT

concoct *vb* to create or think of by clever use of the imagination — see INVENT

concoction *n* something (as a device) created for the first time through the use of the imagination — see INVENTION 1

concomitant *n* something that is found along with something else — see ACCOMPANIMENT

concomitant *adj* present at the same time and place — see COINCIDENT

concord *n* peaceful coexistence — see HARMONY 2

concourse *n* a typically long narrow way connecting parts of a building — see HALL 2

concrete *adj* **1** existing in fact and not merely as a possibility — see ACTUAL
2 relating to or composed of matter — see MATERIAL 1

concrete *vb* to become physically firm or solid — see HARDEN 1

concur *vb* **1** to have or come to the same opinion or point of view — see AGREE 1
2 to occur or exist at the same time — see COINCIDE 1

concurrence *n* **1** the occurrence or existence of several things at once ⟨the *concurrence* of my birthday and the concert by my favorite rock band made my preference for a birthday present pretty obvious⟩
synonyms coexistence, coincidence
related words development, happening, occurrence
2 the act or fact of being of one opinion about something — see AGREEMENT 1
3 the approval by someone in authority for the doing of something — see PERMISSION

concurrent *adj* **1** existing or occurring at the same period of time — see CONTEMPORARY 1
2 present at the same time and place — see COINCIDENT

concurrently *adv* at one and the same time — see TOGETHER 1

concussion *n* a forceful coming together of two things — see IMPACT 1

condemn *vb* **1** to declare to be morally wrong or evil ⟨it is a sign of human progress that slavery, which was once common, is now universally *condemned*⟩
synonyms censure, damn, decry, denounce, execrate, reprehend, reprobate
related words attack, blast, criticize, knock, pan, slam; belittle, deprecate, disparage; doom, sentence; convict; blacklist, excommunicate, ostracize; rebuke, reprimand, reproach; admonish, chide, reprove; berate, lambaste (*or* lambast), scold, upbraid; curse, imprecate; abhor, abominate, detest, hate, loathe, revile
near antonyms approve, endorse (*also* indorse), sanction; eulogize, exalt, extol (*also* extoll), glorify, laud, praise; acclaim, applaud, commend, hail; consecrate, hallow, sanctify; honor, revere, venerate
antonyms bless
2 to express one's unfavorable opinion of the worth or quality of — see CRITICIZE
3 to express public or formal disapproval of — see CENSURE 1
4 to find or pronounce guilty — see CONVICT
5 to impose a judicial punishment on — see SENTENCE

condemnation *n* an often public or formal expression of disapproval — see CENSURE

condensation *n* **1** a shortened version of a written work — see ABRIDGMENT
2 the act or process of reducing the size or volume of something by or as if by pressing — see COMPRESSION

condense *vb* **1** to become smaller in size or volume through the drawing together of particles of matter — see CONTRACT 2
2 to reduce in size or volume by or as if by pressing parts or members together — see COMPRESS 1
3 to increase the amount of (a substance in a mixture) by removing other substances — see CONCENTRATE 1

condensed *adj* not lasting for a considerable time — see SHORT 2

condescend *vb* **1** to descend to a level that is beneath one's dignity ⟨I will not *condescend* to answer the sore loser's charge that I cheated in order to win the race⟩
synonyms deign, stoop
related words debase, degrade, demean, humble, humiliate, lower
near antonyms rise
2 to assume or treat with an air of superiority ⟨wealthy people who tend to be *condescending* toward their poor relations⟩
synonyms lord (it over), patronize
related words cold-shoulder, cut, high-hat, snub

condiment *n* something used to enhance the flavor of cooked or prepared food ⟨the cafeteria's self-serve table has a full array of *condiments*⟩
synonyms seasoning
related words herb, savory, spice; relish, sauce; flavoring

condition *n* **1** a state of being or fitness ⟨a car that was ten years old but in still good *condition*⟩
synonyms estate, fettle, form, kilter, order, repair, shape, trim
related words practice (*also* practise); pass, phase, stage
near antonyms disorder, disrepair
2 something upon which the carrying out of an agreement or offer depends ⟨you'll get a raise in your allowance with the *condition* that you'll do a better job of keeping your room clean⟩
synonyms provision, proviso, qualification, reservation, stipulation
related words strings, terms; prerequisite, requirement, requisite; limitation, modification, restriction; exception, exemption; essential, must, necessity
3 an abnormal state that disrupts a plant's or animal's normal bodily functioning — see DISEASE
4 something necessary, indispensable, or unavoidable — see ESSENTIAL 1
5 something that limits one's freedom of action or choice — see RESTRICTION 1

condition *vb* **1** to bring to a proper or desired state of fitness ⟨the length of time that it takes for runners to *condition* their bodies for a marathon⟩

synonyms season, train
related words fit, prepare, ready; acclimate, acclimatize, break in, orient, orientate; accustom, familiarize, habituate; harden, inure
2 to change (something) so as to make it suitable for a new use or situation — see ADAPT

conditional *adj* determined by something else — see DEPENDENT 2

conditioning *n* energetic movement of the body for the sake of physical fitness — see EXERCISE 1

condole (with) *vb* to have sympathy for — see PITY

condone *vb* to overlook or dismiss as of little importance — see EXCUSE 1

conduct *n* **1** the act or activity of looking after and making decisions about something <the president was happy to leave the *conduct* of foreign affairs to his secretary of state>
synonyms administration, control, direction, governance, government, guidance, handling, management, operation, oversight, regulation, running, superintendence, supervision
related words care, custody, guardianship, protection, tutelage; engineering, machination, manipulation
2 the way or manner in which one conducts oneself — see BEHAVIOR

conduct *vb* **1** to look after and make decisions about <the company's president continues to *conduct* the everyday affairs of the software firm he founded many years ago>
synonyms administer, carry on, control, direct, govern, guide, handle, manage, operate, oversee, regulate, run, superintend, supervise
related words care (for), keep, mind, tend, watch; lead, pilot, steer; guard, protect, safeguard
2 to cause to move to a central point or along a restricted pathway — see CHANNEL
3 to manage the actions of (oneself) in a particular way — see BEHAVE
4 to point out the way for (someone) especially from a position in front — see LEAD 1

conduit *n* **1** a long hollow cylinder for carrying a substance (as a liquid or gas) — see PIPE 1
2 an open man-made passageway for water — see CHANNEL 1

confection *n* a food having a high sugar content — see SWEET 1

confederacy *n* an association of persons, parties, or states for mutual assistance and protection <a *confederacy* of several small nations who had promised to come to one another's aid if any were attacked>
synonyms alliance, bloc, coalition, combination, combine, confederation, federation, league, union
related words cabal, conspiracy, junto; cartel, syndicate, trust; faction, side, wing; association, group, organization; affiliation, cooperative, partnership

confederate *n* **1** one associated with another in wrongdoing — see ACCOMPLICE
2 someone associated with another to give assistance or moral support — see ALLY

confederate *vb* to form or enter into an association that furthers the interests of its members — see ALLY

confederation *n* **1** an association of persons, parties, or states for mutual assistance and protection — see CONFEDERACY
2 the state of having shared interests or efforts (as in social or business matters) — see ASSOCIATION 1

confer *vb* **1** to give the ownership or benefit of (something) formally or publicly <the British monarch continues to *confer* knighthood on those who are outstanding in their fields>
synonyms accord, award, grant
related words bestow, contribute, donate, give, present; furnish, provide, supply; extend, offer, proffer; allocate, appropriate, assign
near antonyms rescind, revoke
2 to exchange viewpoints or seek advice for the purpose of finding a solution to a problem <my parents are going to *confer* with a financial advisor about saving for my college education>
synonyms advise, consult, counsel, parley, powwow, treat
related words debate, deliberate, discuss, hash (over); coach, guide, tutor; recommend, suggest; direct, refer (to)

conference *n* **1** a body of people come together in one place — see GATHERING 1
2 a coming together of a number of persons for a specified purpose — see MEETING 1
3 a meeting featuring a group discussion — see FORUM
4 an exchange of views for the purpose of exploring a subject or deciding an issue — see DISCUSSION 1

confess *vb* to accept the truth or existence of (something) usually reluctantly — see ADMIT

confession *n* an open declaration of something (as a fault or the commission of an offense) about oneself <a *confession* that he had been lying all along>
synonyms acknowledgment (*also* acknowledgement), admission, avowal, concession
related words allowance; betrayal, disclosure, divulgence, revelation; announcement, declaration, proclamation; contrition, regret, remorse, repentance

confidant *n* a person who has a strong liking for and trust in another — see FRIEND 1

confidence *n* **1** great faith in oneself or one's abilities <a lifelong *confidence* that enabled her to achieve great things despite powerful obstacles>
synonyms aplomb, assurance, self-assurance, self-confidence, self-esteem
related words cockiness, complacence, complacency, conceit, conceitedness, ego, egotism, overconfidence, pompousness, pride, self-admiration, self-conceit, self-importance, self-satisfaction, smugness, vainglory, vanity; calmness, composure, coolness, equanimity; self-possession
near antonyms apprehension, doubt, misgiving
antonyms diffidence, self-doubt
2 a state of mind in which one is free from doubt <the *confidence* with which the game show contestant answered every question>
synonyms assurance, assuredness, certainty, certitude, conviction, positiveness, sureness
related words authoritarianism, dogmatism; decisiveness, firmness, resolution
near antonyms hesitancy, hesitation, indecisiveness, irresolution
antonyms doubt, incertitude, nonconfidence, uncertainty
3 firm belief in the integrity, ability, effectiveness, or genuineness of someone or something — see TRUST 1

4 information shared only with another or with a select few — see SECRET 1
confidence game *n* a scheme in which the victim is cheated out of his money after first gaining his trust ⟨the old *confidence game* in which the victims are told that they must pay a fee in order to collect their prize money⟩
synonyms hustle, racket, swindle
related words double cross, fix; gyp, rip-off; squeeze; ruse, subterfuge, trick
confidence man *n* a dishonest person who uses clever means to cheat others out of something of value — see TRICKSTER 1
confident *adj* **1** having or showing great faith in oneself or one's abilities ⟨you'll need to be *confident* —even in the face of rejection—if you want to pursue a career in show business⟩
synonyms assured, secure, self-assured, self-confident
related words hopeful, optimistic, rosy, sanguine, upbeat; complacent, conceited, egoistic, egotistic (*or* egotistical), important, overweening, pompous, prideful, proud, self-conceited, self-important, self-satisfied, smug, stuck-up, vain, vainglorious; calm, collected, composed, cool, placid, self-possessed, serene, tranquil, undisturbed, unperturbed
near antonyms meek, timid, unassertive; modest, unassuming, unpretentious; jittery, jumpy, nervous
antonyms diffident, insecure, self-doubting
2 having or showing a mind free from doubt — see CERTAIN 2
confidential *adj* not known or meant to be known by the general populace — see PRIVATE 1
confiding *adj* having or showing trust in another — see TRUSTING 1
configuration *n* **1** the arrangement of parts that gives something its basic form — see FRAME 1
2 the way in which something is sized, arranged, or organized — see FORMAT 1
3 the way in which the elements of something (as a work of art) are arranged — see COMPOSITION 3
4 the outward appearance of something as distinguished from its substance — see FORM 1
confine *vb* **1** to set bounds or an upper limit for — see LIMIT 1
2 to put in or as if in prison — see IMPRISON
confinement *n* **1** the act of confining or the state of being confined — see INTERNMENT
2 the act or practice of keeping something (as an activity) within certain boundaries — see RESTRICTION 2
confines *n pl* **1** a real or imaginary point beyond which a person or thing cannot go — see LIMIT
2 the line or relatively narrow space that marks the outer limit of something — see BORDER 1
confirm *vb* to give evidence or testimony to the truth or factualness of ⟨several eyewitnesses who can *confirm* the youngster's account of what happened⟩
synonyms bear out, corroborate, substantiate, support, validate, verify, vindicate
related words attest, authenticate, avouch, certify, testify (to), vouch (for), witness; guarantee, warrant; affirm, assert, aver, avow, profess
near antonyms contradict, gainsay; deny, disavow, disclaim
antonyms disprove, rebut, refute
confirmable *adj* capable of being proven as true or real — see VERIFIABLE
confirmation *n* something presented in support of the truth or accuracy of a claim — see PROOF
confirmatory *adj* serving to give support to the truth or factualness of something — see CORROBORATIVE
confirmed *adj* **1** being such by habit and not likely to change — see HABITUAL 1
2 firmly established over time — see INVETERATE 1
confirming *adj* serving to give support to the truth or factualness of something — see CORROBORATIVE
confiscate *vb* to take ownership or control of (something) by right of one's authority ⟨anything that might be used as a weapon will be *confiscated* by the security guards⟩
synonyms expropriate, sequester
related words appropriate, arrogate, preempt, usurp; commandeer, seize, take over
near antonyms release, relinquish, surrender, yield
conflagration *n* a destructive burning — see FIRE
conflict *n* **1** a lack of agreement or harmony — see DISCORD
2 a physical dispute between opposing individuals or groups — see FIGHT 1
3 a state of armed violent struggle between states, nations, or groups — see WAR 1
4 an earnest effort for superiority or victory over another — see CONTEST 1
conflict *vb* to be out of harmony or agreement usually noticeably — see CLASH
conflicting *adj* not being in agreement or harmony — see INCONSISTENT
confluence *n* the coming together of two or more things to the same point — see CONVERGENCE
conform *vb* **1** to be in agreement on every point — see CHECK 1
2 to form a pleasing relationship — see HARMONIZE 1
3 to bring to a state free of conflicts, inconsistencies, or differences — see HARMONIZE 2
4 to change (something) so as to make it suitable for a new use or situation — see ADAPT
conform (to) *vb* to act according to the commands of — see OBEY
conformable *adj* readily giving in to the command or authority of another — see OBEDIENT
conformable (to) *adj* not having or showing any apparent conflict — see CONSISTENT
conformation *n* **1** the outward appearance of something as distinguished from its substance — see FORM 1
2 the way in which something is sized, arranged, or organized — see FORMAT 1
conformity *n* **1** a state of consistency ⟨the simple lifestyle of the Amish is in *conformity* with their ascetic religious beliefs⟩
synonyms accord, accordance, agreement, congruity, consonance, harmony, tune
related words assimilation, integration; oneness, solidarity, togetherness; affinity, empathy, sympathy
near antonyms discrepancy, disparity, dissimilarity
antonyms conflict, disagreement
2 a bending to the authority or control of another — see OBEDIENCE 1

confound *vb* **1** to throw into a state of mental uncertainty — see CONFUSE 1

2 to throw into a state of self-conscious distress — see EMBARRASS 1

confront *vb* to oppose (something hostile or dangerous) with firmness or courage — see FACE 2

confrontation *n* an earnest effort for superiority or victory over another — see CONTEST 1

confuse *vb* **1** to throw into a state of mental uncertainty ⟨the similar-sounding words "censure" and "censor" often *confuse* people⟩

synonyms addle, baffle, befog, befuddle, bemuse, bewilder, confound, disorient, muddle, muddy, mystify, perplex, puzzle

related words stick, stump; abash, discomfit, disconcert, discountenance, embarrass, faze, fluster, mortify, nonplus, rattle; agitate, bother, chagrin, discomfort, discompose, dismay, disquiet, distress, disturb, perturb, stun, unhinge, unsettle, upset; deceive, misguide, mislead

near antonyms assure, reassure, satisfy; enlighten, inform

2 to make (something) unclear to the understanding ⟨stop *confusing* the issue with irrelevant facts⟩

synonyms becloud, befog, blur, cloud, fog, muddy

related words complicate, perplex, sophisticate; entangle, snarl, tangle; disorder, jumble, mess (up), mix (up)

near antonyms simplify, streamline; disentangle, straighten (out), untangle

antonyms clarify

3 to throw into a state of self-conscious distress — see EMBARRASS 1

4 to undo the proper order or arrangement of — see DISORDER

confused *adj* **1** lacking in order, neatness, and often cleanliness — see MESSY

2 suffering from mental confusion — see DIZZY 2

confusion *n* **1** a state of mental uncertainty ⟨the farmer's driving directions to the fairground just left us in total *confusion*⟩

synonyms bafflement, befuddlement, bewilderment, distraction, muddle, mystification, perplexity, puzzlement, whirl

related words abashment, discomfiture, embarrassment, fluster, mortification; agitation, chagrin, discomfort, dismay, disquiet, distress, disturbance, perturbation, upset

near antonyms assurance, certainty, certitude, confidence, conviction, positiveness, sureness

2 a state in which everything is out of order — see CHAOS

3 the emotional state of being made self-consciously uncomfortable — see EMBARRASSMENT 1

confute *vb* to prove to be false — see DISPROVE

congeal *vb* **1** to become physically firm or solid — see HARDEN 1

2 to turn from a liquid into a substance resembling jelly — see COAGULATE

congenial *adj* **1** giving pleasure or contentment to the mind or senses — see PLEASANT

2 having or marked by agreement in feeling or action — see HARMONIOUS 3

congenital *adj* being such from birth or by nature — see NATURAL 1

congest *vb* to prevent passage through — see CLOG 1

conglomerate *n* a group of businesses or enterprises under one control ⟨the huge media *conglomerate* owns TV and radio stations, a cable company, and a movie studio⟩

synonyms empire

related words multinational; cartel, combination, syndicate, trust; chain; association, corporation, organization, pool

conglomerate *vb* **1** to come together into one body or place — see ASSEMBLE 1

2 to gradually form into a layer, pile, or mass — see COLLECT 2

congratulate *vb* to express to (someone) admiration for his or her success or good fortune ⟨let me be the first to *congratulate* you on winning the award⟩

synonyms compliment, felicitate

related words applaud, cheer, commend, hail; extol (*also* extoll), glorify, laud, praise

near antonyms bad-mouth, belittle, decry, disparage, put down; jeer, mock, ridicule, taunt, tease

congratulations *n pl* best wishes — see COMPLIMENTS

congregate *vb* to come together into one body or place — see ASSEMBLE 1

congregation *n* **1** a body of persons gathered for religious worship ⟨the whole *congregation* began to sing with great fervor⟩

synonyms assembly, church

related words laity, parish; communion, denomination, fold, sect

2 a body of people come together in one place — see GATHERING 1

congress *n* **1** the highest lawmaking body of a political unit ⟨the national emergency required a special session of *congress*⟩

synonyms parliament

related words assembly, chamber, council, diet, house, legislature

2 a coming together of a number of persons for a specified purpose — see MEETING 1

3 a group of persons formally joined together for some common interest — see ASSOCIATION 2

congruity *n* a state of consistency — see CONFORMITY 1

congruous *adj* **1** having the parts agreeably related — see HARMONIOUS 2

2 not having or showing any apparent conflict — see CONSISTENT

congruously *adv* in a manner suitable for the occasion or purpose — see PROPERLY

conjectural *adj* existing only as an assumption or speculation — see THEORETICAL 1

conjecture *n* an opinion or judgment based on little or no evidence ⟨the many *conjectures* about the true identity of Jack the Ripper⟩

synonyms guess, supposition, surmise

related words hypothesis, theory, thesis; guesswork, speculation; hunch, intuition; belief, faith

conjecture *vb* **1** to decide the size, amount, number, or distance of (something) without actual measurement — see ESTIMATE 2

2 to form an opinion from little or no evidence — see GUESS 1

conjoin *vb* **1** to come together to form a single unit — see UNITE 1

2 to form or enter into an association that furthers the interests of its members — see ALLY

conjoint *adj* used or done by a number of people as a group — see COLLECTIVE

conjointly *adv* in or by combined action or effort — see TOGETHER 2

conjugal *adj* of or relating to marriage — see MARITAL

conjugate *vb* **1** to come together to form a single unit — see UNITE 1
2 to put or bring together so as to form a new and longer whole — see CONNECT 1

conjunction *n* the coming together of two or more things to the same point — see CONVERGENCE

conjuration *n* a spoken word or set of words believed to have magic power — see SPELL 1

conjure *vb* to make a request to (someone) in an earnest or urgent manner — see BEG

conjure (up) *vb* to call into being through the use of one's inner resources or powers — see SUMMON 2

conjurer *or* **conjuror** *n* **1** a person skilled in using supernatural forces — see MAGICIAN 1
2 one who practices tricks and illusions for entertainment — see MAGICIAN 2

conjuring *n* **1** the power to control natural forces through supernatural means — see MAGIC 1
2 the art or skill of performing tricks or illusions for entertainment — see MAGIC 2

conk (out) *vb* to stop functioning — see FAIL 1

connect *vb* **1** to put or bring together so as to form a new and longer whole ⟨*connect* all the sets of lights and attach them to the branches of the Christmas tree⟩
synonyms chain, compound, conjugate, couple, hitch, hook, join, link, yoke
related words dovetail; concatenate, string; cement, coalesce, combine, fuse, unite
near antonyms divide, part, split
antonyms disconnect, disjoin, separate, unchain, uncouple, unhitch, unlink, unyoke
2 to come together to form a single unit — see UNITE 1
3 to think of (something) in combination — see ASSOCIATE 2

connecting *n* the act or an instance of joining two or more things into one — see UNION 1

connection *n* **1** the fact or state of having something in common ⟨the endless debate about the *connection* between crime and poverty⟩
synonyms association, bearing, kinship, liaison, linkage, relation, relationship
related words correlation, interrelation; materiality, pertinence, relevance; bond, link, tie; affiliation, alliance, union; likeness, resemblance, similarity
2 a place where two or more things are united — see JOINT 1
3 an acquaintance who has influence especially in the business or political world — see CONTACT
4 the act or an instance of joining two or more things into one — see UNION 1
5 the fact or state of being pertinent — see PERTINENCE
6 the state of having shared interests or efforts (as in social or business matters) — see ASSOCIATION 1

connivance *n* a secret agreement or cooperation between two parties for an illegal or dishonest purpose — see COLLUSION

connive *vb* to secretly sympathize with or pretend ignorance of something improper or unlawful ⟨the principal *connived* at all the school absences that were recorded on the day of the city's celebration of its Super Bowl victory⟩
synonyms wink
related words condone, disregard, excuse, ignore, overlook, tolerate
near antonyms disapprove (of), frown (on *or* upon); deny, disallow, refuse

connoisseur *n* a person having a knowledgeable and fine appreciation of the arts ⟨a forthcoming exhibit at the art museum that is eagerly awaited by *connoisseurs* of ancient Greek pottery⟩
synonyms dilettante
related words adept, authority, expert, master; critic, reviewer; amateur, dabbler; collector
near antonyms materialist, philistine

connubial *adj* of or relating to marriage — see MARITAL

conquer *vb* **1** to bring under one's control by force of arms ⟨before his final defeat, Napoleon had managed to *conquer* much of Europe⟩
synonyms dominate, overpower, subdue, subject, subjugate, vanquish
related words beat, crush, defeat, drub, lick, mow (down), rout, smash, thrash, trounce; enslave; break, put down, quell, suppress
near antonyms emancipate, free, liberate, manumit, release
2 to achieve a victory over — see BEAT 2
3 to achieve victory (as in a contest) — see WIN 1

conqueror *n* one that defeats an enemy or opponent — see VICTOR 1

conquest *n* the act or process of bringing someone or something under one's control ⟨the *conquest* of much of North and South America by the Spanish during the 16th century⟩
synonyms dominating, domination, overpowering, subduing, subjecting, subjection, subjugating, subjugation, vanquishing
related words triumph, victory, winning; beating, defeat, drubbing, licking, trouncing; enslavement
near antonyms emancipation, freeing, liberation, manumission, release

conscientious *adj* **1** guided by or in accordance with one's sense of right and wrong ⟨operated on the belief that most people are *conscientious*, the unattended farm stand has a price list and a money drawer for customers to leave payment for their purchases⟩
synonyms ethical, honest, honorable, just, moral, principled, scrupulous
related words good, righteous, upright, virtuous; dutiful, observant, respectful; overconscientious; reliable, trustworthy, trusty
near antonyms unreliable, untrustworthy
antonyms cutthroat, dishonest, dishonorable, immoral, unethical, unjust, unprincipled, unscrupulous
2 taking great care and effort — see PAINSTAKING

conscientiousness *n* strict attentiveness to what one is doing — see CARE 1

conscious *adj* having specified facts or feelings actively impressed on the mind ⟨*conscious* of the fact that my hands were sweating the whole time that I was making my presentation⟩
synonyms alive, aware, cognizant, mindful, sensible, sentient
related words attentive, heedful, observant, regardful, vigilant, watchful
near antonyms inattentive, unheeding, unobservant, unobserving
antonyms insensible, unaware, unconscious, unmindful

consciously *adv* with full awareness of what one is doing — see INTENTIONALLY

conscript *n* a person forced or required to enroll in military service ⟨as the war continued, the body of enlisted soldiers was supplemented by an increasing number of *conscripts*⟩
synonyms draftee, inductee
related words recruit, rookie

conscript *vb* to pick especially for required military service — see DRAFT 1

consecrate *vb* **1** to keep or intend for a special purpose — see DEVOTE 1
2 to make holy through prayers or ritual — see BLESS 1

consecrated *adj* set apart or worthy of veneration by association with God — see HOLY 2

consecration *n* the act of making something holy through religious ritual ⟨the *consecration* of the Host during Communion⟩
synonyms blessing, hallowing, sanctification
related words dedication
near antonyms defilement, desecration, profanation

consecutive *adj* following one after another without others coming in between ⟨the team's winning streak has lasted for seven *consecutive* games⟩
synonyms sequential, succeeding, successional, successive
related words serial; constant, continuous, uninterrupted; ensuing, following, later, next, subsequent

consensus *n* the act or fact of being of one opinion about something — see AGREEMENT 1

consent *n* the approval by someone in authority for the doing of something — see PERMISSION

consequence *n* **1** a condition or occurrence traceable to a cause — see EFFECT 1
2 the quality or state of being important — see IMPORTANCE

consequent *adj* coming as a result — see RESULTANT

consequential *adj* **1** coming as a result — see RESULTANT
2 having great meaning or lasting effect — see IMPORTANT 1

consequently *adv* for this or that reason — see THEREFORE

conservation *n* **1** the careful maintaining and protection of something valuable especially in its natural or original state ⟨everyone has a duty to aid in the *conservation* of our nation's wilderness areas⟩
synonyms preservation
related words care, maintenance, upkeep; salvation, saving; guardianship, protection, safeguarding, safekeeping; economy, husbandry, management
near antonyms neglect, squandering, waste; destruction, ruin; damage, injury
2 the act or activity of keeping something in an existing and usually satisfactory condition — see MAINTENANCE

conservative *adj* **1** tending to favor established ideas, conditions, or institutions ⟨*conservative* baseball fans consider the new ballpark too modern-looking and plain ugly⟩
synonyms old-fashioned, orthodox, reactionary, traditional, unprogressive
related words conventional; faithful, loyal, steadfast, true-blue
near antonyms extremist, radical, revolutionary; nonconformist
antonyms liberal, nonorthodox, nontraditional, progressive, unorthodox
2 not excessively showy — see QUIET 2

conservative *n* a person whose political beliefs are centered on tradition and keeping things the way they are ⟨proposed legislation that was opposed by *conservatives* throughout the state⟩
synonyms reactionary, rightist
related words conformist
near antonyms extremist, radical, revolutionary, revolutionist
antonyms leftist, liberal, progressive

conservatory *n* a glass-enclosed building for growing plants ⟨the college's *conservatory* is entirely devoted to cultivating and displaying orchids⟩
synonyms greenhouse, hothouse
related words cold frame; nursery

conserve *vb* to keep in good condition — see MAINTAIN 1

conserving *n* the act or activity of keeping something in an existing and usually satisfactory condition — see MAINTENANCE

consider *vb* **1** to think of in a particular way ⟨I *consider* him a very good friend⟩
synonyms account, call, count, esteem, hold, rate, reckon, regard, take (for)
related words believe, feel, sense, think; conceive, fancy, imagine
phrases look on (*or* upon)
2 to give serious and careful thought to — see PONDER
3 to have as an opinion — see BELIEVE 2

considerable *adj* **1** sufficiently large in size, amount, or number to merit attention ⟨the *considerable* number of auto accidents that resulted from the surprise snowstorm⟩
synonyms good, goodly, good-sized, healthy, largish, respectable, significant, sizable (*or* sizeable), substantial, tidy
related words big, colossal, enormous, gigantic, great, huge, immense, mammoth
near antonyms piddling, puny, trivial, unimportant; marginal, meager, slight; little, small, tiny
antonyms inconsiderable, insignificant, insubstantial
2 of a size greater than average of its kind — see LARGE

considerably *adv* to a large extent or degree — see GREATLY 2

considerate *adj* **1** given to or made with heedful anticipation of the needs and happiness of others — see THOUGHTFUL 1
2 having or showing a close attentiveness to avoiding danger or trouble — see CAREFUL 1

considerately *adv* with good reason or courtesy — see WELL 4

consideration *n* **1** a careful weighing of the reasons for or against something ⟨after much *consideration* we decided to make an offer on the house⟩
synonyms debate, deliberation, thought
related words cogitation, contemplation, meditation, pondering, rumination; introspection, reflection; agonizing, hesitation, indecision
2 something (as money) that is given or received in return for goods or services — see PAYMENT 2

considered *adj* decided on as a result of careful thought — see DELIBERATE 1

consign *vb* **1** to cause to go or be taken from one place to another — see SEND
2 to put (something) into the possession or safe-keeping of another — see GIVE 2
consist (of) *vb* to be made up of — see COMPRISE 1
consistency *n* the degree to which a fluid can resist flowing ⟨beat the egg whites until they take on the *consistency* of whipped cream⟩
synonyms density, thickness, viscosity
related words compactness, firmness, solidity; ropiness, stickiness
consistent *adj* not having or showing any apparent conflict ⟨the clothes you wear to class must be *consistent* with the school's dress code⟩
synonyms compatible, conformable (to), congruous, consonant, correspondent (with *or* to), harmonious, nonconflicting
related words appropriate, fitting, meet, suitable
phrases of a piece
antonyms conflicting, incompatible, incongruous, inconsistent, inharmonious, unharmonious
consistently *adv* on every relevant occasion — see ALWAYS 1
consolation *n* **1** the giving of hope and strength in times of grief, distress, or suffering ⟨the *consolation* of the grieving family by their pastor⟩
synonyms comforting, consoling, solace, solacing
related words commiseration, condolence, sympathy; counseling (*or* counselling)
2 a feeling of ease from grief or trouble — see COMFORT 1
console *vb* to ease the grief or distress of — see COMFORT 1
consolidate *vb* **1** to bring (something) to a central point or under a single control — see CENTRALIZE
2 to make markedly greater in measure or degree — see INTENSIFY
consolidation *n* the act or an instance of joining two or more things into one — see UNION 1
consoling *n* the giving of hope and strength in times of grief, distress, or suffering — see CONSOLATION 1
consonance *n* **1** a balanced, pleasing, or suitable arrangement of parts — see HARMONY 1
2 a state of consistency — see CONFORMITY 1
consonant *adj* **1** having the parts agreeably related — see HARMONIOUS 2
2 not having or showing any apparent conflict — see CONSISTENT
consort *n* the person to whom another is married — see SPOUSE
consort *vb* to come or be together as friends — see ASSOCIATE 1
conspicuous *adj* **1** likely to attract attention — see NOTICEABLE
2 very noticeable especially for being incorrect or bad — see EGREGIOUS
conspiracy *n* **1** a group involved in secret or criminal activities — see RING 1
2 a secret agreement or cooperation between two parties for an illegal or dishonest purpose — see COLLUSION
3 a secret plan for accomplishing evil or unlawful ends — see PLOT 1
conspire *vb* to engage in a secret plan to accomplish evil or unlawful ends — see PLOT
constable *n* a member of a force charged with law enforcement at the local level — see OFFICER 1
constabulary *n* a body of officers of the law — see POLICE 2
constancy *n* **1** the state of continuing without change ⟨the mistaken notion that there is *constancy* in language—words do indeed change their meanings over time⟩
synonyms changelessness, fixedness, immutability, invariability, stability, steadiness, unchangeableness
related words consistency, regularity, sameness, uniformity; durability, lastingness, permanence
near antonyms inconsistency, irregularity, unevenness; evanescence, impermanence
antonyms changeability, changeableness, instability, mutability, unsteadiness, variability
2 adherence to something to which one is bound by a pledge or duty — see FIDELITY
constant *adj* **1** not undergoing a change in condition ⟨change is the only *constant* thing in the world of fashion⟩
synonyms changeless, stable, stationary, steady, unchanging, unvarying
related words fast, fixed, hard-and-fast, immutable, inflexible, invariable, unalterable, unchangeable; established, set, settled; durable, enduring, lasting, permanent
near antonyms alterable, changeable, flexible, mutable, variable; ephemeral, evanescent, fleeting, momentary, transient, transitory
antonyms changeful, changing, fluctuating, inconstant, unstable, unsteady, varying
2 appearing or occurring repeatedly from time to time — see REGULAR 1
3 firm in one's allegiance to someone or something — see FAITHFUL 1
constantly *adv* **1** many times — see OFTEN
2 on every relevant occasion — see ALWAYS 1
consternation *n* the emotion experienced in the presence or threat of danger — see FEAR
constituent *n* one of the parts that make up a whole — see ELEMENT 1
constitute *vb* **1** to be all the substance of ⟨nine players *constitute* a baseball team⟩
synonyms compose, comprise, form, make up
related words embody, incorporate, integrate; complement, complete, supplement; fill out, flesh (out)
2 to be responsible for the creation and early operation or use of — see FOUND
3 to pick (someone) by one's authority for a specific position or duty — see APPOINT 2
constitution *n* **1** the set of qualities that makes a person, a group of people, or a thing different from others — see NATURE 1
2 the type of body that a person has — see PHYSIQUE
constitutional *n* a relaxed journey on foot for exercise or pleasure — see WALK
constitutionally *adv* by natural character or ability — see NATURALLY 1
constrain *vb* **1** to cause (a person) to give in to pressure — see FORCE
2 to keep from exceeding a desirable degree or level (as of expression) — see CONTROL 1
constraint *n* **1** the checking of one's true feelings and impulses when dealing with others ⟨in civilized society people do not just say or do whatever they feel like—they exercise some *constraint*⟩
synonyms inhibition, repression, reserve, restraint, self-control, self-restraint, suppression

related words control, discipline, self-denial, self-discipline; composure, self-possession; aloofness, detachedness, distance; bashfulness, modesty, shyness; reticence, silence, taciturnity
near antonyms self-indulgence; bluntness, candor, frankness
2 something that limits one's freedom of action or choice — see RESTRICTION 1
3 the use of power to impose one's will on another — see FORCE 2

constrict *vb* **1** to become smaller in size or volume through the drawing together of particles of matter — see CONTRACT 2
2 to reduce in size or volume by or as if by pressing parts or members together — see COMPRESS 1

constriction *n* the act or process of reducing the size or volume of something by or as if by pressing — see COMPRESSION

construct *vb* to form by putting together parts or materials — see BUILD

construction *n* **1** something put together by arranging or connecting an array of parts ⟨the swing set turned out to be a more complicated *construction* than the "some assembly required" warning suggested⟩
synonyms erection, structure
related words arrangement, assembly; frame, framework, skeleton
2 a statement that makes something clear — see EXPLANATION 1

constructive *adj* having a role in deciding something's final form — see FORMATIVE

construe *vb* to make plain or understandable — see EXPLAIN 1

consult *vb* to exchange viewpoints or seek advice for the purpose of finding a solution to a problem — see CONFER 2

consultant *n* a person who gives advice especially professionally ⟨a *consultant* in public relations to a number of large corporations⟩
synonyms adviser (*or* advisor), counselor (*or* counsellor)
related words authority, expert, professional; confidant

consume *vb* **1** to destroy all trace of ⟨massive fires had *consumed* hundreds of square miles of forest⟩
synonyms devour, eat (up)
related words gut; deplete, exhaust, use up; raze, ruin, waste; annihilate, extinguish
2 to make complete use of — see DEPLETE
3 to take in as food — see EAT 1

consummate *adj* **1** having or showing exceptional knowledge, experience, or skill in a field of endeavor — see PROFICIENT
2 having no exceptions or restrictions — see ABSOLUTE 2
3 of the greatest or highest degree or quantity — see ULTIMATE 1

consummate *vb* to bring (something) to a state where nothing remains to be done — see FINISH 1

consummation *n* **1** the last part of a process or action — see FINALE
2 the state of being actual or complete — see FRUITION

contact *n* an acquaintance who has influence especially in the business or political world ⟨an intern who got her summer job in the governor's office through *contacts*⟩
synonyms connection
related words big shot, bigwig, somebody, VIP; go-between, intermediary, mediator

contact *vb* to transmit information or requests to ⟨you can *contact* me at this number⟩
synonyms communicate (with), reach
related words apprise, fill in, inform, notify; buzz, call, phone, ring [*chiefly British*], telephone
phrases get (*or* keep) in touch with

contagious *adj* **1** capable of being passed by physical contact from one person to another ⟨chicken pox, measles, German measles, and other *contagious* diseases⟩
synonyms catching, communicable, transmittable
related words infectious, infective
near antonyms noninfectious
antonyms noncommunicable
2 exciting a similar feeling or reaction in others ⟨the enthusiasm of the new club members was *contagious*⟩
synonyms catching, infectious, spreading
related words palpable, perceptible, tangible; irresistible, overpowering, overwhelming; fetching, inviting, winning

contain *vb* **1** to have within ⟨the top drawer of the cabinet *contains* my stamp collection⟩
synonyms hold
related words accommodate, fit; encase, enclose (*also* inclose), encompass; harbor, house, lodge, shelter
2 to have as part of a whole — see INCLUDE
3 to be made up of — see COMPRISE 1
4 to gain emotional or mental control of — see COLLECT 1
5 to keep from exceeding a desirable degree or level (as of expression) — see CONTROL 1

container *n* something into which a liquid or smaller objects can be put for storage or transportation ⟨save the plastic *containers* from the deli for other uses⟩
synonyms holder, receptacle, vessel
related words cartridge; bin, box, carton, case, crate; bag, pocket, sack; cooler, warmer

contaminant *n* something that is or that makes impure — see IMPURITY

contaminate *vb* to make unfit for use by the addition of something harmful or undesirable ⟨a supply of drinking water that was *contaminated* by a toxic waste dump⟩
synonyms befoul, defile, foul, poison, pollute, taint
related words infect; besmirch, dirty, soil, sully; corrupt, rot, spoil; adulterate, doctor; dilute, water (down)
near antonyms clean, cleanse, purge; filter; disinfect, sanitize
antonyms decontaminate, purify

contaminated *adj* containing foreign or lower-grade substances — see IMPURE

contemplate *vb* **1** to give serious and careful thought to — see PONDER
2 to have in mind as a purpose or goal — see INTEND

contemplation *n* long or deep thinking about spiritual matters ⟨the decision to enter a monastery and to spend one's life in prayer and *contemplation*⟩
synonyms meditation
related words introspection, reflection, retrospection; cogitation, deliberation, musing, pondering, rumination

contemplative *adj* given to or marked by long, quiet thinking ⟨a *contemplative* person who likes to go on solitary walks⟩ ⟨the *contemplative* life of the monks at the abbey⟩
synonyms meditative, melancholy, pensive, reflective, ruminant, thoughtful
related words introspective, retrospective; earnest, serious, sober, somber (*or* sombre); analytic (*or* analytical), logical, rational; deliberate, purposeful
near antonyms flighty, flippant, frivolous; brainless, mindless, silly, thoughtless, unthinking
antonyms unreflective

contemporaneous *adj* existing or occurring at the same period of time — see CONTEMPORARY 1

contemporaneously *adv* at one and the same time — see TOGETHER 1

contemporary *adj* **1** existing or occurring at the same period of time ⟨the absurd notion that early cave dwellers were *contemporary* with the dinosaurs⟩
synonyms coeval, coexistent, coexisting, coextensive, concurrent, contemporaneous, simultaneous, synchronous
related words accompanying, attendant, attending, coincident, concomitant
antonyms noncontemporary
2 being or involving the latest methods, concepts, information, or styles — see MODERN

contemporary *n* a person who lives at the same time or is about the same age as another ⟨Abraham Lincoln and Charles Darwin were exact *contemporaries*, actually being born on the same day in 1809⟩
synonyms coeval
related words accompaniment, companion, concomitant; equal, peer

contempt *n* open dislike for someone or something considered unworthy of one's concern or respect ⟨my undying *contempt* for people who abuse animals⟩
synonyms despite, despitefulness, disdain, scorn
related words abhorrence, abomination, execration, hate, hatred, loathing; cattiness, hatefulness, invidiousness, malevolence, malice, maliciousness, malignancy, malignity, meanness, spite, spitefulness; aversion, disgust, distaste, horror, odium, repugnance, repulsion, revulsion; animosity, antagonism, antipathy, bitterness, enmity, grudge, hostility, jealousy, pique, resentment; bile, jaundice, rancor, spleen, venom, virulence, vitriol
near antonyms acceptance, tolerance; adoration, veneration, worship; affection, fondness, liking
antonyms admiration, esteem, regard, respect

contemptible *adj* **1** arousing or deserving of one's loathing and disgust ⟨the *contemptible* thieves who stole the Christmas gifts intended for needy children⟩
synonyms despicable, lousy, nasty, pitiable, pitiful, scabby, scummy, scurvy, sorry, wretched
related words abhorrent, abominable, detestable, execrable, hateful, loathsome, odious; disgusting, repugnant, repulsive; disgraceful, dishonorable, shameful; base, ignoble, low, mean; shabby, sordid, squalid, vile; cowardly, craven, dastardly
near antonyms high-minded, honorable, noble, principled; commendable, creditable, laudable, praiseworthy
antonyms admirable
2 deserving pitying scorn (as for inadequacy) — see PITIFUL 1
3 not following or in accordance with standards of honor and decency — see IGNOBLE 2

contemptuous *adj* **1** feeling or showing open dislike for someone or something regarded as undeserving of respect or concern ⟨loutish tourists who are *contemptuous* of the ways and traditions of their host countries⟩
synonyms disdainful, scornful
related words discourteous, disrespectful, impudent, insolent; arrogant, cavalier, high-handed; haughty, lofty, lordly, prideful, sniffish, snobbish, supercilious; pompous, self-important, superior
near antonyms deferential, respectful; accepting, tolerant; courteous, polite
antonyms admiring, appreciative
2 intended to make a person or thing seem of little importance or value — see DEROGATORY

contend *vb* **1** to engage in a contest — see COMPETE
2 to state (something) as a reason in support of or against something under consideration — see ARGUE 1
3 to state as a fact usually forcefully — see CLAIM 1

contend (with) *vb* **1** to deal with (something) usually skillfully or efficiently — see HANDLE 1
2 to strive to reduce or eliminate — see FIGHT 2

contender *n* **1** one who seeks an office, honor, position, or award — see CANDIDATE
2 one who strives for the same thing as another — see COMPETITOR

content *adj* feeling that one's needs or desires have been met ⟨are you *content* with your present allowance?⟩
synonyms contented, gratified, happy, pleased, satisfied
related words delighted, glad, joyful, joyous, jubilant; ecstatic, elated, enraptured, euphoric, overjoyed, rapturous, thrilled; appeased, mollified, pacified, placated
near antonyms disaffected, disgruntled; discouraged, disheartened, dispirited
antonyms discontent, discontented, displeased, dissatisfied, malcontent, unhappy

[1]**content** *n* **1** a major object of interest or concern (as in a discussion or artistic composition) — see MATTER 1
2 the amount of something (as subject matter) included — see COVERAGE
3 the largest number or amount that something can hold — see CAPACITY 1

[2]**content** *n* the feeling experienced when one's wishes are met — see PLEASURE 1

content *vb* to give satisfaction to — see PLEASE

contented *adj* feeling that one's needs or desires have been met — see CONTENT

contentedness *n* the feeling experienced when one's wishes are met — see PLEASURE 1

contention *n* an idea or opinion that is put forth in a discussion or debate ⟨my *contention* is that today's lower batting averages are the result of better pitching⟩
synonyms argument, assertion, thesis
related words hypothesis, theory; proposal, proposition; assumption, presupposition, supposition; position, stand

contentious *adj* **1** feeling or displaying eagerness to fight — see BELLIGERENT
2 given to arguing — see ARGUMENTATIVE 1

contentiousness *n* an inclination to fight or quarrel — see BELLIGERENCE

contentment *n* the feeling experienced when one's wishes are met — see PLEASURE 1

contest *n* **1** an earnest effort for superiority or victory over another ⟨the eternal *contest* between the forces of good and the forces of evil⟩
synonyms battle, combat, conflict, confrontation, duel, face-off, rivalry, struggle, tug-of-war, warfare
related words showdown; contention, discord, friction, strife; controversy, debate, disagreement
near antonyms concord, harmony, peace
2 a competitive encounter between individuals or groups carried on for amusement, exercise, or in pursuit of a prize — see GAME 1
3 a physical dispute between opposing individuals or groups — see FIGHT 1

contest *vb* to demand proof of the truth or rightness of — see CHALLENGE 1

contestant *n* one who strives for the same thing as another — see COMPETITOR

contiguity *n* the state or condition of being near — see PROXIMITY

contiguous *adj* having a border in common — see ADJACENT

continent *n* one of the great divisions of land on the globe or the main part of such a division — see MAINLAND

contingency *n* something that might happen — see EVENT 2

contingent *n* a body of persons chosen as representatives of a larger group ⟨our Scout troop sent a large *contingent* to the jamboree⟩
synonyms delegation
related words embassy, legation, mission; crew, detachment, gang, outfit, squad

contingent (on *or* upon) *adj* determined by something else — see DEPENDENT 2

continual *adj* **1** going on and on without any interruptions — see CONTINUOUS
2 occurring or appearing at intervals — see INTERMITTENT 1

continually *adv* **1** many times — see OFTEN
2 on every relevant occasion — see ALWAYS 1

continuance *n* **1** continuing existence — see PERSISTENCE 1
2 uninterrupted or lasting existence — see CONTINUATION

continuation *n* uninterrupted or lasting existence ⟨the *continuation* of high unemployment has cost the government much support⟩
synonyms continuance, duration, endurance, persistence, subsistence
related words elongation, extension, lengthening, prolongation
near antonyms abridgment (*or* abridgement), curtailment, shortening
antonyms ending, termination

continue *vb* **1** to remain indefinitely in existence or in the same state ⟨the heavy snow *continued* throughout the night⟩
synonyms abide, endure, hold (up), hold on, keep up, last, persist, run on
related words linger, remain, stay, stick around, tarry
near antonyms abate, die (down), ebb, let up, moderate, subside, wane
antonyms cease, desist, discontinue, quit, stop
2 to begin again or return to after an interruption — see RESUME

continuous *adj* going on and on without any interruptions ⟨a city that has been under *continuous* bombardment for three days⟩
synonyms ceaseless, continual, incessant, unbroken, unceasing, uninterrupted, unremitting
related words endless, eternal, everlasting, interminable, perpetual, unending; changeless, constant, stable, steady, unchanging, unvarying
near antonyms intermittent, periodic, recurrent, recurring
antonyms noncontinuous

contort *vb* to twist (something) out of a natural or normal shape or condition ⟨the acrobat is able to *contort* his body so that it almost looks like a pretzel⟩
synonyms deform, distort, screw, squinch, warp
related words deface, disfigure; wrench, wrest, wring; coil, curl, twine, wind, wreathe

contortion *n* the twisting of something out of its natural or normal shape or condition ⟨the comedian is renowned for his seemingly endless variety of facial *contortions*⟩
synonyms deformation, distortion, screwing, squinching, warping
related words defacement, disfigurement

contour *n* a line that traces the outer limits of an object or surface — see OUTLINE 1

contract *n* **1** a formal agreement to fulfill an obligation — see GUARANTEE 1
2 an arrangement about action to be taken — see AGREEMENT 2

contract *vb* **1** to become affected with (a disease or disorder) ⟨before vaccines were invented, people lived in fear of *contracting* polio⟩
synonyms catch, come down (with), get, sicken (with), take
related words break out (with); die (from), succumb (to); fail, sink, weaken
near antonyms recover (from), shake (off)
2 to become smaller in size or volume through the drawing together of particles of matter ⟨metal *contracts* at low temperatures⟩
synonyms compress, condense, constrict, shrink
related words collapse, deflate; dry (up), shrivel, wither; decrease, diminish, dwindle, lessen; recede, retreat, withdraw
near antonyms accumulate, grow, increase; balloon, inflate, puff (up)
antonyms expand, swell
3 to reduce in size or volume by or as if by pressing parts or members together — see COMPRESS 1

contraction *n* the act or process of reducing the size or volume of something by or as if by pressing — see COMPRESSION

contradict *vb* **1** to make an assertion that is contrary to one made by (another) ⟨no matter what I say, you always have to *contradict* me⟩
synonyms disagree (with), gainsay
related words challenge, contest, dispute, question; confute, rebut, refute; cross, fight, oppose, resist
near antonyms concur (with); confirm, corroborate, substantiate, verify
antonyms agree (with)
2 to declare not to be true — see DENY 1

contradiction *n* **1** someone or something with qualities or features that seem to conflict with

one another ⟨a loving father as well as a ruthless killer, the gangster is a living *contradiction*⟩
synonyms incongruity, paradox
related words conundrum, enigma, mystery, puzzle, riddle
2 a refusal to confirm the truth of a statement — see DENIAL 2

contradictory *adj* being as different as possible — see OPPOSITE

contraption *n* an interesting and often novel device with a practical use — see GADGET

contrariness *n* refusal to obey — see DISOBEDIENCE

contrariwise *adv* just the opposite being true ⟨the rock singer is hardly a carouser; *contrariwise*, he totally abstains from alcohol⟩
synonyms again, conversely
phrases on the contrary
near antonyms even, indeed, nay, truly, verily, yea

contrary *adj* **1** being as different as possible — see OPPOSITE
2 engaging in or marked by childish misbehavior — see NAUGHTY
3 given to resisting authority or another's control — see DISOBEDIENT

contrary *n* something that is as different as possible from something else — see OPPOSITE

contrast *n* the quality or state of being different — see DIFFERENCE 1

contribute *vb* **1** to make a donation as part of a group effort ⟨would you like to *contribute* to the Thanksgiving fund for needy families?⟩
synonyms chip in, kick in, pitch in
related words bestow, donate, give, present
2 to make a present of — see GIVE 1

contribution *n* a gift of money or its equivalent to a charity, humanitarian cause, or public institution ⟨*contributions* for the victims of the earthquake began pouring in⟩
synonyms alms, benefaction, beneficence, charity, donation, philanthropy
related words offering, tithe; bequest, endowment, legacy; aid, assistance, relief, welfare; grant, subsidy

contrite *adj* **1** feeling sorrow for a wrong that one has done ⟨being *contrite* is not enough to spare you an arrest if you're caught shoplifting⟩
synonyms apologetic, penitent, regretful, remorseful, repentant, rueful, sorry
related words sad, grieving, mournful, sorrowful, woeful
near antonyms merciless, pitiless, ruthless
antonyms impenitent, remorseless, unapologetic, unrepentant
2 suffering from or expressive of a feeling of responsibility for wrongdoing — see GUILTY 2

contriteness *n* a feeling of responsibility for wrongdoing — see GUILT 1

contrition *n* a feeling of responsibility for wrongdoing — see GUILT 1

contrivance *n* **1** an interesting and often novel device with a practical use — see GADGET
2 something (as a device) created for the first time through the use of the imagination — see INVENTION 1

contrive *vb* **1** to create or think of by clever use of the imagination — see INVENT
2 to engage in a secret plan to accomplish evil or unlawful ends — see PLOT
3 to plan out usually with subtle skill or care — see ENGINEER

contrived *adj* lacking in natural or spontaneous quality — see ARTIFICIAL 1

contriver *n* one who creates or introduces something new — see INVENTOR

control *n* **1** a mechanism for adjusting the operation of a device, machine, or system ⟨the *controls* for the player are well marked⟩
synonyms regulator
related words button, dial, key, knob, lever, push button, switch
2 the ability to direct the course of something ⟨after the tail fell off, the plane went out of the pilot's *control*⟩ ⟨firefighters keeping *control* of the blaze⟩
synonyms grasp, hand(s)
related words clutch, grip, hold, mastery; command, dominion, helm; authority, jurisdiction, might, power
3 the act or activity of looking after and making decisions about something — see CONDUCT 1
4 the fact or state of having (something) at one's disposal — see POSSESSION 1
5 the right or means to command or control others — see POWER 1

control *vb* **1** to keep from exceeding a desirable degree or level (as of expression) ⟨you must learn to *control* your temper⟩
synonyms bridle, check, constrain, contain, curb, govern, hold in, inhibit, regulate, rein (in), restrain, tame
related words bottle (up), repress, suppress; arrest, interrupt, stop; block, hinder, impede, obstruct; gag, muzzle, silence
near antonyms liberate, loose, loosen, unleash; air, express, take out, vent
2 to gain emotional or mental control of — see COLLECT 1
3 to exercise authority or power over — see GOVERN 1
4 to look after and make decisions about — see CONDUCT 1

controversy *n* variance of opinion on a matter — see DISAGREEMENT 1

contusion *n* a bodily injury in which small blood vessels are broken but the overlying skin is not ⟨*contusions* occurred as a result of a car accident⟩
synonyms bruise
related words black eye; discoloration

conundrum *n* something hard to understand or explain — see MYSTERY

convalesce *vb* to become healthy and strong again after illness or weakness ⟨the long months that the soldier spent in the hospital slowly *convalescing*⟩
synonyms gain, heal, mend, rally, recover, recuperate, snap back
related words come around, come round, come to, improve, pick up, revive; cheer (up), perk (up); pull through, survive; recruit
near antonyms ail, collapse, come down, sicken; decline, degenerate, deteriorate, fade, fail, languish, sink, waste (away), weaken, wilt, wither, worsen; relapse

convalescence *n* the process or period of gradually regaining one's health and strength ⟨her release from the hospital was followed by a long *convalescence* at home⟩

synonyms comeback, healing, mending, rally, recovery, recuperation, rehabilitation, snapback
related words resuscitation, revival; survival
near antonyms decline, deterioration, failing, languishing, sinking, wasting (away), weakening

convene *vb* **1** to bring together in assembly by or as if by command — see CONVOKE
2 to come together into one body or place — see ASSEMBLE 1

convenience *n* something that adds to one's ease — see COMFORT 2

convenient *adj* situated within easy reach ‹the shopping mall is *convenient* to all of the area's major highways›
synonyms accessible, handy, reachable
related words close, near, nigh; abutting, adjacent, adjoining
near antonyms distant, far, remote
antonyms inaccessible, inconvenient, unhandy, unreachable

convention *n* **1** a coming together of a number of persons for a specified purpose — see MEETING 1
2 a formal agreement between two or more nations or peoples — see TREATY
3 an arrangement about action to be taken — see AGREEMENT 2
4 an inherited or established way of thinking, feeling, or doing — see TRADITION 1

conventional *adj* **1** accepted, used, or practiced by most people — see CURRENT 1
2 based on customs usually handed down from a previous generation — see TRADITIONAL 1
3 following or agreeing with established form, custom, or rules — see FORMAL 1

converge *vb* to come together into one body or place — see ASSEMBLE 1

convergence *n* the coming together of two or more things to the same point ‹the *convergence* of the city's major arteries on a single rotary›
synonyms confluence, conjunction, meeting
related words joining, juncture, merging, union
antonyms divergence

conversant *adj* having information especially as a result of study or experience — see FAMILIAR 2

conversation *n* talking or a talk between two or more people ‹Thomas Jefferson was celebrated for his brilliant, wide-ranging *conversations* with a host of friends and acquaintances›
synonyms colloquy, dialogue (*also* dialog), discourse, discussion, exchange
related words banter, cross fire, give-and-take, repartee; conference, parley, powwow; babble, chat, chatter, chitchat, gabfest, gossip, palaver, prate, prattle, rap, small talk, table talk; roundtable, symposium; debate, deliberation

conversational *adj* **1** fond of talking or conversation — see TALKATIVE
2 having the style and content of everyday conversation — see CHATTY 1
3 used in or suitable for speech and not formal writing — see COLLOQUIAL 1

conversationalist *n* a person who talks constantly — see CHATTERBOX

converse *vb* to engage in casual or rambling conversation — see CHAT

converse (with) *vb* to communicate with by means of spoken words — see TALK (TO)

conversely *adv* just the opposite being true — see CONTRARIWISE

conversion *n* a change in form, appearance, or use ‹the *conversion* of the spare bedroom into a home office was easily accomplished›
synonyms changeover, metamorphosis, transfiguration, transformation
related words shift, transition; adjustment, alteration, modification; redoing, refashioning, remaking, remodeling, revamping, revision, reworking, variation; deformation, disfigurement, distortion, mutation, transmutation; displacement, replacement, substitution, supplantation

convert *n* **1** a person who has recently been persuaded to join a religious sect ‹the *converts* were the most vocal and fervent worshippers in the church›
synonyms proselyte
related words newcomer, novice, recruit
2 one who follows the opinions or teachings of another — see FOLLOWER

convert *vb* **1** to persuade to change to one's religious faith ‹young missionaries who go door-to-door trying to *convert* people›
synonyms proselytize
related words brainwash, influence, sway; propagate
near antonyms dissuade
2 to change in form, appearance, or use ‹the old factory was *converted* into an apartment building›
synonyms make over, metamorphose, transfigure, transform
related words adjust, alter, modify; redo, refashion, remake, remodel, revamp, revise, rework, vary; deform, disfigure, distort, mutate, transmute; displace, replace, substitute, supplant

convey *vb* **1** to cause (something) to pass from one to another — see COMMUNICATE 1
2 to support and take from one place to another — see CARRY 1

conveyance *n* something used to carry goods or passengers ‹the covered wagon was the major *conveyance* that transported settlers and their belongings across the frontier›
synonyms transport, transportation, vehicle
related words carrier, hauler, mover; transit

convict *n* a person convicted as a criminal and serving a prison sentence ‹a warning that the three escaped *convicts* were armed and dangerous›
synonyms jailbird
related words captive, capture, inmate, internee, prisoner

convict *vb* to find or pronounce guilty ‹an accused person is presumed innocent until *convicted* in a court of law›
synonyms condemn
related words censure, denounce, rebuke, reprimand, reproach, reprove; admonish, castigate, chastise; penalize, punish, sentence
near antonyms cite, commend, endorse (*also* indorse); approve, bless, sanction
antonyms absolve, acquit, clear, exonerate, vindicate

conviction *n* **1** a state of mind in which one is free from doubt — see CONFIDENCE 2
2 an idea that is believed to be true or valid without positive knowledge — see OPINION 1

convince *vb* to cause (someone) to agree with a belief or course of action by using arguments or earnest requests — see PERSUADE

convincing *adj* having the power to persuade — see COGENT

convincing *n* the act of reasoning or pleading with someone to accept a belief or course of action — see PERSUASION 1

convivial *adj* likely to seek or enjoy the company of others ⟨the hiking club attracts a wide range of *convivial* people who share a love of the outdoors⟩
synonyms boon, companionable, extroverted (*also* extraverted), gregarious, outgoing, sociable, social
related words cordial, friendly, hospitable; affable, genial, gracious; animated, lively, sprightly, vivacious; communicative, expansive, garrulous, talkative
near antonyms misanthropic; aloof, reserved, standoffish; reticent, silent, taciturn
antonyms antisocial, introverted, reclusive, unsociable

conviviality *n* **1** joyful or festive activity — see MERRYMAKING
2 the quality or state of being social — see SOCIABILITY

convocation *n* **1** a body of people come together in one place — see GATHERING 1
2 a coming together of a number of persons for a specified purpose — see MEETING 1

convoke *vb* to bring together in assembly by or as if by command ⟨*convoked* the leading experts on juvenile delinquency to study the situation⟩
synonyms assemble, call, convene, muster, summon
related words amass, collect, gather, group, round up
near antonyms break up, dissolve

convoluted *adj* having many parts or aspects that are usually interrelated — see COMPLEX 1

convoy *vb* to go along with in order to provide assistance, protection, or companionship — see ACCOMPANY

convulse *vb* to make a series of small irregular or violent movements — see SHAKE 1

convulsion *n* a violent disturbance (as of the political or social order) ⟨the Russian Revolution was one of the major *convulsions* of the 20th century⟩
synonyms cataclysm, paroxysm, storm, tempest, tumult, upheaval, uproar
related words overthrow, overturn, revolution, subversion, upset; fit, seizure, spasm; eruption, flare-up, outbreak, outburst; commotion, furor, fuss, hubbub, hullabaloo, row, ruckus, stew, turmoil; quaking, rocking, shaking, trembling

convulsive *adj* marked by sudden or violent disturbance ⟨the assassination of Martin Luther King was one of the most *convulsive* events of the 1960s⟩
synonyms cataclysmal (*or* cataclysmic), stormy, tempestuous, tumultuous
related words fitful, spasmodic, sporadic
near antonyms calm, peaceful, serene, tranquil

cook *n* a person who prepares food by some manner of heating ⟨the hearty meals prepared by the *cook* at summer camp⟩
synonyms chef, cooker
related words baker

cook (up) *vb* to create or think of by clever use of the imagination — see INVENT

cooker *n* **1** an appliance that prepares food for consumption by heating it ⟨a portable gas-fired *cooker* that's perfect for camping trips⟩
synonyms cookstove, range
related words broiler, fryer (*also* frier), microwave oven, oven, roaster, rotisserie, stove, toaster, toaster oven
2 a person who prepares food by some manner of heating — see COOK

cookery *n* the art or style of preparing food (as in a specified region) ⟨tacos represented my introduction to Mexican *cookery*⟩
synonyms cooking, cuisine

cooking *n* the art or style of preparing food (as in a specified region) — see COOKERY

cookstove *n* an appliance that prepares food for consumption by heating it — see COOKER 1

cool *adj* **1** having or showing a lack of friendliness or interest in others ⟨the locals were *cool* towards outsiders⟩ ⟨the schoolmaster's *cool* manner did not encourage chitchat⟩
synonyms aloof, antisocial, cold, detached, distant, frosty, remote, standoffish, unsociable
related words introverted, reclusive, reserved, withdrawn; misanthropic; apathetic, indifferent, unconcerned; disinterested, incurious, uninterested; reticent, silent, taciturn; diffident, shy, timid
near antonyms companionable, convivial, extroverted (*also* extraverted), gregarious, outgoing; communicative, expansive, garrulous, talkative
antonyms cordial, friendly, sociable, warm
2 free from emotional or mental agitation — see CALM 2
3 having a low or subnormal temperature — see COLD 1
4 lacking in friendliness or warmth of feeling — see COLD 2

cool *vb* **1** to cause to lose heat ⟨*cool* your drinks in the icy mountain stream⟩
synonyms chill, refrigerate
related words air-condition; freeze, ice, quick-freeze, supercool; air-cool, ventilate
near antonyms bake, boil, broil, steam
antonyms heat, warm
2 to become still and orderly — see QUIET 1

coolheaded *adj* free from emotional or mental agitation — see CALM 2

coolheadedness *n* evenness of emotions or temper — see EQUANIMITY

coolish *adj* having a low or subnormal temperature — see COLD 1

coolness *n* evenness of emotions or temper — see EQUANIMITY

coop *n* an enclosure with an open framework for keeping animals — see CAGE

coop (up) *vb* to close or shut in by or as if by barriers — see ENCLOSE 1

cooperate *vb* **1** to participate or assist in a joint effort to accomplish an end ⟨conservation groups *cooperated* with state authorities to find a humane way to manage the area's overpopulation of deer⟩
synonyms collaborate, concert, join, team (up)
related words connive, conspire; affiliate, ally, associate, band, combine, confederate, league, unite
phrases play ball
2 to form or enter into an association that furthers the interests of its members — see ALLY

cooperation *n* **1** the state of having shared interests or efforts (as in social or business matters) — see ASSOCIATION 1

2 the work and activity of a number of persons who individually contribute toward the efficiency of the whole — see TEAMWORK

coordinate *n* one that is equal to another in status, achievement, or value — see EQUAL

coordinate *vb* **1** to bring to a state free of conflicts, inconsistencies, or differences — see HARMONIZE 2

2 to form a pleasing relationship — see HARMONIZE 1

coordination *n* the work and activity of a number of persons who individually contribute toward the efficiency of the whole — see TEAMWORK

cop *n* a member of a force charged with law enforcement at the local level — see OFFICER 1

copacetic *also* **copasetic** *or* **copesetic** *adj* being to one's liking — see SATISFACTORY 1

cope *vb* to meet one's day-to-day needs — see GET ALONG 1

cope (with) *vb* to deal with (something) usually skillfully or efficiently — see HANDLE 1

copious *adj* pouring forth in great amounts — see PROFUSE

cop–out *n* the act or a means of getting or keeping away from something undesirable — see ESCAPE 2

cop out *vb* to break a promise or agreement — see RENEGE

coppice *n* a thick patch of shrubbery, small trees, or underbrush — see THICKET

copse *n* a thick patch of shrubbery, small trees, or underbrush — see THICKET

copulate *vb* to engage in sexual intercourse ⟨the time of year when deer in the wild are likely to *copulate*⟩
synonyms mate, sleep
related words fornicate

copulating *n* sexual union involving penetration of the vagina by the penis — see SEXUAL INTERCOURSE

copulation *n* sexual union involving penetration of the vagina by the penis — see SEXUAL INTERCOURSE

copy *n* something that is made to look exactly like something else ⟨a *copy* of the famous painting "Washington Crossing the Delaware"⟩
synonyms carbon copy, duplicate, duplication, facsimile, imitation, reduplication, replica, replication, reproduction
related words counterfeit, fake, forgery, phony (*also* phoney), sham; dummy, mock-up, simulation; reconstruction, re-creation; image, likeness, semblance, shadow; impression, imprint, print
antonyms original

copy *vb* **1** to make an exact likeness of ⟨for the movie, set designers *copied* the Oval Office in the White House down to the smallest detail⟩
synonyms duplicate, imitate, reduplicate, replicate, reproduce
related words counterfeit, fake, forge; simulate; reconstruct, re-create
near antonyms create, imagine, initiate, invent
antonyms originate
2 to use (someone or something) as the model for one's speech, mannerisms, or behavior — see IMITATE 1

copycat *n* a person who adopts the appearance or behavior of another especially in an obvious way ⟨every rock singer who makes it big soon has a whole cluster of *copycats*⟩
synonyms aper, copyist, imitator
related words parrot

copyist *n* a person who adopts the appearance or behavior of another especially in an obvious way — see COPYCAT

coquettish *adj* affecting shyness or modesty in order to attract masculine interest — see COY 1

cord *n* a length of braided, flexible material that is used for tying or connecting things ⟨a vacuum cleaner with an extra long *cord*⟩
synonyms cable, lace, lacing, line, rope, string, wire
related words guy, lanyard, stay

cordial *adj* **1** having or showing kindly feeling and sincere interest — see FRIENDLY 1
2 showing a natural kindness and courtesy especially in social situations — see GRACIOUS 1

cordiality *n* kindly concern, interest, or support — see GOODWILL 1

core *n* **1** the seat of one's deepest thoughts and emotions ⟨in my very *core* I knew that an injustice was being committed⟩
synonyms breast, heart, quick, soul
related words conscience, mind
phrases bottom of one's heart
2 a thing or place that is of greatest importance to an activity or interest — see CENTER 1
3 the central part or aspect of something under consideration — see CRUX
4 the main or greater part of something as distinguished from its appendages — see BODY 1
5 an area or point that is an equal distance from all points along an edge or outer surface — see CENTER 2

corker *n* something very good of its kind — see JIM-DANDY

corkscrew *adj* turning around an axis like the thread of a screw — see SPIRAL

corn *n* something (as a work of literature or music) that is too sentimental ⟨a story about a lost puppy that was pure *corn*⟩
synonyms mush, schmaltz (*also* schmalz)
related words claptrap, drivel, rubbish, slush

corner *n* **1** a difficult, puzzling, or embarrassing situation from which there is no easy escape — see PREDICAMENT
2 a place where roads meet — see CROSSROAD 1

cornerstone *n* an immaterial thing upon which something else rests — see BASE 1

cornet *n* something shaped like a hollow cone and used as a container ⟨*cornets* of pastry dough that were baked and later filled with cream⟩
synonyms cornucopia, horn
related words funnel, tube

cornucopia *n* something shaped like a hollow cone and used as a container — see CORNET

corny *adj* appealing to the emotions in an obvious and tiresome way ⟨*corny* violin music during the movie's love scenes⟩
synonyms maudlin, mawkish, mushy, saccharine, sappy, schmaltzy, sentimental, sloppy, sugar-coated, sugary
related words dreamy, moonstruck, nostalgic; flat, insipid, tasteless, vapid, watery
near antonyms unadulterated, unvarnished; cynical, hard-boiled, hardheaded
antonyms unsentimental

corollary *n* a condition or occurrence traceable to a cause — see EFFECT 1

coronet *n* a decorative band or wreath worn about

the head as a symbol of victory or honor — see CROWN 1

corporal *adj* of or relating to the human body — see PHYSICAL 1

corporeal *adj* of or relating to the human body — see PHYSICAL 1

corps *n* the body of people in a profession or field of activity ⟨a reporter who is widely respected throughout the press *corps*⟩
synonyms brotherhood, community, fellowship, fraternity
related words calling, profession; association, club, federation, guild (*also* gild), organization, society, sodality

corpse *n* a dead body ⟨the discovery of a *corpse* required a call to the police⟩
synonyms cadaver, carcass, remains
related words deceased, decedent

corpulence *n* the condition of having an excess of body fat ⟨the doctor warned that *corpulence* is unhealthy and not just unattractive⟩
synonyms adiposity, chubbiness, fatness, fleshiness, grossness, obesity, plumpness, portliness, pudginess, rotundity
related words bulkiness, heaviness; huskiness, stoutness; brawniness, burliness
near antonyms fitness, trimness; scrawniness, skinniness
antonyms leanness, slenderness, slimness, thinness

corpulent *adj* having an excess of body fat — see FAT 1

corral *n* an enclosure with an open framework for keeping animals — see CAGE

corral *vb* **1** to close or shut in by or as if by barriers — see ENCLOSE 1
2 to take physical control or possession of (something) suddenly or forcibly — see CATCH

correct *adj* **1** being in agreement with the truth or a fact or a standard ⟨a real brainteaser with only one *correct* solution to it⟩
synonyms accurate, exact, precise, proper, right, so, true
related words legitimate, logical, valid; errorless, faultless, flawless, impeccable, letter-perfect, perfect; rigorous, strict, stringent
near antonyms defective, faulty, flawed, imperfect
antonyms false, improper, inaccurate, incorrect, inexact, untrue, wrong
2 following the established traditions of refined society and good taste — see PROPER 1
3 marked by or showing careful attention to set forms and details — see CEREMONIOUS 1

correct *vb* **1** to remove errors, defects, deficiencies, or deviations from ⟨students who never take the time to *correct* their own compositions before handing them in⟩
synonyms amend, debug, emend, rectify, reform, remedy
related words redraft, redraw, restyle, revise, rework, rewrite; redress, right; ameliorate, better, improve; perfect, polish, touch up; fix, mend, repair; adjust, modulate, regulate; alter, change, modify
near antonyms damage, harm, hurt, impair, injure, mar, spoil; aggravate, worsen
2 to balance with an equal force so as to make ineffective — see OFFSET
3 to inflict a penalty on for a fault or crime — see PUNISH

correctable *adj* capable of being corrected — see REMEDIABLE

correcting *adj* inflicting, involving, or serving as punishment — see PUNITIVE

correction *n* **1** a change designed to correct or improve a written work ⟨here's your theme back with the *corrections* marked in blue⟩
synonyms amendment, emendation
related words cut, deletion; addition, amplification, supplement; alteration, modification, revision; improvement, renovation; clarification, explanation, explication
2 suffering, loss, or hardship imposed in response to a crime or offense — see PUNISHMENT

correctional *adj* inflicting, involving, or serving as punishment — see PUNITIVE

corrective *adj* **1** serving to raise or adjust something to some standard or proper condition ⟨eyeglasses are called *corrective* lenses by the department of motor vehicles⟩
synonyms rectifying, remedial, remedying, reformative, reformatory
related words curative, medicinal, therapeutic; reparative, restorative; beneficial, helpful, salutary, wholesome
2 inflicting, involving, or serving as punishment — see PUNITIVE

corrective *n* something that corrects or counteracts something undesirable — see CURE 1

correctly *adv* in a manner suitable for the occasion or purpose — see PROPERLY

correlate *vb* to think of (something) in combination — see ASSOCIATE 2

correspond *vb* **1** to engage in an exchange of written messages ⟨old friends who have been *corresponding* for years⟩
synonyms write
related words communicate, intercommunicate; airmail, e-mail, telegraph; mail, post; answer, reply
2 to be in agreement on every point — see CHECK 1

correspond (to) *vb* **1** to be the exact counterpart of — see MATCH 1
2 to be the same in meaning or effect — see AMOUNT (TO) 2

correspondence *n* **1** a point which two or more things share in common — see SIMILARITY 2
2 the quality or state of having many qualities in common — see SIMILARITY 1

correspondent *n* a person employed by a newspaper, magazine, or radio or television station to gather, write, or report news — see REPORTER

correspondent *adj* having qualities in common — see ALIKE

correspondent (with *or* to) *adj* not having or showing any apparent conflict — see CONSISTENT

corresponding *adj* having qualities in common — see ALIKE

correspondingly *adv* in like manner — see ALSO 1

corridor *n* a typically long narrow way connecting parts of a building — see HALL 2

corroborate *vb* to give evidence or testimony to the truth or factualness of — see CONFIRM

corroborating *adj* serving to give support to the truth or factualness of something — see CORROBORATIVE

corroboration *n* something presented in support of the truth or accuracy of a claim — see PROOF

corroborative *adj* serving to give support to the truth or factualness of something ⟨the results of the DNA fingerprinting was all the *corroborative* evidence the jury needed to convict⟩

synonyms confirmatory, confirming, corroborating, corroboratory, substantiating, supporting, supportive, verifying, vindicating

related words auxiliary, supplementary; beneficial, helpful

near antonyms contradictory, contrary, counter, opposing

antonyms confuting, disproving, refuting

corroboratory *adj* serving to give support to the truth or factualness of something — see CORROBORATIVE

corrode *vb* to consume or wear away gradually — see EAT 2

corrosion *n* a gradual weakening, loss, or destruction ⟨the *corrosion* of family values that is often brought on by great wealth⟩

synonyms attrition, erosion

related words breakdown, decay, decomposition, disintegration, dissolution

near antonyms gain, increase

antonyms buildup

corrupt *adj* having or showing lowered moral character or standards ⟨*corrupt* businessmen who are out to fleece the public⟩ ⟨*corrupt* business practices that should be investigated⟩

synonyms debased, debauched, decadent, degenerate, degraded, demoralized, depraved, dissipated, dissolute, perverse, perverted, reprobate, warped

related words crooked, cutthroat, dishonest, unethical, unprincipled, unscrupulous; contaminated, spoiled, tainted; bad, evil, immoral, iniquitous, nefarious, sinful, vicious, wicked

near antonyms incorruptible, uncorruptible; ethical, honest, principled; good, moral, righteous, virtuous

antonyms uncorrupted

corrupt *vb* **1** to go through decomposition — see DECAY 1

2 to lower in character or dignity — see DEBASE 1

corrupted *adj* having undergone organic breakdown — see ROTTEN 1

corruptible *adj* open to improper influence and especially bribery — see VENAL

corruption *n* **1** the process by which dead organic matter separates into simpler substances ⟨the ancient Egyptians used special preservatives to spare their dead from complete *corruption*⟩

synonyms breakdown, decay, decomposition, putrefaction, rot, spoilage

related words crumbling, disintegration, dissolution; curdling, fermentation, moldering, souring

near antonyms growth, maturation, ripening

2 a sinking to a state of low moral standards and behavior ⟨the *corruption* of the upper classes eventually led to the fall of the Roman empire⟩

synonyms corruptness, debasement, debauchery, decadence, degeneracy, degeneration, degradation, demoralization, depravity, dissipatedness, dissipation, dissoluteness, perversion

related words evil, immorality, nefariousness, sinfulness, wickedness

near antonyms goodness, morality, righteousness, virtue

3 immoral conduct or practices harmful or offensive to society — see VICE 1

corruptness *n* a sinking to a state of low moral standards and behavior — see CORRUPTION 2

corsair *n* someone who engages in robbery of ships at sea — see PIRATE

cortege *also* **cortège** *n* **1** a body of employees or servants who accompany and wait on a person ⟨the movie star's *cortege* included her hair stylist, makeup artist, personal assistant, and press agent⟩

synonyms following, retinue, suite, train

related words crew, personnel, staff; assistant, attendant, helper, retainer

2 a body of individuals moving along in an orderly and often ceremonial way ⟨the funeral *cortege* of mourners stretched for three city blocks⟩

synonyms parade, procession

related words column, line, string, train

cosmetics *n pl* preparations intended to beautify the face or hair — see MAKEUP 1

cosmic *adj* unusually large — see HUGE

cosmopolitan *adj* having a wide and refined knowledge of the world especially from personal experience — see WORLDLY-WISE

cosmopolitan *n* a person with the outlook, experience, and manners thought to be typical of big city dwellers ⟨as someone who had lived in Paris for a year as an exchange student, she seemed very much the *cosmopolitan* to her old classmates⟩

synonyms metropolitan, sophisticate

related words urbanite; worldling

antonyms bumpkin, hick, provincial, rustic, yokel

cosmos *n* the whole body of things observed or assumed — see UNIVERSE

cost *n* **1** a payment made in the course of achieving a result — see EXPENSE

2 the amount of money that is demanded as payment for something — see PRICE 1

3 the loss or penalty involved in achieving a goal — see PRICE 2

cost *vb* to have a price of ⟨the raffle tickets *cost* a dollar each⟩

synonyms bring, fetch, go (for), sell (for)

related words amount (to), come (to), total; command, exact; ask, demand

costly *adj* commanding a large price ⟨running is one sport that does not require a lot of *costly* equipment⟩

synonyms dear, expensive, high, precious, premium, valuable

related words exorbitant, extravagant, overpriced, prohibitive, steep, stiff, unreasonable; invaluable, priceless

near antonyms moderate, reasonable; valueless, worthless; discounted

antonyms cheap, inexpensive

costume *n* **1** clothing chosen as appropriate for a specific situation — see OUTFIT 1

2 clothing put on to hide one's true identity or imitate someone or something else — see DISGUISE

costume *vb* to outfit with clothes and especially fine or special clothes — see CLOTHE 1

coterie *n* a group of people sharing a common interest and relating together socially — see GANG 2

cotillion *n* a social gathering for dancing — see DANCE

cottage *n* an often small house for recreational or seasonal use ⟨for a month every summer we rent a *cottage* on the ocean⟩

synonyms cabin, camp, chalet, lodge
related words bungalow, cot; hut, shack, shanty

cottony *adj* smooth or delicate in appearance or feel — see SOFT 2

couch *n* a long upholstered piece of furniture designed for several sitters ⟨find yourself a place on the *couch* and make yourself at home⟩
synonyms chesterfield, davenport, divan, lounge, settee, sofa
related words love seat; day bed, sofa bed; bench

couch *vb* to convey in appropriate or telling terms — see PHRASE

cougar *n* a large tawny cat of the wild ⟨in many areas suburban developments have encroached upon the habitat of the *cougar*⟩
synonyms catamount, mountain lion, panther, puma

council *n* **1** a coming together of a number of persons for a specified purpose — see MEETING 1
2 a group of persons formally joined together for some common interest — see ASSOCIATION 2
3 a meeting featuring a group discussion — see FORUM

counsel *n* **1** a person whose profession is to conduct lawsuits for clients or to advise about legal rights and obligations — see LAWYER
2 an opinion suggesting a wise or proper course of action — see ADVICE

counsel *vb* **1** to exchange viewpoints or seek advice for the purpose of finding a solution to a problem — see CONFER 2
2 to give advice and instruction to (someone) regarding the course or process to be followed — see GUIDE 1
3 to give advice to — see ADVISE 1
4 to put forward as one's choice for a wise or proper course of action — see ADVISE 2

counselor *or* **counsellor** *n* **1** a person who gives advice especially professionally — see CONSULTANT
2 a person whose profession is to conduct lawsuits for clients or to advise about legal rights and obligations — see LAWYER

count *n* **1** a total number obtained or recorded by noting each thing as it was being added ⟨my *count* for the number of bird species and subspecies that visited the sanctuary that weekend was 43⟩
synonyms tally
related words score; amount, gross, sum, total, whole
2 a formal claim of criminal wrongdoing against a person — see CHARGE 1

count *vb* **1** to find the sum of (a collection of things) by noting each one as it is being added ⟨*count* the baseball gloves in the storage locker to see if there are enough to go around⟩
synonyms enumerate, number, tell
related words add (up), tally, total; calculate, compute, reckon, table, tabulate; check, mark, tick (off)
2 to be of importance — see MATTER
3 to place reliance or trust — see DEPEND 2
4 to think of in a particular way — see CONSIDER 1

countenance *n* **1** facial appearance regarded as an indication of mood or feeling — see LOOK 1
2 the front part of the head — see FACE 1

countenance *vb* **1** to have a favorable opinion of — see APPROVE (OF)
2 to put up with (something painful or difficult) — see BEAR 2

counter *adj* opposed to one's interests — see ADVERSE 1

counter *vb* to strive to reduce or eliminate — see FIGHT 2

counteract *vb* to balance with an equal force so as to make ineffective — see OFFSET

counteraction *n* a force or influence that makes an opposing force ineffective or less effective — see COUNTERBALANCE

counterattack *n* an attack made to counter an enemy's attack ⟨suddenly the tide of battle turned, and the rebels, who had been falling back, made a furious *counterattack*⟩
synonyms counteroffensive
related words sally, sortie; blitzkrieg, charge; assault, attack, offensive, onslaught

counterbalance *n* a force or influence that makes an opposing force ineffective or less effective ⟨charitable giving is usually a good *counterbalance* to the self-indulgent commercialism of the Christmas season⟩
synonyms balance, canceler (*or* canceller), counteraction, counterpoise, counterweight, equipoise, neutralizer, offset
related words trade-off

counterbalance *vb* to balance with an equal force so as to make ineffective — see OFFSET

counterfeit *adj* being such in appearance only and made or manufactured with the intention of committing fraud ⟨*counterfeit* money that had been passed all over town⟩
synonyms bogus, fake, false, forged, inauthentic, phony (*also* phoney), sham, spurious, unauthentic
related words artificial, factitious, imitation, man-made, mimic, mock, simulated, substitute, synthetic; dummy, nonfunctioning, ornamental; cultured, fabricated, manufactured; deceptive, delusive, misleading
near antonyms natural; actual, true, valid
antonyms authentic, bona fide, genuine, real

counterfeit *n* an imitation that is passed off as genuine — see FAKE 1

counterfeit *vb* **1** to imitate or copy especially in order to deceive — see FAKE 1
2 to present a false appearance of — see FEIGN

counteroffensive *n* an attack made to counter an enemy's attack — see COUNTERATTACK

counterpane *n* a decorative cloth used as a top covering for a bed ⟨a beautiful *counterpane* that was a family heirloom⟩
synonyms bedspread, coverlet, spread
related words comforter, puff, quilt; bedclothes, bedding

counterpart *n* **1** one that is equal to another in status, achievement, or value — see EQUAL
2 something or someone that strongly resembles another — see IMAGE 1

counterpoise *n* a force or influence that makes an opposing force ineffective or less effective — see COUNTERBALANCE

counterpoise *vb* to balance with an equal force so as to make ineffective — see OFFSET

countersign *n* a word or phrase that must be spoken by a person in order to pass a guard — see PASSWORD

counterweight *n* a force or influence that makes an opposing force ineffective or less effective — see COUNTERBALANCE

countless *adj* too many to be counted ⟨I've told you *countless* times not to do that⟩

synonyms innumerable, numberless, uncountable, uncounted, unnumbered, untold
related words endless, infinite, unlimited, vast; many, multitudinous, numerous
near antonyms finite, limited
antonyms countable

count out *vb* to prevent the participation or inclusion of — see EXCLUDE

country *adj* of, relating to, associated with, or typical of open areas with few buildings or people — see RURAL

country *n* **1** the land of one's birth, residence, or citizenship ⟨a great love for my *country*⟩
synonyms fatherland, home, homeland, motherland, sod
related words old country; community, neighborhood
2 the open rural area outside of big towns and cities ⟨out in the *country*, where the air is fresh and the rivers are clean⟩
synonyms countryside, sticks
related words exurbia; backwater, backwoods, bush, frontier, hinterland, up-country; wild, wilderness
near antonyms conurbation, megalopolis, urban sprawl
3 a body of people composed of one or more nationalities usually with its own territory and government — see NATION

countryman *n* **1** a person living in or originally from the same country as another — see COMPATRIOT
2 an awkward or simple person especially from a small town or the country — see HICK

countryseat *n* a large impressive residence — see MANSION

countryside *n* the open rural area outside of big towns and cities — see COUNTRY 2

coup *n* a successful result brought about by hard work — see ACCOMPLISHMENT 1

couple *n* two things of the same or similar kind that match or are considered together — see PAIR

couple *vb* **1** to come together to form a single unit — see UNITE 1
2 to put or bring together so as to form a new and longer whole — see CONNECT 1

coupling *n* **1** a place where two or more things are united — see JOINT 1
2 the act or an instance of joining two or more things into one — see UNION 1

coupon *n* a small sheet of plastic, paper, or paperboard showing that the bearer has a claim to something (as admittance) — see TICKET 1

courage *n* strength of mind to carry on in spite of danger ⟨the moral *courage* to speak out against injustice when no one else will⟩
synonyms bravery, courageousness, daring, dauntlessness, doughtiness, fearlessness, gallantry, greatheartedness, guts, hardihood, heart, heroism, intrepidity, intrepidness, nerve, stoutness, valor
related words backbone, fiber, fortitude, grit, gumption, mettle, pluck, spunk; determination, perseverance, resolution; endurance, stamina, tenacity; audacity, boldness, brazenness, cheek, effrontery, gall, temerity
near antonyms faintheartedness, fearfulness, timidity, timorousness; feebleness, softness, weakness; impotence, ineffectualness; hesitation, indecision, indecisiveness, irresolution
antonyms cowardice, cowardliness, cravenness, dastardliness, spinelessness, yellowness

courageous *adj* feeling or displaying no fear by temperament — see BRAVE

courageousness *n* strength of mind to carry on in spite of danger — see COURAGE

courier *n* one that carries a message or does an errand — see MESSENGER

course *n* **1** a way of acting or proceeding ⟨the president's usual *course* has been to obtain advice from several people and then make up his own mind⟩
synonyms line, policy, procedure, program
related words blueprint, design, plan, scheme, strategy; intent, intention, purpose; approach, direction, path, pathway, tack
2 a series of lectures on a subject ⟨a *course* on American history from the colonial period to the present⟩
synonyms class
related words elective, refresher, seminar; core, curriculum
3 a usually fixed or ordered series of actions or events leading to a result — see PROCESS 1
4 the direction along which something or someone moves — see PATH 1

course *vb* to proceed or move quickly — see HURRY 2

court *n* **1** the residence of a ruler ⟨Hampton *Court* was the residence of King Henry VIII⟩
synonyms palace
related words castle, château, estate, mansion, villa
2 an open space wholly or partly enclosed (as by buildings or walls) ⟨the art museum boasts a glass-sided *court* that is filled with an array of greenery and sculpture⟩
synonyms close, courtyard, enclosure (*also* inclosure), patio, quadrangle, yard
related words place, plaza, square; deck, terrace
3 an assembly of persons for the administration of justice ⟨this *court* is now called to order⟩
synonyms bar, tribunal
related words judiciary; court-martial; inquisition, kangaroo court
4 a public official having authority to decide questions of law — see JUDGE 1

court *vb* **1** to act so as to make (something) more likely ⟨you're *courting* disaster if you keep playing with matches⟩
synonyms ask (for), invite, woo
related words angle (for), fish (for); hunt, search, seek
phrases look for
2 to go on dates that may eventually lead to marriage ⟨they *courted* for a year before getting married⟩
synonyms date
related words romance, spark, woo; escort, see, take out
phrases go steady, make love

courteous *adj* showing consideration, courtesy, and good manners — see POLITE 1

courteously *adv* with good reason or courtesy — see WELL 4

courteousness *n* speech or behavior that is a sign of good breeding — see POLITENESS

courtesy *n* **1** an act of kind assistance — see FAVOR 1
2 an act or utterance that is a customary show of good manners — see CIVILITY 1
3 speech or behavior that is a sign of good breeding — see POLITENESS

courting *n* the series of social engagements shared by a couple looking to get married — see COURTSHIP

courtship *n* the series of social engagements shared by a couple looking to get married ⟨a long-married couple who look back on their whirlwind *courtship* with fondness and laughter⟩
synonyms courting, dating
related words affair, love affair, romance; betrothal, engagement

courtyard *n* an open space wholly or partly enclosed (as by buildings or walls) — see COURT 2

cove *n* a part of a body of water that extends beyond the general shoreline — see GULF 1

covenant *n* **1** a formal agreement between two or more nations or peoples — see TREATY
2 a formal agreement to fulfill an obligation — see GUARANTEE 1
3 an arrangement about action to be taken — see AGREEMENT 2

covenant *vb* to make a solemn declaration of intent — see PROMISE 1

cover *n* **1** a piece placed over an open container to hold in, protect, or conceal its contents ⟨where's the *cover* for the cookie jar?⟩
synonyms cap, lid, top
related words dome, hood, roof; capsule, case, casing, covering, housing, jacket, sheath, shell
2 means or method of defending — see DEFENSE 1
3 something that encloses another thing especially to protect it — see [1]CASE 1

cover *vb* **1** to serve as a replacement usually for a time only ⟨a friend *covered* for me as a hospital volunteer while my family went on vacation⟩
synonyms fill in, pinch-hit, stand in, sub, substitute, take over
related words understudy; relieve, spell; double (as)
2 to form a layer over ⟨by morning a foot of snow *covered* the ground⟩
synonyms blanket, carpet, coat, overlay, overlie, overspread, sheet
related words enclose (*also* inclose), enshroud, envelop, enwrap, mantle, shawl, shroud, swathe, wrap; cloak, clothe, curtain, veil; circle, encircle, encompass
3 to place a protective layer over ⟨*cover* your skin with sunblock so you won't get sunburned⟩
synonyms screen, shield
related words cloak, clothe, veil; disguise, mask, obscure
near antonyms bare, expose, uncover
4 to have (something) as a subject matter — see CONCERN 1
5 to keep secret or shut off from view — see [1]HIDE 2
6 to make one's way through, across, or over — see TRAVERSE
7 to pay continued close attention to (something) for a particular purpose — see MONITOR
8 to drive danger or attack away from — see DEFEND 1

cover (up) *vb* to keep from being publicly known — see SUPPRESS 1

coverage *n* the amount of something (as subject matter) included ⟨the biographical dictionary's *coverage* is limited to people no longer living⟩
synonyms content
related words compass, gamut, range, scope, sweep; membership, participation

covering *n* something that encloses another thing especially to protect it — see [1]CASE 1

coverlet *n* a decorative cloth used as a top covering for a bed — see COUNTERPANE

covert *adj* **1** hidden from view — see SECLUDED
2 undertaken or done so as to escape being observed or known by others — see SECRET 1

covert *n* **1** a place where a person goes to hide — see HIDEOUT
2 a thick patch of shrubbery, small trees, or underbrush — see THICKET

covet *vb* to have an earnest wish to own or enjoy — see DESIRE

coveting *adj* having or marked by an eager and often selfish desire especially for material possessions — see GREEDY 1

covetous *adj* **1** having or marked by an eager and often selfish desire especially for material possessions — see GREEDY 1
2 having or showing mean resentment of another's possessions or advantages — see ENVIOUS

covetousness *n* **1** a painful awareness of another's possessions or advantages and a desire to have them too — see ENVY
2 an intense selfish desire for wealth or possessions — see GREED

cow *vb* to make timid or fearful by or as if by threats — see INTIMIDATE

coward *n* a person who shows a shameful lack of courage in the face of danger ⟨the soldiers who ran as soon as the first shots were fired were branded as *cowards*⟩
synonyms chicken, craven, dastard, poltroon, recreant, sissy
related words defeatist, quitter; pushover, weakling, wimp; snake, sneak
near antonyms daredevil
antonyms hero, stalwart, valiant

cowardice *n* a shameful lack of courage in the face of danger ⟨the *cowardice* shown by political leaders who were willing to give the Nazis whatever they wanted⟩
synonyms cowardliness, cravenness, dastardliness, spinelessness, yellowness
related words diffidence, faintheartedness, fearfulness, timidity, timorousness; carefulness, cautiousness, wariness; bashfulness, shyness; feebleness, softness, weakness
near antonyms audacity, boldness, brazenness; backbone, fiber, fortitude, grit, gumption, mettle, pluck, spunk; determination, perseverance, resolution; endurance, stamina, tenacity
antonyms bravery, courage, courageousness, daring, dauntlessness, doughtiness, fearlessness, gallantry, greatheartedness, guts, hardihood, heart, heroism, intrepidity, intrepidness, nerve, stoutness, valor

cowardliness *n* a shameful lack of courage in the face of danger — see COWARDICE

cowardly *adj* having or showing a shameful lack of courage ⟨a *cowardly* bully who picks on much smaller kids⟩ ⟨vile charges that were made in a *cowardly*, unsigned letter⟩

synonyms chicken, chickenhearted, craven, dastardly, lily-livered, pusillanimous, recreant, spineless, unheroic, yellow

related words diffident, fainthearted, fearful, timid, timorous; afraid, frightened, scared; careful, cautious, wary; bashful, coy, shy; feeble, soft, weak

near antonyms audacious, bold, brazen, cheeky, nervy; plucky, spirited, spunky; determined, resolute

antonyms brave, courageous, daring, dauntless, doughty, fearless, gallant, greathearted, gutsy, hardy, heroic, intrepid, lionhearted, stalwart, stout, stouthearted, valiant, valorous

cowboy *n* a hired hand who tends cattle or horses at a ranch or on the range ⟨*cowboys* were rounding up the cattle for branding⟩

synonyms buckaroo, cowhand, cowman, cowpoke, cowpuncher

related words cowgirl; gaucho, vaquero; horseman, horsewoman, wrangler; cattleman, rancher; herdsman

cower *vb* to draw back or crouch down in fearful submission ⟨the abused dog always *cowered* in the presence of its master⟩

synonyms cringe, grovel, quail

related words flinch, recoil, shrink, squinch; blanch, blench, whiten; fawn, kowtow, toady

cowhand *n* a hired hand who tends cattle or horses at a ranch or on the range — see COWBOY

cowhide *vb* to strike repeatedly with something long and thin or flexible — see WHIP 1

cowman *n* a hired hand who tends cattle or horses at a ranch or on the range — see COWBOY

coworker *n* a fellow worker — see COLLEAGUE

cowpoke *n* a hired hand who tends cattle or horses at a ranch or on the range — see COWBOY

cowpuncher *n* a hired hand who tends cattle or horses at a ranch or on the range — see COWBOY

coy *adj* **1** affecting shyness or modesty in order to attract masculine interest ⟨not wanting him to know that she was interested in him, she acted very *coy* at the dance⟩

synonyms coquettish, demure, kittenish

related words flirtatious; goody-goody, overmodest, priggish, prim, prudish

2 not comfortable around people — see SHY 2

cozen *vb* **1** to cause to believe what is untrue — see DECEIVE

2 to rob by the use of trickery or threats — see FLEECE

cozener *n* a dishonest person who uses clever means to cheat others out of something of value — see TRICKSTER 1

cozy *adj* **1** enjoying physical comfort — see COMFORTABLE 2

2 providing physical comfort — see COMFORTABLE 1

crab *n* an irritable and complaining person — see GROUCH

crab *vb* to express dissatisfaction, pain, or resentment usually tiresomely — see COMPLAIN

crabby *adj* **1** easily irritated or annoyed — see IRRITABLE

2 given to complaining a lot — see FUSSY 1

crack *adj* having or showing exceptional knowledge, experience, or skill in a field of endeavor — see PROFICIENT

crack *n* **1** an irregular usually narrow break in a surface created by pressure ⟨a pebble struck the car's windshield and left a *crack* in it⟩

synonyms chink, cleft, cranny, crevice, fissure, rift, split

related words craze, hairline; fracture, rupture; breach, gap, opening; cut, gash, incision, slit

2 a hard strike with a part of the body or an instrument — see [1]BLOW

3 a loud explosive sound — see CLAP 1

4 an effort to do or accomplish something — see ATTEMPT

5 something said or done to cause laughter — see JOKE 1

crack *vb* **1** to break suddenly with an explosive sound ⟨the tree branch unexpectedly *cracked* under our weight⟩

synonyms pop, snap

related words crackle, hiss, sizzle, sputter; burst, explode, shatter; clack, click, clatter

2 to yield to mental or emotional stress ⟨after hours of tough questioning the suspect finally *cracked* and blurted out a confession⟩

synonyms break (down), flip, freak (out)

phrases go to pieces

3 to change (as a secret message) from code into ordinary language — see DECODE

4 to deliver a blow to (someone or something) usually in a strong vigorous manner — see HIT 1

5 to find an answer for through reasoning — see SOLVE

crackbrain *n* **1** a person judged to be legally or medically insane — see LUNATIC 1

2 a person of odd or whimsical habits — see ECCENTRIC

crackbrained *adj* having or showing a very abnormal or sick state of mind — see INSANE 1

crack down (on) *vb* to put a stop to (something) by the use of force — see QUELL 1

cracked *adj* having or showing a very abnormal or sick state of mind — see INSANE 1

crackerjack *adj* **1** having or showing exceptional knowledge, experience, or skill in a field of endeavor — see PROFICIENT

2 of the very best kind — see EXCELLENT

crackerjack *n* **1** a person with a high level of knowledge or skill in a field — see EXPERT

2 something very good of its kind — see JIM-DANDY

crackpot *n* a person of odd or whimsical habits — see ECCENTRIC

crack–up *n* the violent coming together of two bodies into destructive contact — see CRASH 1

crack up *vb* **1** to declare enthusiastic approval of — see ACCLAIM

2 to praise or publicize lavishly and often excessively — see TOUT 1

craft *n* **1** an occupation requiring skillful use of the hands ⟨the *craft* of cabinetmaking was much admired in colonial times⟩

synonyms handcraft, handicraft, trade

related words art, skill; calling, occupation, profession, vocation

2 a small buoyant structure for travel on water — see BOAT 1

3 the inclination or practice of misleading others through lies or trickery — see DECEIT

4 skill in achieving one's ends through indirect, subtle, or underhanded means — see CUNNING 1

5 subtle or imaginative ability in inventing, devising, or executing something — see SKILL 1

craft *vb* to put (something) into proper and usually carefully worked out written form — see COMPOSE 1

craftiness *n* **1** skill in achieving one's ends through indirect, subtle, or underhanded means — see CUNNING 1
2 the inclination or practice of misleading others through lies or trickery — see DECEIT

craftsman *n* a person whose occupation requires skill with the hands — see ARTISAN

crafty *adj* clever at attaining one's ends by indirect and often deceptive means — see ARTFUL 1

crag *n* a steep wall of rock, earth, or ice — see CLIFF

craggy *adj* having an uneven edge or outline — see RAGGED 1

cram *vb* **1** to fit (something) into a tight space — see CROWD 1
2 to put into (something) as much as can be held or contained — see FILL 1

crammed *adj* containing or seeming to contain the greatest quantity or number possible — see FULL 1

cramp *n* a painful sudden tightening of a muscle ⟨I was suddenly awakened by a *cramp* in my leg⟩
synonyms charley horse, crick, spasm
related words contraction, jerk, stitch, twinge, twitch

cramp *vb* to create difficulty for the work or activity of — see HAMPER

crane *vb* to move from a lower to a higher place or position — see RAISE 1

cranium *n* the case of bone that encloses the brain and supports the jaws of vertebrates — see SKULL

crank *n* **1** a person of odd or whimsical habits — see ECCENTRIC
2 an irritable and complaining person — see GROUCH

crank (up) *vb* to cause to function — see ACTIVATE

crankiness *n* readiness to show annoyance or impatience — see PETULANCE

cranky *adj* **1** difficult to use or operate especially because of size, weight, or design — see CUMBERSOME
2 easily irritated or annoyed — see IRRITABLE
3 given to complaining a lot — see FUSSY 1

cranny *n* an irregular usually narrow break in a surface created by pressure — see CRACK 1

crash *n* **1** the violent coming together of two bodies into destructive contact ⟨the fiery *crash* of two jumbo jet airplanes in midair⟩
synonyms collision, crack-up, smash, smashup, wreck
related words accident; demolishment, destruction, ruin
2 a falling short of one's goals — see FAILURE 2
3 a loud explosive sound — see CLAP 1
4 a forceful coming together of two things — see IMPACT 1

crash *vb* **1** to cause to break with violence and much noise — see SMASH 1
2 to come into usually forceful contact with something — see HIT 2
3 to stop functioning — see FAIL 1

crass *adj* lacking in refinement or good taste — see COARSE 2

crassness *n* the quality or state of lacking refinement or good taste — see VULGARITY 1

crave *vb* to have an earnest wish to own or enjoy — see DESIRE

craven *adj* having or showing a shameful lack of courage — see COWARDLY

craven *n* a person who shows a shameful lack of courage in the face of danger — see COWARD

cravenness *n* a shameful lack of courage in the face of danger — see COWARDICE

craving *n* a strong wish for something — see DESIRE

crawl *vb* **1** to move slowly with the body close to the ground ⟨the time we had to *crawl* through a narrow passageway from one cave to another⟩
synonyms creep, grovel, slither, snake, worm, wriggle
related words crouch, squat; slide; edge, inch, nose; skulk, sneak, steal, tiptoe
2 to move slowly ⟨the weekend traffic on the road to the beach just *crawled*⟩
synonyms creep, drag, inch, plod, poke
related words lumber, shamble, shuffle, tramp, trudge
near antonyms float, glide, sail; hurry, tear
antonyms fly, race, speed, whiz (*or* whizz), zip
3 to move or act slowly — see DELAY 1

crawler *n* someone who moves slowly or more slowly than others — see SLOWPOKE

crawling *adj* moving or proceeding at less than the normal, desirable, or required speed — see SLOW 1

craze *n* a practice or interest that is very popular for a short time — see FAD

craze *vb* to cause to go insane or as if insane ⟨soldiers who had been *crazed* by months of combat and chaos in the countryside⟩
synonyms derange, madden, unbalance, unhinge, unstring
related words agitate, bother, confuse, discompose, disquiet, distract, disturb, perturb, unsettle, upset; annoy, irritate, vex
near antonyms calm, quiet, relax, settle, soothe, tranquilize (*or* tranquillize)

crazed *adj* having or showing a very abnormal or sick state of mind — see INSANE 1

craziness *n* lack of good sense or judgment — see FOOLISHNESS 1

crazy *adj* **1** conceived or made without regard for reason or reality — see FANTASTIC 1
2 having or showing a very abnormal or sick state of mind — see INSANE 1
3 showing or marked by a lack of good sense or judgment — see FOOLISH 1
4 showing urgent desire or interest — see EAGER

crazy (about *or* over) *adj* filled with an intense or excessive love for — see ENAMORED (OF)

creak *n* a harsh grating sound — see RASP

creak *vb* to make a short shrill noise — see SQUEAK

cream *n* individuals carefully selected as being the best of a class — see ELITE

crease *n* a small fold in a soft and otherwise smooth surface — see WRINKLE 1

crease *vb* to develop creases or folds — see WRINKLE 1

create *vb* to be the cause of (a situation, action, or state of mind) — see EFFECT

creation *n* **1** something (as a device) created for the first time through the use of the imagination — see INVENTION 1
2 the whole body of things observed or assumed — see UNIVERSE

creative *adj* **1** having the skill and imagination to create new things ⟨Thomas Edison's status as perhaps America's greatest *creative* genius⟩
synonyms imaginative, ingenious, innovative, inventive, original
related words gifted, inspired, talented; resourceful; fecund, fertile, fruitful, productive, prolific
near antonyms imitative, uninspired; infertile, unproductive
antonyms uncreative, unimaginative, unoriginal
2 showing a use of the imagination and creativity especially in inventing — see CLEVER 1

creativeness *n* the skill and imagination to create new things — see CREATIVITY 1

creativity *n* **1** the skill and imagination to create new things ⟨the arts and crafts fair showed the remarkable *creativity* of local artists and artisans⟩
synonyms creativeness, imaginativeness, ingeniousness, ingenuity, invention, inventiveness, originality
related words resourcefulness; fecundity, fertility, fruitfulness, productiveness, productivity; freshness, newness, novelty; genius, inspiration, talent
near antonyms dryness, dullness (*also* dulness)
2 the ability to form mental images of things that either are not physically present or have never been conceived or created by others — see IMAGINATION

creator *n* **1** a person who establishes a whole new field of endeavor — see FATHER 2
2 *cap* the being worshipped as the creator and ruler of the universe — see DEITY 2

creature *n* **1** a member of the human race — see HUMAN
2 one of the lower animals as distinguished from human beings — see ANIMAL

credence *n* **1** firm belief in the integrity, ability, effectiveness, or genuineness of someone or something — see TRUST 1
2 mental conviction of the truth of some statement or the reality of some being or phenomenon — see BELIEF 1

credentials *n pl* a skill, an ability, or knowledge that makes a person able to do a particular job — see QUALIFICATION 1

credible *adj* worthy of being accepted as true or reasonable — see BELIEVABLE

credit *n* **1** the right to take possession of goods before paying for them ⟨because of their reputation for not paying their bills, no store will extend the family *credit*⟩
synonyms trust
related words installment plan, layaway
2 an asset that brings praise or renown — see GLORY 2
3 mental conviction of the truth of some statement or the reality of some being or phenomenon — see BELIEF 1
4 public acknowledgment or admiration for an achievement — see GLORY 1

credit *vb* **1** to explain (something) as being the result of something else ⟨has to *credit* his success in picking winning lottery numbers to pure luck⟩
synonyms accredit, ascribe, attribute, impute
related words blame, pin (on); associate, connect, link
2 to regard as right or true — see BELIEVE 1

creditable *adj* deserving of high regard or great approval — see ADMIRABLE

credo *n* **1** a body of beliefs and practices regarding the supernatural and the worship of one or more deities — see RELIGION 1
2 the basic beliefs or guiding principles of a person or group — see CREED 1

credulity *n* readiness to believe the claims of others without sufficient evidence ⟨the quack pushing the phony medicine was taking advantage of the *credulity* of people hoping for miracle cures⟩
synonyms credulousness, gullibility, naïveté (*also* naivete)
related words artlessness, simplicity, unsophistication; trust, unwariness
near antonyms sophistication, worldliness; distrust, mistrust, suspicion, wariness; doubt, uncertainty
antonyms incredulity, skepticism

credulousness *n* readiness to believe the claims of others without sufficient evidence — see CREDULITY

creed *n* **1** the basic beliefs or guiding principles of a person or group ⟨central to the *creed* of this organization of medical volunteers is the belief that health care is a basic human right⟩
synonyms credo, doctrine, gospel, ideology, philosophy
related words manifesto
2 a body of beliefs and practices regarding the supernatural and the worship of one or more deities — see RELIGION 1

creek *n* **1** a natural body of running water smaller than a river ⟨the shallow *creek* that runs in back of our house⟩
synonyms brook, brooklet, rill, rivulet, run [*chiefly Midland*], streamlet
related words freshet, runoff; river, stream, watercourse, waterway; canal, millrace, millstream, race
2 *chiefly British* a part of a body of water that extends beyond the general shoreline — see GULF 1

creep *n* a person whose behavior is offensive to others — see JERK 1

creep *vb* **1** to advance gradually beyond the usual or desirable limits — see ENCROACH
2 to move or act slowly — see DELAY 1
3 to move slowly with the body close to the ground — see CRAWL 1
4 to move slowly — see CRAWL 2

creeper *n* someone who moves slowly or more slowly than others — see SLOWPOKE

creeping *adj* moving or proceeding at less than the normal, desirable, or required speed — see SLOW 1

creepy *adj* fearfully and mysteriously strange or fantastic — see EERIE

crest *n* the line formed when two sloping surfaces come together along their topmost edge — see RIDGE

crestfallen *adj* feeling unhappiness — see SAD 1

cretin *n* **1** a person whose behavior is offensive to others — see JERK 1
2 a stupid person — see IDIOT

crevice *n* an irregular usually narrow break in a surface created by pressure — see CRACK 1

crew *n* a group of people working together on a task — see GANG 1

crick *n* a painful sudden tightening of a muscle — see CRAMP

crime *n* **1** activities that are in violation of the laws of the state ⟨a promise by the president to step up the war against *crime*⟩

synonyms criminality, lawbreaking, lawlessness
related words malfeasance, misconduct; wrongdoing; evil, immorality, sin, wickedness; corruption, depravity; malefaction, misdeed, misdoing, offense (*or* offence), transgression, trespass
2 a regrettable or blameworthy act ⟨it's a *crime* to waste food, so give the rest of the pizza to me⟩
synonyms disgrace, pity, shame, sin
related words outrage, scandal
3 a breaking of a moral or legal code — see OFFENSE 1
4 a cause of shame — see DISGRACE 2

criminal *adj* contrary to or forbidden by law — see ILLEGAL 1

criminal *n* a person who has committed a crime ⟨car thieves, pickpockets, burglars, and other *criminals*⟩
synonyms crook, culprit; felon, lawbreaker, malefactor, offender
related words desperado, outlaw; convict, jailbird; perpetrator; evildoer, sinner, transgressor, trespasser, wrongdoer; gangster, gunman, hoodlum, mobster, racketeer, thug; backslider, relapser, repeater

criminality *n* activities that are in violation of the laws of the state — see CRIME 1

crimp *n* **1** a small fold in a soft and otherwise smooth surface — see WRINKLE 1
2 something that makes movement or progress more difficult — see ENCUMBRANCE

crimson *vb* to develop a rosy facial color (as from excitement or embarrassment) — see BLUSH

cringe *vb* to draw back or crouch down in fearful submission — see COWER

crinkle *n* a small fold in a soft and otherwise smooth surface — see WRINKLE 1

crinkle *vb* **1** to create (as by crushing) an irregular mass of creases in — see CRUMPLE 1
2 to develop creases or folds — see WRINKLE 1

cripple *vb* **1** to cause severe or permanent injury to — see MAIM
2 to reduce the soundness, effectiveness, or perfection of — see DAMAGE 1
3 to render powerless, ineffective, or unable to move — see PARALYZE

crisis *n* a time or state of affairs requiring prompt or decisive action — see EMERGENCY

crisp *adj* **1** having a texture that readily breaks into little pieces under pressure ⟨the bag of *crisp* cookies had a lot of crumbs on the bottom⟩
synonyms brittle, crispy, crumbly, flaky, friable, short
related words crunchy; breakable, delicate, fragile
near antonyms elastic, flexible, pliable, pliant, resilient; strong, sturdy, tough
2 being clean and in good order — see NEAT 1
3 marked by the use of few words to convey much information or meaning — see CONCISE

crisply *adv* in a few words — see SHORTLY 1

crispness *n* the quality or state of being marked by or using only few words to convey much meaning — see SUCCINCTNESS

crispy *adj* having a texture that readily breaks into little pieces under pressure — see CRISP 1

crisscross *vb* to make one's way through, across, or over — see TRAVERSE

criterion *n* something set up as an example against which others of the same type are compared — see STANDARD 1

critic *n* **1** a person given to harsh judgments and to finding faults ⟨the president's hard-core *critics* are going to criticize him no matter what he does⟩
synonyms carper, castigator, caviler (*or* caviller), censurer, faultfinder, nitpicker, railer, scold
related words belittler, derider, detractor; pettifogger, quibbler; complainer, crybaby, fusser, whiner
2 a person who makes or expresses a judgment on the quality of offerings in some field of endeavor ⟨the restaurant *critic* said that the fries at that fast-food outlet were the worst that she had ever eaten⟩
synonyms reviewer
related words analyst, columnist, commentator; appraiser, evaluator, judge

critical *adj* **1** given to making or expressing unfavorable judgments about things ⟨adults tend to be *critical* of teenagers' taste in music and movies⟩
synonyms captious, carping, caviling (*or* cavilling), faultfinding, hypercritical, overcritical
related words discerning, discriminating, judicious; demanding, exacting, fastidious, finicky, fussy, particular
near antonyms undiscerning
antonyms uncritical
2 needing immediate attention — see ACUTE 2
3 of the greatest possible importance — see CRUCIAL

criticism *n* an essay evaluating or analyzing something ⟨every *criticism* of the movie has noted that there are major holes in its plot⟩
synonyms notice, review
related words rave; appraisal, assessment, evaluation; analysis, examination, study

criticize *vb* to express one's unfavorable opinion of the worth or quality of ⟨the students who feel the need to *criticize* every single idea by the principal for improving the school⟩
synonyms blame, censure, condemn, denounce, dis [*slang*], fault, knock, pan, reprehend
related words assail, attack, blast, slam, slash; beef, bellyache, carp, complain, crab, croak, fuss, gripe, grouse, growl, grumble, kick, moan, murmur, mutter, repine, squawk, wail, whine, yammer; admonish, chide, rebuke, reprimand, reproach, reprove; berate, castigate, crucify, excoriate, flay, lambaste (*or* lambast), lash, pillory, scold, upbraid; bad-mouth, belittle, disparage, put down
phrases find fault (with), take to task
near antonyms approve, endorse (*also* indorse), recommend, sanction
antonyms extol (*also* extoll), laud, praise

critter *n* one of the lower animals as distinguished from human beings — see ANIMAL

croak *vb* **1** to express dissatisfaction, pain, or resentment usually tiresomely — see COMPLAIN
2 *slang* to stop living — see DIE 1
3 *slang* to deprive of life — see KILL 1

croaker *n* an irritable and complaining person — see GROUCH

croaking *adj* harsh and dry in sound — see HOARSE

crockery *n* articles made of baked clay ⟨a display of beautifully hand-painted *crockery* on the kitchen countertop⟩
synonyms earthenware, pottery, stoneware
related words ceramics; china, porcelain

crone *n* a mean or ugly old woman ⟨a run-down

house that was inhabited by a cantankerous *crone* who kept to herself⟩
synonyms beldam (*or* beldame), hag, witch
related words grandam (*or* grandame); harpy, shrew, virago

crony *n* **1** a person frequently seen in the company of another — see ASSOCIATE 1
2 a person who has a strong liking for and trust in another — see FRIEND 1

crook *n* **1** a person who has committed a crime — see CRIMINAL
2 something that curves or is curved — see BEND 1

crook *vb* **1** to cause to turn away from a straight line — see BEND 1
2 to turn away from a straight line or course — see CURVE 1

crooked *adj* **1** marked by a long series of irregular curves ⟨a long, *crooked* line of people had formed in front of the ticket booth⟩
synonyms bending, curled, curling, curved, curving, devious, serpentine, sinuous, tortuous, twisted, twisting, winding
related words zigzag, zigzagging; circling, coiled, coiling, corkscrew, looping, spiral, spiraling (*or* spiralling), swirling; circuitous, indirect, roundabout; meandering, rambling, wandering
near antonyms direct, linear
antonyms straight, straightaway
2 given to or marked by cheating and deception — see DISHONEST 2
3 inclined or twisted to one side — see AWRY
4 marked by, based on, or done by the use of dishonest methods to acquire something of value — see FRAUDULENT 1

crookedness *n* the inclination or practice of misleading others through lies or trickery — see DECEIT

crop *n* **1** the quantity of an animal or vegetable product gathered at the end of a season ⟨the wheat *crop* is going to be exceptionally large this year⟩
synonyms harvest
related words return, yield
2 a usually small number of persons considered as a unit — see GROUP 2

crop *vb* **1** to look after or assist the growth of by labor and care — see GROW 1
2 to make (as hair) shorter with or as if with the use of shears — see CLIP

crop (up) *vb* to come to one's attention especially gradually or unexpectedly — see ARISE 2

cropper *n* a falling short of one's goals — see FAILURE 2

croquette *n* a small usually rounded mass of minced food that has been fried — see CAKE

cross *adj* easily irritated or annoyed — see IRRITABLE

cross *n* **1** a test of faith, patience, or strength — see TRIAL 1
2 an offspring of parents with different genes especially when of different races, breeds, species, or genera — see HYBRID

cross *vb* **1** to be unfaithful or disloyal to — see BETRAY 1
2 to divide by passing through or across — see INTERSECT
3 to make one's way through, across, or over — see TRAVERSE

cross (out) *vb* to show (something written) to be no longer valid by drawing a cross over or a line through it — see X (OUT)

crossbred *adj* being offspring produced by parents of different races, breeds, species, or genera — see MIXED 1

crossbreed *n* an offspring of parents with different genes especially when of different races, breeds, species, or genera — see HYBRID

cross fire *n* an often noisy or angry expression of differing opinions — see ARGUMENT 1

crossing *n* **1** a journey over water in a vessel — see SAIL
2 a place where roads meet — see CROSSROAD 1

crossness *n* readiness to show annoyance or impatience — see PETULANCE

crossroad *n* **1** *usually* **crossroads** *pl* a place where roads meet ⟨the fast-food chain has a restaurant at practically every *crossroads*⟩
synonyms corner, crossing, intersection
related words overpass, underpass
2 *usually* **crossroads** *pl* a time or state of affairs requiring prompt or decisive action — see EMERGENCY

cross section *n* a number of things selected from a group to stand for the whole — see SAMPLE 1

crossways *adv* in a line or direction running from corner to corner — see CROSSWISE

crosswise *adv* in a line or direction running from corner to corner ⟨first cut the sandwiches *crosswise* and then trim the crusts⟩
synonyms athwart, crossways, obliquely, transversely

crotchet *n* an odd or peculiar habit — see IDIOSYNCRASY

crotchetiness *n* readiness to show annoyance or impatience — see PETULANCE

crotchety *adj* easily irritated or annoyed — see IRRITABLE

crouch *vb* to lie low with the limbs close to the body ⟨the cat *crouched* in the bushes, waiting for the right moment to pounce on the chipmunk⟩
synonyms huddle, hunch, scrunch, squat, squinch
related words curl up

crow *vb* **1** to feel or express joy or triumph — see EXULT
2 to praise or express pride in one's own possessions, qualities, or accomplishments often to excess — see BOAST

crowd *n* **1** a great number of persons or things gathered together ⟨a huge *crowd* of fans was on hand to greet the returning Super Bowl champions⟩
synonyms army, crush, drove, flock, horde, host, legion, mob, multitude, press, swarm, throng
related words masses, rabble, riffraff; gaggle, herd; heap, mountain, pile
2 a group of people sharing a common interest and relating together socially — see GANG 2

crowd *vb* **1** to fit (something) into a tight space ⟨*crowded* all the boats into the harbor before the storm struck⟩
synonyms cram, jam, ram, sandwich, squeeze, stuff, wedge
related words fill, heap, jam-pack, load, pack
2 to move upon or fill (something) in great numbers ⟨cars *crowded* the roads over the long holiday weekend⟩
synonyms flock, mob, swarm, throng
related words beset, infest, invade, overrun; clog, dam, obstruct, plug (up)

3 to gather into a closely packed group — see PRESS 3

crowded *adj* **1** containing or seeming to contain the greatest quantity or number possible — see FULL 1
2 having little space between items or parts — see CLOSE 1

crown *n* **1** a decorative band or wreath worn about the head as a symbol of victory or honor ⟨the *crown* of laurel leaves that is traditionally placed on the winner of the marathon⟩
synonyms coronet, diadem
related words tiara; garland, laurel
2 the position occupied by the one who comes in first in a competition ⟨his lifelong dream of someday winning the heavyweight boxing *crown*⟩
synonyms championship, title
3 the highest part or point — see HEIGHT 1

crown *vb* to bring to a triumphant conclusion ⟨the Olympic Games were *crowned* by spectacular closing ceremonies⟩
synonyms climax, culminate
related words complete, conclude, finish, round (off *or* out), terminate, wrap up

crucial *adj* of the greatest possible importance ⟨water is *crucial* to our survival⟩
synonyms critical, key, pivotal, vital
related words decisive, life-and-death; basic, elementary, fundamental; essential, indispensable, necessary, requisite; pressing, urgent
near antonyms inconsequential, insignificant, trivial, unimportant

crucible *n* a test of faith, patience, or strength — see TRIAL 1

crude *adj* **1** being such as found in nature and not altered by processing or refining ⟨a spill of *crude* oil along a coastline is the worst kind of environmental disaster⟩
synonyms native, natural, raw, undressed, unprocessed, unrefined, untreated
related words undeveloped; roughhewn, unfinished, unpolished; unbaked, uncooked; impure, unfiltered, unpurified
phrases in the rough
near antonyms filtered, pure, purified
antonyms dressed, processed, refined, treated
2 belonging to or characteristic of an early level of skill or development — see PRIMITIVE 1
3 depicting or referring to sexual matters in a way that is unacceptable in polite society — see OBSCENE 1
4 lacking in refinement or good taste — see COARSE 2
5 hastily or roughly constructed — see RUDE 1

crudeness *n* **1** the quality or state of being obscene — see OBSCENITY 1
2 the quality or state of lacking refinement or good taste — see VULGARITY 1

cruel *adj* **1** having or showing the desire to inflict severe pain and suffering on others ⟨a *cruel* dictator who tortured anyone who dared to speak out against him⟩ ⟨*cruel* and unusual punishments are forbidden by the U.S. Constitution⟩
synonyms barbaric, barbarous, brutal, heartless, inhumane, sadistic, savage, vicious, wanton
related words cutthroat, merciless, pitiless, ruthless; fell, ferocious, grim; bloodthirsty, murderous, sanguinary, sanguine; catty, despiteful, hateful, malevolent, malicious, malign, malignant, mean, nasty, spiteful
near antonyms tender, warm, warmhearted; charitable, clement, lenient, merciful, pitying; pacific, peaceable, peaceful
antonyms benign, benignant, compassionate, good-hearted, humane, kind, kindhearted, sympathetic, tenderhearted
2 difficult to endure — see HARSH 1
3 hard to accept or bear especially emotionally — see BITTER 2
4 having or showing a desire to cause someone pain or suffering for the sheer enjoyment of it — see HATEFUL

cruelness *n* the willful infliction of pain and suffering on others — see CRUELTY

cruelty *n* the willful infliction of pain and suffering on others ⟨centuries after he ravaged Europe, Attila the Hun remains notorious for his *cruelty*⟩
synonyms barbarity, brutality, cruelness, heartlessness, inhumanity, sadism, savageness, savagery, viciousness, wantonness
related words mercilessness, ruthlessness; ferocity, fierceness; bloodthirstiness, sanguinity; cattiness, despitefulness, hatefulness, malevolence, maliciousness, malignity, meanness, nastiness, spitefulness
near antonyms tenderness, warmheartedness, warmth; clemency, leniency, mercifulness, mercy, pity
antonyms benignity, compassion, good-heartedness, humanity, kindheartedness, kindness, sympathy

cruise *n* a journey over water in a vessel — see SAIL

cruise *vb* to travel on water in a vessel — see SAIL 1

crumb *n* **1** a very small amount — see PARTICLE 1
2 a very small piece — see BIT 1

crumble *vb* to become worse or of less value — see DETERIORATE

crumbly *adj* having a texture that readily breaks into little pieces under pressure — see CRISP 1

crumple *vb* **1** to create (as by crushing) an irregular mass of creases in ⟨*crumpled* the piece of paper and angrily threw it in the wastebasket⟩
synonyms crinkle, rumple, scrunch, wrinkle
related words corrugate, crease, crimp, fold, furrow, pleat; ripple, ruffle; disarrange, jumble, mess (up), muss (up)
antonyms iron out, smooth
2 to fall down or in as a result of physical pressure — see COLLAPSE 1

crunch *n* a time or state of affairs requiring prompt or decisive action — see EMERGENCY

crunch *vb* to press or strike against or together so as to make a scraping sound — see GRIND 2

crunch (on) *vb* to crush or grind with the teeth — see BITE (ON)

crusade *n* a series of activities undertaken to achieve a goal — see CAMPAIGN

crusader *n* one who is intensely or excessively devoted to a cause — see ZEALOT

crush *n* **1** a strong but often short-lived liking for another person ⟨the *crush* that she had on a boy whom she had met over the summer⟩
synonyms infatuation, passion
related words fixation, obsession; affection, devotion, fondness, love; craze, fad, rage, vogue
2 a great number of persons or things gathered together — see CROWD 1

crush *vb* **1** to cause to become a pulpy mass ⟨dark-

colored grapes that will be *crushed* to make red wine⟩
synonyms mash, pulp, squash
related words press, squeeze; beat, pound, powder, pulverize
2 to achieve a victory over — see BEAT 2
3 to put a stop to (something) by the use of force — see QUELL 1
4 to reduce to fine particles — see POWDER
5 to subject to incapacitating emotional or mental stress — see OVERWHELM 1
6 to apply external pressure on so as to force out the juice or contents of — see PRESS 2

crusher *n* something (as a fact or argument) that is decisive or overwhelming — see CLINCHER

crusty *adj* being or characterized by direct, brief, and potentially rude speech or manner — see BLUNT 1

crux *n* the central part or aspect of something under consideration ⟨the *crux* of the problem is that the school's current budget is totally inadequate⟩
synonyms core, gist, heart, nub, pith, pivot
related words course, direction, drift, tenor; body, essence, substance

cry *n* **1** a loud vocal expression of strong emotion — see SHOUT
2 a natural vocal sound made by an animal — see CALL 1
3 an attention-getting word or phrase used to publicize something (as a campaign or product) — see SLOGAN
4 an earnest request — see PLEA 1

cry *vb* **1** to shed tears often while making meaningless sounds as a sign of pain or distress ⟨some kids started to *cry* even before the doctor had given them their shot⟩
synonyms bawl, blubber, sob, weep
related words grieve, keen, lament, mourn; howl, scream, squall, wail, yowl; pule, whimper, whine; sniffle, snivel; groan, moan, sigh
2 to utter one's distinctive animal sound ⟨we knew that we were getting very close to the ocean when we could hear sea gulls *crying*⟩
synonyms call, sing
3 to speak so as to be heard at a distance — see CALL 1

cry (out) *vb* to utter with a sudden burst of strong feeling — see EXCLAIM

crybaby *n* a person who makes frequent complaints usually about little things ⟨car trips that were often spoiled by a couple of *crybabies* in the back seat⟩
synonyms complainer, fusser, griper, growler, grumbler, whiner
related words malcontent; carper, critic, faultfinder, nitpicker, squawker; bawler, wailer, weeper

cry down *vb* to express scornfully one's low opinion of — see DECRY 1

crying *adj* needing immediate attention — see ACUTE 2

crypt *n* an underground burial chamber ⟨the old church's *crypt* is the final resting place for the president and his beloved wife⟩
synonyms catacomb(s), vault
related words mausoleum, sepulcher (*or* sepulchre), tomb

cryptic *adj* **1** being beyond one's powers to know, understand, or explain — see MYSTERIOUS 1
2 having an often intentionally veiled or uncertain meaning — see OBSCURE 1

crystallize *vb* to take on a definite form — see FORM 1

cub *n* a young person who is between infancy and adulthood — see CHILD 1

cubicle *n* one of the parts into which an enclosed space is divided — see COMPARTMENT

cuckoo *adj* **1** having or showing a very abnormal or sick state of mind — see INSANE 1
2 showing or marked by a lack of good sense or judgment — see FOOLISH 1

cuddle *vb* **1** to lie close — see NUZZLE
2 to sit or recline comfortably or cozily — see SNUGGLE 1

cudgel *n* a heavy rigid stick used as a weapon or for punishment — see CLUB 1

cue *n* **1** a series of persons or things arranged one behind another — see LINE 1
2 a slight or indirect pointing to something (as a solution or explanation) — see HINT 1

cuff *n* a hard strike with a part of the body or an instrument — see [1]BLOW

cuisine *n* the art or style of preparing food (as in a specified region) — see COOKERY

cull *n* something separated from a group or lot for not being as good as the others ⟨the unbruised apples will be packed in bags, and the *culls* will be used for cider⟩
synonyms discard, reject, rejection
related words second, throwaway

cull *vb* to decide to accept (someone or something) from a group of possibilities — see CHOOSE 1

culminate *vb* to bring to a triumphant conclusion — see CROWN

culmination *n* the highest part or point — see HEIGHT 1

culpability *n* responsibility for wrongdoing or failure — see BLAME 1

culpable *adj* **1** deserving reproach or blame — see BLAMEWORTHY
2 responsible for a wrong — see GUILTY 1

culprit *n* a person who has committed a crime — see CRIMINAL

cult *n* **1** a group of people showing intense devotion to a cause, person, or work (as a film) ⟨long after it had gone off the air, the TV series continued to have a huge *cult*⟩
synonyms following
related words discipleship
2 a body of beliefs and practices regarding the supernatural and the worship of one or more deities — see RELIGION 1

cultivate *vb* **1** to come to have gradually — see DEVELOP 2
2 to help the growth or development of — see FOSTER 1
3 to look after or assist the growth of by labor and care — see GROW 1
4 to work by plowing, sowing, and raising crops on — see FARM

cultivated *adj* having or showing a taste for the fine arts and gracious living ⟨the museum's annual gala for charity usually attracts a *cultivated* crowd⟩
synonyms civilized, cultured, genteel, polished, refined
related words cerebral, highbrow, intellectual; educated, erudite, knowledgeable, learned, literate, scholarly, well-read; civil, courteous, mannerly,

polite, well-bred; cosmopolitan, sophisticated, urbane
near antonyms ignorant, illiterate, uneducated, unlettered; lowbrow, unintelligent; coarse, ill-bred, ill-mannered; provincial, rustic, unsophisticated; boorish, churlish, cloddish, clownish, crude, uncouth, vulgar
antonyms philistine, uncivilized, uncultured, unpolished, unrefined

cultivation *n* a high level of taste and enlightenment as a result of extensive intellectual training and exposure to the arts — see CULTURE 1

cultivator *n* a person who cultivates the land and grows crops on it — see FARMER

cultural *adj* of or relating to the fine arts ⟨with its many museums, theaters, and opera and ballet companies, the city is a *cultural* paradise⟩
synonyms artistic
related words aesthetic, tasteful

culture *n* **1** a high level of taste and enlightenment as a result of extensive intellectual training and exposure to the arts ⟨because of its wide reputation as a place of *culture*, Boston became known as "the Athens of America"⟩
synonyms civilization, cultivation, polish, refinement
related words education, erudition, learning, literacy, scholarship; sophistication, urbanity; breeding, gentility, manners; class, elegance, grace, taste; civility, courtesy, politeness
near antonyms ignorance, illiteracy; parochialism, provincialism, unsophistication; boorishness, churlishness, clownishness, coarseness, crudeness, vulgarity
antonyms philistinism
2 the way people live at a particular time and place — see CIVILIZATION 1

culture *vb* to look after or assist the growth of by labor and care — see GROW 1

cultured *adj* having or showing a taste for the fine arts and gracious living — see CULTIVATED

cumbersome *adj* difficult to use or operate especially because of size, weight, or design ⟨a long-handled wrench that is too *cumbersome* for tight spots, like under the sink⟩
synonyms awkward, clumsy, cranky, cumbrous, ungainly, unhandy, unwieldy
related words uncontrollable, unmanageable; bulky, heavy, massive; impracticable, impractical
near antonyms functional, practicable, practical, serviceable, useful
antonyms handy

cumbrous *adj* difficult to use or operate especially because of size, weight, or design — see CUMBERSOME

cummerbund *n* a strip of flexible material (as leather) worn around the waist — see [2]BELT

cumulative *adj* produced by a series of additions of identical or similar things ⟨a *cumulative* weight gain of 20 pounds over the course of a year⟩
synonyms additive, incremental
related words gradual, step-by-step

cunning *adj* **1** clever at attaining one's ends by indirect and often deceptive means — see ARTFUL 1
2 skillful with the hands — see DEXTEROUS 1

cunning *n* **1** skill in achieving one's ends through indirect, subtle, or underhanded means ⟨the *cunning* with which Tom Sawyer was able to get others to whitewash the fence for him⟩
synonyms artfulness, artifice, caginess, canniness, craft, craftiness, deviousness, foxiness, guile, slickness, slyness, sneakiness, subtleness, subtlety, wiliness
related words calculation, care, design; savvy, sharpness, shrewdness; cleverness, ingeniousness, ingenuity, inventiveness; ease, facility, finesse; deceitfulness, duplicity, shiftiness
2 subtle or imaginative ability in inventing, devising, or executing something — see SKILL 1
3 the inclination or practice of misleading others through lies or trickery — see DECEIT

cup *n* a round vessel equipped with a handle and designed for drinking ⟨a large *cup* that can hold almost a pint of hot chocolate⟩
synonyms mug
related words stein, tankard; demitasse, noggin; teacup

cupboard *n* a storage case typically having doors and shelves — see CABINET

cupidity *n* an intense selfish desire for wealth or possessions — see GREED

cur *n* a person whose behavior is offensive to others — see JERK 1

curb *n* something that limits one's freedom of action or choice — see RESTRICTION 1

curb *vb* to keep from exceeding a desirable degree or level (as of expression) — see CONTROL 1

curdy *adj* having small pieces or lumps spread throughout — see CHUNKY 1

cure *n* **1** something that corrects or counteracts something undesirable ⟨a fun hobby is always a good *cure* for boredom⟩
synonyms corrective, remedy
related words cure-all, elixir, panacea; answer, solution; aid, help, relief, succor; balm, palliative
2 a substance or preparation used to treat disease — see MEDICINE

cure *vb* **1** to bring about recovery from ⟨do you have anything that will *cure* my headache?⟩
synonyms heal, remedy
related words allay, alleviate, assuage, relieve; palliate, salve, soothe; ease, lighten, moderate, temper; doctor, treat
near antonyms aggravate, worsen
2 to restore to a healthy condition — see HEAL 1

cure–all *n* something that cures all ills or problems ⟨raising a young person's self-esteem is not the *cure-all* that some people think⟩
synonyms elixir, panacea
related words corrective, cure, remedy

curio *n* **1** a small object displayed for its attractiveness or interest — see KNICKKNACK
2 something strange or unusual that is an object of interest — see CURIOSITY 2

curiosity *n* **1** an eager desire to find out about things that are often none of one's business ⟨the neighbors' *curiosity* about what we paid for our new car was really offensive⟩
synonyms curiousness, inquisitiveness, nosiness
related words attentiveness, concern, interest, regard; inquiry, interrogation, questioning; intrusiveness, obtrusiveness, officiousness; eavesdropping, rubbernecking
near antonyms apathy, disinterestedness, disregard, indifference, unconcern
2 something strange or unusual that is an object of interest ⟨the museum's *curiosities* include items constructed entirely out of toothpicks⟩
synonyms curio, exotic, oddity, rarity
related words marvel, prodigy, wonder; abnor-

mality, anomaly, freak, monster, monstrosity; malformation, mutant, mutation

3 a small object displayed for its attractiveness or interest — see KNICKKNACK

curious *adj* **1** interested in what is not one's own business ⟨*curious* neighbors peered out of their windows as the new people moved in⟩
synonyms inquisitive, nosy (*or* nosey), prying, snoopy
related words interfering, intrusive, meddlesome, meddling, obtrusive, officious; inquisitional, inquisitorial; concerned, interested
near antonyms apathetic, disinterested, indifferent, unconcerned, uninterested
antonyms incurious, uncurious
2 different from the ordinary in a way that causes curiosity or suspicion — see ODD 2
3 noticeably different from what is generally found or experienced — see UNUSUAL 1

curiousness *n* an eager desire to find out about things that are often none of one's business — see CURIOSITY 1

curl *n* a length of hair that forms a loop or series of loops ⟨a young girl with beautiful golden *curls*⟩
synonyms ringlet
related words kink, wave; lock, tress

curl *vb* to follow a circular or spiral course — see WIND

curled *adj* **1** forming or styled into loops — see CURLY
2 marked by a long series of irregular curves — see CROOKED 1

curling *adj* marked by a long series of irregular curves — see CROOKED 1

curl up *vb* to sit or recline comfortably or cozily — see SNUGGLE 1

curly *adj* forming or styled into loops ⟨the boy's naturally *curly* hair⟩
synonyms curled
related words frizzy, kinky, waved, wavy
near antonyms lank, limp
antonyms straight

curmudgeon *n* an irritable and complaining person — see GROUCH

currency *n* something (as pieces of stamped metal or printed paper) customarily and legally used as a medium of exchange, a measure of value, or a means of payment — see MONEY

current *adj* **1** accepted, used, or practiced by most people ⟨the *current* theories on parenting favor allowing children lots of self-expression⟩
synonyms conventional, customary, going, popular, prevailing, prevalent, standard, stock, usual
related words average, common, everyday, normal, ordinary; regular, routine; ubiquitous, universal, widespread; accustomed, wonted; fashionable, in, modish, stylish
near antonyms abnormal, exceptional, extraordinary, uncommon
antonyms nonstandard, unconventional, unpopular, unusual
2 being or involving the latest methods, concepts, information, or styles — see MODERN
3 existing or in progress right now — see PRESENT 1

current *n* **1** a prevailing or general movement or inclination — see TREND 1
2 noticeable movement of air in a particular direction — see [1]WIND 1

currently *adv* at the present time — see NOW 1

curse *n* **1** a prayer that harm will come to someone ⟨the victim's *curse* that the man who robbed her never receive any pleasure from her money⟩
synonyms anathema, execration, imprecation, malediction
related words censure, condemnation, damnation, denunciation; hex, spell
near antonyms citation, commendation, endorsement
antonyms benediction, benison, blessing
2 a disrespectful or indecent word or expression — see SWEARWORD

curse *vb* **1** to ask a divine power to send harm or evil upon ⟨I *curse* the guy who had the idea of having annoying salespeople call up innocent people to sell them things they don't want⟩
synonyms imprecate
related words condemn, damn, denounce, execrate, reprobate; hex, jinx; fulminate (against), rail (against), revile
near antonyms applaud, commend, congratulate
antonyms bless
2 to cause persistent suffering to — see AFFLICT
3 to use offensive or indecent language — see SWEAR 1

cursorily *adv* with excessive or careless speed — see HASTILY 1

cursory *adj* acting or done with excessive or careless speed — see HASTY 1

curt *adj* being or characterized by direct, brief, and potentially rude speech or manner — see BLUNT 1

curtail *vb* **1** to make (as hair) shorter with or as if with the use of shears — see CLIP
2 to make less in extent or duration — see SHORTEN

curtain *n* **1** something that covers or conceals like a piece of cloth — see CLOAK 1
2 curtains *pl* pieces of cloth hung to darken, decorate, or divide a room — see DRAPERY

curtain *vb* to keep secret or shut off from view — see [1]HIDE 2

curvature *n* something that curves or is curved — see BEND 1

curve *n* something that curves or is curved — see BEND 1

curve *vb* **1** to turn away from a straight line or course ⟨after following a straight path most of the way down the mountain, the ski trail abruptly *curves* to the right⟩
synonyms arc, arch, bend, bow, crook, hook, round, sweep, swerve, wheel
related words circle, coil, curl, loop, spiral; turn, twist, wind; deviate, veer
antonyms straighten
2 to cause to turn away from a straight line — see BEND 1

curved *adj* marked by a long series of irregular curves — see CROOKED 1

curving *adj* marked by a long series of irregular curves — see CROOKED 1

cushion *n* something that serves as a protective barrier ⟨used a blanket as a *cushion* between the two tables in the moving van⟩
synonyms buffer, bumper, fender, pad
related words baffle, muffler; padding; safeguard, shield; barricade, cordon

cushion *vb* to lessen the shock of ⟨a substantial nest egg helped to *cushion* the sudden loss of her job⟩

synonyms buffer, gentle, soften
related words baffle, dampen, deaden, dull; moderate, modulate, temper; allay, alleviate, assuage, ease; lighten, mitigate, relieve
near antonyms heighten, intensify, sharpen

cushy *adj* providing physical comfort — see COMFORTABLE 1

cusp *n* the last and usually sharp or tapering part of something long and narrow — see POINT 2

cuss *n* a disrespectful or indecent word or expression — see SWEARWORD

cuss *vb* to use offensive or indecent language — see SWEAR 1

custodian *n* **1** a person who takes care of a property sometimes for an absent owner ⟨the *custodian* made his usual rounds of the building to make sure that everything was OK⟩
synonyms caretaker, guardian, janitor, keeper, warden, watchman
related words curator; sexton; steward
2 a person or group that watches over someone or something — see GUARD 1
3 someone that protects — see PROTECTOR

custody *n* responsibility for the safety and well-being of someone or something ⟨the divorcing parents will share *custody* of the children⟩
synonyms care, guardianship, keeping, safekeeping, trust, ward
related words control, governorship, management, superintendence, supervision

custom *adj* made or fitted to the needs or preferences of a specific customer — see CUSTOM-MADE

custom *n* **1** a usual manner of behaving or doing — see HABIT
2 an inherited or established way of thinking, feeling, or doing — see TRADITION 1

customary *adj* **1** accepted, used, or practiced by most people — see CURRENT 1
2 based on customs usually handed down from a previous generation — see TRADITIONAL 1

customer *n* **1** a person who buys a product or uses a service from a business ⟨the store greatly values its regular *customers*⟩
synonyms client, guest, patron
related words consumer, end user, user; buyer, purchaser; browser, prospect, shopper, window-shopper
near antonyms merchant, seller, vendor (*also* vender)
2 a member of the human race — see HUMAN

customized *adj* made or fitted to the needs or preferences of a specific customer — see CUSTOM-MADE

custom–made *adj* made or fitted to the needs or preferences of a specific customer ⟨an odd-sized window that will require the purchase of *custom-made* curtains⟩
synonyms custom, customized, tailored, tailor-made
related words particular, special, specialized; handcrafted, handmade
antonyms mass-produced, ready-made

cut *n* **1** a piece that has been separated from the whole by cutting ⟨choose *cuts* of meat that have very little visible fat⟩
synonyms cutting, slice
related words chop, cutlet; chunk, hunk, lump; clipping, paring, shaving, snippet; sliver, splinter
2 an individual part of a process, series, or ranking — see DEGREE 1
3 something belonging to, due to, or contributed by an individual member of a group — see SHARE 1

cut *vb* **1** to penetrate with a sharp edge (as a knife) ⟨I *cut* my hand on a piece of broken glass⟩
synonyms gash, incise, rip, slash, slice, slit
related words saw, scissor; cleave, rive, split; pierce, stab; bruise, hack, lacerate, mangle; rend, tear; butcher, carve, dissect; chop, dice, mince; amputate, cut off, sever
2 to fail to attend ⟨a warning that she had been *cutting* too many classes without valid excuses⟩
synonyms miss, skip
related words ignore, neglect, pass over
phrases absent oneself, play hooky
antonyms attend, show up (for)
3 to deliberately ignore or treat rudely — see SNUB 1
4 to make (as hair) shorter with or as if with the use of shears — see CLIP
5 to shorten the standing leafy plant cover of — see MOW 1

cut (across) *vb* to make one's way through, across, or over — see TRAVERSE

cut (down) *vb* to bring down by cutting — see FELL 2

cut (out) *vb* to bring (as an action or operation) to an immediate end — see STOP 1

cut back *vb* **1** to make (as hair) shorter with or as if with the use of shears — see CLIP
2 to make less in extent or duration — see SHORTEN

cute *adj* very pleasing to look at — see BEAUTIFUL

cuteness *n* the qualities in a person or thing that as a whole give pleasure to the senses — see BEAUTY 1

cut in *vb* to cause a disruption in a conversation or discussion — see INTERRUPT

cutlet *n* a small usually rounded mass of minced food that has been fried — see CAKE

cut off *vb* to set or keep apart from others — see ISOLATE

cut out *vb* to stop functioning — see FAIL 1

cut–rate *adj* **1** costing little — see CHEAP 1
2 of low quality — see CHEAP 2

cutter *n* an instrument with a sharp edge for cutting — see KNIFE

cutthroat *adj* not guided by or showing a concern for what is right — see UNPRINCIPLED

cutting *adj* **1** causing intense discomfort to one's skin ⟨a frigid day with a *cutting* wind that made it seem even colder⟩
synonyms biting, bitter, keen, penetrating, piercing, raw, sharp, smarting, stinging
related words brisk, invigorating, nippy, snappy; needlelike, prickly, tingling; caustic, corrosive
near antonyms balmy, gentle, mild, soothing
2 having an edge thin enough to cut or pierce something — see SHARP 1
3 marked by the use of wit that is intended to cause hurt feelings — see SARCASTIC

cutting *n* a piece that has been separated from the whole by cutting — see CUT 1

cut up *vb* to engage in attention-getting playful or boisterous behavior ⟨high-spirited cousins who *cut up* at every family gathering⟩
synonyms act up, clown (around), fool (around),

horse (around), monkey (around), show off, skylark
related words carry on, misbehave; roughhouse; caper, cavort, disport, frisk, frolic, gambol, lark, rollick, romp; carouse, revel, wassail

cycle *n* **1** a series of events or actions that repeat themselves regularly and in the same order ⟨the *cycle* of birth, growth, decline, and death that is experienced by all life forms⟩
synonyms circle, round
related words pattern, syndrome; course, development, progression, run; circuit, loop, ring; rotation, revolution, turn; chain, sequence, series, string, succession, train
2 a long or seemingly long period of time — see AGE 2

cynic *n* a person who distrusts other people and believes that everything is done for selfish reasons ⟨a *cynic* who believes that nobody does a good deed without expecting something in return⟩
synonyms misanthrope, pessimist
related words misogynist; doubter, skeptic; belittler, derider, detractor, scoffer; malcontent; defeatist, quitter
near antonyms optimist; idealist; sentimentalist

cynical *adj* having or showing a deep distrust of human beings and their motives ⟨so *cynical* that he can't understand why anyone would volunteer to help out at a homeless shelter⟩
synonyms misanthropic, pessimistic
related words distrustful, mistrustful, skeptical, suspicious; derisive, mocking, sardonic, scornful; defeatist, fatalistic, negative; ironic (*or* ironical), sarcastic; jaded, sophisticated, worldly-wise; hard-bitten, hard-boiled, unsentimental
near antonyms trustful, trusting, unsuspicious; cheerful, optimistic, rose-colored; ingenuous, innocent, naive (*or* naïve), unsophisticated; idealistic, impractical, romantic; maudlin, mushy, saccharine, sappy, sentimental

cynosure *n* a thing or place that is of greatest importance to an activity or interest — see CENTER 1

czar *also* **tsar** *or* **tzar** *n* a person of rank, power, or influence in a particular field — see MAGNATE

[1]dab *n* a quick thrust — see [1]POKE

[2]dab *n* a very small amount — see PARTICLE 1

dabbler *n* a person who regularly or occasionally engages in an activity without being or becoming an expert at it — see AMATEUR

dad *n* a male human parent — see FATHER 1

daddy *n* a male human parent — see FATHER 1

daffy *adj* **1** having or showing a very abnormal or sick state of mind — see INSANE 1
2 showing or marked by a lack of good sense or judgment — see FOOLISH 1

daft *adj* **1** having or showing a very abnormal or sick state of mind — see INSANE 1
2 showing or marked by a lack of good sense or judgment — see FOOLISH 1

daftness *n* lack of good sense or judgment — see FOOLISHNESS 1

daily *adj* occurring, done, produced, or appearing every day ⟨they made their *daily* stop at the coffee shop after work to relax before dinner⟩
synonyms day-to-day, diurnal
related words alternate, cyclical, intermittent, periodic, recurrent, recurring, regular; continuous, frequent, incessant
near antonyms nightly, nocturnal; monthly, weekly, yearly; erratic, infrequent, irregular; occasional, spasmodic, sporadic; interrupted

daintiness *n* the state or quality of having a delicate structure — see DELICACY 2

dainty *adj* **1** hard to please — see FINICKY
2 having qualities that appeal to a refined taste — see CHOICE
3 satisfying or pleasing because of fineness or mildness — see DELICATE 1

dainty *n* something that is pleasing to eat because it is rare or a luxury — see DELICACY 1

dais *n* a level usually raised surface — see PLATFORM

dale *n* an area of lowland between hills or mountains — see VALLEY

dalliance *n* activity engaged in to amuse oneself — see PLAY 1

dallier *n* someone who moves slowly or more slowly than others — see SLOWPOKE

dally *vb* **1** to engage in activity for amusement — see PLAY 1
2 to move or act slowly — see DELAY 1
3 to show a liking for someone of the opposite sex just for fun — see FLIRT
4 to spend time doing nothing — see IDLE

dallying *adj* moving or proceeding at less than the normal, desirable, or required speed — see SLOW 1

dam *n* a bank of earth constructed to control water ⟨the river backed up behind the *dam* until it formed a new lake⟩
synonyms dike, embankment, levee
related words breakwater, jetty, seawall; breastwork, bulwark, earthwork, rampart; canal, channel, ditch, gutter, trough; lock; barricade, barrier, block; floodgate, sluice

dam *vb* **1** to prevent passage through — see CLOG 1
2 to close up so that no empty spaces remain — see FILL 2

damage *n* **1** something that causes loss or pain — see INJURY 1
2 damages *pl* a sum of money to be paid as a punishment — see FINE
3 damages *pl* payment to another for a loss or injury — see COMPENSATION 1

damage *vb* **1** to reduce the soundness, effectiveness, or perfection of ⟨the explosion in the sewers *damaged* the entire city's water supply⟩
synonyms blemish, break, cripple, deface, disfig-

ure, flaw, harm, hurt, impair, injure, mar, spoil, vitiate
related words enfeeble, undermine, weaken; erode, scour, wash out, wear (away); blight, tarnish; dent, dint; botch, gum (up); lacerate, wound; maim, mangle, mutilate, torment, torture; annihilate, crush, dash, decimate, demolish, destroy, devastate, pulverize, raze, ruin, scourge, shatter, smash, tear down, waste, wipe out, wreck
near antonyms cure, heal, help, rectify, remedy; edit, remodel, revise; ameliorate, better, enhance, improve, meliorate
antonyms fix, mend, patch, rebuild, recondition, reconstruct, renovate, repair, revamp
2 to cause bodily damage to — see INJURE 1

damaging *adj* causing or capable of causing harm — see HARMFUL

dame *n* **1** a dignified usually elderly woman of some rank or authority — see MATRIARCH
2 a woman of high birth or social position — see GENTLEWOMAN

damn *vb* **1** to declare to be morally wrong or evil — see CONDEMN 1
2 to impose a judicial punishment on — see SENTENCE

damp *adj* slightly or moderately wet — see MOIST

damp *vb* to reduce or weaken in strength or feeling — see DULL 1

dampen *vb* **1** to make or become slightly or moderately wet — see MOISTEN
2 to reduce or weaken in strength or feeling — see DULL 1

damper *n* a device on a musical instrument that deadens or softens its tone — see MUTE

dampness *n* the amount of water suspended in the air in tiny droplets — see MOISTURE

damsel *n* a young usually unmarried woman — see GIRL 1

dance *n* a social gathering for dancing ⟨who are you taking to the *dance* Saturday night?⟩
synonyms ball, cotillion, formal, hop, prom
related words blowout, celebration, event, festival, festivity, fete (*or* fête), gala, masquerade, mixer, party, reception, shindig, soiree (*or* soirée)

dance *vb* **1** to perform a series of usually rhythmic bodily movements to music ⟨she liked to *dance* to her favorite rock bands⟩
synonyms foot (it), hoof (it), step
related words prance, strut, trip; gavotte, jig, jitterbug, jive, mambo, polka, tango, tap-dance, waltz; tread
2 to make an irregular series of quick, sudden movements — see FLIT

dandle *vb* to treat with great or excessive care — see BABY

dandy *adj* of the very best kind — see EXCELLENT

dandy *n* **1** a man extremely interested in his clothing and personal appearance ⟨that *dandy* was willing to spend all day and hundreds of dollars just to get the perfect pair of shoes⟩
synonyms buck, dude, fop, gallant
related words coxcomb, popinjay; blade, cavalier; swell; clotheshorse
near antonyms slattern, slob, sloven, slut
2 something very good of its kind — see JIM-DANDY

danger *n* **1** the state of not being protected from injury, harm, or evil ⟨he knew he was in *danger* when he received the threatening phone calls at home⟩
synonyms distress, endangerment, imperilment, jeopardy, peril, risk, trouble
related words exposure, liability, vulnerability; precariousness, threat
near antonyms preservation, salvation; defense, protection; exemption, immunity, impunity
antonyms safeness, safety, security
2 something that may cause injury or harm ⟨she was willing to face the *dangers* of the construction site in order to get her Frisbee back⟩
synonyms hazard, menace, peril, pitfall, risk, threat, trouble
related words snare, trap
near antonyms guard, protection, safeguard, shield, ward

dangerous *adj* involving potential loss or injury ⟨the soldiers were commanded to go on a *dangerous* mission behind enemy lines⟩
synonyms grave, grievous, hazardous, jeopardizing, menacing, parlous, perilous, risky, serious, threatening, unhealthy, unsafe, venturesome
related words insecure, precarious, treacherous, uncertain; chance, haphazard, random; distressing, sickening, unpleasant; ugly, wicked; adverse, bad, baleful, baneful, deleterious, detrimental, evil, harmful, hurtful, ill, inimical, injurious, malignant, nasty, noxious, pernicious, pestilent; deadly, deathly, destructive, dire, fatal, fateful, fell, killer, lethal, mortal, murderous
near antonyms advantageous, beneficial, good
antonyms harmless, innocent, innocuous, safe

dangle *vb* to place on an elevated point without support from below — see HANG 1

dangling *adj* extending freely from a support from above — see DEPENDENT 1

dank *adj* slightly or moderately wet — see MOIST

dapper *adj* being strikingly neat and trim in style or appearance — see SMART 1

dapple *n* a small area that is different (as in color) from the main part — see SPOT 1

dapple *vb* to mark with small spots especially unevenly — see SPOT

dappled *also* **dapple** *adj* **1** marked with spots — see SPOTTED 1
2 having blotches of two or more colors — see PIED

dare *vb* **1** to invite (someone) to take part in a contest or to perform a feat — see CHALLENGE 2
2 to oppose (something hostile or dangerous) with firmness or courage — see FACE 2

daredevil *adj* **1** foolishly adventurous or bold — see FOOLHARDY 1
2 having or showing a lack of concern for the consequences of one's actions — see RECKLESS 1

daring *adj* inclined or willing to take risks — see BOLD 1

daring *n* strength of mind to carry on in spite of danger — see COURAGE

dark *adj* **1** being without light or without much light ⟨a *dark* alley that most people wisely avoided⟩
synonyms darkened, darkish, darkling, darksome, dim, dimmed, dusky, gloomy, murky, obscure, obscured, pitch-black, pitch-dark, somber (*or* sombre)
related words moonless, sunless; cloudy, dull, dulled, lackluster; shadowy, shady; gray (*also* grey), leaden, pale
near antonyms beaming, effulgent, glowing, lambent, radiant, shining; glossy, lustrous, shiny

antonyms bright, brightened, brilliant, illuminated, illumined, light, lighted (*or* lit), lucent, lucid, luminous

2 causing or marked by an atmosphere lacking in cheer — see GLOOMY 1

3 given to keeping one's activities hidden from public observation or knowledge — see SECRETIVE

4 having an often intentionally veiled or uncertain meaning — see OBSCURE 1

5 lacking in education or the knowledge gained from books — see IGNORANT 1

dark *n* **1** a time or place of little or no light ⟨I have a bad habit of running into tables in the *dark*⟩

synonyms blackness, darkness, dusk, gloaming, gloom, murk, night, semidarkness, shade, shadows, twilight, umbra

related words blackout, brownout; shadiness; dullness (*also* dulness), somberness; cloudiness, fogginess, haziness, mistiness, murkiness; dimness, faintness, gloominess, grayness, paleness

near antonyms moonlight, starlight, sunlight; effulgence, radiance, shine, sunshine; incandescence, luminescence, luminosity

antonyms blaze, brightness, brilliance, day, daylight, glare, glow, light, lightness

2 the time from sunset to sunrise when there is no visible sunlight — see NIGHT 1

darken *vb* **1** to take on a gloomy or forbidding look ⟨his face slowly *darkened* as we told him the sad news⟩

synonyms gloom, glower, lower (*also* lour)

related words frown, scowl; glare, stare; brood, mope, pout, sulk; anger, fume, rage, steam; intimidate, menace, threaten

antonyms brighten, cheer (up), lighten, perk (up)

2 to make dark, dim, or indistinct — see CLOUD 1

darkened *adj* being without light or without much light — see DARK 1

darkening *adj* causing or marked by an atmosphere lacking in cheer — see GLOOMY 1

darkish *adj* being without light or without much light — see DARK 1

darkling *adj* **1** being beyond one's powers to know, understand, or explain — see MYSTERIOUS 1

2 being without light or without much light — see DARK 1

3 having an often intentionally veiled or uncertain meaning — see OBSCURE 1

darkness *n* **1** a time or place of little or no light — see DARK 1

2 the quality or state of having a veiled or uncertain meaning — see OBSCURITY 1

3 the time from sunset to sunrise when there is no visible sunlight — see NIGHT 1

darksome *adj* being without light or without much light — see DARK 1

darling *adj* **1** granted special treatment or attention ⟨they poured gifts and affection on their *darling* child⟩

synonyms beloved, cherished, dear, favored, favorite, loved, pet, precious, special, sweet

related words admired, adored, appreciated, esteemed, relished, revered; prized, treasured; preferred

near antonyms despised, detested, disdained, disfavored, disliked, execrated, hated, loathed; abandoned, forgotten, ignored

2 having qualities that tend to make one loved — see LOVABLE

3 giving pleasure or contentment to the mind or senses — see PLEASANT

darling *n* **1** a person or thing that is preferred over others — see FAVORITE

2 a person with whom one is in love — see SWEETHEART

darn *vb* to close up with a series of interlacing stitches — see SEW

dart *n* an act or expression showing scorn and usually intended to hurt another's feelings — see INSULT

dart *vb* to make an irregular series of quick, sudden movements — see FLIT

dash *n* active strength of body or mind — see VIGOR 1

dash *vb* **1** to go at a pace faster than a walk — see RUN 1

2 to proceed or move quickly — see HURRY 2

3 to send through the air especially with a quick forward motion of the arm — see THROW

4 to wet or soil by striking with something liquid or mushy — see SPLASH 2

dashing *adj* inclined or willing to take risks — see BOLD 1

dashingly *adv* **1** in a bright and showy way — see GAILY 3

2 in a strikingly neat and trim manner — see SMARTLY

dastard *n* a person who shows a shameful lack of courage in the face of danger — see COWARD

dastardliness *n* a shameful lack of courage in the face of danger — see COWARDICE

dastardly *adj* having or showing a shameful lack of courage — see COWARDLY

date *n* **1** an agreement to be present at a specified time and place — see ENGAGEMENT 2

2 the period during which something exists, lasts, or is in progress — see DURATION 1

date *vb* **1** to go on a social engagement with ⟨I don't want to *date* him—I'd rather just be friends⟩

synonyms take out

related words accompany, escort, see; court, woo

2 to go on dates that may eventually lead to marriage — see COURT 2

dated *adj* having passed its time of use or usefulness — see OBSOLETE

dateless *adj* **1** dating or surviving from the distant past — see ANCIENT 1

2 lasting forever — see EVERLASTING

dating *n* the series of social engagements shared by a couple looking to get married — see COURTSHIP

datum *n* a single piece of information — see FACT 3

daub *vb* to rub an oily or sticky substance over — see SMEAR 1

daunt *vb* to lessen the courage or confidence of — see DISCOURAGE 1

dauntless *adj* feeling or displaying no fear by temperament — see BRAVE

dauntlessness *n* strength of mind to carry on in spite of danger — see COURAGE

davenport *n* a long upholstered piece of furniture designed for several sitters — see COUCH

dawdle *vb* **1** to move or act slowly — see DELAY 1

2 to spend time doing nothing — see IDLE

dawdler *n* someone who moves slowly or more slowly than others — see SLOWPOKE

dawdling *adj* moving or proceeding at less than the normal, desirable, or required speed — see SLOW 1

dawn *n* **1** the first appearance of light in the morning or the time of its appearance ⟨we stayed up talking until *dawn*⟩
synonyms aurora, cockcrow, dawning, daybreak, daylight, morn, morning, sunrise, sunup
related words day, daytime, light; twilight; forenoon
near antonyms dark, darkness, night, nighttime; afternoon, dusk, evening, gloaming
antonyms nightfall, sundown, sunset
2 the point at which something begins — see BEGINNING
dawn *vb* to come into existence — see BEGIN 2
dawn (on) *vb* to come into the mind of — see OCCUR (TO)
dawning *n* the first appearance of light in the morning or the time of its appearance — see DAWN 1
day *n* **1** the hours of light between one night and the next ⟨during the *day*, we like to go play ball in the park⟩
synonyms daylight, daytime
related words light, sunlight, sunshine; dawn, dawning, daybreak, morn, morning, sunrise, sunset; dusk, evening, gloaming, nightfall, sundown, twilight
near antonyms dark, darkness
antonyms night, nighttime
2 an extent of time associated with a particular person or thing — see AGE 1
daybreak *n* the first appearance of light in the morning or the time of its appearance — see DAWN 1
daydream *n* a conception or image created by the imagination and having no objective reality — see FANTASY 1
daydreaming *n* the state of being lost in thought — see REVERIE
daylight *n* **1** the first appearance of light in the morning or the time of its appearance — see DAWN 1
2 the hours of light between one night and the next — see DAY 1
daytime *n* the hours of light between one night and the next — see DAY 1
day–to–day *adj* occurring, done, produced, or appearing every day — see DAILY
daze *n* a state of mental confusion — see HAZE 2
daze *vb* **1** to make senseless or dizzy by a blow — see STUN 1
2 to overpower with light — see DAZZLE
dazed *adj* suffering from mental confusion — see DIZZY 2
dazzle *n* the quality or state of having or giving off light — see BRILLIANCE 1
dazzle *vb* to overpower with light ⟨skiers were *dazzled* by the glare off of the slopes of freshly packed snow⟩
synonyms bedazzle, blind, daze
related words confuse, overpower, overwhelm, stun
dazzling *adj* giving off or reflecting much light — see BRIGHT 1
deacon *n* a person specially trained and authorized to conduct religious services in a Christian church — see CLERGYMAN
dead *adj* **1** no longer living ⟨I inherited this heirloom from my *dead* great-grandfather⟩
synonyms breathless, deceased, defunct, departed, fallen, gone, late, lifeless
related words extinct; dying, fading, moribund; stillborn; finished, lapsed, terminated; barren, desert; inanimate, insensate, nonliving, unanimated
phrases bitten the dust, passed away, passed on
near antonyms animate, animated; dynamic, lively, thriving, vibrant, vital, vivacious; active, functioning, operative, running
antonyms alive, breathing, going, living
2 depleted in strength, energy, or freshness — see WEARY 1
3 having no exceptions or restrictions — see ABSOLUTE 2
4 lacking in sensation or feeling — see NUMB
5 no longer existing — see EXTINCT
6 not being in a state of use, activity, or employment — see INACTIVE 2
7 of, relating to, or suggestive of death — see DEATHLY 1
dead *adv* **1** in a direct line or course — see DIRECTLY 1
2 to a full extent or degree — see FULLY 1
deaden *vb* to reduce or weaken in strength or feeling — see DULL 1
dead heat *n* a situation in which neither participant in a contest, competition, or struggle comes out ahead of the other — see TIE 1
deadlock *n* a point in a struggle where neither side is capable of winning or willing to give in — see IMPASSE
deadly *adj* likely to cause or capable of causing death ⟨the doctors were alarmed about the outbreak of the *deadly* new virus⟩
synonyms baleful, deathly, fatal, fell, killer, lethal, mortal, murderous, pestilent, vital
related words baneful, destructive, harmful, noxious, pernicious; poisonous, toxic, virulent; dangerous, grave, grievous, hazardous, jeopardizing, menacing, parlous, perilous, risky, serious, threatening, ugly, unhealthy, unsound; capital; bloody, internecine, sanguinary, sanguine
near antonyms beneficial, restorative; nonpoisonous, nontoxic, safe
antonyms healthful, healthy, nonfatal, nonlethal, wholesome
deadly *adv* to a great degree — see VERY 1
deadness *n* the state of being dead — see DEATH 2
deadpan *adj* not expressing any emotion — see BLANK 1
deadwood *n* discarded or useless material — see GARBAGE
deafening *adj* marked by a high volume of sound — see LOUD 1
[1]**deal** *n* a considerable amount — see LOT 2
[2]**deal** *n* **1** an arrangement about action to be taken — see AGREEMENT 2
2 the transfer of ownership of something from one person to another for a price — see SALE
deal *vb* **1** to carry on the business of buying and selling goods or other property — see TRADE 1
2 to talk over or dispute the terms of a purchase — see BARGAIN
deal (in) *vb* to offer for sale to the public — see MARKET
deal (out) *vb* to give out (something) in appropriate amounts or to appropriate individuals — see ADMINISTER 1
deal (with) *vb* **1** to behave toward in a stated way — see TREAT 1

2 to have (something) as a subject matter — see CONCERN 1
dealer *n* **1** a buyer and seller of goods for profit — see MERCHANT
2 the person in a business deal who hands over an item in exchange for money — see VENDOR
dealings *n pl* doings between individuals or groups — see RELATION 1
dean *n* the senior member of a group <the *dean* of the Aspen ski instructors oversaw the training of the rescue team>
synonyms elder, elder statesman, senior
related words better, superior
near antonyms inferior, subordinate, underling; beginner, freshman, newcomer, rookie
antonyms baby
dear *adj* **1** commanding a large price — see COSTLY
2 granted special treatment or attention — see DARLING 1
3 having qualities that tend to make one loved — see LOVABLE
dear *n* a person with whom one is in love — see SWEETHEART
dearth *n* **1** a falling short of an essential or desirable amount or number — see DEFICIENCY
2 the fact or state of being absent — see LACK 1
death *n* **1** the permanent stopping of all the vital bodily activities <we were all saddened by the *death* of our teacher>
synonyms decease, demise, doom, end, passing, quietus
related words casualty, fatality; martyrdom, self-destruction, suicide; annihilation, destruction, ending, expiration, extermination, ruin
near antonyms existence, life; creation
antonyms birth
2 the state of being dead <*death* is one of the few constants in the universe>
synonyms deadness, lifelessness, sleep
antonyms existence, life
3 the act of ceasing to exist <the *death* of the Soviet economic system in the wake of the breakup of the USSR>
synonyms demise, expiration, termination
related words dispersion, dissolution; shutdown; decease, doom, end, ending, passing, quietus; suicide; annihilation, destruction, ruin
near antonyms existence
antonyms beginning, creation, start
deathless *adj* lasting forever — see EVERLASTING
deathlike *adj* of, relating to, or suggestive of death — see DEATHLY 1
deathly *adj* **1** of, relating to, or suggestive of death <his *deathly* pallor suggested that any attempt to find a pulse would be futile>
synonyms dead, deathlike, mortal
related words ghostly, phantom, spectral; inactive, inert, inoperative, lifeless, quiescent, still; macabre; baleful, fatal, fateful, fell, killer, lethal, murderous, pestilent
near antonyms active, alive, living; animated, energetic, lively, vigorous, vivacious; hale, healthy, hearty, robust, sound
2 likely to cause or capable of causing death — see DEADLY
debacle *also* **débâcle** *n* **1** a sudden violent event that brings about great loss or destruction — see DISASTER
2 something that has failed — see FAILURE 3
debar *vb* to prevent the participation or inclusion of — see EXCLUDE
debark *vb* to go ashore from a ship — see DISEMBARK
debase *vb* **1** to lower in character or dignity <we *debased* ourselves when we cheated on the test>
synonyms abase, corrupt, debauch, degrade, demean, deprave, pervert, poison, profane, prostitute, subvert, warp
related words contaminate, pollute, taint; descend; disgrace, humble, humiliate; blemish, damage, deface, destroy, flaw, harm, hurt, impair, mar, ruin, spoil, stain, tarnish, vitiate, wreck; depreciate, downgrade
near antonyms dignify, exalt, honor; amend, improve; cleanse, purify, restore; respect
antonyms elevate, ennoble, uplift
2 to reduce to a lower standing in one's own eyes or in others' eyes — see HUMBLE
debased *adj* having or showing lowered moral character or standards — see CORRUPT
debasement *n* a sinking to a state of low moral standards and behavior — see CORRUPTION 2
debatable *adj* **1** open to question or dispute <it's always *debatable* which college football team is really number one, since there's more than one ranking system>
synonyms disputable, doubtable, doubtful, moot, questionable
related words refutable; controversial, debated, disputed; dubious, inconclusive, indecisive, problematic (*also* problematical), uncertain; academic, hypothetical, speculative, theoretical (*also* theoretic); ambiguous, equivocal
near antonyms irrefutable; certain, definite, positive, sure; unambiguous, unequivocal; absolute, clear, conclusive, decisive; uncontested, undisputed
antonyms incontestable, incontrovertible, indisputable, indubitable, undeniable, unquestionable
2 giving good reason for being doubted, questioned, or challenged — see DOUBTFUL 2
debate *n* **1** a careful weighing of the reasons for or against something — see CONSIDERATION 1
2 variance of opinion on a matter — see DISAGREEMENT 1
debate *vb* **1** to give serious and careful thought to — see PONDER
2 to talk about (an issue) usually from various points of view and for the purpose of arriving at a decision or opinion — see DISCUSS
debater *n* a person who takes part in a dispute — see DISPUTANT
debauch *vb* to lower in character or dignity — see DEBASE 1
debauched *adj* having or showing lowered moral character or standards — see CORRUPT
debaucher *n* a person who has sunk below the normal moral standard — see DEGENERATE
debauchery *n* **1** immoral conduct or practices harmful or offensive to society — see VICE 1
2 a sinking to a state of low moral standards and behavior — see CORRUPTION 2
debilitate *vb* to diminish the physical strength of — see WEAKEN 1
debilitated *adj* lacking bodily strength — see WEAK 1
debilitation *n* **1** a gradual sinking and wasting away of mind or body — see DECLINE 1

2 the quality or state of lacking physical strength or vigor — see WEAKNESS 1

debility *n* the quality or state of lacking physical strength or vigor — see WEAKNESS 1

debonair *adj* having or showing very polished and worldly manners — see SUAVE

debris *n* the portion or bits of something left over or behind after it has been destroyed — see REMAINS 1

debt *n* a breaking of a moral or legal code — see OFFENSE 1

debug *vb* to remove errors, defects, deficiencies, or deviations from — see CORRECT 1

debunk *vb* to reveal the true nature of — see EXPOSE 1

decadence *n* **1** a change to a lower state or level — see DECLINE 2

2 a sinking to a state of low moral standards and behavior — see CORRUPTION 2

decadent *adj* **1** having lost forcefulness, courage, or spirit — see EFFETE 1

2 having or showing lowered moral character or standards — see CORRUPT

decadent *n* a person who has sunk below the normal moral standard — see DEGENERATE

decalogue *n* a collection or system of rules of conduct — see CODE

decamping *n* the act of leaving a place — see DEPARTURE

decampment *n* the act of leaving a place — see DEPARTURE

decapitate *vb* to cut off the head of ⟨he started *decapitating* wildflowers with his walking stick as they strolled through the park⟩

synonyms behead, guillotine

related words prune, shorten, trim; scalp

decay *n* **1** a gradual sinking and wasting away of mind or body — see DECLINE 1

2 the process by which dead organic matter separates into simpler substances — see CORRUPTION 1

decay *vb* **1** to go through decomposition ⟨the logs *decayed* on the rain forest floor⟩ ⟨the atom of plutonium *decayed* in the test chamber⟩

synonyms break down, corrupt, decompose, disintegrate, molder, putrefy, rot, spoil

related words sour, turn; contaminate, defile, pollute, taint; curdle, ferment; crumble, degenerate, deteriorate

phrases go to seed, run to seed

near antonyms develop, grow, mature, ripen; refresh, renew, restore; cleanse, purify; assemble, compose, integrate

2 to become worse or of less value — see DETERIORATE

3 to lose bodily strength or vigor — see WEAKEN 2

decayed *adj* **1** having lost forcefulness, courage, or spirit — see EFFETE 1

2 having undergone organic breakdown — see ROTTEN 1

decaying *n* a gradual sinking and wasting away of mind or body — see DECLINE 1

decease *n* the permanent stopping of all the vital bodily activities — see DEATH 1

decease *vb* to stop living — see DIE 1

deceased *adj* no longer living — see DEAD 1

deceit *n* the inclination or practice of misleading others through lies or trickery ⟨the evil queen in the story was full of *deceit*⟩

synonyms artifice, craft, craftiness, crookedness, cunning, deceitfulness, dishonesty, dissembling, dissimulation, double-dealing, duplicity, fakery, foxiness, guile, wiliness

related words equivocation, prevarication; chicanery, skulduggery (*or* skullduggery), subterfuge, trickery; hypocrisy, insincerity; deviousness, shrewdness; treacherousness, underhandedness, unscrupulousness; covertness, furtiveness, secrecy, shadiness, sneakiness, stealthiness; oiliness, shiftiness, slickness, slipperiness, slyness, smoothness

near antonyms candidness, candor, directness, frankness, ingenuousness, openness, plainness; honesty, probity; reliability, trustworthiness

antonyms artlessness, forthrightness, good faith, guilelessness, sincerity

deceitful *adj* **1** marked by, based on, or done by the use of dishonest methods to acquire something of value — see FRAUDULENT 1

2 tending or having power to deceive — see DECEPTIVE 1

deceitfulness *n* **1** the inclination or practice of misleading others through lies or trickery — see DECEIT

2 the tendency to tell lies — see DISHONESTY 1

deceive *vb* to cause to believe what is untrue ⟨he went to great lengths to *deceive* his younger brother about the nature of his new job at the mall⟩

synonyms beguile, bluff, cozen, delude, dupe, fool, gull, have, hoax, hoodwink, humbug, misguide, misinform, mislead, snow, string along, take in, trick

related words cheat, chisel, defraud, fleece, gyp, hustle, rook, swindle

near antonyms debunk, expose, reveal, show up, uncloak, uncover, unmask; disclose, divulge, tell, unveil; disabuse, disenchant, disillusion; edify, enlighten

antonyms undeceive

deceiving *adj* tending or having power to deceive — see DECEPTIVE 1

decelerate *vb* to cause to move or proceed at a less rapid pace — see SLOW 1

deceleration *n* a usually gradual decrease in the pace or level of activity of something — see SLOWDOWN

decency *n* **1** socially acceptable behavior ⟨the standards of basic *decency* demanded that they help the old lady with her groceries⟩

synonyms decorum, form, propriety

related words civility, courtesy, politeness; dignity, grace, refinement; discretion, prudence; correctness, decorousness, fitness, rightness, seemliness; attention, attentiveness, care, carefulness; goodness, high-mindedness, honesty, morality, probity, rectitude, righteousness, straightness, uprightness, virtue, virtuousness

near antonyms coarseness, crudeness, gracelessness; discourtesy, impoliteness, incivility; imprudence, indiscretion; badness, evil, immorality, wickedness

antonyms impropriety, indecency, indecorum

2 conduct that conforms to an accepted standard of right and wrong — see MORALITY 1

decent *adj* **1** conforming to a high standard of morality or virtue — see GOOD 2

2 following the accepted rules of moral conduct — see HONORABLE 1

3 following the established traditions of refined society and good taste — see PROPER 1

4 free from any trace of the coarse or indecent — see CHASTE
5 of a level of quality that meets one's needs or standards — see ADEQUATE
deceptive *adj* **1** tending or having power to deceive <in his *deceptive* answer about the vehicle's history, the salesman said that the used car had never been hit by another car>
synonyms beguiling, deceitful, deceiving, deluding, delusive, delusory, fallacious, false, misleading, specious
related words devious, guileful, shady, shifty, sly, sneaking, sneaky, trick, tricky, underhand, underhanded; inaccurate, incorrect, wrong; bewildering, confounding, distracting, perplexing, puzzling; crooked, dishonest, double-dealing, faithless, fast, fraudulent, knavish, lying, mendacious, untrustworthy, untruthful; insidious, perfidious, treacherous; artificial, backhanded, feigned, hypocritical, insincere, left-handed, two-faced
near antonyms candid, frank, open, plain; clarifying, elucidative, explanatory, illuminating; revealing, revelatory; honest, trustworthy, truthful
antonyms aboveboard, forthright, straightforward
2 given to or marked by cheating and deception — see DISHONEST 2
decide *vb* **1** to come to a judgment after discussion or consideration <they *decided* to go out for pizza after the movie was over>
synonyms choose, conclude, determine, figure, opt, resolve
related words decree, rule; cull, elect, handpick, pick, prefer, select, single (out), take
phrases make up one's mind
near antonyms abstain, decline, refuse, reject, turn down; delay, hesitate, stall, temporize; shilly-shally, vacillate, waver
2 to give an opinion about (something at issue or in dispute) — see JUDGE 1
3 to come to an agreement or decision concerning the details of — see ARRANGE 1
4 to make final, definite, or beyond dispute — see CLINCH
decided *adj* not subject to misinterpretation or more than one interpretation — see CLEAR 2
decidedness *n* firm or unwavering adherence to one's purpose — see DETERMINATION 1
decimate *vb* to bring to a complete end the physical soundness, existence, or usefulness of — see DESTROY 1
decimation *n* the state or fact of being rendered nonexistent, physically unsound, or useless — see DESTRUCTION
decipher *vb* to change (as a secret message) from code into ordinary language — see DECODE
decision *n* **1** a position arrived at after consideration <after much deliberation, we made a *decision* about what to have on our pizza>
synonyms conclusion, deliverance, determination, diagnosis, judgment (*or* judgement), opinion, resolution, verdict
related words decree, mandate, order; say-so; doom, finding, ruling, sentence; choice, option, selection
near antonyms deadlock, draw, stalemate, standoff, tie
2 firm or unwavering adherence to one's purpose — see DETERMINATION 1
decisive *adj* **1** fully committed to achieving a goal — see DETERMINED 1
2 having the power to persuade — see COGENT
3 serving to put an end to all debate or questioning — see CONCLUSIVE 1
decisiveness *n* firm or unwavering adherence to one's purpose — see DETERMINATION 1
deck *vb* **1** to make more attractive by adding something that is beautiful or becoming — see DECORATE
2 to outfit with clothes and especially fine or special clothes — see CLOTHE 1
declaim *vb* **1** to give a formal often extended talk on a subject — see TALK 1
2 to talk as if giving an important and formal speech — see ORATE 1
declamation *n* a usually formal discourse delivered to an audience — see SPEECH 1
declaration *n* a solemn and often public declaration of the truth or existence of something — see PROTESTATION
declare *vb* **1** to make known openly or publicly — see ANNOUNCE
2 to state as a fact usually forcefully — see CLAIM 1
3 to state clearly and strongly — see ASSERT 1
declension *n* **1** a gradual sinking and wasting away of mind or body — see DECLINE 1
2 a change to a lower state or level — see DECLINE 2
decline *n* **1** a gradual sinking and wasting away of mind or body <her sad *decline* from a robust athlete to an old woman with arthritis>
synonyms debilitation, decay, decaying, declension, degeneration, descent, deterioration, ebbing, enfeeblement, weakening
related words atrophy; exhaustion; drooping, flagging, limping; relapse, setback
near antonyms invigoration, strengthening; progress
antonyms improvement, recovery, revitalization
2 a change to a lower state or level <the *decline* of the Roman Empire>
synonyms decadence, declension, degeneracy, degeneration, degradation, descent, deterioration, downfall, downgrade, fall
related words decay, rotting, spoiling; breakup, crumbling, decomposition, disintegration, dissolution; abasement, debasement; depreciation, lessening; decimation, demolishment, demolition, desolation, destruction, havoc, ruin, ruination; abatement, decrease, decrement, de-escalation, deflation, diminishment, diminution, dip, drop, fall, loss, lowering, reduction, sag, shrinkage
near antonyms advancement, development, evolution, growth; blossoming, flourishing, flowering; renewal, restoration, revitalization; heightening; accretion, accrual, addendum, addition, augmentation, boost, enhancement, gain, increase, increment, raise, supplement
antonyms ascent, rise, upswing
3 a loss of status — see COMEDOWN
4 the amount by which something is lessened — see DECREASE
decline *vb* **1** to show unwillingness to accept, do, engage in, or agree to <he *declined* the invitation to the party> <she *declined* to participate in the soccer game>
synonyms disapprove, negative, refuse, reject, repudiate, spurn, turn down

related words overrule, veto; forbid, prohibit, proscribe; dismiss; abstain, forbear, refrain; deny, dispute, gainsay; balk, stick; abjure, renounce; avoid, bypass, detour
near antonyms condone, countenance, swallow, tolerate; adopt, embrace, receive, take; accede, acquiesce, agree, assent, consent; choose, select; espouse, support
antonyms accept, agree (to), approve
2 to be unwilling to grant — see DENY 2
3 to go to a lower level — see DROP 2
4 to become worse or of less value — see DETERIORATE
5 to grow less in scope or intensity especially gradually — see DECREASE 2
6 to lead or extend downward — see DESCEND 1

declined *adj* bending downward or forward — see NODDING

declining *adj* bending downward or forward — see NODDING

decode *vb* to change (as a secret message) from code into ordinary language ⟨the agents worked into the night to *decode* the transmission from the enemy spy⟩
synonyms break, crack, decipher
related words render, translate; dope (out), figure out, puzzle (out), solve, unravel, work, work out
antonyms cipher, code, encode

decolorize *vb* to make white or whiter by removing color — see WHITEN

decompose *vb* to go through decomposition — see DECAY 1

decomposed *adj* having undergone organic breakdown — see ROTTEN 1

decomposition *n* the process by which dead organic matter separates into simpler substances — see CORRUPTION 1

decorate *vb* to make more attractive by adding something that is beautiful or becoming ⟨they *decorated* the hallway with paintings and tapestries⟩
synonyms adorn, array, beautify, bedeck, bedizen, deck, do, dress, embellish, enrich, garnish, grace, ornament, trim
related words doll up, dress up, trick (out); brighten, freshen, smarten, spruce (up); boss, chase, emboss; embroider, figure, flounce, fringe, garland, hang, lace, wreathe; gild, paint; redecorate, redo
near antonyms simplify, streamline; bare, denude, dismantle, display, divest, expose, reveal, strip, uncover
antonyms blemish, deface, disfigure, mar, scar, spoil

decoration *n* **1** something that decorates or beautifies ⟨they put lots of *decorations* on and around the Christmas tree⟩
synonyms adornment, caparison, embellishment, frill, garnish, ornament, trim
related words finery, frippery; flounce, flourish, furbelow, ruffle; enhancement, enrichment, improvement; embossment, embroidery, fancywork; gilt, glitter; design, figure, pattern; furnishings, regalia, trappings
near antonyms blemish, defacement, disfigurement, scar; blot, spot, stain
2 something given in recognition of achievement — see AWARD

decorative *adj* serving to add beauty ⟨they planted *decorative* flowers all along the path to the cottage⟩
synonyms adorning, beautifying, embellishing, ornamental
related words alluring, appealing, attractive, charming, delightful, glamorous (*also* glamourous), pleasing, prepossessing; beauteous, beautiful, bonny, comely, fair, gorgeous, handsome, lovely, pretty, stunning; detailed, elaborate, fancy, ornate
antonyms functional, utilitarian

decorous *adj* **1** following the established traditions of refined society and good taste — see PROPER 1
2 marked by or showing careful attention to set forms and details — see CEREMONIOUS 1

decorum *n* socially acceptable behavior — see DECENCY 1

decoy *n* something used to attract animals to a hook or into a trap — see BAIT 1

decoy *vb* to lead away from a usual or proper course by offering some pleasure or advantage — see LURE

decrease *n* the amount by which something is lessened ⟨the average *decrease* in the price of milk was five cents per gallon⟩
synonyms abatement, decline, decrement, diminishment, diminution, drop, fall, loss, reduction, shrinkage
related words deduction, dent, depression; slip, slump; curtailment, cut, cutback
near antonyms accretion, accrual, accumulation, addition, supplement; continuation, extension; upswing, uptrend, upturn
antonyms boost, enlargement, gain, increase, increment, raise, rise

decrease *vb* **1** to make smaller in amount, volume, or extent ⟨they *decreased* the amount of water flowing through the pipes in order to prevent an overflow⟩
synonyms abate, de-escalate, diminish, downsize, dwindle, lessen, lower, reduce
related words compress, condense, constrict, contract; abbreviate, abridge, clip, crop, curtail, cut, cut back, cut down, dock, pare, prune, retrench, shorten, slash, trim, truncate, whittle; deflate, shrink; moderate, modify, modulate, qualify
near antonyms blow up, dilate, distend, inflate, swell; elongate, extend, lengthen, prolong, protract; add (to), complement, supplement; enhance, heighten, intensify
antonyms aggrandize, amplify, augment, boost, enlarge, escalate, expand, increase, raise
2 to grow less in scope or intensity especially gradually ⟨the force of the wind slowly *decreased* until the flowers were standing upright again⟩
synonyms abate, decline, de-escalate, die (down), diminish, dwindle, ebb, fall, lessen, let up, lower, moderate, recede, relent, remit, shrink, subside, taper, taper off, wane
related words compress, condense, constrict, contract; evaporate, fade (away), give out, melt (away), peter (out), vanish; slacken, slow (down); alleviate, ease, relax; flag, sink, weaken; cave (in), collapse, deflate, give out
near antonyms appear, emerge, show up; blow up, distend, elongate, lengthen
antonyms accumulate, balloon, build, burgeon, enlarge, escalate, expand, grow, increase, intensify, mount, mushroom, pick up, rise, snowball, soar, swell, wax

decree *n* **1** a statement of what to do that must be obeyed by those concerned — see COMMAND 1

2 an order publicly issued by an authority — see EDICT 1

decree *vb* to give an order — see COMMAND 2

decrement *n* the amount by which something is lessened — see DECREASE

decry *vb* **1** to express scornfully one's low opinion of ⟨scientists were quick to *decry* the claims of the psychic⟩
synonyms bad-mouth, belittle, cry down, deprecate, depreciate, diminish, discount, disparage, minimize, put down, write off
related words abuse, scold; disapprove (of), dislike; censure, condemn, criticize, denounce, reprehend, reprobate; asperse, defame, malign, slander, traduce, vilify; discredit, disgrace
near antonyms approve, countenance, endorse (*also* indorse), favor, recommend, sanction; commend, compliment, eulogize
antonyms acclaim, applaud, exalt, extol (*also* extoll), glorify, laud, magnify, praise
2 to declare to be morally wrong or evil — see CONDEMN 1

decrying *adj* intended to make a person or thing seem of little importance or value — see DEROGATORY

dedicate *vb* to keep or intend for a special purpose — see DEVOTE 1

dedication *n* adherence to something to which one is bound by a pledge or duty — see FIDELITY

deduce *vb* to form an opinion through reasoning and information — see INFER 1

deducible *adj* being or provable by reasoning in which the conclusion follows necessarily from given information — see DEDUCTIVE

deduct *vb* to take away (an amount or number) from a total — see SUBTRACT

deduction *n* **1** something that is or may be subtracted ⟨contestants get a *deduction* from their scores for every incorrect guess⟩
synonyms abatement, discount, reduction
related words kickback, rebate; dent, depreciation; decline, decrement, diminishment, diminution, drop, fall, loss; forfeit, forfeiture, penalty
near antonyms accretion, accrual, augmentation, boost, gain, increase, increment, raise, rise; appreciation
antonyms accession, addition
2 the act or an instance of taking away from a total — see SUBTRACTION
3 an opinion arrived at through a process of reasoning — see CONCLUSION 1

deductive *adj* being or provable by reasoning in which the conclusion follows necessarily from given information ⟨using *deductive* reasoning we must conclude that since everyone eventually dies, sooner or later it's going to be our turn⟩
synonyms deducible, derivable, inferable, reasoned
related words conjectural, hypothetical, purported, supposed, suppositional; academic, speculative, theoretical (*also* theoretic); logical, rational
near antonyms inducible, inductive; absolute, categorical (*also* categoric), definite, explicit, express; instinctive, intuitive; illogical, irrational

deed *n* **1** an act of notable skill, strength, or cleverness — see FEAT 1
2 something done by someone — see ACTION 1

deed *vb* to give over the legal possession or ownership of — see TRANSFER 1

deem *vb* to have as an opinion — see BELIEVE 2

deep *adj* **1** extending far downward or inward ⟨they dropped their bucket down a *deep* well⟩ ⟨the knife made a *deep* cut into the wood⟩
synonyms abysmal, bottomless
related words abyssal, unfathomable; boundless, endless, immeasurable, inestimable, infinite, limitless, measureless, unlimited, vast
near antonyms depthless, two-dimensional; even, flat, flush, horizontal, level, plane, smooth; confined, finite, limited, measured, restricted
antonyms shallow, shoal, skin-deep, superficial, surface
2 having a low musical pitch or range ⟨the tour guide had a very *deep* voice⟩
synonyms bass, low, throaty
related words gruff, hoarse, husky, rough
near antonyms squeaking, squeaky, squealing, thin; earsplitting, penetrating, piercing, strident; peeping, tinny
antonyms acute, high, high-pitched, piping, sharp, shrill, treble
3 being beyond one's powers to know, understand, or explain — see MYSTERIOUS 1
4 difficult for one of ordinary knowledge or intelligence to understand — see PROFOUND 1
5 having an often intentionally veiled or uncertain meaning — see OBSCURE 1
6 extreme in degree, power, or effect — see INTENSE

deep *n* **1** the most intense or characteristic phase of something — see THICK
2 the whole body of salt water that covers nearly three-fourths of the earth — see OCEAN

deepen *vb* to make markedly greater in measure or degree — see INTENSIFY

deep–rooted *adj* firmly established over time — see INVETERATE 1

deep–seated *adj* firmly established over time — see INVETERATE 1

de–escalate *vb* **1** to make smaller in amount, volume, or extent — see DECREASE 1
2 to grow less in scope or intensity especially gradually — see DECREASE 2

deface *vb* **1** to deliberately cause the damage or destruction of another's property — see VANDALIZE 1
2 to reduce the soundness, effectiveness, or perfection of — see DAMAGE 1

defacement *n* deliberate damaging or destroying of another's property — see VANDALISM

defacer *n* a person who damages or destroys property on purpose — see VANDAL

defamation *n* the making of false statements that damage another's reputation — see SLANDER

defamatory *adj* causing or intended to cause unjust injury to a person's good name — see LIBELOUS

defame *vb* to make untrue and harmful statements about — see SLANDER

defaming *n* the making of false statements that damage another's reputation — see SLANDER

default *n* the nonperformance of an assigned or expected action — see FAILURE 1

defeat *n* **1** failure to win a contest ⟨sore losers griping about their *defeat* in the basketball game earlier that week⟩
synonyms beating, drubbing, licking, loss, overthrow, rout, shellacking, trimming, trouncing, whipping
related words collapse, debacle (*also* débâcle),

failure, fizzle, flop, nonsuccess, setback, upset, washout; lurch, shutout
near antonyms accomplishment, achievement; landslide, sweep
antonyms success, triumph, victory, win
2 a falling short of one's goals — see FAILURE 2
defeat *vb* to achieve a victory over — see BEAT 2
defeatist *adj* emphasizing or expecting the worst — see PESSIMISTIC 1
defeatist *n* one who emphasizes bad aspects or conditions and expects the worst — see PESSIMIST 1
defect *n* something that spoils the appearance or completeness of a thing — see BLEMISH
defect (from) *vb* to leave (a cause or party) often in order to take up another ⟨many soldiers *defected from* the rebel army as soon as they realized the uprising was hopeless⟩
synonyms desert, rat (on)
related words abandon, abdicate, abjure, cut off, disown, forsake, quit, reject, renounce, repudiate, spurn; renege; depart, go, leave, withdraw
phrases go back on, walk out on
near antonyms adhere (to), cling (to), stick (to *or* with); cherish, cultivate, foster
defective *adj* having a fault — see FAULTY
defector *n* a person who abandons a cause or organization usually without right — see RENEGADE
defend *vb* **1** to drive danger or attack away from ⟨a solemn oath to *defend* the country at any cost⟩
synonyms cover, guard, protect, safeguard, screen, secure, shield, ward
related words avert, prevent; fend (off), oppose, resist, withstand; battle, contend, fight, war; conserve, keep, preserve, save; buffer, palisade, picket, wall
phrases look out for, stand up for
near antonyms bombard, storm; beset, besiege, overrun; capitulate, cave, submit, yield
antonyms assail, assault, attack
2 to continue to declare to be true or proper despite opposition or objections — see MAINTAIN 2
defendable *adj* capable of being defended with good reasoning against verbal attack — see TENABLE 2
defender *n* someone that protects — see PROTECTOR
defense *n* **1** means or method of defending ⟨thorns are a rose's *defense* against grazing animals⟩
synonyms aegis, ammunition, armor, cover, guard, protection, safeguard, screen, security, shield, wall, ward
related words arm, armament, munitions, weapon, weaponry; fastness, fort, fortress, palisade, stronghold
near antonyms aggression, assault, attack, offense (*or* offence), offensive
2 an explanation that frees one from fault or blame — see EXCUSE
defenseless *adj* lacking protection from danger or resistance against attack — see HELPLESS 1
defenselessness *n* the quality or state of having little resistance to some outside agent — see SUSCEPTIBILITY
defensible *adj* capable of being defended with good reasoning against verbal attack — see TENABLE 1
defensive *adj* intended to resist or prevent attack or aggression ⟨a *defensive* alliance against the aggressors⟩
synonyms protective, self-protective
related words deterrent, preventive; safe, secure
near antonyms aggressive, bellicose, belligerent, combative, contentious, militant, pugnacious, quarrelsome, scrappy, truculent, warlike
antonyms offensive
defensive *n* a position or readiness to oppose actual or expected attack ⟨their harsh words put him on the *defensive*⟩
synonyms guard
related words alert, watch
antonyms offensive
defer *vb* to assign to a later time — see POSTPONE
deference *n* a readiness or willingness to yield to the wishes of others — see COMPLIANCE 1
deferential *adj* marked by or showing proper regard for another's higher status — see RESPECTFUL
deferentially *adv* in manner showing no signs of pride or self-assertion — see LOWLY
defiance *n* **1** refusal to obey — see DISOBEDIENCE
2 the inclination to resist — see RESISTANCE 1
defiant *adj* given to resisting authority or another's control — see DISOBEDIENT
deficiency *n* a falling short of an essential or desirable amount or number ⟨there was a *deficiency* of fresh food in the house⟩
synonyms dearth, deficit, failure, famine, inadequacy, insufficiency, lack, paucity, poverty, scantiness, scarceness, scarcity, shortage, want
related words absence, omission; meagerness, poorness, skimpiness; necessity, need, privation
near antonyms bountifulness, copiousness; excess, overabundance, oversupply, surfeit, surplus
antonyms abundance, adequacy, amplitude, plenitude, plenty, sufficiency
deficient *adj* **1** lacking some necessary part — see INCOMPLETE
2 falling short of a standard — see BAD 1
3 not coming up to a usual standard or meeting a particular need — see SHORT 3
deficit *n* a falling short of an essential or desirable amount or number — see DEFICIENCY
defile *n* a narrow opening between hillsides or mountains that can be used for passage — see CANYON
defile *vb* **1** to make unfit for use by the addition of something harmful or undesirable — see CONTAMINATE
2 to treat (a sacred place or object) shamefully or with great disrespect — see DESECRATE
defilement *n* **1** an act of great disrespect shown to God or to sacred ideas, people, or things — see BLASPHEMY
2 something that is or that makes impure — see IMPURITY
define *vb* **1** to draw or make apparent the outline of — see OUTLINE 1
2 to mark the limits of — see LIMIT 2
3 to point out the chief quality or qualities of an individual or group — see CHARACTERIZE 1
4 to give the rules about (something) clearly and exactly — see PRESCRIBE
defined *adj* having distinct or certain limits — see LIMITED 1
definite *adj* **1** having distinct or certain limits — see LIMITED 1

2 so clearly expressed as to leave no doubt about the meaning — see EXPLICIT
definitely *adv* without any question — see INDEED 1
definitive *adj* **1** being the most accurate and apparently thorough <the *definitive* work on the attack on Pearl Harbor>
synonyms authoritative
related words conclusive, decisive; official; accurate, correct; complete, thorough
2 serving to put an end to all debate or questioning — see CONCLUSIVE 1
3 so clearly expressed as to leave no doubt about the meaning — see EXPLICIT
deflect *vb* to change the course or direction of (something) — see TURN 2
deform *vb* to twist (something) out of a natural or normal shape or condition — see CONTORT
deformation *n* the twisting of something out of its natural or normal shape or condition — see CONTORTION
deformed *adj* badly or imperfectly formed — see MALFORMED
deformity *n* something that spoils the appearance or completeness of a thing — see BLEMISH
defraud *vb* to rob by the use of trickery or threats — see FLEECE
defrauder *n* a dishonest person who uses clever means to cheat others out of something of value — see TRICKSTER 1
defrauding *adj* marked by, based on, or done by the use of dishonest methods to acquire something of value — see FRAUDULENT 1
defrosted *adj* freed from a frozen state by exposure to warmth — see THAWED
deft *adj* skillful with the hands — see DEXTEROUS 1
deftness *n* **1** ease and grace in physical activity — see DEXTERITY 2
2 subtle or imaginative ability in inventing, devising, or executing something — see SKILL 1
defunct *adj* **1** no longer existing — see EXTINCT
2 no longer living — see DEAD 1
defy *vb* **1** to go against the commands, prohibitions, or rules of — see DISOBEY
2 to invite (someone) to take part in a contest or to perform a feat — see CHALLENGE 2
3 to oppose (something hostile or dangerous) with firmness or courage — see FACE 2
4 to refuse to give in to — see RESIST
degeneracy *n* **1** a change to a lower state or level — see DECLINE 2
2 a sinking to a state of low moral standards and behavior — see CORRUPTION 2
degenerate *adj* **1** having lost forcefulness, courage, or spirit — see EFFETE 1
2 having or showing lowered moral character or standards — see CORRUPT
degenerate *n* a person who has sunk below the normal moral standard <the *degenerate* would stop at nothing to get satisfaction>
synonyms backslider, debaucher, decadent, libertine, pervert, profligate
related words delinquent, derelict, incorrigible; blackguard, cad, heel, knave, rascal, miscreant, reprobate, rogue, scoundrel, villain; playboy, satyr
near antonyms saint
degenerate *vb* to become worse or of less value — see DETERIORATE
degeneration *n* **1** a change to a lower state or level — see DECLINE 2
2 a gradual sinking and wasting away of mind or body — see DECLINE 1
3 a sinking to a state of low moral standards and behavior — see CORRUPTION 2
degradation *n* **1** a change to a lower state or level — see DECLINE 2
2 a sinking to a state of low moral standards and behavior — see CORRUPTION 2
degrade *vb* **1** to bring to a lower grade or rank — see DEMOTE
2 to lower in character or dignity — see DEBASE 1
3 to reduce to a lower standing in one's own eyes or in others' eyes — see HUMBLE
degraded *adj* having or showing lowered moral character or standards — see CORRUPT
degrading *adj* intended to make a person or thing seem of little importance or value — see DEROGATORY
degree *n* **1** an individual part of a process, series, or ranking <they completed the project by *degrees*>
synonyms cut, grade, inch, notch, peg, phase, point, stage, step
related words amount, measure, plane; decrement, increment
2 the placement of someone or something in relation to others in a vertical arrangement — see RANK 1
dehydrate *vb* to make dry — see DRY 1
deification *n* excessive admiration of or devotion to a person — see WORSHIP
deify *vb* **1** to love or admire too much — see IDOLIZE
2 to offer honor or respect to (someone) as a divine power — see WORSHIP 1
deifying *adj* reflecting great admiration or devotion — see WORSHIPFUL
deign *vb* to descend to a level that is beneath one's dignity — see CONDESCEND 1
deity *n* **1** a being having superhuman powers and control over a particular part of life or the world <to the ancient Greeks, Zeus was the *deity* who ruled over the sky and weather, and Poseidon was god of the sea>
synonyms divinity, god
related words angel, demigod, demon (*or* daemon), devil, spirit, supernatural
2 *cap* the being worshipped as the creator and ruler of the universe <we prayed to the *Deity* for salvation>
synonyms Allah, Almighty, Creator, Divinity, Father, God, Godhead, Jehovah, Lord, Maker, Providence, Supreme Being
3 the quality or state of being divine — see DIVINITY
dejected *adj* feeling unhappiness — see SAD 1
dejection *n* a state or spell of low spirits — see SADNESS
delay *n* an instance or period of being prevented from going about one's business <there was a *delay* for our boarding while the airplane unloaded incoming passengers>
synonyms detainment, holdup, wait
related words deferment, postponement; reprieve, respite; hesitation, lag, pause, setback, slowdown
near antonyms haste, rush; dispatch, promptness
delay *vb* **1** to move or act slowly <she told them to stop *delaying* and get to bed>

synonyms crawl, creep, dally, dawdle, dillydally, drag, lag, linger, loiter, poke, tarry
related words hang around, hang out, idle, loaf, loll, lounge; amble, ease, inch, lumber, plod, saunter, shuffle, stagger, stroll; decelerate, slow (down *or* up); filibuster, procrastinate, stall, temporize
phrases mark time
near antonyms bowl, breeze, dart, hump, hurtle, hustle, scramble, stampede; gallop, jog, run, sprint, trot; accelerate, quicken, speed up; catch up, fast-forward, outpace, outrun, outstrip, overtake
antonyms barrel, bolt, career, course, dash, fly, hasten, hotfoot (it), hurry, race, rip, rocket, run, rush, scoot, scud, scurry, speed, tear, whirl, whisk, whiz (*or* whizz), zip
2 to assign to a later time — see POSTPONE
3 to create difficulty for the work or activity of — see HAMPER

delectable *adj* **1** giving pleasure or contentment to the mind or senses — see PLEASANT
2 very pleasing to the sense of taste — see DELICIOUS 1

delectably *adv* in a pleasing way — see WELL 5

delectation *n* **1** a source of great satisfaction — see DELIGHT 1
2 the feeling experienced when one's wishes are met — see PLEASURE 1

delegate *n* **1** a person sent on a mission to represent another — see AMBASSADOR
2 a person who acts or does business for another — see AGENT 2

delegate *vb* **1** to appoint as one's representative <he *delegated* his son to go pick up the tickets for him>
synonyms commission, depute, deputize
related words assign, charge; appoint, designate, name, nominate
near antonyms abrogate; abdicate
2 to put (something) into the possession or safekeeping of another — see GIVE 2

delegation *n* **1** a body of persons chosen as representatives of a larger group — see CONTINGENT
2 the granting of power to perform various acts or duties — see COMMISSION 1

delete *vb* to show (something written) to be no longer valid by drawing a cross over or a line through it — see X (OUT)

deleterious *adj* causing or capable of causing harm — see HARMFUL

deletion *n* something left out — see OMISSION

deliberate *adj* **1** decided on as a result of careful thought <the judge made a *deliberate* decision to impose the maximum sentence>
synonyms advised, calculated, considered, measured, reasoned, studied, thoughtful, weighed
related words aforethought, premeditated; educated, informed; intentional, purposeful; designed, intended, planned, projected; careful, meticulous; foresighted, forethoughtful, provident, prudent
near antonyms ill-advised; chance, haphazard, hit-or-miss, random; aimless, desultory, purposeless; hasty, hurried, rushed; abrupt, impetuous, sudden; automatic, extemporaneous, impromptu, instinctive, spontaneous
antonyms casual
2 made, given, or done with full awareness of what one is doing — see INTENTIONAL

deliberate *vb* to give serious and careful thought to — see PONDER

deliberately *adv* with full awareness of what one is doing — see INTENTIONALLY

deliberation *n* **1** a careful weighing of the reasons for or against something — see CONSIDERATION 1
2 an exchange of views for the purpose of exploring a subject or deciding an issue — see DISCUSSION 1

delicacy *n* **1** something that is pleasing to eat because it is rare or a luxury <they were given a plate of *delicacies* while they waited for the queen>
synonyms dainty, goody, tidbit (*also* titbit), treat
related words morsel; candy, dessert, junket, sweet, sweetmeat
2 the state or quality of having a delicate structure <they marvelled at the *delicacy* of a snowflake>
synonyms daintiness, delicateness, exquisiteness, fineness, fragility
related words flimsiness, insubstantiality, wispiness
near antonyms firmness, solidity; strength
antonyms coarseness, crudeness, crudity, roughness, rudeness
3 the tendency to be or state of being squeamish <the urgent need for blood prompted many people to overcome their habitual *delicacy* and become first-time donors>
synonyms qualmishness, queasiness, squeamishness
related words daintiness, fastidiousness, finickiness, fussiness
near antonyms boldness
antonyms indelicacy
4 the quality or state of being very accurate — see PRECISION
5 the quality or state of lacking physical strength or vigor — see WEAKNESS 1

delicate *adj* **1** satisfying or pleasing because of fineness or mildness <a heavy sauce would spoil the *delicate* flavor of this fish>
synonyms dainty, exquisite, refined, subtle
related words choice, elegant, extraordinary, incomparable, peerless, preeminent, prime, rare, select, superior, superlative, supreme, transcendent, unsurpassed; picked, selected; fine, fragile, frail
near antonyms coarse, crude, rough; common, ordinary; average, fair, indifferent, mediocre, medium, middling, run-of-the-mill, second-rate
antonyms robust, strong, sturdy
2 able to sense slight impressions or differences — see ACUTE 1
3 accomplished with trained ability — see SKILLFUL
4 easily broken — see FRAGILE 1
5 easily injured without careful handling — see TENDER 1
6 hard to please — see FINICKY
7 having qualities that appeal to a refined taste — see CHOICE
8 lacking bodily strength — see WEAK 1
9 made or done with extreme care and accuracy — see FINE 2
10 meeting the highest standard of accuracy — see PRECISE 1
11 not harsh or stern especially in manner, nature, or effect — see GENTLE 1

12 requiring exceptional skill or caution in performance or handling — see TRICKY

delicateness *n* **1** the quality or state of lacking physical strength or vigor — see WEAKNESS 1
2 the state or quality of having a delicate structure — see DELICACY 2

delicious *adj* **1** very pleasing to the sense of taste ⟨the family sat down to a *delicious* Thanksgiving dinner⟩
synonyms ambrosial, appetizing, delectable, flavorful, luscious, palatable, savory, scrumptious, tasty, toothsome, yummy
related words digestible, eatable, edible; delightful, heavenly, pleasing; agreeable, gratifying, pleasant; satisfying; choice, dainty, delicate, exquisite, rare
near antonyms banal, boring, commonplace, tedious; noisome, smelly, stinky; noxious, unwholesome; miserable, wretched; abhorrent, abominable, awful, detestable, disagreeable, disgusting, distasteful, foul, horrid, nauseating, offensive, repellent, repugnant, repulsive, sickening, unpleasant
antonyms flat, flavorless, insipid, stale, tasteless, unappetizing, unpalatable
2 giving pleasure or contentment to the mind or senses — see PLEASANT

deliciously *adv* in a pleasing way — see WELL 5

deliciousness *n* the quality of being delicious ⟨the fancy feast was *deliciousness* itself⟩
synonyms lusciousness, savor, savoriness, tastiness

delight *n* **1** a source of great satisfaction ⟨the school play was a *delight* for the parents⟩
synonyms delectation, gas [*slang*], joy, kick, manna, pleasure, treat
related words amusement, diversion, entertainment, fun, recreation; comfort, relief, solace; gratification, indulgence; ambrosia
2 someone or something that provides amusement or enjoyment — see FUN 1
3 the feeling experienced when one's wishes are met — see PLEASURE 1

delight *vb* **1** to feel or express joy or triumph — see EXULT
2 to give satisfaction to — see PLEASE

delight (in) *vb* to take pleasure in — see ENJOY 1

delighted *adj* experiencing pleasure, satisfaction, or delight — see GLAD 1

delightful *adj* **1** giving pleasure or contentment to the mind or senses — see PLEASANT
2 providing amusement or enjoyment — see FUN

delightfully *adv* in a pleasing way — see WELL 5

delimit *vb* to mark the limits of — see LIMIT 2

delineate *vb* **1** to draw or make apparent the outline of — see OUTLINE 1
2 to give a representation or account of in words — see DESCRIBE 1

delineated *adj* producing a mental picture through clear and impressive description — see GRAPHIC 1

delineation *n* **1** a picture using lines to represent the chief features of an object or scene — see DRAWING
2 a vivid representation in words of someone or something — see DESCRIPTION 1

delinquency *n* **1** the nonperformance of an assigned or expected action — see FAILURE 1
2 the quality or state of being late — see LATENESS

delinquent *adj* not arriving, occurring, or settled at the due, usual, or proper time — see LATE 1

deliquesce *vb* to go from a solid to a liquid state — see LIQUEFY

delirious *adj* **1** feeling overwhelming fear or worry — see FRANTIC 1
2 marked by great and often stressful excitement or activity — see FURIOUS 1

delirium *n* a state of wildly excited activity or emotion — see FRENZY

deliver *vb* **1** to free from the penalties or consequences of sin — see SAVE 1
2 to remove from danger or harm — see SAVE 2
3 to give (something) over to the control or possession of another usually under duress — see SURRENDER 1
4 to put (something) into the possession of someone for use or consumption — see FURNISH 2
5 to put (something) into the possession or safekeeping of another — see GIVE 2
6 to turn out as planned or desired — see SUCCEED 1

deliverance *n* **1** the saving from danger or evil — see SALVATION
2 a position arrived at after consideration — see DECISION 1

deliverer *n* **1** a person who delivers goods to customers usually over a regular local route — see DELIVERYMAN
2 one that saves from danger or destruction — see SAVIOR

delivery *n* **1** a freeing from an obligation or responsibility — see RELEASE 1
2 the act or process of giving birth to children — see CHILDBIRTH

deliveryman *n* a person who delivers goods to customers usually over a regular local route ⟨the *deliveryman* dropped off a package for us while we were at the store⟩
synonyms deliverer
related words bearer, carrier, courier, go-between, liaison, messenger

delude *vb* to cause to believe what is untrue — see DECEIVE

deluding *adj* tending or having power to deceive — see DECEPTIVE 1

deluge *n* **1** a great flow of water or of something that overwhelms — see FLOOD
2 a steady falling of water from the sky in significant quantity — see RAIN 1

deluge *vb* to cover or become filled with a flood — see FLOOD

delusion *n* a conception or image created by the imagination and having no objective reality — see FANTASY 1

delusive *adj* tending or having power to deceive — see DECEPTIVE 1

delusory *adj* tending or having power to deceive — see DECEPTIVE 1

deluxe *adj* showing obvious signs of wealth and comfort — see LUXURIOUS

delve (into) *vb* to search through or into — see EXPLORE 1

delving *n* a systematic search for the truth or facts about something — see INQUIRY 1

demagogue *also* **demagog** *n* a person who stirs up public feelings especially of discontent — see AGITATOR

demand *n* **1** something that someone insists upon having ⟨the terrorists presented their list of *demands*⟩
synonyms claim, dun, requisition, ultimatum

related words desire, request, want, wish; drive, need, requirement, stipulation; basic, essential, must; imposition; condition, provision
2 something necessary, indispensable, or unavoidable — see ESSENTIAL 1
demand *vb* **1** to ask for (something) earnestly or with authority ⟨the losing party *demanded* a recount of the votes cast in the election⟩
synonyms call (for), claim, clamor (for), command, enjoin, exact, insist (on), press (for), quest, stipulate (for)
related words ask, plead (for), request, want; cry (for), necessitate, need, require, take, warrant; requisition; impose; badger, dun, hound
near antonyms give up, relinquish, surrender, yield
2 to have as a requirement — see NEED 1
3 to set or receive as a price — see CHARGE 1
demanding *adj* **1** requiring much time, effort, or careful attention ⟨the *demanding* assignment kept them working all night⟩
synonyms arduous, burdensome, challenging, exacting, grueling (*or* gruelling), laborious, onerous, taxing, toilsome
related words difficult, formidable, hard, herculean, rough, rugged, stiff, strenuous, tough; oppressive, trying; rigid, rigorous, severe, stern, strict, stringent
near antonyms easy, effortless, facile, simple, smooth
antonyms light, undemanding
2 hard to please — see FINICKY
3 requiring considerable physical or mental effort — see HARD 2
demarcate *vb* to mark the limits of — see LIMIT 2
demarcation *n* the state of being kept distinct — see SEPARATION 2
[1]**demean** *vb* **1** to lower in character or dignity — see DEBASE 1
2 to reduce to a lower standing in one's own eyes or in others' eyes — see HUMBLE
[2]**demean** *vb* to manage the actions of (oneself) in a particular way — see BEHAVE
demeaning *adj* intended to make a person or thing seem of little importance or value — see DEROGATORY
demeanor *n* the way or manner in which one conducts oneself — see BEHAVIOR
demented *adj* having or showing a very abnormal or sick state of mind — see INSANE 1
dementia *n* a serious mental disorder that prevents one from living a safe and normal life — see INSANITY 1
demerit *n* a defect in character — see FAULT 1
demesne *n* **1** a part or portion having no fixed boundaries — see REGION 1
2 a region of activity, knowledge, or influence — see FIELD 2
3 the area around and belonging to a building — see GROUND 1
demilitarization *n* the reduction or elimination of a country's armed forces or weapons — see DISARMAMENT
demilitarize *vb* to reduce the size and strength of the armed forces of — see DISARM 1
demise *n* **1** the permanent stopping of all the vital bodily activities — see DEATH 1
2 the act of ceasing to exist — see DEATH 3
democracy *n* government in which the supreme power is held by the people and used by them directly or indirectly through representation ⟨under our *democracy* the people have some control over their lives by being able to decide who their political leaders will be⟩
synonyms republic, self-government, self-rule
related words home rule, self-determination; autonomy, sovereignty
near antonyms despotism, dictatorship, monarchy, totalitarianism, tyranny
democratic *adj* of, relating to, or favoring political democracy ⟨the *democratic* system ensured that every citizen's voice was heard⟩
synonyms popular, republican, self-governing, self-ruling
related words representative; libertarian
near antonyms autocratic, despotic, dictatorial, monarchal (*or* monarchial), monarchical (*also* monarchic), tyrannical (*also* tyrannic)
antonyms undemocratic
demolish *vb* **1** to destroy (as a building) completely by knocking down or breaking to pieces ⟨they *demolished* the old warehouse to make room for the new shopping mall⟩
synonyms raze, tear down
related words blow up, dynamite; abolish, annihilate, crack up, crush, dash, decimate, destroy, devastate, devour, dissolve, do in, eradicate, extirpate, finish, flatten, obliterate, overturn, pulverize, ravage, ruin, scourge, smash, total, unmake, waste, wipe out, wreck
near antonyms build, construct, erect, put up, raise; rebuild, renew, renovate, restore; create, fabricate, fashion, forge, form, make, manufacture, shape
2 to bring to a complete end the physical soundness, existence, or usefulness of — see DESTROY 1
3 to cause to break open or into pieces by or as if by an explosive — see BLAST 1
demolishment *n* the state or fact of being rendered nonexistent, physically unsound, or useless — see DESTRUCTION
demolition *n* the state or fact of being rendered nonexistent, physically unsound, or useless — see DESTRUCTION
demon *or* **daemon** *n* an evil spirit ⟨only in rare cases is the ancient rite of exorcism performed to cast out a troublesome *demon*⟩
synonyms devil, fiend, ghoul, imp, incubus
related words apparition, bogey (*also* bogy *or* bogie), familiar, ghost, phantasm, phantom, poltergeist, shade, shadow, specter (*or* spectre), spirit, spook, vision, wraith; brownie, dwarf, elf, faerie (*also* faery), fairy, fay, gnome, goblin, gremlin, hobgoblin, leprechaun, pixie (*also* pixy), puck, sprite, troll; monster, ogre
near antonyms angel
demoniac *also* **demoniacal** *adj* of, relating to, or worthy of an evil spirit — see FIENDISH
demonic *adj* of, relating to, or worthy of an evil spirit — see FIENDISH
demonstrable *adj* capable of being proven as true or real — see VERIFIABLE
demonstrate *vb* **1** to gain full recognition or acceptance of — see ESTABLISH 1
2 to show the existence or truth of by evidence — see PROVE 1
3 to make known (something abstract) through outward signs — see SHOW 2
4 to make plain or understandable — see EXPLAIN 1

5 to show or make clear by using examples — see ILLUSTRATE 1
demonstration *n* **1** a mass meeting for the purpose of displaying or arousing support for a cause or person — see RALLY 2
2 an outward and often exaggerated indication of something abstract (as a feeling) for effect — see SHOW 1
demonstrative *adj* showing feeling freely <my grandmother was always very *demonstrative* when we visited, showering us with hugs and kisses>
synonyms effusive, emotional, uninhibited, unreserved, unrestrained
related words dramatic, histrionic, melodramatic, theatrical; gushing, maudlin, mawkish, mushy, schmaltzy, sentimental; communicative, expansive; extroverted (*also* extraverted), outgoing; affectionate, feeling, intense, loving, passionate, sensitive, soulful, warm; blunt, candid, frank, outspoken, plain
near antonyms constrained; quiet, reticent, silent, taciturn; bashful, modest, retiring, shy; introverted, self-directed; aloof, detached, dispassionate, impassive, indifferent, phlegmatic, stolid, unconcerned, unfeeling; chilly, cold, frigid, glacial, hard-boiled, hardhearted, icy, unfriendly
antonyms inhibited, reserved, restrained, undemonstrative, unemotional
demoralization *n* **1** a sinking to a state of low moral standards and behavior — see CORRUPTION 2
2 the state of being discouraged — see DISCOURAGEMENT
demoralize *vb* **1** to deprive of courage or confidence — see UNNERVE 1
2 to lessen the courage or confidence of — see DISCOURAGE 1
demoralized *adj* having or showing lowered moral character or standards — see CORRUPT
demote *vb* to bring to a lower grade or rank <the court-martial's decision was to *demote* the officer responsible for the failed mission>
synonyms break, bust, degrade, downgrade, reduce
related words can, dismiss, fire, lay off, sack; abase, debase, demean, humble, humiliate, lower
near antonyms hire
antonyms advance, elevate, promote, raise
demount *vb* to take apart — see DISASSEMBLE
demur *n* a feeling or declaration of disapproval or dissent — see OBJECTION
demur *vb* to present an opposing opinion or argument — see OBJECT
demure *adj* **1** affecting shyness or modesty in order to attract masculine interest — see COY 1
2 not comfortable around people — see SHY 2
3 not having or showing any feelings of superiority, self-assertiveness, or showiness — see HUMBLE 1
demureness *n* the absence of any feelings of being better than others — see HUMILITY
den *n* **1** the shelter or resting place of a wild animal <the foxes hid in their *den* until the bear left the area>
synonyms burrow, hole, lair, lodge
related words nest
2 a place where a person goes to hide — see HIDEOUT
denial *n* **1** an unwillingness to grant something asked for <our principal's *denial* of our request to come to school on Halloween dressed in costumes>
synonyms disallowance, nay, no, refusal, rejection
related words decline, rebuff, repudiation; negative
near antonyms acceptance, accession, consent, leave, permission, sufferance
antonyms allowance, grant
2 a refusal to confirm the truth of a statement <the senator issued a flat *denial* of the accusation against her>
synonyms contradiction, disallowance, disavowal, disclaimer, negation, rejection, repudiation
related words disproof, rebuttal, refutation; negative
near antonyms confession; affirmation, assertion, declaration
antonyms acknowledgment (*also* acknowledgement), admission, avowal, confirmation
denizen *n* one who lives permanently in a place — see INHABITANT
denominate *vb* to give a name to — see NAME 1
denomination *n* a word or combination of words by which a person or thing is regularly known — see NAME 1
denotation *n* **1** a word or combination of words by which a person or thing is regularly known — see NAME 1
2 the idea that is conveyed or intended to be conveyed to the mind by language, symbol, or action — see MEANING 1
denotative *adj* indicating something — see INDICATIVE
denote *vb* to communicate or convey (as an idea) to the mind — see MEAN 1
denoting *adj* indicating something — see INDICATIVE
denounce *vb* **1** to declare to be morally wrong or evil — see CONDEMN 1
2 to express one's unfavorable opinion of the worth or quality of — see CRITICIZE
3 to express public or formal disapproval of — see CENSURE 1
dense *adj* **1** having little space between items or parts — see CLOSE 1
2 not having or showing an ability to absorb ideas readily — see STUPID 1
denseness *n* the quality or state of lacking intelligence or quickness of mind — see STUPIDITY 1
density *n* **1** the degree to which a fluid can resist flowing — see CONSISTENCY
2 the quality or state of lacking intelligence or quickness of mind — see STUPIDITY 1
dent *n* a sunken area forming a separate space — see HOLE 2
dented *adj* curved inward — see HOLLOW
denuded *adj* lacking a usual or natural covering — see NAKED 2
denunciation *n* an often public or formal expression of disapproval — see CENSURE
deny *vb* **1** to declare not to be true <the congressman *denied* all charges of wrongdoing>
synonyms contradict, disallow, disavow, disclaim, gainsay, negate, negative, reject, repudiate
related words disown, renounce; challenge, confute, disprove, rebut, refute; disagree (with), dispute

near antonyms accept, adopt, embrace, espouse; affirm, announce, assert, aver, claim, declare, maintain, profess, submit; authenticate, corroborate, substantiate, validate, verify
antonyms acknowledge, admit, allow, avow, concede, confirm, own
2 to be unwilling to grant ⟨he *denied* access to the top secret files to the nosy reporters⟩
synonyms decline, disallow, refuse, reject, withhold
related words rebuff, repel, spurn; check, constrain, hold, keep, restrain, restrict
near antonyms afford, furnish, give, provide, supply
antonyms allow, concede, grant, let, permit
depart *vb* **1** to leave a place often for another — see GO 2
2 to stop living — see DIE 1
departed *adj* **1** no longer existing — see EXTINCT
2 no longer living — see DEAD 1
departing *n* the act of leaving a place — see DEPARTURE
department *n* **1** a large unit of a governmental, business, or educational organization — see DIVISION 2
2 a region of activity, knowledge, or influence — see FIELD 2
departure *n* the act of leaving a place ⟨his sudden *departure* left them wondering if they'd upset him⟩
synonyms decamping, decampment, departing, exit, exiting, farewell, going, leave-taking, lighting out, parting, quitting, walking out
related words flight, retirement, retreat, running away, withdrawal; emigration, evacuation, exodus; egress; abandonment, forsaking, relinquishment
near antonyms advent, coming; entrance, ingress
antonyms arrival
depend *vb* **1** to be determined by, based on, or subject (to) ⟨whether or not we play baseball will *depend* on how much rain we get⟩
synonyms hang, hinge
related words base, establish, found, rest, stay; ground
2 to place reliance or trust ⟨I know I can always *depend* on you for help when I really need it⟩
synonyms count, lean, reckon, rely
related words commit, confide, entrust, trust
phrases bank on, figure on
near antonyms distrust, mistrust
dependability *n* worthiness as the recipient of another's trust or confidence — see RELIABILITY
dependable *adj* worthy of one's trust ⟨Boy Scouts are supposed to be always *dependable*⟩
synonyms good, reliable, responsible, safe, solid, steady, sure, tried, tried-and-true, true, trustworthy, trusty
related words constant, devoted, faithful, fast, loyal, staunch (*or* stanch), steadfast; honest, sincere, single-minded; infallible, unerring; firm, sound, strong; effective, telling; attested, authenticated, confirmed, proven, valid, validated, verified; blameless, irreproachable, unimpeachable, unquestionable
near antonyms disloyal, faithless, false, unfaithful; deceitful, dishonest; doubtful, dubious, questionable, suspect, uncertain, unsound; hazardous, risky; unauthenticated, unconfirmed, untried, unverified
antonyms irresponsible, undependable, unreliable, untrustworthy
dependence *n* **1** the quality or state of needing something or someone ⟨a baby's total *dependence* upon his or her parents for every one of life's needs⟩
synonyms dependency, reliance
related words reciprocity, relativity; confidence, faith, stock, trust
near antonyms autonomy, sovereignty
antonyms independence, self-reliance
2 something or someone to which one looks for support ⟨ultimately rice became the chief *dependence* in that state⟩
synonyms buttress, mainstay, pillar, reliance, standby, support
related words backbone, spine; crutch, prop, stay
dependency *n* the quality or state of needing something or someone — see DEPENDENCE 1
dependent *adj* **1** extending freely from a support from above ⟨the *dependent* willow branches swayed in the gentle breeze⟩
synonyms dangling, hanging, pendent (*or* pendant), pendulous
2 determined by something else ⟨our going to the movies tonight is *dependent* on whether or not we have any money left after we eat out⟩
synonyms conditional, contingent (on *or* upon), subject (to), tentative
related words liable, open, susceptible; limited, modified, qualified, restricted; doubtful, iffy, problematic (*also* problematical), questionable, uncertain
near antonyms absolute, categorical (*also* categoric), ultimate; basal, basic, fundamental, primary
antonyms independent, unconditional
depict *vb* **1** to give a representation or account of in words — see DESCRIBE 1
2 to point out the chief quality or qualities of an individual or group — see CHARACTERIZE 1
3 to present a picture of — see PICTURE 1
depiction *n* a vivid representation in words of someone or something — see DESCRIPTION 1
deplete *vb* to make complete use of ⟨miners *depleted* the vein of copper ore after months of working⟩
synonyms clean (out), consume, drain, exhaust, expend, spend, use up
related words decrease, diminish, lessen, reduce; eat, use; bankrupt, impoverish; cripple, debilitate, disable, enfeeble, sap, undermine, weaken; dry up, empty; dissipate, squander, waste
near antonyms augment, enlarge, increase; bolster, fortify, reinforce, strengthen; rebuild, repair, restore, revive
antonyms renew, replace
deplorable *adj* of a kind to cause great distress — see REGRETTABLE
deplore *vb* **1** to feel or express sorrow for — see LAMENT 1
2 to feel sorry or dissatisfied about — see REGRET
deploring *adj* expressing or suggesting mourning — see MOURNFUL 1
deport *vb* **1** to force to leave a country — see BANISH 1
2 to manage the actions of (oneself) in a particular way — see BEHAVE
deportation *n* the forced removal from a homeland — see EXILE 1

deportee *n* a person forced to emigrate for political reasons — see ÉMIGRÉ 1
deportment *n* the way or manner in which one conducts oneself — see BEHAVIOR
depose *vb* **1** to remove from a position of prominence or power (as a throne) ⟨they *deposed* the dictator after he had bankrupted the country⟩
synonyms dethrone, oust, uncrown, unmake, unseat, unthrone
related words discharge, dismiss; overthrow, usurp, subvert, topple; eject, throw out
near antonyms inaugurate, induct, install, instate, invest; appoint, designate, elect
antonyms crown, enthrone, throne
2 to make a solemn declaration under oath for the purpose of establishing a fact — see TESTIFY
deposit *n* **1** matter that settles to the bottom of a body of liquid ⟨a *deposit* of silt on the river bed⟩
synonyms deposition, dregs, grounds, precipitate, sediment
related words lees; ooze, sludge; dross, slag, waste
2 a collection of things kept available for future use or need — see STORE 1
3 a sum of money set aside for a particular purpose — see FUND 1
deposit *vb* **1** to put in an account ⟨we *deposited* the check in a bank account⟩
synonyms bank
related words cache, hoard, lay away, reserve, salt away, save, squirrel (away), stash, store, stow; invest
near antonyms remove, take out; disburse, expend, lay out, spend
antonyms withdraw
2 to arrange something in a certain spot or position — see PLACE 1
deposition *n* matter that settles to the bottom of a body of liquid — see DEPOSIT 1
depository *n* a building for storing goods — see STOREHOUSE
depot *n* **1** a building for storing goods — see STOREHOUSE
2 a place where military arms are stored — see ARMORY
deprave *vb* to lower in character or dignity — see DEBASE 1
depraved *adj* having or showing lowered moral character or standards — see CORRUPT
depravedness *n* the state or quality of being utterly evil — see ENORMITY 1
depravity *n* **1** a sinking to a state of low moral standards and behavior — see CORRUPTION 2
2 immoral conduct or practices harmful or offensive to society — see VICE 1
3 the state or quality of being utterly evil — see ENORMITY 1
deprecate *vb* **1** to express scornfully one's low opinion of — see DECRY 1
2 to hold an unfavorable opinion of — see DISAPPROVE
deprecation *n* **1** refusal to accept as right or desirable — see DISAPPROVAL
2 the act of making a person or a thing seem little or unimportant — see DEPRECIATION
depreciate *vb* **1** to lower the price or value of ⟨a faded finish will really *depreciate* your car when you decide to trade it in⟩
synonyms cheapen, depress, mark down, write off
related words underrate, undervalue; abate, abridge, compress, contract, de-escalate, deflate, diminish, dwindle, lessen, lower, moderate, reduce, shrink
near antonyms bloat, blow up, inflate; add, aggrandize, amplify, augment, balloon, boost, dilate, enlarge, escalate, expand, extend, heighten, increase, maximize, raise, swell
antonyms appreciate, mark up
2 to express scornfully one's low opinion of — see DECRY 1
depreciation *n* the act of making a person or a thing seem little or unimportant ⟨the boys' *depreciation* of the girls' basketball victories only showed how jealous they were⟩
synonyms belittlement, deprecation, detraction, diminishment, disparagement, put-down
related words aspersion, backbiting, defamation, libel, slander, vilification; derision, mockery, ridicule; abuse, invective, vituperation; censure, condemnation, denunciation
near antonyms acclaim, praise; approbation, approval, commendation
antonyms aggrandizement, ennoblement, exaltation, glorification, magnification
depreciative *adj* intended to make a person or thing seem of little importance or value — see DEROGATORY
depreciatory *adj* intended to make a person or thing seem of little importance or value — see DEROGATORY
depress *vb* **1** to make sad ⟨the thought of failing the test *depressed* me⟩
synonyms burden, oppress, sadden
related words ail, distress, trouble; afflict, torment, torture; discourage, dishearten, dispirit; bother, disquiet, disturb, perturb, upset
near antonyms animate, enliven, invigorate; comfort, console, solace; excite, inspire, stimulate; elate, exhilarate; encourage, hearten; delight, gratify, please
antonyms brighten, buoy, cheer, gladden
2 to cause to fall intentionally or unintentionally — see DROP 1
3 to lower the price or value of — see DEPRECIATE 1
4 to push steadily against with some force — see PRESS 1
depressed *adj* **1** curved inward — see HOLLOW
2 feeling unhappiness — see SAD 1
depressing *adj* **1** causing or marked by an atmosphere lacking in cheer — see GLOOMY 1
2 causing unhappiness — see SAD 2
depression *n* **1** a period of decreased economic activity ⟨during the 1930s the U.S. suffered a great *depression*⟩
synonyms recession, slump
related words crash, panic; stagnation
near antonyms development, growth; advancement, progress
antonyms boom
2 a state or spell of low spirits — see SADNESS
3 a sunken area forming a separate space — see HOLE 2
deprivation *n* the state of being robbed of something normally enjoyed — see PRIVATION
deprived *adj* kept from having the necessities of life or a healthful environment ⟨*deprived* children growing up in the slums⟩
synonyms disadvantaged, underprivileged
related words impoverished, needy, poor; hapless, ill-fated, ill-starred, unfortunate, unlucky

near antonyms fortunate, lucky; affluent, rich, wealthy; coddled, indulged, pampered, spoiled
antonyms privileged

depth *n* **1** distance measured from the top to the bottom of something ⟨be sure to check the *depth* of the water before diving off the dock⟩
synonyms drop
related words lowness; draft, sounding
near antonyms shallowness; altitude, elevation, height
2 the quality of being great in extent (as of insight) ⟨the *depth* of the poet's understanding of human nature has given his works a timeless appeal⟩
synonyms profoundness, profundity
related words discernment, sense, wisdom; brain, intellect, intelligence; acuteness, keenness, penetration, sharpness
near antonyms shallowness, superficiality; smattering
3 the most intense or characteristic phase of something — see THICK

depthless *adj* lacking significant physical depth — see SHALLOW 1

depute *vb* to appoint as one's representative — see DELEGATE 1

deputize *vb* to appoint as one's representative — see DELEGATE 1

deputy *n* **1** a person who acts or does business for another — see AGENT 2
2 a person who helps a more skilled person — see HELPER

derange *vb* **1** to cause to go insane or as if insane — see CRAZE
2 to undo the proper order or arrangement of — see DISORDER

deranged *adj* having or showing a very abnormal or sick state of mind — see INSANE 1

derangement *n* **1** a serious mental disorder that prevents one from living a safe and normal life — see INSANITY 1
2 an act or instance of the order of things being disturbed — see UPSET

derelict *adj* **1** failing to give proper care and attention — see NEGLIGENT
2 left unoccupied or unused — see ABANDONED

dereliction *n* **1** the act of abandoning ⟨the family's shameful *dereliction* of their pets at the end of the summer season⟩
synonyms abandonment, desertion, forsaking
related words defection; discard, dumping, jettison
near antonyms retention
antonyms reclamation
2 failure to take the care that a cautious person usually takes — see NEGLIGENCE 1
3 the nonperformance of an assigned or expected action — see FAILURE 1

deride *vb* to make (someone or something) the object of unkind laughter — see RIDICULE

derision *n* the making of unkind jokes as a way of showing one's scorn for someone or something — see RIDICULE

derisive *adj* so foolish or pointless as to be worthy of scornful laughter — see RIDICULOUS 1

derisory *adj* so foolish or pointless as to be worthy of scornful laughter — see RIDICULOUS 1

derivable *adj* being or provable by reasoning in which the conclusion follows necessarily from given information — see DEDUCTIVE

derivative *adj* taken or created from something original or basic — see SECONDARY 1

derivative *n* something that naturally develops or is developed from something else ⟨the whole field of industrial robots is a *derivative* of technology developed for the space program⟩
synonyms by-product, offshoot, outgrowth, spin-off
related words descendant (*or* descendent); aftermath, consequence, result; aftereffect, side effect; copy, duplicate, facsimile, replica, reproduction
near antonyms archetype, original, prototype; antecedent, cause, determinant
antonyms origin, root, source

derogatory *adj* intended to make a person or thing seem of little importance or value ⟨fans made a steady stream of *derogatory* remarks about the players on the visiting team⟩
synonyms belittling, contemptuous, decrying, degrading, demeaning, depreciative, depreciatory, disdainful, disparaging, scornful, slighting, uncomplimentary
related words aspersing, defamatory, detractive, insulting, libelous, maligning, slandering, slanderous, vilifying; abusive, opprobrious, scurrilous; despiteful, malevolent, malicious, spiteful
near antonyms admiring, adulatory, laudatory; appreciative, respectful
antonyms commendatory, complimentary

descant *vb* **1** to give a formal often extended talk on a subject — see TALK 1
2 to produce musical sounds with the voice — see SING 1

descend *vb* **1** to lead or extend downward ⟨the pathway *descends* to the river bank⟩
synonyms decline, dip, drop, fall, plunge
related words cant, incline, lean, list, recline, slant, slope, tilt, tip
near antonyms even, flatten, level, straighten
antonyms ascend, climb, rise
2 to become worse or of less value — see DETERIORATE
3 to go to a lower level — see DROP 2

descend (on *or* upon) *vb* to take sudden, violent action against — see ATTACK 1

descendant *or* **descendent** *adj* bending downward or forward — see NODDING

descending *adj* bending downward or forward — see NODDING

descent *n* **1** the act or process of going to a lower level or altitude ⟨the airplane began its gradual *descent* to the landing field⟩
synonyms dip, dive, down, drop, fall, nosedive, plunge
related words comedown, downfall, downgrade; sinking
near antonyms advance, headway, progress, progression; betterment, improvement
antonyms ascent, climb, rise, upswing, upturn
2 a gradual sinking and wasting away of mind or body — see DECLINE 1
3 a change to a lower state or level — see DECLINE 2
4 a loss of status — see COMEDOWN
5 a sudden attack on and entrance into hostile territory — see RAID 1
6 the act or action of setting upon with force or violence — see ATTACK 1
7 the line of ancestors from whom a person is descended — see ANCESTRY

describe *vb* **1** to give a representation or account of in words <he tried to *describe* the dream he had last night as accurately as he could>
synonyms delineate, depict, draw, image, paint, picture, portray, sketch
related words characterize, qualify, represent; demonstrate, illustrate; narrate, recite, recount, relate; display, exhibit, show; hint, suggest; draft, outline
near antonyms color, distort, falsify, garble, misrepresent, pervert, twist, warp
2 to give an oral or written account of in some detail — see TELL 1
3 to point out the chief quality or qualities of an individual or group — see CHARACTERIZE 1
description *n* **1** a vivid representation in words of someone or something <we recognized his cousin from his *description*>
synonyms delineation, depiction, picture, portrait, portrayal, sketch
related words account, chronicle, narrative, report, story, tale; demonstration, exemplification, illustration
2 a number of persons or things that are grouped together because they have something in common — see SORT 1
descry *vb* **1** to come upon after searching, study, or effort — see FIND 1
2 to make note of (something) through the use of one's eyes — see SEE 1
desecrate *vb* to treat (a sacred place or object) shamefully or with great disrespect <vandals *desecrated* the cemetery last night with graffiti>
synonyms defile, profane, violate
related words blaspheme, curse, swear; befoul, contaminate, foul, pollute; affront, insult, offend; crush, decimate, demolish, destroy, devastate, ravage, raze, ruin, waste, wreck; despoil, loot, pillage, plunder, raid, ransack, rob, sack, spoil, strip
near antonyms bless, consecrate, dedicate, hallow, sanctify; honor, respect; cleanse, purify
desecration *n* an act of great disrespect shown to God or to sacred ideas, people, or things — see BLASPHEMY
[1]**desert** *n* land that is uninhabited or not fit for crops — see WASTELAND
[2]**desert** *n* suffering, loss, or hardship imposed in response to a crime or offense — see PUNISHMENT
desert *vb* **1** to leave (a cause or party) often in order to take up another — see DEFECT
2 to cause to remain behind — see LEAVE 1
deserted *adj* left unoccupied or unused — see ABANDONED
deserter *n* a person who abandons a cause or organization usually without right — see RENEGADE
desertion *n* the act of abandoning — see DERELICTION 1
deserve *vb* to be or make worthy of (as a reward or punishment) — see EARN 2
deserved *adj* being what is called for by accepted standards of right and wrong — see JUST 1
deserving *adj* having sufficient worth or merit to receive one's honor, esteem, or reward — see WORTHY
desex *vb* to remove the sex organs of — see NEUTER
design *n* **1** a method worked out in advance for achieving some objective — see PLAN 1
2 a secret plan for accomplishing evil or unlawful ends — see PLOT 1
3 something that one hopes or intends to accomplish — see GOAL
4 a unit of decoration that is repeated all over something (as a fabric) — see PATTERN 1
5 the way in which the elements of something (as a work of art) are arranged — see COMPOSITION 3
design *vb* **1** to have in mind as a purpose or goal — see INTEND
2 to work out the details of (something) in advance — see PLAN 1
designate *vb* **1** to decide upon (the time or date for an event) usually from a position of authority — see APPOINT 1
2 to pick (someone) by one's authority for a specific position or duty — see APPOINT 2
3 to give a name to — see NAME 1
designation *n* **1** a word or combination of words by which a person or thing is regularly known — see NAME 1
2 the state or fact of being chosen for a position or duty — see APPOINTMENT 1
designedly *adv* with full awareness of what one is doing — see INTENTIONALLY
designer *n* one who creates or introduces something new — see INVENTOR
desirable *adj* suitable for bringing about a desired result under the circumstances — see EXPEDIENT
desire *n* a strong wish for something <a *desire* for adventure and excitement prompted him to travel to Africa>
synonyms appetite, craving, drive, hankering, hunger, itch, longing, lust, passion, pining, thirst, urge, yearning, yen
related words compulsion, impulse, urge, will, zeal; liking, love, taste; eagerness, impatience; wish, want; necessity, need, requirement; avarice, cupidity, greed, rapacity
near antonyms abhorrence, aversion, disfavor, disgust, dislike, distaste, hatred, repugnance, repulsion; apathy, indifference, unconcern
desire *vb* to have an earnest wish to own or enjoy <he greatly *desired* a new mountain bike for his next birthday>
synonyms ache (for), covet, crave, die (for), hanker (for *or* after), hunger (for), itch (for), long (for), lust (for *or* after), pant (after), pine (for), repine (for), sigh (for), thirst (for), want, wish (for), yearn (for)
related words delight (in), enjoy, fancy, like, relish
near antonyms abhor, abominate, detest, hate, loathe; decline, refuse, reject, spurn
desirous *adj* showing urgent desire or interest — see EAGER
desirousness *n* urgent desire or interest — see EAGERNESS
desist (from) *vb* to bring (as an action or operation) to an immediate end — see STOP 1
desk *n* a large unit of a governmental, business, or educational organization — see DIVISION 2
desolate *adj* **1** causing or marked by an atmosphere lacking in cheer — see GLOOMY 1
2 sad from lack of companionship or separation from others — see LONESOME 1
desolate *vb* to bring to a complete end the physical soundness, existence, or usefulness of — see DESTROY 1
desolation *n* **1** a state or spell of low spirits — see SADNESS

2 land that is uninhabited or not fit for crops — see WASTELAND

3 the state of being unattended to or not cared for — see NEGLECT 1

4 the state or fact of being rendered nonexistent, physically unsound, or useless — see DESTRUCTION

despair *n* **1** utter loss of hope ⟨the endless drought drove the farmers to *despair*⟩

synonyms desperation, despondency, forlornness, hopelessness

related words blues, depression, dejection, desolation, doldrums, dolor, downheartedness, dumps, gloom, melancholy, mopes, oppression, sadness, sorrow, unhappiness; cynicism, pessimism; acceptance, resignation

near antonyms cheer, cheerfulness, sunniness; optimism

antonyms hope, hopefulness

2 the state of being discouraged — see DISCOURAGEMENT

despair *vb* to lose all hope or confidence ⟨we *despaired* when we saw how little time we had left to complete our project⟩

synonyms despond

related words give up, surrender, yield; darken, sadden; grieve, mourn, sorrow; discourage, dishearten, dispirit

near antonyms assure, encourage, hearten, reassure; hope

antonyms brighten, cheer (up), perk (up)

despairing *adj* emphasizing or expecting the worst — see PESSIMISTIC 1

desperation *n* utter loss of hope — see DESPAIR 1

despicable *adj* **1** arousing or deserving of one's loathing and disgust — see CONTEMPTIBLE 1

2 not following or in accordance with standards of honor and decency — see IGNOBLE 2

3 deserving pitying scorn (as for inadequacy) — see PITIFUL 1

despise *vb* **1** to dislike strongly — see HATE

2 to ignore in a disrespectful manner — see SCORN 2

despite *n* **1** open dislike for someone or something considered unworthy of one's concern or respect — see CONTEMPT

2 the desire to cause pain for the satisfaction of doing harm — see MALICE

despite *prep* without being prevented by ⟨we went to the party *despite* the bad weather outside⟩

synonyms notwithstanding, with

phrases in despite of, in spite of

despiteful *adj* having or showing a desire to cause someone pain or suffering for the sheer enjoyment of it — see HATEFUL

despitefully *adv* in a mean or spiteful manner — see NASTILY

despitefulness *n* open dislike for someone or something considered unworthy of one's concern or respect — see CONTEMPT

despoil *vb* to search through with the intent of committing robbery — see RANSACK 1

despond *vb* to lose all hope or confidence — see DESPAIR

despondency *n* **1** a state or spell of low spirits — see SADNESS

2 the state of being discouraged — see DISCOURAGEMENT

3 utter loss of hope — see DESPAIR 1

despondent *adj* feeling unhappiness — see SAD 1

despot *n* a person who uses power or authority in a cruel, unjust, or harmful way ⟨the *despot* threw anyone who dared to criticize his rule into jail⟩

synonyms autocrat, dictator, oppressor, potentate, tyrant

related words dominator, master, overlord, ruler; king, lord, monarch, prince, queen, sovereign; baron, czar (*also* tsar *or* tzar), magnate, mogul, tycoon; authoritarian, disciplinarian, discipliner, martinet

despotic *adj* **1** exercising power or authority without interference by others — see ABSOLUTE 1

2 fond of ordering people around — see BOSSY

despotism *n* a system of government in which the ruler has unlimited power ⟨by the end of the 20th century many countries around the world had rejected *despotism* in favor of democracy⟩

synonyms autocracy, dictatorship, totalitarianism, tyranny

related words monarchy; authoritarianism, fascism; domination, oppression

near antonyms democracy; freedom; anarchy

destine *vb* to determine the fate of in advance ⟨his extreme height seemed to *destine* him for a career in basketball⟩

synonyms doom, fate, foredoom, foreordain, ordain, predestine, predetermine

related words forecast, foretell, predict, prognosticate, prophesy; preconceive, prejudge; condemn, sentence

destiny *n* a state or end that seemingly has been decided beforehand — see FATE 1

destitute *adj* **1** lacking money or material possessions — see POOR 1

2 utterly lacking in something needed, wanted, or expected — see DEVOID 1

destitution *n* the state of lacking sufficient money or material possessions — see POVERTY 1

destroy *vb* **1** to bring to a complete end the physical soundness, existence, or usefulness of ⟨they practically *destroyed* the safe in order to get at the money inside⟩ ⟨their poor scores on the final exam *destroyed* any chance they might have had to pass the course⟩

synonyms annihilate, decimate, demolish, desolate, devastate, do in, extinguish, pulverize, raze, ruin, shatter, smash, tear down, waste, wreck

related words gut; beat, best, clobber, conquer, crush, defeat, lick, master, overbear, overcome, prevail (over), scotch, subdue, surmount, thrash, triumph (over), win (against); blow up, break, damage, deface, disintegrate, dynamite, mangle, mar, mutilate, spoil, vitiate; erode, scour, wash out, wear (away); dismantle, undo, unmake; blot out, eradicate, exterminate, extirpate, obliterate, remove, rub out, stamp (out), wipe out; despoil, loot, pillage, plunder, ravage, sack, vandalize; assassinate, butcher, cut down, dispatch, execute, kill, massacre, murder, slaughter, slay, zap

near antonyms create, invent; fabricate, fashion, forge, form, make, manufacture, shape; bring about, establish, found, institute, organize; conserve, preserve, protect, save; rebuild, reconstruct, remodel, renovate, restore

antonyms build, construct, erect, put up, raise

2 to bring destruction to (something) through violent action — see RAVAGE

3 to deprive of life — see KILL 1

destruction *n* the state or fact of being rendered nonexistent, physically unsound, or useless ⟨the

violent storm resulted in the *destruction* of their tree house⟩
synonyms annihilation, decimation, demolishment, demolition, desolation, devastation, extermination, extinction, havoc, loss, obliteration, ruin, ruination, wastage, wreckage
related words depredation, despoilment, despoliation; breakup, disintegration, dissolution; assassination, execution, killing, massacre, slaughter
near antonyms conservation, preservation, protection; reconstruction, re-creation, remodeling, renovation, restoration
antonyms building, construction, erection, raising

destructive *adj* **1** causing or tending to cause destruction ⟨the *destructive* storm blew down trees all over town, and blew the roof off our neighbor's house⟩
synonyms calamitous, cataclysmal (*or* cataclysmic), devastating, disastrous, ruinous
related words deadly, fatal, lethal, mortal, vital; deleterious, detrimental, harmful, pernicious
near antonyms preservative, protective; creative, formative; harmless, innocuous, inoffensive, nondestructive; ameliorative, helpful, useful
antonyms constructive
2 bringing about ruin or misfortune — see FATAL 1

desultorily *adv* without definite aim, direction, rule, or method — see HIT OR MISS

desultory *adj* **1** lacking a definite plan, purpose, or pattern — see RANDOM
2 passing from one topic to another — see DISCURSIVE

detached *adj* **1** having or showing a lack of friendliness or interest in others — see COOL 1
2 not physically attached to another unit — see SEPARATE 2

detachment *n* **1** lack of favoritism toward one side or another ⟨the judge showed great *detachment* when deciding the controversial case⟩
synonyms disinterestedness, impartiality, neutrality, objectivity
related words equitableness, fairness; apathy, indifference, unconcern; broad-mindedness, open-mindedness, tolerance
near antonyms chauvinism, nepotism; subjectivity; bent, inclination, leaning, penchant, predilection, predisposition, proclivity, propensity, tendency; preconception, prejudgment
antonyms bias, favor, favoritism, one-sidedness, partiality, partisanship, prejudice
2 a small military unit with a special task or function ⟨the general sent a *detachment* ahead to scout the enemy's position⟩
synonyms detail
related words commando, firing squad, paratroops, patrol, picket; battalion, command, company, corps, division, platoon, regiment, squad, troop, wing

detail *n* **1** a separate part in a list, account, or series — see ITEM 1
2 a single piece of information — see FACT 3
3 a small military unit with a special task or function — see DETACHMENT 2

detail *vb* **1** to assign to a place or position — see [2]POST
2 to pick (someone) by one's authority for a specific position or duty — see APPOINT 2
3 to specify one after another — see ENUMERATE 1

detailed *adj* **1** including many small descriptive features ⟨a *detailed* report on all the activities that their Scout troop had been involved in over the past year⟩
synonyms circumstantial, elaborate, full, minute, particularized, thorough
related words enumerated, inventoried, itemized, listed; delineated, specific, specified; abundant, copious; comprehensive, exhausting, exhaustive, thoroughgoing; accurate, exact, precise; complete, entire, replete; distinct, explicit, precise, sharp; inclusive, mapped (out); descriptive, graphic (*also* graphical), picturesque, vivid
near antonyms concise, pithy, short, succinct; abbreviated, abridged, curtailed, cut, pruned, shortened, trimmed; indeterminate, nebulous, nondescript, sketchy, vague; bird's-eye, broad, general, nonspecific, overall, unspecified
antonyms compendious, summary
2 made or done with great care or with much detail — see ELABORATE 1

detailedly *adv* with attention to all aspects or details — see THOROUGHLY 1

detainment *n* an instance or period of being prevented from going about one's business — see DELAY

detect *vb* to come upon after searching, study, or effort — see FIND 1

detectable *adj* able to be perceived by a sense or by the mind — see PERCEPTIBLE

detection *n* the act or process of sighting or learning the existence of something for the first time — see DISCOVERY 1

detective *n* a person whose business is solving crimes and catching criminals or gathering information that is not easy to get ⟨the *detective* tracked the criminals to an abandoned warehouse on the south side of town⟩
synonyms investigator, operative, plainclothesman, shadow, sleuth, tail
related words Federal, G-man, narc (*or* nark) [*slang*]

detector *n* a device that detects some physical quantity and responds usually with a transmitted signal — see SENSOR

deter *vb* to steer (a person) from an activity or course of action — see DISCOURAGE 2

detergent *n* a substance used for cleaning — see CLEANER

deteriorate *vb* to become worse or of less value ⟨the garden slowly *deteriorated* after months of neglect⟩
synonyms crumble, decay, decline, degenerate, descend, ebb, rot, sink, worsen
related words recede, wane; decompose, degrade, disintegrate; sour, spoil; lessen, lower, reduce; debilitate, undermine, weaken
phrases go to pot
near antonyms better, upgrade; enhance, enrich, fortify, heighten, intensify, strengthen; advance, develop, progress
antonyms ameliorate, improve, meliorate

deterioration *n* **1** a gradual sinking and wasting away of mind or body — see DECLINE 1
2 a change to a lower state or level — see DECLINE 2

determinate *adj* **1** having been established and usually not subject to change — see FIXED 1
2 having distinct or certain limits — see LIMITED 1

determination *n* **1** firm or unwavering adherence

to one's purpose ⟨the *determination* with which the pioneers settled the land despite many hardships and setbacks⟩
synonyms decidedness, decision, decisiveness, firmness, granite, purposefulness, resoluteness, resolution, resolve
related words doggedness, obstinacy, perseverance, persistence, stubbornness, tenaciousness, tenacity; backbone, fortitude, grit, pluck
near antonyms uncertainty
antonyms hesitation, indecision, irresolution, vacillation
2 a position arrived at after consideration — see DECISION 1
3 an opinion arrived at through a process of reasoning — see CONCLUSION 1

determine *vb* **1** to give an opinion about (something at issue or in dispute) — see JUDGE 1
2 to come to a judgment after discussion or consideration — see DECIDE 1
3 to come upon after searching, study, or effort — see FIND 1

determined *adj* **1** fully committed to achieving a goal ⟨his *determined* opponent would not be bluffed or shaken⟩
synonyms bent (on *or* upon), bound, decisive, firm, intent, purposeful, resolute, resolved, set
related words certain, cocksure, positive, sure; earnest, serious; steady, unfaltering, unhesitating, unswerving, unwavering
near antonyms doubtful, dubious, uncertain, unsure
antonyms faltering, hesitant, indecisive, irresolute, undetermined, unresolved, vacillating, wavering
2 showing no signs of slackening or yielding in one's purpose — see UNYIELDING 1

determinedly *adv* with great effort or determination — see HARD 1

deterrent *n* something that makes movement or progress more difficult — see ENCUMBRANCE

detest *vb* to dislike strongly — see HATE

detestable *adj* not following or in accordance with standards of honor and decency — see IGNOBLE 2

dethrone *vb* to remove from a position of prominence or power (as a throne) — see DEPOSE 1

detonate *vb* to break open or into pieces usually because of internal pressure — see EXPLODE 1

detonation *n* the act or an instance of exploding — see EXPLOSION 1

detour *vb* **1** to avoid by going around ⟨we had to *detour* the construction zone in order to get to the stadium⟩
synonyms bypass, circumvent, skirt
related words circumnavigate; avoid, dodge, duck, elude, escape, eschew, evade, shake, shun
near antonyms confront, face, meet; accept, court, embrace, pursue, seek, welcome
2 to change one's course or direction — see TURN 3

detraction *n* the act of making a person or a thing seem little or unimportant — see DEPRECIATION

detriment *n* something that causes loss or pain — see INJURY 1

detrimental *adj* causing or capable of causing harm — see HARMFUL

devastate *vb* **1** to bring destruction to (something) through violent action — see RAVAGE
2 to bring to a complete end the physical soundness, existence, or usefulness of — see DESTROY 1
3 to subject to incapacitating emotional or mental stress — see OVERWHELM 1

devastating *adj* causing or tending to cause destruction — see DESTRUCTIVE 1

devastation *n* the state or fact of being rendered nonexistent, physically unsound, or useless — see DESTRUCTION

develop *vb* **1** to gradually become clearer or more detailed ⟨as the story of the bombing *developed*, the scope of the tragedy became more apparent⟩
synonyms evolve, unfold
related words advance, proceed, progress; mature, ripen; materialize
2 to come to have gradually ⟨they *developed* a taste for green olives⟩
synonyms acquire, cultivate, form
related words gain, get, obtain; achieve, attain, reach; foster, nourish, nurture, promote
antonyms lose
3 to become mature — see MATURE
4 to express more fully and in greater detail — see EXPAND 1

developed *adj* being far along in development — see ADVANCED 1

developer *n* one who creates or introduces something new — see INVENTOR

development *n* **1** the act or process of going from the simple or basic to the complex or advanced ⟨the *development* of an idea into a marketable product⟩
synonyms elaboration, evolution, expansion, growth, progress, progression
related words advancement, betterment, improvement, perfection, refinement; maturation
near antonyms decadence, decay, decaying, declension, decline, degeneration, descent, deterioration, downgrade, ebbing, weakening
antonyms regression, retrogression
2 a condition or occurrence traceable to a cause — see EFFECT 1
3 the process of becoming mature — see MATURATION

deviant *adj* departing from some accepted standard of what is normal ⟨some studies show that many violent criminals begin exhibiting *deviant* behavior in early childhood⟩
synonyms aberrant, abnormal, anomalous, atypical, irregular, unnatural
related words extraordinary, preternatural; rare, uncommon, uncustomary, unusual, unwonted; odd, peculiar, strange, weird
near antonyms common, familiar, ordinary; customary, usual, wonted
antonyms natural, normal, regular, standard, typical

deviant *n* a person who does not conform to generally accepted standards or customs — see NONCONFORMIST 1

deviate *vb* to change one's course or direction — see TURN 3

device *n* **1** a clever often underhanded means to achieve an end — see TRICK 1
2 an article intended for use in work — see IMPLEMENT
3 devices *pl* a habitual attraction to some activity or thing — see INCLINATION 1

devil *n* **1** *cap* the supreme personification of evil often represented as the ruler of Hell ⟨the *Devil* is traditionally seen as a being who relentlessly tempts people to commit evil⟩

synonyms Lucifer, Satan
related words deuce, dickens
phrases Prince of Darkness
2 an evil spirit — see DEMON
3 a member of the human race — see HUMAN
4 an appealingly mischievous person — see SCAMP 1
5 a mean, evil, or unprincipled person — see VILLAIN

devilfish *n* any of several extremely large rays <they saw a *devilfish* when they went scuba diving in the Caribbean, but it swam away quickly>
synonyms devil ray, manta, manta ray, sea devil
related words ray, skate

devilish *adj* **1** going beyond a normal or acceptable limit in degree or amount — see EXCESSIVE
2 of, relating to, or worthy of an evil spirit — see FIENDISH
3 tending to or exhibiting reckless playfulness — see MISCHIEVOUS 1

devilishly *adv* beyond a normal or acceptable limit — see TOO 1

devilishness *n* playful, reckless behavior that is not intended to cause serious harm — see MISCHIEF 1

devil–may–care *adj* **1** having a relaxed, casual manner — see EASYGOING 1
2 having or showing a lack of concern or seriousness — see CAREFREE
3 having or showing a lack of concern for the consequences of one's actions — see RECKLESS 1

devilment *n* playful, reckless behavior that is not intended to cause serious harm — see MISCHIEF 1

devil ray *n* any of several extremely large rays — see DEVILFISH

devilry *or* **deviltry** *n* playful, reckless behavior that is not intended to cause serious harm — see MISCHIEF 1

devious *adj* **1** clever at attaining one's ends by indirect and often deceptive means — see ARTFUL 1
2 marked by a long series of irregular curves — see CROOKED 1

deviousness *n* skill in achieving one's ends through indirect, subtle, or underhanded means — see CUNNING 1

devise *vb* to create or think of by clever use of the imagination — see INVENT

deviser *n* one who creates or introduces something new — see INVENTOR

devoid *adj* **1** utterly lacking in something needed, wanted, or expected <the so-called comedy is totally *devoid* of intelligence, originality, and even laughs>
synonyms bereft, destitute, void
related words bare, barren, blank, empty, lacking, stark, vacant, wanting; deficient, fragmental, fragmentary, incomplete, partial; absent, missing
near antonyms filled, full; furnished, provided, supplied
antonyms replete
2 lacking contents that could or should be present — see EMPTY 1

devote *vb* **1** to keep or intend for a special purpose <he *devoted* several hours every weekend to playing with his dog>
synonyms allocate, consecrate, dedicate, earmark, reserve, save
related words hallow, sanctify; commit, confide, consign, entrust
phrases set apart, set aside
2 to occupy (oneself) diligently or with close attention — see APPLY

devoted *adj* **1** feeling or showing love — see LOVING
2 firm in one's allegiance to someone or something — see FAITHFUL 1

devotedness *n* **1** a feeling of strong or constant regard for and dedication to someone — see LOVE 1
2 adherence to something to which one is bound by a pledge or duty — see FIDELITY

devotee *n* a person with a strong and habitual liking for something — see FAN

devotion *n* **1** a feeling of strong or constant regard for and dedication to someone — see LOVE 1
2 adherence to something to which one is bound by a pledge or duty — see FIDELITY
3 belief and trust in and loyalty to God — see FAITH 1

devotional *adj* of, relating to, or used in the practice or worship services of a religion — see RELIGIOUS 1

devour *vb* to destroy all trace of — see CONSUME 1

devout *adj* showing a devotion to God and to a life of virtue — see HOLY 1

devoutness *n* the quality or state of being spiritually pure or virtuous — see HOLINESS

dexterity *n* **1** mental skill or quickness <the ambassador showed great *dexterity* in his handling of the touchy situation>
synonyms adroitness, cleverness, finesse, sleight
related words ability, prowess, talent; competence, efficiency, expertise, know-how, proficiency; ingeniousness, ingenuity, resourcefulness
near antonyms inadequacy, ineptitude, ineptness; slowness, stupidity
2 ease and grace in physical activity <the juggler needed lots of *dexterity* in order to keep all five balls in the air at the same time>
synonyms agility, deftness, nimbleness, sleight, spryness
related words coordination
antonyms awkwardness, clumsiness, gawkiness

dexterous *also* **dextrous** *adj* **1** skillful with the hands <the *dexterous* watchmaker was able to repair the tiny gears and parts in the antique watch>
synonyms clever, cunning, deft, handy
related words agile, flexible, graceful, limber, lissome (*also* lissom), lithe, nimble, spry; coordinated; adept, competent, expert, masterful, masterly, proficient, skilled, skillful; double-jointed, loose-jointed
near antonyms awkward, bungling, clumsy, fumbling, gawky; uncoordinated; incompetent, inept, maladroit
antonyms butterfingered, heavy-handed, unhandy
2 accomplished with trained ability — see SKILLFUL

diabolical *or* **diabolic** *adj* of, relating to, or worthy of an evil spirit — see FIENDISH

diadem *n* a decorative band or wreath worn about the head as a symbol of victory or honor — see CROWN 1

diagnosis *n* a position arrived at after consideration — see DECISION 1

diagonal *adj* running in a slanting direction <the *diagonal* design ran up the wall all the way from the lower left to the upper right-hand corner>
synonyms canted, inclined, leaning, listing,

oblique, pitched, slanted, slantwise, sloped, sloping, tilted, tilting
near antonyms horizontal, vertical; parallel, perpendicular
diagonal *n* the degree to which something rises up from a position level with the horizon — see SLANT
diagram *n* something that visually explains or decorates a text — see ILLUSTRATION 1
dial *vb* to make a telephone call to — see CALL 2
dialect *n* the special terms or expressions of a particular group or field — see TERMINOLOGY
dialogue *also* **dialog** *n* talking or a talk between two or more people — see CONVERSATION
diametric *or* **diametrical** *adj* being as different as possible — see OPPOSITE
diatribe *n* a long angry speech or scolding — see TIRADE
dice *n* a small cube marked on each side with one to six spots and usually played in pairs in various games — see DIE
dice *vb* to cut into small pieces — see CHOP
dicker *vb* to talk over or dispute the terms of a purchase — see BARGAIN
dictate *n* a statement of what to do that must be obeyed by those concerned — see COMMAND 1
dictate *vb* to give an order — see COMMAND 2
dictator *n* a person who uses power or authority in a cruel, unjust, or harmful way — see DESPOT
dictatorial *adj* **1** exercising power or authority without interference by others — see ABSOLUTE 1
2 fond of ordering people around — see BOSSY
3 having or showing a tendency to force one's will on others without any regard to fairness or necessity — see ARBITRARY 1
dictatorship *n* a system of government in which the ruler has unlimited power — see DESPOTISM
diction *n* **1** the clear and accurate pronunciation of words especially in public speaking ⟨the actors had very good *diction*, clearly speaking every single word of the Shakespearean play that they were performing⟩
synonyms articulation, enunciation
related words elocution; speech, wording
2 the way in which something is put into words — see WORDING
dictionary *n* a reference book giving information about the meanings, pronunciations, uses, and origins of words listed in alphabetical order ⟨try to develop the habit of going to the *dictionary* whenever you encounter an unfamiliar word⟩
synonyms lexicon, wordbook
related words glossary, thesaurus, vocabulary
die *n* a small cube marked on each side with one to six spots and usually played in pairs in various games ⟨he rolled the *die*, hoping for a six⟩
synonyms bone(s), dice
die *vb* **1** to stop living ⟨the king *died* of old age after ruling for many years⟩
synonyms croak [*slang*], decease, depart, expire, pass (on), pass away, perish, succumb
related words disappear, fade
phrases bite the dust
near antonyms be, exist, subsist; flourish, prosper, thrive
antonyms breathe, live
2 to come to an end — see CEASE 1
3 to stop functioning — see FAIL 1
die (down) *vb* to grow less in scope or intensity especially gradually — see DECREASE 2
die (for) *vb* to have an earnest wish to own or enjoy — see DESIRE
differ *vb* **1** to be unlike; to not be the same ⟨my brother and I *differ* in looks⟩
synonyms disagree, vary
related words clash, conflict, jar; distinguish, divide, separate
near antonyms blend, harmonize
antonyms accord, agree, conform, correspond
2 to have a different opinion — see DISAGREE 1
difference *n* **1** the quality or state of being different ⟨there's a great *difference* between claiming to care about the environment and living like you really do⟩
synonyms contrast, disagreement, discrepancy, disparateness, disparity, dissimilarity, distinction, distinctiveness, distinctness, diverseness, diversity, unlikeness
related words deviance, divergence; change, modification, variation; conflict, discord, discordance, dissension, dissent, dissidence, disunity, friction, strife; variability, variance; incompatibility, incongruity, incongruousness; disproportion
near antonyms identicalness, identity; analogy, similitude; accordance, agreement, conformity, congruity, correspondence; equality, equivalence, equivalency; parallelism
antonyms alikeness, community, likeness, resemblance, sameness, similarity
2 variance of opinion on a matter — see DISAGREEMENT 1
3 the act, process, or result of making different — see CHANGE
different *adj* **1** being not of the same kind ⟨apples are *different* from oranges⟩
synonyms disparate, dissimilar, distinct, distinctive, distinguishable, diverse, other, unalike, unlike
related words divers, miscellaneous, several, sundry, variant, varied, various; individual, particular, peculiar, single; unequal; disproportionate
near antonyms identical, selfsame; equal, equivalent, tantamount; akin, analogous, comparable, related; homogeneous, uniform
antonyms alike, indistinguishable, like, parallel, same, similar
2 not the same or shared — see SEPARATE 1
differential *adj* favoring, applying, or being unequal treatment of different classes of people — see DISCRIMINATORY
differentiate *vb* to understand or point out the difference — see DISTINGUISH 1
differently *adv* in a different way — see OTHERWISE
difficult *adj* **1** requiring considerable physical or mental effort — see HARD 2
2 requiring exceptional skill or caution in performance or handling — see TRICKY
difficulty *n* **1** something that is a cause for suffering or special effort especially in the attainment of a goal ⟨the many *difficulties* that he encountered on the road from poor orphan to head of a major corporation⟩
synonyms adversity, asperity, hardness, hardship, rigor
related words discomfort, inconvenience, nuisance; affliction, trial, tribulation; knock, misfortune, mishap, tragedy; bar, catch, check, clog, crimp, embarrassment, handicap, hindrance, hitch, hurdle, impediment, interference, let, man-

acle, obstacle, obstruction, rub, shackle, snag, stop, trammel; block, chain, deterrent, encumbrance, fetter, inhibition; hump
near antonyms advantage, break, opportunity
2 something that makes a situation more complicated or difficult — see COMPLICATION 1

diffident *adj* not comfortable around people — see SHY 2

diffuse *adj* using or containing more words than necessary to express an idea — see WORDY

diffuseness *n* the use of too many words to express an idea — see VERBIAGE

dig *n* **1** a quick thrust — see [1]POKE
2 an act or expression showing scorn and usually intended to hurt another's feelings — see INSULT

dig *vb* **1** to hollow out or form (something) by removing earth ⟨a backhoe *dug* a hole in the backyard to make a swimming pool⟩
synonyms excavate, shovel
related words dredge; burrow, claw, grub; dig in; scoop, spade; delve; mine, quarry
near antonyms fill (in); smooth (out *or* over)
2 to take pleasure in — see ENJOY 1
3 *slang* to recognize the meaning of — see COMPREHEND 1

dig (into) *vb* to search through or into — see EXPLORE 1

dig (through) *vb* to look through (as a place) carefully or thoroughly in an effort to find or discover something — see SEARCH 1

dig (up) *vb* to come upon after searching, study, or effort — see FIND 1

digest *n* **1** a short statement of the main points — see SUMMARY
2 a shortened version of a written work — see ABRIDGMENT

digest *vb* to make into a short statement of the main points (as of a report) — see SUMMARIZE

diggings *n pl* the place where one lives — see HOME 1

digit *n* a character used to represent a mathematical value — see NUMBER

dignified *adj* having or showing a serious and reserved manner ⟨the chief justice of the U.S. Supreme Court is always very *dignified* when swearing in the new president⟩ ⟨*dignified* funeral services for the fallen firemen⟩
synonyms august, imposing, solemn, staid, stately
related words decorous, formal, proper, seemly; grim, sober, somber (*or* sombre); aristocratic, lordly, majestic, noble
near antonyms coarse, crass, crude, improper, indecent, uncouth, unseemly, vulgar
antonyms flighty, frivolous, giddy, goofy, silly, undignified

dignify *vb* to enhance the status of — see EXALT

dignity *n* high position within society — see RANK 2

digression *n* a departure from the subject under consideration — see TANGENT

digressive *adj* passing from one topic to another — see DISCURSIVE

dike *n* **1** a bank of earth constructed to control water — see DAM
2 a long narrow channel dug in the earth — see DITCH

dilapidated *adj* showing signs of advanced wear and tear and neglect — see SHABBY 1

dilapidation *n* the state of being unattended to or not cared for — see NEGLECT 1

dilatory *adj* moving or proceeding at less than the normal, desirable, or required speed — see SLOW 1

dilemma *n* a situation in which one has to choose between two or more equally unsatisfactory choices ⟨they were faced with a *dilemma* : either they could spend the night out in the cold or they could walk back into their house and face their father⟩
synonyms quandary
related words deadlock, halt, impasse, quagmire, stalemate, standoff; knot, problem; difficulty, fix, hole, jam, pickle, pinch, plight, predicament, spot
near antonyms breeze, cinch, duck soup, snap

dilettante *adj* lacking or showing a lack of expert skill — see AMATEURISH

dilettante *n* **1** a person having a knowledgeable and fine appreciation of the arts — see CONNOISSEUR
2 a person who regularly or occasionally engages in an activity without being or becoming an expert at it — see AMATEUR

diligence *n* attentive and persistent effort ⟨through the *diligence* and ingenuity of a single detective, the gang's ringleader was finally caught⟩
synonyms assiduity, assiduousness, industriousness, industry
related words application, concentration; doggedness, perseverance, persistence, tenacity, tirelessness
near antonyms carelessness; idleness, indolence, laziness

diligent *adj* involved in often constant activity — see BUSY 1

diligently *adv* with great effort or determination — see HARD 1

dillydally *vb* **1** to move or act slowly — see DELAY 1
2 to spend time doing nothing — see IDLE

dillydallying *adj* moving or proceeding at less than the normal, desirable, or required speed — see SLOW 1

dilute *adj* **1** not containing very much of some important element — see WEAK 3
2 containing foreign or lower-grade substances — see IMPURE

dilute *vb* to alter (something) for the worse with the addition of foreign or lower-grade substances — see ADULTERATE

diluted *adj* **1** not containing very much of some important element — see WEAK 3
2 containing foreign or lower-grade substances — see IMPURE

dim *adj* **1** being without light or without much light — see DARK 1
2 lacking a surface luster or gloss — see MATTE
3 not seen or understood clearly — see FAINT 1

dim *vb* to make dark, dim, or indistinct — see CLOUD 1

dimension *n* **1** the total amount of measurable space or surface occupied by something — see [1]SIZE
2 dimensions *pl* an area over which activity, capacity, or influence extends — see RANGE 2

diminish *vb* **1** to express scornfully one's low opinion of — see DECRY 1
2 to make smaller in amount, volume, or extent — see DECREASE 1
3 to grow less in scope or intensity especially gradually — see DECREASE 2

diminishment *n* **1** the act of making a person or a

thing seem little or unimportant — see DEPRECIATION

2 the amount by which something is lessened — see DECREASE

diminution *n* the amount by which something is lessened — see DECREASE

diminutive *adj* of a size that is less than average — see SMALL 1

diminutive *n* a living thing much smaller than others of its kind — see DWARF 1

diminutiveness *n* the quality or state of being little in size — see SMALLNESS

dimmed *adj* being without light or without much light — see DARK 1

din *n* loud, confused, and usually unharmonious sound — see NOISE 1

din *vb* to say or state again — see REPEAT 1

dine *vb* **1** to take a meal ⟨they *dined* elegantly at the city's finest restaurant before taking in an opera downtown⟩

synonyms eat, fare, feed

related words banquet, feast, fete (*or* fête); board, mess; breakfast, lunch, sup; picnic

2 to entertain with a fancy meal — see FEAST

diner *n* a public establishment where meals are served to paying customers for consumption on the premises — see RESTAURANT

dinghy *n* a boat equipped with one or more sails — see SAILBOAT

dinginess *n* the state or quality of being dirty — see DIRTINESS 1

dingy *adj* not clean — see DIRTY 1

dinky *adj* of a size that is less than average — see SMALL 1

dinner *n* a large fancy meal often accompanied by ceremony or entertainment — see FEAST

dinnerware *n* dishes used for eating or serving food or drink — see TABLEWARE 2

dinning *adj* making loud, confused, and usually unharmonious sounds — see NOISY 1

dint *n* a sunken area forming a separate space — see HOLE 2

dip *n* the act or process of going to a lower level or altitude — see DESCENT 1

dip *vb* **1** to sink or push (something) briefly into or as if into a liquid ⟨he went to *dip* a paper towel in water and clean off the window⟩ ⟨she *dipped* a hand into her pocket and pulled out a piece of candy⟩

synonyms douse, duck, dunk, immerse, souse, submerge, submerse

related words drench, flood, soak, wet; plunge, thrust

2 to lift out with something that holds liquid ⟨they *dipped* water from the bucket to pour into the kettle⟩

synonyms lade, ladle, scoop, spoon

related words bail; deplete, drain, eliminate, exhaust; bleed, draw (off); dish; draw, siphon

near antonyms pour; fill

3 to go to a lower level — see DROP 2

4 to lead or extend downward — see DESCEND 1

5 to take a quick or hasty look — see GLANCE 2

diplomacy *n* the ability to deal with others in touchy situations without offending them — see TACT

diplomatic *adj* having or showing tact — see TACTFUL

dipper *n* a utensil with a bowl and a handle that is used especially in cooking and serving food — see SPOON

dire *adj* **1** being or showing a sign of evil or calamity to come — see OMINOUS

2 causing fear — see FEARFUL

3 needing immediate attention — see ACUTE 2

direct *adj* **1** done or working without something else coming in between ⟨a zoologist whose works are based entirely on her *direct* observation of animals in the wild⟩ ⟨the virus was the *direct* cause of the disease⟩

synonyms firsthand, immediate, primary

related words clinical

antonyms indirect, secondhand

2 free in expressing one's true feelings and opinions — see FRANK

3 going straight to the point clearly and firmly — see STRAIGHTFORWARD 1

direct *adv* in a direct line or course — see DIRECTLY 1

direct *vb* **1** to cause to move to a central point or along a restricted pathway — see CHANNEL

2 to issue orders to (someone) by right of authority — see COMMAND 1

3 to give an order — see COMMAND 2

4 to look after and make decisions about — see CONDUCT 1

5 to point or turn (something) toward a target or goal — see AIM 1

6 to point out the way for (someone) especially from a position in front — see LEAD 1

direction *n* **1** a statement of what to do that must be obeyed by those concerned — see COMMAND 1

2 the act or activity of looking after and making decisions about something — see CONDUCT 1

directive *n* **1** a statement of what to do that must be obeyed by those concerned — see COMMAND 1

2 an order publicly issued by an authority — see EDICT 1

3 a written communication giving information or directions — see MEMORANDUM 1

directly *adv* **1** in a direct line or course ⟨we went *directly* to the school without stopping⟩

synonyms dead, direct, due, plumb, plump, right, straight

phrases as the crow flies

near antonyms circuitously, deviously

antonyms indirectly

2 in an honest and direct manner — see STRAIGHTFORWARD

3 in the same words — see VERBATIM

4 without delay — see IMMEDIATELY

directness *n* the free expression of one's true feelings and opinions — see CANDOR

director *n* a person who manages or directs — see EXECUTIVE

directorial *adj* suited for or relating to the directing of things — see EXECUTIVE

direful *adj* causing fear — see FEARFUL 1

dirge *n* a composition expressing one's grief over a loss — see LAMENT 2

dirt *n* **1** the loose surface material in which plants naturally grow ⟨dig into the *dirt* to a depth of about three inches⟩

synonyms earth, ground, soil

related words clay, duff, dust, gravel, humus, loam, loess, marl, mud, sand, silt, subsoil, topsoil

2 the solid part of our planet's surface as distinguished from the sea and air — see EARTH 2

3 foul matter that mars the purity or cleanliness of something — see FILTH 1
4 the quality or state of being obscene — see OBSCENITY 1

dirtiness *n* **1** the state or quality of being dirty ⟨when the maid arrived, she exclaimed over the *dirtiness* of the china⟩
synonyms dinginess, dustiness, filthiness, foulness, griminess, grubbiness, nastiness, squalidness, uncleanliness, uncleanness
related words impurity; messiness, sloppiness, untidiness; shabbiness; squalor; smuttiness, sootiness
near antonyms purity
antonyms cleanliness, immaculateness, spotlessness
2 the quality or state of being obscene — see OBSCENITY 1

dirty *adj* **1** not clean ⟨after playing in the mud all day, his clothes were very *dirty*⟩
synonyms besmirched, blackened, dingy, dusty, filthy, foul, grimy, grubby, grungy, mucky, muddy, nasty, smutty, soiled, sordid, stained, sullied, unclean, uncleanly
related words contaminated, defiled, impure, polluted, tainted; uncleaned, unsanitary, unsterile, unsterilized, unwashed; discolored; bedraggled, draggled; chaotic, cluttered, confused, disarranged, disarrayed, disheveled (*or* dishevelled), disordered, jumbled, littered, messed, messy, muddled, mussed, mussy, rumpled, scruffy, sloppy, slovenly, unkempt, untidy; shabby, sleazy, squalid; smutty, sooty
near antonyms clear, limpid, pure; cleaned, cleansed, combed, groomed, neat, ordered, orderly, tidy; bleached, purified, whitened; bright, flawless, perfect, shiny, sparkling, unspotted, untouched; taintless, unblemished, undefiled, unpolluted, untainted, wholesome
antonyms clean, cleanly, immaculate, spick-and-span (*or* spic-and-span), spotless, stainless, unsoiled, unstained, unsullied
2 depicting or referring to sexual matters in a way that is unacceptable in polite society — see OBSCENE 1
3 marked by wet and windy conditions — see FOUL 1
4 not being in accordance with the rules or standards of what is fair in sport — see FOUL 2
5 not following or in accordance with standards of honor and decency — see IGNOBLE 2

dirty *vb* to make dirty ⟨she *dirtied* her new shoes when she splashed in the puddle⟩
synonyms befoul, begrime, besmirch, blacken, foul, grime, mire, muddy, smirch, smudge, soil, stain, sully
related words contaminate, defile, pollute, taint; discolor; confuse, disarrange, disarray, dishevel, disorder, jumble, mess, muddle
near antonyms decontaminate, purge, purify; disinfect, sanitize; brush, dry-clean, dust, launder, mop, rinse, scour, scrub, sweep, wash, wipe; brighten, deodorize, freshen, renew, spruce (up); straighten (up), tidy (up)
antonyms clean, cleanse

dis *vb, slang* **1** to cause hurt feelings or deep resentment in — see INSULT
2 to express one's unfavorable opinion of the worth or quality of — see CRITICIZE

disable *vb* **1** to cause severe or permanent injury to — see MAIM
2 to render powerless, ineffective, or unable to move — see PARALYZE

disabled *adj* deprived of the power to perform one or more natural bodily activities ⟨the *disabled* man was unable to climb the stairs without help⟩
synonyms challenged, incapacitated
related words blind, deaf, mute; halt, lame, paralyzed, quadriplegic; immobile, immobilized; ailing, diseased, ill, sick, unfit, unhealthy, unsound, unwell
near antonyms bouncing, chipper, fit, hale, healthy, hearty, robust, sound, well, whole, wholesome
antonyms able-bodied, nondisabled

disabuse *vb* to free from mistaken beliefs or foolish hopes — see DISILLUSION

disadvantage *n* a feature of someone or something that creates difficulty for achieving success ⟨their lack of height was a *disadvantage* on the basketball court⟩
synonyms drawback, handicap, liability, minus, penalty, strike
related words stranglehold; detriment, disability, impairment; failing, shortcoming; bar, catch, check, clog, crimp, embarrassment, hindrance, hitch, hurdle, impediment, interference, let, manacle, obstacle, obstruction, rub, shackle, stop, trammel
near antonyms vantage; head start, jump, lead, margin, start; ascendancy, better, command, control, drop, mastery, predominance, superiority, supremacy, transcendence, upper hand; prerogative, privilege; break, opportunity; aid, assistance, help
antonyms advantage, asset, edge, plus

disadvantaged *adj* kept from having the necessities of life or a healthful environment — see DEPRIVED

disadvantageous *adj* opposed to one's interests — see ADVERSE 1

disaffect *vb* **1** to cause to change from friendly or loving to unfriendly or uncaring — see ESTRANGE
2 to make discontented — see DISCONTENT

disaffection *n* the loss of friendship or affection — see ESTRANGEMENT

disagree *vb* **1** to have a different opinion ⟨she thought we were still headed north on the trail, but I *disagreed*⟩
synonyms differ, dissent
related words clash, collide, conflict, contrast; counter, debate, object, oppose, protest, resist; contest, dispute; argue, bicker, fall out, quarrel
near antonyms accede, accept, acquiesce, comply, consent, subscribe; affiliate, ally, associate, collaborate, collude, compromise, cooperate, get along, side
antonyms agree, assent, concur
2 to be unlike; to not be the same — see DIFFER 1

disagree (with) *vb* to make an assertion that is contrary to one made by (another) — see CONTRADICT 1

disagreeable *adj* **1** having or showing a habitually bad temper — see ILL-TEMPERED
2 not giving pleasure to the mind or senses — see UNPLEASANT

disagreeing *adj* not being in agreement or harmony — see INCONSISTENT

disagreement *n* **1** variance of opinion on a matter ⟨there was some *disagreement* about what the color of the missing sweater actually was⟩
synonyms controversy, debate, difference, disputation, dispute, dissension
related words clash, collision, conflict, contention, discord, strife; discussion; altercation, argument, bicker, falling-out, fight, quarrel
near antonyms acceptance, compliance; concord, peace
antonyms accord, agreement, consensus, harmony, unanimity
2 an often noisy or angry expression of differing opinions — see ARGUMENT 1
3 the quality or state of being different — see DIFFERENCE 1

disallow *vb* **1** to declare not to be true — see DENY 1
2 to be unwilling to grant — see DENY 2

disallowance *n* **1** an unwillingness to grant something asked for — see DENIAL 1
2 a refusal to confirm the truth of a statement — see DENIAL 2

disappear *vb* to cease to be visible ⟨the stranger *disappeared* into the mists, never to be seen again⟩
synonyms dissolve, evanesce, evaporate, fade, flee, go (away), melt, vanish
related words clear, dissipate
near antonyms arrive, break out, come out, emerge, issue, loom, show up
antonyms appear, materialize

disappoint *vb* to fall short in satisfying the expectation or hope of ⟨they were *disappointed* by the outcome of the big game⟩
synonyms cheat, dissatisfy, fail, let down
related words discontent, disgruntle, displease; disenchant, disillusion
near antonyms gladden
antonyms satisfy

disappointment *n* **1** the emotion felt when one's expectations are not met ⟨we felt *disappointment* after failing a test that we thought would be easy⟩
synonyms dismay, dissatisfaction, frustration, letdown
related words disenchantment, disillusionment; blues, dejection, depression, desolateness, desolation, despondency, disconsolateness, distress, doldrums, dolefulness, dolor, downheartedness, dreariness, dumps, gloom, gloominess, joylessness, melancholy, mopes, oppression, sadness, sorrow, unhappiness; alarm, concern, consternation; chagrin, discomfiture
near antonyms bliss, felicity, gladness, happiness, joy
antonyms contentment, gratification, satisfaction
2 something that disappoints ⟨after all the publicity and high expectations, the sequel to the movie blockbuster was a *disappointment*⟩
synonyms bummer, letdown
related words anticlimax, failure, fiasco, fizzle; lemon, loser
near antonyms success, winner; relief

disapprobation *n* refusal to accept as right or desirable — see DISAPPROVAL

disapproval *n* refusal to accept as right or desirable ⟨thus far, every one of her boyfriends has met with her parents' *disapproval*⟩
synonyms deprecation, disapprobation, disfavor, dislike, displeasure
related words blame, censure, criticism, condemnation, denunciation, dressing down, opprobrium, reproach, reprobation; antagonism, antipathy, hostility; belittlement, disparagement, opposition
near antonyms acclaim, commendation, praise; endorsement, sanction; empathy, sympathy
antonyms approbation, approval, favor

disapprove *vb* to show unwillingness to accept, do, engage in, or agree to — see DECLINE 1

disapprove (of) *vb* to hold an unfavorable opinion of ⟨my sister *disapproves of* smoking and refuses to date anyone who thinks it's cool⟩
synonyms deprecate, discountenance, disfavor, dislike, frown (on), reprove
related words blame, censure, condemn, criticize, denounce, reprehend, reprobate; chide, rebuke, reproach, scold
near antonyms endorse (*also* indorse), sanction, support; adore, delight (in), dig, enjoy, fancy, groove (on), love, relish, revel (in)
antonyms approve, favor, like

disarm *vb* **1** to reduce the size and strength of the armed forces of ⟨the defeated nation was *disarmed* so that it would never again be a threat to international order⟩
synonyms demilitarize
related words demobilize
near antonyms equip, mobilize
antonyms arm, militarize
2 to lessen the anger or agitation of — see PACIFY

disarmament *n* the reduction or elimination of a country's armed forces or weapons ⟨the ambassador spoke at length about the possible unilateral *disarmament* of his country⟩
synonyms demilitarization
related words demobilization
near antonyms mobilization
antonyms militarization

disarming *adj* **1** having qualities that tend to make one loved — see LOVABLE
2 likely to win one's affection — see INGRATIATING
3 tending to lessen or avoid conflict or hostility — see PACIFIC 1

disarrange *vb* to undo the proper order or arrangement of — see DISORDER

disarranged *adj* lacking in order, neatness, and often cleanliness — see MESSY

disarrangement *n* a state in which everything is out of order — see CHAOS

disarray *n* a state in which everything is out of order — see CHAOS

disarray *vb* to undo the proper order or arrangement of — see DISORDER

disarrayed *adj* lacking in order, neatness, and often cleanliness — see MESSY

disassemble *vb* to take apart ⟨they had to *disassemble* the television set in order to replace the wiring⟩
synonyms demount, dismantle, dismember, knock down, strike, take down
related words detach, disengage; disconnect, disjoin, disunite, divide, separate
near antonyms build, erect; combine, unite
antonyms assemble, construct, put together

disaster *n* a sudden violent event that brings about great loss or destruction ⟨hurricanes are natural *disasters*⟩

synonyms calamity, cataclysm, catastrophe, debacle (*also* débâcle), tragedy
related words collapse, crash, meltdown; convulsion, paroxysm, upheaval; accident, casualty, fatality; misadventure, mischance, misfortune, mishap, woe; bummer, downer
near antonyms godsend, manna, windfall

disastrous *adj* **1** bringing about ruin or misfortune — see FATAL 1
2 causing or tending to cause destruction — see DESTRUCTIVE 1

disavow *vb* **1** to declare not to be true — see DENY 1
2 to refuse to acknowledge as one's own or as one's responsibility — see DISCLAIM 1

disavowal *n* a refusal to confirm the truth of a statement — see DENIAL 2

disband *vb* **1** to cease to exist or cause to cease to exist as a group or organization <they *disbanded* the committee after the report had been submitted> <the rock group *disbanded* upon finishing the tour>
synonyms break up, disperse, dissolve
near antonyms incorporate; consolidate
antonyms band, join, unite
2 to cause (members of a group) to move widely apart — see SCATTER 1

disbandment *n* an act or process in which something scatters or is scattered — see SCATTERING 1

disbelief *n* refusal to accept as true <their story explaining their absence was met with frank *disbelief*>
synonyms incredulity, unbelief
related words distrust, doubt, mistrust, skepticism, suspicion, uncertainty; denial, rejection, repudiation
near antonyms acceptance, faith; trust
antonyms belief, credence, credit

disbelieve *vb* to think not to be true or real <many *disbelieved* the medium's claims that she could communicate with the spirits of the dead>
synonyms discredit, negate
related words deny, reject, repudiate; distrust, doubt, mistrust, suspect; debunk, disprove; deride, pooh-pooh, scoff (at)
near antonyms trust
antonyms accept, believe, credit, swallow

disbeliever *n* a person who is always ready to doubt or question the truth or existence of something — see SKEPTIC

disbelieving *adj* inclined to doubt or question claims — see SKEPTICAL 1

disburden *vb* **1** to empty or rid of cargo — see UNLOAD 1
2 to set (a person or thing) free of something that encumbers — see RID

disburse *vb* to hand over or use up in payment — see SPEND 1

disbursement *n* **1** a payment made in the course of achieving a result — see EXPENSE
2 the act of offering money in exchange for goods or services — see PAYMENT 1

discard *n* something separated from a group or lot for not being as good as the others — see CULL

discard *vb* to get rid of as useless or unwanted <*discard* an old, torn sweater>
synonyms cast, ditch, dump, fling (off *or* away), jettison, junk, lose, reject, scrap, shed, shuck (off), slough (*also* sluff), throw away, throw out, unload
related words abandon, desert, forsake; dismiss; abolish, annihilate, eliminate, eradicate, expunge, exterminate, extinguish, extirpate, liquidate, remove, root (out), stamp (out), wipe out
phrases dispose of, set aside
near antonyms adopt, embrace, take on; employ, use, utilize; hold, hold back, keep, retain

discarding *n* the getting rid of whatever is unwanted or useless — see DISPOSAL 1

discern *vb* **1** to make note of (something) through the use of one's eyes — see SEE 1
2 to understand or point out the difference — see DISTINGUISH 1

discernible *adj* able to be perceived by a sense or by the mind — see PERCEPTIBLE

discerning *adj* having or showing deep understanding and intelligent application of knowledge — see WISE 1

discernment *n* the ability to understand inner qualities or relationships — see WISDOM 1

discharge *n* **1** a directed propelling of a missile by a firearm or artillery piece — see SHOT
2 a freeing from an obligation or responsibility — see RELEASE 1
3 the termination of the employment of an employee or a work force often temporarily — see LAYOFF
4 the doing of an action — see COMMISSION 2

discharge *vb* **1** to cause (a projectile) to be driven forward with force — see SHOOT 1
2 to empty or rid of cargo — see UNLOAD 1
3 to give what is owed for — see PAY 2
4 to set free (as from slavery or confinement) — see FREE 1
5 to throw or give off — see EMIT 1
6 to cause a weapon to release a missile with great force — see SHOOT 2

disciple *n* one who follows the opinions or teachings of another — see FOLLOWER

disciplinary *adj* inflicting, involving, or serving as punishment — see PUNITIVE

discipline *n* **1** a region of activity, knowledge, or influence — see FIELD 2
2 suffering, loss, or hardship imposed in response to a crime or offense — see PUNISHMENT

discipline *vb* to inflict a penalty on for a fault or crime — see PUNISH

disciplining *adj* inflicting, involving, or serving as punishment — see PUNITIVE

disclaim *vb* **1** to refuse to acknowledge as one's own or as one's responsibility <the prisoner *disclaimed* any part in the prank>
synonyms disavow, disown, repudiate
related words contradict, deny, disallow, gainsay, negate, negative, refuse, reject; challenge, confute, criticize, disprove, rebut, refute; dispute, question
near antonyms accept, adopt, embrace, espouse; admit, concede, confess, grant; affirm, announce, assert, aver, declare, maintain, profess, submit; authenticate, confirm, corroborate, substantiate, validate, verify
antonyms acknowledge, avow, claim, own, recognize
2 to declare not to be true — see DENY 1

disclaimer *n* a refusal to confirm the truth of a statement — see DENIAL 2

disclose *vb* to make known (as information previously kept secret) — see REVEAL 1

disclosure *n* the act or an instance of making

known something previously unknown or concealed — see REVELATION

disco *n* a bar or restaurant offering special nighttime entertainment (as music, dancing, or comedy acts) — see NIGHTCLUB

discomfit *vb* to throw into a state of self-conscious distress — see EMBARRASS 1

discomfiting *adj* causing embarrassment — see AWKWARD 3

discomfiture *n* the emotional state of being made self-consciously uncomfortable — see EMBARRASSMENT 1

discomfort *vb* to trouble the mind of; to make uneasy — see DISTURB 1

discomforting *adj* **1** causing discomfort — see UNCOMFORTABLE 1
2 causing worry or anxiety — see TROUBLESOME

discommode *vb* to cause discomfort to or trouble for — see INCONVENIENCE

discommoding *adj* causing difficulty, discomfort, or annoyance — see INCONVENIENT 1

discompose *vb* **1** to trouble the mind of; to make uneasy — see DISTURB 1
2 to undo the proper order or arrangement of — see DISORDER

discomposing *adj* causing worry or anxiety — see TROUBLESOME

disconcert *vb* to throw into a state of self-conscious distress — see EMBARRASS 1

disconcerting *adj* causing embarrassment — see AWKWARD 3

disconnect *vb* to set or force apart — see SEPARATE 1

disconnected *adj* **1** not clearly or logically connected — see INCOHERENT 1
2 not physically attached to another unit — see SEPARATE 2

disconsolate *adj* feeling unhappiness — see SAD 1

disconsolateness *n* a state or spell of low spirits — see SADNESS

discontent *adj* having a feeling that one has been wronged or thwarted in one's ambitions — see DISCONTENTED

discontent *n* the condition of being dissatisfied with one's life or situation ⟨the rebels tried to stir up *discontent* among the citizens⟩
synonyms discontentedness, discontentment, disgruntlement, displeasure, dissatisfaction
related words bitterness, resentment; disquiet, perturbation, uneasiness; blues, dejection, depression, desolateness, desolation, despondency, disconsolateness, doldrums, dolefulness, dolor, downheartedness, dreariness, dumps; misery, sadness, sorrow, unhappiness, wretchedness
near antonyms bliss, felicity, gladness, happiness, joy, lightheartedness; elatedness, exultation, jubilation, triumph
antonyms contentedness, contentment, pleasure, satisfaction

discontent *vb* to make discontented ⟨the ongoing lack of decent food *discontented* and demoralized the soldiers in the rebel army⟩
synonyms disaffect, disgruntle, displease, dissatisfy
related words alienate, estrange; agitate, discompose, disquiet, disturb, perturb, upset; annoy, irk, irritate, nettle, peeve; depress, sadden
near antonyms delight, gladden, tickle; calm, soothe, tranquilize (*also* tranquillize)
antonyms content, gratify, please, satisfy

discontented *adj* having a feeling that one has been wronged or thwarted in one's ambitions ⟨he was *discontented* with his small role in the school play⟩
synonyms aggrieved, discontent, disgruntled, displeased, dissatisfied, malcontent
related words disappointed, frustrated, unfulfilled; disquieted, disturbed, perturbed, upset; dejected, depressed, despairing, despondent, disconsolate, doleful, down, downcast, downhearted, forlorn, hangdog, inconsolable, joyless, low-spirited, miserable, mournful, sad, sorrowful, unhappy
near antonyms blissful, delighted, glad, happy, joyful, joyous; elated, exultant, jubilant, triumphant
antonyms content, contented, gratified, pleased, satisfied

discontentedness *n* the condition of being dissatisfied with one's life or situation — see DISCONTENT

discontentment *n* the condition of being dissatisfied with one's life or situation — see DISCONTENT

discontinuance *n* the stopping of a process or activity — see END 1

discontinue *vb* **1** to bring (as an action or operation) to an immediate end — see STOP 1
2 to stop doing (something) permanently — see QUIT 2
3 to come to an end — see CEASE 1

discontinuity *n* **1** an open space in a barrier (as a wall or hedge) — see GAP 1
2 a break in continuity — see GAP 2

discontinuous *adj* lacking in steadiness or regularity of occurrence — see FITFUL

discord *n* a lack of agreement or harmony ⟨the *discord* between the two scout leaders threatened to tear our troop apart⟩
synonyms conflict, discordance, dissension, dissent, dissidence, disunity, friction, schism, strife, variance, war, warfare
related words clash, collision, competition, contention; altercation, argument, bicker, brawl, debate, disagreement, dispute, falling-out, fight, hassle, jar, quarrel, row, run-in, scrap, spat, squabble, tiff, wrangle; incompatibility, incongruity, inconsistency, inconsonance; animosity, antagonism, antipathy, enmity, hostility, ill will, rancor
near antonyms concurrence, cooperation
antonyms accord, agreement, concord, concordance, harmony, peace

discordance *n* **1** a lack of agreement or harmony — see DISCORD
2 loud, confused, and usually unharmonious sound — see NOISE 1

discordant *adj* **1** marked by or producing a harsh combination of sounds — see DISSONANT
2 making loud, confused, and usually unharmonious sounds — see NOISY 1
3 feeling or displaying eagerness to fight — see BELLIGERENT
4 not being in agreement or harmony — see INCONSISTENT

discotheque *n* a bar or restaurant offering special nighttime entertainment (as music, dancing, or comedy acts) — see NIGHTCLUB

discount *n* something that is or may be subtracted — see DEDUCTION 1

discount *vb* to express scornfully one's low opinion of — see DECRY 1

discountenance *vb* **1** to hold an unfavorable opinion of — see DISAPPROVE

2 to throw into a state of self-conscious distress — see EMBARRASS 1

discourage *vb* **1** to lessen the courage or confidence of <I didn't let losing *discourage* me from trying again>

synonyms daunt, demoralize, dishearten, dismay, dispirit, unman, unnerve

related words browbeat, bully, cow, intimidate; depress, sadden, weigh; afflict, try; damp, dampen, deaden; distress, trouble; bother, irk, vex, worry; debilitate, enfeeble, undermine, weaken; frighten, horrify, scare

near antonyms buoy (up), cheer, gladden; animate, enliven, invigorate; fortify, reinforce, strengthen; assure, reassure; boost, energize, excite, galvanize, inspire, lift, provoke, quicken, rally, stimulate, stir

antonyms embolden, encourage, hearten, nerve, steel

2 to steer (a person) from an activity or course of action <the higher fines may help *discourage* drivers from speeding on the highway>

synonyms deter, dissuade, inhibit

related words divert

near antonyms egg (on), exhort, goad, prod, urge; impel, induce, prompt

antonyms encourage, persuade

discouragement *n* the state of being discouraged <we tried to avoid *discouragement* after failing the test twice>

synonyms demoralization, despair, despondency, disheartenment, dismay, dispiritedness

related words blues, dejection, depression, dumps, gloom, melancholy, mopes; defeatism, pessimism, resignation

near antonyms optimism, sanguinity

antonyms encouragement

discourse *n* **1** an exchange of views for the purpose of exploring a subject or deciding an issue — see DISCUSSION 1

2 talking or a talk between two or more people — see CONVERSATION

discourse *vb* **1** to give a formal often extended talk on a subject — see TALK 1

2 to talk as if giving an important and formal speech — see ORATE 1

discourteous *adj* showing a lack of manners or consideration for others — see IMPOLITE

discourteousness *n* rude behavior — see DISCOURTESY

discourtesy *n* rude behavior <the courtiers shuddered at the *discourtesy* shown to the king>

synonyms discourteousness, disrespect, impertinence, impoliteness, impudence, incivility, inconsideration, insolence, rudeness, ungraciousness

related words audacity, boldness, brashness, brassiness, sauciness, shamelessness; boorishness, churlishness, clownishness, crudeness, loutishness, vulgarity; abruptness, bluntness, brusqueness, crustiness, curtness, gruffness, sharpness; crabbedness, crossness, disagreeableness, grumpiness, sullenness, surliness; impropriety, inappropriateness, incorrectness, indecency, unfitness, unsuitability; arrogance, conceit, conceitedness, presumption, pretense (*or* pretence), pretension, pretentiousness

near antonyms humility, meekness, modesty; deference, dutifulness, respectfulness, submissiveness; acceptability, appropriateness, correctness, decency, decorousness, fitness, goodness, propriety, respectability, respectableness, rightness, seemliness, suitability, suitableness; affability, cordiality, friendliness, geniality, hospitality; felicitousness, grace, gracefulness

antonyms civility, considerateness, consideration, courtesy, genteelness, gentility, graciousness, politeness, thoughtfulness

discover *vb* **1** to come to an awareness <I was startled to *discover* that my keys were missing>

synonyms ascertain, catch on, find out, hear, learn, realize, see

related words hit (on *or* upon), tumble (to); descry, detect, encounter, espy, spot; dope (out), figure out, puzzle (out); discern, note, observe, perceive; divine

near antonyms miss, overlook; disregard, ignore; forget, unlearn; blanket, blot out, cloak, conceal, cover, curtain, enshroud, hide, mask, occult, screen, shroud, veil

2 to come upon after searching, study, or effort — see FIND 1

3 to make known (as information previously kept secret) — see REVEAL 1

discovery *n* **1** the act or process of sighting or learning the existence of something for the first time <the *discovery* of a new species of starfish>

synonyms detection, finding, spotting, unearthing

related words disclosure, exposure, revelation, uncovering, unveiling; creation, invention; exploration; rediscovery

near antonyms concealment, hiding

2 something discovered <his many zoological *discoveries* included several species of birds>

synonyms find

related words pay dirt, strike, treasure trove; breakthrough

discredit *n* the state of having lost the esteem of others — see DISGRACE 1

discredit *vb* **1** to reduce to a lower standing in one's own eyes or in others' eyes — see HUMBLE

2 to think not to be true or real — see DISBELIEVE

discreditable *adj* not respectable — see DISREPUTABLE

discreet *adj* having or showing good judgment and restraint especially in conduct or speech <he was very *discreet*, only saying what was necessary>

synonyms judicious, prudent

related words cautious, chary, circumspect; foresighted, forethoughtful; discerning, discriminating, sage, sane, sapient, sensible, wise; canny, provident; astute, perspicacious, sagacious, shrewd

near antonyms careless, heedless; improvident, shortsighted; foolish, unwise

antonyms imprudent, indiscreet, injudicious

discreetness *n* the ability to make intelligent decisions especially in everyday matters — see COMMON SENSE

discrepancy *n* the quality or state of being different — see DIFFERENCE 1

discrepant *adj* not being in agreement or harmony — see INCONSISTENT

discrete *adj* not physically attached to another unit — see SEPARATE 2

discreteness *n* the state of being kept distinct — see SEPARATION 2

discretion *n* **1** the ability to make intelligent decisions especially in everyday matters — see COMMON SENSE
2 the power, right, or opportunity to choose — see CHOICE 1

discretionary *adj* subject to one's freedom of choice — see OPTIONAL

discriminate *vb* to understand or point out the difference — see DISTINGUISH 1

discriminating *adj* favoring, applying, or being unequal treatment of different classes of people — see DISCRIMINATORY

discrimination *n* the state of being kept distinct — see SEPARATION 2

discriminational *adj* favoring, applying, or being unequal treatment of different classes of people — see DISCRIMINATORY

discriminative *adj* favoring, applying, or being unequal treatment of different classes of people — see DISCRIMINATORY

discriminatory *adj* favoring, applying, or being unequal treatment of different classes of people ⟨a company that was fined for its *discriminatory* practices in the hiring of women⟩
synonyms differential, discriminating, discriminational, discriminative
related words biased, inequitable, partial, partisan, prejudiced, prejudicial, unequal, unfair, unjust
near antonyms equal, equitable, fair, just; impartial, neutral, objective, unbiased, uncolored, unprejudiced
antonyms nondiscriminatory

discursive *adj* passing from one topic to another ⟨the speaker's *discursive* style made it difficult to understand his point⟩
synonyms desultory, digressive, leaping, maundering, rambling
related words circuitous, deviating, devious, roundabout
near antonyms focused (*also* focussed)

discuss *vb* to talk about (an issue) usually from various points of view and for the purpose of arriving at a decision or opinion ⟨we *discussed* the new proposal for the school stadium⟩
synonyms argue, bandy, chew over, debate, dispute, hash (over), moot, talk over
related words descant (on), lecture (on *or* about), speak (about), talk (about); broach, introduce; forge, hammer (out), thrash (out); consider, deliberate, weigh; reason (with)

discussion *n* **1** an exchange of views for the purpose of exploring a subject or deciding an issue ⟨the *discussion* about the club budget went on for hours⟩
synonyms argument, colloquy, conference, deliberation, discourse, give-and-take, parley, talk
related words debate, dialogue (*also* dialog); forum, meeting, powwow, roundtable, seminar, symposium; chat, conversation, rap
2 talking or a talk between two or more people — see CONVERSATION

disdain *n* open dislike for someone or something considered unworthy of one's concern or respect — see CONTEMPT

disdain *vb* to show contempt for — see SCORN 1

disdainful *adj* **1** feeling or showing open dislike for someone or something regarded as undeserving of respect or concern — see CONTEMPTUOUS 1
2 having or displaying feelings of scorn for what is regarded as beneath oneself — see PROUD 1
3 intended to make a person or thing seem of little importance or value — see DEROGATORY

disease *n* an abnormal state that disrupts a plant's or animal's normal bodily functioning ⟨they caught a rare *disease* while they were traveling in Africa and were sick for weeks⟩
synonyms affection, ailment, bug, complaint, complication, condition, disorder, fever, ill, illness, infirmity, malady, sickness, trouble
related words contagion, contagious disease; infection, infectious disease; deficiency disease; attack, bout, fit, spell; debility, decrepitude, feebleness, frailness, lameness, weakness; malaise, matter; pest, pestilence, plague
near antonyms fitness, healthiness, heartiness, robustness, soundness, wholeness, wholesomeness
antonyms health, wellness

disembark *vb* to go ashore from a ship ⟨the cruise passengers *disembarked* as soon as they got to the terminal in Miami⟩
synonyms debark, land
related words beach; anchor, dock, put in
near antonyms board, get (on); weigh (anchor)
antonyms embark

disembowel *vb* to take the internal organs out of — see GUT

disenchant *vb* to free from mistaken beliefs or foolish hopes — see DISILLUSION

disencumber *vb* **1** to empty or rid of cargo — see UNLOAD 1
2 to set (a person or thing) free of something that encumbers — see RID

disencumbered *adj* no longer burdened with something unpleasant or painful — see FREE 2

disengage *vb* to set free from entanglement or difficulty — see EXTRICATE

disentangle *vb* **1** to separate the various strands of — see UNRAVEL 1
2 to set free from entanglement or difficulty — see EXTRICATE

disfavor *n* **1** a strong feeling of not liking or approving — see DISLIKE 1
2 refusal to accept as right or desirable — see DISAPPROVAL

disfavor *vb* **1** to feel dislike for — see DISLIKE 1
2 to hold an unfavorable opinion of — see DISAPPROVE

disfigure *vb* to reduce the soundness, effectiveness, or perfection of — see DAMAGE 1

disfigurement *n* something that spoils the appearance or completeness of a thing — see BLEMISH

disgorge *vb* to throw out or off (something from within) often violently — see ERUPT 1

disgrace *n* **1** the state of having lost the esteem of others ⟨the players who threw the game were in *disgrace* with their schoolmates⟩
synonyms discredit, dishonor, disrepute, ignominy, infamy, odium, opprobrium, reproach, shame
related words contempt, disdain, scorn; deprecation, disapprobation, disapproval, disfavor; abasement, debasement, debasing, degradation, humbling, humiliation; blot, brand, slur, smirch, spot, stain, stigma
near antonyms admiration, regard; awe, fear, reverence; fame, glory, renown, repute
antonyms esteem, honor, respect

2 a cause of shame ⟨the exposure of his criminal activities was a huge *disgrace* for the councilman⟩
synonyms crime, dishonor, reflection, reproach, scandal
related words brand, smirch, spot, stain, stigma
antonyms credit, honor
3 a regrettable or blameworthy act — see CRIME 2
disgrace *vb* to reduce to a lower standing in one's own eyes or in others' eyes — see HUMBLE
disgraceful *adj* not respectable — see DISREPUTABLE
disgruntle *vb* **1** to cause to change from friendly or loving to unfriendly or uncaring — see ESTRANGE
2 to make discontented — see DISCONTENT
disgruntled *adj* having a feeling that one has been wronged or thwarted in one's ambitions — see DISCONTENTED
disgruntlement *n* **1** the condition of being dissatisfied with one's life or situation — see DISCONTENT
2 the loss of friendship or affection — see ESTRANGEMENT
disguise *n* clothing put on to hide one's true identity or imitate someone or something else ⟨Mardi Gras revelers dressed in a colorful array of outlandish *disguises*⟩
synonyms camouflage, costume, guise
related words domino, mask, veil, vizard; dress, getup, outfit, rig; coloring, cosmetic, makeup, paint
disguise *vb* to change the dress or looks of so as to conceal true identity ⟨the spies *disguised* themselves as harmless tourists⟩
synonyms camouflage, cloak, dress up, mask
related words blanket, blot out, conceal, cover, curtain, enshroud, hide, obscure, occult, screen, shroud, veil; affect, assume, counterfeit, dissemble, dissimulate, feign, pose, pretend, sham, simulate
near antonyms display, exhibit, expose, flaunt, parade, show, uncover, unmask; betray, disclose, discover, reveal
disgust *n* a dislike so strong as to cause stomach upset or queasiness ⟨we turned from the grisly scene with *disgust*⟩
synonyms aversion, distaste, loathing, nausea, repugnance, repulsion, revulsion
related words abhorrence, abomination, execration, hate, hatred; disapproval, disfavor, disinclination, dislike, disliking, displeasure
near antonyms appetite, bent, fondness, like, liking, partiality, penchant, predilection, preference, propensity, taste
disgust *vb* to cause to feel disgust ⟨the usual school lunch *disgusted* us, so we started bringing our lunches from home⟩
synonyms nauseate, repel, repulse, revolt, sicken, turn off
related words displease, distress; appall, horrify; affront, insult, offend, outrage, shock
near antonyms attract, charm, entice, tempt; delight, gratify, please, rejoice, tickle
disgusted *adj* filled with disgust — see SICK 2
dish *n* a usually circular utensil for holding something (as food) ⟨we threw all of the ingredients for the salsa into a *dish* and mixed them together⟩
synonyms vessel
related words bowl, casserole, charger, cup, plate, platter, salver, saucer, tray
dishearten *vb* to lessen the courage or confidence of — see DISCOURAGE 1
disheartenment *n* the state of being discouraged — see DISCOURAGEMENT
dishevel *vb* to undo the proper order or arrangement of — see DISORDER
disheveled *or* **dishevelled** *adj* lacking in order, neatness, and often cleanliness — see MESSY
dishonest *adj* **1** telling or containing lies ⟨*dishonest* kids who lie about their ages in order to get into R-rated movies⟩ ⟨*dishonest* statements about the fight in the locker room⟩
synonyms lying, mendacious, untruthful
related words erroneous, fallacious, false, misleading; double-dealing, hypocritical, two-faced
near antonyms candid, open, straightforward; earnest, sincere, true
antonyms honest, truthful, veracious
2 given to or marked by cheating and deception ⟨*dishonest* car dealers who roll back mileage gauges⟩ ⟨*dishonest* business deals that landed him in jail⟩
synonyms crooked, deceptive, fast, fraudulent, shady, sharp, shifty, underhand, underhanded
related words unconscionable, unethical, unprincipled, unscrupulous; deceitful, deceiving, deluding, delusive, delusory; artful, cunning; devious, furtive, sneaking, sneaky, tricky; insidious, perfidious, treacherous
near antonyms conscientious, honorable, just, scrupulous, upright; forthright, straightforward
antonyms aboveboard, honest, straight
3 marked by, based on, or done by the use of dishonest methods to acquire something of value — see FRAUDULENT 1
dishonesty *n* **1** the tendency to tell lies ⟨if you gain a reputation for *dishonesty*, no one will believe you even when you're telling the truth⟩
synonyms deceitfulness, mendacity, untruthfulness
related words artifice, craft, craftiness, crookedness, cunning, deceit, dissembling, dissimulation, double-dealing, duplicity, fakery, foxiness, guile, wiliness; falseness; hypocrisy
near antonyms honor, incorruptibility; candidness, candor, frankness, good faith, sincerity, straightforwardness; dependability, reliability, reliableness, trustworthiness; accuracy, objectivity; authenticity, correctness, genuineness; credibility
antonyms honesty, integrity, probity, truthfulness, veracity, verity
2 the inclination or practice of misleading others through lies or trickery — see DECEIT
dishonor *n* **1** the state of having lost the esteem of others — see DISGRACE 1
2 a cause of shame — see DISGRACE 2
dishonor *vb* to reduce to a lower standing in one's own eyes or in others' eyes — see HUMBLE
dishonorable *adj* **1** not following or in accordance with standards of honor and decency — see IGNOBLE 2
2 not respectable — see DISREPUTABLE
disillusion *vb* to free from mistaken beliefs or foolish hopes ⟨we were *disillusioned* when we saw how the movie star acted in real life⟩
synonyms disabuse, disenchant, undeceive
related words debunk, expose, show up, uncloak, uncover, unmask; disclose, divulge, tell, unveil
near antonyms beguile, bluff, cozen, delude, dupe, fool, gull, hoax, hoodwink, kid, misguide,

misinform, mislead, misrepresent, snow, take in, trick

disinclination *n* **1** a lack of willingness or desire to do or accept something — see RELUCTANCE
2 a strong feeling of not liking or approving — see DISLIKE 1

disinclined *adj* having doubts about the wisdom of doing something — see HESITANT

disintegrate *vb* to go through decomposition — see DECAY 1

disinter *vb* to remove from place of burial — see EXHUME

disinterested *adj* **1** having or showing a lack of interest or concern — see INDIFFERENT 1
2 marked by justice, honesty, and freedom from bias — see FAIR 2

disinterestedness *n* **1** lack of favoritism toward one side or another — see DETACHMENT 1
2 lack of interest or concern — see INDIFFERENCE

disjoin *vb* to set or force apart — see SEPARATE 1

disjoint *vb* to set or force apart — see SEPARATE 1

disjointed *adj* not clearly or logically connected — see INCOHERENT 1

dislike *n* **1** a strong feeling of not liking or approving ⟨we have a strong *dislike* for olives and wouldn't eat them even if we were paid⟩
synonyms allergy, averseness, aversion, disfavor, disinclination, disliking
related words disgust, distaste, loathing, nausea, repugnance, repulsion, revulsion; abomination, antipathy, detestation, hate, hatred; deprecation, disapproval, displeasure, dissatisfaction; jaundice
near antonyms affection, attachment, love; bent, leaning, penchant, predilection, propensity, tendency
antonyms appetite, fondness, like, liking, partiality, preference, taste
2 refusal to accept as right or desirable — see DISAPPROVAL

dislike *vb* **1** to feel dislike for ⟨the two dogs *disliked* each other the first time they met, and never did become friends⟩
synonyms disfavor
related words abhor, abominate, detest, hate, loathe; condemn, despise, scorn; disapprove (of), frown (on *or* upon), object (to)
near antonyms admire, appreciate, cherish, revere, venerate, worship; prize, treasure, value; drink (in), savor; dote (on), idolize; favor, prefer
antonyms adore, cotton (to), delight (in), dig, enjoy, fancy, groove (on), like, love, relish, revel (in)
2 to hold an unfavorable opinion of — see DISAPPROVE

disliking *n* a strong feeling of not liking or approving — see DISLIKE 1

dislocate *vb* **1** to change the place or position of — see MOVE 1
2 to undo the proper order or arrangement of — see DISORDER

dislocation *n* an act or instance of the order of things being disturbed — see UPSET

disloyal *adj* not true in one's allegiance to someone or something — see FAITHLESS

disloyalty *n* **1** lack of faithfulness especially to one's husband or wife — see INFIDELITY 1
2 the act or fact of violating the trust or confidence of another — see BETRAYAL

dismal *adj* **1** causing or marked by an atmosphere lacking in cheer — see GLOOMY 1
2 causing unhappiness — see SAD 2

dismantle *vb* to take apart — see DISASSEMBLE

dismay *n* **1** the emotion felt when one's expectations are not met — see DISAPPOINTMENT 1
2 the state of being discouraged — see DISCOURAGEMENT

dismay *vb* to lessen the courage or confidence of — see DISCOURAGE 1

dismember *vb* to take apart — see DISASSEMBLE

dismiss *vb* **1** to let go from office, service, or employment ⟨the secretary was *dismissed* after it was discovered that she was stealing office supplies⟩
synonyms can, cashier, fire, muster out, remove, retire, sack
related words downsize, furlough, lay off; boot (out), bounce
near antonyms contract, subcontract
antonyms employ, hire
2 to drive or force out — see EJECT 1

dismissal *n* the termination of the employment of an employee or a work force often temporarily — see LAYOFF

disobedience *n* refusal to obey ⟨they gave up on training the dog to fetch because of his constant *disobedience*⟩
synonyms contrariness, defiance, frowardness, insubordination, intractability, rebelliousness, recalcitrance, refractoriness, unruliness, willfulness
related words disrespect, impudence, insolence, rudeness; doggedness, hardheadedness, mulishness, obstinacy, pertinaciousness, pertinacity, perversity, stubbornness; mischievousness, naughtiness
near antonyms agreeability, amiability; slavishness, submissiveness, subservience
antonyms amenability, compliance, docility, obedience

disobedient *adj* given to resisting authority or another's control ⟨the *disobedient* child refused to eat his vegetables⟩
synonyms balky, contrary, defiant, froward, insubordinate, intractable, rebellious, recalcitrant, refractory, restive, ungovernable, unruly, untoward, wayward, willful (*or* wilful)
related words insurgent, mutinous; dogged, hardheaded, headstrong, mulish, obdurate, obstinate, peevish, pertinacious, pigheaded, self-willed, stubborn, unyielding; obstreperous, uncontrollable, unmanageable, wild; perverse, resistant, wrongheaded; bad, disorderly, errant, misbehaving, mischievous, monkeying, monkeyish, naughty; undisciplined; dissident, nonconformist; disrespectful, ill-mannered, ill-natured, impolite, impudent, insolent, ornery, rude, uncouth
near antonyms acquiescent, agreeable, amiable, deferential, obliging; submissive, yielding; behaved, disciplined, well-bred; courteous, polite, respectful; servile, slavish, subservient; decorous, orderly, proper; controllable, governable, manageable
antonyms amenable, compliant, docile, obedient, tractable

disobey *vb* to go against the commands, prohibitions, or rules of ⟨students who *disobey* their teachers and use cell phones in class⟩ ⟨drivers who consistently *disobey* traffic laws⟩
synonyms defy, rebel (against)
related words mutiny (against), revolt (against);

disregard, ignore, tune out; dismiss, flout, pooh-pooh, reject, scoff (at), scorn, shrug off; break, transgress, violate; combat, contest, dispute, fight, oppose, resist, withstand
near antonyms defer (to), serve, submit (to), surrender (to), yield (to); keep, observe; accede (to), acquiesce (to), agree (to), assent (to), comply (with), conform (to), oblige; attend, hear, heed, listen (to), mark, note, notice, regard, watch
antonyms follow, mind, obey
disoblige *vb* to cause discomfort to or trouble for — see INCONVENIENCE
disobliging *adj* causing difficulty, discomfort, or annoyance — see INCONVENIENT 1
disorder *n* **1** a state in which everything is out of order — see CHAOS
2 an abnormal state that disrupts a plant's or animal's normal bodily functioning — see DISEASE
disorder *vb* to undo the proper order or arrangement of ⟨be careful not to *disorder* the carefully arranged contents of the dresser⟩
synonyms confuse, derange, disarrange, disarray, discompose, dishevel, dislocate, disorganize, disrupt, disturb, hash, jumble, mess (up), mix (up), muddle, muss, rumple, scramble, shuffle, tousle, tumble, upset
related words embroil, entangle, snarl, tangle; agitate, stir (up), unsettle
near antonyms align, line, line up; systematize; adjust, fix
antonyms arrange, array, draw up, marshal, order, organize, range, regulate, straighten (up), tidy
disordered *adj* lacking in order, neatness, and often cleanliness — see MESSY
disorderly *adj* **1** not restrained by or under the control of legal authority — see LAWLESS
2 lacking in order, neatness, and often cleanliness — see MESSY
disorganization *n* a state in which everything is out of order — see CHAOS
disorganize *vb* to undo the proper order or arrangement of — see DISORDER
disorient *vb* to throw into a state of mental uncertainty — see CONFUSE 1
disown *vb* to refuse to acknowledge as one's own or as one's responsibility — see DISCLAIM 1
disparage *vb* to express scornfully one's low opinion of — see DECRY 1
disparagement *n* the act of making a person or a thing seem little or unimportant — see DEPRECIATION
disparaging *adj* intended to make a person or thing seem of little importance or value — see DEROGATORY
disparate *adj* being not of the same kind — see DIFFERENT 1
disparateness *n* the quality or state of being different — see DIFFERENCE 1
disparity *n* the quality or state of being different — see DIFFERENCE 1
dispassionate *adj* marked by justice, honesty, and freedom from bias — see FAIR 2
dispatch *n* **1** a message on paper from one person or group to another — see LETTER
2 a piece of conveyed information — see COMMUNICATION
dispatch *vb* **1** to cause to go or be taken from one place to another — see SEND
2 to deprive of life — see KILL 1
3 to put to death deliberately — see MURDER 1
dispel *vb* to cause (members of a group) to move widely apart — see SCATTER 1
dispensable *adj* not needed by the circumstances or to accomplish an end — see UNNECESSARY
dispensation *n* the act or process of giving out something to each member of a group — see DISTRIBUTION 1
dispense *vb* to give out (something) in appropriate amounts or to appropriate individuals — see ADMINISTER 1
dispersal *n* an act or process in which something scatters or is scattered — see SCATTERING 1
disperse *vb* **1** to cause (members of a group) to move widely apart — see SCATTER 1
2 to cease to exist or cause to cease to exist as a group or organization — see DISBAND 1
dispersion *n* an act or process in which something scatters or is scattered — see SCATTERING 1
dispirit *vb* to lessen the courage or confidence of — see DISCOURAGE 1
dispiritedness *n* **1** a state or spell of low spirits — see SADNESS
2 the state of being discouraged — see DISCOURAGEMENT
displace *vb* **1** to change the place or position of — see MOVE 1
2 to force to leave a country — see BANISH 1
3 to take the place of — see REPLACE 1
displacement *n* the forced removal from a homeland — see EXILE 1
display *n* **1** a public showing of objects of interest — see EXHIBITION 1
2 an outward and often exaggerated indication of something abstract (as a feeling) for effect — see SHOW 1
display *vb* **1** to present so as to invite notice or attention — see SHOW 1
2 to make known (something abstract) through outward signs — see SHOW 2
displease *vb* to make discontented — see DISCONTENT
displeased *adj* having a feeling that one has been wronged or thwarted in one's ambitions — see DISCONTENTED
displeasing *adj* not giving pleasure to the mind or senses — see UNPLEASANT
displeasure *n* **1** refusal to accept as right or desirable — see DISAPPROVAL
2 the condition of being dissatisfied with one's life or situation — see DISCONTENT
disport *vb* **1** to cause (someone) to pass the time agreeably occupied — see AMUSE
2 to engage in activity for amusement — see PLAY 1
3 to play and run about happily — see FROLIC 1
4 to present so as to invite notice or attention — see SHOW 1
disposal *n* **1** the getting rid of whatever is unwanted or useless ⟨trash *disposal* is on Wednesday in our neighborhood⟩
synonyms discarding, disposition, dumping, jettison, junking, removal, riddance, scrapping, throwing away
related words clearance, clearing; decimation, demolishment, demolition, destruction
near antonyms accumulation, acquirement, acquisition, collection, deposit
2 the way objects in space or events in time are arranged or follow one another — see ORDER 1

dispose *vb* **1** to arrange something in a certain spot or position — see PLACE 1
2 to put into a particular arrangement — see ORDER 1

disposed *adj* having a desire or inclination (as for a specified course of action) — see WILLING 1

disposition *n* **1** one's characteristic attitude or mood ⟨he had a cheerful *disposition* and was very rarely depressed⟩
synonyms grain, nature, temper, temperament
related words cheer, frame, humor, mode, mood; attitude, outlook, perspective, point of view, standpoint, viewpoint; emotion, feeling, heart, passion, sentiment; strain; belief, conviction, mind, opinion, persuasion; expression, tone, vein; character, individuality, personality; responsiveness, sensibility, sensitiveness, sensitivity
2 a habitual attraction to some activity or thing — see INCLINATION 1
3 the getting rid of whatever is unwanted or useless — see DISPOSAL 1
4 the way objects in space or events in time are arranged or follow one another — see ORDER 1

disprove *vb* to prove to be false ⟨Magellan's circumnavigation of the globe *disproved* any lingering notions that the earth is flat⟩
synonyms belie, confute, rebut, refute
related words overthrow, overturn
phrases give the lie to
near antonyms evidence, show; demonstrate, display, illustrate, manifest; argue, reason
antonyms confirm, prove, verify

disputable *adj* **1** giving good reason for being doubted, questioned, or challenged — see DOUBTFUL
2 open to question or dispute — see DEBATABLE 2

disputant *n* a person who takes part in a dispute ⟨there were only three *disputants* in the argument, but they made enough noise for a dozen⟩
synonyms arguer, debater, disputer, quarreler (*or* quarreller), squabbler, wrangler
related words advocate, defendant, plaintiff, pleader; nitpicker, pettifogger, quibbler

disputation *n* variance of opinion on a matter — see DISAGREEMENT 1

disputatious *adj* **1** feeling or displaying eagerness to fight — see BELLIGERENT
2 given to arguing — see ARGUMENTATIVE 1

disputatiousness *n* an inclination to fight or quarrel — see BELLIGERENCE

dispute *n* **1** variance of opinion on a matter — see DISAGREEMENT 1
2 an often noisy or angry expression of differing opinions — see ARGUMENT 1

dispute *vb* **1** to demand proof of the truth or rightness of — see CHALLENGE 1
2 to express different opinions about something often angrily — see ARGUE 2
3 to talk about (an issue) usually from various points of view and for the purpose of arriving at a decision or opinion — see DISCUSS

disputer *n* a person who takes part in a dispute — see DISPUTANT

disquiet *n* **1** a disturbed or uneasy state — see UNREST
2 an uneasy state of mind usually over the possibility of an anticipated misfortune or trouble — see ANXIETY 1

disquiet *vb* to trouble the mind of; to make uneasy — see DISTURB 1

disquieting *adj* **1** causing worry or anxiety — see TROUBLESOME
2 marked by or causing agitation or uncomfortable feelings — see NERVOUS 2

disregard *n* lack of interest or concern — see INDIFFERENCE

disregard *vb* **1** to ignore in a disrespectful manner — see SCORN 2
2 to fail to give proper attention to — see NEGLECT 1
3 to overlook or dismiss as of little importance — see EXCUSE 1

disrepair *n* the state of being unattended to or not cared for — see NEGLECT 1

disreputable *adj* not respectable ⟨a *disreputable* Internet retailer that had a record of hundreds of complaints for shoddy merchandise and slow refunds⟩
synonyms discreditable, disgraceful, dishonorable, ignominious, infamous, notorious, shameful
related words bad, immoral, seamy, shady, sordid, unethical, unsavory, wicked; base, contemptible, despicable, detestable, dirty, low, mean, vile, wretched
near antonyms ethical, good, moral
antonyms honorable, reputable, respectable

disrepute *n* the state of having lost the esteem of others — see DISGRACE 1

disrespect *n* rude behavior — see DISCOURTESY

disrobe *vb* to remove clothing from — see UNDRESS

disrobed *adj* lacking or shed of clothing — see NAKED 1

disrupt *vb* to undo the proper order or arrangement of — see DISORDER

disruption *n* an act or instance of the order of things being disturbed — see UPSET

dissatisfaction *n* **1** the condition of being dissatisfied with one's life or situation — see DISCONTENT
2 the emotion felt when one's expectations are not met — see DISAPPOINTMENT 1

dissatisfied *adj* having a feeling that one has been wronged or thwarted in one's ambitions — see DISCONTENTED

dissatisfy *vb* **1** to fall short in satisfying the expectation or hope of — see DISAPPOINT
2 to make discontented — see DISCONTENT

dissect *vb* to identify and examine the basic elements or parts of (something) especially for discovering interrelationships — see ANALYZE

dissection *n* the separation and identification of the parts of a whole — see ANALYSIS 1

dissemble *vb* to take on a false or deceptive appearance — see PRETEND 1

dissembling *n* **1** the inclination or practice of misleading others through lies or trickery — see DECEIT
2 the pretending of having virtues, principles, or beliefs that one in fact does not have — see HYPOCRISY

disseminate *vb* to cause to be known over a considerable area or by many people — see SPREAD 1

dissension *n* **1** a lack of agreement or harmony — see DISCORD
2 variance of opinion on a matter — see DISAGREEMENT 1

dissent *n* **1** a lack of agreement or harmony — see DISCORD

2 departure from a generally accepted theory, opinion, or practice — see HERESY

dissent *vb* to have a different opinion — see DISAGREE 1

dissenter *n* a person who believes or teaches something opposed to accepted beliefs — see HERETIC

dissentient *adj* deviating from commonly accepted beliefs or practices — see HERETICAL

dissenting *adj* deviating from commonly accepted beliefs or practices — see HERETICAL

disservice *n* unfair or inadequate treatment of someone or something or an instance of this ⟨you do a great *disservice* to the professionals at the day-care center when you refer to them as "babysitters"⟩
synonyms injury, injustice, raw deal, wrong
related words insult, offense, outrage; complaint, grievance
near antonyms cricket
antonyms justice

dissever *vb* to set or force apart — see SEPARATE 1

dissidence *n* **1** a lack of agreement or harmony — see DISCORD
2 departure from a generally accepted theory, opinion, or practice — see HERESY

dissident *adj* deviating from commonly accepted beliefs or practices — see HERETICAL

dissident *n* a person who believes or teaches something opposed to accepted beliefs — see HERETIC

dissimilar *adj* being not of the same kind — see DIFFERENT 1

dissimilarity *n* the quality or state of being different — see DIFFERENCE 1

dissimulation *n* **1** the inclination or practice of misleading others through lies or trickery — see DECEIT
2 the pretending of having virtues, principles, or beliefs that one in fact does not have — see HYPOCRISY

dissipate *vb* **1** to cause (members of a group) to move widely apart — see SCATTER 1
2 to use up carelessly — see WASTE 1

dissipated *adj* having or showing lowered moral character or standards — see CORRUPT

dissipatedness *n* a sinking to a state of low moral standards and behavior — see CORRUPTION 2

dissipation *n* **1** a sinking to a state of low moral standards and behavior — see CORRUPTION 2
2 an act or process in which something scatters or is scattered — see SCATTERING 1

dissociate *vb* to set or force apart — see SEPARATE 1

dissolute *adj* having or showing lowered moral character or standards — see CORRUPT

dissoluteness *n* a sinking to a state of low moral standards and behavior — see CORRUPTION 2

dissolution *n* the act or process of a whole separating into two or more parts or pieces — see SEPARATION 1

dissolve *vb* **1** to cease to be visible — see DISAPPEAR
2 to cease to exist or cause to cease to exist as a group or organization — see DISBAND 1
3 to put an end to by formal action — see ABOLISH

dissonant *adj* marked by or producing a harsh combination of sounds ⟨a *dissonant* chorus of noises arose from the busy construction site⟩
synonyms discordant, inharmonious, unmelodious, unmusical
related words blaring, clanging, clashing, clattering, grating, harsh, jangling, jarring, metallic, raspy, raucous, scratching, screeching, shrill, squeaky, strident; disagreeable, unpleasant, unpleasing; atonal, off-key
near antonyms dulcet, euphonious, mellifluous, mellow, melodic, sweet, tuneful; resonant, sonorous; quavering, trilling, warbling; agreeable, appealing, pleasant; cadenced, lilting, lyric, lyrical, rhythmic (*or* rhythmical); chordal, harmonic, homophonic, orchestral, polyphonic, symphonic, tonal
antonyms harmonious, harmonizing, melodious, musical

dissuade *vb* to steer (a person) from an activity or course of action — see DISCOURAGE 2

distance *n* the space or amount of space between two points, lines, surfaces, or objects ⟨the *distance* between the earth and the sun is about 93 million miles⟩
synonyms lead, length, remove, spacing, spread, stretch, way
related words altitude, area, breadth, depth, height, rise, space, volume, width; extension, extent; cast, range, reach, scope, shot, sweep, throw; drop, fall, flight, haul; berth, clearance
phrases a far cry

distant *adj* **1** not close in time or space ⟨the *distant* towers were barely visible in the fog⟩
synonyms away, far, faraway, far-off, remote, removed
related words apart, isolated, obscure, outlying, out-of-the-way, retired, secluded, secret, sequestered
near antonyms adjacent, adjoining, contiguous
antonyms close, near, nearby, nigh
2 having or showing a lack of friendliness or interest in others — see COOL 1

distaste *n* a dislike so strong as to cause stomach upset or queasiness — see DISGUST

distasteful *adj* **1** disagreeable or disgusting to the sense of taste ⟨cod-liver oil is so *distasteful* that it's worse than anything it cures⟩
synonyms unappetizing, unpalatable, unsavory
related words abominable, awful, bad, filthy, foul, horrible, loathsome, nasty, nauseating, noisome, obnoxious, offensive, repellent, repugnant, repulsive, revolting, shocking, sickening; bland, flat, flavorless, insipid, savorless, tasteless
near antonyms appealing, attractive, flavorful, piquant, rich
antonyms appetizing, delectable, delicious, palatable, savory, tasty
2 not giving pleasure to the mind or senses — see UNPLEASANT
3 causing intense displeasure, disgust, or resentment — see OFFENSIVE 1

distill *vb* to remove usually visible impurities from — see CLARIFY 1

distinct *adj* **1** being not of the same kind — see DIFFERENT 1
2 not subject to misinterpretation or more than one interpretation — see CLEAR 2
3 of a particular or exact sort — see EXPRESS 1
4 serving to identify as belonging to an individual or group — see CHARACTERISTIC 1

distinction *n* **1** exceptionally high quality — see EXCELLENCE 1

2 a quality that gives something special worth — see EXCELLENCE 2
3 public acknowledgment or admiration for an achievement — see GLORY 1
4 the fact or state of being above others in rank or importance — see EMINENCE 1
5 something given in recognition of achievement — see AWARD
6 the quality or state of being different — see DIFFERENCE 1
7 the state of being kept distinct — see SEPARATION 2

distinctive *adj* **1** being not of the same kind — see DIFFERENT 1
2 serving to identify as belonging to an individual or group — see CHARACTERISTIC 1

distinctiveness *n* the quality or state of being different — see DIFFERENCE 1

distinctness *n* the quality or state of being different — see DIFFERENCE 1

distinguish *vb* **1** to understand or point out the difference ⟨even at such a young age, he could *distinguish* between right and wrong⟩
synonyms differentiate, discern, discriminate, separate
related words comprehend, grasp, know, understand; divide, part, sever; demarcate, mark (off), set off
near antonyms confound, lump (together), mingle
antonyms confuse, mistake, mix (up)
2 to be an important feature of — see CHARACTERIZE 2
3 to find out or establish the identity of — see IDENTIFY 1
4 to make note of (something) through the use of one's eyes — see SEE 1

distinguishable *adj* **1** able to be perceived by a sense or by the mind — see PERCEPTIBLE
2 being not of the same kind — see DIFFERENT 1

distinguished *adj* standing above others in rank, importance, or achievement — see EMINENT

distinguishing *adj* serving to identify as belonging to an individual or group — see CHARACTERISTIC 1

distort *vb* **1** to change so much as to create a wrong impression or alter the meaning of — see GARBLE
2 to twist (something) out of a natural or normal shape or condition — see CONTORT

distorted *adj* badly or imperfectly formed — see MALFORMED

distortion *n* the twisting of something out of its natural or normal shape or condition — see CONTORTION

distract *vb* **1** to draw the attention or mind to something else ⟨we were *distracted* from our homework by the noise outside⟩
synonyms divert
related words amuse, entertain; stray, wander
near antonyms focus
2 to trouble the mind of; to make uneasy — see DISTURB 1

distraction *n* **1** a state of mental uncertainty — see CONFUSION 1
2 a state of wildly excited activity or emotion — see FRENZY
3 the act or activity of providing pleasure or amusement especially for the public — see ENTERTAINMENT 1

distraught *adj* feeling overwhelming fear or worry — see FRANTIC 1

distress *n* **1** a state of great suffering of body or mind ⟨the upcoming final exam is causing us considerable *distress*⟩ ⟨the survivors were in extreme *distress* after having been stranded on the island for a week with no food⟩
synonyms affliction, agony, anguish, misery, pain, strait(s), torment, torture, tribulation, woe
related words discomfort; cross, crucible, trial; heartbreak, joylessness, sadness, sorrow, unhappiness; emergency, pinch; asperity, difficulty, hardship, rigor; ache, hurt, pang, smarting, soreness, stitch, throe, twinge; danger, jeopardy, trouble
near antonyms comfort, consolation, solace; alleviation, assuagement, ease, relief; peace, security
2 the state of not being protected from injury, harm, or evil — see DANGER 1

distress *vb* to trouble the mind of; to make uneasy — see DISTURB 1

distressful *adj* **1** marked by or causing agitation or uncomfortable feelings — see NERVOUS 2
2 of a kind to cause great distress — see REGRETTABLE

distressing *adj* **1** causing worry or anxiety — see TROUBLESOME
2 of a kind to cause great distress — see REGRETTABLE
3 marked by or causing agitation or uncomfortable feelings — see NERVOUS 2

distribute *vb* to give out (something) in appropriate amounts or to appropriate individuals — see ADMINISTER 1

distribution *n* **1** the act or process of giving out something to each member of a group ⟨we oversaw the *distribution* of medicine to the natives⟩
synonyms allocation, apportionment, dispensation, division, issuance
related words disbursement; reapportionment, redistribution
2 the way objects in space or events in time are arranged or follow one another — see ORDER 1

district *n* an area (as of a city) set apart for some purpose or having some special feature ⟨Independence Hall in Philadelphia's historic *district*⟩
synonyms neighborhood, quarter, section
related words belt, zone; department, division, part; precinct, ward; area, locality, place, region; barrio, enclave, ghetto

distrust *n* a feeling or attitude that one does not know the truth, truthfulness, or trustworthiness of someone or something — see DOUBT

distrust *vb* to have no trust or confidence in ⟨we *distrusted* the stranger when he offered us free candy⟩
synonyms doubt, mistrust, question, suspect
related words disbelieve, discount, discredit, negate
phrases look askance at
near antonyms bank (on *or* upon), count (on *or* upon), depend (on *or* upon), rely (on *or* upon)
antonyms trust

distrustful *adj* **1** inclined to doubt or question claims — see SKEPTICAL 1
2 not feeling sure about the truth, wisdom, or trustworthiness of someone or something — see DOUBTFUL 1

distrustfully *adv* with distrust — see ASKANCE

distrustfulness *n* a feeling or attitude that one

does not know the truth, truthfulness, or trustworthiness of someone or something — see DOUBT

disturb *vb* **1** to trouble the mind of; to make uneasy <all that talk of war *disturbed* us>
synonyms agitate, bother, concern, discomfort, discompose, disquiet, distract, distress, exercise, freak (out), perturb, undo, unhinge, unsettle, upset, worry
related words aggravate, anger, annoy, bug, chafe, chivy, exasperate, fret, gall, get, grate, harass, harry, irk, irritate, nettle, peeve, pester, pique, put out, rile, vex; bedevil, haunt, plague; abash, confound, confuse, discomfit, disconcert, discountenance, embarrass, faze, fluster, mortify, nonplus, rattle; daunt, demoralize, discourage, dishearten, dismay, dispirit
near antonyms allay, alleviate, assuage; appease, conciliate, mollify, pacify, placate, propitiate
antonyms calm, compose, quiet, settle, soothe, tranquilize (*also* tranquillize)
2 to change the place or position of — see MOVE 1
3 to undo the proper order or arrangement of — see DISORDER
4 to thrust oneself upon (another) without invitation — see BOTHER 1
5 to cause discomfort to or trouble for — see INCONVENIENCE

disturbance *n* **1** a state of noisy, confused activity — see COMMOTION
2 an act or instance of the order of things being disturbed — see UPSET
3 the act of making unwelcome intrusions upon another — see ANNOYANCE 1

disturbing *adj* **1** causing annoyance — see ANNOYING
2 causing embarrassment — see AWKWARD 3
3 causing worry or anxiety — see TROUBLESOME
4 marked by or causing agitation or uncomfortable feelings — see NERVOUS 2

disunion *n* the act or process of a whole separating into two or more parts or pieces — see SEPARATION 1

disunite *vb* to set or force apart — see SEPARATE 1

disunited *adj* disagreeing with each other — see DIVIDED

disunity *n* a lack of agreement or harmony — see DISCORD

disuse *n* lack of use <the old farmhouse showed signs of *disuse*>
synonyms idleness, inactivity
related words abandonment, desertion, neglect; dormancy, latency, quiescence
antonyms use

disused *adj* left unoccupied or unused — see ABANDONED

ditch *n* a long narrow channel dug in the earth <after skidding on the ice, our car went right into the *ditch*>
synonyms dike, gutter, trench, trough
related words culvert, drain, draw, gully, ravine; drill, furrow

ditch *vb* to get rid of as useless or unwanted — see DISCARD

dither *n* **1** a state of nervous or irritated concern — see FRET
2 a sense of panic or extreme nervousness — see JITTERS

dithery *adj* feeling or showing uncomfortable feelings of uncertainty — see NERVOUS 1

ditty *n* a short musical composition for the human voice often with instrumental accompaniment — see SONG 1

diurnal *adj* occurring, done, produced, or appearing every day — see DAILY

divan *n* a long upholstered piece of furniture designed for several sitters — see COUCH

dive *n* **1** an act or instance of diving <the penguin took a *dive* off of the ice sheet>
synonyms pitch, plunge
related words dip, immersion, submersion; fall, slip, spill, stumble, tumble; descent, drop; belly flop, header, jackknife
near antonyms jump, leap
2 the act or process of going to a lower level or altitude — see DESCENT 1

dive *vb* to cast oneself head first into deep water <we watched her *dive* in after the drowning man>
synonyms pitch, plunge, sound
related words dip, immerse, submerge; belly flop
near antonyms surface

diverge *vb* **1** to extend outwards from or as if from a central point — see RADIATE 1
2 to go or move in different directions from a central point — see SEPARATE 2

divergence *n* a movement in different directions away from a common point <a growing *divergence* of opinion about that U.S. president's place in history>
synonyms separation
related words difference, disagreement, discrepancy, disparateness, disparity, dissidence, dissimilarity, distinction, distinctiveness, distinctness, diversity, unlikeness
near antonyms accord, agreement; likeness, similarity
antonyms convergence

divers *adj* being of many and various kinds — see MANIFOLD

diverse *adj* being not of the same kind — see DIFFERENT 1

diverseness *n* **1** the quality or state of being composed of many different elements or types — see VARIETY 1
2 the quality or state of being different — see DIFFERENCE 1

diversion *n* **1** someone or something that provides amusement or enjoyment — see FUN 1
2 the act or activity of providing pleasure or amusement especially for the public — see ENTERTAINMENT 1

diversity *n* **1** the quality or state of being composed of many different elements or types — see VARIETY 1
2 the quality or state of being different — see DIFFERENCE 1

divert *vb* **1** to cause (someone) to pass the time agreeably occupied — see AMUSE
2 to change the course or direction of (something) — see TURN 2
3 to draw the attention or mind to something else — see DISTRACT 1

diverting *adj* providing amusement or enjoyment — see FUN

divide *vb* **1** to set or force apart — see SEPARATE 1
2 to go or move in different directions from a central point — see SEPARATE 2

divided *adj* disagreeing with each other <the club members were *divided* on the need for more fundraising>

synonyms disunited, split
phrases at loggerheads, at odds
antonyms undivided, united

dividend *n* something given in addition to what is ordinarily expected or owed — see BONUS

divider *n* something that divides, separates, or marks off — see DIVISION 1

divine *adj* **1** of the very best kind — see EXCELLENT
2 of, relating to, or being God — see HOLY 3

divine *n* a person specially trained and authorized to conduct religious services in a Christian church — see CLERGYMAN

divine *vb* to realize or know about beforehand — see FORESEE

diviner *n* one who predicts future events or developments — see PROPHET

divinity *n* **1** the quality or state of being divine ⟨Henry David Thoreau felt the presence of *divinity* in every part of nature⟩
synonyms deity, godhead, godhood
2 a being having superhuman powers and control over a particular part of life or the world — see DEITY 1
3 *cap* the being worshipped as the creator and ruler of the universe — see DEITY 2

divisible *adj* capable of being split into two or more parts or pieces — see SEPARABLE

division *n* **1** something that divides, separates, or marks off ⟨we poked our heads over the *division* between the yards to see what the fuss was about⟩
synonyms divider, partition
related words barrier, fence, wall; border, boundary, limit
2 a large unit of a governmental, business, or educational organization ⟨the complaints *division* handled all of the calls from the angry townsfolk⟩
synonyms bureau, department, desk, office
3 one of the units into which a whole is divided on the basis of a common characteristic — see CLASS 2
4 the act or process of a whole separating into two or more parts or pieces — see SEPARATION 1
5 the act or process of giving out something to each member of a group — see DISTRIBUTION 1

divorce *vb* to set or force apart — see SEPARATE 1

divulge *vb* to make known (as information previously kept secret) — see REVEAL 1

divulgence *n* the act or an instance of making known something previously unknown or concealed — see REVELATION

dizzy *adj* **1** having a feeling of being whirled about and in danger of falling down ⟨I felt very *dizzy* after I got off of the roller coaster⟩
synonyms giddy, light-headed, reeling, whirling
related words faint, weak; addled, befuddled, confused, dazed
near antonyms clearheaded; stable, steady
2 suffering from mental confusion ⟨he felt *dizzy* from trying to remember all of the dates and names that were sure to be asked on the test⟩
synonyms befuddled, bewildered, confused, dazed, stunned, stupefied
related words senseless, unconscious
phrases at sea
near antonyms alert, conscious
antonyms clearheaded, unconfused
3 moving, proceeding, or acting with great speed — see FAST 1

do *vb* **1** to be fitting or proper ⟨Oh, that outfit just won't *do* for the opera⟩
synonyms befit, fit, go, serve, suit
related words satisfy, suffice; function, work
2 to be enough — see SERVE 2
3 to carry through (as a process) to completion — see PERFORM 1
4 to make more attractive by adding something that is beautiful or becoming — see DECORATE
5 to meet one's day-to-day needs — see GET ALONG 1

doable *adj* capable of being done or carried out — see POSSIBLE 1

docile *adj* readily giving in to the command or authority of another — see OBEDIENT

docility *n* a readiness or willingness to yield to the wishes of others — see COMPLIANCE 1

dock *n* a structure used by boats and ships for taking on or landing cargo and passengers ⟨the boat remained tied up at the *dock* for a week, waiting for the weather to clear⟩
synonyms float, jetty, landing, levee, pier, quay, wharf
related words berth, mooring, slip; dockyard, marina, shipyard

[1]**dock** *vb* to make (as hair) shorter with or as if with the use of shears — see CLIP

[2]**dock** *vb* to stop at or near a place along the shore — see LAND 1

docket *n* a listing of things to be presented or considered (as at a concert or play) — see PROGRAM 1

dockworker *n* one who loads and unloads ships at a port ⟨the *dockworkers* spent all afternoon taking crates off of the ship⟩
synonyms longshoreman, stevedore

doctor *n* a person specially trained in healing human medical disorders ⟨we called a *doctor* as soon as we realized the baby was sick⟩
synonyms medic, physician
related words dermatologist, general practitioner, gynecologist, internist, neurologist, obstetrician, ophthalmologist, orthopedist, pediatrician, specialist, surgeon; intern, resident; nurse, paramedic

doctor *vb* **1** to give medical treatment to ⟨a pledge to *doctor* the burn victims until they were whole again⟩
synonyms treat
related words cure, heal, mend, rehabilitate, remedy; attend, care (for), dose, drug, minister (to), nurse
2 to put into good shape or working order again — see MEND 1

doctrine *n* **1** a statement or body of statements concerning faith or morals proclaimed by a church ⟨the Catholic Church's *doctrine* on the Eucharist⟩
synonyms canon, dogma
related words belief, conviction, tenet; credo, creed, ideology, philosophy, theology; axiom, precept, principle
2 the basic beliefs or guiding principles of a person or group — see CREED 1

document *n* **1** a piece of paper with information written or to be written on it — see FORM 2
2 a written or printed paper giving information about or proof of something — see CERTIFICATE

document *vb* to show the existence or truth of by evidence — see PROVE 1

documentary *adj* restricted to or based on fact — see FACTUAL 1

documentation *n* something presented in support of the truth or accuracy of a claim — see PROOF

dodder *vb* to move forward while swaying from side to side — see STAGGER 1

dodge *n* a clever often underhanded means to achieve an end — see TRICK 1

dodge *vb* **1** to move suddenly aside or to and fro ⟨*dodging* through the crowd on his way to the exit⟩
synonyms duck, sidestep, zigzag
related words avoid, elude, escape, evade, parry, shirk, skirt; deflect, turn; slide, slip
2 to avoid having to comply with (something) especially through cleverness — see CIRCUMVENT 1
3 to get or keep away from (as a responsibility) through cleverness or trickery — see ESCAPE 2

dodger *n* a dishonest person who uses clever means to cheat others out of something of value — see TRICKSTER 1

dodging *n* the act or a means of getting or keeping away from something undesirable — see ESCAPE 2

dodo *n* **1** a person with old-fashioned ideas — see FOGY
2 a stupid person — see IDIOT

doff *vb* to rid oneself of (a garment) — see REMOVE 1

dog *n* a domestic mammal that is related to the wolves and foxes ⟨we got a *dog* from the pound to keep as a pet⟩
synonyms canine, doggy (*or* doggie), hound, pooch
related words cur, mongrel, mutt; bitch; lapdog, pup, puppy, whelp; bird dog, hunter, police dog, sheepdog, sled dog, watchdog, wolf dog, wolfhound

dog *vb* to go after or on the track of — see FOLLOW 2

dog–eared *adj* showing signs of advanced wear and tear and neglect — see SHABBY 1

dogged *adj* **1** continuing despite difficulties, opposition, or discouragement — see PERSISTENT
2 sticking to an opinion, purpose, or course of action in spite of reason, arguments, or persuasion — see OBSTINATE
3 showing no signs of slackening or yielding in one's purpose — see UNYIELDING 1

doggedness *n* a steadfast adherence to an opinion, purpose, or course of action — see OBSTINACY

dogging *n* the act of going after or in the tracks of another — see PURSUIT

doggy *or* **doggie** *n* a domestic mammal that is related to the wolves and foxes — see DOG

dogma *n* a statement or body of statements concerning faith or morals proclaimed by a church — see DOCTRINE 1

do in *vb* **1** to bring to a complete end the physical soundness, existence, or usefulness of — see DESTROY 1
2 to deprive of life — see KILL 1
3 to put to death deliberately — see MURDER 1
4 to use up all the physical energy of — see EXHAUST 1

doing *n* something done by someone — see ACTION 1

doldrums *n pl* **1** a state of temporary inactivity — see ABEYANCE
2 a state or spell of low spirits — see SADNESS
3 the state of being bored — see BOREDOM

dole (out) *vb* to give out (something) in appropriate amounts or to appropriate individuals — see ADMINISTER 1

doleful *adj* **1** expressing or suggesting mourning — see MOURNFUL 1
2 feeling unhappiness — see SAD 1

dolefulness *n* deep sadness especially for the loss of someone or something loved — see SORROW

doll *n* **1** a small figure often of a human being used especially as a child's plaything ⟨there was a row of *dolls* along the shelf in the bedroom⟩
synonyms dolly, puppet
related words rag doll; figure, figurine; plaything, toy
2 a young usually unmarried woman — see GIRL 1

doll up *vb* to put on one's best or formal clothes — see DRESS UP

dolly *n* a small figure often of a human being used especially as a child's plaything — see DOLL 1

dolor *n* deep sadness especially for the loss of someone or something loved — see SORROW

dolorous *adj* expressing or suggesting mourning — see MOURNFUL 1

dolt *n* a stupid person — see IDIOT

doltish *adj* not having or showing an ability to absorb ideas readily — see STUPID 1

doltishness *n* the quality or state of lacking intelligence or quickness of mind — see STUPIDITY 1

domain *n* a region of activity, knowledge, or influence — see FIELD 2

domestic *adj* **1** of or relating to a household or family ⟨the surest way to maintain *domestic* peace and harmony is to have everyone pitch in on chores⟩
synonyms familial, household
related words homelike, homely, homey; residential
2 changed from the wild state so as to become useful and obedient to humans — see TAME 1

domestic *n* **1** a female domestic servant — see MAID 1
2 a person hired to perform household or personal services — see SERVANT

domesticated *adj* changed from the wild state so as to become useful and obedient to humans — see TAME 1

domicile *n* the place where one lives — see HOME 1

domicile *vb* to provide with living quarters or shelter — see HOUSE 1

dominance *n* **1** controlling power or influence over others — see SUPREMACY 1
2 the fact or state of being above others in rank or importance — see EMINENCE 1

dominant *adj* coming before all others in importance — see FOREMOST 1

dominate *vb* **1** to bring under one's control by force of arms — see CONQUER 1
2 to look down on — see OVERLOOK 1
3 to serve as leader of — see LEAD 2

dominating *n* the act or process of bringing someone or something under one's control — see CONQUEST

domination *n* the act or process of bringing someone or something under one's control — see CONQUEST

domineering *adj* fond of ordering people around — see BOSSY

dominie *n* a person specially trained and authorized to conduct religious services in a Christian church — see CLERGYMAN
dominion *n* **1** controlling power or influence over others — see SUPREMACY 1
2 the right or means to command or control others — see POWER 1
don *vb* to place on one's person — see PUT ON 1
donate *vb* to make a present of — see GIVE 1
donation *n* **1** a gift of money or its equivalent to a charity, humanitarian cause, or public institution — see CONTRIBUTION
2 something given to someone without expectation of a return — see GIFT 1
donator *n* one that helps another with gifts or money — see BENEFACTOR
done *adj* brought or having come to an end — see COMPLETE 2
done in *adj* depleted in strength, energy, or freshness — see WEARY 1
donkey *n* **1** a sturdy and patient domestic mammal that is used especially to carry things ⟨we put our bags on the *donkey* and headed down the canyon⟩
synonyms ass, burro, jackass
related words jack, jenny; hinny, mule; pack animal
2 a stupid person — see IDIOT
donor *n* one that helps another with gifts or money — see BENEFACTOR
doom *n* **1** a decision made by a court or tribunal regarding a case it has heard — see SENTENCE
2 a state or end that seemingly has been decided beforehand — see FATE 1
3 the permanent stopping of all the vital bodily activities — see DEATH 1
doom *vb* **1** to determine the fate of in advance — see DESTINE
2 to impose a judicial punishment on — see SENTENCE
door *n* **1** a barrier by which an entry is closed and opened ⟨we locked the *door* to the room so that no one could get in⟩
synonyms gate, hatch, portal
related words Dutch door, French door, lattice, portcullis, postern, trapdoor, wicket
2 the opening through which one can enter or leave a structure ⟨a steady stream of visitors through the front *door*⟩
synonyms doorway, entrance, gate, gateway, way
related words hatch, hatchway
doorkeeper *n* a person who tends a door ⟨the *doorkeeper* held the door open for us so we didn't have to put down our packages⟩
synonyms doorman, gatekeeper, janitor, porter [*chiefly British*]
doorman *n* a person who tends a door — see DOORKEEPER
doorway *n* **1** the means or right of entering or participating in — see ENTRANCE 1
2 the opening through which one can enter or leave a structure — see DOOR 2
dope *n* **1** information not generally available to the public ⟨he gave us the *dope* on the deal taking place that night at the warehouse⟩
synonyms lowdown, scoop, tip
related words dirt, gossip, rumor, story; hint, pointer; information, intelligence, news, tidings, word
2 a stupid person — see IDIOT
dope (out) *vb* to find an answer for through reasoning — see SOLVE
doper *n* a person who regularly uses drugs especially illegally ⟨the *doper* had to go straight, since he couldn't keep a steady job while using drugs⟩
synonyms addict, fiend, junkie (*also* junky), substance abuser, user
related words pothead
dopey *adj* not having or showing an ability to absorb ideas readily — see STUPID 1
dopiness *n* the quality or state of lacking intelligence or quickness of mind — see STUPIDITY 1
dork *n, slang* a stupid person — see IDIOT
dorky *adj, slang* not having or showing an ability to absorb ideas readily — see STUPID 1
dormancy *n* **1** a state of temporary inactivity — see ABEYANCE
2 lack of action or activity — see INACTION
dormant *adj* **1** being in a state of suspended consciousness — see ASLEEP 1
2 not being in a state of use, activity, or employment — see INACTIVE 2
dot *n* a small area that is different (as in color) from the main part — see SPOT 1
dot *vb* **1** to cover by or as if by scattering something over or on — see SCATTER 2
2 to mark with small spots especially unevenly — see SPOT
dote (on) *vb* to love or admire too much — see IDOLIZE
dotted *adj* marked with spots — see SPOTTED 1
dotty *adj* showing or marked by a lack of good sense or judgment — see FOOLISH 1
double *adj* **1** consisting of two members or parts that are usually joined ⟨an egg with a *double* yolk⟩
synonyms binary, bipartite, dual, duplex, twin
related words mated, paired
antonyms single
2 being twice as great or as many ⟨after it was ranked the best in the country, the college had *double* the usual number of applicants⟩
synonyms twofold
double *adv* to two times the amount or degree — see DOUBLY
double *n* something or someone that strongly resembles another — see IMAGE 1
double *vb* **1** to make twice as great or as many ⟨we *doubled* our efforts to find a solution to the problem⟩
synonyms duplicate, redouble
related words compound, multiply; accumulate, balloon, build (up), burgeon, enlarge, escalate, expand, increase, mount, mushroom, proliferate, rise, snowball, swell, wax
2 to lay one part over or against another part of — see FOLD 1
double-cross *vb* to be unfaithful or disloyal to — see BETRAY 1
double cross *n* the act or fact of violating the trust or confidence of another — see BETRAYAL
double-crosser *n* one who betrays a trust or an allegiance — see TRAITOR
double-dealing *adj* **1** marked by, based on, or done by the use of dishonest methods to acquire something of value — see FRAUDULENT 1
2 not being or expressing what one appears to be or express — see INSINCERE
double-dealing *n* the inclination or practice of

misleading others through lies or trickery — see DECEIT

doubly *adv* to two times the amount or degree ⟨we were *doubly* certain of her guilt after we read the article in the newspaper⟩
synonyms double, twice, twofold

doubt *n* a feeling or attitude that one does not know the truth, truthfulness, or trustworthiness of someone or something ⟨from the beginning I had my *doubts* about the new kid in school⟩
synonyms distrust, distrustfulness, incertitude, misgiving, mistrust, mistrustfulness, skepticism, suspicion, uncertainty
related words disbelief, incredulity, unbelief; anxiety, concern; compunction, qualm, scruple
near antonyms credence, faith
antonyms assurance, belief, certainty, certitude, confidence, conviction, sureness, surety, trust

doubt *vb* to have no trust or confidence in — see DISTRUST

doubtable *adj* **1** giving good reason for being doubted, questioned, or challenged — see DOUBTFUL 2
2 open to question or dispute — see DEBATABLE 1

doubter *n* a person who is always ready to doubt or question the truth or existence of something — see SKEPTIC

doubtful *adj* **1** not feeling sure about the truth, wisdom, or trustworthiness of someone or something ⟨he was *doubtful* about the decision to complete the project despite its mounting problems⟩
synonyms distrustful, dubious, mistrustful, skeptical, suspicious, uncertain, unconvinced, undecided, unsettled, unsure
related words diffident, insecure; hesitant, indecisive, irresolute, vacillating, wavering
phrases on the fence
near antonyms assured, confident, sanguine, self-assured; decisive, determined, resolute
antonyms certain, convinced, positive, sure
2 giving good reason for being doubted, questioned, or challenged ⟨the election results were highly *doubtful*, so an investigation was begun⟩
synonyms debatable, disputable, doubtable, dubious, equivocal, fishy, problematic (*also* problematical), questionable, shady, shaky, suspect, suspicious
related words moot; ambiguous, open, unclear; uncertain, undecided, undetermined; far-fetched, flimsy, improbable, unlikely
near antonyms decisive, definitive; clear, obvious, open-and-shut, positive
antonyms certain, incontestable, indisputable, indubitable, sure, undeniable, undoubted, unquestionable
3 not likely to be true or to occur — see IMPROBABLE
4 open to question or dispute — see DEBATABLE 1

doubtfully *adv* with distrust — see ASKANCE

doubting *adj* inclined to doubt or question claims — see SKEPTICAL 1

doubtingly *adv* with distrust — see ASKANCE

doubtless *adj* having or showing a mind free from doubt — see CERTAIN 2

doubtless *adv* **1** without any question — see INDEED 1
2 without much doubt — see PROBABLY

dough *n* something (as pieces of stamped metal or printed paper) customarily and legally used as a medium of exchange, a measure of value, or a means of payment — see MONEY

doughtiness *n* strength of mind to carry on in spite of danger — see COURAGE

doughty *adj* feeling or displaying no fear by temperament — see BRAVE

dour *adj* harsh and threatening in manner or appearance — see GRIM 1

douse *vb* **1** to cause to cease burning — see EXTINGUISH 1
2 to make wet — see WET
3 to sink or push (something) briefly into or as if into a liquid — see DIP 1

doused *adj* containing, covered with, or thoroughly penetrated by water — see WET

dove *n* **1** a person who opposes war or warlike policies ⟨the *doves* were in favor of using the money to improve the school system instead of the army⟩
synonyms pacifist
related words peacemaker
near antonyms militarist; chauvinist, nationalist
antonyms hawk, jingo, warmonger
2 an innocent or gentle person — see LAMB

dovetail *vb* to be in agreement on every point — see CHECK 1

dowager *n* a dignified usually elderly woman of some rank or authority — see MATRIARCH

dowdily *adv* in a careless or unfashionable manner — see SLOPPILY

dowdy *adj* **1** lacking neatness in dress or person — see SLOPPY 1
2 marked by an obvious lack of style or good taste — see TACKY 1

down *adj* **1** brought or having come to an end — see COMPLETE 2
2 directed down — see DOWNCAST 1
3 feeling unhappiness — see SAD 1
4 temporarily suffering from a disorder of the body — see SICK 1

down *adv* toward or in a lower position ⟨the stairs went *down* to the basement⟩
synonyms below, downward, over
related words facedown; low; downgrade, downhill, downstairs
near antonyms aloft
antonyms up, upward (*or* upwards), upwardly

[1]**down** *n* a soft airy substance or covering — see FUZZ

[2]**down** *n* **1** the act or process of going to a lower level or altitude — see DESCENT 1
2 a loss of status — see COMEDOWN

down *vb* **1** to strike (someone) so forcefully as to cause a fall — see FELL 1
2 to take into the stomach through the mouth and throat — see SWALLOW 1

downcast *adj* **1** directed down ⟨her *downcast* gaze made us realize that she was shy⟩
synonyms down, downward, lowered
near antonyms elevated, lifted, raised, uplifted, upward
2 feeling unhappiness — see SAD 1

downer *n* something (as a situation or event) that is depressing ⟨that math exam was a real *downer*⟩
synonyms bummer
related words bore, drag; accident, fatality, mishap, woe; calamity, catastrophe, debacle (*also* débâcle), misfortune, tragedy
near antonyms pick-me-up

downfall *n* **1** a change to a lower state or level — see DECLINE 2
2 a loss of status — see COMEDOWN

downgrade *n* a change to a lower state or level — see DECLINE 2

downgrade *vb* to bring to a lower grade or rank — see DEMOTE

downhearted *adj* feeling unhappiness — see SAD 1

downheartedness *n* a state or spell of low spirits — see SADNESS

downpour *n* a steady falling of water from the sky in significant quantity — see RAIN 1

downright *adj* **1** being or characterized by direct, brief, and potentially rude speech or manner — see BLUNT 1
2 having no exceptions or restrictions — see ABSOLUTE 2

downs *n pl* a broad area of level or rolling treeless country — see PLAIN

downsize *vb* to make smaller in amount, volume, or extent — see DECREASE 1

down–to–earth *adj* willing to see things as they really are and deal with them sensibly — see REALISTIC 1

downward *adv* toward or in a lower position — see DOWN

downward *adj* directed down — see DOWNCAST 1

downwind *adj* being in the direction that the wind is blowing ⟨we were *downwind* of the deer, so it couldn't smell us⟩
synonyms leeward
antonyms upwind, windward

downy *adj* smooth or delicate in appearance or feel — see SOFT 2

doze *n* a short sleep — see [1]NAP

doze *vb* **1** to be in a state of sleep — see SLEEP 1
2 to sleep lightly or briefly — see NAP 1

dozer *n* one who sleeps — see SLEEPER

dozing *adj* being in a state of suspended consciousness — see ASLEEP 1

dozing *n* a natural periodic loss of consciousness during which the body restores itself — see SLEEP 1

drab *adj* causing weariness, restlessness, or lack of interest — see BORING

draft *n* **1** a mass or quantity of something taken up and carried, conveyed, or transported — see LOAD 1
2 the portion of a serving of a beverage that is swallowed at one time — see DRINK 2
3 noticeable movement of air in a particular direction — see [1]WIND 1

draft *vb* **1** to pick especially for required military service ⟨my grandfather was *drafted* to fight in the war, even though he didn't want to go⟩
synonyms conscript
related words impress, press; enlist, enroll (*also* enrol); sign up, volunteer
near antonyms discharge
2 to put (something) into proper and usually carefully worked out written form — see COMPOSE 1

draftee *n* a person forced or required to enroll in military service — see CONSCRIPT

drag *n* **1** someone or something boring ⟨that lecture was such a *drag* that half of the audience fell asleep⟩
synonyms bore
related words bummer, downer; pill
near antonyms gas [*slang*]
2 a passage cleared for public vehicular travel — see WAY 1
3 something that makes movement or progress more difficult — see ENCUMBRANCE
4 the portion of a serving of a beverage that is swallowed at one time — see DRINK 2

drag *vb* **1** to cause to follow by applying steady force on — see PULL 1
2 to move or act slowly — see DELAY 1
3 to move slowly — see CRAWL 2

dragger *n* someone who moves slowly or more slowly than others — see SLOWPOKE

dragging *adj* moving or proceeding at less than the normal, desirable, or required speed — see SLOW 1

drain *vb* **1** to remove (liquid) gradually or completely ⟨we *drained* the water from the tank before cleaning it⟩
synonyms bleed, draw (off), pump, siphon, tap
related words milk; suck; clear, empty, evacuate, exhaust, vacate, void
antonyms fill
2 to make complete use of — see DEPLETE
3 to use up all the physical energy of — see EXHAUST 1

drained *adj* depleted in strength, energy, or freshness — see WEARY 1

drainpipe *n* a pipe or channel for carrying off water from a roof — see GUTTER 1

drama *n* **1** the public performance of plays ⟨he has been interested in *drama* from the first time he ever saw a play⟩
synonyms dramatics, stage, theater (*or* theatre), theatricals
related words boards; acting, footlights; entertainment, show business
2 a written work in which the story is told through speech and action that is intended to be acted out on stage — see PLAY 2

dramatic *adj* **1** having the general quality or effect of a stage performance ⟨the basketball player's *dramatic* announcement of his sudden retirement held everybody spellbound⟩
synonyms histrionic, melodramatic, theatrical
related words affected, emotional, sensational
near antonyms matter-of-fact, monotonous
antonyms undramatic, untheatrical
2 given to or marked by attention-getting behavior suggestive of stage acting — see THEATRICAL 1
3 likely to attract attention — see NOTICEABLE

dramatics *n pl* the public performance of plays — see DRAMA 1

dramatization *n* a written work in which the story is told through speech and action that is intended to be acted out on stage — see PLAY 2

drapery *n* pieces of cloth hung to darken, decorate, or divide a room ⟨the *drapery* for the picture window matched the color of the furniture in the center of the room⟩
synonyms curtains, drapes
related words hanging(s), tapestry, window shade

drapes *n pl* pieces of cloth hung to darken, decorate, or divide a room — see DRAPERY

draw *n* **1** a situation in which neither participant in a contest, competition, or struggle comes out ahead of the other — see TIE 1
2 something that attracts interest — see MAGNET
3 the act or an instance of applying force on something so that it moves in the direction of the force — see PULL 1

draw *vb* **1** to cause to follow by applying steady force on — see PULL 1
2 to give a representation or account of in words — see DESCRIBE 1
3 to receive as return for effort — see EARN 1
4 to take away from a place or position — see REMOVE 2
5 to take the internal organs out of — see GUT

draw (off) *vb* to remove (liquid) gradually or completely — see DRAIN 1

draw (up) *vb* to put (something) into proper and usually carefully worked out written form — see COMPOSE 1

drawback *n* a feature of someone or something that creates difficulty for achieving success — see DISADVANTAGE

drawing *n* a picture using lines to represent the chief features of an object or scene <he made a *drawing* of the tree in his sketchpad while he was waiting for the bus>
synonyms cartoon, delineation, sketch
related words outline, silhouette; caricature, doodle, illustration; depiction, image, likeness, portrait, representation; engraving, etching; blueprint

drawing out *n* the act of making longer — see EXTENSION 1

drawn *adj* stretched with little or no give — see TAUT

draw on *vb* to come near or nearer — see APPROACH 1

draw out *vb* to make longer — see EXTEND 1

draw up *vb* **1** to bring (something) to a standstill — see [1]HALT 1
2 to put into a particular arrangement — see ORDER 1

dread *n* **1** suspicion or fear of future harm or misfortune — see APPREHENSION 1
2 the emotion experienced in the presence or threat of danger — see FEAR

dreadful *adj* **1** causing fear — see FEARFUL 1
2 causing intense displeasure, disgust, or resentment — see OFFENSIVE 1
3 extremely disturbing or repellent — see HORRIBLE 1

dreadfulness *n* the quality of inspiring intense dread or dismay — see HORROR 1

dream *n* **1** a series of often striking pictures created by the imagination during sleep <I had a *dream* last night about flying without any support>
synonyms nightmare, vision
related words daydream, pipe dream, reverie (*also* revery); chimera, delusion, fancy, fantasy (*also* phantasy), figment, hallucination, illusion, mirage, phantasm
2 a conception or image created by the imagination and having no objective reality — see FANTASY 1
3 something that one hopes or intends to accomplish — see GOAL

dream *vb* to form a mental picture of — see IMAGINE 1

dreamer *n* one whose conduct is guided more by the image of perfection than by the real world — see IDEALIST

dreamily *adv* in a pleasing way — see WELL 5

dreamy *adj* **1** giving pleasure or contentment to the mind or senses — see PLEASANT
2 tending to calm the emotions and relieve stress — see SOOTHING 1

drear *adj* **1** causing or marked by an atmosphere lacking in cheer — see GLOOMY 1
2 causing unhappiness — see SAD 2

dreariness *n* a state or spell of low spirits — see SADNESS

dreary *adj* **1** causing or marked by an atmosphere lacking in cheer — see GLOOMY 1
2 causing unhappiness — see SAD 2
3 causing weariness, restlessness, or lack of interest — see BORING

dredge *vb* to look through (as a place) carefully or thoroughly in an effort to find or discover something — see SEARCH 1

dregs *n pl* matter that settles to the bottom of a body of liquid — see DEPOSIT 1

drench *vb* **1** to make wet — see WET
2 to wet thoroughly with liquid — see SOAK 1

drenched *adj* containing, covered with, or thoroughly penetrated by water — see WET

dress *adj* relating to or suitable for wearing to an event requiring elegant dress and manners <the naval commander wore his *dress* uniform to the ball>
synonyms dressy, formal
related words costume; chic, dapper, fashionable, modish, natty, sharp, smart, stylish; custom-made, fitted, tailored; state
near antonyms street; dowdy, unfashionable, unstylish
antonyms casual, informal, sporty

dress *n* **1** a garment with a joined blouse and skirt for a woman or girl <what a lovely *dress* you're wearing today!>
synonyms frock, gown
related words chemise, granny, housedress, jumper, Mother Hubbard, muumuu (*or* mumu), overdress
2 clothing chosen as appropriate for a specific situation — see OUTFIT 1
3 covering for the human body — see CLOTHING

dress *vb* **1** to cover with a bandage — see BANDAGE
2 to make more attractive by adding something that is beautiful or becoming — see DECORATE
3 to make smooth or glossy usually by repeatedly applying surface pressure — see POLISH
4 to outfit with clothes and especially fine or special clothes — see CLOTHE 1
5 to put on one's best or formal clothes — see DRESS UP

dress down *vb* to criticize (someone) severely or angrily especially for personal failings — see SCOLD

dressing *n* **1** a medicated covering used to heal an injury <nurses put a *dressing* over his cuts so they wouldn't get infected>
synonyms plaster, poultice
related words balm, cream, liniment, lotion, ointment, salve, unguent
2 a savory fluid food used as a topping or accompaniment to a main dish — see SAUCE 1

dress up *vb* **1** to put on one's best or formal clothes <we always like to *dress up* when going to parties>
synonyms doll up, dress
related words apparel, array, attire, bedeck, bedizen, caparison, clothe, costume, deck, garb, garment, invest, rig (out), robe
2 to change the dress or looks of so as to conceal true identity — see DISGUISE

dressy *adj* relating to or suitable for wearing to an event requiring elegant dress and manners — see DRESS

dribble *vb* **1** to fall or let fall in or as if in drops — see DRIP
2 to flow in a broken irregular stream — see GURGLE
3 to let saliva or some other substance flow from the mouth — see DROOL

driblet *n* **1** a very small amount — see PARTICLE 1
2 the quantity of fluid that falls naturally in one rounded mass — see DROP 1

drift *n* **1** a pile or ridge of granular matter (as sand or snow) — see [2]BANK
2 a prevailing or general movement or inclination — see TREND 1
3 the idea that is conveyed or intended to be conveyed to the mind by language, symbol, or action — see MEANING 1

drift *vb* **1** to move or proceed smoothly and readily — see FLOW 2
2 to rest or move along the surface of a liquid or in the air — see FLOAT

drifter *n* a person who roams about without a fixed route or destination — see NOMAD

drill *n* something done over and over in order to develop skill — see EXERCISE 2

[1]drill *vb* **1** to make a hole or series of holes in — see PERFORATE
2 to strike with a missile from a gun — see SHOOT 3

[2]drill *vb* to put or set into the ground to grow — see PLANT

drink *n* **1** a liquid suitable for drinking ⟨we went inside to have a *drink* after mowing the lawn⟩
synonyms beverage, libation, quencher
related words potion; pop, soda, soda pop, soft drink; alcohol, brew, intoxicant, liquor, spirits
2 the portion of a serving of a beverage that is swallowed at one time ⟨the thirsty scout took a long *drink* from his canteen⟩
synonyms draft, drag, gulp, nip, quaff, shot, sip, slug, snort, sup, swallow, swig, swill
3 a fermented or distilled beverage that can make a person drunk — see ALCOHOL

drink *vb* **1** to swallow in liquid form ⟨the doctor wants her to *drink* lots of water before the examination⟩
synonyms gulp, guzzle, imbibe, quaff, sip, slurp, sup, swig, swill, toss (down *or* off)
related words lap, lick; consume, down, mouth (down); tipple; toast, wine
2 to take in (something liquid) through small openings — see ABSORB 1

drinkable *adj* suitable for drinking — see POTABLE

drip *n* the quantity of fluid that falls naturally in one rounded mass — see DROP 1

drip *vb* to fall or let fall in or as if in drops ⟨water from the leaky roof was *dripping* all over the floor⟩ ⟨the cracked bottle *dripped* wine⟩
synonyms dribble, trickle
related words bleed, exude, ooze, seep, weep; discharge

dripping *adj* containing, covered with, or thoroughly penetrated by water — see WET

drive *n* **1** a passage cleared for public vehicular travel — see WAY 1
2 a series of activities undertaken to achieve a goal — see CAMPAIGN
3 a strong wish for something — see DESIRE
4 active strength of body or mind — see VIGOR 1
5 readiness to engage in daring or difficult activity — see ENTERPRISE 2

drive *vb* **1** to urge, push, or force onward ⟨cowboys *drove* the herd of cattle from San Antonio to San Francisco⟩
synonyms herd, punch, run
related words shepherd; wrangle; egg, exhort, goad, prick, prod, spur, urge
2 to travel by a motorized vehicle ⟨I'm going to *drive* across the country—want to come?⟩
synonyms automobile, motor
related words roll, wheel; chauffeur, taxi; ride; drag, race
3 to apply force to (someone or something) so that it moves in front of one — see PUSH 1
4 to cause (a person) to give in to pressure — see FORCE
5 to cause to function — see ACTIVATE
6 to set or keep in motion — see MOVE 2

drivel *n* **1** language, behavior, or ideas that are absurd and contrary to good sense — see NONSENSE 1
2 unintelligible or meaningless talk — see GIBBERISH

drivel *vb* **1** to let saliva or some other substance flow from the mouth — see DROOL
2 to speak rapidly, inarticulately, and usually unintelligibly — see BABBLE 1

driver *n* a person who travels by automobile — see MOTORIST

drizzle *n* a light or fine rain ⟨the intermittent *drizzle* was just heavy enough to spoil all of our outdoor activities⟩
synonyms mist, sprinkle
related words precipitation, rainfall, shower
near antonyms cloudburst, deluge, downpour, storm; rainstorm, thunderstorm; monsoon

droll *adj* causing or intended to cause laughter — see FUNNY 1

drollness *n* the amusing quality or element in something — see HUMOR 1

[1]drone *n* a lazy person — see LAZYBONES

[2]drone *n* a monotonous sound like that of an insect in motion — see HUM

drone *vb* to fly, turn, or move rapidly with a fluttering or vibratory sound — see WHIRR

drool *vb* to let saliva or some other substance flow from the mouth ⟨the dog *drooled* when we put the steak down on the floor⟩
synonyms dribble, drivel, salivate, slaver, slobber
related words water; expectorate, spit; foam, froth; sputter

droop *n* the extent to which something hangs or dips below a straight line — see SAG

droop *vb* **1** to be limp from lack of water or vigor ⟨the flowers *drooped* on their stalks in the blazing sun⟩
synonyms flag, hang, loll, sag, wilt
related words slouch, slump; collapse, drop, fall, sink, subside
near antonyms distend, stiffen; rise, straighten
2 to lose bodily strength or vigor — see WEAKEN 2

drooping *adj* bending downward or forward — see NODDING

droopy *adj* **1** bending downward or forward — see NODDING
2 not stiff in structure — see LIMP 1
3 feeling unhappiness — see SAD 1

drop *n* **1** the quantity of fluid that falls naturally in

one rounded mass <a *drop* of water fell from the leaky faucet every few seconds>
synonyms blob, driblet, drip, droplet, glob, globule
related words dewdrop, raindrop, tear; spatter; dribble, trickle
2 distance measured from the top to the bottom of something — see DEPTH 1
3 the act or process of going to a lower level or altitude — see DESCENT 1
4 the amount by which something is lessened — see DECREASE
5 the more favorable condition or position in a competition — see ADVANTAGE 1

drop *vb* **1** to cause to fall intentionally or unintentionally <I *dropped* the fly ball> <*drop* the anchor>
synonyms depress, lower
related words flatten, floor, level; bobble, bungle, foozle, fumble; immerse, sink, submerge
antonyms lift, pick up, raise
2 to go to a lower level <although they start out high, prices for home electronics eventually *drop*>
synonyms decline, descend, dip, fall, lower, nosedive, plummet, plunge, sink, tumble
related words decrease, diminish, lessen; recede, retreat
antonyms arise, lift, rise, soar
3 to bring (as an action or operation) to an immediate end — see STOP 1
4 to stop doing (something) permanently — see QUIT 2
5 to lead or extend downward — see DESCEND 1
6 to put an end to (something planned or previously agreed to) — see CANCEL 1
7 to bring forth from the womb — see BEAR 1
8 to strike (someone) so forcefully as to cause a fall — see FELL 1

drop (by *or* in) *vb* to make a brief visit — see CALL 3

droplet *n* the quantity of fluid that falls naturally in one rounded mass — see DROP 1

dropping *n* **1 droppings** *pl* solid matter discharged from an animal's alimentary canal <the only bad part about owning a rabbit was cleaning the *droppings* out of the cage every night>
synonyms dung, excrement, excreta, feces, slops, waste
related words stool; dunghill, guano, manure, muck; spoor; sewage
2 the act of putting an end to something planned or previously agreed to — see CANCELLATION

dross *n* discarded or useless material — see GARBAGE

droughty *adj* marked by little or no precipitation or humidity — see DRY 1

drove *n* **1** a great number of persons or things gathered together — see CROWD 1
2 a group of domestic animals assembled or herded together — see HERD

drown *vb* **1** to cover or become filled with a flood — see FLOOD
2 to wet thoroughly with liquid — see SOAK 1

drowse *n* a short sleep — see [1]NAP

drowse *vb* to sleep lightly or briefly — see NAP 1

drowsiness *n* the quality or state of desiring or needing sleep — see SLEEPINESS

drowsy *adj* **1** desiring or needing sleep — see SLEEPY 1
2 tending to cause sleep — see HYPNOTIC

drub *vb* **1** to strike repeatedly — see BEAT 1
2 to achieve a victory over — see BEAT 2
3 to defeat by a large margin — see WHIP 2

drubbing *n* failure to win a contest — see DEFEAT 1

drudge *n* a person who does very hard or dull work — see SLAVE 2

drudge *vb* to devote serious and sustained effort — see LABOR

drudger *n* a person who does very hard or dull work — see SLAVE 2

drudgery *n* very hard or unpleasant work — see TOIL

drug *n* a substance or preparation used to treat disease — see MEDICINE

druggist *n* a person who prepares drugs according to a doctor's prescription <she got her prescription for antibiotics filled by the *druggist*>
synonyms apothecary, pharmacist
related words pharmacologist

drugstore *n* a retail store where medicines and miscellaneous articles are sold <we picked up her medicine and some toothpaste at the *drugstore*>
synonyms pharmacy
related words dispensary

drum *n* a metal container in the shape of a cylinder — see CAN

drum *vb* to strike or cause to strike lightly and usually rhythmically — see [1]TAP

drum (out) *vb* to drive or force out — see EJECT 1

drunk *adj* being under the influence of alcohol <several wedding guests who got a little *drunk*>
synonyms drunken, high, inebriate, inebriated, intoxicated, loaded [*slang*], soused, tipsy
related words maudlin; befuddled, stupefied; debauched, dissipated, dissolute
near antonyms abstemious, abstinent, temperate; clearheaded, cool, level, steady
antonyms sober

drunk *n* **1** a person who makes a habit of getting drunk <you can't trust anything that old *drunk* says>
synonyms drunkard, inebriate, soak, sot, souse, tippler
related words alcoholic, substance abuser; drinker
near antonyms abstainer
2 a bout of drinking — see CAROUSE

drunkard *n* a person who makes a habit of getting drunk — see DRUNK 1

drunken *adj* being under the influence of alcohol — see DRUNK

dry *adj* **1** marked by little or no precipitation or humidity <the *dry* climate of the American Southwest>
synonyms arid, droughty, sere, thirsty, waterless
related words baked, dehydrated, parched, sunbaked; rainless
near antonyms drenched, dripping, saturated, soaked, soaking, sodden, sopping, soppy, soused
antonyms damp, dank, humid, moist, wet
2 causing weariness, restlessness, or lack of interest — see BORING

dry *vb* **1** to make dry <they *dried* the grapes to make raisins>
synonyms dehydrate, parch, sear
related words dehumidify; evaporate; shrivel, wither
near antonyms deluge, douse, drench, saturate,

soak, sop, souse; damp, dampen, moisten; rehydrate
antonyms hydrate, wet
2 to lose liveliness, force, or freshness — see WITHER

dryad *n* a mythical goddess represented as a young girl and said to live outdoors — see NYMPH 1

dry run *n* a private performance or session in preparation for a public appearance — see REHEARSAL

dual *adj* consisting of two members or parts that are usually joined — see DOUBLE 1

dub *vb* to give a name to — see NAME 1

dubious *adj* **1** giving good reason for being doubted, questioned, or challenged — see DOUBTFUL 2
2 having doubts about the wisdom of doing something — see HESITANT
3 not likely to be true or to occur — see IMPROBABLE
4 not feeling sure about the truth, wisdom, or trustworthiness of someone or something — see DOUBTFUL 1

dubiously *adv* with distrust — see ASKANCE

duck *vb* **1** to get or keep away from (as a responsibility) through cleverness or trickery — see ESCAPE 2
2 to move suddenly aside or to and fro — see DODGE 1
3 to sink or push (something) briefly into or as if into a liquid — see DIP 1

ducking *n* the act or a means of getting or keeping away from something undesirable — see ESCAPE 2

duck soup *n* something that is easy to do — see CINCH

duct *n* a long hollow cylinder for carrying a substance (as a liquid or gas) — see PIPE 1

dud *n* **1** something that has failed — see FAILURE 3
2 duds *pl* covering for the human body — see CLOTHING

dude *n* **1** a man extremely interested in his clothing and personal appearance — see DANDY 1
2 an adult male human being — see MAN 1

dudgeon *n* the feeling of being offended or resentful after a slight or indignity — see PIQUE

due *adj* **1** having reached the date at which payment is required ⟨the loan is *due* next April⟩
synonyms mature
related words delinquent, outstanding, overdue, owed, owing, receivable, unpaid, unsettled; payable
2 being in accordance with the prescribed, normal, or logical course of events ⟨their train is *due* to arrive in half an hour⟩
synonyms anticipated, awaited, expected, scheduled, slated
near antonyms belated, delinquent, dilatory, latish, overdue, tardy
3 being what is called for by accepted standards of right and wrong — see JUST 1

due *adv* in a direct line or course — see DIRECTLY 1

due (to) *adj* coming as a result — see RESULTANT

duel *n* an earnest effort for superiority or victory over another — see CONTEST 1

due to *prep* as the result of — see BECAUSE OF

dull *adj* **1** lacking sharpness of edge or point ⟨the *dull* knife just bounced off the skin of the tomato without cutting it⟩
synonyms blunt, blunted, dulled, obtuse
related words rounded
near antonyms cutting, edged, edgy, ground, honed, stropped; jagged, needlelike, prickly, spiked, spiky, spiny
antonyms keen, pointed, sharp, sharpened, whetted
2 causing weariness, restlessness, or lack of interest — see BORING
3 covered over by clouds — see OVERCAST
4 lacking a surface luster or gloss — see MATTE
5 lacking intensity of color — see PALE 1
6 not having or showing an ability to absorb ideas readily — see STUPID 1
7 not loud in pitch or volume — see SOFT 1
8 slow to move or act — see INACTIVE 1

dull *vb* **1** to reduce or weaken in strength or feeling ⟨the aspirin *dulled* his headache and he was soon feeling better⟩
synonyms benumb, blunt, damp, dampen, deaden, numb
related words muffle, mute, tone (down); decrease, diminish, lessen, let up (on), reduce, subdue; debilitate, enfeeble, weaken; dwindle, recede, subside, taper (off), wane; alleviate, ease, lighten; abate, moderate
near antonyms amplify, beef (up), boost, consolidate, deepen, enhance, heighten, intensify, magnify, redouble, step up, strengthen; animate, arouse, stimulate
antonyms sharpen, whet
2 to make white or lighter by removing color — see WHITEN

dulled *adj* **1** lacking a surface luster or gloss — see MATTE
2 lacking intensity of color — see PALE 1
3 lacking sharpness of edge or point — see DULL 1

dullness *also* **dulness** *n* the quality or state of lacking intelligence or quickness of mind — see STUPIDITY 1

dumb *adj* **1** deliberately refraining from speech — see SILENT 1
2 not having or showing an ability to absorb ideas readily — see STUPID 1

dumbbell *n* a stupid person — see IDIOT

dumbfound *also* **dumfound** *vb* to make a strong impression on (someone) with something unexpected — see SURPRISE 1

dumbfounded *or* **dumfounded** *adj* **1** affected with sudden and great wonder or surprise — see THUNDERSTRUCK
2 filled with amazement or wonder — see OPENMOUTHED

dumbfounding *or* **dumfounding** *adj* causing a strong emotional reaction because unexpected — see SURPRISING 1

dumbness *n* **1** incapacity for or restraint from speaking — see SILENCE 1
2 the quality or state of lacking intelligence or quickness of mind — see STUPIDITY 1

dummy *n* **1** a stupid person — see IDIOT
2 a three-dimensional representation of the human body used especially for displaying clothes — see MANNEQUIN 1

dump *n* **1** a place where discarded materials (as trash) are dumped ⟨all of the used packaging eventually ends up in the *dump*⟩
synonyms landfill, sanitary landfill
related words pigpen, pigsty

2 a place where military arms are stored — see ARMORY

dump *vb* to get rid of as useless or unwanted — see DISCARD

dumping *n* the getting rid of whatever is unwanted or useless — see DISPOSAL 1

dumps *n pl* a state or spell of low spirits — see SADNESS

dumpy *adj* being compact and broad in build and often short in stature — see STOCKY

dun *n* something that someone insists upon having — see DEMAND 1

dunce *n* a stupid person — see IDIOT

dung *n* solid matter discharged from an animal's alimentary canal — see DROPPING 1

dunk *vb* to sink or push (something) briefly into or as if into a liquid — see DIP 1

duo *n* two things of the same or similar kind that match or are considered together — see PAIR

dupe *n* one who is easily deceived or cheated ⟨the swindler was able to escape with all of the *dupe's* money⟩
synonyms chump, gull, pigeon, sap, sucker, tool
related words victim; schlemiel; butt, derision, laughingstock, mark, mock, mockery; booby, dodo, fool, goose, half-wit, jackass, lunatic, monkey, nincompoop, ninny, nitwit, simpleton, turkey; pushover; loser
near antonyms confidence man, shark, sharper, swindler, trickster

dupe *vb* to cause to believe what is untrue — see DECEIVE

duplex *adj* consisting of two members or parts that are usually joined — see DOUBLE 1

duplicate *adj* resembling another in every respect — see SAME 1

duplicate *n* **1** something or someone that strongly resembles another — see IMAGE 1
2 something that is made to look exactly like something else — see COPY 1

duplicate *vb* **1** to make an exact likeness of — see COPY 1
2 to make or do again — see REPEAT 4
3 to make twice as great or as many — see DOUBLE 1

duplication *n* **1** something or someone that strongly resembles another — see IMAGE 1
2 something that is made to look exactly like something else — see COPY
3 the act of saying or doing over again — see REPEAT

duplicity *n* the inclination or practice of misleading others through lies or trickery — see DECEIT

durability *n* continuing existence — see PERSISTENCE 1

duration *n* **1** the period during which something exists, lasts, or is in progress ⟨for the whole *duration* of the speech the bored audience fidgeted⟩
synonyms date, life, life span, lifetime, run, standing, time
related words spell, stretch; span, tenure, term; hitch, tour, turn
2 uninterrupted or lasting existence — see CONTINUATION

duress *n* the use of power to impose one's will on another — see FORCE 2

during *prep* in the course of ⟨we wrote notes *during* the boring lecture⟩
synonyms over, through, throughout

dusk *n* **1** the time from when the sun begins to set to the onset of total darkness ⟨we stopped playing at *dusk*, since it was getting too dark to see the ball⟩
synonyms evening, eventide, gloaming, nightfall, sundown, sunset, twilight
related words dark, darkness, night, nighttime
near antonyms day, daytime, light
antonyms aurora, cockcrow, dawn, dawning, daybreak, daylight, morn, morning, sunrise, sunup
2 a time or place of little or no light — see DARK 1

dusky *adj* being without light or without much light — see DARK 1

dust *n* **1** discarded or useless material — see GARBAGE
2 the solid part of our planet's surface as distinguished from the sea and air — see EARTH 2

dustiness *n* the state or quality of being dirty — see DIRTINESS 1

dusty *adj* **1** consisting of very small particles — see FINE 1
2 not clean — see DIRTY 1

dutiful *adj* marked by or showing proper regard for another's higher status — see RESPECTFUL

duty *n* **1** a charge usually of money collected by the government from people or businesses for public use — see TAX
2 a piece of work that needs to be done regularly — see CHORE 1
3 something one must do because of prior agreement — see OBLIGATION

dwarf *adj* of a size that is less than average — see SMALL 1

dwarf *n* **1** a living thing much smaller than others of its kind ⟨Shetland ponies are the *dwarfs* of the horse world⟩
synonyms diminutive, midget, mite, peewee, pygmy, runt, scrub, shrimp
related words mini, miniature
near antonyms whale
antonyms behemoth, colossus, giant, jumbo, leviathan, mammoth, monster, titan
2 an imaginary being usually having a small human form and magical powers — see FAIRY

dwarf *vb* to hold back the normal growth of — see STUNT

dwarfish *adj* of a size that is less than average — see SMALL 1

dwell *vb* **1** to continue to be in a place for a significant amount of time — see STAY 1
2 to have a home — see LIVE 1

dweller *n* one who lives permanently in a place — see INHABITANT

dwelling *n* the place where one lives — see HOME 1

dwindle *vb* **1** to make smaller in amount, volume, or extent — see DECREASE 1
2 to grow less in scope or intensity especially gradually — see DECREASE 2

dye *n* a substance used to color other materials — see PIGMENT

dye *vb* to give color or a different color to — see COLOR 1

dyestuff *n* a substance used to color other materials — see PIGMENT

dying *adj* nearly dead — see MORIBUND

dynamic *adj* **1** having active strength of body or mind — see VIGOROUS 1
2 marked by or uttered with forcefulness — see EMPHATIC 1

dyspeptic *adj* having or showing a habitually bad temper — see ILL-TEMPERED

each *adj* being one of a group ⟨*each* park visitor receives a free souvenir⟩
synonyms any, every
related words all; several, various; particular; respective, specific
phrases each and every

each *adv* for each one — see APIECE

eager *adj* showing urgent desire or interest ⟨Tom was *eager* to try out his new pair of skis⟩
synonyms agog, anxious, ardent, athirst, avid, crazy, desirous, enthusiastic, excited, gung ho, hot, hungry, impatient, keen, nuts, raring, solicitous, thirsty, voracious
related words engaged, interested; hung up, obsessed; ambitious, covetous, craving, hankering, longing, pining; restive, restless; disposed, inclined, ready, unreluctant, willing
phrases champing at the bit
near antonyms incurious, unconcerned, uninterested; aloof, detached, disinterested; impassive, stolid; halfhearted, lackadaisical, languid, languorous, spiritless; averse, disinclined, hesitant, loath (*or* loth), reluctant, unwilling
antonyms apathetic, indifferent, uneager

eagerness *n* urgent desire or interest ⟨students with an *eagerness* to learn⟩
synonyms appetite, ardor, avidity, desirousness, enthusiasm, excitement, hunger, impatience, keenness, thirst
related words alacrity, quickness; ambition, gusto, zest
near antonyms unconcern; aloofness, detachment; impassivity, languor
antonyms apathy, indifference

ear *n* a state of being aware — see ATTENTION 2

earliest *adj* coming before all others in time or order — see FIRST 1

early *adj* **1** relating to or occurring near the beginning of a process, series, or time period ⟨*early* birds of the Jurassic period⟩
synonyms ancient, primal, primeval, primitive, primordial
related words aged, antediluvian, antiquated, antique, hoary
near antonyms advanced, complex
antonyms late
2 occurring before the usual or expected time ⟨we had an *early* dinner so as not to miss the concert⟩
synonyms inopportune, precocious, premature, unseasonable, untimely
related words unanticipated, unexpected; abrupt, sudden
near antonyms slow, tardy; anticipated, expected
antonyms late

early *adv* before the usual or expected time ⟨that year spring arrived *early*⟩
synonyms beforehand, inopportunely, precociously, prematurely, unseasonably
related words immediately, promptly, punctually; betimes, seasonably
near antonyms belatedly, tardily
antonyms late

earmark *vb* to keep or intend for a special purpose — see DEVOTE 1

earn *vb* **1** to receive as return for effort ⟨for years I've *earned* pocket money by mowing lawns⟩
synonyms acquire, attain, capture, carry, draw, gain, garner, get, land, make, obtain, procure, realize, secure, win
related words clear, net; accomplish, achieve, notch (up), score; accumulate, draw, rack up; catch, pick up; occupy, take over; reacquire, recapture, regain, remake
phrases come by
near antonyms give up, hand over, part (with), relinquish, surrender, yield
antonyms forfeit, lose
2 to be or make worthy of (as a reward or punishment) ⟨you've *earned* the afternoon off after all that hard work⟩
synonyms deserve, merit, rate
related words entitle, qualify

earnest *adj* not joking or playful in mood or manner — see SERIOUS 1

earnestness *n* a mental state free of jesting or trifling ⟨practiced the art of acting with great *earnestness*⟩
synonyms gravity, intentness, seriousness, soberness, sobriety, solemnity
related words deliberation, determination, firmness, purposefulness, resolve; absorption, attentiveness, concentration, engrossment
near antonyms lightness, shallowness, superficiality; dalliance, dilettantism
antonyms frivolity, levity, lightheartedness

earnings *n pl* **1** an increase usually measured in money that comes from labor, business, or property — see INCOME
2 the amount of money left when expenses are subtracted from the total amount received — see PROFIT 1

earshot *n* range of hearing ⟨babysitters should remain within *earshot* of young children⟩
synonyms hearing, sound
related words volume; distance, sight

earsplitting *adj* marked by a high volume of sound — see LOUD 1

earth *n* **1** the celestial body on which we live ⟨environmentalists who are committed to preserving the *earth*⟩
synonyms globe, planet, world
related words cosmos, creation, universe; orb, sphere; macrocosm, microcosm
2 the solid part of our planet's surface as distinguished from the sea and air ⟨after nearly drowning, I was glad to feel the *earth* under my feet⟩
synonyms dirt, dust, ground, land, soil
related words continent, landmass; island, isthmus, mainland, peninsula
3 the loose surface material in which plants naturally grow — see DIRT 1

earthenware *n* articles made of baked clay — see CROCKERY

earthlike *adj* consisting or suggestive of earth — see EARTHY 1

earthly *adj* having to do with life on earth especially as opposed to that in heaven ⟨a sermon against our obsession with *earthly* pursuits⟩
synonyms carnal, fleshly, material, mundane, temporal, terrestrial, worldly
related words bodily, corporal, corporeal, physical; daily, diurnal; unspiritual

near antonyms celestial, empyreal, empyrean; divine, spiritual, utopian; extraterrestrial
antonyms heavenly, nontemporal

earthquake *n* a shaking of the earth ⟨the San Andreas Fault is notorious for its *earthquakes*⟩
synonyms quake, tremor
related words shock; cataclysm, convulsion, upheaval

earthy *adj* **1** consisting or suggestive of earth ⟨the unmistakably *earthy* aroma of a greenhouse⟩
synonyms earthlike, loamy
related words clayey, dusty, muddy, sandy
2 willing to see things as they really are and deal with them sensibly — see REALISTIC 1

ease *n* **1** reduction of or freedom from pain ⟨the sunburn medication brought me instant *ease*⟩
synonyms alleviation, comfort, relief
related words appeasement, assuagement, decrease, diminishment, moderation, mollification; calming, salving, soothing
near antonyms discomfort, unrest; agony, anguish, pain
2 carefree freedom from constraint — see ABANDON
3 freedom from activity or labor — see [1]REST 1

ease *vb* **1** to free from obstruction or difficulty ⟨measures intended to *ease* the flow of traffic during rush hour⟩
synonyms facilitate, loosen (up), smooth, unclog
related words accelerate, expedite, hasten, speed; advance, further, promote; aid, assist, help, improve
phrases pave the way (for)
near antonyms hinder, impede; retard
antonyms complicate
2 to make less taut — see SLACKEN
3 to make more bearable or less severe — see HELP 2

easily *adv* without difficulty ⟨a skater who *easily* executes even the most difficult jumps⟩
synonyms effortlessly, facilely, fluently, freely, handily, lightly, painlessly, readily, smoothly
related words ably, adeptly, adroitly, competently, dexterously, efficiently, expertly, proficiently, skillfully; instinctively, intuitively, naturally, spontaneously
near antonyms awkwardly, clumsily, gracelessly, ineptly, maladroitly; painfully, painstakingly
antonyms arduously, laboriously

easy *adj* **1** involving minimal difficulty or effort ⟨a minor problem with an *easy* solution⟩
synonyms effortless, facile, fluent, fluid, light, painless, ready, simple, smooth, snap, soft
related words apparent, clear, distinct, evident, manifest, obvious, plain; clear-cut, straightforward, uncomplicated
near antonyms painful, troublesome; abstruse, complex, complicated, intricate, knotty
antonyms arduous, difficult, hard, labored
2 readily taken advantage of ⟨senior citizens who are *easy* prey for scam artists⟩
synonyms exploitable, gullible, naive (*or* naïve), susceptible, trusting
related words credulous, trustful, uncritical, unsuspecting, unsuspicious; artless, simple, unsophisticated
near antonyms critical, cynical, mistrustful, skeptical, suspicious; sophisticated
3 providing physical comfort — see COMFORTABLE 1

easygoing *adj* **1** having a relaxed, casual manner ⟨counselors at the summer camp are pretty *easygoing*⟩
synonyms affable, breezy, devil-may-care, happy-go-lucky, laid-back, low-pressure
related words carefree, lackadaisical, nonchalant, unaffected, unconcerned; familiar, homey, informal; lax, lenient, permissive, soft
near antonyms ceremonious, decorous, formal, rigid, strict
antonyms uptight
2 not bound by rigid standards ⟨boys are pretty *easygoing* about housekeeping⟩
synonyms flexible, lax, loose, relaxed, slack, unrestrained, unrestricted
related words careless, heedless, negligent, slipshod, sloppy, slovenly, unfussy
near antonyms constrained, restrained, restricted, rigid, strict, tight; exact, fussy, meticulous, scrupulous
antonyms rigorous
3 having or showing a lack of concern or seriousness — see CAREFREE

eat *vb* **1** to take in as food ⟨having gone all day without food, we greedily *ate* the hamburgers⟩
synonyms consume, ingest
related words digest, down, mouth (down), swallow; bolt, devour, gobble (up *or* down), gorge, gulp, wolf; chew, gnaw (at *or* on), lap, lick, nibble (on); relish, savor, taste; banquet, dine, feast, gormandize, pig out; dispatch, polish off; breakfast, lunch, sup; munch, snack
2 to consume or wear away gradually ⟨the pot's protective coating was *eaten* away by the acid⟩
synonyms bite (at), corrode, erode, fret
related words break down, break up, decompose, disintegrate, dissolve; destroy, ruin, wreck
3 to take a meal — see DINE 1

eat (up) *vb* to destroy all trace of — see CONSUME 1

eatable *adj* suitable for use as food — see EDIBLE

eatables *n pl* substances intended to be eaten — see FOOD

eavesdrop (on) *vb* to listen to (another in private conversation) ⟨a nosy traveler who likes to *eavesdrop on* his fellow airline passengers⟩
synonyms listen in (on), overhear
related words bug, tap, wiretap; monitor, snoop, spy; hear, hearken

eaves trough *n* a pipe or channel for carrying off water from a roof — see GUTTER 1

ebb *vb* **1** to become worse or of less value — see DETERIORATE
2 to grow less in scope or intensity especially gradually — see DECREASE 2

ebbing *n* a gradual sinking and wasting away of mind or body — see DECLINE 1

ebony *adj* having the color of soot or coal — see BLACK 1

eccentric *n* a person of odd or whimsical habits ⟨an *eccentric* who designed his house to look like a Scottish castle⟩
synonyms character, codger, crackbrain, crackpot, crank, kook, nut, oddball, screwball, weirdo
related words bohemian, maverick, nonconformist; coot, rarity; freak
near antonyms conformer, conformist, follower, sheep

eccentricity *n* an odd or peculiar habit — see IDIOSYNCRASY

ecclesiastic *n* a person specially trained and authorized to conduct religious services in a Christian church — see CLERGYMAN

ecclesiastical *or* **ecclesiastic** *adj* of or relating to a church ⟨*ecclesiastical* laws that have been in existence for centuries⟩
synonyms churchly
related words divine, holy, religious, sacramental; apostolic, canonical, clerical, episcopal, evangelical, ministerial, papal, pastoral, patriarchal, pontifical, priestly, rabbinical, sacerdotal
near antonyms lay, profane, secular, temporal

echo *vb* **1** to continue or be repeated in a series of reflected sound waves — see REVERBERATE
2 to say after another — see REPEAT 3

eclipse *vb* to be greater, better, or stronger than — see SURPASS 1

economical *adj* careful in the management of money or resources — see FRUGAL

economize *vb* to avoid unnecessary waste or expense ⟨in tough times people learn how to *economize*⟩
synonyms save, scrimp, skimp
related words conserve, husband, manage; scrape; cut back, cut down, retrench
near antonyms dissipate, fritter (away), squander, throw away
antonyms waste

economizing *adj* careful in the management of money or resources — see FRUGAL

economy *n* careful management of material resources ⟨people on fixed incomes are used to practicing *economy*⟩
synonyms frugality, husbandry, providence, scrimping, skimping, thrift
related words conservation, saving; miserliness, stinginess; discretion, prudence
near antonyms extravagance, improvidence, lavishness, prodigality, squandering
antonyms wastefulness

ecstasy *n* a state of overwhelming usually pleasurable emotion ⟨actors are typically in *ecstasy* upon winning an Oscar⟩
synonyms elation, euphoria, exhilaration, heaven, intoxication, paradise, rapture, rhapsody, transport
related words exaltation; bliss, blissfulness, delight, enchantment, gladness, happiness, joy, joyfulness, pleasure; reverie, trance; inspiration; fervor, frenzy, madness, passion
near antonyms blues, dejection, despondency, doldrums, downheartedness, dumps, melancholy, mopes
antonyms depression

ecstatic *adj* experiencing or marked by overwhelming usually pleasurable emotion ⟨a football player who was *ecstatic* upon receiving a full athletic scholarship to the college of his choice⟩
synonyms elated, enraptured, entranced, euphoric, exhilarated, intoxicated, rapturous, rhapsodic (*also* rhapsodical)
related words exultant, jubilant, triumphant; enthusiastic, excited, gung ho, thrilled; blissful, delighted, glad, gratified, happy, joyful, joyous, pleased, satisfied, tickled
near antonyms blue, dejected, despondent, disconsolate, disheartened, downhearted, melancholy
antonyms depressed

Eden *n* a place or state of great happiness — see PARADISE 1

edge *n* **1** a harsh or sharp quality ⟨the teacher's voice had a sarcastic *edge* as she welcomed the tardy student to class⟩
synonyms acidity, acridness, acrimoniousness, acrimony, acuteness, asperity, bite, bitterness, harshness, keenness, poignancy, pungency, roughness, sharpness, tartness
related words ginger, punch, spice, tang; severity, shrillness, virulence; pointedness, thorniness
2 the line or relatively narrow space that marks the outer limit of something — see BORDER 1
3 the more favorable condition or position in a competition — see ADVANTAGE 1

edge *vb* to make sharp or sharper — see SHARPEN

edged *adj* having an edge thin enough to cut or pierce something — see SHARP 1

edgewise *adv* with one side faced forward — see SIDEWAYS

edginess *n* a state of nervousness marked by sudden jerky movements — see JUMPINESS

edgy *adj* **1** feeling or showing uncomfortable feelings of uncertainty — see NERVOUS 1
2 having an edge thin enough to cut or pierce something — see SHARP 1

edible *adj* suitable for use as food ⟨*edible* plant products⟩
synonyms eatable, esculent
related words absorbable, chewable, digestible; nourishing, nutritious, nutritive; appetizing, delicious, flavorful, palatable, savory, succulent, tasty, toothsome
near antonyms indigestible, nondigestible
antonyms inedible

edibles *n pl* substances intended to be eaten — see FOOD

edict *n* **1** an order publicly issued by an authority ⟨the school board's *edict* put a new student dress code into effect⟩
synonyms decree, directive, fiat, ruling
related words call, decision, judgment (*or* judgement); announcement, declaration, dictum, manifesto, proclamation, pronouncement; canon, encyclical
2 a statement of what to do that must be obeyed by those concerned — see COMMAND 1

edifice *n* **1** a large, magnificent, or massive building ⟨the U.S. Capitol is one of our nation's most impressive *edifices*⟩
synonyms hall, palace, tower
related words construction, erection, structure; castle, château, estate, manor, mansion, villa; mausoleum, memorial, monument
2 something built as a dwelling, shelter, or place for human activity — see BUILDING

edify *vb* to provide (someone) with moral or spiritual understanding — see ENLIGHTEN 2

edit *vb* to prepare for publication by correcting, rewriting, or updating ⟨the publisher *edited* a new version of its best-selling school dictionary⟩
synonyms redraft, revamp, revise, rework
related words amend, correct, emend, rectify; collect, compile; issue, print, publish

educate *vb* **1** to cause to acquire knowledge or skill in some field — see TEACH
2 to provide (someone) with moral or spiritual understanding — see ENLIGHTEN 2

educated *adj* having or displaying advanced knowledge or education ⟨*educated* people are

often more aware and tolerant of cultural and ethnic diversity〉
synonyms erudite, knowledgeable, learned, literate, scholarly, well-read
related words civilized, cultivated, cultured; cerebral, highbrow, intellectual; polished, refined, well-bred; academic, bookish, didactic, pedantic, professorial; instructed, schooled, skilled, trained; homeschooled, self-educated, self-taught; briefed, enlightened, informed, versed
near antonyms uncivilized, uncultivated, uncultured; lowbrow, unintelligent; ill-bred, unpolished, unrefined; uninformed
antonyms ignorant, illiterate, uneducated

education *n* **1** the act or process of imparting knowledge or skills to another 〈a teacher who devoted herself to the *education* of children with special needs〉
synonyms instruction, schooling, teaching, training, tutelage, tutoring
related words coaching, conditioning, cultivation, preparation, readying; development, direction, guidance, nurturance, nurturing; edification, enlightenment, improvement
2 the understanding and information gained from being educated 〈a person whose extensive *education* was obvious to all who met him〉
synonyms erudition, knowledge, learnedness, learning, scholarship, science
related words culture, edification, enlightenment; literacy, reading; bookishness, pedantry
near antonyms ignorance, illiteracy

educational *adj* **1** providing useful information or knowledge — see INFORMATIVE
2 of or relating to schooling or learning especially at an advanced level — see ACADEMIC

educative *adj* providing useful information or knowledge — see INFORMATIVE

educator *n* a person whose occupation is to give formal instruction in a school — see TEACHER

educe *vb* to draw out (something hidden, latent, or reserved) 〈the gift of a puppy finally *educed* a response from the shy boy〉
synonyms elicit, evoke, raise
related words drag, dredge (up), extort, pull, wangle, wrest, wring; gain, get, obtain, procure, secure; expose, reveal, uncover
near antonyms miss, overlook, pass over

eerie *adj* fearfully and mysteriously strange or fantastic 〈*eerie* noises would occasionally come from locked rooms in the castle〉
synonyms creepy, haunting, spooky, uncanny, unearthly, weird
related words ghostly, spectral; odd, strange, uncommon, unusual; preternatural, supernatural; enigmatic (*also* enigmatical), inscrutable, mysterious, puzzling; dreadful, fearsome, horrible, horrifying, terrible, terrifying
near antonyms common, commonplace, everyday, normal, ordinary, usual

efface *vb* to destroy all traces of — see ANNIHILATE 1

effect *n* **1** a condition or occurrence traceable to a cause 〈better health is always one of the *effects* of improved hygiene〉
synonyms aftereffect, aftermath, conclusion, consequence, corollary, development, fate, fruit, issue, outcome, outgrowth, product, result, resultant, sequel, sequence, upshot
related words ramification; denouement, repercussion; conclusion, end; by-product, side effect
phrases matter of course
near antonyms consideration, determinant, factor; base, basis, foundation, ground, groundwork
antonyms antecedent, cause, occasion, reason
2 the power to bring about a result on another 〈religion has a profound *effect* on our lives〉
synonyms impact, influence, mark, repercussion, sway
related words authority, clout, prestige, weight; command, domination, dominion; consequence, importance, significance
3 effects *pl* transportable items that one owns — see POSSESSION 2

effect *vb* to be the cause of (a situation, action, or state of mind) 〈classroom discussions designed to *effect* a change in racial attitudes〉
synonyms bring about, cause, create, effectuate, engender, generate, induce, make, produce, prompt, result (in), spawn, work, yield
related words decide, determine; begin, establish, father, found, inaugurate, initiate, institute, introduce, set, set up; advance, encourage, forward, foster, promote; enact, render, turn out
phrases bring forth, give rise to
near antonyms impede, limit, restrict; dampen, repress, smother, stifle, suppress; arrest, check, curb, restrain, retard; can, kill, snuff (out), still; abolish, demolish, destroy, extinguish, liquidate, quash, quell, quench

effective *adj* **1** producing or capable of producing a desired result 〈an *effective* treatment of the once-dreaded disease〉
synonyms effectual, efficacious, efficient, fruitful, potent, productive
related words adequate, capable, competent; adept, expert, masterly, proficient, skilled, skillful; cogent, convincing, killer, sound, striking, telling, valid; active, dynamic; operative, useful, working; feasible, practical, realizable, workable
near antonyms incapable, incompetent, inexpert, unqualified; abortive, bootless, futile, vain; empty, hollow, idle, pointless; inoperative, useless, worthless
antonyms fruitless, ineffective, ineffectual, inefficient, unproductive
2 having the power to persuade — see COGENT

effectiveness *n* **1** the capacity to persuade — see COGENCY 1
2 the power to produce a desired result — see EFFICACY
3 the quality of an utterance that provokes interest and produces an effect — see [1]PUNCH 1

effectual *adj* producing or capable of producing a desired result — see EFFECTIVE 1

effectualness *n* the power to produce a desired result — see EFFICACY

effectuate *vb* to be the cause of (a situation, action, or state of mind) — see EFFECT

effeminate *adj* having or displaying qualities more suitable for women than for men 〈a comedian deliberately affecting *effeminate* mannerisms〉
synonyms feminine, girlish, sissy, unmanly, womanish, womanlike, womanly
related words old-maidish, overnice, spinsterish; dandyish, foppish, sappy
antonyms manlike, manly, mannish, masculine

effervescent *adj* joyously unrestrained — see EXUBERANT

effete *adj* **1** having lost forcefulness, courage, or spirit ⟨the soft, *effete* society that marked the final years of the Roman empire⟩
synonyms decadent, decayed, degenerate, overripe, washed-up
related words decaying, declining, dying, failing, waning; soft, weak; dissolute, immoral
2 depleted in strength, energy, or freshness — see WEARY 1
3 lacking bodily strength — see WEAK 1
4 lacking strength of will or character — see WEAK 2

efficacious *adj* producing or capable of producing a desired result — see EFFECTIVE 1

efficaciousness *n* the power to produce a desired result — see EFFICACY

efficacy *n* the power to produce a desired result ⟨questioned the *efficacy* of the alarms in actually preventing auto theft⟩
synonyms effectiveness, effectualness, efficaciousness, efficiency, productiveness
related words ability, capability, capacity; potency, strength
near antonyms inability, inadequacy, incompetence
antonyms ineffectiveness, ineffectualness, inefficiency

efficiency *n* the power to produce a desired result — see EFFICACY

efficient *adj* producing or capable of producing a desired result — see EFFECTIVE 1

effort *n* the active use of energy in producing a result ⟨the finished parade float was well worth the *effort*⟩
synonyms elbow grease, exertion, expenditure, labor, pains, sweat, trouble, while, work
related words drudgery, grind, toil, travail; dint, energy; force, might, muscle, power, puissance; attempt, endeavor, essay
near antonyms adroitness, ease, facility, fluency, smoothness; idleness, inaction, inactivity, indolence, inertia, languor, laziness

effortless *adj* involving minimal difficulty or effort — see EASY 1

effortlessly *adv* without difficulty — see EASILY

effrontery *n* shameless boldness ⟨the little squirt had the *effrontery* to deny eating any cookies, even with the crumbs still on his lips⟩
synonyms audacity, brashness, brass, brassiness, brazenness, cheek, cheekiness, chutzpah (*also* chutzpa *or* hutzpah *or* hutzpa), gall, nerve, nerviness, pertness, presumption, presumptuousness, sauce, sauciness, temerity
related words arrogance, assurance, cockiness, confidence, overconfidence, sanguinity, self-assurance, self-confidence; impertinence, impudence, insolence, rudeness
near antonyms bashfulness, diffidence, hesitancy, modesty, shyness, timidity

effulgence *n* the quality or state of having or giving off light — see BRILLIANCE 1

effulgent *adj* giving off or reflecting much light — see BRIGHT 1

effusive *adj* showing feeling freely — see DEMONSTRATIVE

egg (on) *vb* to try to persuade (someone) through earnest appeals to follow a course of action — see URGE

ego *n* **1** a reasonable or justifiable sense of one's worth or importance — see PRIDE 1
2 an often unjustified feeling of being pleased with oneself or with one's situation or achievements — see COMPLACENCE

egocentric *adj* overly concerned with one's own desires, needs, or interests ⟨the cult attracts *egocentric* people who are preoccupied with reaching their potential as individuals⟩
synonyms egoistic, egotistic (*or* egotistical), self-centered, selfish, self-seeking
related words complacent, conceited, self-conceited, self-directed, self-important, self-indulgent, self-satisfied, smug, vain
near antonyms altruistic, generous, greathearted, magnanimous, self-sacrificing
antonyms selfless

egoism *n* excessive interest in oneself ⟨because of her *egoism*, she never gave a thought to asking how the others felt⟩
synonyms egotism, self-centeredness, self-interest, selfishness, self-regard
related words conceit, self-admiration, self-conceit, self-esteem, self-importance, self-indulgence, self-respect, self-satisfaction, self-sufficiency
near antonyms altruism, generosity, magnanimity, self-sacrifice
antonyms selflessness

egoistic *adj* **1** having too high an opinion of oneself — see CONCEITED
2 overly concerned with one's own desires, needs, or interests — see EGOCENTRIC

egotism *n* **1** an often unjustified feeling of being pleased with oneself or with one's situation or achievements — see COMPLACENCE
2 excessive interest in oneself — see EGOISM

egotistic *or* **egotistical** *adj* **1** having too high an opinion of oneself — see CONCEITED
2 overly concerned with one's own desires, needs, or interests — see EGOCENTRIC

egregious *adj* very noticeable especially for being incorrect or bad ⟨the student's theme was marred by a number of *egregious* errors in spelling⟩
synonyms blatant, conspicuous, flagrant, glaring, gross, obvious, patent, pronounced, rank, striking
related words clear, distinct, evident, notable, outstanding, plain, salient; absolute, arrant, downright, out-and-out, outright, sheer, stark, utter; abominable, atrocious, awful, deplorable, execrable, heinous, monstrous, outrageous, preposterous, shameful, shocking
near antonyms imperceptible, inconspicuous; insignificant, slight, trifling, trivial; concealed, hidden, invisible

egress *n* a place or means of going out — see EXIT 1

ejaculate *vb* to utter with a sudden burst of strong feeling — see EXCLAIM

eject *vb* **1** to drive or force out ⟨we quickly *ejected* the unwanted guest from our party⟩
synonyms banish, boot (out), bounce, cast (out), chase, dismiss, drum (out), expel, extrude, oust, rout, run off, throw out
related words deport, displace, dispossess, evict, exile, expatriate, ostracize, shut out; discharge, fire, sack
phrases send packing
near antonyms accept, admit, receive, take in; welcome; entertain, harbor, house, lodge, shelter
2 to throw out or off (something from within) often violently — see ERUPT 1

eke out *vb* to get with great difficulty ⟨*eked out* a living from the family's small farm⟩
synonyms scrape, scrounge, squeeze, wrest, wring
related words acquire, earn, gain, obtain, procure, secure

elaborate *adj* **1** made or done with great care or with much detail ⟨*elaborate* festivities for the 200th anniversary of the town's founding⟩
synonyms complex, complicated, detailed, fancy, intricate, involved, sophisticated
related words elegant, grand, ornate, magnificent, splendid; extravagant, flamboyant, frilly, grandiose, ostentatious, overwrought; labyrinthine
near antonyms modest, plain, uncomplicated, unsophisticated
antonyms simple
2 including many small descriptive features — see DETAILED 1
3 having many parts or aspects that are usually interrelated — see COMPLEX 1

elaborate (on) *vb* **1** to add to the interest of by including made-up details — see EMBROIDER
2 to express more fully and in greater detail — see EXPAND 1

elaborateness *n* the state or quality of having many interrelated parts or aspects — see COMPLEXITY 1

elaboration *n* **1** the act or process of going from the simple or basic to the complex or advanced — see DEVELOPMENT 1
2 the representation of something in terms that go beyond the facts — see EXAGGERATION

elapse *vb* to come to an end — see CEASE 1

elastic *adj* **1** able to revert to original size and shape after being stretched, squeezed, or twisted ⟨*elastic* rubber bands⟩
synonyms flexible, resilient, rubberlike, rubbery, springy, stretch, stretchable, supple
related words adaptable, ductile, malleable, moldable, plastic, pliable, pliant; limber, lissome (*also* lissom), lithe
near antonyms firm, hard, solid; brittle, crisp, friable
antonyms inelastic, inflexible, nonelastic, rigid, stiff
2 capable of being readily changed — see FLEXIBLE 1

elate *vb* to fill with great joy ⟨the winning of the state basketball championship *elated* the whole student body⟩
synonyms elevate, enrapture, exhilarate, overjoy, transport
related words excite, inspire, stimulate, uplift; delight, gladden, gratify, please
near antonyms demoralize, discourage, dishearten, dispirit; distress, oppress, sadden
antonyms depress

elated *adj* experiencing or marked by overwhelming usually pleasurable emotion — see ECSTATIC

elation *n* a state of overwhelming usually pleasurable emotion — see ECSTASY

elbow *vb* to force one's way — see PRESS 4

elbow grease *n* the active use of energy in producing a result — see EFFORT

elbowroom *n* an extent or area available for or used up by some activity or thing — see ROOM 1

elder *n* **1** a person of advanced years — see SENIOR CITIZEN
2 one who is above another in rank, station, or office — see SUPERIOR
3 one who is older than another — see SENIOR 1
4 the senior member of a group — see DEAN

elderly *adj* being of advanced years and especially past middle age ⟨*elderly* people who stay active are usually the healthiest and the happiest⟩
synonyms aged, aging, ancient, geriatric, long-lived, old, older, senior
related words adult, grown-up, mature, middle-aged; pensioned, retired, superannuated; matriarchal, patriarchal, venerable; doddering, senile, tottery
near antonyms youngish; adolescent, immature, juvenile, puerile
antonyms young, youthful

elder statesman *n* the senior member of a group — see DEAN

elect *adj* singled out from a number or group as more to one's liking — see SELECT 1

elect *n* individuals carefully selected as being the best of a class — see ELITE

elect *vb* to decide to accept (someone or something) from a group of possibilities — see CHOOSE 1

election *n* the act or process of selecting — see SELECTION 1

elective *adj* subject to one's freedom of choice — see OPTIONAL

electric *adj* causing great emotional or mental stimulation — see EXCITING 1

electrify *vb* to cause a pleasurable stimulation of the feelings — see THRILL

electrifying *adj* causing great emotional or mental stimulation — see EXCITING 1

elegance *n* dignified or restrained beauty of form, appearance, or style ⟨the *elegance* of the hotel's French furnishings⟩
synonyms class, elegancy, grace, gracefulness, handsomeness, majesty, refinement, stateliness
related words grandeur, lavishness, luxuriousness, magnificence, ornateness, richness, splendor; artfulness, chic, polish, sophistication, taste, tastefulness; choiceness, classicism, dignity, exquisiteness, restraint, simplicity; affectedness, grandiosity, pretentiousness
near antonyms coarseness, crudeness, flashiness, garishness, gaudiness, gracelessness, grotesqueness, tastelessness, tawdriness

elegancy *n* dignified or restrained beauty of form, appearance, or style — see ELEGANCE

elegant *adj* **1** having or showing elegance ⟨the most *elegant* First Lady in the nation's history⟩ ⟨the bride's *elegant* gown received nothing but praise⟩
synonyms graceful, handsome, majestic, refined, stately, tasteful
related words grand, lavish, luxurious, magnificent, ornate, rich, splendid; artful, genteel, polished, sophisticated; classic, exquisite, restrained, simple; chic, fashionable, posh, smart, stylish; affected, grandiose, pretentious
near antonyms coarse, crude, flashy, garish, gaudy, grotesque, tacky, tawdry
antonyms graceless, inelegant, tasteless, unhandsome
2 having qualities that appeal to a refined taste — see CHOICE

elegiac *adj* causing or marked by an atmosphere lacking in cheer — see GLOOMY 1

elegy *n* a composition expressing one's grief over a loss — see LAMENT 2

element *n* **1** one of the parts that make up a whole ⟨a free press is an essential *element* of a democracy⟩
synonyms component, constituent, factor, ingredient, member
related words detail, item, particular, point; aspect, characteristic, facet, feature, trait; division, fragment, particle, piece, portion, section, sector, segment
near antonyms aggregate, composite, compound, sum, total, totality
antonyms whole
2 elements *pl* general or basic truths on which other truths or theories can be based — see PRINCIPLES 1
elemental *adj* of or relating to the simplest facts or theories of a subject — see ELEMENTARY
elementary *adj* of or relating to the simplest facts or theories of a subject ⟨students who do not have even an *elementary* knowledge of geography⟩
synonyms basic, elemental, essential, fundamental, rudimentary, underlying
related words primal, primary, prime; primitive; beginning, introductory, preliminary
near antonyms complex, sophisticated; detailed, extensive, intricate
antonyms advanced
elephantine *adj* unusually large — see HUGE
elevate *vb* **1** to fill with great joy — see ELATE
2 to move from a lower to a higher place or position — see RAISE 1
3 to move higher in rank or position — see PROMOTE 1
elevated *adj* **1** being positioned above a surface ⟨an *elevated* monorail that transports visitors all over the theme park⟩
synonyms lifted, raised, uplifted, upraised
related words aerial, suspended; erect, upright
near antonyms low-lying
antonyms sunken
2 very dignified in form, tone, or style ⟨the *elevated* language of Lincoln's Gettysburg Address⟩
synonyms eloquent, formal, high-flown, lofty, majestic, stately, towering
related words bombastic, declamatory, florid, flowery, grandiloquent, highfalutin, pompous, stilted
near antonyms casual, colloquial, conversational, informal, slangy; coarse, crude, indecent, vulgar
antonyms low, undignified
3 being at a higher level than average — see HIGH 2
4 having, characterized by, or arising from a dignified and generous nature — see NOBLE 2
5 located at a greater height than average or usual — see HIGH 3
elevation *n* **1** a raising or a state of being raised to a higher rank or position — see ADVANCEMENT 1
2 an area of high ground — see HEIGHT 4
3 the distance of something or someone from bottom to top — see HEIGHT 3
4 the most extreme or advanced point — see HEIGHT 2
elf *n* an imaginary being usually having a small human form and magical powers — see FAIRY
elfin *adj* having an often mysterious or magical power to attract — see FASCINATING 1
elfish *adj* given to good-natured joking or teasing — see PLAYFUL
elicit *vb* to draw out (something hidden, latent, or reserved) — see EDUCE
eliminate *vb* to prevent the participation or inclusion of — see EXCLUDE
elite *n* individuals carefully selected as being the best of a class ⟨the winners of this science award represent the *elite* of our high schools⟩
synonyms best, choice, cream, elect, fat, flower, pick, prime, upper crust
related words aristocracy, (the) establishment, gentry, nobility, society, (the) top, upper class
phrases cream of the crop
near antonyms commoners, masses, rank and file
elixir *n* something that cures all ills or problems — see CURE-ALL
elliptic *or* **elliptical** *adj* having the shape of an egg — see OVAL
elocution *n* the art of speaking in public eloquently and effectively — see ORATORY 1
elongate *vb* to make longer — see EXTEND 1
elongated *adj* of great extent from end to end — see LONG 1
elongation *n* the act of making longer — see EXTENSION 1
eloquence *n* the art or power of speaking or writing in a forceful and convincing way ⟨the *eloquence* of Martin Luther King's "I Have a Dream" speech⟩
synonyms articulateness, poetry, rhetoric
related words expression, expressiveness; declamation, elocution, oratory; forcefulness, meaningfulness, persuasiveness; ardor, fervor, passion, power
eloquent *adj* **1** able to express oneself clearly and well — see ARTICULATE
2 clearly conveying a special meaning (as one's mood) — see EXPRESSIVE
3 very dignified in form, tone, or style — see ELEVATED 2
else *adj* resulting in an increase in amount or number — see ADDITIONAL
else *adv* in a different way — see OTHERWISE
elucidate *vb* to make plain or understandable — see EXPLAIN 1
elucidation *n* a statement that makes something clear — see EXPLANATION 1
elucidative *adj* serving to explain — see EXPLANATORY
elude *vb* to get or keep away from (as a responsibility) through cleverness or trickery — see ESCAPE 2
eluding *n* the act or a means of getting or keeping away from something undesirable — see ESCAPE 2
elusive *adj* hard to find, capture, or isolate ⟨the giant squid is one of the ocean's most *elusive* inhabitants⟩
synonyms evasive, fugitive, slippery
related words cagey (*also* cagy), shifty; ephemeral, evanescent, fleeting, momentary, passing, short-lived, transitory; unavailable, unobtainable
near antonyms accessible, approachable, attainable, available, obtainable
elvish *adj* tending to or exhibiting reckless playfulness — see MISCHIEVOUS 1
Elysian *adj* of, relating to, or suggesting heaven — see CELESTIAL
Elysium *n* **1** a dwelling place of perfect bliss for the soul after death — see HEAVEN 1

2 a place or state of great happiness — see PARADISE 1
emaciated *adj* suffering extreme weight loss as a result of hunger or disease ⟨the *emaciated* bodies of the survivors of the concentration camps⟩
synonyms cadaverous, gaunt, haggard, skeletal, wasted
related words bony, rawboned, scrawny, skinny, thin; starved, underfed, undernourished; shriveled, withered, wizened
near antonyms beefy, brawny, burly, fit, hale, healthy, hearty, husky; chubby, corpulent, fat, fleshy, heavyset, plump, portly, stocky, thickset
emancipate *vb* to set free (as from slavery or confinement) — see FREE 1
emancipation *n* the act of setting free from slavery — see LIBERATION
emasculate *vb* to deprive of courage or confidence — see UNNERVE 1
embankment *n* a bank of earth constructed to control water — see DAM
embargo *n* an order that something not be done or used — see PROHIBITION 2
embark (on *or* upon) *vb* to take the first step in (a process or course of action) — see BEGIN 1
embarrass *vb* **1** to throw into a state of self-conscious distress ⟨the young soldier was *embarrassed* by the public praise for his heroism⟩
synonyms abash, confound, confuse, discomfit, disconcert, discountenance, faze, fluster, mortify, nonplus, rattle
related words agitate, bother, chagrin, discomfort, discompose, dismay, disquiet, distress, disturb, perturb, unhinge, unsettle, upset; debase, degrade, demean, humble, humiliate
near antonyms calm, comfort, console, relieve, soothe; buoy, cheer, embolden, encourage, hearten; assure, reassure
2 to create difficulty for the work or activity of — see HAMPER
embarrassing *adj* causing embarrassment — see AWKWARD 3
embarrassment *n* **1** the emotional state of being made self-consciously uncomfortable ⟨experienced the great *embarrassment* of tripping while on stage⟩
synonyms abashment, confusion, discomfiture, fluster, mortification
related words agitation, bother, chagrin, discomfort, discomposure, dismay, disquiet, distress, disturbance, perturbation, uneasiness, upset; debasement, degradation, humiliation
near antonyms aplomb, assurance, composure, confidence, coolness, equanimity, poise, self-assurance, self-confidence, self-possession
2 something that makes movement or progress more difficult — see ENCUMBRANCE
embed *also* **imbed** *vb* to set solidly in or as if in surrounding matter — see ENTRENCH
embellish *vb* **1** to add to the interest of by including made-up details — see EMBROIDER
2 to make more attractive by adding something that is beautiful or becoming — see DECORATE
embellishing *adj* serving to add beauty — see DECORATIVE
embellishment *n* **1** something that decorates or beautifies — see DECORATION 1
2 the representation of something in terms that go beyond the facts — see EXAGGERATION
embitter *vb* to implant bitter feelings in ⟨the family refused to allow their collision with a drunk driver *embitter* them⟩
synonyms antagonize, envenom
related words aggravate, anger, enrage, incense, infuriate, madden; alienate, disaffect, disgruntle, estrange; sour
near antonyms endear, ingratiate; appease, assuage, mollify, pacify, placate, propitiate; sweeten
embittered *adj* having or showing deep-seated resentment — see BITTER 1
emblem *n* a device, design, or figure used as an identifying mark ⟨the oil company uses a scallop shell as its *emblem*⟩
synonyms hallmark, logo, symbol, trademark
related words icon, pictograph; badge, coat of arms, crest, insignia; monogram, stamp, token
emblematic *also* **emblematical** *adj* having the function or meaning of a symbol — see SYMBOLIC
embodiment *n* a visible representation of something abstract (as a quality) ⟨Mother Theresa was often regarded as the *embodiment* of selfless devotion to others⟩
synonyms epitome, incarnation, manifestation, personification
related words exemplification, incorporation, substantiation; essence, quintessence; archetype, exemplar, model, paradigm, pattern; acme, apex, culmination, peak, pinnacle, summit, zenith
embody *vb* **1** to make a part of a body or system ⟨concepts of moral behavior that we should *embody* into our daily life⟩
synonyms assimilate, incorporate, integrate
related words amalgamate, blend, combine, commingle, fuse, intermingle, merge, mingle
2 to represent in visible form ⟨George Washington *embodied* so many of the virtues that Americans hold dear⟩
synonyms epitomize, incarnate, manifest, materialize, personalize, personify, substantiate
related words actualize, realize; symbolize; exemplify, illustrate
embolden *vb* to fill with courage or strength of purpose — see ENCOURAGE 1
emboldened *adj* inclined or willing to take risks — see BOLD 1
embosom *vb* to surround or cover closely — see ENFOLD 1
embower *vb* to surround or cover closely — see ENFOLD 1
embrace *vb* **1** to put one's arms around and press tightly ⟨upon being finally reunited, the overjoyed father *embraced* his son⟩
synonyms clasp, enfold, grasp, hug
related words cling, cradle, grab, grip, hold; embosom, encircle, entwine, envelop; fold, lock, twine, wrap; cuddle, fondle, nestle, nuzzle, pat, pet, snuggle, stroke
2 to surround or cover closely — see ENFOLD 1
3 to take for one's own use (something originated by another) — see ADOPT
4 receive or accept gladly or readily — see WELCOME
5 to have as part of a whole — see INCLUDE
embroider *vb* to add to the interest of by including made-up details ⟨Dad likes to *embroider* his fishing stories⟩
synonyms color, elaborate (on), embellish, exaggerate, magnify, pad, stretch
related words amplify, enhance, enlarge (upon),

expand, flesh (out); fudge, hedge; overdo, overdraw, overemphasize, overplay, overstate; caricature; satirize
near antonyms belittle, minimize, play (down), understate
embroidering *n* the representation of something in terms that go beyond the facts — see EXAGGERATION
embroidery *n* decorative stitching done on cloth with the use of a needle — see NEEDLEWORK
embroil *vb* to place in conflict or difficulties ⟨the town has been *embroiled* in controversy over the building of the huge shopping mall⟩
synonyms bog (down), mire
related words enmesh, ensnare, entangle, entrap, snare, tangle, trap
near antonyms emancipate, free, liberate, release
emend *vb* to remove errors, defects, deficiencies, or deviations from — see CORRECT 1
emendation *n* a change designed to correct or improve a written work — see CORRECTION 1
emerge *vb* to come to one's attention especially gradually or unexpectedly — see ARISE 2
emergency *n* a time or state of affairs requiring prompt or decisive action ⟨an alert, quick-thinking girl who is good to have around in an *emergency*⟩
synonyms clutch, crisis, crossroad(s), crunch, exigency, head, juncture, zero hour
related words contingency, possibility; climax, landmark, milestone, turning point; condition, pass, situation, strait; deadlock, impasse, stalemate; corner, fix, hole, hot water, jam, pinch, predicament, scrape, spot
emigrant *n* one that leaves one place to settle in another ⟨a city teeming with *emigrants* from many lands⟩
synonyms émigré (*also* emigré), immigrant, migrant, settler
related words defector, deportee, evacuee, exile, expatriate, refugee; alien, foreigner, noncitizen, nonnative; colonist, newcomer, squatter
near antonyms aborigine, native; citizen, inhabitant, national, resident
antonyms nonimmigrant
émigré *also* **emigré** *n* **1** a person forced to emigrate for political reasons ⟨the revolution resulted in a flood of *émigrés* into neighboring countries⟩
synonyms deportee, evacuee, exile, expatriate, refugee
related words alien, fugitive; castoff, outcast, pariah; loyalist, patriot
2 one that leaves one place to settle in another — see EMIGRANT
eminence *n* **1** the fact or state of being above others in rank or importance ⟨the *eminence* of the Nobel Prize in the field of awards and prizes⟩
synonyms distinction, dominance, noteworthiness, preeminence, superiority
related words celebrity, fame, famousness, glory, honor, renown, reputation, repute; authority, greatness, influence, power, weight
near antonyms insignificance, unimportance; inferiority, mediocrity; obscurity
2 an area of high ground — see HEIGHT 4
eminent *adj* standing above others in rank, importance, or achievement ⟨many *eminent* surgeons are on the hospital's staff⟩
synonyms distinguished, illustrious, noble, notable, noteworthy, outstanding, preeminent, prestigious, signal, star, superior
related words celebrated, famed, famous, glorious, honored, renowned, reputable; infamous, notorious; dominant, paramount, predominant
near antonyms insignificant, minor, unimportant; average, inferior, mediocre; obscure, uncelebrated, unsung
emissary *n* a person sent on a mission to represent another — see AMBASSADOR
emit *vb* **1** to throw or give off ⟨the cabin's chimney *emitted* smoke⟩
synonyms cast (off), discharge, exhale, expel, issue, release, shoot, vent
related words eliminate, evacuate, excrete, exude, ooze, secrete; gush, pour, spew
near antonyms absorb, inhale
2 to send forth using the vocal chords — see UTTER 1
emolument *n* the money paid regularly to a person for labor or services — see WAGE
emotion *n* **1** a subjective response to a person, thing, or situation — see FEELING 1
2 depth of feeling — see ARDOR 1
emotional *adj* **1** having or expressing great depth of feeling — see FERVENT
2 having the power to affect the feelings or sympathies — see MOVING
3 showing feeling freely — see DEMONSTRATIVE
emphasis *n* **1** a special notice or importance given to something ⟨a prep school with a long-established *emphasis* on sports⟩
synonyms accent, accentuation, stress, weight
related words attention, concentration, consideration, heed, note, regard; value, worth; consequence, import, moment, significance; precedence, primacy, priority
near antonyms apathy, disregard, indifference
2 the quality or state of being forceful (as in expression) — see VEHEMENCE 1
emphasize *vb* to indicate the importance of by giving prominent display ⟨supermarket tabloids that *emphasize* sensational news stories⟩
synonyms accent, accentuate, feature, highlight, play (up), point (up), stress, underline, underscore
related words focus, identify, pinpoint, spotlight; advertise, boost, plug, promote, publicize
near antonyms tone (down), understate; belittle, discount, disparage, minimize
antonyms play (down)
emphatic *adj* **1** marked by or uttered with forcefulness ⟨the governor issued an *emphatic* denial of all charges⟩
synonyms aggressive, assertive, dynamic, energetic, forceful, resounding, strenuous, vehement, vigorous
related words decided, insistent, marked, pointed; arresting, compelling, conspicuous, noticeable, striking; absolute, categorical (*also* categoric), clear, plain, unambiguous, unequivocal
near antonyms guarded, mild, weak, wishy-washy; ambiguous, equivocal; understated
antonyms unemphatic
2 likely to attract attention — see NOTICEABLE
empire *n* a group of businesses or enterprises under one control — see CONGLOMERATE
empirical *adj* based on observation or experience ⟨guidelines for raising children that are based on *empirical* evidence⟩
synonyms experimental, objective, observational

related words actual, factual, genuine, hard, real; accepted, established, tried, tried-and-true; indisputable, undeniable; demonstrable, provable, verifiable
near antonyms conjectural, hypothetical, speculative; unproven, unsubstantiated, unverified
antonyms nonempirical, theoretical (*also* theoretic)

employ *n* the state of being provided with a paying job — see HIRE 1

employ *vb* **1** to provide with a paying job ⟨a new factory that will *employ* 500 people⟩
synonyms engage, hire, retain, take on
related words recruit, sign on; keep
near antonyms furlough, lay off
antonyms can, discharge, dismiss, fire, sack
2 to put into action or service — see USE 1

employable *adj* capable of or suitable for being used for a particular purpose — see USABLE 1

employed *adj* involved in often constant activity — see BUSY 1

employee *n* one who works for another for wages or a salary ⟨an employer who was loved and admired by generations of *employees*⟩
synonyms hand, hireling, jobholder, worker
related words assistant, cog, flunky (*also* flunkey), subordinate, underling, yes-man; drudge, grub, laborer, navvy [*chiefly British*], toiler, workingman, workman; associate, colleague, coworker
near antonyms boss, superior, supervisor
antonyms employer

employment *n* **1** the act or practice of employing something for a particular purpose — see USE 1
2 the activity by which one regularly makes a living — see OCCUPATION
3 the state of being provided with a paying job — see HIRE 1

emporium *n* an establishment where goods are sold to consumers — see SHOP 1

empower *vb* to give official or legal power to — see AUTHORIZE 1

emptiness *n* **1** a need or desire for food — see HUNGER 1
2 empty space — see VACANCY 1
3 the quality or state of being empty — see VACANCY 2

empty *adj* **1** lacking contents that could or should be present ⟨the refrigerator is *empty*, so we'll have to eat out⟩
synonyms bare, blank, devoid, stark, vacant, void
related words barren, hollow; available, clear, free, open; unfilled, unfurnished; unattended, uninhabited, unoccupied; abandoned, deserted, emptied, forsaken, vacated; depleted, drained, dry, exhausted
near antonyms complete; replete; furnished, provided, supplied; filled, occupied; flush, overflowing, packed, teeming
antonyms full
2 feeling a desire or need for food — see HUNGRY 1
3 having no meaning — see MEANINGLESS
4 having no usefulness — see WORTHLESS
5 producing no results — see FUTILE

empty *vb* to remove the contents of ⟨*empty* the room before starting to paint the ceiling⟩
synonyms clear, evacuate, vacate, void
related words deplete, drain, eliminate, exhaust; bleed, draw (off); clean, flush, purge, scour, sweep
antonyms fill, load

empyreal *adj* of, relating to, or suggesting heaven — see CELESTIAL

empyrean *adj* of, relating to, or suggesting heaven — see CELESTIAL

emulate *vb* to use (someone or something) as the model for one's speech, mannerisms, or behavior — see IMITATE 1

emulative *adj* using or marked by the use of something else as a basis or model — see IMITATIVE

enable *vb* **1** to make able or possible ⟨my new glasses *enable* me to read⟩
synonyms allow, let, permit
related words fit, prepare, qualify, ready; approve, endorse (*also* indorse), sanction; condition, equip
near antonyms inhibit, preclude; disallow, enjoin, forbid, prohibit
antonyms prevent
2 to give official or legal power to — see AUTHORIZE 1

enact *vb* to put into effect through legislative or authoritative action ⟨Congress *enacts* all laws relating to foreign trade and immigration⟩
synonyms lay down, legislate, make, pass
related words bring about, effect; allow, authorize, permit, sanction; decree, dictate, proclaim; administer, execute; approve, confirm, ratify
near antonyms abolish, abrogate, annul, cancel, invalidate, nullify; overturn, reverse
antonyms repeal, rescind, revoke

enactment *n* **1** a rule of conduct or action laid down by a governing authority and especially a legislator — see LAW 1
2 the doing of an action — see COMMISSION 2

enamored (of) *adj* filled with an intense or excessive love for ⟨many teenage girls became *enamored of* the movie idol for his boyish good looks⟩
synonyms crazy (about *or* over), enraptured (by), infatuated (with), mad (about), nuts (about)
related words hung up, obsessed; foolish, silly, wild; bewitched, captivated, charmed, enchanted, entranced, fascinated
phrases sweet on
near antonyms cool, detached, unimpressed; disenchanted, disillusioned

encamp *vb* **1** to live in a camp or the outdoors — see CAMP
2 to provide with living quarters or shelter — see HOUSE 1

encampment *n* a place where a group of people live for a short time in tents or cabins — see CAMP 1

encapsulate *vb* to make into a short statement of the main points (as of a report) — see SUMMARIZE

encapsulation *n* a short statement of the main points — see SUMMARY

encase *vb* to close or shut in by or as if by barriers — see ENCLOSE 1

enchain *vb* to confine or restrain with or as if with chains — see BIND 1

enchant *vb* **1** to attract or delight as if by magic — see CHARM 1
2 to cast a spell on — see BEWITCH 1
3 to hold the attention of as if by a spell — see ENTHRALL 1

enchanted *adj* being or appearing to be under a magic spell ⟨an *enchanted* isle of the South Pacific⟩
synonyms bewitched, charmed, entranced, magic, magical, spellbound

related words dreamy, fairy, fairylike; fantastic, miraculous, utopian, wondrous; hypnotized, mesmerized; captivated, fascinated

enchanter *n* a person skilled in using supernatural forces — see MAGICIAN 1

enchanting *adj* having an often mysterious or magical power to attract — see FASCINATING 1

enchantment *n* **1** a spoken word or set of words believed to have magic power — see SPELL 1

2 the power of irresistible attraction — see CHARM 2

3 the power to control natural forces through supernatural means — see MAGIC 1

enchantress *n* **1** a woman believed to have often harmful supernatural powers — see WITCH 1

2 a woman whom men find irresistibly attractive — see SIREN

encircle *vb* **1** to pass completely around <communication satellites *encircling* the earth>

synonyms circle, circumnavigate, compass, girdle, girth, loop, orbit, ring, round

related words cross, perambulate, traverse

2 to form a circle around — see SURROUND

enclose *also* **inclose** *vb* **1** to close or shut in by or as if by barriers <dogs who spend the day *enclosed* in small cages>

synonyms cage, closet, coop (up), corral, encase, envelop, fence (in), hedge, hem, house, immure, pen, wall (in)

related words bound, circumscribe, confine, contain, limit, restrict; encircle, encompass, ring, surround

2 to form a circle around — see SURROUND

3 to surround or cover closely — see ENFOLD 1

enclosure *also* **inclosure** *n* an open space wholly or partly enclosed (as by buildings or walls) — see COURT 2

encomium *n* a formal expression of praise <the *encomiums* bestowed on a teacher at her retirement ceremonies>

synonyms accolade, citation, commendation, eulogy, homage, paean, panegyric, salutation, tribute

related words award, decoration, honor, prize; acclaim, acclamation, approval, compliment, recommendation; applause, plaudits; bravo, hallelujah

near antonyms censure, condemnation, denunciation, indictment, rebuke, reprimand, reproof; admonition, correction, lecture, sermon

encompass *vb* **1** to form a circle around — see SURROUND

2 to have as part of a whole — see INCLUDE

3 to surround or cover closely — see ENFOLD 1

encounter *n* a brief clash between enemies or rivals <survived an *encounter* with the school bully at the local park>

synonyms brush, hassle, run-in, scrape, skirmish

related words argument, fight, quarrel, row, spat, squabble, tiff; battle, brawl, fray, wrangle

encounter *vb* **1** to come upon face-to-face or as if face-to-face — see MEET 1

2 to come upon unexpectedly or by chance — see HAPPEN (ON *OR* UPON)

3 to enter into contest or conflict with — see ENGAGE 2

encourage *vb* **1** to fill with courage or strength of purpose <a pep talk that *encouraged* the team to get out there and win>

synonyms buoy (up), cheer (up), comfort, embolden, hearten, inspire, steel

related words animate, enliven, invigorate; fortify, reinforce, strengthen; assure, reassure; boost, energize, excite, galvanize, provoke, quicken, rally, stimulate, stir

near antonyms demoralize, depress, sadden; debilitate, enfeeble, undermine, weaken

antonyms daunt, discourage, dishearten, dispirit

2 to help the growth or development of — see FOSTER 1

3 to rouse to strong feeling or action — see PROVOKE 1

4 to try to persuade (someone) through earnest appeals to follow a course of action — see URGE

encouragement *n* something that arouses action or activity — see IMPULSE

encouraging *adj* **1** having qualities which inspire hope — see HOPEFUL 1

2 making one feel good inside — see HEARTWARMING

3 pointing toward a happy outcome — see FAVORABLE 2

encroach *vb* to advance gradually beyond the usual or desirable limits <each year the sea continues to *encroach* upon the island's beaches>

synonyms creep, inch, worm

related words snake, sneak; entrench (*also* intrench), impinge, infringe, intrude, invade; overpass, overreach, overrun, overshoot, overstep

encrust *also* **incrust** *vb* to cover with a hardened layer <refrigerator shelves that were *encrusted* with the residue of many spills>

synonyms cake, rime

related words besmear, coat, smear, spread; cover, daub; coagulate, congeal, harden

encumber *vb* **1** to create difficulty for the work or activity of — see HAMPER

2 to place a weight or burden on — see LOAD 1

encumbrance *n* something that makes movement or progress more difficult <without the *encumbrance* of a heavy backpack, I could sprint along the trail>

synonyms bar, block, chain, clog, crimp, deterrent, drag, embarrassment, fetter, handicap, hindrance, hurdle, impediment, inhibition, interference, let, manacle, obstacle, obstruction, shackles, stop, stumbling block, trammel

related words catch, hitch, rub, snag; hobble; arrest, check, constraint, curb, rein, restraint, stop; delay, holdup; burden, load; danger, hazard, peril; adversity, difficulty, disadvantage, hardship

near antonyms catalyst, goad, impetus, incentive, spur, stimulant, stimulus; advantage, edge; break

antonyms aid, assistance, benefit, help

encyclopedic *also* **encyclopaedic** *adj* covering everything or all important points <a tour guide with an *encyclopedic* knowledge of New York City and its people>

synonyms compendious, complete, comprehensive, full, global, inclusive, in-depth, omnibus, panoramic, universal

related words broad, catholic, extensive, far-reaching, general, overall, sweeping, vast, wide; blanket, indiscriminate, unrestricted

near antonyms circumscribed, limited, narrow, restricted, specialized; exact, precise; individual, singular, specific

end *n* **1** the stopping of a process or activity <the *end* of hostilities brought general rejoicing>

synonyms cessation, close, closure, conclusion, discontinuance, ending, expiration, finish, halt, lapse, shutdown, shutoff, stop, stoppage, surcease, termination

related words abeyance, interruption, moratorium, suspension

near antonyms extension, persistence, prolongation

antonyms continuation

2 a real or imaginary point beyond which a person or thing cannot go — see LIMIT

3 an unused or unwanted piece or item typically of small size or value — see [1]SCRAP 1

4 something that one hopes or intends to accomplish — see GOAL

5 the last and usually sharp or tapering part of something long and narrow — see POINT 2

6 the last part of a process or action — see FINALE

7 the line or relatively narrow space that marks the outer limit of something — see BORDER 1

8 the permanent stopping of all the vital bodily activities — see DEATH 1

end *vb* **1** to bring (an event) to a natural or appropriate stopping point — see CLOSE 3

2 to bring (as an action or operation) to an immediate end — see STOP 1

3 to come to an end — see CEASE 1

endanger *vb* to place in danger ⟨a reckless use of fireworks that *endangered* the lives of many people⟩

synonyms adventure, compromise, gamble (with), hazard, imperil, jeopardize, menace, risk, venture

related words intimidate, threaten; expose; subject; chance, wager

near antonyms guard, protect, shelter, shield; preserve, resume, save

endangered *adj* being in a situation where one is likely to meet with harm — see LIABLE 1

endangerment *n* the state of not being protected from injury, harm, or evil — see DANGER 1

endearing *adj* **1** having qualities that tend to make one loved — see LOVABLE

2 likely to win one's affection — see INGRATIATING

endeavor *n* an effort to do or accomplish something — see ATTEMPT

endeavor *vb* **1** to devote serious and sustained effort — see LABOR

2 to make an effort to do — see ATTEMPT

ended *adj* brought or having come to an end — see COMPLETE 2

endemic *adj* belonging to a particular place by birth or origin — see NATIVE 1

ending *n* **1** the last part of a process or action — see FINALE

2 the stopping of a process or activity — see END 1

endless *adj* **1** being or seeming to be without limits — see INFINITE

2 lasting forever — see EVERLASTING

endorse *also* **indorse** *vb* to promote the interests or cause of — see SUPPORT 1

endow *vb* **1** to furnish with something freely or naturally ⟨a young performer *endowed* with a great singing voice⟩

synonyms endue, invest

related words equip, provide, supply; bestow, confer; accord, award, grant; empower, enable, enhance, enrich, heighten; bless, favor, grace; bequeath, will

near antonyms dispossess, divest, strip; deplete, drain, exhaust; skimp, stint

2 to furnish (as an institution) with a regular source of income ⟨a wealthy businessman who *endowed* several museums⟩

synonyms finance, fund, subsidize

related words establish, found, organize; bequeath, contribute, donate, subscribe, support; award, grant; back, promote, sponsor

near antonyms draw, receive; subsist

3 to provide money for — see FINANCE 1

endowment *n* a special and usually inborn ability — see TALENT

endue *vb* to furnish with something freely or naturally — see ENDOW 1

endurable *adj* capable of being endured — see BEARABLE

endurance *n* **1** continuing existence — see PERSISTENCE 1

2 uninterrupted or lasting existence — see CONTINUATION

endure *vb* **1** to come to a knowledge of (something) by living through it — see EXPERIENCE

2 to put up with (something painful or difficult) — see BEAR 2

3 to remain indefinitely in existence or in the same state — see CONTINUE 1

enemy *n* one that is hostile toward another ⟨a beloved minister with no known *enemies*⟩

synonyms adversary, antagonist, foe, opponent

related words archenemy; (the) opposition; nemesis; bane, bête noire; assailant, attacker, combatant, invader; competitor, emulator, rival

near antonyms ally, collaborator, colleague, confederate, friendly, partner; adherent, disciple, follower; backer, benefactor, supporter

antonyms friend

energetic *adj* **1** having active strength of body or mind — see VIGOROUS 1

2 having much high-spirited energy and movement — see LIVELY 1

3 marked by or uttered with forcefulness — see EMPHATIC 1

energetically *adv* in a vigorous and forceful manner — see HARD 3

energize *vb* to give life, vigor, or spirit to — see ANIMATE

energized *adj* made or become fresh in spirits or vigor — see NEW 4

energy *n* **1** active strength of body or mind — see VIGOR 1

2 something with a usable capacity for doing work — see FUEL

3 the ability to exert effort for the accomplishment of a task — see POWER 2

enervate *vb* to diminish the physical strength of — see WEAKEN 1

enervated *adj* **1** lacking bodily energy or motivation — see LISTLESS

2 lacking bodily strength — see WEAK 1

enfeeble *vb* to diminish the physical strength of — see WEAKEN 1

enfeebled *adj* lacking bodily strength — see WEAK 1

enfeeblement *n* **1** a gradual sinking and wasting away of mind or body — see DECLINE 1

2 the quality or state of lacking physical strength or vigor — see WEAKNESS 1

enfold *vb* **1** to surround or cover closely ⟨darkness began to *enfold* the lonely house on the hill⟩

synonyms embosom, embower, embrace, enclose (*also* inclose), encompass, enshroud, envelop, enwrap, invest, lap, mantle, shroud, swathe, veil, wrap
related words curtain, drape; encase; swaddle; blanket, overlay, overspread; camouflage, cloak, disguise, mask; circle, encircle, encompass
near antonyms bare, denude, expose, strip
2 to put one's arms around and press tightly — see EMBRACE 1

enforce *vb* to carry out effectively ⟨the duty of the police is to *enforce* the law⟩
synonyms administer, apply, execute, implement
related words effect, effectuate; discharge, fulfill (*or* fulfil), render; cite, invoke; enact, legislate; honor, observe; prosecute; promulgate
near antonyms disregard, ignore, neglect

enfranchise *vb* to set free (as from slavery or confinement) — see FREE 1

enfranchisement *n* **1** the act of setting free from slavery — see LIBERATION
2 the right to formally express one's position or will in an election — see VOTE 1

engage *vb* **1** to hold the attention of ⟨the challenging jigsaw puzzle *engaged* us all evening⟩
synonyms absorb, busy, engross, enthrall (*or* enthral), fascinate, grip, immerse, interest, intrigue, involve, occupy
related words allure, attract, bewitch, captivate, charm, enchant; hypnotize, mesmerize; monopolize, preoccupy
near antonyms bore, jade, pall, tire, weary
2 to enter into contest or conflict with ⟨the daring young captain was eager to *engage* the enemy⟩
synonyms battle, encounter, face, meet, take on
related words emulate, rival; contend, fight, oppose
near antonyms elude, escape, evade; retreat
3 to obligate by prior agreement — see PLEDGE 1
4 to provide with a paying job — see EMPLOY 1
5 to take or get the temporary use of (something) for a set sum — see HIRE 1

engaged *adj* **1** involved in often constant activity — see BUSY 1
2 pledged in marriage ⟨the *engaged* couple make a charming pair⟩
synonyms affianced, betrothed
related words committed
antonyms unengaged

engagement *n* **1** the act or state of being engaged to be married ⟨the fun couple recently announced their *engagement*⟩
synonyms betrothal, espousal, troth
antonyms disengagement
2 an agreement to be present at a specified time and place ⟨a lifelong practice of marking all of my *engagements* on a weekly calendar⟩
synonyms appointment, date, rendezvous, tryst
related words arrangement; invitation; interview; get-together, meeting; call, visit; schedule
3 the state of being provided with a paying job — see HIRE 1

engaging *adj* **1** having an often mysterious or magical power to attract — see FASCINATING 1
2 holding the attention or provoking interest — see INTERESTING

engender *vb* to be the cause of (a situation, action, or state of mind) — see EFFECT

engine *n* a device that changes energy into mechanical motion ⟨a car with a 200-horsepower *engine*⟩
synonyms machine, motor
related words converter, transformer; appliance, mechanism; equipment; mill

engineer *vb* to plan out usually with subtle skill or care ⟨the mayor *engineered* an agreement to have a major league team play in our city⟩
synonyms contrive, finagle, finesse, frame, machinate, maneuver, manipulate, mastermind, negotiate, wangle
related words intrigue, plot, scheme; connive; concoct, cook (up), hatch; captain, command, conduct, direct, handle, manage, quarterback, run; gerrymander
near antonyms blow, bobble, botch, bungle, butcher, flub, fumble, gum (up), louse up, mangle, mess (up), mishandle, muff

engrave *vb* **1** to cut (as letters or designs) on a hard surface ⟨*engraved* the birth and death dates on the tombstone⟩
synonyms etch, grave, incise, inscribe
related words carve, chisel, sculpt, sculpture; chase; score
2 to produce a vivid impression of ⟨a scar that forever *engraved* the killer's face in the witness's mind⟩
synonyms etch, impress, imprint, ingrain
related words imbue, implant, inculcate, infuse, instill

engross *vb* to hold the attention of — see ENGAGE 1

engrossed *adj* having the mind fixed on something — see ATTENTIVE

engrossing *adj* holding the attention or provoking interest — see INTERESTING

engrossment *n* a focusing of the mind on something — see ATTENTION 1

engulf *vb* to cover or become filled with a flood — see FLOOD

enhance *vb* **1** to make better — see IMPROVE
2 to make markedly greater in measure or degree — see INTENSIFY

enhancement *n* an instance of notable progress in the development of knowledge, technology, or skill — see ADVANCE 2

enigma *n* something hard to understand or explain — see MYSTERY

enigmatic *also* **enigmatical** *adj* **1** being beyond one's powers to know, understand, or explain — see MYSTERIOUS 1
2 having an often intentionally veiled or uncertain meaning — see OBSCURE 1

enjoin *vb* **1** to ask for (something) earnestly or with authority — see DEMAND 1
2 to issue orders to (someone) by right of authority — see COMMAND 1
3 to order not to do or use or to be done or used — see FORBID

enjoining *n* the act of ordering that something not be done or used — see PROHIBITION 1

enjoy *vb* **1** to take pleasure in ⟨TV and videos are OK, but we still *enjoy* seeing movies on the big screen⟩
synonyms adore, delight (in), dig, fancy, groove (on), like, love, relish, revel (in)
related words admire, appreciate, cherish, revere, venerate, worship; prize, treasure, value; devour, drink (in), savor; dote (on), idolize; cotton (to), favor, prefer

phrases be partial to, get a kick (*or* charge) out of, go for, have a soft spot for, take to
near antonyms abhor, abominate, detest, dislike, hate, loathe; condemn, despise, scorn
2 to keep, control, or experience as one's own — see HAVE 1

enjoyable *adj* **1** giving pleasure or contentment to the mind or senses — see PLEASANT
2 providing amusement or enjoyment — see FUN

enjoyment *n* the feeling experienced when one's wishes are met — see PLEASURE 1

enlarge *vb* **1** to become greater in extent, volume, amount, or number — see INCREASE 2
2 to make greater in size, amount, or number — see INCREASE 1

enlarge (on) *vb* to express more fully and in greater detail — see EXPAND 1

enlighten *vb* **1** to give information to ‹the lecturer at the planetarium *enlightened* us about the latest astronomical discoveries›
synonyms acquaint, advise, apprise, brief, clue, familiarize, fill in, inform, instruct, tell, wise (up)
related words clarify, clear (up), construe, elucidate, explain, explicate, expound, illuminate, illustrate, interpret, spell out; announce, disclose, report; disabuse, disenchant, disillusion
near antonyms misinform, mislead
2 to provide (someone) with moral or spiritual understanding ‹many people around the world have been *enlightened* by the teachings of Gautama Buddha›
synonyms edify, educate, nurture
related words elevate, ennoble, lift, uplift; better, improve, transform; exalt, glorify, transfigure
near antonyms confuse, perplex, puzzle; becloud, cloud, darken, obscure

enlist (in) *vb* to become a member of — see ENTER 2

enliven *vb* to give life, vigor, or spirit to — see ANIMATE

enmesh *vb* to catch or hold as if in a net — see ENTANGLE 2

enmity *n* a deep-seated ill will ‹*enmity* had existed between the two families for generations›
synonyms animosity, antagonism, antipathy, bitterness, gall, grudge, hostility, jaundice, rancor
related words hate, hatred, loathing; vindictiveness, virulence, vitriol; alienation, disaffection, estrangement; abhorrence, aversion, repugnance, repulsion; disgust, horror; conflict, coolness, friction, strain, tension; discord, unfriendliness; malice, malignancy, malignity, spite, spitefulness, venom
near antonyms amiability, amicability, civility, cordiality, friendliness, hospitality, neighborliness; comity, empathy, friendship, goodwill, sympathy, understanding
antonyms amity

ennoble *vb* to enhance the status of — see EXALT

ennui *n* the state of being bored — see BOREDOM

enormity *n* **1** the state or quality of being utterly evil ‹the *enormity* of the crimes committed by the Nazis›
synonyms atrociousness, atrocity, badness, depravedness, depravity, evilness, heinousness, monstrosity, nefariousness, sinfulness, vileness, wickedness
related words accursedness, baseness, devilishness, execrableness, fiendishness, hellishness; corruption, decadence, degeneracy; immorality; infamy, notoriety
near antonyms morality; chasteness, innocence, purity
antonyms goodness, righteousness, virtuousness
2 the quality or state of being very large — see IMMENSITY

enormous *adj* unusually large — see HUGE

enormously *adv* to a large extent or degree — see GREATLY 2

enormousness *n* the quality or state of being very large — see IMMENSITY

enough *adv* **1** in or to a degree or quantity that meets one's requirements or satisfaction ‹the elevator is big *enough* to hold everyone›
synonyms adequately, satisfactorily, sufficiently
related words acceptably, decently, fairly, moderately, passably, tolerably; abundantly, amply; commensurately, proportionately
antonyms inadequately, insufficiently, unsatisfactorily
2 to some degree or extent — see FAIRLY

enrage *vb* to make angry — see ANGER

enraged *adj* feeling or showing anger — see ANGRY

enrapture *vb* **1** to fill with great joy — see ELATE
2 to fill with overwhelming emotion (as wonder or delight) — see ENTRANCE

enraptured *adj* experiencing or marked by overwhelming usually pleasurable emotion — see ECSTATIC

enraptured (by) *adj* filled with an intense or excessive love for — see ENAMORED (OF)

enrich *vb* **1** to make better — see IMPROVE
2 to make more attractive by adding something that is beautiful or becoming — see DECORATE

enroll *also* **enrol** *vb* **1** to enter in a list or roll ‹the school *enrolls* about 800 students›
synonyms inscribe, list, matriculate, register
related words catalog (*or* catalogue), itemize, tabulate, tally; file, index; book, log, post; program, schedule; check in
near antonyms cancel, delete, exclude, expel, expunge, reject; omit, overlook
2 to put (someone or something) on a list — see [1]LIST 2

enroll (in) *vb* to become a member of — see ENTER 2

enrollment *n* the number of individuals registered — see REGISTRATION

ensconce *vb* **1** to establish or place comfortably or snugly ‹the kids had contentedly *ensconced* themselves on the couch before the TV›
synonyms install, lodge, perch, roost, settle
related words curl up; park, plant; anchor, bivouac, camp; burrow; locate, situate
2 to put into a hiding place — see [1]HIDE 1

enshrine *vb* to enhance the status of — see EXALT

enshroud *vb* **1** to keep secret or shut off from view — see [1]HIDE 2
2 to surround or cover closely — see ENFOLD 1

ensign *n* a piece of cloth with a special design that is used as an emblem or for signaling — see FLAG 1

enslavement *n* the state of being a slave — see SLAVERY 1

ensnare *vb* to catch or hold as if in a net — see ENTANGLE 2

ensuing *adj* **1** being the one that comes immediately after another — see NEXT

2 being, occurring, or carried out at a time after something else — see SUBSEQUENT

ensure *vb* to make sure, certain, or safe ⟨regulations that *ensure* the wholesomeness of our food⟩
synonyms assure, cinch, guarantee, guaranty, insure, secure
related words attest, certify, vouch, warrant, witness; pledge, promise, swear
near antonyms enfeeble, undermine, weaken

entail *vb* to have as part of a whole — see INCLUDE

entangle *vb* **1** to twist together into a usually confused mass ⟨in the process of taking down the Christmas tree, we managed to *entangle* the string of lights into a hopeless mess of wires⟩
synonyms interlace, intertwine, interweave, knot, snarl, tangle
related words weave, wind, wreathe; braid, plait
antonyms disentangle
2 to catch or hold as if in a net ⟨the young runaway gradually became *entangled* in a web of lies⟩
synonyms enmesh, ensnare, entrap, mesh, snare, tangle, trap
related words bag, capture, collar; embroil, implicate, involve, mire
near antonyms extricate, untangle; detach, disengage; clear, free, liberate
antonyms disentangle

entanglement *n* something that catches and holds — see WEB 1

enter *vb* **1** to go or come in or into ⟨the hikers *entered* the cave with considerable caution⟩
synonyms access, penetrate, pierce
related words barge (in), breeze (in), burst (in *or* into), waltz (in); drop (in), pop (in)
phrases set foot in, step in
antonyms depart, exit, leave
2 to become a member of ⟨patriotic young men and women *entering* the armed services⟩
synonyms enlist (in), enroll (in), join, sign on (for), sign up (for)
related words reenlist, reenroll, reenter
3 to put (someone or something) on a list — see ^{1}LIST 2

enter (into *or* upon) *vb* to take the first step in (a process or course of action) — see BEGIN 1

enterprise *n* **1** a commercial or industrial activity or organization ⟨the booming economy witnessed the launch of many small *enterprises*⟩
synonyms business, company, concern, establishment, firm, house, outfit
related words conglomerate, corporation, multinational; association, cartel, chain, combine, syndicate, trust; agency, dealer, outlet
2 readiness to engage in daring or difficult activity ⟨the *enterprise* shown by the early developers and promoters of personal computers⟩
synonyms aggressiveness, ambition, drive, go, hustle, initiative
related words gumption, pluck, snap, spirit, spunk, starch; assertiveness, self-reliance; energy, hardihood, pep, vigor, vitality
near antonyms inactivity, inertia, passivity; diffidence, faintheartedness, timidity; hesitation, reluctance; indolence, laziness, lethargy
3 a risky undertaking — see GAMBLE

enterprising *adj* **1** having or showing a bold forcefulness in the pursuit of a goal — see AGGRESSIVE 1
2 inclined or willing to take risks — see BOLD 1

entertain *vb* **1** to cause (someone) to pass the time agreeably occupied — see AMUSE
2 to give serious and careful thought to — see PONDER
3 to keep in one's mind or heart — see HARBOR 1

entertaining *adj* providing amusement or enjoyment — see FUN

entertainment *n* **1** the act or activity of providing pleasure or amusement especially for the public ⟨a variety show was staged as *entertainment* for the scouts at the jamboree⟩
synonyms amusement, distraction, diversion, recreation
related words show business; delectation, delight, enjoyment, joy, mirth; gratification, relaxation, relief, satisfaction; exhibition, performance, presentation, production, show, spectacle; escapism
2 someone or something that provides amusement or enjoyment — see FUN 1

enthrall *or* **enthral** *vb* **1** to hold the attention of as if by a spell ⟨*enthralled* by the flickering fire in the hearth, we lost all track of time⟩
synonyms arrest, enchant, fascinate, grip, hypnotize, mesmerize, spellbind
related words enrapture, entrance, thrill; beguile, bewitch, charm; absorb, engage, engross, involve
phrases cast a spell on
2 to fill with overwhelming emotion (as wonder or delight) — see ENTRANCE
3 to hold the attention of — see ENGAGE 1

enthralled *adj* having the mind fixed on something — see ATTENTIVE

enthralling *adj* holding the attention or provoking interest — see INTERESTING

enthrallment *n* a focusing of the mind on something — see ATTENTION 1

enthuse *vb* to make an exaggerated display of affection or enthusiasm — see GUSH 2

enthusiasm *n* **1** a practice or interest that is very popular for a short time — see FAD
2 urgent desire or interest — see EAGERNESS

enthusiast *n* a person with a strong and habitual liking for something — see FAN

enthusiastic *adj* showing urgent desire or interest — see EAGER

enthusiastically *adv* in an enthusiastic manner — see SKY-HIGH

entice *vb* to lead away from a usual or proper course by offering some pleasure or advantage — see LURE

enticement *n* **1** something that persuades one to perform an action for pleasure or gain — see LURE 1
2 the act or pressure of giving in to a desire especially when ill-advised — see TEMPTATION 1

entire *adj* **1** not divided or scattered among several areas of interest or concern — see WHOLE 1
2 not lacking any part or member that properly belongs to it — see COMPLETE 1

entirely *adv* to a full extent or degree — see FULLY 1

entitle *vb* **1** to give a right to ⟨the card *entitles* my grandmother to the discount for senior citizens⟩
synonyms authorize, qualify
related words empower, enable, license (*also* licence); approve, endorse (*also* indorse); allow, let, permit; certify, ratify, sanction, validate
antonyms disqualify
2 to give a name to — see NAME 1

entity *n* one that has a real and independent exis-

tence ⟨the question of whether extrasensory perception will ever be a scientifically recognized *entity*⟩
synonyms being, individual, object, something, substance, thing
related words body; material, matter, stuff

entomb *vb* to place (a dead body) in the earth, a tomb, or the sea — see BURY 1

entombing *n* the act or ceremony of putting a dead body in its final resting place — see BURIAL

entombment *n* the act or ceremony of putting a dead body in its final resting place — see BURIAL

entrails *n pl* the internal organs of the body — see GUT 1

entrance *n* **1** the means or right of entering or participating in ⟨*entrance* to the club is by invitation only⟩
synonyms access, admission, admittance, doorway, entrée (*or* entree), entry, gateway
related words approval, certification, qualification
2 the opening through which one can enter or leave a structure — see DOOR 2

entrance *vb* to fill with overwhelming emotion (as wonder or delight) ⟨a production of *The Nutcracker* ballet that will *entrance* audiences⟩
synonyms carry away, enrapture, enthrall (*or* enthral), overjoy, ravish, transport
related words delight, gladden, gratify, please, satisfy; bewitch, captivate, charm, enchant, fascinate; elate, excite, exhilarate, stir

entranced *adj* **1** being or appearing to be under a magic spell — see ENCHANTED
2 experiencing or marked by overwhelming usually pleasurable emotion — see ECSTATIC

entrancing *adj* having an often mysterious or magical power to attract — see FASCINATING 1

entrap *vb* to catch or hold as if in a net — see ENTANGLE 2

entreat *vb* to make a request to (someone) in an earnest or urgent manner — see BEG

entreating *adj* asking humbly — see SUPPLIANT

entreaty *n* an earnest request — see PLEA 1

entrée *or* **entree** *n* the means or right of entering or participating in — see ENTRANCE 1

entrench *also* **intrench** *vb* to set solidly in or as if in surrounding matter ⟨a father who *entrenched* in our minds the belief that hard work pays off⟩
synonyms embed (*also* imbed), fix, implant, ingrain, lodge, root
related words imbue, infuse, instill; establish, place, put, settle, stick
near antonyms eliminate, eradicate; eject, expel; detach, disconnect, disengage, remove
antonyms dislodge, root (out), uproot

entrenched *also* **intrenched** *adj* firmly established over time — see INVETERATE 1

entrust *vb* **1** to give a task, duty, or responsibility to ⟨we *entrusted* our financial adviser with the investment of all of our savings⟩
synonyms assign, charge, commission, trust
related words confer, impose; commit, consign, delegate, relegate; allocate, allot; authorize, empower, invest
2 to put (something) into the possession or safekeeping of another — see GIVE 2

entry *n* **1** the entrance room of a building — see HALL 1
2 the means or right of entering or participating in — see ENTRANCE 1

entryway *n* the entrance room of a building — see HALL 1

entwine *vb* to follow a circular or spiral course — see WIND

enumerate *vb* **1** to specify one after another ⟨I proceeded to *enumerate* the reasons why my allowance needed raising⟩
synonyms detail, itemize, list, numerate, rehearse, tick (off)
related words outline; tabulate, tally; catalog (*or* catalogue), inventory; chart, diagram, graph; calculate, compute, estimate, figure, reckon; cite, mention, name
2 to find the sum of (a collection of things) by noting each one as it is being added — see COUNT 1
3 to make a list of — see [1]LIST 1

enunciate *vb* **1** to utter clearly and distinctly — see ARTICULATE 1
2 to make known openly or publicly — see ANNOUNCE

enunciation *n* the clear and accurate pronunciation of words especially in public speaking — see DICTION 1

envelop *vb* **1** to close or shut in by or as if by barriers — see ENCLOSE 1
2 to surround or cover closely — see ENFOLD 1

envenom *vb* to implant bitter feelings in — see EMBITTER

envenomed *adj* containing or contaminated with a substance capable of injuring or killing a living thing — see POISONOUS

envious *adj* having or showing mean resentment of another's possessions or advantages ⟨a family that is *envious* of their neighbors' big house⟩
synonyms covetous, invidious, jaundiced, jealous, resentful
related words begrudging, grudging; avaricious, grasping, greedy; distrustful, suspicious; malicious, petty, spiteful
phrases green with envy
near antonyms generous, kind, kindhearted; altruistic, benevolent, charitable; well-meaning

enviousness *n* a painful awareness of another's possessions or advantages and a desire to have them too — see ENVY

environment *n* the circumstances, conditions, or objects by which one is surrounded ⟨the joys of growing up in the *environment* that a small town offers⟩
synonyms atmosphere, climate, environs, medium, milieu, setting, surroundings
related words backdrop, background, context; element; situation, status; habitat

environs *n pl* **1** the area around a city ⟨the city and its *environs* total about a million in population⟩
synonyms exurbia, outskirts, purlieu, suburbia
related words backwater, backwoods, hinterland
2 the circumstances, conditions, or objects by which one is surrounded — see ENVIRONMENT

envisage *vb* to form a mental picture of — see IMAGINE 1

envoy *n* **1** a person sent on a mission to represent another — see AMBASSADOR
2 a person who acts or does business for another — see AGENT 2

envy *n* a painful awareness of another's possessions or advantages and a desire to have them too ⟨her *envy* of her neighbor's fancy clothes wrecked their friendship⟩

synonyms covetousness, enviousness, invidiousness, jealousy, resentment
related words animosity, enmity, hatred, ill will; malice, maliciousness, spitefulness
near antonyms benevolence, goodwill, kindness, sympathy

enwrap *vb* to surround or cover closely — see ENFOLD 1

ephemeral *adj* lasting only for a short time — see MOMENTARY

epicure *n* a person with refined tastes in food and wine ⟨Thomas Jefferson was one of America's first great *epicures*⟩
synonyms gourmand, gourmet
related words connoisseur, dilettante; savorer
near antonyms glutton, gorger, hog, trencherman

epigram *n* an often stated observation regarding something from common experience — see SAYING

epigrammatic *adj* marked by the use of few words to convey much information or meaning — see CONCISE

episode *n* something that happens — see EVENT 1

episodic *adj* appearing in parts or numbers that follow regularly — see SERIAL

epistle *n* a message on paper from one person or group to another — see LETTER

epithet *n* **1** a descriptive or familiar name given instead of or in addition to the one belonging to an individual — see NICKNAME
2 an act or expression showing scorn and usually intended to hurt another's feelings — see INSULT

epitome *n* **1** a short statement of the main points — see SUMMARY
2 a visible representation of something abstract (as a quality) — see EMBODIMENT
3 the most perfect type or example — see QUINTESSENCE 1

epitomize *vb* **1** to make into a short statement of the main points (as of a report) — see SUMMARIZE
2 to represent in visible form — see EMBODY 2

epoch *n* an extent of time associated with a particular person or thing — see AGE 1

equable *adj* marked by temperatures that are neither too high nor too low — see CLEMENT

equal *vb* **1** to produce something equal to (as in quality or value) ⟨no one has *equaled* Shakespeare's plays⟩
synonyms match, meet, tie
related words beat, excel, outdo, surpass, top; amount (to), approach, touch; measure (up), rival
2 to be the same in meaning or effect — see AMOUNT (TO) 2
3 to be the exact counterpart of — see MATCH 1

equal *adj* **1** marked by justice, honesty, and freedom from bias — see FAIR 2
2 resembling another in every respect — see SAME 1

equal *n* one that is equal to another in status, achievement, or value ⟨a basketball player who truly has no *equal* in his sport⟩
synonyms coordinate, counterpart, equivalent, fellow, like, match, parallel, peer, rival
related words analogue (*or* analog); double, mate, twin; associate, colleague, companion, partner; competitor

equality *n* the state or fact of being exactly the same in number, amount, status, or quality — see EQUIVALENCE

equalize *vb* to make equal in amount, degree, or status ⟨a plan to *equalize* educational opportunities for all the state's children, rich and poor alike⟩
synonyms balance, equate, even, level
related words accommodate, adjust, compensate, fit; homogenize, normalize, regularize, standardize; democratize

equanimity *n* evenness of emotions or temper ⟨an Olympic diver who always displays remarkable *equanimity* on the platform⟩
synonyms aplomb, calmness, composure, coolheadedness, coolness, imperturbability, placidity, self-possession, serenity, tranquillity (*or* tranquility)
related words assurance, confidence, poise, self-assurance, self-confidence; apathy, detachment, indifference, phlegm
near antonyms alarm, anxiety, apprehension, disquiet; excitability, nervousness; disturbance
antonyms agitation, discomposure, perturbation

equate *vb* **1** to regard or represent as equal or comparable ⟨a value system that *equates* money with success⟩
synonyms compare, liken
related words associate, connect, join, link, match; group, lump (together)
near antonyms differentiate, discriminate, distinguish
2 to describe as similar — see COMPARE 1
3 to make equal in amount, degree, or status — see EQUALIZE

equatorial *adj* being near the equator — see LOW 1

equilibrium *n* a condition in which opposing forces are equal to one another — see BALANCE 1

equine *n* a large hoofed domestic animal that is used for carrying or drawing loads and for riding — see HORSE

equip *vb* **1** to make competent (as by training, skill, or ability) for a particular office or function — see QUALIFY 2
2 to provide (someone) with what is needed for a task or activity — see FURNISH 1

equipage *n* a horse-drawn wheeled vehicle for carrying passengers — see CARRIAGE 1

equipment *n* items needed for the performance of a task or activity ⟨the *equipment* for the polar expedition included ships, instruments, sleds, dogs, and provisions⟩
synonyms accoutrements (*or* accouterments), apparatus, gear, material(s), matériel (*or* materiel), outfit, paraphernalia, tackle
related words accessories, attachments, fittings; baggage, belongings, impedimenta; appliances, facilities, instruments, machinery, tools; apparel, attire, habiliments, raiment, trappings; battery

equipoise *n* **1** a condition in which opposing forces are equal to one another — see BALANCE 1
2 a force or influence that makes an opposing force ineffective or less effective — see COUNTERBALANCE

equitable *adj* marked by justice, honesty, and freedom from bias — see FAIR 2

equity *n* the act or practice of giving to others what is their due — see JUSTICE 1

equivalence *n* the state or fact of being exactly the same in number, amount, status, or quality ⟨moviegoers who mistakenly believe that there is an *equivalence* between the personality of an actor and that of his character⟩

synonyms equality, equivalency, par, parity, sameness
related words compatibility, correlation, correspondence; likeness, similarity; exchangeability, interchangeability
near antonyms difference, discrepancy, disparity, divergence; incompatibility; dissimilarity, unlikeness
antonyms inequality
equivalency *n* the state or fact of being exactly the same in number, amount, status, or quality — see EQUIVALENCE
equivalent *n* one that is equal to another in status, achievement, or value — see EQUAL
equivocal *adj* **1** giving good reason for being doubted, questioned, or challenged — see DOUBTFUL 2
2 having an often intentionally veiled or uncertain meaning — see OBSCURE 1
equivocalness *n* the quality or state of having a veiled or uncertain meaning — see OBSCURITY 1
equivocate *vb* to avoid giving a definite answer or position <the candidate *equivocated* as long as he could on controversial issues>
synonyms fudge, hedge, pussyfoot
related words dodge, duck, evade, sidestep, skirt; bypass, circumvent; cavil, quibble
phrases beat around (*or* about) the bush, dance around, hem and haw
equivocation *n* the quality or state of having a veiled or uncertain meaning — see OBSCURITY 1
era *n* an extent of time associated with a particular person or thing — see AGE 1
eradicate *vb* to destroy all traces of — see ANNIHILATE 1
ere *prep* earlier than — see BEFORE 1
erect *adj* rising straight up <a lone tree remained *erect* after the terrible tornado had passed>
synonyms perpendicular, plumb, raised, standing, upright, upstanding, vertical
related words elevated, lifted, upended, upraised; freestanding
near antonyms prostrate, supine; hanging, sagging, slanted, slanting
antonyms flat, recumbent
erect *vb* **1** to fix in an upright position <the tribes of the Pacific Northwest *erected* totem poles in front of their dwellings>
synonyms pitch, put up, raise, rear, set up, upend, upraise
related words brace, buttress, prop (up), shore (up), support; elevate, hoist, lift
near antonyms demolish, flatten, knock down, level, raze, tear down
2 to form by putting together parts or materials — see BUILD
erection *n* something put together by arranging or connecting an array of parts — see CONSTRUCTION 1
ergo *adv* for this or that reason — see THEREFORE
erode *vb* **1** to consume or wear away gradually — see EAT 2
2 to damage or diminish by continued friction — see ABRADE 1
erosion *n* a gradual weakening, loss, or destruction — see CORROSION
erotic *adj* of, relating to, or expressing sexual attraction <the *erotic* aspects of the story of Beauty and the Beast>
synonyms amatory, amorous, sexy
related words carnal, sensual, sensuous; bawdy, lascivious, lewd, lustful, obscene, prurient, spicy
err *vb* to commit an offense — see OFFEND 1
errant *adj* **1** engaging in or marked by childish misbehavior — see NAUGHTY
2 traveling from place to place — see ITINERANT
erratic *adj* **1** lacking a definite plan, purpose, or pattern — see RANDOM
2 lacking in steadiness or regularity of occurrence — see FITFUL
3 not staying constant — see UNEVEN 2
erratically *adv* without definite aim, direction, rule, or method — see HIT OR MISS
erroneous *adj* not being in agreement with what is true — see FALSE 1
erroneously *adv* in a mistaken or inappropriate way — see WRONGLY
erroneousness *n* the quality or state of being false — see FALLACY 2
error *n* **1** an unintentional departure from truth or accuracy <a report on the earthquake contained several unfortunate *errors*>
synonyms blunder, fault, flub, fumble, goof, inaccuracy, lapse, miscue, misstep, mistake, oversight, slip, slipup, stumble
related words boner, howler; foul-up, muff; misapprehension, miscalculation, misconception, misjudgment, misstatement, misunderstanding
near antonyms accuracy, correctness, precision
2 a breaking of a moral or legal code — see OFFENSE 1
3 a false idea or belief — see FALLACY 1
erstwhile *adj* having been such at some previous time — see FORMER
erudite *adj* **1** having or displaying advanced knowledge or education — see EDUCATED
2 suggestive of the vocabulary used in books — see BOOKISH
erudition *n* the understanding and information gained from being educated — see EDUCATION 2
erupt *vb* **1** to throw out or off (something from within) often violently <the volcano *erupted* clouds of poisonous gas and tons of hot ash>
synonyms belch, disgorge, eject, expel, jet, spew, spout, spurt
related words gush, pour, stream, surge; emanate, issue, spring; discharge, emit, fire; cast, fling, heave, hurl, launch, pitch, toss
near antonyms bottle (up), contain, restrain, shut (in *or* up)
2 to develop suddenly and violently <a fire *erupted*, and flames soon engulfed the room>
synonyms break out, burst (forth), explode, flame, flare (up)
related words burgeon, mushroom, snowball; blow up, detonate, touch off
eruption *n* **1** a sudden intense expression of strong feeling — see OUTBURST 1
2 the act or an instance of exploding — see EXPLOSION 1
escalate *vb* **1** to become greater in extent, volume, amount, or number — see INCREASE 2
2 to make greater in size, amount, or number — see INCREASE 1
escalated *adj* being at a higher level than average — see HIGH 2
escapade *n* a playful or mischievous act intended as a joke — see PRANK
escape *n* **1** the act or an instance of getting free

from danger or confinement ⟨a daring prison *escape*⟩
synonyms flight, getaway, lam, slip
related words deliverance, liberation, redemption, release, rescue, salvation
near antonyms imprisonment, incarceration; custody, detention, hold, holding, retention; danger, hazard, jeopardy, peril, risk
2 the act or a means of getting or keeping away from something undesirable ⟨the reading of science fiction novels as an *escape* from boring reality⟩
synonyms avoidance, cop-out, dodging, ducking, eluding, eschewing, evasion, out, shaking, shunning
related words bypassing, circumvention; averting, deflection, prevention
near antonyms abidance, endurance, submission, toleration

escape *vb* **1** to get free from a dangerous or confining situation ⟨everyone managed to *escape* from the burning building in time⟩
synonyms abscond, clear out, flee, fly, get away, get out, lam, run away, run off
related words avoid, elude, evade, lose, shun; decamp, depart, exit, leave; disentangle, extricate; emancipate, free, liberate, redeem, release
phrases fly the coop, free oneself
near antonyms abide, linger, remain, stay, tarry; come back, return
2 to get or keep away from (as a responsibility) through cleverness or trickery ⟨a judge who is very determined not to let criminals *escape* punishment⟩
synonyms avoid, dodge, duck, elude, eschew, evade, shake, shirk, shun
related words miss; avert, deflect, divert, obviate, parry, prevent, ward (off); debar, exclude, preclude; bypass, circumvent, skirt; foil, frustrate, outwit, thwart
phrases get around, have nothing to do with, shy away from, steer clear of
near antonyms accept, court, embrace, pursue, seek, welcome; catch, contract, incur

escarpment *n* a steep wall of rock, earth, or ice — see CLIFF

eschew *vb* to get or keep away from (as a responsibility) through cleverness or trickery — see ESCAPE 2

eschewing *n* the act or a means of getting or keeping away from something undesirable — see ESCAPE 2

escort *n* one that accompanies another for protection, guidance, or as a courtesy ⟨the mayor served as the First Lady's *escort* for her tour of the city⟩
synonyms attendant, companion, guard, guide
related words chaperone (*or* chaperon), squire; shadow, sidekick; conductor, leader, pilot

escort *vb* to go along with in order to provide assistance, protection, or companionship — see ACCOMPANY

esculent *adj* suitable for use as food — see EDIBLE

esoteric *adj* difficult for one of ordinary knowledge or intelligence to understand — see PROFOUND 1

especial *adj* of a particular or exact sort — see EXPRESS 1

especially *adv* to a great degree — see VERY 1

espionage *n* the secret gathering of information on others ⟨the acts of *espionage* on behalf of the Confederacy carried on by Belle Boyd and Rose Greenhow⟩
synonyms spying
related words dope, goods, lowdown; counterintelligence, intelligence; observation, reconnaissance, surveillance; bugging, eavesdropping, wiretapping

espousal *n* **1** a ceremony in which two people are united in matrimony — see WEDDING
2 the act or state of being engaged to be married — see ENGAGEMENT 1

espouse *vb* **1** to give in marriage — see MARRY 2
2 to take as a spouse — see MARRY 3

esprit *n* active strength of body or mind — see VIGOR 1

espy *vb* to make note of (something) through the use of one's eyes — see SEE 1

essay *n* **1** a short piece of writing typically expressing a point of view ⟨school *essays* on what it means to be a patriot⟩
synonyms article, composition, paper, theme
related words column, commentary, editorial, feature, report, review, write-up; dissertation, thesis; tract, treatise; discourse, discussion, exposition, study
2 an effort to do or accomplish something — see ATTEMPT

essay *vb* to make an effort to do — see ATTEMPT

essence *n* the quality or qualities that make a thing what it is ⟨the belief that power ultimately rests with the people is the very *essence* of democracy⟩
synonyms essentiality, nature, quintessence, soul, stuff, substance
related words heart, spirit; center, core, keynote, marrow, pith, seat; embodiment, epitome, incarnation, manifestation, personification; aspect, attribute, feature, property; gist, kernel, nub

essential *adj* **1** impossible to do without ⟨a well-stocked public library is *essential* for the well-being of a community⟩
synonyms all-important, imperative, indispensable, integral, necessary, needed, needful, required, requisite, vital
related words prerequisite; compulsory, mandatory, obligatory; important, momentous, significant; basic, central, fundamental, key, organic; insistent, persistent, pressing, urgent
near antonyms undesired, unwanted; inconsequential, insignificant, unimportant; excess, extra, superfluous, surplus
antonyms dispensable, needless, nonessential, unnecessary, unneeded
2 of or relating to the simplest facts or theories of a subject — see ELEMENTARY
3 being a part of the innermost nature of a person or thing — see INHERENT

essential *n* **1** something necessary, indispensable, or unavoidable ⟨the *essentials* for success include a willingness to work and the right attitude⟩
synonyms condition, demand, must, necessity, need, requirement, requisite
related words precondition, prerequisite; advantage, edge, plus
near antonyms extra, extravagance, frill, luxury, superfluity
antonyms nonessential, nonnecessity
2 essentials *pl* general or basic truths on which other truths or theories can be based — see PRINCIPLES 1

essentiality *n* the quality or qualities that make a thing what it is — see ESSENCE

establish *vb* **1** to gain full recognition or acceptance of ⟨the teenagers accused of shoplifting were able to *establish* their innocence⟩
synonyms demonstrate, prove, show, substantiate
related words attest, authenticate, bear out, document, evidence, support, sustain, uphold; confirm, corroborate, justify, validate, verify
phrases prove beyond a reasonable doubt
near antonyms confute, discredit, invalidate, rebut, refute
antonyms disprove
2 to show the existence or truth of by evidence — see PROVE 1
3 to be responsible for the creation and early operation or use of — see FOUND

establisher *n* a person who establishes a whole new field of endeavor — see FATHER 2

establishment *n* **1** a building, room, or suite of rooms occupied by a service business — see PLACE 2
2 a commercial or industrial activity or organization — see ENTERPRISE 1
3 a public organization with a particular purpose or function — see INSTITUTION 1
4 a structure that is designed and built for a particular purpose — see FACILITY

estate *n* **1** a large impressive residence — see MANSION
2 a state of being or fitness — see CONDITION 1
3 one of the segments of society into which people are grouped — see CLASS 1

esteem *n* a feeling of great approval and liking — see ADMIRATION 1

esteem *vb* **1** to think of in a particular way — see CONSIDER 1
2 to think very highly or favorably of — see ADMIRE

esteemed *adj* having a good reputation especially in a field of knowledge — see RESPECTABLE 1

estimate *n* **1** the act of placing a value on the nature, character, or quality of something ⟨what we owe our war veterans is beyond *estimate*⟩
synonyms appraisal, appraisement, assessment, estimation, evaluation, reckoning, valuation
related words calculation, computation, measurement
2 an opinion on the nature, character, or quality of something — see ESTIMATION 1

estimate *vb* **1** to make an approximate or tentative judgment regarding ⟨experts *estimated* the value of the painting at a million dollars⟩
synonyms appraise, assess, evaluate, rate, set, value
related words adjudge, deem, judge; ascertain, determine, discover, learn; price, prize; decide, settle; analyze, assay, survey, test; reappraise, reassess, reevaluate, revalue
2 to decide the size, amount, number, or distance of (something) without actual measurement ⟨we *estimated* the snowfall to be about a foot⟩
synonyms calculate, call, conjecture, figure, gauge (*also* gage), guess, judge, make, place, put, reckon, suppose
near antonyms calibrate, measure, scale; compute

estimation *n* **1** an opinion on the nature, character, or quality of something ⟨the teacher's *estimation* of her student's scientific aptitude proved to be well-founded when he won a national science award⟩
synonyms appraisal, appraisement, assessment, estimate, evaluation, judgment (*or* judgement)
related words impression, notion, perception; confidence, faith, stock, trust
2 the act of placing a value on the nature, character, or quality of something — see ESTIMATE 1
3 a feeling of great approval and liking — see ADMIRATION 1

estrange *vb* to cause to change from friendly or loving to unfriendly or uncaring ⟨Carrie's tendency to tattle *estranged* her classmates⟩
synonyms alienate, disaffect, disgruntle, sour
related words antagonize, embitter, envenom; aggravate, anger, enrage, incense, infuriate, madden; disunite, divide, separate, sever, sunder; disappoint, disenchant, disillusion
near antonyms endear, ingratiate; appease, conciliate, mollify, pacify, propitiate
antonyms reconcile

estrangement *n* the loss of friendship or affection ⟨a silly quarrel that eventually resulted in a complete and lasting *estrangement* between the onetime friends⟩
synonyms alienation, disaffection, disgruntlement, souring
related words antagonism, embitterment, envenoming; aggravation, incensing, infuriation; disunion, division, divorce, schism, separation; disenchantment, disillusionment
near antonyms endearment, ingratiation; appeasement, conciliation, mollification, pacification, propitiation
antonyms reconciliation

estuary *n* a part of a body of water that extends beyond the general shoreline — see GULF 1

etch *vb* **1** to cut (as letters or designs) on a hard surface — see ENGRAVE 1
2 to produce a vivid impression of — see ENGRAVE 2

eternal *adj* lasting forever — see EVERLASTING

eternally *adv* for all time — see EVER 1

eternity *n* **1** endless time ⟨the question whether the universe will end someday or continue to exist in *eternity*⟩
synonyms infinity, perpetuity
related words boundlessness, endlessness, interminableness, permanence, timelessness
2 unending existence after death ⟨a firm belief in the *eternity* of the soul⟩
synonyms afterlife, hereafter, immortality
related words otherworld
phrases life after death
3 a long or seemingly long period of time — see AGE 2

ethereal *adj* resembling air in lightness — see AIRY 1

ethical *adj* **1** conforming to a high standard of morality or virtue — see GOOD 2
2 following the accepted rules of moral conduct — see HONORABLE 1
3 guided by or in accordance with one's sense of right and wrong — see CONSCIENTIOUS 1

ethics *n pl* the code of good conduct for an individual or group ⟨the *ethics* of scouting require scouts to be loyal, clean, and reverent⟩
synonyms morality, morals, principles, standards
related words customs, etiquette, manners, mores; beliefs, dogma, faith, tenets

ethnic *adj* of, relating to, or reflecting the traits exhibited by a group of people with a common ancestry and culture — see RACIAL

etiquette *n* personal conduct or behavior as evaluated by an accepted standard of appropriateness for a social or professional setting — see MANNER 1

eulogy *n* a formal expression of praise — see ENCOMIUM

euphonious *adj* **1** having a pleasantly flowing quality suggestive of music — see LYRIC 1
2 having a pleasing mixture of notes — see HARMONIOUS 1

euphoria *n* a state of overwhelming usually pleasurable emotion — see ECSTASY

euphoric *adj* experiencing or marked by overwhelming usually pleasurable emotion — see ECSTATIC

evacuate *vb* to remove the contents of — see EMPTY

evacuee *n* a person forced to emigrate for political reasons — see ÉMIGRÉ 1

evade *vb* to get or keep away from (as a responsibility) through cleverness or trickery — see ESCAPE 2

evaluate *vb* to make an approximate or tentative judgment regarding — see ESTIMATE 1

evaluation *n* **1** an opinion on the nature, character, or quality of something — see ESTIMATION 1
2 the act of placing a value on the nature, character, or quality of something — see ESTIMATE 1

evanesce *vb* to cease to be visible — see DISAPPEAR

evanescent *adj* lasting only for a short time — see MOMENTARY

evaporate *vb* to cease to be visible — see DISAPPEAR

evasion *n* the act or a means of getting or keeping away from something undesirable — see ESCAPE 2

evasive *adj* hard to find, capture, or isolate — see ELUSIVE

even *adj* **1** being neither more nor less than a certain amount, number, or extent <the distance to town is an *even* mile>
synonyms exact, flat, precise, round
near antonyms approximate, comparative, relative
2 having a surface without bends, breaks, or irregularities — see LEVEL
3 resembling another in every respect — see SAME 1

even *adv* not merely this but also <the blue whale is a huge, *even* awesome animal by any measure>
synonyms indeed, nay, truly, verily, yea
related words assuredly, certainly, decidedly, definitely, positively, really, surely, undeniably, unquestionably
phrases in fact, in reality, in truth

even *vb* **1** to make free from breaks, curves, or bumps <*even* the filling before adding the top layer of the cake>
synonyms flatten, level, plane, smooth
related words clip, crop, pare, prune, shave, trim; lay, spread; card, comb, rake
near antonyms coarsen, rumple, wrinkle
antonyms rough, roughen
2 to make equal in amount, degree, or status — see EQUALIZE

evening *n* the time from when the sun begins to set to the onset of total darkness — see DUSK 1

event *n* **1** something that happens <dinnertime was devoted to talking over the day's *events*, not to watching television>
synonyms affair, circumstance, episode, hap, happening, incident, occasion, occurrence, thing
related words coincidence, fluke, freak; landmark, milestone, page, phenomenon, turning point; adventure, experience; accident, crisis, emergency, juncture; achievement, deed, exploit, feat; news, tidings
2 something that might happen <in the *event* of rain, graduation ceremonies will be held indoors>
synonyms case, contingency, eventuality, possibility
related words probability; chance, risk
3 a competitive encounter between individuals or groups carried on for amusement, exercise, or in pursuit of a prize — see GAME 1
4 a social gathering — see PARTY 1

eventful *adj* having great meaning or lasting effect — see IMPORTANT 1

eventide *n* the time from when the sun begins to set to the onset of total darkness — see DUSK 1

eventuality *n* **1** something that can develop or become actual — see POTENTIAL
2 something that might happen — see EVENT 2

eventually *adv* at a later time — see YET 1

ever *adv* **1** for all time <the name of Benedict Arnold will *ever* be linked with treason>
synonyms always, aye (*also* ay), eternally, everlastingly, evermore, forever, forevermore, permanently, perpetually
related words enduringly, long, perennially
phrases forever and a day, forever and ever, for good, to (*or* until) the end of time
antonyms never, nevermore
2 in any way or respect — see AT ALL
3 on every relevant occasion — see ALWAYS 1

everlasting *adj* lasting forever <valentines typically express the giver's *everlasting* love and devotion>
synonyms ceaseless, dateless, deathless, endless, eternal, immortal, permanent, perpetual, undying, unending
related words durable, enduring, lasting, persistent; imperishable, indestructible; timeless; abiding, steadfast, steady, unfailing, unfaltering
near antonyms ephemeral, evanescent, fleeting, momentary, passing, short-lived, transitory
antonyms impermanent, mortal, temporary

everlastingly *adv* for all time — see EVER 1

evermore *adv* for all time — see EVER 1

every *adj* being one of a group — see EACH

everybody *pron* every person <*everybody* must do what his or her conscience dictates>
synonyms all, everyone
phrases each and everyone, one and all
antonyms nobody

everyday *adj* **1** being of the type that is encountered in the normal course of events — see ORDINARY 1
2 having to do with the practical details of regular life — see MUNDANE 1
3 not designed for special occasions — see CASUAL 1
4 often observed or encountered — see COMMON 1

everyone *pron* every person — see EVERYBODY

everyplace *adv* in every place or in all places — see EVERYWHERE

everywhere *adv* in every place or in all places ⟨freedom and happiness are the goals of people *everywhere*⟩
synonyms all over, everyplace, throughout
phrases all over the place (*or* map), far and near, far and wide, high and low, in every corner (*or* quarter)
antonyms nowhere

evidence *n* something presented in support of the truth or accuracy of a claim — see PROOF

evident *adj* **1** appearing to be true on the basis of evidence that may or may not be confirmed — see APPARENT 1
2 not subject to misinterpretation or more than one interpretation — see CLEAR 2

evidently *adv* to all outward appearances — see APPARENTLY

evil *adj* **1** causing or capable of causing harm — see HARMFUL
2 not conforming to a high moral standard; morally unacceptable — see BAD 2

evil *n* that which is morally unacceptable ⟨our free will allows us to choose between good and *evil*⟩
synonyms bad, evildoing, ill, immorality, iniquity, sin, villainy, wrong
related words atrociousness, badness, evilness, heinousness, nefariousness, sinfulness, vileness, wickedness; devilry (*or* deviltry), fiendishness; cancer, decay, rot, squalor; corruption, debauchery, degeneracy, depravity, indecency, perversion; abomination, anathema, taboo (*also* tabu)
near antonyms integrity, probity, rectitude, uprightness; goodness, righteousness, virtuousness
antonyms good, morality, right, virtue

evildoer *n* **1** a person who commits moral wrongs ⟨if good people stand by and do nothing, *evildoers* will triumph⟩
synonyms malefactor, sinner, wrongdoer
related words criminal, crook, felon, lawbreaker, miscreant, reprobate, transgressor, villain
near antonyms angel, saint
2 a mean, evil, or unprincipled person — see VILLAIN

evildoing *n* that which is morally unacceptable — see EVIL

evilness *n* the state or quality of being utterly evil — see ENORMITY 1

evince *vb* to make known (something abstract) through outward signs — see SHOW 2

eviscerate *vb* to take the internal organs out of — see GUT

evocative *adj* provoking a memory or mental association — see SUGGESTIVE 2

evoke *vb* to draw out (something hidden, latent, or reserved) — see EDUCE

evolution *n* the act or process of going from the simple or basic to the complex or advanced — see DEVELOPMENT 1

evolve *vb* to gradually become clearer or more detailed — see DEVELOP 1

evolved *adj* being far along in development — see ADVANCED 1

exact *adj* **1** being in agreement with the truth or a fact or a standard — see CORRECT 1
2 being neither more nor less than a certain amount, number, or extent — see EVEN 1
3 following an original exactly — see FAITHFUL 2
4 made or done with extreme care and accuracy — see FINE 2
5 meeting the highest standard of accuracy — see PRECISE 1

exact *vb* **1** to ask for (something) earnestly or with authority — see DEMAND 1
2 to establish or apply as a charge or penalty — see IMPOSE
3 to get (as money) by the use of force or threats — see EXTORT

exacting *adj* **1** hard to please — see FINICKY
2 not allowing for any exceptions or loosening of standards — see RIGID 1
3 requiring considerable physical or mental effort — see HARD 2
4 requiring much time, effort, or careful attention — see DEMANDING 1

exactitude *n* the quality or state of being very accurate — see PRECISION

exactly *adv* **1** as stated or indicated without the slightest difference ⟨we will meet at *exactly* six o'clock⟩
synonyms just, precisely, right, sharp, smack-dab, squarely
2 in a like manner — see JUST 1
3 in the same words — see VERBATIM
4 without any relaxation of standards or precision — see STRICTLY

exactness *n* the quality or state of being very accurate — see PRECISION

exaggerate *vb* **1** to add to the interest of by including made-up details — see EMBROIDER
2 to describe or express in too strong terms — see OVERSTATE

exaggeration *n* the representation of something in terms that go beyond the facts ⟨their *exaggeration* was such that a rainstorm became a hurricane⟩
synonyms caricature, coloring, elaboration, embellishment, embroidering, hyperbole, magnification, overstatement, padding, stretching
related words amplification, enhancement; fabrication, misrepresentation; fudging, hedging
near antonyms belittlement, disparagement, minimizing
antonyms understatement

exalt *vb* to enhance the status of ⟨popular support and media hype have *exalted* Super Bowl Sunday to the level of a national holiday⟩
synonyms aggrandize, dignify, ennoble, enshrine, glorify, magnify
related words boost, elevate, lift, promote, raise, upgrade, uplift; heighten, intensify; idealize, romanticize, sanitize, sugarcoat; canonize, deify; acclaim, extol (*also* extoll), honor, laud, praise
near antonyms belittle, decry, depreciate, detract, disparage, minimize
antonyms abase, degrade, demean, humble, humiliate

exam *n* a set of questions or problems designed to assess knowledge, skills, or intelligence — see EXAMINATION 1

examination *n* **1** a set of questions or problems designed to assess knowledge, skills, or intelligence ⟨applicants to the prep school are required to take an *examination*⟩
synonyms exam, quiz, test
related words catechism; audition; final; checkup, inspection, review; inquiry, interrogation, investigation, probe, research

2 a systematic search for the truth or facts about something — see INQUIRY 1

3 a close look at or over someone or something in order to judge condition — see INSPECTION

examine *vb* **1** to put a series of questions to ⟨the defense attorney was eager to *examine* her star witness⟩

synonyms grill, interrogate, pump, query, question, quiz

related words debrief; cross-examine; catechize; annoy, harass, hound, pester

phrases give the third degree to

2 to look over closely (as for judging quality or condition) — see INSPECT

example *n* one of a group or collection that shows what the whole is like ⟨a war bonnet that is a fine *example* of Native American handicraft⟩

synonyms case, exemplar, illustration, instance, representative, sample, specimen

related words cross section; evidence, indication, manifestation, sign

phrases case in point

exasperate *vb* to disturb the peace of mind of (someone) especially by repeated disagreeable acts — see IRRITATE 1

exasperating *adj* causing annoyance — see ANNOYING

exasperation *n* **1** something that is a source of irritation — see ANNOYANCE 3

2 the feeling of impatience or anger caused by another's repeated disagreeable acts — see ANNOYANCE 2

excavate *vb* to hollow out or form (something) by removing earth — see DIG 1

exceed *vb* to go beyond the limit of ⟨by resorting to corporal punishment, the teacher had *exceeded* his authority⟩

synonyms overreach, overrun, overshoot, overstep, surpass

related words encroach, entrench (*also* intrench), infringe, invade, trespass; overdo, overuse, overwork

exceedingly *also* **exceeding** *adv* to a great degree — see VERY 1

excel *vb* to be greater, better, or stronger than — see SURPASS 1

excellence *n* **1** exceptionally high quality ⟨the annual awards honor *excellence* in children's literature⟩

synonyms distinction, excellency, greatness, preeminence, superbness, superiority, supremacy

related words faultlessness, flawlessness, impeccability, perfection; goodness, value, worth; consequence, importance, notability

near antonyms averageness, badness, inferiority, mediocrity, ordinariness, worthlessness

2 a quality that gives something special worth ⟨the particular *excellence* of down in clothing and sleeping bags is its lightness⟩

synonyms distinction, excellency, merit, value, virtue

related words advantage, edge, superiority

near antonyms blemish, defect, failing, fault, flaw

antonyms deficiency

excellency *n* **1** a quality that gives something special worth — see EXCELLENCE 2

2 exceptionally high quality — see EXCELLENCE 1

excellent *adj* of the very best kind ⟨fast-food fans rate this chain's fries as *excellent*⟩

synonyms A1, bang-up, banner, boss [*slang*], capital, classic, crackerjack, dandy, divine, fabulous, fine, first-class, first-rate, grand, great, groovy, heavenly, jim-dandy, keen, marvelous (*or* marvellous), mean, neat, nifty, noble, par excellence, prime, sensational, splendid, stellar, sterling, superb, superior, superlative, supernal, swell, terrific, tip-top, top, top-notch, unsurpassed, wonderful

related words acceptable, adequate, all right, decent, good, OK, passable, satisfactory, tolerable; better, exceptional, fancy, high-grade, premium, special

phrases out of sight

near antonyms bad, inferior, low-grade, substandard, unsatisfactory; mediocre, second-class, second-rate; atrocious, execrable, vile, wretched

antonyms poor

except *also* **excepting** *conj* if it were not for the fact that ⟨I'd go, *except* it's too far⟩

synonyms but, only, saving, yet

except *also* **excepting** *prep* not including ⟨the store is open daily *except* Sundays⟩

synonyms aside from, bar, barring, beside, besides, but, except for, excluding, outside, outside of, save, saving

except *vb* to prevent the participation or inclusion of — see EXCLUDE

except for *prep* not including — see EXCEPT

exceptionable *adj* provoking or likely to provoke protest — see OBJECTIONABLE

exceptional *adj* being out of the ordinary ⟨an *exceptional* amount of snow fell in March⟩

synonyms aberrant, abnormal, atypical, extraordinary, freak, odd, peculiar, phenomenal, rare, singular, uncommon, uncustomary, unique, unusual, unwonted

related words conspicuous, notable, noticeable, outstanding, prominent, remarkable, salient, striking; bizarre, deviant, eccentric, outlandish, quaint, strange, weird; incomprehensible, inconceivable, incredible, unimaginable, unthinkable

near antonyms everyday, familiar, frequent

antonyms common, customary, normal, ordinary, typical, unexceptional, usual

excerpt *n* a part taken from a longer work ⟨we'll read an *excerpt* from the novel⟩

synonyms extract, passage

related words snippet; citation, quotation; context; selection

excess *adj* being over what is needed — see SPARE 1

excess *n* the state or an instance of going beyond what is usual, proper, or needed ⟨a new television season with an *excess* of wisecracking teenagers⟩

synonyms fat, overabundance, overage, overflow, overkill, overmuch, oversupply, superabundance, superfluity, surfeit, surplus

related words abundance, bounty, plentitude, plenty, profusion, sufficiency; overproduction, overstock

near antonyms dearth, lack, scarcity

antonyms deficiency, deficit, insufficiency

excessive *adj* going beyond a normal or acceptable limit in degree or amount ⟨nerdy hackers who spend an *excessive* amount of time sitting in front of their computers⟩

synonyms devilish, exorbitant, extravagant, extreme, immoderate, inordinate, lavish, overmuch, overweening, steep, stiff, towering, unconscionable, undue

related words boundless, endless, immeasurable, infinite, limitless; intolerable, unbearable, unjustifiable, unwarranted; improper, inappropriate, thick, unseemly
near antonyms deficient, inadequate, insufficient; minimal, minimum
antonyms moderate, modest, reasonable, temperate

excessively *adv* beyond a normal or acceptable limit — see TOO 1

exchange *n* **1** a giving or taking of one thing of value in return for another ⟨*exchanges* of commemorative pins are common among Olympic athletes⟩
synonyms barter, commutation, swap, trade, truck
related words replacement, substitution; reciprocation, recompense, requital; bargain, deal, horse trade, negotiation, transaction; bargaining, dealing, dickering, haggling, horse trading; logrolling
2 talking or a talk between two or more people — see CONVERSATION

exchange *vb* to give up (something) and take something else in return — see CHANGE 3

excitable *adj* easily excited by nature ⟨an *excitable* child who needed a stable home life⟩
synonyms flighty, fluttery, high-strung, jittery, jumpy, nervous, skittish, spooky
related words hot-blooded, mercurial, temperamental, unstable, volatile, volcanic; anxious, edgy, jumpy, nervy, tense, uptight; emotional, hypersensitive, intense, sensitive, soulful; dramatic, histrionic, melodramatic; irascible, irritable, prickly, testy, touchy
near antonyms calm, collected, cool, serene, tranquil; easy, easygoing, laid-back, relaxed
antonyms unflappable

excite *vb* **1** to cause a pleasurable stimulation of the feelings — see THRILL
2 to rouse to strong feeling or action — see PROVOKE 1

excited *adj* **1** being in a state of increased activity or agitation — see FEVERISH 1
2 showing urgent desire or interest — see EAGER

excitement *n* **1** something that arouses a strong response from another — see PROVOCATION 1
2 urgent desire or interest — see EAGERNESS

exciter *n* a person who stirs up public feelings especially of discontent — see AGITATOR

exciting *adj* **1** causing great emotional or mental stimulation ⟨an *exciting*, come-from-behind victory for the underdogs in the last game of the World Series⟩
synonyms breathtaking, electric, electrifying, exhilarating, galvanizing, inspiring, rip-roaring, rousing, stimulating, stirring, thrilling
related words arresting, interesting, intriguing, provocative, tantalizing; absorbing, engrossing, gripping, riveting; moving, poignant, touching; enchanting, enthralling, fascinating, spellbinding
near antonyms boring, tedious, tiresome; dreary, dull, humdrum, monotonous, uninteresting
antonyms unexciting
2 serving or likely to arouse a strong reaction — see PROVOCATIVE

exclaim *vb* to utter with a sudden burst of strong feeling ⟨the whole team *exclaimed* with one voice, "We won!"⟩
synonyms blurt (out), bolt, cry (out), ejaculate
related words blunder, leak; bellow, bleat, crow, holler, hoot, howl, roar, shout, whoop, yowl; interject

exclude *vb* to prevent the participation or inclusion of ⟨troublemakers were *excluded* from the club⟩
synonyms ban, bar, count out, debar, eliminate, except, rule out
related words blackball, blacklist, ostracize; banish, deport, exile, expel, oust, throw out; block, hinder, impede, obstruct; cease, discontinue, halt, suspend; deter, stave off, ward (off)
near antonyms accept, entertain, receive, welcome
antonyms admit, include

excluding *prep* not including — see EXCEPT

exclusive *adj* **1** belonging only to the one person, unit, or group named — see SOLE 1
2 not divided or scattered among several areas of interest or concern — see WHOLE 1

exclusively *adv* for nothing other than — see SOLELY 1

excoriate *vb* to criticize harshly and usually publicly — see ATTACK 2

excrement *n* solid matter discharged from an animal's alimentary canal — see DROPPING 1

excrescence *n* an abnormal mass of tissue — see GROWTH 1

excreta *n pl* solid matter discharged from an animal's alimentary canal — see DROPPING 1

excruciating *adj* **1** intensely or unbearably painful ⟨those who publicly disagreed with the government were subjected to *excruciating* torture⟩
synonyms agonizing, harrowing, racking, tormenting, torturing, torturous
related words acute, exquisite, extreme, fierce, intense, vehement, violent; piercing, sharp, shooting, stabbing, stinging, tearing, tingling
2 causing intense mental or physical distress — see SHARP 2
3 difficult to endure — see HARSH 1
4 hard to accept or bear especially emotionally — see BITTER 2

exculpate *vb* to free from a charge of wrongdoing ⟨I will present evidence that will *exculpate* my client⟩
synonyms absolve, acquit, clear, exonerate, vindicate
related words atone (for), expiate; discharge, liberate, redeem, release, unburden; condone, excuse, forgive, pardon, remit; avenge, redress, revenge
near antonyms accuse, arraign, charge, impeach, indict; convict
antonyms incriminate

excursion *n* **1** a short trip for pleasure ⟨our weekend *excursions* have been to all parts of our home state⟩
synonyms jaunt, junket, outing, sally
related words journey, travel(s); circuit, tour; expedition, odyssey, safari; detour; hike, peregrination, trek, walk; pilgrimage
2 a departure from the subject under consideration — see TANGENT

excursionist *n* a person who travels for pleasure — see TOURIST

excusable *adj* worthy of forgiveness — see VENIAL

excuse *n* an explanation that frees one from fault or blame ⟨a whole evening of must-see TV is no *excuse* for not having your homework done⟩

synonyms alibi, defense, justification, plea, reason
related words guise, pretense (*or* pretence), pretext, rationale, rationalization; cop-out, out; acknowledgment (*also* acknowledgement), apology, atonement, confession
excuse *vb* **1** to overlook or dismiss as of little importance ⟨the student's theme is so good that I'm willing to *excuse* the spelling errors⟩
synonyms brush (aside *or* off), condone, disregard, forgive, gloss (over), gloze (over), ignore, pardon, pass over, remit, shrug off, wink (at)
related words explain, justify, rationalize, whitewash; absolve, acquit, clear, exculpate, exonerate, vindicate
phrases forgive and forget
near antonyms heed, mark, mind, note, object (to)
2 to be an acceptable reason for — see JUSTIFY 1
3 to make (something) seem less bad by offering excuses — see PALLIATE 1
execrable *adj* **1** extremely unsatisfactory — see WRETCHED 1
2 of low quality — see CHEAP 2
execrate *vb* **1** to declare to be morally wrong or evil — see CONDEMN 1
2 to dislike strongly — see HATE
execration *n* **1** a prayer that harm will come to someone — see CURSE 1
2 a very strong dislike — see HATE 1
execute *vb* **1** to carry out effectively — see ENFORCE
2 to carry through (as a process) to completion — see PERFORM 1
3 to put to death deliberately — see MURDER 1
execution *n* the doing of an action — see COMMISSION 2
executive *adj* suited for or relating to the directing of things ⟨the *executive* skills needed to manage a large business office⟩
synonyms administrative, directorial, managerial, supervisory
related words bureaucratic, governmental, ministerial, official, parliamentary; regulatory; authoritarian, despotic, dictatorial
executive *n* a person who manages or directs ⟨a program that teaches company *executives* how to better manage their staffs⟩
synonyms administrator, director, manager, superintendent, supervisor
related words officer, official; commissioner, minister; boss, chief, head, leader, president
exemplar *n* **1** one of a group or collection that shows what the whole is like — see EXAMPLE
2 someone of such unequaled perfection as to deserve imitation — see IDEAL 1
3 the most perfect type or example — see QUINTESSENCE 1
exemplary *adj* constituting, serving as, or worthy of being a pattern to be imitated — see MODEL
exemplify *vb* to show or make clear by using examples — see ILLUSTRATE 1
exemption *n* freedom from punishment, harm, or loss — see IMPUNITY
exercise *n* **1** energetic movement of the body for the sake of physical fitness ⟨the doctor ordered plenty of fresh air and *exercise*⟩
synonyms activity, conditioning, exertion
related words training, warm-up, workout; toning, trimming; aerobics, bodybuilding, calisthenics, isometrics, weight lifting; physical therapy
2 something done over and over in order to develop skill ⟨a young piano student dutifully going through the standard finger *exercises*⟩
synonyms drill, practice (*also* practise), routine, training, workout
related words assignment, homework, lesson
3 the act or practice of employing something for a particular purpose — see USE 1
exercise *vb* **1** to bring to bear especially forcefully or effectively — see EXERT
2 to do over and over so as to become skilled — see PRACTICE
3 to put into action or service — see USE 1
4 to trouble the mind of; to make uneasy — see DISTURB 1
exert *vb* to bring to bear especially forcefully or effectively ⟨parental involvement has been shown to *exert* the most influence over a child's success in school⟩
synonyms apply, exercise, ply, put out, wield
related words employ, use, utilize
exertion *n* **1** energetic movement of the body for the sake of physical fitness — see EXERCISE 1
2 the active use of energy in producing a result — see EFFORT
exfoliate *vb* to cast (a natural bodily covering or appendage) aside — see SHED 1
exhale *vb* **1** to let or force out of the lungs ⟨before answering, the suspect *exhaled* a cloud of cigarette smoke⟩
synonyms blow (out), breathe (out), expire
related words expectorate
antonyms inhale, inspire
2 to throw or give off — see EMIT 1
exhaust *vb* **1** to use up all the physical energy of ⟨the long day at the county fair had *exhausted* everyone⟩
synonyms burn out, do in, drain, fag, fatigue, tire, tucker (out), wash out, wear, wear out, weary
related words debilitate, enervate, enfeeble, sap, waste, weaken
phrases wear to a frazzle
near antonyms activate, energize, invigorate, strengthen, vitalize; relax, rest, unwind
2 to make complete use of — see DEPLETE
exhausted *adj* depleted in strength, energy, or freshness — see WEARY 1
exhaustion *n* a complete depletion of energy or strength — see FATIGUE
exhaustive *adj* trying all possibilities ⟨after an *exhaustive* search of our house, we still hadn't found the cat⟩
synonyms all-out, clean, complete, comprehensive, full-scale, out-and-out, thorough, thoroughgoing, total
related words broad, extensive, far-reaching, in-depth, wide; general, global, inclusive
near antonyms aimless, desultory, haphazard, hit-or-miss, random; cursory, shallow, slipshod, superficial; limited, narrow, restricted
exhaustively *adv* with attention to all aspects or details — see THOROUGHLY 1
exhibit *n* a public showing of objects of interest — see EXHIBITION 1
exhibit *vb* to present so as to invite notice or attention — see SHOW 1
exhibition *n* **1** a public showing of objects of interest ⟨an *exhibition* of valuable and fascinating artifacts from a recovered pirate ship⟩

synonyms display, exhibit, exposition, fair, show
related words demonstration, performance, presentation, production; extravaganza, pageant, spectacle; auction, offering, sale
2 an outward and often exaggerated indication of something abstract (as a feeling) for effect — see SHOW 1
exhilarate *vb* **1** to cause a pleasurable stimulation of the feelings — see THRILL
2 to fill with great joy — see ELATE
exhilarated *adj* experiencing or marked by overwhelming usually pleasurable emotion — see ECSTATIC
exhilarating *adj* causing great emotional or mental stimulation — see EXCITING 1
exhilaration *n* **1** a pleasurably intense stimulation of the feelings — see THRILL
2 a state of overwhelming usually pleasurable emotion — see ECSTASY
exhort *vb* to try to persuade (someone) through earnest appeals to follow a course of action — see URGE
exhume *vb* to remove from place of burial ⟨the remains of John Paul Jones were *exhumed* in Paris and transported with great ceremony to the U.S. Naval Academy⟩
synonyms disinter, unearth
antonyms bury, entomb, inter
exigency *n* a time or state of affairs requiring prompt or decisive action — see EMERGENCY
exile *n* **1** the forced removal from a homeland ⟨the *exile* of French settlers from Nova Scotia resulted in the birth of the Cajun community in the U.S.⟩
synonyms banishment, deportation, displacement, expatriation, expulsion
related words ostracism; extradition; dispersion, scattering; emigration, migration; evacuation
near antonyms repatriation, return; immigration
2 a person forced to emigrate for political reasons — see ÉMIGRÉ 1
exile *vb* to force to leave a country — see BANISH 1
exist *vb* to have life — see BE 1
existence *n* the fact of being or of being real ⟨the *existence* of UFOs is something that people continue to argue about⟩
synonyms actuality, reality, subsistence
related words genuineness, realness; activity, animation, life; currency, presence, prevalence
near antonyms absence, dearth, lack, want
antonyms nonexistence
existent *adj* **1** existing in fact and not merely as a possibility — see ACTUAL
2 having being at the present time — see EXTANT 1
existing *adj* having being at the present time — see EXTANT 1
exit *n* **1** a place or means of going out ⟨all of the building's *exits* were being watched by security guards⟩
synonyms egress, issue, outlet
related words escape, release; opening, passage, vent
near antonyms access, entrée (*or* entree)
antonyms entrance, entry, entryway, ingress
2 the act of leaving a place — see DEPARTURE
exit *vb* to leave a place often for another — see GO 2
exiting *n* the act of leaving a place — see DEPARTURE
exodus *n* a flowing or going out — see OUTFLOW
exonerate *vb* to free from a charge of wrongdoing — see EXCULPATE
exorbitant *adj* going beyond a normal or acceptable limit in degree or amount — see EXCESSIVE
exorbitantly *adv* beyond a normal or acceptable limit — see TOO 1
exotic *adj* excitingly or mysteriously unusual ⟨the dream of someday traveling to *exotic* lands⟩
synonyms fantastic, glamorous (*also* glamourous), marvelous (*or* marvellous), outlandish, romantic, strange
related words colorful, picturesque, quaint; alien, foreign; distant, faraway, remote; alluring, captivating, enchanting, fascinating
exotic *n* something strange or unusual that is an object of interest — see CURIOSITY 2
expand *vb* **1** to express more fully and in greater detail ⟨an article on the First Ladies that the author later *expanded* into a book⟩
synonyms amplify, develop, elaborate (on), enlarge (on)
related words add (to), complement, supplement; discourse, expatiate, ramble, run on
near antonyms compress, contract; outline, summarize, sum up
antonyms abbreviate, abridge, condense, shorten
2 to make greater in size, amount, or number — see INCREASE 1
3 to arrange the parts of (something) over a wider area — see OPEN 3
4 to become greater in extent, volume, amount, or number — see INCREASE 2
expanse *n* a wide space or area ⟨the great explorers who crossed the vast *expanse* of the ocean in small ships⟩
synonyms breadth, extent, reach, spread, stretch
related words domain, field, sphere, territory; compass, range, scope, sweep; gamut, scale, spectrum; depth, emptiness, void; distance, extension, latitude, length, span; amplitude, immensity, magnitude
expansion *n* **1** something added (as by growth) — see INCREASE 1
2 the act or process of going from the simple or basic to the complex or advanced — see DEVELOPMENT 1
expansive *adj* having considerable extent — see EXTENSIVE
expatiate *vb* to give a formal often extended talk on a subject — see TALK 1
expatriate *n* a person forced to emigrate for political reasons — see ÉMIGRÉ 1
expatriate *vb* to force to leave a country — see BANISH 1
expatriation *n* the forced removal from a homeland — see EXILE 1
expect *vb* to believe in the future occurrence of (something) ⟨we *expect* their arrival late this afternoon⟩
synonyms anticipate, await, hope (for), watch (for)
related words bank on, count (on *or* upon), depend (on *or* upon), rely (on *or* upon); envisage, foresee; foretell, predict, prophesy; assume, presume, presuppose; contemplate, eye, view
phrases look for, look forward to
near antonyms doubt, question
expectant *adj* **1** having or showing signs of eagerly awaiting something ⟨*expectant* crowds gathered

at the spot where the President was scheduled to make an appearance⟩
synonyms agape, agog, anticipatory
related words open-eyed, openmouthed; alert, vigilant, watchful; anxious, breathless, eager, enthusiastic, raring; impatient, restive, restless
near antonyms apathetic, indifferent, unconcerned, unimpressed, uninterested, unmoved
2 containing unborn young within the body — see PREGNANT 1

expected *adj* being in accordance with the prescribed, normal, or logical course of events — see DUE 2

expedient *adj* suitable for bringing about a desired result under the circumstances ⟨made the *expedient* decision to sell the land to whomever offered the most money⟩
synonyms advisable, desirable, judicious, politic, prudent, tactical, wise
related words advantageous, beneficial, profitable; useful, utilitarian; feasible, possible, practicable, practical; opportune, seasonable, timely; opportunistic, self-seeking
near antonyms impractical, unfeasible, unprofitable; inopportune, unseasonable, untimely
antonyms imprudent, inadvisable, inexpedient, injudicious, unwise

expedient *n* **1** a temporary replacement — see MAKESHIFT
2 an action planned or taken to achieve a desired result — see MEASURE 1
3 something that one uses to accomplish an end especially when the usual means is not available — see RESOURCE 1

expedition *n* a going from one place to another usually of some distance — see JOURNEY

expeditious *adj* having or showing the ability to respond without delay or hesitation — see QUICK 1

expel *vb* **1** to drive or force out — see EJECT 1
2 to throw or give off — see EMIT 1
3 to throw out or off (something from within) often violently — see ERUPT 1

expend *vb* **1** to hand over or use up in payment — see SPEND 1
2 to make complete use of — see DEPLETE

expenditure *n* **1** a payment made in the course of achieving a result — see EXPENSE
2 the active use of energy in producing a result — see EFFORT

expense *n* a payment made in the course of achieving a result ⟨they spared no *expense* in building the house of their dreams⟩
synonyms cost, disbursement, expenditure, outgo, outlay
related words overhead; outflow; spending money; charge, price, rate, tab, tariff, toll

expensive *adj* commanding a large price — see COSTLY

expensively *adv* in a luxurious manner — see HIGH

experience *n* **1** knowledge gained by actually doing or living through something ⟨the hospital is looking for nurses with operating-room *experience*⟩
synonyms expertise, know-how, proficiency, savvy, skills
related words background; command, mastery; acquaintance, familiarity, intimacy
near antonyms ignorance, unawareness, unfamiliarity
antonyms inexperience
2 an exciting or noteworthy event that one experiences firsthand — see ADVENTURE

experience *vb* to come to a knowledge of (something) by living through it ⟨eventually we all have to *experience* the loss of a loved one⟩
synonyms endure, feel, have, know, see, suffer, sustain, taste, undergo
related words encounter, meet; accept, receive
phrases go through

experienced *adj* having or showing exceptional knowledge, experience, or skill in a field of endeavor — see PROFICIENT

experiment *n* a procedure or operation carried out to resolve an uncertainty ⟨Benjamin Franklin's famous *experiment* in which he flew a kite in a thunderstorm to see if lightning and electricity were identical⟩
synonyms experimentation, test, trial
related words trial and error; dry run, shakedown; exercise, practice (*also* practise), rehearsal, tryout, workout; crucible, ordeal; attempt, effort, try

experimental *adj* **1** made or done as an experiment ⟨an *experimental* procedure for patients suffering from leukemia⟩
synonyms pilot, trial
related words developmental, investigative, preparatory; preliminary, provisional, temporary, tentative; conjectural, hypothetical, speculative, theoretical (*also* theoretic); untested, untried; unproved, unproven
near antonyms accepted, established, standard; tested, tried; advanced, developed; proved, proven; conclusive, decisive, definitive, final, permanent
2 based on observation or experience — see EMPIRICAL

experimentation *n* a procedure or operation carried out to resolve an uncertainty — see EXPERIMENT

expert *adj* **1** accomplished with trained ability — see SKILLFUL
2 having or showing exceptional knowledge, experience, or skill in a field of endeavor — see PROFICIENT

expert *n* a person with a high level of knowledge or skill in a field ⟨*experts* at the crime lab were able to tell the sex, race, and approximate age of the murderer⟩
synonyms ace, adept, artist, authority, crackerjack, maestro, master, past master, scholar, shark, virtuoso, whiz, wizard
related words pro, professional; specialist; addict, aficionado, buff, devotee, enthusiast, fan; craftsman, journeyman; jack-of-all-trades
near antonyms apprentice, beginner, neophyte, novice; dabbler, dilettante; layman, nonprofessional
antonyms amateur

expertise *n* knowledge gained by actually doing or living through something — see EXPERIENCE 1

expertly *adv* in a skillful or expert manner — see WELL 3

expiate *vb* to make up for (an offense) ⟨Yom Kippur is the holy day on which Jews are expected to *expiate* sins committed during the past year⟩
synonyms atone (for)
related words compensate, recompense, reimburse, remunerate, repay; amend, correct, rectify, redress; propitiate
phrases make amends for, make good for

expiration *n* **1** the act of ceasing to exist — see DEATH 3
2 the stopping of a process or activity — see END 1

expire *vb* **1** to come to an end — see CEASE 1
2 to let or force out of the lungs — see EXHALE 1
3 to stop living — see DIE 1

expired *adj* no longer existing — see EXTINCT

explain *vb* **1** to make plain or understandable ⟨write an essay that *explains* the meaning of the poem⟩
synonyms clarify, clear (up), construe, demonstrate, elucidate, explicate, expound, illuminate, illustrate, interpret, spell out
related words decipher, decode; analyze, break down; disentangle, undo, unravel, unscramble, untangle; resolve, solve; define, specify
phrases get across
near antonyms befog, cloud; confound, confuse
antonyms obscure
2 to give the reason for or cause of ⟨can you *explain* your very odd behavior at the wedding reception?⟩
synonyms account (for), explain away, rationalize
related words condone, excuse, forgive, justify; absolve, acquit, exculpate, exonerate, vindicate

explainable *adj* capable of having the reason for or cause of determined — see SOLVABLE

explain away *vb* to give the reason for or cause of — see EXPLAIN 2

explanation *n* **1** a statement that makes something clear ⟨an *explanation* of photosynthesis that the whole class was able to understand⟩
synonyms clarification, construction, elucidation, explication, exposition, illumination, illustration, interpretation
related words paraphrase, restatement, translation; deciphering, decoding; disentanglement, unscrambling; analysis; definition, meaning; demonstration, enactment; justification, rationale, rationalization, reasoning
2 a statement given to explain a belief or act — see REASON 1

explanatory *adj* serving to explain ⟨the *explanatory* section has as its heading "Using Your Dictionary"⟩
synonyms elucidative, expository, illuminative, illustrative, interpretive
related words analytic (*also* analytical), demonstrative, discursive; exculpatory

expletive *n* a disrespectful or indecent word or expression — see SWEARWORD

explicable *adj* capable of having the reason for or cause of determined — see SOLVABLE

explicate *vb* to make plain or understandable — see EXPLAIN 1

explication *n* a statement that makes something clear — see EXPLANATION 1

explicit *adj* so clearly expressed as to leave no doubt about the meaning ⟨*explicit* instructions about what to do in an emergency⟩
synonyms clear-cut, definite, definitive, express, specific, unambiguous, unequivocal
related words avowed, declared, stated; categorical (*also* categoric), complete, comprehensive, exhaustive, full; certain, sure, unmistakable; clear, distinct, lucid; exact, precise; direct, literal, plain, simple, straightforward; comprehensible, intelligible, understandable
near antonyms cryptic, dark, enigmatic (*also* enigmatical), obscure, unclear; imprecise, inaccurate, incorrect, inexact; incomprehensible, unintelligible
antonyms implicit, implied, inferred; ambiguous, circuitous; equivocal, indefinite

explicitness *n* **1** careful thoroughness of detail — see PARTICULARITY 1
2 clearness of expression — see SIMPLICITY 2

explode *vb* **1** to break open or into pieces usually because of internal pressure ⟨the building was wrecked when a powerful bomb *exploded*⟩
synonyms blow up, burst, detonate, go off, pop
related words fragment, shatter, smash, splinter; discharge, fire, shoot; balloon, burgeon, mushroom
near antonyms collapse, fizzle
antonyms implode
2 to cause to break open or into pieces by or as if by an explosive — see BLAST 1
3 to develop suddenly and violently — see ERUPT 2

exploit *n* **1** an act of notable skill, strength, or cleverness — see FEAT 1
2 something done by someone — see ACTION 1

exploit *vb* **1** to take unfair advantage of ⟨a student who *exploits* his friend's good nature by always sponging off him⟩
synonyms abuse, capitalize (on), cash in (on), impose (on *or* upon), play (on *or* upon), use
related words manipulate, mistreat; bleed, cheat, fleece, overcharge, skin, soak, stick; commercialize
2 to control or take advantage of by artful, unfair, or insidious means — see MANIPULATE 1
3 to put into action or service — see USE 1

exploitable *adj* **1** capable of or suitable for being used for a particular purpose — see USABLE 1
2 readily taken advantage of — see EASY 2

exploration *n* a systematic search for the truth or facts about something — see INQUIRY 1

explore *vb* **1** to search through or into ⟨let's *explore* new ways of raising money for the school band⟩
synonyms delve (into), dig (into), inquire (into), investigate, look (into), probe, research
related words examine, inspect, sift, study, view; browse, peruse, scan, skim (through), thumb (through)
2 to go into or range over for purposes of discovery ⟨we must continue to *explore* the depths of the ocean⟩
synonyms hunt, probe, prospect, search
related words reconnoiter (*or* reconnoitre), scout; disclose, discover, reveal, unearth; fathom, plumb, sound

explosion *n* **1** the act or an instance of exploding ⟨the *explosion* of the first atomic bomb at Hiroshima⟩
synonyms blast, bursting, detonation, eruption
related words discharge, firing, shooting; blowout, flare-up; bang, boom, pop
antonyms implosion
2 a sudden intense expression of strong feeling — see OUTBURST 1
3 an outburst or display of excited anger — see TANTRUM

explosive *adj* **1** extreme in degree, power, or effect — see INTENSE

2 marked by bursts of destructive force or intense activity — see VIOLENT 1

exponent *n* a person who actively supports or favors a cause ⟨*exponents* of space exploration called for more missions to the outer reaches of the solar system⟩
synonyms advocate, apostle, backer, booster, champion, friend, promoter, proponent, supporter
related words loyalist, partisan, stalwart; adherent, cohort, disciple, follower; expounder, interpreter; cheerleader
near antonyms enemy, foe, rival; belittler, critic, faultfinder
antonyms adversary, antagonist, opponent

expose *vb* **1** to reveal the true nature of ⟨a well-researched article that *exposes* the UFO story as a hoax⟩
synonyms debunk, show up, uncloak, uncover, unmask
related words discredit, disprove; disclose, divulge, tell, unveil
near antonyms conceal, hide, secrete
antonyms camouflage, cloak, disguise, mask
2 to make known (as information previously kept secret) — see REVEAL 1
3 to make known (something abstract) through outward signs — see SHOW 2
4 to present so as to invite notice or attention — see SHOW 1

exposed *adj* **1** being in a situation where one is likely to meet with harm — see LIABLE 1
2 lacking a usual or natural covering — see NAKED 2
3 lacking protection from danger or resistance against attack — see HELPLESS 1

exposition *n* **1** a public showing of objects of interest — see EXHIBITION 1
2 a series of explanations or observations on something (as an event) — see COMMENTARY
3 a statement that makes something clear — see EXPLANATION 1

expository *adj* serving to explain — see EXPLANATORY

expostulate (with) *vb* to present an opposing opinion or argument — see OBJECT

expostulation *n* a feeling or declaration of disapproval or dissent — see OBJECTION

exposure *n* **1** the state of being left without shelter or protection against something harmful ⟨some people avoid situations in which there is a high level of *exposure* to germs⟩
synonyms liability, openness, vulnerability
related words susceptibility; defenselessness, helplessness, weakness; danger, jeopardy, peril, risk
near antonyms protection, safeguarding, sheltering, shielding
2 the act or an instance of making known something previously unknown or concealed — see REVELATION

expound *vb* to make plain or understandable — see EXPLAIN 1

express *adj* **1** of a particular or exact sort ⟨a trip to the supermarket with the *express* purpose of buying milk⟩
synonyms distinct, especial, precise, set, special, specific
related words lone, only, separate, single, sole, solitary; distinctive, exclusive, individual, peculiar, unique; limited, restricted; specified
near antonyms general, generic, nonexclusive, universal
antonyms nonspecific
2 so clearly expressed as to leave no doubt about the meaning — see EXPLICIT

express *vb* **1** to make known (as an idea, emotion, or opinion) ⟨in a true democracy, a person can freely *express* his or her views⟩
synonyms air, give, look, sound, state, vent, ventilate, voice
related words advertise, announce, declare, enunciate, proclaim; broadcast, circulate, disseminate, publish; describe, write, write up; sound off, speak out, speak up; chime in; communicate, convey, put across, put over; offer, submit
phrases put forth
near antonyms censor, restrain, restrict
antonyms stifle, suppress
2 to apply external pressure on so as to force out the juice or contents of — see PRESS 2
3 to communicate or convey (as an idea) to the mind — see MEAN 1
4 to convey in appropriate or telling terms — see PHRASE

expression *n* **1** an act, process, or means of putting something into words ⟨the poem is his *expression* of his grief upon the loss of his beloved dog⟩
synonyms articulation, formulation, statement, utterance, voice
related words outlet, vent; observation, reflection, remark, thought; speech, tongue
2 facial appearance regarded as an indication of mood or feeling — see LOOK 1
3 a pronounceable series of letters having a distinct meaning especially in a particular field — see WORD 1
4 a sequence of words having a specific meaning — see PHRASE

expressionless *adj* not expressing any emotion — see BLANK 1

expressive *adj* clearly conveying a special meaning (as one's mood) ⟨the teacher's *expressive* sigh showed that she had heard that excuse many times before⟩
synonyms eloquent, meaning, meaningful, pregnant, revealing, significant, suggestive
related words graphic (*also* graphical), pictorial, vivid; evocative, redolent, reminiscent; sententious, weighty; flavorful, rich

expressway *n* a passage cleared for public vehicular travel — see WAY 1

expropriate *vb* to take ownership or control of (something) by right of one's authority — see CONFISCATE

expulsion *n* the forced removal from a homeland — see EXILE 1

expunge *vb* to destroy all traces of — see ANNIHILATE 1

expurgate *vb* to remove objectionable parts from — see CENSOR

exquisite *adj* **1** extreme in degree, power, or effect — see INTENSE
2 having qualities that appeal to a refined taste — see CHOICE
3 satisfying or pleasing because of fineness or mildness — see DELICATE 1

exquisiteness *n* the state or quality of having a delicate structure — see DELICACY 2

extant *adj* **1** having being at the present time ⟨a

celebrated author who is generally regarded as America's greatest novelist *extant*⟩
synonyms alive, existent, existing, living
related words active, busy, flourishing, functioning, operating, working
near antonyms defunct, destroyed, exterminated; departed, gone, lost; nonexistent; idle, inactive, inert
antonyms dead, extinct
2 existing or in progress right now — see PRESENT 1

extemporaneous *adj* made or done without previous thought or preparation ⟨caught by surprise, I had to make an *extemporaneous* speech at the awards banquet⟩
synonyms ad-lib, extempore, impromptu, improvised, offhand, offhanded, snap, spur-of-the-moment, unconsidered, unplanned, unpremeditated, unprepared, unrehearsed
related words automatic, impulsive, instinctive, involuntary, spontaneous; casual, informal, unauthorized
near antonyms deliberate, intended, intentional
antonyms considered, planned, premeditated, prepared, rehearsed

extempore *adj* made or done without previous thought or preparation — see EXTEMPORANEOUS

extemporize *vb* to perform, make, or do without preparation — see IMPROVISE

extend *vb* **1** to make longer ⟨our guests from out of town *extended* their visit by a week⟩
synonyms draw out, elongate, lengthen, prolong, protract, stretch
related words amplify, enlarge, expand, increase; attenuate, thin
near antonyms decrease, diminish, lessen, reduce; thicken
antonyms abbreviate, abridge, curtail, cut, cut back, shorten
2 to put before another for acceptance or consideration — see OFFER 1
3 to arrange the parts of (something) over a wider area — see OPEN 3
4 to be positioned along a certain course or in a certain direction — see RUN 3
5 to make greater in size, amount, or number — see INCREASE 1

extended *adj* **1** expressing one thing in terms normally used for another — see FIGURATIVE
2 having considerable extent — see EXTENSIVE
3 lasting for a considerable time — see LONG 2
4 of great extent from end to end — see LONG 1

extended family *n* those who live as a family in one house — see HOUSEHOLD

extension *n* **1** the act of making longer ⟨the board's *extension* of the school year drew howls of protest⟩
synonyms drawing out, elongation, lengthening, prolongation, prolonging, stretching
antonyms abbreviation, abridgment (*or* abridgement), curtailment, cutback, shortening
2 a smaller structure added to a main building — see ANNEX

extensive *adj* having considerable extent ⟨a rock hound whose *extensive* reading enables him to identify just about any rock or mineral⟩
synonyms broad, expansive, extended, far-flung, far-reaching, wide, widespread
related words comprehensive, general, global, inclusive; boundless, endless, limitless, unlimited; capacious, commodious, roomy, spacious
near antonyms circumscribed, limited, restricted
antonyms narrow

extensively *adv* to a large extent or degree — see GREATLY 2

extent *n* **1** a real or imaginary point beyond which a person or thing cannot go — see LIMIT
2 a wide space or area — see EXPANSE
3 an area over which activity, capacity, or influence extends — see RANGE 2
4 the total amount of measurable space or surface occupied by something — see [1]SIZE

extenuate *vb* to make (something) seem less bad by offering excuses — see PALLIATE 1

exterior *adj* situated on the outside or farther out — see OUTER

exterior *n* an outer part or layer ⟨the *exterior* of the tooth consists of very hard enamel⟩
synonyms face, outside, skin, surface, veneer
related words facade (*also* façade), front, top; cover, covering, facing; appearance, disguise, guise, mask, semblance, show
antonyms inside, interior

exterminate *vb* to destroy all traces of — see ANNIHILATE 1

extermination *n* the state or fact of being rendered nonexistent, physically unsound, or useless — see DESTRUCTION

external *adj* situated on the outside or farther out — see OUTER

extinct *adj* no longer existing ⟨a few overgrown ruins are all that remain of that once mighty but now *extinct* civilization⟩
synonyms bygone, dead, defunct, departed, expired, gone, vanished
related words nonexistent; dying, faded, moribund; collapsed, fallen, overthrown; antiquated, dated, obsolete, passé; finished, lapsed, terminated; lost, missing
near antonyms active, dynamic, thriving, vibrant
antonyms alive, existent, existing, extant, living

extinction *n* the state or fact of being rendered nonexistent, physically unsound, or useless — see DESTRUCTION

extinguish *vb* **1** to cause to cease burning ⟨the fire in the skillet was quickly *extinguished* by slamming the lid on⟩
synonyms douse, put out, quench, snuff (out)
related words choke, smother, suffocate; stamp (out)
antonyms fire, ignite, inflame, kindle
2 to bring to a complete end the physical soundness, existence, or usefulness of — see DESTROY 1

extirpate *vb* to destroy all traces of — see ANNIHILATE 1

extol *also* **extoll** *vb* to proclaim the glory of — see PRAISE 1

extort *vb* to get (as money) by the use of force or threats ⟨a school bully who was used to *extorting* lunch money from weaker kids⟩
synonyms exact, wrest, wring
related words bleed, fleece, gouge, milk, skin, squeeze; cheat, gyp, racketeer, swindle; coerce, compel, force

extortioner *n* a person who gets money from another by using force or threats — see RACKETEER

extortionist *n* a person who gets money from another by using force or threats — see RACKETEER

extra *adj* being over what is needed — see SPARE 1

extra *adv* to a great degree — see VERY 1
extra *n* **1** an interchangeable part or piece of equipment that is kept on hand for replacement of an original — see SPARE
2 something adding to pleasure or comfort but not absolutely necessary — see LUXURY 1
3 something given in addition to what is ordinarily expected or owed — see BONUS
extract *n* a part taken from a longer work — see EXCERPT
extract *vb* to draw out by force or with effort ⟨*extracted* a splinter from my hand⟩
synonyms prize, pry, pull, root (out), tear (out), uproot, wrest, yank
related words remove, take (out), withdraw
near antonyms implant, insert, install, instill; cram, jam, ram, stuff, wedge
extraction *n* the line of ancestors from whom a person is descended — see ANCESTRY
extraneous *adj* **1** not being a vital part of or belonging to something — see EXTRINSIC
2 not having anything to do with the matter at hand — see IRRELEVANT
extraneousness *n* the quality or state of not having anything to do with the matter at hand — see IRRELEVANCE
extraordinary *adj* **1** being out of the ordinary — see EXCEPTIONAL
2 noticeably different from what is generally found or experienced — see UNUSUAL 1
extrapolate *vb* to form an opinion through reasoning and information — see INFER 1
extrasensory perception *n* the power of seeing or knowing about things that are not present to the senses — see CLAIRVOYANCE
extravagance *n* **1** the quality or fact of being free or wasteful in the expenditure of money ⟨Hollywood stars are famous for the *extravagance* of their parties⟩
synonyms lavishness, prodigality, wastefulness
related words bountifulness, generosity, liberality; improvidence, squandering; indulgence, overindulgence, self-indulgence; excess, immoderacy, overkill
near antonyms austerity, moderation, restraint, temperance
antonyms economy, frugality
2 an instance of spending money or resources without care or restraint — see WASTE 1
extravagant *adj* **1** given to spending money freely or foolishly — see PRODIGAL
2 going beyond a normal or acceptable limit in degree or amount — see EXCESSIVE
extravagantly *adv* in a luxurious manner — see HIGH
extreme *adj* **1** most distant from a center ⟨spacecraft that is specially designed to explore the *extreme* edge of our solar system⟩
synonyms farthermost, farthest, furthermost, furthest, outermost, outmost, remotest, ultimate, utmost
near antonyms intermediate, medial, median, mid, middle, middlemost, midmost
antonyms inmost, innermost, nearest
2 being very far from the center of public opinion ⟨their *extreme* political views attracted only a small band of followers⟩
synonyms extremist, fanatic (*or* fanatical), rabid, radical, revolutionary, revolutionist, ultra
related words subversive, violent, wild; reactionary
near antonyms conservative, moderate, temperate; conventional, orthodox, traditional; liberal, progressive
antonyms middle-of-the-road
3 going beyond a normal or acceptable limit in degree or amount — see EXCESSIVE
extremely *adv* to a great degree — see VERY 1
extremist *adj* being very far from the center of public opinion — see EXTREME 2
extremist *n* a person who favors rapid and sweeping changes especially in laws and methods of government — see RADICAL
extricate *vb* to set free from entanglement or difficulty ⟨you've woven such a web of lies that it's hard to see how you can *extricate* yourself now⟩
synonyms clear, disengage, disentangle, free, liberate, release, untangle
related words deliver, redeem, rescue, save; disburden, disencumber, unburden; unravel, unsnarl, untie, untwine
near antonyms block, hamper, hinder, impede, obstruct; burden, encumber, load, weigh
antonyms embroil, entangle
extrinsic *adj* not being a vital part of or belonging to something ⟨the fact that the ring belonged to your grandmother is *extrinsic* to its value to a jeweler⟩
synonyms adventitious, alien, extraneous, foreign
related words exterior, external, outside; immaterial, inapplicable, insignificant, irrelevant; nonessential, unessential, unnecessary
near antonyms congenital, deep-seated, inborn, inbred; inside, interior, internal; basic, essential, necessary
antonyms inherent, innate, intrinsic
extroverted *also* **extraverted** *adj* likely to seek or enjoy the company of others — see CONVIVIAL
extrude *vb* to drive or force out — see EJECT 1
exuberance *n* the quality or state of having abundant or intense activity — see VITALITY 1
exuberant *adj* joyously unrestrained ⟨*exuberant* crowds rushed to greet the returning national champions in collegiate basketball⟩
synonyms bubbly, buoyant, effervescent, frolicsome, high-spirited, vivacious
related words extroverted (*also* extraverted), outgoing, uninhibited; carefree, insouciant, joyful, lighthearted, lively, sprightly; boisterous, raucous, rollicking, rowdy; giddy, light-headed, silly; ecstatic, euphoric, rapturous; audacious, bold, brash, brazen, impertinent, impudent, insolent, saucy
near antonyms constrained, inhibited, repressed, restrained, subdued; impassive, phlegmatic, stoic (*or* stoical), stolid; depressed, dour, glum, morose, surly
antonyms low-spirited, noneffervescent, sullen
exuberantly *adv* **1** in a quick and spirited manner — see GAILY 2
2 in an enthusiastic manner — see SKY-HIGH
exude *vb* to flow forth slowly through small openings ⟨a sticky resin *exudes* from the bark of the tree⟩
synonyms bleed, ooze, percolate, seep, strain, sweat, weep
related words dribble, drip, trickle; discharge, emit, give off, vent; emanate, flow, spring
near antonyms flood, gush, pour, stream, surge

exult *vb* to feel or express joy or triumph ⟨the winners of the Super Bowl spent the next week *exulting* in their victory⟩
synonyms crow, delight, glory, joy, rejoice, triumph
related words gloat; boast, brag; flaunt, parade, show off, strut, swagger
near antonyms bemoan, bewail, grieve, lament, weep

exultant *adj* having or expressing feelings of joy or triumph ⟨the *exultant* winner of the award for best country artist of the year⟩
synonyms exulting, glorying, jubilant, rejoicing, triumphant
related words ecstatic, elated, euphoric; arrogant, boastful, cocky; conquering, victorious, winning
near antonyms crestfallen, defeated, dejected, depressed, disconsolate, dispirited, downcast

exulting *adj* having or expressing feelings of joy or triumph — see EXULTANT

exurbia *n* the area around a city — see ENVIRONS 1

eye *n* **1** a circular strip — see RING 2
2 a state of being aware — see ATTENTION 2
3 a thing or place that is of greatest importance to an activity or interest — see CENTER 1
4 an idea that is believed to be true or valid without positive knowledge — see OPINION 1
5 an instance of looking especially briefly — see LOOK 2
6 the ability to see — see EYESIGHT

eye *vb* **1** to keep one's eyes on — see WATCH 1
2 to make note of (something) through the use of one's eyes — see SEE 1

eye–catching *adj* likely to attract attention — see NOTICEABLE

eyeful *n* a lovely woman — see BEAUTY 2

eyeglasses *n pl* a pair of lenses set in a frame that is held in place with ear supports and which are usually worn to correct vision — see GLASSES 1

eyeless *adj* lacking the power of sight — see BLIND

eye–opening *adj* **1** causing a strong emotional reaction because unexpected — see SURPRISING 1
2 causing wonder or astonishment — see MARVELOUS 1

eyesight *n* the ability to see ⟨the keen *eyesight* of a bird of prey⟩
synonyms eye, sight, vision
related words myopia, nearsightedness; farsightedness; astigmatism

eyesore *n* something unpleasant to look at ⟨the old abandoned house was a neighborhood *eyesore*⟩
synonyms fright, horror, mess, monstrosity, sight
related words blot, smear, smudge, spot, stain

eyespot *n* a small area that is different (as in color) from the main part — see SPOT 1

fable *n* **1** a story intended to teach a basic truth or moral about life — see ALLEGORY
2 a traditional but unfounded story that gives the reason for a current custom, belief, or fact of nature — see MYTH 1
3 something that is the product of the imagination — see FICTION

fabled *adj* based on, described in, or being a myth — see MYTHICAL 1

fabric *n* a woven or knitted material (as of cotton or nylon) — see CLOTH

fabricate *vb* **1** to bring into being by combining, shaping, or transforming materials — see MAKE 1
2 to create or think of by clever use of the imagination — see INVENT
3 to form by putting together parts or materials — see BUILD
4 to make a statement one knows to be untrue — see LIE 1

fabrication *n* **1** a statement known by its maker to be untrue and made in order to deceive — see LIE
2 something that is the product of the imagination — see FICTION

fabricator *n* a person who tells lies — see LIAR

fabulous *adj* **1** based on, described in, or being a myth — see MYTHICAL 1
2 causing wonder or astonishment — see MARVELOUS 1
3 not real and existing only in the imagination — see IMAGINARY
4 of the very best kind — see EXCELLENT

facade *also* **façade** *n* **1** a forward part or surface — see FRONT 1
2 a display of emotion or behavior that is insincere or intended to deceive — see MASQUERADE

face *n* **1** the front part of the head ⟨the criminal hid his *face* from the news cameras as he slumped into the patrol car⟩
synonyms countenance, kisser [*slang*], mug, puss [*slang*], visage
related words appearance, features, lineaments, looks; expression, physiognomy
2 a forward part or surface — see FRONT 1
3 a twisting of the facial features in disgust or disapproval — see GRIMACE
4 an outer part or layer — see EXTERIOR
5 facial appearance regarded as an indication of mood or feeling — see LOOK 1
6 outward and often deceptive indication — see APPEARANCE 2

face *vb* **1** to stand or sit with the face or front toward ⟨the house *faces* the sparkling blue waters of the Pacific Ocean⟩
synonyms front, look (toward), point (toward)
related words abut, adjoin, border, meet, neighbor, touch; command, dominate, overlook
2 to oppose (something hostile or dangerous) with firmness or courage ⟨movie superheroes who are ever ready to *face* danger without blinking an eye⟩
synonyms beard, brave, brazen, breast, confront, dare, defy, outbrave
related words encounter, meet; accost, approach; repel, resist, withstand; battle, combat, contend (with), fight, oppose, square (off)
phrases stand up to

near antonyms avoid, eschew, shun; elude, escape, evade
antonyms dodge, duck, shirk, sidestep
3 to cover with something that protects — see SHEATHE
4 to enter into contest or conflict with — see ENGAGE 2

face–off *n* an earnest effort for superiority or victory over another — see CONTEST 1

facet *n* a certain way in which something appears or may be regarded — see ASPECT 1

facetious *adj* **1** given to or marked by mature intelligent humor — see WITTY
2 making light of something usually regarded as serious or sacred — see FLIPPANT

facetiousness *n* a lack of seriousness often at an improper time — see FRIVOLITY 1

face–to–face *adv* in person and usually privately — see TÊTE-À-TÊTE

facile *adj* **1** having or showing a lack of depth of understanding or character — see SUPERFICIAL 2
2 involving minimal difficulty or effort — see EASY 1

facilely *adv* without difficulty — see EASILY

facilitate *vb* to free from obstruction or difficulty — see EASE 1

facility *n* a structure that is designed and built for a particular purpose ⟨the city is known for its outstanding medical *facilities*⟩
synonyms complex, establishment, installation
related words building, edifice; institute, institution; business, company, concern, outfit

facsimile *n* **1** something or someone that strongly resembles another — see IMAGE 1
2 something that is made to look exactly like something else — see COPY

fact *n* **1** the quality of being actual ⟨scientists deal in the realm of *fact*, not speculation⟩
synonyms actuality, factuality, materiality, reality
related words authenticity, genuineness, truth
near antonyms fancy, fantasy (*also* phantasy), fiction; fictitiousness
antonyms unreality
2 something that actually exists ⟨once considered a wild fantasy, the Internet is now a *fact* of everyday life⟩
synonyms case, materiality, reality
related words certainty, inevitability; circumstance, event, occurrence, phenomenon; element, item, particular, thing
near antonyms eventuality, possibility, potentiality, probability
antonyms fantasy (*also* phantasy), fiction, illusion
3 a single piece of information ⟨a book of little-known *facts* about famous people⟩
synonyms datum, detail, nicety, particular, particularity, point
related words article, item; element, ingredient, part; aspect, facet, factor; evidence, exhibit; database, information, knowledge
near antonyms error, fallacy, falsehood, misconception, myth

faction *n* a group of people acting together within a larger group ⟨several *factions* within the environmental movement have joined forces⟩
synonyms bloc, body, coalition, party, sect, set, side, wing
related words crew, gang, pack, team; denomination, persuasion, schism

factitious *adj* **1** being such in appearance only and made with or manufactured from usually cheaper materials — see IMITATION
2 lacking in natural or spontaneous quality — see ARTIFICIAL 1

factor *n* **1** a person who acts or does business for another — see AGENT 2
2 one of the parts that make up a whole — see ELEMENT 1

factory *n* a building or set of buildings for the manufacturing of goods ⟨the new *factory* will create hundreds of much-needed jobs⟩
synonyms manufactory, mill, plant, shop, works, workshop
related words sweatshop; workroom; yard

factual *adj* **1** restricted to or based on fact ⟨a *factual* biography of George Washington that scoffs at the story about the cherry tree⟩
synonyms documentary, hard, historical, literal, matter-of-fact, nonfictional, objective, true
related words actual, authentic, genuine, real; documented, established; reliable, verifiable; demonstrable, provable; incontestable, incontrovertible, indisputable, irrefutable, undeniable, unquestionable; plain, simple, unexaggerated; certain, undoubted
near antonyms hypothetical, speculative, theoretical (*also* theoretic); fabulous, fanciful, imaginary, legendary, mythical (*or* mythic); embroidered, exaggerated
antonyms fictional, fictionalized, fictitious, nondocumentary, nonhistorical
2 existing in fact and not merely as a possibility — see ACTUAL

factuality *n* **1** agreement with fact or reality — see TRUTH
2 the quality of being actual — see FACT 1

faculty *n* **1** a natural ability of the mind or body — see POWER 3
2 a special and usually inborn ability — see TALENT
3 the physical or mental power to do something — see ABILITY

fad *n* a practice or interest that is very popular for a short time ⟨the *fad* for that kind of music had long passed⟩
synonyms craze, enthusiasm, fashion, go, last word, mode, rage, sensation, style, trend, vogue
related words crush, infatuation; fervor, passion; furor, fuss, hullabaloo, to-do, uproar; bandwagon, crusade, cult, movement; novelty, wrinkle; caprice, fancy, whim
near antonyms classic, standard

fade *vb* **1** to cease to be visible — see DISAPPEAR
2 to make white or whiter by removing color — see WHITEN

faded *adj* lacking intensity of color — see PALE 1

faerie *also* **faery** *n* an imaginary being usually having a small human form and magical powers — see FAIRY

fag *n* a person who does very hard or dull work — see SLAVE 2

fag *vb* **1** to devote serious and sustained effort — see LABOR
2 to use up all the physical energy of — see EXHAUST 1

fag end *n* an unused or unwanted piece or item typically of small size or value — see [1]SCRAP 1

fail *vb* **1** to stop functioning ⟨my video camera

failed just as I was about to shoot the big moment⟩
synonyms break, break down, conk (out), crash, cut out, die, give out, stall
related words fizzle, sputter, wheeze; malfunction
antonyms start (up)
2 to be unsuccessful ⟨despite all the publicity, the movie *failed* miserably at the box office⟩
synonyms collapse, flop, flunk, fold, wash out
related words flounder, struggle; decline, slip, slump, wane
phrases fall flat
near antonyms flourish, prosper, thrive
antonyms succeed
3 to fall short in satisfying the expectation or hope of — see DISAPPOINT
4 to lose bodily strength or vigor — see WEAKEN 2
5 to miss the opportunity or obligation — see NEGLECT 3

failing *n* a defect in character — see FAULT 1

failure *n* **1** the nonperformance of an assigned or expected action ⟨your *failure* to check the batteries in the smoke detector could have tragic results⟩
synonyms default, delinquency, dereliction, neglect, negligence, oversight
related words carelessness, heedlessness, laxity
near antonyms compliance, discharge, fulfillment
2 a falling short of one's goals ⟨the *failure* of the school's fund-raising drive was a big disappointment to all⟩
synonyms collapse, crash, cropper, defeat, fizzle, nonsuccess
related words futility, uselessness; ineffectiveness, ineffectualness; deficiency, inadequacy, insufficiency; disappointment, letdown, setback
antonyms accomplishment, achievement, success
3 something that has failed ⟨the students' first attempt to build a homemade rocket was a disappointing *failure*⟩
synonyms bummer, bust, catastrophe, debacle (*also* débâcle), dud, fiasco, fizzle, flop, lemon, loser, turkey, washout
related words also-ran, disappointment, has-been; botch, hash, mess, muddle, shambles
near antonyms corker, crackerjack, dandy, jim-dandy, phenomenon
antonyms blockbuster, hit, smash, success, winner
4 a falling short of an essential or desirable amount or number — see DEFICIENCY

faint *adj* **1** not seen or understood clearly ⟨after wandering in the woods for hours, we had only a *faint* idea of where we were⟩
synonyms bleary, dim, foggy, fuzzy, hazy, indefinite, indistinct, indistinguishable, murky, nebulous, obscure, opaque, shadowy, unclear, undefined, undetermined, vague
related words dark, dusky, gloomy; impalpable, inappreciable, intangible, invisible; incomprehensible, inexplicable, mysterious, puzzling
near antonyms bright, distinct, evident, obvious; certain, firm, strong, sure
antonyms clear, definite
2 lacking bodily strength — see WEAK 1

faint *n* a temporary or permanent state of unconsciousness ⟨shocking news can cause a person to fall into a *faint*⟩
synonyms blackout, coma, insensibility, knockout, swoon
related words daze, stupor, trance; drowsiness, narcosis, sleep, somnolence

faint *vb* to lose consciousness ⟨the kind of person who *faints* at the sight of blood⟩
synonyms black out, pass out, swoon
related words break down, collapse
antonyms come around, come round, come to, revive

fainthearted *adj* easily frightened — see SHY 1

faintheartedness *n* lack of willingness to assert oneself and take risks — see TIMIDITY

faintness *n* the quality or state of lacking physical strength or vigor — see WEAKNESS 1

fair *adj* **1** not stormy or cloudy ⟨we prayed that there would be *fair* weather during our vacation at the beach⟩
synonyms clear, cloudless, sunny, sunshiny, unclouded
related words balmy, clement, gentle, mild, temperate; calm, halcyon, peaceful, placid, tranquil; fine, pleasant
near antonyms harsh, inclement, severe; blustering, blustery, breezy, gusty; foggy, hazy, misty
antonyms bleak, cloudy, dirty, foul, nasty, overcast, rainy, raw, rough, squally, stormy, sunless
2 marked by justice, honesty, and freedom from bias ⟨a commanding officer who enjoyed the respect of his soldiers because his decisions were always *fair*⟩
synonyms disinterested, dispassionate, equal, equitable, impartial, just, nonpartisan, objective, square, unbiased, unprejudiced
related words candid, frank, forthright, open, straightforward; balanced, rational, reasonable
near antonyms deceitful, deceptive, dishonest; arbitrary, unconscionable, unreasonable
antonyms biased, inequitable, partisan, prejudiced, unequal, unjust
3 following or according to the rules ⟨a hockey player who is respected for his *fair* play⟩
synonyms clean, legal, sportsmanlike, sportsmanly
related words just, law-abiding; ethical, moral, principled; honorable, irreproachable, unimpeachable
near antonyms immoral, unethical, unprincipled, unscrupulous
antonyms dirty, foul, nasty, unfair, unsportsmanlike
4 of light complexion ⟨*fair* people tend to sunburn easily⟩
synonyms light
related words ashen, pale, pallid, pasty, peaked, sallow, wan, white
antonyms black, brunet (*or* brunette), dark, swarthy
5 having qualities which inspire hope — see HOPEFUL 1
6 of a pale yellow or yellowish brown color — see BLOND
7 of average to below average quality — see MEDIOCRE 1
8 very pleasing to look at — see BEAUTIFUL

fair *n* a public showing of objects of interest — see EXHIBITION 1

fairly *adv* to some degree or extent ⟨for someone without professional training, she sings *fairly* well⟩
synonyms enough, kind of, like, moderately,

more or less, pretty, quite, rather, relatively, something, somewhat, sort of
related words acceptably, decently, passably, tolerably
near antonyms awfully, exceedingly (*also* exceeding), exceptionally, extremely, greatly, surpassingly, very

fairness *n* the qualities in a person or thing that as a whole give pleasure to the senses — see BEAUTY 1

fairy *n* an imaginary being usually having a small human form and magical powers ⟨*fairies* are part of the folklore of many countries and cultures⟩
synonyms brownie, dwarf, elf, faerie (*also* faery), fay, gnome, goblin, gremlin, hobgoblin, leprechaun, pixie (*also* pixy), puck, sprite, troll
related words changeling; imp; banshee, ghoul, ogre

fairy tale *n* a statement known by its maker to be untrue and made in order to deceive — see LIE

faith *n* **1** belief and trust in and loyalty to God ⟨a people who are known for their strong and steadfast *faith*⟩
synonyms devotion, piety, religion
related words devoutness, piousness, religiousness; adoration, reverence, veneration, worship
near antonyms disbelief, doubt, unbelief
antonyms atheism, godlessness
2 a body of beliefs and practices regarding the supernatural and the worship of one or more deities — see RELIGION 1
3 adherence to something to which one is bound by a pledge or duty — see FIDELITY
4 firm belief in the integrity, ability, effectiveness, or genuineness of someone or something — see TRUST 1
5 mental conviction of the truth of some statement or the reality of some being or phenomenon — see BELIEF 1

faithful *adj* **1** firm in one's allegiance to someone or something ⟨fans of the Chicago Cubs are famously *faithful*⟩
synonyms constant, devoted, fast, good, loyal, pious, staunch (*or* stanch), steadfast, steady, true, true-blue
related words dependable, dutiful, reliable, tried, trustworthy; unfaltering, unhesitating, unwavering; determined, intent, resolute; confirmed, dyed-in-the-wool, inveterate, sworn; ardent, fervent, fervid, impassioned, passionate
near antonyms undependable, unreliable, untrustworthy; faltering, hesitant, vacillating, wavering; dubious, irresolute, uncertain; apathetic, dispassionate, uninterested
antonyms disloyal, faithless, false, fickle, inconstant, perfidious, recreant, traitorous, treacherous, unfaithful, untrue
2 following an original exactly ⟨a *faithful* filming of Robert Louis Stevenson's novel *Treasure Island*⟩
synonyms accurate, authentic, exact, precise, right, strict, true, veracious
related words lifelike, realistic; careful, conscientious, meticulous, punctilious, scrupulous; authoritative; bona fide, genuine, real
near antonyms careless, slack, slipshod, slovenly
antonyms false, imprecise, inaccurate, inauthentic, inexact, loose, unfaithful

faithfulness *n* adherence to something to which one is bound by a pledge or duty — see FIDELITY

faithless *adj* not true in one's allegiance to someone or something ⟨*faithless* friends who deserted him in his time of need⟩
synonyms disloyal, false, fickle, inconstant, perfidious, recreant, traitorous, treacherous, unfaithful, untrue
related words undependable, unreliable, untrustworthy; faltering, hesitant, vacillating, wavering; dubious, irresolute, uncertain; apathetic, dispassionate, uninterested
near antonyms dependable, reliable, tried, trustworthy; unfaltering, unhesitating, unwavering; determined, intent, resolute; confirmed, dyed-in-the-wool, inveterate, sworn; ardent, fervent, fervid, impassioned, passionate
antonyms constant, devoted, faithful, fast, loyal, staunch (*or* stanch), steadfast, steady, true

faithlessness *n* **1** lack of faithfulness especially to one's husband or wife — see INFIDELITY 1
2 the act or fact of violating the trust or confidence of another — see BETRAYAL

fake *adj* **1** being such in appearance only and made with or manufactured from usually cheaper materials — see IMITATION
2 being such in appearance only and made or manufactured with the intention of committing fraud — see COUNTERFEIT
3 lacking in natural or spontaneous quality — see ARTIFICIAL 1

fake *n* **1** an imitation that is passed off as genuine ⟨experts declared that one of the museum's prized paintings was actually a *fake*⟩
synonyms counterfeit, forgery, hoax, humbug, phony (*also* phoney), sham
related words copy, reproduction; dummy; fraud, imposture, swindle; simulation, synthetic
near antonyms original
2 one who makes false claims of identity or expertise — see IMPOSTOR

fake *vb* **1** to imitate or copy especially in order to deceive ⟨pranksters *faked* giant footprints and then claimed that they had seen Bigfoot⟩
synonyms counterfeit, forge
related words simulate; crib, plagiarize; adulterate, doctor, fudge, juggle, manipulate, tamper (with); concoct, cook (up), fabricate, invent
2 to present a false appearance of — see FEIGN

faker *n* one who makes false claims of identity or expertise — see IMPOSTOR

fakery *n* the inclination or practice of misleading others through lies or trickery — see DECEIT

fall *n* **1** the act of going down from an upright position suddenly and involuntarily ⟨a bad *fall* that resulted in several broken bones⟩
synonyms slip, spill, stumble, tumble
related words header, pratfall; trip; descent, dive, plunge, slide; free-fall
2 a change to a lower state or level — see DECLINE 2
3 a loss of status — see COMEDOWN
4 the act or process of going to a lower level or altitude — see DESCENT 1
5 the amount by which something is lessened — see DECREASE
6 *usually* **falls** *pl* a fall of water usually from a great height — see WATERFALL

fall *vb* **1** to go down from an upright position suddenly and involuntarily ⟨better sand that walkway before somebody *falls* on the ice⟩
synonyms slip, stumble, topple, trip, tumble

related words collapse, crumple, drop, keel over, slump (over); nose-dive, plunge, precipitate
antonyms get up, rise, stand (up), uprise
2 to yield to the control or power of enemy forces ⟨the city *fell* after weeks of merciless bombardment⟩
synonyms capitulate, give up, knuckle under, submit, succumb, surrender
related words bow, buckle, cave (in), collapse; hand over, relinquish, yield; lose; fail, fold
near antonyms fight, oppose, resist, withstand; beat, overcome, win; prevail, triumph
antonyms stand
3 to go to a lower level — see DROP 2
4 to grow less in scope or intensity especially gradually — see DECREASE 2
5 to lead or extend downward — see DESCEND 1

fallacious *adj* **1** not using or following good reasoning — see ILLOGICAL
2 tending or having power to deceive — see DECEPTIVE 1

fallaciousness *n* the quality or state of being false — see FALLACY 2

fallacy *n* **1** a false idea or belief ⟨the once-common *fallacy* that girls just weren't any good at math⟩
synonyms error, falsehood, falsity, illusion, misconception, myth, old wives' tale, untruth
related words superstition; distortion, inaccuracy, misinterpretation, misrepresentation, misstatement, misunderstanding; sophism, sophistry; fib, lie, story, tale
antonyms truth, verity
2 the quality or state of being false ⟨the *fallacy* of the notion of spontaneous generation was demonstrated by the Dutch naturalist Leeuwenhoek⟩
synonyms erroneousness, fallaciousness, falseness, falsity, untruth
related words speciousness, spuriousness; deception, deceptiveness, delusion
near antonyms accuracy, correctness, factualness, genuineness
antonyms truth

fall back *vb* to move back or away (as from something difficult, dangerous, or disagreeable) — see RETREAT 1

fallen *adj* no longer living — see DEAD 1

fall guy *n* a person or thing taking the blame for others — see SCAPEGOAT

falling–out *n* an often noisy or angry expression of differing opinions — see ARGUMENT 1

fall out *vb* to express different opinions about something often angrily — see ARGUE 2

fallow *adj* not being in a state of use, activity, or employment — see INACTIVE 2

false *adj* **1** not being in agreement with what is true ⟨early reports about the explosion contained much *false* information⟩
synonyms erroneous, inaccurate, incorrect, inexact, invalid, off, unsound, untrue, untruthful, wrong
related words specious, spurious; deceptive, delusive, delusory, distorted, fallacious, misleading; amiss, askew, awry; deceitful, dishonest, fraudulent, lying, mendacious, untruthful; unconfirmed, unproven, untested; fabricated, invented, made-up, trumped-up
near antonyms confirmed, demonstrated, established, proven, tested
antonyms accurate, correct, errorless, factual, right, sound, true, valid
2 being such in appearance only and made with or manufactured from usually cheaper materials — see IMITATION
3 being such in appearance only and made or manufactured with the intention of committing fraud — see COUNTERFEIT
4 lacking in natural or spontaneous quality — see ARTIFICIAL 1
5 marked by, based on, or done by the use of dishonest methods to acquire something of value — see FRAUDULENT 1
6 not true in one's allegiance to someone or something — see FAITHLESS
7 tending or having power to deceive — see DECEPTIVE 1

falsehood *n* **1** a false idea or belief — see FALLACY 1
2 a statement known by its maker to be untrue and made in order to deceive — see LIE

falseness *n* **1** lack of faithfulness especially to one's husband or wife — see INFIDELITY 1
2 the act or fact of violating the trust or confidence of another — see BETRAYAL
3 the quality or state of being false — see FALLACY 2

falsify *vb* to change so much as to create a wrong impression or alter the meaning of — see GARBLE

falsity *n* **1** a false idea or belief — see FALLACY 1
2 a statement known by its maker to be untrue and made in order to deceive — see LIE
3 lack of faithfulness especially to one's husband or wife — see INFIDELITY 1
4 the act or fact of violating the trust or confidence of another — see BETRAYAL
5 the quality or state of being false — see FALLACY 2

falter *vb* **1** to show uncertainty about the right course of action — see HESITATE
2 to swing unsteadily back and forth or from side to side — see TEETER 1

faltering *n* the act or an instance of pausing because of uncertainty about the right course of action — see HESITATION

fame *n* the fact or state of being known to the public ⟨many go to Hollywood in search of *fame* and fortune⟩
synonyms celebrity, notoriety, renown
related words infamy; name, report, reputation, repute; cachet, position, prestige, rank, standing, stature; distinction, eminence, glory, greatness, honor, illustriousness, note, preeminence, prominence; acclaim, acknowledgment (*also* acknowledgement), praise, recognition; adoration, idolization
near antonyms disgrace, dishonor, disrepute, ignominy, odium, opprobrium, shame; unimportance
antonyms anonymity, obscurity

famed *adj* widely known — see FAMOUS

familial *adj* of or relating to a household or family — see DOMESTIC 1

familiar *adj* **1** closely acquainted ⟨the little inside jokes that people who have long been *familiar* like to share⟩
synonyms bosom, chummy, close, friendly, intimate, thick
related words affable, boon, companionable, convivial, cordial, genial, gracious, hearty; gregarious, sociable, social; comfortable, cozy, easy, snug; amicable, neighborly; confidential, secre-

tive; affectionate, dear, devoted, fond, loving, warm
near antonyms aloof, cold, cool, reserved, standoffish, unfriendly, unsociable, withdrawn
antonyms distant
2 having information especially as a result of study or experience ⟨book editors who are *familiar* with what is being taught in the schools⟩
synonyms abreast, acquainted, conversant, informed, knowledgeable, up, up-to-date, versed
related words aware, cognizant, conscious, heedful, mindful
phrases in the know
near antonyms unaware, unconscious, unmindful; blind, oblivious, unknowing, unwitting
antonyms ignorant, unacquainted, unfamiliar, uninformed
3 often observed or encountered — see COMMON 1
4 showing a lack of proper social reserve or modesty — see PRESUMPTUOUS 1

familiar *n* a person who has a strong liking for and trust in another — see FRIEND 1

familiarity *n* **1** the state of being in a very personal or private relationship ⟨the elderly couple enjoys a *familiarity* that is the result of many years of happy marriage⟩
synonyms chumminess, closeness, inseparability, intimacy, nearness
related words immediacy; affinity, kinship; commitment, devotion; affection, fondness, love; constancy, faithfulness, fidelity; amity, fellowship, friendship, goodwill; affability, conviviality, cordiality, geniality
near antonyms aloofness, coldness, coolness, reserve
antonyms distance
2 a socially improper or unsuitable act or remark — see IMPROPRIETY 2
3 knowledge gained by personal experience — see ACQUAINTANCE

familiarize *vb* **1** to give information to — see ENLIGHTEN 1
2 to impart knowledge of a new thing or situation to — see ACQUAINT 1

family *n* **1** a group of persons who come from the same ancestor ⟨the Adams *family* made remarkable contributions to American life for more than two centuries⟩
synonyms blood, clan, folks, house, kin, kindred, kinfolk, kinsfolk, line, lineage, people, race, stock, tribe
related words nuclear family; extended family, kith; brood; descendant (*or* descendent), issue, offspring, progeny, scion, seed; clansman, kinsman, kinswoman, relative; dynasty
near antonyms ancestry, birth, descent, extraction, origin, pedigree
2 one of the units into which a whole is divided on the basis of a common characteristic — see CLASS 2

family tree *n* the line of ancestors from whom a person is descended — see ANCESTRY

famine *n* a falling short of an essential or desirable amount or number — see DEFICIENCY

famished *adj* feeling a desire or need for food — see HUNGRY 1

famishment *n* a need or desire for food — see HUNGER 1

famous *adj* widely known ⟨a book about some of the most *famous* people of the last century⟩
synonyms celebrated, famed, noted, notorious, prominent, renowned, star, well-known
related words fabled, fabulous, legendary; infamous; distinguished, eminent, exceptional, great, illustrious, leading, notable, outstanding, prestigious, remarkable; important, significant; favorite, popular, preferred; estimable, honorable, reputable, respectable; formidable, redoubtable
near antonyms insignificant, unimportant; inconspicuous; undistinguished, unexceptional; unpopular
antonyms anonymous, obscure, unknown

fan *n* a person with a strong and habitual liking for something ⟨life-long *fans* of country and western music⟩
synonyms addict, aficionado, buff, bug, devotee, enthusiast, fanatic, fancier, fiend, freak, lover, maniac, nut
related words groupie; admirer, collector, connoisseur, dilettante; authority, expert; cultist, disciple, follower, votary; backer, patron, promoter, supporter; partisan, zealot; booster, rooter, well-wisher; faddist
near antonyms belittler, carper, critic, detractor

fan (out) *vb* **1** to arrange the parts of (something) over a wider area — see OPEN 3
2 to extend outwards from or as if from a central point — see RADIATE 1

fanatic *n* **1** a person with a strong and habitual liking for something — see FAN
2 one who is intensely or excessively devoted to a cause — see ZEALOT

fanatic *or* **fanatical** *adj* being very far from the center of public opinion — see EXTREME 2

fancier *n* a person with a strong and habitual liking for something — see FAN

fanciful *adj* **1** conceived or made without regard for reason or reality — see FANTASTIC 1
2 not real and existing only in the imagination — see IMAGINARY

fancy *adj* made or done with great care or with much detail — see ELABORATE 1

fancy *n* **1** a conception or image created by the imagination and having no objective reality — see FANTASY 1
2 a sudden impulsive and apparently unmotivated idea or action — see WHIM
3 positive regard for something — see LIKING
4 the ability to form mental images of things that either are not physically present or have never been conceived or created by others — see IMAGINATION

fancy *vb* **1** to form a mental picture of — see IMAGINE 1
2 to take pleasure in — see ENJOY 1

fanny *n* the part of the body upon which someone sits — see BUTTOCKS

fantastic *adj* **1** conceived or made without regard for reason or reality ⟨a *fantastic* scheme for getting rich quick⟩
synonyms absurd, bizarre, crazy, fanciful, foolish, insane, nonsensical, preposterous, unreal, wild
related words inconceivable, incredible, unbelievable; extravagant, grotesque; eccentric, odd, peculiar, strange, weird; farcical, laughable, ludicrous, ridiculous
antonyms realistic, reasonable

2 excitingly or mysteriously unusual — see EXOTIC
3 not real and existing only in the imagination — see IMAGINARY
4 too extraordinary or improbable to believe — see INCREDIBLE

fantasy *also* **phantasy** *n* **1** a conception or image created by the imagination and having no objective reality ⟨a constant daydreamer who started to believe his own *fantasies*⟩
synonyms chimera, conceit, daydream, delusion, dream, fancy, figment, hallucination, illusion, phantasm, pipe dream, unreality, vision
related words mirage; brainchild, idea; concoction, fabrication, fiction, invention; envisaging, imaging, visualization
near antonyms actuality, fact, reality
2 the ability to form mental images of things that either are not physically present or have never been conceived or created by others — see IMAGINATION
3 something that is the product of the imagination — see FICTION

far *adj* **1** lasting for a considerable time — see LONG 2
2 not close in time or space — see DISTANT 1

far *adv* to a great degree — see VERY 1

faraway *adj* not close in time or space — see DISTANT 1

farce *n* **1** a poor, insincere, or insulting imitation of something — see MOCKERY 1
2 humorous entertainment — see COMEDY

farcical *adj* **1** causing or intended to cause laughter — see FUNNY 1
2 so foolish or pointless as to be worthy of scornful laughter — see RIDICULOUS 1

fare *n* substances intended to be eaten — see FOOD

fare *vb* **1** to meet one's day-to-day needs — see GET ALONG 1
2 to move forward along a course — see GO 1
3 to take a meal — see DINE 1

farewell *adj* given, taken, or performed at parting — see PARTING 1

farewell *n* **1** an expression of good wishes at parting — see GOOD-BYE
2 the act of leaving a place — see DEPARTURE
3 the act or process of two or more persons going off in different directions — see PARTING

far–fetched *adj* not likely to be true or to occur — see IMPROBABLE

far–flung *adj* having considerable extent — see EXTENSIVE

farm *n* a piece of land and its buildings used to grow crops or raise livestock ⟨a *farm* that has been in the same family for five generations⟩
synonyms farmstead, grange, ranch
related words cropland, farmland, farmyard; farmhouse, homestead, manor, plantation; croft [*chiefly British*], station; garden, orchard

farm *vb* to work by plowing, sowing, and raising crops on ⟨we're planning on *farming* 50 acres the first year⟩
synonyms cultivate, tend, till
related words crop, plant; harvest, reap; harrow, hoe

farmer *n* a person who cultivates the land and grows crops on it ⟨a young *farmer* whose family has been growing wheat for many generations⟩
synonyms agriculturist (*or* agriculturalist), agronomist, cultivator, grower, planter, tiller
related words farmhand, gleaner, harvester, reaper; crofter [*chiefly British*], cropper, sharecropper; homesteader, nester [*West*]; granger; rancher, ranchero, ranchman

farming *adj* engaged in or concerned with agriculture — see AGRICULTURAL

farming *n* the science or occupation of cultivating the soil, producing crops, and raising livestock — see AGRICULTURE

farmstead *n* a piece of land and its buildings used to grow crops or raise livestock — see FARM

far–off *adj* not close in time or space — see DISTANT 1

far–out *adj* different from the ordinary in a way that causes curiosity or suspicion — see ODD 2

far–reaching *adj* having considerable extent — see EXTENSIVE

farsighted *adj* having or showing awareness of and preparation for the future — see FORESIGHTED

farsightedness *n* concern or preparation for the future — see FORESIGHT 2

farther *adj* resulting in an increase in amount or number — see ADDITIONAL

farther *adv* at or to a greater distance or more advanced point ⟨they had traveled *farther* down the Colorado River than any previous explorers⟩
synonyms beyond, further, yon, yonder

farthermost *adj* most distant from a center — see EXTREME 1

farthest *adj* most distant from a center — see EXTREME 1

fascinate *vb* **1** to attract or delight as if by magic — see CHARM 1
2 to hold the attention of as if by a spell — see ENTHRALL 1
3 to hold the attention of — see ENGAGE 1

fascinating *adj* **1** having an often mysterious or magical power to attract ⟨the *fascinating* cities and peoples of central Asia have been intriguing travelers at least since the time of Marco Polo⟩
synonyms alluring, appealing, attractive, bewitching, captivating, charming, elfin, enchanting, engaging, entrancing, fetching, glamorous (*also* glamourous), luring, magnetic, seductive
related words enthralling, gripping, hypnotizing, mesmerizing, riveting, spellbinding; enticing, tantalizing, tempting; exciting, haunting, interesting, intriguing, titillating; beckoning, inviting, winning; darling, delightful, pleasing
near antonyms boring, irksome, tedious, tiresome; abhorrent, distasteful, invidious, loathsome, obnoxious, offensive
antonyms repellant, repelling, repugnant, repulsive, revolting
2 holding the attention or provoking interest — see INTERESTING

fascination *n* the power of irresistible attraction — see CHARM 2

fashion *n* **1** a practice or interest that is very popular for a short time — see FAD
2 a distinctive way of putting ideas into words — see STYLE 1
3 a usual manner of behaving or doing — see HABIT
4 the means or procedure for doing something — see METHOD

fashion *vb* to bring into being by combining, shaping, or transforming materials — see MAKE 1

fashionable *adj* **1** being in the latest or current fashion — see STYLISH

2 enjoying widespread favor or approval — see POPULAR 1

fashionableness *n* the state of enjoying widespread approval — see POPULARITY

fast *adj* **1** moving, proceeding, or acting with great speed ⟨the *fast* pace of construction resulted in our new house being done ahead of schedule⟩
synonyms breakneck, breathless, brisk, dizzy, fleet, fleet-footed, flying, hasty, lightning, nippy, quick, rapid, rapid-fire, rattling, snappy, speedy, swift, whirlwind
related words expeditious, prompt, ready; hurried, quickened; breathtaking; energetic, strenuous, strong, vigorous
near antonyms crawling, dawdling, laggard, lingering, plodding, poky (*or* pokey), slowish, sluggish, unhurried; deliberate, leisurely, measured; dilatory, late
antonyms slow
2 firm in one's allegiance to someone or something — see FAITHFUL 1
3 firmly positioned in place and difficult to dislodge — see TIGHT 2
4 given to or marked by cheating and deception — see DISHONEST 2
5 marked by the ability to withstand stress without structural damage or distortion — see STABLE 1

fast *adv* **1** with great speed ⟨run as *fast* as you can to get help⟩
synonyms apace, briskly, fleetly, full tilt, hastily, posthaste, presto, pronto, quick, quickly, rapidly, snappily, soon, speedily, swift, swiftly
related words immediately, promptly, readily; impetuously, impulsively, rashly, recklessly; abruptly, suddenly; energetically, vigorously
phrases at full tilt, by leaps and bounds, in short order
near antonyms laggardly, lingeringly, ploddingly, sluggishly; deliberately, leisurely
antonyms slow, slowly
2 to a full extent or degree — see FULLY 1

fasten *vb* **1** to cause (something) to hold to another ⟨use this paperclip to *fasten* your picture to the application form⟩
synonyms affix, attach, fix
related words adhere, bolt, clamp, clasp, clinch, clip, glue, hang, harness, lace, lash, latch, nail, paste, pin, rivet, screw, staple, stick, strap, tack, tie, yoke; connect, join, link, unite; reattach, refasten, refix
near antonyms part, separate, sever; loose, loosen
antonyms detach, undo, unfasten
2 to put securely in place or in a desired position ⟨don't forget to *fasten* all the lines on your tent⟩
synonyms anchor, catch, clamp, fix, hitch, moor, secure, set
related words embed (*also* imbed), entrench (*also* intrench), implant, ingrain, lodge, wedge
near antonyms extract, pry, yank
antonyms loose, loosen, unfasten, unloose, unloosen
3 to fix (as one's attention) steadily toward a central objective — see CONCENTRATE 2

fastidious *adj* hard to please — see FINICKY

fastness *n* **1** a high rate of movement or performance — see SPEED
2 a structure or place from which one can resist attack — see FORT
3 adherence to something to which one is bound by a pledge or duty — see FIDELITY

fat *adj* **1** having an excess of body fat ⟨the popular image of Santa Claus as a *fat* man in a red suit⟩
synonyms chubby, corpulent, fleshy, full, gross, obese, overweight, plump, portly, pudgy, roly-poly, rotund, round, tubby
related words beefy, bulky, chunky, heavy, heavyset, stocky, stout, thick, thickset, weighty; brawny, burly, husky; dumpy, squat, stubby; paunchy, potbellied; flabby, soft; buxom
near antonyms angular, bony, gaunt, lank, lanky, rawboned, sinewy, skinny; cadaverous, haggard, skeletal, wasted; puny, scraggy, scrawny, slight; reedy, twiggy, willowy
antonyms lean, slender, slim, spare, thin
2 containing or seeming to contain the greatest quantity or number possible — see FULL 1
3 having a greater than usual measure across — see WIDE 1
4 having or being of relatively great depth or extent from one surface to its opposite — see THICK 1
5 producing abundantly — see FERTILE
6 yielding a profit — see PROFITABLE 1

fat *n* **1** individuals carefully selected as being the best of a class — see ELITE
2 the state or an instance of going beyond what is usual, proper, or needed — see EXCESS

fatal *adj* **1** bringing about ruin or misfortune ⟨I made the *fatal* mistake of sharing my secret with the school's biggest blabbermouth⟩
synonyms calamitous, cataclysmal (*or* cataclysmic), catastrophic, destructive, disastrous, fateful, ruinous, unfortunate
related words hapless, ill-fated, ill-starred, luckless
near antonyms fluky, fortuitous, fortunate, happy, lucky, providential; auspicious, bright, encouraging, golden, heartening, hopeful, promising, propitious
2 likely to cause or capable of causing death — see DEADLY

fatality *n* a person or thing harmed, lost, or destroyed — see CASUALTY 1

fate *n* **1** a state or end that seemingly has been decided beforehand ⟨the belief that it was this country's *fate* to extend from sea to sea⟩
synonyms circumstance, destiny, doom, fortune, lot, portion
related words accident, chance, hazard, luck; predestination; consequence, effect, issue, outcome, result, upshot
2 a condition or occurrence traceable to a cause — see EFFECT 1

fate *vb* to determine the fate of in advance — see DESTINE

fateful *adj* bringing about ruin or misfortune — see FATAL 1

fathead *n* a stupid person — see IDIOT

father *n* **1** a male human parent ⟨the special relationship that exists between *fathers* and sons⟩
synonyms dad, daddy, old man, pa, papa, pop
related words patriarch
2 a person who establishes a whole new field of endeavor ⟨Sir Isaac Newton is regarded by many as the *father* of modern science⟩
synonyms author, begetter, creator, establisher, founder, generator, inaugurator, initiator, instituter (*or* institutor), originator

related words conceiver, contriver, designer, formulator, innovator, inventor, spawner; builder, maker, producer; developer, pioneer, researcher; organizer, promoter; encourager, inspiration, inspirer
near antonyms disciple, follower, supporter
3 a person specially trained and authorized to conduct religious services in a Christian church — see CLERGYMAN
4 a person who is several generations earlier in an individual's line of descent — see ANCESTOR 1
5 *cap* the being worshipped as the creator and ruler of the universe — see DEITY 2
father *vb* to become the father of ⟨Paul Revere somehow found room in his small house for the large family he had *fathered*⟩
synonyms beget, get, sire
related words breed, multiply, procreate, propagate, reproduce, spawn; bear, engender, generate, produce
fatherland *n* the land of one's birth, residence, or citizenship — see COUNTRY 1
fathom *vb* to measure the depth of (as a body of water) typically with a weighted line — see [2]SOUND 1
fatigue *n* a complete depletion of energy or strength ⟨the day-long battle against the blaze left firefighters in a state of utter *fatigue*⟩
synonyms burnout, collapse, exhaustion, lassitude, prostration, tiredness, weariness
related words debilitation, enervation, faintness, feebleness, weakness; languor, lethargy, listlessness; sluggishness, slumber, stupor, torpor; apathy, inertia, passivity
near antonyms energy, go, liveliness, pep, vigor, vitality; might, potency, strength
antonyms refreshment, rejuvenation, revitalization
fatigue *vb* to use up all the physical energy of — see EXHAUST 1
fatigued *adj* depleted in strength, energy, or freshness — see WEARY 1
fatness *n* the condition of having an excess of body fat — see CORPULENCE
fatty *adj* containing animal fat especially in unusual amounts ⟨*fatty* ground beef that was the cheapest available⟩
synonyms adipose
related words greasy, oily
near antonyms fibrous, gristly, stringy, tough; nonfat
antonyms lean
fatuity *n* **1** a foolish act or idea — see FOLLY 1
2 lack of good sense or judgment — see FOOLISHNESS 1
3 the quality or state of lacking intelligence or quickness of mind — see STUPIDITY 1
fatuous *adj* **1** not having or showing an ability to absorb ideas readily — see STUPID 1
2 showing or marked by a lack of good sense or judgment — see FOOLISH 1
faucet *n* a fixture for controlling the flow of a liquid ⟨don't forget to turn off the *faucet*⟩
synonyms cock, gate, spigot, stopcock, tap, valve
related words hydrant, spout
fault *n* **1** a defect in character ⟨the common *fault* of being quick to judge others⟩
synonyms demerit, failing, foible, frailty, shortcoming, vice, weakness
related words blot, spot, stain; blemish, deficiency, flaw; Achilles' heel; corruption, depravity, evil, immorality, sinfulness, wickedness
near antonyms excellence, perfection; goodness, integrity, morality, probity, rectitude, righteousness
antonyms merit, virtue
2 an unintentional departure from truth or accuracy — see ERROR 1
3 responsibility for wrongdoing or failure — see BLAME 1
4 something that spoils the appearance or completeness of a thing — see BLEMISH
5 the state of being held as the cause of something that needs to be set right — see RESPONSIBILITY 1
fault *vb* to express one's unfavorable opinion of the worth or quality of — see CRITICIZE
faultfinder *n* a person given to harsh judgments and to finding faults — see CRITIC 1
faultfinding *adj* given to making or expressing unfavorable judgments about things — see CRITICAL 1
faultily *adv* in a mistaken or inappropriate way — see WRONGLY
faultless *adj* **1** being entirely without fault or flaw — see PERFECT 1
2 free from guilt or blame — see INNOCENT 2
faultlessly *adv* without any flaws or errors — see PERFECTLY 1
faultlessness *n* the quality or state of being free from guilt or blame — see INNOCENCE 1
faulty *adj* having a fault ⟨the cause of the plane crash was traced to *faulty* wiring⟩
synonyms bad, defective, flawed, imperfect
related words fallible; blemished, broken, damaged, defaced, disfigured, impaired, injured, marred, spoiled; deficient, inadequate, incomplete, insufficient, wanting
near antonyms complete, entire, intact, whole; undamaged, unimpaired, unspoiled
antonyms faultless, flawless, impeccable, perfect
favor *n* **1** an act of kind assistance ⟨a good and generous friend who is always doing *favors* for others⟩
synonyms boon, courtesy, grace, indulgence, kindness, mercy, service, turn
related words dispensation, waiver; advantage, benefit, blessing, godsend, manna; liberty, license (*or* licence), privilege
near antonyms hindrance, impediment, obstacle
2 a feeling of great approval and liking — see ADMIRATION 1
3 an acceptance of something as satisfactory — see APPROVAL 1
4 an attitude that always favors one way of feeling or acting especially without considering any other possibilities — see BIAS
5 positive regard for something — see LIKING
6 the state of enjoying widespread approval — see POPULARITY
favor *vb* **1** to do a service or favor for — see OBLIGE 1
2 to have a favorable opinion of — see APPROVE (OF)
3 to show partiality toward — see PREFER 1
favorable *adj* **1** expressing approval ⟨*favorable* reviews for the movie were few⟩
synonyms admiring, applauding, appreciative, approving, commendatory, complimentary, friendly, good, positive

related words eulogistic, laudatory, praiseful; respectful, supportive; adulatory, worshipful
near antonyms captious, carping, caviling (*or* cavilling), censuring, hypercritical, overcritical
antonyms adverse, disapproving, negative, unappreciative, uncomplimentary, unfavorable, unfriendly
2 pointing toward a happy outcome ⟨*favorable* conditions for opening a new business⟩
synonyms auspicious, bright, encouraging, golden, heartening, hopeful, promising, propitious
related words fortunate, happy, lucky, providential; advantageous, beneficial, profitable
near antonyms unfortunate, unhappy, unlucky; calamitous, catastrophic, disastrous, fatal, ruinous
antonyms discouraging, disheartening, futureless, hopeless, inauspicious, unfavorable, unpromising
3 conferring benefits; promoting or contributing to personal or social well-being — see BENEFICIAL
4 showing or expressing acceptance or approval — see POSITIVE

favorably *adv* in a pleasing way — see WELL 5

favored *adj* **1** granted special treatment or attention — see DARLING 1
2 singled out from a number or group as more to one's liking — see SELECT 1

favorite *adj* granted special treatment or attention — see DARLING 1

favorite *n* a person or thing that is preferred over others ⟨the youngest child was always Mother's *favorite*⟩
synonyms darling, minion, pet, preference
related words beloved, dear; jewel, prize, treasure
near antonyms abomination, anathema, bête noire, bugbear

fawn *vb* to use flattery or the doing of favors in order to win approval especially from a superior ⟨a student who could not wait to *fawn* over the new teacher⟩
synonyms fuss, kowtow, toady
related words drool, gush, slaver, slobber; endear, ingratiate; court, woo; adulate, idolize, worship; blandish, cajole, coax, flatter, soft-soap; cower, cringe, grovel; abase, debase, demean; defer, submit, yield
phrases curry favor
near antonyms despise, disdain, scorn; gibe (*or* jibe), jeer, scoff; brave, challenge, defy

fawner *n* a person who flatters another in order to get ahead — see SYCOPHANT

fay *adj* given to good-natured joking or teasing — see PLAYFUL

fay *n* an imaginary being usually having a small human form and magical powers — see FAIRY

faze *vb* to throw into a state of self-conscious distress — see EMBARRASS 1

fealty *n* adherence to something to which one is bound by a pledge or duty — see FIDELITY

fear *n* the emotion experienced in the presence or threat of danger ⟨the sight of the headless horseman filled the schoolmaster with *fear*⟩
synonyms alarm, anxiety, apprehension, consternation, dread, fearfulness, fright, horror, panic, terror, trepidation
related words phobia; creeps, jitters, nervousness, willies; pang, qualm, twinge; agitation, discomposure, disquiet, perturbation; concern, dismay, worry; cowardice, faintheartedness, timidity, timorousness
near antonyms aplomb, assurance, boldness, confidence, self-assurance, self-confidence; courage, dauntlessness, fearlessness, fortitude

fear *vb* to experience concern or anxiety — see WORRY 1

fearful *adj* **1** causing fear ⟨the *fearful* roar of a lion⟩
synonyms alarming, dire, direful, dreadful, fearsome, forbidding, formidable, frightening, frightful, hair-raising, horrendous, horrible, horrifying, intimidating, redoubtable, scary, shocking, terrible, terrifying
related words daunting, disconcerting, discouraging, dismaying, disquieting, distressing, disturbing, perturbing, startling, threatening, troubling, trying; creepy, eerie (*also* eery), weird; ghastly, gruesome, nightmarish
near antonyms comforting, consoling, inviting, reassuring, soothing; nonthreatening
2 easily frightened — see SHY 1
3 extreme in degree, power, or effect — see INTENSE
4 filled with fear or dread — see AFRAID 1

fearfulness *n* the emotion experienced in the presence or threat of danger — see FEAR

fearless *adj* feeling or displaying no fear by temperament — see BRAVE

fearlessness *n* strength of mind to carry on in spite of danger — see COURAGE

fearsome *adj* causing fear — see FEARFUL 1

feasible *adj* capable of being done or carried out — see POSSIBLE 1

feast *n* a large fancy meal often accompanied by ceremony or entertainment ⟨some 90 Native Americans showed up for the *feast* put on by the Pilgrims at Plymouth⟩
synonyms banquet, dinner, feed, spread
related words chow, repast; blowout, festival, fete (*or* fête), gala, party, shindig; festivity; barbecue, clambake, cookout, fry, luau, roast

feast *vb* to entertain with a fancy meal ⟨the returning war heroes were *feasted* all over the country⟩
synonyms banquet, dine, junket, regale
related words cater, feed; fete (*or* fête), honor

feat *n* **1** an act of notable skill, strength, or cleverness ⟨Washington's legendary *feat* of tossing a silver dollar across the Rappahannock River⟩
synonyms deed, exploit, stunt, trick
related words accomplishment, achievement, coup; adventure; performance
2 something done by someone — see ACTION 1

feather *n* **1** a number of persons or things that are grouped together because they have something in common — see SORT 1
2 dressy clothing — see FINERY

featherbrained *adj* lacking in seriousness or maturity — see GIDDY 1

feathery *adj* having little weight — see [1]LIGHT 1

feature *n* something that sets apart an individual from others of the same kind — see CHARACTERISTIC

feature *vb* to indicate the importance of by giving prominent display — see EMPHASIZE

feces *n pl* solid matter discharged from an animal's alimentary canal — see DROPPING 1

fecund *adj* producing abundantly — see FERTILE

fed up *adj* having one's patience, interest, or pleasure exhausted — see WEARY 2

federate *vb* to form or enter into an association that furthers the interests of its members — see ALLY

federation *n* an association of persons, parties, or states for mutual assistance and protection — see CONFEDERACY

fee *n* the amount of money that is demanded as payment for something — see PRICE 1

feeble *adj* lacking bodily strength — see WEAK 1

feebleness *n* the quality or state of lacking physical strength or vigor — see WEAKNESS 1

feed *n* **1** a large fancy meal often accompanied by ceremony or entertainment — see FEAST
2 food eaten or prepared for eating at one time — see MEAL

feed *vb* **1** to provide food or meals for ⟨a charity dedicated to *feeding* the hungry⟩
synonyms board, cater, provision
related words serve, wait; nourish, nurture; banquet, dine, feast, regale; mess
2 to put (something) into the possession of someone for use or consumption — see FURNISH 2
3 to take a meal — see DINE 1

feed (on) *vb* to seize and eat (something) as prey — see PREY

feel *n* an indefinite physical response to a stimulus — see SENSATION 1

feel *vb* **1** to have a vague awareness of ⟨I *feel* trouble brewing in the town⟩
synonyms perceive, scent, see, sense, smell, taste
related words behold, discern, observe, view; ascertain, discover, learn; anticipate, expect, foresee
2 to come into bodily contact with (something) so as to perceive a slight pressure on the skin — see TOUCH 1
3 to come to a knowledge of (something) by living through it — see EXPERIENCE
4 to have as an opinion — see BELIEVE 2
5 to search for something blindly or uncertainly — see GROPE

feel (for) *vb* to have sympathy for — see PITY

feeling *n* **1** a subjective response to a person, thing, or situation ⟨an overall *feeling* of happiness about their new home⟩
synonyms emotion, passion, sentiment
related words impression, perception, sense; attitude, outlook, perspective, viewpoint; belief, opinion, view; responsiveness, sensibility, sensitiveness, sensitivity
2 feelings *pl* general emotional condition ⟨a remark that thoughtlessly hurt her *feelings*⟩
synonyms heartstrings, passions, sensibilities
related words cheer, frame, humor, mode, mood, temper
3 an idea that is believed to be true or valid without positive knowledge — see OPINION 1
4 an indefinite physical response to a stimulus — see SENSATION 1
5 sorrow or the capacity to feel sorrow for another's suffering or misfortune — see SYMPATHY 1
6 the capacity for feeling for another's unhappiness or misfortune — see HEART 1

feign *vb* to present a false appearance of ⟨I would never *feign* illness just to get out of a test⟩
synonyms affect, assume, counterfeit, fake, pretend, profess, put on, sham, simulate
related words act, dissemble, impersonate, masquerade; forge, imitate; camouflage, conceal, disguise, mask; bluff, feint; malinger

feigned *adj* **1** lacking in natural or spontaneous quality — see ARTIFICIAL 1
2 not being or expressing what one appears to be or express — see INSINCERE

felicitate *vb* to express to (someone) admiration for his or her success or good fortune — see CONGRATULATE

felicitations *n pl* best wishes — see COMPLIMENTS

felicitous *adj* **1** giving pleasure or contentment to the mind or senses — see PLEASANT
2 meeting the requirements of a purpose or situation — see FIT 1

felicitously *adv* in a pleasing way — see WELL 5

felicitousness *n* the quality or state of being especially suitable or fitting — see APPROPRIATENESS

felicity *n* **1** a feeling or state of well-being and contentment — see HAPPINESS 1
2 something that provides happiness or does good for a person or thing — see BLESSING 2

feline *n* a small domestic animal known for catching mice — see CAT 1

fell *adj* **1** likely to cause or capable of causing death — see DEADLY
2 violently unfriendly or aggressive in disposition — see FIERCE 1

fell *vb* **1** to strike (someone) so forcefully as to cause a fall ⟨a boxer who was often *felled* in the first round⟩
synonyms bowl (down *or* over), down, drop, floor, knock (down *or* over), level
related words hit, jab, poke, punch, smite, sock, strike, whack
2 to bring down by cutting ⟨the settlers began the daunting task of *felling* the mighty trees that blanketed the island⟩
synonyms chop (down), cut (down), hew, mow
related words bulldoze, flatten, level, raze, tear down
3 to deprive of life — see KILL 1

fellow *n* **1** a male romantic companion — see BOYFRIEND
2 a person frequently seen in the company of another — see ASSOCIATE 1
3 an adult male human being — see MAN 1
4 either of a pair matched in one or more qualities — see MATE 1
5 one that is equal to another in status, achievement, or value — see EQUAL

fellowship *n* **1** a friendly relationship marked by ready communication and mutual understanding — see RAPPORT
2 a group of persons formally joined together for some common interest — see ASSOCIATION 2
3 kindly concern, interest, or support — see GOODWILL 1
4 the body of people in a profession or field of activity — see CORPS
5 the feeling of closeness and friendship that exists between companions — see COMPANIONSHIP

female *adj* of, relating to, or marked by qualities traditionally associated with women — see FEMININE 1

female *n* an adult female human being — see WOMAN

feminine *adj* **1** of, relating to, or marked by qualities traditionally associated with women ⟨the *feminine* furnishings suggested that the bedroom was intended for a girl⟩
synonyms female, womanish, womanlike, womanly

related words effeminate, girlish, sissy, unmanly; ladylike; distaff, petticoat
near antonyms boyish, hoydenish, tomboyish; gentlemanly
antonyms male, manlike, manly, mannish, masculine
2 having or displaying qualities more suitable for women than for men — see EFFEMINATE
fen *n* spongy land saturated or partially covered with water — see SWAMP
fence *n* a physical object that blocks the way — see BARRIER
fence (in) *vb* to close or shut in by or as if by barriers — see ENCLOSE 1
fend (off) *vb* to drive back — see REPEL 1
fender *n* something that serves as a protective barrier — see CUSHION
feral *adj* living outdoors without taming or domestication by humans — see WILD 1
ferment *n* a disturbed or uneasy state — see UNREST
ferment *vb* to cause or encourage the development of — see INCITE 1
ferocious *adj* **1** extreme in degree, power, or effect — see INTENSE
2 marked by bursts of destructive force or intense activity — see VIOLENT 1
3 violently unfriendly or aggressive in disposition — see FIERCE 1
ferry *vb* to support and take from one place to another — see CARRY 1
fertile *adj* producing abundantly ⟨the *fertile* mind of Leonardo da Vinci explored art, architecture, engineering, mathematics, and many other fields⟩
synonyms fat, fecund, fruitful, luxuriant, productive, prolific, rich
related words bearing, producing, yielding; abounding, abundant, bountiful; copious, plenteous, plentiful; blooming, bursting, flourishing, swarming, teeming, thriving; creative, inventive, original
near antonyms meager (*or* meagre), scant, scanty, skimpy, spare, sparse
antonyms barren, infertile, sterile, unfruitful, unproductive
fervency *n* depth of feeling — see ARDOR 1
fervent *adj* having or expressing great depth of feeling ⟨a *fervent* speech that called for tolerance and compassion for those who are different⟩
synonyms ardent, blazing, burning, charged, emotional, fervid, feverish, fiery, flaming, glowing, hot-blooded, impassioned, passionate, red-hot, vehement, warm, warm-blooded
related words gushing, maudlin, mawkish, mushy, sentimental; histrionic, melodramatic; enthusiastic, gung ho, zealous; enamored, infatuated, obsessed
phrases on fire
near antonyms detached, dry, impersonal, objective; reserved, undemonstrative
antonyms cold, cool, dispassionate, impassive, unemotional
fervid *adj* having or expressing great depth of feeling — see FERVENT
fervidness *n* depth of feeling — see ARDOR 1
fervor *n* depth of feeling — see ARDOR 1
festival *n* a time or program of special events and entertainment in honor of something ⟨tourists flock to the town for its annual strawberry *festival*⟩
synonyms carnival, celebration, festivity, fete (*or* fête), fiesta, gala, jubilee
related words jamboree, jollification, merrymaking, revel, revelry; exhibit, exhibition, exposition, fair, show; exercises, honors
festive *adj* indicative of or marked by high spirits or good humor — see MERRY
festivity *n* **1** a mood characterized by high spirits and amusement and often accompanied by laughter — see MIRTH
2 a time or program of special events and entertainment in honor of something — see FESTIVAL
3 joyful or festive activity — see MERRYMAKING
fetch *vb* to have a price of — see COST
fetching *adj* having an often mysterious or magical power to attract — see FASCINATING 1
fetch up *vb* to bring (something) to a standstill — see [1]HALT 1
fete *or* **fête** *vb* to show appreciation, respect, or affection for (someone) with a public celebration — see HONOR
fete *or* **fête** *n* **1** a social gathering — see PARTY 1
2 a time or program of special events and entertainment in honor of something — see FESTIVAL
fetid *adj* having an unpleasant smell — see MALODOROUS
fetish *also* **fetich** *n* **1** something about which one is constantly thinking or concerned — see FIXATION
2 something worn or kept to bring good luck or keep away evil — see CHARM 1
fetter *n* **1** something that limits one's freedom of action or choice — see RESTRICTION 1
2 something that makes movement or progress more difficult — see ENCUMBRANCE
3 something that physically prevents free movement — see BOND 1
fetter *vb* **1** to confine or restrain with or as if with chains — see BIND 1
2 to create difficulty for the work or activity of — see HAMPER
fettle *n* a state of being or fitness — see CONDITION 1
fever *n* an abnormal state that disrupts a plant's or animal's normal bodily functioning — see DISEASE
feverish *adj* **1** being in a state of increased activity or agitation ⟨scary stories that were the product of a *feverish* imagination⟩
synonyms agitated, excited, frenzied, heated, hectic, overactive, overwrought
related words ardent, burning, fervent, fiery, impassioned; high-strung, jittery, jumpy, nervous
phrases keyed up
near antonyms calm, composed, cool, serene, tranquil
2 having or expressing great depth of feeling — see FERVENT
3 marked by great and often stressful excitement or activity — see FURIOUS 1
few *n* a small number ⟨a *few* of the songs on the album are good, but most are forgettable⟩
synonyms handful, scattering, smattering, sprinkle, sprinkling
related words minority
near antonyms majority, most; abundance, excess, plenty, surplus
antonyms army, crowd, flock, horde, host, legion, many, mountain, multitude
fiancé *n* the person to whom one is engaged to be married — see BETROTHED

fiancée *n* the person to whom one is engaged to be married — see BETROTHED
fiasco *n* something that has failed — see FAILURE 3
fiat *n* an order publicly issued by an authority — see EDICT 1
fib *n* a statement known by its maker to be untrue and made in order to deceive — see LIE
fib *vb* to make a statement one knows to be untrue — see LIE 1
fibber *n* a person who tells lies — see LIAR
fiber *n* the strength of mind that enables a person to endure pain or hardship — see FORTITUDE
fibrous *adj* resembling or having the texture of a mass of strings — see STRINGY
fickle *adj* **1** likely to change frequently, suddenly, or unexpectedly ⟨a *fickle* friendship that was on and off over the years⟩
synonyms capricious, changeable, changeful, flickery, fluctuating, fluid, inconstant, mercurial, mutable, temperamental, uncertain, unpredictable, unsettled, unstable, unsteady, variable, volatile
related words aimless, erratic, haphazard, irregular, random; hesitating, shilly-shallying, vacillating, wavering; undependable, unreliable, untrustworthy; adaptable, mobile, protean, versatile
near antonyms equable, even, uniform; abiding, durable, lasting, permanent, persistent; dependable, reliable, trustworthy
antonyms certain, changeless, constant, immutable, invariable, settled, stable, steady, unchangeable
2 not true in one's allegiance to someone or something — see FAITHLESS
fiction *n* something that is the product of the imagination ⟨most stories about famous outlaws of the Old West are *fictions* that have little or nothing to do with fact⟩
synonyms fable, fabrication, fantasy (*also* phantasy), figment, invention
related words anecdote, narrative, novel, story, tale, yarn; falsehood, fib, lie, misrepresentation, untruth
near antonyms actuality, reality
antonyms fact
fictional *adj* not real and existing only in the imagination — see IMAGINARY
fictitious *adj* not real and existing only in the imagination — see IMAGINARY
fiddle *vb* to make jerky or restless movements — see FIDGET
fiddle (around) *vb* to spend time in aimless activity ⟨we spent the snow day just *fiddling around*⟩
synonyms fool (around), mess (around), monkey (around), play, potter (around), putter (around), trifle
related words dally, dawdle, dillydally, hang around, hang out, idle, loaf, loll, lounge; clown (around), horse (around); tinker
near antonyms buckle (down)
fiddle (with) *vb* to handle thoughtlessly, ignorantly, or mischievously — see TAMPER
fiddlesticks *n pl* language, behavior, or ideas that are absurd and contrary to good sense — see NONSENSE 1
fidelity *n* adherence to something to which one is bound by a pledge or duty ⟨they have never wavered in their *fidelity* to the cause of freedom⟩
synonyms allegiance, constancy, dedication, devotedness, devotion, faith, faithfulness, fastness, fealty, loyalty, steadfastness
related words affection, attachment, fondness; determination, firmness, resolution; dependability, reliability, trustworthiness
near antonyms alienation, disaffection, estrangement, separation
antonyms disloyalty, faithlessness, falseness, inconstancy, infidelity, perfidiousness, perfidy, treachery
fidget *vb* to make jerky or restless movements ⟨small children are likely to *fidget* in church⟩
synonyms fiddle, jerk, squirm, toss, twitch, wiggle, wriggle, writhe
related words flit, flutter, twitter; quake, quiver, shake, shiver, tremble; pace
near antonyms relax, rest, unwind
fidgets *n pl* a state of nervousness marked by sudden jerky movements — see JUMPINESS
fie *interj* how surprising, doubtful, or unbelievable — see NO
field *n* **1** a small area of usually open land ⟨a *field* that is the frequent site of neighborhood softball games⟩
synonyms clearing, ground, lot, parcel, plat, plot, tract
related words common(s); grass, green, greensward, lawn; glade, grassland, heath, lea, meadow, moor, pasture
2 a region of activity, knowledge, or influence ⟨the first woman to enter the *field* of medicine⟩
synonyms area, arena, demesne, department, discipline, domain, line, province, realm, specialty, sphere
related words study, subject; territory, turf; business, occupation, profession, pursuit, racket, vocation
3 a part or portion having no fixed boundaries — see REGION 1
fiend *n* **1** a mean, evil, or unprincipled person — see VILLAIN
2 a person who regularly uses drugs especially illegally — see DOPER
3 a person with a strong and habitual liking for something — see FAN
4 an evil spirit — see DEMON
fiendish *adj* of, relating to, or worthy of an evil spirit ⟨a *fiendish* delight in playing cruel tricks⟩
synonyms demoniac (*also* demoniacal), demonic, devilish, diabolical (*or* diabolic), satanic
related words hellish, infernal; baleful, evil, sinister; malevolent, malicious, malignant; heinous, monstrous; barbarous, cruel, ferocious, inhuman, savage, vicious
near antonyms celestial, heavenly; beneficent, benevolent, benign, benignant; godly, holy, saintly
antonyms angelic
fierce *adj* **1** violently unfriendly or aggressive in disposition ⟨the Vikings had a well-earned reputation for being *fierce* warriors⟩
synonyms fell, ferocious, grim, savage, vicious
related words bellicose, belligerent, pugnacious, warlike; contentious, quarrelsome, truculent; menacing, threatening; bestial, brute, inhuman, inhumane; barbaric, uncivilized, wild; heartless, implacable, merciless, pitiless, relentless, ruthless, unrelenting, wanton; bloodthirsty, bloody, murderous; rapacious, ravenous, voracious
near antonyms amicable, congenial, friendly; compliant, submissive, tame, unaggressive; com-

passionate, kind, merciful; pacific, peaceable, peaceful; amiable, complaisant, obliging; human, humane; civilized, cultured
antonyms gentle, mild
2 extreme in degree, power, or effect — see INTENSE
3 harsh and threatening in manner or appearance — see GRIM 1
4 having or showing a bold forcefulness in the pursuit of a goal — see AGGRESSIVE 1
5 marked by bursts of destructive force or intense activity — see VIOLENT 1
6 marked by great and often stressful excitement or activity — see FURIOUS 1

fierceness *n* the quality or state of being forceful (as in expression) — see VEHEMENCE 1

fiery *adj* **1** being on fire — see ABLAZE 1
2 having a notably high temperature — see HOT 1
3 having or expressing great depth of feeling — see FERVENT
4 marked by a lively display of strong feeling — see SPIRITED 1

fiesta *n* a time or program of special events and entertainment in honor of something — see FESTIVAL

fight *n* **1** a physical dispute between opposing individuals or groups ⟨a troubled youth who got into one *fight* after another⟩
synonyms battle, clash, combat, conflict, contest, fracas, fray, hassle, scrap, scrimmage, scuffle, skirmish, struggle, tussle
related words pitched battle; brawl, free-for-all, melee; fisticuffs; confrontation, duel, face-off; altercation, argument, disagreement, quarrel, row, wrangle
2 a forceful effort to reach a goal or objective — see STRUGGLE 1
3 an inclination to fight or quarrel — see BELLIGERENCE
4 an often noisy or angry expression of differing opinions — see ARGUMENT 1

fight *vb* **1** to oppose (someone) in physical conflict ⟨a proud people who have fiercely *fought* all invaders of their homeland⟩
synonyms battle, clash (with), combat, scrimmage (with), skirmish (with), war (against)
related words duel; bash, batter, beat, buffet, hit, punch, slug, strike; box, spar; brawl; grapple, scuffle, tussle, wrestle; bump, collide
phrases fall foul (of)
near antonyms give up, submit, surrender
2 to strive to reduce or eliminate ⟨a civil rights leader who dedicated his life to *fighting* prejudice⟩
synonyms battle, combat, contend (with), counter, oppose
related words baffle, foil, frustrate, resist, thwart, withstand; confront, defy, face, meet
near antonyms abide, bear, endure, suffer; advocate, back, support, uphold
antonyms advance, encourage, foster, further, promote
3 to engage in a contest — see COMPETE
4 to express different opinions about something often angrily — see ARGUE 2
5 to refuse to give in to — see RESIST

fighter *n* **1** a person engaged in military service — see SOLDIER
2 one that engages in the sport of fighting with the fists — see BOXER

figment *n* **1** a conception or image created by the imagination and having no objective reality — see FANTASY 1
2 something that is the product of the imagination — see FICTION

figurative *adj* expressing one thing in terms normally used for another ⟨the *figurative* meaning of "allergy" is "a feeling of dislike"⟩
synonyms extended, metaphorical
related words allegorical, emblematic (*also* emblematical), symbolic (*also* symbolical); euphemistic
near antonyms nonsymbolic
antonyms literal, nonfigurative

figure *n* **1** a character used to represent a mathematical value — see NUMBER
2 a line that traces the outer limits of an object or surface — see OUTLINE 1
3 a person who is widely known and usually much talked about — see CELEBRITY 1
4 a small statue — see FIGURINE
5 a three-dimensional representation of the human body used especially for displaying clothes — see MANNEQUIN 1
6 a unit of decoration that is repeated all over something (as a fabric) — see PATTERN 1
7 something that visually explains or decorates a text — see ILLUSTRATION 1
8 the amount of money that is demanded as payment for something — see PRICE 1
9 the outward appearance of something as distinguished from its substance — see FORM 1
10 the type of body that a person has — see PHYSIQUE
11 figures *pl* the act or process of performing mathematical operations to find a value — see CALCULATION

figure *vb* **1** to come to a judgment after discussion or consideration — see DECIDE 1
2 to decide the size, amount, number, or distance of (something) without actual measurement — see ESTIMATE 2
3 to determine (a value) by doing the necessary mathematical operations — see CALCULATE 1
4 to have as an opinion — see BELIEVE 2

figure out *vb* to find an answer for through reasoning — see SOLVE

figurine *n* a small statue ⟨his collection of *figurines* includes toy soldiers from every war that America has fought⟩
synonyms figure, statuette
related words doll, marionette, puppet; bust, figurehead; carving, model, sculpture; dummy, form, mannequin
antonyms colossus

figuring *n* the act or process of performing mathematical operations to find a value — see CALCULATION

filch *vb* to take (something) without right and with an intent to keep — see STEAL 1

file *n* a series of persons or things arranged one behind another — see LINE 1

[1]file *vb* to make smooth by friction — see GRIND 1

[2]file *vb* to move along with a steady regular step especially in a group — see MARCH 1

fill *n* soft material that is used to fill the hollow parts of something — see FILLING

fill *vb* **1** to put into (something) as much as can be held or contained ⟨*fill* the basket with apples⟩
synonyms charge, cram, heap, jam, jam-pack, load, pack, stuff

related words flood, glut, swamp; crowd, crush, press, ram, shove, squash, squeeze; refill, reload, repack
near antonyms lighten
antonyms empty
2 to close up so that no empty spaces remain ⟨before starting to paint, *fill* all the cracks with putty⟩
synonyms block, bung, dam, pack, plug, stop, stuff
related words choke, clog, obstruct; caulk, chink
near antonyms excavate, hollow (out), scoop (out)
3 to do what is required by the terms of — see FULFILL 1

filled *adj* containing or seeming to contain the greatest quantity or number possible — see FULL 1

filler *n* soft material that is used to fill the hollow parts of something — see FILLING

fill in *vb* **1** to give information to — see ENLIGHTEN 1
2 to serve as a replacement usually for a time only — see COVER 1

filling *n* soft material that is used to fill the hollow parts of something ⟨the *filling* for the parka is goose down⟩
synonyms fill, filler, padding, stuffing
related words interlining, lining, wadding; cushion

film *n* **1** a story told by means of a series of continuously projected pictures and a sound track — see MOVIE 1
2 the art or business of making a movie — see MOVIE 2

filmy *adj* **1** being of a material lacking in sturdiness or substance — see FLIMSY 1
2 very thin and easy to see through — see SHEER 1

filter *vb* **1** to pass through a filter — see STRAIN 2
2 to remove usually visible impurities from — see CLARIFY 1

filth *n* **1** foul matter that mars the purity or cleanliness of something ⟨the *filth* in the restaurant's kitchen was unbelievable⟩
synonyms dirt, grime, muck, smut, soil
related words scum, sewage, slime, sludge, swill; garbage, refuse, trash; soot; dirtiness, filthiness, foulness, griminess, grubbiness, nastiness, squalidness, uncleanliness, uncleanness
near antonyms cleanliness, cleanness
2 the quality or state of being obscene — see OBSCENITY 1

filthiness *n* **1** the quality or state of being obscene — see OBSCENITY 1
2 the state or quality of being dirty — see DIRTINESS 1

filthy *adj* **1** depicting or referring to sexual matters in a way that is unacceptable in polite society — see OBSCENE 1
2 not clean — see DIRTY 1

finagle *vb* to plan out usually with subtle skill or care — see ENGINEER

final *adj* **1** following all others of the same kind in order or time — see LAST
2 having been established and usually not subject to change — see FIXED 1

finale *n* the last part of a process or action ⟨the *finale* to the festivities was a grand display of fireworks⟩
synonyms close, closing, conclusion, consummation, end, ending, finis, finish, windup
related words apex, climax, crescendo, culmination, peak, summit, zenith; aftermath, anticlimax, coda, epilogue, postscript; tag end, tail end
near antonyms introduction, overture, prelude, prologue
antonyms beginning, dawn, opening, start

finalize *vb* to bring (something) to a state where nothing remains to be done — see FINISH 1

finally *adv* at a later time — see YET 1

finance *vb* **1** to provide money for ⟨a local business kindly *financed* the high school band's trip to New York City⟩
synonyms capitalize, endow, fund, stake, subsidize, underwrite
related words grubstake; aid, back, patronize, sponsor, support
2 to furnish (as an institution) with a regular source of income — see ENDOW 2

finances *n pl* available money — see FUND 2

financial *adj* of or relating to money, banking, or investments ⟨the *financial* world was watching the stock market closely⟩
synonyms fiscal, monetary, pecuniary
related words capitalist (*or* capitalistic), commercial, economic

find *n* something discovered — see DISCOVERY 2

find *vb* **1** to come upon after searching, study, or effort ⟨we finally *found* the information after searching dozens of Internet sites⟩
synonyms ascertain, descry, detect, determine, dig (up), discover, find out, get, hit (on *or* upon), hunt (down *or* up), learn, locate, run down, scare up, scout (up), track (down)
related words espy, sight, spot; look for, search (for *or* out), seek
near antonyms lose, mislay, misplace
antonyms miss, overlook, pass over
2 to come upon unexpectedly or by chance — see HAPPEN (ON *OR* UPON)

finding *n* **1** a decision made by a court or tribunal regarding a case it has heard — see SENTENCE
2 the act or process of sighting or learning the existence of something for the first time — see DISCOVERY 1

find out *vb* **1** to come to an awareness — see DISCOVER 1
2 to come upon after searching, study, or effort — see FIND 1

fine *adj* **1** consisting of very small particles ⟨the *fine* sand found on the island's beaches⟩
synonyms dusty, floury, powdery
related words smooth; filtered, pulverized, refined
near antonyms rough; unfiltered, unrefined; gravelly, gritty, sandy; pebbly, rocky, stony (*also* stoney); lumpy, mealy
antonyms coarse, grainy, granular, granulated
2 made or done with extreme care and accuracy ⟨the *fine* distinction between bravery and recklessness⟩
synonyms delicate, exact, hairline, hairsplitting, minute, nice, refined, subtle
related words nitpicking, quibbling; petty, piddling, trifling, trivial; fastidious, finicky, fussy, particular
near antonyms apparent, clear, obvious; broad, indefinite; careless, slapdash, slipshod, sloppy
antonyms coarse, inexact, rough
3 being of less than usual width — see NARROW 1
4 being to one's liking — see SATISFACTORY 1
5 free from added matter — see PURE 1

6 meeting the highest standard of accuracy — see PRECISE 1
7 of a level of quality that meets one's needs or standards — see ADEQUATE
8 of a size that is less than average — see SMALL 1
9 of the very best kind — see EXCELLENT

fine *adv* in a satisfactory way — see WELL 1

fine *n* a sum of money to be paid as a punishment ⟨a $50 *fine* for speeding⟩
synonyms damages, forfeit, forfeiture, mulct, penalty
related words reparations; award, compensation; indemnity

fine *vb* to establish or apply as a charge or penalty — see IMPOSE

fineness *n* **1** the quality or state of being little in size — see SMALLNESS
2 the quality or state of being very accurate — see PRECISION
3 the state or quality of having a delicate structure — see DELICACY 2

finery *n* dressy clothing ⟨the guests arrived at the wedding in all their *finery*⟩
synonyms array, best, bravery, caparison, feather, frippery, full dress, gaiety (*also* gayety), regalia
related words apparel, attire, costume, duds, raiment
near antonyms rags, tatters

finesse *n* mental skill or quickness — see DEXTERITY 1

finesse *vb* to plan out usually with subtle skill or care — see ENGINEER

finicky *adj* hard to please ⟨cats have a reputation for being *finicky* eaters⟩
synonyms choosy (*or* choosey), dainty, delicate, demanding, exacting, fastidious, fussy, nice, oldmaidish, particular, picky
related words discerning, discriminating, insightful, knowledgeable; carping, critical; careful, meticulous, punctilious, scrupulous; queasy (*also* queazy), squeamish; peevish, petulant, prickly, touchy
near antonyms affable, breezy, devil-may-care, happy-go-lucky, laid-back; flexible, lax, loose; lenient, permissive; uncritical
antonyms undemanding, unfussy

finis *n* the last part of a process or action — see FINALE

finish *n* **1** the last part of a process or action — see FINALE
2 the stopping of a process or activity — see END 1

finish *vb* **1** to bring (something) to a state where nothing remains to be done ⟨we should *finish* the painting of the house by tomorrow⟩
synonyms complete, consummate, finalize, perfect
related words follow through, see out, stick out; accomplish, achieve, effect; discharge, execute, fulfill (*or* fulfil), perform; machine, polish, refine, round (off *or* out), shine, touch up
near antonyms abandon, desert, drop, forsake, quit
2 to bring (an event) to a natural or appropriate stopping point — see CLOSE 3
3 to come to an end — see CEASE 1

finished *adj* brought or having come to an end — see COMPLETE 2

finite *adj* **1** having a limit ⟨our nation's natural resources are abundant, but they are also *finite*⟩
synonyms limited
related words confined, restricted; definable, defined, definite, determinate; decided, established, fixed, set; exact, precise, specific
near antonyms unconfined, unrestricted; indefinite, indeterminate, undefinable, undefined
antonyms boundless, infinite, unbounded, unlimited
2 having distinct or certain limits — see LIMITED 1

fire *n* a destructive burning ⟨a number of suspicious *fires* in the neighborhood recently⟩
synonyms conflagration, holocaust, inferno
related words blaze, flare-up; backfire, bonfire, forest fire, wildfire; arson

fire *vb* **1** to cause (a projectile) to be driven forward with force — see SHOOT 1
2 to cause a weapon to release a missile with great force — see SHOOT 2
3 to give life, vigor, or spirit to — see ANIMATE
4 to let go from office, service, or employment — see DISMISS 1
5 to send through the air especially with a quick forward motion of the arm — see THROW
6 to set (something) on fire — see BURN 2

fire (up) *vb* to rouse to strong feeling or action — see PROVOKE 1

firearm *n* a portable weapon from which a shot is discharged by gunpowder — see GUN 1

firebrand *n* a person who stirs up public feelings especially of discontent — see AGITATOR

firebug *n* a person who deliberately and unlawfully sets fire to a building or other property — see ARSONIST

fireproof *adj* incapable of being burned — see INCOMBUSTIBLE

fireside *n* the place where one lives — see HOME 1

fireworks *n pl* an outburst or display of excited anger — see TANTRUM

firing *n* a directed propelling of a missile by a firearm or artillery piece — see SHOT

firkin *n* an enclosed wooden vessel for holding beverages — see CASK

firm *adj* **1** not showing weakness or uncertainty ⟨a friendly fellow with a ready smile and a *firm* handshake⟩
synonyms forceful, hearty, iron, lusty, robust, solid, stout, strong, sturdy, vigorous
related words mighty, powerful, tough, unyielding; animated, energetic, lively, spirited; certain, confident, sanguine, sure
near antonyms feeble, fragile, frail; limp, listless, spiritless
antonyms uncertain, weak
2 having a consistency that does not easily yield to pressure ⟨cold butter that was too *firm* to spread⟩
synonyms compact, hard, rigid, solid, stiff, unyielding
related words case-hardened, compacted, compressed, hardened, indurated, stiffened, tempered; close, dense, heavy, thick, thickset; inelastic, inflexible, ramrod, unbending; compressed, condensed; sturdy, substantial; impenetrable, impermeable, nonporous
near antonyms loose, scattered, thin; bendable, elastic, flexible, malleable, pliable; flaccid, floppy, limp, slack; airy, light; permeable, porous
antonyms flabby, soft, spongy, squashy, squishy
3 firmly positioned in place and difficult to dislodge — see TIGHT 2

4 fully committed to achieving a goal — see DETERMINED 1
5 having been established and usually not subject to change — see FIXED 1
6 marked by the ability to withstand stress without structural damage or distortion — see STABLE 1

firm *n* a commercial or industrial activity or organization — see ENTERPRISE 1

firm (up) *vb* to become physically firm or solid — see HARDEN 1

firmament *n* the expanse of air surrounding the earth — see SKY

firmly *adv* in a vigorous and forceful manner — see HARD 3

firmness *n* **1** firm or unwavering adherence to one's purpose — see DETERMINATION 1
2 the ability to withstand force or stress without being distorted, dislodged, or damaged — see STABILITY 1

first *adj* **1** coming before all others in time or order <the much-studied *first*—and last—voyage of the *Titanic*>
synonyms earliest, inaugural, initial, maiden, original, pioneer, premier
related words ancient, early, primal, primary, primeval, primitive, primordial; antecedent, preceding, previous
near antonyms advanced, late; ensuing, following, subsequent, succeeding
antonyms final, last, terminal, ultimate
2 coming before all others in importance — see FOREMOST 1
3 highest in rank or authority — see HEAD

first *adv* **1** as a substitute — see INSTEAD
2 by choice or preference — see RATHER 1

first–class *adj* of the very best kind — see EXCELLENT

firsthand *adj* done or working without something else coming in between — see DIRECT 1

firstly *adv* in the beginning — see ORIGINALLY

first–rate *adj* of the very best kind — see EXCELLENT

firth *n* a part of a body of water that extends beyond the general shoreline — see GULF 1

fiscal *adj* of or relating to money, banking, or investments — see FINANCIAL

fish *vb* to search for something blindly or uncertainly — see GROPE

fishy *adj* giving good reason for being doubted, questioned, or challenged — see DOUBTFUL 2

fissure *n* an irregular usually narrow break in a surface created by pressure — see CRACK 1

fit *adj* **1** meeting the requirements of a purpose or situation <clothing that is *fit* for horseback riding>
synonyms applicable, appropriate, apt, becoming, befitting, felicitous, fitting, good, happy, meet, proper, right, suitable
related words just, justified, right; needed, required, requisite; able, capable, competent, qualified, trained; acceptable, adequate, decent, satisfactory, tolerable; correct, decorous, respectable, seemly
near antonyms incompetent, unqualified, untrained; inadequate, intolerable, unacceptable, unsatisfactory; incorrect, indecorous, unseemly
antonyms improper, inapplicable, inappropriate, inapt, infelicitous, unhappy, unsuitable, wrong
2 being in a state of fitness for some experience or action — see READY 1
3 capable of or suitable for being used for a particular purpose — see USABLE 1
4 enjoying health and vigor — see HEALTHY 1
5 having the required skills for an acceptable level of performance — see COMPETENT

fit *n* **1** a sudden experiencing of a physical or mental disorder — see ATTACK 2
2 a sudden intense expression of strong feeling — see OUTBURST 1
3 an outburst or display of excited anger — see TANTRUM

fit *vb* **1** to be fitting or proper — see DO 1
2 to be in agreement on every point — see CHECK 1
3 to change (something) so as to make it suitable for a new use or situation — see ADAPT
4 to make competent (as by training, skill, or ability) for a particular office or function — see QUALIFY 2
5 to make or have room for — see ACCOMMODATE 1
6 to make ready in advance — see PREPARE 1

fit (in *or* into) *vb* to put among or between others — see INSERT

fit (out) *vb* to provide (someone) with what is needed for a task or activity — see FURNISH 1

fitful *adj* lacking in steadiness or regularity of occurrence <a night of *fitful* sleep did not leave me feeling well rested the next morning>
synonyms casual, choppy, discontinuous, erratic, intermittent, irregular, occasional, spasmodic, sporadic, spotty, unsteady
related words convulsive, sudden, violent; broken, disconnected, fragmentary, interrupted; desultory, haphazard, hit-or-miss, random; changing, fluctuating, unstable, varying, wavering; changeable, fickle, variable
near antonyms equable, even, stable, uniform; unchanging, unvarying, unwavering; methodical, orderly, systematic
antonyms constant, continuous, regular, steady

fitness *n* **1** the condition of being sound in body — see HEALTH
2 the quality or state of being especially suitable or fitting — see APPROPRIATENESS

fitting *adj* meeting the requirements of a purpose or situation — see FIT 1

fittingly *adv* in a manner suitable for the occasion or purpose — see PROPERLY

fittingness *n* the quality or state of being especially suitable or fitting — see APPROPRIATENESS

fix *n* **1** a difficult, puzzling, or embarrassing situation from which there is no easy escape — see PREDICAMENT
2 something given or promised in order to improperly influence a person's conduct or decision — see BRIBE

fix *vb* **1** to arrange something in a certain spot or position — see PLACE 1
2 to cause (something) to hold to another — see FASTEN 1
3 to come to an agreement or decision concerning the details of — see ARRANGE 1
4 to decide upon (the time or date for an event) usually from a position of authority — see APPOINT 1
5 to make ready in advance — see PREPARE 1
6 to put into good shape or working order again — see MEND 1

7 to put securely in place or in a desired position — see FASTEN 2
8 to set solidly in or as if in surrounding matter — see ENTRENCH
fixable *adj* capable of being corrected — see REMEDIABLE
fixation *n* something about which one is constantly thinking or concerned <their weight is an unfortunate *fixation* for many teenagers>
synonyms fetish (*also* fetich), idée fixe, mania, obsession, preoccupation, prepossession
related words complex, hang-up, problem; compulsion, craving, enthusiasm, fascination, infatuation, passion; idiosyncrasy, quirk; penchant, predilection, proclivity
near antonyms apathy, indifference, unconcern
fixed *adj* **1** having been established and usually not subject to change <the baseball card dealer's prices were *fixed*, so bargaining was not an option>
synonyms certain, determinate, final, firm, flat, frozen, hard, hard-and-fast, set, settled, stable
related words nonadjustable, nonnegotiable, unchangeable; constant, steady, unchanging, uniform, unwavering; definite, exact, explicit, specific; stated, stipulated
near antonyms adjustable, changeable, negotiable; indefinite, unspecified
2 not capable of changing or being changed — see INFLEXIBLE 1
fixedness *n* the state of continuing without change — see CONSTANCY 1
fizz *n* a sound similar to the speech sound \s\ stretched out — see HISS 1
fizz *vb* to make a sound like that of stretching out the speech sound \s\ — see HISS
fizzle *n* **1** a falling short of one's goals — see FAILURE 2
2 something that has failed — see FAILURE 3
fjord *or* **fiord** *n* a part of a body of water that extends beyond the general shoreline — see GULF 1
flabbergast *vb* to make a strong impression on (someone) with something unexpected — see SURPRISE 1
flabbergasted *adj* **1** affected with sudden and great wonder or surprise — see THUNDERSTRUCK
2 filled with amazement or wonder — see OPENMOUTHED
flabbergasting *adj* causing a strong emotional reaction because unexpected — see SURPRISING 1
flabby *adj* giving easily to the touch — see SOFT 3
flaccid *adj* not stiff in structure — see LIMP 1
flag *n* **1** a piece of cloth with a special design that is used as an emblem or for signaling <the *flags* of both countries were prominently displayed at the treaty signing>
synonyms banner, colors, ensign, guidon, jack, pennant, pennon, standard, streamer
related words bunting; black flag, Jolly Roger, union jack, white flag; semaphore, signaler; badge, coat of arms, crest, insignia
2 an object intended to give public notice or warning — see SIGNAL 1
[1]**flag** *vb* **1** to be limp from lack of water or vigor — see DROOP
2 to lose bodily strength or vigor — see WEAKEN 2
[2]**flag** *vb* to direct or notify by a movement or gesture — see MOTION
flagellate *vb* to strike repeatedly with something long and thin or flexible — see WHIP 1
flagon *n* a handled container for holding and pouring liquids that usually has a lip or a spout — see PITCHER
flagrant *adj* very noticeable especially for being incorrect or bad — see EGREGIOUS
flail *vb* **1** to move or cause to move with a striking motion — see FLAP
2 to strike repeatedly with something long and thin or flexible — see WHIP 1
flair *n* a special and usually inborn ability — see TALENT
flake *n* a small flat piece separated from a whole — see CHIP 1
flaky *adj* having a texture that readily breaks into little pieces under pressure — see CRISP 1
flamboyance *n* excessive or unnecessary display — see OSTENTATION
flamboyant *adj* **1** likely to attract attention — see NOTICEABLE
2 excessively showy — see GAUDY
flamboyantly *adv* in a bright and showy way — see GAILY 3
flame *n* a person with whom one is in love — see SWEETHEART
flame *vb* **1** to be on fire especially brightly — see BURN 1
2 to develop suddenly and violently — see ERUPT 2
3 to shine with a bright harsh light — see GLARE 1
4 to shoot forth bursts of light — see FLASH 1
flaming *adj* **1** being on fire — see ABLAZE 1
2 having or expressing great depth of feeling — see FERVENT
flammable *adj* capable of catching or being set on fire — see COMBUSTIBLE
flank *n* a place, space, or direction away from or beyond a central point or line — see SIDE 1
flank *vb* to be adjacent to — see ADJOIN 1
flanking *adj* having a border in common — see ADJACENT
flap *vb* to move or cause to move with a striking motion <the stirring sight of a huge flock of geese *flapping* their wings>
synonyms beat, flail, flop, flutter, whip
related words bang, batter, buffet, knock, pound, smack, spank, thump; flick, flicker, flit; oscillate, sway, swing; undulate, wave; palpitate, pulse, throb
flapjack *n* a flat cake made from thin batter and cooked on both sides (as on a griddle) — see PANCAKE
flare *n* **1** a sudden and usually temporary growth of activity — see OUTBREAK
2 a sudden intense expression of strong feeling — see OUTBURST 1
3 the steady giving off of the form of radiation that makes vision possible — see LIGHT 1
flare *vb* to shine with a bright harsh light — see GLARE 1
flare (out) *vb* to arrange the parts of (something) over a wider area — see OPEN 3
flare (up) *vb* **1** to become very angry — see BLOW UP
2 to develop suddenly and violently — see ERUPT 2
flare–up *n* **1** a sudden and usually temporary growth of activity — see OUTBREAK
2 a sudden intense expression of strong feeling — see OUTBURST 1

flash *adj* lasting only for a short time — see MOMENTARY
flash *n* **1** a sudden and usually temporary growth of activity — see OUTBREAK
2 a sudden intense expression of strong feeling — see OUTBURST 1
3 a very small space of time — see INSTANT
4 something extraordinary or surprising — see WONDER 1
flash *vb* **1** to shoot forth bursts of light ⟨the actress's diamond necklace *flashed* as she hurried on stage to accept the award⟩
synonyms flame, glance, gleam, glimmer, glint, glisten, glister, glitter, scintillate, shimmer, sparkle, twinkle, wink
related words beam, radiate, shine; bedazzle, blind, daze, dazzle; blaze, burn, flare, glare, glow
2 to present so as to invite notice or attention — see SHOW 1
3 to shine with light at regular intervals — see BLINK 1
flashily *adv* in a bright and showy way — see GAILY 3
flashiness *n* excessive or unnecessary display — see OSTENTATION
flashy *adj* **1** attractively eye-catching in style — see JAZZY 1
2 excessively showy — see GAUDY
flat *adj* **1** being neither more nor less than a certain amount, number, or extent — see EVEN 1
2 causing weariness, restlessness, or lack of interest — see BORING
3 having a surface without bends, breaks, or irregularities — see LEVEL
4 having been established and usually not subject to change — see FIXED 1
5 having no exceptions or restrictions — see ABSOLUTE 2
6 lacking a surface luster or gloss — see MATTE
7 lacking in qualities that make for spirit and character — see WISHY-WASHY 1
8 lacking in taste or flavor — see INSIPID 1
flat *adv* to a full extent or degree — see FULLY 1
flat *n, chiefly British* a room or set of rooms in a private house or a block used as a separate dwelling place — see APARTMENT 1
flatten *vb* to make free from breaks, curves, or bumps — see EVEN 1
flatter *vb* **1** to praise too much ⟨the billionaire had an army of assistants who *flattered* him at every opportunity⟩
synonyms adulate, blarney, overpraise, soft-soap
related words blandish, cajole, coax, wheedle; fawn, kowtow, toady; idolize, worship; eulogize, extol (*also* extoll), laud, praise; applaud, commend, compliment; congratulate, felicitate; drool, gush, slaver, slobber; endear, ingratiate; court, woo
near antonyms bad-mouth, belittle, decry, depreciate, disparage, put down
2 to think highly of (oneself) — see PRIDE
flattery *n* excessive praise ⟨a talk show host who is known for charming her guests with *flattery*⟩
synonyms adulation, blarney, overpraise, soft soap
related words allurements, blandishments, endearments; compliments; congratulations, felicitations, greetings, regards, respects; adoration, idolatry, worship; cajolery, endearment, ingratiation; acclaim, applause, commendation, praise
near antonyms bad-mouthing, belittlement, depreciation, detraction, disparagement, put-down
flatware *n* eating and serving utensils — see TABLEWARE 1
flaunt *vb* to present so as to invite notice or attention — see SHOW 1
flaunting *n* an outward and often exaggerated indication of something abstract (as a feeling) for effect — see SHOW 1
flavor *n* **1** a special quality or impression associated with something — see AURA
2 something (as a spice or herb) that adds an agreeable or interesting taste to food — see SEASONING 1
3 the property of a substance that can be identified by the sense of taste — see TASTE 1
flavor *vb* to make more pleasant to the taste by adding something intensely flavored — see SEASON 1
flavorful *adj* very pleasing to the sense of taste — see DELICIOUS 1
flavoring *n* something (as a spice or herb) that adds an agreeable or interesting taste to food — see SEASONING 1
flavorless *adj* lacking in taste or flavor — see INSIPID 1
flaw *n* something that spoils the appearance or completeness of a thing — see BLEMISH
flaw *vb* to reduce the soundness, effectiveness, or perfection of — see DAMAGE 1
flawed *adj* having a fault — see FAULTY
flawless *adj* being entirely without fault or flaw — see PERFECT 1
flawlessly *adv* without any flaws or errors — see PERFECTLY 1
flaxen *adj* of a pale yellow or yellowish brown color — see BLOND
flay *vb* **1** to criticize (someone) severely or angrily especially for personal failings — see SCOLD
2 to remove the natural covering of — see PEEL
fleck *n* **1** a small area that is different (as in color) from the main part — see SPOT 1
2 a very small piece — see BIT 1
fleck *vb* to mark with small spots especially unevenly — see SPOT
flecked *adj* marked with spots — see SPOTTED 1
fledgling *n* a person who is just starting out in a field of activity — see BEGINNER
flee *vb* **1** to cease to be visible — see DISAPPEAR
2 to get free from a dangerous or confining situation — see ESCAPE 1
3 to hasten away from something dangerous or frightening — see RUN 2
fleece *n* the hairy covering of a mammal especially when fine, soft, and thick — see FUR 1
fleece *vb* to rob by the use of trickery or threats ⟨swindlers who use the telephone to *fleece* senior citizens out of their savings⟩
synonyms bleed, cheat, chisel, cozen, defraud, gyp, hustle, mulct, rook, shortchange, skin, squeeze, stick, sting, swindle, victimize
related words extort, wrench, wrest, wring; gouge, overcharge, soak; exploit, milk; deceive, dupe, fool, gull, trick; rope (in); betray, double-cross
fleecy *adj* covered with or as if with hair — see HAIRY 1
fleet *adj* moving, proceeding, or acting with great speed — see FAST 1
fleet *n* a group of vehicles traveling together or

under one management ⟨a *fleet* of buses rolling down the highway⟩
synonyms armada, caravan, cavalcade, line, motorcade, train
related words convoy, flotilla, navy; column, cortege (*also* cortège), parade, procession

fleet–footed *adj* moving, proceeding, or acting with great speed — see FAST 1

fleeting *adj* lasting only for a short time — see MOMENTARY

fleetly *adv* with great speed — see FAST 1

fleetness *n* a high rate of movement or performance — see SPEED

flesh *n* animal and especially mammal tissue used as food — see MEAT 1

fleshiness *n* **1** the condition of having an excess of body fat — see CORPULENCE
2 the quality or state of being full of juice — see SUCCULENCE

fleshly *adj* **1** having to do with life on earth especially as opposed to that in heaven — see EARTHLY
2 of or relating to the human body — see PHYSICAL 1
3 pleasing to the physical senses — see SENSUAL

fleshy *adj* **1** full of juice — see JUICY
2 having an excess of body fat — see FAT 1

flexible *adj* **1** capable of being readily changed ⟨fortunately, Mom has a very *flexible* schedule for her office job⟩
synonyms adaptable, adjustable, alterable, changeable, elastic, fluid, malleable, modifiable, variable
related words changing, fluctuating, inconstant, unstable, unsteady, varying
near antonyms constant, stable, steady, unchanging, uniform, unvarying
antonyms established, fixed, immutable, inelastic, inflexible, invariable, nonmalleable, ramrod, set, unalterable, unchangeable
2 not bound by rigid standards — see EASYGOING 2
3 able to bend easily without breaking — see WILLOWY
4 able to revert to original size and shape after being stretched, squeezed, or twisted — see ELASTIC 1

flick *vb* to make an irregular series of quick, sudden movements — see FLIT

flicker *n* a sudden and usually temporary growth of activity — see OUTBREAK

flicker *vb* to make an irregular series of quick, sudden movements — see FLIT

flickery *adj* likely to change frequently, suddenly, or unexpectedly — see FICKLE 1

flier *or* **flyer** *n* **1** a risky undertaking — see GAMBLE
2 one who flies or is qualified to fly an aircraft or spacecraft — see PILOT
3 a short printed publication with no cover or with a paper cover — see PAMPHLET

[1]**flight** *n* the act or an instance of getting free from danger or confinement — see ESCAPE 1

[2]**flight** *n* travel through the air by the use of wings ⟨for centuries people had been fascinated by the *flight* of birds⟩
synonyms flying
related words aviation; aeronautics; ballooning, gliding, skydiving, soaring

flightiness *n* **1** a lack of seriousness often at an improper time — see FRIVOLITY 1
2 a state of nervousness marked by sudden jerky movements — see JUMPINESS

flighty *adj* **1** easily excited by nature — see EXCITABLE
2 lacking in seriousness or maturity — see GIDDY 1

flimsy *adj* **1** being of a material lacking in sturdiness or substance ⟨a *flimsy* scarf that was more for decoration than for warmth⟩
synonyms filmy, gauzy, gossamer, gossamery, insubstantial, unsubstantial
related words dainty, delicate, fine; feeble, fragile, frail; sheer, transparent
near antonyms durable, lasting, tough; coarse, heavy, rough, rude
antonyms sturdy, substantial
2 not likely to be true or to occur — see IMPROBABLE

flinch *vb* to draw back in fear, pain, or disgust ⟨there are some patients who *flinch* at the mere sight of a needle⟩
synonyms blench, quail, recoil, shrink, wince
related words blanch, pale, whiten; quake, quiver, shake, shudder, tremble; crouch, squinch; jerk, start, twitch; recede, retire, retreat, withdraw; falter, hesitate, reel, waver
near antonyms advance, approach, near; confront, challenge, defy, face

fling *n* **1** a time or instance of carefree fun ⟨most families spend Labor Day weekend having one last summer *fling*⟩
synonyms binge, frolic, gambol, lark, revel, rollick, romp, spree
related words caper, escapade, prank; antic, monkeyshine(s), shenanigans; field day; festivity, merriment, merrymaking; enjoyment, indulgence, pleasure, self-indulgence; amusement, diversion, entertainment, recreation
2 an effort to do or accomplish something — see ATTEMPT

fling *vb* to send through the air especially with a quick forward motion of the arm — see THROW

fling (off *or* away) *vb* to get rid of as useless or unwanted — see DISCARD

flinty *adj* **1** given to exacting standards of discipline and self-restraint — see SEVERE 1
2 harsh and threatening in manner or appearance — see GRIM 1

flip *adj* making light of something usually regarded as serious or sacred — see FLIPPANT

flip *vb* **1** to become very angry — see BLOW UP
2 to change the position of (an object) so that the opposite side or end is showing — see REVERSE 2
3 to yield to mental or emotional stress — see CRACK 2

flippancy *n* a lack of seriousness often at an improper time — see FRIVOLITY 1

flippant *adj* making light of something usually regarded as serious or sacred ⟨his *flippant* comment that the poor save on taxes offended many people⟩
synonyms facetious, flip, pert, smart, smart-alecky (*or* smart-aleck)
related words flighty, frivolous; cheeky, cocky, cute, fresh, impertinent, impish, impudent, mischievous, playful, roguish, sassy, saucy, waggish; disrespectful, rude; breezy, casual, glib, inappropriate, thoughtless
near antonyms grave, serious, sober, solemn, somber (*or* sombre)
antonyms earnest, sincere

flirt *vb* to show a liking for someone of the opposite sex just for fun ⟨the servers at that restaurant *flirt* with all the customers⟩
synonyms dally, frivol, trifle
related words josh, kid, put on, razz, rib, tease; fool, lead on, string along; play (with), toy (with)

flit *vb* to make an irregular series of quick, sudden movements ⟨bargain hunters at the flea market *flitted* from table to table like hummingbirds in a garden⟩
synonyms dance, dart, flick, flicker, flutter, zip
related words dash, fly, sail, shoot, speed, sprint, zoom; scamper, scud, scurry, scuttle, skip, skitter; meander, ramble, roam, wander
near antonyms float, hang, hover

float *n* a structure used by boats and ships for taking on or landing cargo and passengers — see DOCK

float *vb* to rest or move along the surface of a liquid or in the air ⟨a canoe *floating* down the river⟩ ⟨particles of dust *floating* in the air⟩
synonyms drift, glide, hang, hover, poise, ride, sail, waft
related words bob, dangle, suspend; buoy; balloon, raft
near antonyms dive, lunge, plunge; dip, immerse, submerge, submerse
antonyms settle, sink

flock *n* **1** a great number of persons or things gathered together — see CROWD 1
2 a group of domestic animals assembled or herded together — see HERD

flock *vb* to move upon or fill (something) in great numbers — see CROWD 2

flog *vb* **1** to strike repeatedly with something long and thin or flexible — see WHIP 1
2 to strike repeatedly — see BEAT 1

flogger *n* a long thin or flexible tool for striking — see WHIP

flood *n* a great flow of water or of something that overwhelms ⟨a *flood* nearly wiped out the town⟩ ⟨a *flood* of messages on my computer⟩
synonyms cataclysm, cataract, deluge, flood tide, inundation, overflow, spate, torrent
related words current, river, stream, tide; discharge, flush, gush, outflow, outpouring; flux, inflow, influx; engulfment, washout; avalanche; cascade, waterfall; excess, glut, overabundance, overage, overkill, overmuch, oversupply, superabundance, superfluity, surfeit, surplus
near antonyms dribble, drip, trickle
antonyms drought

flood *vb* to cover or become filled with a flood ⟨the lowlands were completely *flooded*⟩ ⟨angry calls *flooded* the radio station⟩
synonyms deluge, drown, engulf, inundate, overflow, overwhelm, submerge, submerse, swamp
related words overcome, overrun; flow, flush, gush, pour, sluice, spout, spurt, stream; douse, drench, soak, wet
near antonyms dehydrate, dry, parch
antonyms drain

flood tide *n* a great flow of water or of something that overwhelms — see FLOOD

floor *n* the surface upon which a body of water lies — see BOTTOM 2

floor *vb* **1** to cause an often unpleasant surprise for — see SHOCK 1
2 to make a strong impression on (someone) with something unexpected — see SURPRISE 1
3 to strike (someone) so forcefully as to cause a fall — see FELL 1
4 to subject to incapacitating emotional or mental stress — see OVERWHELM 1

flop *n* something that has failed — see FAILURE 3

flop *vb* **1** to throw or set down clumsily or casually ⟨they *flopped* themselves onto the couch to watch the game⟩ ⟨*flopped* the bag of groceries onto the counter⟩
synonyms plop, plump, plunk
related words fling, heave, sling, toss; ensconce, install, plant, settle
2 to be unsuccessful — see FAIL 2
3 to move or cause to move with a striking motion — see FLAP

floppy *adj* not stiff in structure — see LIMP 1

flora *n* green leaves or plants — see GREENERY 1

floral *adj* of or relating to flowers ⟨wallpaper with a *floral* pattern for the bedroom⟩
synonyms flowered, flowery
related words florid; abloom

florid *adj* **1** elaborately and often excessively decorated — see ORNATE
2 full of fine words and fancy expressions — see FLOWERY 1
3 having a healthy reddish skin tone — see RUDDY

floss *n* a soft airy substance or covering — see FUZZ

flounce *n* a strip of fabric gathered or pleated on one edge and used as trimming — see RUFFLE

flounder *vb* **1** to make progress in a clumsy, struggling manner ⟨unprepared choristers who *floundered* helplessly through the musical number⟩
synonyms limp, lumber, plod, stumble, trudge
related words shamble, shuffle; wallow, welter; falter, lurch, reel, stagger, sway, teeter, totter; blunder, fumble, muddle
near antonyms coast, fly, glide, sail, zip, zoom
2 to move heavily or clumsily — see LUMBER 1

flourish *vb* **1** to grow vigorously — see THRIVE 1
2 to reach a desired level of accomplishment — see SUCCEED 2

flourishing *adj* **1** having attained a desired end or state of good fortune — see SUCCESSFUL 1
2 marked by much life, movement, or activity — see ALIVE 2
3 marked by vigorous growth and well-being especially economically — see PROSPEROUS 1

floury *adj* consisting of very small particles — see FINE 1

flout *vb* to ignore in a disrespectful manner — see SCORN 2

flow *vb* **1** to move in a stream ⟨water was *flowing* over the dam at a tremendous rate⟩
synonyms pour, roll, run, stream
related words arise, emanate, issue, spring; course, race, rush; gush, spout, spurt; deluge, engulf, flood, inundate, overflow, swamp; cascade, dribble, drip, gutter, riffle, ripple, trickle; flush, wash out
near antonyms clot, coagulate, congeal, gel, harden, set
antonyms back up
2 to move or proceed smoothly and readily ⟨as everyone relaxed, the conversation really started to *flow*⟩
synonyms bowl, breeze, coast, drift, glide, roll, sail, skim, slide, slip, stream, sweep, whisk

related words fly, race, rush, speed
near antonyms limp, lumber, plod, stumble, trudge; shamble, shuffle; stamp, stomp, stump, tramp; labor, toil
antonyms flounder, struggle

flower *n* **1** the usually showy plant part that produces seeds ⟨*flowers* are always a thoughtful gift⟩
synonyms bloom, blossom
related words bud, floret; bouquet, nosegay, posy; arrangement, boutonniere, corsage, garland, lei, spray, wreath
2 a state or time of great activity, thriving, or achievement — see BLOOM 1
3 individuals carefully selected as being the best of a class — see ELITE

flower *vb* to produce flowers — see BLOOM

flowered *adj* of or relating to flowers — see FLORAL

flowery *adj* **1** full of fine words and fancy expressions ⟨the *flowery* verses that always appear on valentines⟩
synonyms florid, grandiloquent, highfalutin, high-flown, high-sounding
related words affected, grandiose, inflated, pompous, pretentious, stilted; excessive, flattering, fulsome; boastful, bombastic; elevated, eloquent, lofty
near antonyms prosaic, unpoetic; bald, direct, matter-of-fact, plain, plainspoken, simple, stark, straightforward, unadorned; natural, unaffected, unpretentious
2 of or relating to flowers — see FLORAL

flowing *adj* capable of moving like a liquid — see FLUID 1

flub *n* an unintentional departure from truth or accuracy — see ERROR 1

flub *vb* to make or do (something) in a clumsy or unskillful way — see BOTCH

fluctuate *vb* to pass from one form, state, or level to another — see CHANGE 2

fluctuating *adj* **1** likely to change frequently, suddenly, or unexpectedly — see FICKLE 1
2 not staying constant — see UNEVEN 2

fluent *adj* **1** able to express oneself clearly and well — see ARTICULATE
2 capable of moving like a liquid — see FLUID 1
3 involving minimal difficulty or effort — see EASY 1

fluently *adv* without difficulty — see EASILY

fluff *n* a soft airy substance or covering — see FUZZ

fluffy *adj* resembling air in lightness — see AIRY 1

fluid *adj* **1** capable of moving like a liquid ⟨warm the jam until it is *fluid*, then spread it over the cake⟩
synonyms flowing, fluent, liquid
related words diluted, thin, watery, weak
near antonyms clotted, coagulated, gelatinous, gelled, jelled, jellied, thick; gluey, glutinous, gooey, gummy, viscous
antonyms hard, solid
2 capable of being readily changed — see FLEXIBLE 1
3 involving minimal difficulty or effort — see EASY 1
4 likely to change frequently, suddenly, or unexpectedly — see FICKLE 1

fluky *adj* **1** coming or happening by good luck especially unexpectedly — see FORTUNATE 1
2 happening by chance — see ACCIDENTAL

flume *n* **1** a narrow opening between hillsides or mountains that can be used for passage — see CANYON
2 an open man-made passageway for water — see CHANNEL 1

flunk *vb* to be unsuccessful — see FAIL 2

flunky *also* **flunkey** *n* **1** a person hired to perform household or personal services — see SERVANT
2 a person who flatters another in order to get ahead — see SYCOPHANT

fluorescence *n* the steady giving off of the form of radiation that makes vision possible — see LIGHT 1

flurry *n* **1** a sudden and usually temporary growth of activity — see OUTBREAK
2 a sudden brief rush of wind — see GUST 1

flush *adj* **1** having a healthy reddish skin tone — see RUDDY
2 having a surface without bends, breaks, or irregularities — see LEVEL
3 having active strength of body or mind — see VIGOROUS 1
4 having goods, property, or money in abundance — see RICH 1
5 possessing or covered with great numbers or amounts of something specified — see RIFE

flush *n* **1** a rosy appearance of the cheeks — see BLOOM 2
2 a state or time of great activity, thriving, or achievement — see BLOOM 1
3 a sudden intense expression of strong feeling — see OUTBURST 1

flush *vb* **1** to pour liquid over or through in order to cleanse ⟨use this cleaner to *flush* the drain in the sink⟩
synonyms irrigate, rinse, sluice, wash
related words deluge, engulf, flood, inundate, swamp; flow, gush, rush, stream; douche, hose; drench, saturate, soak; douse, slosh, splash
2 to develop a rosy facial color (as from excitement or embarrassment) — see BLUSH

fluster *n* **1** a state of nervous or irritated concern — see FRET
2 the emotional state of being made self-consciously uncomfortable — see EMBARRASSMENT 1

fluster *vb* to throw into a state of self-conscious distress — see EMBARRASS 1

flustering *adj* causing embarrassment — see AWKWARD 3

flutter *n* a sudden and usually temporary growth of activity — see OUTBREAK

flutter *vb* **1** to make an irregular series of quick, sudden movements — see FLIT
2 to move or cause to move with a striking motion — see FLAP

fluttery *adj* easily excited by nature — see EXCITABLE

flux *n* a flowing or coming in — see INFLUX

flux *vb* to go from a solid to a liquid state — see LIQUEFY

fly *vb* **1** to move through the air with or as if with outstretched wings ⟨the Wright brothers realized mankind's age-old wish to *fly*⟩
synonyms glide, plane, soar, wing
related words drift, float, hang, hover, waft; coast, cruise, sail, sweep; dart, flit, flutter; catapult, jet, orbit, rocket
2 to get free from a dangerous or confining situation — see ESCAPE 1
3 to proceed or move quickly — see HURRY 2

4 to hasten away from something dangerous or frightening — see RUN 2

flying *adj* **1** acting or done with excessive or careless speed — see HASTY 1
2 moving, proceeding, or acting with great speed — see FAST 1

flying *n* travel through the air by the use of wings — see [1]FLIGHT

flyspeck *n* a very small piece — see BIT 1

foam *n* a light mass of fine bubbles formed in or on a liquid ⟨a steaming cup of hot cocoa with a sprinkling of marshmallows drifting through the *foam*⟩
synonyms froth, head, lather, spume, suds, surf
related words mousse; mist, spindrift, spray; scum

foaming *adj* feeling or showing anger — see ANGRY

foamy *adj* covered with, consisting of, or resembling foam ⟨*foamy* milk shakes⟩
synonyms frothy, lathery, sudsy
related words bubbly, effervescent, fizzy, sparkling; soapy

focus *n* a thing or place that is of greatest importance to an activity or interest — see CENTER 1

focus *vb* to fix (as one's attention) steadily toward a central objective — see CONCENTRATE 2

focused *also* **focussed** *adj* **1** having the mind fixed on something — see ATTENTIVE
2 not divided or scattered among several areas of interest or concern — see WHOLE 1

foe *n* one that is hostile toward another — see ENEMY

fog *n* **1** a state of mental confusion — see HAZE 2
2 an atmospheric condition in which suspended particles in the air rob it of its transparency — see HAZE 1

fog *vb* **1** to make (something) unclear to the understanding — see CONFUSE 2
2 to make dark, dim, or indistinct — see CLOUD 1

foggy *adj* **1** filled with or dimmed by fine particles (as of dust or water) in suspension — see HAZY 1
2 not seen or understood clearly — see FAINT 1

fogy *also* **fogey** *n* a person with old-fashioned ideas ⟨old *fogies* who said that rap music would never last⟩
synonyms antediluvian, dodo, fossil, fuddy-duddy, reactionary, stick-in-the-mud
related words conservative, rightist, tory; old hand, old-timer, veteran; old maid
near antonyms liberal, progressive, radical
antonyms modern

foible *n* a defect in character — see FAULT 1

foil *vb* to prevent from achieving a goal — see FRUSTRATE

foist *vb* to offer (something fake, useless, or inferior) as genuine, useful, or valuable ⟨shopkeepers who *foist* shoddy souvenirs on unsuspecting tourists⟩
synonyms palm off, pass off
related words force, impose, inflict; counterfeit, fake, forge; distort, falsify, misrepresent

fold *n* a group of people sharing a common interest and relating together socially — see GANG 2

fold *vb* **1** to lay one part over or against another part of ⟨*fold* the blanket so that it will fit inside the trunk⟩
synonyms double
related words overlap, overlay, overlie; collapse, telescope; close, shut
antonyms extend, open, spread, unfold
2 to be unsuccessful — see FAIL 2

folder *n* a short printed publication with no cover or with a paper cover — see PAMPHLET

foliage *n* green leaves or plants — see GREENERY 1

folk *n* **1 folks** *pl* a group of persons who come from the same ancestor — see FAMILY 1
2 one of the segments of society into which people are grouped — see CLASS 1
3 folks *pl* human beings in general — see PEOPLE 1

folklore *n* the body of customs, beliefs, stories, and sayings associated with a people, thing, or place ⟨the Scottish Highlands are rich in *folklore*⟩
synonyms legend, lore, myth, mythology, tradition
related words information, knowledge, wisdom; anecdote, fable, folktale, old wives' tale, tale, yarn

follow *vb* **1** to come after in time ⟨a wrap-up always *follows* the Super Bowl broadcast⟩
synonyms postdate, succeed, supervene
related words displace, replace, supersede, supplant; ensue
antonyms antedate, precede, predate
2 to go after or on the track of ⟨let's *follow* the boys to their hiding place⟩
synonyms chase, dog, hound, pursue, shadow, tag, tail, trace, track, trail
related words accompany, chaperone (*or* chaperon), escort; hunt, search (for), seek; eye, observe, watch
near antonyms head
antonyms guide, lead, pilot
3 to act according to the commands of — see OBEY
4 to make one's way through, across, or over — see TRAVERSE
5 to take notice of and be guided by — see HEED 1

follower *n* one who follows the opinions or teachings of another ⟨the *followers* of Gandhi have spread his philosophy of nonviolence all over the world⟩
synonyms adherent, convert, disciple, partisan, pupil, votary
related words apostle; faithful, loyalist; advocate, backer, champion, supporter; scholar, student; ideologist, sectarian; admirer, cultist, devotee, enthusiast, fan, idolater (*or* idolator), worshipper (*or* worshiper), zealot; flunky (*also* flunkey), hanger-on, henchman, lackey, satellite, stooge, sycophant, toady, yes-man
near antonyms apostate, defector, renegade, traitor, turncoat
antonyms leader

following *prep* subsequent to in time or order — see AFTER

following *adj* being the one that comes immediately after another — see NEXT

following *n* **1** a body of employees or servants who accompany and wait on a person — see CORTEGE 1
2 a group of people showing intense devotion to a cause, person, or work (as a film) — see CULT 1
3 the act of going after or in the tracks of another — see PURSUIT

follow through *vb* to carry through (as a process) to completion — see PERFORM 1

folly *n* **1** a foolish act or idea ⟨the American purchase of Alaska was originally considered a grand *folly*⟩

synonyms absurdity, asininity, fatuity, foolery, idiocy, imbecility, inanity, insanity, lunacy, stupidity
related words absurdness, craziness, foolishness, madness, senselessness, witlessness; monkeyshine(s), shenanigans, tomfoolery; drivel, humbug, nonsense, twaddle; blunder, bungle, flub, goof, howler
near antonyms discretion, forethought, prudence, sagacity, wisdom; brainstorm, inspiration
2 lack of good sense or judgment — see FOOLISHNESS 1
3 language, behavior, or ideas that are absurd and contrary to good sense — see NONSENSE 1

foment *vb* to cause or encourage the development of — see INCITE 1

fomenter *n* a person who stirs up public feelings especially of discontent — see AGITATOR

fond *adj* **1** having a liking or affection <even lots of city people are *fond* of country music>
synonyms attached, inclined, partial
related words crazy (about *or* over), enamored, enraptured, gone (on), infatuated, mad (about), nuts (about); desirous, eager, enthusiastic, excited, gung ho, keen
near antonyms apathetic, cool, indifferent, uninterested; contemptuous, disdainful, scornful; antagonistic, antipathetic, hostile; alienated, disaffected, disenchanted, estranged
antonyms allergic, averse, disinclined
2 feeling or showing love — see LOVING

fondle *vb* to touch or handle in a tender or loving manner <a cat who enjoys being *fondled* by his loving owners>
synonyms caress, love, pat, pet, stroke
related words cuddle, nestle, nose, nuzzle, snuggle; cradle, embrace, enfold, hug; bounce, dandle; knead, massage; baby, coddle, indulge, mollycoddle, pamper, spoil

fondness *n* **1** a feeling of strong or constant regard for and dedication to someone — see LOVE 1
2 positive regard for something — see LIKING

food *n* substances intended to be eaten <a simple, little restaurant with excellent *food*>
synonyms bread, chow, eatables, edibles, fare, foodstuffs, grub, meat, provender, provisions, table, viands, victuals, vittles
related words rations; aliment, nutriment; diet, nurture, sustenance; mess, pap; feed, fodder, forage, slop, swill; feast, meal, refreshments, repast, spread; board; dish, plate, serving
near antonyms poison

foodstuffs *n pl* substances intended to be eaten — see FOOD

fool *n* **1** a person who lacks good sense or judgment <only a *fool* would attempt to climb that mountain unprepared>
synonyms booby, goose, half-wit, jackass, lunatic, nincompoop, ninny, nitwit, nut, simpleton, turkey, yo-yo
related words daredevil; madman, madwoman; blockhead, cretin, dodo, dolt, dope, dumbbell, dummy, dunce, idiot, imbecile, moron; featherbrain, scatterbrain; butt, dupe, laughingstock, mockery, monkey; chump, loser, schlemiel
near antonyms sage, thinker; brain, genius
2 a person formerly kept in a royal or noble household to amuse with jests and pranks <a king's *fool* could get away with saying things that others in the palace couldn't>
synonyms jester, motley
related words buffoon, clown, comedian, comedienne, comic, cutup, harlequin, zany

fool *vb* **1** to cause to believe what is untrue — see DECEIVE
2 to make jokes — see JOKE

fool (around) *vb* **1** to engage in attention-getting playful or boisterous behavior — see CUT UP
2 to spend time in aimless activity — see FIDDLE (AROUND)

fool (with) *vb* to handle thoughtlessly, ignorantly, or mischievously — see TAMPER

foolery *n* **1** a foolish act or idea — see FOLLY 1
2 wildly playful or mischievous behavior — see HORSEPLAY

foolhardy *adj* **1** foolishly adventurous or bold <hikers who were *foolhardy* enough to remain on the summit during a thunderstorm>
synonyms brash, daredevil, madcap, overbold, overconfident, reckless
related words adventuresome, adventurous, audacious, bold, daring, venturesome, venturous; brave, courageous, dauntless, fearless, intrepid, lionhearted, stouthearted, undaunted, valiant; hotheaded; impetuous, impulsive, rash; brainless, foolish, harebrained, scatterbrained; careless, heedless, thoughtless; hasty, headlong, precipitate
near antonyms unadventurous, unambitious; fainthearted, timid, timorous; calm, cool, levelheaded, sensible; alert, intelligent, quick-witted, sharp
antonyms careful, cautious, heedful, prudent
2 having or showing a lack of concern for the consequences of one's actions — see RECKLESS 1

fooling *adj* marked by or expressive of mild or good-natured teasing — see QUIZZICAL

foolish *adj* **1** showing or marked by a lack of good sense or judgment <*foolish* people who thought that the world would end in the year 2000> <a *foolish* scheme that was supposed to make us all rich>
synonyms absurd, asinine, balmy, brainless, cockeyed, crazy, cuckoo, daffy, daft, dotty, fatuous, harebrained, half-witted, insane, jerky, kooky, loony (*also* looney), lunatic, mad, nonsensical, nutty, preposterous, sappy, screwball, senseless, silly, simpleminded, stupid, unwise, wacky, weak-minded, witless, zany
related words dumb, idiotic, imbecilic, moronic; fallacious, illogical, invalid, irrational, unreasonable; farcical, laughable, ludicrous, ridiculous
near antonyms brainy, bright, clever, intelligent, smart; logical, rational, reasonable, valid
antonyms judicious, prudent, sage, sane, sapient, sensible, sound, wise
2 conceived or made without regard for reason or reality — see FANTASTIC 1

foolishness *n* **1** lack of good sense or judgment <the *foolishness* of going off to search for the fountain of youth>
synonyms absurdity, asininity, balminess, brainlessness, craziness, daftness, fatuity, folly, inanity, insanity, lunacy, madness, nonsensicalness, nuttiness, preposterousness, senselessness, silliness, simplicity, wackiness, witlessness, zaniness
related words idiocy, imbecility, stupidity; fallacy, irrationality, unreasonableness; laughableness, ludicrousness, ridiculousness
near antonyms logicalness, rationality, reasonableness, validity
antonyms prudence, sageness, sanity, sapience, sensibleness, soundness, wisdom

2 language, behavior, or ideas that are absurd and contrary to good sense — see NONSENSE 1
3 the quality or state of lacking intelligence or quickness of mind — see STUPIDITY 1
foot *n* the lowest part, place, or point — see BOTTOM 3
foot *vb* to give what is owed for — see PAY 2
foot (it) *vb* **1** to go on foot — see WALK
2 to perform a series of usually rhythmic bodily movements to music — see DANCE 1
foot (up) *vb* to combine (numbers) into a single sum — see ADD 2
foothold *n* a place from which an advance (as for military operations) is made — see BASE 2
footing *n* **1** an immaterial thing upon which something else rests — see BASE 1
2 position with regard to conditions and circumstances — see SITUATION 1
3 the placement of someone or something in relation to others in a vertical arrangement — see RANK 1
footloose *adj* **1** not bound, confined, or detained by force — see FREE 3
2 not held back by rules, duties, or worries — see FREEWHEELING
footpath *n* a rough course or way formed by or as if by repeated footsteps — see TRAIL 1
footprint *n* the mark or impression made by a foot <mysterious *footprints* along the beach>
synonyms footstep, step
related words hoofprint; spoor, track; sign, trace, vestige
footstep *n* the mark or impression made by a foot — see FOOTPRINT
foozle *vb* to make or do (something) in a clumsy or unskillful way — see BOTCH
fop *n* a man extremely interested in his clothing and personal appearance — see DANDY 1
for *conj* for the reason that — see SINCE
forage *vb* to feed on grass or herbs — see [1]GRAZE
forage (for) *vb* to go in search of — see SEEK 1
foray *n* a sudden attack on and entrance into hostile territory — see RAID 1
foray (into) *vb* to enter for conquest or plunder — see INVADE
forbear *vb* to resist the temptation of <she's old enough to make her own decisions, so we must *forbear* criticizing her taste in clothes>
synonyms abstain (from), forgo (*also* forego), keep (from), refrain (from)
related words avoid, eschew, shun; check, constrain, curb, inhibit; deny, refuse, withhold; buck, combat, fight
near antonyms capitulate, knuckle under, submit, surrender
antonyms give in (to), succumb (to), yield (to)
forbearance *n* the capacity to endure what is difficult or disagreeable without complaining — see PATIENCE
forbearing *adj* accepting pains or hardships calmly or without complaint — see PATIENT 1
forbid *vb* to order not to do or use or to be done or used <smoking is *forbidden* throughout the building> <we *forbid* you to see him>
synonyms ban, bar, enjoin, interdict, outlaw, prohibit, proscribe
related words deter, discourage, dissuade; repress, suppress; halt, preclude, prevent, stop; embargo, exclude, rule out, shut out; debar, deprive, disallow, reject, veto; check, curb, inhibit, restrain; block, hinder, impede, obstruct
near antonyms approve, endorse (*also* indorse), sanction; authorize, license (*also* licence); abet, encourage, promote, support; bid, command, order; abide, bear, endure, tolerate
antonyms allow, let, permit, suffer
forbidden *adj* that may not be permitted — see IMPERMISSIBLE
forbidding *adj* **1** causing fear — see FEARFUL 1
2 harsh and threatening in manner or appearance — see GRIM 1
forbidding *n* the act of ordering that something not be done or used — see PROHIBITION 1
force *n* **1** a body of persons at work or available for work <the nation's labor *force*>
synonyms help, manpower, personnel, pool, staff
related words labor, proletariat, rank and file; band, company, crew, gang, outfit, party, team; employee, helper, hireling, worker
2 the use of power to impose one's will on another <a cruel tyrant who disbanded the parliament and ruled by *force*>
synonyms coercion, compulsion, constraint, duress, pressure
related words browbeating, bulldozing, bullying; fear, intimidation, menace, sword, terror, terrorism, threat, violence; might, muscle, strength; hardheadedness, self-will, willfulness; strain, stress
near antonyms agreement, approval, consent, permission; persuasion, reason
3 the ability to exert effort for the accomplishment of a task — see POWER 2
4 the capacity to persuade — see COGENCY 1
5 the quality of an utterance that provokes interest and produces an effect — see [1]PUNCH 1
6 the use of brute strength to cause harm to a person or property — see VIOLENCE
force *vb* to cause (a person) to give in to pressure <*forced* the natives to sell their land> <hunger *forced* the refugees to steal>
synonyms coerce, compel, constrain, drive, make, muscle, obligate, oblige, press, pressure
related words browbeat, bulldoze, bully; high-pressure, intimidate, menace, terrorize, threaten
near antonyms allow, let, permit; convince, induce, persuade
forced *adj* **1** forcing one's compliance or participation by or as if by law — see MANDATORY
2 lacking in natural or spontaneous quality — see ARTIFICIAL 1
3 not made or done willingly or by choice — see INVOLUNTARY 1
forceful *adj* **1** having the power to persuade — see COGENT
2 marked by or uttered with forcefulness — see EMPHATIC 1
3 not showing weakness or uncertainty — see FIRM 1
4 having power over the minds or behavior of others — see INFLUENTIAL 1
forcefully *adv* in a vigorous and forceful manner — see HARD 3
forcefulness *n* **1** the capacity to persuade — see COGENCY 1
2 the quality of an utterance that provokes interest and produces an effect — see [1]PUNCH 1
3 the quality or state of being forceful (as in expression) — see VEHEMENCE 1

forcibly *adv* in a vigorous and forceful manner — see HARD 3
ford *n* a place where a body of water (as a sea or river) is shallow — see SHOAL
forearm *vb* to prepare (oneself) mentally or emotionally — see FORTIFY 1
forebear *also* **forbear** *n* a person who is several generations earlier in an individual's line of descent — see ANCESTOR 1
forebode *also* **forbode** *vb* to show signs of a favorable or successful outcome — see BODE
foreboding *adj* being or showing a sign of evil or calamity to come — see OMINOUS
foreboding *n* **1** a feeling that something bad will happen — see PREMONITION
2 something believed to be a sign or warning of a future event — see OMEN
3 suspicion or fear of future harm or misfortune — see APPREHENSION 1
forecast *n* a declaration that something will happen in the future — see PREDICTION
forecast *vb* to tell of or describe beforehand — see FORETELL
forecaster *n* one who predicts future events or developments — see PROPHET
forecasting *n* a declaration that something will happen in the future — see PREDICTION
foredoom *vb* to determine the fate of in advance — see DESTINE
forefather *n* a person who is several generations earlier in an individual's line of descent — see ANCESTOR 1
forefront *n* the leading or most important part of a movement ⟨a politician who was in the *forefront* of women's rights⟩
synonyms vanguard
related words spearhead
near antonyms rank and file
forego *vb* to go or come before in time — see PRECEDE
foregoer *n* **1** one that announces or indicates the later arrival of another — see FORERUNNER 1
2 something belonging to an earlier time from which something else was later developed — see ANCESTOR 2
foregoing *adj* going before another in time or order — see PREVIOUS
forehanded *adj* having or showing awareness of and preparation for the future — see FORESIGHTED
foreign *adj* **1** being, relating to, or characteristic of a country other than one's own ⟨more Americans should take an interest in *foreign* languages⟩
synonyms alien, nonnative
related words imported, introduced, naturalized, transplanted; international, multicultural, multinational; distant, far-off, overseas, remote; bizarre, exotic, outlandish, strange
near antonyms endemic, local; aboriginal, indigenous
antonyms domestic, native
2 not being a vital part of or belonging to something — see EXTRINSIC
foreigner *n* a person who is not native to or known to a community — see STRANGER
foreknow *vb* to realize or know about beforehand — see FORESEE
foreknowledge *n* the special ability to see or know about events before they actually occur — see FORESIGHT 1
foreman *n* the person (as an employer or supervisor) who tells people and especially workers what to do — see BOSS
foremost *adj* **1** coming before all others in importance ⟨Albert Einstein is regarded by many as the *foremost* figure of the 20th century⟩
synonyms arch, cardinal, central, chief, dominant, first, grand, greatest, highest, key, leading, main, paramount, predominant, preeminent, premier, primary, principal, sovereign, supreme
related words distinguished, eminent, notable, noteworthy, illustrious, outstanding, prestigious, stellar, superior; important, major, momentous, significant; incomparable, matchless, unequaled (*or* unequalled), unparalleled, unsurpassed
near antonyms inconsequential, insignificant, minor, trivial, unimportant; collateral, inferior, secondary, subordinate, subsidiary
antonyms last, least
2 highest in rank or authority — see HEAD
forename *n* a name that is placed before one's family name ⟨a long string of *forenames* was given to the latest addition to the royal family⟩
synonyms Christian name, given name
related words appellation, denomination, designation; epithet, handle, nickname, sobriquet (*also* soubriquet); alias, nom de plume, pen name, pseudonym
forenoon *n* the time from sunrise until noon — see MORNING 1
foreordain *vb* to determine the fate of in advance — see DESTINE
forepart *n* a forward part or surface — see FRONT 1
forerunner *n* **1** one that announces or indicates the later arrival of another ⟨the return of the swallows is traditionally regarded as a *forerunner* of spring⟩
synonyms angel, foregoer, harbinger, herald, precursor
related words foreboder, foreshadower, foretaste, forewarning; advertiser, announcer, crier, proclaimer; courier, messenger, runner; augury, omen, portent, presage; mark, sign, symptom; bellwether
2 something belonging to an earlier time from which something else was later developed — see ANCESTOR 2
foresee *vb* to realize or know about beforehand ⟨a freak accident that no one could possibly have *foreseen*⟩
synonyms anticipate, divine, foreknow
related words augur, forecast, foretell, presage, prognosticate, prophesy; envisage, foreshadow, prefigure, visualize; forewarn; preview; descry, discern, perceive; apprehend, dread, fear
foreseeing *adj* having or showing awareness of and preparation for the future — see FORESIGHTED
foreseer *n* one who predicts future events or developments — see PROPHET
foreshadow *vb* to give a slight indication of beforehand ⟨a series of small tremors that *foreshadowed* the massive earthquake the next day⟩
synonyms prefigure
related words anticipate, foreknow, foresee; forecast, foretell, predict, prognosticate, prophesy; forewarn; augur, bode, forebode (*also* forbode), portend, presage, promise; connote, hint, imply, insinuate, intimate, suggest
foreshadowing *n* something believed to be a sign or warning of a future event — see OMEN

foresight *n* **1** the special ability to see or know about events before they actually occur ⟨a mysterious woman who claims to have the gift of *foresight*⟩
synonyms foreknowledge, prescience
related words premonition, presentiment; clairvoyance, extrasensory perception, sixth sense; omniscience; divination
2 concern or preparation for the future ⟨had the *foresight* to realize the global importance of the Internet⟩
synonyms farsightedness, foresightedness, forethought, prescience, providence
related words precaution, premeditation; discretion, insight, prudence, sagacity, wisdom
near antonyms hindsight
antonyms improvidence, shortsightedness

foresighted *adj* having or showing awareness of and preparation for the future ⟨the *foresighted* conservationists who worked to create the national park system⟩
synonyms farsighted, forehanded, foreseeing, forethoughtful, prescient, provident
related words careful, cautious; insightful, perceptive, prudent, sage, wise
near antonyms careless, heedless, incautious
antonyms improvident, shortsighted

foresightedness *n* concern or preparation for the future — see FORESIGHT 2

forest *n* a dense growth of trees and shrubs covering a large area ⟨the endless *forest* that the first European settlers encountered⟩
synonyms timber, timberland, wood(s), woodland
related words coppice, copse, grove, scrubland, stand, thicket; greenwood, wildwood; woodlot

forestall *vb* to keep from happening by taking action in advance — see PREVENT

forestallment *n* the act or practice of keeping something from happening — see PREVENTION

foretell *vb* to tell of or describe beforehand ⟨a 16th century astrologer who, some claim, accurately *foretold* 20th century events⟩
synonyms augur, forecast, predict, presage, prognosticate, prophesy
related words forewarn; bode, forebode (*also* forbode), portend; anticipate, divine, foreknow, foresee; announce, declare, proclaim
near antonyms recount, relate, report

foreteller *n* one who predicts future events or developments — see PROPHET

foretelling *n* a declaration that something will happen in the future — see PREDICTION

forethought *n* concern or preparation for the future — see FORESIGHT 2

forethoughtful *adj* having or showing awareness of and preparation for the future — see FORESIGHTED

forever *adv* **1** for all time — see EVER 1
2 on every relevant occasion — see ALWAYS 1

forevermore *adv* for all time — see EVER 1

forewarn *vb* to give notice to beforehand especially of danger or risk — see WARN

forewarning *n* the act or an instance of telling beforehand of danger or risk — see WARNING 1

foreword *n* a short section (as of a book) that leads to or explains the main part — see INTRODUCTION

forfeit *n* a sum of money to be paid as a punishment — see FINE

forfeiture *n* a sum of money to be paid as a punishment — see FINE

forgather *or* **foregather** *vb* to come together into one body or place — see ASSEMBLE 1

[1]**forge** *vb* **1** to imitate or copy especially in order to deceive — see FAKE 1
2 to produce or bring about especially by long or repeated effort — see HAMMER (OUT)
3 to shape with a hammer — see HAMMER 1

[2]**forge** *vb* to move forward along a course — see GO 1

forged *adj* being such in appearance only and made or manufactured with the intention of committing fraud — see COUNTERFEIT

forgery *n* an imitation that is passed off as genuine — see FAKE 1

forget *vb* **1** to be unable to recall or think of ⟨I *forget* exactly on which street that the house is⟩
synonyms unlearn
related words lose, miss; blank; disregard, ignore, neglect, overlook
near antonyms reminisce; remind
antonyms mind [*chiefly dialect*], recall, recollect, remember
2 to fail to give proper attention to — see NEGLECT 1
3 to leave undone or unattended to especially through carelessness — see NEGLECT 2
4 to miss the opportunity or obligation — see NEGLECT 3

forgetful *adj* inclined to forget what one has learned or to do what one should ⟨we become more *forgetful* as we get older⟩
synonyms absentminded
related words absent, abstracted, lost, oblivious, preoccupied, unmindful; amnesiac, senile; lax, neglectful, negligent, remiss, slack; careless, heedless, inconsiderate, thoughtless
near antonyms alert, keen, sharp; careful, conscientious, heedful, thoughtful
antonyms retentive

forgetfulness *n* a state of being disregardful or unconscious of one's surroundings, concerns, or obligations — see OBLIVION

forgivable *adj* worthy of forgiveness — see VENIAL

forgive *vb* **1** to cease to have feelings of anger or bitterness toward ⟨it is not easy to *forgive* those who have hurt us⟩
synonyms pardon
related words absolve, acquit, clear, exculpate, exonerate, vindicate; remit, shrive; condone, disregard, excuse, ignore, pass over, shrug off
near antonyms smart; despise, detest, dislike, hate, loathe; avenge, redress, revenge
antonyms resent
2 to overlook or dismiss as of little importance — see EXCUSE 1

forgiveness *n* release from the guilt or penalty of an offense — see PARDON

forgo *also* **forego** *vb* to resist the temptation of — see FORBEAR

forgotten *adj* left unoccupied or unused — see ABANDONED

fork *vb* to go or move in different directions from a central point — see SEPARATE 2

forlorn *adj* **1** feeling unhappiness — see SAD 1
2 sad from lack of companionship or separation from others — see LONESOME 1

forlornness *n* **1** a state or spell of low spirits — see SADNESS
2 utter loss of hope — see DESPAIR 1

form *n* **1** the outward appearance of something as

distinguished from its substance ⟨carved the block of wood into the *form* of a duck⟩
synonyms cast, configuration, conformation, figure, geometry, shape
related words contour, outline, profile, silhouette; framework, skeleton, situation; arrangement, layout, organization, pattern, plan, setup
near antonyms composition, material, matter, stuff, substance
2 a piece of paper with information written or to be written on it ⟨I filled out all the *forms* for applying to the school⟩
synonyms blank, document, paper
related words instrument, writ
3 personal conduct or behavior as evaluated by an accepted standard of appropriateness for a social or professional setting — see MANNER 1
4 a state of being or fitness — see CONDITION 1
5 a three-dimensional representation of the human body used especially for displaying clothes — see MANNEQUIN 1
6 an oft-repeated action or series of actions performed in accordance with tradition or a set of rules — see RITE
7 socially acceptable behavior — see DECENCY 1
8 the means or procedure for doing something — see METHOD
9 the type of body that a person has — see PHYSIQUE
10 the way in which the elements of something (as a work of art) are arranged — see COMPOSITION 3

form *vb* **1** to take on a definite form ⟨my ideas on the subject are just starting to *form*⟩
synonyms crystallize, jell, shape (up), solidify
related words coalesce, cohere, fuse; combine, connect, join, unite
near antonyms break down, decompose, disintegrate
2 to be all the substance of — see CONSTITUTE 1
3 to bring into being by combining, shaping, or transforming materials — see MAKE 1
4 to come into existence — see BEGIN 2
5 to come to have gradually — see DEVELOP 2

formal *adj* **1** following or agreeing with established form, custom, or rules ⟨a *formal* meeting of the school board⟩ ⟨a *formal* contract that was legally binding⟩
synonyms ceremonial, ceremonious, conventional, orthodox, regular, routine
related words authorized, certified, official; accepted, correct, decorous, proper; formalistic, ritual, ritualistic; methodical, orderly, systematic
near antonyms unauthorized, unofficial; improper, incorrect, indecorous
antonyms informal, irregular, unceremonious, unconventional, unorthodox
2 being something in name or form only — see NOMINAL 1
3 marked by or showing careful attention to set forms and details — see CEREMONIOUS 1
4 relating to or suitable for wearing to an event requiring elegant dress and manners — see DRESS
5 very dignified in form, tone, or style — see ELEVATED 2

formal *n* a social gathering for dancing — see DANCE

formality *n* **1** an act or utterance that is a customary show of good manners — see CIVILITY 1
2 an oft-repeated action or series of actions performed in accordance with tradition or a set of rules — see RITE

formalize *vb* to make agree with a single established standard or model — see STANDARDIZE

format *n* **1** the way in which something is sized, arranged, or organized ⟨the book's *format* is very user-friendly⟩
synonyms arrangement, configuration, conformation, formation, layout, setup
related words design, plan, scheme; composition, constitution, makeup; build, construction, structure
2 the way in which the elements of something (as a work of art) are arranged — see COMPOSITION 3

formation *n* the way in which something is sized, arranged, or organized — see FORMAT 1

formative *adj* having a role in deciding something's final form ⟨a teacher who was a *formative* influence on generations of students⟩
synonyms constructive, productive
related words causal, creative; consequential, influential
antonyms nonconstructive, nonproductive, unproductive

former *adj* having been such at some previous time ⟨the coach is a *former* professional baseball player⟩
synonyms erstwhile, late, old, onetime, past, sometime, whilom
related words bygone, dead, extinct
near antonyms contemporary, current, present; future, prospective

formidable *adj* **1** causing fear — see FEARFUL 1
2 requiring considerable physical or mental effort — see HARD 2

formless *adj* having no definite or recognizable form ⟨a *formless* mass of clay that the potter transformed into an attractive bowl⟩
synonyms amorphous, shapeless, unformed, unshaped, unstructured
related words characterless, featureless, nondescript; chaotic, disorganized, incoherent, unordered, unorganized; fuzzy, hazy, indeterminate, indistinct, obscure, unclear, vague
near antonyms coherent, ordered, organized; clear, definite, distinct
antonyms formed, shaped, structured

formulaic *adj* using or marked by the use of something else as a basis or model — see IMITATIVE

formulate *vb* **1** to convey in appropriate or telling terms — see PHRASE
2 to put (something) into proper and usually carefully worked out written form — see COMPOSE 1

formulation *n* an act, process, or means of putting something into words — see EXPRESSION 1

formulator *n* one who creates or introduces something new — see INVENTOR

forsake *vb* to cause to remain behind — see LEAVE 1

forsaken *adj* left unoccupied or unused — see ABANDONED

forsaking *n* the act of abandoning — see DERELICTION 1

forsooth *adv* **1** to tell the truth — see ACTUALLY 1
2 without any question — see INDEED 1

fort *n* a structure or place from which one can resist attack ⟨a series of *forts* along the frontier⟩
synonyms bastion, citadel, fastness, fortification, fortress, hold, stronghold

related words breastwork, bulwark, parapet, rampart; bunker, dugout

forte *n* something for which a person shows a special talent ⟨doing funny impressions of people has always been my *forte*⟩
synonyms speciality, specialty
related words area, demesne, department, discipline, domain, field, line, province, realm, sphere; element; aptness, bent, faculty, flair, genius, gift, knack, talent

forth *adv* **1** toward a point ahead in space or time — see ONWARD 1
2 toward or at a point lying in advance in space or time — see ALONG

forthcoming *adj* being soon to appear or take place ⟨everyone's excited about the *forthcoming* school vacation⟩
synonyms approaching, coming, imminent, impending, nearing, oncoming, pending, upcoming
related words future; anticipated, awaited, expected, foreseen, predicted
near antonyms bygone, former, past
antonyms late, recent

forthright *adj* **1** free in expressing one's true feelings and opinions — see FRANK
2 going straight to the point clearly and firmly — see STRAIGHTFORWARD 1

forthrightly *adv* in an honest and direct manner — see STRAIGHTFORWARD

forthrightness *n* the free expression of one's true feelings and opinions — see CANDOR

forthwith *adv* without delay — see IMMEDIATELY

fortification *n* a structure or place from which one can resist attack — see FORT

fortify *vb* **1** to prepare (oneself) mentally or emotionally ⟨Kelly *fortified* herself for the basketball tournament with a series of confidence-boosting exercises⟩
synonyms brace, forearm, nerve, ready, steel, strengthen
related words harden, inure, season, toughen; bolster, boost, buoy (up), buttress, prop (up), reinforce, support, sustain; embolden, encourage, hearten; rally, rouse, stir
near antonyms demoralize, discourage, dishearten, unnerve; debilitate, enfeeble, undermine, weaken
2 to increase the ability of (as a muscle) to exert physical force — see STRENGTHEN 1
3 to make able to withstand physical hardship, strain, or exposure — see HARDEN 2

fortitude *n* the strength of mind that enables a person to endure pain or hardship ⟨it was only with the greatest *fortitude* that the Pilgrims were able to survive their first winter in Plymouth⟩
synonyms backbone, fiber, grit, guts, pluck, spunk
related words determination, purposefulness, resoluteness, resolution; bravery, courage, fearlessness, intrepidity; endurance, stamina, tolerance; heart, mettle, spirit; audacity, boldness, brass, cheek, chutzpah (*also* chutzpa *or* hutzpah *or* hutzpa), effrontery, hardihood, nerve, temerity
near antonyms indecisiveness, irresoluteness, irresolution, vacillation; cowardliness, cravenness, faintheartedness, timidity, timorousness
antonyms spinelessness

fortress *n* a structure or place from which one can resist attack — see FORT

fortuitous *adj* **1** coming or happening by good luck especially unexpectedly — see FORTUNATE 1
2 happening by chance — see ACCIDENTAL

fortunate *adj* **1** coming or happening by good luck especially unexpectedly ⟨in a *fortunate* turn of events, the motel had one last vacancy⟩
synonyms fluky, fortuitous, happy, lucky, providential
related words convenient, opportune, seasonable, timely; unexpected, unforeseen, unlooked-for; accidental, chance, coincidental; auspicious, bright, fair, promising, propitious; benign, favorable, golden, good; advantageous, beneficial, profitable
near antonyms inconvenient, inopportune, unseasonable, untimely; anticipated, expected, foreseen; deliberate, intentional, planned; inauspicious, unpromising
antonyms luckless, unfortunate, unhappy, unlucky
2 having good luck — see LUCKY 1

fortunateness *n* success that is partly the result of chance — see LUCK 1

fortune *n* **1** what is going to happen to someone in the time ahead ⟨the telephone psychic proceeded to tell me my *fortune*—at great length⟩
synonyms future
related words circumstance, destiny, doom, lot, portion; futurities, outlook, prospect
near antonyms present
antonyms past
2 a very large amount of money ⟨the billionaire's huge mansion must have cost a *fortune*⟩
synonyms king's ransom, mint, wad
related words heap, pile, pot; bonanza, mine, treasure trove; assets, property, riches, wealth
antonyms mite, pittance
3 a state or end that seemingly has been decided beforehand — see FATE 1
4 success that is partly the result of chance — see LUCK 1
5 the total of one's money and property — see WEALTH 1

fortune–teller *n* one who predicts future events or developments — see PROPHET

forty winks *n pl* a short sleep — see [1]NAP

forum *n* a meeting featuring a group discussion ⟨a public *forum* called to find out how residents felt about a large high school being built in their neighborhood⟩
synonyms colloquy, conference, council, panel, parley, powwow, roundtable, seminar, symposium
related words caucus, town meeting; assembly, conclave, congregation, congress, convention, convocation, synod; debate, deliberation; brainstorming

forward *adv* **1** toward or at a point lying in advance in space or time — see ALONG
2 toward a point ahead in space or time — see ONWARD 1

forward *adj* showing a lack of proper social reserve or modesty — see PRESUMPTUOUS 1

forward *vb* to help the growth or development of — see FOSTER 1

fossil *n* a person with old-fashioned ideas — see FOGY

foster *vb* **1** to help the growth or development of ⟨the head librarian firmly declared that it is indeed the duty of local government to *foster* learning and a love of reading⟩

synonyms advance, cultivate, encourage, forward, further, nourish, nurture, promote
related words back, champion, support, uphold; endow, finance, fund, patronize, subsidize; abet, aid, assist; advertise, boost, plug, publicize, tout; agitate (for), campaign (for), work (for)
near antonyms forbid, prevent, prohibit; battle, combat, counter, fight, oppose; repress, stifle, suppress; arrest, check, halt, retard
antonyms discourage, frustrate, hinder, inhibit
2 to bring to maturity through care and education — see BRING UP 1

foul *adj* **1** marked by wet and windy conditions <the *foul* weather brought out the windbreakers and rain slickers as everyone braced for a day of rough sailing>
synonyms bleak, dirty, inclement, nasty, raw, rough, squally, stormy, tempestuous, turbulent
related words blustering, blustery, breezy, gusty, windblown, windswept; cloudy, overcast, sunless; rainy, snowy; foggy, hazy, misty
near antonyms clear, cloudless, rainless, sunny; balmy, calm, halcyon, peaceful, placid
antonyms clement, fair
2 not being in accordance with the rules or standards of what is fair in sport <an aggressive hockey player who is known for his *foul* play and readiness for a fight>
synonyms dirty, illegal, unfair, unsportsmanlike
related words dishonorable, shabby, shameful; ignoble, low, mean, ungentlemanly; immoral, unethical, unjust, unprincipled, unrighteous, unscrupulous
near antonyms just, law-abiding; ethical, moral, principled, righteous; honorable, irreproachable, unimpeachable
antonyms clean, fair, legal, sportsmanlike, sportsmanly
3 causing intense displeasure, disgust, or resentment — see OFFENSIVE 1
4 depicting or referring to sexual matters in a way that is unacceptable in polite society — see OBSCENE 1
5 having an unpleasant smell — see MALODOROUS
6 not clean — see DIRTY 1

foul *vb* **1** to make dirty — see DIRTY
2 to make unfit for use by the addition of something harmful or undesirable — see CONTAMINATE

foulness *n* **1** the quality or state of being obscene — see OBSCENITY 1
2 the state or quality of being dirty — see DIRTINESS 1

foul play *n* **1** the intentional and unlawful taking of another person's life — see HOMICIDE
2 the use of brute strength to cause harm to a person or property — see VIOLENCE

foul–up *n* an instance of confusion <there was a *foul-up* with our mail order, and not one item arrived as ordered>
synonyms mix-up
related words bobble, botch, bungle, fumble; blunder, error, flub, goof, mistake, slipup; chaos, confusion, disarrangement, disarray, disorder, hash, jumble, mess, muddle, shambles

foul up *vb* to make or do (something) in a clumsy or unskillful way — see BOTCH

found *vb* to be responsible for the creation and early operation or use of <John Harvard did not actually *found* the university that now bears his name>
synonyms constitute, establish, inaugurate, initiate, innovate, institute, introduce, launch, pioneer, set up, start
related words author, father, originate; create, invent, produce; construct, erect, put up; develop, enlarge, expand; endow, finance, fund, subsidize; arrange, organize, systematize
near antonyms abolish, annihilate, annul, nullify; end, finish, stop, terminate
antonyms close (down), phase out, shut (up)

foundation *n* **1** a public organization with a particular purpose or function — see INSTITUTION 1
2 an immaterial thing upon which something else rests — see BASE 1

founder *n* a person who establishes a whole new field of endeavor — see FATHER 2

foursquare *adj* **1** free in expressing one's true feelings and opinions — see FRANK
2 going straight to the point clearly and firmly — see STRAIGHTFORWARD 1

foursquare *adv* in an honest and direct manner — see STRAIGHTFORWARD

fox *vb* to get the better of through cleverness — see OUTWIT

foxiness *n* **1** skill in achieving one's ends through indirect, subtle, or underhanded means — see CUNNING 1
2 the inclination or practice of misleading others through lies or trickery — see DECEIT

foxy *adj* clever at attaining one's ends by indirect and often deceptive means — see ARTFUL 1

foyer *n* **1** a centrally located room in a building that serves as a gathering or waiting area or as a passageway into the interior <theatergoers crowded the *foyer* during the play's intermission>
synonyms hall, lobby
related words entry, entryway, hallway, vestibule; concourse, corridor, gallery, passageway; antechamber, anteroom, waiting room
2 the entrance room of a building — see HALL 1

fracas *n* **1** a physical dispute between opposing individuals or groups — see FIGHT 1
2 a rough and often noisy fight usually involving several people — see BRAWL 1

fractionation *n* the act or process of a whole separating into two or more parts or pieces — see SEPARATION 1

fracture *vb* to cause to separate into pieces usually suddenly or forcibly — see BREAK 1

fragile *adj* **1** easily broken <attaching the beautiful but *fragile* ornaments to the Christmas tree is always a touchy operation>
synonyms breakable, delicate, frail
related words dainty, fine, gossamer; flimsy, slight, tenuous; brittle, crisp, crumbly, flaky, friable, short; feeble, infirm, weak; inelastic, inflexible, stiff
near antonyms firm, solid, substantial; elastic, flexible, resilient
antonyms nonbreakable, strong, sturdy, tough, unbreakable
2 easily injured without careful handling — see TENDER 1

fragility *n* the state or quality of having a delicate structure — see DELICACY 2

fragment *n* a broken or irregular part of something that often remains incomplete <charred *fragments*

of the exploded rocket were scattered over a huge area of ground⟩
synonyms bit, piece, scrap
related words shred, tatter; end, leftover, remainder, remnant; part, portion, section, segment

fragment *vb* to cause to separate into pieces usually suddenly or forcibly — see BREAK 1

fragmental *adj* lacking some necessary part — see INCOMPLETE

fragmentary *adj* lacking some necessary part — see INCOMPLETE

fragrance *n* a sweet or pleasant smell ⟨the *fragrance* of lilac trees in full bloom⟩
synonyms aroma, bouquet, incense, perfume, redolence, scent, spice
related words odor
antonyms reek, stench, stink

fragrant *adj* having a pleasant smell ⟨the balsam fir is a favorite as a Christmas tree because it is so *fragrant*⟩
synonyms ambrosial, aromatic, perfumed, redolent, savory, scented, sweet
related words flowery, fruity, pungent, spicy; odoriferous, odorous; clean, fresh, pure
near antonyms odorless, unscented; fusty, musty, stale; gamy (*or* gamey)
antonyms fetid, foul, malodorous, noisome, putrid, rancid, rank, reeking, reeky, smelly, stinking, stinky, strong

frail *adj* **1** easily broken — see FRAGILE 1
2 easily injured without careful handling — see TENDER 1
3 lacking bodily strength — see WEAK 1
4 lacking strength of will or character — see WEAK 2

frailness *n* **1** the quality or state of lacking physical strength or vigor — see WEAKNESS 1
2 the quality or state of lacking strength of will or character — see WEAKNESS 2

frailty *n* **1** a defect in character — see FAULT 1
2 the quality or state of lacking physical strength or vigor — see WEAKNESS 1
3 the quality or state of lacking strength of will or character — see WEAKNESS 2

frame *n* **1** the arrangement of parts that gives something its basic form ⟨now that the *frame* has been built, we have a better idea of the size of our new house⟩
synonyms configuration, framework, shell, skeleton, structure
related words lattice, network; contour, figure, outline, profile, shape, silhouette; chassis
2 a state of mind dominated by a particular emotion — see MOOD 1
3 the type of body that a person has — see PHYSIQUE

frame *vb* **1** to bring into being by combining, shaping, or transforming materials — see MAKE 1
2 to plan out usually with subtle skill or care — see ENGINEER
3 to put (something) into proper and usually carefully worked out written form — see COMPOSE 1
4 to work out the details of (something) in advance — see PLAN 1

framework *n* the arrangement of parts that gives something its basic form — see FRAME 1

franchise *n* the right to formally express one's position or will in an election — see VOTE 1

frank *adj* free in expressing one's true feelings and opinions ⟨our ballet teacher is very *frank* about telling her students whether she thinks they have the talent for a career in dance⟩
synonyms candid, direct, forthright, foursquare, free-spoken, honest, open, openhearted, outspoken, plain, plainspoken, straight, straightforward, unguarded, unreserved
related words artless, earnest, sincere; outgoing, uninhibited, unrestrained; vocal, vociferous; abrupt, bluff, blunt, brusque, curt, gruff, sharp; impolite, inconsiderate, rude, tactless, undiplomatic, unsubtle
near antonyms inhibited, reserved, restrained; close-mouthed, reticent, tight-lipped; ambiguous, circuitous, equivocal, evasive; diplomatic, politic, tactful; civil, considerate, courteous, polite
antonyms dissembling

frankly *adv* to tell the truth — see ACTUALLY 1

frankness *n* the free expression of one's true feelings and opinions — see CANDOR

frantic *adj* **1** feeling overwhelming fear or worry ⟨the *frantic* parents were searching all over the fairgrounds for their lost child⟩
synonyms agitated, delirious, distraught, frenzied, hysterical
related words alarmed, anxious, disquieted, disturbed, troubled, upset, worried, wrought (up); berserk, crazed, demented, deranged, mad, maniacal (*also* maniac); raging, ranting, raving
near antonyms calm, peaceful, serene, tranquil; cool, coolheaded, undisturbed, unperturbed, untroubled
antonyms collected, composed, self-possessed
2 marked by great and often stressful excitement or activity — see FURIOUS 1

frantically *adv* in a confused and reckless manner — see HELTER-SKELTER 1

fraternal *adj* of, relating to, or befitting brothers ⟨there was a *fraternal* bond between the two boys all throughout their school years⟩
synonyms brotherly
related words familial, sisterly; chummy, friendly, neighborly

fraternity *n* **1** a group of persons formally joined together for some common interest — see ASSOCIATION 2
2 the body of people in a profession or field of activity — see CORPS

fraternize *vb* **1** to come or be together as friends — see ASSOCIATE 1
2 to take part in social activities — see SOCIALIZE

fraud *n* one who makes false claims of identity or expertise — see IMPOSTOR

fraudulent *adj* **1** marked by, based on, or done by the use of dishonest methods to acquire something of value ⟨hoping to get millions from the insurance company, the man made the *fraudulent* claim that he had been seriously injured in the accident⟩
synonyms crooked, deceitful, defrauding, dishonest, double-dealing, false
related words deceptive, misleading, specious
near antonyms legitimate, true, valid
antonyms aboveboard, honest, truthful
2 given to or marked by cheating and deception — see DISHONEST 2

fraught *adj* possessing or covered with great numbers or amounts of something specified — see RIFE

fray *n* **1** a forceful effort to reach a goal or objective — see STRUGGLE 1

2 a physical dispute between opposing individuals or groups — see FIGHT 1
3 a rough and often noisy fight usually involving several people — see BRAWL 1

fray *vb* to damage or diminish by continued friction — see ABRADE 1

frayed *adj* worn or torn into or as if into rags — see RAGGED 2

freak *adj* being out of the ordinary — see EXCEPTIONAL

freak *n* **1** a person, thing, or event that is not normal ⟨that snowstorm in April was a *freak*, since our weather is usually much balmier by then⟩
synonyms abnormality, anomaly, monster, monstrosity
related words malformation, mutant, mutation; character, crackbrain, crackpot, eccentric, kook, oddball, screwball, weirdo; deviant; maverick, nonconformist
near antonyms sample, specimen; standard
antonyms average, norm
2 a person with a strong and habitual liking for something — see FAN
3 a sudden impulsive and apparently unmotivated idea or action — see WHIM

freak (out) *vb* **1** to trouble the mind of; to make uneasy — see DISTURB 1
2 to yield to mental or emotional stress — see CRACK 2

freakish *adj* prone to sudden illogical changes of mind, ideas, or actions — see WHIMSICAL

freakishness *n* an inclination to sudden illogical changes of mind, ideas, or actions — see WHIMSICALITY

freckle *vb* to mark with small spots especially unevenly — see SPOT

freckled *adj* marked with spots — see SPOTTED 1

free *adj* **1** not being under the rule or control of another ⟨the 20th century saw many African countries become *free* after many years of European rule⟩
synonyms autonomous, independent, self-governing, separate, sovereign
related words freeborn; delivered, emancipated, freed, liberated, manumitted, redeemed, released; unconquered, ungoverned, unruled, unsupervised; empowered, enfranchised; democratic, republican
near antonyms captive, conquered, enslaved, subdued, subjugated; inferior, subordinate, subservient
antonyms dependent, subject, unfree
2 no longer burdened with something unpleasant or painful ⟨after our son arrived home safely, we were grateful to be *free* from worry⟩
synonyms disencumbered, quit, unburdened
related words delivered, freed, liberated, released; unhampered, unimpeded
3 not bound, confined, or detained by force ⟨all of the animals in the game preserve are *free* to roam all over its vast area⟩
synonyms footloose, loose, unbound, unconfined, unrestrained
related words escaped; uncaged, unchained, unfettered, unleashed; uncaught; unanchored, unbolted, undone, unfastened, untied; clear, disengaged, unengaged
phrases at large, at liberty
near antonyms caught; caged, chained, leashed; anchored, bolted, fastened, shackled, tied
antonyms bound, confined, restrained, unfree
4 not costing or charging anything ⟨although the museum normally charges admission, on Wednesdays it is *free* to all⟩
synonyms complimentary, gratis, gratuitous
related words nominal; discretionary, freewill, optional, voluntary; honorary, uncompensated, unpaid
near antonyms paid
5 allowing passage without obstruction — see OPEN 1
6 giving or sharing in abundance and without hesitation — see GENEROUS 1
7 not being in a state of use, activity, or employment — see INACTIVE 2
8 showing a lack of proper social reserve or modesty — see PRESUMPTUOUS 1

free *vb* **1** to set free (as from slavery or confinement) ⟨a global crusade to *free* Nelson Mandela from a South African prison had emerged⟩
synonyms discharge, emancipate, enfranchise, liberate, loose, loosen, manumit, release, spring, unbind, uncage, unchain, unfetter
related words bail (out), deliver, parole, ransom, redeem, rescue; disengage, disentangle, extricate
near antonyms manacle, shackle, trammel; immure, imprison, incarcerate, intern, jail; conquer, enslave, subdue, subjugate
antonyms bind, confine, enchain, fetter, restrain
2 to arrange clear passage of (something) by removing obstructions — see OPEN 2
3 to rid the surface of (as an area) from things in the way — see CLEAR 1
4 to set (a person or thing) free of something that encumbers — see RID
5 to set free from entanglement or difficulty — see EXTRICATE

freebie *or* **freebee** *n* something given to someone without expectation of a return — see GIFT 1

freebooter *n* someone who engages in robbery of ships at sea — see PIRATE

freedom *n* **1** the state of being free from the control or power of another ⟨we owe our *freedom* to the untold numbers of soldiers who have fought in our nation's wars since its founding⟩
synonyms autonomy, independence, liberty, self-government, sovereignty
related words emancipation, enfranchisement, liberation, manumission, release
near antonyms captivity, enchainment, enslavement, imprisonment, incarceration, subjugation
antonyms dependence, subjection
2 the right to act or move freely ⟨as special guests of the owners, the youngsters had full *freedom* of the resort and its private beach⟩
synonyms authorization, free hand, latitude, license (*or* licence), run
related words authority, mandate, power; range, room, space

free-for-all *adj* freely available for use or participation by all — see OPEN 2

free-for-all *n* a rough and often noisy fight usually involving several people — see BRAWL 1

free hand *n* the right to act or move freely — see FREEDOM 2

freehanded *adj* giving or sharing in abundance and without hesitation — see GENEROUS 1

freeing *n* the act of setting free from slavery — see LIBERATION

freely *adv* **1** of one's own free will — see VOLUNTARILY
2 without difficulty — see EASILY

free–spoken *adj* free in expressing one's true feelings and opinions — see FRANK

freestanding *adj* not physically attached to another unit — see SEPARATE 2

freeway *n* a passage cleared for public vehicular travel — see WAY 1

freewheeling *adj* not held back by rules, duties, or worries ⟨James Bond has long been the model of the *freewheeling* hero who encounters danger and excitement in every corner of the globe⟩
synonyms footloose
related words easygoing, nonchalant, relaxed; unattached, uncommitted; unbridled, ungoverned, unrestrained; uninhibited, unsuppressed; self-assured, self-confident, self-reliant
near antonyms attached, committed
antonyms tied

freewill *adj* **1** made, given, or done with one's own free will — see INTENTIONAL 1
2 done, made, or given with one's own free will — see VOLUNTARY 1

free will *n* the act or power of making one's own choices or decisions ⟨all of the workers at the homeless shelter are unpaid and are there of their own *free will*⟩
synonyms accord, choice, option, self-determination, volition, will
related words election, preference; inclination, penchant, predilection, predisposition
near antonyms coercion, compulsion, constraint, duress, force

freeze *n* a weather condition marked by low temperatures — see COLD

freeze *vb* to become physically firm or solid — see HARDEN 1

freezing *adj* having a low or subnormal temperature — see COLD 1

freight *n* a mass or quantity of something taken up and carried, conveyed, or transported — see LOAD 1

frenetic *adj* marked by great and often stressful excitement or activity — see FURIOUS 1

frenzied *adj* **1** being in a state of increased activity or agitation — see FEVERISH 1
2 feeling overwhelming fear or worry — see FRANTIC 1
3 marked by great and often stressful excitement or activity — see FURIOUS 1

frenziedly *adv* in a confused and reckless manner — see HELTER-SKELTER 1

frenzy *n* a state of wildly excited activity or emotion ⟨in its *frenzy* to flee the danger the crowd became uncontrollable, and a number of people were trampled to death⟩
synonyms agitation, delirium, distraction, furor, furore, fury, hysteria, rage, rampage, uproar
related words chaos, confusion, disorder, turmoil; clamor, commotion, hubbub, hurly-burly, tumult
near antonyms calm, peacefulness, serenity, tranquillity (*or* tranquility)

frequency *n* the fact or state of happening often ⟨the *frequency* of twins in that family is remarkable⟩
synonyms commonness, prevalence
related words constancy, continualness, regularity; appearance, incidence, occurrence
antonyms infrequency, uncommonness, unusualness

frequent *adj* **1** appearing or occurring repeatedly from time to time — see REGULAR 1
2 often observed or encountered — see COMMON 1

frequent *vb* to go to or spend time in often ⟨like their counterparts elsewhere, the town's teenagers like to *frequent* the local malls⟩
synonyms hang around (in), hang out (at), haunt, resort (to), visit
related words attend, take in; infest, invade, swarm, overrun; drop (in *or* by), pop (in), run (in), stop (in *or* by); sojourn (at), stay (at), stop (over), tarry (in)
near antonyms elude, escape, evade
antonyms avoid, shun

frequenter *n* a person who visits another — see GUEST 1

frequently *adv* many times — see OFTEN

fresh *adj* **1** being in an original and unused or unspoiled state ⟨the restaurant uses only really *fresh* ingredients in all of its dishes⟩
synonyms brand-new, pristine, virgin
related words unaltered, unblemished, unbruised, uncontaminated, undamaged, undefiled, unharmed, unhurt, unimpaired, uninjured, unpolluted, unsoiled, unspoiled, unsullied, untainted, untouched, unused, unworn
near antonyms blemished, bruised, damaged, defiled, harmed, hurt, impaired, injured, soiled, sullied, tainted; faded, shopworn, used, worn; contaminated, polluted, spoiled
antonyms stale
2 displaying or marked by rude boldness — see NERVY 1
3 not known or experienced before — see NEW 2

freshen *vb* to bring back to a former condition or vigor — see RENEW 1

freshened *adj* made or become fresh in spirits or vigor — see NEW 4

freshly *adv* not long ago — see NEWLY

freshman *n* a person who is just starting out in a field of activity — see BEGINNER

freshness *n* the quality or appeal of being new — see NOVELTY 1

fret *n* a state of nervous or irritated concern ⟨one of my customers always gets into a *fret* if I'm so much as 15 minutes late delivering his newspaper⟩
synonyms dither, fluster, fuss, huff, lather, pother, stew, tizzy, twitter
related words dudgeon, pique; alarm, panic; ado, agitation, delirium, distraction, furor, hysteria, uproar; nervous breakdown

fret *vb* **1** to consume or wear away gradually — see EAT 2
2 to damage or diminish by continued friction — see ABRADE 1
3 to experience concern or anxiety — see WORRY 1

friable *adj* having a texture that readily breaks into little pieces under pressure — see CRISP 1

friary *n* a residence for men under religious vows — see MONASTERY

friction *n* a lack of agreement or harmony — see DISCORD

frictionless *adj* having or marked by agreement in feeling or action — see HARMONIOUS 3

friend *n* **1** a person who has a strong liking for and

trust in another ⟨really close *friends* who like to do everything together and are always sharing secrets⟩
synonyms buddy, chum, comrade, confidant, crony, familiar, intimate, pal
related words acquaintance; associate, cohort, colleague, companion, fellow, hearty, hobnobber, mate, partner, peer; brother, sister; accomplice, ally, collaborator, confederate; benefactor, supporter, sympathizer, well-wisher; friendly
near antonyms adversary, antagonist, opponent, rival; archenemy, nemesis
antonyms enemy, foe
2 a person who actively supports or favors a cause — see EXPONENT

friendliness *n* kindly concern, interest, or support — see GOODWILL 1

friendly *adj* **1** having or showing kindly feeling and sincere interest ⟨all of the kids at Stacy's new school seemed *friendly*⟩ ⟨as a *friendly* gesture, we presented our new neighbors with a plate of homemade cookies⟩
synonyms amicable, companionable, comradely, cordial, genial, hearty, neighborly, warm, warm-hearted
related words affable, approachable, gracious; convivial, gregarious, hospitable, sociable, social; jolly, jovial, merry; extroverted (*also* extraverted), outgoing; brotherly, fraternal, sisterly; close, familiar, intimate; affectionate, devoted, loving
near antonyms cold, cool, frigid; bellicose, belligerent, contentious, quarrelsome
antonyms antagonistic, hostile, unfriendly
2 closely acquainted — see FAMILIAR 1
3 expressing approval — see FAVORABLE 1

friendship *n* kindly concern, interest, or support — see GOODWILL 1

fright *n* **1** something unpleasant to look at — see EYESORE
2 the emotion experienced in the presence or threat of danger — see FEAR

frighten *vb* to strike with fear ⟨around the campfire the campers tried to *frighten* one another with ghostly legends and grisly tales⟩
synonyms affright, alarm, horrify, panic, scare, shock, spook, startle, terrify, terrorize
related words appall, dismay; amaze, astound, awe; chill, daunt, demoralize, dispirit, unman, unnerve; discompose, disconcert, disquiet, disturb, perturb, upset
near antonyms cheer, comfort, console, solace, soothe; embolden, encourage, hearten
antonyms reassure

frightened *adj* filled with fear or dread — see AFRAID 1

frightening *adj* causing fear — see FEARFUL 1

frightful *adj* **1** causing fear — see FEARFUL 1
2 extremely disturbing or repellent — see HORRIBLE 1

frightfully *adv* to a great degree — see VERY 1

frightfulness *n* the quality of inspiring intense dread or dismay — see HORROR 1

frigid *adj* **1** having a low or subnormal temperature — see COLD 1
2 lacking in friendliness or warmth of feeling — see COLD 2

frill *n* **1** a strip of fabric gathered or pleated on one edge and used as trimming — see RUFFLE
2 something adding to pleasure or comfort but not absolutely necessary — see LUXURY 1
3 something that decorates or beautifies — see DECORATION 1

fringe *n* the line or relatively narrow space that marks the outer limit of something — see BORDER 1

fringe *vb* **1** to be adjacent to — see ADJOIN 1
2 to serve as a border for — see BORDER

fringing *adj* having a border in common — see ADJACENT

frippery *n* **1** dressy clothing — see FINERY
2 something of little importance — see TRIFLE

frisk *vb* to play and run about happily — see FROLIC 1

friskiness *n* a natural disposition for playful behavior — see PLAYFULNESS

frisky *adj* **1** given to good-natured joking or teasing — see PLAYFUL
2 having much high-spirited energy and movement — see LIVELY 1

fritter *n* a small usually rounded mass of minced food that has been fried — see CAKE

fritter (away) *vb* to use up carelessly — see WASTE 1

frivol *vb* to show a liking for someone of the opposite sex just for fun — see FLIRT

frivolity *n* a lack of seriousness often at an improper time ⟨the boys were scolded for joking during the funeral service, which was hardly the time for *frivolity*⟩
synonyms facetiousness, flightiness, flippancy, frivolousness, levity, light-headedness, lightness
related words cheerfulness, gaiety (*also* gayety), glee, high-spiritedness, lightheartedness, merriment, mirth
near antonyms gloom, melancholy, moroseness, sadness, sullenness
synonyms gravity, intentness, seriousness, soberness, sobriety

frivolous *adj* **1** lacking importance — see UNIMPORTANT
2 lacking in seriousness or maturity — see GIDDY 1

frivolousness *n* a lack of seriousness often at an improper time — see FRIVOLITY 1

frock *n* a garment with a joined blouse and skirt for a woman or girl — see DRESS 1

frolic *n* **1** a playful or mischievous act intended as a joke — see PRANK
2 a time or instance of carefree fun — see FLING 1
3 activity engaged in to amuse oneself — see PLAY 1

frolic *vb* **1** to play and run about happily ⟨scores of swimmers were *frolicking* in the ocean surf along the beach⟩
synonyms caper, cavort, disport, frisk, gambol, lark, rollick, romp, sport
related words bound, leap, skip, spring, tumble; curvet, dance, prance; carouse, revel, roister; carry on, fool (around), horse (around); clown, cut up; joyride, roughhouse, skylark
phrases kick up one's heels
near antonyms mope, stew, sulk
2 to engage in activity for amusement — see PLAY 1

frolicking *n* activity engaged in to amuse oneself — see PLAY 1

frolicsome *adj* **1** given to good-natured joking or teasing — see PLAYFUL
2 joyously unrestrained — see EXUBERANT

front *n* **1** a forward part or surface ⟨the *front* of the

church features a magnificent stained-glass window⟩
synonyms exterior, facade (*also* façade), face, forepart, outside, skin, surface, veneer
near antonyms innards, inside, interior
antonyms back, rear, reverse
2 a display of emotion or behavior that is insincere or intended to deceive — see MASQUERADE

front *vb* to stand or sit with the face or front toward — see FACE 1

frontier *n* **1** a region along the dividing line between two countries ⟨the Apaches were once feared on both sides of the U.S.-Mexico *frontier*⟩
synonyms border, borderland, march
related words no-man's-land
2 a rural region that forms the edge of the settled or developed part of a country ⟨Alaska has been called America's last *frontier*⟩
synonyms backwater, backwoods, bush, hinterland, up-country
related words country, countryside, sticks

frontiersman *n* a person who settles in a new region ⟨the *frontiersmen* were willing to brave harsh living conditions in order to achieve a better life⟩
synonyms colonist, colonizer, homesteader, pioneer, settler
related words explorer, pathfinder, trailblazer

frost *n* a covering of tiny ice crystals on a cold surface ⟨the wintertime routine of scraping the *frost* off the car's windshield every morning⟩
synonyms hoar, hoarfrost, rime
related words frostwork

frosty *adj* **1** having a low or subnormal temperature — see COLD 1
2 having or showing a lack of friendliness or interest in others — see COOL 1
3 lacking in friendliness or warmth of feeling — see COLD 2

froth *n* a light mass of fine bubbles formed in or on a liquid — see FOAM

frothy *adj* covered with, consisting of, or resembling foam — see FOAMY

froward *adj* **1** engaging in or marked by childish misbehavior — see NAUGHTY
2 given to resisting authority or another's control — see DISOBEDIENT
3 given to resisting control or discipline by others — see UNCONTROLLABLE

frowardness *n* refusal to obey — see DISOBEDIENCE

frown *n* a twisting of the facial features in disgust or disapproval — see GRIMACE

frown *vb* to look with anger or disapproval ⟨the principal just stood there and *frowned* at the student who, once again, was in trouble⟩
synonyms glare, gloom, glower, lower (*also* lour), scowl
related words gape, gaze, ogle, stare; grimace, pout; growl, snarl, sneer
phrases look daggers
antonyms beam, smile

frown (on) *vb* to hold an unfavorable opinion of — see DISAPPROVE

frowsy *or* **frowzy** *adj* lacking neatness in dress or person — see SLOPPY 1

frozen *adj* **1** firmly positioned in place and difficult to dislodge — see TIGHT 2
2 having been established and usually not subject to change — see FIXED 1

frugal *adj* careful in the management of money or resources ⟨by being *frugal*, the family is able to stretch its monthly budget⟩
synonyms economical, economizing, provident, scrimping, sparing, thrifty
related words conserving, preserving, saving; forehanded, foresighted, prudent; penny-wise; cheap, close, closefisted, miserly, niggardly, parsimonious, stingy, stinting, tight, tightfisted
near antonyms improvident, shortsighted; freehanded, generous, liberal, openhanded, unsparing; extravagant, indulgent, lavish
antonyms prodigal, wasteful

frugality *n* careful management of material resources — see ECONOMY

fruit *n* **1** a condition or occurrence traceable to a cause — see EFFECT 1
2 something produced by physical or intellectual effort — see PRODUCT 1

fruitful *adj* **1** producing abundantly — see FERTILE
2 producing or capable of producing a desired result — see EFFECTIVE 1

fruition *n* the state of being actual or complete ⟨when she landed the lead in a Broadway play, a lifelong dream was brought to *fruition*⟩
synonyms accomplishment, achievement, actuality, attainment, consummation, fulfillment, realization
antonyms naught (*also* nought), nonfulfillment

fruitless *adj* producing no results — see FUTILE

frustrate *vb* to prevent from achieving a goal ⟨a multitude of conflicting opinions *frustrated* me in my attempt to find a computer that best suits my needs⟩
synonyms baffle, balk, beat, checkmate, foil, thwart
related words bar, block, hinder, impede, obstruct; arrest, check, halt, stop; forestall, obviate, preclude; negate, neutralize, nullify; counteract, offset; conquer, defeat, overcome
near antonyms abet, aid, assist; ease, facilitate, smooth;
antonyms advance, cultivate, encourage, forward, foster, further, nurture, promote

frustrating *adj* causing annoyance — see ANNOYING

frustration *n* **1** something that is a source of irritation — see ANNOYANCE 3
2 the emotion felt when one's expectations are not met — see DISAPPOINTMENT 1
3 the feeling of impatience or anger caused by another's repeated disagreeable acts — see ANNOYANCE 2

fuddy–duddy *n* a person with old-fashioned ideas — see FOGY

fudge *n* **1** language, behavior, or ideas that are absurd and contrary to good sense — see NONSENSE 1
2 unintelligible or meaningless talk — see GIBBERISH

fudge *vb* **1** to avoid giving a definite answer or position — see EQUIVOCATE
2 to use dishonest methods to achieve a goal — see CHEAT 1

fuel *n* something with a usable capacity for doing work ⟨such fossil *fuels* as coal, petroleum, and natural gas⟩
synonyms energy, power
related words kindling, propellant

fugitive *adj* **1** hard to find, capture, or isolate — see ELUSIVE
2 lasting only for a short time — see MOMENTARY

fulfill *or* **fulfil** *vb* **1** to do what is required by the terms of ⟨the football player must remain with the team one more year to *fulfill* his contract⟩
synonyms answer, comply (with), fill, keep, meet, redeem, satisfy
related words complete, conclude, finalize, finish; accomplish, achieve, bring about, bring off, effect; discharge, execute, perform
phrases abide by, make good
near antonyms disregard, ignore, neglect, overlook, slight
antonyms breach, break, violate
2 to carry through (as a process) to completion — see PERFORM 1

fulfilling *adj* making one feel good inside — see HEARTWARMING

fulfillment *n* **1** the doing of an action — see COMMISSION 2
2 the state of being actual or complete — see FRUITION

full *adj* **1** containing or seeming to contain the greatest quantity or number possible ⟨at the start of the game everyone was *full* of energy and hope⟩ ⟨the boy's bedroom is *full* of sports trophies and medals⟩
synonyms brimful, brimming, bursting, chock-full (*or* chockful), crammed, crowded, fat, filled, jammed, jam-packed, loaded, packed, stuffed
related words overcrowded, overfilled, overflowing, overfull, overloaded, overstuffed; abounding, fraught, replete, rife, swarming, teeming
near antonyms deficient, incomplete, insufficient, short; depleted, drained, exhausted
antonyms bare, blank, devoid, empty, stark, vacant, void
2 of the highest degree ⟨even at the age of eighteen he hadn't reached his *full* height⟩ ⟨a boat going at *full* speed⟩
synonyms greatest, maximum, top, topmost, utmost
related words high
near antonyms low
antonyms least, lowest, minimal, minimum
3 having one's appetite completely satisfied ⟨even the heartiest eaters are sure to be *full* when they leave that restaurant⟩
synonyms sated, satiate, satiated, stuffed, surfeited
related words glutted, gorged, overfed, overfull, overstuffed
near antonyms underfed, undernourished
antonyms empty, hungry, starving
4 covering everything or all important points — see ENCYCLOPEDIC
5 having an abundance of some characteristic quality (as flavor) — see FULL-BODIED
6 having an excess of body fat — see FAT 1
7 including many small descriptive features — see DETAILED 1
8 not lacking any part or member that properly belongs to it — see COMPLETE 1

full *adv* **1** to a full extent or degree — see FULLY 1
2 to a great degree — see VERY 1

full *n* a complete amount of something — see WHOLE

full blast *adv* with all power or resources being used ⟨Mom and Dad arrived home to find the stereo going *full blast* and the kitchen a mess⟩
synonyms all out, full steam ahead, full tilt, tooth and nail
related words completely, fully, totally; extremely, utterly
phrases in full career, to the hilt

full–blooded *adj* of unmixed ancestry — see PUREBRED

full–blown *adj* fully grown or developed — see MATURE 1

full–bodied *adj* having an abundance of some characteristic quality (as flavor) ⟨after that huge Sunday brunch, Mom and Dad needed a *full-bodied* coffee⟩
synonyms concentrated, full, potent, rich, robust, strong
related words heavy; straight, undiluted, unmixed
near antonyms diluted, watered (down), watery
antonyms light, mild, thin, weak

full dress *n* dressy clothing — see FINERY

full–fledged *adj* fully grown or developed — see MATURE 1

full–grown *adj* fully grown or developed — see MATURE 1

full–scale *adj* trying all possibilities — see EXHAUSTIVE

full steam ahead *adv* with all power or resources being used — see FULL BLAST

full tilt *adv* **1** with all power or resources being used — see FULL BLAST
2 with great speed — see FAST 1

fully *adv* **1** to a full extent or degree ⟨only with daybreak did we *fully* realize the extent of the damage from the storm⟩
synonyms all, altogether, clean, completely, dead, entirely, fast, flat, full, perfectly, plumb [*chiefly dialect*], quite, thoroughly, totally, utterly, well, wholly
related words absolutely, categorically, unqualifiedly; by and large, chiefly, generally, largely, mainly, more or less, mostly, predominately, primarily, principally
phrases at length, to pieces, to the hilt
near antonyms barely, hardly, just, scarcely
antonyms partially, partly
2 with attention to all aspects or details — see THOROUGHLY 1

fulminate *vb* to talk loudly and wildly — see RANT

fulmination *n* harsh insulting language — see ABUSE 1

fulsome *adj* overly or insincerely flattering ⟨the player's *fulsome* praise for the coach showed just how hard he was trying to be named captain of the team⟩
synonyms adulatory, gushing, unctuous
related words drooling, slavering, slobbering; cloying, sickening; demonstrative, effusive, mushy; hypocritical, insincere, sanctimonious; endearing, ingratiating; extravagant, lavish, unrestrained; abundant, copious, profuse
near antonyms earnest, genuine, heartfelt, sincere, unfeigned

fumble *n* an unintentional departure from truth or accuracy — see ERROR 1

fumble *vb* **1** to make or do (something) in a clumsy or unskillful way — see BOTCH
2 to search for something blindly or uncertainly — see GROPE

fumbled *adj* showing or marked by a lack of skill

and tact (as in dealing with a situation) — see AWKWARD 2

fume *vb* **1** to be excited or emotionally stirred up with anger — see BOIL 1
2 to express one's anger usually violently — see RAGE 1

fuming *adj* feeling or showing anger — see ANGRY

fun *adj* providing amusement or enjoyment ⟨there were so many *fun* things to do at summer camp that I really hated to leave⟩
synonyms amusing, delightful, diverting, enjoyable, entertaining, pleasurable
related words agreeable, beguiling, pleasant; funny, hilarious, humorous; gay, happy, jolly, merry; exciting, stimulating, thrilling
near antonyms disagreeable, unpleasant
antonyms boring, dull

fun *n* **1** someone or something that provides amusement or enjoyment ⟨theme parks with their rides, shows, and games are great *fun* for the whole family⟩
synonyms delight, diversion, entertainment, pleasure, recreation
related words binge, fling, frolic, gambol, lark, revel, rollick, romp, spree; carousing, festivity, gaiety (*also* gayety), hilarity, merrymaking, revelry; picnic; laugh, riot, scream
antonyms bore, bummer, downer, drag
2 an attitude or manner not to be taken seriously ⟨when I said that playing the piano like that could get you arrested, I only said it in *fun*⟩
synonyms game, jest, play, sport
related words facetiousness, flippancy, levity
near antonyms earnestness, gravity, seriousness
antonyms earnest
3 activity engaged in to amuse oneself — see PLAY 1

fun *vb* to make jokes — see JOKE

function *n* **1** a social gathering — see PARTY 1
2 an assignment at which one regularly works for pay — see JOB 1
3 the action for which a person or thing is specially fitted or used or for which a thing exists — see ROLE

function *vb* to have a certain purpose ⟨the heart *functions* as a pump for the blood⟩
synonyms act, perform, serve, work
related words operate, run; control, direct, manage

functional *adj* **1** being in effective operation — see ACTIVE 1
2 capable of being put to use or account — see PRACTICAL 1
3 capable of or suitable for being used for a particular purpose — see USABLE 1

functionary *n* **1** a person who holds a public office — see OFFICIAL
2 a worker in a government agency — see BUREAUCRAT

functioning *adj* being in effective operation — see ACTIVE 1

fund *n* **1** a sum of money set aside for a particular purpose ⟨our club has a *fund* for parties—which we like to have as often as possible⟩
synonyms account, budget, deposit, kitty, nest egg, pool
related words chest, coffer(s); assets, savings, savings account; bankroll, cache, collection, hoard, reserve, treasure; petty cash, pin money, pocket money, spending money
2 funds *pl* available money ⟨my *funds* were a little low, so I asked my favorite lending institution—Dad—for a small advance on my allowance⟩
synonyms bankroll, finances, pocket, resources, wherewithal
related words cash, money; assets, capital, means, wealth; purse, treasury
3 the number of individuals or amount of something available at any given time — see SUPPLY

fund *vb* **1** to furnish (as an institution) with a regular source of income — see ENDOW 2
2 to provide money for — see FINANCE 1

fundamental *adj* of or relating to the simplest facts or theories of a subject — see ELEMENTARY

fundamentals *n pl* general or basic truths on which other truths or theories can be based — see PRINCIPLES 1

funeral *adj* expressing or suggesting mourning — see MOURNFUL 1

funeral director *n* a person who manages funerals and prepares the dead for burial or cremation ⟨the *funeral director* instructed the pallbearers on how to proceed⟩
synonyms mortician, undertaker
related words embalmer

funereal *adj* causing or marked by an atmosphere lacking in cheer — see GLOOMY 1

funnel *vb* to cause to move to a central point or along a restricted pathway — see CHANNEL

funniness *n* the amusing quality or element in something — see HUMOR 1

funning *adj* marked by or expressive of mild or good-natured teasing — see QUIZZICAL

funny *adj* **1** causing or intended to cause laughter ⟨a very *funny* movie that had audiences rolling in the aisles⟩
synonyms antic, comic, comical, droll, farcical, hilarious, humorous, hysterical, laughable, ludicrous, ridiculous, riotous, risible, screaming, sidesplitting, uproarious
related words amusing, diverting, entertaining; clownish, slapstick, zany; facetious, flip, flippant, pert, smart, smart-alecky (*or* smart-aleck); jocular, playful, waggish; priceless, rich, whimsical, witty; gleeful, merry, mirthful
near antonyms grave, serious, sober, solemn, somber (*or* sombre); affecting, moving, poignant, touching, tragic; lachrymose, mournful, sad, tearful
antonyms humorless, lame, uncomic, unfunny
2 different from the ordinary in a way that causes curiosity or suspicion — see ODD 2
3 noticeably different from what is generally found or experienced — see UNUSUAL 1

funny *n* a series of drawings that tell a story or part of a story — see COMIC STRIP

fur *n* **1** the hairy covering of a mammal especially when fine, soft, and thick ⟨the chinchilla is known for its exceptionally soft *fur*⟩
synonyms coat, fleece, hair, pelage, pile, wool
related words hide, pelt, skin
2 a soft airy substance or covering — see FUZZ
3 the outer covering of an animal removed for its commercial value — see HIDE 1

furbelow *n* a strip of fabric gathered or pleated on one edge and used as trimming — see RUFFLE

furious *adj* **1** marked by great and often stressful excitement or activity ⟨everyone worked at a *furious* pace in order to get the float ready for the parade⟩

synonyms delirious, feverish, fierce, frantic, frenetic, frenzied, mad, rabid, violent, wild
related words concentrated, high-pressured, intense, vehement; excessive, extreme, inordinate; crazy, demented, insane, irrational
near antonyms calm, peaceful, quiet, subdued, tranquil; moderate, reasonable, temperate; casual, easygoing, low-pressure
antonyms relaxed
2 extreme in degree, power, or effect — see INTENSE
3 feeling or showing anger — see ANGRY
4 marked by bursts of destructive force or intense activity — see VIOLENT 1

furlough *n* the termination of the employment of an employee or a work force often temporarily — see LAYOFF

furnish *vb* **1** to provide (someone) with what is needed for a task or activity <the students were *furnished* with brushes, crayons, pencils, and various other art supplies>
synonyms accoutre (*or* accouter), equip, fit (out), outfit, rig, supply
related words stock, store; bestow, donate, give, present; deal, dispense, distribute, dole (out); allocate, allot, assign
near antonyms deprive, dispossess, divest, strip
2 to put (something) into the possession of someone for use or consumption <we'll gladly *furnish* the food for any out-of-town guests>
synonyms deliver, feed, give, hand, hand over, provide, supply
related words administer, dispense, distribute, dole (out), mete (out), parcel (out); cede, deed, transfer
near antonyms conserve, preserve, save
antonyms hold (back), keep (back), reserve, retain, withhold

furnishings *n pl* the movable articles in a room — see FURNITURE

furniture *n* the movable articles in a room <we bought all new *furniture* for our new house>
synonyms appointments, cabinetwork, furnishings, movables (*or* moveables)
related words effects, goods, possessions
near antonyms fixtures

furor *n* **1** a state of noisy, confused activity — see COMMOTION
2 a state of wildly excited activity or emotion — see FRENZY
3 an intense emotional state of displeasure with someone or something — see ANGER

furore *n* **1** a state of noisy, confused activity — see COMMOTION
2 a state of wildly excited activity or emotion — see FRENZY

furrow *n* a small fold in a soft and otherwise smooth surface — see WRINKLE 1

furrow *vb* **1** to cut into and turn over the sod of (a piece of land) using a bladed implement — see PLOW 1
2 to develop creases or folds — see WRINKLE 1

furry *adj* **1** covered with or as if with hair — see HAIRY 1
2 made of or resembling hair — see HAIRY 2

further *adj* resulting in an increase in amount or number — see ADDITIONAL

further *adv* **1** at or to a greater distance or more advanced point — see FARTHER
2 in addition to what has been said — see MORE 1

further *vb* to help the growth or development of — see FOSTER 1

furtherance *n* forward movement in time or place — see ADVANCE 1

furthermore *adv* in addition to what has been said — see MORE 1

furthermost *adj* most distant from a center — see EXTREME 1

furthest *adj* most distant from a center — see EXTREME 1

furtive *adj* **1** given to acting in secret and to concealing one's intentions — see SNEAKY 1
2 undertaken or done so as to escape being observed or known by others — see SECRET 1

fury *n* **1** a bad-tempered scolding woman — see SHREW
2 a state of wildly excited activity or emotion — see FRENZY
3 an intense emotional state of displeasure with someone or something — see ANGER

fuse *vb* **1** to come together to form a single unit — see UNITE 1
2 to go from a solid to a liquid state — see LIQUEFY
3 to turn into a single mass that is more or less the same throughout — see BLEND 1

fusillade *n* a rapid or overwhelming outpouring of many things at once — see BARRAGE

fusion *n* a distinct entity formed by the combining of two or more different things — see BLEND

fuss *n* **1** a feeling or declaration of disapproval or dissent — see OBJECTION
2 a state of nervous or irritated concern — see FRET
3 a state of noisy, confused activity — see COMMOTION
4 an expression of dissatisfaction, pain, or resentment — see COMPLAINT 1

fuss *vb* **1** to express dissatisfaction, pain, or resentment usually tiresomely — see COMPLAIN
2 to make an exaggerated display of affection or enthusiasm — see GUSH 2
3 to make often peevish criticisms or objections about matters that are minor, unimportant, or irrelevant — see QUIBBLE
4 to use flattery or the doing of favors in order to win approval especially from a superior — see FAWN

fusser *n* **1** a person who makes frequent complaints usually about little things — see CRYBABY
2 an irritable and complaining person — see GROUCH

fussy *adj* **1** given to complaining a lot <the kids riding in the back were *fussy* passengers, always asking "Are we there yet?">
synonyms crabby, cranky, grouchy, grumpy, querulous
related words fidgety, restive, restless, squirmy, uneasy; discontented, disgruntled, displeased, dissatisfied; fretful, nervous, worrisome; cantankerous, crotchety, irascible, irritable, ornery
near antonyms amiable, genial, good-humored, good-natured, good-tempered; accommodating, complaisant, obliging; easygoing, laid-back, relaxed
antonyms uncomplaining
2 hard to please — see FINICKY
3 taking great care and effort — see PAINSTAKING

fusty *adj* having an unpleasant smell — see MALODOROUS

futile *adj* producing no results ⟨the prison is so well guarded that all attempts to escape have been *futile*⟩
synonyms abortive, bootless, empty, fruitless, ineffective, ineffectual, unavailing, unproductive, unprofitable, unsuccessful, useless, vain
related words hollow, idle, meaningless, pointless, worthless; hopeless, impossible; inadequate, insufficient
phrases in vain, of no avail
near antonyms meaningful, worthwhile; adequate, sufficient
antonyms effective, effectual, efficacious, efficient, fruitful, productive, profitable, successful

future *adj* of a time after the present ⟨we must preserve our national parks in all their glory so that *future* generations can experience the majesty of nature⟩
synonyms coming, unborn
related words approaching, forthcoming, imminent, impending, nearing, oncoming, pending, upcoming; later, posterior, subsequent; anticipated, awaited, expected, planned, predicted, projected; eventual, final, last, ultimate
near antonyms ancient, olden
antonyms bygone, past

future *n* **1** time that is to come ⟨in the *future*, there may be medical discoveries that are beyond our fondest dreams⟩
synonyms by-and-by, futurity, hereafter, offing
related words eventuality, finality; posterity
near antonyms yesterday, yesteryear; antiquity, old, yore
antonyms past
2 what is going to happen to someone in the time ahead — see FORTUNE 1

futurist *n* one who predicts future events or developments — see PROPHET

futurity *n* time that is to come — see FUTURE 1

fuzz *n* a soft airy substance or covering ⟨a comfortable old sweater with clumps of *fuzz* all over it⟩
synonyms down, floss, fluff, fur, lint, nap, pile
related words batting

fuzzy *adj* **1** made of or resembling hair — see HAIRY 2
2 not clearly expressed — see VAGUE 1
3 not seen or understood clearly — see FAINT 1

G

gab *vb* to engage in casual or rambling conversation — see CHAT

gabble *n* unintelligible or meaningless talk — see GIBBERISH

gabble *vb* **1** to engage in casual or rambling conversation — see CHAT
2 to speak rapidly, inarticulately, and usually unintelligibly — see BABBLE 1

gabbler *n* a person who talks constantly — see CHATTERBOX

gabby *adj* fond of talking or conversation — see TALKATIVE

gabfest *n* friendly, informal conversation or an instance of this — see CHAT

gad (about) *vb* to move about from place to place aimlessly — see WANDER

gadabout *n* a person who roams about without a fixed route or destination — see NOMAD

gadfly *n* one who is obnoxiously annoying — see NUISANCE 1

gadget *n* an interesting and often novel device with a practical use ⟨she tried out a new *gadget* for weeding the garden⟩
synonyms appliance, contraption, contrivance, gimmick, gizmo (*or* gismo), jigger
related words implement, instrument, tool, utensil; ingenuity, innovation, invention; accessory, adjunct; mechanism, trick

gaffe *n* a socially improper or unsuitable act or remark — see IMPROPRIETY 2

gag *n* something said or done to cause laughter — see JOKE 1

gag *vb* **1** to discharge the contents of the stomach through the mouth — see VOMIT
2 to experience complete or partial blockage of the windpipe — see CHOKE 2

gage *n* something given or held to assure that the giver will keep a promise — see PLEDGE 1

gaiety *also* **gayety** *n* **1** dressy clothing — see FINERY
2 joyful or festive activity — see MERRYMAKING

gaily *also* **gayly** *adv* **1** in a cheerful or happy manner ⟨we sat around the table, *gaily* teasing each other and laughing about the good old days⟩
synonyms cheerfully, happily, heartily, jocosely, jovially, merrily, mirthfully
related words blithely, blithesomely, breezily, brightly, buoyantly; cheerily, gladly, gladsomely, sanguinely, sunnily; good-humoredly, good-naturedly
near antonyms abjectly, dejectedly, despondently, disconsolately, dispiritedly, wretchedly; dolefully, dolorously, forlornly, mournfully, plaintively, sorrowfully; dourly, glumly, sternly, sulkily, sullenly; dismally, drearily, gloomily
antonyms bleakly, cheerlessly, darkly, heavily, miserably, morosely, unhappily
2 in a quick and spirited manner ⟨children *gaily* running to the buses on the last day of school⟩
synonyms animatedly, animately, exuberantly, high-spiritedly, jauntily, pertly, sprightly, trippingly
related words friskily, playfully, skittishly, sportively; briskly, crisply, snappily, springily; breezily, cockishly; allegro
near antonyms idly, indolently, lazily, slothfully; heavily, inactively, listlessly
antonyms dully, inanimately, sluggishly, tardily
3 in a bright and showy way ⟨the Mexican dancers were *gaily* dressed in lavish, bright costumes⟩
synonyms dashingly, flamboyantly, flashily, jauntily, rakishly, swankily

related words garishly, gaudily, loud, loudly, ostentatiously; fancily, gallantly, ornately; nattily, neatly, smartly; conspicuously, luridly, spectacularly, strikingly; gorgeously, splendidly
near antonyms inconspicuously, unobtrusively, unpretentiously; chastely, demurely, homely, modestly; plainly, simply; colorlessly, dirtily, drably, dully; bleakly, severely, somberly
antonyms conservatively, plain, quietly

gain *n* **1** something added (as by growth) — see INCREASE 1
2 the amount of money left when expenses are subtracted from the total amount received — see PROFIT 1
3 gains *pl* an increase usually measured in money that comes from labor, business, or property — see INCOME

gain *vb* **1** to increase in ⟨as the car coasted downhill, it gradually *gained* speed and momentum⟩
synonyms build (up), gather, grow (in), pick up
related words accrue, accumulate, amass; excite, stimulate; enhance, enrich, maximize; boost, jack (up), mount, step up
near antonyms abate, diminish (in), dip, dwindle, fall (in), lessen, taper, taper off
antonyms decrease (in), lose
2 to receive as return for effort — see EARN 1
3 to become healthy and strong again after illness or weakness — see CONVALESCE

gainful *adj* yielding a profit — see PROFITABLE 1

gainsay *vb* **1** to declare not to be true — see DENY 1
2 to make an assertion that is contrary to one made by (another) — see CONTRADICT 1

gal *n* **1** a woman with whom one is in love — see GIRLFRIEND
2 a young usually unmarried woman — see GIRL 1

gala *n* a time or program of special events and entertainment in honor of something — see FESTIVAL

gale *n* a sudden intense expression of strong feeling — see OUTBURST 1

gall *n* **1** a deep-seated ill will — see ENMITY
2 shameless boldness — see EFFRONTERY

gall *vb* **1** to damage or diminish by continued friction — see ABRADE 1
2 to disturb the peace of mind of (someone) especially by repeated disagreeable acts — see IRRITATE 1
3 to make sore by continued rubbing — see CHAFE 1

gallant *adj* **1** feeling or displaying no fear by temperament — see BRAVE
2 having, characterized by, or arising from a dignified and generous nature — see NOBLE 2
3 large and impressive in size, grandeur, extent, or conception — see GRAND 1

gallant *n* **1** a man extremely interested in his clothing and personal appearance — see DANDY 1
2 a man who courts a woman usually with the goal of marrying her — see SUITOR 1

gallantly *adv* in a manner befitting a person of the highest character and ideals — see GREATLY 1

gallantry *n* strength of mind to carry on in spite of danger — see COURAGE

gallery *n* **1** a building or part of a building in which objects of interest are displayed — see MUSEUM
2 a typically long narrow way connecting parts of a building — see HALL 2

galling *adj* **1** causing annoyance — see ANNOYING
2 hard to accept or bear especially emotionally — see BITTER 2

gallivant *also* **galavant** *vb* to move about from place to place aimlessly — see WANDER

gallivanting *also* **galavanting** *adj* traveling from place to place — see ITINERANT

gallop *vb* to go at a pace faster than a walk — see RUN 1

galore *adj* pouring forth in great amounts — see PROFUSE

galvanize *vb* to cause a pleasurable stimulation of the feelings — see THRILL

galvanizing *adj* causing great emotional or mental stimulation — see EXCITING 1

gamble *n* a risky undertaking ⟨would never take a *gamble* on such a poorly researched business deal⟩
synonyms chance, enterprise, flier (*or* flyer), speculation, venture
related words bet, hazard, stake, wager; liberty; dark horse, long shot, play

gamble *vb* to risk (something) on the outcome of an uncertain event — see BET

gamble (on) *vb* to take a chance on — see RISK 1

gamble (with) *vb* to place in danger — see ENDANGER

gambler *n* one that bets (as on the outcome of a contest or sports event) — see BETTOR

gambol *n* a time or instance of carefree fun — see FLING 1

gambol *vb* to play and run about happily — see FROLIC 1

game *adj* having a desire or inclination (as for a specified course of action) — see WILLING 1

game *n* **1** a competitive encounter between individuals or groups carried on for amusement, exercise, or in pursuit of a prize ⟨decided he would indulge in a friendly basketball *game* with his friends before dinner⟩
synonyms bout, competition, contest, event, match, meet, sweepstakes, tournament, tourney
related words athletics, sport; battle, conflict, scrimmage, skirmish, struggle, tug-of-war, tussle; championship, final, nightcap, play-off, semifinal; derby, field day, open; marathon, race; heat, round, run, set; rally, volley; rubber, runoff, sudden death; dead heat, photo finish, seesaw; classic
2 a method worked out in advance for achieving some objective — see PLAN 1
3 an attitude or manner not to be taken seriously — see FUN 2

gameness *n* cheerful readiness to do something — see ALACRITY

gamut *n* the distance or extent between possible extremes — see RANGE 3

gander *n* an instance of looking especially briefly — see LOOK 2

gang *n* **1** a group of people working together on a task ⟨a *gang* of neighborhood residents spent the weekend cleaning up the park⟩
synonyms band, company, crew, outfit, party, squad, team
related words army, battalion, brigade, corps, troop; force, host, posse, stable, troupe; administration, department, help, personnel, staff
2 a group of people sharing a common interest and relating together socially ⟨the whole *gang* went out for pizza⟩ ⟨the school's computer hackers had their own little *gang*⟩

synonyms body, bunch, circle, clan, clique, community, coterie, crowd, fold, lot, ring, set
related words bevy, covey, flock, herd, horde, mob, swarm, throng; club, college, fellowship, guild (*also* gild), league, organization, society; cohort, pack; camp, faction, sect, side, tribe; mess, squad; brotherhood, fraternity, order, sisterhood, sodality, sorority; commune; alliance, bloc, coalition, confederation, congress, council, federation, union
near antonyms loner; individualist
3 a group involved in secret or criminal activities — see RING 1

gangling *adj* being tall, thin and usually loose-jointed — see LANKY

gangly *adj* being tall, thin and usually loose-jointed — see LANKY

gangster *n* a violent, brutal person who is often a member of an organized gang — see HOODLUM

gaol *n, chiefly British* a place of confinement for persons held in lawful custody — see JAIL

gap *n* **1** an open space in a barrier (as a wall or hedge) <there were several visible *gaps* in the wall where the drywall had pulled away from the wall framing>
synonyms breach, break, discontinuity, gulf, hole, interval, opening, rent, rift, separation
related words chink, cleft, crack, cranny, crevice, fissure; notch, slit, slot, split; interspace, pore, space; abyss, aperture, cavity, chasm, gape, orifice; fracture, rupture, severance, sundering
2 a break in continuity <there was a 15-minute *gap* between the two televised sporting events>
synonyms discontinuity, hiatus, interim, interlude, intermission, interruption, interval
related words caesura, pause, space; lapse, suspension; lull, recess, respite, rest
near antonyms continuum, run, stretch; procession, progression
antonyms continuation, continuity
3 a narrow opening between hillsides or mountains that can be used for passage — see CANYON

gape *vb* to look long and hard in wonder or surprise <she *gaped* openmouthed at the young man in the mall with purple and green hair>
synonyms gawk, gaze, goggle, peer, rubberneck, stare
related words glare, gloat, glower; eye, observe, watch; leer, ogle
near antonyms glance, glimpse, peek, peep; browse, dip (into), scan; blink, wink

garb *n* clothing chosen as appropriate for a specific situation — see OUTFIT 1

garb *vb* to outfit with clothes and especially fine or special clothes — see CLOTHE 1

garbage *n* discarded or useless material <the stray dogs were looking for leftover food in the family's *garbage*>
synonyms chaff, deadwood, dross, dust, junk, litter, refuse, riffraff, rubbish, scrap, trash, waste
related words offal, sewage, slop, swill, wash; debris, detritus, rubble, ruins; lumber, odds and ends; flotsam, jetsam; castoff, cull, discard, reject, throwaway; nothing, straw, two bits
near antonyms catch, treasure, treasure trove
antonyms find, prize

garble *vb* to change so much as to create a wrong impression or alter the meaning of <the candidate complained that his views had been deliberately *garbled* by his opponent>
synonyms color, distort, falsify, misinterpret, misrepresent, misstate, pervert, twist, warp
related words belie, camouflage, disguise, mask, veil; complicate, confound, confuse, mix up; mystify, obscure, puzzle; equivocate, fib, lie, palter, prevaricate
near antonyms clarify, clear (up), explain, illuminate, illustrate, interpret, spell out; decipher

garden *adj* **1** being of the type that is encountered in the normal course of events — see ORDINARY 1
2 often observed or encountered — see COMMON 1

garish *adj* excessively showy — see GAUDY

garishness *n* excessive or unnecessary display — see OSTENTATION

garment *vb* to outfit with clothes and especially fine or special clothes — see CLOTHE 1

garner *vb* **1** to bring together in one body or place — see GATHER 1
2 to receive as return for effort — see EARN 1

garnish *n* something that decorates or beautifies — see DECORATION 1

garnish *vb* to make more attractive by adding something that is beautiful or becoming — see DECORATE

garrote *or* **garotte** *vb* to keep (someone) from breathing by exerting pressure on the windpipe — see CHOKE 1

garrulous *adj* fond of talking or conversation — see TALKATIVE

gas *n* **1** boastful speech or writing — see BOMBAST 1
2 language that is impressive-sounding but not meaningful or sincere — see RHETORIC 1
3 *slang* a source of great satisfaction — see DELIGHT 1

gas *vb* to engage in casual or rambling conversation — see CHAT

gaseous *adj* marked by the use of impressive-sounding but mostly meaningless words and phrases — see RHETORICAL

gash *n* a long deep cut <got a *gash* in his knee that required four stitches>
synonyms incision, laceration, rent, rip, slash, slit, tear
related words abrasion, score, scrape, scratch; injury, wound

gash *vb* to penetrate with a sharp edge (as a knife) — see CUT 1

gasp *vb* to breathe hard, quickly, or with difficulty <the runner was *gasping* by the end of the marathon>
synonyms blow, hyperventilate, pant, puff, wheeze
related words choke, gulp, huff; exhale, expire
phrases to be out of breath

gassy *adj* marked by the use of impressive-sounding but mostly meaningless words and phrases — see RHETORICAL

gate *n* **1** a barrier by which an entry is closed and opened — see DOOR 1
2 the opening through which one can enter or leave a structure — see DOOR 2
3 a fixture for controlling the flow of a liquid — see FAUCET

gatekeeper *n* a person who tends a door — see DOORKEEPER

gateway *n* **1** something that allows someone to achieve a desired goal — see PASSPORT

2 the means or right of entering or participating in — see ENTRANCE 1
3 the opening through which one can enter or leave a structure — see DOOR 2
gather *vb* **1** to bring together in one body or place ⟨he *gathered* the leftovers from the table and gave them to the dog⟩ ⟨let's *gather* the students and have them line up on the playground before going in from recess⟩
synonyms accumulate, amass, assemble, collect, concentrate, garner, group, lump, pick up, round up, scrape (together)
related words agglomerate, aggregate, ball, bunch, cluster, huddle; heap, pile, stack; muster, raise, rally; flock, herd, hive, pack, press, swarm, throng, troop; congregate, forgather (*or* foregather), meet, rendezvous; affiliate, ally, combine, connect, join, link, merge, unite; arrange, organize, systematize; regather, regroup
phrases get together
near antonyms break up, disband, disintegrate, dissolve, separate, sever, split (up); dismiss, send
antonyms dispel, disperse, dissipate, scatter
2 to catch or collect (a crop or natural resource) for human use — see HARVEST
3 to come together into one body or place — see ASSEMBLE 1
4 to form an opinion through reasoning and information — see INFER 1
5 to gradually form into a layer, pile, or mass — see COLLECT 2
6 to increase in — see GAIN 1
gather (up) *vb* to call into being through the use of one's inner resources or powers — see SUMMON 2
gathering *n* **1** a body of people come together in one place ⟨the President spoke before the *gathering* of student leaders⟩
synonyms assemblage, assembly, conference, congregation, convocation, meeting, muster
related words aggregation, collection, conglomeration; company, coterie, gang, pack; caucus, forum, market, panel, rally, symposium, synod; crowd, flock, horde, legion, multitude, press, swarm, throng; crush, mob, rabble
2 a coming together of a number of persons for a specified purpose — see MEETING 1
3 a mass or quantity that has piled up or that has been gathered — see ACCUMULATION 1
gauche *adj* lacking social grace and assurance — see AWKWARD 1
gaud *n* a small object displayed for its attractiveness or interest — see KNICKKNACK
gaudiness *n* excessive or unnecessary display — see OSTENTATION
gaudy *adj* excessively showy ⟨the bright purple sequined miniskirt she wore to the wedding was *gaudy*⟩
synonyms flamboyant, flashy, garish, glitzy, loud, ostentatious, splashy, swank (*or* swanky), tawdry
related words meretricious, pretentious; graceless, inelegant, tacky, tasteless, vulgar; bedizened, extravagant, fancy, florid, glittery, spectacular; lurid, ornate, overdone, overwrought
near antonyms appropriate, fitting, proper; inconspicuous, muted, restrained, subdued, toned (down), unobtrusive; elegant, graceful, tasteful; modest, plain, simple, unpretentious
antonyms conservative, quiet, understated
gauge *also* **gage** *vb* **1** to decide the size, amount, number, or distance of (something) without actual measurement — see ESTIMATE 2
2 to find out the size, extent, or amount of — see MEASURE
gaunt *adj* suffering extreme weight loss as a result of hunger or disease — see EMACIATED
gauntlet *also* **gantlet** *n* a test of faith, patience, or strength — see TRIAL
gauzy *adj* **1** being of a material lacking in sturdiness or substance — see FLIMSY 1
2 very thin and easy to see through — see SHEER 1
gawk *n* a big clumsy often slow-witted person — see OAF
gawk *vb* to look long and hard in wonder or surprise — see GAPE
gawky *adj* lacking in physical ease and grace in movement or in the use of the hands — see CLUMSY 1
gay *adj* **1** having much high-spirited energy and movement — see LIVELY 1
2 having or showing a lack of concern or seriousness — see CAREFREE
3 indicative of or marked by high spirits or good humor — see MERRY
4 having or showing a good mood or disposition — see CHEERFUL 1
5 serving to lift one's spirits — see CHEERFUL 2
gaze *vb* to look long and hard in wonder or surprise — see GAPE
gazette *n* a publication that appears at regular intervals — see JOURNAL
gear *n* items needed for the performance of a task or activity — see EQUIPMENT
gel *vb* to turn from a liquid into a substance resembling jelly — see COAGULATE
gelatinous *adj* being of such a thick consistency as to readily cling to objects upon contact — see STICKY 1
gem *n* **1** a usually valuable stone cut and polished for ornament ⟨a ring set with diamonds and other precious *gems*⟩
synonyms brilliant, gemstone, jewel
related words birthstone; baguette, cameo, scarab, solitaire, teardrop; paste, rhinestone, zircon
near antonyms rough
2 someone or something unusually desirable — see PRIZE 1
gemstone *n* a usually valuable stone cut and polished for ornament — see GEM 1
genealogy *n* the line of ancestors from whom a person is descended — see ANCESTRY
general *adj* **1** belonging or relating to the whole ⟨a *general* increase in postage rates⟩ ⟨there's been a *general* improvement in the economy⟩
synonyms blanket, common, generic, global, overall, universal
related words broad, collective, comprehensive, extensive, pervasive, sweeping, ubiquitous, wholesale, wide, widespread; complete, full, plenary; planetary, worldwide
near antonyms component, constituent; cross-sectional, divisional, fragmentary, partial; local, localized, regional, sectional
antonyms individual, particular
2 relating to the main elements and not to specific details ⟨gave the *general* impression of being kindhearted⟩ ⟨a *general* course of study in American history⟩

synonyms all-around (*also* all-round), bird's-eye, broad, nonspecific, overall
related words comprehensive, inclusive; absolute, boundless, expansive, extensive, infinite, panoramic, sweeping, vast, wide; indeterminate, nebulous, nondescript, vague; nonspecific, unlimited, unrestricted, unspecified
near antonyms limited, restricted, specified; distinct, explicit, precise, sharp; comprehensive, elaborate, full, mapped (out), thorough; enumerated, inventoried, itemized, listed; individual, singular; particular, peculiar
antonyms delineated, detailed, particularized, specific
3 held by or applicable to a majority of the people ⟨it was the *general* opinion that the politician was a liar⟩ ⟨the *general* mood of the nation was one of hope and optimism⟩
synonyms common, public, popular, prevailing, vulgar
related words unanimous, universal; pop; everyday, familiar, household, usual, well-known; contemporary, current, present; dominant, predominant, preponderant; characteristic, typical; pandemic, pervasive, prevalent, rife, widespread; communal, shared
near antonyms rare, strange, unknown, unusual; distinctive, especial, idiosyncratic, peculiar, special, unique; individual, separate, singular; nonpublic, personal, private
antonyms uncommon, unpopular
4 not limited or specialized in application or purpose ⟨a new kitchen tool of *general* usefulness⟩
synonyms all-around (*also* all-round), all-purpose, unlimited, unqualified, unrestricted, unspecialized
related words broad, wide; nonspecific, unspecified, vague
near antonyms bounded, circumscribed, confined, definite, demarcated, determinate, finite, qualified
antonyms limited, restricted, specialized, technical

generality *n* **1** an idea or statement about all of the members of a group or all the instances of a situation — see GENERALIZATION
2 the main or greater part of something as distinguished from its appendages — see BODY 1

generalization *n* an idea or statement about all of the members of a group or all the instances of a situation ⟨the *generalization* that children who like violent entertainment grow up to be violent criminals⟩
synonyms aphorism, generality, maxim, stereotype
related words concept, conception, notion; precept, rule, rule of thumb; adage, proverb, saw, saying; cliché, commonplace, platitude, truism; hypothesis, proposition, theory

generally *adv* **1** according to the usual course of things — see NATURALLY 2
2 for the most part — see CHIEFLY

generate *vb* to be the cause of (a situation, action, or state of mind) — see EFFECT

generator *n* a person who establishes a whole new field of endeavor — see FATHER 2

generic *adj* belonging or relating to the whole — see GENERAL 1

generosity *n* the quality or state of being generous — see LIBERALITY

generous *adj* **1** giving or sharing in abundance and without hesitation ⟨a civic leader who is very *generous* with his money and time⟩
synonyms bounteous, bountiful, charitable, free, freehanded, liberal, munificent, openhanded, unselfish, unsparing
related words extravagant, handsome, lavish, profuse, unstinting; altruistic, beneficent, benevolent, hospitable, humanitarian, philanthropic; compassionate, good-hearted, greathearted, kindly, magnanimous, openhearted
near antonyms mean, petty, small; frugal, spare, sparing, thrifty; chary, stinting; acquisitive, avaricious, avid, coveting, covetous, desirous, grasping, hoggish, itchy, mercenary, rapacious; begrudging, envious, grudging, resentful
antonyms cheap, close, closefisted, miserly, niggardly, parsimonious, penurious, selfish, stingy, tight, tightfisted, uncharitable
2 being more than enough without being excessive — see PLENTIFUL

generously *adv* in a generous manner — see WELL 2

genesis *n* the point at which something begins — see BEGINNING

genetic *also* **genetical** *adj* genetically passed or capable of being passed from parent to offspring — see HEREDITARY

genial *adj* **1** having an easygoing and pleasing manner especially in social situations — see AMIABLE
2 having or showing kindly feeling and sincere interest — see FRIENDLY 1
3 showing a natural kindness and courtesy especially in social situations — see GRACIOUS 1

geniality *n* the state or quality of having a pleasant or agreeable manner in socializing with others — see AMIABILITY 1

genius *n* **1** a very smart person ⟨the 16-year-old college graduate was considered to be a *genius*⟩
synonyms brain, intellect, thinker, whiz, wizard
related words egghead, highbrow, intellectual; master, virtuoso; ace, crackerjack, natural; sage, savant
near antonyms ignoramus, illiterate, know-nothing; ass, donkey, fool, jackass; beast, boor, cad, churl, clown, creep, cretin, cur, heel, jerk, louse, lout, skunk, snake, stinker
antonyms blockhead, dodo, dolt, dope, dumbbell, dummy, dunce, fathead, goon, half-wit, idiot, imbecile, knothead, moron, nitwit, numskull (*or* numbskull), pinhead
2 a special and usually inborn ability — see TALENT
3 a habitual attraction to some activity or thing — see INCLINATION 1
4 the set of qualities that makes a person, a group of people, or a thing different from others — see NATURE 1

gent *n* an adult male human being — see MAN 1

genteel *adj* **1** following the established traditions of refined society and good taste — see PROPER 1
2 having or showing a taste for the fine arts and gracious living — see CULTIVATED
3 of high birth, rank, or station — see NOBLE 1
4 showing consideration, courtesy, and good manners — see POLITE 1

gentile *n* a person who does not worship the God of the Bible — see HEATHEN 1

gentility *n* speech or behavior that is a sign of good breeding — see POLITENESS

gentle *adj* **1** not harsh or stern especially in manner, nature, or effect ⟨use a *gentle* detergent on that delicate silk blouse⟩ ⟨the pastor had a *gentle* disposition that calmed everyone he met⟩
synonyms balmy, benign, bland, delicate, light, mellow, mild, soft, soothing, tender
related words sleek, slick, smooth; calm, pacific, peaceful, placid, quiet, serene, tranquil; clement, compassionate, easy, lenient, merciful; buffering, cushioning, softening
near antonyms exquisite, fierce, intense, powerful, severe; forceful, forcible, savage, violent; roughened, rugged, strong; abrading, irritating, roughening; grim, gruff, rude, stiff; heavy-handed, oppressive, tyrannical (*also* tyrannic)
antonyms abrasive, caustic, coarse, hard, harsh, rough, scathing, stern, ungentle
2 marked by temperatures that are neither too high nor too low — see CLEMENT
3 of high birth, rank, or station — see NOBLE 1

gentle *vb* to lessen the shock of — see CUSHION

gentleman *n* **1** a man of high birth or social position ⟨many of the signers of the Declaration of Independence were *gentlemen* who were risking everything⟩
synonyms aristocrat, grandee, noble, nobleman, patrician
related words squire; cavalier, knight; don, nawab, seigneur, seignior, sheikh (*or* sheik); baron, baronet, count, duke, earl, esquire, lord, marquess, marquis, prince, thane, viscount; czar (*also* tsar *or* tzar), magnate, mogul, nabob; socialite, swell
near antonyms boor, churl, cotter (*or* cottar), fellah, peasant, peon; commoner, plebeian; proletarian; toiler
2 an adult male human being — see MAN 1
3 an honorable and courteous man — see CAVALIER

gentlewoman *n* a woman of high birth or social position ⟨in the 19th century a number of American *gentlewomen* used their wealth and influence to further abolitionism, women's rights, and other worthy causes⟩
synonyms dame, lady, noblewoman
related words ladyship, madam; baroness, countess, duchess, marchioness; czarina (*also* tsarina *or* tzarina), empress, queen; dowager, matriarch, matron, mistress

gentry *n* the highest class in a society — see ARISTOCRACY

genuine *adj* **1** being exactly as appears or as claimed — see AUTHENTIC 1
2 free from any intent to deceive or impress others — see GUILELESS

genuinely *adv* in actual fact — see VERY 2

geometry *n* the outward appearance of something as distinguished from its substance — see FORM 1

geriatric *adj* being of advanced years and especially past middle age — see ELDERLY

germane *adj* having to do with the matter at hand — see PERTINENT

germfree *adj* free from filth, infection, or dangers to health — see SANITARY

gestation *n* the state of containing unborn young within the body — see PREGNANCY

gesticulation *n* a movement of the body or limbs that expresses or emphasizes an idea or feeling — see GESTURE 1

gesture *n* **1** a movement of the body or limbs that expresses or emphasizes an idea or feeling ⟨a teenager who often shrugs her shoulders in a *gesture* of indifference⟩
synonyms gesticulation, pantomime, sign, signal
related words beck, flourish, shrug, wave; body language, posture; indication, motion
2 an act or utterance that is a customary show of good manners — see CIVILITY 1

gesture *vb* to direct or notify by a movement or gesture — see MOTION

get *vb* **1** to acquire complete knowledge, understanding, or skill in — see LEARN 1
2 to become affected with (a disease or disorder) — see CONTRACT 1
3 to become the father of — see FATHER
4 to cause (someone) to agree with a belief or course of action by using arguments or earnest requests — see PERSUADE
5 to come upon after searching, study, or effort — see FIND 1
6 to disturb the peace of mind of (someone) especially by repeated disagreeable acts — see IRRITATE 1
7 to eventually have as a state or quality — see BECOME
8 to receive as return for effort — see EARN 1
9 to recognize the meaning of — see COMPREHEND 1
10 to take physical control or possession of (something) suddenly or forcibly — see CATCH 1
11 to leave a place often for another — see GO 2

get along *vb* **1** to meet one's day-to-day needs ⟨most college students can *get along* with just a few hours of sleep at night⟩
synonyms cope, do, fare, get by, get on, make out, manage, shift
related words carry on, contrive, fend, handle, scrape (by *or* through), survive; eke out, scrape (out), scrounge, squeeze, wrest, wring; afford, swing
phrases make shift
near antonyms collapse, fail, fall short, fizzle, flounder; decline, peter (out), slump, wane; give up
2 to move forward along a course — see GO 1

getaway *n* the act or an instance of getting free from danger or confinement — see ESCAPE 1

get by *vb* to meet one's day-to-day needs — see GET ALONG 1

get off *vb* **1** to leave a place often for another — see GO 2
2 to take the first step in (a process or course of action) — see BEGIN 1

get on *vb* to meet one's day-to-day needs — see GET ALONG 1

get out *vb* **1** to become known ⟨news of the rock star's secret wedding *got out* to the news media⟩
synonyms come out, leak (out), out, spread
related words break, develop, transpire, unfold; circulate, disclose, reveal, spill, tell
near antonyms hush (up), suppress; conceal, disguise, hide, mask; secrete
2 to get free from a dangerous or confining situation — see ESCAPE 1
3 to produce and release for distribution in printed form — see PUBLISH 1

get–together *n* **1** a coming together of a number of persons for a specified purpose — see MEETING 1
2 a social gathering — see PARTY 1

getup *n* clothing chosen as appropriate for a specific situation — see OUTFIT 1

get up *vb* to leave one's bed — see ARISE 1

gewgaw *n* a small object displayed for its attractiveness or interest — see KNICKKNACK

ghastliness *n* the quality of inspiring intense dread or dismay — see HORROR 1

ghastly *adj* extremely disturbing or repellent — see HORRIBLE 1

ghost *n* the soul of a dead person thought of especially as appearing to living people ⟨looked for *ghosts* in the graveyard on Halloween⟩
synonyms apparition, bogey (*also* bogy *or* bogie), phantasm, phantom, poltergeist, shade, shadow, specter (*or* spectre), spirit, spook, vision, wraith
related words banshee, demon (*or* daemon), familiar (*or* familiar spirit), genie, imp, incubus, puck; vampire, zombie

ghoul *n* an evil spirit — see DEMON

giant *adj* unusually large — see HUGE

giant *n* something that is unusually large and powerful ⟨the Great Pyramids of Egypt are *giants*⟩
synonyms behemoth, blockbuster, colossus, jumbo, leviathan, mammoth, monster, titan, whale, whopper
related words amazon; bulk, hulk; heavyweight
near antonyms lightweight, weakling, wimp, wisp; nonentity, twerp, whippersnapper
antonyms dwarf, midget, mini, miniature, peewee, pygmy, runt, shrimp

gibber *vb* to speak rapidly, inarticulately, and usually unintelligibly — see BABBLE 1

gibberish *n* unintelligible or meaningless talk ⟨was so excited he could only talk *gibberish*⟩
synonyms babble, blabber, bunk, claptrap, drivel, fudge, gabble, gobbledygook (*also* gobbledegook), hogwash, jabber, jabberwocky, jazz, moonshine, mumbo jumbo, nonsense, piffle, prattle, rigmarole, rot
related words abracadabra; chatter, clatter, gab, gibber, prate, tattle, twaddle; double-talk, hocus-pocus, jive; gas, hot air, wind

gibe *or* **jibe** *vb* to make (someone or something) the object of unkind laughter — see RIDICULE

giddy *adj* **1** lacking in seriousness or maturity ⟨the *giddy* youngsters continued to laugh, joke, and make faces during the ceremonies⟩
synonyms featherbrained, flighty, frivolous, goofy, harebrained, light-headed, puerile, scatterbrained, silly
related words fatuous, foolish, inane, nonsensical, thoughtless, witless; crazy, daffy, daft, exuberant, flippant, fluttery, light, lighthearted, playful; sappy, shallow, superficial
near antonyms grave, melancholy, somber (*or* sombre), thoughtful; dignified, heavy, no-nonsense, sedate, severe, solemn, staid
antonyms earnest, serious, serious-minded, sober
2 having a feeling of being whirled about and in danger of falling down — see DIZZY 1

gift *n* **1** something given to someone without expectation of a return ⟨gave him a *gift* for his birthday⟩
synonyms bestowal, donation, freebie (*or* freebee), giveaway, lagniappe, largess (*or* largesse), present, presentation
related words alms, benefaction, beneficence, benevolence, charity, contribution, dole, generosity, offering, philanthropy; grant, subsidy; remembrance, tribute; bonus, boon, windfall; favor, valentine; gratuity, tip; award, prize, reward; bequest, legacy; sacrifice
near antonyms advance, loan; bribe, sop
2 a special and usually inborn ability — see TALENT

gigantic *adj* unusually large — see HUGE

giggle *n* an explosive sound that is a sign of amusement — see LAUGH 1

gimmick *n* **1** a clever often underhanded means to achieve an end — see TRICK 1
2 an interesting and often novel device with a practical use — see GADGET

ginger *n* active strength of body or mind — see VIGOR 1

gingerbread *adj* elaborately and often excessively decorated — see ORNATE

gingerly *adj* having or showing a close attentiveness to avoiding danger or trouble — see CAREFUL 1

gingery *adj* **1** having active strength of body or mind — see VIGOROUS 1
2 marked by a lively display of strong feeling — see SPIRITED 1

gird *vb* **1** to encircle or bind with or as if with a belt ⟨for the celebration of the heroes' return, well-wishers *girded* hundreds of trees with yellow ribbons⟩ ⟨she *girded* her waist with a delicate sash⟩
synonyms band, belt, girdle, girt, girth, wrap
related words tie up, truss; circle, loop, wind, wreathe; bandage, swathe; chain, cord, enchain, lash, rope, shackle, tape, wire
near antonyms loose, loosen, unbind, unchain, undo, unfasten, unlash, untie, unwind
antonyms unwrap
2 to gather into a tight mass by means of a line or cord — see TIE 1

girdle *n* a strip of flexible material (as leather) worn around the waist — see [2]BELT

girdle *vb* **1** to encircle or bind with or as if with a belt — see GIRD 1
2 to pass completely around — see ENCIRCLE 1

girl *n* **1** a young usually unmarried woman ⟨a book that discusses the special challenges that *girls* face as they enter their teenage years⟩
synonyms bobby-soxer, chick [*slang*], damsel, doll, gal, lass, lassie, mademoiselle, maid, maiden, miss
related words gamine; hoyden, tomboy; hussy; ingenue; belle, deb, debutante, sylph; schoolgirl; teenybopper; senorita (*or* señorita)
2 a woman with whom one is in love — see GIRLFRIEND

girlfriend *n* a woman with whom one is in love ⟨he proposed to his *girlfriend* of seven years⟩
synonyms gal, girl, ladylove
related words mistress; beloved, darling, dear, favorite, flame, honey, love, lover, sweet, sweetheart, valentine

girlish *adj* having or displaying qualities more suitable for women than for men — see EFFEMINATE

girt *vb* to encircle or bind with or as if with a belt — see GIRD 1

girth *n* the distance around a round body — see CIRCUMFERENCE 1

girth *vb* **1** to encircle or bind with or as if with a belt — see GIRD 1
2 to pass completely around — see ENCIRCLE 1

gist *n* the central part or aspect of something under consideration — see CRUX

give *vb* **1** to make a present of ⟨tutors *gave* their time to help students after school⟩
synonyms bestow, contribute, donate, present
related words chip in, kick in, pitch in; award, confer, dole (out), endow; afford, furnish, provide; lavish, regale; aid, assist, benefit, help; administer, dispense, impart, issue, render; extend, offer, pay, proffer, tender; sacrifice
near antonyms hold, keep, pocket, retain, withhold; preserve, save; advance, lend, loan; sell
2 to put (something) into the possession or safekeeping of another ⟨*gave* my camera to my father to hold while I went swimming⟩
synonyms commend, commit, consign, delegate, deliver, entrust, hand over, leave, pass, transfer, transmit, trust, turn over, vest
related words confer, grant; assign, deal (out), dispense, disperse, distribute, divide; release, relinquish, submit, surrender, turn in, yield; bequeath, hand down, will; advance, lend, loan; furnish, supply
near antonyms detain, hold back, reserve, withhold; own, possess; accept, receive, take in; occupy, take, take over
antonyms hold, keep, retain
3 to bring before the public in performance or exhibition — see PRESENT 1
4 to fall down or in as a result of physical pressure — see COLLAPSE 1
5 to hand over or use up in payment — see SPEND 1
6 to make known (as an idea, emotion, or opinion) — see EXPRESS 1
7 to occupy (oneself) diligently or with close attention — see APPLY 2
8 to produce as revenue — see YIELD 2
9 to put (something) into the possession of someone for use or consumption — see FURNISH 2
10 to put before another for acceptance or consideration — see OFFER 1

give–and–take *n* **1** an exchange of views for the purpose of exploring a subject or deciding an issue — see DISCUSSION 1
2 the act or practice of each side giving up something in order to reach an agreement — see CONCESSION 1
3 good-natured teasing or exchanging of clever remarks — see BANTER

giveaway *n* something given to someone without expectation of a return — see GIFT 1

give away *vb* to make known (something abstract) through outward signs — see SHOW 2

give in *vb* **1** to give up and cease resistance (as to a liking, temptation, or habit) — see YIELD 1
2 to cease resistance (as to another's arguments, demands, or control) — see YIELD 3

given *adj* **1** being in the habit or custom — see ACCUSTOMED
2 having a tendency to be or act in a certain way — see PRONE 1

given name *n* a name that is placed before one's family name — see FORENAME

give out *vb* to stop functioning — see FAIL 1

give up *vb* **1** to give (something) over to the control or possession of another usually under duress — see SURRENDER 1
2 to stop doing (something) permanently — see QUIT 2
3 to yield to the control or power of enemy forces — see FALL 2

giving *n* the act of offering money in exchange for goods or services — see PAYMENT 1

gizmo *or* **gismo** *n* an interesting and often novel device with a practical use — see GADGET

glacial *adj* **1** having a low or subnormal temperature — see COLD 1
2 lacking in friendliness or warmth of feeling — see COLD 2

glad *adj* **1** experiencing pleasure, satisfaction, or delight ⟨the husband was *glad* to see his wife again, after so long an absence⟩
synonyms blissful, delighted, gratified, happy, joyful, joyous, pleased, satisfied, tickled
related words beaming, blithe, blithesome, buoyant, cheerful, cheery, gay, gladsome, lighthearted, sunny, upbeat; gleeful, jocund, jolly, jovial, laughing, merry, mirthful, smiling; carried away, ecstatic, elated, enraptured, entranced, euphoric, exhilarated, intoxicated, rapturous, rhapsodic; exuberant, exultant, jubilant, rapt, rejoicing, thrilled; hopeful, optimistic, rosy, sanguine
near antonyms abject, aggrieved, anguished, blue, brokenhearted, dejected, depressed, despondent, disconsolate, disheartened, downcast, downhearted, forlorn, melancholy; doleful, dolorous, lachrymose, mournful, plaintive, sorrowful, sorry, woeful; black, dark, desolate, dispirited, gloomy, glum, gray (*also* grey), grieved, heartbroken, heartsick, miserable, woebegone, wretched
antonyms displeased, joyless, sad, unhappy, unsatisfied
2 having a desire or inclination (as for a specified course of action) — see WILLING 1
3 serving to lift one's spirits — see CHEERFUL 2

gladden *vb* to give satisfaction to — see PLEASE

gladdening *adj* making one feel good inside — see HEARTWARMING

gladiatorial *adj* feeling or displaying eagerness to fight — see BELLIGERENT

gladness *n* **1** a feeling or state of well-being and contentment — see HAPPINESS 1
2 the feeling experienced when one's wishes are met — see PLEASURE 1

gladsome *adj* having or showing a good mood or disposition — see CHEERFUL 1

glamorize *also* **glamourize** *vb* to represent or think of as better than reality — see IDEALIZE

glamorous *also* **glamourous** *adj* **1** excitingly or mysteriously unusual — see EXOTIC
2 having an often mysterious or magical power to attract — see FASCINATING 1

glamour *also* **glamor** *n* the power of irresistible attraction — see CHARM 2

glance *n* an instance of looking especially briefly — see LOOK 2

glance *vb* **1** to strike and fly off at an angle ⟨the basketball *glanced* off the rim⟩ ⟨her wild pitch *glanced* off my shoulder and landed in the dugout⟩
synonyms bounce, carom, rebound, ricochet, skim, skip
related words brush, graze, nudge, shave, sweep; bump, contact, hit, kiss, touch; sideswipe; reflect
2 to take a quick or hasty look ⟨just *glanced* at the instructions before assembling the bike⟩ ⟨*glanced* over his shoulder to see if she was still there⟩
synonyms browse, dip, glimpse, peek, skim
related words peep; blink, squint; look over, scan
near antonyms examine, overlook, oversee, ques-

tion, survey; study, view; peer, pry; gawk, goggle, rubberneck; leer, ogle
antonyms gaze, stare
3 to shoot forth bursts of light — see FLASH 1
glare *n* the steady giving off of the form of radiation that makes vision possible — see LIGHT 1
glare *vb* **1** to shine with a bright harsh light ⟨the spotlight *glared* down on the suspect as the police questioned him relentlessly⟩
synonyms beat, blaze, burn, flame, flare
related words beam, glow, radiate; flash, glance, gleam, glimmer, glint, glisten, glister, glitter, scintillate, shimmer, sparkle, twinkle; bedazzle, blind, daze, dazzle
2 to look with anger or disapproval — see FROWN
glaring *adj* very noticeable especially for being incorrect or bad — see EGREGIOUS
glasses *n pl* a pair of lenses set in a frame that is held in place with ear supports and which are usually worn to correct vision ⟨I'm a little nearsighted, so I'm going to need *glasses*⟩
synonyms eyeglasses, specs, spectacles
related words bifocals; monocle, pince-nez; sunglasses; goggles; contact lens
gleam *n* the steady giving off of the form of radiation that makes vision possible — see LIGHT 1
gleam *vb* to shoot forth bursts of light — see FLASH 1
glee *n* a mood characterized by high spirits and amusement and often accompanied by laughter — see MIRTH
glee club *n* an organized group of singers — see CHORUS 1
gleeful *adj* indicative of or marked by high spirits or good humor — see MERRY
gleefulness *n* a mood characterized by high spirits and amusement and often accompanied by laughter — see MIRTH
glide *vb* **1** to move or proceed smoothly and readily — see FLOW 2
2 to move through the air with or as if with outstretched wings — see FLY 1
3 to rest or move along the surface of a liquid or in the air — see FLOAT
glimmer *n* a very small amount — see PARTICLE 1
glimmer *vb* to shoot forth bursts of light — see FLASH 1
glimpse *n* an instance of looking especially briefly — see LOOK 2
glimpse *vb* to take a quick or hasty look — see GLANCE 2
glint *vb* to shoot forth bursts of light — see FLASH 1
glisten *vb* to shoot forth bursts of light — see FLASH 1
glistening *adj* having a shiny surface or finish — see GLOSSY
glister *vb* to shoot forth bursts of light — see FLASH 1
glitter *vb* to shoot forth bursts of light — see FLASH 1
glitz *n* excessive or unnecessary display — see OSTENTATION
glitzy *adj* excessively showy — see GAUDY
gloaming *n* **1** a time or place of little or no light — see DARK 1
2 the time from when the sun begins to set to the onset of total darkness — see DUSK 1
glob *n* **1** a small uneven mass — see LUMP 1
2 the quantity of fluid that falls naturally in one rounded mass — see DROP 1
global *adj* **1** belonging or relating to the whole — see GENERAL 1
2 covering everything or all important points — see ENCYCLOPEDIC
3 having every part of the surface the same distance from the center — see ROUND 1
globe *n* **1** a more or less round body or mass — see [1]BALL 1
2 the celestial body on which we live — see EARTH 1
globule *n* the quantity of fluid that falls naturally in one rounded mass — see DROP 1
gloom *n* **1** a state or spell of low spirits — see SADNESS
2 a time or place of little or no light — see DARK 1
gloom *vb* **1** to look with anger or disapproval — see FROWN
2 to take on a gloomy or forbidding look — see DARKEN 1
gloominess *n* a state or spell of low spirits — see SADNESS
gloomy *adj* **1** causing or marked by an atmosphere lacking in cheer ⟨the cold rain made for a *gloomy* day⟩
synonyms black, bleak, cheerless, comfortless, dark, darkening, depressing, desolate, dismal, drear, dreary, elegaic, funereal, glum, gray (*also* grey), miserable, morbid, morose, murky, saturnine, sepulchral, somber (*or* sombre), sullen, wretched
related words dejected, depressed, despondent, disconsolate, droopy, inconsolable, low, melancholy, sad, unhappy, woebegone, woeful; discomfiting, discouraging, disheartening, dismaying, dispiriting, distressful, distressing, upsetting; desperate, hopeless, pessimistic; lamentable, lugubrious, mournful, sorrowful; cloudy, colorless, drab, dull; dour, grim, lowering (*also* louring), menacing, negative, oppressive, threatening
near antonyms blithe, blithesome, buoyant, gay, jocund, jolly, joyful, joyous, merry, mirthful; encouraging, hopeful, optimistic; lighthearted, lightsome
antonyms bright, cheerful, cheering, cheery, comforting, cordial, gay, festive, friendly, heartwarming, sunshiny
2 feeling unhappiness — see SAD 1
3 being without light or without much light — see DARK 1
glorify *vb* **1** to enhance the status of — see EXALT
2 to offer honor or respect to (someone) as a divine power — see WORSHIP 1
3 to praise or publicize lavishly and often excessively — see TOUT 1
4 to proclaim the glory of — see PRAISE 1
5 to represent or think of as better than reality — see IDEALIZE
glorious *adj* large and impressive in size, grandeur, extent, or conception — see GRAND 1
gloriously *adv* in a pleasing way — see WELL 5
gloriousness *n* impressiveness of beauty on a large scale — see MAGNIFICENCE
glory *n* **1** public acknowledgment or admiration for an achievement ⟨the drama teacher gave the stage crew all the *glory* for the successful production⟩
synonyms acclaim, accolade, credit, distinction, homage, honor, laurels

related words celebrity, fame, renown, repute; compliment, encomium, eulogy, panegyric, toast, tribute; acclamation, ovation, plaudit, praise, rave, rhapsody; citation, commendation, note, recommendation; elevation, exaltation, glorification

2 an asset that brings praise or renown ⟨the new computer lab was the *glory* of the middle school⟩

synonyms boast, credit, honor, jewel, pride, treasure

related words pièce de résistance, showpiece; attraction, feature, highlight; distinction, excellence, merit, value, virtue

phrases a feather in one's cap

near antonyms disgrace, dishonor; blemish, blot, defect, shame, slur, smirch, smudge, stain, stigma; eyesore, fright, horror, mess

3 impressiveness of beauty on a large scale — see MAGNIFICENCE

glory *vb* to feel or express joy or triumph — see EXULT

glorying *adj* having or expressing feelings of joy or triumph — see EXULTANT

gloss *n* brightness created by light reflected from a surface — see SHINE 1

gloss *vb* to make smooth or glossy usually by repeatedly applying surface pressure — see POLISH

gloss (over) *vb* **1** to make (something) seem less bad by offering excuses — see PALLIATE 1

2 to overlook or dismiss as of little importance — see EXCUSE 1

glossy *adj* having a shiny surface or finish ⟨the *glossy* finish on the gym floor⟩ ⟨a sports car with an interior upholstered with *glossy* leather⟩

synonyms buffed, burnished, glistening, lustrous, polished, rubbed, satin, satiny, sleek

related words silken, silky, slick, slippery; glassy, glazed, lacquered, shellacked, varnished; gleaming, glittering, reflective, shining

near antonyms lackluster

antonyms dim, dull, flat, lusterless, matte (*also* mat *or* matt)

glow *n* the steady giving off of the form of radiation that makes vision possible — see LIGHT 1

glow *vb* **1** to be on fire especially brightly — see BURN 1

2 to develop a rosy facial color (as from excitement or embarrassment) — see BLUSH

glower *vb* **1** to look with anger or disapproval — see FROWN

2 to take on a gloomy or forbidding look — see DARKEN 1

glowing *adj* **1** giving off or reflecting much light — see BRIGHT 1

2 having a healthy reddish skin tone — see RUDDY

3 having or being an outward sign of good feelings (as of love, confidence, or happiness) — see RADIANT 1

4 having or expressing great depth of feeling — see FERVENT

gloze (over) *vb* **1** to make (something) seem less bad by offering excuses — see PALLIATE 1

2 to overlook or dismiss as of little importance — see EXCUSE 1

glue *n* a substance used to stick things together ⟨used *glue* to stick the photo in the album⟩

synonyms adhesive, cement, size

related words epoxy, epoxy resin, library paste, mucilage, superglue; dope, goo, gum

gluey *adj* being of such a thick consistency as to readily cling to objects upon contact — see STICKY 1

glum *adj* **1** causing or marked by an atmosphere lacking in cheer — see GLOOMY 1

2 feeling unhappiness — see SAD 1

3 given to or displaying a resentful silence and often irritability — see SULKY

glut *vb* to fill with food to capacity — see GORGE 1

glutinous *adj* being of such a thick consistency as to readily cling to objects upon contact — see STICKY 1

glutton *n* one who eats greedily or too much ⟨he's such a *glutton* that he ate the whole cake⟩

synonyms gorger, gormandizer, gourmand, hog, overeater, stuffer, swiller

related words feaster, trencherman; muncher; guzzler

near antonyms dieter, nibbler, picker

gluttonous *adj* having a huge appetite — see VORACIOUS 1

gnash *vb* to press or strike against or together so as to make a scraping sound — see GRIND 2

gnaw (on) *vb* to crush or grind with the teeth — see BITE (ON)

gnawer *n* one who is obnoxiously annoying — see NUISANCE 1

gnome *n* an imaginary being usually having a small human form and magical powers — see FAIRY

go *adj* being in a state of fitness for some experience or action — see READY 1

go *n* **1** a practice or interest that is very popular for a short time — see FAD

2 active strength of body or mind — see VIGOR 1

3 an effort to do or accomplish something — see ATTEMPT

4 readiness to engage in daring or difficult activity — see ENTERPRISE 2

go *vb* **1** to move forward along a course ⟨everything is *going* according to our plans⟩

synonyms advance, fare, forge, get along, march, proceed, progress

related words accelerate, fast-forward, speed; approach, near; journey, pass, repair, run, travel, wend; actuate, drive, impel, propel, push; do, go off, take out

phrases gain ground

near antonyms arrest, balk, block, check, detain, halt, hinder, hold back, impede, nip, obstruct, slow (down *or* up), stem; repress, retard, stunt, suppress; delay, interrupt, stall; cramp, hamper, inhibit; cease, let up, pause; regress

antonyms remain, stand, stay, stop

2 to leave a place often for another ⟨will *go* on vacation at the end of the year⟩ ⟨decided it would be better to *go* before she got any angrier⟩

synonyms begone, clear out, depart, exit, get, get off, move, pull (out), quit, sally (forth), shove (off), take off, walk out

related words set out, start, strike out; abscond, decamp, escape, evacuate, flee, fly, get out, run away, scat, scram, skip; go out, light out, step out; abandon, desert, forsake, vacate; emigrate; remove, retire, retreat, withdraw

phrases beat it

near antonyms abide, dwell, lodge, remain, settle, stay, tarry; approach, close, near; hit, land, reach

antonyms arrive, come, show up, turn up

3 to be fitting or proper — see DO 1

4 to be in agreement on every point — see CHECK 1
5 to be positioned along a certain course or in a certain direction — see RUN 3
6 to eventually have as a state or quality — see BECOME
7 to fall down or in as a result of physical pressure — see COLLAPSE 1
8 to have or be in a usual or proper place — see BELONG 1
9 to lose bodily strength or vigor — see WEAKEN 2
10 to make one's way through, across, or over — see TRAVERSE
11 to occur within a continuous range of variation — see RUN 4
12 to risk (something) on the outcome of an uncertain event — see BET

go (for) *vb* to have a price of — see COST

go (on) *vb* to take place — see HAPPEN

go (to) *vb* to use or seek out as a source of aid, relief, or advantage — see RESORT (TO) 1

goad *n* something that arouses action or activity — see IMPULSE

goad *vb* **1** to try to persuade (someone) through earnest appeals to follow a course of action — see URGE
2 to urge or push forward with or as if with a pointed object — see PROD 1

goal *n* something that one hopes or intends to accomplish ⟨graduating from high school with honors is one of my main *goals*⟩
synonyms aim, ambition, aspiration, design, dream, end, intent, intention, mark, meaning, object, objective, plan, pretension, purpose, target, thing
related words plot, project, scheme; desire, hope, wish; destination, terminus
near antonyms means, method, way

goat *n* a person or thing taking the blame for others — see SCAPEGOAT

[1]**gob** *n* **1** a small uneven mass — see LUMP 1
2 gobs *pl* a considerable amount — see LOT 2

[2]**gob** *n* one who operates or navigates a seagoing vessel — see SAILOR

gobbet *n* a small uneven mass — see LUMP 1

gobbledygook *also* **gobbledegook** *n* unintelligible or meaningless talk — see GIBBERISH

go–between *n* **1** one that carries a message or does an errand — see MESSENGER
2 one who works with opposing sides in order to bring about an agreement — see MEDIATOR

goblin *n* an imaginary being usually having a small human form and magical powers — see FAIRY

god *n* **1** a being having superhuman powers and control over a particular part of life or the world — see DEITY 1
2 *cap* the being worshipped as the creator and ruler of the universe — see DEITY 2

goddess *n* a lovely woman — see BEAUTY 2

godhead *n* **1** the quality or state of being divine — see DIVINITY
2 *cap* the being worshipped as the creator and ruler of the universe — see DEITY 2

godhood *n* the quality or state of being divine — see DIVINITY

godless *adj* lacking religious emotions, principles, or practices — see IRRELIGIOUS

godlike *adj* of, relating to, or being God — see HOLY 3

godliness *n* the quality or state of being spiritually pure or virtuous — see HOLINESS

godly *adj* showing a devotion to God and to a life of virtue — see HOLY 1

godsend *n* something that provides happiness or does good for a person or thing — see BLESSING 2

Godspeed *n* an expression of good wishes at parting — see GOOD-BYE

go–getter *n* an ambitious person who eagerly goes after what is desired ⟨a *go-getter* with his sights set on the presidency⟩
synonyms hummer, hustler, live wire, powerhouse, rustler, self-starter
related words dasher; doer, enterpriser; he-man
near antonyms dawdler, idler, loafer, lounger, putterer, trifler; goldbrick, malingerer, procrastinator, shirker, slacker; drone, lazybones, sluggard; dallier, laggard, lingerer, loiterer, slowpoke, stick-in-the-mud; ignorer, ne'er-do-well, neglecter; daydreamer, dreamer; dropout, quitter

go–getting *adj* **1** having a strong desire for personal advancement — see AMBITIOUS 1
2 having or showing a bold forcefulness in the pursuit of a goal — see AGGRESSIVE 1

go–getting *n* eager desire for personal advancement — see AMBITION 1

goggle *vb* to look long and hard in wonder or surprise — see GAPE

going *adj* **1** accepted, used, or practiced by most people — see CURRENT 1
2 being in effective operation — see ACTIVE 1
3 having attained a desired end or state of good fortune — see SUCCESSFUL 1

going *n* **1** forward movement in time or place — see ADVANCE 1
2 the act of leaving a place — see DEPARTURE

gold *n* something (as pieces of stamped metal or printed paper) customarily and legally used as a medium of exchange, a measure of value, or a means of payment — see MONEY

goldbrick *n* one who deliberately avoids work or duty — see SLACKER

golden *adj* **1** having qualities which inspire hope — see HOPEFUL 1
2 marked by conspicuously full and rich sounds or tones — see RESONANT
3 marked by vigorous growth and well-being especially economically — see PROSPEROUS 1
4 of a pale yellow or yellowish brown color — see BLOND
5 pointing toward a happy outcome — see FAVORABLE 2

golden–ager *n* a person of advanced years — see SENIOR CITIZEN

golden mean *n* a middle point between extremes — see MEAN 1

gone *adj* **1** no longer existing — see EXTINCT
2 no longer living — see DEAD 1
3 no longer possessed — see LOST

good *adj* **1** based on sound reasoning or information ⟨had enough information to make a *good* assessment of the situation⟩
synonyms commonsense, hard, informed, just, justified, levelheaded, logical, rational, reasonable, reasoned, sensible, sober, solid, valid, well-founded
related words actual, real, true; certain, sure; certified, validated, verified; confirmed, corroborated, substantiated; cogent, convincing, credible
near antonyms unsubstantiated, unsupported, un-

warranted; flimsy, implausible, unconvincing, weak; fallacious, false, misled
antonyms groundless, illogical, invalid, irrational, nonrational, nonsensical, nonvalid, unfounded, ungrounded, uninformed, unjustified, unreasonable, unsound
2 conforming to a high standard of morality or virtue <a *good* person who seldom did wrong> <*good* behavior will earn you the respect of others>
synonyms decent, ethical, honest, honorable, just, moral, right, righteous, right-minded, straight, upright, virtuous
related words correct, decorous, proper, seemly; high-minded, noble, principled; commendable, creditable, exemplary, legitimate; esteemed, law-abiding, reputable, respected, upstanding, worthy; blameless, clean, guiltless, immaculate, incorruptible, innocent, inoffensive, irreproachable, unobjectionable; lily-white, pure, scrupulous, spotless, uncorrupted, unerring; goody-goody, moralistic, sanctimonious, self-righteous
near antonyms improper, incorrect, indecorous, naughty, unbecoming, unseemly; corrupt, debased, debauched, degenerate, depraved, dissolute, perverted, reprobate; unprincipled, unscrupulous; atrocious, infamous, villainous; base, low, mean, vicious, vile; blameworthy, objectionable, offensive; iniquitous, nefarious; errant, erring, fallen
antonyms bad, black, dishonest, dishonorable, evil, evil-minded, immoral, indecent, sinful, unethical, unrighteous, wicked, wrong
3 according to the rules of logic — see LOGICAL 1
4 being to one's liking — see SATISFACTORY 1
5 expressing approval — see FAVORABLE 1
6 firm in one's allegiance to someone or something — see FAITHFUL 1
7 giving pleasure or contentment to the mind or senses — see PLEASANT
8 having or showing exceptional knowledge, experience, or skill in a field of endeavor — see PROFICIENT
9 having sufficient worth or merit to receive one's honor, esteem, or reward — see WORTHY
10 having the required skills for an acceptable level of performance — see COMPETENT
11 meeting the requirements of a purpose or situation — see FIT 1
12 showing or expressing acceptance or approval — see POSITIVE
13 sufficiently large in size, amount, or number to merit attention — see CONSIDERABLE 1
14 worthy of one's trust — see DEPENDABLE

good *adv* in a satisfactory way — see WELL 1

good *n* **1** something that provides happiness or does good for a person or thing — see BLESSING 2
2 the state of doing well especially in relation to one's happiness or success — see WELFARE
3 goods *pl* products that are bought and sold in business — see MERCHANDISE

Good Book *n* a book made up of the writings accepted by Christians as coming from God — see BIBLE

good–bye *or* **good-by** *n* an expression of good wishes at parting <said our *good-byes* and headed for home>
synonyms adieu, au revoir, bon voyage, farewell, Godspeed
related words leave-taking, send-off
near antonyms greeting(s), salutation, salute; welcome
antonyms hello

good–hearted *adj* having or marked by sympathy and consideration for others — see HUMANE 1

goodly *adj* **1** of a size greater than average of its kind — see LARGE
2 sufficiently large in size, amount, or number to merit attention — see CONSIDERABLE 1

good–natured *adj* having an easygoing and pleasing manner especially in social situations — see AMIABLE

good–naturedness *n* **1** a desire or disposition to please — see COMPLAISANCE
2 the state or quality of having a pleasant or agreeable manner in socializing with others — see AMIABILITY 1

goodness *n* conduct that conforms to an accepted standard of right and wrong — see MORALITY 1

good–sized *adj* **1** of a size greater than average of its kind — see LARGE
2 sufficiently large in size, amount, or number to merit attention — see CONSIDERABLE 1

good–tempered *adj* having an easygoing and pleasing manner especially in social situations — see AMIABLE

good–temperedness *n* the state or quality of having a pleasant or agreeable manner in socializing with others — see AMIABILITY 1

goodwill *n* **1** kindly concern, interest, or support <the long tradition of *goodwill* that exists between the United States and Canada>
synonyms amity, benevolence, cordiality, fellowship, friendliness, friendship, kindliness
related words camaraderie, community, companionship, comradeship; civility, comity, concord, harmony, rapport; charity, generosity, neighborliness; affinity, communion, empathy, sympathy, tolerance; altruism, philanthropy, selflessness
near antonyms disfavor, intolerance; animosity, antagonism, antipathy, enmity, hate, hatred, hostility, incivility, malice, rancor
antonyms ill will, malevolence
2 cheerful readiness to do something — see ALACRITY

goody *n* something that is pleasing to eat because it is rare or a luxury — see DELICACY 1

gooey *adj* being of such a thick consistency as to readily cling to objects upon contact — see STICKY 1

goof *n* an unintentional departure from truth or accuracy — see ERROR 1

go off *vb* to break open or into pieces usually because of internal pressure — see EXPLODE 1

goofy *adj* lacking in seriousness or maturity — see GIDDY 1

goon *n* **1** a stupid person — see IDIOT
2 a violent, brutal person who is often a member of an organized gang — see HOODLUM

goose *n* a person who lacks good sense or judgment — see FOOL 1

goose egg *n* the numerical symbol 0 or the absence of number or quantity represented by it — see ZERO 1

go over *vb* to turn out as planned or desired — see SUCCEED 1

gore *vb* to penetrate or hold (something) with a pointed object — see IMPALE

gorge *n* a narrow opening between hillsides or

mountains that can be used for passage — see CANYON

gorge *vb* **1** to fill with food to capacity ⟨they *gorged* themselves on the four pies Aunt Martha brought for Thanksgiving⟩
synonyms glut, sate, stuff, surfeit
related words gobble, gormandize, pig out; gulp, guzzle; cloy, fill; banquet, feast, regale
near antonyms diet, fast
2 to eat greedily or to excess ⟨the kids *gorged* on Halloween candy when they got home from trick-or-treating⟩
synonyms gormandize, overeat, pig out, swill
related words devour, glut, sate, stuff, surfeit, wolf; banquet, feast, regale; bolt, cram, gulp, guzzle
near antonyms nibble, peck, pick, taste

gorgeous *adj* very pleasing to look at — see BEAUTIFUL

gorgeousness *n* the qualities in a person or thing that as a whole give pleasure to the senses — see BEAUTY 1

gorger *n* one who eats greedily or too much — see GLUTTON

gormandize *vb* to eat greedily or to excess — see GORGE 2

gormandizer *n* one who eats greedily or too much — see GLUTTON

gory *adj* containing, smeared, or stained with blood — see BLOODY 1

gospel *n* the basic beliefs or guiding principles of a person or group — see CREED 1

gossamer *adj* **1** being of a material lacking in sturdiness or substance — see FLIMSY 1
2 resembling air in lightness — see AIRY 1
3 very thin and easy to see through — see SHEER 1

gossamery *adj* **1** being of a material lacking in sturdiness or substance — see FLIMSY 1
2 resembling air in lightness — see AIRY 1
3 very thin and easy to see through — see SHEER 1

gossip *n* friendly, informal conversation or an instance of this — see CHAT

gossip *vb* to relate sometimes questionable or secret information of a personal nature ⟨likes to *gossip* with others about our neighbors' arguments⟩
synonyms blab, talk, tattle
related words bandy (about), circulate, noise (about), rumor; disclose, divulge, reveal, tell; hint, imply, insinuate, intimate, let on, suggest; inform, report, snitch, squeal, tip (off); babble, spill; confide
phrases spill the beans
near antonyms clam up, shut up

gossipy *adj* having the style and content of everyday conversation — see CHATTY 1

gouge *vb* to charge (someone) too much for goods or services — see OVERCHARGE 1

gourmand *n* **1** a person with refined tastes in food and wine — see EPICURE
2 one who eats greedily or too much — see GLUTTON

gourmet *n* a person with refined tastes in food and wine — see EPICURE

govern *vb* **1** to exercise authority or power over ⟨the president is elected in order to *govern* the country⟩
synonyms boss, captain, command, control, preside (over), rule
related words conduct, direct, head, lead; administer, manage, oversee, regulate, superintend, supervise; dictate, dominate, domineer, lord (it over), master, oppress, reign (over), tyrannize; conquer, subdue, subjugate
2 to keep from exceeding a desirable degree or level (as of expression) — see CONTROL 1
3 to look after and make decisions about — see CONDUCT 1

governance *n* **1** lawful control over the affairs of a political unit (as a nation) — see RULE 2
2 the act or activity of looking after and making decisions about something — see CONDUCT 1

government *n* **1** lawful control over the affairs of a political unit (as a nation) — see RULE 2
2 the act or activity of looking after and making decisions about something — see CONDUCT 1

gown *n* a garment with a joined blouse and skirt for a woman or girl — see DRESS 1

gown *vb* to outfit with clothes and especially fine or special clothes — see CLOTHE 1

grab *n* an instance of theft — see THEFT 2

grab *vb* to take physical control or possession of (something) suddenly or forcibly — see CATCH 1

grace *n* **1** an act of kind assistance — see FAVOR 1
2 dignified or restrained beauty of form, appearance, or style — see ELEGANCE

grace *vb* to make more attractive by adding something that is beautiful or becoming — see DECORATE

graceful *adj* **1** moving easily ⟨the *graceful* ballerina effortlessly leapt across the dance floor⟩
synonyms agile, light, light-footed, lissome (*also* lissom), lithe, lithesome, nimble, spry
related words flexible, limber, loose-jointed, pliable, pliant, supple; adroit, deft, dexterous (*also* dextrous); fleet-footed, surefooted
near antonyms inflexible, rigid, stiff; bungling, inept, maladroit
antonyms awkward, clumsy, gawky, graceless, lumbering, ungainly, ungraceful
2 having or showing elegance — see ELEGANT 1

gracefulness *n* dignified or restrained beauty of form, appearance, or style — see ELEGANCE

graceless *adj* **1** lacking in physical ease and grace in movement or in the use of the hands — see CLUMSY 1
2 lacking social grace and assurance — see AWKWARD 1
3 not appropriate for a particular occasion or situation — see INAPPROPRIATE

gracious *adj* **1** showing a natural kindness and courtesy especially in social situations ⟨a *gracious* teacher who made the new student feel welcome⟩
synonyms affable, cordial, genial, hospitable, sociable
related words agreeable, amiable, benignant, congenial, convivial, friendly, kind, kindly, neighborly; accommodating, obliging; considerate, courteous, polite, thoughtful; sophisticated, urbane; approachable, attentive, outgoing
near antonyms boorish, churlish; abrupt, blunt, brusque, curt, gruff, sharp, snippy; antisocial, disagreeable, discourteous, ill-mannered, impolite, rude, sullen, surly, uncivil, unfriendly, unkind, unmannerly; crabbed, crabby, cross, crusty, grumpy
antonyms inhospitable, ungracious, unsociable

2 having an easygoing and pleasing manner especially in social situations — see AMIABLE
3 showing consideration, courtesy, and good manners — see POLITE 1

graciousness *n* **1** speech or behavior that is a sign of good breeding — see POLITENESS
2 the state or quality of having a pleasant or agreeable manner in socializing with others — see AMIABILITY 1

gradational *adj* proceeding or changing by steps or degrees — see GRADUAL

gradationally *adv* by small steps or amounts — see GRADUALLY

grade *n* **1** an individual part of a process, series, or ranking — see DEGREE 1
2 degree of excellence — see QUALITY 1
3 one of the units into which a whole is divided on the basis of a common characteristic — see CLASS 2
4 something set up as an example against which others of the same type are compared — see STANDARD 1
5 the degree to which something rises up from a position level with the horizon — see SLANT

grade *vb* **1** to arrange or assign according to type — see CLASSIFY 1
2 to take or have a certain position within a group arranged in vertical classes — see RANK 1

gradient *n* the degree to which something rises up from a position level with the horizon — see SLANT

gradual *adj* proceeding or changing by steps or degrees ⟨a *gradual* drop in gas prices will take place over the next several months⟩
synonyms gradational, incremental, phased, piecemeal, step-by-step
related words progressive, stepped, tapered; imperceptible, inching
near antonyms abrupt, acute, sharp; changeable, dynamic, volatile
antonyms sudden

gradually *adv* by small steps or amounts ⟨*gradually* worked his way down the class roster⟩ ⟨add the sugar to the beaten egg whites *gradually* to make the meringue⟩
synonyms gradationally, little by little, piece by piece, piecemeal
related words hierarchically, increasingly, progressively; fractionally, imperceptibly; slowly
near antonyms acutely, sharply, steeply, unprogressively; hastily, precipitously
antonyms abruptly, suddenly

graduation *n* a scheme of rank or order — see [3]SCALE 1

grain *n* **1** a very small piece — see BIT 1
2 one's characteristic attitude or mood — see DISPOSITION 1

grainy *adj* made up of large particles — see COARSE 1

grand *adj* **1** large and impressive in size, grandeur, extent, or conception ⟨the *grand* ceremonies that typically mark the opening of the Olympic Games⟩
synonyms august, baronial, gallant, glorious, grandiose, heroic, imposing, magnificent, majestic, monumental, noble, proud, regal, royal, splendid, stately
related words colossal, monstrous, prodigious, stupendous, tremendous; kingly, lordly, princely, queenly; awesome, awful, cosmic, sublime, wondrous; formidable, impressive, prepossessing, redoubtable; marvelous (*or* marvellous), superb, terrific, wonderful; extravagant, lavish, luxurious, opulent, sumptuous; gorgeous, resplendent, splendiferous; extraordinary, killer, remarkable, sensational, striking; celestial, divine, heavenly
near antonyms lowly, modest, unprepossessing; average, common, mediocre, ordinary, run-of-the-mill, second-rate; abject, mean, meretricious, shabby, sordid; insignificant, measly, paltry, petty, puny, trifling, trivial
antonyms humble, unheroic, unimposing, unimpressive
2 coming before all others in importance — see FOREMOST 1
3 not lacking any part or member that properly belongs to it — see COMPLETE 1
4 of a size greater than average of its kind — see LARGE
5 of high birth, rank, or station — see NOBLE 1
6 of the very best kind — see EXCELLENT
7 unusually large — see HUGE

grandee *n* a man of high birth or social position — see GENTLEMAN 1

grandeur *n* impressiveness of beauty on a large scale — see MAGNIFICENCE

grandfather *n* a person who is several generations earlier in an individual's line of descent — see ANCESTOR 1

grandiloquence *n* **1** boastful speech or writing — see BOMBAST 1
2 language that is impressive-sounding but not meaningful or sincere — see RHETORIC 1

grandiloquent *adj* **1** full of fine words and fancy expressions — see FLOWERY 1
2 marked by the use of impressive-sounding but mostly meaningless words and phrases — see RHETORICAL

grandiose *adj* **1** large and impressive in size, grandeur, extent, or conception — see GRAND 1
2 self-consciously trying to present an appearance of grandeur or importance — see PRETENTIOUS 1

grandiosity *n* the quality or state of appearing or trying to appear more important or more valuable than is the case — see PRETENSE 1

grandly *adv* **1** in a luxurious manner — see HIGH
2 in a manner befitting a person of the highest character and ideals — see GREATLY 1

grandness *n* **1** impressiveness of beauty on a large scale — see MAGNIFICENCE
2 the quality or state of being large in size — see LARGENESS

grange *n* a piece of land and its buildings used to grow crops or raise livestock — see FARM

granite *n* firm or unwavering adherence to one's purpose — see DETERMINATION 1

grant *n* a sum of money allotted for a specific use by official or formal action — see APPROPRIATION

grant *vb* **1** to accept the truth or existence of (something) usually reluctantly — see ADMIT
2 to give the ownership or benefit of (something) formally or publicly — see CONFER 1

granting *n* the approval by someone in authority for the doing of something — see PERMISSION

granular *adj* made up of large particles — see COARSE 1

granulated *adj* made up of large particles — see COARSE 1

granule *n* a very small piece — see BIT 1

graphic *also* **graphical** *adj* **1** producing a mental picture through clear and impressive description <the report offered many *graphic* details about the huge earthquake that rocked the area>
synonyms delineated, pictorial, picturesque, vivid
related words depicted, descriptive, expressive; concrete, explicit, specific; faithful, lifelike, natural, realistic; fresh, incisive, sharp
near antonyms indeterminate, nebulous, obscure, sketchy, unclear, vague; blurry, dark, dim, muddy, murky, shadowy
2 consisting of or relating to pictures — see PICTORIAL 1
graphic *n* something that visually explains or decorates a text — see ILLUSTRATION 1
grapple *n* the act or manner of holding — see HOLD 1
grapple *vb* **1** to seize and attempt to unbalance one another for the purpose of achieving physical mastery — see WRESTLE
2 to take physical control or possession of (something) suddenly or forcibly — see CATCH 1
grapple (with) *vb* to deal with (something) usually skillfully or efficiently — see HANDLE 1
grasp *n* **1** the ability to direct the course of something — see CONTROL 2
2 the act or manner of holding — see HOLD 1
3 the knowledge gained from the process of coming to know or understand something — see COMPREHENSION
grasp *vb* **1** to have a practical understanding of — see KNOW 1
2 to put one's arms around and press tightly — see EMBRACE 1
3 to reach for and take hold of by embracing with the fingers or arms — see TAKE 1
4 to recognize the meaning of — see COMPREHEND 1
grasping *adj* having or marked by an eager and often selfish desire especially for material possessions — see GREEDY 1
grassland *n* a broad area of level or rolling treeless country — see PLAIN
grate *vb* **1** to disturb the peace of mind of (someone) especially by repeated disagreeable acts — see IRRITATE 1
2 to pass roughly and noisily over or against a surface — see SCRAPE 1
3 to press or strike against or together so as to make a scraping sound — see GRIND 2
grateful *adj* **1** feeling or expressing gratitude <was *grateful* for her neighbor's help after she broke her foot>
synonyms appreciative, obliged, thankful
related words beholden, indebted; gratified, pleased; thanking
antonyms thankless, unappreciative, ungrateful, unthankful
2 giving pleasure or contentment to the mind or senses — see PLEASANT
gratefulness *n* acknowledgment of having received something good from another — see THANKS
gratification *n* the feeling experienced when one's wishes are met — see PLEASURE 1
gratified *adj* **1** experiencing pleasure, satisfaction, or delight — see GLAD 1
2 feeling that one's needs or desires have been met — see CONTENT
gratify *vb* **1** to give in to (a desire) — see INDULGE
2 to give satisfaction to — see PLEASE
gratifying *adj* **1** giving pleasure or contentment to the mind or senses — see PLEASANT
2 making one feel good inside — see HEARTWARMING
grating *adj* **1** disagreeable to one's aesthetic or artistic sense — see HARSH 2
2 harsh and dry in sound — see HOARSE
gratis *adj* not costing or charging anything — see FREE 4
gratitude *n* acknowledgment of having received something good from another — see THANKS
gratuitous *adj* **1** not costing or charging anything — see FREE 4
2 not needed by the circumstances or to accomplish an end — see UNNECESSARY
gratuity *n* **1** a small sum of money given for a service over and above what is due — see [2]TIP 1
2 something given in addition to what is ordinarily expected or owed — see BONUS
grave *adj* **1** having a matter of importance as its topic — see SERIOUS 2
2 involving potential loss or injury — see DANGEROUS
3 not joking or playful in mood or manner — see SERIOUS 1
grave *n* a final resting place for a dead person <put flowers on his mother's *grave*>
synonyms sepulcher (*or* sepulchre), sepulture, tomb
related words catacomb, charnel, crypt, mausoleum, vault; cemetery, churchyard, graveyard, potter's field; barrow, mound, tumulus
grave *vb* to cut (as letters or designs) on a hard surface — see ENGRAVE 1
gravel *adj* harsh and dry in sound — see HOARSE
gravelly *adj* harsh and dry in sound — see HOARSE
gravestone *n* a shaped stone laid over or erected near a grave and usually bearing an inscription to identify and preserve the memory of the deceased — see TOMBSTONE
graveyard *n* a piece of land used for burying the dead — see CEMETERY
gravid *adj* containing unborn young within the body — see PREGNANT 1
gravity *n* a mental state free of jesting or trifling — see EARNESTNESS
gravy *n* **1** a savory fluid food used as a topping or accompaniment to a main dish — see SAUCE 1
2 something given in addition to what is ordinarily expected or owed — see BONUS
gray *also* **grey** *adj* **1** of the color gray <the *gray* elephant and the gaudily dressed circus performer created a striking contrast>
synonyms grayish, leaden, pewter, silver, silvery, slate, slaty, steely
related words achromatic, neutral; dirty, dull, faded, washed-out; ashen, ashy, chalky, livid, mousy (*or* mousey), pale, white, whitish; chocolate, dun, sandy, sepia; brindled, grizzled, hoar, hoary
near antonyms ablaze, bright, deep, gay, rich; chromatic, colored
2 causing or marked by an atmosphere lacking in cheer — see GLOOMY 1
grayish *adj* of the color gray — see GRAY 1
gray matter *n* the ability to learn and understand or to deal with problems — see INTELLIGENCE 1

[1]**graze** *vb* to feed on grass or herbs <cows *grazing* in the meadow>
synonyms browse, forage, pasture
related words eat, feed, nibble

[2]**graze** *vb* **1** to damage by rubbing against a sharp or rough surface — see SCRAPE 2
2 to pass lightly across or touch gently especially in passing — see BRUSH

grease *vb* to coat (something) with a slippery substance in order to reduce friction — see LUBRICATE

greased *adj* having or being a surface so smooth as to make sliding or falling likely — see SLICK 1

greasy *adj* having or being a surface so smooth as to make sliding or falling likely — see SLICK 1

great *adj* **1** having or showing exceptional knowledge, experience, or skill in a field of endeavor — see PROFICIENT
2 having, characterized by, or arising from a dignified and generous nature — see NOBLE 2
3 lasting for a considerable time — see LONG 2
4 of a size greater than average of its kind — see LARGE
5 of the very best kind — see EXCELLENT

greatcoat *n* a warm outdoor coat — see OVERCOAT

greatest *adj* **1** coming before all others in importance — see FOREMOST 1
2 of the highest degree — see FULL 2

greathearted *adj* **1** feeling or displaying no fear by temperament — see BRAVE
2 having, characterized by, or arising from a dignified and generous nature — see NOBLE 2

greatheartedness *n* strength of mind to carry on in spite of danger — see COURAGE

greatly *adv* **1** in a manner befitting a person of the highest character and ideals <as commander of the Union army's first black regiment, Robert Gould Shaw died as *greatly* as he had lived>
synonyms gallantly, grandly, heroically, highmindedly, honorably, magnanimously, nobly
related words loftily, venerably; magnificently, majestically
near antonyms abominably, contemptibly, despicably, detestably, hatefully; degenerately
antonyms basely, dishonorably, ignobly
2 to a large extent or degree <Todd has *greatly* increased the scope of his theme on civic responsibility>
synonyms astronomically, broadly, colossally, considerably, enormously, extensively, hugely, largely, massively, monstrously, much, sizably, stupendously, tremendously, utterly, vastly
related words appreciably, noticeably, significantly; abundantly, amply, copiously, healthily, plentifully
near antonyms modestly; fractionally; imperceptibly, infinitesimally, insignificantly, invisibly, microscopically, minutely, negligibly; barely, hardly, just, scarcely
antonyms little, slightly
3 to a great degree — see VERY 1

greatness *n* **1** exceptionally high quality — see EXCELLENCE 1
2 the quality or state of being large in size — see LARGENESS

greed *n* an intense selfish desire for wealth or possessions <don't let *greed* for riches control you>
synonyms acquisitiveness, avarice, avariciousness, avidity, covetousness, cupidity, greediness, rapaciousness, rapacity
related words materialism, possessiveness; appetite, craving, hankering, hunger, itch, longing, lust, passion, ravenousness, thirst, voracity, yearning, yen
near antonyms contentment, fulfillment, satisfaction; bounteousness, bounty, charity, generosity, generousness, liberality, openhandedness, openheartedness, unselfishness

greediness *n* an intense selfish desire for wealth or possessions — see GREED

greedy *adj* **1** having or marked by an eager and often selfish desire especially for material possessions <a young rocker who was *greedy* for fame and riches> <the *greedy* exploitation of the land by developers>
synonyms acquisitive, avaricious, avid, coveting, covetous, grasping, mercenary, rapacious
related words materialistic, philistine; desirous, eager, itchy, miserly; hoggish, piggish, swinish; devouring, gluttonous, gobbling, insatiable, ravenous, unquenchable, voracious; discontent, discontented, malcontent, unquenched, unsatisfied; begrudging, grudging, resentful
near antonyms bounteous, bountiful, charitable, freehanded, generous, greathearted, handsome, liberal, munificent, openhanded, openhearted, unselfish, unsparing; controlled, moderate, restrained, temperate; content, sated, satisfied
2 having a huge appetite — see VORACIOUS 1

green *adj* **1** covered with a thick, healthy natural growth — see LUSH 1
2 lacking in adult experience or maturity — see CALLOW
3 lacking in worldly wisdom or informed judgment — see NAIVE 1
4 lacking the warm skin color indicative of or associated with good health — see SICKLY 2

green *n* green leaves or plants — see GREENERY 1

greenback *n* a piece of printed paper used as money — see [1]BILL 2

greenery *n* green leaves or plants <Scottish highlands covered with lush *greenery*>
synonyms flora, foliage, green, herbage, leafage, vegetation, verdure
related words grassland, prairie; underbrush, undergrowth

greenhorn *n* a person who is just starting out in a field of activity — see BEGINNER

greenhouse *n* a glass-enclosed building for growing plants — see CONSERVATORY

greenness *n* the quality or state of being simple and sincere — see NAÏVETÉ 1

greeting *n* **1** an expression of goodwill upon meeting — see HELLO
2 greetings *pl* best wishes — see COMPLIMENT

gregarious *adj* likely to seek or enjoy the company of others — see CONVIVIAL

gregariousness *n* the quality or state of being social — see SOCIABILITY

gremlin *n* an imaginary being usually having a small human form and magical powers — see FAIRY

griddle cake *n* a flat cake made from thin batter and cooked on both sides (as on a griddle) — see PANCAKE

grief *n* deep sadness especially for the loss of someone or something loved — see SORROW

grievance *n* **1** a lingering ill will towards a person for a real or imagined wrong — see GRUDGE 1

2 an expression of dissatisfaction, pain, or resentment — see COMPLAINT 1

grieve *vb* to feel deep sadness or mental pain ⟨*grieved* over the lost cat⟩
synonyms agonize, bleed, hurt, mourn, sorrow, suffer
related words ache, long (for), pine (away); rack, torment, torture; bemoan, bewail, deplore, lament, rue; bawl, cry, groan, howl, keen, moan, take on, wail, weep, yammer
near antonyms beam, cheer, exult, joy, laugh, overjoy, ravish, rejoice; comfort, console

grieve (for) *vb* to feel or express sorrow for — see LAMENT 1

grieving *adj* expressing or suggesting mourning — see MOURNFUL 1

grievous *adj* **1** difficult to endure — see HARSH 1
2 hard to accept or bear especially emotionally — see BITTER 2
3 involving potential loss or injury — see DANGEROUS
4 of a kind to cause great distress — see REGRETTABLE

grievously *adv* with feelings of bitterness or grief — see HARD 2

grill *n* a public establishment where meals are served to paying customers for consumption on the premises — see RESTAURANT

grill *vb* to put a series of questions to — see EXAMINE 1

grim *adj* **1** harsh and threatening in manner or appearance ⟨a *grim* and desolate landscape⟩ ⟨a *grim* and short-tempered shopkeeper who didn't exactly invite friendly conversation⟩
synonyms austere, dour, fierce, flinty, forbidding, gruff, intimidating, lowering (*also* louring), rough, rugged, severe, stark, steely, stern, ungentle
related words bleak, cold, hostile, unfriendly; adamant, determined, firm, resolute, steadfast, unflinching; fixed, hard, immovable, implacable, inflexible, obdurate, rigid, set, stiff, unbending, uncompromising, unyielding; immutable, unchangeable; black, cheerless, dark, gloomy, glum, joyless, moody, morose, sulky, sullen, surly; brooding, grave, melancholy, serious, sober, solemn, somber (*or* sombre), unsmiling, weighty
near antonyms bland, meek, mellow, soft; easy, quiet, tranquil; agreeable, bright, cheerful, inviting, pleasant, pleasing, sweet; glad, happy, lighthearted, merry, mirthful, sunny; featherbrained, flighty, frivolous, giddy, goofy, light-headed, playful
antonyms benign, benignant, gentle, mild, tender
2 difficult to endure — see HARSH 1
3 showing no signs of slackening or yielding in one's purpose — see UNYIELDING 1
4 violently unfriendly or aggressive in disposition — see FIERCE 1

grimace *n* a twisting of the facial features in disgust or disapproval ⟨made a *grimace* when he tasted the medicine⟩
synonyms face, frown, lower (*also* lour), mouth, pout, scowl
related words flinch, squinch, wince; growl, snarl; simper, smirk; scoff, sneer; glare, glower, look, stare
near antonyms grin, smile

grimace *vb* to distort one's face — see MUG 1

grime *n* foul matter that mars the purity or cleanliness of something — see FILTH 1

grime *vb* to make dirty — see DIRTY

griminess *n* the state or quality of being dirty — see DIRTINESS 1

grimy *adj* not clean — see DIRTY 1

grin *vb* to express an emotion (as amusement) by curving the lips upward — see SMILE 1

grind *n* **1** a harsh grating sound — see RASP
2 a person slavishly devoted to intellectual or academic pursuits — see NERD
3 very hard or unpleasant work — see TOIL

grind *vb* **1** to make smooth by friction ⟨after they are *ground* and polished, these stones can be used for jewelry⟩
synonyms buff, file, hone, rasp, rub, sand
related words plane, scrape; sandblast, scour; burnish, polish; sharpen, whet; regrind
near antonyms coarsen, roughen
2 to press or strike against or together so as to make a scraping sound ⟨everyone in the car winced when the driver *ground* the gears trying to shift into second⟩
synonyms crunch, gnash, grate, grit, scrape, scrunch
related words creak, groan, rasp, scratch; clash, jangle, jar
3 to make sharp or sharper — see SHARPEN
4 to make smooth or glossy usually by repeatedly applying surface pressure — see POLISH
5 to pass roughly and noisily over or against a surface — see SCRAPE 1
6 to reduce to fine particles — see POWDER

grind (out) *vb* to produce or bring about especially by long or repeated effort — see HAMMER (OUT)

grinder *n* a large sandwich on a long split roll — see SUBMARINE

grip *n* **1** a bag carried by hand and designed to hold a traveler's clothing and personal articles — see TRAVELING BAG
2 the act or manner of holding — see HOLD 1
3 the knowledge gained from the process of coming to know or understand something — see COMPREHENSION
4 the right or means to command or control others — see POWER 1

grip *vb* **1** to have or keep in one's hands — see HOLD 1
2 to hold the attention of as if by a spell — see ENTHRALL 1
3 to hold the attention of — see ENGAGE 1
4 to reach for and take hold of by embracing with the fingers or arms — see TAKE 1

gripe *n* an expression of dissatisfaction, pain, or resentment — see COMPLAINT 1

gripe *vb* to express dissatisfaction, pain, or resentment usually tiresomely — see COMPLAIN

griper *n* **1** a person who makes frequent complaints usually about little things — see CRYBABY
2 an irritable and complaining person — see GROUCH

gripping *adj* holding the attention or provoking interest — see INTERESTING

grisliness *n* the quality of inspiring intense dread or dismay — see HORROR 1

grisly *adj* extremely disturbing or repellent — see HORRIBLE 1

grit *n* the strength of mind that enables a person to endure pain or hardship — see FORTITUDE

grit *vb* to press or strike against or together so as to make a scraping sound — see GRIND 2

groan *n* **1** a crying out in grief — see LAMENT 1
2 a long low sound indicating pain or grief — see MOAN 1

groan *vb* to utter a moan — see MOAN 1

grog *n* a fermented or distilled beverage that can make a person drunk — see ALCOHOL

groggery *n* a place of business where alcoholic beverages are sold to be consumed on the premises — see BARROOM

grogshop *n* a place of business where alcoholic beverages are sold to be consumed on the premises — see BARROOM

groomed *adj* being clean and in good order — see NEAT 1

groove *n* an established and often automatic or monotonous series of actions followed when engaging in some activity — see ROUTINE 1

groove *vb* to mark with or as if with a line or groove — see SCORE 1

groove (on) *vb* to take pleasure in — see ENJOY 1

groovy *adj* of the very best kind — see EXCELLENT

grope *vb* to search for something blindly or uncertainly ⟨*groped* for her car keys⟩ ⟨*groping* for the right answer⟩
synonyms feel, fish, fumble
related words cast about, hunt, look, reach, seek (out); clutch, grab, scrabble, snatch

gross *adj* **1** depicting or referring to sexual matters in a way that is unacceptable in polite society — see OBSCENE 1
2 having an excess of body fat — see FAT 1
3 lacking in refinement or good taste — see COARSE 2
4 very noticeable especially for being incorrect or bad — see EGREGIOUS

grossness *n* **1** the condition of having an excess of body fat — see CORPULENCE
2 the quality or state of being obscene — see OBSCENITY 1
3 the quality or state of lacking refinement or good taste — see VULGARITY 1

grot *n* a naturally formed underground chamber with an opening to the surface — see CAVE

grotesque *adj* **1** disagreeable to one's aesthetic or artistic sense — see HARSH 2
2 unpleasant to look at — see UGLY 1

grotto *n* a naturally formed underground chamber with an opening to the surface — see CAVE

grouch *n* an irritable and complaining person ⟨an uncle who is a real *grouch* when he's sick⟩
synonyms bear, complainer, crab, crank, croaker, curmudgeon, fusser, griper, grouser, growler, grumbler, grump, murmurer, mutterer, whiner
related words fulminator, malcontent, sorehead; killjoy, party pooper, spoilsport; defeatist, pessimist; faultfinder, kicker, nagger, nitpicker, quibbler
near antonyms optimist; rejoicer

grouchiness *n* readiness to show annoyance or impatience — see PETULANCE

grouchy *adj* **1** easily irritated or annoyed — see IRRITABLE
2 given to complaining a lot — see FUSSY 1

ground *adj* having an edge thin enough to cut or pierce something — see SHARP 1

ground *n* **1 grounds** *pl* the area around and belonging to a building ⟨an escorted tour of the White House and its surrounding *grounds*⟩
synonyms demesne, park, premises, yard
related words acres, estate, land, lot, parcel, plot, property, real estate, realty; campus; backyard, churchyard, dooryard, schoolyard
2 grounds *pl* matter that settles to the bottom of a body of liquid — see DEPOSIT 1
3 grounds *pl* something (as a belief) that serves as the basis for another thing — see REASON 2
4 a small area of usually open land — see FIELD 1
5 an immaterial thing upon which something else rests — see BASE 1
6 the loose surface material in which plants naturally grow — see DIRT 1
7 the physical conditions or features that form the setting against which something is viewed — see BACKGROUND 1
8 the solid part of our planet's surface as distinguished from the sea and air — see EARTH 2

ground *vb* to find a basis — see BASE

grounded *adj* resting on the shore or bottom of a body of water — see AGROUND

groundless *adj* having no basis in reason or fact ⟨please stop making *groundless* accusations against the teachers you dislike⟩ ⟨fears of a strike proved *groundless*⟩
synonyms invalid, nonvalid, unfounded, ungrounded, unreasonable, unsubstantiated, unsupported, unwarranted
related words illogical, irrational, nonlogical, unconscionable, unsound; fallacious, false, misled, wrong; gratuitous, uncalled-for, unnecessary; flimsy, implausible, misleading, specious, unconvincing, unsatisfying, untenable, weak; ill-advised, unreasoned; inconsistent; absurd, asinine, foolish, meaningless, nonsensical, preposterous, senseless, silly; insane, nutty, mad, wacky
near antonyms certified, validated, verified; confirmed, corroborated; informed, logical, rational; commonsense, sane, sensible, sober, wise; actual, genuine, real, true; certain, sure; clear, cogent, compelling, convincing, credible, persuasive, plausible, satisfying, solid
antonyms good, hard, just, justified, reasonable, reasoned, substantiated, valid, well-founded

ground plan *n* a method worked out in advance for achieving some objective — see PLAN 1

ground rule *n* a statement spelling out the proper procedure or conduct for an activity — see RULE 1

groundwork *n* an immaterial thing upon which something else rests — see BASE 1

group *n* **1** a number of things considered as a unit ⟨car buffs stood around admiring a *group* of classic cars in the parking lot⟩
synonyms array, assemblage, bank, batch, battery, block, bunch, clump, cluster, collection, grouping, huddle, knot, lot, package, parcel, passel, set, suite
related words accumulation, aggregate, aggregation, conglomeration; agglomeration, assortment, hodgepodge, jumble, miscellany, mixture, odds and ends, sundries, variety; series, suit
phrases the whole kit and caboodle
near antonyms entity, item, single, unit
2 a usually small number of persons considered as a unit ⟨the next *group* of guests were being seated for dinner⟩
synonyms array, batch, battery, body, bunch, cluster, crop, grouping, huddle, knot, lot, parcel, party, passel
related words assembly, congregation, gathering, organization; circle, clan, clique, coterie, fellow-

ship, gang, ring, set; faction, guild (*also* gild), order, school, sect; brigade, crew, outfit, platoon, posse; alliance, bloc, coalition, confederacy, confederation, federation, league, union; bevy, covey
phrases the whole kit and caboodle
near antonyms individual, single
3 one of the units into which a whole is divided on the basis of a common characteristic — see CLASS 2
group *vb* **1** to arrange or assign according to type — see CLASSIFY 1
2 to bring together in one body or place — see GATHER 1
grouping *n* **1** a number of things considered as a unit — see GROUP 1
2 a usually small number of persons considered as a unit — see GROUP 2
grouse *vb* to express dissatisfaction, pain, or resentment usually tiresomely — see COMPLAIN
grouser *n* an irritable and complaining person — see GROUCH
grovel *vb* **1** to draw back or crouch down in fearful submission — see COWER
2 to move slowly with the body close to the ground — see CRAWL 1
grow *vb* **1** to look after or assist the growth of by labor and care <a dedicated home gardener who *grows* tomatoes in her small garden every summer>
synonyms crop, cultivate, culture, promote, raise, rear, tend
related words breed, produce, propagate; plant, sow; gather, glean, harvest, reap; germinate, quicken, root, sprout
near antonyms kill; dig, extirpate, pick, pluck, pull (up), uproot; cut, hay, mow
2 to become mature — see MATURE
3 to eventually have as a state or quality — see BECOME
grow (in) *vb* to increase in — see GAIN 1
grower *n* a person who cultivates the land and grows crops on it — see FARMER
growl *vb* **1** to express dissatisfaction, pain, or resentment usually tiresomely — see COMPLAIN
2 to make a long loud deep noise or cry — see ROAR
3 to make a low heavy rolling sound — see RUMBLE
growler *n* **1** a person who makes frequent complaints usually about little things — see CRYBABY
2 an irritable and complaining person — see GROUCH
grown–up *n* a fully grown person — see ADULT
growth *n* **1** an abnormal mass of tissue <found a *growth* on the dog's neck under her collar>
synonyms excrescence, lump, neoplasm, tumor
related words outgrowth; cancer, carcinoma, lymphoma, malignancy, melanoma; cyst, tubercle, wart
2 the act or process of going from the simple or basic to the complex or advanced — see DEVELOPMENT 1
3 the process of becoming mature — see MATURATION
grow up *vb* to become mature — see MATURE
grub *n* substances intended to be eaten — see FOOD
grub *vb* to devote serious and sustained effort — see LABOR
grubber *n* a person who does very hard or dull work — see SLAVE 2
grubbiness *n* the state or quality of being dirty — see DIRTINESS 1
grubby *adj* not clean — see DIRTY 1
grudge *n* **1** a lingering ill will towards a person for a real or imagined wrong <he's had a *grudge* against her ever since she snubbed him at the dance>
synonyms grievance, resentment, score
related words condemnation; offense (*or* offence), umbrage; complaint; peeve, pique
2 a deep-seated ill will — see ENMITY
grueling *or* **gruelling** *adj* **1** requiring considerable physical or mental effort — see HARD 2
2 requiring much time, effort, or careful attention — see DEMANDING 1
gruesome *adj* extremely disturbing or repellent — see HORRIBLE 1
gruesomeness *n* the quality of inspiring intense dread or dismay — see HORROR 1
gruff *adj* **1** harsh and dry in sound — see HOARSE
2 harsh and threatening in manner or appearance — see GRIM 1
grumble *n* an expression of dissatisfaction, pain, or resentment — see COMPLAINT 1
grumble *vb* **1** to express dissatisfaction, pain, or resentment usually tiresomely — see COMPLAIN
2 to make a low heavy rolling sound — see RUMBLE
grumbler *n* **1** a person who makes frequent complaints usually about little things — see CRYBABY
2 an irritable and complaining person — see GROUCH
grump *n* an irritable and complaining person — see GROUCH
grumpiness *n* readiness to show annoyance or impatience — see PETULANCE
grumpy *adj* **1** easily irritated or annoyed — see IRRITABLE
2 given to complaining a lot — see FUSSY 1
grungy *adj* **1** not clean — see DIRTY 1
2 showing signs of advanced wear and tear and neglect — see SHABBY 1
grunt *n* speech that is not clear enough to be understood — see MUMBLE
grunt *vb* to speak softly and unclearly — see MUMBLE
grunting *n* speech that is not clear enough to be understood — see MUMBLE
guarantee *n* **1** a formal agreement to fulfill an obligation <the contractors gave us a written *guarantee* that the work on the house would be done by Christmas>
synonyms bond, contract, covenant, guaranty, surety, warranty
related words oath, pledge, vow, word; bargain, compact, pact, treaty; assurance, insurance; bail, deposit, pawn, security
2 something given or held to assure that the giver will keep a promise — see PLEDGE 1
guarantee *vb* **1** to assume responsibility for the satisfactory quality or performance of — see WARRANT 1
2 to make sure, certain, or safe — see ENSURE
guarantor *n* a person who takes the responsibility for some other person or thing — see SPONSOR
guaranty *n* **1** a formal agreement to fulfill an obligation — see GUARANTEE 1
2 something given or held to assure that the giver will keep a promise — see PLEDGE 1

guaranty *vb* to make sure, certain, or safe — see ENSURE

guard *n* **1** a person or group that watches over someone or something ⟨checked in with the security *guard* at the gate⟩

synonyms custodian, guardian, keeper, lookout, picket, sentinel, sentry, warden, warder, watch, watchman

related words observer, patrol, spotter, watchdog; bodyguard, convoy, defender, escort, honor guard

2 a position or readiness to oppose actual or expected attack — see DEFENSIVE

3 a protective device (as on a weapon) to prevent accidental operation — see SAFETY 2

4 means or method of defending — see DEFENSE 1

5 one that accompanies another for protection, guidance, or as a courtesy — see ESCORT

6 someone that protects — see PROTECTOR

guard *vb* to drive danger or attack away from — see DEFEND 1

guard (against) *vb* to be cautious of or on guard against — see BEWARE (OF)

guarded *adj* having or showing a close attentiveness to avoiding danger or trouble — see CAREFUL 1

guardian *n* **1** a person or group that watches over someone or something — see GUARD 1

2 a person who takes care of a property sometimes for an absent owner — see CUSTODIAN 1

guardianship *n* responsibility for the safety and well-being of someone or something — see CUSTODY

guardrail *n* a protective barrier consisting of a horizontal bar and its supports — see RAILING

guardroom *n* a place of confinement for persons held in lawful custody — see JAIL

guess *n* an opinion or judgment based on little or no evidence — see CONJECTURE

guess *vb* **1** to form an opinion from little or no evidence ⟨though she does not speak with an accent, I would still *guess* that she is a foreigner⟩

synonyms assume, conjecture, presume, speculate, suppose, surmise, suspect, suspicion [*chiefly dialect*]

related words conclude, deduce, gather, infer; hypothesize, theorize; believe, conceive, expect, imagine, reckon [*chiefly dialect*], take, think

near antonyms demonstrate, establish, prove; ascertain, determine, find out

2 to decide the size, amount, number, or distance of (something) without actual measurement — see ESTIMATE 2

3 to have as an opinion — see BELIEVE 2

guest *n* **1** a person who visits another ⟨invited the afternoon *guests* to stay for dinner⟩

synonyms caller, frequenter, visitant, visitor

related words company; crasher, hanger-on

near antonyms denizen, dweller, habitant, inhabitant, occupant, resident, resider

2 a person who buys a product or uses a service from a business — see CUSTOMER 1

guffaw *n* an explosive sound that is a sign of amusement — see LAUGH 1

guidance *n* **1** an opinion suggesting a wise or proper course of action — see ADVICE

2 the act or activity of looking after and making decisions about something — see CONDUCT 1

3 the duty or function of watching or guarding for the sake of proper direction or control — see SUPERVISION 1

guide *n* one that accompanies another for protection, guidance, or as a courtesy — see ESCORT

guide *vb* **1** to give advice and instruction to (someone) regarding the course or process to be followed ⟨the famous chef *guided* her through the creation of the wedding cake, showing her how to ice the layers, fashion the elaborate decorations, and assemble the whole shebang⟩

synonyms coach, counsel, lead, mentor, pilot, shepherd, show, tutor

related words direct, steer; accompany, escort, see; oversee, superintend, supervise; drill, train; brief, enlighten, inform; instruct, school, teach; inculcate, indoctrinate; cultivate, foster, nurture

2 to look after and make decisions about — see CONDUCT 1

3 to point out the way for (someone) especially from a position in front — see LEAD 1

guidon *n* a piece of cloth with a special design that is used as an emblem or for signaling — see FLAG 1

guild *also* **gild** *n* a group of persons formally joined together for some common interest — see ASSOCIATION 2

guile *n* **1** skill in achieving one's ends through indirect, subtle, or underhanded means — see CUNNING 1

2 the inclination or practice of misleading others through lies or trickery — see DECEIT

guileful *adj* clever at attaining one's ends by indirect and often deceptive means — see ARTFUL 1

guileless *adj* free from any intent to deceive or impress others ⟨she was an easy-going, *guileless* young woman who was comfortable just being herself⟩

synonyms artless, genuine, honest, ingenuous, innocent, naive (*or* naïve), natural, real, simple, sincere, true, unaffected, unpretending, unpretentious

related words childlike, impressionable, inexperienced, malleable, persuadable, simpleminded, unsophisticated, unworldly; unforced, unstudied; candid, frank, free, openhearted, plain, plainspoken, single-minded; trustful, trusting

phrases on the level

near antonyms sophisticated, worldly, worldly-wise; crooked, deceitful, deceptive, devious, double-dealing, hypocritical, two-faced; arch, calculating, canny, crafty, cunning, designing, scheming, sharp, shifty, shrewd, slick, slippery, sly, tricky, underhanded, wily; flattering, mealymouthed, smooth, sycophantic, unctuous; feigned, forced, strained

antonyms affected, artful, artificial, assuming, dishonest, dissembling, dissimulating, fake, false, guileful, insincere, phony (*also* phoney), pretentious

guilelessly *adv* without any attempt to impress by deception or exaggeration — see NATURALLY 3

guilelessness *n* the quality or state of being simple and sincere — see NAÏVETÉ 1

guillotine *vb* to cut off the head of — see DECAPITATE

guilt *n* **1** a feeling of responsibility for wrongdoing ⟨he was wracked with *guilt* after he accidentally broke his sister's antique grandfather clock⟩

synonyms contriteness, contrition, penitence, re-

gret, remorse, remorsefulness, repentance, rue, self-reproach, shame
related words compunction, misgiving, qualm, scruple; blame, fault, responsibility; chagrin, embarrassment; anguish, distress, grief, sadness, sorrow
antonyms impenitence, remorselessness
2 responsibility for wrongdoing or failure — see BLAME 1

guiltless *adj* free from guilt or blame — see INNOCENT 2

guiltlessness *n* the quality or state of being free from guilt or blame — see INNOCENCE 1

guilty *adj* **1** responsible for a wrong ⟨he was found *guilty* on all charges brought against him⟩
synonyms blamable, culpable
related words blameworthy, censurable, impeachable, indictable, punishable, reprehensible, reproachable; accused, arraigned, impeached, implicated, indicted; accountable, answerable; condemned, convicted
phrases at fault
near antonyms absolved, acquitted, exonerated, vindicated; faultless, impeccable, irreproachable, unimpeachable
antonyms blameless, guiltless, innocent
2 suffering from or expressive of a feeling of responsibility for wrongdoing ⟨she was burdened with a *guilty* conscience after stealing the newspaper from the newsstand⟩
synonyms ashamed, contrite, hangdog, penitent, remorseful, repentant, shamed, shamefaced
related words apologetic, sorry; regretful, rueful; penitential; blushing, chagrined, embarrassed, sheepish
near antonyms unapologetic; brazen, cheeky, impudent
antonyms impenitent, remorseless, shameless, unashamed, unrepentant

guise *n* **1** a display of emotion or behavior that is insincere or intended to deceive — see MASQUERADE
2 clothing chosen as appropriate for a specific situation — see OUTFIT 1
3 clothing put on to hide one's true identity or imitate someone or something else — see DISGUISE
4 outward and often deceptive indication — see APPEARANCE 2

gulch *n* a narrow opening between hillsides or mountains that can be used for passage — see CANYON

gulf *n* **1** a part of a body of water that extends beyond the general shoreline ⟨dipped our feet in the warm waters of the *gulf*⟩
synonyms bay, bight, cove, creek [*chiefly British*], estuary, firth, fjord (*or* fiord), inlet, loch [*Scottish*]
related words harbor, port, road(s), roadstead; narrow, sound, strait; bayou
2 an immeasurable depth or space — see ABYSS
3 a narrow opening between hillsides or mountains that can be used for passage — see CANYON
4 an open space in a barrier (as a wall or hedge) — see GAP 1

gull *n* one who is easily deceived or cheated — see DUPE

gull *vb* to cause to believe what is untrue — see DECEIVE

gullibility *n* readiness to believe the claims of others without sufficient evidence — see CREDULITY

gullible *adj* readily taken advantage of — see EASY 2

gulp *n* the portion of a serving of a beverage that is swallowed at one time — see DRINK 2

gulp *vb* to swallow in liquid form — see DRINK 1

gummy *adj* being of such a thick consistency as to readily cling to objects upon contact — see STICKY 1

gun *n* **1** a portable weapon from which a shot is discharged by gunpowder ⟨while her father preferred hunting with a crossbow, she preferred a *gun*⟩
synonyms arm, firearm, piece, small arm
related words forty-five (*or* .45), gat [*slang*], handgun, pistol, revolver, rod [*slang*], six-gun, six-shooter, zip gun; blunderbuss, flintlock, harquebus (*or* arquebus), matchlock, musket, muzzle-loader, rifle, shotgun; automatic, machine gun, repeater, submachine gun, tommy gun; speargun
2 guns *pl* large firearms (as cannon or rockets) — see ARTILLERY

gun *vb* to strike with a missile from a gun — see SHOOT 3

gung ho *adj* showing urgent desire or interest — see EAGER

gurgle *vb* to flow in a broken irregular stream ⟨the tiny stream *gurgled* down the rocky slope and joined the larger river at the bottom of the hill⟩
synonyms bubble, dribble, lap, plash, ripple, splash, trickle, wash
related words eddy, purl, swirl; swash, swish, whish; drip, drop; gush, jet, rush, spout, spurt, squirt
near antonyms run
antonyms pour, roll, stream

gush *n* **1** a flowing or going out — see OUTFLOW
2 a sudden intense expression of strong feeling — see OUTBURST 1

gush *vb* **1** to flow out in great quantities or with force ⟨the dam cracked and water *gushed* from the break⟩
synonyms jet, pour, rush, spew, spout, spurt, squirt
related words cascade, issue, roll, run, stream; plash, slosh, splash; surge, swell; flush, sluice; deluge, engulf, flood, inundate, overflow, overwhelm, submerge, swamp
near antonyms spatter, sprinkle; exude, leak, ooze, seep, weep
antonyms dribble, drip, drop, trickle
2 to make an exaggerated display of affection or enthusiasm ⟨he *gushed* about his favorite basketball player, calling him "the best there ever was"⟩
synonyms enthuse, fuss, rave, rhapsodize, slobber
related words dote (on), fawn; emote

gushing *adj* **1** overly or insincerely flattering — see FULSOME
2 pouring forth in great amounts — see PROFUSE

gust *n* **1** a sudden brief rush of wind ⟨a *gust* tore her umbrella from her grip and blew it down the street⟩
synonyms blast, blow, flurry, williwaw
related words breeze, zephyr; air, breath, waft; puff, whiff; gale, hurricane, squall, tempest, tornado, windstorm; northeaster, norther, northerly, northwester, southeaster, southwester, westerly
2 a sudden intense expression of strong feeling — see OUTBURST 1

gusty *adj* marked by strong wind or more wind than usual — see WINDY 1

gut *n* **1 guts** *pl* the internal organs of the body ⟨dissected the frog and looked at its *guts*⟩
synonyms entrails, innards, inside(s), viscera, vitals
related words bowel(s), intestine(s); giblet(s), variety meat
2 guts *pl* strength of mind to carry on in spite of danger — see COURAGE
3 guts *pl* the strength of mind that enables a person to endure pain or hardship — see FORTITUDE
4 the part of the body between the chest and the pelvis — see STOMACH

gut *vb* to take the internal organs out of ⟨you'll need to *gut* the fish and wash it out before you can cook it⟩
synonyms clean, disembowel, draw, eviscerate
related words bone, dress; cut, excise, extract, remove, withdraw; transplant

gutsy *adj* inclined or willing to take risks — see BOLD 1

gutter *n* **1** a pipe or channel for carrying off water from a roof ⟨one of his chores is to clean leaves and sticks out of the *gutters* before winter sets in⟩
synonyms drainpipe, eaves trough, spout, trough, waterspout
related words drain, flume, sluice; conduit, duct
2 a long narrow channel dug in the earth — see DITCH

guy *n* **1** a member of the human race — see HUMAN
2 an adult male human being — see MAN 1

guzzle *vb* to swallow in liquid form — see DRINK 1

gym *n* a building or room used for sports activities and exercising ⟨decided to get up early and go to the *gym* to lift weights⟩
synonyms gymnasium, spa
related words arena, bowl, coliseum, colosseum, stadium

gymnasium *n* a building or room used for sports activities and exercising — see GYM

gyp *vb* to rob by the use of trickery or threats — see FLEECE

gyrate *vb* to move in circles around an axis or center — see SPIN 1

gyration *n* a rapid turning about on an axis or central point — see SPIN 1

habiliment *n, usually* **habiliments** *pl* covering for the human body — see CLOTHING

habit *n* a usual manner of behaving or doing ⟨it was his *habit* to rise early⟩
synonyms custom, fashion, pattern, practice (*also* practise), trick, way, wont
related words addiction; disposition; bent, inclination, proclivity, tendency, turn; convention, form, mode, style; usage; manners, mores; groove, rote, routine, rut; affectation, airs, pose; attribute, characteristic, mark, trait; oddity, peculiarity, quirk, singularity, tic; strangeness, weirdness

habitable *adj* suitable for living in — see LIVABLE

habitant *n* one who lives permanently in a place — see INHABITANT

habitat *n* the place where a plant or animal is usually or naturally found — see HOME 2

habitation *n* the place where one lives — see HOME 1

habitual *adj* **1** being such by habit and not likely to change ⟨Sarah admits she's an *habitual* procrastinator, but she still manages to complete her assignments on time⟩
synonyms chronic, confirmed, inveterate
related words incorrigible, unregenerate; born, natural; persistent, regular, steady, unfailing; addicted; accustomed, habituated, used; deep-rooted, entrenched (*also* intrenched), inbred, inherent, innate
near antonyms unaccustomed, unused; occasional
2 appearing or occurring repeatedly from time to time — see REGULAR 1

habituated *adj* being in the habit or custom — see ACCUSTOMED

hacienda *n* a large impressive residence — see MANSION

[1]hack *n* a V-shaped cut usually on an edge or a surface — see NOTCH 1

[2]hack *n* an automobile that carries passengers for a fare usually determined by the distance traveled — see TAXI

hackney *adj* used or heard so often as to be dull — see STALE

hackneyed *adj* used or heard so often as to be dull — see STALE

hag *n* **1** a mean or ugly old woman — see CRONE
2 a woman believed to have often harmful supernatural powers — see WITCH 1

haggard *adj* suffering extreme weight loss as a result of hunger or disease — see EMACIATED

haggle *vb* to talk over or dispute the terms of a purchase — see BARGAIN

hail *n* **1** a heavy fall of objects — see RAIN 2
2 a rapid or overwhelming outpouring of many things at once — see BARRAGE

hail *vb* **1** to declare enthusiastic approval of — see ACCLAIM
2 to demand or request the presence or service of — see SUMMON 1

hair *n* **1** a very small distance or degree ⟨a race that was won by a *hair*⟩
synonyms ace, hairbreadth (*or* hairsbreadth), inch
related words bit, crumb, jot, mite, particle, smidgen, trace, trifle
2 the hairy covering of a mammal especially when fine, soft, and thick — see FUR 1

hairbreadth *or* **hairsbreadth** *n* a very small distance or degree — see HAIR 1

hairline *adj* **1** being of less than usual width — see NARROW 1
2 made or done with extreme care and accuracy — see FINE 2
3 meeting the highest standard of accuracy — see PRECISE 1

hair–raising *adj* causing fear — see FEARFUL 1
hairsplitting *adj* made or done with extreme care and accuracy — see FINE 2
hairy *adj* **1** covered with or as if with hair ‹a *hairy* spider›
synonyms bristly, fleecy, furry, hirsute, rough, shaggy, unshorn, wooliy (*also* wooly)
related words bearded, mustachioed, whiskered; downy, fluffy, fuzzy, nappy
near antonyms beardless, shaved, shaven
antonyms bald, furless, hairless, shorn, smooth
2 made of or resembling hair ‹enough *hairy* clumps around the house to make another cat› ‹a *hairy* mass of fiberglass insulation›
synonyms furry, fuzzy, rough, shaggy, woolly (*also* wooly)
related words downy, fluffy, nappy
halcyon *adj* free from storms or physical disturbance — see CALM 1
hale *adj* enjoying health and vigor — see HEALTHY 1
hale *vb* to cause to follow by applying steady force on — see PULL 1
half *adv* in any way or respect — see AT ALL
half *n* **1** one of two equal or nearly equal parts ‹to be fair, we each get *half* the pie›
synonyms moiety
related words hemisphere, meridian, semicircle; component, division, fraction, part, piece, portion, section, segment
near antonyms aggregate, whole
2 either of a pair matched in one or more qualities — see MATE 1
halfhearted *adj* showing little or no interest or enthusiasm — see TEPID 1
halfway *adj* **1** lacking some necessary part — see INCOMPLETE
2 occupying a position equally distant from the ends or extremes — see MIDDLE 1
half–wit *n* **1** a person who lacks good sense or judgment — see FOOL 1
2 a stupid person — see IDIOT
half–witted *adj* **1** not having or showing an ability to absorb ideas readily — see STUPID 1
2 showing or marked by a lack of good sense or judgment — see FOOLISH 1
hall *n* **1** the entrance room of a building ‹the guests hung their coats in the *hall*›
synonyms entry, entryway, foyer, lobby, vestibule
related words antechamber, anteroom, waiting room; doorway, entrance, threshold
2 a typically long narrow way connecting parts of a building ‹the bedroom is at the end of the *hall*›
synonyms concourse, corridor, gallery, hallway, passage, passageway
related words arcade, breezeway, cloister
3 a large room or building for enclosed public gatherings ‹the concert *hall* was full›
synonyms arena, auditorium, theater (*or* theatre)
related words amphitheater, hippodrome, house, playhouse; ballroom; lyceum; chamber, senate
4 a centrally located room in a building that serves as a gathering or waiting area or as a passageway into the interior — see FOYER 1
5 a large impressive residence — see MANSION
6 a large, magnificent, or massive building — see EDIFICE 1
hallmark *n* a device, design, or figure used as an identifying mark — see EMBLEM
hallow *vb* to make holy through prayers or ritual — see BLESS 1
hallowed *adj* **1** deserving honor and respect especially by reason of age — see VENERABLE 1
2 set apart or worthy of veneration by association with God — see HOLY 2
hallowing *n* the act of making something holy through religious ritual — see CONSECRATION
hallucination *n* a conception or image created by the imagination and having no objective reality — see FANTASY 1
hallway *n* a typically long narrow way connecting parts of a building — see HALL 2
halt *n* **1** a point in a struggle where neither side is capable of winning or willing to give in — see IMPASSE
2 the stopping of a process or activity — see END 1
¹halt *vb* **1** to bring (something) to a standstill ‹traffic was *halted* by the parade›
synonyms arrest, catch, check, draw up, fetch up, hold up, stall, stay, still, stop
related words balk, block, blockade, dam, detain, hinder, hold, hold back, impede, obstruct, stem; conclude, end, terminate; call, discontinue, suspend; clamp down, rein (in), squash, squelch, stamp, stanch (*also* staunch), stunt, suppress, turn back
near antonyms carry on, continue, follow through, keep on, keep up, run on; advance, fare, move, proceed, progress, wend; actuate, budge, drive, impel, propel, push, stir
2 to bring (as an action or operation) to an immediate end — see STOP 1
3 to come to an end — see CEASE 1
²halt *vb* to walk while favoring one leg — see LIMP 1
hammer *vb* **1** to shape with a hammer ‹medieval artisans *hammered* brass into bowls and trays which they embossed with elaborate designs›
synonyms beat, forge, pound
related words chase, fashion, form, knead, model, mold, work; coin, mint, stamp; carve, chisel, hew, sculpt, sculpture
2 to deliver a blow to (someone or something) usually in a strong vigorous manner — see HIT 1
3 to strike repeatedly — see BEAT 1
hammer (out) *vb* to produce or bring about especially by long or repeated effort ‹the school committee *hammered out* a new sports-participation policy with input from students, parents, and administrators›
synonyms build (up), carve (out), forge, grind (out), work out
related words cobble (together *or* up), create, construct, fabricate, fashion, form, frame, manufacture, model, shape, tailor; conceive, concoct, contrive, cook (up), devise, hatch, invent, originate; bring forth, effect; accomplish, achieve, bring off
near antonyms demolish, destroy, dismantle, raze, tear down; ruin, undo, unmake, wreck
hamper *vb* to create difficulty for the work or activity of ‹fallen branches *hampered* the hikers as they made their way along the narrow path›
synonyms clog, cramp, delay, embarrass, encumber, fetter, handicap, hinder, hobble, hold back, hold up, impede, inhibit, interfere (with), manacle, obstruct, shackle, tie up, trammel
related words arrest, brake, check, constrain, curb, rein, restrain, snag; bind, chain, handcuff, leash, muzzle, strap, tether, tie; barricade, block,

blockade, dam, head (off), plug; balk, choke, hurt, repress, retard, stifle, straiten, strangle, stunt; baffle, foil, frustrate, interrupt, sabotage, thwart; bog (down), confine, hedge (in), hem (in), limit, tie (down)
phrases cramp one's style, give a hard time
near antonyms clear, make way, open, unclog, unplug, unstop; free, liberate, release, untie; loosen, smooth; further, promote
antonyms aid, assist, facilitate, help

hams *n pl* the part of the body upon which someone sits — see BUTTOCKS

hamstring *vb* to render powerless, ineffective, or unable to move — see PARALYZE

hand *n* **1** a certain way in which something appears or may be regarded — see ASPECT 1
2 a place, space, or direction away from or beyond a central point or line — see SIDE 1
3 an arrow-shaped piece on a dial or scale for registering information — see POINTER 1
4 one who works for another for wages or a salary — see EMPLOYEE
5 the form or style of a particular person's writing — see HANDWRITING 1
6 *usually* **hands** *pl* the ability to direct the course of something — see CONTROL 2
7 hands *pl* the fact or state of having (something) at one's disposal — see POSSESSION 1

hand *vb* **1** to put (something) into the possession of someone for use or consumption — see FURNISH 2
2 to shift possession of (something) from one person to another — see PASS 1

handbag *n* **1** a bag carried by hand and designed to hold a traveler's clothing and personal articles — see TRAVELING BAG
2 a container for carrying money and small personal items — see PURSE

handbook *n* a book used for instruction in a subject — see TEXTBOOK

handcraft *n* an occupation requiring skillful use of the hands — see CRAFT 1

handcuff *vb* to confine or restrain with or as if with chains — see BIND 1

handcuff *n usually* **handcuffs** *pl* something that physically prevents free movement — see BOND 1

handful *n* a small number — see FEW

handicap *n* **1** a feature of someone or something that creates difficulty for achieving success — see DISADVANTAGE
2 something that makes movement or progress more difficult — see ENCUMBRANCE

handicap *vb* to create difficulty for the work or activity of — see HAMPER

handicraft *n* an occupation requiring skillful use of the hands — see CRAFT 1

handicrafter *n* a person whose occupation requires skill with the hands — see ARTISAN

handily *adv* without difficulty — see EASILY

handiwork *n* something produced by physical or intellectual effort — see PRODUCT 1

handkerchief *n* a scarf worn on the head — see BANDANNA

handle *n* a word or combination of words by which a person or thing is regularly known — see NAME 1

handle *vb* **1** to deal with (something) usually skillfully or efficiently <as host of a live TV talk show, she must *handle* any situation that comes up>
synonyms contend (with), cope (with), grapple (with), manage, maneuver, manipulate, negotiate, swing, treat
related words bring off, carry out, pull, swing; command, direct, guide, steer; control, regulate, run
phrases have a grip on
near antonyms botch, bungle, goof (up), louse up, mess (up)
antonyms fumble, muddle (through)
2 to behave toward in a stated way — see TREAT 1
3 to control the mechanical operation of — see OPERATE 1
4 to look after and make decisions about — see CONDUCT 1

handling *n* the act or activity of looking after and making decisions about something — see CONDUCT 1

hand over *vb* **1** to give (something) over to the control or possession of another usually under duress — see SURRENDER 1
2 to put (something) into the possession of someone for use or consumption — see FURNISH 2
3 to put (something) into the possession or safekeeping of another — see GIVE 2
4 to shift possession of (something) from one person to another — see PASS 1

handpick *vb* to decide to accept (someone or something) from a group of possibilities — see CHOOSE 1

handsome *adj* **1** having or showing elegance — see ELEGANT 1
2 of a size greater than average of its kind — see LARGE
3 very pleasing to look at — see BEAUTIFUL

handsomely *adv* in a generous manner — see WELL 2

handsomeness *n* **1** dignified or restrained beauty of form, appearance, or style — see ELEGANCE
2 the qualities in a person or thing that as a whole give pleasure to the senses — see BEAUTY 1

hand-to-mouth *adj* less plentiful than what is normal, necessary, or desirable — see MEAGER

handwriting *n* **1** the form or style of a particular person's writing <she immediately recognized the *handwriting* on the envelope as that of her old college roommate>
synonyms hand, penmanship, script
related words scratch, scrawl, scribble; backhand, print; autograph, signature
2 writing done by hand <most students are taught the value of good *handwriting*>
synonyms calligraphy, longhand, manuscript, penmanship, script
related words lettering; shorthand
antonyms print, type

handy *adj* **1** situated within easy reach — see CONVENIENT
2 skillful with the hands — see DEXTEROUS 1

hang *vb* **1** to place on an elevated point without support from below <*hang* your coats on the coat rack in the hall>
synonyms dangle, sling, suspend, swing
related words hook, pin, tack; drape, festoon, garland, string; extend (out), jut, project, stick out; overhang, protrude; cascade, depend, fall
2 to be determined by, based on, or subject (to) — see DEPEND 1
3 to be limp from lack of water or vigor — see DROOP 1

4 to rest or move along the surface of a liquid or in the air — see FLOAT

hang (over) *vb* to remain poised to inflict harm, danger, or distress on — see THREATEN

hang around *vb* **1** to come or be together as friends — see ASSOCIATE 1

2 to continue to be in a place for a significant amount of time — see STAY 1

3 to spend time doing nothing — see IDLE

hang around (in) *vb* to go to or spend time in often — see FREQUENT

hang back *vb* to show uncertainty about the right course of action — see HESITATE

hangdog *adj* suffering from or expressive of a feeling of responsibility for wrongdoing — see GUILTY 2

hanger–on *n* a person who is supported or seeks support from another without making an adequate return — see LEECH

hanging *adj* **1** bending downward or forward — see NODDING

2 extending freely from a support from above — see DEPENDENT 1

hang on (to) *vb* **1** to continue to have in one's possession or power — see KEEP 2

2 to have or keep in one's hands — see HOLD 1

hangout *n* a place for spending time or for socializing ⟨Jake's favorite *hangout* is the local community center⟩

synonyms haunt, rendezvous, resort

related words camp, canteen, club, clubhouse, den, harbor, haven, nest, refuge, retreat

hang out *vb* to spend time doing nothing — see IDLE

hang out (at) *vb* to go to or spend time in often — see FREQUENT

hanker (for *or* after) *vb* to have an earnest wish to own or enjoy — see DESIRE

hankering *n* a strong wish for something — see DESIRE

hanky–panky *n* the use of clever underhanded actions to achieve an end — see TRICKERY

hap *n* **1** something that happens — see EVENT 1

2 the uncertain course of events — see CHANCE 1

hap *vb* to take place — see HAPPEN

haphazard *adj* lacking a definite plan, purpose, or pattern — see RANDOM

haphazard *adv* without definite aim, direction, rule, or method — see HIT OR MISS

haphazardly *adv* without definite aim, direction, rule, or method — see HIT OR MISS

hapless *adj* having, prone to, or marked by bad luck — see UNLUCKY

happen *vb* to take place ⟨did anything exciting *happen* over the summer?⟩

synonyms be, befall, betide, chance, come, come about, go (on), hap, occur, pass, transpire

related words arise, crop (up), develop, materialize, spring (up); intervene; fall out, go off, proceed, turn out

phrases come to pass

happen (on *or* upon) *vb* to come upon unexpectedly or by chance ⟨*happened on* the filming of a movie⟩

synonyms chance (upon), encounter, find, hit (upon), meet, stumble (on *or* onto)

related words confront, face; discover, turn up

phrases bump into, come across, run across, run into

happen (upon) *vb* to come upon face-to-face or as if face-to-face — see MEET 1

happening *n* **1** an exciting or noteworthy event that one experiences firsthand — see ADVENTURE

2 something that happens — see EVENT 1

happily *adv* **1** in a cheerful or happy manner — see GAILY 1

2 in a manner suitable for the occasion or purpose — see PROPERLY

happiness *n* **1** a feeling or state of well-being and contentment ⟨Marta's *happiness* was complete when she got her very own horse⟩

synonyms blessedness, bliss, blissfulness, felicity, gladness, joy

related words elatedness, elation, exhilaration, exultation, intoxication; ecstasy, euphoria, heaven, rapture, rapturousness; delectation, delight, enjoyment, pleasure; cheer, cheerfulness, exuberance, gaiety (*also* gayety), gladsomeness, glee, gleefulness, jollity, joyfulness, joyousness, jubilation, lightheartedness; content, contentedness, gratification, satisfaction

near antonyms anguish, desolation, joylessness, sorrow, woe, woefulness; blues, dejection, depression, despondency, disheartenment, dispiritedness, doldrums, downheartedness, gloom, gloominess, melancholy, mournfulness

antonyms misery, sadness, unhappiness, wretchedness

2 the feeling experienced when one's wishes are met — see PLEASURE 1

happy *adj* **1** coming or happening by good luck especially unexpectedly — see FORTUNATE 1

2 experiencing pleasure, satisfaction, or delight — see GLAD 1

3 feeling that one's needs or desires have been met — see CONTENT

4 having good luck — see LUCKY 1

5 meeting the requirements of a purpose or situation — see FIT 1

happy–go–lucky *adj* **1** having a relaxed, casual manner — see EASYGOING 1

2 having or showing a lack of concern or seriousness — see CAREFREE

harangue *n* **1** a long angry speech or scolding — see TIRADE

2 a usually formal discourse delivered to an audience — see SPEECH 1

harangue *vb* **1** to give a formal often extended talk on a subject — see TALK 1

2 to talk as if giving an important and formal speech — see ORATE 1

harassment *n* the act of making unwelcome intrusions upon another — see ANNOYANCE 1

harbinger *n* one that announces or indicates the later arrival of another — see FORERUNNER 1

harbor *n* **1** a part of a body of water protected and deep enough to be a place of safety for ships ⟨the tanker stayed in Boston *harbor* three days to undergo repairs⟩

synonyms anchorage, harborage, haven, port

related words seaport; arm, bay, bight, cove, creek [*chiefly British*], estuary, firth, fjord (*or* fiord), gulf, inlet, loch [*Scottish*], narrow, roads, roadstead; canal, channel, sound, strait

2 something (as a building) that offers cover from the weather or protection from danger — see SHELTER

harbor *vb* **1** to keep in one's mind or heart ⟨Grand-

pa *harbored* a grudge against his first boss for nearly 50 years⟩
synonyms bear, cherish, entertain, have, hold, nurse
related words cultivate, foster, nurture, sustain, support; carry, keep, maintain, preserve, remember, retain, treasure; cleave (to), cling (to), hang on (to), stick (to)
near antonyms disregard, drop, forget, ignore, neglect, overlook; abjure, decline, deny, disdain, refuse, reject, repudiate, scorn; abandon, desert, discard, forsake, give up, quit, renounce, throw out
2 to provide with living quarters or shelter — see HOUSE 1
3 to be or provide a shelter for — see SHELTER 1

harborage *n* **1** a part of a body of water protected and deep enough to be a place of safety for ships — see HARBOR 1
2 something (as a building) that offers cover from the weather or protection from danger — see SHELTER

hard *adj* **1** having or showing a lack of sympathy or tender feelings ⟨a *hard* man, who never had a kind word for anyone⟩
synonyms callous, cold-blooded, hard-boiled, hardhearted, heartless, inhuman, inhumane, insensate, insensitive, merciless, obdurate, pitiless, ruthless, soulless, stony (*also* stoney), uncharitable, unfeeling, unmerciful, unsparing, unsympathetic
related words inconsiderate, thoughtless, uncaring, unfriendly, unloving, unthinking; grim, hard-bitten, harsh, heavy-handed, oppressive, rough, severe, stern, tough, ungentle; abusive, acrimonious, disagreeable, hateful, ill-natured, ill-tempered, malevolent, malicious, mean, rancorous, spiteful, surly, virulent; barbarous, bestial, brutal, brutish, cruel, evil-minded, savage, vicious
near antonyms benevolent, benignant, gentle, kind; clement, lenient, mild; cordial, friendly, good-natured, good-tempered, gracious; tolerant, understanding; affectionate, loving
antonyms charitable, compassionate, humane, merciful, sensitive, softhearted, sympathetic, tender, tenderhearted, warm, warmhearted
2 requiring considerable physical or mental effort ⟨clearing land is *hard* work⟩ ⟨a *hard* Spanish test⟩
synonyms arduous, demanding, difficult, exacting, formidable, grueling (*or* gruelling), herculean, killer, laborious, murderous, rough, severe, stiff, strenuous, tall, toilsome, tough
related words abstract, abstruse, complex, complicated, insoluble, intricate, involved, knotty, problematic (*also* problematical), recondite, serious, spiny, thorny, ticklish, tricky, stubborn; burdensome, exhausting, labored, onerous, oppressive, problem, sore, stressful, taxing, tight, trying, uphill; annoying, bothersome, distressing, irksome, troublesome, vexatious; grievous, grim, heavy, strict, stringent; brutal, cruel, inhuman, painful
near antonyms achievable, clear, doable, elementary, manageable, uncomplicated; comforting, gentle, painless, relaxed, smooth, soothing
antonyms easy, effortless, facile, simple, soft, undemanding
3 able to withstand hardship, strain, or exposure — see HARDY 1
4 based on sound reasoning or information — see GOOD 1
5 difficult to endure — see HARSH 1
6 extreme in degree, power, or effect — see INTENSE
7 given to exacting standards of discipline and self-restraint — see SEVERE 1
8 having a consistency that does not easily yield to pressure — see FIRM 2
9 having been established and usually not subject to change — see FIXED 1
10 having or showing deep-seated resentment — see BITTER 1
11 sticking to an opinion, purpose, or course of action in spite of reason, arguments, or persuasion — see OBSTINATE
12 restricted to or based on fact — see FACTUAL 1

hard *adv* **1** with great effort or determination ⟨we took a much-needed break after working *hard* all week⟩ ⟨a *hard* -won victory⟩
synonyms arduously, assiduously, determinedly, diligently, hardly, indefatigably, industriously, intensely, intensively, intently, laboriously, mightily, sedulously, slavishly, strenuously, tirelessly
related words actively, animatedly, briskly, busily, dynamically, energetically, feverishly, spiritedly, vehemently, vigorously, zealously; continuously, ploddingly, steadily, unabatedly, unrelentingly, unremittingly; ardently, attentively, conscientiously, earnestly, exhaustively, meticulously, painstakingly, seriously, thoroughly
near antonyms casually, desultorily, indolently, lackadaisically, languidly, lazily, listlessly, shiftlessly, sluggishly, spiritlessly, tiredly, wearily
2 with feelings of bitterness or grief ⟨took the news of their grandfather's death *hard*⟩
synonyms agonizingly, bitterly, grievously, hardly, mournfully, painfully, regretfully, resentfully, ruefully, sadly, sorely, sorrowfully, unhappily, woefully, wretchedly
related words abjectly, dejectedly, despondently, dispiritedly; blackly, darkly, distressfully, distressingly, forlornly, gloomily, miserably; acutely, harshly, keenly, poignantly, severely, sharply; cruelly, hurtfully, ill, rancorously
near antonyms cheerfully, cheerily, delightedly, gaily (*also* gayly), gleefully, good-naturedly, lightheartedly, merrily; blithely, calmly, casually, dispassionately, easily, indifferently, lightly, nonchalantly, unconcernedly; favorably, well
antonyms gladly, happily, joyfully, joyously
3 in a vigorous and forceful manner ⟨Terry hit the ball *hard* and it soared out of bounds⟩ ⟨the wind blew *hard* all day⟩
synonyms energetically, firmly, forcefully, forcibly, mightily, powerfully, stiffly, stoutly, strenuously, strongly, sturdily, vigorously
related words robustly, sharply, vehemently, violently; animatedly, briskly, crisply, dynamically, heartily, lustily, snappily, spiritedly, vivaciously; decidedly, determinedly, directly, emphatically, fast, fixedly, intensively, intently, resolutely, rigidly, smartly, solidly, soundly, squarely, steadfastly, steadily, surely; aggressively, assertively, manfully, potently
phrases with might and main
near antonyms delicately, faintly, frailly, shakily; indirectly, languidly, listlessly, spiritlessly; impotently, ineffectively, ineffectually, nervelessly, spinelessly, uncertainly
antonyms feebly, gently, softly, weakly

4 at, within, or to a short distance or time — see NEAR 1
5 in a manner so as to cause loss or suffering — see HARDLY 1

hard–and–fast *adj* **1** having been established and usually not subject to change — see FIXED 1
2 not capable of changing or being changed — see INFLEXIBLE 1

hard–bitten *adj* able to withstand hardship, strain, or exposure — see HARDY 1

hard–boiled *adj* having or showing a lack of sympathy or tender feelings — see HARD 1

hard–core *adj* firmly established over time — see INVETERATE 1

harden *vb* **1** to become physically firm or solid ⟨waited for the bubbly caramel-and-nut sauce to cool and *harden* into peanut brittle⟩
synonyms concrete, congeal, firm (up), freeze, set, solidify
related words cake, callus, encrust (*also* incrust); coagulate, clot, gel, jell, jelly, stiffen, thicken; calcify, crystallize, ossify, petrify; anneal, case harden, temper
near antonyms deliquesce, dissolve, flux, fuse, liquefy, melt, smelt, thaw
antonyms soften
2 to make able to withstand physical hardship, strain, or exposure ⟨pioneer women who had been *hardened* by years of living on the plains⟩
synonyms fortify, inure, season, steel, strengthen, toughen
related words acclimate, acclimatize, adapt, adjust; anneal, temper; invigorate, vitalize; immunize; bolster, boost, brace, buttress, forearm, prop (up), reinforce, support; break in, limber (up), train; accustom, condition, habituate, naturalize
near antonyms emasculate, enervate, enfeeble, exhaust, sap, weaken; cripple, debilitate, incapacitate; sensitize
antonyms soften
3 to increase the ability of (as a muscle) to exert physical force — see STRENGTHEN 1

hardened *adj* **1** able to withstand hardship, strain, or exposure — see HARDY 1
2 sticking to an opinion, purpose, or course of action in spite of reason, arguments, or persuasion — see OBSTINATE

hardheaded *adj* **1** having or showing a practical cleverness or judgment — see SHREWD
2 sticking to an opinion, purpose, or course of action in spite of reason, arguments, or persuasion — see OBSTINATE
3 willing to see things as they really are and deal with them sensibly — see REALISTIC 1

hardheadedness *n* a steadfast adherence to an opinion, purpose, or course of action — see OBSTINACY

hardhearted *adj* **1** having or showing a lack of sympathy or tender feelings — see HARD 1
2 sticking to an opinion, purpose, or course of action in spite of reason, arguments, or persuasion — see OBSTINATE

hardihood *n* **1** active strength of body or mind — see VIGOR 1
2 strength of mind to carry on in spite of danger — see COURAGE

hardly *adv* **1** in a manner so as to cause loss or suffering ⟨the new judge vowed to deal *hardly* with repeat offenders⟩
synonyms hard, harshly, ill, oppressively, roughly, severely, sternly, stiffly
related words callously, cold-bloodedly, hardheartedly, heartlessly, inhumanely, inhumanly, insensately, insensitively, mercilessly, obdurately, pitilessly, ruthlessly, tyrannically, uncharitably, unfeelingly, unmercifully, unsparingly; abusively, brutally, brutishly, savagely, viciously; aggressively, assertively, decidedly, determinedly, firmly, grimly, gruffly, resolutely, strongly, toughly
near antonyms benevolently, benignantly, considerately, cordially, graciously, kindly, lovingly, tenderly; charitably, compassionately, humanely, mercifully, softheartedly, sympathetically, tolerantly, understandingly
antonyms clemently, gently, leniently, lightly, mildly, softly
2 certainly not ⟨it's *hardly* surprising that our team won, considering how weak the opponents were⟩
synonyms no, none, no way, scarcely
related words near, never, nothing, nowhere, nowise
phrases by no means, nothing doing, on no account
near antonyms awful, awfully, enormously, exceedingly (*also* exceeding), extremely, greatly, highly, hugely, immensely, mighty, most, quite, terribly, very; assuredly, clearly, perfectly, plainly, positively, really, truly, unequivocally, unquestionably, utterly; doubtless, more or less, mostly, rather, slightly, somewhat
antonyms absolutely, certainly, completely, definitely, positively, surely
3 by a very small margin — see JUST 2
4 with feelings of bitterness or grief — see HARD 2
5 with great effort or determination — see HARD 1

hardness *n* **1** something that is a cause for suffering or special effort especially in the attainment of a goal — see DIFFICULTY 1
2 the quality or state of being demanding or unyielding (as in discipline or criticism) — see SEVERITY

hardship *n* something that is a cause for suffering or special effort especially in the attainment of a goal — see DIFFICULTY 1

hardy *adj* **1** able to withstand hardship, strain, or exposure ⟨chrysanthemums are *hardy* enough to survive a light frost⟩ ⟨the men and women who settled the West were a *hardy* lot⟩
synonyms hard, hard-bitten, hardened, inured, rugged, stout, strong, sturdy, tough, toughened, vigorous
related words flinty, leathery, resilient, stalwart; durable, enduring, everlasting, immortal, imperishable, lasting, permanent, stable, staunch (*or* stanch), staying, tenacious, unyielding; flourishing, prospering, thriving; able-bodied, brawny, muscular; fit, fortified, hale, healthy, husky, lusty, red-blooded, robust, sound, strapping, virile; annealed, seasoned, tempered
near antonyms emasculated, enervated, enfeebled, exhausted, run-down, sapped, wasted, weakened, worn, worn out; crippled, debilitated, diseased, incapacitated, infirm, unsound; fragile, frail, puny; resistless, sensitive, susceptible, unresistant, vulnerable, yielding; mortal, perishable, temporary, transient
antonyms delicate, nonhardy, soft, tender, weak
2 inclined or willing to take risks — see BOLD 1

harebrained *adj* **1** lacking in seriousness or maturity — see GIDDY 1
2 showing or marked by a lack of good sense or judgment — see FOOLISH 1
hark *vb* to pay attention especially through the act of hearing — see LISTEN
hark back (to) *vb* to bring back to mind — see REMEMBER
harlequin *n* a comically dressed performer (as at a circus) who entertains with playful tricks and ridiculous behavior — see CLOWN 1
harlot *n* a woman who engages in sexual activities for money — see PROSTITUTE
harlotry *n* the practice of engaging in sexual activities for money — see PROSTITUTION
harm *n* something that causes loss or pain — see INJURY 1
harm *vb* **1** to cause bodily damage to — see INJURE 1
2 to reduce the soundness, effectiveness, or perfection of — see DAMAGE 1
harmful *adj* causing or capable of causing harm ⟨DDT has been proven extremely *harmful* to the environment⟩
synonyms adverse, bad, baleful, baneful, damaging, deleterious, detrimental, evil, hurtful, ill, injurious, mischievous, noxious, pernicious, prejudicial
related words hostile, inimical, unfriendly; contagious, deadly, infectious, pestilent, pestilential, poisonous, venomous; insidious, menacing, ominous, sinister, threatening; dangerous, hazardous, imperiling, jeopardizing, parlous, perilous, risky, unsafe, unsound; nasty, noisome, unhealthful, unhealthy, unwholesome; destructive, fatal, lethal, malignant, ruinous
near antonyms advantageous, beneficial, useful; favorable, good, propitious; curative, healthful, healthy, helpful, palliative, remedial, salubrious, salutary, wholesome; secure, sound; benign, benignant; noncorrosive, nondestructive, nonfatal, noninfectious, nonlethal, nonpoisonous, nonpolluting, nontoxic, nonvenomous
antonyms harmless, innocent, innocuous, inoffensive, safe
harmless *adj* not causing injury or hurt ⟨a perfectly *harmless* little spider⟩
synonyms innocent, innocuous, inoffensive, safe, white
related words healthful, healthy, salubrious, wholesome; benign, benignant; sound, trustworthy; gentle, gracious, mild; nonthreatening, painless, unobjectionable; noncorrosive, nondestructive, nonfatal, noninfectious, nonlethal, nonpoisonous, nonpolluting, nontoxic, nonvenomous
near antonyms poisonous, venomous; menacing, ominous, sinister, threatening; dangerous, hazardous, imperiling, jeopardizing, parlous, perilous, risky, unsafe, unsound; nasty, noisome, unhealthful, unhealthy, unwholesome; offensive, painful, scathing, wounding; deadly, fatal, lethal, ruinous; contaminated, corrosive, malignant, noxious, pestilent, polluted, tainted
antonyms adverse, bad, baleful, baneful, damaging, deleterious, detrimental, evil, harmful, hurtful, ill, injurious, mischievous, noxious, pernicious, prejudicial
harmonious *adj* **1** having a pleasing mixture of notes ⟨the naturally *harmonious* sounds of a forest glen in springtime⟩
synonyms euphonious, harmonizing, melodious, musical, symphonic, tuneful
related words blending, chiming, flowing, mellifluous; dulcet, mellow, melodic, sweet; echoing, resonant, sonorous; quavering, trilling, warbling; agreeable, appealing, pleasant; cadenced, lilting, lyric, lyrical, rhythmic (*or* rhythmical); chordal, harmonic, homophonic, orchestral, polyphonic, tonal
near antonyms blaring, clanging, clashing, clattering, grating, harsh, jangling, jarring, metallic, raspy, raucous, scratching, screeching, shrill, squeaky, strident; disagreeable, unpleasant, unpleasing; atonal, off-key
antonyms discordant, dissonant, inharmonious, unharmonious, unmelodious, unmusical
2 having the parts agreeably related ⟨a *harmonious* arrangement of archways and doorways in the palace courtyard⟩
synonyms balanced, congruous, consonant
related words even, proportioned, regular, symmetrical (*or* symmetric); aesthetic (*or* esthetic), artistic, becoming, elegant, graceful, tasteful; agreeable, felicitous, pleasant, pleasing, satisfying; compatible, coordinated, correspondent, matched, matching
near antonyms asymmetrical, disordered, irregular, skewed, unequal, uneven, unsymmetrical; distasteful, graceless, inartistic, inelegant, tasteless, unaesthetic, unbecoming, ungraceful, unlovely; disagreeable, displeasing, dissatisfying, infelicitous, unfortunate, unpleasant, unsightly; clashing, conflicting, disunited, incompatible, uncoordinated
antonyms incongruous, inharmonious, unbalanced
3 having or marked by agreement in feeling or action ⟨an unusually *harmonious* meeting among the leaders resulted in a quick peace agreement⟩
synonyms agreeable, amicable, compatible, congenial, frictionless, kindred, unanimous, united
related words pacific, peaceable, peaceful; collaborating, cooperative, symbiotic; noncompetitive, nonconflicting, uncompetitive; sympathetic, tolerant, understanding; affable, amiable, cordial, friendly, genial, neighborly; collaborating
near antonyms antagonistic, antipathetic, clashing, conflicting, hostile, inimical, unfriendly; belligerent, contentious, quarrelsome; contradicting, contradictory, contrary, opposing, opposite; competing, competitive, rivaling (*or* rivalling)
antonyms disagreeable, disunited, incompatible, inharmonious, uncongenial
4 not having or showing any apparent conflict — see CONSISTENT
harmonize *vb* **1** to form a pleasing relationship ⟨the color of the walls *harmonized* nicely with the blue tones in the carpet⟩
synonyms agree, blend, conform, coordinate
related words balance, correlate, correspond, dovetail, match; meet, parallel; bond, coalesce, cohere, conjoin, fuse, merge, square, tally
near antonyms contradict, contrast, counter, differ, diverge, jar; cancel (out), counteract, negate, offset
antonyms clash, collide, conflict
2 to bring to a state free of conflicts, inconsistencies, or differences ⟨an attempt to *harmonize* the New Testament version of events with the accounts of the ancient Romans⟩

synonyms accommodate, conciliate, conform, coordinate, key, reconcile
related words adapt, attune, tune; blend, combine, connect, correlate, dovetail, fit, fuse, integrate, join, match, merge, orchestrate, pair, square, suit, synchronize, synthesize, unify, unite; align, arrange, array, balance, equalize, even, order, proportion, regularize, standardize
near antonyms confuse, disarray, disorder, disorganize, disrupt, disturb, skew, upset
antonyms alienate, disjoin
3 to be in agreement on every point — see CHECK 1

harmonizing *adj* having a pleasing mixture of notes — see HARMONIOUS 1

harmony *n* **1** a balanced, pleasing, or suitable arrangement of parts ⟨her face had an angelic *harmony* that fascinated the leading painters of her day⟩
synonyms balance, coherence, consonance, proportion, symmetry, symphony, unity
related words coordination, correlation, correspondence, equalization, equilibrium, evenness, order, orderliness, regularity, uniformity
near antonyms confusion, disorganization, dissonance, disturbance, tension; disconnectedness, disjointedness, incompatibility; irregularity, unevenness
antonyms asymmetry, discordance, disproportion, disunity, imbalance, incoherence
2 peaceful coexistence ⟨Mary Beth was determined to live in *harmony* with her new stepsister⟩
synonyms comity, compatibility, concord, peace
related words amity, congeniality, fellowship, fraternization, friendship; collaboration, reciprocity, symbiosis; consensus, unanimity, unity; affinity, connection, empathy, kinship, oneness, rapport, solidarity, sympathy, understanding; peacefulness, serenity, tranquillity (*or* tranquility)
near antonyms antagonism, antipathy, enmity, hatred, hostility, unfriendliness; alienation, breach, divorce, estrangement, rupture, schism, severance; dissent, dissidence; disturbance, strife, turmoil
antonyms conflict, discord, dissension
3 a state of consistency — see CONFORMITY 1

harness *vb* to put into action or service — see USE 1

harpoon *vb* to penetrate or hold (something) with a pointed object — see IMPALE

harpy *n* a bad-tempered scolding woman — see SHREW

harrow *vb* to cause persistent suffering to — see AFFLICT

harrowing *adj* **1** hard to accept or bear especially emotionally — see BITTER 2
2 intensely or unbearably painful — see EXCRUCIATING 1

harrying *n* the act of making unwelcome intrusions upon another — see ANNOYANCE 1

harsh *adj* **1** difficult to endure ⟨*harsh* conditions in the refugee camp⟩
synonyms bitter, brutal, burdensome, cruel, excruciating, grievous, grim, hard, heavy, inhuman, murderous, onerous, oppressive, rough, rugged, severe, stiff, tough, trying
related words austere, bleak, comfortless, discomforting, forbidding, hostile, inhospitable, Spartan, uncomfortable; biting, inclement, intemperate; rigorous, strict, stringent; agonizing, heartbreaking, heartrending, painful, wretched; crushing, grinding, overwhelming, wearing; insufferable, insupportable, intolerable, unbearable, unendurable; harrowing, tortuous; bad, disagreeable, hostile, unfriendly, unpleasant
near antonyms comfortable, cozy, luxurious, snug; agreeable, friendly, genial, hospitable, pleasant; peaceful, relaxing, reposeful, restful; bearable, endurable, painless, tolerable; balmy, calm, clement, gentle, mild, moderate, temperate
antonyms easy, light, soft
2 disagreeable to one's aesthetic or artistic sense ⟨the *harsh* lighting in the cafeteria makes the food look slightly off-color⟩
synonyms grating, grotesque, jarring, unaesthetic
related words flashy, garish, gaudy, loud, tawdry; tacky, tasteless, vulgar; inartistic, unartistic; artless, clumsy, crude, graceless, inelegant, rude; uncouth, uncultured, unrefined; disgusting, gross, obscene, repugnant, repulsive, ugly; disagreeable, jolting, unpleasant, unpleasing; blaring, clashing, discordant, dissonant, inharmonious, off-key, jangling, raspy, raucous, unharmonious, unmelodious, unmusical; bizarre, kinky, odd, outlandish, shocking
near antonyms artful, artistic; attractive, beautiful, becoming, comely; agreeable, appealing, felicitous, good, harmonious, harmonizing, pleasing, seemly; calming, comforting, soothing; softened, subdued; cultured, elegant, graceful, gracious, polished, refined, tasteful
antonyms aesthetic (*or* esthetic)
3 causing discomfort — see UNCOMFORTABLE 1
4 given to exacting standards of discipline and self-restraint — see SEVERE 1
5 hard to accept or bear especially emotionally — see BITTER 2

harshly *adv* in a manner so as to cause loss or suffering — see HARDLY 1

harshness *n* **1** a harsh or sharp quality — see EDGE 1
2 the quality or state of being demanding or unyielding (as in discipline or criticism) — see SEVERITY

harum–scarum *adv* in a confused and reckless manner — see HELTER-SKELTER 1

harvest *n* the quantity of an animal or vegetable product gathered at the end of a season — see CROP 1

harvest *vb* to catch or collect (a crop or natural resource) for human use ⟨*harvest* salmon from nearby rivers⟩ ⟨every year we *harvest* corn from our own garden⟩
synonyms gather, pick, reap
related words clam, fish, seal, shrimp, whale; accumulate, garner; glean; cut, hay, mow; bag, capture, hunt, net, snare, trap; crop, grow, raise
near antonyms plant, seed, sow

hash *n* an unorganized collection or mixture of various things — see MISCELLANY 1

hash *vb* **1** to cut into small pieces — see CHOP
2 to undo the proper order or arrangement of — see DISORDER

hash (over) *vb* to talk about (an issue) usually from various points of view and for the purpose of arriving at a decision or opinion — see DISCUSS

hassle *n* **1** a brief clash between enemies or rivals — see ENCOUNTER
2 a physical dispute between opposing individuals or groups — see FIGHT 1

3 an often noisy or angry expression of differing opinions — see ARGUMENT 1
4 something that is a source of irritation — see ANNOYANCE 3
hassle *vb* **1** to attack repeatedly with mean put-downs or insults — see TEASE 2
2 to express different opinions about something often angrily — see ARGUE 2
haste *n* **1** a high rate of movement or performance — see SPEED
2 excited and often showy or disorderly speed — see HURRY 1
hasten *vb* **1** to cause to move or proceed fast or faster — see HURRY 1
2 to proceed or move quickly — see HURRY 2
hastily *adv* **1** with excessive or careless speed ⟨the *hastily* put together report contained a lot of errors⟩
synonyms cursorily, headlong, hotfoot, hurriedly, pell-mell, precipitately, precipitously, rashly
related words headily, hotheadedly, impatiently, impetuously, impulsively, recklessly, thoughtlessly; automatically, glancingly, haphazardly; impromptu, spontaneously; abruptly, suddenly; offhand, offhandedly
phrases on the spur of the moment
near antonyms calculatingly, circumspectly, designedly; falteringly, hesitantly, hesitatingly, tentatively; leisurely, slowly
antonyms deliberately, studiedly
2 with great speed — see FAST 1
hastiness *n* excited and often showy or disorderly speed — see HURRY 1
hasty *adj* **1** acting or done with excessive or careless speed ⟨Anna later regretted her *hasty* decision to sell her car⟩
synonyms cursory, flying, headlong, hurried, pell-mell, precipitate, precipitous, rash, rushed
related words breakneck, breathtaking; headstrong, heady, hotheaded, impatient, impetuous, impulsive, madcap, reckless, unadvised; quick, rapid, speedy, swift; impromptu, makeshift, offhand, offhanded, slap-dash, snap, spontaneous, spur-of-the-moment; abrupt, sudden
near antonyms calculated, calculating, measured; circumspect, foresighted, forethoughtful; drawn-out, extended, long-term, prolonged; faltering, hesitant, hesitating, tentative; dallying, dawdling, laggard, leisurely, poky (*or* pokey), shilly-shallying, slow
antonyms deliberate, unhurried
2 moving, proceeding, or acting with great speed — see FAST 1
hat *n* a covering for the head usually having a shaped crown ⟨Paul brought back warm fur *hats* for everyone from Russia⟩
synonyms cap, headdress, headgear, headpiece, lid [*slang*]
related words beret, biretta, boater, bonnet, bowler, derby, fedora, fez, hard hat, helm, helmet, homburg, hood, leghorn, miter, nightcap, panama, pillbox, poke bonnet, shako, skullcap, sombrero, sou'wester, Stetson, stocking cap, stovepipe, sunbonnet, tam-o'-shanter, top hat, topper, toque, turban; war bonnet; coronet, crown, diadem, headband, tiara; babushka, coif, kerchief, mantilla, scarf, shawl, tallith, veil, wimple
hatch *n* a barrier by which an entry is closed and opened — see DOOR 1
hatch *vb* to cover and warm eggs to hatch them — see SET 1
hate *n* **1** a very strong dislike ⟨*hate* can sometimes be replaced with tolerance when people meet face to face⟩
synonyms abhorrence, abomination, execration, hatred, loathing
related words cattiness, despite, despitefulness, hatefulness, invidiousness, malevolence, malice, maliciousness, malignancy, malignity, meanness, spite, spitefulness; aversion, disgust, distaste, horror, odium, repugnance, repulsion, revulsion; animosity, antagonism, antipathy, bitterness, contempt, disdain, enmity, grudge, hostility, jealousy, pique, resentment, scorn; bile, jaundice, rancor, spleen, venom, virulence, vitriol
near antonyms appetite, inclination, liking; adoration, veneration, worship; acceptance, tolerance; passion, relish, taste
antonyms affection, devotion, fondness, love
2 something or someone that is hated ⟨the Alaska pipeline is a pet *hate* of environmentalists⟩
synonyms abhorrence, abomination, anathema, antipathy, aversion, bête noire
related words dread, hang-up, horror, phobia; bogey (*also* bogy *or* bogie), bugaboo, bugbear; adversary, enemy; annoyance, grievance, hassle, nuisance, peeve
near antonyms beloved, darling, dear, honey; delight, enjoyment, felicity, joy, pleasure; favorite, like, preference; treasure
antonyms love
hate *vb* to dislike strongly ⟨Pete *hated* the farm and dreamed of working in the city⟩
synonyms abhor, abominate, despise, detest, execrate, loathe
related words deplore, deprecate, disapprove (of), discountenance, disdain, disfavor, scorn
phrases have it in for
near antonyms fancy, favor, like, prefer; enjoy, relish; adore, esteem, idolize, revere, venerate, worship; cherish, prize, treasure
antonyms love
hateful *adj* having or showing a desire to cause someone pain or suffering for the sheer enjoyment of it ⟨a *hateful* bully who loved to pick on little kids⟩ ⟨Janet's *hateful* remarks drove Penny to tears⟩
synonyms catty, cruel, despiteful, malevolent, malicious, malign, malignant, mean, nasty, spiteful, virulent
related words devious, scoundrelly, scurvy, snakelike; acrimonious, bitter, envious, jaundiced, jealous, rancorous, resentful; contemptuous, deprecating, disdainful, obnoxious, opprobrious, scornful, snide, unkind, unkindly, unloving; baleful, baneful, evil; harsh, hostile, inimical; acrid, caustic, scathing, venomous
near antonyms compassionate, good, good-hearted, kind, kindhearted, kindly, sympathetic, warm, warmhearted; affable, agreeable, amiable, cordial, friendly, genial, gracious, nice, pleasant; affectionate, amorous, sweet, tender, tenderhearted; altruistic, high-minded, humanitarian, magnanimous, noble, philanthropic
antonyms benevolent, benign, benignant, loving, unmalicious
hatefully *adv* in a mean or spiteful manner — see NASTILY

hatefulness *n* the desire to cause pain for the satisfaction of doing harm — see MALICE
hatred *n* a very strong dislike — see HATE 1
haughtiness *n* an exaggerated sense of one's importance that shows itself in the making of excessive or unjustified claims — see ARROGANCE
haughty *adj* **1** having a feeling of superiority that shows itself in an overbearing attitude — see ARROGANT
2 having or displaying feelings of scorn for what is regarded as beneath oneself — see PROUD 1
haul *n* **1** the total amount collected or obtained especially at one time ⟨the trick-or-treaters showed off their *haul*⟩
synonyms catch, take, yield
related words bag; earnings, gain, gross, income, net, payoff, proceeds, profit, receipts, return, revenue, winnings; booty, loot, plunder, spoils, swag; appropriation, collection
near antonyms deduction, loss, subtraction
2 a mass or quantity of something taken up and carried, conveyed, or transported — see LOAD 1
3 the act or an instance of applying force on something so that it moves in the direction of the force — see PULL 1
haul *vb* **1** to cause to follow by applying steady force on — see PULL 1
2 to support and take from one place to another — see CARRY 1
haunches *n pl* the part of the body upon which someone sits — see BUTTOCKS
haunt *n* a place for spending time or for socializing — see HANGOUT
haunt *vb* to go to or spend time in often — see FREQUENT
haunting *adj* fearfully and mysteriously strange or fantastic — see EERIE
have *vb* **1** to keep, control, or experience as one's own ⟨Aunt Chloe *has* 31 pairs of red shoes⟩
synonyms command, enjoy, hold, occupy, own, possess, retain
related words keep, reserve, withhold; bear, carry; boast, show off, sport
near antonyms abandon, cede, disclaim, disown, hand over, relinquish, renounce, surrender, yield; discard, dump; decline, reject, repudiate, spurn; need, require
antonyms lack, want
2 to agree to receive whether willingly or reluctantly — see TAKE 2
3 to bring forth from the womb — see BEAR 1
4 to cause to believe what is untrue — see DECEIVE
5 to come to a knowledge of (something) by living through it — see EXPERIENCE
6 to give permission for or to approve of — see ALLOW 1
7 to influence someone with a bribe — see BRIBE
8 to keep in one's mind or heart — see HARBOR 1
have (to) *vb* to be under necessity or obligation to — see NEED 2
haven *n* **1** a part of a body of water protected and deep enough to be a place of safety for ships — see HARBOR 1
2 something (as a building) that offers cover from the weather or protection from danger — see SHELTER
havoc *n* **1** a state in which everything is out of order — see CHAOS
2 the state or fact of being rendered nonexistent, physically unsound, or useless — see DESTRUCTION
hawk *n* one who urges or attempts to cause a war — see WARMONGER
hawk *vb* to sell from place to place usually in small quantities — see PEDDLE
hawker *n* one who sells things outdoors — see PEDDLER
hazard *n* **1** something that may cause injury or harm — see DANGER 2
2 the uncertain course of events — see CHANCE 1
hazard *vb* **1** to place in danger — see ENDANGER
2 to take a chance on — see RISK 1
hazardous *adj* involving potential loss or injury — see DANGEROUS
haze *n* **1** an atmospheric condition in which suspended particles in the air rob it of its transparency ⟨Jim could barely make out the tall buildings through the *haze*⟩
synonyms fog, mist, murk, reek, smog, soup
related words cloud, fume, miasma, smoke, steam
2 a state of mental confusion ⟨people wandered around in a *haze* in the days following the earthquake⟩
synonyms daze, fog, muddle, spin
related words reverie, stupor, trance; befuddlement, bewilderment, perplexity, puzzlement; delirium, malaise, paralysis; cloudiness, fogginess
near antonyms alertness, levelheadedness
haze *vb* to make dark, dim, or indistinct — see CLOUD 1
hazed *adj* covered over by clouds — see OVERCAST
hazy *adj* **1** filled with or dimmed by fine particles (as of dust or water) in suspension ⟨*hazy* skies made it dangerous to fly⟩ ⟨the *hazy* sunshine so common in August⟩
synonyms beclouded, befogged, clouded, cloudy, foggy, misty, murky, smoggy, soupy
related words overcast, rainy, stormy, thick; dirty, miry, mucky, muddy, slimy, slushy, turbid; smoky (*also* smokey), sooty; filmy, milky, opaque
near antonyms bright, clean; fair, rainless, sunny, sunshiny; translucent, transparent
antonyms clear, cloudless, limpid, pellucid, unclouded
2 covered over by clouds — see OVERCAST
3 not seen or understood clearly — see FAINT 1
head *adj* highest in rank or authority ⟨Mr. Pendergast, *head* editor at the TV station for 17 years, has hired and fired innumerable staff members⟩
synonyms chief, commanding, first, foremost, high, lead, leading, managing, preeminent, premier, presiding, primary, prime, principal, supreme
related words high-level, senior; controlling, directing, officiating, overseeing, reigning, ruling, supervisory; main, major, paramount, predominant; dominant, grand, superior, topmost, upmost, upper, uppermost
phrases in charge
near antonyms inferior, last, lesser, lower, lowly, second, secondary, subordinate; assistant, assisting, coadjutor, deputy, junior, under
head *n* **1** the upper or front part of the body that contains the brain, the major sense organs, and the mouth ⟨I hit my *head* as I went through the low doorway⟩
synonyms noddle, noggin, pate, poll
related words cranium, crown, scalp, skull

2 the place of leadership or command ⟨every year a different parent is placed at the *head* of the troop's cookie drive⟩
synonyms chair, headship, helm, rein
related words chieftainship, commandership, directorship; forefront, lead, preferment; chairmanship, deanship, dictatorship, governorship, kingship, mastership, mastery, presidency, superintendency; dominance, dominion, jurisdiction, sovereignty, sway, upper hand; eminence, height, pedestal, pinnacle, seat, throne, top
near antonyms ranks
3 a light mass of fine bubbles formed in or on a liquid — see FOAM
4 a member of the human race — see HUMAN
5 a time or state of affairs requiring prompt or decisive action — see EMERGENCY
6 the beginning part of a stream — see HEADWATER
7 the highest part or point — see HEIGHT 1
8 the normal or healthy condition of the mental abilities — see MIND 2
9 the part of a person that feels, thinks, perceives, wills, and especially reasons — see MIND 1
10 the person (as an employer or supervisor) who tells people and especially workers what to do — see BOSS

head *vb* **1** to go on a specified course or in a certain direction ⟨the migrant workers were *heading* for California for the grape harvest⟩
synonyms bear, make
related words aim, bend, direct, point, turn; put, put out, set forth, set off, set out, strike, take off; face, orient, steer; about-face, back, come about, come round, cut, incline, put about, reverse, swerve, tack, veer, yaw, wheel
2 to be at the front of — see LEAD 3
3 to be in charge of — see BOSS 1
4 to be positioned along a certain course or in a certain direction — see RUN 3
5 to point or turn (something) toward a target or goal — see AIM
6 to serve as leader of — see LEAD 2

headache *n* **1** a dull, unpleasant, or difficult piece of work — see CHORE 2
2 something that is a source of irritation — see ANNOYANCE 3

headdress *n* a covering for the head usually having a shaped crown — see HAT

headgear *n* a covering for the head usually having a shaped crown — see HAT

heading *n* a word or series of words often in larger letters placed at the beginning of a passage or at the top of a page in order to introduce or categorize ⟨Fran found the recipe for turkey gumbo under the *heading* "stews" rather than under "soups"⟩
synonyms caption, headline, rubric, title
related words guide word, legend; greeting, salutation; superscript, superscription; subhead, subheading, subtitle

headland *n* **1** an area of high ground jutting out into a body of water beyond the line of the coast ⟨the lighthouse, situated on a narrow, rocky *headland,* commands an expansive view of the coast⟩
synonyms point, promontory
related words cape, peninsula; breakwater, jetty, levee; spit
2 an area of land that juts out into a body of water — see [2]CAPE

headline *n* a word or series of words often in larger letters placed at the beginning of a passage or at the top of a page in order to introduce or categorize — see HEADING

headlong *adj* acting or done with excessive or careless speed — see HASTY 1

headlong *adv* with excessive or careless speed — see HASTILY 1

headman *n* the person (as an employer or supervisor) who tells people and especially workers what to do — see BOSS

headpiece *n* a covering for the head usually having a shaped crown — see HAT

headquarters *n pl* **1** a place from which authority is exercised — see SEAT 1
2 the place from which a commander runs operations — see COMMAND 3

headship *n* **1** the duty or function of watching or guarding for the sake of proper direction or control — see SUPERVISION 1
2 the place of leadership or command — see HEAD 2

headstone *n* a shaped stone laid over or erected near a grave and usually bearing an inscription to identify and preserve the memory of the deceased — see TOMBSTONE

headstrong *adj* **1** given to resisting control or discipline by others — see UNCONTROLLABLE
2 sticking to an opinion, purpose, or course of action in spite of reason, arguments, or persuasion — see OBSTINATE

headwater *n usually* **headwaters** *pl* the beginning part of a stream ⟨the first exploration of the Missouri River from its mouth to its *headwaters* was made by Meriwether Lewis and William Clark in the early 1800s⟩
synonyms head, source
related words fountain, fountainhead, geyser, hot spring, spring, thermal spring, wellspring

headway *n* forward movement in time or place — see ADVANCE 1

heal *vb* **1** to restore to a healthy condition ⟨a low-fat vegetarian diet, moderate exercise, and stress management help *heal* a diseased heart⟩ ⟨*heal* the sick⟩
synonyms cure, mend, rehabilitate
related words attend (to), care (for), doctor, minister (to), nurse, treat; fortify, rejuvenate, renew, resuscitate, revive; alleviate, fix, relieve, remedy, repair
phrases take care of
near antonyms damage, disable, harm, hurt, impair, injure, lacerate, lame, maim, mangle, mutilate, wound; afflict, ail, debilitate, enervate, enfeeble, lay up, sap, sicken, waste, weaken
2 to become healthy and strong again after illness or weakness — see CONVALESCE
3 to bring about recovery from — see CURE 1

healing *n* the process or period of gradually regaining one's health and strength — see CONVALESCENCE

health *n* the condition of being sound in body ⟨Sam gradually regained his *health* after a long bout with cholera⟩
synonyms fitness, healthiness, heartiness, robustness, soundness, wellness, wholeness, wholesomeness
related words fettle, shape; cleanliness, hygiene; hardiness, lustiness, ruggedness, stamina, strength, toughness, vigor, vigorousness, vitality;

bloom, flush, flushness; activeness, agility, liveliness, spryness; weal, welfare, well-being
near antonyms debility, decrepitude, feebleness, frailness, infirmity, lameness, weakness; ailment, condition, disease, disorder, malady, trouble
antonyms illness, sickness, unhealthiness, unsoundness

healthful *adj* good for the health ⟨one of the most *healthful* forms of exercise is a brisk walk⟩
synonyms healthy, restorative, salubrious, salutary, wholesome
related words alleviative, corrective, curative, remedial, tonic; advantageous, beneficial, useful; antiseptic, clean, hygienic, sanitary; nonfattening, nonpoisonous, nontoxic
near antonyms deleterious, injurious, pernicious; infectious, poisonous, toxic; insanitary, unhygienic, unsanitary
antonyms insalubrious, noxious, unhealthful, unhealthy, unwholesome

healthiness *n* the condition of being sound in body — see HEALTH

healthy *adj* **1** enjoying health and vigor ⟨always a hard worker, Grandma has remained *healthy* into her eighties⟩
synonyms able-bodied, bouncing, chipper, fit, hale, hearty, robust, sound, well, whole, wholesome
related words hardy, lusty, rugged, stalwart, strong, sturdy, tough; nondisabled, nonhandicapped, uncrippled; active, agile, lively, sprightly, spry, vigorous, vital; blooming, clean-cut, flourishing, flush, thriving; all right, good, right
phrases in fine fettle
near antonyms decrepit, enfeebled, feeble, infirm, run-down, sickened, sickly, weak, weakened, weakly, worn-out; challenged, crippled, debilitated, disabled, incapacitated, lame; delicate, fragile, frail; undernourished; afflicted, troubled; bad, poorly
antonyms ailing, diseased, ill, sick, unfit, unhealthy, unsound, unwell
2 good for the health — see HEALTHFUL
3 sufficiently large in size, amount, or number to merit attention — see CONSIDERABLE 1

heap *n* **1** a considerable amount — see LOT 2
2 a quantity of things thrown or stacked on one another — see [1]PILE 1

heap *vb* **1** to give readily and in large quantities — see RAIN 2
2 to gradually form into a layer, pile, or mass — see COLLECT 2
3 to lay or throw on top of one another — see PILE
4 to put into (something) as much as can be held or contained — see FILL 1

hear *vb* **1** to come to an awareness — see DISCOVER 1
2 to pay attention especially through the act of hearing — see LISTEN

hearing *n* range of hearing — see EARSHOT

hearken *vb* to pay attention especially through the act of hearing — see LISTEN

heart *n* **1** the capacity for feeling for another's unhappiness or misfortune ⟨when her parents refused her request for a puppy, Jessica asked, "Have you no *heart* ?"⟩
synonyms charity, commiseration, compassion, feeling, humanity, kindheartedness, kindliness, kindness, mercy, pity, softheartedness, sympathy
related words responsiveness, sensitivity; affection, love, regard; affinity, empathy, rapport; altruism, benevolence, benignity, generosity, goodwill, humanitarianism, philanthropy
near antonyms callousness, coldness, indifference, unconcern; cruelty, harshness; animosity, antipathy, dislike, hatred, hostility
antonyms hardheartedness, inhumanity, mercilessness
2 the body of knowledge that has been retained in one's mind or the use of it ⟨Dan can recite the entire Declaration of Independence by *heart*⟩
synonyms memory, rote
related words association, conning, memorization
3 a thing or place that is of greatest importance to an activity or interest — see CENTER 1
4 strength of mind to carry on in spite of danger — see COURAGE
5 the central part or aspect of something under consideration — see CRUX
6 the seat of one's deepest thoughts and emotions — see CORE 1

heartache *n* deep sadness especially for the loss of someone or something loved — see SORROW

heartbreak *n* deep sadness especially for the loss of someone or something loved — see SORROW

heartbreaking *adj* **1** causing unhappiness — see SAD 2
2 of a kind to cause great distress — see REGRETTABLE
3 deserving of one's pity — see PATHETIC 1

heartbroken *adj* **1** feeling unhappiness — see SAD 1
2 expressing or suggesting mourning — see MOURNFUL 1

hearten *vb* to fill with courage or strength of purpose — see ENCOURAGE 1

heartening *adj* **1** having qualities which inspire hope — see HOPEFUL 1
2 making one feel good inside — see HEARTWARMING
3 pointing toward a happy outcome — see FAVORABLE 2

hearth *n* the place where one lives — see HOME 1

hearthstone *n* the place where one lives — see HOME 1

heartily *adv* in a cheerful or happy manner — see GAILY 1

heartiness *n* the condition of being sound in body — see HEALTH

heartless *adj* **1** having or showing a lack of sympathy or tender feelings — see HARD 1
2 having or showing the desire to inflict severe pain and suffering on others — see CRUEL 1

heartlessness *n* the willful infliction of pain and suffering on others — see CRUELTY

heartrending *adj* **1** causing unhappiness — see SAD 2
2 hard to accept or bear especially emotionally — see BITTER 2
3 of a kind to cause great distress — see REGRETTABLE
4 deserving of one's pity — see PATHETIC 1

heartsick *adj* feeling unhappiness — see SAD 1

heartsickness *n* a state or spell of low spirits — see SADNESS

heartsore *adj* feeling unhappiness — see SAD 1

heartstrings *n pl* general emotional condition — see FEELING 2

heartwarming *adj* making one feel good inside ⟨Sarah appreciated the *heartwarming* welcome she received from her relatives in Israel⟩

synonyms cheering, comforting, encouraging, fulfilling, gladdening, gratifying, heartening, rewarding, satisfying
related words affecting, inspiring, moving, poignant, stirring, touching; edifying, elevating, uplifting; sympathetic, tender; kind, kindly, loving, warm; exciting, exhilarating, rousing, stimulating, thrilling; pleasing, welcoming
near antonyms cheerless, depressing, disappointing, discouraging, disgruntling, disheartening, displeasing, dissatisfying, saddening; cold, unfeeling, unfriendly, unkind, unloving, unpleasant
antonyms depressing, discouraging, disheartening, dispiriting

hearty *adj* **1** characterized by unqualified enthusiasm ⟨Frank expressed *hearty* approval of his aunt's suggestion to rendezvous in Tokyo⟩
synonyms wholehearted
related words single-minded; ardent, avid, eager, enthusiastic, excited, exuberant, gung ho, impassioned, keen, raring, vehement, warm, zealous; alacritous, immediate, prompt, ready, willing, unhesitating; animated, energetic, lively, spirited, vigorous; absolute, bona fide, genuine, unaffected, undisguised, unequivocal, unrestrained
near antonyms apathetic, disinterested, indifferent, uninterested; lackadaisical, listless, perfunctory, spiritless, uneager, unenthusiastic, unexcited; equivocal, hesitant, qualified, tentative, uncertain; delayed, dilatory, doubtful, hedging, hesitating; forced, reluctant, resistant, unwilling
antonyms grudging, halfhearted, lukewarm, tepid
2 enjoying health and vigor — see HEALTHY 1
3 having or showing kindly feeling and sincere interest — see FRIENDLY 1
4 not showing weakness or uncertainty — see FIRM 1

heat *n* depth of feeling — see ARDOR 1

heat *vb* to cause to have or give off heat to a moderate degree — see WARM 1

heated *adj* **1** being in a state of increased activity or agitation — see FEVERISH 1
2 having or giving off heat to a moderate degree — see WARM 1

heathen *adj* not civilized — see SAVAGE 1

heathen *n* **1** a person who does not worship the God of the Bible ⟨a missionary sent to distant lands to convert the *heathens*⟩
synonyms gentile, idolater (*or* idolator), pagan
related words atheist, infidel, nonbeliever, non-Christian, unbeliever; polytheist, theist
near antonyms Christian, Jew, Muslim
2 an uncivilized person ⟨European colonizers, who considered the New World peoples to be *heathens*, forced them to conform to European ways⟩
synonyms barbarian, savage
related words Neanderthal, primitive

heathenish *adj* not civilized — see SAVAGE 1

heave *vb* **1** to lift with effort ⟨I *heaved* my duffel bag into the bus's overhead compartment⟩
synonyms boost, heft, hoist, jack (up)
related words elevate, hike, raise, rear, up, uplift, upraise
near antonyms drop, lower; sink, submerge, submerse
2 to discharge the contents of the stomach through the mouth — see VOMIT
3 to move from a lower to a higher place or position — see RAISE 1
4 to send through the air especially with a quick forward motion of the arm — see THROW

heaven *n* **1** a dwelling place of perfect bliss for the soul after death ⟨prayed that the souls of the deceased would go to *heaven*⟩
synonyms Elysium, kingdom come, paradise
related words empyrean; glory; otherworld
phrases on high
near antonyms inferno; limbo, purgatory; hades, netherworld, underworld
antonyms hell, perdition
2 a place or state of great happiness — see PARADISE 1
3 a state of overwhelming usually pleasurable emotion — see ECSTASY
4 *usually* **heavens** *pl* the expanse of air surrounding the earth — see SKY

heavenly *adj* **1** of the very best kind — see EXCELLENT
2 of, relating to, or being God — see HOLY 3
3 of, relating to, or suggesting heaven — see CELESTIAL
4 giving pleasure or contentment to the mind or senses — see PLEASANT

heavily *adv* to a great degree — see VERY 1

heaviness *n* **1** the amount that something weighs — see WEIGHT 1
2 the state or quality of being heavy — see WEIGHTINESS 1

heavy *adj* **1** having great weight ⟨this trunk full of books is much too *heavy* for one person to lift⟩
synonyms hefty, massive, ponderous, weighty
related words burdensome, leaden, lumpish; bulky, elephantine, outsize; overweight, top-heavy; solid, substantial
near antonyms airy, ethereal, feathery, gossamer, gossamery; flimsy, fluffy, insubstantial
antonyms light, lightweight, weightless
2 causing weariness, restlessness, or lack of interest — see BORING
3 containing much seasoning, fat, or sugar — see RICH 2
4 covered over by clouds — see OVERCAST
5 difficult to endure — see HARSH 1
6 extreme in degree, power, or effect — see INTENSE
7 having a matter of importance as its topic — see SERIOUS 2

heavy *n* a mean, evil, or unprincipled person — see VILLAIN

heavy–handed *adj* **1** given to exacting standards of discipline and self-restraint — see SEVERE 1
2 lacking in physical ease and grace in movement or in the use of the hands — see CLUMSY 1

heavyset *adj* being compact and broad in build and often short in stature — see STOCKY

heckle *vb* to attack repeatedly with mean put-downs or insults — see TEASE 2

heckler *n* a person who causes repeated emotional pain, distress, or annoyance to another — see TORMENTOR

hectic *adj* being in a state of increased activity or agitation — see FEVERISH 1

hectically *adv* in a confused and reckless manner — see HELTER-SKELTER 1

hector *vb* to make timid or fearful by or as if by threats — see INTIMIDATE

hedge *n* a physical object that blocks the way — see BARRIER

hedge *vb* **1** to avoid giving a definite answer or position — see EQUIVOCATE
2 to close or shut in by or as if by barriers — see ENCLOSE 1

heed *n* **1** a state of being aware — see ATTENTION 2
2 strict attentiveness to what one is doing — see CARE 1

heed *vb* **1** to take notice of and be guided by ⟨if Paul had *heeded* his brother's advice, he might not have gotten lost⟩
synonyms follow, listen (to), mind, note, observe, regard, watch
related words consider, contemplate, mull, ponder, weigh; comply (with), keep, obey, respect; hark (to), hear, hearken (to); mark, notice, see
near antonyms brush (off), dismiss, pooh-pooh, scorn, shrug off; defy, flout; slight, snub
antonyms disregard, ignore, tune out
2 to pay attention especially through the act of hearing — see LISTEN

heedful *adj* having or showing a close attentiveness to avoiding danger or trouble — see CAREFUL 1

heedfulness *n* **1** a close attentiveness to avoiding danger — see CAUTION 1
2 strict attentiveness to what one is doing — see CARE 1

heedless *adj* not paying or showing close attention especially for the purpose of avoiding trouble — see CARELESS 1

heedlessness *n* failure to take the care that a cautious person usually takes — see NEGLIGENCE 1

heel *n* a person whose behavior is offensive to others — see JERK 1

heel *vb* to set or cause to be at an angle — see LEAN 1

heft *n* the amount that something weighs — see WEIGHT 1

heft *vb* **1** to lift with effort — see HEAVE 1
2 to move from a lower to a higher place or position — see RAISE 1

heftiness *n* **1** the quality or state of being large in size — see LARGENESS
2 the state or quality of being heavy — see WEIGHTINESS 1

hefty *adj* **1** having great weight — see HEAVY 1
2 of a size greater than average of its kind — see LARGE

height *n* **1** the highest part or point ⟨many regard the painting of the Sistine Chapel as the *height* of Michelangelo's career⟩
synonyms acme, apex, climax, crown, culmination, head, high-water mark, meridian, peak, pinnacle, summit, tip-top, top, zenith
related words bloom, flood tide, flower, glory, heyday; high; cap, ceiling, crest, roof; crescendo, extremity, maximum, tip, vertex
near antonyms abyss, base, foot; minimum
antonyms bottom, nadir
2 the most extreme or advanced point ⟨the student's defiant use of a cell phone during class was regarded by the teacher as the *height* of insolence⟩
synonyms depth, extremity, limit
related words consummation, epitome, quintessence, ultimate
3 the distance of something or someone from bottom to top ⟨the average *height* of the players on the volleyball team is well over six feet⟩
synonyms altitude, elevation, stature
related words rise; highness, loftiness, tallness
4 an area of high ground ⟨Gulliver, standing on a *height* near the shore, saw an island suspended above the sea⟩
synonyms altitude(s), elevation, eminence, highland, hill, mound, prominence, rise, upland
related words alp, mount, mountain, peak; butte, mesa, plateau, table, tableland; cliff, crag, precipice, tor; ridge, sierra; dome, sugarloaf; foothill, hillock, knob, knoll; down
near antonyms dale, dell, dingle, glen, hollow, vale, valley; basin, bottom, bottomland, fen, flat, floodplain, plain, tidewater
antonyms lowland
5 the most intense or characteristic phase of something — see THICK

heighten *vb* **1** to make markedly greater in measure or degree — see INTENSIFY
2 to move from a lower to a higher place or position — see RAISE 1

heightened *adj* being at a higher level than average — see HIGH 2

heinousness *n* the state or quality of being utterly evil — see ENORMITY 1

heir *n* a person who has the right to inherit property ⟨upon his death, Mr. Parkworth's property was divided evenly among his *heirs*, four sons and three daughters⟩
synonyms inheritor, legatee
related words claimant; heir apparent, successor; heiress; assignee, beneficiary, grantee; descendant (*or* descendent), scion (*also* cion)

helical *adj* turning around an axis like the thread of a screw — see SPIRAL

hell *n* **1** the place of punishment for the wicked after death ⟨condemned to *hell* for their sins⟩
synonyms perdition
related words inferno; purgatory; hades, netherworld, underworld
near antonyms empyrean; glory
antonyms Elysium, heaven, kingdom come, paradise
2 a situation or state that causes great suffering and unhappiness ⟨picking cotton under the hot summer sun was *hell*⟩
synonyms agony, horror, misery, murder, nightmare, torment, torture
related words cross, ordeal, trial, tribulation; gall, thorn; bummer, downer, drag
near antonyms delight, diversion, entertainment, fun, pleasure, recreation; lark, picnic, riot
antonyms heaven, paradise
3 a place of uproar or confusion — see MADHOUSE 2
4 a state in which everything is out of order — see CHAOS

hellion *n* an appealingly mischievous person — see SCAMP 1

hello *n* an expression of goodwill upon meeting ⟨we said our *hellos* and got right down to business⟩
synonyms greeting, salutation, salute, welcome
related words amenities, civilities, pleasantries; regards, respects, wishes
antonyms adieu, bon voyage, farewell, Godspeed, good-bye (*or* good-by)

helm *n* the place of leadership or command — see HEAD 2

helmsman *n* the person (as an employer or supervisor) who tells people and especially workers what to do — see BOSS

help *n* **1** an act or instance of helping ⟨Andrew didn't get any *help* with his homework⟩
synonyms aid, assist, assistance, backing, boost, lift, support
related words advancement, encouragement, facilitation, forwarding, furtherance, furthering, nurturance; benefaction, patronage, promotion, sponsorship; advice, care, counsel, guidance, mentoring; attendance, attention, service; beneficence, charity, favor, kindness, philanthropy; relief, succor
near antonyms constraint, frustration, inhibition, interference, obstruction, repression, restraint; deterrence, discouragement
antonyms hindrance
2 a thing that helps ⟨the computer is a great *help* for writing reports⟩
synonyms advantage, aid, benefit, boon
related words lift, pick-me-up; support, sustenance; blessing, godsend, windfall; recourse, resort, resource; asset
near antonyms constraint, inhibitor, liability, obstacle, obstruction, restraint, stranglehold
antonyms disadvantage, drawback, hindrance, impediment
3 a body of persons at work or available for work — see FORCE 1

help *vb* **1** to provide (someone) with what is useful or necessary to achieve an end ⟨Mary Beth flew to Chicago to *help* her dad when he moved into an apartment⟩
synonyms abet, aid, assist, back, prop (up), support
related words advance, facilitate, forward, foster, further; champion, endorse (*also* indorse), patronize, promote, sponsor; attend, care (for), comfort, minister (to), succor; bolster, boost, buttress, reinforce; advise, counsel, guide, mentor, nurture; bail out, deliver, rescue, save; embolden, encourage, hearten; benefit, favor, profit, serve
phrases to stand one in good stead
near antonyms balk, bar, block, constrain, hamper, hold back, impede, inhibit, obstruct, restrain, strangle; baffle, foil, frustrate, interfere, oppose, sabotage, thwart; desert, disappoint, fail, let down; discourage, dishearten; repress, retard, stifle, straiten, stunt; damage, harm, hurt, injure
antonyms hinder
2 to make more bearable or less severe ⟨the new ointment didn't *help* Josh's sunburn one bit⟩
synonyms allay, alleviate, assuage, ease, mitigate, mollify, palliate, relieve, soothe
related words abate, lighten, moderate, soften, temper; cure, heal, remedy; amend, correct, emend, fix, mend, rectify, reform, repair; ameliorate, better, enhance, enrich, improve, meliorate, perfect, refine
near antonyms harm, hurt, impair, injure; heighten, intensify, sharpen
antonyms aggravate
3 to keep from happening by taking action in advance — see PREVENT

helper *n* a person who helps a more skilled person ⟨over the summer Chris worked as a carpenter's *helper*⟩
synonyms adjutant, aid, aide, apprentice, assistant, coadjutor, deputy, helpmate, helpmeet, mate, sidekick
related words attendant, handmaiden (*also* handmaid), maid, maidservant, scullion, servant; auxiliary, subordinate, underling; employee, hand, help, hireling, laborer, worker

helpful *adj* conferring benefits; promoting or contributing to personal or social well-being — see BENEFICIAL

helpless *adj* **1** lacking protection from danger or resistance against attack ⟨after the storm we found a *helpless* baby bird that had fallen out of its nest⟩
synonyms defenseless, exposed, susceptible, undefended, unguarded, unprotected, unresistant, unshielded, vulnerable
related words indefensible, untenable; uncovered, unsafe, unsheltered; overcome, preyed (on *or* upon); disarmed, passive, resistless, unarmed; feeble, frail, weak; abandoned, marooned
phrases in the lurch
near antonyms defensible; covered, fortified, safe, secure, screened, sheltered; armed, armored; immune, impenetrable, impregnable, invincible, strong, unassailable, unbeatable, unconquerable
antonyms guarded, invulnerable, protected, resistant, shielded
2 unable to act or achieve one's purpose — see POWERLESS

helpmate *n* **1** a person who helps a more skilled person — see HELPER
2 the female partner in a marriage — see WIFE

helpmeet *n* **1** a person who helps a more skilled person — see HELPER
2 the female partner in a marriage — see WIFE

helter–skelter *adv* **1** in a confused and reckless manner ⟨the sheep ran *helter-skelter* inside their pen when the coyote appeared in their midst⟩
synonyms amok (*or* amuck), berserk, frantically, frenziedly, harum-scarum, hectically, madly, pell-mell, wild, wildly
related words agitatedly, confusedly, crazily, desperately, feverishly, skittishly, uncontrollably; heedlessly, hotheadedly, recklessly, wantonly; chaotically, riotously, tumultuously, turbulently; aimlessly, haphazardly, hit-or-miss
near antonyms calmly, collectedly, composedly, coolly, imperturbably, peacefully, placidly, serenely, unconcernedly; meekly, mildly, passively, tamely; methodically, orderly, systematically
2 without definite aim, direction, rule, or method — see HIT OR MISS

hem *vb* to close or shut in by or as if by barriers — see ENCLOSE 1

hence *adv* **1** for this or that reason — see THEREFORE
2 from this or that place — see AWAY

henceforth *adv* from this point on ⟨*henceforth,* there will be no more prolonged coffee breaks⟩
synonyms henceforward, hereafter

henceforward *adv* from this point on — see HENCEFORTH

henpeck *vb* to subject (someone) to constant scoldings and sharp reminders — see NAG

herald *n* one that announces or indicates the later arrival of another — see FORERUNNER 1

herbage *n* green leaves or plants — see GREENERY 1

herculean *adj* **1** requiring considerable physical or mental effort — see HARD 2
2 unusually large — see HUGE

herd *n* **1** a group of domestic animals assembled or

herded together <the great *herds* of cattle that cowboys once drove across the plains>
synonyms drove, flock
related words colony, covey, gaggle, pack, school, swarm
2 the body of the community as contrasted with the elite — see MASS 1

herd *vb* to urge, push, or force onward — see DRIVE 1

herder *n* a tender of livestock <the nomadic reindeer *herders* of Siberia live in reindeer-skin tents>
synonyms herdsman
related words buckaroo, cowboy, cowgirl, cowhand, cowherd, cowman, cowpoke, cowpuncher, gaucho, ranchero, vaquero; shepherd, sheepherder, shepherdess; goatherd; wrangler; drover

herdsman *n* a tender of livestock — see HERDER

hereafter *adv* from this point on — see HENCEFORTH

hereafter *n* **1** time that is to come — see FUTURE 1
2 unending existence after death — see ETERNITY 2

hereditary *adj* genetically passed or capable of being passed from parent to offspring <eye and hair color are *hereditary*>
synonyms genetic (*also* genetical), heritable, inborn, inheritable, inherited
related words congenital, inbred, inherent, innate, native, natural
near antonyms acquired

heresy *n* departure from a generally accepted theory, opinion, or practice <the *heresy* of asserting that Shakespeare was not a great writer>
synonyms dissent, dissidence, heterodoxy, nonconformity
related words error, fallacy, falsehood, misbelief, misconception, myth; apostasy, defection, schism, sectarianism, separatism; deviance, deviation, unconventionality; disagreement, discord, dissension
near antonyms agreement, conformation, conventionality
antonyms conformity, orthodoxy

heretic *n* a person who believes or teaches something opposed to accepted beliefs <Galileo was condemned as a *heretic* for supporting Copernicus's thesis that the earth revolves around the sun and not vice versa>
synonyms dissenter, dissident, nonconformist
related words apostate, defector, renegade; schismatic, sectarian, separatist; disbeliever, infidel, unbeliever; bohemian, individualist
near antonyms believer
antonyms conformer, conformist

heretical *adj* deviating from commonly accepted beliefs or practices <the belief that women should be allowed to have careers outside the home was once considered *heretical*>
synonyms dissentient, dissenting, dissident, heterodox nonconformist, nonorthodox, unconventional, unorthodox
related words nontraditional; apostate, defecting, renegade; schismatic, sectarian, separatist
antonyms conforming, conformist, conventional, orthodox

heretofore *adv* up to this or that time — see HITHERTO

heritable *adj* genetically passed or capable of being passed from parent to offspring — see HEREDITARY

heritage *n* something that is or may be inherited — see INHERITANCE

hermit *n* a person who lives away from others — see RECLUSE

hero *n* a large sandwich on a long split roll — see SUBMARINE

heroic *adj* **1** feeling or displaying no fear by temperament — see BRAVE
2 large and impressive in size, grandeur, extent, or conception — see GRAND 1
3 unusually large — see HUGE

heroically *adv* in a manner befitting a person of the highest character and ideals — see GREATLY 1

heroism *n* strength of mind to carry on in spite of danger — see COURAGE

hesitance *n* **1** a lack of willingness or desire to do or accept something — see RELUCTANCE
2 the act or an instance of pausing because of uncertainty about the right course of action — see HESITATION

hesitancy *n* **1** a lack of willingness or desire to do or accept something — see RELUCTANCE
2 the act or an instance of pausing because of uncertainty about the right course of action — see HESITATION

hesitant *adj* having doubts about the wisdom of doing something <Ivan was *hesitant* about lending CDs to his friends after he'd lost several of them that way>
synonyms afraid, disinclined, dubious, indisposed, loath (*or* loth), reluctant
related words uneager, unenthusiastic; averse, unwilling; doubtful, faltering, irresolute, questioning, uncertain, undecided, unsure, vacillating, wobbly; fainthearted, shy, timid
near antonyms eager, enthusiastic, glad, happy, keen; ready, willing; certain, decided, resolute, sure, unquestioning
antonyms disposed, inclined

hesitate *vb* to show uncertainty about the right course of action <Keri didn't *hesitate* before answering the question>
synonyms falter, hang back, shilly-shally, stagger, teeter, vacillate, waver, wobble
related words haw, hem; dally, dawdle, delay, linger, procrastinate, pause, wait; back down, chicken (out); consider, debate, deliberate, ponder, weigh; oscillate; equivocate, hedge, pussyfoot
near antonyms budge, stir; advance, continue
antonyms dive (in), plunge (in)

hesitation *n* the act or an instance of pausing because of uncertainty about the right course of action <one moment's *hesitation* on my part, and the elusive butterfly was lost to me forever>
synonyms faltering, hesitance, hesitancy, indecision, irresolution, shilly-shallying, vacillation, wavering, wobbling
related words delay, hawing, procrastination, waiting; consideration, debate, deliberation, doubt, incertitude, indetermination, uncertainty; avoidance, equivocation; aversion, disinclination, indisposition, reluctance, unwillingness; faintheartedness, shyness, timidness
near antonyms certainty, certitude, confidence, decisiveness, determination, firmness, resoluteness, resolution, sureness; alacrity, eagerness, readiness

heterodox *adj* deviating from commonly accepted beliefs or practices — see HERETICAL

heterodoxy *n* departure from a generally accepted theory, opinion, or practice — see HERESY

heterogeneous *adj* consisting of many things of different sorts — see MISCELLANEOUS

het up *adj* feeling or showing uncomfortable feelings of uncertainty — see NERVOUS 1

hew *vb* **1** to bring down by cutting — see FELL 2
2 to hold to something firmly as if by adhesion — see STICK 1

hew (to) *vb* to give steadfast support to — see ADHERE

hex *n* **1** a woman believed to have often harmful supernatural powers — see WITCH 1
2 something that brings bad luck — see JINX

hex *vb* to cast a spell on — see BEWITCH 1

heyday *n* a state or time of great activity, thriving, or achievement — see BLOOM 1

hiatus *n* a break in continuity — see GAP 2

hick *n* an awkward or simple person especially from a small town or the country ⟨city dwellers who looked down on their cousins from northern Maine as *hicks*⟩
synonyms bumpkin, clodhopper, countryman, hillbilly, provincial, rustic, yokel
related words boor, clod, gawk, lout, oaf; greenhorn, tenderfoot; peasant, peon; mountaineer
near antonyms slicker, smoothy (*or* smoothie); suburbanite, urbanite
antonyms cosmopolitan, sophisticate

hide *n* **1** the outer covering of an animal removed for its commercial value ⟨seal *hides* are used by Eskimos to make footwear, boats, shelters, bags, and clothing⟩
synonyms fur, leather, pelt, skin
related words badger, beaver, chamois, chinchilla, ermine, fisher, fox, mink, muskrat, otter, Persian lamb, rabbit, raccoon (*also* racoon), sable, seal, silver fox; bearskin, buckskin, calfskin, coonskin, cowhide, deerskin, doeskin, goatskin, horsehide, kidskin, lambskin, pigskin, rawhide, sealskin, sharkskin, sheepskin, snakeskin; fleece, mouton; alligator; cordovan, morocco, patent leather, suede
2 the hairless natural covering of an animal prepared for use — see LEATHER 1

[1]hide *vb* **1** to put into a hiding place ⟨the thief *hid* the stolen jewelry under the floorboards⟩
synonyms bury, cache, conceal, ensconce, secrete
related words hoard, squirrel (away), stash; entomb, inter
near antonyms bare, expose, reveal, show, uncover, unmask, unveil, unwrap; flaunt, parade, show off; disinter, unearth
antonyms display, exhibit
2 to keep secret or shut off from view ⟨he tried to *hide* his criminal past⟩ ⟨she *hid* the cat's litter box behind a screen⟩
synonyms blanket, blot out, cloak, conceal, cover, curtain, enshroud, mask, obscure, occult, screen, shroud, veil
related words camouflage, cover (up), disguise, smother; gild, gloss (over), varnish, whitewash; becloud, bedim, befog, cloud, darken, eclipse, overcast, overshadow, shade
near antonyms bring out, present; clarify, illuminate; advertise, air, broadcast, proclaim, publicize
antonyms bare, disclose, display, divulge, expose, reveal, show, uncloak, uncover, unmask, unveil
3 to strike repeatedly with something long and thin or flexible — see WHIP 1

[2]hide *vb* to strike repeatedly — see BEAT 1

hideaway *n* a place where a person goes to hide — see HIDEOUT

hideous *adj* **1** causing intense displeasure, disgust, or resentment — see OFFENSIVE 1
2 extremely disturbing or repellent — see HORRIBLE 1
3 unpleasant to look at — see UGLY 1

hideousness *n* the quality of inspiring intense dread or dismay — see HORROR 1

hideout *n* a place where a person goes to hide ⟨they found the stolen jewels under the floorboards in the thief's *hideout,* a cabin deep in the woods⟩
synonyms concealment, covert, den, hideaway, lair, nest
related words blind, cover, nook, recess; hangout, harbor, haunt, haven, refuge, retreat, shelter

hiding *n* the placing of something out of sight — see CONCEALMENT 1

higgledy–piggledy *adj* lacking in order, neatness, and often cleanliness — see MESSY

high *adj* **1** extending to a great distance upward ⟨Mt. Everest is the *highest* mountain in the world⟩
synonyms lofty, tall, towering
related words dominant, dominating, eminent, prominent; elevated, lifted, raised, uplifted, upswept; high-rise, statuesque
near antonyms flat, stubby, stumpy
antonyms low, low-lying, short, squat
2 being at a higher level than average ⟨gasoline prices are *high* right now⟩ ⟨a *high* fever⟩ ⟨people with *high* incomes⟩
synonyms advanced, elevated, escalated, heightened, increased, jacked (up), raised, up
related words extreme, full, maximized, maximum, peaked, sky-high, utmost; inflated, over, overfilled, overflowing, overfull, overlarge, overloaded, oversize (*or* oversized)
near antonyms decreased, depressed, dropped, receded, under
antonyms down, low
3 located at a greater height than average or usual ⟨an eagle's nest *high* on the cliff⟩ ⟨an old house with *high* ceilings⟩
synonyms airy, elevated
related words aerial, ascendant, ascending, soaring; overhead, overlooking, raised, upheld, uplifted, upraised; topmost, upmost, upper, uppermost, upward
near antonyms depressed, descendant (*or* descendent), descending, down, dropped, fallen, grounded, lowered, sunken; lowermost, nethermost, undermost; abreast, even, level
antonyms low, low-lying
4 being far along in development — see ADVANCED 1
5 being under the influence of alcohol — see DRUNK
6 commanding a large price — see COSTLY
7 having, characterized by, or arising from a dignified and generous nature — see NOBLE 2
8 highest in rank or authority — see HEAD

high *n* the expanse of air surrounding the earth — see SKY

high *adv* in a luxurious manner ⟨after he won the lottery Philip lived *high* until all the money was gone⟩
synonyms expensively, extravagantly, grandly,

lavishly, luxuriously, opulently, richly, sumptuously
related words imposingly, impressively, magnificently, splendidly; grandiosely, ostentatiously, pretentiously; affluently, comfortably, fine; immoderately, indulgently, intemperately, prodigally, wantonly, wastefully
near antonyms unassumingly, unpretentiously; cheaply, economically, frugally, inexpensively, meagerly, poorly, skimpily, sparely, sparingly, thriftily; conservatively, moderately, prudently, reasonably, restrainedly, sensibly, temperately
antonyms austerely, humbly, modestly, plainly, simply

highborn *adj* of high birth, rank, or station — see NOBLE 1

highbrow *adj* much given to learning and thinking — see INTELLECTUAL 1

higher *adj* being far along in development — see ADVANCED 1

highest *adj* **1** being at a point or level higher than all others — see TOP 1
2 coming before all others in importance — see FOREMOST 1

highfalutin *adj* **1** full of fine words and fancy expressions — see FLOWERY 1
2 having a feeling of superiority that shows itself in an overbearing attitude — see ARROGANT
3 having or displaying feelings of scorn for what is regarded as beneath oneself — see PROUD 1
4 self-consciously trying to present an appearance of grandeur or importance — see PRETENTIOUS 1

high–flown *adj* **1** full of fine words and fancy expressions — see FLOWERY 1
2 very dignified in form, tone, or style — see ELEVATED 2

high–handed *adj* **1** having a feeling of superiority that shows itself in an overbearing attitude — see ARROGANT
2 having or showing a tendency to force one's will on others without any regard to fairness or necessity — see ARBITRARY 1

high–hat *adj* having a feeling of superiority that shows itself in an overbearing attitude — see ARROGANT

high–hat *vb* to show contempt for — see SCORN 1

high jinks *n pl* wildly playful or mischievous behavior — see HORSEPLAY

highland *n* an area of high ground — see HEIGHT 4

highlight *vb* to indicate the importance of by giving prominent display — see EMPHASIZE

highly *adv* to a great degree — see VERY 1

high–minded *adj* having, characterized by, or arising from a dignified and generous nature — see NOBLE 2

high–mindedly *adv* in a manner befitting a person of the highest character and ideals — see GREATLY 1

high noon *n* the middle of the day — see NOON

high–pitched *adj* having a high musical pitch or range — see SHRILL

high–pressure *adj* having or showing a bold forcefulness in the pursuit of a goal — see AGGRESSIVE 1

highroad *n* a passage cleared for public vehicular travel — see WAY 1

high–sounding *adj* full of fine words and fancy expressions — see FLOWERY 1

high–spirited *adj* **1** joyously unrestrained — see EXUBERANT
2 marked by a lively display of strong feeling — see SPIRITED 1

high–spiritedly *adv* in a quick and spirited manner — see GAILY 2

high–strung *adj* easily excited by nature — see EXCITABLE

high–water mark *n* the highest part or point — see HEIGHT 1

highway *n* a passage cleared for public vehicular travel — see WAY 1

hijack *also* **highjack** *vb* to take control of (a vehicle) by force — see COMMANDEER 1

hike *vb* to move from a lower to a higher place or position — see RAISE 1

hilarious *adj* causing or intended to cause laughter — see FUNNY 1

hilariousness *n* the amusing quality or element in something — see HUMOR 1

hilarity *n* a mood characterized by high spirits and amusement and often accompanied by laughter — see MIRTH

hill *n* **1** a quantity of things thrown or stacked on one another — see [1]PILE 1
2 an area of high ground — see HEIGHT 4

hill *vb* to form into a pile or ridge of earth — see MOUND 1

hillbilly *n* an awkward or simple person especially from a small town or the country — see HICK

hind *adj* being at or in the part of something opposite the front part — see BACK

hinder *vb* to create difficulty for the work or activity of — see HAMPER

hindmost *adj* **1** being at or in the part of something opposite the front part — see BACK
2 following all others of the same kind in order or time — see LAST

hindrance *n* **1** something that makes movement or progress more difficult — see ENCUMBRANCE
2 something that stands in the way of one's progress or achievement — see OBSTACLE 1

hinge *vb* to be determined by, based on, or subject (to) — see DEPEND 1

hint *n* **1** a slight or indirect pointing to something (as a solution or explanation) ⟨can't you give me some *hint* as to where you're taking me?⟩
synonyms clue, cue, indication, inkling, intimation, lead, suggestion
related words breath, flicker, glimmer, glimpse, mention, scent, whiff, wind; hunch, idea, inspiration, notion; allusion, implication, inference, innuendo, insinuation; evidence, mark, overtone, pointer, sign, signal, telltale, token; assistance, nod, prompt, tip, tip-off, wink; feeling, foreboding, intuition, premonition, presentiment, suspicion; augury, foreshadower, foretaste, omen, portent, prefigurement, symptom
near antonyms answer, solution
2 a piece of advice or useful information especially from an expert — see [1]TIP 1
3 a very small amount — see PARTICLE 1

hint *vb* to convey an idea indirectly ⟨Cecilia kept *hinting* that she wanted an invitation to Patty's party⟩
synonyms allude, imply, indicate, infer, insinuate, intimate, suggest
related words advert, mention, point, refer, signal, signify; smack (of), smell (of)
near antonyms announce, declare, proclaim; elucidate, explain, spell out

hinterland *n* a rural region that forms the edge of

the settled or developed part of a country — see FRONTIER 2

hip *adj* having inside information — see WISE 2

hire *n* **1** the state of being provided with a paying job ⟨college graduates seeking *hire* by big corporations⟩
synonyms employ, employment, engagement
related words appointment, assignment, conscription, enlistment, recruitment; incumbency, tenure; occupation, place, position, post, situation, work
near antonyms boot, discharge, dismissal, firing, removal, sack; demotion, suspension; furlough, layoff, leave, liberty, retirement
antonyms joblessness, unemployment
2 the money paid regularly to a person for labor or services — see WAGE

hire *vb* **1** to take or get the temporary use of (something) for a set sum ⟨the Young's *hired* a limousine for their daughter's wedding⟩
synonyms charter, engage, lease, rent
related words sublease, sublet; check out; arrange (for), bespeak, book, contract (for), order, reserve, sign up (for)
2 to provide with a paying job — see EMPLOY 1

hireling *n* one who works for another for wages or a salary — see EMPLOYEE

hirsute *adj* covered with or as if with hair — see HAIRY 1

hiss *n* **1** a sound similar to the speech sound \s\ stretched out ⟨the *hiss* of air escaping from a balloon⟩
synonyms fizz, sizzle, swish, whish, whiz (*or* whizz)
related words wheeze, whistle, whoosh, zip; sibilant
2 a vocal sound made to express scorn or disapproval — see CATCALL

hiss *vb* to make a sound like that of stretching out the speech sound \s\ ⟨the frightened kitten *hissed* at us when we tried to pick it up⟩
synonyms fizz, sizzle, swish, whish, whiz (*or* whizz)
related words wheeze, whistle, whoosh, zip; bubble, effervesce; buzz, drone, hum

historian *n* a student or writer of history ⟨*historians* are still trying to sort out fact from fiction in the story of Kateri Tekakwitha, the Lily of the Mohawks⟩
synonyms annalist, chronicler
related words autobiographer, biographer; archivist, chronologist, genealogist

historical *adj* restricted to or based on fact — see FACTUAL 1

history *n* **1** an account of important events in the order in which they happened ⟨a *history* of the American civil rights movement during the 1960s⟩
synonyms annals, chronicle, record
related words autobiography, diary, journal, memoir, reminiscence(s); biography, life; epic, legend, narrative, saga, story, tale; archives, documentation, log, register, report; chronology, genealogy
2 a relating of events usually in the order in which they happened — see ACCOUNT 1
3 the events or experience of former times — see PAST

histrionic *adj* **1** given to or marked by attention-getting behavior suggestive of stage acting — see THEATRICAL 1
2 having the general quality or effect of a stage performance — see DRAMATIC 1

hit *n* **1** a person or thing that is successful ⟨the new babysitter turned out to be a great *hit* with the kids⟩
synonyms blockbuster, megahit, smash, success, winner
related words corker, crackerjack, dandy, jim-dandy, pip, prizewinner; gem, jewel, treasure; marvel, phenomenon, sensation, wonder; coup, triumph, victory
near antonyms disappointment, fizzle, lemon, loser
antonyms bummer, bust, catastrophe, debacle (*also* débâcle), dud, failure, fiasco, flop, turkey, washout
2 a hard strike with a part of the body or an instrument — see [1]BLOW

hit *vb* **1** to deliver a blow to (someone or something) usually in a strong vigorous manner ⟨a good carpenter *hits* a nail just two or three times to drive it in⟩
synonyms bang, bash, bat, belt, bludgeon, bop, bust, clap, clobber, clout, crack, hammer, knock, paste, pound, punch, rap, slam, slap, slog, slug, smack, smite, sock, strike, swat, swipe, thump, thwack, wallop, whack, whale, zap
related words batter, beat, buffet, bung, chop, drub, lace, lambaste (*or* lambast), lick, mangle, maul, pelt, pepper, pummel, rough; bunt, flick, stroke, tap; bump, butt, jab, jostle, kick, knee, poke, prod, push, shove, stamp; bowl (over), knock (down); cane, club, cudgel, flail, flog, lash, slash, spear, stab, switch, thrash, whip; brain
2 to come into usually forceful contact with something ⟨when she fell on the ice, she *hit* hard and badly bruised her elbow⟩
synonyms bang, bash, bump, collide, crash, impact, impinge, knock, ram, slam, smash, strike, swipe, thud
related words bounce, carom, glance, rebound, ricochet, skim, skip; contact, land, touch; brush, graze, kiss, nudge, scrape, shave, sweep; bulldoze, jostle, muscle, press, push
near antonyms miss, skirt
3 to obtain (as a goal) through effort — see ACHIEVE 1

hit (on *or* upon) *vb* to come upon after searching, study, or effort — see FIND 1

hit (upon) *vb* to come upon unexpectedly or by chance — see HAPPEN (ON *OR* UPON)

hitch *n* a fixed period of time during which a person holds a job or position — see TERM 1

hitch *vb* **1** to move or cause to move with a sharp quick motion — see JERK 1
2 to put or bring together so as to form a new and longer whole — see CONNECT 1
3 to put securely in place or in a desired position — see FASTEN 2
4 to travel by securing free rides — see HITCHHIKE

hitcher *n* one who hitchhikes — see HITCHHIKER

hitchhike *vb* to travel by securing free rides ⟨Andrew *hitchhiked* from Baltimore to attend his sister's wedding in New Jersey⟩
synonyms hitch, thumb
related words bum; stow away; hijack (*also* highjack)

hitchhiker *n* one who hitchhikes ⟨on the highway

out of town we picked up a *hitchhiker* who was trying to get to his sister's wedding⟩
synonyms hitcher
related words stowaway; hijacker
hither *adj* being the less far of two — see NEAR 1
hitherto *adv* up to this or that time ⟨at the talent show Kyle revealed his *hitherto* unknown gift for doing impressions⟩
synonyms heretofore, theretofore, thus far, yet
related words before, formerly, previously
near antonyms afterward (*or* afterwards), later, subsequently; hereupon, thereupon
antonyms henceforth, henceforward, hereafter, thenceforth, thenceforward (*also* thenceforwards), thereafter
hit–or–miss *adj* lacking a definite plan, purpose, or pattern — see RANDOM
hit or miss *adv* without definite aim, direction, rule, or method ⟨Angelo was learning Spanish *hit or miss,* mostly just by hearing his friends speak it⟩
synonyms aimlessly, anyhow, anyway, anywise, desultorily, erratically, haphazard, haphazardly, helter-skelter, irregularly, randomly
related words capriciously, carelessly, casually, indiscriminately, informally, offhand, offhandedly, promiscuously, whimsically; accidentally, fortuitously, inadvertently, unconsciously, unintentionally, unwittingly; disconnectedly, disjointedly, fitfully, intermittently, spottily, unpredictably; higgledy-piggledy, topsy-turvy
phrases at random
near antonyms carefully, formally, meticulously, orderly, punctiliously; deliberately, intentionally, purposefully, purposely
antonyms methodically, systematically
hoagie *n* a large sandwich on a long split roll — see SUBMARINE
hoar *adj* dating or surviving from the distant past — see ANCIENT 1
hoar *n* a covering of tiny ice crystals on a cold surface — see FROST
hoard *n* **1** a supply stored up and often hidden away ⟨Dad was upset when Mom put his entire *hoard* of empty yogurt containers in the recycling bin⟩
synonyms cache, stash, stockpile, store
related words coffers, deposit, funds, nest egg, savings, sinking fund, treasure; inventory, reserve, reservoir, stock; provisions, resources; accumulation, collection; repertory
2 a collection of things kept available for future use or need — see STORE 1
hoard *vb* to put (something of future use or value) in a safe or secret place ⟨Dad's been *hoarding* empty yogurt containers all winter, with the intention of using them to start seedlings in the spring⟩
synonyms cache, lay away, lay up, put by, salt away, squirrel (away), stash, stockpile, store, stow
related words accumulate, acquire, amass, assemble, collect, concentrate, garner, gather, round up, scrape (together); heap, pile, stack; conserve, husband, preserve; bank, deposit, hold, keep, reserve, retain, save, stock, withhold; conceal, ensconce, secrete
phrases set aside
near antonyms discard, dump, throw away, throw out; consume, squander, use up, waste; hand over, relinquish, surrender; blow, dissipate, fritter (away), lavish, misspend, run through, spend; deplete, exhaust, expend; dispel, disperse, dissipate, scatter
hoarfrost *n* a covering of tiny ice crystals on a cold surface — see FROST
hoarse *adj* harsh and dry in sound ⟨the dying man spoke in a *hoarse* whisper⟩
synonyms coarse, croaking, grating, gravel, gravelly, gruff, husky, rasping, raspy, scratchy, throaty
related words guttural; abrasive, cacophonous, discordant, grinding, jarring, rough, scraping, scratching; cawing, raucous, squawking, strident; choked, cracked, strained, strangled
near antonyms gentle, gliding, golden, liquid, mellifluous, mellow, sweet, tender; satiny, silken, smooth, soft, velvety
hoary *adj* dating or surviving from the distant past — see ANCIENT 1
hoax *n* an imitation that is passed off as genuine — see FAKE 1
hoax *vb* to cause to believe what is untrue — see DECEIVE
hoaxer *n* **1** a dishonest person who uses clever means to cheat others out of something of value — see TRICKSTER 1
2 one who makes false claims of identity or expertise — see IMPOSTOR
hob *n* playful, reckless behavior that is not intended to cause serious harm — see MISCHIEF 1
hobble *vb* **1** to create difficulty for the work or activity of — see HAMPER
2 to walk while favoring one leg — see LIMP 1
hobgoblin *n* **1** an imaginary being usually having a small human form and magical powers — see FAIRY
2 something or someone that causes fear or dread especially without reason — see BOGEY 1
hobnob *vb* **1** to come or be together as friends — see ASSOCIATE 1
2 to take part in social activities — see SOCIALIZE
hobnobber *n* a person frequently seen in the company of another — see ASSOCIATE 1
hobo *n* a homeless wanderer who may beg or steal for a living — see TRAMP
hock *vb* to leave as a guarantee of repayment of a loan — see PAWN
hodgepodge *n* an unorganized collection or mixture of various things — see MISCELLANY 1
hog *n* one who eats greedily or too much — see GLUTTON
hoggish *adj* having a huge appetite — see VORACIOUS 1
hogshead *n* an enclosed wooden vessel for holding beverages — see CASK
hogwash *n* **1** language, behavior, or ideas that are absurd and contrary to good sense — see NONSENSE 1
2 unintelligible or meaningless talk — see GIBBERISH
hoist *vb* **1** to lift with effort — see HEAVE 1
2 to move from a lower to a higher place or position — see RAISE 1
hold *n* **1** the act or manner of holding ⟨make sure you have a firm *hold* on the chain saw before you turn it on⟩
synonyms clasp, grapple, grasp, grip
related words anchorage, leverage, purchase; grab, seizure; foothold, footing, toehold; embrace, hug
near antonyms release, relinquishment

2 a structure or place from which one can resist attack — see FORT
3 the right or means to command or control others — see POWER 1

hold *vb* **1** to have or keep in one's hands ⟨this casserole dish is too hot to *hold,* so grab a potholder⟩
synonyms clench, cling (to), clutch, grip, hang on (to), hold on (to)
related words bear, carry; catch, grapple, nab, seize, snatch, take; feel, finger, handle, paw; clasp, embrace, grasp, hug
near antonyms drop, give, hand, unclasp, unhand; release, relinquish
2 to continue to have in one's possession or power — see KEEP 2
3 to have as an opinion — see BELIEVE 2
4 to have within — see CONTAIN 1
5 to keep in one's mind or heart — see HARBOR 1
6 to keep, control, or experience as one's own — see HAVE 1
7 to make or have room for — see ACCOMMODATE 1
8 to reach for and take hold of by embracing with the fingers or arms — see TAKE 1
9 to think of in a particular way — see CONSIDER 1

hold (up) *vb* **1** to continue to operate or to meet one's needs — see HOLD OUT
2 to remain indefinitely in existence or in the same state — see CONTINUE 1

hold back *vb* to create difficulty for the work or activity of — see HAMPER

holder *n* **1** one who has a legal or rightful claim to ownership — see PROPRIETOR
2 something into which a liquid or smaller objects can be put for storage or transportation — see CONTAINER

hold in *vb* to keep from exceeding a desirable degree or level (as of expression) — see CONTROL 1

holding *n* **1** a decision made by a court or tribunal regarding a case it has heard — see SENTENCE
2 *usually* **holdings** *pl* transportable items that one owns — see POSSESSION 2

hold off (on) *vb* to assign to a later time — see POSTPONE

hold on *vb* **1** to remain indefinitely in existence or in the same state — see CONTINUE 1
2 to remain in place in readiness or expectation of something — see WAIT

hold on (to) *vb* to have or keep in one's hands — see HOLD 1

hold out *vb* to continue to operate or to meet one's needs ⟨we hoped our supply of firewood would *hold out* until power was restored⟩ ⟨luckily, the old outboard motor *held out* till we made it to shore⟩
synonyms hold (up), last, keep up, prevail, survive
related words bear up, carry on, cope, endure, go, hang in, persevere; continue, draw out, hang on, linger, persist, remain, stretch
near antonyms break down, collapse, conk (out), crash, die, expire, stall, stop; run down, wane
antonyms fail, fizzle, give out, go out, peter (out), run out

holdup *n* an instance or period of being prevented from going about one's business — see DELAY

hold up *vb* **1** to assign to a later time — see POSTPONE
2 to bring (something) to a standstill — see [1]HALT 1
3 to create difficulty for the work or activity of — see HAMPER

hole *n* **1** a place in a surface allowing passage into or through a thing ⟨Mark was beside himself after seeing that his little sister had punched *holes* in his homework⟩
synonyms aperture, opening, orifice, perforation
related words chink, cleft, crack, cranny, crevice, cut, breach, break, fissure, gash, notch, rent, rift, rupture, slash, slit, split; gap, slot, space; exit, mouth, outlet, pore, vent; entrance, inlet, intake; pinprick, punch, puncture; armhole, buttonhole, knothole, peephole, pinhole, wormhole
near antonyms fill, filler, filling, patch, plug, seal, stopper; barrier, blockage, obstacle, obstruction
2 a sunken area forming a separate space ⟨Ann dug a *hole* big enough to plant the tree⟩
synonyms cavity, concavity, dent, depression, dint, hollow, indentation, pit, recess
related words burrow, cave, cavern, ditch, excavation, furrow, groove, trench, trough; basin, bowl, valley; alcove, cleft, niche, nook, opening, recess, socket; alveolus, dimple, gouge, notch, impression, pocket; chuckhole, crater, posthole, pothole, sinkhole, wallow, waterhole, well; abyss, chasm, gulf, vacuity, vacuum, void
near antonyms hill, mound, projection, rise; bump, lump, pimple, swell, swelling, tumor
antonyms bulge, convexity, protrusion, protuberance
3 a difficult, puzzling, or embarrassing situation from which there is no easy escape — see PREDICAMENT
4 a dirty or messy place — see PIGPEN
5 an open space in a barrier (as a wall or hedge) — see GAP 1
6 the shelter or resting place of a wild animal — see DEN 1

hole *vb* to make a hole or series of holes in — see PERFORATE

holiday *n, chiefly British* a period during which the usual routine of school or work is suspended — see VACATION

holiday *vb* to take or spend a vacation — see VACATION

holiness *n* the quality or state of being spiritually pure or virtuous ⟨known throughout the world for his *holiness,* the prophet was visited daily by hundreds of pilgrims⟩
synonyms blessedness, devoutness, godliness, piety, piousness, sainthood, saintliness, saintship, sanctity
related words asceticism, devotion, morality, prayerfulness, religiousness, spirituality; righteousness, virtuousness
near antonyms blasphemousness, irreverence, sacrilegiousness; depravity, sinfulness, wickedness
antonyms godlessness, impiety, ungodliness, unholiness

holler *n* a loud vocal expression of strong emotion — see SHOUT

holler *vb* to speak so as to be heard at a distance — see CALL 1

hollow *adj* curved inward ⟨there's a *hollow* spot in the mattress where Jim sleeps⟩
synonyms concave, dented, depressed, indented, recessed, sunken

related words alveolar, cavernous, cuplike, cupped; dimpled, pockmarked; compressed, condensed, contracted, diminished, reduced
near antonyms ballooning, bloated, blown up, bulbous, distended, enlarged, expanded, extended, inflated, jutting, projecting, puffed (up), puffy, risen, swollen; domed, globular, rounded, spherical
antonyms bulging, convex, protruding, protuberant
hollow *n* **1** a sunken area forming a separate space — see HOLE 2
2 an area of lowland between hills or mountains — see VALLEY
holocaust *n* a destructive burning — see FIRE
holy *adj* **1** showing a devotion to God and to a life of virtue ⟨the *holy* monk spent many hours on his knees in prayer⟩
synonyms devout, godly, pious, religious, sainted, saintly
related words ascetic, prayerful, reverent, reverential, spiritual, worshipful; beatified, blessed, canonized, venerable; angelic (*or* angelical), cherubic; chaste, pure, righteous, virtuous
near antonyms blasphemous, desecrating, irreverent, profane, sacrilegious, unspiritual; backsliding, unfaithful; sinful, sinning, wicked
antonyms faithless, godless, impious, irreligious, ungodly, unholy
2 set apart or worthy of veneration by association with God ⟨the Torah contains the *holy* writings of Judaism⟩
synonyms blessed, consecrated, hallowed, sacred, sacrosanct, sanctified
related words adored, enshrined, glorified, revered, venerated, worshipped (*also* worshiped); ceremonial, liturgical, priestly, religious, ritual, spiritual; biblical, scriptural
near antonyms nonreligious, unspiritual; earthly, mundane, secular, temporal, worldly
antonyms unconsecrated, unhallowed, unsanctified
3 of, relating to, or being God ⟨the *Holy* Trinity⟩
synonyms blessed, divine, godlike, heavenly, sacred, supernatural
related words eternal, everlasting, immortal; almighty, omnipotent, omniscient, supreme
near antonyms human, mortal
4 not to be violated, criticized, or tampered with — see SACRED 1
Holy Writ *n* a book made up of the writings accepted by Christians as coming from God — see BIBLE
homage *n* **1** a formal expression of praise — see ENCOMIUM
2 public acknowledgment or admiration for an achievement — see GLORY 1
hombre *n* an adult male human being — see MAN 1
home *n* **1** the place where one lives ⟨as we entered his 34-room mansion, Ernest said, "Welcome to my humble *home* !"⟩
synonyms abode, diggings, domicile, dwelling, fireside, habitation, hearth, hearthstone, house, lodging, pad, place, quarters, residence, roof
related words accommodations, housing, nest, residency, shelter; bungalow, cabin, chalet, cottage; duplex, ranch, split level, town house, tract house, triplex; apartment, apartment house, condominium, flat, tenement, tenement house, walk-up; penthouse, salon, suite; barracks, boardinghouse, dorm, dormitory, lodgment (*or* lodgement), lodging house, room(s), rooming house; castle, château, country seat, estate, manor, manor house, mansion, palace, villa; farmhouse, grange, hacienda, homestead, ranch house; houseboat, mobile home, motor home, trailer; hermitage, manse, parsonage, vicarage; hovel, hut, shack
2 the place where a plant or animal is usually or naturally found ⟨the American south, the *home* of the armadillo⟩
synonyms habitat, niche, range, territory
related words element, environment, environs, haunt, locality, milieu, neighborhood, setting, surroundings
3 the land of one's birth, residence, or citizenship — see COUNTRY 1
homeboy *n* a violent, brutal person who is often a member of an organized gang — see HOODLUM
homeland *n* the land of one's birth, residence, or citizenship — see COUNTRY 1
homely *adj* unpleasant to look at — see UGLY 1
homesteader *n* a person who settles in a new region — see FRONTIERSMAN
homicidal *adj* eager for or marked by the shedding of blood, extreme violence, or killing — see BLOODTHIRSTY
homicide *n* the intentional and unlawful taking of another person's life ⟨the missing man was thought to be the victim of a *homicide,* but his body was never found⟩
synonyms foul play, murder, slaying
related words killing, manslaughter; bloodshed, butchery, carnage, decimation, destruction, massacre, slaughter; assassination, execution; euthanasia, mercy killing
homily *n* a public speech usually by a member of the clergy for the purpose of giving moral guidance or uplift — see SERMON
homogenize *vb* to make agree with a single established standard or model — see STANDARDIZE
Homo sapiens *n* the human race — see MANKIND
hone *vb* **1** to make sharp or sharper — see SHARPEN
2 to make smooth by friction — see GRIND 1
honed *adj* having an edge thin enough to cut or pierce something — see SHARP 1
honest *adj* **1** being in the habit of telling the truth — see TRUTHFUL
2 conforming to a high standard of morality or virtue — see GOOD 2
3 following the accepted rules of moral conduct — see HONORABLE 1
4 free from any intent to deceive or impress others — see GUILELESS
5 free in expressing one's true feelings and opinions — see FRANK
6 guided by or in accordance with one's sense of right and wrong — see CONSCIENTIOUS 1
honestly *adv* to tell the truth — see ACTUALLY 1
honesty *n* **1** devotion to telling the truth ⟨George Washington has gone down in history for his *honesty*⟩
synonyms integrity, probity, truthfulness, veracity, verity
related words honor, incorruptibility; candidness, candor, frankness, good faith, sincerity, straightforwardness; dependability, reliability, reliableness, trustworthiness; accuracy, objectivity; authenticity, correctness, genuineness; credibility

near antonyms deception, dissembling, dissimulation, duplicity, fakery, falseness, falsity, fraudulentness, hypocrisy, insincerity; beguilement, craftiness, cunning, furtiveness, guile, insidiousness, oiliness, slickness, slipperiness, slyness, smoothness, trickery, underhandedness, wiliness; equivocation, prevarication; exaggeration, inaccuracy
antonyms deceit, deceitfulness, dishonesty, lying, mendacity, untruthfulness
2 conduct that conforms to an accepted standard of right and wrong — see MORALITY 1
3 faithfulness to high moral standards — see HONOR 1

honey *n* a person with whom one is in love — see SWEETHEART

honor *n* **1** faithfulness to high moral standards ⟨the mayor, a man of *honor,* never broke a promise to the voters⟩
synonyms honesty, integrity, probity, rectitude, righteousness, uprightness
related words blamelessness, character, conscientiousness, decency, fairness, high-mindedness, incorruptibility, justice, morality, nobility, reputability, respectability, scrupulousness, virtue, virtuousness
near antonyms corruptibility, corruption, corruptness, debasement, decadence, degeneracy, depravity, disgracefulness, disreputableness, dissipation, dissoluteness, looseness, perversion, profligacy, shamelessness, venality; blameworthiness, criminality, crookedness, dishonesty, immorality, unrighteousness, unscrupulousness; knavery, rascality, roguishness; meanness, reprehensibleness, rottenness, sinfulness, vileness, villainy, wretchedness
antonyms baseness, lowness
2 an asset that brings praise or renown — see GLORY 2
3 public acknowledgment or admiration for an achievement — see GLORY 1
4 something given in recognition of achievement — see AWARD
5 something granted as a special favor — see PRIVILEGE

honor *vb* to show appreciation, respect, or affection for (someone) with a public celebration ⟨the newlyweds were *honored* with a dinner given by the bride's grandmother⟩
synonyms fete (*or* fête), recognize
related words acknowledge, cite, commend, compliment, credit, thank; extol (*also* extoll), glorify, laud, praise; acclaim, applaud, cheer, hail, salute; celebrate, commemorate, memorialize, observe; congratulate, felicitate
near antonyms bad-mouth, defame, libel, malign, slander; boo, hiss, hoot, jeer; censure, condemn, damn, denounce, reprobate; mock, put down, ridicule, slight

honorable *adj* **1** following the accepted rules of moral conduct ⟨the only *honorable* thing to do is to admit that you were wrong and apologize⟩
synonyms decent, ethical, honest, just, noble, principled, respectable, righteous, upright, upstanding
related words decorous, proper, seemly; blameless, guiltless, irreproachable, unassailable, unimpeachable; chivalrous, high-minded, right-minded; conscientious, fair, good, incorruptible, moral, reputable, respected, scrupulous, uncorrupted, virtuous
near antonyms bad, blackguardly, corrupt, criminal, crooked, immoral, iniquitous, knavish, mean, rascally, reprehensible, roguish, rotten, scoundrelly, sinful; unfair, unscrupulous, vile, villainous, wicked, wretched; blamable, blameworthy, censurable; debased, debauched, decadent, degenerate, depraved, disgraceful, disreputable, dissipated, dissolute, libertine, loose, perverted, profligate, reprobate, shameful, unscrupulous, venal
antonyms base, dishonest, ignoble, low, unethical, unjust, unprincipled, unrighteous
2 conforming to a high standard of morality or virtue — see GOOD 2
3 guided by or in accordance with one's sense of right and wrong — see CONSCIENTIOUS 1

honorably *adv* in a manner befitting a person of the highest character and ideals — see GREATLY 1

[1]hood *n* a violent, brutal person who is often a member of an organized gang — see HOODLUM

[2]hood *n* something that covers or conceals like a piece of cloth — see CLOAK 1

hoodlum *n* a violent, brutal person who is often a member of an organized gang ⟨a couple of *hoodlums* held up the convenience store⟩
synonyms bully, gangster, goon, homeboy, hood, mobster, mug, punk, roughneck, rowdy, ruffian, thug, tough, toughie
related words cutthroat, scoundrel, villain; assassin, bandit, bravo, brigand, criminal, crook, desperado, felon, gunman, highwayman, lawbreaker, mafioso, outlaw, perpetrator, pickpocket, racketeer, robber, swindler, thief

hoodoo *n* something that brings bad luck — see JINX

hoodwink *vb* to cause to believe what is untrue — see DECEIVE

hoof (it) *vb* **1** to go on foot — see WALK
2 to perform a series of usually rhythmic bodily movements to music — see DANCE 1

hook *n* a hard strike with a part of the body or an instrument — see [1]BLOW

hook *vb* **1** to cause to turn away from a straight line — see BEND 1
2 to put or bring together so as to form a new and longer whole — see CONNECT 1
3 to take (something) without right and with an intent to keep — see STEAL 1
4 to take physical control or possession of (something) suddenly or forcibly — see CATCH 1
5 to turn away from a straight line or course — see CURVE 1

hookup *n* the state of having shared interests or efforts (as in social or business matters) — see ASSOCIATION 1

hoop *n* a circular strip — see RING 2

hoosegow *n* a place of confinement for persons held in lawful custody — see JAIL

hoot *n* **1** a loud vocal expression of strong emotion — see SHOUT
2 a vocal sound made to express scorn or disapproval — see CATCALL
3 the smallest amount or part imaginable — see JOT

hop *n* **1** a social gathering for dancing — see DANCE
2 an act of leaping into the air — see JUMP 1

hop *vb* **1** to move with a light bouncing step — see SKIP 1

2 to propel oneself upward or forward into the air — see JUMP 1

hope (for) *vb* to believe in the future occurrence of (something) — see EXPECT

hopeful *adj* **1** having qualities which inspire hope <economists are offering a *hopeful* forecast for a healthy economy in the coming year>
synonyms auspicious, bright, encouraging, fair, golden, heartening, likely, optimistic, promising, propitious, rose-colored, rosy, upbeat
related words cheering, comforting, reassuring; assured, confident, decisive, doubtless, positive, sure, unhesitating; bullish, favorable, good
near antonyms cheerless, comfortless; doubtful, dubious, uncertain; bearish, grim, negative, unfavorable
antonyms bleak, dark, desperate, discouraging, disheartening, dismal, dreary, gloomy, hopeless, inauspicious, pessimistic, unlikely, unpromising
2 pointing toward a happy outcome — see FAVORABLE 2

hopeful *n* one who seeks an office, honor, position, or award — see CANDIDATE

hopeless *adj* **1** not capable of being cured or reformed <a *hopeless* optimist who looked for the good in everyone and everything> <a *hopeless* criminal who spent most of his life in jail>
synonyms incorrigible, incurable, irrecoverable, irredeemable, irremediable, irretrievable, unrecoverable, unredeemable
related words irreparable, irreversible; unpromising; impenitent, unreformed, unregenerate, unrepentant
near antonyms reversible; promising; penitent, repentant; repairable, reparable, salvageable
antonyms correctable, curable, reclaimable, recoverable, redeemable, reformable, remediable, retrievable
2 emphasizing or expecting the worst — see PESSIMISTIC 1
3 incapable of being solved or accomplished — see IMPOSSIBLE

hopelessness *n* utter loss of hope — see DESPAIR 1

horde *n* a great number of persons or things gathered together — see CROWD 1

horn *n* something shaped like a hollow cone and used as a container — see CORNET

horrendous *adj* **1** causing fear — see FEARFUL 1
2 causing intense displeasure, disgust, or resentment — see OFFENSIVE 1
3 extremely disturbing or repellent — see HORRIBLE 1

horrible *adj* **1** extremely disturbing or repellent <a *horrible* car accident that left eyewitnesses in a state of shock>
synonyms appalling, atrocious, awful, dreadful, frightful, ghastly, grisly, gruesome, hideous, horrendous, horrid, horrifying, lurid, macabre, monstrous, nightmarish, shocking, terrible
related words bloodcurdling, dire, direful, fearful, fearsome, forbidding, formidable, frightening, hair-raising, terrifying; abhorrent, deplorable, disagreeable, disgusting, distasteful, loathsome, nauseating, obnoxious, offensive, repugnant, repulsive, revolting, sickening; abominable, evil, foul, heinous, noxious, odious, unspeakable, vile
near antonyms agreeable, appealing, attractive, enticing, inviting; cheering, comforting, soothing
2 causing fear — see FEARFUL 1
3 causing intense displeasure, disgust, or resentment — see OFFENSIVE 1

horrid *adj* **1** causing intense displeasure, disgust, or resentment — see OFFENSIVE 1
2 extremely disturbing or repellent — see HORRIBLE 1

horridness *n* the quality of inspiring intense dread or dismay — see HORROR 1

horrified *adj* filled with fear or dread — see AFRAID 1

horrify *vb* to strike with fear — see FRIGHTEN

horrifying *adj* **1** causing fear — see FEARFUL 1
2 extremely disturbing or repellent — see HORRIBLE 1

horror *n* **1** the quality of inspiring intense dread or dismay <it's difficult to even begin to comprehend the *horror* of the Holocaust>
synonyms atrociousness, atrocity, awfulness, dreadfulness, frightfulness, ghastliness, grisliness, gruesomeness, hideousness, horridness, monstrosity, repulsiveness
related words badness, baseness, diabolicalness, evil, foulness, heinousness, immorality, iniquity, invidiousness, nefariousness, ungodliness, viciousness, vileness, wickedness; accursedness, cursedness, deplorableness, despicableness, detestableness, execrableness, hatefulness, loathsomeness, reprehensibleness; creepiness, eeriness, fearfulness, fearsomeness, ghostliness, scariness; agony, hellishness, misery, torment, torture
near antonyms agreeableness, delightfulness, pleasantness; allurement, appeal, attraction, attractiveness, desirability, desirableness
2 a situation or state that causes great suffering and unhappiness — see HELL 2
3 something unpleasant to look at — see EYESORE
4 the emotion experienced in the presence or threat of danger — see FEAR

horse *n* a large hoofed domestic animal that is used for carrying or drawing loads and for riding <the mounted police stable their *horses* in the city park>
synonyms equine, nag, steed
related words colt, filly, foal, gelding, mare, stallion; bronco, mustang, pony; charger, courser, cow pony, mount, palfrey, prancer, quarter horse, racehorse, saddle horse, trotter, war-horse, workhorse; bay, black, buckskin, chestnut, dun, palomino, pinto, roan, sorrel; cob, jade, plug

horse (around) *vb* to engage in attention-getting playful or boisterous behavior — see CUT UP

horseplay *n* wildly playful or mischievous behavior <when he saw us spraying each other with the hose instead of washing the car, Dad yelled, "Cut out the *horseplay*!">
synonyms clowning, foolery, high jinks, horsing (around), monkeying, monkeyshines, roughhouse, roughhousing, shenanigans, skylarking, tomfoolery
related words buffoonery, clownishness, foolishness, funning, jesting, joking, nonsense, waggery; boisterousness, rowdiness; devilry (*or* deviltry), impishness, mischief, mischievousness, prankishness, roguishness, trickery; cavorting, frivolity, frolicking, gamboling (*or* gambolling), merrymaking, playfulness, revelry, roistering, romping, sporting, sportiveness

horse sense *n* the ability to make intelligent decisions especially in everyday matters — see COMMON SENSE

horse–trade *vb* to talk over or dispute the terms of a purchase — see BARGAIN
horsewhip *vb* to strike repeatedly with something long and thin or flexible — see WHIP 1
horsing (around) *n* wildly playful or mischievous behavior — see HORSEPLAY
hose *n* a close-fitting covering for the foot and leg — see STOCKING
hospice *n* a place that provides rooms and usually a public dining room for overnight guests — see HOTEL
hospitable *adj* showing a natural kindness and courtesy especially in social situations — see GRACIOUS 1
host *n* **1** a great number of persons or things gathered together — see CROWD 1
2 a large body of men and women organized for land warfare — see ARMY 1
hostel *n* a place that provides rooms and usually a public dining room for overnight guests — see HOTEL
hostelry *n* a place that provides rooms and usually a public dining room for overnight guests — see HOTEL
hostile *adj* **1** marked by opposition or ill will ⟨our landlord has a *hostile* attitude toward foreigners and refuses to rent to them⟩
synonyms antagonistic, inhospitable, inimical, jaundiced, negative, unfriendly, unsympathetic
related words adverse, bellicose, belligerent, clashing, conflicting, contentious, contrary, opposed, pugnacious, quarrelsome, resisting; antisocial, cold, cool, disagreeable, disapproving, distant, frigid, icy, biased, prejudiced; discourteous, impolite, rude, surly, uncivil, unfavorable, unkind, unpleasant, unsociable; acrimonious, antipathetic, bitter, hateful, malevolent, opprobrious, rancorous, spiteful, unloving, vindictive, virulent
near antonyms affable, amiable, amicable, companionable, convivial, cordial, civil, genial, gracious, gregarious, neighborly, pleasant, sociable, social, warm; affectionate, devoted, kind, loving, nice, sweet; accepting, agreeable, approving, benign, empathetic, favorable, understanding, warmhearted, welcoming
antonyms friendly, hospitable, sympathetic
2 opposed to one's interests — see ADVERSE 1
hostility *n* **1** a deep-seated ill will — see ENMITY
2 hostilities *pl* a state of armed violent struggle between states, nations, or groups — see WAR 1
hot *adj* **1** having a notably high temperature ⟨the casserole, just out of the oven, was too *hot* to eat⟩
synonyms broiling, burning, fiery, piping hot, red-hot, roasting, scalding, scorching, searing, sultry, superheated, sweltering, torrid
related words blazing, glowing, molten, sizzling; heated, overheated, reheated, warmed; snug, toasty, warm; feverish, flushed, inflamed; muggy, steamy, summery, tropical
near antonyms chilly, cool, frosty, nippy, snowy, subzero, wintry; cooled, refrigerated, unheated, unthawed; benumbed, numb, shivering; lukewarm, temperate, tepid
antonyms arctic, chill, chilled, cold, freezing, frigid, frozen, glacial, ice-cold, iced, icy
2 being or involving the latest methods, concepts, information, or styles — see MODERN
3 enjoying widespread favor or approval — see POPULAR 1
4 marked by bursts of destructive force or intense activity — see VIOLENT 1
5 showing urgent desire or interest — see EAGER
hot air *n* **1** boastful speech or writing — see BOMBAST 1
2 language that is impressive-sounding but not meaningful or sincere — see RHETORIC 1
hot–blooded *adj* having or expressing great depth of feeling — see FERVENT
hotcake *n* a flat cake made from thin batter and cooked on both sides (as on a griddle) — see PANCAKE
hotchpotch *n* an unorganized collection or mixture of various things — see MISCELLANY 1
hotel *n* a place that provides rooms and usually a public dining room for overnight guests ⟨for their 50th anniversary they stayed at one of the finest *hotels* in San Francisco⟩
synonyms caravansary (*or* caravanserai), hospice, hostel, hostelry, inn, lodge, public house, tavern
related words bed-and-breakfast; accommodations, lodgings, rest; motel, motor court, resort, spa, youth hostel; camp, campground; bunkhouse, dorm, dormitory; boardinghouse, lodging house, rooming house
hotfoot *adv* with excessive or careless speed — see HASTILY 1
hotfoot (it) *vb* to proceed or move quickly — see HURRY 2
hothouse *n* a glass-enclosed building for growing plants — see CONSERVATORY
hotness *n* the state of enjoying widespread approval — see POPULARITY
hot war *n* a state of armed violent struggle between states, nations, or groups — see WAR 1
hound *n* a domestic mammal that is related to the wolves and foxes — see DOG
hound *vb* **1** to go after or on the track of — see FOLLOW 2
2 to subject (someone) to constant scoldings and sharp reminders — see NAG
hounding *n* the act of going after or in the tracks of another — see PURSUIT
house *n* **1** a commercial or industrial activity or organization — see ENTERPRISE 1
2 a group of persons who come from the same ancestor — see FAMILY 1
3 the place where one lives — see HOME 1
4 those who live as a family in one house — see HOUSEHOLD
house *vb* **1** to provide with living quarters or shelter ⟨some of the freshmen were temporarily *housed* in the gym while the new dorm was being finished⟩
synonyms accommodate, billet, board, bunk, chamber, domicile, encamp, harbor, lodge, put up, quarter, roof, shelter, take in
related words ensconce, home, roost, secure, stable, tent
near antonyms eject, evict
2 to close or shut in by or as if by barriers — see ENCLOSE 1
house cat *n* a small domestic animal known for catching mice — see CAT 1
household *adj* **1** of or relating to a household or family — see DOMESTIC 1
2 often observed or encountered — see COMMON 1
household *n* those who live as a family in one

house ⟨a *household* that consists of a single mom, her two kids, and her widowed mother⟩
synonyms extended family, house, ménage
related words folks, kin, kindred, kinfolk, kinsfolk, kith; brood; nuclear family; clan, community
housekeeper *n* a female domestic servant — see MAID 1
housemaid *n* a female domestic servant — see MAID 1
housing *n* something that encloses another thing especially to protect it — see [1]CASE 1
hovel *n* a small, simply constructed, and often temporary dwelling — see SHACK
hover *vb* to rest or move along the surface of a liquid or in the air — see FLOAT
hover (over) *vb* to remain poised to inflict harm, danger, or distress on — see THREATEN
howbeit *adv* in spite of that — see HOWEVER
howbeit *conj* in spite of the fact that — see ALTHOUGH
however *adv* in spite of that ⟨I'm all out of eggs; *however,* I can still make us a nice breakfast⟩
synonyms howbeit, nevertheless, nonetheless, notwithstanding, still, though, withal, yet
related words after all, anyhow, regardless
howl *n* **1** a crying out in grief — see LAMENT 1
2 a loud vocal expression of strong emotion — see SHOUT
3 a violent shouting — see CLAMOR 1
howl *vb* **1** to make a long loud mournful sound ⟨several coyotes began *howling* close by as the sun went down⟩ ⟨the wind *howled* on the open plain⟩
synonyms bay, keen, wail, yowl
related words bawl, caterwaul, squall, yawp (*or* yaup), yell, yelp
2 to cry out loudly and emotionally — see SCREAM
hoydenish *adj* having qualities or traits that are traditionally considered inappropriate for a girl or woman — see UNFEMININE
hub *n* a thing or place that is of greatest importance to an activity or interest — see CENTER 1
hubbub *n* **1** a state of noisy, confused activity — see COMMOTION
2 a violent shouting — see CLAMOR 1
huckster *n* one who sells things outdoors — see PEDDLER
huddle *n* **1** a coming together of a number of persons for a specified purpose — see MEETING 1
2 a number of things considered as a unit — see GROUP 1
3 a usually small number of persons considered as a unit — see GROUP 2
huddle *vb* **1** to gather into a closely packed group — see PRESS 3
2 to lie low with the limbs close to the body — see CROUCH
hue *n* a property that becomes apparent when light falls on an object and by which things that are identical in form can be distinguished — see COLOR 1
hue and cry *n* a violent shouting — see CLAMOR 1
huff *n* **1** a state of nervous or irritated concern — see FRET
2 an outburst or display of excited anger — see TANTRUM
3 the feeling of being offended or resentful after a slight or indignity — see PIQUE
huffiness *n* readiness to show annoyance or impatience — see PETULANCE
hug *vb* to put one's arms around and press tightly — see EMBRACE 1
huge *adj* unusually large ⟨the old stadium was replaced by a *huge* new one that seats 100,000 spectators⟩
synonyms astronomical (*also* astronomic), bumper, colossal, cosmic, elephantine, enormous, giant, gigantic, grand, herculean, heroic, immense, jumbo, king-size (*or* king-sized), mammoth, massive, monster, monstrous, monumental, mountainous, prodigious, super, titanic, tremendous, vast, vasty, whacking, whopping
related words big, bulky, considerable, extensive, good, goodly, good-sized, great, gross, handsome, hefty, hulking, largish, major, sizable (*or* sizeable), substantial, voluminous; august, formidable, grandiose, imposing, lofty, majestic; cavernous, monolithic, overwhelming, staggering, stupendous, towering; boundless, cosmic, immeasurable, infinite
near antonyms little, petite, pint-size (*or* pint-sized), puny, small, smallish, undersized
antonyms bitty, diminutive, microscopic (*or* microscopical), midget, miniature, minute, pocket, pygmy, teeny, teeny-weeny, tiny, wee
hugely *adv* **1** to a great degree — see VERY 1
2 to a large extent or degree — see GREATLY 2
hugeness *n* the quality or state of being very large — see IMMENSITY
hugger–mugger *adj* **1** lacking in order, neatness, and often cleanliness — see MESSY
2 undertaken or done so as to escape being observed or known by others — see SECRET 1
hulk *n* a big clumsy often slow-witted person — see OAF
hulking *adj* **1** of a size greater than average of its kind — see LARGE
2 strongly and heavily built — see [1]HUSKY
hull *vb* to remove the natural covering of — see PEEL
hullabaloo *n* **1** a state of noisy, confused activity — see COMMOTION
2 a violent shouting — see CLAMOR 1
hum *n* a monotonous sound like that of an insect in motion ⟨we heard the *hum* of an outboard motor and a few minutes later the small craft came into sight⟩
synonyms buzz, chirr, drone, purr, thrum, whir (*also* whirr), whiz (*or* whizz), zoom
related words babble, coo, gurgle, hiss, moan, murmur, rustle, sigh, whisper; whish, zing, zip
near antonyms bawl, howl, roar, scream, screech, shriek
hum *vb* to fly, turn, or move rapidly with a fluttering or vibratory sound — see WHIRR
human *adj* relating to or characteristic of human beings ⟨it's *human* nature to care about what people think of us⟩
synonyms mortal, natural
related words anthropoid, hominid, humanlike, humanoid
near antonyms angelic (*or* angelical), divine, godlike, superhuman, supernatural; immortal, omnipotent, omniscient; animal, beastly, bestial, brute; inhuman, robotic
antonyms nonhuman
human *n* a member of the human race ⟨*humans* are the only mammals not endowed with a natu-

ral defense against the elements, such as fur or a thick hide⟩
synonyms being, bird, body, creature, customer, devil, guy, head, individual, life, man, mortal, party, person, scout, sort, soul, specimen, thing, wight
related words hominid, homo, humanoid; brother, fellow, fellowman, neighbor; celebrity, personage, personality, self, somebody
near antonyms animal, beast, brute

humane *adj* **1** having or marked by sympathy and consideration for others ⟨*humane* guards who treated the prisoners decently⟩ ⟨the Geneva conventions spelled out standards for *humane* treatment of prisoners of war⟩
synonyms beneficent, benevolent, benignant, compassionate, good-hearted, kind, kindhearted, kindly, softhearted, sympathetic, tender, tenderhearted, warmhearted
related words attentive, considerate, thoughtful; affable, benign, cordial, friendly, gentle, good, good-natured, good-tempered, gracious, mild, nice, pleasant; clement, forbearing, forgiving, lenient, merciful, soft; patient, pitying, tolerant, understanding; altruistic, brotherly, charitable, generous, greathearted, humanitarian, magnanimous, noble, openhearted, philanthropic, unselfish, unsparing
near antonyms merciless, pitiless, ruthless; inconsiderate, insensitive, thoughtless, uncaring, unthinking; grim, hard-boiled, harsh, heavy-handed, severe, stern, tough, unsentimental; hateful, malevolent, malicious, mean, spiteful, virulent
antonyms barbarous, bestial, brutal, brutish, callous, cold-blooded, cruel, hardhearted, heartless, inhuman, inhumane, insensate, savage, unfeeling, unkind, unkindly, unsympathetic
2 having or showing the capacity for sharing the feelings of another — see SYMPATHETIC 1

humanitarian *adj* having or showing a concern for the welfare of others — see CHARITABLE 1

humanity *n* **1** human beings in general — see PEOPLE 1
2 the capacity for feeling for another's unhappiness or misfortune — see HEART 1
3 the human race — see MANKIND

humankind *n* **1** human beings in general — see PEOPLE 1
2 the human race — see MANKIND

humble *adj* **1** not having or showing any feelings of superiority, self-assertiveness, or showiness ⟨a medical scientist who remained remarkably *humble* even after winning the Nobel Prize⟩ ⟨even though she'd been twice proven wrong, Janet's attitude was still far from *humble*⟩
synonyms demure, lowly, meek, modest, retiring, unassuming, unpretentious
related words acquiescent, compliant, deferential, resigned, submissive, unaggressive, unassertive, yielding; cowering, cringing, shrinking; ingenuous, naive (*or* naïve), plain, simple, unaffected; bashful, diffident, mousy (*or* mousey), overmodest, passive, quiet, reserved, shy, subdued, timid, unobtrusive
near antonyms aggressive, assertive, audacious, bold, brash, brassy, cheeky, forward; cocksure, cocky, confident, overconfident, self-confident; egocentric, egoistic, self-centered, self-satisfied; boastful, bombastic, vain, vainglorious; condescending, disdainful, dominant, dominating, domineering, imperious, lofty, lordly, magisterial, masterful, overbearing, patronizing, pontificating; flamboyant, flaunting, highfalutin, parading, ostentatious, showy
antonyms arrogant, conceited, egotistic (*or* egotistical), haughty, high-hat, pompous, presumptuous, pretentious, prideful, proud, self-assertive, self-conceited, self-important, stuck-up, supercilious, superior
2 belonging to the class of people of low social or economic rank — see IGNOBLE 1

humble *vb* to reduce to a lower standing in one's own eyes or in others' eyes ⟨Philip was utterly *humbled* by a crushing defeat in the first round of the state chess tournament⟩
synonyms abase, debase, degrade, demean, discredit, disgrace, dishonor, humiliate, lower, shame, smirch, take down
related words abash, discomfit, discountenance, embarrass, fluster, mortify; belittle, castigate, criticize, decry, depreciate, detract, disparage, minimize, put down, ridicule; bad-mouth, defame, defile, libel, malign, slander; affront, insult; censure, condemn, damn, denounce, reprobate
near antonyms acclaim, applaud, boast, celebrate, cite, commend, compliment, congratulate, decorate, eulogize, extol (*also* extoll), fete (*or* fête), hail, honor, laud, praise, salute, tout; acknowledge, recognize; highlight, play up, spotlight; dignify, ennoble, enshrine, glorify, magnify; lift, promote, raise, upgrade, uplift
antonyms aggrandize, elevate, exalt

humbleness *n* the absence of any feelings of being better than others — see HUMILITY

humbly *adv* in manner showing no signs of pride or self-assertion — see LOWLY

humbug *n* **1** an imitation that is passed off as genuine — see FAKE 1
2 language, behavior, or ideas that are absurd and contrary to good sense — see NONSENSE 1
3 one who makes false claims of identity or expertise — see IMPOSTOR

humbug *vb* to cause to believe what is untrue — see DECEIVE

humbuggery *n* language, behavior, or ideas that are absurd and contrary to good sense — see NONSENSE 1

humdrum *adj* causing weariness, restlessness, or lack of interest — see BORING

humid *adj* containing or characterized by an uncomfortable amount of moisture ⟨the air was so *humid* that our beach towels hanging on the line never really got dry⟩
synonyms muggy, sticky, sultry
related words summery, sweltering, torrid; semitropical (*also* semitropic), subtropical (*also* subtropic), tropic, tropical; close, heavy, oppressive, smothering, stifling, stuffy, suffocating; clammy, damp, dank, moist; drenched, dripping, soaked, sodden, soggy, sopping, soppy, waterlogged, wet
near antonyms bracing, cool, crisp, fresh, invigorating, refreshing; arid, baked, burned, burnt, dehydrated, desert, droughty, dusty, parched, scorched, seared, semiarid, sere, thirsty
antonyms dry

humidity *n* the amount of water suspended in the air in tiny droplets — see MOISTURE

humiliate *vb* to reduce to a lower standing in one's own eyes or in others' eyes — see HUMBLE

humility *n* the absence of any feelings of being

better than others ‹displaying genuine *humility*, the peace activist accepted the Nobel Prize on behalf of all who have worked to end the violence›
synonyms demureness, humbleness, lowliness, meekness, modesty, retiringness
related words acquiescence, compliance, deference, resignedness, submission, submissiveness; ingenuousness, naïveté (*also* naivete); directness, plainness, simpleness; bashfulness, diffidence, passiveness, passivity, quietness, reserve, reservedness, shyness, timidity, timidness
near antonyms aggressiveness, assertiveness; audaciousness, boldness, brashness, brassiness, cheek, cheekiness, cockiness, forwardness, overconfidence, presumptuousness, temerity; impudence, insolence, nerve; boastfulness, self-centeredness, self-satisfaction; vanity, vaingloriousness; condescension, disdain, imperiousness, lordliness, masterfulness; flamboyance, ostentation, ostentatiousness, showiness
antonyms arrogance, conceit, egoism, egotism, haughtiness, pompousness, pretense (*or* pretence), pretension, pretentiousness, pride, pridefulness, superciliousness, superiority

hummer *n* an ambitious person who eagerly goes after what is desired — see GO-GETTER

humming *adj* marked by much life, movement, or activity — see ALIVE 2

humor *n* **1** the amusing quality or element in something ‹Sarah failed to see any *humor* in being chased by the dog, but Tom thought it was quite funny›
synonyms drollness, funniness, hilariousness, humorousness, richness
related words amusement, enjoyment, fun, pleasure; absurdity, irony, laughableness, ludicrousness, ridiculousness; burlesque, caricature, comedy, farce, jest, lampoon, parody, satire, slapstick
near antonyms agony, anguish, heartache, misery, sorrow, woe
antonyms pathos
2 humorous entertainment — see COMEDY
3 a state of mind dominated by a particular emotion — see MOOD 1

humor *vb* to give in to (a desire) — see INDULGE

humorist *n* a person (as a writer) noted for or specializing in humor ‹Mark Twain is perhaps America's most beloved *humorist*›
synonyms card, comedian, comic, jester, joker, jokester, wag, wit
related words comedienne, entertainer; banterer, cut up, kidder, practical joker, prankster, teaser, wisecracker; buffoon, clown, fool, harlequin, zany; caricaturist, lampooner, parodist, satirist

humorless *adj* not joking or playful in mood or manner — see SERIOUS 1

humorous *adj* **1** causing or intended to cause laughter — see FUNNY 1
2 given to or marked by mature intelligent humor — see WITTY

humorousness *n* the amusing quality or element in something — see HUMOR 1

hump *vb* **1** to devote serious and sustained effort — see LABOR
2 to proceed or move quickly — see HURRY 2

hunch *vb* to lie low with the limbs close to the body — see CROUCH

hung *also* **hanged** *adj* bending downward or forward — see NODDING

hunger *n* **1** a need or desire for food ‹no amount of *hunger* would induce me to eat octopus›
synonyms appetite, emptiness, famishment
related words rapaciousness, ravenousness, voracity; malnutrition, starvation, undernourishment; craving, sweet tooth; stomach; famine, fast, hunger strike; gluttony, gourmandism, greed, hoggishness
near antonyms fill, fullness, glut, repletion, satiation, satiety, satisfaction
2 a strong wish for something — see DESIRE
3 urgent desire or interest — see EAGERNESS

hunger (for) *vb* to have an earnest wish to own or enjoy — see DESIRE

hungry *adj* **1** feeling a desire or need for food ‹John was still *hungry* after eating only a muffin for breakfast›
synonyms empty, famished, starved, starving
related words rapacious, ravenous, voracious, wolfish; malnourished, underfed, undernourished; gluttonous, gormandizing, greedy, hoggish, insatiable, piggish
near antonyms engorged, glutted, gorged, overfed, overfull, replete, sated, satiated, stuffed, surfeited
antonyms full, satisfied
2 showing urgent desire or interest — see EAGER

hung up *adj* **1** having extreme or relentless concern ‹Stephanie's parents are already *hung up* about her getting into a good college, and she's only six years old›
synonyms obsessed
related words absorbed, anxious, concerned, distracted, engaged, engrossed, full, involved, occupied, prepossessed, preoccupied, worried; ardent, crazy, fervent, fervid, foolish, impassioned, nuts, passionate, silly
near antonyms apathetic, cool, detached, dispassionate, unconcerned, unenthusiastic, uninterested, uninvolved
2 feeling or showing uncomfortable feelings of uncertainty — see NERVOUS 1

hunk *n* a small uneven mass — see LUMP 1

hunt *n* an act or process of looking carefully or thoroughly for someone or something — see SEARCH

hunt *vb* **1** to seek out (game) for food or sport ‹Indians of the plains *hunted* buffalo for food, clothing, and shelter›
synonyms chase, stalk
related words capture, drag, net, snare, trap; ferret, dog, hawk, hound; pursue, run down, track, trail; gun (for), harpoon, kill, shoot; poach
2 to go in search of — see SEEK 1
3 to go into or range over for purposes of discovery — see EXPLORE 2

hunt (down *or* up) *vb* to come upon after searching, study, or effort — see FIND 1

hunt (through) *vb* to look through (as a place) carefully or thoroughly in an effort to find or discover something — see SEARCH 1

hunter *n* a person who hunts game ‹*hunters* must have a license to shoot deer›
synonyms huntsman
related words huntress, sportsman, sportswoman; archer, gunner; falconer, hawker; hunter-gatherer, trapper; poacher

huntsman *n* a person who hunts game — see HUNTER

hurdle *n* something that makes movement or progress more difficult — see ENCUMBRANCE

hurl *vb* to send through the air especially with a quick forward motion of the arm — see THROW

hurly–burly *n* a state of noisy, confused activity — see COMMOTION

hurried *adj* acting or done with excessive or careless speed — see HASTY 1

hurriedly *adv* with excessive or careless speed — see HASTILY 1

hurry *n* **1** excited and often showy or disorderly speed ⟨after all her *hurry* to get her history report done on time, Elizabeth learned that it wasn't due till the following week⟩
synonyms haste, hastiness, hustle, precipitation, precipitousness, rush
related words bustle, flurry, flutter, scurry, scuttle, stir, whirl; beeline, dash, scramble, stampede; hotheadedness, impetuosity, impetuousness, impulsiveness, rashness; fleetness, quickness, rapidity, rapidness, speed, speediness, swiftness; celerity, dispatch, expeditiousness, promptness
near antonyms dilatoriness, lateness, pokiness, procrastination, slowness; languor, leisureliness, lethargy, sluggishness, torpor; inaction, inactivity, inertia, inertness, quiescence
antonyms deliberateness, deliberation
2 a high rate of movement or performance — see SPEED

hurry *vb* **1** to cause to move or proceed fast or faster ⟨the new nursing staff was *hurried* through the orientation because they were so desperately needed on the ward⟩
synonyms accelerate, hasten, quicken, rush, speed (up), whisk
related words drive, goad, prod, propel, push, race, spur, stir, urge; advance, aid, dispatch, ease, encourage, expedite, facilitate, forward, further
near antonyms delay, hamper, hinder, restrain; brake, check, stay
antonyms decelerate, retard, slow (down)
2 to proceed or move quickly ⟨if we *hurry,* we'll make the four o'clock train⟩
synonyms barrel, bolt, bowl, breeze, career, course, dash, fly, hasten, hotfoot (it), hump, hurtle, hustle, pelt, race, rip, rocket, run, rush, rustle, scoot, scurry, scuttle, shoot, speed, step (along), tear, trot, whirl, whisk, zip, zoom
related words dart, flit, scamper, scud, scuffle; stampede, streak, whiz (*or* whizz); gallop, jog, sprint; accelerate, quicken; catch up, fast-forward, outpace, outrun, outstrip, overtake
phrases shake a leg
near antonyms dally, dawdle, drag, lag, linger, loiter, tarry; amble, lumber, plod, saunter, shuffle, stroll; decelerate, slow (down *or* up)
antonyms crawl, creep, poke

hurt *n* something that causes loss or pain — see INJURY 1

hurt *vb* **1** to feel or cause physical pain ⟨my head *hurts*⟩ ⟨a bad sprain that really *hurts*⟩ ⟨I *hurt* all over⟩
synonyms ache, pain, smart
related words bleed, bite, burn, chafe, cramp, fester, itch, nag, pinch, pound, rack, sting, swell, throb, tingle, twinge; agonize, suffer
2 to reduce the soundness, effectiveness, or perfection of — see DAMAGE 1
3 to cause bodily damage to — see INJURE 1
4 to feel deep sadness or mental pain — see GRIEVE

hurtful *adj* **1** causing or capable of causing harm — see HARMFUL
2 hard to accept or bear especially emotionally — see BITTER 2

hurting *adj* causing or feeling bodily pain — see PAINFUL 1

hurtle *vb* **1** to proceed or move quickly — see HURRY 2
2 to send through the air especially with a quick forward motion of the arm — see THROW

husband *n* the male partner in a marriage ⟨she and her *husband* just celebrated their 50th wedding anniversary⟩
synonyms man, old man
related words consort, mate, partner, spouse; bridegroom, groom; widower

husbandry *n* **1** careful management of material resources — see ECONOMY
2 the science or occupation of cultivating the soil, producing crops, and raising livestock — see AGRICULTURE

hush *n* **1** a state of freedom from storm or disturbance — see CALM
2 the near or complete absence of sound — see SILENCE 2

hush *vb* **1** to become still and orderly — see QUIET 1
2 to stop talking — see SHUT UP
3 to stop the noise or speech of — see SILENCE 1

hush (up) *vb* to keep from being publicly known — see SUPPRESS 1

hushed *adj* **1** free from disturbing noise or uproar — see QUIET 1
2 free from storms or physical disturbance — see CALM 1
3 mostly or entirely without sound — see SILENT 3
4 not known or meant to be known by the general populace — see PRIVATE 1

husk *n* something that encloses another thing especially to protect it — see [1]CASE 1

husk *vb* to remove the natural covering of — see PEEL

[1]**husky** *adj* strongly and heavily built ⟨a *husky* weight lifter⟩
synonyms beefy, brawny, burly, hulking
related words able-bodied, athletic, heavy, hefty, herculean, mighty, muscle-bound, muscular, powerful, robust, rugged, stalwart, strapping, strong, sturdy; chunky, compact, heavyset, solid, squat, squatty, stocky, thickset; dumpy, lumpish, portly, pudgy, stout
near antonyms lean, light, lightweight, slender, slight, slim, svelte, sylphlike, thin, willowy; bony, gangling, gangly, gaunt, gawky, lanky, scrawny, skinny, spare, twiggy; sinewy, spidery, wiry; delicate, emaciated, fragile, frail, puny, weakly

[2]**husky** *adj* harsh and dry in sound — see HOARSE

hustle *n* **1** a scheme in which the victim is cheated out of his money after first gaining his trust — see CONFIDENCE GAME
2 excited and often showy or disorderly speed — see HURRY 1
3 readiness to engage in daring or difficult activity — see ENTERPRISE 2

hustle *vb* **1** to devote serious and sustained effort — see LABOR
2 to proceed or move quickly — see HURRY 2
3 to rob by the use of trickery or threats — see FLEECE

hustler *n* an ambitious person who eagerly goes after what is desired — see GO-GETTER

hut *n* a small, simply constructed, and often temporary dwelling — see SHACK

hutch *n* **1** a small, simply constructed, and often temporary dwelling — see SHACK
2 a storage case typically having doors and shelves — see CABINET

hybrid *adj* being offspring produced by parents of different races, breeds, species, or genera — see MIXED 1

hybrid *n* an offspring of parents with different genes especially when of different races, breeds, species, or genera ⟨a tangelo is a *hybrid* of the tangerine and the grapefruit⟩
synonyms cross, crossbreed, mongrel
related words mulatto
near antonyms purebred, thoroughbred

hygienic *adj* free from filth, infection, or dangers to health — see SANITARY

hymn *n* a religious song ⟨our Sunday church services always open with a *hymn*⟩
synonyms anthem, canticle, carol, chorale, psalm, spiritual
related words dirge, lament, requiem, threnody; Gloria Patri, hallelujah, paean; mass, oratorio; processional, recessional

hymnal *n* a book of hymns ⟨*hymnals* are distributed among the congregation before the church service so everyone can join in the singing⟩
synonyms hymnbook, psalmody
related words breviary, missal, Psalter, songster

hymnbook *n* a book of hymns — see HYMNAL

hyperbole *n* the representation of something in terms that go beyond the facts — see EXAGGERATION

hypercritical *adj* given to making or expressing unfavorable judgments about things — see CRITICAL 1

hyperventilate *vb* to breathe hard, quickly, or with difficulty — see GASP

hypnosis *n* the art or act of inducing in a person a sleep-like state during which he or she readily follows suggestions ⟨with *hypnosis* there's some question as to just how involuntary the actions of the hypnotized person really are⟩
synonyms hypnotism, mesmerism
related words bewitchment, enchantment, spellbinding

hypnotic *adj* tending to cause sleep ⟨her eyes soon grew heavy from the *hypnotic* rhythm of the train's wheels⟩
synonyms drowsy, narcotic, opiate, slumberous (*or* slumbrous)
related words depressant, relaxant, sedative, tranquilizing (*also* tranquillizing); calming, lulling, quieting, relaxing, restful, settling, soothing; analgesic, anesthetic, anesthetizing, benumbing, deadening, dulling, numbing; hypnotizing, mesmerizing, stupefying
near antonyms arousing, awakening, energizing, invigorating, rousing, stimulating, wakening, waking
antonyms stimulant

hypnotism *n* the art or act of inducing in a person a sleep-like state during which he or she readily follows suggestions — see HYPNOSIS

hypnotize *vb* to hold the attention of as if by a spell — see ENTHRALL 1

hypocrisy *n* the pretending of having virtues, principles, or beliefs that one in fact does not have ⟨the *hypocrisy* of people who claim to care about the environment but ride around in gas-guzzlers⟩
synonyms cant, dissembling, dissimulation, insincerity, piousness, sanctimoniousness
related words deception, deceptiveness, dishonesty, falsity, pretense, pretension, pretentiousness, self-righteousness, self-satisfaction; duplicity, fakery, falseness, fraudulentness, shamming; artificiality, glibness, oiliness, smoothness, unctuousness
near antonyms candor, honesty, openness, probity, straightforwardness, truthfulness; artlessness, guilelessness, naturalness, unaffectedness
antonyms genuineness, sincerity

hypocritical *adj* not being or expressing what one appears to be or express — see INSINCERE

hypodermic *n* a slender hollow instrument by which material is put into or taken from the body through the skin — see NEEDLE 1

hypodermic needle *n* a slender hollow instrument by which material is put into or taken from the body through the skin — see NEEDLE 1

hypodermic syringe *n* a slender hollow instrument by which material is put into or taken from the body through the skin — see NEEDLE 1

hypothesis *n* an idea that is the starting point for making a case or conducting an investigation — see THEORY

hypothetical *adj* existing only as an assumption or speculation — see THEORETICAL 1

hysteria *n* a state of wildly excited activity or emotion — see FRENZY

hysterical *adj* **1** causing or intended to cause laughter — see FUNNY 1
2 feeling overwhelming fear or worry — see FRANTIC 1

ice–cold *adj* having a low or subnormal temperature — see COLD 1

icy *adj* **1** having a low or subnormal temperature — see COLD 1
2 lacking in friendliness or warmth of feeling — see COLD 2

idea *n* something imagined or pictured in the mind ⟨my *idea* of the perfect vacation spot is an unspoiled beach⟩
synonyms concept, conception, image, impression, notion, picture, thought
related words apprehension, premonition, presentiment; chimera, illusion, phantasm; caprice, conceit, fancy, freak, notion, vagary, whim; observa-

tion, perception, reflection; assumption, belief, conclusion, conviction; conjecture, guess, hunch, hypothesis, speculation, supposition, surmise, theory; brainstorm, inspiration
near antonyms actuality, fact, reality

ideal *adj* being entirely without fault or flaw — see PERFECT 1

ideal *n* **1** someone of such unequaled perfection as to deserve imitation ⟨she's our *ideal* of the concerned, caring physician⟩
synonyms beau ideal, classic, exemplar, model, nonpareil, paragon
related words role model; embodiment, epitome, incarnation, manifestation, personification; archetype, example, paradigm, pattern; guideline, principle, rule; gauge (*also* gage), standard, touchstone; essence, quintessence; acme, apex, culmination, peak, pinnacle, summit, zenith
2 the most perfect type or example — see QUINTESSENCE 1

idealist *n* one whose conduct is guided more by the image of perfection than by the real world ⟨an *idealist* sees the best in everyone, regardless of how they behave⟩
synonyms dreamer, romantic, romanticist, utopian, visionary
related words sentimentalist; daydreamer, optimist, theorist; perfectionist; thinker
near antonyms cynic, defeatist, pessimist
antonyms pragmatist, realist

idealize *vb* to represent or think of as better than reality ⟨he had a tendency to *idealize* his heroes and believe they could do no wrong⟩
synonyms glamorize (*also* glamourize), glorify, romanticize
related words daydream, imagine, romance, theorize, vision; better, perfect
near antonyms blame, condemn, criticize, denounce; worsen

ideally *adv* without any flaws or errors — see PERFECTLY 1

idée fixe *n* something about which one is constantly thinking or concerned — see FIXATION

identical *adj* **1** being one and not another — see SAME 2
2 resembling another in every respect — see SAME 1

identicalness *n* the state of being exactly alike — see IDENTITY 1

identify *vb* **1** to find out or establish the identity of ⟨with a quick look at everyone's tongue, Mom was able to *identify* the person who had sneaked a piece of blueberry pie⟩
synonyms distinguish, pinpoint, single (out)
related words diagnose; determine, find; locate, pick out, place, recognize, spot; check, examine, inspect, investigate, notice, observe, scrutinize; betray, disclose, discover, reveal
near antonyms camouflage, conceal, disguise, hide; counterfeit, feign, sham, simulate
2 to think of (something) in combination — see ASSOCIATE 2

identifying *adj* serving to identify as belonging to an individual or group — see CHARACTERISTIC 1

identity *n* **1** the state of being exactly alike ⟨although the covers of the two paperback editions of the novel are different, there's a complete *identity* in the texts⟩
synonyms identicalness, sameness
related words oneness; homogeneity, homology; equality, equivalence; accordance, agreement, conformity, congruity, correspondence, likeness, resemblance, similarity
near antonyms alteration, change, modification, variation; distinction, distinctiveness, distinctness, exoticness, individuality, separateness, separation, uniqueness, unusualness; deviance, divergence; variance; incompatibility, incongruity, incongruousness; contrast
antonyms difference, disagreement, discrepancy, disparateness, disparity, dissimilarity, unlikeness
2 the set of qualities that make a person different from other people — see INDIVIDUALITY

ideology *n* the basic beliefs or guiding principles of a person or group — see CREED 1

idiocy *n* a foolish act or idea — see FOLLY 1

idiom *n* a sequence of words having a specific meaning — see PHRASE

idiosyncrasy *n* an odd or peculiar habit ⟨his only *idiosyncrasy* was collecting pencil erasers and making little dolls out of them⟩
synonyms crotchet, eccentricity, mannerism, oddity, peculiarity, quirk, singularity, trick
related words affectation, airs; attribute, characteristic, mark, property, trait; custom, habit, pattern, practice (*also* practise), way, wont; addiction; abnormality, perversion; disposition, genius, leaning, partiality; bent, inclination, penchant, predilection, predisposition, proclivity, propensity, tendency, turn; attitude, character, humor, identity, individuality, nature, personality, temperament
near antonyms conformity, sameness

idiot *n* a stupid person ⟨only an *idiot* would jump off a bridge just because their friends told them to⟩
synonyms blockhead, cretin, dodo, dolt, donkey, dope, dork [*slang*], dumbbell, dummy, dunce, fathead, goon, half-wit, ignoramus, imbecile, jackass, knothead, moron, nincompoop, ninny, nitwit, numskull (*or* numbskull), pinhead, simpleton, stock, turkey
related words booby, fool, goose, loony (*also* looney), lunatic, madman, nut, zany; loser; gawk; featherbrain, scatterbrain; beast, boor, cad, churl, clown, creep, cur, heel, jerk, skunk, snake, stinker, villain
near antonyms egghead, intellectual, sage, thinker
antonyms brain, genius

idle *vb* to spend time doing nothing ⟨she likes to *idle* during the summer even though her parents always tell her to get out and do something⟩
synonyms dally, dawdle, dillydally, hang around, hang out, loaf, loll, lounge
related words fiddle, fool, mess, monkey, play, potter, putter, trifle; estivate, hibernate; lag, linger, loiter, poke, relax, rest, tarry; amble, mosey, saunter, stroll; bum, furlough, goldbrick, malinger
phrases kill time, lie around, mark time, waste time
near antonyms drudge, grind, grub, hump, hustle, labor, moil, peg, plod, plow, plug, slave, sweat, toil, travail, work; apply, buckle (down); exert, put out

idle *adj* **1** not being in a state of use, activity, or employment — see INACTIVE 2
2 not easily aroused to action or work — see LAZY

idleness *n* **1** an inclination not to do work or engage in activities — see LAZINESS

2 lack of action or activity — see INACTION
3 lack of use — see DISUSE
idler *n* a lazy person — see LAZYBONES
idolater *or* **idolator** *n* a person who does not worship the God of the Bible — see HEATHEN 1
idolatry *n* excessive admiration of or devotion to a person — see WORSHIP
idolization *n* excessive admiration of or devotion to a person — see WORSHIP
idolize *vb* to love or admire too much ⟨she *idolized* her big sister⟩
synonyms adore, adulate, canonize, deify, dote (on), worship
related words appreciate, cherish, esteem, prize, treasure, value; fancy, favor, like, prefer; regard; respect, revere, venerate; approve, endorse (*also* indorse), support
near antonyms abhor, abominate, despise, detest, disdain, dislike, hate, loathe; belittle, deprecate, disparage, put down
idolizing *adj* reflecting great admiration or devotion — see WORSHIPFUL
ignitable *adj* capable of catching or being set on fire — see COMBUSTIBLE
ignite *vb* to set (something) on fire — see BURN 2
ignited *adj* being on fire — see ABLAZE 1
ignoble *adj* **1** belonging to the class of people of low social or economic rank ⟨an *ignoble* child cannot grow up to be king⟩
synonyms baseborn, common, humble, inferior, low, lower-class, lowly, mean, plebeian, proletarian, vulgar
related words bourgeois, middle-class; peasant, plain, poor, simple, working-class
near antonyms eminent, illustrious, notable, prominent
antonyms aristocratic, high, highborn, lofty, noble, wellborn
2 not following or in accordance with standards of honor and decency ⟨cheating on a test is an *ignoble* act and can get you expelled⟩
synonyms base, contemptible, despicable, detestable, dirty, dishonorable, low, mean, snide, sordid, vile, wretched
related words bad, black, evil, foul, immoral, iniquitous, wicked, wrong; cruel, nasty, vicious; blamable, blameworthy, censurable, reprehensible; corrupt, debased, debauched, degenerate, depraved, dissolute, perverted; atrocious, villainous; unethical, unprincipled, unscrupulous; discreditable, disgraceful, disreputable, ignominious, shameful
near antonyms ethical, honest, just, principled, righteous, right-minded, scrupulous; commendable, excellent, exemplary, good, moral, right; decent, proper, reputable, respectable, seemly; blameless, guiltless; incorruptible, irreproachable; uncorrupted, unerring
antonyms high, high-minded, honorable, lofty, noble, straight, upright, venerable, virtuous
ignominious *adj* not respectable — see DISREPUTABLE
ignominy *n* the state of having lost the esteem of others — see DISGRACE 1
ignoramus *n* a stupid person — see IDIOT
ignorance *n* **1** the state of being unaware or uninformed ⟨*ignorance* of the law is no excuse⟩
synonyms obliviousness, unawareness, unfamiliarity
related words callowness, greenness, inexperience, innocence, naïveté (*also* naivete), rawness, simpleness, unsophistication
near antonyms experience, know-how; sophistication
antonyms acquaintance, awareness, familiarity
2 the state of being unlearned ⟨with such vast sums spent on education, the level of *ignorance* among graduating seniors is a national disgrace⟩
synonyms illiteracy
related words brainlessness, dumbness, idiocy, imbecility, stupidity; philistinism; foolishness, mindlessness, senselessness, witlessness
near antonyms education, instruction, training; enlightenment, knowledge; erudition, scholarship
antonyms learning, literacy
ignorant *adj* **1** lacking in education or the knowledge gained from books ⟨the teacher was committed to educating the children of those poor, *ignorant* farmers⟩
synonyms benighted, dark, illiterate, nonliterate, simple, uneducated, uninstructed, unlearned, unlettered, unread, unschooled, untaught, untutored
related words lowbrow, uncultivated, uncultured; callow, green, inexperienced, innocent, naive (*or* naïve); unsophisticated; raw, untrained; brainless, dumb, idiotic, imbecilic, moronic, stupid, witless; foolish, senseless, silly
near antonyms brilliant, intelligent, smart; experienced, expert, trained; erudite, learned, scholarly; cultivated, cultured, highbrow, intellectual; sophisticated; acquainted, aware, familiar
antonyms educated, knowledgeable, literate, schooled
2 not informed about or aware of something ⟨he was *ignorant* of their plans⟩
synonyms oblivious, unacquainted, unaware, unconscious, ungrounded, uninformed, unknowing, unmindful, unwitting
related words uneducated, unschooled, untaught; absent, absentminded, abstracted, heedless, inattentive
near antonyms conversant, educated, knowledgeable, schooled, taught; heedful, observant; sensitive, sentient
antonyms acquainted, aware, cognizant, conscious, conversant, grounded, informed, knowing, mindful, witting
ignore *vb* **1** to fail to give proper attention to — see NEGLECT 1
2 to overlook or dismiss as of little importance — see EXCUSE 1
ilk *n* a number of persons or things that are grouped together because they have something in common — see SORT 1
ill *adj* **1** affected with nausea — see NAUSEOUS
2 causing or capable of causing harm — see HARMFUL
3 temporarily suffering from a disorder of the body — see SICK 1
ill *adv* in a manner so as to cause loss or suffering — see HARDLY 1
ill *n* **1** an abnormal state that disrupts a plant's or animal's normal bodily functioning — see DISEASE
2 that which is morally unacceptable — see EVIL
ill–advised *adj* showing poor judgment especially in personal relationships or social situations — see INDISCREET

ill–bred *adj* **1** lacking in refinement or good taste — see COARSE 2
2 showing a lack of manners or consideration for others — see IMPOLITE

illegal *adj* **1** contrary to or forbidden by law ⟨it is *illegal* to steal⟩
synonyms criminal, illegitimate, illicit, unlawful, wrongful
related words bad, evil, immoral, shameful, sinful, unethical, wicked, wrong; blamable, blameworthy, censurable, reprehensible; banned, barred, disallowed, discouraged, forbidden, interdicted, outlawed, prohibited, proscribed; unauthorized, unlicensed, unsanctioned; corrupt, unprincipled, unscrupulous, villainous
near antonyms ethical, good, just, principled, right, righteous, virtuous; allowed, permitted; authorized, licensed (*also* licenced); approved, endorsed, sanctioned; abetted, encouraged, promoted, suggested, supported; correct, decent, decorous, proper, seemly
antonyms lawful, legal, legitimate
2 not being in accordance with the rules or standards of what is fair in sport — see FOUL 2

illegitimate *adj* **1** born to a father and mother who are not married ⟨despite being *illegitimate*, Alexander Hamilton rose to greatness⟩
synonyms baseborn, bastard, misbegotten
related words fatherless, motherless; adopted, orphaned
antonyms legitimate
2 contrary to or forbidden by law — see ILLEGAL 1

ill–fated *adj* having, prone to, or marked by bad luck — see UNLUCKY

ill–favored *adj* unpleasant to look at — see UGLY 1

ill–humored *adj* having or showing a habitually bad temper — see ILL-TEMPERED

illicit *adj* contrary to or forbidden by law — see ILLEGAL 1

illimitable *adj* being or seeming to be without limits — see INFINITE

illiteracy *n* the state of being unlearned — see IGNORANCE 2

illiterate *adj* lacking in education or the knowledge gained from books — see IGNORANT 1

ill–mannered *adj* showing a lack of manners or consideration for others — see IMPOLITE

ill–natured *adj* having or showing a habitually bad temper — see ILL-TEMPERED

illness *n* **1** an abnormal state that disrupts a plant's or animal's normal bodily functioning — see DISEASE
2 the condition of not being in good health — see SICKNESS 1

illogical *adj* not using or following good reasoning ⟨the *illogical* claim that playing basketball makes people taller because one sees so many tall players⟩ ⟨*illogical* people are likely to believe every sensational claim on TV⟩
synonyms fallacious, invalid, irrational, nonrational, unreasonable, unreasoning, unsound, weak
related words misleading, specious; ill-advised, unconsidered, unreasoned; inconsistent; absurd, asinine, foolish, meaningless, nonsensical, preposterous, senseless, silly; odd, peculiar, strange, unusual, weird; insane, mad, nutty, wacky; disordered, disorganized, rambling, random; unconvincing, unsatisfying; inexplicable, unaccountable, unexplainable
near antonyms commonsense, sane, sensible, sober, wise; enlightened, informed, just, justified, reasoned; ordered, organized; clear, cogent, compelling, convincing, credible, persuasive, plausible, satisfying, solid; certain, sure, true; confirmed, corroborated, demonstrated, established, substantiated, validated, well-founded
antonyms logical, rational, reasonable, sound, valid

ill–starred *adj* having, prone to, or marked by bad luck — see UNLUCKY

ill–tempered *adj* having or showing a habitually bad temper ⟨an *ill-tempered* cat will scratch⟩
synonyms bearish, bilious, cantankerous, disagreeable, dyspeptic, ill-humored, ill-natured, ornery, splenetic, surly
related words choleric, crabby, cranky, crotchety, fussy, grouchy, grumpy, querulous; irascible, irritable, peevish, petulant, quick-tempered, snappish, testy, touchy; argumentative, contentious, contrary; angry, exasperated, indignant, irate, mad, upset, uptight; depressed, dour, glum, morose, sullen
near antonyms agreeable, amicable, congenial, friendly, pleasant; benign, gentle, kind, nice, sweet; bubbly, cheerful, cheery, effervescent, exuberant, high-spirited, lighthearted, lively, joyful, vivacious; content, glad, happy; calm, placid, serene; long-suffering, patient, tolerant
antonyms amiable, good-natured, good-tempered

ill–treat *vb* to inflict physical or emotional harm upon — see ABUSE 1

illuminate *vb* **1** to supply with light ⟨a floor lamp *illuminates* a living room rather nicely⟩
synonyms illumine, irradiate, light, lighten
related words brighten; beam, beat (down), radiate, shine; floodlight; highlight, spotlight; blaze, burn, fire, flame, glare, glow, ignite, incinerate, kindle; bedazzle, blind, daze, dazzle; gleam, glisten, glitter
near antonyms dim, dull, obscure; cover, shroud, veil; douse, extinguish, put out, quench, snuff (out)
antonyms blacken, darken
2 to make plain or understandable — see EXPLAIN 1

illuminated *adj* filled with much light — see BRIGHT 2

illumination *n* **1** a statement that makes something clear — see EXPLANATION 1
2 the quality or state of having or giving off light — see BRILLIANCE 1
3 the steady giving off of the form of radiation that makes vision possible — see LIGHT 1

illuminative *adj* serving to explain — see EXPLANATORY

illumine *vb* to supply with light — see ILLUMINATE 1

illumined *adj* filled with much light — see BRIGHT 2

ill–use *vb* to inflict physical or emotional harm upon — see ABUSE 1

illusion *n* **1** a conception or image created by the imagination and having no objective reality — see FANTASY 1
2 a false idea or belief — see FALLACY 1

illustrate *vb* **1** to show or make clear by using examples ⟨she *illustrated* her point with a story about her last experiment and the results it provided⟩

synonyms demonstrate, exemplify, instance
related words cite, mention, quote; name, specify; analyze, break down; clarify, clear (up), explain, explicate, expound; edify, elucidate, enlighten; illuminate; construe, interpret; simplify, spell out; detail, enumerate, list
near antonyms becloud, blur, cloud, darken, fog, muddy, obscure; confuse, perplex, puzzle
2 to make plain or understandable — see EXPLAIN 1

illustration *n* **1** something that visually explains or decorates a text ⟨the book on birds had gorgeous *illustrations*⟩
synonyms diagram, figure, graphic, plate
related words drawing, illumination, image, pictogram, pictograph, picture; caption, key, legend; depiction, portrait, portrayal, representation; clarification, elucidation, explanation, explication, exposition
2 a statement that makes something clear — see EXPLANATION 1
3 a two-dimensional design intended to look like a person or thing — see PICTURE 1
4 one of a group or collection that shows what the whole is like — see EXAMPLE

illustrative *adj* serving to explain — see EXPLANATORY

illustrious *adj* standing above others in rank, importance, or achievement — see EMINENT

image *n* **1** something or someone that strongly resembles another ⟨the girl is growing up to be the perfect *image* of her mother⟩
synonyms carbon copy, counterpart, double, duplicate, duplication, facsimile, likeness, match, picture, replica, ringer, spit
related words effigy, portrait, portrayal; companion, counterpart, fellow, mate; equal, equivalent, identical twin; analogue (*or* analog), parallel
near antonyms antithesis, converse, opposite, reverse
2 a two-dimensional design intended to look like a person or thing — see PICTURE 1
3 something imagined or pictured in the mind — see IDEA

image *vb* **1** to present a picture of — see PICTURE 1
2 to give a representation or account of in words — see DESCRIBE 1
3 to reproduce or show (an exact likeness) as a mirror would — see REFLECT

imaginary *adj* not real and existing only in the imagination ⟨his *imaginary* friend had purple hair⟩
synonyms chimerical, fabulous, fanciful, fantastic, fictional, fictitious, imagined, invented, made-up, make-believe, mythical (*or* mythic), phantasmal, phantom, pretend, unreal
related words fabled, legendary, romantic; abstract, hypothetical, theoretical (*also* theoretic); unbelievable, unconvincing, unlikely; conceived, envisaged, pictured, visualized; deceptive, delusional, delusive, hallucinatory, illusory; concocted, fabricated
near antonyms authentic, genuine, true; factual, verifiable, verified; believable, convincing, realistic; corporeal, material, physical, solid, substantial; palpable, tangible
antonyms actual, existent, existing, real

imagination *n* the ability to form mental images of things that either are not physically present or have never been conceived or created by others ⟨a cartoonist needs a good *imagination* in order to think up and draw interesting cartoons⟩
synonyms creativity, fancy, fantasy (*also* phantasy), imaginativeness, invention, inventiveness
related words brainstorm, brainstorming, inspiration; fecundity, fertility; ingenuity, originality; versatility; chimera, daydream, delusion, dream, figment, hallucination, illusion, mirage, phantasm, pipe dream; envisaging, visualization
near antonyms literalness

imaginative *adj* **1** having the skill and imagination to create new things — see CREATIVE 1
2 showing a use of the imagination and creativity especially in inventing — see CLEVER 1

imaginativeness *n* **1** the ability to form mental images of things that either are not physically present or have never been conceived or created by others — see IMAGINATION
2 the skill and imagination to create new things — see CREATIVITY 1

imagine *vb* **1** to form a mental picture of ⟨she *imagined* meeting the members of her favorite rock band face-to-face⟩
synonyms conceive, dream, envisage, fancy, picture, vision, visualize
related words daydream, stargaze; hallucinate; reflect, relive, reminisce; contemplate, meditate, muse, ponder, ruminate; concoct, fabricate, invent, make up, manufacture, plan, project
2 to have as an opinion — see BELIEVE 2

imagined *adj* not real and existing only in the imagination — see IMAGINARY

imbecile *n* a stupid person — see IDIOT

imbecility *n* a foolish act or idea — see FOLLY 1

imbibe *vb* **1** to swallow in liquid form — see DRINK 1
2 to take in (something liquid) through small openings — see ABSORB 1

imbue *vb* to cause (as a person) to become filled or saturated with a certain quality or principle — see INFUSE

imitate *vb* **1** to use (someone or something) as the model for one's speech, mannerisms, or behavior ⟨teenage boys who *imitate* whichever rock stars are hot⟩
synonyms ape, copy, emulate, mime, mimic
related words burlesque, caricature, lampoon, mock, parody, travesty; impersonate, perform, play; pantomime
2 to copy or exaggerate (someone or something) in order to make fun of — see MIMIC 1
3 to make an exact likeness of — see COPY 1

imitation *adj* being such in appearance only and made with or manufactured from usually cheaper materials ⟨you have to be careful not to buy an *imitation* diamond passed off as the real thing⟩
synonyms artificial, factitious, bogus, fake, false, man-made, mimic, mock, sham, simulated, substitute, synthetic
related words dummy, phony (*also* phoney); cultured, manufactured; unauthentic; adulterated, doctored, fudged, juggled, manipulated, tampered (with); concocted, fabricated; counterfeit, deceptive, forged, fraudulent, misleading; affected, feigned, pseudo, spurious
near antonyms authentic, bona fide, legitimate, true; premium, quality, valuable; pure, unadulterated
antonyms genuine, natural, real

imitation *n* something that is made to look exactly like something else — see COPY
imitative *adj* using or marked by the use of something else as a basis or model ⟨your writing style tends to be *imitative* of whichever author you've recently read⟩
synonyms apish, emulative, formulaic, mimetic, mimic, slavish, unoriginal
related words copied, cribbed, plagiarized; artificial, bogus, factitious, fake, false, imitation, manmade, mock, sham, simulated, substitute, synthetic; duplicated, photocopied, reduplicated, reproduced, transcribed; backup; counterfeit, deceptive, forged, fraudulent, misleading; uninspired
near antonyms authentic, bona fide, legitimate, true; genuine, natural, real; classic, ideal, model
antonyms archetypal, original
imitator *n* **1** a person who adopts the appearance or behavior of another especially in an obvious way — see COPYCAT
2 a person who imitates another's voice and mannerisms for comic effect — see MIMIC
immaculate *adj* **1** free from any trace of the coarse or indecent — see CHASTE
2 free from dirt or stain — see CLEAN 1
immaterial *adj* **1** not composed of matter ⟨it is only possible to study *immaterial* forces like gravity by observing their effects on the physical world⟩
synonyms bodiless, incorporeal, insubstantial, nonmaterial, nonphysical, spiritual, unsubstantial
related words metaphysical, supernatural; impalpable, insensible, intangible, invisible; airy, diaphanous, ethereal, tenuous, thin, vaporous
near antonyms animal, carnal, fleshly; detectable, discernable, noticeable, observable, palpable, sensible, tangible, visible; bulky, heavy, massive, solid
antonyms bodily, corporeal, material, physical, substantial
2 not having anything to do with the matter at hand — see IRRELEVANT
immature *adj* **1** being in the early stage of life, growth, or development — see YOUNG
2 having or showing the annoying qualities (as silliness) associated with children — see CHILDISH
3 lacking in adult experience or maturity — see CALLOW
immeasurable *adj* being or seeming to be without limits — see INFINITE
immediacy *n* the state or condition of being near — see PROXIMITY
immediate *adj* **1** done or occurring without any noticeable lapse in time — see INSTANTANEOUS
2 done or working without something else coming in between — see DIRECT 1
3 done, carried out, or given without delay — see PROMPT 1
4 not being distant in time, space, or significance — see CLOSE 2
immediately *adv* without delay ⟨if you don't leave *immediately*, you'll be late for school and probably get in trouble⟩
synonyms directly, forthwith, instantly, now, promptly, pronto, right away, right now, straightaway, straightway
related words away, freely; anon, momentarily, shortly, soon; apace, briskly, fast, fleetly, full-tilt, posthaste, quick, quickly, rapidly, readily, snappily, speedily, swift, swiftly; abruptly, presto, suddenly, unexpectedly; hastily, impetuously, impulsively, rashly, recklessly; exactly, opportunely, punctually, seasonably
phrases at once, on the line, on the spot
near antonyms slowly; late, tardily
immense *adj* unusually large — see HUGE
immenseness *n* the quality or state of being very large — see IMMENSITY
immensity *n* the quality or state of being very large ⟨the *immensity* of the mountain was awe-inspiring, especially up close⟩
synonyms enormity, enormousness, hugeness, immenseness, magnitude, massiveness, vastness
related words bigness, extensiveness, greatness, largeness, voluminousness, weightiness; awesomeness, grandness, stupendousness; excessiveness, extravagance, extremeness, immoderacy
near antonyms littleness, puniness, smallness; triviality, unimportance
antonyms diminutiveness, minuteness, tininess
immerse *vb* **1** to hold the attention of — see ENGAGE 1
2 to sink or push (something) briefly into or as if into a liquid — see DIP 1
immersed *adj* having the mind fixed on something — see ATTENTIVE
immersing *adj* holding the attention or provoking interest — see INTERESTING
immersion *n* a focusing of the mind on something — see ATTENTION 1
immigrant *n* one that leaves one place to settle in another — see EMIGRANT
imminent *adj* **1** giving signs of immediate occurrence ⟨a storm is *imminent,* so you should seek shelter now⟩
synonyms impending, pending, threatening
related words approaching, coming, forthcoming, future, near, nearing, oncoming, upcoming; brewing, gathering; likely, possible, probable; inevitable, unavoidable; menacing, ominous, portentous; anticipated, awaited, expected, foreseen, predicted
near antonyms distant, far-off, remote; eventual, ultimate; bygone, former, past; late, recent
2 being soon to appear or take place — see FORTHCOMING
immobile *adj* **1** fixed in a place or position — see STATIONARY 1
2 incapable of moving or being moved — see IMMOVABLE 1
immobilize *vb* to render powerless, ineffective, or unable to move — see PARALYZE
immoderate *adj* going beyond a normal or acceptable limit in degree or amount — see EXCESSIVE
immodest *adj* showing a lack of proper social reserve or modesty — see PRESUMPTUOUS 1
immolate *vb* to give up as an offering to a god — see SACRIFICE
immolation *n* something offered to a god — see SACRIFICE
immoral *adj* **1** not conforming to a high moral standard; morally unacceptable — see BAD 2
2 not guided by or showing a concern for what is right — see UNPRINCIPLED
immorality *n* **1** immoral conduct or practices harmful or offensive to society — see VICE 1
2 that which is morally unacceptable — see EVIL
immortal *adj* lasting forever — see EVERLASTING
immortality *n* unending existence after death — see ETERNITY 2

immortalize *vb* to give eternal or lasting existence to — see PERPETUATE

immovable *adj* **1** incapable of moving or being moved ⟨that boulder is *immovable,* even with a bulldozer⟩
synonyms immobile, irremovable, nonmotile, nonmoving, unbudging, unmovable
related words motionless, moveless, static, stationary, still, unmoving; fast, fixed, rooted, steadfast, stuck, wedged
near antonyms portable, removable, transferable, transportable
antonyms mobile, motile, movable (*or* moveable), moving
2 sticking to an opinion, purpose, or course of action in spite of reason, arguments, or persuasion — see OBSTINATE

immunity *n* freedom from punishment, harm, or loss — see IMPUNITY

immure *vb* **1** to close or shut in by or as if by barriers — see ENCLOSE 1
2 to put in or as if in prison — see IMPRISON

immurement *n* the act of confining or the state of being confined — see INTERNMENT

immutability *n* the state of continuing without change — see CONSTANCY 1

immutable *adj* not capable of changing or being changed — see INFLEXIBLE 1

imp *n* **1** an appealingly mischievous person — see SCAMP 1
2 an evil spirit — see DEMON

impact *n* **1** a forceful coming together of two things ⟨the glass shattered on *impact* with the floor⟩
synonyms bump, collision, concussion, crash, jar, jolt, shock, smash, strike, wallop
related words blow, buffet, hit, knock, punch, rap, slap, thump; bashing, battering, bludgeoning, clobbering, hammering, lambasting, licking, pounding, pummelling, thrashing; contact, encounter, meeting, touch
2 the power to bring about a result on another — see EFFECT 2
3 the quality of an utterance that provokes interest and produces an effect — see [1]PUNCH 1

impact *vb* **1** to act upon (a person or a person's feelings) so as to cause a response — see [1]AFFECT 1
2 to come into usually forceful contact with something — see HIT 2

impair *vb* to reduce the soundness, effectiveness, or perfection of — see DAMAGE 1

impale *vb* to penetrate or hold (something) with a pointed object ⟨*impale* a marshmallow or two on that stick and let's start toasting⟩
synonyms gore, harpoon, lance, pierce, puncture, skewer, spear, spike, stab, stick, transfix
related words spindle; perforate; jab, poke, prick, punch, thrust; cut, knife, slice

impalpable *adj* **1** not capable of being perceived by the sense of touch — see INTANGIBLE
2 not perceptible by a sense or by the mind — see IMPERCEPTIBLE

impart *vb* to cause (something) to pass from one to another — see COMMUNICATE 1

impartial *adj* marked by justice, honesty, and freedom from bias — see FAIR 2

impartiality *n* lack of favoritism toward one side or another — see DETACHMENT 1

impassable *adj* impossible to get through or into — see IMPENETRABLE 1

impasse *n* a point in a struggle where neither side is capable of winning or willing to give in ⟨if we cannot ever agree on which movie to see tonight, we are at an *impasse*⟩
synonyms deadlock, halt, stalemate, standstill
related words dead end; bottleneck, corner, dilemma, fix, hole, jam, pickle, pinch, plight, predicament, quagmire, quandary, spot; difficulty; problem

impassioned *adj* having or expressing great depth of feeling — see FERVENT

impassive *adj* **1** not feeling or showing emotion ⟨she remained *impassive* as they told her the bad news⟩
synonyms apathetic, cold-blooded, phlegmatic, stoic (*or* stoical), stolid, undemonstrative, unemotional
related words cold, cool, dispassionate, unmoved; calm, collected, composed; imperturbable, unflappable; reserved, reticent, taciturn; blank, deadpan, dry, empty, expressionless, inexpressive, vacant, wooden; enigmatic (*also* enigmatical), impenetrable, inscrutable; aloof, detached, unconcerned, unsentimental; impersonal, objective, unresponsive; hardhearted, pitiless, unfeeling; inconsiderate, thoughtless
near antonyms blazing, burning, fiery, flaming, glowing, red-hot; ardent, enthusiastic, gung ho, zealous; gushing, maudlin, mawkish, mushy, sentimental; dramatic, histrionic, melodramatic; compassionate, responsive, sympathetic; reactive, sensitive
antonyms demonstrative, emotional, fervent, fervid, hot-blooded, impassioned, passionate
2 not expressing any emotion — see BLANK 1

impassivity *n* a lack of emotion or emotional expressiveness — see APATHY 1

impatience *n* urgent desire or interest — see EAGERNESS

impatient *adj* **1** showing urgent desire or interest — see EAGER
2 unable or unwilling to endure — see INTOLERANT 1

impeach *vb* to make a claim of wrongdoing against — see ACCUSE

impeccability *n* the quality or state of being free from guilt or blame — see INNOCENCE 1

impeccable *adj* **1** being entirely without fault or flaw — see PERFECT 1
2 free from guilt or blame — see INNOCENT 2

impeccably *adv* without any flaws or errors — see PERFECTLY 1

impecunious *adj* lacking money or material possessions — see POOR 1

impecuniousness *n* the state of lacking sufficient money or material possessions — see POVERTY 1

impede *vb* to create difficulty for the work or activity of — see HAMPER

impediment *n* something that makes movement or progress more difficult — see ENCUMBRANCE

impel *vb* to set or keep in motion — see MOVE 2

impend *vb* to be about to happen — see LOOM

impend (over) *vb* to remain poised to inflict harm, danger, or distress on — see THREATEN

impending *adj* **1** being soon to appear or take place — see FORTHCOMING
2 giving signs of immediate occurrence — see IMMINENT 1

impenetrable *adj* **1** impossible to get through or into ⟨the ancient temple was surrounded by vast stretches of *impenetrable* jungle⟩

synonyms impassable, impermeable, impervious
related words close, compact, dense, thick; compressed, condensed; sturdy, substantial, tough; firm, frozen, hard, solid, stiff; inflexible, rigid, unbending, unyielding
near antonyms soft, squishy; bendable, elastic, flexible, giving, malleable, pliable, yielding; absorbent, porous
antonyms negotiable, passable, penetrable, permeable
2 being beyond one's powers to know, understand, or explain — see MYSTERIOUS 1
3 impossible to understand — see INCOMPREHENSIBLE
4 not allowing penetration (as by gas, liquid, or light) — see TIGHT 1

impenitent *adj* not sorry for having done wrong — see REMORSELESS

imperative *adj* **1** forcing one's compliance or participation by or as if by law — see MANDATORY
2 impossible to do without — see ESSENTIAL 1
3 needing immediate attention — see ACUTE 2

imperceptible *adj* not perceptible by a sense or by the mind <a slight difference in hue between the two glasses that's *imperceptible* unless they're placed side by side>
synonyms impalpable, inappreciable, indistinguishable, insensible
related words inaudible, intangible, invisible; inconspicuous, indistinct, unnoticeable, unseeable, unseen; faint, insignificant, slight, trivial; buried, concealed, covert, disguised, hidden, obscure, shrouded, unapparent, vague
near antonyms audible, observable, tangible, visible; clear, conspicuous, evident, eye-catching, manifest, noticeable, obvious, plain, prominent, striking; apparent, distinct, significant, straightforward
antonyms appreciable, discernible, palpable, perceptible, sensible

imperfect *adj* having a fault — see FAULTY

imperfection *n* something that spoils the appearance or completeness of a thing — see BLEMISH

imperil *vb* to place in danger — see ENDANGER

imperilment *n* the state of not being protected from injury, harm, or evil — see DANGER 1

imperious *adj* **1** fond of ordering people around — see BOSSY
2 having a feeling of superiority that shows itself in an overbearing attitude — see ARROGANT
3 having or showing a tendency to force one's will on others without any regard to fairness or necessity — see ARBITRARY 1
4 needing immediate attention — see ACUTE 2

imperiousness *n* an exaggerated sense of one's importance that shows itself in the making of excessive or unjustified claims — see ARROGANCE

imperishable *adj* impossible to destroy — see INDESTRUCTIBLE

impermanent *adj* **1** intended to last, continue, or serve for a limited time — see TEMPORARY 1
2 lasting only for a short time — see MOMENTARY

impermeable *adj* **1** impossible to get through or into — see IMPENETRABLE 1
2 not allowing penetration (as by gas, liquid, or light) — see TIGHT 1

impermissible *adj* that may not be permitted <chewing gum is an *impermissible* activity in school>
synonyms banned, barred, forbidden, interdicted, outlawed, prohibited, proscribed, taboo (*also* tabu)
related words intolerable, unacceptable, unbearable, unendurable; illegal, illegitimate, illicit, improper, inappropriate, unadvisable, unauthorized, unlawful, unlicensed, unmentionable; unseemly, unsuitable; objectionable; disallowed, disapproved, discouraged; refused, rejected, revoked, unsanctioned, vetoed; repressed, suppressed; precluded, prevented, stopped; excluded, ruled out, shut out; blocked, hindered, impeded, obstructed
near antonyms acceptable, bearable, endurable, tolerable; accepted, accredited, allowed, appropriate, approved, authorized, certified, endorsed, lawful, legal, legitimate, licensed (*also* licenced), OK (*or* okay), permitted, warranted; accorded, granted, sanctioned, vouchsafed; brooked, condoned, countenanced; encouraged, promoted, supported; commanded, mandatory, ordered, required; proper, seemly, suitable, tolerated, unobjectionable
antonyms allowable, licensable, permissible, permissive, sufferable

impersonate *vb* **1** to pretend to be (what one is not) in appearance or behavior <a school intruder was caught trying to *impersonate* a teacher>
synonyms masquerade (as), play, pose (as)
related words ape, copy, imitate, mime, mimic, mock, parody, travesty; act, perform, portray
2 to present a portrayal or performance of — see ACT 1

impersonator *n* **1** a person who imitates another's voice and mannerisms for comic effect — see MIMIC
2 one who acts professionally (as in a play, movie, or television show) — see ACTOR

impertinence *n* **1** disrespectful or argumentative talk given in response to a command or request — see BACK TALK
2 rude behavior — see DISCOURTESY

impertinent *adj* **1** displaying or marked by rude boldness — see NERVY 1
2 showing a lack of manners or consideration for others — see IMPOLITE

imperturbability *n* evenness of emotions or temper — see EQUANIMITY

imperturbable *adj* not easily panicked or upset — see UNFLAPPABLE

impervious *adj* **1** not allowing penetration (as by gas, liquid, or light) — see TIGHT 1
2 impossible to get through or into — see IMPENETRABLE 1

impetus *n* something that arouses action or activity — see IMPULSE

impiety *n* an act of great disrespect shown to God or to sacred ideas, people, or things — see BLASPHEMY

impinge *vb* to come into usually forceful contact with something — see HIT 2

impious *adj* not showing proper reverence for the holy or sacred — see IRREVERENT

impish *adj* tending to or exhibiting reckless playfulness — see MISCHIEVOUS 1

impishness *n* **1** a natural disposition for playful behavior — see PLAYFULNESS
2 playful, reckless behavior that is not intended to cause serious harm — see MISCHIEF 1

implacable *adj* **1** sticking to an opinion, purpose, or course of action in spite of reason, arguments, or persuasion — see OBSTINATE

2 showing no signs of slackening or yielding in one's purpose — see UNYIELDING 1

implant *vb* to set solidly in or as if in surrounding matter — see ENTRENCH

implausible *adj* too extraordinary or improbable to believe — see INCREDIBLE

implement *n* an article intended for use in work <gardening *implements* such as hoes, spades, and pruners>
synonyms device, instrument, tool, utensil
related words apparatus, appliance, mechanism; contraption, contrivance, gadget, gizmo (*or* gismo), jigger

implement *vb* to carry out effectively — see ENFORCE

implementation *n* the doing of an action — see COMMISSION 2

implicit *adj* understood although not put into words <the *implicit* agreement in the outing club is that every member pays his or her own way on all trips>
synonyms implied, tacit, unexpressed, unspoken, unvoiced, wordless
related words inferred; unannounced, undeclared, unsaid, untold; hinted, intimated, suggested
near antonyms apparent, blatant, evident, obvious, plain, straightforward; unambiguous, unequivocal, unmistakable
antonyms explicit, express, expressed, spoken, stated

implied *adj* understood although not put into words — see IMPLICIT

implore *vb* to make a request to (someone) in an earnest or urgent manner — see BEG

imploring *adj* asking humbly — see SUPPLIANT

imply *vb* to convey an idea indirectly — see HINT

impolite *adj* showing a lack of manners or consideration for others <the librarian was shocked that anyone could be so *impolite* as to continue talking despite repeated warnings to be quiet>
synonyms discourteous, ill-bred, ill-mannered, impertinent, inconsiderate, rude, thoughtless, uncalled-for, uncivil, ungracious, unmannerly
related words audacious, bold, bold-faced, brash, brassy, disrespectful, impudent, insolent, saucy, shameless; boorish, churlish, clownish, loutish, uncouth, vulgar; undiplomatic, unsportsmanlike; abrupt, blunt, brusque, crusty, curt, gruff, sharp, snippy; antisocial, crabbed, cross, disagreeable, grumpy, sullen, surly; improper, inappropriate, incorrect, indecent, indecorous, unseemly; arrogant, conceited, presumptuous, pretentious
near antonyms humble, meek, modest, unassertive; deferential, dutiful, respectful, submissive, yielding; acceptable, appropriate, becoming, befitting, correct, decent, decorous, fit, fitting, good, meet, proper, respectable, right, seemly, suitable; affable, cordial, friendly, genial, hospitable, sociable; felicitous, graceful
antonyms civil, considerate, courteous, genteel, gracious, mannerly, polite, thoughtful, well-bred

impoliteness *n* rude behavior — see DISCOURTESY

import *n* 1 the quality or state of being important — see IMPORTANCE
2 the idea that is conveyed or intended to be conveyed to the mind by language, symbol, or action — see MEANING 1

import *vb* 1 to be of importance — see MATTER
2 to communicate or convey (as an idea) to the mind — see MEAN 1

importance *n* the quality or state of being important <a final exam has great *importance*>
synonyms consequence, import, magnitude, moment, significance, weight, weightiness
related words celebrity, distinction, eminence, fame, note, noteworthiness, notoriety, preeminence, prominence, renown; store, substance, value, worth, worthiness; gravity, seriousness; authority, potency, power; mark, name, report, reputation, repute; cachet, position, prestige, rank, standing, stature; glory, greatness, honor, illustriousness
near antonyms paltriness, pettiness, worthlessness; disgrace, dishonor, disrepute, ignominy, odium, opprobrium, shame; anonymity; obscurity
antonyms insignificance, littleness, slightness, smallness, triviality, unimportance

important *adj* 1 having great meaning or lasting effect <the discovery of penicillin was a very *important* event in the history of medicine>
synonyms big, consequential, eventful, major, material, meaningful, momentous, significant, substantial, weighty
related words decisive, fatal, fateful, strategic; earnest, grave, serious, sincere; distinctive, exceptional, impressive, outstanding, prominent, remarkable; valuable, worthwhile, worthy; distinguished, eminent, great, illustrious, preeminent, prestigious; famous, notorious, renowned; all-important, critical, crucial
near antonyms inconsiderable, minor, paltry, petty, worthless; anonymous, nameless, obscure, uncelebrated, unknown
antonyms insignificant, little, minor, slight, small, trivial, unimportant
2 having great power or influence <Rachel Carson was an *important* figure in the environmental movement>
synonyms influential, mighty, potent, powerful, puissant, significant, strong
related words high-level, senior, top; able, capable, competent, effective, efficient; authoritarian, autocratic, despotic, dictatorial, magisterial, tyrannical (*also* tyrannic); distinguished, dominant, eminent, famous, great, illustrious, notorious, preeminent, prestigious, renowned; dynamic, energetic, forceful, robust, sturdy, tough, vigorous
near antonyms feeble, flimsy, frail, infirm; anonymous, obscure; incapable, incompetent, ineffective, inept, unfit, useless
antonyms impotent, insignificant, little, powerless, unimportant, weak
3 having a feeling of superiority that shows itself in an overbearing attitude — see ARROGANT
4 having too high an opinion of oneself — see CONCEITED

importune *vb* to make a request to (someone) in an earnest or urgent manner — see BEG

impose *vb* to establish or apply as a charge or penalty <every town *imposes* a fine for speeding>
synonyms assess, charge, exact, fine, lay, levy, put
related words dock, mulct, penalize, tax; extort, shake down, wrest, wring; bleed, fleece, gouge, milk, skin, squeeze; coerce, compel, force; inflict, wreak; set; reapply, reimpose, relay
near antonyms abate, diminish, lessen; forgive, release
antonyms remit

impose (on *or* upon) *vb* to take unfair advantage of — see EXPLOIT 1

imposing *adj* **1** having or showing a serious and reserved manner — see DIGNIFIED
2 large and impressive in size, grandeur, extent, or conception — see GRAND 1

imposition *n* a charge usually of money collected by the government from people or businesses for public use — see TAX

impossible *adj* incapable of being solved or accomplished ⟨the seemingly *impossible* problem of world hunger⟩ ⟨fitting everything in my backpack seemed an *impossible* task⟩
synonyms hopeless, unachievable, unattainable, unsolvable
related words impracticable, impractical; doubtful, dubious, far-fetched, improbable, unlikely; implausible, inconceivable, incredible, unbelievable, unthinkable; futile, useless; absurd, fantastic, outlandish, preposterous, ridiculous
near antonyms practicable, practical, reasonable; likely, probable; acceptable, believable, conceivable, credible, plausible
antonyms achievable, attainable, doable, feasible, possible, realizable, workable

impost *n* a charge usually of money collected by the government from people or businesses for public use — see TAX

impostor *or* **imposter** *n* one who makes false claims of identity or expertise ⟨the man who claimed to be a prince turned out to be an *impostor*⟩
synonyms charlatan, fake, faker, fraud, hoaxer, humbug, mountebank, phony (*also* phoney), pretender, quack
related words imitator, impersonator, mimic; actor, bluffer, counterfeiter, deceiver, dissembler, duper, feigner, misleader, trickster; poseur
near antonyms adept, expert, master, professional, virtuoso, whiz, wizard

impotence *n* the lack of sufficient ability, power, or means — see INABILITY

impotent *adj* **1** not able to produce fruit or offspring — see STERILE 1
2 unable to act or achieve one's purpose — see POWERLESS

impoverished *adj* **1** lacking money or material possessions — see POOR 1
2 producing inferior or only a small amount of vegetation — see BARREN 1

impoverishment *n* the state of lacking sufficient money or material possessions — see POVERTY 1

impracticable *adj* not capable of being put to use or account — see IMPRACTICAL

impractical *adj* not capable of being put to use or account ⟨the flimsy little toy shovel was cute, but completely *impractical* for digging up tree stumps⟩
synonyms impracticable, inoperable, nonpractical, unusable, unworkable, useless
related words unsuitable; inaccessible, unattainable, unavailable, unobtainable, unreachable; dead, dormant, fallow, free, idle, inactive, inert, inoperative, latent; arrested, interrupted, suspended; unrealistic
near antonyms accessible, available, obtainable, reachable; all-around (*also* all-round), handy; active, alive, busy, employed, functioning, operating, operative, running, working
antonyms applicable, feasible, functional, operable, operational, practicable, practical, usable, useful, workable

imprecate *vb* to ask a divine power to send harm or evil upon — see CURSE 1

imprecation *n* a prayer that harm will come to someone — see CURSE 1

imprecise *adj* not precisely correct — see INEXACT 1

impregnable *adj* incapable of being defeated, overcome, or subdued — see INVINCIBLE

impregnate *vb* to wet thoroughly with liquid — see SOAK 1

impress *n* a perceptible trace left by pressure — see PRINT 1

impress *vb* **1** to act upon (a person or a person's feelings) so as to cause a response — see [1]AFFECT 1
2 to produce a vivid impression of — see ENGRAVE 2

impression *n* **1** a perceptible trace left by pressure — see PRINT 1
2 something imagined or pictured in the mind — see IDEA

impressionist *n* a person who imitates another's voice and mannerisms for comic effect — see MIMIC

impressive *adj* having the power to affect the feelings or sympathies — see MOVING

imprimatur *n* an acceptance of something as satisfactory — see APPROVAL 1

imprint *n* **1** a mark or series of marks left on a surface by something that has passed along it — see TRACK 1
2 a perceptible trace left by pressure — see PRINT 1

imprint *vb* to produce a vivid impression of — see ENGRAVE 2

imprison *vb* to put in or as if in prison ⟨in this society, we try to *imprison* criminals so that they can't do any more harm⟩
synonyms commit, confine, immure, incarcerate, intern, jail, jug, lock (up)
related words constrain, limit, restrain, restrict, shut; apprehend, arrest, capture, catch, detain; impress, shanghai; hold, keep; enslave, subjugate
near antonyms emancipate, manumit
antonyms discharge, free, liberate, release

imprisoned *adj* taken and held prisoner — see CAPTIVE

imprisonment *n* the act of confining or the state of being confined — see INTERNMENT

improbable *adj* not likely to be true or to occur ⟨it is *improbable* that we will be allowed to stay out all night⟩
synonyms doubtful, dubious, far-fetched, flimsy, questionable, unapt, unlikely
related words implausible, impossible, inconceivable, incredible, last, unbelievable, unthinkable; absurd, outlandish, preposterous, ridiculous; outside, remote, slight
near antonyms believable, conceivable, credible, plausible; possible; liable
antonyms likely, probable

impromptu *adj* made or done without previous thought or preparation — see EXTEMPORANEOUS

improper *adj* not appropriate for a particular occasion or situation — see INAPPROPRIATE

improperly *adv* in a mistaken or inappropriate way — see WRONGLY

impropriety *n* **1** the quality or state of not being so-

cially proper ⟨the *impropriety* of the song that the campers sang for the visitors was embarrassing⟩
synonyms inappropriateness, incorrectness, indecency, unfitness
related words coarseness, crudeness; imprudence, indiscretion
near antonyms discretion, prudence; etiquette
antonyms appropriateness, correctness, decency, decorousness, fitness, propriety, rightness, seemliness, suitability
2 a socially improper or unsuitable act or remark ⟨such *improprieties* as asking people how much money they make⟩
synonyms familiarity, gaffe, indiscretion, solecism
related words blunder, error, flub, fumble, goof, lapse, miscue, misstep, mistake, slip, slipup, stumble; discourtesy, incivility, offense (*or* offence); boner, howler, screamer; foul-up, muff; misapprehension, miscalculation, misconception, misjudgment, misstatement, misunderstanding
near antonyms manners, proprieties
antonyms amenity, civility, courtesy, formality, gesture

improve *vb* to make better ⟨a little salt would *improve* this bland food⟩
synonyms ameliorate, amend, better, enhance, enrich, meliorate, perfect, refine
related words correct, emend, rectify, reform, remedy; help; edit, revise; upgrade; fortify, intensify, strengthen; retouch, touch up
near antonyms damage, harm, hurt, impair, injure, spoil, tarnish; blemish, blight, deface, disfigure, flaw, mar; diminish, lessen, lower, reduce
antonyms worsen

improved *adj* being far along in development — see ADVANCED 1

improvement *n* an instance of notable progress in the development of knowledge, technology, or skill — see ADVANCE 2

improvident *adj* not thinking about and providing for the future ⟨the *improvident* view that the wearing away of the ozone layer need not concern us⟩
synonyms myopic, shortsighted
related words careless, heedless, imprudent, incautious, injudicious, unwise; extravagant, prodigal, profligate, spendthrift, thriftless, unthrifty; indulgent, lavish, reckless, wasteful
near antonyms careful, judicious, prudent, sensible, wise; economical, economizing, frugal, scrimping, sparing, thrifty; conserving, preserving, saving
antonyms farsighted, forehanded, foreseeing, foresighted, forethoughtful, provident

improvise *vb* to perform, make, or do without preparation ⟨since the award was a complete surprise, I *improvised* an acceptance speech⟩
synonyms ad-lib, extemporize
related words concoct, contrive, cook (up), devise, hatch, invent, make up, think up; cobble (together *or* up), dash (off)
near antonyms arrange, prepare, ready; consider, contemplate, ponder, study, think; practice (*or* practise), rehearse

improvised *adj* made or done without previous thought or preparation — see EXTEMPORANEOUS

imprudent *adj* showing poor judgment especially in personal relationships or social situations — see INDISCREET

impudence *n* **1** disrespectful or argumentative talk given in response to a command or request — see BACK TALK
2 rude behavior — see DISCOURTESY

impudent *adj* displaying or marked by rude boldness — see NERVY 1

impulse *n* something that arouses action or activity ⟨the new auto factory was just the *impulse* that the local economy needed⟩
synonyms boost, encouragement, goad, impetus, incentive, incitement, instigation, momentum, motivation, provocation, spur, stimulant, stimulus, yeast
related words inducement, invitation; cause, consideration, motive, reason

impulsive *adj* **1** caused by or suggestive of an irresistible urge — see COMPULSIVE
2 prone to sudden illogical changes of mind, ideas, or actions — see WHIMSICAL

impulsiveness *n* an inclination to sudden illogical changes of mind, ideas, or actions — see WHIMSICALITY

impunity *n* freedom from punishment, harm, or loss ⟨she mistakenly believed that she could insult people with *impunity*⟩
synonyms exemption, immunity
related words armor, defense, guard, protection, safeguard, safety, security, shield; buffer, bumper, screen; absolution, absolving, dispensation, forgiveness
near antonyms exposure, liability, susceptibility, vulnerability

impure *adj* containing foreign or lower-grade substances ⟨be careful, because *impure* motor oil can damage your car's engine⟩
synonyms adulterated, alloyed, contaminated, dilute, diluted, polluted, tainted, thinned, weakened
related words befouled, besmirched, corrupted, debased, defiled, dirtied, fouled, soiled, spoiled, sullied; blended, commingled, incorporated, intermingled, intermixed, merged, mingled, mixed; coalesced, combined, compounded; cheapened, doctored
near antonyms clarified, filtered, purified, refined; neat, plain, straight; concentrated, strong; uncombined; pasteurized
antonyms pure, unadulterated, unalloyed, uncontaminated, undiluted, unpolluted, untainted

impurity *n* something that is or that makes impure ⟨*impurities* in the water made it cloudy⟩
synonyms adulterant, contaminant, defilement, pollutant
related words blot, blotch, spot, stain, taint; dirt, filth, grime; blemish, defect, disfigurement, fault, flaw; abnormality, imperfection, irregularity
near antonyms clarifier, filter, purifier, refiner; cleanliness, immaculateness, purity

impute *vb* to explain (something) as being the result of something else — see CREDIT 1

in *adj* **1** being in the latest or current fashion — see STYLISH
2 enjoying widespread favor or approval — see POPULAR 1

in *adv* at, within, or to a short distance or time — see NEAR 1

inability *n* the lack of sufficient ability, power, or means ⟨the apparent *inability* of young children to sit still⟩
synonyms impotence, inadequacy, incapability,

incapacity, incompetence, ineptitude, powerlessness
related words inaptitude; ineffectiveness, ineffectualness, inefficiency
near antonyms aptitude, bent, flair, talent; effectiveness, effectualness, efficaciousness, efficiency; fitness, suitability; power, strength
antonyms ability, adequacy, capability, capacity, competence, potency

inaccessible *adj* hard or impossible to get to or get at ⟨my pen is *inaccessible* now that it's fallen down the crack behind my desk⟩
synonyms inconvenient, unapproachable, unattainable, unavailable, unobtainable, unreachable, untouchable
related words distant, far, faraway, far-off, remote, removed; apart, hidden, isolated, out-of-the-way, secluded
near antonyms close, near, nearby
antonyms accessible, approachable, attainable, convenient, obtainable, reachable

inaccuracy *n* an unintentional departure from truth or accuracy — see ERROR 1

inaccurate *adj* **1** not being in agreement with what is true — see FALSE 1
2 not precisely correct — see INEXACT 1

inaccurately *adv* in a mistaken or inappropriate way — see WRONGLY

inaction *n* lack of action or activity ⟨as a result of the park department's *inaction*, the city's pools are not ready to open for the summer⟩
synonyms dormancy, idleness, inactivity, inertness, nonaction, quiescence
related words indolence, languor, lassitude, laziness, lethargy, listlessness, sleepiness, sloth, sluggishness
near antonyms animateness, briskness, liveliness, sprightliness; business, diligence, employment, industriousness, occupation
antonyms action, activeness, activity

inactive *adj* **1** slow to move or act ⟨it's easiest to catch snakes early in the morning, while they're still cold and *inactive*⟩
synonyms dull, inert, lethargic, quiescent, sleepy, sluggish, torpid
related words apathetic, indolent, languorous, lazy, lazyish, listless, slothful; dormant, inanimate, motionless, sedentary, static, still; dead; dopey, drugged
near antonyms busy, engaged, occupied, working; animated, dynamic, energetic, lively, sprightly, vigorous; assiduous, diligent, hardworking, industrious
antonyms active
2 not being in a state of use, activity, or employment ⟨an *inactive* oil well⟩
synonyms dead, dormant, fallow, free, idle, inert, inoperative, latent, off, vacant
related words arrested, interrupted, suspended; asleep, lifeless, quiescent, sleepy; inoperable, unusable, unworkable, useless; dead, dull, slow
phrases out of commission
near antonyms functional, operable, operational, workable; assiduous, industrious; energetic, vigorous; feasible, practical, usable, useful, viable
antonyms active, alive, busy, employed, functioning, on, operating, operative, running, working

inactivity *n* **1** lack of action or activity — see INACTION
2 lack of use — see DISUSE

inadequacy *n* **1** a falling short of an essential or desirable amount or number — see DEFICIENCY
2 the lack of sufficient ability, power, or means — see INABILITY

inadequate *adj* not coming up to a usual standard or meeting a particular need — see SHORT 3

inadequately *adv* in an unsatisfactory way — see BADLY

inadvertent *adj* happening by chance — see ACCIDENTAL

inadvisable *adj* showing poor judgment especially in personal relationships or social situations — see INDISCREET

inane *adj* having no meaning — see MEANINGLESS

inanity *n* **1** a foolish act or idea — see FOLLY 1
2 lack of good sense or judgment — see FOOLISHNESS 1

inapplicability *n* the quality or state of not having anything to do with the matter at hand — see IRRELEVANCE

inapplicable *adj* not having anything to do with the matter at hand — see IRRELEVANT

inappreciable *adj* not perceptible by a sense or by the mind — see IMPERCEPTIBLE

inappropriate *adj* not appropriate for a particular occasion or situation ⟨a bathing suit is *inappropriate* dress for strolling the streets of this seaside village⟩
synonyms graceless, improper, inapt, incongruous, incorrect, indecorous, inept, infelicitous, unapt, unbecoming, unfit, unhappy, unseemly, unsuitable, wrong
related words inopportune, unfortunate, unseasonable, untimely; immaterial, irrelevant; incompatible, uncongenial, unharmonious; bad, naughty, sinful; blamable, blameworthy, censurable; banned, barred, disallowed; forbidden, interdicted, outlawed, prohibited, proscribed; awkward, gauche, ungraceful; unacceptable, unsatisfactory
near antonyms fortunate, opportune, seasonable, timely; apt, material, relevant; compatible, congenial, harmonious; allowed, authorized, permitted; approved, endorsed, licensed (*also* licenced), sanctioned; abetted, encouraged, promoted, supported; acceptable, adequate, satisfactory; commendable, creditable, exemplary; blameless, irreproachable
antonyms appropriate, becoming, befitting, correct, decorous, felicitous, fit, fitting, genteel, happy, meet, proper, right, seemly, suitable

inappropriately *adv* in a mistaken or inappropriate way — see WRONGLY

inappropriateness *n* **1** the quality or state of being unsuitable or unfitting ⟨I cannot even begin to describe the *inappropriateness* of such language for the dinner table⟩
synonyms inaptness, incorrectness, infelicity, unfitness, wrongness
related words inadmissibility, inapplicability, extraneousness, inadequacy, irrelevance, meaninglessness, pointlessness, senselessness; inauspiciousness, intolerability, undesirability, undesirableness, unsatisfactorability, uselessness
near antonyms admissibility, applicability, bearing, connection, materiality, pertinence, pointedness, relevance
antonyms appropriateness, aptness, correctness, felicitousness, felicity, fitness, fittingness, rightness, seemliness, suitability, suitableness

2 the quality or state of not being socially proper — see IMPROPRIETY 1
inapt *adj* not appropriate for a particular occasion or situation — see INAPPROPRIATE
inaptly *adv* in a mistaken or inappropriate way — see WRONGLY
inaptness *n* the quality or state of being unsuitable or unfitting — see INAPPROPRIATENESS 1
inarticulate *adj* unable to speak — see MUTE 1
inasmuch as *conj* for the reason that — see SINCE
inaugural *adj* coming before all others in time or order — see FIRST 1
inaugural *n* the process or an instance of being formally placed in an office or organization — see INSTALLATION 1
inaugurate *vb* **1** to be responsible for the creation and early operation or use of — see FOUND
2 to put into an office or welcome into an organization with special ceremonies — see INSTALL 1
inauguration *n* the process or an instance of being formally placed in an office or organization — see INSTALLATION 1
inaugurator *n* a person who establishes a whole new field of endeavor — see FATHER 2
inauspicious *adj* being or showing a sign of evil or calamity to come — see OMINOUS
inauthentic *adj* being such in appearance only and made or manufactured with the intention of committing fraud — see COUNTERFEIT
inborn *adj* **1** being a part of the innermost nature of a person or thing — see INHERENT
2 genetically passed or capable of being passed from parent to offspring — see HEREDITARY
inbred *adj* being a part of the innermost nature of a person or thing — see INHERENT
incandescence *n* the steady giving off of the form of radiation that makes vision possible — see LIGHT 1
incandescent *adj* giving off or reflecting much light — see BRIGHT 1
incantation *n* a spoken word or set of words believed to have magic power — see SPELL 1
incapability *n* the lack of sufficient ability, power, or means — see INABILITY
incapable *adj* lacking qualities (as knowledge, skill, or ability) required to do a job — see INCOMPETENT
incapacitate *vb* to render powerless, ineffective, or unable to move — see PARALYZE
incapacitated *adj* deprived of the power to perform one or more natural bodily activities — see DISABLED
incapacity *n* the lack of sufficient ability, power, or means — see INABILITY
incarcerate *vb* to put in or as if in prison — see IMPRISON
incarcerated *adj* taken and held prisoner — see CAPTIVE
incarceration *n* the act of confining or the state of being confined — see INTERNMENT
incarnate *vb* to represent in visible form — see EMBODY 2
incarnation *n* a visible representation of something abstract (as a quality) — see EMBODIMENT
incautious *adj* not paying or showing close attention especially for the purpose of avoiding trouble — see CARELESS 1
incautiousness *n* failure to take the care that a cautious person usually takes — see NEGLIGENCE 1
incendiary *n* **1** a person who deliberately and unlawfully sets fire to a building or other property — see ARSONIST
2 a person who stirs up public feelings especially of discontent — see AGITATOR
incense *n* a sweet or pleasant smell — see FRAGRANCE
incense *vb* to make angry — see ANGER
incensed *adj* feeling or showing anger — see ANGRY
incentive *n* something that arouses action or activity — see IMPULSE
inception *n* the point at which something begins — see BEGINNING
incertitude *n* a feeling or attitude that one does not know the truth, truthfulness, or trustworthiness of someone or something — see DOUBT
incessant *adj* going on and on without any interruptions — see CONTINUOUS
incessantly *adv* on every relevant occasion — see ALWAYS 1
inch *n* **1** a very small distance or degree — see HAIR 1
2 an individual part of a process, series, or ranking — see DEGREE 1
inch *vb* **1** to advance gradually beyond the usual or desirable limits — see ENCROACH
2 to move slowly — see CRAWL 2
incident *n* something that happens — see EVENT 1
incidental *adj* happening by chance — see ACCIDENTAL
incipiency *n* the point at which something begins — see BEGINNING
incise *vb* **1** to cut (as letters or designs) on a hard surface — see ENGRAVE 1
2 to penetrate with a sharp edge (as a knife) — see CUT 1
incision *n* a long deep cut — see GASH
incite *vb* **1** to cause or encourage the development of <the rock band's failure to show up *incited* a riot, as the crowd had waited for hours>
synonyms abet, ferment, foment, instigate, provoke, raise, stir (up), whip (up)
related words forward, foster, further, promote, sow, stimulate; set off, trigger; excite, galvanize, inflame, inspire, motivate, rouse; activate, energize, quicken, vitalize
near antonyms check, curb, discourage, inhibit, restrain; calm, soothe, subdue, tranquilize (*also* tranquillize)
2 to rouse to strong feeling or action — see PROVOKE 1
incitement *n* **1** something that arouses a strong response from another — see PROVOCATION 1
2 something that arouses action or activity — see IMPULSE
inciter *n* a person who stirs up public feelings especially of discontent — see AGITATOR
inciting *adj* serving or likely to arouse a strong reaction — see PROVOCATIVE
incivility *n* rude behavior — see DISCOURTESY
inclement *adj* marked by wet and windy conditions — see FOUL 1
inclination *n* **1** a habitual attraction to some activity or thing <her natural *inclination* to help people in need>
synonyms bent, devices, disposition, genius, leaning, partiality, penchant, predilection, predisposition, proclivity, propensity, tendency, turn
related words bias, prejudice; aptitude, faculty,

flair, gift, knack, talent; addiction, fondness, liking; forte, speciality, specialty; convention, custom, habit, pattern, practice (*also* practise), routine, trick, way, wont; oddity, peculiarity, quirk, singularity
near antonyms aversion, dislike, distaste; impartiality, neutrality, objectivity; apathy, disinterestedness, indifference
2 the act of positioning or an instance of being positioned at an angle — see TILT
3 the degree to which something rises up from a position level with the horizon — see SLANT

incline *n* the degree to which something rises up from a position level with the horizon — see SLANT

incline *vb* **1** to set or cause to be at an angle — see LEAN 1
2 to show a liking or proneness (for something) — see LEAN 2

inclined *adj* **1** having a desire or inclination (as for a specified course of action) — see WILLING 1
2 having a liking or affection — see FOND 1
3 having a tendency to be or act in a certain way — see PRONE 1
4 running in a slanting direction — see DIAGONAL

inclining *adj* bending downward or forward — see NODDING

include *vb* to have as part of a whole ⟨the test *included* some hard essay questions⟩
synonyms carry, comprehend, contain, embrace, encompass, entail, involve, number, take in
related words comprise, consist (of); have, hold, own, possess; admit, receive; compose, constitute, form, make; assimilate, embody, incorporate, integrate
near antonyms bar, debar, preclude, prevent, prohibit; deny, refuse, reject; eliminate, except, rule out; lose, mislay, misplace
antonyms exclude, omit

inclusive *adj* covering everything or all important points — see ENCYCLOPEDIC

incognito *adj* not named or identified by a name — see NAMELESS 1

incoherent *adj* **1** not clearly or logically connected ⟨the thriller's *incoherent* plot left movie audiences wondering who did what⟩
synonyms disconnected, disjointed, unconnected
related words baffling, bewildering, confounding, confused, confusing, disordered, disorderly, disorganized, muddled, perplexing, puzzling; disconcerting, frustrating; fallacious, illogical, inconsistent, invalid, irrational, unsound; absurd, asinine, eccentric, foolish, odd, peculiar, strange, unreasonable, unusual, weird; meaningless, nonsensical, nutty, preposterous, ridiculous, senseless, silly; unconvincing, unsatisfying; inexplicable, unaccountable, unexplainable
near antonyms ordered, orderly, organized; logical, rational, reasonable, sensible, solid, sound, valid; cogent, compelling, convincing, persuasive, plausible, satisfying; clear, lucid, perspicuous
antonyms coherent, connected
2 consisting of particles that do not stick together — see LOOSE 2

incombustible *adj* incapable of being burned ⟨we keep our important papers in an *incombustible* safe in the basement⟩
synonyms fireproof, noncombustible, nonflammable, noninflammable, uninflammable
related words nonexplosive
near antonyms ablaze, afire, blazing, burning, fiery; consumable; explosive, incendiary, volcanic
antonyms burnable, combustible, flammable, ignitable, inflammable

income *n* an increase usually measured in money that comes from labor, business, or property ⟨her summer job gave her some extra *income*⟩
synonyms earnings, gain(s), proceeds, profit, return, revenue, yield
related words killing, windfall; salary, tips, wages; capital, finances, funds, money
near antonyms cost, expenditures, expenses, outgo, outlay

incommode *vb* to cause discomfort to or trouble for — see INCONVENIENCE

incommoding *adj* causing difficulty, discomfort, or annoyance — see INCONVENIENT 1

incommunicable *adj* beyond the power to describe — see INDESCRIBABLE

incomparable *adj* having no equal or rival for excellence or desirability — see ONLY 1

incompatible *adj* not being in agreement or harmony — see INCONSISTENT

incompetence *n* the lack of sufficient ability, power, or means — see INABILITY

incompetent *adj* lacking qualities (as knowledge, skill, or ability) required to do a job ⟨an *incompetent* carpenter had built the deck, and the railings were loose already⟩
synonyms incapable, inept, inexpert, unfit, unqualified, unskilled, unskillful
related words ineffective, ineffectual, inefficient; callow, green, inexperienced, raw; unequipped, unprepared, untrained; useless, worthless; ineligible; wanting
near antonyms prepared, ready, trained; experienced, practiced (*or* practised), seasoned, veteran
antonyms able, capable, competent, expert, fit, qualified, skilled, skillful

incomplete *adj* lacking some necessary part ⟨an *incomplete* puzzle that has several pieces missing⟩
synonyms deficient, fragmental, fragmentary, halfway, partial
related words broken, damaged, flawed, impaired, imperfect, injured, marred, spoiled; sketchy, uncompleted, unfinished
near antonyms flawless, perfect, unbroken, undamaged, unimpaired, uninjured, unmarred; completed, finished
antonyms complete, entire, full, intact, whole

incompletely *adv* in some measure or degree — see PARTLY

incomprehensible *adj* impossible to understand ⟨rocket science is *incomprehensible* to most people⟩
synonyms impenetrable, unfathomable, unintelligible
related words abstruse, enigmatic (*also* enigmatical), esoteric, inscrutable, recondite; cryptic, mysterious, obscure; unanswerable, unknowable; baffling, bewildering, confounding, confusing, mystifying, perplexing, puzzling
near antonyms basic, elementary, rudimentary; easy, simple; coherent, connected, ordered, orderly, organized; clear, cogent, compelling, convincing, lucid, perspicuous, plain, straightforward
antonyms fathomable, intelligible, understandable

inconceivable *adj* too extraordinary or improbable to believe — see INCREDIBLE
incongruity *n* someone or something with qualities or features that seem to conflict with one another — see CONTRADICTION 1
incongruous *adj* **1** not appropriate for a particular occasion or situation — see INAPPROPRIATE
2 not being in agreement or harmony — see INCONSISTENT
inconsequential *adj* **1** lacking importance — see UNIMPORTANT
2 so small or unimportant as to warrant little or no attention — see NEGLIGIBLE
inconsiderable *adj* **1** lacking importance — see UNIMPORTANT
2 so small or unimportant as to warrant little or no attention — see NEGLIGIBLE 1
inconsiderate *adj* showing a lack of manners or consideration for others — see IMPOLITE
inconsideration *n* rude behavior — see DISCOURTESY
inconsistent *adj* not being in agreement or harmony ⟨*inconsistent* theories make it difficult to settle on one explanation⟩
synonyms clashing, conflicting, disagreeing, discordant, discrepant, incompatible, incongruous, inharmonious
related words irreconcilable; antagonistic, antithetical, contradictory, contrary, opposing, opposite
near antonyms akin, like, similar
antonyms agreeing, compatible, congruous, consistent, consonant, harmonious, nonconflicting
inconsolable *adj* feeling unhappiness — see SAD 1
inconspicuous *adj* not readily seen or noticed — see UNOBTRUSIVE
inconstancy *n* lack of faithfulness especially to one's husband or wife — see INFIDELITY 1
inconstant *adj* **1** likely to change frequently, suddenly, or unexpectedly — see FICKLE 1
2 not true in one's allegiance to someone or something — see FAITHLESS
incontestable *adj* not capable of being challenged or proved wrong — see IRREFUTABLE
incontestably *adv* without any question — see INDEED 1
incontrovertible *adj* not capable of being challenged or proved wrong — see IRREFUTABLE
incontrovertibly *adv* without any question — see INDEED 1
inconvenience *n* something that is a source of irritation — see ANNOYANCE 3
inconvenience *vb* to cause discomfort to or trouble for ⟨he *inconvenienced* his sister by moving into her tiny apartment⟩
synonyms discommode, disoblige, disturb, incommode, trouble
related words burden, encumber, saddle, weigh; hamper, hamstring, hinder, hobble, impede; aggravate, anger, annoy, bother, bug, exasperate, gall, get, nettle, peeve, pique, put out, rile, vex; grate, inflame, provoke; agitate, perturb, upset
near antonyms aid, assist, help; ease, facilitate; appease, conciliate, mollify, pacify, placate; delight, gladden, gratify, please; comfort, console, content
antonyms accommodate, oblige
inconvenient *adj* **1** causing difficulty, discomfort, or annoyance ⟨the unexpected visitors showed up at an *inconvenient* time⟩
synonyms awkward, discommoding, disobliging, incommoding
related words bothersome, burdensome, onerous, troublesome; annoying, exasperating, irritating
near antonyms acceptable, bearable, tolerable; advantageous, desirable, good, helpful
antonyms convenient
2 hard or impossible to get to or get at — see INACCESSIBLE
incorporate *vb* **1** to make a part of a body or system — see EMBODY 1
2 to turn into a single mass that is more or less the same throughout — see BLEND 1
incorporeal *adj* not composed of matter — see IMMATERIAL 1
incorrect *adj* **1** having an opinion that does not agree with truth or the facts ⟨you're *incorrect* about the date of the final exam—it's next Tuesday, not Wednesday⟩
synonyms mistaken, wrong
related words confused, misguided, misled; erroneous, false; deceived, deluded, tricked
phrases all wet, full of it
near antonyms informed; accurate, exact, precise
antonyms correct, right
2 not appropriate for a particular occasion or situation — see INAPPROPRIATE
3 not being in agreement with what is true — see FALSE 1
incorrectly *adv* in a mistaken or inappropriate way — see WRONGLY
incorrectness *n* **1** the quality or state of being unsuitable or unfitting — see INAPPROPRIATENESS 1
2 the quality or state of not being socially proper — see IMPROPRIETY 1
incorrigible *adj* not capable of being cured or reformed — see HOPELESS 1
increase *n* **1** something added (as by growth) ⟨shortly after he turned 12, he had a sudden height *increase*⟩
synonyms accretion, accrual, addendum, addition, augmentation, boost, expansion, gain, increment, plus, proliferation, raise, rise, supplement
related words accumulation; complement; appendix, continuation, extension, uptrend, upturn; jump
near antonyms deduction
antonyms abatement, decrease, diminishment, lessening, lowering, reduction
2 the act or process of becoming greater in number — see MULTIPLICATION
increase *vb* **1** to make greater in size, amount, or number ⟨if you *increase* the number by two, how much do you have now?⟩
synonyms add (to), aggrandize, amplify, augment, boost, compound, enlarge, escalate, expand, extend, multiply, raise, swell, up
related words skyrocket; blow up, dilate, distend, inflate; elongate, lengthen, prolong, protract; enhance, heighten, intensify, magnify; complement, supplement; beef (up), reinforce, strengthen; maximize; accumulate, amass, collect; follow up, parlay
near antonyms abbreviate, abridge, curtail, shorten; compress, condense, constrict, cut back, retrench
antonyms abate, contract, decrease, diminish, lessen, lower, reduce, subtract (from)
2 to become greater in extent, volume, amount,

or number ⟨the number of Internet users *increased* rapidly during the 1990s⟩
synonyms accumulate, appreciate, balloon, build (up), burgeon, enlarge, escalate, expand, mount, multiply, mushroom, proliferate, rise, snowball, swell, wax
related words rocket, skyrocket; heighten, intensify; blow up, distend, inflate; crest, peak, surge
antonyms contract, decrease, diminish, lessen, wane

increased *adj* being at a higher level than average — see HIGH 2

incredible *adj* too extraordinary or improbable to believe ⟨she came in on Monday with an *incredible* story about monsters eating her homework⟩
synonyms fantastic, implausible, inconceivable, unbelievable, unconvincing, unimaginable, unthinkable
related words doubtful, dubious, far-fetched, fishy, flimsy, questionable, suspect, unlikely, unreasonable; hopeless, impossible; absurd, outlandish, preposterous, ridiculous; indefensible, insupportable, untenable
near antonyms likely, possible, probable; reasonable
antonyms believable, conceivable, convincing, credible, imaginable, plausible

incredulity *n* refusal to accept as true — see DISBELIEF

incredulous *adj* inclined to doubt or question claims — see SKEPTICAL 1

increment *n* something added (as by growth) — see INCREASE 1

incremental *adj* **1** proceeding or changing by steps or degrees — see GRADUAL
2 produced by a series of additions of identical or similar things — see CUMULATIVE

incriminate *vb* to make a claim of wrongdoing against — see ACCUSE

incubate *vb* to cover and warm eggs to hatch them — see SET 1

incubus *n* an evil spirit — see DEMON

inculcate *vb* to cause (as a person) to become filled or saturated with a certain quality or principle — see INFUSE

incumbent *adj* forcing one's compliance or participation by or as if by law — see MANDATORY

incurable *adj* not capable of being cured or reformed — see HOPELESS 1

incurious *adj* having or showing a lack of interest or concern — see INDIFFERENT 1

incursion *n* a sudden attack on and entrance into hostile territory — see RAID 1

indecency *n* **1** the quality or state of being obscene — see OBSCENITY 1
2 the quality or state of not being socially proper — see IMPROPRIETY 1

indecent *adj* depicting or referring to sexual matters in a way that is unacceptable in polite society — see OBSCENE 1

indecision *n* the act or an instance of pausing because of uncertainty about the right course of action — see HESITATION

indecorous *adj* not appropriate for a particular occasion or situation — see INAPPROPRIATE

indeed *interj* how surprising, doubtful, or unbelievable — see NO

indeed *adv* **1** without any question ⟨I know that you can *indeed* do better than that⟩
synonyms assuredly, certainly, definitely, doubtless, forsooth, incontestably, incontrovertibly, indisputably, really, surely, truly, undeniably, undoubtedly, unquestionably
related words conceivably, likely, perhaps, possibly, probably; clearly, obviously, unmistakably
phrases by all means, for sure
2 not merely this but also — see EVEN

indefatigable *adj* showing no signs of weariness even after long hard effort — see TIRELESS

indefatigably *adv* with great effort or determination — see HARD 1

indefensible *adj* too bad to be excused or justified — see INEXCUSABLE

indefinable *adj* beyond the power to describe — see INDESCRIBABLE

indefinite *adj* **1** being or seeming to be without limits — see INFINITE
2 not clearly expressed — see VAGUE 1
3 not seen or understood clearly — see FAINT 1

indelicacy *n* the quality or state of lacking refinement or good taste — see VULGARITY 1

indelicateness *n* the quality or state of lacking refinement or good taste — see VULGARITY 1

indemnification *n* payment to another for a loss or injury — see COMPENSATION 1

indemnify *vb* to provide (someone) with a just payment for loss or injury — see COMPENSATE 1

indemnity *n* payment to another for a loss or injury — see COMPENSATION 1

indentation *n* **1** a sunken area forming a separate space — see HOLE 2
2 a V-shaped cut usually on an edge or a surface — see NOTCH 1

indented *adj* curved inward — see HOLLOW

independence *n* **1** the ability to care for one's self — see SELF-SUFFICIENCY
2 the state of being free from the control or power of another — see FREEDOM 1

independent *adj* **1** able to take care of oneself without outside help — see SELF-SUFFICIENT
2 not being under the rule or control of another — see FREE 1

independently *adv* without aid or support — see ALONE 1

in–depth *adj* covering everything or all important points — see ENCYCLOPEDIC

indescribable *adj* beyond the power to describe ⟨the *indescribable* immensity of Mount Everest⟩
synonyms incommunicable, indefinable, ineffable, inexpressible, nameless, unspeakable, unutterable
related words inconceivable, incredible, unbelievable, unimaginable, unthinkable; characterless, featureless, nondescript
near antonyms conceivable, imaginable, thinkable
antonyms communicable, definable, expressible, speakable

indestructible *adj* impossible to destroy ⟨diamonds are widely considered to be *indestructible,* because they are one of the hardest known substances⟩
synonyms imperishable, inextinguishable
related words incorruptible; deathless, immortal, perpetual, undying; indelible; durable, enduring, lasting, permanent, unbreakable; strong, sturdy, tough
near antonyms mortal; impermanent, transient, transitory; breakable, delicate, flimsy, fragile, frail
antonyms destructible, extinguishable, perishable

index *n* an arrow-shaped piece on a dial or scale for registering information — see POINTER 1

index *vb* to put (someone or something) on a list — see [1]LIST 2

Indian *n* a member of any of the native peoples of the western hemisphere usually not including the Eskimos — see AMERICAN INDIAN

indicate *vb* to convey an idea indirectly — see HINT

indication *n* a slight or indirect pointing to something (as a solution or explanation) — see HINT 1

indicative *adj* indicating something ⟨a wide-eyed look that is *indicative* of his constant curiosity⟩
synonyms denotative, denoting, significant, signifying, telltale
related words alluding, allusive, referring; characteristic, symptomatic; demonstrative, exhibiting, expressive; symbolic (*also* symbolical); connoting, hinting, implying, insinuating, suggestive

indicator *n* an arrow-shaped piece on a dial or scale for registering information — see POINTER 1

indict *vb* to make a claim of wrongdoing against — see ACCUSE

indictment *n* a formal claim of criminal wrongdoing against a person — see CHARGE 1

indifference *n* lack of interest or concern ⟨he felt only *indifference* towards his schoolwork⟩
synonyms apathy, casualness, disinterestedness, disregard, insouciance, nonchalance, unconcern
related words halfheartedness, lukewarmness; carelessness, heedlessness, recklessness, unawareness; lethargy, listlessness; calmness, detachment, dispassion; callousness, hardheartedness, hardness, insensitivity; impassivity, phlegm; aloofness, coldness
near antonyms attentiveness, awareness, conscientiousness, heedfulness; sensitivity, warmheartedness; bias, partiality, prejudice; ardor, fervency, passion, warmth, zeal
antonyms concern, interest, regard

indifferent *adj* **1** having or showing a lack of interest or concern ⟨*indifferent* about the result of the football game⟩
synonyms apathetic, casual, disinterested, incurious, insouciant, nonchalant, perfunctory, unconcerned, uncurious, uninterested
related words halfhearted, lukewarm; aloof, cold, numb, remote, unemotional; calm, detached, dispassionate; careless, heedless, mindless; impassive, phlegmatic, stoic (*or* stoical), stolid; lethargic, listless; unawed, undazzled, unimpressed
near antonyms attentive, aware, conscientious, heedful, mindful; caring, sensitive, warmhearted; ardent, fervent, passionate, warm, zealous
antonyms concerned, interested
2 of average to below average quality — see MEDIOCRE 1

indigence *n* the state of lacking sufficient money or material possessions — see POVERTY 1

indigenous *adj* belonging to a particular place by birth or origin — see NATIVE 1

indigent *adj* lacking money or material possessions — see POOR 1

indignant *adj* feeling or showing anger — see ANGRY

indignation *n* an intense emotional state of displeasure with someone or something — see ANGER

indignity *n* an act or expression showing scorn and usually intended to hurt another's feelings — see INSULT

indirect *adj* not straightforward or direct ⟨the cab driver took a very *indirect* route to the hotel⟩ ⟨a long-winded, *indirect* answer to a very simple question⟩
synonyms circuitous, circular, roundabout
related words crooked, serpentine, sinuous, tortuous, twisting, winding; meandering, rambling, wandering; circumlocutory, long-winded, prolix, verbose; deceitful, deceptive, devious, dishonest, duplicitous, insidious, misleading, sneaky, underhand, underhanded; calculating, crafty, cunning, subtle, tricky
near antonyms candid, forthright, frank, honest, open, plain, unconcealed, undisguised
antonyms direct, straight, straightforward

indiscreet *adj* showing poor judgment especially in personal relationships or social situations ⟨telling a friend's secrets is *indiscreet,* and unkind as well⟩
synonyms ill-advised, imprudent, inadvisable, injudicious, tactless, unadvisable, unwise
related words dumb, idiotic, moronic, stupid; inconsiderate, thoughtless; ill-mannered, improper, inappropriate, indecorous, unbecoming, uncivil, unseemly; foolish, harebrained, nonsensical, preposterous, senseless, silly
near antonyms intelligent, logical, rational, sensible, smart, sound; appropriate, becoming, civil, decorous, proper, seemly; sage, sane, sapient
antonyms advisable, discreet, judicious, prudent, tactful, wise

indiscretion *n* a socially improper or unsuitable act or remark — see IMPROPRIETY 2

indispensable *adj* impossible to do without — see ESSENTIAL 1

indisposed *adj* **1** having doubts about the wisdom of doing something — see HESITANT
2 temporarily suffering from a disorder of the body — see SICK 1

indisposition *n* the condition of not being in good health — see SICKNESS 1

indisputable *adj* not capable of being challenged or proved wrong — see IRREFUTABLE

indisputably *adv* without any question — see INDEED 1

indistinct *adj* not seen or understood clearly — see FAINT 1

indistinguishable *adj* **1** not perceptible by a sense or by the mind — see IMPERCEPTIBLE
2 not seen or understood clearly — see FAINT 1
3 resembling another in every respect — see SAME 1

individual *adj* **1** of, relating to, or belonging to a single person ⟨everyone has his or her own *individual* opinion about the subject, but you will have to work together⟩
synonyms individualized, particular, peculiar, personal, personalized, private, privy, separate, singular, unique
related words characteristic, distinctive, intimate; identifying, idiosyncratic; special, specific; independent, nonconformist, self-directed, self-sufficient; custom, customized, specialized
near antonyms broad, prevailing, prevalent, widespread; common, normal, regular, typical
antonyms general, generic, popular, public, shared, universal
2 not the same or shared — see SEPARATE 1
3 serving to identify as belonging to an individual or group — see CHARACTERISTIC 1

individual *n* **1** a member of the human race — see HUMAN
2 one that has a real and independent existence — see ENTITY

individualist *n* a person who does not conform to generally accepted standards or customs — see NONCONFORMIST 1

individuality *n* the set of qualities that make a person different from other people ⟨her *individuality* showed through in everything she did⟩
synonyms character, identity, personality, selfhood, self-identity
related words distinctiveness, oneness, peculiarity, separateness, singleness, singularity, uniqueness; disposition, humor, nature, temper, temperament; independence
near antonyms conformity, conventionality

individualized *adj* of, relating to, or belonging to a single person — see INDIVIDUAL 1

indoctrinate *vb* to cause to acquire knowledge or skill in some field — see TEACH

indolence *n* an inclination not to do work or engage in activities — see LAZINESS

indolent *adj* not easily aroused to action or work — see LAZY

indomitable *adj* incapable of being defeated, overcome, or subdued — see INVINCIBLE

indubitable *adj* not capable of being challenged or proved wrong — see IRREFUTABLE

induce *vb* **1** to be the cause of (a situation, action, or state of mind) — see EFFECT
2 to cause (someone) to agree with a belief or course of action by using arguments or earnest requests — see PERSUADE

inducement *n* the act of reasoning or pleading with someone to accept a belief or course of action — see PERSUASION 1

inducing *n* the act of reasoning or pleading with someone to accept a belief or course of action — see PERSUASION 1

induct *vb* to put into an office or welcome into an organization with special ceremonies — see INSTALL 1

inductee *n* a person forced or required to enroll in military service — see CONSCRIPT

induction *n* the process or an instance of being formally placed in an office or organization — see INSTALLATION 1

indulge *vb* to give in to (a desire) ⟨the grandparents generally *indulged* the child's wishes⟩
synonyms cater (to), gratify, humor
related words bask, luxuriate, revel, wallow; coddle, mollycoddle, pamper, spoil; delight, please, pleasure; sate, satiate, satisfy
near antonyms bridle, check, constrain, curb, inhibit, restrain, stifle

indulgence *n* **1** an act of kind assistance — see FAVOR 1
2 something adding to pleasure or comfort but not absolutely necessary — see LUXURY 1

industrious *adj* involved in often constant activity — see BUSY 1

industriously *adv* with great effort or determination — see HARD 1

industriousness *n* attentive and persistent effort — see DILIGENCE

industry *n* attentive and persistent effort — see DILIGENCE

inebriate *adj* being under the influence of alcohol — see DRUNK 1

inebriate *n* a person who makes a habit of getting drunk — see DRUNK

inebriated *adj* being under the influence of alcohol — see DRUNK

ineffable *adj* beyond the power to describe — see INDESCRIBABLE

ineffective *adj* **1** not producing the desired result ⟨an *ineffective* effort to move the bookcase⟩
synonyms ineffectual, inefficient, inexpedient
related words abortive, bootless, fruitless, futile, nonproductive, pointless, unavailing, unproductive, unprofitable, unsuccessful, useless, worthless
near antonyms availing, beneficial, helpful, productive, profitable, successful, useful, worthwhile
antonyms effective, effectual, efficacious, efficient, expedient
2 producing no results — see FUTILE

ineffectual *adj* **1** not producing the desired result — see INEFFECTIVE 1
2 producing no results — see FUTILE

inefficient *adj* not producing the desired result — see INEFFECTIVE 1

inelegant *adj* **1** lacking social grace and assurance — see AWKWARD 1
2 marked by an obvious lack of style or good taste — see TACKY 1

inept *adj* **1** lacking qualities (as knowledge, skill, or ability) required to do a job — see INCOMPETENT
2 not appropriate for a particular occasion or situation — see INAPPROPRIATE
3 showing or marked by a lack of skill and tact (as in dealing with a situation) — see AWKWARD 2

ineptitude *n* the lack of sufficient ability, power, or means — see INABILITY

inequity *n* the state of being unfair or unjust — see INJUSTICE 1

inert *adj* **1** not being in a state of use, activity, or employment — see INACTIVE 2
2 slow to move or act — see INACTIVE 1

inertia *n* an inclination not to do work or engage in activities — see LAZINESS

inertness *n* lack of action or activity — see INACTION

inescapable *adj* impossible to avoid or evade — see INEVITABLE

inescapably *adv* because of necessity — see NEEDS

inevitable *adj* impossible to avoid or evade ⟨getting wet is *inevitable* if you are going to try to give your dog a bath⟩
synonyms certain, inescapable, necessary, sure, unavoidable
related words decided, definite, settled; likely, possible, probable; destined, fated, foreordained, predestined, predetermined, preordained; inexorable, relentless, unremitting
phrases in the bag
near antonyms preventable (*also* preventible); doubtful, dubious, questionable, shaky, unclear; undecided, unsettled; undependable, unreliable; improbable, unlikely
antonyms avoidable, escapable, uncertain, unsure

inevitably *adv* because of necessity — see NEEDS

inexact *adj* **1** not precisely correct ⟨a thousand is an *inexact* figure for the number of islands in the St. Lawrence River⟩
synonyms imprecise, inaccurate, loose
related words approximate; erroneous, false, in-

correct, off, wrong; general, indefinable, indefinite, indeterminate, indistinct, undefined, undetermined, unsettled, vague; faulty, flawed, mistaken; specious; distorted, fallacious, misleading; doubtful, dubious, questionable, uncertain; inconclusive, indecisive; debatable, disputable; invalidated, unconfirmed, unsubstantiated, unsupported
near antonyms certain, incontestable, indubitable, positive, sure, undeniable, unquestionable; correct, errorless, factual, right, sound, true, valid; clear-cut, decisive, definable, defined, definite; incontrovertible, indisputable, irrefutable; absolute, unqualified; confirmed, corroborated, determined, established, substantiated, supported, validated
antonyms accurate, dead, exact, precise
2 not being in agreement with what is true — see FALSE 1

inexcusable *adj* too bad to be excused or justified ⟨spitting at a teacher is *inexcusable* behavior and will be severely punished⟩
synonyms indefensible, unforgivable, unjustifiable, unpardonable, unwarrantable
related words insufferable, insupportable, intolerable, unbearable, unendurable; abominable, atrocious, heinous, monstrous, outrageous, scandalous, shocking; egregious, flagrant, glaring, gross, rank; unacceptable, untenable; black, evil, iniquitous, vicious, wicked; base, contemptible, deplorable, despicable, dirty, execrable, ignoble, reprobate, vile, wretched; cruel, nasty; blamable, blameworthy, censurable, reprehensible; banned, barred, condemned, disallowed, forbidden, interdicted, outlawed, prohibited, proscribed
near antonyms acceptable, tolerable; authorized, legal, permissible; allowed, permitted, tolerated; approved, endorsed, sanctioned; abetted, encouraged, promoted, supported; ethical, good, moral, virtuous
antonyms defensible, excusable, forgivable, justifiable, pardonable

inexhaustible *adj* showing no signs of weariness even after long hard effort — see TIRELESS

inexpedient *adj* not producing the desired result — see INEFFECTIVE 1

inexpensive *adj* costing little — see CHEAP 1

inexperienced *adj* **1** lacking in adult experience or maturity — see CALLOW
2 lacking or showing a lack of expert skill — see AMATEURISH

inexpert *adj* **1** lacking or showing a lack of expert skill — see AMATEURISH
2 lacking qualities (as knowledge, skill, or ability) required to do a job — see INCOMPETENT
3 showing or marked by a lack of skill and tact (as in dealing with a situation) — see AWKWARD 2

inexplicable *adj* impossible to explain ⟨an *inexplicable* desire for ice cream at two in the morning⟩
synonyms unaccountable, unexplainable
related words indefinable, indescribable, inexpressible; enigmatic (*also* enigmatical), impenetrable, incomprehensible, inscrutable, mysterious, unfathomable, unknowable; irrational, unreasonable, unsound; foolish, mindless, senseless; absurd, odd, peculiar, strange, unusual, weird
near antonyms logical, rational, reasonable, understandable; sane, sensible, wise; compelling, convincing, persuasive, plausible, satisfying; confirmed, corroborated, determined, established, explained, substantiated, validated
antonyms accountable, explainable, explicable

inexpressible *adj* beyond the power to describe — see INDESCRIBABLE

inexpressive *adj* not expressing any emotion — see BLANK 1

inextinguishable *adj* impossible to destroy — see INDESTRUCTIBLE

infallible *adj* **1** not being or likely to be wrong ⟨a teacher with an *infallible* memory for names⟩
synonyms unerring, unfailing
related words errorless, faultless, flawless, impeccable; certain, foolproof, perfect, sure; dependable, reliable
near antonyms defective, faulty, flawed, imperfect; undependable, unreliable
antonyms fallible
2 not likely to fail ⟨an *infallible* cure for hiccups⟩
synonyms certain, sure, unfailing
related words dependable, reliable, surefire; deadly, unerring
near antonyms doubtful, questionable, uncertain
antonyms fallible

infamous *adj* not respectable — see DISREPUTABLE

infamy *n* the state of having lost the esteem of others — see DISGRACE 1

infant *n* a recently born person — see BABY

infantile *adj* having or showing the annoying qualities (as silliness) associated with children — see CHILDISH

infatuated (with) *adj* filled with an intense or excessive love for — see ENAMORED (OF)

infatuation *n* a strong but often short-lived liking for another person — see CRUSH 1

infectious *adj* exciting a similar feeling or reaction in others — see CONTAGIOUS 2

infelicitous *adj* not appropriate for a particular occasion or situation — see INAPPROPRIATE

infelicity *n* the quality or state of being unsuitable or unfitting — see INAPPROPRIATENESS 1

infer *vb* **1** to form an opinion through reasoning and information ⟨he *inferred* that she had left because her coat was gone⟩
synonyms conclude, deduce, extrapolate, gather, judge, reason, understand
related words conjecture, guess, speculate, surmise; construe, interpret; contemplate, rationalize, think; ascertain, dope (out), find out
phrases draw a conclusion
2 to convey an idea indirectly — see HINT

inferable *adj* being or provable by reasoning in which the conclusion follows necessarily from given information — see DEDUCTIVE

inference *n* an opinion arrived at through a process of reasoning — see CONCLUSION 1

inferior *adj* **1** situated lower down ⟨creatures that inhabit the dark, *inferior* depths of the ocean⟩
synonyms lower, nether
related words lowest, nethermost; underlying
near antonyms highest, uppermost; overhanging, overhead
antonyms higher, superior, upper
2 of little or less value or merit ⟨a girl who has always felt *inferior* to her older sister⟩
synonyms mean, minor, secondary, second-class, second-rate
related words junior, lesser, lower, petty, smaller, subordinate, under; average, common, fair, mid-

dling, ordinary; amiss, bad, defective, unsatisfactory, wrong; deficient, inadequate, insufficient, unacceptable; littler, slighter, smaller; jerkwater, one-horse, two-bit
near antonyms major, more, primary, senior; choice, exceptional, first-class, first-rate, high-grade, premium, prime; acceptable, adequate, sufficient
antonyms greater, higher, superior
3 belonging to the class of people of low social or economic rank — see IGNOBLE 1
4 falling short of a standard — see BAD 1
5 having not so great importance or rank as another — see LESSER
6 of low quality — see CHEAP 2

inferior *n* one who is of lower rank and typically under the authority of another — see UNDERLING

inferno *n* a destructive burning — see FIRE

infertile *adj* **1** not able to produce fruit or offspring — see STERILE 1
2 producing inferior or only a small amount of vegetation — see BARREN 1

infest *vb* to spread or swarm over in a troublesome manner ⟨called in an exterminator because the house was *infested* with ants⟩
synonyms overrun
related words beset, overspread, overwhelm; abound, crawl, teem; annoy, pester, plague; contaminate, infect

infidelity *n* **1** lack of faithfulness especially to one's husband or wife ⟨*infidelity* can lead to divorce⟩
synonyms disloyalty, faithlessness, falseness, falsity, inconstancy, perfidiousness, perfidy, unfaithfulness
related words adultery; betrayal, double-cross, double-dealing, duplicity, sellout, treachery, treason; deceit, deception, lying
near antonyms staunchness, steadfastness; dependability, reliability; honesty, trustworthiness
antonyms allegiance, constancy, devotedness, devotion, faith, faithfulness, fealty, fidelity, loyalty
2 the act or fact of violating the trust or confidence of another — see BETRAYAL

infiltrate *vb* to introduce in a gradual, secret, or clever way — see INSINUATE

infinite *adj* being or seeming to be without limits ⟨the *infinite* expanse of outer space⟩
synonyms boundless, endless, illimitable, immeasurable, indefinite, limitless, measureless, unbounded, unfathomable, unlimited
related words abysmal, bottomless; countless, incalculable, inestimable, innumerable, unmeasured; inexhaustible; far-flung, immense, vast
near antonyms fathomable, measurable; depthless, shallow, superficial
antonyms bounded, circumscribed, confined, definite, finite, limited, restricted

infinitesimal *adj* very small in size — see TINY

infinity *n* endless time — see ETERNITY 1

infirm *adj* lacking bodily strength — see WEAK 1

infirmity *n* **1** an abnormal state that disrupts a plant's or animal's normal bodily functioning — see DISEASE
2 the quality or state of lacking physical strength or vigor — see WEAKNESS 1

inflame *vb* **1** to make angry — see ANGER
2 to set (something) on fire — see BURN 2

inflamed *adj* **1** being on fire — see ABLAZE 1
2 feeling or showing anger — see ANGRY

inflammable *adj* capable of catching or being set on fire — see COMBUSTIBLE

inflexibility *n* the quality or state of being demanding or unyielding (as in discipline or criticism) — see SEVERITY

inflexible *adj* **1** not capable of changing or being changed ⟨the *inflexible* law of gravity⟩
synonyms fixed, hard-and-fast, immutable, invariable, unalterable, unchangeable
related words changeless, constant, determinate, established, set, settled, stable, steadfast, steady, unaltered, unchanging, unvarying; immovable, unmovable
near antonyms adaptable, adjustable; fickle, fluctuating, inconstant, uncertain, unstable, varying
antonyms alterable, changeable, flexible, mutable, variable
2 incapable of or highly resistant to bending — see STIFF 1
3 not allowing for any exceptions or loosening of standards — see RIGID 1
4 sticking to an opinion, purpose, or course of action in spite of reason, arguments, or persuasion — see OBSTINATE

inflow *n* a flowing or coming in — see INFLUX

influence *n* **1** the power to direct the thinking or behavior of others usually indirectly ⟨a mayor who doesn't hesitate to use her *influence* to get business leaders behind civic improvements⟩
synonyms authority, clout, pull, sway, weight
related words command, dominance, dominion, mastery, predominance, scepter, sovereignty, supremacy; consequence, eminence, importance, moment; impact, impression, mark
near antonyms helplessness, impotence, powerlessness, weakness
2 the power to bring about a result on another — see EFFECT 2

influence *vb* to act upon (a person or a person's feelings) so as to cause a response — see [1]AFFECT 1

influential *adj* **1** having power over the minds or behavior of others ⟨in light of the effect that they have had, religious leaders such as Jesus and Muḥammad must be regarded as among the most *influential* people ever⟩
synonyms authoritative, forceful, weighty
related words controlling, dominating, masterful; dominant, predominant, sovereign, supreme; eminent, important, momentous
near antonyms helpless, impotent, powerless, weak; incapable, unable
2 having great power or influence — see IMPORTANT 2

influx *n* a flowing or coming in ⟨a sudden *influx* of people⟩
synonyms flux, inflow, inrush
related words deluge, flood, flow, inundation, overflow, spate, torrent; rush, stampede; flow, river, stream, tide
near antonyms emigration, exodus, flight
antonyms outflow, outpouring

inform *vb* **1** to give information (as to the authorities) about another's improper or unlawful activities — see SQUEAL 1
2 to give information to — see ENLIGHTEN 1

informal *adj* **1** not rigidly following established form, custom, or rules ⟨an *informal* meeting allowed everyone to get acquainted⟩

synonyms irregular, unceremonious, unconventional, unorthodox
related words unauthorized, unofficial; casual, easygoing, lax, loose, relaxed
near antonyms correct, decorous, proper; constrained, inhibited, restrained, rigid, stiff, stuffy, uptight
antonyms ceremonial, ceremonious, conventional, formal, orthodox, regular, routine
2 not designed for special occasions — see CASUAL 1
3 used in or suitable for speech and not formal writing — see COLLOQUIAL 1

informant *n* a person who provides secret information about another's wrongdoing — see INFORMER

information *n* a report of recent events or facts not previously known — see NEWS

informational *adj* providing useful information or knowledge — see INFORMATIVE

informative *adj* providing useful information or knowledge ⟨some Web sites for family vacation resorts are very *informative* and some are practically useless⟩
synonyms educational, educative, informational, instructional, instructive
related words comprehensive, detailed, full; edifying, elucidative, enlightening, explanatory, illuminating; chatty, gossipy, newsy; availing, beneficial, constructive, helpful, profitable; practical, serviceable, usable, useful, worthwhile
near antonyms impractical, unhelpful, unusable, useless
antonyms uninstructive

informed *adj* **1** based on sound reasoning or information — see GOOD 1
2 having information especially as a result of study or experience — see FAMILIAR 2

informer *n* a person who provides secret information about another's wrongdoing ⟨the *informer* who told the police about that conspiracy angered a lot of dangerous people⟩
synonyms betrayer, informant, snitcher, squealer, stool pigeon, talebearer, tattler, tattletale, telltale
related words collaborator; blabbermouth, gossip, gossiper; snoop, snooper, spy; notifier

infraction *n* a failure to uphold the requirements of law, duty, or obligation — see BREACH 1

infrequent *adj* not often occurring or repeated ⟨a shut-in who made *infrequent* trips to the store⟩
synonyms occasional, rare, sporadic
related words scarce, scattered, uncommon, unique, unusual; choppy, discontinuous, erratic, fitful, intermittent, irregular, spasmodic, spotty, unsteady
near antonyms common, ordinary, routine
antonyms frequent

infrequently *adv* not often — see SELDOM

infringe *vb* to fail to keep — see VIOLATE 1

infringement *n* a failure to uphold the requirements of law, duty, or obligation — see BREACH 1

infuriate *vb* to make angry — see ANGER

infuriated *adj* feeling or showing anger — see ANGRY

infuse *vb* to cause (as a person) to become filled or saturated with a certain quality or principle ⟨parents who *infuse* their children with strong moral values⟩
synonyms imbue, inculcate, ingrain, inoculate, invest, steep, suffuse
related words animate, enliven, invigorate; implant, instill, plant; impregnate, permeate, pervade, saturate; deluge, drown, fill, flood, inundate, overwhelm, submerge
near antonyms deprive, divest, strip; clear, empty; eliminate, remove, take away

ingenious *adj* **1** having the skill and imagination to create new things — see CREATIVE 1
2 showing a use of the imagination and creativity especially in inventing — see CLEVER 1

ingeniousness *n* the skill and imagination to create new things — see CREATIVITY 1

ingenuity *n* the skill and imagination to create new things — see CREATIVITY 1

ingenuous *adj* **1** free from any intent to deceive or impress others — see GUILELESS
2 lacking in worldly wisdom or informed judgment — see NAIVE 1

ingenuously *adv* without any attempt to impress by deception or exaggeration — see NATURALLY 3

ingenuousness *n* the quality or state of being simple and sincere — see NAÏVETÉ 1

ingest *vb* **1** to take in as food — see EAT 1
2 to take into the stomach through the mouth and throat — see SWALLOW 1

ingrain *vb* **1** to cause (as a person) to become filled or saturated with a certain quality or principle — see INFUSE
2 to produce a vivid impression of — see ENGRAVE 2
3 to set solidly in or as if in surrounding matter — see ENTRENCH

ingrained *adj* being a part of the innermost nature of a person or thing — see INHERENT

ingratiating *adj* likely to win one's affection ⟨one of the orphans had a most *ingratiating* smile⟩
synonyms disarming, endearing, winning, winsome
related words adorable, charming, likable, lovable; affecting, poignant, touching; adulatory, deferential, groveling (*or* grovelling), kowtowing, obsequious, servile, sycophantic; drooling, slavering, slobbering; soapy, sugary, unctuous
near antonyms alienating, disaffecting, displeasing; repugnant, repulsive; arrogant, disdainful, haughty, insolent, proud, scornful

ingredient *n* one of the parts that make up a whole — see ELEMENT 1

inhabitable *adj* suitable for living in — see LIVABLE

inhabitant *n* one who lives permanently in a place ⟨the *inhabitants* of the town don't like the tourists⟩
synonyms denizen, dweller, habitant, occupant, resident, resider
related words aborigine, native; citizen, national, subject; colonist, émigré (*also* emigré), migrant, newcomer, settler; burgher, townie, villager
near antonyms alien, foreigner; guest, tourist, visitor; defector, escaper, evacuee, exile, expatriate, refugee
antonyms transient

inharmonious *adj* **1** not being in agreement or harmony — see INCONSISTENT
2 marked by or producing a harsh combination of sounds — see DISSONANT

inherent *adj* being a part of the innermost nature of a person or thing ⟨an *inherent* concept of justice⟩
synonyms essential, inborn, inbred, ingrained, innate, integral, intrinsic, natural

related words basic, constitutional, elemental, fundamental; congenital, hereditary, inherited, inmost, inner, interior; internal; characteristic, distinctive, peculiar; normal, regular, typical
near antonyms alien, foreign; accidental, coincidental, incidental; acquired; superficial, surface; exterior, external
antonyms adventitious, extraneous, extrinsic

inherently *adv* by natural character or ability — see NATURALLY 1

inheritable *adj* genetically passed or capable of being passed from parent to offspring — see HEREDITARY

inheritance *n* something that is or may be inherited ⟨a sense of humor was her *inheritance* from her mother⟩
synonyms bequest, birthright, heritage, legacy, patrimony
related words heirloom; bestowal, gift, offering, present

inherited *adj* genetically passed or capable of being passed from parent to offspring — see HEREDITARY

inheritor *n* a person who has the right to inherit property — see HEIR

inhibit *vb* **1** to create difficulty for the work or activity of — see HAMPER
2 to keep from exceeding a desirable degree or level (as of expression) — see CONTROL 1
3 to steer (a person) from an activity or course of action — see DISCOURAGE 2

inhibition *n* **1** the checking of one's true feelings and impulses when dealing with others — see CONSTRAINT 1
2 something that makes movement or progress more difficult — see ENCUMBRANCE

inhospitable *adj* marked by opposition or ill will — see HOSTILE 1

inhuman *adj* **1** difficult to endure — see HARSH 1
2 having or showing a lack of sympathy or tender feelings — see HARD 1

inhumane *adj* **1** having or showing a lack of sympathy or tender feelings — see HARD 1
2 having or showing the desire to inflict severe pain and suffering on others — see CRUEL 1

inhumanity *n* the willful infliction of pain and suffering on others — see CRUELTY

inimical *adj* **1** marked by opposition or ill will — see HOSTILE 1
2 opposed to one's interests — see ADVERSE 1

inimitable *adj* having no equal or rival for excellence or desirability — see ONLY 1

iniquitous *adj* not conforming to a high moral standard; morally unacceptable — see BAD 2

iniquity *n* **1** immoral conduct or practices harmful or offensive to society — see VICE 1
2 that which is morally unacceptable — see EVIL

initial *adj* coming before all others in time or order — see FIRST 1

initially *adv* in the beginning — see ORIGINALLY

initiate *vb* **1** to be responsible for the creation and early operation or use of — see FOUND
2 to impart knowledge of a new thing or situation to — see ACQUAINT 1
3 to put into an office or welcome into an organization with special ceremonies — see INSTALL 1

initiation *n* the process or an instance of being formally placed in an office or organization — see INSTALLATION 1

initiative *n* readiness to engage in daring or difficult activity — see ENTERPRISE 2

initiator *n* a person who establishes a whole new field of endeavor — see FATHER 2

inject *vb* to put among or between others — see INSERT

injudicious *adj* showing poor judgment especially in personal relationships or social situations — see INDISCREET

injure *vb* **1** to cause bodily damage to ⟨*injured* himself while skiing⟩
synonyms damage, harm, hurt, wound
related words batter, bruise, contuse, gash, gore, lacerate, scald, scar, scathe, tear; cripple, lame, maim, mangle, mutilate; afflict, torment, torture; lay up; blemish, impair, mar, scrape, spoil
near antonyms cure, fix, heal, mend, remedy
2 to reduce the soundness, effectiveness, or perfection of — see DAMAGE 1

injurious *adj* causing or capable of causing harm — see HARMFUL

injury *n* **1** something that causes loss or pain ⟨the harsh words were the worst *injury*⟩
synonyms damage, detriment, harm, hurt
related words disservice, injustice, outrage, wrong; affront, dart, indignity, insult, offense (*or* offence); crippling, mayhem, mutilation; defacement, disablement, disability, disfigurement; abrasion, bruise, bump, contusion, scald, scar, scathe, scrape, scratch, sear
near antonyms healing, recovery; cure, fix, remedy
2 unfair or inadequate treatment of someone or something or an instance of this — see DISSERVICE

injustice *n* **1** the state of being unfair or unjust ⟨the *injustice* of the coach's accusation that I'd been lazy frustrated and angered me⟩
synonyms inequity, unfairness, unjustness
related words dirtiness, foulness
antonyms equity, fairness, justice
2 unfair or inadequate treatment of someone or something or an instance of this — see DISSERVICE

inkling *n* a slight or indirect pointing to something (as a solution or explanation) — see HINT 1

inlet *n* a part of a body of water that extends beyond the general shoreline — see GULF 1

inn *n* a place that provides rooms and usually a public dining room for overnight guests — see HOTEL

innards *n pl* the internal organs of the body — see GUT 1

innate *adj* being a part of the innermost nature of a person or thing — see INHERENT

innately *adv* by natural character or ability — see NATURALLY 1

inner *adj* **1** situated farther in ⟨an *inner* area of the national park that is some distance from the nearest road⟩
synonyms inside, interior, internal, inward
related words inmost, innermost; central, mid, middle
near antonyms outermost, outmost
antonyms exterior, external, outer, outside, outward
2 of or relating to the mind — see MENTAL 1

innocence *n* **1** the quality or state of being free from guilt or blame ⟨the accused criminal eventually proved her *innocence* and was released⟩

synonyms blamelessness, faultlessness, guiltlessness, impeccability
related words decency, goodness, honesty, incorruptibility, integrity, righteousness, uprightness, virtuousness; morality, virtue; chastity, purity; harmlessness, inoffensiveness
near antonyms blame, fault, responsibility; corruption, criminality, depravity, evil, immorality, reprehensibleness, sinfulness, wickedness; harmfulness, offensiveness
antonyms blameworthiness, culpability, guilt, guiltiness
2 the quality or state of being simple and sincere — see NAÏVETÉ 1

innocent *adj* **1** free from sin ⟨an *innocent* baby⟩
synonyms pure
related words chaste, moral, virtuous; immaculate, spotless, unblemished, unstained, unsullied; decent, ethical, good, honest, honorable, righteous, upright, virtuous; blameless, guiltless
near antonyms lascivious, lewd, lustful, unchaste; evil, immoral, iniquitous, reprobate, unrighteous, wicked; corrupt, debased, debauched, degenerate, depraved, dissolute, erring, fallen, lost, perverted; condemned, damned
antonyms impure, sinful
2 free from guilt or blame ⟨the robbery suspect was found to be *innocent*⟩
synonyms blameless, clear, faultless, guiltless, impeccable, irreproachable
related words absolved, acquitted, cleared, exonerated, vindicated; ethical, law-abiding, moral, righteous, upright, virtuous
phrases in the clear
near antonyms blamable, blameworthy, censurable, culpable, impeachable, indictable, punishable; accused, impeached, indicted; condemned, convicted; hangdog, shamed, shamefaced
antonyms guilty
3 free from any intent to deceive or impress others — see GUILELESS
4 lacking in worldly wisdom or informed judgment — see NAIVE 1
5 not causing injury or hurt — see HARMLESS

innocent *n* an innocent or gentle person — see LAMB

innocently *adv* **1** without any attempt to impress by deception or exaggeration — see NATURALLY 3
2 with purity of thought and deed — see PURELY

innocuous *adj* not causing injury or hurt — see HARMLESS

innovate *vb* to be responsible for the creation and early operation or use of — see FOUND

innovation *n* something (as a device) created for the first time through the use of the imagination — see INVENTION 1

innovative *adj* having the skill and imagination to create new things — see CREATIVE 1

innovator *n* one who creates or introduces something new — see INVENTOR

innumerable *adj* too many to be counted — see COUNTLESS

inoculate *vb* to cause (as a person) to become filled or saturated with a certain quality or principle — see INFUSE

inoffensive *adj* not causing injury or hurt — see HARMLESS

inoperable *adj* **1** not being in working order ⟨we have several *inoperable* cars on the property⟩
synonyms inoperative, malfunctioning, nonfunctional, nonfunctioning, nonoperating
related words broken; off; deactivated, deadlocked, ineffective, ineffectual, nonproductive, unproductive, unusable, unworkable, useless
phrases on the blink, out of commission
near antonyms effective, effectual, employable, performing, producing, productive, serving, usable, useful, viable, workable
antonyms functional, functioning, operable, operating, operational, operative, running, working
2 not capable of being put to use or account — see IMPRACTICAL

inoperative *adj* **1** not being in a state of use, activity, or employment — see INACTIVE 2
2 not being in working order — see INOPERABLE 1

inopportune *adj* occurring before the usual or expected time — see EARLY 2

inopportunely *adv* before the usual or expected time — see EARLY

inordinate *adj* going beyond a normal or acceptable limit in degree or amount — see EXCESSIVE

inordinately *adv* beyond a normal or acceptable limit — see TOO 1

inquest *n* a systematic search for the truth or facts about something — see INQUIRY 1

inquire (into) *vb* to search through or into — see EXPLORE 1

inquire (of) *vb* to put a question or questions to — see ASK 1

inquiry *n* **1** a systematic search for the truth or facts about something ⟨an *inquiry* into the origins of the universe⟩
synonyms delving, examination, exploration, inquest, inquisition, investigation, probe, probing, research, study
related words quest; audit, check; checkup, diagnosis, inspection; hearing, interrogation, trial; feeler, query, question; poll, questionnaire; challenge, cross-examination, grilling, quiz
2 an act or instance of asking for information — see QUESTION 2

inquisition *n* a systematic search for the truth or facts about something — see INQUIRY 1

inquisitive *adj* interested in what is not one's own business — see CURIOUS 1

inquisitiveness *n* an eager desire to find out about things that are often none of one's business — see CURIOSITY 1

inroad *n* a sudden attack on and entrance into hostile territory — see RAID 1

inrush *n* a flowing or coming in — see INFLUX

insane *adj* **1** having or showing a very abnormal or sick state of mind ⟨only an *insane* person would jump off a skyscraper⟩
synonyms balmy, bananas, batty, crackbrained, cracked, crazed, crazy, cuckoo, daffy, daft, demented, deranged, loco, loony (*also* looney), lunatic, mad, maniacal (*also* maniac), mental, moonstruck, nuts, nutty, screwy, unbalanced, unsound, wacky
related words dotty, off; aberrant, delusional, disordered; eccentric, odd, queer, strange; foolish, senseless, witless; irrational, unreasonable; berserk, delirious; depressed; distraught, frantic, frenzied, hysterical
phrases around the bend, off one's rocker, out of one's head (*or* mind)

near antonyms clear, lucid, rational, reasonable; judicious, sensible, wise; healthy, normal
antonyms balanced, sane, sound
2 conceived or made without regard for reason or reality — see FANTASTIC 1
3 showing or marked by a lack of good sense or judgment — see FOOLISH 1

insanity *n* **1** a serious mental disorder that prevents one from living a safe and normal life ⟨his *insanity* requires that he spend the rest of his life in a mental hospital⟩
synonyms aberration, dementia, derangement, lunacy, madness, mania
related words irrationality, unreasonableness; delirium, frenzy, hysteria; neurosis, psychosis, schizophrenia; delusion, hallucination, obsession, phobia; abnormality, unsoundness
near antonyms lucidity, rationality, reasonableness; normality, soundness
antonyms mind, saneness, sanity
2 a foolish act or idea — see FOLLY 1
3 lack of good sense or judgment — see FOOLISHNESS 1

inscribe *vb* **1** to cut (as letters or designs) on a hard surface — see ENGRAVE 1
2 to enter in a list or roll — see ENROLL 1
3 to put (someone or something) on a list — see [1]LIST 2

inscrutable *adj* **1** being beyond one's powers to know, understand, or explain — see MYSTERIOUS 1
2 having an often intentionally veiled or uncertain meaning — see OBSCURE 1

insecure *adj* not tightly fastened, tied, or stretched — see LOOSE 1

insecurity *n* the quality or state of not being firmly fixed in position — see INSTABILITY

insensate *adj* having or showing a lack of sympathy or tender feelings — see HARD 1

insensibility *n* **1** a lack of emotion or emotional expressiveness — see APATHY 1
2 a temporary or permanent state of unconsciousness — see FAINT

insensible *adj* **1** having lost consciousness — see UNCONSCIOUS 1
2 not perceptible by a sense or by the mind — see IMPERCEPTIBLE

insensitive *adj* **1** having or showing a lack of sympathy or tender feelings — see HARD 1
2 lacking in sensation or feeling — see NUMB

inseparability *n* the state of being in a very personal or private relationship — see FAMILIARITY 1

insert *vb* to put among or between others ⟨*inserted* a book in its proper place on the shelf⟩
synonyms fit (in *or* into), inject, insinuate, interject, interpolate, interpose, introduce
related words inlay, inset, install, weave, work (in); cram, sandwich, shove, thrust, wedge; add, append, attach
near antonyms eject, eliminate, exclude, expel, extract, withdraw; deduct, detach, subtract; reject

inside *adj* **1** not known or meant to be known by the general populace — see PRIVATE 1
2 situated farther in — see INNER 1

inside *n* **1** an interior or internal part ⟨the *inside* of the clock features an amazingly complex mechanism⟩
synonyms interior, within
related words bowels, guts, innards; stuffing; recesses; center, core, heart
near antonyms border, boundary, brim, brink, edge, end, extremity, fringe, limit, lip, margin, perimeter, periphery, rim
antonyms exterior, outside
2 *usually* **insides** *pl* the internal organs of the body — see GUT 1

insight *n* the ability to understand inner qualities or relationships — see WISDOM 1

insightful *adj* having or showing deep understanding and intelligent application of knowledge — see WISE 1

insignificant *adj* **1** lacking importance — see UNIMPORTANT
2 so small or unimportant as to warrant little or no attention — see NEGLIGIBLE 1

insincere *adj* not being or expressing what one appears to be or express ⟨the *insincere* compliments of a spiteful gossip⟩
synonyms artificial, backhanded, double-dealing, feigned, hypocritical, left-handed, mealy, mealy-mouthed, two-faced, unctuous
related words empty, hollow, meaningless; deceitful, devious, dishonest, untruthful; facile, glib, superficial; bogus, counterfeit, fake, false, phony (*also* phoney), sham; facetious, jocular
near antonyms candid, direct, forthright, frank, open, plain, straightforward
antonyms genuine, heartfelt, honest, sincere, unfeigned

insincerity *n* the pretending of having virtues, principles, or beliefs that one in fact does not have — see HYPOCRISY

insinuate *vb* **1** to introduce in a gradual, secret, or clever way ⟨the spy *insinuated* himself into the terrorist organization⟩
synonyms infiltrate, slip, sneak, work (in), worm
related words creep, edge, wiggle; insert, interpolate, interpose, introduce
2 to convey an idea indirectly — see HINT
3 to put among or between others — see INSERT

insipid *adj* **1** lacking in taste or flavor ⟨an apple pie with a mushy, *insipid* filling that strongly resembled soggy cardboard⟩
synonyms flat, flavorless, savorless, tasteless
related words bland, dilute, thin, watery, weak; plain, unflavored
near antonyms disgusting, distasteful, loathsome, sickening, unappetizing, unpalatable; appetizing, delectable, delicious, palatable, toothsome; piquant, seasoned, spicy; flavored; heavy, rich
antonyms flavorful, savory, tasty
2 lacking in qualities that make for spirit and character — see WISHY-WASHY 1

insist *vb* to state as a fact usually forcefully — see CLAIM 1

insist (on) *vb* to ask for (something) earnestly or with authority — see DEMAND 1

insistence *n* a solemn and often public declaration of the truth or existence of something — see PROTESTATION

insistent *adj* continuing despite difficulties, opposition, or discouragement — see PERSISTENT

insolence *n* **1** disrespectful or argumentative talk given in response to a command or request — see BACK TALK
2 rude behavior — see DISCOURTESY

insolent *adj* displaying or marked by rude boldness — see NERVY 1

insouciance *n* lack of interest or concern — see INDIFFERENCE

insouciant *adj* **1** having or showing a lack of concern or seriousness — see CAREFREE
2 having or showing a lack of interest or concern — see INDIFFERENT 1

inspect *vb* to look over closely (as for judging quality or condition) ⟨*inspected* the animal before the show⟩
synonyms audit, check (out), examine, review, scan, scrutinize, survey
related words notice, observe, watch; peruse, pore (over); analyze, dissect; delve (into), explore, investigate, probe, research, study; categorize, classify
phrases go over
near antonyms skim; glance (at *or* over); miss, overlook

inspection *n* a close look at or over someone or something in order to judge condition ⟨a room *inspection* should include looking under the bed⟩
synonyms audit, check, checkup, examination, review, scan, scrutiny, survey
related words analysis, dissection; exploration, investigation, probe, research, study; inquisition, interrogation; perusal; observation, surveillance, watch

inspire *vb* to fill with courage or strength of purpose — see ENCOURAGE 1

inspiring *adj* causing great emotional or mental stimulation — see EXCITING 1

instability *n* the quality or state of not being firmly fixed in position ⟨the *instability* of the bridge became apparent when it suddenly collapsed⟩
synonyms insecurity, precariousness, shakiness, unsteadiness
related words insubstantiality, unsoundness; changeability, inconstancy, mutability
near antonyms firmness, soundness, substantiality
antonyms fixedness, security, stability, steadiness

install *vb* **1** to put into an office or welcome into an organization with special ceremonies ⟨*installed* her as the new principal⟩
synonyms baptize, inaugurate, induct, initiate, instate, invest
related words swear in; accept, admit, receive, take in; enlist, enroll (*also* enrol)
near antonyms can, discharge, fire, terminate; muster out
2 to establish or place comfortably or snugly — see ENSCONCE 1

installation *n* **1** the process or an instance of being formally placed in an office or organization ⟨the *installation* of a new president takes place once every four years⟩
synonyms baptism, inaugural, inauguration, induction, initiation, installment, investiture
related words enlistment, enrollment; promotion
near antonyms discharge, removal
2 a structure that is designed and built for a particular purpose — see FACILITY

installment *n* the process or an instance of being formally placed in an office or organization — see INSTALLATION 1

instance *n* one of a group or collection that shows what the whole is like — see EXAMPLE

instance *vb* **1** to give as an example — see QUOTE 1
2 to make reference to or speak about briefly but specifically — see MENTION 1
3 to show or make clear by using examples — see ILLUSTRATE 1

instant *adj* **1** done or occurring without any noticeable lapse in time — see INSTANTANEOUS
2 needing immediate attention — see ACUTE 2

instant *n* a very small space of time ⟨it all happened in an *instant*⟩
synonyms flash, jiffy, minute, moment, second, shake, split second, trice, twinkle, twinkling, wink
related words microsecond, nanosecond; snatch, spurt
near antonyms aeon (*or* eon), age, eternity; infinity, lifetime

instantaneous *adj* done or occurring without any noticeable lapse in time ⟨the thunder following the lightning was nearly *instantaneous*⟩
synonyms immediate, instant, straightaway
related words summary; fast, hit-and-run, prompt, quick, rapid, speedy, swift
near antonyms dilatory, tardy; slow, sluggish; prolonged, protracted; deferred, delayed

instantly *adv* without delay — see IMMEDIATELY

instate *vb* to put into an office or welcome into an organization with special ceremonies — see INSTALL 1

instead *adv* as a substitute ⟨I was offered a ride, but I chose to walk *instead*⟩
synonyms first, rather
related words alternately, alternatively

instigate *vb* **1** to cause or encourage the development of — see INCITE 1
2 to rouse to strong feeling or action — see PROVOKE 1

instigating *adj* serving or likely to arouse a strong reaction — see PROVOCATIVE

instigation *n* **1** something that arouses a strong response from another — see PROVOCATION 1
2 something that arouses action or activity — see IMPULSE

instigator *n* a person who stirs up public feelings especially of discontent — see AGITATOR

instinctive *adj* done instantly and without conscious thought or decision — see AUTOMATIC 1

instinctual *adj* done instantly and without conscious thought or decision — see AUTOMATIC 1

institute *n* **1** a group of persons formally joined together for some common interest — see ASSOCIATION 2
2 a public organization with a particular purpose or function — see INSTITUTION 1

institute *vb* to be responsible for the creation and early operation or use of — see FOUND

instituter *or* **institutor** *n* a person who establishes a whole new field of endeavor — see FATHER 2

institution *n* **1** a public organization with a particular purpose or function ⟨a charitable *institution* devoted to raising funds to feed the hungry⟩
synonyms establishment, foundation, institute
related words body, collective, group; corporation, enterprise; charity, philanthropy; think tank
2 a group of persons formally joined together for some common interest — see ASSOCIATION 2

instruct *vb* **1** to cause to acquire knowledge or skill in some field — see TEACH
2 to give information to — see ENLIGHTEN 1
3 to issue orders to (someone) by right of authority — see COMMAND 1

instruction *n* **1** a statement of what to do that must be obeyed by those concerned — see COMMAND 1
2 the act or process of imparting knowledge or skills to another — see EDUCATION 1

instructional *adj* providing useful information or knowledge — see INFORMATIVE
instructive *adj* providing useful information or knowledge — see INFORMATIVE
instructor *n* a person whose occupation is to give formal instruction in a school — see TEACHER
instrument *n* **1** a written or printed paper giving information about or proof of something — see CERTIFICATE
2 an article intended for use in work — see IMPLEMENT
3 something used to achieve an end — see AGENT 1
instrumentalist *n* a person who plays a musical instrument — see MUSICIAN 1
instrumentality *n* something used to achieve an end — see AGENT 1
insubordinate *adj* given to resisting authority or another's control — see DISOBEDIENT
insubordination *n* refusal to obey — see DISOBEDIENCE
insubstantial *adj* **1** being of a material lacking in sturdiness or substance — see FLIMSY 1
2 not composed of matter — see IMMATERIAL 1
insufferable *adj* more than can be put up with — see UNBEARABLE
insufficiency *n* a falling short of an essential or desirable amount or number — see DEFICIENCY
insufficient *adj* not coming up to a usual standard or meeting a particular need — see SHORT 3
insular *adj* not broad or open in views or opinions — see NARROW 2
insulate *vb* to set or keep apart from others — see ISOLATE
insulation *n* the state of being alone or kept apart from others — see ISOLATION
insult *n* an act or expression showing scorn and usually intended to hurt another's feelings ⟨yelling an *insult* at the bully was not a very smart thing to do⟩
synonyms affront, barb, dart, dig, epithet, indignity, name, offense (*or* offence), outrage, put-down, sarcasm, slight, slur
related words gibe (*or* jibe), jeer, sneer, taunt; abuse, invective, vituperation; disapproval, opprobrium; disgrace, dishonor, shame; attack, criticism, slam; torment, torture
near antonyms accolade, commendation, compliment; acclaim, applause, praise; adulation, flattery
insult *vb* to cause hurt feelings or deep resentment in ⟨*insulted* the people by saying their home was ugly⟩
synonyms affront, dis [*slang*], offend, outrage, slight, wound
related words cut, snub; displease, distress, disturb, hurt, pain, trouble, upset; jeer, mock, ridicule, sneer (at), taunt; defame, disparage, libel, malign, revile, slander, slur, smear; oppress, persecute, torment, torture
near antonyms acclaim, applaud, approve, hail; commend, compliment, eulogize, praise; adulate, flatter; exalt, glorify, honor; delight, gratify, please, satisfy
insupportable *adj* more than can be put up with — see UNBEARABLE
insure *vb* to make sure, certain, or safe — see ENSURE
insurgency *n* open fighting against authority (as one's own government) — see REBELLION
insurgent *adj* taking part in a rebellion — see REBELLIOUS 1
insurgent *n* a person who rises up against authority — see REBEL
insurmountable *adj* incapable of being defeated, overcome, or subdued — see INVINCIBLE
insurrection *n* open fighting against authority (as one's own government) — see REBELLION
insurrectionary *adj* taking part in a rebellion — see REBELLIOUS 1
insurrectionary *n* a person who rises up against authority — see REBEL
insurrectionist *n* a person who rises up against authority — see REBEL
intact *adj* not lacking any part or member that properly belongs to it — see COMPLETE 1
intangible *adj* not capable of being perceived by the sense of touch ⟨electrical energy is completely *intangible*⟩
synonyms impalpable
related words bodiless, immaterial, incorporeal, insubstantial, unsubstantial; ethereal, spiritual, unreal
near antonyms tactile; corporeal, physical; embodied, material, real, solid, substantial
antonyms palpable, tangible, touchable
integer *n* a character used to represent a mathematical value — see NUMBER
integral *adj* **1** being a part of the innermost nature of a person or thing — see INHERENT
2 impossible to do without — see ESSENTIAL 1
3 not lacking any part or member that properly belongs to it — see COMPLETE 1
integrate *vb* **1** to make a part of a body or system — see EMBODY 1
2 to turn into a single mass that is more or less the same throughout — see BLEND 1
integrity *n* **1** conduct that conforms to an accepted standard of right and wrong — see MORALITY 1
2 devotion to telling the truth — see HONESTY 1
3 faithfulness to high moral standards — see HONOR 1
intellect *n* **1** a very smart person — see GENIUS 1
2 the ability to learn and understand or to deal with problems — see INTELLIGENCE 1
intellectual *adj* **1** much given to learning and thinking ⟨as the daughter of college professors, she's used to being around *intellectual* people⟩
synonyms cerebral, highbrow
related words cultivated, cultured; erudite, learned, literate, scholarly, well-read; academic, bookish, professorial; didactic, pedantic; high-hat, snobbish, snobby, snooty; educated, schooled; brainy, bright, brilliant, clever, intelligent, quick-witted, smart
near antonyms uncultivated, uncultured; ignorant, illiterate, uneducated, unlettered, unread; dumb, foolish, idiotic, moronic, slow, stupid, unintelligent
antonyms lowbrow, nonintellectual
2 of or relating to the mind — see MENTAL 1
intelligence *n* **1** the ability to learn and understand or to deal with problems ⟨high scores on this test supposedly demonstrate great *intelligence*⟩
synonyms brain(s), gray matter, intellect, reason, sense
related words acumen, alertness, astuteness, discernment, insight, judgment (*or* judgement), mentality, perception, perspicacity; sagacity, sapience, wisdom, wit; head, mind, skull

near antonyms denseness, density, doltishness, dopiness, dullness (*also* dulness), dumbness, fatuity, feeblemindedness, foolishness, idiocy, imbecility, senselessness, simpleness, slowness, stupidity

2 a report of recent events or facts not previously known — see NEWS

intelligent *adj* **1** having or showing quickness of mind ⟨the dolphin is considered one of the most *intelligent* animals⟩ ⟨running for help was an *intelligent* response to the emergency⟩

synonyms alert, brainy, bright, brilliant, clever, keen, nimble, quick, quick-witted, sharp, sharp-witted, smart

related words apt, ingenious, resourceful; acute, astute, discerning, insightful, knowing, perceptive, perspicacious, sagacious, sapient, savvy, wise; cerebral, erudite, highbrow, knowledgeable, learned, literate, scholarly, well-read; educated, informed, schooled, skilled, trained; creative, inventive, judicious, prudent, sage, sane, sapient, sensible, sound, wise; crafty, cunning, foxy, shrewd, wily; logical, rational, reasonable

near antonyms retarded; foolish, idiotic, imbecile, imbecilic, moronic, silly, witless; ignorant, illiterate, lowbrow, nonintellectual, unacademic, uneducated, uninformed

antonyms brainless, dense, doltish, dorky, dull, dumb, mindless, obtuse, simple, slow, stupid, thick, unintelligent

2 having the ability to reason — see RATIONAL 1

intemperate *adj* showing no signs of being under control — see RAMPANT 1

intend *vb* to have in mind as a purpose or goal ⟨he *intends* to be the president of a large corporation someday⟩

synonyms aim, aspire, contemplate, design, mean, meditate, plan, propose

related words dream, hope, wish; consider, debate, mull (over), ponder; attempt, endeavor, strive, struggle, try; plot, scheme; accomplish, achieve, effect, execute, perform

phrases figure on

intended *n* the person to whom one is engaged to be married — see BETROTHED

intense *adj* extreme in degree, power, or effect ⟨the *intense* cold of the polar regions⟩

synonyms deep, explosive, exquisite, fearful, ferocious, fierce, furious, hard, heavy, intensive, profound, terrible, vehement, vicious, violent

related words accentuated, aggravated, concentrated, deepened; emphasized, enhanced, heightened, intensified, magnified; stressed; exhaustive, thorough; harsh, rigorous, severe

near antonyms feeble, weak; shallow, superficial; moderated, qualified; alleviated, eased, lightened, toned (down); abated, decreased, diminished, lessened, reduced, subdued

antonyms light, moderate, soft

intensely *adv* with great effort or determination — see HARD 1

intensify *vb* to make markedly greater in measure or degree ⟨*intensified* her efforts to move that bookcase by herself⟩

synonyms amplify, beef (up), boost, consolidate, deepen, enhance, heighten, magnify, redouble, step up, strengthen

related words broaden, enlarge, expand, extend, lengthen; accelerate, hasten, quicken; accentuate, emphasize, stress; augment, reinforce, supplement; maximize; enliven, jazz (up); aggravate, exacerbate

near antonyms decrease, diminish, lessen, let up (on), reduce, subdue, tone (down), weaken; dwindle, recede, subside, taper (off), wane; alleviate, ease, lighten

antonyms abate, moderate

intensity *n* **1** depth of feeling — see ARDOR 1

2 the quality or state of being forceful (as in expression) — see VEHEMENCE 1

intensive *adj* extreme in degree, power, or effect — see INTENSE

intensively *adv* with great effort or determination — see HARD 1

intent *adj* **1** fully committed to achieving a goal — see DETERMINED 1

2 having the mind fixed on something — see ATTENTIVE

intent *n* **1** something that one hopes or intends to accomplish — see GOAL

2 the idea that is conveyed or intended to be conveyed to the mind by language, symbol, or action — see MEANING 1

intention *n* something that one hopes or intends to accomplish — see GOAL

intentional *adj* made, given, or done with full awareness of what one is doing ⟨I'm fairly sure that your "accidental" attack on your sister with a water balloon was really *intentional*⟩

synonyms deliberate, purposeful, willful (*or* wilful)

related words knowing, witting; designed, intended, planned; conscious; advised, calculated, considered, measured, reasoned, studied, thoughtful, weighed; premeditated; discretionary, elective, optional, volunteer

near antonyms inadvertent, unwitting; accidental, chance, haphazard, hit-or-miss, incidental, random; aimless, desultory, purposeless; abrupt, impetuous, sudden; coerced, forced, involuntary; compulsory, mandatory, necessary, nonelective, obligatory, ordered, required; casual; extemporaneous, impromptu, impulsive, instinctive, spontaneous, unforced, unpremeditated

antonyms unintentional

intentionally *adv* with full awareness of what one is doing ⟨the witness *intentionally* gave misleading answers to the questions⟩

synonyms consciously, deliberately, designedly, knowingly, purposefully, purposely, willfully, wittingly

related words calculatingly, studiedly; voluntarily, willingly

phrases on purpose

near antonyms accidentally, incidentally, randomly; involuntarily, unwillingly; impulsively, instinctively, spontaneously

antonyms inadvertently, unconsciously, unintentionally, unknowingly, unwittingly

intently *adv* with great effort or determination — see HARD 1

intentness *n* a mental state free of jesting or trifling — see EARNESTNESS

inter *vb* to place (a dead body) in the earth, a tomb, or the sea — see BURY 1

interaction *n* doings between individuals or groups — see RELATION 1

intercede *vb* to act as a go-between for opposing sides — see INTERVENE

intercessor *n* one who works with opposing sides

in order to bring about an agreement — see MEDIATOR
intercommunicate *vb* to engage in an exchange of information or ideas — see COMMUNICATE 2
intercourse *n* **1** doings between individuals or groups — see RELATION 1
2 sexual union involving penetration of the vagina by the penis — see SEXUAL INTERCOURSE
interdict *n* an order that something not be done or used — see PROHIBITION 2
interdict *vb* to order not to do or use or to be done or used — see FORBID
interdicted *adj* that may not be permitted — see IMPERMISSIBLE
interdicting *n* the act of ordering that something not be done or used — see PROHIBITION 1
interdiction *n* **1** an order that something not be done or used — see PROHIBITION 2
2 the act of ordering that something not be done or used — see PROHIBITION 1
interest *n* **1** a legal right to participation in the advantages, profits, and responsibility of something ⟨all of the workers at the food cooperative have an *interest* in it⟩
synonyms claim, share, stake
related words ownership, part, partnership, possession, title
2 the state of doing well especially in relation to one's happiness or success — see WELFARE
interest *vb* to hold the attention of — see ENGAGE 1
interesting *adj* holding the attention or provoking interest ⟨the history lecture was so *interesting* that I didn't fall asleep after all⟩
synonyms absorbing, arresting, engaging, engrossing, enthralling, fascinating, gripping, immersing, intriguing, involving, riveting
related words breathtaking, electric, electrifying, exciting, exhilarating, galvanizing, inspiring, rousing, stimulating, stirring, thrilling; provocative, tantalizing; emphatic, showy, splashy, striking; alluring, attractive, bewitching, captivating, charming, enchanting, spellbinding; hypnotizing, mesmerizing; curious, odd, unusual, weird; amazing, astonishing, astounding, eye-opening, fabulous, marvelous (*or* marvellous), surprising, wonderful, wondrous; amusing, entertaining
near antonyms tiresome, tiring, wearisome, wearying; unexciting; dreary, humdrum, pedestrian; demoralizing, discouraging, disheartening, dispiriting
antonyms boring, drab, dry, dull, heavy, monotonous, tedious, uninteresting
interfere *vb* to interest oneself in what is not one's concern ⟨a strong resentment of outsiders who *interfered* with their traditional ways of doing things⟩
synonyms butt in, intrude, meddle, mess, nose, obtrude, poke, pry, snoop
related words intercede, interpose, intervene; encroach, infringe, invade, trespass; fiddle, fool, monkey, play, tamper
near antonyms avoid, eschew, shun; disregard, ignore, neglect, overlook
interfere (with) *vb* to create difficulty for the work or activity of — see HAMPER
interference *n* something that makes movement or progress more difficult — see ENCUMBRANCE
interferer *n* a person who meddles in the affairs of others — see BUSYBODY
interfering *adj* thrusting oneself where one is not welcome or invited — see INTRUSIVE
interim *adj* intended to last, continue, or serve for a limited time — see TEMPORARY 1
interim *n* a break in continuity — see GAP 2
interior *adj* situated farther in — see INNER 1
interior *n* an interior or internal part — see INSIDE 1
interject *vb* to put among or between others — see INSERT
interlace *vb* **1** to cause to twine about one another — see INTERTWINE 1
2 to scatter or set here and there among other things — see THREAD 1
3 to twist together into a usually confused mass — see ENTANGLE 1
interloper *n* a person who meddles in the affairs of others — see BUSYBODY
interlude *n* a break in continuity — see GAP 2
intermediary *adj* occupying a position equally distant from the ends or extremes — see MIDDLE 1
intermediary *n* one who works with opposing sides in order to bring about an agreement — see MEDIATOR
intermediate *adj* **1** being about midway between extremes of amount or size — see MIDDLE 2
2 occupying a position equally distant from the ends or extremes — see MIDDLE 1
interment *n* the act or ceremony of putting a dead body in its final resting place — see BURIAL
intermingle *vb* to turn into a single mass that is more or less the same throughout — see BLEND 1
intermission *n* a break in continuity — see GAP 2
intermittent *adj* **1** occurring or appearing at intervals ⟨*intermittent* showers had me opening and closing my umbrella all day long⟩
synonyms continual, periodic, periodical, recurrent, recurring
related words alternate, alternating, cyclic (*or* cyclical), rhythmic (*or* rhythmical), seasonal, serial; erratic, fitful, irregular, occasional, spasmodic, sporadic, spotty, unsteady
near antonyms eternal, everlasting, interminable, perpetual
antonyms constant, continuous, incessant, unceasing
2 lacking in steadiness or regularity of occurrence — see FITFUL
intermix *vb* to turn into a single mass that is more or less the same throughout — see BLEND 1
intermixture *n* a distinct entity formed by the combining of two or more different things — see BLEND
intern *vb* to put in or as if in prison — see IMPRISON
internal *adj* situated farther in — see INNER 1
interned *adj* taken and held prisoner — see CAPTIVE
internee *n* one that has been taken and held in confinement — see CAPTIVE
internment *n* the act of confining or the state of being confined ⟨the *internment* of Americans of Japanese descent during World War II is one of the more shameful chapters in United States history⟩
synonyms captivity, confinement, immurement, imprisonment, incarceration
related words bondage, enslavement, servitude; restraint, restriction; arrest, capture, entrapment; custody, detainment, detention

near antonyms emancipation, liberation, manumission, redemption, release; freedom, independence, liberty
interpenetrate *vb* to spread throughout — see PERMEATE
interpolate *vb* to put among or between others — see INSERT
interpose *vb* **1** to act as a go-between for opposing sides — see INTERVENE
2 to cause a disruption in a conversation or discussion — see INTERRUPT
3 to put among or between others — see INSERT
interposer *n* one who works with opposing sides in order to bring about an agreement — see MEDIATOR
interpret *vb* to make plain or understandable — see EXPLAIN 1
interpretation *n* a statement that makes something clear — see EXPLANATION 1
interpretive *adj* serving to explain — see EXPLANATORY
interring *n* the act or ceremony of putting a dead body in its final resting place — see BURIAL
interrogate *vb* **1** to put a question or questions to — see ASK 1
2 to put a series of questions to — see EXAMINE 1
interrupt *vb* to cause a disruption in a conversation or discussion ⟨it's rude to *interrupt* when someone is making an important point⟩
synonyms break (in), chime in, cut in, interpose, intrude
related words barge (in), bother; add, chip in, contribute, put in
interruption *n* **1** a break in continuity — see GAP 2
2 a momentary halt in an activity — see PAUSE
intersect *vb* to divide by passing through or across ⟨the highway *intersects* that road⟩
synonyms bisect, cross
related words crisscross
intersection *n* a place where roads meet — see CROSSROAD 1
intersperse *vb* to scatter or set here and there among other things — see THREAD 1
intertwine *vb* **1** to cause to twine about one another ⟨*intertwined* two different colors of yarn⟩
synonyms interlace, interweave, lace
related words blend, fuse, join, link, mix
near antonyms disentangle, uncoil, untangle, untwine, unwind
2 to twist together into a usually confused mass — see ENTANGLE
interval *n* **1** a break in continuity — see GAP 2
2 an open space in a barrier (as a wall or hedge) — see GAP 1
intervene *vb* to act as a go-between for opposing sides ⟨*intervened* in the argument before any real harm was done⟩
synonyms intercede, interpose, mediate
related words butt in, interfere, intrude, meddle, obtrude, pry, snoop; arbitrate, moderate, negotiate; barge (in), bother; break (in), chime in, cut in; infringe, invade, trespass
near antonyms stand by; avoid, eschew, shun; disregard, ignore, overlook
interweave *vb* **1** to cause to twine about one another — see INTERTWINE 1
2 to scatter or set here and there among other things — see THREAD 1
3 to twist together into a usually confused mass — see ENTANGLE 1
intimacy *n* the state of being in a very personal or private relationship — see FAMILIARITY 1
intimate *adj* **1** closely acquainted — see FAMILIAR 1
2 not known or meant to be known by the general populace — see PRIVATE 1
intimate *n* a person who has a strong liking for and trust in another — see FRIEND 1
intimate *vb* to convey an idea indirectly — see HINT
intimation *n* a slight or indirect pointing to something (as a solution or explanation) — see HINT 1
intimidate *vb* to make timid or fearful by or as if by threats ⟨refusing to be *intimidated* by the manager's harsh stare, I demanded my money back⟩
synonyms browbeat, bully, cow, hector
related words affright, alarm, frighten, horrify, scare, shock, spook, startle, terrify; menace, terrorize, threaten; badger, harass, hound; bulldoze, coerce, compel, constrain, dragoon, force, make, oblige, press, pressure; demoralize, unman, unnerve; discompose, disconcert, disquiet, distress, disturb, perturb, upset
near antonyms cheer, comfort, console, reassure, solace, soothe; embolden, encourage, hearten, steel; convince, persuade
intimidating *adj* **1** causing fear — see FEARFUL 1
2 harsh and threatening in manner or appearance — see GRIM 1
intimidator *n* a person who teases, threatens, or hurts smaller or weaker persons — see BULLY 1
intolerable *adj* more than can be put up with — see UNBEARABLE
intolerant *adj* **1** unable or unwilling to endure ⟨*intolerant* of pain⟩
synonyms impatient
related words uncompromising, unforgiving, unyielding; complaining, fussing, griping, grumbling, protesting, squawking, whining
near antonyms accepting, forgiving, long-suffering, resigned, uncomplaining, willing; indulgent
antonyms abiding, enduring, forbearing, patient, tolerant
2 unwilling to grant other people social rights or to accept other viewpoints ⟨*intolerant* people supported racism⟩
synonyms bigoted, narrow, narrow-minded, prejudiced, small-minded
related words conservative, hidebound, old-fashioned, reactionary; insular, parochial, provincial; biased, one-sided, partial, partisan
near antonyms extreme, progressive, radical; impartial, objective, unbiased
antonyms broad-minded, liberal, open-minded, tolerant, unprejudiced
intone *vb* to utter in musical or drawn out tones — see CHANT 1
intoxicant *n* a fermented or distilled beverage that can make a person drunk — see ALCOHOL
intoxicate *vb* to cause a pleasurable stimulation of the feelings — see THRILL
intoxicated *adj* **1** being under the influence of alcohol — see DRUNK
2 experiencing or marked by overwhelming usually pleasurable emotion — see ECSTATIC
intoxication *n* a state of overwhelming usually pleasurable emotion — see ECSTASY
intractability *n* refusal to obey — see DISOBEDIENCE

intractable *adj* **1** given to resisting authority or another's control — see DISOBEDIENT
2 given to resisting control or discipline by others — see UNCONTROLLABLE

intrepid *adj* feeling or displaying no fear by temperament — see BRAVE

intrepidity *n* strength of mind to carry on in spite of danger — see COURAGE

intrepidness *n* strength of mind to carry on in spite of danger — see COURAGE

intricacy *n* **1** something that makes a situation more complicated or difficult — see COMPLICATION 1
2 the state or quality of having many interrelated parts or aspects — see COMPLEXITY 1

intricate *adj* **1** having many parts or aspects that are usually interrelated — see COMPLEX 1
2 made or done with great care or with much detail — see ELABORATE 1

intrigue *n* a secret plan for accomplishing evil or unlawful ends — see PLOT 1

intrigue *vb* **1** to engage in a secret plan to accomplish evil or unlawful ends — see PLOT
2 to hold the attention of — see ENGAGE 1

intriguing *adj* holding the attention or provoking interest — see INTERESTING

intrinsic *adj* being a part of the innermost nature of a person or thing — see INHERENT

intrinsically *adv* by natural character or ability — see NATURALLY 1

introduce *vb* **1** to make (one person) known (to another) socially ⟨a friend *introduced* him to the woman who later became his wife⟩
synonyms acquaint, present
related words address, greet, hail, meet
2 to present or bring forward for discussion ⟨the moderator *introduced* a new topic for the debate⟩
synonyms bring up, broach, moot, raise
related words allude (to), cite, mention, name, refer (to); offer, propose, suggest; air, express, speak (of), talk (about), vent, ventilate; interject, interrupt; debate, discuss, thrash (out *or* over)
near antonyms censor, hush (up), quiet, silence, suppress
3 to be responsible for the creation and early operation or use of — see FOUND
4 to impart knowledge of a new thing or situation to — see ACQUAINT 1
5 to put among or between others — see INSERT

introducer *n* one who creates or introduces something new — see INVENTOR

introduction *n* a short section (as of a book) that leads to or explains the main part ⟨a famous person wrote the *introduction* to that new textbook⟩
synonyms foreword, preamble, preface, prelude, prologue
related words beginning, commencement, initiation, opening, origin, origination, outset, start
near antonyms postscript; aftermath; cessation, close, closing, conclusion, end, finale, finish, stop, termination
antonyms epilogue

introductory *adj* coming before the main part or item usually to introduce or prepare for what follows — see PRELIMINARY

introverted *adj* not comfortable around people — see SHY 2

intrude *vb* **1** to cause a disruption in a conversation or discussion — see INTERRUPT
2 to interest oneself in what is not one's concern — see INTERFERE

intrude (upon) *vb* to thrust oneself upon (another) without invitation — see BOTHER 1

intruder *n* a person who meddles in the affairs of others — see BUSYBODY

intruding *adj* thrusting oneself where one is not welcome or invited — see INTRUSIVE

intrusive *adj* thrusting oneself where one is not welcome or invited ⟨that *intrusive* neighbor never knocks before coming in⟩
synonyms interfering, intruding, meddlesome, meddling, nosy (*or* nosey), obtrusive, officious, presumptuous, prying, snoopy
related words bold, brazen, impertinent, impudent, insolent, rude; invading, trespassing; curious, inquisitive; annoying, harassing, pestiferous
near antonyms quiet, reserved, reticent, retiring, silent, taciturn, withdrawn; inhibited, restrained, subdued
antonyms unobtrusive

inundate *vb* to cover or become filled with a flood — see FLOOD

inundation *n* a great flow of water or of something that overwhelms — see FLOOD

inure *vb* to make able to withstand physical hardship, strain, or exposure — see HARDEN 2

inured *adj* able to withstand hardship, strain, or exposure — see HARDY 1

invade *vb* to enter for conquest or plunder ⟨a superpower that had a tendency to *invade* and take over smaller and weaker countries⟩
synonyms foray (into), overrun, raid
related words despoil, loot, maraud, pillage, plunder, ravage, sack; conquer, crush, overcome, overpower, overwhelm, subdue, subjugate; assail, assault, attack; battle, combat, fight, war (with); encroach, infringe, trespass; besiege, blockade; occupy
near antonyms defend, guard, protect, shield; oppose, resist, withstand; capitulate (to), cede (to), submit (to), succumb (to), surrender (to), yield (to)

invader *n* one that starts armed conflict against another especially without reasonable cause — see AGGRESSOR

[1]**invalid** *adj* chronically or repeatedly suffering from poor health — see SICKLY 1

[2]**invalid** *adj* **1** having no legal or binding force — see NULL 1
2 not being in agreement with what is true — see FALSE 1
3 not using or following good reasoning — see ILLOGICAL
4 having no basis in reason or fact — see GROUNDLESS

invalidate *vb* to put an end to by formal action — see ABOLISH

invariability *n* the state of continuing without change — see CONSTANCY 1

invariable *adj* not capable of changing or being changed — see INFLEXIBLE 1

invariably *adv* on every relevant occasion — see ALWAYS 1

invariant *adj* not varying — see UNIFORM

invasion *n* a sudden attack on and entrance into hostile territory — see RAID 1

invective *n* harsh insulting language — see ABUSE 1

invent *vb* to create or think of by clever use of the imagination ⟨they *invented* an explanation for the

broken vase that would satisfy their grandmother⟩
synonyms concoct, contrive, cook (up), devise, fabricate, make up, manufacture, think (up)
related words coin, contrive, create, design, hatch, produce; daydream, dream, fantasize; conceive, envisage, imagine, picture, visualize
near antonyms copy, duplicate, imitate, mimic, replicate

invented *adj* not real and existing only in the imagination — see IMAGINARY

invention *n* **1** something (as a device) created for the first time through the use of the imagination ⟨his clever *invention* made people's lives easier⟩
synonyms coinage, concoction, contrivance, creation, innovation, wrinkle
related words contraption, device, gadget, gizmo (*or* gismo), novelty; design, product, work; dream, fantasy (*also* phantasy), picture, vision; conception, imagining, origination
near antonyms copy, duplicate, imitation
2 something that is the product of the imagination — see FICTION
3 the ability to form mental images of things that either are not physically present or have never been conceived or created by others — see IMAGINATION
4 the skill and imagination to create new things — see CREATIVITY 1

inventive *adj* having the skill and imagination to create new things — see CREATIVE 1

inventiveness *n* **1** the ability to form mental images of things that either are not physically present or have never been conceived or created by others — see IMAGINATION
2 the skill and imagination to create new things — see CREATIVITY 1

inventor *n* one who creates or introduces something new ⟨the *inventor* of the electric light bulb⟩
synonyms contriver, designer, developer, deviser, formulator, innovator, introducer, originator
related words author, creator, establisher, father, founder, inaugurator, originator; pioneer, researcher; builder, maker, producer; dreamer
near antonyms copier, duplicator, imitator

inventory *vb* to make a list of — see [1]LIST 1

invert *vb* to change the position of (an object) so that the opposite side or end is showing — see REVERSE 2

invertebrate *adj* lacking strength of will or character — see WEAK 2

invest *vb* **1** to cause (as a person) to become filled or saturated with a certain quality or principle — see INFUSE
2 to furnish with something freely or naturally — see ENDOW 1
3 to give official or legal power to — see AUTHORIZE 1
4 to outfit with clothes and especially fine or special clothes — see CLOTHE 1
5 to put into an office or welcome into an organization with special ceremonies — see INSTALL 1
6 to surround (as a fortified place) with armed forces for the purpose of capturing or preventing commerce and communication — see BESIEGE
7 to surround or cover closely — see ENFOLD 1

investigate *vb* to search through or into — see EXPLORE 1

investigation *n* a systematic search for the truth or facts about something — see INQUIRY 1

investigator *n* a person whose business is solving crimes and catching criminals or gathering information that is not easy to get — see DETECTIVE

investiture *n* the process or an instance of being formally placed in an office or organization — see INSTALLATION 1

investment *n* the cutting off of an area by military means to stop the flow of people or supplies — see BLOCKADE

inveterate *adj* **1** firmly established over time ⟨he has an *inveterate* tendency to tell tall tales that began when he was just a little boy⟩
synonyms confirmed, deep-rooted, deep-seated, entrenched (*also* intrenched), hard-core, rooted, settled
related words fixed, immutable, set; implanted, inculcated, instilled; inborn, inbred, inherent, innate, natural; accustomed, chronic, customary, habitual, regular, typical, usual; abiding, enduring, lifelong, persistent, persisting
near antonyms brief, ephemeral, fleeting, impermanent, momentary, short-lived, temporary, transient
2 being such by habit and not likely to change — see HABITUAL 1

invidious *adj* having or showing mean resentment of another's possessions or advantages — see ENVIOUS

invidiousness *n* a painful awareness of another's possessions or advantages and a desire to have them too — see ENVY

invigorate *vb* to give life, vigor, or spirit to — see ANIMATE

invigorated *adj* made or become fresh in spirits or vigor — see NEW 4

invigorating *adj* having a renewing effect on the state of the body or mind — see TONIC

invincible *adj* incapable of being defeated, overcome, or subdued ⟨an *invincible* wrestler who has never lost a match⟩
synonyms impregnable, indomitable, insurmountable, invulnerable, unbeatable, unconquerable
related words inviolable, unassailable, untouchable; armored, defended, guarded, protected, safe, safeguarded, secure, shielded; unbeaten, unconquered, undefeated, unsubdued
near antonyms exposed, imperiled, insecure, liable, open, susceptible, unguarded, unprotected, unsafe, unshielded; defenseless, helpless, powerless, weak
antonyms surmountable, vulnerable

inviolable *adj* not to be violated, criticized, or tampered with — see SACRED 1

invite *vb* to act so as to make (something) more likely — see COURT 1

invoice *n* a record of goods sold or services performed together with the costs due — see [1]BILL 1

involuntary *adj* **1** not made or done willingly or by choice ⟨my long stays on the sidelines during our football games were strictly *involuntary*⟩
synonyms coerced, forced, unintended, unintentional, unwilling
related words accidental, unplanned, unpremeditated; automatic, impulsive, instinctive, spontaneous, unprompted; inadvertent, unconscious, unknowing, unwitting
near antonyms advised, conscious, considered, knowing, planned, premeditated, purposeful; volitional

antonyms deliberate, intentional, unforced, voluntary, willful (*or* wilful), willing
2 done instantly and without conscious thought or decision — see AUTOMATIC 1
3 forcing one's compliance or participation by or as if by law — see MANDATORY

involution *n* the state or quality of having many interrelated parts or aspects — see COMPLEXITY 1

involve *vb* **1** to be the business or affair of — see CONCERN 2
2 to have as part of a whole — see INCLUDE
3 to hold the attention of — see ENGAGE 1

involved *adj* **1** having many parts or aspects that are usually interrelated — see COMPLEX 1
2 made or done with great care or with much detail — see ELABORATE 1

involving *adj* holding the attention or provoking interest — see INTERESTING

invulnerable *adj* incapable of being defeated, overcome, or subdued — see INVINCIBLE

inward *adj* situated farther in — see INNER 1

in–your–face *adj* having or showing a bold forcefulness in the pursuit of a goal — see AGGRESSIVE 1

iota *n* the smallest amount or part imaginable — see JOT

irascibility *n* readiness to show annoyance or impatience — see PETULANCE

irascible *adj* easily irritated or annoyed — see IRRITABLE

irate *adj* feeling or showing anger — see ANGRY

irateness *n* an intense emotional state of displeasure with someone or something — see ANGER

ire *n* an intense emotional state of displeasure with someone or something — see ANGER

ireful *adj* feeling or showing anger — see ANGRY

irk *vb* to disturb the peace of mind of (someone) especially by repeated disagreeable acts — see IRRITATE 1

irksome *adj* causing annoyance — see ANNOYING

iron *adj* not showing weakness or uncertainty — see FIRM 1

irons *n pl* something that physically prevents free movement — see BOND 1

irradiate *vb* to supply with light — see ILLUMINATE 1

irrational *adj* not using or following good reasoning — see ILLOGICAL

irrecoverable *adj* **1** not capable of being cured or reformed — see HOPELESS 1
2 not capable of being repaired, regained, or undone — see IRREPARABLE

irredeemable *adj* **1** not capable of being cured or reformed — see HOPELESS 1
2 not capable of being repaired, regained, or undone — see IRREPARABLE

irrefutable *adj* not capable of being challenged or proved wrong <the *irrefutable* reply of "Because I like it!">
synonyms incontestable, incontrovertible, indisputable, indubitable, unanswerable, undeniable, unquestionable
related words certain, definite, positive, sure; unambiguous, unequivocal; absolute, clear, conclusive, decisive; uncontested, undisputed
near antonyms controversial, debated, disputed; doubtful, dubious, inconclusive, indecisive, uncertain; ambiguous, equivocal
antonyms answerable, debatable, disputable, questionable

irregular *adj* **1** departing from some accepted standard of what is normal — see DEVIANT
2 lacking in steadiness or regularity of occurrence — see FITFUL
3 not having a level or smooth surface — see UNEVEN 1
4 not rigidly following established form, custom, or rules — see INFORMAL 1
5 not staying constant — see UNEVEN 2

irregularly *adv* without definite aim, direction, rule, or method — see HIT OR MISS

irrelevance *n* the quality or state of not having anything to do with the matter at hand <the *irrelevance* of the comment brought conversation to a standstill>
synonyms extraneousness, inapplicability
related words inappropriateness, inaptness, unfitness, unsuitability; insignificance, unimportance; pointlessness, uselessness
near antonyms bearing, connection; appropriateness, aptness, fitness, suitability; importance, significance; usefulness
antonyms applicability, materiality, pertinence, relevance

irrelevant *adj* not having anything to do with the matter at hand <*irrelevant* questions that merely disrupted the classroom lesson>
synonyms extraneous, immaterial, inapplicable
related words inconsequential, insignificant, unimportant; meaningless, pointless, senseless, useless; inappropriate, inapt, unsuitable
phrases beside the point
near antonyms important, meaningful, significant; sensible, useful; appropriate, apt, fit, suitable
antonyms applicable, apposite, apropos, germane, material, pertinent, relevant

irreligious *adj* lacking religious emotions, principles, or practices <raised in an *irreligious* family where the subject of God was never even discussed>
synonyms godless, nonreligious
related words ungodly, unholy; blasphemous, impious, irreverent, sacrilegious; agnostic, atheistic; unconsecrated, unhallowed; profane, secular, worldly
near antonyms devout, godly, holy, pious, prayerful, reverent, worshipful, worshipping (*also* worshiping); sanctimonious
antonyms religious

irremediable *adj* **1** not capable of being cured or reformed — see HOPELESS 1
2 not capable of being repaired, regained, or undone — see IRREPARABLE

irremovable *adj* incapable of moving or being moved — see IMMOVABLE 1

irreparable *adj* not capable of being repaired, regained, or undone <*irreparable* damage to the car>
synonyms irrecoverable, irredeemable, irremediable, irretrievable, irreversible, unrecoverable, unredeemable
related words irreplaceable, irrevocable; unredeemed, unrepaired
near antonyms corrected, fixed, recovered, remedied, repaired
antonyms fixable, redeemable, remediable, retrievable

irreproachable *adj* **1** free from guilt or blame — see INNOCENT 2
2 being entirely without fault — see PERFECT 1

irresolution *n* the act or an instance of pausing because of uncertainty about the right course of action — see HESITATION

irresponsible *adj* having or showing a lack of concern for the consequences of one's actions — see RECKLESS 1

irretrievable *adj* **1** not capable of being cured or reformed — see HOPELESS 1
2 not capable of being repaired, regained, or undone — see IRREPARABLE

irreverence *n* an act of great disrespect shown to God or to sacred ideas, people, or things — see BLASPHEMY

irreverent *adj* not showing proper reverence for the holy or sacred ⟨*irreverent* behavior during church services⟩
synonyms blasphemous, impious, profane, sacrilegious
related words agnostic, atheistic; godless, irreligious, nonreligious, secular; ungodly, unholy; unconsecrated, unhallowed, unsanctified
near antonyms devout, godly, holy, prayerful, religious, worshipful, worshipping (*also* worshiping); consecrated, hallowed, sanctified
antonyms pious, reverent

irreversible *adj* not capable of being repaired, regained, or undone — see IRREPARABLE

irrigate *vb* to pour liquid over or through in order to cleanse — see FLUSH 1

irritability *n* readiness to show annoyance or impatience — see PETULANCE

irritable *adj* easily irritated or annoyed ⟨that *irritable* old man always yells at people to stay off of his lawn⟩
synonyms choleric, crabby, cranky, cross, crotchety, grouchy, grumpy, irascible, peevish, perverse, pettish, petulant, quick-tempered, short-tempered, snappish, snappy, snippy, testy, waspish
related words bearish, bilious, cantankerous, disagreeable, dyspeptic, ill-humored, ill-natured, ill-tempered, ornery, surly; sensitive, sulky, thin-skinned, touchy; hot-blooded, passionate
phrases out of sorts
near antonyms affable, cordial, friendly, genial, sociable; amiable, good-natured, good-tempered, well-disposed; carefree, easygoing, relaxed; obliging, patient, tolerant, uncomplaining, understanding

irritableness *n* readiness to show annoyance or impatience — see PETULANCE

irritant *n* something that is a source of irritation — see ANNOYANCE 3

irritate *vb* **1** to disturb the peace of mind of (someone) especially by repeated disagreeable acts ⟨constant chatter *irritated* the student, who was trying to concentrate on a hard assignment⟩
synonyms aggravate, annoy, bother, bug, chafe, exasperate, gall, get, grate, irk, nettle, peeve, persecute, pique, put out, rasp, rile, vex
related words hassle, heckle; nag; inflame, provoke, rouse; bait, harass, harry, pester; anger, enrage, incense, infuriate, madden; agitate, disturb, fret, perturb, upset; affront, insult, offend, outrage
phrases rub the wrong way
near antonyms appease, conciliate, mollify, oblige, pacify, placate, propitiate; delight, gladden, gratify, please, satisfy; comfort, console, content, quiet, soothe
2 to make sore by continued rubbing — see CHAFE 1

irritating *adj* causing annoyance — see ANNOYING

irritation *n* the feeling of impatience or anger caused by another's repeated disagreeable acts — see ANNOYANCE 2

irruption *n* a sudden attack on and entrance into hostile territory — see RAID 1

island *n* a fairly small area of land completely surrounded by water ⟨they're taking a trip to an *island* in Hawaii for vacation⟩
synonyms isle, islet
related words barrier reef, cay, coral reef, key; archipelago, atoll; cape, headland, peninsula, promontory
near antonyms continent, main, mainland

isle *n* a fairly small area of land completely surrounded by water — see ISLAND

islet *n* a fairly small area of land completely surrounded by water — see ISLAND

isolate *vb* to set or keep apart from others ⟨*isolated* her in a corner for a five-minute punishment after she threw a book at her friend⟩
synonyms cut off, insulate, seclude, segregate, separate, sequester
related words quarantine; confine, immure, incarcerate, intern, jail, lock (up), restrain, restrict; detach, disengage, remove; detain, hold, keep
near antonyms associate, connect, join, link, unite; discharge, free, liberate, loose, release
antonyms desegregate, integrate

isolated *adj* hidden from view — see SECLUDED

isolation *n* the state of being alone or kept apart from others ⟨*isolation* always made the sociable child lonely⟩
synonyms insulation, secludedness, seclusion, segregation, separateness, sequestration, solitariness, solitude
related words loneliness, lonesomeness; confinement, incarceration, internment, quarantine; retirement, withdrawal
near antonyms companionship, company

issuance *n* the act or process of giving out something to each member of a group — see DISTRIBUTION 1

issue *n* **1** a condition or occurrence traceable to a cause — see EFFECT 1
2 a place or means of going out — see EXIT 1
3 the descendants of a person, animal, or plant — see OFFSPRING

issue *vb* **1** to produce and release for distribution in printed form — see PUBLISH 1
2 to throw or give off — see EMIT 1

Italian sandwich *n* a large sandwich on a long split roll — see SUBMARINE

itch *n* a strong wish for something — see DESIRE

itch (for) *vb* to have an earnest wish to own or enjoy — see DESIRE

item *n* **1** a separate part in a list, account, or series ⟨she got all the *items* on her grocery list except cereal⟩
synonyms detail, particular, point
related words article, belonging, object, stuff, thing; characteristic, constituent, element, feature; ingredient; division, particle, piece, portion, section, segment
near antonyms aggregate, composite, compound, conglomerate; entirety, sum, total, totality, whole
2 a report of recent events or facts not previously known — see NEWS

itemize *vb* **1** to make a list of — see [1]LIST 1
2 to specify one after another — see ENUMERATE 1
itinerant *adj* traveling from place to place <an *itinerant* musician can see a lot of the world>
synonyms errant, gallivanting (*also* galavanting), nomad (*or* nomadic), peripatetic, ranging, roaming, roving, vagabond, vagrant, wandering, wayfaring
related words drifting, footloose, meandering, rambling; sauntering, strolling, traipsing, walking
near antonyms immobile, settled, stationary

jab *n* a quick thrust — see [1]POKE
jabber *n* unintelligible or meaningless talk — see GIBBERISH
jabber *vb* **1** to engage in casual or rambling conversation — see CHAT
2 to speak rapidly, inarticulately, and usually unintelligibly — see BABBLE 1
jabberer *n* a person who talks constantly — see CHATTERBOX
jabberwocky *n* unintelligible or meaningless talk — see GIBBERISH
jack *n* **1** *slang* something (as pieces of stamped metal or printed paper) customarily and legally used as a medium of exchange, a measure of value, or a means of payment — see MONEY
2 a piece of cloth with a special design that is used as an emblem or for signaling — see FLAG 1
3 an adult male human being — see MAN 1
4 one who operates or navigates a seagoing vessel — see SAILOR
jack (up) *vb* **1** to lift with effort — see HEAVE 1
2 to move from a lower to a higher place or position — see RAISE 1
jackass *n* **1** a person who lacks good sense or judgment — see FOOL 1
2 a stupid person — see IDIOT
3 a sturdy and patient domestic mammal that is used especially to carry things — see DONKEY 1
jacked (up) *adj* being at a higher level than average — see HIGH 2
jacket *n* something that encloses another thing especially to protect it — see [1]CASE 1
jackpot *n* the total of the bets at stake at one time — see POT 1
jack–tar *n* one who operates or navigates a seagoing vessel — see SAILOR
jade *vb* to make weary and restless by being dull or monotonous — see [2]BORE
jaded *adj* **1** depleted in strength, energy, or freshness — see WEARY 1
2 having one's patience, interest, or pleasure exhausted — see WEARY 2
jading *adj* causing weariness, restlessness, or lack of interest — see BORING
jagged *adj* **1** having an uneven edge or outline — see RAGGED 1
2 not having a level or smooth surface — see UNEVEN 1
jail *n* a place of confinement for persons held in lawful custody <sentenced to three years in *jail* for his crime>
synonyms brig, gaol [*chiefly British*], guardroom, hoosegow, jug, lockup, pen, penitentiary, prison, stockade
related words bull pen; concentration camp, prison camp; dungeon, keep; reformatory, reform school
near antonyms freedom
jail *vb* to put in or as if in prison — see IMPRISON
jailbird *n* a person convicted as a criminal and serving a prison sentence — see CONVICT
jailed *adj* taken and held prisoner — see CAPTIVE
jam *n* a difficult, puzzling, or embarrassing situation from which there is no easy escape — see PREDICAMENT
jam *vb* **1** to fit (something) into a tight space — see CROWD 1
2 to prevent passage through — see CLOG 1
3 to put into (something) as much as can be held or contained — see FILL 1
jammed *adj* **1** containing or seeming to contain the greatest quantity or number possible — see FULL 1
2 firmly positioned in place and difficult to dislodge — see TIGHT 2
jam–pack *vb* to put into (something) as much as can be held or contained — see FILL 1
jam–packed *adj* **1** containing or seeming to contain the greatest quantity or number possible — see FULL 1
2 having little space between items or parts — see CLOSE 1
janitor *n* **1** a person who takes care of a property sometimes for an absent owner — see CUSTODIAN 1
2 a person who tends a door — see DOORKEEPER
jar *n* **1** a forceful coming together of two things — see IMPACT 1
2 something that makes a strong impression because it is so unexpected — see SURPRISE 1
jar *vb* to be out of harmony or agreement usually noticeably — see CLASH
jargon *n* the special terms or expressions of a particular group or field — see TERMINOLOGY
jarring *adj* disagreeable to one's aesthetic or artistic sense — see HARSH 2
jaundice *n* a deep-seated ill will — see ENMITY
jaundiced *adj* **1** having or showing mean resentment of another's possessions or advantages — see ENVIOUS
2 marked by opposition or ill will — see HOSTILE 1
jaunt *n* a short trip for pleasure — see EXCURSION 1
jauntily *adv* **1** in a bright and showy way — see GAILY 3
2 in a quick and spirited manner — see GAILY 2
jaunty *adj* having much high-spirited energy and movement — see LIVELY 1

javelin *n* a weapon with a long straight handle and sharp head or blade — see SPEAR

jaw *vb* **1** to criticize (someone) severely or angrily especially for personal failings — see SCOLD
2 to engage in casual or rambling conversation — see CHAT

jazz *n* unintelligible or meaningless talk — see GIBBERISH

jazz (up) *vb* to give life, vigor, or spirit to — see ANIMATE

jazziness *n* the quality or state of having abundant or intense activity — see VITALITY 1

jazzy *adj* **1** attractively eye-catching in style ⟨that's a *jazzy* bathing suit, with all those spangles⟩
synonyms flashy, snazzy, splashy
related words cool, hip, neat; à la mode (*also* a la mode), chic, dashing; faddish, fashionable, in, modish, posh, ritzy, sharp, smart, snappy, spruce, stylish; custom, designer; garish, gaudy, loud, rakish, wild
near antonyms classic, elegant, genteel, polished, refined, sophisticated, stately, swank; plain, quiet, restrained, simple, understated
2 having much high-spirited energy and movement — see LIVELY 1

jealous *adj* **1** intolerant of rivalry or unfaithfulness ⟨became *jealous* whenever she paid attention to anyone but him⟩
synonyms possessive
related words controlling, demanding, grasping; covetous, envious, invidious, jaundiced; distrustful, mistrustful, suspicious
phrases green with envy
near antonyms undemanding; tolerant, trustful, trusting, understanding
2 having or showing mean resentment of another's possessions or advantages — see ENVIOUS

jealousy *n* a painful awareness of another's possessions or advantages and a desire to have them too — see ENVY

jeer *n* a vocal sound made to express scorn or disapproval — see CATCALL

jeer *vb* to make (someone or something) the object of unkind laughter — see RIDICULE

Jehovah *n* the being worshipped as the creator and ruler of the universe — see DEITY 2

jell *vb* **1** to take on a definite form — see FORM 1
2 to turn from a liquid into a substance resembling jelly — see COAGULATE

jelly *vb* to turn from a liquid into a substance resembling jelly — see COAGULATE

jeopardize *vb* to place in danger — see ENDANGER

jeopardizing *adj* involving potential loss or injury — see DANGEROUS

jeopardy *n* the state of not being protected from injury, harm, or evil — see DANGER 1

jerk *n* **1** a person whose behavior is offensive to others ⟨his constant rudeness and insensitivity made everyone think he was a real *jerk*⟩
synonyms beast, boor, cad, churl, clown, creep, cretin, cur, heel, joker, louse, lout, skunk, slob, snake, stinker
related words brute, Neanderthal, savage; rascal, rogue, scamp, villain; fool, jackass, nincompoop, nitwit; blockhead, dolt, goon, idiot
near antonyms hero, idol, role model
2 the act or an instance of applying force on something so that it moves in the direction of the force — see PULL 1

jerk *vb* **1** to move or cause to move with a sharp quick motion ⟨I *jerked* to one side to avoid getting hit⟩ ⟨*jerked* the leash to get the dog's attention⟩
synonyms buck, hitch, jolt, twitch, yank
related words bump, jounce, lurch, stagger; jiggle, shake; lug, pull, tug; pluck, tweak; grab, snap, snatch, wrench, wrest, wring
2 to make jerky or restless movements — see FIDGET

jerky *adj* **1** marked by a series of sharp quick motions ⟨made *jerky* progress walking with the new crutches⟩
synonyms bumpy, rough
related words choppy, erratic, fitful, irregular, spasmodic, spastic, unsteady
near antonyms calm, placid, smooth, steady, still
2 showing or marked by a lack of good sense or judgment — see FOOLISH 1

jest *n* **1** an attitude or manner not to be taken seriously — see FUN 2
2 something said or done to cause laughter — see JOKE 1

jest *vb* to make jokes — see JOKE

jester *n* **1** a person (as a writer) noted for or specializing in humor — see HUMORIST
2 a person formerly kept in a royal or noble household to amuse with jests and pranks — see FOOL 2

jesting *adj* marked by or expressive of mild or good-natured teasing — see QUIZZICAL

jesting *n* good-natured teasing or exchanging of clever remarks — see BANTER

jet *vb* **1** to flow out in great quantities or with force — see GUSH 1
2 to throw out or off (something from within) often violently — see ERUPT 1

jettison *n* the getting rid of whatever is unwanted or useless — see DISPOSAL 1

jettison *vb* to get rid of as useless or unwanted — see DISCARD

jetty *n* a structure used by boats and ships for taking on or landing cargo and passengers — see DOCK

jewel *n* **1** a usually valuable stone cut and polished for ornament — see GEM 1
2 an asset that brings praise or renown — see GLORY 2
3 someone or something unusually desirable — see PRIZE 1

jibe *vb* to be in agreement on every point — see CHECK 1

jiffy *n* a very small space of time — see INSTANT

jig *n* a clever often underhanded means to achieve an end — see TRICK 1

jigger *n* an interesting and often novel device with a practical use — see GADGET

jiggling *n* a series of slight movements by a body back and forth or from side to side — see VIBRATION

jim–dandy *adj* of the very best kind — see EXCELLENT

jim–dandy *n* something very good of its kind ⟨the brand new car was a *jim-dandy*⟩
synonyms beauty, corker, crackerjack, dandy, knockout, nifty, pip
related words marvel, wonder; gem, jewel, treasure
near antonyms disappointment, failure, lemon, loser

jimmy *vb* to raise, move, or pull apart with or as if with a lever — see [1]PRY 1

jingle *n* **1** a series of short high ringing sounds — see TINKLE

2 a short musical composition for the human voice often with instrumental accompaniment — see SONG 1

jingle *vb* to make a repeated sharp light ringing sound ⟨the bell on the kitten's collar *jingled* as she walked⟩

synonyms chink, clink, tinkle

related words clack, clang, clank; clatter, rattle; ding, jangle, ping, ring

jingo *n* **1** one who shows excessive favoritism towards his or her country — see NATIONALIST

2 one who urges or attempts to cause a war — see WARMONGER

jingoism *n* excessive favoritism towards one's own country — see CHAUVINISM

jinx *n* something that brings bad luck ⟨believed the broken mirror was a *jinx*⟩

synonyms hex, hoodoo

related words curse, evil eye, spell; augury, omen, portent

near antonyms amulet, charm, talisman

jitters *n pl* a sense of panic or extreme nervousness ⟨always got the *jitters* right before a test⟩

synonyms dither, nerves, shakes, shivers, willies

related words cold sweat, creeps; anxiety, fear, hysteria; frazzle, nervous breakdown

near antonyms aplomb, composure, coolheadedness, equanimity, imperturbability, self-possession

jittery *adj* **1** easily excited by nature — see EXCITABLE

2 feeling or showing uncomfortable feelings of uncertainty — see NERVOUS 1

jive *vb* **1** to make fun of in a good-natured way — see TEASE 1

2 to make jokes — see JOKE

job *n* **1** an assignment at which one regularly works for pay ⟨a high-paying *job* as a banker⟩

synonyms appointment, berth, billet, capacity, function, place, position, post, situation

related words business, employment, occupation, profession; work; office, spot; calling, pursuit, vocation; line, racket; engagement; livelihood, living; assignment, mission, task

near antonyms avocation; joblessness, unemployment

2 a piece of work that needs to be done regularly — see CHORE 1

3 a specific task with which a person or group is charged — see MISSION

4 the action for which a person or thing is specially fitted or used or for which a thing exists — see ROLE

jobholder *n* one who works for another for wages or a salary — see EMPLOYEE

jocose *adj* indicative of or marked by high spirits or good humor — see MERRY

jocosely *adv* in a cheerful or happy manner — see GAILY 1

jocular *adj* given to or marked by mature intelligent humor — see WITTY

jocund *adj* indicative of or marked by high spirits or good humor — see MERRY

jog *vb* **1** to go at a pace faster than a walk — see RUN 1

2 to make short up-and-down movements — see NOD

joggle *vb* to make a series of small irregular or violent movements — see SHAKE 1

join *vb* **1** to be adjacent to — see ADJOIN 1

2 to become a member of — see ENTER 2

3 to come together to form a single unit — see UNITE 1

4 to participate or assist in a joint effort to accomplish an end — see COOPERATE 1

5 to put or bring together so as to form a new and longer whole — see CONNECT 1

joining *adj* having a border in common — see ADJACENT

joint *adj* used or done by a number of people as a group — see COLLECTIVE

joint *n* **1** a place where two or more things are united ⟨the leak was found at a *joint* in the pipe⟩

synonyms connection, coupling, junction, juncture

related words crux, link, tie; interconnection, intersection; abutment, articulation; seam, suture; concourse, confluence, meeting; union

near antonyms crack, separation

2 a building, room, or suite of rooms occupied by a service business — see PLACE 2

jointly *adv* in or by combined action or effort — see TOGETHER 2

joke *n* **1** something said or done to cause laughter ⟨he was known for his hilarious *jokes*⟩

synonyms crack, gag, jest, laugh, pleasantry, quip, sally, waggery, wisecrack, witticism

related words funning, joking, wisecracking; antic, buffoonery, caper, monkeyshine(s), prank; caricature, lampoon, parody, put-on; banter, persiflage, raillery, repartee; facetiousness, funniness, hilariousness, humorousness; barb, humor, wit, wordplay

2 a poor, insincere, or insulting imitation of something — see MOCKERY 1

joke *vb* to make jokes ⟨he was known for his ability to *joke*⟩

synonyms banter, fool, fun, jest, jive, josh, kid, quip, wisecrack

related words chaff, mock, rally, razz, rib, ridicule, tease; caricature, lampoon, parody, satirize; amuse, divert, entertain

joker *n* **1** a person (as a writer) noted for or specializing in humor — see HUMORIST

2 a person whose behavior is offensive to others — see JERK 1

3 an adult male human being — see MAN 1

jokester *n* a person (as a writer) noted for or specializing in humor — see HUMORIST

joking *adj* marked by or expressive of mild or good-natured teasing — see QUIZZICAL

jollification *n* joyful or festive activity — see MERRYMAKING

jollity *n* joyful or festive activity — see MERRYMAKING

jolly *adj* indicative of or marked by high spirits or good humor — see MERRY

jolly *adv* to a great degree — see VERY 1

jolt *n* **1** a forceful coming together of two things — see IMPACT 1

2 something that makes a strong impression because it is so unexpected — see SURPRISE 1

jolt *vb* **1** to make a series of small irregular or violent movements — see SHAKE 1

2 to move or cause to move with a sharp quick motion — see JERK 1

3 to cause an often unpleasant surprise for — see SHOCK 1

josh *vb* **1** to make fun of in a good-natured way — see TEASE 1
2 to make jokes — see JOKE

joshing *adj* marked by or expressive of mild or good-natured teasing — see QUIZZICAL

joshing *n* good-natured teasing or exchanging of clever remarks — see BANTER

jot *n* the smallest amount or part imaginable ⟨it's obvious that he doesn't have a *jot* of interest in history⟩
synonyms hoot, iota, lick, modicum, rap, tittle, whit
related words ace, bit, crumb, dab, driblet, glimmer, hint, little, mite, nip, ounce, peanuts, ray, scruple, shade, shadow, shred, smidgen, snap, speck, spot, sprinkling, strain, streak, suspicion, touch, trace

jot (down) *vb* to make a written note of — see RECORD 1

jounce *vb* **1** to make a series of small irregular or violent movements — see SHAKE 1
2 to make short up-and-down movements — see NOD

journal *n* a publication that appears at regular intervals ⟨a monthly scientific *journal*⟩
synonyms gazette, magazine, newspaper, organ, paper, periodical, review
related words annual, bimonthly, biweekly, daily, monthly, quarterly, semimonthly, semiweekly, weekly, yearbook; broadside, extra, sheet, tabloid

journalist *n* a person employed by a newspaper, magazine, or radio or television station to gather, write, or report news — see REPORTER

journey *n* a going from one place to another usually of some distance ⟨they were hungry and tired after their long *journey*⟩
synonyms expedition, passage, peregrination, travel(s), trek, trip
related words errand, excursion, flight, hop, jaunt, junket, outing, sally, tour; cruise, sail, voyage; drive, ride, spin; odyssey, pilgrimage, progress, quest, safari

journey *vb* to take a trip especially of some distance — see TRAVEL 1

jovial *adj* indicative of or marked by high spirits or good humor — see MERRY

joviality *n* a mood characterized by high spirits and amusement and often accompanied by laughter — see MIRTH

jovially *adv* in a cheerful or happy manner — see GAILY 1

joy *n* **1** a feeling or state of well-being and contentment — see HAPPINESS 1
2 a source of great satisfaction — see DELIGHT 1

joy *vb* to feel or express joy or triumph — see EXULT

joyful *adj* experiencing pleasure, satisfaction, or delight — see GLAD 1

joyless *adj* feeling unhappiness — see SAD 1

joylessness *n* a state or spell of low spirits — see SADNESS

joyous *adj* experiencing pleasure, satisfaction, or delight — see GLAD 1

jubilant *adj* having or expressing feelings of joy or triumph — see EXULTANT

jubilee *n* a time or program of special events and entertainment in honor of something — see FESTIVAL

judge *n* **1** a person who impartially decides or resolves a dispute or controversy ⟨their father always played the role of *judge* when there was a disagreement⟩
synonyms arbiter, arbitrator, referee, umpire
related words justice, magistrate; intermediary, mediator, negotiator; conciliator, go-between, peacemaker, reconciler; decider
2 a public official having authority to decide questions of law ⟨the *judge* gave the defendant a suspended sentence⟩
synonyms bench, court, justice, magistrate
related words justice of the peace
near antonyms claimant, plaintiff; defendant

judge *vb* **1** to give an opinion about (something at issue or in dispute) ⟨the committee will *judge* the case based on the evidence⟩
synonyms adjudge, adjudicate, arbitrate, decide, determine, referee, rule (on), settle, umpire
related words consider, hear, ponder, weigh; size (up); mediate, moderate, negotiate; prosecute, try; find (for *or* against)
near antonyms equivocate, skirt
2 to decide the size, amount, number, or distance of (something) without actual measurement — see ESTIMATE 2
3 to form an opinion through reasoning and information — see INFER 1

judgment *or* **judgement** *n* **1** a decision made by a court or tribunal regarding a case it has heard — see SENTENCE
2 a position arrived at after consideration — see DECISION 1
3 an idea that is believed to be true or valid without positive knowledge — see OPINION 1
4 an opinion on the nature, character, or quality of something — see ESTIMATION 1

judicious *adj* **1** having or showing good judgment and restraint especially in conduct or speech — see DISCREET
2 suitable for bringing about a desired result under the circumstances — see EXPEDIENT

jug *n* **1** a place of confinement for persons held in lawful custody — see JAIL
2 a handled container for holding and pouring liquids that usually has a lip or a spout — see PITCHER

jug *vb* to put in or as if in prison — see IMPRISON

jugglery *n* the use of clever underhanded actions to achieve an end — see TRICKERY

juiciness *n* the quality or state of being full of juice — see SUCCULENCE

juicy *adj* full of juice ⟨she bit into the *juicy* orange⟩
synonyms fleshy, pulpy, succulent
related words sappy, watery
near antonyms dehydrated, dry, withered

jumble *n* **1** a state in which everything is out of order — see CHAOS
2 an unorganized collection or mixture of various things — see MISCELLANY 1

jumble *vb* to undo the proper order or arrangement of — see DISORDER

jumbled *adj* lacking in order, neatness, and often cleanliness — see MESSY

jumbo *adj* unusually large — see HUGE

jumbo *n* something that is unusually large and powerful — see GIANT

jump *n* **1** an act of leaping into the air ⟨her first *jump* from an airplane at the age of 12⟩
synonyms bound, hop, leap, spring, vault
related words bounce, lope, skip; caper, gambol; attack, pounce; dive, pitch, plunge

2 the more favorable condition or position in a competition — see ADVANTAGE 1

jump *vb* **1** to propel oneself upward or forward into the air ⟨*jumped* across the ditch⟩
synonyms bound, hop, leap, spring, vault
related words bounce, hurdle, lope, skip; buck; caper, cavort, frolic, gambol, romp; attack, pounce; shoot, skyrocket
2 to move suddenly and sharply (as in surprise) — see START 1

jump (on) *vb* **1** to take sudden, violent action against — see ATTACK 1
2 to criticize harshly and usually publicly — see ATTACK 2

jumpiness *n* a state of nervousness marked by sudden jerky movements ⟨the police detective interpreted the suspect's *jumpiness* as a sign of guilt⟩
synonyms edginess, fidgets, flightiness, restiveness, skittishness
related words agitation, anxiety, anxiousness, apprehension, apprehensiveness, disquiet, feverishness, nervousness, perturbation, uneasiness, upset, worry; nerves, tenseness, tension; dither, jitters, shakes, shivers, willies
near antonyms confidence, self-assurance, self-confidence, sureness; control, self-control; aplomb, calm, calmness, collectedness, composure, coolheadedness, coolness, ease, easiness, equanimity, imperturbability, self-possession

jumpy *adj* **1** easily excited by nature — see EXCITABLE
2 feeling or showing uncomfortable feelings of uncertainty — see NERVOUS 1

junction *n* **1** a place where two or more things are united — see JOINT 1
2 the act or an instance of joining two or more things into one — see UNION 1

juncture *n* **1** a particular and often important moment in time — see POINT 1
2 a place where two or more things are united — see JOINT 1
3 a time or state of affairs requiring prompt or decisive action — see EMERGENCY

junior *adj* having not so great importance or rank as another — see LESSER

junior *n* one who is of lower rank and typically under the authority of another — see UNDERLING

junk *n* discarded or useless material — see GARBAGE

junk *vb* to get rid of as useless or unwanted — see DISCARD

junket *n* a short trip for pleasure — see EXCURSION 1

junket *vb* to entertain with a fancy meal — see FEAST

junkie *also* **junky** *n* a person who regularly uses drugs especially illegally — see DOPER

junking *n* the getting rid of whatever is unwanted or useless — see DISPOSAL 1

junky *adj* **1** having no usefulness — see WORTHLESS
2 of low quality — see CHEAP 2

junto *n* a group of persons formally joined together for some common interest — see ASSOCIATION 2

jurisdiction *n* lawful control over the affairs of a political unit (as a nation) — see RULE 2

just *adj* **1** being what is called for by accepted standards of right and wrong ⟨a *just* punishment should fit the crime⟩
synonyms deserved, due, merited, right, rightful, warranted
related words applicable, appropriate, apt, fit, fitting, meet, proper, requisite, suitable; lawful, legal; accurate, correct
near antonyms incoherent, irrelevant; improper, inapplicable, inappropriate, inapt, inequitable; arbitrary, despotic
antonyms undeserved, undue, unjust, unwarranted
2 based on sound reasoning or information — see GOOD 1
3 conforming to a high standard of morality or virtue — see GOOD 2
4 following the accepted rules of moral conduct — see HONORABLE 1
5 guided by or in accordance with one's sense of right and wrong — see CONSCIENTIOUS 1
6 marked by justice, honesty, and freedom from bias — see FAIR 2

just *adv* **1** in a like manner ⟨you can do it *just* the way they do⟩
synonyms exactly, precisely
related words as well, dead, even, expressly, perfectly
phrases to a T
near antonyms slightly, somewhat, vaguely
2 by a very small margin ⟨I was *just* over the minimum height requirement for admittance to the amusement park ride⟩
synonyms barely, hardly, marginally, scarcely, slightly
related words minimally, minutely; approximately, more or less, roughly, somewhat
near antonyms definitely, easily, plainly, positively, quite, unquestionably; abundantly, completely, copiously, generously, greatly
antonyms considerably, significantly, substantially, well
3 nothing more than ⟨I was *just* kidding⟩
synonyms but, merely, only, simply
4 as stated or indicated without the slightest difference — see EXACTLY 1
5 for nothing other than — see SOLELY 1
6 not long ago — see NEWLY

justice *n* **1** the act or practice of giving to others what is their due ⟨they felt that *justice* had been done in the case⟩
synonyms equity, right
related words fairness, impartiality; goodness, virtue; honor; decorum
near antonyms bias, partiality, prejudice; corruption, foul play; crime
antonyms inequity, injustice, wrong
2 a public official having authority to decide questions of law — see JUDGE 1

justifiable *adj* capable of being defended with good reasoning against verbal attack — see TENABLE 1

justification *n* an explanation that frees one from fault or blame — see EXCUSE

justified *adj* based on sound reasoning or information — see GOOD 1

justify *vb* **1** to be an acceptable reason for ⟨you seem to think that losing a basketball game *justifies* a temper tantrum⟩
synonyms excuse
related words account (for), explain, rationalize; brush (aside *or* off), condone, disregard, forgive, gloss (over), ignore, pardon, pass over, remit, shrug off, wink (at)

2 to continue to declare to be true or proper despite opposition or objections — see MAINTAIN 2
jut *n* a part that sticks out from the general mass of something — see BULGE
jut *vb* to extend outward beyond a usual point — see BULGE
juvenile *adj* **1** being in the early stage of life, growth, or development — see YOUNG
2 having or showing the annoying qualities (as silliness) associated with children — see CHILDISH
3 lacking in adult experience or maturity — see CALLOW
juvenile *n* a young person who is between infancy and adulthood — see CHILD 1
juxtaposed *adj* having a border in common — see ADJACENT

keelhaul *vb* to criticize (someone) severely or angrily especially for personal failings — see SCOLD
keen *adj* **1** able to sense slight impressions or differences — see ²ACUTE 1
2 causing intense discomfort to one's skin — see CUTTING 1
3 having an edge thin enough to cut or pierce something — see SHARP 1
4 having or showing quickness of mind — see INTELLIGENT 1
5 of the very best kind — see EXCELLENT
6 showing urgent desire or interest — see EAGER
keen *n* a crying out in grief — see LAMENT 1
keen *vb* to make a long loud mournful sound — see HOWL 1
keenness *n* **1** a harsh or sharp quality — see EDGE 1
2 urgent desire or interest — see EAGERNESS
keep *vb* **1** to act properly in relation to ⟨*keep* the Sabbath by not working⟩
synonyms celebrate, commemorate, observe
related words bless, consecrate, sanctify, solemnize; honor, laud, praise; obey, respect, revere, reverence, venerate; remember
phrases live up to
near antonyms disregard, forget, ignore, neglect, overlook
antonyms break, transgress, violate
2 to continue to have in one's possession or power ⟨the money is yours to *keep*⟩ ⟨*keep* my secret and don't tell it to anyone⟩
synonyms hang on (to), hold, reserve, retain, withhold
related words conserve, preserve, save; enjoy, have, own, possess; conduct, control, detain, direct; bear, harbor
near antonyms abandon, cede, yield; contribute, donate, give; discard, dump; decline, reject, repudiate, spurn
antonyms hand over, relinquish, surrender
3 to do what is required by the terms of — see FULFILL 1
4 to place somewhere for safekeeping or ready availability — see STORE 1
keep (from) *vb* to resist the temptation of — see FORBEAR
keep (to) *vb* to give steadfast support to — see ADHERE
keeper *n* **1** a person or group that watches over someone or something — see GUARD 1
2 a person who takes care of a property sometimes for an absent owner — see CUSTODIAN 1
keeping *n* **1** responsibility for the safety and well-being of someone or something — see CUSTODY
2 the fact or state of having (something) at one's disposal — see POSSESSION 1
keepsake *n* something that serves to keep alive the memory of a person or event — see MEMORIAL
keep up *vb* **1** to continue to operate or to meet one's needs — see HOLD OUT
2 to keep in good condition — see MAINTAIN 1
3 to remain indefinitely in existence or in the same state — see CONTINUE 1
keg *n* an enclosed wooden vessel for holding beverages — see CASK
kerchief *n* a scarf worn on the head — see BANDANNA
kerf *n* a V-shaped cut usually on an edge or a surface — see NOTCH 1
key *adj* **1** coming before all others in importance — see FOREMOST 1
2 of the greatest possible importance — see CRUCIAL
key *n* **1** an explanatory list of the symbols on a map or chart — see LEGEND 1
2 something that allows someone to achieve a desired goal — see PASSPORT
key *vb* to bring to a state free of conflicts, inconsistencies, or differences — see HARMONIZE 2
keystone *n* an immaterial thing upon which something else rests — see BASE 1
kibitzer *n* a person who meddles in the affairs of others — see BUSYBODY
kick *n* **1** a pleasurably intense stimulation of the feelings — see THRILL
2 a source of great satisfaction — see DELIGHT 1
3 a feeling or declaration of disapproval or dissent — see OBJECTION
kick *vb* **1** to express dissatisfaction, pain, or resentment usually tiresomely — see COMPLAIN
2 to present an opposing opinion or argument — see OBJECT
kick in *vb* to make a donation as part of a group effort — see CONTRIBUTE 1
kick off *vb* to take the first step in (a process or course of action) — see BEGIN 1
kid *n* a young person who is between infancy and adulthood — see CHILD 1
kid *vb* **1** to make fun of in a good-natured way — see TEASE 1
2 to make jokes — see JOKE
kidding *adj* marked by or expressive of mild or good-natured teasing — see QUIZZICAL

kiddish *adj* having or showing the annoying qualities (as silliness) associated with children — see CHILDISH
kidnap *vb* to carry a person away by unlawful force or against his or her will ⟨the child was *kidnapped* and held for ransom⟩
synonyms abduct
related words impress, shanghai, waylay; snatch, spirit
phrases make away with
near antonyms deliver, ransom, redeem, rescue; restore, return
kill *vb* **1** to deprive of life ⟨the soldier was *killed* in battle⟩
synonyms croak [*slang*], destroy, dispatch, do in, fell, slay
related words annihilate, blot out, butcher, decimate, massacre, slaughter, wipe out; cut down, finish, nip, snuff; assassinate, execute, murder, smite
phrases do away with
near antonyms restore, resurrect, resuscitate, revive; nurture
antonyms animate
2 to reject by or as if by a vote — see NEGATIVE 1
3 to show (something written) to be no longer valid by drawing a cross over or a line through it — see X (OUT)
killer *adj* **1** likely to cause or capable of causing death — see DEADLY
2 requiring considerable physical or mental effort — see HARD 2
killer *n* a person who kills another person — see ASSASSIN
killjoy *n* a person who spoils the pleasure of others ⟨his constant negative attitude made him a real *killjoy* when others were trying to have fun⟩
synonyms party pooper, spoilsport
related words fuddy-duddy, goody-goody, old maid, stick-in-the-mud; defeatist, pessimist; complainer, grouch, sorehead, whiner
near antonyms cutup, live wire; carouser, celebrant, celebrator, merrymaker, reveler (*or* reveller), roisterer; libertine, playboy, rake
kilter *n* a state of being or fitness — see CONDITION 1
kin *n* **1** a group of persons who come from the same ancestor — see FAMILY 1
2 a person connected with another by blood or marriage — see RELATIVE
kind *adj* **1** given to or made with heedful anticipation of the needs and happiness of others — see THOUGHTFUL 1
2 having or marked by sympathy and consideration for others — see HUMANE 1
kind *n* **1** a number of persons or things that are grouped together because they have something in common — see SORT 1
2 one of the units into which a whole is divided on the basis of a common characteristic — see CLASS 2
kindhearted *adj* having or marked by sympathy and consideration for others — see HUMANE 1
kindheartedness *n* the capacity for feeling for another's unhappiness or misfortune — see HEART 1
kindle *vb* to set (something) on fire — see BURN 2
kindled *adj* being on fire — see ABLAZE 1
kindliness *n* **1** kindly concern, interest, or support — see GOODWILL 1
2 the capacity for feeling for another's unhappiness or misfortune — see HEART 1
kindly *adj* having or marked by sympathy and consideration for others — see HUMANE 1
kindly *adv* with good reason or courtesy — see WELL 4
kindness *n* **1** an act of kind assistance — see FAVOR 1
2 the capacity for feeling for another's unhappiness or misfortune — see HEART 1
kind of *adv* to some degree or extent — see FAIRLY
kindred *adj* **1** having a close connection like that between family members — see RELATED
2 having or marked by agreement in feeling or action — see HARMONIOUS 3
kindred *n* a group of persons who come from the same ancestor — see FAMILY 1
kinfolk *n pl* a group of persons who come from the same ancestor — see FAMILY 1
king *n* a person of rank, power, or influence in a particular field — see MAGNATE
kingdom come *n* a dwelling place of perfect bliss for the soul after death — see HEAVEN 1
kingly *adj* fit for or worthy of a royal ruler — see MONARCHICAL
kingpin *n* the person (as an employer or supervisor) who tells people and especially workers what to do — see BOSS
king–size *or* **king–sized** *adj* **1** unusually large — see HUGE
2 of great extent from end to end — see LONG 1
king's ransom *n* a very large amount of money — see FORTUNE 2
kinky *adj* different from the ordinary in a way that causes curiosity or suspicion — see ODD 2
kinsfolk *n pl* a group of persons who come from the same ancestor — see FAMILY 1
kinship *n* the fact or state of having something in common — see CONNECTION 1
kinsman *n* a person connected with another by blood or marriage — see RELATIVE
kirk *n, chiefly Scottish* a building for public worship and especially Christian worship — see CHURCH 1
kiss *vb* **1** to touch one another with the lips as a sign of love ⟨it's traditional for couples to *kiss* under the mistletoe at Christmastime⟩
synonyms make out, pet, smooch
related words smack; caress, fondle, hug; bill, cuddle, nestle, snuggle
2 to pass lightly across or touch gently especially in passing — see BRUSH
kisser *n, slang* **1** the front part of the head — see FACE 1
2 the opening through which food passes into the body of an animal — see MOUTH 1
kittenish *adj* affecting shyness or modesty in order to attract masculine interest — see COY 1
¹kitty *n* a small domestic animal known for catching mice — see CAT 1
²kitty *n* a sum of money set aside for a particular purpose — see FUND 1
knack *n* a special and usually inborn ability — see TALENT
knapsack *n* a soft-sided case designed for carrying belongings especially on the back — see PACK 1
knave *n* a mean, evil, or unprincipled person — see VILLAIN
knavery *n* playful, reckless behavior that is not intended to cause serious harm — see MISCHIEF 1

knavish *adj* tending to or exhibiting reckless playfulness — see MISCHIEVOUS 1

knell *vb* to make the clear sound heard when metal vibrates — see RING 1

knickknack *n* a small object displayed for its attractiveness or interest ⟨a variety of pretty porcelain *knickknacks* adorned the mantel⟩
synonyms bauble, curio, curiosity, gaud, gewgaw, novelty, ornamental, trinket
related words bric-a-brac, trumpery; trifle; figurine, objet d'art, ornament; souvenir

knife *n* an instrument with a sharp edge for cutting ⟨be careful in using the *knife* to split open the cardboard box⟩
synonyms blade, cutter
related words bayonet, bolo, bowie knife, dagger, dirk, machete, pocketknife, poniard, stiletto, switchblade; saber, steel, sword; scalpel

knob *n* a small uneven mass — see LUMP 1

knock *n* **1** a hard strike with a part of the body or an instrument — see [1]BLOW
2 bad luck or an example of this — see MISFORTUNE

knock *vb* **1** to come into usually forceful contact with something — see HIT 2
2 to deliver a blow to (someone or something) usually in a strong vigorous manner — see HIT 1
3 to express one's unfavorable opinion of the worth or quality of — see CRITICIZE

knock (about) *vb* to move about from place to place aimlessly — see WANDER

knock (down *or* over) *vb* to strike (someone) so forcefully as to cause a fall — see FELL 1

knockabout *adj* being rough or noisy in a high-spirited way — see BOISTEROUS

knock down *vb* to take apart — see DISASSEMBLE

knock off *vb* **1** to bring (as an action or operation) to an immediate end — see STOP 1
2 to stop doing (something) permanently — see QUIT 2

knockout *adj* very pleasing to look at — see BEAUTIFUL

knockout *n* **1** a lovely woman — see BEAUTY 2
2 a temporary or permanent state of unconsciousness — see FAINT
3 something very good of its kind — see JIM-DANDY

knot *n* **1** a number of things considered as a unit — see GROUP 1
2 a small rounded mass of swollen tissue — see BUMP 1
3 a uniting or binding force or influence — see BOND 2
4 a usually small number of persons considered as a unit — see GROUP 2
5 something that requires thought and skill for resolution — see PROBLEM 1

knot *vb* to twist together into a usually confused mass — see ENTANGLE 1

knothead *n* a stupid person — see IDIOT

knotty *adj* **1** having many parts or aspects that are usually interrelated — see COMPLEX 1
2 requiring exceptional skill or caution in performance or handling — see TRICKY

know *vb* **1** to have a practical understanding of ⟨he *knows* several languages⟩
synonyms comprehend, grasp, understand
related words appreciate, apprehend, fathom, perceive; have, possess
near antonyms misapprehend, misconceive, misinterpret, misunderstand
2 to come to a knowledge of (something) by living through it — see EXPERIENCE

know–how *n* knowledge gained by actually doing or living through something — see EXPERIENCE 1

knowing *adj* **1** having inside information — see WISE 2
2 having or showing a practical cleverness or judgment — see SHREWD

knowingly *adv* with full awareness of what one is doing — see INTENTIONALLY

knowledge *n* **1** a body of facts learned by study or experience ⟨the forest ranger shared some of his vast *knowledge* of the woods with us⟩
synonyms lore, science, wisdom
related words information, intelligence, lowdown, news; data, evidence, facts; acquaintance, awareness, familiarity, literacy
near antonyms ignorance, inexperience, unfamiliarity
2 the understanding and information gained from being educated — see EDUCATION 2

knowledgeable *adj* **1** having information especially as a result of study or experience — see FAMILIAR 2
2 having or displaying advanced knowledge or education — see EDUCATED

knuckle under *vb* **1** to cease resistance (as to another's arguments, demands, or control) — see YIELD 3
2 to yield to the control or power of enemy forces — see FALL 2

kook *n* a person of odd or whimsical habits — see ECCENTRIC

kooky *adj* showing or marked by a lack of good sense or judgment — see FOOLISH 1

kowtow *vb* to use flattery or the doing of favors in order to win approval especially from a superior — see FAWN

label *n* a slip (as of paper or cloth) that is attached to something to identify or describe it ⟨on its frame the painting had a *label* with its title and the name of the artist⟩
synonyms marker, tag, ticket
related words caption, legend; brand, emblem, logo, mark, symbol; badge, decal, plaque, seal, stamp, sticker

label *vb* **1** to attach an identifying slip to ⟨he *labeled* all of the poisonous materials with the familiar skull and crossbones⟩
synonyms mark, tag, ticket

related words caption, earmark, stamp; call, designate, identify, name, tab; brand, stigmatize
2 to give a name to — see NAME 1

labor *n* **1** a dull, unpleasant, or difficult piece of work — see CHORE 2
2 the active use of energy in producing a result — see EFFORT
3 very hard or unpleasant work — see TOIL
4 the act or process of giving birth to children — see CHILDBIRTH

labor *vb* to devote serious and sustained effort ⟨he *labored* most of the evening over the difficult homework assignment⟩
synonyms drudge, endeavor, fag, grub, hump, hustle, moil, peg (away), plod, plow, plug, slave, slog, strain, strive, struggle, sweat, toil, travail, work
related words apply (oneself), attempt, buckle (down), hammer (away), pitch in; attack, drive; essay, try; exercise, exert, overexert, overwork; eke out, grind (out), put out, scratch; trudge, wade; employ, ply, use, utilize, wield
near antonyms break, ease (up), let up, slacken; bum, goldbrick, idle, loaf, lounge, shirk, slack (off); dawdle, poke, tarry; relax, rest; disport, frolic, gambol, play, recreate, rollick, romp, sport
antonyms dabble, fiddle (around), fool (around), mess (around), putter (around)

laborer *n* a person who does very hard or dull work — see SLAVE 2

laborious *adj* **1** involved in often constant activity — see BUSY 1
2 requiring considerable physical or mental effort — see HARD 2
3 requiring much time, effort, or careful attention — see DEMANDING 1

laboriously *adv* with great effort or determination — see HARD 1

laborsaving *adj* designed to replace or decrease human labor and especially physical labor ⟨a new *laborsaving* device let us clean the house in half the time⟩
synonyms automated, automatic, robotic, self-acting
related words mechanical, motorized; computerized; aiding, helping; easing, relieving; timesaving

labyrinth *n* a confusing and complicated arrangement of passages — see MAZE

labyrinthine *adj* having many parts or aspects that are usually interrelated — see COMPLEX 1

lace *n* **1** a length of braided, flexible material that is used for tying or connecting things — see CORD
2 a length of something formed of three or more strands woven together — see BRAID

lace *vb* **1** to cause to twine about one another — see INTERTWINE 1
2 to scatter or set here and there among other things — see THREAD 1
3 to strike repeatedly — see BEAT 1

laceration *n* a long deep cut — see GASH

lachrymose *adj* given to expressing strong emotion (as sorrow) by readily shedding tears — see TEARFUL 1

lacing *n* **1** a length of braided, flexible material that is used for tying or connecting things — see CORD
2 a length of something formed of three or more strands woven together — see BRAID

lack *n* **1** the fact or state of being absent ⟨the *lack* of news about the fate of the soldiers was frustrating⟩
synonyms absence, dearth, want
related words deficiency, deficit, inadequacy, insufficiency, meagerness, paucity, poverty, scantiness, scarceness, scarcity, shortage, skimpiness; deprivation, loss, necessity, need, needfulness, omission; privation; vacuum, void
near antonyms abundance, amplitude, bounty, plenitude, plenty, wealth; adequacy, sufficiency; excess, overabundance, oversupply, surfeit, surplus; deluge, flood; heap, mountain, peck, pile, pot, quantity, raft, stack, volume, wad; fund, pool, stock, supply; hoard, stockpile
antonyms presence
2 a falling short of an essential or desirable amount or number — see DEFICIENCY
3 a state of being without something necessary, desirable, or useful — see NEED 1

lackadaisical *adj* lacking bodily energy or motivation — see LISTLESS

lackey *n* a person hired to perform household or personal services — see SERVANT

lacking *adj* **1** not coming up to a usual standard or meeting a particular need — see SHORT 3
2 not present or in evidence — see ABSENT 2

laconic *adj* **1** marked by the use of few words to convey much information or meaning — see CONCISE
2 tending not to speak frequently (as by habit or inclination) — see SILENT 2

laconically *adv* in a few words — see SHORTLY 1

lad *n* **1** a male person who has not yet reached adulthood — see BOY
2 an adult male human being — see MAN 1

ladder *n* a scheme of rank or order — see [3]SCALE 1

laddie *n* a male person who has not yet reached adulthood — see BOY

lade *vb* **1** to lift out with something that holds liquid — see DIP 2
2 to place a weight or burden on — see LOAD 1

lading *n* a mass or quantity of something taken up and carried, conveyed, or transported — see LOAD 1

ladle *n* a utensil with a bowl and a handle that is used especially in cooking and serving food — see SPOON

ladle *vb* to lift out with something that holds liquid — see DIP 2

lady *n* **1** an adult female human being — see WOMAN
2 the female partner in a marriage — see WIFE
3 a woman of high birth or social position — see GENTLEWOMAN

ladylove *n* a woman with whom one is in love — see GIRLFRIEND

lag *vb* **1** to lose bodily strength or vigor — see WEAKEN 2
2 to move or act slowly — see DELAY 1

laggard *adj* moving or proceeding at less than the normal, desirable, or required speed — see SLOW 1

laggard *n* someone who moves slowly or more slowly than others — see SLOWPOKE

laggardly *adv* at a pace that is less than usual, desirable, or expected — see SLOW

lagger *n* someone who moves slowly or more slowly than others — see SLOWPOKE

lagging *adj* moving or proceeding at less than the normal, desirable, or required speed — see SLOW

lagniappe *n* **1** something given in addition to what is ordinarily expected or owed — see BONUS
2 something given to someone without expectation of a return — see GIFT 1
laid–back *adj* having a relaxed, casual manner — see EASYGOING 1
lair *n* **1** a place where a person goes to hide — see HIDEOUT
2 the shelter or resting place of a wild animal — see DEN 1
lam *n* the act or an instance of getting free from danger or confinement — see ESCAPE 1
lam *vb* to get free from a dangerous or confining situation — see ESCAPE 1
lamb *n* an innocent or gentle person ⟨the new guys at football camp were *lambs* who hardly knew what awaited them⟩
synonyms angel, dove, innocent, sheep
related words fledgling, greenhorn, ingenue (*or* ingénue); cherub, saint; mollycoddle, sissy, softy (*or* softie), weakling, wimp; dupe, pigeon, sap, sucker
near antonyms bully, roughneck, rowdy, tough; beast, boor, cad, churl, clown, creep, cretin, cur, heel, jerk; shark, skunk, snake, stinker; rascal, rogue, scamp, villain
antonyms wolf
lambaste *or* **lambast** *vb* **1** to criticize (someone) severely or angrily especially for personal failings — see SCOLD
2 to criticize harshly and usually publicly — see ATTACK 2
3 to strike repeatedly — see BEAT 1
lambent *adj* giving off or reflecting much light — see BRIGHT 1
lame *vb* to cause severe or permanent injury to — see MAIM
lamella *n* a small thin piece of material that resembles an animal scale — see ²SCALE
lament *n* **1** a crying out in grief ⟨the national *lament* that was heard when President Kennedy was assassinated⟩
synonyms groan, howl, keen, lamentation, moan, plaint, wail
related words grieving, mourning, weeping; regret; complaint, outcry, protest
near antonyms cheering, laughing, smiling
antonyms exultation, rejoicing
2 a composition expressing one's grief over a loss ⟨a poem that is her *lament* for her late grandmother⟩
synonyms dirge, elegy, requiem, threnody
related words taps
near antonyms encomium, eulogy, paean, panegyric
lament *vb* **1** to feel or express sorrow for ⟨she *lamented* the loss of her beloved pet⟩
synonyms bemoan, bewail, deplore, grieve (for), mourn, wail (for)
related words elegize; complain (about), cry (for), groan (about), keen, moan, weep; regret, rue; deprecate, disapprove (of)
near antonyms beam, cheer, laugh, smile; boast, brag, crow
antonyms exult (in), glory (in), rejoice (in)
2 to feel sorry or dissatisfied about — see REGRET
lamentable *adj* **1** expressing or suggesting mourning — see MOURNFUL 1
2 of a kind to cause great distress — see REGRETTABLE
lamentation *n* a crying out in grief — see LAMENT 1
lamina *n* a small thin piece of material that resembles an animal scale — see ²SCALE
lamp *n* something that provides illumination — see LIGHT 2
lampoon *n* a creative work that uses sharp humor to point up the foolishness of a person, institution, or human nature in general — see SATIRE
lance *n* a weapon with a long straight handle and sharp head or blade — see SPEAR
lance *vb* to penetrate or hold (something) with a pointed object — see IMPALE
land *n* **1** a body of people composed of one or more nationalities usually with its own territory and government — see NATION
2 a broad geographical area — see REGION 2
3 the solid part of our planet's surface as distinguished from the sea and air — see EARTH 2
land *vb* **1** to stop at or near a place along the shore ⟨the Pilgrims *landed* at Plymouth after exploring Cape Cod Bay⟩
synonyms anchor, dock
related words moor, tie up; beach, ground; harbor; arrive, reach; debark, disembark
phrases drop anchor, make port
near antonyms embark, launch, sail
2 to get to a destination — see COME 2
3 to go ashore from a ship — see DISEMBARK
4 to come to rest after descending from the air — see ALIGHT
5 to receive as return for effort — see EARN 1
6 to take physical control or possession of (something) suddenly or forcibly — see CATCH 1
landfill *n* a place where discarded materials (as trash) are dumped — see DUMP 1
landing *n* a structure used by boats and ships for taking on or landing cargo and passengers — see DOCK
landlord *n* the owner of land or housing that is rented to another ⟨agreed to pay the *landlord* the rent on the first Monday of each month⟩
synonyms lessor, renter
related words landlady; laird, landholder, landowner; host, proprietor; slumlord
antonyms lessee, lodger, tenant
landmark *n* a point in a chain of events at which an important change (as in one's fortunes) occurs — see TURNING POINT
language *n* **1** the stock of words, pronunciation, and grammar used by a people as their basic means of communication ⟨Great Britain, the United States, Australia, and other countries where English is the dominant *language*⟩
synonyms lingo, mother tongue, speech, tongue, vocabulary
related words argot, cant, dialect, idiom, jargon, parlance, patois, patter, pidgin, slang, vernacular; colloquialism, localism, regionalism; terminology
2 the special terms or expressions of a particular group or field — see TERMINOLOGY
3 the way in which something is put into words — see WORDING
languid *adj* **1** lacking bodily energy or motivation — see LISTLESS
2 lacking bodily strength — see WEAK 1
3 moving or proceeding at less than the normal, desirable, or required speed — see SLOW 1
languish *vb* to lose bodily strength or vigor — see WEAKEN 2

languishing *adj* lacking bodily energy or motivation — see LISTLESS
languor *n* the quality or state of lacking physical strength or vigor — see WEAKNESS 1
languorous *adj* lacking bodily energy or motivation — see LISTLESS
lank *adj* not stiff in structure — see LIMP 1
lanky *adj* being tall, thin and usually loose-jointed <the *lanky* basketball star was great at slam-dunking>
synonyms gangling, gangly, rangy, spindling, spindly
related words angular, bony, gaunt, lank, rawboned, scrawny, skinny; lean, slender, slim, spare, thin; racy, reedy, spidery, stringy, twiggy, wiry; spindle-shanked
near antonyms chubby, chunky, heavyset, pudgy, squat, stocky, stout, stubby, stumpy, sturdy, thick-bodied, thickset; muscle-bound
lap *n* a portion of a trip — see LEG 2
1lap *vb* **1** to flow along or against — see WASH 1
2 to flow in a broken irregular stream — see GURGLE
3 to move with a splashing motion — see SLOSH
2lap *vb* **1** to lie over parts of one another — see OVERLAP
2 to surround or cover closely — see ENFOLD 1
lapping *n* a partial covering of one thing by an adjoining thing — see OVERLAP
lapse *n* **1** a change in status for the worse usually temporarily — see REVERSE 1
2 an unintentional departure from truth or accuracy — see ERROR 1
3 the stopping of a process or activity — see END 1
lapse *vb* to come to an end — see CEASE 1
larceny *n* the unlawful taking and carrying away of property without the consent of its owner — see THEFT 1
large *adj* of a size greater than average of its kind <he was hungry, so he ordered the *large* pizza>
synonyms big, bulky, considerable, goodly, good-sized, grand, great, handsome, hefty, hulking, largish, outsize (*also* outsized), oversize (*or* oversized), sizable (*or* sizeable), substantial, tidy, voluminous
related words astronomical (*also* astronomic), bumper, cavernous, colossal, enormous, gigantic, gross, heroic, huge, immense, jumbo, king-size (*or* king-sized), major, mammoth, massive, monolithic, monstrous, monumental, prodigious, staggering, stupendous, super, tremendous, vast, vasty, whacking, whopping; excessive, exorbitant, extravagant, extreme, immoderate, inordinate; abundant, ample, appreciable, copious, plentiful; fat, thick; capacious, commodious, roomy, spacious
near antonyms diminutive, microscopic (*or* microscopical), midget, miniature, minute, pint-size (*or* pint-sized), pocket-size (*also* pocket-sized), pygmy, smallish, teeny, teeny-weeny, tiny, wee; petite, slender, slight, slim, thin
antonyms little, puny, small, undersized
largely *adv* **1** for the most part — see CHIEFLY
2 to a large extent or degree — see GREATLY 2
largeness *n* the quality or state of being large in size <I was impressed by the *largeness* of the portions at the new restaurant>
synonyms bigness, bulkiness, grandness, greatness, heftiness, substantiality, voluminousness
related words enormity, enormousness, extensiveness, grossness, healthiness, hugeness, immenseness, immensity, magnitude, massiveness, stupendousness, vastness; excessiveness, extravagance, extremeness, immoderacy; abundance, ampleness, bountifulness, copiousness, liberality; adequacy, sufficiency; weightiness
near antonyms diminutiveness, minuteness, tininess; slightness; meagerness, poorness, scantiness, scarceness, scarcity, skimpiness, slenderness, slimness, spareness, sparseness, stinginess; deficiency, inadequacy
antonyms fineness, littleness, puniness, smallness
largess *or* **largesse** *n* **1** something given to someone without expectation of a return — see GIFT 1
2 the quality or state of being generous — see LIBERALITY
largish *adj* **1** of a size greater than average of its kind — see LARGE
2 sufficiently large in size, amount, or number to merit attention — see CONSIDERABLE 1
lariat *n* a rope or long leather thong with a noose used especially for catching livestock — see LASSO
lark *n* a time or instance of carefree fun — see FLING 1
lark *vb* to play and run about happily — see FROLIC 1
larva *n* a young wingless often wormlike form (as a grub or caterpillar) that hatches from the egg of many insects <the *larva* looked ugly, but it was destined to hatch into a beautiful butterfly>
synonyms naiad, nymph
lascivious *adj* **1** depicting or referring to sexual matters in a way that is unacceptable in polite society — see OBSCENE 1
2 having a strong sexual desire — see LUSTFUL
lasciviousness *n* the quality or state of being obscene — see OBSCENITY 1
lash *n* a long thin or flexible tool for striking — see WHIP
lash *vb* to strike repeatedly with something long and thin or flexible — see WHIP 1
lass *n* a young usually unmarried woman — see GIRL 1
lassie *n* a young usually unmarried woman — see GIRL 1
lassitude *n* a complete depletion of energy or strength — see FATIGUE
lasso *n* a rope or long leather thong with a noose used especially for catching livestock <the cowpuncher skillfully tossed the *lasso* around the calf's neck>
synonyms lariat, reata, riata
last *adj* following all others of the same kind in order or time <*last* one in the pool is a rotten egg>
synonyms closing, concluding, final, hindmost, latest, latter, rearmost, terminal, terminating, ultimate
related words consequent, ensuing, eventual, following, succeeding; conclusive, crowning, decisive, definitive; farthest, furthest, remotest; lowermost, lowest, nethermost; endmost, extreme, outermost, outmost; penultimate
near antonyms eminent, premier, superior
antonyms beginning, earliest, first, inaugural, initial, maiden, opening, original, primary, starting
last *vb* **1** to continue to operate or to meet one's needs — see HOLD OUT

2 to remain indefinitely in existence or in the same state — see CONTINUE 1

last word *n* a practice or interest that is very popular for a short time — see FAD

late *adj* **1** not arriving, occurring, or settled at the due, usual, or proper time ⟨I ran as fast as I could, but was still *late* for class⟩
synonyms behind, behindhand, belated, delinquent, latish, overdue, tardy
related words delayed, detained, postponed; dilatory, laggard, slow, sluggish
near antonyms opportune, seasonable, timely; prompt, punctual
antonyms early, premature
2 having been such at some previous time — see FORMER
3 no longer living — see DEAD 1

late *adv* not long ago — see NEWLY

lately *adv* not long ago — see NEWLY

latency *n* a state of temporary inactivity — see ABEYANCE

lateness *n* the quality or state of being late ⟨we were unable to get into the movie due to our *lateness* in arriving⟩
synonyms belatedness, delinquency, tardiness
related words dilatoriness, sluggishness
near antonyms promptness, punctuality
antonyms earliness

latent *adj* not being in a state of use, activity, or employment — see INACTIVE 2

later *adj* being, occurring, or carried out at a time after something else — see SUBSEQUENT

later *adv* following in time or place — see AFTER

lateral *adj* of, relating to, or located on one side — see SIDE

latest *adj* following all others of the same kind in order or time — see LAST

lather *n* **1** a light mass of fine bubbles formed in or on a liquid — see FOAM
2 a state of nervous or irritated concern — see FRET

lathery *adj* covered with, consisting of, or resembling foam — see FOAMY

latish *adj* not arriving, occurring, or settled at the due, usual, or proper time — see LATE 1

latitude *n* the right to act or move freely — see FREEDOM 2

latrine *n* a room furnished with a fixture for flushing body waste — see TOILET

latter *adj* following all others of the same kind in order or time — see LAST

laud *vb* **1** to declare enthusiastic approval of — see ACCLAIM
2 to proclaim the glory of — see PRAISE 1

laudable *adj* deserving of high regard or great approval — see ADMIRABLE

laugh *n* **1** an explosive sound that is a sign of amusement ⟨the child's frown turned into a *laugh* when he saw the clown⟩
synonyms cackle, chortle, chuckle, giggle, guffaw, laughter, snicker, snigger, titter
related words crow, whoop; grin, simper, smile, smirk
near antonyms cry, groan, moan, sob, wail
2 someone or something that is very funny — see SCREAM
3 something said or done to cause laughter — see JOKE 1

laugh *vb* to express scornful amusement by means of facial contortions — see SNEER

laugh (at) *vb* to make (someone or something) the object of unkind laughter — see RIDICULE

laughable *adj* **1** causing or intended to cause laughter — see FUNNY 1
2 so foolish or pointless as to be worthy of scornful laughter — see RIDICULOUS 1

laughing *adj* indicative of or marked by high spirits or good humor — see MERRY

laughingstock *n* a person or thing that is made fun of ⟨his nerdy clothes made him the *laughingstock* of the schoolyard⟩
synonyms butt, mark, mock, mockery, target
related words chump, dupe, fall guy, fool, gull, monkey, pigeon, sap, sucker, victim
near antonyms favorite, darling, pet

laughter *n* an explosive sound that is a sign of amusement — see LAUGH 1

launch *n* **1** a rising from a surface at the start of a flight (as of a rocket) — see LIFT-OFF
2 the point at which something begins — see BEGINNING

launch *vb* **1** to be responsible for the creation and early operation or use of — see FOUND
2 to take the first step in (a process or course of action) — see BEGIN 1
3 to send through the air especially with a quick forward motion of the arm — see THROW

laurels *n pl* public acknowledgment or admiration for an achievement — see GLORY 1

lavaliere *also* **lavalliere** *n* an ornament worn on a chain around the neck or wrist — see PENDANT

lavatory *n* a room furnished with a fixture for flushing body waste — see TOILET

lave *vb* to flow along or against — see WASH 1

lavish *adj* **1** going beyond a normal or acceptable limit in degree or amount — see EXCESSIVE
2 pouring forth in great amounts — see PROFUSE
3 showing obvious signs of wealth and comfort — see LUXURIOUS

lavish *vb* **1** to give readily and in large quantities — see RAIN 2
2 to use up carelessly — see WASTE 1

lavishly *adv* in a luxurious manner — see HIGH

lavishness *n* the quality or fact of being free or wasteful in the expenditure of money — see EXTRAVAGANCE 1

law *n* **1** a rule of conduct or action laid down by a governing authority and especially a legislator ⟨a record number of *laws* were passed in that legislative session⟩
synonyms act, enactment, ordinance, statute
related words decree, directive, edict, fiat, ruling; bylaw, regulation, rule; amendment, bill, legislation; common law, martial law; prohibition, restriction; canon, encyclical
2 a collection or system of rules of conduct — see CODE
3 the department of government that keeps order, fights crime, and enforces statutes — see POLICE 1

law–abiding *adj* readily giving in to the command or authority of another — see OBEDIENT

lawbreaker *n* a person who has committed a crime — see CRIMINAL

lawbreaking *adj* not restrained by or under the control of legal authority — see LAWLESS

lawbreaking *n* **1** a breaking of a moral or legal code — see OFFENSE 1
2 activities that are in violation of the laws of the state — see CRIME 1

lawful *adj* permitted by law — see LEGAL 1
lawfulness *n* the quality or state of being legal — see LEGALITY
lawgiver *n* a member of an organized body of persons having the authority to make laws — see LEGISLATOR
lawless *adj* not restrained by or under the control of legal authority <the *lawless* rioters were destroying everything in sight>
synonyms anarchic, disorderly, lawbreaking, unruly
related words defiant, insubordinate, mutinous, rebellious, refractory, riotous; undisciplined; criminal, illegal, illegitimate, illicit, unlawful, wrongful
near antonyms lawful, legal, legalized, legitimate
antonyms law-abiding, orderly
lawlessness *n* **1** a state in which there is widespread wrongdoing and disregard for rules and authority — see ANARCHY
2 activities that are in violation of the laws of the state — see CRIME 1
lawmaker *n* a member of an organized body of persons having the authority to make laws — see LEGISLATOR
lawsuit *n* a court case for enforcing a right or claim <she filed a *lawsuit* against the moving company that was responsible for breaking her furniture>
synonyms action, proceeding, suit
related words litigation; case, cause, complaint
lawyer *n* a person whose profession is to conduct lawsuits for clients or to advise about legal rights and obligations <their *lawyers* told them that they couldn't use the park for the concert without permission from the city>
synonyms advocate, attorney, counsel, counselor (*or* counsellor)
related words pettifogger, shyster; district attorney, prosecutor; solicitor; jurist; lawgiver, lawmaker, legislator, solon
lax *adj* **1** failing to give proper care and attention — see NEGLIGENT
2 not bound by rigid standards — see EASYGOING 2
3 not tightly fastened, tied, or stretched — see LOOSE 1
laxness *n* failure to take the care that a cautious person usually takes — see NEGLIGENCE 1
lay *n* **1** a rhythmic series of musical tones arranged to give a pleasing effect — see MELODY
2 a short musical composition for the human voice often with instrumental accompaniment — see SONG 1
lay *vb* **1** to arrange something in a certain spot or position — see PLACE 1
2 to cause to come to rest at the bottom (as of a liquid) — see SETTLE 1
3 to establish or apply as a charge or penalty — see IMPOSE
4 to make ready in advance — see PREPARE 1
5 to put a layer of on a surface — see SPREAD 2
6 to risk (something) on the outcome of an uncertain event — see BET
lay away *vb* to put (something of future use or value) in a safe or secret place — see HOARD
lay down *vb* **1** to put into effect through legislative or authoritative action — see ENACT
2 to state clearly and strongly — see ASSERT 1
3 to give the rules about (something) clearly and exactly — see PRESCRIBE
layoff *n* the termination of the employment of an employee or a work force often temporarily <many people lost their jobs in the *layoff*>
synonyms discharge, dismissal, furlough
related words closing, shutdown; downsizing
lay off *vb* to bring (as an action or operation) to an immediate end — see STOP 1
lay off (of) *vb* to stop doing (something) permanently — see QUIT 2
layout *n* **1** the way in which something is sized, arranged, or organized — see FORMAT 1
2 the way in which the elements of something (as a work of art) are arranged — see COMPOSITION 3
lay out *vb* **1** to hand over or use up in payment — see SPEND 1
2 to work out the details of (something) in advance — see PLAN 1
layover *n* a brief halt in a journey — see STOP 1
lay up *vb* to put (something of future use or value) in a safe or secret place — see HOARD
laziness *n* an inclination not to do work or engage in activities <although she often talks about ambitious household projects, nothing even gets started because of her *laziness*>
synonyms idleness, indolence, inertia, shiftlessness, sloth
related words apathy, languor, lassitude, lethargy, listlessness, sluggishness; goldbricking, loafing
near antonyms enterprise, initiative; assiduity, diligence, perseverance; energy, pep, vigor, vim, vitality
antonyms drive, industriousness, industry
lazy *adj* not easily aroused to action or work <the *lazy* dog just wanted to lie on the couch all day and sleep>
synonyms idle, indolent, shiftless, slothful
related words apathetic, languorous, lazyish, lethargic, listless, sluggish, torpid
near antonyms ambitious, diligent, enterprising, zealous; dynamic, energetic, exuberant, lively, vigorous
antonyms industrious
lazybones *n pl* a lazy person <he's a *lazybones* who is never willing to do any work>
synonyms drone, idler, loafer, slouch, slug, sluggard
related words bum, ne'er-do-well; sleepyhead; dawdler, laggard, putterer, slowpoke, stick-in-the-mud, trifler; goldbrick, malingerer, shirker, slacker; dallier, lingerer, loiterer, lounger, saunterer; delayer, procrastinator; dropout, quitter
near antonyms live wire, powerhouse
antonyms doer, go-getter, hummer, hustler, rustler, self-starter
lea *n* open land over which livestock may roam and feed — see RANGE 1
lead *adj* highest in rank or authority — see HEAD
lead *n* **1** the person who has the most important role in a play, movie, or TV show — see STAR 2
2 the space or amount of space between two points, lines, surfaces, or objects — see DISTANCE
3 a piece of advice or useful information especially from an expert — see [1]TIP 1
4 a slight or indirect pointing to something (as a solution or explanation) — see HINT 1
lead *vb* **1** to point out the way for (someone) especially from a position in front <the tour guide *led* the group through the museum>

synonyms conduct, direct, guide, marshal, pilot, route, show, steer, usher
related words precede; accompany, attend, chaperone (*or* chaperon), convoy, escort, see; control, manage
near antonyms dog, hound, shadow, tail, tailgate
antonyms follow, trail
2 to serve as leader of ⟨the honor of *leading* the soccer squad⟩
synonyms boss, captain, command, dominate, head, spearhead
related words control, direct, govern, handle, manage, oversee, regulate, superintend, supervise
near antonyms bow (to), comply (with), defer (to), follow, obey, serve, submit (to), yield (to)
3 to be at the front of ⟨the marching band *led* the parade⟩
synonyms head
related words precede; announce, herald; accompany, attend, escort, usher
near antonyms conclude, end, finish, stop, terminate; tail, tailgate; dog, follow, trail
4 to be positioned along a certain course or in a certain direction — see RUN 3
5 to give advice and instruction to (someone) regarding the course or process to be followed — see GUIDE 1

leaden *adj* **1** causing weariness, restlessness, or lack of interest — see BORING
2 of the color gray — see GRAY 1

leader *n* **1** a long hollow cylinder for carrying a substance (as a liquid or gas) — see PIPE 1
2 the person (as an employer or supervisor) who tells people and especially workers what to do — see BOSS

leading *adj* **1** coming before all others in importance — see FOREMOST 1
2 highest in rank or authority — see HEAD

lead on *vb* to lead away from a usual or proper course by offering some pleasure or advantage — see LURE

leafage *n* green leaves or plants — see GREENERY 1

leaflet *n* a short printed publication with no cover or with a paper cover — see PAMPHLET

leafy *adj* covered with a thick, healthy natural growth — see LUSH 1

league *n* **1** a group of persons formally joined together for some common interest — see ASSOCIATION 2
2 an association of persons, parties, or states for mutual assistance and protection — see CONFEDERACY

league *vb* to form or enter into an association that furthers the interests of its members — see ALLY

leak (out) *vb* to become known — see GET OUT 1

lean *adj* having a noticeably small amount of body fat — see THIN 1

lean *n* the degree to which something rises up from a position level with the horizon — see SLANT

lean *vb* **1** to set or cause to be at an angle ⟨just *lean* the ladder against the tree and climb up it⟩
synonyms angle, cant, cock, heel, incline, list, slant, slope, tilt, tip
related words bank; bend, deviate, swerve, veer; decline, descend, recline, retreat
near antonyms even, flatten, level, straighten
2 to show a liking or proneness (for something) ⟨his diet *leans* toward greasy food⟩
synonyms incline, run, tend, trend
related words go, gravitate; indicate, point, suggest
near antonyms avoid, shun, shy (from *or* away from)
3 to place reliance or trust — see DEPEND 2

lean (toward) *vb* to show partiality toward — see PREFER 1

leaning *adj* running in a slanting direction — see DIAGONAL

leaning *n* **1** a prevailing or general movement or inclination — see TREND 1
2 a habitual attraction to some activity or thing — see INCLINATION 1

leap *n* an act of leaping into the air — see JUMP 1

leap *vb* to propel oneself upward or forward into the air — see JUMP 1

leaping *adj* passing from one topic to another — see DISCURSIVE

learn *vb* **1** to acquire complete knowledge, understanding, or skill in ⟨after months of trying, he finally *learned* the dance steps⟩
synonyms get, master, pick up
related words apprehend, comprehend, grasp, know, understand; absorb, assimilate, digest, imbibe; ascertain, descry, detect, determine, dig up, discern, discover, examine, find out, hear, hit (on *or* upon), run down, scare up, search (for), see, track (down), tumble (to), unearth; major (in), study; memorize
phrases get the hang (*or* knack) of
near antonyms forget, misunderstand; miss, overlook; disregard, ignore, neglect
antonyms unlearn
2 to come to an awareness — see DISCOVER 1
3 to come upon after searching, study, or effort — see FIND 1
4 to commit to memory — see MEMORIZE

learned *adj* **1** having or displaying advanced knowledge or education — see EDUCATED
2 suggestive of the vocabulary used in books — see BOOKISH

learnedness *n* the understanding and information gained from being educated — see EDUCATION 2

learning *n* the understanding and information gained from being educated — see EDUCATION 2

lease *vb* **1** to give the possession and use of (something) in return for periodic payment — see RENT 1
2 to take or get the temporary use of (something) for a set sum — see HIRE 1

least *adj* being the least in amount, number, or size possible — see MINIMAL

leather *n* **1** the hairless natural covering of an animal prepared for use ⟨the company claims to use only the finest *leathers* for its shoes and handbags⟩
synonyms hide, skin
related words coat, fleece, fur, pelt; alligator, buckskin, calfskin, chamois, cordovan, cowhide, deerskin, doeskin, goatskin, horsehide, kid, kidskin, lambskin, morocco, pigskin, seal, sharkskin, sheepskin, snakeskin, suede
2 the outer covering of an animal removed for its commercial value — see HIDE 1

leathery *adj* not easily chewed — see TOUGH 1

leave *n* **1** a period during which the usual routine of school or work is suspended — see VACATION
2 the approval by someone in authority for the doing of something — see PERMISSION

leave *vb* **1** to cause to remain behind ⟨you can

leave your lunch in the refrigerator while we're outside⟩ ⟨lovers who promise never to *leave* one another⟩
synonyms abandon, desert, forsake, maroon, quit
related words discard, ditch, dump, fling, jettison, junk, scrap, shed, shuck (off), throw away, throw out; deliver, give up, hand over, relinquish, surrender, yield; retreat (from), take off (from), vacate, withdraw (from); abjure, cut off, disown, reject, renounce, repudiate, separate (from); sacrifice; distance; disregard, forget, ignore, neglect
phrases walk out on
near antonyms harbor, have, hold, keep, own, possess, reserve, retain, withhold; redeem, rescue, save
antonyms reclaim
2 to give by means of a will ⟨I'm going to *leave* all of my possessions to my children⟩
synonyms bequeath, will
related words deed; hand down, pass (down); devise
3 to give up (a job or office) — see QUIT 1
4 to put (something) into the possession or safekeeping of another — see GIVE 2

leave off *vb* **1** to bring (as an action or operation) to an immediate end — see STOP 1
2 to come to an end — see CEASE 1

leave–taking *n* **1** the act of leaving a place — see DEPARTURE
2 the act or process of two or more persons going off in different directions — see PARTING 1

leavings *n pl* a remaining group or portion — see REMAINDER 1

lecture *vb* **1** to criticize (someone) severely or angrily especially for personal failings — see SCOLD
2 to give a formal often extended talk on a subject — see TALK 1

leech *n* a person who is supported or seeks support from another without making an adequate return ⟨whenever the gang went out for pizza, the *leech* in the group always had an excuse for not paying his fair share⟩
synonyms hanger-on, parasite, sponge, sponger
related words dependent; deadbeat, idler; flunky (*also* flunkey), henchman, lackey, satellite, stooge, sycophant, toady, yes-man; cheapskate, miser, niggard, piker, scrooge, skinflint, tightwad
near antonyms benefactor, philanthropist, supporter

leer (at) *vb* to look at in a flirtatious or desiring way — see OGLE

leery *adj* inclined to doubt or question claims — see SKEPTICAL 1

leeward *adj* being in the direction that the wind is blowing — see DOWNWIND

left *n* a political belief stressing progress, the essential goodness of humankind, and individual freedom — see LIBERALISM

left–handed *adj* not being or expressing what one appears to be or express — see INSINCERE

leftover *n* an unused or unwanted piece or item typically of small size or value — see [1]SCRAP 1

leftovers *n* a remaining group or portion — see REMAINDER 1

leg *n* **1** a lower limb of an animal ⟨he broke his *leg* when he accidentally stepped in that gopher hole⟩
synonyms pin
related words member; foreleg, forelimb; calf, drumstick, shank, shin, thigh
2 a portion of a trip ⟨on the first *leg* of the cruise they went south to the Caribbean⟩
synonyms lap, stage
related words layover, stopover

leg (it) *vb* to go on foot — see WALK

legacy *n* something that is or may be inherited — see INHERITANCE

legal *adj* **1** permitted by law ⟨drinking is only *legal* if you are 21 years old⟩
synonyms lawful, legitimate
related words allowable, authorized, noncriminal, permissible; justifiable, warrantable; regulation, statutory; good, innocent, proper, right
near antonyms bad, corrupt, evil, immoral, iniquitous, reprobate, sinful, wicked, wrong; banned, criminal, forbidden, guilty, outlawed, prohibited, unauthorized, unjust; nonconstitutional, unconstitutional
antonyms illegal, illegitimate, illicit, unlawful, wrongful
2 following or according to the rules — see FAIR 3

legality *n* the quality or state of being legal ⟨the senator questioned the *legality* of the proposed program⟩
synonyms lawfulness, legitimacy
related words rightfulness, rightness; permissibility, permissibleness
near antonyms badness, immorality, iniquity, sinfulness, unjustness, wickedness, wrongness; criminality, unconstitutionality
antonyms illegality, illegitimacy, unlawfulness, wrongfulness

legal tender *n* something (as pieces of stamped metal or printed paper) customarily and legally used as a medium of exchange, a measure of value, or a means of payment — see MONEY

legate *n* a person sent on a mission to represent another — see AMBASSADOR

legatee *n* a person who has the right to inherit property — see HEIR

legend *n* **1** an explanatory list of the symbols on a map or chart ⟨the *legend* indicated that a large circle represented each city, while a small circle stood for a small town⟩
synonyms key
related words scale; caption; guide, table
2 an explanation or description accompanying a pictorial illustration — see CAPTION 1
3 a traditional but unfounded story that gives the reason for a current custom, belief, or fact of nature — see MYTH 1
4 the body of customs, beliefs, stories, and sayings associated with a people, thing, or place — see FOLKLORE

legendary *adj* based on, described in, or being a myth — see MYTHICAL 1

legerdemain *n* **1** the art or skill of performing tricks or illusions for entertainment — see MAGIC 2
2 the use of clever underhanded actions to achieve an end — see TRICKERY

legion *n* **1** a large body of men and women organized for land warfare — see ARMY 1
2 a great number of persons or things gathered together — see CROWD 1

legionary *n* a person engaged in military service — see SOLDIER

legionnaire *n* a person engaged in military service — see SOLDIER

legislate *vb* to put into effect through legislative or authoritative action — see ENACT

legislator *n* a member of an organized body of persons having the authority to make laws ⟨the *legislators* met in an all-night session to hammer out the details of the bill⟩
synonyms lawgiver, lawmaker, solon
related words assemblyman, assemblywoman; congressman, congresswoman; senator

legitimacy *n* the quality or state of being legal — see LEGALITY

legitimate *adj* permitted by law — see LEGAL 1

lei *n* an ornamental chain or string (as of beads) worn around the neck — see NECKLACE

leisure *n* freedom from activity or labor — see [1]REST 1

leisurely *adj* moving or proceeding at less than the normal, desirable, or required speed — see SLOW 1

leisurely *adv* at a pace that is less than usual, desirable, or expected — see SLOW

lemon *n* something that has failed — see FAILURE 3

lend *vb* to give to another for temporary use with the understanding that it or a like thing will be returned ⟨I can *lend* you my copy of the textbook until the weekend⟩ ⟨can you *lend* me five dollars?⟩
synonyms advance, loan
related words furnish, give, grant; lease, let [*chiefly British*], rent
near antonyms receive, take
antonyms borrow

length *n* the space or amount of space between two points, lines, surfaces, or objects — see DISTANCE

lengthen *vb* to make longer — see EXTEND 1

lengthening *n* the act of making longer — see EXTENSION 1

lengthy *adj* **1** of great extent from end to end — see LONG 1
2 lasting for a considerable time — see LONG 2

lenience *n* kind, gentle, or compassionate treatment especially towards someone who is undeserving of it — see MERCY 1

leniency *n* kind, gentle, or compassionate treatment especially towards someone who is undeserving of it — see MERCY 1

lenity *n* kind, gentle, or compassionate treatment especially towards someone who is undeserving of it — see MERCY 1

leprechaun *n* an imaginary being usually having a small human form and magical powers — see FAIRY

less *adj* having not so great importance or rank as another — see LESSER

lessen *vb* **1** to make smaller in amount, volume, or extent — see DECREASE 1
2 to grow less in scope or intensity especially gradually — see DECREASE 2

lesser *adj* having not so great importance or rank as another ⟨it was the *lesser* evil of the two choices⟩
synonyms inferior, junior, less, lower, minor, smaller, subordinate, under
related words little, mean, small; minute, petty; jerkwater, one-horse, second-class, second-rate, two-bit; secondary, subsidiary
near antonyms exceptional, first-class, first-rate
antonyms greater, higher, major, more, primary, prime, senior, superior

lesson *n* something assigned to be read or studied ⟨your *lesson* for tonight will be the chapter on chemical reactions⟩
synonyms assignment, reading
related words homework, schoolwork; lecture; drill, exercise, practice (*also* practise); etude, study

lessor *n* the owner of land or housing that is rented to another — see LANDLORD

let *n* something that makes movement or progress more difficult — see ENCUMBRANCE

let *vb* **1** to give permission to — see ALLOW
2 *chiefly British* to give the possession and use of (something) in return for periodic payment — see RENT 1
3 to make able or possible — see ENABLE 1

letdown *n* **1** the emotion felt when one's expectations are not met — see DISAPPOINTMENT 1
2 something that disappoints — see DISAPPOINTMENT 2

let down *vb* to fall short in satisfying the expectation or hope of — see DISAPPOINT

lethal *adj* likely to cause or capable of causing death — see DEADLY

lethargic *adj* slow to move or act — see INACTIVE 1

let on *vb* to take on a false or deceptive appearance — see PRETEND 1

letter *n* a message on paper from one person or group to another ⟨he wrote her a *letter* every week she was away⟩
synonyms dispatch, epistle, memo, memorandum, missive, note
related words airmail, card, electronic mail, e-mail, junk mail, mail, postal card, postcard; communication, report; encyclical

letter carrier *n* a person who delivers mail — see POSTMAN

letter–perfect *adj* being entirely without fault or flaw — see PERFECT 1

letup *n* a usually gradual decrease in the pace or level of activity of something — see SLOWDOWN

let up *vb* **1** to come to an end — see CEASE 1
2 to grow less in scope or intensity especially gradually — see DECREASE 2

levee *n* **1** a bank of earth constructed to control water — see DAM
2 a structure used by boats and ships for taking on or landing cargo and passengers — see DOCK

level *adj* having a surface without bends, breaks, or irregularities ⟨looked for a *level* place to land the plane⟩
synonyms even, flat, flush, plane, smooth
related words exact, uniform; aligned, regular, true; horizontal, tabular; plumb, straight, vertical
near antonyms inexact, irregular, unaligned; undulating, wavy
antonyms bumpy, coarse, lumpy, rough, uneven

level *n* the placement of someone or something in relation to others in a vertical arrangement — see RANK 1

level *vb* **1** to make equal in amount, degree, or status — see EQUALIZE
2 to make free from breaks, curves, or bumps — see EVEN 1
3 to point or turn (something) toward a target or goal — see AIM 1
4 to strike (someone) so forcefully as to cause a fall — see FELL 1

levelheaded *adj* based on sound reasoning or information — see GOOD 1

levelheadedness *n* the ability to make intelligent decisions especially in everyday matters — see COMMON SENSE
lever *vb* to raise, move, or pull apart with or as if with a lever — see [1]PRY 1
leviathan *n* something that is unusually large and powerful — see GIANT
levity *n* a lack of seriousness often at an improper time — see FRIVOLITY 1
levy *n* a charge usually of money collected by the government from people or businesses for public use — see TAX
levy *vb* to establish or apply as a charge or penalty — see IMPOSE
lewd *adj* **1** depicting or referring to sexual matters in a way that is unacceptable in polite society — see OBSCENE 1
2 having a strong sexual desire — see LUSTFUL
3 hinting at or intended to call to mind matters regarded as indecent — see SUGGESTIVE 1
lewdness *n* the quality or state of being obscene — see OBSCENITY 1
lexical *adj* of or relating to words or language — see VERBAL 1
lexicon *n* a reference book giving information about the meanings, pronunciations, uses, and origins of words listed in alphabetical order — see DICTIONARY
liability *n* **1** a feature of someone or something that creates difficulty for achieving success — see DISADVANTAGE
2 the state of being held as the cause of something that needs to be set right — see RESPONSIBILITY 1
3 the state of being left without shelter or protection against something harmful — see EXPOSURE 1
liable *adj* **1** being in a situation where one is likely to meet with harm <because of his frail constitution, he's *liable* to diseases>
synonyms endangered, exposed, open, sensitive, subject (to), susceptible, vulnerable
related words likely, prone; uncovered, undefended, unguarded, unprotected, unscreened, unsecured, unsheltered, unshielded
phrases in jeopardy
near antonyms covered, guarded, protected, safeguarded, screened, secured, sheltered, shielded, warded
antonyms invulnerable, unexposed
2 being the one who must meet an obligation or suffer the consequences for failing to do so — see RESPONSIBLE 1
liaison *n* **1** the fact or state of having something in common — see CONNECTION 1
2 the state of having shared interests or efforts (as in social or business matters) — see ASSOCIATION 1
liar *n* a person who tells lies <she knew he was a *liar* when he started claiming that he was an astronaut>
synonyms fabricator, fibber, prevaricator, storyteller
related words defamer, libeler (*or* libeller), slanderer; perjurer; distorter, falsifier; equivocator, palterer; gossip, gossiper, talebearer; charlatan, cheat, cheater, confidence man, counterfeiter, cozener, deceiver, defrauder, dissembler, dissimulator, double-dealer, fraud, hustler, mountebank, pretender
near antonyms square shooter
libation *n* a liquid suitable for drinking — see DRINK 1
libel *n* the making of false statements that damage another's reputation — see SLANDER
libel *vb* to make untrue and harmful statements about — see SLANDER
libeling *n* the making of false statements that damage another's reputation — see SLANDER
libelous *or* **libellous** *adj* causing or intended to cause unjust injury to a person's good name <*libelous* statements about a celebrity for which the tabloid was sued>
synonyms defamatory, scandalous, slanderous
related words erroneous, false, inaccurate, incorrect, inexact, invalid, off, unsound, untrue, wrong; depreciative, depreciatory, derogatory, detractive, disparaging, uncomplimentary, unfavorable; invidious, objectionable; maligning, traducing, vilifying; hateful, malevolent, malicious, spiteful
near antonyms appreciative, complimentary, favorable; adulatory, commendatory, eulogistic, laudatory; accurate, correct, errorless, factual, right, sound, true, valid
liberal *adj* **1** not bound by traditional ways or beliefs <parents who take a very *liberal* attitude toward letting their children stay out late>
synonyms broad-minded, nonconventional, nonorthodox, nontraditional, open-minded, progressive, radical, unconventional, unorthodox
related words advanced, contemporary, modern; forbearing, indulgent, lenient, permissive, tolerant; extreme; impartial, objective, unbiased
near antonyms hard, rigid, strict; doctrinal, dogmatic; bigoted, intolerant, narrow-minded; reactionary
antonyms conservative, conventional, nonprogressive, old-fashioned, orthodox, traditional
2 being more than enough without being excessive — see PLENTIFUL
3 giving or sharing in abundance and without hesitation — see GENEROUS 1
liberalism *n* a political belief stressing progress, the essential goodness of humankind, and individual freedom <*liberalism* had always claimed to stand for the greatest social good>
synonyms left
related words radicalism, socialism
antonyms conservatism, right
liberality *n* the quality or state of being generous <already known for his *liberality*, the billionaire continued to give away record amounts of money>
synonyms bountifulness, bounty, generosity, largess (*or* largesse), openhandedness, openheartedness, philanthropy, unselfishness
related words beneficence, charity; kindness; gift, gratuity, lagniappe; tribute; extravagance, improvidence, lavishness, prodigality, wastefulness; spendthrift; dissipating, squandering
near antonyms conserving, economizing, economy, frugality, husbandry, providence, scrimping, skimping, thrift; conservation, saving; husbanding, managing; scraping; cutting back
antonyms cheapness, closeness, meanness, miserliness, parsimony, penuriousness, pinching, stinginess, tightness
liberally *adv* in a generous manner — see WELL 2
liberate *vb* **1** to set free (as from slavery or confinement) — see FREE 1

2 to set free from entanglement or difficulty — see EXTRICATE

liberation *n* the act of setting free from slavery ⟨the *liberation* of the slaves was one of the key results of the Civil War⟩
synonyms emancipation, enfranchisement, freeing, manumission
related words deliverance, redemption, salvation; autonomy, freedom, independence, liberty, self-government, sovereignty
near antonyms bondage, serfdom, servitude, thralldom (*or* thraldom), yoke; captivity, enchainment, imprisonment, incarceration; conquest, subjugation
antonyms enslavement

libertine *n* a person who has sunk below the normal moral standard — see DEGENERATE

liberty *n* the state of being free from the control or power of another — see FREEDOM 1

library *n* **1** a place where books, periodicals, and records are kept for use but not for sale ⟨I went to the *library* to do some research for my report⟩
synonyms archive
related words stacks
2 an organized group of objects acquired and maintained for study, exhibition, or personal pleasure — see COLLECTION 1

licensable *adj* that may be permitted — see PERMISSIBLE

license *also* **licence** *vb* to give official or legal power to — see AUTHORIZE 1

license *or* **licence** *n* **1** the approval by someone in authority for the doing of something — see PERMISSION
2 the granting of power to perform various acts or duties — see COMMISSION 1
3 the right to act or move freely — see FREEDOM 2

licentious *adj* having a strong sexual desire — see LUSTFUL

licentiousness *n* immoral conduct or practices harmful or offensive to society — see VICE 1

lick *n* **1** a hard strike with a part of the body or an instrument — see [1]BLOW
2 a very small amount — see PARTICLE 1
3 the smallest amount or part imaginable — see JOT

lick *vb* **1** to strike repeatedly — see BEAT 1
2 to achieve a victory over — see BEAT 2

licking *n* failure to win a contest — see DEFEAT 1

lid *n* **1** a piece placed over an open container to hold in, protect, or conceal its contents — see COVER 1
2 *slang* a covering for the head usually having a shaped crown — see HAT

lie *n* a statement known by its maker to be untrue and made in order to deceive ⟨he wanted to deny the accusation, but he couldn't tell a *lie*⟩
synonyms fabrication, fairy tale, falsehood, falsity, fib, mendacity, prevarication, story, tale, untruth, whopper
related words distortion, exaggeration, half-truth; ambiguity, equivocation; defamation, libel, slander; perjury; bluff, pose, pretense (*or* pretence); humbug, jive, nonsense; fallacy, misconception, myth; misinformation, misrepresentation, misstatement; deceit, deceitfulness, dishonesty, duplicity, fraudulence
near antonyms fact, truism, verity; honesty, truthfulness, veracity; authentication, confirmation, substantiation, validation, verification
antonyms truth

lie *vb* **1** to make a statement one knows to be untrue ⟨would I *lie* to you about that?⟩
synonyms fabricate, fib, prevaricate
related words forswear, perjure; equivocate, fudge, palter; beguile, cozen, deceive, delude, dupe, fool, gull, hoax, hoodwink, kid, snow, take in, trick; defame, libel, slander, traduce; falsify, misrepresent, misstate; distort, garble; dissemble, dissimulate; misguide, misinform, mislead
phrases tell stories (*or* tales)
near antonyms assert, swear, testify; authenticate, confirm, substantiate, validate, verify
2 to be positioned along a certain course or in a certain direction — see RUN 3
3 to occupy a place or location — see STAND 1

lie detector *n* an instrument for detecting physical signs of the tension that goes with lying ⟨hooked the suspect up to a *lie detector* before interrogating him about the robbery⟩
synonyms polygraph

life *n* **1** a history of a person's life — see BIOGRAPHY
2 a member of the human race — see HUMAN
3 active strength of body or mind — see VIGOR 1
4 the period during which something exists, lasts, or is in progress — see DURATION 1
5 the way people live at a particular time and place — see CIVILIZATION 1

lifeless *adj* no longer living — see DEAD 1

lifelessness *n* the state of being dead — see DEATH 2

lifelike *adj* closely resembling the object imitated — see NATURAL 2

life span *n* the period during which something exists, lasts, or is in progress — see DURATION 1

lifestyle *n* the way people live at a particular time and place — see CIVILIZATION 1

lifetime *n* the period during which something exists, lasts, or is in progress — see DURATION 1

lift *n* **1** an act or instance of helping — see HELP 1
2 a means of getting to a destination in a vehicle driven by another — see RIDE

lift *vb* **1** to move from a lower to a higher place or position — see RAISE 1
2 to move or extend upward — see ASCEND

lifted *adj* being positioned above a surface — see ELEVATED 1

lift–off *n* a rising from a surface at the start of a flight (as of a rocket) ⟨everyone was quiet in the control room as they waited for *lift-off*⟩
synonyms launch, takeoff
near antonyms crash; splashdown
antonyms landing

ligature *n* **1** something that physically prevents free movement — see BOND 1
2 a uniting or binding force or influence — see BOND 2

[1]**light** *adj* **1** having little weight ⟨the suitcase was as *light* as a feather after all the clothes fell out⟩
synonyms airy, feathery, lightweight, underweight, weightless
related words bantam, diminutive, little, minute, small, smallish, puny, tiny, undersized, wee; flimsy, fragile, insubstantial; petite, slender, slight, slim, thin
near antonyms big, considerable, extensive, goodly, good-sized, great, handsome, huge, hulking,

jumbo, king-size (*or* king-sized), large, largish, massive, oversize (*or* oversized), sizable (*or* sizeable), substantial, super, voluminous, whacking; bulky, cumbersome, unwieldy
antonyms heavy, hefty, leaden, overweight, ponderous, weighty
2 involving minimal difficulty or effort — see EASY 1
3 less plentiful than what is normal, necessary, or desirable — see MEAGER
4 moving easily — see GRACEFUL 1
5 not harsh or stern especially in manner, nature, or effect — see GENTLE 1
6 resembling air in lightness — see AIRY 1

[2]light *adj* **1** filled with much light — see BRIGHT 2
2 lacking intensity of color — see PALE 1
3 of light complexion — see FAIR 4

light *n* **1** the steady giving off of the form of radiation that makes vision possible ⟨he read poetry by the *light* of the moon⟩
synonyms blaze, flare, fluorescence, glare, gleam, glow, illumination, incandescence, luminescence, radiance, shine
related words flash, glimmer, glint, glitter, scintillation, shimmer, sparkle, twinkle; daylight, moonlight, sunlight; afterglow, aureole, aurora, beam, ray, shaft, streak, stream; glisten, gloss, luster (*or* lustre), polish, reflection, sheen
near antonyms blackness, dark, darkness, dimness, dusk, duskiness, gloom, night, shadow
2 something that provides illumination ⟨turn off the *light* when you go to bed⟩
synonyms beacon, lamp
related words arc lamp (*also* arc light), candelabra, candelabrum, candle, chandelier, dark lantern, electric, flare, flash, flashbulb, flashcube, flashlight, floodlight, fluorescent lamp, gaslight, headlight, incandescent lamp, klieg light (*or* kleig light), lantern, light bulb, lighthouse, lighting, sconce, spotlight, streetlight
3 a person who is widely known and usually much talked about — see CELEBRITY 1

[1]light *vb* to come to rest after descending from the air — see ALIGHT

[2]light *vb* **1** to set (something) on fire — see BURN 2
2 to supply with light — see ILLUMINATE 1

lighted *or* **lit** *adj* **1** filled with much light — see BRIGHT 2
2 being on fire — see ABLAZE 1

lighten *vb* to supply with light — see ILLUMINATE 1

light–footed *adj* moving easily — see GRACEFUL 1

light–headed *adj* **1** having a feeling of being whirled about and in danger of falling down — see DIZZY 1
2 lacking in seriousness or maturity — see GIDDY 1

light–headedness *n* a lack of seriousness often at an improper time — see FRIVOLITY 1

lighthearted *adj* having or showing a lack of concern or seriousness — see CAREFREE

lightheartedness *n* carefree freedom from constraint — see ABANDON

lighting out *n* the act of leaving a place — see DEPARTURE

lightly *adv* without difficulty — see EASILY

[1]lightness *n* **1** the state or quality of having little weight ⟨the first thing I noticed about the little bird was its *lightness*; I could hardly tell I was holding it in my hand⟩
synonyms slightness, weightlessness
related words airiness, delicacy, etherealness; flimsiness, fluffiness, insubstantiality
near antonyms solidity, solidness, substantiality
antonyms heaviness, heftiness, massiveness, ponderousness, weightiness
2 a lack of seriousness often at an improper time — see FRIVOLITY 1

[2]lightness *n* the quality or state of having or giving off light — see BRILLIANCE 1

lightning *adj* moving, proceeding, or acting with great speed — see FAST 1

lightsome *adj* having or showing a good mood or disposition — see CHEERFUL 1

lightweight *adj* having little weight — see [1]LIGHT 1

lightweight *n* a person of no importance or influence — see NOBODY

like *adj* having qualities in common — see ALIKE

like *adv* to some degree or extent — see FAIRLY

like *conj* the way it would be or one would do if — see AS IF

[1]like *n* **1** a number of persons or things that are grouped together because they have something in common — see SORT 1
2 one that is equal to another in status, achievement, or value — see EQUAL

[2]like *n* positive regard for something — see LIKING

like *vb* **1** to wish to have ⟨I'd *like* another slice of pizza, but I've already eaten more than I should have⟩
synonyms care (for), want
related words adore, delight (in), dig, enjoy, fancy, groove (on), like, love, relish, revel (in); covet, crave, die (for), wish (for), yearn (for)
2 to show partiality toward — see PREFER 1
3 to take pleasure in — see ENJOY 1
4 to see fit — see CHOOSE 2

likelihood *n* the quality or state of being likely to occur — see PROBABILITY 1

likeliness *n* the quality or state of being likely to occur — see PROBABILITY 1

likely *adj* **1** having a high chance of occurring ⟨if you don't do well in school, your *likely* fate is a low-paying job⟩
synonyms probable
related words conceivable, earthly, imaginable, possible, potential; apt, bound, certain, doubtless, inescapable, inevitable, necessary, sure, unavoidable
near antonyms impossible, inconceivable, unimaginable
antonyms doubtful, dubious, improbable, questionable, unlikely
2 having qualities which inspire hope — see HOPEFUL 1
3 worthy of being accepted as true or reasonable — see BELIEVABLE

likely *adv* without much doubt — see PROBABLY

liken *vb* **1** to describe as similar — see COMPARE 1
2 to regard or represent as equal or comparable — see EQUATE 1

likeness *n* **1** a two-dimensional design intended to look like a person or thing — see PICTURE 1
2 something or someone that strongly resembles another — see IMAGE 1
3 the quality or state of having many qualities in common — see SIMILARITY 1

likewise *adv* **1** in addition to what has been said — see MORE 1
2 in like manner — see ALSO 1

liking *n* positive regard for something ⟨I have a *liking* for dark chocolate⟩
synonyms appetite, fancy, favor, fondness, like, love, partiality, preference, relish, shine, taste, use
related words craving, desire, longing, thirst, yen; enthusiasm, interest, passion; bias, prejudice; bent, inclination, leaning, propensity, tendency; weakness
near antonyms apathy, disinclination; indifference, unconcern
antonyms aversion, disfavor, dislike, distaste, hatred, loathing

lily–livered *adj* having or showing a shameful lack of courage — see COWARDLY

limb *n* a major outgrowth from the main stem of a woody plant — see BRANCH 1

limber *adj* able to bend easily without breaking — see WILLOWY

limit *n* a real or imaginary point beyond which a person or thing cannot go ⟨there was no *limit* to the number of challenges they faced⟩
synonyms bound, boundary, ceiling, confines, end, extent, limitation, line, termination
related words extremity, fag end; border, brim, edge, margin, rim, verge; outside; bar, barrier, fence, hedge, restraint, stop, wall

limit *vb* **1** to set bounds or an upper limit for ⟨*limit* the note to a few words⟩
synonyms circumscribe, confine, restrict
related words bar, block, hinder, impede, obstruct; constrict, contract, lessen, narrow, pinch, squeeze, tighten; quell, repress, suppress; number; modify, qualify
near antonyms broaden, expand, widen; overextend, overreach
antonyms exceed
2 to mark the limits of ⟨adjectives *limit* the meanings of nouns⟩
synonyms bound, circumscribe, define, delimit, demarcate, mark (out), terminate
related words control, determine, govern; delineate, describe

limitation *n* **1** a real or imaginary point beyond which a person or thing cannot go — see LIMIT
2 something that limits one's freedom of action or choice — see RESTRICTION 1
3 the act or practice of keeping something (as an activity) within certain boundaries — see RESTRICTION 2

limited *adj* **1** having distinct or certain limits ⟨to avoid overcrowding, the number of tickets to the outdoor concerts is *limited*⟩
synonyms bounded, circumscribed, defined, definite, determinate, finite, measured, narrow, restricted
related words modified, qualified; detailed, exact, precise, specific; confined, constricted, moderate, modest; minute, puny, small, tiny; determined, fixed, settled
near antonyms bottomless, countless, incalculable, inestimable, inexhaustible, innumerable, unfathomable; general, indeterminate, nebulous, vague; enlarged, escalated, expanded; considerable, copious, plentiful; big, bulky, bumper, extensive, goodly, good-sized, great, handsome, hefty, hulking, jumbo, king-size (*or* king-sized), large, largish, oversize (*or* oversized), respectable, sizable (*or* sizeable), substantial, super, vast, voluminous, whacking; epic, grandiose, major; ample, broad, comprehensive, cosmopolitan, expansive, global, inclusive, universal, whole
antonyms boundless, dimensionless, endless, illimitable, immeasurable, indefinite, infinite, limitless, measureless, unbounded, undefined, unlimited, unmeasured
2 having a limit — see FINITE 1

limitless *adj* being or seeming to be without limits — see INFINITE

limp *adj* **1** not stiff in structure ⟨his broken arm was *limp* as he held it against his side⟩
synonyms droopy, flaccid, floppy, lank, yielding
related words flabby, mushy, semisoft, soft, squashy, squishy; delicate, flimsy, insubstantial; elastic, flexible, lax, loose, pliant, relaxed, resilient, springy, stretchy, supple
near antonyms firm, hard, indurated, solid, sound, strong; brittle, crisp; compact, dense, substantial
antonyms inflexible, resilient, rigid, stiff, sturdy, tense; firm, hard, indurated, solid, sound, strong
2 depleted in strength, energy, or freshness — see WEARY 1
3 lacking bodily energy or motivation — see LISTLESS

limp *vb* **1** to walk while favoring one leg ⟨she *limped* all day after stubbing her toe on the lawn sprinkler⟩
synonyms halt, hobble
related words hitch; blunder, falter, lurch, shuffle, stagger, stumble, teeter, totter, waver, wobble; dodder
near antonyms breeze, glide, sail
antonyms stride
2 to make progress in a clumsy, struggling manner — see FLOUNDER 1

limpid *adj* easily seen through — see CLEAR 1

limpidity *n* the state or quality of being easily seen through — see CLARITY 1

limpidness *n* the state or quality of being easily seen through — see CLARITY 1

line *n* **1** a series of persons or things arranged one behind another ⟨we waited in the *line* for lunch for what seemed like hours⟩
synonyms column, cue, file, queue, range, string, train
related words echelon, rank, row, tier; progression, sequence, succession; array
2 a way of acting or proceeding — see COURSE 1
3 the activity by which one regularly makes a living — see OCCUPATION
4 a region of activity, knowledge, or influence — see FIELD 2
5 a real or imaginary point beyond which a person or thing cannot go — see LIMIT
6 a long hollow cylinder for carrying a substance (as a liquid or gas) — see PIPE 1
7 a length of braided, flexible material that is used for tying or connecting things — see CORD
8 a group of vehicles traveling together or under one management — see FLEET
9 the direction along which something or someone moves — see PATH 1
10 a group of persons who come from the same ancestor — see FAMILY 1
11 the line of ancestors from whom a person is descended — see ANCESTRY

lineage *n* **1** the line of ancestors from whom a person is descended — see ANCESTRY
2 a group of persons who come from the same ancestor — see FAMILY 1

linear *adj* free from irregularities (as curves, bends, or angles) in course — see STRAIGHT 1
linger *vb* to move or act slowly — see DELAY 1
lingerer *n* someone who moves slowly or more slowly than others — see SLOWPOKE
lingo *n* **1** the stock of words, pronunciation, and grammar used by a people as their basic means of communication — see LANGUAGE 1
2 the special terms or expressions of a particular group or field — see TERMINOLOGY
linguistic *adj* of or relating to words or language — see VERBAL 1
link *n* **1** a rod-shaped portion of seasoned ground meat in a casing — see SAUSAGE
2 a uniting or binding force or influence — see BOND 2
link *vb* **1** to put or bring together so as to form a new and longer whole — see CONNECT 1
2 to think of (something) in combination — see ASSOCIATE 2
link (up) *vb* to come together to form a single unit — see UNITE 1
linkage *n* the fact or state of having something in common — see CONNECTION 1
linking *n* the act or an instance of joining two or more things into one — see UNION 1
linkup *n* the state of having shared interests or efforts (as in social or business matters) — see ASSOCIATION 1
lint *n* a soft airy substance or covering — see FUZZ
lionhearted *adj* feeling or displaying no fear by temperament — see BRAVE
liquefy *vb* to go from a solid to a liquid state <the steel *liquefied* in the intense heat of the forge>
synonyms deliquesce, flux, fuse, melt, run, thaw
related words found, gutter, smelt, try; dissolve, render; soften, thin
near antonyms clot, coagulate, congeal, gel, jell, jelly, thicken
antonyms harden, set, solidify
liquid *adj* **1** capable of moving like a liquid — see FLUID 1
2 easily seen through — see CLEAR 1
liquidate *vb* **1** to destroy all traces of — see ANNIHILATE 1
2 to put to death deliberately — see MURDER 1
3 to give what is owed for — see PAY 2
liquor *n* a fermented or distilled beverage that can make a person drunk — see ALCOHOL
lissome *also* **lissom** *adj* **1** moving easily — see GRACEFUL 1
2 able to bend easily without breaking — see WILLOWY
1list *n* a record of a series of items (as names or titles) usually arranged according to some system <we put eggs, sour cream, tomatoes, roast beef, and cheddar cheese on the shopping *list*>
synonyms canon, catalog (*or* catalogue), checklist, listing, menu, register, registry, roll, roster, schedule, table
related words agenda, bibliography, compilation, directory, docket, glossary, index, inventory, manifest, payroll; calendar, chronology, timetable
2list *n* the act of positioning or an instance of being positioned at an angle — see TILT
3list *n* a long narrow piece of material — see STRIP
1list *vb* **1** to make a list of <he *listed* the people on the team>
synonyms enumerate, inventory, itemize, numerate
related words count, mark, number; check (off), tick (off)
2 to put (someone or something) on a list <her number isn't *listed* in the phone book>
synonyms catalog (*or* catalogue), enroll (*also* enrol), enter, index, inscribe, put down, record, register, schedule, slate
related words book, file, note; classify, compile, tabulate; reschedule
near antonyms delete
3 to enter in a list or roll — see ENROLL 1
4 to specify one after another — see ENUMERATE 1
2list *vb* to set or cause to be at an angle — see LEAN 1
listen *vb* to pay attention especially through the act of hearing <would you *listen* to what I have to say?>
synonyms attend, hark, hear, hearken, heed, mind
phrases prick up one's ears
near antonyms discount, disregard
antonyms ignore, tune out
listen (to) *vb* to take notice of and be guided by — see HEED 1
listen in (on) *vb* to listen to (another in private conversation) — see EAVESDROP (ON)
listing *adj* **1** inclined or twisted to one side — see AWRY
2 running in a slanting direction — see DIAGONAL
listing *n* a record of a series of items (as names or titles) usually arranged according to some system — see 1LIST
listless *adj* lacking bodily energy or motivation <when I had the flu, I felt *listless* and worn-out>
synonyms enervated, lackadaisical, languid, languishing, languorous, limp, spiritless
related words indolent, lazy, slothful; lethargic, logy, sleepy, sluggish, torpid; exhausted, tired, weary; feeble, frail, weak; apathetic, impassive, phlegmatic, stolid; careless, heedless, thoughtless, unwary; inactive, inert
near antonyms active, dynamic, industrious; avid, eager, enthusiastic, keen, lively, vivacious; cheerful, chipper, perky, up; agog, alert, awake, dapper, open-eyed, sleepless, vigilant, watchful, wide-awake
antonyms ambitious, animated, energetic, enterprising, motivated
listlessness *n* the state of being bored — see BOREDOM
literal *adj* restricted to or based on fact — see FACTUAL 1
literary *adj* suggestive of the vocabulary used in books — see BOOKISH
literate *adj* having or displaying advanced knowledge or education — see EDUCATED
lithe *adj* **1** able to bend easily without breaking — see WILLOWY
2 moving easily — see GRACEFUL 1
lithesome *adj* moving easily — see GRACEFUL 1
litter *n* **1** an unorganized collection or mixture of various things — see MISCELLANY 1
2 discarded or useless material — see GARBAGE
littered *adj* lacking in order, neatness, and often cleanliness — see MESSY
little *adj* **1** having relatively little height — see SHORT 1
2 lacking importance — see UNIMPORTANT

3 not broad or open in views or opinions — see NARROW 2
4 not lasting for a considerable time — see SHORT 2
5 of a size that is less than average — see SMALL 1

little *adv* **1** in a very small quantity or degree ⟨we had *little* more than we needed to survive in the wilderness⟩
synonyms negligibly, nominally, slightly
related words meagerly, scantily; barely, hardly, just, marginally, minimally, scarcely
phrases a bit
near antonyms completely, entirely, purely, thoroughly, totally, utterly; eminently, exceptionally; appreciably, discernibly, noticeably, palpably; abundantly, plentifully; generously, handsomely, liberally; astronomically, grandly, hugely, monstrously, monumentally
antonyms awful, awfully, beastly, considerably, deadly, especially, exceedingly (*also* exceeding), extensively, extra, extremely, far, frightfully, full, greatly, heavily, highly, jolly, mightily, mighty, mortally, most, much, particularly, rattling, real, right, significantly, so, something, substantially, super, terribly, too, very, whacking
2 not often — see SELDOM

little *n* a very small amount — see PARTICLE 1

little by little *adv* by small steps or amounts — see GRADUALLY

littleness *n* the quality or state of being little in size — see SMALLNESS

littlest *adj* being the least in amount, number, or size possible — see MINIMAL

livable *also* **liveable** *adj* suitable for living in ⟨after adding some furniture and painting the walls, the apartment was *livable*⟩
synonyms habitable, inhabitable
related words comfortable, cozy, homelike, homey, intimate, snug; deluxe, lavish, luxuriant, luxurious, plush, sumptuous; opulent, palatial, rich; acceptable, bearable, endurable, sufferable, supportable, sustainable, tolerable
near antonyms uncomfortable; humble, Spartan; economical, frugal, spare, thrifty; intolerable, unacceptable, unbearable, unendurable, insupportable
antonyms uninhabitable, unlivable

live *adj* having or showing life — see ALIVE 1

live *vb* **1** to have a home ⟨he *lived* next door to the hospital⟩
synonyms abide, dwell, reside
related words lodge, settle, stay; frequent, hang out (at), haunt; inhabit, occupy; people, populate; lease, rent, sublet, tenant
2 to have life — see BE 1

liveliness *n* the quality or state of having abundant or intense activity — see VITALITY 1

lively *adj* **1** having much high-spirited energy and movement ⟨the *lively* puppy was racing around the dining room floor chasing after people's shoelaces⟩
synonyms active, animate, animated, bouncing, brisk, energetic, frisky, gay, jaunty, jazzy, peppy, perky, pert, racy, snappy, spanking, sparky, spirited, sprightly, springy, vital, vivacious, zippy
related words dapper, dashing, spiffy; agog, alert, awake, open-eyed, up, wide-awake; agile, nimble, spry; bright, buoyant, cheerful, chipper, effervescent, upbeat; eager, enthusiastic, keen; frolicsome, impish, playful; bubbly, exuberant, high-spirited; high-strung, nervous, skittish
phrases on the go
near antonyms indolent, lazy, unambitious; inert, lethargic, sleepy, sluggish, tired, torpid, weary; apathetic, impassive, phlegmatic, stolid; boring, dull, irksome, tedious
antonyms dead, inactive, inanimate, lackadaisical, languid, languishing, languorous, lifeless, limp, listless, spiritless, unanimated
2 marked by much life, movement, or activity — see ALIVE 2

liven (up) *vb* to give life, vigor, or spirit to — see ANIMATE

livery *n* the distinctive clothing worn by members of a particular group — see UNIFORM

live wire *n* an ambitious person who eagerly goes after what is desired — see GO-GETTER

livid *adj* lacking a healthy skin color — see PALE 2

living *adj* **1** being in effective operation — see ACTIVE 1
2 having being at the present time — see EXTANT 1
3 having or showing life — see ALIVE 1

load *n* **1** a mass or quantity of something taken up and carried, conveyed, or transported ⟨they placed a *load* of grain on the truck going to Florida⟩
synonyms burden, cargo, draft, freight, haul, lading, loading, payload, weight
related words consignment, boatload, carload, shipload, truckload; ballast, deadweight; overload, surcharge; bale, bundle, pack, package, packet, parcel, shipment; manifest; body, bulk, mass
2 loads *pl* a considerable amount — see LOT 2

load *vb* **1** to place a weight or burden on ⟨students complaining that their teachers were *loading* them with work⟩
synonyms burden, encumber, lade, lumber, saddle, weight
related words clog, clutter, fill, heap; press, weigh; strain, tax; overburden, overload, overtax, surcharge; handicap; afflict, oppress
near antonyms alleviate, ease, lighten, relieve
antonyms disencumber, unburden, unload
2 to put into (something) as much as can be held or contained — see FILL 1

loaded *adj* **1** containing or seeming to contain the greatest quantity or number possible — see FULL 1
2 having goods, property, or money in abundance — see RICH 1
3 *slang* being under the influence of alcohol — see DRUNK

loading *n* a mass or quantity of something taken up and carried, conveyed, or transported — see LOAD 1

loaf *vb* to spend time doing nothing — see IDLE

loafer *n* a lazy person — see LAZYBONES

loamy *adj* consisting or suggestive of earth — see EARTHY 1

loan *vb* to give to another for temporary use with the understanding that it or a like thing will be returned — see LEND

loath *or* **loth** *adj* having doubts about the wisdom of doing something — see HESITANT

loathe *vb* to dislike strongly — see HATE

loathing *n* **1** a dislike so strong as to cause stomach upset or queasiness — see DISGUST
2 a very strong dislike — see HATE 1

loathsome *adj* causing intense displeasure, disgust, or resentment — see OFFENSIVE 1

lob *vb* to send through the air especially with a quick forward motion of the arm — see THROW

lobby *n* **1** a centrally located room in a building that serves as a gathering or waiting area or as a passageway into the interior — see FOYER 1
2 the entrance room of a building — see HALL 1

local *n* a local unit of an organization — see CHAPTER

locale *n* the area or space occupied by or intended for something — see PLACE 1

locality *n* the area or space occupied by or intended for something — see PLACE 1

locate *vb* to come upon after searching, study, or effort — see FIND 1

location *n* the area or space occupied by or intended for something — see PLACE 1

loch *n, Scottish* a part of a body of water that extends beyond the general shoreline — see GULF 1

lock (up) *vb* to put in or as if in prison — see IMPRISON

locker *n* **1** a covered rectangular container for storing or transporting things — see CHEST
2 a storage case typically having doors and shelves — see CABINET

lockup *n* a place of confinement for persons held in lawful custody — see JAIL

loco *adj* having or showing a very abnormal or sick state of mind — see INSANE 1

locus *n* the area or space occupied by or intended for something — see PLACE 1

locution *n* a distinctive way of putting ideas into words — see STYLE 1

lodestone *n* something that attracts interest — see MAGNET

lodge *n* **1** a place that provides rooms and usually a public dining room for overnight guests — see HOTEL
2 an often small house for recreational or seasonal use — see COTTAGE
3 the meeting place of an organization — see CLUB 2
4 the shelter or resting place of a wild animal — see DEN 1

lodge *vb* to provide with living quarters or shelter — see HOUSE 1
2 to establish or place comfortably or snugly — see ENSCONCE 1
3 to set solidly in or as if in surrounding matter — see ENTRENCH

lodged *adj* firmly positioned in place and difficult to dislodge — see TIGHT 2

lodger *n* one who rents a room or apartment in another's house — see TENANT

lodging *n* **1** the place where one lives — see HOME 1
2 lodgings *pl* a room or set of rooms in a private house or a block used as a separate dwelling place — see APARTMENT 1

loft *vb* to send through the air especially with a quick forward motion of the arm — see THROW

loftiest *adj* being at a point or level higher than all others — see TOP 1

loftiness *n* an exaggerated sense of one's importance that shows itself in the making of excessive or unjustified claims — see ARROGANCE

lofty *adj* **1** extending to a great distance upward — see HIGH 1
2 having a feeling of superiority that shows itself in an overbearing attitude — see ARROGANT
3 having or displaying feelings of scorn for what is regarded as beneath oneself — see PROUD 1
4 having, characterized by, or arising from a dignified and generous nature — see NOBLE 2
5 very dignified in form, tone, or style — see ELEVATED 2

log *vb* to make a written note of — see RECORD 1

logger *n* a person whose job is to cut down trees — see LUMBERJACK

logic *n* the thought processes that have been established as leading to valid solutions to problems ⟨I tried to use *logic* to figure out the solution to the puzzle⟩
synonyms reason, reasoning, sense
related words cogency, coherence, rationality, thought; analysis; deduction, induction
near antonyms incoherence, insanity, irrationality

logical *adj* **1** according to the rules of logic ⟨the lawyer won the case with a *logical* argument about the motives of the suspect⟩
synonyms analytic (*or* analytical), coherent, good, rational, reasonable, sensible, sound, valid
related words sane; thoughtful; scientific
near antonyms specious; crazy, insane; senseless, thoughtless
antonyms illogical, incoherent, invalid, irrational, unreasonable, unsound
2 based on sound reasoning or information — see GOOD 1

logo *n* a device, design, or figure used as an identifying mark — see EMBLEM

logy *adj* depleted in strength, energy, or freshness — see WEARY 1

loiter *vb* to move or act slowly — see DELAY 1

loiterer *n* someone who moves slowly or more slowly than others — see SLOWPOKE

loll *vb* **1** to be limp from lack of water or vigor — see DROOP 1
2 to refrain from labor or exertion — see REST 1
3 to spend time doing nothing — see IDLE

lone *adj* **1** being the one or ones of a class with no other members — see ONLY 2
2 not being in the company of others — see ALONE 1

lonely *adj* **1** not being in the company of others — see ALONE 1
2 sad from lack of companionship or separation from others — see LONESOME 1

loner *n* a person who does not conform to generally accepted standards or customs — see NONCONFORMIST 1

lonesome *adj* **1** sad from lack of companionship or separation from others ⟨a *lonesome* kitten left at the pound by its owners⟩
synonyms desolate, forlorn, lonely, lorn
related words friendless; abandoned, deserted, forgotten, forsaken, neglected; alone, lone, solitary; only, sole
near antonyms accompanied, attended, escorted
2 not being in the company of others — see ALONE 1

lone wolf *n* a person who does not conform to generally accepted standards or customs — see NONCONFORMIST 1

long *adj* **1** of great extent from end to end ⟨giraffes

have *long* necks to help them reach leaves on tall trees⟩
synonyms elongated, extended, king-size (*or* king-sized), lengthy
related words extensive, far-reaching, longish, outstretched; oblong, rectangular; big, considerable, good-sized, hefty, hulking, jumbo, large, largish, oversize (*or* oversized), sizable (*or* sizeable), substantial, super
near antonyms abbreviated, abridged, curtailed, diminished, shortened; diminutive, little, minute, puny, small, smallish, tiny, undersized, wee
antonyms brief, short
2 lasting for a considerable time ⟨summer vacation seemed *long*, but we had to go back to school soon enough⟩
synonyms extended, far, great, lengthy, long-lived, long-range, long-term, marathon
related words endless, everlasting, interminable, persistent; longish, overlong, prolonged, protracted; permanent
near antonyms abrupt, sudden; abbreviated, condensed, curtailed; ephemeral, fleeting, momentary, transient, transitory; impermanent
antonyms brief, short, short-lived, short-range, short-term

long (for) *vb* to have an earnest wish to own or enjoy — see DESIRE

longhand *n* writing done by hand — see HANDWRITING 2

longing *n* a strong wish for something — see DESIRE

long–lived *adj* **1** being of advanced years and especially past middle age — see ELDERLY
2 lasting for a considerable time — see LONG 2

long–range *adj* lasting for a considerable time — see LONG 2

longshoreman *n* one who loads and unloads ships at a port — see DOCKWORKER

long–suffering *adj* accepting pains or hardships calmly or without complaint — see PATIENT 1

long–suffering *n* the capacity to endure what is difficult or disagreeable without complaining — see PATIENCE

long–term *adj* lasting for a considerable time — see LONG 2

long–winded *adj* using or containing more words than necessary to express an idea — see WORDY

long–windedness *n* the use of too many words to express an idea — see VERBIAGE

look *n* **1** facial appearance regarded as an indication of mood or feeling ⟨you should have seen the *look* on your face when we yelled "Surprise!"⟩
synonyms cast, countenance, expression, face, visage
related words frown, grimace, mouth, scowl; air, appearance, aspect, bearing, demeanor, manner, mien
2 an instance of looking especially briefly ⟨she gave the junk mail a quick *look* before throwing it in the garbage pail⟩
synonyms cast, eye, gander, glance, glimpse, peek, peep, regard, sight, view
related words gape, gaze, glare, leer, ogle, stare; squint
3 the outward form of someone or something especially as indicative of a quality — see APPEARANCE 1
4 looks *pl* the qualities in a person or thing that as a whole give pleasure to the senses — see BEAUTY 1

look *vb* **1** to give the impression of being — see SEEM
2 to make known (as an idea, emotion, or opinion) — see EXPRESS 1

look (at) *vb* to make note of (something) through the use of one's eyes — see SEE 1

look (into) *vb* to search through or into — see EXPLORE 1

look (toward) *vb* to stand or sit with the face or front toward — see FACE 1

looking glass *n* a smooth or polished surface (as of glass) that forms images by reflection — see MIRROR

lookout *n* **1** a high place or structure from which a wide view is possible ⟨we went up to the *lookout* on the top of the hill to watch the fireworks⟩
synonyms observatory, outlook
related words aerie, crow's nest, tower, watchtower
2 all that can be seen from a certain point — see VIEW 1
3 the act or state of being constantly attentive and responsive to signs of opportunity, activity, or danger — see VIGILANCE
4 a person or group that watches over someone or something — see GUARD 1

look up *vb* to go in search of — see SEEK 1

loom *vb* to be about to happen ⟨he could tell that trouble was *looming* when the bullies swaggered into the park⟩
synonyms brew, impend
related words advance, approach, close in, draw on, gather, near; lower (*also* lour), menace, threaten
near antonyms die down, diminish, disappear, dwindle, fade, vanish, wane; fall back, pass, recede, retreat, withdraw

loony *n* a person judged to be legally or medically insane — see LUNATIC 1

loony *also* **looney** *adj* **1** showing or marked by a lack of good sense or judgment — see FOOLISH 1
2 having or showing a very abnormal or sick state of mind — see INSANE 1

loop *n* a circular strip — see RING 2

loop *vb* to pass completely around — see ENCIRCLE 1

loose *adj* **1** not tightly fastened, tied, or stretched ⟨secure your neckerchief with a *loose* knot⟩
synonyms insecure, lax, loosened, relaxed, slack, slackened, unsecured
related words detached, free, unattached, unbound, undone, unfastened, untied; baggy; nonrestrictive
near antonyms constrained, restrained; attached, bound, fastened, tied
antonyms taut, tense, tight
2 consisting of particles that do not stick together ⟨the car wheels slipped on the *loose* gravel in the driveway⟩
synonyms incoherent, unconsolidated
related words nonadhesive; disconnected, disjointed, separate, unconnected; coarse, granular, rough
near antonyms connected, solid; compacted, compressed; adhesive, gluey, sticky
antonyms coherent, compact, dense, packed
3 not bound by rigid standards — see EASYGOING 2

4 not bound, confined, or detained by force — see FREE 3
5 not precisely correct — see INEXACT 1
loose *vb* 1 to cause (a projectile) to be driven forward with force — see SHOOT 1
2 to find emotional release for — see TAKE OUT 1
3 to set free (as from slavery or confinement) — see FREE 1
4 to set free (from a state of being held in check) — see RELEASE 1
loosen *vb* 1 to make less taut — see SLACKEN
2 to set free (as from slavery or confinement) — see FREE 1
3 to set free (from a state of being held in check) — see RELEASE 1
loosen (up) *vb* to free from obstruction or difficulty — see EASE 1
loosened *adj* not tightly fastened, tied, or stretched — see LOOSE 1
loot *n* valuables stolen or taken by force ⟨the burglar was caught when he stopped to examine the *loot* from the robbery⟩
synonyms booty, plunder, spoil, swag
related words prize; catch, haul, take; pilferage; windfall
loot *vb* to search through with the intent of committing robbery — see RANSACK 1
lop (off) *vb* to make (as hair) shorter with or as if with the use of shears — see CLIP
lope *vb* to move with a light bouncing step — see SKIP 1
lopsided *adj* inclined or twisted to one side — see AWRY
loquacious *adj* fond of talking or conversation — see TALKATIVE
Lord *n* the being worshipped as the creator and ruler of the universe — see DEITY 2
lord (it over) *vb* to assume or treat with an air of superiority — see CONDESCEND 2
lordliness *n* an exaggerated sense of one's importance that shows itself in the making of excessive or unjustified claims — see ARROGANCE
lordly *adj* 1 having a feeling of superiority that shows itself in an overbearing attitude — see ARROGANT
2 having or displaying feelings of scorn for what is regarded as beneath oneself — see PROUD 1
3 having, characterized by, or arising from a dignified and generous nature — see NOBLE 2
lore *n* 1 a body of facts learned by study or experience — see KNOWLEDGE 1
2 the body of customs, beliefs, stories, and sayings associated with a people, thing, or place — see FOLKLORE
lorn *adj* sad from lack of companionship or separation from others — see LONESOME 1
lose *vb* 1 to be unable to find or have at hand ⟨I always *lose* my keys⟩
synonyms mislay, misplace
near antonyms have
antonyms find, locate
2 to get rid of as useless or unwanted — see DISCARD
loser *n* something that has failed — see FAILURE 3
loss *n* 1 the act or an instance of not having or being able to find ⟨he was upset over the *loss* of his bike⟩
synonyms mislaying, misplacement
related words deprivation, dispossession; forfeit, forfeiture, penalty; sacrifice; bereavement
antonyms acquisition, gain
2 a person or thing harmed, lost, or destroyed — see CASUALTY 1
3 failure to win a contest — see DEFEAT 1
4 the amount by which something is lessened — see DECREASE
5 the state of being robbed of something normally enjoyed — see PRIVATION
6 the state or fact of being rendered nonexistent, physically unsound, or useless — see DESTRUCTION
lost *adj* no longer possessed ⟨they searched all over the house for the *lost* keys⟩
synonyms gone, mislaid, misplaced, missing
related words absent, castaway; irrecoverable, irretrievable; forgotten, unknown
near antonyms cherished, protected, treasured
antonyms owned, possessed, retained
lot *n* 1 a small piece of land that is developed or available for development ⟨we often played in the vacant *lot* down at the end of the street⟩
synonyms parcel, plat, plot, property, tract
related words patch; frontage; lease; development; real estate
2 a considerable amount ⟨they needed to do a *lot* of studying for the test⟩
synonyms abundance, barrel, bucket, bushel, deal, gobs, heap, loads, mass, mountain, much, oodles, peck, pile, plenitude, plenty, pot, profusion, quantity, raft, reams, scads, stack, volume, wad, wealth
related words embarrassment, excess, overabundance, overage, overkill, overmuch, oversupply, superabundance, superfluity, surfeit, surplus; deluge, flood, overflow
near antonyms atom, crumb, fragment, grain, iota, jot, modicum, molecule, particle, scrap, shred, tittle, whit; scattering, smattering; drop, morsel, shot; piece, portion, section; absence, dearth, lack, paucity, poverty, scarceness, scarcity, shortage, want; deficiency, deficit, inadequacy, insufficiency, meagerness, scantiness, skimpiness
antonyms ace, bit, dab, driblet, glimmer, hint, lick, little, mite, mouthful, ounce, peanuts, pinch, scruple, smidgen, speck, spot, sprinkling, suspicion, taste, touch, trace
3 a small area of usually open land — see FIELD 1
4 a number of things considered as a unit — see GROUP 1
5 a state or end that seemingly has been decided beforehand — see FATE 1
6 a group of people sharing a common interest and relating together socially — see GANG 2
7 a usually small number of persons considered as a unit — see GROUP 2
loud *adj* 1 marked by a high volume of sound ⟨*loud* music that could be heard all over the neighborhood⟩
synonyms blaring, blasting, booming, clamorous, clangorous, deafening, earsplitting, piercing, resounding, ringing, roaring, sonorous, stentorian, thunderous
related words brazen, dinning, discordant, noisy, obstreperous, raucous, rip-roaring, vociferous; grating, harsh, shrill, strident
near antonyms dead, quiet, silent, still; dreamy, peaceful, restful, soothing, tranquil; softened, toned (down)
antonyms gentle, low, soft
2 excessively showy — see GAUDY

lounge *n* a long upholstered piece of furniture designed for several sitters — see COUCH
lounge *vb* **1** to refrain from labor or exertion — see REST 1
2 to spend time doing nothing — see IDLE
louse *n* a person whose behavior is offensive to others — see JERK 1
louse up *vb* to make or do (something) in a clumsy or unskillful way — see BOTCH
lousy *adj* **1** arousing or deserving of one's loathing and disgust — see CONTEMPTIBLE 1
2 falling short of a standard — see BAD 1
3 extremely unsatisfactory — see WRETCHED 1
4 of low quality — see CHEAP 2
lout *n* **1** a big clumsy often slow-witted person — see OAF
2 a person whose behavior is offensive to others — see JERK 1
loutish *adj* having or showing crudely insensitive or impolite manners — see CLOWNISH
lovable *adj* having qualities that tend to make one loved ⟨she was a *lovable* child, always helpful and kind⟩
synonyms adorable, darling, dear, disarming, endearing, precious, sweet, winning
related words embraceable, kissable; beloved, cherished, treasured; attractive, beautiful, desirable, lovely; captivating, charming, fascinating; admirable, likable (*or* likeable), reputable, respectable; affable, agreeable, cheerful, cordial, friendly, genial, gracious, kind, pleasant; delightful, pleasing
near antonyms unloved; contemptible, disagreeable, disgusting, distasteful, heinous, horrible, offensive, unlikable, unpleasant; frightful, grotesque, hideous, ill-favored, monstrous, ogreish, repellent (*also* repellant), repugnant, repulsive; ugly, unattractive, unsightly, vile
antonyms abhorrent, abominable, detestable, hateful, odious, unlovable
love *n* **1** a feeling of strong or constant regard for and dedication to someone ⟨her *love* for her children was truly selfless⟩
synonyms affection, attachment, devotedness, devotion, fondness, passion
related words appetite, favor, like, liking, partiality, preference, taste; craving, crush, desire, infatuation, longing, lust, yearning; ardor, eagerness, enthusiasm, fervor, zeal; esteem, regard, respect; adoration, idolatry, worship; allegiance, fealty, fidelity, loyalty
near antonyms allergy, animosity, antipathy, aversion, disfavor, dislike; abhorrence, disgust, repugnance, repulsion, revulsion; misanthropy
antonyms abomination, hate, hatred, loathing, rancor
2 a person with whom one is in love — see SWEETHEART
3 positive regard for something — see LIKING
love *vb* **1** to hold dear ⟨patriots who *loved* their country well enough to die for it⟩
synonyms appreciate, cherish, prize, treasure, value
related words delight (in), dig, enjoy, fancy, groove (on), like, relish, revel (in); admire, esteem, regard, respect, revere, reverence, venerate; enshrine, memorialize; adore, dote (on), idolize, worship
phrases set store (by *or* on)
near antonyms undervalue; abhor, abominate, despise, detest, execrate, hate, loathe; disdain, scorn, scout; belittle, decry, deprecate, depreciate, disparage; abandon, forget, neglect
2 to feel passion, devotion, or tenderness for ⟨a husband who *loves* his wife more than anything⟩
synonyms adore, cherish, worship
related words idealize, idolize; revere, reverence, venerate; delight (in), dote (on)
phrases fall for, lose one's heart (to)
near antonyms antagonize, displease; disapprove (of), disfavor, dislike; disgust, repulse, turn off
antonyms abhor, abominate, despise, detest, execrate, hate, loathe
3 to take pleasure in — see ENJOY 1
4 to touch or handle in a tender or loving manner — see FONDLE
love affair *n* a brief romantic relationship — see AFFAIR 1
loved *adj* granted special treatment or attention — see DARLING 1
loveliness *n* the qualities in a person or thing that as a whole give pleasure to the senses — see BEAUTY 1
lovely *adj* very pleasing to look at — see BEAUTIFUL
lover *n* a person with a strong and habitual liking for something — see FAN
loving *adj* feeling or showing love ⟨they were a *loving* family, supporting each other when times were bad⟩
synonyms adoring, affectionate, devoted, fond, tender, tenderhearted
related words caring, compassionate, considerate, cordial, doting, forgiving, friendly, kind, warmhearted; ardent, fervent, impassioned, passionate, warm; amatory, amorous, erotic; enamored, infatuated, lovesick; mushy, romantic, sentimental; brotherly, fatherly, motherly, sisterly
near antonyms aloof, detached, hardhearted, indifferent, pitiless, reserved, uncaring, unfeeling; disaffected, unconcerned, uninvolved; cold, frigid, unfriendly; hard-boiled, unromantic, unsentimental
antonyms unloving
low *adj* **1** being near the equator ⟨we took a cruise to the *low* northern latitudes⟩
synonyms equatorial, tropical
near antonyms temperate
antonyms polar
2 belonging to or characteristic of an early level of skill or development — see PRIMITIVE 1
3 belonging to the class of people of low social or economic rank — see IGNOBLE 1
4 feeling unhappiness — see SAD 1
5 having a low musical pitch or range — see DEEP 2
6 having relatively little height — see SHORT 1
7 lacking bodily strength — see WEAK 1
8 lacking in refinement or good taste — see COARSE 2
9 not following or in accordance with standards of honor and decency — see IGNOBLE 2
10 not loud in pitch or volume — see SOFT 1
11 costing little — see CHEAP 1
lowbred *adj* lacking in refinement or good taste — see COARSE 2
lowbrow *adj* lacking in refinement or good taste — see COARSE 2
lowbrow *n* a person who is chiefly interested in

material comfort and is hostile or indifferent to art and culture — see PHILISTINE

lowdown *n* information not generally available to the public — see DOPE 1

lower *adj* **1** having not so great importance or rank as another — see LESSER
2 situated lower down — see INFERIOR 1

[1]**lower** *vb* **1** to cause to fall intentionally or unintentionally — see DROP 1
2 to go to a lower level — see DROP 2
3 to make smaller in amount, volume, or extent — see DECREASE 1
4 to grow less in scope or intensity especially gradually — see DECREASE 2
5 to reduce to a lower standing in one's own eyes or in others' eyes — see HUMBLE

[2]**lower** *also* **lour** *vb* **1** to take on a gloomy or forbidding look — see DARKEN 1
2 to look with anger or disapproval — see FROWN

lower *also* **lour** *n* a twisting of the facial features in disgust or disapproval — see GRIMACE

lower–class *adj* belonging to the class of people of low social or economic rank — see IGNOBLE 1

lowered *adj* directed down — see DOWNCAST 1

lowering *also* **louring** *adj* **1** covered over by clouds — see OVERCAST
2 harsh and threatening in manner or appearance — see GRIM 1

lowest *adj* being the least in amount, number, or size possible — see MINIMAL

low–grade *adj* of low quality — see CHEAP 2

lowliness *n* the absence of any feelings of being better than others — see HUMILITY

lowly *adj* **1** belonging to the class of people of low social or economic rank — see IGNOBLE 1
2 not having or showing any feelings of superiority, self-assertiveness, or showiness — see HUMBLE 1

lowly *adv* in manner showing no signs of pride or self-assertion ⟨the courtier bowed *lowly* before his king during the ceremony⟩
synonyms deferentially, humbly, meekly, modestly, sheepishly, submissively
related words fearfully, timidly; bashfully, diffidently, shyly; civilly, courteously, politely, respectfully
near antonyms fearlessly; discourteously, disdainfully, disrespectfully, impertinently, rashly, recklessly, saucily; impolitely, impudently, rudely, ungraciously
antonyms arrogantly, audaciously, boldly, brashly, brazenly, contemptuously, haughtily, pridefully, proudly, scornfully, swaggeringly

low–lying *adj* having relatively little height — see SHORT 1

lowness *n* **1** the quality or state of lacking refinement or good taste — see VULGARITY 1
2 the quality or state of lacking physical strength or vigor — see WEAKNESS 1

low–pressure *adj* having a relaxed, casual manner — see EASYGOING 1

low–spirited *adj* feeling unhappiness — see SAD 1

loyal *adj* firm in one's allegiance to someone or something — see FAITHFUL 1

loyalist *n* a person who loves his or her country and supports its interests and policies — see PATRIOT

loyalty *n* adherence to something to which one is bound by a pledge or duty — see FIDELITY

lozenge *n* a small mass containing medicine to be taken orally — see PILL

lubber *n* a big clumsy often slow-witted person — see OAF

lubberly *adj* lacking in physical ease and grace in movement or in the use of the hands — see CLUMSY 1

lubricate *vb* to coat (something) with a slippery substance in order to reduce friction ⟨it's not a good idea to use olive oil to *lubricate* the gears in an appliance⟩
synonyms grease, oil, slick, wax
near antonyms coarsen, rough, roughen

lubricated *adj* having or being a surface so smooth as to make sliding or falling likely — see SLICK 1

lucent *adj* **1** easily seen through — see CLEAR 1
2 giving off or reflecting much light — see BRIGHT 1

lucid *adj* **1** giving off or reflecting much light — see BRIGHT 1
2 having full use of one's mind and control over one's actions — see SANE
3 not subject to misinterpretation or more than one interpretation — see CLEAR 2

lucidity *n* **1** clearness of expression — see SIMPLICITY 2
2 the quality or state of having or giving off light — see BRILLIANCE 1

lucidness *n* clearness of expression — see SIMPLICITY 2

Lucifer *n* the supreme personification of evil often represented as the ruler of Hell — see DEVIL 1

luck *n* **1** success that is partly the result of chance ⟨some people have all the *luck*⟩
synonyms fortunateness, fortune, luckiness
related words break, fluke, godsend, hit, serendipity, strike, windfall; chance, opportunity; coup, stroke
near antonyms knock, misadventure, mishap; adversity, curse, sorrow, tragedy, trouble; calamity, cataclysm, catastrophe, disaster; defeat, failure, fizzle, nonsuccess; accident, casualty; disappointment, letdown, setback; circumstance, destiny, doom, fate, lot, portion
antonyms mischance, misfortune, unluckiness
2 the uncertain course of events — see CHANCE 1

luckiness *n* success that is partly the result of chance — see LUCK 1

luckless *adj* having, prone to, or marked by bad luck — see UNLUCKY

lucky *adj* **1** having good luck ⟨the *lucky* gambler walked out of the casino with $10,000⟩
synonyms fortunate, happy
related words blessed, favored, gifted, privileged; fair, golden, promising
near antonyms cursed, disadvantaged
antonyms hapless, ill-fated, ill-starred, luckless, star-crossed, unfortunate, unhappy, unlucky
2 coming or happening by good luck especially unexpectedly — see FORTUNATE 1

lucrative *adj* yielding a profit — see PROFITABLE 1

lucre *n* **1** something (as pieces of stamped metal or printed paper) customarily and legally used as a medium of exchange, a measure of value, or a means of payment — see MONEY
2 the amount of money left when expenses are subtracted from the total amount received — see PROFIT 1

ludicrous *adj* **1** causing or intended to cause laughter — see FUNNY 1
2 so foolish or pointless as to be worthy of scornful laughter — see RIDICULOUS 1

lug *n* a big clumsy often slow-witted person — see OAF
lug *vb* **1** to cause to follow by applying steady force on — see PULL 1
2 to support and take from one place to another — see CARRY 1
lugubrious *adj* expressing or suggesting mourning — see MOURNFUL 1
lukewarm *adj* **1** having or giving off heat to a moderate degree — see WARM 1
2 showing little or no interest or enthusiasm — see TEPID 1
lukewarmness *n* the quality or state of being moderate in temperature — see WARMTH 1
lull *n* a momentary halt in an activity — see PAUSE
lulling *adj* tending to calm the emotions and relieve stress — see SOOTHING 1
lumber *n* tree logs as prepared for human use — see WOOD
lumber *vb* **1** to move heavily or clumsily ⟨the elephant *lumbered* through the jungle⟩
synonyms barge, clump, flounder, lump, pound, scuff, scuffle, shamble, shuffle, stamp, stomp, stumble, stump, tramp, tromp
related words drag, flop, haul; labor, plod, trudge; careen, lurch, stagger, sway, teeter, totter, waddle, weave, wobble
near antonyms float, hover, waft
antonyms breeze, coast, glide, slide, waltz, whisk
2 to make progress in a clumsy, struggling manner — see FLOUNDER 1
3 to make a low heavy rolling sound — see RUMBLE
4 to place a weight or burden on — see LOAD 1
lumbering *adj* lacking in physical ease and grace in movement or in the use of the hands — see CLUMSY 1
lumberjack *n* a person whose job is to cut down trees ⟨the sawmill gets most of its business from the *lumberjacks* up north⟩
synonyms logger
related words sawyer; forester
luminary *n* **1** a ball-shaped gaseous celestial body that shines by its own light — see STAR 1
2 a person who is widely known and usually much talked about — see CELEBRITY 1
luminescence *n* the steady giving off of the form of radiation that makes vision possible — see LIGHT 1
luminosity *n* the quality or state of having or giving off light — see BRILLIANCE 1
luminous *adj* giving off or reflecting much light — see BRIGHT 1
lump *n* **1** a small uneven mass ⟨she dumped a *lump* of clay on the table and started to sculpt⟩
synonyms blob, chunk, clod, clump, glob, gob, gobbet, hunk, knob, nub, nubble, nugget, wad
related words bead, drop, globule; block, body, bulk; particle, piece, portion; bit, chip, crumb, morsel, scrap
2 a small rounded mass of swollen tissue — see BUMP 1
3 an abnormal mass of tissue — see GROWTH 1
lump *vb* **1** to bring together in one body or place — see GATHER 1
2 to move heavily or clumsily — see LUMBER 1
lumpish *adj* lacking in physical ease and grace in movement or in the use of the hands — see CLUMSY 1
lumpy *adj* **1** having small pieces or lumps spread throughout — see CHUNKY 1
2 not having a level or smooth surface — see UNEVEN 1
lunacy *n* **1** a foolish act or idea — see FOLLY 1
2 a serious mental disorder that prevents one from living a safe and normal life — see INSANITY 1
3 lack of good sense or judgment — see FOOLISHNESS 1
lunatic *adj* **1** having or showing a very abnormal or sick state of mind — see INSANE 1
2 showing or marked by a lack of good sense or judgment — see FOOLISH 1
lunatic *n* **1** a person judged to be legally or medically insane ⟨the *lunatic* was committed to an institution after running naked through the department store⟩
synonyms crackbrain, loony (*also* looney), maniac, neurotic, nut, psychopath, psychotic
related words madman, madwoman; deviant; paranoid, schizophrenic; character, crackpot, crank, eccentric, kook, oddball, screwball; case, patient
2 a person who lacks good sense or judgment — see FOOL 1
lurch *vb* **1** to make a series of unsteady side-to-side motions — see ROCK 1
2 to move forward while swaying from side to side — see STAGGER 1
lure *n* **1** something that persuades one to perform an action for pleasure or gain ⟨the promise of easy money is always the *lure* for some people to take up a life of crime⟩
synonyms allurement, bait, enticement, temptation, turn-on
related words appeal, call; attraction, goad, incentive, inducement, persuasion, seduction, spur; decoy, snare, trap
near antonyms caution, warning
2 something used to attract animals to a hook or into a trap — see BAIT 1
3 the act or pressure of giving in to a desire especially when ill-advised — see TEMPTATION 1
lure *vb* to lead away from a usual or proper course by offering some pleasure or advantage ⟨the hunter *lured* the lion into the open with the antelope carcass⟩
synonyms allure, beguile, decoy, entice, lead on, seduce, tempt
related words inveigle, persuade, rope (in), snow; catch, ensnare, entrap, snare; captivate, charm, enchant
near antonyms caution, ward (off), warn; drive (away *or* off), repulse, turn away
lurid *adj* **1** extremely disturbing or repellent — see HORRIBLE 1
2 lacking a healthy skin color — see PALE 2
3 arousing a strong and usually superficial interest or emotional reaction — see SENSATIONAL 1
luring *adj* having an often mysterious or magical power to attract — see FASCINATING 1
lurk *vb* to move about in a sly or secret manner — see SNEAK 1
lurker *n* someone who acts in a sly and secret manner — see SNEAK
luscious *adj* **1** very pleasing to the sense of taste — see DELICIOUS 1
2 pleasing to the physical senses — see SENSUAL
3 giving pleasure or contentment to the mind or senses — see PLEASANT

lusciousness *n* the quality of being delicious — see DELICIOUSNESS

lush *adj* **1** covered with a thick healthy natural growth ⟨they loved to go for picnics in the *lush* woodlands⟩
synonyms green, leafy, luxuriant, overgrown, verdant
related words fat, fecund, fertile, fruitful, productive, rich; dense, tangled
near antonyms bleak, depleted, infertile, poor, unproductive; arid, dead, desert, dry, parched
antonyms barren, leafless
2 growing thickly and vigorously — see RANK 1

lust (for *or* after) *vb* to have an earnest wish to own or enjoy — see DESIRE

lust *n* a strong wish for something — see DESIRE

luster *or* **lustre** *n* brightness created by light reflected from a surface — see SHINE 1

lusterless *adj* lacking a surface luster or gloss — see MATTE

lustful *adj* having a strong sexual desire ⟨the *lustful* student was always chasing after girls⟩
synonyms lascivious, lewd, licentious, passionate, wanton
related words prurient; dissipated, dissolute, libertine; corrupt, debauched, depraved, immoral, indecent
near antonyms celibate, chaste, decent, modest, moral, pure, virtuous; monastic, monkish; maidenly, virginal; innocent, lily-white

lustiness *n* the quality or state of having abundant or intense activity — see VITALITY 1

lustrous *adj* **1** giving off or reflecting much light — see BRIGHT 1
2 having a shiny surface or finish — see GLOSSY

lusty *adj* **1** having active strength of body or mind — see VIGOROUS 1
2 not showing weakness or uncertainty — see FIRM 1

luxuriant *adj* **1** covered with a thick, healthy natural growth — see LUSH 1
2 growing thickly and vigorously — see RANK 1
3 producing abundantly — see FERTILE
4 showing obvious signs of wealth and comfort — see LUXURIOUS

luxurious *adj* showing obvious signs of wealth and comfort ⟨the *luxurious* apartment was filled with the latest electronic gadgets and fine works of art⟩
synonyms deluxe, lavish, luxuriant, opulent, palatial, plush, sumptuous
related words costly, expensive; rich; extravagant, grandiose, ostentatious, pretentious, showy; awesome, awful, beautiful, gorgeous, grand, imposing, impressive, magnificent, majestic, splendid, stately; comfortable, cozy, homelike, homey, snug
near antonyms economical, frugal, meager (*or* meagre), spare, thrifty
antonyms ascetic, austere, humble, Spartan

luxuriously *adv* in a luxurious manner — see HIGH

luxury *n* something adding to pleasure or comfort but not absolutely necessary ⟨a private yacht is a *luxury*⟩
synonyms amenity, comfort, extra, frill, indulgence, superfluity
related words extravagance; dainty, delicacy, treat; accessory, option
antonyms basic, essential, fundamental, necessity, requirement
2 something that adds to one's ease — see COMFORT 2

lying *adj* telling or containing lies — see DISHONEST 1

lynx–eyed *adj* having unusually keen vision — see SHARP-EYED

lyric *adj* **1** having a pleasantly flowing quality suggestive of music ⟨they performed a slow, *lyric* dance for the audience⟩
synonyms euphonious, lyrical, mellifluous, mellow, melodic, melodious, musical
related words dulcet, golden, sweet
near antonyms disconnected, staccato; discordant, grating, harsh, jarring, strident
2 having qualities suggestive of poetry — see POETIC

lyric *n* **1** a composition using rhythm and often rhyme to create a lyrical effect — see POEM
2 a short musical composition for the human voice often with instrumental accompaniment — see SONG 1

lyrical *adj* **1** having a pleasantly flowing quality suggestive of music — see LYRIC 1
2 having qualities suggestive of poetry — see POETIC

ma *n* a female human parent — see MOTHER

macabre *adj* extremely disturbing or repellent — see HORRIBLE 1

Machiavellian *adj* not guided by or showing a concern for what is right — see UNPRINCIPLED

machinate *vb* **1** to engage in a secret plan to accomplish evil or unlawful ends — see PLOT
2 to plan out usually with subtle skill or care — see ENGINEER

machination *n* a secret plan for accomplishing evil or unlawful ends — see PLOT 1

machine *n* **1** a device that changes energy into mechanical motion — see ENGINE
2 a self-propelled passenger vehicle on wheels — see CAR

machinery *n* something used to achieve an end — see AGENT 1

mackintosh *or* **macintosh** *n chiefly British* a coat made of water-resistant material — see RAINCOAT

macrocosm *n* the whole body of things observed or assumed — see UNIVERSE

mad *adj* **1** feeling or showing anger — see ANGRY
2 having or showing a very abnormal or sick state of mind — see INSANE 1
3 marked by great and often stressful excitement or activity — see FURIOUS 1

4 showing or marked by a lack of good sense or judgment — see FOOLISH 1

mad (about) *adj* filled with an intense or excessive love for — see ENAMORED (OF)

madcap *adj* foolishly adventurous or bold — see FOOLHARDY 1

madden *vb* **1** to cause to go insane or as if insane — see CRAZE
2 to make angry — see ANGER

maddening *adj* causing annoyance — see ANNOYING

mademoiselle *n* a young usually unmarried woman — see GIRL 1

made–up *adj* not real and existing only in the imagination — see IMAGINARY

madhouse *n* **1** a place where insane people are cared for ⟨it was hard to believe that this place with the bright cheery walls was really a *madhouse*⟩
synonyms asylum
related words institution; hospice, hospital, sanatorium, sanitarium; home
2 a place of uproar or confusion ⟨our house is always a *madhouse* on school mornings, with five kids and two dogs running around⟩
synonyms babel, bedlam, circus, hell
related words commotion, havoc, pandemonium, racket, ruckus, tumult, turmoil; clamor, clatter, din, hubbub, noise; chaos, confusion, disarrangement, disarray, disorder, maelstrom, mess, muss
near antonyms heaven, paradise, utopia; order, orderliness, organization; calm, peace; hush, quiet, silence, soundlessness, stillness

madly *adv* **1** in a confused and reckless manner — see HELTER-SKELTER 1
2 in an enthusiastic manner — see SKY-HIGH

madness *n* **1** a serious mental disorder that prevents one from living a safe and normal life — see INSANITY 1
2 lack of good sense or judgment — see FOOLISHNESS 1

maelstrom *n* water moving rapidly in a circle with a hollow in the center — see WHIRLPOOL

maestro *n* a person with a high level of knowledge or skill in a field — see EXPERT

Mafia *n* a group involved in secret or criminal activities — see RING 1

magazine *n* **1** a building for storing goods — see STOREHOUSE
2 a place where military arms are stored — see ARMORY
3 a publication that appears at regular intervals — see JOURNAL

magic *adj* **1** being or appearing to be under a magic spell — see ENCHANTED
2 having seemingly supernatural qualities or powers — see MYSTIC 1

magic *n* **1** the power to control natural forces through supernatural means ⟨he claimed that he could summon a storm through *magic*⟩
synonyms bewitchment, black art, black magic, conjuring, enchantment, mojo, necromancy, sorcery, voodooism, witchcraft, witchery, wizardry
related words abracadabra, amulet, charm, fetish (*also* fetich), mascot, phylactery, talisman; curse, hex, incantation, jinx, spell; augury, divining, forecasting, foreknowing, foreseeing, foretelling, fortune-telling, predicting, presaging, prognosticating, prophesying, soothsaying; hoodoo, occultism, spiritualism; augur, omen; exorcism; alchemy
near antonyms science
2 the art or skill of performing tricks or illusions for entertainment ⟨they hired someone to do *magic* for their child's tenth birthday party⟩
synonyms conjuring, legerdemain
related words deception, trickery
phrases sleight of hand
3 the power of irresistible attraction — see CHARM 2

magical *adj* **1** being or appearing to be under a magic spell — see ENCHANTED
2 being so extraordinary or abnormal as to suggest powers which violate the laws of nature — see SUPERNATURAL 2
3 having seemingly supernatural qualities or powers — see MYSTIC 1

magician *n* **1** a person skilled in using supernatural forces ⟨the *magician* was able to turn birds purple with a simple spell⟩
synonyms charmer, conjurer (*or* conjuror), enchanter, necromancer, sorcerer, voodoo, witch, wizard
related words enchantress, hag, hex, sorceress, warlock; medicine man; foreseer, fortune-teller, prognosticator, prophesier, prophet, soothsayer; medium; exorcist
2 one who practices tricks and illusions for entertainment ⟨the famous *magician's* best trick was always pulling a rabbit out of a hat⟩
synonyms conjurer (*or* conjuror), prestidigitator, trickster
related words charmer, enchanter, enchantress

magistrate *n* a public official having authority to decide questions of law — see JUDGE 1

magnanimous *adj* having, characterized by, or arising from a dignified and generous nature — see NOBLE 2

magnanimously *adv* in a manner befitting a person of the highest character and ideals — see GREATLY 1

magnate *n* a person of rank, power, or influence in a particular field ⟨the film studio *magnate* had movie stars at his beck and call⟩
synonyms baron, czar (*also* tsar *or* tzar), king, mogul, prince, tycoon
related words big shot, bigwig, figure, nabob, notable, personage, VIP; celebrity, personality, star; moneybags, plutocrat

magnet *n* something that attracts interest ⟨the giant theme park is a *magnet* for tourists to the area⟩
synonyms attraction, draw, lodestone
related words capital, cynosure, mecca; allure, allurement, bait, enticement, fascination, lure, temptation, turn-on; appeal, call; incentive, inducement, persuasion, spur

magnetic *adj* having an often mysterious or magical power to attract — see FASCINATING 1

magnetism *n* the power of irresistible attraction — see CHARM 2

magnetize *vb* to attract or delight as if by magic — see CHARM 1

magnification *n* the representation of something in terms that go beyond the facts — see EXAGGERATION

magnificence *n* impressiveness of beauty on a large scale ⟨the *magnificence* of the great castle hallway is beyond description⟩
synonyms augustness, brilliance, gloriousness, glory, grandeur, grandness, majesty, nobility, no-

bleness, resplendence, splendor, stateliness, stupendousness, sublimeness, superbness
related words awesomeness, marvelousness, wondrousness; lavishness, luxuriance, luxury, opulence, sumptuousness; grandiosity, ostentation, pretentiousness; flashiness, gaudiness, ornateness, showiness; extraordinariness, remarkableness

magnificent *adj* large and impressive in size, grandeur, extent, or conception — see GRAND 1

magnify *vb* **1** to add to the interest of by including made-up details — see EMBROIDER
2 to enhance the status of — see EXALT
3 to make markedly greater in measure or degree — see INTENSIFY
4 to proclaim the glory of — see PRAISE 1

magnitude *n* **1** the quality or state of being important — see IMPORTANCE
2 the quality or state of being very large — see IMMENSITY
3 the total amount of measurable space or surface occupied by something — see [1]SIZE

magnum opus *n* something (as a work of art) that is a great achievement and often its creator's greatest achievement — see MASTERPIECE

magpie *n* a person who talks constantly — see CHATTERBOX

maid *n* **1** a female domestic servant ⟨they hired a *maid* to do the housework after the baby was born⟩
synonyms charwoman, domestic, housekeeper, housemaid, maidservant
related words attendant, chambermaid, handmaiden (*also* handmaid), lady-in-waiting; nursemaid
2 a young usually unmarried woman — see GIRL 1

maiden *adj* **1** coming before all others in time or order — see FIRST 1
2 never having had sexual relations — see VIRGIN 1

maiden *n* a young usually unmarried woman — see GIRL 1

maidservant *n* a female domestic servant — see MAID 1

mail *n* communications or parcels sent or carried through the postal system ⟨whenever they were separated, the lovers always sent each other lots of *mail*⟩
synonyms matter, parcel post, post [*chiefly British*]
related words electronic mail, e-mail; dispatch, epistle, message, missive, note, postcard; airmail, rural free delivery, special delivery; junk mail

mail *vb* to send through the postal system ⟨if you don't *mail* that letter soon, it's going to arrive late⟩
synonyms post
related words airmail; address, consign; direct, dispatch, forward, remit, route, ship, transmit, transport; register
near antonyms receive

mail carrier *n* a person who delivers mail — see POSTMAN

mailman *n* a person who delivers mail — see POSTMAN

maim *vb* to cause severe or permanent injury to ⟨on-the-job accidents *maim* far too many workers every year⟩
synonyms cripple, disable, lame, mutilate
related words dismember, hamstring, hobble; batter, bruise, bung (up), mangle, maul, rough (up); gore, lacerate, wound; disfigure, scar; break, damage, harm, hurt, impair, injure; bash, beat, belt, bludgeon, buffet, drub, hammer, lace, lambaste (*or* lambast), lick, paste, pelt, pound, pummel, thump; bang, box, hit, punch, slap, smack, smash, sock, spank, swat, swipe, thrash, thwack, whack; flog, lash, wallop, whip; kill, murder; torment, torture
near antonyms cure, heal, remedy; doctor, fix, mend, patch; rebuild, recondition, reconstruct, rejuvenate, renew, renovate, repair, restore

main *adj* coming before all others in importance — see FOREMOST 1

main *n* **1** muscular strength — see MUSCLE 1
2 one of the great divisions of land on the globe or the main part of such a division — see MAINLAND
3 the main or greater part of something as distinguished from its appendages — see BODY 1

mainland *n* one of the great divisions of land on the globe or the main part of such a division ⟨the boat back to the *mainland* leaves once every two days⟩
synonyms continent, main
related words subcontinent, supercontinent
near antonyms island, isle, islet; atoll, barrier reef, cay, coral reef, key; cape, headland, peninsula, promontory

mainly *adv* for the most part — see CHIEFLY

mainstay *n* something or someone to which one looks for support — see DEPENDENCE 2

maintain *vb* **1** to keep in good condition ⟨he repairs and *maintains* antique cars as a hobby⟩
synonyms conserve, keep up, preserve, save
related words support, sustain; care (for), husband, manage; defend, guard, protect, safeguard, screen, shield; cure, fix, heal, remedy; mend, patch, rebuild, reconstruct
near antonyms disregard, ignore, neglect; break, damage, destroy, harm, hurt, impair, injure, ruin, wreck
2 to continue to declare to be true or proper despite opposition or objections ⟨part of debating is learning to *maintain* your position in the face of harsh challenges⟩
synonyms defend, justify, support, uphold
related words advocate, champion, espouse; confirm, vindicate, warrant; affirm, assert, avow, claim, contend, declare, insist, proclaim, profess, state; argue, debate, discuss; emphasize, stress, underline, underscore
near antonyms abandon, forsake, recant, retract, take back, withdraw; controvert, disprove, rebut, refute
3 to pay the living expenses of — see SUPPORT 2
4 to state (something) as a reason in support of or against something under consideration — see ARGUE 1
5 to state as a fact usually forcefully — see CLAIM 1

maintainable *adj* capable of being defended with good reasoning against verbal attack — see TENABLE 1

maintenance *n* the act or activity of keeping something in an existing and usually satisfactory condition ⟨I was hired to perform basic *maintenance* until the property could be sold⟩
synonyms conservation, conserving, preservation, preserving, upkeep
related words support, sustaining; care, guardian-

ship; defense, guarding, protection, safeguarding, safekeeping
near antonyms dereliction, ignoring, neglect; damage, destruction, harm, hurt, injury, ruin

majestic *adj* **1** having or showing elegance — see ELEGANT 1
2 large and impressive in size, grandeur, extent, or conception — see GRAND 1
3 very dignified in form, tone, or style — see ELEVATED 2

majesty *n* **1** a dignified bearing or appearance befitting royalty <even as a child, the princess possessed a certain *majesty* that would later serve her well>
synonyms augustness, stateliness
related words high-mindedness, magnanimity, nobility; haughtiness, lordliness, pompousness; dignity, poise; grandeur, grandness, greatness, impressiveness, magnificence, resplendence, splendor
2 dignified or restrained beauty of form, appearance, or style — see ELEGANCE
3 impressiveness of beauty on a large scale — see MAGNIFICENCE

major *adj* having great meaning or lasting effect — see IMPORTANT 1

majority *n* the state of being fully grown or developed — see MATURITY

make *vb* **1** to bring into being by combining, shaping, or transforming materials <will you help me *make* the dough for the cookies?>
synonyms fabricate, fashion, form, frame, manufacture, produce
related words assemble, build, construct, erect, make up, put up, raise, rear, structure, throw up; craft, handcraft; forge, mold, shape; prefabricate; create, invent, originate; establish, father, institute, organize; concoct, contrive, cook up, design, devise, imagine, think (up); conceive, envisage, picture, visualize; refashion, remake, remanufacture
phrases put together
near antonyms disassemble, dismantle, take apart; break up, dismember; abolish, annihilate, demolish, destroy, devastate, eradicate, exterminate, extinguish, flatten, pulverize, raze, ruin, shatter, smash, wreck; break, damage, harm, hurt, impair; blow up, explode
2 to obtain (as a goal) through effort — see ACHIEVE 1
3 to be the cause of (a situation, action, or state of mind) — see EFFECT
4 to carry through (as a process) to completion — see PERFORM 1
5 to cause (a person) to give in to pressure — see FORCE
6 to decide the size, amount, number, or distance of (something) without actual measurement — see ESTIMATE 2
7 to form by putting together parts or materials — see BUILD
8 to give the impression of being — see SEEM
9 to go on a specified course or in a certain direction — see HEAD 1
10 to put into effect through legislative or authoritative action — see ENACT
11 to receive as return for effort — see EARN 1
12 to recognize the meaning of — see COMPREHEND 1

make–believe *adj* not real and existing only in the imagination — see IMAGINARY

make out *vb* **1** to meet one's day-to-day needs — see GET ALONG 1
2 to recognize the meaning of — see COMPREHEND 1
3 to touch one another with the lips as a sign of love — see KISS 1

make over *vb* **1** to change in form, appearance, or use — see CONVERT 2
2 to give over the legal possession or ownership of — see TRANSFER 1
3 to make different in some way — see CHANGE 1

Maker *n* the being worshipped as the creator and ruler of the universe — see DEITY 2

makeshift *adj* taking the place of one that came before — see NEW 1

makeshift *n* a temporary replacement <when his belt broke, he used string as a *makeshift* until he could get home to replace it>
synonyms expedient, stopgap
related words recourse, refuge, resort; alternate, backup, standby, stand-in, substitute, understudy
near antonyms archetype, original, prototype

makeup *n* **1** preparations intended to beautify the face or hair <she never left the house without applying her *makeup* and arranging her jewelry>
synonyms cosmetics, paint
related words greasepaint; camouflage; cold cream, cream, eye shadow, kohl, lipstick, lotion, mascara, oil, powder, rouge, vanishing cream
2 the way in which the elements of something (as a work of art) are arranged — see COMPOSITION 3

make up *vb* **1** to be all the substance of — see CONSTITUTE 1
2 to create or think of by clever use of the imagination — see INVENT
3 to form by putting together parts or materials — see BUILD

make up (for) *vb* to balance with an equal force so as to make ineffective — see OFFSET

making *n* the basic elements from which something can be developed <she had all the *makings* of an excellent leader, but she needed some experience first>
synonyms material, raw material, stuff, substance
related words possibility, potential, potentiality; matter

maladroit *adj* showing or marked by a lack of skill and tact (as in dealing with a situation) — see AWKWARD 2

malady *n* an abnormal state that disrupts a plant's or animal's normal bodily functioning — see DISEASE

malcontent *adj* having a feeling that one has been wronged or thwarted in one's ambitions — see DISCONTENTED

male *adj* considered characteristic of or appropriate for men — see MASCULINE

male *n* an adult male human being — see MAN 1

malediction *n* a prayer that harm will come to someone — see CURSE 1

malefaction *n* a breaking of a moral or legal code — see OFFENSE 1

malefactor *n* **1** a person who commits moral wrongs — see EVILDOER 1
2 a person who has committed a crime — see CRIMINAL

malevolence *n* the desire to cause pain for the satisfaction of doing harm — see MALICE

malevolent *adj* having or showing a desire to cause someone pain or suffering for the sheer enjoyment of it — see HATEFUL
malevolently *adv* in a mean or spiteful manner — see NASTILY
malfeasance *n* improper or illegal behavior — see MISCONDUCT
malformed *adj* badly or imperfectly formed <a clay sculpture of an eagle that was so *malformed* that it looked more like a feathered football>
synonyms deformed, distorted, misshapen, monstrous, shapeless
related words defaced, disfigured; aberrant, abnormal, freakish, mutant; asymmetrical (*or* asymmetric), crooked, disproportionate, irregular, lopsided, nonsymmetrical, overbalanced, unbalanced, unequal; horrible, horrific, terrible; ugly, unattractive
near antonyms flawless, perfect
antonyms shapely
malfunctioning *adj* not being in working order — see INOPERABLE 1
malice *n* the desire to cause pain for the satisfaction of doing harm <there was no reason other than pure *malice* to spread such disgusting lies all over school>
synonyms cattiness, despite, hatefulness, malevolence, maliciousness, malignancy, malignity, meanness, nastiness, spite, spitefulness, spleen, venom, viciousness
related words abusiveness, cruelty; abhorrence, abomination, execration, hate, hatred, loathing; animosity, antagonism, antipathy, bitterness, enmity, grudge, hostility, ill will, jaundice, rancor, resentment; despicableness, invidiousness; vengefulness, vindictiveness; aversion, disgust, distaste, horror, repugnance, repulsion, revulsion; contempt, disdain; jealousy, pique, resentment, scorn; bile, rancor, virulence, vitriol
near antonyms devotion, love, passion; amiability, amicability, amity, civility, cordiality, friendliness, hospitality; adoration, ardor, infatuation, veneration, worship; affection, charity, kindliness; comity, empathy, friendship, goodwill, sympathy, understanding
malicious *adj* having or showing a desire to cause someone pain or suffering for the sheer enjoyment of it — see HATEFUL
maliciously *adv* in a mean or spiteful manner — see NASTILY
maliciousness *n* the desire to cause pain for the satisfaction of doing harm — see MALICE
malign *adj* having or showing a desire to cause someone pain or suffering for the sheer enjoyment of it — see HATEFUL
malign *vb* to make untrue and harmful statements about — see SLANDER
malignancy *n* the desire to cause pain for the satisfaction of doing harm — see MALICE
malignant *adj* having or showing a desire to cause someone pain or suffering for the sheer enjoyment of it — see HATEFUL
malignantly *adv* in a mean or spiteful manner — see NASTILY
maligning *n* the making of false statements that damage another's reputation — see SLANDER
malignity *n* the desire to cause pain for the satisfaction of doing harm — see MALICE
malleability *n* the quality or state of being easily molded — see PLASTICITY
malleable *adj* **1** capable of being easily molded or modeled — see PLASTIC
2 capable of being readily changed — see FLEXIBLE 1
malodorous *adj* having an unpleasant smell <the garbage became quite *malodorous* after it sat there for two weeks>
synonyms fetid, foul, fusty, musty, noisome, rank, reeking, reeky, smelly, stinking, stinky, strong
related words putrid, rancid, stale; bad, disgusting, offensive, repulsive, revolting, vile; decayed, decaying, decomposed, decomposing, rotted, rotten, rotting, spoiled, spoiling; dirty, filthy, nasty, noxious; odoriferous, odorous
near antonyms flowery, fruity, spicy, woodsy
antonyms ambrosial, aromatic, fragrant, perfumed, redolent, savory, scented, sweet
maltreat *vb* **1** to inflict physical or emotional harm upon — see ABUSE 1
2 to abuse physically — see MANHANDLE 1
mama *n* a female human parent — see MOTHER
mammoth *adj* unusually large — see HUGE
mammoth *n* something that is unusually large and powerful — see GIANT
mammy *n* a female human parent — see MOTHER
man *n* **1** an adult male human being <the children always feel better when there's a *man* or a woman around>
synonyms bloke [*chiefly British*], buck, cat [*slang*], chap [*chiefly British*], dude, fellow, gent, gentleman, guy, hombre, jack, joker, lad, male
related words master, mister, sir
2 a male romantic companion — see BOYFRIEND
3 a member of the human race — see HUMAN
4 the human race — see MANKIND
5 the male partner in a marriage — see HUSBAND
manacle *n* **1** something that physically prevents free movement — see BOND 1
2 something that makes movement or progress more difficult — see ENCUMBRANCE
manacle *vb* **1** to confine or restrain with or as if with chains — see BIND 1
2 to create difficulty for the work or activity of — see HAMPER
manage *vb* **1** to deal with (something) usually skillfully or efficiently — see HANDLE 1
2 to look after and make decisions about — see CONDUCT 1
3 to meet one's day-to-day needs — see GET ALONG 1
management *n* the act or activity of looking after and making decisions about something — see CONDUCT 1
manager *n* a person who manages or directs — see EXECUTIVE
managerial *adj* suited for or relating to the directing of things — see EXECUTIVE
managing *adj* highest in rank or authority — see HEAD
man–at–arms *n* a person engaged in military service — see SOLDIER
mandate *n* the granting of power to perform various acts or duties — see COMMISSION 1
mandatory *adj* forcing one's compliance or participation by or as if by law <the tests are *mandatory* for all students wishing to graduate>
synonyms compulsory, forced, imperative, incumbent, involuntary, necessary, nonelective, obligatory, peremptory, required

related words all-important, essential, indispensable, needed, requisite; insistent, persistent, pressing, urgent; demanded, enforced; coercive
near antonyms chosen, discretionary; dispensable, unnecessary, unneeded, unwanted; inconsequential, insignificant, nonessential, unimportant
antonyms elective, optional, voluntary

maneuver *vb* **1** to deal with (something) usually skillfully or efficiently — see HANDLE 1
2 to plan out usually with subtle skill or care — see ENGINEER

manful *adj* feeling or displaying no fear by temperament — see BRAVE

mangle *vb* to make or do (something) in a clumsy or unskillful way — see BOTCH

mangy *adj* showing signs of advanced wear and tear and neglect — see SHABBY 1

manhandle *vb* **1** to abuse physically <charges that the police *manhandled* peaceful protesters>
synonyms maltreat, maul, mishandle, rough (up)
related words abuse, ill-treat, ill-use, mistreat, misuse; roughhouse, wrestle; bash, batter, beat, buffet, drub, lambaste (*or* lambast), lick, pound, pummel, slap, thrash; harm, hurt, injure, wound; oppress, persecute, wrong; ambush, assail, attack; clobber, fight, gang up (on), hit, jump, knock; torment, torture
near antonyms caress, fondle, pet; coddle, mollycoddle, pamper; care (for), foster, nurture
2 to inflict physical or emotional harm upon — see ABUSE 1

manhood *n* the set of qualities considered appropriate for or characteristic of men — see VIRILITY

mania *n* **1** a serious mental disorder that prevents one from living a safe and normal life — see INSANITY 1
2 something about which one is constantly thinking or concerned — see FIXATION

maniac *n* **1** a person judged to be legally or medically insane — see LUNATIC 1
2 a person with a strong and habitual liking for something — see FAN

maniacal *also* **maniac** *adj* having or showing a very abnormal or sick state of mind — see INSANE 1

manifest *adj* not subject to misinterpretation or more than one interpretation — see CLEAR 2

manifest *vb* **1** to make known (something abstract) through outward signs — see SHOW 2
2 to represent in visible form — see EMBODY 2

manifestation *n* a visible representation of something abstract (as a quality) — see EMBODIMENT

manifold *adj* being of many and various kinds <the *manifold* attractions of that state make it an ideal destination for a family vacation>
synonyms divers, multifarious, myriad
related words multiform, multiple, multiplex, multitudinous; heterogeneous, miscellaneous, mixed, sundry, various; different, diverse, unlike, varied
near antonyms homogeneous, monolithic, unmixed, unvaried; alike, identical, same; distinct, distinctive, individual, separate; alone, lone, only, sole, solitary; singular, unique

manikin *or* **mannikin** *n* **1** a three-dimensional representation of the human body used especially for displaying clothes — see MANNEQUIN 1
2 a person who poses with or wears merchandise (as clothes) often for pictorial advertising — see MODEL 2

manipulate *vb* **1** to control or take advantage of by artful, unfair, or insidious means <*manipulated* their parents into agreeing to let them stay out later by telling their mother that their father agreed, and vice versa>
synonyms exploit, play (upon)
related words engineer, finagle, jockey, maneuver; beguile, bluff, cozen, deceive, delude, dupe, fool, gull, hoax, hoodwink, kid, snow, take in, trick; intrigue, machinate, plot, scheme; arrange, contrive, devise, finesse, mastermind; cheat, chisel, defraud, fleece, gyp, hustle, swindle
2 to deal with (something) usually skillfully or efficiently — see HANDLE 1
3 to plan out usually with subtle skill or care — see ENGINEER

mankind *n* the human race <all of *mankind* stands to gain if world peace is finally achieved>
synonyms Homo sapiens, humanity, humankind, man
related words being, body, creature, fellowman, human, individual, mortal, party, person

manlike *adj* **1** considered characteristic of or appropriate for men — see MASCULINE
2 having qualities or traits that are traditionally considered inappropriate for a girl or woman — see UNFEMININE

manliness *n* the set of qualities considered appropriate for or characteristic of men — see VIRILITY

manly *adj* considered characteristic of or appropriate for men — see MASCULINE

man–made *adj* being such in appearance only and made with or manufactured from usually cheaper materials — see IMITATION

manna *n* **1** a source of great satisfaction — see DELIGHT 1
2 something that provides happiness or does good for a person or thing — see BLESSING 2

mannequin *n* **1** a three-dimensional representation of the human body used especially for displaying clothes <the *mannequin* over there looks so real>
synonyms dummy, figure, form, manikin (*or* mannikin)
related words doll
2 a person who poses with or wears merchandise (as clothes) often for pictorial advertising — see MODEL 2

manner *n* **1 manners** *pl* personal conduct or behavior as evaluated by an accepted standard of appropriateness for a social or professional setting <her table *manners* were so impeccable that she even knew how to use all five forks>
synonyms etiquette, form, mores, proprieties
related words amenities, civilities, pleasantries; bearing, demeanor, deportment; courtesy, decorum, mannerliness, politeness; formalities, protocol, rules; air, attitude, carriage, poise, polish, pose, posture, presence; custom, habit, pattern, practice (*also* practise), trick, way, wont; convention, fashion, mode, style
2 a distinctive way of putting ideas into words — see STYLE 1
3 a number of persons or things that are grouped together because they have something in common — see SORT 1
4 the means or procedure for doing something — see METHOD

mannerism *n* an odd or peculiar habit — see IDIOSYNCRASY

mannerliness *n* speech or behavior that is a sign of good breeding — see POLITENESS
mannerly *adj* showing consideration, courtesy, and good manners — see POLITE 1
mannish *adj* **1** considered characteristic of or appropriate for men — see MASCULINE
2 having qualities or traits that are traditionally considered inappropriate for a girl or woman — see UNFEMININE
manor *n* a large impressive residence — see MANSION
manor house *n* a large impressive residence — see MANSION
manpower *n* a body of persons at work or available for work — see FORCE 1
mansion *n* a large impressive residence ⟨if I ever win the lottery, I'm going to buy a *mansion* in the mountains⟩
synonyms castle, château, countryseat, estate, hacienda, hall, manor, manor house, palace, villa
related words showplace; abode, domicile, dwelling, habitation, hearth, home, house, lodging(s), pad, place; housing, nest, quarter(s), residency, roof; aerie, penthouse; salon, suite, townhouse
man–size *or* **man–sized** *adj* considered characteristic of or appropriate for men — see MASCULINE
manta *n* any of several extremely large rays — see DEVILFISH
manta ray *n* any of several extremely large rays — see DEVILFISH
mantilla *n* a scarf worn on the head — see BANDANNA
mantle *n* **1** a sleeveless garment worn so as to hang over the shoulders, arms, and back — see [1]CAPE
2 something that covers or conceals like a piece of cloth — see CLOAK 1
mantle *vb* to surround or cover closely — see ENFOLD 1
manual *n* a book used for instruction in a subject — see TEXTBOOK
manufactory *n* a building or set of buildings for the manufacturing of goods — see FACTORY
manufacture *vb* **1** to bring into being by combining, shaping, or transforming materials — see MAKE 1
2 to create or think of by clever use of the imagination — see INVENT
manumission *n* the act of setting free from slavery — see LIBERATION
manumit *vb* to set free (as from slavery or confinement) — see FREE 1
manuscript *n* writing done by hand — see HANDWRITING 2
many *adj* being of a large but indefinite number ⟨a journey of *many* miles begins with a single step⟩
synonyms multiple, multiplex, multitudinous, numerous
related words countless, innumerable, numberless, uncountable, unnumbered, untold; several, some; miscellaneous, mixed, sundry, various; divers, manifold, multifarious, myriad
near antonyms countable, limited
antonyms few
map *n* an illustration of certain features of a geographical area ⟨there is a *map* of the United States on the wall over there⟩
synonyms chart
related words graph, graphic; relief map
map (out) *vb* to work out the details of (something) in advance — see PLAN 1
mar *vb* **1** to affect slightly with something morally bad or undesirable — see TAINT 1
2 to reduce the soundness, effectiveness, or perfection of — see DAMAGE 1
marathon *adj* lasting for a considerable time — see LONG 2
maraud *vb* to search through with the intent of committing robbery — see RANSACK 1
marble *vb* to mark with small spots especially unevenly — see SPOT 1
marbled *adj* having blotches of two or more colors — see PIED
march *n* **1** a region along the dividing line between two countries — see FRONTIER 1
2 forward movement in time or place — see ADVANCE 1
march *vb* **1** to move along with a steady regular step especially in a group ⟨the band had to practice for hours to be able to *march* in perfect step⟩
synonyms file, pace, parade, stride
related words goose-step; perambulate, step, traipse, tread; hike, tramp; lumber, plod, stamp, stomp, stride, trudge
near antonyms amble, meander, ramble, stroll, wander
2 to move forward along a course — see GO 1
margin *n* the line or relatively narrow space that marks the outer limit of something — see BORDER 1
margin *vb* to serve as a border for — see BORDER
marginally *adv* by a very small margin — see JUST 2
marine *adj* **1** of or relating to the sea ⟨he loves collecting little *marine* creatures while at the beach⟩
synonyms maritime, oceanic, pelagic
related words abyssal, deep-sea, deepwater, saltwater; admiralty, nautical, naval; undersea, underwater; hydrographic, oceanographic
2 of or relating to navigation of the sea ⟨a collection of *marine* instruments, including a sextant⟩
synonyms maritime, nautical, navigational
related words admiralty, naval; oceangoing, seafaring, seagoing; hydrographic, oceanographic
mariner *n* one who operates or navigates a seagoing vessel — see SAILOR
marital *adj* of or relating to marriage ⟨neither of them ever forgot their *marital* vows, no matter how hard things sometimes were⟩
synonyms conjugal, connubial, married, matrimonial, nuptial, wedded
related words espoused, matched, mated; bridal; wifely; affianced, betrothed, committed, engaged, pledged, promised
maritime *adj* **1** of or relating to navigation of the sea — see MARINE 2
2 of or relating to the sea — see MARINE 1
mark *n* **1** a person or thing that is made fun of — see LAUGHINGSTOCK
2 a person or thing that is the object of abuse, criticism, or ridicule — see TARGET 1
3 overall quality as seen or judged by people in general — see REPUTATION
4 something set up as an example against which others of the same type are compared — see STANDARD 1
5 something that one hopes or intends to accomplish — see GOAL
6 something that sets apart an individual from others of the same kind — see CHARACTERISTIC

7 something that spoils the appearance or completeness of a thing — see BLEMISH

8 the power to bring about a result on another — see EFFECT 2

mark *vb* **1** to attach an identifying slip to — see LABEL 1

2 to be an important feature of — see CHARACTERIZE 2

3 to make a written note of — see RECORD 1

mark (out) *vb* to mark the limits of — see LIMIT 2

mark down *vb* to lower the price or value of — see DEPRECIATE 1

marked *adj* likely to attract attention — see NOTICEABLE

marker *n* a slip (as of paper or cloth) that is attached to something to identify or describe it — see LABEL

market *vb* to offer for sale to the public ⟨local farmers *market* their garden-fresh produce in roadside stands all over the valley⟩

synonyms deal (in), merchandise, put up, retail, sell, vend

related words wholesale; hawk, peddle; barter, distribute, exchange, export, handle, trade, traffic (in); advertise, ballyhoo, boost, plug, promote, tout; bargain, chaffer, dicker, haggle, horse-trade, palter; auction; provide, supply; keep, stock

antonyms buy, purchase

marketable *adj* **1** fit to be offered for sale ⟨you'll need to clean that car up a bit before it's *marketable*⟩

synonyms salable (*or* saleable)

related words commercial, profitable; costly, fancy, fine, high-grade, precious, premium, prime, valuable; dear, expensive, extravagant

near antonyms damaged, shopworn; cheap, useless, worthless; bad, inferior, low-grade, substandard, unsatisfactory

antonyms nonsalable, unmarketable, unsalable

2 fit or likely to be sold especially on a large scale — see COMMERCIAL

marketplace *n* the buying and selling of goods especially on a large scale and between different places — see COMMERCE

market value *n* the amount of money for which something will find a buyer — see VALUE 1

marksman *n* a person skilled in shooting at a target ⟨only the best *marksmen* can hit the bull's-eye at 500 feet⟩

synonyms sharpshooter, shooter, shot

related words rifleman, trapshooter; gunman, gunner, sniper

maroon *vb* to cause to remain behind — see LEAVE 1

marriage *n* **1** a union representing a special kind of social and legal partnership between two people ⟨some religions consider *marriage* a sacrament⟩

synonyms match, matrimony, wedlock

related words bigamy, monogamy, polygamy; intermarriage, miscegenation, remarriage; attachment, commitment, relationship; betrothal, engagement, espousal, hand, pledge, promise, proposal, troth

near antonyms annulment, divorce, separation

2 a ceremony in which two people are united in matrimony — see WEDDING

married *adj* of or relating to marriage — see MARITAL

marry *vb* **1** to perform the ceremony of marriage for ⟨they chose a very nice priest to *marry* them⟩

synonyms wed

related words match, mate; conjoin, connect, unite; affiance

2 to give in marriage ⟨they worried about the cost of *marrying* off five daughters⟩

synonyms espouse, match, wed

related words commit, engage; affiance, betroth, pledge, promise

3 to take as a spouse ⟨he *married* his girlfriend three years ago, and they've been happy ever since⟩

synonyms espouse, wed

related words affiance, betroth, commit, engage, pledge, promise, propose; remarry

near antonyms separate (from)

antonyms divorce

4 to take a spouse ⟨she had always believed she would never *marry*, but fate proved her wrong⟩

synonyms wed

related words couple, mate; pair off, remarry

phrases tie the knot

near antonyms divorce, separate

5 to come together to form a single unit — see UNITE 1

marsh *n* spongy land saturated or partially covered with water — see SWAMP

marshal *vb* **1** to assemble and make ready for action — see MOBILIZE

2 to point out the way for (someone) especially from a position in front — see LEAD 1

3 to put into a particular arrangement — see ORDER 1

marshaling *or* **marshalling** *n* an act of gathering forces together to renew or attempt an effort — see RALLY 1

marshland *n* spongy land saturated or partially covered with water — see SWAMP

martial *adj* **1** of, relating to, or suitable for war or a warrior ⟨the young recruit looked all grown up in his new *martial* uniform⟩

synonyms military, soldierly

related words aggressive, bellicose, combative, contentious, guerrilla, pugnacious, quarrelsome, scrappy, truculent, warlike; belligerent, militant, warring; antagonistic, argumentative, fierce, gladiatorial, hot-tempered; mercenary

near antonyms civil, civilian, nonmilitary; conciliatory, nonviolent, pacific, peaceable, peaceful; affable, amiable, amicable, benevolent, complaisant, cordial, easygoing, friendly, genial, good-natured, gracious, ingratiating, obliging

antonyms unsoldierly

2 of or relating to the armed services — see MILITARY 1

martyr *vb* to cause persistent suffering to — see AFFLICT

marvel *n* something extraordinary or surprising — see WONDER 1

marveling *or* **marvelling** *adj* filled with amazement or wonder — see OPENMOUTHED

marvelous *or* **marvellous** *adj* **1** causing wonder or astonishment ⟨the sheer immensity of the ancient ruin known as Stonehenge is *marvelous* to behold⟩

synonyms amazing, astonishing, astounding, awesome, awful, eye-opening, fabulous, miraculous, portentous, prodigious, staggering, stunning, stupendous, sublime, surprising, wonderful, wondrous

related words incomprehensible, inconceivable,

incredible, unbelievable, unimaginable, unthinkable; extraordinary, phenomenal, rare, sensational, spectacular; singular, uncommon, unique, unusual, unwonted; conspicuous, notable, noticeable, outstanding, remarkable; impressive, striking; animating, energizing, enlightening, enlivening, exciting, galvanizing, invigorating, stimulating; alluring, attracting, attractive, beguiling, bewitching, captivating, charming, enchanting, entertaining, enthralling, fascinating, interesting
near antonyms unimpressive, uninspiring, unremarkable; boring, dull, jading, monotonous, tedious, tiring, uninspired, uninteresting, wearisome, weary, wearying; common, customary, mundane, normal, ordinary, typical, unexceptional, usual; draining, enervating, exhausting, fatiguing, wearing; debilitating, enfeebling; demoralizing, discouraging, disheartening, dispiriting
2 excitingly or mysteriously unusual — see EXOTIC
3 of the very best kind — see EXCELLENT

mascot *n* something worn or kept to bring good luck or keep away evil — see CHARM 1

masculine *adj* considered characteristic of or appropriate for men ⟨some people consider chest hair to be a particularly appealing *masculine* trait⟩
synonyms male, manlike, manly, mannish, man-size (*or* man-sized), virile
related words boyish, tomboyish
near antonyms girlish, sissy; feminine, womanish, womanlike, womanly; emasculated, impotent, weakened
antonyms effeminate, unmanly, unmasculine

masculinity *n* the set of qualities considered appropriate for or characteristic of men — see VIRILITY

mash *vb* **1** to apply external pressure on so as to force out the juice or contents of — see PRESS 2
2 to cause to become a pulpy mass — see CRUSH 1

mask *n* **1** a cover or partial cover for the face used to disguise oneself ⟨he loved his gorilla *mask* so much that he even tried to sleep with it on⟩
synonyms vizard
related words camouflage, disguise; bill, cloak, domino, hood, veil, visor (*also* vizor)
2 something that covers or conceals like a piece of cloth — see CLOAK 1

mask *vb* **1** to change the dress or looks of so as to conceal true identity — see DISGUISE
2 to keep secret or shut off from view — see [1]HIDE 2

masquerade *n* a display of emotion or behavior that is insincere or intended to deceive ⟨although she was deeply bored, she maintained a *masquerade* of polite interest as her guest droned on⟩
synonyms act, airs, charade, facade (*also* façade), front, guise, pose, pretense (*or* pretence), put-on, semblance, show
related words appearance, color, gloss; camouflage, cloak, disguise; affectation, deceit, deception, double-dealing, duplicity, fraud, guile; betrayal, double cross, faithlessness, falseness, falsity, infidelity, perfidy, treachery, treason, unfaithfulness; excuse, pretext
near antonyms candor, frankness, openheartedness, sincerity

masquerade (as) *vb* to pretend to be (what one is not) in appearance or behavior — see IMPERSONATE 1

mass *n* **1 masses** *pl* the body of the community as contrasted with the elite ⟨the *masses* demanded the elimination of tax breaks for the rich⟩
synonyms commoners, herd, mob, people, plebeians, populace, rank and file
related words proletariat, rabble, riffraff, scum, trash; bourgeoisie, middle class; public
near antonyms aristocracy, gentry, nobility, upper class, upper crust
antonyms elite
2 a considerable amount — see LOT 2
3 a distinct and separate portion of matter — see BODY 2
4 the main or greater part of something as distinguished from its appendages — see BODY 1

massacre *n* the killing of a large number of people ⟨the infamous *massacre* of more than 200 Sioux at Wounded Knee, South Dakota⟩
synonyms butchery, carnage, slaughter
related words bloodshed, foul play, homicide, killing, manslaughter, murder, slaying; mortality; annihilation, decimation, demolishing, destruction, devastation, eradication, extermination; genocide; assassination, execution

massacre *vb* to kill on a large scale ⟨the country's rival ethnic groups began *massacring* one another⟩
synonyms butcher, mow (down), slaughter
related words assassinate, execute, murder, slay; annihilate, decimate, demolish, destroy, devastate, eradicate, exterminate, waste, wipe out

massive *adj* **1** having great weight — see HEAVY 1
2 unusually large — see HUGE

massively *adv* to a large extent or degree — see GREATLY 2

massiveness *n* **1** the quality or state of being very large — see IMMENSITY
2 the state or quality of being heavy — see WEIGHTINESS 1

mass-produced *adj* made beforehand in large numbers — see READY-MADE

master *adj* having or showing exceptional knowledge, experience, or skill in a field of endeavor — see PROFICIENT

master *n* **1** a person with a high level of knowledge or skill in a field — see EXPERT
2 one that defeats an enemy or opponent — see VICTOR 1
3 the person (as an employer or supervisor) who tells people and especially workers what to do — see BOSS

master *vb* **1** to achieve a victory over — see BEAT 2
2 to acquire complete knowledge, understanding, or skill in — see LEARN 1

masterful *adj* **1** accomplished with trained ability — see SKILLFUL 1
2 fond of ordering people around — see BOSSY
3 having a feeling of superiority that shows itself in an overbearing attitude — see ARROGANT
4 having or showing exceptional knowledge, experience, or skill in a field of endeavor — see PROFICIENT

masterfully *adv* in a skillful or expert manner — see WELL 3

masterfulness *n* **1** subtle or imaginative ability in inventing, devising, or executing something — see SKILL 1
2 an exaggerated sense of one's importance that shows itself in the making of excessive or unjustified claims — see ARROGANCE

masterly *adj* **1** accomplished with trained ability — see SKILLFUL 1
2 having or showing exceptional knowledge, experience, or skill in a field of endeavor — see PROFICIENT

mastermind *vb* to plan out usually with subtle skill or care — see ENGINEER

masterpiece *n* something (as a work of art) that is a great achievement and often its creator's greatest achievement ⟨Michelangelo's frescoes in the Sistine Chapel are often considered to be his *masterpieces*⟩
synonyms classic, magnum opus
related words pièce de résistance, showpiece; blockbuster, success; gem, jewel, prize, treasure
near antonyms debacle (*also* débâcle), disaster, failure, fiasco, fizzle, turkey

mastership *n* a highly developed skill in or knowledge of something — see COMMAND 2

mastery *n* **1** a highly developed skill in or knowledge of something — see COMMAND 2
2 the right or means to command or control others — see POWER 1

masticate *vb* to crush or grind with the teeth — see BITE (ON)

match *n* **1** a competitive encounter between individuals or groups carried on for amusement, exercise, or in pursuit of a prize — see GAME 1
2 a union representing a special kind of social and legal partnership between two people — see MARRIAGE 1
3 either of a pair matched in one or more qualities — see MATE 1
4 one that is equal to another in status, achievement, or value — see EQUAL
5 something or someone that strongly resembles another — see IMAGE 1

match *vb* **1** to be the exact counterpart of ⟨does this handbag's shade of blue *match* my navy blue pants?⟩ ⟨the rare blood type that exactly *matched* that of the transplant recipient⟩
synonyms correspond (to), equal, parallel
related words blend (with), coordinate (with), go (with), harmonize (with); complement, supplement; counterbalance, counterpoise; echo, mirror, repeat; amount (to), approach, near; measure (up), partake (of), rival, suggest
2 to give in marriage — see MARRY 2
3 to produce something equal to (as in quality or value) — see EQUAL 1

matching *adj* having qualities in common — see ALIKE

matchless *adj* having no equal or rival for excellence or desirability — see ONLY 1

mate *n* **1** either of a pair matched in one or more qualities ⟨have you seen the *mate* to this glove anywhere?⟩
synonyms companion, fellow, half, match, twin
related words coordinate; counterpart, equal, equivalent, like, parallel, peer, rival; carbon copy, double, duplicate, identical twin, ringer; analogue (*or* analog), similarity
near antonyms antithesis, converse, opposite, reverse
2 a person frequently seen in the company of another — see ASSOCIATE 1
3 *chiefly British* a person who helps a more skilled person — see HELPER
4 the person to whom another is married — see SPOUSE

mate *vb* to engage in sexual intercourse — see COPULATE

material *adj* **1** relating to or composed of matter ⟨there's no *material* evidence, such as a dead body, that a murder has been committed⟩
synonyms concrete, physical, substantial
related words bodily, carnal, corporal, corporeal, fleshly; appreciable, detectable, discernible, noticeable, observable, palpable, perceptible, sensible, tangible; objective, phenomenal; bulky, heavy, massive, solid, weighty
near antonyms bodiless, disembodied, incorporeal; ethereal, insubstantial, unsubstantial; impalpable, imperceptible, insensible, intangible, invisible, unnoticeable; airy, diaphanous, tenuous, thin, vaporous; metaphysical, spiritual
antonyms immaterial, nonmaterial, nonphysical
2 having great meaning or lasting effect — see IMPORTANT 1
3 having to do with life on earth especially as opposed to that in heaven — see EARTHLY
4 having to do with the matter at hand — see PERTINENT
5 of or relating to the human body — see PHYSICAL 1

material *n* **1** the basic elements from which something can be developed — see MAKING
2 *usually* **materials** *pl* items needed for the performance of a task or activity — see EQUIPMENT

materialist *n* a person who is chiefly interested in material comfort and is hostile or indifferent to art and culture — see PHILISTINE

materiality *n* **1** something that actually exists — see FACT 2
2 the fact or state of being pertinent — see PERTINENCE
3 the quality of being actual — see FACT 1

materialize *vb* **1** to come into existence — see BEGIN 2
2 to come into view — see APPEAR 1
3 to come to one's attention especially gradually or unexpectedly — see ARISE 2
4 to represent in visible form — see EMBODY 2

matériel *or* **materiel** *n* items needed for the performance of a task or activity — see EQUIPMENT

maternal *adj* of, relating to, or characteristic of a mother — see MOTHERLY

maternity *n* motherly character or qualities ⟨she had such *maternity* at such a young age that all her classmates went to her for comfort⟩
synonyms motherliness
related words nurturance; fertility, fruitfulness, productivity, richness

mathematical *adj* meeting the highest standard of accuracy — see PRECISE 1

mating *n* sexual union involving penetration of the vagina by the penis — see SEXUAL INTERCOURSE

matriarch *n* a dignified usually elderly woman of some rank or authority ⟨even though she was 87, the *matriarch* of the family knew everything that was going on⟩
synonyms dame, dowager, matron
related words grandam (*or* grandame); headmistress, mistress; ma, mama, mammy, mom, momma

matriculate *vb* to enter in a list or roll — see ENROLL 1

matrimonial *adj* of or relating to marriage — see MARITAL

matrimony *n* a union representing a special kind of

social and legal partnership between two people — see MARRIAGE 1

matron *n* a dignified usually elderly woman of some rank or authority — see MATRIARCH

matte *also* **mat** *or* **matt** *adj* lacking a surface luster or gloss ⟨I chose a paint with a *matte* finish so the walls wouldn't be too shiny⟩
synonyms dim, dull, dulled, flat, lusterless
related words tarnished, unpolished; cloudy, dingy, dirty, drab, mousy (*or* mousey), muddy; gray (*also* grey), leaden, pale; dark, darkened, dimmed, dusky, gloomy, murky, obscure, obscured, somber (*or* sombre)
near antonyms buffed, burnished, glazed, lacquered, polished, shellacked, varnished; satin, satiny; silken, silky; slick, slippery; gleaming, glimmering, glinting, glistening, glittering, scintillating, shimmering, shining, sparkling, twinkling; beaming, bedazzling, bright, brightened, brilliant, dazzling, effulgent, lucent, lucid, luminous, radiant, shining
antonyms glossy, lustrous, shiny, sleek

matter *n* **1** a major object of interest or concern (as in a discussion or artistic composition) ⟨that is not relevant to the *matter* under discussion⟩
synonyms content, motif, motive, question, subject, theme, topic
related words idea, point, purpose; issue, problem; body, bulk, burden, core, crux, fundamental, generality, gist, heart, kernel, keynote, main, marrow, mass, nub, nucleus, pith, purport, quick, staple, substance, sum; basis; bottom, essential, essentiality; affair, argument, debate
near antonyms aside, digression, interjection, parenthesis, tangent
2 something to be dealt with ⟨we must take care of this *matter* before it becomes a real problem⟩
synonyms affair, business, thing
related words problem; crisis, crossroad, emergency, exigency, juncture, strait, zero hour; concern, trouble, worry; care, lookout, responsibility; deadlock, impasse, stalemate; corner, fix, hole, hot water, pinch, predicament, scrape, spot
3 communications or parcels sent or carried through the postal system — see MAIL
4 something that requires thought and skill for resolution — see PROBLEM 1

matter *vb* to be of importance ⟨she believes that doing well in school really does *matter*⟩
synonyms count, import, mean, signify, weigh
related words affect, influence, sway; add up (to), amount (to)
phrases carry weight, cut ice

matter–of–fact *adj* **1** restricted to or based on fact — see FACTUAL 1
2 willing to see things as they really are and deal with them sensibly — see REALISTIC 1

maturation *n* the process of becoming mature ⟨a flower's *maturation* from bud to full bloom can take weeks⟩
synonyms development, growth, maturing, ripening
related words blossoming, flourishing, flowering; mellowing, softening
near antonyms decadence, decline, declining, deterioration; fading, shriveling, waning, wilting, withering; death, dying, expiring, perishing; regression, retrogression, reversion

mature *adj* **1** fully grown or developed ⟨I like pears when they're still hard, before they're *mature*⟩
synonyms adult, full-blown, full-fledged, full-grown, matured, ripe, ripened
related words aged, aging (*or* ageing), old; golden, mellow
near antonyms blooming, blossoming, burgeoning, flourishing, flowering; undeveloped, unfinished, unformed
antonyms green, immature, juvenile, unripened, young, youthful
2 having reached the date at which payment is required — see DUE 1

mature *vb* to become mature ⟨a young figure skater whose talent is still *maturing*⟩
synonyms age, develop, grow, grow up, progress, ripen
related words mellow, soften; bloom, blossom, burgeon, flourish, flower; open, unfold; advance, evolve
near antonyms decline, deteriorate; dry, fade, shrivel, wane, wilt, wither; regress, retrogress, revert; backslide, lapse, return

matured *adj* fully grown or developed — see MATURE 1

maturing *n* the process of becoming mature — see MATURATION

maturity *n* the state of being fully grown or developed ⟨people are legally considered to have reached *maturity* at eighteen years old in the United States⟩
synonyms adulthood, majority
related words manhood, womanhood; bloom, flush, heyday, prime; middle age, seniority

maudlin *adj* appealing to the emotions in an obvious and tiresome way — see CORNY

maul *vb* **1** to abuse physically — see MANHANDLE 1
2 to strike repeatedly — see BEAT 1

maunder *vb* **1** to move about from place to place aimlessly — see WANDER
2 to talk at length without sticking to a topic or getting to a point — see RAMBLE 1

maundering *adj* passing from one topic to another — see DISCURSIVE

maverick *n* a person who does not conform to generally accepted standards or customs — see NONCONFORMIST 1

mawkish *adj* appealing to the emotions in an obvious and tiresome way — see CORNY

mawkishness *n* the state or quality of having an excess of tender feelings (as of love, nostalgia, or compassion) — see SENTIMENTALITY

maxim *n* **1** an idea or statement about all of the members of a group or all the instances of a situation — see GENERALIZATION
2 an often stated observation regarding something from common experience — see SAYING

maximum *adj* **1** of the greatest or highest degree or quantity — see ULTIMATE 1
2 of the highest degree — see FULL 2

maximum *n* the greatest amount, number, or part — see MOST

maybe *adv* it is possible — see PERHAPS

mayhap *adv* it is possible — see PERHAPS

maze *n* a confusing and complicated arrangement of passages ⟨the mansion had a beautifully landscaped *maze* constructed of tall cypresses⟩
synonyms labyrinth
related words meander; jungle, quagmire; knot, snarl, tangle, web; entanglement, entrapment, snare, trap

meager *or* **meagre** *adj* less plentiful than what is

normal, necessary, or desirable ‹ever since he started the diet, his dinners have been more *meager* than he would like›
synonyms hand-to-mouth, light, niggardly, poor, scant, scanty, scarce, skimpy, slender, slim, spare, sparse, stingy
related words deficient, inadequate, insufficient, lacking, wanting; bare, mere, minimum; slight, small; barren, infertile, sterile, unfruitful, unproductive
near antonyms adequate, enough, sufficient; fat, fecund, fertile, fruitful, prolific, rich; lavish, luxuriant; blooming, bursting, flourishing, swarming, teeming, thriving
antonyms abundant, ample, bountiful, copious, generous, liberal, plenteous, plentiful

meal *n* food eaten or prepared for eating at one time ‹all she wants to do is sit quietly after the large Thanksgiving *meal*›
synonyms chow, feed, mess, repast, table
related words board; breakfast, buffet, dinner, lunch, luncheon, refreshments, smorgasbord, snack, supper, tea; bite, gulp, morsel, serving, taste; banquet, feast, spread; bake, barbecue, clambake, cookout, fry, luau, picnic, potluck, roast

mealy *adj* not being or expressing what one appears to be or express — see INSINCERE

mealymouthed *adj* not being or expressing what one appears to be or express — see INSINCERE

mean *adj* **1** belonging to the class of people of low social or economic rank — see IGNOBLE 1
2 giving or sharing as little as possible — see STINGY 1
3 having or showing a desire to cause someone pain or suffering for the sheer enjoyment of it — see HATEFUL
4 not following or in accordance with standards of honor and decency — see IGNOBLE 2
5 of little or less value or merit — see INFERIOR 2
6 of the very best kind — see EXCELLENT
7 showing signs of advanced wear and tear and neglect — see SHABBY 1

mean *n* **1** a middle point between extremes ‹that candidate's moderate views were seen as the *mean* that voters were looking for›
synonyms golden mean, medium, middle, midpoint
related words arithmetic mean, average; median, norm, par, standard
near antonyms maximum, minimum
2 means *pl* an action planned or taken to achieve a desired result — see MEASURE 1
3 means *pl* something used to achieve an end — see AGENT 1
4 means *pl* the total of one's money and property — see WEALTH 1

mean *vb* **1** to communicate or convey (as an idea) to the mind ‹the national anthem *means* various things to various people›
synonyms denote, express, import, signify, spell
related words connote, imply, suggest; add up (to), amount (to); hint, insinuate, intimate; embody, epitomize, personify, represent, symbolize; advert, allude (to), mention, refer (to); indicate, point (to), signal; announce, declare; elucidate, explain
2 to be of importance — see MATTER
3 to have in mind as a purpose or goal — see INTEND

meander *vb* to move about from place to place aimlessly — see WANDER

meaning *adj* clearly conveying a special meaning (as one's mood) — see EXPRESSIVE

meaning *n* **1** the idea that is conveyed or intended to be conveyed to the mind by language, symbol, or action ‹the unmistakable *meaning* of the skier's upraised arms as he finished his spectacular run›
synonyms denotation, drift, import, intent, purport, sense, significance, signification
related words connotation; hint, implication, intimation, suggestion; message, tenor, theme; bottom, essence, essentiality, nature, soul, stuff; acceptance, definition; burden, crux, gist; core, heart, kernel, marrow, nub, nucleus, pith, point, quick; matter, motif, motive, subject, topic
2 something that one hopes or intends to accomplish — see GOAL

meaningful *adj* **1** clearly conveying a special meaning (as one's mood) — see EXPRESSIVE
2 having great meaning or lasting effect — see IMPORTANT 1

meaningless *adj* having no meaning ‹this is an utterly *meaningless* bit of nonsense›
synonyms empty, inane, pointless, senseless
related words insignificant, trivial, unimportant; absurd, asinine, balmy, brainless, crazy, daffy, daft, dotty, fatuous, foolish, half-witted, harebrained, insane, jerky, kooky, loony (*also* looney), lunatic, mad, mindless, nonsensical, nutty, preposterous, sappy, silly, unintelligent, unwise, wacky, weak-minded, witless, zany; irrational, unreasonable; aimless, haphazard, purposeless
near antonyms eloquent, expressive, pregnant, revealing, suggestive, telling; logical, rational, reasonable, valid
antonyms meaningful

meanly *adv* in a mean or spiteful manner — see NASTILY

meanness *n* the desire to cause pain for the satisfaction of doing harm — see MALICE

measly *adj* so small or unimportant as to warrant little or no attention — see NEGLIGIBLE 1

measure *n* **1** an action planned or taken to achieve a desired result ‹such new security *measures* as metal detectors at all the entrances›
synonyms expedient, means, move, shift, step
related words act, deed, doing, feat, thing; procedure, proceeding, process; accomplishment, achievement, exploit; activity, affair, business, dealing, enterprise, event; attempt, endeavor, essay, initiative, operation, undertaking; effort, exertion, labor, pains, trouble, work; project, proposal, proposition; makeshift, resort, resource, stopgap
2 a given or particular mass or aggregate of matter — see AMOUNT
3 something set up as an example against which others of the same type are compared — see STANDARD 1
4 the recurrent pattern formed by a series of sounds having a regular rise and fall in intensity — see RHYTHM
5 the total amount of measurable space or surface occupied by something — see [1]SIZE

measure *vb* to find out the size, extent, or amount of ‹for this experiment, you need to carefully *measure* all the chemicals before you mix them together›

synonyms gauge (*also* gage), scale, span
related words weigh; calibrate; lay off, mark (off); calculate, compute, figure, reckon, work out; conjecture, estimate, guess, judge, suppose; add up, sum, tally, total; ascertain, discover, dope (out), figure out, find out

measured *adj* **1** decided on as a result of careful thought — see DELIBERATE 1
2 having distinct or certain limits — see LIMITED 1
3 marked by or occurring with a noticeable regularity in the rise and fall of sound — see RHYTHMIC

measureless *adj* being or seeming to be without limits — see INFINITE

measurement *n* the total amount of measurable space or surface occupied by something — see [1]SIZE

measure up (to) *vb* to come near or nearer to in character or quality — see APPROXIMATE

meat *n* **1** animal and especially mammal tissue used as food ⟨we need to go shopping; there's only enough *meat* in the freezer for one more dinner⟩
synonyms flesh
related words game, poultry, variety meat
2 substances intended to be eaten — see FOOD

mecca *n* a thing or place that is of greatest importance to an activity or interest — see CENTER 1

mechanical *adj* **1** done instantly and without conscious thought or decision — see AUTOMATIC 1
2 lacking in natural or spontaneous quality — see ARTIFICIAL 1

medal *n* a piece of metal given in honor of a special event, a person, or an achievement ⟨the display case held an impressive array of military *medals* from World War II⟩
synonyms medallion, order
related words decoration, honor; crown, insignia, laurel, ribbon, title; badge, button, chevron, cockade, color, ensign, rosette; distinction; award, prize, trophy; citation, commendation

medallion *n* a piece of metal given in honor of a special event, a person, or an achievement — see MEDAL

meddle *vb* to interest oneself in what is not one's concern — see INTERFERE

meddler *n* a person who meddles in the affairs of others — see BUSYBODY

meddlesome *adj* thrusting oneself where one is not welcome or invited — see INTRUSIVE

meddling *adj* thrusting oneself where one is not welcome or invited — see INTRUSIVE

medial *adj* occupying a position equally distant from the ends or extremes — see MIDDLE 1

median *adj* **1** being about midway between extremes of amount or size — see MIDDLE 2
2 occupying a position equally distant from the ends or extremes — see MIDDLE 1

mediate *vb* to act as a go-between for opposing sides — see INTERVENE

mediator *n* one who works with opposing sides in order to bring about an agreement ⟨if you two cannot resolve this argument on your own, we'll have to bring in a *mediator*⟩
synonyms arbiter, arbitrator, conciliator, go-between, intercessor, intermediary, interposer, middleman, peacemaker
related words moderator; bargainer, negotiator; appeaser, pacifier, reconciler; broker; agent, attorney, deputy, factor, procurator, proxy; liaison; ambassador, emissary, envoy, messenger; delegate, representative; busybody, interferer, meddler; judge, referee, umpire; adviser (*or* advisor), counselor

medic *n* a person specially trained in healing human medical disorders — see DOCTOR

medication *n* a substance or preparation used to treat disease — see MEDICINE

medicine *n* a substance or preparation used to treat disease ⟨if you don't take all the doses of your *medicine*, you might get sick again⟩
synonyms cure, drug, medication, pharmaceutical, physic, remedy, specific
related words botanical, patent medicine, prescription; cordial, tonic; miracle drug, wonder drug; capsule, pill, tablet; injection, shot; liniment, lotion, ointment, potion, poultice, salve; syrup, tincture; antibiotic, antiseptic, serum

mediocre *adj* **1** of average to below average quality ⟨your grades are *mediocre* and barely acceptable⟩
synonyms common, fair, indifferent, medium, middling, ordinary, passable, run-of-the-mill, second-rate, so-so
related words acceptable, adequate, all right, alright, decent, OK (*or* okay), reasonable, satisfactory, sufficient, sufficing, tolerable; moderate, modest; presentable, respectable; minimal, unexceptional; fine, good, nice
near antonyms distinguished, excellent, exceptional, exquisite, first-class, first-rate, matchless, maximum, optimal, optimum, outstanding, peerless, preeminent, special, superior, supreme, topnotch; unmatched, unparalleled, unsurpassed; deficient, inadequate, insufficient, lacking, unacceptable, unsatisfactory, wanting
2 of low quality — see CHEAP 2

meditate *vb* **1** to give serious and careful thought to — see PONDER
2 to have in mind as a purpose or goal — see INTEND

meditation *n* long or deep thinking about spiritual matters — see CONTEMPLATION

meditative *adj* given to or marked by long, quiet thinking — see CONTEMPLATIVE

medium *adj* **1** being about midway between extremes of amount or size — see MIDDLE 2
2 occupying a position equally distant from the ends or extremes — see MIDDLE 1
3 of average to below average quality — see MEDIOCRE 1

medium *n* **1** a middle point between extremes — see MEAN 1
2 something used to achieve an end — see AGENT 1
3 the circumstances, conditions, or objects by which one is surrounded — see ENVIRONMENT

medley *n* an unorganized collection or mixture of various things — see MISCELLANY 1

meek *adj* not having or showing any feelings of superiority, self-assertiveness, or showiness — see HUMBLE 1

meekly *adv* in manner showing no signs of pride or self-assertion — see LOWLY

meekness *n* the absence of any feelings of being better than others — see HUMILITY

meet *adj* meeting the requirements of a purpose or situation — see FIT 1

meet *n* a competitive encounter between individuals or groups carried on for amusement, exercise, or in pursuit of a prize — see GAME 1

meet *vb* **1** to come upon face-to-face or as if face-to-face ⟨we never once *met* another car on that lonely country road⟩
synonyms chance (upon), encounter, happen (upon), stumble (upon)
related words accost, confront; face, greet, salute; collide (with), crash (into); crisscross, cross, pass; hit (upon), light (upon), tumble (to)
phrases bump into
near antonyms avoid, elude, escape, evade, shun
2 to come together into one body or place — see ASSEMBLE 1
3 to come upon unexpectedly or by chance — see HAPPEN (ON *OR* UPON)
4 to do what is required by the terms of — see FULFILL 1
5 to enter into contest or conflict with — see ENGAGE 2
6 to produce something equal to (as in quality or value) — see EQUAL 1
7 to put up with (something painful or difficult) — see BEAR 2

meeting *n* **1** a coming together of a number of persons for a specified purpose ⟨there will be another committee *meeting* next week to discuss the parish fair⟩
synonyms assembly, conference, congress, convention, convocation, council, gathering, get-together, huddle, powwow, roundtable, seminar
related words caucus, conclave, synod; demonstration, rally; conversation, dialogue (*also* dialog), discourse, discussion, palaver, talk; negotiation, parley; audience, interview, session
2 a body of people come together in one place — see GATHERING 1
3 the coming together of two or more things to the same point — see CONVERGENCE

meetly *adv* in a manner suitable for the occasion or purpose — see PROPERLY

megahit *n* a person or thing that is successful — see HIT 1

megalopolis *n* a thickly settled, highly populated area — see CITY

melancholy *adj* **1** causing unhappiness — see SAD 2
2 feeling unhappiness — see SAD 1
3 given to or marked by long, quiet thinking — see CONTEMPLATIVE

melancholy *n* a state or spell of low spirits — see SADNESS

mélange *n* an unorganized collection or mixture of various things — see MISCELLANY 1

melee *n* a rough and often noisy fight usually involving several people — see BRAWL 1

meliorate *vb* to make better — see IMPROVE

mellifluous *adj* having a pleasantly flowing quality suggestive of music — see LYRIC 1

mellow *adj* **1** having a pleasantly flowing quality suggestive of music — see LYRIC 1
2 not harsh or stern especially in manner, nature, or effect — see GENTLE 1

melodic *adj* having a pleasantly flowing quality suggestive of music — see LYRIC 1

melodious *adj* **1** having a pleasantly flowing quality suggestive of music — see LYRIC 1
2 having a pleasing mixture of notes — see HARMONIOUS 1

melodramatic *adj* **1** given to or marked by attention-getting behavior suggestive of stage acting — see THEATRICAL 1
2 having the general quality or effect of a stage performance — see DRAMATIC 1

melody *n* a rhythmic series of musical tones arranged to give a pleasing effect ⟨this week, we'll learn to play a more complicated *melody* on the saxophone⟩
synonyms air, lay, song, strain, tune, warble
related words descant; cadence, measure, meter, rhythm; ballad, ditty, hymn, lyric, madrigal

melt *vb* **1** to cease to be visible — see DISAPPEAR
2 to go from a solid to a liquid state — see LIQUEFY

member *n* **1** one of the parts that make up a whole — see ELEMENT 1
2 one of the pieces from which something is designed to be assembled — see PART 1

memento *n* something that serves to keep alive the memory of a person or event — see MEMORIAL

memo *n* **1** a message on paper from one person or group to another — see LETTER
2 a usually brief written reminder — see NOTE 1
3 a written communication giving information or directions — see MEMORANDUM 1

memoir *n* a history of a person's life — see BIOGRAPHY

memorandum *n* **1** a written communication giving information or directions ⟨I'm waiting for the *memorandum* that will explain the new vacation policy⟩
synonyms directive, memo, notice
related words announcement, declaration, proclamation, pronouncement; charge, command, dictate; directions, instructions, orders, word; encyclical, epistle, letter, mail, message, missive, note
2 a message on paper from one person or group to another — see LETTER
3 a usually brief written reminder — see NOTE 1

memorial *adj* serving to preserve the memory of a person, thing, or an event — see COMMEMORATIVE

memorial *n* something that serves to keep alive the memory of a person or event ⟨the Vietnam War *Memorial* is a starkly beautiful testimonial to the bravery of the soldiers who served in Vietnam⟩
synonyms commemorative, keepsake, memento, monument, remembrance, reminder, souvenir, token
related words memorabilia; relic, vestige; cairn, landmark, marker; testimonial, tribute

memorialize *vb* to be a memorial of — see COMMEMORATE 1

memorializing *adj* serving to preserve the memory of a person, thing, or an event — see COMMEMORATIVE

memorize *vb* to commit to memory ⟨everyone has to *memorize* a poem for next week⟩
synonyms con, learn, study
related words recall, recollect, relive, remember, reminisce, retain; accept, apprehend, comprehend, get, grasp, understand; absorb, digest
near antonyms forget; ignore, neglect, overlook
antonyms unlearn

memory *n* **1** the power or process of recalling what has been previously learned or experienced ⟨a photographic *memory* makes taking tests entirely too easy⟩
synonyms mind, recollection, remembrance, reminiscence
related words contemplation, musing, reflection,

retrospection, thinking; awareness, cognizance, consciousness; apprehension, comprehension, understanding
near antonyms forgetfulness
2 a particular act or instance of recalling or the thing remembered ⟨I have only the vaguest *memory* of the family vacation we took the year I turned three⟩
synonyms recall, recollection, remembrance, reminiscence
related words flashback; memento, memorial, reminder, souvenir, token; association
3 the body of knowledge that has been retained in one's mind or the use of it — see HEART 2

menace *n* something that may cause injury or harm — see DANGER 2

menace *vb* **1** to place in danger — see ENDANGER
2 to remain poised to inflict harm, danger, or distress on — see THREATEN

menacing *adj* **1** being or showing a sign of evil or calamity to come — see OMINOUS
2 involving potential loss or injury — see DANGEROUS

ménage *n* those who live as a family in one house — see HOUSEHOLD

mend *vb* **1** to put into good shape or working order again ⟨that shirt will be as good as new when I'm finished *mending* it⟩
synonyms doctor, fix, patch, recondition, renovate, repair, revamp
related words overhaul, rebuild, reconstruct, refurbish; aid, cure, heal, help; condition, prepare, ready; care (for), maintain, service; rejuvenate, renew, restore; adjust, correct, modify, rectify, redress, reform, right; ameliorate, better, improve, meliorate
near antonyms break, damage, harm, hurt, impair, injure, mar, ruin, spoil, wreck; cripple, disable
2 to become healthy and strong again after illness or weakness — see CONVALESCE
3 to restore to a healthy condition — see HEAL 1

mendacious *adj* telling or containing lies — see DISHONEST 1

mendacity *n* **1** a statement known by its maker to be untrue and made in order to deceive — see LIE
2 the tendency to tell lies — see DISHONESTY 1

mendicant *n* a person who lives by public begging — see BEGGAR

mending *n* the process or period of gradually regaining one's health and strength — see CONVALESCENCE

menial *n* a person hired to perform household or personal services — see SERVANT

menstruation *n* an occurrence of menstruating — see PERIOD 1

mental *adj* **1** of or relating to the mind ⟨a funny *mental* image made him laugh out loud⟩
synonyms cerebral, inner, intellectual, psychological (*also* psychologic)
related words cognitive, conscious; psychic (*also* psychical), telepathic; spiritual; alert, brainy, bright, clever, intelligent, quick-witted, rational, reasoning, smart, thinking
near antonyms bodily, carnal, corporal, corporeal, fleshly, physical, somatic
2 having or showing a very abnormal or sick state of mind — see INSANE 1

mention *vb* **1** to make reference to or speak about briefly but specifically ⟨you only *mentioned* in passing some of your accomplishments⟩
synonyms advert (to), cite, instance, name, note, notice, quote, refer (to), specify, touch (on *or* upon)
related words allude (to), hint (at), imply, infer, intimate, suggest; point (out), signal, signify; denominate, designate; indicate; bring up, broach, interject, interpolate, interpose, introduce; infiltrate, insinuate, worm; announce, declare, pronounce; elucidate, explain
near antonyms disregard, ignore, neglect, overlook, pass over, slight
2 to give as an example — see QUOTE 1

mentor *vb* to give advice and instruction to (someone) regarding the course or process to be followed — see GUIDE 1

menu *n* **1** a list of foods served at or available for a meal ⟨the *menu* at the fancy restaurant listed many dishes that I had never heard of⟩
synonyms bill of fare
related words chow, cuisine, fare, grub
2 a record of a series of items (as names or titles) usually arranged according to some system — see [1]LIST

mercenary *adj* having or marked by an eager and often selfish desire especially for material possessions — see GREEDY 1

merchandise *n* products that are bought and sold in business ⟨we stock only the finest-quality *merchandise* in this store⟩
synonyms commodities, goods, wares
related words line; export, import; inventory, staples, stock, stuff

merchandise *vb* to offer for sale to the public — see MARKET

merchandiser *n* **1** a buyer and seller of goods for profit — see MERCHANT
2 the person in a business deal who hands over an item in exchange for money — see VENDOR

merchant *n* a buyer and seller of goods for profit ⟨free trade agreements that are favored by *merchants* on both sides of the border⟩
synonyms dealer, merchandiser, trader, tradesman, trafficker
related words businessman; buyer, purchaser; hawker, peddler (*also* pedlar); retailer, seller, shopkeeper, storekeeper, vendor (*also* vender); jobber, middleman, wholesaler; distributor, provider, supplier

mercifulness *n* kind, gentle, or compassionate treatment especially towards someone who is undeserving of it — see MERCY 1

merciless *adj* having or showing a lack of sympathy or tender feelings — see HARD 1

mercurial *adj* likely to change frequently, suddenly, or unexpectedly — see FICKLE 1

mercy *n* **1** kind, gentle, or compassionate treatment especially towards someone who is undeserving of it ⟨always show your enemies *mercy*, because it makes you a better person⟩
synonyms charity, clemency, lenience, leniency, lenity, mercifulness, quarter
related words humanitarianism, philanthropy; empathy, pity, sympathy, understanding; commiseration, favor, grace; benevolence, care, compassion, gentleness, goodness, goodwill, kindliness, kindness, meekness, mildness, niceness, softness, tenderness; altruism, generosity, magnanimity, nobility; affection, devotion, love, worship
near antonyms reprisal, retaliation, retribution, revenge, vengeance; venom, vindictiveness, viru-

lence, vitriol; brutality, cruelty, savagery, violence; castigation, chastisement, punishment, scolding; abhorrence, abomination, execration, hate, hatred, loathing; cattiness, malevolence, malice, malignity, meanness, spite, spitefulness, spleen; animosity, antagonism, antipathy, bitterness, enmity, grudge, hostility, jealousy, pique, resentment; bile, jaundice, rancor; hatefulness, invidiousness; coarseness, grimness, hardness, harshness, roughness
2 an act of kind assistance — see FAVOR 1
3 the capacity for feeling for another's unhappiness or misfortune — see HEART 1

mere *n, chiefly British* a small often deep body of water — see [1]POOL

mere *adj* being this and no more ⟨the *mere* idea of your traveling alone to Europe is ridiculous⟩
synonyms bare, very
related words absolute, sheer, simple, stark, utter; alone, only, singular, sole, solitary, solo, unique

merely *adv* nothing more than — see JUST 3

merge *vb* to turn into a single mass that is more or less the same throughout — see BLEND 1

merging *n* the act or an instance of joining two or more things into one — see UNION 1

meridian *n* the highest part or point — see HEIGHT 1

merit *n* **1** a quality that gives something special worth — see EXCELLENCE 2
2 the relative usefulness or importance of something as judged by specific qualities — see WORTH 1

merit *vb* to be or make worthy of (as a reward or punishment) — see EARN 2

merited *adj* being what is called for by accepted standards of right and wrong — see JUST 1

meritorious *adj* **1** deserving of high regard or great approval — see ADMIRABLE
2 having sufficient worth or merit to receive one's honor, esteem, or reward — see WORTHY

merrily *adv* in a cheerful or happy manner — see GAILY 1

merriment *n* **1** a mood characterized by high spirits and amusement and often accompanied by laughter — see MIRTH
2 joyful or festive activity — see MERRYMAKING

merriness *n* a mood characterized by high spirits and amusement and often accompanied by laughter — see MIRTH

merry *adj* indicative of or marked by high spirits or good humor ⟨Santa Claus has *merry*, twinkling blue eyes⟩
synonyms blithesome, festive, gay, gleeful, jocose, jocund, jolly, jovial, laughing, mirthful, sunny
related words amused, beaming, chuckling, giggling, smiling; bright, buoyant, carefree, cheerful, cheery, chipper, lighthearted, lightsome, upbeat; animated, jaunty, lively, perky, sprightly, vivacious; blessed, blissful, delighted, ecstatic, elated, enraptured, entranced, euphoric, exhilarated, exuberant, exultant, gladsome, happy, high, joyful, joyous, jubilant, overjoyed, radiant, rapturous, ravished, thrilled; amusing, facetious, flippant, funny, hilarious, jesting, joking, joshing, playful, witty; careless, cavalier, devil-may-care, easygoing, happy-go-lucky, insouciant, unconcerned; hopeful, optimistic, rosy, sanguine
near antonyms abject, aggrieved, anguished, blue, brokenhearted, dejected, depressed, despondent, disconsolate, disheartened, dispirited, downcast, downhearted, forlorn, heartbroken, heartsick, melancholy, sad, sorrowful, unhappy; crying, groaning, moaning, sobbing, wailing; discontented, disgruntled, moody; doleful, dolorous, joyless, lachrymose, mournful, plaintive, sorry, woeful; black, dark, desolate, gloomy, glum, gray (*also* grey); miserable, woebegone, wretched; dull, lethargic, listless, sluggish, torpid

merrymaker *n* one who engages in merrymaking especially in honor of a special occasion — see CELEBRANT

merrymaking *n* joyful or festive activity ⟨Christmas Eve is always an occasion of much *merrymaking* at our home⟩
synonyms conviviality, festivity, gaiety (*also* gayety), jollification, jollity, merriment, reveling, revelry
related words carousal, carouse; delight, diversion, entertainment, fun, pleasure, recreation, riot; glee, gleefulness, joviality, merriness, mirth, mirthfulness; carnival, celebration, party, revel; frolicking, gamboling, rollicking, romping; enjoyment, happiness, joy; binge, fling, frolic, gambol, lark, rollick, romp, spree; buffoonery, clownishness, flippancy, frivolity, funning, jesting, jocularity, joking, joshing, levity, lightheartedness, playfulness; zaniness
near antonyms blackness, darkness, gloominess, glumness, grief, grieving, heartbreak, miserableness, misery, mournfulness, mourning, wretchedness; anguish, dejection, depression, despondence, forlornness, melancholy, sorrow, unhappiness

mesa *n* a broad flat area of elevated land — see PLATEAU

mesh *n* a fabric made of strands loosely twisted, knotted, or woven together at regular intervals — see [1]NET 1

mesh *vb* to catch or hold as if in a net — see ENTANGLE 2

mesmerism *n* the art or act of inducing in a person a sleep-like state during which he or she readily follows suggestions — see HYPNOSIS

mesmerize *vb* to hold the attention of as if by a spell — see ENTHRALL 1

mess *n* **1** a state in which everything is out of order — see CHAOS
2 food eaten or prepared for eating at one time — see MEAL
3 something unpleasant to look at — see EYESORE

mess *vb* to interest oneself in what is not one's concern — see INTERFERE

mess (around) *vb* to spend time in aimless activity — see FIDDLE (AROUND)

mess (up) *vb* **1** to make or do (something) in a clumsy or unskillful way — see BOTCH
2 to undo the proper order or arrangement of — see DISORDER

mess (with) *vb* to handle thoughtlessly, ignorantly, or mischievously — see TAMPER

message *n* a piece of conveyed information — see COMMUNICATION

messed *adj* lacking in order, neatness, and often cleanliness — see MESSY

messenger *n* one that carries a message or does an errand ⟨the *messenger* comes by twice a day to pick up packages⟩
synonyms courier, go-between, page, runner

related words forerunner, harbinger, herald; agent, ambassador, delegate, deputy, emissary, envoy, representative; bearer, carrier, deliveryman, letter carrier, mail carrier, mailman

messy *adj* lacking in order, neatness, and often cleanliness ⟨you cannot go out to play until you clean up this *messy* room and put away all your toys⟩
synonyms chaotic, cluttered, confused, disarranged, disarrayed, disheveled (*or* dishevelled), disordered, disorderly, higgledy-piggledy, hugger-mugger, jumbled, littered, messed, muddled, mussed, mussy, pell-mell, rumpled, sloppy, topsy-turvy, tousled, tumbled, unkempt, untidy, upside-down
related words besmirched, blackened, dingy, dirty, filthy, foul, grimy, grubby, grungy, mucky, nasty, soiled, spotted, squalid, stained, sullied, unclean, uncleanly; dowdy, frowsy (*or* frowzy), slatternly, slovenly, uncombed; wrinkled; contaminated, defiled, polluted, tainted; knotted, snarled, tangled; seedy, shabby, sleazy, sordid; neglected, neglectful, negligent
phrases at sixes and sevens
near antonyms clean, cleaned, cleanly, hygienic, immaculate, sparkling, spick-and-span (*or* spic-and-span), spotless, stainless, unsoiled, unsullied; methodical, systematic; careful, fastidious, fussy, meticulous; combed, groomed, manicured; taintless, undefiled, unpolluted, untainted, wholesome
antonyms neat, ordered, orderly, organized, shipshape, snug, tidied, tidy, trim

metamorphose *vb* to change in form, appearance, or use — see CONVERT 2

metamorphosis *n* a change in form, appearance, or use — see CONVERSION

metaphor *n* an elaborate or fanciful way of expressing something — see CONCEIT 1

metaphorical *adj* expressing one thing in terms normally used for another — see FIGURATIVE

metaphysical *adj* of, relating to, or being part of a reality beyond the observable physical universe — see SUPERNATURAL 1

mete (out) *vb* to give out (something) in appropriate amounts or to appropriate individuals — see ADMINISTER 1

meter *n* the recurrent pattern formed by a series of sounds having a regular rise and fall in intensity — see RHYTHM

method *n* the means or procedure for doing something ⟨all experiments must be conducted using the proper scientific *method*⟩
synonyms approach, fashion, form, manner, strategy, style, system, tack, tactics, technique, way
related words mode; blueprint, design, game, ground plan, intrigue, layout, line, plan, plot, program, route, scheme; expedient, move, shift, step; practice (*also* practise), process, routine; project, proposal, proposition; policy

methodical *adj* following a set method, arrangement, or pattern ⟨a *methodical* study plan that included lists of points to memorize⟩
synonyms orderly, organized, regular, systematic, systematized
related words regularized, standardized; accurate, correct, exact, precise; detailed, specific; businesslike
near antonyms chaotic, disordered, disorderly, unordered
antonyms disorganized, haphazard, irregular, unsystematic

meticulous *adj* taking great care and effort — see PAINSTAKING

metric *adj* marked by or occurring with a noticeable regularity in the rise and fall of sound — see RHYTHMIC

metrical *adj* marked by or occurring with a noticeable regularity in the rise and fall of sound — see RHYTHMIC

metropolis *n* a thickly settled, highly populated area — see CITY

metropolitan *n* a person with the outlook, experience, and manners thought to be typical of big city dwellers — see COSMOPOLITAN

mettlesome *adj* marked by a lively display of strong feeling — see SPIRITED 1

mewl *vb* to utter feeble plaintive cries — see WHIMPER

microminiature *adj* very small in size — see TINY

microscopic *also* **microscopical** *adj* very small in size — see TINY

mid *adj* occupying a position equally distant from the ends or extremes — see MIDDLE 1

mid *prep* in or into the middle of — see AMONG

midday *n* the middle of the day — see NOON

middle *adj* **1** occupying a position equally distant from the ends or extremes ⟨you must mark the exact *middle* point of each of these lines in order to solve the problem⟩
synonyms halfway, intermediary, intermediate, medial, median, medium, mid, middlemost, midmost, midway
related words equidistant; central, inmost, inner, innermost, nearest
near antonyms outer, peripheral
antonyms extreme, farthest, farthermost, furthermost, furthest, outermost, outmost, remotest, utmost
2 being about midway between extremes of amount or size ⟨a house that is *middle* -sized for that neighborhood⟩ ⟨a man of *middle* height⟩
synonyms average, intermediate, median, medium, moderate, modest
related words reasonable; common, commonplace, conventional, normal, popular, regular, routine, standard, typical, usual; passable, tolerable
near antonyms excessive, extreme; rare, strange, uncommon, unusual; distinctive, idiosyncratic, special, unique; individual, peculiar, private

middle *n* **1** a middle point between extremes — see MEAN 1
2 an area or point that is an equal distance from all points along an edge or outer surface — see CENTER 2
3 the middle region of the human body — see MIDRIFF
4 the most intense or characteristic phase of something — see THICK

middleman *n* one who works with opposing sides in order to bring about an agreement — see MEDIATOR

middlemost *adj* occupying a position equally distant from the ends or extremes — see MIDDLE 1

middle-of-the-road *adj* avoiding major social change or extreme political ideas — see MODERATE 2

middling *adj* of average to below average quality — see MEDIOCRE 1

midget *n* a living thing much smaller than others of its kind — see DWARF 1

midmost *adj* occupying a position equally distant from the ends or extremes — see MIDDLE 1

midpoint *n* **1** a middle point between extremes — see MEAN 1

2 an area or point that is an equal distance from all points along an edge or outer surface — see CENTER 2

midriff *n* the middle region of the human body ⟨*midriff*-baring tops are popular this summer⟩

synonyms middle, waist, waistline

related words abdomen, torso, trunk

midst *n* **1** an area or point that is an equal distance from all points along an edge or outer surface — see CENTER 2

2 the most intense or characteristic phase of something — see THICK

midst *prep* in or into the middle of — see AMONG

midway *adj* occupying a position equally distant from the ends or extremes — see MIDDLE 1

mien *n* the outward form of someone or something especially as indicative of a quality — see APPEARANCE 1

might *n* the ability to exert effort for the accomplishment of a task — see POWER 2

mightily *adv* **1** to a great degree — see VERY 1

2 with great effort or determination — see HARD 1

3 in a vigorous and forceful manner — see HARD 3

mighty *adj* having great power or influence — see IMPORTANT 2

mighty *adv* to a great degree — see VERY 1

migrant *adj* having a way of life that involves moving from one region to another typically on a seasonal basis — see MIGRATORY

migrant *n* one that leaves one place to settle in another — see EMIGRANT

migratory *adj* having a way of life that involves moving from one region to another typically on a seasonal basis ⟨most of the apple crop is picked by *migratory* workers⟩ ⟨*migratory* birds heading south for the winter⟩

synonyms migrant, mobile

related words errant, itinerant, nomadic, peripatetic, ranging, roaming, roving, traveling (*or* travelling), vagabond, vagrant, wandering, wayfaring; ambulatory, drifting, footloose, gallivanting (*also* galavanting), lingering, meandering, rambling, sauntering, strolling, traipsing, walking

near antonyms immobile, stationary; established, fast, fixed, rooted, set, settled

antonyms nonmigratory, resident

mild *adj* **1** marked by temperatures that are neither too high nor too low — see CLEMENT

2 not harsh or stern especially in manner, nature, or effect — see GENTLE 1

milestone *n* a point in a chain of events at which an important change (as in one's fortunes) occurs — see TURNING POINT

milieu *n* the circumstances, conditions, or objects by which one is surrounded — see ENVIRONMENT

militancy *n* an inclination to fight or quarrel — see BELLIGERENCE

militant *adj* **1** feeling or displaying eagerness to fight — see BELLIGERENT

2 having or showing a bold forcefulness in the pursuit of a goal — see AGGRESSIVE 1

militant *n* one who is intensely or excessively devoted to a cause — see ZEALOT

militarist *n* one who urges or attempts to cause a war — see WARMONGER

military *adj* **1** of or relating to the armed services ⟨the colonel testified that revealing any more information would have required giving away *military* secrets⟩

synonyms martial, service

related words naval; GI, gladiatorial, mercenary, soldierly; aggressive, bellicose, combative, contentious, militant, militaristic, pugnacious, quarrelsome, scrappy, truculent, warlike

near antonyms civilian

antonyms nonmilitary

2 of, relating to, or suitable for war or a warrior — see MARTIAL 1

military *n* the combined army, air force, and navy of a nation — see ARMED FORCES

mill *n* a building or set of buildings for the manufacturing of goods — see FACTORY

mime *n* an actor in a story performed silently and entirely by body movements ⟨that annoying *mime* on the sidewalk is pretending to be in an invisible box again⟩

synonyms mimic, mummer, pantomime, pantomimist

related words entertainer, performer, player, trouper; imitator, impersonator, impressionist

mime *vb* to use (someone or something) as the model for one's speech, mannerisms, or behavior — see IMITATE 1

mimetic *adj* using or marked by the use of something else as a basis or model — see IMITATIVE

mimic *adj* **1** being such in appearance only and made with or manufactured from usually cheaper materials — see IMITATION

2 using or marked by the use of something else as a basis or model — see IMITATIVE

mimic *n* **1** a person who imitates another's voice and mannerisms for comic effect ⟨a gifted *mimic* who can do a terrific imitation of anyone's voice⟩

synonyms imitator, impersonator, impressionist

related words caricaturist, lampooner, mocker, parodist, satirist; mime, mummer, pantomimist; entertainer, performer, player, trouper; parrot

2 an actor in a story performed silently and entirely by body movements — see MIME

mimic *vb* **1** to copy or exaggerate (someone or something) in order to make fun of ⟨the comedian was famous for *mimicking* the President's distinctive lisp⟩

synonyms burlesque, caricature, imitate, mock, parody, take off (on), travesty

related words lampoon, satirize; deride, ridicule; ape, parrot; duplicate, emulate, replicate, reproduce; act, counterfeit, dissemble, fake, feign, pretend, sham, simulate; elaborate, embellish, embroider, exaggerate, magnify, pad, stretch; amplify, enhance, enlarge (upon), expand, flesh (out), overdraw, overstate; mime, pantomime; impersonate, perform, play

2 to use (someone or something) as the model for one's speech, mannerisms, or behavior — see IMITATE 1

mince *vb* to cut into small pieces — see CHOP

mind *vb* **1** to pay attention especially through the act of hearing — see LISTEN

2 *chiefly dialect* to bring back to mind — see REMEMBER

3 to act according to the commands of — see OBEY
4 to be cautious of or on guard against — see BEWARE (OF)
5 to have an interest or concern for — see CARE
6 to take charge of especially on behalf of another — see ²TEND 1
7 to take notice of and be guided by — see HEED 1

mind *n* **1** the part of a person that feels, thinks, perceives, wills, and especially reasons ⟨scientists still disagree about exactly where the *mind* is located⟩
synonyms cerebrum, head
related words brain, gray matter, intellect, intelligence, reason; acumen, alertness, astuteness, brilliance, insight, judgment (*or* judgement), mentality, perception, perspicacity, sagacity, sapience, wisdom, wit; awareness, cognizance, consciousness, self-awareness, self-consciousness
2 the normal or healthy condition of the mental abilities ⟨everyone used to tease him and tell him he was out of his *mind* when he swore he'd seen a flying saucer⟩
synonyms head, reason, saneness, sanity, wit
related words rationality, reasonableness, sense; health, healthfulness, healthiness, wholesomeness; lucidity, lucidness, normality, soundness; wisdom
near antonyms delusion, hallucination; delirium, frenzy, hysteria
antonyms derangement, insanity, lunacy, madness, mania
3 an idea that is believed to be true or valid without positive knowledge — see OPINION 1
4 the power or process of recalling what has been previously learned or experienced — see MEMORY 1

mindful *adj* having specified facts or feelings actively impressed on the mind — see CONSCIOUS

mindless *adj* **1** not having or showing an ability to absorb ideas readily — see STUPID 1
2 not paying or showing close attention especially for the purpose of avoiding trouble — see CARELESS 1

mindlessness *n* the quality or state of lacking intelligence or quickness of mind — see STUPIDITY 1

mine *n* a usually concealed explosive device designed to go off when disturbed — see BOOBY TRAP 1

mine *vb* to place hidden explosive devices in or under ⟨the troops *mined* the field before they gave it up to the enemy⟩
synonyms boobytrap
related words blow up, bomb; ambush, snare, trap; attack

mingle *vb* **1** to turn into a single mass that is more or less the same throughout — see BLEND 1
2 to take part in social activities — see SOCIALIZE

miniature *adj* very small in size — see TINY

miniature *n* an exact representation of something in greatly reduced size — see MODEL 1

minimal *adj* being the least in amount, number, or size possible ⟨the beached whales were returned to the sea with only *minimal* loss of life⟩
synonyms least, littlest, lowest, minimum, slightest
related words fewer, lesser, low, slight, small, smaller
near antonyms highest
antonyms full, greatest, largest, maximum, top, topmost, utmost

minimize *vb* to express scornfully one's low opinion of — see DECRY 1

minimum *adj* being the least in amount, number, or size possible — see MINIMAL

minion *n* a person or thing that is preferred over others — see FAVORITE

minister *n* **1** a person sent on a mission to represent another — see AMBASSADOR
2 a person specially trained and authorized to conduct religious services in a Christian church — see CLERGYMAN

minister (to) *vb* to attend to the needs and comforts of — see NURSE 1

ministerial *adj* of, relating to, or characteristic of the clergy — see CLERICAL

minor *adj* **1** having not so great importance or rank as another — see LESSER
2 of little or less value or merit — see INFERIOR 2
3 lacking importance — see UNIMPORTANT

minstrel *n* a person who writes poetry — see POET

minstrelsy *n* writing that uses rhythm, vivid language, and often rhyme to provoke an emotional response — see POETRY 1

mint *n* a very large amount of money — see FORTUNE 2

minus *n* a feature of someone or something that creates difficulty for achieving success — see DISADVANTAGE

minus *prep* not having — see WITHOUT 1

minute *adj* **1** including many small descriptive features — see DETAILED 1
2 lacking importance — see UNIMPORTANT
3 so small or unimportant as to warrant little or no attention — see NEGLIGIBLE 1
4 made or done with extreme care and accuracy — see FINE 2
5 very small in size — see TINY

minute *n* a very small space of time — see INSTANT

minutely *adv* with attention to all aspects or details — see THOROUGHLY 1

miracle *n* something extraordinary or surprising — see WONDER 1

miraculous *adj* **1** being so extraordinary or abnormal as to suggest powers which violate the laws of nature — see SUPERNATURAL 2
2 causing wonder or astonishment — see MARVELOUS 1

mire *n* **1** soft wet earth — see MUD
2 spongy land saturated or partially covered with water — see SWAMP

mire *vb* **1** to make dirty — see DIRTY
2 to place in conflict or difficulties — see EMBROIL

mirror *n* a smooth or polished surface (as of glass) that forms images by reflection ⟨breaking a *mirror* is supposed to bring seven years of bad luck⟩
synonyms looking glass
related words pier glass; reflector

mirror *vb* to reproduce or show (an exact likeness) as a mirror would — see REFLECT

mirth *n* a mood characterized by high spirits and amusement and often accompanied by laughter ⟨as charming as your mutual *mirth* is, could you refrain from nudging each other and giggling during class?⟩
synonyms cheer, cheerfulness, cheeriness, festivity, glee, gleefulness, hilarity, joviality, merriment, merriness, mirthfulness

related words frivolity, levity; carnival, gaiety (*also* gayety), jollification, jollity, reveling, revelry; brightness, buoyancy, good-humoredness, good-naturedness, humor, sunniness; insouciance, lightheartedness, playfulness; buffoonery, clownishness, flippancy, funning, jesting, jocularity, joking, joshing; animation, jauntiness, liveliness, perkiness, vivacity; joyfulness, joyousness, jubilance, rejoicing; frolicking, gamboling (*or* gambolling), rollicking, romping
near antonyms blues, dejection, depression, despondence, forlornness, sadness, sorrow, unhappiness; bile, gloom, melancholy, sourness, spleen; earnestness, graveness, gravity, grimness, seriousness, soberness, solemnity; discontent, disgruntlement, moodiness; dolefulness, dolorousness, joylessness, mournfulness, plaintiveness, woe, woefulness; blackness, darkness, gloominess, glumness; desolateness, desolation; heartbreak, miserableness, misery, mourning, wretchedness

mirthful *adj* indicative of or marked by high spirits or good humor — see MERRY

mirthfully *adv* in a cheerful or happy manner — see GAILY 1

mirthfulness *n* a mood characterized by high spirits and amusement and often accompanied by laughter — see MIRTH

miry *adj* full of or covered with soft wet earth — see MUDDY 1

misadventure *n* bad luck or an example of this — see MISFORTUNE

misanthrope *n* a person who distrusts other people and believes that everything is done for selfish reasons — see CYNIC

misanthropic *adj* having or showing a deep distrust of human beings and their motives — see CYNICAL

misapplication *n* incorrect or improper use — see MISUSE

misapply *vb* to put to a bad or improper use ⟨you've *misapplied* the theorem to certain problems that require a different formula⟩ ⟨kids who *misapply* their boundless energy and get into trouble⟩
synonyms abuse, misuse, pervert, profane, prostitute
related words degrade, twist; mismanage; corrupt, debase, desecrate
near antonyms apply, employ, use, utilize; respect

misapprehend *vb* to fail to understand the true or actual meaning of — see MISUNDERSTAND

misapprehension *n* **1** a failure to understand correctly — see MISUNDERSTANDING 1
2 a wrong judgment — see MISTAKE 1

misappropriate *vb* to take (something) without right and with an intent to keep — see STEAL 1

misbegotten *adj* born to a father and mother who are not married — see ILLEGITIMATE 1

misbehave *vb* to behave badly ⟨if the two of you *misbehave* in public like that again, you'll have to go to bed early for a week⟩
synonyms act up, carry on
related words misconduct; disobey; clown (around), cut up, fool (around), horse (around); show off; roughhouse
phrases raise Cain, run riot
near antonyms obey; acquit, act, bear, comport, demean, deport, quit; comply, conform; check, collect, compose, constrain, contain, control, curb, handle, inhibit, move, quiet, repress, restrain

misbehaving *adj* engaging in or marked by childish misbehavior — see NAUGHTY

misbehavior *n* improper or illegal behavior — see MISCONDUCT

miscalculate *vb* to make an incorrect judgment regarding ⟨they *miscalculated* how difficult the long trip would be⟩
synonyms misconceive, misjudge, mistake
related words misconstrue, misinterpret, misunderstand; overestimate, overrate, overvalue; underestimate, underrate, undervalue; miscount

miscarry *vb* to go wrong ⟨the scheme to save the dolphins *miscarried*, and all were lost⟩
synonyms misfire
related words miss; break down, conk (out), crash, die, fail, stall; fizzle, flop, flunk, fold, wash out; flounder, struggle; decline, slip, slump, wane
phrases fall flat, fall short
near antonyms prevail, succeed; flourish, prosper, thrive

miscellaneous *adj* consisting of many things of different sorts ⟨the bottom of the drawer was always a *miscellaneous* accumulation of odds and ends⟩
synonyms assorted, heterogeneous, mixed, motley, patchwork, promiscuous, varied
related words manifold, multifarious; multiple, multiplex, myriad; disparate, divergent, diverse, sundry, various; chaotic, cluttered, confused, disarranged, disarrayed, disheveled (*or* dishevelled), disordered, jumbled, littered, messed, messy, muddled; amalgamated, blended, combined, conglomerated, fused, incorporated, intermingled, intermixed, merged, mingled; unclassified, unsorted
near antonyms monolithic, uniform; alike, identical, like, same; distinct, distinctive, individual, separate
antonyms homogeneous

miscellaneousness *n* the quality or state of being composed of many different elements or types — see VARIETY 1

miscellany *n* **1** an unorganized collection or mixture of various things ⟨the box from the attic contained a *miscellany* of old records, family photo albums, and long-forgotten love letters⟩
synonyms assortment, clutter, hash, hodgepodge, hotchpotch, jumble, litter, medley, mélange, mishmash, motley, muddle, potpourri, rummage, scramble, shuffle, tumble, variety, welter
related words notions, odds and ends, sundries; accumulation, aggregation, conglomeration; catchall, patchwork; admixture, amalgam, blend, combination, composite, compound, fusion, intermixture, mix, mixture; chaos, confusion, disarrangement, disarray, disorder, mess, muddle, shambles; knot, snarl, tangle
phrases odds and ends
2 a collection of writings — see ANTHOLOGY

mischance *n* **1** a chance and usually sudden event bringing loss or injury — see ACCIDENT 1
2 bad luck or an example of this — see MISFORTUNE

mischief *n* **1** playful, reckless behavior that is not intended to cause serious harm ⟨the children claimed that setting off a firecracker was harmless *mischief*, but they got a lecture anyway⟩
synonyms devilishness, devilment, devilry (*or*

deviltry), hob, impishness, knavery, mischievousness, rascality, roguishness, shenanigans, waggery, wickedness
related words diabolicalness, naughtiness; friskiness, playfulness, sportiveness; chicanery, hanky-panky, trickery; high jinks, monkeyshines, skylarking, tomfoolery; antic, caper, practical joke; aggravation, annoyance, exasperation, irritation
near antonyms gravity, seriousness, solemnity
2 a natural disposition for playful behavior — see PLAYFULNESS
3 an appealingly mischievous person — see SCAMP 1

mischievous *adj* **1** tending to or exhibiting reckless playfulness ‹the children had been so *mischievous* that we had to pay the babysitter extra and then clean up the mess›
synonyms devilish, elvish, impish, knavish, pixieish, prankish, rascally, roguish, sly, waggish, wicked
related words antic, coltish, frisky, kittenish, playful, sportive; gay, happy, lighthearted, whimsical; energetic, lively, spirited, sprightly; artful, cunning, tricky; misbehaving, naughty; pestering, riling, teasing
near antonyms grave, grim, sober, solemn, stern
2 engaging in or marked by childish misbehavior — see NAUGHTY
3 causing or capable of causing harm — see HARMFUL

mischievousness *n* **1** a natural disposition for playful behavior — see PLAYFULNESS
2 playful, reckless behavior that is not intended to cause serious harm — see MISCHIEF 1

misconceive *vb* to make an incorrect judgment regarding — see MISCALCULATE

misconception *n* a false idea or belief — see FALLACY 1

misconduct *n* improper or illegal behavior ‹some rough play got the hockey player fined for *misconduct* on the ice›
synonyms malfeasance, misbehavior, misdoing, wrongdoing
related words crime, malefaction, misdeed, sin, wrong; malpractice; familiarity, gaffe, impropriety, indiscretion; blunder, error, fault, flub, fumble, goof, lapse, miscue, misstep, mistake, slip, slipup, stumble

misconduct *vb* to manage badly — see MISMANAGE

misconstruction *n* a failure to understand correctly — see MISUNDERSTANDING 1

misconstrue *vb* to fail to understand the true or actual meaning of — see MISUNDERSTAND

misconstruing *n* a failure to understand correctly — see MISUNDERSTANDING 1

miscreant *n* a mean, evil, or unprincipled person — see VILLAIN

miscue *n* an unintentional departure from truth or accuracy — see ERROR 1

misdeed *n* a breaking of a moral or legal code — see OFFENSE 1

misdoing *n* **1** a breaking of a moral or legal code — see OFFENSE 1
2 improper or illegal behavior — see MISCONDUCT

miser *n* a mean grasping person who is usually stingy with money ‹the *miser* liked to sit and play with his money›
synonyms cheapskate, niggard, piker, scrooge, skinflint, tightwad
related words hoarder, saver
near antonyms prodigal, profligate, spender, spendthrift, squanderer, waster, wastrel

miserable *adj* **1** causing or marked by an atmosphere lacking in cheer — see GLOOMY 1
2 feeling unhappiness — see SAD 1
3 of low quality — see CHEAP 2
4 showing signs of advanced wear and tear and neglect — see SHABBY 1
5 deserving of one's pity — see PATHETIC 1

miserliness *n* the quality of being overly sparing with money — see PARSIMONY

misery *n* **1** a situation or state that causes great suffering and unhappiness — see HELL 2
2 a state of great suffering of body or mind — see DISTRESS 1

misfire *vb* to go wrong — see MISCARRY

misfortune *n* bad luck or an example of this ‹through sheer *misfortune* our car got a flat tire and we were late› ‹our *misfortunes* of the last year included the loss of a beloved pet›
synonyms adversity, knock, misadventure, mischance, mishap
related words calamity, cataclysm, catastrophe, disaster; tragedy; affliction, hardship, trial, tribulation; distress, misery, suffering, unhappiness; defeat, failure, fizzle, nonsuccess; curse, sorrow, trouble; accident, casualty; disappointment, letdown, setback; circumstance, destiny, doom, fate, lot, portion
near antonyms break, chance, fluke, godsend, hit, opportunity, stroke, windfall; accomplishment, achievement, success
antonyms fortune, luck

misgiving *n* **1** a feeling or attitude that one does not know the truth, truthfulness, or trustworthiness of someone or something — see DOUBT
2 an uneasy feeling about the rightness of what one is doing or going to do — see QUALM
3 suspicion or fear of future harm or misfortune — see APPREHENSION 1

misgovern *vb* to manage badly — see MISMANAGE

misguide *vb* to cause to believe what is untrue — see DECEIVE

mishandle *vb* **1** to inflict physical or emotional harm upon — see ABUSE 1
2 to abuse physically — see MANHANDLE 1
3 to manage badly — see MISMANAGE

mishap *n* **1** a chance and usually sudden event bringing loss or injury — see ACCIDENT 1
2 bad luck or an example of this — see MISFORTUNE

mishmash *n* an unorganized collection or mixture of various things — see MISCELLANY 1

misinform *vb* to cause to believe what is untrue — see DECEIVE

misinterpret *vb* **1** to change so much as to create a wrong impression or alter the meaning of — see GARBLE
2 to fail to understand the true or actual meaning of — see MISUNDERSTAND

misinterpretation *n* a failure to understand correctly — see MISUNDERSTANDING 1

misjudge *vb* to make an incorrect judgment regarding — see MISCALCULATE

misjudging *n* a wrong judgment — see MISTAKE 1

misjudgment *n* a wrong judgment — see MISTAKE 1

mislaid *adj* no longer possessed — see LOST

mislay *vb* to be unable to find or have at hand — see LOSE 1

mislaying *n* the act or an instance of not having or being able to find — see LOSS 1

mislead *vb* to cause to believe what is untrue — see DECEIVE

misleading *adj* tending or having power to deceive — see DECEPTIVE 1

mismanage *vb* to manage badly ⟨the business was *mismanaged* so seriously that it had to declare bankruptcy⟩
synonyms misconduct, misgovern, mishandle, misrule
related words abuse, ill-treat, ill-use, maltreat, mistreat, misuse; damage, harm, hurt, violate
near antonyms govern, handle, manage, rule; care (for), nurture; aid, help, protect, rescue

misplace *vb* to be unable to find or have at hand — see LOSE 1

misplaced *adj* no longer possessed — see LOST

misplacement *n* the act or an instance of not having or being able to find — see LOSS 1

misread *vb* to fail to understand the true or actual meaning of — see MISUNDERSTAND

misreading *n* a failure to understand correctly — see MISUNDERSTANDING 1

misrepresent *vb* **1** to change so much as to create a wrong impression or alter the meaning of — see GARBLE
2 to give a false idea of — see BELIE 1

misrule *n* a state in which there is widespread wrongdoing and disregard for rules and authority — see ANARCHY

misrule *vb* to manage badly — see MISMANAGE

miss *n* a young usually unmarried woman — see GIRL 1

miss *vb* **1** to fail to attend — see CUT 2
2 to fail to understand the true or actual meaning of — see MISUNDERSTAND

misshapen *adj* badly or imperfectly formed — see MALFORMED

missing *adj* **1** no longer possessed — see LOST
2 not present or in evidence — see ABSENT 2
3 not at a certain place — see ABSENT 1

mission *n* a specific task with which a person or group is charged ⟨your *mission* is to clean up the house before company arrives⟩
synonyms assignment, charge, job, operation, post
related words burden, chore, duty, need, obligation, requirement, responsibility; labor, work; commitment, pledge, promise; appointment, designation, nomination; compulsion, constraint, restraint

missive *n* a message on paper from one person or group to another — see LETTER

misspend *vb* to use up carelessly — see WASTE 1

misstate *vb* to change so much as to create a wrong impression or alter the meaning of — see GARBLE

misstep *n* an unintentional departure from truth or accuracy — see ERROR 1

mist *n* **1** a light or fine rain — see DRIZZLE
2 an atmospheric condition in which suspended particles in the air rob it of its transparency — see HAZE 1

mist *vb* to make dark, dim, or indistinct — see CLOUD 1

mistake *n* **1** a wrong judgment ⟨I made a *mistake* when I assumed that you were the one who broke the window⟩
synonyms misapprehension, misjudging, misjudgment
related words blunder, error, fault, flub, fumble, goof, inaccuracy, lapse, miscue, misstep, slipup, stumble; foul-up, muff; miscalculation, misstatement; misconception, misconstruction, misconstruing, misinterpretation
2 an unintentional departure from truth or accuracy — see ERROR 1

mistake *vb* **1** to fail to understand the true or actual meaning of — see MISUNDERSTAND
2 to make an incorrect judgment regarding — see MISCALCULATE

mistaken *adj* having an opinion that does not agree with truth or the facts — see INCORRECT 1

mistakenly *adv* in a mistaken or inappropriate way — see WRONGLY

mistreat *vb* to inflict physical or emotional harm upon — see ABUSE 1

mistrust *n* a feeling or attitude that one does not know the truth, truthfulness, or trustworthiness of someone or something — see DOUBT

mistrust *vb* to have no trust or confidence in — see DISTRUST

mistrustful *adj* **1** inclined to doubt or question claims — see SKEPTICAL 1
2 not feeling sure about the truth, wisdom, or trustworthiness of someone or something — see DOUBTFUL 1

mistrustfully *adv* with distrust — see ASKANCE

mistrustfulness *n* a feeling or attitude that one does not know the truth, truthfulness, or trustworthiness of someone or something — see DOUBT

misty *adj* filled with or dimmed by fine particles (as of dust or water) in suspension — see HAZY 1

misunderstand *vb* to fail to understand the true or actual meaning of ⟨you *misunderstood* that poem because you didn't look up the words you didn't know⟩
synonyms misapprehend, misconstrue, misinterpret, misread, miss, mistake
related words misconceive
antonyms apprehend, catch, comprehend, conceive, fathom, grasp, know, make out, penetrate, perceive, savvy, see, seize, take in, understand

misunderstanding *n* **1** a failure to understand correctly ⟨people once thought that there were canals on Mars because of a common *misunderstanding* of a report by an Italian astronomer⟩
synonyms misapprehension, misconstruction, misconstruing, misinterpretation, misreading
related words misconception, mistake
near antonyms appreciation, apprehension, comprehension, conception, grasp, knowledge, perception, understanding; awareness, consciousness, realization
2 an often noisy or angry expression of differing opinions — see ARGUMENT 1

misusage *n* incorrect or improper use — see MISUSE

misuse *n* incorrect or improper use ⟨the warranty for this dryer is null and void if you subject the product to deliberate *misuse*⟩
synonyms abuse, misapplication, misusage, perversion
related words mishandling, mismanagement, mismanaging; maltreatment, mistreatment; damage,

destruction, ruin, spoiling, wrecking; corruption, debasement, desecration, profanation, prostitution
near antonyms application, employment, use, utilization
misuse *vb* **1** to put to a bad or improper use — see MISAPPLY
2 to inflict physical or emotional harm upon — see ABUSE 1
mite *n* **1** a very small sum of money ⟨I have only a *mite* left to buy lunch for the rest of the week⟩
synonyms peanuts, pittance, shoestring, song
related words petty cash, pin money, pocket money, spending money
near antonyms capital, means, wherewithal; opulence, riches, treasure, wealth; heap, pile, pot; bonanza, mine, treasure trove, treasury
antonyms fortune, king's ransom, mint, wad
2 a living thing much smaller than others of its kind — see DWARF 1
3 a very small amount — see PARTICLE 1
mitigate *vb* to make more bearable or less severe — see HELP 2
mix *n* a distinct entity formed by the combining of two or more different things — see BLEND
mix *vb* **1** to turn into a single mass that is more or less the same throughout — see BLEND 1
2 to take part in social activities — see SOCIALIZE
mix (up) *vb* to undo the proper order or arrangement of — see DISORDER
mixed *adj* **1** being offspring produced by parents of different races, breeds, species, or genera ⟨our *mixed* dog has a greyhound's body but the features of a collie⟩
synonyms crossbred, hybrid, mongrel
related words dihybrid, trihybrid; crossbred, crossed, hybridized, interbred, outcrossed
near antonyms pedigreed; inbred
antonyms full-blooded, purebred, thoroughbred
2 consisting of many things of different sorts — see MISCELLANEOUS
mixture *n* a distinct entity formed by the combining of two or more different things — see BLEND
mix–up *n* an instance of confusion — see FOUL-UP
moan *n* **1** a long low sound indicating pain or grief ⟨she uttered an agonized *moan* and clutched her stomach⟩
synonyms groan, wail
related words blubbering, crying, sniveling, sobbing, weeping, whimpering, whining, yammering; keen, lament; bawl, cry, howl, shriek, squall, whimper, whine, yelp, yowl
near antonyms cackle, chuckle, chortle, giggle, guffaw, laugh, snicker, titter
2 a crying out in grief — see LAMENT 1
moan *vb* **1** to utter a moan ⟨he *moaned* and cried for days after his dog died⟩
synonyms groan, wail
related words cry, blubber, sob, weep; sniff, snivel, whimper, whine; bemoan, bewail, deplore, keen, lament, rue; bleed, grieve, mourn, sorrow, suffer; bawl, howl, shriek, squall, yammer, yelp, yowl
near antonyms cackle, chuckle, chortle, giggle, guffaw, laugh, snicker, titter
2 to express dissatisfaction, pain, or resentment usually tiresomely — see COMPLAIN
mob *n* **1** a great number of persons or things gathered together — see CROWD 1
2 a group involved in secret or criminal activities — see RING 1
3 the body of the community as contrasted with the elite — see MASS 1
mob *vb* to move upon or fill (something) in great numbers — see CROWD 2
mobile *adj* **1** capable of being moved especially with ease — see MOVABLE
2 having a way of life that involves moving from one region to another typically on a seasonal basis — see MIGRATORY
mobile home *n* a motor vehicle that is specially equipped for living while traveling — see CAMPER
mobilization *n* an act of gathering forces together to renew or attempt an effort — see RALLY 1
mobilize *vb* to assemble and make ready for action ⟨we are prepared to *mobilize* the troops on very short notice⟩
synonyms marshal, muster, rally
related words arrange, line up, order, organize; call (up), convene, summon; activate
near antonyms disarrange, disorder, disorganize; deactivate, dismiss
antonyms demobilize
mobster *n* a violent, brutal person who is often a member of an organized gang — see HOODLUM
mock *adj* **1** being such in appearance only and made with or manufactured from usually cheaper materials — see IMITATION
2 lacking in natural or spontaneous quality — see ARTIFICIAL 1
mock *n* a person or thing that is made fun of — see LAUGHINGSTOCK
mock *vb* **1** to copy or exaggerate (someone or something) in order to make fun of — see MIMIC 1
2 to make (someone or something) the object of unkind laughter — see RIDICULE
mocker *n* a person who causes repeated emotional pain, distress, or annoyance to another — see TORMENTOR
mockery *n* **1** a poor, insincere, or insulting imitation of something ⟨the resort's Old West show for tourists is a *mockery* of Native American culture⟩
synonyms caricature, farce, joke, parody, sham, travesty
related words burlesque, comedy; lampoon, take-off; counterfeit, fake, feigning, pretense (*or* pretence), simulation
near antonyms homage, tribute
2 a person or thing that is made fun of — see LAUGHINGSTOCK
3 the making of unkind jokes as a way of showing one's scorn for someone or something — see RIDICULE
mod *adj* being or involving the latest methods, concepts, information, or styles — see MODERN
[1]**mode** *n* **1** a distinctive way of putting ideas into words — see STYLE 1
2 a state of mind dominated by a particular emotion — see MOOD 1
[2]**mode** *n* a practice or interest that is very popular for a short time — see FAD
model *adj* constituting, serving as, or worthy of being a pattern to be imitated ⟨why can't you be like your sister, who is such a well-behaved *model* child?⟩
synonyms archetypal, classic, exemplary, paradigmatic, quintessential
related words ideal, nonpareil, special, unique; absolute, flawless, impeccable, perfect; bang-up,

banner, capital, dandy, fine, first-class, first-rate, grand, great, groovy, jim-dandy, par excellence, prime, superb, superior, superlative, terrific, tiptop, top, top-notch, unsurpassed, wonderful; exceptional, fancy, high-grade
near antonyms bad, poor, substandard, unsatisfactory; atrocious, execrable, wretched; deficient, disappointing, failed, inadequate, inferior, poor; average, normal, ordinary, representative, typical; mediocre, second-class, second-rate

model *n* **1** an exact representation of something in greatly reduced size ‹the dollhouse was a tiny, perfect *model* of the family's actual house›
synonyms miniature
related words copy, duplicate, duplication, imitation, replica, replication, reproduction; dwarf, midget, mini, pygmy
near antonyms archetype, original, prototype; blowup, enlargement
2 a person who poses with or wears merchandise (as clothes) often for pictorial advertising ‹the most famous *models* can earn thousands of dollars an hour›
synonyms manikin, mannequin
related words figure, form; doll, dummy
3 someone of such unequaled perfection as to deserve imitation — see IDEAL 1

moderate *adj* **1** avoiding extremes in behavior or expression ‹he was only a *moderate* drinker, stopping after a couple of glasses of wine›
synonyms temperate
related words controlled, curbed, disciplined, restrained, self-controlled; calculated, deliberate, measured; rational, reasonable; average, mediocre, medium, modest, ordinary, run-of-the-mill, so-so; normal, ordinary, regular, routine, typical, usual
near antonyms excessive, extreme, inordinate, radical; irrational, unreasonable; extremist, fanatic (*or* fanatical), rabid, radical
antonyms immoderate, intemperate
2 avoiding major social change or extreme political ideas ‹the principal's *moderate* position on cell phones is that students can use them at school but only for emergencies›
synonyms middle-of-the-road
related words conventional, orthodox, traditional, rational, reasonable; neutral
near antonyms excessive; conservative, reactionary, rightist; leftist, liberal, progressive; fanatic (*or* fanatical), revolutionary, revolutionist, subversive, violent; agitating, fomenting, incendiary, inciting, instigating, provocative, provoking; rabble-rousing; dissenting
antonyms extremist, radical
3 being about midway between extremes of amount or size — see MIDDLE 2
4 marked by temperatures that are neither too high nor too low — see CLEMENT

moderate *vb* to grow less in scope or intensity especially gradually — see DECREASE 2

moderately *adv* to some degree or extent — see FAIRLY

moderateness *n* an avoidance of extremes in one's actions, beliefs, or habits — see TEMPERANCE

moderation *n* an avoidance of extremes in one's actions, beliefs, or habits — see TEMPERANCE

moderator *n* a person in charge of a meeting — see CHAIR 1

modern *adj* being or involving the latest methods, concepts, information, or styles ‹this hairstyle is absolutely the most *modern* fashion out there›
synonyms contemporary, current, hot, mod, modernistic, new, newfangled, new-fashioned, present-day, red-hot, space-age, ultramodern, up-to-date
related words fashionable, in, modish, stylish; last, latest; modernized, updated; futuristic, nontraditional
near antonyms anachronistic; aged, age-old, ancient, antediluvian, hoary, old, venerable; bygone, former, late, olden, past; antique, historic, historical; obsolete, outmoded, outworn; old-world; discarded, disused, moth-eaten; forgotten, remote; ageless, dateless, timeless
antonyms antiquated, archaic, dated, fusty, musty, noncontemporary, oldfangled, old-fashioned, old-time, out-of-date, passé

modern *n* a person with very modern ideas ‹the leaders of the American suffragists were originally regarded by many people as uppity *moderns* who should have stayed in their place›
synonyms ultramodernist
related words leftist, liberal, progressive; extremist, radical; bohemian
near antonyms conservative, rightist, Tory; old hand, old-timer, veteran
antonyms antediluvian, dodo, fogy (*also* fogey), fossil, fuddy-duddy, reactionary, stick-in-the-mud

modernistic *adj* being or involving the latest methods, concepts, information, or styles — see MODERN

modest *adj* **1** being about midway between extremes of amount or size — see MIDDLE 2
2 free from any trace of the coarse or indecent — see CHASTE
3 not comfortable around people — see SHY 2
4 not having or showing any feelings of superiority, self-assertiveness, or showiness — see HUMBLE 1

modestly *adv* **1** in manner showing no signs of pride or self-assertion — see LOWLY
2 with purity of thought and deed — see PURELY

modesty *n* **1** the absence of any feelings of being better than others — see HUMILITY
2 the quality or state of being morally pure — see CHASTITY

modicum *n* the smallest amount or part imaginable — see JOT

modifiable *adj* capable of being readily changed — see FLEXIBLE 1

modification *n* the act, process, or result of making different — see CHANGE

modify *vb* **1** to limit the meaning of (as a noun) — see QUALIFY 1
2 to make different in some way — see CHANGE 1

modish *adj* **1** being in the latest or current fashion — see STYLISH
2 enjoying widespread favor or approval — see POPULAR 1

modishness *n* the state of enjoying widespread approval — see POPULARITY

mogul *n* a person of rank, power, or influence in a particular field — see MAGNATE

moiety *n* one of two equal or nearly equal parts — see HALF 1

moil *vb* to devote serious and sustained effort — see LABOR

moist *adj* slightly or moderately wet ‹luckily, my

new suede shoes are only a bit *moist* after I accidentally wore them in the rain⟩
synonyms damp, dank
related words dewy; clammy; humid, muggy, sticky; sultry, summery, sweltering, torrid, tropical; dripping, drenched, saturated, soaked, soaking, sodden, soggy, sopping, soppy, steeped, water-logged
near antonyms arid, dry, waterless; baked, burned, burnt, dehydrated, desert, droughty, dusty, parched, scorched, seared, sere

moisten *vb* to make or become slightly or moderately wet ⟨*moisten* the cloth before cleaning with it⟩
synonyms dampen
related words drench, saturate, soak, steep; humidify; dip, immerge, immerse
near antonyms dehumidify, dehydrate, parch, scorch, sear
antonyms dry

moisture *n* the amount of water suspended in the air in tiny droplets ⟨dew is really just *moisture* from the air that condenses and collects when the temperature drops at night⟩
synonyms dampness, humidity
related words mugginess, stickiness, stuffiness; sultriness; clamminess, dankness, sogginess, wetness
near antonyms aridity, dehydration, dryness

mojo *n* **1** something worn or kept to bring good luck or keep away evil — see CHARM 1
2 the power to control natural forces through supernatural means — see MAGIC 1

molder *vb* to go through decomposition — see DECAY 1

molecule *n* a very small piece — see BIT 1

mollify *vb* **1** to lessen the anger or agitation of — see PACIFY
2 to make more bearable or less severe — see HELP 2

mollifying *adj* tending to lessen or avoid conflict or hostility — see PACIFIC 1

mollycoddle *n* a person without strength of character — see WEAKLING 2

mollycoddle *vb* to treat with great or excessive care — see BABY

molt *vb* to cast (a natural bodily covering or appendage) aside — see SHED 1

mom *n* a female human parent — see MOTHER

moment *n* **1** a particular point at which an event takes place — see OCCASION 1
2 the quality or state of being important — see IMPORTANCE
3 a very small space of time — see INSTANT
4 the time currently existing or in progress — see PRESENT 1

momentarily *adv* at or within a short time — see SHORTLY 2

momentary *adj* lasting only for a short time ⟨the pain of the flu shot was only *momentary*⟩
synonyms ephemeral, evanescent, flash, fleeting, fugitive, impermanent, passing, short-lived, temporary, transient, transitory
related words brief, short; acting, interim
near antonyms lifelong
antonyms enduring, eternal, everlasting, lasting, long-lived, permanent, perpetual

momentous *adj* having great meaning or lasting effect — see IMPORTANT 1

momentum *n* something that arouses action or activity — see IMPULSE

momma *n* a female human parent — see MOTHER

monarch *n* one who rules over a people with a sole, supreme, and usually hereditary authority ⟨the ruling *monarch* of Britain at that time was Queen Elizabeth I⟩
synonyms autocrat, ruler, sovereign
related words czar (*also* tsar *or* tzar), emperor, empress, kaiser, king, lord, mogul, prince, queen, satrap, sultan; authoritarian, despot, dictator, overlord, potentate, tyrant; royalty

monarchal *or* **monarchial** *adj* fit for or worthy of a royal ruler — see MONARCHICAL

monarchical *also* **monarchic** *adj* fit for or worthy of a royal ruler ⟨guests who stay in the hotel's most expensive suite live in *monarchical* splendor⟩
synonyms kingly, monarchal (*or* monarchial), princely, queenly, regal, royal
related words aristocratic, baronial, imperial, lordly, noble, patrician

monastery *n* a residence for men under religious vows ⟨Gregory Mendel worked out his concepts of genetics by doing breeding experiments using pea plants in the *monastery's* garden⟩
synonyms abbey, cloister, friary, priory
related words house; convent, nunnery; lamasery

monetary *adj* of or relating to money, banking, or investments — see FINANCIAL

money *n* something (as pieces of stamped metal or printed paper) customarily and legally used as a medium of exchange, a measure of value, or a means of payment ⟨are you sure you have enough *money* to buy all that?⟩
synonyms bread [*slang*], cash, chips, currency, dough, gold, jack [*slang*], legal tender, lucre, pelf, tender, wampum [*slang*]
related words change, coinage, specie; paper money, scrip; banknote, cashier's check, check, draft, money order, note; bill, buck, dollar, greenback; bankroll, capital, finances, funds; mite, pittance; bundle, fortune, king's ransom, mint, wad; abundance, means, opulence, riches, treasure, wealth; resources, wherewithal; pin money, pocket money, spending money

moneyed *or* **monied** *adj* having goods, property, or money in abundance — see RICH 1

mongrel *adj* being offspring produced by parents of different races, breeds, species, or genera — see MIXED 1

mongrel *n* an offspring of parents with different genes especially when of different races, breeds, species, or genera — see HYBRID

monitor *vb* to pay continued close attention to (something) for a particular purpose ⟨police regularly *monitor* that road to record traffic density and catch speeders⟩
synonyms cover, watch
related words eye; behold, look, regard, see; gape, gawk, gaze, glare, goggle, peer, stare; glance, glimpse, peek, peep
phrases keep an eye on

monkey *n* an appealingly mischievous person — see SCAMP 1

monkey (around) *vb* **1** to engage in attention-getting playful or boisterous behavior — see CUT UP
2 to spend time in aimless activity — see FIDDLE (AROUND)

monkey (with) *vb* to handle thoughtlessly, ignorantly, or mischievously — see TAMPER

monkeying *n* wildly playful or mischievous behavior — see HORSEPLAY

monkeyshines *n pl* wildly playful or mischievous behavior — see HORSEPLAY

monochromatic *adj* having or consisting of a single color ⟨although marble and bronze sculptures are *monochromatic*, they can be amazingly lifelike⟩
synonyms solid
related words colored, colorful, pigmented; chromatic
near antonyms dappled (*also* dapple), marbled, shaded; mottled, piebald, pied, pinto; barred, brindled (*or* brindle); checkered, patterned, plaid, striped
antonyms motley, multicolored, polychromatic, varicolored, variegated

monopolize *vb* to have complete control over ⟨it is illegal in the United States to *monopolize* an entire industry or product⟩ ⟨you shouldn't *monopolize* that toy while your friends are waiting to play with it⟩
synonyms sew up
related words corner, hog; absorb, consume, engross; have, hold, own, possess; control, direct, govern, manage, reign (over), rule

monotonous *adj* causing weariness, restlessness, or lack of interest — see BORING

monotonousness *n* a tedious lack of variety — see MONOTONY

monotony *n* a tedious lack of variety ⟨the *monotony* of the cafeteria's selections was almost as bad as the quality⟩
synonyms monotonousness, sameness
related words uniformity; boredom, dullness (*also* dulness), ennui, restlessness, tediousness, tedium, tiresomeness, weariness, wearisomeness
near antonyms diversity, multiplicity, variety; variability, variation; absorption, engagement, engrossment, enthrallment, fascination, grip, interest, intrigue; animation, excitement, invigoration, stimulation

monster *adj* unusually large — see HUGE

monster *n* **1** a strange or horrible and often frightening creature ⟨both children insisted that their parents check under the bed for *monsters* every night⟩
synonyms monstrosity, ogre
related words ogre; bête noire, bogey (*also* bogy *or* bogie), bugaboo, bugbear; banshee, bogeyman, demon (*or* daemon), devil, fiend, fright, imp, incubus; horror, terror; abomination, anathema; abnormality, freak; mutant, mutation
2 a person, thing, or event that is not normal — see FREAK 1
3 a mean, evil, or unprincipled person — see VILLAIN 1
4 something that is unusually large and powerful — see GIANT

monstrosity *n* **1** a person, thing, or event that is not normal — see FREAK 1
2 a strange or horrible and often frightening creature — see MONSTER 1
3 something unpleasant to look at — see EYESORE
4 the quality of inspiring intense dread or dismay — see HORROR 1
5 the state or quality of being utterly evil — see ENORMITY 1

monstrous *adj* **1** badly or imperfectly formed — see MALFORMED
2 extremely disturbing or repellent — see HORRIBLE 1
3 unusually large — see HUGE

monstrously *adv* **1** beyond a normal or acceptable limit — see TOO 1
2 to a large extent or degree — see GREATLY 2

monthlies *n pl* an occurrence of menstruating — see PERIOD 1

monument *n* **1** a shaped stone laid over or erected near a grave and usually bearing an inscription to identify and preserve the memory of the deceased — see TOMBSTONE
2 something that serves to keep alive the memory of a person or event — see MEMORIAL

monumental *adj* **1** large and impressive in size, grandeur, extent, or conception — see GRAND 1
2 unusually large — see HUGE

mooch *vb* to move about from place to place aimlessly — see WANDER

mood *n* **1** a state of mind dominated by a particular emotion ⟨losing my favorite sweater left me in a bad *mood* for the rest of the day⟩
synonyms cheer, frame, humor, mode, spirit, temper
related words attitude, outlook, perspective, standpoint, viewpoint; emotion, feeling, heart, passion, sentiment; strain; belief, conviction, mind, opinion; expression, tone, vein; character, disposition, individuality, personality, temperament; responsiveness, sensibility, sensitiveness, sensitivity
2 a special quality or impression associated with something — see AURA

moody *adj* frequently influenced by moods and especially bad moods ⟨teenagers are often both *moody* and changeable⟩
synonyms temperamental
related words capricious, changeable, changeful, fickle, fluctuating, fluid, inconstant, mercurial, mutable, uncertain, unsettled, unstable, unsteady, variable, volatile, whimsical
near antonyms equable, even; changeless, constant, settled, stable, steady, unchanging

moonshine *n* **1** illegally produced liquor ⟨during Prohibition, *moonshine* and "bathtub gin" were made secretly⟩
synonyms bootleg
related words alcohol, booze, drink, grog, spirits
2 a fermented or distilled beverage that can make a person drunk — see ALCOHOL
3 unintelligible or meaningless talk — see GIBBERISH

moonstruck *adj* having or showing a very abnormal or sick state of mind — see INSANE 1

moor *vb* to put securely in place or in a desired position — see FASTEN 2

moot *adj* open to question or dispute — see DEBATABLE 1

moot *vb* **1** to present or bring forward for discussion — see INTRODUCE 2
2 to talk about (an issue) usually from various points of view and for the purpose of arriving at a decision or opinion — see DISCUSS

mope *vb* **1** to move about from place to place aimlessly — see WANDER
2 to silently go about in a bad mood — see SULK

mopes *n pl* a state or spell of low spirits — see SADNESS

moral *adj* **1** conforming to a high standard of morality or virtue — see GOOD 2

2 guided by or in accordance with one's sense of right and wrong — see CONSCIENTIOUS 1

moralist *n* a person who is greatly concerned with seemly behavior and morality especially regarding sexual matters — see PRUDE

morality *n* **1** conduct that conforms to an accepted standard of right and wrong ⟨the candidate claimed to be the best choice because of his unswerving *morality*⟩
synonyms character, decency, goodness, honesty, integrity, probity, rectitude, righteousness, uprightness, virtue, virtuousness
related words high-mindedness, honor, incorruptibility; appropriateness, correctness, decorousness, decorum, etiquette, fitness, propriety, seemliness; ethics, morals
near antonyms impropriety, indecency, indiscretion; debauchery, degeneracy, degradation, depravity, perversion; crookedness, dishonesty, underhandedness, unscrupulousness; lowness, meanness, viciousness, vileness; corruption, sin
antonyms badness, evil, immorality, wickedness
2 the code of good conduct for an individual or group — see ETHICS

morally *adv* with purity of thought and deed — see PURELY

morals *n pl* the code of good conduct for an individual or group — see ETHICS

morass *n* spongy land saturated or partially covered with water — see SWAMP

morbid *adj* causing or marked by an atmosphere lacking in cheer — see GLOOMY 1

mordant *adj* marked by the use of wit that is intended to cause hurt feelings — see SARCASTIC

more *adj* resulting in an increase in amount or number — see ADDITIONAL

more *adv* **1** in addition to what has been said ⟨the sci-fi movie was totally unbelievable and, what's *more*, it was boring⟩
synonyms additionally, again, also, besides, further, furthermore, likewise, moreover, then, too, withal, yet
phrases as well, in addition to, to boot
2 to a greater or higher extent ⟨the boxers for this bout are *more* evenly matched than the last two were⟩
synonyms better

more or less *adv* **1** very close to but not completely — see ALMOST
2 to some degree or extent — see FAIRLY

moreover *adv* in addition to what has been said — see MORE 1

mores *n pl* personal conduct or behavior as evaluated by an accepted standard of appropriateness for a social or professional setting — see MANNER 1

moribund *adj* nearly dead ⟨with its run-down look and empty aisles, the business appeared *moribund*⟩
synonyms dying
related words expiring, fading, passing away, sinking; decadent, declining, deteriorating; dead, deceased, defunct, departed, gone, passed away; terminal
near antonyms alive, animate, living; being, breathing, existing, subsisting, surviving; flourishing, prospering, thriving

morn *n* **1** the first appearance of light in the morning or the time of its appearance — see DAWN 1
2 the time from sunrise until noon — see MORNING 1

morning *n* **1** the time from sunrise until noon ⟨I hate getting up in the *morning* to go to school⟩
synonyms forenoon, morn
related words aurora, dawn, dawning, daybreak, daylight; cockcrow, sunrise, sunup; day, daytime, light
near antonyms dark, darkness, night, nighttime, twilight; dusk, evening, nightfall, sundown, sunset; afternoon
2 the first appearance of light in the morning or the time of its appearance — see DAWN 1
3 the point at which something begins — see BEGINNING

moron *n* a stupid person — see IDIOT

morose *adj* causing or marked by an atmosphere lacking in cheer — see GLOOMY 1

morsel *n* **1** a small piece or quantity of food ⟨I suppose you can have dessert, since you only left a couple *morsels* on your plate⟩
synonyms bite, mouthful, nibble, taste, tidbit (*also* titbit)
related words snack; appetizer, hors d'oeuvre; bit, chew, crumb, dab, driblet, hint, lick, nubbin, nugget, pinch, scrap, shred, smidgen (*also* smidgeon *or* smidgin), speck, spot, sprinkling, suspicion, touch, trace; dash, drop; gulp, swallow, swig
2 a very small piece — see BIT 1

mortal *adj* **1** likely to cause or capable of causing death — see DEADLY
2 of, relating to, or suggestive of death — see DEATHLY 1
3 relating to or characteristic of human beings — see HUMAN

mortal *n* a member of the human race — see HUMAN

mortally *adv* to a great degree — see VERY 1

mortician *n* a person who manages funerals and prepares the dead for burial or cremation — see FUNERAL DIRECTOR

mortification *n* the emotional state of being made self-consciously uncomfortable — see EMBARRASSMENT 1

mortify *vb* to throw into a state of self-conscious distress — see EMBARRASS 1

[1]**most** *adv* to a great degree — see VERY 1

[2]**most** *adv* very close to but not completely — see ALMOST

most *adj* of the greatest or highest degree or quantity — see ULTIMATE 1

most *n* the greatest amount, number, or part ⟨this room will accommodate 50 people at the *most*⟩
synonyms maximum, outside
related words best, utmost
antonyms least, minimum

mostly *adv* for the most part — see CHIEFLY

mote *n* a very small piece — see BIT 1

moth–eaten *adj* **1** having passed its time of use or usefulness — see OBSOLETE
2 showing signs of advanced wear and tear and neglect — see SHABBY 1
3 used or heard so often as to be dull — see STALE

mother *n* a female human parent ⟨he dreaded telling his *mother* that her favorite figurine had gotten broken⟩
synonyms ma, mama, mammy, mom, momma, mum [*chiefly British*]
related words matriarch, matron

mother *vb* to attend to the needs and comforts of — see NURSE 1

motherland *n* the land of one's birth, residence, or citizenship — see COUNTRY 1

motherliness *n* motherly character or qualities — see MATERNITY

motherly *adj* of, relating to, or characteristic of a mother ⟨she showed a sweet *motherly* tenderness toward the tiny kitten she was taking care of⟩
synonyms maternal
related words parental; female, feminine, womanish, womanlike, womanly; matriarchal, matronly; caring, giving, nurturing

mother tongue *n* the stock of words, pronunciation, and grammar used by a people as their basic means of communication — see LANGUAGE 1

motif *n* **1** a major object of interest or concern (as in a discussion or artistic composition) — see MATTER 1
2 a unit of decoration that is repeated all over something (as a fabric) — see PATTERN 1

motion *n* the act or an instance of changing position — see MOVEMENT 1

motion *vb* to direct or notify by a movement or gesture ⟨the referee *motioned* the team captains to confer with him on the sideline⟩
synonyms beckon, flag, gesture, signal, wave
related words gesticulate, pantomime, sign; signalize; acquaint, advise, inform, relate, tell; flourish, shrug

motionlessly *adv* without motion — see STILL 1

motion picture *n* **1** a story told by means of a series of continuously projected pictures and a sound track — see MOVIE 1
2 motion pictures *pl* the art or business of making a movie — see MOVIE 2

motivation *n* something that arouses action or activity — see IMPULSE

motive *n* **1** a major object of interest or concern (as in a discussion or artistic composition) — see MATTER 1
2 a unit of decoration that is repeated all over something (as a fabric) — see PATTERN 1
3 something (as a belief) that serves as the basis for another thing — see REASON 2

motley *adj* **1** consisting of many things of different sorts — see MISCELLANEOUS
2 marked by a variety of usually vivid colors — see COLORFUL

motley *n* **1** a person formerly kept in a royal or noble household to amuse with jests and pranks — see FOOL 2
2 an unorganized collection or mixture of various things — see MISCELLANY 1

motor *n* **1** a device that changes energy into mechanical motion — see ENGINE
2 a self-propelled passenger vehicle on wheels — see CAR

motor *vb* to travel by a motorized vehicle — see DRIVE 2

motorboat *n* a boat equipped with a motor ⟨*motorboats* are banned on the lake because they are a hazard to swimmers⟩
synonyms powerboat, speedboat
related words cabin cruiser, cruiser, runabout

motorcade *n* a group of vehicles traveling together or under one management — see FLEET

motorcar *n* a self-propelled passenger vehicle on wheels — see CAR

motor home *n* a motor vehicle that is specially equipped for living while traveling — see CAMPER

motorist *n* a person who travels by automobile ⟨environmental organizations suggest that *motorists* get together and carpool to avoid using several cars and adding to pollution⟩
synonyms automobilist, driver
related words operator; chauffeur; carpooler

motor vehicle *n* a self-propelled passenger vehicle on wheels — see CAR

mottle *n* a small area that is different (as in color) from the main part — see SPOT 1

mottle *vb* to mark with small spots especially unevenly — see SPOT

mottled *adj* **1** having blotches of two or more colors — see PIED
2 marked with spots — see SPOTTED 1

mound *n* **1** a pile or ridge of granular matter (as sand or snow) — see [2]BANK
2 a quantity of things thrown or stacked on one another — see [1]PILE 1
3 an area of high ground — see HEIGHT 4

mound *vb* **1** to form into a pile or ridge of earth ⟨he likes to sit on the beach and *mound* sand into sand castles⟩
synonyms bank, hill
related words heap, pile, pyramid, stack; embank; bunch, bundle, clump, lump, mass, wad; accumulate, amass, assemble, collect, gather, group
2 to lay or throw on top of one another — see PILE

[1]**mount** *n* an elevation of land higher than a hill — see MOUNTAIN 1

[2]**mount** *n* something that holds up or serves as a foundation for something else — see SUPPORT 1

mount *vb* **1** to become greater in extent, volume, amount, or number — see INCREASE 2
2 to bring before the public in performance or exhibition — see PRESENT 1
3 to move or extend upward — see ASCEND

mountain *n* **1** an elevation of land higher than a hill ⟨my cousin likes to climb *mountains* just because she can⟩
synonyms alp, mount, peak
related words mountain range, seamount; mountaintop, pinnacle, precipice, summit
near antonyms basin, bowl, depression, hollow, vale, valley
2 a considerable amount — see LOT 2
3 a quantity of things thrown or stacked on one another — see [1]PILE 1

mountain lion *n* a large tawny cat of the wild — see COUGAR

mountainous *adj* unusually large — see HUGE

mountebank *n* one who makes false claims of identity or expertise — see IMPOSTOR

mounting *n* something that holds up or serves as a foundation for something else — see SUPPORT 1

mourn *vb* **1** to feel deep sadness or mental pain — see GRIEVE
2 to feel or express sorrow for — see LAMENT 1

mournful *adj* **1** expressing or suggesting mourning ⟨she had such a *mournful* expression that someone teasingly asked if her dog had died⟩
synonyms anguished, bemoaning, bewailing, deploring, doleful, dolorous, funeral, grieving, heartbroken, lamentable, lugubrious, plaintive, regretful, rueful, sorrowful, sorry, wailing, weeping, woeful
related words elegiac, melancholy; dejected, de-

pressed, despondent, disconsolate, dispirited, downcast, downhearted, heartsick, inconsolable; careworn, sad, unhappy, woebegone; bawling, crying, groaning, howling, keening, moaning, yammering; bleeding, suffering; black, bleak, cheerless, comfortless, dark, darkening, desolate, dismal, dreary, funereal, gloomy, glum, gray (*also* grey), joyless, low, miserable, moody, morbid, morose, pathetic, pessimistic, piteous, saturnine, somber (*or* sombre), sullen, wretched
near antonyms delighted, exulting, glorying, happy, joyful, rejoicing, triumphant; bright, cheerful, cheering, cheery; laughing, smiling; blithe, blithesome, buoyant, gay, jocund, jolly, joyous, lighthearted, merry, mirthful; encouraging, hopeful, optimistic
2 feeling unhappiness — see SAD 1

mournfully *adv* with feelings of bitterness or grief — see HARD 2

mouse *vb* to move about in a sly or secret manner — see SNEAK 1

mousy *or* **mousey** *adj* easily frightened — see SHY 1

mouth *n* **1** the opening through which food passes into the body of an animal ⟨the baby chicks opened their *mouths* very wide and chirped piteously when their mother came back with worms⟩
synonyms kisser [*slang*], mug
related words countenance, face, puss [*slang*], visage; muzzle; jaws, mandible, maxilla; gullet, maw
2 a twisting of the facial features in disgust or disapproval — see GRIMACE

mouth *vb* to speak softly and unclearly — see MUMBLE

mouth (off) *vb* to talk as if giving an important and formal speech — see ORATE 1

mouthful *n* a small piece or quantity of food — see MORSEL 1

mouthpiece *n* a person who speaks for another or for a group — see SPOKESPERSON

movable *or* **moveable** *adj* capable of being moved especially with ease ⟨any furniture that is not *movable* will be covered with protective cloths by the painters⟩
synonyms mobile, portable
related words adjustable, flexible, modular; removable, transferable, transportable; motile, moving; unsteady, unstable; manageable
near antonyms motionless, moveless, static, stationary, still, stuck, unmoving, wedged; fast, fixed, rooted, steadfast
antonyms immobile, immovable, irremovable, unmovable

movables *or* **moveables** *n pl* **1** the movable articles in a room — see FURNITURE
2 transportable items that one owns — see POSSESSION 2

move *n* **1** an action planned or taken to achieve a desired result — see MEASURE 1
2 the act or an instance of changing position — see MOVEMENT 1

move *vb* **1** to change the place or position of ⟨I need you to *move* all your books off the chair before company gets here⟩
synonyms budge, dislocate, displace, disturb, remove, shift, transfer, transpose
related words bear, carry, convey, drive, haul, transmit, transport; transplant; replace, supersede, supplant; alter, make over, modify, redo, refashion, remake, remodel, revamp, revise, rework, vary
near antonyms fix, freeze, set, stabilize
2 to set or keep in motion ⟨the hands of the wall clock are *moved* by battery⟩
synonyms actuate, drive, impel, propel, work
related words activate, motivate, provoke; abet, ferment, foment, incite, raise, stir (up), whip (up); set off, trigger; excite, galvanize, inflame, inspire, motivate, rouse
near antonyms check, curb, inhibit, restrain
3 to change one's position ⟨don't *move* while I'm trying to draw your portrait⟩
synonyms budge, shift, stir
related words fidget, jiggle, squirm, twitch, wiggle, writhe; rouse
near antonyms remain, stay; stabilize
antonyms freeze
4 to act upon (a person or a person's feelings) so as to cause a response — see ^{1}AFFECT 1
5 to rouse to strong feeling or action — see PROVOKE 1
6 to cause (someone) to agree with a belief or course of action by using arguments or earnest requests — see PERSUADE
7 to cause to function — see ACTIVATE
8 to leave a place often for another — see GO 2

movement *n* **1** the act or an instance of changing position ⟨a sudden *movement* in the far corner of the room made her turn in that direction⟩
synonyms motion, move, shift, shifting, stir, stirring
related words dislocation, migration, relocation; locomotion, mobility, motility; fiddling, fidgeting, squirming, twitching, wriggling, writhing; flailing, flapping, waving
near antonyms immobility; inertia, inertness, stillness; ending, finish, halt, pause, stop, termination
antonyms motionlessness
2 a series of activities undertaken to achieve a goal — see CAMPAIGN

movie *n* **1** a story told by means of a series of continuously projected pictures and a sound track ⟨there was much excitement when it was announced that the popular children's book would be turned into a *movie*⟩
synonyms film, motion picture, moving picture, picture
related words animated cartoon, cartoon, docudrama, documentary, feature
2 movies *pl* the art or business of making a movie ⟨many a small-town girl has gone to Hollywood, dreaming of making it big in the *movies*⟩
synonyms cinema, film, motion pictures, pictures, screen
related words show business

moving *adj* having the power to affect the feelings or sympathies ⟨he gave a truly *moving* graduation speech that had some graduates in tears⟩
synonyms affecting, emotional, impressive, poignant, stirring, touching
related words eloquent, expressive, meaningful, significant; demonstrative, excitable, feeling, passionate, responsive, sensitive; exciting, provoking, rousing, stimulating; dramatic, histrionic, melodramatic, theatrical
near antonyms cold, cool, detached, dispassionate; deadpan
antonyms unemotional, unimpressive

moving picture *n* a story told by means of a series of continuously projected pictures and a sound track — see MOVIE 1

mow *vb* **1** to shorten the standing leafy plant cover of <you really should *mow* the lawn before it gets much higher>
synonyms cut
related words clip, crop, dock, lop, manicure, pare, prune, trim; shave, shear
2 to bring down by cutting — see FELL 2

mow (down) *vb* to kill on a large scale — see MASSACRE

much *adv* **1** to a great degree — see VERY 1
2 to a large extent or degree — see GREATLY 2
3 very close to but not completely — see ALMOST

much *n* a considerable amount — see LOT 2

muck *n* **1** foul matter that mars the purity or cleanliness of something — see FILTH 1
2 soft wet earth — see MUD

mucky *adj* **1** full of or covered with soft wet earth — see MUDDY 1
2 not clean — see DIRTY 1

mud *n* soft wet earth <we cannot play softball today because the field turned to *mud* after last night's heavy rain>
synonyms mire, muck, ooze, slime, slop, sludge, slush
related words gumbo, silt; clay, dirt, gravel, humus, loam, sand, soil

muddle *n* **1** a state in which everything is out of order — see CHAOS
2 a state of mental confusion — see HAZE 2
3 a state of mental uncertainty — see CONFUSION 1
4 an unorganized collection or mixture of various things — see MISCELLANY 1

muddle *vb* **1** to throw into a state of mental uncertainty — see CONFUSE 1
2 to undo the proper order or arrangement of — see DISORDER

muddled *adj* lacking in order, neatness, and often cleanliness — see MESSY

muddy *adj* **1** full of or covered with soft wet earth <please do not walk in the house with *muddy* boots on, as you will get the carpet dirty>
synonyms miry, mucky, oozy, slimy, sludgy, slushy
related words clayey, loamy, silty; bedraggled; dirty, filthy, foul, grimy, grubby, grungy, impure, squalid, unclean, uncleanly
near antonyms clean, cleanly, immaculate, spotless, unsoiled, unsullied
2 having visible particles in liquid suspension — see CLOUDY 1
3 not clean — see DIRTY 1

muddy *vb* **1** to throw into a state of mental uncertainty — see CONFUSE 1
2 to make (something) unclear to the understanding — see CONFUSE 2
3 to make dirty — see DIRTY

muff *vb* to make or do (something) in a clumsy or unskillful way — see BOTCH

muffle *vb* to deaden the sound of <the walls *muffled* their conversation so that only a low murmur was heard>
synonyms mute
related words insulate, soundproof; dampen, mellow, soften, subdue, tone (down); baffle; smother
near antonyms amplify, enhance, heighten, increase, magnify, strengthen

mug *n* **1** a round vessel equipped with a handle and designed for drinking — see CUP
2 a violent, brutal person who is often a member of an organized gang — see HOODLUM
3 the front part of the head — see FACE 1
4 the opening through which food passes into the body of an animal — see MOUTH 1

mug *vb* **1** to distort one's face <every time their picture was snapped, both children *mugged* by sticking out their tongues or scrunching up their faces>
synonyms grimace
related words pout; contort, deform, twist, warp; frown, glare, gloom, glower, lower (*also* lour), scowl; gape, gaze, ogle, stare; growl, snarl, sneer; simper, smirk
phrases make faces
near antonyms beam, grin, smile
2 to take a photograph of — see PHOTOGRAPH

muggy *adj* containing or characterized by an uncomfortable amount of moisture — see HUMID

mulct *n* a sum of money to be paid as a punishment — see FINE

mulct *vb* to rob by the use of trickery or threats — see FLEECE

mulish *adj* sticking to an opinion, purpose, or course of action in spite of reason, arguments, or persuasion — see OBSTINATE

mulishness *n* a steadfast adherence to an opinion, purpose, or course of action — see OBSTINACY

mull (over) *vb* to give serious and careful thought to — see PONDER

multicolored *adj* marked by a variety of usually vivid colors — see COLORFUL

multifarious *adj* being of many and various kinds — see MANIFOLD

multiple *adj* being of a large but indefinite number — see MANY

multiplex *adj* being of a large but indefinite number — see MANY

multiplication *n* the act or process of becoming greater in number <there's been a steady *multiplication* in our attic of old video equipment since the revolution in consumer electronics>
synonyms accumulating, accumulation, addition, increase, proliferation
related words doubling, quadrupling, tripling; growth, rise, spread; enlargement, escalation, expansion; amplification, distention, inflation; accretion, accrual, augmentation; extension, lengthening
near antonyms compressing, compression, condensation, condensing, constricting, constriction, contracting, contraction, diminishing, diminishment, lessening, lowering, shrinking; retrenching, retrenchment, shortening
antonyms decrease

multiply *vb* **1** to bring forth offspring — see PROCREATE
2 to make greater in size, amount, or number — see INCREASE 1
3 to become greater in extent, volume, amount, or number — see INCREASE 2

multitude *n* a great number of persons or things gathered together — see CROWD 1

multitudinous *adj* being of a large but indefinite number — see MANY

mum *n, chiefly British* a female human parent — see MOTHER

mum *adj* deliberately refraining from speech — see SILENT 1

mumble *n* speech that is not clear enough to be understood <please answer the question without your usual *mumble* and try to use complete sentences>
synonyms grunt, grunting, murmur, murmuring, mutter, muttering
related words undertone, whisper; babble, babbling, blab, blabbing, chatter, chattering, drivel, driveling (*or* drivelling), gabble, gabbling, jabber, jabbering, maundering, prattle, prattling, rambling

mumble *vb* to speak softly and unclearly <I can't understand you if you *mumble*>
synonyms grunt, mouth, murmur, mutter
related words babble, blab, chatter, drivel, gabble, gibber, jabber, maunder, prattle, ramble; breathe, gasp, pant, whisper
near antonyms articulate, enunciate
antonyms speak out, speak up

mumbo jumbo *n* unintelligible or meaningless talk — see GIBBERISH

mummer *n* **1** an actor in a story performed silently and entirely by body movements — see MIME
2 one who acts professionally (as in a play, movie, or television show) — see ACTOR

mundane *adj* **1** having to do with the practical details of regular life <they didn't want to be bothered with *mundane* concerns like doing the dishes while on vacation>
synonyms everyday, prosaic, workaday
related words earthly, temporal, worldly; average, common, commonplace, customary, familiar, garden, normal, ordinary, plain, popular, routine, run-of-the-mill, typical, unexceptional, unremarkable, usual; frequent, habitual, regular; expected, predictable
near antonyms high-minded, lofty, noble, sublime; aberrant, abnormal, atypical; exceptional, extraordinary, odd, peculiar, phenomenal, rare, singular, special, uncommon, uncustomary, unique, unusual, unwonted; bizarre, curious, funny, odd, outlandish, quaint, remarkable, strange, weird
2 having to do with life on earth especially as opposed to that in heaven — see EARTHLY

municipality *n* a thickly settled, highly populated area — see CITY

munificent *adj* giving or sharing in abundance and without hesitation — see GENEROUS 1

munificently *adv* in a generous manner — see WELL 2

murder *n* **1** a situation or state that causes great suffering and unhappiness — see HELL 2
2 the intentional and unlawful taking of another person's life — see HOMICIDE

murder *vb* **1** to put to death deliberately <those people made me so mad I felt like I wanted to *murder* them>
synonyms dispatch, do in, execute, liquidate, slay
related words blot out, destroy, fell, kill, smite, zap; assassinate; butcher, massacre, mow (down), slaughter; annihilate, eliminate, eradicate, exterminate, wipe out
phrases do away with
2 to make or do (something) in a clumsy or unskillful way — see BOTCH

murderer *n* a person who kills another person — see ASSASSIN

murdering *adj* eager for or marked by the shedding of blood, extreme violence, or killing — see BLOODTHIRSTY

murderous *adj* **1** difficult to endure — see HARSH 1
2 requiring considerable physical or mental effort — see HARD 2
3 likely to cause or capable of causing death — see DEADLY
4 eager for or marked by the shedding of blood, extreme violence, or killing — see BLOODTHIRSTY

murk *n* **1** a time or place of little or no light — see DARK 1
2 an atmospheric condition in which suspended particles in the air rob it of its transparency — see HAZE 1

murkiness *n* the quality or state of having a veiled or uncertain meaning — see OBSCURITY 1

murky *adj* **1** being without light or without much light — see DARK 1
2 causing or marked by an atmosphere lacking in cheer — see GLOOMY 1
3 filled with or dimmed by fine particles (as of dust or water) in suspension — see HAZY 1
4 having an often intentionally veiled or uncertain meaning — see OBSCURE 1
5 not seen or understood clearly — see FAINT 1

murmur *n* **1** an expression of dissatisfaction, pain, or resentment — see COMPLAINT 1
2 speech that is not clear enough to be understood — see MUMBLE

murmur *vb* **1** to express dissatisfaction, pain, or resentment usually tiresomely — see COMPLAIN
2 to speak softly and unclearly — see MUMBLE

murmurer *n* an irritable and complaining person — see GROUCH

murmuring *n* speech that is not clear enough to be understood — see MUMBLE

muscle *n* **1** muscular strength <I'm going to need someone with real *muscle* to help me move all this furniture>
synonyms brawn, main
related words force, might, potency, power, puissance, sinew
near antonyms impotence, weakness
2 the ability to exert effort for the accomplishment of a task — see POWER 2

muscle *vb* **1** to cause (a person) to give in to pressure — see FORCE
2 to force one's way — see PRESS 4

muscular *adj* **1** marked by a well-developed musculature <Olympic runners tend to have very *muscular* legs>
synonyms brawny, sinewy
related words wiry; powerful, strong; beefy, burly, hefty, hulking, husky; able-bodied, athletic, herculean, mighty, robust, rugged, stalwart, strapping, sturdy
near antonyms nonathletic; delicate, feeble, fragile, frail, weak, weakly, wimpy; light, lightweight, slight; lean, slender, slim, svelte, sylphlike, thin, willowy; emaciated, gaunt, lank, rawboned, spare
antonyms scrawny, skinny
2 having muscles capable of exerting great physical force — see STRONG 1

museum *n* a building or part of a building in which objects of interest are displayed <we're taking a trip to the *Museum* of Natural History as a special treat for science class>
synonyms gallery, salon

related words archives, collection, library; display, exhibition; studio

mush *n* **1** something (as a work of literature or music) that is too sentimental — see CORN
2 the state or quality of having an excess of tender feelings (as of love, nostalgia, or compassion) — see SENTIMENTALITY

mushroom *vb* to become greater in extent, volume, amount, or number — see INCREASE 2

mushy *adj* **1** appealing to the emotions in an obvious and tiresome way — see CORNY
2 giving easily to the touch — see SOFT 3

musical *adj* **1** having a pleasantly flowing quality suggestive of music — see LYRIC 1
2 having a pleasing mixture of notes — see HARMONIOUS 1

musicale *n* an entertainment featuring singing or the playing of musical instruments — see CONCERT

musician *n* **1** a person who plays a musical instrument ⟨the violinist was a famous and exquisitely talented *musician*⟩
synonyms instrumentalist, player
related words artist, performer; maestro, virtuoso; accompanist, recitalist, soloist; accordionist, bassoonist, clarinetist (*or* clarinettist), cornetist (*or* cornettist), drummer, fiddler, flautist, flutist, guitarist, harpist, oboist, organ-grinder, organist, percussionist, pianist, piper, saxophonist, trombonist, trumpeter, violinist
2 a person who writes musical compositions — see COMPOSER

muskeg *n* spongy land saturated or partially covered with water — see SWAMP

muss *vb* to undo the proper order or arrangement of — see DISORDER

mussed *adj* lacking in order, neatness, and often cleanliness — see MESSY

mussy *adj* lacking in order, neatness, and often cleanliness — see MESSY

must *n* something necessary, indispensable, or unavoidable — see ESSENTIAL 1

must *vb* to be under necessity or obligation to — see NEED 2

muster *n* a body of people come together in one place — see GATHERING 1

muster *vb* **1** to assemble and make ready for action — see MOBILIZE
2 to bring together in assembly by or as if by command — see CONVOKE

muster out *vb* to let go from office, service, or employment — see DISMISS 1

musty *adj* **1** having an unpleasant smell — see MALODOROUS
2 used or heard so often as to be dull — see STALE

mutable *adj* likely to change frequently, suddenly, or unexpectedly — see FICKLE 1

mutate *vb* to pass from one form, state, or level to another — see CHANGE 2

mute *adj* **1** unable to speak ⟨the child is both deaf and *mute* because her hearing was lost at birth⟩
synonyms inarticulate, speechless, voiceless
related words tongue-tied; incoherent, incomprehensible; closemouthed, laconic, taciturn, tight-lipped, uncommunicative; mum, nonspeaking, quiet, silent, wordless
near antonyms communicative, gabby, garrulous, loquacious, talkative, talky, vocal; expatiating, speaking out, speaking up; articulating, speaking, talking; articulate, eloquent, fluent, voluble
2 deliberately refraining from speech — see SILENT 1

mute *n* a device on a musical instrument that deadens or softens its tone ⟨I got in trouble for practicing my trumpet at three in the morning when the *mute* fell out, and I woke everyone up⟩
synonyms damper
related words muffler, quieter, softener

mute *vb* **1** to stop the noise or speech of — see SILENCE 1
2 to deaden the sound of — see MUFFLE

muted *adj* **1** mostly or entirely without sound — see SILENT 3
2 not excessively showy — see QUIET 2

muteness *n* incapacity for or restraint from speaking — see SILENCE 1

mutilate *vb* to cause severe or permanent injury to — see MAIM

mutineer *n* a person who rises up against authority — see REBEL

mutinous *adj* taking part in a rebellion — see REBELLIOUS 1

mutiny *n* open fighting against authority (as one's own government) — see REBELLION

mutiny *vb* to rise up against established authority — see REBEL

mutter *n* speech that is not clear enough to be understood — see MUMBLE

mutter *vb* **1** to express dissatisfaction, pain, or resentment usually tiresomely — see COMPLAIN
2 to speak softly and unclearly — see MUMBLE

mutterer *n* an irritable and complaining person — see GROUCH

muttering *n* speech that is not clear enough to be understood — see MUMBLE

mutual *adj* used or done by a number of people as a group — see COLLECTIVE

myopic *adj* **1** able to see near things more clearly than distant ones — see NEARSIGHTED
2 not thinking about and providing for the future — see IMPROVIDENT

myriad *adj* being of many and various kinds — see MANIFOLD

mysterious *adj* **1** being beyond one's powers to know, understand, or explain ⟨the huge stone statues on Easter Island are ancient, *mysterious*, and haunting⟩
synonyms cryptic, darkling, deep, enigmatic (*also* enigmatical), impenetrable, inscrutable, mystic, occult, uncanny
related words dark, murky, obscure, shadowy, vague; ambiguous, equivocal; incomprehensible, unfathomable, unintelligible; inexplicable, unaccountable, unexplainable; unanswerable, unknowable; metaphysical, mystical, supernatural; abstruse, esoteric, recondite; baffling, bewildering, confounding, confusing, mystifying, perplexing, puzzling
near antonyms fathomable, intelligible, understandable; clear, obvious, open-and-shut, plain, straightforward, transparent
2 having an often intentionally veiled or uncertain meaning — see OBSCURE 1

mystery *n* something hard to understand or explain ⟨why my sister dyed her hair bright blue is still a *mystery* to my parents⟩
synonyms conundrum, enigma, mystification, puzzle, puzzlement, riddle, secret
related words brainteaser, challenge, perplexity, poser, problem, stumper

mystic *adj* **1** having seemingly supernatural qualities or powers ⟨the notion that a cat has nine lives is based upon the belief that nine is a *mystic* number⟩
synonyms magic, magical, occult, weird
related words bewitched, enchanted, spellbound; bewitching, charming, conjuring, enchanting, wiling; awesome, extraordinary, marvelous (*or* marvellous), wondrous; divining, forecasting, foreknowing, foreseeing, foretelling, fortunetelling, predicting, presaging, prognosticating, prophesying, soothsaying
near antonyms commonplace, ordinary, unremarkable
2 being beyond one's powers to know, understand, or explain — see MYSTERIOUS 1
3 having an often intentionally veiled or uncertain meaning — see OBSCURE 1

mystification *n* **1** a state of mental uncertainty — see CONFUSION 1
2 something hard to understand or explain — see MYSTERY

mystify *vb* to throw into a state of mental uncertainty — see CONFUSE 1

myth *n* **1** a traditional but unfounded story that gives the reason for a current custom, belief, or fact of nature ⟨according to an ancient Greek *myth*, humans acquired fire from a giant who had stolen it from heaven⟩
synonyms fable, legend
related words allegory, parable; fabrication, fantasy (*also* phantasy), fiction, figment, invention; narrative, saga, story, tale, yarn
2 the body of customs, beliefs, stories, and sayings associated with a people, thing, or place — see FOLKLORE
3 a false idea or belief — see FALLACY 1

mythical *or* **mythic** *adj* **1** based on, described in, or being a myth ⟨for years the Spanish conquistadors searched for the *mythical* El Dorado, a place of unimaginable riches⟩
synonyms fabled, fabulous, legendary
related words famed, romanticized, storied; fabricated, fantastic, fantastical, fictional, fictitious; fanciful; allegorical, mythological
near antonyms actual, real; historical; factual, true
2 not real and existing only in the imagination — see IMAGINARY

mythology *n* the body of customs, beliefs, stories, and sayings associated with a people, thing, or place — see FOLKLORE

nab *vb* **1** to take or keep under one's control by authority of law — see ARREST 1
2 to take physical control or possession of (something) suddenly or forcibly — see CATCH 1

nag *n* a large hoofed domestic animal that is used for carrying or drawing loads and for riding — see HORSE

nag *vb* to subject (someone) to constant scoldings and sharp reminders ⟨she kept *nagging* him to fix the furnace before the weather got any colder⟩
synonyms henpeck, hound, needle
related words carp (at), fuss (about *or* over), nitpick; annoy, badger, bait, bother, bug, chivy, harass, harry, hassle, irk, pester, plague, ride, vex, yap (at); egg, goad, incite, prod, prompt, spur, urge; exhort, insist, press, pressure, push; blandish, cajole, coax, wheedle; beg, importune, plead
near antonyms compliment; commend, laud, praise, recommend, tout; acclaim, applaud, eulogize, extol (*also* extoll)

naiad *n* **1** a mythical goddess represented as a young girl and said to live outdoors — see NYMPH 1
2 a young wingless often wormlike form (as a grub or caterpillar) that hatches from the egg of many insects — see LARVA

nail *vb* to take physical control or possession of (something) suddenly or forcibly — see CATCH 1

naive *or* **naïve** *adj* **1** lacking in worldly wisdom or informed judgment ⟨a first-time buyer who was so *naive* that he believed the salesman and paid good money for the rusty and broken-down car⟩
synonyms green, ingenuous, innocent, simple, simpleminded, uncritical, unknowing, unsophisticated, unsuspecting, unsuspicious, unwary, unworldly, wide-eyed
related words callow, dewy, inexperienced, raw; childlike, idealistic, impractical; believing, credulous, gullible, susceptible, trustful, trusting, unguarded; beguiled, duped, gulled, tricked; careless, heedless
near antonyms critical, doubting, incredulous, skeptical, suspecting, suspicious, unconvinced; careful, cautious, guarded, leery, wary, watchful; down-to-earth, hardheaded, pragmatic (*also* pragmatical), realistic, sober
antonyms cynical, experienced, knowing, sophisticated, worldly, worldly-wise
2 free from any intent to deceive or impress others — see GUILELESS
3 readily taken advantage of — see EASY 2

naively *adv* without any attempt to impress by deception or exaggeration — see NATURALLY 3

naïveté *also* **naivete** *n* **1** the quality or state of being simple and sincere ⟨her *naïveté* led her to leave her new bike outside the mall unchained while she shopped⟩
synonyms artlessness, greenness, guilelessness, ingenuousness, innocence, naturalness, simpleness, simplicity, unsophistication, unworldliness
related words candor, frankness, genuineness, honesty, openness, sincerity, straightforwardness; callowness, childishness, inexperience, rawness; carelessness, heedlessness; ignorance, obliviousness, unawareness; credulity, credulousness, gullibility; idealism, impracticality, optimism
near antonyms affectedness, artificiality, pretentiousness; deviousness, dishonesty, insincerity; disbelief, doubtfulness, incredulity, suspicious-

ness; carefulness, caution, wariness; pessimism, skepticism; maturity
antonyms artfulness, cynicism, sophistication, worldliness
2 readiness to believe the claims of others without sufficient evidence — see CREDULITY

naked *adj* **1** lacking or shed of clothing ⟨had recurrent nightmares about being *naked* in public⟩
synonyms bare, disrobed, nude, stripped, unclad, unclothed, undressed
related words denuded, peeled; raw, stark; unveiled
near antonyms covered, veiled; arrayed, caparisoned, decked (out), rigged (out), tricked (out); vested; decent
antonyms appareled (*or* apparelled), attired, clad, clothed, dressed, garbed, invested, robed, suited
2 lacking a usual or natural covering ⟨the winter trees were *naked* without their colorful fall leaves⟩
synonyms bald, bare, denuded, exposed, open, peeled, stripped, uncovered
related words displayed, revealed; hairless, shaven; disrobed, unclad, unclothed, undressed; skinned; divested; unprotected, unsheltered
near antonyms mantled; overgrown, overrun, overspread; bearded, hairy
antonyms covered
3 free from all additions or embellishment — see PLAIN 1

name *adj* having a good reputation especially in a field of knowledge — see RESPECTABLE 1

name *n* **1** a word or combination of words by which a person or thing is regularly known ⟨introduced himself and then asked what my *name* was⟩
synonyms appellation, cognomen, denomination, denotation, designation, handle, title
related words christian name, forename, given name; family name, maiden name, surname; epithet, nickname, sobriquet (*also* soubriquet); alias, nom de plume, pen name, pseudonym; binomial, vernacular; misnomer; label, trademark
2 an act or expression showing scorn and usually intended to hurt another's feelings — see INSULT
3 outward and often deceptive indication — see APPEARANCE 2
4 overall quality as seen or judged by people in general — see REPUTATION

name *vb* **1** to give a name to ⟨decided to *name* her new puppy "Bubbles"⟩
synonyms baptize, call, christen, denominate, designate, dub, entitle, label, style, term, title
related words denote, specify; miscall, misname; nickname; rename
2 to make reference to or speak about briefly but specifically — see MENTION 1
3 to pick (someone) by one's authority for a specific position or duty — see APPOINT 2
4 to decide to accept (someone or something) from a group of possibilities — see CHOOSE 1
5 to decide upon (the time or date for an event) usually from a position of authority — see APPOINT 1

nameless *adj* **1** not named or identified by a name ⟨the victim of the crime will remain *nameless* to protect his privacy⟩ ⟨*nameless* editors who write TV listings in the newspaper⟩
synonyms anonymous, incognito, unbaptized, unchristened, unidentified, unnamed, untitled
related words unspecified; obscure, uncelebrated, unheard-of, unknown, unnoted, unremarkable
near antonyms denominated, designated, specified; labeled (*or* labelled), tabbed, titled; celebrated, famed, famous, known, notable, noted, noteworthy, remarkable, renowned, well-known
antonyms baptized, christened, dubbed, named, termed
2 beyond the power to describe — see INDESCRIBABLE
3 not widely known — see OBSCURE 2

namer *n* someone with the right or responsibility for making a selection — see SELECTOR

[1]**nap** *n* a short sleep ⟨so tired that she needed to take a refreshing *nap* before soccer practice⟩
synonyms catnap, doze, drowse, forty winks, siesta, snooze, wink
related words repose, rest; slumber; bed

[2]**nap** *n* a soft airy substance or covering — see FUZZ

nap *vb* **1** to sleep lightly or briefly ⟨decided to let the kids *nap* for a few more minutes before waking them⟩
synonyms catnap, doze, drowse, slumber, snooze
related words relax, repose, rest; couch, lay, lie, roost; lull
near antonyms arise, arouse, awake, awaken, get up, rise, rouse, uprise, wake (up), waken
2 be in a state of sleep — see SLEEP 1

napping *adj* being in a state of suspended consciousness — see ASLEEP 1

napping *n* a natural periodic loss of consciousness during which the body restores itself — see SLEEP 1

narcotic *adj* **1** tending to calm the emotions and relieve stress — see SOOTHING 1
2 tending to cause sleep — see HYPNOTIC

narrate *vb* to give an oral or written account of in some detail — see TELL 1

narrative *n* **1** a relating of events usually in the order in which they happened — see ACCOUNT 1
2 a work with imaginary characters and events that is shorter and usually less complex than a novel — see STORY 1

narrow *adj* **1** being of less than usual width ⟨found a *narrow* opening in the fence that he was able to squeeze through⟩
synonyms fine, hairline, needlelike, skinny, slender, slim, thin
related words attenuated, elongated, linear; close, compressed, condensed, constricted, contracted, squeezed, tight, tightened; reedy, stalky, stringy, twiggy, wispy; spare
near antonyms chunky, squat, stocky, stumpy, thick, thickset; bulky, massive
antonyms broad, fat, wide
2 not broad or open in views or opinions ⟨a *narrow* person who thought that anyone who owned a television was morally corrupt⟩
synonyms insular, little, parochial, petty, provincial, sectarian, small, small-minded
related words inflexible, obdurate, obstinate, rigid, set, stubborn, unyielding, wrongheaded; bigoted, intolerant, narrow-minded; biased, discriminating, discriminatory, jaundiced, one-sided, partial, partisan, prejudiced; old-fashioned, reactionary, stodgy, straitlaced (*or* straightlaced); dogmatic, opinionated; limited
near antonyms impartial, nonpartisan, objective, unbiased, unprejudiced

antonyms broad-minded, catholic, cosmopolitan, liberal, open, open-minded, receptive, tolerant
3 having distinct or certain limits — see LIMITED 1
4 showing little difference in the standing of the competitors — see CLOSE 3
5 unwilling to grant other people social rights or to accept other viewpoints — see INTOLERANT 2

narrow–minded *adj* unwilling to grant other people social rights or to accept other viewpoints — see INTOLERANT 2

narrows *n pl* a narrow body of water between two land masses — see CHANNEL 2

nastily *adv* in a mean or spiteful manner ⟨he *nastily* stuck his foot out and tripped the front runner because he couldn't stand to see her win⟩
synonyms cattily, despitefully, hatefully, malevolently, maliciously, malignantly, meanly, spitefully, viciously, villainously, virulently, wickedly
related words contemptuously, deprecatingly, disdainfully, scornfully; acrimoniously, antagonistically, caustically, hostilely, invidiously, obnoxiously, rancorously, venomously; bitterly, enviously, jealously, resentfully; balefully, callously, cruelly, hardheartedly, heartlessly, inhumanely, mercilessly, pitilessly, ruthlessly, soullessly, unfeelingly; disagreeably, ill, ungraciously, unkindly; ill-naturedly, inconsiderately, insensitively, thoughtlessly; diabolically, fiendishly; misanthropically
near antonyms affably, agreeably, amiably, cordially, genially, good-humoredly, good-naturedly, graciously, nicely, pleasantly; altruistically, humanely; considerately, feelingly, lovingly, mercifully, sensitively, softheartedly, solicitously, soulfully, thoughtfully; compassionately, sympathetically; angelically, divinely, sweetly, tenderly
antonyms benevolently, benignantly, good-heartedly, kindheartedly, kindly

nastiness *n* **1** the desire to cause pain for the satisfaction of doing harm — see MALICE
2 the quality or state of being obscene — see OBSCENITY 1
3 the state or quality of being dirty — see DIRTINESS 1

nasty *adj* **1** arousing or deserving of one's loathing and disgust — see CONTEMPTIBLE 1
2 causing intense displeasure, disgust, or resentment — see OFFENSIVE 1
3 causing or feeling bodily pain — see PAINFUL 1
4 depicting or referring to sexual matters in a way that is unacceptable in polite society — see OBSCENE 1
5 having or showing a desire to cause someone pain or suffering for the sheer enjoyment of it — see HATEFUL
6 marked by wet and windy conditions — see FOUL 1
7 not clean — see DIRTY 1
8 not giving pleasure to the mind or senses — see UNPLEASANT

nation *n* a body of people composed of one or more nationalities usually with its own territory and government ⟨the American people became one *nation* when they adopted the Constitution in 1789⟩
synonyms commonwealth, country, land, sovereignty, state
related words city-state; domain, dominion, empire, kingdom, realm, republic; duchy, dukedom, principality, seigniory (*or* seignory), sultanate; democracy, dictatorship, monarchy, oligarchy, sovereign, theocracy; colony, dependency, province, settlement, soil; fatherland, homeland, motherland; power, superpower

national *adj* of or relating to a nation ⟨played the home team's *national* anthem before the start of the soccer game⟩
synonyms civil, public, state
related words civic, federal, municipal; government, governmental; domestic, internal; democratic, republican; nationwide
near antonyms global, international; alien, external, foreign
antonyms nonnational

national *n* a person who owes allegiance to a government and is protected by it — see CITIZEN 1

nationalism *n* **1** excessive favoritism towards one's own country — see CHAUVINISM
2 love and support for one's country — see PATRIOTISM

nationalist *adj* having or showing love and support for one's country — see PATRIOTIC

nationalist *n* one who shows excessive favoritism towards his or her country ⟨a staunch *nationalist* who favored any policy that would give the country more power in the international arena⟩
synonyms chauvinist, jingo
related words loyalist, patriot; hawk, warmonger
near antonyms internationalist; neutralist

nationalistic *adj* having or showing love and support for one's country — see PATRIOTIC

native *adj* **1** belonging to a particular place by birth or origin ⟨though she now lived in the Northeast, she was a *native* Midwesterner⟩
synonyms aboriginal, born, endemic, indigenous
related words domestic, local; original
near antonyms imported, introduced, transplanted; alien, exotic, foreign, strange; expatriate, immigrant
antonyms nonnative
2 being such as found in nature and not altered by processing or refining — see CRUDE 1

Native American *n* a member of any of the native peoples of the western hemisphere usually not including the Eskimos — see AMERICAN INDIAN

nativity *n* the act or instance of being born — see BIRTH 1

nattily *adv* in a strikingly neat and trim manner — see SMARTLY

natty *adj* being strikingly neat and trim in style or appearance — see SMART 1

natural *adj* **1** being such from birth or by nature ⟨from his first visits to the wading pool, we could tell he loved water and was a *natural* swimmer⟩
synonyms born, congenital
related words chronic, confirmed, habitual, ingrained, inveterate, proper, regular; constitutional, consummate; elemental, elementary, essential, hereditary, inborn, inherent, innate, intimate, intrinsic, native; instinctual, intuitive
near antonyms cultivated, developed, trained; alien, foreign, unnatural
antonyms nonnatural
2 closely resembling the object imitated ⟨the display of stuffed birds and plastic plants actually looked very *natural*⟩
synonyms lifelike, near, realistic
related words alike, like, living, matching; akin, analogous, approximate, comparable, resembling; accurate, close, faithful, true; convincing

near antonyms dissimilar, off, unalike, unlike; incomparable, unmatched; contrasted, contrasting, different, disparate; fake, mock, phony (*also* phoney), sham
antonyms nonnatural, nonrealistic, unrealistic
3 being a part of the innermost nature of a person or thing — see INHERENT
4 being such as found in nature and not altered by processing or refining — see CRUDE 1
5 existing without human habitation or cultivation — see WILD 2
6 free from any intent to deceive or impress others — see GUILELESS
7 relating to or characteristic of human beings — see HUMAN

naturally *adv* **1** by natural character or ability ⟨tour guides who are *naturally* outgoing and can easily approach and converse with strangers⟩
synonyms constitutionally, inherently, innately, intrinsically
related words elementally, essentially, fundamentally; instinctively, intuitively; intimately
near antonyms artificially, unnaturally
2 according to the usual course of things ⟨we *naturally* like to be as comfortable as possible⟩
synonyms commonly, generally, normally, ordinarily, typically, usually
related words customarily, habitually, regularly, routinely; familiarly; conventionally, traditionally
phrases of course
near antonyms oddly, peculiarly, queerly, strangely; anomalously, irregularly; radically
antonyms abnormally, atypically, extraordinarily, uncommonly, unusually
3 without any attempt to impress by deception or exaggeration ⟨he tried to act *naturally* around the girl he had a crush on⟩
synonyms artlessly, guilelessly, ingenuously, innocently, naively, sincerely, unaffectedly, unfeignedly, unpretentiously
related words genuinely, honestly, simply, truly; freely, openheartedly, openly; candidly, frankly, matter-of-factly; informally, relaxedly, unceremoniously
near antonyms artfully, cannily, deceitfully, deceptively, deviously, dishonestly, falsely; archly, calculatingly, craftily, cunningly, furtively, insidiously, sharply, shiftily, slickly, slyly, underhand, underhanded, underhandedly; flatteringly, sycophantically, unctuously
antonyms affectedly, artificially, hypocritically, insincerely, pretentiously, unnaturally

naturalness *n* **1** carefree freedom from constraint — see ABANDON
2 the quality or state of being simple and sincere — see NAÏVETÉ 1

nature *n* **1** the set of qualities that makes a person, a group of people, or a thing different from others ⟨it was the violent *nature* of his stories that got them banned from school libraries⟩ ⟨her *nature* was such that lying was never an option for her⟩ ⟨the stoic *nature* of these people enables them to endure one calamity after another⟩
synonyms character, complexion, constitution, genius, personality, tone
related words distinctiveness, distinctness, individuality, singularity, uniqueness; attribute, characteristic, earmark, feature, flavor, hallmark, mark, point, property, savor, stamp, trait; disposition, grain, sort, temper, temperament; composition, makeup; essence, essentiality, soul, spirit, stuff, substance; habit, way
2 that part of the physical world that is removed from human habitation ⟨needed to get out of the office and be out in *nature* to clear his head⟩
synonyms open, open air, outdoors, out-of-doors, wild, wilderness
related words backwoods, bush, country, frontier, hinterland, sticks, up-country; outside, without; badland, barren, desert, waste, wasteland
3 a number of persons or things that are grouped together because they have something in common — see SORT 1
4 one's characteristic attitude or mood — see DISPOSITION 1
5 the quality or qualities that make a thing what it is — see ESSENCE
6 the whole body of things observed or assumed — see UNIVERSE

naught *also* **nought** *n* the numerical symbol 0 or the absence of number or quantity represented by it — see ZERO 1

naughty *adj* engaging in or marked by childish misbehavior ⟨told her to act her age and stop throwing temper tantrums like a *naughty* little girl⟩
synonyms bad, contrary, errant, froward, misbehaving, mischievous
related words defiant, disrespectful, ill-mannered, ill-natured, impolite, improper, impudent, indecorous, insolent, rude, uncouth, unmannerly; disobedient, headstrong, intractable, obstreperous, recalcitrant, refractory, transgressing, unruly, untoward, willful (*or* wilful); balky, restive, uncontrollable, ungovernable, wayward, wild; arch, elfish, impish, monkeying, monkeyish, ornery, pixieish, prankish, rascally, roguish, waggish; dissolute, perverse, wrongheaded; disorderly, rowdy, ruffianly; corrupt, evil, wicked; insurgent, mutinous, rebellious; disobliging, inconsiderate, selfish, thoughtless, unkind, unkindly; babyish, childish, immature, infantile, puerile
near antonyms acquiescent, compliant, complying, dutiful, obedient, submissive; clean, correct, decent, decorous, moral, proper, respectable; considerate, courteous, kindly, mannerly, polite, thoughtful; angelic, divine, heavenly; amenable, docile, governable, tractable; amiable, complaisant, good-natured, obliging, pleasant; discreet, modest; grown-up, mature
antonyms behaved, behaving, nice, orderly

nausea *n* **1** a disturbed condition of the stomach in which one feels like vomiting ⟨symptoms include fever accompanied by a loss of appetite and *nausea*⟩
synonyms qualmishness, queasiness, queerness, sickness, squeamishness
related words qualm; airsickness, morning sickness, motion sickness, seasickness
2 a dislike so strong as to cause stomach upset or queasiness — see DISGUST

nauseate *vb* to cause to feel disgust — see DISGUST

nauseated *adj* **1** affected with nausea — see NAUSEOUS
2 filled with disgust — see SICK 2

nauseating *adj* causing intense displeasure, disgust, or resentment — see OFFENSIVE 1

nauseous *adj* affected with nausea ⟨after eating the last four pieces of the two-week-old pizza, he was feeling a little *nauseous*⟩

synonyms ill, nauseated, qualmish, queasy (*also* queazy), queer, queerish, sick, sickish, squeamish
related words green, peaked, sickly; unsettled, upset, woozy
near antonyms settled; healthy, well

nautical *adj* of or relating to navigation of the sea — see MARINE 2

navigable *adj* capable of being traveled on — see PASSABLE 1

navigate *vb* to travel on water in a vessel — see SAIL 1

navigational *adj* of or relating to navigation of the sea — see MARINE 2

navigator *n* one who operates or navigates a seagoing vessel — see SAILOR

nay *adv* not merely this but also — see EVEN

nay *n* **1** a vote or decision against something — see NO 1
2 an unwillingness to grant something asked for — see DENIAL 1

Neanderthal *adj* not civilized — see SAVAGE 1

near *adj* **1** being the less far of two ⟨grab the comforter from the *near* side of the bed⟩
synonyms closer, hither, nigher, this
related words fore, forward, front, inside
near antonyms distant, remote, remoter; back, outside
antonyms far, farther, further, opposite, other, that
2 being such only when compared to something else — see COMPARATIVE
3 closely resembling the object imitated — see NATURAL 2
4 not being distant in time, space, or significance — see CLOSE 2

near *adv* **1** at, within, or to a short distance or time ⟨the campers were cold, so they moved *nearer* to the campfire⟩ ⟨as summer draws *near*, we usually start planning our annual vacation⟩
synonyms around, by, close, hard, in, nearby, nigh
related words hereabouts (*or* hereabout), thereabouts (*or* thereabout); along, alongside
phrases at close quarters, at hand
2 to a close degree ⟨copy the artist's drawing into your own sketchbook as *near* as you can⟩
synonyms closely, nearly
near antonyms distantly, remotely
3 very close to but not completely — see ALMOST

near *prep* close to — see AROUND 1

near *vb* **1** to come near or nearer — see APPROACH 1
2 to move closer to — see COME 1

nearby *adj* not being distant in time, space, or significance — see CLOSE 2

nearby *adv* at, within, or to a short distance or time — see NEAR 1

nearing *adj* being soon to appear or take place — see FORTHCOMING

nearly *adv* **1** to a close degree — see NEAR 2
2 very close to but not completely — see ALMOST

nearness *n* **1** the state of being in a very personal or private relationship — see FAMILIARITY 1
2 the state or condition of being near — see PROXIMITY

nearsighted *adj* able to see near things more clearly than distant ones ⟨I am a little *nearsighted* and need to wear glasses to drive⟩
synonyms myopic, shortsighted
related words astigmatic
antonyms farsighted

neat *adj* **1** being clean and in good order ⟨keep the kitchen *neat* so the cook doesn't have to work around piles of dirty dishes⟩
synonyms crisp, groomed, orderly, picked up, shipshape, snug, tidied, tidy, trim, uncluttered
related words dapper, natty, prim, saucy, smart, spiffy, spruce; immaculate, spick-and-span (*or* spic-and-span), spotless; rakish, sleek, streamlined, taut; organized, straight, systematic
near antonyms seedy, shabby, slipshod, sloppy; dirty, filthy, foul, nasty, sordid, squalid; frowzy, rumpled, tousled, tumbled; disorganized, unsystematic
antonyms disheveled (*or* dishevelled), disordered, disorderly, messy, mussed, mussy, slovenly, unkempt, untidy
2 free from added matter — see PURE 1
3 of the very best kind — see EXCELLENT

nebulous *adj* **1** having an often intentionally veiled or uncertain meaning — see OBSCURE 1
2 not seen or understood clearly — see FAINT 1

nebulousness *n* the quality or state of having a veiled or uncertain meaning — see OBSCURITY 1

necessarily *adv* because of necessity — see NEEDS

necessary *adj* **1** forcing one's compliance or participation by or as if by law — see MANDATORY
2 impossible to avoid or evade — see INEVITABLE
3 impossible to do without — see ESSENTIAL 1

necessitate *vb* to have as a requirement — see NEED 1

necessity *n* something necessary, indispensable, or unavoidable — see ESSENTIAL 1

necklace *n* an ornamental chain or string (as of beads) worn around the neck ⟨found a lovely *necklace* to match the bracelet and ring her mother had given her⟩
synonyms choker, lei
related words rope, strand; bangle, lavaliere (*also* lavalliere), locket, pendant (*also* pendent)

necromancer *n* a person skilled in using supernatural forces — see MAGICIAN 1

necromancy *n* the power to control natural forces through supernatural means — see MAGIC 1

need *n* **1** a state of being without something necessary, desirable, or useful ⟨when it came time to wrap the presents, he found he was in *need* of adhesive tape⟩
synonyms absence, lack, needfulness, want
related words deficiency, deficit, inadequacy, insufficiency; dearth, meagerness, paucity, poverty, scantiness, scarceness, scarcity, shortage, skimpiness; defect, minus; deprivation, famishment, privation; demand, essential, necessity, requirement, requisite
near antonyms adequacy, enough, sufficiency; fund, pool, stock, supply; excess, fill, overabundance, oversupply, plenty, surfeit, surplus; hoard, stockpile
2 something necessary, indispensable, or unavoidable — see ESSENTIAL 1
3 something one must do because of prior agreement — see OBLIGATION
4 the state of lacking sufficient money or material possessions — see POVERTY 1

need *vb* **1** to have as a requirement ⟨a national crisis that *needs* a strong leader to solve it⟩
synonyms demand, necessitate, require, take, want, warrant

related words entail, involve; ask, beg, claim, clamor (for), cry (for); lack; command, enjoin, exact, insist, press, quest, stipulate

phrases call for

near antonyms own, possess

antonyms have, hold

2 to be under necessity or obligation to ⟨you *need* not stand when she enters the room⟩

synonyms have (to), must, ought (to), shall, should

related words will

needed *adj* impossible to do without — see ESSENTIAL 1

needful *adj* impossible to do without — see ESSENTIAL 1

needfulness *n* a state of being without something necessary, desirable, or useful — see NEED 1

neediness *n* the state of lacking sufficient money or material possessions — see POVERTY 1

needle *n* **1** a slender hollow instrument by which material is put into or taken from the body through the skin ⟨the nurse inserted the *needle* into his vein and collected some blood for testing⟩

synonyms hypodermic, hypodermic needle, hypodermic syringe, syringe

2 an arrow-shaped piece on a dial or scale for registering information — see POINTER 1

needle *vb* **1** to attack repeatedly with mean put-downs or insults — see TEASE 2

2 to subject (someone) to constant scoldings and sharp reminders — see NAG

needlelike *adj* being of less than usual width — see NARROW 1

needler *n* a person who causes repeated emotional pain, distress, or annoyance to another — see TORMENTOR

needless *adj* not needed by the circumstances or to accomplish an end — see UNNECESSARY

needlework *n* decorative stitching done on cloth with the use of a needle ⟨a school outing to the museum to see an exhibition of 18th century *needlework*⟩

synonyms embroidery

related words crewel, cross-stitch, needlepoint; hemstitch, fagoting (*or* faggoting), smocking; fancywork

needs *adv* because of necessity ⟨the dangers of global warming must *needs* be recognized—and recognized soon—by the industrialized nations of the world⟩

synonyms inescapably, inevitably, necessarily, perforce, unavoidably

related words involuntarily

antonyms unnecessarily

needy *adj* lacking money or material possessions — see POOR 1

ne'er *adv* at no time — see NEVER 1

nefarious *adj* not conforming to a high moral standard; morally unacceptable — see BAD 2

nefariousness *n* the state or quality of being utterly evil — see ENORMITY 1

negate *vb* **1** to declare not to be true — see DENY 1

2 to put an end to by formal action — see ABOLISH

3 to think not to be true or real — see DISBELIEVE

negation *n* a refusal to confirm the truth of a statement — see DENIAL 2

negative *adj* **1** marked by opposition or ill will — see HOSTILE 1

2 opposed to one's interests — see ADVERSE 1

negative *n* **1** a vote or decision against something — see NO 1

2 something that is as different as possible from something else — see OPPOSITE

negative *vb* **1** to reject by or as if by a vote ⟨though the rebuttal was very eloquent, he *negatived* it in favor of the first argument⟩ ⟨she *negatived* pizza for dinner, noting that they had already had it for three nights that week⟩

synonyms blackball, kill, veto

related words decline, disallow, disapprove, dismiss, refuse; blacklist

near antonyms admit, allow, approve, assent (to), pass, sanction; elect, support

antonyms confirm, ratify

2 to declare not to be true — see DENY 1

3 to show unwillingness to accept, do, engage in, or agree to — see DECLINE 1

neglect *n* **1** the state of being unattended to or not cared for ⟨the barn sat in *neglect* until it finally fell down⟩

synonyms desolation, dilapidation, disrepair, seediness

related words inattention, negligence; abandonment, desertion; decay, decrepitude, dereliction, deterioration, disintegration, ruin, ruination

near antonyms conservation, preservation

antonyms repair

2 the nonperformance of an assigned or expected action — see FAILURE 1

neglect *vb* **1** to fail to give proper attention to ⟨the news media *neglected* the real issues of the campaign and focused on personalities⟩

synonyms disregard, forget, ignore, overlook, overpass, pass over, slight, slur (over)

related words fail; miss, omit; brush (aside *or* off), reject, shrug off, slough (off); disdain, pooh-pooh, scorn; scant, skimp

near antonyms appreciate, cherish, prize, treasure, value; cultivate, foster, nurse, nurture; pamper; remember; listen (to), watch; follow, mark, note, notice, observe, remark

antonyms attend (to), heed, mind, regard, tend (to)

2 to leave undone or unattended to especially through carelessness ⟨she plays too much and *neglects* her homework⟩ ⟨I've *neglected* my garden, and now it's overgrown with weeds⟩

synonyms forget, shirk

related words slack (off)

near antonyms carry out, do, execute, perform; accomplish, achieve

antonyms attend (to), remember

3 to miss the opportunity or obligation ⟨the job applicant *neglected* to mention his criminal record⟩

synonyms fail, forget, omit

related words disregard, ignore, overlook, overpass, pass over, slight; slide, slip; default; skip

near antonyms heed, mind, remember; keep, observe; carry out, do, execute, perform, practice (*or* practise); discharge, fulfill (*or* fulfil), meet, satisfy; comply (with)

neglected *adj* showing signs of advanced wear and tear and neglect — see SHABBY 1

neglectful *adj* failing to give proper care and attention — see NEGLIGENT

neglecting *adj* failing to give proper care and attention — see NEGLIGENT

negligence *n* **1** failure to take the care that a cautious person usually takes ⟨exhibiting his usual *negligence*, he failed to set the emergency brake, and the car rolled down the steep hill and crashed into the telephone pole⟩
synonyms carelessness, dereliction, heedlessness, incautiousness, laxness, remissness, slackness
related words foolhardiness, rashness, recklessness, wildness; neglect, omission; delinquency, irresponsibility, malfeasance, malpractice, misconduct; misdirection, mishandling, mismanagement; forgetfulness, inattention, inattentiveness, obliviousness, shortsightedness, unwariness
near antonyms alertness, attention, attentiveness, awareness; circumspection, observance, vigilance, watchfulness; responsibility, responsibleness
antonyms care, carefulness, caution, cautiousness, heedfulness
2 the nonperformance of an assigned or expected action — see FAILURE 1

negligent *adj* failing to give proper care and attention ⟨has been *negligent* in taking care of the neighbor's dog, repeatedly forgetting to feed the poor animal⟩
synonyms careless, derelict, lax, neglectful, neglecting, remiss, slack
related words heedless, incautious, irresponsible, reckless, wild; unguarded, unwary; forgetful; disregardful, disregarding, inattentive, oblivious, thoughtless, unheeding, unmindful, unthinking; apathetic, disinterested, indifferent, unconcerned, uninterested; delinquent; loose
near antonyms meticulous, painstaking, punctilious; cautious, chary, circumspect, gingerly, guarded; alert, heedful, heeding, mindful, observant, regardful, regarding, vigilant, wary, watchful; foresighted, forethoughtful, provident, responsible; thinking, thoughtful; concerned, interested
antonyms attentive, careful, conscientious

negligible *adj* **1** so small or unimportant as to warrant little or no attention ⟨the two cents in change was such a *negligible* sum that she left the store without collecting the pennies from the cashier⟩
synonyms inconsequential, inconsiderable, insignificant, measly, minute, nominal, paltry, petty, picayune, piddling, slight, trifling, trivial
related words inferior, mean; imperceptible, inappreciable; little, puny, tiny; hairsplitting, nitpicking, pettifogging; one-horse, small-fry, two-bit
near antonyms serious, substantial, weighty; eventful, momentous; conspicuous, noteworthy, prominent, outstanding, remarkable, striking; appreciable, discernible, measurable
antonyms big, consequential, considerable, important, material, significant
2 lacking importance — see UNIMPORTANT
3 small in degree — see REMOTE 1

negligibly *adv* in a very small quantity or degree — see LITTLE 1

negotiable *adj* capable of being traveled on — see PASSABLE 1

negotiate *vb* **1** to bring about through discussion and compromise ⟨wanted to *negotiate* a higher salary before she accepted the job offer⟩
synonyms arrange, concert, conclude
related words settle (on *or* upon); bargain, chaffer, deal, dicker, haggle, horse-trade, palter; agree; contract, covenant; argue, debate, discuss, hammer (out), hash (over), reason, talk, talk over, work out
2 to deal with (something) usually skillfully or efficiently — see HANDLE 1
3 to plan out usually with subtle skill or care — see ENGINEER
4 to talk over or dispute the terms of a purchase — see BARGAIN

negotiation *n* the act or practice of each side giving up something in order to reach an agreement — see CONCESSION 1

neigh *vb* to make the cry typical of a horse ⟨the horses *neighed* when the rider came into the barn⟩
synonyms nicker, whinny

neighborhood *n* **1** an area (as of a city) set apart for some purpose or having some special feature — see DISTRICT
2 the people living in a particular area — see COMMUNITY 1

neighboring *adj* not being distant in time, space, or significance — see CLOSE 2

neighborly *adj* having or showing kindly feeling and sincere interest — see FRIENDLY 1

nemesis *n* **1** one who inflicts punishment in return for an injury or offense ⟨Batman is the Joker's main *nemesis* and always foils his wicked plots⟩
synonyms avenger, castigator, chastiser, punisher, scourge, vigilante
related words revenger; redresser, righter; requiter
near antonyms ransomer, redeemer, vindicator
2 suffering, loss, or hardship imposed in response to a crime or offense — see PUNISHMENT

neophyte *n* a person who is just starting out in a field of activity — see BEGINNER

neoplasm *n* an abnormal mass of tissue — see GROWTH 1

nerd *n* a person slavishly devoted to intellectual or academic pursuits ⟨was such a *nerd* she stayed home from the party to study for the exam on Monday⟩
synonyms bookworm, grind
related words egghead, highbrow, intellectual; brain, genius; scholar
near antonyms slacker, underachiever; lowbrow

nerve *n* **1** shameless boldness — see EFFRONTERY
2 strength of mind to carry on in spite of danger — see COURAGE
3 nerves *pl* a sense of panic or extreme nervousness — see JITTERS

nerve *vb* to prepare (oneself) mentally or emotionally — see FORTIFY 1

nerved *adj* inclined or willing to take risks — see BOLD 1

nerveless *adj* **1** lacking strength of will or character — see WEAK 2
2 not easily panicked or upset — see UNFLAPPABLE

nerviness *n* shameless boldness — see EFFRONTERY

nervous *adj* **1** feeling or showing uncomfortable feelings of uncertainty ⟨he was *nervous* about how he would do at the varsity basketball tryouts⟩
synonyms aflutter, anxious, dithery, edgy, het up, hung up, jittery, jumpy, nervy, perturbed, tense, troubled, uneasy, unquiet, upset, uptight, worried

related words aggrieved, bothered, concerned, disquieted, distraught, distressed, disturbed; apprehensive, foreboding, hesitant, misgiving; fretful, fretting, stewing, vexed; qualmish, qualmy; flustered, twittered, undone, unnerved, unstrung; obsessed, preoccupied, restless; fidgety, flighty, fluttery, high-strung, skittish, spooky
phrases keyed up, on edge, on pins and needles
near antonyms confident, self-assured, self-confident, sure; controlled, self-controlled
antonyms calm, collected, cool, easy, nerveless, relaxed
2 marked by or causing agitation or uncomfortable feelings ⟨a *nervous* silence filled the room as the teacher handed out the graded exams⟩
synonyms agitating, anxious, disquieting, distressful, distressing, disturbing, restless, tense, unnerving, unsettling, worrisome
related words bothersome, troublesome; foreboding, misgiving; discouraging, disheartening, strained; restive, restless, unrestful; awkward, embarrassing
near antonyms restful; pacific
antonyms calming, comfortable, easy, peaceful, quiet, quieting, tranquil
3 easily excited by nature — see EXCITABLE

nervousness *n* an uneasy state of mind usually over the possibility of an anticipated misfortune or trouble — see ANXIETY 1

nervy *adj* **1** displaying or marked by rude boldness ⟨the *nervy* waiter held up the small tip and called out to the departing customers, "Hope it doesn't break the bank!"⟩
synonyms arch, bold, bold-faced, brash, brassy, brazen, cheeky, cocky, fresh, impertinent, impudent, insolent, sassy, saucy
related words assertive, forward, obtrusive; audacious, defiant, disrespectful; shameless, unabashed, unblushing; bluff, blunt, curt; facetious, flip, flippant, pert, smart, smart-alecky (*or* smart-aleck)
near antonyms demure, humble, modest; courteous, genteel, mannerly, polite, proper; deferential, respectful; abashed, ashamed, blushing, embarrassed; gentle, mild; inconspicuous, unobtrusive
antonyms meek, mousy (*or* mousey), retiring, shy, timid
2 feeling or showing uncomfortable feelings of uncertainty — see NERVOUS 1
3 inclined or willing to take risks — see BOLD 1

nest *n* a place where a person goes to hide — see HIDEOUT

nest egg *n* a sum of money set aside for a particular purpose — see FUND 1

nestle *vb* **1** to lie close — see NUZZLE
2 to sit or recline comfortably or cozily — see SNUGGLE 1

[1]**net** *n* **1** a fabric made of strands loosely twisted, knotted, or woven together at regular intervals ⟨the basketball didn't go into the basket, it just hit the *net*⟩
synonyms mesh, netting, network
related words web, webbing; grille (*also* grill), lattice, screen, screening; filigree, lace
2 a device or scheme for capturing another by surprise — see TRAP 1
3 something that catches and holds — see WEB 1

[2]**net** *n* the amount of money left when expenses are subtracted from the total amount received — see PROFIT 1

nether *adj* situated lower down — see INFERIOR 1

netting *n* a fabric made of strands loosely twisted, knotted, or woven together at regular intervals — see [1]NET 1

nettle *vb* to disturb the peace of mind of (someone) especially by repeated disagreeable acts — see IRRITATE 1

nettling *adj* causing annoyance — see ANNOYING

network *n* **1** a fabric made of strands loosely twisted, knotted, or woven together at regular intervals — see [1]NET 1
2 something made up of many interdependent or related parts — see SYSTEM 1

neurotic *n* a person judged to be legally or medically insane — see LUNATIC 1

neuter *vb* to remove the sex organs of ⟨Dad agreed to buy us the dog on the condition that we have her *neutered* so she couldn't have puppies⟩
synonyms alter, desex
related words castrate, emasculate, geld; spay; sterilize

neutral *adj* not favoring or joined to either side in a quarrel, contest, or war ⟨Sweden remained *neutral* during World War II, refusing to join either side of the conflict⟩
synonyms nonpartisan, unallied
related words autonomous, independent, sovereign, unaffiliated; nonbelligerent; individualistic; disinterested, evenhanded, fair, impartial, unbiased, uninfluenced, unprejudiced; bipartisan
near antonyms biased, partial, partisan, prejudiced, unfair; affiliated, associated, federated; belligerent
antonyms allied, confederate

neutrality *n* lack of favoritism toward one side or another — see DETACHMENT 1

neutralize *vb* to balance with an equal force so as to make ineffective — see OFFSET

neutralizer *n* a force or influence that makes an opposing force ineffective or less effective — see COUNTERBALANCE

never *adv* **1** at no time ⟨I have *never* been out of the country⟩
synonyms ne'er
related words nevermore; not; infrequently, little, rarely, seldom
near antonyms eternally, everlastingly, evermore, invariably; frequently, often, recurrently, repeatedly
antonyms always, constantly, continuously, endlessly, ever, forever, perpetually
2 not in any degree, way, or under any condition ⟨though she turned down his offer of marriage twice, he was *never* convinced that she did not love him⟩
synonyms no, none, nothing, noway (*or* noways), nowise
related words nowhere near
phrases by no means, in no wise, nothing doing, on no account
near antonyms completely, extremely, full, fully, par excellence, right, very; altogether, exactly; somehow, someway (*also* someways); out
antonyms anyhow, anyway, anywise, at all, ever, half, however

nevertheless *adv* in spite of that — see HOWEVER

new *adj* **1** taking the place of one that came before ⟨after my bike was stolen, my scooter became my *new* mode of transportation⟩
synonyms backup, makeshift, substitute

related words alternate, alternative; different, other, separate; extra, spare; another, second; utility; successive; equivalent
near antonyms first, former; equal, identical, same; lasting, permanent
antonyms original
2 not known or experienced before ⟨Spanish was a *new* course of study for her⟩ ⟨the Americas were *new* lands for the European explorers⟩
synonyms fresh, novel, original, strange, unaccustomed, unfamiliar, unheard-of, unknown, unprecedented
related words innovative, unique; nontraditional, unconventional, untried, unused, unworn
near antonyms conventional, established, traditional, tried, tried-and-true; derivative, imitative
antonyms familiar, old, time-honored, tired
3 recently made and never used before ⟨that unique scent that is the telltale sign of a *new* car⟩
synonyms brand-new, spick-and-span (*or* spic-and-span), unused
related words clean, fresh, pristine, unspoiled; untouched; newfangled, new-fashioned; natural, raw, virgin, unprocessed, untreated, unworked
near antonyms dirty, soiled, spoiled, stale; aged, beat-up, old, worn
antonyms hand-me-down, second hand, used
4 made or become fresh in spirits or vigor ⟨a little rest made him a *new* man after the exhausting basketball game⟩
synonyms energized, freshened, invigorated, reanimated, recreated, reenergized, refreshed, regenerated, renewed, resuscitated, revived
related words animated, enlivened, exhilarated, jazzed (up); resurrected; rested, untired, unwearied
near antonyms tired, weary; dampened, deadened; emasculated, unmanned; demoralized, disheartened, dispirited
antonyms drained, enervated, exhausted, weakened
5 being or involving the latest methods, concepts, information, or styles — see MODERN

new *adv* not long ago — see NEWLY

newborn *n* a recently born person — see BABY

newcomer *n* a person who is just starting out in a field of activity — see BEGINNER

newfangled *adj* being or involving the latest methods, concepts, information, or styles — see MODERN

new-fashioned *adj* being or involving the latest methods, concepts, information, or styles — see MODERN

newly *adv* not long ago ⟨as soon as he left the room, his dog jumped on the *newly* made bed and rumpled it again⟩
synonyms freshly, just, late, lately, new, now, only, recently
related words latterly
phrases of late
near antonyms ago, before, earlier, early, erstwhile, formerly, previously; heretofore, hitherto
antonyms anciently

newness *n* the quality or appeal of being new — see NOVELTY 1

news *n pl* a report of recent events or facts not previously known ⟨dropped by to give me the latest *news* about her daughter⟩
synonyms information, intelligence, item, story, tidings, word
related words announcement, communication, message; dope, lowdown, scoop, tidbit (*also* titbit), tip; gossip, rumor, tale, tattle; feedback

newspaper *n* a publication that appears at regular intervals — see JOURNAL

newsy *adj* having the style and content of everyday conversation — see CHATTY 1

next *adj* being the one that comes immediately after another ⟨my house is the *next* one⟩ ⟨turn at the *next* street, not this one⟩ ⟨she was *next* in line for concert tickets⟩
synonyms coming, ensuing, following, succeeding
related words consecutive, sequential, successive; posterior, subsequent; immediate; second
phrases on deck
near antonyms anterior, former; past; last
antonyms antecedent, foregoing, precedent, preceding, previous, prior

next-door *adj* not being distant in time, space, or significance — see CLOSE 2

next to *adv* very close to but not completely — see ALMOST

next to *prep* close to — see AROUND 1

nib *n* the jaws of a bird together with their hornlike covering — see BEAK

nibble *n* a small piece or quantity of food — see MORSEL 1

nibble *vb* to crush or grind with the teeth — see BITE (ON)

nice *adj* **1** following the established traditions of refined society and good taste — see PROPER 1
2 giving pleasure or contentment to the mind or senses — see PLEASANT
3 hard to please — see FINICKY
4 having an easygoing and pleasing manner especially in social situations — see AMIABLE
5 made or done with extreme care and accuracy — see FINE 2

nicely *adv* **1** in a pleasing way — see WELL 5
2 in a satisfactory way — see WELL 1
3 with good reason or courtesy — see WELL 4

niceness *n* the state or quality of having a pleasant or agreeable manner in socializing with others — see AMIABILITY 1

nicety *n* a single piece of information — see FACT 3

niche *n* **1** a hollowed-out space in a wall ⟨statues of various saints occupy the *niches* lining the abbey's many corridors⟩
synonyms alcove, nook, recess
related words corner, cranny, cubbyhole; cubicle; dent, indentation
2 the place where a plant or animal is usually or naturally found — see HOME 2

nick *n* a V-shaped cut usually on an edge or a surface — see NOTCH 1

nicker *vb* to make the cry typical of a horse — see NEIGH

nickname *n* a descriptive or familiar name given instead of or in addition to the one belonging to an individual ⟨his wavy hair earned him the *nickname* "Curly" early in life⟩
synonyms alias, cognomen, epithet, sobriquet (*also* soubriquet)
related words appellation, denomination, denotation, designation, handle, label, title; nom de plume, pen name, pseudonym

nifty *adj* of the very best kind — see EXCELLENT

nifty *n* something very good of its kind — see JIM-DANDY

niggard *adj* giving or sharing as little as possible — see STINGY 1
niggard *n* a mean grasping person who is usually stingy with money — see MISER
niggardly *adj* **1** giving or sharing as little as possible — see STINGY 1
2 less plentiful than what is normal, necessary, or desirable — see MEAGER
nigh *adj* not being distant in time, space, or significance — see CLOSE 2
nigh *adv* **1** at, within, or to a short distance or time — see NEAR 1
2 very close to but not completely — see ALMOST
nigher *adj* being the less far of two — see NEAR 1
night *adj* of, relating to, or occurring in the night — see NOCTURNAL
night *n* **1** the time from sunset to sunrise when there is no visible sunlight ⟨loved to sit outside at *night* and watch the stars⟩
synonyms dark, darkness, nighttime
related words dusk, evening, gloaming, nightfall, twilight; midnight
near antonyms dawn, daybreak, forenoon, morning; high noon, midday, noon, noonday, noontide, noontime; afternoon
antonyms day, daytime
2 a time or place of little or no light — see DARK 1
nightclub *n* a bar or restaurant offering special nighttime entertainment (as music, dancing, or comedy acts) ⟨decided to go dancing at a local *nightclub* after the long dinner and movie⟩
synonyms cabaret, café (*also* cafe), disco, discotheque, roadhouse
related words barroom, pub [*chiefly British*], public house [*chiefly British*], saloon, tavern; dive, speakeasy; canteen
nightdress *n* a loose pullover garment worn in bed — see NIGHTGOWN
nightfall *n* the time from when the sun begins to set to the onset of total darkness — see DUSK 1
nightgown *n* a loose pullover garment worn in bed ⟨decided to buy a flannel *nightgown* instead of pajamas⟩
synonyms nightdress, nightshirt
related words nightclothes; pajamas, pj's, pyjamas [*chiefly British*]; nightcap; lingerie
nightly *adj* of, relating to, or occurring in the night — see NOCTURNAL
nightmare *n* **1** a series of often striking pictures created by the imagination during sleep — see DREAM 1
2 a situation or state that causes great suffering and unhappiness — see HELL 2
nightmarish *adj* extremely disturbing or repellent — see HORRIBLE 1
nightshirt *n* a loose pullover garment worn in bed — see NIGHTGOWN
nightstick *n* a heavy rigid stick used as a weapon or for punishment — see CLUB 1
nighttime *adj* of, relating to, or occurring in the night — see NOCTURNAL
nighttime *n* the time from sunset to sunrise when there is no visible sunlight — see NIGHT 1
nil *n* the numerical symbol 0 or the absence of number or quantity represented by it — see ZERO 1
nimble *adj* **1** having or showing quickness of mind — see INTELLIGENT 1
2 moving easily — see GRACEFUL 1
nimbleness *n* ease and grace in physical activity — see DEXTERITY 2
nincompoop *n* **1** a person who lacks good sense or judgment — see FOOL 1
2 a stupid person — see IDIOT
ninny *n* **1** a person who lacks good sense or judgment — see FOOL 1
2 a stupid person — see IDIOT
[1]**nip** *n* **1** a very small amount — see PARTICLE 1
2 an uncomfortable degree of coolness — see CHILL
[2]**nip** *n* the portion of a serving of a beverage that is swallowed at one time — see DRINK 2
nip *vb* **1** to make (as hair) shorter with or as if with the use of shears — see CLIP
2 to squeeze tightly between two surfaces, edges, or points — see PINCH 1
3 to take (something) without right and with an intent to keep — see STEAL 1
nip and tuck *adj* showing little difference in the standing of the competitors — see CLOSE 3
nipper *n* a male person who has not yet reached adulthood — see BOY
nipping *adj* having a low or subnormal temperature — see COLD 1
nippy *adj* **1** having a low or subnormal temperature — see COLD 1
2 having a powerfully stimulating odor or flavor — see SHARP 3
3 moving, proceeding, or acting with great speed — see FAST 1
4 uncomfortably cool — see CHILLY 1
nitpick *vb* to make often peevish criticisms or objections about matters that are minor, unimportant, or irrelevant — see QUIBBLE
nitpicker *n* a person given to harsh judgments and to finding faults — see CRITIC 1
nitwit *n* **1** a person who lacks good sense or judgment — see FOOL 1
2 a stupid person — see IDIOT
no *interj* how surprising, doubtful, or unbelievable ⟨*no*—you can't possibly mean that I failed that test! I studied for days!⟩
synonyms ah, aha, fie, indeed, pshaw, well, what, why
related words gee, ha, hello, hey, lo, oh; fiddlesticks, phooey, pooh; there; oops, ugh; egad, gad, the deuce, the devil, the dickens, zounds
no *adv* **1** not in any degree, way, or under any condition — see NEVER 2
2 certainly not — see HARDLY 2
no *n* **1** a vote or decision against something ⟨though I wanted spaghetti for dinner, the consensus was a decisive *no*⟩
synonyms nay, negative
related words con; blackball, veto; denial, negation, refusal
near antonyms pro; acceptance, approval, grace
antonyms positive, yea, yes
2 an unwillingness to grant something asked for — see DENIAL 1
nobility *n* impressiveness of beauty on a large scale — see MAGNIFICENCE
noble *adj* **1** of high birth, rank, or station ⟨despite his *noble* background, the prince is known for his unpretentious way with common people⟩
synonyms aristocratic, genteel, gentle, grand, highborn, patrician, upper-class, wellborn
related words high, lofty, superior; elevated, ennobled, exalted; gentlemanly, kingly, knightly, lady-

like, lordly, princely, queenly, regal, royal; high-level, senior
near antonyms inferior, knavish; bastard, illegitimate; ordinary, plain; abased, degraded; junior, subordinate
antonyms baseborn, common, humble, ignoble, low, lower-class, lowly, mean, plebeian
2 having, characterized by, or arising from a dignified and generous nature ⟨the factory owner had a kind, *noble* disposition that showed in his unstinting generosity toward the poor⟩ ⟨our country was founded on the *noble* ideas that are put forth in the founding fathers' writings⟩
synonyms chivalrous, elevated, gallant, great, greathearted, high, high-minded, lofty, lordly, magnanimous, sublime
related words ennobled, exalted, glorified; heroic, honorable, venerable, worthy; knightly, princely, regal; moving, inspiring, uplifting; august, magnificent, majestic
near antonyms sordid, squalid, vile, wretched; abominable, contemptible, despicable, detestable, hateful, offensive, repulsive, ugly; dastardly, dirty, lousy, sorry; little, mean, narrow, small-minded; degrading, discreditable, humiliating, ignominious; coarse, crude, vulgar
antonyms base, debased, degenerate, degraded, ignoble, low
3 following the accepted rules of moral conduct — see HONORABLE 1
4 large and impressive in size, grandeur, extent, or conception — see GRAND 1
5 of the very best kind — see EXCELLENT
6 standing above others in rank, importance, or achievement — see EMINENT

noble *n* a man of high birth or social position — see GENTLEMAN 1

nobleman *n* a man of high birth or social position — see GENTLEMAN 1

nobleness *n* impressiveness of beauty on a large scale — see MAGNIFICENCE

noblewoman *n* a woman of high birth or social position — see GENTLEWOMAN

nobly *adv* in a manner befitting a person of the highest character and ideals — see GREATLY 1

nobody *n* a person of no importance or influence ⟨she felt like a *nobody* until she won the National Spelling Bee⟩
synonyms lightweight, nonentity, nothing, shrimp, twerp, whippersnapper, zero, zilch
related words least; inferior, mediocrity, obscurity; figurehead, puppet
near antonyms chief, head, lead, leader; celebrity, luminary, notable, personality, star, superstar; authority, superior; great power, party, power
antonyms big shot, bigwig, eminence, figure, magnate, nabob, personage, somebody, VIP

nobody *pron* no person ⟨there is *nobody* home⟩ ⟨*nobody* wants to clean up that mess⟩
synonyms none, no one
near antonyms anybody, anyone; somebody, someone
antonyms everybody, everyone

nocturnal *adj* of, relating to, or occurring in the night ⟨he bought a new telescope so he could pursue his favorite *nocturnal* hobby of astronomy⟩
synonyms night, nightly, nighttime
related words late; midnight, overnight
near antonyms noon
antonyms daily, diurnal

nod *vb* to make short up-and-down movements ⟨though she couldn't see the rain, she knew it had started because she could see the flowers *nod* as raindrops hit them⟩
synonyms bob, bobble, jog, jounce, pump, seesaw
related words jerk, jiggle, shake, wiggle, wobble; oscillate, rock, sway, swing, undulate; drop, duck

nodding *adj* bending downward or forward ⟨some students, with *nodding* heads, were falling asleep during the boring lecture⟩
synonyms bowed, bowing, declined, declining, descendant (*or* descendent), descending, drooping, droopy, hanging, hung (*also* hanged), inclining, pendulous, sagging, stooping
related words floppy, limp; dangling, falling, pendent (*or* pendant), suspended; dipping, sinking, slumping
near antonyms erect, inflexible, rigid, stiff; elevated, raised, upraised
antonyms unbending, upright

noddle *n* the upper or front part of the body that contains the brain, the major sense organs, and the mouth — see HEAD 1

node *n* a small rounded mass of swollen tissue — see BUMP 1

nodule *n* a small rounded mass of swollen tissue — see BUMP 1

Noel *n* the season celebrating Christmas — see YULETIDE

noggin *n* the upper or front part of the body that contains the brain, the major sense organs, and the mouth — see HEAD 1

no–good *adj* having no usefulness — see WORTHLESS

no–good *n* a mean, evil, or unprincipled person — see VILLAIN

noise *n* **1** loud, confused, and usually unharmonious sound ⟨the blaring *noise* of traffic on Fifth Avenue made casual conversation impossible⟩
synonyms bluster, cacophony, clamor, clangor, din, discordance, racket, roar
related words discord, dissonance; commotion, furor, hubbub, hullabaloo, hurly-burly, rumpus, tumult, uproar; babel; clatter, jangle; bang, blast, boom, clap, crack, crash
near antonyms calm, hush, lull; quietude, serenity, tranquillity (*or* tranquility)
antonyms quiet, silence, still, stillness
2 a violent shouting — see CLAMOR 1

noise (about) *vb* to make (as a piece of information) the subject of common talk without any authority or confirmation of accuracy — see RUMOR

noiseless *adj* mostly or entirely without sound — see SILENT 3

noisome *adj* **1** bad for the well-being of the body — see UNHEALTHY 1
2 causing intense displeasure, disgust, or resentment — see OFFENSIVE 1
3 having an unpleasant smell — see MALODOROUS

noisy *adj* **1** making loud, confused, and usually unharmonious sounds ⟨the *noisy* crowd moved up the street, shouting louder as they went along⟩
synonyms clangorous, dinning, discordant
related words cacophonous, dissonant; resounding, sonorous; clamorous, uproarious; blatant, obstreperous, strident, vociferous; blaring, booming, brassy, brazen, clanging, earsplitting

near antonyms calm, hushed
antonyms noiseless, quiet, silent, soundless, still
2 full of or characterized by the presence of noise ⟨the crowded auditorium was *noisy*, packed with excited theatergoers eager for the show to start⟩ ⟨the manufacturing company was a *noisy* place, so we wore ear protection while we toured⟩
synonyms clamorous, clangorous, clattering, clattery, resounding
related words resonant, sonorous; buzzing, humming, murmuring; blustery, boisterous, raucous, rip-roaring, roaring, roistering, romping, rowdy; tumultuous, uproarious, woolly (*also* wooly); obstreperous, vociferous
near antonyms calm, peaceful, serene, tranquil
antonyms hushed, noiseless, quiet, silent, soundless, stilled, stilly

nomad *or* **nomadic** *adj* traveling from place to place — see ITINERANT

nomad *n* a person who roams about without a fixed route or destination ⟨after college she became quite the *nomad*, backpacking through Europe with no particular destination⟩
synonyms drifter, gadabout, rambler, roamer, rover, stroller, vagabond, wanderer, wayfarer
related words laggard, straggler; lingerer, loiterer, sojourner; bum, hobo, tramp; sightseer, traveler (*or* traveller); transient, vagrant; ambler, saunterer
near antonyms homebody; denizen, dweller, habitant, inhabitant, resident, settler

nominal *adj* **1** being something in name or form only ⟨he was the *nominal* head of state—everyone knew the country was actually run by one of his advisers⟩
synonyms formal, paper, titular
related words so-called; phantom, virtual
near antonyms actual, real, true
2 so small or unimportant as to warrant little or no attention — see NEGLIGIBLE 1

nominally *adv* in a very small quantity or degree — see LITTLE 1

nonaction *n* lack of action or activity — see INACTION

nonbinding *adj* having no legal or binding force — see NULL 1

nonchalance *n* lack of interest or concern — see INDIFFERENCE

nonchalant *adj* having or showing a lack of interest or concern — see INDIFFERENT 1

noncombustible *adj* incapable of being burned — see INCOMBUSTIBLE

nonconflicting *adj* not having or showing any apparent conflict — see CONSISTENT

nonconformist *adj* deviating from commonly accepted beliefs or practices — see HERETICAL

nonconformist *n* **1** a person who does not conform to generally accepted standards or customs ⟨always the *nonconformist*, she insisted on wearing red on St. Patrick's Day and not green like everyone else⟩
synonyms bohemian, deviant, individualist, loner, lone wolf, maverick
related words character, codger, crackbrain, crackpot, crank, eccentric, freak, kook, nut, oddball, screwball, weirdo; misfit, outsider; anomaly
near antonyms adherent, follower, supporter; sheep
antonyms conformer, conformist
2 a person who believes or teaches something opposed to accepted beliefs — see HERETIC

nonconformity *n* departure from a generally accepted theory, opinion, or practice — see HERESY

nonconventional *adj* not bound by traditional ways or beliefs — see LIBERAL 1

none *adv* **1** certainly not — see HARDLY 2
2 not in any degree, way, or under any condition — see NEVER 2

none *pron* no person — see NOBODY

nonelective *adj* forcing one's compliance or participation by or as if by law — see MANDATORY

nonentity *n* a person of no importance or influence — see NOBODY

nonessential *adj* not needed by the circumstances or to accomplish an end — see UNNECESSARY

nonetheless *adv* in spite of that — see HOWEVER

nonexistent *adj* not present or in evidence — see ABSENT 2

nonfictional *adj* restricted to or based on fact — see FACTUAL 1

nonflammable *adj* incapable of being burned — see INCOMBUSTIBLE

nonfunctional *adj* not being in working order — see INOPERABLE 1

nonfunctioning *adj* not being in working order — see INOPERABLE 1

noninflammable *adj* incapable of being burned — see INCOMBUSTIBLE

nonliterary *adj* used in or suitable for speech and not formal writing — see COLLOQUIAL 1

nonliterate *adj* lacking in education or the knowledge gained from books — see IGNORANT 1

nonmaterial *adj* not composed of matter — see IMMATERIAL 1

nonmotile *adj* incapable of moving or being moved — see IMMOVABLE 1

nonmoving *adj* **1** fixed in a place or position — see STATIONARY 1
2 incapable of moving or being moved — see IMMOVABLE 1

nonnative *adj* being, relating to, or characteristic of a country other than one's own — see FOREIGN 1

nonnative *n* a person who is not native to or known to a community — see STRANGER

no–nonsense *adj* not joking or playful in mood or manner — see SERIOUS 1

nonoperating *adj* not being in working order — see INOPERABLE 1

nonorthodox *adj* **1** deviating from commonly accepted beliefs or practices — see HERETICAL
2 not bound by traditional ways or beliefs — see LIBERAL 1

nonpareil *adj* having no equal or rival for excellence or desirability — see ONLY 1

nonpareil *n* someone of such unequaled perfection as to deserve imitation — see IDEAL 1

nonpartisan *adj* **1** marked by justice, honesty, and freedom from bias — see FAIR 2
2 not favoring or joined to either side in a quarrel, contest, or war — see NEUTRAL

nonphysical *adj* not composed of matter — see IMMATERIAL 1

nonplus *vb* to throw into a state of self-conscious distress — see EMBARRASS 1

nonpractical *adj* not capable of being put to use or account — see IMPRACTICAL

nonprofessional *adj* lacking or showing a lack of expert skill — see AMATEURISH

nonpublic *adj* not known or meant to be known by the general populace — see PRIVATE 1
nonrational *adj* not using or following good reasoning — see ILLOGICAL
nonrealistic *adj* using elements of form (as color, line, or texture) with little or no attempt at creating a realistic picture — see ABSTRACT 2
nonreligious *adj* **1** lacking religious emotions, principles, or practices — see IRRELIGIOUS
2 not involving religion or religious matters — see PROFANE 1
nonresistant *adj* receiving or enduring without offering resistance — see PASSIVE
nonsense *n* **1** language, behavior, or ideas that are absurd and contrary to good sense ⟨told him to stop his mischievous *nonsense* and start behaving properly⟩ ⟨the discussion about building a time machine was complete *nonsense*⟩ ⟨a hundred years ago, the idea that man could walk on the moon was regarded as impractical *nonsense*⟩
synonyms bunk, claptrap, drivel, fiddlesticks, folly, foolishness, fudge, hogwash, humbug, humbuggery, piffle, rot, senselessness, silliness, slush, stupidity, trash
related words absurdity, asininity, fatuity, foolery, idiocy, imbecility, inanity, insanity, lunacy; absurdness, craziness, foolishness, madness, senselessness, witlessness; monkeyshines, shenanigans, tomfoolery; gas, hot air, jazz, moonshine, rigmarole, twaddle; double-talk
near antonyms levelheadedness, rationality, reasonability, reasonableness, sensibleness; common sense, horse sense, sense; discernment, judgment (*or* judgement), wisdom
2 unintelligible or meaningless talk — see GIBBERISH
nonsensical *adj* **1** conceived or made without regard for reason or reality — see FANTASTIC 1
2 showing or marked by a lack of good sense or judgment — see FOOLISH 1
nonsensicalness *n* lack of good sense or judgment — see FOOLISHNESS 1
nonspecific *adj* relating to the main elements and not to specific details — see GENERAL 2
nonsuccess *n* a falling short of one's goals — see FAILURE 2
nontraditional *adj* not bound by traditional ways or beliefs — see LIBERAL 1
nonvalid *adj* **1** having no legal or binding force — see NULL 1
2 having no basis in reason or fact — see GROUNDLESS
nonviolent *adj* not involving violence or force — see PEACEFUL 2
nook *n* a hollowed-out space in a wall — see NICHE 1
noon *n* the middle of the day ⟨we eat a big lunch around *noon* then have dinner in the evening⟩
synonyms high noon, midday, noonday, noontide, noontime
related words forenoon, morning; afternoon, evening
noonday *n* the middle of the day — see NOON
no one *pron* no person — see NOBODY
noontide *n* the middle of the day — see NOON
noontime *n* the middle of the day — see NOON
norm *n* what is typical of a group, class, or series — see AVERAGE
normal *adj* **1** being of the type that is encountered in the normal course of events — see ORDINARY 1
2 having full use of one's mind and control over one's actions — see SANE
3 having or showing the qualities associated with the members of a particular group or kind — see TYPICAL 1
normal *n* what is typical of a group, class, or series — see AVERAGE
normalcy *n* the state or fact of being the way things usually are — see NORMALITY
normality *n* the state or fact of being the way things usually are ⟨the county slowly has returned to *normality* after a week of flash flooding⟩
synonyms normalcy, status quo
related words groove, routine, rut; currency, prevalence; conventionality; orderliness, peace
near antonyms irregularity, uncommonness, unusualness; disorderliness, disruptiveness; disruption, disturbance; anomalousness, deviance; exceptionalness, extraordinariness, noteworthiness, remarkableness; unconventionality
antonyms abnormality
normalize *vb* to make agree with a single established standard or model — see STANDARDIZE
normally *adv* according to the usual course of things — see NATURALLY 2
nose *vb* **1** to become aware of by means of the sense organs in the nose — see SMELL 1
2 to interest oneself in what is not one's concern — see INTERFERE
nosedive *n* the act or process of going to a lower level or altitude — see DESCENT 1
nose–dive *vb* to go to a lower level — see DROP 2
nosegay *n* a bunch of flowers — see BOUQUET 1
nosiness *n* an eager desire to find out about things that are often none of one's business — see CURIOSITY 1
nosy *or* **nosey** *adj* **1** interested in what is not one's own business — see CURIOUS 1
2 thrusting oneself where one is not welcome or invited — see INTRUSIVE
notable *adj* standing above others in rank, importance, or achievement — see EMINENT
notable *n* a person who is widely known and usually much talked about — see CELEBRITY 1
notation *n* a usually brief written reminder — see NOTE 1
notch *n* **1** a V-shaped cut usually on an edge or a surface ⟨lifted up the fence rail and put it in the *notch* cut into the post⟩
synonyms chip, hack, indentation, kerf, nick
related words punch; groove, score; slit, slot
2 a narrow opening between hillsides or mountains that can be used for passage — see CANYON
3 an individual part of a process, series, or ranking — see DEGREE 1
note *n* **1** a usually brief written reminder ⟨I'll make a *note* to myself so I don't forget to pick up some milk on the way home⟩
synonyms memo, memorandum, notation
related words memoir, minutes, report; line; document, writing
2 a message on paper from one person or group to another — see LETTER
3 a natural vocal sound made by an animal — see CALL 1
4 a piece of printed paper used as money — see [1]BILL 2
5 a special quality or impression associated with something — see AURA

6 overall quality as seen or judged by people in general — see REPUTATION
7 a briefly expressed opinion — see REMARK
note *vb* **1** to make a statement of one's opinion — see REMARK 1
2 to make a written note of — see RECORD 1
3 to make note of (something) through the use of one's eyes — see SEE 1
4 to make reference to or speak about briefly but specifically — see MENTION 1
5 to take notice of and be guided by — see HEED 1
noted *adj* widely known — see FAMOUS
notepad *n* a number of sheets of writing paper glued together at one edge — see PAD 1
noteworthiness *n* the fact or state of being above others in rank or importance — see EMINENCE 1
noteworthy *adj* standing above others in rank, importance, or achievement — see EMINENT
nothing *adv* not in any degree, way, or under any condition — see NEVER 2
nothing *n* **1** a person of no importance or influence — see NOBODY
2 something of little importance — see TRIFLE
3 the numerical symbol 0 or the absence of number or quantity represented by it — see ZERO 1
notice *n* **1** a published statement informing the public of a matter of general interest — see ANNOUNCEMENT
2 a state of being aware — see ATTENTION 2
3 a written communication giving information or directions — see MEMORANDUM 1
4 an essay evaluating or analyzing something — see CRITICISM
5 the act or an instance of telling beforehand of danger or risk — see WARNING 1
notice *vb* **1** to make note of (something) through the use of one's eyes — see SEE 1
2 to make reference to or speak about briefly but specifically — see MENTION 1
noticeable *adj* likely to attract attention <the stain on the new carpet was quite *noticeable,* and nothing we did made it any lighter>
synonyms arresting, bold, catchy, conspicuous, dramatic, emphatic, eye-catching, flamboyant, marked, prominent, pronounced, remarkable, showy, splashy, striking
related words detectable, discernible, observable, perceptible, visible; outstanding, salient; distinguished, eminent, impressive, notable, noteworthy; highlighted, spotlighted; flagrant, glaring, screaming; flashy, garish, gaudy, glitzy, jazzy, loud, meretricious, swank (*or* swanky), tawdry; high-falutin, ostentatious, pretentious; extravagant, fancy, florid, glittery, spectacular; opulent, ornate, overdone, overwrought; absorbing, engrossing, enthralling, fascinating, interesting, riveting
near antonyms subtle; concealed, hidden, shrouded; dim, faint, obscure; insignificant, undistinguished, unimportant; modest, unaffected, unassuming, unpretentious; conservative, plain, quiet, simple, unaffected, understated; muted, restrained, subdued, subtle, toned-down
antonyms inconspicuous, unemphatic, unnoticeable, unobtrusive, unremarkable
notification *n* a published statement informing the public of a matter of general interest — see ANNOUNCEMENT
notion *n* **1 notions** *pl* small useful items <the fabric store had a wide variety of thread, pins, buttons, and other *notions*>
synonyms novelties, odds and ends, sundries
related words bauble(s), bric-a-brac, gewgaw(s), knickknack(s), trinket(s); hodgepodge, miscellany, variety
2 a sudden impulsive and apparently unmotivated idea or action — see WHIM
3 an idea that is believed to be true or valid without positive knowledge — see OPINION 1
4 something imagined or pictured in the mind — see IDEA
notoriety *n* the fact or state of being known to the public — see FAME
notorious *adj* **1** not respectable — see DISREPUTABLE
2 widely known — see FAMOUS
notwithstanding *adv* in spite of that — see HOWEVER
notwithstanding *prep* without being prevented by — see DESPITE
nourish *vb* **1** to help the growth or development of — see FOSTER 1
2 to supply with nourishment — see SUSTAIN 1
nourishing *adj* providing the substances necessary for health and bodily growth — see NUTRITIOUS
novel *adj* not known or experienced before — see NEW 2
novelette *n* a work with imaginary characters and events that is shorter and usually less complex than a novel — see STORY 1
novella *n* a work with imaginary characters and events that is shorter and usually less complex than a novel — see STORY 1
novelty *n* **1** the quality or appeal of being new <the *novelty* of having a cat quickly wore off>
synonyms freshness, newness, originality
related words strangeness, unfamiliarity, unusualness; progressiveness; up-to-dateness; departure, divergence, innovation, offshoot, shoot
near antonyms banality, commonness, familiarity, staleness
2 novelties *pl* small useful items — see NOTION 1
3 a small object displayed for its attractiveness or interest — see KNICKKNACK
novice *n* a person who is just starting out in a field of activity — see BEGINNER
now *adv* **1** at the present time <that company doesn't make those toys *now* because they are unsafe>
synonyms anymore, currently, nowadays, presently, right now, today
related words here
near antonyms away, far, farthest, remotest; heretofore, hitherto, since; ago, previously
antonyms before, formerly, long, once, then
2 not long ago — see NEWLY
3 on some occasions — see SOMETIMES
4 without delay — see IMMEDIATELY
now *conj* for the reason that — see SINCE
now *n* the time currently existing or in progress — see PRESENT 1
nowadays *adv* at the present time — see NOW 1
noway *or* **noways** *adv* not in any degree, way, or under any condition — see NEVER 2
no way *adv* certainly not — see HARDLY 2
nowise *adv* not in any degree, way, or under any condition — see NEVER 2
noxious *adj* **1** bad for the well-being of the body — see UNHEALTHY 1

2 causing or capable of causing harm — see HARMFUL

nth *adj* of the greatest or highest degree or quantity — see ULTIMATE 1

nub *n* **1** a small uneven mass — see LUMP 1
2 the central part or aspect of something under consideration — see CRUX

nubbin *n* a very small piece — see BIT 1

nubble *n* a small uneven mass — see LUMP 1

nubbly *adj* having small pieces or lumps spread throughout — see CHUNKY 1

nubby *adj* having small pieces or lumps spread throughout — see CHUNKY 1

nucleus *n* a thing or place that is of greatest importance to an activity or interest — see CENTER 1

nude *adj* lacking or shed of clothing — see NAKED 1

nudge *vb* to pass lightly across or touch gently especially in passing — see BRUSH

nugget *n* a small uneven mass — see LUMP 1

nuisance *n* **1** one who is obnoxiously annoying ⟨my little brother was being a *nuisance* by poking and prodding me throughout the long car trip⟩
synonyms annoyance, annoyer, bother, gadfly, gnawer, persecutor, pest, tease, teaser
related words headache; harrier, heckler; hassle, plague; molester, tormentor, torturer
near antonyms charmer, smoothy (*or* smoothie)
2 something that is a source of irritation — see ANNOYANCE 3

null *adj* **1** having no legal or binding force ⟨the contract was *null* because the other person forgot to sign it⟩
synonyms invalid, nonbinding, nonvalid, null and void, void
related words illegal; useless, worthless; ineffective, ineffectual
near antonyms legal; working
antonyms binding, good, valid
2 having no usefulness — see WORTHLESS

null and void *adj* having no legal or binding force — see NULL 1

nullify *vb* to put an end to by formal action — see ABOLISH

numb *adj* lacking in sensation or feeling ⟨I sat in one position too long and now my feet are *numb*⟩
synonyms asleep, benumbed, dead, insensitive, numbed, unfeeling
related words chilled, nipped; anesthetized, deadened, drugged, stupefied; insensible, senseless, unconscious; inanimate, insensate
near antonyms awake
antonyms feeling, sensitive

numb *vb* to reduce or weaken in strength or feeling — see DULL 1

numbed *adj* lacking in sensation or feeling — see NUMB

number *n* a character used to represent a mathematical value ⟨asked him to write out the equation in *numbers*, not letters⟩
synonyms digit, figure, integer, numeral, whole number
related words decimal, fraction; cipher; symbol

number *vb* **1** to find the sum of (a collection of things) by noting each one as it is being added — see COUNT 1
2 to have a total of — see AMOUNT (TO) 1
3 to have as part of a whole — see INCLUDE

numberless *adj* too many to be counted — see COUNTLESS

numbing *adj* having a low or subnormal temperature — see COLD 1

numbness *n* a lack of emotion or emotional expressiveness — see APATHY 1

numeral *n* a character used to represent a mathematical value — see NUMBER

numerate *vb* **1** to make a list of — see [1]LIST 1
2 to specify one after another — see ENUMERATE 1

numerous *adj* being of a large but indefinite number — see MANY

numskull *or* **numbskull** *n* a stupid person — see IDIOT

nuptial *adj* of or relating to marriage — see MARITAL

nuptial *n, usually* **nuptials** *pl* a ceremony in which two people are united in matrimony — see WEDDING

nurse *n* a girl or woman employed to care for a young child or children ⟨sent his little son back to his *nurse* so that he could return to his study to work⟩
synonyms babysitter, nursemaid, nurser, sitter
related words mammy; governess

nurse *vb* **1** to attend to the needs and comforts of ⟨took some time to *nurse* his grandmother, helping her get from one room to the other and making sure she was warm⟩
synonyms care (for), minister (to), mother
related words cure, heal, remedy; doctor, treat; aid, conserve, preserve, provide (for), support; baby, coddle, mollycoddle, pamper, spoil; cater (to), humor; indulge
phrases look after, look out for, look to, see to, take care of
near antonyms brush (aside *or* off), forget, ignore, neglect, overlook, slight
2 to keep in one's mind or heart — see HARBOR 1
3 to treat with great or excessive care — see BABY

nursemaid *n* a girl or woman employed to care for a young child or children — see NURSE

nurser *n* a girl or woman employed to care for a young child or children — see NURSE

nurture *vb* **1** to help the growth or development of — see FOSTER 1
2 to provide (someone) with moral or spiritual understanding — see ENLIGHTEN 2
3 to supply with nourishment — see SUSTAIN 1

nut *n* **1** a person of odd or whimsical habits — see ECCENTRIC
2 a person who lacks good sense or judgment — see FOOL 1
3 a person with a strong and habitual liking for something — see FAN
4 a person judged to be legally or medically insane — see LUNATIC 1

nutrient *adj* providing the substances necessary for health and bodily growth — see NUTRITIOUS

nutritional *adj* providing the substances necessary for health and bodily growth — see NUTRITIOUS

nutritious *adj* providing the substances necessary for health and bodily growth ⟨opted for a *nutritious* snack and bought an apple instead of a candy bar⟩
synonyms nourishing, nutrient, nutritional, nutritive
related words dietary, dietetic; beneficial, healthful, healthy, restorative, salubrious, salutary, wholesome

near antonyms insalubrious, unhealthful, unhealthy, unwholesome
antonyms nonnutritious

nutritive *adj* providing the substances necessary for health and bodily growth — see NUTRITIOUS

nuts *adj* **1** having or showing a very abnormal or sick state of mind — see INSANE 1
2 showing urgent desire or interest — see EAGER

nuts (about) *adj* filled with an intense or excessive love for — see ENAMORED (OF)

nuttiness *n* lack of good sense or judgment — see FOOLISHNESS 1

nutty *adj* **1** having or showing a very abnormal or sick state of mind — see INSANE 1
2 showing or marked by a lack of good sense or judgment — see FOOLISH 1

nuzzle *vb* to lie close ⟨newborn puppies *nuzzling* against their mother to stay warm⟩
synonyms cuddle, nestle, snuggle
related words curl up; crouch, huddle
near antonyms blench, flinch, quail, recoil, shrink, shy, start, wince

nymph *n* **1** a mythical goddess represented as a young girl and said to live outdoors ⟨she bought the book of fairy tales for the beautiful engravings of *nymphs* and fairies featured between the stories⟩
synonyms dryad, naiad, oread
related words mermaid, siren
2 a young wingless often wormlike form (as a grub or caterpillar) that hatches from the egg of many insects — see LARVA

oaf *n* a big clumsy often slow-witted person ⟨it is not polite to call your brother a stupid *oaf*⟩
synonyms clod, gawk, hulk, lout, lubber, lug
related words chump, loser, schlemiel, turkey; ass, blockhead, dolt, donkey, dope, dumbbell, dummy, goon, half-wit, idiot, ignoramus, imbecile, jackass, moron, nincompoop, ninny, nitwit, simpleton; beast, boor, brute, cad, churl, clown, creep, cretin, cur, heel, louse, skunk, snake, stinker, villain; booby, fool, goose, loony (*also* looney), lunatic, madman, nut; featherbrain, scatterbrain; rascal, rogue, scamp
near antonyms brain, genius; egghead, intellectual, sage, thinker

oafish *adj* not having or showing an ability to absorb ideas readily — see STUPID 1

oafishness *n* the quality or state of lacking intelligence or quickness of mind — see STUPIDITY 1

oar *vb* to move a boat by means of oars — see [1]ROW

oarsman *n* a person who drives a boat forward by means of oars ⟨the only *oarsman* in a rowboat designed for two⟩
synonyms rower, sculler
related words coxswain, crewman; puller, sailor

oath *n* a person's solemn declaration that he or she will do or not do something — see PROMISE

obduracy *n* a steadfast adherence to an opinion, purpose, or course of action — see OBSTINACY

obdurate *adj* **1** having or showing a lack of sympathy or tender feelings — see HARD 1
2 sticking to an opinion, purpose, or course of action in spite of reason, arguments, or persuasion — see OBSTINATE

obedience *n* **1** a bending to the authority or control of another ⟨the drill sergeant demanded complete and unquestioning *obedience* from the recruits⟩
synonyms compliance, conformity, observance, submission, subordination
related words acquiescence, agreeability, amenability; docility, submissiveness; capitulation, surrender, yielding; servility, slavishness, subservience; inhibition, repression, restraint, suppression; control, discipline, order
near antonyms contrariness, frowardness, intractability, rebelliousness, recalcitrance, refractoriness; disrespect, impudence, insolence, rudeness; insurgency, insurrection, mutiny, revolt; hardheadedness, mulishness, obstinacy, perversity, stubbornness, willfulness; misbehavior, mischievousness, naughtiness; dissent, dissidence
antonyms disobedience, insubordination, noncompliance, rebelling, rebellion
2 a readiness or willingness to yield to the wishes of others — see COMPLIANCE 1

obedient *adj* readily giving in to the command or authority of another ⟨that boy is so *obedient* that he does everything the first time he is asked⟩
synonyms amenable, compliant, conformable, docile, law-abiding, submissive, tractable
related words acquiescent, agreeable, amiable, obliging; surrendering, yielding; obsequious, servile, slavish, subservient; decorous, disciplined, mannerly, orderly; constrained, curbed, inhibited, repressed, restrained; controllable, governable, manageable; gentle, meek, mild
near antonyms insurgent, mutinous; dogged, hardheaded, headstrong, mulish, obdurate, obstinate, peevish, pigheaded, self-willed, stubborn, unyielding, willful (*or* wilful); obstreperous, restive, uncontrollable, ungovernable, unmanageable, wild; balky, defiant, perverse, resistant, wayward; bad, disorderly, errant, misbehaving, mischievous, naughty; ill-bred, undisciplined; dissident, nonconformist; disrespectful, ill-mannered, impolite, impudent, insolent, rude
antonyms contrary, disobedient, froward, insubordinate, intractable, rebellious, recalcitrant, refractory, unruly

obese *adj* having an excess of body fat — see FAT 1

obesity *n* the condition of having an excess of body fat — see CORPULENCE

obey *vb* to act according to the commands of ⟨it is important to *obey* your teachers immediately in the case of an emergency⟩ ⟨most people *obey* the law and wear their seat belts⟩
synonyms comply (with), conform (to), follow, mind, observe

related words defer (to), submit (to), surrender (to), yield (to); accede (to), acquiesce (to), agree (to), assent (to); attend, hear, heed, listen (to), mark, note, notice, regard, watch
phrases abide by
near antonyms challenge, dare; rebel (against); defy; direct, lead; brush off, disregard, ignore, overlook, overpass, pass over, tune out, wink (at); dismiss, pooh-pooh, shrug off; break, transgress, violate; deride, flout, scorn
antonyms disobey

object *n* **1** something material that can be perceived by the senses ⟨I kept tripping over countless little *objects* scattered about the darkened room⟩
synonyms thing
related words article, item, piece; being, entity, substance; commodity, good, ware; accessory, accompaniment, bauble, curio; knickknack, spangle, token, trinket
2 one that has a real and independent existence — see ENTITY
3 something that one hopes or intends to accomplish — see GOAL

object *vb* to present an opposing opinion or argument ⟨they *objected* to the conductor's insistence that their train tickets were not valid⟩
synonyms demur, expostulate (with), kick, protest, remonstrate (with)
related words cavil, quibble; challenge, dare, defy; conflict (with), debate, dispute, hassle, quarrel, squabble, wrangle; complain, inveigh (against); balk (at), stick (at); censure, criticize, denounce; disobey, rebel (against); demonstrate (against)
phrases take exception
near antonyms approve, sanction; accept; accede (to), acquiesce (to), agree (with), assent (to); comply (with), obey; advocate, champion, defend, maintain, support, sustain, uphold

objection *n* a feeling or declaration of disapproval or dissent ⟨pardon me, but I have an *objection* to any plan that requires staying out all night⟩
synonyms challenge, complaint, demur, expostulation, fuss, protest, question, remonstrance
related words compunction, doubt, misgiving, qualm, scruple; difficulty, misunderstanding; cavil, quibble; argument, conflict, debate, dispute, dissent, hassle, quarrel, squabble; censure, criticism; defiance, disobedience, rebellion
near antonyms willingness; approval, sanction; acceptance, acquiescence, agreement, assent; compliance, obedience

objectionable *adj* provoking or likely to provoke protest ⟨that T-shirt displays *objectionable* images which are not appropriate for school⟩
synonyms censurable, exceptionable, obnoxious, offensive, reprehensible
related words bawdy, coarse, crude, dirty, filthy, foul, gross, indecent, lewd, nasty, obscene, smutty, vulgar; blamable, blameworthy, lascivious, pornographic, ribald, scurrilous; debasing, perverted, profane; racy, salty, suggestive; unacceptable, undesirable, unwanted, unwelcome; abhorrent, disgusting, loathsome, repellent (*also* repellant), repugnant, repulsive, revolting; disagreeable, displeasing, distasteful, unpleasant; bad, execrable, lousy, miserable; atrocious, infamous; indecent, indecorous, unbecoming; earthy, unprintable; naughty, wicked
near antonyms acceptable, agreeable, pleasant, pleasing, welcome; good; approved, endorsed, sanctioned; abetted, encouraged, promoted, supported; becoming, correct, decent, decorous, exemplary, seemly; blameless, commendable, creditable; immaculate, perfect, pure, spotless
antonyms inoffensive, unobjectionable

objective *adj* **1** based on observation or experience — see EMPIRICAL
2 marked by justice, honesty, and freedom from bias — see FAIR 2
3 restricted to or based on fact — see FACTUAL 1

objective *n* something that one hopes or intends to accomplish — see GOAL

objectivity *n* lack of favoritism toward one side or another — see DETACHMENT 1

obligate *vb* to cause (a person) to give in to pressure — see FORCE

obligation *n* something one must do because of prior agreement ⟨their financial *obligations* keep them from giving to charities as much as they would like⟩
synonyms burden, charge, commitment, duty, need, responsibility
related words pledge, promise; arrangement, prearrangement, setup; compact, contract, covenant, pact; payment, tribute; compulsion, constraint, restraint; must, requirement; coercion, duress, force; appointment, engagement, reservation
near antonyms grace, postponement, stay; discharge, exemption, release, waiver; alternative, choice, option, pick, preference, selection

obligatory *adj* forcing one's compliance or participation by or as if by law — see MANDATORY

oblige *vb* **1** to do a service or favor for ⟨I would appreciate it greatly if you could *oblige* me by bringing a dessert to the party⟩
synonyms accommodate, favor
related words humor, indulge; coddle, mollycoddle, pamper; appease, conciliate, mollify, pacify, placate; delight, gladden, gratify, please, satisfy; abet, aid, assist, help, support; attend, care (for), minister (to), relieve, succor
near antonyms bother, discommode, disturb, incommode, inconvenience, trouble; burden, encumber, saddle, weigh; desert, disappoint, fail, let down; constrain, hamper, hamstring, hinder, hobble, hold back, impede, obstruct, restrain; frustrate, oppose, sabotage, thwart
antonyms disoblige
2 to cause (a person) to give in to pressure — see FORCE

obliged *adj* feeling or expressing gratitude — see GRATEFUL 1

oblique *adj* **1** inclined or twisted to one side — see AWRY
2 running in a slanting direction — see DIAGONAL

obliquely *adv* in a line or direction running from corner to corner — see CROSSWISE

obliterate *vb* to destroy all traces of — see ANNIHILATE 1

obliteration *n* the state or fact of being rendered nonexistent, physically unsound, or useless — see DESTRUCTION

oblivion *n* a state of being disregardful or unconscious of one's surroundings, concerns, or obligations ⟨for two weeks each year the stressed-out couple enjoy the blissful *oblivion* that comes with a vacation at the beach⟩

synonyms forgetfulness, obliviousness
related words ignorance, unawareness, unconsciousness, unfamiliarity
near antonyms memory, recall, recollection, remembrance; alertness, awareness, cognizance, consciousness

oblivious *adj* not informed about or aware of something — see IGNORANT 2

obliviousness *n* **1** a state of being disregardful or unconscious of one's surroundings, concerns, or obligations — see OBLIVION
2 the state of being unaware or uninformed — see IGNORANCE 1

obnoxious *adj* **1** causing intense displeasure, disgust, or resentment — see OFFENSIVE 1
2 provoking or likely to provoke protest — see OBJECTIONABLE

obscene *adj* **1** depicting or referring to sexual matters in a way that is unacceptable in polite society ⟨*obscene* language and artwork is forbidden in this school⟩
synonyms bawdy, coarse, crude, dirty, filthy, foul, gross, indecent, lascivious, lewd, nasty, pornographic, ribald, smutty, unprintable, vulgar, wanton
related words earthy, racy, salty, suggestive; indecorous, unbecoming; debasing, perverted, profane; naughty, wicked; exceptionable, objectionable, unacceptable, undesirable, unwanted, unwelcome; abhorrent, disgusting, loathsome, offensive, repellent (*also* repellant), repugnant, repulsive, revolting; distasteful, obnoxious, unpleasant; blamable, blameworthy, censurable, reprehensible; atrocious, infamous; abusive, scurrilous
near antonyms priggish, prim, prudish, puritanical, straitlaced (*or* straightlaced), Victorian; correct, decorous, genteel, polite, proper, seemly; innocuous, inoffensive; acceptable, agreeable, desirable, pleasant, pleasing, welcome; appropriate, becoming, fit, meet, suitable; immaculate, perfect, pure, spotless; approved, endorsed, sanctioned
antonyms clean, decent
2 causing intense displeasure, disgust, or resentment — see OFFENSIVE 1

obscenity *n* **1** the quality or state of being obscene ⟨the issue of whether *obscenity* is a fundamental part of rap music⟩
synonyms bawdiness, coarseness, crudeness, dirt, dirtiness, filth, filthiness, foulness, grossness, indecency, lasciviousness, lewdness, nastiness, ribaldry, smuttiness, vulgarity
related words raciness, saltiness, suggestiveness; perversion, profanity; naughtiness, wickedness; loathsomeness, offensiveness, repulsiveness; distastefulness, obnoxiousness, unpleasantness
near antonyms priggishness, primness, prudery, prudishness, puritanism; correctness, decency, decorousness, decorum, seemliness; appropriateness, fitness, suitability, suitableness; immaculateness, perfection, purity, spotlessness
2 a disrespectful or indecent word or expression — see SWEARWORD

obscure *adj* **1** having an often intentionally veiled or uncertain meaning ⟨a fantasy writer who likes to put lots of *obscure* references and images in her tales of wizards and warlocks⟩
synonyms ambiguous, cryptic, dark, darkling, deep, enigmatic (*also* enigmatical), equivocal, inscrutable, murky, mysterious, mystic, nebulous, occult
related words abstruse, esoteric, recondite; bleary, cloudy, dim, faint, foggy, fuzzy, hazy, indefinite, indistinct, indistinguishable, shadowy, unclear, uncertain, undefined, undetermined, vague; impenetrable, incomprehensible; inexplicable; eerie, uncanny, weird; impalpable, inappreciable, intangible, invisible; unanswerable, unknowable; baffling, bewildering, confounding, confusing, mystifying, perplexing, puzzling, unfathomable; difficult, complex, complicated, obtuse
near antonyms comprehensible, fathomable, intelligible, knowable, understandable; bright, distinct, evident; certain, firm, strong, sure; defined, determined; direct, straightforward; definite, exact, explicit; appreciable, palpable, tangible, visible; blatant, patent, unmistakable
antonyms clear, obvious, plain, unambiguous, unequivocal
2 not widely known ⟨he's an *obscure* artist now, but he's sure to be famous someday⟩
synonyms anonymous, nameless, uncelebrated, unknown, unnoted, unsung
related words insignificant, minor, unimportant; undistinguished, unexceptional; unpopular; faceless
near antonyms fabled, fabulous, legendary; infamous; distinguished, eminent, exceptional, great, illustrious, leading, notable, outstanding, prestigious, remarkable; important, significant; favorite, popular, preferred; estimable, honorable, reputable, respectable; influential, major
antonyms celebrated, famed, famous, noted, notorious, prominent, renowned, well-known
3 being without light or without much light — see DARK 1
4 not seen or understood clearly — see FAINT 1

obscure *vb* **1** to keep secret or shut off from view — see [1]HIDE 2
2 to make dark, dim, or indistinct — see CLOUD 1

obscured *adj* being without light or without much light — see DARK 1

obscurity *n* **1** the quality or state of having a veiled or uncertain meaning ⟨the 16th-century astrologer's predictions are so filled with *obscurity* that people can interpret them any way they want⟩
synonyms ambiguity, ambiguousness, darkness, equivocalness, equivocation, murkiness, nebulousness, opacity
related words cloudiness, dimness, faintness, fogginess, fuzziness, haziness, indefiniteness, indistinctness, uncertainty, vagueness; impenetrability, incomprehensibility; deepness, profoundness; intangibility, invisibility; abstruseness; complexity, complication, difficulty, obtuseness
near antonyms comprehensibility, intelligibility; brightness, distinctness; certainty, surety; definiteness, exactness, explicitness; directness, straightforwardness; palpability, tangibility, visibility
antonyms clarity, clearness, obviousness, plainness
2 the quality or state of being mostly or completely unknown ⟨the singer languished in relative *obscurity* for years before becoming famous⟩
synonyms anonymity
related words oblivion; inconspicuousness, invisibility; insignificance, unimportance; unpopularity

near antonyms name, report, reputation, repute; popularity; importance, significance; distinction, eminence, glory, greatness, honor, illustriousness, note, preeminence, prominence; cachet, position, prestige, rank, standing, stature; acclaim, acknowledgment (*also* acknowledgement), praise, recognition; adoration, idolization
antonyms celebrity, fame, notoriety, renown

observable *adj* capable of being seen — see VISIBLE

observance *n* **1** an act of following a custom, rule, or law ⟨the *observance* of this family tradition would make your grandmother very happy⟩
synonyms observation
related words attention, heed, notice; respecting, upholding
near antonyms infraction, offense (*or* offence), sin, trespass, wrong; disregard, forgetting, ignoring, neglect, overlooking; delinquency, dereliction
antonyms breach, infringement, nonobservance, transgression, violation
2 an oft-repeated action or series of actions performed in accordance with tradition or a set of rules — see RITE
3 a bending to the authority or control of another — see OBEDIENCE 1
4 a state of being aware — see ATTENTION 2

observation *n* **1** a state of being aware — see ATTENTION 2
2 an act of following a custom, rule, or law — see OBSERVANCE 1

observational *adj* based on observation or experience — see EMPIRICAL

observatory *n* a high place or structure from which a wide view is possible — see LOOKOUT 1

observe *vb* **1** to act according to the commands of — see OBEY
2 to act properly in relation to — see KEEP 1
3 to keep one's eyes on — see WATCH 1
4 to make a statement of one's opinion — see REMARK 1
5 to make note of (something) through the use of one's eyes — see SEE 1
6 to take notice of and be guided by — see HEED 1

obsessed *adj* having extreme or relentless concern — see HUNG UP 1

obsession *n* something about which one is constantly thinking or concerned — see FIXATION

obsessive *adj* caused by or suggestive of an irresistible urge — see COMPULSIVE

obsolete *adj* having passed its time of use or usefulness ⟨the abacus was considered *obsolete* once the electronic calculator was invented⟩
synonyms antiquated, archaic, dated, moth-eaten, outdated, outmoded, out-of-date, outworn, passé
related words aging, obsolescent; discarded, disused, superannuated, worn-out; inoperable, unusable, unworkable, useless; dead, defunct, extinct; dormant, fallow, free, idle, inactive, inert, inoperative, latent; ancient, antediluvian, antique, fusty, musty, old, oldfangled, old-fashioned, old-time, old-world; aged, age-old, hoary, venerable; bygone, erstwhile, former, late, past; historic, historical
near antonyms contemporary, current, mod, modern, new, newfangled, new-fashioned, present-day, recent, ultramodern, up-to-date; fresh; modernized, refurbished, remodeled, renewed; functional, operable, operational, workable; active, alive, busy, employed, functioning, operating, operative

obstacle *n* something that makes movement or progress more difficult — see ENCUMBRANCE

obstinacy *n* a steadfast adherence to an opinion, purpose, or course of action ⟨the mindless *obstinacy* of those people who continue to insist that the earth is flat⟩
synonyms doggedness, hardheadedness, mulishness, obduracy, peevishness, persistence, pertinaciousness, pertinacity, self-will, stubbornness, tenaciousness, tenacity, willfulness
related words perverseness, perversity, resistance, waywardness, wrongheadedness; hardness, inflexibility, relentlessness, sternness, strictness; certainty, determination, firmness; inexorability, resolve, rigidity, rigidness, steadfastness; contrariness, defiance, disobedience, insubordination, recalcitrance
near antonyms broad-mindedness, open-mindedness, reasonableness, receptivity; acceptance, acquiescence, flexibility, pliability; compliance, docility, obedience; submission, surrender, willingness, yielding; slavishness, subservience

obstinate *adj* sticking to an opinion, purpose, or course of action in spite of reason, arguments, or persuasion ⟨the child was *obstinate* about wanting that specific toy, despite being offered several others⟩
synonyms adamant, adamantine, dogged, hard, hardened, hardheaded, hardhearted, headstrong, immovable, implacable, inflexible, mulish, obdurate, opinionated, ossified, pat, peevish, pertinacious, perverse, pigheaded, rigid, self-willed, stubborn, unbending, uncompromising, unrelenting, unyielding, willful (*or* wilful)
related words hidebound, narrow-minded; resistant, wayward, wrongheaded; persistent, tenacious; iron, relentless; grim, severe, stern, strict; determined, firm, inexorable, resolved, single-minded, steadfast, sure, unflinching; contrary, disobedient, froward, insubordinate, intractable, recalcitrant, refractory, uncooperative, ungovernable, unmanageable, unruly; defiant, insurgent, mutinous; indomitable, invincible, unconquerable; confirmed, inveterate, unregenerate; demanding, exacting
near antonyms docile, law-abiding, obedient, submissive, tractable; accepting, receptive, responsive, willing; governable, manageable, reasonable, temperate; slavish, subservient
antonyms acquiescent, agreeable, amenable, compliant, complying, flexible, pliable, pliant, relenting, yielding

obstreperous *adj* engaging in or marked by loud and insistent cries especially of protest — see VOCIFEROUS

obstruct *vb* **1** to create difficulty for the work or activity of — see HAMPER
2 to prevent passage through — see CLOG 1

obstruction *n* something that makes movement or progress more difficult — see ENCUMBRANCE

obtain *vb* to receive as return for effort — see EARN 1

obtainable *adj* possible to get — see AVAILABLE 1

obtrude *vb* to interest oneself in what is not one's concern — see INTERFERE

obtrusive *adj* thrusting oneself where one is not welcome or invited — see INTRUSIVE
obtuse *adj* **1** lacking sharpness of edge or point — see DULL 1
2 not having or showing an ability to absorb ideas readily — see STUPID 1
obtuseness *n* the quality or state of lacking intelligence or quickness of mind — see STUPIDITY 1
obviate *vb* to keep from happening by taking action in advance — see PREVENT
obviating *n* the act or practice of keeping something from happening — see PREVENTION
obvious *adj* **1** not subject to misinterpretation or more than one interpretation — see CLEAR 2
2 very noticeable especially for being incorrect or bad — see EGREGIOUS
occasion *n* **1** a particular point at which an event takes place ⟨the *occasion* of our last meeting with our old friend was several years ago, unfortunately⟩
synonyms moment, time
related words flash, instant, jiffy, minute, second, shake, split second, trice, twinkle, wink; while
2 a favorable combination of circumstances, time, and place — see OPPORTUNITY
3 someone or something responsible for a result — see CAUSE 1
4 something that happens — see EVENT 1
occasional *adj* **1** lacking in steadiness or regularity of occurrence — see FITFUL
2 not often occurring or repeated — see INFREQUENT
occasionally *adv* on some occasions — see SOMETIMES
occult *adj* **1** being beyond one's powers to know, understand, or explain — see MYSTERIOUS 1
2 having an often intentionally veiled or uncertain meaning — see OBSCURE 1
3 having seemingly supernatural qualities or powers — see MYSTIC 1
occult *vb* to keep secret or shut off from view — see [1]HIDE 2
occupant *n* one who lives permanently in a place — see INHABITANT
occupation *n* the activity by which one regularly makes a living ⟨my primary *occupation* is as a stockbroker, but I'm a drummer in a rock band on the weekends⟩
synonyms calling, employment, line, profession, trade, vocation, work
related words racket; art, craft, handicraft; appointment, assignment, berth, billet, duty, function, job, office, place, position, post, situation; business, engagement, livelihood, living
near antonyms avocation, hobby, pursuit
occupied *adj* involved in often constant activity — see BUSY 1
occupy *vb* **1** to hold the attention of — see ENGAGE 1
2 to keep, control, or experience as one's own — see HAVE 1
occur *vb* to take place — see HAPPEN
occur (to) *vb* to come into the mind of ⟨it didn't *occur to* me to ask until much later⟩
synonyms dawn (on), strike
related words appear, arrive, come, emerge, materialize; con, learn, memorize; recall, recollect, remember, reminisce
near antonyms forget, unlearn; disregard, neglect, overlook
occurrence *n* something that happens — see EVENT 1
ocean *n* the whole body of salt water that covers nearly three-fourths of the earth ⟨the Vikings explored the *ocean* in small open boats, beginning in the eighth century⟩
synonyms blue, brine, deep, sea, seven seas
related words high seas, main, waters; basin; Davy Jones's locker
oceanic *adj* of or relating to the sea — see MARINE 1
ocular *adj* of, relating to, or used in vision — see VISUAL 1
odd *adj* **1** being one of a pair or set without a corresponding mate ⟨somehow, there's always at least one *odd* sock that comes out of the dryer⟩
synonyms unmatched, unpaired
related words alone, lone, only, single, singular, sole, solitary
antonyms matched, paired
2 different from the ordinary in a way that causes curiosity or suspicion ⟨one girl dyed her hair purple with pink polka dots, which was a rather *odd* effect⟩
synonyms bizarre, curious, far-out, funny, kinky, outlandish, out-of-the-way, outré, peculiar, quaint, queer, queerish, quirky, remarkable, screwy, strange, wacky, way-out, weird, wild
related words aberrant, abnormal, atypical, extraordinary, fantastic, flaky, freak, freakish, idiosyncratic, phenomenal, singular, unique, unusual, unwonted; conspicuous, notable, noticeable, outstanding, prominent, salient, striking; atrocious, outrageous, shocking; nonconformist, unconventional, unorthodox; eccentric, idiosyncratic; rare, uncommon, uncustomary; baffling, bewildering, confounding, mystifying, perplexing, puzzling
near antonyms average, commonplace, everyday, garden, ordinary, prosaic, routine, run-of-the-mill, typical, unexceptional, unremarkable, usual, workaday; conformist, conservative, conventional; expected, familiar, predictable; common, customary, frequent, habitual, regular, wonted
3 being out of the ordinary — see EXCEPTIONAL
4 noticeably different from what is generally found or experienced — see UNUSUAL 1
oddball *n* a person of odd or whimsical habits — see ECCENTRIC
oddity *n* **1** an odd or peculiar habit — see IDIOSYNCRASY
2 something strange or unusual that is an object of interest — see CURIOSITY 2
oddment *n* an unused or unwanted piece or item typically of small size or value — see [1]SCRAP 1
odds *n pl* a measure of how often an event will occur instead of another — see PROBABILITY 2
odds and ends *n pl* **1** small useful items — see NOTION 1
2 a remaining group or portion — see REMAINDER 1
odious *adj* causing intense displeasure, disgust, or resentment — see OFFENSIVE 1
odium *n* the state of having lost the esteem of others — see DISGRACE 1
odor *n* the quality of a thing that makes it perceptible to the sense organs in the nose — see SMELL
of *prep* **1** earlier than — see BEFORE 1
2 having to do with — see ABOUT 1
off *adv* from this or that place — see AWAY

off *adj* **1** falling short of a standard — see BAD 1

2 not being in a state of use, activity, or employment — see INACTIVE 2

3 not being in agreement with what is true — see FALSE 1

4 small in degree — see REMOTE 1

offbeat *adj* noticeably different from what is generally found or experienced — see UNUSUAL 1

offend *vb* **1** to commit an offense ⟨since this is the first time you've *offended,* we'll let you off lightly⟩

synonyms err, sin, transgress, trespass

related words breach, break, infringe, violate; backslide, lapse

phrases break the law, fall from grace

near antonyms forgive, justify; repent

2 to cause hurt feelings or deep resentment in — see INSULT

offender *n* a person who has committed a crime — see CRIMINAL

offense *or* **offence** *n* **1** a breaking of a moral or legal code ⟨wartime *offenses* that are crimes against all of humanity⟩

synonyms breach, crime, debt, error, lawbreaking, malefaction, misdeed, misdoing, sin, transgression, trespass, violation, wrongdoing

related words felony, misdemeanor; fault, foible, peccadillo; break, infringement; immorality, iniquity, sinfulness, vice, wickedness; criminality, illegality, lawlessness, unlawfulness

near antonyms blamelessness, faultlessness, guiltlessness, innocence; goodness, morality, righteousness, virtue, virtuousness

2 the act or action of setting upon with force or violence — see ATTACK 1

3 an act or expression showing scorn and usually intended to hurt another's feelings — see INSULT

4 the feeling of being offended or resentful after a slight or indignity — see PIQUE

offensive *adj* **1** causing intense displeasure, disgust, or resentment ⟨I find your disrespectful attitude toward religion very *offensive*⟩ ⟨the smell of rotting food is quite *offensive*⟩

synonyms abhorrent, abominable, appalling, awful, distasteful, dreadful, foul, hideous, horrendous, horrible, horrid, loathsome, nasty, nauseating, noisome, obnoxious, obscene, odious, repellent (*also* repellant), repugnant, repulsive, revolting, scandalous, shocking, sickening, ugly

related words exceptionable, objectionable; disagreeable, unpleasant; contemptible, despicable, detestable, hateful; unhealthy, unwholesome; execrable, lousy, miserable; atrocious, heinous, unspeakable; barbarous, unchristian, uncivilized, ungodly, unholy

near antonyms acceptable, agreeable, attractive, delectable, delightful, desirable, likable (*or* likeable), pleasant, pleasing, welcome; unobjectionable; healthy, wholesome

antonyms inoffensive

2 provoking or likely to provoke protest — see OBJECTIONABLE

offensive *n* the act or action of setting upon with force or violence — see ATTACK 1

offer *n* something which is presented for consideration — see PROPOSAL

offer *vb* **1** to put before another for acceptance or consideration ⟨I *offered* my boss an alternative to the plan that required me to work overtime⟩

synonyms extend, give, proffer, tender

related words pose, propose

near antonyms accept, receive, take; decline, refuse, reject; retract, withdraw; consider, contemplate, mull (over), ponder, study, think (over)

2 to set before the mind for consideration — see PROPOSE 1

3 to bring before the public in performance or exhibition — see PRESENT 1

4 to give up as an offering to a god — see SACRIFICE

offering *n* something offered to a god — see SACRIFICE

offhand *adj* made or done without previous thought or preparation — see EXTEMPORANEOUS

offhanded *adj* made or done without previous thought or preparation — see EXTEMPORANEOUS

office *n* a large unit of a governmental, business, or educational organization — see DIVISION 2

officeholder *n* a person who holds a public office — see OFFICIAL

officer *n* **1** a member of a force charged with law enforcement at the local level ⟨if you are ever lost, find the nearest *officer* and ask for help⟩

synonyms bobby [*British*], bull [*slang*], constable, cop, policeman, police officer

related words patrolman, policewoman; detective, inspector, plainclothesman; marshal, sheriff, trooper; captain, lieutenant, sergeant

2 a person who holds a public office — see OFFICIAL

official *adj* ordered or allowed by those in authority ⟨the *official* languages for those Olympic Games were French and English⟩

synonyms authorized, sanctioned

related words legal, permissible; approved, endorsed; abetted, encouraged, promoted, suggested, supported; certified, licensed (*also* licenced); authoritative, canonical, ex officio; semiofficial

near antonyms illegal, illicit, unlawful; unapproved, unendorsed, unlicensed

antonyms unauthorized, unofficial, unsanctioned

official *n* a person who holds a public office ⟨some of our best public *officials* do their jobs quietly and are never in the news⟩

synonyms functionary, officeholder, officer, public servant

related words bureaucrat; administrator, commissioner, director, executive, manager, superintendent, supervisor; chair, chairman

officious *adj* thrusting oneself where one is not welcome or invited — see INTRUSIVE

offing *n* time that is to come — see FUTURE 1

offset *n* a force or influence that makes an opposing force ineffective or less effective — see COUNTERBALANCE

offset *vb* to balance with an equal force so as to make ineffective ⟨if you get a high grade on this quiz, it will *offset* the D from your last one⟩

synonyms annul, cancel (out), compensate (for), correct, counteract, counterbalance, counterpoise, make up (for), neutralize

related words invalidate, negate, nullify; atone (for); outweigh, redeem; redress, relieve, remedy; override, overrule

offshoot *n* **1** a branch of a main stem especially of a plant ⟨we knew the rose bush had survived the winter when it began producing *offshoots* and turning green again⟩

synonyms outgrowth, shoot

related words excrescence, growth; bough, limb, twig; bud, floret; spray, sprig
2 something that naturally develops or is developed from something else — see DERIVATIVE

offspring *n* the descendants of a person, animal, or plant ⟨the racehorse's *offspring* all proved to be very good racers as well⟩ ⟨the couple celebrated their 50th wedding anniversary surrounded by three generations of *offspring*⟩
synonyms issue, posterity, progeny, seed, spawn
related words brood, hatch, litter, young; child, scion (*also* cion)
near antonyms ancestor, antecedent, forebear (*also* forbear), forefather, parent

offstage *adj or adv* off or away from the part of the stage visible to the audience ⟨please wait until you are *offstage* to start changing costumes⟩
synonyms backstage
related words upstage
phrases behind the scenes

oft *adv* many times — see OFTEN

often *adv* many times ⟨I seem to stumble *often* when I try to walk in high heels⟩
synonyms constantly, continually, frequently, oft, oftentimes (*or* ofttimes), repeatedly
related words always, consistently, continuously, perpetually; afresh, again, anew; commonly, ordinarily, regularly, routinely; intermittently, periodically, recurrently; generally, usually
phrases again and again, over and over, time after time, time and again
near antonyms occasionally, sometimes, sporadically, never; once
antonyms infrequently, rarely, seldom

oftentimes *or* **ofttimes** *adv* many times — see OFTEN

ogle *vb* to look at in a flirtatious or desiring way ⟨I do wish you two would stop *ogling* each other during class⟩
synonyms leer (at)
related words eye, gape, gawk, gaze, glare, goggle, peer, rubberneck, stare

ogre *n* **1** a strange or horrible and often frightening creature — see MONSTER 1
2 something or someone that causes fear or dread especially without reason — see BOGEY 1

oh *n* the numerical symbol 0 or the absence of number or quantity represented by it — see ZERO 1

oil *n* a picture created with usually oil paint — see PAINTING

oil *vb* to coat (something) with a slippery substance in order to reduce friction — see LUBRICATE

oiled *adj* having or being a surface so smooth as to make sliding or falling likely — see SLICK 1

oil painting *n* a picture created with usually oil paint — see PAINTING

oilskin *n* a coat made of water-resistant material — see RAINCOAT

OK *or* **okay** *adj* **1** being to one's liking — see SATISFACTORY 1
2 of a level of quality that meets one's needs or standards — see ADEQUATE

OK *or* **okay** *adv* **1** in a satisfactory way — see WELL 1
2 used to express agreement — see YES

OK *or* **okay** *n* an acceptance of something as satisfactory — see APPROVAL 1

OK *or* **okay** *vb* **1** to give official acceptance of something as satisfactory — see APPROVE
2 to have a favorable opinion of — see APPROVE (OF)

old *adj* **1** being of advanced years and especially past middle age — see ELDERLY
2 dating or surviving from the distant past — see ANCIENT 1
3 having been such at some previous time — see FORMER

older *adj* being of advanced years and especially past middle age — see ELDERLY

oldfangled *adj* pleasantly reminiscent of an earlier time — see OLD-FASHIONED 1

old–fashioned *adj* **1** pleasantly reminiscent of an earlier time ⟨an elegant, *old-fashioned* bun that was held in place with pearl hairpins⟩
synonyms antique, oldfangled, old-time, old-world, quaint
related words antiquated, obsolete; historic, historical, olden, traditional; outdated, outmoded, out-of-date, outworn, passé; dated, fusty, moth-eaten, musty; aged, age-old, ancient, antediluvian, fossilized, hoary, venerable; bygone, erstwhile, former, late, past; forgotten, remote; ageless, dateless; timeless
near antonyms fresh, new, up-to-date; chic, fashionable, smart, stylish; modernized, refurbished, remodeled, renewed
antonyms contemporary, hot, mod, modern, newfangled, new-fashioned, ultramodern
2 tending to favor established ideas, conditions, or institutions — see CONSERVATIVE 1

old hand *n* a person with long experience in a specified area — see VETERAN

old–maidish *adj* hard to please — see FINICKY

old man *n* **1** a male human parent — see FATHER 1
2 the male partner in a marriage — see HUSBAND

oldster *n* a person of advanced years — see SENIOR CITIZEN

old–time *adj* pleasantly reminiscent of an earlier time — see OLD-FASHIONED 1

old–timer *n* **1** a person of advanced years — see SENIOR CITIZEN
2 a person with long experience in a specified area — see VETERAN

old wives' tale *n* a false idea or belief — see FALLACY 1

old–world *adj* pleasantly reminiscent of an earlier time — see OLD-FASHIONED 1

omen *n* something believed to be a sign or warning of a future event ⟨some people believe that a black cat crossing your path is an *omen* that something bad is about to happen to you⟩
synonyms augury, auspice, boding, foreboding, foreshadowing, portent, prefiguring, presage
related words forerunner, harbinger, herald, precursor; foretaste, hint, inkling, intimation, suggestion; forewarning; forecast, foretelling, prediction, prognostication, prophecy; badge, mark, note, token

ominous *adj* being or showing a sign of evil or calamity to come ⟨that comment about downsizing from the company president sounded *ominous*⟩
synonyms baleful, dire, foreboding, inauspicious, menacing, portentous, sinister, threatening
related words black, dark, gloomy; unfavorable, unpromising; ill-fated, ill-starred, star-crossed, unfortunate, unlucky; evil, malign, malignant
near antonyms auspicious, benign, favorable, promising, propitious

omission *n* something left out ⟨the disk contains a selection of deleted scenes, and a couple of the *omissions* greatly add to the intelligibility of the movie's plot⟩
synonyms deletion
related words elimination; blank, skip; lapse, slip; deduction, reduction, subtraction
near antonyms inclusion; accretion, accrual, addendum, addition, augmentation, boost, gain, increase, increment, raise, rise, supplement

omit *vb* to miss the opportunity or obligation — see NEGLECT 3

omnibus *adj* covering everything or all important points — see ENCYCLOPEDIC

omnipotent *adj* having unlimited power or authority ⟨the nearly universal religious belief that God is *omnipotent* and can do anything⟩
synonyms all-powerful, almighty
related words great, sovereign, supreme, towering, transcendent; authoritative, chief, majestic, masterful; mighty, potent, powerful, strong; divine, godlike
near antonyms helpless, impotent, powerless; limited, restricted

omnipresent *adj* present in all places and at all times ⟨seeking some much-needed relief from the *omnipresent* noise of the big city⟩
synonyms ubiquitous, universal
related words boundless, endless, illimitable, immeasurable, indefinite, infinite, limitless, measureless, unbounded, unfathomable, unlimited
near antonyms bounded, circumscribed, confined, finite, limited, restricted

on *adj* being in effective operation — see ACTIVE 1

on *adv* **1** toward a point ahead in space or time — see ONWARD 1
2 toward or at a point lying in advance in space or time — see ALONG

on *prep* **1** having to do with — see ABOUT 1
2 in or into contact with — see AGAINST

oncoming *adj* being soon to appear or take place — see FORTHCOMING

one *adj* known but not named — see CERTAIN 1

one-dimensional *adj* having or showing a lack of depth of understanding or character — see SUPERFICIAL 2

onerous *adj* **1** difficult to endure — see HARSH 1
2 requiring much time, effort, or careful attention — see DEMANDING 1

one-sided *adj* inclined to favor one side over another — see PARTIAL 1

one-sidedness *n* an attitude that always favors one way of feeling or acting especially without considering any other possibilities — see BIAS

onetime *adj* having been such at some previous time — see FORMER

ongoing *adj* **1** being in progress or development ⟨we do seem to be making some headway on that *ongoing* project⟩ ⟨the ever *ongoing* quest for knowledge by men and women of science⟩
synonyms afoot, proceeding, under way
related words functioning, happening, operating, working; afloat, alive, going; advancing, gaining
near antonyms receding, regressing, retrogressing
antonyms arrested, halted, stalled, stopped
2 existing or in progress right now — see PRESENT 1

only *adj* **1** having no equal or rival for excellence or desirability ⟨the *only* way to really appreciate the beauty of the forest is to walk through it⟩
synonyms incomparable, inimitable, matchless, nonpareil, peerless, unequaled (*or* unequalled), unexampled, unmatched, unparalleled, unrivaled (*or* unrivalled), unsurpassable, unsurpassed
related words singular, unique; exceptional, extraordinary, rare, uncommon, unusual; A1, bang-up, banner, boss [*slang*], capital, classic, dandy, excellent, fabulous, fine, first-class, first-rate, grand, great, groovy, jim-dandy, keen, marvelous (*or* marvellous), mean, neat, par excellence, prime, superb, superior, superlative, terrific, tip-top, top-notch; better, preferred; exceptional, fancy, high-grade, special
near antonyms common, everyday, normal, ordinary, usual; inferior, lesser, worse, worst; bad, low, lower; low-grade, substandard, unsatisfactory; mediocre, second-class, second-rate; atrocious, execrable, wretched
2 being the one or ones of a class with no other members ⟨that is the *only* possible right answer⟩ ⟨we were the *only* passengers on the tour bus⟩
synonyms alone, lone, singular, sole, solitary, special, unique
related words solo, unaccompanied, unattended; incomparable, inimitable, matchless, peerless, unequaled (*or* unequalled), unmatched, unparalleled, unrivaled (*or* unrivalled), unsurpassable, unsurpassed; distinct, distinctive, individual, separate
near antonyms manifold, multifarious, myriad; assorted, heterogenous, miscellaneous, mixed, motley

only *adv* **1** for nothing other than — see SOLELY 1
2 not long ago — see NEWLY
3 nothing more than — see JUST 3

only *conj* if it were not for the fact that — see EXCEPT

onrush *n* forward movement in time or place — see ADVANCE 1

onset *n* **1** the act or action of setting upon with force or violence — see ATTACK 1
2 the point at which something begins — see BEGINNING

onslaught *n* the act or action of setting upon with force or violence — see ATTACK 1

onward *also* **onwards** *adv* **1** toward a point ahead in space or time ⟨we must continue to move *onward,* or we will die in this desert⟩
synonyms ahead, forth, forward, on
near antonyms backward
2 toward or at a point lying in advance in space or time — see ALONG

oodles *n* a considerable amount — see LOT 2

ooze *n* soft wet earth — see MUD

ooze *vb* to flow forth slowly through small openings — see EXUDE 1

oozy *adj* full of or covered with soft wet earth — see MUDDY 1

opacity *n* the quality or state of having a veiled or uncertain meaning — see OBSCURITY 1

opaque *adj* not seen or understood clearly — see FAINT 1

open *adj* **1** allowing passage without obstruction ⟨thank you for clearing out the hallway so that it's *open* again⟩
synonyms clear, cleared, free, unclogged, unclosed, unobstructed, unstopped
related words emptied, unoccupied, vacant; exposed, revealed; gaping, wide, yawning; unbarred, unbolted, unclasped, unfastened, unlatched, un-

locked, unsealed; unbuttoned, unclenched, unfolded, unfurled, unzipped
near antonyms constricted, cramped, encumbered, hampered, hindered, impeded, interfered (with), trammeled; barricaded, blockaded, dammed
antonyms blocked, clogged, closed, jammed, obstructed, plugged, shut, stopped, stuffed, uncleared
2 freely available for use or participation by all ⟨the beach's *open* sand castle-building contest that every year attracts competitors of all ages and abilities⟩
synonyms free-for-all, public, unrestricted
related words collective, common, communal, shared; accessible, available, free; unregulated
near antonyms limited; inaccessible, unavailable
antonyms closed, exclusive, off-limits, private, restricted
3 being in a situation where one is likely to meet with harm — see LIABLE 1
4 free in expressing one's true feelings and opinions — see FRANK
5 lacking a usual or natural covering — see NAKED 2
6 not known by only a select few — see PUBLIC 1
7 not yet settled or decided — see PENDING 1
8 willing to consider new or different ideas — see OPEN-MINDED 1

open *n* that part of the physical world that is removed from human habitation — see NATURE 2

open *vb* **1** to change from a closed to an open position ⟨please *open* the door to let the cat out⟩
synonyms unclose
related words unbar, unbolt, unclasp, unfasten, unlatch, unlock; unbutton, unclench, unfold, unfurl, unzip; disengage, release, slip
near antonyms bar, bolt, clasp, fasten, latch, lock; button (up), zip (up)
antonyms close, shut
2 to arrange clear passage of (something) by removing obstructions ⟨we need to *open* this drain that's clogged with hair⟩
synonyms clear, free, unclog, unstop
related words ease, facilitate, loosen (up), smooth
near antonyms constrict, encumber, hamper, hinder, impede, interfere (with), obstruct, trammel; barricade, blockade
antonyms block, clog (up), close, dam (up), plug (up), stop
3 to arrange the parts of (something) over a wider area ⟨when we got too close, the cardinal *opened* its wings and flew to a higher branch⟩
synonyms expand, extend, fan (out), flare (out), spread (out), stretch (out), outspread, outstretch, unfold
related words overspread
near antonyms compact, compress, condense, reduce
antonyms close, contract, fold
4 to rid the surface of (as an area) from things in the way — see CLEAR 1
5 to take the first step in (a process or course of action) — see BEGIN 1

open–air *adj* of, relating to, or held in the open air — see OUTDOORS

open air *n* that part of the physical world that is removed from human habitation — see NATURE 2

open–and–shut *adj* not subject to misinterpretation or more than one interpretation — see CLEAR 2

open–eyed *adj* paying close attention usually for the purpose of anticipating approaching danger or opportunity — see ALERT 1

openhanded *adj* giving or sharing in abundance and without hesitation — see GENEROUS 1

openhandedness *n* the quality or state of being generous — see LIBERALITY

openhearted *adj* free in expressing one's true feelings and opinions — see FRANK

openheartedness *n* **1** the free expression of one's true feelings and opinions — see CANDOR
2 the quality or state of being generous — see LIBERALITY

opening *n* **1** a favorable combination of circumstances, time, and place — see OPPORTUNITY
2 a place in a surface allowing passage into or through a thing — see HOLE 1
3 an open space in a barrier (as a wall or hedge) — see GAP 1

open–minded *adj* **1** willing to consider new or different ideas ⟨all I ask is that you try to be *open-minded* when we present our suggestions⟩
synonyms broad-minded, open, receptive
related words impartial, neutral, objective, unbiased, unprejudiced; easygoing, tolerant; calm, detached, dispassionate; amenable, compliant; impressionable, suggestible, susceptible; persuadable, persuasible
near antonyms biased, one-sided, partial, partisan, prejudiced; bigoted, intolerant
antonyms narrow-minded
2 not bound by traditional ways or beliefs — see LIBERAL 1

openmouthed *adj* filled with amazement or wonder ⟨I was *openmouthed* at the stunning view from the mountaintop⟩
synonyms amazed, astonished, astounded, awed, awestruck, dumbfounded (*or* dumfounded), flabbergasted, marveling (*or* marvelling), wondering
related words startled, surprised; bemused, bewildered, puzzled; overwhelmed, staggered, stunned, stupefied
near antonyms unimpressed; disinterested, incurious, indifferent, unconcerned, uninterested; dispassionate, emotionless, impassive, unemotional; bored, jaded

openness *n* **1** the free expression of one's true feelings and opinions — see CANDOR
2 the state of being left without shelter or protection against something harmful — see EXPOSURE 1

open sesame *n* something that allows someone to achieve a desired goal — see PASSPORT

operable *adj* capable of or suitable for being used for a particular purpose — see USABLE 1

operate *vb* **1** to control the mechanical operation of ⟨do not *operate* heavy machinery, including cars, after taking this medication⟩
synonyms handle, run, work
related words use; maneuver, manipulate, ply, wield; command, control, direct, drive, guide, pilot, steer
2 to look after and make decisions about — see CONDUCT 1
3 to produce a desired effect — see ACT 2
4 to put into action or service — see USE 1

operating *adj* being in effective operation — see ACTIVE 1

operation *n* **1** a specific task with which a person or group is charged — see MISSION
2 a usually fixed or ordered series of actions or events leading to a result — see PROCESS 1
3 the act or activity of looking after and making decisions about something — see CONDUCT 1
4 the act or practice of employing something for a particular purpose — see USE 1

operational *adj* being in effective operation — see ACTIVE 1

operative *adj* being in effective operation — see ACTIVE 1

operative *n* **1** a person who tries secretly to obtain information for one country in the territory of another usually unfriendly country — see SPY
2 a person whose business is solving crimes and catching criminals or gathering information that is not easy to get — see DETECTIVE

opiate *adj* tending to cause sleep — see HYPNOTIC

opine *vb* to make a statement of one's opinion — see REMARK 1

opinion *n* **1** an idea that is believed to be true or valid without positive knowledge ⟨my *opinion* is that such interference was unnecessary⟩
synonyms belief, conviction, eye, feeling, judgment (*or* judgement), mind, notion, persuasion, sentiment, verdict, view
related words say; impression, perception, take; attitude; assumption, presumption, presupposition; conclusion, decision, determination; deliverance, esteem, estimate, estimation; credence, credit, faith; concept, conception, idea, thought; position, stand; comment, observation, reflection, remark; conjecture, guess, hunch, hypothesis, surmise, theory; advice, recommendation, suggestion; angle, outlook, perspective, point of view, shoes, slant, standpoint, viewpoint
near antonyms fact, truth
2 a position arrived at after consideration — see DECISION 1

opinionated *adj* sticking to an opinion, purpose, or course of action in spite of reason, arguments, or persuasion — see OBSTINATE

opponent *n* **1** one that takes a position opposite another in a competition or conflict ⟨in martial arts, before the match begins, always bow to your *opponent*⟩
synonyms adversary, antagonist, rival
related words equal, match; enemy, foe; archenemy, nemesis; competitor, contestant; bane, bête noire, curse; assailant, attacker, combatant, invader
near antonyms accomplice, ally, confederate, partner; advocate, champion, exponent, proponent, supporter
2 one that is hostile toward another — see ENEMY

opportune *adj* especially suitable for a certain time — see TIMELY 1

opportunist *n* one who does things only for his own benefit and with little regard for right and wrong — see SELF-SEEKER

opportunity *n* a favorable combination of circumstances, time, and place ⟨this art school could be a wonderful *opportunity* for you to finally develop your talent for painting⟩
synonyms chance, occasion, opening, room
related words break; play, way; juncture, pass

oppose *vb* **1** to refuse to give in to — see RESIST
2 to strive to reduce or eliminate — see FIGHT 2

opposite *adj* being as different as possible ⟨your suggestion that we hold the meeting at night is precisely *opposite* to our original plan for a nice breakfast⟩
synonyms antipodal, antipodean, antithetical, contradictory, contrary, diametric (*or* diametrical), polar
related words adverse, negative, unfavorable; antagonistic, antipathetic, counter, hostile; converse, inverse, reverse; disparate, dissimilar, divergent, unalike, unlike
near antonyms alike, analogous, like, similar; equivalent, identical, same; synonymous
antonyms noncontradictory

opposite *n* something that is as different as possible from something else ⟨no matter what I say, you insist on the *opposite*⟩
synonyms antipode, antithesis, contrary, negative, reverse
related words negation; antonym; converse, inverse
near antonyms synonym; analogue, counterpart; carbon copy, copy, duplicate, replica

opposition *n* the inclination to resist — see RESISTANCE 1

oppress *vb* **1** to make sad — see DEPRESS 1
2 to subject to incapacitating emotional or mental stress — see OVERWHELM 1

oppression *n* a state or spell of low spirits — see SADNESS

oppressive *adj* difficult to endure — see HARSH 1

oppressively *adv* in a manner so as to cause loss or suffering — see HARDLY 1

oppressor *n* **1** a person who causes repeated emotional pain, distress, or annoyance to another — see TORMENTOR
2 a person who uses power or authority in a cruel, unjust, or harmful way — see DESPOT

opprobrium *n* the state of having lost the esteem of others — see DISGRACE 1

opt *vb* to come to a judgment after discussion or consideration — see DECIDE 1

opt (for) *vb* to decide to accept (someone or something) from a group of possibilities — see CHOOSE 1

optic *adj* of, relating to, or used in vision — see VISUAL 1

optical *adj* of, relating to, or used in vision — see VISUAL 1

optimism *n* an inclination to believe in the most favorable outcome ⟨your perpetual *optimism* even when things look bleak⟩
synonyms sanguinity
related words brightness, cheerfulness, perkiness, sunniness; hope, hopefulness, rosiness; idealism
near antonyms pessimism, skepticism; cynicism; desperation, discouragement, disheartenment, hopelessness; bleakness, cheerlessness, dreariness, gloom, gloominess; pragmatism, realism

optimistic *adj* having qualities which inspire hope — see HOPEFUL 1

option *n* **1** the act or power of making one's own choices or decisions — see FREE WILL
2 the power, right, or opportunity to choose — see CHOICE 1

optional *adj* subject to one's freedom of choice ⟨certain activities are *optional,* and you may choose not to participate if you wish⟩
synonyms discretionary, elective, voluntary
related words alternative, chosen; dispensable, unnecessary, unneeded, unwanted

near antonyms essential, indispensable, necessary, requisite
antonyms compulsory, mandatory, nonelective, obligatory, required

opulence *n* the total of one's money and property — see WEALTH 1

opulent *adj* **1** having goods, property, or money in abundance — see RICH 1
2 showing obvious signs of wealth and comfort — see LUXURIOUS

opulently *adv* in a luxurious manner — see HIGH

opus *n* a literary, musical, or artistic production — see COMPOSITION 1

oral *adj* **1** created by the body's organs of sound — see VOCAL
2 made or carried on through speaking rather than in writing — see VERBAL 2

orate *vb* **1** to talk as if giving an important and formal speech ⟨politicians will *orate* lengthily at any opportunity⟩
synonyms declaim, discourse, harangue, mouth (off)
related words rant, rave; lecture, preach; advertise, announce, broadcast, declare, proclaim, pronounce; speak, talk
2 to give a formal often extended talk on a subject — see TALK 1

oration *n* a usually formal discourse delivered to an audience — see SPEECH 1

oratorical *adj* marked by the use of impressive-sounding but mostly meaningless words and phrases — see RHETORICAL

oratory *n* **1** the art of speaking in public eloquently and effectively ⟨this debate class will teach you all to be skilled at *oratory*⟩
synonyms elocution
related words bombast, grandiloquence; rhetoric; discourse, speech, talk
2 language that is impressive-sounding but not meaningful or sincere — see RHETORIC 1

orb *n* a more or less round body or mass — see [1]BALL 1

orbit *vb* to pass completely around — see ENCIRCLE 1

orchestra *n* a usually large group of musicians playing together — see [2]BAND 1

ordain *vb* **1** to determine the fate of in advance — see DESTINE
2 to give an order — see COMMAND 2

ordeal *n* a test of faith, patience, or strength — see TRIAL 1

order *n* **1** the way objects in space or events in time are arranged or follow one another ⟨you always keep your books in perfect alphabetical *order*⟩ ⟨we haven't found out the *order* of the speeches yet⟩
synonyms arrangement, array, disposal, disposition, distribution, ordering, sequence, setup
related words continuity; precedence, priority; chain, progression, succession; series; aligning, alignment, lining up; design, layout, pattern, structure, system
near antonyms confusion, disorder, disorganization, disruption, upset; disconnection, disjointedness
2 a group of persons formally joined together for some common interest — see ASSOCIATION 2
3 a number of persons or things that are grouped together because they have something in common — see SORT 1
4 a piece of metal given in honor of a special event, a person, or an achievement — see MEDAL
5 a state of being or fitness — see CONDITION 1
6 a statement of what to do that must be obeyed by those concerned — see COMMAND 1
7 one of the segments of society into which people are grouped — see CLASS 1
8 one of the units into which a whole is divided on the basis of a common characteristic — see CLASS 2

order *vb* **1** to put into a particular arrangement ⟨I've *ordered* all of my CDs according to type of music⟩ ⟨he likes to *order* his life so that there are few surprises⟩
synonyms arrange, array, classify, codify, dispose, draw up, marshal, organize, range, systematize
related words groom, make up, spruce (up), straighten (up), tidy (up); unscramble; align, line, line up, queue; alphabetize, file; emplace, place, set; display, lay out, map (out)
antonyms derange, disarrange, disarray, disorder, mess (up), muss (up), rumple, upset
2 to give a request or demand for ⟨they *ordered* hamburgers for lunch⟩
synonyms ask (for), request, requisition
related words commission, solicit; charter, hire, license (*also* licence)
phrases call for
3 to give an order — see COMMAND 2
4 to issue orders to (someone) by right of authority — see COMMAND 1

ordering *n* **1** a scheme of rank or order — see [3]SCALE 1
2 the way objects in space or events in time are arranged or follow one another — see ORDER 1

orderly *adj* **1** being clean and in good order — see NEAT 1
2 following a set method, arrangement, or pattern — see METHODICAL

ordinance *n* a rule of conduct or action laid down by a governing authority and especially a legislator — see LAW 1

ordinarily *adv* according to the usual course of things — see NATURALLY 2

ordinary *adj* **1** being of the type that is encountered in the normal course of events ⟨it was a perfectly *ordinary* and undistinguished shirt⟩
synonyms average, common, commonplace, everyday, garden, normal, prosaic, routine, run-of-the-mill, standard, unexceptional, unremarkable, usual, workaday
related words regular, typical; familiar, homely, plain, popular, vulgar; natural; customary, wonted; insignificant, trivial, unimportant; customary, frequent, habitual; expected, predictable
near antonyms curious, funny, peculiar, quaint, queer; aberrant, atypical, irregular; rare, scarce; fantastic, phenomenal; bizarre, far-out, outrageous, outré, weird, wild; eccentric, idiosyncratic, nonconformist, unconventional, unorthodox; freak, freakish; conspicuous, notable, outstanding, prominent, salient, signal, striking; singular, unique
antonyms abnormal, exceptional, extraordinary, odd, out-of-the-way, strange, unusual
2 of average to below average quality — see MEDIOCRE 1
3 often observed or encountered — see COMMON 1

ordnance *n* large firearms (as cannon or rockets) — see ARTILLERY

oread *n* a mythical goddess represented as a young girl and said to live outdoors — see NYMPH 1

organ *n* **1** a publication that appears at regular intervals — see JOURNAL
2 something used to achieve an end — see AGENT 1

organization *n* a group of persons formally joined together for some common interest — see ASSOCIATION 2

organize *vb* to put into a particular arrangement — see ORDER 1

organized *adj* following a set method, arrangement, or pattern — see METHODICAL

orient *vb* to impart knowledge of a new thing or situation to — see ACQUAINT 1

orientate *vb* to impart knowledge of a new thing or situation to — see ACQUAINT 1

orifice *n* a place in a surface allowing passage into or through a thing — see HOLE 1

origin *n* the line of ancestors from whom a person is descended — see ANCESTRY

original *adj* **1** coming before all others in time or order — see FIRST 1
2 having the skill and imagination to create new things — see CREATIVE 1
3 not known or experienced before — see NEW 2

original *n* something from which copies are made ⟨please make copies to hand out, but keep the *original*⟩
synonyms archetype, prototype
related words example, paradigm, pattern; beau ideal, exemplar, classic, ideal, model, nonpareil, paragon; blueprint, draft
near antonyms copy, imitation, replica, reproduction; counterfeit, fake, forgery, sham

originality *n* **1** the quality or appeal of being new — see NOVELTY 1
2 the skill and imagination to create new things — see CREATIVITY 1

originally *adv* in the beginning ⟨we *originally* planned to go out tonight, but we changed our minds⟩
synonyms firstly, initially, primarily
related words incipiently; primitively
phrases at first
near antonyms finally, lastly, ultimately

originate *vb* to come into existence — see BEGIN 2

originator *n* **1** one who creates or introduces something new — see INVENTOR
2 a person who establishes a whole new field of endeavor — see FATHER 2

orison *n* an address to God or a deity — see PRAYER 1

ornament *n* something that decorates or beautifies — see DECORATION 1

ornament *vb* to make more attractive by adding something that is beautiful or becoming — see DECORATE

ornamental *adj* serving to add beauty — see DECORATIVE

ornamental *n* a small object displayed for its attractiveness or interest — see KNICKKNACK

ornate *adj* elaborately and often excessively decorated ⟨an *ornate* gambling casino that is designed to look like an Italian palace⟩
synonyms bedizened, florid, gingerbread, overdecorated, overwrought
related words arabesque, baroque, rococo; extravagant, flamboyant, spectacular, splashy; flashy, garish, gaudy, glitzy, loud, ostentatious, pretentious, showy, swank, tawdry; elaborate, extreme; adorned, arrayed, beautified, bedecked, decked, decorated, dressed, embellished, enriched, garnished, ornamented, trimmed; flowery, frilly, lacy; enhanced, heightened, intensified; bossed, chased, emblazoned, embossed, embroidered, flounced, fringed, garlanded, gilded, laced, wreathed
near antonyms bare, denuded, exposed, naked, stripped, uncovered; modest, simple, unassuming, unpretentious; conservative, muted, quiet, restrained, subdued, tasteful, toned-down, understated, unobtrusive
antonyms austere, plain, severe, stark, unadorned

ornery *adj* having or showing a habitually bad temper — see ILL-TEMPERED

orthodox *adj* **1** following or agreeing with established form, custom, or rules — see FORMAL 1
2 tending to favor established ideas, conditions, or institutions — see CONSERVATIVE 1

oscillation *n* a series of slight movements by a body back and forth or from side to side — see VIBRATION

ossified *adj* sticking to an opinion, purpose, or course of action in spite of reason, arguments, or persuasion — see OBSTINATE

ostensible *adj* appearing to be true on the basis of evidence that may or may not be confirmed — see APPARENT 1

ostensibly *adv* to all outward appearances — see APPARENTLY

ostentation *n* excessive or unnecessary display ⟨the sheer *ostentation* of the rock star's mansion was overwhelming⟩
synonyms flamboyance, flashiness, garishness, gaudiness, glitz, ostentatiousness, pretentiousness, showiness, swank
related words extravaganza, pageant, parade, show; dazzle, pageantry, spectacle; adornment, decoration, dressing, embellishment, garnishment, ornamentation, trimming; extravagance, fanciness, luxuriousness, opulence, richness, sumptuousness; loudness, luridness; meretriciousness, tawdriness, vulgarity
near antonyms conservativeness, moderation, modesty, restraint, simplicity, understatement; elegance, gracefulness, tastefulness
antonyms austerity, plainness, severity

ostentatious *adj* **1** excessively showy — see GAUDY
2 self-consciously trying to present an appearance of grandeur or importance — see PRETENTIOUS 1

ostentatiousness *n* excessive or unnecessary display — see OSTENTATION

other *adj* **1** being not of the same kind — see DIFFERENT 1
2 resulting in an increase in amount or number — see ADDITIONAL

other *adv* in a different way — see OTHERWISE

otherwise *adv* in a different way ⟨a serious student who always does his best, for his conscience will not let him do *otherwise*⟩
synonyms differently, else, other
related words diversely, variously
near antonyms similarly
antonyms likewise

ought (to) *vb* to be under necessity or obligation to — see NEED 2

ounce *n* a very small amount — see PARTICLE 1

oust *vb* **1** to drive or force out — see EJECT 1
2 to remove from a position of prominence or power (as a throne) — see DEPOSE 1

out *adv* **1** in or into the open air — see OUTDOORS
2 with one's normal voice speaking the words — see ALOUD

out *adj* not at a certain place — see ABSENT 1

out *n* the act or a means of getting or keeping away from something undesirable — see ESCAPE 2

out *vb* to become known — see GET OUT 1

out–and–out *adj* **1** having no exceptions or restrictions — see ABSOLUTE 2
2 trying all possibilities — see EXHAUSTIVE

outbrave *vb* to oppose (something hostile or dangerous) with firmness or courage — see FACE 2

outbreak *n* a sudden and usually temporary growth of activity ⟨there was an immediate *outbreak* of paper shuffling and a pretense of work when the teacher re-entered the room⟩
synonyms burst, flare, flare-up, flash, flicker, flurry, flutter, outburst, spurt
related words binge, jag, spree; boost, increase, pickup, upswing, upturn; epidemic, eruption, explosion, paroxysm; deluge, flood, rush, spate, surge; commotion, furor, uproar
near antonyms calm, doldrums, slump

outburst *n* **1** a sudden intense expression of strong feeling ⟨when the coach suddenly started crying hysterically, everyone was shocked by the unexpected *outburst*⟩
synonyms agony, burst, eruption, explosion, fit, flare, flare-up, flash, flush, gale, gush, gust, paroxysm, spasm, storm
related words blowup, grouch, rage, tantrum; ecstasy, rapture, transport; delirium, frenzy, furor
2 a sudden and usually temporary growth of activity — see OUTBREAK

outcast *n* one who is cast out or rejected by society ⟨they were convinced that they would become total *outcasts* if they didn't buy the newest fashions⟩
synonyms castaway, castoff, pariah, reject
related words untouchable; outsider; deportee, exile
near antonyms insider

outcome *n* a condition or occurrence traceable to a cause — see EFFECT 1

outcry *n* a violent shouting — see CLAMOR 1

outdated *adj* having passed its time of use or usefulness — see OBSOLETE

outdistance *vb* to be greater, better, or stronger than — see SURPASS 1

outdo *vb* to be greater, better, or stronger than — see SURPASS 1

outdoor *also* **outdoors** *adj* of, relating to, or held in the open air ⟨an *outdoor* picnic is always at the mercy of the weather, of course⟩
synonyms open-air, out-of-door (*or* out-of-doors)
related words airy; exterior, external, outer, outside, outward; outermost, outmost
near antonyms inner, inside, interior, internal, inward; inmost, innermost
antonyms indoor

outdoors *adv* in or into the open air ⟨please wait until you're *outdoors* to run around and scream⟩
synonyms out, outside
related words without
near antonyms in, inside, within
antonyms indoors

outdoors *n* that part of the physical world that is removed from human habitation — see NATURE 2

outer *adj* situated on the outside or farther out ⟨the *outer* edge of the blade of your figure skate always wears out faster than the inner because you use it more⟩
synonyms exterior, external, outside, outward
related words outermost, outlying, outmost; superficial, surface
near antonyms inmost, innermost
antonyms inner, inside, interior, internal, inward

outermost *adj* most distant from a center — see EXTREME 1

outfit *n* **1** clothing chosen as appropriate for a specific situation ⟨you'll need a special *outfit* for the scout troop⟩ ⟨do you want to buy a new *outfit* for the Halloween party?⟩
synonyms costume, dress, garb, getup, guise, togs
related words apparel, attire, clothes, duds, raiment; fashion, mode, style; array, caparison, vestments
2 a commercial or industrial activity or organization — see ENTERPRISE 1
3 a group of people working together on a task — see GANG 1
4 items needed for the performance of a task or activity — see EQUIPMENT
5 the distinctive clothing worn by members of a particular group — see UNIFORM

outfit *vb* to provide (someone) with what is needed for a task or activity — see FURNISH 1

outflow *n* a flowing or going out ⟨there was an immediate *outflow* of students from the door when the bell rang⟩
synonyms exodus, gush, outpouring
related words drain, flow; ebb, reflux; rush, stampede; emigration, flight; discharge, emanation, emission
near antonyms deluge, flood, inundation, overflow, spate, torrent; flow, river, stream, tide
antonyms flux, inflow, influx, inrush

outfox *vb* to get the better of through cleverness — see OUTWIT

outgo *n* a payment made in the course of achieving a result — see EXPENSE

outgoing *adj* likely to seek or enjoy the company of others — see CONVIVIAL

outgrowth *n* **1** a branch of a main stem especially of a plant — see OFFSHOOT 1
2 a condition or occurrence traceable to a cause — see EFFECT 1
3 something that naturally develops or is developed from something else — see DERIVATIVE

outing *n* a short trip for pleasure — see EXCURSION 1

outlander *n* a person who is not native to or known to a community — see STRANGER

outlandish *adj* **1** different from the ordinary in a way that causes curiosity or suspicion — see ODD 2
2 excitingly or mysteriously unusual — see EXOTIC

outlast *vb* to last longer than ⟨I truly hope this car will *outlast* our previous one⟩ ⟨your work will probably *outlast* you⟩
synonyms outlive, outwear
related words survive; outstay; abide (beyond), endure (past), hold (past), hold out (past), last (beyond), persist (beyond); draw out, perpetuate; succeed

outlaw *vb* to order not to do or use or to be done or used — see FORBID

outlawed *adj* that may not be permitted — see IMPERMISSIBLE

outlawing *n* the act of ordering that something not be done or used — see PROHIBITION 1

outlay *n* a payment made in the course of achieving a result — see EXPENSE

outlet *n* a place or means of going out — see EXIT 1

outline *n* **1** a line that traces the outer limits of an object or surface ⟨place your hand on the paper and draw an *outline* around it⟩
synonyms contour, figure, silhouette
related words delineation, sketch; profile, skyline; form, cast, configuration, conformation, geometry, shape; framework, skeleton
2 a short statement of the main points — see SUMMARY

outline *vb* **1** to draw or make apparent the outline of ⟨she carefully *outlined* the tree before she started drawing in the leaves⟩
synonyms define, delineate, silhouette, sketch, trace
related words line; bound, fringe, margin, skirt; edge, hem, rim, trim; frame; circle, compass, encircle, girdle, girth, loop, ring, round, surround; chart, diagram, draw, map (out)
2 to make into a short statement of the main points (as of a report) — see SUMMARIZE

outlive *vb* to last longer than — see OUTLAST

outlook *n* **1** a high place or structure from which a wide view is possible — see LOOKOUT 1
2 a way of looking at or thinking about something — see POINT OF VIEW
3 all that can be seen from a certain point — see VIEW 1

out loud *adv* with one's normal voice speaking the words — see ALOUD

outmaneuver *vb* to get the better of through cleverness — see OUTWIT

outmoded *adj* having passed its time of use or usefulness — see OBSOLETE

outmost *adj* most distant from a center — see EXTREME 1

out–of–date *adj* having passed its time of use or usefulness — see OBSOLETE

out–of–door *or* **out-of-doors** *adj* of, relating to, or held in the open air — see OUTDOORS

out–of–doors *n* that part of the physical world that is removed from human habitation — see NATURE 2

out–of–the–way *adj* different from the ordinary in a way that causes curiosity or suspicion — see ODD 2

outpouring *n* a flowing or going out — see OUTFLOW

output *n* something produced by physical or intellectual effort — see PRODUCT 1

outrage *n* **1** an act or expression showing scorn and usually intended to hurt another's feelings — see INSULT
2 an intense emotional state of displeasure with someone or something — see ANGER

outrage *vb* **1** to cause hurt feelings or deep resentment in — see INSULT
2 to make angry — see ANGER

outraged *adj* feeling or showing anger — see ANGRY

outrank *vb* to be greater in importance than — see OUTWEIGH

outré *adj* different from the ordinary in a way that causes curiosity or suspicion — see ODD 2

outright *adj* having no exceptions or restrictions — see ABSOLUTE 2

outset *n* the point at which something begins — see BEGINNING

outshine *vb* to be greater, better, or stronger than — see SURPASS 1

outside *adj* **1** situated on the outside or farther out — see OUTER
2 small in degree — see REMOTE 1

outside *adv* in or into the open air — see OUTDOORS

outside *n* **1** an outer part or layer — see EXTERIOR
2 the greatest amount, number, or part — see MOST

outside *prep* **1** not including — see EXCEPT
2 out of the reach or sphere of — see BEYOND 2

outside of *prep* **1** not including — see EXCEPT
2 out of the reach or sphere of — see BEYOND 2

outsider *n* a person who is not native to or known to a community — see STRANGER

outsize *also* **outsized** *adj* **1** unusually large — see HUGE
2 of a size greater than average of its kind — see LARGE

outskirts *n pl* the area around a city — see ENVIRONS 1

outsmart *vb* to get the better of through cleverness — see OUTWIT

outspoken *adj* free in expressing one's true feelings and opinions — see FRANK

outspread *vb* to arrange the parts of (something) over a wider area — see OPEN 3

outstanding *adj* **1** not yet paid ⟨there are several *outstanding* bills left, but at least we paid the rest⟩
synonyms overdue, owed, owing, payable, unpaid, unsettled
related words due, mature
near antonyms prepaid
antonyms cleared, liquidated, paid (off *or* up), repaid, settled
2 standing above others in rank, importance, or achievement — see EMINENT

outstretch *vb* to arrange the parts of (something) over a wider area — see OPEN 3

outstrip *vb* to be greater, better, or stronger than — see SURPASS 1

outward *adj* situated on the outside or farther out — see OUTER

outwear *vb* to last longer than — see OUTLAST

outweigh *vb* to be greater in importance than ⟨the need to finish your homework *outweighs* your desire to see your favorite TV show⟩
synonyms outrank, overbalance, overshadow, overweigh
related words count, import, matter, mean, signify, weigh; dwarf; exceed, outstrip, surpass, transcend

outwit *vb* to get the better of through cleverness ⟨a plan to *outwit* their opponents at their own game⟩
synonyms fox, outfox, outsmart, outmaneuver, overreach
related words outguess, second-guess; baffle, balk, circumvent, foil, frustrate, thwart; cozen, deceive, dupe, fool, gull, trick; conquer, defeat, lick, overcome; bar, block, hinder, impede, obstruct

outworn *adj* having passed its time of use or usefulness — see OBSOLETE

oval *adj* having the shape of an egg ⟨the *Oval* Office in the White House⟩
synonyms elliptic (*or* elliptical), ovate, ovoid
ovate *adj* having the shape of an egg — see OVAL
ovation *n* enthusiastic and usually public expression of approval — see APPLAUSE
over *adj* brought or having come to an end — see COMPLETE 2
over *adv* **1** from one side to the other of an intervening space ⟨let's swim *over* to that island⟩
synonyms across, through
related words clear
2 yet another time — see AGAIN 1
3 to or in a higher place — see ABOVE
4 from beginning to end — see THROUGH 1
5 toward or in a lower position — see DOWN
over *prep* **1** higher than — see ABOVE
2 in the course of — see DURING
3 on or to the farther side of — see BEYOND 1
4 to the opposite side of — see ACROSS
5 in random positions within the boundaries of — see AROUND 2
overabundance *n* the state or an instance of going beyond what is usual, proper, or needed — see EXCESS
overactive *adj* being in a state of increased activity or agitation — see FEVERISH 1
overage *n* the state or an instance of going beyond what is usual, proper, or needed — see EXCESS
overall *adj* **1** belonging or relating to the whole — see GENERAL 1
2 relating to the main elements and not to specific details — see GENERAL 2
overall *adv* for the most part — see CHIEFLY
over and above *prep* in addition to — see BESIDES 1
overbalance *vb* to be greater in importance than — see OUTWEIGH
overbear *vb* to achieve a victory over — see BEAT 2
overbearing *adj* fond of ordering people around — see BOSSY
overbold *adj* foolishly adventurous or bold — see FOOLHARDY 1
overburden *vb* to fill or load to excess — see OVERLOAD
overcast *adj* covered over by clouds ⟨the dark, *overcast* sky made the whole day seem depressing⟩
synonyms beclouded, clouded, cloudy, dull, hazed, hazy, heavy, lowering (*also* louring), overclouded
related words bedimmed, befogged, blackened, darkened, darksome, dim, dimmed, dulled, dusky, misty, murky, obscure, obscured, overshadowed; sunless; black, bleak, cheerless, dark, desolate, dismal, drear, dreary, funereal, gloomy, glum, gray (*also* grey), somber (*or* sombre), sullen
near antonyms sunny, sunshiny; brightened, brilliant, dazzling, illuminated, illumined, lighted (*or* lit), lightened, radiant, shiny
antonyms clear, cloudless
overcast *vb* to make dark, dim, or indistinct — see CLOUD 1
overcharge *vb* **1** to charge (someone) too much for goods or services ⟨I think that store may have *overcharged* us for the shoes, which were supposed to be on sale⟩
synonyms gouge, soak, sting, surcharge
related words cheat, defraud, stick; clip, fleece, skin
antonyms undercharge
2 to fill or load to excess — see OVERLOAD
overcloud *vb* to make dark, dim, or indistinct — see CLOUD 1
overclouded *adj* covered over by clouds — see OVERCAST
overcoat *n* a warm outdoor coat ⟨put your *overcoat* on—it's freezing out there!⟩
synonyms greatcoat, surcoat, topcoat
related words chesterfield, frock coat, mackinaw, ulster; jacket, parka; oilskin, raincoat, sou'wester; wrap
near antonyms undercoat
overcome *vb* **1** to achieve a victory over — see BEAT 2
2 to subject to incapacitating emotional or mental stress — see OVERWHELM 1
overconfident *adj* foolishly adventurous or bold — see FOOLHARDY 1
overcritical *adj* given to making or expressing unfavorable judgments about things — see CRITICAL 1
overdecorated *adj* elaborately and often excessively decorated — see ORNATE
overdo *vb* to describe or express in too strong terms — see OVERSTATE
overdraw *vb* to describe or express in too strong terms — see OVERSTATE
overdue *adj* **1** not arriving, or occurring, or settled at the due, usual, or proper time — see LATE 1
2 not yet paid — see OUTSTANDING 1
overeat *vb* to eat greedily or to excess — see GORGE 2
overeater *n* one who eats greedily or too much — see GLUTTON
overestimate *vb* to place too high a value on ⟨they *overestimated* their ability to do the work on such short notice⟩
synonyms overrate, overvalue
related words appreciate, cherish, prize, treasure, value; admire, esteem, regard, respect; adore, idolize, revere, reverence, venerate, worship
near antonyms belittle, decry, depreciate, disparage; despise, disdain, scorn; abhor, abominate, detest, loathe
antonyms underestimate, underrate, undervalue
overfamiliar *adj* showing a lack of proper social reserve or modesty — see PRESUMPTUOUS 1
overfill *vb* **1** to fill or load to excess — see OVERLOAD
2 to flow over the brim or top of — see OVERFLOW 1
overflow *n* **1** a great flow of water or of something that overwhelms — see FLOOD
2 the state or an instance of going beyond what is usual, proper, or needed — see EXCESS
overflow *vb* **1** to flow over the brim or top of ⟨the tea in the cup *overflowed* onto the saucer⟩
synonyms overfill, run over
related words boil over, spill, well (up); flow, flush, gush, pour, sluice, spout, spurt, stream; deluge, drown, engulf, flood, inundate, overwhelm, submerge, submerse, swamp; wash (over); brim, cascade, slop, slosh
near antonyms recede
2 to cover or become filled with a flood — see FLOOD

overgrown *adj* covered with a thick, healthy natural growth — see LUSH 1
overhang *n* a part that sticks out from the general mass of something — see BULGE
overhang *vb* **1** to extend outward beyond a usual point — see BULGE
2 to remain poised to inflict harm, danger, or distress on — see THREATEN
overhaul *vb* to move fast enough to get even with — see OVERTAKE
overhead *adv* to or in a higher place — see ABOVE
overhear *vb* to listen to (another in private conversation) — see EAVESDROP (ON)
overjoy *vb* **1** to fill with overwhelming emotion (as wonder or delight) — see ENTRANCE
2 to fill with great joy — see ELATE
overkill *n* the state or an instance of going beyond what is usual, proper, or needed — see EXCESS
overlap *n* a partial covering of one thing by an adjoining thing ⟨the orthodontist will try to fix that *overlap* of two of your upper incisors⟩
synonyms lapping, overlaying, overlying, overspreading
related words shingling
overlap *vb* to lie over parts of one another ⟨there were so many papers on the desk that many of them *overlapped*⟩
synonyms lap, overlay, overlie, overspread
related words shingle
overlay *vb* **1** to form a layer over — see COVER 2
2 to lie over parts of one another — see OVERLAP
overlaying *n* a partial covering of one thing by an adjoining thing — see OVERLAP
overlie *vb* **1** to lie over parts of one another — see OVERLAP
2 to form a layer over — see COVER 2
overload *vb* to fill or load to excess ⟨try not to *overload* your backpack, or you could end up with back problems⟩
synonyms overburden, overcharge, overfill
related words stuff; burden, charge, encumber, lade, load, lumber, saddle, weight
near antonyms lighten, unburden, unload
overlook *vb* **1** to look down on ⟨the fortress *overlooks* the city⟩
synonyms command, dominate
related words face, front
2 to fail to give proper attention to — see NEGLECT 1
overly *adv* beyond a normal or acceptable limit — see TOO 1
overlying *n* a partial covering of one thing by an adjoining thing — see OVERLAP
overmaster *vb* to subject to incapacitating emotional or mental stress — see OVERWHELM 1
overmatch *vb* to achieve a victory over — see BEAT 2
overmuch *adj* going beyond a normal or acceptable limit in degree or amount — see EXCESSIVE
overmuch *adv* beyond a normal or acceptable limit — see TOO 1
overmuch *n* the state or an instance of going beyond what is usual, proper, or needed — see EXCESS
overpass *vb* to fail to give proper attention to — see NEGLECT 1
overpower *vb* **1** to bring under one's control by force of arms — see CONQUER 1
2 to subject to incapacitating emotional or mental stress — see OVERWHELM 1
overpowering *n* the act or process of bringing someone or something under one's control — see CONQUEST
overpraise *n* excessive praise — see FLATTERY
overpraise *vb* to praise too much — see FLATTER 1
overrate *vb* to place too high a value on — see OVERESTIMATE
overreach *vb* **1** to get the better of through cleverness — see OUTWIT
2 to go beyond the limit of — see EXCEED
overripe *adj* having lost forcefulness, courage, or spirit — see EFFETE 1
overrun *vb* **1** to enter for conquest or plunder — see INVADE
2 to go beyond the limit of — see EXCEED
3 to spread or swarm over in a troublesome manner — see INFEST
oversee *vb* **1** to look after and make decisions about — see CONDUCT 1
2 to be in charge of — see BOSS 1
3 to take charge of especially on behalf of another — see [2]TEND 1
overshadow *vb* **1** to make dark, dim, or indistinct — see CLOUD 1
2 to be greater in importance than — see OUTWEIGH
overshoot *vb* to go beyond the limit of — see EXCEED
oversight *n* **1** the act or activity of looking after and making decisions about something — see CONDUCT 1
2 an unintentional departure from truth or accuracy — see ERROR 1
3 the duty or function of watching or guarding for the sake of proper direction or control — see SUPERVISION 1
4 the nonperformance of an assigned or expected action — see FAILURE 1
oversize *or* **oversized** *adj* **1** unusually large — see HUGE
2 of a size greater than average of its kind — see LARGE
overspread *vb* **1** to form a layer over — see COVER 2
2 to lie over parts of one another — see OVERLAP
overspreading *n* a partial covering of one thing by an adjoining thing — see OVERLAP
overstate *vb* to describe or express in too strong terms ⟨it appears you've somewhat *overstated* your computer skills, if you can't find the "on" button!⟩
synonyms exaggerate, overdo, overdraw, put on
related words color, elaborate, embellish, embroider, magnify, pad, stretch; fudge, hedge; overemphasize, overplay
near antonyms belittle, minimize, play down
antonyms understate
overstatement *n* the representation of something in terms that go beyond the facts — see EXAGGERATION
overstep *vb* to go beyond the limit of — see EXCEED
oversupply *n* the state or an instance of going beyond what is usual, proper, or needed — see EXCESS
overtake *vb* to move fast enough to get even with ⟨she had to hurry to *overtake* her friends, who had forgotten their umbrellas⟩ ⟨the thunderstorm *overtook* them suddenly⟩

synonyms catch up (with), overhaul
related words chase, pursue; gain, reach; pass, surpass
near antonyms fall short

overthrow *n* failure to win a contest — see DEFEAT 1

overtop *vb* to be greater, better, or stronger than — see SURPASS 1

overturn *vb* to turn on one's side or upside down — see CAPSIZE

overvalue *vb* to place too high a value on — see OVERESTIMATE

overweening *adj* **1** having too high an opinion of oneself — see CONCEITED
2 going beyond a normal or acceptable limit in degree or amount — see EXCESSIVE
3 having a feeling of superiority that shows itself in an overbearing attitude — see ARROGANT

overweigh *vb* to be greater in importance than — see OUTWEIGH

overweight *adj* having an excess of body fat — see FAT 1

overwhelm *vb* **1** to subject to incapacitating emotional or mental stress ⟨just the thought of how much work there is to do *overwhelms* me⟩
synonyms carry away, crush, devastate, floor, oppress, overcome, overmaster, overpower, prostrate, snow under, swamp, whelm
related words deluge, drown; confute, defeat, refute; demoralize, distress, disturb, rock, shatter, stagger, unman, unnerve, upset
2 to cover or become filled with a flood — see FLOOD

overwrought *adj* **1** being in a state of increased activity or agitation — see FEVERISH 1
2 elaborately and often excessively decorated — see ORNATE

ovoid *adj* having the shape of an egg — see OVAL

owed *adj* not yet paid — see OUTSTANDING 1

owing *adj* not yet paid — see OUTSTANDING 1

owing to *prep* as the result of — see BECAUSE OF

own *vb* to keep, control, or experience as one's own — see HAVE 1

own (up) *vb* to accept the truth or existence of (something) usually reluctantly — see ADMIT

owner *n* one who has a legal or rightful claim to ownership — see PROPRIETOR

pa *n* a male human parent — see FATHER 1

pace *vb* to move along with a steady regular step especially in a group — see MARCH 1

pacific *adj* **1** tending to lessen or avoid conflict or hostility ⟨as a *pacific* gesture, we invited our feuding neighbors to our backyard barbecue⟩
synonyms appeasing, conciliating, conciliatory, disarming, mollifying, pacifying, peacemaking, placating, propitiatory
related words endearing, ingratiating; peaceable, peaceful; nonbelligerent, unaggressive, unassertive; calming, comforting, quieting, soothing; obliging, satisfying; affable, amiable, amicable, benevolent, gentle, kind, kindly; submissive, surrendering, yielding
near antonyms aggravating, annoying, exasperating, inflammatory, irritating, nettling, offensive, provocative, provoking, vexing; engaging, incensing, infuriating, maddening; antagonistic, hostile; aggressive, assertive, bellicose, belligerent, combative, contentious, pugnacious, quarrelsome, scrappy, truculent; martial, militant, military, warlike
antonyms antagonizing
2 inclined to live in peace and to avoid war — see PEACEFUL 1

pacifist *n* a person who opposes war or warlike policies — see DOVE 1

pacify *vb* to lessen the anger or agitation of ⟨the only thing that would *pacify* the child and end the tantrum was a new toy⟩
synonyms appease, conciliate, disarm, mollify, placate, propitiate
related words calm, comfort, console, content, quiet, soothe; endear (to), ingratiate; delight, gladden, gratify, please; blarney, flatter, overpraise, soft-soap; assuage, quench, sate, satiate, satisfy; cater (to), humor, indulge; blandish, cajole, coax, wheedle; coddle, mollycoddle, pamper, spoil
near antonyms aggravate, annoy, bother, bug, chafe, cross, exasperate, gall, get, grate, irk, irritate, nettle, peeve, pique, put out, rankle, rile, roil, ruffle, vex; provoke, rouse; harass, harry, pester; agitate, distress, disturb, fret, perturb, upset; affront, insult, offend
antonyms anger, enrage, incense, infuriate, madden, outrage

pacifying *adj* **1** tending to calm the emotions and relieve stress — see SOOTHING 1
2 tending to lessen or avoid conflict or hostility — see PACIFIC 1

pack *n* **1** a soft-sided case designed for carrying belongings especially on the back ⟨part of basic training is becoming accustomed to taking very long hikes with an eighty-pound *pack*⟩
synonyms backpack, knapsack, rucksack
related words haversack; grip, luggage, suitcase, traveling bag
2 a wrapped or sealed case containing an item or set of items — see PACKAGE 1

pack *vb* **1** to close up so that no empty spaces remain — see FILL 2
2 to put into (something) as much as can be held or contained — see FILL 1
3 to support and take from one place to another — see CARRY 1
4 to wear or have on one's person — see CARRY 2

pack (off) *vb* to cause to go or be taken from one place to another — see SEND

package *n* **1** a wrapped or sealed case containing an item or set of items ⟨Mom needed our help carrying all the *packages* and bags home from the store⟩

synonyms bundle, pack, packet, parcel
related words bag, poke [*chiefly Southern and Midland*], pouch, sack; box, container, crate
2 a number of things considered as a unit — see GROUP 1
packed *adj* **1** containing or seeming to contain the greatest quantity or number possible — see FULL 1
2 having little space between items or parts — see CLOSE 1
packet *n* a wrapped or sealed case containing an item or set of items — see PACKAGE 1
pact *n* **1** a formal agreement between two or more nations or peoples — see TREATY
2 an arrangement about action to be taken — see AGREEMENT 2
pad *n* **1** a number of sheets of writing paper glued together at one edge <we'll need to buy a new *pad* for telephone messages soon>
synonyms notepad, tablet
related words album, notebook, scrapbook; booklet, pamphlet
2 a place set aside for sleeping — see BED 1
3 something that serves as a protective barrier — see CUSHION
4 the place where one lives — see HOME 1
pad *vb* **1** to add to the interest of by including made-up details — see EMBROIDER
2 to go on foot — see WALK
padding *n* **1** soft material that is used to fill the hollow parts of something — see FILLING
2 the representation of something in terms that go beyond the facts — see EXAGGERATION
paddle *vb* to move a boat by means of oars — see [1]ROW
padre *n* a person specially trained and authorized to conduct religious services in a Christian church — see CLERGYMAN
paean *n* a formal expression of praise — see ENCOMIUM
pagan *n* a person who does not worship the God of the Bible — see HEATHEN 1
page *n* one that carries a message or does an errand — see MESSENGER
pageant *n* a staged presentation often with music that consists of a procession of narrated or enacted scenes <we always put on a Christmas *pageant* every year>
synonyms cavalcade
related words tableau; kaleidoscope, montage, panorama; drama, play; demonstration, performance, presentation, production; exhibition, extravaganza, show, spectacle; parade
pail *n* a round container that is open at the top and outfitted with a handle <fetch me a *pail* full of water, please>
synonyms bucket
related words cauldron, kettle, pot; canteen, flagon, jar, jug, pitcher; bail, hod; tank, tub, vat
pain *n* **1** a sharp unpleasant sensation usually felt in some specific part of the body <the child was crying because of a *pain* in her knee>
synonyms ache, pang, prick, smart, sting, stitch, throe, tingle, twinge
related words discomfort, distress, soreness, tenderness; agony, anguish, misery, suffering, torment, torture; inflammation, swelling; damage, harm, hurt, injury; backache, bellyache, charley horse, colic, earache, gripe, headache, stomachache, toothache
near antonyms comfort, ease
2 a state of great suffering of body or mind — see DISTRESS 1
3 pains *pl* strict attentiveness to what one is doing — see CARE 1
4 pains *pl* the active use of energy in producing a result — see EFFORT
pain *vb* to feel or cause physical pain — see HURT 1
painful *adj* **1** causing or feeling bodily pain <her broken arm was too *painful* for her to go on the trip>
synonyms aching, hurting, nasty, sore
related words damaging, harmful, hurtful, injurious; raw, tender; bleeding, burning, chafing, cramping, festering; itching, nagging, pinching, pricking, prickling, smarting, stinging; inflamed, swollen; threatening, wounding
near antonyms curative, healing, helping, remedial
antonyms painless
2 hard to accept or bear especially emotionally — see BITTER 2
painfully *adv* with feelings of bitterness or grief — see HARD 2
painkiller *n* something (as a drug) that relieves pain <a lot of *painkillers* have turned out to be addictive substances for patients>
synonyms analgesic, anesthetic
related words sedative, tranquilizer (*also* tranquillizer); narcotic, opiate
painless *adj* involving minimal difficulty or effort — see EASY 1
painlessly *adv* without difficulty — see EASILY
painstaking *adj* taking great care and effort <she was always *painstaking* about her homework>
synonyms careful, conscientious, fussy, meticulous
related words assiduous, diligent, indefatigable, persevering, sedulous; exhaustive, thorough, thoroughgoing; attentive, observant, vigilant, watchful; accurate, precise; critical, demanding, discriminating, exacting, finicky, particular; cautious, chary, circumspect, gingerly, guarded, heedful, wary; deliberate, plodding, slow; studied, thoughtful; all-out, determined, dogged, intensive, tenacious, tireless, zealous
near antonyms cursory; heedless, inattentive, incautious, mindless, unguarded, unsafe, unwary; lax, neglectful, negligent, slipshod, sloppy, slovenly; imprecise; inaccurate, uncritical, undemanding, undiscriminating; bold, impetuous, rash, reckless; apathetic, indifferent, lackadaisical, lazy
antonyms careless
paint *n* preparations intended to beautify the face or hair — see MAKEUP 1
paint *vb* **1** to give a representation or account of in words — see DESCRIBE 1
2 to give color or a different color to — see COLOR 1
painting *n* a picture created with usually oil paint <the Mona Lisa is a beautiful *painting* of a woman with a most mysterious smile>
synonyms canvas, oil, oil painting
related words fresco, mural, panorama; cartoon, drawing, etching, pastel, sketch, watercolor, work; masterpiece; pièce de résistance, showpiece
phrases work of art
pair *n* two things of the same or similar kind that match or are considered together <a *pair* of blue

socks⟩ ⟨the cheerleader and the computer nerd make quite a *pair* together⟩
synonyms brace, couple, duo, twain, twosome
related words span, yoke; partnership, team; companion, complement, doublet, fellow, half, match, mate, twin; counterpart, equal, equivalent, like, parallel, peer

pal *n* a person who has a strong liking for and trust in another — see FRIEND 1

pal (around) *vb* to come or be together as friends — see ASSOCIATE 1

palace *n* **1** a large impressive residence — see MANSION
2 a large, magnificent, or massive building — see EDIFICE 1
3 the residence of a ruler — see COURT 1

palatable *adj* **1** being to one's liking — see SATISFACTORY 1
2 giving pleasure or contentment to the mind or senses — see PLEASANT
3 very pleasing to the sense of taste — see DELICIOUS 1

palatial *adj* showing obvious signs of wealth and comfort — see LUXURIOUS

palaver *n* friendly, informal conversation or an instance of this — see CHAT

palaver *vb* to engage in casual or rambling conversation — see CHAT

pale *adj* **1** lacking intensity of color ⟨we chose a very *pale* pink for the walls of the room⟩
synonyms dull, dulled, faded, light, pastel, washed-out
related words flat, lackluster, lusterless, matte (*also* mat *or* matt); dim, faint; dirty, muddy; achromatic, colorless, uncolored, undyed, unpainted, unstained; blanched, bleached, washed, white, whitened; gray (*also* grey), indistinct, neutral
near antonyms bright, brilliant, vibrant, vivid; chromatic, colored, dyed, painted, stained, tinged, tinted; colorful, multicolored, polychromatic, polychrome, varicolored, variegated; flashy, garish, gaudy, loud, showy, splashy
antonyms dark, deep, gay, rich
2 lacking a healthy skin color ⟨after a week with the flu, she was deathly *pale* and noticeably thinner⟩
synonyms ashen, ashy, blanched, cadaverous, livid, lurid, paled, pallid, pasty, peaked, wan
related words sallow, sick, sickly, waxen, waxy; white, whitened; deathlike; anemic, bloodless; untanned
near antonyms blooming, blushing, flushed, glowing, pink
antonyms florid, flush, rubicund, ruddy, sanguine

pale *vb* to make white or whiter by removing color — see WHITEN

paled *adj* lacking a healthy skin color — see PALE 2

palisade *n* a steep wall of rock, earth, or ice — see CLIFF

palliate *vb* **1** to make (something) seem less bad by offering excuses ⟨don't try to *palliate* your constant lying by claiming that everybody lies⟩
synonyms excuse, extenuate, gloss (over), gloze (over), whitewash
related words sugarcoat, varnish; apologize, atone, confess; explain, justify, rationalize; alleviate, lessen, lighten, mitigate, moderate, soften, temper; absolve, acquit, clear, exculpate, exonerate, vindicate
2 to make more bearable or less severe — see HELP 2

pallid *adj* lacking a healthy skin color — see PALE 2

palm off *vb* to offer (something fake, useless, or inferior) as genuine, useful, or valuable — see FOIST

palmy *adj* **1** having attained a desired end or state of good fortune — see SUCCESSFUL 1
2 marked by vigorous growth and well-being especially economically — see PROSPEROUS 1

palpable *adj* **1** able to be perceived by a sense or by the mind — see PERCEPTIBLE
2 capable of being perceived by the sense of touch — see TANGIBLE
3 not subject to misinterpretation or more than one interpretation — see CLEAR 2

palpitate *vb* to expand and contract in a rhythmic manner — see PULSATE

palpitation *n* a rhythmic expanding and contracting — see PULSATION

palsy *n* complete or partial loss of physical function (as motion or sensation) in a part of the body — see PARALYSIS

palter *vb* to talk over or dispute the terms of a purchase — see BARGAIN

paltry *adj* so small or unimportant as to warrant little or no attention — see NEGLIGIBLE 1

pamper *vb* to treat with great or excessive care — see BABY

pamphlet *n* a short printed publication with no cover or with a paper cover ⟨*pamphlets* about common safety precautions that we all can put into use⟩
synonyms booklet, brochure, circular, flier (*or* flyer), folder, leaflet
related words advertisement, catalog (*or* catalogue); tract; paperback, pocket book; guidebook, handbook, instructions, manual

pan *vb* to express one's unfavorable opinion of the worth or quality of — see CRITICIZE

panacea *n* something that cures all ills or problems — see CURE-ALL

pancake *n* a flat cake made from thin batter and cooked on both sides (as on a griddle) ⟨every Sunday morning, we have *pancakes* and bacon for breakfast⟩
synonyms flapjack, griddle cake, hotcake, slapjack
related words crepe (*or* crêpe); waffle

pandemonium *n* a state of noisy, confused activity — see COMMOTION

panegyric *n* a formal expression of praise — see ENCOMIUM

panel *n* **1** a meeting featuring a group discussion — see FORUM
2 a select group of persons assigned to consider or take action on some matter — see COMMITTEE

pang *n* a sharp unpleasant sensation usually felt in some specific part of the body — see PAIN 1

panhandler *n* a person who lives by public begging — see BEGGAR

panic *n* the emotion experienced in the presence or threat of danger — see FEAR

panic *vb* to strike with fear — see FRIGHTEN

panorama *n* all that can be seen from a certain point — see VIEW 1

panoramic *adj* covering everything or all important points — see ENCYCLOPEDIC

pan out *vb* **1** to come to be — see COME OUT 1

2 to turn out as planned or desired — see SUCCEED 1
pant *vb* to breathe hard, quickly, or with difficulty — see GASP
pant (after) *vb* to have an earnest wish to own or enjoy — see DESIRE
pantaloons *n pl* an outer garment covering each leg separately from waist to ankle — see PANTS
panther *n* a large tawny cat of the wild — see COUGAR
pantomime *n* **1** a movement of the body or limbs that expresses or emphasizes an idea or feeling — see GESTURE 1
2 an actor in a story performed silently and entirely by body movements — see MIME
pantomimist *n* an actor in a story performed silently and entirely by body movements — see MIME
pants *n pl* an outer garment covering each leg separately from waist to ankle ⟨you'll need a nice pair of *pants* for the job interview⟩
synonyms breeches, pantaloons, slacks, trousers
related words corduroys, denims, jeans; hose, legging (*or* leggin), pantsuit
papa *n* a male human parent — see FATHER 1
paper *adj* being something in name or form only — see NOMINAL 1
paper *n* **1** a piece of paper with information written or to be written on it — see FORM 2
2 a publication that appears at regular intervals — see JOURNAL
3 a short piece of writing done as a school exercise — see COMPOSITION 2
4 a short piece of writing typically expressing a point of view — see ESSAY 1
par *n* **1** something set up as an example against which others of the same type are compared — see STANDARD 1
2 the state or fact of being exactly the same in number, amount, status, or quality — see EQUIVALENCE
3 what is typical of a group, class, or series — see AVERAGE
parable *n* a story intended to teach a basic truth or moral about life — see ALLEGORY
parade *n* a body of individuals moving along in an orderly and often ceremonial way — see CORTEGE 2
parade *vb* **1** to move along with a steady regular step especially in a group — see MARCH 1
2 to present so as to invite notice or attention — see SHOW 1
paradigmatic *adj* constituting, serving as, or worthy of being a pattern to be imitated — see MODEL
paradise *n* **1** a place or state of great happiness ⟨Susan's idea of *paradise* was a world where no one had to go to work⟩
synonyms Eden, Elysium, heaven, utopia
related words dreamland, fairyland, promised land, wonderland; bliss, euphoria, gladness, joy
antonyms hell
2 a dwelling place of perfect bliss for the soul after death — see HEAVEN 1
3 a state of overwhelming usually pleasurable emotion — see ECSTASY
paradox *n* someone or something with qualities or features that seem to conflict with one another — see CONTRADICTION 1
paragon *n* someone of such unequaled perfection as to deserve imitation — see IDEAL 1
parallel *adj* having qualities in common — see ALIKE
parallel *n* **1** a point which two or more things share in common — see SIMILARITY 2
2 one that is equal to another in status, achievement, or value — see EQUAL
parallel *vb* to be the exact counterpart of — see MATCH 1
parallelism *n* the quality or state of having many qualities in common — see SIMILARITY 1
paralysis *n* complete or partial loss of physical function (as motion or sensation) in a part of the body ⟨the car accident left one athlete with *paralysis* from the waist down⟩
synonyms palsy
related words cerebral palsy, multiple sclerosis, poliomyelitis; debilitation, debility, decrepitude, enfeeblement, feebleness, frailness, weakness; infirmity, lameness; disability, impairment
near antonyms mobility, motility, sensation
paralytic *adj* affected with paralysis ⟨at first, he would not accept that he was now *paralytic* and needed help⟩
synonyms paralyzed
related words challenged, crippled, disabled, handicapped, maimed, mutilated; hobbled, lame, lamed; impaired, incapacitated; hamstrung; debilitated, decrepit, enfeebled, feeble, infirm, weak, weakened
near antonyms able-bodied
paralyze *vb* to render powerless, ineffective, or unable to move ⟨a blizzard *paralyzed* the city for two days⟩
synonyms cripple, disable, hamstring, immobilize, incapacitate, prostrate
related words attenuate, debilitate, enfeeble, sap, undermine, weaken; hobble, lame; maim, mutilate
near antonyms energize, galvanize, vitalize; fortify, strengthen; empower; refresh, rejuvenate, restore
paralyzed *adj* affected with paralysis — see PARALYTIC
paramount *adj* **1** coming before all others in importance — see FOREMOST 1
2 of the greatest or highest degree or quantity — see ULTIMATE 1
paraphernalia *n* **1** items needed for the performance of a task or activity — see EQUIPMENT
2 transportable items that one owns — see POSSESSION 2
paraphrase *n* an instance of expressing something in different words ⟨your essays on human rights should have some original thought and not be simply a *paraphrase* of what's in the textbook⟩
synonyms rephrasing, restatement, restating, rewording, translating, translation
related words rehash; summary
near antonyms copy, transcript, transcription
antonyms quotation, quote
paraphrase *vb* to express something (as a text or statement) in different words ⟨could you *paraphrase* your diagnosis of my medical condition, using simpler language?⟩
synonyms rephrase, restate, reword, translate
related words summarize
near antonyms repeat; copy, reproduce, transcribe
antonyms quote
parasite *n* a person who is supported or seeks sup-

port from another without making an adequate return — see LEECH
parboil *vb* to cook in a liquid heated to the point that it gives off steam — see BOIL 2
parcel *n* **1** a number of things considered as a unit — see GROUP 1
2 a small area of usually open land — see FIELD 1
3 a small piece of land that is developed or available for development — see LOT 1
4 a usually small number of persons considered as a unit — see GROUP 2
5 a wrapped or sealed case containing an item or set of items — see PACKAGE 1
parcel (out) *vb* to give out (something) in appropriate amounts or to appropriate individuals — see ADMINISTER 1
parcel post *n* communications or parcels sent or carried through the postal system — see MAIL
parch *vb* to make dry — see DRY 1
pardon *n* release from the guilt or penalty of an offense 〈the criminal is hoping for a Presidential *pardon*〉
synonyms absolution, amnesty, forgiveness, remission, remittal
related words parole; acquittal, exculpation, exoneration, vindication; exemption, immunity, impunity, indemnity; commutation, commuting, reprieve
near antonyms conviction, sentence; assessment, charge, fine, imposition, levying; castigation, chastening, chastisement, condemnation
antonyms penalty, punishment, retribution
pardon *vb* **1** to cease to have feelings of anger or bitterness toward — see FORGIVE 1
2 to overlook or dismiss as of little importance — see EXCUSE 1
pardonable *adj* worthy of forgiveness — see VENIAL
pare *vb* to make (as hair) shorter with or as if with the use of shears — see CLIP
parentage *n* the line of ancestors from whom a person is descended — see ANCESTRY
parenthood *n* the caring for a child by its parents — see PARENTING
parenting *n* the caring for a child by its parents 〈as the big day approaches, the expectant couple are starting to get worried about their fitness for *parenting*〉
synonyms parenthood
related words raising, rearing, upbringing; fatherhood, fathering, paternity; maternity, motherhood, mothering
par excellence *adj* of the very best kind — see EXCELLENT
pariah *n* one who is cast out or rejected by society — see OUTCAST
parity *n* the state or fact of being exactly the same in number, amount, status, or quality — see EQUIVALENCE
park *n* the area around and belonging to a building — see GROUND 1
parley *n* **1** a meeting featuring a group discussion — see FORUM
2 an exchange of views for the purpose of exploring a subject or deciding an issue — see DISCUSSION 1
parley *vb* to exchange viewpoints or seek advice for the purpose of finding a solution to a problem — see CONFER 2
parliament *n* the highest lawmaking body of a political unit — see CONGRESS 1
parlor *n* a building, room, or suite of rooms occupied by a service business — see PLACE 2
parlous *adj* involving potential loss or injury — see DANGEROUS
parochial *adj* not broad or open in views or opinions — see NARROW 2
parody *n* **1** a work that imitates and exaggerates another work for comic effect 〈the musical was a *parody* of *Romeo and Juliet*, with silly songs during the sad scenes〉
synonyms burlesque, caricature, spoof, takeoff
related words lampoon, mockery, satire, travesty; comedy, farce, sketch, slapstick, squib; distortion, exaggeration; imitation, impersonation, mimicking
near antonyms archetype, original, prototype
2 a poor, insincere, or insulting imitation of something — see MOCKERY 1
parody *vb* to copy or exaggerate (someone or something) in order to make fun of — see MIMIC 1
paroxysm *n* **1** a sudden intense expression of strong feeling — see OUTBURST 1
2 a violent disturbance (as of the political or social order) — see CONVULSION
parrot *vb* to say after another — see REPEAT 3
parsimonious *adj* giving or sharing as little as possible — see STINGY 1
parsimony *n* the quality of being overly sparing with money 〈her *parsimony* was so extreme that she'd walk five miles to the store to save a few cents on gas〉
synonyms cheapness, closeness, miserliness, penuriousness, pinching, stinginess, tightness
related words conserving, economizing, economy, frugality, husbandry, providence, scrimping, skimping, thrift; conservation, saving; husbanding, managing
near antonyms extravagance, lavishness; dissipation, improvidence, prodigality, squandering, wastefulness
antonyms generosity, liberality, openhandedness, openheartedness, philanthropy
parson *n* a person specially trained and authorized to conduct religious services in a Christian church — see CLERGYMAN
part *adv* in some measure or degree — see PARTLY
part *n* **1** one of the pieces from which something is designed to be assembled 〈the model car came in several small *parts* that had to be assembled〉
synonyms member, partition, portion, section, segment
related words component, constituent, element, factor, ingredient, moiety, parcel; cut, length; bit, fragment, particle, scrap
near antonyms whole; aggregate, composite, compound, sum, total, totality
2 something belonging to, due to, or contributed by an individual member of a group — see SHARE 1
3 the action for which a person or thing is specially fitted or used or for which a thing exists — see ROLE
4 *usually* **parts** *pl* a broad geographical area — see REGION 2
part *vb* to set or force apart — see SEPARATE 1
partake *vb* to take a share or part 〈we should all *partake* of this fine meal together〉
synonyms participate, share

related words endure, experience, feel, see, taste, undergo; encounter, meet; accept, receive

partaker *n* one who takes part in something — see PARTICIPANT

partial *adj* **1** inclined to favor one side over another ⟨that judge is always *partial* to the defense, so be careful⟩
synonyms biased, one-sided, partisan, prejudiced
related words jaundiced, unfriendly, unsympathetic; colored, distorted, misrepresented, warped; convinced, influenced, persuaded, predisposed, prepossessed, swayed; affected, concerned, interested
near antonyms open, open-minded, persuasible, receptive; fair, honest, just, reasonable; bipartisan; autonomous, independent, unallied; aloof, detached, dispassionate, hardheaded, impersonal, objective, unemotional; apathetic, indifferent, unenthusiastic, uninterested
antonyms evenhanded, impartial, neutral, nonpartisan, unbiased, unprejudiced
2 having a liking or affection — see FOND 1
3 lacking some necessary part — see INCOMPLETE

partiality *n* **1** an attitude that always favors one way of feeling or acting especially without considering any other possibilities — see BIAS
2 a habitual attraction to some activity or thing — see INCLINATION 1
3 positive regard for something — see LIKING

partially *adv* in some measure or degree — see PARTLY

participant *n* one who takes part in something ⟨he seemed to be a willing *participant* in the prank⟩
synonyms partaker, participator, party, sharer
related words actor; accessory, aide, assistant, helper; colleague, partner
near antonyms bystander, looker-on, observer, onlooker, spectator, watcher
antonyms nonparticipant

participate *vb* to take a share or part — see PARTAKE

participator *n* one who takes part in something — see PARTICIPANT

particle *n* **1** a very small amount ⟨I did all but a *particle* of my work⟩
synonyms ace, bit, crumb, dab, driblet, glimmer, hint, lick, little, mite, nip, ounce, peanuts, ray, scruple, shade, shadow, shred, smidgen (*also* smidgeon *or* smidgin), snap, spark, speck, spot, sprinkling, strain, streak, suspicion, touch, trace
related words iota, jot, modicum, tittle, whit; atom, dot, fleck, flyspeck, grain, granule, molecule, morsel, mote, nubbin, patch, scrap; dash, drop, pinch; part, portion, section; bite, nibble, taste; handful, scattering, smattering; dose, shot; chip, flake, fragment, shard, shiver, sliver, smithereens, splinter; shred, tatter; clipping, paring, shaving
near antonyms abundance, barrel, bucket, bushel, deal, gobs, heaps, loads, mass, mountain, much, peck, pile, plenty, profusion, quantity, raft, scads, stack, wad, wealth; volume; embarrassment, excess, overabundance, overage, overflow, overkill, overmuch, oversupply, superabundance, superfluity, surfeit, surplus; chunk, hunk, lump, slab
2 a very small piece — see BIT 1

particular *adj* **1** hard to please — see FINICKY
2 of, relating to, or belonging to a single person — see INDIVIDUAL 1
3 tending to select carefully — see SELECTIVE

particular *n* **1** a separate part in a list, account, or series — see ITEM 1
2 a single piece of information — see FACT 3

particularity *n* **1** careful thoroughness of detail ⟨with great *particularity* she described the qualities she's looking for in a boyfriend⟩
synonyms explicitness, specificity
related words attentiveness, care, carefulness, conscientiousness, finickiness, fussiness, meticulousness; alertness, cautiousness, circumspection, heedfulness, safeness; discrimination; accuracy, exactitude, exactness, precision
near antonyms imprecision, inaccuracy, inexactness; indistinctness, vagueness
antonyms generality
2 a single piece of information — see FACT 3

particularized *adj* including many small descriptive features — see DETAILED 1

particularly *adv* to a great degree — see VERY 1

parting *adj* given, taken, or performed at parting ⟨she gave him a *parting* gift to remember her by⟩
synonyms farewell, valedictory
related words final, last, ultimate; departing, leaving

parting *n* **1** the act or process of two or more persons going off in different directions ⟨although their *parting* was sad, they knew they would see each other again⟩
synonyms farewell, leave-taking, separation
related words departure, egress, exit, exiting, exodus, going, leaving, quitting, running away; decampment, flight, withdrawal; abandonment, desertion, forsaking
near antonyms reunion; arrival, greeting, welcome; gathering, joining, meeting
2 the act of leaving a place — see DEPARTURE

partisan *adj* inclined to favor one side over another — see PARTIAL 1

partisan *n* **1** one who follows the opinions or teachings of another — see FOLLOWER
2 one who is intensely or excessively devoted to a cause — see ZEALOT

partisanship *n* an attitude that always favors one way of feeling or acting especially without considering any other possibilities — see BIAS

partition *n* **1** one of the pieces from which something is designed to be assembled — see PART 1
2 something that divides, separates, or marks off — see DIVISION 1
3 the act or process of a whole separating into two or more parts or pieces — see SEPARATION 1

partly *adv* in some measure or degree ⟨you're only *partly* right⟩
synonyms incompletely, part, partially
related words in part
near antonyms absolutely, dead, downright, plain, plumb, utterly
antonyms completely, entirely, totally, wholly

partner *n* the person to whom another is married — see SPOUSE

partnership *n* the state of having shared interests or efforts (as in social or business matters) — see ASSOCIATION 1

parturition *n* the act or process of giving birth to children — see CHILDBIRTH

party *n* **1** a social gathering ⟨we're all invited to the big *party* to celebrate the end of the term⟩
synonyms affair, blowout, event, fete (*or* fête), function, get-together, reception, shindig
related words ball, formal, prom; celebration,

gala, occasion; orgy, saturnalia; benefit, clambake, hen party, housewarming, masquerade, mixer, shower, salon, soiree (*or* soirée), stag, tea
2 a group of people acting together within a larger group — see FACTION
3 a group of people working together on a task — see GANG 1
4 a member of the human race — see HUMAN
5 a usually small number of persons considered as a unit — see GROUP 2
6 one who takes part in something — see PARTICIPANT

party pooper *n* a person who spoils the pleasure of others — see KILLJOY

pass *n* **1** a narrow opening between hillsides or mountains that can be used for passage — see CANYON
2 a passage cleared for public vehicular travel — see WAY 1
3 a small sheet of plastic, paper, or paperboard showing that the bearer has a claim to something (as admittance) — see TICKET 1
4 an effort to do or accomplish something — see ATTEMPT

pass *vb* **1** to shift possession of (something) from one person to another <could you please *pass* me the phone?>
synonyms hand, hand over, reach, transfer
related words relay; bear, carry; finger, handle, paw; cede, give, give up, release, relinquish, surrender
2 to come to an end — see CEASE 1
3 to put (something) into the possession or safekeeping of another — see GIVE 2
4 to put into effect through legislative or authoritative action — see ENACT
5 to take place — see HAPPEN

pass (on) *vb* to stop living — see DIE 1

pass (over) *vb* to make one's way through, across, or over — see TRAVERSE

passable *adj* **1** capable of being traveled on <after the snowstorm, the roads might not be *passable* for the morning ride to school>
synonyms navigable, negotiable
related words clear, cleared, open, unclogged, unobstructed
near antonyms blocked, choked, clogged, closed, congested, dammed, jammed, obstructed; barricaded, blockaded
antonyms impassable
2 capable of being passed into or through — see PENETRABLE
3 of a level of quality that meets one's needs or standards — see ADEQUATE
4 of average to below average quality — see MEDIOCRE 1

passably *adv* in a satisfactory way — see WELL 1

passage *n* **1** an established course for traveling from one place to another <the long *passage* down the Atlantic seaboard, around Cape Horn, and up the Pacific Coast to California>
synonyms approach, avenue, path, route, way
related words bypath, byway, lane; bypass, drive, freeway, highway, road, street, thoroughfare; trace, track, trail; airway; channel, watercourse, waterway; door, doorway, gate, gateway, portal
2 a going from one place to another usually of some distance — see JOURNEY
3 a journey over water in a vessel — see SAIL
4 a part taken from a longer work — see EXCERPT
5 forward movement in time or place — see ADVANCE 1

passageway *n* **1** a passage cleared for public vehicular travel — see WAY 1
2 a typically long narrow way connecting parts of a building — see HALL 2

pass away *vb* to stop living — see DIE 1

passé *adj* having passed its time of use or usefulness — see OBSOLETE

passel *n* **1** a number of things considered as a unit — see GROUP 1
2 a usually small number of persons considered as a unit — see GROUP 2

passing *adj* lasting only for a short time — see MOMENTARY

passing *n* the permanent stopping of all the vital bodily activities — see DEATH 1

passion *n* **1** a feeling of strong or constant regard for and dedication to someone — see LOVE 1
2 a strong but often short-lived liking for another person — see CRUSH 1
3 a strong wish for something — see DESIRE
4 a subjective response to a person, thing, or situation — see FEELING 1
5 depth of feeling — see ARDOR 1
6 passions *pl* general emotional condition — see FEELING 2

passionate *adj* **1** having a strong sexual desire — see LUSTFUL
2 having or expressing great depth of feeling — see FERVENT

passive *adj* receiving or enduring without offering resistance <the student body was surprisingly *passive* about having recess shortened>
synonyms acquiescent, nonresistant, resigned, tolerant, tolerating, unresistant, unresisting, yielding
related words forbearing, long-suffering, patient, uncomplaining; agreeable, amenable, compliant, complying, conformist, docile, guidable, law-abiding, obedient, subordinate, tractable, willing; submissive, surrendering; amiable, obliging; slavish, subservient; disciplined, governable, manageable; apathetic, uncaring, unresponsive
near antonyms defiant; contrary, disobedient, insubordinate, insurgent, intractable, mutinous, rebellious, recalcitrant, refractory, uncontrollable, ungovernable, unruly; balky, perverse, wayward, wrongheaded; headstrong, willful (*or* wilful); indomitable; undisciplined, unmanageable; dissident, nonconformist
antonyms protesting, resistant, resisting, unyielding

pass off *vb* to offer (something fake, useless, or inferior) as genuine, useful, or valuable — see FOIST

pass out *vb* to lose consciousness — see FAINT

pass over *vb* **1** to fail to give proper attention to — see NEGLECT 1
2 to overlook or dismiss as of little importance — see EXCUSE 1

passport *n* something that allows someone to achieve a desired goal <meeting that movie director could be your *passport* to a big acting career>
synonyms gateway, key, open sesame
related words password; accomplishment, achievement, success; manner, means, method, system, technique, way; blueprint, design, plan, scheme, strategy

password *n* a word or phrase that must be spoken

by a person in order to pass a guard ⟨the *password* for the dance party will be changed next week⟩
synonyms countersign, watchword
related words shibboleth, sign; signal; hint, indication

past *adj* having been such at some previous time — see FORMER

past *n* the events or experience of former times ⟨we spent a pleasant evening recalling the *past* together⟩
synonyms auld lang syne, history, yesterday, yesteryear, yore
related words bygone; flashback; annals, chronicle, record; memoir; antiquity
near antonyms future, tomorrow; present

past *prep* on or to the farther side of — see BEYOND 1

paste *vb* to deliver a blow to (someone or something) usually in a strong vigorous manner — see HIT 1

pastel *adj* lacking intensity of color — see PALE 1

past master *n* a person with a high level of knowledge or skill in a field — see EXPERT

pastoral *adj* **1** of, relating to, associated with, or typical of open areas with few buildings or people — see RURAL
2 of, relating to, or characteristic of the clergy — see CLERICAL

pasturage *n* open land over which livestock may roam and feed — see RANGE 1

pasture *n* open land over which livestock may roam and feed — see RANGE 1

pasture *vb* to feed on grass or herbs — see [1]GRAZE

pasty *adj* lacking a healthy skin color — see PALE 2

pat *adj* sticking to an opinion, purpose, or course of action in spite of reason, arguments, or persuasion — see OBSTINATE

pat *vb* to touch or handle in a tender or loving manner — see FONDLE

patch *n* **1** a small area that is different (as in color) from the main part — see SPOT 1
2 a very small piece — see BIT 1

patch *vb* to put into good shape or working order again — see MEND 1

patch (together) *vb* to make or assemble roughly or hastily — see COBBLE (TOGETHER)

patchwork *adj* consisting of many things of different sorts — see MISCELLANEOUS

pate *n* the upper or front part of the body that contains the brain, the major sense organs, and the mouth — see HEAD 1

patent *adj* **1** not subject to misinterpretation or more than one interpretation — see CLEAR 2
2 very noticeable especially for being incorrect or bad — see EGREGIOUS

path *n* **1** the direction along which something or someone moves ⟨try to stay out of the *path* of the golf balls while playing⟩ ⟨I tripped over a rock directly in my *path*⟩
synonyms course, line, pathway, route, steps, track, way
related words circle, circuit, loop, orbit; flight path, trajectory; ascent, descent
2 a rough course or way formed by or as if by repeated footsteps — see TRAIL 1
3 an established course for traveling from one place to another — see PASSAGE 1

pathetic *adj* **1** deserving of one's pity ⟨the plight of the homeless family was quite *pathetic*⟩
synonyms heartbreaking, heartrending, miserable, piteous, pitiable, pitiful, poor, rueful, sorry, wretched
related words deplorable, lamentable, regrettable; emotional, impressive, inspiring; affecting, moving, poignant, stirring, touching; awful, horrible, terrible; distressing, disturbing, upsetting; grievous, sad, sorrowful, woeful
near antonyms unimpressive, uninspiring
2 causing unhappiness — see SAD 2

pathway *n* **1** a rough course or way formed by or as if by repeated footsteps — see TRAIL 1
2 the direction along which something or someone moves — see PATH 1

patience *n* the capacity to endure what is difficult or disagreeable without complaining ⟨my mother is endowed with nearly endless *patience*⟩
synonyms forbearance, long-suffering, sufferance, tolerance
related words acquiescence, resignation; passiveness, passivity; amenability, compliance, conformism, docility, obedience, subordination, tractability, willingness; discipline, self-control; submission, submissiveness
near antonyms defiance; contrariness, disobedience, insubordination, intractability, recalcitrance, resistance, willfulness
antonyms impatience

patient *adj* **1** accepting pains or hardships calmly or without complaint ⟨you were very *patient* about having to wait for me for so long⟩
synonyms forbearing, long-suffering, stoic (*or* stoical), tolerant, uncomplaining
related words lenient; acquiescent, passive, resigned, unresistant, unresisting, yielding; agreeable, amenable, compliant, complying, conformist, docile, law-abiding, obedient, submissive, subordinate, tractable, willing; slavish, subservient; amiable, obliging; collected, composed; constrained, contained, curbed, inhibited, repressed, restrained; disciplined, self-contained, self-controlled; apathetic, uncaring, unresponsive
near antonyms bored, tired, weary; defiant, resistant; contrary, disobedient, insubordinate, intractable, rebellious, recalcitrant, refractory, ungovernable, unmanageable, unruly
antonyms complaining, fed up, impatient, protesting
2 continuing despite difficulties, opposition, or discouragement — see PERSISTENT

patient *n* an individual awaiting or under medical care and treatment ⟨the nurse asked the *patient* to change into a paper gown⟩
synonyms case
related words inpatient, outpatient; sufferer, victim; convalescent, nursling

patio *n* an open space wholly or partly enclosed (as by buildings or walls) — see COURT 2

patois *n* the special terms or expressions of a particular group or field — see TERMINOLOGY

patrician *adj* of high birth, rank, or station — see NOBLE 1

patrician *n* a man of high birth or social position — see GENTLEMAN 1

patrimony *n* something that is or may be inherited — see INHERITANCE

patriot *n* a person who loves his or her country and supports its interests and policies ⟨the contention that true *patriots* would be willing to do anything for their country⟩

synonyms loyalist
related words chauvinist; jingoist, nationalist; compatriot, countryman
near antonyms collaborator, quisling, spy, traitor; betrayer, deserter, recreant; renegade

patriotic *adj* having or showing love and support for one's country ⟨hanging a flag outside is a *patriotic* gesture⟩
synonyms nationalist, nationalistic
related words chauvinist; jingoistic; constant, devoted, faithful, loyal, staunch (*or* stanch), steadfast, steady, true; ardent, fervent, fervid, impassioned, passionate
near antonyms traitorous, treasonous; disaffected, disloyal, faithless, false, fickle, inconstant, perfidious, recreant, treacherous, unfaithful
antonyms unpatriotic

patriotism *n* love and support for one's country ⟨her *patriotism* was so great that she quit her job to work for the war effort⟩
synonyms nationalism
related words chauvinism; jingoism; allegiance, constancy, devotion, faithfulness, fealty, loyalty, staunchness, steadfastness; fervency, fervidness, passion
near antonyms desertion, treason; disaffection, disloyalty, faithlessness, falseness, fickleness, inconstancy, perfidiousness, treachery, unfaithfulness

patron *n* **1** a person who buys a product or uses a service from a business — see CUSTOMER 1
2 a person who takes the responsibility for some other person or thing — see SPONSOR
3 one that helps another with gifts or money — see BENEFACTOR

patronize *vb* **1** to assume or treat with an air of superiority — see CONDESCEND 2
2 to promote the interests or cause of — see SUPPORT 1

patter *vb* to engage in casual or rambling conversation — see CHAT

patter *n* the special terms or expressions of a particular group or field — see TERMINOLOGY

pattern *n* **1** a unit of decoration that is repeated all over something (as a fabric) ⟨a quilt with tiny pink roses as the *pattern*⟩
synonyms design, figure, motif, motive
related words device; adornment, caparison, decoration, embellishment, frill, garnish, ornament, trim
2 a usual manner of behaving or doing — see HABIT
3 an established and often automatic or monotonous series of actions followed when engaging in some activity — see ROUTINE 1
4 the way in which the elements of something (as a work of art) are arranged — see COMPOSITION 3

patty *also* **pattie** *n* a small usually rounded mass of minced food that has been fried — see CAKE

paucity *n* a falling short of an essential or desirable amount or number — see DEFICIENCY

paunch *n* an enlarged or bulging abdomen — see POTBELLY

pauperism *n* the state of lacking sufficient money or material possessions — see POVERTY 1

pause *n* a momentary halt in an activity ⟨there was a brief *pause* for applause in her speech⟩
synonyms break, breath, breather, interruption, lull, recess
related words time-out; interim, interlude, intermission, interval, respite, rest; cessation, discontinuance, ending, expiration, finishing, lapse, stopping, termination; abeyance, moratorium, surcease, suspension; discontinuity, gap, hiatus
near antonyms continuation, endurance, persistence, progress, progression; extension, prolongation

pause *vb* to come to a temporary halt in one's activity ⟨he *paused* for a moment to tie his shoe⟩
synonyms break
related words break in, interrupt; cease, discontinue, end, finish, stop, terminate; knock off, lay off, quit; lapse, let up
near antonyms continue, persist; advance, progress; extend, prolong, stretch

pawn *n* **1** one that is or can be used to further the purposes of another ⟨she disliked being a *pawn* in her friends' power games⟩
synonyms puppet, tool
related words chump, dupe, foil, gull, sucker, victim; minion, stooge; yes-man
2 something given or held to assure that the giver will keep a promise — see PLEDGE 1

pawn *vb* to leave as a guarantee of repayment of a loan ⟨he *pawned* his watch in order to pay off his gambling debt⟩
synonyms hock, pledge
related words deposit, mortgage; bond
near antonyms buy (back), redeem, win (back)

pay *n* **1** the money paid regularly to a person for labor or services — see WAGE
2 something (as money) that is given or received in return for goods or services — see PAYMENT 2

pay *vb* **1** to give (someone) the sum of money owed for goods or services received ⟨we need to *pay* the cashier and then we can leave⟩
synonyms compensate, recompense, remunerate
related words reimburse, repay, requite; pay off, pay up, prepay
2 to give what is owed for ⟨you ought to *pay* that bill before it's overdue⟩
synonyms clear, discharge, foot, liquidate, pay off, pay up, quit, recompense, settle, spring (for), stand
antonyms repudiate
3 to hand over or use up in payment — see SPEND 1
4 to produce as revenue — see YIELD 2

payable *adj* not yet paid — see OUTSTANDING 1

paying *adj* yielding a profit — see PROFITABLE 1

paying *n* the act of offering money in exchange for goods or services — see PAYMENT 1

payload *n* a mass or quantity of something taken up and carried, conveyed, or transported — see LOAD 1

payment *n* **1** the act of offering money in exchange for goods or services ⟨they are very prompt in the *payment* of their credit card bills⟩
synonyms compensation, disbursement, giving, paying, remitment, remittance, remuneration
related words rendering, tendering; reimbursement, repayment; paying off, paying up, prepayment; overpayment
near antonyms underpayment
antonyms nonpayment, repudiation
2 something (as money) that is given or received in return for goods or services ⟨their *payment* for mowing the lawn was $20⟩ ⟨we finally mailed our last car *payment* last week⟩

synonyms compensation, consideration, pay, recompense, remittance, remuneration, requital
related words salary, stipend, wage(s); disbursement, expenditure, outlay; rebate, refund; indemnity, recoupment, redress, reparation, restitution; adjustment, settlement; deposit; reimbursement, repayment; prepayment; overpayment; rent, rental
3 the money paid regularly to a person for labor or services — see WAGE

payoff *n* the amount of money left when expenses are subtracted from the total amount received — see PROFIT 1

pay off *vb* to give what is owed for — see PAY 2

pay up *vb* to give what is owed for — see PAY 2

peace *n* **1** a state without war ⟨after a long and bitter war, the troubled region finally achieved *peace*⟩
synonyms peacefulness
related words accord, amity, concord, harmony; calm, quiet, serenity, tranquillity (*or* tranquility); order, stability; pacification
near antonyms conflict, contention, discord, dissidence, strife, trouble; tumult, turmoil, unrest, upheaval; fighting, warfare; action, battle, combat
antonyms war
2 a state of freedom from storm or disturbance — see CALM
3 peaceful coexistence — see HARMONY 2

peaceable *adj* **1** inclined to live in peace and to avoid war — see PEACEFUL 1
2 not involving violence or force — see PEACEFUL 2

peaceful *adj* **1** inclined to live in peace and to avoid war ⟨a *peaceful* tribe that had quietly inhabited these shores for centuries before the arrival of the Europeans⟩
synonyms pacific, peaceable
related words calm, mild, neutral, quiet, relaxed, serene, tranquil; affable, amiable, amicable, benevolent, gentle, kind, kindly; nonbelligerent, unaggressive; submissive, yielding
near antonyms militaristic; aggressive, bellicose, belligerent, combative, contentious, discordant, pugnacious, quarrelsome, scrappy, truculent; antagonistic, argumentative, fierce, gladiatorial, hostile, hot-tempered
antonyms warlike
2 not involving violence or force ⟨UN officials struggled to find a *peaceful* solution to the troublesome conflict⟩
synonyms nonviolent, peaceable
related words conciliatory, pacific, peacemaking; nonbelligerent, unaggressive, unassertive; appeasing, conciliating, mollifying, pacifying, placating; calming, quieting, soothing
near antonyms armed, martial, militant, military, warlike; aggressive, assertive, bellicose, belligerent, combative, contentious, quarrelsome; antagonistic, argumentative, fierce, gladiatorial, hostile; tempestuous, volcanic
antonyms forced, violent
3 free from disturbing noise or uproar — see QUIET 1
4 free from storms or physical disturbance — see CALM 1

peacefulness *n* **1** a state of freedom from storm or disturbance — see CALM
2 a state without war — see PEACE 1

peacemaker *n* one who works with opposing sides in order to bring about an agreement — see MEDIATOR

peacemaking *adj* tending to lessen or avoid conflict or hostility — see PACIFIC 1

peak *n* **1** an elevation of land higher than a hill — see MOUNTAIN 1
2 the highest part or point — see HEIGHT 1
3 the projecting front part of a hat or cap — see VISOR

peaked *adj* **1** lacking a healthy skin color — see PALE 2
2 tapering to a thin tip — see POINTED 1
3 temporarily suffering from a disorder of the body — see SICK 1

peal *vb* to make the clear sound heard when metal vibrates — see RING 1

peanuts *n pl* **1** a very small amount — see PARTICLE 1
2 a very small sum of money — see MITE 1

pearl *n* someone or something unusually desirable — see PRIZE 1

pebbly *adj* not having a level or smooth surface — see UNEVEN 1

peck *n* a considerable amount — see LOT 2

peculiar *adj* **1** being out of the ordinary — see EXCEPTIONAL
2 different from the ordinary in a way that causes curiosity or suspicion — see ODD 2
3 noticeably different from what is generally found or experienced — see UNUSUAL 1
4 of, relating to, or belonging to a single person — see INDIVIDUAL 1
5 serving to identify as belonging to an individual or group — see CHARACTERISTIC 1

peculiarity *n* **1** an odd or peculiar habit — see IDIOSYNCRASY
2 something that sets apart an individual from others of the same kind — see CHARACTERISTIC

pecuniary *adj* of or relating to money, banking, or investments — see FINANCIAL

pedagogue *n* a person whose occupation is to give formal instruction in a school — see TEACHER

peddle *vb* to sell from place to place usually in small quantities ⟨he traveled around the country *peddling* Bibles⟩
synonyms hawk
related words retail, wholesale; deal (in), distribute, high-pressure, hustle, market, merchandise, trade (in), vend

peddler *also* **pedlar** *n* one who sells things outdoors ⟨the *peddler* on the street corner selling baseball caps⟩
synonyms hawker, huckster
related words dealer, merchandiser, seller, vendor (*also* vender); concessionaire; black marketeer, bootlegger, fence, fencer, hustler, smuggler, trader
near antonyms buyer, purchaser; consumer, end user, user

pedestrian *adj* causing weariness, restlessness, or lack of interest — see BORING

pedigree *n* the line of ancestors from whom a person is descended — see ANCESTRY

pedigreed *adj* of unmixed ancestry — see PUREBRED

peek *n* an instance of looking especially briefly — see LOOK 2

peek *vb* to take a quick or hasty look — see GLANCE 2

peel *vb* to remove the natural covering of ⟨she *peeled* an apple with great care⟩
synonyms bark, flay, hull, husk, shell, shuck, skin
related words bare, denude, expose, scale, strip; pare

peel (off) *vb* to rid oneself of (a garment) — see REMOVE 1

peeled *adj* lacking a usual or natural covering — see NAKED 2

peep *n* an instance of looking especially briefly — see LOOK 2

peep *vb* to make a short sharp sound like a small bird — see CHIRP

peer *n* one that is equal to another in status, achievement, or value — see EQUAL

peer *vb* to look long and hard in wonder or surprise — see GAPE

peerless *adj* having no equal or rival for excellence or desirability — see ONLY 1

peeve *n* **1** something that is a source of irritation — see ANNOYANCE 3
2 the feeling of being offended or resentful after a slight or indignity — see PIQUE

peeve *vb* to disturb the peace of mind of (someone) especially by repeated disagreeable acts — see IRRITATE 1

peeving *adj* causing annoyance — see ANNOYING

peevish *adj* **1** easily irritated or annoyed — see IRRITABLE
2 sticking to an opinion, purpose, or course of action in spite of reason, arguments, or persuasion — see OBSTINATE

peevishness *n* **1** a steadfast adherence to an opinion, purpose, or course of action — see OBSTINACY
2 readiness to show annoyance or impatience — see PETULANCE

peewee *n* a living thing much smaller than others of its kind — see DWARF 1

peg *n* an individual part of a process, series, or ranking — see DEGREE 1

peg *vb* **1** to arrange or assign according to type — see CLASSIFY 1
2 to send through the air especially with a quick forward motion of the arm — see THROW

peg (away) *vb* to devote serious and sustained effort — see LABOR

pelage *n* the hairy covering of a mammal especially when fine, soft, and thick — see FUR 1

pelagic *adj* of or relating to the sea — see MARINE 1

pelf *n* something (as pieces of stamped metal or printed paper) customarily and legally used as a medium of exchange, a measure of value, or a means of payment — see MONEY

pellet *n* a usually round or cone-shaped little piece of lead made to be fired from a firearm — see BULLET

pell–mell *adj* **1** acting or done with excessive or careless speed — see HASTY 1
2 lacking in order, neatness, and often cleanliness — see MESSY

pell–mell *adv* **1** in a confused and reckless manner — see HELTER-SKELTER 1
2 with excessive or careless speed — see HASTILY 1

pellucid *adj* easily seen through — see CLEAR 1

pelt *n* the outer covering of an animal removed for its commercial value — see HIDE 1

pelt *vb* **1** to proceed or move quickly — see HURRY 2
2 to send through the air especially with a quick forward motion of the arm — see THROW
3 to strike repeatedly — see BEAT 1

pen *n* **1** a place of confinement for persons held in lawful custody — see JAIL
2 an enclosure with an open framework for keeping animals — see CAGE

pen *vb* **1** to close or shut in by or as if by barriers — see ENCLOSE 1
2 to compose and set down on paper the words of — see WRITE 1

penal *adj* inflicting, involving, or serving as punishment — see PUNITIVE

penalize *vb* to inflict a penalty on for a fault or crime — see PUNISH

penalizing *adj* inflicting, involving, or serving as punishment — see PUNITIVE

penalty *n* **1** a feature of someone or something that creates difficulty for achieving success — see DISADVANTAGE
2 a sum of money to be paid as a punishment — see FINE
3 suffering, loss, or hardship imposed in response to a crime or offense — see PUNISHMENT

penchant *n* a habitual attraction to some activity or thing — see INCLINATION 1

pencil (in) *vb* to compose and set down on paper the words of — see WRITE 1

pendant *also* **pendent** *n* an ornament worn on a chain around the neck or wrist ⟨Navajo necklaces with *pendants* finely crafted in genuine sky-blue turquoise⟩
synonyms bangle, charm, lavalier (*also* lavalliere)
related words locket, teardrop

pendent *or* **pendant** *adj* extending freely from a support from above — see DEPENDENT 1

pending *adj* **1** not yet settled or decided ⟨a decision is *pending* about whether to buy computers or sports equipment with this money⟩
synonyms open, undecided, undetermined, unresolved, unsettled
related words hanging; arguable, debatable, disputable, moot, uncertain, unsure
near antonyms confirmed, established; certain, sure
antonyms decided, determined, resolved, settled
2 being soon to appear or take place — see FORTHCOMING
3 giving signs of immediate occurrence — see IMMINENT 1

pendulous *adj* **1** bending downward or forward — see NODDING
2 extending freely from a support from above — see DEPENDENT 1

penetrable *adj* capable of being passed into or through ⟨unfortunately, our netting proved to be a rather *penetrable* barrier that allowed in our cabin a steady stream of mosquitoes⟩
synonyms passable, permeable, porous
related words absorbent
near antonyms airtight, watertight; close, compact, dense, thick
antonyms impassable, impenetrable, impermeable, impervious, nonporous

penetrate *vb* to go or come in or into — see ENTER 1

penetrating *adj* causing intense discomfort to one's skin — see CUTTING 1

peninsula *n* an area of land that juts out into a body of water — see [2]CAPE
penitence *n* a feeling of responsibility for wrongdoing — see GUILT 1
penitent *adj* **1** feeling sorrow for a wrong that one has done — see CONTRITE 1
2 suffering from or expressive of a feeling of responsibility for wrongdoing — see GUILTY 2
penitentiary *n* a place of confinement for persons held in lawful custody — see JAIL
penman *n* a person who creates a written work — see AUTHOR 1
penmanship *n* **1** the form or style of a particular person's writing — see HANDWRITING 1
2 writing done by hand — see HANDWRITING 2
pennant *n* a piece of cloth with a special design that is used as an emblem or for signaling — see FLAG 1
penniless *adj* lacking money or material possessions — see POOR 1
pennon *n* a piece of cloth with a special design that is used as an emblem or for signaling — see FLAG 1
pensive *adj* given to or marked by long, quiet thinking — see CONTEMPLATIVE
penstock *n* a long hollow cylinder for carrying a substance (as a liquid or gas) — see PIPE 1
penthouse *n* a smaller structure added to a main building — see ANNEX
penumbra *n* partial darkness due to the obstruction of light rays — see SHADE 1
penurious *adj* **1** giving or sharing as little as possible — see STINGY 1
2 lacking money or material possessions — see POOR 1
penuriousness *n* **1** the quality of being overly sparing with money — see PARSIMONY
2 the state of lacking sufficient money or material possessions — see POVERTY 1
penury *n* the state of lacking sufficient money or material possessions — see POVERTY 1
peon *n* a person who does very hard or dull work — see SLAVE 2
people *n pl* **1** human beings in general ⟨despite the horrors she witnessed, Anne Frank never lost her faith in *people*⟩
synonyms folks, humanity, humankind, public, society, world
related words crowd, masses, mob, populace, proletariat, rabble, riffraff
2 the body of the community as contrasted with the elite — see MASS 1
3 a group of persons who come from the same ancestor — see FAMILY 1
pep *n* active strength of body or mind — see VIGOR 1
pep (up) *vb* to give life, vigor, or spirit to — see ANIMATE
pepper *vb* **1** to cover by or as if by scattering something over or on — see SCATTER 2
2 to mark with small spots especially unevenly — see SPOT
peppery *adj* marked by a lively display of strong feeling — see SPIRITED 1
peppiness *n* the quality or state of having abundant or intense activity — see VITALITY 1
peppy *adj* **1** having active strength of body or mind — see VIGOROUS 1
2 having much high-spirited energy and movement — see LIVELY 1
per *prep* using the means or agency of — see BY 2
perambulation *n* a relaxed journey on foot for exercise or pleasure — see WALK
per capita *adv* for each one — see APIECE
perceive *vb* **1** to have a vague awareness of — see FEEL 1
2 to make note of (something) through the use of one's eyes — see SEE 1
3 to recognize the meaning of — see COMPREHEND 1
percentage *n* a measure of how often an event will occur instead of another — see PROBABILITY 2
perceptible *adj* able to be perceived by a sense or by the mind ⟨you should note a *perceptible* temperature change when you add the second element⟩
synonyms appreciable, detectable, discernible, distinguishable, palpable, sensible
related words audible, observable, tangible, visible; clear, conspicuous, evident, eye-catching, manifest, noticeable, obvious, plain, prominent, striking; apparent, distinct, significant, straightforward
near antonyms inaudible, intangible, invisible; inconspicuous, indistinct, unnoticeable; faint, insignificant, slight, trivial; buried, concealed, covert, disguised, hidden, obscure, shrouded, vague
antonyms impalpable, imperceptible, inappreciable, indistinguishable, insensible
perception *n* **1** the ability to understand inner qualities or relationships — see WISDOM 1
2 the knowledge gained from the process of coming to know or understand something — see COMPREHENSION
perceptive *adj* **1** able to sense slight impressions or differences — see ACUTE 1
2 having or showing deep understanding and intelligent application of knowledge — see WISE 1
perceptiveness *n* the ability to understand inner qualities or relationships — see WISDOM 1
perch *vb* **1** to come to rest after descending from the air — see ALIGHT
2 to establish or place comfortably or snugly — see ENSCONCE 1
perchance *adv* it is possible — see PERHAPS
percolate *vb* to flow forth slowly through small openings — see EXUDE
percolate (into) *vb* to spread throughout — see PERMEATE
perdition *n* the place of punishment for the wicked after death — see HELL 1
peregrinate *vb* to take a trip especially of some distance — see TRAVEL 1
peregrination *n* a going from one place to another usually of some distance — see JOURNEY
peremptoriness *n* an exaggerated sense of one's importance that shows itself in the making of excessive or unjustified claims — see ARROGANCE
peremptory *adj* **1** fond of ordering people around — see BOSSY
2 forcing one's compliance or participation by or as if by law — see MANDATORY
3 having a feeling of superiority that shows itself in an overbearing attitude — see ARROGANT
4 having or showing a tendency to force one's will on others without any regard to fairness or necessity — see ARBITRARY 1
perfect *adj* **1** being entirely without fault or flaw ⟨a stunningly *perfect* performance—not the slightest

mistake—won her the gold medal in women's figure skating⟩
synonyms absolute, faultless, flawless, ideal, impeccable, irreproachable, letter-perfect, unblemished
related words consummate, expert, masterly; classic, dandy, excellent, fabulous, fine, first-class, first-rate, grand, great, marvelous (*or* marvellous), prime, superb, superior, superlative, terrific, top, top-notch, unsurpassed; completed, finished, perfected, polished; complete, entire, intact, whole; immaculate, unbruised, undamaged, unimpaired, uninjured, unmarred, unspoiled; exceptional, fancy, high-grade, special; accurate, correct, exact, precise; infallible, unerring, unfailing
near antonyms deficient, inadequate, incomplete, insufficient, wanting; unfinished, unpolished; fallible; blemished, blighted, broken, damaged, defaced, disfigured, impaired, injured, marred, spoiled, vitiated; atrocious, execrable, wretched; imprecise, inaccurate, incorrect, inexact, wrong
antonyms bad, censurable, defective, faulty, flawed, imperfect, reproachable
2 having no exceptions or restrictions — see ABSOLUTE 2
3 not lacking any part or member that properly belongs to it — see COMPLETE 1
perfect *vb* **1** to bring (something) to a state where nothing remains to be done — see FINISH 1
2 to make better — see IMPROVE
perfection *n* the most perfect type or example — see QUINTESSENCE 1
perfectly *adv* **1** without any flaws or errors ⟨you did that handspring *perfectly* on your first try⟩
synonyms faultlessly, flawlessly, ideally, impeccably
related words excellently, fabulously, finely, grandly, greatly, marvelously, superbly, superiorly, superlatively, terrifically; exceptionally, fancily, specially
phrases to a nicety, to a T, to a turn
near antonyms deficiently, inadequately, incompletely, insufficiently; fallibly; atrociously, execrably, wretchedly
antonyms badly, defectively, faultily, imperfectly
2 to a full extent or degree — see FULLY 1
perfidious *adj* not true in one's allegiance to someone or something — see FAITHLESS
perfidiousness *n* lack of faithfulness especially to one's husband or wife — see INFIDELITY 1
perfidy *n* **1** lack of faithfulness especially to one's husband or wife — see INFIDELITY 1
2 the act or fact of violating the trust or confidence of another — see BETRAYAL
perforate *vb* to make a hole or series of holes in ⟨he *perforated* the sheet with his pencil and put it in his binder⟩
synonyms bore, drill, hole, pierce, punch, puncture
related words broach, tap; poke, prick; penetrate; burrow (into), excavate, gouge, groove, hollow; break, cut, gash, notch, rend, rupture, slash, slit, split
near antonyms fill, patch, plug, seal
perforation *n* **1** a mark or small hole made by a pointed instrument — see PRICK 1
2 a place in a surface allowing passage into or through a thing — see HOLE 1
perforce *adv* because of necessity — see NEEDS
perform *vb* **1** to carry through (as a process) to completion ⟨she *performed* the task quickly and expertly⟩
synonyms accomplish, achieve, carry out, commit, compass, do, execute, follow through, fulfill (*or* fulfil), make
related words bring about, effect, effectuate, implement; engage (in), practice (*or* practise); work (at); reduplicate, reenact, repeat; actualize, attain, realize; complete, end, finish, wind up
phrases go through
near antonyms fail; skimp, slight, slur
2 to have a certain purpose — see FUNCTION
3 to present a portrayal or performance of — see ACT 1
4 to produce a desired effect — see ACT 2
performance *n* the doing of an action — see COMMISSION 2
perfume *n* a sweet or pleasant smell — see FRAGRANCE
perfume *vb* to fill or infuse with a pleasant odor or odor-releasing substance — see SCENT 1
perfumed *adj* having a pleasant smell — see FRAGRANT
perfunctory *adj* having or showing a lack of interest or concern — see INDIFFERENT 1
perhaps *adv* it is possible ⟨*perhaps* we will not have to take this exam, but I doubt it⟩
synonyms conceivably, maybe, mayhap, perchance, possibly
related words likely, probably; certainly, doubtless, surely, undoubtedly; presumably
peril *n* **1** something that may cause injury or harm — see DANGER 2
2 the state of not being protected from injury, harm, or evil — see DANGER 1
perilous *adj* involving potential loss or injury — see DANGEROUS
perimeter *n* the line or relatively narrow space that marks the outer limit of something — see BORDER 1
period *n* **1** an occurrence of menstruating ⟨girls having their *period* will be excused from gym class⟩
synonyms menstruation, monthlies
related words menses
2 an extent of time associated with a particular person or thing — see AGE 1
periodic *adj* **1** appearing in parts or numbers that follow regularly — see SERIAL
2 appearing or occurring repeatedly from time to time — see REGULAR 1
3 occurring or appearing at intervals — see INTERMITTENT 1
periodical *adj* **1** appearing in parts or numbers that follow regularly — see SERIAL
2 occurring or appearing at intervals — see INTERMITTENT 1
periodical *n* a publication that appears at regular intervals — see JOURNAL
peripatetic *adj* traveling from place to place — see ITINERANT
peripheral *adj* available to supply something extra when needed — see AUXILIARY
periphery *n* the line or relatively narrow space that marks the outer limit of something — see BORDER 1
perish *vb* to stop living — see DIE 1
perk (up) *vb* **1** to become glad or hopeful — see CHEER (UP) 1

2 to move from a lower to a higher place or position — see RAISE 1

perky *adj* having much high-spirited energy and movement — see LIVELY 1

permanent *adj* lasting forever — see EVERLASTING

permanently *adv* for all time — see EVER 1

permeable *adj* capable of being passed into or through — see PENETRABLE

permeate *vb* to spread throughout ⟨the smell of freshly baked bread *permeated* the house⟩
synonyms interpenetrate, percolate (into), pervade, suffuse, transfuse
related words diffuse (through), impregnate, pass (into), penetrate; fill (up); drench, infuse, saturate, soak, steep; flood, glut

permissible *adj* that may be permitted ⟨fortunately, that is a *permissible* shortcut to the answer⟩
synonyms admissible, allowable, licensable
related words acceptable, bearable, endurable, tolerable; accredited, allowed, authorized, certified, endorsed, licensed (*also* licenced), OK (*or* okay), permitted, sanctioned, warranted; mandatory, ordered, required
near antonyms intolerable, unacceptable, unbearable, unendurable; objectionable; denied, disallowed, refused, rejected, vetoed; repressed, suppressed; outlawed
antonyms banned, barred, forbidden, impermissible, inadmissible, interdicted, prohibited, proscribed

permission *n* the approval by someone in authority for the doing of something ⟨she asked for *permission* to have a piece of candy⟩ ⟨the President granted *permission* for the foreign diplomats to have special quarters⟩
synonyms allowance, authorization, clearance, concurrence, consent, granting, leave, license (*or* licence), sanction, sufferance
related words imprimatur, seal, signature, stamp; accreditation, certification; liberty, pass; concession, patent, permit; acceptance, acquiescence, agreement, assent, OK (*or* okay); accord, grant
near antonyms denial, refusal, rejection, revocation; taboo; injunction, veto; deterrence, discouragement, repression, suppression; ban, embargo, exclusion
antonyms interdiction, prohibition, proscription

permit *vb* **1** to give permission for or to approve of — see ALLOW 1
2 to give permission to — see ALLOW 2
3 to make able or possible — see ENABLE 1

pernicious *adj* causing or capable of causing harm — see HARMFUL

perpendicular *adj* rising straight up — see ERECT

perpetration *n* the doing of an action — see COMMISSION 2

perpetual *adj* lasting forever — see EVERLASTING

perpetually *adv* **1** for all time — see EVER 1
2 on every relevant occasion — see ALWAYS 1

perpetuate *vb* to give eternal or lasting existence to ⟨we hope to *perpetuate* this holiday tradition⟩
synonyms immortalize
related words commemorate, memorialize; celebrate, enshrine, honor; conserve, keep up, maintain, preserve, support, sustain; defend, guard, protect, safeguard
near antonyms extinguish, put out, snuff (out); annihilate, crush, decimate, demolish, destroy, devastate; eradicate, erase, expunge, extirpate, obliterate, wipe out

perpetuity *n* endless time — see ETERNITY 1

perplex *vb* **1** to make complex or difficult — see COMPLICATE
2 to throw into a state of mental uncertainty — see CONFUSE 1

perplexity *n* a state of mental uncertainty — see CONFUSION 1

perquisite *n* **1** a small sum of money given for a service over and above what is due — see [2]TIP 1
2 something given in addition to what is ordinarily expected or owed — see BONUS

persecute *vb* **1** to cause persistent suffering to — see AFFLICT
2 to disturb the peace of mind of (someone) especially by repeated disagreeable acts — see IRRITATE 1

persecutor *n* **1** a person who causes repeated emotional pain, distress, or annoyance to another — see TORMENTOR
2 one who is obnoxiously annoying — see NUISANCE 1

persevere *vb* to continue despite difficulties, opposition, or discouragement ⟨although he was frustrated by the lack of financial resources and support, he *persevered* in his scientific research⟩
synonyms carry on, persist
related words hang on; follow through; knuckle down
phrases hang in there
near antonyms give up, quit, surrender, yield; falter, hesitate, vacillate, waver

persevering *adj* continuing despite difficulties, opposition, or discouragement — see PERSISTENT

persiflage *n* good-natured teasing or exchanging of clever remarks — see BANTER

persist *vb* **1** to continue despite difficulties, opposition, or discouragement — see PERSEVERE
2 to remain indefinitely in existence or in the same state — see CONTINUE 1

persistence *n* **1** continuing existence ⟨the *persistence* of the child's fever made us start to worry⟩
synonyms continuance, durability, endurance
related words longevity, staying power, tenacity; permanence; survival; continuation
near antonyms discontinuance; cessation, desisting, ending, finish, quitting, stop
2 uninterrupted or lasting existence — see CONTINUATION
3 a steadfast adherence to an opinion, purpose, or course of action — see OBSTINACY

persistent *adj* continuing despite difficulties, opposition, or discouragement ⟨although his first attempts were unsuccessful, he was *persistent* in his pursuit of a career in rock music⟩
synonyms dogged, insistent, patient, persevering, pertinacious, tenacious
related words assured, certain, dedicated, determined, firm, intent, positive, resolute, resolved, single-minded, sure; hardheaded, headstrong, mulish, obdurate, obstinate, opinionated, peevish, perverse, pigheaded, self-willed, stubborn, unyielding; unfaltering, unhesitating, unwavering; resistant, wayward, wrongheaded; constant, devoted, faithful, good, loyal, staunch (*or* stanch), steadfast, steady, true; indomitable, unconquerable; hard, inflexible, relentless, stern, unbending, unrelenting, unyielding
near antonyms quitting, surrendering, yielding;

faltering, hesitant, hesitating, irresolute, vacillating, wavering; disloyal, faithless, false, fickle, inconstant, perfidious, traitorous, treacherous
person *n* a member of the human race — see HUMAN
personage *n* a person who is widely known and usually much talked about — see CELEBRITY 1
personal *adj* of, relating to, or belonging to a single person — see INDIVIDUAL 1
personality *n* **1** a person who is widely known and usually much talked about — see CELEBRITY 1
2 the set of qualities that make a person different from other people — see INDIVIDUALITY
3 the set of qualities that makes a person, a group of people, or a thing different from others — see NATURE 1
personalize *vb* to represent in visible form — see EMBODY 2
personalized *adj* of, relating to, or belonging to a single person — see INDIVIDUAL 1
personally *adv* in person and usually privately — see TÊTE-À-TÊTE
personalty *n* transportable items that one owns — see POSSESSION 2
personification *n* a visible representation of something abstract (as a quality) — see EMBODIMENT
personify *vb* to represent in visible form — see EMBODY 2
personnel *n* a body of persons at work or available for work — see FORCE 1
perspective *n* a way of looking at or thinking about something — see POINT OF VIEW
perspicuity *n* clearness of expression — see SIMPLICITY 2
perspicuous *adj* not subject to misinterpretation or more than one interpretation — see CLEAR 2
perspicuousness *n* clearness of expression — see SIMPLICITY 2
persuade *vb* to cause (someone) to agree with a belief or course of action by using arguments or earnest request <she *persuaded* us that she can indeed communicate with the dead> <he *persuaded* his teachers to grant an extension>
synonyms argue, convince, get, induce, move, prevail (on *or* upon), satisfy, talk (into), win (over)
related words cajole, coax, exhort, urge; lead on, seduce, snow, tempt; incline, influence, move, prompt, sell, sway; attract, bring, draw, entice, interest; chew over, converse, debate, discuss, dispute, hash (over), moot; reason (with)
near antonyms dissuade
persuading *n* the act of reasoning or pleading with someone to accept a belief or course of action — see PERSUASION 1
persuasion *n* **1** the act of reasoning or pleading with someone to accept a belief or course of action <the suffragists' gradual *persuasion* of the American people that voting rights had to be extended to women>
synonyms convincing, inducement, inducing, persuading, suasion
related words cajolery, coaxing, exhortation, urging; seduction, tempting; influencing, prompting, swaying; lobbying, pressuring
2 a body of beliefs and practices regarding the supernatural and the worship of one or more deities — see RELIGION 1
3 an idea that is believed to be true or valid without positive knowledge — see OPINION 1
persuasive *adj* having the power to persuade — see COGENT
persuasiveness *n* the capacity to persuade — see COGENCY 1
pert *adj* **1** having much high-spirited energy and movement — see LIVELY 1
2 making light of something usually regarded as serious or sacred — see FLIPPANT
pertain *vb* **1** to be the property of a person or group of persons — see BELONG 2
2 to have a relation or connection — see APPLY 1
pertain (to) *vb* to have (something) as a subject matter — see CONCERN 1
pertinacious *adj* **1** continuing despite difficulties, opposition, or discouragement — see PERSISTENT
2 sticking to an opinion, purpose, or course of action in spite of reason, arguments, or persuasion — see OBSTINATE
pertinaciousness *n* a steadfast adherence to an opinion, purpose, or course of action — see OBSTINACY
pertinacity *n* a steadfast adherence to an opinion, purpose, or course of action — see OBSTINACY
pertinence *n* the fact or state of being pertinent <job applicants should question the *pertinence* of any questions about their personal lives>
synonyms applicability, bearing, connection, materiality, relevance, relevancy
related words appropriateness, aptness, fitness, suitability; importance, significance; usefulness
near antonyms inappropriateness, inaptness, unfitness, unsuitability; insignificance, unimportance; pointlessness, uselessness
antonyms extraneousness, inapplicability, irrelevance
pertinent *adj* having to do with the matter at hand <he impressed the jury with his concise, *pertinent* answers to the attorney's questions>
synonyms applicable, apposite, apropos, germane, material, pointed, relative, relevant
related words appropriate, apt, fit, fitting, suitable; important, meaningful, significant; sensible, useful; admissible, allowable
phrases in point, to the point
near antonyms inconsequential, insignificant, unimportant; meaningless, purposeless, senseless, useless; inappropriate, inapt, unsuitable; inadmissible
antonyms extraneous, immaterial, inapplicable, irrelevant, pointless
pertly *adv* in a quick and spirited manner — see GAILY 2
pertness *n* shameless boldness — see EFFRONTERY
perturb *vb* to trouble the mind of; to make uneasy — see DISTURB 1
perturbation *n* an uneasy state of mind usually over the possibility of an anticipated misfortune or trouble — see ANXIETY 1
perturbed *adj* feeling or showing uncomfortable feelings of uncertainty — see NERVOUS 1
perturbing *adj* causing worry or anxiety — see TROUBLESOME
peruse *vb* to go over and mentally take in the content of — see READ
pervade *vb* to spread throughout — see PERMEATE
perverse *adj* **1** easily irritated or annoyed — see IRRITABLE
2 having or showing lowered moral character or standards — see CORRUPT

3 sticking to an opinion, purpose, or course of action in spite of reason, arguments, or persuasion — see OBSTINATE

perverseness *n* readiness to show annoyance or impatience — see PETULANCE

perversion *n* **1** a sinking to a state of low moral standards and behavior — see CORRUPTION 2
2 incorrect or improper use — see MISUSE

perversity *n* readiness to show annoyance or impatience — see PETULANCE

pervert *n* a person who has sunk below the normal moral standard — see DEGENERATE

pervert *vb* **1** to change so much as to create a wrong impression or alter the meaning of — see GARBLE
2 to lower in character or dignity — see DEBASE 1
3 to put to a bad or improper use — see MISAPPLY

perverted *adj* having or showing lowered moral character or standards — see CORRUPT

pessimist *n* **1** one who emphasizes bad aspects or conditions and expects the worst ⟨she's such a *pessimist* that she's convinced she'll fail every test⟩
synonyms defeatist
related words cynic, fatalist; pragmatist, realist
near antonyms dreamer, idealist, romantic, utopian, visionary; sentimentalist
antonyms optimist
2 a person who distrusts other people and believes that everything is done for selfish reasons — see CYNIC

pessimistic *adj* **1** emphasizing or expecting the worst ⟨with that *pessimistic* attitude, it's no wonder you're depressed⟩
synonyms defeatist, despairing, hopeless
related words cynical, fatalistic; desperate, discouraging, disheartening, inauspicious, unlikely, unpromising; bleak, cheerless, comfortless, dismal, dreary, gloomy; grim; contrary, hostile, negative
near antonyms auspicious, encouraging, fair, heartening, likely, promising, propitious; cheering, comforting, reassuring; favorable, good, positive; idealist, romantic, utopian, visionary
antonyms hopeful, optimistic, rose-colored, rosy, upbeat
2 having or showing a deep distrust of human beings and their motives — see CYNICAL

pest *n* **1** a widespread disease resulting in a high rate of death — see PLAGUE
2 one who is obnoxiously annoying — see NUISANCE 1
3 something that is a source of irritation — see ANNOYANCE 3

pester *vb* to thrust oneself upon (another) without invitation — see BOTHER 1

pestering *n* the act of making unwelcome intrusions upon another — see ANNOYANCE 1

pestilence *n* a widespread disease resulting in a high rate of death — see PLAGUE

pestilent *adj* likely to cause or capable of causing death — see DEADLY

pesty *adj* causing annoyance — see ANNOYING

pet *adj* granted special treatment or attention — see DARLING 1

pet *n* **1** a person or thing that is preferred over others — see FAVORITE
2 a state of resentful silence or irritability — see SULK

pet *vb* **1** to touch or handle in a tender or loving manner — see FONDLE
2 to touch one another with the lips as a sign of love — see KISS 1

petition *n* an earnest request — see PLEA 1

petition *vb* to make a request to (someone) in an earnest or urgent manner — see BEG

petitioner *n* one who asks earnestly for a favor or gift — see SUPPLICANT

pettish *adj* easily irritated or annoyed — see IRRITABLE

pettishness *n* readiness to show annoyance or impatience — see PETULANCE

petty *adj* **1** not broad or open in views or opinions — see NARROW 2
2 so small or unimportant as to warrant little or no attention — see NEGLIGIBLE 1

petulance *n* readiness to show annoyance or impatience ⟨I do not appreciate your *petulance* and eagerness to argue⟩
synonyms biliousness, crankiness, crossness, crotchetiness, grouchiness, grumpiness, huffiness, irascibility, irritability, irritableness, peevishness, perverseness, perversity, pettishness, testiness, waspishness
related words cantankerousness, disagreeableness, dyspepsia, fretfulness, orneriness, sulkiness, surliness; aggression, aggressiveness, bellicosity, belligerence, combativeness, contentiousness, contrariness, disputatiousness, fight, pugnacity, scrappiness, truculence; fussiness, querulousness, rudeness; oversensitiveness, sensitivity; antagonism, fierceness, hostility, unfriendliness; anger, exasperation, rage, wrath; hot-bloodedness, passion
near antonyms forbearance, patience, tolerance, understanding; affability, amicability, cordiality, friendliness, sociability; amiability, good-humoredness, good-naturedness, good-temperedness; coolness, serenity, tranquility; easygoingness, gentleness, kindliness, mildness

petulant *adj* easily irritated or annoyed — see IRRITABLE

pewter *adj* of the color gray — see GRAY 1

phantasm *n* **1** a conception or image created by the imagination and having no objective reality — see FANTASY 1
2 the soul of a dead person thought of especially as appearing to living people — see GHOST

phantasmal *adj* not real and existing only in the imagination — see IMAGINARY

phantom *adj* not real and existing only in the imagination — see IMAGINARY

phantom *n* the soul of a dead person thought of especially as appearing to living people — see GHOST

pharmaceutical *n* a substance or preparation used to treat disease — see MEDICINE

pharmacist *n* a person who prepares drugs according to a doctor's prescription — see DRUGGIST

pharmacy *n* a retail store where medicines and miscellaneous articles are sold — see DRUGSTORE

phase *n* **1** a certain way in which something appears or may be regarded — see ASPECT 1
2 an individual part of a process, series, or ranking — see DEGREE 1

phased *adj* proceeding or changing by steps or degrees — see GRADUAL

phenomenal *adj* **1** being out of the ordinary — see EXCEPTIONAL
2 being so extraordinary or abnormal as to sug-

gest powers which violate the laws of nature — see SUPERNATURAL 2

phenomenon *n* something extraordinary or surprising — see WONDER 1

philanthropic *adj* having or showing a concern for the welfare of others — see CHARITABLE 1

philanthropy *n* **1** a gift of money or its equivalent to a charity, humanitarian cause, or public institution — see CONTRIBUTION

2 the giving of necessities and especially money to the needy — see CHARITY 1

3 the quality or state of being generous — see LIBERALITY

philharmonic *n* a usually large group of musicians playing together — see [2]BAND 1

philistine *n* a person who is chiefly interested in material comfort and is hostile or indifferent to art and culture ⟨the town's *philistines* who think that spending on the arts is a waste of taxpayers' money⟩

synonyms lowbrow, materialist

related words capitalist, plutocrat; boor, cad, churl, clown, creep, cur, jerk, lout

near antonyms highbrow; egghead, intellectual, sage, thinker; brain, genius

philosophy *n* the basic beliefs or guiding principles of a person or group — see CREED 1

phlegm *n* a lack of emotion or emotional expressiveness — see APATHY 1

phlegmatic *adj* not feeling or showing emotion — see IMPASSIVE 1

phone *vb* to make a telephone call to — see CALL 2

phony *also* **phoney** *adj* **1** being such in appearance only and made or manufactured with the intention of committing fraud — see COUNTERFEIT

2 lacking in natural or spontaneous quality — see ARTIFICIAL 1

phony *also* **phoney** *n* **1** an imitation that is passed off as genuine — see FAKE 1

2 one who makes false claims of identity or expertise — see IMPOSTOR

photo *n* a picture created from an image recorded on a light-sensitive surface by a camera — see PHOTOGRAPH

photo *vb* to take a photograph of — see PHOTOGRAPH

photograph *n* a picture created from an image recorded on a light-sensitive surface by a camera ⟨the old *photograph* was faded but still clear enough to make out⟩

synonyms photo, print, shot, snap, snapshot

related words blowup, close-up, enlargement, still; daguerreotype, monochrome, tintype

photograph *vb* to take a photograph of ⟨we *photographed* the baby birds frequently⟩

synonyms mug, photo, shoot, snap

related words image, picture, retake; film, videotape

phrases capture on film

photographer *n* one who takes photographs ⟨we'll need to choose a *photographer* for the wedding⟩

synonyms shooter, shutterbug

related words cinematographer

phrase *n* a sequence of words having a specific meaning ⟨draw a literal representation of the *phrase* "to rain cats and dogs"⟩

synonyms expression, idiom

related words cliché; locution, term; epithet, expletive, name; byword, cry, motto, shibboleth, slogan, watchword; archaism, colloquialism, euphemism, modernism, neologism, provincialism, vulgarism

phrases figure of speech

phrase *vb* to convey in appropriate or telling terms ⟨he had trouble thinking of how to *phrase* his question for the visiting dignitary⟩

synonyms articulate, clothe, couch, express, formulate, put, say, state, word

related words craft, frame; hint, imply, insinuate, intimate, suggest; paraphrase, rephrase, restate, reword, summarize, translate; communicate, disclose, speak, tell; describe, render, write up

phraseology *n* **1** a distinctive way of putting ideas into words — see STYLE 1

2 the way in which something is put into words — see WORDING

phrasing *n* the way in which something is put into words — see WORDING

phylactery *n* something worn or kept to bring good luck or keep away evil — see CHARM 1

physic *n* a substance or preparation used to treat disease — see MEDICINE

physical *adj* **1** of or relating to the human body ⟨*physical* sensations such as heat and pain⟩

synonyms animal, bodily, carnal, corporal, corporeal, fleshly, material, somatic

related words anatomic (*or* anatomical), physiological; sensual, sensuous; hand-to-hand

near antonyms intellectual, mental, psychological (*also* psychologic); bodiless, immaterial, incorporeal, spiritual; ethereal, metaphysical, psychic (*also* psychical)

antonyms nonmaterial, nonphysical

2 relating to or composed of matter — see MATERIAL 1

physician *n* a person specially trained in healing human medical disorders — see DOCTOR

physique *n* the type of body that a person has ⟨she had a well-toned *physique*⟩

synonyms build, constitution, figure, form, frame, shape

related words anatomy, structure

picayune *adj* so small or unimportant as to warrant little or no attention — see NEGLIGIBLE 1

pick *n* **1** a person or thing that is chosen — see CHOICE 2

2 individuals carefully selected as being the best of a class — see ELITE

3 the power, right, or opportunity to choose — see CHOICE 1

pick *vb* **1** to catch or collect (a crop or natural resource) for human use — see HARVEST

2 to decide to accept (someone or something) from a group of possibilities — see CHOOSE 1

picked *adj* singled out from a number or group as more to one's liking — see SELECT 1

picked up *adj* being clean and in good order — see NEAT 1

picker *n* someone with the right or responsibility for making a selection — see SELECTOR

picket *n* a person or group that watches over someone or something — see GUARD 1

picking *n* the act or process of selecting — see SELECTION 1

pickle *n* a difficult, puzzling, or embarrassing situation from which there is no easy escape — see PREDICAMENT

pick up *vb* **1** to acquire complete knowledge, understanding, or skill in — see LEARN 1

2 to bring together in one body or place — see GATHER 1
3 to get possession of (something) by giving money in exchange for — see BUY
4 to increase in — see GAIN 1
5 to move from a lower to a higher place or position — see RAISE 1
6 to take or keep under one's control by authority of law — see ARREST 1

picky *adj* **1** hard to please — see FINICKY
2 tending to select carefully — see SELECTIVE

picnic *n* something that is easy to do — see CINCH

pictorial *adj* **1** consisting of or relating to pictures ⟨he's planning to do a primarily *pictorial* report on Africa⟩
synonyms graphic (*also* graphical), visual
related words photographic, video; drawn, painted, represented; illustrative; pictographic
2 producing a mental picture through clear and impressive description — see GRAPHIC 1

picture *n* **1** a two-dimensional design intended to look like a person or thing ⟨she produced a beautiful *picture* of her mother using watercolors⟩
synonyms illustration, image, likeness
related words delineation, depiction, representation; portrait; drawing, finger painting; etching, silhouette, sketch, watercolor; caricature, cartoon, doodle; collage, montage, photograph; hieroglyphic, ideogram; pictograph
2 a story told by means of a series of continuously projected pictures and a sound track — see MOVIE 1
3 a vivid representation in words of someone or something — see DESCRIPTION 1
4 position with regard to conditions and circumstances — see SITUATION 1
5 something or someone that strongly resembles another — see IMAGE 1
6 something imagined or pictured in the mind — see IDEA
7 pictures *pl* the art or business of making a movie — see MOVIE 2

picture *vb* **1** to present a picture of ⟨the famous painting that *pictures* the Founding Fathers signing the Declaration of Independence⟩
synonyms depict, image, portray, represent
related words delineate, describe, render; outline, sketch; illustrate, show; caricature
2 to form a mental picture of — see IMAGINE 1
3 to give a representation or account of in words — see DESCRIBE 1

picturesque *adj* producing a mental picture through clear and impressive description — see GRAPHIC 1

piddling *adj* so small or unimportant as to warrant little or no attention — see NEGLIGIBLE 1

piebald *adj* having blotches of two or more colors — see PIED

piece *n* **1** a broken or irregular part of something that often remains incomplete — see FRAGMENT
2 a literary, musical, or artistic production — see COMPOSITION 1
3 a portable weapon from which a shot is discharged by gunpowder — see GUN 1

piece *vb* to form by putting together parts or materials — see BUILD

piece by piece *adv* by small steps or amounts — see GRADUALLY

piecemeal *adj* proceeding or changing by steps or degrees — see GRADUAL

piecemeal *adv* **1** by small steps or amounts — see GRADUALLY
2 into parts or to pieces — see APART

pied *adj* having blotches of two or more colors ⟨although the mother's was pure black, the foal's coat was *pied*⟩
synonyms blotched, dappled (*also* dapple), marbled, mottled, piebald, pinto, splotched, spotted
related words shaded; checkered, motley, multicolored, polychromatic, polychrome, varicolored, variegated; blotted, brindled (*or* brindle), specked, speckled, streaked; colored, colorful, pigmented; dotted, peppered, sprinkled; stippled; discolored, dyed, marked, stained; flecked, streaked; bespattered, spattered
near antonyms monochromatic, solid

pier *n* **1** a structure used by boats and ships for taking on or landing cargo and passengers — see DOCK
2 an upright shaft that supports an overhead structure — see PILLAR 1

pierce *vb* **1** to go or come in or into — see ENTER 1
2 to make a hole or series of holes in — see PERFORATE
3 to penetrate or hold (something) with a pointed object — see IMPALE

piercing *adj* **1** causing intense discomfort to one's skin — see CUTTING 1
2 marked by a high volume of sound — see LOUD 1

piety *n* **1** belief and trust in and loyalty to God — see FAITH 1
2 the quality or state of being spiritually pure or virtuous — see HOLINESS

piffle *n* **1** language, behavior, or ideas that are absurd and contrary to good sense — see NONSENSE 1
2 unintelligible or meaningless talk — see GIBBERISH

pigeon *n* one who is easily deceived or cheated — see DUPE

piggish *adj* having a huge appetite — see VORACIOUS 1

pigheaded *adj* sticking to an opinion, purpose, or course of action in spite of reason, arguments, or persuasion — see OBSTINATE

pigment *n* a substance used to color other materials ⟨I'm running out of the black *pigment*⟩
synonyms color, coloring, dye, dyestuff, stain, tincture
related words cast, hue, shade, tinge, tint, tone

pig out *vb* to eat greedily or to excess — see GORGE 2

pigpen *n* a dirty or messy place ⟨your room is a *pigpen* —so clean it up!⟩
synonyms hole, pigsty, shambles
related words chaos, confusion, disarrangement, disarray, disorder, jumble, mess, muddle; dump; clutter, litter, mishmash

pigsty *n* a dirty or messy place — see PIGPEN

[1]**pike** *n* a passage cleared for public vehicular travel — see WAY 1

[2]**pike** *n* a weapon with a long straight handle and sharp head or blade — see SPEAR

[3]**pike** *n* the last and usually sharp or tapering part of something long and narrow — see POINT 2

piker *n* a mean grasping person who is usually stingy with money — see MISER

pikestaff *n* a weapon with a long straight handle and sharp head or blade — see SPEAR

pilaster *n* an upright shaft that supports an overhead structure — see PILLAR 1

[1]**pile** *n* **1** a quantity of things thrown or stacked on one another ⟨a large *pile* of newspapers that needed to be disposed of⟩
synonyms cock, heap, hill, mound, mountain, rick, stack
related words bank, bar, drift, embankment; pyramid; barrow, cairn, pyre; accumulation, aggregate, assemblage, collection, conglomeration, gathering, grouping, hoard, jumble
2 a considerable amount — see LOT 2

[2]**pile** *n* **1** a soft airy substance or covering — see FUZZ
2 the hairy covering of a mammal especially when fine, soft, and thick — see FUR 1

pile *vb* to lay or throw on top of one another ⟨*piled* all the clothes on the chair before putting them away⟩
synonyms heap, mound, stack
related words bank; layer, pyramid; accumulate, amass, assemble, collect, gather, group, mass; bunch, clump, lump
antonyms unpile

pile (up) *vb* to gradually form into a layer, pile, or mass — see COLLECT 2

pilfer *vb* to take (something) without right and with an intent to keep — see STEAL 1

pilgrimage *vb* to take a trip especially of some distance — see TRAVEL 1

pill *n* a small mass containing medicine to be taken orally ⟨you'll have to take one of these *pills* every six hours for your flu⟩
synonyms capsule, lozenge, tablet
related words drug, medication, pharmaceutical, specific; miracle drug, wonder drug; potion, preparation; dosage, dose, drop, sleeping pill, tranquilizer (*also* tranquillizer)

pillage *vb* to search through with the intent of committing robbery — see RANSACK 1

pillar *n* **1** an upright shaft that supports an overhead structure ⟨the ancient Greek temple boasted graceful marble *pillars* with richly ornamented tops⟩
synonyms column, pier, pilaster, post, stanchion
related words caryatid, pedestal; buttress, flying buttress; needle, obelisk
2 something or someone to which one looks for support — see DEPENDENCE 2

pilot *adj* made or done as an experiment — see EXPERIMENTAL 1

pilot *n* one who flies or is qualified to fly an aircraft or spacecraft ⟨the airline is seeking experienced *pilots* to fly the new airplane⟩
synonyms airman, aviator, birdman, flier (*or* flyer)
related words ace, bush pilot, copilot, test pilot

pilot *vb* **1** to give advice and instruction to (someone) regarding the course or process to be followed — see GUIDE 1
2 to point out the way for (someone) especially from a position in front — see LEAD 1

pin *n* a lower limb of an animal — see LEG 1

pinch *n* an instance of theft — see THEFT 2
2 the act of taking or holding under one's control by authority of law — see ARREST

pinch *vb* **1** to squeeze tightly between two surfaces, edges, or points ⟨the zipper on those jeans always *pinches* me⟩
synonyms nip
related words clasp, clutch, grasp, grip
near antonyms drop, free, loose, loosen, release
2 to take (something) without right and with an intent to keep — see STEAL 1
3 to take or keep under one's control by authority of law — see ARREST 1

pincher *n* one who steals — see THIEF

pinch–hit *vb* to serve as a replacement usually for a time only — see COVER 1

pinch hitter *n* a person or thing that takes the place of another — see SUBSTITUTE

pinching *adj* giving or sharing as little as possible — see STINGY 1

pinching *n* the quality of being overly sparing with money — see PARSIMONY

pine (for) *vb* to have an earnest wish to own or enjoy — see DESIRE

pinhead *n* a stupid person — see IDIOT

pinhole *n* a mark or small hole made by a pointed instrument — see PRICK 1

pining *n* a strong wish for something — see DESIRE

pinnacle *n* the highest part or point — see HEIGHT 1

pinpoint *adj* meeting the highest standard of accuracy — see PRECISE 1

pinpoint *vb* to find out or establish the identity of — see IDENTIFY 1

pinprick *n* a mark or small hole made by a pointed instrument — see PRICK 1

pinto *adj* having blotches of two or more colors — see PIED

pint–size *or* **pint–sized** *adj* of a size that is less than average — see SMALL 1

pioneer *adj* coming before all others in time or order — see FIRST 1

pioneer *n* a person who settles in a new region — see FRONTIERSMAN

pioneer *vb* to be responsible for the creation and early operation or use of — see FOUND

pious *adj* **1** firm in one's allegiance to someone or something — see FAITHFUL 1
2 showing a devotion to God and to a life of virtue — see HOLY 1

piousness *n* **1** the pretending of having virtues, principles, or beliefs that one in fact does not have — see HYPOCRISY
2 the quality or state of being spiritually pure or virtuous — see HOLINESS

pip *n* something very good of its kind — see JIM-DANDY

pipe *n* **1** a long hollow cylinder for carrying a substance (as a liquid or gas) ⟨the plumber came and fixed the water *pipe* that was leaking⟩
synonyms channel, conduit, duct, leader, line, penstock, trough, tube
related words drain, drainpipe, funnel, hydrant, main, smokestack, spout, stovepipe, tile, waterspout; pipeline, piping
2 an enclosed wooden vessel for holding beverages — see CASK

pipe *vb* **1** to cause to move to a central point or along a restricted pathway — see CHANNEL
2 to make a short sharp sound like a small bird — see CHIRP

pipe dream *n* a conception or image created by the imagination and having no objective reality — see FANTASY 1

pipeline *n* a direct way of passing along information or supplies ⟨an equipment hauler serves as the columnist's *pipeline* for gossip about the rock band⟩ ⟨the battle was ultimately lost because the enemy had destroyed our *pipeline* for resupply⟩

synonyms channel

related words conduit; grapevine, outlet; fountainhead, origin, source, wellspring; supplier; connection, contact

piping *adj* having a high musical pitch or range — see SHRILL

piping hot *adj* having a notably high temperature — see HOT 1

piquancy *n* the quality or state of being stimulating to the mind or senses ⟨a talk show host known for the quickness and *piquancy* of his wit⟩ ⟨I appreciated the *piquancy* of the peppers in the sauce⟩

synonyms pungency, zest

related words raciness, spiciness; fieriness, hotness; acuteness, keenness, sharpness; provocativeness; excitement, invigoration, stimulation, thrill; flavor, savor, tastiness

near antonyms flatness, tastelessness; dullness (*also* dulness), monotonousness, predictability, tediousness; blandness, thinness, weakness

antonyms insipidity

piquant *adj* sharp and pleasantly stimulating to the mind or senses ⟨a *piquant* tidbit of information about the new neighbors⟩ ⟨the *piquant* cuisine of India boasts some highly spiced dishes⟩

synonyms pungent, zesty

related words racy, spicy; fiery, hot; acute, keen; biting, bitter, cutting, mordant, trenchant; animating, energizing, enlightening, exciting, galvanizing, invigorating, provocative; appetizing, delectable, delicious, palatable, toothsome; flavorful, savory, tasty; absorbing, engaging, engrossing, enthralling, fascinating, gripping, interesting, intriguing

near antonyms flat, flavorless, savorless, tasteless; banal, boring, dull, monotonous, pedestrian, predictable, tedious, tiring, uninteresting, wearisome, wearying; bland, dilute, thin, watery, weak

antonyms insipid

pique *n* the feeling of being offended or resentful after a slight or indignity ⟨she's still in a *pique* over being snubbed by a so-called friend at the party⟩

synonyms dudgeon, huff, offense (*or* offence), peeve, resentment, umbrage

related words aggravation, anger, annoyance, bother, discomfort, exasperation, frustration, irritation, vexation; agitation, angriness, displeasure, distress, disturbance, indignation, irateness, ire, outrage, perturbation, upset; dander, temper; fit, pet, sulk(s), tantrum, tizzy; affront, insult

near antonyms satisfaction; appeasement, mollification, pacification; delight, pleasure

pique *vb* **1** to disturb the peace of mind of (someone) especially by repeated disagreeable acts — see IRRITATE 1

2 to rouse to strong feeling or action — see PROVOKE 1

piquing *adj* serving or likely to arouse a strong reaction — see PROVOCATIVE

piracy *n* the act or pursuit of robbing ships at sea ⟨many countries have harsh penalties for *piracy* now⟩

synonyms pirating

related words depredation, despoilment, despoliation, looting, marauding, pillaging, plunder, plundering, raiding, robbery; privateering; burglary, housebreaking, stealing, thieving; hijacking (*also* highjacking), rustling

pirate *n* someone who engages in robbery of ships at sea ⟨Sir Francis Drake was a British *pirate* who preyed on Spanish ships with the permission of the British queen⟩

synonyms buccaneer, corsair, freebooter, rover

related words looter, marauder, pillager, plunderer, raider, robber; privateer; burglar, housebreaker, stealer, thief; hijacker, rustler

pirating *n* the act or pursuit of robbing ships at sea — see PIRACY

pirouette *n* a rapid turning about on an axis or central point — see SPIN 1

pirouette *vb* to move in circles around an axis or center — see SPIN 1

pit *n* a sunken area forming a separate space — see HOLE 2

pit–a–pat *vb* to expand and contract in a rhythmic manner — see PULSATE

pitch *n* **1** an act or instance of diving — see DIVE 1

2 the degree to which something rises up from a position level with the horizon — see SLANT

pitch *vb* **1** to fix in an upright position — see ERECT 1

2 to cast oneself head first into deep water — see DIVE

3 to make a series of unsteady side-to-side motions — see ROCK 1

4 to send through the air especially with a quick forward motion of the arm — see THROW

pitch–black *adj* **1** being without light or without much light — see DARK 1

2 having the color of soot or coal — see BLACK 1

pitch–dark *adj* **1** being without light or without much light — see DARK 1

2 having the color of soot or coal — see BLACK 1

pitched *adj* running in a slanting direction — see DIAGONAL

pitcher *n* a handled container for holding and pouring liquids that usually has a lip or a spout ⟨please bring me the *pitcher* full of lemonade from the table⟩

synonyms flagon, jug

related words carafe, decanter; bucket, pail, pot; canteen, cup, flask, mug, stein; barrel, cask, hogshead, pipe, puncheon

pitch in *vb* to make a donation as part of a group effort — see CONTRIBUTE 1

pitchy *adj* having the color of soot or coal — see BLACK 1

piteous *adj* deserving of one's pity — see PATHETIC 1

pitfall *n* **1** a danger or difficulty that is hidden or not easily recognized ⟨buying a house can be full of *pitfalls* for the unwary⟩

synonyms booby trap, catch, snag

related words snare, trap, web; hazard, peril, risk; bombshell, surprise; bait, lure

2 something that may cause injury or harm — see DANGER 2

pith *n* the central part or aspect of something under consideration — see CRUX

pithily *adv* in a few words — see SHORTLY 1

pithiness *n* the quality or state of being marked by or using only few words to convey much meaning — see SUCCINCTNESS

pithy *adj* marked by the use of few words to convey much information or meaning — see CONCISE

pitiable *adj* **1** arousing or deserving of one's loathing and disgust — see CONTEMPTIBLE 1
2 deserving pitying scorn (as for inadequacy) — see PITIFUL 1
3 deserving of one's pity — see PATHETIC 1

pitiful *adj* **1** deserving pitying scorn (as for inadequacy) <that is a *pitiful* attempt at an essay on patriotism; you'll have to do it over>
synonyms contemptible, despicable, pitiable, sorry
related words deplorable, discreditable, disgraceful, disreputable, infamous, notorious; abhorrent, abominable, detestable, hateful, odious; bad, inferior, poor; disgusting, dishonorable, shameful; unworthy, worthless; scandalous, shocking, sordid, unsavory
near antonyms admirable, creditable, laudable, meritorious, praiseworthy; notable, noteworthy, noticeable, outstanding, reputable, worthy; excellent; flawless, perfect; honorable, noble; honest, straight
antonyms decent, presentable, respectable
2 arousing or deserving of one's loathing and disgust — see CONTEMPTIBLE 1
3 deserving of one's pity — see PATHETIC 1

pitiless *adj* having or showing a lack of sympathy or tender feelings — see HARD 1

pittance *n* a very small sum of money — see MITE 1

pitter–patter *vb* to expand and contract in a rhythmic manner — see PULSATE

pity *n* **1** a regrettable or blameworthy act — see CRIME 2
2 the capacity for feeling for another's unhappiness or misfortune — see HEART 1

pity *vb* to have sympathy for <I always *pity* the people who have to work in this freezing weather>
synonyms bleed (for), commiserate (with), condole (with), feel (for), sympathize (with)
related words care (for); grieve (for), sorrow (for); love; tolerate, understand
near antonyms disregard, ignore, neglect, overlook; dislike, hate, scorn

pivot *n* the central part or aspect of something under consideration — see CRUX

pivot *vb* to move (something) in a curved or circular path on or as if on an axis — see TURN 1

pivotal *adj* of the greatest possible importance — see CRUCIAL

pixie *also* **pixy** *n* an imaginary being usually having a small human form and magical powers — see FAIRY

pixieish *adj* tending to or exhibiting reckless playfulness — see MISCHIEVOUS 1

placard *n* a sheet bearing an announcement for posting in a public place — see POSTER

placard *vb* **1** to affix (as a notice) to or on a suitable place — see [1]POST 1
2 to make known openly or publicly — see ANNOUNCE

placate *vb* to lessen the anger or agitation of — see PACIFY

placating *adj* tending to lessen or avoid conflict or hostility — see PACIFIC 1

place *n* **1** the area or space occupied by or intended for something <the *place* chosen for the picnic> <there's the *place* where I left my umbrella>
synonyms locale, locality, location, locus, point, position, site, spot
related words scene; region, section, sector
2 a building, room, or suite of rooms occupied by a service business <we're going to our favorite *place* to eat>
synonyms establishment, joint, parlor, salon
related words spot, station; facility, installation; studio; den, dive, hole
3 an assignment at which one regularly works for pay — see JOB 1
4 an extent or area available for or used up by some activity or thing — see ROOM 1
5 the action for which a person or thing is specially fitted or used or for which a thing exists — see ROLE
6 the place where one lives — see HOME 1
7 the placement of someone or something in relation to others in a vertical arrangement — see RANK 1

place *vb* **1** to arrange something in a certain spot or position <he carefully *placed* the flowers in a vase>
synonyms deposit, dispose, fix, lay, position, put, set, set up, situate, stick
related words rearrange, reorder; orient; establish, locate, settle; assemble, collect; carry; berth, park; affix, anchor, wedge; lay out, line up, queue, rank; set down
near antonyms relocate, remove, take; banish; displace, replace, supplant
2 to arrange or assign according to type — see CLASSIFY 1
3 to decide the size, amount, number, or distance of (something) without actual measurement — see ESTIMATE 2
4 to take or have a certain position within a group arranged in vertical classes — see RANK 1

placid *adj* **1** free from emotional or mental agitation — see CALM 2
2 free from storms or physical disturbance — see CALM 1

placidity *n* **1** a state of freedom from storm or disturbance — see CALM
2 evenness of emotions or temper — see EQUANIMITY

plague *n* a widespread disease resulting in a high rate of death <the Black Death was a *plague* that killed about one third of Europe's population in the Middle Ages>
synonyms pest, pestilence
related words epidemic, pandemic; affection, affliction, contagion, contagious disease, infection, infectious disease, infirmity, malady; curse, scourge

plague *vb* to cause persistent suffering to — see AFFLICT

plain *adj* **1** free from all additions or embellishment <I like my hamburgers *plain*, with no ketchup or relish> <just give us the *plain* facts and none of your snide comments>
synonyms bald, bare, naked, simple, unadorned, undecorated, unvarnished
related words chaste, modest; unexaggerated, unsophisticated; denuded, divested, stripped; dry, laconic, terse; unpretentious; austere, bleak, severe, spartan, stark; inconspicuous, muted, restrained, subdued, toned (down), unobtrusive; conservative, quiet, understated
near antonyms flamboyant, flashy, garish, gaudy, glittery, glitzy, loud, ostentatious, showy, splashy, swank (*or* swanky), tawdry; bedizened, florid, lurid, ornate; exaggerated, overdecorated, over-

done, overwrought; baroque, extravagant, rococo; arrayed, bedecked, decked-out, dressed, garnished, trimmed
antonyms adorned, decorated, embellished, fancy, ornamented
2 free from added matter — see PURE 1
3 free in expressing one's true feelings and opinions — see FRANK
4 going straight to the point clearly and firmly — see STRAIGHTFORWARD 1
5 not subject to misinterpretation or more than one interpretation — see CLEAR 2

plain *adv* in an honest and direct manner — see STRAIGHTFORWARD

plain *n* a broad area of level or rolling treeless country ⟨the first settlers in that area lived on the vast *plains* in lonely log cabins⟩
synonyms down, grassland, prairie, savanna (*also* savannah), steppe, tundra, veld (*or* veldt)
related words pampas; floodplain; bottom, bottomland, flat, lowland; plateau, table, tableland, upland

plainclothesman *n* a person whose business is solving crimes and catching criminals or gathering information that is not easy to get — see DETECTIVE

plainly *adv* in an honest and direct manner — see STRAIGHTFORWARD

plainness *n* **1** the free expression of one's true feelings and opinions — see CANDOR
2 the quality or state of having a form or structure of few parts or elements — see SIMPLICITY 1

plainspoken *adj* free in expressing one's true feelings and opinions — see FRANK

plaint *n* **1** a crying out in grief — see LAMENT 1
2 an expression of dissatisfaction, pain, or resentment — see COMPLAINT 1

plaintiff *n* the person in a legal proceeding who makes a charge of wrongdoing against another — see COMPLAINANT

plaintive *adj* expressing or suggesting mourning — see MOURNFUL 1

plait *n* a length of something formed of three or more strands woven together — see BRAID

plait *vb* to form into a braid — see BRAID

plan *n* **1** a method worked out in advance for achieving some objective ⟨there is a contingency *plan* in the office for handling almost any emergency⟩
synonyms arrangement, blueprint, design, game, ground plan, program, project, scheme, strategy, system
related words collusion, conspiracy, plot; maneuver, ruse, stratagem, subterfuge, trick; means, method, tactic, technique, way; conception, idea, proposal; aim, intention, purpose; diagram, formula, layout, map, policy, recipe, setup
2 something that one hopes or intends to accomplish — see GOAL

plan *vb* **1** to work out the details of (something) in advance ⟨we *planned* the school dance down to the smallest detail⟩
synonyms arrange, blueprint, calculate, chart, design, frame, lay out, map (out), project, schematize, scheme (out)
related words conspire, intrigue, machinate; draft, outline, sketch; aim, figure, intend, mean; contemplate, meditate, premeditate
2 to have in mind as a purpose or goal — see INTEND

plane *adj* having a surface without bends, breaks, or irregularities — see LEVEL

plane *vb* **1** to make free from breaks, curves, or bumps — see EVEN 1
2 to move through the air with or as if with outstretched wings — see FLY 1

planet *n* the celestial body on which we live — see EARTH 1

plant *n* a building or set of buildings for the manufacturing of goods — see FACTORY

plant *vb* to put or set into the ground to grow ⟨I'll *plant* the marigold seeds in the spring⟩
synonyms drill, put in, seed, sow
related words bed; replant, transplant; scatter; pot
near antonyms gather, harvest, reap

plantation *n* a settlement in a new country or region — see COLONY 1

planter *n* a person who cultivates the land and grows crops on it — see FARMER

plash *vb* **1** to flow in a broken irregular stream — see GURGLE
2 to move with a splashing motion — see SLOSH
3 to wet or soil by striking with something liquid or mushy — see SPLASH 2

plaster *n* a medicated covering used to heal an injury — see DRESSING 1

plastic *adj* capable of being easily molded or modeled ⟨Silly Putty is famous for being very *plastic*⟩
synonyms malleable
related words adaptable; ductile, pliable, pliant, supple, willowy; elastic, flexible, resilient, workable; bending, giving, tractable, yielding
near antonyms inflexible, rigid, stiff

plasticity *n* the quality or state of being easily molded ⟨we chose that type of clay for its greater *plasticity*⟩
synonyms malleability
related words adaptability; pliability, suppleness; elasticity, flexibility, resilience
near antonyms inflexibility, rigidity, stiffness

plat *n* **1** a small area of usually open land — see FIELD 1
2 a small piece of land that is developed or available for development — see LOT 1

plate *n* **1** a small thin piece of material that resembles an animal scale — see [2]SCALE
2 something that visually explains or decorates a text — see ILLUSTRATION 1

plateau *n* a broad flat area of elevated land ⟨Native Americans have inhabited the *plateau* for centuries⟩
synonyms mesa, table, tableland
related words butte, dome, height, highland, upland

platform *n* a level usually raised surface ⟨you'll have to stand up there on the *platform* for your speech⟩
synonyms dais, podium, rostrum, stage, stand
related words altar, pulpit; balcony

platitude *n* an idea or expression that has been used by many people — see COMMONPLACE

plaudit *n usually* **plaudits** *pl* enthusiastic and usually public expression of approval — see APPLAUSE

plausible *adj* worthy of being accepted as true or reasonable — see BELIEVABLE

play *n* **1** activity engaged in to amuse oneself ⟨it's such a delight to watch the children in their *play*⟩

synonyms dalliance, frolic, frolicking, fun, recreation, relaxation, rollicking, sport
related words gamboling, romping; amusement, diversion, entertainment; delight, enjoyment, pleasure; friskiness, playfulness, sportiveness, wantonness; devilment, devilry (*or* deviltry), hob, impishness, mischief, mischievousness, rascality, roguishness, waggery; binge, fling, lark, revel, spree; hilarity, merrymaking, revelry; buffoonery, horseplay, tomfoolery
near antonyms drudgery, labor, work; duty, obligation, responsibility
2 a written work in which the story is told through speech and action that is intended to be acted out on stage ⟨we'll be putting on a school *play* using that stage⟩
synonyms drama, dramatization
related words comedy, melodrama, musical, musical comedy, tragedy, tragicomedy; magnum opus, opus, work; adaptation
3 an attitude or manner not to be taken seriously — see FUN 2
4 the act or practice of employing something for a particular purpose — see USE 1

play *vb* **1** to engage in activity for amusement ⟨you need some time to run and *play* in the yard after that hard work⟩
synonyms dally, disport, frolic, recreate, rollick, sport
related words gambol, romp; dabble, trifle; amuse, divert, entertain; delight, please; dabble, mess (around), putter; bum (around), dawdle, goldbrick, idle, loaf, lounge (around *or* about), relax, rest, slack (off); jest, joke, tease
near antonyms drudge, labor, plod, plug (away), slave, strain, strive, struggle, sweat, toil, work
2 to present a portrayal or performance of — see ACT 1
3 to pretend to be (what one is not) in appearance or behavior — see IMPERSONATE 1
4 to spend time in aimless activity — see FIDDLE (AROUND)

play (on *or* upon) *vb* to take unfair advantage of — see EXPLOIT 1

play (up) *vb* to indicate the importance of by giving prominent display — see EMPHASIZE

play (upon) *vb* to control or take advantage of by artful, unfair, or insidious means — see MANIPULATE 1

play (with) *vb* to handle thoughtlessly, ignorantly, or mischievously — see TAMPER

played out *adj* depleted in strength, energy, or freshness — see WEARY 1

player *n* **1** a person who plays a musical instrument — see MUSICIAN 1
2 one who acts professionally (as in a play, movie, or television show) — see ACTOR

playful *adj* given to good-natured joking or teasing ⟨the little girl was lighthearted and *playful*⟩
synonyms antic, coltish, elfish, fay, frisky, frolicsome, rollicking, sportive
related words kittenish; gay, happy, lighthearted, whimsical; energetic, lively, spirited, sprightly; devilish, knavish, rascally; amusing, diverting, enjoyable, entertaining, fun, pleasurable; dabbling, frivolous, trifling; delightful, pleasant, pleasing; jesting, joking, teasing
near antonyms dutiful, responsible; grave, grim, serious, solemn, somber (*or* sombre), stern, stolid; no-nonsense, priggish, starchy, stuffy; decorous, formal, proper, sedate, staid; guarded, inhibited, restrained
antonyms earnest, serious-minded, sober

playfulness *n* a natural disposition for playful behavior ⟨the *playfulness* of the kitten can be quite amusing⟩
synonyms friskiness, impishness, mischief, mischievousness, prankishness, sportiveness
related words devilment, devilry (*or* deviltry), hob, rascality, waggery; devilishness, diabolicalness, knavery; frivolousness; energy, liveliness, sprightliness; gaiety (*also* gayety), lightheartedness, whimsicality
near antonyms graveness, grimness, seriousness, solemnity, sternness; priggishness, starchiness, stuffiness; constraint, restraint, self-control
antonyms earnestness, soberness

playhouse *n* a building or part of a building where movies are shown — see THEATER 1

plea *n* **1** an earnest request ⟨the student made an impassioned *plea* for more time to finish the test⟩
synonyms appeal, cry, entreaty, petition, prayer, solicitation, suit, supplication
related words application; call, demand, insistence
2 an explanation that frees one from fault or blame — see EXCUSE

plead *vb* to state (something) as a reason in support of or against something under consideration — see ARGUE 1

plead (for) *vb* to make a request for — see ASK (FOR) 1

plead (to) *vb* to make a request to (someone) in an earnest or urgent manner — see BEG

pleader *n* one who asks earnestly for a favor or gift — see SUPPLICANT

pleading *adj* asking humbly — see SUPPLIANT

pleasant *adj* giving pleasure or contentment to the mind or senses ⟨the massage was extremely *pleasant* and relaxing⟩
synonyms agreeable, congenial, darling, delectable, delicious, delightful, dreamy, enjoyable, felicitous, good, grateful, gratifying, heavenly, luscious, nice, palatable, pleasing, pleasurable, satisfying, welcome
related words alluring, attractive, desirable, inviting, tempting; charming, enchanting, fascinating; calming, comforting, soothing; affable, amiable, amusing, cheerful, cheery, genial, goodly, good-natured, gracious, hospitable, kindly, personable; blissful, glad, happy, joyous; elating, exhilarating, intoxicating; ecstatic, euphoric, rapturous
near antonyms abominable, horrid, miserable, wretched; disgusting, distasteful, obnoxious, offensive, repellent (*also* repellant), repugnant, repulsive; abhorrent, detestable, hateful, odious; boring, commonplace, dull, flat, insipid, irksome, stale, tedious; displeasing, dissatisfying; depressing, disheartening, dismal, dreary, gloomy; black, blue, dejected, depressed, despondent, disconsolate, down, downcast, downhearted, forlorn, hangdog, heartbreaking, heartrending, heartsick, heartsore, inconsolable, joyless, lachrymose, low-spirited, sad, unhappy; bemoaning, bewailing, deploring, doleful, dolorous, grieving, lugubrious, mournful, plaintive, regretful, rueful, sorrowful, wailing, weeping; aggravating, annoying, exasperating, irritating, peeving, perturbing, vexing; forbidding; hostile, intimidating; angering, enraging, incensing, inflaming, infuriating, maddening, out-

raging, rankling, riling; distressing, disturbing, upsetting
antonyms disagreeable, unpalatable, unpleasant, unwelcome
pleasantly *adv* in a pleasing way — see WELL 5
pleasantness *n* the state or quality of having a pleasant or agreeable manner in socializing with others — see AMIABILITY 1
pleasantry *n* something said or done to cause laughter — see JOKE 1
please *vb* to give satisfaction to ⟨fresh flowers *please* me greatly⟩
synonyms content, delight, gladden, gratify, rejoice, satisfy, suit, warm
related words appease, mollify, pacify, placate, soothe; assuage, quench, sate, satiate; excite, tickle, titillate; overjoy, thrill; calm, comfort; cater (to), humor, indulge; coddle, mollycoddle, pamper, spoil
near antonyms aggravate, annoy, bother, bug, chafe, cross, exasperate, gall, get, grate, irk, irritate, nettle, peeve, perturb, pique, put out, ruffle, vex; anger, enrage, incense, inflame, infuriate, madden, outrage, rankle, rile, roil; provoke, rouse; agitate, distress, disturb, fret, upset; harass, harry, pester; affront, insult, offend
antonyms displease
pleased *adj* **1** experiencing pleasure, satisfaction, or delight — see GLAD 1
2 feeling that one's needs or desires have been met — see CONTENT
pleasing *adj* giving pleasure or contentment to the mind or senses — see PLEASANT
pleasingly *adv* in a pleasing way — see WELL 5
pleasurable *adj* **1** giving pleasure or contentment to the mind or senses — see PLEASANT
2 providing amusement or enjoyment — see FUN
pleasure *n* **1** the feeling experienced when one's wishes are met ⟨nothing gives me more *pleasure* than a hot meal after a long day⟩
synonyms content, contentedness, contentment, delectation, delight, enjoyment, gladness, gratification, happiness, relish, satisfaction
related words bliss, felicity, glee, gleefulness, joy; amusement, diversion, entertainment; elatedness, elation, exhilaration, exultation, intoxication; ecstasy, euphoria, heaven, rapture; cheer, cheerfulness, exuberance, gaiety (*also* gayety), jollity, joyfulness, jubilation; comfort, ease, restfulness
near antonyms misery, sadness, unhappiness, wretchedness; anguish, desolation, joylessness, sorrow, woe; dejection, depression, despondency, dispiritedness, gloom, melancholy; aggravation, annoyance, exasperation, irritation, pique, vexation; anger, fury, rage; agitation, distress, disturbance, upset; discomfort, restlessness, uneasiness
antonyms discontent, discontentedness, discontentment, displeasure, dissatisfaction, unhappiness
2 a source of great satisfaction — see DELIGHT 1
3 someone or something that provides amusement or enjoyment — see FUN 1
pleat *vb* to form into a braid — see BRAID
plebeian *adj* belonging to the class of people of low social or economic rank — see IGNOBLE 1
plebeians *n pl* the body of the community as contrasted with the elite — see MASS 1
pledge *n* **1** something given or held to assure that the giver will keep a promise ⟨I was required to leave my keys as a *pledge* that I would bring the car back⟩
synonyms gage, guarantee, guaranty, pawn, security
related words bail, bond; deposit, down payment; surety, warranty; oath, promise, word; commitment, compact, contract, covenant; recognizance
2 a person's solemn declaration that he or she will do or not do something — see PROMISE
pledge *vb* **1** to obligate by prior agreement ⟨I would love to go to dinner with you, but I've *pledged* myself to a play with my parents that night⟩
synonyms commit, engage, troth
related words affiance, betroth, plight, promise, swear, vow; contract, enlist, enroll (*also* enrol), sign on, sign up
near antonyms renege
2 to leave as a guarantee of repayment of a loan — see PAWN
3 to make a solemn declaration of intent — see PROMISE 1
plenary *adj* not lacking any part or member that properly belongs to it — see COMPLETE 1
plenitude *n* **1** a considerable amount — see LOT 2
2 an amount or supply more than sufficient to meet one's needs — see PLENTY 1
plenteous *adj* being more than enough without being excessive — see PLENTIFUL
plentiful *adj* being more than enough without being excessive ⟨a *plentiful* amount of strawberries that will be more than enough for a couple of pies⟩
synonyms abundant, ample, bountiful, comfortable, generous, liberal, plenteous
related words abounding, overflowing, replete, rich, rife, teeming, wealthy; adequate, enough, sufficient; fat, fecund, fertile, fruitful, prolific; copious, galore, lavish, profuse; luxuriant
near antonyms deficient, inadequate, insufficient, lacking, wanting; meager (*or* meagre), niggardly, stingy; skimpy; least, minimum; light, slight, small; barren, infertile, sterile, unfruitful, unproductive
antonyms bare, minimal, scant
plentitude *n* an amount or supply more than sufficient to meet one's needs — see PLENTY 1
plenty *n* **1** an amount or supply more than sufficient to meet one's needs ⟨you'll have *plenty* of time to do your science project⟩
synonyms abundance, plenitude, plentitude, superabundance, wealth
related words adequacy, competence, competency, enough, sufficiency; amplitude, liberality; excess, overflow, overkill, oversupply, superfluity, surfeit, surplus; fecundity, fertility, fruitfulness, richness; lavishness, luxuriance
near antonyms paucity, poverty, scarcity; barrenness, infertility, sterility
antonyms deficiency, inadequacy, insufficiency
2 a considerable amount — see LOT 2
pliable *adj* able to bend easily without breaking — see WILLOWY
pliant *adj* able to bend easily without breaking — see WILLOWY
plod *vb* **1** to devote serious and sustained effort — see LABOR
2 to make progress in a clumsy, struggling manner — see FLOUNDER 1
3 to move slowly — see CRAWL 2

plop *vb* to throw or set down clumsily or casually — see FLOP 1

plot *n* **1** a secret plan for accomplishing evil or unlawful ends <they uncovered a *plot* to assassinate the President just in time>
synonyms conspiracy, design, intrigue, machination, scheme
related words frame-up; manipulation, subterfuge, trickery; artifice, contrivance, maneuver, stratagem, trick; cabal, confederacy, ring; game, gimmick, racket; ground plan, program, strategy, system; collusion, complicity, connivance, conniving
2 a small area of usually open land — see FIELD 1
3 a small piece of land that is developed or available for development — see LOT 1

plot *vb* to engage in a secret plan to accomplish evil or unlawful ends <mobsters were caught *plotting* to take over the company>
synonyms conspire, contrive, intrigue, machinate, scheme
related words brew, concoct, cook (up), hatch; connive; engineer, jockey, maneuver, manipulate; design, frame, lay out, map, plan, shape

plow *vb* **1** to cut into and turn over the sod of (a piece of land) using a bladed implement <we'll have to get out there and *plow* and plant both fields before it rains>
synonyms break, furrow
related words cultivate, till; fallow; harrow, hoe, rake
2 to devote serious and sustained effort — see LABOR

ploy *n* a clever often underhanded means to achieve an end — see TRICK 1

pluck *n* **1** the act or an instance of applying force on something so that it moves in the direction of the force — see PULL 1
2 the strength of mind that enables a person to endure pain or hardship — see FORTITUDE

plug *vb* **1** to close up so that no empty spaces remain — see FILL 2
2 to devote serious and sustained effort — see LABOR
3 to provide publicity for — see PUBLICIZE 1
4 to strike with a missile from a gun — see SHOOT 3

plug (up) *vb* to prevent passage through — see CLOG 1

plugger *n* a person who does very hard or dull work — see SLAVE 2

plum *n* someone or something unusually desirable — see PRIZE 1

plumb *adj* rising straight up — see ERECT

plumb *adv* **1** in a direct line or course — see DIRECTLY 1
2 *chiefly dialect* to a full extent or degree — see FULLY 1

plumb *vb* to measure the depth of (as a body of water) typically with a weighted line — see [2]SOUND 1

plume *n* something given in recognition of achievement — see AWARD

plume *vb* to think highly of (oneself) — see PRIDE

plummet *vb* to go to a lower level — see DROP 2

plump *adj* having an excess of body fat — see FAT 1

plump *adv* in a direct line or course — see DIRECTLY 1

plump *vb* to throw or set down clumsily or casually — see FLOP 1

plumpness *n* the condition of having an excess of body fat — see CORPULENCE

plunder *n* valuables stolen or taken by force — see LOOT

plunder *vb* to search through with the intent of committing robbery — see RANSACK 1

plunge *n* **1** an act or instance of diving — see DIVE 1
2 the act or process of going to a lower level or altitude — see DESCENT 1

plunge *vb* **1** to cast oneself head first into deep water — see DIVE
2 to go to a lower level — see DROP 2
3 to lead or extend downward — see DESCEND 1

plunk *vb* to throw or set down clumsily or casually — see FLOP 1

plus *n* something added (as by growth) — see INCREASE 1

plush *adj* showing obvious signs of wealth and comfort — see LUXURIOUS

ply *vb* to bring to bear especially forcefully or effectively — see EXERT

poach *vb* to cook in a liquid heated to the point that it gives off steam — see BOIL 2

po'boy *also* **poor boy** *n* a large sandwich on a long split roll — see SUBMARINE

pocket *adj* of a size that is less than average — see SMALL 1

pocket *n* available money — see FUND 2

pocket *vb* **1** to refrain from openly showing or uttering — see SUPPRESS 2
2 to take (something) without right and with an intent to keep — see STEAL 1

pocketbook *n* a container for carrying money and small personal items — see PURSE

pocket–size *also* **pocket–sized** *adj* of a size that is less than average — see SMALL 1

pockmark *n* something that spoils the appearance or completeness of a thing — see BLEMISH

pod *n* something that encloses another thing especially to protect it — see [1]CASE 1

podium *n* a level usually raised surface — see PLATFORM

poem *n* a composition using rhythm and often rhyme to create a lyrical effect <your assignment is to write two *poems* about springtime>
synonyms lyric, song, verse
related words rhyme (*also* rime); ballad, lay; elegy, English sonnet, epic, epigram, haiku, jingle, lament, limerick, ode, psalm, sonnet; blank verse, free verse, minstrelsy, poesy, poetry

poesy *n* writing that uses rhythm, vivid language, and often rhyme to provoke an emotional response — see POETRY 1

poet *n* a person who writes poetry <Emily Dickinson is famous as the *poet* who rarely left the house but often journeyed to the depths of the human heart>
synonyms bard, minstrel, versifier
related words poetess; poet laureate; troubadour; epigrammatist, rhymer, sonneteer

poetic *adj* having qualities suggestive of poetry <your description of the sun setting over the Grand Canyon was a particularly *poetic* piece of writing>
synonyms lyric, lyrical, poetical
related words metric, metrical, rhyming, rhythmic (*or* rhythmical); rhapsodic (*also* rhapsodical);

florid, flowery, grandiloquent, highfalutin, high-flown, ornate; figurative, metaphorical, symbolic (*also* symbolical)
near antonyms factual, literal, matter-of-fact
antonyms prosaic, prose, unpoetic

poetical *adj* having qualities suggestive of poetry — see POETIC

poetry *n* **1** writing that uses rhythm, vivid language, and often rhyme to provoke an emotional response ⟨not all *poetry* has to rhyme⟩
synonyms minstrelsy, poesy, song, verse
related words rhyme (*also* rime); blank verse, free verse
antonyms prose
2 the art or power of speaking or writing in a forceful and convincing way — see ELOQUENCE

poignancy *n* a harsh or sharp quality — see EDGE 1

poignant *adj* having the power to affect the feelings or sympathies — see MOVING

point *n* **1** a particular and often important moment in time ⟨it was at that *point* that I had to stop and check on the experiment⟩
synonyms juncture
related words flash, instant, jiffy, minute, moment, second, shake, split second, trice, twinkle, wink; bit, spell, stretch, while; brink, threshold, verge
2 the last and usually sharp or tapering part of something long and narrow ⟨be careful with the *point* on that umbrella, or you could hurt someone⟩
synonyms apex, cusp, end, pike, tip
related words prong, tine; barb, jag, prickle, snag, spike, sticker
3 a separate part in a list, account, or series — see ITEM 1
4 a single piece of information — see FACT 3
5 a small area that is different (as in color) from the main part — see SPOT 1
6 an area of high ground jutting out into a body of water beyond the line of the coast — see HEADLAND 1
7 an area of land that juts out into a body of water — see [2]CAPE
8 an individual part of a process, series, or ranking — see DEGREE 1
9 something that sets apart an individual from others of the same kind — see CHARACTERISTIC
10 the area or space occupied by or intended for something — see PLACE 1
11 the quality of an utterance that provokes interest and produces an effect — see [1]PUNCH 1

point (toward) *vb* to stand or sit with the face or front toward — see FACE 1

point (up) *vb* to indicate the importance of by giving prominent display — see EMPHASIZE

pointed *adj* **1** tapering to a thin tip ⟨the snake plant's long *pointed* leaves make it an easily recognized houseplant⟩
synonyms peaked, sharp, tipped
related words barbed, jagged, pronged, spiky
near antonyms dull, rounded
antonyms blunt
2 having to do with the matter at hand — see PERTINENT

pointer *n* **1** an arrow-shaped piece on a dial or scale for registering information ⟨the *pointer* on my bathroom scale must be stuck—I know I lost weight⟩
synonyms hand, index, indicator, needle
related words dial, face, gauge (*also* gage)
2 a piece of advice or useful information especially from an expert — see [1]TIP 1

pointless *adj* having no meaning — see MEANINGLESS

point of view *n* a way of looking at or thinking about something ⟨who actually has the right to possession of that wilderness area depends on your *point of view*⟩
synonyms angle, outlook, perspective, shoes, slant, standpoint, viewpoint
related words interpretation, spin; belief, conviction, eye, feeling, judgment (*or* judgement), mind, notion, opinion, perception, persuasion, sentiment, verdict, view; impression, take; wavelength; side; attitude, position, posture, stand

poise *n* a condition in which opposing forces are equal to one another — see BALANCE 1

poise *vb* to rest or move along the surface of a liquid or in the air — see FLOAT

poison *adj* containing or contaminated with a substance capable of injuring or killing a living thing — see POISONOUS

poison *n* a substance that by chemical action can kill or injure a living thing ⟨the only way to get rid of rats is to leave out *poison*⟩
synonyms bane, toxin, venom
related words cancer, contagion, disease, virus; fungicide, germicide, herbicide, insecticide
near antonyms antidote, antivenin; cure; cure-all, elixir, panacea

poison *vb* **1** to affect slightly with something morally bad or undesirable — see TAINT 1
2 to make unfit for use by the addition of something harmful or undesirable — see CONTAMINATE
3 to lower in character or dignity — see DEBASE 1

poisoned *adj* containing or contaminated with a substance capable of injuring or killing a living thing — see POISONOUS

poisonous *adj* containing or contaminated with a substance capable of injuring or killing a living thing ⟨some evil person was leaving out *poisonous* meat for neighborhood dogs to eat⟩
synonyms envenomed, poison, poisoned, toxic, venomous
related words contagious, infectious; deleterious, harmful, hurtful, injurious, malignant, noxious, virulent; unhealthful, unhealthy, unwholesome; calamitous, deadly, fatal, lethal, murderous
near antonyms beneficial, curative, healthful, healthy, helpful, palliative, remedial, salubrious, salutary, wholesome; benign, harmless, innocuous, inoffensive; nonfatal, nonlethal
antonyms nonpoisonous, nontoxic, nonvenomous

[1]**poke** *n* a quick thrust ⟨please stop giving the cat *pokes* while it's trying to sleep⟩
synonyms dab, dig, jab
related words punch; stab, stick; push, shove; jam, jerk, jog, nudge

[2]**poke** *n* *chiefly Southern & Midland* a container made of a flexible material (as paper or plastic) — see BAG 1

poke *vb* **1** to extend outward beyond a usual point — see BULGE
2 to interest oneself in what is not one's concern — see INTERFERE
3 to move or act slowly — see DELAY 1
4 to move slowly — see CRAWL 2

poking *adj* moving or proceeding at less than the normal, desirable, or required speed — see SLOW 1

poky *or* **pokey** *adj* moving or proceeding at less than the normal, desirable, or required speed — see SLOW 1

polar *adj* **1** being as different as possible — see OPPOSITE
2 having a low or subnormal temperature — see COLD 1

police *n* **1** the department of government that keeps order, fights crime, and enforces statutes ⟨the appearance of a ransom note meant that the teenager's disappearance was now a matter for the *police*⟩
synonyms law
related words judiciary, jurisprudence, justice
2 a body of officers of the law ⟨the National Guard will serve as backup for the metropolitan *police* in the event of violent protests⟩
synonyms constabulary, police force
related words constable, cop, gendarme, officer, policeman, police officer, policewoman, trooper

police force *n* a body of officers of the law — see POLICE 2

policeman *n* a member of a force charged with law enforcement at the local level — see OFFICER 1

police officer *n* a member of a force charged with law enforcement at the local level — see OFFICER 1

policy *n* a way of acting or proceeding — see COURSE 1

polish *n* **1** a high level of taste and enlightenment as a result of extensive intellectual training and exposure to the arts — see CULTURE 1
2 brightness created by light reflected from a surface — see SHINE 1

polish *vb* to make smooth or glossy usually by repeatedly applying surface pressure ⟨you'll need to *polish* your shoes with a clean rag before the performance⟩
synonyms buff, burnish, dress, gloss, grind, rub, shine, smooth
related words sleek, slick; coat, glaze; finish, veneer; brighten; rasp, sand, sandblast, sandpaper, scour, scrape, scrub
near antonyms rough (up), roughen, scuff (up)

polished *adj* **1** having a shiny surface or finish — see GLOSSY
2 having or showing a taste for the fine arts and gracious living — see CULTIVATED

polite *adj* **1** showing consideration, courtesy, and good manners ⟨it's only *polite* to hold the door for the person behind you⟩
synonyms civil, courteous, genteel, gracious, mannerly, well-bred
related words attentive, considerate, thoughtful; chivalrous, courtly, gallant; ceremonial, ceremonious; formal, suave, unctuous, urbane; elegant, refined; deferential, dutiful, respectful, submissive, yielding; acceptable, appropriate, becoming, befitting, correct, decent, decorous, fit, fitting, good, meet, proper, respectable, right, seemly, suitable; affable, cordial, friendly, genial, hospitable, sociable; felicitous, graceful; humble, meek, modest, unassertive
near antonyms heedless, inconsiderate, thoughtless; audacious, bold, bold-faced, brash, brassy, disrespectful, impertinent, impudent, insolent, saucy, shameless; boorish, churlish, clownish, loutish, uncouth, vulgar; casual, informal, unceremonious; improper, inappropriate, incorrect, indecent, indecorous, uncalled-for, unrespectable, unseemly; arrogant, conceited, presumptuous, pretentious
antonyms discourteous, ill-bred, ill-mannered, impolite, inconsiderate, rude, thoughtless, uncivil, ungracious, unmannerly
2 following the established traditions of refined society and good taste — see PROPER 1

politeness *n* speech or behavior that is a sign of good breeding ⟨the little girl's *politeness* greatly impressed her teacher⟩
synonyms civility, courteousness, courtesy, gentility, graciousness, mannerliness
related words attentiveness, consideration, thoughtfulness; ceremonialness, ceremoniousness, ceremony, formality; chivalrousness, chivalry, courtliness, gallantry; breeding, manners; suaveness, unctuousness, urbanity; elegance, refinement; deference, respect; decency, decorousness, decorum, propriety, respectability, seemliness; affability, cordiality, friendliness, geniality, hospitality, sociability; felicitousness, gracefulness; humility, meekness, modesty, shyness
near antonyms audaciousness, audacity, boldness, brashness, brassiness, disrespect, impertinence, impudence, insolence, sauciness, shamelessness; boorishness, churlishness, clownishness, loutishness, vulgarity; casualness, informality; impropriety, inappropriateness, incorrectness, indecency; inconsideration, thoughtlessness; arrogance, conceit, presumption, pretentiousness
antonyms discourteousness, discourtesy, impoliteness, incivility, rudeness, ungraciousness

politic *adj* suitable for bringing about a desired result under the circumstances — see EXPEDIENT

poll *n* the upper or front part of the body that contains the brain, the major sense organs, and the mouth — see HEAD 1

poll *vb* to go around and approach (people) with a request for opinions or information — see CANVASS

pollutant *n* something that is or that makes impure — see IMPURITY

pollute *vb* to make unfit for use by the addition of something harmful or undesirable — see CONTAMINATE

polluted *adj* containing foreign or lower-grade substances — see IMPURE

poltergeist *n* the soul of a dead person thought of especially as appearing to living people — see GHOST

poltroon *n* a person who shows a shameful lack of courage in the face of danger — see COWARD

polychromatic *adj* marked by a variety of usually vivid colors — see COLORFUL

polychrome *adj* marked by a variety of usually vivid colors — see COLORFUL

polygraph *n* an instrument for detecting physical signs of the tension that goes with lying — see LIE DETECTOR

pommel *vb* to strike repeatedly — see BEAT 1

pompous *adj* **1** having a feeling of superiority that shows itself in an overbearing attitude — see ARROGANT
2 having too high an opinion of oneself — see CONCEITED
3 self-consciously trying to present an appearance of grandeur or importance — see PRETENTIOUS 1

pompousness *n* **1** an exaggerated sense of one's importance that shows itself in the making of excessive or unjustified claims — see ARROGANCE
2 an often unjustified feeling of being pleased with oneself or with one's situation or achievements — see COMPLACENCE

ponder *vb* to give serious and careful thought to ⟨I'm *pondering* whether or not I should join another club⟩
synonyms chew over, cogitate, consider, contemplate, debate, deliberate, entertain, meditate, mull (over), question, ruminate, study, think (about *or* over), weigh
related words muse (upon), reflect (on *or* upon), reminisce; conclude, reason; second-guess, speculate; brood (about *or* over), fret (about *or* over), obsess (about *or* over); believe, conceive, opine; absorb, assimilate, digest, drink (in)
phrases cudgel one's brains
near antonyms disregard, ignore, overlook, slight; dismiss, pooh-pooh (*also* pooh), reject

ponderous *adj* **1** causing weariness, restlessness, or lack of interest — see BORING
2 having great weight — see HEAVY 1

ponderousness *n* the state or quality of being heavy — see WEIGHTINESS 1

pooch *n* a domestic mammal that is related to the wolves and foxes — see DOG

¹pool *n* a small often deep body of water ⟨when it rains, that small *pool* grows to almost the size of a lake⟩
synonyms mere [*chiefly British*], puddle
related words basin, hole, sinkhole; swimming pool; lake

²pool *n* **1** a body of persons at work or available for work — see FORCE 1
2 the number of individuals or amount of something available at any given time — see SUPPLY
3 a sum of money set aside for a particular purpose — see FUND 1
4 the total of the bets at stake at one time — see POT 1

poor *adj* **1** lacking money or material possessions ⟨every year, we make up a basket of food at Thanksgiving for a *poor* family in the neighborhood⟩
synonyms beggared, broke, destitute, impecunious, impoverished, indigent, needy, penniless, penurious, poverty-stricken, stone-broke
related words deprived, disadvantaged, underprivileged; bankrupt, bankrupted, insolvent; depressed, pinched, reduced, straitened; low, short
phrases hard up
near antonyms comfortable, prosperous
antonyms affluent, flush, moneyed (*or* monied), opulent, rich, wealthy, well-heeled, well-off, well-to-do
2 producing inferior or only a small amount of vegetation — see BARREN 1
3 less plentiful than what is normal, necessary, or desirable — see MEAGER
4 falling short of a standard — see BAD 1
5 of low quality — see CHEAP 2
6 deserving of one's pity — see PATHETIC 1

poorly *adj* temporarily suffering from a disorder of the body — see SICK 1

poorly *adv* in an unsatisfactory way — see BADLY

poorness *n* the state of lacking sufficient money or material possessions — see POVERTY 1

¹pop *n* a loud explosive sound — see CLAP 1

²pop *n* a male human parent — see FATHER 1

pop *vb* **1** to break open or into pieces usually because of internal pressure — see EXPLODE 1
2 to break suddenly with an explosive sound — see CRACK 1
3 to cause to break open or into pieces by or as if by an explosive — see BLAST 1
4 to strike with a missile from a gun — see SHOOT 3

pop (in) *vb* to make a brief visit — see CALL 3

populace *n* the body of the community as contrasted with the elite — see MASS 1

popular *adj* **1** enjoying widespread favor or approval ⟨bell-bottom jeans were *popular* in the seventies⟩
synonyms fashionable, hot, in, modish, popularized, vogue
related words favorite, preferred; desirable, liked, wanted; celebrated, famed, famous, noted, notorious, prominent, renowned, well-known; fabled, fabulous, legendary; leading, notable, outstanding, remarkable; important, significant
near antonyms washed-up; despised, detested, disliked, hated, rejected; insignificant, unimportant; indistinguished, unexceptional; anonymous, nameless, obscure, unknown; inconspicuous
antonyms out, unpopular
2 accepted, used, or practiced by most people — see CURRENT 1
3 held by or applicable to a majority of the people — see GENERAL 3
4 of, relating to, or favoring political democracy — see DEMOCRATIC

popularity *n* the state of enjoying widespread approval ⟨the sudden *popularity* of low-cut blouses horrified my mother⟩
synonyms fashionableness, favor, hotness, modishness, vogue
related words craze, fad, mode, rage, style, trend; bandwagon; fame, notoriety, prominence, renown; enthusiasm, fervor, passion
near antonyms oblivion, obscurity
antonyms disfavor, unpopularity

popularized *adj* enjoying widespread favor or approval — see POPULAR 1

pore (over) *vb* to go over and mentally take in the content of — see READ

pornographic *adj* depicting or referring to sexual matters in a way that is unacceptable in polite society — see OBSCENE 1

porous *adj* capable of being passed into or through — see PENETRABLE

port *n* a part of a body of water protected and deep enough to be a place of safety for ships — see HARBOR 1

portable *adj* capable of being moved especially with ease — see MOVABLE

portal *n* a barrier by which an entry is closed and opened — see DOOR 1

portent *n* **1** something believed to be a sign or warning of a future event — see OMEN
2 something extraordinary or surprising — see WONDER 1

portentous *adj* **1** being or showing a sign of evil or calamity to come — see OMINOUS
2 causing wonder or astonishment — see MARVELOUS 1

porter *n chiefly British* a person who tends a door — see DOORKEEPER

portion *n* **1** a state or end that seemingly has been decided beforehand — see FATE 1
2 one of the pieces from which something is designed to be assembled — see PART 1
3 something belonging to, due to, or contributed by an individual member of a group — see SHARE 1

portion *vb* to give out (something) in appropriate amounts or to appropriate individuals — see ADMINISTER 1

portliness *n* the condition of having an excess of body fat — see CORPULENCE

portly *adj* having an excess of body fat — see FAT 1

portmanteau *n* a bag carried by hand and designed to hold a traveler's clothing and personal articles — see TRAVELING BAG

portrait *n* a vivid representation in words of someone or something — see DESCRIPTION 1

portray *vb* **1** to give a representation or account of in words — see DESCRIBE 1
2 to point out the chief quality or qualities of an individual or group — see CHARACTERIZE 1
3 to present a picture of — see PICTURE 1
4 to present a portrayal or performance of — see ACT 1

portrayal *n* a vivid representation in words of someone or something — see DESCRIPTION 1

pose *n* a display of emotion or behavior that is insincere or intended to deceive — see MASQUERADE

pose *vb* to set before the mind for consideration — see PROPOSE 1

pose (as) *vb* to pretend to be (what one is not) in appearance or behavior — see IMPERSONATE 1

position *n* **1** an assignment at which one regularly works for pay — see JOB 1
2 the action for which a person or thing is specially fitted or used or for which a thing exists — see ROLE
3 the area or space occupied by or intended for something — see PLACE 1
4 the place where someone is assigned to stand or remain — see STATION 1
5 the placement of someone or something in relation to others in a vertical arrangement — see RANK 1

position *vb* to arrange something in a certain spot or position — see PLACE 1

positive *adj* **1** expressing approval — see FAVORABLE 1
2 having or showing a mind free from doubt — see CERTAIN 2

positiveness *n* a state of mind in which one is free from doubt — see CONFIDENCE 2

possess *vb* to keep, control, or experience as one's own — see HAVE 1

possession *n* **1** the fact or state of having (something) at one's disposal ⟨a student who was found to have several overdue library books in his *possession*⟩
synonyms control, hands, keeping
related words ownership, proprietorship; authority, command, dominion, mastery, power; enjoyment, repossession, retention; claiming, collaring, commandeering, confiscation, procurement
near antonyms dispossession, relinquishment, surrendering, transferal
antonyms nonpossession
2 possessions *pl* transportable items that one owns ⟨we packed up all of our *possessions* and moved to a new house⟩
synonyms belongings, chattels, effects, holdings, movables (*or* moveables), paraphernalia, personalty, things
related words treasures, valuables; junk, stuff; appointments, fixtures, furnishings; property, tangibles; collateral
near antonyms real estate

possessive *adj* intolerant of rivalry or unfaithfulness — see JEALOUS 1

possessor *n* one who has a legal or rightful claim to ownership — see PROPRIETOR

possibility *n* **1** something that can develop or become actual — see POTENTIAL
2 something that might happen — see EVENT 2

possible *adj* **1** capable of being done or carried out ⟨I think that building the entire set in two days is *possible*, if difficult⟩
synonyms achievable, attainable, doable, feasible, practicable, realizable, viable, workable
related words practical, reasonable, sensible; likely, probable; acceptable, believable, conceivable, creditable, plausible; available, usable
near antonyms impractical, unrealistic; doubtful, dubious, far-fetched, improbable, unlikely; implausible, inconceivable, incredible, unbelievable; futile, useless, vain; absurd, fantastic, outlandish, preposterous, ridiculous; unthinkable
antonyms hopeless, impossible, impracticable, unachievable, unattainable, unworkable
2 existing only as a possibility and not in fact — see POTENTIAL

possibly *adv* it is possible — see PERHAPS

[1]**post** *n chiefly British* communications or parcels sent or carried through the postal system — see MAIL

[2]**post** *n* **1** a specific task with which a person or group is charged — see MISSION
2 the place where someone is assigned to stand or remain — see STATION 1
3 an assignment at which one regularly works for pay — see JOB 1

[3]**post** *n* an upright shaft that supports an overhead structure — see PILLAR 1

[1]**post** *vb* **1** to affix (as a notice) to or on a suitable place ⟨the student organizations always *post* their announcements on the cafeteria walls⟩
synonyms placard
related words nail, plaster, tack (up); advertise, announce, blaze, broadcast, call, declare, proclaim, promulgate, publicize, publish
near antonyms remove, take down
2 to make known openly or publicly — see ANNOUNCE

[2]**post** *vb* to assign to a place or position ⟨the police are planning to *post* an officer outside the hospital room of the witness⟩
synonyms detail, station
related words set; appoint; place, position

[3]**post** *vb* to send through the postal system — see MAIL

postdate *vb* to come after in time — see FOLLOW 1

poster *n* a sheet bearing an announcement for posting in a public place ⟨we put up a hundred *posters* announcing the concert⟩
synonyms bill, placard
related words billboard, sign, signboard; broadside, flier (*or* flyer), handbill, handout, playbill;

ad, advertisement, announcement, bulletin, dispatch, release

posterior *adj* **1** being at or in the part of something opposite the front part — see BACK
2 being, occurring, or carried out at a time after something else — see SUBSEQUENT

posterior *n* the part of the body upon which someone sits — see BUTTOCKS

posterity *n* the descendants of a person, animal, or plant — see OFFSPRING

posthaste *adv* with great speed — see FAST 1

posthumous *adj* occurring after one's death ⟨the soldier was awarded a *posthumous* medal for valor⟩
synonyms postmortem
related words belated, delayed, late

posting *n* a published statement informing the public of a matter of general interest — see ANNOUNCEMENT

postman *n* a person who delivers mail ⟨the *postman* comes at around nine every morning⟩
synonyms letter carrier, mail carrier, mailman
related words messenger; postmaster

postmortem *adj* occurring after one's death — see POSTHUMOUS

postmortem *n* examination of a dead body especially to find out the cause of death — see AUTOPSY

postmortem examination *n* examination of a dead body especially to find out the cause of death — see AUTOPSY

postpone *vb* to assign to a later time ⟨we'll have to *postpone* the decision until we have all the information⟩
synonyms defer, delay, hold off (on), hold up, put off, shelve
related words suspend; hesitate, pause, stay; detain, retard, slow; extend, lengthen, prolong, protract, stretch (out); wait
near antonyms act, deal (with), decide (upon), do, work (on)

postulate *n* something taken as being true or factual and used as a starting point for a course of action or reasoning — see ASSUMPTION

postulate *vb* to take as true or as a fact without actual proof — see ASSUME 2

posture *n* **1** a general way of holding the body ⟨a good upright *posture* will prevent backaches⟩
synonyms carriage, stance
related words attention; body language; pose, seat; bearing, behavior, conduct, demeanor, deportment; air, poise, presence; aspect, look, mien
2 position with regard to conditions and circumstances — see SITUATION 1

posy *n* a bunch of flowers — see BOUQUET 1

pot *n* **1** the total of the bets at stake at one time ⟨everyone got a bit nervous when the *pot* was more than a hundred dollars⟩
synonyms jackpot, pool
related words fund, kitty; bet, stake, wager
2 a considerable amount — see LOT 2

potable *adj* suitable for drinking ⟨around here, the only *potable* water comes from wells⟩
synonyms drinkable
related words clean, fresh, pure, uncontaminated, unpolluted; nonpoisonous
near antonyms contaminated, dirty, foul, polluted; poison, poisonous, toxic; unhealthful, unhealthy, unwholesome
antonyms undrinkable

potbelly *n* an enlarged or bulging abdomen ⟨he began exercising to get rid of his growing *potbelly* and tighten up his stomach⟩
synonyms paunch
related words belly, breadbasket [*slang*], gut, stomach, tummy; chubbiness, corpulence, fat, fatness, fleshiness, obesity, overweight, paunchiness, plumpness, portliness, pudginess; chunkiness, heaviness, stoutness

potency *n* the ability to exert effort for the accomplishment of a task — see POWER 2

potent *adj* **1** having an abundance of some characteristic quality (as flavor) — see FULL-BODIED
2 having great power or influence — see IMPORTANT 2
3 producing or capable of producing a desired result — see EFFECTIVE 1

potentate *n* a person who uses power or authority in a cruel, unjust, or harmful way — see DESPOT

potential *adj* existing only as a possibility and not in fact ⟨I can see a few *potential* problems with getting a puppy, but we'll wait and see if they come up⟩
synonyms possible
related words conceivable, imaginable, plausible, thinkable; likely, probable; conjectural, hypothetical, suppositional, theoretical (*also* theoretic); alleged, assumed, purported, reputed, supposed; achievable, attainable, doable, feasible, practicable, viable, workable
near antonyms authenticated, confirmed, demonstrated, established, proven, substantiated; authentic, bona fide, genuine, true
antonyms actual, existent, factual, real

potential *n* something that can develop or become actual ⟨a time when cloning was merely a *potential* and the stuff of science fiction⟩
synonyms eventuality, possibility, potentiality
related words likelihood, probability; latency
near antonyms actuality, reality; certainty

potentiality *n* something that can develop or become actual — see POTENTIAL

pother *n* **1** a state of nervous or irritated concern — see FRET
2 a state of noisy, confused activity — see COMMOTION

potpourri *n* an unorganized collection or mixture of various things — see MISCELLANY 1

potter (around) *vb* to spend time in aimless activity — see FIDDLE (AROUND)

potterer *n* a person who regularly or occasionally engages in an activity without being or becoming an expert at it — see AMATEUR

potter's field *n* a piece of land used for burying the dead — see CEMETERY

pottery *n* articles made of baked clay — see CROCKERY

pouch *n* a container made of a flexible material (as paper or plastic) — see BAG 1

poultice *n* a medicated covering used to heal an injury — see DRESSING 1

pounce (on *or* upon) *vb* to take sudden, violent action against — see ATTACK 1

pound *n* **1** a hard strike with a part of the body or an instrument — see [1]BLOW
2 an enclosure with an open framework for keeping animals — see CAGE

pound *vb* **1** to move heavily or clumsily — see LUMBER 1

2 to deliver a blow to (someone or something) usually in a strong vigorous manner — see HIT 1
3 to strike repeatedly — see BEAT 1
4 to shape with a hammer — see HAMMER 1

pour *vb* **1** to cause to flow in a stream ‹she lifted the teakettle and *poured* some hot water through the spout›
synonyms stream
related words ladle, spoon; cascade, trickle; deluge, flood, inundate, overflow
2 to move in a stream — see FLOW 1
3 to flow out in great quantities or with force — see GUSH 1
4 to fall as water in a continuous stream of drops from the clouds — see RAIN 1
5 to give readily and in large quantities — see RAIN 2

pouring *adj* marked by or abounding with rain — see RAINY

pout *n* **1** a twisting of the facial features in disgust or disapproval — see GRIMACE
2 pouts *pl* a state of resentful silence or irritability — see SULK

pout *vb* to silently go about in a bad mood — see SULK

pouting *adj* given to or displaying a resentful silence and often irritability — see SULKY

poverty *n* **1** the state of lacking sufficient money or material possessions ‹he dreamed of finding a good job and working his way out of *poverty* and debt›
synonyms beggary, destitution, impecuniousness, impoverishment, indigence, need, neediness, pauperism, penuriousness, penury, poorness, want
related words misery, woe, wretchedness; exigency, necessity; austerity, deprivation, privation; bankruptcy, insolvency; belt-tightening, pinching, straitening
near antonyms luxury, prosperity
antonyms affluence, opulence, richness, wealthiness
2 a falling short of an essential or desirable amount or number — see DEFICIENCY

poverty–stricken *adj* lacking money or material possessions — see POOR 1

powder *vb* to reduce to fine particles ‹you have to *powder* the antibiotic tablet and mix it with food›
synonyms atomize, crush, grind, pulverize
related words grate; crumble, crunch; break, bust, dash, fracture, fragment; shatter, smash, splinter; mill

powdery *adj* consisting of very small particles — see FINE 1

power *n* **1** the right or means to command or control others ‹the principal has nearly complete *power* over this school›
synonyms arm, authority, clutch, command, control, dominion, grip, hold, mastery, sway
related words clout, influence, pull, weight; jurisdiction; direction, management; dominance, predominance, sovereignty, supremacy; prerogative, privilege, right; eminence, importance, moment
near antonyms helplessness, weakness
antonyms impotence, powerlessness
2 the ability to exert effort for the accomplishment of a task ‹the corporation has the *power* to accomplish almost anything› ‹you'll need to build a bit more *power* in order to be a star pitcher›
synonyms energy, force, might, muscle, potency, puissance, sinew, strength, vigor
related words aptitude, capability, capacity, competence, competency; adequacy, effectiveness, effectualness, usefulness
near antonyms disability, inability, inaptitude, incapability, incapacity, incompetence, incompetency; ineffectiveness, ineffectualness, uselessness; helplessness, paralysis
antonyms impotence, powerlessness, weakness
3 a natural ability of the mind or body ‹dogs have a very highly developed *power* of smell›
synonyms faculty
related words function; capability, capacity; aptitude, endowment, flair, genius, gift, instinct, knack, talent
near antonyms inability, incapability, incapacity; inaptitude, inaptness, ineptness
4 something with a usable capacity for doing work — see FUEL

powerboat *n* a boat equipped with a motor — see MOTORBOAT

powerful *adj* having great power or influence — see IMPORTANT 2

powerfully *adv* in a vigorous and forceful manner — see HARD 3

powerhouse *n* an ambitious person who eagerly goes after what is desired — see GO-GETTER

powerless *adj* unable to act or achieve one's purpose ‹I wish I could help you, but I am *powerless* in this situation›
synonyms helpless, impotent, weak
related words incapable, incompetent, ineffective, ineffectual, inept, unfit, useless; feeble, frail, infirm, passive, spineless, supine, unaggressive
near antonyms able, capable, competent, effective, efficient; authoritarian, autocratic, despotic, dictatorial, magisterial, tyrannical (*also* tyrranic); dominant, dynamic, energetic, forceful, robust, sturdy, tough, vigorous; important, major, significant; high-level, senior, top
antonyms mighty, potent, powerful, puissant, strong

powerlessness *n* the lack of sufficient ability, power, or means — see INABILITY

powwow *n* **1** a coming together of a number of persons for a specified purpose — see MEETING 1
2 a meeting featuring a group discussion — see FORUM

powwow *vb* to exchange viewpoints or seek advice for the purpose of finding a solution to a problem — see CONFER 2

practicable *adj* **1** capable of being done or carried out — see POSSIBLE 1
2 capable of being put to use or account — see PRACTICAL 1
3 capable of or suitable for being used for a particular purpose — see USABLE 1

practical *adj* **1** capable of being put to use or account ‹a *practical* and simple solution for the town's waste disposal› ‹she has some *practical* information on sight-seeing in San Francisco›
synonyms applicable, functional, practicable, serviceable, usable, useful, workable, working
related words down-to-earth, pragmatic (*also* pragmatical), utilitarian; accessible, available, obtainable, reachable; all-around (*also* all-round), handy; active, alive, busy, employed, functioning, operating, operative
near antonyms abstract, academic, theoretical (*also* theoretic); inaccessible, unattainable, unavailable, unobtainable, unreachable; unsuitable

antonyms impracticable, impractical, unusable, unworkable, useless
2 willing to see things as they really are and deal with them sensibly — see REALISTIC 1
practical joke *n* a playful or mischievous act intended as a joke — see PRANK
practically *adv* very close to but not completely — see ALMOST
practice *also* **practise** *n* **1** a private performance or session in preparation for a public appearance — see REHEARSAL
2 a usual manner of behaving or doing — see HABIT
3 something done over and over in order to develop skill — see EXERCISE 2
practice *or* **practise** *vb* to do over and over so as to become skilled ⟨in order to play the guitar well, you need to *practice* fingering every single day⟩
synonyms exercise, rehearse
related words prepare (for), train (with); drill, repeat; work (at *or* on); review, study
practiced *or* **practised** *adj* **1** having or showing exceptional knowledge, experience, or skill in a field of endeavor — see PROFICIENT
2 accomplished with trained ability — see SKILLFUL
pragmatic *also* **pragmatical** *adj* willing to see things as they really are and deal with them sensibly — see REALISTIC 1
prairie *n* a broad area of level or rolling treeless country — see PLAIN
praise *vb* **1** to proclaim the glory of ⟨hymns that *praise* God⟩
synonyms bless, extol (*also* extoll), glorify, laud, magnify
related words adore, deify, idolize, worship; acclaim, applaud, commend, compliment, hail, salute; celebrate, cheer, eulogize, rhapsodize; cite; flatter; crack up, recommend, tout
near antonyms blame, censure, reprehend, reprobate; criticize, reprove; admonish, chide, rebuke, reprimand, reproach; castigate, lambaste (*or* lambast)
2 to declare enthusiastic approval of — see ACCLAIM
praiseworthy *adj* deserving of high regard or great approval — see ADMIRABLE
prance *vb* to walk with exaggerated arm and leg movements — see STRUT 1
prank *n* a playful or mischievous act intended as a joke ⟨as a *prank*, several students managed to change all the classroom clocks to different times⟩
synonyms antic, caper, escapade, frolic, practical joke, trick
related words skylarking; adventure, experience, game, lark, time; high jinks, horseplay, play, roughhousing, rowdiness; shenanigans, tomfoolery; joking, kidding, teasing; gambit, hoax, maneuver, ploy; deed, feat, mission, performance, stunt; caprice, conceit, fancy, vagary, whim, whimsy; deceit, deception, delusion, fooling, fraud, hoodwinking, ruse, sham, stratagem, subterfuge, trickery, wile
prankish *adj* tending to or exhibiting reckless playfulness — see MISCHIEVOUS 1
prankishness *n* a natural disposition for playful behavior — see PLAYFULNESS
prate *vb* to engage in casual or rambling conversation — see CHAT
prattle *n* unintelligible or meaningless talk — see GIBBERISH
prattle *vb* **1** to engage in casual or rambling conversation — see CHAT
2 to speak rapidly, inarticulately, and usually unintelligibly — see BABBLE 1
prattler *n* a person who talks constantly — see CHATTERBOX
pray *vb* to make a request to (someone) in an earnest or urgent manner — see BEG
prayer *n* **1** an address to God or a deity ⟨he always directed a bedside *prayer* to God before going to sleep⟩
synonyms orison
related words collect, grace, invocation, litany, thanksgiving; evensong, matins, vespers; appeal, begging, beseeching, entreaty, imploring, petition, pleading, request, soliciting, suit, supplication
2 an earnest request — see PLEA 1
prayerful *adj* asking humbly — see SUPPLIANT
preacher *n* a person specially trained and authorized to conduct religious services in a Christian church — see CLERGYMAN
preamble *n* a short section (as of a book) that leads to or explains the main part — see INTRODUCTION
precariousness *n* the quality or state of not being firmly fixed in position — see INSTABILITY
precautionary *adj* concerned with or serving to keep something from happening — see PREVENTIVE
precede *vb* to go or come before in time ⟨there are two speeches which will *precede* yours⟩
synonyms antedate, forego, predate
antonyms follow, succeed
precedence *n* the right to one's attention before other things considered less important — see PRIORITY
precedent *adj* going before another in time or order — see PREVIOUS
preceding *adj* going before another in time or order — see PREVIOUS
preceptor *n* a person whose occupation is to give formal instruction in a school — see TEACHER
precious *adj* **1** commanding a large price — see COSTLY
2 granted special treatment or attention — see DARLING 1
3 having qualities that tend to make one loved — see LOVABLE
precipice *n* a steep wall of rock, earth, or ice — see CLIFF
precipitate *adj* acting or done with excessive or careless speed — see HASTY 1
precipitate *n* matter that settles to the bottom of a body of liquid — see DEPOSIT 1
precipitate *vb* to fall as water in a continuous stream of drops from the clouds — see RAIN 1
precipitately *adv* with excessive or careless speed — see HASTILY 1
precipitating *adj* marked by or abounding with rain — see RAINY
precipitation *n* excited and often showy or disorderly speed — see HURRY 1
precipitous *adj* **1** acting or done with excessive or careless speed — see HASTY 1
2 having an incline approaching the perpendicular — see STEEP 1
precipitously *adv* with excessive or careless speed — see HASTILY 1

precipitousness *n* excited and often showy or disorderly speed — see HURRY 1

précis *n* a short statement of the main points — see SUMMARY

precise *adj* **1** meeting the highest standard of accuracy ⟨a machine which takes very *precise* measurements⟩
synonyms accurate, close, delicate, exact, fine, hairline, mathematical, pinpoint, rigorous
related words correct, right, strict, true; definite, definitive; nice, subtle; careful, fastidious, finicky
near antonyms approximate, round; false, incorrect, untrue, wrong; careless, loose; indefinite, unclear, vague; doubtful, dubious, questionable, unreliable, untrustworthy
antonyms coarse, imprecise, inaccurate, inexact, rough
2 being in agreement with the truth or a fact or a standard — see CORRECT 1
3 being neither more nor less than a certain amount, number, or extent — see EVEN 1
4 following an original exactly — see FAITHFUL 2
5 of a particular or exact sort — see EXPRESS 1

precisely *adv* **1** as stated or indicated without the slightest difference — see EXACTLY 1
2 in a like manner — see JUST 1
3 without any relaxation of standards or precision — see STRICTLY

preciseness *n* the quality or state of being very accurate — see PRECISION

precision *n* the quality or state of being very accurate ⟨the company that measures TV ratings prides itself on the *precision* of its calculations⟩
synonyms accuracy, closeness, delicacy, exactitude, exactness, fineness, preciseness, rigorousness, veracity
related words correctness, rightness, strictness, truth; definiteness, definitiveness; nicety, subtlety; care, carefulness, fastidiousness
near antonyms approximation, roundness; falseness, falsity, incorrectness, wrongness; carelessness, guesswork, looseness; indefiniteness, unclearness, vagueness
antonyms coarseness, impreciseness, imprecision, inaccuracy, inexactness, roughness

preclude *vb* to keep from happening by taking action in advance — see PREVENT

precluding *n* the act or practice of keeping something from happening — see PREVENTION

precocious *adj* occurring before the usual or expected time — see EARLY 2

precociously *adv* before the usual or expected time — see EARLY

preconception *n* an attitude, belief, or impression formed in advance of actual experience of something — see PREPOSSESSION 1

precursor *n* **1** one that announces or indicates the later arrival of another — see FORERUNNER 1
2 something belonging to an earlier time from which something else was later developed — see ANCESTOR 2

predaceous *or* **predacious** *adj* living by killing and eating other animals — see PREDATORY

predate *vb* to go or come before in time — see PRECEDE

predatory *adj* living by killing and eating other animals ⟨hawks are *predatory* and pose a danger to rabbits and other pets⟩
synonyms predaceous (*or* predacious), rapacious
related words carnivorous; aggressive, deadly, ferocious, fierce, savage, violent; untamed, wild
near antonyms herbivorous, vegetarian; gentle, submissive, tame

predecessor *n* something belonging to an earlier time from which something else was later developed — see ANCESTOR 2

predestine *vb* to determine the fate of in advance — see DESTINE

predetermine *vb* to determine the fate of in advance — see DESTINE

predicament *n* a difficult, puzzling, or embarrassing situation from which there is no easy escape ⟨if you had told the truth in the first place, we wouldn't be in this *predicament*⟩
synonyms corner, fix, hole, jam, pickle, spot
related words difficulty, dilemma, hot water, pinch, plight, quagmire, quandary, scrape, trouble; deadlock, halt, impasse, stalemate, standstill; clutch, crisis, crossroad, emergency, exigency, juncture, strait

predicate *vb* to find a basis — see BASE

predict *vb* to tell of or describe beforehand — see FORETELL

predicting *n* a declaration that something will happen in the future — see PREDICTION

prediction *n* a declaration that something will happen in the future ⟨we were all amazed when the fortune-teller's *predictions* turned out to be true⟩
synonyms auguring, cast, forecast, forecasting, foretelling, predicting, presaging, prognosis, prognosticating, prognostication, prophecy, soothsaying
related words augury, omen, portent, sign; anticipation, foreknowledge; foresight; conjecture, guess, surmise

predictive *adj* being a sign of a later course of events — see PROPHETIC

predilection *n* a habitual attraction to some activity or thing — see INCLINATION 1

predisposition *n* a habitual attraction to some activity or thing — see INCLINATION 1

predominance *n* controlling power or influence over others — see SUPREMACY 1

predominant *adj* coming before all others in importance — see FOREMOST 1

predominantly *adv* for the most part — see CHIEFLY

preeminence *n* **1** exceptionally high quality — see EXCELLENCE 1
2 controlling power or influence over others — see SUPREMACY 1
3 the fact or state of being above others in rank or importance — see EMINENCE 1

preeminent *adj* **1** coming before all others in importance — see FOREMOST 1
2 highest in rank or authority — see HEAD
3 standing above others in rank, importance, or achievement — see EMINENT

preempt *vb* to take or make use of without authority or right — see APPROPRIATE 1

preface *n* a short section (as of a book) that leads to or explains the main part — see INTRODUCTION

prefer *vb* **1** to show partiality toward ⟨I generally *prefer* chocolate ice cream over vanilla⟩
synonyms favor, lean (toward), like
related words adore, cotton (to), delight (in), dig, enjoy, fancy, groove (on), relish, revel (in); choose, cull, handpick, name, pick, select, single

(out), take; covet, crave, desire, want, wish (for); bias, prejudice; incline (towards), tend (to); admire, appreciate, cherish, prize, treasure, value
phrases be partial to
near antonyms disfavor, dislike; abhor, abominate, detest, hate, loathe; decline, refuse, reject, turn down; discard, jettison, throw away, throw out
2 to decide to accept (someone or something) from a group of possibilities — see CHOOSE 1
preferably *adv* by choice or preference — see RATHER 1
preference *n* **1** a person or thing that is preferred over others — see FAVORITE
2 positive regard for something — see LIKING
3 the power, right, or opportunity to choose — see CHOICE 1
preferment *n* a raising or a state of being raised to a higher rank or position — see ADVANCEMENT 1
preferred *adj* singled out from a number or group as more to one's liking — see SELECT 1
prefigure *vb* to give a slight indication of beforehand — see FORESHADOW
prefiguring *n* something believed to be a sign or warning of a future event — see OMEN
pregnancy *n* the state of containing unborn young within the body <an elephant's *pregnancy* can last almost a year>
synonyms gestation
related words conception; begetting, breeding, generation, siring, spawning
near antonyms barrenness, infertility
pregnant *adj* **1** containing unborn young within the body <we only realized that our cat had been *pregnant* when she unexpectedly delivered three kittens>
synonyms expectant, gravid
related words childbearing; brooding; conceiving, impregnated
phrases with child, with young
near antonyms barren, infertile; aborting, miscarrying; delivered
antonyms nonpregnant
2 clearly conveying a special meaning (as one's mood) — see EXPRESSIVE
prejudgment *n* an attitude, belief, or impression formed in advance of actual experience of something — see PREPOSSESSION 1
prejudice *n* **1** an attitude that always favors one way of feeling or acting especially without considering any other possibilities — see BIAS
2 hatred of or discrimination against a person or persons based on their race — see RACISM 2
prejudice *vb* to cause to have often negative opinions formed without sufficient knowledge <all the bad stories I had heard about that teacher *prejudiced* me against him even before the first class>
synonyms bias
related words dispose, incline, predispose; influence, prepossess; convince, persuade, suggest
prejudiced *adj* **1** inclined to favor one side over another — see PARTIAL 1
2 unwilling to grant other people social rights or to accept other viewpoints — see INTOLERANT 2
prejudicial *adj* **1** causing or capable of causing harm — see HARMFUL
2 opposed to one's interests — see ADVERSE 1
preliminary *adj* coming before the main part or item usually to introduce or prepare for what follows <we need to do some *preliminary* research in order to properly focus the experiment>
synonyms introductory, preparatory
related words introducing, prefacing, preparing, readying; premonitory, warning; basic, fundamental; ahead, early, former, preceding, previous, prior
near antonyms after, behind, following, subsequent
prelude *n* a short section (as of a book) that leads to or explains the main part — see INTRODUCTION
premature *adj* occurring before the usual or expected time — see EARLY 2
prematurely *adv* before the usual or expected time — see EARLY
premier *adj* **1** coming before all others in time or order — see FIRST 1
2 highest in rank or authority — see HEAD
3 coming before all others in importance — see FOREMOST 1
premise *n* **1** something taken as being true or factual and used as a starting point for a course of action or reasoning — see ASSUMPTION
2 premises *pl* the area around and belonging to a building — see GROUND 1
premise *vb* to take as true or as a fact without actual proof — see ASSUME 2
premium *adj* commanding a large price — see COSTLY
premium *n* something given in recognition of achievement — see AWARD
premonition *n* a feeling that something bad will happen <she had a *premonition* that her cat would somehow get hurt that day>
synonyms foreboding, presage, presentiment
related words anticipation, foreknowledge; insight, intuition; augury, omen, portent, sign; impression, suspicion; anxiety, apprehension, care, concern, disquiet, doubt, dread, fear, misgiving, unease, worry; foresight
preoccupation *n* something about which one is constantly thinking or concerned — see FIXATION
preoccupied *adj* lost in thought and unaware of one's surroundings or actions — see ABSENT-MINDED 1
preparatory *adj* coming before the main part or item usually to introduce or prepare for what follows — see PRELIMINARY
prepare *vb* **1** to make ready in advance <I think I *prepared* myself well for this test> <we *prepared* the classroom for the important visitors by getting rid of some unsightly clutter>
synonyms fit, fix, lay, ready
related words brace, fortify, steel; batten, gather, gear (up), mount, train; boot (up), prime; arrange, set, spread; arm, equip, furnish, outfit, provide, supply; incline, predispose; draft, draw (up), frame; warm (up)
2 to make competent (as by training, skill, or ability) for a particular office or function — see QUALIFY 2
3 to put (something) into proper and usually carefully worked out written form — see COMPOSE 1
prepared *adj* being in a state of fitness for some experience or action — see READY 1
prepossession *n* **1** an attitude, belief, or impression formed in advance of actual experience of something <the foreign tourists' *prepossessions* about life in the U.S. had been formed by many hours of American TV shows>

synonyms preconception, prejudgment
related words bias, prejudice; conjecture, hypothesis, imagining, predetermination, presumption, presupposition, speculation, supposition, theorizing, theory; concept, thought
2 something about which one is constantly thinking or concerned — see FIXATION
preposterous *adj* **1** conceived or made without regard for reason or reality — see FANTASTIC 1
2 showing or marked by a lack of good sense or judgment — see FOOLISH 1
3 so foolish or pointless as to be worthy of scornful laughter — see RIDICULOUS 1
preposterousness *n* lack of good sense or judgment — see FOOLISHNESS 1
prerogative *n* something to which one has a just claim — see RIGHT 1
presage *n* **1** a feeling that something bad will happen — see PREMONITION
2 something believed to be a sign or warning of a future event — see OMEN
presage *vb* to tell of or describe beforehand — see FORETELL
presaging *n* a declaration that something will happen in the future — see PREDICTION
prescience *n* **1** the special ability to see or know about events before they actually occur — see FORESIGHT 1
2 concern or preparation for the future — see FORESIGHT 2
prescient *adj* having or showing awareness of and preparation for the future — see FORESIGHTED
prescribe *vb* to give the rules about (something) clearly and exactly ⟨in chess, you can move the various pieces only in certain *prescribed* ways⟩
synonyms define, lay down, specify
related words decree, dictate, ordain; assign, direct, fix, set, settle; arrange, order; choose, select; adjure, bid, charge, command, enjoin, instruct, tell; conduct, control, lead, manage; coerce, constrain, force; oblige, require
presence *n* **1** a position within view ⟨men should watch their language when in the *presence* of ladies⟩
synonyms sight
related words nearness, proximity
2 the outward form of someone or something especially as indicative of a quality — see APPEARANCE 1
present *adj* **1** existing or in progress right now ⟨I am very busy at the *present* moment⟩
synonyms current, extant, ongoing, present-day
related words contemporary, mod, modern, new, newfangled, new-fashioned, now, recent, red-hot, space-age, ultramodern, up-to-date; being, breathing, existing, living
near antonyms done, ended, finished, over; ancient, antediluvian, antiquated, antique, archaic, dated, fusty, musty, noncontemporary, obsolete, old, oldfangled, old-fashioned, old-time, out-of-date, outworn, passé; bygone, erstwhile, formerly
antonyms ago, past; future
2 being within the confines of a specified place ⟨all of you are required to be *present* for every class⟩
synonyms attending
related words accompanying, observing, participating; available; abounding; latent; breathing, existing, existent, extant, live
phrases in attendance, on hand
near antonyms departed, gone, retired; nonexistent; AWOL, truant; dead, departed, lost, vanished; delayed, late, overdue, tardy
antonyms absent, away, missing, out
present *n* **1** the time currently existing or in progress ⟨I cannot talk to you at *present*, but perhaps in a few minutes⟩
synonyms moment, now, today
related words phase, stage, state; tonight, tomorrow
near antonyms yesterday, yesteryear
antonyms past; future
2 something given to someone without expectation of a return — see GIFT 1
present *vb* **1** to bring before the public in performance or exhibition ⟨we will *present* a performance of *Our Town* this week⟩
synonyms carry, give, mount, offer, stage
related words display, exhibit, show; preview; act, impersonate, perform, play, portray; depict, dramatize, enact, render, represent; extend, proffer, tender
2 to make (one person) known (to another) socially — see INTRODUCE 1
3 to make a present of — see GIVE 1
presentation *n* something given to someone without expectation of a return — see GIFT 1
present–day *adj* **1** being or involving the latest methods, concepts, information, or styles — see MODERN
2 existing or in progress right now — see PRESENT 1
presentiment *n* a feeling that something bad will happen — see PREMONITION
presently *adv* **1** at or within a short time — see SHORTLY 2
2 at the present time — see NOW 1
preservation *n* **1** the act or activity of keeping something in an existing and usually satisfactory condition — see MAINTENANCE
2 the careful maintaining and protection of something valuable especially in its natural or original state — see CONSERVATION 1
preserve *vb* to keep in good condition — see MAINTAIN 1
preserving *n* the act or activity of keeping something in an existing and usually satisfactory condition — see MAINTENANCE
president *n* a person in charge of a meeting — see CHAIR 1
preside (over) *vb* to exercise authority or power over — see GOVERN 1
presiding *adj* highest in rank or authority — see HEAD
press *n* a great number of persons or things gathered together — see CROWD 1
press *vb* **1** to push steadily against with some force ⟨an old doorbell that requires you to *press* the button hard⟩
synonyms bear (down on), depress, shove, weigh (on *or* upon)
related words compress, squash, squeeze; compel, force, pressure; lean (on *or* against), muscle; drive, propel, thrust; compact, constrict, contract, crush, scrunch, wring; cram, jam, jampack, pack, stuff, wedge
2 to apply external pressure on so as to force out the juice or contents of ⟨my family will only drink juice from freshly *pressed* oranges⟩
synonyms crush, express, mash, squeeze

related words pulp, puree; extract, extrude

3 to gather into a closely packed group ⟨everyone *pressed* around me to see the pictures⟩

synonyms bunch, cluster, crowd, huddle

related words assemble, collect, congregate, flock, gather, herd, swarm, throng; encircle, mob, surround; embrace, hug

4 to force one's way ⟨we continued to *press* deeper and deeper into the tangled rain forest⟩

synonyms bulldoze, elbow, muscle, push

related words jostle; ram, shove, thrust

5 to cause (a person) to give in to pressure — see FORCE

6 to try to persuade (someone) through earnest appeals to follow a course of action — see URGE

press (for) *vb* to ask for (something) earnestly or with authority — see DEMAND 1

pressing *adj* needing immediate attention — see ACUTE 2

pressure *n* **1** the burden on one's emotional or mental well-being created by demands on one's time — see STRESS 1

2 the use of power to impose one's will on another — see FORCE 2

pressure *vb* to cause (a person) to give in to pressure — see FORCE

prestidigitator *n* one who practices tricks and illusions for entertainment — see MAGICIAN 2

prestigious *adj* **1** having a good reputation especially in a field of knowledge — see RESPECTABLE 1

2 standing above others in rank, importance, or achievement — see EMINENT

presto *adv* with great speed — see FAST 1

presumably *adv* **1** to all outward appearances — see APPARENTLY

2 without much doubt — see PROBABLY

presume *vb* **1** to form an opinion from little or no evidence — see GUESS 1

2 to take as true or as a fact without actual proof — see ASSUME 2

presumed *adj* appearing to be true on the basis of evidence that may or may not be confirmed — see APPARENT 1

presuming *adj* showing a lack of proper social reserve or modesty — see PRESUMPTUOUS 1

presumption *n* **1** shameless boldness — see EFFRONTERY

2 something taken as being true or factual and used as a starting point for a course of action or reasoning — see ASSUMPTION

presumptuous *adj* **1** showing a lack of proper social reserve or modesty ⟨it's a little *presumptuous* of you to assume that I'm your new best friend just because I invited you along⟩

synonyms bold, familiar, forward, free, immodest, overfamiliar, presuming

related words arrogant, complacent, conceited, egoistic, egotistic (*or* egotistical), important, overweening, pompous, prideful, proud, self-assertive, self-conceited, self-important, self-satisfied, smug, uppity, vain, vainglorious; cavalier, disdainful, haughty, lordly, pretentious, snobbish, stuck-up, supercilious, superior; audacious, brash, brassy, brazen, fresh, impertinent, impudent, pert, saucy; confident, self-assured, self-confident, sure; boastful, braggart, bragging; domineering, high-handed, imperious; self-centered, selfish

near antonyms humble, meek, unassertive; bashful, retiring, shy; diffident, self-doubting

antonyms modest, unassuming

2 having a feeling of superiority that shows itself in an overbearing attitude — see ARROGANT

3 thrusting oneself where one is not welcome or invited — see INTRUSIVE

presumptuousness *n* **1** an exaggerated sense of one's importance that shows itself in the making of excessive or unjustified claims — see ARROGANCE

2 shameless boldness — see EFFRONTERY

presuppose *vb* to take as true or as a fact without actual proof — see ASSUME 2

presupposition *n* something taken as being true or factual and used as a starting point for a course of action or reasoning — see ASSUMPTION

pretend *adj* not real and existing only in the imagination — see IMAGINARY

pretend *vb* **1** to take on a false or deceptive appearance ⟨I *pretended* that I was scared of the vacuum cleaner⟩

synonyms dissemble, let on

related words act, impersonate, masquerade, play, pose; affect, assume, counterfeit, fake, feign, profess, put on, simulate; camouflage, conceal, disguise, mask; bluff, feint

phrases make a pretense, make a show, make believe, put on an act, put up a front

2 to present a false appearance of — see FEIGN

pretended *adj* lacking in natural or spontaneous quality — see ARTIFICIAL 1

pretender *n* one who makes false claims of identity or expertise — see IMPOSTOR

pretense *or* **pretence** *n* **1** the quality or state of appearing or trying to appear more important or more valuable than is the case ⟨she seemed to be a very down-to-earth woman who was completely free of *pretense*⟩

synonyms affectation, affectedness, grandiosity, pretension, pretentiousness

related words arrogance, complacency, conceit, egotism, pride, self-assertion, self-conceit, self-importance, self-satisfaction, smugness, vaingloriousness, vainglory, vainness, vanity; disdain, haughtiness, lordliness, snobbery, snobbishness, superciliousness, superiority; confidence, presumption, self-assurance, self-confidence, sureness; boastfulness, braggadocio; aggressiveness, assertiveness, audaciousness, boldness, brassiness, cheekiness, cockiness, forwardness, impudence, insolence, rudeness; grandiloquence; flashiness, gaudiness, ostentation, show, showiness

near antonyms demureness, humbleness, humility, meekness, modesty; bashfulness, diffidence, shyness, timidity; naturalness, sincerity

2 a display of emotion or behavior that is insincere or intended to deceive — see MASQUERADE

3 an entitlement to something — see CLAIM 1

4 an exaggerated sense of one's importance that shows itself in the making of excessive or unjustified claims — see ARROGANCE

pretension *n* **1** an entitlement to something — see CLAIM 1

2 an exaggerated sense of one's importance that shows itself in the making of excessive or unjustified claims — see ARROGANCE

3 the quality or state of appearing or trying to appear more important or more valuable than is the case — see PRETENSE 1

4 something that one hopes or intends to accomplish — see GOAL

pretentious *adj* **1** self-consciously trying to present an appearance of grandeur or importance ⟨the *pretentious* hosts served caviar at their party, even though they themselves dislike it⟩
synonyms affected, grandiose, highfalutin, ostentatious, pompous
related words grandiloquent, high-sounding, sententious; arrogant, complacent, conceited, egoistic, egotistic (*or* egotistical), important, overweening, prideful, proud, self-assertive, self-conceited, self-important, self-satisfied, smug, uppity, vain, vainglorious; cavalier, disdainful, haughty, lordly, snobbish, snobby, stuck-up, supercilious, superior; confident, self-assured, self-confident, sure; boastful, braggart, bragging; aggressive, assertive, audacious, bold, brassy, cheeky, cocky, forward, impudent, insolent, rude; flashy, flaunting, gaudy, showy
near antonyms demure, homely, humble, lowly, meek, retiring, unassertive, unassuming; bashful, diffident, mousy (*or* mousey), overmodest, passive, quiet, reserved, shy, timid
antonyms modest, unpretentious
2 having a feeling of superiority that shows itself in an overbearing attitude — see ARROGANT

pretentiousness *n* **1** an exaggerated sense of one's importance that shows itself in the making of excessive or unjustified claims — see ARROGANCE
2 excessive or unnecessary display — see OSTENTATION
3 the quality or state of appearing or trying to appear more important or more valuable than is the case — see PRETENSE 1

preternatural *adj* of, relating to, or being part of a reality beyond the observable physical universe — see SUPERNATURAL 1

prettiness *n* the qualities in a person or thing that as a whole give pleasure to the senses — see BEAUTY 1

pretty *adj* very pleasing to look at — see BEAUTIFUL

pretty *adv* to some degree or extent — see FAIRLY

prevail *vb* **1** to achieve victory (as in a contest) — see WIN 1
2 to continue to operate or to meet one's needs — see HOLD OUT

prevail (on *or* upon) *vb* to cause (someone) to agree with a belief or course of action by using arguments or earnest requests — see PERSUADE

prevail (over) *vb* to achieve a victory over — see BEAT 2

prevailing *adj* **1** accepted, used, or practiced by most people — see CURRENT 1
2 held by or applicable to a majority of the people — see GENERAL 3

prevalence *n* the fact or state of happening often — see FREQUENCY

prevalent *adj* accepted, used, or practiced by most people — see CURRENT 1

prevaricate *vb* to make a statement one knows to be untrue — see LIE 1

prevarication *n* a statement known by its maker to be untrue and made in order to deceive — see LIE

prevaricator *n* a person who tells lies — see LIAR

prevent *vb* to keep from happening by taking action in advance ⟨a lot of problems would have been *prevented* if we'd just prepared better⟩
synonyms avert, forestall, help, obviate, preclude
related words anticipate, provide; negate, neutralize, nullify; avoid, save; baffle, balk, checkmate, deter, foil, frustrate, thwart; bar, block, hamper, hinder, impede, interfere (with), retard, stall; deflect, fend (off), head (off), stave off, stop, ward (off); avoid, circumvent, dodge, elude, escape, evade; forbid, inhibit, prohibit; arrest, check, halt, stop; counteract, offset
near antonyms abet, aid, assist; ease, facilitate, smooth; advance, cultivate, encourage, forward, foster, further, nurture, promote; allow, leave, let, permit

preventative *adj* concerned with or serving to keep something from happening — see PREVENTIVE

prevention *n* the act or practice of keeping something from happening ⟨good crowd control is crucial to the *prevention* of riots⟩
synonyms averting, forestallment, obviating, precluding
related words avoidance, circumvention; negation, neutralization, nullification; baffling, balking, checkmate, debarment, determent, deterrence, foiling, frustration, thwarting; bar, block, hindrance, interference; interdiction, prohibition
near antonyms aid, assistance; facilitation; advancement, cultivation, encouragement, nurture, promotion

preventive *adj* concerned with or serving to keep something from happening ⟨if you start taking this *preventive* medicine now, you may not get sick after all⟩
synonyms precautionary, preventative
related words deterrent, deterring; negating, neutralizing, nullifying; baffling, balking, foiling, frustrating, thwarting; blocking, hampering, hindering, impeding, retardant, stalling
near antonyms abetting, aiding, assisting; easing, facilitating, smoothing; encouraging, forwarding, fostering, furthering, nurturing, promoting

previous *adj* going before another in time or order ⟨the new instructor should consult with the *previous* teacher about the lesson plans⟩ ⟨the *previous* math problem also included a reference to store discounts⟩
synonyms antecedent, anterior, foregoing, precedent, preceding, prior
related words advance, early, premature; earliest, first, inaugural, initial, maiden, original, pioneer; preexisting; introductory, preliminary; erstwhile, former, whilom
near antonyms advanced, late; final, last, terminal, ultimate
antonyms after, ensuing, following, subsequent, succeeding

previously *adv* so as to precede something in order of time — see AHEAD 1

previous to *prep* earlier than — see BEFORE 1

prey *n* an animal that is hunted or killed ⟨rabbits are common *prey* for owls and hawks⟩
synonyms chase, quarry
related words game; kill, victim; creature, critter, beast, brute; target
near antonyms carnivore; chaser, hunter, pursuer; killer, murderer
antonyms predator

prey (on *or* upon) *vb* to seize and eat (something) as prey ⟨a fox has been *preying on* the chickens⟩
synonyms feed (on, upon, *or* off)
related words chase, hunt, pursue; destroy, dispatch, do in, fell, kill, slay

price *n* **1** the amount of money that is demanded as payment for something ⟨I really wanted to buy that shirt, but the *price* was more money than I had⟩
synonyms charge, cost, fee, figure
related words list price, market value, rate, tariff, unit price; carrying charge, overcharge, surcharge; deduction, discount, markdown, reduction, sale; deposit; down payment; account, bill, check, invoice, tab
2 the loss or penalty involved in achieving a goal ⟨I finished the essay, but the *price* was losing a night's sleep⟩
synonyms cost
related words expense, toll; forfeit, penalty, sacrifice
3 something offered or given in return for a service performed — see REWARD

prick *n* **1** a mark or small hole made by a pointed instrument ⟨the immunization shot left a *prick* on my arm that turned into a bruise⟩
synonyms perforation, pinhole, pinprick, punch, puncture, stab
related words gouge, groove, hollow; break, cut, gash, notch, rupture, slash, slit
2 a sharp unpleasant sensation usually felt in some specific part of the body — see PAIN 1

prickly *adj* likely to cause a scratch — see SCRATCHY 1

pride *n* **1** a reasonable or justifiable sense of one's worth or importance ⟨finishing that survival course gave me a real sense of *pride* and confidence in my abilities⟩
synonyms ego, pridefulness, self-esteem, self-regard, self-respect
related words confidence, self-assurance, self-confidence; dignity, face, honor, prestige
near antonyms disgrace, humiliation, shame; demureness, humbleness, humility, modesty; diffidence, meekness, shyness, timidity, timidness
2 an asset that brings praise or renown — see GLORY 2
3 an often unjustified feeling of being pleased with oneself or with one's situation or achievements — see COMPLACENCE

pride *vb* to think highly of (oneself) ⟨he *prides* himself on the quality of his writing⟩
synonyms flatter, plume
related words boast, brag, vaunt; congratulate, felicitate

prideful *adj* **1** having or displaying feelings of scorn for what is regarded as beneath oneself — see PROUD 1
2 having too high an opinion of oneself — see CONCEITED

pridefulness *n* **1** a reasonable or justifiable sense of one's worth or importance — see PRIDE 1
2 an often unjustified feeling of being pleased with oneself or with one's situation or achievements — see COMPLACENCE

priest *n* a person specially trained and authorized to conduct religious services in a Christian church — see CLERGYMAN

priestly *adj* of, relating to, or characteristic of the clergy — see CLERICAL

prim *adj* given to or marked by very conservative standards regarding personal behavior or morals — see STRAITLACED

primal *adj* relating to or occurring near the beginning of a process, series, or time period — see EARLY 1

primarily *adv* **1** in the beginning — see ORIGINALLY
2 for the most part — see CHIEFLY

primary *adj* **1** coming before all others in importance — see FOREMOST 1
2 done or working without something else coming in between — see DIRECT 1
3 highest in rank or authority — see HEAD

prime *adj* **1** highest in rank or authority — see HEAD
2 of the very best kind — see EXCELLENT

prime *n* **1** a state or time of great activity, thriving, or achievement — see BLOOM 1
2 individuals carefully selected as being the best of a class — see ELITE

primer *n* a book used for instruction in a subject — see TEXTBOOK

primeval *adj* relating to or occurring near the beginning of a process, series, or time period — see EARLY 1

primitive *adj* **1** belonging to or characteristic of an early level of skill or development ⟨*primitive* wooden tools were used before the Iron Age⟩
synonyms crude, low, rude, rudimentary
related words basic, simple, uncomplicated; homely, homespun, unsophisticated; early, primeval, primordial; backward, underdeveloped, undeveloped; aged, ancient, antediluvian, antiquated, antique, dated, fusty, hoary, musty, obsolete, old, oldfangled, old-fashioned, old-time, out-of-date, outworn, passé, past
near antonyms complex, complicated, intricate, involved, sophisticated; full-blown, full-grown, grown, mature, matured, perfected, ripe, ripened; civilized, cultivated, enlightened, refined; contemporary, current, latest, mod, modern, new, newfangled, new-fashioned, novel, now, present-day, space-age, ultramodern, up-to-date
antonyms advanced, developed, evolved, higher
2 relating to or occurring near the beginning of a process, series, or time period — see EARLY 1

primordial *adj* relating to or occurring near the beginning of a process, series, or time period — see EARLY 1

prince *n* a person of rank, power, or influence in a particular field — see MAGNATE

princely *adj* fit for or worthy of a royal ruler — see MONARCHICAL

principal *adj* **1** coming before all others in importance — see FOREMOST 1
2 highest in rank or authority — see HEAD

principal *n* the person who has the most important role in a play, movie, or TV show — see STAR 2

principally *adv* for the most part — see CHIEFLY

principled *adj* **1** following the accepted rules of moral conduct — see HONORABLE 1
2 guided by or in accordance with one's sense of right and wrong — see CONSCIENTIOUS 1

principles *n pl* **1** general or basic truths on which other truths or theories can be based ⟨if you don't learn the *principles* of algebra now, you won't understand much later on⟩
synonyms basics, elements, essentials, fundamentals, rudiments
related words basis, foundation, groundwork; nitty-gritty; belief, canon, doctrine, dogma, faith, philosophy; axiom, law, precept, tenet; rule, standard; theorem

near antonyms details, trivia
2 the code of good conduct for an individual or group — see ETHICS

print *n* **1** a perceptible trace left by pressure ⟨one telltale sign that I had been napping was the *print* left by the chenille bedspread on my cheek⟩
synonyms impress, impression, imprint, stamp
related words dent, hollow, indentation; mark, sign
2 a picture created from an image recorded on a light-sensitive surface by a camera — see PHOTOGRAPH

print *vb* to produce and release for distribution in printed form — see PUBLISH 1

prior *adj* going before another in time or order — see PREVIOUS

priority *n* the right to one's attention before other things considered less important ⟨the principal has decided to give your request *priority*, so you'll have a meeting early tomorrow morning⟩
synonyms precedence, right-of-way
related words preference; urgency; ascendancy, preeminence, primacy, supremacy; transcendence; order, progression, sequence, succession

prior to *prep* earlier than — see BEFORE 1

priory *n* a residence for men under religious vows — see MONASTERY

prison *n* a place of confinement for persons held in lawful custody — see JAIL

prisoner *n* one that has been taken and held in confinement — see CAPTIVE

pristine *adj* being in an original and unused or unspoiled state — see FRESH 1

private *adj* **1** not known or meant to be known by the general populace ⟨that he is planning to retire is *private* information until he makes a public announcement⟩
synonyms confidential, hushed, inside, intimate, nonpublic, privy, secret
related words classified, top secret; unadvertised, unannounced, undisclosed, unmentioned; clandestine, collusive, conspiratorial, covert; surreptitious, undercover, underhand, underhanded; personal; closeted, concealed, hidden; repressed, silenced, stifled, suppressed
near antonyms well-known; advertised, aired, announced, blazed, broadcast, declared, disclosed, divulged, enunciated, heralded, proclaimed, professed, promulgated, publicized, published, reported, spotlighted; general, popular, prevailing, vulgar; prevalent, rife, widespread; communal, shared
antonyms common, open, public
2 undertaken or done so as to escape being observed or known by others — see SECRET 1
3 of, relating to, or belonging to a single person — see INDIVIDUAL 1

privation *n* the state of being robbed of something normally enjoyed ⟨the constant *privation* of sleep was starting to affect my schoolwork⟩
synonyms deprivation, loss
related words lack, need, want; dispossession; denial, forfeit, forfeiture, penalty, sacrifice; bereavement
near antonyms ownership, possession; accumulation, acquiring, gain

privilege *n* something granted as a special favor ⟨you will have the *privilege* of leading the line today⟩
synonyms appanage, boon, concession, honor
related words courtesy; claim, entitlement, right; birthright; perquisite, prerogative; charter, grant, patent; exemption, immunity, waiver
near antonyms duty, obligation, responsibility

privy *adj* **1** not known or meant to be known by the general populace — see PRIVATE 1
2 undertaken or done so as to escape being observed or known by others — see SECRET 1
3 of, relating to, or belonging to a single person — see INDIVIDUAL 1

prize *n* **1** someone or something unusually desirable ⟨in her parents' view, her current boyfriend is certainly no *prize*⟩
synonyms catch, gem, jewel, pearl, plum, treasure
related words find, godsend, goody, valuable, windfall; booty, loot, spoil; glory, pride; jackpot, treasure trove
near antonyms lemon, loser
2 something given in recognition of achievement — see AWARD

[1]**prize** *vb* **1** to draw out by force or with effort — see EXTRACT
2 to raise, move, or pull apart with or as if with a lever — see [1]PRY 1

[2]**prize** *vb* to hold dear — see LOVE 1

prizefighter *n* one that engages in the sport of fighting with the fists — see BOXER

probability *n* **1** the quality or state of being likely to occur ⟨the plot of the movie thriller was exciting and surprising but woefully lacking in *probability*⟩
synonyms likelihood, likeliness
related words credibility, plausibility; liability; feasibility, feasibleness, possibility, potentiality, reasonability, viability
near antonyms doubtfulness, dubiousness; impracticability, impracticality; implausibility, incredibility
antonyms improbability, unlikelihood, unlikeliness
2 a measure of how often an event will occur instead of another ⟨the *probability* of flipping a coin and getting heads fifty times in a row is not good⟩
synonyms chance, odds, percentage
related words outlook, prospect; possibility, potential, potentiality

probable *adj* **1** worthy of being accepted as true or reasonable — see BELIEVABLE
2 having a high chance of occurring — see LIKELY 1

probably *adv* without much doubt ⟨we would *probably* win that bet⟩
synonyms doubtless, likely, presumably
related words mayhap, perchance, perhaps, possibly; conceivably, imaginably, plausibly, practically, reasonably; potentially; assuredly, certainly, clearly, conclusively, decisively, definitely, definitively, indubitably, positively, surely
near antonyms implausibly, inconceivably, incredibly, unbelievably
antonyms improbably

probe *n* a systematic search for the truth or facts about something — see INQUIRY 1

probe *vb* **1** to search through or into — see EXPLORE 1
2 to go into or range over for purposes of discovery — see EXPLORE 2

probing *n* a systematic search for the truth or facts about something — see INQUIRY 1

probity *n* **1** conduct that conforms to an accepted standard of right and wrong — see MORALITY 1
2 devotion to telling the truth — see HONESTY 1
3 faithfulness to high moral standards — see HONOR 1

problem *n* **1** something that requires thought and skill for resolution ⟨the *problem* of world hunger⟩
synonyms case, knot, matter, trouble
related words issue, question; challenge; corner, fix, hole, hot water, jam, pickle, predicament, situation; glitch, hitch, snag; conundrum, enigma, mystery, puzzle, puzzlement, riddle; brainteaser, perplexer, poser, stumper
antonyms answer, solution
2 an interrogative expression often used to test knowledge — see QUESTION 1
3 something that is a source of irritation — see ANNOYANCE 3

problematic *also* **problematical** *adj* **1** requiring exceptional skill or caution in performance or handling — see TRICKY
2 giving good reason for being doubted, questioned, or challenged — see DOUBTFUL 2

procedure *n* **1** a usually fixed or ordered series of actions or events leading to a result — see PROCESS 1
2 a way of acting or proceeding — see COURSE 1

proceed *vb* to move forward along a course — see GO 1

proceed (along) *vb* to make one's way through, across, or over — see TRAVERSE

proceeding *adj* being in progress or development — see ONGOING 1

proceeding *n* **1** a court case for enforcing a right or claim — see LAWSUIT
2 a usually fixed or ordered series of actions or events leading to a result — see PROCESS 1

proceeds *n pl* **1** an increase usually measured in money that comes from labor, business, or property — see INCOME
2 the amount of money left when expenses are subtracted from the total amount received — see PROFIT 1

process *n* **1** a usually fixed or ordered series of actions or events leading to a result ⟨the *process* by which the elastic fibers spun by silkworms is turned into soft, lustrous cloth⟩
synonyms course, operation, procedure, proceeding
related words fashion, manner, method, mode, style, system, technique, way; approach, blueprint, design, game plan, layout, plan, plot, program, scheme, strategy; accomplishment, achievement, attainment, enterprise, performance, undertaking, work; activity, functioning, movement
2 forward movement in time or place — see ADVANCE 1

procession *n* **1** a body of individuals moving along in an orderly and often ceremonial way — see CORTEGE 2
2 forward movement in time or place — see ADVANCE 1

proclaim *vb* to make known openly or publicly — see ANNOUNCE

proclivity *n* a habitual attraction to some activity or thing — see INCLINATION 1

procreate *vb* to bring forth offspring ⟨in life science class we learned how animals *procreate*⟩
synonyms breed, multiply, propagate, reproduce
related words bear, beget, engender, generate, get, mother, parent, produce, sire; hatch, spawn

procurable *adj* possible to get — see AVAILABLE 1

procurator *n* a person who acts or does business for another — see AGENT 2

procure *vb* to receive as return for effort — see EARN 1

prod *vb* **1** to urge or push forward with or as if with a pointed object ⟨my sister keeps *prodding* me with her pencil to move along faster⟩
synonyms goad, spur
related words chuck, jab, jog, nudge, poke; bore, drill, pierce, prick, punch, puncture, stab, stick; drive, propel
2 to try to persuade (someone) through earnest appeals to follow a course of action — see URGE

prodigal *adj* given to spending money freely or foolishly ⟨the *prodigal* child always spent her allowance the minute she got it⟩
synonyms extravagant, profligate, spendthrift, squandering, thriftless, unthrifty, wasteful
related words improvident, myopic, shortsighted; bountiful, generous, lavish, liberal, openhanded, openhearted, philanthropic; careless, heedless, imprudent, incautious, injudicious, unwise; indulgent, reckless, self-indulgent, splurging, wanton
near antonyms cheap, close, mean, miserly, niggardly, parsimonious, penurious, pinching, spare, sparing, stingy, tight, tightfisted; careful, judicious, prudent, sensible, wise; farsighted, forehanded, foresighted, forethoughtful, provident
antonyms conserving, economical, economizing, frugal, scrimping, skimping, thrifty

prodigal *n* someone who carelessly spends money ⟨the million-dollar lottery winner was such a *prodigal* that there was no money left after a few years⟩
synonyms profligate, spender, spendthrift, squanderer, waster, wastrel
near antonyms miser, skinflint, tightwad; conserver, saver
antonyms economizer

prodigality *n* **1** an instance of spending money or resources without care or restraint — see WASTE 1
2 the quality or fact of being free or wasteful in the expenditure of money — see EXTRAVAGANCE 1

prodigious *adj* **1** causing wonder or astonishment — see MARVELOUS 1
2 unusually large — see HUGE

prodigy *n* something extraordinary or surprising — see WONDER 1

produce *n* something produced by physical or intellectual effort — see PRODUCT 1

produce *vb* **1** to be the cause of (a situation, action, or state of mind) — see EFFECT
2 to bring forth from the womb — see BEAR 1
3 to bring into being by combining, shaping, or transforming materials — see MAKE 1

product *n* **1** something produced by physical or intellectual effort ⟨that book is the *product* of years of work⟩ ⟨a rebuilt car which is the *product* of several people's labor⟩
synonyms affair, fruit, handiwork, output, produce, production, thing, work, yield
related words article, commodity, object; goods, line, merchandise, wares; handcraft, handicraft; aftereffect, aftermath, conclusion, consequence,

development, effect, issue, outcome, result, upshot; by-product, derivative, offshoot, outgrowth, residual, side effect, spin-off
2 a condition or occurrence traceable to a cause — see EFFECT 1
production *n* something produced by physical or intellectual effort — see PRODUCT 1
productive *adj* **1** having a role in deciding something's final form — see FORMATIVE
2 producing abundantly — see FERTILE
3 producing or capable of producing a desired result — see EFFECTIVE 1
productiveness *n* the power to produce a desired result — see EFFICACY
profane *adj* **1** not involving religion or religious matters ⟨it was hard to juggle the requirements of church and our more *profane* duties⟩
synonyms secular, temporal
related words atheistic, godless, irreligious, pagan; lay, nonclerical; nondenominational, nonsectarian; earthly, mundane, terrestrial, worldly; material, physical, substantial; bodily, carnal, corporal, fleshly; blasphemous, impious, irreverent, sacrilegious; unconsecrated, unhallowed, unsanctified
near antonyms divine, spiritual; consecrated, hallowed, holy, sanctified; churchly, devout, godly, pious, prayerful, reverent, worshipful; ethereal, insubstantial, metaphysical, unsubstantial; bodiless, immaterial, incorporeal, nonphysical
antonyms religious, sacred
2 not showing proper reverence for the holy or sacred — see IRREVERENT
profane *vb* **1** to lower in character or dignity — see DEBASE 1
2 to put to a bad or improper use — see MISAPPLY
3 to treat (a sacred place or object) shamefully or with great disrespect — see DESECRATE
profess *vb* **1** to present a false appearance of — see FEIGN
2 to state clearly and strongly — see ASSERT 1
3 to state as a fact usually forcefully — see CLAIM 1
profession *n* **1** a solemn and often public declaration of the truth or existence of something — see PROTESTATION
2 the activity by which one regularly makes a living — see OCCUPATION
proffer *n* something which is presented for consideration — see PROPOSAL
proffer *vb* **1** to put before another for acceptance or consideration — see OFFER 1
2 to set before the mind for consideration — see PROPOSE 1
proficiency *n* **1** a highly developed skill in or knowledge of something — see COMMAND 2
2 knowledge gained by actually doing or living through something — see EXPERIENCE 1
proficient *adj* having or showing exceptional knowledge, experience, or skill in a field of endeavor ⟨she is quite *proficient* at computer repair⟩ ⟨a *proficient* rendition of a difficult piano piece⟩
synonyms accomplished, ace, adept, consummate, crack, crackerjack, experienced, expert, good, great, master, masterful, masterly, practiced (*or* practised), skilled, skillful, versed, veteran, virtuoso
related words adroit, clever, deft, dexterous (*also* dextrous), handy; gifted, talented; experienced, polished, refined; effective, effectual, efficient, workmanlike; able, capable, competent, fit, qualified; educated, knowledgeable, schooled, taught, trained, tutored; all-around (*also* all-round), well-rounded; long-term, old
near antonyms incapable, incompetent, inept, unable, unfit, unqualified; artless, crude, rude; ineffective, ineffectual, inefficient; ungifted, untalented; ignorant, unschooled, untaught, untrained, untutored; beginning, green, inexperienced, new, raw, untested, untried; rough, unpolished
antonyms amateur, amateurish, inexperienced, inexpert, unexperienced, unpracticed, unprofessional, unseasoned, unskilled, unskillful
proficiently *adv* in a skillful or expert manner — see WELL 3
profit *n* **1** the amount of money left when expenses are subtracted from the total amount received ⟨after we deducted the cost of sugar, lemons, and paper cups, the *profit* from a day of lemonade sales was about $20⟩
synonyms earnings, gain, lucre, net, payoff, proceeds, return
related words killing, windfall; gross; compensation, emolument, income, pay, payment, remittal, requital, salary, wages; interest, return, yield; (the) black; royalty
near antonyms cost, expenditure, expense, loss, outgo, outlay
2 an increase usually measured in money that comes from labor, business, or property — see INCOME
profit *vb* to provide with something useful or desirable — see BENEFIT
profitable *adj* **1** yielding a profit ⟨selling lemonade turned out to be a *profitable* venture⟩
synonyms fat, gainful, lucrative, paying, remunerative
related words advantageous, beneficial, rewarding, useful, worthwhile
antonyms unprofitable
2 conferring benefits; promoting or contributing to personal or social well-being — see BENEFICIAL
profligate *adj* given to spending money freely or foolishly — see PRODIGAL
profligate *n* **1** someone who carelessly spends money — see PRODIGAL
2 a person who has sunk below the normal moral standard — see DEGENERATE
profound *adj* **1** difficult for one of ordinary knowledge or intelligence to understand ⟨a *profound* observation about good and evil that few listeners fully grasped⟩
synonyms abstruse, deep, esoteric, recondite
related words erudite, learned, scholarly; academic, pedantic; complex, complicated, hard; darkling, enigmatic (*also* enigmatical), inscrutable, mysterious, mystic, uncanny; impenetrable, incomprehensible, unfathomable, unintelligible; ambiguous, cryptic; unanswerable, unknowable; baffling, bewildering, confounding, confusing, mystifying, perplexing, puzzling
near antonyms easy, facile, simple, straightforward; comprehensible, fathomable, intelligible, understandable; clear, obvious, plain
antonyms shallow
2 extreme in degree, power, or effect — see INTENSE
3 having no exceptions or restrictions — see ABSOLUTE 2
profoundness *n* the quality of being great in extent (as of insight) — see DEPTH 2

profundity *n* the quality of being great in extent (as of insight) — see DEPTH 2

profuse *adj* pouring forth in great amounts ⟨we received *profuse* thanks for our efforts⟩ ⟨a *profuse* rush of water from the collapsing dike⟩

synonyms copious, galore, gushing, lavish, riotous

related words abounding, abundant, ample, bounteous, bountiful, liberal, plenteous, plentiful; extravagant, luxuriant; fat, fecund, fertile; free, liberal, munificent, openhanded, unsparing, unstinting; excessive, immoderate; adequate, complete, enough, sufficient

near antonyms meager, niggardly, poor, scant, scanty, spare, sparse, stingy; deficient, inadequate, incomplete, insufficient, lacking, unsatisfactory, wanting; bare, mere, minimal; slight, small

antonyms dribbling, trickling

profusion *n* a considerable amount — see LOT 2

progeny *n* the descendants of a person, animal, or plant — see OFFSPRING

prognosis *n* a declaration that something will happen in the future — see PREDICTION

prognosticate *vb* to tell of or describe beforehand — see FORETELL

prognosticating *n* a declaration that something will happen in the future — see PREDICTION

prognostication *n* a declaration that something will happen in the future — see PREDICTION

prognosticator *n* one who predicts future events or developments — see PROPHET

program *n* **1** a listing of things to be presented or considered (as at a concert or play) ⟨the *program* will tell us the scheduled order of musical numbers⟩

synonyms agenda, calendar, docket, schedule, timetable

related words card, exercises; arrangement, order, organization

2 a method worked out in advance for achieving some objective — see PLAN 1

3 a way of acting or proceeding — see COURSE 1

progress *n* **1** forward movement in time or place — see ADVANCE 1

2 the act or process of going from the simple or basic to the complex or advanced — see DEVELOPMENT 1

progress *vb* **1** to become mature — see MATURE

2 to move forward along a course — see GO 1

progression *n* **1** a series of things linked together — see CHAIN 1

2 forward movement in time or place — see ADVANCE 1

3 the act or process of going from the simple or basic to the complex or advanced — see DEVELOPMENT 1

progressive *adj* **1** being far along in development — see ADVANCED 1

2 not bound by traditional ways or beliefs — see LIBERAL 1

prohibit *vb* to order not to do or use or to be done or used — see FORBID

prohibited *adj* that may not be permitted — see IMPERMISSIBLE

prohibiting *n* the act of ordering that something not be done or used — see PROHIBITION 1

prohibition *n* **1** the act of ordering that something not be done or used ⟨the principal's *prohibition* against the use of cell phones in the school building met with unanimous approval by the teachers⟩

synonyms banning, barring, enjoining, forbidding, interdicting, interdiction, outlawing, prohibiting, proscribing, proscription

related words bidding, charging, decreeing, dictation, direction, instruction; deterrence, discouragement, dissuading; repression, suppression; coercion, compulsion, constraint, force

near antonyms allowance, permission, sufferance, toleration; approval, endorsement; encouragement, promotion, support; compliance, obedience

2 an order that something not be done or used ⟨the school issued a *prohibition* against wearing clothing with obscene and provocative slogans⟩

synonyms ban, embargo, interdict, interdiction, proscription, veto

related words taboo (*also* tabu); injunction; constraint, inhibition, limitation, restraint, restriction; deterrent, discouragement; repression, suppression; prevention; denial, disallowance, negation, refusal, rejection; objection, protest

near antonyms sufferance, tolerance, toleration; allowance, allowing, authorization, consent, granting, leave, letting, license (*or* licence), licensing, permission, permitting, sanctioning; approval, endorsement; enabling, encouragement, facilitation, promotion, support; compliance, obedience; accession, acquiescence, agreement, assent

antonyms prescription

project *n* a method worked out in advance for achieving some objective — see PLAN 1

project *vb* **1** to extend outward beyond a usual point — see BULGE

2 to work out the details of (something) in advance — see PLAN 1

projection *n* a part that sticks out from the general mass of something — see BULGE

proletarian *adj* belonging to the class of people of low social or economic rank — see IGNOBLE 1

proletariat *n* people looked down upon as ignorant and of the lowest class — see RABBLE

proliferate *vb* to become greater in extent, volume, amount, or number — see INCREASE 2

proliferation *n* **1** something added (as by growth) — see INCREASE 1

2 the act or process of becoming greater in number — see MULTIPLICATION

prolific *adj* producing abundantly — see FERTILE

prolix *adj* using or containing more words than necessary to express an idea — see WORDY

prolixity *n* the use of too many words to express an idea — see VERBIAGE

prologue *n* a short section (as of a book) that leads to or explains the main part — see INTRODUCTION

prolong *vb* to make longer — see EXTEND 1

prolongation *n* the act of making longer — see EXTENSION 1

prolonging *n* the act of making longer — see EXTENSION 1

prom *n* a social gathering for dancing — see DANCE

prominence *n* an area of high ground — see HEIGHT 4

prominent *adj* **1** likely to attract attention — see NOTICEABLE

2 widely known — see FAMOUS

promiscuous *adj* consisting of many things of different sorts — see MISCELLANEOUS

promise *n* a person's solemn declaration that he or she will do or not do something ⟨he gave a *promise* that he would arrive on time⟩
synonyms oath, pledge, troth, vow, word
related words appointment, arrangement, commitment, engagement; compact, contract, covenant; assurance, guarantee, guaranty; bail, bond, deposit, gage, pawn, security, token, warranty

promise *vb* **1** to make a solemn declaration of intent ⟨I *promised* not to fight with my sister⟩
synonyms covenant, pledge, swear, vow
related words affiance, betroth, plight, troth; accede, agree, assent, consent; contract, engage, guarantee, undertake; affirm, assert, aver, avouch, avow, declare, insist, warrant
phrases give one's word
2 to show signs of a favorable or successful outcome — see BODE

promising *adj* **1** having qualities which inspire hope — see HOPEFUL 1
2 pointing toward a happy outcome — see FAVORABLE 2

promontory *n* **1** an area of high ground jutting out into a body of water beyond the line of the coast — see HEADLAND 1
2 an area of land that juts out into a body of water — see [2]CAPE

promote *vb* **1** to move higher in rank or position ⟨the Navy *promoted* her to captain for her record of outstanding performance⟩
synonyms advance, elevate, raise, upgrade
related words forward, further; aggrandize, boost, heighten, improve, lift, uplift; commission, ennoble, knight; acclaim, applaud, celebrate, cite, commend, compliment, congratulate, decorate; eulogize, extol (*also* extoll), glorify, hail, honor, laud, praise, salute
near antonyms depose, dethrone, dismiss, expel, impeach, oust, overthrow, remove, unmake, unseat; demean, disgrace, dishonor, humble, humiliate, mortify, shame, take down; censure, condemn, damn, denounce, reprobate
antonyms abase, degrade, demote, downgrade, lower, reduce
2 to help the growth or development of — see FOSTER 1
3 to look after or assist the growth of by labor and care — see GROW 1
4 to provide publicity for — see PUBLICIZE 1

promoter *n* a person who actively supports or favors a cause — see EXPONENT

promotion *n* a raising or a state of being raised to a higher rank or position — see ADVANCEMENT 1

prompt *adj* **1** done, carried out, or given without delay ⟨*prompt* treatment of snakebites is always advisable⟩
synonyms immediate, punctual, timely
related words apt, quick, ready, willing; opportune, seasonable; early
near antonyms delinquent, latish, overdue; behind, behindhand, delayed, detained; dilatory, laggard, slow
antonyms belated, late, tardy
2 having or showing the ability to respond without delay or hesitation — see QUICK 1

prompt *vb* **1** to be the cause of (a situation, action, or state of mind) — see EFFECT
2 to try to persuade (someone) through earnest appeals to follow a course of action — see URGE

promptitude *n* the quality or habit of arriving on time ⟨the teacher's *promptitude* was such that you could set your watch by his morning arrival⟩
synonyms promptness, punctuality, timeliness
related words aptness, quickness, readiness, willingness; earliness
near antonyms belatedness, lateness; slowness
antonyms tardiness

promptly *adv* without delay — see IMMEDIATELY

promptness *n* the quality or habit of arriving on time — see PROMPTITUDE

promulgate *vb* to make known openly or publicly — see ANNOUNCE

prone *adj* **1** having a tendency to be or act in a certain way ⟨he was *prone* to emotional outbursts under stress⟩
synonyms apt, given, inclined, tending
related words choosing, preferring; disposed, likely, predisposed, willing
near antonyms averse, disinclined, indisposed, loath (*or* loth), unwilling
2 lying with the face downwards ⟨stretched out *prone* on the bed for a backrub⟩
synonyms prostrate
related words flat, recumbent; reclining, reposing; horizontal
near antonyms erect, raised, standing, upright, upstanding, vertical
antonyms supine

proneness *n* an established pattern of behavior — see TENDENCY 1

pronounced *adj* **1** likely to attract attention — see NOTICEABLE
2 very noticeable especially for being incorrect or bad — see EGREGIOUS

pronto *adv* **1** with great speed — see FAST 1
2 without delay — see IMMEDIATELY

proof *n* something presented in support of the truth or accuracy of a claim ⟨she presented *proof* that she had not cheated⟩
synonyms attestation, confirmation, corroboration, documentation, evidence, substantiation, testament, testimony, validation, witness
related words (the) goods; certificate, document, exhibit; demonstration, illustration; authentication, identification, manifestation, verification
near antonyms rebuttal, refutation; accusation, allegation, charge; assumption, conjecture, guess, presumption, surmise, suspicion
antonyms disproof

prop (up) *vb* **1** to hold up or serve as a foundation for — see SUPPORT 3
2 to provide (someone) with what is useful or necessary to achieve an end — see HELP 1

propagate *vb* **1** to bring forth offspring — see PROCREATE
2 to cause to be known over a considerable area or by many people — see SPREAD 1

propel *vb* **1** to apply force to (someone or something) so that it moves in front of one — see PUSH 1
2 to cause to function — see ACTIVATE
3 to set or keep in motion — see MOVE 2

propensity *n* **1** an established pattern of behavior — see TENDENCY 1
2 a habitual attraction to some activity or thing — see INCLINATION 1

proper *adj* **1** following the established traditions of refined society and good taste ⟨the formal ball called for *proper* attire—tuxedos and full-length gowns only⟩

synonyms correct, decent, decorous, genteel, nice, polite, respectable, seemly
related words acceptable, adequate, satisfactory, tolerable; dress, dressy, formal; dignified, elegant, gracious; priggish, prim, stuffy; apt, material, relevant; compatible, congenial, harmonious; allowed, authorized, kosher, permitted
near antonyms intolerable, unacceptable, unsatisfactory; casual, grungy, informal; seedy, shabby, tacky; banned, barred, disallowed; forbidden, interdicted, outlawed, prohibited, proscribed; awkward, gauche, ungraceful
antonyms improper, incorrect, indecent, indecorous, unbecoming, unseemly
2 being in agreement with the truth or a fact or a standard — see CORRECT 1
3 marked by or showing careful attention to set forms and details — see CEREMONIOUS 1
4 meeting the requirements of a purpose or situation — see FIT 1
5 serving to identify as belonging to an individual or group — see CHARACTERISTIC 1

properly *adv* in a manner suitable for the occasion or purpose <the scouts were *properly* dressed for a week of camping>
synonyms appropriately, congruously, correctly, fittingly, happily, meetly, rightly, suitably
related words well; acceptably, adequately, passably, satisfactorily, tolerably; decently, decorously
near antonyms unacceptably, unsatisfactorily; inopportunely, unfortunately, unseasonably; inaptly, irrelevantly; awkwardly, ungracefully
antonyms improperly, inappropriately, incongruously, incorrectly, unsuitably, wrongly

property *n* **1** a small piece of land that is developed or available for development — see LOT 1
2 something that sets apart an individual from others of the same kind — see CHARACTERISTIC

prophecy *n* a declaration that something will happen in the future — see PREDICTION

prophesier *n* one who predicts future events or developments — see PROPHET

prophesy *vb* to tell of or describe beforehand — see FORETELL

prophet *n* one who predicts future events or developments <a *prophet* who swore he could see wars before they happened>
synonyms augur, diviner, forecaster, foreseer, foreteller, fortune-teller, futurist, prognosticator, prophesier, seer, soothsayer
related words prophetess; mystic, oracle; astrologer

prophetic *or* **prophetical** *adj* being a sign of a later course of events <the breaking of the cereal bowl was a *prophetic* start to a day filled with accidents and foul-ups>
synonyms predictive
related words baleful, dire, foreboding, menacing, portentous, sinister, threatening; inauspicious, unpromising; oracular; revelatory, telling
near antonyms auspicious, promising, propitious, rosy

propitiate *vb* to lessen the anger or agitation of — see PACIFY

propitiatory *adj* tending to lessen or avoid conflict or hostility — see PACIFIC 1

propitious *adj* **1** having qualities which inspire hope — see HOPEFUL 1
2 pointing toward a happy outcome — see FAVORABLE 2

proponent *n* a person who actively supports or favors a cause — see EXPONENT

proportion *n* **1** a balanced, pleasing, or suitable arrangement of parts — see HARMONY 1
2 something belonging to, due to, or contributed by an individual member of a group — see SHARE 1
3 the relationship in quantity, amount, or size between two or more things — see RATIO
4 the total amount of measurable space or surface occupied by something — see [1]SIZE

proportional *adj* corresponding in size, amount, extent, or degree <each child receives an allowance *proportional* to his or her age and needs>
synonyms commensurate, proportionate
related words balanced, symmetrical; correlative, reciprocal; contingent, dependent, relative; akin, comparable, similar
phrases in proportion
near antonyms asymmetrical (*or* asymmetric), distorted, irregular, lopsided, nonsymmetrical, twisted, unsymmetrical; unbalanced
antonyms disproportionate

proportionate *adj* corresponding in size, amount, extent, or degree — see PROPORTIONAL

proposal *n* something which is presented for consideration <the city council is accepting *proposals* for ways to use that land>
synonyms offer, proffer, proposition, suggestion
related words feeler, overture; motion; advancement, nomination, recommendation; presentation, submission, tender; arrangement, game, ground plan, layout, line, plan, plot, project, strategy, system; conception, idea, notion, thought

propose *vb* **1** to set before the mind for consideration <he *proposed* that we go for a walk this afternoon>
synonyms advance, offer, pose, proffer, propound, suggest, vote
related words move; nominate, recommend; present, submit, tender; file, lay, lodge; arrange, calculate, chart, contrive, cover, frame, map, plan, plot, shape
phrases put forward
2 to have in mind as a purpose or goal — see INTEND

proposition *n* **1** an idea that is the starting point for making a case or conducting an investigation — see THEORY
2 something which is presented for consideration — see PROPOSAL

propound *vb* to set before the mind for consideration — see PROPOSE 1

proprieties *n pl* personal conduct or behavior as evaluated by an accepted standard of appropriateness for a social or professional setting — see MANNER 1

proprietor *n* one who has a legal or rightful claim to ownership <I am the sole *proprietor* of my car>
synonyms holder, owner, possessor
related words homeowner, landowner
near antonyms squatter; lessee, renter, tenant

propriety *n* socially acceptable behavior — see DECENCY 1

prorate *vb* to give out (something) in appropriate amounts or to appropriate individuals — see ADMINISTER 1

prosaic *adj* **1** being of the type that is encountered in the normal course of events — see ORDINARY 1

2 having to do with the practical details of regular life — see MUNDANE 1

proscribe *vb* to order not to do or use or to be done or used — see FORBID

proscribed *adj* that may not be permitted — see IMPERMISSIBLE

proscribing *n* the act of ordering that something not be done or used — see PROHIBITION 1

proscription *n* **1** the act of ordering that something not be done or used — see PROHIBITION 1
2 an order that something not be done or used — see PROHIBITION 2

proselyte *n* a person who has recently been persuaded to join a religious sect — see CONVERT 1

proselytize *vb* to persuade to change to one's religious faith — see CONVERT 1

prospect *n* **1** all that can be seen from a certain point — see VIEW 1
2 one who seeks an office, honor, position, or award — see CANDIDATE

prospect *vb* to go into or range over for purposes of discovery — see EXPLORE 2

prosper *vb* **1** to grow vigorously — see THRIVE 1
2 to reach a desired level of accomplishment — see SUCCEED 2

prospering *adj* marked by vigorous growth and well-being especially economically — see PROSPEROUS 1

prosperous *adj* **1** marked by vigorous growth and well-being especially economically ⟨a *prosperous* business that will soon be expanding⟩
synonyms booming, flourishing, golden, palmy, prospering, roaring, successful, thriving
related words affluent, moneyed (*or* monied), opulent, rich, substantial, wealthy, well-heeled, well-off, well-to-do; comfortable
near antonyms declining, dying, failing, floundering, languishing, struggling; bankrupt, bankrupted, insolvent
antonyms unsuccessful
2 having attained a desired end or state of good fortune — see SUCCESSFUL 1
3 growing thickly and vigorously — see RANK 1

prostitute *n* a woman who engages in sexual activities for money ⟨the town was horrified to discover that she had once been a *prostitute*⟩
synonyms harlot, whore
related words coquette, flirt, libertine, siren, tempter, temptress, wench

prostitute *vb* **1** to lower in character or dignity — see DEBASE 1
2 to put to a bad or improper use — see MISAPPLY

prostitution *n* the practice of engaging in sexual activities for money ⟨*prostitution* is illegal in most states⟩
synonyms harlotry

prostrate *adj* **1** depleted in strength, energy, or freshness — see WEARY 1
2 lacking bodily strength — see WEAK 1
3 lying with the face downwards — see PRONE 2

prostrate *vb* **1** to diminish the physical strength of — see WEAKEN 1
2 to render powerless, ineffective, or unable to move — see PARALYZE
3 to subject to incapacitating emotional or mental stress — see OVERWHELM 1

prostrated *adj* lacking bodily strength — see WEAK 1

prostration *n* a complete depletion of energy or strength — see FATIGUE

protean *adj* able to do many different kinds of things — see VERSATILE

protect *vb* to drive danger or attack away from — see DEFEND 1

protection *n* **1** means or method of defending — see DEFENSE 1
2 someone that protects — see PROTECTOR
3 the state of not being exposed to danger — see SAFETY 1

protective *adj* intended to resist or prevent attack or aggression — see DEFENSIVE

protector *n* someone that protects ⟨a bigger girl served as her *protector* against bullies at school⟩
synonyms custodian, defender, guard, protection
related words bodyguard, champion; keeper, lookout, sentinel, sentry, warden, warder, watch, watchdog, watchman; conserver, keeper, preserver, saver

protest *n* a feeling or declaration of disapproval or dissent — see OBJECTION

protest *vb* **1** to state as a fact usually forcefully — see CLAIM 1
2 to present an opposing opinion or argument — see OBJECT

protestation *n* a solemn and often public declaration of the truth or existence of something ⟨the governor went on television to make a passionate *protestation* of his innocence in the bribery scandal⟩
synonyms affirmation, assertion, avouchment, avowal, claim, declaration, insistence, profession
related words announcement, declaration, proclamation, pronouncement; argument, justification, rationalization, reason; confirmation, vindication
near antonyms disclaimer; challenge, dispute, question; confutation, disproof, rebuttal, refutation; contradiction, denial, negation
antonyms disavowal

prototype *n* something from which copies are made — see ORIGINAL

protract *vb* to make longer — see EXTEND 1

protrude *vb* to extend outward beyond a usual point — see BULGE

protrusion *n* a part that sticks out from the general mass of something — see BULGE

protuberance *n* a part that sticks out from the general mass of something — see BULGE

proud *adj* **1** having or displaying feelings of scorn for what is regarded as beneath oneself ⟨the unemployed woman was too *proud* to take a job as a maid⟩
synonyms disdainful, haughty, highfalutin, lofty, lordly, prideful, superior
related words complacent, conceited, egoistic, egotistic (*or* egotistical), important, self-assertive, self-conceited, self-important, self-satisfied, smug, uppity, vain, vainglorious; arrogant, pretentious, snobbish, stuck-up, supercilious; cavalier, overbearing, overweening, peremptory, swaggering; high-sounding, pompous; condescending, patronizing; cocky, overconfident, presumptuous; bloated, boastful, bombastic; audacious, bold, brash, brassy, cheeky, cocksure, forward, impertinent, impudent, saucy; confident, presuming, self-assured, self-confident, sure; domineering, high-handed, imperious; self-centered, selfish; dominating, magisterial, masterful
near antonyms demure, homely, meek, unassuming, unpretentious; bashful, retiring, shy, timid;

diffident, self-doubting; acquiescent, compliant, deferential, resigned, submissive, unassertive, yielding; apologetic, cowering, cringing, shrinking; passive, quiet, reserved, subdued, unobtrusive

antonyms humble, lowly, modest

2 having too high an opinion of oneself — see CONCEITED

3 large and impressive in size, grandeur, extent, or conception — see GRAND 1

provable *adj* capable of being proven as true or real — see VERIFIABLE

prove *vb* **1** to show the existence or truth of by evidence ⟨the prosecutor used DNA evidence to *prove* the defendant's guilt⟩

synonyms demonstrate, document, establish, substantiate, validate

related words back (up), buttress, corroborate; evidence, evince, record, support, witness; adduce, attest, authenticate, certify, identify; confirm, sustain, verify; clinch, nail, settle; depose, testify

near antonyms challenge, dispute, object; allege, assume, conjecture, guess, presume, surmise, suspect

antonyms disprove, rebut, refute

2 to come to be — see COME OUT 1

3 to gain full recognition or acceptance of — see ESTABLISH 1

provender *n* substances intended to be eaten — see FOOD

proverb *n* an often stated observation regarding something from common experience — see SAYING

provide *vb* to put (something) into the possession of someone for use or consumption — see FURNISH 2

provide (for) *vb* to pay the living expenses of — see SUPPORT 2

providence *n* **1** careful management of material resources — see ECONOMY

2 concern or preparation for the future — see FORESIGHT 2

3 *cap* the being worshipped as the creator and ruler of the universe — see DEITY 2

provident *adj* **1** careful in the management of money or resources — see FRUGAL

2 having or showing awareness of and preparation for the future — see FORESIGHTED

providential *adj* coming or happening by good luck especially unexpectedly — see FORTUNATE 1

province *n* a region of activity, knowledge, or influence — see FIELD 2

provincial *adj* not broad or open in views or opinions — see NARROW 2

provincial *n* an awkward or simple person especially from a small town or the country — see HICK

provision *n* **1** something upon which the carrying out of an agreement or offer depends — see CONDITION 2

2 provisions *pl* substances intended to be eaten — see FOOD

provision *vb* to provide food or meals for — see FEED 1

provisional *adj* intended to last, continue, or serve for a limited time — see TEMPORARY 1

proviso *n* something upon which the carrying out of an agreement or offer depends — see CONDITION 2

provocation *n* **1** something that arouses a strong response from another ⟨Dad only gets angry from the greatest of *provocations*⟩

synonyms excitement, incitement, instigation, stimulant, stimulation, stimulus

related words encouragement, goad, incentive, inducement, jog, prod, spur; induction, inspiration, motivation; aggravation, annoyance, bother, exasperation, frustration, hassle, headache, irritant, nuisance, peeve, pest

near antonyms subduing

2 something that arouses action or activity — see IMPULSE

provocative *adj* serving or likely to arouse a strong reaction ⟨a *provocative* editorial that sparked a heated discussion⟩

synonyms exciting, inciting, instigating, piquing, provoking, stimulating

related words explosive, fiery, incendiary, inflammatory, triggering; inducing, inspirational, inspiring, motivating; jeering, taunting, teasing; activating, energizing, galvanizing, quickening, vitalizing; angering, enraging, maddening, upsetting; aggravating, annoying, bothersome, exasperating, galling, irksome, irritating, pesky, vexatious, vexing

near antonyms subduing

provoke *vb* **1** to rouse to strong feeling or action ⟨his teasing finally *provoked* her to anger⟩ ⟨a strong chilling breeze *provoked* the picnickers to move inside⟩

synonyms arouse, encourage, excite, fire (up), incite, instigate, move, pique, stimulate, stir

related words fan, inflame, kindle, trigger; activate, energize, galvanize, induce, inspire, motivate, quicken, vitalize; abet, ferment, foment, raise, whip (up); anger, enrage, madden, upset; jeer, taunt, tease; aggravate, annoy, bother, exasperate, gall, get, irritate, vex

near antonyms calm, soothe, subdue, tranquilize (*also* tranquillize)

2 to cause or encourage the development of — see INCITE 1

provoking *adj* serving or likely to arouse a strong reaction — see PROVOCATIVE

proximity *n* the state or condition of being near ⟨the *proximity* of the curtains to the fireplace was a cause of concern to the safety inspector⟩

synonyms closeness, contiguity, immediacy, nearness

related words abutment, juxtaposition

antonyms distance, remoteness

proxy *n* a person who acts or does business for another — see AGENT 2

prude *n* a person who is greatly concerned with seemly behavior and morality especially regarding sexual matters ⟨it's not true that only a *prude* would object to being pressured for physical intimacy⟩

synonyms moralist, puritan

related words goody-goody; fuddy-duddy, old maid, prig, spoilsport

near antonyms libertarian, libertine

prudence *n* the ability to make intelligent decisions especially in everyday matters — see COMMON SENSE

prudent *adj* **1** having or showing good judgment and restraint especially in conduct or speech — see DISCREET

2 suitable for bringing about a desired result under the circumstances — see EXPEDIENT

prudery *n* a tendency to care a great deal about seemly behavior and morals especially in sexual

matters ⟨such *prudery* regarding artistic depictions of the nude has no place on a college campus⟩
synonyms prudishness, puritanism
related words priggishness, primness; morality, virtue
near antonyms libertarianism

prudish *adj* given to or marked by very conservative standards regarding personal behavior or morals — see STRAITLACED

prudishness *n* a tendency to care a great deal about seemly behavior and morals especially in sexual matters — see PRUDERY

prune *vb* to make (as hair) shorter with or as if with the use of shears — see CLIP

[1]**pry** *vb* **1** to raise, move, or pull apart with or as if with a lever ⟨it took some effort to *pry* up the trap door⟩
synonyms jimmy, lever, prize
related words elevate, hoist, lift, uplift; break, break up, detach, disengage, disjoin, divide, part, pull, separate; shift
near antonyms connect, join
2 to draw out by force or with effort — see EXTRACT

[2]**pry** *vb* to interest oneself in what is not one's concern — see INTERFERE

prying *adj* **1** interested in what is not one's own business — see CURIOUS 1
2 thrusting oneself where one is not welcome or invited — see INTRUSIVE

psalm *n* a religious song — see HYMN

psalmody *n* a book of hymns — see HYMNAL

pseudo *adj* lacking in natural or spontaneous quality — see ARTIFICIAL 1

pseudonym *n* a fictitious or assumed name ⟨the most notorious serial killer of the 19th century remains known only by the *pseudonym* of Jack the Ripper⟩
synonyms alias
related words nom de plume, pen name; appellation, designation; misnomer; epithet, nickname, sobriquet (*also* soubriquet)

pshaw *interj* how surprising, doubtful, or unbelievable — see NO

psyche *n* an immaterial force within a human being thought to give the body life, energy, and power — see SOUL 1

psychological *also* **psychologic** *adj* of or relating to the mind — see MENTAL 1

psychopath *n* a person judged to be legally or medically insane — see LUNATIC 1

psychotic *n* a person judged to be legally or medically insane — see LUNATIC 1

pub *n* a place of business where alcoholic beverages are sold to be consumed on the premises — see BARROOM

public *adj* **1** not known by only a select few ⟨it was *public* knowledge that they were expecting a baby⟩
synonyms open
related words general, popular; unclassified, well-known; advertised, aired, announced, broadcast, declared, disclosed, divulged, heralded, posted, proclaimed, promulgated, publicized, published, spotlighted; current, prevalent, rife, widespread; communal, shared; reported, reputed, rumored
near antonyms classified; unadvertised, unannounced, undisclosed; clandestine, collusive, conspiratorial, covert; surreptitious, undercover, underhand, underhanded; intimate, personal; concealed, repressed, reserved, silenced, stifled, suppressed, withheld; recanted, retracted, revoked
antonyms confidential, private, privy, secret
2 freely available for use or participation by all — see OPEN 2
3 of or relating to a nation — see NATIONAL
4 held by or applicable to a majority of the people — see GENERAL 3
5 used or done by a number of people as a group — see COLLECTIVE

public *n* human beings in general — see PEOPLE 1

public house *n* **1** a place that provides rooms and usually a public dining room for overnight guests — see HOTEL
2 *chiefly British* a place of business where alcoholic beverages are sold to be consumed on the premises — see BARROOM

publicity *n* newsworthy information released to the media that is designed to gain public attention or support for a person, business, or cause ⟨an endless flow of *publicity* for our charity event resulted in a great turnout⟩
synonyms ballyhoo
related words ad, advertisement, commercial, message, plug, promotion, spot, word; banner, bill, billboard, placard, poster, sign; advertising, marketing, propaganda; pronouncement, publication, release; broadcast, bulletin, dispatch, newscast, report, story; testimonial, write-up

publicize *vb* **1** to provide publicity for ⟨the movie studios widely *publicized* their summer blockbusters⟩
synonyms ballyhoo, plug, promote, tout
related words advertise; push; acclaim, hail, laud, praise; recommend, review; announce, broadcast, publish
2 to make known openly or publicly — see ANNOUNCE

public servant *n* **1** a person who holds a public office — see OFFICIAL
2 a worker in a government agency — see BUREAUCRAT

publish *vb* **1** to produce and release for distribution in printed form ⟨our local animal shelter *publishes* a newsletter⟩
synonyms get out, issue, print
related words serialize; contribute, edit, syndicate; manufacture, produce; distribute, market
near antonyms censor, suppress
2 to make known openly or publicly — see ANNOUNCE

puck *n* an imaginary being usually having a small human form and magical powers — see FAIRY

puddle *n* a small often deep body of water — see [1]POOL

pudginess *n* the condition of having an excess of body fat — see CORPULENCE

pudgy *adj* having an excess of body fat — see FAT 1

puerile *adj* **1** having or showing the annoying qualities (as silliness) associated with children — see CHILDISH
2 lacking in adult experience or maturity — see CALLOW
3 lacking in seriousness or maturity — see GIDDY 1

puff *n* a slight or gentle movement of air — see BREEZE 1

puff *vb* to breathe hard, quickly, or with difficulty — see GASP

pugilist *n* one that engages in the sport of fighting with the fists — see BOXER

pugnacious *adj* feeling or displaying eagerness to fight — see BELLIGERENT

pugnacity *n* an inclination to fight or quarrel — see BELLIGERENCE

puissance *n* the ability to exert effort for the accomplishment of a task — see POWER 2

puissant *adj* having great power or influence — see IMPORTANT 2

pule *vb* to utter feeble plaintive cries — see WHIMPER

pull *n* **1** the act or an instance of applying force on something so that it moves in the direction of the force ⟨I gave the door such a *pull* that when it suddenly opened, I nearly fell backwards⟩
synonyms draw, haul, jerk, pluck, tug, wrench, yank
related words drag, tow; hitch, jerk, twitch; grab, snatch
near antonyms heave, shove, thrust
antonyms push
2 the power to direct the thinking or behavior of others usually indirectly — see INFLUENCE 1

pull *vb* **1** to cause to follow by applying steady force on ⟨a team of horses *pulling* a heavy wagon⟩
synonyms drag, draw, hale, haul, lug, tow, tug
related words attract; jerk, yank; carry, convey, ferry, move, transport
near antonyms shove, thrust
antonyms drive, propel, push
2 to draw out by force or with effort — see EXTRACT
3 to injure by overuse, misuse, or pressure — see STRAIN 1

pull (out) *vb* to leave a place often for another — see GO 2

pulp *vb* to cause to become a pulpy mass — see CRUSH 1

pulpiness *n* the quality or state of being full of juice — see SUCCULENCE

pulpy *adj* **1** full of juice — see JUICY
2 giving easily to the touch — see SOFT 3

pulsate *vb* to expand and contract in a rhythmic manner ⟨the heart muscle *pulsates* regularly to pump blood⟩
synonyms beat, palpitate, pit-a-pat, pitter-patter, pulse, throb
related words fluctuate, oscillate, vibrate; quiver, tremble

pulsation *n* a rhythmic expanding and contracting ⟨you should press against the artery in your wrist and count the *pulsations* to calculate your heart rate⟩
synonyms beat, palpitation, pulse, throb
related words fluctuation, oscillation, vibration; quiver, tremble, tremor

pulse *n* a rhythmic expanding and contracting — see PULSATION

pulse *vb* to expand and contract in a rhythmic manner — see PULSATE

pulverize *vb* **1** to bring to a complete end the physical soundness, existence, or usefulness of — see DESTROY 1
2 to reduce to fine particles — see POWDER

puma *n* a large tawny cat of the wild — see COUGAR

pummel *vb* to strike repeatedly — see BEAT 1

pump *vb* **1** to make short up-and-down movements — see NOD
2 to put a series of questions to — see EXAMINE 1
3 to remove (liquid) gradually or completely — see DRAIN 1

[1]punch *n* **1** the quality of an utterance that provokes interest and produces an effect ⟨the real *punch* of the speech came in its closing lines⟩
synonyms cogency, effectiveness, force, forcefulness, impact, point
related words payoff; importance, significance; appeal, attraction, charm, fascination
2 active strength of body or mind — see VIGOR 1
3 a hard strike with a part of the body or an instrument — see [1]BLOW

[2]punch *n* a mark or small hole made by a pointed instrument — see PRICK 1

punch *vb* **1** to deliver a blow to (someone or something) usually in a strong vigorous manner — see HIT 1
2 to make a hole or series of holes in — see PERFORATE
3 to urge, push, or force onward — see DRIVE 1

puncheon *n* an enclosed wooden vessel for holding beverages — see CASK

punctual *adj* done, carried out, or given without delay — see PROMPT 1

punctuality *n* the quality or habit of arriving on time — see PROMPTITUDE

puncture *n* a mark or small hole made by a pointed instrument — see PRICK 1

puncture *vb* **1** to make a hole or series of holes in — see PERFORATE
2 to penetrate or hold (something) with a pointed object — see IMPALE

pungency *n* **1** a harsh or sharp quality — see EDGE 1
2 the quality or state of being stimulating to the mind or senses — see PIQUANCY

pungent *adj* **1** having a powerfully stimulating odor or flavor — see SHARP 3
2 marked by the use of wit that is intended to cause hurt feelings — see SARCASTIC
3 sharp and pleasantly stimulating to the mind or senses — see PIQUANT

puniness *n* the quality or state of being little in size — see SMALLNESS

punish *vb* to inflict a penalty on for a fault or crime ⟨the child was *punished* for breaking dishes on purpose⟩ ⟨if caught, the thief will be severely *punished*⟩
synonyms castigate, chasten, chastise, correct, discipline, penalize
related words assess, charge, dock, fine, impose, levy, mulct; convict, sentence; condemn, damn, denounce; criticize, reprove; wreak
near antonyms forfeit; get off, ransom, release; commute, reprieve; absolve, acquit, exculpate, exonerate, vindicate
antonyms excuse, pardon, spare

punisher *n* one who inflicts punishment in return for an injury or offense — see NEMESIS 1

punishment *n* suffering, loss, or hardship imposed in response to a crime or offense ⟨the child's *punishment* was confiscation of his toys for a day⟩
synonyms castigation, chastisement, correction, desert, discipline, nemesis, penalty, wrath
related words reprisal, retaliation, retribution, revenge, vengeance; assessment, charge, fine, mulct;

example, sentence; confinement, imprisonment, incarceration; condemnation, damnation, denouncement; criticism, reproof
near antonyms amnesty, indemnity, pardon, parole; acquittal, exculpation, exoneration, vindication; exemption, immunity, impunity; release; commutation, reprieve; absolution, forgiveness, remission, remitment; condonation, disregard, overlooking

punitive *adj* inflicting, involving, or serving as punishment ⟨any misbehavior was immediately met with a *punitive* response⟩ ⟨the company had to pay a million dollars in *punitive* damages⟩
synonyms castigating, chastening, chastising, correcting, correctional, corrective, disciplinary, disciplining, penal, penalizing
related words retaliatory, retributive, retributory, revengeful; vengeful, wrathful
near antonyms compensatory; acquitting, exculpating, exculpatory, exonerating, vindicating; absolving, condoning, pardoning, remitting; commuting, reprieving

punk *adj* **1** falling short of a standard — see BAD 1
2 extremely unsatisfactory — see WRETCHED 1
3 temporarily suffering from a disorder of the body — see SICK 1

punk *n* a violent, brutal person who is often a member of an organized gang — see HOODLUM

puny *adj* of a size that is less than average — see SMALL 1

pupil *n* **1** one who attends a school — see STUDENT
2 one who follows the opinions or teachings of another — see FOLLOWER

puppet *n* **1** a small figure often of a human being used especially as a child's plaything — see DOLL 1
2 one that is or can be used to further the purposes of another — see PAWN 1

purchasable *adj* open to improper influence and especially bribery — see VENAL

purchase *vb* to get possession of (something) by giving money in exchange for — see BUY

pure *adj* **1** free from added matter ⟨I'm allergic to any jewelry that isn't *pure* silver⟩ ⟨the solution must be kept *pure* for the experiment to work⟩
synonyms absolute, fine, neat, plain, purified, refined, straight, unadulterated, unalloyed, undiluted, unmixed
related words clarified, filtered, refined; clean, uncontaminated, uncorrupted, undefiled, unpolluted, untainted; rendered, tried; concentrated, full-bodied, strong; uncombined
near antonyms befouled, besmirched, contaminated, corrupted, debased, defiled, fouled, polluted, soiled, spoiled, sullied, tainted; amalgamated, blended, coalesced, combined, commingled, compounded, incorporated, intermingled, intermixed, merged, mingled; conjoined, fused, joined, linked, united; cheapened, doctored, watered (down)
antonyms adulterated, alloyed, diluted, impure, mixed
2 free from any trace of the coarse or indecent — see CHASTE
3 free from sin — see INNOCENT 1
4 having no exceptions or restrictions — see ABSOLUTE 2

purebred *adj* of unmixed ancestry ⟨that horse is a *purebred* Arabian⟩
synonyms full-blooded, pedigreed, thoroughbred
related words inbred
near antonyms crossbred, crossed, hybridized, interbred, outcrossed
antonyms hybrid, mixed, mongrel

purely *adv* with purity of thought and deed ⟨the devout girl vowed to live her life *purely* and in the service of God⟩
synonyms chastely, innocently; morally, righteously; modestly, virtuously
related words decently, decorously, properly; priggishly, primly, prudishly
near antonyms indecently, obscenely, vulgarly; lasciviously, lewdly, lustfully
antonyms evilly, immorally, impurely, sinfully, wickedly

purge *vb* to free from moral guilt or blemish especially ceremonially — see PURIFY 1

purification *n* the act or fact of freeing from sin or moral guilt ⟨some people must undergo a ritual *purification* after certain activities⟩
synonyms cleansing, sanctification
related words rebirth, regeneration, restoration; grace, redemption, salvation; absolution, forgiveness, remission; acquittal, clearance, clearing, exoneration, vindication; atonement, expiation
near antonyms blasphemy, defilement, desecration, profanation, violation; corruption, debasement, perversion; contamination, pollution, sullying, tarnishing

purified *adj* free from added matter — see PURE 1

purify *vb* **1** to free from moral guilt or blemish especially ceremonially ⟨Catholics go to confession to be *purified*⟩
synonyms cleanse, purge, sanctify
related words amend, improve, refine; heal, regenerate, restore; elevate, ennoble, uplift; absolve, acquit, clear, exonerate, vindicate
near antonyms corrupt, debase, debauch, defile, degrade, demean, deprave, pervert, stain, warp; poison, profane, prostitute; sully, tarnish
2 to remove usually visible impurities from — see CLARIFY 1

puritan *n* a person who is greatly concerned with seemly behavior and morality especially regarding sexual matters — see PRUDE

puritanical *adj* given to or marked by very conservative standards regarding personal behavior or morals — see STRAITLACED

puritanism *n* a tendency to care a great deal about seemly behavior and morals especially in sexual matters — see PRUDERY

purity *n* the quality or state of being morally pure — see CHASTITY

purlieus *n pl* the area around a city — see ENVIRONS 1

purloin *vb* to take (something) without right and with an intent to keep — see STEAL 1

purloiner *n* one who steals — see THIEF

purport *n* the idea that is conveyed or intended to be conveyed to the mind by language, symbol, or action — see MEANING 1

purpose *n* **1** something that one hopes or intends to accomplish — see GOAL
2 the action for which a person or thing is specially fitted or used or for which a thing exists — see ROLE

purposeful *adj* **1** fully committed to achieving a goal — see DETERMINED 1

2 made, given, or done with full awareness of what one is doing — see INTENTIONAL

purposefully *adv* with full awareness of what one is doing — see INTENTIONALLY

purposefulness *n* firm or unwavering adherence to one's purpose — see DETERMINATION 1

purposely *adv* with full awareness of what one is doing — see INTENTIONALLY

purr *n* a monotonous sound like that of an insect in motion — see HUM

purse *n* a container for carrying money and small personal items ⟨I left my *purse* at home, so I can't buy anything after all⟩
synonyms bag, handbag, pocketbook
related words billfold, wallet; compact, vanity; poke, pouch, sack; backpack, haversack, knapsack, rucksack

pursue *vb* **1** to go after or on the track of — see FOLLOW 2
2 to go in search of — see SEEK 1

pursuing *n* the act of going after or in the tracks of another — see PURSUIT

pursuit *n* the act of going after or in the tracks of another ⟨the constant *pursuit* of the rock band by a horde of screaming fans as they roamed about the city⟩
synonyms chase, chasing, dogging, following, hounding, pursuing, shadowing, tagging, tailing, tracing, tracking, trailing
related words tagging along; path, track, trail; search, seeking

push *vb* **1** to apply force to (someone or something) so that it moves in front of one ⟨I had to *push* my damaged bike all the way home⟩
synonyms drive, propel, shove, thrust
related words impel, move; bear (down), compress, depress, jam, pressure, squash, squeeze, weigh (upon); bulldoze, compel, force, lean (on *or* against), muscle, ram
2 to force one's way — see PRESS 4

pushover *n* something that is easy to do — see CINCH

pusillanimous *adj* having or showing a shameful lack of courage — see COWARDLY

[1]**puss** *n slang* the front part of the head — see FACE 1

[2]**puss** *n* a small domestic animal known for catching mice — see CAT 1

pussy *n* a small domestic animal known for catching mice — see CAT 1

pussyfoot *vb* **1** to avoid giving a definite answer or position — see EQUIVOCATE
2 to move about in a sly or secret manner — see SNEAK 1

put *vb* **1** to arrange something in a certain spot or position — see PLACE 1
2 to convey in appropriate or telling terms — see PHRASE
3 to decide the size, amount, number, or distance of (something) without actual measurement — see ESTIMATE 2
4 to establish or apply as a charge or penalty — see IMPOSE

put by *vb* to put (something of future use or value) in a safe or secret place — see HOARD

put–down *n* **1** an act or expression showing scorn and usually intended to hurt another's feelings — see INSULT
2 the act of making a person or a thing seem little or unimportant — see DEPRECIATION

put down *vb* **1** to express scornfully one's low opinion of — see DECRY 1
2 to make a written note of — see RECORD 1
3 to put (someone or something) on a list — see [1]LIST 2
4 to put a stop to (something) by the use of force — see QUELL 1

put in *vb* to put or set into the ground to grow — see PLANT

put off *vb* **1** to assign to a later time — see POSTPONE
2 to rid oneself of (a garment) — see REMOVE 1

put–on *adj* lacking in natural or spontaneous quality — see ARTIFICIAL 1

put–on *n* a display of emotion or behavior that is insincere or intended to deceive — see MASQUERADE

put on *vb* **1** to place on one's person ⟨I *put on* a coat and shoes to go outside⟩
synonyms don, slip (on *or* into), throw (on)
related words apparel, array, attire, bedeck, bedizen, bundle up, caparison, clothe, doll up, dress, garb, rig, robe, suit, trick, uniform; overdress
near antonyms disrobe, strip, undress
antonyms doff, remove, take off
2 to describe or express in too strong terms — see OVERSTATE
3 to present a false appearance of — see FEIGN

put out *vb* **1** to bring to bear especially forcefully or effectively — see EXERT
2 to cause to cease burning — see EXTINGUISH 1
3 to disturb the peace of mind of (someone) especially by repeated disagreeable acts — see IRRITATE 1

putrefaction *n* the process by which dead organic matter separates into simpler substances — see CORRUPTION 1

putrefied *adj* having undergone organic breakdown — see ROTTEN 1

putrefy *vb* to go through decomposition — see DECAY 1

putrid *adj* having undergone organic breakdown — see ROTTEN 1

putter (around) *vb* to spend time in aimless activity — see FIDDLE (AROUND)

putterer *n* a person who regularly or occasionally engages in an activity without being or becoming an expert at it — see AMATEUR

put up *vb* **1** to fix in an upright position — see ERECT 1
2 to form by putting together parts or materials — see BUILD
3 to offer for sale to the public — see MARKET
4 to provide with living quarters or shelter — see HOUSE 1

puzzle *n* something hard to understand or explain — see MYSTERY

puzzle *vb* to throw into a state of mental uncertainty — see CONFUSE 1

puzzle (out) *vb* to find an answer for through reasoning — see SOLVE

puzzlement *n* **1** a state of mental uncertainty — see CONFUSION 1
2 something hard to understand or explain — see MYSTERY

pygmy *adj* of a size that is less than average — see SMALL 1

pygmy *n* a living thing much smaller than others of its kind — see DWARF 1

quack *n* one who makes false claims of identity or expertise — see IMPOSTOR
quadrangle *n* an open space wholly or partly enclosed (as by buildings or walls) — see COURT 2
quaff *n* the portion of a serving of a beverage that is swallowed at one time — see DRINK 2
quaff *vb* to swallow in liquid form — see DRINK 1
quail *vb* **1** to draw back in fear, pain, or disgust — see FLINCH
2 to draw back or crouch down in fearful submission — see COWER
quaint *adj* **1** different from the ordinary in a way that causes curiosity or suspicion — see ODD 2
2 pleasantly reminiscent of an earlier time — see OLD-FASHIONED 1
quake *n* a shaking of the earth — see EARTHQUAKE
quake *vb* to make a series of small irregular or violent movements — see SHAKE 1
quaking *adj* marked by or given to small uncontrollable bodily movements — see SHAKY 1
qualification *n* **1** a skill, an ability, or knowledge that makes a person able to do a particular job ⟨the fashion firm was looking for an applicant who could list superior sewing skills among his or her *qualifications*⟩
synonyms capability, credentials, stuff
related words command, expertise, mastery, proficiency; ability, capacity, competence, competency, facility, faculty; flair, genius, gift, talent; forte, specialty; fitness, suitability, suitableness; makings, potentiality
2 something upon which the carrying out of an agreement or offer depends — see CONDITION 2
qualified *adj* having the required skills for an acceptable level of performance — see COMPETENT
qualify *vb* **1** to limit the meaning of (as a noun) ⟨*qualifying* the noun "adventure" in the title of your story with a descriptive adjective would make it more attention-grabbing⟩
synonyms modify, restrict
related words alter, distort, twist; narrow; compare, conjugate, decline, inflect
near antonyms broaden, expand, widen
2 to make competent (as by training, skill, or ability) for a particular office or function ⟨raising five children has *qualified* her to be an advice columnist on parenting⟩
synonyms equip, fit, prepare, ready, season
related words accustom, adapt, adjust, condition, groom, habituate, shape, tailor, train; authorize, entitle; empower, enable
3 to give a right to — see ENTITLE 1
4 to give official or legal power to — see AUTHORIZE 1
quality *n* **1** degree of excellence ⟨we expect a high *quality* of service in such a fancy restaurant⟩
synonyms caliber (*or* calibre), class, grade, rate
related words hallmark, standard; mark; footing, place, position, rank, standing, stature, status
2 high position within society — see RANK 2
3 something that sets apart an individual from others of the same kind — see CHARACTERISTIC
qualm *n* an uneasy feeling about the rightness of what one is doing or going to do ⟨she had no *qualms* about selling her old term papers to other students, even though it was against the academic honor code⟩
synonyms compunction, misgiving, scruple
related words conscience; distrust, doubt, mistrust, suspicion, uncertainty; qualmishness, unease, uneasiness; reluctance, unwillingness; demur, objection, protest; guilt, regret, remorse, self-reproach, shame; contrition, penitence, repentance
near antonyms aplomb, assurance, certainty, certitude, confidence, conviction, self-assurance, self-confidence, sureness
qualmish *adj* affected with nausea — see NAUSEOUS
qualmishness *n* **1** a disturbed condition of the stomach in which one feels like vomiting — see NAUSEA 1
2 the tendency to be or state of being squeamish — see DELICACY 3
quandary *n* a situation in which one has to choose between two or more equally unsatisfactory choices — see DILEMMA
quantity *n* **1** a considerable amount — see LOT 2
2 a given or particular mass or aggregate of matter — see AMOUNT
quarrel *n* an often noisy or angry expression of differing opinions — see ARGUMENT 1
quarrel *vb* to express different opinions about something often angrily — see ARGUE 2
quarreler *or* **quarreller** *n* a person who takes part in a dispute — see DISPUTANT
quarrelsome *adj* **1** feeling or displaying eagerness to fight — see BELLIGERENT
2 given to arguing — see ARGUMENTATIVE 1
quarry *n* an animal that is hunted or killed — see PREY
quarter *n* **1** an area (as of a city) set apart for some purpose or having some special feature — see DISTRICT
2 kind, gentle, or compassionate treatment especially towards someone who is undeserving of it — see MERCY 1
3 the place where someone is assigned to stand or remain — see STATION 1
4 quarters *pl* the place where one lives — see HOME 1
quarter *vb* to provide with living quarters or shelter — see HOUSE 1
[1]**quash** *vb* to put a stop to (something) by the use of force — see QUELL 1
[2]**quash** *vb* to put an end to by formal action — see ABOLISH
quaver *vb* to sing with the alternation of two musical tones — see WARBLE
quavery *adj* marked by or given to small uncontrollable bodily movements — see SHAKY 1
quay *n* a structure used by boats and ships for taking on or landing cargo and passengers — see DOCK
queasiness *n* **1** a disturbed condition of the stomach in which one feels like vomiting — see NAUSEA 1
2 the tendency to be or state of being squeamish — see DELICACY 3
queasy *also* **queazy** *adj* affected with nausea — see NAUSEOUS

queenly *adj* fit for or worthy of a royal ruler — see MONARCHICAL

queer *adj* **1** affected with nausea — see NAUSEOUS
2 different from the ordinary in a way that causes curiosity or suspicion — see ODD 2
3 noticeably different from what is generally found or experienced — see UNUSUAL 1

queerish *adj* **1** affected with nausea — see NAUSEOUS
2 different from the ordinary in a way that causes curiosity or suspicion — see ODD 2

queerness *n* a disturbed condition of the stomach in which one feels like vomiting — see NAUSEA 1

quell *vb* **1** to put a stop to (something) by the use of force ⟨the National Guard was called in to help *quell* the late-night disturbances downtown⟩
synonyms clamp down (on), crack down (on), crush, put down, quash, repress, silence, snuff (out), squash, squelch, subdue, suppress
related words douse, extinguish, put out, quench; smother, stifle, strangle; annihilate, destroy, smash; exterminate, obliterate, wipe out; conquer, overcome, overwhelm, subjugate, vanquish
near antonyms abet, aid, assist, help, support; incite, instigate, provoke, stir; advance, encourage, foster, further, promote
2 to stop the noise or speech of — see SILENCE 1

quench *vb* **1** to cause to cease burning — see EXTINGUISH 1
2 to put a complete end to (a physical need or desire) — see SATISFY 1

quencher *n* a liquid suitable for drinking — see DRINK 1

querulous *adj* given to complaining a lot — see FUSSY 1

query *n* an act or instance of asking for information — see QUESTION 2

query *vb* **1** to demand proof of the truth or rightness of — see CHALLENGE 1
2 to put a question or questions to — see ASK 1
3 to put a series of questions to — see EXAMINE 1

quest *n* an act or process of looking carefully or thoroughly for someone or something — see SEARCH

quest *vb* **1** to ask for (something) earnestly or with authority — see DEMAND 1
2 to go in search of — see SEEK 1
3 to make a request for — see ASK (FOR) 1

question *n* **1** an interrogative expression often used to test knowledge ⟨because I have missed so many classes, I had a hard time answering every *question* on today's surprise quiz⟩
synonyms problem
related words brainteaser, conundrum, poser, puzzle, quiz, riddle, stickler, stumper
near antonyms answer, response, solution
2 an act or instance of asking for information ⟨after reading the brief statement to the reporters, the lawyer ended the press conference by saying, "No more *questions*, please"⟩ ⟨the dozens of *questions* researched by the reference librarians⟩
synonyms call, inquiry, request, query
related words questionnaire, survey; inquisition, interrogating, interrogation, questioning
3 a feeling or declaration of disapproval or dissent — see OBJECTION
4 a major object of interest or concern (as in a discussion or artistic composition) — see MATTER 1

question *vb* **1** to demand proof of the truth or rightness of — see CHALLENGE 1
2 to give serious and careful thought to — see PONDER
3 to have no trust or confidence in — see DISTRUST
4 to put a question or questions to — see ASK 1
5 to put a series of questions to — see EXAMINE 1

questionable *adj* **1** giving good reason for being doubted, questioned, or challenged — see DOUBTFUL 2
2 not likely to be true or to occur — see IMPROBABLE
3 open to question or dispute — see DEBATABLE 1

questioner *n* a person who is always ready to doubt or question the truth or existence of something — see SKEPTIC

questioning *adj* inclined to doubt or question claims — see SKEPTICAL 1

queue *n* a series of persons or things arranged one behind another — see LINE 1

quibble *vb* to make often peevish criticisms or objections about matters that are minor, unimportant, or irrelevant ⟨he spent the entire evening *quibbling* about the historical inaccuracies in the television series on World War II⟩
synonyms carp, cavil, fuss, nitpick
related words criticize, fault; beef, bellyache, complain, crab, croak, gripe, grouse, growl, grumble, moan, squawk, wail, whine, yammer; murmur, mutter
phrases split hairs
near antonyms applaud, commend, compliment, praise, recommend; approve, back, endorse (*also* indorse), support

quick *adj* **1** having or showing the ability to respond without delay or hesitation ⟨she was a *quick* wit, always ready with a pun or joke when the moment called for one⟩
synonyms alacritous, alert, expeditious, prompt, ready, willing
related words receptive, responsive; immediate, instant, instantaneous, summary; fast, hit-and-run, rapid, speedy, swift; eager, keen, sharp; apt, clever, smart
near antonyms unresponsive; dull, indolent, laggard, lazy, logy, slothful, slow, sluggish, tardy; dormant, idle, inactive, inert
2 having or showing quickness of mind — see INTELLIGENT 1
3 moving, proceeding, or acting with great speed — see FAST 1

quick *adv* with great speed — see FAST 1

quick *n* the seat of one's deepest thoughts and emotions — see CORE 1

quicken *vb* **1** to cause to move or proceed fast or faster — see HURRY 1
2 to give life, vigor, or spirit to — see ANIMATE

quickly *adv* with great speed — see FAST 1

quickness *n* a high rate of movement or performance — see SPEED

quick–tempered *adj* easily irritated or annoyed — see IRRITABLE

quick–witted *adj* having or showing quickness of mind — see INTELLIGENT 1

quiescence *n* **1** a state of temporary inactivity — see ABEYANCE
2 lack of action or activity — see INACTION

quiescent *adj* slow to move or act — see INACTIVE 1

quiet *adj* **1** free from disturbing noise or uproar ⟨left the din of the rock concert and went to a

quiet restaurant where we could hear one another talk⟩
synonyms calm, hushed, peaceful, restful, serene, still, stilly, tranquil
related words noiseless, silent, soundless; speechless, wordless; dead, motionless, quiescent; muffled, muted, quieted
near antonyms crazy, tempestuous, wild
antonyms boisterous, clamorous, clattery, deafening, loud, noisy, raucous, rip-roaring, roistering, romping, rowdy, tumultuous, uproarious, woolly (*also* wooly)
2 not excessively showy ⟨she decided to wear a *quiet* business suit to the interview instead of her blue satin party dress⟩
synonyms conservative, muted, restrained, subdued, toned-down, understated, unpretentious
related words appropriate, fit, fitting, proper, suitable; modest, plain, simple, unadorned; inconspicuous, unobtrusive; tasteful; drab, mousy (*or* mousey); practical, sensible
near antonyms meretricious; graceless, inelegant, tacky, tasteless, vulgar; baroque, fancy, frilly, gilded, ornate, rococo; overdecorated, overdone, overwrought
antonyms flamboyant, flashy, garish, gaudy, glitzy, loud, ostentatious, splashy, swank (*or* swanky), tawdry
3 free from storms or physical disturbance — see CALM 1
4 hidden from view — see SECLUDED
5 mostly or entirely without sound — see SILENT 3
6 not loud in pitch or volume — see SOFT 1
quiet *n* **1** a state of freedom from storm or disturbance — see CALM
2 the near or complete absence of sound — see SILENCE 2
quiet *adv* without motion — see STILL 1
quiet *vb* **1** to become still and orderly ⟨told his rowdy class to *quiet* down during the lesson⟩
synonyms calm (down), cool, hush, settle (down)
related words relax, tranquilize (*also* tranquillize), unwind
near antonyms agitate, discompose, disrupt, disturb, provoke, rile, ruffle, stir; annoy, irritate
antonyms act up, carry on, cut up
2 to free from distress or disturbance — see CALM 1
quiet (down) *vb* to stop talking — see SHUT UP
quieted *adj* mostly or entirely without sound — see SILENT 3
quieting *adj* tending to calm the emotions and relieve stress — see SOOTHING 1
quietly *adv* without motion — see STILL 1
quietness *n* **1** a state of freedom from storm or disturbance — see CALM
2 the near or complete absence of sound — see SILENCE 2
quietude *n* **1** a state of freedom from storm or disturbance — see CALM
2 the near or complete absence of sound — see SILENCE 2
quietus *n* **1** a freeing from an obligation or responsibility — see RELEASE 1
2 the permanent stopping of all the vital bodily activities — see DEATH 1
quintessence *n* **1** the most perfect type or example ⟨the Parthenon in Greece was considered the *quintessence* of the perfectly proportioned building⟩
synonyms beau ideal, classic, epitome, exemplar, ideal, perfection
related words archetype, model, prototype; paradigm, standard; nonpareil, paragon; embodiment, incarnation, personification; acme, height, last word, ultimate, zenith
2 the quality or qualities that make a thing what it is — see ESSENCE
quintessential *adj* constituting, serving as, or worthy of being a pattern to be imitated — see MODEL
quip *n* something said or done to cause laughter — see JOKE 1
quip *vb* to make jokes — see JOKE
quirk *n* an odd or peculiar habit — see IDIOSYNCRASY
quirky *adj* different from the ordinary in a way that causes curiosity or suspicion — see ODD 2
quisling *n* one who betrays a trust or an allegiance — see TRAITOR
quit *adj* no longer burdened with something unpleasant or painful — see FREE 2
quit *vb* **1** to give up (a job or office) ⟨decided to *quit* his job at the fast-food restaurant⟩
synonyms leave, resign (from), retire (from), step down (from)
related words abandon, vacate; drop out (of), throw up
phrases give notice
near antonyms hire (out *or* on)
antonyms stay (at)
2 to stop doing (something) permanently ⟨told her it was high time she *quit* smoking⟩
synonyms discontinue, drop, give up, knock off, lay off (of)
related words break off, break up, close, conclude, end, expire, finish; pause, taper off; throw up; cease, desist, leave off
phrases have done (with)
near antonyms go, run on; hang on, hold on, persevere, persist; follow through, see out; resume; preserve, stay
antonyms carry on, continue, keep, keep up, maintain
3 to bring (as an action or operation) to an immediate end — see STOP 1
4 to cause to remain behind — see LEAVE 1
5 to cease resistance (as to another's arguments, demands, or control) — see YIELD 3
6 to come to an end — see CEASE 1
7 to give what is owed for — see PAY 2
8 to leave a place often for another — see GO 2
9 to manage the actions of (oneself) in a particular way — see BEHAVE
quite *adv* **1** to a full extent or degree — see FULLY 1
2 to some degree or extent — see FAIRLY
quittance *n* **1** a freeing from an obligation or responsibility — see RELEASE 1
2 payment to another for a loss or injury — see COMPENSATION 1
quitting *n* the act of leaving a place — see DEPARTURE
quiver *n* an instance of shaking involuntarily with fear or cold — see SHIVER 1
quiver *vb* to make a series of small irregular or violent movements — see SHAKE 1
quivering *n* a series of slight movements by a body

back and forth or from side to side — see VIBRATION

quiz *vb* **1** to put a question or questions to — see ASK 1
2 to put a series of questions to — see EXAMINE 1

quiz *n* **1** a person who causes repeated emotional pain, distress, or annoyance to another — see TORMENTOR
2 a set of questions or problems designed to assess knowledge, skills, or intelligence — see EXAMINATION 1

quizzer *n* a person who causes repeated emotional pain, distress, or annoyance to another — see TORMENTOR

quizzical *adj* marked by or expressive of mild or good-natured teasing ⟨my puns are usually greeted with loud *quizzical* groans by my so-called friends⟩
synonyms bantering, chaffing, fooling, funning, jesting, joking, joshing, kidding, rallying, razzing, ribbing
related words bandying, quipping; deriding, derisive, derisory, jeering, mocking, ridiculing, taunting; contemptuous, sarcastic, scornful

quota *n* something belonging to, due to, or contributed by an individual member of a group — see SHARE 1

quotation *n* a passage referred to, repeated, or offered as an example ⟨the beautiful autumn day brought to mind this *quotation* from Thoreau: "So live in each season as it passes; breathe the air, drink the drink, taste the fruit, and resign yourself to the influences of each"⟩
synonyms citation, quote
related words allusion, reference; excerpt, extract; line, part, section

quote *n* a passage referred to, repeated, or offered as an example — see QUOTATION

quote *vb* **1** to give as an example ⟨I could *quote* to you a hundred instances in the past when you've lied to me⟩
synonyms adduce, cite, instance, mention
related words exemplify, represent; illustrate, refer (to); document, substantiate
2 to make reference to or speak about briefly but specifically — see MENTION 1
3 to say after another — see REPEAT 3

rabble *n* people looked down upon as ignorant and of the lowest class ⟨the crown prince was reminded that even the *rabble* of the realm deserved his attention and compassion⟩
synonyms proletariat, riffraff, scum, trash
related words dregs; herd, masses, mob, people, populace, public, rank and file; bourgeoisie, middle class, working class
near antonyms elect, establishment; gentlefolk, nobility
antonyms aristocracy, elite, gentry, society, upper class, upper crust

rabble–rouser *n* a person who stirs up public feelings especially of discontent — see AGITATOR

rabid *adj* **1** being very far from the center of public opinion — see EXTREME 2
2 feeling or showing anger — see ANGRY
3 marked by bursts of destructive force or intense activity — see VIOLENT 1
4 marked by great and often stressful excitement or activity — see FURIOUS 1

race *n* a group of persons who come from the same ancestor — see FAMILY 1

race *vb* **1** to engage in a contest — see COMPETE
2 to proceed or move quickly — see HURRY 2

raceway *n* an open man-made passageway for water — see CHANNEL 1

racial *adj* of, relating to, or reflecting the traits exhibited by a group of people with a common ancestry and culture ⟨humanitarian aid workers are often given special training to help them understand the *racial* differences between them and the people they will be serving⟩
synonyms ethnic, tribal
related words familial; folk; kin, kindred; cultural, multicultural, national

racialism *n* **1** the belief that certain races of people are by birth and nature superior to others — see RACISM 1
2 hatred of or discrimination against a person or persons based on their race — see RACISM 2

racialist *n* a person who believes that one race should control all others — see SUPREMACIST

racism *n* **1** the belief that certain races of people are by birth and nature superior to others ⟨Hitler's declaration of his belief in a "master race" was the first indication of the inherent *racism* of the Nazi movement⟩
synonyms racialism
related words apartheid, segregation; eugenics
near antonyms desegregation, integration
2 hatred of or discrimination against a person or persons based on their race ⟨the 1963 bombing of the Sixteenth Street Baptist Church in Birmingham, Alabama, was one of the most notorious incidents of *racism* that occurred during the civil rights movement of the 1960s⟩
synonyms prejudice, racialism
related words apartheid, jim crow, segregation; bigotry, intolerance, narrow-mindedness, narrowness

racist *n* a person who believes that one race should control all others — see SUPREMACIST

rack *vb* **1** to cause persistent suffering to — see AFFLICT
2 to injure by overuse, misuse, or pressure — see STRAIN 1

racket *n* **1** a scheme in which the victim is cheated out of his money after first gaining his trust — see CONFIDENCE GAME
2 loud, confused, and usually unharmonious sound — see NOISE 1

racketeer *n* a person who gets money from another by using force or threats ⟨the *racketeer* threat-

ened to have his thugs vandalize the shop if the shopkeeper didn't pay him a monthly bribe⟩
synonyms blackmailer, extortioner, extortionist
related words crook, gangster, hoodlum, mafioso, mobster; bully, ruffian, thug; cheat, cheater, chiseler, confidence man, defrauder, double-dealer, gouger, gyp, hustler, profiteer, shark, sharper, swindler

racking *adj* intensely or unbearably painful — see EXCRUCIATING 1

rack up *vb* to gain (as points or runs in a game) as credit towards one's total number of points — see SCORE 2

racy *adj* **1** having much high-spirited energy and movement — see LIVELY 1
2 hinting at or intended to call to mind matters regarded as indecent — see SUGGESTIVE 1

radiance *n* **1** the quality or state of having or giving off light — see BRILLIANCE 1
2 the steady giving off of the form of radiation that makes vision possible — see LIGHT 1

radiant *adj* **1** having or being an outward sign of good feelings (as of love, confidence, or happiness) ⟨left the interview with a *radiant* smile on her face, confident she had gotten the job⟩ ⟨a *radiant* bride⟩
synonyms aglow, beaming, glowing, sunny
related words brilliant, dazzling, effulgent, gleaming, luminous, refulgent, shining, starry; blithe, blithesome, bright, cheerful, cheery, chipper, gay, gladsome, lightsome, merry, mirthful, optimistic, upbeat; jocund, jovial, laughing, smiling; blooming, rosy
near antonyms flat, listless, stoic (*or* stoical), unemotional; dark, darkening, depressing, dismal, gloomy, glum, gray (*also* grey), melancholy, sullen; frowning, glaring, glowering, lowering (*also* louring), scowling
2 giving off or reflecting much light — see BRIGHT 1

radiate *vb* **1** to extend outwards from or as if from a central point ⟨the heat *radiating* from the fire⟩ ⟨the spokes of a bicycle wheel *radiate* from the hub towards the rim⟩
synonyms branch, diverge, fan (out)
related words diffuse, dispel, disperse, dissipate; fork, stem; divide, separate, split; scatter, splay, spread; arise, derive, emanate, flow, issue, proceed, spring
near antonyms approach, close in (on), near; center (on), centralize
antonyms concentrate, converge, focus, funnel, meet
2 to emit rays of light — see SHINE 1

radical *adj* **1** being very far from the center of public opinion — see EXTREME 2
2 not bound by traditional ways or beliefs — see LIBERAL 1

radical *n* a person who favors rapid and sweeping changes especially in laws and methods of government ⟨*radicals* staged large, violent protests in the hopes of toppling the government⟩
synonyms extremist, revolutionary, revolutionist
related words leftist, red; progressive, reformer; anarchist, subversive; agitator, insurgent, insurrectionist, rebel; secessionist, separatist
near antonyms conservative, reactionary, rightist, Tory
antonyms moderate

raffish *adj* lacking in refinement or good taste — see COARSE 2

raffishness *n* the quality or state of lacking refinement or good taste — see VULGARITY 1

raft *n* a considerable amount — see LOT 2

rage *n* **1** a state of wildly excited activity or emotion — see FRENZY
2 an intense emotional state of displeasure with someone or something — see ANGER
3 a practice or interest that is very popular for a short time — see FAD

rage *vb* **1** to express one's anger usually violently ⟨the bad call prompted the coach to *rage* about the refereeing, even throwing his clipboard at one referee⟩
synonyms bristle, fume, storm
related words blow up, flare (up), flip; bluster, carry on, fulminate, rampage, rant, rave, take on; burn, foam, seethe, smolder, steam; chafe, fret, stew
near antonyms allay, appease, pacify, soothe; check, collect, compose, contain, curb, hold in, rein, repress, restrain, smother, subdue, suppress; moderate, tone (down), temper; ease, let up, relax; calm, cool, hush, quell, quiet, settle, still
2 to be excited or emotionally stirred up with anger — see BOIL 1

ragged *adj* **1** having an uneven edge or outline ⟨the Rocky Mountains cut an angular, *ragged* profile against the sky, in contrast to the rounded silhouette of the rolling, green Adirondack Mountains⟩
synonyms broken, craggy, jagged, scraggly, scraggy
related words saw-toothed, serrate, serrated; harsh, rough, rugged; irregular, nonuniform
near antonyms regular, uniform; flat, level, plane
antonyms clean, even, smooth, unbroken
2 worn or torn into or as if into rags ⟨finally convinced her to throw away her favorite pair of jeans, *ragged* from decades of yard work⟩
synonyms frayed, raggedy, ratty, seedy, shabby, tattered, threadbare, worn-out
related words dowdy, scruffy; dingy, faded; shredded; holey, patchy
3 not having a level or smooth surface — see UNEVEN 1
4 wearing torn or worn out clothes — see TATTERED 1

raggedy *adj* **1** wearing torn or worn out clothes — see TATTERED 1
2 worn or torn into or as if into rags — see RAGGED 2

rags *n pl* covering for the human body — see CLOTHING

ragtag *adj* wearing torn or worn out clothes — see TATTERED 1

raid *n* **1** a sudden attack on and entrance into hostile territory ⟨repeated Viking *raids* wore down the defenses of the seaside village⟩
synonyms descent, foray, incursion, inroad, invasion, irruption
related words pillage, plunder; aggression, assault, offense (*or* offence), offensive, onset, onslaught, siege, storm, strike; charge, sally, sortie; ambuscade, ambush, surprise; air raid, blitz, blitzkrieg, bombardment
2 the act or action of setting upon with force or violence — see ATTACK 1

raid *vb* **1** to enter for conquest or plunder — see INVADE

2 to take sudden, violent action against — see ATTACK 1

raider *n* one that starts armed conflict against another especially without reasonable cause — see AGGRESSOR

rail *n* **1** a protective barrier consisting of a horizontal bar and its supports — see RAILING
2 a roadway overlaid with parallel steel rails over which trains travel — see RAILROAD

rail (at *or* against) *vb* to criticize (someone) severely or angrily especially for personal failings — see SCOLD

railer *n* a person given to harsh judgments and to finding faults — see CRITIC 1

railing *n* a protective barrier consisting of a horizontal bar and its supports ‹had to put a *railing* on the balcony when the baby started walking›
synonyms balustrade, banister, guardrail, rail
related words handrail; taffrail; bar; fender

raillery *n* good-natured teasing or exchanging of clever remarks — see BANTER

railroad *n* a roadway overlaid with parallel steel rails over which trains travel ‹Grandpa used to walk along the main *railroad* in town to get to school›
synonyms rail, railway, road
related words el, elevated, elevated railroad; monorail

railway *n* a roadway overlaid with parallel steel rails over which trains travel — see RAILROAD

raiment *n* covering for the human body — see CLOTHING

rain *n* **1** a steady falling of water from the sky in significant quantity ‹Mom yelled at us to come in out of the *rain* before we caught cold›
synonyms cloudburst, deluge, downpour, rainfall, rainstorm, storm, wet
related words precipitation, shower; thunderstorm
near antonyms drizzle, mist, sprinkle
2 a heavy fall of objects ‹the Norman invaders fled when the castle's defenders threw a *rain* of stones down upon them›
synonyms hail, shower, storm
related words barrage, broadside, cannonade, fusillade, salvo, volley; flood, gush, rush, spate, torrent; eruption, outbreak, outburst

rain *vb* **1** to fall as water in a continuous stream of drops from the clouds ‹it started *raining* this morning and hasn't let up since›
synonyms pour, precipitate, storm
related words shower; hail, squall; deluge, flood
phrases rain cats and dogs
near antonyms drizzle, mist, spit, sprinkle
2 to give readily and in large quantities ‹she *rained* praise upon her graduating students› ‹the squadron *rained* bombs on the enemy's fortifications›
synonyms heap, lavish, pour, shower
related words gush, stream; flood, inundate, overflow; bombard, hail
near antonyms hold back, keep, reserve, retain, withhold

raincoat *n* a coat made of water-resistant material ‹grabbed my umbrella and *raincoat* before going out in the thunderstorm›
synonyms mackintosh (*or* macintosh) [*chiefly British*], oilskin, slicker, waterproof [*chiefly British*]
related words rainwear; poncho, sou'wester, trench coat

rainfall *n* a steady falling of water from the sky in significant quantity — see RAIN 1

rainstorm *n* a steady falling of water from the sky in significant quantity — see RAIN 1

rainy *adj* marked by or abounding with rain ‹found that the cold, *rainy* weather made his joints swell and ache›
synonyms pouring, precipitating, stormy, wet
related words drizzling, drizzly, misty, spitting, sprinkling
near antonyms dry

raise *n* something added (as by growth) — see INCREASE 1

raise *vb* **1** to move from a lower to a higher place or position ‹asked the students to *raise* their hands if they knew the answer›
synonyms boost, crane, elevate, heave, heft, heighten, hike, hoist, jack (up), lift, perk (up), pick up, up, uphold, uplift, upraise
related words ascend, mount, rise; rear, upend
near antonyms descend, fall, pitch, plunge, slip; bear, depress, press, push; sink, submerge
antonyms drop, lower
2 to bring to maturity through care and education — see BRING UP 1
3 to cause or encourage the development of — see INCITE 1
4 to draw out (something hidden, latent, or reserved) — see EDUCE
5 to fix in an upright position — see ERECT 1
6 to form by putting together parts or materials — see BUILD
7 to look after or assist the growth of by labor and care — see GROW 1
8 to make greater in size, amount, or number — see INCREASE 1
9 to move higher in rank or position — see PROMOTE 1
10 to present or bring forward for discussion — see INTRODUCE 2

raised *adj* **1** being at a higher level than average — see HIGH 2
2 being positioned above a surface — see ELEVATED 1
3 rising straight up — see ERECT

rake *vb* to look through (as a place) carefully or thoroughly in an effort to find or discover something — see SEARCH 1

rakishly *adv* in a bright and showy way — see GAILY 3

rally *n* **1** an act of gathering forces together to renew or attempt an effort ‹in a last-minute *rally* the Confederates at Bull Run were able to turn a near defeat into an upset victory›
synonyms marshaling (*or* marshalling), mobilization, rallying
related words call-up, summons; convening, muster, mustering
2 a mass meeting for the purpose of displaying or arousing support for a cause or person ‹a huge *rally* for the candidate on the eve of the election›
synonyms demonstration
related words assembly, convention, gathering; march; protest, sit-down, sit-down strike, sit-in, strike
3 the process or period of gradually regaining one's health and strength — see CONVALESCENCE

[1]**rally** *vb* **1** to assemble and make ready for action — see MOBILIZE
2 to become healthy and strong again after illness or weakness — see CONVALESCE
3 to regain a former or normal state — see RECOVER 2

[2]**rally** *vb* to make fun of in a good-natured way — see TEASE 1

rallying *n* an act of gathering forces together to renew or attempt an effort — see RALLY 1

rallying *adj* marked by or expressive of mild or good-natured teasing — see QUIZZICAL

ram *vb* **1** to come into usually forceful contact with something — see HIT 2
2 to fit (something) into a tight space — see CROWD 1

ramble *n* a relaxed journey on foot for exercise or pleasure — see WALK

ramble *vb* **1** to talk at length without sticking to a topic or getting to a point ⟨the teenagers sat around the pizza parlor, *rambling* on about dating, homework, movies, and the local football team⟩
synonyms maunder, rattle, run on
related words deviate, digress, stray, wander; sidetrack; blab, chatter, gab, gabble, jabber, patter, prate, prattle
2 to move about from place to place aimlessly — see WANDER

rambler *n* a person who roams about without a fixed route or destination — see NOMAD

rambling *adj* **1** passing from one topic to another — see DISCURSIVE
2 using or containing more words than necessary to express an idea — see WORDY

rambunctious *adj* being rough or noisy in a high-spirited way — see BOISTEROUS

ramify *vb* to set or force apart — see SEPARATE 1

rampage *n* a state of wildly excited activity or emotion — see FRENZY

rampant *adj* **1** showing no signs of being under control ⟨the mayor promised to put a stop to the *rampant* crime that plagued the city⟩
synonyms intemperate, unbridled, unchecked, uncontrolled, uncurbed, ungoverned, unhampered, unhindered, unrestrained
related words uncontrollable, ungovernable; immoderate; riotous, uninhibited, wild
near antonyms moderate, tempered
antonyms checked, controlled, curbed, hampered, hindered, restrained, temperate
2 growing thickly and vigorously — see RANK 1

ramrod *adj* given to exacting standards of discipline and self-restraint — see SEVERE 1

ranch *n* a piece of land and its buildings used to grow crops or raise livestock — see FARM

rancor *n* a deep-seated ill will — see ENMITY

rancorous *adj* having or showing deep-seated resentment — see BITTER 1

random *adj* lacking a definite plan, purpose, or pattern ⟨since we were new in town, our choice of a vet for our dog was entirely *random*⟩
synonyms aimless, arbitrary, desultory, erratic, haphazard, hit-or-miss, scattered, slapdash, stray
related words accidental, casual, chance, fluky, fortuitous, inadvertent, incidental, lucky, unconsidered, unintended, unintentional, unplanned, unpremeditated; irregular, sporadic, spot; objectless, purposeless; indiscriminate, unsystematic; unaimed, undirected
near antonyms established, fixed, regular, set, stable, steady; constant, continuous, even; arranged, managed, orchestrated, ordered, planned; aware, conscious, deliberate, purposeful, thoughtful
antonyms methodical, nonrandom, orderly, systematic

randomly *adv* without definite aim, direction, rule, or method — see HIT OR MISS

range *n* **1** open land over which livestock may roam and feed ⟨knew exactly how many head of cattle were turned out on the *range* that morning to graze⟩
synonyms lea, pasturage, pasture
related words ranch, station; feedlot, stockyard, yard; grassland, pampas, prairie, savanna (*also* savannah), steppe
2 an area over which activity, capacity, or influence extends ⟨didn't know she had such a wide *range* of knowledge until I talked to her⟩
synonyms amplitude, breadth, compass, dimension(s), extent, reach, realm, scope, sweep, width
related words gamut, spectrum, spread; domain, field, sphere; horizon, panorama
3 the distance or extent between possible extremes ⟨an actor who can go through the full *range* of emotion, from joy to sorrow, in mere minutes⟩
synonyms gamut, scale, spectrum, spread, stretch
related words measure, pitch, scale; amplitude, compass, dimension(s), extent, reach, realm, scope, sweep, width
4 a relaxed journey on foot for exercise or pleasure — see WALK
5 a series of persons or things arranged one behind another — see LINE 1
6 an appliance that prepares food for consumption by heating it — see COOKER 1
7 the place where a plant or animal is usually or naturally found — see HOME 2

range *vb* **1** to arrange or assign according to type — see CLASSIFY 1
2 to move about from place to place aimlessly — see WANDER
3 to occur within a continuous range of variation — see RUN 4
4 to put into a particular arrangement — see ORDER 1

ranging *adj* traveling from place to place — see ITINERANT

rangy *adj* being tall, thin and usually loose-jointed — see LANKY

rank *adj* **1** growing thickly and vigorously ⟨covered with trumpet vines so *rank* you couldn't see the trellis beneath them⟩
synonyms lush, luxuriant, prosperous, rampant, weedy
related words lavish, profuse; overgrown, overrun; close, dense, thick
near antonyms dormant; blighted, stunted
antonyms sparse
2 having an unpleasant smell — see MALODOROUS
3 very noticeable especially for being incorrect or bad — see EGREGIOUS

rank *n* **1** the placement of someone or something in relation to others in a vertical arrangement ⟨attained the highest *rank* in Boy Scouting⟩
synonyms degree, footing, level, place, position, ranking, situation, standing, station, status

related words condition, echelon, estate, order, walk; capacity, function; rating
2 high position within society ⟨was born a woman of *rank* who socialized only with other members of the elite⟩
synonyms class, dignity, quality, standing
related words gentility, gentleness, nobility, nobleness; grandness, highness, loftiness; distinction, precedence, preeminence, primacy; caste, position, station, status; preferment
near antonyms debasement, degradation; subordinateness, subordination; baseness, commonness, inferiority, lowliness, lowness
3 a series of people or things arranged side by side — see ROW 1
4 *usually* **ranks** *pl* one of the units into which a whole is divided on the basis of a common characteristic — see CLASS 2

rank *vb* **1** to take or have a certain position within a group arranged in vertical classes ⟨my favorite pitcher *ranks* first in the league for number of consecutive outs⟩
synonyms be, grade, place, rate
related words seed; count; class, classify, set, sort; install, instate
2 to arrange or assign according to type — see CLASSIFY 1

rank and file *n* the body of the community as contrasted with the elite — see MASS 1

ranking *n* **1** a scheme of rank or order — see [3]SCALE 1
2 the placement of someone or something in relation to others in a vertical arrangement — see RANK 1

rankle *vb* to make angry — see ANGER

rankling *adj* causing annoyance — see ANNOYING

ransack *vb* **1** to search through with the intent of committing robbery ⟨it was clear that the thieves who had *ransacked* the museum were professionals—they bypassed most of the exhibits and went straight for the vaults⟩
synonyms despoil, loot, maraud, pillage, plunder, sack, strip
related words burglarize; comb, hunt, rake, rifle, rummage; harry, raid; ravish
2 to look through (as a place) carefully or thoroughly in an effort to find or discover something — see SEARCH 1

ransom *vb* to free from captivity or punishment by paying a price ⟨the prince emptied the treasury to *ransom* his son from the kidnappers⟩
synonyms redeem
related words bail; deliver, rescue, save; emancipate, liberate; recover, regain, retrieve; release; buy; salvage

rant *n* **1** a long angry speech or scolding — see TIRADE
2 boastful speech or writing — see BOMBAST 1

rant *vb* to talk loudly and wildly ⟨when the salesclerk gave him incorrect change, he began *ranting* about the sorry state of math education today⟩
synonyms bluster, fulminate, rave, spout
related words sound off, speak out, speak up; blare, blurt out, bolt; declaim, harangue, mouth, orate, pontificate; carry on, rage, storm, take on
near antonyms grunt, murmur, mutter, slur; breathe, whisper

[1]**rap** *n* **1** a formal claim of criminal wrongdoing against a person — see CHARGE 1
2 a hard strike with a part of the body or an instrument — see [1]BLOW
3 responsibility for wrongdoing or failure — see BLAME 1

[2]**rap** *n* friendly, informal conversation or an instance of this — see CHAT

[3]**rap** *n* the smallest amount or part imaginable — see JOT

[1]**rap** *vb* to deliver a blow to (someone or something) usually in a strong vigorous manner — see HIT 1
2 to strike or cause to strike lightly and usually rhythmically — see [1]TAP

[2]**rap** *vb* to engage in casual or rambling conversation — see CHAT

rapacious *adj* **1** having a huge appetite — see VORACIOUS 1
2 living by killing and eating other animals — see PREDATORY
3 having or marked by an eager and often selfish desire especially for material possessions — see GREEDY 1

rapaciousness *n* an intense selfish desire for wealth or possessions — see GREED

rapacity *n* an intense selfish desire for wealth or possessions — see GREED

rapid *adj* moving, proceeding, or acting with great speed — see FAST 1

rapid–fire *adj* moving, proceeding, or acting with great speed — see FAST 1

rapidity *n* a high rate of movement or performance — see SPEED

rapidly *adv* with great speed — see FAST 1

rapidness *n* a high rate of movement or performance — see SPEED

rapport *n* a friendly relationship marked by ready communication and mutual understanding ⟨his good *rapport* with his students was one of the reasons why the school board named him Teacher of the Year⟩
synonyms communion, fellowship, rapprochement
related words accord, agreement, concord, harmony; oneness, solidarity, togetherness, unity; affinity, empathy, sympathy, understanding; amity, chumminess, companionship, friendship; reciprocity, symbiosis
near antonyms alienation, disaffection, estrangement; coldness, cold shoulder, distance, iciness; animosity, antagonism, enmity, hostility, rancor, spite

rapprochement *n* a friendly relationship marked by ready communication and mutual understanding — see RAPPORT

rapscallion *n* **1** a mean, evil, or unprincipled person — see VILLAIN
2 an appealingly mischievous person — see SCAMP 1

rapt *adj* having the mind fixed on something — see ATTENTIVE

rapture *n* a state of overwhelming usually pleasurable emotion — see ECSTASY

rapturous *adj* experiencing or marked by overwhelming usually pleasurable emotion — see ECSTATIC

rare *adj* **1** being out of the ordinary — see EXCEPTIONAL
2 having qualities that appeal to a refined taste — see CHOICE
3 not often occurring or repeated — see INFREQUENT

4 noticeably different from what is generally found or experienced — see UNUSUAL 1

rarely *adv* not often — see SELDOM

raring *adj* showing urgent desire or interest — see EAGER

rarity *n* something strange or unusual that is an object of interest — see CURIOSITY 2

rascal *n* **1** a mean, evil, or unprincipled person — see VILLAIN

2 an appealingly mischievous person — see SCAMP 1

rascality *n* playful, reckless behavior that is not intended to cause serious harm — see MISCHIEF 1

rascally *adj* tending to or exhibiting reckless playfulness — see MISCHIEVOUS 1

rash *adj* acting or done with excessive or careless speed — see HASTY 1

rashly *adv* with excessive or careless speed — see HASTILY 1

rasp *n* a harsh grating sound ⟨the rusted lock opened with a *rasp*⟩

synonyms creak, grind, scrape, scratch

related words clash, jangle, jar; croak; blast, bleat, bray, screech

rasp *vb* **1** to make smooth by friction — see GRIND 1

2 to pass roughly and noisily over or against a surface — see SCRAPE 1

3 to disturb the peace of mind of (someone) especially by repeated disagreeable acts — see IRRITATE 1

raspberry *n* a vocal sound made to express scorn or disapproval — see CATCALL

rasping *adj* harsh and dry in sound — see HOARSE

raspy *adj* harsh and dry in sound — see HOARSE

rat (on) *vb* to leave (a cause or party) often in order to take up another — see DEFECT

rate *n* **1** degree of excellence — see QUALITY 1

2 the relationship in quantity, amount, or size between two or more things — see RATIO

[1]**rate** *vb* **1** to be or make worthy of (as a reward or punishment) — see EARN 2

2 to make an approximate or tentative judgment regarding — see ESTIMATE 1

3 to take or have a certain position within a group arranged in vertical classes — see RANK 1

4 to think of in a particular way — see CONSIDER 1

[2]**rate** *vb* to criticize (someone) severely or angrily especially for personal failings — see SCOLD

rather *adv* **1** by choice or preference ⟨I would *rather* go to the movies than stay at home⟩

synonyms first, preferably, readily, soon, willingly

related words alternately, alternatively, either, instead; electively, optionally; desirably, gladly, wishfully; voluntarily

near antonyms reluctantly; forcibly, willy-nilly

antonyms involuntarily, unwillingly

2 as a substitute — see INSTEAD

3 to some degree or extent — see FAIRLY

ratify *vb* to give official acceptance of something as satisfactory — see APPROVE

ratio *n* the relationship in quantity, amount, or size between two or more things ⟨the *ratio* of students to teachers in my school is nine to one⟩

synonyms proportion, rate

related words average; frequency; correspondence; percentage

near antonyms disproportion

ration *vb* to give as a share or portion — see ALLOT

rational *adj* **1** having the ability to reason ⟨human beings are *rational* creatures⟩

synonyms intelligent, reasonable, reasoning, thinking

related words analytic (*or* analytical), logical; brainy, cerebral, highbrow, intellectual; cognitive, mental; practical, sane, sensible

near antonyms brainless, mindless, stupid; illogical

antonyms irrational, nonrational, unintelligent, unreasonable, unreasoning, unthinking

2 according to the rules of logic — see LOGICAL 1

3 based on sound reasoning or information — see GOOD 1

rationale *n* a statement given to explain a belief or act — see REASON 1

rationalize *vb* to give the reason for or cause of — see EXPLAIN 2

rattle *vb* **1** to make a series of short sharp noises ⟨the children tromped through the kitchen, making the plates on the shelf *rattle*⟩

synonyms clack, clatter

related words chink, chirp, clank, click, clink; clang, clash, crash; spatter, sputter

2 to engage in casual or rambling conversation — see CHAT

3 to talk at length without sticking to a topic or getting to a point — see RAMBLE 1

4 to throw into a state of self-conscious distress — see EMBARRASS 1

rattling *adj* moving, proceeding, or acting with great speed — see FAST 1

rattling *adv* to a great degree — see VERY 1

ratty *adj* **1** showing signs of advanced wear and tear and neglect — see SHABBY 1

2 worn or torn into or as if into rags — see RAGGED 2

raucous *adj* being rough or noisy in a high-spirited way — see BOISTEROUS

ravage *vb* to bring destruction to (something) through violent action ⟨Hurricane Andrew *ravaged* Louisiana and Florida in 1992, causing $19 billion in damage⟩

synonyms destroy, devastate, ruin, scourge

related words despoil, foray, harry, loot, maraud, pillage, plunder, sack, strip; annihilate, desolate, extirpate, obliterate, smash, waste, wipe out, wreck; decimate, mow; demolish, raze; crush, overpower, overrun, overthrow, overwhelm

near antonyms recondition, recover, redeem, rehabilitate, restore

rave *vb* to make an exaggerated display of affection or enthusiasm — see GUSH 2

2 to talk loudly and wildly — see RANT

rave *n, often* **raves** *pl* enthusiastic and usually public expression of approval — see APPLAUSE

ravel (out) *vb* to separate the various strands of — see UNRAVEL 1

raven *adj* having the color of soot or coal — see BLACK 1

ravenous *adj* having a huge appetite — see VORACIOUS 1

ravine *n* a narrow opening between hillsides or mountains that can be used for passage — see CANYON

ravish *vb* to fill with overwhelming emotion (as wonder or delight) — see ENTRANCE

ravishing *adj* very pleasing to look at — see BEAUTIFUL

raw *adj* **1** not cooked ⟨you should wash your hands after handling *raw* chicken⟩
synonyms uncooked
related words unbaked, unheated; rare; underdone
near antonyms well-done; overdone; baked, boiled, braised, broiled, fried, grilled, heated, roasted, sautéed
antonyms cooked
2 being such as found in nature and not altered by processing or refining — see CRUDE 1
3 lacking in adult experience or maturity — see CALLOW
4 marked by wet and windy conditions — see FOUL 1
5 uncomfortably cool — see CHILLY 1
6 causing intense discomfort to one's skin — see CUTTING 1

raw deal *n* unfair or inadequate treatment of someone or something or an instance of this — see DISSERVICE

rawhide *vb* to strike repeatedly with something long and thin or flexible — see WHIP 1

raw material *n* the basic elements from which something can be developed — see MAKING

rawness *n* an uncomfortable degree of coolness — see CHILL

ray *n* **1** a narrow sharply defined line of light radiating from an object — see SHAFT 1
2 a very small amount — see PARTICLE 1

raze *vb* **1** to bring to a complete end the physical soundness, existence, or usefulness of — see DESTROY 1
2 to destroy (as a building) completely by knocking down or breaking to pieces — see DEMOLISH 1

razz *vb* to make fun of in a good-natured way — see TEASE 1

razzing *adj* marked by or expressive of mild or good-natured teasing — see QUIZZICAL

reach *n* **1** a wide space or area — see EXPANSE
2 an area over which activity, capacity, or influence extends — see RANGE 2

reach *vb* **1** to shift possession of (something) from one person to another — see PASS 1
2 to transmit information or requests to — see CONTACT

reachable *adj* situated within easy reach — see CONVENIENT

reacquire *vb* to get again in one's possession — see RECOVER 1

react *vb* to act or behave in response (as to a stimulus or influence) ⟨it was my first touchdown, and I didn't know how to *react* to the cheers of the crowd⟩
synonyms reply, respond
related words answer, return; retaliate; construe, interpret, read, take, understand
near antonyms act, behave; affect, cause, draw, effect

reaction *n* action or behavior that is done in return to other action or behavior ⟨we were startled by her extreme *reaction* to the bad grade⟩
synonyms reply, response, take
related words answer, return; backlash; rebound; revulsion, rise; jerk, start, twitch
near antonyms action, behavior; cause, effect

reactionary *adj* tending to favor established ideas, conditions, or institutions — see CONSERVATIVE

reactionary *n* **1** a person whose political beliefs are centered on tradition and keeping things the way they are — see CONSERVATIVE 1
2 a person with old-fashioned ideas — see FOGY

read *vb* to go over and mentally take in the content of ⟨he always *reads* the newspaper in the morning as he eats breakfast⟩
synonyms peruse, pore (over)
related words browse, dip (into), leaf (through), scan, skim, thumb (through); slog (through), wade (through); reread; proofread; decipher; review, study; apprehend, comprehend, get, grasp, make, make out, perceive, see, understand

readdress *vb* to consider again especially with the possibility of change or reversal — see RECONSIDER

readily *adv* **1** by choice or preference — see RATHER 1
2 without difficulty — see EASILY

reading *n* something assigned to be read or studied — see LESSON

ready *adj* **1** being in a state of fitness for some experience or action ⟨after studying for a whole month, she felt *ready* for the final exam⟩
synonyms fit, go, prepared, set
related words conditioned, primed; braced, fortified, steeled; qualified, trained
near antonyms unqualified, untrained
antonyms half-cocked, unprepared, unready
2 having a desire or inclination (as for a specified course of action) — see WILLING 1
3 having or showing the ability to respond without delay or hesitation — see QUICK 1
4 involving minimal difficulty or effort — see EASY 1

ready *vb* **1** to make competent (as by training, skill, or ability) for a particular office or function — see QUALIFY 2
2 to make ready in advance — see PREPARE 1
3 to prepare (oneself) mentally or emotionally — see FORTIFY 1

ready–made *adj* made beforehand in large numbers ⟨the store was full of inexpensive *ready-made* clothing⟩
synonyms mass-produced, store
related words ready-to-wear; commercial; prefabricated
near antonyms handcrafted, handmade, homemade; tailored, tailor-made
antonyms custom, custom-made

real *adj* **1** being exactly as appears or as claimed — see AUTHENTIC 1
2 existing in fact and not merely as a possibility — see ACTUAL
3 free from any intent to deceive or impress others — see GUILELESS

real *adv* to a great degree — see VERY 1

realistic *adj* **1** willing to see things as they really are and deal with them sensibly ⟨our guidance counselor encouraged us to be more *realistic* in our job choices, so we reluctantly gave up the idea of becoming professional snake charmers⟩
synonyms down-to-earth, earthy, hardheaded, matter-of-fact, practical, pragmatic (*also* pragmatical)
related words philistine, utilitarian; logical, nononsense, rational, reasonable, sane, sensible, sound; hard-boiled, unromantic, unsentimental; cynical, disillusioned
near antonyms fanciful, fantastic, imaginative; ro-

mantic, sentimental; illogical, insane, irrational, unreasonable; theoretical (*also* theoretic)
antonyms idealistic, impractical, unrealistic, utopian, visionary
2 closely resembling the object imitated — see NATURAL 2
reality *n* **1** something that actually exists — see FACT 2
2 the fact of being or of being real — see EXISTENCE
3 the quality of being actual — see FACT 1
realizable *adj* capable of being done or carried out — see POSSIBLE 1
realization *n* the state of being actual or complete — see FRUITION
realize *vb* **1** to come to an awareness — see DISCOVER 1
2 to receive as return for effort — see EARN 1
really *adv* **1** in actual fact — see VERY 2
2 to tell the truth — see ACTUALLY 1
3 without any question — see INDEED 1
realm *n* **1** a region of activity, knowledge, or influence — see FIELD 2
2 an area over which activity, capacity, or influence extends — see RANGE 2
reams *n pl* a considerable amount — see LOT 2
reanalyze *vb* to consider again especially with the possibility of change or reversal — see RECONSIDER
reanimate *vb* to bring back to life, practice, or activity — see REVIVE 1
reanimated *adj* made or become fresh in spirits or vigor — see NEW 4
reanimation *n* the act or an instance of bringing something back to life, public attention, or vigorous activity — see REVIVAL
reap *vb* to catch or collect (a crop or natural resource) for human use — see HARVEST
reappraisal *n* a usually critical look at a past event — see REVIEW 1
rear *adj* being at or in the part of something opposite the front part — see BACK
rear *n* the part of the body upon which someone sits — see BUTTOCKS
rear *vb* **1** to bring to maturity through care and education — see BRING UP 1
2 to fix in an upright position — see ERECT 1
3 to form by putting together parts or materials — see BUILD
4 to look after or assist the growth of by labor and care — see GROW 1
rearmost *adj* following all others of the same kind in order or time — see LAST
rearward *adj* **1** being at or in the part of something opposite the front part — see BACK
2 directed, turned, or done toward the back — see BACKWARD
reason *n* **1** a statement given to explain a belief or act ⟨gave a good *reason* for her seemingly suspicious behavior⟩
synonyms argument, case, explanation, rationale
related words alibi, defense, excuse, justification; appeal, plea; guise, pretense (*or* pretence), pretext, rationalization
2 something (as a belief) that serves as the basis for another thing ⟨a firm belief that we are here on earth to help others is the *reason* for her tireless volunteer work⟩
synonyms grounds, motive, wherefore, why
related words antecedent, cause, occasion
3 an explanation that frees one from fault or blame — see EXCUSE
4 someone or something responsible for a result — see CAUSE 1
5 the ability to learn and understand or to deal with problems — see INTELLIGENCE 1
6 the normal or healthy condition of the mental abilities — see MIND 2
7 the thought processes that have been established as leading to valid solutions to problems — see LOGIC
reason *vb* **1** to form an opinion through reasoning and information — see INFER 1
2 to state (something) as a reason in support of or against something under consideration — see ARGUE 1
reasonable *adj* **1** according to the rules of logic — see LOGICAL 1
2 based on sound reasoning or information — see GOOD 1
3 costing little — see CHEAP 1
4 having the ability to reason — see RATIONAL 1
reasonably *adv* with good reason or courtesy — see WELL 4
reasoned *adj* **1** based on sound reasoning or information — see GOOD 1
2 being or provable by reasoning in which the conclusion follows necessarily from given information — see DEDUCTIVE
3 decided on as a result of careful thought — see DELIBERATE 1
reasoning *adj* having the ability to reason — see RATIONAL 1
reasoning *n* the thought processes that have been established as leading to valid solutions to problems — see LOGIC
reassure *vb* to ease the grief or distress of — see COMFORT 1
reata *n* a rope or long leather thong with a noose used especially for catching livestock — see LASSO
rebel *n* a person who rises up against authority ⟨the *rebel* would not submit peacefully, even after he was captured⟩
synonyms insurgent, insurrectionary, insurrectionist, mutineer, red, revolter, revolutionary, revolutionist, revolutionizer
related words challenger, defier, resister; anarchist; extremist, malcontent, radical
near antonyms loyalist, supporter; counterrevolutionary, counterrevolutionist
rebel *vb* to rise up against established authority ⟨the colonists *rebelled* when the unfair tax was imposed⟩
synonyms mutiny, revolt
related words defy, disobey; revolutionize
near antonyms obey, submit; attend, serve
rebel (against) *vb* to go against the commands, prohibitions, or rules of — see DISOBEY
rebellion *n* open fighting against authority (as one's own government) ⟨the *rebellion* would have failed if not for the aid sent by other countries⟩
synonyms insurgency, insurrection, mutiny, revolt, revolution, uprising
related words coup, coup d'état, overthrow; sedition, treachery, treason; sabotage, subversion
near antonyms counterrevolution
rebellious *adj* **1** taking part in a rebellion ⟨the *rebellious* troops fought a pitched battle with divisions still loyal to the government⟩

synonyms insurgent, insurrectionary, mutinous, revolutionary
related words seditious, traitorous, treacherous, treasonous
near antonyms loyal; obedient
2 given to resisting authority or another's control — see DISOBEDIENT
rebelliousness *n* refusal to obey — see DISOBEDIENCE
rebirth *n* the act or an instance of bringing something back to life, public attention, or vigorous activity — see REVIVAL
rebound *vb* **1** to regain a former or normal state — see RECOVER 2
2 to strike and fly off at an angle — see GLANCE 1
rebuff *n* treatment that is deliberately unfriendly — see COLD SHOULDER
rebuke *n* an often public or formal expression of disapproval — see CENSURE
rebuke *vb* **1** to criticize (someone) usually gently so as to correct a fault ⟨*rebuked* the toddler for his habit of telling fibs⟩
synonyms admonish, chide, reprimand, reproach, reprove
related words berate, castigate, chew out, dress down, flay, jaw, keelhaul, lambaste (*or* lambast), lecture, rail (at *or* against), scold, score, upbraid; abuse, assail, attack, bad-mouth, blame, blast, censure, condemn, criticize, crucify, denounce, dis [*slang*], excoriate, fault, knock, lash, pan, reprehend, slam; belittle, disparage, mock, put down; ridicule, scoff, scorn
near antonyms approve, endorse (*also* indorse), sanction; extol (*also* extoll), laud, praise
2 to criticize (someone) severely or angrily especially for personal failings — see SCOLD
3 to express public or formal disapproval of — see CENSURE 1
rebut *vb* to prove to be false — see DISPROVE
recalcitrance *n* refusal to obey — see DISOBEDIENCE
recalcitrant *adj* **1** given to resisting authority or another's control — see DISOBEDIENT
2 given to resisting control or discipline by others — see UNCONTROLLABLE
recall *n* **1** a particular act or instance of recalling or the thing remembered — see MEMORY 2
2 the act of putting an end to something planned or previously agreed to — see CANCELLATION
recall *vb* **1** to bring back to mind — see REMEMBER
2 to put an end to (something planned or previously agreed to) — see CANCEL 1
recant *vb* to solemnly or formally reject or go back on (as something formerly adhered to) — see ABJURE
recap *n* a short statement of the main points — see SUMMARY
recap *vb* to make into a short statement of the main points (as of a report) — see SUMMARIZE
recapitulate *vb* to make into a short statement of the main points (as of a report) — see SUMMARIZE
recapitulation *n* a short statement of the main points — see SUMMARY
recapture *vb* to get again in one's possession — see RECOVER 1
recast *vb* to make different in some way — see CHANGE 1
recede *vb* **1** to grow less in scope or intensity especially gradually — see DECREASE 2
2 to move back or away (as from something difficult, dangerous, or disagreeable) — see RETREAT 1
recently *adv* not long ago — see NEWLY
receptacle *n* something into which a liquid or smaller objects can be put for storage or transportation — see CONTAINER
reception *n* a social gathering — see PARTY 1
receptive *adj* willing to consider new or different ideas — see OPEN-MINDED 1
recess *n* **1** a hollowed-out space in a wall — see NICHE 1
2 a period during which the usual routine of school or work is suspended — see VACATION
3 a momentary halt in an activity — see PAUSE
4 a sunken area forming a separate space — see HOLE 2
recess *vb* to bring to a formal close for a period of time — see ADJOURN
recessed *adj* curved inward — see HOLLOW
recession *n* **1** a period of decreased economic activity — see DEPRESSION 1
2 an act of moving away especially from something difficult, dangerous, or disagreeable — see RETREAT 1
reciprocal *adj* related to each other in such a way that one completes the other — see COMPLEMENTARY
recite *vb* **1** to give an oral or written account of in some detail — see TELL 1
2 to give from memory — see REPEAT 2
reckless *adj* **1** having or showing a lack of concern for the consequences of one's actions ⟨the *reckless* skiers were making everyone nervous by schussing down the mountainside at lightning speed⟩
synonyms daredevil, devil-may-care, foolhardy, irresponsible
related words adventurous, bold, daring, venturesome; hasty, headlong, hotheaded, impetuous, precipitate, rash, wild; nonchalant, unconcerned, unworried; careless, heedless, inattentive, incautious, unheeding; inconsiderate, thoughtless, unthinking
near antonyms careful, cautious, circumspect, heedful; overcareful, overcautious, timid
antonyms responsible
2 foolishly adventurous or bold — see FOOLHARDY 1
reckon *vb* **1** to decide the size, amount, number, or distance of (something) without actual measurement — see ESTIMATE 2
2 *chiefly dialect* to have as an opinion — see BELIEVE 2
3 to determine (a value) by doing the necessary mathematical operations — see CALCULATE 1
4 to place reliance or trust — see DEPEND 2
5 to think of in a particular way — see CONSIDER 1
reckoning *n* **1** the act of placing a value on the nature, character, or quality of something — see ESTIMATE 1
2 the act or process of performing mathematical operations to find a value — see CALCULATION
reclaim *vb* **1** to get again in one's possession — see RECOVER 1
2 to make better in behavior or character — see REFORM 1

3 to obtain (a raw material) by separating it from a by-product or waste product — see RECYCLE
reclamation *n* the act or process of getting something back — see RECOVERY 1
recluse *n* a person who lives away from others <he was sick of cities and crowds, so he decided to go live by himself in the woods as a *recluse*>
synonyms anchorite, hermit, solitary
related words homebody, shut-in; monk
near antonyms socialite
recognize *vb* to show appreciation, respect, or affection for (someone) with a public celebration — see HONOR
recoil *vb* to draw back in fear, pain, or disgust — see FLINCH
recollect *vb* to bring back to mind — see REMEMBER
re–collect *vb* **1** to gain emotional or mental control of — see COLLECT 1
2 to get again in one's possession — see RECOVER 1
recollection *n* **1** a particular act or instance of recalling or the thing remembered — see MEMORY 2
2 the power or process of recalling what has been previously learned or experienced — see MEMORY 1
recommend *vb* to put forward as one's choice for a wise or proper course of action — see ADVISE 2
recompense *n* **1** payment to another for a loss or injury — see COMPENSATION 1
2 something (as money) that is given or received in return for goods or services — see PAYMENT 2
recompense *vb* **1** to give (someone) the sum of money owed for goods or services received — see PAY 1
2 to give what is owed for — see PAY 2
3 to provide (someone) with a just payment for loss or injury — see COMPENSATE 1
reconceive *vb* to consider again especially with the possibility of change or reversal — see RECONSIDER
reconcile *vb* to bring to a state free of conflicts, inconsistencies, or differences — see HARMONIZE 2
recondite *adj* difficult for one of ordinary knowledge or intelligence to understand — see PROFOUND 1
recondition *vb* to put into good shape or working order again — see MEND 1
reconsider *vb* to consider again especially with the possibility of change or reversal <the new information forced the general to *reconsider* his plan of attack>
synonyms readdress, reanalyze, reconceive, reevaluate, reexamine, rethink, review, reweigh
related words reappraise, reassess; amend, correct, emend, rectify, reform, remedy, revise
phrases change one's mind (about), go over, think better of, view in a new light
near antonyms assert, defend, maintain, uphold
reconsideration *n* a usually critical look at a past event — see REVIEW 1
record *n* **1** a relating of events usually in the order in which they happened — see ACCOUNT 1
2 an account of important events in the order in which they happened — see HISTORY 1
record *vb* **1** to make a written note of <the reporter *recorded* the events of the evening in her notebook for later reference>
synonyms jot (down), log, mark, note, put down, register, set down
related words chronicle; chalk (up), score; rerecord
2 to put (someone or something) on a list — see [1]LIST 2
recount *vb* to give an oral or written account of in some detail — see TELL 1
recoup *vb* **1** to get again in one's possession — see RECOVER 1
2 to provide (someone) with a just payment for loss or injury — see COMPENSATE 1
recoupment *n* **1** payment to another for a loss or injury — see COMPENSATION 1
2 the act or process of getting something back — see RECOVERY 1
recourse *n* something that one uses to accomplish an end especially when the usual means is not available — see RESOURCE 1
recover *vb* **1** to get again in one's possession <after fishing around in the garbage for ten minutes, I was able to *recover* my lost keys>
synonyms reacquire, recapture, reclaim, re-collect, recoup, regain, repossess, retake, retrieve
related words recruit, replenish; redeem, repurchase; rescue
phrases get back
near antonyms lose, mislay, misplace
2 to regain a former or normal state <after a disastrous first half, the team was able to *recover* toward the end of the game and manage a win>
synonyms rally, rebound, snap back
related words reanimate, revitalize, revive
phrases make a comeback
near antonyms decline, fail, worsen
3 to become healthy and strong again after illness or weakness — see CONVALESCE
4 to obtain (a raw material) by separating it from a by-product or waste product — see RECYCLE
recovery *n* **1** the act or process of getting something back <the *recovery* of the sunken boat took over a week>
synonyms reclamation, recoupment, repossession, retrieval
related words recruitment, replenishment; redemption, rescue
near antonyms loss, misplacement
2 the process or period of gradually regaining one's health and strength — see CONVALESCENCE
recreant *adj* **1** having or showing a shameful lack of courage — see COWARDLY
2 not true in one's allegiance to someone or something — see FAITHLESS
recreant *n* **1** a person who abandons a cause or organization usually without right — see RENEGADE
2 a person who shows a shameful lack of courage in the face of danger — see COWARD
3 one who betrays a trust or an allegiance — see TRAITOR
recreate *vb* **1** to bring back to a former condition or vigor — see RENEW 1
2 to engage in activity for amusement — see PLAY 1
recreated *adj* made or become fresh in spirits or vigor — see NEW 4
recreation *n* **1** activity engaged in to amuse oneself — see PLAY 1
2 someone or something that provides amusement or enjoyment — see FUN 1
3 the act or activity of providing pleasure or

amusement especially for the public — see ENTERTAINMENT 1
recruit *n* a person who is just starting out in a field of activity — see BEGINNER
rectifiable *adj* capable of being corrected — see REMEDIABLE
rectify *vb* to remove errors, defects, deficiencies, or deviations from — see CORRECT 1
rectifying *adj* serving to raise or adjust something to some standard or proper condition — see CORRECTIVE 1
rectitude *n* **1** conduct that conforms to an accepted standard of right and wrong — see MORALITY 1
2 faithfulness to high moral standards — see HONOR 1
recuperate *vb* to become healthy and strong again after illness or weakness — see CONVALESCE
recuperation *n* the process or period of gradually regaining one's health and strength — see CONVALESCENCE
recurrent *adj* occurring or appearing at intervals — see INTERMITTENT 1
recurring *adj* occurring or appearing at intervals — see INTERMITTENT 1
recycle *vb* to obtain (a raw material) by separating it from a by-product or waste product ⟨*recycling* the aluminum from pop cans is environmentally sound⟩
synonyms reclaim, recover
related words reuse; process
red *n* a person who rises up against authority — see REBEL
red–blooded *adj* having active strength of body or mind — see VIGOROUS 1
redden *vb* to develop a rosy facial color (as from excitement or embarrassment) — see BLUSH
redeem *vb* **1** to do what is required by the terms of — see FULFILL 1
2 to free from captivity or punishment by paying a price — see RANSOM
3 to free from the penalties or consequences of sin — see SAVE 1
4 to make better in behavior or character — see REFORM 1
redeemer *n* one that saves from danger or destruction — see SAVIOR
red–hot *adj* **1** being or involving the latest methods, concepts, information, or styles — see MODERN
2 having a notably high temperature — see HOT 1
3 having or expressing great depth of feeling — see FERVENT
redo *vb* **1** to make different in some way — see CHANGE 1
2 to make or do again — see REPEAT 4
redoing *n* the act, process, or result of making different — see CHANGE
redolence *n* **1** a sweet or pleasant smell — see FRAGRANCE
2 the quality of a thing that makes it perceptible to the sense organs in the nose — see SMELL
redolent *adj* having a pleasant smell — see FRAGRANT
redouble *vb* **1** to make markedly greater in measure or degree — see INTENSIFY
2 to make twice as great or as many — see DOUBLE 1
redoubtable *adj* causing fear — see FEARFUL 1
redraft *vb* to prepare for publication by correcting, rewriting, or updating — see EDIT
redress *n* payment to another for a loss or injury — see COMPENSATION 1
reduce *vb* **1** to bring to a lower grade or rank — see DEMOTE
2 to make smaller in amount, volume, or extent — see DECREASE 1
reduction *n* **1** something that is or may be subtracted — see DEDUCTION 1
2 the amount by which something is lessened — see DECREASE
redundancy *n* the use of too many words to express an idea — see VERBIAGE
reduplicate *vb* **1** to make an exact likeness of — see COPY 1
2 to make or do again — see REPEAT 4
reduplication *n* **1** something that is made to look exactly like something else — see COPY
2 the act of saying or doing over again — see REPEAT
reecho *vb* to continue or be repeated in a series of reflected sound waves — see REVERBERATE
reek *n* **1** a strong unpleasant smell — see STINK
2 an atmospheric condition in which suspended particles in the air rob it of its transparency — see HAZE 1
reek *vb* to give off an extremely unpleasant smell — see STINK
reeking *adj* having an unpleasant smell — see MALODOROUS
reeky *adj* having an unpleasant smell — see MALODOROUS
reel *n* a rapid turning about on an axis or central point — see SPIN 1
reel *vb* **1** to be in a confused state as if from being twirled around — see SPIN 2
2 to move forward while swaying from side to side — see STAGGER 1
reeling *adj* having a feeling of being whirled about and in danger of falling down — see DIZZY 1
reenergized *adj* made or become fresh in spirits or vigor — see NEW 4
reevaluate *vb* to consider again especially with the possibility of change or reversal — see RECONSIDER
reexamination *n* a usually critical look at a past event — see REVIEW 1
reexamine *vb* to consider again especially with the possibility of change or reversal — see RECONSIDER
refashion *vb* to make different in some way — see CHANGE 1
refashioning *n* the act, process, or result of making different — see CHANGE
refer *vb* to have a relation or connection — see APPLY 1
refer (to) *vb* **1** to make reference to or speak about briefly but specifically — see MENTION 1
2 to use or seek out as a source of aid, relief, or advantage — see RESORT (TO) 1
referee *vb* to give an opinion about (something at issue or in dispute) — see JUDGE 1
reference *n* relation to or concern with something specified — see RESPECT 1
refine *vb* to make better — see IMPROVE
refined *adj* **1** being far along in development — see ADVANCED 1
2 free from added matter — see PURE 1
3 having or showing a taste for the fine arts and gracious living — see CULTIVATED
4 having or showing elegance — see ELEGANT 1

5 made or done with extreme care and accuracy — see FINE 2
6 satisfying or pleasing because of fineness or mildness — see DELICATE 1
refinement *n* **1** an instance of notable progress in the development of knowledge, technology, or skill — see ADVANCE 2
2 a high level of taste and enlightenment as a result of extensive intellectual training and exposure to the arts — see CULTURE 1
3 dignified or restrained beauty of form, appearance, or style — see ELEGANCE
reflect *vb* to reproduce or show (an exact likeness) as a mirror would ⟨her face was *reflected* in the waters of the still pond⟩
synonyms image, mirror
related words copy, duplicate, imitate, reduplicate, repeat, replicate, reproduce
reflection *n* **1** a briefly expressed opinion — see REMARK
2 a cause of shame — see DISGRACE 2
reflective *adj* given to or marked by long, quiet thinking — see CONTEMPLATIVE
reform *vb* **1** to make better in behavior or character ⟨a *reformed* criminal who is now a productive member of society⟩
synonyms reclaim, redeem, rehabilitate
related words amend, improve; cleanse, purify, restore
near antonyms abase, corrupt, debauch, degrade, demean, demoralize, deprave, pervert, poison, profane, prostitute, subvert, warp
2 to remove errors, defects, deficiencies, or deviations from — see CORRECT 1
reformative *adj* serving to raise or adjust something to some standard or proper condition — see CORRECTIVE 1
reformatory *adj* serving to raise or adjust something to some standard or proper condition — see CORRECTIVE 1
refractoriness *n* refusal to obey — see DISOBEDIENCE
refractory *adj* **1** given to resisting authority or another's control — see DISOBEDIENT
2 given to resisting control or discipline by others — see UNCONTROLLABLE
refrain *n* a part of a song or hymn that is repeated every so often — see CHORUS 2
refrain (from) *vb* to resist the temptation of — see FORBEAR
refresh *vb* to bring back to a former condition or vigor — see RENEW 1
refreshed *adj* made or become fresh in spirits or vigor — see NEW 4
refreshen *vb* to bring back to a former condition or vigor — see RENEW 1
refreshing *adj* having a renewing effect on the state of the body or mind — see TONIC
refrigerate *vb* to cause to lose heat — see COOL 1
refuge *n* something (as a building) that offers cover from the weather or protection from danger — see SHELTER
refugee *n* a person forced to emigrate for political reasons — see ÉMIGRÉ 1
refulgence *n* the quality or state of having or giving off light — see BRILLIANCE 1
refulgent *adj* giving off or reflecting much light — see BRIGHT 1
refund *vb* to make a return payment to — see REPAY
refusal *n* an unwillingness to grant something asked for — see DENIAL 1
refuse *n* discarded or useless material — see GARBAGE
refuse *vb* **1** to be unwilling to grant — see DENY 2
2 to show unwillingness to accept, do, engage in, or agree to — see DECLINE 1
refute *vb* to prove to be false — see DISPROVE
regain *vb* to get again in one's possession — see RECOVER 1
regal *adj* **1** fit for or worthy of a royal ruler — see MONARCHICAL
2 large and impressive in size, grandeur, extent, or conception — see GRAND 1
regale *vb* **1** to cause (someone) to pass the time agreeably occupied — see AMUSE
2 to entertain with a fancy meal — see FEAST
regalia *n* dressy clothing — see FINERY
regard *n* **1** a feeling of great approval and liking — see ADMIRATION 1
2 an instance of looking especially briefly — see LOOK 2
3 relation to or concern with something specified — see RESPECT 1
4 **regards** *pl* best wishes — see COMPLIMENT
regard *vb* **1** to make note of (something) through the use of one's eyes — see SEE 1
2 to take notice of and be guided by — see HEED 1
3 to think of in a particular way — see CONSIDER 1
4 to think very highly or favorably of — see ADMIRE
regardful *adj* marked by or showing proper regard for another's higher status — see RESPECTFUL
regarding *prep* having to do with — see ABOUT 1
regardless *adv* in spite of everything ⟨the weather looked bad, but they were resolved to go on with their picnic *regardless*⟩
synonyms anyhow, anyway
related words nevertheless
phrases in any case, no matter
regenerate *vb* **1** to bring back to a former condition or vigor — see RENEW 1
2 to bring back to life, practice, or activity — see REVIVE 1
regenerated *adj* made or become fresh in spirits or vigor — see NEW 4
regeneration *n* the act or an instance of bringing something back to life, public attention, or vigorous activity — see REVIVAL
regime *also* **régime** *n* lawful control over the affairs of a political unit (as a nation) — see RULE 2
regimen *n* lawful control over the affairs of a political unit (as a nation) — see RULE 2
region *n* **1** a part or portion having no fixed boundaries ⟨if you look in the upper left *region* of the sky, you can see the constellation Orion⟩
synonyms area, demesne, field, zone
related words section; locale, locality, location, locus, place, point, position, site, spot
2 a broad geographical area ⟨corn is mostly grown in the central *regions* of the country⟩
synonyms belt, land, part(s), tract, zone
related words district, territory
[1]**register** *n* a person whose job is to keep records — see CLERK 1
[2]**register** *n* a record of a series of items (as names or titles) usually arranged according to some system — see [1]LIST

register *vb* **1** to enter in a list or roll — see ENROLL 1
2 to make a written note of — see RECORD 1
3 to put (someone or something) on a list — see [1]LIST 2
registrar *n* a person whose job is to keep records — see CLERK 1
registration *n* the number of individuals registered <there was a large *registration* for the popular swim classes at the community center>
synonyms enrollment, registry
related words class
registry *n* **1** a record of a series of items (as names or titles) usually arranged according to some system — see [1]LIST
2 the number of individuals registered — see REGISTRATION
regress *vb* to go back to a previous and usually lower state or level <in extreme circumstances, people sometimes *regress* to the behavior they exhibited in childhood>
synonyms retrogress, revert
related words backslide, lapse, relapse; return
near antonyms grow, mature, ripen
antonyms advance, develop, evolve, progress
regression *n* the act or an instance of going back to an earlier and lower level especially of intelligence or behavior <the *regression* to really childish behavior that boys often undergo when put in large groups>
synonyms retrogression, reversion
related words backslide, lapse, relapse; return; nondevelopment
near antonyms growth, maturation, ripening
antonyms advancement, development, evolution, progression
regret *n* a feeling of responsibility for wrongdoing — see GUILT 1
regret *vb* to feel sorry or dissatisfied about <we *regret* any inconvenience that we may have caused you>
synonyms bemoan, deplore, lament, repent, rue
related words bewail, grieve (for), mourn, sorrow (for)
regretful *adj* **1** expressing or suggesting mourning — see MOURNFUL 1
2 feeling sorrow for a wrong that one has done — see CONTRITE 1
regretfully *adv* with feelings of bitterness or grief — see HARD 2
regrettable *adj* of a kind to cause great distress <the explorers forged ahead despite the *regrettable* loss of some of their companions>
synonyms deplorable, distressful, distressing, grievous, heartbreaking, heartrending, lamentable, unfortunate, woeful
related words affecting, moving, poignant, touching; awful, dire, dreadful, fearful, terrible; horrible, horrifying, intolerable, overwhelming, shocking, sickening, unbearable; miserable, pitiful, wretched; calamitous, disastrous
near antonyms gratifying, pleasing, rewarding, satisfying; comforting, encouraging, heartening; cheering, heartwarming, inspiring; fortunate, happy, lucky
regular *adj* **1** appearing or occurring repeatedly from time to time <what with one or another of our pets having problems, we've been *regular* visitors at the animal hospital>
synonyms constant, frequent, habitual, periodic, repeated, steady
related words chronic, confirmed, inveterate; expected, usual
near antonyms unexpected, unusual
antonyms inconstant, infrequent, irregular
2 following a set method, arrangement, or pattern — see METHODICAL
3 following or agreeing with established form, custom, or rules — see FORMAL 1
4 having no exceptions or restrictions — see ABSOLUTE 2
5 having or showing the qualities associated with the members of a particular group or kind — see TYPICAL 1
regular *n* a person engaged in military service — see SOLDIER
regularize *vb* to make agree with a single established standard or model — see STANDARDIZE
regulate *vb* **1** to keep from exceeding a desirable degree or level (as of expression) — see CONTROL 1
2 to look after and make decisions about — see CONDUCT 1
regulation *n* **1** a statement spelling out the proper procedure or conduct for an activity — see RULE 1
2 the act or activity of looking after and making decisions about something — see CONDUCT 1
3 the duty or function of watching or guarding for the sake of proper direction or control — see SUPERVISION 1
regulator *n* a mechanism for adjusting the operation of a device, machine, or system — see CONTROL 1
rehabilitate *vb* **1** to make better in behavior or character — see REFORM 1
2 to restore to a healthy condition — see HEAL 1
rehabilitation *n* the process or period of gradually regaining one's health and strength — see CONVALESCENCE
rehearsal *n* a private performance or session in preparation for a public appearance <we made a few mistakes in *rehearsal*, but we were pretty sure that we'd be okay on opening night>
synonyms dry run, practice (*also* practise), trial
related words dress rehearsal; preview; drill, exercise
rehearse *vb* **1** to do over and over so as to become skilled — see PRACTICE
2 to give an oral or written account of in some detail — see TELL 1
3 to say or state again — see REPEAT 1
4 to specify one after another — see ENUMERATE 1
reimburse *vb* to make a return payment to — see REPAY
rein *n* the place of leadership or command — see HEAD 2
rein (in) *vb* to keep from exceeding a desirable degree or level (as of expression) — see CONTROL 1
reiterate *vb* **1** to make or do again — see REPEAT 4
2 to say or state again — see REPEAT 1
reiteration *n* the act of saying or doing over again — see REPEAT
reiterative *adj* marked by repetition — see REPETITIVE
reject *n* **1** one who is cast out or rejected by society — see OUTCAST

2 something separated from a group or lot for not being as good as the others — see CULL

reject *vb* **1** to be unwilling to grant — see DENY 2
2 to declare not to be true — see DENY 1
3 to get rid of as useless or unwanted — see DISCARD
4 to show unwillingness to accept, do, engage in, or agree to — see DECLINE 1

rejected *adj* left unoccupied or unused — see ABANDONED

rejection *n* **1** a refusal to confirm the truth of a statement — see DENIAL 2
2 an unwillingness to grant something asked for — see DENIAL 1
3 something separated from a group or lot for not being as good as the others — see CULL

rejoice *vb* **1** to feel or express joy or triumph — see EXULT
2 to give satisfaction to — see PLEASE

rejoicing *adj* having or expressing feelings of joy or triumph — see EXULTANT

rejoin *vb* to speak or write in reaction to a question or to another reaction — see ANSWER 1

rejoinder *n* something spoken or written in reaction especially to a question — see ANSWER 1

rejuvenate *vb* **1** to bring back to a former condition or vigor — see RENEW 1
2 to bring back to life, practice, or activity — see REVIVE 1

rejuvenation *n* the act or an instance of bringing something back to life, public attention, or vigorous activity — see REVIVAL

rekindle *vb* to bring back to life, practice, or activity — see REVIVE 1

relate *vb* **1** to form a close personal relationship — see COMMUNE
2 to give an oral or written account of in some detail — see TELL 1
3 to have a relation or connection — see APPLY 1
4 to think of (something) in combination — see ASSOCIATE 2

related *adj* having a close connection like that between family members <the *related* fields of anthropology and archaeology>
synonyms affiliated, akin, allied, kindred
related words associated, connected; alike, analogous, comparable, correspondent, corresponding, like, matching, parallel, resembling, similar, such, suchlike; identical, same; germane, pertinent, relevant
near antonyms different, disparate, dissimilar, distinct, distinctive, distinguishable, diverse, other, unalike, unlike
antonyms unrelated

relation *n* **1 relations** *pl* doings between individuals or groups <*relations* between the rival newspapers remained friendly despite their competition for the same stories>
synonyms dealings, interaction, intercourse
related words interrelationship
2 a person connected with another by blood or marriage — see RELATIVE
3 the fact or state of having something in common — see CONNECTION 1
4 the state of having shared interests or efforts (as in social or business matters) — see ASSOCIATION 1

relationship *n* **1** the fact or state of having something in common — see CONNECTION 1
2 the state of having shared interests or efforts (as in social or business matters) — see ASSOCIATION 1

relative *adj* **1** being such only when compared to something else — see COMPARATIVE
2 having to do with the matter at hand — see PERTINENT

relative *n* a person connected with another by blood or marriage <it's always fun to see all your *relatives* at a big family gathering>
synonyms kin, kinsman, relation
related words in-law; kinswoman; blood, clan, family, folk, house, kindred, kinfolk, kinsfolk, line, lineage, people, race, stock, tribe

relatively *adv* to some degree or extent — see FAIRLY

relax *vb* **1** to get rid of nervous tension or anxiety <she took deep breaths to *relax* before going on stage>
synonyms unwind
related words loosen (up), unbend; repose, rest; alleviate, comfort, ease, relieve; calm, compose, cool, quiet, settle
antonyms tense (up)
2 to make less taut — see SLACKEN
3 to refrain from labor or exertion — see REST 1

relaxation *n* **1** activity engaged in to amuse oneself — see PLAY 1
2 freedom from activity or labor — see [1]REST 1

relaxed *adj* **1** enjoying physical comfort — see COMFORTABLE 2
2 not bound by rigid standards — see EASYGOING 2
3 not tightly fastened, tied, or stretched — see LOOSE 1

relaxing *adj* tending to calm the emotions and relieve stress — see SOOTHING 1

release *n* **1** a freeing from an obligation or responsibility <after they declared bankruptcy, the bank agreed to a *release* from their debt>
synonyms delivery, discharge, quietus, quittance
related words exemption, immunity, waiver
2 a document containing a declaration of an intentional giving up of a right, claim, or privilege — see WAIVER
3 a published statement informing the public of a matter of general interest — see ANNOUNCEMENT

release *vb* **1** to set free (from a state of being held in check) <he *released* his anger with a great yell of frustration>
synonyms loose, loosen, uncork, unleash, unlock, unloose, unloosen
related words discharge, emancipate, enfranchise, free, liberate, manumit, spring, unbind, uncage, unchain, unfetter; air, express, vent
near antonyms manacle, shackle, trammel; bind, confine, enchain, fetter
antonyms bridle, check, constrain, contain, control, curb, govern, hold in, inhibit, regulate, rein (in), restrain, tame
2 to find emotional release for — see TAKE OUT 1
3 to set free (as from slavery or confinement) — see FREE 1
4 to set free from entanglement or difficulty — see EXTRICATE
5 to throw or give off — see EMIT 1

relent *vb* to grow less in scope or intensity especially gradually — see DECREASE 2

relentless *adj* showing no signs of slackening or yielding in one's purpose — see UNYIELDING 1

relevance *n* the fact or state of being pertinent — see PERTINENCE

relevancy *n* the fact or state of being pertinent — see PERTINENCE

relevant *adj* having to do with the matter at hand — see PERTINENT

reliability *n* worthiness as the recipient of another's trust or confidence ⟨we never had to question the *reliability* of the park rangers in an emergency⟩
synonyms dependability, reliableness, solidity, solidness, sureness, trustworthiness
related words infallibility
near antonyms doubtfulness, dubiousness

reliable *adj* worthy of one's trust — see DEPENDABLE

reliableness *n* worthiness as the recipient of another's trust or confidence — see RELIABILITY

reliance *n* **1** something or someone to which one looks for support — see DEPENDENCE 2
2 the quality or state of needing something or someone — see DEPENDENCE 1

relic *n* **1** a tiny often physical indication of something lost or vanished — see VESTIGE
2 something belonging to or surviving from an earlier period — see ANTIQUE

relief *n* **1** a feeling of ease from grief or trouble — see COMFORT 1
2 a person or thing that takes the place of another — see SUBSTITUTE
3 reduction of or freedom from pain — see EASE 1

relieve *vb* **1** to make more bearable or less severe — see HELP 2
2 to set (a person or thing) free of something that encumbers — see RID

religion *n* **1** a body of beliefs and practices regarding the supernatural and the worship of one or more deities ⟨the Jewish *religion* has followers in many parts of the globe⟩
synonyms credo, creed, cult, faith, persuasion
related words church, communion, denomination, sect; belief, doctrine, dogma, theology; monotheism, polytheism, theism
near antonyms agnosticism, atheism, secularism
2 belief and trust in and loyalty to God — see FAITH 1

religious *adj* **1** of, relating to, or used in the practice or worship services of a religion ⟨J.S. Bach wrote some of the most beautiful *religious* music in the world⟩
synonyms devotional, sacred, spiritual
related words blessed, consecrated, hallowed, holy, sacrosanct, sanctified; liturgical, ritual, sacramental
near antonyms earthly, mundane, worldly; irreligious, semireligious
antonyms nonreligious, profane, secular
2 showing a devotion to God and to a life of virtue — see HOLY 1

relinquish *vb* **1** to give (something) over to the control or possession of another usually under duress — see SURRENDER 1
2 to give up (as a position of authority) formally — see ABDICATE

relinquishment *n* the usually forced yielding of one's person or possessions to the control of another — see SURRENDER

relish *n* **1** positive regard for something — see LIKING
2 the feeling experienced when one's wishes are met — see PLEASURE 1

relish *vb* to take pleasure in — see ENJOY 1

reluctance *n* a lack of willingness or desire to do or accept something ⟨the mice showed an odd *reluctance* to eat the cheese we had put out for them⟩
synonyms disinclination, hesitance, hesitancy, unwillingness
related words faltering, hesitation, indecision, irresolution, shilly-shallying, staggering, vacillation, wavering, wobbling; distrust, distrustfulness, doubt, incertitude, misgiving, mistrust, mistrustfulness, skepticism, suspicion, uncertainty
near antonyms certainty, certitude, sureness, surety
antonyms inclination, willingness

reluctant *adj* having doubts about the wisdom of doing something — see HESITANT

rely *vb* to place reliance or trust — see DEPEND 2

remain *vb* to continue to be in a place for a significant amount of time — see STAY 1

remainder *n* **1** a remaining group or portion ⟨the *remainder* of the pills were saved in case they were needed later⟩
synonyms balance, leavings, leftovers, odds and ends, remains, remnant, residue, rest
related words fragment, scrap; oddment, scraping(s), stub, stump; excess, surplus
near antonyms bulk, most
2 an unused or unwanted piece or item typically of small size or value — see [1]SCRAP 1

remains *n pl* **1** the portion or bits of something left over or behind after it has been destroyed ⟨the *remains* of the house ripped apart by the tornado littered the block for weeks afterward⟩
synonyms ashes, debris, residue, rubble, ruins, wreck, wreckage
related words detritus, flotsam, jetsam; garbage, refuse, trash
2 a dead body — see CORPSE
3 a remaining group or portion — see REMAINDER 1

remake *vb* **1** to make different in some way — see CHANGE 1
2 to make or do again — see REPEAT 4

remaking *n* the act, process, or result of making different — see CHANGE

remark *n* a briefly expressed opinion ⟨the speaker made some short *remarks* about the new museum before officially opening the doors to visitors⟩
synonyms comment, note, observation, reflection
related words analysis, commentary, exposition; annotation; belief, conviction, eye, feeling, judgment (*or* judgement), mind, notion, opinion, persuasion, sentiment, verdict, view

remark *vb* **1** to make a statement of one's opinion ⟨he *remarked* on the attractiveness of the background music in the restaurant⟩
synonyms comment, note, observe, opine
related words articulate, express, say, speak, state, talk, tell, utter, verbalize, vocalize
2 to make note of (something) through the use of one's eyes — see SEE 1

remarkable *adj* **1** different from the ordinary in a way that causes curiosity or suspicion — see ODD 2
2 likely to attract attention — see NOTICEABLE

remediable *adj* capable of being corrected ⟨the problems with the local transportation system were severe but still *remediable*⟩

synonyms correctable, fixable, rectifiable, repairable, reparable
related words amendable, improvable, resolvable; redeemable
near antonyms irredeemable, irretrievable, unrecoverable
antonyms incorrigible, irremediable, irreparable

remedial *adj* serving to raise or adjust something to some standard or proper condition — see CORRECTIVE 1

remedy *n* **1** a substance or preparation used to treat disease — see MEDICINE
2 something that corrects or counteracts something undesirable — see CURE 1

remedy *vb* **1** to bring about recovery from — see CURE 1
2 to remove errors, defects, deficiencies, or deviations from — see CORRECT 1

remedying *adj* serving to raise or adjust something to some standard or proper condition — see CORRECTIVE 1

remember *vb* to bring back to mind ⟨I *remember* the fun we had last summer very clearly, but I can't *remember* anything I learned in school yesterday⟩
synonyms hark back (to), mind [*chiefly dialect*], recall, recollect, reminisce (about), think (of)
related words recapture, recur; educe, elicit, evoke, extract, remind; relive
phrases look back (on *or* upon)
near antonyms disregard, ignore, neglect, overlook; lose, miss; blank (out)
antonyms forget, unlearn

remembrance *n* **1** a particular act or instance of recalling or the thing remembered — see MEMORY 2
2 something that serves to keep alive the memory of a person or event — see MEMORIAL
3 the power or process of recalling what has been previously learned or experienced — see MEMORY 1

reminder *n* something that serves to keep alive the memory of a person or event — see MEMORIAL

reminisce (about) *vb* to bring back to mind — see REMEMBER

reminiscence *n* **1** a particular act or instance of recalling or the thing remembered — see MEMORY 2
2 the power or process of recalling what has been previously learned or experienced — see MEMORY 1

reminiscent *adj* provoking a memory or mental association — see SUGGESTIVE 2

remiss *adj* failing to give proper care and attention — see NEGLIGENT

remission *n* release from the guilt or penalty of an offense — see PARDON

remissness *n* failure to take the care that a cautious person usually takes — see NEGLIGENCE 1

remit *vb* **1** to grow less in scope or intensity especially gradually — see DECREASE 2
2 to overlook or dismiss as of little importance — see EXCUSE 1

remitment *n* the act of offering money in exchange for goods or services — see PAYMENT 1

remittable *adj* worthy of forgiveness — see VENIAL

remittal *n* release from the guilt or penalty of an offense — see PARDON

remittance *n* **1** something (as money) that is given or received in return for goods or services — see PAYMENT 2
2 the act of offering money in exchange for goods or services — see PAYMENT 1

remnant *n* **1** a remaining group or portion — see REMAINDER 1
2 an unused or unwanted piece or item typically of small size or value — see [1]SCRAP 1

remodel *vb* to make different in some way — see CHANGE 1

remodeling *n* the act, process, or result of making different — see CHANGE

remonstrance *n* a feeling or declaration of disapproval or dissent — see OBJECTION

remonstrate (with) *vb* to present an opposing opinion or argument — see OBJECT

remorse *n* a feeling of responsibility for wrongdoing — see GUILT 1

remorseful *adj* **1** feeling sorrow for a wrong that one has done — see CONTRITE 1
2 suffering from or expressive of a feeling of responsibility for wrongdoing — see GUILTY 2

remorsefulness *n* a feeling of responsibility for wrongdoing — see GUILT 1

remorseless *adj* not sorry for having done wrong ⟨the *remorseless* killer was sentenced to life in prison without chance of parole⟩
synonyms impenitent, unrepentant
related words compassionless, cruel, merciless, pitiless, ruthless, unmerciful; shameless, unashamed
near antonyms ashamed, hangdog, shamed, shamefaced
antonyms contrite, guilty, penitent, regretful, remorseful, repentant, sorry

remote *adj* **1** small in degree ⟨there's a *remote* chance that it'll rain today, so I brought an umbrella⟩
synonyms negligible, off, outside, slight, slim, small
near antonyms great, large; distinct, significant
antonyms good
2 having or showing a lack of friendliness or interest in others — see COOL 1
3 hidden from view — see SECLUDED
4 not close in time or space — see DISTANT 1

remotest *adj* most distant from a center — see EXTREME 1

removal *n* the getting rid of whatever is unwanted or useless — see DISPOSAL 1

remove *n* the space or amount of space between two points, lines, surfaces, or objects — see DISTANCE

remove *vb* **1** to rid oneself of (a garment) ⟨I *removed* my coat as soon as I got inside⟩
synonyms doff, peel (off), put off, take off
related words husk, shed
near antonyms wear
antonyms don, put on, slip (into)
2 to take away from a place or position ⟨he carefully *removed* the old manuscript from the shelf⟩
synonyms clear, draw, withdraw
related words demount, dislodge; abstract, cut, extract, pull; move, shift, transfer
near antonyms mount
antonyms place, put
3 to change the place or position of — see MOVE 1
4 to let go from office, service, or employment — see DISMISS 1

removed *adj* not close in time or space — see DISTANT 1
remunerate *vb* **1** to give (someone) the sum of money owed for goods or services received — see PAY 1
2 to provide (someone) with a just payment for loss or injury — see COMPENSATE 1
remuneration *n* **1** the act of offering money in exchange for goods or services — see PAYMENT 1
2 payment to another for a loss or injury — see COMPENSATION 1
3 something (as money) that is given or received in return for goods or services — see PAYMENT 2
remunerative *adj* yielding a profit — see PROFITABLE 1
rend *vb* to cause (something) to separate into jagged pieces by violently pulling at it — see TEAR 1
render *vb* to give (something) over to the control or possession of another usually under duress — see SURRENDER 1
rendezvous *vb* to come together into one body or place — see ASSEMBLE 1
rendezvous *n* **1** a place for spending time or for socializing — see HANGOUT
2 an agreement to be present at a specified time and place — see ENGAGEMENT 2
renegade *n* a person who abandons a cause or organization usually without right ⟨a band of *renegades* who had deserted their infantry units and were making their way to Mexico⟩
synonyms defector, deserter, recreant
related words betrayer, double-crosser, quisling, traitor, turncoat; chicken, coward, craven, dastard, poltroon; defier, insurgent, insurrectionary, insurrectionist, mutineer, rebel, red, revolter, revolutionary, revolutionist, revolutionizer
near antonyms adherent, disciple, follower, zealot
antonyms loyalist
renege *vb* to break a promise or agreement ⟨Dad promised to take me out for ice cream on the weekend, only to *renege* on Saturday morning⟩
synonyms back down, back off, cop out
related words chicken (out); disavow, recall, recant, retract, take back, withdraw
phrases go back on
near antonyms follow through; fulfill (*or* fulfil), honor
renew *vb* **1** to bring back to a former condition or vigor ⟨the trip to New York *renewed* our enthusiasm for travel⟩
synonyms freshen, recreate, refresh, refreshen, regenerate, rejuvenate, restore, revitalize, revive
related words make over, refurbish, rehabilitate, remake, remodel, renovate; refill, replenish, resupply
2 to begin again or return to after an interruption — see RESUME
3 to bring back to life, practice, or activity — see REVIVE 1
renewal *n* the act or an instance of bringing something back to life, public attention, or vigorous activity — see REVIVAL
renewed *adj* made or become fresh in spirits or vigor — see NEW 4
renounce *vb* **1** to give up (as a position of authority) formally — see ABDICATE
2 to solemnly or formally reject or go back on (as something formerly adhered to) — see ABJURE
renouncement *n* the act or practice of giving up or rejecting something once enjoyed or desired — see RENUNCIATION
renovate *vb* to put into good shape or working order again — see MEND 1
renown *n* the fact or state of being known to the public — see FAME
renowned *adj* widely known — see FAMOUS
rent *n* **1** a long deep cut — see GASH
2 an open space in a barrier (as a wall or hedge) — see GAP 1
rent *vb* **1** to give the possession and use of (something) in return for periodic payment ⟨we *rented* the apartment to a college student for $500 a month⟩
synonyms lease, let [*chiefly British*]
related words charter, hire; lodge; sublease, sublet
2 to take or get the temporary use of (something) for a set sum — see HIRE 1
renter *n* **1** one who rents a room or apartment in another's house — see TENANT
2 the owner of land or housing that is rented to another — see LANDLORD
renunciation *n* the act or practice of giving up or rejecting something once enjoyed or desired ⟨his *renunciation* of his smoking habit pleased his whole family⟩
synonyms abnegation, renouncement, repudiation, self-denial
related words denial, refusal; relinquishment, resignation, surrender
near antonyms acceptance; adoption, embrace, espousal
antonyms indulgence, self-indulgence
reopen *vb* to begin again or return to after an interruption — see RESUME
repair *n* a state of being or fitness — see CONDITION 1
repair *vb* to put into good shape or working order again — see MEND 1
repairable *adj* capable of being corrected — see REMEDIABLE
reparable *adj* capable of being corrected — see REMEDIABLE
reparation *n* payment to another for a loss or injury — see COMPENSATION 1
repartee *n* **1** a quick witty response — see RETORT 1
2 good-natured teasing or exchanging of clever remarks — see BANTER
repast *n* food eaten or prepared for eating at one time — see MEAL
repay *vb* to make a return payment to ⟨I *repaid* my friend the twenty dollars he had lent me⟩
synonyms refund, reimburse
related words quit, satisfy, settle
phrases pay back
repeal *n* the act of putting an end to something planned or previously agreed to — see CANCELLATION
repeal *vb* **1** to put an end to (something planned or previously agreed to) — see CANCEL 1
2 to put an end to by formal action — see ABOLISH
repeat *n* the act of saying or doing over again ⟨the news story will be broadcast on the six o'clock show, with a *repeat* on the 11 o'clock newscast⟩
synonyms duplication, reduplication, reiteration, repetition, replication
related words rerun

repeat *vb* **1** to say or state again ⟨I *repeated* the address over and over until I had it memorized⟩
synonyms din, rehearse, reiterate
related words echo, parrot; mouth
2 to give from memory ⟨*repeated* correctly all the verses she had memorized⟩
synonyms recite, say
related words declaim, mouth, orate, speak
near antonyms read
3 to say after another ⟨now *repeat* the oath after me⟩
synonyms echo, parrot, quote
related words mouth; copy, imitate, mimic
4 to make or do again ⟨try not to *repeat* your mistakes⟩
synonyms duplicate, redo, reduplicate, reiterate, remake, replicate
related words renew

repeated *adj* appearing or occurring repeatedly from time to time — see REGULAR 1

repeatedly *adv* many times — see OFTEN

repel *vb* **1** to drive back ⟨the defenders *repelled* the attacking army after several hours of fierce fighting⟩
synonyms fend (off), repulse, stave off
related words hold off, resist, withstand; deflect, ward (off); rebuff, snub, spurn
near antonyms welcome
2 to cause to feel disgust — see DISGUST
3 to refuse to give in to — see RESIST

repelled *adj* filled with disgust — see SICK 2

repellent *also* **repellant** *adj* causing intense displeasure, disgust, or resentment — see OFFENSIVE 1

repent *vb* to feel sorry or dissatisfied about — see REGRET

repentance *n* a feeling of responsibility for wrongdoing — see GUILT 1

repentant *adj* **1** feeling sorrow for a wrong that one has done — see CONTRITE 1
2 suffering from or expressive of a feeling of responsibility for wrongdoing — see GUILTY 2

repercussion *n* the power to bring about a result on another — see EFFECT 2

repetition *n* the act of saying or doing over again — see REPEAT

repetitious *adj* marked by repetition — see REPETITIVE

repetitive *adj* marked by repetition ⟨the *repetitive* lyrics of so many rock songs⟩
synonyms reiterative, repetitious

rephrase *vb* to express something (as a text or statement) in different words — see PARAPHRASE

rephrasing *n* an instance of expressing something in different words — see PARAPHRASE

repine *vb* to express dissatisfaction, pain, or resentment usually tiresomely — see COMPLAIN

repine (for) *vb* to have an earnest wish to own or enjoy — see DESIRE

replace *vb* **1** to take the place of ⟨the old street lights were *replaced* with more energy-efficient models⟩
synonyms displace, substitute, supersede, supplant
related words preempt, usurp
2 to bring, send, or put back to a former or proper place — see RETURN 1

replacement *n* a person or thing that takes the place of another — see SUBSTITUTE

replete *adj* possessing or covered with great numbers or amounts of something specified — see RIFE

replica *n* **1** something or someone that strongly resembles another — see IMAGE 1
2 something that is made to look exactly like something else — see COPY

replicate *vb* **1** to make an exact likeness of — see COPY 1
2 to make or do again — see REPEAT 4

replication *n* **1** something that is made to look exactly like something else — see COPY
2 the act of saying or doing over again — see REPEAT

reply *n* **1** action or behavior that is done in return to other action or behavior — see REACTION
2 something spoken or written in reaction especially to a question — see ANSWER 1

reply *vb* **1** to act or behave in response (as to a stimulus or influence) — see REACT
2 to speak or write in reaction to a question or to another reaction — see ANSWER 1

report *n* **1** a loud explosive sound — see CLAP 1
2 a relating of events usually in the order in which they happened — see ACCOUNT 1
3 overall quality as seen or judged by people in general — see REPUTATION

report *vb* to give an oral or written account of in some detail — see TELL 1

reporter *n* a person employed by a newspaper, magazine, or radio or television station to gather, write, or report news ⟨the *reporter* was careful to ask as many questions as possible without annoying anyone⟩
synonyms correspondent, journalist
related words announcer, broadcaster, newscaster, newsman, newspaperman; anchor, anchorman, anchorperson, anchorwoman, legman; columnist, commentator, copyreader, editor, sportswriter, staffer

repose *n* **1** a natural periodic loss of consciousness during which the body restores itself — see SLEEP 1
2 a state of freedom from storm or disturbance — see CALM
3 freedom from activity or labor — see [1]REST 1

repose *vb* to refrain from labor or exertion — see REST 1

repository *n* a building for storing goods — see STOREHOUSE

repossess *vb* to get again in one's possession — see RECOVER 1

repossession *n* the act or process of getting something back — see RECOVERY 1

reprehend *vb* **1** to declare to be morally wrong or evil — see CONDEMN 1
2 to express one's unfavorable opinion of the worth or quality of — see CRITICIZE

reprehensible *adj* **1** deserving reproach or blame — see BLAMEWORTHY
2 provoking or likely to provoke protest — see OBJECTIONABLE

represent *vb* **1** to point out the chief quality or qualities of an individual or group — see CHARACTERIZE 1
2 to present a picture of — see PICTURE 1
3 to serve as a material counterpart of — see SYMBOLIZE 1

representative *n* **1** a person who acts or does business for another — see AGENT 2

2 a person sent on a mission to represent another — see AMBASSADOR
3 one of a group or collection that shows what the whole is like — see EXAMPLE
representative *adj* **1** having or showing the qualities associated with the members of a particular group or kind — see TYPICAL 1
2 having the function or meaning of a symbol — see SYMBOLIC
repress *vb* **1** to put a stop to (something) by the use of force — see QUELL 1
2 to refrain from openly showing or uttering — see SUPPRESS 2
repression *n* the checking of one's true feelings and impulses when dealing with others — see CONSTRAINT 1
reprimand *n* an often public or formal expression of disapproval — see CENSURE
reprimand *vb* **1** to criticize (someone) severely or angrily especially for personal failings — see SCOLD
2 to criticize (someone) usually gently so as to correct a fault — see REBUKE 1
3 to express public or formal disapproval of — see CENSURE 1
reprisal *n* the act or an instance of paying back an injury with an injury — see REVENGE
reproach *n* **1** a cause of shame — see DISGRACE 2
2 an often public or formal expression of disapproval — see CENSURE
3 the state of having lost the esteem of others — see DISGRACE 1
reproach *vb* **1** to criticize (someone) severely or angrily especially for personal failings — see SCOLD
2 to criticize (someone) usually gently so as to correct a fault — see REBUKE 1
3 to express public or formal disapproval of — see CENSURE 1
reproachable *adj* deserving reproach or blame — see BLAMEWORTHY
reprobate *adj* having or showing lowered moral character or standards — see CORRUPT
reprobate *n* a mean, evil, or unprincipled person — see VILLAIN
reprobate *vb* to declare to be morally wrong or evil — see CONDEMN 1
reproduce *vb* **1** to bring forth offspring — see PROCREATE
2 to make an exact likeness of — see COPY 1
reproduction *n* something that is made to look exactly like something else — see COPY
reproof *n* an often public or formal expression of disapproval — see CENSURE
reprove *vb* **1** to criticize (someone) usually gently so as to correct a fault — see REBUKE 1
2 to express public or formal disapproval of — see CENSURE 1
3 to hold an unfavorable opinion of — see DISAPPROVE
republic *n* government in which the supreme power is held by the people and used by them directly or indirectly through representation — see DEMOCRACY
republican *adj* of, relating to, or favoring political democracy — see DEMOCRATIC
repudiate *vb* **1** to declare not to be true — see DENY 1
2 to refuse to acknowledge as one's own or as one's responsibility — see DISCLAIM 1
3 to show unwillingness to accept, do, engage in, or agree to — see DECLINE 1
repudiation *n* **1** a refusal to confirm the truth of a statement — see DENIAL 2
2 the act or practice of giving up or rejecting something once enjoyed or desired — see RENUNCIATION
repugnance *n* a dislike so strong as to cause stomach upset or queasiness — see DISGUST
repugnant *adj* causing intense displeasure, disgust, or resentment — see OFFENSIVE 1
repulse *n* treatment that is deliberately unfriendly — see COLD SHOULDER
repulse *vb* **1** to cause to feel disgust — see DISGUST
2 to drive back — see REPEL 1
repulsed *adj* filled with disgust — see SICK 2
repulsion *n* a dislike so strong as to cause stomach upset or queasiness — see DISGUST
repulsive *adj* causing intense displeasure, disgust, or resentment — see OFFENSIVE 1
repulsiveness *n* the quality of inspiring intense dread or dismay — see HORROR 1
reputable *adj* having a good reputation especially in a field of knowledge — see RESPECTABLE 1
reputation *n* overall quality as seen or judged by people in general ⟨the college's athletic department has a good *reputation*, but the school's science facilities are a bit lacking⟩
synonyms character, mark, name, note, report, repute
related words credit, honor; celebrity, fame, notoriety, renown
near antonyms infamy
repute *n* overall quality as seen or judged by people in general — see REPUTATION
reputed *adj* **1** appearing to be true on the basis of evidence that may or may not be confirmed — see APPARENT 1
2 having a good reputation especially in a field of knowledge — see RESPECTABLE 1
request *n* an act or instance of asking for information — see QUESTION 2
request *vb* **1** to give a request or demand for — see ORDER 2
2 to make a request for — see ASK (FOR) 1
3 to make a request of — see ASK 2
requiem *n* a composition expressing one's grief over a loss — see LAMENT 2
require *vb* to have as a requirement — see NEED 1
required *adj* **1** forcing one's compliance or participation by or as if by law — see MANDATORY
2 impossible to do without — see ESSENTIAL 1
requirement *n* something necessary, indispensable, or unavoidable — see ESSENTIAL 1
requisite *adj* impossible to do without — see ESSENTIAL 1
requisite *n* something necessary, indispensable, or unavoidable — see ESSENTIAL 1
requisition *n* something that someone insists upon having — see DEMAND 1
requisition *vb* to give a request or demand for — see ORDER 2
requital *n* **1** payment to another for a loss or injury — see COMPENSATION 1
2 something (as money) that is given or received in return for goods or services — see PAYMENT 2
3 the act or an instance of paying back an injury with an injury — see REVENGE
requite *vb* **1** to provide (someone) with a just payment for loss or injury — see COMPENSATE 1

2 to punish in kind the wrongdoer responsible for — see AVENGE

rescind *vb* **1** to put an end to (something planned or previously agreed to) — see CANCEL 1
2 to put an end to by formal action — see ABOLISH

rescission *n* the act of putting an end to something planned or previously agreed to — see CANCELLATION

rescue *vb* to remove from danger or harm — see SAVE 2

rescuer *n* one that saves from danger or destruction — see SAVIOR

research *n* a systematic search for the truth or facts about something — see INQUIRY 1

research *vb* to search through or into — see EXPLORE 1

resemblance *n* **1** a point which two or more things share in common — see SIMILARITY 2
2 the quality or state of having many qualities in common — see SIMILARITY 1

resembling *adj* having qualities in common — see ALIKE

resentful *adj* **1** having or showing deep-seated resentment — see BITTER 1
2 having or showing mean resentment of another's possessions or advantages — see ENVIOUS

resentfully *adv* with feelings of bitterness or grief — see HARD 2

resentment *n* **1** a lingering ill will towards a person for a real or imagined wrong — see GRUDGE 1
2 a painful awareness of another's possessions or advantages and a desire to have them too — see ENVY
3 the feeling of being offended or resentful after a slight or indignity — see PIQUE

reservation *n* something upon which the carrying out of an agreement or offer depends — see CONDITION 2

reserve *n* **1** the checking of one's true feelings and impulses when dealing with others — see CONSTRAINT 1
2 a collection of things kept available for future use or need — see STORE
3 a person or thing that takes the place of another — see SUBSTITUTE
4 an interchangeable part or piece of equipment that is kept on hand for replacement of an original — see SPARE

reserve *vb* **1** to arrange to have something (as a hotel room) held for one's future use <we made sure to *reserve* a kennel for our dog several months before the start of the family vacation>
synonyms bespeak, book
related words earmark; contract, engage, retain
2 to continue to have in one's possession or power — see KEEP 2
3 to keep or intend for a special purpose — see DEVOTE 1

reserved *adj* tending not to speak frequently (as by habit or inclination) — see SILENT 2

reside *vb* to have a home — see LIVE 1

residence *n* the place where one lives — see HOME 1

resident *n* one who lives permanently in a place — see INHABITANT

resider *n* one who lives permanently in a place — see INHABITANT

residue *n* **1** the portion or bits of something left over or behind after it has been destroyed — see REMAINS 1
2 a remaining group or portion — see REMAINDER 1

resign *vb* to give up (as a position of authority) formally — see ABDICATE

resign (from) *vb* to give up (a job or office) — see QUIT 1

resigned *adj* receiving or enduring without offering resistance — see PASSIVE

resilient *adj* able to revert to original size and shape after being stretched, squeezed, or twisted — see ELASTIC 1

resist *vb* to refuse to give in to <it is important to *resist* the temptation to run away from your problems>
synonyms buck, defy, fight, oppose, repel, withstand
related words battle, combat, contend (with), counter; contest, dispute; baffle, balk, foil, frustrate, thwart; check, counter, hinder, obstruct, stem
antonyms bow (to), capitulate (to), give in (to), submit (to), succumb (to), surrender (to), yield (to)

resistance *n* **1** the inclination to resist <there was much *resistance* to the idea of removing our baseball caps while eating>
synonyms defiance, opposition
related words demur, objection, protest, remonstrance; compunction, misgiving, reservation; disobedience, noncompliance
near antonyms compliance, obedience; acceptance, approval
antonyms acquiescence
2 a secret organization in a conquered country fighting against enemy forces <soldiers from the *resistance* were captured after a short battle outside the foreign ministry>
synonyms underground
related words cabal, conspiracy

resolute *adj* fully committed to achieving a goal — see DETERMINED 1

resoluteness *n* firm or unwavering adherence to one's purpose — see DETERMINATION 1

resolution *n* **1** a position arrived at after consideration — see DECISION 1
2 firm or unwavering adherence to one's purpose — see DETERMINATION 1

resolvable *adj* capable of having the reason for or cause of determined — see SOLVABLE

resolve *n* firm or unwavering adherence to one's purpose — see DETERMINATION 1

resolve *vb* **1** to come to a judgment after discussion or consideration — see DECIDE 1
2 to find an answer for through reasoning — see SOLVE
3 to set or force apart — see SEPARATE 1

resolved *adj* fully committed to achieving a goal — see DETERMINED 1

resonant *adj* marked by conspicuously full and rich sounds or tones <the orator's *resonant* voice filled the hall>
synonyms golden, resounding, reverberant, reverberating, ringing, round, sonorous, vibrant
related words deep, full, mellifluous, mellow, rich; loud, powerful, stentorian, thundering, thunderous
near antonyms cavernous, hollow; faint, low, murmurous, muted, smothered, soft, weak; thin, tinny

resonate *vb* to continue or be repeated in a series of reflected sound waves — see REVERBERATE

resort (to) *vb* **1** to use or seek out as a source of aid, relief, or advantage ⟨we were so desperate for better grades on our homework that we were forced to *resort to* spending all our evenings at the library⟩
synonyms go (to), refer (to), turn (to)
related words employ, use, utilize; depend (on), rely (on)
phrases fall back on
2 to go to or spend time in often — see FREQUENT

resort *n* **1** a place for spending time or for socializing — see HANGOUT
2 something that one uses to accomplish an end especially when the usual means is not available — see RESOURCE 1

resound *vb* to continue or be repeated in a series of reflected sound waves — see REVERBERATE

resounding *adj* **1** full of or characterized by the presence of noise — see NOISY 2
2 marked by a high volume of sound — see LOUD 1
3 marked by conspicuously full and rich sounds or tones — see RESONANT
4 marked by or uttered with forcefulness — see EMPHATIC 1

resource *n* **1** something that one uses to accomplish an end especially when the usual means is not available ⟨we used every possible *resource* to raise the funds needed to save our town's oldest house⟩
synonyms expedient, recourse, resort
related words hope, opportunity, possibility, relief; makeshift, replacement, stopgap, substitute
2 resources *pl* available money — see FUND 2

respect *n* **1** relation to or concern with something specified ⟨with *respect* to your application⟩
synonyms reference, regard
2 a feeling of great approval and liking — see ADMIRATION 1
3 respects *pl* best wishes — see COMPLIMENT

respect *vb* to think very highly or favorably of — see ADMIRE

respectable *adj* **1** having a good reputation especially in a field of knowledge ⟨no *respectable* dietician would advise people to eat just one kind of food⟩
synonyms esteemed, name, prestigious, reputable, reputed, respected
related words honorable, worthy; creditable, good, praiseworthy; celebrated, distinguished, famed, famous, honored, illustrious, notable, prominent, renowned, well-known
antonyms disreputable, loose
2 following the accepted rules of moral conduct — see HONORABLE 1
3 following the established traditions of refined society and good taste — see PROPER 1
4 of a level of quality that meets one's needs or standards — see ADEQUATE
5 sufficiently large in size, amount, or number to merit attention — see CONSIDERABLE 1

respected *adj* having a good reputation especially in a field of knowledge — see RESPECTABLE 1

respectful *adj* marked by or showing proper regard for another's higher status ⟨the children were remarkably *respectful* while in the President's office⟩
synonyms deferential, dutiful, regardful
related words reverent, reverential, venerating, worshipful; fawning, groveling (*or* grovelling), obsequious, servile, subservient, sycophantic, toadying; civil, courteous, gracious, polite
near antonyms abusive, insulting, offensive; contemptuous, impudent, irreverent; discourteous, insolent, rude, uncivil
antonyms disrespectful

respecting *prep* having to do with — see ABOUT 1

respective *adj* not the same or shared — see SEPARATE 1

respire *vb* to inhale and exhale air — see BREATHE 1

resplendence *n* impressiveness of beauty on a large scale — see MAGNIFICENCE

respond *vb* **1** to act or behave in response (as to a stimulus or influence) — see REACT
2 to speak or write in reaction to a question or to another reaction — see ANSWER 1

response *n* **1** action or behavior that is done in return to other action or behavior — see REACTION
2 something spoken or written in reaction especially to a question — see ANSWER 1

responsibility *n* **1** the state of being held as the cause of something that needs to be set right ⟨*responsibility* for the accident lies with the driver who was speeding⟩
synonyms blame, fault, liability
related words accountability
2 something one must do because of prior agreement — see OBLIGATION

responsible *adj* **1** being the one who must meet an obligation or suffer the consequences for failing to do so ⟨each student is *responsible* for getting his or her own homework done on time⟩
synonyms accountable, answerable, liable
related words beholden, indebted, obligated, obliged
near antonyms exempt, immune
antonyms irresponsible, unaccountable
2 worthy of one's trust — see DEPENDABLE

[1]rest *n* **1** freedom from activity or labor ⟨I'm looking forward to enjoying some *rest* at the end of the school term⟩
synonyms ease, leisure, relaxation, repose
related words catnapping, dozing, napping, resting, sleep, slumber, slumbering, snoozing; quiet, silence, stillness; calm, peace, peacefulness, placidity, restfulness, serenity, tranquillity (*or* tranquility)
near antonyms pressure, strain, stress, tension
antonyms exertion, labor, toil, work
2 a natural periodic loss of consciousness during which the body restores itself — see SLEEP 1

[2]rest *n* a remaining group or portion — see REMAINDER 1

rest *vb* **1** to refrain from labor or exertion ⟨a beach resort that caters to gung ho exercisers and athletes as well as vacationers who just want to *rest*⟩
synonyms bask, loll, lounge, relax, repose
related words bum, goldbrick, idle, loaf, slack (off)
near antonyms drudge, grub, hump, hustle, labor, moil, peg (away), plod, plow, plug, slave, slog, strain, strive, struggle, sweat, toil, travail, work; exercise, work out
2 be in a state of sleep — see SLEEP 1
3 to find a basis — see BASE

restart *vb* to begin again or return to after an interruption — see RESUME

restate *vb* to express something (as a text or statement) in different words — see PARAPHRASE

restatement *n* an instance of expressing something in different words — see PARAPHRASE

restating *n* an instance of expressing something in different words — see PARAPHRASE

restaurant *n* a public establishment where meals are served to paying customers for consumption on the premises ⟨when we get sick of cooking dinner at home, we like to go out to eat at a nice *restaurant*⟩
synonyms café (*also* cafe), diner, grill
related words cafeteria, coffeehouse, garden, luncheonette, lunchroom, snack bar, tearoom; bar, barroom, inn, tavern

restful *adj* free from disturbing noise or uproar — see QUIET 1

restfulness *n* a state of freedom from storm or disturbance — see CALM

resting *adj* being in a state of suspended consciousness — see ASLEEP 1

resting *n* a natural periodic loss of consciousness during which the body restores itself — see SLEEP 1

restitution *n* payment to another for a loss or injury — see COMPENSATION 1

restive *adj* **1** given to resisting authority or another's control — see DISOBEDIENT
2 lacking or denying rest — see RESTLESS 1

restiveness *n* **1** a disturbed or uneasy state — see UNREST
2 a state of nervousness marked by sudden jerky movements — see JUMPINESS

restless *adj* **1** lacking or denying rest ⟨the worried mother spent a *restless* night, tossing and turning in bed for hours⟩
synonyms restive, uneasy, unquiet, unrestful
related words agitated, distressed, disturbed, perturbed, troubled, unsettled; aflutter, anxious, dithery, edgy, fidgety, het up, hung up, jittery, jumpy, nervous, nervy, tense, upset, uptight, worried
near antonyms calm, easy, peaceful, quiet, relaxing, tranquil
antonyms restful
2 marked by or causing agitation or uncomfortable feelings — see NERVOUS 2

restlessness *n* **1** a disturbed or uneasy state — see UNREST
2 the state of being bored — see BOREDOM

restorative *adj* **1** good for the health — see HEALTHFUL
2 having a renewing effect on the state of the body or mind — see TONIC

restore *vb* **1** to bring back to a former condition or vigor — see RENEW 1
2 to bring, send, or put back to a former or proper place — see RETURN 1

restrain *vb* **1** to keep from exceeding a desirable degree or level (as of expression) — see CONTROL 1
2 to take or keep under one's control by authority of law — see ARREST 1

restrained *adj* not excessively showy — see QUIET 2

restraint *n* **1** the checking of one's true feelings and impulses when dealing with others — see CONSTRAINT 1
2 something that limits one's freedom of action or choice — see RESTRICTION 1
3 the power to control one's actions, impulses, or emotions — see WILL 1

restrict *vb* **1** to set bounds or an upper limit for — see LIMIT 1
2 to limit the meaning of (as a noun) — see QUALIFY 1

restricted *adj* having distinct or certain limits — see LIMITED 1

restriction *n* **1** something that limits one's freedom of action or choice ⟨my parents placed several *restrictions* on the party we were planning⟩
synonyms check, condition, constraint, curb, fetter, limitation, restraint
related words exception, proviso, qualification, reservation, stipulation, strings
near antonyms freedom, latitude
2 the act or practice of keeping something (as an activity) within certain boundaries ⟨the *restriction* of surfing to the southern end of the beach rankled some surfers⟩
synonyms confinement, limitation
related words constraint, restraint; isolation, segregation

rest room *n* a room furnished with a fixture for flushing body waste — see TOILET

result *n* **1** a condition or occurrence traceable to a cause — see EFFECT 1
2 something attained by mental effort and especially by computation — see ANSWER 2

result (in) *vb* to be the cause of (a situation, action, or state of mind) — see EFFECT

resultant *adj* coming as a result ⟨frequent trips to the ice cream parlor and the *resultant* gain in weight were starting to affect my tennis game⟩
synonyms attendant, consequent, consequential, due (to)
related words accompanying, coincident, concomitant
near antonyms causal

resultant *n* a condition or occurrence traceable to a cause — see EFFECT 1

resume *vb* to begin again or return to after an interruption ⟨we *resumed* the game as soon as the rain had passed⟩
synonyms continue, renew, reopen, restart
related words resuscitate, revive
near antonyms complete, conclude, consummate, end, finalize, finish; belay, break, can, cease, check, cut, desist, discontinue, drop, halt, knock off, leave off, quit, scuttle, shut off, stay, stop, terminate

résumé *or* **resume** *also* **resumé** *n* a short statement of the main points — see SUMMARY

resurgence *n* the act or an instance of bringing something back to life, public attention, or vigorous activity — see REVIVAL

resurrect *vb* to bring back to life, practice, or activity — see REVIVE 1

resurrection *n* the act or an instance of bringing something back to life, public attention, or vigorous activity — see REVIVAL

resuscitate *vb* to bring back to life, practice, or activity — see REVIVE 1

resuscitated *adj* made or become fresh in spirits or vigor — see NEW 4

resuscitation *n* the act or an instance of bringing something back to life, public attention, or vigorous activity — see REVIVAL

retail *vb* to offer for sale to the public — see MARKET

retain *vb* **1** to continue to have in one's possession or power — see KEEP 2
2 to keep, control, or experience as one's own — see HAVE 1
3 to provide with a paying job — see EMPLOY 1

retainer *n* a person hired to perform household or personal services — see SERVANT

retake *vb* to get again in one's possession — see RECOVER 1

retaliate *vb* to punish in kind the wrongdoer responsible for — see AVENGE

retaliation *n* the act or an instance of paying back an injury with an injury — see REVENGE

retard *vb* to cause to move or proceed at a less rapid pace — see SLOW 1

retardation *n* a usually gradual decrease in the pace or level of activity of something — see SLOWDOWN

retarding *n* a usually gradual decrease in the pace or level of activity of something — see SLOWDOWN

retch *vb* to discharge the contents of the stomach through the mouth — see VOMIT

rethink *vb* to consider again especially with the possibility of change or reversal — see RECONSIDER

reticent *adj* **1** given to keeping one's activities hidden from public observation or knowledge — see SECRETIVE
2 tending not to speak frequently (as by habit or inclination) — see SILENT 2

retinue *n* a body of employees or servants who accompany and wait on a person — see CORTEGE 1

retire *vb* **1** to go to one's bed in order to sleep — see BED
2 to let go from office, service, or employment — see DISMISS 1
3 to move back or away (as from something difficult, dangerous, or disagreeable) — see RETREAT 1

retire (from) *vb* to give up (a job or office) — see QUIT 1

retired *adj* hidden from view — see SECLUDED

retirement *n* an act of moving away especially from something difficult, dangerous, or disagreeable — see RETREAT 1

retiring *adj* **1** not comfortable around people — see SHY 2
2 not having or showing any feelings of superiority, self-assertiveness, or showiness — see HUMBLE 1

retiringness *n* the absence of any feelings of being better than others — see HUMILITY

retort *n* **1** a quick witty response ⟨the clever boy responded to the bully's threat with a rude *retort*⟩
synonyms comeback, repartee, riposte
related words back talk; crack, quip, sally, wisecrack, witticism; cut, insult, put-down
2 something spoken or written in reaction especially to a question — see ANSWER 1

retort *vb* to speak or write in reaction to a question or to another reaction — see ANSWER 1

retract *vb* to solemnly or formally reject or go back on (as something formerly adhered to) — see ABJURE

retreat *n* **1** an act of moving away especially from something difficult, dangerous, or disagreeable ⟨we made a strategic *retreat* when we realized that we were outnumbered⟩
synonyms recession, retirement, revulsion, withdrawal
related words flinch, recoil, shrinking
antonyms advancement
2 something (as a building) that offers cover from the weather or protection from danger — see SHELTER

retreat *vb* **1** to move back or away (as from something difficult, dangerous, or disagreeable) ⟨we *retreated* to the safety of the cellar at the first sign of the tornado⟩
synonyms back (away), fall back, recede, retire, withdraw
related words flinch, recoil, shrink; chicken (out); back down, backtrack; abandon, depart, evacuate, go, leave, quit, vacate
phrases give way, lose ground
near antonyms beard, brave, brazen, breast, confront, dare, defy, face, outbrave
antonyms advance
2 to hasten away from something dangerous or frightening — see RUN 2

retribution *n* the act or an instance of paying back an injury with an injury — see REVENGE

retrieval *n* the act or process of getting something back — see RECOVERY 1

retrieve *vb* to get again in one's possession — see RECOVER 1

retrograde *adj* directed, turned, or done toward the back — see BACKWARD

retrogress *vb* to go back to a previous and usually lower state or level — see REGRESS

retrogression *n* the act or an instance of going back to an earlier and lower level especially of intelligence or behavior — see REGRESSION

retrospect *n* a usually critical look at a past event — see REVIEW 1

retrospection *n* a usually critical look at a past event — see REVIEW 1

return *n* **1** something spoken or written in reaction especially to a question — see ANSWER 1
2 an increase usually measured in money that comes from labor, business, or property — see INCOME
3 the amount of money left when expenses are subtracted from the total amount received — see PROFIT 1

return *vb* **1** to bring, send, or put back to a former or proper place ⟨when I'm done reading a book, I always *return* it to the very shelf I got it from⟩
synonyms replace, restore
near antonyms remove, take
2 to produce as revenue — see YIELD 2
3 to speak or write in reaction to a question or to another reaction — see ANSWER 1

revamp *vb* **1** to make different in some way — see CHANGE 1
2 to prepare for publication by correcting, rewriting, or updating — see EDIT
3 to put into good shape or working order again — see MEND 1

revamping *n* the act, process, or result of making different — see CHANGE

reveal *vb* **1** to make known (as information previously kept secret) ⟨at the end of the book, the detective *reveals* the identity of the mysterious stranger⟩
synonyms bare, disclose, discover, divulge, ex-

pose, spill, tell, unbosom, uncloak, uncover, unmask, unveil
related words debunk, show up; unclothe, undrape; advertise, announce, blaze, broadcast, declare, placard, post, proclaim, promulgate, publicize, publish, sound; betray, blab, give away, leak, let on; inform, squeal, talk; communicate, impart, relate; acknowledge, admit, avow, concede, confess, own; disinter, unearth
phrases spill the beans (about)
near antonyms camouflage, disguise; gild, gloss (over), varnish, whitewash; becloud, bedim, befog, cloud, darken, eclipse, obscure, overcast, overshadow, shade
antonyms cloak, conceal, cover (up), enshroud, hide, mask, shroud, veil
2 to make known (something abstract) through outward signs — see SHOW 2

revealing *adj* clearly conveying a special meaning (as one's mood) — see EXPRESSIVE

revel *n* a time or instance of carefree fun — see FLING 1

revel (in) *vb* to take pleasure in — see ENJOY 1

revelation *n* the act or an instance of making known something previously unknown or concealed ⟨the *revelation* of the movie star's secret marriage by the tabloids⟩ ⟨a new biography of the former president that contains several shocking *revelations*⟩
synonyms disclosure, divulgence, exposure
related words bombshell, surprise; acknowledgment (*also* acknowledgement), admission, avowal, concession, confession
near antonyms concealment, cover-up

reveler *or* **reveller** *n* one who engages in merrymaking especially in honor of a special occasion — see CELEBRANT

reveling *n* joyful or festive activity — see MERRYMAKING

revelry *n* joyful or festive activity — see MERRYMAKING

revenge *n* the act or an instance of paying back an injury with an injury ⟨my *revenge* on the bully who stole my lunch money was the talk of the whole school⟩
synonyms reprisal, requital, retaliation, retribution, vengeance
related words counter, counterattack, counteroffensive; castigation, chastisement, correction; desert(s), discipline, nemesis, penalty, punishment, wrath; amends, compensation, indemnification, indemnity, quittance, recompense, recoupment, redress, remuneration, reparation(s), restitution
near antonyms clemency, grace, leniency, lenity, mercy; forgiveness, pardon, remission

revenge *vb* to punish in kind the wrongdoer responsible for — see AVENGE

revengeful *adj* likely to seek revenge — see VINDICTIVE

revenue *n* an increase usually measured in money that comes from labor, business, or property — see INCOME

reverberant *adj* marked by conspicuously full and rich sounds or tones — see RESONANT

reverberate *vb* to continue or be repeated in a series of reflected sound waves ⟨a room with nothing but hard surfaces will cause the music from your audio system to *reverberate*⟩
synonyms echo, reecho, resonate, resound, sound
near antonyms damp, dampen, deaden, dull, quiet

reverberating *adj* marked by conspicuously full and rich sounds or tones — see RESONANT

revere *vb* to offer honor or respect to (someone) as a divine power — see WORSHIP 1

revered *adj* deserving honor and respect especially by reason of age — see VENERABLE 1

reverence *vb* to offer honor or respect to (someone) as a divine power — see WORSHIP 1

reverend *adj* deserving honor and respect especially by reason of age — see VENERABLE 1

reverend *n* a person specially trained and authorized to conduct religious services in a Christian church — see CLERGYMAN

reverie *also* **revery** *n* the state of being lost in thought ⟨unfortunately, I was deep in *reverie* when the teacher called my name⟩
synonyms daydreaming, study, trance, woolgathering
related words contemplation, meditation, musing; absentmindedness, absorption, abstraction, preoccupation; chimera, conceit, daydream, delusion, dream, fancy, fantasy (*also* phantasy), figment, hallucination, illusion, phantasm, pipe dream, unreality, vision

reversal *n* a change in status for the worse usually temporarily — see REVERSE 1

reverse *n* **1** a change in status for the worse usually temporarily ⟨the loss of my paper route was just the first of my financial *reverses* since the start of the new year⟩
synonyms lapse, reversal, setback
related words disappointment, frustration, letdown; comedown, decline, descent, down, downfall, fall; turnabout, turnaround; recession, regression, retrogression, reversion; relapse; breakdown, collapse, crash, meltdown, ruin, undoing
near antonyms status quo
2 something that is as different as possible from something else — see OPPOSITE

reverse *vb* **1** to change (as an opinion) to the contrary ⟨the principal refused to *reverse* his decision regarding the use of cellular phones⟩
synonyms switch
related words abrogate, overturn, repeal, rescind, revoke, strike (down); countermand, about-face, backtrack, revert
near antonyms maintain, support, uphold
2 to change the position of (an object) so that the opposite side or end is showing ⟨when one side of the cleaning cloth gets dirty, just *reverse* it⟩ ⟨you can *reverse* the jacket for a whole new look⟩
synonyms flip, invert, turn (over)
related words transpose; exchange, interchange, shift, switch; overturn, upset

reversion *n* the act or an instance of going back to an earlier and lower level especially of intelligence or behavior — see REGRESSION

revert *vb* to go back to a previous and usually lower state or level — see REGRESS

review *n* **1** a usually critical look at a past event ⟨a *review* of yesterday's football game gave us a lot of good ideas on how to improve for the next one⟩
synonyms reappraisal, reconsideration, reexamination, retrospect, retrospection
related words recap, recapitulation, rehash
near antonyms preview

2 a close look at or over someone or something in order to judge condition — see INSPECTION
3 a publication that appears at regular intervals — see JOURNAL
4 an essay evaluating or analyzing something — see CRITICISM
review *vb* 1 to consider again especially with the possibility of change or reversal — see RECONSIDER
2 to look over closely (as for judging quality or condition) — see INSPECT
reviewer *n* a person who makes or expresses a judgment on the quality of offerings in some field of endeavor — see CRITIC 2
revise *n* the act, process, or result of making different — see CHANGE
revise *vb* 1 to make different in some way — see CHANGE 1
2 to prepare for publication by correcting, rewriting, or updating — see EDIT
revision *n* the act, process, or result of making different — see CHANGE
revitalization *n* the act or an instance of bringing something back to life, public attention, or vigorous activity — see REVIVAL
revitalize *vb* 1 to bring back to a former condition or vigor — see RENEW 1
2 to bring back to life, practice, or activity — see REVIVE 1
revival *n* the act or an instance of bringing something back to life, public attention, or vigorous activity <there was a *revival* of interest in the author's classic horror stories after a film version of his best-known story was released>
synonyms reanimation, rebirth, regeneration, rejuvenation, renewal, resurgence, resurrection, resuscitation, revitalization
related words renaissance, renascence; reactivation; rally, recovery, recuperation
near antonyms death, expiration, extinction
revive *vb* 1 to bring back to life, practice, or activity <an effort to *revive* the once-common custom of celebrating May 1 as a springtime festival of games and dances>
synonyms reanimate, regenerate, rejuvenate, rekindle, renew, resurrect, resuscitate, revitalize
related words reactivate, restart
near antonyms extinguish, quench, suppress
2 to bring back to a former condition or vigor — see RENEW 1
3 to gain consciousness again — see COME TO
revived *adj* made or become fresh in spirits or vigor — see NEW 4
reviving *adj* having a renewing effect on the state of the body or mind — see TONIC
revocation *n* the act of putting an end to something planned or previously agreed to — see CANCELLATION
revoke *vb* to put an end to (something planned or previously agreed to) — see CANCEL 1
revolt *n* open fighting against authority (as one's own government) — see REBELLION
revolt *vb* 1 to cause to feel disgust — see DISGUST
2 to rise up against established authority — see REBEL
revolted *adj* filled with disgust — see SICK 2
revolter *n* a person who rises up against authority — see REBEL
revolting *adj* causing intense displeasure, disgust, or resentment — see OFFENSIVE 1
revolution *n* 1 a rapid turning about on an axis or central point — see SPIN 1
2 open fighting against authority (as one's own government) — see REBELLION
revolutionary *adj* 1 being very far from the center of public opinion — see EXTREME 2
2 taking part in a rebellion — see REBELLIOUS 1
revolutionary *n* 1 a person who favors rapid and sweeping changes especially in laws and methods of government — see RADICAL
2 a person who rises up against authority — see REBEL
revolutionist *adj* being very far from the center of public opinion — see EXTREME 2
revolutionist *n* 1 a person who favors rapid and sweeping changes especially in laws and methods of government — see RADICAL
2 a person who rises up against authority — see REBEL
revolutionizer *n* a person who rises up against authority — see REBEL
revolve *vb* 1 to move (something) in a curved or circular path on or as if on an axis — see TURN 1
2 to move in circles around an axis or center — see SPIN 1
revulsion *n* 1 a dislike so strong as to cause stomach upset or queasiness — see DISGUST
2 an act of moving away especially from something difficult, dangerous, or disagreeable — see RETREAT 1
reward *n* something offered or given in return for a service performed <there was a *reward* of twenty dollars for the return of her missing cat>
synonyms bounty, price
related words bonus, lagniappe, premium; bonanza, jackpot, treasure trove; award, decoration, distinction, honor, plume, premium, prize; gratuity, tip; desert(s), wages
reward *vb* to give something as a token of gratitude or admiration for a service or achievement <the firefighters were *rewarded* by the city for their heroic actions with vacations>
synonyms award
related words cite, decorate, honor, remember; compensate, pay, recompense, requite; reimburse, repay; acclaim, applaud, commend, compliment, hail, praise, salute
rewarding *adj* making one feel good inside — see HEARTWARMING
reweigh *vb* to consider again especially with the possibility of change or reversal — see RECONSIDER
reword *vb* to express something (as a text or statement) in different words — see PARAPHRASE
rewording *n* an instance of expressing something in different words — see PARAPHRASE
rework *vb* 1 to make different in some way — see CHANGE 1
2 to prepare for publication by correcting, rewriting, or updating — see EDIT
reworking *n* the act, process, or result of making different — see CHANGE
rhapsodic *also* **rhapsodical** *adj* experiencing or marked by overwhelming usually pleasurable emotion — see ECSTATIC
rhapsodically *adv* in an enthusiastic manner — see SKY-HIGH
rhapsodize *vb* to make an exaggerated display of affection or enthusiasm — see GUSH 2

rhapsody *n* a state of overwhelming usually pleasurable emotion — see ECSTASY

rhetoric *n* **1** language that is impressive-sounding but not meaningful or sincere ⟨the mayor's promise to fight drugs was just *rhetoric*, since there was no money in the city budget for a drug program⟩
synonyms bombast, gas, grandiloquence, hot air, oratory, wind
related words claptrap, drivel, gibberish, hogwash, humbug, jabberwocky, jazz, moonshine, nonsense; affectedness, floweriness, grandiosity, loftiness, pomposity, pretension, pretentiousness; verboseness, verbosity, windiness, wordiness
2 the art or power of speaking or writing in a forceful and convincing way — see ELOQUENCE

rhetorical *adj* marked by the use of impressive-sounding but mostly meaningless words and phrases ⟨an essay on civic duty that was mostly *rhetorical*, full of flowery quotations but providing nothing helpful⟩
synonyms bombastic, gaseous, gassy, grandiloquent, oratorical, windy
related words elevated, florid, flowery, grandiose, highfalutin, high-flown, high-sounding, inflated, lofty, pompous, pretentious, stilted; overdone, verbose, wordy
near antonyms eloquent, well-spoken; bald, direct, matter-of-fact, plain, plainspoken, simple, stark, straightforward, unadorned, unaffected, unpretentious

rhythm *n* the recurrent pattern formed by a series of sounds having a regular rise and fall in intensity ⟨the steady *rhythm* of the rain falling on the roof⟩
synonyms beat, cadence, measure, meter
related words accent, accentuation, emphasis, stress; drum, throb; lilt, movement, sway; hexameter, pentameter, tetrameter, trimeter

rhythmic *or* **rhythmical** *adj* marked by or occurring with a noticeable regularity in the rise and fall of sound ⟨lulled to sleep by the *rhythmic* sound of her mother's voice reading the Bible⟩
synonyms cadenced, measured, metric, metrical
related words even, regular, steady, uniform; lilting, musical, swaying
antonyms unmeasured, unrhythmic

riata *n* a rope or long leather thong with a noose used especially for catching livestock — see LASSO

rib *vb* to make fun of in a good-natured way — see TEASE 1

ribald *adj* **1** depicting or referring to sexual matters in a way that is unacceptable in polite society — see OBSCENE 1
2 hinting at or intended to call to mind matters regarded as indecent — see SUGGESTIVE 1

ribaldry *n* the quality or state of being obscene — see OBSCENITY 1

ribbing *adj* marked by or expressive of mild or good-natured teasing — see QUIZZICAL

ribbon *n* a long narrow piece of material — see STRIP

rich *adj* **1** having goods, property, or money in abundance ⟨Tanya's dad works as chauffeur for the *richest* man in town, a big oil baron⟩
synonyms affluent, flush, loaded, moneyed (*or* monied), opulent, wealthy, well-heeled, well-off, well-to-do
related words comfortable, propertied, prosperous, successful; flourishing, prospering, thriving; advantaged, blessed, privileged
near antonyms deprived, disadvantaged, underprivileged; bankrupt, bankrupted, beggared, broke, indebted, insolvent, pauperized, ruined, stone-broke; depressed, pinched, reduced, straitened; low, short
antonyms destitute, impecunious, impoverished, indigent, needy, penniless, penurious, poor, poverty-stricken
2 containing much seasoning, fat, or sugar ⟨stay away from *rich* foods before you sing tonight⟩
synonyms heavy
related words buttery, fat, fatty, greasy, oily; caloric, calorific, fattening; cloying, filling, overfilling, satiating, sating; spicy, sugary; creamy, sauced
near antonyms natural, plain, simple; unseasoned; diet, nonfattening, slimming; nonfat
antonyms light
3 having an abundance of some characteristic quality (as flavor) — see FULL-BODIED
4 producing abundantly — see FERTILE

riches *n* the total of one's money and property — see WEALTH 1

richly *adv* in a luxurious manner — see HIGH

richness *n* the amusing quality or element in something — see HUMOR 1

rick *n* a quantity of things thrown or stacked on one another — see [1]PILE 1

ricochet *vb* to strike and fly off at an angle — see GLANCE 1

rid *vb* to set (a person or thing) free of something that encumbers ⟨worked two jobs to *rid* himself of debt⟩
synonyms clear, disburden, disencumber, free, relieve, unburden
related words discharge, emancipate, enfranchise, liberate, loose, loosen, manumit, release, spring, unbind, uncage, unchain, unfetter; bail (out), deliver, redeem, rescue; disengage, disentangle, extricate
near antonyms bog (down), fetter, restrain, shackle, subject, weigh (down), weight (down)
antonyms burden, encumber, saddle

riddance *n* the getting rid of whatever is unwanted or useless — see DISPOSAL 1

riddle *n* something hard to understand or explain — see MYSTERY

riddle *vb* to find an answer for through reasoning — see SOLVE

ride *n* a means of getting to a destination in a vehicle driven by another ⟨Laurie sometimes gets a *ride* to school from her neighbor⟩
synonyms lift, transportation
related words drive, spin, turn; joyride; conveyance, passage, transit, transport

ride *vb* **1** to attack repeatedly with mean put-downs or insults — see TEASE 2
2 to make fun of in a good-natured way — see TEASE 1
3 to rest or move along the surface of a liquid or in the air — see FLOAT

ride (out) *vb* to come safely through — see SURVIVE 1

ridge *n* the line formed when two sloping surfaces come together along their topmost edge ⟨pigeons roosting along the *ridge* of the roof⟩
synonyms crest
related words divide; backbone, chine, ridgepole,

spine; eminence, peak, prominence, promontory, rise

ridicule *n* the making of unkind jokes as a way of showing one's scorn for someone or something ⟨the early efforts by the suffragists to obtain voting rights for women were met with *ridicule*⟩
synonyms derision, mockery
related words contempt, disdain, scorn; belittlement, deprecation, disparagement; insult, put-down; laughter, snickering; burlesque, caricature, mimicry, satire
near antonyms applause, approval, commendation, praise

ridicule *vb* to make (someone or something) the object of unkind laughter ⟨the term "big bang theory" was originally coined to *ridicule* the belief that the universe was created by a giant explosion⟩
synonyms deride, gibe (*or* jibe), jeer, laugh (at), mock, scout
related words scoff (at), scorn, sneer (at); bad-mouth, belittle, decry, disparage, pooh-pooh (*also* pooh), put down; chaff, jive, josh, kid, quiz, rally, razz, rib, ride, tease; bait, bug, harass, harry, hassle, heckle, needle, pester, target, taunt, torment; ape, burlesque, caricature, imitate, lampoon, mimic, parody, parrot, satirize, take off (on), travesty
phrases make fun of, poke fun at
near antonyms applaud, approve, commend, endorse (*also* indorse), sanction

ridiculer *n* a person who causes repeated emotional pain, distress, or annoyance to another — see TORMENTOR

ridiculous *adj* **1** so foolish or pointless as to be worthy of scornful laughter ⟨a movie thriller with such a *ridiculous* plot that it gets only guffaws from audiences⟩
synonyms absurd, comical, derisive, derisory, farcical, laughable, ludicrous, preposterous, risible, silly
related words asinine, brainless, dumb, fatuous, foolish, half-witted, harebrained, idiotic, imbecilic, inane, jerky, moronic, nonsensical, simple-minded, stupid, unwise, weak-minded, witless; balmy, cockeyed, crazy, cuckoo, daffy, daft, dotty, insane, kooky, loony (*also* looney), lunatic, mad, nutty, screwball, senseless, wacky; fantastic, far-fetched, inconceivable, incredible, unbelievable, unreal, unreasonable
near antonyms earnest, serious, solemn; believable, conceivable, credible, logical, rational, realistic, reasonable, sensible
2 causing or intended to cause laughter — see FUNNY 1

rife *adj* possessing or covered with great numbers or amounts of something specified ⟨our school is *rife* with rumors about the incoming principal⟩
synonyms abounding, flush, fraught, replete, swarming, teeming, thick, thronging
related words brimming, bulging, bursting, chock-full (*or* chockful), crammed, crowded, fat, filled, full, jammed, jam-packed, loaded, packed, saturated, stuffed; clogged, congested, overcrowded, overfilled, overflowing, overfull, overloaded, overstuffed, surfeited; alive, animated, astir, bustling, busy, buzzing, humming, lively
near antonyms bare, barren, blank, devoid, empty, stark, vacant, void; depleted, drained, exhausted; deficient, incomplete, insufficient, short

riffraff *n* **1** discarded or useless material — see GARBAGE
2 people looked down upon as ignorant and of the lowest class — see RABBLE

rifle *vb* to look through (as a place) carefully or thoroughly in an effort to find or discover something — see SEARCH 1

rift *n* **1** an irregular usually narrow break in a surface created by pressure — see CRACK 1
2 an open space in a barrier (as a wall or hedge) — see GAP 1

rig *n* a horse-drawn wheeled vehicle for carrying passengers — see CARRIAGE 1

rig *vb* to provide (someone) with what is needed for a task or activity — see FURNISH 1

rig (out) *vb* to outfit with clothes and especially fine or special clothes — see CLOTHE 1

right *adj* **1** following an original exactly — see FAITHFUL 2
2 being exactly as appears or as claimed — see AUTHENTIC 1
3 being in agreement with the truth or a fact or a standard — see CORRECT 1
4 being what is called for by accepted standards of right and wrong — see JUST 1
5 conforming to a high standard of morality or virtue — see GOOD 2
6 free from irregularities (as curves, bends, or angles) in course — see STRAIGHT 1
7 having full use of one's mind and control over one's actions — see SANE
8 meeting the requirements of a purpose or situation — see FIT 1

right *adv* **1** as stated or indicated without the slightest difference — see EXACTLY 1
2 in a direct line or course — see DIRECTLY 1
3 to a great degree — see VERY 1

right *n* **1** something to which one has a just claim ⟨everyone has the *right* to life, liberty, and the pursuit of happiness⟩
synonyms appanage, birthright, prerogative
related words due, entitlement, perquisite, privilege
2 an entitlement to something — see CLAIM 1
3 the act or practice of giving to others what is their due — see JUSTICE 1

right away *adv* without delay — see IMMEDIATELY

righteous *adj* **1** conforming to a high standard of morality or virtue — see GOOD 2
2 following the accepted rules of moral conduct — see HONORABLE 1

righteously *adv* with purity of thought and deed — see PURELY

righteousness *n* **1** conduct that conforms to an accepted standard of right and wrong — see MORALITY 1
2 faithfulness to high moral standards — see HONOR 1

rightful *adj* being what is called for by accepted standards of right and wrong — see JUST 1

rightist *n* a person whose political beliefs are centered on tradition and keeping things the way they are — see CONSERVATIVE

rightly *adv* in a manner suitable for the occasion or purpose — see PROPERLY

right–minded *adj* conforming to a high standard of morality or virtue — see GOOD 2

rightness *n* the quality or state of being especially suitable or fitting — see APPROPRIATENESS

right now *adv* **1** at the present time — see NOW 1
2 without delay — see IMMEDIATELY

right–of–way *n* the right to one's attention before other things considered less important — see PRIORITY

rigid *adj* **1** not allowing for any exceptions or loosening of standards ⟨*rigid* enforcement of drug laws⟩
synonyms exacting, inflexible, rigorous, strict, stringent, uncompromising
related words close, conscientious, scrupulous, undeviating; adamant, adamantine, determined, dogged, firm, relentless, resolved, single-minded, steadfast, stubborn, tenacious, unbending, unflinching; immovable, implacable, unrelenting, unyielding; austere, demanding, flinty, grim, hard, hardened, hardhearted, harsh, ironbound, severe, stern, tough
near antonyms acquiescent, compliant, compromising, pliable, pliant, relenting, yielding; easy, easygoing, gentle, indulgent, kindly, lenient, merciful, mild, pampering, soft, spoiling, tolerant
antonyms flexible, lax, loose, relaxed
2 given to exacting standards of discipline and self-restraint — see SEVERE 1
3 having a consistency that does not easily yield to pressure — see FIRM 2
4 incapable of or highly resistant to bending — see STIFF 1
5 sticking to an opinion, purpose, or course of action in spite of reason, arguments, or persuasion — see OBSTINATE
6 stretched with little or no give — see TAUT

rigidity *n* the quality or state of being demanding or unyielding (as in discipline or criticism) — see SEVERITY

rigidly *adv* without any relaxation of standards or precision — see STRICTLY

rigidness *n* the quality or state of being demanding or unyielding (as in discipline or criticism) — see SEVERITY

rigmarole *n* unintelligible or meaningless talk — see GIBBERISH

rigor *n* something that is a cause for suffering or special effort especially in the attainment of a goal — see DIFFICULTY 1

rigorous *adj* **1** given to exacting standards of discipline and self-restraint — see SEVERE 1
2 meeting the highest standard of accuracy — see PRECISE 1
3 not allowing for any exceptions or loosening of standards — see RIGID 1

rigorously *adv* without any relaxation of standards or precision — see STRICTLY

rigorousness *n* **1** the quality or state of being demanding or unyielding (as in discipline or criticism) — see SEVERITY
2 the quality or state of being very accurate — see PRECISION

rile *vb* to disturb the peace of mind of (someone) especially by repeated disagreeable acts — see IRRITATE 1

rile *vb* to make angry — see ANGER

riled *adj* feeling or showing anger — see ANGRY

riling *adj* causing annoyance — see ANNOYING

rill *n* a natural body of running water smaller than a river — see CREEK 1

rim *n* the line or relatively narrow space that marks the outer limit of something — see BORDER 1

rim *vb* to serve as a border for — see BORDER

rime *n* a covering of tiny ice crystals on a cold surface — see FROST

rime *vb* to cover with a hardened layer — see ENCRUST

ring *n* **1** a group involved in secret or criminal activities ⟨a *ring* of counterfeiters passing phony $20 bills⟩
synonyms cabal, conspiracy, gang, Mafia, mob, syndicate
related words circle, clan, clique, coterie, crowd; junta, oligarchy
2 a circular strip ⟨a metal *ring* encircled the barrel⟩
synonyms band, circle, eye, hoop, loop, round
related words belt, cincture, collar, girdle; wreath; coil, spiral
3 a communication by telephone — see CALL 3
4 a group of people sharing a common interest and relating together socially — see GANG 2
5 something with a perfectly round circumference — see CIRCLE 1

ring *vb* **1** to make the clear sound heard when metal vibrates ⟨I didn't hear the doorbell *ring*⟩
synonyms chime, knell, peal, toll
related words clang, clank, ding, jangle, jingle, ping, tinkle; resound, reverberate
2 to form a circle around — see SURROUND
3 to pass completely around — see ENCIRCLE 1

ring (up) *vb, chiefly British* to make a telephone call to — see CALL 2

ringer *n* something or someone that strongly resembles another — see IMAGE 1

ringing *adj* **1** marked by a high volume of sound — see LOUD 1
2 marked by conspicuously full and rich sounds or tones — see RESONANT

ringlet *n* a length of hair that forms a loop or series of loops — see CURL

rinse *vb* to pour liquid over or through in order to cleanse — see FLUSH 1

riot *n* someone or something that is very funny — see SCREAM

riotous *adj* **1** causing or intended to cause laughter — see FUNNY 1
2 pouring forth in great amounts — see PROFUSE

rip *n* a long deep cut — see GASH

rip *vb* **1** to cause (something) to separate into jagged pieces by violently pulling at it — see TEAR 1
2 to penetrate with a sharp edge (as a knife) — see CUT 1
3 to proceed or move quickly — see HURRY 2
4 to separate or remove by forceful pulling — see TEAR 2

ripe *adj* fully grown or developed — see MATURE 1

ripen *vb* to become mature — see MATURE

ripened *adj* fully grown or developed — see MATURE 1

ripening *n* the process of becoming mature — see MATURATION

rip–off *n* an instance of theft — see THEFT 2

rip off *vb* **1** to remove valuables from (a place) unlawfully — see ROB
2 to take (something) without right and with an intent to keep — see STEAL 1

riposte *n* a quick witty response — see RETORT 1

ripple *vb* to flow in a broken irregular stream — see GURGLE

rip–roaring *adj* causing great emotional or mental stimulation — see EXCITING 1

rise *n* **1** a raising or a state of being raised to a higher rank or position — see ADVANCEMENT 1
2 an area of high ground — see HEIGHT 4
3 an upward slope — see ASCENT 2
4 something added (as by growth) — see INCREASE 1
5 the act or an instance of rising or climbing up — see ASCENT 1

rise *vb* **1** to become greater in extent, volume, amount, or number — see INCREASE 2
2 to leave one's bed — see ARISE 1
3 to move or extend upward — see ASCEND

risible *adj* **1** causing or intended to cause laughter — see FUNNY 1
2 so foolish or pointless as to be worthy of scornful laughter — see RIDICULOUS 1

rising *n* the act or an instance of rising or climbing up — see ASCENT 1

risk *n* **1** something that may cause injury or harm — see DANGER 2
2 the state of not being protected from injury, harm, or evil — see DANGER 1

risk *vb* **1** to take a chance on ⟨Colette didn't want to *risk* running out of film on her trip, so she brought along a dozen rolls⟩
synonyms chance, gamble (on), hazard, venture
related words brave, challenge, dare, defy, face; compromise, endanger, imperil, jeopardize, menace; expose, subject; bet (on), wager
2 to place in danger — see ENDANGER

risky *adj* involving potential loss or injury — see DANGEROUS

rite *n* an oft-repeated action or series of actions performed in accordance with tradition or a set of rules ⟨the annual summer *rite* of loading up the car for the big family vacation⟩
synonyms ceremonial, ceremony, form, formality, observance, ritual, solemnity
related words amenities, civility, decorum, etiquette, graces, proprieties; convention, custom, habit, manners, mores, practice (*also* practise), standard, tradition, way; celebration, service

ritual *n* an oft-repeated action or series of actions performed in accordance with tradition or a set of rules — see RITE

rival *n* **1** one that is equal to another in status, achievement, or value — see EQUAL
2 one that takes a position opposite another in a competition or conflict — see OPPONENT 1
3 one who strives for the same thing as another — see COMPETITOR

rivalry *n* an earnest effort for superiority or victory over another — see CONTEST 1

rive *vb* to cause (something) to separate into jagged pieces by violently pulling at it — see TEAR 1

rivet *vb* to fix (as one's attention) steadily toward a central objective — see CONCENTRATE 2

riveting *adj* holding the attention or provoking interest — see INTERESTING

rivulet *n* a natural body of running water smaller than a river — see CREEK 1

road *n* **1** a passage cleared for public vehicular travel — see WAY 1
2 a roadway overlaid with parallel steel rails over which trains travel — see RAILROAD

roadhouse *n* a bar or restaurant offering special nighttime entertainment (as music, dancing, or comedy acts) — see NIGHTCLUB

roadway *n* a passage cleared for public vehicular travel — see WAY 1

roam *vb* to move about from place to place aimlessly — see WANDER

roamer *n* a person who roams about without a fixed route or destination — see NOMAD

roaming *adj* traveling from place to place — see ITINERANT

roar *n* **1** a violent shouting — see CLAMOR 1
2 loud, confused, and usually unharmonious sound — see NOISE 1

roar *vb* to make a long loud deep noise or cry ⟨its engine *roared* as the car sped away⟩
synonyms bellow, boom, growl, thunder
related words grumble, roll, rumble; blare, blast, peal, scream, screech, shriek, squall; cry, holler, hoot, shout, whoop, yell; caterwaul, howl, wail, yowl
near antonyms mumble, murmur, mutter, whisper; squeak, whimper

roaring *adj* **1** marked by a high volume of sound — see LOUD 1
2 marked by vigorous growth and well-being especially economically — see PROSPEROUS 1

roast *vb* to make fun of in a good-natured way — see TEASE 1

roasting *adj* having a notably high temperature — see HOT 1

rob *vb* to remove valuables from (a place) unlawfully ⟨in jail for *robbing* a bank⟩
synonyms burglarize, rip off, steal (from)
related words despoil, loot, pillage, plunder, sack, spoil, strip; bleed, break in, cheat, chisel, cozen, defraud, exploit, fleece, gyp, mulct, rook, squeeze, stick, swindle; hold up, mug, stick up

robber *n* one who steals — see THIEF

robbery *n* the unlawful taking and carrying away of property without the consent of its owner — see THEFT 1

robe *vb* to outfit with clothes and especially fine or special clothes — see CLOTHE 1

robotic *adj* designed to replace or decrease human labor and especially physical labor — see LABOR-SAVING

robust *adj* **1** enjoying health and vigor — see HEALTHY 1
2 having active strength of body or mind — see VIGOROUS 1
3 having an abundance of some characteristic quality (as flavor) — see FULL-BODIED
4 not showing weakness or uncertainty — see FIRM 1

robustness *n* **1** the condition of being sound in body — see HEALTH
2 the quality or state of having abundant or intense activity — see VITALITY 1

rock *vb* **1** to make a series of unsteady side-to-side motions ⟨the boat was *rocking* so much that Rosa felt seasick⟩
synonyms careen, lurch, pitch, roll, seesaw, sway, toss, wobble
related words blunder, dodder, falter, flounder, halt, hitch, hobble, jerk, reel, stagger, stumble, teeter, toddle, totter, tumble, waddle, weave; oscillate, undulate, wag, waggle
2 to swing unsteadily back and forth or from side to side — see TEETER 1

rock bottom *n* the lowest part, place, or point — see BOTTOM 3

rocket *vb* **1** to proceed or move quickly — see HURRY 2
2 to rise abruptly and rapidly — see SKYROCKET

rod *n* **1** a heavy rigid stick used as a weapon or for punishment — see CLUB 1
2 a straight piece (as of wood or metal) that is longer than it is wide — see BAR 1
rogue *n* **1** a mean, evil, or unprincipled person — see VILLAIN
2 an appealingly mischievous person — see SCAMP 1
roguish *adj* tending to or exhibiting reckless playfulness — see MISCHIEVOUS 1
roguishness *n* playful, reckless behavior that is not intended to cause serious harm — see MISCHIEF 1
roil *vb* **1** to be in a state of violent rolling motion — see SEETHE 1
2 to make angry — see ANGER
roiled *adj* **1** feeling or showing anger — see ANGRY
2 having visible particles in liquid suspension — see CLOUDY 1
roisterer *n* one who engages in merrymaking especially in honor of a special occasion — see CELEBRANT
role *also* **rôle** *n* the action for which a person or thing is specially fitted or used or for which a thing exists ⟨in science class we're studying the *role* of sunlight in the body's production of vitamin D⟩
synonyms capacity, function, job, part, place, position, purpose, task, work
related words affair, business, concern, involvement, participation; niche, office, post, situation; calling, occupation, pursuit, vocation; activity, assignment, charge, commission, duty, mission, responsibility, service, use
roll *n* **1** a rapid turning about on an axis or central point — see SPIN 1
2 a record of a series of items (as names or titles) usually arranged according to some system — see [1]LIST
roll *vb* **1** to form into a round compact mass — see WAD
2 to make a low heavy rolling sound — see RUMBLE
3 to make a series of unsteady side-to-side motions — see ROCK 1
4 to move (something) in a curved or circular path on or as if on an axis — see TURN 1
5 to move in a stream — see FLOW 1
6 to move in circles around an axis or center — see SPIN 1
7 to move or proceed smoothly and readily — see FLOW 2
rollick *n* a time or instance of carefree fun — see FLING 1
rollick *vb* **1** to engage in activity for amusement — see PLAY 1
2 to play and run about happily — see FROLIC 1
rollicking *adj* given to good-natured joking or teasing — see PLAYFUL
rollicking *n* activity engaged in to amuse oneself — see PLAY 1
roly-poly *adj* having an excess of body fat — see FAT 1
romance *n* a brief romantic relationship — see AFFAIR 1
romantic *adj* excitingly or mysteriously unusual — see EXOTIC
romantic *n* one whose conduct is guided more by the image of perfection than by the real world — see IDEALIST
romanticist *n* one whose conduct is guided more by the image of perfection than by the real world — see IDEALIST
romanticize *vb* to represent or think of as better than reality — see IDEALIZE
romp *n* a time or instance of carefree fun — see FLING 1
romp *vb* to play and run about happily — see FROLIC 1
roof *n* **1** a raised covering over something for decoration or protection — see CANOPY
2 the place where one lives — see HOME 1
roof *vb* to provide with living quarters or shelter — see HOUSE 1
rook *vb* to rob by the use of trickery or threats — see FLEECE
rookie *n* a person who is just starting out in a field of activity — see BEGINNER
room *n* **1** an extent or area available for or used up by some activity or thing ⟨need more *room* to do a cartwheel⟩ ⟨made *room* for him on the bench⟩
synonyms elbowroom, place, space, way
related words capacity, range, scope; clearance, freedom, latitude, leeway, play
2 an area within a building that has been set apart from surrounding space by a wall ⟨finally had a *room* to himself when his brother went off to college⟩
synonyms apartment, cell, chamber, closet
related words accommodation, berth, booth, cabin, compartment, cubicle
3 a favorable combination of circumstances, time, and place — see OPPORTUNITY
roomer *n* one who rents a room or apartment in another's house — see TENANT
roomy *adj* more than adequate or average in capacity — see SPACIOUS
roost *vb* **1** to come to rest after descending from the air — see ALIGHT
2 to establish or place comfortably or snugly — see ENSCONCE 1
root *vb* to set solidly in or as if in surrounding matter — see ENTRENCH
root (out) *vb* **1** to destroy all traces of — see ANNIHILATE 1
2 to draw out by force or with effort — see EXTRACT
rooted *adj* firmly established over time — see INVETERATE 1
rope *n* a length of braided, flexible material that is used for tying or connecting things — see CORD
ropy *adj* being of a consistency that resists flow — see THICK 2
roquelaure *n* a sleeveless garment worn so as to hang over the shoulders, arms, and back — see [1]CAPE
rose-colored *adj* having qualities which inspire hope — see HOPEFUL 1
roster *n* a record of a series of items (as names or titles) usually arranged according to some system — see [1]LIST
rostrum *n* a level usually raised surface — see PLATFORM
rosy *adj* **1** having a healthy reddish skin tone — see RUDDY
2 having qualities which inspire hope — see HOPEFUL 1
rot *n* **1** language, behavior, or ideas that are absurd and contrary to good sense — see NONSENSE 1

2 the process by which dead organic matter separates into simpler substances — see CORRUPTION 1
3 unintelligible or meaningless talk — see GIBBERISH
rot *vb* **1** to become worse or of less value — see DETERIORATE
2 to go through decomposition — see DECAY 1
rotate *vb* **1** to move (something) in a curved or circular path on or as if on an axis — see TURN 1
2 to move in circles around an axis or center — see SPIN 1
rotation *n* a rapid turning about on an axis or central point — see SPIN 1
rote *n* **1** an established and often automatic or monotonous series of actions followed when engaging in some activity — see ROUTINE 1
2 the body of knowledge that has been retained in one's mind or the use of it — see HEART 2
rotten *adj* **1** having undergone organic breakdown ⟨*rotten*, smelly meat that should have been refrigerated⟩
synonyms addled, bad, corrupted, decayed, decomposed, putrefied, putrid, spoiled
related words curdled, fermented, rancid, sour, soured, turned; contaminated, defiled, fouled, polluted, tainted; corroded, crumbled, degenerated, deteriorated, disintegrated; decaying, decomposing, moldering, moldy, putrefying, rotting
near antonyms fresh, good, preserved; pristine, uncontaminated, undefiled, unpolluted, unspoiled, untainted, untouched
2 falling short of a standard — see BAD 1
3 not conforming to a high moral standard; morally unacceptable — see BAD 2
4 not giving pleasure to the mind or senses — see UNPLEASANT
5 extremely unsatisfactory — see WRETCHED 1
6 of low quality — see CHEAP 2
rotund *adj* having an excess of body fat — see FAT 1
rotundity *n* the condition of having an excess of body fat — see CORPULENCE
rough *adj* **1** covered with or as if with hair — see HAIRY 1
2 marked by bursts of destructive force or intense activity — see VIOLENT 1
3 marked by wet and windy conditions — see FOUL 1
4 not having a level or smooth surface — see UNEVEN 1
5 requiring considerable physical or mental effort — see HARD 2
6 difficult to endure — see HARSH 1
7 harsh and threatening in manner or appearance — see GRIM 1
8 hastily or roughly constructed — see RUDE 1
9 lacking in refinement or good taste — see COARSE 2
10 made of or resembling hair — see HAIRY 2
11 marked by a series of sharp quick motions — see JERKY 1
rough (up) *vb* to abuse physically — see MANHANDLE 1
roughened *adj* not having a level or smooth surface — see UNEVEN 1
roughhewn *adj* **1** hastily or roughly constructed — see RUDE 1
2 lacking in refinement or good taste — see COARSE 2
3 lacking social grace and assurance — see AWKWARD 1
roughhouse *n* wildly playful or mischievous behavior — see HORSEPLAY
roughhousing *n* wildly playful or mischievous behavior — see HORSEPLAY
roughly *adv* in a manner so as to cause loss or suffering — see HARDLY 1
roughneck *n* a violent, brutal person who is often a member of an organized gang — see HOODLUM
roughness *n* **1** a harsh or sharp quality — see EDGE 1
2 the quality or state of lacking refinement or good taste — see VULGARITY 1
round *adj* **1** having every part of the surface the same distance from the center ⟨*round* golf balls⟩ ⟨the earth is not perfectly *round*⟩
synonyms global, spherical
related words annular, circular, disklike (*or* disclike), ringlike; curved, looped, spiral; balled, rotund, rounded, roundish; elliptic (*or* elliptical), oval, ovate, ovoid
2 having an excess of body fat — see FAT 1
3 marked by conspicuously full and rich sounds or tones — see RESONANT
4 being neither more nor less than a certain amount, number, or extent — see EVEN 1
round *adv* **1** from beginning to end — see THROUGH 1
2 on all sides or in every direction — see AROUND 1
3 toward the opposite direction — see AROUND 2
round *n* **1** a circular strip — see RING 2
2 a series of events or actions that repeat themselves regularly and in the same order — see CYCLE 1
3 something with a perfectly round circumference — see CIRCLE 1
round *prep* in random positions within the boundaries of — see AROUND 2
round *vb* **1** to form into a round compact mass — see WAD
2 to pass completely around — see ENCIRCLE 1
3 to turn away from a straight line or course — see CURVE 1
round (off *or* out) *vb* **1** to bring (an event) to a natural or appropriate stopping point — see CLOSE 3
2 to serve as a completing element to — see COMPLEMENT
roundabout *adj* not straightforward or direct — see INDIRECT
roundly *adv* with attention to all aspects or details — see THOROUGHLY 1
roundtable *n* **1** a coming together of a number of persons for a specified purpose — see MEETING 1
2 a meeting featuring a group discussion — see FORUM
roundup *n* a short statement of the main points — see SUMMARY
round up *vb* to bring together in one body or place — see GATHER 1
rouse *vb* **1** to cause to stop sleeping — see WAKE 1
2 to cease to be asleep — see WAKE 2
rousing *adj* causing great emotional or mental stimulation — see EXCITING 1
rout *n* failure to win a contest — see DEFEAT 1
rout *vb* **1** to achieve a victory over — see BEAT 2
2 to defeat by a large margin — see WHIP 2
3 to drive or force out — see EJECT 1

route *n* 1 a passage cleared for public vehicular travel — see WAY 1
2 an established course for traveling from one place to another — see PASSAGE 1
3 the direction along which something or someone moves — see PATH 1
route *vb* to point out the way for (someone) especially from a position in front — see LEAD 1
routine *adj* 1 being of the type that is encountered in the normal course of events — see ORDINARY 1
2 following or agreeing with established form, custom, or rules — see FORMAL 1
3 often observed or encountered — see COMMON 1
routine *n* 1 an established and often automatic or monotonous series of actions followed when engaging in some activity <part of my morning *routine* is drinking a cup of hot chocolate while waiting for the bus>
synonyms groove, pattern, rote, rut, treadmill
related words custom, fashion, habit, practice (*also* practise), trick, wont; approach, manner, method, procedure, strategy, style, tack, way; design, plan, program, scheme; convention, policy, tradition
2 something done over and over in order to develop skill — see EXERCISE 2
rove *vb* to move about from place to place aimlessly — see WANDER
rover *n* 1 a person who roams about without a fixed route or destination — see NOMAD
2 someone who engages in robbery of ships at sea — see PIRATE
roving *adj* traveling from place to place — see ITINERANT
row *n* 1 a series of people or things arranged side by side <stood in a *row* to have their picture taken> <three *rows* of eight jelly beans equals 24 jelly beans>
synonyms bank, rank
related words chain, column, cue, file, line, procession, queue, string, train; echelon, tier; array, sequence
2 a passage cleared for public vehicular travel — see WAY 1
3 a rough and often noisy fight usually involving several people — see BRAWL 1
4 a state of noisy, confused activity — see COMMOTION
5 an often noisy or angry expression of differing opinions — see ARGUMENT 1
¹row *vb* to move a boat by means of oars <*rowed* around the lake>
synonyms oar, paddle, scull
related words canoe; pole, punt
²row *vb* to express different opinions about something often angrily — see ARGUE 2
rowdy *adj* being rough or noisy in a high-spirited way — see BOISTEROUS
rowdy *n* a violent, brutal person who is often a member of an organized gang — see HOODLUM
rower *n* a person who drives a boat forward by means of oars — see OARSMAN
royal *adj* 1 fit for or worthy of a royal ruler — see MONARCHICAL
2 large and impressive in size, grandeur, extent, or conception — see GRAND 1
rub *vb* 1 to damage or diminish by continued friction — see ABRADE 1
2 to make smooth by friction — see GRIND 1
3 to make smooth or glossy usually by repeatedly applying surface pressure — see POLISH
rubbed *adj* having a shiny surface or finish — see GLOSSY
rubberlike *adj* able to revert to original size and shape after being stretched, squeezed, or twisted — see ELASTIC 1
rubberneck *vb* to look long and hard in wonder or surprise — see GAPE
rubbery *adj* able to revert to original size and shape after being stretched, squeezed, or twisted — see ELASTIC 1
rubbish *n* discarded or useless material — see GARBAGE
rubbishy *adj* of low quality — see CHEAP 2
rubble *n* the portion or bits of something left over or behind after it has been destroyed — see REMAINS 1
rubicund *adj* having a healthy reddish skin tone — see RUDDY
rub out *vb* to destroy all traces of — see ANNIHILATE 1
rubric *n* a word or series of words often in larger letters placed at the beginning of a passage or at the top of a page in order to introduce or categorize — see HEADING
rucksack *n* a soft-sided case designed for carrying belongings especially on the back — see PACK 1
ruckus *n* 1 a rough and often noisy fight usually involving several people — see BRAWL 1
2 a state of noisy, confused activity — see COMMOTION
ruction *n* 1 a rough and often noisy fight usually involving several people — see BRAWL 1
2 a state of noisy, confused activity — see COMMOTION
ruddy *adj* having a healthy reddish skin tone <his *ruddy* complexion runs in the family>
synonyms blooming, florid, flush, glowing, rosy, rubicund, sanguine
related words bronzed, brown, suntanned, tanned; flushed, pink, pinkish, warm; cherubic
near antonyms ashen, ashy, pale, pallid, pasty, sallow, wan, waxen, waxy; blanched, white, whitened; anemic, peaked, sick, sickly; bloodless, cadaverous, deathlike
rude *adj* 1 hastily or roughly constructed <a *rude* shelter built from unfinished logs by some forgotten pioneer>
synonyms artless, clumsy, crude, rough, roughhewn, unrefined
related words defective, faulty, flawed, imperfect; imprecise, inexact; inartistic, undressed, unfinished, unpolished, unworked; amateur, amateurish, inexpert, unprofessional, unskilled, unskillful; primitive, rudimentary
near antonyms faultless, finished, meticulous, perfected, polished, well-done; adept, adroit, dexterous (*also* dextrous), expert, masterful, masterly, neat, practiced (*or* practised), skillful, workmanlike; artful, artistic, sophisticated; exact, precise
antonyms refined
2 belonging to or characteristic of an early level of skill or development — see PRIMITIVE 1
3 lacking in refinement or good taste — see COARSE 2
4 not civilized — see SAVAGE 1
5 showing a lack of manners or consideration for others — see IMPOLITE

rudeness *n* **1** rude behavior — see DISCOURTESY
2 the quality or state of lacking refinement or good taste — see VULGARITY 1

rudimentary *adj* **1** belonging to or characteristic of an early level of skill or development — see PRIMITIVE 1
2 of or relating to the simplest facts or theories of a subject — see ELEMENTARY

rudiments *n pl* general or basic truths on which other truths or theories can be based — see PRINCIPLES 1

rue *n* a feeling of responsibility for wrongdoing — see GUILT 1

rue *vb* to feel sorry or dissatisfied about — see REGRET

rueful *adj* **1** expressing or suggesting mourning — see MOURNFUL 1
2 feeling sorrow for a wrong that one has done — see CONTRITE 1
3 deserving of one's pity — see PATHETIC 1

ruefully *adv* with feelings of bitterness or grief — see HARD 2

ruffian *n* a violent, brutal person who is often a member of an organized gang — see HOODLUM

ruffle *n* a strip of fabric gathered or pleated on one edge and used as trimming ⟨likes lace curtains without *ruffles* and chintz curtains with *ruffles*⟩
synonyms flounce, frill, furbelow
related words border, edging, fringe, trim; pleat, ruff; bunting, skirting

rugged *adj* **1** able to withstand hardship, strain, or exposure — see HARDY 1
2 difficult to endure — see HARSH 1
3 harsh and threatening in manner or appearance — see GRIM 1
4 having muscles capable of exerting great physical force — see STRONG 1
5 not having a level or smooth surface — see UNEVEN 1

ruin *n* **1** the state or fact of being rendered nonexistent, physically unsound, or useless — see DESTRUCTION
2 ruins *pl* the portion or bits of something left over or behind after it has been destroyed — see REMAINS 1

ruin *vb* **1** to cause to lose one's fortune and become unable to pay one's debts ⟨*ruined* by the Great Chicago Fire of 1871, the industrialist was forced to sell his mansion and start all over again⟩
synonyms bankrupt, bust
related words beggar, impoverish, pauperize; break, reduce, straiten; clean (out), wipe out
near antonyms enrich, richen
2 to bring destruction to (something) through violent action — see RAVAGE
3 to bring to a complete end the physical soundness, existence, or usefulness of — see DESTROY 1

ruination *n* the state or fact of being rendered nonexistent, physically unsound, or useless — see DESTRUCTION

ruinous *adj* **1** bringing about ruin or misfortune — see FATAL 1
2 causing or tending to cause destruction — see DESTRUCTIVE 1

rule *n* **1** a statement spelling out the proper procedure or conduct for an activity ⟨read the *rules* that are posted before you use the pool⟩
synonyms bylaw, ground rule, regulation
related words code, constitution, decalogue; act, law, ordinance, statute; command, decree, dictate, directive, edict, fiat, order; axiom, fundamental, maxim, precept; moral, principle, value; prohibition, restriction; convention, custom, habit, manners, mores, practice (*also* practise), tradition, way; blueprint, canon, formula, guide, guideline, recipe, standard
2 lawful control over the affairs of a political unit (as a nation) ⟨the years during which Russia was under Communist *rule*⟩
synonyms administration, authority, governance, government, jurisdiction, regime (*also* régime), regimen
related words reign; dominion, power, sovereignty, supremacy, sway; command, leadership; direction, management, regulation, superintendence, supervision; dictatorship, domination, mastery, oppression, subjugation, tyranny

rule *vb* to exercise authority or power over — see GOVERN

rule (on) *vb* to give an opinion about (something at issue or in dispute) — see JUDGE 1

rule out *vb* to prevent the participation or inclusion of — see EXCLUDE

ruler *n* one who rules over a people with a sole, supreme, and usually hereditary authority — see MONARCH

ruling *n* **1** a decision made by a court or tribunal regarding a case it has heard — see SENTENCE
2 an order publicly issued by an authority — see EDICT 1

rumble *vb* to make a low heavy rolling sound ⟨when thunder *rumbled* in the distant sky, we wisely began packing up our stuff⟩
synonyms growl, grumble, lumber, roll
related words boom, drum, thunder

ruminant *adj* given to or marked by long, quiet thinking — see CONTEMPLATIVE

ruminate *vb* to give serious and careful thought to — see PONDER

rummage *n* an unorganized collection or mixture of various things — see MISCELLANY 1

rummage *vb* to look through (as a place) carefully or thoroughly in an effort to find or discover something — see SEARCH 1

rumor *vb* to make (as a piece of information) the subject of common talk without any authority or confirmation of accuracy ⟨for years people have been *rumoring* the principal's imminent retirement⟩
synonyms bruit (about), circulate, noise (about), whisper
related words bandy (about), blab, gossip; disclose, divulge, report, reveal, tell; hint, imply, insinuate, intimate, let on, suggest; broadcast, promulgate, propagate, spread

rump *n* the part of the body upon which someone sits — see BUTTOCKS

rumple *vb* **1** to create (as by crushing) an irregular mass of creases in — see CRUMPLE 1
2 to develop creases or folds — see WRINKLE 1
3 to undo the proper order or arrangement of — see DISORDER

rumpled *adj* lacking in order, neatness, and often cleanliness — see MESSY

rumpus *n* a state of noisy, confused activity — see COMMOTION

run *n* **1** a prevailing or general movement or inclination — see TREND 1
2 *chiefly Midland* a natural body of running water smaller than a river — see CREEK 1

3 the period during which something exists, lasts, or is in progress — see DURATION 1
4 the right to act or move freely — see FREEDOM 2

run *vb* **1** to go at a pace faster than a walk ⟨*ran* all the way to the bus stop, but still missed the bus⟩
synonyms dash, gallop, jog, scamper, sprint, trip, trot
related words bound, canter, leap, lope, skip, spring; foot (it), hoof (it), hotfoot (it), leg (it); nip, race, scuttle, step (along)
near antonyms amble, lumber, plod, saunter, shamble, shuffle, stroll; crawl, creep, poke; plod, trudge; hobble, limp
2 to hasten away from something dangerous or frightening ⟨rather than *run* from a black bear, it's better to hold your ground and make lots of noise⟩
synonyms bolt, break, flee, fly, retreat, run away, run off
related words abscond, clear out, decamp, elope, escape, light out, retreat, scat, scram, skip (out)
phrases beat it, turn tail
near antonyms beard, brave, confront, dare, defy, face
3 to be positioned along a certain course or in a certain direction ⟨the road *runs* along the river for a while⟩
synonyms extend, go, head, lead, lie
related words cross, cut, pass; follow, span, traverse
4 to occur within a continuous range of variation ⟨the electric bill *runs* between 30 and 50 dollars a month⟩
synonyms go, range, vary
related words alternate, move, shift; change, mutate; extend, reach, stretch, sweep
5 to move in a stream — see FLOW 1
6 to proceed or move quickly — see HURRY 2
7 to show a liking or proneness (for something) — see LEAN 2
8 to urge, push, or force onward — see DRIVE 1
9 to control the mechanical operation of — see OPERATE 1
10 to eventually have as a state or quality — see BECOME
11 to go from a solid to a liquid state — see LIQUEFY
12 to look after and make decisions about — see CONDUCT 1
13 to cause to function — see ACTIVATE

run away *vb* **1** to get free from a dangerous or confining situation — see ESCAPE 1
2 to hasten away from something dangerous or frightening — see RUN 2

run–down *adj* **1** showing signs of advanced wear and tear and neglect — see SHABBY 1
2 temporarily suffering from a disorder of the body — see SICK 1

run down *vb* to come upon after searching, study, or effort — see FIND 1

run–in *n* a brief clash between enemies or rivals — see ENCOUNTER

runner *n* one that carries a message or does an errand — see MESSENGER

running *adj* being in effective operation — see ACTIVE 1

running *n* the act or activity of looking after and making decisions about something — see CONDUCT 1

runny *adj* having an overly soft liquid consistency ⟨*runny* scrambled eggs⟩
synonyms soupy, watery
related words flowing, fluid, liquefied; dilute, diluted, thin, thinned, watered (down), weak; slushy, soggy, wet
near antonyms syrupy, viscid, viscous; creamy, heavy, thick, thickened, thickish; gelatinous, gluey, glutinous, gooey, gummy, sticky

run off *vb* **1** to drive or force out — see EJECT 1
2 to get free from a dangerous or confining situation — see ESCAPE 1
3 to hasten away from something dangerous or frightening — see RUN 2

run–of–the–mill *adj* **1** being of the type that is encountered in the normal course of events — see ORDINARY 1
2 of average to below average quality — see MEDIOCRE 1

run on *vb* **1** to engage in casual or rambling conversation — see CHAT
2 to remain indefinitely in existence or in the same state — see CONTINUE 1
3 to talk at length without sticking to a topic or getting to a point — see RAMBLE 1

run over *vb* to flow over the brim or top of — see OVERFLOW 1

runt *n* a living thing much smaller than others of its kind — see DWARF 1

run through *vb* to use up carelessly — see WASTE 1

rural *adj* of, relating to, associated with, or typical of open areas with few buildings or people ⟨grew up in a *rural* community where more than half the people were farmers⟩ ⟨a painter noted for his *rural* landscapes⟩
synonyms bucolic, country, pastoral, rustic
related words countrified (*also* countryfied), provincial; agrarian, agricultural
near antonyms citified, urbanized; metropolitan, municipal; nonagricultural, nonfarm
antonyms urban

rush *n* **1** excited and often showy or disorderly speed — see HURRY 1
2 the act or action of setting upon with force or violence — see ATTACK 1

rush *vb* **1** to cause to move or proceed fast or faster — see HURRY 1
2 to flow out in great quantities or with force — see GUSH 1
3 to proceed or move quickly — see HURRY 2
4 to take sudden, violent action against — see ATTACK 1

rushed *adj* acting or done with excessive or careless speed — see HASTY 1

rustic *adj* of, relating to, associated with, or typical of open areas with few buildings or people — see RURAL

rustic *n* an awkward or simple person especially from a small town or the country — see HICK

rustle *vb* to proceed or move quickly — see HURRY 2

rustler *n* an ambitious person who eagerly goes after what is desired — see GO-GETTER

rut *n* an established and often automatic or monotonous series of actions followed when engaging in some activity — see ROUTINE 1

ruthless *adj* having or showing a lack of sympathy or tender feelings — see HARD 1

sable *adj* having the color of soot or coal — see BLACK 1

saccharine *adj* appealing to the emotions in an obvious and tiresome way — see CORNY

sacerdotal *adj* of, relating to, or characteristic of the clergy — see CLERICAL

sack *n* **1** a container made of a flexible material (as paper or plastic) — see BAG 1
2 a place set aside for sleeping — see BED 1

sack *vb* **1** to let go from office, service, or employment — see DISMISS 1
2 to search through with the intent of committing robbery — see RANSACK 1

sacred *adj* **1** not to be violated, criticized, or tampered with ⟨we took a *sacred* oath not to let anyone find our hideout⟩
synonyms holy, inviolable, sacrosanct, unassailable, untouchable
related words inviolate, pure; privileged, protected, shielded; exempt, immune
near antonyms blasphemous, irreverent, profane
2 of, relating to, or being God — see HOLY 3
3 of, relating to, or used in the practice or worship services of a religion — see RELIGIOUS 1
4 set apart or worthy of veneration by association with God — see HOLY 2

sacrifice *n* something offered to a god ⟨the herders selected their best lamb as a *sacrifice* in order to receive blessings from their god⟩
synonyms immolation, offering, victim
related words holocaust; contribution, donation

sacrifice *vb* to give up as an offering to a god ⟨in the Old Testament Abraham was willing to *sacrifice* even his son to God⟩
synonyms immolate, offer
related words consecrate, dedicate, devote; give, surrender, yield

sacrilege *n* an act of great disrespect shown to God or to sacred ideas, people, or things — see BLASPHEMY

sacrilegious *adj* not showing proper reverence for the holy or sacred — see IRREVERENT

sacristy *n* a room in a church building for sacred furnishings (as vestments) ⟨our choir robes were stored in the *sacristy*⟩
synonyms vestry
related words cloakroom

sacrosanct *adj* **1** not to be violated, criticized, or tampered with — see SACRED 1
2 set apart or worthy of veneration by association with God — see HOLY 2

sad *adj* **1** feeling unhappiness ⟨movies in which the hero dies always make us feel *sad*⟩
synonyms bad, blue, brokenhearted, crestfallen, dejected, depressed, despondent, disconsolate, doleful, down, downcast, downhearted, droopy, forlorn, gloomy, glum, heartbroken, heartsick, heartsore, inconsolable, joyless, low, low-spirited, melancholy, miserable, mournful, saddened, sorrowful, sorry, unhappy, woebegone, woeful, wretched
related words aggrieved, distressed, troubled; despairing, hopeless; disappointed, discouraged, disheartened, dispirited; suicidal; dolorous, lugubrious, plaintive, tearful; regretful, rueful; grieving, wailing, weeping; black, bleak, cheerless, comfortless, dark, darkening, depressing, desolate, dismal, drear, dreary, funereal, gray (*also* grey), morbid, morose, murky, saturnine, somber (*or* sombre), sullen
near antonyms ecstatic, elated, enraptured, entranced, euphoric, exhilarated, exuberant, exultant; blithe, blithesome, gay, jocund, jolly, jovial, lightsome, merry, mirthful; excited, thrilled; hopeful, optimistic; encouraged, heartened; animated, jaunty, lively, perky, sprightly, vivacious; content, gratified, pleased, satisfied; beaming, grinning, laughing, smiling; boon, carefree, careless, cavalier, devil-may-care, easygoing, happy-go-lucky, insouciant, lighthearted, unconcerned
antonyms blissful, buoyant, buoyed, cheerful, cheery, chipper, delighted, glad, gladdened, gladsome, gleeful, happy, joyful, joyous, jubilant, sunny, upbeat
2 causing unhappiness ⟨the *sad* news about our uncle's death made my father cry⟩
synonyms depressing, dismal, drear, dreary, heartbreaking, heartrending, melancholy, pathetic, saddening, sorry, tearful, teary
related words discomforting, discomposing, disquieting, distressing, disturbing, perturbing; affecting, moving, poignant, touching; discouraging, disheartening, dispiriting
near antonyms heartening, heartwarming, inspiring, stimulating, stirring, uplifting; agreeable, pleasant, pleasurable; exhilarating, thrilling
antonyms cheering, cheery, glad, happy

sadden *vb* to make sad — see DEPRESS 1

saddened *adj* feeling unhappiness — see SAD 1

saddening *adj* causing unhappiness — see SAD 2

saddle *vb* to place a weight or burden on — see LOAD 1

sadism *n* the willful infliction of pain and suffering on others — see CRUELTY

sadistic *adj* having or showing the desire to inflict severe pain and suffering on others — see CRUEL 1

sadly *adv* with feelings of bitterness or grief — see HARD 2

sadness *n* a state or spell of low spirits ⟨she was filled with *sadness* at the thought of having to leave her family⟩
synonyms blues, dejection, depression, desolation, despondency, disconsolateness, dispiritedness, doldrums, downheartedness, dreariness, dumps, forlornness, gloom, gloominess, heartsickness, joylessness, melancholy, mopes, oppression, unhappiness
related words melancholia, self-pity; anguish, dolor, grief, sorrow; dolefulness, mournfulness, somberness, sorrowfulness, woefulness; agony, distress, pain; misery, woe, wretchedness; discouragement, disheartenment; moodiness; despair, desperation, hopelessness; boredom, ennui, tedium
near antonyms gaiety (*also* gayety), gayness, glee, gleefulness, humor, jollity, joviality, lightheartedness, merriment, mirth, mirthfulness; cheer, cheerfulness, hopefulness, optimism, sunniness; content, contentedness, contentment, satisfaction; delight, gratification
antonyms bliss, blissfulness, ecstasy, elatedness,

elation, euphoria, exhilaration, exuberance, exultation, felicity, gladness, gladsomeness, happiness, heaven, intoxication, joy, joyfulness, joyousness, jubilation, rapture, rapturousness

safe *adj* **1** not exposed to the threat of loss or injury ⟨the minute the rain started, we ran to a place where we were *safe* from getting wet⟩
synonyms all right, alright, secure
related words hale, healthy, intact, sound, well, whole; scatheless, unharmed, unhurt, uninjured, unscathed
near antonyms damaged, harmed, hurt, injured, scathed, wounded
antonyms endangered, imperiled, insecure, liable, threatened, unsafe, vulnerable
2 providing safety ⟨we tried to find a *safe* place to hide the candy⟩
synonyms secure, snug
related words guarding, protecting, safeguarding, sheltering, shielding; defended, guarded, protected, sheltered, shielded; impregnable, inviolable, invulnerable, unassailable, unconquerable
near antonyms undefended, unguarded, unprotected, vulnerable
antonyms dangerous, hazardous, insecure, risky, unsafe
3 having or showing a close attentiveness to avoiding danger or trouble — see CAREFUL 1
4 not causing injury or hurt — see HARMLESS
5 worthy of one's trust — see DEPENDABLE

safe *n* a specially reinforced container to keep valuables safe ⟨the hotel recommended that we keep all our valuables in its *safe* during our stay⟩
synonyms coffer, safe-deposit box, strongbox
related words vault; locker, storeroom, treasury; footlocker, trunk

safe–deposit box *n* a specially reinforced container to keep valuables safe — see SAFE

safeguard *n* means or method of defending — see DEFENSE 1

safeguard *vb* to drive danger or attack away from — see DEFEND 1

safekeeping *n* responsibility for the safety and well-being of someone or something — see CUSTODY

safeness *n* the state of not being exposed to danger — see SAFETY 1

safety *n* **1** the state of not being exposed to danger ⟨we were lucky to make it to *safety* just as the lions broke loose from their cage at the zoo⟩
synonyms protection, safeness, security
related words aegis, defense, guardianship, ward; guard, safeguard, screen, shield; asylum, harbor, haven, refuge, retreat, shelter; inviolability, invulnerability
near antonyms hazard, risk, threat; instability, precariousness
antonyms danger, distress, endangerment, imperilment, jeopardy, peril, trouble
2 a protective device (as on a weapon) to prevent accidental operation ⟨the gun couldn't be fired as long as the *safety* was on⟩
synonyms guard
related words lock

sag *n* the extent to which something hangs or dips below a straight line ⟨if there's too much *sag* in the rod, the curtains will drag on the floor⟩
synonyms droop, slack, slackness
related words laxity, laxness, looseness
near antonyms tautness, tenseness, tension, tightness

sag *vb* **1** to be limp from lack of water or vigor — see DROOP 1
2 to decline gradually from a standard level — see SLIP 1
3 to lose bodily strength or vigor — see WEAKEN 2

sagacious *adj* having or showing deep understanding and intelligent application of knowledge — see WISE 1

sagaciousness *n* the ability to understand inner qualities or relationships — see WISDOM 1

sagacity *n* the ability to understand inner qualities or relationships — see WISDOM 1

sage *adj* having or showing deep understanding and intelligent application of knowledge — see WISE 1

sage *n* a person of deep wisdom or learning ⟨the young prince visited the *sage* to learn the meaning of life⟩
synonyms savant, scholar
related words brain, egghead, genius, highbrow, intellectual, thinker; guru, mahatma; rabbi; master, mentor, teacher
near antonyms blockhead, dodo, dolt, donkey, dope, dumbbell, dummy, dunce, fathead, fool, goon, half-wit, idiot, ignoramus, imbecile, jackass, knothead, know-nothing, moron, nincompoop, ninny, nitwit, numskull (*or* numbskull), pinhead, simpleton, stock, turkey

sageness *n* the ability to understand inner qualities or relationships — see WISDOM 1

sagging *adj* bending downward or forward — see NODDING

sail *n* a journey over water in a vessel ⟨we went for a brief *sail* on the bay to relax⟩
synonyms crossing, cruise, passage, voyage

sail *vb* **1** to travel on water in a vessel ⟨I can't *sail* when there's any breeze at all because I get seasick easily⟩
synonyms boat, cruise, navigate, voyage
related words yacht; coast; log
phrases make sail
2 to move or proceed smoothly and readily — see FLOW 2
3 to rest or move along the surface of a liquid or in the air — see FLOAT

sailboat *n* a boat equipped with one or more sails ⟨we were stuck in the *sailboat* for an hour until the wind came up and we could move again⟩
synonyms bark, dinghy, windjammer
related words brigantine, caravel, catboat, clipper, corvette, cutter, frigate, galleon, galley, junk, ketch, lugger, outrigger, pinnace, schooner, shallop, ship, sloop, square-rigger, xebec, yacht, yawl; bottom, craft, vessel

sailor *n* one who operates or navigates a seagoing vessel ⟨the *sailors* were glad to be arriving in port after their long voyage⟩
synonyms gob, jack, jack-tar, mariner, navigator, salt, sea dog, seafarer, seaman, swab, tar
related words crewman, deckhand

saint *vb* to declare to be a saint and worthy of public respect ⟨Brigid of Sweden was *sainted* in October of 1391⟩
synonyms canonize
related words deify, worship; consecrate, hallow, sanctify; beatify, venerate

sainted *adj* showing a devotion to God and to a life of virtue — see HOLY 1

sainthood *n* the quality or state of being spiritually pure or virtuous — see HOLINESS

saintliness *n* the quality or state of being spiritually pure or virtuous — see HOLINESS

saintly *adj* showing a devotion to God and to a life of virtue — see HOLY 1

saintship *n* the quality or state of being spiritually pure or virtuous — see HOLINESS

salable *or* **saleable** *adj* **1** fit or likely to be sold especially on a large scale — see COMMERCIAL
2 fit to be offered for sale — see MARKETABLE 1

salary *n* the money paid regularly to a person for labor or services — see WAGE

sale *n* the transfer of ownership of something from one person to another for a price ⟨my neighbor tried to make a *sale*, but no one was interested in buying his old car⟩
synonyms deal, trade, transaction
related words auction; haggle, negotiation; bargain, buy; purchase; clearance; fair; garage sale, rummage sale, yard sale

salesclerk *n* a person employed to sell goods or services especially in a store — see SALESPERSON

salesman *n* a person employed to sell goods or services especially in a store — see SALESPERSON

salesperson *n* a person employed to sell goods or services especially in a store ⟨we asked a *salesperson* to see if they had any shoes in the stockroom in our size⟩
synonyms clerk, salesclerk, salesman
related words salespeople; saleswoman

saline *adj* of, relating to, or containing salt — see SALTY 1

salinity *n* the quality or state of being salty — see SALTINESS

saliva *n* the fluid that is secreted into the mouth by certain glands ⟨our mouths filled with *saliva* when we smelled the delicious dinner⟩
synonyms slobber, spit, spittle
related words foam, froth; expectoration, sputum

salivate *vb* to let saliva or some other substance flow from the mouth — see DROOL

sallow *adj* lacking the warm skin color indicative of or associated with good health — see SICKLY 2

sally *n* **1** a short trip for pleasure — see EXCURSION 1
2 something said or done to cause laughter — see JOKE 1

sally (forth) *vb* to leave a place often for another — see GO 2

salon *n* **1** a building or part of a building in which objects of interest are displayed — see MUSEUM
2 a building, room, or suite of rooms occupied by a service business — see PLACE 2

saloon *n* a place of business where alcoholic beverages are sold to be consumed on the premises — see BARROOM

salt *adj* of, relating to, or containing salt — see SALTY 1

salt *n* one who operates or navigates a seagoing vessel — see SAILOR

salt away *vb* to put (something of future use or value) in a safe or secret place — see HOARD

saltiness *n* the quality or state of being salty ⟨the *saltiness* of the pretzels went well with the soda pop we were drinking⟩
synonyms brininess, salinity, saltness
near antonyms purity; sweetness

saltness *n* the quality or state of being salty — see SALTINESS

salty *adj* **1** of, relating to, or containing salt ⟨*salty* sea water is safe to swim in, but you really shouldn't swallow it⟩
synonyms briny, saline, salt
related words brackish
near antonyms sweet; clear, pure
2 hinting at or intended to call to mind matters regarded as indecent — see SUGGESTIVE 1

salubrious *adj* good for the health — see HEALTHFUL

salutary *adj* **1** conferring benefits; promoting or contributing to personal or social well-being — see BENEFICIAL
2 good for the health — see HEALTHFUL

salutation *n* **1** a formal expression of praise — see ENCOMIUM
2 an expression of goodwill upon meeting — see HELLO

salute *n* an expression of goodwill upon meeting — see HELLO

salute *vb* to declare enthusiastic approval of — see ACCLAIM

salvation *n* the saving from danger or evil ⟨we spent the night in the jungle praying for *salvation* from the dangerous animals⟩
synonyms deliverance
related words ransom, recovery, redemption, rescue; extrication; defense, protection, safeguarding; conservation, preservation

salvo *n* a rapid or overwhelming outpouring of many things at once — see BARRAGE

same *adj* **1** resembling another in every respect ⟨I bought the *same* shirt at the mall for five dollars less⟩
synonyms coequal, duplicate, equal, even, identical, indistinguishable
related words akin, alike, analogous, comparable, correspondent, corresponding, equivalent, like, matching, parallel, similar, such, suchlike, tantamount
near antonyms disparate, diverse, varied, various; distinct, distinctive
antonyms different, dissimilar, distinguishable, other, unalike, unlike
2 being one and not another ⟨that's the *same* guy I saw down at the beach yesterday⟩
synonyms identical, selfsame, very
near antonyms disparate, dissimilar, distinct, distinctive, distinguishable, diverse, unalike, unlike, varied, various
antonyms another, different, other

sameness *n* **1** a tedious lack of variety — see MONOTONY
2 the state of being exactly alike — see IDENTITY 1
3 the state or fact of being exactly the same in number, amount, status, or quality — see EQUIVALENCE

sample *n* **1** a number of things selected from a group to stand for the whole ⟨based on a *sample* of the menu items, we decided that this was the best restaurant in town⟩
synonyms cross section
related words case, example, exemplar, illustration, instance, representative, specimen; selection
2 one of a group or collection that shows what the whole is like — see EXAMPLE

sample *vb* to put (something) to a test — see TRY (OUT) 1

sanctification *n* **1** the act of making something

holy through religious ritual — see CONSECRATION

2 the act or fact of freeing from sin or moral guilt — see PURIFICATION

sanctified *adj* set apart or worthy of veneration by association with God — see HOLY 2

sanctify *vb* **1** to free from moral guilt or blemish especially ceremonially — see PURIFY 1

2 to make holy through prayers or ritual — see BLESS 1

sanctimoniousness *n* the pretending of having virtues, principles, or beliefs that one in fact does not have — see HYPOCRISY

sanction *n* the approval by someone in authority for the doing of something — see PERMISSION

sanction *vb* to give official acceptance of something as satisfactory — see APPROVE

sanctioned *adj* ordered or allowed by those in authority — see OFFICIAL

sanctity *n* the quality or state of being spiritually pure or virtuous — see HOLINESS

sanctuary *n* **1** a place that is considered sacred (as within a religion) — see SHRINE

2 something (as a building) that offers cover from the weather or protection from danger — see SHELTER

sanctum *n* **1** a place that is considered sacred (as within a religion) — see SHRINE

2 something (as a building) that offers cover from the weather or protection from danger — see SHELTER

sand *vb* to make smooth by friction — see GRIND 1

sandwich *vb* to fit (something) into a tight space — see CROWD 1

sandy *adj* of a pale yellow or yellowish brown color — see BLOND

sane *adj* having full use of one's mind and control over one's actions ⟨the court ruled that the woman was indeed *sane* when she made out her will⟩

synonyms balanced, clearheaded, lucid, normal, right, stable

related words clear, logical, rational, reasonable; judicious, levelheaded, sensible, wise; healthy, sound

near antonyms balmy, bananas, batty, crackbrained, cracked, cuckoo, daffy, daft, dotty, loco [*slang*], loony (*also* looney), moonstruck, nuts, nutty, off, screwy, wacky; aberrant, disordered; delusional, neurotic, paranoid, psychotic, schizophrenic; eccentric, odd, queer, strange; foolish, senseless, witless; irrational, unreasonable; berserk, delirious; depressed, despondent; distraught, frantic, frenzied, hysterical

antonyms crazed, crazy, demented, deranged, insane, lunatic, mad, maniacal (*also* maniac), mental, unbalanced, unsound

saneness *n* the normal or healthy condition of the mental abilities — see MIND 2

sanguinary *adj* eager for or marked by the shedding of blood, extreme violence, or killing — see BLOODTHIRSTY

sanguine *adj* **1** eager for or marked by the shedding of blood, extreme violence, or killing — see BLOODTHIRSTY

2 having a healthy reddish skin tone — see RUDDY

3 having or showing a mind free from doubt — see CERTAIN 2

sanguinity *n* an inclination to believe in the most favorable outcome — see OPTIMISM

sanitary *adj* free from filth, infection, or dangers to health ⟨the nurse made sure that everything in the room was *sanitary* so that the baby wouldn't get sick⟩

synonyms aseptic, germfree, hygienic, sterile

related words antibacterial, antibiotic, antiseptic, germicidal; clean, immaculate, spick-and-span (*or* spic-and-span), spotless, stainless, unsoiled, unsullied; beneficial, healthful, healthy, restorative, salubrious, salutary, wholesome

near antonyms pathogenic; bedraggled, besmirched, dingy, dirty, draggled, dusty, filthy, foul, grimy, grubby, grungy, mucky, muddy, nasty, soiled, sordid, stained, sullied, unclean, uncleanly; insalubrious, noxious, unhealthful, unhealthy, unwholesome

antonyms insanitary, unhygienic, unsanitary

sanitary landfill *n* a place where discarded materials (as trash) are dumped — see DUMP 1

sanity *n* the normal or healthy condition of the mental abilities — see MIND 2

sans *prep* not having — see WITHOUT 1

sap *n* **1** active strength of body or mind — see VIGOR 1

2 one who is easily deceived or cheated — see DUPE

sap *vb* to diminish the physical strength of — see WEAKEN 1

sapience *n* the ability to understand inner qualities or relationships — see WISDOM 1

sapient *adj* having or showing deep understanding and intelligent application of knowledge — see WISE 1

sapped *adj* lacking bodily strength — see WEAK 1

sappiness *n* the state or quality of having an excess of tender feelings (as of love, nostalgia, or compassion) — see SENTIMENTALITY

sappy *adj* **1** appealing to the emotions in an obvious and tiresome way — see CORNY

2 showing or marked by a lack of good sense or judgment — see FOOLISH 1

sarcasm *n* an act or expression showing scorn and usually intended to hurt another's feelings — see INSULT

sarcastic *adj* marked by the use of wit that is intended to cause hurt feelings ⟨her *sarcastic* comments that my singing reminded her of the time her dog was sick⟩

synonyms acrid, biting, caustic, cutting, mordant, pungent, sardonic, satiric (*or* satirical), scalding, scathing, sharp, smart-alecky (*or* smart-aleck), tart

related words acid, acidic, cross, sour; incisive, trenchant; cynical, dry, ironic, wry; facetious, flippant, tongue-in-cheek; acrimonious, bitter, resentful; harsh, rough, severe, stringent; concise, crisp, curt, pithy, succinct, terse; backhanded, insincere

near antonyms amusing, droll, merry, playful, sportive, waggish; gentle, mild; bland; good-humored, good-natured; diplomatic, polite, smooth, suave, urbane; affable, cordial, genial, gracious

sardonic *adj* marked by the use of wit that is intended to cause hurt feelings — see SARCASTIC

sash *n* a strip of flexible material (as leather) worn around the waist — see [2]BELT

sass *n* disrespectful or argumentative talk given in response to a command or request — see BACK TALK

sassy *adj* displaying or marked by rude boldness — see NERVY 1
Satan *n* the supreme personification of evil often represented as the ruler of Hell — see DEVIL 1
satanic *adj* of, relating to, or worthy of an evil spirit — see FIENDISH
sate *vb* **1** to fill with food to capacity — see GORGE 1
2 to put a complete end to (a physical need or desire) — see SATISFY 1
sated *adj* having one's appetite completely satisfied — see FULL 3
satiate *adj* having one's appetite completely satisfied — see FULL 3
satiate *vb* to put a complete end to (a physical need or desire) — see SATISFY 1
satiated *adj* having one's appetite completely satisfied — see FULL 3
satin *adj* **1** having a shiny surface or finish — see GLOSSY
2 smooth or delicate in appearance or feel — see SOFT 2
satiny *adj* **1** having a shiny surface or finish — see GLOSSY
2 smooth or delicate in appearance or feel — see SOFT 2
satire *n* a creative work that uses sharp humor to point up the foolishness of a person, institution, or human nature in general ⟨a *satire* about the music industry in which a handsome but untalented youth is turned into a rock star⟩
synonyms lampoon
related words burlesque, caricature, parody, spoof, takeoff; comedy, farce, sketch, slapstick, squib; derision, ridicule; mockery, travesty
satiric *or* **satirical** *adj* marked by the use of wit that is intended to cause hurt feelings — see SARCASTIC
satisfaction *n* **1** the feeling experienced when one's wishes are met — see PLEASURE 1
2 payment to another for a loss or injury — see COMPENSATION 1
satisfactorily *adv* **1** in a satisfactory way — see WELL 1
2 in or to a degree or quantity that meets one's requirements or satisfaction — see ENOUGH 1
satisfactoriness *n* the quality or state of meeting one's needs adequately — see SUFFICIENCY
satisfactory *adj* **1** being to one's liking ⟨we found the meal most *satisfactory*⟩
synonyms agreeable, all right, alright, copacetic (*also* copasetic *or* copesetic), fine, good, OK (*or* okay), palatable
related words delectable, delicious, delightful, dreamy, felicitous, gratifying, nice, pleasant, pleasing, scrumptious, welcome; acceptable, adequate, decent, passable, tolerable
antonyms disagreeable, unsatisfactory
2 of a level of quality that meets one's needs or standards — see ADEQUATE
satisfied *adj* **1** experiencing pleasure, satisfaction, or delight — see GLAD 1
2 feeling that one's needs or desires have been met — see CONTENT
satisfy *vb* **1** to put a complete end to (a physical need or desire) ⟨they *satisfied* their hunger after the game with a big pasta dinner⟩
synonyms assuage, quench, sate, satiate
related words cater (to), gratify, indulge; alleviate, lighten, relieve
near antonyms arouse, excite, pique, stimulate; tantalize, tease
2 to cause (someone) to agree with a belief or course of action by using arguments or earnest requests — see PERSUADE
3 to do what is required by the terms of — see FULFILL 1
4 to give satisfaction to — see PLEASE
satisfying *adj* **1** giving pleasure or contentment to the mind or senses — see PLEASANT
2 having the power to persuade — see COGENT
3 making one feel good inside — see HEARTWARMING
satisfyingly *adv* in a pleasing way — see WELL 5
saturate *vb* to wet thoroughly with liquid — see SOAK 1
saturated *adj* containing, covered with, or thoroughly penetrated by water — see WET
saturnine *adj* causing or marked by an atmosphere lacking in cheer — see GLOOMY 1
sauce *n* **1** a savory fluid food used as a topping or accompaniment to a main dish ⟨the chef poured *sauce* over the meat just before he served it⟩
synonyms dressing, gravy
related words condiment, relish, seasoning; fixing(s), garnish, topping; dip, marinade
2 disrespectful or argumentative talk given in response to a command or request — see BACK TALK
3 shameless boldness — see EFFRONTERY
sauciness *n* shameless boldness — see EFFRONTERY
saucy *adj* displaying or marked by rude boldness — see NERVY 1
saunter *n* a relaxed journey on foot for exercise or pleasure — see WALK
sausage *n* a rod-shaped portion of seasoned ground meat in a casing ⟨a couple of *sausages* and eggs make a good breakfast⟩
synonyms link
related words bologna, frankfurter, hot dog, knockwurst, liverwurst, pepperoni, salami, wiener
savage *adj* **1** not civilized ⟨Tarzan is usually portrayed as a noble but *savage* warrior of the jungle⟩
synonyms barbarous, heathen, heathenish, Neanderthal, rude, uncivil, uncivilized, uncultivated, wild
related words coarse, crude, primitive, rough; uncouth, uncultured
near antonyms cultured, enlightened, humane, sophisticated; genteel, polite, refined, urbane, well-bred
antonyms civilized
2 having or showing the desire to inflict severe pain and suffering on others — see CRUEL 1
3 living outdoors without taming or domestication by humans — see WILD 1
4 violently unfriendly or aggressive in disposition — see FIERCE 1
savage *n* **1** a mean, evil, or unprincipled person — see VILLAIN 1
2 an uncivilized person — see HEATHEN 2
savageness *n* the willful infliction of pain and suffering on others — see CRUELTY
savagery *n* the willful infliction of pain and suffering on others — see CRUELTY
savanna *also* **savannah** *n* a broad area of level or rolling treeless country — see PLAIN

savant *n* a person of deep wisdom or learning — see SAGE

save *prep* not including — see EXCEPT

save *vb* **1** to free from the penalties or consequences of sin ⟨the Christian belief that Jesus lived and died to *save* humanity⟩
synonyms deliver, redeem
related words reclaim, reform; forgive, pardon, remit; bless, hallow; consecrate, purify, sanctify
2 to remove from danger or harm ⟨the fire fighter *saved* my brother from the burning building⟩
synonyms bail out, deliver, rescue
related words salvage; emancipate, free, liberate, manumit, release; disentangle, extricate; recover
antonyms compromise, endanger, imperil, jeopardize
3 to avoid unnecessary waste or expense — see ECONOMIZE
4 to keep in good condition — see MAINTAIN 1
5 to keep or intend for a special purpose — see DEVOTE 1

saver *n* one that saves from danger or destruction — see SAVIOR

saving *conj* if it were not for the fact that — see EXCEPT

saving *prep* not including — see EXCEPT

savior *or* **saviour** *n* one that saves from danger or destruction ⟨the policeman proved to be our *savior*, arriving on the scene just as we were about to be mugged⟩
synonyms deliverer, redeemer, rescuer, saver
related words custodian, defender, guard, guardian, keeper, lookout, protector, sentinel, sentry, warden, warder, watch, watchman

savor *n* **1** the property of a substance that can be identified by the sense of taste — see TASTE 1
2 the quality of being delicious — see DELICIOUSNESS

savor *vb* to make more pleasant to the taste by adding something intensely flavored — see SEASON 1

savoriness *n* the quality of being delicious — see DELICIOUSNESS

savorless *adj* lacking in taste or flavor — see INSIPID 1

savory *adj* **1** having a pleasant smell — see FRAGRANT
2 very pleasing to the sense of taste — see DELICIOUS 1

savvy *n* knowledge gained by actually doing or living through something — see EXPERIENCE 1

saw *n* an often stated observation regarding something from common experience — see SAYING

saw–toothed *adj* notched or toothed along the edge — see SERRATED

say *vb* **1** to express (a thought or emotion) in words ⟨why don't you just *say* what's on your mind?⟩
synonyms articulate, speak, state, talk, tell, utter, verbalize, vocalize
related words air, discuss, express, give, look, sound, state, vent, ventilate, voice; advertise, announce, blaze, broadcast, declare, enunciate, proclaim, publicize, publish; affirm, allege, assert, aver, avouch, avow; breathe, drawl, gasp, mouth, murmur, shout, splutter, spout, whisper; couch, formulate, phrase, put, word; comment, remark
phrases put into words
near antonyms stifle, suppress
2 to convey in appropriate or telling terms — see PHRASE
3 to give from memory — see REPEAT 2

say *n* the right to express a wish, choice, or opinion — see VOICE 1

saying *n* an often stated observation regarding something from common experience ⟨there's an old *saying* that you should let sleeping dogs lie⟩
synonyms adage, aphorism, byword, epigram, maxim, proverb, saw
related words cliché, commonplace, platitude; expression, felicity; axiom, motto, precept, truism, truth; observation, reflection, remark

scabby *adj* arousing or deserving of one's loathing and disgust — see CONTEMPTIBLE 1

scads *n pl* a considerable amount — see LOT 2

scalawag *or* **scallywag** *n* a mean, evil, or unprincipled person — see VILLAIN

scalding *adj* **1** having a notably high temperature — see HOT 1
2 marked by the use of wit that is intended to cause hurt feelings — see SARCASTIC

[1]**scale** *n* a device for measuring weight ⟨I hate getting on the bathroom *scale*⟩
synonyms balance
related words gravimeter

[2]**scale** *n* a small thin piece of material that resembles an animal scale ⟨*scales* of mica were embedded in the granite⟩
synonyms lamella, lamina, plate
related words chip, flake, sliver, splinter

[3]**scale** *n* **1** a scheme of rank or order ⟨a student who scored very highly on a standard intelligence *scale*⟩
synonyms graduation, ladder, ordering, ranking
related words arrangement, array, disposal, disposition, distribution, order, sequence, series
2 the distance or extent between possible extremes — see RANGE 3

scale *vb* to find out the size, extent, or amount of — see MEASURE

scaly *adj* composed of or covered with scales ⟨the snake's *scaly* skin was dry to the touch⟩
synonyms squamous
related words scalelike
near antonyms smooth
antonyms scaleless

scamp *n* **1** an appealingly mischievous person ⟨those little *scamps* are always getting into trouble, but no one has the heart to punish them⟩
synonyms devil, hellion, imp, mischief, monkey, rapscallion, rascal, rogue, urchin
related words cutup, madcap, skylarker; ragamuffin; brat, disrupter, nuisance; juvenile delinquent; gamin, gamine
near antonyms beast, boor, cad, churl, clown, creep, cretin, cur, heel, joker, louse, lout, skunk, snake, stinker; knave, scalawag (*or* scallywag), scoundrel, villain
2 a mean, evil, or unprincipled person — see VILLAIN

scamper *vb* to go at a pace faster than a walk — see RUN 1

scan *n* a close look at or over someone or something in order to judge condition — see INSPECTION

scan *vb* to look over closely (as for judging quality or condition) — see INSPECT

scandal *n* a cause of shame — see DISGRACE 2

scandalous *adj* **1** causing intense displeasure, disgust, or resentment — see OFFENSIVE 1

2 causing or intended to cause unjust injury to a person's good name — see LIBELOUS

scant *adj* less plentiful than what is normal, necessary, or desirable — see MEAGER

scant *vb* to use or give out in stingy amounts — see SPARE

scantiness *n* a falling short of an essential or desirable amount or number — see DEFICIENCY

scanty *adj* less plentiful than what is normal, necessary, or desirable — see MEAGER

scapegoat *n* a person or thing taking the blame for others ⟨companies often use the economy as a *scapegoat* to avoid taking responsibility for dropping sales⟩
synonyms fall guy, goat, whipping boy
related words victim; butt, dupe, fool, laughingstock, mockery, monkey; excuse

scar *n* something that spoils the appearance or completeness of a thing — see BLEMISH

scarce *adj* **1** less plentiful than what is normal, necessary, or desirable — see MEAGER
2 not coming up to a usual standard or meeting a particular need — see SHORT 3

scarcely *adv* **1** by a very small margin — see JUST 2
2 certainly not — see HARDLY 2

scarceness *n* a falling short of an essential or desirable amount or number — see DEFICIENCY

scarcity *n* a falling short of an essential or desirable amount or number — see DEFICIENCY

scare *vb* to strike with fear — see FRIGHTEN

scared *adj* filled with fear or dread — see AFRAID 1

scare up *vb* to come upon after searching, study, or effort — see FIND 1

scarp *n* a steep wall of rock, earth, or ice — see CLIFF

scary *adj* **1** causing fear — see FEARFUL 1
2 easily frightened — see SHY 1

scathe *vb* to criticize harshly and usually publicly — see ATTACK 2

scathing *adj* marked by the use of wit that is intended to cause hurt feelings — see SARCASTIC

scatter *vb* **1** to cause (members of a group) to move widely apart ⟨the noise of the backfiring car *scattered* the pigeons⟩
synonyms clear out, disband, dispel, disperse, dissipate
related words break up, isolate, part, segregate, separate, split up; diffuse, disseminate, diverge, spread
near antonyms agglutinate, conglomerate; unify, unite
antonyms assemble, cluster, collect, concentrate, congregate, gather
2 to cover by or as if by scattering something over or on ⟨the hillside was *scattered* with wildflowers⟩
synonyms bestrew, dot, pepper, sow, spray, sprinkle, strew
related words blanket, dust; stud; dapple, fleck, speckle, spot, stipple

scatterbrained *adj* lacking in seriousness or maturity — see GIDDY 1

scattered *adj* lacking a definite plan, purpose, or pattern — see RANDOM

scattering *n* **1** an act or process in which something scatters or is scattered ⟨the *scattering* of the protesters suddenly turned violent and chaotic⟩
synonyms disbandment, dispersal, dispersion, dissipation
near antonyms assembly, collection, concentration, gathering
2 a small number — see FEW

scenario *n* the written form of a story prepared for film production — see SCREENPLAY

scene *n* **1** the place and time in which the action for a portion of a dramatic work (as a movie) is set ⟨the first *scene* was the kitchen of a fancy restaurant during dinner⟩
synonyms background, setting
related words backdrop, scenery, set; tableau
2 an outburst or display of excited anger — see TANTRUM
3 position with regard to conditions and circumstances — see SITUATION 1
4 the array of painted backgrounds and furnishings used for a scene in a stage production — see SCENERY

scenery *n* the array of painted backgrounds and furnishings used for a scene in a stage production ⟨the *scenery* in the high school production was all handmade⟩
synonyms scene, set
related words backdrop, drop; background, setting; prop, property

scent *n* **1** a sweet or pleasant smell — see FRAGRANCE
2 the quality of a thing that makes it perceptible to the sense organs in the nose — see SMELL 1

scent *vb* **1** to fill or infuse with a pleasant odor or odor-releasing substance ⟨fancy bars of soap *scented* with lavender⟩
synonyms perfume
near antonyms deodorize
2 to become aware of by means of the sense organs in the nose — see SMELL
3 to have a vague awareness of — see FEEL 1

scented *adj* having a pleasant smell — see FRAGRANT

schedule *n* **1** a listing of things to be presented or considered (as at a concert or play) — see PROGRAM 1
2 a record of a series of items (as names or titles) usually arranged according to some system — see [1]LIST

schedule *vb* to put (someone or something) on a list — see [1]LIST 2

scheduled *adj* being in accordance with the prescribed, normal, or logical course of events — see DUE 2

schematize *vb* to work out the details of (something) in advance — see PLAN 1

scheme *n* **1** a clever often underhanded means to achieve an end — see TRICK 1
2 a secret plan for accomplishing evil or unlawful ends — see PLOT 1
3 a method worked out in advance for achieving some objective — see PLAN 1

scheme *vb* to engage in a secret plan to accomplish evil or unlawful ends — see PLOT

scheme (out) *vb* to work out the details of (something) in advance — see PLAN 1

schism *n* **1** a lack of agreement or harmony — see DISCORD
2 the act or process of a whole separating into two or more parts or pieces — see SEPARATION 1

schmaltz *also* **schmalz** *n* something (as a work of literature or music) that is too sentimental — see CORN

schmaltzy *adj* appealing to the emotions in an obvious and tiresome way — see CORNY

scholar *n* **1** a person of deep wisdom or learning — see SAGE
2 a person with a high level of knowledge or skill in a field — see EXPERT
3 one who attends a school — see STUDENT

scholarly *adj* **1** having or displaying advanced knowledge or education — see EDUCATED
2 of or relating to schooling or learning especially at an advanced level — see ACADEMIC

scholarship *n* the understanding and information gained from being educated — see EDUCATION 2

scholastic *adj* of or relating to schooling or learning especially at an advanced level — see ACADEMIC

school *n* a place or establishment for teaching and learning ⟨one of the first *schools* in the country to admit girls as students⟩
synonyms academy, seminary
related words elementary school, grammar school, high school, junior high school, middle school, preparatory school, public school, secondary school, trade school; Sunday school, yeshiva (*also* yeshivah)

school *vb* to cause to acquire knowledge or skill in some field — see TEACH

schooling *n* the act or process of imparting knowledge or skills to another — see EDUCATION 1

schoolteacher *n* a person whose occupation is to give formal instruction in a school — see TEACHER

science *n* **1** a body of facts learned by study or experience — see KNOWLEDGE 1
2 the understanding and information gained from being educated — see EDUCATION 2

scintillate *vb* **1** to give off sparks — see SPARK 1
2 to shoot forth bursts of light — see FLASH 1

scoffer *n* a person who causes repeated emotional pain, distress, or annoyance to another — see TORMENTOR

scold *n* a person given to harsh judgments and to finding faults — see CRITIC 1

scold *vb* to criticize (someone) severely or angrily especially for personal failings ⟨he *scolded* the kids for not cleaning up the mess they had made in the kitchen⟩
synonyms berate, castigate, chew out, dress down, flay, jaw, keelhaul, lambaste (*or* lambast), lecture, rail (at *or* against), rate, rebuke, reprimand, reproach, score, upbraid
related words admonish, chide, remonstrate (with), reprove; abuse, assail, attack, bad-mouth, blame, blast, censure, condemn, criticize, crucify, denounce, dis [*slang*], excoriate, fault, knock, lash, pan, reprehend, slam; belittle, disparage, mock, put down; ridicule, scoff, scorn
phrases read the riot act (to), take to task
near antonyms approve, endorse (*also* indorse), sanction; extol (*also* extoll), laud, praise

scoop *n* **1** a utensil with a bowl and a handle that is used especially in cooking and serving food — see SPOON
2 information not generally available to the public — see DOPE 1

scoop *vb* to lift out with something that holds liquid — see DIP 2

scoot *vb* to proceed or move quickly — see HURRY 2

scope *n* an area over which activity, capacity, or influence extends — see RANGE 2

scorch *vb* to burn on the surface ⟨the picnickers kept *scorching* their marshmallows, deliberately sticking their skewers into the licking flames of the campfire⟩
synonyms char, sear, singe
related words fire, ignite, inflame, kindle, light; bake, cremate, incinerate; scald, scathe

scorching *adj* having a notably high temperature — see HOT 1

score *n* a lingering ill will towards a person for a real or imagined wrong — see GRUDGE 1

score *vb* **1** to mark with or as if with a line or groove ⟨the glassblower *scored* the glass rod first so that it would break cleanly⟩
synonyms groove, scribe, seam
related words abrade, file, graze, rasp, scarify, scratch
2 to gain (as points or runs in a game) as credit towards one's total number of points ⟨he *scored* the winning goal in the final minute of play⟩
synonyms rack up, tally
related words triumph, win; best, defeat
near antonyms lose
3 to obtain (as a goal) through effort — see ACHIEVE 1
4 to criticize (someone) severely or angrily especially for personal failings — see SCOLD

scorn *n* open dislike for someone or something considered unworthy of one's concern or respect — see CONTEMPT

scorn *vb* **1** to show contempt for ⟨*scorned* the religious traditions of their ancestors⟩
synonyms disdain, high-hat, slight, sniff (at), snub
related words scout; abhor, despise, detest, hate, loathe; disapprove (of), discountenance, disfavor, frown (on *or* upon)
phrases look down on, sneeze at
near antonyms cherish, prize, treasure, value; admire, esteem; revere, venerate, worship; accept, appreciate, approve (of), care (for), countenance, favor, OK (*or* okay), subscribe (to)
antonyms honor, respect
2 to ignore in a disrespectful manner ⟨she *scorned* the suggestions of her classmates for the parade float⟩
synonyms despise, disregard, flout
related words dismiss, forget, ignore, neglect, overlook, overpass, pass over, slight, slur (over)
near antonyms accept, approve; use

scorner *n* a person who causes repeated emotional pain, distress, or annoyance to another — see TORMENTOR

scornful *adj* **1** feeling or showing open dislike for someone or something regarded as undeserving of respect or concern — see CONTEMPTUOUS 1
2 intended to make a person or thing seem of little importance or value — see DEROGATORY

Scot *n* a person born or living in Scotland ⟨my grandfather was a *Scot*, but my grandmother was Welsh⟩
synonyms Scotchman, Scotsman, Scottie

Scotch *adj* of, relating to, or characteristic of the people of Scotland — see SCOTTISH

Scotchman *n* a person born or living in Scotland — see SCOT

Scots *adj* of, relating to, or characteristic of the people of Scotland — see SCOTTISH

Scotsman *n* a person born or living in Scotland — see SCOT
Scottie *n* a person born or living in Scotland — see SCOT
Scottish *adj* of, relating to, or characteristic of the people of Scotland ⟨golf was originally a *Scottish* game⟩
synonyms Scotch, Scots
scoundrel *n* a mean, evil, or unprincipled person — see VILLAIN
scour *vb* to look through (as a place) carefully or thoroughly in an effort to find or discover something — see SEARCH 1
scourge *n* **1** a long thin or flexible tool for striking — see WHIP
2 one who inflicts punishment in return for an injury or offense — see NEMESIS 1
scourge *vb* **1** to bring destruction to (something) through violent action — see RAVAGE
2 to strike repeatedly with something long and thin or flexible — see WHIP 1
scout *n* a member of the human race — see HUMAN
scout *vb* to make (someone or something) the object of unkind laughter — see RIDICULE
scout (up) *vb* to come upon after searching, study, or effort — see FIND 1
scowl *n* a twisting of the facial features in disgust or disapproval — see GRIMACE
scowl *vb* to look with anger or disapproval — see FROWN
scrabble *n* a forceful effort to reach a goal or objective — see STRUGGLE 1
scraggly *adj* having an uneven edge or outline — see RAGGED 1
scraggy *adj* **1** having an uneven edge or outline — see RAGGED 1
2 not having a level or smooth surface — see UNEVEN 1
scramble *n* an unorganized collection or mixture of various things — see MISCELLANY 1
scramble *vb* **1** to move (as up or over something) often with the help of the hands in holding or pulling — see CLIMB 1
2 to undo the proper order or arrangement of — see DISORDER
[1]**scrap** *n* **1** an unused or unwanted piece or item typically of small size or value ⟨only a *scrap* of silk was left on the sewing table after they had finished the project⟩
synonyms end, fag end, leftover, oddment, remainder, remnant, stub
related words leavings, odds and ends, remains, residual, residue, scraping(s), stump; balance, rest; chip, flake, fragment, piece, sliver, splinter; ribbon(s), shred, tatter
near antonyms whole
2 a broken or irregular part of something that often remains incomplete — see FRAGMENT
3 a physical dispute between opposing individuals or groups — see FIGHT 1
4 a very small piece — see BIT 1
5 discarded or useless material — see GARBAGE
[2]**scrap** *n* an often noisy or angry expression of differing opinions — see ARGUMENT 1
[1]**scrap** *vb* to express different opinions about something often angrily — see ARGUE 2
[2]**scrap** *vb* to get rid of as useless or unwanted — see DISCARD

scrape *n* **1** a brief clash between enemies or rivals — see ENCOUNTER
2 a harsh grating sound — see RASP
scrape *vb* **1** to pass roughly and noisily over or against a surface ⟨the rusty old gate *scraped* whenever anyone managed to open it⟩
synonyms grate, grind, rasp, scratch
related words rub; groan, whine
near antonyms glide, skate, slide
2 to damage by rubbing against a sharp or rough surface ⟨she *scraped* her knee when she fell down⟩
synonyms abrade, graze, scratch, scuff
related words bark, skin; chafe, fret, gall; claw, cut, lacerate; bruise, contuse
near antonyms polish, smooth, soften, wax
3 to get with great difficulty — see EKE OUT
4 to press or strike against or together so as to make a scraping sound — see GRIND 2
scrape (together) *vb* to bring together in one body or place — see GATHER 1
scrappiness *n* an inclination to fight or quarrel — see BELLIGERENCE
scrapping *n* the getting rid of whatever is unwanted or useless — see DISPOSAL 1
scrappy *adj* **1** feeling or displaying eagerness to fight — see BELLIGERENT
2 given to arguing — see ARGUMENTATIVE 1
scratch *n* a harsh grating sound — see RASP
scratch *vb* **1** to damage by rubbing against a sharp or rough surface — see SCRAPE 2
2 to pass roughly and noisily over or against a surface — see SCRAPE 1
3 to write or draw hastily or carelessly — see SCRIBBLE
scratch (out) *vb* **1** to compose and set down on paper the words of — see WRITE 1
2 to show (something written) to be no longer valid by drawing a cross over or a line through it — see X (OUT)
scratchy *adj* **1** likely to cause a scratch ⟨*scratchy* shrubbery that's intended to keep kids and pets off the old man's property⟩
synonyms brambly, prickly, thistly, thorny
related words burred; coarse, jagged, rough; irritating, itchy, stinging
near antonyms polished, smooth, soft, soothing; gentle
2 harsh and dry in sound — see HOARSE
scrawl *vb* to write or draw hastily or carelessly — see SCRIBBLE
scream *n* someone or something that is very funny ⟨that new comedy is a *scream*⟩
synonyms laugh, riot
related words howler; crack, gag, jest, joke, pleasantry, quip, sally, waggery, wisecrack, witticism; caution, sight
near antonyms bummer, downer
scream *vb* to cry out loudly and emotionally ⟨we *screamed* when the roller coaster began its thirty foot plunge⟩
synonyms howl, screech, shriek, shrill, squall, squeal, yelp, yell
related words bay, caterwaul, keen, squawk, wail, yawp (*or* yaup), yowl; bawl, call, cry, holler, shout, vociferate
near antonyms murmur, mutter, whisper
screaming *adj* **1** arousing a strong and usually superficial interest or emotional reaction — see SENSATIONAL 1

2 causing or intended to cause laughter — see FUNNY 1

screech *vb* to cry out loudly and emotionally — see SCREAM

screeching *adj* having a high musical pitch or range — see SHRILL

screen *n* **1** the art or business of making a movie — see MOVIE 2

2 means or method of defending — see DEFENSE 1

screen *vb* **1** to drive danger or attack away from — see DEFEND 1

2 to keep secret or shut off from view — see [1]HIDE 2

3 to pass through a filter — see STRAIN 2

4 to place a protective layer over — see COVER 3

screenplay *n* the written form of a story prepared for film production ⟨each actor was given a copy of the *screenplay* to study⟩

synonyms scenario, script

related words story, text

screw *vb* to twist (something) out of a natural or normal shape or condition — see CONTORT

screwball *adj* showing or marked by a lack of good sense or judgment — see FOOLISH 1

screwball *n* a person of odd or whimsical habits — see ECCENTRIC

screwing *n* the twisting of something out of its natural or normal shape or condition — see CONTORTION

screwlike *adj* turning around an axis like the thread of a screw — see SPIRAL

screwy *adj* **1** different from the ordinary in a way that causes curiosity or suspicion — see ODD 2

2 having or showing a very abnormal or sick state of mind — see INSANE 1

scribble *vb* to write or draw hastily or carelessly ⟨she *scribbled* a quick note on the pad by the door before leaving⟩

synonyms scratch, scrawl

related words doodle; jot (down); ink, inscribe, letter, pen, pencil, print, write

scribe *n* a person whose job is to keep records — see CLERK 1

scribe *vb* to mark with or as if with a line or groove — see SCORE 1

scrimmage *n* a physical dispute between opposing individuals or groups — see FIGHT 1

scrimmage (with) *vb* to oppose (someone) in physical conflict — see FIGHT 1

scrimp *vb* to avoid unnecessary waste or expense — see ECONOMIZE

scrimping *adj* careful in the management of money or resources — see FRUGAL

scrimping *n* careful management of material resources — see ECONOMY

script *n* **1** the form or style of a particular person's writing — see HANDWRITING 1

2 the written form of a story prepared for film production — see SCREENPLAY

3 writing done by hand — see HANDWRITING 2

Scripture *n* a book made up of the writings accepted by Christians as coming from God — see BIBLE

scrooge *n* a mean grasping person who is usually stingy with money — see MISER

scrounge *vb* to get with great difficulty — see EKE OUT

scrub *n* a living thing much smaller than others of its kind — see DWARF 1

scruffy *adj* showing signs of advanced wear and tear and neglect — see SHABBY 1

scrumptious *adj* very pleasing to the sense of taste — see DELICIOUS 1

scrunch *vb* **1** to create (as by crushing) an irregular mass of creases in — see CRUMPLE 1

2 to lie low with the limbs close to the body — see CROUCH

3 to press or strike against or together so as to make a scraping sound — see GRIND 2

scruple *n* **1** a very small amount — see PARTICLE 1

2 a very small piece — see BIT 1

3 an uneasy feeling about the rightness of what one is doing or going to do — see QUALM

scrupulous *adj* guided by or in accordance with one's sense of right and wrong — see CONSCIENTIOUS 1

scrupulousness *n* strict attentiveness to what one is doing — see CARE 1

scrutinize *vb* to look over closely (as for judging quality or condition) — see INSPECT

scrutiny *n* a close look at or over someone or something in order to judge condition — see INSPECTION

scuff *vb* **1** to damage by rubbing against a sharp or rough surface — see SCRAPE 2

2 to move heavily or clumsily — see LUMBER 1

scuffle *n* a physical dispute between opposing individuals or groups — see FIGHT 1

scuffle *vb* **1** to move heavily or clumsily — see LUMBER 1

2 to seize and attempt to unbalance one another for the purpose of achieving physical mastery — see WRESTLE

scull *vb* to move a boat by means of oars — see [1]ROW

sculler *n* a person who drives a boat forward by means of oars — see OARSMAN

sculpt *vb* to create a three-dimensional representation of (something) using solid material ⟨I *sculpted* a figure of a giraffe out of clay in art class today⟩

synonyms carve, sculpture

related words chisel, engrave, etch, grave, incise, inscribe; cast, form, model, mold, shape

sculpture *vb* to create a three-dimensional representation of (something) using solid material — see SCULPT

scum *n* people looked down upon as ignorant and of the lowest class — see RABBLE

scummy *adj* arousing or deserving of one's loathing and disgust — see CONTEMPTIBLE 1

scurry *vb* to proceed or move quickly — see HURRY 2

scurvy *adj* arousing or deserving of one's loathing and disgust — see CONTEMPTIBLE 1

scuttle *vb* to proceed or move quickly — see HURRY 2

sea *n* the whole body of salt water that covers nearly three-fourths of the earth — see OCEAN

sea devil *n* any of several extremely large rays — see DEVILFISH

sea dog *n* one who operates or navigates a seagoing vessel — see SAILOR

seafarer *n* one who operates or navigates a seagoing vessel — see SAILOR

seam *vb* to mark with or as if with a line or groove — see SCORE 1

seaman *n* one who operates or navigates a seagoing vessel — see SAILOR

sear *vb* **1** to burn on the surface — see SCORCH
2 to make dry — see DRY 1

search *n* an act or process of looking carefully or thoroughly for someone or something ⟨the *search* for the lost puppy took hours⟩
synonyms hunt, quest
related words chase, pursuit; reconnaissance, scout; canvas, survey; exploration, probe; forage

search *vb* **1** to look through (as a place) carefully or thoroughly in an effort to find or discover something ⟨we *searched* the closet for half an hour until we found the missing shoe⟩
synonyms comb, dig (through), dredge, hunt (through), rake, ransack, rifle, rummage, scour
related words audit, check (out), examine, inspect, investigate, review, scan, scrutinize, survey; ascertain, descry, detect, determine, discover, ferret (out), find, find out, get, hit (on *or* upon), learn, locate, run down, scare up, track (down); explore, probe, prospect, skirmish, snoop; browse, glance (over), look over; peruse, study
near antonyms hide; abandon, lose; ignore, neglect
2 to go into or range over for purposes of discovery — see EXPLORE 2

search (for *or* out) *vb* to go in search of — see SEEK 1

searing *adj* having a notably high temperature — see HOT 1

season *vb* **1** to make more pleasant to the taste by adding something intensely flavored ⟨the chef *seasoned* the vegetables as soon as they came out of the oven⟩
synonyms flavor, savor, spice
related words enhance, enrich, sauce; salt, pepper
2 to bring to a proper or desired state of fitness — see CONDITION 1
3 to make able to withstand physical hardship, strain, or exposure — see HARDEN 2
4 to make competent (as by training, skill, or ability) for a particular office or function — see QUALIFY 2

seasonable *adj* especially suitable for a certain time — see TIMELY 1

seasoning *n* **1** something (as a spice or herb) that adds an agreeable or interesting taste to food ⟨the stew was too bland before they added the *seasoning*⟩
synonyms flavor, flavoring, spice
related words sauce
2 something used to enhance the flavor of cooked or prepared food — see CONDIMENT

seat *n* **1** a place from which authority is exercised ⟨all applications had to be submitted at the county *seat* for proper processing⟩
synonyms command, headquarters
related words center, home; capital
2 the part of the body upon which someone sits — see BUTTOCKS
3 a thing or place that is of greatest importance to an activity or interest — see CENTER 1

seat *vb* to cause to sit down ⟨the usher *seated* them in the third row⟩
synonyms set down, sit
related words ensconce, settle; lay, lie, rest; place, put; recline, repose

seclude *vb* to set or keep apart from others — see ISOLATE

secluded *adj* hidden from view ⟨we stayed in a *secluded* resort, far away from the regular tourist crowds⟩
synonyms cloistered, covert, isolated, quiet, remote, retired, secret, sheltered
related words lonely, reclusive, solitary; private
near antonyms obvious, visible; exposed

secludedness *n* the state of being alone or kept apart from others — see ISOLATION

seclusion *n* the state of being alone or kept apart from others — see ISOLATION

second *n* a very small space of time — see INSTANT

secondary *adj* **1** taken or created from something original or basic ⟨history textbooks are *secondary* sources for historical information and do not represent original research⟩
synonyms derivative, secondhand
related words unoriginal; consequent, resultant
near antonyms fundamental, nonderivative; first, primary
antonyms basic, original
2 of little or less value or merit — see INFERIOR 2

second–class *adj* of little or less value or merit — see INFERIOR 2

secondhand *adj* taken or created from something original or basic — see SECONDARY 1

second–rate *adj* **1** of average to below average quality — see MEDIOCRE 1
2 of little or less value or merit — see INFERIOR 2
3 of low quality — see CHEAP 2

secrecy *n* the practice or habit of keeping secrets or keeping one's affairs secret ⟨in picking helpers for a surprise party, you'd very much want to choose people known for their *secrecy*⟩
synonyms closeness, secretiveness
related words discreetness, discretion, prudence; circumspection, wariness; reserve, reticence, silence, taciturnity; furtiveness, shiftiness, slyness, sneakiness, underhandedness; concealment, stealth, subterfuge
near antonyms candor, frankness, honesty, openness; imprudence, indiscretion

secret *adj* **1** undertaken or done so as to escape being observed or known by others ⟨a *secret* operation to rescue captive soldiers behind enemy lines⟩
synonyms clandestine, covert, furtive, hugger-mugger, private, privy, sneak, sneaking, sneaky, stealthy, surreptitious, undercover, underground, underhand, underhanded
related words classified, confidential, restricted, top secret, undisclosed; concealed, hidden, secreted, subterranean, unadvertised, unexposed
near antonyms acknowledged, avowed; aboveboard, straightforward, unconcealed, undisguised; unclassified, unrestricted; clear, evident, manifest, obvious, patent, plain
antonyms open, overt, public
2 working on missions in which one's objectives, activities, or true identity are not publicly revealed ⟨*secret* agents whose wartime exploits were known only by top government officials⟩
synonyms undercover
related words covert, private, secretive, subterranean
near antonyms overt
3 hidden from view — see SECLUDED
4 not known or meant to be known by the general populace — see PRIVATE 1

secret *n* **1** information shared only with another or

with a select few ⟨they're best friends and are constantly sharing *secrets*⟩
synonyms confidence
related words dope, lowdown
near antonyms open secret
2 something hard to understand or explain — see MYSTERY

secrete *vb* to put into a hiding place — see [1]HIDE 1

secretion *n* the placing of something out of sight — see CONCEALMENT 1

secretive *adj* given to keeping one's activities hidden from public observation or knowledge ⟨the intelligence agency remained *secretive* despite the media's demands for more openness in government⟩
synonyms close, closemouthed, dark, reticent, uncommunicative
related words quiet, reserved, silent, taciturn, tight-lipped; discreet, prudent; clandestine, covert, furtive, hugger-mugger, secret, sneak, sneaky, stealthy, surreptitious, undercover, underhand, underhanded
near antonyms candid, frank, honest; blunt, outspoken, tactless
antonyms communicative, open

secretiveness *n* the practice or habit of keeping secrets or keeping one's affairs secret — see SECRECY

sect *n* a group of people acting together within a larger group — see FACTION

sectarian *adj* not broad or open in views or opinions — see NARROW 2

section *n* **1** an area (as of a city) set apart for some purpose or having some special feature — see DISTRICT
2 one of the pieces from which something is designed to be assembled — see PART 1

secular *adj* not involving religion or religious matters — see PROFANE 1

secure *adj* **1** firmly positioned in place and difficult to dislodge — see TIGHT 2
2 having or showing great faith in oneself or one's abilities — see CONFIDENT 1
3 not exposed to the threat of loss or injury — see SAFE 1
4 providing safety — see SAFE 2

secure *vb* **1** to drive danger or attack away from — see DEFEND 1
2 to make sure, certain, or safe — see ENSURE
3 to put securely in place or in a desired position — see FASTEN 2
4 to receive as return for effort — see EARN 1

security *n* **1** means or method of defending — see DEFENSE 1
2 something given or held to assure that the giver will keep a promise — see PLEDGE 1
3 the state of not being exposed to danger — see SAFETY 1

sedate *adj* not joking or playful in mood or manner — see SERIOUS 1

sedative *adj* tending to calm the emotions and relieve stress — see SOOTHING 1

sediment *n* matter that settles to the bottom of a body of liquid — see DEPOSIT 1

sediment *vb* to cause to come to rest at the bottom (as of a liquid) — see SETTLE 1

seduce *vb* to lead away from a usual or proper course by offering some pleasure or advantage — see LURE

seducer *n* one that tries to get a person to give in to a desire — see TEMPTER

seduction *n* the act or pressure of giving in to a desire especially when ill-advised — see TEMPTATION 1

seductive *adj* having an often mysterious or magical power to attract — see FASCINATING 1

seductiveness *n* the power of irresistible attraction — see CHARM 2

seductress *n* a woman whom men find irresistibly attractive — see SIREN

sedulous *adj* involved in often constant activity — see BUSY 1

sedulously *adv* with great effort or determination — see HARD 1

see *vb* **1** to make note of (something) through the use of one's eyes ⟨out of the corner of my eye I *saw* the deer run into the woods⟩
synonyms behold, descry, discern, distinguish, espy, eye, look (at), note, notice, observe, perceive, regard, remark, sight, spy, view, witness
related words identify, make out, pick out; attend (to), consider, heed, mark, mind; study, watch; examine, inspect, scan, scrutinize, survey; glance (at), glimpse, peer (at)
phrases get a load of [*slang*], lay eyes on, set eyes on
near antonyms disregard, ignore, neglect, overpass, pass over; miss, overlook
2 to come to a knowledge of (something) by living through it — see EXPERIENCE
3 to come to an awareness — see DISCOVER 1
4 to have a vague awareness of — see FEEL 1
5 to make a social call upon — see VISIT 1
6 to recognize the meaning of — see COMPREHEND 1

seeable *adj* capable of being seen — see VISIBLE

seed *n* the descendants of a person, animal, or plant — see OFFSPRING

seed *vb* to put or set into the ground to grow — see PLANT

seediness *n* the state of being unattended to or not cared for — see NEGLECT 1

seedy *adj* **1** showing signs of advanced wear and tear and neglect — see SHABBY 1
2 worn or torn into or as if into rags — see RAGGED 2

seeing *conj* for the reason that — see SINCE

seek *vb* **1** to go in search of ⟨the knights of the Round Table fervently *sought* the Holy Grail⟩
synonyms cast about (for), cast around (for), forage (for), hunt, look up, pursue, quest, search (for *or* out)
related words ferret (out), root (out)
phrases look for
near antonyms hide, lose; ignore, neglect
2 to make a request for — see ASK (FOR) 1
3 to make an effort to do — see ATTEMPT

seeker *n* one who seeks an office, honor, position, or award — see CANDIDATE

seem *vb* to give the impression of being ⟨I tried to cheer them up because they *seemed* depressed⟩
synonyms act, appear, look, make, sound
related words dissemble, pretend; resemble, suggest; hint, imply, insinuate

seeming *adj* appearing to be true on the basis of evidence that may or may not be confirmed — see APPARENT 1

seemingly *adv* to all outward appearances — see APPARENTLY

seemliness *n* the quality or state of being especially suitable or fitting — see APPROPRIATENESS

seemly *adj* following the established traditions of refined society and good taste — see PROPER 1

seep *vb* to flow forth slowly through small openings — see EXUDE

seer *n* one who predicts future events or developments — see PROPHET

seesaw *vb* **1** to make a series of unsteady side-to-side motions — see ROCK 1
2 to make short up-and-down movements — see NOD

seethe *vb* **1** to be in a state of violent rolling motion ⟨the water *seethed* with schools of feeding piranha⟩
synonyms boil, churn, roil
related words reel, spin, swirl, whirl; agitate, stir
near antonyms abate, calm, subside
2 to be excited or emotionally stirred up with anger — see BOIL 1

segment *n* one of the pieces from which something is designed to be assembled — see PART 1

segregate *vb* to set or keep apart from others — see ISOLATE

segregation *n* the state of being alone or kept apart from others — see ISOLATION

seize *vb* **1** to recognize the meaning of — see COMPREHEND 1
2 to take or keep under one's control by authority of law — see ARREST 1
3 to take physical control or possession of (something) suddenly or forcibly — see CATCH 1

seizure *n* a sudden experiencing of a physical or mental disorder — see ATTACK 2

seldom *adv* not often ⟨we *seldom* go to the theater downtown because its prices are so high⟩
synonyms infrequently, little, rarely
related words ne'er, never
phrases hardly ever
near antonyms generally, usually; always, constantly, continuously, endlessly, eternally, ever, everlastingly, evermore, forever, invariably; recurrently, repeatedly
antonyms frequently, often

select *adj* **1** singled out from a number or group as more to one's liking ⟨they use only *select* beans to make their coffee⟩
synonyms chosen, elect, favored, picked, preferred, selected
related words fashionable; exclusive; culled, screened, weeded (out), winnowed (out)
near antonyms average, common, commonplace, ordinary, run-of-the-mill
2 having qualities that appeal to a refined taste — see CHOICE

select *vb* to decide to accept (someone or something) from a group of possibilities — see CHOOSE 1

selected *adj* singled out from a number or group as more to one's liking — see SELECT 1

selecting *n* the act or process of selecting — see SELECTION 1

selection *n* **1** the act or process of selecting ⟨his *selection* of a running mate was a long, tedious affair⟩
synonyms choice, choosing, election, picking, selecting
related words option; appointment, assignment, designation, naming, nomination
2 a person or thing that is chosen — see CHOICE 2

selective *adj* tending to select carefully ⟨we were highly *selective* about the music we listened to while trying out loudspeakers⟩
synonyms choosy (*or* choosey), particular, picky
related words fastidious, finicky, fussy; discerning, discriminating, judicious
near antonyms indiscriminate
antonyms nonselective

selector *n* someone with the right or responsibility for making a selection ⟨the librarians who are the *selectors* of the annual award for best children's book⟩
synonyms chooser, namer, picker
related words elector, voter

self–acting *adj* designed to replace or decrease human labor and especially physical labor — see LABORSAVING

self–admiration *n* an often unjustified feeling of being pleased with oneself or with one's situation or achievements — see COMPLACENCE

self–assertive *adj* having or showing a bold forcefulness in the pursuit of a goal — see AGGRESSIVE 1

self–assurance *n* great faith in oneself or one's abilities — see CONFIDENCE 1

self–assured *adj* having or showing great faith in oneself or one's abilities — see CONFIDENT 1

self–centered *adj* overly concerned with one's own desires, needs, or interests — see EGOCENTRIC

self–centeredness *n* excessive interest in oneself — see EGOISM

self–conceit *n* an often unjustified feeling of being pleased with oneself or with one's situation or achievements — see COMPLACENCE

self–conceited *adj* having too high an opinion of oneself — see CONCEITED

self–confidence *n* great faith in oneself or one's abilities — see CONFIDENCE 1

self–confident *adj* having or showing great faith in oneself or one's abilities — see CONFIDENT 1

self–containment *n* the power to control one's actions, impulses, or emotions — see WILL 1

self–control *n* **1** the power to control one's actions, impulses, or emotions — see WILL 1
2 the checking of one's true feelings and impulses when dealing with others — see CONSTRAINT 1

self–denial *n* the act or practice of giving up or rejecting something once enjoyed or desired — see RENUNCIATION

self–destruction *n* the act of deliberately killing oneself — see SUICIDE

self–determination *n* the act or power of making one's own choices or decisions — see FREE WILL

self–discipline *n* the power to control one's actions, impulses, or emotions — see WILL 1

self–esteem *n* **1** a reasonable or justifiable sense of one's worth or importance — see PRIDE 1
2 an often unjustified feeling of being pleased with oneself or with one's situation or achievements — see COMPLACENCE
3 great faith in oneself or one's abilities — see CONFIDENCE 1

self–governing *adj* **1** not being under the rule or control of another — see FREE 1
2 of, relating to, or favoring political democracy — see DEMOCRATIC

self–government *n* **1** government in which the supreme power is held by the people and used by them directly or indirectly through representation — see DEMOCRACY

2 the power to control one's actions, impulses, or emotions — see WILL 1
3 the state of being free from the control or power of another — see FREEDOM 1
selfhood *n* the set of qualities that make a person different from other people — see INDIVIDUALITY
self-identity *n* the set of qualities that make a person different from other people — see INDIVIDUALITY
self-importance *n* **1** an exaggerated sense of one's importance that shows itself in the making of excessive or unjustified claims — see ARROGANCE
2 an often unjustified feeling of being pleased with oneself or with one's situation or achievements — see COMPLACENCE
self-important *adj* having too high an opinion of oneself — see CONCEITED
self-interest *n* excessive interest in oneself — see EGOISM
selfish *adj* overly concerned with one's own desires, needs, or interests — see EGOCENTRIC
selfishness *n* excessive interest in oneself — see EGOISM
self-possessed *adj* free from emotional or mental agitation — see CALM 2
self-possession *n* **1** evenness of emotions or temper — see EQUANIMITY
2 the power to control one's actions, impulses, or emotions — see WILL 1
self-protective *adj* intended to resist or prevent attack or aggression — see DEFENSIVE
self-regard *n* **1** excessive interest in oneself — see EGOISM
2 a reasonable or justifiable sense of one's worth or importance — see PRIDE 1
self-reliance *n* the ability to care for one's self — see SELF-SUFFICIENCY
self-reliant *adj* able to take care of oneself without outside help — see SELF-SUFFICIENT
self-reproach *n* a feeling of responsibility for wrongdoing — see GUILT 1
self-respect *n* a reasonable or justifiable sense of one's worth or importance — see PRIDE 1
self-restraint *n* **1** the power to control one's actions, impulses, or emotions — see WILL 1
2 the checking of one's true feelings and impulses when dealing with others — see CONSTRAINT 1
self-rule *n* government in which the supreme power is held by the people and used by them directly or indirectly through representation — see DEMOCRACY
self-ruling *adj* of, relating to, or favoring political democracy — see DEMOCRATIC
selfsame *adj* being one and not another — see SAME 2
self-satisfaction *n* an often unjustified feeling of being pleased with oneself or with one's situation or achievements — see COMPLACENCE
self-satisfied *adj* having too high an opinion of oneself — see CONCEITED
self-seeker *n* one who does things only for his own benefit and with little regard for right and wrong ⟨he was accused of being a *self-seeker*, of being nice only to people who could do him favors⟩
synonyms opportunist, temporizer
related words egoist, egotist; conniver, machinator, plotter, schemer
self-seeking *adj* **1** having a strong desire for personal advancement — see AMBITIOUS 1
2 overly concerned with one's own desires, needs, or interests — see EGOCENTRIC
self-starter *n* an ambitious person who eagerly goes after what is desired — see GO-GETTER
self-sufficiency *n* the ability to care for one's self ⟨*self-sufficiency* is a goal that all teenagers should work towards⟩
synonyms independence, self-reliance, self-support
related words autonomy, self-determination; potency, power, resilience, strength
near antonyms helplessness, impotence, inadequacy, weakness
antonyms dependence, reliance
self-sufficient *adj* able to take care of oneself without outside help ⟨the college student worked nights so that he would be *self-sufficient*⟩
synonyms independent, self-reliant, self-supporting
related words potent, powerful, resilient, strong
near antonyms helpless, inadequate, insufficient; impotent, weak
antonyms dependent, reliant
self-support *n* the ability to care for one's self — see SELF-SUFFICIENCY
self-supporting *adj* able to take care of oneself without outside help — see SELF-SUFFICIENT
self-will *n* a steadfast adherence to an opinion, purpose, or course of action — see OBSTINACY
self-willed *adj* sticking to an opinion, purpose, or course of action in spite of reason, arguments, or persuasion — see OBSTINATE
sell *vb* to offer for sale to the public — see MARKET
sell (for) *vb* to have a price of — see COST
sell (out) *vb* to be unfaithful or disloyal to — see BETRAY 1
seller *n* the person in a business deal who hands over an item in exchange for money — see VENDOR
sellout *n* the act or fact of violating the trust or confidence of another — see BETRAYAL
semblance *n* **1** a display of emotion or behavior that is insincere or intended to deceive — see MASQUERADE
2 outward and often deceptive indication — see APPEARANCE 2
semidarkness *n* a time or place of little or no light — see DARK 1
seminar *n* **1** a coming together of a number of persons for a specified purpose — see MEETING 1
2 a meeting featuring a group discussion — see FORUM
seminary *n* a place or establishment for teaching and learning — see SCHOOL
send *vb* to cause to go or be taken from one place to another ⟨they promised to *send* the package in the morning⟩
synonyms consign, pack (off), ship, transfer, transmit, transport
related words convey, deliver, hand over; advance, drop, launch, remit; address, forward; bestow, contribute, donate, give, present
near antonyms acquire, draw, earn, gain, garner, get, obtain, procure, secure
antonyms accept, receive
senior *adj* being of advanced years and especially past middle age — see ELDERLY
senior *n* **1** one who is older than another ⟨since the man next door is my *senior* by a number of years, I always address him as "Mr. Barton"⟩

synonyms elder
related words ancestor, forerunner, predecessor
near antonyms contemporary, peer; descendant (*or* descendent), successor
antonyms junior
2 one who is above another in rank, station, or office — see SUPERIOR
3 the senior member of a group — see DEAN

senior citizen *n* a person of advanced years <more and more *senior citizens* are living active, rewarding lives>
synonyms ancient, elder, golden-ager, oldster, old-timer
related words senior; graybeard, patriarch; beldam (*or* beldame), grandam (*or* grandame); adult, grown-up
near antonyms adolescent, minor; child, cub, juvenile, kid
antonyms youngster, youth

sensation *n* **1** an indefinite physical response to a stimulus <we felt just the barest *sensation* of warmth when we leaned against the radiator>
synonyms feel, feeling, sense
related words impression, perception; hint, suggestion
2 a practice or interest that is very popular for a short time — see FAD
3 something extraordinary or surprising — see WONDER 1

sensational *adj* **1** arousing a strong and usually superficial interest or emotional reaction <the *sensational* news story caused a stir, but after a few days everyone forgot about it>
synonyms lurid, screaming
related words colorful, juicy, racy; dramatic, histrionic, melodramatic, theatrical; coarse, vulgar
near antonyms innocuous, inoffensive; dignified, formal, proper, restrained
2 of or relating to physical sensation or the senses — see SENSORY
3 of the very best kind — see EXCELLENT

sense *n* **1** an indefinite physical response to a stimulus — see SENSATION 1
2 the ability to learn and understand or to deal with problems — see INTELLIGENCE 1
3 the ability to make intelligent decisions especially in everyday matters — see COMMON SENSE
4 the idea that is conveyed or intended to be conveyed to the mind by language, symbol, or action — see MEANING 1
5 the thought processes that have been established as leading to valid solutions to problems — see LOGIC

sense *vb* to have a vague awareness of — see FEEL 1

senseless *adj* **1** having lost consciousness — see UNCONSCIOUS 1
2 having no meaning — see MEANINGLESS
3 not having or showing an ability to absorb ideas readily — see STUPID 1
4 showing or marked by a lack of good sense or judgment — see FOOLISH 1

senselessness *n* **1** lack of good sense or judgment — see FOOLISHNESS 1
2 language, behavior, or ideas that are absurd and contrary to good sense — see NONSENSE 1
3 the quality or state of lacking intelligence or quickness of mind — see STUPIDITY 1

sensibilities *n* general emotional condition — see FEELING 2

sensible *adj* **1** able to be perceived by a sense or by the mind — see PERCEPTIBLE
2 according to the rules of logic — see LOGICAL 1
3 based on sound reasoning or information — see GOOD 1
4 having specified facts or feelings actively impressed on the mind — see CONSCIOUS

sensibleness *n* the ability to make intelligent decisions especially in everyday matters — see COMMON SENSE

sensitive *adj* **1** able to sense slight impressions or differences — see ACUTE 1
2 being in a situation where one is likely to meet with harm — see LIABLE 1
3 easily injured without careful handling — see TENDER 1
4 of or relating to physical sensation or the senses — see SENSORY

sensor *n* a device that detects some physical quantity and responds usually with a transmitted signal <the thief accidentally triggered the motion *sensor*, which alerted the police>
synonyms detector
related words eye; electric eye, photoelectric cell; alarm, trigger

sensory *adj* of or relating to physical sensation or the senses <trying to listen to music while watching the TV and eating dinner caused a sort of *sensory* overload>
synonyms sensational, sensitive, sensuous
related words afferent, receptive; sensual
near antonyms extrasensory, intuitional

sensual *adj* pleasing to the physical senses <the *sensual* feel of a velvet shirt against the skin>
synonyms carnal, fleshly, luscious, sensuous, voluptuous
related words bodily, corporeal; agreeable, delectable, delicious, delightful, dreamy, gratifying, palatable, pleasant, pleasing, pleasurable, scrumptious; epicurean, luxurious, self-indulgent
near antonyms harsh, painful, uncomfortable

sensuous *adj* **1** of or relating to physical sensation or the senses — see SENSORY
2 pleasing to the physical senses — see SENSUAL

sentence *n* a decision made by a court or tribunal regarding a case it has heard <the court-martial pronounced a *sentence* of not guilty on all counts of cowardice>
synonyms doom, finding, holding, judgment (*or* judgement), ruling
related words verdict; injunction; decree, edict, order; declaration, deliverance, dictum, pronouncement; conclusion, decision, determination, opinion, resolution; discipline, penalty, punishment

sentence *vb* to impose a judicial punishment on <the judge *sentenced* him to a fine of fifty dollars and time served>
synonyms condemn, damn, doom
related words adjudge, judge; castigate, chasten, chastise, correct, discipline, penalize, punish; conclude, decide, determine, find, opine, resolve

sentient *adj* having specified facts or feelings actively impressed on the mind — see CONSCIOUS

sentiment *n* **1** a subjective response to a person, thing, or situation — see FEELING 1
2 an idea that is believed to be true or valid without positive knowledge — see OPINION 1

sentimental *adj* appealing to the emotions in an obvious and tiresome way — see CORNY

sentimentalism *n* the state or quality of having an excess of tender feelings (as of love, nostalgia, or compassion) — see SENTIMENTALITY

sentimentality *n* the state or quality of having an excess of tender feelings (as of love, nostalgia, or compassion) ⟨the *sentimentality* of the story of star-crossed lovers only made it even more popular with moviegoers⟩
synonyms mawkishness, mush, sappiness, sentimentalism, sloppiness
related words emotion; sentiment; corn, schmaltz (*also* schmalz)
near antonyms cynicism, hardheadedness, hardheartedness

sentinel *n* a person or group that watches over someone or something — see GUARD 1

sentry *n* a person or group that watches over someone or something — see GUARD 1

separable *adj* capable of being split into two or more parts or pieces ⟨the outdated belief that the atom is the smallest particle of matter and is not *separable*⟩
synonyms divisible
related words detachable
near antonyms combinable, joinable
antonyms indivisible, inseparable

separate *adj* **1** not the same or shared ⟨we stayed in *separate* apartments on our vacation⟩
synonyms different, individual, respective
related words disparate, dissimilar, distinct, distinctive, distinguishable, diverse, unalike, varied
near antonyms identical, selfsame, very
antonyms same
2 not physically attached to another unit ⟨the housing development has 200 *separate* homes, each with its own enclosed yard⟩
synonyms detached, disconnected, discrete, freestanding, single, unattached, unconnected
related words independent, self-contained; individual, private
antonyms attached, connected, joined
3 not being under the rule or control of another — see FREE 1
4 of, relating to, or belonging to a single person — see INDIVIDUAL 1

separate *vb* **1** to set or force apart ⟨we tried to *separate* the gluey pages, but they were stuck tight⟩
synonyms break up, disconnect, disjoin, disjoint, dissever, dissociate, disunite, divide, divorce, part, ramify, resolve, sever, split, sunder, uncouple, unlink, unyoke
related words decompose, disassemble, dissolve; bisect, fractionate, halve, quarter, segment, subdivide; break, rend, rip, rupture, tear; cut off, insulate, isolate, seclude, segregate, sequester; detach, disengage, disentangle, untie
near antonyms assemble, associate, blend, combine, mingle, mix; connect, couple; unify; accumulate, agglutinate, attach, bind, cement, close, fasten, fuse, stick, weld
antonyms join, link, unify, unite
2 to go or move in different directions from a central point ⟨the searchers *separated* in order to cover more ground⟩
synonyms branch (out), diverge, divide, fork
related words bestrew, broadcast, clear out, disband, dispel, disperse, dissipate, distribute, scatter, sow; distance, recede, retreat
near antonyms assemble, gather, meet
antonyms converge, join
3 to arrange or assign according to type — see CLASSIFY 1
4 to set or keep apart from others — see ISOLATE
5 to understand or point out the difference — see DISTINGUISH 1

separateness *n* the state of being alone or kept apart from others — see ISOLATION

separation *n* **1** the act or process of a whole separating into two or more parts or pieces ⟨the *separation* of Czechoslovakia into the Czech Republic and Slovakia⟩
synonyms breakup, dissolution, disunion, division, fractionation, partition, schism, split
related words breach, rupture; decomposition, disassembly, segmentation, subdivision; dispersal, scattering; administration, apportionment, distribution; isolation, seclusion, segregation, sequestration
near antonyms assemblage, association; attachment, connection, link, linkage, linkup; combination, fusion
antonyms unification, union
2 the state of being kept distinct ⟨the *separation* of church and state is an important concept in the United States⟩
synonyms demarcation, discreteness, discrimination, distinction
related words differentiation
near antonyms blurring, confusion
3 a movement in different directions away from a common point — see DIVERGENCE
4 an open space in a barrier (as a wall or hedge) — see GAP 1
5 the act or process of two or more persons going off in different directions — see PARTING 1

sepulcher *or* **sepulchre** *n* a final resting place for a dead person — see GRAVE

sepulchral *adj* causing or marked by an atmosphere lacking in cheer — see GLOOMY 1

sepulture *n* **1** a final resting place for a dead person — see GRAVE
2 the act or ceremony of putting a dead body in its final resting place — see BURIAL

sequel *n* a condition or occurrence traceable to a cause — see EFFECT 1

sequence *n* **1** a condition or occurrence traceable to a cause — see EFFECT 1
2 a series of things linked together — see CHAIN 1
3 the way objects in space or events in time are arranged or follow one another — see ORDER 1

sequential *adj* following one after another without others coming in between — see CONSECUTIVE

sequester *vb* **1** to set or keep apart from others — see ISOLATE
2 to take ownership or control of (something) by right of one's authority — see CONFISCATE

sequestration *n* the state of being alone or kept apart from others — see ISOLATION

sere *adj* marked by little or no precipitation or humidity — see DRY 1

serene *adj* **1** free from disturbing noise or uproar — see QUIET 1
2 free from emotional or mental agitation — see CALM 2
3 free from storms or physical disturbance — see CALM 1

sereneness *n* a state of freedom from storm or disturbance — see CALM

serenity *n* **1** a state of freedom from storm or disturbance — see CALM
2 evenness of emotions or temper — see EQUANIMITY

serial *adj* appearing in parts or numbers that follow regularly ⟨"Uncle Tom's Cabin" first appeared as a *serial* novel from 1851 to 1852⟩
synonyms episodic, periodic, periodical
related words sequential; recurrent, regular

serious *adj* **1** not joking or playful in mood or manner ⟨our parents were quite *serious* when they told us not to stay out too late⟩
synonyms earnest, grave, humorless, no-nonsense, sedate, severe, sober, solemn, staid, uncomic, unfunny, unsmiling, weighty
related words harsh, stern, strict; dignified, distinguished, elevated, serious-minded
near antonyms antic, comic, comical, droll, farcical, funny, hilarious, hysterical, laughable, light, light-headed, ludicrous, ridiculous, risible, riotous, screaming, side-splitting, uproarious; featherbrained, flighty, frivolous, goofy, harebrained, lighthearted, puerile, scatterbrained; absurd, asinine, balmy, brainless, cockeyed, crazy, cuckoo, daffy, daft, dotty, fatuous, foolish, half-witted, insane, jerky, kooky, loony (*also* looney), lunatic, mad, nonsensical, nutty, preposterous, sappy, screwball, senseless, silly, unwise, wacky, weak-minded, witless, zany
antonyms facetious, flip, flippant, humorous, jesting, jocular, joking, playful
2 having a matter of importance as its topic ⟨a very *serious* film that dealt with the aftermath of the Gulf War⟩
synonyms grave, heavy, weighty
related words big, consequential, eventful, important, major, material, meaningful, momentous, significant, substantial
near antonyms insignificant, little, minor, slight, small, trivial, unimportant
antonyms light
3 involving potential loss or injury — see DANGEROUS

seriousness *n* a mental state free of jesting or trifling — see EARNESTNESS

sermon *n* a public speech usually by a member of the clergy for the purpose of giving moral guidance or uplift ⟨a *sermon* whose message was that we should love our neighbors as much as we love ourselves⟩
synonyms homily
related words lecture, speech; lesson

serpent *n* a limbless reptile with a long body — see SNAKE 1

serpentine *adj* marked by a long series of irregular curves — see CROOKED 1

serrate *adj* notched or toothed along the edge — see SERRATED

serrated *adj* notched or toothed along the edge ⟨you should use a *serrated* knife when cutting bread, so you don't squash the loaf⟩
synonyms saw-toothed, serrate
related words wavy
near antonyms flat, smooth

serried *adj* having little space between items or parts — see CLOSE 1

servant *n* a person hired to perform household or personal services ⟨the wealthy family had *servants* to clean and cook for them⟩
synonyms domestic, flunky (*also* flunkey), lackey, menial, retainer, steward
related words butler, footman, groom, houseboy, man, majordomo, manservant, servitor, valet; handmaiden (*also* handmaid), housekeeper, housemaid, lady-in-waiting, maid, maidservant, wench, woman; attendant, follower
near antonyms boss, captain, chief, foreman, head, headman, helmsman, kingpin, leader, taskmaster
antonyms master

serve *vb* **1** to be a servant for ⟨he *served* his master faithfully for twenty years⟩
synonyms slave (for), work (for)
phrases wait on, wait upon
2 to be enough ⟨they made the pasta *serve* for eight guests⟩
synonyms do, suffice
related words answer, suit; assuage, content, quench, sate, satiate, satisfy
3 to be fitting or proper — see DO 1
4 to behave toward in a stated way — see TREAT 1
5 to have a certain purpose — see FUNCTION
6 to provide with something useful or desirable — see BENEFIT

server *n* a person who serves food or drink ⟨we had barely finished ordering when the *server* brought our salads⟩
synonyms waiter
related words waitress; bartender; steward, stewardess

service *adj* of or relating to the armed services — see MILITARY 1

service *n* **1** an act of kind assistance — see FAVOR 1
2 the capacity for being useful for some purpose — see USE 2
3 the combined army, air force, and navy of a nation — see ARMED FORCES

serviceability *n* the capacity for being useful for some purpose — see USE 2

serviceable *adj* **1** capable of being put to use or account — see PRACTICAL 1
2 capable of or suitable for being used for a particular purpose — see USABLE 1

serviceableness *n* the capacity for being useful for some purpose — see USE 2

serviceman *n* a person engaged in military service — see SOLDIER

servility *n* the state of being a slave — see SLAVERY 1

servitude *n* the state of being a slave — see SLAVERY 1

set *adj* **1** being in a state of fitness for some experience or action — see READY 1
2 firmly positioned in place and difficult to dislodge — see TIGHT 2
3 fully committed to achieving a goal — see DETERMINED 1
4 having been established and usually not subject to change — see FIXED 1
5 of a particular or exact sort — see EXPRESS 1

set *n* **1** a group of people acting together within a larger group — see FACTION
2 a group of people sharing a common interest and relating together socially — see GANG 2
3 a number of things considered as a unit — see GROUP 1
4 one of the units into which a whole is divided on the basis of a common characteristic — see CLASS 2

5 the array of painted backgrounds and furnishings used for a scene in a stage production — see SCENERY

set *vb* **1** to cover and warm eggs to hatch them ⟨the hen *set* for days⟩
synonyms brood, hatch, incubate, sit
related words lay, spawn; pip
2 to decide upon (the time or date for an event) usually from a position of authority — see APPOINT 1
3 to make an approximate or tentative judgment regarding — see ESTIMATE 1
4 *chiefly dialect* to rest on the buttocks or haunches — see SIT 1
5 to point or turn (something) toward a target or goal — see AIM 1
6 to come to an agreement or decision concerning the details of — see ARRANGE 1
7 to put securely in place or in a desired position — see FASTEN 2
8 to turn from a liquid into a substance resembling jelly — see COAGULATE
9 to arrange something in a certain spot or position — see PLACE 1
10 to become physically firm or solid — see HARDEN 1

setback *n* a change in status for the worse usually temporarily — see REVERSE 1

set down *vb* **1** to cause to sit down — see SEAT
2 to make a written note of — see RECORD 1

set in *vb* to come into existence — see BEGIN 2

set off *vb* to cause to function — see ACTIVATE

settee *n* a long upholstered piece of furniture designed for several sitters — see COUCH

setting *n* **1** the circumstances, conditions, or objects by which one is surrounded — see ENVIRONMENT
2 the place and time in which the action for a portion of a dramatic work (as a movie) is set — see SCENE 1

settle *vb* **1** to cause to come to rest at the bottom (as of a liquid) ⟨the light rain will *settle* the dust in the air⟩ ⟨careful handling will *settle* the lees in the bottom of the wine bottle⟩
synonyms lay, sediment
related words filter, screen, sieve, sift, strain; resettle
near antonyms disturb, mix, stir
antonyms raise
2 to give an opinion about (something at issue or in dispute) — see JUDGE 1
3 to come to an agreement or decision concerning the details of — see ARRANGE 1
4 to come to rest after descending from the air — see ALIGHT
5 to establish or place comfortably or snugly — see ENSCONCE 1
6 to free from distress or disturbance — see CALM 1
7 to gain emotional or mental control of — see COLLECT 1
8 to give what is owed for — see PAY 2
9 to make final, definite, or beyond dispute — see CLINCH
10 to stop the noise or speech of — see SILENCE 1

settle (down) *vb* to become still and orderly — see QUIET 1

settled *adj* **1** firmly established over time — see INVETERATE 1
2 having been established and usually not subject to change — see FIXED 1

settlement *n* an arrangement about action to be taken — see AGREEMENT 2

settler *n* **1** a person who settles in a new region — see FRONTIERSMAN
2 one that leaves one place to settle in another — see EMIGRANT

setup *n* **1** the way in which something is sized, arranged, or organized — see FORMAT 1
2 the way objects in space or events in time are arranged or follow one another — see ORDER 1

set up *vb* **1** to arrange something in a certain spot or position — see PLACE 1
2 to be responsible for the creation and early operation or use of — see FOUND
3 to fix in an upright position — see ERECT 1
4 to form by putting together parts or materials — see BUILD

seven seas *n pl* the whole body of salt water that covers nearly three-fourths of the earth — see OCEAN

sever *vb* to set or force apart — see SEPARATE 1

severe *adj* **1** given to exacting standards of discipline and self-restraint ⟨a *severe*, uncompromising teacher who locked the classroom door precisely when the bell rang and let no one in afterward⟩
synonyms austere, authoritarian, flinty, hard, harsh, heavy-handed, ramrod, rigid, rigorous, stern, strict
related words demanding, exacting; uncharitable, unforgiving; adamant, adamantine, hardened, hardhearted, immovable, implacable, inflexible, ossified, unbending, uncompromising, unyielding; dour, gruff; ascetic, monastic; browbeating, bullying; determined, firm, resolved, single-minded, steadfast, unflinching; dogged, intractable, obstinate, relentless
near antonyms easy, easygoing, laid-back, undemanding; charitable, kind, merciful, patient, soft, softhearted; accepting, compromising, yielding; responsive, willing; acquiescent, agreeable, amenable, compliant, flexible, pliable, pliant
antonyms forbearing, indulgent, lax, lenient, tolerant
2 harsh and threatening in manner or appearance — see GRIM 1
3 not joking or playful in mood or manner — see SERIOUS 1
4 difficult to endure — see HARSH 1
5 requiring considerable physical or mental effort — see HARD 2

severely *adv* in a manner so as to cause loss or suffering — see HARDLY 1

severity *n* the quality or state of being demanding or unyielding (as in discipline or criticism) ⟨Jane's parents were legendary for the *severity* of their discipline—she never got away with so much as a white lie⟩
synonyms hardness, harshness, inflexibility, rigidity, rigidness, rigorousness, sternness, strictness
related words hardheartedness, implacability, obduracy; dourness, gruffness; asceticism, austerity, monasticism; determination, firmness, resolve, steadfastness; obstinacy, stubbornness
near antonyms forbearance, indulgence, kindness, lenience, patience, softness, tenderness, tolerance; responsiveness, willingness; compliance, pliability
antonyms flexibility, gentleness, laxness, mildness

sew *vb* to close up with a series of interlacing stitches ⟨luckily, Mom was able to *sew* the tear in my pants so skillfully that they looked as good as new⟩
synonyms darn, stitch
related words mend, patch, repair; baste, ease, fell, finish, overcast; crochet, knit, quilt
sew up *vb* to have complete control over — see MONOPOLIZE
sex *n* sexual union involving penetration of the vagina by the penis — see SEXUAL INTERCOURSE
sexual intercourse *n* sexual union involving penetration of the vagina by the penis ⟨many people believe that it's best to wait to experience *sexual intercourse* until you're mature enough to handle it⟩
synonyms coitus, copulating, copulation, intercourse, mating, sex, sexual relations
related words fornication; safe sex; sexuality
phrases making love
sexual relations *n pl* sexual union involving penetration of the vagina by the penis — see SEXUAL INTERCOURSE
sexy *adj* of, relating to, or expressing sexual attraction — see EROTIC
shabby *adj* **1** showing signs of advanced wear and tear and neglect ⟨*shabby* wallpaper that was peeling from the walls⟩
synonyms dilapidated, dog-eared, grungy, mangy, mean, miserable, moth-eaten, neglected, ratty, run-down, scruffy, seedy, tacky, threadbare
related words abandoned, desolate, forlorn; broken-down, decrepit, worn-out; bedraggled, dingy, ragged, tattered; decaying, deteriorated, deteriorating, ramshackle; broken, damaged, destroyed, harmed, hurt, impaired, injured, ruined, wrecked
phrases gone to seed
near antonyms brand-new, fresh, new; cared-for, kept-up, maintained; mended, patched, rebuilt, reconstructed; smart, spiffy, spruce
2 worn or torn into or as if into rags — see RAGGED 2
shack *n* a small, simply constructed, and often temporary dwelling ⟨a farmer's *shack* out in the fields that's used for lambing and as a shelter from storms⟩
synonyms cabin, camp, hovel, hut, hutch, shanty
related words lean-to, shed; cot, cottage, lodge; cabana; bungalow, chalet; hogan, wickiup, wigwam
shackle *n* **1** something that physically prevents free movement — see BOND 1
2 shackles *pl* something that makes movement or progress more difficult — see ENCUMBRANCE
shackle *vb* **1** to confine or restrain with or as if with chains — see BIND 1
2 to create difficulty for the work or activity of — see HAMPER
shade *n* **1** partial darkness due to the obstruction of light rays ⟨it was hard to see in the *shade* after being in the brilliant sunlight⟩ ⟨the trees cast *shade*⟩
synonyms penumbra, shadiness, shadow, umbra
related words blackness, dimness, duskiness, gloominess, murkiness, obscurity, somberness; cloudiness, dullness (*also* dulness)
near antonyms brightness, brilliance, effulgence, illumination, incandescence, light, lightness, lucidity, lucidness, luminosity, radiance
2 a time or place of little or no light — see DARK 1
3 a property that becomes apparent when light falls on an object and by which things that are identical in form can be distinguished — see COLOR 1
4 a very small amount — see PARTICLE 1
5 the soul of a dead person thought of especially as appearing to living people — see GHOST
shade *vb* to shelter (something) from light and heat ⟨the trees *shaded* us quite nicely from the noonday sun⟩
synonyms shadow
related words cloud, darken, dim, dull; canopy, cover, protect, screen
near antonyms illuminate, light, lighten; expose
shaded *adj* protected from the sun's rays — see SHADY 1
shadiness *n* partial darkness due to the obstruction of light rays — see SHADE 1
shadow *n* **1** a person whose business is solving crimes and catching criminals or gathering information that is not easy to get — see DETECTIVE
2 partial darkness due to the obstruction of light rays — see SHADE 1
3 shadows *pl* a time or place of little or no light — see DARK 1
4 a tiny often physical indication of something lost or vanished — see VESTIGE
5 a very small amount — see PARTICLE 1
6 the soul of a dead person thought of especially as appearing to living people — see GHOST
shadow *vb* **1** to go after or on the track of — see FOLLOW 2
2 to make dark, dim, or indistinct — see CLOUD 1
3 to shelter (something) from light and heat — see SHADE
shadowed *adj* protected from the sun's rays — see SHADY 1
shadowing *n* the act of going after or in the tracks of another — see PURSUIT
shadowy *adj* **1** not seen or understood clearly — see FAINT 1
2 protected from the sun's rays — see SHADY 1
shady *adj* **1** protected from the sun's rays ⟨a lovely *shady* spot in the park that was pleasantly cool⟩
synonyms shaded, shadowed, shadowy
related words canopied, covered, sheltered; cloudy; dark, darkened, darkish, darkling, darksome, dim, dimmed, dusky, gloomy, moonless, murky, obscure, obscured, pitch-black, pitch-dark, somber (*or* sombre), sunless
near antonyms bedazzling, bright, brightened, brilliant, dazzling, effulgent, illuminated, illumined, incandescent, light, lighted (*or* lit), lucent, lucid, luminous; beaming, lambent, radiant, shining; lustrous
antonyms sunny
2 given to or marked by cheating and deception — see DISHONEST 2
3 giving good reason for being doubted, questioned, or challenged — see DOUBTFUL 2
4 given to acting in secret and to concealing one's intentions — see SNEAKY 1
shaft *n* **1** a narrow sharply defined line of light radiating from an object ⟨*shafts* of late-afternoon sunlight pierced the blinds and streaked the floor⟩
synonyms beam, ray
related words moonbeam, sunbeam; laser, spotlight
2 a weapon with a long straight handle and sharp head or blade — see SPEAR

shaggy *adj* **1** covered with or as if with hair — see HAIRY 1
2 made of or resembling hair — see HAIRY 2

shake *vb* **1** to make a series of small irregular or violent movements ⟨the bus rattled and *shook* as it barreled down a rutted road⟩
synonyms agitate, convulse, joggle, jolt, jounce, quake, quiver, shudder, vibrate, wobble
related words rock, sway; quaver, shiver, tremble; dodder, waver; flicker, fluctuate, flutter, oscillate, wave; beat, palpitate, pit-a-pat, pitter-patter, pulsate, pulse, throb
2 to get or keep away from (as a responsibility) through cleverness or trickery — see ESCAPE 2

shake *n* **1** a very small space of time — see INSTANT
2 shakes *pl* a sense of panic or extreme nervousness — see JITTERS

shake up *vb* to cause an often unpleasant surprise for — see SHOCK 1

shakiness *n* the quality or state of not being firmly fixed in position — see INSTABILITY

shaking *adj* marked by or given to small uncontrollable bodily movements — see SHAKY 1

shaking *n* **1** a series of slight movements by a body back and forth or from side to side — see VIBRATION
2 the act or a means of getting or keeping away from something undesirable — see ESCAPE 2

shaky *adj* **1** marked by or given to small uncontrollable bodily movements ⟨the old man's hands were so *shaky* that I was afraid he'd drop the glass⟩
synonyms quaking, quavery, shaking, shuddering, shuddery, tottery, trembling, tremulous, wobbling, wobbly
related words shivering, shivery
near antonyms controlled, firm, settled, stable, steady
2 giving good reason for being doubted, questioned, or challenged — see DOUBTFUL 2

shall *vb* to be under necessity or obligation to — see NEED 2

shallow *adj* **1** lacking significant physical depth ⟨the dog quickly dug a *shallow* hole that was barely deep enough to accommodate his bone⟩
synonyms depthless, shoal
related words skin-deep, superficial, surface; fathomable, measurable; finite, limited, measured, restricted; even, flat, flush, horizontal, level, plane, smooth
near antonyms abysmal, abyssal, bottomless, boundless, endless, immeasurable, inestimable, infinite, limitless, measureless, unfathomable, unlimited, vast; navigable
antonyms deep
2 having or showing a lack of depth of understanding or character — see SUPERFICIAL 2

shallow *n, usually* **shallows** *pl* a place where a body of water (as a sea or river) is shallow — see SHOAL

sham *adj* **1** being such in appearance only and made with or manufactured from usually cheaper materials — see IMITATION
2 being such in appearance only and made or manufactured with the intention of committing fraud — see COUNTERFEIT
3 lacking in natural or spontaneous quality — see ARTIFICIAL 1

sham *n* **1** a poor, insincere, or insulting imitation of something — see MOCKERY 1
2 an imitation that is passed off as genuine — see FAKE 1

sham *vb* to present a false appearance of — see FEIGN

shamble *vb* to move heavily or clumsily — see LUMBER 1

shambles *n pl* **1** a dirty or messy place — see PIGPEN
2 a state in which everything is out of order — see CHAOS

shame *n* **1** a feeling of responsibility for wrongdoing — see GUILT 1
2 a regrettable or blameworthy act — see CRIME 2
3 the state of having lost the esteem of others — see DISGRACE 1

shame *vb* to reduce to a lower standing in one's own eyes or in others' eyes — see HUMBLE

shamed *adj* suffering from or expressive of a feeling of responsibility for wrongdoing — see GUILTY 2

shamefaced *adj* suffering from or expressive of a feeling of responsibility for wrongdoing — see GUILTY 2

shameful *adj* not respectable — see DISREPUTABLE

shanty *n* a small, simply constructed, and often temporary dwelling — see SHACK

shape *n* **1** a state of being or fitness — see CONDITION 1
2 the outward appearance of something as distinguished from its substance — see FORM 1
3 the type of body that a person has — see PHYSIQUE

shape *vb* to change (something) so as to make it suitable for a new use or situation — see ADAPT

shape (up) *vb* to take on a definite form — see FORM 1

shapeless *adj* **1** badly or imperfectly formed — see MALFORMED
2 having no definite or recognizable form — see FORMLESS

share *n* **1** something belonging to, due to, or contributed by an individual member of a group ⟨my *share* of the lottery winnings is over a million dollars⟩ ⟨Sue's *share* of the bill comes to $13.44⟩
synonyms allotment, allowance, cut, part, portion, proportion, quota
related words lot, ration; commission, percentage; member, partition, section, segment
near antonyms aggregate, composite, compound, sum, total, totality; whole
2 a legal right to participation in the advantages, profits, and responsibility of something — see INTEREST 1

share *vb* to take a share or part — see PARTAKE

shared *adj* used or done by a number of people as a group — see COLLECTIVE

sharer *n* one who takes part in something — see PARTICIPANT

shark *n* **1** a dishonest person who uses clever means to cheat others out of something of value — see TRICKSTER 1
2 a person with a high level of knowledge or skill in a field — see EXPERT

sharp *adj* **1** having an edge thin enough to cut or pierce something ⟨be careful, as that knife is *sharp* enough to slice off a finger⟩
synonyms cutting, edged, edgy, ground, honed, keen, sharpened, stropped, trenchant, whetted

related words clawlike; jabbing, jagged, lacerating, piercing, scratching, stabbing
near antonyms rounded, seamless, smooth; soft; even, flat, level, slick
antonyms blunt, blunted, dull, dulled, obtuse
2 causing intense mental or physical distress ⟨sudden *sharp* pains in your right lower belly can be a sign of appendicitis⟩
synonyms acute, agonizing, biting, excruciating, smart, smarting
related words bitter, cutting, keen, penetrating, piercing, raw, stinging; afflicting, distressing, disturbing, upsetting; cruel, grievous, harsh, heartrending, hurtful, lacerating, painful, paralyzing, severe, tormenting, torturous; insufferable, insupportable, intolerable, unacceptable, unbearable, unsupportable; appalling, awful, bad, dire, dreadful, ghastly, horrible, miserable, nasty, rotten, terrible, vile, wretched
near antonyms painless; acceptable, bearable, endurable, supportable, sustainable, tolerable; livable (*also* liveable), sufferable
antonyms dull
3 having a powerfully stimulating odor or flavor ⟨the cheese is so *sharp* that its rank aroma can practically clear a room⟩
synonyms nippy, pungent, strong
related words acid, acidic; acrid, bitter, harsh; piquant, spicy, tart, zesty; putrid, rancid, rank; acute, keen; animating, energizing, exciting, galvanizing, invigorating, provocative; appetizing, delectable, delicious, palatable, toothsome; flavorful, savory, tasty
near antonyms aged, mellow; gentle, soft; flat, flavorless, insipid; savorless, tasteless; dilute, thin, watery, weak
antonyms bland, mild, smooth
4 tapering to a thin tip — see POINTED 1
5 being in the latest or current fashion — see STYLISH
6 being strikingly neat and trim in style or appearance — see SMART 1
7 causing intense discomfort to one's skin — see CUTTING 1
8 given to or marked by cheating and deception — see DISHONEST 2
9 having or showing a practical cleverness or judgment — see SHREWD
10 having or showing quickness of mind — see INTELLIGENT 1
11 marked by the use of wit that is intended to cause hurt feelings — see SARCASTIC
12 able to sense slight impressions or differences — see ACUTE 1
13 uncomfortably cool — see CHILLY 1

sharp *adv* as stated or indicated without the slightest difference — see EXACTLY 1

sharpen *vb* to make sharp or sharper ⟨you need to *sharpen* your penknife's blade frequently in order to be able to whittle properly⟩
synonyms edge, grind, hone, strop, whet
related words file
near antonyms buff, burnish, gloss, polish, round, smooth
antonyms blunt, dull

sharpened *adj* having an edge thin enough to cut or pierce something — see SHARP 1

sharper *n* a dishonest person who uses clever means to cheat others out of something of value — see TRICKSTER 1

sharp–eyed *adj* having unusually keen vision ⟨a very *sharp-eyed* child found the last Easter egg, which was hidden in the flower arrangement⟩
synonyms clear-sighted, lynx-eyed
related words sighted; alert, attentive, aware, observant, observing, vigilant, watchful
near antonyms blind, eyeless, sightless, stone-blind, unseeing; astigmatic, myopic, nearsighted, shortsighted; unobservant, unobserving; purblind

sharply *adv* in a strikingly neat and trim manner — see SMARTLY

sharpness *n* **1** a harsh or sharp quality — see EDGE 1
2 an uncomfortable degree of coolness — see CHILL

sharpshooter *n* a person skilled in shooting at a target — see MARKSMAN

sharp–witted *adj* **1** having or showing a practical cleverness or judgment — see SHREWD
2 having or showing quickness of mind — see INTELLIGENT 1

shatter *vb* **1** to bring to a complete end the physical soundness, existence, or usefulness of — see DESTROY 1
2 to cause to break open or into pieces by or as if by an explosive — see BLAST 1
3 to cause to break with violence and much noise — see SMASH 1

shave *vb* **1** to make (as hair) shorter with or as if with the use of shears — see CLIP
2 to pass lightly across or touch gently especially in passing — see BRUSH

shaver *n* a male person who has not yet reached adulthood — see BOY

shear *vb* to make (as hair) shorter with or as if with the use of shears — see CLIP

sheath *n* something that encloses another thing especially to protect it — see [1]CASE 1

sheathe *vb* to cover with something that protects ⟨sometimes shipbuilders *sheathe* a ship's bottom with copper for extra protection from barnacles and other threats⟩
synonyms face
related words apparel, array, clothe, dress, garb, robe; side, skin; embosom, embower, embrace, encase, enclose (*also* inclose), encompass, enshroud, envelop, enwrap, invest, lap, mantle, shroud, surround, swathe, veil, wrap; blanket, overlay, overspread
near antonyms bare, denude, expose, strip

shed *vb* **1** to cast (a natural bodily covering or appendage) aside ⟨a snake's skin doesn't grow as the snake does, so every so often the snake will *shed* its old skin⟩
synonyms exfoliate, molt, slough (*also* sluff)
related words flake, peel, scale; discard
2 to get rid of as useless or unwanted — see DISCARD

sheen *n* brightness created by light reflected from a surface — see SHINE 1

sheep *n* an innocent or gentle person — see LAMB

sheepish *adj* not comfortable around people — see SHY 2

sheepishly *adv* in manner showing no signs of pride or self-assertion — see LOWLY

sheer *adj* **1** very thin and easy to see through ⟨we had to get window shades because passersby could see right through our *sheer* curtains⟩
synonyms filmy, gauzy, gossamer, gossamery, transparent

related words clear, limpid, liquid, lucent, pellucid; lucid, translucent; dainty, delicate, flimsy, fragile, frail; colorless, uncolored
near antonyms opaque; cloudy, foggy, hazy, misty, murky, smoky (*also* smokey); drab, dull, lackluster, lusterless
2 having no exceptions or restrictions — see ABSOLUTE 2
3 having an incline approaching the perpendicular — see STEEP 1
sheer *vb* **1** to change one's course or direction — see TURN 3
2 to depart abruptly from a straight line or course — see SWERVE 1
sheet *vb* to form a layer over — see COVER 2
shell *n* **1** something that encloses another thing especially to protect it — see [1]CASE 1
2 the arrangement of parts that gives something its basic form — see FRAME 1
shell *vb* **1** to remove the natural covering of — see PEEL
2 to use bombs or artillery against — see BOMBARD
shellacking *n* failure to win a contest — see DEFEAT 1
shell–shocked *adj* suffering from high levels of physical and especially psychological stress — see STRESSED-OUT
shelter *n* something (as a building) that offers cover from the weather or protection from danger ⟨the sudden fierce storm forced us to run to the nearest *shelter*⟩
synonyms asylum, harbor, harborage, haven, refuge, retreat, sanctuary, sanctum
related words anchorage, mooring, port; cover, screen; abode, diggings, domicile, dwelling, habitation, house, housing, lodging, lodgment (*or* lodgement), pad, place, quarters, residence, rest, roof; den, lair, hermitage, hideaway, hideout; fastness, fort, fortress, palisade, stronghold; lean-to, shed, windbreak
shelter *vb* **1** to be or provide a shelter for ⟨the abandoned barn *shelters* a colony of stray cats⟩
synonyms harbor
related words cover, defend, protect, safeguard, screen, shield, ward; domicile, house, place; shade, shadow
near antonyms expose
2 to provide with living quarters or shelter — see HOUSE 1
sheltered *adj* hidden from view — see SECLUDED
shelve *vb* to assign to a later time — see POSTPONE
shenanigans *n pl* **1** playful, reckless behavior that is not intended to cause serious harm — see MISCHIEF 1
2 wildly playful or mischievous behavior — see HORSEPLAY
shepherd *vb* to give advice and instruction to (someone) regarding the course or process to be followed — see GUIDE 1
shibboleth *n* **1** an attention-getting word or phrase used to publicize something (as a campaign or product) — see SLOGAN
2 an idea or expression that has been used by many people — see COMMONPLACE
shield *n* means or method of defending — see DEFENSE 1
shield *vb* **1** to drive danger or attack away from — see DEFEND 1
2 to place a protective layer over — see COVER 3
shift *n* **1** an action planned or taken to achieve a desired result — see MEASURE 1
2 the act or an instance of changing position — see MOVEMENT 1
shift *vb* **1** to change the place or position of — see MOVE 1
2 to change one's position — see MOVE 3
3 to pass from one form, state, or level to another — see CHANGE 2
4 to give up (something) and take something else in return — see CHANGE 3
5 to meet one's day-to-day needs — see GET ALONG 1
shifting *n* the act or an instance of changing position — see MOVEMENT 1
shiftless *adj* not easily aroused to action or work — see LAZY
shiftlessness *n* an inclination not to do work or engage in activities — see LAZINESS
shifty *adj* **1** given to acting in secret and to concealing one's intentions — see SNEAKY 1
2 given to or marked by cheating and deception — see DISHONEST 2
shillelagh *n* a heavy rigid stick used as a weapon or for punishment — see CLUB 1
shilly–shally *vb* to show uncertainty about the right course of action — see HESITATE
shilly–shallying *n* the act or an instance of pausing because of uncertainty about the right course of action — see HESITATION
shimmer *vb* to shoot forth bursts of light — see FLASH 1
shindig *n* a social gathering — see PARTY 1
shindy *n* a state of noisy, confused activity — see COMMOTION
shine *n* **1** brightness created by light reflected from a surface ⟨the troop inspector insisted on nothing less than a dazzling *shine* from every pair of shoes in the line of review⟩
synonyms gloss, luster (*or* lustre), polish, sheen
related words glare, gleam, glimmer, glint, glisten, glow, shimmer; flicker, sparkle, twinkle; illumination, irradiation; iridescence, luminescence; brightness, brilliance, luminosity, radiance; finish, glaze
near antonyms dimness, dinginess, dirtiness, drabness, dullness (*also* dulness), flatness; grayness, paleness; cloudiness, gloom, murkiness, obscurity, somberness
2 the steady giving off of the form of radiation that makes vision possible — see LIGHT 1
3 positive regard for something — see LIKING
shine *vb* **1** to emit rays of light ⟨the sun appears to *shine* particularly brightly in summer because that is when it's closest to the Earth⟩
synonyms beam, radiate
related words blaze, burn, fire, flame, gleam, glimmer, glint, glisten, glitter, glow, shimmer; blink, flare, flash, flicker, scintillate, sparkle, twinkle, wink; beat (down), glare; brighten, illuminate, illumine, irradiate, light, lighten; bedazzle, blind, daze, dazzle
near antonyms blacken, darken; lower (*also* lour)
2 to make smooth or glossy usually by repeatedly applying surface pressure — see POLISH
shining *adj* giving off or reflecting much light — see BRIGHT 1
shiny *adj* giving off or reflecting much light — see BRIGHT 1
ship *n* a large craft for travel by water ⟨we chose

to spend our vacation on a cruise *ship* traveling through the Caribbean⟩
synonyms boat, vessel
related words argosy, containership, corvette, cruiser, cutter, destroyer, ferryboat, flagship, freighter, icebreaker, ironclad, lightship, liner, man-of-war, merchantman, merchant ship, packet, steamer, supertanker, tanker, trader, tramp, transport, warship

ship *vb* to cause to go or be taken from one place to another — see SEND

shippable *adj* capable of being taken from one place to another by public carrier ⟨only boxes of five pounds and under are *shippable* by the postal service⟩
synonyms transferable, transmittable, transportable
related words addressable
antonyms nontransferable, receivable

shipshape *adj* being clean and in good order — see NEAT 1

shipwreck *n* the destruction or loss of a ship ⟨the *shipwreck* of much of the Spanish Armada ended Spain's plans for invading England⟩
synonyms shipwrecking, wreck, wreckage, wrecking
related words beaching, grounding, stranding; foundering, sinking
near antonyms salvage, salvaging

shipwreck *vb* to cause irreparable damage to (a ship) by running aground or sinking ⟨the helmsman fell asleep at the wheel and *shipwrecked* his yacht on the rocks⟩
synonyms strand, wreck
related words beach; founder, sink
near antonyms salvage

shipwrecking *n* the destruction or loss of a ship — see SHIPWRECK

shirk *vb* **1** to get or keep away from (as a responsibility) through cleverness or trickery — see ESCAPE 2
2 to leave undone or unattended to especially through carelessness — see NEGLECT 2

shirker *n* one who deliberately avoids work or duty — see SLACKER

shirty *adj, chiefly British* feeling or showing anger — see ANGRY

shiver *n* **1** an instance of shaking involuntarily with fear or cold ⟨Joe experienced a sudden *shiver* when confronted with the sight of the dark basement⟩
synonyms quiver, shudder, tremble
related words agitation, convulsing, jolt, quake, shake, tremor, vibration, wobble; fluctuation, flutter, oscillation, wave; beat, palpitation, pulsation, pulse, throb
2 shivers *pl* a sense of panic or extreme nervousness — see JITTERS

shivery *adj* having a low or subnormal temperature — see COLD 1

shoal *adj* lacking significant physical depth — see SHALLOW 1

shoal *n* a place where a body of water (as a sea or river) is shallow ⟨the *shoals* off Nantucket Island are famous as the final resting places of many ill-fated ships⟩
synonyms ford, shallows
related words bank, bar, sandbank, sandbar
near antonyms trench; abyss, deep, depth

shock *n* **1** a forceful coming together of two things — see IMPACT 1
2 the state of being strongly impressed by something unexpected or unusual — see SURPRISE 2

shock *vb* **1** to cause an often unpleasant surprise for ⟨Mom was *shocked* by the terrible news that her cousin had died in an accident⟩ ⟨Jack was *shocked* to find out that his grades were much lower than he realized⟩
synonyms appall, bowl (over), floor, jolt, shake up
related words affright, alarm, dismay, frighten, horrify, panic, scare, spook, startle, terrify, terrorize; disgust, nauseate, repel, revolt, sicken, turn off; displease, offend, outrage, scandalize; amaze, astound, awe; chill, daunt, demoralize, dispirit, unman, unnerve; discompose, disconcert, disquiet, disturb, perturb, unsettle, upset; crush, overpower, overwhelm
phrases knock for a loop
near antonyms cushion; delight, gratify, please, rejoice, tickle; charm, entice, tempt; cheer, comfort, console, solace, soothe; reassure
2 to make a strong impression on (someone) with something unexpected — see SURPRISE 1
3 to strike with fear — see FRIGHTEN

shocked *adj* **1** affected with sudden and great wonder or surprise — see THUNDERSTRUCK
2 filled with disgust — see SICK 2

shocking *adj* **1** causing a strong emotional reaction because unexpected — see SURPRISING 1
2 causing fear — see FEARFUL 1
3 causing intense displeasure, disgust, or resentment — see OFFENSIVE 1
4 extremely disturbing or repellent — see HORRIBLE 1

shoddy *adj* of low quality — see CHEAP 2

shoes *n pl* a way of looking at or thinking about something — see POINT OF VIEW

shoestring *n* a very small sum of money — see MITE 1

shoot *n* a branch of a main stem especially of a plant — see OFFSHOOT 1

shoot *vb* **1** to cause (a projectile) to be driven forward with force ⟨BB guns *shoot* small round metal pellets⟩
synonyms blast, discharge, fire, loose
related words launch, project; blaze (at), snipe (at); cast, catapult, fling, heave, hurl, pelt, pitch, sling, throw, toss
2 to cause a weapon to release a missile with great force ⟨soldiers train extensively to learn to *shoot* accurately and quickly⟩
synonyms blast, discharge, fire
related words blaze, pepper, snipe
3 to strike with a missile from a gun ⟨hunters can *shoot* deer only during the legally specified open season⟩
synonyms drill, gun, plug, pop
related words blaze, pepper; blast (at), fire (at); pick off; overshoot; snipe (at); croak [*slang*], destroy, dispatch, do in, fell, kill, slay; annihilate, blot out, butcher, decimate, massacre, slaughter, wipe out
4 to proceed or move quickly — see HURRY 2
5 to take a photograph of — see PHOTOGRAPH
6 to throw or give off — see EMIT 1

shoot (up) *vb* to rise abruptly and rapidly — see SKYROCKET

shooter *n* **1** a person skilled in shooting at a target — see MARKSMAN

2 one who takes photographs — see PHOTOGRAPHER

shop *n* **1** *also* **shoppe** an establishment where goods are sold to consumers ⟨the only *shop* which carries that game is halfway across the state⟩
synonyms bazaar, emporium, store
related words market, marketplace, outlet, showroom; boutique, department store, dime store, five-and-ten, thrift shop, variety store
2 a building or set of buildings for the manufacturing of goods — see FACTORY

[1]shore *n* something that holds up or serves as a foundation for something else — see SUPPORT 1

[2]shore *n* the usually sandy or gravelly land bordering a body of water — see BEACH

shore (up) *vb* to hold up or serve as a foundation for — see SUPPORT 3

short *adj* **1** having relatively little height ⟨a lot of boys are *shorter* than the girls in middle school, but they quickly catch up by high school⟩
synonyms little, low, low-lying
related words dwarf, dwarfish; petite, slight; diminutive, little, pint-size (*or* pint-sized), small, smallish; bantam, bitty, dinky, miniature, minimized, minute, puny, teeny, teeny-weeny, tiny, undersized, wee; dumpy, flat, scrubby, squat, squatty, stubby, stumpy, stunted
near antonyms elevated, lifted, raised, uplifted, upswept; high-rise, statuesque; gangling, gangly, lanky, rangy
antonyms high, lofty, tall, towering
2 not lasting for a considerable time ⟨fortunately for those of us in the hot sun, the graduation speech was *short* and to the point⟩
synonyms brief, condensed, little
related words abbreviated, abridged, curtailed, cut-back, shortened; compact, condensed; abrupt, sudden; ephemeral, fleeting, momentary, short-lived, transient, transitory; impermanent; compendious, concise, crisp, epigrammatic, laconic, pithy, succinct, summary, terse; short-range, short-term
near antonyms endless, everlasting, interminable, persistent, unending; longish, overlong, prolonged, protracted; permanent; enlarged, expanded, supplemented; long-range, long-term
antonyms extended, great, lengthy, long, long-lived, marathon
3 not coming up to a usual standard or meeting a particular need ⟨regrettably, the art supplies are *short* this year, so you'll have to share⟩
synonyms deficient, inadequate, insufficient, lacking, scarce, shy, wanting
related words hand-to-mouth, light, meager, niggardly, poor, scant, scanty, skimpy, slender, slim, spare, sparse, stingy; bare, mere, minimum; slight, small
near antonyms abundant, ample, bounteous, bountiful, copious, generous, liberal, plenteous, plentiful; enlarged, expanded, supplemented; abounding, overflowing, teeming; lavish, luxuriant, rich; big, considerable, hefty, jumbo, large, largish, oversize (*or* oversized), sizable (*or* sizeable), substantial, super
antonyms adequate, enough, sufficient
4 having a texture that readily breaks into little pieces under pressure — see CRISP 1

short *adv* with great suddenness ⟨the bicyclist ahead of me unexpectedly pulled up *short* and I plowed into him⟩
synonyms abruptly, suddenly
related words quickly; surprisingly, unexpectedly
near antonyms gradually, slowly; hesitantly

shortage *n* a falling short of an essential or desirable amount or number — see DEFICIENCY

shortchange *vb* to rob by the use of trickery or threats — see FLEECE

shortcoming *n* a defect in character — see FAULT 1

shorten *vb* to make less in extent or duration ⟨we decided to *shorten* the distance we had to walk home by cutting across the neighbor's lawn⟩ ⟨if Grandma has to go shopping today, you'll need to *shorten* your visit⟩
synonyms abbreviate, abridge, curtail, cut back
related words digest, summarize; abate, compress, constrict, contract, cut, cut down, pare, prune, trim; decrease, de-escalate, deflate, diminish, dock, dwindle, lessen, lower, moderate, modify, reduce, retrench, shrink, slash, taper
near antonyms enlarge, expand, supplement; add, aggrandize, amplify, augment, balloon, boost, dilate, escalate, heighten, increase, maximize, raise; blow up, distend, inflate, swell
antonyms elongate, extend, lengthen, prolong, protract

short–lived *adj* lasting only for a short time — see MOMENTARY

shortly *adv* **1** in a few words ⟨the sudden closing of the restaurant was announced only with a *shortly* worded sign: "Out of Business"⟩
synonyms briefly, compactly, concisely, crisply, laconically, pithily, succinctly, summarily, tersely
related words aphoristically; exactly, precisely; abruptly, bluntly, brusquely, curtly
phrases in a nutshell
near antonyms redundantly, repetitiously
antonyms diffusely, long-windedly, verbosely, wordily
2 at or within a short time ⟨the test will begin *shortly*, so don't go too far away to find a bathroom⟩
synonyms anon, momentarily, presently, soon
related words directly, forthwith, immediately, instantly, now, promptly, pronto, right away, right now, straightaway
phrases by and by

shortness *n* the condition of being short — see BREVITY 1

shortsighted *adj* **1** able to see near things more clearly than distant ones — see NEARSIGHTED
2 not thinking about and providing for the future — see IMPROVIDENT

short story *n* a work with imaginary characters and events that is shorter and usually less complex than a novel — see STORY 1

short–tempered *adj* easily irritated or annoyed — see IRRITABLE

short–term *adj* intended to last, continue, or serve for a limited time — see TEMPORARY 1

shot *n* **1** a directed propelling of a missile by a firearm or artillery piece ⟨cannon operators often had to use several *shots* to figure out the range of their targets⟩
synonyms blasting, discharge, firing
related words potshot; barrage, bombardment, broadside, burst, cannonade, fusillade, hail, salvo, storm, volley
2 an effort to do or accomplish something — see ATTEMPT

3 a picture created from an image recorded on a light-sensitive surface by a camera — see PHOTOGRAPH

4 a person skilled in shooting at a target — see MARKSMAN

5 the portion of a serving of a beverage that is swallowed at one time — see DRINK 2

should *vb* to be under necessity or obligation to — see NEED 2

shoulder *vb* to take to or upon oneself — see ASSUME 1

shout *n* a loud vocal expression of strong emotion ⟨Jason gave a sudden *shout* of surprise when the shower abruptly turned ice-cold⟩
synonyms cry, holler, hoot, howl, yell, yowl, whoop
related words scream, screech, shriek, squall, squeak, squeal, yelp; bellow, clamor, roar; caterwaul, wail
near antonyms mumble, murmur, mutter; gasp, whimper, whisper

shout *vb* to speak so as to be heard at a distance — see CALL 1

shove *vb* **1** to apply force to (someone or something) so that it moves in front of one — see PUSH 1
2 to push steadily against with some force — see PRESS 1

shove (off) *vb* to leave a place often for another — see GO 2

shovel *vb* to hollow out or form (something) by removing earth — see DIG 1

show *n* **1** an outward and often exaggerated indication of something abstract (as a feeling) for effect ⟨the children made a *show* of disgust when confronted with asparagus⟩
synonyms demonstration, display, exhibition, flaunting
related words act, pretense (*or* pretence), simulation; affectation, pose, sham; betrayal, disclosure
2 a display of emotion or behavior that is insincere or intended to deceive — see MASQUERADE
3 outward and often deceptive indication — see APPEARANCE 2
4 a public showing of objects of interest — see EXHIBITION 1

show *vb* **1** to present so as to invite notice or attention ⟨Julie made sure she *showed* the test paper with a big A on it to everyone in her family⟩
synonyms display, disport, exhibit, expose, flash, flaunt, parade, show off, sport, strut, unveil
related words brandish, flourish; advertise, air, broadcast, proclaim, publicize; divulge, talk (about), tell (of); bare, discover, reveal, uncloak, uncover
near antonyms camouflage, disguise, mask; conceal, cover, curtain, enshroud, hide, obscure, occult, shroud, veil
2 to make known (something abstract) through outward signs ⟨John's expressive face *shows* his every thought and emotion clearly⟩
synonyms bespeak, betray, demonstrate, display, expose, evince, give away, manifest, reveal
related words bare, disclose, unbosom, uncloak, uncover; advertise, air, broadcast, proclaim, publicize
near antonyms belie, misrepresent; distort, falsify, garble, twist; camouflage, disguise; gild, gloss (over), varnish, whitewash; conceal, counterfeit, cover, hide, mask, obscure, veil
3 to gain full recognition or acceptance of — see ESTABLISH 1
4 to give advice and instruction to (someone) regarding the course or process to be followed — see GUIDE 1
5 to point out the way for (someone) especially from a position in front — see LEAD 1

shower *n* **1** a heavy fall of objects — see RAIN 2
2 a rapid or overwhelming outpouring of many things at once — see BARRAGE

shower *vb* to give readily and in large quantities — see RAIN 2

showiness *n* excessive or unnecessary display — see OSTENTATION

show off *vb* **1** to engage in attention-getting playful or boisterous behavior — see CUT UP
2 to present so as to invite notice or attention — see SHOW 1

show up *vb* **1** to come into view — see APPEAR 1
2 to get to a destination — see COME 2
3 to reveal the true nature of — see EXPOSE 1

showy *adj* likely to attract attention — see NOTICEABLE

shred *n* a very small amount — see PARTICLE 1

shred *vb* to cause (something) to separate into jagged pieces by violently pulling at it — see TEAR 1

shrew *n* a bad-tempered scolding woman ⟨Rip Van Winkle went off into mountains to escape his wife, a *shrew* who made his life miserable⟩
synonyms fury, harpy, termagant, virago
related words carper, castigator, censurer, caviler (*or* caviller), critic, faultfinder, nitpicker, railer, scold; belittler, derider, detractor; pettifogger, quibbler

shrewd *adj* having or showing a practical cleverness or judgment ⟨a *shrewd* used car dealer who knew how to make the best possible deal⟩ ⟨*shrewd* investments that paid off big⟩
synonyms astute, canny, clear-sighted, hardheaded, knowing, sharp, sharp-witted, smart
related words artful, cagey (*also* cagy), crafty, cunning, devious, foxy, guileful, slick, sly, subtle, wily; discerning, insightful, perceptive, perspicacious, sagacious, sage, sapient, wise; experienced, veteran; discriminating, discriminative; agile, alert, brainy, bright, brilliant, clever, intelligent, keen, quick, quick-witted; apt, ingenious, resourceful; informed, knowledgeable, well-read
near antonyms artless, guileless, ingenuous, innocent, naive (*or* naïve); exploitable, gullible; undiscerning, unperceptive, unwise; dense, dull, obtuse; brainless, dumb, feebleminded, simple, slow, stupid, unintelligent, weak-minded; foolish, idiotic, imbecilic, moronic, silly, simple, thoughtless, witless; ignorant, uninformed
antonyms unknowing

shriek *vb* to cry out loudly and emotionally — see SCREAM

shrieking *adj* having a high musical pitch or range — see SHRILL

shrill *adj* having a high musical pitch or range ⟨the *shrill* sound of a policeman's whistle⟩
synonyms acute, high-pitched, piping, screeching, shrieking, squeaking, squeaky, treble, whistling
related words peeping, thin, tinny; piercing, ear-splitting, piercing, penetrating, strident; squealing, whining, yelping
near antonyms gruff
antonyms bass, deep, low, throaty

shrill *vb* to cry out loudly and emotionally — see SCREAM

shrimp *n* **1** a living thing much smaller than others of its kind — see DWARF 1
2 a person of no importance or influence — see NOBODY

shrine *n* a place that is considered sacred (as within a religion) ⟨for centuries pilgrims have traveled to the *shrine* of Saint Thomas à Becket in Canterbury, England⟩
synonyms sanctuary, sanctum
related words reliquary

shrink *vb* **1** to become smaller in size or volume through the drawing together of particles of matter — see CONTRACT 2
2 to draw back in fear, pain, or disgust — see FLINCH
3 to grow less in scope or intensity especially gradually — see DECREASE 2

shrinkage *n* the amount by which something is lessened — see DECREASE

shroud *n* something that covers or conceals like a piece of cloth — see CLOAK 1

shroud *vb* **1** to keep secret or shut off from view — see [1]HIDE 2
2 to make dark, dim, or indistinct — see CLOUD 1
3 to surround or cover closely — see ENFOLD 1

shrug off *vb* to overlook or dismiss as of little importance — see EXCUSE 1

shuck *vb* to remove the natural covering of — see PEEL

shuck (off) *vb* to get rid of as useless or unwanted — see DISCARD

shudder *n* an instance of shaking involuntarily with fear or cold — see SHIVER 1

shudder *vb* to make a series of small irregular or violent movements — see SHAKE 1

shuddering *adj* marked by or given to small uncontrollable bodily movements — see SHAKY 1

shuddering *n* a series of slight movements by a body back and forth or from side to side — see VIBRATION

shuddery *adj* marked by or given to small uncontrollable bodily movements — see SHAKY 1

shuffle *n* an unorganized collection or mixture of various things — see MISCELLANY 1

shuffle *vb* **1** to move heavily or clumsily — see LUMBER 1
2 to undo the proper order or arrangement of — see DISORDER

shun *vb* to get or keep away from (as a responsibility) through cleverness or trickery — see ESCAPE 2

shunning *n* the act or a means of getting or keeping away from something undesirable — see ESCAPE 2

shush *vb* to stop the noise or speech of — see SILENCE 1

shut *vb* **1** to position (something) so as to prevent passage through an opening — see CLOSE 1
2 to stop the operations of — see CLOSE 2

shutdown *n* the stopping of a process or activity — see END 1

shutoff *n* the stopping of a process or activity — see END 1

shut off *vb* to bring (as an action or operation) to an immediate end — see STOP 1

shutterbug *n* one who takes photographs — see PHOTOGRAPHER

shut up *vb* to stop talking ⟨it's not polite to tell your classmates to *shut up*, even if you disagree with them⟩
synonyms clam up, hush, quiet (down)
related words calm (down), cool (down), settle (down); haw, hem
antonyms speak, talk

shy *adj* **1** easily frightened ⟨a *shy* cat who hid under the bed every time she heard any loud noise⟩
synonyms fainthearted, fearful, mousy (*or* mousey), scary, skittish, timid, timorous
related words chicken, chickenhearted, cowardly, craven, dastardly, lily-livered, jittery, jumpy, pusillanimous, spineless, unheroic, yellow; anxious, apprehensive, nervous; afraid, alarmed, horrified, panicked, panicky, scared, shocked, spooked, startled, terrified, terrorized
near antonyms brave, courageous, dauntless, doughty, fearless, gallant, greathearted, heroic, intrepid, lionhearted, stalwart, stout, stouthearted, valiant, valorous; assured, confident, self-assured, self-confident; determined, firm, game, plucky, resolute, unflinching, unswerving; mettlesome, spirited, spunky
antonyms adventuresome, adventurous, audacious, bold, daring, dashing, gutsy, hardy, venturous, venturesome
2 not comfortable around people ⟨a *shy* person who finds talking to anyone but a close friend to be an awkward and unpleasant experience⟩
synonyms bashful, coy, demure, diffident, introverted, modest, retiring, sheepish
related words antisocial, unsociable, unsocial; awkward, embarrassed, self-conscious, unadventurous, unassertive, unenterprising; inhibited, reserved, uneasy, uptight
near antonyms convivial, sociable, social; bold, dashing, forceful; brash, forward, uninhibited, unreserved
antonyms extroverted (*also* extraverted), immodest, outgoing
3 not coming up to a usual standard or meeting a particular need — see SHORT 3

sick *adj* **1** temporarily suffering from a disorder of the body ⟨Jessie was *sick* with a cold on Monday and had to stay home from school⟩
synonyms ailing, bad, down, ill, indisposed, peaked, poorly, punk, run-down, sickened, unhealthy, unsound, unwell
related words nauseated, nauseous, qualmish, queasy (*also* queazy), sickish, squeamish; airsick, carsick, seasick, dizzy, light-hearted, woozy; achy, feverish; diseased, disordered; feeble, frail, infirm, sickly, weak, weakly; afflicted, troubled; challenged, crippled, debilitated, disabled, incapacitated, lame
phrases out of sorts, under the weather
near antonyms cured; better, convalescing, improved, mending, recovering, recuperating, rehabilitated; hardy, hearty, lusty, robust, rugged, stalwart, strong, tough; blooming, bouncing, flourishing, flush, thriving
antonyms chipper, hale, healthful, healthy, sound, well, whole, wholesome
2 filled with disgust ⟨it makes me *sick* to think of someone hurting a helpless animal⟩
synonyms disgusted, nauseated, repelled, repulsed, revolted, shocked, sickened, squeamish
related words angry, displeased, mad, upset
near antonyms delighted, pleased, thrilled; be-

guiled, bewitched, captivated, charmed, enchanted, enthralled, fascinated, mesmerized
3 affected with nausea — see NAUSEOUS
4 having one's patience, interest, or pleasure exhausted — see WEARY 2

sicken *vb* to cause to feel disgust — see DISGUST

sicken (with) *vb* to become affected with (a disease or disorder) — see CONTRACT 1

sickened *adj* **1** temporarily suffering from a disorder of the body — see SICK 1
2 filled with disgust — see SICK 2

sickening *adj* causing intense displeasure, disgust, or resentment — see OFFENSIVE 1

sickish *adj* affected with nausea — see NAUSEOUS

sickly *adj* chronically or repeatedly suffering from poor health ⟨a *sickly* foal that seemed to catch everything that the other horses had⟩
synonyms ailing, invalid, weakly
related words bedridden; delicate, fragile, frail; dying, fading, incurable, moribund; challenged, crippled, debilitated, incapacitated, lame; decrepit, enfeebled, feeble, infirm, weak, weakened, worn-out
near antonyms able-bodied, nondisabled, nonhandicapped
antonyms healthy, well

sickness *n* **1** the condition of not being in good health ⟨Jamie pleaded *sickness* and tried to stay home from school every single time there was a spelling test scheduled⟩
synonyms illness, indisposition, unhealthiness, unsoundness
related words malaise; ailment, condition, disease, disorder, malady, trouble, upset; debility, decrepitude, feebleness, frailness, infirmity, lameness
near antonyms fettle, fitness, shape; hardiness, heartiness, lustiness, robustness, ruggedness, stamina, strength, toughness, vigor, vigorousness, vitality; bloom, flush, flushness; weal, welfare, well-being
antonyms health, healthiness, soundness, wellness, wholeness, wholesomeness
2 an abnormal state that disrupts a plant or animal's normal bodily functioning — see DISEASE 1
3 a disturbed condition of the stomach in which one feels like vomiting — see NAUSEA 1

side *adj* of, relating to, or located on one side ⟨please bring all deliveries to the *side* door⟩
synonyms lateral
related words left, right; one-sided

side *n* **1** a place, space, or direction away from or beyond a central point or line ⟨will everyone who wants to sign up for volleyball please stand off to this *side* of the gym?⟩
synonyms flank, hand
related words direction, face, outside, underpart, underside; lee, leeward, windward; left, right
2 a certain way in which something appears or may be regarded — see ASPECT 1
3 a group of people acting together within a larger group — see FACTION

sideboard *n* a storage case typically having doors and shelves — see CABINET

sidekick *n* a person who helps a more skilled person — see HELPER

side–splitting *adj* causing or intended to cause laughter — see FUNNY 1

sidestep *vb* **1** to avoid having to comply with (something) especially through cleverness — see CIRCUMVENT 1
2 to move suddenly aside or to and fro — see DODGE 1

sideways *adv* with one side faced forward ⟨I had to walk *sideways* to get between the two towering piles of boxes⟩
synonyms broadside, edgewise, sidewise
related words aslant, obliquely, indirectly; laterally, sideward (*or* sidewards)
near antonyms dead, direct, right, straight

sidewise *adv* with one side faced forward — see SIDEWAYS

siege *n* **1** a sudden experiencing of a physical or mental disorder — see ATTACK 2
2 the cutting off of an area by military means to stop the flow of people or supplies — see BLOCKADE

siesta *n* a short sleep — see [1]NAP

sigh *vb* to take in and let out a deep audible breath or to make a similar sound ⟨Mom always used to *sigh* loudly whenever she found a mess on the floor⟩ ⟨a breeze *sighed* through the leaves⟩
synonyms sough
related words gasp, huff, pant, puff, wheeze; breathe, respire; exhale, expire, inhale, inspire; yawn

sigh (for) *vb* to have an earnest wish to own or enjoy — see DESIRE

sight *n* **1** a position within view — see PRESENCE 1
2 an instance of looking especially briefly — see LOOK 2
3 something unpleasant to look at — see EYESORE
4 the ability to see — see EYESIGHT

sight *vb* to make note of (something) through the use of one's eyes — see SEE 1

sightless *adj* lacking the power of sight — see BLIND

sightly *adj* very pleasing to look at — see BEAUTIFUL

sightseer *n* a person who travels for pleasure — see TOURIST

sign *n* **1** a movement of the body or limbs that expresses or emphasizes an idea or feeling — see GESTURE 1
2 a written or printed mark that is meant to convey information to the reader — see CHARACTER 1

sign *vb* to write one's name on (as a document) ⟨you'll have to *sign* the contract for it to be legal⟩
synonyms autograph
related words countersign, endorse (*also* indorse), register, sign on; author, pen, pencil (in), scratch (out), scrawl, scribble, write

signal *adj* standing above others in rank, importance, or achievement — see EMINENT

signal *n* **1** an object intended to give public notice or warning ⟨stop signs are *signals* for vehicles to come to a full stop—not suggestions for slowing down, as some drivers seem to think⟩
synonyms flag, tocsin
2 a movement of the body or limbs that expresses or emphasizes an idea or feeling — see GESTURE 1

signal *vb* to direct or notify by a movement or gesture — see MOTION

significance *n* **1** the idea that is conveyed or intended to be conveyed to the mind by language, symbol, or action — see MEANING 1
2 the quality or state of being important — see IMPORTANCE

significant *adj* **1** clearly conveying a special meaning (as one's mood) — see EXPRESSIVE

2 indicating something — see INDICATIVE
3 having great meaning or lasting effect — see IMPORTANT 1
4 having great power or influence — see IMPORTANT 2
5 sufficiently large in size, amount, or number to merit attention — see CONSIDERABLE 1

signification *n* the idea that is conveyed or intended to be conveyed to the mind by language, symbol, or action — see MEANING 1

signify *vb* **1** to be of importance — see MATTER
2 to communicate or convey (as an idea) to the mind — see MEAN 1

signifying *adj* indicating something — see INDICATIVE

sign on (for) *vb* to become a member of — see ENTER 2

sign up (for) *vb* to become a member of — see ENTER 2

silence *n* **1** incapacity for or restraint from speaking ⟨the teacher expects complete *silence* from everyone during all tests⟩
synonyms dumbness, muteness, speechlessness, stillness
related words inarticulateness, voicelessness; reserve, reticence, reticency, taciturnity
near antonyms communication, speaking, talking; eloquence, fluency, volubility; chattiness, garrulousness, loquaciousness, loquacity, talkativeness; verboseness, verbosity, windiness, wordiness
2 the near or complete absence of sound ⟨the *silence* of the garden was refreshing after the din of the party inside⟩
synonyms hush, quiet, quietness, quietude, still, stillness
related words calm, lull, peacefulness, tranquillity (*or* tranquility)
near antonyms din, clamor, hubbub, racket, tumult, uproar
antonyms noise, sound

silence *vb* **1** to stop the noise or speech of ⟨the instructor quickly *silenced* anyone who tried to interrupt⟩ ⟨we need to have a repairman come and *silence* that door alarm⟩
synonyms hush, mute, quell, settle, shush, still
near antonyms agitate, stir
2 to put a stop to (something) by the use of force — see QUELL 1

silent *adj* **1** deliberately refraining from speech ⟨the *silent* child had to be prompted to say hello⟩
synonyms dumb, mum, mute, speechless, uncommunicative
related words inarticulate, tongue-tied; nonvocal, voiceless
near antonyms articulate, eloquent, fluent, voluble; gabby, garrulous, loquacious, talkative, talky; outspoken, unreserved, vocal
antonyms communicative, speaking, talking
2 tending not to speak frequently (as by habit or inclination) ⟨a naturally *silent* boy, he was often overshadowed by his louder siblings⟩
synonyms closemouthed, laconic, reserved, reticent, taciturn, tight-lipped, uncommunicative
related words inhibited, introverted, restrained; sedate, self-contained, sober, staid
near antonyms free-spoken, outspoken, vocal; blabby, gossipy, talebearing; long-winded, verbose, windy, wordy
antonyms chatty, communicative, conversational, gabby, garrulous, loquacious, talkative, talky, unreserved
3 mostly or entirely without sound ⟨the room was so *silent* that you could have heard a pin drop⟩
synonyms hushed, muted, noiseless, quiet, quieted, soundless, still
related words peaceful, tranquil
antonyms noisy, unquiet

silhouette *n* a line that traces the outer limits of an object or surface — see OUTLINE 1

silhouette *vb* to draw or make apparent the outline of — see OUTLINE 1

silken *adj* smooth or delicate in appearance or feel — see SOFT 2

silky *adj* smooth or delicate in appearance or feel — see SOFT 2

silliness *n* **1** lack of good sense or judgment — see FOOLISHNESS 1
2 language, behavior, or ideas that are absurd and contrary to good sense — see NONSENSE 1

silly *adj* **1** lacking in seriousness or maturity — see GIDDY 1
2 showing or marked by a lack of good sense or judgment — see FOOLISH 1
3 so foolish or pointless as to be worthy of scornful laughter — see RIDICULOUS 1

silver *adj* of the color gray — see GRAY 1

silver *n* eating and serving utensils — see TABLEWARE 1

silverware *n* eating and serving utensils — see TABLEWARE 1

silvery *adj* of the color gray — see GRAY 1

similar *adj* having qualities in common — see ALIKE

similarity *n* **1** the quality or state of having many qualities in common ⟨the *similarity* between the two essays is too great to be coincidental — one student virtually copied the other⟩
synonyms alikeness, community, correspondence, likeness, parallelism, resemblance, similitude
related words analogousness; equivalence, equivalency, parity; identicalness, identity, sameness; correlation, relationship; exchangeability, interchangeability; accordance, agreement, compatibility, conformity, congruity
near antonyms inequality; conflict, disagreement, discrepancy, disparity, variance; incompatibility, incongruity, incongruousness
antonyms dissimilarity, unlikeness
2 a point which two or more things share in common ⟨the only *similarity* between this project and the last one is that both will involve some lab work⟩
synonyms correspondence, parallel, resemblance, similitude
related words counterpart, equal, equivalent
near antonyms difference, discrepancy; deviance, divergence; change, modification, variation
antonyms dissimilarity

similarly *adv* in like manner — see ALSO 1

similitude *n* **1** the quality or state of having many qualities in common — see SIMILARITY 1
2 a point which two or more things share in common — see SIMILARITY 2

simmer *vb* to cook in a liquid heated to the point that it gives off steam — see BOIL 2

simple *adj* **1** free from all additions or embellishment — see PLAIN 1

2 free from any intent to deceive or impress others — see GUILELESS
3 having no exceptions or restrictions — see ABSOLUTE 2
4 involving minimal difficulty or effort — see EASY 1
5 lacking in worldly wisdom or informed judgment — see NAIVE 1
6 lacking in education or the knowledge gained from books — see IGNORANT 1
7 not having or showing an ability to absorb ideas readily — see STUPID 1

simpleminded *adj* 1 lacking in worldly wisdom or informed judgment — see NAIVE 1
2 showing or marked by a lack of good sense or judgment — see FOOLISH 1

simpleness *n* 1 the quality or state of being simple and sincere — see NAÏVETÉ 1
2 the quality or state of lacking intelligence or quickness of mind — see STUPIDITY 1

simpleton *n* 1 a person who lacks good sense or judgment — see FOOL 1
2 a stupid person — see IDIOT

simplicity *n* 1 the quality or state of having a form or structure of few parts or elements ⟨the *simplicity* of this machine should enable everyone to learn how to use it⟩
synonyms plainness, unsophistication
related words homogeneity, unity
antonyms complexity, complication, elaborateness, intricacy, sophistication
2 clearness of expression ⟨the *simplicity* of this poem is beautiful⟩
synonyms clarity, explicitness, lucidity, lucidness, perspicuity, perspicuousness
related words incisiveness, directness, forthrightness, openness, straightforwardness
near antonyms ambiguity, equivocalness; incomprehensibility, unintelligibility; circuitousness, deviousness, indirectness, indistinctness; dimness, disjointedness, incoherence; faintness, fuzziness, muddiness, nebulousness, vagueness
antonyms obscurity
3 lack of good sense or judgment — see FOOLISHNESS 1
4 the quality or state of being simple and sincere — see NAÏVETÉ 1

simplify *vb* to make less complex ⟨you need to *simplify* this process somewhat or you'll never finish it today⟩
synonyms streamline
related words oversimplify; prune, strip (down), trim; purify, refine
near antonyms elaborate
antonyms complicate, perplex, sophisticate

simply *adv* 1 for nothing other than — see SOLELY 1
2 nothing more than — see JUST 3

simulate *vb* to present a false appearance of — see FEIGN

simulated *adj* 1 being such in appearance only and made with or manufactured from usually cheaper materials — see IMITATION
2 lacking in natural or spontaneous quality — see ARTIFICIAL 1

simultaneous *adj* existing or occurring at the same period of time — see CONTEMPORARY 1

simultaneously *adv* at one and the same time — see TOGETHER 1

sin *n* 1 a breaking of a moral or legal code — see OFFENSE 1
2 that which is morally unacceptable — see EVIL
3 immoral conduct or practices harmful or offensive to society — see VICE 1
4 a regrettable or blameworthy act — see CRIME 2

sin *vb* to commit an offense — see OFFEND 1

since *conj* for the reason that ⟨*since* I've done all my chores today, I should be allowed to go out and play⟩
synonyms as, because, for, inasmuch as, now, seeing, whereas
phrases as long as (*or* so long as), in view (*or* light) of the fact

sincere *adj* free from any intent to deceive or impress others — see GUILELESS

sincerely *adv* without any attempt to impress by deception or exaggeration — see NATURALLY 3

sinew *n* the ability to exert effort for the accomplishment of a task — see POWER 2

sinewy *adj* 1 having muscles capable of exerting great physical force — see STRONG 1
2 marked by a well-developed musculature — see MUSCULAR 1

sinful *adj* not conforming to a high moral standard; morally unacceptable — see BAD 2

sinfulness *n* the state or quality of being utterly evil — see ENORMITY 1

sing *vb* 1 to produce musical sounds with the voice ⟨it's relatively rare to find actors who can also *sing* well⟩
synonyms carol, chant, descant, vocalize
related words belt, croon, harmonize, hum, lilt, quaver, scat, sharp, slur, trill, troll, warble, yodel; serenade
2 to utter in musical or drawn out tones — see CHANT 1
3 to utter one's distinctive animal sound — see CRY 2

singe *vb* to burn on the surface — see SCORCH

singer *n* one who sings ⟨a famous opera *singer* will be performing tomorrow⟩
synonyms caroler (*or* caroller), songster, vocalist, vocalizer, voice
related words harmonizer, hummer, warbler, yodeler; serenader; cantor, chorist; songstress

single *adj* 1 not married ⟨there was such a shortage of *single* men in the neighborhood that he had his pick of girlfriends⟩
synonyms unattached, unmarried, unwed
related words fancy-free, footloose; marriageable, unmated, unpaired; divorced, separated
near antonyms mated, paired; affianced, betrothed, committed, engaged, pledged, promised; remarried
antonyms attached, espoused, married, wed
2 belonging only to the one person, unit, or group named — see SOLE 1
3 not physically attached to another unit — see SEPARATE 2

single (out) *vb* 1 to decide to accept (someone or something) from a group of possibilities — see CHOOSE 1
2 to find out or establish the identity of — see IDENTIFY 1

single–handedly *adv* without aid or support — see ALONE 1

singly *adv* without aid or support — see ALONE 1

singular *adj* 1 being out of the ordinary — see EXCEPTIONAL

2 noticeably different from what is generally found or experienced — see UNUSUAL 1

3 of, relating to, or belonging to a single person — see INDIVIDUAL 1

4 being the one or ones of a class with no other members — see ONLY 2

singularity *n* an odd or peculiar habit — see IDIOSYNCRASY

sinister *adj* being or showing a sign of evil or calamity to come — see OMINOUS

sink *vb* **1** to become worse or of less value — see DETERIORATE

2 to go to a lower level — see DROP 2

sinner *n* a person who commits moral wrongs — see EVILDOER 1

sinuous *adj* marked by a long series of irregular curves — see CROOKED 1

sip *n* the portion of a serving of a beverage that is swallowed at one time — see DRINK 2

sip *vb* to swallow in liquid form — see DRINK 1

siphon *vb* **1** to remove (liquid) gradually or completely — see DRAIN 1

2 to cause to move to a central point or along a restricted pathway — see CHANNEL

sire *vb* to become the father of — see FATHER

siren *n* a woman whom men find irresistibly attractive ⟨one of history's most famous *sirens*, Cleopatra charmed both Julius Caesar and Mark Antony⟩

synonyms enchantress, seductress, temptress

related words charmer, seducer

sissy *adj* having or displaying qualities more suitable for women than for men — see EFFEMINATE

sissy *n* a person who shows a shameful lack of courage in the face of danger — see COWARD

sit *vb* **1** to rest on the buttocks or haunches ⟨everybody needs to *sit* down, or no one will be able to see the movie⟩

synonyms set [*chiefly dialect*]

related words perch; lounge, slouch, sprawl, squat, straddle

near antonyms arise, get up, rise, stand

2 to cause to sit down — see SEAT

3 to cover and warm eggs to hatch them — see SET 1

4 to occupy a place or location — see STAND 1

site *n* the area or space occupied by or intended for something — see PLACE 1

sitter *n* a girl or woman employed to care for a young child or children — see NURSE

sitting duck *n* a person or thing that is the object of abuse, criticism, or ridicule — see TARGET 1

situate *vb* to arrange something in a certain spot or position — see PLACE 1

situation *n* **1** position with regard to conditions and circumstances ⟨the school's *situation* is improving with additional financial help⟩

synonyms footing, picture, posture, scene, status

related words rank, standing; place, spot, state; score, status quo

2 an assignment at which one regularly works for pay — see JOB 1

3 the placement of someone or something in relation to others in a vertical arrangement — see RANK 1

sixth sense *n* the power of seeing or knowing about things that are not present to the senses — see CLAIRVOYANCE

sizable *or* **sizeable** *adj* **1** of a size greater than average of its kind — see LARGE

2 sufficiently large in size, amount, or number to merit attention — see CONSIDERABLE 1

sizably *adv* to a large extent or degree — see GREATLY 2

size *n* the total amount of measurable space or surface occupied by something ⟨we worried that the immense *size* of the sofa would make getting it through the doorway impossible⟩

synonyms dimension, extent, magnitude, measure, measurement, proportion

related words area; capaciousness, commodiousness, roominess, spaciousness; ampleness, amplitude, bigness, bulk, bulkiness, enormousness, grandness, greatness, grossness, heftiness, hugeness, immenseness, immensity, largeness, mass, massiveness, monstrousness, stupendousness, tremendousness, vastness, volume, voluminousness

size *n* a substance used to stick things together — see GLUE

sizzle *n* a sound similar to the speech sound \s\ stretched out — see HISS 1

sizzle *vb* to make a sound like that of stretching out the speech sound \s\ — see HISS

skeletal *adj* suffering extreme weight loss as a result of hunger or disease — see EMACIATED

skeleton *n* the arrangement of parts that gives something its basic form — see FRAME 1

skeptic *n* a person who is always ready to doubt or question the truth or existence of something ⟨the demand by *skeptics* that believers in Bigfoot produce some hard evidence of that hairy humanoid⟩

synonyms disbeliever, doubter, questioner, unbeliever

related words cynic, misanthrope, pessimist; derider, ridiculer, scoffer

near antonyms chump, dupe, gull, pigeon, sucker

skeptical *adj* **1** inclined to doubt or question claims ⟨it's good to be *skeptical* about what you see on TV⟩

synonyms disbelieving, distrustful, doubting, incredulous, leery, mistrustful, questioning, suspecting, suspicious, unbelieving

related words paranoid; critical, puzzled, quizzical; careful, cautious, guarded, leery, wary, watchful; cynical, experienced, knowing, sophisticated, worldly, worldly-wise; curious, inquiring, inquisitive, nosy (*or* nosey), snoopy; uncertain, unconvinced, undecided, undetermined, unsettled, unsure; hesitant

near antonyms green, ingenuous, innocent, naive (*or* naïve), simple, simpleminded, unknowing, unsophisticated, unworldly, wide-eyed; certain, confident, positive, sure; callow, inexperienced, raw; childlike, idealistic, impractical; beguiled, deceived, duped, gulled, tricked; careless, heedless, unsuspecting, unsuspicious, unwary

antonyms credulous, gullible, trustful, trusting, uncritical, unquestioning

2 not feeling sure about the truth, wisdom, or trustworthiness of someone or something — see DOUBTFUL 1

skeptically *adv* with distrust — see ASKANCE

skepticism *n* a feeling or attitude that one does not know the truth, truthfulness, or trustworthiness of someone or something — see DOUBT

sketch *n* **1** a picture using lines to represent the chief features of an object or scene — see DRAWING

2 a vivid representation in words of someone or something — see DESCRIPTION 1

sketch *vb* **1** to draw or make apparent the outline of — see OUTLINE 1
2 to give a representation or account of in words — see DESCRIBE 1
skewed *adj* inclined or twisted to one side — see AWRY
skewer *vb* to penetrate or hold (something) with a pointed object — see IMPALE
skill *n* **1** subtle or imaginative ability in inventing, devising, or executing something <with unbelievable *skill*, the expert in origami transformed a few sheets of paper into a menagerie of exotic animals>
synonyms adeptness, adroitness, art, artfulness, artifice, artistry, cleverness, craft, cunning, deftness, masterfulness, skillfulness
related words dexterity, ease, finesse, handiness; experience, expertise, expertness, know-how, proficiency; creativity, ingenuity, inventiveness, knowledge, learning; aptitude, bent, flair, gift, knack, talent
near antonyms amateurishness, awkwardness, clumsiness, crudeness, rudeness; inability, inadequacy, incapability, incapacity, incompetence, ineffectiveness, ineffectualness, inefficiency
antonyms artlessness, ineptitude, ineptness, maladroitness
2 skills *pl* knowledge gained by actually doing or living through something — see EXPERIENCE 1
skilled *adj* having or showing exceptional knowledge, experience, or skill in a field of endeavor — see PROFICIENT
skillful *adj* **1** accomplished with trained ability <the ice skater performed a *skillful* and graceful series of jumps>
synonyms adroit, artful, delicate, dexterous (*also* dextrous), expert, masterful, masterly, practiced (*or* practised), virtuoso, workmanlike
related words facile, smooth; artistic, creative, fancy, ingenious, neat; adept, clever, cunning; able, adequate, capable, competent
near antonyms awkward, clumsy, crude; ineffective, ineffectual; incompetent, inept
antonyms amateur, amateurish, artless, rude, unprofessional, unskillful
2 having or showing exceptional knowledge, experience, or skill in a field of endeavor — see PROFICIENT
skillfully *adv* in a skillful or expert manner — see WELL 3
skillfulness *n* subtle or imaginative ability in inventing, devising, or executing something — see SKILL 1
skim *vb* **1** to move or proceed smoothly and readily — see FLOW 2
2 to pass lightly across or touch gently especially in passing — see BRUSH
3 to strike and fly off at an angle — see GLANCE 1
4 to take a quick or hasty look — see GLANCE 2
skimp *vb* to avoid unnecessary waste or expense — see ECONOMIZE
skimp (on) *vb* to use or give out in stingy amounts — see SPARE
skimping *n* careful management of material resources — see ECONOMY
skimpy *adj* less plentiful than what is normal, necessary, or desirable — see MEAGER
skin *n* **1** an outer part or layer — see EXTERIOR
2 the outer covering of an animal removed for its commercial value — see HIDE 1
3 the hairless natural covering of an animal prepared for use — see LEATHER 1
skin *vb* **1** to remove the natural covering of — see PEEL
2 to rob by the use of trickery or threats — see FLEECE
skin–deep *adj* **1** lying on or affecting only the outer layer of something — see SUPERFICIAL 1
2 having or showing a lack of depth of understanding or character — see SUPERFICIAL 2
skinflint *n* a mean grasping person who is usually stingy with money — see MISER
skinny *adj* **1** being of less than usual width — see NARROW 1
2 having a noticeably small amount of body fat — see THIN 1
skip *vb* **1** to move with a light bouncing step <children *skipping* across the playground>
synonyms bound, hop, lope, trip
related words caper, frisk, gambol, romp; skim, skitter; jump, leap, vault
near antonyms lumber, plod, trudge
2 to fail to attend — see CUT 2
3 to strike and fly off at an angle — see GLANCE 1
skipper *n* a person in overall command of a ship — see CAPTAIN 1
skirmish *n* **1** a brief clash between enemies or rivals — see ENCOUNTER
2 a physical dispute between opposing individuals or groups — see FIGHT
skirmish (with) *vb* to oppose (someone) in physical conflict — see FIGHT 1
skirt *n* the line or relatively narrow space that marks the outer limit of something — see BORDER 1
skirt *vb* **1** to avoid by going around — see DETOUR 1
2 to avoid having to comply with (something) especially through cleverness — see CIRCUMVENT 1
3 to be adjacent to — see ADJOIN 1
4 to serve as a border for — see BORDER
skirting *adj* having a border in common — see ADJACENT
skittish *adj* **1** easily excited by nature — see EXCITABLE
2 easily frightened — see SHY 1
skittishness *n* a state of nervousness marked by sudden jerky movements — see JUMPINESS
skulk *vb* to move about in a sly or secret manner — see SNEAK 1
skulker *n* someone who acts in a sly and secret manner — see SNEAK
skull *n* the case of bone that encloses the brain and supports the jaws of vertebrates <anthropologists just found the *skull* of a prehistoric man in the desert>
synonyms cranium
related words braincase; death's-head; head, noddle, noggin, pate, poll; crown, scalp
skunk *n* a person whose behavior is offensive to others — see JERK 1
skunk *vb* **1** to defeat by a large margin — see WHIP 2
2 to achieve a victory over — see BEAT 2
sky *n* the expanse of air surrounding the earth <the *sky* usually looks deep blue on a bright clear day>
synonyms blue, firmament, heaven(s), high
related words horizon, skyline
sky–high *adv* in an enthusiastic manner <some re-

viewers had praised the movie *sky-high*, but we thought that it was just a so-so comedy>
synonyms enthusiastically, exuberantly, madly, rhapsodically
related words avidly, eagerly, excitedly, impatiently, keenly; fanatically, rabidly, zealously
near antonyms aloofly, disinterestedly, impassively, incuriously; hesitantly, reluctantly, unwillingly
antonyms apathetically, indifferently, lukewarmly, perfunctorily

skylark *vb* to engage in attention-getting playful or boisterous behavior — see CUT UP

skylarking *n* wildly playful or mischievous behavior — see HORSEPLAY

skyrocket *vb* to rise abruptly and rapidly <the price of candy bars in the vending machine has *skyrocketed* over the past few months>
synonyms rocket, shoot (up), soar, zoom
related words accumulate, appreciate, balloon, build (up), burgeon, enlarge, escalate, expand, increase, mount, multiply, mushroom, proliferate, snowball, swell, wax; crest, peak, surge; heighten, intensify
near antonyms collapse, fall; contract, decrease, diminish, drop, lessen, wane
antonyms nose-dive, plummet, plunge, slump, tumble

skyward *adv* to or in a higher place — see ABOVE

slack *adj* **1** failing to give proper care and attention — see NEGLIGENT
2 not bound by rigid standards — see EASYGOING 2
3 not tightly fastened, tied, or stretched — see LOOSE 1

slack *n* **1** the extent to which something hangs or dips below a straight line — see SAG
2 slacks *pl* an outer garment covering each leg separately from waist to ankle — see PANTS

slack *vb* to make less taut — see SLACKEN

slacken *vb* to make less taut <you'll need to *slacken* the rope a bit to get it free of that post>
synonyms ease, loosen, relax, slack
related words detach, free, unbind, undo, unfasten, untie
near antonyms attach, bind, fasten, tie; constrain, restrain
antonyms strain, stretch, tense, tighten

slackened *adj* not tightly fastened, tied, or stretched — see LOOSE 1

slacker *n* one who deliberately avoids work or duty <there will be no *slackers* tolerated in this group—anyone who doesn't do their share will get booted out>
synonyms goldbrick, shirker
related words malingerer; dropout, quitter; drone, idler, lazybones, loafer, slouch, slug, sluggard; dallier, lingerer, loiterer, lounger, saunterer; dawdler, laggard, putterer, slowpoke
near antonyms live wire, powerhouse; doer, go-getter, hummer, hustler, rustler, self-starter

slackness *n* **1** failure to take the care that a cautious person usually takes — see NEGLIGENCE 1
2 the extent to which something hangs or dips below a straight line — see SAG

slam *n* **1** a hard strike with a part of the body or an instrument — see BLOW 1
2 a loud explosive sound — see CLAP 1

slam *vb* **1** to shove into a closed position with force and noise <the sulky child ran into her room and *slammed* the door loudly>
synonyms bang
related words close, shut, stop; bar, batten (down), bolt, chain, fasten, latch, lock, seal, secure
near antonyms open; unbar, unbolt, unfasten, unlatch, unlock, unseal
2 to deliver a blow to (someone or something) usually in a strong vigorous manner — see HIT 1
3 to come into usually forceful contact with something — see HIT 2
4 to criticize harshly and usually publicly — see ATTACK 2

slander *n* the making of false statements that damage another's reputation <unhappy that she hadn't won, the girl resorted to *slander* and claimed that the winner's science project had actually been done by his father>
synonyms aspersing, blackening, defamation, defaming, libel, libeling, maligning, smearing, traducing, vilification, vilifying
related words aspersion, innuendo, smear; backbiting, detraction; abuse, invective, vituperation; attack, criticism, censure, denunciation; contempt, disdain, scorn; belittlement, disparagement; cattiness, despite, hatefulness, malevolence, malice, maliciousness, malignancy, malignity, meanness, nastiness, spite, spitefulness, spleen, venom, viciousness
near antonyms acclaim, accolade, applause, commendation, praise; esteem, honor, respect; adulation, flattery; adoration, reverence, veneration, worship

slander *vb* to make untrue and harmful statements about <for some reason, that newspaper seems determined to *slander* one particular celebrity>
synonyms asperse, blacken, defame, libel, malign, smear, traduce, vilify
related words belittle, detract, disparage; discredit, disgrace, dishonor, shame; abase, debase, degrade, humble, humiliate; disdain, scorn
near antonyms exalt, glorify, honor; acclaim, applaud, commend, praise; esteem, respect; admire, regard; adore, revere, venerate, worship

slanderous *adj* causing or intended to cause unjust injury to a person's good name — see LIBELOUS

slang *n* the special terms or expressions of a particular group or field — see TERMINOLOGY

slant *n* **1** the degree to which something rises up from a position level with the horizon <the road has just enough of a *slant* to make bicycling up it a little strenuous>
synonyms cant, diagonal, grade, gradient, inclination, incline, lean, pitch, slope, tilt, upgrade
related words ascent, bank, climb, rise
near antonyms declension, declination, decline, declivity, descent, dip, downgrade, fall, receding
2 a way of looking at or thinking about something — see POINT OF VIEW

slant *vb* to set or cause to be at an angle — see LEAN 1

slanted *adj* **1** inclined or twisted to one side — see AWRY
2 running in a slanting direction — see DIAGONAL

slanting *adj* inclined or twisted to one side — see AWRY

slantways *adv* so as to slant — see SLANTWISE

slantwise *adj* **1** inclined or twisted to one side — see AWRY

2 running in a slanting direction — see DIAGONAL

slantwise *adv* so as to slant ⟨be careful not to lay the first boards *slantwise*, or the whole bookcase won't be straight⟩

synonyms slantways

related words down, downward (*or* downwards), up, upward (*or* upwards)

slap *n* a hard strike with a part of the body or an instrument — see [1]BLOW

slap *vb* to deliver a blow to (someone or something) usually in a strong vigorous manner — see HIT 1

slapdash *adj* lacking a definite plan, purpose, or pattern — see RANDOM

slapjack *n* a flat cake made from thin batter and cooked on both sides (as on a griddle) — see PANCAKE

slapstick *n* humorous entertainment — see COMEDY

slash *n* a long deep cut — see GASH

slash *vb* **1** to penetrate with a sharp edge (as a knife) — see CUT 1

2 to strike repeatedly with something long and thin or flexible — see WHIP 1

slate *adj* of the color gray — see GRAY 1

slate *vb* to put (someone or something) on a list — see [1]LIST 2

slated *adj* being in accordance with the prescribed, normal, or logical course of events — see DUE 2

slaty *adj* of the color gray — see GRAY 1

slaughter *n* the killing of a large number of people — see MASSACRE

slaughter *vb* to kill on a large scale — see MASSACRE

slave *n* **1** a person who is considered the property of another person ⟨many American *slaves* reached freedom in the North through the network known as the Underground Railroad⟩

synonyms bondman, bondsman, chattel, thrall

related words helot, serf; attendant, domestic, drudge, lackey, menial, servant

near antonyms freedman; enslaver, slave driver, slaveholder, slaver; master, taskmaster

antonyms freeman

2 a person who does very hard or dull work ⟨unappreciated office *slaves* who perform the necessary but tedious task of filing paperwork⟩

synonyms drudge, drudger, fag, grubber, laborer, peon, plugger, slogger, toiler, worker

related words workhorse; coolie, serf

near antonyms goldbrick, shirker; drone, idler, lazybones, loafer, slouch, slug, sluggard

slave *vb* to devote serious and sustained effort — see LABOR

slave (for) *vb* to be a servant for — see SERVE 1

slave driver *n* a boss who assigns much work — see TASKMASTER 1

slaver *vb* to let saliva or some other substance flow from the mouth — see DROOL

slavery *n* **1** the state of being a slave ⟨a child born into *slavery* was considered simply another addition to the master's wealth and property⟩

synonyms bondage, enslavement, servility, servitude, thrall, thralldom (*or* thraldom), yoke

related words peonage, serfdom; dependence, subjection, subjugation; captivity, enchainment, imprisonment, incarceration

near antonyms emancipation, enfranchisement, liberation, manumission; autonomy, independence, self-government, sovereignty

antonyms freedom, liberty

2 very hard or unpleasant work — see TOIL

slavish *adj* using or marked by the use of something else as a basis or model — see IMITATIVE

slavishly *adv* with great effort or determination — see HARD 1

slay *vb* **1** to deprive of life — see KILL 1

2 to put to death deliberately — see MURDER 1

slaying *n* the intentional and unlawful taking of another person's life — see HOMICIDE

sleazy *adj* of low quality — see CHEAP 2

sleek *adj* having a shiny surface or finish — see GLOSSY

sleep *n* **1** a natural periodic loss of consciousness during which the body restores itself ⟨eight hours of *sleep* or more are necessary for children and teenagers to function⟩

synonyms catnapping, dozing, napping, repose, rest, resting, slumber, slumbering, snoozing

related words catnap, doze, drowse, forty winks, nap, siesta, snooze, wink; oversleeping; dreaming, rapid eye movement

near antonyms insomnia, sleeplessness

antonyms consciousness, wakefulness

2 the state of being dead — see DEATH 2

sleep *vb* **1** be in a state of sleep ⟨the baby *slept* for the entire length of the car trip⟩

synonyms catnap, doze, nap, rest, slumber, snooze

related words drowse (off), nod (off); oversleep; dream, hibernate

near antonyms arise, arouse, awake, rise

2 to engage in sexual intercourse — see COPULATE

sleeper *n* one who sleeps ⟨Joe is a restless *sleeper* who always wakes up with the covers kicked off⟩

synonyms dozer, slumberer

related words nodder

near antonyms insomniac; riser, waker

sleepiness *n* the quality or state of desiring or needing sleep ⟨Sarah suffered such *sleepiness* in class that there were days when she could hardly keep her eyes open⟩

synonyms drowsiness, somnolence

related words lassitude, lethargy, sluggishness, torpor; dozing, resting, sleeping, slumbering; oversleeping

near antonyms awareness, consciousness

antonyms insomnia, sleeplessness, wakefulness

sleeping *adj* being in a state of suspended consciousness — see ASLEEP 1

sleepless *adj* not sleeping or able to sleep — see WAKEFUL

sleepy *adj* **1** desiring or needing sleep ⟨the *sleepy* children were carried up to bed⟩

synonyms drowsy, slumberous (*or* slumbrous), somnolent

related words asleep, dormant, dozing, resting, sleeping, slumbering; nodding, yawning

near antonyms restive, restless, sleepless

antonyms alert, awake, conscious, wakeful, wide-awake

2 slow to move or act — see INACTIVE 1

sleight *n* **1** a clever often underhanded means to achieve an end — see TRICK 1

2 mental skill or quickness — see DEXTERITY 1

3 ease and grace in physical activity — see DEXTERITY 2

slender *adj* **1** being of less than usual width — see NARROW 1
2 having a noticeably small amount of body fat — see THIN 1
3 less plentiful than what is normal, necessary, or desirable — see MEAGER

sleuth *n* a person whose business is solving crimes and catching criminals or gathering information that is not easy to get — see DETECTIVE

slice *n* a piece that has been separated from the whole by cutting — see CUT 1

slice *vb* **1** to cut into long slender pieces — see SLIVER
2 to penetrate with a sharp edge (as a knife) — see CUT 1

slick *adj* **1** having or being a surface so smooth as to make sliding or falling likely ⟨roads are often *slick* during the first hour of a rainstorm⟩
synonyms greased, greasy, lubricated, oiled, slicked, slippery, slithery
related words brushed, buffed, burnished, glossed, ground, polished, rubbed, shined; coated, glazed, waxed; soapy, waxy; rasped, sandblasted, sanded, sandpapered, scoured, scraped, scrubbed
near antonyms coarsened, rough, roughened, scuffed, uneven
2 clever at attaining one's ends by indirect and often deceptive means — see ARTFUL 1

slick *vb* to coat (something) with a slippery substance in order to reduce friction — see LUBRICATE

slicked *adj* having or being a surface so smooth as to make sliding or falling likely — see SLICK 1

slicker *n* a coat made of water-resistant material — see RAINCOAT

slickness *n* skill in achieving one's ends through indirect, subtle, or underhanded means — see CUNNING 1

slide *vb* **1** to move about in a sly or secret manner — see SNEAK 1
2 to move or proceed smoothly and readily — see FLOW 2

slight *adj* **1** lacking bodily strength — see WEAK 1
2 lacking importance — see UNIMPORTANT
3 of a size that is less than average — see SMALL 1
4 so small or unimportant as to warrant little or no attention — see NEGLIGIBLE 1
5 small in degree — see REMOTE 1

slight *n* an act or expression showing scorn and usually intended to hurt another's feelings — see INSULT

slight *vb* **1** to cause hurt feelings or deep resentment in — see INSULT
2 to deliberately ignore or treat rudely — see SNUB 1
3 to show contempt for — see SCORN 1
4 to fail to give proper attention to — see NEGLECT 1

slightest *adj* being the least in amount, number, or size possible — see MINIMAL

slighting *adj* intended to make a person or thing seem of little importance or value — see DEROGATORY

slightly *adv* **1** by a very small margin — see JUST 2
2 in a very small quantity or degree — see LITTLE 1

slightness *n* **1** the quality or state of being little in size — see SMALLNESS
2 the state or quality of having little weight — see [1]LIGHTNESS 1

slim *adj* **1** being of less than usual width — see NARROW 1
2 having a noticeably small amount of body fat — see THIN 1
3 less plentiful than what is normal, necessary, or desirable — see MEAGER
4 small in degree — see REMOTE 1

slime *n* soft wet earth — see MUD

slimy *adj* full of or covered with soft wet earth — see MUDDY 1

[1]**sling** *vb* to place on an elevated point without support from below — see HANG 1

[2]**sling** *vb* to send through the air especially with a quick forward motion of the arm — see THROW

slink *vb* to move about in a sly or secret manner — see SNEAK 1

[1]**slip** *n* a long narrow piece of material — see STRIP

[2]**slip** *n* **1** an unintentional departure from truth or accuracy — see ERROR 1
2 the act of going down from an upright position suddenly and involuntarily — see FALL 1
3 the act or an instance of getting free from danger or confinement — see ESCAPE 1

slip *vb* **1** to decline gradually from a standard level ⟨Susie's grades *slipped* somewhat after she joined five after-school activities⟩
synonyms sag
related words drop, fall, slump; flag, sink, slacken, slow (down), weaken; abate, contract, decrease, de-escalate, die (down), diminish, dwindle, ebb, lessen, let up, lower, moderate, recede, relent, shrink, subside, taper, taper off, wane
near antonyms rocket, shoot (up), soar; balloon, burgeon, enlarge, escalate, expand, increase, mount, multiply, mushroom, proliferate, snowball, swell, wax; crest, peak, surge
2 to go down from an upright position suddenly and involuntarily — see FALL 1
3 to introduce in a gradual, secret, or clever way — see INSINUATE
4 to move about in a sly or secret manner — see SNEAK 1
5 to move or proceed smoothly and readily — see FLOW 2

slip (on *or* into) *vb* to place on one's person — see PUT ON 1

slippery *adj* **1** given to acting in secret and to concealing one's intentions — see SNEAKY 1
2 hard to find, capture, or isolate — see ELUSIVE
3 having or being a surface so smooth as to make sliding or falling likely — see SLICK 1

slipup *n* an unintentional departure from truth or accuracy — see ERROR 1

slit *n* a long deep cut — see GASH

slit *vb* to penetrate with a sharp edge (as a knife) — see CUT 1

slither *vb* to move slowly with the body close to the ground — see CRAWL 1

slithery *adj* having or being a surface so smooth as to make sliding or falling likely — see SLICK 1

sliver *n* a small flat piece separated from a whole — see CHIP 1

sliver *vb* to cut into long slender pieces ⟨carefully *slivered* the rattan stems into strips for basketry⟩
synonyms slice, splinter
related words chip, chop, dice, hash, mince; saw, scissor; cleave, rive, split; gash, incise, rip, slash, slit

slob *n* **1** a dirty or sloppy person ⟨only a *slob* would let his bedroom get so messy that his own mother couldn't remember what the floor looked like⟩
synonyms sloven
related words slattern, slut
near antonyms cleaner
antonyms old maid
2 a person whose behavior is offensive to others — see JERK 1

slobber *n* the fluid that is secreted into the mouth by certain glands — see SALIVA

slobber *vb* **1** to let saliva or some other substance flow from the mouth — see DROOL
2 to make an exaggerated display of affection or enthusiasm — see GUSH 2

slog *vb* **1** to deliver a blow to (someone or something) usually in a strong vigorous manner — see HIT 1
2 to devote serious and sustained effort — see LABOR

slogan *n* an attention-getting word or phrase used to publicize something (as a campaign or product) ⟨within days, virtually everyone was familiar with the newest advertising *slogan* for that brand of soda⟩
synonyms cry, shibboleth, watchword
related words tag line; expression, idiom; cliché; maxim, motto

slogger *n* a person who does very hard or dull work — see SLAVE 2

slop *n* **1** soft wet earth — see MUD
2 slops *pl* solid matter discharged from an animal's alimentary canal — see DROPPING 1

slope *n* the degree to which something rises up from a position level with the horizon — see SLANT

slope *vb* to set or cause to be at an angle — see LEAN 1

sloped *adj* running in a slanting direction — see DIAGONAL

sloping *adj* running in a slanting direction — see DIAGONAL

sloppily *adv* in a careless or unfashionable manner ⟨everyone dressed *sloppily* for the task of cleaning out the garage⟩
synonyms dowdily, slovenly, unstylishly
related words slatternly; chaotically, messily, untidily; shabbily, sleazily; dingily, dirtily, filthily, foully, grubbily, nastily
near antonyms neatly, orderly, tidily; fashionably, modishly; carefully, fastidiously, fussily, meticulously; cleanly, immaculately, spotlessly
antonyms nattily, sharply, smartly, sprucely

sloppiness *n* the state or quality of having an excess of tender feelings (as of love, nostalgia, or compassion) — see SENTIMENTALITY

sloppy *adj* **1** lacking neatness in dress or person ⟨a *sloppy* child who always seems to have spilled something on his clothes⟩
synonyms dowdy, frowsy (*or* frowzy), slovenly, unkempt, untidy
related words slatternly, sluttish; chaotic, cluttered, confused, disarranged, disheveled (*or* dishevelled), disordered, messed, messy, muddled, mussed, mussy, rumpled, uncombed, wrinkled; shabby, sleazy; besmirched, blackened, dingy, dirty, filthy, foul, grimy, grubby, grungy, mucky, nasty, soiled, spotted, squalid, stained, sullied, unclean, uncleanly
near antonyms chic, fashionable, modish, stylish; combed, groomed; neat, ordered, orderly, tidy; careful, fastidious, fussy, meticulous; clean, cleaned, cleanly, immaculate, sparkling, spotless, stainless, unsoiled, unsullied
antonyms dapper, dashing, dolled up, sharp, smart, spruce
2 lacking in order, neatness, and often cleanliness — see MESSY
3 appealing to the emotions in an obvious and tiresome way — see CORNY

slosh *vb* to move with a splashing motion ⟨the baby gurgled contentedly as the water *sloshed* gently around him in the bathtub⟩
synonyms lap, plash, splash, swash
related words babble, bubble, gurgle, ripple

sloth *n* an inclination not to do work or engage in activities — see LAZINESS

slothful *adj* not easily aroused to action or work — see LAZY

slouch *n* a lazy person — see LAZYBONES

slough *also* **slue** *n* spongy land saturated or partially covered with water — see SWAMP

slough *also* **sluff** *vb* **1** to cast (a natural bodily covering or appendage) aside — see SHED 1
2 to get rid of as useless or unwanted — see DISCARD

sloven *n* a dirty or sloppy person — see SLOB 1

slovenly *adj* lacking neatness in dress or person — see SLOPPY 1

slovenly *adv* in a careless or unfashionable manner — see SLOPPILY

slow *adj* **1** moving or proceeding at less than the normal, desirable, or required speed ⟨because of the holiday, traffic to the beach was particularly *slow*⟩ ⟨*slow* readers⟩
synonyms crawling, creeping, dallying, dawdling, dilatory, dillydallying, dragging, laggard, lagging, languid, leisurely, poking, poky (*or* pokey), sluggish, tardy, unhurried
related words deliberate, measured; inactive, inert, lethargic, loafing, lounging; lingering, loitering, tarrying; ambling, inching, plodding, shuffling, strolling; decelerating, slowing; filibustering, procrastinating, stalling
near antonyms expeditious, prompt, ready; accelerated, hastened, quickened; hurried, rushed
antonyms barreling, bolting, breakneck, breathless, brisk, careering, dizzy, fast, fleet, flying, hasty, hurrying, lightning, quick, racing, rapid, rocketing, running, rushing, scooting, scudding, scurrying, snappy, speeding, speedy, swift, whirling, whirlwind, whisking, zipping
2 not having or showing an ability to absorb ideas readily — see STUPID 1

slow *adv* at a pace that is less than usual, desirable, or expected ⟨you need to go *slow* with this experiment, or you'll make mistakes⟩
synonyms laggardly, leisurely, slowly, sluggishly, tardily
related words carefully, cautiously, deliberately, purposefully; ploddingly
near antonyms immediately, posthaste, presto, promptly, pronto, readily, soon; impetuously, impulsively, rashly, recklessly; abruptly, suddenly
antonyms apace, briskly, fast, fleetly, full tilt, hastily, quick, quickly, rapidly, snappily, speedily, swift, swiftly

slow *vb* to cause to move or proceed at a less rapid pace ⟨if you don't *slow* your delivery down a bit, your speech will be over too soon⟩

synonyms brake, decelerate, retard
related words halt, stop; encumber, hamper, handicap, hinder, hobble, hold back, hold up, impede, inhibit, obstruct, tie up; arrest, check, constrain, curb, rein, restrain; baffle, foil, frustrate, sabotage, thwart
near antonyms drive, encourage, goad, propel, push, spur, stir, urge; advance, aid, dispatch, ease, expedite, facilitate, forward, further, help
antonyms accelerate, hasten, hurry, quicken, rush, speed (up), step up

slowdown *n* a usually gradual decrease in the pace or level of activity of something <disease experts are encouraged by the recent *slowdown* in the spread of the virus>
synonyms braking, deceleration, letup, retardation, retarding
related words decline, drop, slump; ebb, remission, retreat, wane; flagging, weakening; arrest, check, halt, stoppage; collapse, crash, fall, plunge
antonyms acceleration, hastening, quickening

slowly *adv* at a pace that is less than usual, desirable, or expected — see SLOW

slowness *n* the quality or state of lacking intelligence or quickness of mind — see STUPIDITY 1

slowpoke *n* someone who moves slowly or more slowly than others <quit being such a *slowpoke* this morning, or you'll be late>
synonyms crawler, creeper, dallier, dawdler, dragger, laggard, lagger, lingerer, loiterer, snail, stick-in-the-mud, straggler
related words latecomer; drone, idler, lazybones, loafer, lounger, slouch, slug, sluggard; delayer, procrastinator
near antonyms go-getter, hustler, scrambler; hurrier, rusher, speeder
antonyms speedster

sludge *n* soft wet earth — see MUD

sludgy *adj* full of or covered with soft wet earth — see MUDDY 1

[1]**slug** *n* a hard strike with a part of the body or an instrument — see [1]BLOW

[2]**slug** *n* **1** a lazy person — see LAZYBONES
2 the portion of a serving of a beverage that is swallowed at one time — see DRINK 2

slug *vb* to deliver a blow to (someone or something) usually in a strong vigorous manner — see HIT 1

sluggard *n* a lazy person — see LAZYBONES

sluggish *adj* **1** moving or proceeding at less than the normal, desirable, or required speed — see SLOW 1
2 slow to move or act — see INACTIVE 1

sluggishly *adv* at a pace that is less than usual, desirable, or expected — see SLOW

sluice *vb* to pour liquid over or through in order to cleanse — see FLUSH 1

slumber *n* a natural periodic loss of consciousness during which the body restores itself — see SLEEP 1

slumber *vb* **1** be in a state of sleep — see SLEEP 1
2 to sleep lightly or briefly — see NAP 1

slumberer *n* one who sleeps — see SLEEPER

slumbering *adj* being in a state of suspended consciousness — see ASLEEP 1

slumbering *n* a natural periodic loss of consciousness during which the body restores itself — see SLEEP 1

slumberous *or* **slumbrous** *adj* **1** desiring or needing sleep — see SLEEPY 1
2 tending to cause sleep — see HYPNOTIC

slump *n* a period of decreased economic activity — see DEPRESSION 1

slur *n* an act or expression showing scorn and usually intended to hurt another's feelings — see INSULT

slur (over) *vb* to fail to give proper attention to — see NEGLECT 1

slurp *vb* to swallow in liquid form — see DRINK 1

slush *n* **1** language, behavior, or ideas that are absurd and contrary to good sense — see NONSENSE 1
2 soft wet earth — see MUD

slushy *adj* full of or covered with soft wet earth — see MUDDY 1

sly *adj* **1** clever at attaining one's ends by indirect and often deceptive means — see ARTFUL 1
2 given to acting in secret and to concealing one's intentions — see SNEAKY 1
3 tending to or exhibiting reckless playfulness — see MISCHIEVOUS 1

slyness *n* skill in achieving one's ends through indirect, subtle, or underhanded means — see CUNNING 1

smack *n* a hard strike with a part of the body or an instrument — see [1]BLOW

smack *vb* to deliver a blow to (someone or something) usually in a strong vigorous manner — see HIT 1

smack–dab *adv* as stated or indicated without the slightest difference — see EXACTLY 1

small *adj* **1** of a size that is less than average <a *small* cat who never weighed more than five pounds>
synonyms bantam, diminutive, dinky, dwarf, dwarfish, fine, little, pint-size (*or* pint-sized), pocket, pocket-size (*also* pocket-sized), puny, pygmy, slight, smallish, undersized
related words petite; scrubby, stunted; bitty, inappreciable, infinitesimal, micro, microscopic (*also* microscopical), midget, miniature, miniaturized, minute, teeny, teeny-weeny, tiny, wee; underweight; meager (*or* meagre), niggardly, poor, scant, scanty, scarce, skimpy, slender, slim, spare, sparse, stingy; deficient, inadequate, insufficient, lacking, wanting
near antonyms bulky, hefty, hulking, massive, voluminous; cavernous, colossal, elephantine, enormous, giant, gigantic, gross, Herculean, heroic, huge, immense, jumbo, mammoth, monolithic, monstrous, monumental, prodigious, staggering, stupendous, tremendous, vast; abundant, ample, appreciable, bountiful, copious, generous, healthy, liberal, plenteous, plentiful; fat, thick; broad, wide; boundless, cosmic, immeasurable, infinite; adequate, enough, sufficient
antonyms big, bumper, considerable, goodly, good-sized, grand, great, handsome, king-size (*or* king-sized), large, largish, outsize (*also* outsized), oversize (*or* oversized), sizable (*or* sizeable), substantial, super, whacking, whopping
2 small in degree — see REMOTE 1
3 lacking importance — see UNIMPORTANT
4 not broad or open in views or opinions — see NARROW 2

small arm *n* a portable weapon from which a shot is discharged by gunpowder — see GUN 1

smaller *adj* having not so great importance or rank as another — see LESSER

small–fry *adj* lacking importance — see UNIMPORTANT

smallish *adj* of a size that is less than average — see SMALL 1

small–minded *adj* **1** unwilling to grant other people social rights or to accept other viewpoints — see INTOLERANT 2
2 not broad or open in views or opinions — see NARROW 2

smallness *n* the quality or state of being little in size ⟨my grandmother was surprised by the *smallness* of the latest electronic devices⟩
synonyms diminutiveness, fineness, littleness, puniness, slightness
related words minuteness, tininess; meagerness, poorness, scantiness, scarceness, scarcity, skimpiness, slenderness, slimness, spareness, sparseness, stinginess; deficiency, inadequacy
near antonyms enormity, enormousness, grossness, hugeness, immenseness, immensity, stupendousness; extensiveness, vastness; excessiveness, extravagance, extremeness, immoderacy; abundance, ampleness, bountifulness, copiousness, healthiness, liberality; adequacy, sufficiency; heaviness, heftiness, weightiness; bulkiness, massiveness, voluminousness
antonyms bigness, grandness, greatness, largeness, magnitude

small talk *n* friendly, informal conversation or an instance of this — see CHAT

smart *adj* **1** being strikingly neat and trim in style or appearance ⟨dressed in their *smart* new uniforms, the cadets proudly paraded around the grounds of the military school⟩
synonyms dapper, natty, sharp, spruce
related words dressy, elegant, formal; neat, orderly, tidy; fashionable, modish, stylish; careful, fastidious, fussy, meticulous; clean, immaculate, spotless
near antonyms messy, untidy; shabby, sleazy; dingy, dirty, filthy, foul, grimy, grubby, nasty; dowdy, inelegant, unfashionable, unstylish
antonyms sloppy, slovenly
2 being in the latest or current fashion — see STYLISH
3 causing intense mental or physical distress — see SHARP 2
4 given to or marked by mature intelligent humor — see WITTY
5 making light of something usually regarded as serious or sacred — see FLIPPANT
6 having or showing a practical cleverness or judgment — see SHREWD
7 having or showing quickness of mind — see INTELLIGENT 1
8 having a wide and refined knowledge of the world especially from personal experience — see WORLDLY-WISE

smart *n* a sharp unpleasant sensation usually felt in some specific part of the body — see PAIN 1

smart *vb* to feel or cause physical pain — see HURT 1

smart aleck *n* a person who likes to show off in a clever but annoying way ⟨some *smart aleck* in the audience kept shouting clever insults at the speaker⟩
synonyms smarty (*or* smartie), wiseacre, wise guy
related words know-it-all; wisecracker; hotshot, show-off

smart–alecky *or* **smart–aleck** *adj* **1** making light of something usually regarded as serious or sacred — see FLIPPANT
2 marked by the use of wit that is intended to cause hurt feelings — see SARCASTIC

smarting *adj* **1** causing intense discomfort to one's skin — see CUTTING 1
2 causing intense mental or physical distress — see SHARP 2

smartly *adv* in a strikingly neat and trim manner ⟨the *smartly* dressed scouts marched at the head of the Memorial Day parade⟩
synonyms dashingly, nattily, sharply, sprucely
related words neatly, orderly, tidily, trimly; elegantly, fashionably, modishly, stylishly, swankily; carefully, fastidiously, fussily, meticulously; cleanly, immaculately, spotlessly
near antonyms dowdily, inelegantly, unstylishly; slatternly; messily, untidily; shabbily, sleazily; dingily, dirtily, filthily, foully, grubbily, nastily
antonyms sloppily, slovenly

smarty *or* **smartie** *n* a person who likes to show off in a clever but annoying way — see SMART ALECK

smash *n* **1** a forceful coming together of two things — see IMPACT 1
2 the violent coming together of two bodies into destructive contact — see CRASH 1
3 a hard strike with a part of the body or an instrument — see [1]BLOW
4 a loud explosive sound — see CLAP 1
5 a person or thing that is successful — see HIT 1

smash *vb* **1** to cause to break with violence and much noise ⟨deliberately *smashed* a glass against the brick fireplace⟩
synonyms crash, shatter
related words bust, fracture, fragment; bash, demolish, destroy, pulverize, ruin, wreck; shiver, splinter, split; crack, crunch, crush, snap
2 to cause to break open or into pieces by or as if by an explosive — see BLAST 1
3 to bring to a complete end the physical soundness, existence, or usefulness of — see DESTROY 1
4 to come into usually forceful contact with something — see HIT 2

smashup *n* the violent coming together of two bodies into destructive contact — see CRASH 1

smattering *n* a small number — see FEW

smear *vb* **1** to rub an oily or sticky substance over ⟨the toddler gleefully *smeared* her hair and face with maple syrup⟩
synonyms anoint, bedaub, besmear, daub
related words coat, paint, plaster; grease, oil; gum, lard, pitch, tar; begrime, besmirch, blacken, dirty, foul, grime, mire, muddy, smirch, smudge, soil, stain, sully
2 to make untrue and harmful statements about — see SLANDER

smearing *n* the making of false statements that damage another's reputation — see SLANDER

smell *n* the quality of a thing that makes it perceptible to the sense organs in the nose ⟨the *smell* of vanilla is supposed to be very soothing⟩
synonyms odor, redolence, scent, sniff
related words whiff; aroma, bouquet, fragrance, perfume; ambrosia, lusciousness, savor, savoriness, spice, tang; acridness, fetidness, foulness, noisomeness, rancidity, rankness, stench, stink; incense, musk

smell *vb* **1** to become aware of by means of the sense organs in the nose ⟨we *smelled* the aroma of freshly baked cookies as soon as we walked in the house⟩
synonyms nose, scent, sniff, whiff
related words breathe, drink (in), inhale
2 to have a vague awareness of — see FEEL 1
smelly *adj* having an unpleasant smell — see MALODOROUS
smidgen *also* **smidgeon** *or* **smidgin** *n* a very small amount — see PARTICLE 1
smile *vb* **1** to express an emotion (as amusement) by curving the lips upward ⟨he *smiled* in pleasure when he saw the giant sign welcoming him home⟩
synonyms beam, grin
related words laugh, simper; smirk, sneer
near antonyms grimace; frown, glare, glower, scowl
2 to express scornful amusement by means of facial contortions — see SNEER
smirch *n* a mark of guilt or disgrace — see STAIN 1
smirch *vb* **1** to make dirty — see DIRTY
2 to reduce to a lower standing in one's own eyes or in others' eyes — see HUMBLE
smite *vb* to deliver a blow to (someone or something) usually in a strong vigorous manner — see HIT 1
smog *n* an atmospheric condition in which suspended particles in the air rob it of its transparency — see HAZE 1
smoggy *adj* filled with or dimmed by fine particles (as of dust or water) in suspension — see HAZY 1
smooch *vb* to touch one another with the lips as a sign of love — see KISS 1
smooth *adj* **1** having or showing very polished and worldly manners — see SUAVE
2 involving minimal difficulty or effort — see EASY 1
3 having a surface without bends, breaks, or irregularities — see LEVEL
smooth *vb* **1** to free from obstruction or difficulty — see EASE 1
2 to make free from breaks, curves, or bumps — see EVEN 1
3 to make smooth or glossy usually by repeatedly applying surface pressure — see POLISH
smoothly *adv* without difficulty — see EASILY
smother *vb* **1** to be or cause to be killed by lack of breathable air ⟨you should never play inside discarded appliances because you could become trapped and *smother*⟩
synonyms choke, stifle, strangle, suffocate
related words garrote (*or* garotte), throttle; asphyxiate; drown
near antonyms breathe, exhale, expire, inhale, inspire
2 to refrain from openly showing or uttering — see SUPPRESS 2
smudge *vb* to make dirty — see DIRTY
smug *adj* having too high an opinion of oneself — see CONCEITED
smugness *n* an often unjustified feeling of being pleased with oneself or with one's situation or achievements — see COMPLACENCE
smut *n* foul matter that mars the purity or cleanliness of something — see FILTH 1
smuttiness *n* the quality or state of being obscene — see OBSCENITY 1
smutty *adj* **1** depicting or referring to sexual matters in a way that is unacceptable in polite society — see OBSCENE 1
2 not clean — see DIRTY 1
snag *n* a danger or difficulty that is hidden or not easily recognized — see PITFALL 1
snail *n* someone who moves slowly or more slowly than others — see SLOWPOKE
snake *n* **1** a limbless reptile with a long body ⟨*snakes* are cold-blooded, so they regulate their body temperature by alternately basking in sunlight and seeking shade⟩
synonyms serpent, viper
related words adder, anaconda, asp, blacksnake, boa, bull snake, bushmaster, cobra, constrictor, copperhead, coral snake, cottonmouth moccasin, diamondback rattlesnake, fer-de-lance, garter snake, glass snake, gopher snake, green snake, hognose snake, indigo snake, king cobra, king snake, krait, mamba, milk snake, pit viper, puff adder, python, racer, rat snake, rattlesnake, sea serpent, sidewinder, water moccasin, water snake
2 a person whose behavior is offensive to others — see JERK 1
snake *vb* **1** to move about in a sly or secret manner — see SNEAK 1
2 to move slowly with the body close to the ground — see CRAWL 1
snap *adj* **1** involving minimal difficulty or effort — see EASY 1
2 made or done without previous thought or preparation — see EXTEMPORANEOUS
snap *n* **1** a loud explosive sound — see CLAP 1
2 a picture created from an image recorded on a light-sensitive surface by a camera — see PHOTOGRAPH
3 active strength of body or mind — see VIGOR 1
4 a weather condition marked by low temperatures — see COLD
5 a very small amount — see PARTICLE 1
6 something that is easy to do — see CINCH
snap *vb* **1** to speak sharply or irritably ⟨the shopkeeper finally *snapped* at one customer who couldn't seem to make up his mind⟩
synonyms bark, snarl
related words shout, yell; blow up, explode
2 to break suddenly with an explosive sound — see CRACK 1
3 to take a photograph of — see PHOTOGRAPH
snap (up) *vb* to take physical control or possession of (something) suddenly or forcibly — see CATCH 1
snapback *n* the process or period of gradually regaining one's health and strength — see CONVALESCENCE
snap back *vb* **1** to become healthy and strong again after illness or weakness — see CONVALESCE
2 to regain a former or normal state — see RECOVER 2
snappily *adv* with great speed — see FAST 1
snappish *adj* easily irritated or annoyed — see IRRITABLE
snappy *adj* **1** being in the latest or current fashion — see STYLISH
2 easily irritated or annoyed — see IRRITABLE
3 having a low or subnormal temperature — see COLD 1
4 having much high-spirited energy and movement — see LIVELY 1

5 moving, proceeding, or acting with great speed — see FAST 1

snapshot *n* a picture created from an image recorded on a light-sensitive surface by a camera — see PHOTOGRAPH

snare *n* **1** a device or scheme for capturing another by surprise — see TRAP 1
2 something that catches and holds — see WEB 1

snare *vb* **1** to catch or hold as if in a net — see ENTANGLE 2
2 to take physical control or possession of (something) suddenly or forcibly — see CATCH 1

[1]**snarl** *vb* to speak sharply or irritably — see SNAP 1

[2]**snarl** *vb* to twist together into a usually confused mass — see ENTANGLE 1

snatch *vb* to take physical control or possession of (something) suddenly or forcibly — see CATCH 1

snatching *n* an instance of theft — see THEFT 2

snazzy *adj* attractively eye-catching in style — see JAZZY 1

sneak *adj* undertaken or done so as to escape being observed or known by others — see SECRET 1

sneak *n* someone who acts in a sly and secret manner ⟨"Why, you little *sneak*," Mom exclaimed, "you made my birthday present right under my nose!"⟩
synonyms lurker, skulker
related words skunk, snake; sharper, slicker, swindler; stalker

sneak *vb* **1** to move about in a sly or secret manner ⟨the little kids *sneak* around upstairs when they're supposed to be in bed⟩
synonyms lurk, mouse, pussyfoot, skulk, slide, slink, slip, snake, steal
related words crawl, creep, edge, inch, worm; pad, tiptoe
2 to introduce in a gradual, secret, or clever way — see INSINUATE

sneakiness *n* skill in achieving one's ends through indirect, subtle, or underhanded means — see CUNNING 1

sneaking *adj* **1** given to acting in secret and to concealing one's intentions — see SNEAKY 1
2 undertaken or done so as to escape being observed or known by others — see SECRET 1

sneaky *adj* **1** given to acting in secret and to concealing one's intentions ⟨the *sneaky* little girl was clearly up to something⟩
synonyms furtive, shady, shifty, slippery, sly, sneaking, stealthy
related words devious, guileful; close, close-mouthed, reticent, secretive; clandestine, covert, dark; deceitful, deceiving, deceptive, tricky, underhand, underhanded; crooked, dishonest, double-dealing, two-faced; lying, mendacious, untrustworthy, untruthful; insidious, perfidious, treacherous
near antonyms aboveboard, forthright, straightforward; candid, frank, open, plain; honest, trustworthy, truthful
2 undertaken or done so as to escape being observed or known by others — see SECRET 1

sneer *vb* to express scornful amusement by means of facial contortions ⟨the most popular girl in school *sneered* every time she saw the "nerds"⟩
synonyms laugh, smile, snicker, snigger
related words sniff, snort; catcall, hoot, insult, jeer, mock, ridicule; decry, despise, disdain; scorn

snicker *n* an explosive sound that is a sign of amusement — see LAUGH 1

snicker *vb* to express scornful amusement by means of facial contortions — see SNEER

snide *adj* not following or in accordance with standards of honor and decency — see IGNOBLE 2

sniff *n* the quality of a thing that makes it perceptible to the sense organs in the nose — see SMELL

sniff *vb* to become aware of by means of the sense organs in the nose — see SMELL 1

sniff (at) *vb* to show contempt for — see SCORN 1

snigger *n* an explosive sound that is a sign of amusement — see LAUGH 1

snigger *vb* to express scornful amusement by means of facial contortions — see SNEER

snip *vb* to make (as hair) shorter with or as if with the use of shears — see CLIP

snippet *n* a very small piece — see BIT 1

snippy *adj* **1** being or characterized by direct, brief, and potentially rude speech or manner — see BLUNT 1
2 easily irritated or annoyed — see IRRITABLE

[1]**snitch** *vb* to give information (as to the authorities) about another's improper or unlawful activities — see SQUEAL 1

[2]**snitch** *vb* to take (something) without right and with an intent to keep — see STEAL 1

snitcher *n* a person who provides secret information about another's wrongdoing — see INFORMER

snoop *vb* to interest oneself in what is not one's concern — see INTERFERE

snoopy *adj* **1** interested in what is not one's own business — see CURIOUS 1
2 thrusting oneself where one is not welcome or invited — see INTRUSIVE

snooze *n* a short sleep — see NAP

snooze *vb* **1** be in a state of sleep — see SLEEP 1
2 to sleep lightly or briefly — see [1]NAP 1

snoozing *n* a natural periodic loss of consciousness during which the body restores itself — see SLEEP 1

snort *n* **1** a vocal sound made to express scorn or disapproval — see CATCALL
2 the portion of a serving of a beverage that is swallowed at one time — see DRINK 2

snow *vb* to cause to believe what is untrue — see DECEIVE

snowball *vb* to become greater in extent, volume, amount, or number — see INCREASE 2

snow under *vb* **1** to defeat by a large margin — see WHIP 2
2 to subject to incapacitating emotional or mental stress — see OVERWHELM 1

snub *n* treatment that is deliberately unfriendly — see COLD SHOULDER

snub *vb* **1** to deliberately ignore or treat rudely ⟨the snob in town always *snubbed* anyone she thought was beneath her⟩
synonyms cold-shoulder, cut, slight
related words ostracize; brush (aside *or* off), disdain, rebuff, reject, repulse; disregard, forget, neglect, overlook, overpass, pass over, shrug off
2 to show contempt for — see SCORN 1

snuff (out) *vb* **1** to cause to cease burning — see EXTINGUISH 1
2 to destroy all traces of — see ANNIHILATE 1
3 to put a stop to (something) by the use of force — see QUELL 1

snug *adj* **1** being clean and in good order — see NEAT 1
2 providing physical comfort — see COMFORTABLE 1
3 enjoying physical comfort — see COMFORTABLE 2
4 firmly positioned in place and difficult to dislodge — see TIGHT 2
5 providing safety — see SAFE 2

snug *vb* to sit or recline comfortably or cozily — see SNUGGLE 1

snuggle *vb* **1** to sit or recline comfortably or cozily ⟨it's particularly nice to *snuggle* next to the fire on a snowy day⟩
synonyms cuddle, curl up, nestle, snug
related words huddle
2 to lie close — see NUZZLE

so *adj* being in agreement with the truth or a fact or a standard — see CORRECT 1

so *adv* **1** for this or that reason — see THEREFORE
2 in like manner — see ALSO 1
3 to a great degree — see VERY 1

soak *n* a person who makes a habit of getting drunk — see DRUNK 1

soak *vb* **1** to wet thoroughly with liquid ⟨we ran for home as soon as the rain started, but our clothes still ended up *soaked*⟩
synonyms drench, drown, impregnate, saturate, sop, souse, steep
related words marinate; presoak; dip, immerse, inundate, submerge; bathe, douse, wash, water, wet; infiltrate, penetrate, permeate
near antonyms dehydrate, dry; drain, empty, void
antonyms wring (out)
2 to charge (someone) too much for goods or services — see OVERCHARGE 1
3 to make wet — see WET

soak (up) *vb* to take in (something liquid) through small openings — see ABSORB 1

soaked *adj* containing, covered with, or thoroughly penetrated by water — see WET

soaking *adj* containing, covered with, or thoroughly penetrated by water — see WET

soap *n* a substance used for cleaning — see CLEANER

soar *n* the act or an instance of rising or climbing up — see ASCENT 1

soar *vb* **1** to move or extend upward — see ASCEND
2 to move through the air with or as if with outstretched wings — see FLY 1
3 to rise abruptly and rapidly — see SKYROCKET

sob *vb* to shed tears often while making meaningless sounds as a sign of pain or distress — see CRY 1

sober *adj* **1** not having one's mind affected by alcohol ⟨it's important to stay *sober* if you're going to be driving a car⟩
synonyms clearheaded, straight
related words abstemious, abstinent, dry, temperate
near antonyms alcoholic
antonyms befuddled, dissipated, drunk, drunken, high, inebriate, inebriated, intoxicated, loaded [*slang*], soused, tipsy
2 based on sound reasoning or information — see GOOD 1
3 not joking or playful in mood or manner — see SERIOUS 1

soberness *n* a mental state free of jesting or trifling — see EARNESTNESS

sobriety *n* a mental state free of jesting or trifling — see EARNESTNESS

sobriquet *also* **soubriquet** *n* a descriptive or familiar name given instead of or in addition to the one belonging to an individual — see NICKNAME

sociability *n* the quality or state of being social ⟨her *sociability* was called into question when she said she hated parties⟩
synonyms conviviality, gregariousness
related words amiability, friendliness, neighborliness; camaraderie, companionship, fellowship; boldness, brashness, extroversion (*or* extraversion), forwardness, immodesty
near antonyms bashfulness, coyness, diffidence, shyness, timidity, timidness; introversion; modesty

sociable *adj* **1** likely to seek or enjoy the company of others — see CONVIVIAL
2 showing a natural kindness and courtesy especially in social situations — see GRACIOUS 1

social *adj* likely to seek or enjoy the company of others — see CONVIVIAL

socialize *vb* to take part in social activities ⟨he likes to *socialize* with his coworkers after work ends⟩
synonyms associate, fraternize, hobnob, mingle, mix
phrases rub elbows, rub shoulders
near antonyms avoid, eschew, shun; slight, snub

society *n* **1** a group of persons formally joined together for some common interest — see ASSOCIATION 2
2 human beings in general — see PEOPLE 1
3 the feeling of closeness and friendship that exists between companions — see COMPANIONSHIP
4 the way people live at a particular time and place — see CIVILIZATION 1

sock *n* **1** a close-fitting covering for the foot and leg — see STOCKING
2 a hard strike with a part of the body or an instrument — see [1]BLOW

sock *vb* to deliver a blow to (someone or something) usually in a strong vigorous manner — see HIT 1

sod *n* the land of one's birth, residence, or citizenship — see COUNTRY 1

sodality *n* a group of persons formally joined together for some common interest — see ASSOCIATION 2

sodden *adj* containing, covered with, or thoroughly penetrated by water — see WET

sofa *n* a long upholstered piece of furniture designed for several sitters — see COUCH

soft *adj* **1** not loud in pitch or volume ⟨*soft* music played in the background while we ate⟩
synonyms dull, low, quiet
related words dead, silent, still; dreamy, peaceful, restful, soothing, tranquil; muffled, muted, softened, toned (down)
near antonyms brazen, dinning, discordant, noisy, obstreperous, raucous, rip-roaring, vociferous; grating, harsh, shrill, strident
antonyms blaring, blasting, booming, clamorous, clangorous, deafening, earsplitting, loud, piercing, resounding, ringing, roaring, sonorous, stentorian, thunderous
2 smooth or delicate in appearance or feel ⟨I like this sweater the best because it is so *soft* and comfortable⟩

synonyms cottony, downy, satin, satiny, silken, silky, velvety
related words creamy; delicate, fine, slick, smooth
near antonyms bumpy, lumpy, pebbly; broken, jagged, ragged, rugged; grainy, granular, gritty
antonyms coarse, harsh, rough, scratchy
3 giving easily to the touch <*soft* mattresses make it very easy to fall asleep, but they have a tendency to get lumpy>
synonyms flabby, mushy, pulpy, spongy, squashy, squishy
related words unhardened; doughy, fleshy; droopy, flaccid, floppy, lank, limp, slack, yielding; compressible, malleable, pliable, pliant, workable
near antonyms inflexible, resilient, rigid, stiff, tense; resistant, sound, strong, sturdy, tough, unyielding; hardened, indurated, tempered
antonyms firm, hard, solid
4 involving minimal difficulty or effort — see EASY 1
5 lacking bodily strength — see WEAK 1
6 lacking strength of will or character — see WEAK 2
7 not harsh or stern especially in manner, nature, or effect — see GENTLE 1
8 providing physical comfort — see COMFORTABLE 1

soften *vb* **1** to diminish the physical strength of — see WEAKEN 1
2 to lessen the shock of — see CUSHION

softened *adj* lacking bodily strength — see WEAK 1

softhearted *adj* having or marked by sympathy and consideration for others — see HUMANE 1

softheartedness *n* the capacity for feeling for another's unhappiness or misfortune — see HEART 1

softness *n* the quality or state of lacking strength of will or character — see WEAKNESS 2

soft–soap *vb* **1** to get (someone) to do something by gentle urging, special attention, or flattery — see COAX
2 to praise too much — see FLATTER 1

soft soap *n* excessive praise — see FLATTERY

softy *or* **softie** *n* a person lacking in physical strength — see WEAKLING 1

soggy *adj* containing, covered with, or thoroughly penetrated by water — see WET

soil *n* **1** foul matter that mars the purity or cleanliness of something — see FILTH 1
2 the loose surface material in which plants naturally grow — see DIRT 1
3 the solid part of our planet's surface as distinguished from the sea and air — see EARTH 2

soil *vb* to make dirty — see DIRTY

soiled *adj* not clean — see DIRTY 1

sojourn *n* a temporary residing as another's guest — see VISIT 1

sojourn *vb* to reside as a temporary guest — see VISIT 2

solace *n* **1** a feeling of ease from grief or trouble — see COMFORT 1
2 the giving of hope and strength in times of grief, distress, or suffering — see CONSOLATION 1

solace *vb* to ease the grief or distress of — see COMFORT 1

solacing *n* the giving of hope and strength in times of grief, distress, or suffering — see CONSOLATION 1

solar plexus *n* the part of the body between the chest and the pelvis — see STOMACH

soldier *n* a person engaged in military service <one of the goals of war is to keep as many *soldiers* as possible from being killed>
synonyms fighter, legionary, legionnaire, man-at-arms, regular, serviceman, warrior
related words servicewoman; cavalier, cuirassier, dragoon, trooper; dogface, doughboy, footman, foot soldier, infantryman; commando, marine, ranger; artilleryman, musketeer, rifleman; archer, lancer, spearman; Confederate, Continental, Federal, GI, guardsman, Rough Rider; guerilla, irregular, partisan; combatant, noncombatant; mercenary, soldier of fortune; veteran, war-horse; conscript, draftee, recruit; reservist
antonyms civilian

soldierly *adj* of, relating to, or suitable for war or a warrior — see MARTIAL 1

sole *adj* **1** belonging only to the one person, unit, or group named <the landowner has *sole* rights to the property, so he can do whatever he wants to with it>
synonyms exclusive, single, unshared
related words proprietary
near antonyms joint, mutual, shared
antonyms nonexclusive
2 being the one or ones of a class with no other members — see ONLY 2

solecism *n* a socially improper or unsuitable act or remark — see IMPROPRIETY 2

solely *adv* **1** for nothing other than <I fight *solely* for my country, not for money!>
synonyms alone, exclusively, just, only, simply
related words mainly, mostly, primarily
near antonyms additionally, also, likewise
2 without aid or support — see ALONE 1

solemn *adj* **1** having or showing a serious and reserved manner — see DIGNIFIED
2 not joking or playful in mood or manner — see SERIOUS 1

solemnity *n* **1** a mental state free of jesting or trifling — see EARNESTNESS
2 an oft-repeated action or series of actions performed in accordance with tradition or a set of rules — see RITE

solicit *vb* **1** to go around and approach (people) with a request for opinions or information — see CANVASS
2 to make a request for — see ASK (FOR) 1
3 to make a request of — see ASK 2
4 to make a request to (someone) in an earnest or urgent manner — see BEG

solicitation *n* an earnest request — see PLEA 1

soliciting *adj* asking humbly — see SUPPLIANT

solicitor *n* **1** one that tries to get a person to give in to a desire — see TEMPTER
2 one who asks earnestly for a favor or gift — see SUPPLICANT

solicitous *adj* **1** given to or made with heedful anticipation of the needs and happiness of others — see THOUGHTFUL 1
2 showing urgent desire or interest — see EAGER

solicitude *n* an uneasy state of mind usually over the possibility of an anticipated misfortune or trouble — see ANXIETY 1

solid *adj* **1** based on sound reasoning or information — see GOOD 1
2 having a consistency that does not easily yield to pressure — see FIRM 2
3 having or consisting of a single color — see MONOCHROMATIC

4 not showing weakness or uncertainty — see FIRM 1
5 worthy of one's trust — see DEPENDABLE
solidify *vb* **1** to become physically firm or solid — see HARDEN 1
2 to take on a definite form — see FORM 1
solidity *n* worthiness as the recipient of another's trust or confidence — see RELIABILITY
solidness *n* worthiness as the recipient of another's trust or confidence — see RELIABILITY
solitariness *n* the state of being alone or kept apart from others — see ISOLATION
solitary *adj* **1** being the one or ones of a class with no other members — see ONLY 2
2 not being in the company of others — see ALONE 1
solitary *n* a person who lives away from others — see RECLUSE
solitude *n* the state of being alone or kept apart from others — see ISOLATION
solo *adj* not being in the company of others — see ALONE 1
solon *n* a member of an organized body of persons having the authority to make laws — see LEGISLATOR
soluble *adj* capable of having the reason for or cause of determined — see SOLVABLE
solution *n* something attained by mental effort and especially by computation — see ANSWER 2
solvable *adj* capable of having the reason for or cause of determined ⟨I'm sure that the mystery of what happened to the missing pizza is *solvable*⟩
synonyms answerable, explainable, explicable, resolvable, soluble
related words analyzable, decipherable; feasible, workable
near antonyms impossible
antonyms inexplicable, insoluble, unexplainable, unsolvable
solve *vb* to find an answer for through reasoning ⟨it took me half an hour to *solve* the logic puzzle⟩
synonyms answer, break, crack, dope (out), figure out, puzzle (out), resolve, riddle, unravel, work, work out
related words clear (up), iron out, straighten (out), unscramble, untangle, untie; divine, guess; decipher, decode
somatic *adj* of or relating to the human body — see PHYSICAL 1
somber *or* **sombre** *adj* **1** being without light or without much light — see DARK 1
2 causing or marked by an atmosphere lacking in cheer — see GLOOMY 1
some *adj* known but not named — see CERTAIN 1
some *adv* very close to but not completely — see ALMOST
somebody *n* a person who is widely known and usually much talked about — see CELEBRITY 1
someday *adv* at a later time — see YET 1
something *adv* **1** to a great degree — see VERY 1
2 to some degree or extent — see FAIRLY
something *n* one that has a real and independent existence — see ENTITY
sometime *adj* having been such at some previous time — see FORMER
sometime *adv* at a later time — see YET 1
sometimes *adv* on some occasions ⟨*sometimes* I like to go skiing, and *sometimes* I prefer to stay inside where it's warm⟩
synonyms now, occasionally
related words intermittently, periodically; infrequently, rarely, seldom; irregularly, sporadically
phrases at times, from time to time, now and then, once in a while
near antonyms frequently, often, oftentimes (*or* ofttimes); commonly, ordinarily, regularly, usually; always, constantly, invariably; continually, continuously, incessantly, perpetually, unceasingly, uninterruptedly; endlessly, ever, interminably
somewhat *adv* to some degree or extent — see FAIRLY
somnolence *n* the quality or state of desiring or needing sleep — see SLEEPINESS
somnolent *adj* desiring or needing sleep — see SLEEPY 1
song *n* **1** a short musical composition for the human voice often with instrumental accompaniment ⟨she sang a short *song* for the talent show⟩
synonyms ballad, ditty, jingle, lay, lyric, vocal
related words anthem, canticle, carol, chorale, hymn, noel, psalm, spiritual; dirge, lament, requiem, threnody; hallelujah, paean; aria, barcarole (*or* barcarolle), blues, cantata, chantey (*or* chanty), chorus, croon, descant, glee, lullaby, madrigal, motet, part-song, pop, rocker, round, roundelay, serenade, troll
2 a composition using rhythm and often rhyme to create a lyrical effect — see POEM
3 a rhythmic series of musical tones arranged to give a pleasing effect — see MELODY
4 a very small sum of money — see MITE 1
5 writing that uses rhythm, vivid language, and often rhyme to provoke an emotional response — see POETRY 1
songster *n* one who sings — see SINGER
songwriter *n* a person who writes musical compositions — see COMPOSER
sonny *n* a male person who has not yet reached adulthood — see BOY
sonorous *adj* **1** marked by a high volume of sound — see LOUD 1
2 marked by conspicuously full and rich sounds or tones — see RESONANT
soon *adv* **1** at or within a short time — see SHORTLY 2
2 by choice or preference — see RATHER 1
3 with great speed — see FAST 1
soothe *vb* **1** to ease the grief or distress of — see COMFORT 1
2 to free from distress or disturbance — see CALM 1
3 to make more bearable or less severe — see HELP 2
soothing *adj* **1** tending to calm the emotions and relieve stress ⟨the *soothing* music eventually put the entire yoga class in the proper mood⟩
synonyms calming, comforting, dreamy, lulling, narcotic, pacifying, quieting, relaxing, sedative, tranquilizing (*also* tranquillizing)
related words hypnotic, opiate; anesthetic, deadening, depressant, numbing
near antonyms energizing, invigorating, stimulant, stimulating; aggravating, annoying, bothersome, exasperating, galling, grating, irksome, irritating, troublesome, vexing
2 not harsh or stern especially in manner, nature, or effect — see GENTLE 1
soothsayer *n* one who predicts future events or developments — see PROPHET

soothsaying *n* a declaration that something will happen in the future — see PREDICTION
sop *n* something given or promised in order to improperly influence a person's conduct or decision — see BRIBE
sop *vb* to wet thoroughly with liquid — see SOAK 1
sophisticate *n* a person with the outlook, experience, and manners thought to be typical of big city dwellers — see COSMOPOLITAN
sophisticate *vb* to make complex or difficult — see COMPLICATE
sophisticated *adj* **1** having a wide and refined knowledge of the world especially from personal experience — see WORLDLY-WISE
2 having many parts or aspects that are usually interrelated — see COMPLEX 1
3 having or showing very polished and worldly manners — see SUAVE
4 made or done with great care or with much detail — see ELABORATE 1
sophistication *n* the state or quality of having many interrelated parts or aspects — see COMPLEXITY 1
soppy *adj* containing, covered with, or thoroughly penetrated by water — see WET
sorcerer *n* a person skilled in using supernatural forces — see MAGICIAN 1
sorceress *n* a woman believed to have often harmful supernatural powers — see WITCH 1
sorcery *n* the power to control natural forces through supernatural means — see MAGIC 1
sordid *adj* **1** not clean — see DIRTY 1
2 not following or in accordance with standards of honor and decency — see IGNOBLE 2
sore *adj* **1** causing or feeling bodily pain — see PAINFUL 1
2 feeling or showing anger — see ANGRY
3 having or showing deep-seated resentment — see BITTER 1
sorely *adv* with feelings of bitterness or grief — see HARD 2
sorriness *n* deep sadness especially for the loss of someone or something loved — see SORROW
sorrow *n* deep sadness especially for the loss of someone or something loved ⟨he felt great *sorrow* at the loss of his beloved pet⟩
synonyms affliction, anguish, dolefulness, dolor, grief, heartache, heartbreak, sorriness, woe
related words agony, distress, pain, suffering, torment; blues, dejection, depression, desolateness, desolation, despondency, disconsolateness, dispiritedness, distress, doldrums, downheartedness, dreariness, dumps, forlornness, gloom, gloominess, heartsickness, joylessness, melancholy, miserableness, misery, mopes, oppression, sadness, unhappiness, wretchedness; regret, remorse, rue
near antonyms gaiety (*also* gayety), gayness, humor, jollity, joviality, lightheartedness, merriment, merrymaking, mirth, mirthfulness; hopefulness, optimism; enjoyment; content, contentedness
antonyms blessedness, bliss, blissfulness, cheer, cheerfulness, cheeriness, delight, ecstasy, elatedness, elation, euphoria, exhilaration, exuberance, exultation, gladness, gladsomeness, glee, gleefulness, happiness, joy, joyfulness, joyousness, jubilation, pleasure, rapture, rapturousness
sorrow *vb* to feel deep sadness or mental pain — see GRIEVE
sorrowful *adj* **1** expressing or suggesting mourning — see MOURNFUL 1
2 feeling unhappiness — see SAD 1
sorrowfully *adv* with feelings of bitterness or grief — see HARD 2
sorry *adj* **1** arousing or deserving of one's loathing and disgust — see CONTEMPTIBLE 1
2 causing unhappiness — see SAD 2
3 deserving pitying scorn (as for inadequacy) — see PITIFUL 1
4 feeling sorrow for a wrong that one has done — see CONTRITE 1
5 feeling unhappiness — see SAD 1
6 expressing or suggesting mourning — see MOURNING 1
7 deserving of one's pity — see PATHETIC 1
sort *n* **1** a number of persons or things that are grouped together because they have something in common ⟨I prefer jackets with zippers to the *sort* that close with buttons⟩
synonyms breed, class, description, feather, ilk, kind, like, manner, nature, order, type
related words model; sample, specimen; bracket, category, division, family, grade, group, lot, persuasion, rank(s), set
2 a member of the human race — see HUMAN
sort *vb* to arrange or assign according to type — see CLASSIFY 1
sort of *adv* to some degree or extent — see FAIRLY
so–so *adj* of average to below average quality — see MEDIOCRE 1
so–so *adv* in a satisfactory way — see WELL 1
sot *n* a person who makes a habit of getting drunk — see DRUNK 1
sough *vb* to take in and let out a deep audible breath or to make a similar sound — see SIGH
soul *n* **1** an immaterial force within a human being thought to give the body life, energy, and power ⟨many religions teach that the *soul* is immortal⟩
synonyms psyche, spirit
related words life, vitality
near antonyms body, flesh
2 a member of the human race — see HUMAN
3 the quality or qualities that make a thing what it is — see ESSENCE
4 the seat of one's deepest thoughts and emotions — see CORE 1
soulless *adj* having or showing a lack of sympathy or tender feelings — see HARD 1
sound *adj* **1** according to the rules of logic — see LOGICAL 1
2 enjoying health and vigor — see HEALTHY 1
3 marked by the ability to withstand stress without structural damage or distortion — see STABLE 1
sound *n* **1** a narrow body of water between two land masses — see CHANNEL 2
2 range of hearing — see EARSHOT
[1]**sound** *vb* **1** to continue or be repeated in a series of reflected sound waves — see REVERBERATE
2 to give the impression of being — see SEEM
3 to make known (as an idea, emotion, or opinion) — see EXPRESS 1
4 to make known openly or publicly — see ANNOUNCE
[2]**sound** *vb* **1** to measure the depth of (as a body of water) typically with a weighted line ⟨the pilot *sounded* the river to make sure we weren't in any danger of running aground⟩
synonyms fathom, plumb

related words gauge (*also* gage), measure, scale
2 to cast oneself head first into deep water — see DIVE

soundless *adj* mostly or entirely without sound — see SILENT 3

soundness *n* **1** the ability to withstand force or stress without being distorted, dislodged, or damaged — see STABILITY 1
2 the condition of being sound in body — see HEALTH

sound off *vb* to voice one's opinions freely with force — see SPEAK UP

soup *n* an atmospheric condition in which suspended particles in the air rob it of its transparency — see HAZE 1

soupy *adj* **1** filled with or dimmed by fine particles (as of dust or water) in suspension — see HAZY 1
2 having an overly soft liquid consistency — see RUNNY

sour *adj* **1** causing or characterized by the one of the four basic taste sensations that is produced chiefly by acids ⟨the *sour* candy made our mouths all wrinkly inside⟩
synonyms acid, acidic, tart, vinegary
related words dry, soured, unsweetened; pungent, sharp, tangy; astringent, puckery; acetic; hyperacid
near antonyms sweet; bland, smooth
2 not giving pleasure to the mind or senses — see UNPLEASANT

sour *vb* to cause to change from friendly or loving to unfriendly or uncaring — see ESTRANGE

source *n* the beginning part of a stream — see HEADWATER

souring *n* the loss of friendship or affection — see ESTRANGEMENT

souse *n* a person who makes a habit of getting drunk — see DRUNK 1

souse *vb* **1** to make wet — see WET
2 to sink or push (something) briefly into or as if into a liquid — see DIP 1
3 to wet thoroughly with liquid — see SOAK 1

soused *adj* **1** being under the influence of alcohol — see DRUNK
2 containing, covered with, or thoroughly penetrated by water — see WET

souvenir *n* something that serves to keep alive the memory of a person or event — see MEMORIAL

sovereign *adj* **1** coming before all others in importance — see FOREMOST 1
2 not being under the rule or control of another — see FREE 1

sovereign *n* one who rules over a people with a sole, supreme, and usually hereditary authority — see MONARCH

sovereignty *n* **1** the state of being free from the control or power of another — see FREEDOM 1
2 a body of people composed of one or more nationalities usually with its own territory and government — see NATION

sow *vb* **1** to cover by or as if by scattering something over or on — see SCATTER 2
2 to put or set into the ground to grow — see PLANT

spa *n* a building or room used for sports activities and exercising — see GYM

space *n* **1** an extent or area available for or used up by some activity or thing — see ROOM 1
2 an indefinite but usually short period of time — see WHILE 1

space–age *adj* being or involving the latest methods, concepts, information, or styles — see MODERN

spacing *n* the space or amount of space between two points, lines, surfaces, or objects — see DISTANCE

spacious *adj* more than adequate or average in capacity ⟨almost all of the guests were able to fit into the *spacious* living room⟩
synonyms ample, capacious, commodious, roomy
related words broad, wide; big, bulky, considerable, generous, goodly, good-sized, grand, great, handsome, hefty, hulking, king-size (*or* king-sized), large, largish, outsize (*also* outsized), oversize (*or* oversized), sizable (*or* sizeable), substantial, super, voluminous; enormous, immense, vast; expansive, extended, extensive; boundless, limitless, unbounded
near antonyms confined, cramped, limited, narrow, restricted; small, snug, tight, tiny

span *vb* to find out the size, extent, or amount of — see MEASURE

spank *n* a hard strike with a part of the body or an instrument — see [1]BLOW

spanking *adj* having much high-spirited energy and movement — see LIVELY 1

spare *adj* **1** being over what is needed ⟨I had some *spare* time to kill, so I cleaned up my room a bit⟩
synonyms excess, extra, superfluous, supernumerary, surplus
related words accessory, additional, supplemental, supplementary; dispensable, extraneous, gratuitous, needless, nonessential, unessential, unnecessary, unneeded, unwanted
near antonyms inadequate, insufficient, meager, scant, scanty, scarce, short, sparse
2 giving or sharing as little as possible — see STINGY 1
3 having a noticeably small amount of body fat — see THIN 1
4 less plentiful than what is normal, necessary, or desirable — see MEAGER

spare *n* an interchangeable part or piece of equipment that is kept on hand for replacement of an original ⟨first we took the burnt light bulb out, and then we replaced it with the *spare*⟩
synonyms extra, reserve
related words backup, substitute; stock; copy, double, duplicate, replacement
near antonyms archetype, original

spare *vb* to use or give out in stingy amounts ⟨I'll have a banana split and don't *spare* the whipped cream⟩
synonyms scant, skimp (on), stint (on)
related words dole (out), mete (out), portion (out), ration (out); pinch, shortchange
near antonyms lavish, rain

sparing *adj* **1** careful in the management of money or resources — see FRUGAL
2 giving or sharing as little as possible — see STINGY 1

spark *n* a very small amount — see PARTICLE 1

spark *vb* **1** to give off sparks ⟨the broken radio *sparked* and smoked the instant it was plugged in⟩
synonyms scintillate, sparkle
related words flash; burn
2 to cause to function — see ACTIVATE

sparkle *vb* **1** to give off sparks — see SPARK 1
2 to shoot forth bursts of light — see FLASH 1

sparky *adj* having much high-spirited energy and movement — see LIVELY 1
sparse *adj* less plentiful than what is normal, necessary, or desirable — see MEAGER
spasm *n* **1** a painful sudden tightening of a muscle — see CRAMP
2 a sudden intense expression of strong feeling — see OUTBURST 1
spasmodic *adj* lacking in steadiness or regularity of occurrence — see FITFUL
spat *n* an often noisy or angry expression of differing opinions — see ARGUMENT 1
spat *vb* to express different opinions about something often angrily — see ARGUE 2
spate *n* a great flow of water or of something that overwhelms — see FLOOD
spatter *vb* **1** to cause (something liquid or mushy) to move along in sheets — see SPLASH 1
2 to wet or soil by striking with something liquid or mushy — see SPLASH 2
spawn *n* the descendants of a person, animal, or plant — see OFFSPRING
spawn *vb* to be the cause of (a situation, action, or state of mind) — see EFFECT
speak *vb* **1** to express (a thought or emotion) in words — see SAY 1
2 to give a formal often extended talk on a subject — see TALK 1
speak (to *or* with) *vb* to communicate with by means of spoken words — see TALK 1
speaker *n* **1** a person in charge of a meeting — see CHAIR 1
2 a person who speaks for another or for a group — see SPOKESPERSON
speak out *vb* to voice one's opinions freely with force — see SPEAK UP
speak up *vb* to voice one's opinions freely with force <she's never been afraid to *speak up* in class>
synonyms sound off, speak out, spout (off)
related words bawl, call, cry, holler, shout, sing (out), vociferate, yell; articulate, enunciate
phrases speak one's mind
near antonyms hush, suppress; quiet
spear *n* a weapon with a long straight handle and sharp head or blade <the Roman gladiator thrust his *spear* triumphantly into the lion's side>
synonyms javelin, lance, pike, pikestaff, shaft
related words dart, spike; gaff, halberd, harpoon, trident
spear *vb* to penetrate or hold (something) with a pointed object — see IMPALE
spearhead *vb* to serve as leader of — see LEAD 2
special *adj* **1** being the one or ones of a class with no other members — see ONLY 2
2 granted special treatment or attention — see DARLING 1
3 of a particular or exact sort — see EXPRESS 1
speciality *n* something for which a person shows a special talent — see FORTE
specialized *adj* used by or intended for experts in a particular field of knowledge — see TECHNICAL
specialty *n* **1** a region of activity, knowledge, or influence — see FIELD 2
2 something for which a person shows a special talent — see FORTE
species *n* one of the units into which a whole is divided on the basis of a common characteristic — see CLASS 2
specific *adj* **1** of a particular or exact sort — see EXPRESS 1
2 so clearly expressed as to leave no doubt about the meaning — see EXPLICIT
specific *n* a substance or preparation used to treat disease — see MEDICINE
specificity *n* careful thoroughness of detail — see PARTICULARITY 1
specify *vb* **1** to give the rules about (something) clearly and exactly — see PRESCRIBE
2 to make reference to or speak about briefly but specifically — see MENTION 1
specimen *n* **1** a member of the human race — see HUMAN
2 one of a group or collection that shows what the whole is like — see EXAMPLE
specious *adj* tending or having power to deceive — see DECEPTIVE 1
speck *n* **1** a small area that is different (as in color) from the main part — see SPOT 1
2 a very small amount — see PARTICLE 1
3 a very small piece — see BIT 1
speck *vb* to mark with small spots especially unevenly — see SPOT
speckle *n* a small area that is different (as in color) from the main part — see SPOT 1
speckle *vb* to mark with small spots especially unevenly — see SPOT
speckled *adj* marked with spots — see SPOTTED 1
specs *n pl* a pair of lenses set in a frame that is held in place with ear supports and which are usually worn to correct vision — see GLASSES 1
spectacles *n pl* a pair of lenses set in a frame that is held in place with ear supports and which are usually worn to correct vision — see GLASSES 1
specter *or* **spectre** *n* the soul of a dead person thought of especially as appearing to living people — see GHOST
spectrum *n* the distance or extent between possible extremes — see RANGE 3
speculate *vb* to form an opinion from little or no evidence — see GUESS 1
speculation *n* a risky undertaking — see GAMBLE
speculative *adj* existing only as an assumption or speculation — see THEORETICAL 1
speech *n* **1** a usually formal discourse delivered to an audience <the guest of honor gave a short *speech* in appreciation of the award>
synonyms address, declamation, harangue, oration, talk
related words diatribe, rant, tirade; eulogy, panegyric, tribute; keynote address, lecture; homily, sermon; monologue, soliloquy; pitch, presentation, spiel
2 the stock of words, pronunciation, and grammar used by a people as their basic means of communication — see LANGUAGE 1
speechless *adj* **1** deliberately refraining from speech — see SILENT 1
2 unable to speak — see MUTE 1
speechlessness *n* incapacity for or restraint from speaking — see SILENCE 1
speed *n* a high rate of movement or performance <we did our homework with as much *speed* as possible so we could go to the movies>
synonyms celerity, fastness, fleetness, haste, hurry, quickness, rapidity, rapidness, speediness, swiftness, velocity
related words clip, pace, rate, tempo; drive, hustle; acceleration, rush; dispatch, expedition, expeditiousness, promptness
near antonyms languidness, languor, leisureliness,

lethargy, torpor; reluctance; deliberateness, deliberation
antonyms slowness, sluggishness

speed *vb* to proceed or move quickly — see HURRY 2

speed (up) *vb* to cause to move or proceed fast or faster — see HURRY 1

speedboat *n* a boat equipped with a motor — see MOTORBOAT

speedily *adv* with great speed — see FAST 1

speediness *n* a high rate of movement or performance — see SPEED

speedy *adj* moving, proceeding, or acting with great speed — see FAST 1

spell *n* **1** a spoken word or set of words believed to have magic power <the witch cast a *spell* that turned the prince into a toad>
synonyms bewitchment, charm, conjuration, enchantment, incantation
related words curse, hex, jinx; black magic, conjuring, magic, mojo, necromancy, sorcery, voodooism, witchcraft, witchery, wizardry
2 a sudden experiencing of a physical or mental disorder — see ATTACK 2
3 an indefinite but usually short period of time — see WHILE 1

spell *vb* **1** to cast a spell on — see BEWITCH 1
2 to communicate or convey (as an idea) to the mind — see MEAN 1

spellbind *vb* to hold the attention of as if by a spell — see ENTHRALL 1

spellbound *adj* being or appearing to be under a magic spell — see ENCHANTED

spell out *vb* to make plain or understandable — see EXPLAIN 1

spend *vb* **1** to hand over or use up in payment <I always end up *spending* too much money at the mall>
synonyms disburse, expend, give, lay out, pay
related words lavish, rain; blow; squander, waste
near antonyms cache, hoard, save; acquire, earn, make
2 to make complete use of — see DEPLETE
3 to use up carelessly — see WASTE 1

spender *n* someone who carelessly spends money — see PRODIGAL

spendthrift *adj* given to spending money freely or foolishly — see PRODIGAL

spendthrift *n* someone who carelessly spends money — see PRODIGAL

spent *adj* depleted in strength, energy, or freshness — see WEARY 1

spew *vb* **1** to flow out in great quantities or with force — see GUSH 1
2 to throw out or off (something from within) often violently — see ERUPT 1

sphere *n* **1** a more or less round body or mass — see [1]BALL 1
2 a region of activity, knowledge, or influence — see FIELD 2

spherical *adj* having every part of the surface the same distance from the center — see ROUND 1

spice *n* **1** a sweet or pleasant smell — see FRAGRANCE
2 something (as a spice or herb) that adds an agreeable or interesting taste to food — see SEASONING 1

spice *vb* to make more pleasant to the taste by adding something intensely flavored — see SEASON 1

spick-and-span *or* **spic-and-span** *adj* **1** free from dirt or stain — see CLEAN 1
2 recently made and never used before — see NEW 3

spicy *adj* hinting at or intended to call to mind matters regarded as indecent — see SUGGESTIVE 1

spigot *n* a fixture for controlling the flow of a liquid — see FAUCET

spike *vb* to penetrate or hold (something) with a pointed object — see IMPALE

spill *n* the act of going down from an upright position suddenly and involuntarily — see FALL 1

spill *vb* to make known (as information previously kept secret) — see REVEAL 1

spin *n* **1** a rapid turning about on an axis or central point <the ice skater moved into a tight *spin* at the end of her routine>
synonyms gyration, pirouette, reel, revolution, roll, rotation, twirl, wheel, whirl
related words circuit, circulation; coil, curl, curve, spiral, twist; circle, orbit; eddy, swirl
2 a state of mental confusion — see HAZE 2

spin *vb* **1** to move in circles around an axis or center <after *spinning* around three times blindfolded, I tried to pin the tail on the donkey and almost fell over>
synonyms gyrate, pirouette, revolve, roll, rotate, turn, twirl, wheel, whirl
related words coil, curl, curve, round, spiral, twine, twist, wind; circle, orbit
2 to be in a confused state as if from being twirled around <my head *spun* as I contemplated all the possible problems this could cause>
synonyms reel, swim, whirl
near antonyms calm, collect; settle, steady
3 to move (something) in a curved or circular path on or as if on an axis — see TURN 1

spinal column *n* a column of bones supporting the trunk of a vertebrate animal — see SPINE

spindling *adj* being tall, thin and usually loose-jointed — see LANKY

spindly *adj* being tall, thin and usually loose-jointed — see LANKY

spine *n* a column of bones supporting the trunk of a vertebrate animal <he hurt his *spine* in the accident, but the doctor says he'll be walking again in no time>
synonyms backbone, chine, spinal column, vertebral column
related words back, spinal cord, vertebra

spineless *adj* **1** lacking strength of will or character — see WEAK 2
2 having or showing a shameful lack of courage — see COWARDLY

spinelessness *n* **1** the quality or state of lacking strength of will or character — see WEAKNESS 2
2 a shameful lack of courage in the face of danger — see COWARDICE

spin-off *n* something that naturally develops or is developed from something else — see DERIVATIVE

spiny *adj* requiring exceptional skill or caution in performance or handling — see TRICKY

spiral *adj* turning around an axis like the thread of a screw <a *spiral* staircase takes visitors up into the Statue of Liberty>
synonyms coiling, corkscrew, helical, screwlike, winding
related words curving, curling, twisting
near antonyms lineal, linear, straight

spiral *vb* to follow a circular or spiral course — see WIND
spirit *n* **1** an immaterial force within a human being thought to give the body life, energy, and power — see SOUL 1
2 a state of mind dominated by a particular emotion — see MOOD 1
3 the soul of a dead person thought of especially as appearing to living people — see GHOST
4 spirits *pl* a fermented or distilled beverage that can make a person drunk — see ALCOHOL
spirited *adj* **1** marked by a lively display of strong feeling ‹the town meeting featured a *spirited* debate about the proposed ban on skateboarding in the plaza downtown›
synonyms fiery, gingery, high-spirited, mettlesome, peppery, spunky
related words animate, animated, bouncing, bouncy, brisk, energetic, frisky, jaunty, jazzy, peppy, perky, pert, racy, snappy, spanking, sparky, sprightly, springy, vital, vivacious, zippy; ardent, fervent, impassioned, passionate
near antonyms boring, dull, lifeless
antonyms spiritless
2 having much high-spirited energy and movement — see LIVELY 1
spiritless *adj* lacking bodily energy or motivation — see LISTLESS
spiritual *adj* **1** not composed of matter — see IMMATERIAL 1
2 of, relating to, or used in the practice or worship services of a religion — see RELIGIOUS 1
spiritual *n* a religious song — see HYMN
¹spit *n* an area of land that juts out into a body of water — see ²CAPE
²spit *n* **1** something or someone that strongly resembles another — see IMAGE 1
2 the fluid that is secreted into the mouth by certain glands — see SALIVA
spite *n* the desire to cause pain for the satisfaction of doing harm — see MALICE
spiteful *adj* having or showing a desire to cause someone pain or suffering for the sheer enjoyment of it — see HATEFUL
spitefully *adv* in a mean or spiteful manner — see NASTILY
spitefulness *n* the desire to cause pain for the satisfaction of doing harm — see MALICE
spittle *n* the fluid that is secreted into the mouth by certain glands — see SALIVA
spit up *vb* to discharge the contents of the stomach through the mouth — see VOMIT
splash *vb* **1** to cause (something liquid or mushy) to move along in sheets ‹I always *splash* water at my sister when we go to the pool›
synonyms spatter
related words dabble, lap, plash, wash
2 to wet or soil by striking with something liquid or mushy ‹the bus *splashed* us as it passed›
synonyms bespatter, dash, plash, spatter, splatter
related words drench, drown, impregnate, saturate, soak, sop, souse, steep; bathe, douse, wash, water, wet; throw; spray; slop, sprinkle; squirt
3 to flow along or against — see WASH 1
4 to flow in a broken irregular stream — see GURGLE
5 to move with a splashing motion — see SLOSH
splashy *adj* **1** likely to attract attention — see NOTICEABLE
2 attractively eye-catching in style — see JAZZY 1
3 excessively showy — see GAUDY
splatter *vb* to wet or soil by striking with something liquid or mushy — see SPLASH 2
spleen *n* **1** an intense emotional state of displeasure with someone or something — see ANGER
2 the desire to cause pain for the satisfaction of doing harm — see MALICE
splendid *adj* **1** large and impressive in size, grandeur, extent, or conception — see GRAND 1
2 of the very best kind — see EXCELLENT
splendidly *adv* in a pleasing way — see WELL 5
splendor *n* **1** impressiveness of beauty on a large scale — see MAGNIFICENCE
2 the quality or state of having or giving off light — see BRILLIANCE 1
splenetic *adj* having or showing a habitually bad temper — see ILL-TEMPERED
splint *n* a small flat piece separated from a whole — see CHIP 1
splinter *n* a small flat piece separated from a whole — see CHIP 1
splinter *vb* to cut into long slender pieces — see SLIVER
split *adj* disagreeing with each other — see DIVIDED
split *n* **1** an irregular usually narrow break in a surface created by pressure — see CRACK 1
2 the act or process of a whole separating into two or more parts or pieces — see SEPARATION 1
split *vb* to set or force apart — see SEPARATE 1
split second *n* a very small space of time — see INSTANT
splotch *n* a small area that is different (as in color) from the main part — see SPOT 1
splotch *vb* to mark with small spots especially unevenly — see SPOT
splotched *adj* having blotches of two or more colors — see PIED
splotchy *adj* marked with spots — see SPOTTED 1
spoil *n* valuables stolen or taken by force — see LOOT
spoil *vb* **1** to affect slightly with something morally bad or undesirable — see TAINT 1
2 to go through decomposition — see DECAY 1
3 to reduce the soundness, effectiveness, or perfection of — see DAMAGE 1
4 to treat with great or excessive care — see BABY
spoilage *n* the process by which dead organic matter separates into simpler substances — see CORRUPTION 1
spoiled *adj* having undergone organic breakdown — see ROTTEN 1
spoilsport *n* a person who spoils the pleasure of others — see KILLJOY
spoken *adj* made or carried on through speaking rather than in writing — see VERBAL 2
spokesman *n* a person who speaks for another or for a group — see SPOKESPERSON
spokesperson *n* a person who speaks for another or for a group ‹the *spokesperson* for the protesting students presented their demands to the principal›
synonyms mouthpiece, speaker, spokesman
related words spokeswoman; sayer, talker; agent, delegate, deputy, representative
sponge *n* a person who is supported or seeks support from another without making an adequate return — see LEECH

sponge *vb* to take in (something liquid) through small openings — see ABSORB 1
sponger *n* a person who is supported or seeks support from another without making an adequate return — see LEECH
spongy *adj* giving easily to the touch — see SOFT 3
sponsor *n* a person who takes the responsibility for some other person or thing ⟨you need a *sponsor* to recommend you in order to get into the exclusive country club⟩
synonyms backer, guarantor, patron, surety
related words chaperone (*or* chaperon); advocate, champion, supporter; benefactor; coach, mentor, teacher
spontaneity *n* carefree freedom from constraint — see ABANDON
spontaneous *adj* done instantly and without conscious thought or decision — see AUTOMATIC 1
spoof *n* a work that imitates and exaggerates another work for comic effect — see PARODY 1
spook *n* **1** a person who tries secretly to obtain information for one country in the territory of another usually unfriendly country — see SPY
2 the soul of a dead person thought of especially as appearing to living people — see GHOST
spook *vb* to strike with fear — see FRIGHTEN
spooked *adj* filled with fear or dread — see AFRAID 1
spooky *adj* **1** easily excited by nature — see EXCITABLE
2 fearfully and mysteriously strange or fantastic — see EERIE
spoon *n* a utensil with a bowl and a handle that is used especially in cooking and serving food ⟨it's easier to eat soup with a *spoon* than with a fork⟩
synonyms dipper, ladle, scoop
related words skimmer
spoon *vb* to lift out with something that holds liquid — see DIP 2
sporadic *adj* **1** lacking in steadiness or regularity of occurrence — see FITFUL
2 not often occurring or repeated — see INFREQUENT
sport *n* **1** activity engaged in to amuse oneself — see PLAY 1
2 an attitude or manner not to be taken seriously — see FUN 2
sport *vb* **1** to engage in activity for amusement — see PLAY 1
2 to play and run about happily — see FROLIC 1
3 to present so as to invite notice or attention — see SHOW 1
sportive *adj* given to good-natured joking or teasing — see PLAYFUL
sportiveness *n* a natural disposition for playful behavior — see PLAYFULNESS
sportsmanlike *adj* following or according to the rules — see FAIR 3
sportsmanly *adj* following or according to the rules — see FAIR 3
spot *n* **1** a small area that is different (as in color) from the main part ⟨in summer the white coat of the snow leopard is studded with brownish black *spots*⟩
synonyms blotch, dapple, dot, eyespot, fleck, mottle, patch, point, speck, speckle, splotch
related words birthmark, freckle, mole; blot, mark, smear, smudge, stain; spatter, splash
2 a difficult, puzzling, or embarrassing situation from which there is no easy escape — see PREDICAMENT
3 a mark of guilt or disgrace — see STAIN 1
4 a very small amount — see PARTICLE 1
5 the area or space occupied by or intended for something — see PLACE 1
spot *vb* to mark with small spots especially unevenly ⟨to give the effect of sunlight on water, the artist *spotted* the lake in his painting with flecks of gold paint⟩
synonyms blotch, dapple, dot, fleck, freckle, marble, mottle, pepper, speck, speckle, splotch, sprinkle, stipple
related words blot, dye, stain; streak, stripe; intersperse, stud; bespatter, spatter
spotless *adj* free from dirt or stain — see CLEAN 1
spotted *adj* **1** marked with spots ⟨the *spotted* tablecloth clashed with the stripes on the wallpaper⟩
synonyms dappled (*also* dapple), dotted, flecked, freckled, mottled, speckled, splotchy, spotty, stippled, variegated
related words spangled; marbled, moiré (*or* moire), veined; motley, multicolored; piebald, roan
near antonyms solid
2 having blotches of two or more colors — see PIED
spotting *n* the act or process of sighting or learning the existence of something for the first time — see DISCOVERY 1
spotty *adj* **1** lacking in steadiness or regularity of occurrence — see FITFUL
2 marked with spots — see SPOTTED 1
spouse *n* the person to whom another is married ⟨employees and their *spouses* are covered by the health plan⟩
synonyms consort, mate, partner
related words husband, man, old man; lady, wife
near antonyms single; bachelor; maid, maiden, spinster
spout *n* a pipe or channel for carrying off water from a roof — see GUTTER 1
spout *vb* **1** to flow out in great quantities or with force — see GUSH 1
2 to talk loudly and wildly — see RANT
3 to throw out or off (something from within) often violently — see ERUPT 1
spout (off) *vb* to voice one's opinions freely with force — see SPEAK UP
spray *vb* to cover by or as if by scattering something over or on — see SCATTER 2
spread *n* **1** a decorative cloth used as a top covering for a bed — see COUNTERPANE
2 a large fancy meal often accompanied by ceremony or entertainment — see FEAST
3 a wide space or area — see EXPANSE
4 the distance or extent between possible extremes — see RANGE 3
5 the space or amount of space between two points, lines, surfaces, or objects — see DISTANCE
spread *vb* **1** to cause to be known over a considerable area or by many people ⟨*spread* the news!⟩
synonyms broadcast, circulate, disseminate, propagate
related words radiate, sprawl; diffuse, dispense, disperse, dissipate, scatter, sow; communicate, pass (on), transmit
near antonyms conceal, hide, hold (in), secrete; contain, limit, restrict
2 to put a layer of on a surface ⟨we *spread* the fer-

tilizer over the lawn evenly until it was fully covered⟩
synonyms apply, lay
related words dab, daub, plaster, smear; blanket, carpet, coat, cover, layer, overlay, overlie, overspread, sheet, surface
near antonyms peel, strip, uncover
3 to become known — see GET OUT 1
4 to cause (something) to pass from one to another — see COMMUNICATE 1
spread (out) *vb* to arrange the parts of (something) over a wider area — see OPEN 3
spreading *adj* exciting a similar feeling or reaction in others — see CONTAGIOUS 2
spree *n* a time or instance of carefree fun — see FLING 1
sprightliness *n* the quality or state of having abundant or intense activity — see VITALITY 1
sprightly *adv* in a quick and spirited manner — see GAILY 2
sprightly *adj* having much high-spirited energy and movement — see LIVELY 1
spring *n* an act of leaping into the air — see JUMP 1
spring *vb* **1** to come into existence — see BEGIN 2
2 to propel oneself upward or forward into the air — see JUMP 1
3 to set free (as from slavery or confinement) — see FREE 1
spring (for) *vb* to give what is owed for — see PAY 2
spring (up) *vb* to come to one's attention especially gradually or unexpectedly — see ARISE 2
springy *adj* **1** able to revert to original size and shape after being stretched, squeezed, or twisted — see ELASTIC 1
2 having much high-spirited energy and movement — see LIVELY 1
sprinkle *n* **1** a light or fine rain — see DRIZZLE
2 a small number — see FEW
sprinkle *vb* **1** to cover by or as if by scattering something over or on — see SCATTER 2
2 to mark with small spots especially unevenly — see SPOT
sprinkling *n* **1** a small number — see FEW
2 a very small amount — see PARTICLE 1
sprint *vb* to go at a pace faster than a walk — see RUN 1
sprite *n* an imaginary being usually having a small human form and magical powers — see FAIRY
spruce *adj* being strikingly neat and trim in style or appearance — see SMART 1
sprucely *adv* in a strikingly neat and trim manner — see SMARTLY
spry *adj* moving easily — see GRACEFUL 1
spryness *n* ease and grace in physical activity — see DEXTERITY 2
spume *n* a light mass of fine bubbles formed in or on a liquid — see FOAM
spunk *n* the strength of mind that enables a person to endure pain or hardship — see FORTITUDE
spunky *adj* marked by a lively display of strong feeling — see SPIRITED 1
spur *n* something that arouses action or activity — see IMPULSE
spur *vb* to urge or push forward with or as if with a pointed object — see PROD 1
spurious *adj* **1** being such in appearance only and made or manufactured with the intention of committing fraud — see COUNTERFEIT
2 lacking in natural or spontaneous quality — see ARTIFICIAL 1
spurn *vb* to show unwillingness to accept, do, engage in, or agree to — see DECLINE 1
spur-of-the-moment *adj* made or done without previous thought or preparation — see EXTEMPORANEOUS
spurt *n* a sudden and usually temporary growth of activity — see OUTBREAK
spurt *vb* **1** to flow out in great quantities or with force — see GUSH 1
2 to throw out or off (something from within) often violently — see ERUPT 1
sputter *vb* to speak rapidly, inarticulately, and usually unintelligibly — see BABBLE 1
spy *n* a person who tries secretly to obtain information for one country in the territory of another usually unfriendly country ⟨the government *spy* risked his life every day to get vital information back to his country⟩
synonyms operative, spook
related words counterspy, shadow
phrases secret agent, undercover agent
spy *vb* to make note of (something) through the use of one's eyes — see SEE 1
spying *n* the secret gathering of information on others — see ESPIONAGE
squabble *n* an often noisy or angry expression of differing opinions — see ARGUMENT 1
squabble *vb* to express different opinions about something often angrily — see ARGUE 2
squabbler *n* a person who takes part in a dispute — see DISPUTANT
squad *n* a group of people working together on a task — see GANG 1
squalidness *n* the state or quality of being dirty — see DIRTINESS 1
squall *n* **1** a disturbance of the atmosphere accompanied by wind and often by precipitation (as rain or snow) — see STORM 1
2 a state of noisy, confused activity — see COMMOTION
squall *vb* to cry out loudly and emotionally — see SCREAM
squally *adj* marked by wet and windy conditions — see FOUL 1
squamous *adj* composed of or covered with scales — see SCALY
squander *vb* to use up carelessly — see WASTE 1
squanderer *n* someone who carelessly spends money — see PRODIGAL
squandering *adj* given to spending money freely or foolishly — see PRODIGAL
square *adj* marked by justice, honesty, and freedom from bias — see FAIR 2
square *vb* **1** to be in agreement on every point — see CHECK 1
2 to influence someone with a bribe — see BRIBE
squarely *adv* as stated or indicated without the slightest difference — see EXACTLY 1
squash *vb* **1** to cause to become a pulpy mass — see CRUSH 1
2 to put a stop to (something) by the use of force — see QUELL 1
squashy *adj* giving easily to the touch — see SOFT 3
squat *adj* being compact and broad in build and often short in stature — see STOCKY
squat *vb* to lie low with the limbs close to the body — see CROUCH

squatty *adj* being compact and broad in build and often short in stature — see STOCKY

squawk *n* an expression of dissatisfaction, pain, or resentment — see COMPLAINT 1

squawk *vb* to express dissatisfaction, pain, or resentment usually tiresomely — see COMPLAIN

squeak *vb* to make a short shrill noise ⟨a loose board that *squeaked* every time we walked on the floor⟩
synonyms creak
related words cheep, peep; scream, screech, shriek, shrill, sing, squeal, yelp, yip

squeaking *adj* having a high musical pitch or range — see SHRILL

squeaky *adj* having a high musical pitch or range — see SHRILL

squeal *vb* **1** to give information (as to the authorities) about another's improper or unlawful activities ⟨as soon as the stool pigeon got to the police station, he *squealed* to the police about the whole smuggling operation⟩
synonyms inform, snitch, talk, tell
related words betray, give away, rat (on), turn in; blab, tattle; tip (off)
2 to cry out loudly and emotionally — see SCREAM

squealer *n* a person who provides secret information about another's wrongdoing — see INFORMER

squeamish *adj* **1** affected with nausea — see NAUSEOUS
2 filled with disgust — see SICK 2

squeamishness *n* **1** a disturbed condition of the stomach in which one feels like vomiting — see NAUSEA 1
2 the tendency to be or state of being squeamish — see DELICACY 3

squeeze *vb* **1** to apply external pressure on so as to force out the juice or contents of — see PRESS 2
2 to fit (something) into a tight space — see CROWD 1
3 to get with great difficulty — see EKE OUT
4 to reduce in size or volume by or as if by pressing parts or members together — see COMPRESS 1
5 to rob by the use of trickery or threats — see FLEECE

squeezing *n* the act or process of reducing the size or volume of something by or as if by pressing — see COMPRESSION

squelch *vb* to put a stop to (something) by the use of force — see QUELL 1

squinch *vb* **1** to lie low with the limbs close to the body — see CROUCH
2 to twist (something) out of a natural or normal shape or condition — see CONTORT

squinching *n* the twisting of something out of its natural or normal shape or condition — see CONTORTION

squire *vb* to go along with in order to provide assistance, protection, or companionship — see ACCOMPANY

squirm *vb* to make jerky or restless movements — see FIDGET

squirrel (away) *vb* to put (something of future use or value) in a safe or secret place — see HOARD

squirt *vb* to flow out in great quantities or with force — see GUSH 1

squishy *adj* giving easily to the touch — see SOFT 3

stab *n* **1** a mark or small hole made by a pointed instrument — see PRICK 1
2 an effort to do or accomplish something — see ATTEMPT

stab *vb* to penetrate or hold (something) with a pointed object — see IMPALE

stability *n* **1** the ability to withstand force or stress without being distorted, dislodged, or damaged ⟨the bridge was designed with such great *stability* that it supposedly will not collapse even under the harshest weather conditions⟩
synonyms firmness, soundness, steadiness, strength, sturdiness
related words dependability, durability, reliability; solidity, solidness; cohesion, toughness
near antonyms insecurity, weakness
antonyms instability, unsoundness, unsteadiness
2 the state of continuing without change — see CONSTANCY 1

stable *adj* **1** marked by the ability to withstand stress without structural damage or distortion ⟨the tower was *stable* enough to withstand the strongest winds without collapsing⟩
synonyms fast, firm, sound, stalwart, strong, sturdy
related words dependable, durable, reliable; solid; cohesive, tough
near antonyms insecure, weak
antonyms unsound, unstable, unsteady
2 having been established and usually not subject to change — see FIXED 1
3 having full use of one's mind and control over one's actions — see SANE
4 not undergoing a change in condition — see CONSTANT 1

stack *n* **1** a considerable amount — see LOT 2
2 a quantity of things thrown or stacked on one another — see [1]PILE 1

stack *vb* to lay or throw on top of one another — see PILE

stack up (against *or* with) *vb* to come near or nearer to in character or quality — see APPROXIMATE

stadium *n* a large usually roofless building for sporting events with tiers of seats for spectators ⟨the football game will be held at the new *stadium*, which seats 100,000 people⟩
synonyms bowl, circus, coliseum, colosseum
related words gym, gymnasium, spa; arena, hippodrome

staff *n* **1** a body of persons at work or available for work — see FORCE 1
2 a heavy rigid stick used as a weapon or for punishment — see CLUB 1

stage *n* **1** a level usually raised surface — see PLATFORM
2 a portion of a trip — see LEG 2
3 an individual part of a process, series, or ranking — see DEGREE 1
4 the public performance of plays — see DRAMA 1

stage *vb* to bring before the public in performance or exhibition — see PRESENT 1

stagger *vb* **1** to move forward while swaying from side to side ⟨I was so tired last night that I just *staggered* upstairs to bed without eating dinner⟩
synonyms careen, dodder, lurch, reel, teeter, totter, waddle
related words rock, sway, weave, wobble; clump, flounder, lumber, lump, pound, scuff, scuffle, shamble, shuffle, stamp, stomp, stumble, tramp, tromp

2 to show uncertainty about the right course of action — see HESITATE
staggering *adj* causing wonder or astonishment — see MARVELOUS 1
staid *adj* **1** not joking or playful in mood or manner — see SERIOUS 1
2 having or showing a serious and reserved manner — see DIGNIFIED
stain *n* **1** a mark of guilt or disgrace ⟨the *stain* of this cowardly act would haunt him for the rest of his career⟩
synonyms blot, brand, smirch, spot, stigma, taint
related words discredit, disgrace, dishonor, disrepute, guilt, ignominy, infamy, odium, opprobrium, reproach, shame
near antonyms award, credit, honor
2 a substance used to color other materials — see PIGMENT
stain *vb* **1** to affect slightly with something morally bad or undesirable — see TAINT 1
2 to give color or a different color to — see COLOR 1
3 to make dirty — see DIRTY
stained *adj* not clean — see DIRTY 1
stainless *adj* free from dirt or stain — see CLEAN 1
stake *n* **1** a legal right to participation in the advantages, profits, and responsibility of something — see INTEREST 1
2 the money or thing risked on the outcome of an uncertain event — see BET
stake *vb* **1** to provide money for — see FINANCE 1
2 to risk (something) on the outcome of an uncertain event — see BET
stale *adj* used or heard so often as to be dull ⟨viewers were bored by the *stale* story lines of the new crop of sitcoms⟩
synonyms banal, commonplace, hackney, hackneyed, moth-eaten, musty, stereotyped, threadbare, tired, trite
related words canned, unimaginative, uninspired, unoriginal; normal, ordinary, rote, routine, standard, stock, typical, usual; boring, drab, dreary, dry, dull, flat, heavy, humdrum, jading, leaden, monotonous, pedestrian, ponderous, prosaic, tame, tedious, tiresome, tiring, unanimated, undramatic, uninteresting, vapid, wearisome, weary, wearying; corny, maudlin, mawkish, mushy, saccharine, sappy, schmaltzy, sentimental, sloppy, sugarcoated, sugary
near antonyms animating, energizing, enlivening, exciting, galvanizing, invigorating, stimulating; absorbing, engaging, engrossing, gripping, interesting, intriguing, involving; atypical, extraordinary, uncommon, unusual
antonyms fresh, new, original
stalemate *n* **1** a point in a struggle where neither side is capable of winning or willing to give in — see IMPASSE
2 a situation in which neither participant in a contest, competition, or struggle comes out ahead of the other — see TIE 1
stalk *vb* **1** to seek out (game) for food or sport — see HUNT 1
2 to walk with exaggerated arm and leg movements — see STRUT 1
stall *vb* **1** to bring (something) to a standstill — see [1]HALT 1
2 to stop functioning — see FAIL 1
stalwart *adj* **1** feeling or displaying no fear by temperament — see BRAVE
2 having muscles capable of exerting great physical force — see STRONG 1
3 marked by the ability to withstand stress without structural damage or distortion — see STABLE 1
stamp *n* a perceptible trace left by pressure — see PRINT 1
stamp *vb* **1** to move heavily or clumsily — see LUMBER 1
2 to tread on heavily so as to crush or injure — see TRAMPLE
stamp (out) *vb* to destroy all traces of — see ANNIHILATE 1
stance *n* a general way of holding the body — see POSTURE 1
stanchion *n* an upright shaft that supports an overhead structure — see PILLAR 1
stand *n* a level usually raised surface — see PLATFORM
stand *vb* **1** to occupy a place or location ⟨the monument *stands* in the middle of the town plaza⟩
synonyms be, lie, sit
related words command, overlook; remain, rest, stay; await, wait; post, station
2 to put up with (something painful or difficult) — see BEAR 2
3 to give what is owed for — see PAY 2
standard *adj* **1** accepted, used, or practiced by most people — see CURRENT 1
2 being of the type that is encountered in the normal course of events — see ORDINARY 1
3 having or showing the qualities associated with the members of a particular group or kind — see TYPICAL 1
standard *n* **1** something set up as an example against which others of the same type are compared ⟨the animation in that movie set the *standard* against which all later animated cartoons were judged⟩
synonyms benchmark, criterion, grade, mark, measure, par, touchstone, yardstick
related words rule; case, example, instance; acme, apex, meridian, peak, pinnacle, summit, zenith
near antonyms aberration, abnormality, deviation
2 a piece of cloth with a special design that is used as an emblem or for signaling — see FLAG 1
3 what is typical of a group, class, or series — see AVERAGE
4 standards *pl* the code of good conduct for an individual or group — see ETHICS
standardize *vb* to make agree with a single established standard or model ⟨the plan is to *standardize* the test for reading comprehension so that we can see how students across the state compare⟩
synonyms formalize, homogenize, normalize, regularize
related words codify, organize, systematize; average, equalize, even; accredit, certify; control, govern, regulate; coordinate, harmonize, integrate, reconcile, synthesize
near antonyms customize, individualize, tailor
standby *n* something or someone to which one looks for support — see DEPENDENCE 2
stand–in *n* a person or thing that takes the place of another — see SUBSTITUTE
stand in *vb* to serve as a replacement usually for a time only — see COVER 1
standing *adj* **1** fixed in a place or position — see STATIONARY 1
2 rising straight up — see ERECT

standing *n* **1** high position within society — see RANK 2
2 the period during which something exists, lasts, or is in progress — see DURATION 1
3 the placement of someone or something in relation to others in a vertical arrangement — see RANK 1
standoff *n* a situation in which neither participant in a contest, competition, or struggle comes out ahead of the other — see TIE 1
standoffish *adj* having or showing a lack of friendliness or interest in others — see COOL 1
standout *n* a person who is widely known and usually much talked about — see CELEBRITY 1
stand out *vb* to extend outward beyond a usual point — see BULGE
standpoint *n* a way of looking at or thinking about something — see POINT OF VIEW
standstill *n* a point in a struggle where neither side is capable of winning or willing to give in — see IMPASSE
staple *n* the main or greater part of something as distinguished from its appendages — see BODY 1
star *adj* **1** of or relating to the stars — see STELLAR 1
2 standing above others in rank, importance, or achievement — see EMINENT
3 widely known — see FAMOUS
star *n* **1** a ball-shaped gaseous celestial body that shines by its own light ⟨it's difficult to see the *stars* at night in the middle of the city because of all the streetlights⟩
synonyms luminary, sun
related words constellation; dwarf, fixed star, giant star, lodestar (*also* loadstar), neutron star, nova, red giant, supernova, variable star, white dwarf
2 the person who has the most important role in a play, movie, or TV show ⟨when the *star* of the school play came down with the flu on opening night, her understudy got to go on⟩
synonyms lead, principal
related words leading lady, leading man; superstar; ingenue (*or* ingénue), starlet
near antonyms extra, supernumerary
3 a person who is widely known and usually much talked about — see CELEBRITY 1
starch *n* active strength of body or mind — see VIGOR 1
starchy *adj* marked by or showing careful attention to set forms and details — see CEREMONIOUS 1
star–crossed *adj* having, prone to, or marked by bad luck — see UNLUCKY
stare *vb* to look long and hard in wonder or surprise — see GAPE
stark *adj* **1** harsh and threatening in manner or appearance — see GRIM 1
2 having no exceptions or restrictions — see ABSOLUTE 2
3 lacking contents that could or should be present — see EMPTY 1
4 producing inferior or only a small amount of vegetation — see BARREN 1
starry *adj* of or relating to the stars — see STELLAR 1
start *n* the point at which something begins — see BEGINNING
start *vb* **1** to move suddenly and sharply (as in surprise) ⟨I *started* from my chair when I heard the sudden scream⟩
synonyms bolt, jump, startle
related words jerk, twitch; flinch, recoil; bound, leap, spring; react, respond
2 to be responsible for the creation and early operation or use of — see FOUND
3 to cause to function — see ACTIVATE
4 to come into existence — see BEGIN 2
5 to extend outward beyond a usual point — see BULGE
6 to take the first step in (a process or course of action) — see BEGIN 1
startle *vb* **1** to make a strong impression on (someone) with something unexpected — see SURPRISE 1
2 to move suddenly and sharply (as in surprise) — see START 1
3 to strike with fear — see FRIGHTEN
startling *adj* causing a strong emotional reaction because unexpected — see SURPRISING 1
starved *adj* feeling a desire or need for food — see HUNGRY 1
starving *adj* feeling a desire or need for food — see HUNGRY 1
stash *n* a supply stored up and often hidden away — see HOARD 1
stash *vb* to put (something of future use or value) in a safe or secret place — see HOARD
stashing *n* the placing of something out of sight — see CONCEALMENT 1
state *adj* of or relating to a nation — see NATIONAL
state *n* a body of people composed of one or more nationalities usually with its own territory and government — see NATION
state *vb* **1** to convey in appropriate or telling terms — see PHRASE
2 to express (a thought or emotion) in words — see SAY 1
3 to make known (as an idea, emotion, or opinion) — see EXPRESS 1
state house *n* the building in which a state legislature meets — see CAPITOL
stateliness *n* **1** a dignified bearing or appearance befitting royalty — see MAJESTY 1
2 dignified or restrained beauty of form, appearance, or style — see ELEGANCE
3 impressiveness of beauty on a large scale — see MAGNIFICENCE
stately *adj* **1** having or showing a serious and reserved manner — see DIGNIFIED
2 having or showing elegance — see ELEGANT 1
3 large and impressive in size, grandeur, extent, or conception — see GRAND 1
4 very dignified in form, tone, or style — see ELEVATED 2
statement *n* **1** a record of goods sold or services performed together with the costs due — see [1]BILL 1
2 an act, process, or means of putting something into words — see EXPRESSION 1
3 something that is said — see WORD 2
static *adj* fixed in a place or position — see STATIONARY 1
station *n* **1** the place where someone is assigned to stand or remain ⟨the soldiers remained at their *station* even though a huge enemy force was approaching⟩
synonyms position, post, quarter

related words assignment, detail
2 a regular stopping place ⟨the historic house was once a *station* on the Underground Railroad, the network that helped slaves reach freedom in the North⟩
synonyms stop, way station
related words depot, terminal; layover, stopover
3 the placement of someone or something in relation to others in a vertical arrangement — see RANK 1

station *vb* to assign to a place or position — see ²POST

stationary *adj* **1** fixed in a place or position ⟨a *stationary* bicycle is good for exercise, but you won't enjoy the scenery very much⟩
synonyms immobile, nonmoving, standing, static
related words immovable, irremovable, nonmotile, unmovable; frozen, motionless, stagnant, still, unbudging
near antonyms motile
antonyms mobile, movable (*or* moveable), moving, nonstationary
2 not undergoing a change in condition — see CONSTANT 1

statuette *n* a small statue — see FIGURINE

stature *n* the distance of something or someone from bottom to top — see HEIGHT 3

status *n* **1** position with regard to conditions and circumstances — see SITUATION 1
2 the placement of someone or something in relation to others in a vertical arrangement — see RANK 1

status quo *n* the state or fact of being the way things usually are — see NORMALITY

statute *n* a rule of conduct or action laid down by a governing authority and especially a legislator — see LAW 1

staunch *or* **stanch** *adj* firm in one's allegiance to someone or something — see FAITHFUL 1

stave off *vb* to drive back — see REPEL 1

¹stay *n* a temporary residing as another's guest — see VISIT 1

²stay *n* something that holds up or serves as a foundation for something else — see SUPPORT 1

stay *vb* **1** to continue to be in a place for a significant amount of time ⟨let's *stay* inside this pavilion until it stops raining⟩
synonyms abide, dwell, hang around, remain, stick around, tarry
related words await, hang on, hold on, wait; dally, linger, loiter; keep
antonyms go, leave, quit
2 to bring (something) to a standstill — see ¹HALT 1
3 to hold up or serve as a foundation for — see SUPPORT 3
4 to remain in place in readiness or expectation of something — see WAIT
5 to reside as a temporary guest — see VISIT 2

steadfast *adj* firm in one's allegiance to someone or something — see FAITHFUL 1

steadfastness *n* adherence to something to which one is bound by a pledge or duty — see FIDELITY

steadiness *n* **1** the ability to withstand force or stress without being distorted, dislodged, or damaged — see STABILITY 1
2 the state of continuing without change — see CONSTANCY 1

steady *adj* **1** firm in one's allegiance to someone or something — see FAITHFUL 1
2 appearing or occurring repeatedly from time to time — see REGULAR 1
3 not undergoing a change in condition — see CONSTANT 1
4 not varying — see UNIFORM
5 worthy of one's trust — see DEPENDABLE

steal *n* something bought or offered for sale at a desirable price — see BARGAIN 1

steal *vb* **1** to take (something) without right and with an intent to keep ⟨the guy who tried to *steal* my car was sentenced to a year in jail⟩
synonyms appropriate, filch, hook, misappropriate, nip, pilfer, pinch, pocket, purloin, rip off, snitch, swipe, thieve
related words burglarize, fleece, rob; loot, pillage, plunder, sack; hijack (*or* highjack); pick, rifle; poach, rustle, shoplift; collar, grab, grasp, nail, seize, snatch, take; mooch, sponge; abduct, kidnap, shanghai, spirit
phrases make away with, run off with, walk off with
near antonyms buy, purchase; bestow, contribute, donate, give, present
2 to move about in a sly or secret manner — see SNEAK 1

steal (from) *vb* to remove valuables from (a place) unlawfully — see ROB

stealer *n* one who steals — see THIEF

stealing *n* the unlawful taking and carrying away of property without the consent of its owner — see THEFT 1

stealthy *adj* **1** given to acting in secret and to concealing one's intentions — see SNEAKY 1
2 undertaken or done so as to escape being observed or known by others — see SECRET 1

steam *vb* to be excited or emotionally stirred up with anger — see BOIL 1

steaming *adj* feeling or showing anger — see ANGRY

steed *n* a large hoofed domestic animal that is used for carrying or drawing loads and for riding — see HORSE

steel *n* a hand weapon with a length of metal sharpened on one or both sides and usually tapered to a sharp point — see SWORD

steel *vb* **1** to fill with courage or strength of purpose — see ENCOURAGE 1
2 to make able to withstand physical hardship, strain, or exposure — see HARDEN 2
3 to prepare (oneself) mentally or emotionally — see FORTIFY 1

steely *adj* **1** harsh and threatening in manner or appearance — see GRIM 1
2 of the color gray — see GRAY 1

steep *adj* **1** having an incline approaching the perpendicular ⟨a very *steep* rock face that was nearly impossible to climb⟩
synonyms abrupt, bold, precipitous, sheer
related words perpendicular, plumb, straight, vertical; craggy, hilly, mountainous, scarped; angled, canted, cocked, heeled, inclined, listed, slanted, sloped, tilted, tipped
near antonyms gentle, gradual, moderate; even, flat, flush, horizontal, level, plane, smooth, unruffled, unwrinkled
antonyms easy
2 going beyond a normal or acceptable limit in degree or amount — see EXCESSIVE

steep *vb* **1** to cause (as a person) to become filled

or saturated with a certain quality or principle — see INFUSE
2 to wet thoroughly with liquid — see SOAK 1

steer *vb* to point out the way for (someone) especially from a position in front — see LEAD 1

stellar *adj* **1** of or relating to the stars ⟨humankind's dream of *stellar* navigation is hampered by the vast distances between the stars, even in our own galaxy⟩
synonyms astral, star, starry
related words celestial, empyrean, heavenly; astronomical (*also* astronomic), astrophysical; astronautic (*or* astronautical); starlike, star-spangled
2 of the very best kind — see EXCELLENT

stench *n* a strong unpleasant smell — see STINK

stentorian *adj* marked by a high volume of sound — see LOUD 1

step *n* **1** an action planned or taken to achieve a desired result — see MEASURE 1
2 an individual part of a process, series, or ranking — see DEGREE 1
3 the mark or impression made by a foot — see FOOTPRINT
4 steps *pl* the direction along which something or someone moves — see PATH 1

step *vb* **1** to go on foot — see WALK
2 to perform a series of usually rhythmic bodily movements to music — see DANCE 1

step (along) *vb* to proceed or move quickly — see HURRY 2

step–by–step *adj* proceeding or changing by steps or degrees — see GRADUAL

step down (from) *vb* **1** to give up (a job or office) — see QUIT 1
2 to give up (as a position of authority) formally — see ABDICATE

steppe *n* a broad area of level or rolling treeless country — see PLAIN

step up *vb* to make markedly greater in measure or degree — see INTENSIFY

stereotype *n* an idea or statement about all of the members of a group or all the instances of a situation — see GENERALIZATION

stereotyped *adj* used or heard so often as to be dull — see STALE

sterile *adj* **1** not able to produce fruit or offspring ⟨*sterile* couples sometimes choose to adopt needy children⟩ ⟨the apple tree turned out to be *sterile*, never yielding a crop of apples⟩
synonyms barren, impotent, infertile, unfruitful
related words altered, desexed, neutered, sterilized; castrated, emasculated, gelded; spayed; fruitless, unproductive
near antonyms fecund, luxuriant, productive, prolific; enriched, fertilized, rich; impregnated, pregnant; potent; bearing, producing, yielding; blooming, bursting, flourishing, swarming, teeming
antonyms fat, fertile, fruitful
2 free from filth, infection, or dangers to health — see SANITARY

sterling *adj* of the very best kind — see EXCELLENT

stern *adj* **1** given to exacting standards of discipline and self-restraint — see SEVERE 1
2 harsh and threatening in manner or appearance — see GRIM 1

sternly *adv* in a manner so as to cause loss or suffering — see HARDLY 1

sternness *n* the quality or state of being demanding or unyielding (as in discipline or criticism) — see SEVERITY

stevedore *n* one who loads and unloads ships at a port — see DOCKWORKER

stew *n* **1** a state of nervous or irritated concern — see FRET
2 a state of noisy, confused activity — see COMMOTION

stew *vb* **1** to cook in a liquid heated to the point that it gives off steam — see BOIL 2
2 to experience concern or anxiety — see WORRY 1

steward *n* a person hired to perform household or personal services — see SERVANT

stick *vb* **1** to hold to something firmly as if by adhesion ⟨those magnets are strong enough to *stick* well to the refrigerator⟩
synonyms adhere, cleave, cling, hew
related words bind, cohere, fasten, fuse, glue, unite
near antonyms loosen; drop, fall
2 to arrange something in a certain spot or position — see PLACE 1
3 to penetrate or hold (something) with a pointed object — see IMPALE
4 to rob by the use of trickery or threats — see FLEECE

stick (to *or* with) *vb* to give steadfast support to — see ADHERE

stick around *vb* to continue to be in a place for a significant amount of time — see STAY 1

stick–in–the–mud *n* **1** a person with old-fashioned ideas — see FOGY
2 someone who moves slowly or more slowly than others — see SLOWPOKE

stick out *vb* **1** to extend outward beyond a usual point — see BULGE
2 to put up with (something painful or difficult) — see BEAR 2

sticks *n pl* the open rural area outside of big towns and cities — see COUNTRY 2

sticky *adj* **1** being of such a thick consistency as to readily cling to objects upon contact ⟨the *sticky* maple syrup was a mess to clean up⟩
synonyms adhesive, gelatinous, gluey, glutinous, gooey, gummy, viscid, viscous
related words ropy, tacky; adherent, tenacious
antonyms nonadhesive, nonviscous
2 containing or characterized by an uncomfortable amount of moisture — see HUMID

stiff *adj* **1** incapable of or highly resistant to bending ⟨use a *stiff* piece of paper for the project⟩
synonyms inflexible, rigid, stiffened, unyielding
related words inelastic; firm, hard, solid, sound, strong; brittle, crisp; compact, dense, substantial; arthritic, rheumatic; nonelastic, nonmalleable
near antonyms elastic, resilient, springy, stretchy, workable; malleable; droopy, flabby, flaccid, mushy, semisoft, soft, squashy, squishy; lank, limber, limp, lissome (*also* lissom), lithe, willowy
antonyms flexible, floppy, pliable, pliant, supple, yielding
2 difficult to endure — see HARSH 1
3 going beyond a normal or acceptable limit in degree or amount — see EXCESSIVE
4 having a consistency that does not easily yield to pressure — see FIRM 2
5 lacking social grace and assurance — see AWKWARD 1

6 requiring considerable physical or mental effort — see HARD 2

stiffened *adj* incapable of or highly resistant to bending — see STIFF 1

stiffly *adv* **1** in a manner so as to cause loss or suffering — see HARDLY 1
2 in a vigorous and forceful manner — see HARD 3

stifle *vb* **1** to be or cause to be killed by lack of breathable air — see SMOTHER 1
2 to refrain from openly showing or uttering — see SUPPRESS 2

stifling *adj* lacking fresh air — see STUFFY 1

stigma *n* a mark of guilt or disgrace — see STAIN 1

still *adj* **1** free from disturbing noise or uproar — see QUIET 1
2 free from storms or physical disturbance — see CALM 1
3 mostly or entirely without sound — see SILENT 3

still *adv* **1** without motion ⟨now, you have to sit very *still* while the hairdresser cuts your hair⟩
synonyms motionlessly, quiet, quietly
related words immovably; inactively
near antonyms movably
2 in spite of that — see HOWEVER

still *n* **1** a state of freedom from storm or disturbance — see CALM
2 the near or complete absence of sound — see SILENCE 2

still *vb* **1** to bring (something) to a standstill — see [1]HALT 1
2 to free from distress or disturbance — see CALM 1
3 to stop the noise or speech of — see SILENCE 1

stillness *n* **1** a state of freedom from storm or disturbance — see CALM
2 incapacity for or restraint from speaking — see SILENCE 1
3 the near or complete absence of sound — see SILENCE 2

stilly *adj* **1** free from disturbing noise or uproar — see QUIET 1
2 free from storms or physical disturbance — see CALM 1

stilted *adj* lacking social grace and assurance — see AWKWARD 1

stimulant *n* **1** something that arouses a strong response from another — see PROVOCATION 1
2 something that arouses action or activity — see IMPULSE

stimulate *vb* **1** to give life, vigor, or spirit to — see ANIMATE
2 to rouse to strong feeling or action — see PROVOKE 1

stimulating *adj* **1** causing great emotional or mental stimulation — see EXCITING 1
2 having a renewing effect on the state of the body or mind — see TONIC
3 serving or likely to arouse a strong reaction — see PROVOCATIVE

stimulation *n* something that arouses a strong response from another — see PROVOCATION 1

stimulative *adj* having a renewing effect on the state of the body or mind — see TONIC

stimulus *n* **1** something that arouses a strong response from another — see PROVOCATION 1
2 something that arouses action or activity — see IMPULSE

sting *n* a sharp unpleasant sensation usually felt in some specific part of the body — see PAIN 1

sting *vb* **1** to charge (someone) too much for goods or services — see OVERCHARGE 1
2 to rob by the use of trickery or threats — see FLEECE

stinginess *n* the quality of being overly sparing with money — see PARSIMONY

stinging *adj* causing intense discomfort to one's skin — see CUTTING 1

stingy *adj* **1** giving or sharing as little as possible ⟨until his redemption, Ebenezer Scrooge is the classic example of a very *stingy*, heartless miser⟩
synonyms cheap, close, closefisted, mean, niggard, niggardly, parsimonious, penurious, pinching, spare, sparing, stinting, tight, tightfisted, uncharitable
related words careful, chary, conserving, economical, economizing, frugal, saving, scrimping, skimping, thrifty; acquisitive, avaricious, avid, coveting, covetous, desirous, grasping, greedy, hoggish, itchy, mercenary, rapacious, selfish, shabby, small, sordid; begrudging, envious, grudging, resentful; inhospitable
near antonyms altruistic, selfless, unselfish; extravagant, free, handsome, lavish, profuse; beneficent, benevolent, hospitable, humanitarian, philanthropic; compassionate, good-hearted, greathearted, kindly, magnanimous, openhearted; thriftless, unthrifty; dissipating, frittering, prodigal, profligate, spendthrift, splurging, squandering, wasteful, wasting
antonyms bounteous, bountiful, charitable, freehanded, generous, liberal, munificent, openhanded, unsparing, unstinting
2 less plentiful than what is normal, necessary, or desirable — see MEAGER

stink *n* a strong unpleasant smell ⟨the *stink* of burned plastic lingered in the kitchen for days after we accidentally melted a spatula on the stove⟩
synonyms reek, stench
related words acridness, fetidness, foulness, fustiness, malodorousness, mustiness, rancidity, rankness, staleness; badness, vileness; dirt, dirtiness, filth, filthiness, nastiness; odor, redolence, scent, sniff
near antonyms floweriness, lusciousness, savoriness, spiciness, sweetness; bouquet; ambrosia
antonyms aroma, fragrance, perfume

stink *vb* to give off an extremely unpleasant smell ⟨the dog *stinks* because she tangled with a skunk again⟩
synonyms reek
related words exhale, savor, smell; decay, decompose, rot, spoil; disgust, offend, repulse, revolt

stinker *n* a person whose behavior is offensive to others — see JERK 1

stinking *adj* having an unpleasant smell — see MALODOROUS

stinky *adj* having an unpleasant smell — see MALODOROUS

stint *n* **1** a fixed period of time during which a person holds a job or position — see TERM 1
2 a piece of work that needs to be done regularly — see CHORE 1

stint (on) *vb* to use or give out in stingy amounts — see SPARE

stinting *adj* giving or sharing as little as possible — see STINGY 1

stipend *n* the money paid regularly to a person for labor or services — see WAGE

stipple *vb* to mark with small spots especially unevenly — see SPOT

stippled *adj* marked with spots — see SPOTTED 1

stipulate (for) *vb* to ask for (something) earnestly or with authority — see DEMAND 1

stipulation *n* something upon which the carrying out of an agreement or offer depends — see CONDITION 2

stir *n* **1** a state of noisy, confused activity — see COMMOTION
2 the act or an instance of changing position — see MOVEMENT 1

stir *vb* **1** to cause (as a liquid) to move about in a circle especially repeatedly ⟨the recipe says to *stir* the mixture carefully until it's properly blended⟩
synonyms agitate, churn, swirl, whirl
related words beat, paddle, whip, whisk; reel, shake, wheel
2 to change one's position — see MOVE 3
3 to rouse to strong feeling or action — see PROVOKE 1

stir (up) *vb* to cause or encourage the development of — see INCITE 1

stirring *adj* **1** causing great emotional or mental stimulation — see EXCITING 1
2 having the power to affect the feelings or sympathies — see MOVING

stirring *n* the act or an instance of changing position — see MOVEMENT 1

stitch *n* a sharp unpleasant sensation usually felt in some specific part of the body — see PAIN 1

stitch *vb* to close up with a series of interlacing stitches — see SEW

stock *adj* accepted, used, or practiced by most people — see CURRENT 1

stock *n* **1** a group of persons who come from the same ancestor — see FAMILY 1
2 a stupid person — see IDIOT
3 firm belief in the integrity, ability, effectiveness, or genuineness of someone or something — see TRUST 1
4 the line of ancestors from whom a person is descended — see ANCESTRY

stockade *n* a place of confinement for persons held in lawful custody — see JAIL

stocking *n* a close-fitting covering for the foot and leg ⟨be sure to wear your thick wool *stockings* if it's cold today⟩
synonyms hose, sock
related words hosiery; anklet, bobby socks, bootee

stockpile *n* a supply stored up and often hidden away — see HOARD 1

stockpile *vb* to put (something of future use or value) in a safe or secret place — see HOARD

stocky *adj* being compact and broad in build and often short in stature ⟨he was a tough, *stocky* little boy, muscular and solid⟩
synonyms chunky, dumpy, heavyset, squat, squatty, stout, stubby, stumpy, thickset
related words beefy, brawny, bulky, burly, husky, sturdy, thick, thickish, weighty; chubby, corpulent, fat, fleshy, full, gross, heavy, obese, overweight, plump, portly, pudgy, roly-poly, rotund, round, tubby; paunchy, potbellied; flabby, soft
near antonyms delicate, fragile, frail, puny; lean, skinny, slender, slim, spare, thin; angular, bony, gaunt, lank, lanky, rawboned, sinewy; scraggy, scrawny, slight; anorexic, cadaverous, emaciated, haggard, skeletal, wasted; spindly, twiggy, waspish, weedy, willowy, wiry

stodgy *adj* causing weariness, restlessness, or lack of interest — see BORING

stoic *or* **stoical** *adj* **1** accepting pains or hardships calmly or without complaint — see PATIENT 1
2 not feeling or showing emotion — see IMPASSIVE 1

stolid *adj* **1** not expressing any emotion — see BLANK 1
2 not feeling or showing emotion — see IMPASSIVE 1

stomach *n* the part of the body between the chest and the pelvis ⟨please don't lean on my *stomach*—I just had a big meal⟩
synonyms abdomen, belly, breadbasket [*slang*], gut, solar plexus, tummy
related words middle, midriff, waist; paunch, potbelly; thorax

stomach *vb* to put up with (something painful or difficult) — see BEAR 2

stomachache *n* abdominal pain especially when focused in the digestive organs ⟨you can stay home from school tomorrow if you still have a *stomachache*⟩
synonyms bellyache
related words colic, cramps

stomp *vb* **1** to move heavily or clumsily — see LUMBER 1
2 to tread on heavily so as to crush or injure — see TRAMPLE

stone blind *adj* lacking the power of sight — see BLIND

stone–broke *adj* lacking money or material possessions — see POOR 1

stoneware *n* articles made of baked clay — see CROCKERY

stony *also* **stoney** *adj* having or showing a lack of sympathy or tender feelings — see HARD 1

stool pigeon *n* a person who provides secret information about another's wrongdoing — see INFORMER

stoop *vb* to descend to a level that is beneath one's dignity — see CONDESCEND 1

stooping *adj* bending downward or forward — see NODDING

stop *n* **1** a brief halt in a journey ⟨our guide called for a *stop* at the trail hut to eat and rest a bit⟩
synonyms layover, stopover
related words break, pause, rest
2 a regular stopping place — see STATION 2
3 something that makes movement or progress more difficult — see ENCUMBRANCE
4 the stopping of a process or activity — see END 1

stop *vb* **1** to bring (as an action or operation) to an immediate end ⟨please *stop* that running in the library⟩
synonyms break, break off, can, cease, cut (out), desist (from), discontinue, drop, end, halt, knock off, lay off, leave off, quit, shut off
related words complete, conclude, finish; close (down); deactivate; block, blockade, dam, delay, detain, hinder, hold, hold back, impede, obstruct, stem; call, suspend; arrest, brake, check, clamp down, rein (in), squash, squelch, stamp, stanch (*also* staunch), stunt, suppress, turn back; pause, stay, suspend; abolish, abort, annul, demolish, destroy, dissolve, kill, ruin, scuttle, snuff

phrases have done with, put the kibosh on
near antonyms carry on, continue, follow through, keep up, run on; advance, proceed, progress; actuate, drive, impel, propel, stir
2 to bring (something) to a standstill — see [1]HALT 1
3 to close up so that no empty spaces remain — see FILL 2
4 to come to an end — see CEASE 1

stop (by *or* in) *vb* to make a brief visit — see CALL 3

stop (up) *vb* to prevent passage through — see CLOG 1

stopcock *n* a fixture for controlling the flow of a liquid — see FAUCET

stopgap *n* a temporary replacement — see MAKESHIFT

stopover *n* a brief halt in a journey — see STOP 1

stoppage *n* the stopping of a process or activity — see END 1

storage *n* a building for storing goods — see STOREHOUSE

store *adj* made beforehand in large numbers — see READY-MADE

store *n* **1** a collection of things kept available for future use or need ⟨Dad has a *store* of funny stories for when conversation lags at company parties⟩
synonyms cache, deposit, hoard, reserve
related words budget, fund, nest egg, pool, reservoir, stock, stockpile, supply; accumulation, assemblage, collection, gathering
2 a supply stored up and often hidden away — see HOARD 1
3 an establishment where goods are sold to consumers — see SHOP 1

store *vb* **1** to place somewhere for safekeeping or ready availability ⟨we decided to *store* the lawn mower in the shed instead of the garage⟩
synonyms keep, stow
related words garage, house; file, pack, shelve
2 to put (something of future use or value) in a safe or secret place — see HOARD

storehouse *n* a building for storing goods ⟨the company has a large *storehouse* filled with lumber for manufacturing its line of furniture⟩
synonyms depository, depot, magazine, repository, storage, stowage, warehouse
related words cache, stockroom, storeroom; bank, bin, container, locker, safe-deposit box, strongbox; arsenal, dump

storm *n* **1** a disturbance of the atmosphere accompanied by wind and often by precipitation (as rain or snow) ⟨a winter *storm* bringing about six inches of snow⟩
synonyms squall, tempest
related words blizzard, hail storm, ice storm, northeaster, norther, rainstorm, sandstorm, snowstorm, southeaster, southwester, thunderstorm, windstorm; cyclone, hurricane, typhoon
2 a heavy fall of objects — see RAIN 2
3 a rapid or overwhelming outpouring of many things at once — see BARRAGE
4 a state of noisy, confused activity — see COMMOTION
5 a steady falling of water from the sky in significant quantity — see RAIN 1
6 a sudden intense expression of strong feeling — see OUTBURST 1
7 a violent disturbance (as of the political or social order) — see CONVULSION

storm *vb* **1** to express one's anger usually violently — see RAGE 1
2 to fall as water in a continuous stream of drops from the clouds — see RAIN 1
3 to take sudden, violent action against — see ATTACK 1

stormy *adj* **1** marked by bursts of destructive force or intense activity — see VIOLENT 1
2 marked by or abounding with rain — see RAINY
3 marked by sudden or violent disturbance — see CONVULSIVE
4 marked by turmoil or disturbance especially of natural elements — see WILD 3
5 marked by wet and windy conditions — see FOUL 1

story *n* **1** a work with imaginary characters and events that is shorter and usually less complex than a novel ⟨if you go right to bed, Daddy will read a *story* to you⟩
synonyms narrative, novelette, novella, short story, tale, yarn
related words exemplum, fable, parable; anecdote, joke; fairy tale, folktale, legend, myth, romance; account, annals, chronicle, history, record, report
2 a brief account of something interesting that happened especially to one personally ⟨Grandpa is always telling *stories* about what it was like growing up on a farm⟩
synonyms anecdote, tale, yarn
related words episode, event, happening, incident, occurrence; recital, recitation
3 a report of recent events or facts not previously known — see NEWS
4 a relating of events usually in the order in which they happened — see ACCOUNT 1
5 a rumor or report of a personal or sensational nature — see TALE 1
6 a statement known by its maker to be untrue and made in order to deceive — see LIE

storyteller *n* a person who tells lies — see LIAR

stout *adj* **1** able to withstand hardship, strain, or exposure — see HARDY 1
2 being compact and broad in build and often short in stature — see STOCKY
3 feeling or displaying no fear by temperament — see BRAVE
4 having muscles capable of exerting great physical force — see STRONG 1
5 not showing weakness or uncertainty — see FIRM 1

stouthearted *adj* feeling or displaying no fear by temperament — see BRAVE

stoutly *adv* in a vigorous and forceful manner — see HARD 3

stoutness *n* strength of mind to carry on in spite of danger — see COURAGE

stow *vb* **1** to place somewhere for safekeeping or ready availability — see STORE 1
2 to put (something of future use or value) in a safe or secret place — see HOARD

stowage *n* a building for storing goods — see STOREHOUSE

straggler *n* someone who moves slowly or more slowly than others — see SLOWPOKE

straight *adj* **1** free from irregularities (as curves, bends, or angles) in course ⟨in the wide, open spaces of the West some rural roads are incredibly *straight*⟩

synonyms linear, right, straightaway, straightforward
related words unbent, uncurled, untwisted; direct, undeviating, unswerving
near antonyms bowed, rounded; entwined, kinked, swirled, turned, turning, twined, twining, twisted, twisting, veering, warped; bending, coiled, coiling, corkscrew, curled, curling, curved, curving, looped, looping, spiral, spiraling (*or* spiralling), winding; meandering, weaving; devious, serpentine, sinuous, zigzag, zigzagging
antonyms crooked
2 conforming to a high standard of morality or virtue — see GOOD 2
3 free from added matter — see PURE 1
4 free in expressing one's true feelings and opinions — see FRANK
5 going straight to the point clearly and firmly — see STRAIGHTFORWARD 1
6 not having one's mind affected by alcohol — see SOBER 1

straight *adv* **1** in a direct line or course — see DIRECTLY 1
2 in an honest and direct manner — see STRAIGHTFORWARD

straightaway *adj* **1** done or occurring without any noticeable lapse in time — see INSTANTANEOUS
2 free from irregularities (as curves, bends, or angles) in course — see STRAIGHT 1

straightaway *adv* without delay — see IMMEDIATELY

straighten *vb* to cause to follow a line that is without bends or curls ⟨*straighten* that extension cord—it should be just long enough to reach the wall outlet⟩
synonyms unbend, uncurl
related words uncoil, unwind; disentangle, untangle, untwine, untwist
near antonyms arc, bend, bow, hook, round; entwine, kink, swirl, turn, twine, twist; coil, loop, spiral, wind
antonyms bend, crook, curl, curve

straightforward *also* **straightforwards** *adv* in an honest and direct manner ⟨she finally told him *straightforward* that she wasn't interested in a date⟩
synonyms directly, forthrightly, foursquare, plain, plainly, straight, straightforwardly
related words candidly, frankly, honestly, openheartedly, openly, unguardedly, unreservedly; artlessly, earnestly, sincerely; abruptly, bluntly, brusquely, curtly, gruffly, sharply; impolitely, inconsiderately, rudely, tactlessly; truthfully, veraciously
near antonyms long-windedly, verbosely, wordily; civilly, courteously, diplomatically, politely, tactfully; deceitfully, mendaciously, untruthfully; erroneously, fallaciously, falsely, hypocritically, insincerely; ambiguously, circuitously, equivocally, evasively, indirectly

straightforward *adj* **1** going straight to the point clearly and firmly ⟨a *straightforward* account of the football game with no digressions or personal comments⟩
synonyms direct, forthright, foursquare, plain, straight
related words aboveboard, candid, frank, free-spoken, honest, open, openhearted, outspoken, plainspoken, unguarded, unreserved; artless, earnest, sincere; uninhibited, unrestrained; abrupt, bluff, blunt, brusque, curt, gruff, sharp; impolite, inconsiderate, rude, tactless, undiplomatic; true, truthful, veracious
near antonyms circumlocutory, long-winded, prolix, verbose, wordy; inhibited, reserved, restrained; civil, courteous, polite, tactful; deceitful, lying, mendacious, untruthful; erroneous, fallacious, false; ambiguous, equivocal, evasive, misleading; double-dealing, hypocritical, two-faced
antonyms circuitous, indirect, roundabout
2 free from irregularities (as curves, bends, or angles) in course — see STRAIGHT 1
3 free in expressing one's true feelings and opinions — see FRANK

straightforwardly *adv* in an honest and direct manner — see STRAIGHTFORWARD

straightforwardness *n* the free expression of one's true feelings and opinions — see CANDOR

straightway *adv* without delay — see IMMEDIATELY

[1]**strain** *n* **1** the line of ancestors from whom a person is descended — see ANCESTRY
2 a rhythmic series of musical tones arranged to give a pleasing effect — see MELODY
3 a very small amount — see PARTICLE 1

[2]**strain** *n* the burden on one's emotional or mental well-being created by demands on one's time — see STRESS 1

strain *vb* **1** to injure by overuse, misuse, or pressure ⟨in order to lift something heavy, squat down and lift with your legs, or you'll *strain* your back⟩
synonyms pull, rack, stretch, wrench
related words fray, tax, weaken; damage, harm, hurt, impair, wound; batter, bruise, tear; cripple, lame, mangle, mutilate
2 to pass through a filter ⟨better *strain* that coffee carefully to get all the grounds out⟩
synonyms filter, screen
related words percolate; refilter
3 to devote serious and sustained effort — see LABOR
4 to flow forth slowly through small openings — see EXUDE
5 to subject (a personal quality or faculty) to often excessive stress — see TRY (OUT) 2

strained *adj* lacking in natural or spontaneous quality — see ARTIFICIAL 1

strait *n* **1** a narrow body of water between two land masses — see CHANNEL 2
2 *often* **straits** *pl* a state of great suffering of body or mind — see DISTRESS 1

straitlaced *or* **straightlaced** *adj* given to or marked by very conservative standards regarding personal behavior or morals ⟨a very *straitlaced* old lady who believed women shouldn't even show a bare ankle in public⟩
synonyms prim, prudish, puritanical
related words priggish, staid, stuffy; genteel, proper, refined; decent, honest, moral, right, righteous, upright, virtuous
near antonyms liberated, permissive; bad, immoral, improper, indecent, lax, loose, wicked; debauched, degenerate, degraded, depraved, perverted

strand *n* the usually sandy or gravelly land bordering a body of water — see BEACH

strand *vb* to cause irreparable damage to (a ship) by running aground or sinking — see SHIPWRECK

stranded *adj* resting on the shore or bottom of a body of water — see AGROUND

strange *adj* **1** different from the ordinary in a way that causes curiosity or suspicion — see ODD 2
2 excitingly or mysteriously unusual — see EXOTIC
3 not known or experienced before — see NEW 2
4 noticeably different from what is generally found or experienced — see UNUSUAL 1

stranger *n* a person who is not native to or known to a community <the people of the island are quick to make *strangers* feel at home>
synonyms foreigner, nonnative, outlander, outsider
related words alien; outcast, pariah; drifter, transient, wanderer
near antonyms buddy, chum, comrade, confidant, crony, familiar, friend, intimate, pal; acquaintance, associate, cohort, colleague, companion, fellow, hearty, hobnobber, mate, partner, peer; adversary, antagonist, enemy, foe, opponent, rival; archenemy, nemesis; citizen, inhabitant, resident
antonyms native

strangle *vb* **1** to be or cause to be killed by lack of breathable air — see SMOTHER 1
2 to keep (someone) from breathing by exerting pressure on the windpipe — see CHOKE 1
3 to refrain from openly showing or uttering — see SUPPRESS 2

stratagem *n* a clever often underhanded means to achieve an end — see TRICK 1

strategy *n* **1** a method worked out in advance for achieving some objective — see PLAN 1
2 the means or procedure for doing something — see METHOD

stratum *n* one of the segments of society into which people are grouped — see CLASS 1

straw *adj* of a pale yellow or yellowish brown color — see BLOND

stray *adj* lacking a definite plan, purpose, or pattern — see RANDOM

streak *n* **1** a line or long narrow section differing in color from the background — see STRIPE
2 a very small amount — see PARTICLE 1

streak *vb* to make stripes on — see STRIPE

streaked *adj* having stripes — see STRIPED

stream *vb* **1** to cause to flow in a stream — see POUR 1
2 to move in a stream — see FLOW 1
3 to move or proceed smoothly and readily — see FLOW 2

streamer *n* a piece of cloth with a special design that is used as an emblem or for signaling — see FLAG 1

streamlet *n* a natural body of running water smaller than a river — see CREEK 1

streamline *vb* to make less complex — see SIMPLIFY

street *n* a passage cleared for public vehicular travel — see WAY 1

strength *n* **1** the ability to exert effort for the accomplishment of a task — see POWER 2
2 the ability to withstand force or stress without being distorted, dislodged, or damaged — see STABILITY 1

strengthen *vb* **1** to increase the ability of (as a muscle) to exert physical force <lifting weights every day will eventually *strengthen* your muscles> <the Army makes new recruits run for miles in order to *strengthen* them>
synonyms beef (up), fortify, harden, toughen
related words anneal, temper; firm (up), tone (up); energize, invigorate, vitalize; restrengthen
near antonyms cripple, incapacitate, paralyze; damage, harm, hurt, impair, injure; break down, wear out; sap, undermine
antonyms debilitate, enervate, enfeeble, weaken
2 to make able to withstand physical hardship, strain, or exposure — see HARDEN 2
3 to make markedly greater in measure or degree — see INTENSIFY
4 to prepare (oneself) mentally or emotionally — see FORTIFY 1

strenuous *adj* **1** marked by or uttered with forcefulness — see EMPHATIC 1
2 requiring considerable physical or mental effort — see HARD 2

strenuously *adv* **1** in a vigorous and forceful manner — see HARD 3
2 with great effort or determination — see HARD 1

stress *n* **1** the burden on one's emotional or mental well-being created by demands on one's time <with a full-time job and her college courses, the young woman is under a lot of *stress* right now>
synonyms pressure, strain, tension
related words load, weight; anxiety, concern, uneasiness, worry; aggravation, anger, annoyance, exasperation, irritation, persecution, trouble
near antonyms comfort, consolation
2 a special notice or importance given to something — see EMPHASIS 1

stress *vb* to indicate the importance of by giving prominent display — see EMPHASIZE

stressed–out *adj* suffering from high levels of physical and especially psychological stress <I'm becoming *stressed-out* from trying to keep up with the demands of my school work and the grueling workouts for the football team>
synonyms shell-shocked
related words burned-out (*or* burnt-out), exhausted, tired, worn-out; undone, unmanned, unnerved, unstrung; edgy, nervous, tense, uneasy; agitated, disturbed, perturbed, troubled, upset; aggravated, angry, annoyed, exasperated, irritated
near antonyms relaxed, rested

stretch *adj* able to revert to original size and shape after being stretched, squeezed, or twisted — see ELASTIC 1

stretch *n* **1** a wide space or area — see EXPANSE
2 an indefinite but usually short period of time — see WHILE 1
3 the distance or extent between possible extremes — see RANGE 3
4 the space or amount of space between two points, lines, surfaces, or objects — see DISTANCE

stretch *vb* **1** to add to the interest of by including made-up details — see EMBROIDER
2 to injure by overuse, misuse, or pressure — see STRAIN 1
3 to make longer — see EXTEND 1
4 to subject (a personal quality or faculty) to often excessive stress — see TRY (OUT) 2

stretch (out) *vb* to arrange the parts of (something) over a wider area — see OPEN 3

stretchable *adj* able to revert to original size and shape after being stretched, squeezed, or twisted — see ELASTIC 1

stretching *n* **1** the act of making longer — see EXTENSION 1
2 the representation of something in terms that go beyond the facts — see EXAGGERATION

strew *vb* to cover by or as if by scattering something over or on — see SCATTER 2

strict *adj* **1** following an original exactly — see FAITHFUL 2
2 given to exacting standards of discipline and self-restraint — see SEVERE 1
3 not allowing for any exceptions or loosening of standards — see RIGID 1

strictly *adv* without any relaxation of standards or precision ⟨*strictly* speaking, Columbus did not discover America—the people living there had long known about it⟩ ⟨the rules must be *strictly* obeyed⟩
synonyms exactly, precisely, rigidly, rigorously
related words carefully, conscientiously, meticulously, scrupulously
antonyms imprecisely, inexactly, loosely

strictness *n* the quality or state of being demanding or unyielding (as in discipline or criticism) — see SEVERITY

stricture *n* an often public or formal expression of disapproval — see CENSURE

stride *vb* to move along with a steady regular step especially in a group — see MARCH 1

strife *n* a lack of agreement or harmony — see DISCORD

strike *n* **1** a work stoppage by a body of workers intended to force an employer to meet their demands ⟨the nurses will go on *strike* tomorrow unless they're finally given a pay raise⟩
synonyms walkout
related words shutdown, shutoff, sit-down, slowdown; lockout
2 the act or action of setting upon with force or violence — see ATTACK 1
3 a feature of someone or something that creates difficulty for achieving success — see DISADVANTAGE
4 a forceful coming together of two things — see IMPACT 1

strike *vb* **1** to refuse to work in order to force an employer to meet demands ⟨the union is calling for its members to *strike* until the mining company agrees to meet safety standards⟩
synonyms walk out
related words knock off, lay off; leave, quit, resign; decamp, depart, exit, go, leave, light out, part
2 to act upon (a person or a person's feelings) so as to cause a response — see [1]AFFECT 1
3 to come into the mind of — see OCCUR (TO)
4 to come into usually forceful contact with something — see HIT 2
5 to deliver a blow to (someone or something) usually in a strong vigorous manner — see HIT 1
6 to take apart — see DISASSEMBLE
7 to take sudden, violent action against — see ATTACK 1

strike (into) *vb* to take the first step in (a process or course of action) — see BEGIN 1

strike (out) *vb* to show (something written) to be no longer valid by drawing a cross over or a line through it — see X (OUT)

striking *adj* **1** likely to attract attention — see NOTICEABLE
2 very noticeable especially for being incorrect or bad — see EGREGIOUS

string *n* **1** a length of braided, flexible material that is used for tying or connecting things — see CORD
2 a series of persons or things arranged one behind another — see LINE 1
3 a series of things linked together — see CHAIN 1

string *vb* to put together into a series by means of or as if by means of a thread — see THREAD 2

string along *vb* to cause to believe what is untrue — see DECEIVE

stringent *adj* not allowing for any exceptions or loosening of standards — see RIGID 1

stringy *adj* resembling or having the texture of a mass of strings ⟨*stringy* hair that clearly needed a good washing⟩
synonyms fibrous
related words knotty, ropy, thready; sinewy, wiry

strip *n* a long narrow piece of material ⟨now tear the paper into *strips* and fold them up carefully⟩
synonyms list, ribbon, slip
related words band, bandage, belt, binding, strap, swath, tape

strip *vb* **1** to remove clothing from — see UNDRESS
2 to search through with the intent of committing robbery — see RANSACK 1

stripe *n* a line or long narrow section differing in color from the background ⟨the United States flag has seven red *stripes*⟩
synonyms band, bar, streak
related words blaze, crossbar, pinstripe

stripe *vb* to make stripes on ⟨the children carefully *striped* the paper with red and blue paint⟩
synonyms band, bar, streak
related words blaze

striped *adj* having stripes ⟨the zebra is a black-and-white *striped* animal⟩
synonyms barred, streaked
related words corded, tabby

stripling *n* a male person who has not yet reached adulthood — see BOY

stripped *adj* **1** lacking a usual or natural covering — see NAKED 2
2 lacking or shed of clothing — see NAKED 1

strive *vb* **1** to devote serious and sustained effort — see LABOR
2 to make an effort to do — see ATTEMPT

stroke *n* a hard strike with a part of the body or an instrument — see [1]BLOW

stroke *vb* to touch or handle in a tender or loving manner — see FONDLE

stroke (out) *vb* to show (something written) to be no longer valid by drawing a cross over or a line through it — see X (OUT)

stroll *n* a relaxed journey on foot for exercise or pleasure — see WALK

stroller *n* a person who roams about without a fixed route or destination — see NOMAD

strong *adj* **1** having muscles capable of exerting great physical force ⟨I need some *strong* people to help me move furniture⟩
synonyms brawny, muscular, rugged, sinewy, stalwart, stout
related words forceful, mighty, potent, powerful, puissant; able-bodied, athletic, fit, trim; beefy, burly, husky, strapping; masculine, virile; hard, inured, strengthened, sturdy, tough, toughened; energetic, energized, invigorated, lusty, red-blooded, robust, vigorous, vitalized; hale, healthy, hearty, sound
near antonyms challenged, disabled, incapacitated, paralyzed; impotent, powerless; puny, slight, small, unfit, unhealthy
antonyms delicate, feeble, frail, weak, wimpy

2 able to withstand hardship, strain, or exposure — see HARDY 1

3 having a powerfully stimulating odor or flavor — see SHARP 3

4 having an abundance of some characteristic quality (as flavor) — see FULL-BODIED

5 having an unpleasant smell — see MALODOROUS

6 having great power or influence — see IMPORTANT 2

7 having the power to persuade — see COGENT

8 marked by the ability to withstand stress without structural damage or distortion — see STABLE 1

9 not showing weakness or uncertainty — see FIRM 1

strongbox *n* a specially reinforced container to keep valuables safe — see SAFE

stronghold *n* a structure or place from which one can resist attack — see FORT

strongly *adv* in a vigorous and forceful manner — see HARD 3

strop *vb* to make sharp or sharper — see SHARPEN

stropped *adj* having an edge thin enough to cut or pierce something — see SHARP 1

structure *n* **1** something built as a dwelling, shelter, or place for human activity — see BUILDING

2 something put together by arranging or connecting an array of parts — see CONSTRUCTION 1

3 the arrangement of parts that gives something its basic form — see FRAME 1

struggle *n* **1** a forceful effort to reach a goal or objective ⟨a physically challenged child's determined *struggle* to make straight A's in school⟩

synonyms battle, fight, fray, scrabble

related words effort, exertion, labor, pains, trouble, work; drudgery, grind, sweat, toil, travail; combat, conflict, contest, strife, tussle, war, warfare; attempt, endeavor, essay, try

2 a physical dispute between opposing individuals or groups — see FIGHT 1

3 an earnest effort for superiority or victory over another — see CONTEST 1

struggle *vb* to devote serious and sustained effort — see LABOR

strut *vb* **1** to walk with exaggerated arm and leg movements ⟨the toy soldiers in the Christmas pageant *strutted* stiffly across the stage⟩

synonyms prance, stalk, swagger

related words flounce, mince, traipse; pussyfoot, tiptoe; parade, promenade; pad, step, tread; pace, stride; lumber, lurch, pound, shamble, shuffle, stagger

2 to present so as to invite notice or attention — see SHOW 1

stub *n* an unused or unwanted piece or item typically of small size or value — see [1]SCRAP 1

stubborn *adj* sticking to an opinion, purpose, or course of action in spite of reason, arguments, or persuasion — see OBSTINATE

stubbornness *n* a steadfast adherence to an opinion, purpose, or course of action — see OBSTINACY

stubby *adj* being compact and broad in build and often short in stature — see STOCKY

stuck *adj* firmly positioned in place and difficult to dislodge — see TIGHT 2

stuck–up *adj* having too high an opinion of oneself — see CONCEITED

student *n* one who attends a school ⟨a straight-A *student* at the local high school⟩

synonyms pupil, scholar

related words schoolboy, schoolchild, schoolgirl; schoolfellow, schoolmate; collegian, postgraduate, undergraduate; freshman, junior, senior, sophomore; underclassman, upperclassman

studied *adj* decided on as a result of careful thought — see DELIBERATE 1

study *n* **1** a systematic search for the truth or facts about something — see INQUIRY 1

2 the state of being lost in thought — see REVERIE

study *vb* **1** to use the mind to acquire knowledge ⟨you'll have to *study* hard and learn all about the Revolutionary War in order to pass the history test⟩

synonyms bone (up)

related words cram; analyze, deduce, find out; learn, read; research, restudy

phrases go over, go through

2 to commit to memory — see MEMORIZE

3 to give serious and careful thought to — see PONDER

stuff *n* **1** a skill, an ability, or knowledge that makes a person able to do a particular job — see QUALIFICATION 1

2 the basic elements from which something can be developed — see MAKING

3 the quality or qualities that make a thing what it is — see ESSENCE

stuff *vb* **1** to close up so that no empty spaces remain — see FILL 2

2 to fill with food to capacity — see GORGE 1

3 to fit (something) into a tight space — see CROWD 1

4 to prevent passage through — see CLOG 1

5 to put into (something) as much as can be held or contained — see FILL 1

stuffed *adj* **1** containing or seeming to contain the greatest quantity or number possible — see FULL 1

2 having one's appetite completely satisfied — see FULL 3

stuffer *n* one who eats greedily or too much — see GLUTTON

stuffing *n* soft material that is used to fill the hollow parts of something — see FILLING

stuffy *adj* **1** lacking fresh air ⟨the house was so *stuffy* after being closed up for a month⟩

synonyms breathless, close, stifling, suffocating

related words airless, unventilated; heavy, oppressive, thick

near antonyms bracing, brisk, invigorating, refreshed, sweet; ventilated

antonyms airy, breezy

2 causing weariness, restlessness, or lack of interest — see BORING

stumble *n* **1** an unintentional departure from truth or accuracy — see ERROR 1

2 the act of going down from an upright position suddenly and involuntarily — see FALL 1

stumble *vb* **1** to go down from an upright position suddenly and involuntarily — see FALL 1

2 to make progress in a clumsy, struggling manner — see FLOUNDER 1

3 to move heavily or clumsily — see LUMBER 1

stumble (on *or* onto) *vb* to come upon unexpectedly or by chance — see HAPPEN (ON *OR* UPON)

stumble (upon) *vb* to come upon face-to-face or as if face-to-face — see MEET 1

stumbling block *n* something that makes progress

or movement more difficult — see ENCUMBRANCE

stump *vb* **1** to move heavily or clumsily — see LUMBER 1
2 to invite (someone) to take part in a contest or to perform a feat — see CHALLENGE 2

stumpy *adj* being compact and broad in build and often short in stature — see STOCKY

stun *vb* **1** to make senseless or dizzy by a blow ⟨a powerful uppercut to the jaw *stunned* the boxer and sent him crashing to the canvas⟩
synonyms daze
related words deaden, knock out, paralyze; benumb, numb, stupefy; bowl (over), knock (down)
phrases knock for a loop
2 to make a strong impression on (someone) with something unexpected — see SURPRISE 1

stunned *adj* **1** affected with sudden and great wonder or surprise — see THUNDERSTRUCK
2 suffering from mental confusion — see DIZZY 2

stunner *n* **1** a lovely woman — see BEAUTY 2
2 something that makes a strong impression because it is so unexpected — see SURPRISE 1

stunning *adj* **1** causing a strong emotional reaction because unexpected — see SURPRISING 1
2 causing wonder or astonishment — see MARVELOUS 1
3 very pleasing to look at — see BEAUTIFUL

stunt *n* an act of notable skill, strength, or cleverness — see FEAT 1

stunt *vb* to hold back the normal growth of ⟨unfortunately, an unusually dry summer seems to have permanently *stunted* the tree⟩
synonyms dwarf, suppress
related words arrest, catch, check, halt, hold up, stall, stay, still, stop; balk, block, hold back, impede, obstruct, stem
near antonyms advance, boost, encourage, forward, promote

stupefied *adj* **1** affected with sudden and great wonder or surprise — see THUNDERSTRUCK
2 suffering from mental confusion — see DIZZY 2

stupefy *vb* to make a strong impression on (someone) with something unexpected — see SURPRISE 1

stupefying *adj* causing a strong emotional reaction because unexpected — see SURPRISING 1

stupendous *adj* causing wonder or astonishment — see MARVELOUS 1

stupendously *adv* to a large extent or degree — see GREATLY 2

stupendousness *n* impressiveness of beauty on a large scale — see MAGNIFICENCE

stupid *adj* **1** not having or showing an ability to absorb ideas readily ⟨it's not nice to constantly call your brother *stupid* and ugly⟩ ⟨don't ask *stupid* questions⟩
synonyms brainless, dense, doltish, dopey, dorky [*slang*], dull, dumb, fatuous, half-witted, mindless, oafish, obtuse, senseless, simple, slow, thick, thickheaded, unintelligent, vacuous, weak-minded, witless
related words feebleminded, retarded, simpleminded; foolish, idiotic, imbecile, imbecilic, moronic; ignorant, illiterate, lowbrow, uneducated, uninformed, untaught, unthinking; absurd, asinine, balmy, cockeyed, crazy, cuckoo, daffy, daft, dotty, harebrained, insane, kooky, loony (*also* looney), lunatic, mad, nonsensical, nutty, preposterous, sappy, screwball, silly, unwise, wacky, zany; fallacious, illogical, invalid, irrational, unreasonable
near antonyms ingenious, resourceful; acute, astute, discerning, insightful, keen, knowing, perceptive, perspicacious, sagacious, sage, sapient, savvy, wise; cerebral, erudite, highbrow, intellectual, knowledgeable, learned, literate, scholarly, thinking, well-read; educated, informed, schooled, skilled, trained; crafty, cunning, foxy, shrewd, wily; judicious, prudent, sane, sensible, sound; logical, rational, reasonable, valid
antonyms apt, brainy, bright, brilliant, clever, intelligent, keen, nimble, quick, quick-witted, sharp, sharp-witted, smart
2 causing weariness, restlessness, or lack of interest — see BORING
3 showing or marked by a lack of good sense or judgment — see FOOLISH 1

stupidity *n* **1** the quality or state of lacking intelligence or quickness of mind ⟨the *stupidity* of the dialogue between the two romantic leads had movie audiences giggling uncontrollably⟩
synonyms brainlessness, denseness, density, doltishness, dopiness, dullness (*also* dulness), dumbness, fatuity, foolishness, mindlessness, oafishness, obtuseness, senselessness, simpleness, slowness, stupidness, vacuity, witlessness
related words absurdity, asininity, balminess, craziness, daftness, folly, idiocy, inanity, insanity, lunacy, madness, nonsensicalness, nuttiness, preposterousness, silliness, simplicity, wackiness, zaniness; fallacy, irrationality, unreasonableness
near antonyms acumen, alertness, astuteness, discernment, insight, judgment (*or* judgement), perception, perspicacity; sagacity, sageness, sapience, wisdom, wit; logicalness, rationality, reasonableness, soundness, validity
antonyms braininess, brightness, brilliance, cleverness, intelligence, keenness, quickness, quickwittedness, sharpness, smartness
2 a foolish act or idea — see FOLLY 1
3 language, behavior, or ideas that are absurd and contrary to good sense — see NONSENSE 1

stupidness *n* the quality or state of lacking intelligence or quickness of mind — see STUPIDITY 1

sturdily *adv* in a vigorous and forceful manner — see HARD 3

sturdiness *n* the ability to withstand force or stress without being distorted, dislodged, or damaged — see STABILITY 1

sturdy *adj* **1** able to withstand hardship, strain, or exposure — see HARDY 1
2 marked by the ability to withstand stress without structural damage or distortion — see STABLE 1
3 not showing weakness or uncertainty — see FIRM 1

style *n* **1** a distinctive way of putting ideas into words ⟨I correctly identified the quotation because I recognized Mark Twain's inimitable *style*⟩
synonyms fashion, locution, manner, mode, phraseology, tone, vein
related words delivery, elocution; archaism, colloquialism, regionalism; acceptation, connotation, denotation, idiom
2 the means or procedure for doing something — see METHOD
3 a practice or interest that is very popular for a short time — see FAD

style *vb* to give a name to — see NAME 1

styleless *adj* marked by an obvious lack of style or good taste — see TACKY 1
stylish *adj* being in the latest or current fashion <a pretty, *stylish* dress>
synonyms à la mode (*also* a la mode), chic, fashionable, in, modish, sharp, smart, snappy
related words dapper, dashing, natty, rakish, spiffy, spruce; posh, ritzy, swank (*or* swanky); elegant, graceful, handsome, majestic, refined, sophisticated, stately, tasteful, understated; dandyish, dudish, foppish; classic, exquisite, quiet, restrained, simple; affected, grandiose, pretentious
near antonyms tacky, unattractive, unbecoming; graceless, inelegant, tasteless, unhandsome; frowsy (*or* frowzy), sloppy, slovenly, unkempt, untidy; disheveled (*or* dishevelled), messy, mussy, rumpled, wrinkled; shabby, sleazy
antonyms dowdy, outmoded, styleless, unfashionable, unstylish
suasion *n* the act of reasoning or pleading with someone to accept a belief or course of action — see PERSUASION 1
suave *adj* having or showing very polished and worldly manners <the *suave* gentleman was a great favorite of the elegant ladies who attended parties at the embassy>
synonyms debonair, smooth, sophisticated, urbane
related words glib, slick, unctuous; civilized, cultivated, cultured, graceful, poised, polished, refined; cosmopolitan, smart, worldly-wise; experienced, knowing, practiced (*or* practised), schooled, seasoned; amiable, appealing, attractive; assured, calm, collected, composed, confident, cool, placid, secure, self-assured, self-confident, self-possessed, serene, tranquil, undisturbed, unperturbed
near antonyms awkward, clumsy, gauche, graceless, stiff, stilted, uncomfortable, uneasy, ungraceful, wooden; callow, green, inexperienced, raw; parochial, provincial, roughhewn, rustic; inelegant, philistine, uncivilized, uncultured, unrefined; unsophisticated, unworldly; gawky, lubberly, stodgy, ungainly; diffident, insecure
antonyms boorish, churlish, clownish, loutish, uncouth
[1]**sub** *n* a large sandwich on a long split roll — see SUBMARINE
[2]**sub** *n* a person or thing that takes the place of another — see SUBSTITUTE
sub *vb* to serve as a replacement usually for a time only — see COVER 1
subdue *vb* **1** to achieve a victory over — see BEAT 2
2 to bring under one's control by force of arms — see CONQUER 1
3 to put a stop to (something) by the use of force — see QUELL 1
subdued *adj* not excessively showy — see QUIET 2
subduer *n* one that defeats an enemy or opponent — see VICTOR 1
subduing *n* the act or process of bringing someone or something under one's control — see CONQUEST
subject *n* **1** a major object of interest or concern (as in a discussion or artistic composition) — see MATTER 1
2 a person who owes allegiance to a government and is protected by it — see CITIZEN 1
subject *vb* to bring under one's control by force of arms — see CONQUER 1
subject (to) *adj* **1** determined by something else — see DEPENDENT 2
2 being in a situation where one is likely to meet with harm — see LIABLE 1
subjecting *n* the act or process of bringing someone or something under one's control — see CONQUEST
subjection *n* the act or process of bringing someone or something under one's control — see CONQUEST
subjugate *vb* to bring under one's control by force of arms — see CONQUER 1
subjugating *n* the act or process of bringing someone or something under one's control — see CONQUEST
subjugation *n* the act or process of bringing someone or something under one's control — see CONQUEST
sublime *adj* **1** causing wonder or astonishment — see MARVELOUS 1
2 having, characterized by, or arising from a dignified and generous nature — see NOBLE 2
sublimeness *n* impressiveness of beauty on a large scale — see MAGNIFICENCE
submarine *adj* living, lying, or occurring below the surface of the water — see UNDERWATER
submarine *n* a large sandwich on a long split roll <always orders a roast beef *submarine* with the works>
synonyms grinder, hero, hoagie, Italian sandwich, po'boy (*also* poor boy), sub
submerge *vb* **1** to cover or become filled with a flood — see FLOOD
2 to sink or push (something) briefly into or as if into a liquid — see DIP 1
submerged *adj* living, lying, or occurring below the surface of the water — see UNDERWATER
submerse *vb* **1** to cover or become filled with a flood — see FLOOD
2 to sink or push (something) briefly into or as if into a liquid — see DIP 1
submission *n* **1** a bending to the authority or control of another — see OBEDIENCE 1
2 the usually forced yielding of one's person or possessions to the control of another — see SURRENDER
submissive *adj* readily giving in to the command or authority of another — see OBEDIENT
submissively *adv* in manner showing no signs of pride or self-assertion — see LOWLY
submissiveness *n* a readiness or willingness to yield to the wishes of others — see COMPLIANCE 1
submit *vb* **1** to cease resistance (as to another's arguments, demands, or control) — see YIELD 3
2 to give up and cease resistance (as to a liking, temptation, or habit) — see YIELD 1
3 to yield to the control or power of enemy forces — see FALL 2
submitting *n* the usually forced yielding of one's person or possessions to the control of another — see SURRENDER
subordinate *adj* having not so great importance or rank as another — see LESSER
subordinate *n* one who is of lower rank and typically under the authority of another — see UNDERLING
subordination *n* a bending to the authority or control of another — see OBEDIENCE 1

subpoena *n* a written notice ordering a person to appear in court — see SUMMONS

subscribe (to) *vb* to have a favorable opinion of — see APPROVE (OF)

subsequent *adj* being, occurring, or carried out at a time after something else ⟨I'll do the first problem as an example, but all *subsequent* efforts must be done on your own⟩
synonyms after, ensuing, later, posterior
related words behind, belated, delayed, late, slow; eventual, last, ultimate; following
near antonyms advance, early, premature
antonyms antecedent, anterior, fore, precedent, preceding, previous, prior

subsequently *adv* following in time or place — see AFTER

subside *vb* to grow less in scope or intensity especially gradually — see DECREASE 2

subsidize *vb* **1** to furnish (as an institution) with a regular source of income — see ENDOW 2
2 to provide money for — see FINANCE 1

subsidy *n* a sum of money allotted for a specific use by official or formal action — see APPROPRIATION

subsist *vb* to have life — see BE 1

subsistence *n* **1** the fact of being or of being real — see EXISTENCE
2 uninterrupted or lasting existence — see CONTINUATION

substance *n* **1** the basic elements from which something can be developed — see MAKING
2 the quality or qualities that make a thing what it is — see ESSENCE
3 the total of one's money and property — see WEALTH 1
4 one that has a real and independent existence — see ENTITY

substance abuser *n* a person who regularly uses drugs especially illegally — see DOPER

substandard *adj* falling short of a standard — see BAD 1

substantial *adj* **1** having great meaning or lasting effect — see IMPORTANT 1
2 of a size greater than average of its kind — see LARGE
3 relating to or composed of matter — see MATERIAL 1
4 sufficiently large in size, amount, or number to merit attention — see CONSIDERABLE 1

substantiality *n* the quality or state of being large in size — see LARGENESS

substantially *adv* for the most part — see CHIEFLY

substantiate *vb* **1** to gain full recognition or acceptance of — see ESTABLISH 1
2 to give evidence or testimony to the truth or factualness of — see CONFIRM
3 to represent in visible form — see EMBODY 2
4 to show the existence or truth of by evidence — see PROVE 1

substantiating *adj* serving to give support to the truth or factualness of something — see CORROBORATIVE

substantiation *n* something presented in support of the truth or accuracy of a claim — see PROOF

substitute *adj* **1** being such in appearance only and made with or manufactured from usually cheaper materials — see IMITATION
2 taking the place of one that came before — see NEW 1

substitute *n* a person or thing that takes the place of another ⟨you'll be getting a *substitute* until your regular teacher is feeling better⟩ ⟨if you like, you can use nuts as a *substitute* for coconut in that recipe⟩
synonyms backup, pinch hitter, relief, replacement, reserve, stand-in, sub
related words alternate, understudy; apology, makeshift, stopgap; agent, attorney, commissary, delegate, deputy, envoy, factor, procurator, proxy, representative, surrogate; assistant, second

substitute *vb* **1** to give up (something) and take something else in return — see CHANGE 3
2 to serve as a replacement usually for a time only — see COVER 1
3 to take the place of — see REPLACE 1

subterfuge *n* the use of clever underhanded actions to achieve an end — see TRICKERY

subtle *adj* **1** clever at attaining one's ends by indirect and often deceptive means — see ARTFUL 1
2 made or done with extreme care and accuracy — see FINE 2
3 satisfying or pleasing because of fineness or mildness — see DELICATE 1

subtleness *n* skill in achieving one's ends through indirect, subtle, or underhanded means — see CUNNING 1

subtlety *n* skill in achieving one's ends through indirect, subtle, or underhanded means — see CUNNING 1

subtract *vb* to take away (an amount or number) from a total ⟨if you *subtract* 10 from 23, you get 13⟩ ⟨you can *subtract* the time you spent daydreaming from your total homework time⟩
synonyms deduct, take off
related words decrease, diminish, discount, downsize, lessen, lower, reduce; abbreviate, abridge, clip, crop, curtail, cut, cut back, cut down, dock, pare, prune, retrench, shorten, slash, trim, truncate, whittle
near antonyms adjoin, annex, append, tack (on); add (to), complement, supplement; enhance, heighten, intensify; aggrandize, amplify, augment, boost, enlarge, escalate, expand, increase, raise
antonyms add

subtraction *n* the act or an instance of taking away from a total ⟨the dog was responsible for the unexplained *subtraction* in the number of potato chips on my sister's plate⟩
synonyms deduction
related words discount; abatement, decline, decrement, diminishment, diminution, drop, fall, loss, reduction, shrinkage; curtailment, cut, cutback
near antonyms boost, enlargement, gain, increase, increment, raise, rise; accretion, accrual, accumulation, addendum, appendix, supplement
antonyms addition

suburbia *n* the area around a city — see ENVIRONS 1

subvert *vb* to lower in character or dignity — see DEBASE 1

succeed *vb* **1** to turn out as planned or desired ⟨the advertising campaign that finally *succeeded* used humor to sell the product⟩
synonyms click, deliver, go over, pan out, work out
related words catch on; flourish, prosper, thrive
phrases catch fire
near antonyms languish; flounder, struggle; decline, slip, slump, wane

antonyms collapse, fail, flop, flunk, fold, wash out
2 to reach a desired level of accomplishment <if you want to *succeed* in show business, you have to feel comfortable in front of an audience>
synonyms flourish, prosper, thrive
related words prevail, triumph, win
phrases get ahead, make good, make it
near antonyms flounder, struggle
antonyms fail
3 to come after in time — see FOLLOW 1
succeeding *adj* **1** being the one that comes immediately after another — see NEXT
2 following one after another without others coming in between — see CONSECUTIVE
success *n* **1** a person or thing that is successful — see HIT 1
2 a successful result brought about by hard work — see ACCOMPLISHMENT 1
successful *adj* **1** having attained a desired end or state of good fortune <the family runs several *successful* restaurants>
synonyms flourishing, going, palmy, prosperous, thriving, triumphant
related words coming, promising; booming, growing, roaring, robust
near antonyms futureless, hopeless, inauspicious, no-good; collapsing, failing, flopping, flunking, folding, washing-out; declining, slipping, slumping, waning; bankrupt, destroyed, ruined, wrecked
antonyms failed, unsuccessful
2 marked by vigorous growth and well-being especially economically — see PROSPEROUS 1
successional *adj* following one after another without others coming in between — see CONSECUTIVE
successive *adj* following one after another without others coming in between — see CONSECUTIVE
succinct *adj* marked by the use of few words to convey much information or meaning — see CONCISE
succinctly *adv* in a few words — see SHORTLY 1
succinctness *n* the quality or state of being marked by or using only few words to convey much meaning <Caesar's observation, "I came, I saw, I conquered," is famous for its *succinctness*>
synonyms brevity, briefness, compactness, conciseness, crispness, pithiness, terseness
related words abruptness, bluntness, brusqueness, curtness, shortness
near antonyms redundancy, repetitiousness
antonyms diffuseness, long-windedness, prolixity, verbosity, wordiness
succulence *n* the quality or state of being full of juice <the *succulence* of the apple was such that the first bite sent juice running down my chin>
synonyms fleshiness, juiciness, pulpiness
related words sap, sappiness
succulent *adj* full of juice — see JUICY
succumb *vb* **1** to cease resistance (as to another's arguments, demands, or control) — see YIELD 3
2 to give up and cease resistance (as to a liking, temptation, or habit) — see YIELD 1
3 to stop living — see DIE 1
4 to yield to the control or power of enemy forces — see FALL 2
such *adj* having qualities in common — see ALIKE
suchlike *adj* having qualities in common — see ALIKE
suck (up) *vb* to take in (something liquid) through small openings — see ABSORB 1
sucker *n* one who is easily deceived or cheated — see DUPE
suddenly *adv* **1** with great suddenness — see SHORT
2 without warning — see UNAWARES
suds *n* a light mass of fine bubbles formed in or on a liquid — see FOAM
sudsy *adj* covered with, consisting of, or resembling foam — see FOAMY
sue (for) *vb* to make a request for — see ASK (FOR) 1
suer *n* the person in a legal proceeding who makes a charge of wrongdoing against another — see COMPLAINANT
suffer *vb* **1** to give permission to — see ALLOW 2
2 to come to a knowledge of (something) by living through it — see EXPERIENCE
3 to feel deep sadness or mental pain — see GRIEVE
4 to give permission for or to approve of — see ALLOW 1
sufferable *adj* capable of being endured — see BEARABLE
sufferance *n* **1** the approval by someone in authority for the doing of something — see PERMISSION
2 the capacity to endure what is difficult or disagreeable without complaining — see PATIENCE
suffice *vb* to be enough — see SERVE 2
sufficiency *n* the quality or state of meeting one's needs adequately <the *sufficiency* of the portions is such that you will leave the restaurant with a full stomach but without doggie bags>
synonyms acceptability, adequacy, satisfactoriness
related words appropriateness, correctness, fitness, goodness, properness, rightness, seemliness, suitability, suitableness; bountifulness, copiousness; excess, overabundance, oversupply, surfeit, surplus; abundance, amplitude, plenitude, plenty
near antonyms lack, want; dearth, shortage; meagerness, paucity, poorness, poverty, rareness, rarity, scantiness, scarceness, scarcity, skimpiness; necessity, need, privation
antonyms inadequacy, insufficiency
sufficiently *adv* in or to a degree or quantity that meets one's requirements or satisfaction — see ENOUGH 1
suffocate *vb* to be or cause to be killed by lack of breathable air — see SMOTHER 1
suffocating *adj* lacking fresh air — see STUFFY 1
suffrage *n* the right to formally express one's position or will in an election — see VOTE 1
suffuse *vb* **1** to cause (as a person) to become filled or saturated with a certain quality or principle — see INFUSE
2 to spread throughout — see PERMEATE
sugarcoated *adj* appealing to the emotions in an obvious and tiresome way — see CORNY
sugary *adj* appealing to the emotions in an obvious and tiresome way — see CORNY
suggest *vb* **1** to convey an idea indirectly — see HINT
2 to put forward as one's choice for a wise or proper course of action — see ADVISE 2
3 to set before the mind for consideration — see PROPOSE 1
suggestion *n* **1** a slight or indirect pointing to

something (as a solution or explanation) — see HINT 1

2 something which is presented for consideration — see PROPOSAL

suggestive *adj* **1** hinting at or intended to call to mind matters regarded as indecent ⟨making *suggestive* remarks to one's classmates will not be tolerated⟩

synonyms bawdy, lewd, racy, ribald, salty, spicy

related words leering; coarse, crude, earthy, foul, gross; dirty, filthy, lascivious, nasty, obscene, pornographic, smutty, unprintable, vulgar; indecorous, unbecoming; naughty, wicked; exceptionable, objectionable, unacceptable, undesirable, unwanted, unwelcome

near antonyms clean, decent; innocuous, inoffensive; priggish, prim, prudish, puritanical, straitlaced (*or* straightlaced), Victorian; correct, decorous, genteel, polite, proper, seemly; acceptable, agreeable, desirable, pleasant, pleasing, welcome; appropriate, becoming, fit, meet, suitable; immaculate, pure, spotless

2 provoking a memory or mental association ⟨a haunting and *suggestive* song about a long-lost love⟩

synonyms evocative, reminiscent

related words eloquent, expressive, meaningful, significant; affecting, emotional, moving, poignant, stirring, touching; exciting, provocative, provoking, rousing, stimulating

3 clearly conveying a special meaning (as one's mood) — see EXPRESSIVE

suicide *n* the act of deliberately killing oneself ⟨teenagers are more prone to *suicide* because they mistakenly believe their troubles are insurmountable⟩

synonyms self-destruction

related words martyrdom; foul play, homicide, murder, slaying; killing, manslaughter; assassination, execution; euthanasia, mercy killing

suit *n* **1** a court case for enforcing a right or claim — see LAWSUIT

2 an earnest request — see PLEA 1

suit *vb* **1** to be fitting or proper — see DO 1

2 to give satisfaction to — see PLEASE

3 to outfit with clothes and especially fine or special clothes — see CLOTHE 1

suitability *n* the quality or state of being especially suitable or fitting — see APPROPRIATENESS

suitable *adj* **1** having the required skills for an acceptable level of performance — see COMPETENT

2 meeting the requirements of a purpose or situation — see FIT 1

suitableness *n* the quality or state of being especially suitable or fitting — see APPROPRIATENESS

suitably *adv* in a manner suitable for the occasion or purpose — see PROPERLY

suitcase *n* a bag carried by hand and designed to hold a traveler's clothing and personal articles — see TRAVELING BAG

suite *n* **1** a body of employees or servants who accompany and wait on a person — see CORTEGE 1

2 a number of things considered as a unit — see GROUP 1

3 a room or set of rooms in a private house or a block used as a separate dwelling place — see APARTMENT 1

suitor *n* **1** a man who courts a woman usually with the goal of marrying her ⟨my sister finally married her *suitor* of six years on Sunday⟩

synonyms gallant, swain, wooer

related words beau, boyfriend, fellow, man; admirer, crush, steady; beloved, darling, dear, favorite, flame, honey, love, lover, sweet, sweetheart, valentine; date, escort; fiancé, intended

2 one who asks earnestly for a favor or gift — see SUPPLICANT

sulk *n* a state of resentful silence or irritability ⟨a child sitting in a *sulk* over a minor disagreement⟩

synonyms pet, pouts, sulkiness, sullenness

related words blues, dumps, mopes; surliness; biliousness, crankiness, crossness, crotchetiness, grouchiness, grumpiness, irascibility, irritability, peevishness, perverseness, perversity, pettishness, petulance, testiness, waspishness; cantankerousness, disagreeableness, orneriness

near antonyms sociability; cheerfulness, gaiety (*also* gayety), gladsomeness, good-humoredness, high-spiritedness, lightheartedness, perkiness

sulk *vb* to silently go about in a bad mood ⟨the toddler *sulked* all day whenever he didn't get his way⟩

synonyms mope, pout

related words brood, dwell (on), mull (over), muse (over), ponder; frown, glower, lower (*also* lour), scowl; carry on, take on

sulkiness *n* a state of resentful silence or irritability — see SULK

sulky *adj* given to or displaying a resentful silence and often irritability ⟨our teenage daughter turns *sulky* if we refuse to let her borrow the car⟩

synonyms glum, pouting, sullen, surly

related words dour, gloomy, morose; choleric, crabby, cranky, cross, crotchety, grouchy, grumpy, irascible, irritable, peevish, perverse, pettish, petulant, quick-tempered, short-tempered, snappy, snippy, testy, waspish; brooding, moping; bearish, bilious, cantankerous, disagreeable, dyspeptic, ill-humored, ill-natured, ill-tempered, ornery; sensitive, temperamental, thin-skinned, touchy

near antonyms sociable; cheerful, cheery, gladsome, good-humored, good-natured, perky

sullen *adj* **1** causing or marked by an atmosphere lacking in cheer — see GLOOMY 1

2 given to or displaying a resentful silence and often irritability — see SULKY

sullenness *n* a state of resentful silence or irritability — see SULK

sullied *adj* not clean — see DIRTY 1

sully *vb* to make dirty — see DIRTY

sultry *adj* **1** containing or characterized by an uncomfortable amount of moisture — see HUMID

2 having a notably high temperature — see HOT 1

sum *n* **1** a complete amount of something — see WHOLE

2 a short statement of the main points — see SUMMARY

sum *vb* to combine (numbers) into a single sum — see ADD 2

sum (to *or* into) *vb* to have a total of — see AMOUNT (TO) 1

summarily *adv* in a few words — see SHORTLY 1

summarization *n* a short statement of the main points — see SUMMARY

summarize *vb* to make into a short statement of the main points (as of a report) ⟨the closing minute of the newscast *summarizes* the main story of the day⟩

synonyms abstract, digest, encapsulate, epito-

mize, outline, recap, recapitulate, sum up, wrap up
related words abridge, condense, curtail, shorten; downsize, shrink; concentrate, consolidate; simplify, streamline
near antonyms amplify, elaborate (on *or* upon), enlarge (on *or* upon), expand
summary *adj* marked by the use of few words to convey much information or meaning — see CONCISE
summary *n* a short statement of the main points ⟨many book reports choose to begin with a *summary* of the book⟩
synonyms abstract, digest, encapsulation, epitome, outline, précis, recap, recapitulation, résumé (*or* resume *also* resumé), roundup, sum, summarization, synopsis
related words abbreviation, abridgment (*or* abridgement), condensation, curtailment, shortening; brief; rundown; simplification, streamlining
near antonyms amplification, enlargement, expansion
summation *n* a complete amount of something — see WHOLE
summit *n* the highest part or point — see HEIGHT 1
summon *vb* **1** to demand or request the presence or service of ⟨without explanation, the principal *summoned* me to his office⟩
synonyms call, hail
related words cite, subpoena; assemble, convene, convoke, muster; ask, bid, invite; command, order, request, requisition; beckon, demand, invoke
phrases send for
near antonyms dismiss, send (away), turn away
2 to call into being through the use of one's inner resources or powers ⟨managed to *summon* a bright smile despite the gloomy day⟩
synonyms conjure (up), gather (up)
related words educe, elicit, evoke, raise
3 to bring together in assembly by or as if by command — see CONVOKE
summons *n* a written notice ordering a person to appear in court ⟨if you ignore a court *summons*, you will be fined⟩
synonyms subpoena
related words warrant, writ
sumptuous *adj* showing obvious signs of wealth and comfort — see LUXURIOUS
sumptuously *adv* in a luxurious manner — see HIGH
sum up *vb* to make into a short statement of the main points (as of a report) — see SUMMARIZE
sun *n* **1** the light given off by the star around which the planet Earth revolves ⟨be sure to wear sunscreen if you plan to spend more than a few minutes in the *sun*⟩
synonyms sunlight, sunshine
related words sunburst; daylight
near antonyms cloudiness; penumbra, shade, shadiness, shadow, umbra
2 a ball-shaped gaseous celestial body that shines by its own light — see STAR 1
sunder *vb* to set or force apart — see SEPARATE 1
sundown *n* the time from when the sun begins to set to the onset of total darkness — see DUSK 1
sundowner *n, Australian* a homeless wanderer who may beg or steal for a living — see TRAMP
sundries *n pl* small useful items — see NOTION 1
sunken *adj* **1** curved inward — see HOLLOW
2 living, lying, or occurring below the surface of the water — see UNDERWATER
sunlight *n* the light given off by the star around which the planet Earth revolves — see SUN 1
sunny *adj* **1** having or being an outward sign of good feelings (as of love, confidence, or happiness) — see RADIANT 1
2 having or showing a good mood or disposition — see CHEERFUL 1
3 indicative of or marked by high spirits or good humor — see MERRY
4 not stormy or cloudy — see FAIR 1
sunrise *n* the first appearance of light in the morning or the time of its appearance — see DAWN 1
sunset *n* the time from when the sun begins to set to the onset of total darkness — see DUSK 1
sunshine *n* the light given off by the star around which the planet Earth revolves — see SUN 1
sunshiny *adj* not stormy or cloudy — see FAIR 1
sunup *n* the first appearance of light in the morning or the time of its appearance — see DAWN 1
sup *n* the portion of a serving of a beverage that is swallowed at one time — see DRINK 2
sup *vb* to swallow in liquid form — see DRINK 1
super *adj* unusually large — see HUGE
super *adv* to a great degree — see VERY 1
superabundance *n* **1** an amount or supply more than sufficient to meet one's needs — see PLENTY 1
2 the state or an instance of going beyond what is usual, proper, or needed — see EXCESS
superb *adj* of the very best kind — see EXCELLENT
superbness *n* **1** exceptionally high quality — see EXCELLENCE 1
2 impressiveness of beauty on a large scale — see MAGNIFICENCE
supercilious *adj* having a feeling of superiority that shows itself in an overbearing attitude — see ARROGANT
superciliousness *n* an exaggerated sense of one's importance that shows itself in the making of excessive or unjustified claims — see ARROGANCE
superficial *adj* **1** lying on or affecting only the outer layer of something ⟨a *superficial* scratch that barely even broke the skin⟩
synonyms skin-deep, surface
related words depthless, shallow, shoal; two-dimensional
near antonyms deep, deep-rooted, deep-seated; subcutaneous, subterranean
2 having or showing a lack of depth of understanding or character ⟨a *superficial* analysis of how movie and video violence affects young people⟩
synonyms facile, one-dimensional, shallow, skin-deep
related words cursory, hasty, sketchy; aimless, desultory, haphazard, hit-or-miss, random; limited, narrow, restricted
near antonyms discerning, penetrating; definitive, hard; broad, complete, comprehensive, exhaustive, extensive, far-reaching, wide; general, global, inclusive; detailed, in-depth; critical
antonyms deep, profound
superfluity *n* **1** something adding to pleasure or comfort but not absolutely necessary — see LUXURY 1
2 the state or an instance of going beyond what is usual, proper, or needed — see EXCESS

superfluous *adj* being over what is needed — see SPARE 1

superheated *adj* having a notably high temperature — see HOT 1

superhuman *adj* **1** being so extraordinary or abnormal as to suggest powers which violate the laws of nature — see SUPERNATURAL 2
2 of, relating to, or being part of a reality beyond the observable physical universe — see SUPERNATURAL 1

superintend *vb* **1** to be in charge of — see BOSS 1
2 to look after and make decisions about — see CONDUCT 1
3 to take charge of especially on behalf of another — see ²TEND 1

superintendence *n* **1** the act or activity of looking after and making decisions about something — see CONDUCT 1
2 the duty or function of watching or guarding for the sake of proper direction or control — see SUPERVISION 1

superintendency *n* the duty or function of watching or guarding for the sake of proper direction or control — see SUPERVISION 1

superintendent *n* a person who manages or directs — see EXECUTIVE

superior *adj* **1** having a feeling of superiority that shows itself in an overbearing attitude — see ARROGANT
2 having or displaying feelings of scorn for what is regarded as beneath oneself — see PROUD 1
3 of the very best kind — see EXCELLENT
4 standing above others in rank, importance, or achievement — see EMINENT

superior *n* one who is above another in rank, station, or office <if a customer is rude to you, report it to your *superior* and they'll handle it>
synonyms better, elder, senior
related words boss, chief, head, leader, master
near antonyms assistant, deputy
antonyms inferior, subordinate, underling

superiority *n* **1** an exaggerated sense of one's importance that shows itself in the making of excessive or unjustified claims — see ARROGANCE
2 exceptionally high quality — see EXCELLENCE 1
3 the fact or state of being above others in rank or importance — see EMINENCE 1

superlative *adj* of the very best kind — see EXCELLENT

supernal *adj* **1** of the very best kind — see EXCELLENT
2 of, relating to, or suggesting heaven — see CELESTIAL

supernatural *adj* **1** of, relating to, or being part of a reality beyond the observable physical universe <Susie believes in ghosts, guardian angels, and other *supernatural* beings>
synonyms metaphysical, preternatural, superhuman, unearthly
related words occult; extrasensory; celestial, divine, heavenly
antonyms natural
2 being so extraordinary or abnormal as to suggest powers which violate the laws of nature <he seems to read books with *supernatural* speed>
synonyms magical, miraculous, phenomenal, superhuman, uncanny, unearthly
related words bizarre, curious, far-out, funny, kinky, outlandish, out-of-the-way, outrageous, outré, peculiar, quaint, queer, queerish, quirky, remarkable, screwy, strange, wacky, way-out, weird, wild; baffling, bewildering, confounding, mystifying, perplexing, puzzling, shocking; aberrant, abnormal, atypical, extraordinary, fantastic, flaky, freak, freakish, idiosyncratic, rare, singular, uncommon, unique, unusual, unwonted; unconventional, uncustomary, unorthodox; conspicuous, notable, noticeable, outstanding, prominent, salient, striking
near antonyms average, commonplace, everyday, garden, ordinary, prosaic, routine, run-of-the-mill, typical, unexceptional, unremarkable, usual, workaday; expected, familiar, predictable; common, customary, frequent, habitual, regular, wonted
3 of, relating to, or being God — see HOLY 3

supernumerary *adj* being over what is needed — see SPARE 1

supersede *vb* to take the place of — see REPLACE 1

superstar *n* a person who is widely known and usually much talked about — see CELEBRITY 1

supervene *vb* to come after in time — see FOLLOW 1

supervise *vb* **1** to be in charge of — see BOSS 1
2 to look after and make decisions about — see CONDUCT 1
3 to take charge of especially on behalf of another — see ²TEND 1

supervision *n* **1** the duty or function of watching or guarding for the sake of proper direction or control <our French teacher has *supervision* of all activities of the French Club>
synonyms care, charge, guidance, headship, oversight, regulation, superintendence, superintendency
related words monitoring, observing; administration, control, direction, management, running; leadership, piloting, shepherding, steering; government, reign, rule; aegis, guardianship, protection, tutelage
2 the act or activity of looking after and making decisions about something — see CONDUCT 1

supervisor *n* a person who manages or directs — see EXECUTIVE

supervisory *adj* suited for or relating to the directing of things — see EXECUTIVE

supplant *vb* to take the place of — see REPLACE 1

supple *adj* **1** able to bend easily without breaking — see WILLOWY
2 able to revert to original size and shape after being stretched, squeezed, or twisted — see ELASTIC 1

supplement *n* **1** something added (as by growth) — see INCREASE 1
2 something that serves to complete or make up for a deficiency in something else — see COMPLEMENT 1

supplemental *adj* available to supply something extra when needed — see AUXILIARY

supplementary *adj* **1** available to supply something extra when needed — see AUXILIARY
2 related to each other in such a way that one completes the other — see COMPLEMENTARY

suppliant *adj* asking humbly <the *suppliant* student pleaded for a second chance>
synonyms beseeching, entreating, imploring, pleading, prayerful, soliciting, supplicant, supplicating
related words importunate, insistent, persistent

suppliant *n* one who asks earnestly for a favor or gift — see SUPPLICANT
supplicant *adj* asking humbly — see SUPPLIANT
supplicant *n* one who asks earnestly for a favor or gift ⟨the new governor soon had to deal with a long line of *supplicants* asking for jobs and other political favors⟩
synonyms petitioner, pleader, solicitor, suitor, suppliant
related words beggar, mendicant, panhandler; asker, requester, suer
supplicate *vb* to make a request to (someone) in an earnest or urgent manner — see BEG
supplicating *adj* asking humbly — see SUPPLIANT
supplication *n* an earnest request — see PLEA 1
supply *n* the number of individuals or amount of something available at any given time ⟨the *supply* of grown-ups willing to coach soccer seems to be shrinking⟩
synonyms budget, fund, pool
related words reserve, reservoir, resource; cache, hoard, stockpile; refill, renewal, replacement; kitty, nest egg, pot, purse; source, well, wellspring
supply *vb* **1** to provide (someone) with what is needed for a task or activity — see FURNISH 1
2 to put (something) into the possession of someone for use or consumption — see FURNISH 2
support *n* **1** something that holds up or serves as a foundation for something else ⟨if you don't add a couple more *supports* to that tower of blocks, it's going to fall down⟩
synonyms brace, bulwark, buttress, mount, mounting, shore, stay, underpinning
related words column, pedestal, pilaster, pillar; arch, bracket, cantilever; crutch, mainstay, peg, post, stake, stanchion, stand, stilt, truss; base, foundation, frame
2 an act or instance of helping — see HELP 1
3 something or someone to which one looks for support — see DEPENDENCE 2
support *vb* **1** to promote the interests or cause of ⟨my parents *support* the local schools both by volunteering and by fiercely opposing funding cuts at town meetings⟩
synonyms advocate, back, champion, endorse (*also* indorse), patronize
related words adopt, embrace, espouse; abet, aid, assist, prop (up), second; bolster, boost, buttress, reinforce; bail out, deliver, rescue, save
phrases stand up for
near antonyms baffle, foil, frustrate, interfere, oppose, sabotage, thwart; desert, disappoint, fail, let down
2 to pay the living expenses of ⟨a young widow *supporting* a sick mother as well as two small children on a teacher's salary⟩
synonyms maintain, provide (for)
related words finance, fund, stake
phrases foot the bills for, take care of
3 to hold up or serve as a foundation for ⟨pillars *supporting* the bridge⟩
synonyms bear, bolster, brace, buttress, carry, prop (up), shore (up), stay, underpin, uphold
related words steady, truss, underlie
4 to continue to declare to be true or proper despite opposition or objections — see MAINTAIN 2
5 to give evidence or testimony to the truth or factualness of — see CONFIRM
6 to provide (someone) with what is useful or necessary to achieve an end — see HELP 1
7 to put up with (something painful or difficult) — see BEAR 2
supportable *adj* **1** capable of being defended with good reasoning against verbal attack — see TENABLE 1
2 capable of being endured — see BEARABLE
3 capable of being proven as true or real — see VERIFIABLE
supporter *n* **1** a person who actively supports or favors a cause — see EXPONENT
2 someone associated with another to give assistance or moral support — see ALLY
supporting *adj* serving to give support to the truth or factualness of something — see CORROBORATIVE
supportive *adj* serving to give support to the truth or factualness of something — see CORROBORATIVE
suppose *vb* **1** to decide the size, amount, number, or distance of (something) without actual measurement — see ESTIMATE 2
2 to form an opinion from little or no evidence — see GUESS 1
3 to have as an opinion — see BELIEVE 2
4 to take as true or as a fact without actual proof — see ASSUME 2
supposed *adj* appearing to be true on the basis of evidence that may or may not be confirmed — see APPARENT 1
supposedly *adv* to all outward appearances — see APPARENTLY
supposition *n* **1** an idea that is the starting point for making a case or conducting an investigation — see THEORY
2 an opinion or judgment based on little or no evidence — see CONJECTURE
3 something taken as being true or factual and used as a starting point for a course of action or reasoning — see ASSUMPTION
suppositional *adj* existing only as an assumption or speculation — see THEORETICAL 1
suppress *vb* **1** to keep from being publicly known ⟨the government tried to *suppress* the truth about that incident⟩
synonyms cover (up), hush (up)
related words censor, silence; repress, smother, squash, squelch, stifle
phrases keep a lid on
near antonyms debunk, expose, reveal, show up, uncloak, uncover, unmask; disclose, divulge, tell, unveil; broadcast, circulate, publish, spread; describe, narrate, recite, recount, rehearse, relate, report
2 to refrain from openly showing or uttering ⟨he managed to *suppress* a scream at the sight of the dead body⟩ ⟨*suppressed* her anger⟩
synonyms choke (back), pocket, repress, smother, stifle, strangle, swallow
related words control, govern, handle, manage; bridle, check, curb, hold back, quell; bottle up, contain, hold in; muffle, squelch
near antonyms loose, release, take out, unleash, vent
3 to hold back the normal growth of — see STUNT
4 to put a stop to (something) by the use of force — see QUELL 1
suppression *n* the checking of one's true feelings and impulses when dealing with others — see CONSTRAINT 1
supremacist *n* a person who believes that one race

should control all others ‹white *supremacists* were arrested for painting racial slurs on a church›
synonyms racialist, racist
related words segregationist; bigot

supremacy *n* **1** controlling power or influence over others ‹the Roman empire had *supremacy* over the entire Mediterranean world›
synonyms ascendancy, dominance, dominion, predominance, preeminence
related words primacy, superiority; lordship, scepter, sovereignty; arm, authority, clutch, command, control, grip, hold, mastery, sway; takeover; direction, jurisdiction, management; clout, pull, weight; eminence, importance, moment; prerogative, privilege, right
near antonyms helplessness, weakness; impotence, powerlessness
2 exceptionally high quality — see EXCELLENCE 1

supreme *adj* **1** highest in rank or authority — see HEAD
2 coming before all others in importance — see FOREMOST 1
3 of the greatest or highest degree or quantity — see ULTIMATE 1

Supreme Being *n* the being worshipped as the creator and ruler of the universe — see DEITY 2

surcease *n* the stopping of a process or activity — see END 1

surcharge *vb* to charge (someone) too much for goods or services — see OVERCHARGE 1

surcoat *n* a warm outdoor coat — see OVERCOAT

sure *adj* **1** having or showing a mind free from doubt — see CERTAIN 2
2 impossible to avoid or evade — see INEVITABLE
3 not likely to fail — see INFALLIBLE 2
4 worthy of one's trust — see DEPENDABLE

surely *adv* without any question — see INDEED 1

sureness *n* **1** a state of mind in which one is free from doubt — see CONFIDENCE 2
2 worthiness as the recipient of another's trust or confidence — see RELIABILITY

surety *n* **1** a formal agreement to fulfill an obligation — see GUARANTEE 1
2 a person who takes the responsibility for some other person or thing — see SPONSOR

surf *n* a light mass of fine bubbles formed in or on a liquid — see FOAM

surface *adj* lying on or affecting only the outer layer of something — see SUPERFICIAL 1

surface *n* an outer part or layer — see EXTERIOR

surface *vb* **1** to come to one's attention especially gradually or unexpectedly — see ARISE 2
2 to penetrate the surface (as of water) from below — see BROACH 1

surfeit *n* the state or an instance of going beyond what is usual, proper, or needed — see EXCESS

surfeit *vb* to fill with food to capacity — see GORGE 1

surfeited *adj* having one's appetite completely satisfied — see FULL 3

surge *n* a moving ridge on the surface of water — see WAVE

surly *adj* **1** given to or displaying a resentful silence and often irritability — see SULKY
2 having or showing a habitually bad temper — see ILL-TEMPERED

surmise *n* an opinion or judgment based on little or no evidence — see CONJECTURE

surmise *vb* to form an opinion from little or no evidence — see GUESS 1

surmount *vb* to achieve a victory over — see BEAT 2

surpass *vb* **1** to be greater, better, or stronger than ‹she always tried to *surpass* her older brother at anything he did›
synonyms beat, better, eclipse, excel, outdistance, outdo, outshine, outstrip, overtop, top, transcend
related words exceed, outpace, outrun, overpass; best, clobber, conquer, crush, defeat, drub, lick, master, overcome, overmatch, prevail (over), rout, skunk, subdue, surmount, thrash, trim, triumph (over), trounce, wallop, whip, win (against), worst; outweigh, overbear, overshadow
phrases go one better
near antonyms lose (to)
2 to go beyond the limit of — see EXCEED

surplus *adj* being over what is needed — see SPARE 1

surplus *n* the state or an instance of going beyond what is usual, proper, or needed — see EXCESS

surprise *also* **surprize** *vb* **1** to make a strong impression on (someone) with something unexpected ‹I was very *surprised* when my parents offered to pay for guitar lessons›
synonyms amaze, astonish, astound, bowl (over), dumbfound (*also* dumfound), flabbergast, floor, shock, startle, stun, stupefy
related words befuddle, bewilder, confound, confuse, discomfit, disconcert, dismay, muddle, nonplus, perplex
phrases knock for a loop, take aback, take by surprise
2 to lie in wait for and attack by surprise — see AMBUSH

surprise *n* **1** something that makes a strong impression because it is so unexpected ‹the birthday party was such a complete *surprise* that Jane was speechless for a moment›
synonyms bolt, bombshell, jar, jolt, stunner
related words shock, thunderclap; revelation, shocker
2 the state of being strongly impressed by something unexpected or unusual ‹Danny stared in utter *surprise* at the deer in his living room›
synonyms amazement, astonishment, shock
related words awe, wonder, wonderment; startle; bewilderment, confusion, discomfiture, dismay
3 a scheme in which hidden persons wait to attack by surprise — see AMBUSH 1

surprising *adj* **1** causing a strong emotional reaction because unexpected ‹the *surprising* news that they were going to have a baby had them rushing to buy nursery furniture›
synonyms amazing, astonishing, astounding, dumbfounding (*or* dumfounding), eye-opening, flabbergasting, shocking, startling, stunning, stupefying
related words unannounced, unanticipated, unexpected, unforeseen; awesome, awful, breathtaking, fabulous, marvelous (*or* marvellous), miraculous, portentous, prodigious, staggering, stupendous, sublime, wonderful, wondrous; extraordinary, phenomenal, rare, sensational, spectacular; befuddling, bewildering, confounding, confusing, discomfiting, disconcerting, dismaying, muddling, nonplussing, perplexing; incomprehensible, inconceivable, incredible, unbelievable, unimaginable, unthinkable; singular, uncommon, unique, unusual, unwonted; conspic-

uous, notable, noticeable, outstanding, remarkable; impressive, striking
near antonyms common, customary, mundane, normal, ordinary, typical, unexceptional, unremarkable, usual
2 causing wonder or astonishment — see MARVELOUS 1

surrender *n* the usually forced yielding of one's person or possessions to the control of another ⟨the police demanded the *surrender* of all hostages as a condition for allowing the hijackers safe passage out of the country⟩
synonyms capitulating, capitulation, relinquishment, submission, submitting
related words acceptance, acquiescence, concession; compromise; appeasement, conciliation; capture, fall
near antonyms resistance

surrender *vb* **1** to give (something) over to the control or possession of another usually under duress ⟨Annie *surrendered* the doll to her mother after a brief struggle⟩ ⟨the commander *surrendered* the garrison without having fired a single shot⟩
synonyms cede, deliver, give up, hand over, relinquish, render, turn over, yield
related words commit, consign, entrust; waive; renounce, resign; abandon, desert, discard, forsake, shed
near antonyms keep, retain, withhold
2 to cease resistance (as to another's arguments, demands, or control) — see YIELD 3
3 to give up (as a position of authority) formally — see ABDICATE
4 to give up and cease resistance (as to a liking, temptation, or habit) — see YIELD 1
5 to yield to the control or power of enemy forces — see FALL 2

surreptitious *adj* undertaken or done so as to escape being observed or known by others — see SECRET 1

surround *vb* to form a circle around ⟨she was *surrounded* by cheering fans within moments of scoring the winning goal⟩
synonyms circle, encircle, enclose (*also* inclose), encompass, ring
related words fence (in), hem (in), wall; besiege, entrench (*also* intrench), invest

surroundings *n pl* the circumstances, conditions, or objects by which one is surrounded — see ENVIRONMENT

surveillance *n* the act or state of being constantly attentive and responsive to signs of opportunity, activity, or danger — see VIGILANCE

survey *n* a close look at or over someone or something in order to judge condition — see INSPECTION

survey *vb* **1** to go around and approach (people) with a request for opinions or information — see CANVASS
2 to look over closely (as for judging quality or condition) — see INSPECT

survive *vb* **1** to come safely through ⟨the cat miraculously *survived* a two-story fall⟩
synonyms ride (out), weather
related words outlast, outlive; pull through; abide, continue, endure, hang on, last, lead, persist; be, breathe, exist, live, subsist; flourish, prosper, thrive
near antonyms croak [*slang*], decease, depart, die, expire, pass (on), pass away, perish, succumb; disappear, evaporate, fade, vanish; cease, end, stop
2 to continue to operate or to meet one's needs — see HOLD OUT

susceptibility *n* the quality or state of having little resistance to some outside agent ⟨Carol's unfortunate *susceptibility* to viruses meant she was nearly always sick⟩ ⟨Stephen had a well-known *susceptibility* to anyone with a pathetic story⟩
synonyms defenselessness, vulnerability, weakness
related words helplessness, powerlessness; passiveness, passivity; feebleness, frailness; exposure, liability, openness, sensitivity; receptiveness, receptivity; easiness, gullibility, näiveté (*also* naivete); credulity, credulousness
near antonyms immunity; impenetrability, indomitability, indomitableness, invincibility
antonyms invulnerability

susceptible *adj* **1** being in a situation where one is likely to meet with harm — see LIABLE 1
2 lacking protection from danger or resistance against attack — see HELPLESS 1
3 readily taken advantage of — see EASY 2

suspect *adj* giving good reason for being doubted, questioned, or challenged — see DOUBTFUL 2

suspect *vb* **1** to form an opinion from little or no evidence — see GUESS 1
2 to have no trust or confidence in — see DISTRUST

suspecting *adj* inclined to doubt or question claims — see SKEPTICAL 1

suspend *vb* **1** to bring to a formal close for a period of time — see ADJOURN
2 to place on an elevated point without support from below — see HANG 1

suspense *n* a state of temporary inactivity — see ABEYANCE

suspension *n* a state of temporary inactivity — see ABEYANCE

suspicion *vb, chiefly dialect* to form an opinion from little or no evidence — see GUESS 1

suspicion *n* **1** a feeling or attitude that one does not know the truth, truthfulness, or trustworthiness of someone or something — see DOUBT
2 a very small amount — see PARTICLE 1

suspicious *adj* **1** giving good reason for being doubted, questioned, or challenged — see DOUBTFUL 2
2 inclined to doubt or question claims — see SKEPTICAL 1
3 not feeling sure about the truth, wisdom, or trustworthiness of someone or something — see DOUBTFUL 1

suspiciously *adv* with distrust — see ASKANCE

sustain *vb* **1** to supply with nourishment ⟨a granola bar will *sustain* you long enough to last until lunch⟩
synonyms nourish, nurture
related words sate, satiate, satisfy; cloy, fill, surfeit; fortify, strengthen; feed; board, cater, provision
2 to come to a knowledge of (something) by living through it — see EXPERIENCE
3 to put up with (something painful or difficult) — see BEAR 2

sustainable *adj* **1** capable of being defended with good reasoning against verbal attack — see TENABLE 1

2 capable of being proven as true or real — see VERIFIABLE
3 capable of being endured — see BEARABLE

swab *n* one who operates or navigates a seagoing vessel — see SAILOR

swag *n* valuables stolen or taken by force — see LOOT

swagger *vb* **1** to praise or express pride in one's own possessions, qualities, or accomplishments often to excess — see BOAST
2 to walk with exaggerated arm and leg movements — see STRUT 1

swain *n* **1** a male romantic companion — see BOYFRIEND
2 a man who courts a woman usually with the goal of marrying her — see SUITOR 1

swallow *n* the portion of a serving of a beverage that is swallowed at one time — see DRINK 2

swallow *vb* **1** to take into the stomach through the mouth and throat ⟨try not to *swallow* the toothpaste, because it's not good for you⟩
synonyms down, ingest
related words drink, imbibe, sip; bolt, devour, gobble (up *or* down), gulp; consume, eat, mouth (down); gorge, scarf, scoff, wolf; chew, gnaw (at *or* on), lap, lick, nibble (on); dispatch, polish off
2 to refrain from openly showing or uttering — see SUPPRESS 2
3 to regard as right or true — see BELIEVE 1

swamp *n* spongy land saturated or partially covered with water ⟨be careful in the *swamp*, because alligators sometimes lurk there⟩
synonyms bog, fen, marsh, marshland, mire, morass, muskeg, slough (*also* slue), swampland
related words quagmire; muck, mud, ooze, slime, slop, sludge, slush

swamp *vb* **1** to cover or become filled with a flood — see FLOOD
2 to subject to incapacitating emotional or mental stress — see OVERWHELM 1

swampland *n* spongy land saturated or partially covered with water — see SWAMP

swank *or* **swanky** *adj* excessively showy — see GAUDY

swank *n* excessive or unnecessary display — see OSTENTATION

swankily *adv* in a bright and showy way — see GAILY 3

swap *n* a giving or taking of one thing of value in return for another — see EXCHANGE 1

swap *vb* to give up (something) and take something else in return — see CHANGE 3

swarm *n* a great number of persons or things gathered together — see CROWD 1

swarm *vb* to move upon or fill (something) in great numbers — see CROWD 2

swarming *adj* possessing or covered with great numbers or amounts of something specified — see RIFE

swash *vb* to move with a splashing motion — see SLOSH

swat *n* a hard strike with a part of the body or an instrument — see [1]BLOW

swat *vb* to deliver a blow to (someone or something) usually in a strong vigorous manner — see HIT 1

swathe *vb* to surround or cover closely — see ENFOLD 1

sway *n* **1** the power to bring about a result on another — see EFFECT 2
2 the power to direct the thinking or behavior of others usually indirectly — see INFLUENCE 1
3 the right or means to command or control others — see POWER 1

sway *vb* **1** to act upon (a person or a person's feelings) so as to cause a response — see [1]AFFECT 1
2 to make a series of unsteady side-to-side motions — see ROCK 1

swear *vb* **1** to use offensive or indecent language ⟨you're not allowed to *swear* in this house⟩
synonyms blaspheme, curse, cuss
related words confound, damn, execrate, imprecate; fulminate, rail, rant
2 to make a solemn declaration of intent — see PROMISE 1
3 to make a solemn declaration under oath for the purpose of establishing a fact — see TESTIFY

swearword *n* a disrespectful or indecent word or expression ⟨this is a list of *swearwords* that will not be permitted in my classroom⟩
synonyms curse, cuss, expletive, obscenity, vulgarism
related words profanity; execration, imprecation, malediction; epithet, name; oath

sweat *n* **1** the active use of energy in producing a result — see EFFORT
2 very hard or unpleasant work — see TOIL

sweat *vb* **1** to devote serious and sustained effort — see LABOR
2 to experience concern or anxiety — see WORRY 1
3 to work hard and long — see TOIL
4 to flow forth slowly through small openings — see EXUDE

sweep *n* an area over which activity, capacity, or influence extends — see RANGE 2

sweep *vb* **1** to move or proceed smoothly and readily — see FLOW 2
2 to turn away from a straight line or course — see CURVE 1

sweepstakes *n pl* a competitive encounter between individuals or groups carried on for amusement, exercise, or in pursuit of a prize — see GAME 1

sweet *adj* **1** granted special treatment or attention — see DARLING 1
2 having a pleasant smell — see FRAGRANT
3 having an easygoing and pleasing manner especially in social situations — see AMIABLE
4 having qualities that tend to make one loved — see LOVABLE

sweet *n* **1** a food having a high sugar content ⟨remember to brush your teeth after eating *sweets*⟩
synonyms confection, sweetmeat
related words confectionery; candy, dessert, pastry
2 a person with whom one is in love — see SWEETHEART

sweetheart *n* a person with whom one is in love ⟨I married my high-school *sweetheart* as soon as we both finished college⟩
synonyms beloved, darling, dear, flame, honey, love, sweet
related words beau, boyfriend, fellow, lover, man, swain; gal, girl, girlfriend, ladylove, mistress; date, escort; gallant, suitor, wooer; groom, husband; fiancé, intended; admirer, crush, steady

sweetmeat *n* a food having a high sugar content — see SWEET 1

sweetness *n* the state or quality of having a pleas-

ant or agreeable manner in socializing with others — see AMIABILITY 1
swell *adj* of the very best kind — see EXCELLENT
swell *n* a moving ridge on the surface of water — see WAVE
swell *vb* **1** to become greater in extent, volume, amount, or number — see INCREASE 2
2 to make greater in size, amount, or number — see INCREASE 1
swelling *n* a small rounded mass of swollen tissue — see BUMP 1
sweltering *adj* having a notably high temperature — see HOT 1
swerve *vb* **1** to depart abruptly from a straight line or course <the car *swerved* sharply to avoid the squirrel in the road>
synonyms sheer, veer, yaw
related words skew, slew (*also* slue); arc, arch, bend, bow, crook, curve, hook, round, sweep, wheel; circle, coil, curl, loop, spiral; turn, twist, wind; deviate, stray, wander, waver
antonyms straighten
2 to turn away from a straight line or course — see CURVE 1
3 to cause to turn away from a straight line — see BEND 1
swift *adj* moving, proceeding, or acting with great speed — see FAST 1
swift *adv* with great speed — see FAST 1
swiftly *adv* with great speed — see FAST 1
swiftness *n* a high rate of movement or performance — see SPEED
swig *n* the portion of a serving of a beverage that is swallowed at one time — see DRINK 2
swig *vb* to swallow in liquid form — see DRINK 1
swill *n* the portion of a serving of a beverage that is swallowed at one time — see DRINK 2
swill *vb* **1** to eat greedily or to excess — see GORGE 2
2 to swallow in liquid form — see DRINK 1
swiller *n* one who eats greedily or too much — see GLUTTON
swim *vb* to be in a confused state as if from being twirled around — see SPIN 2
swimmingly *adv* in a pleasing way — see WELL 5
swindle *n* a scheme in which the victim is cheated out of his money after first gaining his trust — see CONFIDENCE GAME
swindle *vb* to rob by the use of trickery or threats — see FLEECE
swindler *n* a dishonest person who uses clever means to cheat others out of something of value — see TRICKSTER 1
swing *vb* **1** to change one's course or direction — see TURN 3
2 to change the course or direction of (something) — see TURN 2
3 to deal with (something) usually skillfully or efficiently — see HANDLE 1
4 to move (something) in a curved or circular path on or as if on an axis — see TURN 1
5 to place on an elevated point without support from below — see HANG 1
swipe *n* a hard strike with a part of the body or an instrument — see [1]BLOW
swipe *vb* **1** to come into usually forceful contact with something — see HIT 2
2 to deliver a blow to (someone or something) usually in a strong vigorous manner — see HIT 1
3 to take (something) without right and with an intent to keep — see STEAL 1
swiping *n* an instance of theft — see THEFT 2
swirl *vb* **1** to cause (as a liquid) to move about in a circle especially repeatedly — see STIR 1
2 to move (something) in a curved or circular path on or as if on an axis — see TURN 1
swish *n* a sound similar to the speech sound \s\ stretched out — see HISS 1
swish *vb* to make a sound like that of stretching out the speech sound \s\ — see HISS
switch *n* **1** a long thin or flexible tool for striking — see WHIP
2 a quick jerky movement from side to side or up and down — see WAG 1
switch *vb* **1** to give up (something) and take something else in return — see CHANGE 3
2 to move from side to side or up and down with quick jerky motions — see WAG
3 to strike repeatedly with something long and thin or flexible — see WHIP 1
4 to change (as an opinion) to the contrary — see REVERSE 1
swoon *n* a temporary or permanent state of unconsciousness — see FAINT
swoon *vb* to lose consciousness — see FAINT
sword *n* a hand weapon with a length of metal sharpened on one or both sides and usually tapered to a sharp point <once upon a time dueling with *swords* was the gentlemanly way to settle a point of honor>
synonyms blade, steel
related words broadsword, cutlass, rapier, saber (*or* sabre), scimitar
sycophant *n* a person who flatters another in order to get ahead <my teacher isn't fooled by the class *sycophants*, who are always telling her what a wonderful teacher she is>
synonyms fawner, flunky (*also* flunkey), toady
related words yes-man; hanger-on, leech, parasite, sponge, sponger; henchman, lackey, minion, satellite, slave, stooge; admirer, cultist, devotee, enthusiast, fan, groveler (*or* groveller), idolater (*or* idolator), worshipper (*or* worshiper), zealot; adherent, convert, disciple, follower, partisan, pupil, votary
symbol *n* **1** a device, design, or figure used as an identifying mark — see EMBLEM
2 a written or printed mark that is meant to convey information to the reader — see CHARACTER 1
symbolic *also* **symbolical** *adj* having the function or meaning of a symbol <the teddy bear in the story was intended to be *symbolic* of a mother's love>
synonyms emblematic (*also* emblematical), representative
related words figurative, metaphorical; allegorical
antonyms nonsymbolic
symbolize *vb* to serve as a material counterpart of <the flag *symbolizes* our country>
synonyms represent
related words embody, epitomize, incarnate, manifest, materialize, personalize, personify; exemplify, illustrate
phrases stand for
symmetry *n* a balanced, pleasing, or suitable arrangement of parts — see HARMONY 1
sympathetic *adj* **1** having or showing the capacity for sharing the feelings of another <a *sympathetic* smile> <Jane was always a *sympathetic* listener>

synonyms compassionate, humane, understanding
related words gentle, sensitive, softhearted, tender, tenderhearted, warm, warmhearted; benevolent, benignant, charitable, kind; clement, lenient, merciful; cordial, friendly, good-natured, good-tempered, gracious; affectionate, loving
near antonyms inconsiderate, insensitive, thoughtless, unthinking; uncaring, unloving; merciless, pitiless, ruthless; grim, hard-bitten, hard-boiled, harsh, oppressive, rough, severe, stern, tough, ungentle; abusive, acrimonious, disagreeable, hateful, ill-natured, ill-tempered, malevolent, malicious, mean, rancorous, spiteful, surly, virulent
antonyms callous, cold-blooded, hardhearted, heartless, inhuman, inhumane, unfeeling, unsympathetic
2 having or marked by sympathy and consideration for others — see HUMANE 1

sympathize (with) *vb* to have sympathy for — see PITY

sympathizer *n* someone associated with another to give assistance or moral support — see ALLY

sympathy *n* **1** sorrow or the capacity to feel sorrow for another's suffering or misfortune ⟨although I'd never lost a relative, I felt great *sympathy* for the classmate whose grandfather died⟩
synonyms commiseration, compassion, feeling
related words condolence, regret; humanity, kind-heartedness, kindliness, kindness, mercy, pity, softheartedness; affinity, empathy, rapport, sensitivity; altruism, benevolence, benignity, charity, generosity, goodwill, humanitarianism, philanthropy
near antonyms indifference, insensitivity, unconcern; cruelty, harshness; animosity, antipathy, dislike, hatred, hostility
antonyms callousness, hardheartedness, heartlessness
2 the capacity for feeling for another's unhappiness or misfortune — see HEART 1

symphonic *adj* having a pleasing mixture of notes — see HARMONIOUS 1

symphony *n* **1** a balanced, pleasing, or suitable arrangement of parts — see HARMONY 1
2 a usually large group of musicians playing together — see [2]BAND 1

symphony orchestra *n* a usually large group of musicians playing together — see [2]BAND 1

symposium *n* a meeting featuring a group discussion — see FORUM

symptomatic *adj* serving to identify as belonging to an individual or group — see CHARACTERISTIC 1

synchronous *adj* existing or occurring at the same period of time — see CONTEMPORARY 1

syndicate *n* **1** a group involved in secret or criminal activities — see RING 1
2 a number of businesses or enterprises united for commercial advantage — see CARTEL

synopsis *n* a short statement of the main points — see SUMMARY

synthetic *adj* being such in appearance only and made with or manufactured from usually cheaper materials — see IMITATION

syringe *n* a slender hollow instrument by which material is put into or taken from the body through the skin — see NEEDLE 1

syrupy *adj* being of a consistency that resists flow — see THICK 2

system *n* **1** something made up of many interdependent or related parts ⟨the national highway *system* allows travel from one end of the country to the other⟩ ⟨the democratic *system* of checks and balances in government⟩
synonyms complex, network
related words interlacement, Internet, net, web; aggregate, conglomerate, totality, whole
2 a method worked out in advance for achieving some objective — see PLAN 1
3 the means or procedure for doing something — see METHOD

systematic *adj* following a set method, arrangement, or pattern — see METHODICAL

systematize *vb* to put into a particular arrangement — see ORDER 1

systematized *adj* following a set method, arrangement, or pattern — see METHODICAL

tab *n* **1** a record of goods sold or services performed together with the costs due — see [1]BILL 1
2 the amount owed at a bar or restaurant or the slip of paper stating the amount — see CHECK 1

tabernacle *n* a building for public worship and especially Christian worship — see CHURCH 1

table *n* **1** a leg-mounted piece of furniture with a broad flat top designed for the serving of food ⟨we sat at the kitchen *table*, playing cards for hours on end⟩
synonyms board
related words coffee table, refectory table; bar, counter; buffet, sideboard
2 food eaten or prepared for eating at one time — see MEAL
3 a broad flat area of elevated land — see PLATEAU
4 a record of a series of items (as names or titles) usually arranged according to some system — see [1]LIST
5 substances intended to be eaten — see FOOD

tableland *n* a broad flat area of elevated land — see PLATEAU

tablet *n* **1** a number of sheets of writing paper glued together at one edge — see PAD 1
2 a small mass containing medicine to be taken orally — see PILL

table talk *n* friendly, informal conversation or an instance of this — see CHAT

tableware *n* **1** eating and serving utensils ⟨we ran short of *tableware*, so Emily went next door and borrowed some forks and knives⟩
synonyms flatware, silver, silverware
related words place setting, setting; silver plate;

cutlery; chopstick, fork, knife, spoon, tablespoon, teaspoon

2 dishes used for eating or serving food or drink ⟨Betty would take out her good *tableware* only on special occasions, as when the mayor came to dinner⟩

synonyms dinnerware

related words setting; china, chinaware, crockery, earthenware, porcelain, pottery, stoneware, ware; crystal, glassware; plate, saucer; cup, glass, goblet, mug, teacup; bowl, casserole, charger, platter, tureen

taboo *also* **tabu** *adj* that may not be permitted — see IMPERMISSIBLE

tacit *adj* understood although not put into words — see IMPLICIT

taciturn *adj* tending not to speak frequently (as by habit or inclination) — see SILENT 2

tack *n* the means or procedure for doing something — see METHOD

tack (on) *vb* to join (something) to a mass, quantity, or number so as to bring about an overall increase — see ADD 1

tackle *n* items needed for the performance of a task or activity — see EQUIPMENT

tackle *vb* to start work on energetically — see ATTACK 3

tacky *adj* **1** marked by an obvious lack of style or good taste ⟨it was *tacky* to wear sneakers, but Tracey's dress shoes hurt her feet⟩ ⟨*tacky* plastic flowers⟩

synonyms cheesy, dowdy, inelegant, styleless, tasteless, trashy, unfashionable, unstylish

related words inappropriate, incorrect, unbecoming, unseemly, unsuitable, wrong; outmoded, out-of-date, passé; coarse, crude, unrefined, vulgar; cheap, common, inferior, junky, lousy, low-grade, second-rate, shoddy, sleazy, tawdry; gaudy, loud, ostentatious, overdone, showy, splashy

near antonyms appropriate, becoming, correct, fitting, proper, right, seemly, suitable; genteel, handsome, neat, quiet, refined, understated; contemporary, modern, up-to-date

antonyms elegant, fashionable, modish, ritzy, smart, stylish, tasteful

2 showing signs of advanced wear and tear and neglect — see SHABBY 1

tact *n* the ability to deal with others in touchy situations without offending them ⟨with supreme *tact*, Isabel suggested to her neighbor that her flower garden was probably not the best place for his dog to use as a bathroom⟩

synonyms diplomacy, tactfulness

related words considerateness, consideration, courtesy, delicacy, graciousness, thoughtfulness; civility, etiquette, mannerliness, manners, politeness; charm, gallantry, gentility, grace, gracefulness, suaveness, suavity; adroitness, deftness, dexterity, finesse; deference, regard, respect

near antonyms discourteousness, discourtesy, inconsiderateness, inconsideration, indelicacy, thoughtlessness, ungraciousness, unthoughtfulness; impoliteness, incivility; boorishness, brashness, brassiness, loutishness; awkwardness, gauchness, gracelessness, maladroitness; disregard, disrespect, impertinence, impudence, insolence, rudeness

antonyms tactlessness

tactful *adj* having or showing tact ⟨Allie tried to be *tactful* when asked to comment on the short story that a classmate had written⟩

synonyms diplomatic

related words considerate, courteous, delicate, gracious, thoughtful; civil, mannerly, polite; charming, gallant, genteel, suave; deferential, regardful, respectful

near antonyms discourteous, inconsiderate, indelicate, thoughtless, ungracious, unthoughtful; ill-bred, ill-mannered, impolite, uncivil, unmannerly; boorish, brash, brassy, loutish; disregardful, disrespectful, impertinent, impudent, insolent, rude

antonyms tactless, undiplomatic

tactfulness *n* the ability to deal with others in touchy situations without offending them — see TACT

tactical *adj* suitable for bringing about a desired result under the circumstances — see EXPEDIENT

tactics *n pl* the means or procedure for doing something — see METHOD

tactless *adj* showing poor judgment especially in personal relationships or social situations — see INDISCREET

tad *n* a male person who has not yet reached adulthood — see BOY

tag *n* a slip (as of paper or cloth) that is attached to something to identify or describe it — see LABEL

tag *vb* **1** to attach an identifying slip to — see LABEL 1

2 to go after or on the track of — see FOLLOW 2

tagging *n* the act of going after or in the tracks of another — see PURSUIT

tail *n* a person whose business is solving crimes and catching criminals or gathering information that is not easy to get — see DETECTIVE

tail *vb* to go after or on the track of — see FOLLOW 2

tailing *n* the act of going after or in the tracks of another — see PURSUIT

tailored *adj* made or fitted to the needs or preferences of a specific customer — see CUSTOM-MADE

tailor–made *adj* made or fitted to the needs or preferences of a specific customer — see CUSTOM-MADE

taint *n* a mark of guilt or disgrace — see STAIN 1

taint *vb* **1** to affect slightly with something morally bad or undesirable ⟨criticism of her sister's singing that was *tainted* by envy⟩ ⟨a tendency toward conceitedness *taints* that athlete's status as a role model⟩

synonyms blemish, mar, poison, spoil, stain, tarnish, touch, vitiate

related words besmear, besmirch, blacken, cloud, dirty, discolor, smear, smirch, smudge, smut, soil, sully, tar; color, distort, twist; damage, deface, flaw, harm, hurt, impair; destroy, ruin, wreck

near antonyms cleanse, purify; elevate, ennoble, uplift

2 to make unfit for use by the addition of something harmful or undesirable — see CONTAMINATE

tainted *adj* containing foreign or lower-grade substances — see IMPURE

take *n* **1** action or behavior that is done in return to other action or behavior — see REACTION

2 the total amount collected or obtained especially at one time — see HAUL 1

take *vb* **1** to reach for and take hold of by embrac-

ing with the fingers or arms ⟨*take* my hand, or we'll get separated in this crowd⟩
synonyms clasp, grasp, grip, hold
related words clench, cling (to), clutch, hang on (to), hold on (to); catch, nab, seize, snatch
phrases lay hold of
near antonyms discharge, drop, free, liberate, release; give, hand, relinquish, unhand
2 to agree to receive whether willingly or reluctantly ⟨will you *take* that call?⟩ ⟨*took* a cut in pay⟩
synonyms accept, have
related words accede (to), assent (to), concede (to), consent (to), OK (*or* okay); acquiesce (to), bow (to), capitulate (to), give in (to), submit (to), succumb (to), surrender (to), yield (to); bear, endure, shoulder, tolerate, swallow; adopt, embrace, welcome
near antonyms dissent (to), object (to), oppose, protest; hold off, resist, withstand
antonyms decline, refuse, reject, spurn, turn down
3 to become affected with (a disease or disorder) — see CONTRACT 1
4 to decide to accept (someone or something) from a group of possibilities — see CHOOSE 1
5 to get possession of (something) by giving money in exchange for — see BUY
6 to have as a requirement — see NEED 1
7 to make or have room for — see ACCOMMODATE 1
8 to produce a desired effect — see ACT 2
9 to put up with (something painful or difficult) — see BEAR 2

take (for) *vb* to think of in a particular way — see CONSIDER 1

take back *vb* to solemnly or formally reject or go back on (as something formerly adhered to) — see ABJURE

take down *vb* **1** to reduce to a lower standing in one's own eyes or in others' eyes — see HUMBLE
2 to take apart — see DISASSEMBLE

take in *vb* **1** to cause to believe what is untrue — see DECEIVE
2 to have as part of a whole — see INCLUDE
3 to provide with living quarters or shelter — see HOUSE 1

takeoff *n* **1** a rising from a surface at the start of a flight (as of a rocket) — see LIFT-OFF
2 a work that imitates and exaggerates another work for comic effect — see PARODY 1

take off *vb* **1** to leave a place often for another — see GO 2
2 to rid oneself of (a garment) — see REMOVE 1
3 to take away (an amount or number) from a total — see SUBTRACT

take off (on) *vb* to copy or exaggerate (someone or something) in order to make fun of — see MIMIC 1

take on *vb* **1** to enter into contest or conflict with — see ENGAGE 2
2 to provide with a paying job — see EMPLOY 1

take out *vb* **1** to find emotional release for ⟨*took out* his frustrations by splitting a cord of firewood⟩
synonyms loose, release, unleash, vent
phrases give way (to)
near antonyms control, govern, handle, manage; bridle, check, contain, curb, hold back, hold in, quell, restrain, smother; allay, lull, quiet, soothe, still; choke, inhibit, muffle, pocket, repress, stifle, strangle, swallow
antonyms bottle (up), repress, suppress
2 to go on a social engagement with — see DATE 1

take over *vb* **1** to serve as a replacement usually for a time only — see COVER 1
2 to take to or upon oneself — see ASSUME 1

take up *vb* to take for one's own use (something originated by another) — see ADOPT

taking *adj* very pleasing to look at — see BEAUTIFUL

tale *n* **1** a rumor or report of a personal or sensational nature ⟨don't believe the *tales* you hear about our neighbor's kid⟩
synonyms story, whisper
related words dirt, gossip, scuttlebutt, talebearing, talk, tattle; defamation, libel, slander; hearsay; fabrication, fairy tale, falsehood, falsity, fib, lie
2 a brief account of something interesting that happened especially to one personally — see STORY 2
3 a statement known by its maker to be untrue and made in order to deceive — see LIE
4 a work with imaginary characters and events that is shorter and usually less complex than a novel — see STORY 1

talebearer *n* a person who provides secret information about another's wrongdoing — see INFORMER

talent *n* a special and usually inborn ability ⟨Liza's musical *talent* was already apparent by the time she was five⟩ ⟨Jim's *talent* for coming up with really funny answers⟩
synonyms aptitude, endowment, faculty, flair, genius, gift, knack
related words bent, inclination, leaning, partiality, penchant, predilection, predisposition, proclivity, propensity, turn; ear, eye, head, mind, nose; feel, hang, instinct, touch, way; capability, competence, facility, proficiency, skill; capacity, power, potential
near antonyms disability, handicap, inability, incapacity; shortcoming, weakness

talisman *n* something worn or kept to bring good luck or keep away evil — see CHARM 1

talk *n* **1** a usually formal discourse delivered to an audience — see SPEECH 1
2 an exchange of views for the purpose of exploring a subject or deciding an issue — see DISCUSSION 1
3 friendly, informal conversation or an instance of this — see CHAT

talk *vb* **1** to give a formal often extended talk on a subject ⟨detective Connolly often *talks* at school assemblies about safety⟩
synonyms declaim, descant, discourse, expatiate, harangue, lecture, orate, speak
related words recite, soliloquize; mouth, spout; filibuster; stump; eulogize
phrases hold forth, take the floor
2 to engage in casual or rambling conversation — see CHAT
3 to express (a thought or emotion) in words — see SAY 1
4 to give information (as to the authorities) about another's improper or unlawful activities — see SQUEAL 1
5 to relate sometimes questionable or secret information of a personal nature — see GOSSIP

talk (into) *vb* to cause (someone) to agree with a

belief or course of action by using arguments or earnest request — see PERSUADE 1

talk (to) *vb* to communicate with by means of spoken words ⟨Patty had never *talked to* a real live cowboy before⟩
synonyms chat (with), converse (with), speak (to *or* with)
related words accost, address, greet, hail, herald; inform, notify, tell
phrases engage in conversation

talkative *adj* fond of talking or conversation ⟨a *talkative* outgoing tour guide showed our school group around the city⟩
synonyms chatty, conversational, gabby, garrulous, loquacious, talky
related words communicative, expansive; demonstrative, effusive, gushing; outspoken, unreserved, vocal; articulate, fluent, glib, voluble; blabby, gossipy, talebearing; long-winded, prolix, verbose, windy, wordy; extroverted (*also* extraverted), gregarious, outgoing, sociable
near antonyms quiet, shy; mum, mute, silent, speechless, tongue-tied, wordless; evasive, nonvocal, secretive, self-contained, uncommunicative; aloof, introverted, unsociable, withdrawn
antonyms closemouthed, laconic, reserved, reticent, taciturn, tight-lipped

talker *n* a person who talks constantly — see CHATTERBOX

talk over *vb* to talk about (an issue) usually from various points of view and for the purpose of arriving at a decision or opinion — see DISCUSS

talky *adj* fond of talking or conversation — see TALKATIVE

tall *adj* **1** extending to a great distance upward — see HIGH 1
2 requiring considerable physical or mental effort — see HARD 2

tally *n* a total number obtained or recorded by noting each thing as it was being added — see COUNT 1

tally *vb* **1** to be in agreement on every point — see CHECK 1
2 to gain (as points or runs in a game) as credit towards one's total number of points — see SCORE 2

tame *adj* **1** changed from the wild state so as to become useful and obedient to humans ⟨every evening, a Canada goose is at the food trough with our *tame* geese⟩
synonyms domestic, domesticated, tamed
related words broken, housebroken, trained; docile, gentle
near antonyms unbroken, untrained
antonyms feral, nondomesticated, undomesticated, untamed, wild
2 causing weariness, restlessness, or lack of interest — see BORING

tame *vb* to keep from exceeding a desirable degree or level (as of expression) — see CONTROL 1

tamed *adj* changed from the wild state so as to become useful and obedient to humans — see TAME 1

tamper (with) *vb* to handle thoughtlessly, ignorantly, or mischievously ⟨someone has *tampered with* my computer files⟩
synonyms fiddle (with), fool (with), mess (with), monkey (with), play (with), tinker (with)
related words alter, doctor, manhandle, manipulate, misuse; butt in, interfere, intrude, meddle

tan *vb* to strike repeatedly with something long and thin or flexible — see WHIP 1

tangent *n* a departure from the subject under consideration ⟨in the middle of her description of her dog's symptoms, she went off on a *tangent* about its cute behavior⟩
synonyms digression, excursion
related words aside, parenthesis; rambling; circuitousness, circularity, circumlocution

tangible *adj* capable of being perceived by the sense of touch ⟨a firm belief in the existence of the soul, even though it is not at all *tangible*⟩
synonyms palpable, touchable
related words tactile; corporeal, physical; actual, concrete, embodied, existent, material, real, substantial; discernible, observable, perceptible, sensible
near antonyms bodiless, immaterial, incorporeal, insubstantial, nonmaterial, nonphysical, unsubstantial; abstract, ethereal, spiritual, unreal
antonyms impalpable, intangible

tangle *vb* **1** to catch or hold as if in a net — see ENTANGLE 2
2 to twist together into a usually confused mass — see ENTANGLE 1

tantrum *n* an outburst or display of excited anger ⟨had a *tantrum* when he found his little sister using his model paints⟩
synonyms blowup, explosion, fireworks, fit, huff, scene
related words eruption, flare-up, outburst, storm, uproar; agitation, delirium, distraction, frenzy, furor, furore, fury, hysteria, rage, rampage, uproar; convulsion(s), paroxysm, seizure, spasm, upheaval; reaction, rise; dander, temper; pet, pouts, sulk(s)

tap *n* a fixture for controlling the flow of a liquid — see FAUCET

[1]tap *vb* to strike or cause to strike lightly and usually rhythmically ⟨*tapped* her foot in time to the music⟩ ⟨kept *tapping* the desk with his pencil⟩
synonyms beat, drum, rap, thrum
related words bang, hammer, hit, knock, pound, thud, thump, thwack, whack; chink, clatter, clink, ping; pat; chuck, clap, flick, tip

[2]tap *vb* to remove (liquid) gradually or completely — see DRAIN 1

taper *vb* to grow less in scope or intensity especially gradually — see DECREASE 2

taper off *vb* to grow less in scope or intensity especially gradually — see DECREASE 2

tar *n* one who operates or navigates a seagoing vessel — see SAILOR

tardily *adv* at a pace that is less than usual, desirable, or expected — see SLOW

tardiness *n* the quality or state of being late — see LATENESS

tardy *adj* **1** moving or proceeding at less than the normal, desirable, or required speed — see SLOW 1
2 not arriving, occurring, or settled at the due, usual, or proper time — see LATE 1

target *n* **1** a person or thing that is the object of abuse, criticism, or ridicule ⟨Cinderella became the *target* of her stepsisters' envy⟩
synonyms butt, mark, sitting duck, victim
related words laughingstock, mockery; fall guy, goat, scapegoat, whipping boy
near antonyms gossip, gossiper, talebearer, tattler, tattletale, troublemaker; defamer, libeler (*or* li-

beller), traducer; baiter, heckler, needler, ribber, taunter, teaser, tormentor; derider, insulter, mocker, ridiculer, scoffer, scorner; caricaturist, lampooner, parodist, satirist
2 a person or thing that is made fun of — see LAUGHINGSTOCK
3 something that one hopes or intends to accomplish — see GOAL

tarnish *vb* to affect slightly with something morally bad or undesirable — see TAINT 1

tarry *vb* **1** to continue to be in a place for a significant amount of time — see STAY 1
2 to move or act slowly — see DELAY 1
3 to reside as a temporary guest — see VISIT 2

tart *adj* **1** causing or characterized by the one of the four basic taste sensations that is produced chiefly by acids — see SOUR 1
2 marked by the use of wit that is intended to cause hurt feelings — see SARCASTIC

tartness *n* **1** a harsh or sharp quality — see EDGE 1
2 biting sharpness of feeling or expression — see ACRIMONY 1

task *n* **1** a piece of work that needs to be done regularly — see CHORE 1
2 the action for which a person or thing is specially fitted or used or for which a thing exists — see ROLE

taskmaster *n* **1** a boss who assigns much work ⟨pitiless *taskmaster* that he was, Ebenezer Scrooge only reluctantly let his ill-paid clerk have Christmas day off⟩
synonyms slave driver
related words enslaver; authoritarian, disciplinarian, discipliner, martinet, stickler; despot, dictator, oppressor, tyrant; dominator, overlord
2 the person (as an employer or supervisor) who tells people and especially workers what to do — see BOSS

taste *n* **1** the property of a substance that can be identified by the sense of taste ⟨Nora can't stand the *taste* of cherry-flavored cough syrup⟩
synonyms flavor, savor
related words relish, smack, tang; savoriness, tastiness; aftertaste
2 a small piece or quantity of food — see MORSEL 1
3 positive regard for something — see LIKING

taste *vb* **1** to come to a knowledge of (something) by living through it — see EXPERIENCE
2 to have a vague awareness of — see FEEL 1

tasteful *adj* having or showing elegance — see ELEGANT 1

tasteless *adj* **1** lacking in refinement or good taste — see COARSE 2
2 lacking in taste or flavor — see INSIPID 1
3 marked by an obvious lack of style or good taste — see TACKY 1

tastelessness *n* the quality or state of lacking refinement or good taste — see VULGARITY 1

tastiness *n* the quality of being delicious — see DELICIOUSNESS

tasty *adj* very pleasing to the sense of taste — see DELICIOUS 1

tatter *vb* to cause (something) to separate into jagged pieces by violently pulling at it — see TEAR 1

tattered *adj* **1** wearing torn or worn out clothes ⟨arrived at the refugee camp *tattered* and exhausted⟩
synonyms ragged, raggedy, ragtag
related words bedraggled, scruffy, shabby, threadbare
near antonyms decked (out), dolled up, dressed up; spiffy
2 worn or torn into or as if into rags — see RAGGED 2

tattle *vb* to relate sometimes questionable or secret information of a personal nature — see GOSSIP

tattler *n* a person who provides secret information about another's wrongdoing — see INFORMER

tattletale *n* a person who provides secret information about another's wrongdoing — see INFORMER

taunt *vb* to attack repeatedly with mean put-downs or insults — see TEASE 2

taunter *n* a person who causes repeated emotional pain, distress, or annoyance to another — see TORMENTOR

taut *adj* stretched with little or no give ⟨a *taut* clothesline⟩
synonyms drawn, rigid, tense, tight
related words firm, inflexible, stiff, tightened, unrelaxed, unyielding
near antonyms drooping, droopy, flaccid, floppy, hanging, lank, limp, loosened, relaxed, slackened, yielding
antonyms lax, loose, slack

tavern *n* **1** a place of business where alcoholic beverages are sold to be consumed on the premises — see BARROOM
2 a place that provides rooms and usually a public dining room for overnight guests — see HOTEL

tawdry *adj* excessively showy — see GAUDY

tawny *adj* of a pale yellow or yellowish brown color — see BLOND

tax *n* a charge usually of money collected by the government from people or businesses for public use ⟨the state sales *tax* boosted the final cost of my new computer⟩
synonyms assessment, duty, imposition, impost, levy
related words custom(s), excise, income tax, poll tax, sales tax, tariff, toll, tribute, withholding tax; surcharge, surtax; revenue

tax *vb* to subject (a personal quality or faculty) to often excessive stress — see TRY (OUT) 2

taxi *n* an automobile that carries passengers for a fare usually determined by the distance traveled — see TAXI

taxicab *n* an automobile that carries passengers for a fare usually determined by the distance traveled ⟨took a *taxicab* to the airport⟩
synonyms cab, hack, taxi
related words hackney; limousine; rickshaw (*also* ricksha)

taxing *adj* requiring much time, effort, or careful attention — see DEMANDING 1

teach *vb* to cause to acquire knowledge or skill in some field ⟨*taught* us about the basics of organic gardening⟩
synonyms educate, indoctrinate, instruct, school, train, tutor
related words coach, mentor, drill, fit, ground, prepare, prime, qualify; direct, guide, lead, rear; catechize, lecture, moralize, preach; implant, inculcate, instill (*also* instil); homeschool; edify, enlighten; brief, familiarize, impart (to), inform, verse; initiate, introduce, show; reeducate, retrain

teacher *n* a person whose occupation is to give formal instruction in a school ⟨a young man who ar-

dently wants to become a *teacher* and teach first grade⟩
synonyms educator, instructor, pedagogue, preceptor, schoolteacher
related words headmaster, master, schoolmaster; headmistress, schoolmarm (*or* schoolma'am), schoolmistress; coach, guide, guru, trainer; mentor, tutor; drillmaster; dean, don, professor; pedant; governess, homeschooler; catechist, lecturer, moralizer, preacher

teaching *n* the act or process of imparting knowledge or skills to another — see EDUCATION 1

team *n* a group of people working together on a task — see GANG 1

team (up) *vb* to participate or assist in a joint effort to accomplish an end — see COOPERATE 1

teamwork *n* the work and activity of a number of persons who individually contribute toward the efficiency of the whole ⟨it takes *teamwork* to pull off a successful fund-raiser⟩
synonyms collaboration, cooperation, coordination
related words fellowship, partnership; community, mutualism, symbiosis; synergism; communion, oneness, solidarity, togetherness, unity

tear *n* a long deep cut — see GASH

tear *vb* **1** to cause (something) to separate into jagged pieces by violently pulling at it ⟨angrily *tore* the letter to shreds⟩
synonyms rend, rip, rive, shred, tatter
related words break, cleave, rupture, split; cut, gash, incise, lacerate, slash; butcher, dismember, dissect, hack, mangle
2 to separate or remove by forceful pulling ⟨*tore* the book from his hand⟩
synonyms rip, wrench, wrest, yank
related words grab, nab, seize, snap (up), snatch; lop (off), nip, jerk; amputate, cut (off), dissever, sever; force, pry
near antonyms reattach
3 to proceed or move quickly — see HURRY 2

tear (out) *vb* to draw out by force or with effort — see EXTRACT

tear down *vb* **1** to bring to a complete end the physical soundness, existence, or usefulness of — see DESTROY 1
2 to destroy (as a building) completely by knocking down or breaking to pieces — see DEMOLISH 1

tearful *adj* **1** given to expressing strong emotion (as sorrow) by readily shedding tears ⟨a *tearful* woman who can be counted on to cry at every wedding, anniversary, and funeral⟩
synonyms lachrymose, teary
related words emotional; maudlin, mawkish, sentimental; bawling, blubbering, crying, keening, sniffling, sniveling, sobbing, wailing, weeping, whimpering; bemoaning, bewailing; doleful, dolorous, grieving, mournful, plaintive; funereal, gloomy, lugubrious; brokenhearted, sad, sorrowful, woeful
near antonyms grinning, laughing, smiling; blithe, blithesome, cheerful, cheery, gay, happy, lighthearted, lightsome, merry, mirthful, sunny
2 causing unhappiness — see SAD 2

teary *adj* **1** causing unhappiness — see SAD 2
2 given to expressing strong emotion (as sorrow) by readily shedding tears — see TEARFUL 1

tease *n* **1** a person who causes repeated emotional pain, distress, or annoyance to another — see TORMENTOR
2 one who is obnoxiously annoying — see NUISANCE 1

tease *vb* **1** to make fun of in a good-natured way ⟨Hilary liked to *tease* her twin brother about his girlfriend⟩
synonyms chaff, jive, josh, kid, rally, razz, rib, ride, roast
related words banter, joke; fool, fun, string along; jest, quip, wisecrack
2 to attack repeatedly with mean put-downs or insults ⟨some of the boys *teased* Michael because his parents were hog farmers⟩
synonyms bait, bug, hassle, heckle, needle, ride, taunt
related words haze; gibe (*or* jibe), mock, ridicule; annoy, bother, chafe, fret, nag, nettle, irritate, gall, get, gnaw (at), pester, trouble, vex; aggravate, exasperate, goad, test, try; aggrieve, agitate, bedevil, beleaguer, discomfort, disturb, perturb; badger, dog, hound; browbeat, bully, hector; harass, harry, persecute, plague, terrorize, torment, torture
phrases pick on

teaser *n* **1** a person who causes repeated emotional pain, distress, or annoyance to another — see TORMENTOR
2 one who is obnoxiously annoying — see NUISANCE 1

teasing *n* the act of making unwelcome intrusions upon another — see ANNOYANCE 1

technical *adj* used by or intended for experts in a particular field of knowledge ⟨although the owner's manual for the receiver was supposedly written for the average consumer, it's filled with *technical* language⟩
synonyms specialized
related words esoteric, especial, exclusive, limited, narrow, peculiar, restricted, special, specific, unique; authoritative, expert, professional, specialist (*or* specialistic)
near antonyms common, generalized, generic, nonexclusive, nonspecific, ordinary, universal; inexpert, lay, nonprofessional, unprofessional
antonyms general, nonspecialized, nontechnical

technique *n* the means or procedure for doing something — see METHOD

tedious *adj* causing weariness, restlessness, or lack of interest — see BORING

tedium *n* the state of being bored — see BOREDOM

teeming *adj* possessing or covered with great numbers or amounts of something specified — see RIFE

teeny *adj* very small in size — see TINY

teeny–weeny *adj* very small in size — see TINY

teeter *vb* **1** to swing unsteadily back and forth or from side to side ⟨*teetered* at the edge of the pool⟩
synonyms falter, rock, totter, waver, wobble
related words flounder, lurch, stumble, toddle; quaver, tremble; careen, reel, stagger, weave
2 to move forward while swaying from side to side — see STAGGER 1
3 to show uncertainty about the right course of action — see HESITATE

telephone *vb* to make a telephone call to — see CALL 2

tell *vb* **1** to give an oral or written account of in some detail ⟨*told* the story of how they had met⟩

synonyms describe, narrate, recite, recount, rehearse, relate, report
related words deliver, give, state, utter, voice; detail, enumerate, itemize, particularize; disclose, divulge, reveal; delineate, depict, express, render, sketch
2 to express (a thought or emotion) in words — see SAY 1
3 to find the sum of (a collection of things) by noting each one as it is being added — see COUNT 1
4 to give information (as to the authorities) about another's improper or unlawful activities — see SQUEAL 1
5 to give information to — see ENLIGHTEN 1
6 to issue orders to (someone) by right of authority — see COMMAND 1
7 to make known (as information previously kept secret) — see REVEAL 1

tell (on) *vb* to act upon (a person or a person's feelings) so as to cause a response — see [1]AFFECT 1

telling *adj* having the power to persuade — see COGENT

telltale *adj* indicating something — see INDICATIVE

telltale *n* a person who provides secret information about another's wrongdoing — see INFORMER

temerity *n* shameless boldness — see EFFRONTERY

temperance *n* an avoidance of extremes in one's actions, beliefs, or habits ⟨Mr. Grindell attributes his ripe old age to *temperance* in all things, especially eating and drinking⟩
synonyms moderateness, moderation, temperateness
related words constraint, control, discipline, restraint, self-control, self-discipline; asceticism, austerity, frugality, mortification, sacrifice, self-denial, self-deprivation; abnegation, abstention, avoidance, eschewal, forbearance; modesty, rationality, reasonableness; abstinence, soberness, sobriety
near antonyms excess, superfluity; extremeness, extremity; unconstraint, unrestraint; extremism, radicalness; irrationality, unreasonableness
antonyms excessiveness, immoderacy, intemperance, intemperateness

temper *n* **1** a special quality or impression associated with something — see AURA
2 a state of mind dominated by a particular emotion — see MOOD 1
3 one's characteristic attitude or mood — see DISPOSITION 1

temperament *n* one's characteristic attitude or mood — see DISPOSITION 1

temperamental *adj* **1** frequently influenced by moods and especially bad moods — see MOODY
2 likely to change frequently, suddenly, or unexpectedly — see FICKLE 1

temperate *adj* **1** avoiding extremes in behavior or expression — see MODERATE 1
2 marked by temperatures that are neither too high nor too low — see CLEMENT

temperateness *n* an avoidance of extremes in one's actions, beliefs, or habits — see TEMPERANCE

tempest *n* **1** a disturbance of the atmosphere accompanied by wind and often by precipitation (as rain or snow) — see STORM 1
2 a violent disturbance (as of the political or social order) — see CONVULSION

tempestuous *adj* **1** marked by bursts of destructive force or intense activity — see VIOLENT 1
2 marked by sudden or violent disturbance — see CONVULSIVE
3 marked by turmoil or disturbance especially of natural elements — see WILD 3
4 marked by wet and windy conditions — see FOUL 1

temple *n* a building for public worship and especially Christian worship — see CHURCH 1

temporal *adj* **1** having to do with life on earth especially as opposed to that in heaven — see EARTHLY
2 not involving religion or religious matters — see PROFANE 1

temporary *adj* **1** intended to last, continue, or serve for a limited time ⟨summer workers look for *temporary* accommodations in private homes⟩ ⟨a *temporary* cook until a permanent replacement can be found⟩
synonyms impermanent, interim, provisional, short-term
related words acting; alternate, proxy, substitute; expedient, improvised, makeshift; intermediary, intermediate, transitional; ephemeral, short-lived, transitory; conditional, contingent, limited, qualified, short-range, tentative; replaceable, terminable
near antonyms final, fixed, set, settled; unconditional, unlimited, unqualified; extended, lasting, long-range, standing; dateless, endless, enduring, eternal, everlasting, perpetual, timeless, unending
antonyms long-term, permanent
2 lasting only for a short time — see MOMENTARY

temporizer *n* one who does things only for his own benefit and with little regard for right and wrong — see SELF-SEEKER

tempt *vb* to lead away from a usual or proper course by offering some pleasure or advantage — see LURE

temptation *n* **1** the act or pressure of giving in to a desire especially when ill-advised ⟨resisted the *temptation* to go sailing and did his chores instead⟩
synonyms allurement, enticement, lure, seduction
related words appeal, attraction; beckoning, invitation; inducement, influence, persuasion, power, sway
2 something that persuades one to perform an action for pleasure or gain — see LURE 1

tempter *n* one that tries to get a person to give in to a desire ⟨there is no greater *tempter* to put off studying than my dog when he wants to play⟩
synonyms baiter, seducer, solicitor
related words enchantress, siren, temptress; briber, inducer, persuader; corrupter (*or* corruptor), debaucher, undoer

temptress *n* a woman whom men find irresistibly attractive — see SIREN

tenable *adj* **1** capable of being defended against physical attack ⟨the soldiers' encampment on the open plain was not *tenable*, so they retreated to higher ground⟩
synonyms defensible
related words defended, guarded, protected, safeguarded, secure, secured, shielded; impregnable, indomitable, invincible, inviolable, invulnerable, unassailable, unbeatable, unconquerable, untouchable
near antonyms assailable, exposed, insecure, li-

able, open, susceptible, undefended, unguarded, unprotected, unsecured, unshielded; defenseless, helpless, powerless, vulnerable, weak
antonyms indefensible, untenable
2 capable of being defended with good reasoning against verbal attack ⟨the *tenable* theory that a giant meteor strike set off a chain of events resulting in the demise of the dinosaurs⟩
synonyms defendable, defensible, justifiable, maintainable, supportable, sustainable
related words rational, reasonable, sensible; acceptable, admissible, allowable, exceptionable, legitimate, passable, unobjectionable, viable, warrantable; confirmable, provable, verifiable; explainable, explicable
near antonyms absurd, irrational, ridiculous; extreme, outrageous, unreasonable; groundless, objectionable, unacceptable, unfounded; inexplicable, unexplainable
antonyms indefensible, insupportable, unjustifiable, untenable

tenacious *adj* continuing despite difficulties, opposition, or discouragement — see PERSISTENT

tenaciousness *n* a steadfast adherence to an opinion, purpose, or course of action — see OBSTINACY

tenacity *n* a steadfast adherence to an opinion, purpose, or course of action — see OBSTINACY

tenant *n* one who rents a room or apartment in another's house ⟨the laundry in the basement is for *tenants* only⟩
synonyms boarder, lodger, renter, roomer
related words roommate; guest, visitor; occupant, resident, resider
near antonyms landholder, landowner, proprietor; landlady; slumlord; host, innkeeper
antonyms landlord

[1]tend *vb* to show a liking or proneness (for something) — see LEAN 2

[2]tend *vb* **1** to take charge of especially on behalf of another ⟨*tend* the store while I run an errand⟩
synonyms attend, care (for), mind, oversee, superintend, supervise
related words direct, manage; guard, patrol, protect, safeguard; baby, baby-sit, chaperone (*or* chaperon), mother, shepherd
phrases look after, see to
near antonyms abandon, disregard, forget, ignore, neglect
2 to look after or assist the growth of by labor and care — see GROW 1
3 to work by plowing, sowing, and raising crops on — see FARM

tendency *n* **1** an established pattern of behavior ⟨a *tendency* to drop things⟩ ⟨a *tendency* to make snap judgements⟩
synonyms aptness, proneness, propensity, way
related words bent, disposition, inclination, leaning, penchant, predilection, predisposition, proclivity; custom, habit, pattern, practice (*also* practise), routine, wont; oddity, peculiarity, quirk, singularity, trick
near antonyms averseness, disinclination, indisposition
2 a prevailing or general movement or inclination — see TREND 1
3 a habitual attraction to some activity or thing — see INCLINATION 1

tender *adj* **1** easily injured without careful handling ⟨a *tender* wound⟩ ⟨*tender* plants that cannot take the cold⟩ ⟨*tender* pride that got bruised when his girlfriend dumped him⟩
synonyms delicate, fragile, frail, sensitive
related words breakable, brittle; flimsy, puny, soft, weak; nonhardy, perishable, resistless, susceptible, unresistant, vulnerable, yielding
near antonyms durable, firm, flinty, hard, hardy, resistant, robust, rugged, solid, sound, stiff, stout, strong, sturdy, substantial; nonbreakable, unbreakable; hardened, inured, strengthened, tempered, toughened
antonyms tough
2 feeling or showing love — see LOVING
3 having or marked by sympathy and consideration for others — see HUMANE 1
4 lacking bodily strength — see WEAK 1
5 not harsh or stern especially in manner, nature, or effect — see GENTLE 1

tender *n* something (as pieces of stamped metal or printed paper) customarily and legally used as a medium of exchange, a measure of value, or a means of payment — see MONEY

tender *vb* to put before another for acceptance or consideration — see OFFER 1

tenderfoot *n* a person who is just starting out in a field of activity — see BEGINNER

tenderhearted *adj* **1** feeling or showing love — see LOVING
2 having or marked by sympathy and consideration for others — see HUMANE 1

tending *adj* having a tendency to be or act in a certain way — see PRONE 1

tenement *n* a room or set of rooms in a private house or a block used as a separate dwelling place — see APARTMENT 1

tense *adj* **1** feeling or showing uncomfortable feelings of uncertainty — see NERVOUS 1
2 marked by or causing agitation or uncomfortable feelings — see NERVOUS 2
3 stretched with little or no give — see TAUT

tension *n* the burden on one's emotional or mental well-being created by demands on one's time — see STRESS 1

tent *n* a raised covering over something for decoration or protection — see CANOPY

tentative *adj* determined by something else — see DEPENDENT 2

tenure *n* a fixed period of time during which a person holds a job or position — see TERM 1

tepid *adj* **1** showing little or no interest or enthusiasm ⟨the proposed table tennis club met with only a *tepid* response⟩
synonyms halfhearted, lukewarm, uneager, unenthusiastic
related words apathetic, disinterested, dispassionate, indifferent, neutral, uncaring, uninterested; lackadaisical, languid, listless, perfunctory, undemonstrative, unemotional, unresponsive; unfeeling, unsympathetic; chill, chilly, cold, cool, frigid, frosty, glacial, icy, unfriendly, wintry
near antonyms agog, ardent, avid, exuberant, gung ho, impassioned, raring; engaged, engrossed, interested; ready, willing; cordial, friendly, genial, warmhearted
antonyms eager, enthusiastic, hearty, keen, passionate, warm, wholehearted
2 having or giving off heat to a moderate degree — see WARM 1

term *n* **1** a fixed period of time during which a per-

son holds a job or position ⟨elected for a two-year *term* as mayor⟩
synonyms hitch, stint, tenure, tour
related words shift, watch; go, turn; duration, standing, time; cycle, span, spell, stretch; life, life span, lifetime
2 a pronounceable series of letters having a distinct meaning especially in a particular field — see WORD 1
term *vb* to give a name to — see NAME 1
termagant *n* a bad-tempered scolding woman — see SHREW
terminal *adj* following all others of the same kind in order or time — see LAST
terminate *vb* **1** to bring (an event) to a natural or appropriate stopping point — see CLOSE 3
2 to come to an end — see CEASE 1
3 to mark the limits of — see LIMIT 2
terminated *adj* brought or having come to an end — see COMPLETE 2
terminating *adj* following all others of the same kind in order or time — see LAST
termination *n* **1** a real or imaginary point beyond which a person or thing cannot go — see LIMIT
2 the act of ceasing to exist — see DEATH 3
3 the stopping of a process or activity — see END 1
terminology *n* the special terms or expressions of a particular group or field ⟨the *terminology* favored by sportscasters⟩ ⟨medical *terminology* that can be hard for the patient to understand⟩
synonyms argot, cant, dialect, jargon, language, lingo, patois, patter, slang, vocabulary
related words colloquialism, idiom, localism, parlance, pidgin, provincialism, regionalism, speech, vernacular; journalese
terrestrial *adj* having to do with life on earth especially as opposed to that in heaven — see EARTHLY
terrible *adj* **1** causing fear — see FEARFUL 1
2 extreme in degree, power, or effect — see INTENSE
3 extremely disturbing or repellent — see HORRIBLE 1
4 extremely unsatisfactory — see WRETCHED 1
5 of low quality — see CHEAP 2
terribly *adv* to a great degree — see VERY 1
terrific *adj* of the very best kind — see EXCELLENT
terrified *adj* filled with fear or dread — see AFRAID 1
terrify *vb* to strike with fear — see FRIGHTEN
terrifying *adj* causing fear — see FEARFUL 1
territory *n* the place where a plant or animal is usually or naturally found — see HOME 2
terror *n* the emotion experienced in the presence or threat of danger — see FEAR
terrorize *vb* to strike with fear — see FRIGHTEN
terrorized *adj* filled with fear or dread — see AFRAID 1
terse *adj* marked by the use of few words to convey much information or meaning — see CONCISE
tersely *adv* in a few words — see SHORTLY 1
terseness *n* the quality or state of being marked by or using only few words to convey much meaning — see SUCCINCTNESS
test *n* **1** a procedure or operation carried out to resolve an uncertainty — see EXPERIMENT
2 a set of questions or problems designed to assess knowledge, skills, or intelligence — see EXAMINATION 1
test *vb* **1** to put (something) to a test — see TRY (OUT) 1
2 to subject (a personal quality or faculty) to often excessive stress — see TRY (OUT) 2
testament *n* something presented in support of the truth or accuracy of a claim — see PROOF
testify *vb* to make a solemn declaration under oath for the purpose of establishing a fact ⟨Mrs. Pattle was called to *testify* against the man whom she saw stealing her neighbor's car⟩
synonyms attest, depose, swear, witness
related words vouch; vow, promise
phrases bear witness
testify (to) *vb* to declare (something) to be true or genuine — see CERTIFY 1
testimony *n* something presented in support of the truth or accuracy of a claim — see PROOF
testiness *n* readiness to show annoyance or impatience — see PETULANCE
testy *adj* easily irritated or annoyed — see IRRITABLE
tête-à-tête *adv* in person and usually privately ⟨met *tête-à-tête* with the student's parents to discuss his disciplinary problems in class⟩
synonyms face-to-face, personally
related words familiarly, intimately; confidentially, secretly; directly, immediately
phrases in private
near antonyms distantly, indirectly; openly, publicly
tête-à-tête *n* friendly, informal conversation or an instance of this — see CHAT
text *n* a book used for instruction in a subject — see TEXTBOOK
textbook *n* a book used for instruction in a subject ⟨new, up-to-date middle school science *textbooks*⟩
synonyms handbook, manual, primer, text
related words schoolbook; grammar, reader, speller; tract, treatise; dictionary, lexicon, vocabulary, wordbook; encyclopedia, reference; bible, guide, guidebook
textile *n* a woven or knitted material (as of cotton or nylon) — see CLOTH
thankful *adj* feeling or expressing gratitude — see GRATEFUL 1
thankfulness *n* acknowledgment of having received something good from another — see THANKS
thankless *adj* not showing gratitude ⟨a *thankless* guest who complained that my home cooking was not to her liking⟩
synonyms unappreciative, ungrateful
related words rude, thoughtless, ungracious
near antonyms beholden, indebted; gratified, pleased; courteous, gracious, thoughtful
antonyms appreciative, grateful, obliged, thankful
2 not likely to be appreciated by those who benefit ⟨the *thankless* job of cleaning up after a party⟩
synonyms unappreciated
related words uncredited, underrated, undervalued, unnoticed, unrecognized, unrewarded, unsung, unvalued
near antonyms credited, esteemed, honored, prized, recognized, regarded, rewarded, valued; creditable, meritorious, praiseworthy
antonyms appreciated, thanked

thanks *n pl* acknowledgment of having received something good from another ⟨to express our *thanks*, we'd like to present you with this plaque⟩
synonyms appreciation, appreciativeness, gratefulness, gratitude, thankfulness
related words thanksgiving; gratification, indebtedness, satisfaction; acknowledgment (*also* acknowledgement), recognition, tribute
antonyms ingratitude, thanklessness, ungratefulness
thaw *vb* to go from a solid to a liquid state — see LIQUEFY
thawed *adj* freed from a frozen state by exposure to warmth ⟨recommends cooking *thawed* fish within 24 hours⟩
synonyms defrosted, unfrozen
related words liquefied, melted, molten; deiced; heated, warmed
near antonyms chilled, iced, refrigerated; quick-frozen, refrozen, supercooled; congealed, glaciated, semisolid; frostbitten, frosty, icy
antonyms frozen, unthawed
theater *or* **theatre** *n* **1** a building or part of a building where movies are shown ⟨there's still one *theater* in town that shows movies for two dollars⟩
synonyms cinema, playhouse
related words nickelodeon; multiplex; drive-in
2 the public performance of plays — see DRAMA 1
3 a large room or building for enclosed public gatherings — see HALL 3
theatrical *adj* **1** given to or marked by attention-getting behavior suggestive of stage acting ⟨after stepping out of their hired limousine, the prom couple made a *theatrical* entrance in their evening clothes⟩
synonyms dramatic, histrionic, melodramatic
related words overacted, overdone, sensational, staged; conspicuous, elaborate, flamboyant, grandiose, ostentatious, showy; affected, artificial, exaggerated, formal, mannered, pretentious, self-conscious, studied, unnatural
near antonyms nondramatic, nontheatrical, unaffected, underplayed, unpretentious; muted, restrained, subdued, toned (down); conservative, discreet, inconspicuous; modest, quiet, plain, simple
antonyms undramatic, untheatrical
2 having the general quality or effect of a stage performance — see DRAMATIC 1
theatricals *n pl* the public performance of plays — see DRAMA 1
theft *n* **1** the unlawful taking and carrying away of property without the consent of its owner ⟨*theft* has never been a big problem at our school⟩
synonyms larceny, robbery, stealing, thievery
related words burglary, housebreaking; embezzlement, embezzling, graft, misappropriation; filching, pilfering, purloining, shoplifting; abduction, hijacking, kidnapping, shanghaiing; despoilment, despoliation, looting, pillage, plundering, rapine; poaching, rustling, smuggling; banditry, piracy
2 an instance of theft ⟨the police found the stolen car an hour after the *theft* was reported⟩
synonyms grab, pinch, rip-off, snatching, swiping
related words burglary, holdup, mugging, stickup; confidence game, con game
theme *n* **1** a major object of interest or concern (as in a discussion or artistic composition) — see MATTER 1
2 a short piece of writing done as a school exercise — see COMPOSITION 2
3 a short piece of writing typically expressing a point of view — see ESSAY 1
then *adv* in addition to what has been said — see MORE 1
theoretical *also* **theoretic** *adj* **1** existing only as an assumption or speculation ⟨the merits of the new testing procedures are purely *theoretical*, since no one has ever used them before⟩
synonyms conjectural, hypothetical, speculative, suppositional
related words alleged, assumed, presumed, presupposed, proposed, supposed, unproved, unproven, untested; academic, debatable, moot; abstract, conceptual, intellectual; nonclinical, nonpractical; nonempirical
near antonyms clinical, practical; concrete, defined, definite, distinct; attested, authenticated, confirmed, demonstrated, established, proven, substantiated, tested, time-tested, validated, verified; empirical (*also* empiric), observational
antonyms actual, factual, real
2 dealing with or expressing a quality or idea — see ABSTRACT 1
theory *n* an idea that is the starting point for making a case or conducting an investigation ⟨set out to prove her *theory* that people can't really taste any difference between colas, so they buy according to the product's image⟩
synonyms hypothesis, proposition, supposition
related words assumption, concession, premise, presumption, presupposition; generalization, guess, guesswork, inference, speculation, surmise; proffer, proposal, suggestion; feeling, hunch, impression, inkling, notion, suspicion; abstraction, concept, conception
near antonyms assurance, certainty, fact, knowledge
thereafter *adv* following in time or place — see AFTER
therefore *adv* for this or that reason ⟨it's snowing hard; *therefore* I think we should stay home⟩
synonyms accordingly, consequently, ergo, hence, so, thereupon, thus, wherefore
theretofore *adv* up to this or that time — see HITHERTO
thereupon *adv* for this or that reason — see THEREFORE
thesis *n* an idea or opinion that is put forth in a discussion or debate — see CONTENTION
thick *adj* **1** having or being of relatively great depth or extent from one surface to its opposite ⟨a *thick* board was laid across the pit⟩
synonyms chunky, fat
related words bulky, dense, hefty, thickish; broad, deep, wide
near antonyms narrow, shallow
antonyms skinny, slender, slim, thin
2 being of a consistency that resists flow ⟨*thick* maple syrup for pancakes⟩
synonyms ropy, syrupy, viscid, viscous
related words creamy, heavy, slushy, thickened, thickish, turbid, undiluted; gluey, glutinous, sticky; gelatinous, gooey, gummy, jellylike; concentrated, condensed
near antonyms flowing, fluid; dilute, diluted, liquid, watered (down), weak
antonyms runny, soupy, thin, watery
3 closely acquainted — see FAMILIAR 1

4 having a greater than usual measure across — see WIDE 1
5 having little space between items or parts — see CLOSE 1
6 not having or showing an ability to absorb ideas readily — see STUPID 1
7 possessing or covered with great numbers or amounts of something specified — see RIFE

thick *n* the most intense or characteristic phase of something ⟨in the *thick* of winter many Northerners are dreaming of tropical islands⟩
synonyms deep, depth, height, middle, midst
related words center, heart

thicket *n* a thick patch of shrubbery, small trees, or underbrush ⟨flushed a pheasant from a *thicket* of willows⟩
synonyms brake, brushwood, chaparral, coppice, copse, covert
related words canebrake; brush, bush, scrub, scrubland; bramble, jungle, tangle; grove, hedge, stand, woodlot; forest, greenwood, wildwood, wood, woodland

thickheaded *adj* not having or showing an ability to absorb ideas readily — see STUPID 1

thickness *n* the degree to which a fluid can resist flowing — see CONSISTENCY

thickset *adj* being compact and broad in build and often short in stature — see STOCKY

thief *n* one who steals ⟨sentenced the *thief* who stole Mrs. Stuckey's rosebushes to 30 hours of community service in the municipal rose garden⟩
synonyms pincher, purloiner, robber, stealer
related words burglar, housebreaker; embezzler, grafter; kleptomaniac; pickpocket, pilferer, rifler, shoplifter; abductor, hijacker, kidnapper, skyjacker; despoiler, looter, plunderer, ransacker, ravisher; poacher, rustler, smuggler; bandit, highwayman, pirate; grabber, mugger

thieve *vb* to take (something) without right and with an intent to keep — see STEAL 1

thievery *n* the unlawful taking and carrying away of property without the consent of its owner — see THEFT 1

thin *adj* **1** having a noticeably small amount of body fat ⟨after her bout with pneumonia, she looked *thinner*⟩
synonyms lean, skinny, slender, slim, spare
related words angular, bony, rawboned, scraggy, scrawny, sinewy; lank, lanky, rangy, reedy, spindling, spindly, twiggy, waspish, weedy, willowy, wiry; anorexic, cadaverous, emaciated, gaunt, haggard, pinched, skeletal, wasted, wizened; puny, meager (*or* meagre), slight
near antonyms beefy, bulky, chunky, fleshy, heavy, heavyset, stocky, stout, thick, thickset, weighty; brawny, burly, husky; dumpy, pudgy, roly-poly, squat, stubby; paunchy, potbellied; flabby, soft; buxom; fleshed-out, full, round
antonyms chubby, corpulent, fat, gross, obese, overweight, plump, portly, rotund, tubby
2 being of less than usual width — see NARROW 1
3 not containing very much of some important element — see WEAK 3

thin *vb* to alter (something) for the worse with the addition of foreign or lower-grade substances — see ADULTERATE

thing *n* **1** a member of the human race — see HUMAN
2 one that has a real and independent existence — see ENTITY
3 something done by someone — see ACTION 1
4 something material that can be perceived by the senses — see OBJECT 1
5 something produced by physical or intellectual effort — see PRODUCT 1
6 something that happens — see EVENT 1
7 something that one hopes or intends to accomplish — see GOAL
8 something to be dealt with — see MATTER 2
9 things *pl* transportable items that one owns — see POSSESSION 2

think *vb* to have as an opinion — see BELIEVE 2

think (about *or* over) *vb* to give serious and careful thought to — see PONDER

think (of) *vb* to bring back to mind — see REMEMBER

think (up) *vb* to create or think of by clever use of the imagination — see INVENT

thinker *n* a very smart person — see GENIUS 1

thinking *adj* having the ability to reason — see RATIONAL 1

thinned *adj* **1** containing foreign or lower-grade substances — see IMPURE
2 not containing very much of some important element — see WEAK 3

thirst *n* **1** a strong wish for something — see DESIRE
2 urgent desire or interest — see EAGERNESS

thirst (for) *vb* to have an earnest wish to own or enjoy — see DESIRE

thirsty *adj* **1** marked by little or no precipitation or humidity — see DRY 1
2 showing urgent desire or interest — see EAGER

this *adj* being the less far of two — see NEAR 1

thistly *adj* likely to cause a scratch — see SCRATCHY 1

thorn *n* something that is a source of irritation — see ANNOYANCE 3

thorny *adj* **1** likely to cause a scratch — see SCRATCHY 1
2 requiring exceptional skill or caution in performance or handling — see TRICKY

thorough *adj* **1** having no exceptions or restrictions — see ABSOLUTE 2
2 including many small descriptive features — see DETAILED 1
3 trying all possibilities — see EXHAUSTIVE

thoroughbred *adj* of unmixed ancestry — see PUREBRED

thoroughfare *n* a passage cleared for public vehicular travel — see WAY 1

thoroughgoing *adj* **1** having no exceptions or restrictions — see ABSOLUTE 2
2 trying all possibilities — see EXHAUSTIVE

thoroughly *adv* **1** with attention to all aspects or details ⟨they searched the grounds *thoroughly* for any sign of the intruder⟩
synonyms completely, comprehensively, detailedly, exhaustively, fully, minutely, roundly, totally
related words all-out, full blast, intensively; broadly, extensively, generally, globally, widely; conclusively, consummately, definitely, perfectly
phrases in detail
near antonyms aimlessly, desultorily, haphazardly, hit-or-miss, randomly; cursorily, imperfectly, inadequately, narrowly, shallowly, sketchily, summarily, superficially; indeterminately, nebulously, vaguely
2 to a full extent or degree — see FULLY 1

though *conj* in spite of the fact that — see ALTHOUGH
though *adv* in spite of that — see HOWEVER
thought *n* **1** a careful weighing of the reasons for or against something — see CONSIDERATION 1
2 something imagined or pictured in the mind — see IDEA
thoughtful *adj* **1** given to or made with heedful anticipation of the needs and happiness of others ⟨a *thoughtful* offer to watch the neighbors' children on moving day⟩ ⟨a *thoughtful* aunt who never forgets the birthday of a niece or nephew⟩
synonyms attentive, considerate, kind, solicitous
related words brotherly, good, good-hearted, helpful, hospitable, kindhearted, kindly, neighborly, nice; caring, compassionate, sympathetic, tender; chivalrous, courteous, courtly, gallant, gracious, polite; diplomatic, tactful; deferential, dutiful, obliging, regardful, respectful; altruistic, beneficent, benevolent, benignant, humane, selfless, unselfish; charitable, generous, magnanimous
near antonyms inattentive, uncaring, unheeding; inhospitable, unkind, unkindly, unneighborly; ill-bred, ill-mannered, impolite, rude, uncivil, uncourteous, unmannerly; unhelpful, unobliging; malevolent, malicious, mean, spiteful
antonyms heedless, inconsiderate, thoughtless, unthinking
2 decided on as a result of careful thought — see DELIBERATE 1
3 given to or marked by long, quiet thinking — see CONTEMPLATIVE
thoughtfully *adv* with good reason or courtesy — see WELL 4
thoughtless *adj* showing a lack of manners or consideration for others — see IMPOLITE
thrall *n* **1** a person who is considered the property of another person — see SLAVE 1
2 the state of being a slave — see SLAVERY 1
thralldom *or* **thraldom** *n* the state of being a slave — see SLAVERY 1
thrash *vb* **1** to achieve a victory over — see BEAT 2
2 to defeat by a large margin — see WHIP 2
3 to strike repeatedly with something long and thin or flexible — see WHIP 1
4 to strike repeatedly — see BEAT 1
thread *vb* **1** to scatter or set here and there among other things ⟨this history book *threads* excerpts from the diaries of pioneer women into its account of the settlement of the West⟩
synonyms interlace, intersperse, interweave, lace, weave, wreathe
related words insert, intermingle, mingle, mix; alternate, juxtapose; amalgamate, assimilate, blend, combine, commingle, embody, fuse, incorporate, integrate, merge
2 to put together into a series by means of or as if by means of a thread ⟨the reporter *threaded* his newspaper articles about the basketball team into a book that was essentially a chronicle of their championship season⟩
synonyms concatenate, string
related words chain, connect, join, link, unite; interlace, intersperse, intertwine, interweave, lace, weave, wreathe
threadbare *adj* **1** showing signs of advanced wear and tear and neglect — see SHABBY 1
2 used or heard so often as to be dull — see STALE
3 worn or torn into or as if into rags — see RAGGED 2
threat *n* something that may cause injury or harm — see DANGER 2
threaten *vb* to remain poised to inflict harm, danger, or distress on ⟨unless the home fans' unacceptable behavior and name-calling stops, the possibility of expulsion from the league *threatens* the school's basketball team⟩
synonyms hang (over), hover (over), impend (over), menace, overhang
related words endanger, hazard, imperil, jeopardize
threatening *adj* **1** giving signs of immediate occurrence — see IMMINENT 1
2 being or showing a sign of evil or calamity to come — see OMINOUS
3 involving potential loss or injury — see DANGEROUS
threefold *adj* having three units or parts — see TRIPLE
threesome *n* a group of three ⟨the *threesome* from Crystal Falls—Jocelyn, Katie, and Lynn—missed their plane and joined up with the rest of the group the next day⟩
synonyms triad, trinity, trio, triple, triplet, triumvirate
related words trilogy; triplicate; triplex
threnody *n* a composition expressing one's grief over a loss — see LAMENT 2
threshold *n* the point at which something begins — see BEGINNING
thrift *n* careful management of material resources — see ECONOMY
thriftless *adj* given to spending money freely or foolishly — see PRODIGAL
thrifty *adj* careful in the management of money or resources — see FRUGAL
thrill *n* a pleasurably intense stimulation of the feelings ⟨everyone gets a real *thrill* out of the Independence Day fireworks⟩
synonyms bang, exhilaration, kick, titillation
related words arousal, electrification, intoxication, stimulation; jolt, shock, surprise; delectation, delight, enjoyment, joy, lift, pleasure; amusement, diversion, entertainment, fun, treat
thrill *vb* to cause a pleasurable stimulation of the feelings ⟨was *thrilled* by the news of Betsy's promotion⟩
synonyms electrify, excite, exhilarate, galvanize, intoxicate, titillate, turn on
related words arouse, incite, inspire, provoke, stimulate; bewitch, captivate, charm, delight, enchant, enthrall (*or* enthral), hypnotize, mesmerize, rivet, spellbind; interest, intrigue, tantalize
near antonyms bore, jade, pall, tire, weary; deject, demoralize, discourage, dishearten, dispirit
thrilling *adj* causing great emotional or mental stimulation — see EXCITING 1
thrive *vb* **1** to grow vigorously ⟨these plants *thrive* with relatively little sunlight⟩
synonyms burgeon, flourish, prosper
related words luxuriate, overgrow, proliferate, shoot up; germinate, root, sprout; bloom, flower, fruit, produce, propagate, regenerate, seed
2 to reach a desired level of accomplishment — see SUCCEED 2
thriving *adj* **1** having attained a desired end or state of good fortune — see SUCCESSFUL 1
2 marked by much life, movement, or activity — see ALIVE 2

3 marked by vigorous growth and well-being especially economically — see PROSPEROUS 1
throaty *adj* **1** harsh and dry in sound — see HOARSE
2 having a low musical pitch or range — see DEEP 2
throb *n* a rhythmic expanding and contracting — see PULSATION
throb *vb* to expand and contract in a rhythmic manner — see PULSATE
throe *n* a sharp unpleasant sensation usually felt in some specific part of the body — see PAIN 1
throng *n* a great number of persons or things gathered together — see CROWD 1
throng *vb* to move upon or fill (something) in great numbers — see CROWD 2
thronging *adj* possessing or covered with great numbers or amounts of something specified — see RIFE
throttle *vb* to keep (someone) from breathing by exerting pressure on the windpipe — see CHOKE 1
through *adv* **1** from beginning to end ⟨read the letter *through* twice⟩ ⟨never once missed class the whole year *through*⟩
synonyms around, over, round, throughout
2 from one side to the other of an intervening space — see OVER 1
through *prep* **1** in or into the middle of — see AMONG
2 in random positions within the boundaries of — see AROUND 2
3 in the course of — see DURING
4 to the opposite side of — see ACROSS
5 along the way of — see BY 1
6 as the result of — see BECAUSE OF
7 using the means or agency of — see BY 2
through *adj* brought or having come to an end — see COMPLETE 2
throughout *prep* **1** in random positions within the boundaries of — see AROUND 2
2 in the course of — see DURING
throughout *adv* **1** from beginning to end — see THROUGH 1
2 in every place or in all places — see EVERYWHERE
throw *vb* to send through the air especially with a quick forward motion of the arm ⟨*threw* a life preserver to the drowning man⟩
synonyms cast, catapult, chuck, dash, fire, fling, heave, hurl, hurtle, launch, lob, loft, peg, pelt, pitch, sling, toss
related words bowl, flip, hook, pass, roll, shoot: buck, eject, impel, precipitate, project, propel, rifle, thrust
throw (on) *vb* to place on one's person — see PUT ON 1
throw away *vb* **1** to get rid of as useless or unwanted — see DISCARD
2 to use up carelessly — see WASTE 1
throwing away *n* the getting rid of whatever is unwanted or useless — see DISPOSAL 1
throw out *vb* **1** to drive or force out — see EJECT 1
2 to get rid of as useless or unwanted — see DISCARD
throw up *vb* **1** to discharge the contents of the stomach through the mouth — see VOMIT
2 to make or assemble roughly or hastily — see COBBLE (TOGETHER)
thrum *n* a monotonous sound like that of an insect in motion — see HUM
thrum *vb* to strike or cause to strike lightly and usually rhythmically — see [1]TAP
thrust *vb* to apply force to (someone or something) so that it moves in front of one — see PUSH 1
thud *n* a hard strike with a part of the body or an instrument — see [1]BLOW
thud *vb* to come into usually forceful contact with something — see HIT 2
thug *n* a violent, brutal person who is often a member of an organized gang — see HOODLUM
thumb *vb* to travel by securing free rides — see HITCHHIKE
thump *n* a hard strike with a part of the body or an instrument — see [1]BLOW
thump *vb* **1** to deliver a blow to (someone or something) usually in a strong vigorous manner — see HIT 1
2 to strike repeatedly — see BEAT 1
thunder *vb* to make a long loud deep noise or cry — see ROAR
thunderous *adj* marked by a high volume of sound — see LOUD 1
thunderstruck *adj* affected with sudden and great wonder or surprise ⟨Colin was *thunderstruck* when his parents told him he was adopted⟩
synonyms amazed, astonished, astounded, awestruck, bowled over, dumbfounded (*or* dumfounded), flabbergasted, shocked, stunned, stupefied
related words startled, surprised; aghast, appalled, dismayed, horrified; bewildered, confused, dazed, overwhelmed; agape, awed, awesome, openmouthed, wide-eyed, widemouthed
near antonyms casual, nonchalant, unruffled
antonyms unawed
thus *adv* for this or that reason — see THEREFORE
thus far *adv* up to this or that time — see HITHERTO
thwack *n* **1** a hard strike with a part of the body or an instrument — see [1]BLOW
2 a loud explosive sound — see CLAP 1
thwack *vb* to deliver a blow to (someone or something) usually in a strong vigorous manner — see HIT 1
thwart *vb* to prevent from achieving a goal — see FRUSTRATE
tick (off) *vb* to specify one after another — see ENUMERATE 1
ticket *n* **1** a small sheet of plastic, paper, or paperboard showing that the bearer has a claim to something (as admittance) ⟨only people with *tickets* will be allowed past the front gates⟩
synonyms check, coupon, pass
related words certificate, note, token, voucher
2 a slip (as of paper or cloth) that is attached to something to identify or describe it — see LABEL
ticket *vb* to attach an identifying slip to — see LABEL 1
tickled *adj* experiencing pleasure, satisfaction, or delight — see GLAD 1
ticklish *adj* requiring exceptional skill or caution in performance or handling — see TRICKY
tidbit *also* **titbit** *n* **1** something that is pleasing to eat because it is rare or a luxury — see DELICACY 1
2 a small piece or quantity of food — see MORSEL 1
tide *n* a prevailing or general movement or inclination — see TREND 1
tidied *adj* being clean and in good order — see NEAT 1

tidings *n pl* a report of recent events or facts not previously known — see NEWS
tidy *adj* **1** being clean and in good order — see NEAT 1
2 of a size greater than average of its kind — see LARGE
3 sufficiently large in size, amount, or number to merit attention — see CONSIDERABLE 1
tie *n* **1** a situation in which neither participant in a contest, competition, or struggle comes out ahead of the other <the competition for first place in the dessert division ended in a *tie* between the chocolate pecan pie and the walnut fudge tart>
synonyms dead heat, draw, stalemate, standoff
related words deadlock, impasse; photo finish; toss-up
2 a uniting or binding force or influence — see BOND 2
tie *vb* **1** to gather into a tight mass by means of a line or cord <*tied* the newspapers into a bundle>
synonyms band, bind, gird, truss
related words cinch, cord, rope, strap, thread, wire; lash, leash, tether; interlace, intertwine, interweave, lace; entangle, knot, snarl, tangle, twist; coil, wind
near antonyms undo, unfasten, unlace, unlash, unloose, unloosen, unthread; unleash, untether; disentangle, uncoil, untangle, untwine, untwist, unwind
antonyms unbind, untie
2 to produce something equal to (as in quality or value) — see EQUAL 1
tie–up *n* the state of having shared interests or efforts (as in social or business matters) — see ASSOCIATION 1
tie up *vb* to create difficulty for the work or activity of — see HAMPER
tiff *n* an often noisy or angry expression of differing opinions — see ARGUMENT 1
tight *adj* **1** not allowing penetration (as by gas, liquid, or light) <a *tight* hull that was no match for an iceberg>
synonyms impenetrable, impermeable, impervious
related words close, compact, dense, snug, thick; airtight, hermetic, watertight; lightproof, soundproof, waterproof
near antonyms absorbent, leaky, porous, unsealed
antonyms penetrable, permeable
2 firmly positioned in place and difficult to dislodge <a *tight* screw that won't come loose> <a jar with a *tight* lid>
synonyms fast, firm, frozen, jammed, lodged, secure, set, snug, stuck, wedged
related words bonded, cemented, glued; anchored, clamped; embedded, entrenched (*also* intrenched), implanted; attached, bound, fastened, secured; immovable, unyielding
near antonyms detached, dislodged, freed, loosened, unattached, unbound, undone, unfastened, unsecured; movable (*or* moveable), yielding
antonyms insecure, loose
3 giving or sharing as little as possible — see STINGY 1
4 having little space between items or parts — see CLOSE 1
5 showing little difference in the standing of the competitors — see CLOSE 3
6 stretched with little or no give — see TAUT
tightfisted *adj* giving or sharing as little as possible — see STINGY 1
tight–lipped *adj* tending not to speak frequently (as by habit or inclination) — see SILENT 2
tightness *n* the quality of being overly sparing with money — see PARSIMONY
tightwad *n* a mean grasping person who is usually stingy with money — see MISER
till *vb* to work by plowing, sowing, and raising crops on — see FARM
tiller *n* a person who cultivates the land and grows crops on it — see FARMER
tilt *n* the act of positioning or an instance of being positioned at an angle <indicated her approval with a slight forward *tilt* of her head>
synonyms angling, bend, cock, inclination, list, tip
related words turn, twist, veer; bow, dip, nod
tilt *vb* to set or cause to be at an angle — see LEAN 1
tilted *adj* **1** inclined or twisted to one side — see AWRY
2 running in a slanting direction — see DIAGONAL
tilting *adj* running in a slanting direction — see DIAGONAL
timber *n* **1** a dense growth of trees and shrubs covering a large area — see FOREST
2 tree logs as prepared for human use — see WOOD
timberland *n* a dense growth of trees and shrubs covering a large area — see FOREST
time *n* **1** a particular point at which an event takes place — see OCCASION 1
2 an exciting or noteworthy event that one experiences firsthand — see ADVENTURE
3 an extent of time associated with a particular person or thing — see AGE 1
4 the period during which something exists, lasts, or is in progress — see DURATION 1
timeliness *n* the quality or habit of arriving on time — see PROMPTITUDE
timely *adj* **1** especially suitable for a certain time <a *timely* invitation to lunch that came just as I was starting to feel hungry>
synonyms opportune, seasonable
related words appropriate, apt, fit, fitting, meet, pat, proper, relevant, suitable; fortunate, lucky, propitious; anticipated, expected; prompt, punctual, undelayed
near antonyms improper, inappropriate, irrelevant, unfit, unsuitable; unfortunate, unlucky; behind, behindhand, belated, delayed, delinquent, late, latish, overdue, postponed, slow, tardy; anticipatory, early, precocious, premature; abrupt, sudden, unanticipated, unexpected
antonyms inopportune, unseasonable, untimely
2 done, carried out, or given without delay — see PROMPT 1
timepiece *n* a device to measure time <the only *timepiece* she used at the cabin was a garden sundial>
synonyms chronometer, clock, timer
related words alarm clock, atomic clock, cuckoo clock, grandfather clock, time clock; hourglass, sandglass, sundial, water clock; chronograph, stopwatch, watch
timer *n* a device to measure time — see TIMEPIECE
timetable *n* a listing of things to be presented or

considered (as at a concert or play) — see PROGRAM 1

timid *adj* easily frightened — see SHY 1

timidity *n* lack of willingness to assert oneself and take risks <none of the scouts showed the least *timidity* about rappeling down the cliff>
synonyms faintheartedness, timidness, timorousness
related words bashfulness, constraint, embarrassment, inhibition, restraint, shyness, skittishness; hesitation, indecision, indecisiveness, irresoluteness, irresolution; alarm, anxiety, apprehension, concern, discomposure, dismay, fear, panic, upset, worry; cowardice, cowardliness, cravenness, spinelessness, yellowness
near antonyms assurance, confidence, self-assurance, self-confidence; composure, coolness, insouciance, nonchalance, unconcern; backbone, decisiveness, determination, fiber, firmness, fortitude, gameness, grit, gumption, mettle, resoluteness, resolution, spunk; bravery, courage, courageousness, daring, dauntlessness, doughtiness, fearlessness, intrepidity, intrepidness
antonyms audaciousness, audacity, boldness, guts, nerve

timidness *n* lack of willingness to assert oneself and take risks — see TIMIDITY

timorous *adj* easily frightened — see SHY 1

timorousness *n* lack of willingness to assert oneself and take risks — see TIMIDITY

tincture *n* a substance used to color other materials — see PIGMENT

tinge *n* a property that becomes apparent when light falls on an object and by which things that are identical in form can be distinguished — see COLOR 1

tinge *vb* to give color or a different color to — see COLOR 1

tingle *n* a sharp unpleasant sensation usually felt in some specific part of the body — see PAIN 1

tinker (with) *vb* to handle thoughtlessly, ignorantly, or mischievously — see TAMPER

tinkle *n* a series of short high ringing sounds <Mrs. Mouse ignored the warning *tinkle* of the cat's bell, and now her children are orphans>
synonyms chime(s), jingle, tintinnabulation
related words clatter, jangle, rattle; chink, clang, clank, clink, dingdong, ping, ring, toll; chirr, ripple, trill, warble

tinkle *vb* to make a repeated sharp light ringing sound — see JINGLE

tint *vb* to give color or a different color to — see COLOR 1

tint *n* a property that becomes apparent when light falls on an object and by which things that are identical in form can be distinguished — see COLOR 1

tintinnabulation *n* a series of short high ringing sounds — see TINKLE

tiny *adj* very small in size <the forest ranger showed us how every square foot of forest is alive with *tiny* creatures>
synonyms atomic, bitty, infinitesimal, microminiature, microscopic (*also* microscopical), miniature, minute, teeny, teeny-weeny, wee
related words diminutive, dwarf, little, midget, model, petite, pocket, pocket-size (*also* pocket-sized), pygmy, small, smallish; dinky, dwarfish, insignificant, pint-size (*or* pint-sized), puny, scrubby, undersized
near antonyms big, bulky, bumper, considerable, extensive, good, goodly, good-sized, grand, great, gross, handsome, hefty, hulking, jumbo, king-size (*or* king-sized), large, largish, major, outsize (*also* outsized), oversize (*or* oversized), sizable (*or* sizeable), substantial, super, whacking, whopping; formidable, grandiose, imposing, lofty, majestic, monolithic, staggering, stupendous, towering; boundless, cavernous, immeasurable, infinite, vast, vasty, voluminous
antonyms astronomical (*also* astronomic), colossal, cosmic, elephantine, enormous, giant, gigantic, herculean, heroic, huge, immense, mammoth, massive, monster, monstrous, monumental, mountainous, prodigious, titanic, tremendous

[1]tip *n* **1** a piece of advice or useful information especially from an expert <got some *tips* from a horticulturist on how to get my violets to bloom>
synonyms hint, lead, pointer
related words advice, advisement, assistance, counsel, guidance, recommendation, suggestion; caution, cautioning, sign, signal, telltale, tip-off, warning; brief, direction, feedback, instruction, observation; prompt, reminder, urging; answer, clue, solution
2 information not generally available to the public — see DOPE 1

[2]tip *n* **1** a small sum of money given for a service over and above what is due <gave our waiter an extra large *tip* for such fantastic service>
synonyms gratuity, perquisite
related words donation, gift, lagniappe, largess (*or* largesse), present; bonus, favor, reward; contribution, offering
2 something given in addition to what is ordinarily expected or owed — see BONUS

[3]tip *n* the act of positioning or an instance of being positioned at an angle — see TILT

[4]tip *n* the last and usually sharp or tapering part of something long and narrow — see POINT 2

tip *vb* to set or cause to be at an angle — see LEAN 1

tipped *adj* tapering to a thin tip — see POINTED 1

tipping *adj* inclined or twisted to one side — see AWRY

tippler *n* a person who makes a habit of getting drunk — see DRUNK 1

tipsy *adj* being under the influence of alcohol — see DRUNK

tip–top *adj* of the very best kind — see EXCELLENT

tip–top *n* the highest part or point — see HEIGHT 1

tirade *n* a long angry speech or scolding <after the inspection by the health department, Jay had to listen to his boss's *tirade* about keeping the restaurant's kitchen cleaner>
synonyms diatribe, harangue, rant
related words assault, attack, invective, lambasting, lashing, tongue-lashing, vituperation; berating, chewing out, rebuke, reprimand, reproach, reproof; abuse, castigation, censure, condemnation, criticism, denunciation; belittlement, deprecation, depreciation, disparagement, dissing; excoriation, execration, revilement; admonishment, admonition, lecture, sermon
near antonyms encomium, eulogy, panegyric, rhapsody, tribute; acclaim, acclamation, accolade, citation, homage, honor, praise; approval, blessing, commendation, endorsement, sanction; ovation, plaudit, rave

tire *vb* **1** to diminish the physical strength of — see WEAKEN 1
2 to make weary and restless by being dull or monotonous — see [2]BORE
3 to use up all the physical energy of — see EXHAUST 1

tired *adj* **1** depleted in strength, energy, or freshness — see WEARY 1
2 having one's patience, interest, or pleasure exhausted — see WEARY 2
3 used or heard so often as to be dull — see STALE

tiredness *n* **1** a complete depletion of energy or strength — see FATIGUE
2 the state of being bored — see BOREDOM

tireless *adj* showing no signs of weariness even after long hard effort ⟨a *tireless* advocate for human rights⟩
synonyms indefatigable, inexhaustible, unflagging, untiring, unwearying, weariless
related words assiduous, conscientious, diligent, meticulous, painstaking, sedulous; determined, dogged, patient, persevering, persistent, pertinacious, plodding, relentless, steadfast, steady, stubborn, tenacious, unabating, unfailing, unfaltering, unflinching, unrelenting, unremitting, unwavering; active, busy, dynamic, energetic, feverish, spirited, vigorous; hard, industrious, intense, laborious, slavish, strenuous
near antonyms indolent, lackadaisical, laggard, lazy, listless, shiftless, slothful, sluggish; apathetic, casual, desultory, languid, spiritless; beat, broken, burned-out (*or* burnt-out), done in, drained, enervated, jaded, overtaxed, overworked, played out, sapped, spent, tuckered (out), wearied, worn-out

tirelessly *adv* with great effort or determination — see HARD 1

tiresome *adj* causing weariness, restlessness, or lack of interest — see BORING

tiring *adj* causing weariness, restlessness, or lack of interest — see BORING

titan *n* something that is unusually large and powerful — see GIANT

titanic *adj* unusually large — see HUGE

titillate *vb* to cause a pleasurable stimulation of the feelings — see THRILL

titillation *n* a pleasurably intense stimulation of the feelings — see THRILL

title *n* **1** a word or combination of words by which a person or thing is regularly known — see NAME 1
2 a word or series of words often in larger letters placed at the beginning of a passage or at the top of a page in order to introduce or categorize — see HEADING
3 the position occupied by the one who comes in first in a competition — see CROWN 2

title *vb* to give a name to — see NAME 1

titter *n* an explosive sound that is a sign of amusement — see LAUGH 1

tittle *n* **1** a very small piece — see BIT 1
2 the smallest amount or part imaginable — see JOT

titular *adj* being something in name or form only — see NOMINAL 1

tizzy *n* a state of nervous or irritated concern — see FRET

to *prep* earlier than — see BEFORE 1

toady *n* a person who flatters another in order to get ahead — see SYCOPHANT

toady *vb* to use flattery or the doing of favors in order to win approval especially from a superior — see FAWN

toast *vb* to cause to have or give off heat to a moderate degree — see WARM 1

toasty *adj* having or giving off heat to a moderate degree — see WARM 1

tocsin *n* **1** an object intended to give public notice or warning — see SIGNAL 1
2 something that tells of approaching danger or risk — see WARNING 2

today *adv* at the present time — see NOW 1

today *n* the time currently existing or in progress — see PRESENT 1

to–do *n* a state of noisy, confused activity — see COMMOTION

together *adv* **1** at one and the same time ⟨the two packages, although sent on different days, arrived *together*⟩
synonyms coincidentally, coincidently, concurrently, contemporaneously, simultaneously
related words close, immediately, narrowly, near
phrases at once
near antonyms apart, independently, individually, singly; consecutively, successively
antonyms separately
2 in or by combined action or effort ⟨working *together*, we can get this project done on time⟩
synonyms conjointly, jointly
related words collectively, mutually, reciprocally, unanimously, unitedly; cooperatively, symbiotically
phrases in concert
antonyms apart, independently, individually, separately, severally, singly, unilaterally

togs *n pl* **1** clothing chosen as appropriate for a specific situation — see OUTFIT 1
2 covering for the human body — see CLOTHING

toil *n* very hard or unpleasant work ⟨after years of *toil* in a sweatshop, Kim was finally able to start her own dressmaking business⟩
synonyms drudgery, grind, labor, slavery, sweat, travail
related words effort, exertion, pains, struggle, trouble; chore, duty, job, obligation, responsibility; routine, tedium, treadmill
near antonyms ease, leisure, relaxation, repose, rest; amusement, diversion, entertainment, recreation, sport; idleness, inactivity, inertia, inertness
antonyms fun, play

toil *vb* to devote serious and sustained effort — see LABOR

toiler *n* a person who does very hard or dull work — see SLAVE 2

toilet *n* a room furnished with a fixture for flushing body waste ⟨we were directed to the *toilets* in the church basement⟩
synonyms bath, bathroom, latrine, lavatory, rest room, washroom, water closet
related words commode; outhouse, privy

toilsome *adj* **1** requiring considerable physical or mental effort — see HARD 2
2 requiring much time, effort, or careful attention — see DEMANDING 1

token *n* something that serves to keep alive the memory of a person or event — see MEMORIAL

tolerable *adj* **1** capable of being endured — see BEARABLE
2 of a level of quality that meets one's needs or standards — see ADEQUATE

tolerably *adv* in a satisfactory way — see WELL 1

tolerance *n* the capacity to endure what is difficult or disagreeable without complaining — see PATIENCE

tolerant *adj* **1** accepting pains or hardships calmly or without complaint — see PATIENT 1
2 receiving or enduring without offering resistance — see PASSIVE

tolerate *vb* to put up with (something painful or difficult) — see BEAR 2

tolerating *adj* receiving or enduring without offering resistance — see PASSIVE

toll *vb* to make the clear sound heard when metal vibrates — see RING 1

tomb *n* a final resting place for a dead person — see GRAVE

tomboyish *adj* having qualities or traits that are traditionally considered inappropriate for a girl or woman — see UNFEMININE

tombstone *n* a shaped stone laid over or erected near a grave and usually bearing an inscription to identify and preserve the memory of the deceased <the many *tombstones* marking the graves of children in the old cemetery reveal the harshness of pioneer life>
synonyms gravestone, headstone, monument
related words cross, marker, plaque, stone, table, tablet; monolith, obelisk, pillar; memorial, shrine

tome *n* a set of printed sheets of paper bound together between covers and forming a work of fiction or nonfiction — see BOOK 1

tomfoolery *n* wildly playful or mischievous behavior — see HORSEPLAY

tone *n* **1** a distinctive way of putting ideas into words — see STYLE 1
2 a property that becomes apparent when light falls on an object and by which things that are identical in form can be distinguished — see COLOR 1
3 the set of qualities that makes a person, a group of people, or a thing different from others — see NATURE 1

toned–down *adj* not excessively showy — see QUIET 2

tongue *n* the stock of words, pronunciation, and grammar used by a people as their basic means of communication — see LANGUAGE 1

tonic *adj* having a renewing effect on the state of the body or mind <breathe in clear *tonic* mountain air> <never underestimate the *tonic* power of humor on a sick person>
synonyms bracing, invigorating, refreshing, restorative, reviving, stimulating, stimulative, vitalizing
related words conditioning, strengthening; animating, exhilarating, exhilarative, quickening, sharp; corrective, curative, curing, medicinal, rectifying, reformative, reformatory, remedial, remedying, reparative, therapeutic; beneficial, healthful, healthy, helpful, salubrious, salutary, wholesome
near antonyms deadening, debilitating, enervating, enfeebling, exhausting, numbing, sapping, weakening

too *adv* **1** beyond a normal or acceptable limit <Ryan thought the test was *too* hard, but, on the other hand, he hadn't studied for it>
synonyms devilishly, excessively, exorbitantly, inordinately, monstrously, overly, overmuch, unacceptably, unduly
related words extravagantly, immoderately, intemperately; extortionately, inexcusably, intolerably, unbearably, unconscionably, unreasonably; improperly, inappropriately; abnormally, extraordinarily, freakishly, singularly, uncommonly, uncustomarily, unusually; astronomically, considerably, eminently, especially, exceedingly, exceptionally, extensively, extra, extremely, incredibly, remarkably, significantly, substantially, super, very, whacking
phrases to a fault
near antonyms acceptably, moderately, modestly, reasonably, temperately; barely, hardly, just, marginally, minimally, scarcely
antonyms deficiently, inadequately, insufficiently
2 in addition to what has been said — see MORE 1
3 to a great degree — see VERY 1

tool *n* **1** an article intended for use in work — see IMPLEMENT
2 one that is or can be used to further the purposes of another — see PAWN 1
3 one who is easily deceived or cheated — see DUPE

tooth and nail *adv* with all power or resources being used — see FULL BLAST

toothsome *adj* very pleasing to the sense of taste — see DELICIOUS 1

top *adj* **1** being at a point or level higher than all others <an office in the *top* story of the building> <the *top* student in our graduating class>
synonyms highest, loftiest, topmost, upmost, uppermost
related words higher, loftier, upper; maximized, maximum, peaked, utmost; chief, first, foremost, head, leading, predominant, preeminent, premier, principal; dominant, dominating, eminent, prominent, towering; elevated, escalated, heightened, jacked (up), lifted, raised, uplifted, upraised
near antonyms below, lower, under; low, lowered, low-lying, sunken
antonyms lowermost, lowest, nethermost, undermost
2 of the greatest or highest degree or quantity — see ULTIMATE 1
3 of the highest degree — see FULL 2
4 of the very best kind — see EXCELLENT

top *n* **1** a piece placed over an open container to hold in, protect, or conceal its contents — see COVER 1
2 the highest part or point — see HEIGHT 1

top *vb* to be greater, better, or stronger than — see SURPASS 1

topcoat *n* a warm outdoor coat — see OVERCOAT

topic *n* a major object of interest or concern (as in a discussion or artistic composition) — see MATTER 1

topmost *adj* **1** being at a point or level higher than all others — see TOP 1
2 of the highest degree — see FULL 2

top–notch *adj* of the very best kind — see EXCELLENT

topper *n* something (as a fact or argument) that is decisive or overwhelming — see CLINCHER

topple *vb* to go down from an upright position suddenly and involuntarily — see FALL 1

topsy–turvy *adj* lacking in order, neatness, and often cleanliness — see MESSY

torment *n* **1** a situation or state that causes great suffering and unhappiness — see HELL 2
2 a state of great suffering of body or mind — see DISTRESS 1

torment *vb* to cause persistent suffering to — see AFFLICT

tormenting *adj* **1** hard to accept or bear especially emotionally — see BITTER 2
2 intensely or unbearably painful — see EXCRUCIATING 1

tormentor *n* a person who causes repeated emotional pain, distress, or annoyance to another <Phillip was relieved when his *tormentor* moved away, and he no longer had to take pains to avoid the bully>
synonyms baiter, heckler, mocker, needler, oppressor, persecutor, quiz, quizzer, ridiculer, scoffer, scorner, taunter, tease, teaser, torturer
related words belittler, derider, detractor, insulter; smart aleck, smarty (*or* smartie), wiseacre, wiseguy; lampooner, satirist; accuser, blamer, troublemaker; assailant, attacker, molester; bother, disturber, pest
near antonyms defender, deliverer, protector, rescuer, saviour; comforter, consoler, solace, soother, succorer

torpid *adj* **1** lacking bodily strength — see WEAK 1
2 slow to move or act — see INACTIVE 1

torrent *n* a great flow of water or of something that overwhelms — see FLOOD

torrid *adj* having a notably high temperature — see HOT 1

tortuous *adj* marked by a long series of irregular curves — see CROOKED 1

torture *n* **1** a situation or state that causes great suffering and unhappiness — see HELL 2
2 a state of great suffering of body or mind — see DISTRESS 1

torture *vb* to cause persistent suffering to — see AFFLICT

torturer *n* a person who causes repeated emotional pain, distress, or annoyance to another — see TORMENTOR

torturing *adj* intensely or unbearably painful — see EXCRUCIATING 1

torturous *adj* intensely or unbearably painful — see EXCRUCIATING 1

toss *vb* **1** to make a series of unsteady side-to-side motions — see ROCK 1
2 to make jerky or restless movements — see FIDGET
3 to send through the air especially with a quick forward motion of the arm — see THROW

toss (down *or* off) *vb* to swallow in liquid form — see DRINK 1

total *adj* **1** having no exceptions or restrictions — see ABSOLUTE 2
2 not lacking any part or member that properly belongs to it — see COMPLETE 1
3 trying all possibilities — see EXHAUSTIVE

total *n* a complete amount of something — see WHOLE

total *vb* **1** to have a total of — see AMOUNT (TO) 1
2 to combine (numbers) into a single sum — see ADD 2

totalitarianism *n* a system of government in which the ruler has unlimited power — see DESPOTISM

totality *n* a complete amount of something — see WHOLE

totally *adv* **1** to a full extent or degree — see FULLY 1
2 with attention to all aspects or details — see THOROUGHLY 1

tote *vb* to support and take from one place to another — see CARRY 1

totter *vb* **1** to move forward while swaying from side to side — see STAGGER 1
2 to swing unsteadily back and forth or from side to side — see TEETER 1

tottery *adj* marked by or given to small uncontrollable bodily movements — see SHAKY 1

touch *n* a very small amount — see PARTICLE 1

touch *vb* **1** to come into bodily contact with (something) so as to perceive a slight pressure on the skin <be careful not to *touch* this pan—it's still hot>
synonyms feel
related words caress, embrace, finger, fondle, hug, paw, rub, stroke; brush, graze; clasp, clench, cling (to), clutch, grasp, grip, handle, hold, palm; chuck, clap, dab, flick, pat, tag, tap, tip; hit, knock, pound, rap, whack
2 to act upon (a person or a person's feelings) so as to cause a response — see [1]AFFECT 1
3 to affect slightly with something morally bad or undesirable — see TAINT 1
4 to be adjacent to — see ADJOIN 1
5 to be the business or affair of — see CONCERN 2

touch (on *or* upon) *vb* to make reference to or speak about briefly but specifically — see MENTION 1

touchable *adj* capable of being perceived by the sense of touch — see TANGIBLE

touch down *vb* to come to rest after descending from the air — see ALIGHT

touching *adj* **1** having a border in common — see ADJACENT
2 having the power to affect the feelings or sympathies — see MOVING

touch off *vb* to cause to function — see ACTIVATE

touchstone *n* something set up as an example against which others of the same type are compared — see STANDARD 1

touchy *adj* requiring exceptional skill or caution in performance or handling — see TRICKY

tough *adj* **1** not easily chewed <her steak was so *tough* that she suggested the waiter use it as a hockey puck>
synonyms chewy, leathery
related words fibrous, gristly, sinewy, stringy; brittle, crunchy, hard
near antonyms mushy, soft
antonyms tender
2 able to withstand hardship, strain, or exposure — see HARDY 1
3 difficult to endure — see HARSH 1
4 requiring considerable physical or mental effort — see HARD 2
5 requiring exceptional skill or caution in performance or handling — see TRICKY

tough *n* a violent, brutal person who is often a member of an organized gang — see HOODLUM

toughen *vb* **1** to increase the ability of (as a muscle) to exert physical force — see STRENGTHEN 1
2 to make able to withstand physical hardship, strain, or exposure — see HARDEN 2

toughened *adj* able to withstand hardship, strain, or exposure — see HARDY 1

toughie *n* a violent, brutal person who is often a member of an organized gang — see HOODLUM

tour *n* a fixed period of time during which a person holds a job or position — see TERM 1

tour *vb* to take a trip especially of some distance — see TRAVEL 1
tourist *n* a person who travels for pleasure <*tourists* from all over like to take pictures of the alligators in the bayou>
synonyms excursionist, sightseer, traveler (*or* traveller), tripper [*chiefly British*]
related words holidayer, vacationer, vacationist; guest, visitor; transient; journeyer, pilgrim, wayfarer
tournament *n* a competitive encounter between individuals or groups carried on for amusement, exercise, or in pursuit of a prize — see GAME 1
tourney *n* a competitive encounter between individuals or groups carried on for amusement, exercise, or in pursuit of a prize — see GAME 1
tousle *vb* to undo the proper order or arrangement of — see DISORDER
tousled *adj* lacking in order, neatness, and often cleanliness — see MESSY
tout *vb* **1** to praise or publicize lavishly and often excessively <a new cleaning agent *touted* as the only product a homeowner needs for all his or her cleaning chores>
synonyms ballyhoo, crack up, glorify, trumpet
related words advance, advertise, announce, boost, herald, offer, plug, promote, publicize; assert, aver, claim, declare, lay down, make out, proclaim, pronounce
2 to declare enthusiastic approval of — see ACCLAIM
3 to provide publicity for — see PUBLICIZE 1
tow *vb* to cause to follow by applying steady force on — see PULL 1
toward *or* **towards** *prep* having to do with — see ABOUT 1
tower *n* a large, magnificent, or massive building — see EDIFICE 1
towering *adj* **1** extending to a great distance upward — see HIGH 1
2 going beyond a normal or acceptable limit in degree or amount — see EXCESSIVE
3 very dignified in form, tone, or style — see ELEVATED 2
town *n* a thickly settled, highly populated area — see CITY
townie *n* a person who lives in a town on a permanent basis — see BURGHER
toxic *adj* containing or contaminated with a substance capable of injuring or killing a living thing — see POISONOUS
toxin *n* a substance that by chemical action can kill or injure a living thing — see POISON
trace *n* **1** a mark or series of marks left on a surface by something that has passed along it — see TRACK 1
2 a passage cleared for public vehicular travel — see WAY 1
3 a rough course or way formed by or as if by repeated footsteps — see TRAIL 1
4 a tiny often physical indication of something lost or vanished — see VESTIGE
5 a very small amount — see PARTICLE 1
trace *vb* **1** to draw or make apparent the outline of — see OUTLINE 1
2 to go after or on the track of — see FOLLOW 2
tracing *n* the act of going after or in the tracks of another — see PURSUIT
track *n* **1** a mark or series of marks left on a surface by something that has passed along it <a muddy *track* across the kitchen floor>
synonyms imprint, trace, trail
related words footprint, footstep, path, print, step, tread; artifact, evidence, leavings, mark, relic, remainder, remain(s), reminder, remnant, residual, residue, sign, spoor, telltale, token, vestige; clue, cue, hint, indication, inkling, intimation, suggestion; scent, shadow, whiff
2 a rough course or way formed by or as if by repeated footsteps — see TRAIL 1
3 the direction along which something or someone moves — see PATH 1
track *vb* to go after or on the track of — see FOLLOW 2
track (down) *vb* to come upon after searching, study, or effort — see FIND 1
tracking *n* the act of going after or in the tracks of another — see PURSUIT
tract *n* **1** a broad geographical area — see REGION 2
2 a small area of usually open land — see FIELD 1
3 a small piece of land that is developed or available for development — see LOT 1
tractable *adj* readily giving in to the command or authority of another — see OBEDIENT
trade *n* **1** a giving or taking of one thing of value in return for another — see EXCHANGE 1
2 an occupation requiring skillful use of the hands — see CRAFT 1
3 the activity by which one regularly makes a living — see OCCUPATION
4 the buying and selling of goods especially on a large scale and between different places — see COMMERCE
5 the transfer of ownership of something from one person to another for a price — see SALE
trade *vb* **1** to carry on the business of buying and selling goods or other property <the U.S. agreed to *trade* with China>
synonyms deal, traffic
related words bargain, barter, horse-trade, negotiate, transact; auction, exchange, merchandise, rebuy, resell, swap; buy, purchase; distribute, market, peddle, retail, sell, supply, vend, wholesale; bootleg, fence, smuggle; corner, monopolize, undersell; invest, speculate
near antonyms boycott
2 to give up (something) and take something else in return — see CHANGE 3
trademark *n* **1** a device (as a word) identifying the maker of a piece of merchandise and legally reserved for the exclusive use of that person or company <*Kleenex* is a *trademark* for a cleansing tissue>
synonyms brand
related words hallmark, imprint, label, logo, mark, name, service mark, stamp; copyright, patent
2 a device, design, or figure used as an identifying mark — see EMBLEM
trader *n* a buyer and seller of goods for profit — see MERCHANT
tradesman *n* **1** a buyer and seller of goods for profit — see MERCHANT
2 a person whose occupation requires skill with the hands — see ARTISAN
tradition *n* **1** an inherited or established way of thinking, feeling, or doing <the town *tradition* of

having the oldest resident ride at the head of the parade⟩
synonyms convention, custom
related words ethic, form, mode, mores, norm, values; birthright, inheritance, legacy; folklore, lore, superstition; culture, heritage, lifestyle
2 the body of customs, beliefs, stories, and sayings associated with a people, thing, or place — see FOLKLORE

traditional *adj* **1** based on customs usually handed down from a previous generation ⟨Ruben had a *traditional* Passover meal at his grandparents' house⟩
synonyms classical, conventional, customary
related words authentic, established, fixed, historical; common, habitual, orthodox, usual; ancestral, historic, old-time, old-world; aged, age-old, ancient, hoary, old, venerable; ageless, dateless, immemorial, timeless
near antonyms contemporary, current, modern, modernized, new, present-day, updated, up-to-date; futuristic, hot, latest, mod, modernistic, newfangled, new-fashioned, red-hot, space-age, ultramodern; nonconformist, nonorthodox, original, progressive, revolutionary, unorthodox, unusual
antonyms nontraditional, unconventional, uncustomary
2 tending to favor established ideas, conditions, or institutions — see CONSERVATIVE 1

traduce *vb* to make untrue and harmful statements about — see SLANDER

traducing *n* the making of false statements that damage another's reputation — see SLANDER

traffic *n* the buying and selling of goods especially on a large scale and between different places — see COMMERCE

traffic *vb* to carry on the business of buying and selling goods or other property — see TRADE 1

trafficker *n* a buyer and seller of goods for profit — see MERCHANT

tragedy *n* a sudden violent event that brings about great loss or destruction — see DISASTER

trail *n* **1** a rough course or way formed by or as if by repeated footsteps ⟨took a *trail* through the woods to get to the main road⟩
synonyms footpath, path, pathway, trace, track
related words bridle path; towpath; bypath, byroad, byway, passageway, walkway; detour, shortcut; course, passage, road, route, run, runway, way
2 a mark or series of marks left on a surface by something that has passed along it — see TRACK 1

trail *vb* to go after or on the track of — see FOLLOW 2

trailer *n* a motor vehicle that is specially equipped for living while traveling — see CAMPER

trailing *n* the act of going after or in the tracks of another — see PURSUIT

train *n* **1** a body of employees or servants who accompany and wait on a person — see CORTEGE 1
2 a group of vehicles traveling together or under one management — see FLEET
3 a series of persons or things arranged one behind another — see LINE 1
4 a series of things linked together — see CHAIN 1

train *vb* **1** to bring to a proper or desired state of fitness — see CONDITION 1
2 to cause to acquire knowledge or skill in some field — see TEACH
3 to fix (as one's attention) steadily toward a central objective — see CONCENTRATE 2
4 to point or turn (something) toward a target or goal — see AIM 1

trainer *n* a person who trains performers or athletes — see COACH

training *n* **1** something done over and over in order to develop skill — see EXERCISE 2
2 the act or process of imparting knowledge or skills to another — see EDUCATION 1

traipse *vb* **1** to go on foot — see WALK
2 to move about from place to place aimlessly — see WANDER

trait *n* something that sets apart an individual from others of the same kind — see CHARACTERISTIC

traitor *n* one who betrays a trust or an allegiance ⟨accused by her family of being a *traitor* when she sold their traditionally animal-friendly business to a competitor known to use animals for testing its products⟩
synonyms apostate, betrayer, double-crosser, quisling, recreant, turncoat
related words collaborationist, collaborator, subversive; conspirator, intriguer, plotter, schemer; defector, deserter, renegade; blabbermouth, gossip, gossiper, informant, informer, rat, snitcher, talebearer, talker, tattler, tattletale

traitorous *adj* not true in one's allegiance to someone or something — see FAITHLESS

trammel *n* something that makes movement or progress more difficult — see ENCUMBRANCE

trammel *vb* **1** to confine or restrain with or as if with chains — see BIND 1
2 to create difficulty for the work or activity of — see HAMPER

tramp *n* a homeless wanderer who may beg or steal for a living ⟨the police encouraged the *tramps* who were sleeping in the park to spend the bitterly cold night in the homeless shelter⟩
synonyms bum, hobo, sundowner [*Australian*], vagabond, vagrant
related words drifter, roamer, transient; beggar, derelict; dodger, malingerer, shirker, slacker; gamine, ragamuffin, urchin, waif

tramp *vb* **1** to move heavily or clumsily — see LUMBER 1
2 to tread on heavily so as to crush or injure — see TRAMPLE

trample *vb* to tread on heavily so as to crush or injure ⟨Isabel looked out her window and beheld the neighbor's Labrador retriever *trampling* her begonias⟩
synonyms stamp, stomp, tramp, tromp
related words override, run down, run over, step (on); mash, smash, squash; boot, kick

trance *n* the state of being lost in thought — see REVERIE

tranquil *adj* **1** free from disturbing noise or uproar — see QUIET 1
2 free from emotional or mental agitation — see CALM 2
3 free from storms or physical disturbance — see CALM 1

tranquilize *also* **tranquillize** *vb* to free from distress or disturbance — see CALM 1

tranquilizing *also* **tranquillizing** *adj* tending to calm the emotions and relieve stress — see SOOTHING 1

tranquillity *or* **tranquility** *n* **1** a state of freedom from storm or disturbance — see CALM

2 evenness of emotions or temper — see EQUANIMITY
transaction *n* the transfer of ownership of something from one person to another for a price — see SALE
transcend *vb* to be greater, better, or stronger than — see SURPASS 1
transfer *vb* **1** to give over the legal possession or ownership of ⟨Claire's grandfather agreed to *transfer* certain stocks to her when she turned 18⟩
synonyms alienate, assign, cede, deed, make over
related words bequeath, hand down, leave, pass down, will; bestow, confer, contribute, deliver, donate, grant, hand over, move, pass, present, release, relinquish, surrender, turn in, turn over, transmit, vest, yield; consign, entrust, trust; lease, lend, loan, rent
2 to cause (something) to pass from one to another — see COMMUNICATE 1
3 to cause to go or be taken from one place to another — see SEND
4 to change the place or position of — see MOVE 1
5 to put (something) into the possession or safekeeping of another — see GIVE 2
6 to shift possession of (something) from one person to another — see PASS 1
transferable *adj* capable of being taken from one place to another by public carrier — see SHIPPABLE
transfiguration *n* a change in form, appearance, or use — see CONVERSION
transfigure *vb* to change in form, appearance, or use — see CONVERT 2
transfix *vb* to penetrate or hold (something) with a pointed object — see IMPALE
transform *vb* to change in form, appearance, or use — see CONVERT 2
transformation *n* a change in form, appearance, or use — see CONVERSION
transfuse *vb* **1** to cause (something) to pass from one to another — see COMMUNICATE 1
2 to spread throughout — see PERMEATE
transgress *vb* **1** to commit an offense — see OFFEND 1
2 to fail to keep — see VIOLATE 1
transgression *n* **1** a breaking of a moral or legal code — see OFFENSE 1
2 a failure to uphold the requirements of law, duty, or obligation — see BREACH 1
transient *adj* lasting only for a short time — see MOMENTARY
transitory *adj* lasting only for a short time — see MOMENTARY
translate *vb* to express something (as a text or statement) in different words — see PARAPHRASE
translating *n* an instance of expressing something in different words — see PARAPHRASE
translation *n* an instance of expressing something in different words — see PARAPHRASE
transmit *vb* **1** to cause (something) to pass from one to another — see COMMUNICATE 1
2 to cause to go or be taken from one place to another — see SEND
3 to put (something) into the possession or safekeeping of another — see GIVE 2
transmittable *adj* **1** capable of being passed by physical contact from one person to another — see CONTAGIOUS 1
2 capable of being taken from one place to another by public carrier — see SHIPPABLE
transparency *n* the state or quality of being easily seen through — see CLARITY 1
transparent *adj* **1** easily seen through — see CLEAR 1
2 not subject to misinterpretation or more than one interpretation — see CLEAR 2
3 very thin and easy to see through — see SHEER 1
transpire *vb* to take place — see HAPPEN
transport *n* **1** a state of overwhelming usually pleasurable emotion — see ECSTASY
2 something used to carry goods or passengers — see CONVEYANCE
transport *vb* **1** to cause to go or be taken from one place to another — see SEND
2 to fill with great joy — see ELATE
3 to fill with overwhelming emotion (as wonder or delight) — see ENTRANCE
4 to force to leave a country — see BANISH 1
5 to support and take from one place to another — see CARRY 1
transportable *adj* capable of being taken from one place to another by public carrier — see SHIPPABLE
transportation *n* **1** a means of getting to a destination in a vehicle driven by another — see RIDE
2 something used to carry goods or passengers — see CONVEYANCE
transpose *vb* to change the place or position of — see MOVE 1
transversely *adv* in a line or direction running from corner to corner — see CROSSWISE
trap *n* **1** a device or scheme for capturing another by surprise ⟨undercover agents devised a *trap* to catch the counterfeiters⟩ ⟨a bear *trap*⟩
synonyms ambush, net, snare, web
related words entanglement, entrapment; booby trap, catch, hazard, pitfall, snag; deception, ploy, ruse, subterfuge, trick
2 a scheme in which hidden persons wait to attack by surprise — see AMBUSH 1
trap *vb* **1** to catch or hold as if in a net — see ENTANGLE 2
2 to take physical control or possession of (something) suddenly or forcibly — see CATCH 1
trash *n* **1** discarded or useless material — see GARBAGE
2 language, behavior, or ideas that are absurd and contrary to good sense — see NONSENSE 1
3 people looked down upon as ignorant and of the lowest class — see RABBLE
trashy *adj* **1** marked by an obvious lack of style or good taste — see TACKY 1
2 of low quality — see CHEAP 2
travail *n* very hard or unpleasant work — see TOIL
travail *vb* to devote serious and sustained effort — see LABOR
travel *vb* **1** to take a trip especially of some distance ⟨loves to *travel* and has been to 34 countries⟩
synonyms journey, peregrinate, pilgrimage, tour, trek, voyage
related words gallivant (*also* galavant), hop, jaunt, knock (about), ramble, roam, rove, traipse, wander; cruise, drive, fly, jet, motor, navigate, sail
2 to make one's way through, across, or over — see TRAVERSE
travel *n, often* **travels** *pl* a going from one place to another usually of some distance — see JOURNEY
traveler *or* **traveller** *n* a person who travels for pleasure — see TOURIST

traveling bag *n* a bag carried by hand and designed to hold a traveler's clothing and personal articles ⟨*traveling bags* made of lightweight but tough fabrics⟩
synonyms carryall, grip, handbag, portmanteau, suitcase
related words carpetbag, duffel bag, kit; backpack, haversack, knapsack, rucksack; attaché case, valise; baggage, bags, luggage

traverse *vb* to make one's way through, across, or over ⟨Julie watched the spider *traverse* the entire wall from floor to ceiling⟩
synonyms cover, crisscross, cross, cut (across), follow, go, pass (over), proceed (along), travel
related words hike, tread, walk; ride

travesty *n* a poor, insincere, or insulting imitation of something — see MOCKERY 1

travesty *vb* to copy or exaggerate (someone or something) in order to make fun of — see MIMIC 1

treacherous *adj* not true in one's allegiance to someone or something — see FAITHLESS

treachery *n* the act or fact of violating the trust or confidence of another — see BETRAYAL

tread *vb* to go on foot — see WALK

treadmill *n* an established and often automatic or monotonous series of actions followed when engaging in some activity — see ROUTINE 1

treason *n* the act or fact of violating the trust or confidence of another — see BETRAYAL

treasure *n* **1** an asset that brings praise or renown — see GLORY 2
2 someone or something unusually desirable — see PRIZE 1

treasure *vb* to hold dear — see LOVE 1

treat *n* **1** a source of great satisfaction — see DELIGHT 1
2 something that is pleasing to eat because it is rare or a luxury — see DELICACY 1

treat *vb* **1** to behave toward in a stated way ⟨she tries to *treat* all of her students fairly and equally, regardless of her personal feelings toward them⟩
synonyms act (toward), be (to), deal (with), handle, serve, use
related words consider, regard; react (to), respond (to)
2 to deal with (something) usually skillfully or efficiently — see HANDLE 1
3 to exchange viewpoints or seek advice for the purpose of finding a solution to a problem — see CONFER 2
4 to give medical treatment to — see DOCTOR 1

treat (of) *vb* to have (something) as a subject matter — see CONCERN 1

treaty *n* a formal agreement between two or more nations or peoples ⟨in accordance with a *treaty* between the United States and the tribes of the Pacific Northwest, commercial fishing of certain kinds of salmon is limited to Native Americans⟩
synonyms accord, alliance, compact, convention, covenant, pact
related words bargain, charter, contract, deal, settlement, understanding

treble *adj* **1** having a high musical pitch or range — see SHRILL
2 having three units or parts — see TRIPLE

trek *n* a going from one place to another usually of some distance — see JOURNEY

trek *vb* to take a trip especially of some distance — see TRAVEL 1

tremble *n* an instance of shaking involuntarily with fear or cold — see SHIVER 1

trembling *adj* marked by or given to small uncontrollable bodily movements — see SHAKY 1

trembling *n* a series of slight movements by a body back and forth or from side to side — see VIBRATION

tremendous *adj* unusually large — see HUGE

tremendously *adv* to a large extent or degree — see GREATLY 2

tremor *n* a shaking of the earth — see EARTHQUAKE

tremulous *adj* marked by or given to small uncontrollable bodily movements — see SHAKY 1

trench *n* a long narrow channel dug in the earth — see DITCH

trenchant *adj* having an edge thin enough to cut or pierce something — see SHARP 1

trend *n* **1** a prevailing or general movement or inclination ⟨according to the survey, there's a growing *trend* for companies to run their own day-care centers for the benefit of employees⟩
synonyms current, drift, leaning, run, tendency, tide, wind
related words curve, shift, swing, turn; custom, habit, propensity, tenor, way
2 a practice or interest that is very popular for a short time — see FAD

trend *vb* to show a liking or proneness (for something) — see LEAN 2

trepidation *n* the emotion experienced in the presence or threat of danger — see FEAR

trespass *n* **1** a breaking of a moral or legal code — see OFFENSE 1
2 a failure to uphold the requirements of law, duty, or obligation — see BREACH 1

trespass *vb* to commit an offense — see OFFEND 1

triad *n* a group of three — see THREESOME

triadic *adj* having three units or parts — see TRIPLE

trial *adj* made or done as an experiment — see EXPERIMENTAL 1

trial *n* **1** a test of faith, patience, or strength ⟨Nancy found living with her cousin a real *trial* and couldn't wait for the summer to end⟩
synonyms cross, crucible, gauntlet (*also* gantlet), ordeal
related words adversity, affliction, asperity, misfortune, mishap, privation, tragedy, tribulation, trouble, vicissitude, woe; challenge, complication, difficulty, grief, hardship, rigor; annoyance, discomfort, inconvenience, nuisance
2 a private performance or session in preparation for a public appearance — see REHEARSAL
3 a procedure or operation carried out to resolve an uncertainty — see EXPERIMENT
4 an effort to do or accomplish something — see ATTEMPT

tribal *adj* of, relating to, or reflecting the traits exhibited by a group of people with a common ancestry and culture — see RACIAL

tribe *n* a group of persons who come from the same ancestor — see FAMILY 1

tribulation *n* a state of great suffering of body or mind — see DISTRESS 1

tribunal *n* an assembly of persons for the administration of justice — see COURT 3

tribute *n* a formal expression of praise — see ENCOMIUM

trice *n* a very small space of time — see INSTANT

trick *n* **1** a clever often underhanded means to

achieve an end <used every *trick* in the book to get out of appearing in the fashion show featuring clothes for teens>
synonyms artifice, device, dodge, gimmick, jig, ploy, scheme, sleight, stratagem, wile
related words bluff, deception, feint; fraud, hoax, swindle
2 a playful or mischievous act intended as a joke — see PRANK
3 a usual manner of behaving or doing — see HABIT
4 an act of notable skill, strength, or cleverness — see FEAT 1
5 an odd or peculiar habit — see IDIOSYNCRASY

trick *vb* to cause to believe what is untrue — see DECEIVE

trickery *n* the use of clever underhanded actions to achieve an end <Delia resorted to *trickery*—even loading up the fishing equipment—to induce her dog into the car for his vet appointment>
synonyms artifice, chicanery, hanky-panky, jugglery, legerdemain, subterfuge, wile
related words artfulness, caginess, craftiness, cunning, deviousness, foxiness, shadiness, sharpness, shiftiness, slickness, slipperiness, slyness, sneakiness, treachery, underhandedness, wiliness; deceit, deceitfulness, deception, deceptiveness, dishonesty, dissimulation, double-dealing, duplicity, guile, hypocrisy, insincerity; fakery, humbuggery, imposture, quackery; design, plotting, scheming, secrecy, stealth

trickle *vb* **1** to fall or let fall in or as if in drops — see DRIP
2 to flow in a broken irregular stream — see GURGLE

trickster *n* **1** a dishonest person who uses clever means to cheat others out of something of value <a heartless *trickster* swindled the elderly woman out of her life savings>
synonyms cheat, cheater, confidence man, cozener, defrauder, dodger, hoaxer, shark, sharper, swindler
related words double-crosser, double-dealer; bluffer, charlatan, fake, faker, humbug, imposter, mountebank, pretender, quack; adventurer, fox, knave, prankster, rascal, rogue; slicker, smoothy (*or* smoothie); plotter, schemer, sneak
2 one who practices tricks and illusions for entertainment — see MAGICIAN 2

tricky *adj* requiring exceptional skill or caution in performance or handling <a *tricky* musical passage for the woodwind section>
synonyms catchy, delicate, difficult, knotty, problematic (*also* problematical), spiny, thorny, ticklish, touchy, tough
related words abstract, abstruse, complex, complicated, hard, intricate, involved, recondite; stubborn, troublesome, vexatious, vexing; burdensome, demanding, discommoding, exacting, importunate, inconvenient, onerous, oppressive, painful
near antonyms easy, manageable, painless, straightforward, uncomplicated, undemanding, untroublesome

tried *adj* worthy of one's trust — see DEPENDABLE

tried–and–true *adj* worthy of one's trust — see DEPENDABLE

trifle *n* something of little importance <let us not speak of *trifles* when our nation may be going to war>
synonyms child's play, frippery, nothing, triviality
related words naught, nothingness, smoke, zero; molehill, peanuts, pittance, song, straw, two bits; nonsense, trivia

trifle *vb* **1** to show a liking for someone of the opposite sex just for fun — see FLIRT
2 to spend time in aimless activity — see FIDDLE (AROUND)

trifling *adj* **1** lacking importance — see UNIMPORTANT
2 so small or unimportant as to warrant little or no attention — see NEGLIGIBLE 1

trigger *vb* to cause to function — see ACTIVATE

trill *vb* to sing with the alternation of two musical tones — see WARBLE

trim *adj* being clean and in good order — see NEAT 1

trim *n* **1** a state of being or fitness — see CONDITION 1
2 something that decorates or beautifies — see DECORATION 1

trim *vb* **1** to achieve a victory over — see BEAT 2
2 to defeat by a large margin — see WHIP 2
3 to make (as hair) shorter with or as if with the use of shears — see CLIP
4 to make more attractive by adding something that is beautiful or becoming — see DECORATE

trimmer *n* one that defeats an enemy or opponent — see VICTOR 1

trimming *n* failure to win a contest — see DEFEAT 1

trinity *n* a group of three — see THREESOME

trinket *n* a small object displayed for its attractiveness or interest — see KNICKKNACK

trio *n* a group of three — see THREESOME

trip *n* a going from one place to another usually of some distance — see JOURNEY

trip *vb* **1** to go at a pace faster than a walk — see RUN 1
2 to go down from an upright position suddenly and involuntarily — see FALL 1
3 to move with a light bouncing step — see SKIP 1

tripartite *adj* having three units or parts — see TRIPLE

triple *adj* having three units or parts <a *triple* scoop of chocolate ice cream>
synonyms threefold, treble, triadic, tripartite, triplex
related words triplicate

triple *n* a group of three — see THREESOME

triplet *n* a group of three — see THREESOME

triplex *adj* having three units or parts — see TRIPLE

tripper *n, chiefly British* a person who travels for pleasure — see TOURIST

trippingly *adv* in a quick and spirited manner — see GAILY 2

trite *adj* used or heard so often as to be dull — see STALE

triumph *n* **1** a successful result brought about by hard work — see ACCOMPLISHMENT 1
2 an instance of defeating an enemy or opponent — see VICTORY

triumph *vb* **1** to achieve victory (as in a contest) — see WIN 1
2 to feel or express joy or triumph — see EXULT

triumph (over) *vb* to achieve a victory over — see BEAT 2

triumphant *adj* **1** having attained a desired end or state of good fortune — see SUCCESSFUL 1

2 having or expressing feelings of joy or triumph — see EXULTANT
triumvirate *n* a group of three — see THREESOME
trivial *adj* **1** lacking importance — see UNIMPORTANT
2 so small or unimportant as to warrant little or no attention — see NEGLIGIBLE 1
triviality *n* something of little importance — see TRIFLE
troll *n* an imaginary being usually having a small human form and magical powers — see FAIRY
tromp *vb* **1** to move heavily or clumsily — see LUMBER 1
2 to tread on heavily so as to crush or injure — see TRAMPLE
troop *n* **1** an organized group of stage performers — see COMPANY 1
2 troops *pl* the combined army, air force, and navy of a nation — see ARMED FORCES
tropical *adj* being near the equator — see LOW 1
trot *vb* **1** to go at a pace faster than a walk — see RUN 1
2 to proceed or move quickly — see HURRY 2
troth *n* **1** a person's solemn declaration that he or she will do or not do something — see PROMISE
2 the act or state of being engaged to be married — see ENGAGEMENT 1
troth *vb* to obligate by prior agreement — see PLEDGE 1
trouble *n* **1** an abnormal state that disrupts a plant's or animal's normal bodily functioning — see DISEASE
2 something that may cause injury or harm — see DANGER 2
3 something that requires thought and skill for resolution — see PROBLEM 1
4 the active use of energy in producing a result — see EFFORT
5 the state of not being protected from injury, harm, or evil — see DANGER 1
trouble *vb* **1** to experience concern or anxiety — see WORRY 1
2 to cause discomfort to or trouble for — see INCONVENIENCE
troubled *adj* feeling or showing uncomfortable feelings of uncertainty — see NERVOUS 1
troublesome *adj* causing worry or anxiety <the *troublesome* news that there will be more cuts in the school budget>
synonyms discomforting, discomposing, disquieting, distressing, disturbing, perturbing, troubling, troublous, unsettling, upsetting, worrisome
related words daunting, demoralizing, discomfiting, disconcerting, discouraging, disheartening, dismaying, dispiriting
near antonyms calming, quieting, settling, soothing
antonyms reassuring, untroublesome
troubling *adj* causing worry or anxiety — see TROUBLESOME
troublous *adj* causing worry or anxiety — see TROUBLESOME
trough *n* **1** a long hollow cylinder for carrying a substance (as a liquid or gas) — see PIPE 1
2 a long narrow channel dug in the earth — see DITCH
3 a pipe or channel for carrying off water from a roof — see GUTTER 1
trounce *vb* **1** to achieve a victory over — see BEAT 2
2 to defeat by a large margin — see WHIP 2
trouncing *n* failure to win a contest — see DEFEAT 1
troupe *n* an organized group of stage performers — see COMPANY 1
trouper *n* one who acts professionally (as in a play, movie, or television show) — see ACTOR
trousers *n pl* an outer garment covering each leg separately from waist to ankle — see PANTS
truce *n* a temporary stopping of fighting <both sides agreed to a 24-hour *truce* beginning at midnight on Christmas Eve>
synonyms armistice, cease-fire
related words accord, reconciliation; peace, peacetime
truck *n* a giving or taking of one thing of value in return for another — see EXCHANGE 1
truculence *n* an inclination to fight or quarrel — see BELLIGERENCE
truculent *adj* feeling or displaying eagerness to fight — see BELLIGERENT
trudge *vb* to make progress in a clumsy, struggling manner — see FLOUNDER 1
true *adj* **1** being exactly as appears or as claimed — see AUTHENTIC 1
2 being in agreement with the truth or a fact or a standard — see CORRECT 1
3 existing in fact and not merely as a possibility — see ACTUAL
4 firm in one's allegiance to someone or something — see FAITHFUL 1
5 following an original exactly — see FAITHFUL 2
6 free from any intent to deceive or impress others — see GUILELESS
7 restricted to or based on fact — see FACTUAL 1
8 worthy of one's trust — see DEPENDABLE
true–blue *adj* firm in one's allegiance to someone or something — see FAITHFUL 1
truism *n* an idea or expression that has been used by many people — see COMMONPLACE
truly *adv* **1** not merely this but also — see EVEN
2 to tell the truth — see ACTUALLY 1
3 without any question — see INDEED 1
trumpery *adj* of low quality — see CHEAP 2
trumpet *vb* to praise or publicize lavishly and often excessively — see TOUT 1
truncheon *n* a heavy rigid stick used as a weapon or for punishment — see CLUB 1
trunk *n* a covered rectangular container for storing or transporting things — see CHEST
truss *vb* to gather into a tight mass by means of a line or cord — see TIE 1
trust *n* **1** firm belief in the integrity, ability, effectiveness, or genuineness of someone or something <a relationship of mutual *trust* between lawyer and client>
synonyms confidence, credence, faith, stock
related words acceptance, assurance, assuredness, certainty, certitude, conviction, positiveness, sureness; credit, dependence, hope, reliance
near antonyms disbelief, incredulity, unbelief; doubt, dubiousness, incertitude, nonconfidence, skepticism, suspicion, uncertainty
antonyms distrust, mistrust
2 a number of businesses or enterprises united for commercial advantage — see CARTEL
3 responsibility for the safety and well-being of someone or something — see CUSTODY
4 the right to take possession of goods before paying for them — see CREDIT 1

trust *vb* **1** to give a task, duty, or responsibility to — see ENTRUST 1
2 to put (something) into the possession or safekeeping of another — see GIVE 2
3 to regard as right or true — see BELIEVE 1
trustful *adj* having or showing trust in another — see TRUSTING 1
trusting *adj* **1** having or showing trust in another ⟨Delia couldn't look into her dog's *trusting* eyes as she drove him to the vet⟩
synonyms confiding, trustful
related words artless, childlike, credulous, guileless, gullible, innocent, naive (*also* naïve), simple, unsophisticated; dependent, hopeful, reliant; accepting, believing, certain, confident, convinced, overconfident, secure, sure, unquestioning, unsuspecting, unsuspicious, unwary
near antonyms disbelieving, incredulous, unbelieving, unconvinced, unpersuaded; hesitant, leery, oversuspicious, skeptical, suspicious, uncertain, unsure, wary
antonyms distrustful, doubtful, doubting, mistrustful
2 readily taken advantage of — see EASY 2
trustworthiness *n* worthiness as the recipient of another's trust or confidence — see RELIABILITY
trustworthy *adj* worthy of one's trust — see DEPENDABLE
trusty *adj* worthy of one's trust — see DEPENDABLE
truth *n* agreement with fact or reality ⟨there is no *truth* to her accusation that Emory cheated on the test⟩
synonyms factuality, verity
related words accuracy, actuality, authenticity, correctness; credibility, honesty, trustworthiness, truthfulness, veracity; dependability, reliability
near antonyms erroneousness, fallaciousness, fallacy; falsehood, fiction, inaccuracy, incorrectness; deceit, dishonesty, mendacity, untruthfulness
antonyms falseness, falsity, untruth
truthful *adj* being in the habit of telling the truth ⟨a *truthful* youngster who wouldn't just make up a story like that⟩
synonyms honest, veracious
related words candid, frank, open, plainspoken; believable, credible, veritable, true; conscientious, moral, principled, scrupulous; dependable, reliable, trustworthy, trusty
near antonyms fallacious, false, untrue; unbelievable, undependable, unreliable, untrustworthy; bluffing, dissembling, dissimulating, duplicitous, equivocating, hypocritical, insincere, posing, pretending; artful, deceitful, deceptive, devious, slick, slippery, sly, sneaky, treacherous, tricky, underhanded, wily
antonyms dishonest, fibbing, lying, mendacious, prevaricating, untruthful
truthfully *adv* to tell the truth — see ACTUALLY 1
truthfulness *n* devotion to telling the truth — see HONESTY 1
try *n* an effort to do or accomplish something — see ATTEMPT
try *vb* to make an effort to do — see ATTEMPT
try (out) *vb* **1** to put (something) to a test ⟨want to *try out* my new skateboard?⟩ ⟨*tried* his skill at archery⟩
synonyms sample, test
related words check out, examine, experiment (with), explore, feel (out), research
2 to subject (a personal quality or faculty) to often excessive stress ⟨you're *trying* my patience⟩
synonyms strain, stretch, tax, test
related words demand, exact, importune, press, pressure, push; aggravate, agitate, exasperate, get (to), gnaw (at), grate, harass, harry, hassle, irk, irritate, pain, pester
trying *adj* difficult to endure — see HARSH 1
tryst *n* an agreement to be present at a specified time and place — see ENGAGEMENT 2
tubby *adj* having an excess of body fat — see FAT 1
tube *n* a long hollow cylinder for carrying a substance (as a liquid or gas) — see PIPE 1
tucker (out) *vb* to use up all the physical energy of — see EXHAUST 1
tuckered (out) *adj* depleted in strength, energy, or freshness — see WEARY 1
tug *n* the act or an instance of applying force on something so that it moves in the direction of the force — see PULL 1
tug *vb* to cause to follow by applying steady force on — see PULL 1
tug–of–war *n* an earnest effort for superiority or victory over another — see CONTEST 1
tumble *n* **1** an unorganized collection or mixture of various things — see MISCELLANY 1
2 the act of going down from an upright position suddenly and involuntarily — see FALL 1
tumble *vb* **1** to go down from an upright position suddenly and involuntarily — see FALL 1
2 to go to a lower level — see DROP 2
3 to undo the proper order or arrangement of — see DISORDER
tumble (to) *vb* to recognize the meaning of — see COMPREHEND 1
tumbled *adj* lacking in order, neatness, and often cleanliness — see MESSY
tummy *n* the part of the body between the chest and the pelvis — see STOMACH
tumor *n* an abnormal mass of tissue — see GROWTH 1
tumult *n* **1** a state of noisy, confused activity — see COMMOTION
2 a violent disturbance (as of the political or social order) — see CONVULSION
3 a violent shouting — see CLAMOR 1
tumultuous *adj* **1** marked by sudden or violent disturbance — see CONVULSIVE
2 marked by turmoil or disturbance especially of natural elements — see WILD 3
tundra *n* a broad area of level or rolling treeless country — see PLAIN
tune *n* **1** a rhythmic series of musical tones arranged to give a pleasing effect — see MELODY
2 a state of consistency — see CONFORMITY 1
tuneful *adj* having a pleasing mixture of notes — see HARMONIOUS 1
turbid *adj* having visible particles in liquid suspension — see CLOUDY 1
turbulent *adj* **1** marked by bursts of destructive force or intense activity — see VIOLENT 1
2 marked by turmoil or disturbance especially of natural elements — see WILD 3
3 marked by wet and windy conditions — see FOUL 1
turkey *n* **1** a person who lacks good sense or judgment — see FOOL 1
2 a stupid person — see IDIOT
3 something that has failed — see FAILURE 3

turmoil *n* **1** a disturbed or uneasy state — see UNREST
2 a state of noisy, confused activity — see COMMOTION
turn *n* **1** a relaxed journey on foot for exercise or pleasure — see WALK
2 an act of kind assistance — see FAVOR 1
3 a habitual attraction to some activity or thing — see INCLINATION 1
4 something that curves or is curved — see BEND 1
turn *vb* **1** to move (something) in a curved or circular path on or as if on an axis <*turned* the doorknob as quietly as possible>
synonyms pivot, revolve, roll, rotate, spin, swing, swirl, twirl, twist, wheel, whirl
related words screw, unscrew; twiddle; crank, reel, wind; circulate
2 to change the course or direction of (something) <the dog *turned* the stampeding flock of sheep around> <he *turned* his cart uphill>
synonyms deflect, divert, swing, veer, wheel, whip
related words avert, move, rechannel, shift, shunt, sidetrack, switch, transfer; swivel, twist, whirl, zigzag; bend, curve, sway; reverse, turn back
3 to change one's course or direction <we *turned* left at the light> <the storm unexpectedly *turned* south and missed our area>
synonyms detour, deviate, sheer, swing, turn off, veer
related words tack, zigzag; double (back), turn back
4 to eventually have as a state or quality — see BECOME
5 to move in circles around an axis or center — see SPIN 1
turn (over) *vb* to change the position of (an object) so that the opposite side or end is showing — see REVERSE 2
turn (to) *vb* to use or seek out as a source of aid, relief, or advantage — see RESORT (TO) 1
turncoat *n* one who betrays a trust or an allegiance — see TRAITOR
turn down *vb* to show unwillingness to accept, do, engage in, or agree to — see DECLINE 1
turn in *vb* to go to one's bed in order to sleep — see BED
turning point *n* a point in a chain of events at which an important change (as in one's fortunes) occurs <the *turning point* came when Victor finally admitted he was a werewolf>
synonyms climax, landmark, milestone
related words break, clincher, highlight; conversion, metamorphosis, transfiguration, transformation, turnabout, turnaround; clutch, crisis, crossroad(s), crunch, emergency, exigency, head, juncture, zero hour
turn off *vb* **1** to cause to feel disgust — see DISGUST
2 to change one's course or direction — see TURN 3
turn–on *n* something that persuades one to perform an action for pleasure or gain — see LURE 1
turn on *vb* **1** to cause a pleasurable stimulation of the feelings — see THRILL
2 to cause to function — see ACTIVATE
turn out *vb* to come to be — see COME OUT 1
turn over *vb* **1** to give (something) over to the control or possession of another usually under duress — see SURRENDER 1
2 to put (something) into the possession or safekeeping of another — see GIVE 2
turnpike *n* a passage cleared for public vehicular travel — see WAY 1
turn up *vb* **1** to come into view — see APPEAR 1
2 to get to a destination — see COME 2
tussle *n* a physical dispute between opposing individuals or groups — see FIGHT 1
tussle *vb* to seize and attempt to unbalance one another for the purpose of achieving physical mastery — see WRESTLE
tutelage *n* the act or process of imparting knowledge or skills to another — see EDUCATION 1
tutor *vb* **1** to cause to acquire knowledge or skill in some field — see TEACH
2 to give advice and instruction to (someone) regarding the course or process to be followed — see GUIDE 1
tutoring *n* the act or process of imparting knowledge or skills to another — see EDUCATION 1
twain *n* two things of the same or similar kind that match or are considered together — see PAIR
tweet *vb* to make a short sharp sound like a small bird — see CHIRP
twerp *n* a person of no importance or influence — see NOBODY
twice *adv* to two times the amount or degree — see DOUBLY
twilight *n* **1** a time or place of little or no light — see DARK 1
2 the time from when the sun begins to set to the onset of total darkness — see DUSK 1
twin *adj* consisting of two members or parts that are usually joined — see DOUBLE 1
twin *n* either of a pair matched in one or more qualities — see MATE 1
twine *vb* to follow a circular or spiral course — see WIND
twinge *n* a sharp unpleasant sensation usually felt in some specific part of the body — see PAIN 1
twinkle *n* a very small space of time — see INSTANT
twinkle *vb* **1** to shine with light at regular intervals — see BLINK 1
2 to shoot forth bursts of light — see FLASH 1
twinkling *n* a very small space of time — see INSTANT
twirl *n* a rapid turning about on an axis or central point — see SPIN 1
twirl *vb* **1** to move (something) in a curved or circular path on or as if on an axis — see TURN 1
2 to move in circles around an axis or center — see SPIN 1
twist *n* a forceful rotating or pulling motion for the purpose of dislodging something — see WRENCH 1
twist *vb* **1** to change so much as to create a wrong impression or alter the meaning of — see GARBLE
2 to follow a circular or spiral course — see WIND
3 to move (something) in a curved or circular path on or as if on an axis — see TURN 1
4 to move by or as if by a forceful rotation — see WRENCH 1
twisted *adj* marked by a long series of irregular curves — see CROOKED 1
twisting *adj* marked by a long series of irregular curves — see CROOKED 1
twisting *n* a forceful rotating or pulling motion for the purpose of dislodging something — see WRENCH 1

twitch *vb* **1** to make jerky or restless movements — see FIDGET
2 to move or cause to move with a sharp quick motion — see JERK 1
twitching *n* a series of slight movements by a body back and forth or from side to side — see VIBRATION
twitter *n* a state of nervous or irritated concern — see FRET
twitter *vb* **1** to engage in casual or rambling conversation — see CHAT
2 to make a short sharp sound like a small bird — see CHIRP
two–faced *adj* not being or expressing what one appears to be or express — see INSINCERE
twofold *adj* being twice as great or as many — see DOUBLE 2
twosome *n* two things of the same or similar kind that match or are considered together — see PAIR
tycoon *n* a person of rank, power, or influence in a particular field — see MAGNATE
type *n* **1** a number of persons or things that are grouped together because they have something in common — see SORT 1
2 one of the units into which a whole is divided on the basis of a common characteristic — see CLASS 2
typical *adj* **1** having or showing the qualities associated with the members of a particular group or kind ⟨*typical* behavior for a two-year-old⟩
synonyms archetypal, average, characteristic, normal, regular, representative, standard
related words common, conventional, customary, ordinary, usual, wonted; expected, familiar, habitual, predictable, routine, unexceptional, unremarkable; predominant, preponderant
near antonyms uncommon, unconventional, uncustomary, unusual, unwonted; distinctive, especial, exceptional, extraordinary, infrequent, noteworthy, rare, remarkable, singular, special, unexpected, unfamiliar, unique, unpredictable; eccentric, idiosyncratic, nonconformist, peculiar, unknown, unorthodox; curious, funny, odd, queer, strange; bizarre, fantastic, far-out, freak, freakish, out-of-the-way, outrageous, outré, unnatural, weird, wild
antonyms aberrant, abnormal, anomalous, atypical, deviant, irregular, nonrepresentative, nontypical
2 serving to identify as belonging to an individual or group — see CHARACTERISTIC 1
typically *adv* according to the usual course of things — see NATURALLY 2
tyrannical *also* **tyrannic** *adj* **1** exercising power or authority without interference by others — see ABSOLUTE 1
2 fond of ordering people around — see BOSSY
tyrannous *adj* **1** exercising power or authority without interference by others — see ABSOLUTE 1
2 fond of ordering people around — see BOSSY
tyranny *n* a system of government in which the ruler has unlimited power — see DESPOTISM
tyrant *n* a person who uses power or authority in a cruel, unjust, or harmful way — see DESPOT
tyro *n* a person who is just starting out in a field of activity — see BEGINNER

U

ubiquitous *adj* **1** often observed or encountered — see COMMON 1
2 present in all places and at all times — see OMNIPRESENT
ugly *adj* **1** unpleasant to look at ⟨her first attempt at painting was pretty *ugly* —a portrait of her sister that was not at all flattering⟩
synonyms grotesque, hideous, homely, ill-favored, unappealing, unattractive, unbeautiful, unhandsome, unlovely, unpleasing, unpretty, unsightly, vile
related words disgusting, repugnant, repulsive, revolting; unimposing, unprepossessing, unimpressive; plain, unaesthetic, unbecoming, unshapely
near antonyms becoming, bonny [*chiefly British*], cute, shapely; imposing, impressive, prepossessing
antonyms attractive, beauteous, beautiful, comely, cute, fair, gorgeous, handsome, lovely, pretty, stunning, taking
2 causing intense displeasure, disgust, or resentment — see OFFENSIVE 1
ultimate *adj* **1** of the greatest or highest degree or quantity ⟨the *ultimate* speed yet attained by a land-based vehicle⟩
synonyms consummate, maximum, most, nth, paramount, supreme, top, utmost, uttermost
related words unequaled (*or* unequalled), unmatched, unparalleled, unrivaled (*or* unrivalled), unsurpassed; topmost, upmost, uppermost
near antonyms littlest, smallest; lowest
antonyms least, minimal, minimum
2 following all others of the same kind in order or time — see LAST
3 most distant from a center — see EXTREME 1
ultimately *adv* at a later time — see YET 1
ultimatum *n* something that someone insists upon having — see DEMAND 1
ultra *adj* being very far from the center of public opinion — see EXTREME 2
ultramodern *adj* being or involving the latest methods, concepts, information, or styles — see MODERN
ultramodernist *n* a person with very modern ideas — see MODERN
umbra *n* **1** a time or place of little or no light — see DARK 1
2 partial darkness due to the obstruction of light rays — see SHADE 1
umbrage *n* the feeling of being offended or resentful after a slight or indignity — see PIQUE
umpire *vb* to give an opinion about (something at issue or in dispute) — see JUDGE 1
unabashed *adj* not embarrassed or ashamed ⟨*unabashed* by their booing and hissing, he continued with his performance⟩

synonyms unashamed, unblushing, unembarrassed
related words prideful, proud; bold, brassy, brazen, impudent, insolent, saucy, shameless; unapologetic, undaunted, undeterred, undismayed; unblinking, unflinching, unshrinking
near antonyms discomfited, disconcerted, nonplussed (*also* nonplused)
antonyms abashed, ashamed, embarrassed, shamefaced, sheepish

unacceptable *adj* falling short of a standard — see BAD 1

unacceptably *adv* **1** beyond a normal or acceptable limit — see TOO 1
2 in an unsatisfactory way — see BADLY

unacclimated *adj* not having acquired a habit or tolerance — see UNUSED 1

unaccompanied *adj* not being in the company of others — see ALONE 1

unaccountable *adj* impossible to explain — see INEXPLICABLE

unaccustomed *adj* **1** not having acquired a habit or tolerance — see UNUSED 1
2 not known or experienced before — see NEW 2
3 noticeably different from what is generally found or experienced — see UNUSUAL 1

unachievable *adj* incapable of being solved or accomplished — see IMPOSSIBLE

unacquainted *adj* not informed about or aware of something — see IGNORANT 2

unadapted *adj* not having acquired a habit or tolerance — see UNUSED 1

unadjusted *adj* not having acquired a habit or tolerance — see UNUSED 1

unadorned *adj* free from all additions or embellishment — see PLAIN 1

unadulterated *adj* **1** free from added matter — see PURE 1
2 having no exceptions or restrictions — see ABSOLUTE 2

unadvisable *adj* showing poor judgment especially in personal relationships or social situations — see INDISCREET

unaesthetic *adj* disagreeable to one's aesthetic or artistic sense — see HARSH 2

unaffected *adj* free from any intent to deceive or impress others — see GUILELESS

unaffectedly *adv* without any attempt to impress by deception or exaggeration — see NATURALLY 3

unaided *adv* without aid or support — see ALONE 1

unalike *adj* being not of the same kind — see DIFFERENT 1

unallied *adj* not favoring or joined to either side in a quarrel, contest, or war — see NEUTRAL

unalloyed *adj* **1** free from added matter — see PURE 1
2 having no exceptions or restrictions — see ABSOLUTE 2

unalterable *adj* not capable of changing or being changed — see INFLEXIBLE 1

unambiguous *adj* **1** not subject to misinterpretation or more than one interpretation — see CLEAR 2
2 so clearly expressed as to leave no doubt about the meaning — see EXPLICIT

unanimated *adj* causing weariness, restlessness, or lack of interest — see BORING

unanimity *n* the act or fact of being of one opinion about something — see AGREEMENT 1

unanimous *adj* having or marked by agreement in feeling or action — see HARMONIOUS 3

unanswerable *adj* not capable of being challenged or proved wrong — see IRREFUTABLE

unanticipated *adj* not expected — see UNEXPECTED

unappealing *adj* unpleasant to look at — see UGLY 1

unappeasable *adj* showing no signs of slackening or yielding in one's purpose — see UNYIELDING 1

unappetizing *adj* disagreeable or disgusting to the sense of taste — see DISTASTEFUL 1

unappreciated *adj* not likely to be appreciated by those who benefit — see THANKLESS 2

unappreciative *adj* not showing gratitude — see THANKLESS 1

unapproachable *adj* hard or impossible to get to or get at — see INACCESSIBLE

unapt *adj* **1** not appropriate for a particular occasion or situation — see INAPPROPRIATE
2 not likely to be true or to occur — see IMPROBABLE

unashamed *adj* not embarrassed or ashamed — see UNABASHED

unasked *adj* not searched or asked for — see UNSOUGHT

unassailable *adj* not to be violated, criticized, or tampered with — see SACRED 1

unassisted *adv* without aid or support — see ALONE 1

unassuming *adj* not having or showing any feelings of superiority, self-assertiveness, or showiness — see HUMBLE 1

unattached *adj* **1** not married — see SINGLE 1
2 not physically attached to another unit — see SEPARATE 2

unattainable *adj* **1** hard or impossible to get to or get at — see INACCESSIBLE
2 incapable of being solved or accomplished — see IMPOSSIBLE

unattractive *adj* unpleasant to look at — see UGLY 1

unauthentic *adj* being such in appearance only and made or manufactured with the intention of committing fraud — see COUNTERFEIT

unavailable *adj* hard or impossible to get to or get at — see INACCESSIBLE

unavailing *adj* producing no results — see FUTILE

unavoidable *adj* impossible to avoid or evade — see INEVITABLE

unavoidably *adv* because of necessity — see NEEDS

unaware *adj* not informed about or aware of something — see IGNORANT 2

unaware *adv* without warning — see UNAWARES

unawareness *n* the state of being unaware or uninformed — see IGNORANCE 1

unawares *adv* without warning <the thunderstorm caught us *unawares*, and we scrambled to get off the ridge as lightning started to flash>
synonyms aback, suddenly, unaware, unexpectedly
related words abruptly, short
phrases all of a sudden
near antonyms slowly; obviously

unbalance *vb* to cause to go insane or as if insane — see CRAZE

unbalanced *adj* **1** having or showing a very abnormal or sick state of mind — see INSANE 1

2 not being in or able to maintain a state of balance — see UNSTABLE 1
unbaptized *adj* not named or identified by a name — see NAMELESS 1
unbearable *adj* more than can be put up with <this heat is *unbearable* —when are we going to get air-conditioning?>
synonyms insufferable, insupportable, intolerable, unendurable, unsupportable
related words unacceptable; crushing, overwhelming; comfortless, harsh, painful, uncomfortable
near antonyms acceptable; adequate
antonyms endurable, sufferable, supportable, tolerable
unbeatable *adj* incapable of being defeated, overcome, or subdued — see INVINCIBLE
unbeautiful *adj* unpleasant to look at — see UGLY 1
unbecoming *adj* not appropriate for a particular occasion or situation — see INAPPROPRIATE
unbeknownst *also* **unbeknown** *adj* happening or existing without one's knowledge — see UNKNOWN 1
unbelief *n* refusal to accept as true — see DISBELIEF
unbelievable *adj* too extraordinary or improbable to believe — see INCREDIBLE
unbeliever *n* a person who is always ready to doubt or question the truth or existence of something — see SKEPTIC
unbelieving *adj* inclined to doubt or question claims — see SKEPTICAL
unbend *vb* to cause to follow a line that is without bends or curls — see STRAIGHTEN
unbending *adj* sticking to an opinion, purpose, or course of action in spite of reason, arguments, or persuasion — see OBSTINATE
unbiased *adj* marked by justice, honesty, and freedom from bias — see FAIR 2
unbidden *also* **unbid** *adj* not searched or asked for — see UNSOUGHT
unbind *vb* **1** to disengage the knotted parts of — see UNTIE
2 to set free (as from slavery or confinement) — see FREE 1
unblemished *adj* being entirely without fault or flaw — see PERFECT 1
unblock *vb* to rid the surface of (as an area) from things in the way — see CLEAR 1
unblushing *adj* not embarrassed or ashamed — see UNABASHED
unborn *adj* of a time after the present — see FUTURE
unbosom *vb* to make known (as information previously kept secret) — see REVEAL 1
unbound *adj* not bound, confined, or detained by force — see FREE 3
unbounded *adj* being or seeming to be without limits — see INFINITE
unbraid *vb* to separate the various strands of — see UNRAVEL 1
unbridled *adj* showing no signs of being under control — see RAMPANT 1
unbroken *adj* **1** going on and on without any interruptions — see CONTINUOUS
2 living outdoors without taming or domestication by humans — see WILD 1
unbudging *adj* incapable of moving or being moved — see IMMOVABLE 1
unburden *vb* **1** to empty or rid of cargo — see UNLOAD 1
2 to set (a person or thing) free of something that encumbers — see RID
unburdened *adj* no longer burdened with something unpleasant or painful — see FREE 2
uncage *vb* to set free (as from slavery or confinement) — see FREE 1
uncalled–for *adj* **1** not needed by the circumstances or to accomplish an end — see UNNECESSARY
2 showing a lack of manners or consideration for others — see IMPOLITE
uncanny *adj* **1** being beyond one's powers to know, understand, or explain — see MYSTERIOUS 1
2 being so extraordinary or abnormal as to suggest powers which violate the laws of nature — see SUPERNATURAL 2
3 fearfully and mysteriously strange or fantastic — see EERIE
uncataloged *adj* not appearing on a list — see UNLISTED
unceasing *adj* going on and on without any interruptions — see CONTINUOUS
uncelebrated *adj* not widely known — see OBSCURE 2
unceremonious *adj* not rigidly following established form, custom, or rules — see INFORMAL 1
uncertain *adj* **1** likely to change frequently, suddenly, or unexpectedly — see FICKLE 1
2 not feeling sure about the truth, wisdom, or trustworthiness of someone or something — see DOUBTFUL 1
uncertainty *n* a feeling or attitude that one does not know the truth, truthfulness, or trustworthiness of someone or something — see DOUBT
unchain *vb* to set free (as from slavery or confinement) — see FREE 1
unchangeable *adj* not capable of changing or being changed — see INFLEXIBLE 1
unchangeableness *n* the state of continuing without change — see CONSTANCY 1
unchanging *adj* **1** not undergoing a change in condition — see CONSTANT 1
2 not varying — see UNIFORM
uncharitable *adj* **1** giving or sharing as little as possible — see STINGY 1
2 having or showing a lack of sympathy or tender feelings — see HARD 1
unchecked *adj* showing no signs of being under control — see RAMPANT 1
unchristened *adj* not named or identified by a name — see NAMELESS 1
uncivil *adj* **1** not civilized — see SAVAGE 1
2 showing a lack of manners or consideration for others — see IMPOLITE
uncivilized *adj* not civilized — see SAVAGE
unclad *adj* lacking or shed of clothing — see NAKED 1
unclean *adj* not clean — see DIRTY 1
uncleanliness *n* the state or quality of being dirty — see DIRTINESS 1
uncleanly *adj* not clean — see DIRTY 1
uncleanness *n* the state or quality of being dirty — see DIRTINESS 1
unclear *adj* **1** not clearly expressed — see VAGUE 1
2 not seen or understood clearly — see FAINT 1
uncloak *vb* **1** to make known (as information previously kept secret) — see REVEAL 1
2 to reveal the true nature of — see EXPOSE 1

unclog *vb* **1** to arrange clear passage of (something) by removing obstructions — see OPEN 2
2 to free from obstruction or difficulty — see EASE 1
unclogged *adj* allowing passage without obstruction — see OPEN 1
unclose *vb* to change from a closed to an open position — see OPEN 1
unclosed *adj* allowing passage without obstruction — see OPEN 1
unclothe *vb* to remove clothing from — see UNDRESS
unclothed *adj* lacking or shed of clothing — see NAKED 1
unclouded *adj* not stormy or cloudy — see FAIR 1
uncluttered *adj* being clean and in good order — see NEAT 1
uncolored *adj* lacking an addition of color — see COLORLESS
uncomfortable *adj* **1** causing discomfort <unfortunately, dressing up for the dance meant wearing an *uncomfortable* shirt>
synonyms comfortless, discomforting, harsh
related words aching, hurting, nasty, painful, sore; distressing, disturbing, upsetting; awkward, cumbersome, inconvenient, ungainly; uneasy
near antonyms easy, soothing; cozy, snug
antonyms comfortable
2 causing embarrassment — see AWKWARD 3
3 lacking social grace and assurance — see AWKWARD 1
uncomic *adj* not joking or playful in mood or manner — see SERIOUS 1
uncommon *adj* **1** being out of the ordinary — see EXCEPTIONAL
2 noticeably different from what is generally found or experienced — see UNUSUAL 1
uncommunicative *adj* **1** deliberately refraining from speech — see SILENT 1
2 given to keeping one's activities hidden from public observation or knowledge — see SECRETIVE
3 tending not to speak frequently (as by habit or inclination) — see SILENT 2
uncomplaining *adj* accepting pains or hardships calmly or without complaint — see PATIENT 1
uncomplimentary *adj* intended to make a person or thing seem of little importance or value — see DEROGATORY
uncompromising *adj* **1** not allowing for any exceptions or loosening of standards — see RIGID 1
2 sticking to an opinion, purpose, or course of action in spite of reason, arguments, or persuasion — see OBSTINATE
unconcern *n* lack of interest or concern — see INDIFFERENCE
unconcerned *adj* **1** having or showing a lack of concern or seriousness — see CAREFREE
2 having or showing a lack of interest or concern — see INDIFFERENT 1
unconditional *adj* having no exceptions or restrictions — see ABSOLUTE 2
unconfined *adj* not bound, confined, or detained by force — see FREE 3
uncongenial *adj* not giving pleasure to the mind or senses — see UNPLEASANT
unconnected *adj* **1** not clearly or logically connected — see INCOHERENT 1
2 not physically attached to another unit — see SEPARATE 2
unconquerable *adj* incapable of being defeated, overcome, or subdued — see INVINCIBLE
unconscionable *adj* **1** going beyond a normal or acceptable limit in degree or amount — see EXCESSIVE
2 not guided by or showing a concern for what is right — see UNPRINCIPLED
unconscious *adj* **1** having lost consciousness <the guard was knocked *unconscious* by a blow to the head>
synonyms cold, insensible, senseless
related words semiconscious; anesthetized
near antonyms alert, awake, aware, up
antonyms conscious
2 not informed about or aware of something — see IGNORANT 2
unconsidered *adj* made or done without previous thought or preparation — see EXTEMPORANEOUS
unconsolidated *adj* consisting of particles that do not stick together — see LOOSE 2
uncontrollable *adj* given to resisting control or discipline by others <the *uncontrollable* child kept throwing tantrums in public and creating scenes>
synonyms froward, headstrong, intractable, recalcitrant, refractory, ungovernable, unmanageable, unruly, untoward, wayward, willful (*or* wilful)
related words contrary, incorrigible, obstinate, perverse, self-willed, stubborn; undisciplined, unpunished; uncontrolled, ungoverned, wild; boisterous, rambunctious, rowdy; disobedient, insubordinate, rebellious; misbehaving, naughty
phrases out of hand
near antonyms docile, obedient, well-behaved; compliant, submissive, yielding
antonyms controllable, governable, tractable
uncontrolled *adj* showing no signs of being under control — see RAMPANT 1
unconventional *adj* **1** deviating from commonly accepted beliefs or practices — see HERETICAL
2 not bound by traditional ways or beliefs — see LIBERAL 1
3 not rigidly following established form, custom, or rules — see INFORMAL 1
unconvinced *adj* not feeling sure about the truth, wisdom, or trustworthiness of someone or something — see DOUBTFUL 1
unconvincing *adj* too extraordinary or improbable to believe — see INCREDIBLE
uncooked *adj* not cooked — see RAW 1
uncordial *adj* lacking in friendliness or warmth of feeling — see COLD 2
uncork *vb* to set free (from a state of being held in check) — see RELEASE 1
uncountable *adj* too many to be counted — see COUNTLESS
uncounted *adj* too many to be counted — see COUNTLESS
uncouple *vb* to set or force apart — see SEPARATE 1
uncouth *adj* **1** having or showing crudely insensitive or impolite manners — see CLOWNISH
2 lacking in refinement or good taste — see COARSE 2
uncover *vb* **1** to make known (as information previously kept secret) — see REVEAL 1
2 to reveal the true nature of — see EXPOSE 1
uncovered *adj* lacking a usual or natural covering — see NAKED 2

uncritical *adj* lacking in worldly wisdom or informed judgment — see NAIVE 1
uncrown *vb* to remove from a position of prominence or power (as a throne) — see DEPOSE 1
unctuous *adj* **1** not being or expressing what one appears to be or express — see INSINCERE
2 overly or insincerely flattering — see FULSOME
uncultivated *adj* **1** existing without human habitation or cultivation — see WILD 2
2 lacking in refinement or good taste — see COARSE 2
3 not civilized — see SAVAGE 1
uncultured *adj* lacking in refinement or good taste — see COARSE 2
uncurbed *adj* showing no signs of being under control — see RAMPANT 1
uncurious *adj* having or showing a lack of interest or concern — see INDIFFERENT 1
uncurl *vb* to cause to follow a line that is without bends or curls — see STRAIGHTEN
uncustomary *adj* **1** being out of the ordinary — see EXCEPTIONAL
2 noticeably different from what is generally found or experienced — see UNUSUAL 1
undaunted *adj* feeling or displaying no fear by temperament — see BRAVE
undeceive *vb* to free from mistaken beliefs or foolish hopes — see DISILLUSION
undecided *adj* **1** not yet settled or decided — see PENDING 1
2 not feeling sure about the truth, wisdom, or trustworthiness of someone or something — see DOUBTFUL 1
undecorated *adj* free from all additions or embellishment — see PLAIN 1
undefended *adj* lacking protection from danger or resistance against attack — see HELPLESS 1
undefined *adj* not seen or understood clearly — see FAINT 1
undemonstrative *adj* not feeling or showing emotion — see IMPASSIVE 1
undeniable *adj* not capable of being challenged or proved wrong — see IRREFUTABLE
undeniably *adv* without any question — see INDEED 1
under *adj* having not so great importance or rank as another — see LESSER
under *adv* in or to a lower place — see BELOW 1
under *prep* in a lower position than — see BELOW
underbelly *n* the side or part facing downward from something — see BOTTOM 1
underbody *n* the side or part facing downward from something — see BOTTOM 1
underclothes *n pl* clothing intended to be worn underneath other clothing — see UNDERWEAR
underclothing *n* clothing intended to be worn underneath other clothing — see UNDERWEAR
undercover *adj* **1** undertaken or done so as to escape being observed or known by others — see SECRET 1
2 working on missions in which one's objectives, activities, or true identity are not publicly revealed — see SECRET 2
undergarments *n pl* clothing intended to be worn underneath other clothing — see UNDERWEAR
undergo *vb* to come to a knowledge of (something) by living through it — see EXPERIENCE
underground *adj* undertaken or done so as to escape being observed or known by others — see SECRET 1
underground *n* a secret organization in a conquered country fighting against enemy forces — see RESISTANCE 2
underhand *adj* **1** given to or marked by cheating and deception — see DISHONEST 2
2 undertaken or done so as to escape being observed or known by others — see SECRET 1
underhanded *adj* **1** given to or marked by cheating and deception — see DISHONEST 2
2 undertaken or done so as to escape being observed or known by others — see SECRET 1
underline *vb* to indicate the importance of by giving prominent display — see EMPHASIZE
underling *n* one who is of lower rank and typically under the authority of another <he instructed his *underlings* to carry out the order immediately>
synonyms inferior, junior, subordinate
related words attendant, follower, retainer; domestic, menial, steward; flunky (*also* flunkey), henchman, lackey, minion; adjutant, aid, aide, assistant, coadjutor, deputy, second; helpmate, helpmeet, mate, sidekick
near antonyms boss, captain, chief, foreman, head, headman, helmsman, kingpin, leader, master, taskmaster
antonyms senior, superior
underlying *adj* of or relating to the simplest facts or theories of a subject — see ELEMENTARY
underneath *adv* in or to a lower place — see BELOW 1
underpin *vb* to hold up or serve as a foundation for — see SUPPORT 3
underpinning *n* **1** an immaterial thing upon which something else rests — see BASE 1
2 something that holds up or serves as a foundation for something else — see SUPPORT 1
underprivileged *adj* kept from having the necessities of life or a healthful environment — see DEPRIVED
underscore *vb* to indicate the importance of by giving prominent display — see EMPHASIZE
underside *n* the side or part facing downward from something — see BOTTOM 1
undersized *adj* of a size that is less than average — see SMALL 1
understand *vb* **1** to form an opinion through reasoning and information — see INFER 1
2 to have a practical understanding of — see KNOW 1
3 to recognize the meaning of — see COMPREHEND 1
understanding *adj* having or showing the capacity for sharing the feelings of another — see SYMPATHETIC 1
understanding *n* **1** an arrangement about action to be taken — see AGREEMENT 2
2 the knowledge gained from the process of coming to know or understand something — see COMPREHENSION
understated *adj* not excessively showy — see QUIET 2
undersurface *n* the side or part facing downward from something — see BOTTOM 1
undertake *vb* to take to or upon oneself — see ASSUME 1
undertaker *n* a person who manages funerals and prepares the dead for burial or cremation — see FUNERAL DIRECTOR
underwater *adj* living, lying, or occurring below the surface of the water <*underwater* plants don't

require as much light to grow as surface plants⟩ ⟨*underwater* exploring takes a long time because you can't move quickly⟩
synonyms aquatic, submarine, submerged, sunken
related words oceanic; abysmal, abyssal, deep, deep-sea, deepwater

under way *adj* being in progress or development — see ONGOING 1

underwear *n* clothing intended to be worn underneath other clothing ⟨*underwear* has got to be the most boring thing that one could ever receive as a birthday present!⟩
synonyms underclothes, underclothing, undergarments, undies
related words lingerie; pantie (*or* panty), slip, underskirt; briefs, drawers, long johns, pants, shorts, underdrawers, underpants, undershirt, union suit; nightdress, nightgown, nightshirt, pajamas, pj's
near antonyms outerwear

underweight *adj* having little weight — see [1]LIGHT 1

underwrite *vb* to provide money for — see FINANCE 1

undesired *adj* not searched or asked for — see UNSOUGHT

undetermined *adj* **1** not seen or understood clearly — see FAINT 1
2 not yet settled or decided — see PENDING 1

undeviating *adj* not varying — see UNIFORM

undies *n pl* clothing intended to be worn underneath other clothing — see UNDERWEAR

undiluted *adj* free from added matter — see PURE 1

undisturbed *adj* free from emotional or mental agitation — see CALM 2

undivided *adj* not divided or scattered among several areas of interest or concern — see WHOLE 1

undo *vb* **1** to deprive of courage or confidence — see UNNERVE 1
2 to disengage the knotted parts of — see UNTIE
3 to trouble the mind of; to make uneasy — see DISTURB 1

undomesticated *adj* living outdoors without taming or domestication by humans — see WILD 1

undoubtedly *adv* without any question — see INDEED 1

undress *vb* to remove clothing from ⟨Mom *undressed* the mud-covered little toddler and plopped her in the bath⟩
synonyms disrobe, strip, unclothe
related words bare, denude, divest, expose, uncover, undrape, unveil; bark, flay, peel, skin
near antonyms apparel, array, attire, caparison, clothe, costume, cover, deck, dress, feather, garb, garment, invest, rig (out), vest; cloak, mantle; drape, swaddle, swathe; accoutre (*or* accouter), equip, furnish, outfit
antonyms dress, gown, robe

undressed *adj* **1** being such as found in nature and not altered by processing or refining — see CRUDE 1
2 lacking or shed of clothing — see NAKED 1

undue *adj* going beyond a normal or acceptable limit in degree or amount — see EXCESSIVE

unduly *adv* beyond a normal or acceptable limit — see TOO 1

undyed *adj* lacking an addition of color — see COLORLESS

undying *adj* lasting forever — see EVERLASTING

uneager *adj* showing little or no interest or enthusiasm — see TEPID 1

unearth *vb* to remove from place of burial — see EXHUME

unearthing *n* the act or process of sighting or learning the existence of something for the first time — see DISCOVERY 1

unearthly *adj* **1** being so extraordinary or abnormal as to suggest powers which violate the laws of nature — see SUPERNATURAL 2
2 fearfully and mysteriously strange or fantastic — see EERIE
3 of, relating to, or being part of a reality beyond the observable physical universe — see SUPERNATURAL 1

uneasiness *n* **1** a disturbed or uneasy state — see UNREST
2 an uneasy state of mind usually over the possibility of an anticipated misfortune or trouble — see ANXIETY 1

uneasy *adj* **1** feeling or showing uncomfortable feelings of uncertainty — see NERVOUS 1
2 lacking or denying rest — see RESTLESS 1
3 lacking social grace and assurance — see AWKWARD 1

uneducated *adj* lacking in education or the knowledge gained from books — see IGNORANT 1

unembarrassed *adj* not embarrassed or ashamed — see UNABASHED

unemotional *adj* not feeling or showing emotion — see IMPASSIVE 1

unending *adj* lasting forever — see EVERLASTING

unendurable *adj* more than can be put up with — see UNBEARABLE

unenjoyable *adj* not giving pleasure to the mind or senses — see UNPLEASANT

unenthusiastic *adj* showing little or no interest or enthusiasm — see TEPID 1

unequal *adj* not staying constant — see UNEVEN 2

unequaled *or* **unequalled** *adj* having no equal or rival for excellence or desirability — see ONLY 1

unequivocal *adj* **1** having no exceptions or restrictions — see ABSOLUTE 2
2 not subject to misinterpretation or more than one interpretation — see CLEAR 2
3 so clearly expressed as to leave no doubt about the meaning — see EXPLICIT

unerring *adj* not being or likely to be wrong — see INFALLIBLE 1

unessential *adj* not needed by the circumstances or to accomplish an end — see UNNECESSARY

unethical *adj* **1** not conforming to a high moral standard; morally unacceptable — see BAD 2
2 not guided by or showing a concern for what is right — see UNPRINCIPLED

uneven *adj* **1** not having a level or smooth surface ⟨we had to plane and sand down the *uneven* wooden board before we could paint it⟩
synonyms broken, bumpy, coarse, irregular, jagged, lumpy, pebbly, ragged, rough, roughened, rugged, scraggy
related words lopsided, unbalanced; inexact, irregular, unaligned; rutted, rutty, undulating, wavy; burred, harsh, nubbly, nubby, scraggly, scratchy; nonuniform
near antonyms exact, uniform; aligned, regular, true; horizontal, tabular; plumb, straight, vertical; flush
antonyms even, flat, level, plane, smooth

2 not staying constant <the level of attendance at the ball park has been very *uneven* this season>
synonyms changing, erratic, fluctuating, irregular, unequal, unstable, unsteady, varying
related words capricious, changeable, changeful, choppy, fickle, fluid, inconsistent, inconstant, mercurial, mutable, uncertain, unsettled, variable, volatile
antonyms changeless, constant, stable, steady, unchanging, unvarying
3 inclined or twisted to one side — see AWRY

unexampled *adj* having no equal or rival for excellence or desirability — see ONLY 1

unexceptional *adj* being of the type that is encountered in the normal course of events — see ORDINARY 1

unexpected *adj* not expected <the pop quiz was *unexpected*, but fortunately I was prepared>
synonyms unanticipated, unforeseen, unlooked-for
related words unintended, unplanned; improbable, unlikely; startling, surprising
near antonyms predicted, prophesied
antonyms anticipated, expected, foreseen

unexpectedly *adv* without warning — see UNAWARES

unexplainable *adj* impossible to explain — see INEXPLICABLE

unexpressed *adj* understood although not put into words — see IMPLICIT

unfailing *adj* **1** not being or likely to be wrong — see INFALLIBLE 1
2 not likely to fail — see INFALLIBLE 2

unfailingly *adv* on every relevant occasion — see ALWAYS 1

unfair *adj* not being in accordance with the rules or standards of what is fair in sport — see FOUL 2

unfairness *n* the state of being unfair or unjust — see INJUSTICE 1

unfaithful *adj* not true in one's allegiance to someone or something — see FAITHLESS

unfaithfulness *n* **1** lack of faithfulness especially to one's husband or wife — see INFIDELITY 1
2 the act or fact of violating the trust or confidence of another — see BETRAYAL

unfamiliar *adj* not known or experienced before — see NEW 2

unfamiliarity *n* the state of being unaware or uninformed — see IGNORANCE 1

unfashionable *adj* marked by an obvious lack of style or good taste — see TACKY 1

unfasten *vb* to disengage the knotted parts of — see UNTIE

unfathomable *adj* **1** being or seeming to be without limits — see INFINITE
2 impossible to understand — see INCOMPREHENSIBLE

unfavorable *adj* opposed to one's interests — see ADVERSE 1

unfeeling *adj* **1** having or showing a lack of sympathy or tender feelings — see HARD 1
2 lacking in sensation or feeling — see NUMB

unfeignedly *adv* without any attempt to impress by deception or exaggeration — see NATURALLY 3

unfeminine *adj* having qualities or traits that are traditionally considered inappropriate for a girl or woman <in bygone days pants were considered *unfeminine*, and even women bicycling were expected to wear skirts>
synonyms hoydenish, manlike, mannish, tomboyish, unladylike, unwomanly
related words gentlemanly, male, manly, masculine
near antonyms effeminate, girlish, sissy, unmanly, unmasculine, womanish, womanlike; distaff, petticoat
antonyms female, feminine, ladylike, womanly

unfetter *vb* to set free (as from slavery or confinement) — see FREE 1

unfit *adj* **1** lacking qualities (as knowledge, skill, or ability) required to do a job — see INCOMPETENT
2 not appropriate for a particular occasion or situation — see INAPPROPRIATE

unfitness *n* **1** the quality or state of being unsuitable or unfitting — see INAPPROPRIATENESS 1
2 the quality or state of not being socially proper — see IMPROPRIETY 1

unflagging *adj* showing no signs of weariness even after long hard effort — see TIRELESS

unflappable *adj* not easily panicked or upset <the *unflappable* teacher never even blinked when the wall map came crashing down>
synonyms imperturbable, nerveless, unshakable
related words calm, collected, composed, cool, coolheaded, nonchalant, placid, self-possessed, serene, tranquil, undisturbed, unperturbed, unruffled, unshaken, untroubled, unworried
near antonyms panicky; aflutter, anxious, dithery, edgy, het up, hung up, jittery, jumpy, nervous, nervy, perturbed, shaky, tense, troubled, uneasy, upset, uptight, worried
antonyms perturbable, shakable

unfledged *adj* lacking in adult experience or maturity — see CALLOW

unflinching *adj* showing no signs of slackening or yielding in one's purpose — see UNYIELDING 1

unfold *vb* **1** to arrange the parts of (something) over a wider area — see OPEN 3
2 to gradually become clearer or more detailed — see DEVELOP 1
3 to produce flowers — see BLOOM

unforced *adj* done, made, or given with one's own free will — see VOLUNTARY 1

unforeseen *adj* not expected — see UNEXPECTED

unforgivable *adj* too bad to be excused or justified — see INEXCUSABLE

unformed *adj* having no definite or recognizable form — see FORMLESS

unfortunate *adj* **1** bringing about ruin or misfortune — see FATAL 1
2 having, prone to, or marked by bad luck — see UNLUCKY
3 of a kind to cause great distress — see REGRETTABLE

unfounded *adj* having no basis in reason or fact — see GROUNDLESS

unfriendly *adj* **1** lacking in friendliness or warmth of feeling — see COLD 2
2 marked by opposition or ill will — see HOSTILE 1
3 opposed to one's interests — see ADVERSE 1

unfrozen *adj* freed from a frozen state by exposure to warmth — see THAWED

unfruitful *adj* not able to produce fruit or offspring — see STERILE 1

unfunny *adj* not joking or playful in mood or manner — see SERIOUS 1

ungainly *adj* **1** difficult to use or operate especial-

ly because of size, weight, or design — see CUMBERSOME
2 lacking in physical ease and grace in movement or in the use of the hands — see CLUMSY 1
ungentle *adj* harsh and threatening in manner or appearance — see GRIM 1
ungodly *adj* falling short of a standard — see BAD 1
ungovernable *adj* **1** given to resisting authority or another's control — see DISOBEDIENT
2 given to resisting control or discipline by others — see UNCONTROLLABLE
ungoverned *adj* showing no signs of being under control — see RAMPANT 1
ungraceful *adj* lacking social grace and assurance — see AWKWARD 1
ungracious *adj* showing a lack of manners or consideration for others — see IMPOLITE
ungraciousness *n* rude behavior — see DISCOURTESY
ungrateful *adj* not showing gratitude — see THANKLESS 1
ungrounded *adj* **1** having no basis in reason or fact — see GROUNDLESS
2 not informed about or aware of something — see IGNORANT 2
unguarded *adj* **1** free in expressing one's true feelings and opinions — see FRANK
2 lacking protection from danger or resistance against attack — see HELPLESS 1
3 not paying or showing close attention especially for the purpose of avoiding trouble — see CARELESS 1
unhampered *adj* showing no signs of being under control — see RAMPANT 1
unhandsome *adj* unpleasant to look at — see UGLY 1
unhandy *adj* **1** difficult to use or operate especially because of size, weight, or design — see CUMBERSOME
2 lacking in physical ease and grace in movement or in the use of the hands — see CLUMSY 1
unhappily *adv* with feelings of bitterness or grief — see HARD 2
unhappiness *n* a state or spell of low spirits — see SADNESS
unhappy *adj* **1** feeling unhappiness — see SAD 1
2 having, prone to, or marked by bad luck — see UNLUCKY
3 not appropriate for a particular occasion or situation — see INAPPROPRIATE
unhealthful *adj* bad for the well-being of the body — see UNHEALTHY 1
unhealthiness *n* the condition of not being in good health — see SICKNESS 1
unhealthy *adj* **1** bad for the well-being of the body ⟨we knew that the junk food at the carnival was *unhealthy*, but it tasted so good!⟩
synonyms noisome, noxious, unhealthful, unwholesome
related words insanitary, unhygienic, unsanitary; nonnutritious; poisonous, toxic; fatal, lethal, mortal
near antonyms hygienic, sanitary; nutritious
antonyms healthful, healthy
2 involving potential loss or injury — see DANGEROUS
3 temporarily suffering from a disorder of the body — see SICK 1
unheard–of *adj* not known or experienced before — see NEW 2
unheroic *adj* having or showing a shameful lack of courage — see COWARDLY
unhindered *adj* showing no signs of being under control — see RAMPANT 1
unhinge *vb* **1** to cause to go insane or as if insane — see CRAZE
2 to trouble the mind of; to make uneasy — see DISTURB 1
unhurried *adj* moving or proceeding at less than the normal, desirable, or required speed — see SLOW 1
unidentified *adj* **1** known but not named — see CERTAIN 1
2 not named or identified by a name — see NAMELESS 1
unification *n* the act or an instance of joining two or more things into one — see UNION 1
uniform *adj* not varying ⟨with flat-screen TVs, picture sharpness is *uniform* over the entire screen, even in the corners⟩
synonyms invariant, steady, unchanging, undeviating, unvarying, unwavering
related words immutable, invariable, unalterable, unchangeable
antonyms changing, deviating, varying
uniform *n* the distinctive clothing worn by members of a particular group ⟨the band *uniform* was brown with red and white stripes⟩
synonyms livery, outfit
related words fatigues, full dress, regimentals; costume, finery, regalia
unify *vb* **1** to bring (something) to a central point or under a single control — see CENTRALIZE
2 to come together to form a single unit — see UNITE 1
unimaginable *adj* too extraordinary or improbable to believe — see INCREDIBLE
unimportant *adj* lacking importance ⟨we figured that the details were *unimportant* as long as we got the basic design correct⟩
synonyms frivolous, inconsequential, inconsiderable, insignificant, little, minor, minute, negligible, slight, small, small-fry, trifling, trivial
related words jerkwater, one-horse; paltry, petty, worthless; anonymous, nameless, obscure, uncelebrated, unknown
near antonyms decisive, fatal, fateful; distinctive, exceptional, impressive, outstanding, prominent, remarkable; valuable, worthwhile, worthy; distinguished, eminent, great, illustrious, preeminent, prestigious; famous, notorious, renowned; all-important, basic, essential, fundamental
antonyms big, consequential, eventful, important, major, material, meaningful, momentous, significant, substantial, weighty
uninflammable *adj* incapable of being burned — see INCOMBUSTIBLE
uninformed *adj* not informed about or aware of something — see IGNORANT 2
uninhibited *adj* showing feeling freely — see DEMONSTRATIVE
uninstructed *adj* lacking in education or the knowledge gained from books — see IGNORANT 1
unintelligent *adj* not having or showing an ability to absorb ideas readily — see STUPID 1
unintelligible *adj* impossible to understand — see INCOMPREHENSIBLE

unintended *adj* **1** happening by chance — see ACCIDENTAL
2 not made or done willingly or by choice — see INVOLUNTARY 1
unintentional *adj* **1** happening by chance — see ACCIDENTAL
2 not made or done willingly or by choice — see INVOLUNTARY 1
uninterested *adj* having or showing a lack of interest or concern — see INDIFFERENT 1
uninteresting *adj* causing weariness, restlessness, or lack of interest — see BORING
uninterrupted *adj* going on and on without any interruptions — see CONTINUOUS
uninvited *adj* not searched or asked for — see UNSOUGHT
union *n* **1** the act or an instance of joining two or more things into one ⟨the *union* of East Germany and West Germany that became possible after the fall of communism⟩
synonyms combination, combining, connecting, connection, consolidation, coupling, junction, linking, merging, unification
related words amalgamation, blend, commingling, compounding, fusion, intermingling, intermixture, mingling, mix, mixture; reunification, reunion
near antonyms detachment, divorcement, separation, severance
antonyms breakup, disconnection, dissolution, disunion, division, parting, partition, schism, split
2 an association of persons, parties, or states for mutual assistance and protection — see CONFEDERACY
3 the state of having shared interests or efforts (as in social or business matters) — see ASSOCIATION 1
unique *adj* **1** of, relating to, or belonging to a single person — see INDIVIDUAL 1
2 being out of the ordinary — see EXCEPTIONAL
3 being the one or ones of a class with no other members — see ONLY 2
4 noticeably different from what is generally found or experienced — see UNUSUAL 1
unison *n* the act or fact of being of one opinion about something — see AGREEMENT 1
unite *vb* **1** to come together to form a single unit ⟨using the microscope, we watched the water droplets *unite* into a single pool⟩
synonyms associate, coalesce, combine, conjoin, conjugate, connect, couple, fuse, join, link (up), marry, unify
related words mate, yoke; ally, confederate, league; chain, compound, hitch, hook; congregate, gather, meet; recombine, rejoin, reunify, reunite
near antonyms detach, disconnect, disjoin, disjoint, dissociate, disunite, divide, divorce, fractionate, isolate, resolve, uncouple, unyoke; disband, disperse, scatter
antonyms break up, dissever, part, section, separate, sever, split, sunder, unlink
2 to bring (something) to a central point or under a single control — see CENTRALIZE
3 to form or enter into an association that furthers the interests of its members — see ALLY
united *adj* **1** having or marked by agreement in feeling or action — see HARMONIOUS 3
2 used or done by a number of people as a group — see COLLECTIVE
unity *n* a balanced, pleasing, or suitable arrangement of parts — see HARMONY 1
universal *adj* **1** able to do many different kinds of things — see VERSATILE
2 belonging or relating to the whole — see GENERAL 1
3 covering everything or all important points — see ENCYCLOPEDIC
4 present in all places and at all times — see OMNIPRESENT
universe *n* the whole body of things observed or assumed ⟨the theory that the *universe* is constantly expanding⟩
synonyms cosmos, creation, macrocosm, nature, world
related words existence, reality
near antonyms nothingness, void
unjustifiable *adj* too bad to be excused or justified — see INEXCUSABLE
unjustness *n* the state of being unfair or unjust — see INJUSTICE 1
unkempt *adj* **1** lacking in order, neatness, and often cleanliness — see MESSY
2 lacking neatness in dress or person — see SLOPPY 1
unknowing *adj* **1** lacking in worldly wisdom or informed judgment — see NAIVE 1
2 not informed about or aware of something — see IGNORANT 2
unknown *adj* **1** happening or existing without one's knowledge ⟨*unknown* to me was the fact that while I was out, my family was hurriedly preparing a surprise birthday party⟩
synonyms unbeknownst (*also* unbeknown)
related words unperceived, unrecognized, unsuspected; unaware, unconscious, unmindful; unknowing, unsuspecting, unwitting; ignorant, unacquainted, unfamiliar
2 not known or experienced before — see NEW 2
3 not widely known — see OBSCURE 2
unlade *vb* to empty or rid of cargo — see UNLOAD 1
unladylike *adj* having qualities or traits that are traditionally considered inappropriate for a girl or woman — see UNFEMININE
unlash *vb* to disengage the knotted parts of — see UNTIE
unlawful *adj* contrary to or forbidden by law — see ILLEGAL 1
unlearn *vb* to be unable to recall or think of — see FORGET 1
unlearned *adj* lacking in education or the knowledge gained from books — see IGNORANT 1
unleash *vb* **1** to set free (from a state of being held in check) — see RELEASE 1
2 to find emotional release for — see TAKE OUT 1
unlettered *adj* lacking in education or the knowledge gained from books — see IGNORANT 1
unlike *adj* being not of the same kind — see DIFFERENT 1
unlikely *adj* not likely to be true or to occur — see IMPROBABLE
unlikeness *n* the quality or state of being different — see DIFFERENCE 1
unlimited *adj* **1** being or seeming to be without limits — see INFINITE
2 not limited or specialized in application or purpose — see GENERAL 4
unlink *vb* to set or force apart — see SEPARATE 1
unlisted *adj* not appearing on a list ⟨she kept her

phone number *unlisted* so as to reduce the number of unwanted calls⟩
synonyms uncataloged, unrecorded, unregistered
related words unwritten; unidentified, unspecified; undisclosed, unknown, unrevealed
antonyms cataloged (*or* catalogued), listed, recorded, registered

unliterary *adj* used in or suitable for speech and not formal writing — see COLLOQUIAL 1

unload *vb* **1** to empty or rid of cargo ⟨the dockworkers *unloaded* the ship⟩
synonyms disburden, discharge, disencumber, unburden, unlade, unpack
related words free, lighten, relieve; clear, empty, evacuate, vacate, void
near antonyms charge, cram, fill, heap, jam, jampack, stuff
antonyms load, pack
2 to get rid of as useless or unwanted — see DISCARD

unlock *vb* to set free (from a state of being held in check) — see RELEASE 1

unlooked–for *adj* not expected — see UNEXPECTED

unloose *vb* to set free (from a state of being held in check) — see RELEASE 1

unloosen *vb* to set free (from a state of being held in check) — see RELEASE 1

unlovely *adj* **1** not giving pleasure to the mind or senses — see UNPLEASANT
2 unpleasant to look at — see UGLY 1

unlucky *adj* having, prone to, or marked by bad luck ⟨the *unlucky* campers had rain all week⟩ ⟨I'm so *unlucky* I don't bother to play the lottery⟩ ⟨an *unlucky* throw of the dice⟩
synonyms hapless, ill-fated, ill-starred, luckless, star-crossed, unfortunate, unhappy
related words adverse, ill, inauspicious, unfavorable, unpromising, untoward; calamitous, catastrophic, disastrous; damned, doomed, tragic
near antonyms blessed, favored, gifted, privileged; auspicious, fair, favorable, golden, promising, propitious
antonyms fortunate, happy, lucky

unmake *vb* to remove from a position of prominence or power (as a throne) — see DEPOSE 1

unman *vb* **1** to deprive of courage or confidence — see UNNERVE 1
2 to lessen the courage or confidence of — see DISCOURAGE 1

unmanageable *adj* given to resisting control or discipline by others — see UNCONTROLLABLE

unmanly *adj* having or displaying qualities more suitable for women than for men — see EFFEMINATE

unmannerly *adj* showing a lack of manners or consideration for others — see IMPOLITE

unmarried *adj* not married — see SINGLE 1

unmask *vb* **1** to make known (as information previously kept secret) — see REVEAL 1
2 to reveal the true nature of — see EXPOSE 1

unmatched *adj* **1** being one of a pair or set without a corresponding mate — see ODD 1
2 having no equal or rival for excellence or desirability — see ONLY 1

unmelodious *adj* marked by or producing a harsh combination of sounds — see DISSONANT

unmerciful *adj* having or showing a lack of sympathy or tender feelings — see HARD 1

unmindful *adj* not informed about or aware of something — see IGNORANT 2

unmistakable *adj* not subject to misinterpretation or more than one interpretation — see CLEAR 2

unmitigated *adj* having no exceptions or restrictions — see ABSOLUTE 2

unmixed *adj* free from added matter — see PURE 1

unmoral *adj* not guided by or showing a concern for what is right — see UNPRINCIPLED

unmovable *adj* incapable of moving or being moved — see IMMOVABLE 1

unmusical *adj* marked by or producing a harsh combination of sounds — see DISSONANT

unnamed *adj* **1** known but not named — see CERTAIN 1
2 not named or identified by a name — see NAMELESS 1

unnatural *adj* **1** departing from some accepted standard of what is normal — see DEVIANT
2 lacking in natural or spontaneous quality — see ARTIFICIAL 1

unnecessary *adj* not needed by the circumstances or to accomplish an end ⟨a hair dryer was an *unnecessary* item on a trip to the desert⟩
synonyms dispensable, gratuitous, needless, nonessential, uncalled-for, unessential, unwarranted
related words discretionary, elective, optional; extra, extraneous, irrelevant, redundant, superfluous
near antonyms all-important, crucial, important, vital; imperative, pressing, urgent
antonyms essential, indispensable, necessary, needed, needful, required

unnerve *vb* **1** to deprive of courage or confidence ⟨the riding accident so *unnerved* me that for a while I was afraid to get back on a horse⟩
synonyms demoralize, emasculate, undo, unman, unstring
related words debilitate, enervate, enfeeble, weaken; prostrate, sap, soften, tire, waste; frighten, scare, terrify, terrorize; daunt, discourage, dishearten, dismay, dispirit; craze, derange, madden, unbalance, unhinge; discompose, disquiet, disturb, faze, perturb, unsettle, upset
near antonyms fortify, strengthen; embolden, encourage, hearten
antonyms nerve
2 to lessen the courage or confidence of — see DISCOURAGE 1

unnerving *adj* marked by or causing agitation or uncomfortable feelings — see NERVOUS 2

unnoted *adj* not widely known — see OBSCURE 2

unnoticeable *adj* not readily seen or noticed — see UNOBTRUSIVE

unnumbered *adj* too many to be counted — see COUNTLESS

unobstructed *adj* allowing passage without obstruction — see OPEN 1

unobtainable *adj* hard or impossible to get to or get at — see INACCESSIBLE

unobtrusive *adj* not readily seen or noticed ⟨the notice that an 18% tip would be automatically added was so *unobtrusive* we almost didn't see it at the bottom of the menu⟩
synonyms inconspicuous, unnoticeable
related words unnoticed; impalpable, imperceptible, inappreciable, indistinguishable, insensible; faint, indistinct, obscure; concealed, hidden

near antonyms arresting, eye-catching, showy, striking; apparent, blatant, clear, distinct, evident, manifest, obvious, plain, unmistakable
antonyms conspicuous, noticeable
unoriginal *adj* using or marked by the use of something else as a basis or model — see IMITATIVE
unorthodox *adj* **1** deviating from commonly accepted beliefs or practices — see HERETICAL
2 not bound by traditional ways or beliefs — see LIBERAL 1
3 not rigidly following established form, custom, or rules — see INFORMAL 1
unpack *vb* to empty or rid of cargo — see UNLOAD 1
unpaid *adj* not yet paid — see OUTSTANDING 1
unpainted *adj* lacking an addition of color — see COLORLESS
unpaired *adj* being one of a pair or set without a corresponding mate — see ODD 1
unpalatable *adj* disagreeable or disgusting to the sense of taste — see DISTASTEFUL 1
unparalleled *adj* having no equal or rival for excellence or desirability — see ONLY 1
unpardonable *adj* too bad to be excused or justified — see INEXCUSABLE
unperturbed *adj* free from emotional or mental agitation — see CALM 2
unplanned *adj* **1** happening by chance — see ACCIDENTAL
2 made or done without previous thought or preparation — see EXTEMPORANEOUS
unpleasant *adj* not giving pleasure to the mind or senses <the burnt pot roast had a very *unpleasant* odor>
synonyms bad, disagreeable, displeasing, distasteful, nasty, rotten, sour, uncongenial, unlovely, unpleasing, unsatisfying, unwelcome
related words abhorrent, abominable, appalling, awful, beastly, disgusting, dreadful, foul, hideous, horrendous, horrible, horrid, invidious, loathsome, nauseating, noisome, obnoxious, obscene, odious, repellent (*also* repellant), repugnant, repulsive, revolting, scandalous, shocking, sickening, ugly, villainous; annoying, galling, irritating, vexing
near antonyms delectable, delicious, delightful, dreamy, felicitous; affable, amiable, friendly, genial, good-natured, good-tempered, gracious, sweet, well-disposed
antonyms agreeable, congenial, good, grateful, gratifying, nice, palatable, pleasant, pleasing, pleasurable, satisfying, welcome
unpleasing *adj* **1** not giving pleasure to the mind or senses — see UNPLEASANT
2 unpleasant to look at — see UGLY 1
unpolished *adj* lacking in refinement or good taste — see COARSE 2
unprecedented *adj* not known or experienced before — see NEW 2
unpredictable *adj* likely to change frequently, suddenly, or unexpectedly — see FICKLE 1
unprejudiced *adj* marked by justice, honesty, and freedom from bias — see FAIR 2
unpremeditated *adj* **1** happening by chance — see ACCIDENTAL
2 made or done without previous thought or preparation — see EXTEMPORANEOUS
unprepared *adj* made or done without previous thought or preparation — see EXTEMPORANEOUS
unpretending *adj* free from any intent to deceive or impress others — see GUILELESS
unpretentious *adj* **1** free from any intent to deceive or impress others — see GUILELESS
2 not excessively showy — see QUIET 2
3 not having or showing any feelings of superiority, self-assertiveness, or showiness — see HUMBLE 1
unpretentiously *adv* without any attempt to impress by deception or exaggeration — see NATURALLY 3
unpretty *adj* unpleasant to look at — see UGLY 1
unprincipled *adj* not guided by or showing a concern for what is right <the *unprincipled* businessman made a lot of money—and didn't care how he made it>
synonyms cutthroat, immoral, Machiavellian, unconscionable, unethical, unmoral, unscrupulous
related words calculating, intriguing, opportunistic, scheming; merciless, pitiless, remorseless, ruthless; crooked, deceitful, dishonest; corrupt, debased, debauched, decadent, degenerate, degraded, demoralized, depraved, dissipated
near antonyms good, just, noble, righteous, virtuous
antonyms ethical, moral, principled, scrupulous
unprintable *adj* depicting or referring to sexual matters in a way that is unacceptable in polite society — see OBSCENE 1
unprocessed *adj* being such as found in nature and not altered by processing or refining — see CRUDE 1
unproductive *adj* **1** producing inferior or only a small amount of vegetation — see BARREN 1
2 producing no results — see FUTILE
unprofessional *adj* lacking or showing a lack of expert skill — see AMATEURISH
unprofitable *adj* producing no results — see FUTILE
unprogressive *adj* tending to favor established ideas, conditions, or institutions — see CONSERVATIVE 1
unprotected *adj* lacking protection from danger or resistance against attack — see HELPLESS 1
unqualified *adj* **1** having no exceptions or restrictions — see ABSOLUTE 2
2 lacking qualities (as knowledge, skill, or ability) required to do a job — see INCOMPETENT
3 not limited or specialized in application or purpose — see GENERAL 4
unquestionable *adj* not capable of being challenged or proved wrong — see IRREFUTABLE
unquestionably *adv* without any question — see INDEED 1
unquiet *adj* **1** feeling or showing uncomfortable feelings of uncertainty — see NERVOUS 1
2 lacking or denying rest — see RESTLESS 1
unravel *vb* **1** to separate the various strands of <it took us forever to *unravel* the jumbled mass of Christmas tree lights>
synonyms disentangle, ravel (out), unbraid, unsnarl, untangle, untwine, untwist
related words smooth, straighten (out); undo, unlace, unstring, unthread, untie, unwind
near antonyms braid, knot, lace, tie, wind
antonyms entangle, snarl, tangle
2 to find an answer for through reasoning — see SOLVE
unreachable *adj* hard or impossible to get to or get at — see INACCESSIBLE

unread *adj* lacking in education or the knowledge gained from books — see IGNORANT 1
unreal *adj* **1** conceived or made without regard for reason or reality — see FANTASTIC 1
2 not real and existing only in the imagination — see IMAGINARY
unreality *n* a conception or image created by the imagination and having no objective reality — see FANTASY 1
unreasonable *adj* **1** having no basis in reason or fact — see GROUNDLESS
2 not using or following good reasoning — see ILLOGICAL
unreasoning *adj* not using or following good reasoning — see ILLOGICAL
unrecorded *adj* not appearing on a list — see UNLISTED
unrecoverable *adj* **1** not capable of being cured or reformed — see HOPELESS 1
2 not capable of being repaired, regained, or undone — see IRREPARABLE
unredeemable *adj* **1** not capable of being cured or reformed — see HOPELESS 1
2 not capable of being repaired, regained, or undone — see IRREPARABLE
unrefined *adj* **1** being such as found in nature and not altered by processing or refining — see CRUDE 1
2 hastily or roughly constructed — see RUDE 1
3 lacking in refinement or good taste — see COARSE 2
unregistered *adj* not appearing on a list — see UNLISTED
unrehearsed *adj* made or done without previous thought or preparation — see EXTEMPORANEOUS
unrelenting *adj* **1** sticking to an opinion, purpose, or course of action in spite of reason, arguments, or persuasion — see OBSTINATE
2 showing no signs of slackening or yielding in one's purpose — see UNYIELDING 1
unremarkable *adj* being of the type that is encountered in the normal course of events — see ORDINARY 1
unremitting *adj* going on and on without any interruptions — see CONTINUOUS
unrepentant *adj* not sorry for having done wrong — see REMORSELESS
unreserved *adj* **1** free in expressing one's true feelings and opinions — see FRANK
2 showing feeling freely — see DEMONSTRATIVE
unresistant *adj* **1** lacking protection from danger or resistance against attack — see HELPLESS 1
2 receiving or enduring without offering resistance — see PASSIVE
unresisting *adj* receiving or enduring without offering resistance — see PASSIVE
unresolved *adj* not yet settled or decided — see PENDING 1
unrest *n* a disturbed or uneasy state ⟨*unrest* gripped the city as the people nervously awaited the expected bombardment⟩ ⟨his stomach *unrest* was just a sign of stage fright⟩
synonyms disquiet, ferment, restiveness, restlessness, turmoil, uneasiness
related words fidgets; agitation, commotion, confusion, tumult, turbulence, upheaval; anarchy, chaos, disorder
near antonyms order, orderliness
antonyms calm, ease, peace, quiet
unrestful *adj* lacking or denying rest — see RESTLESS 1
unrestrained *adj* **1** not bound by rigid standards — see EASYGOING 2
2 not bound, confined, or detained by force — see FREE 3
3 showing feeling freely — see DEMONSTRATIVE
4 showing no signs of being under control — see RAMPANT 1
unrestraint *n* carefree freedom from constraint — see ABANDON
unrestricted *adj* **1** freely available for use or participation by all — see OPEN 2
2 not bound by rigid standards — see EASYGOING 2
3 not limited or specialized in application or purpose — see GENERAL 4
unrighteous *adj* not conforming to a high moral standard; morally unacceptable — see BAD 2
unripe *adj* lacking in adult experience or maturity — see CALLOW
unripened *adj* lacking in adult experience or maturity — see CALLOW
unrivaled *or* **unrivalled** *adj* having no equal or rival for excellence or desirability — see ONLY 1
unruliness *n* refusal to obey — see DISOBEDIENCE
unruly *adj* **1** given to resisting authority or another's control — see DISOBEDIENT
2 given to resisting control or discipline by others — see UNCONTROLLABLE
3 not restrained by or under the control of legal authority — see LAWLESS
unsafe *adj* **1** involving potential loss or injury — see DANGEROUS
2 not paying or showing close attention especially for the purpose of avoiding trouble — see CARELESS 1
unsatisfactorily *adv* in an unsatisfactory way — see BADLY
unsatisfactory *adj* falling short of a standard — see BAD 1
unsatisfying *adj* not giving pleasure to the mind or senses — see UNPLEASANT
unsavory *adj* **1** disagreeable or disgusting to the sense of taste — see DISTASTEFUL 1
2 not conforming to a high moral standard; morally unacceptable — see BAD 2
unsay *vb* to solemnly or formally reject or go back on (as something formerly adhered to) — see ABJURE
unschooled *adj* lacking in education or the knowledge gained from books — see IGNORANT 1
unscrupulous *adj* not guided by or showing a concern for what is right — see UNPRINCIPLED
unseasonable *adj* occurring before the usual or expected time — see EARLY 2
unseasonably *adv* before the usual or expected time — see EARLY
unseat *vb* to remove from a position of prominence or power (as a throne) — see DEPOSE 1
unsecured *adj* not tightly fastened, tied, or stretched — see LOOSE 1
unseemly *adj* not appropriate for a particular occasion or situation — see INAPPROPRIATE
unselfish *adj* giving or sharing in abundance and without hesitation — see GENEROUS 1
unselfishness *n* the quality or state of being generous — see LIBERALITY
unsettle *vb* to trouble the mind of; to make uneasy — see DISTURB 1

unsettled *adj* **1** likely to change frequently, suddenly, or unexpectedly — see FICKLE 1
2 not yet paid — see OUTSTANDING 1
3 not yet settled or decided — see PENDING 1
4 not feeling sure about the truth, wisdom, or trustworthiness of someone or something — see DOUBTFUL 1

unsettling *adj* **1** causing worry or anxiety — see TROUBLESOME
2 marked by or causing agitation or uncomfortable feelings — see NERVOUS 2

unshakable *adj* not easily panicked or upset — see UNFLAPPABLE

unshaken *adj* free from emotional or mental agitation — see CALM 2

unshaped *adj* having no definite or recognizable form — see FORMLESS

unshared *adj* belonging only to the one person, unit, or group named — see SOLE 1

unshielded *adj* lacking protection from danger or resistance against attack — see HELPLESS 1

unshorn *adj* covered with or as if with hair — see HAIRY 1

unsightly *adj* unpleasant to look at — see UGLY 1

unskilled *adj* **1** lacking or showing a lack of expert skill — see AMATEURISH
2 lacking qualities (as knowledge, skill, or ability) required to do a job — see INCOMPETENT

unskillful *adj* **1** lacking qualities (as knowledge, skill, or ability) required to do a job — see INCOMPETENT
2 lacking or showing a lack of expert skill — see AMATEURISH

unsmiling *adj* not joking or playful in mood or manner — see SERIOUS 1

unsnarl *vb* to separate the various strands of — see UNRAVEL 1

unsociable *adj* having or showing a lack of friendliness or interest in others — see COOL 1

unsoiled *adj* free from dirt or stain — see CLEAN 1

unsolicited *adj* not searched or asked for — see UNSOUGHT

unsolvable *adj* incapable of being solved or accomplished — see IMPOSSIBLE

unsophisticated *adj* lacking in worldly wisdom or informed judgment — see NAIVE 1

unsophistication *n* **1** the quality or state of being simple and sincere — see NAÏVETÉ 1
2 the quality or state of having a form or structure of few parts or elements — see SIMPLICITY 1

unsought *adj* not searched or asked for ⟨the meddling neighbor insisted on giving us *unsought* advice⟩
synonyms unasked, unbidden (*also* unbid), undesired, uninvited, unsolicited, unwanted, unwelcome
related words objectionable, offensive, unacceptable, undesirable; uncalled-for, unnecessary
near antonyms necessary, needed, required
antonyms desired, solicited, wanted, welcome

unsound *adj* **1** having or showing a very abnormal or sick state of mind — see INSANE 1
2 not being in agreement with what is true — see FALSE 1
3 not using or following good reasoning — see ILLOGICAL
4 temporarily suffering from a disorder of the body — see SICK 1

unsoundness *n* the condition of not being in good health — see SICKNESS 1

unsparing *adj* **1** giving or sharing in abundance and without hesitation — see GENEROUS 1
2 having or showing a lack of sympathy or tender feelings — see HARD 1

unspeakable *adj* beyond the power to describe — see INDESCRIBABLE

unspecialized *adj* not limited or specialized in application or purpose — see GENERAL 4

unspecified *adj* known but not named — see CERTAIN 1

unspoken *adj* understood although not put into words — see IMPLICIT

unsportsmanlike *adj* not being in accordance with the rules or standards of what is fair in sport — see FOUL 2

unstable *adj* **1** not being in or able to maintain a state of balance ⟨when we put the books down on the *unstable* desk, the whole stack went crashing to the floor⟩
synonyms unbalanced, unsteady
related words rickety, shaky, tottery, wobbly; cockeyed, lopsided, uneven
near antonyms even, level, straight; sound, sturdy, substantial
antonyms balanced, stable, steady
2 likely to change frequently, suddenly, or unexpectedly — see FICKLE 1
3 not staying constant — see UNEVEN 2

unstained *adj* lacking an addition of color — see COLORLESS

unsteadiness *n* the quality or state of not being firmly fixed in position — see INSTABILITY

unsteady *adj* **1** lacking in steadiness or regularity of occurrence — see FITFUL
2 likely to change frequently, suddenly, or unexpectedly — see FICKLE 1
3 not being in or able to maintain a state of balance — see UNSTABLE 1
4 not staying constant — see UNEVEN 2

unstop *vb* to arrange clear passage of (something) by removing obstructions — see OPEN 2

unstopped *adj* allowing passage without obstruction — see OPEN 1

unstring *vb* **1** to cause to go insane or as if insane — see CRAZE
2 to deprive of courage or confidence — see UNNERVE 1

unstructured *adj* having no definite or recognizable form — see FORMLESS

unstylish *adj* marked by an obvious lack of style or good taste — see TACKY 1

unstylishly *adv* in a careless or unfashionable manner — see SLOPPILY

unsubstantial *adj* **1** not composed of matter — see IMMATERIAL 1
2 being of a material lacking in sturdiness or substance — see FLIMSY 1
3 lacking bodily strength — see WEAK 1

unsubstantiated *adj* having no basis in reason or fact — see GROUNDLESS

unsuccessful *adj* producing no results — see FUTILE

unsuitable *adj* not appropriate for a particular occasion or situation — see INAPPROPRIATE

unsuitably *adv* in a mistaken or inappropriate way — see WRONGLY

unsullied *adj* free from dirt or stain — see CLEAN 1

unsung *adj* not widely known — see OBSCURE 2

unsupportable *adj* more than can be put up with — see UNBEARABLE

unsupported *adj* having no basis in reason or fact — see GROUNDLESS
unsure *adj* not feeling sure about the truth, wisdom, or trustworthiness of someone or something — see DOUBTFUL 1
unsurpassable *adj* having no equal or rival for excellence or desirability — see ONLY 1
unsurpassed *adj* **1** having no equal or rival for excellence or desirability — see ONLY 1
2 of the very best kind — see EXCELLENT
unsuspecting *adj* lacking in worldly wisdom or informed judgment — see NAIVE 1
unsuspicious *adj* lacking in worldly wisdom or informed judgment — see NAIVE 1
unsympathetic *adj* **1** having or showing a lack of sympathy or tender feelings — see HARD 1
2 lacking in friendliness or warmth of feeling — see COLD 2
3 marked by opposition or ill will — see HOSTILE 1
4 opposed to one's interests — see ADVERSE 1
untamed *adj* **1** existing without human habitation or cultivation — see WILD 2
2 living outdoors without taming or domestication by humans — see WILD 1
untangle *vb* **1** to separate the various strands of — see UNRAVEL 1
2 to set free from entanglement or difficulty — see EXTRICATE
untaught *adj* lacking in education or the knowledge gained from books — see IGNORANT 1
unthinkable *adj* too extraordinary or improbable to believe — see INCREDIBLE
unthrifty *adj* given to spending money freely or foolishly — see PRODIGAL
unthrone *vb* to remove from a position of prominence or power (as a throne) — see DEPOSE 1
untidy *adj* **1** lacking in order, neatness, and often cleanliness — see MESSY
2 lacking neatness in dress or person — see SLOPPY 1
untie *vb* to disengage the knotted parts of ⟨she always made sure to *untie* her shoelaces before removing her shoes⟩
synonyms unbind, undo, unfasten, unlash
related words unbraid, unlace; disentangle, ravel, unbraid, unravel, unsnarl, untangle, unwind; loose, loosen
near antonyms braid, interlace, interweave, lace, wind; entangle, snarl, tangle
antonyms bind, fasten, knot, lash, tie
untimely *adj* occurring before the usual or expected time — see EARLY 2
untiring *adj* showing no signs of weariness even after long hard effort — see TIRELESS
untitled *adj* not named or identified by a name — see NAMELESS 1
untold *adj* too many to be counted — see COUNTLESS
untouchable *adj* **1** hard or impossible to get to or get at — see INACCESSIBLE
2 not to be violated, criticized, or tampered with — see SACRED 1
untoward *adj* **1** given to resisting authority or another's control — see DISOBEDIENT
2 given to resisting control or discipline by others — see UNCONTROLLABLE
untreated *adj* being such as found in nature and not altered by processing or refining — see CRUDE 1
untroubled *adj* **1** free from emotional or mental agitation — see CALM 2
2 free from storms or physical disturbance — see CALM 1
untrue *adj* **1** not being in agreement with what is true — see FALSE 1
2 not true in one's allegiance to someone or something — see FAITHLESS
untruth *n* **1** a false idea or belief — see FALLACY 1
2 a statement known by its maker to be untrue and made in order to deceive — see LIE
3 the quality or state of being false — see FALLACY 2
untruthful *adj* **1** not being in agreement with what is true — see FALSE 1
2 telling or containing lies — see DISHONEST 1
untruthfulness *n* the tendency to tell lies — see DISHONESTY 1
untutored *adj* lacking in education or the knowledge gained from books — see IGNORANT 1
untwine *vb* to separate the various strands of — see UNRAVEL 1
untwist *vb* to separate the various strands of — see UNRAVEL 1
unusable *adj* not capable of being put to use or account — see IMPRACTICAL
unused *adj* **1** not having acquired a habit or tolerance ⟨while in Mexico we tried to stay out of the sun because we were simply *unused* to the tropical heat⟩
synonyms unacclimated, unaccustomed, unadapted, unadjusted
related words unhardened, unseasoned
near antonyms unaffected, uninfluenced
antonyms acclimated, accustomed, adapted, adjusted, habituated, used
2 recently made and never used before — see NEW 3
unusual *adj* **1** noticeably different from what is generally found or experienced ⟨finding some *unusual* shells by the high-tide mark, we brought them home for our collection⟩
synonyms curious, extraordinary, funny, odd, offbeat, peculiar, queer, rare, singular, strange, unaccustomed, uncommon, uncustomary, unique, weird
related words bizarre, eccentric, far-out, outlandish, outré, way-out; aberrant, abnormal, atypical, exceptional, irregular; newsworthy, notable, noteworthy, noticeable, particular, remarkable, special
near antonyms unexceptional; expected, predictable; familiar, normal, regular, typical
antonyms common, ordinary, usual
2 being out of the ordinary — see EXCEPTIONAL
unutterable *adj* beyond the power to describe — see INDESCRIBABLE
unvarnished *adj* free from all additions or embellishment — see PLAIN 1
unvarying *adj* **1** not undergoing a change in condition — see CONSTANT 1
2 not varying — see UNIFORM
unveil *vb* **1** to make known (as information previously kept secret) — see REVEAL 1
2 to present so as to invite notice or attention — see SHOW 1
unvoiced *adj* understood although not put into words — see IMPLICIT
unwanted *adj* not searched or asked for — see UNSOUGHT

unwarrantable *adj* too bad to be excused or justified — see INEXCUSABLE

unwarranted *adj* **1** not needed by the circumstances or to accomplish an end — see UNNECESSARY

2 having no basis in reason or fact — see GROUNDLESS

unwary *adj* **1** lacking in worldly wisdom or informed judgment — see NAIVE 1

2 not paying or showing close attention especially for the purpose of avoiding trouble — see CARELESS 1

unwavering *adj* not varying — see UNIFORM

unwearying *adj* showing no signs of weariness even after long hard effort — see TIRELESS

unwed *adj* not married — see SINGLE 1

unwelcome *adj* **1** not giving pleasure to the mind or senses — see UNPLEASANT

2 not searched or asked for — see UNSOUGHT

unwell *adj* temporarily suffering from a disorder of the body — see SICK 1

unwholesome *adj* bad for the well-being of the body — see UNHEALTHY 1

unwieldy *adj* difficult to use or operate especially because of size, weight, or design — see CUMBERSOME

unwilling *adj* not made or done willingly or by choice — see INVOLUNTARY 1

unwillingness *n* a lack of willingness or desire to do or accept something — see RELUCTANCE

unwind *vb* to get rid of nervous tension or anxiety — see RELAX 1

unwise *adj* **1** showing or marked by a lack of good sense or judgment — see FOOLISH 1

2 showing poor judgment especially in personal relationships or social situations — see INDISCREET

unwitting *adj* **1** happening by chance — see ACCIDENTAL

2 not informed about or aware of something — see IGNORANT 2

unwomanly *adj* having qualities or traits that are traditionally considered inappropriate for a girl or woman — see UNFEMININE

unwonted *adj* being out of the ordinary — see EXCEPTIONAL

unworkable *adj* not capable of being put to use or account — see IMPRACTICAL

unworldliness *n* the quality or state of being simple and sincere — see NAÏVETÉ 1

unworldly *adj* lacking in worldly wisdom or informed judgment — see NAIVE 1

unworried *adj* free from emotional or mental agitation — see CALM 2

unwritten *adj* made or carried on through speaking rather than in writing — see VERBAL 2

unyielding *adj* **1** showing no signs of slackening or yielding in one's purpose 〈the pioneers faced the challenge of settling the frontier with *unyielding* courage〉

synonyms determined, dogged, grim, implacable, relentless, unappeasable, unflinching, unrelenting

related words hardheaded, headstrong, mulish, obdurate, opinionated, peevish, pertinacious, perverse, pigheaded, self-willed, stubborn, uncooperative, willful (*or* wilful); merciless, ruthless, unforgiving

near antonyms slackening, softening, yielding; impotent, invertebrate, slack, spineless, weak

2 having a consistency that does not easily yield to pressure — see FIRM 2

3 incapable of or highly resistant to bending — see STIFF 1

4 sticking to an opinion, purpose, or course of action in spite of reason, arguments, or persuasion — see OBSTINATE

unyoke *vb* to set or force apart — see SEPARATE 1

up *adj* **1** being at a higher level than average — see HIGH 2

2 brought or having come to an end — see COMPLETE 2

3 having information especially as a result of study or experience — see FAMILIAR 2

up *vb* **1** to make greater in size, amount, or number — see INCREASE 1

2 to move from a lower to a higher place or position — see RAISE 1

3 to move or extend upward — see ASCEND

upbeat *adj* **1** having or showing a good mood or disposition — see CHEERFUL 1

2 having qualities which inspire hope — see HOPEFUL 1

upbraid *vb* to criticize (someone) severely or angrily especially for personal failings — see SCOLD

upcoming *adj* being soon to appear or take place — see FORTHCOMING

up–country *n* a rural region that forms the edge of the settled or developed part of a country — see FRONTIER 2

upend *vb* to fix in an upright position — see ERECT 1

upgrade *n* **1** an upward slope — see ASCENT 2

2 a raising or a state of being raised to a higher rank or position — see ADVANCEMENT 1

3 the degree to which something rises up from a position level with the horizon — see SLANT

upgrade *vb* to move higher in rank or position — see PROMOTE 1

upheaval *n* a violent disturbance (as of the political or social order) — see CONVULSION

uphold *vb* **1** to continue to declare to be true or proper despite opposition or objections — see MAINTAIN 2

2 to hold up or serve as a foundation for — see SUPPORT 3

3 to move from a lower to a higher place or position — see RAISE 1

upkeep *n* the act or activity of keeping something in an existing and usually satisfactory condition — see MAINTENANCE

upland *n* an area of high ground — see HEIGHT 4

uplift *vb* to move from a lower to a higher place or position — see RAISE 1

uplifted *adj* being positioned above a surface — see ELEVATED 1

upmost *adj* being at a point or level higher than all others — see TOP 1

upon *prep* in or into contact with — see AGAINST

upper–class *adj* of high birth, rank, or station — see NOBLE 1

upper class *n* the highest class in a society — see ARISTROCRACY

upper crust *n* **1** individuals carefully selected as being the best of a class — see ELITE

2 the highest class in a society — see ARISTROCRACY

upper hand *n* the more favorable condition or position in a competition — see ADVANTAGE 1

uppermost *adj* being at a point or level higher than all others — see TOP 1
uppish *adj* having a feeling of superiority that shows itself in an overbearing attitude — see ARROGANT
uppity *adj* having a feeling of superiority that shows itself in an overbearing attitude — see ARROGANT
upraise *vb* **1** to move from a lower to a higher place or position — see RAISE 1
2 to fix in an upright position — see ERECT 1
upraised *adj* being positioned above a surface — see ELEVATED 1
upright *adj* **1** conforming to a high standard of morality or virtue — see GOOD 2
2 following the accepted rules of moral conduct — see HONORABLE 1
3 rising straight up — see ERECT
uprightness *n* **1** conduct that conforms to an accepted standard of right and wrong — see MORALITY 1
2 faithfulness to high moral standards — see HONOR 1
uprise *vb* **1** to leave one's bed — see ARISE 1
2 to move or extend upward — see ASCEND
uprising *n* open fighting against authority (as one's own government) — see REBELLION
uproar *n* **1** a state of noisy, confused activity — see COMMOTION
2 a state of wildly excited activity or emotion — see FRENZY
3 a violent disturbance (as of the political or social order) — see CONVULSION
4 a violent shouting — see CLAMOR 1
uproarious *adj* causing or intended to cause laughter — see FUNNY 1
uproot *vb* to draw out by force or with effort — see EXTRACT
upset *adj* feeling or showing uncomfortable feelings of uncertainty — see NERVOUS 1
upset *n* an act or instance of the order of things being disturbed <the move to a new town is just the latest in a series of *upsets* for my family over the last year>
synonyms derangement, dislocation, disruption, disturbance
related words convulsion, revolution, upheaval
upset *vb* **1** to trouble the mind of; to make uneasy — see DISTURB 1
2 to turn on one's side or upside down — see CAPSIZE
3 to undo the proper order or arrangement of — see DISORDER
upsetting *adj* causing worry or anxiety — see TROUBLESOME
upshot *n* a condition or occurrence traceable to a cause — see EFFECT 1
upside–down *adj* lacking in order, neatness, and often cleanliness — see MESSY
upstanding *adj* **1** following the accepted rules of moral conduct — see HONORABLE 1
2 rising straight up — see ERECT
upsweep *vb* to move or extend upward — see ASCEND
uptight *adj* feeling or showing uncomfortable feelings of uncertainty — see NERVOUS 1
up–to–date *adj* **1** being or involving the latest methods, concepts, information, or styles — see MODERN
2 having information especially as a result of study or experience — see FAMILIAR 2
upturn *vb* to move or extend upward — see ASCEND
urbane *adj* having or showing very polished and worldly manners — see SUAVE
urbanize *vb* to accustom to the ways of the city — see CITIFY
urchin *n* an appealingly mischievous person — see SCAMP 1
urge *n* a strong wish for something — see DESIRE
urge *vb* to try to persuade (someone) through earnest appeals to follow a course of action <our teacher *urged* us to do a good job on the assignment>
synonyms egg (on), encourage, exhort, goad, press, prod, prompt
related words drive, propel, spur, stimulate; hurry, hustle, push, rush; beseech, implore, importune; blandish, cajole, coax, soft-soap, wheedle; high-pressure, nag, needle, pressure; foment, incite, instigate, provoke, stir (up)
near antonyms deter, discourage, dissuade; brake, check, constrain, curb, hold back, inhibit, restrain
urgent *adj* needing immediate attention — see ACUTE 2
usable *adj* **1** capable of or suitable for being used for a particular purpose <although the spade was *usable* as a snow shovel, it didn't do a very good job>
synonyms available, employable, exploitable, fit, functional, operable, practicable, serviceable, useful
related words applicable, relevant; doable, feasible; reusable
near antonyms outdated, outmoded
antonyms impracticable, inoperable, nonfunctional, unavailable, unemployable, unusable
2 capable of being put to use or account — see PRACTICAL 1
usage *n* the act or practice of employing something for a particular purpose — see USE 1
use *n* **1** the act or practice of employing something for a particular purpose <the *use* of boom boxes was strictly prohibited in the park>
synonyms application, employment, exercise, operation, play, usage
related words exertion; reuse
near antonyms disuse
2 the capacity for being useful for some purpose <the broken grill wasn't going to be of much *use* in cooking the hamburgers>
synonyms account, avail, service, serviceability, serviceableness, usefulness, utility
related words advantage, benefit, gain; aid, assistance, help; applicability, appropriateness, fitness, relevance; profit, value, worth
near antonyms inapplicability, inappropriateness
antonyms uselessness, worthlessness
3 positive regard for something — see LIKING
use *vb* **1** to put into action or service <I think I'm going to need to *use* the large hammer for this project>
synonyms apply, employ, exercise, exploit, harness, operate, utilize
related words handle, manipulate, wield; direct, run, work; recycle, reuse
phrases draw on (*or* upon), make use of
near antonyms ignore, neglect; misapply, misuse

2 to behave toward in a stated way — see TREAT 1
3 to take unfair advantage of — see EXPLOIT 1

used *adj* being in the habit or custom — see ACCUSTOMED

useful *adj* **1** capable of being put to use or account — see PRACTICAL 1
2 capable of or suitable for being used for a particular purpose — see USABLE 1

usefulness *n* the capacity for being useful for some purpose — see USE 2

useless *adj* **1** not capable of being put to use or account — see IMPRACTICAL
2 producing no results — see FUTILE

user *n* a person who regularly uses drugs especially illegally — see DOPER

use up *vb* to make complete use of — see DEPLETE

usher *vb* to point out the way for (someone) especially from a position in front — see LEAD 1

usual *adj* **1** accepted, used, or practiced by most people — see CURRENT 1
2 being of the type that is encountered in the normal course of events — see ORDINARY 1
3 often observed or encountered — see COMMON 1

usually *adv* according to the usual course of things — see NATURALLY 2

usurp *vb* to take or make use of without authority or right — see APPROPRIATE 1

utensil *n* an article intended for use in work — see IMPLEMENT

utility *n* the capacity for being useful for some purpose — see USE 2

utilize *vb* to put into action or service — see USE 1

utmost *adj* **1** most distant from a center — see EXTREME 1
2 of the greatest or highest degree or quantity — see ULTIMATE 1
3 of the highest degree — see FULL 2

utopia *n* a place or state of great happiness — see PARADISE 1

utopian *n* one whose conduct is guided more by the image of perfection than by the real world — see IDEALIST

utter *adj* having no exceptions or restrictions — see ABSOLUTE 2

utter *vb* **1** to send forth using the vocal chords <she tried not to *utter* a sound as the doctor gave her a flu shot>
synonyms emit
related words blurt (out), ejaculate, exclaim; gasp, groan, heave, hoot, moan, pant, quaver, snarl, sob, sputter, squawk, squeak, squeal, stammer, stutter, whimper, yowl; mouth, whisper
2 to express (a thought or emotion) in words — see SAY 1

utterance *n* **1** an act, process, or means of putting something into words — see EXPRESSION 1
2 something that is said — see WORD 2

uttered *adj* created by the body's organs of sound — see VOCAL

utterly *adv* **1** to a full extent or degree — see FULLY 1
2 to a large extent or degree — see GREATLY 2

uttermost *adj* of the greatest or highest degree or quantity — see ULTIMATE 1

vacancy *n* **1** empty space <the vast *vacancy* that exists between our solar system and the nearest star having its own orbiting planets>
synonyms blank, blankness, emptiness, vacuity, void
related words nothingness; vacuum; bareness, barrenness, bleakness, desolateness, hollowness
near antonyms fullness, repleteness
2 the quality or state of being empty <the *vacancy* of the cavernous gymnasium was eerily apparent to me as I shot baskets alone>
synonyms bareness, emptiness, vacuity
related words hollowness; blankness, vacuum, void; barrenness, bleakness, desolateness; availability, clearness, openness; depletion, dryness, exhaustion
near antonyms completeness; abundance, fatness, repleteness
antonyms fullness

vacant *adj* **1** lacking contents that could or should be present — see EMPTY 1
2 not being in a state of use, activity, or employment — see INACTIVE 2
3 not expressing any emotion — see BLANK 1

vacate *vb* to remove the contents of — see EMPTY

vacated *adj* left unoccupied or unused — see ABANDONED

vacation *n* a period during which the usual routine of school or work is suspended <we take a *vacation* at the beach for a week every year>
synonyms break, holiday [*chiefly British*], leave, recess
related words furlough, liberty; breather, relaxation, respite, rest; interim, intermission, interval; feast, holy day, legal holiday; honeymoon; idling, loafing, lounging, slacking off
near antonyms routine, work

vacation *vb* to take or spend a vacation <Sue is hoping to *vacation* in Spain this summer>
synonyms holiday
related words escape, get away; break, ease up, let up, relax, rest; bum, goldbrick, idle, loaf, lounge, slack off
near antonyms drudge, endeavor, grub, hump, hustle, labor, moil, peg (away), plod, plow, plug, slave, slog, strain, strive, struggle, sweat, toil, travail, work

vacillate *vb* to show uncertainty about the right course of action — see HESITATE

vacillation *n* the act or an instance of pausing because of uncertainty about the right course of action — see HESITATION

vacuity *n* **1** empty space — see VACANCY 1
2 the quality or state of being empty — see VACANCY 2

3 the quality or state of lacking intelligence or quickness of mind — see STUPIDITY 1

vacuous *adj* not having or showing an ability to absorb ideas readily — see STUPID 1

vagabond *adj* traveling from place to place — see ITINERANT

vagabond *n* **1** a homeless wanderer who may beg or steal for a living — see TRAMP

2 a person who roams about without a fixed route or destination — see NOMAD

vagary *n* a sudden impulsive and apparently unmotivated idea or action — see WHIM

vagrant *adj* traveling from place to place — see ITINERANT

vagrant *n* a homeless wanderer who may beg or steal for a living — see TRAMP

vague *adj* **1** not clearly expressed ⟨Johnny gave as *vague* a reply to the test question as he could, hoping for partial credit⟩

synonyms fuzzy, indefinite, unclear

related words ambiguous, cryptic, dark, enigmatic (*also* enigmatical), equivocal, murky, nebulous, obscure, unintelligible; bleary, dim, faint, foggy, hazy, indeterminate, indistinguishable, uncertain, undefinable, undefined, undetermined; inexplicable, inscrutable, mysterious; baffling, bewildering, confounding, confusing, mystifying, perplexing, puzzling, unfathomable

near antonyms candid, direct, forthright, foursquare, frank, honest, open, openhearted, outspoken, plainspoken, straight, straightforward, unguarded; obvious, plain, unambiguous, understandable, unequivocal; comprehensible, fathomable, intelligible; defined, distinct; blatant, patent, unmistakable

antonyms clear, definite, explicit, specific

2 not seen or understood clearly — see FAINT 1

vain *adj* **1** having too high an opinion of oneself — see CONCEITED

2 producing no results — see FUTILE

vainglorious *adj* having too high an opinion of oneself — see CONCEITED

vaingloriousness *n* an often unjustified feeling of being pleased with oneself or with one's situation or achievements — see COMPLACENCE

vainglory *n* an often unjustified feeling of being pleased with oneself or with one's situation or achievements — see COMPLACENCE

vainness *n* an often unjustified feeling of being pleased with oneself or with one's situation or achievements — see COMPLACENCE

vale *n* an area of lowland between hills or mountains — see VALLEY

valedictory *adj* given, taken, or performed at parting — see PARTING

valiant *adj* feeling or displaying no fear by temperament — see BRAVE

valid *adj* **1** according to the rules of logic — see LOGICAL 1

2 based on sound reasoning or information — see GOOD 1

validate *vb* **1** to give evidence or testimony to the truth or factualness of — see CONFIRM

2 to show the existence or truth of by evidence — see PROVE 1

validation *n* something presented in support of the truth or accuracy of a claim — see PROOF

valley *n* an area of lowland between hills or mountains ⟨the *valley* will be the first to flood if the river rises⟩

synonyms dale, hollow, vale

related words canyon, dell, depression, dingle, glen, ravine, rift valley; basin, bowl

near antonyms alp, mount, peak; mountain range; mountaintop, pinnacle, precipice, summit

valor *n* strength of mind to carry on in spite of danger — see COURAGE

valorous *adj* feeling or displaying no fear by temperament — see BRAVE

valuable *adj* commanding a large price — see COSTLY

valuation *n* **1** the act of placing a value on the nature, character, or quality of something — see ESTIMATE 1

2 the amount of money for which something will find a buyer — see VALUE 1

3 the relative usefulness or importance of something as judged by specific qualities — see WORTH 1

value *n* **1** the amount of money for which something will find a buyer ⟨the real *value* of that house is close to a million dollars⟩

synonyms market value, valuation, worth

related words charge, cost, fee, figure, price; appraisal, assessment, estimate, estimation, evaluation; face value, list price, unit price

2 a quality that gives something special worth — see EXCELLENCE 2

3 the relative usefulness or importance of something as judged by specific qualities — see WORTH 1

value *vb* **1** to hold dear — see LOVE 1

2 to make an approximate or tentative judgment regarding — see ESTIMATE 1

valueless *adj* having no usefulness — see WORTHLESS

valve *n* a fixture for controlling the flow of a liquid — see FAUCET

vandal *n* a person who damages or destroys property on purpose ⟨a group of *vandals* broke into school and painted graffiti on the walls⟩

synonyms defacer

related words demolisher, desecrater (*or* desecrator), despoiler, destroyer, dynamiter, ravager, ruiner, saboteur, wrecker; looter, pillager, plunderer, spoiler

near antonyms conserver, preserver, protector, saver

vandalism *n* deliberate damaging or destroying of another's property ⟨anyone guilty of *vandalism* to school property will be expelled⟩

synonyms defacement

related words demolishing, demolishment, desecrating, desecration, despoiling, despoilment, destruction, ravaging, ruin, ruination, wrecking; sabotage; looting, pillaging, plunder, plundering, sacking

near antonyms conservation, preservation, protection, saving

vandalize *vb* to deliberately cause the damage or destruction of another's property ⟨he decided to *vandalize* the store because the owner had kicked him out⟩

synonyms deface

related words desecrate, violate; break, damage, despoil, harm, hurt, impair, mar, shatter, spoil; demolish, destroy, devastate, ravage, raze, ruin, scourge, smash, tear down, waste, wipe out, wreck; sabotage; loot, pillage, plunder, sack

near antonyms conserve, preserve, protect, save; build, rebuild

vanguard *n* the leading or most important part of a movement — see FOREFRONT

vanish *vb* to cease to be visible — see DISAPPEAR

vanished *adj* no longer existing — see EXTINCT

vanity *n* an often unjustified feeling of being pleased with oneself or with one's situation or achievements — see COMPLACENCE

vanquish *vb* to bring under one's control by force of arms — see CONQUER 1

vanquisher *n* one that defeats an enemy or opponent — see VICTOR 1

vanquishing *n* the act or process of bringing someone or something under one's control — see CONQUEST

vantage *n* the more favorable condition or position in a competition — see ADVANTAGE 1

variable *adj* **1** capable of being readily changed — see FLEXIBLE 1
2 likely to change frequently, suddenly, or unexpectedly — see FICKLE 1

variance *n* a lack of agreement or harmony — see DISCORD

variation *n* the act, process, or result of making different — see CHANGE

varicolored *adj* marked by a variety of usually vivid colors — see COLORFUL

varied *adj* consisting of many things of different sorts — see MISCELLANEOUS

variegated *adj* **1** marked by a variety of usually vivid colors — see COLORFUL
2 marked with spots — see SPOTTED 1

variety *n* **1** the quality or state of being composed of many different elements or types ⟨the sheer *variety* of the city's ethnic restaurants was dazzling⟩
synonyms assortment, diverseness, diversity, miscellaneousness, variousness
related words heterogeneousness; disparateness, disparity, dissimilarity, distinction, distinctiveness, distinctness, unlikeness
near antonyms homogeneity, likeness, sameness, similarity; fewness, paucity
2 an unorganized collection or mixture of various things — see MISCELLANY 1

variousness *n* the quality or state of being composed of many different elements or types — see VARIETY 1

varlet *n* a mean, evil, or unprincipled person — see VILLAIN

vary *vb* **1** to be unlike; to not be the same — see DIFFER 1
2 to make different in some way — see CHANGE 1
3 to occur within a continuous range of variation — see RUN 4
4 to pass from one form, state, or level to another — see CHANGE 2

varying *adj* not staying constant — see UNEVEN 2

vast *adj* unusually large — see HUGE

vastly *adv* to a large extent or degree — see GREATLY 2

vastness *n* the quality or state of being very large — see IMMENSITY

vasty *adj* unusually large — see HUGE

[1]**vault** *n* an underground burial chamber — see CRYPT

[2]**vault** *n* an act of leaping into the air — see JUMP 1

vault *vb* to propel oneself upward or forward into the air — see JUMP 1

veer *vb* **1** to change one's course or direction — see TURN 3
2 to change the course or direction of (something) — see TURN 2
3 to depart abruptly from a straight line or course — see SWERVE 1

vegetation *n* green leaves or plants — see GREENERY 1

vehemence *n* **1** the quality or state of being forceful (as in expression) ⟨the *vehemence* in her voice when she said that she never gossiped surprised me⟩
synonyms aggressiveness, assertiveness, emphasis, fierceness, forcefulness, intensity, vigorousness
related words potency, power, strength; eloquence; fervency, insistence, passion, warmth; absoluteness, clearness, incisiveness, plainness
near antonyms ambiguity, equivocation
antonyms feebleness, mildness, weakness
2 depth of feeling — see ARDOR 1

vehement *adj* **1** marked by or uttered with forcefulness — see EMPHATIC 1
2 extreme in degree, power, or effect — see INTENSE
3 having or expressing great depth of feeling — see FERVENT

vehicle *n* **1** something used to achieve an end — see AGENT 1
2 something used to carry goods or passengers — see CONVEYANCE

veil *n* something that covers or conceals like a piece of cloth — see CLOAK 1

veil *vb* **1** to keep secret or shut off from view — see [1]HIDE 2
2 to surround or cover closely — see ENFOLD 1

vein *n* a distinctive way of putting ideas into words — see STYLE 1

veld *or* **veldt** *n* a broad area of level or rolling treeless country — see PLAIN

velocity *n* a high rate of movement or performance — see SPEED

velvety *adj* smooth or delicate in appearance or feel — see SOFT 2

venal *adj* open to improper influence and especially bribery ⟨that judge is known for being *venal* and easily bought⟩
synonyms bribable, corruptible, purchasable
related words hack, mercenary; crooked, cutthroat, dishonest, unethical, unprincipled, unscrupulous; corrupt, debased, debauched, degenerate, degraded, demoralized, depraved, dissipated, dissolute, perverse, perverted, warped; bad, evil, immoral, iniquitous, nefarious, sinful, vicious, wicked
near antonyms ethical, honest, principled; good, moral, righteous, virtuous
antonyms incorruptible, uncorruptible

vend *vb* to offer for sale to the public — see MARKET

vendor *also* **vender** *n* the person in a business deal who hands over an item in exchange for money ⟨we're thinking of making a deal with that other software *vendor*⟩
synonyms dealer, merchandiser, seller
related words auctioneer, concessionaire; blackmarketer, bootlegger, fence, fencer, hustler, smuggler, trader; distributor, retailer; sacrificer; wholesaler; hawker, huckster, peddler (*also* pedlar); salesclerk, salesman, salesperson, saleswom-

an; exporter, handler; bargainer, haggler, horse trader, palterer
near antonyms consumer, end user, user
antonyms buyer, purchaser

veneer *n* an outer part or layer — see EXTERIOR

venerable *adj* **1** deserving honor and respect especially by reason of age ⟨the *venerable* old man was a cherished source of advice and wisdom for the villagers⟩
synonyms hallowed, revered, reverend, venerated
related words honorable, reputable, respectable; honored, respected, reverenced; admirable, estimable, redoubtable; good, moral, righteous
near antonyms bad, discreditable, disgraceful, dishonorable, disreputable, ignominious, infamous, loose, notorious, shameful; immoral, seamy, shady, sordid, unsavory, vile, wicked; base, contemptible, despicable, detestable, dirty, low, mean, wretched
2 dating or surviving from the distant past — see ANCIENT 1

venerate *vb* to offer honor or respect to (someone) as a divine power — see WORSHIP 1

venerated *adj* deserving honor and respect especially by reason of age — see VENERABLE 1

vengeance *n* the act or an instance of paying back an injury with an injury — see REVENGE

vengeful *adj* likely to seek revenge — see VINDICTIVE

venial *adj* worthy of forgiveness ⟨stealing pencils is a *venial* offense⟩
synonyms excusable, forgivable, pardonable, remittable
related words justifiable, redeemable; allowable; insignificant, minor, trifling, trivial; harmless, tolerable
near antonyms abominable, criminal, damning, evil, heinous; sinful, vile, wicked
antonyms inexcusable, mortal, unforgivable, unpardonable

venom *n* **1** a substance that by chemical action can kill or injure a living thing — see POISON
2 the desire to cause pain for the satisfaction of doing harm — see MALICE

venomous *adj* containing or contaminated with a substance capable of injuring or killing a living thing — see POISONOUS

vent *vb* **1** to find emotional release for — see TAKE OUT 1
2 to make known (as an idea, emotion, or opinion) — see EXPRESS 1
3 to throw or give off — see EMIT 1

ventilate *vb* to make known (as an idea, emotion, or opinion) — see EXPRESS 1

venture *n* a risky undertaking — see GAMBLE

venture *vb* **1** to place in danger — see ENDANGER
2 to take a chance on — see RISK 1

venturesome *adj* **1** inclined or willing to take risks — see BOLD 1
2 involving potential loss or injury — see DANGEROUS

venturous *adj* inclined or willing to take risks — see BOLD 1

veracious *adj* **1** being in the habit of telling the truth — see TRUTHFUL
2 following an original exactly — see FAITHFUL 2

veracity *n* **1** devotion to telling the truth — see HONESTY 1
2 the quality or state of being very accurate — see PRECISION

verbal *adj* **1** of or relating to words or language ⟨the child didn't yet have the *verbal* skills needed to tell the doctor about the pain he was experiencing⟩
synonyms lexical, linguistic
related words communicative, conversational
2 made or carried on through speaking rather than in writing ⟨a *verbal* agreement carries less force than a written contract⟩
synonyms oral, spoken, unwritten
related words implicit, informal; articulated, verbalized; given, pronounced, said, sounded, stated, told, voiced
near antonyms explicit, formal
antonyms written

verbalize *vb* to express (a thought or emotion) in words — see SAY 1

verbatim *adv* in the same words ⟨you can't just copy the encyclopedia article *verbatim* for your report—that's plagiarism⟩
synonyms directly, exactly
related words accurately, precisely; identically; literally
phrases word for word
near antonyms basically, essentially; carelessly, freely, imprecisely, inaccurately, loosely
antonyms inexactly

verbiage *n* the use of too many words to express an idea ⟨teachers loathe the *verbiage* that students resort to in order to pad a paper⟩
synonyms circumlocution, diffuseness, longwindedness, prolixity, redundancy, verboseness, verbosity, windiness, wordiness
related words circuitousness, circularity; tautology; reiteration, repetition, repetitiousness; embellishment, embroidering, exaggeration, hyperbole
near antonyms brevity, briefness, compactness, conciseness, crispness, pithiness, succinctness, terseness

verbose *adj* using or containing more words than necessary to express an idea — see WORDY

verboseness *n* the use of too many words to express an idea — see VERBIAGE

verbosity *n* the use of too many words to express an idea — see VERBIAGE

verdant *adj* covered with a thick, healthy natural growth — see LUSH 1

verdict *n* **1** a position arrived at after consideration — see DECISION 1
2 an idea that is believed to be true or valid without positive knowledge — see OPINION 1

verdure *n* green leaves or plants — see GREENERY 1

verge (on)*vb* **1** to be adjacent to — see ADJOIN 1
2 to come very close to being — see BORDER (ON)

verge *n* the line or relatively narrow space that marks the outer limit of something — see BORDER 1

verging *adj* having a border in common — see ADJACENT

verifiable *adj* capable of being proven as true or real ⟨we're not sure whether that's a *verifiable* hypothesis⟩ ⟨you need a *verifiable* note from your doctor to be excused from gym class⟩
synonyms confirmable, demonstrable, provable, supportable, sustainable
related words certifiable, documentable, warrantable; excusable, justifiable; alleged, assumed,

conjectured, guessed, presumed, surmised, suspected
near antonyms debatable, disputable, refutable
antonyms insupportable, unsupportable
verify *vb* to give evidence or testimony to the truth or factualness of — see CONFIRM
verifying *adj* serving to give support to the truth or factualness of something — see CORROBORATIVE
verily *adv* **1** to tell the truth — see ACTUALLY 1
2 not merely this but also — see EVEN
veritably *adv* in actual fact — see VERY 2
verity *n* **1** agreement with fact or reality — see TRUTH
2 devotion to telling the truth — see HONESTY 1
vernacular *adj* used in or suitable for speech and not formal writing — see COLLOQUIAL 1
versatile *adj* able to do many different kinds of things ⟨a *versatile* baseball player can play any position⟩ ⟨this tool is *versatile* enough to serve as a wrench or pliers⟩
synonyms adaptable, all-around (*also* all-round), protean, universal
related words multipurpose; well-rounded; able, ace, adept, experienced, expert, masterful, skilled, skillful; adjustable, alterable, changeable, elastic, flexible, fluid, malleable, modifiable, variable
near antonyms limited; amateur, inexperienced
verse *n* **1** a composition using rhythm and often rhyme to create a lyrical effect — see POEM
2 writing that uses rhythm, vivid language, and often rhyme to provoke an emotional response — see POETRY 1
versed *adj* **1** having information especially as a result of study or experience — see FAMILIAR 2
2 having or showing exceptional knowledge, experience, or skill in a field of endeavor — see PROFICIENT
versifier *n* a person who writes poetry — see POET
vertebral column *n* a column of bones supporting the trunk of a vertebrate animal — see SPINE
vertical *adj* rising straight up — see ERECT
verve *adj* active strength of body or mind — see VIGOR 1
very *adj* **1** being one and not another — see SAME 2
2 being this and no more — see MERE
3 existing in fact and not merely as a possibility — see ACTUAL
very *adv* **1** to a great degree ⟨that was a *very* brave thing to do⟩
synonyms awful, awfully, beastly, deadly, especially, exceedingly (*also* exceeding), extra, extremely, far, frightfully, full, greatly, heavily, highly, hugely, jolly, mightily, mighty, mortally, most, much, particularly, rattling, real, right, so, something, super, terribly, too, whacking
related words completely, entirely, purely, thoroughly, totally, utterly; eminently, exceptionally; considerably, extensively, significantly, substantially; appreciably, discernibly, noticeably, palpably; abundantly, plentifully; astronomically, grandly, monstrously, monumentally
phrases by far, far and away, good and, in particular
near antonyms meagerly, scantily; barely, hardly, just, marginally, minimally, scarcely
antonyms little, negligibly, nominally, slightly
2 in actual fact ⟨the *very* same thing happened to me⟩
synonyms actually, authentically, genuinely, really, veritably
related words accurately, exactly, just, precisely, right, sharp, smack-dab, squarely; almost, nearly, practically; literally, truly
phrases in truth
near antonyms apparently, ostensibly, outwardly, seemingly
antonyms professedly, supposedly
vessel *n* **1** a large craft for travel by water — see SHIP
2 a small buoyant structure for travel on water — see BOAT 1
3 a usually circular utensil for holding something (as food) — see DISH
4 something into which a liquid or smaller objects can be put for storage or transportation — see CONTAINER
vest *vb* to put (something) into the possession or safekeeping of another — see GIVE 2
vestibule *n* the entrance room of a building — see HALL 1
vestige *n* a tiny often physical indication of something lost or vanished ⟨a few strange words carved on a tree were the only *vestige* of the lost colony of Roanoke⟩
synonyms relic, shadow, trace
related words memento, remembrance, reminder; artifact; afterimage, aftertaste; balance, oddment, remainder, remnant, scrap, scraping(s); leavings, remains, residual, residue, rest
vestry *n* a room in a church building for sacred furnishings (as vestments) — see SACRISTY
vet *n* a person with long experience in a specified area — see VETERAN
veteran *adj* having or showing exceptional knowledge, experience, or skill in a field of endeavor — see PROFICIENT
veteran *n* a person with long experience in a specified area ⟨as a *veteran* of politics, she is often consulted by eager young hopefuls⟩
synonyms old hand, old-timer, vet
related words war-horse; expert, master, pro, professional
near antonyms apprentice, cub; boot, novitiate; amateur, dilettante; learner, student, trainee; candidate, entrant, probationer
antonyms beginner, colt, fledgling, freshman, greenhorn, neophyte, newcomer, novice, recruit, rookie, tenderfoot, tyro
veto *n* an order that something not be done or used — see PROHIBITION 2
veto *vb* to reject by or as if by a vote — see NEGATIVE 1
vex *vb* to disturb the peace of mind of (someone) especially by repeated disagreeable acts — see IRRITATE 1
vexation *n* **1** the act of making unwelcome intrusions upon another — see ANNOYANCE 1
2 the feeling of impatience or anger caused by another's repeated disagreeable acts — see ANNOYANCE 2
vexatious *adj* causing annoyance — see ANNOYING
vexing *adj* causing annoyance — see ANNOYING
via *prep* along the way of — see BY 1
viable *adj* capable of being done or carried out — see POSSIBLE 1
viands *n pl* substances intended to be eaten — see FOOD
vibrancy *n* the quality or state of having abundant or intense activity — see VITALITY 1

vibrant *adj* **1** marked by much life, movement, or activity — see ALIVE 2
2 marked by conspicuously full and rich sounds or tones — see RESONANT

vibrate *vb* to make a series of small irregular or violent movements — see SHAKE 1

vibration *n* a series of slight movements by a body back and forth or from side to side ⟨the *vibration* of the floor caused by thundering feet in the hallway⟩
synonyms jiggling, oscillation, quivering, shaking, shuddering, trembling, twitching
related words jiggle, palpitation, shake, shudder, tremor, twitch

vice *n* **1** immoral conduct or practices harmful or offensive to society ⟨that section of the city is legendary for crime and *vice*⟩
synonyms corruption, debauchery, depravity, immorality, iniquity, licentiousness, sin
related words bad, badness, blackness, evil, evildoing, ill, wickedness, wrong, villainy; atrociousness, evilness, heinousness, nefariousness, sinfulness, unscrupulousness, viciousness, vileness; devilry (*or* deviltry), fiendishness; corruptness, debasement, degeneracy, degeneration, depravedness, dissolution; indecency, lasciviousness, lewdness, looseness, perversion; abomination, anathema, taboo (*also* tabu); criminality, reprehensibleness; baseness, despicableness, dirtiness, lowness, meanness; lousiness, miserableness, wretchedness
near antonyms good, right; honesty, honor, integrity, legitimacy, probity, rectitude, scrupulousness, uprightness; goodness, righteousness, virtuousness; blamelessness; chastity, innocence, perfection, pureness, purity, spotlessness; cleanness, correctness, decency, decorousness, propriety, rightness, seemliness
antonyms morality, virtue
2 a defect in character — see FAULT 1

vicious *adj* **1** extreme in degree, power, or effect — see INTENSE
2 having or showing the desire to inflict severe pain and suffering on others — see CRUEL 1
3 not conforming to a high moral standard; morally unacceptable — see BAD 2
4 violently unfriendly or aggressive in disposition — see FIERCE 1

viciously *adv* in a mean or spiteful manner — see NASTILY

viciousness *n* **1** the desire to cause pain for the satisfaction of doing harm — see MALICE
2 the willful infliction of pain and suffering on others — see CRUELTY

victim *n* **1** a person or thing harmed, lost, or destroyed — see CASUALTY 1
2 a person or thing that is the object of abuse, criticism, or ridicule — see TARGET 1
3 something offered to a god — see SACRIFICE

victimize *vb* to rob by the use of trickery or threats — see FLEECE

victor *n* **1** one that defeats an enemy or opponent ⟨the computer is usually the *victor* in a chess match against a human opponent⟩
synonyms beater, conqueror, master, subduer, trimmer, vanquisher, whipper, winner
related words champion, finalist; ruler, subjugator
near antonyms pushover, quitter; failure, flop, washout
antonyms loser
2 the person who comes in first in a competition — see CHAMPION 1

victory *n* an instance of defeating an enemy or opponent ⟨with great effort, our team managed an upset *victory* in the final moments⟩
synonyms triumph, win
related words conquest, mastery, subjugation, vanquishing; landslide, shutout, sweep; success; takeover
near antonyms upset; collapse, debacle (*also* débâcle), failure, fizzle, flop, folding, nonsuccess, washout; decline, slip, slump, wane; lurch, setback
antonyms beating, defeat, licking, loss, overthrow, rout, shellacking, trimming, whipping

victuals *n pl* substances intended to be eaten — see FOOD

vie *vb* to engage in a contest — see COMPETE

view *n* **1** all that can be seen from a certain point ⟨the *view* of the mountains from the inn's porch is spectacular⟩
synonyms lookout, outlook, panorama, prospect, vista
related words landscape, scene, scenery; ken, sight
2 an idea that is believed to be true or valid without positive knowledge — see OPINION 1
3 an instance of looking especially briefly — see LOOK 2

view *vb* to make note of (something) through the use of one's eyes — see SEE 1

viewpoint *n* a way of looking at or thinking about something — see POINT OF VIEW

vigilance *n* the act or state of being constantly attentive and responsive to signs of opportunity, activity, or danger ⟨eternal *vigilance* is the price of freedom⟩
synonyms alertness, attentiveness, lookout, surveillance, watch, watchfulness
related words aliveness, awareness, consciousness, sensitivity; heedfulness, observance, observation; sleeplessness, wakefulness; care, carefulness, caution, chariness, wariness; preparation, readiness
near antonyms absentmindedness, absorption, abstraction, daydreaming, daze, distraction; engrossment, obliviousness, preoccupation; unawareness, unconsciousness; carelessness, heedlessness, inattention, inattentiveness; unwariness

vigilant *adj* paying close attention usually for the purpose of anticipating approaching danger or opportunity — see ALERT 1

vigilante *n* one who inflicts punishment in return for an injury or offense — see NEMESIS 1

vigor *n* **1** active strength of body or mind ⟨she was picked for the soccer team because of her *vigor* and enthusiasm⟩
synonyms bounce, dash, drive, energy, esprit, ginger, go, hardihood, life, pep, punch, sap, snap, starch, verve, vim, vitality, zing, zip
related words animation, briskness, jauntiness, liveliness, spiritedness, sprightliness, vivaciousness, vivacity; ardor, fervor, fire, passion, zeal; main, might, muscle, potency, power, puissance, strength; brawniness, fitness, hardiness, huskiness, virility; haleness, health, healthiness, soundness, wellness
near antonyms indolence, laziness; debilitation, debility, delicacy, delicateness, disablement, enfeeblement, faintness, feebleness, frailness, frailty, impotence, infirmity, powerlessness, puniness,

slightness, softness, tenderness, weakness; enervation, exhaustion, prostration
antonyms lethargy, listlessness, sluggishness
2 the ability to exert effort for the accomplishment of a task — see POWER 2
vigorous *adj* **1** having active strength of body or mind ⟨he remains healthy and *vigorous* despite being over eighty years old⟩
synonyms dynamic, energetic, flush, gingery, lusty, peppy, red-blooded, robust, vital
related words animated, lively, spirited, sprightly, vivacious; energized, enlivened, invigorated, vitalized; firm, fortified, mettlesome, mighty, powerful, puissant, strong; refreshed, rejuvenated, revitalized; able-bodied, beefy, brawny, fit, fortified, hardy, husky, rugged, stalwart, stout, strapping, sturdy, tough; hale, healthy, sound; capable, competent
near antonyms delicate, effete, enervated, faint, feeble, frail, infirm, weak, weakened; impotent, powerless, prostrate, prostrated, sapped, tired; indolent, lackadaisical, languid, lazy; invertebrate, nerveless, soft, spineless, wimpy; ill, unhealthy, unsound, unwell; broken-down, debilitated, decrepit, disabled, wasted, worn-out
antonyms lethargic, listless, sluggish, torpid
2 able to withstand hardship, strain, or exposure — see HARDY 1
3 marked by or uttered with forcefulness — see EMPHATIC 1
4 not showing weakness or uncertainty — see FIRM 1
vigorously *adv* in a vigorous and forceful manner — see HARD 3
vigorousness *n* the quality or state of being forceful (as in expression) — see VEHEMENCE 1
vile *adj* **1** not conforming to a high moral standard; morally unacceptable — see BAD 2
2 not following or in accordance with standards of honor and decency — see IGNOBLE 2
3 unpleasant to look at — see UGLY 1
vileness *n* the state or quality of being utterly evil — see ENORMITY 1
vilification *n* the making of false statements that damage another's reputation — see SLANDER
vilify *vb* to make untrue and harmful statements about — see SLANDER
vilifying *n* the making of false statements that damage another's reputation — see SLANDER
villa *n* a large impressive residence — see MANSION
villager *n* a person who lives in a town on a permanent basis — see BURGHER
villain *n* a mean, evil, or unprincipled person ⟨only a heartless *villain* would kidnap a baby for ransom⟩
synonyms beast, brute, devil, evildoer, fiend, heavy, knave, miscreant, monster, no-good, rapscallion, rascal, reprobate, rogue, savage, scalawag (*or* scallywag), scamp, scoundrel, varlet, wretch
related words blackguard; criminal, crook, culprit, felon, lawbreaker, malefactor, offender, transgressor; perpetrator, sinner, trespasser, wrongdoer; cad, heel; bravo, desperado, outlaw; convict, jailbird; assassin, cutthroat, gangster, gunman, hoodlum, racketeer, ruffian, thug; ne'er-do-well, trash
near antonyms angel, saint; hero
villainous *adj* not conforming to a high moral standard; morally unacceptable — see BAD 2
villainously *adv* in a mean or spiteful manner — see NASTILY
villainy *n* that which is morally unacceptable — see EVIL
vim *n* active strength of body or mind — see VIGOR 1
vindicate *vb* **1** to free from a charge of wrongdoing — see EXCULPATE
2 to give evidence or testimony to the truth or factualness of — see CONFIRM
vindicating *adj* serving to give support to the truth or factualness of something — see CORROBORATIVE
vindictive *adj* likely to seek revenge ⟨be careful not to annoy the *vindictive* old woman who lives down the street⟩
synonyms revengeful, vengeful
related words avenging; resentful, uncharitable, unforgiving; catty, cruel, despiteful, hateful, malevolent, malicious, malign, malignant, mean, nasty, sadistic, spiteful, vicious, virulent; grim, implacable, merciless, relentless, unrelenting; baleful, baneful, evil; harsh, hostile, inimical
near antonyms charitable, forgiving, merciful, relenting; benevolent, benign, benignant, loving; brotherly, compassionate, good, good-hearted, kind, kindhearted, kindly, sympathetic, warm, warmhearted; altruistic, humane, humanitarian, philanthropic; sweet, tender, tenderhearted; high-minded, magnanimous, noble
vinegary *adj* causing or characterized by the one of the four basic taste sensations that is produced chiefly by acids — see SOUR 1
violate *vb* **1** to fail to keep ⟨you *violated* the school rule against swearing at sporting events⟩
synonyms breach, break, infringe, transgress
related words disobey, rebel; brush off, disregard, ignore, overlook, overpass, pass over, tune out, wink (at); dismiss, pooh-pooh (*also* pooh), scorn, shrug off; defy, resist, withstand
near antonyms defer (to), serve, submit (to), surrender (to), yield (to); attend, hear, heed, listen (to), mark, note, notice, regard, watch
antonyms comply (with), conform (to), follow, mind, obey, observe
2 to treat (a sacred place or object) shamefully or with great disrespect — see DESECRATE
violation *n* **1** a breaking of a moral or legal code — see OFFENSE 1
2 a failure to uphold the requirements of law, duty, or obligation — see BREACH 1
violence *n* the use of brute strength to cause harm to a person or property ⟨the police believe that the woman died of natural causes rather than as a result of *violence*⟩
synonyms force, foul play
related words coercion, compulsion, constraint, duress, pressure; damage, detriment, harm, hurt, impairment, injury; crippling, maiming, mayhem, mutilation; assault, attack, bashing, battering, battery, batting, beating, belting, bludgeoning, buffeting, clubbing, drubbing, flogging, hammering, lacing, licking, mauling, pelting, pommeling, pounding, pummeling, thrashing, thumping, walloping, whaling, whipping; onslaught, outbreak, outrage, paroxysm, rampage, revolt, riot, shock, terror, threat, turbulence, upheaval, uproar; browbeating, bulldozing, bullying
near antonyms pacifism
antonyms nonviolence

violent *adj* **1** marked by bursts of destructive force or intense activity ⟨a *violent* fight that left several people badly hurt⟩
synonyms explosive, ferocious, fierce, furious, hot, rabid, rough, stormy, tempestuous, turbulent, volcanic
related words brutal, savage, vicious; antagonistic, hostile; aggressive, assertive, bellicose, belligerent, combative, contentious, gladiatorial, quarrelsome; frantic, frenzied, mad; destructive, ruinous
near antonyms calm, pacific, serene, tranquil; nonbelligerent, unaggressive, unassertive
antonyms nonviolent, peaceable, peaceful
2 extreme in degree, power, or effect — see INTENSE
3 marked by great and often stressful excitement or activity — see FURIOUS 1

VIP *n* a person who is widely known and usually much talked about — see CELEBRITY 1

viper *n* a limbless reptile with a long body — see SNAKE 1

virago *n* a bad-tempered scolding woman — see SHREW

virgin *adj* **1** never having had sexual relations ⟨*virgin* boys are sometimes unfairly teased⟩
synonyms maiden, virginal
related words chaste, modest, pure; innocent, untouched; abstinent, celibate; unmarried, unwed
2 being in an original and unused or unspoiled state — see FRESH 1

virginal *adj* never having had sexual relations — see VIRGIN 1

virile *adj* considered characteristic of or appropriate for men — see MASCULINE

virility *n* the set of qualities considered appropriate for or characteristic of men ⟨many cultures value *virility* as a sign of power⟩
synonyms manhood, manliness, masculinity
related words maleness; boyishness, mannishness, tomboyishness
near antonyms girlishness; femaleness; girlhood, maidenhood
antonyms femininity

virtually *adv* very close to but not completely — see ALMOST

virtue *n* **1** a quality that gives something special worth — see EXCELLENCE 2
2 conduct that conforms to an accepted standard of right and wrong — see MORALITY 1

virtuoso *adj* **1** accomplished with trained ability — see SKILLFUL
2 having or showing exceptional knowledge, experience, or skill in a field of endeavor — see PROFICIENT

virtuoso *n* a person with a high level of knowledge or skill in a field — see EXPERT

virtuous *adj* conforming to a high standard of morality or virtue — see GOOD 2

virtuously *adv* with purity of thought and deed — see PURELY

virtuousness *n* conduct that conforms to an accepted standard of right and wrong — see MORALITY 1

virulence *n* biting sharpness of feeling or expression — see ACRIMONY 1

virulent *adj* having or showing a desire to cause someone pain or suffering for the sheer enjoyment of it — see HATEFUL

virulently *adv* in a mean or spiteful manner — see NASTILY

visage *n* **1** facial appearance regarded as an indication of mood or feeling — see LOOK 1
2 the front part of the head — see FACE 1

viscera *n pl* the internal organs of the body — see GUT 1

viscid *adj* **1** being of a consistency that resists flow — see THICK 2
2 being of such a thick consistency as to readily cling to objects upon contact — see STICKY 1

viscosity *n* the degree to which a fluid can resist flowing — see CONSISTENCY

viscous *adj* **1** being of a consistency that resists flow — see THICK 2
2 being of such a thick consistency as to readily cling to objects upon contact — see STICKY 1

visible *adj* capable of being seen ⟨the *visible* light spectrum runs from red to violet⟩
synonyms apparent, observable, seeable, visual
related words external, outer, outward; detectable, discernible, noticeable, perceptible; clear, conspicuous, evident, eye-catching, manifest, obvious, plain, prominent, striking
near antonyms disappeared, dissolved, evanesced, evaporated, melted, vanished; imperceptible, inconspicuous, indistinct, unnoticeable; faint, insignificant, slight, vague; buried, concealed, covert, disguised, hidden, latent, obscure, shrouded
antonyms invisible, unseeable

vision *n* **1** a conception or image created by the imagination and having no objective reality — see FANTASY 1
2 a series of often striking pictures created by the imagination during sleep — see DREAM 1
3 the ability to see — see EYESIGHT
4 the soul of a dead person thought of especially as appearing to living people — see GHOST

vision *vb* to form a mental picture of — see IMAGINE 1

visionary *n* one whose conduct is guided more by the image of perfection than by the real world — see IDEALIST

visit *n* **1** a temporary residing as another's guest ⟨my aunt always looks forward to her week-long annual *visit* with her mother⟩
synonyms sojourn, stay
related words field trip; layover, stopover
2 a coming to see another briefly for social or business reasons — see CALL 2

visit *vb* **1** to make a social call upon ⟨the club ladies make a point of *visiting* everyone who moves into the neighborhood⟩
synonyms call (on *or* upon), see
related words look up, seek (out); frequent, hang out (at), haunt
phrases drop in on
near antonyms brush (off), cold-shoulder, ignore, snub
2 to reside as a temporary guest ⟨Johnny loves it when his friend Susie comes to *visit* for a month every summer⟩
synonyms sojourn, stay, tarry
related words frequent, hang out (at), haunt; inhabit, occupy
near antonyms abide, dwell, live, reside
3 to engage in casual or rambling conversation — see CHAT
4 to go to or spend time in often — see FREQUENT
5 to make a brief visit — see CALL 3

visitant *n* a person who visits another — see GUEST

visitation *n* a coming to see another briefly for social or business reasons — see CALL 2
visitor *n* a person who visits another — see GUEST 1
visor *also* **vizor** *n* the projecting front part of a hat or cap ⟨the *visor* of her baseball cap shades her eyes nicely⟩
synonyms bill, brim, peak
related words shade
vista *n* all that can be seen from a certain point — see VIEW 1
visual *adj* **1** of, relating to, or used in vision ⟨the eyes are the primary *visual* organs in humans⟩
synonyms ocular, optic, optical
related words seeing, sighted; focusing
antonyms nonvisual
2 capable of being seen — see VISIBLE
3 consisting of or relating to pictures — see PICTORIAL 1
visualize *vb* to form a mental picture of — see IMAGINE 1
vital *adj* **1** having active strength of body or mind — see VIGOROUS 1
2 having much high-spirited energy and movement — see LIVELY 1
3 impossible to do without — see ESSENTIAL 1
4 likely to cause or capable of causing death — see DEADLY
5 of the greatest possible importance — see CRUCIAL
vitality *n* **1** the quality or state of having abundant or intense activity ⟨a city known for the *vitality* of its entertainment and sports scenes⟩
synonyms animation, briskness, exuberance, jazziness, liveliness, lustiness, peppiness, robustness, sprightliness, vibrancy
related words buoyancy, jauntiness, springiness; brightness, cheer, cheerfulness, effervescence, vivacity, vivaciousness; eagerness, enthusiasm, keenness, spiritedness; friskiness, impishness, pertness, playfulness
near antonyms indolence, laziness; languor, lethargy, limpness, listlessness, sleepiness, sluggishness, torpor, weariness; apathy, impassivity; dullness (*or* dulness), tediousness, tedium
antonyms inactivity, lifelessness
2 active strength of body or mind — see VIGOR 1
vitalize *vb* to give life, vigor, or spirit to — see ANIMATE
vitalizing *adj* having a renewing effect on the state of the body or mind — see TONIC
vitals *n pl* the internal organs of the body — see GUT 1
vitiate *vb* **1** to affect slightly with something morally bad or undesirable — see TAINT 1
2 to reduce the soundness, effectiveness, or perfection of — see DAMAGE 1
vitriol *n* **1** biting sharpness of feeling or expression — see ACRIMONY 1
2 harsh insulting language — see ABUSE 1
vittles *n pl* substances intended to be eaten — see FOOD
vituperate *vb* to criticize harshly and usually publicly — see ATTACK 2
vituperation *n* harsh insulting language — see ABUSE 1
vivacious *adj* **1** having much high-spirited energy and movement — see LIVELY 1
2 joyously unrestrained — see EXUBERANT
vivid *adj* producing a mental picture through clear and impressive description — see GRAPHIC 1
vivify *vb* to give life, vigor, or spirit to — see ANIMATE
vizard *n* a cover or partial cover for the face used to disguise oneself — see MASK 1
vocabulary *n* **1** the special terms or expressions of a particular group or field — see TERMINOLOGY
2 the stock of words, pronunciation, and grammar used by a people as their basic means of communication — see LANGUAGE 1
vocal *adj* created by the body's organs of sound ⟨our cat is given to making strange *vocal* noises in the dead of night⟩
synonyms oral, uttered, voiced
related words articulate, articulated, spoken; breathed, drawled, gasped, mouthed, mumbled, murmured, muttered, shouted, spluttered, sputtered, whispered
near antonyms inarticulate; mute, quiet, silent; unexpressed, unspoken, unuttered, unvoiced
antonyms nonvocal
vocal *n* a short musical composition for the human voice often with instrumental accompaniment — see SONG 1
vocalist *n* one who sings — see SINGER
vocalize *vb* **1** to express (a thought or emotion) in words — see SAY 1
2 to produce musical sounds with the voice — see SING 1
vocalizer *n* one who sings — see SINGER
vocation *n* the activity by which one regularly makes a living — see OCCUPATION
vociferate *vb* to speak so as to be heard at a distance — see CALL 1
vociferous *adj* engaging in or marked by loud and insistent cries especially of protest ⟨*vociferous* opponents of the bill protested angrily outside the chambers of the legislature⟩
synonyms blatant, clamorous, obstreperous
related words clangorous, dinning, discordant, noisy; loudmouthed, outspoken, vocal; boisterous, rowdy, uproarious; cacophonous, dissonant, shrill, strident; blaring, booming, brassy, brazen
near antonyms noiseless, quiet, silent, soundless, still; calm, hushed, subdued
vogue *adj* enjoying widespread favor or approval — see POPULAR 1
vogue *n* **1** a practice or interest that is very popular for a short time — see FAD
2 the state of enjoying widespread approval — see POPULARITY
voice *n* **1** the right to express a wish, choice, or opinion ⟨everyone will have a *voice* in the decision of where to go for our field trip⟩
synonyms say, vote
related words part, role, share; enfranchisement, franchise, suffrage; judgment (*or* judgement), say-so; belief, conviction, opinion, sentiment, view
2 an act, process, or means of putting something into words — see EXPRESSION 1
3 one who sings — see SINGER
voice *vb* to make known (as an idea, emotion, or opinion) — see EXPRESS 1
voiced *adj* created by the body's organs of sound — see VOCAL
voiceless *adj* unable to speak — see MUTE 1
void *vb* to put an end to by formal action — see ABOLISH
void *adj* **1** having no legal or binding force — see NULL 1

2 lacking contents that could or should be present — see EMPTY 1
3 utterly lacking in something needed, wanted, or expected — see DEVOID 1
void *n* empty space — see VACANCY 1
void *vb* to remove the contents of — see EMPTY
volatile *adj* likely to change frequently, suddenly, or unexpectedly — see FICKLE 1
volcanic *adj* marked by bursts of destructive force or intense activity — see VIOLENT 1
volition *n* the act or power of making one's own choices or decisions — see FREE WILL
volley *n* a rapid or overwhelming outpouring of many things at once — see BARRAGE
volume *n* **1** a considerable amount — see LOT 2
2 a given or particular mass or aggregate of matter — see AMOUNT
3 a set of printed sheets of paper bound together between covers and forming a work of fiction or nonfiction — see BOOK 1
voluminous *adj* of a size greater than average of its kind — see LARGE
voluminousness *n* the quality or state of being large in size — see LARGENESS
voluntarily *adv* of one's own free will 〈you took part in this *voluntarily*, so you have no cause to complain〉
synonyms freely, willingly
related words consciously, knowingly, wittingly
phrases of one's own accord
near antonyms unconsciously, unknowingly, unwittingly
antonyms involuntarily, unwillingly
voluntary *adj* **1** done, made, or given with one's own free will 〈a *voluntary* contribution to the school's fund-raising drive〉
synonyms freewill, unforced, volunteer, willing
related words discretionary, elective, nonobligatory, optional; impulsive, instinctive, spontaneous, unforced, unpremeditated; conscious, deliberate, intentional, knowing, willful (*or* wilful)
near antonyms compulsory, mandatory, necessary, nonelective, obligatory, ordered, required
antonyms coerced, forced, involuntary
2 subject to one's freedom of choice — see OPTIONAL
volunteer *adj* done, made, or given with one's own free will — see VOLUNTARY 1
voluptuous *adj* pleasing to the physical senses — see SENSUAL
vomit *vb* to discharge the contents of the stomach through the mouth 〈the children with the flu *vomited* every time they tried to eat something〉
synonyms gag, heave, retch, spit up, throw up
related words disgorge, regurgitate; eject, expel, spew
voodoo *n* a person skilled in using supernatural forces — see MAGICIAN 1
voodooism *n* the power to control natural forces through supernatural means — see MAGIC 1
voracious *adj* **1** having a huge appetite 〈it seemed like the *voracious* kitten was eating her weight in food every day〉
synonyms gluttonous, greedy, hoggish, piggish, rapacious, ravenous
related words hearty, wolfish; devouring, gobbling, gorging, gormandizing, insatiable, unquenchable; empty, famished, hungry, starved, starving; malnourished, underfed, undernourished
near antonyms full, content, sated, satisfied
2 showing urgent desire or interest — see EAGER
vortex *n* water moving rapidly in a circle with a hollow in the center — see WHIRLPOOL
votary *n* one who follows the opinions or teachings of another — see FOLLOWER
vote *n* **1** the right to formally express one's position or will in an election 〈in the United States, women were granted the *vote* by the Nineteenth Amendment in 1920〉
synonyms enfranchisement, franchise, suffrage
related words say, voice
antonyms disenfranchisement
2 a piece of paper indicating a person's preferences in an election — see BALLOT
3 the right to express a wish, choice, or opinion — see VOICE 1
vote *vb* to set before the mind for consideration — see PROPOSE 1
vouch (for)*vb* to declare (something) to be true or genuine — see CERTIFY 1
vow *n* a person's solemn declaration that he or she will do or not do something — see PROMISE
vow *vb* to make a solemn declaration of intent — see PROMISE 1
voyage *n* a journey over water in a vessel — see SAIL
voyage *vb* **1** to take a trip especially of some distance — see TRAVEL 1
2 to travel on water in a vessel — see SAIL 1
vulgar *adj* **1** belonging to the class of people of low social or economic rank — see IGNOBLE 1
2 depicting or referring to sexual matters in a way that is unacceptable in polite society — see OBSCENE 1
3 held by or applicable to a majority of the people — see GENERAL 3
4 lacking in refinement or good taste — see COARSE 2
5 used in or suitable for speech and not formal writing — see COLLOQUIAL 1
vulgarism *n* a disrespectful or indecent word or expression — see SWEARWORD
vulgarity *n* **1** the quality or state of lacking refinement or good taste 〈our cousins' general *vulgarity* and poor manners irritate my mother〉
synonyms coarseness, commonness, crassness, crudeness, grossness, indelicacy, indelicateness, lowness, raffishness, roughness, rudeness, tastelessness
related words boorishness, churlishness, clownishness, loutishness; insensitivity, thoughtlessness; gracelessness, tackiness
near antonyms courtliness; elegance, grace, graciousness; consideration, sensitivity, thoughtfulness
antonyms cultivation, gentility, polish, refinement, tastefulness
2 the quality or state of being obscene — see OBSCENITY 1
vulnerability *n* **1** the quality or state of having little resistance to some outside agent — see SUSCEPTIBILITY
2 the state of being left without shelter or protection against something harmful — see EXPOSURE 1
vulnerable *adj* **1** being in a situation where one is likely to meet with harm — see LIABLE 1
2 lacking protection from danger or resistance against attack — see HELPLESS 1

wackiness *n* lack of good sense or judgment — see FOOLISHNESS 1

wacky *adj* **1** different from the ordinary in a way that causes curiosity or suspicion — see ODD 2
2 having or showing a very abnormal or sick state of mind — see INSANE 1
3 showing or marked by a lack of good sense or judgment — see FOOLISH 1

wad *n* **1** a considerable amount — see LOT 2
2 a small uneven mass — see LUMP 1
3 a very large amount of money — see FORTUNE 2

wad *vb* to form into a round compact mass ⟨she *wadded* up the paper and threw it in the wastebasket⟩
synonyms agglomerate, ball, roll, round
related words clump, lump; bead
near antonyms open, spread, unfold
antonyms unroll

waddle *vb* to move forward while swaying from side to side — see STAGGER 1

wade (into) *vb* to start work on energetically — see ATTACK 3

waft *n* a slight or gentle movement of air — see BREEZE 1

waft *vb* to rest or move along the surface of a liquid or in the air — see FLOAT

wag *n* **1** a quick jerky movement from side to side or up and down ⟨the dog gave its tail a single *wag* before it flopped back down⟩
synonyms switch, waggle
related words oscillation, swing; flap, flutter, wave; jerk, shake, twitch, wiggle
2 a person (as a writer) noted for or specializing in humor — see HUMORIST

wag *vb* to move from side to side or up and down with quick jerky motions ⟨the cat's tail *wagged* back and forth in annoyance⟩
synonyms switch, waggle
related words oscillate, swing; beat, flail, flap, flop, whip; flick, flicker, flutter, wave; jerk, shake, twitch, wiggle

wage *n, often* **wages** *pl* the money paid regularly to a person for labor or services ⟨the *wage* you earn is more than enough to support us comfortably⟩
synonyms emolument, hire, pay, payment, salary, stipend
related words minimum wage, take-home pay; compensation, recompense, remittance, remuneration, requital, return; check, commission, paycheck; recoupment, redress, reparation, restitution; reimbursement, repayment; profit, takings, yield

wager *n* the money or thing risked on the outcome of an uncertain event — see BET

wager *vb* to risk (something) on the outcome of an uncertain event — see BET

wagerer *n* one that bets (as on the outcome of a contest or sports event) — see BETTOR

waggery *n* **1** playful, reckless behavior that is not intended to cause serious harm — see MISCHIEF 1
2 something said or done to cause laughter — see JOKE 1

waggish *adj* tending to or exhibiting reckless playfulness — see MISCHIEVOUS 1

waggle *n* a quick jerky movement from side to side or up and down — see WAG 1

waggle *vb* to move from side to side or up and down with quick jerky motions — see WAG

wagon *n* a wheeled usually horse-drawn vehicle used for hauling — see CART

wail *n* **1** a crying out in grief — see LAMENT 1
2 a long low sound indicating pain or grief — see MOAN 1

wail *vb* **1** to express dissatisfaction, pain, or resentment usually tiresomely — see COMPLAIN
2 to make a long loud mournful sound — see HOWL 1
3 to utter a moan — see MOAN 1

wail (for) *vb* to feel or express sorrow for — see LAMENT 1

wailing *adj* expressing or suggesting mourning — see MOURNFUL 1

wain *n* a wheeled usually horse-drawn vehicle used for hauling — see CART

waist *n* the middle region of the human body — see MIDRIFF

waistline *n* the middle region of the human body — see MIDRIFF

wait *n* an instance or period of being prevented from going about one's business — see DELAY

wait *vb* to remain in place in readiness or expectation of something ⟨hurry up, as your sisters are already at the door *waiting* for you⟩
synonyms await, bide, hold on, stay
related words hang around, linger, stick around; anticipate, expect
phrases bide one's time

waiter *n* a person who serves food or drink — see SERVER

waiver *n* a document containing a declaration of an intentional giving up of a right, claim, or privilege ⟨before the hospital will treat you, you have to sign a *waiver* in which you give up your right to sue⟩
synonyms release
related words dispensation, exemption; abdication, relinquishment, renouncement; renunciation, surrender

wake *vb* **1** to cause to stop sleeping ⟨my banging around in the kitchen *woke* the cat⟩
synonyms arouse, awake, awaken, rouse, waken
related words raise, revive; reawake, reawaken; agitate, disturb, excite, provoke, stimulate, stir
near antonyms hypnotize, mesmerize; lay (down)
antonyms lull
2 to cease to be asleep ⟨I *woke* with a start when the door slammed⟩
synonyms arouse, awake, awaken, rouse, waken
related words arise, get up, rise, uprise; watch; revive; reawake, reawaken; shift, stir
near antonyms catnap, doze, drop (off), nap, nod, sleep, slumber, snooze; bed (down), couch, retire, turn in; oversleep

wakeful *adj* not sleeping or able to sleep ⟨the mother remained *wakeful* until her child returned home⟩
synonyms awake, sleepless, wide-awake
related words aroused, awakened, roused, wakened; aware, conscious; revived; reawakened
near antonyms drowsy, nodding, sleepy, slumber-

ous, somnolent; dreaming; hypnotized, mesmerized
antonyms asleep, dormant, dozing, napping, resting, sleeping, slumbering
waken *vb* **1** to cause to stop sleeping — see WAKE 1
2 to cease to be asleep — see WAKE 2
walk *n* a relaxed journey on foot for exercise or pleasure <we went for a long *walk* outside because it was such a nice night>
synonyms constitutional, perambulation, ramble, range, saunter, stroll, turn
related words parade, promenade; expedition, hike, march, peregrination, tramp, travel, trek, trip; excursion, jaunt, junket, outing, sally, spin, tour; pilgrimage, progress, safari
walk *vb* to go on foot <I *walked* slowly to school>
synonyms foot (it), hoof (it), leg (it), pad, step, traipse, tread
related words parade, promenade; march, pace, stride; hike, peregrinate, trek; amble, perambulate, ramble, saunter, stroll, wander; clump, stomp, stump, tramp, tromp; plod, trudge; hobble, limp; mince, prance, pussyfoot, tiptoe; stalk, strut, swagger; lumber, lurch, pound, shamble, shuffle, stagger; nip, trip, trot
walking out *n* the act of leaving a place — see DEPARTURE
walkout *n* a work stoppage by a body of workers intended to force an employer to meet their demands — see STRIKE 1
walk out *vb* **1** to leave a place often for another — see GO 2
2 to refuse to work in order to force an employer to meet demands — see STRIKE 1
wall *n* **1** a physical object that blocks the way — see BARRIER
2 means or method of defending — see DEFENSE 1
wall (in) *vb* to close or shut in by or as if by barriers — see ENCLOSE 1
wallop *n* **1** a forceful coming together of two things — see IMPACT 1
2 a hard strike with a part of the body or an instrument — see [1]BLOW
wallop *vb* **1** to strike repeatedly — see BEAT 1
2 to achieve a victory over — see BEAT 2
3 to defeat by a large margin — see WHIP 2
4 to deliver a blow to (someone or something) usually in a strong vigorous manner — see HIT 1
wampum *n slang* something (as pieces of stamped metal or printed paper) customarily and legally used as a medium of exchange, a measure of value, or a means of payment — see MONEY
wan *adj* lacking a healthy skin color — see PALE 2
wander *vb* to move about from place to place aimlessly <we just went outside and *wandered* around until it was time to go>
synonyms gad (about), gallivant (*also* galavant), knock (about), maunder, meander, mooch, mope, ramble, range, roam, rove, traipse
related words amble, saunter, stroll; bum, hobo; straggle, stray; prowl, tramp, travel
wanderer *n* a person who roams about without a fixed route or destination — see NOMAD
wandering *adj* traveling from place to place — see ITINERANT
wane *vb* to grow less in scope or intensity especially gradually — see DECREASE 2
wangle *vb* to plan out usually with subtle skill or care — see ENGINEER
want *n* **1** the fact or state of being absent — see LACK 1
2 a falling short of an essential or desirable amount or number — see DEFICIENCY
3 a state of being without something necessary, desirable, or useful — see NEED 1
4 the state of lacking sufficient money or material possessions — see POVERTY 1
want *vb* **1** to have an earnest wish to own or enjoy — see DESIRE
2 to have as a requirement — see NEED 1
3 to see fit — see CHOOSE 2
4 to wish to have — see LIKE 1
wanting *adj* **1** falling short of a standard — see BAD 1
2 not coming up to a usual standard or meeting a particular need — see SHORT 3
3 not present or in evidence — see ABSENT 2
wanting *prep* not having — see WITHOUT 1
wanton *adj* **1** depicting or referring to sexual matters in a way that is unacceptable in polite society — see OBSCENE 1
2 having a strong sexual desire — see LUSTFUL
3 having or showing the desire to inflict severe pain and suffering on others — see CRUEL 1
wantonness *n* the willful infliction of pain and suffering on others — see CRUELTY
war *n* **1** a state of armed violent struggle between states, nations, or groups <the United States declared *war* on Japan after the bombing of Pearl Harbor>
synonyms conflict, hostilities, hot war
related words civil war, cold war, holy war, limited war, world war; action, battle, engagement; combat, fighting, warfare; belligerency; wartime
near antonyms demilitarization, demobilization, disarmament; pacification; cease-fire, truce; calm, peacefulness, tranquility
antonyms peace
2 a lack of agreement or harmony — see DISCORD
war (against) *vb* to oppose (someone) in physical conflict — see FIGHT 1
warble *n* a rhythmic series of musical tones arranged to give a pleasing effect — see MELODY
warble *vb* to sing with the alternation of two musical tones <the skylark *warbled* prettily outside our window>
synonyms quaver, trill
related words slur; yodel; belt, carol, chant, chorus, croon, descant, harmonize, troll, vocalize; lilt, scat
ward *n* **1** means or method of defending — see DEFENSE 1
2 responsibility for the safety and well-being of someone or something — see CUSTODY
ward *vb* to drive danger or attack away from — see DEFEND 1
warden *n* **1** a person or group that watches over someone or something — see GUARD 1
2 a person who takes care of a property sometimes for an absent owner — see CUSTODIAN 1
warder *n* a person or group that watches over someone or something — see GUARD 1
warehouse *n* a building for storing goods — see STOREHOUSE
wares *n pl* products that are bought and sold in business — see MERCHANDISE
warfare *n* **1** a lack of agreement or harmony — see DISCORD

2 an earnest effort for superiority or victory over another — see CONTEST 1

wariness *n* a close attentiveness to avoiding danger — see CAUTION 1

warlike *adj* feeling or displaying eagerness to fight — see BELLIGERENT

warm *adj* **1** having or giving off heat to a moderate degree ⟨the pan was still *warm*, but no longer too hot to touch⟩
synonyms heated, lukewarm, tepid, toasty, warmed
related words thawed; broiling, burning, fiery, hot, piping hot, red-hot, roasting, scalding, scorching, searing, sultry, sweltering, torrid; overheated, roasted, superheated, sweltering; blazing, glowing, molten, sizzling; reheated
near antonyms arctic, bitter, bleak, chill, chilly, cold, freezing, frigid, frosty, glacial, ice-cold, iced, icy, nippy, polar, raw, sharp, snappy, snowy, subfreezing, subzero, wintry; unthawed; frosted; benumbed, nipped, numb
antonyms chilled, cool, cooled, refrigerated, unheated
2 having or expressing great depth of feeling — see FERVENT
3 having or showing kindly feeling and sincere interest — see FRIENDLY 1
4 showing or expressing acceptance or approval — see POSITIVE

warm *vb* **1** to cause to have or give off heat to a moderate degree ⟨you'll need to *warm* the food in the microwave⟩
synonyms heat, toast
related words overheat, superheat; reheat; burn, char, fire, scald, scorch, sear
near antonyms freeze, frost, ice
antonyms chill, cool, refrigerate
2 to give satisfaction to — see PLEASE

warm–blooded *adj* having or expressing great depth of feeling — see FERVENT

warmed *adj* having or giving off heat to a moderate degree — see WARM 1

warmhearted *adj* **1** having or marked by sympathy and consideration for others — see HUMANE 1
2 having or showing kindly feeling and sincere interest — see FRIENDLY 1

warmness *n* the quality or state of being moderate in temperature — see WARMTH 1

warmonger *n* one who urges or attempts to cause a war ⟨fortunately, the *warmongers* met with overwhelming opposition⟩
synonyms hawk, jingo, militarist
related words agitator, firebrand, fomenter, instigator, rabble-rouser; belligerent, combatant, militant; chauvinist
near antonyms peacemaker
antonyms dove, pacifist

warmth *n* **1** the quality or state of being moderate in temperature ⟨the cozy *warmth* of the inn's parlor was a welcome relief from the wintry weather outside⟩
synonyms lukewarmness, warmness
related words glow, radiance; heat, hotness, sultriness, stuffiness
near antonyms bitterness, bleakness, cold, coldness, frigidity, frostiness, iciness, rawness, sharpness; frost
antonyms chill, chilliness, coolness
2 depth of feeling — see ARDOR 1

warn *vb* to give notice to beforehand especially of danger or risk ⟨Dad *warned* us that if we continued playing so rough, someone was sure to get hurt⟩
synonyms alert, caution, forewarn
related words augur, forecast, foretell, predict, presage, prognosticate, prophesy; advise, apprise, inform, notify; admonish; bode, forebode, portend
near antonyms imperil, risk

warning *adj* serving as or offering a warning — see CAUTIONARY

warning *n* **1** the act or an instance of telling beforehand of danger or risk ⟨she delivered a strict *warning* that anyone who was caught cheating would get expelled⟩
synonyms admonition, alarm, alert, caution, forewarning, notice
related words auguring, augury, forecasting, foretelling, predicting, prediction, presaging, prognosticating, prophecy, prophesying; apprising, informing, notification, notifying; advice, counsel, guidance, recommendation, suggestion; announcement, declaration
2 something that tells of approaching danger or risk ⟨the ominously darkening sky was a *warning* that a tornado was approaching⟩
synonyms caution, tocsin
related words omen, portent; notification; buoy, knell, sign, signal; foretaste, foretoken; announcement, declaration

warp *vb* **1** to change so much as to create a wrong impression or alter the meaning of — see GARBLE
2 to lower in character or dignity — see DEBASE 1
3 to twist (something) out of a natural or normal shape or condition — see CONTORT

warped *adj* having or showing lowered moral character or standards — see CORRUPT

warping *n* the twisting of something out of its natural or normal shape or condition — see CONTORTION

warrant *vb* **1** to assume responsibility for the satisfactory quality or performance of ⟨the computer company unconditionally *warrants* all of its products for one full year⟩
synonyms guarantee
related words attest, authenticate, avouch, certify, testify (to), vouch (for), witness; assure, bond, contract, covenant; pledge, plight, swear, vow; adhere, assert, declare, insist; insure
2 to give official acceptance of something as satisfactory — see APPROVE
3 to have as a requirement — see NEED 1
4 to state as a fact usually forcefully — see CLAIM 1

warranted *adj* being what is called for by accepted standards of right and wrong — see JUST 1

warranty *n* a formal agreement to fulfill an obligation — see GUARANTEE 1

warrior *n* a person engaged in military service — see SOLDIER

wary *adj* having or showing a close attentiveness to avoiding danger or trouble — see CAREFUL 1

wash *vb* **1** to flow along or against ⟨crystal-clear waters gently *wash* the island's unspoiled beaches⟩
synonyms lap, lave, splash
related words gurgle, ripple, slosh
2 to flow in a broken irregular stream — see GURGLE
3 to make wet — see WET

4 to pour liquid over or through in order to cleanse — see FLUSH 1
washed *adj* containing, covered with, or thoroughly penetrated by water — see WET
washed–out *adj* lacking intensity of color — see PALE 1
washed–up *adj* having lost forcefulness, courage, or spirit — see EFFETE 1
washout *n* something that has failed — see FAILURE 3
wash out *vb* **1** to be unsuccessful — see FAIL 2
2 to make white or whiter by removing color — see WHITEN
3 to use up all the physical energy of — see EXHAUST 1
washroom *n* a room furnished with a fixture for flushing body waste — see TOILET
waspish *adj* easily irritated or annoyed — see IRRITABLE
waspishness *n* readiness to show annoyance or impatience — see PETULANCE
wassail *n* a bout of drinking — see CAROUSE
wastage *n* the state or fact of being rendered nonexistent, physically unsound, or useless — see DESTRUCTION
waste *adj* producing inferior or only a small amount of vegetation — see BARREN 1
waste *n* **1** an instance of spending money or resources without care or restraint ⟨it seems like a *waste* to spend my entire paycheck on a bigger TV⟩
synonyms extravagance, prodigality
related words indulgence, luxury, splurge; loss, wastage; generosity, liberality, openhandedness, profligacy; improvidence, shortsightedness; overindulgence, self-indulgence; excess, immoderacy, overkill; carelessness, heedlessness, imprudence, incautiousness; recklessness
near antonyms necessity; economizing, economy, frugality, saving, scrimping, skimping; austerity, moderation, restraint, temperance, temperateness
2 discarded or useless material — see GARBAGE
3 land that is uninhabited or not fit for crops — see WASTELAND
4 solid matter discharged from an animal's alimentary canal — see DROPPING 1
waste *vb* **1** to use up carelessly ⟨he *wasted* most of his allowance by buying comic books⟩
synonyms blow, dissipate, fritter (away), lavish, misspend, run through, spend, squander, throw away
related words splurge; consume, deplete, exhaust, impoverish; indulge, overindulge; disburse, expend, lay out
near antonyms economize, scrimp, skimp; preserve, protect, save; hoard, lay up
antonyms conserve
2 to bring to a complete end the physical soundness, existence, or usefulness of — see DESTROY 1
3 to diminish the physical strength of — see WEAKEN 1
waste (away) *vb* to lose bodily strength or vigor — see WEAKEN 2
wasted *adj* **1** lacking bodily strength — see WEAK 1
2 suffering extreme weight loss as a result of hunger or disease — see EMACIATED
wasteful *adj* given to spending money freely or foolishly — see PRODIGAL
wastefulness *n* the quality or fact of being free or wasteful in the expenditure of money — see EXTRAVAGANCE 1
wasteland *n* land that is uninhabited or not fit for crops ⟨with proper irrigation and fertilizer, they turned the desert *wasteland* into a fertile plain⟩
synonyms barren, desert, desolation, waste
related words badland; bush, brush; dust bowl; hinterland, upland; open, open air, outdoors, out-of-doors; nature, wild, wilderness
waster *n* someone who carelessly spends money — see PRODIGAL
wastrel *n* someone who carelessly spends money — see PRODIGAL
watch *n* **1** a person or group that watches over someone or something — see GUARD 1
2 the act or state of being constantly attentive and responsive to signs of activity, opportunity, or danger — see VIGILANCE
watch *vb* **1** to keep one's eyes on ⟨I turned my head to continue *watching* the bird as it flew away⟩
synonyms eye, observe
related words behold, look, regard, see, view; gape, gawk, gaze, glare, goggle, peer, rubberneck, stare; guard, wake, ward; monitor, read; spy; glance, glimpse, peek, peep
near antonyms blink, wink
2 to take notice of and be guided by — see HEED 1
3 to pay continued close attention to (something) for a particular purpose — see MONITOR
4 to have an interest or concern for — see CARE
watch (for) *vb* to believe in the future occurrence of (something) — see EXPECT
watchful *adj* paying close attention usually for the purpose of anticipating approaching danger or opportunity — see ALERT 1
watchfulness *n* the act or state of being constantly attentive and responsive to signs of opportunity, activity, or danger — see VIGILANCE
watchman *n* **1** a person or group that watches over someone or something — see GUARD 1
2 a person who takes care of a property sometimes for an absent owner — see CUSTODIAN 1
watch out (for) *vb* to be cautious of or on guard against — see BEWARE (OF)
watchword *n* **1** a word or phrase that must be spoken by a person in order to pass a guard — see PASSWORD
2 an attention-getting word or phrase used to publicize something (as a campaign or product) — see SLOGAN
water *vb* to make wet — see WET
water (down) *vb* to alter (something) for the worse with the addition of foreign or lower-grade substances — see ADULTERATE
water closet *n* a room furnished with a fixture for flushing body waste — see TOILET
watercourse *n* an open man-made passageway for water — see CHANNEL 1
watercraft *n* a small buoyant structure for travel on water — see BOAT 1
watered *adj* containing, covered with, or thoroughly penetrated by water — see WET
waterfall *n* a fall of water usually from a great height ⟨I used to like to throw sticks in the stream and watch them go over the *waterfall*⟩
synonyms cascade, cataract, fall(s)
related words rapid(s), white water; eddy, riffle; undertow, vortex, whirlpool

waterless *adj* marked by little or no precipitation or humidity — see DRY 1

waterlogged *adj* containing, covered with, or thoroughly penetrated by water — see WET

waterproof *n chiefly British* a coat made of water-resistant material — see RAINCOAT

waterproof *adj* made of or treated with material that does not allow water to penetrate ⟨luckily, my backpack is *waterproof*, so my notes didn't get wet⟩
synonyms waterproofed, watertight
related words rainproof; water-repellent, water-resistant; nonabsorbent, nonporous
near antonyms absorbent, porous

waterproofed *adj* made of or treated with material that does not allow water to penetrate — see WATERPROOF

waterspout *n* a pipe or channel for carrying off water from a roof — see GUTTER 1

watertight *adj* made of or treated with material that does not allow water to penetrate — see WATERPROOF

waterway *n* an open man-made passageway for water — see CHANNEL 1

watery *adj* **1** containing, covered with, or thoroughly penetrated by water — see WET
2 having an overly soft liquid consistency — see RUNNY
3 not containing very much of some important element — see WEAK 3

wave *n* a moving ridge on the surface of water ⟨the toddler was almost knocked down by the *waves* created by the speedboat⟩
synonyms billow, surge, swell
related words sea(s); breaker, whitecap; curl; comber, roller; eddy, riffle, ripple, wavelet; tidal wave, tsunami; undertow, vortex, whirlpool

wave *vb* to direct or notify by a movement or gesture — see MOTION

waver *vb* **1** to show uncertainty about the right course of action — see HESITATE
2 to swing unsteadily back and forth or from side to side — see TEETER 1

wavering *n* the act or an instance of pausing because of uncertainty about the right course of action — see HESITATION

wax *vb* **1** to become greater in extent, volume, amount, or number — see INCREASE 2
2 to coat (something) with a slippery substance in order to reduce friction — see LUBRICATE
3 to eventually have as a state or quality — see BECOME

way *n* **1** a passage cleared for public vehicular travel ⟨the town honored the local sports hero by naming after him a short *way* connecting two shopping centers⟩
synonyms artery, avenue, boulevard, drag, drive, expressway, freeway, highroad, highway, pass, passageway, pike, road, roadway, route, row, street, thoroughfare, trace, turnpike
related words causeway; alley, alleyway, bystreet, byway, catwalk, court, lane, place; approach, concourse, path, walkway; access; dead end; aisle, corridor, course, line; track, trail; channel; corduroy, tarmac; crossroad; bypass, overpass, underpass; cloverleaf, rotary
2 a usual manner of behaving or doing — see HABIT
3 an established course for traveling from one place to another — see PASSAGE 1
4 an established pattern of behavior — see TENDENCY 1
5 an extent or area available for or used up by some activity or thing — see ROOM 1
6 the direction along which something or someone moves — see PATH 1
7 the means or procedure for doing something — see METHOD
8 the opening through which one can enter or leave a structure — see DOOR 2
9 the power, right, or opportunity to choose — see CHOICE 1
10 the space or amount of space between two points, lines, surfaces, or objects — see DISTANCE

wayfarer *n* a person who roams about without a fixed route or destination — see NOMAD

wayfaring *adj* traveling from place to place — see ITINERANT

waylay *vb* to lie in wait for and attack by surprise — see AMBUSH

way–out *adj* different from the ordinary in a way that causes curiosity or suspicion — see ODD 2

way station *n* a regular stopping place — see STATION 2

wayward *adj* **1** given to resisting authority or another's control — see DISOBEDIENT
2 given to resisting control or discipline by others — see UNCONTROLLABLE

weak *adj* **1** lacking bodily strength ⟨the little boy was simply too *weak* to lift the box⟩
synonyms debilitated, delicate, effete, enervated, enfeebled, faint, feeble, frail, infirm, languid, low, prostrate, prostrated, sapped, slight, soft, softened, tender, torpid, unsubstantial, wasted, weakened, wimpy
related words challenged, disabled, incapacitated; paralyzed; broken-down, decrepit, worn out; impotent, powerless, puny; breakable, flimsy, fragile; dizzy, groggy, rocky, unsteady, woozy; exhausted, tired, weary; damaged, harmed, hurt, impaired, injured; resistless, susceptible, unresistant, vulnerable, yielding
near antonyms able-bodied, athletic, beefy, brawny, fit, husky, muscular, sinewy, strapping, virile; hard, hardy, lusty, robust, sturdy, tough; fortified, hardened, inured, strengthened, toughened; energetic, energized, invigorated, vigorous, vitalized; hale, healthy, sound; capable, competent; convalescing, recovering, recuperating
antonyms mighty, powerful, rugged, stalwart, stout, strong
2 lacking strength of will or character ⟨the opinion that overweight people are just *weak* individuals who easily give in to temptation⟩
synonyms characterless, effete, frail, invertebrate, nerveless, soft, spineless, weakened, wimpy, wishy-washy
related words forceless, ineffective, ineffectual; impotent, powerless; emasculated, unnerved; pliable, submissive; corrupt, unprincipled, unscrupulous, villainous; cowardly, craven, lily-livered
near antonyms ethical, good, moral, principled, right, righteous, upright, virtuous; determined, mettlesome, resolute; courageous, stalwart, stouthearted
antonyms backboned, firm, strong, tough
3 not containing very much of some important element ⟨the coffee came out too *weak* because I didn't put enough ground beans in⟩

synonyms dilute, diluted, thin, thinned, watery, weakened
related words adulterated, watered (down)
near antonyms enriched, fortified; concentrated, condensed, evaporated
antonyms full-bodied, rich, strong
4 not using or following good reasoning — see ILLOGICAL
5 unable to act or achieve one's purpose — see POWERLESS

weaken *vb* **1** to diminish the physical strength of ⟨several days of hardship in the desert had *weakened* them⟩
synonyms debilitate, enervate, enfeeble, prostrate, sap, soften, tire, waste
related words cripple, disable, incapacitate; deplete, depress, exhaust, impoverish, unman, wash out; damage, harm, hurt, impair, injure; break down, wear out; paralyze
near antonyms energize, invigorate, vitalize; harden, season, toughen
antonyms beef (up), fortify, recruit, strengthen
2 to lose bodily strength or vigor ⟨the bodybuilder *weakened* once she eased off on her workouts⟩
synonyms decay, droop, fail, flag, go, lag, languish, sag, waste (away), wilt
related words break down, wear out; yield
near antonyms convalesce, recover, recuperate; gain
2 to alter (something) for the worse with the addition of foreign or lower-grade substances — see ADULTERATE

weakened *adj* **1** containing foreign or lower-grade substances — see IMPURE
2 lacking bodily strength — see WEAK 1
3 lacking strength of will or character — see WEAK 2
4 not containing very much of some important element — see WEAK 3

weakening *n* a gradual sinking and wasting away of mind or body — see DECLINE 1

weakling *n* **1** a person lacking in physical strength ⟨he was a *weakling* until high school, when he started working out to put on muscle⟩
synonyms softy (*or* softie), wimp
related words pushover, sissy
antonyms powerhouse
2 a person without strength of character ⟨only a *weakling* would be willing to lie to save himself from punishment⟩
synonyms mollycoddle, wimp
related words coward, mouse
antonyms stalwart

weakly *adj* chronically or repeatedly suffering from poor health — see SICKLY 1

weak-minded *adj* **1** not having or showing an ability to absorb ideas readily — see STUPID 1
2 showing or marked by a lack of good sense or judgment — see FOOLISH 1

weakness *n* **1** the quality or state of lacking physical strength or vigor ⟨the flu left me with such *weakness* that I could hardly stand⟩
synonyms debilitation, debility, delicacy, delicateness, enfeeblement, faintness, feebleness, frailness, frailty, infirmity, languor, lowness
related words decay, decrepitude; breakdown, collapse, exhaustion, nervous breakdown, prostration; defenselessness, helplessness; softness, tenderness; disablement, incapacitation; damage, harm, hurt, impairment, injury
near antonyms energy, vitality; brawniness, fitness, huskiness, virility; hardness, ruggedness, stoutness, sturdiness, toughness; haleness, health, healthiness, soundness
antonyms hardihood, hardiness, robustness, strength, vigor
2 the quality or state of lacking strength of will or character ⟨in a moment of *weakness* he shoplifted the comic book⟩
synonyms frailness, frailty, softness, spinelessness
related words collapse; failing, flaw, foibles, peccadillo; evil, immorality, wickedness; corruption, corruptness
near antonyms discipline, self-discipline; goodness, morality, rightness, righteousness, uprightness, virtuousness
antonyms backbone, firmness, fortitude, mettle, resoluteness, strength
3 a defect in character — see FAULT 1
4 the quality or state of having little resistance to some outside agent — see SUSCEPTIBILITY

weal *n* the state of doing well especially in relation to one's happiness or success — see WELFARE

wealth *n* **1** the total of one's money and property ⟨her *wealth* increased to the point where she could afford several luxurious homes⟩
synonyms assets, capital, fortune, means, opulence, riches, substance, wherewithal
related words belongings, chattels, effects, holdings, paraphernalia, possessions, things; finances, money; king's ransom, mint, wad; abundance, affluence, prosperity, success; treasure, valuables; accession, acquisition, personalty, property; nest egg, reserve, resources, savings, treasury; collateral; heap, pile, pot; bonanza, mine, treasure trove
near antonyms debts, liabilities; indebtedness
2 a considerable amount — see LOT 2
3 an amount or supply more than sufficient to meet one's needs — see PLENTY 1

wealthy *adj* having goods, property, or money in abundance — see RICH 1

wear *n* **1** the result of long and hard use ⟨after several years, the carpet was finally showing *wear*⟩
synonyms wear and tear
related words abrasion, corrosion, erosion, erasure; decomposition, disintegration
near antonyms fixing, mending, patching, rebuilding, reconditioning, reconstruction, renovation, repair, revamping
2 covering for the human body — see CLOTHING

wear *vb* **1** to use up all the physical energy of — see EXHAUST 1
2 to damage or diminish by continued friction — see ABRADE 1

wear and tear *n* the result of long and hard use — see WEAR 1

wearied *adj* **1** depleted in strength, energy, or freshness — see WEARY 1
2 having one's patience, interest, or pleasure exhausted — see WEARY 2

weariless *adj* showing no signs of weariness even after long hard effort — see TIRELESS

weariness *n* **1** a complete depletion of energy or strength — see FATIGUE
2 the state of being bored — see BOREDOM

wearisome *adj* causing weariness, restlessness, or lack of interest — see BORING

wear out *vb* to use up all the physical energy of — see EXHAUST 1

weary *adj* **1** depleted in strength, energy, or fresh-

ness ⟨I am just too *weary* to do any more work tonight⟩
synonyms beat, burned-out (*or* burnt-out), bushed, dead, done in, drained, effete, exhausted, fatigued, jaded, limp, logy, played out, prostrate, spent, tired, tuckered (out), wearied, worn, worn-out
related words overtaxed, overworked; run-down; debilitated, enervated, enfeebled, sapped, weakened
phrases worn to a frazzle
near antonyms refreshed, rejuvenated, relaxed, rested, revitalized; active, energetic, invigorated, strengthened, strong, tireless, vitalized
antonyms untired
2 having one's patience, interest, or pleasure exhausted ⟨I am totally *weary* of this constant bickering⟩
synonyms bored, fed up, jaded, sick, tired, wearied
related words apathetic, disinterested, uninterested; glutted, sated, satiated, surfeited; dejected, demoralized, discouraged, disheartened, dispirited; beat, burned-out (*or* burnt-out), bushed, done in, drained, enervated, exhausted, fatigued, limp, played out, tuckered, worn-out; annoyed, frustrated, irritated; disgusted, nauseated, repulsed
near antonyms animated, energized, enlivened, excited, galvanized, invigorated, stimulated, vitalized; amused, entertained; beguiled, bewitched, captivated, charmed, enchanted, enthralled, fascinated, hypnotized, mesmerized; delighted, pleased, thrilled
antonyms absorbed, engaged, engrossed, gripped, interested, intrigued
3 causing weariness, restlessness, or lack of interest — see BORING

weary *vb* **1** to make weary and restless by being dull or monotonous — see [2]BORE
2 to use up all the physical energy of — see EXHAUST 1

wearying *adj* causing weariness, restlessness, or lack of interest — see BORING

weather *vb* to come safely through — see SURVIVE 1

weave *vb* to scatter or set here and there among other things — see THREAD 1

web *n* **1** something that catches and holds ⟨he was caught in the *web* of branches⟩ ⟨she was trapped by her own *web* of lies⟩
synonyms entanglement, net, snare
related words mesh, trap; knot, snarl, tangle; labyrinth, maze; cobweb, spiderweb
2 a device or scheme for capturing another by surprise — see TRAP 1

wed *vb* **1** to give in marriage — see MARRY 2
2 to perform the ceremony of marriage for — see MARRY 1
3 to take a spouse — see MARRY 4
4 to take as a spouse — see MARRY 3

wedded *adj* of or relating to marriage — see MARITAL

wedding *n* a ceremony in which two people are united in matrimony ⟨they chose to have the *wedding* outdoors in the spring⟩
synonyms bridal, espousal, marriage, nuptial(s)
related words match, matrimony, wedlock; reception; engagement, hand, pledge, promise, proposal, troth

wedge *vb* to fit (something) into a tight space — see CROWD 1

wedged *adj* firmly positioned in place and difficult to dislodge — see TIGHT 2

wedlock *n* a union representing a special kind of social and legal partnership between two people — see MARRIAGE 1

wee *adj* very small in size — see TINY

weedy *adj* growing thickly and vigorously — see RANK 1

weep *vb* **1** to flow forth slowly through small openings — see EXUDE
2 to shed tears often while making meaningless sounds as a sign of pain or distress — see CRY 1

weeping *adj* expressing or suggesting mourning — see MOURNFUL 1

weigh *vb* **1** to be of importance — see MATTER
2 to give serious and careful thought to — see PONDER

weigh (on *or* upon) *vb* to push steadily against with some force — see PRESS 1

weighed *adj* decided on as a result of careful thought — see DELIBERATE 1

weight *n* **1** the amount that something weighs ⟨I'm not allowed to lift anything with a *weight* of over ten pounds⟩
synonyms heaviness, heft
related words mass; tonnage; deadweight; heftiness, massiveness, ponderousness, weightiness; solidity, solidness, substantiality; burdensomeness, cumbersomeness
2 the quality or state of being important — see IMPORTANCE
3 a mass or quantity of something taken up and carried, conveyed, or transported — see LOAD 1
4 a special notice or importance given to something — see EMPHASIS 1
5 the main or greater part of something as distinguished from its appendages — see BODY 1
6 the power to direct the thinking or behavior of others usually indirectly — see INFLUENCE 1

weight *vb* to place a weight or burden on — see LOAD 1

weightiness *n* **1** the state or quality of being heavy ⟨the *weightiness* of the bookcase made it difficult to move⟩
synonyms avoirdupois, heaviness, heftiness, massiveness, ponderousness
related words overweight; solidity, solidness, substantiality; bulk, bulkiness, hugeness; burdensomeness, cumbersomeness
near antonyms airiness, delicacy, etherealness; flimsiness, fluffiness, insubstantiality, slightness
antonyms lightness, weightlessness
2 the quality or state of being important — see IMPORTANCE

weightless *adj* having little weight — see [1]LIGHT 1

weightlessness *n* the state or quality of having little weight — see [1]LIGHTNESS 1

weighty *adj* **1** having a matter of importance as its topic — see SERIOUS 2
2 having great meaning or lasting effect — see IMPORTANT 1
3 having great weight — see HEAVY 1
4 not joking or playful in mood or manner — see SERIOUS 1
5 having power over the minds or behavior of others — see INFLUENTIAL 1

weird *adj* **1** different from the ordinary in a way that causes curiosity or suspicion — see ODD 2

2 fearfully and mysteriously strange or fantastic — see EERIE
3 having seemingly supernatural qualities or powers — see MYSTIC 1
4 noticeably different from what is generally found or experienced — see UNUSUAL 1
weirdo *n* a person of odd or whimsical habits — see ECCENTRIC
welcome *adj* giving pleasure or contentment to the mind or senses — see PLEASANT
welcome *n* an expression of goodwill upon meeting — see HELLO
welcome *vb* receive or accept gladly or readily ⟨the eager recruits *welcomed* every new project with which they were presented⟩
synonyms embrace
related words adopt, espouse, take up; greet, hail; enjoy, like, prefer; choose, cull, decide (on), elect, handpick, name, opt (for), pick, select, single (out), take
near antonyms decline, refuse, reject, turn down
welfare *n* the state of doing well especially in relation to one's happiness or success ⟨the social worker was pleased at the improvement in the child's *welfare*⟩
synonyms good, interest, weal, well-being
related words prosperity, success, successfulness; fitness, health, healthiness, robustness, soundness, wellness, wholeness, wholesomeness; bliss, felicity, happiness, joy; advantage, benefit, gain, sake; content, contentedness, gratification, satisfaction
near antonyms unhealthiness, unsoundness; misery, sadness, unhappiness, wretchedness
well *adv* 1 in a satisfactory way ⟨our current system for dividing household chores works *well*, so let's keep it⟩
synonyms acceptably, adequately, all right, fine, good, nicely, OK (*or* okay), passably, satisfactorily, so-so, tolerably
related words appropriately, congruously, correctly, decently, decorously, felicitously, fittingly, meetly, rightly, seemly, suitably
near antonyms unbearably; inappropriately, incorrectly, indecently, unsuitably
antonyms bad, badly, inadequately, intolerably, poorly, unacceptably, unsatisfactorily
2 in a generous manner ⟨the warm and gracious couple always treat overnight guests *well*⟩
synonyms bountifully, generously, handsomely, liberally, munificently
related words considerately, courteously, hospitably, kindly, nicely, reasonably, thoughtfully; affably, amiably, cheerfully, cheerily, genially, good-naturedly, graciously
near antonyms contemptuously, disdainfully, rudely, scornfully; obnoxiously, provocatively; coldly, coolly, frigidly, hostilely; angrily, belligerently
antonyms stingily
3 in a skillful or expert manner ⟨she plays the piano very *well*⟩
synonyms ably, adeptly, capably, competently, expertly, masterfully, proficiently, skillfully
related words aptly; adroitly, deftly, dexterously
near antonyms inaptly
antonyms incapably, incompetently, inefficiently, ineptly, inexpertly, poorly, unskillfully
4 with good reason or courtesy ⟨we cannot *well* get out of going to your cousin's wedding⟩
synonyms considerately, courteously, kindly, nicely, reasonably, thoughtfully
related words pleasantly; excusably, justifiably
near antonyms contemptuously, disdainfully, rudely, scornfully
5 in a pleasing way ⟨the day went *well*, despite the rough beginning⟩
synonyms agreeably, delectably, deliciously, delightfully, dreamily, favorably, felicitously, gloriously, nicely, pleasantly, pleasingly, satisfyingly, splendidly, swimmingly
related words finely, grandly; advantageously, helpfully; fortunately, happily, luckily; prosperously, successfully
antonyms badly
6 to a full extent or degree — see FULLY 1
well *adj* enjoying health and vigor — see HEALTHY 1
well *interj* how surprising, doubtful, or unbelievable — see NO
well–being *n* the state of doing well especially in relation to one's happiness or success — see WELFARE
wellborn *adj* of high birth, rank, or station — see NOBLE 1
well–bred *adj* showing consideration, courtesy, and good manners — see POLITE 1
well–disposed *adj* having an easygoing and pleasing manner especially in social situations — see AMIABLE
well–founded *adj* based on sound reasoning or information — see GOOD 1
well–heeled *adj* having goods, property, or money in abundance — see RICH 1
well–known *adj* widely known — see FAMOUS
wellness *n* the condition of being sound in body — see HEALTH
well–nigh *adv* very close to but not completely — see ALMOST
well–off *adj* having goods, property, or money in abundance — see RICH 1
well–read *adj* having or displaying advanced knowledge or education — see EDUCATED
well–spoken *adj* able to express oneself clearly and well — see ARTICULATE
well–to–do *adj* having goods, property, or money in abundance — see RICH 1
welter *n* 1 a state of noisy, confused activity — see COMMOTION
2 an unorganized collection or mixture of various things — see MISCELLANY 1
wet *adj* containing, covered with, or thoroughly penetrated by water ⟨I left the car windows open while it rained, and the seats got all *wet*⟩
synonyms awash, bathed, doused, drenched, dripping, saturated, soaked, soaking, sodden, soggy, soppy, soused, washed, watered, waterlogged, watery
related words deluged, drowned, flooded, inundated, overflowed; submerged, swamped; hydrated; dipped, dunked, splashed; aqueous; steeped; flushed, irrigated, laved, rinsed, sluiced; clammy, damp, dank, humid, moist
near antonyms waterproof, water-resistant, water-repellent, watertight; baked, dehydrated, freeze-dried; droughty, parched, sere, sunbaked, thirsty; wrung
antonyms arid, dry, unwatered, waterless
2 marked by or abounding with rain — see RAINY

wet *n* a steady falling of water from the sky in significant quantity — see RAIN 1

wet *vb* to make wet ⟨you need to *wet* your hair thoroughly first⟩
synonyms bathe, douse, drench, soak, souse, wash, water
related words damp, dampen, humidify, hydrate, moisten; deluge, drown, flood, inundate, overflow; submerge, swamp; splash; impregnate, saturate, steep; flush, irrigate, lave, rinse, sluice; dip, dunk
near antonyms bake, dehydrate, evaporate, freeze-dry, parch; wring; dehumidify
antonyms dry

whack *n* **1** an effort to do or accomplish something — see ATTEMPT
2 a hard strike with a part of the body or an instrument — see ^{1}BLOW
3 a loud explosive sound — see CLAP 1

whack *vb* to deliver a blow to (someone or something) usually in a strong vigorous manner — see HIT 1

whacking *adj* unusually large — see HUGE

whacking *adv* to a great degree — see VERY 1

whale *n* something that is unusually large and powerful — see GIANT

whale *vb* **1** to deliver a blow to (someone or something) usually in a strong vigorous manner — see HIT 1
2 to strike repeatedly with something long and thin or flexible — see WHIP 1
3 to strike repeatedly — see BEAT 1

wharf *n* a structure used by boats and ships for taking on or landing cargo and passengers — see DOCK

what *interj* how surprising, doubtful, or unbelievable — see NO

wheedle *vb* to get (someone) to do something by gentle urging, special attention, or flattery — see COAX

wheel *n* a rapid turning about on an axis or central point — see SPIN 1

wheel *vb* **1** to change the course or direction of (something) — see TURN 2
2 to move (something) in a curved or circular path on or as if on an axis — see TURN 1
3 to move in circles around an axis or center — see SPIN 1
4 to turn away from a straight line or course — see CURVE 1

wheeze *vb* to breathe hard, quickly, or with difficulty — see GASP

whelm *vb* to subject to incapacitating emotional or mental stress — see OVERWHELM 1

when *conj* in spite of the fact that — see ALTHOUGH

where *adv* at, in, or to what place ⟨*where* will you be tonight?⟩
synonyms whereabouts (*also* whereabout), whither
related words wherever

whereabouts *also* **whereabout** *adv* at, in, or to what place — see WHERE

whereas *conj* for the reason that — see SINCE

wherefore *adv* for this or that reason — see THEREFORE

wherefore *n* something (as a belief) that serves as the basis for another thing — see REASON 2

wherewithal *n* **1** available money — see FUND 2
2 the total of one's money and property — see WEALTH 1

whet *vb* to make sharp or sharper — see SHARPEN

whetted *adj* having an edge thin enough to cut or pierce something — see SHARP 1

whiff *vb* to become aware of by means of the sense organs in the nose — see SMELL 1

while *conj* in spite of the fact that — see ALTHOUGH

while *n* **1** an indefinite but usually short period of time ⟨we stayed at school for a *while* longer⟩
synonyms bit, space, spell, stretch
related words lapse; season, span; day, epoch, era; flash, instant, jiffy, minute, moment, second, shake, spurt, trice, twinkle, twinkling, wink; aeon (*or* eon), age, eternity; interim, interlude, intermission, interval
2 the active use of energy in producing a result — see EFFORT

whilom *adj* having been such at some previous time — see FORMER

whilst *conj chiefly British* in spite of the fact that — see ALTHOUGH

whim *n* a sudden impulsive and apparently unmotivated idea or action ⟨on a *whim,* we stopped at the roadside stand to get ice cream⟩
synonyms caprice, fancy, freak, notion, vagary, whimsy (*also* whimsey)
related words capriciousness, freakishness, whimsicality; conceit; concept, conception, image, impression, picture, thought; brainstorm, inspiration

whimper *vb* to utter feeble plaintive cries ⟨the dog *whimpered* to be let in⟩
synonyms mewl, pule
related words fuss, snivel, snuffle, whine; bawl, cry, weep; peep, squeak; yelp; mumble, murmur, mutter
near antonyms scream, screech, shriek, squeal; howl, squall, wail, yowl; call, caterwaul, squawk; bellow, roar

whimsical *adj* prone to sudden illogical changes of mind, ideas, or actions ⟨it's hard to make plans with my *whimsical* best friend⟩
synonyms capricious, freakish, impulsive
related words mercurial, moody, temperamental, volatile; eccentric, flaky, quirky; arbitrary, erratic, fickle, inconstant, irregular, willful (*or* wilful); impractical, quixotic, romantic
near antonyms equable; levelheaded, logical, practical, reasonable, sensible; fast, fixed, hard-and-fast, immutable, inflexible, invariable, unalterable, unchangeable; changeless, constant, established, set, settled, stable, steadfast, steady, unchanging, unvarying

whimsicality *n* an inclination to sudden illogical changes of mind, ideas, or actions ⟨her *whimsicality* made her unpredictable⟩
synonyms capriciousness, freakishness, impulsiveness
related words moodiness, volatility; eccentricity, flakiness; changeability, unpredictability; arbitrariness, fickleness, inconstancy, irregularity, willfulness; changeability, flexibility, mutability, variability
near antonyms levelheadedness, practicality, reasonableness; fastness, fixedness, immutability, inflexibility, invariability; changelessness, constancy, stability, steadfastness, steadiness

whimsy *also* **whimsey** *n* a sudden impulsive and

apparently unmotivated idea or action — see WHIM

whine *vb* to express dissatisfaction, pain, or resentment usually tiresomely — see COMPLAIN

whiner *n* **1** a person who makes frequent complaints usually about little things — see CRYBABY

2 an irritable and complaining person — see GROUCH

whinny *vb* to make the cry typical of a horse — see NEIGH

whip *n* a long thin or flexible tool for striking ⟨please do not use your belt as a *whip*⟩

synonyms flogger, lash, scourge, switch

related words blacksnake, cat-o'-nine-tails, cowhide, crop, knout, quirt, rawhide, strap; cane, club, cudgel, flail; stripe

whip *vb* **1** to strike repeatedly with something long and thin or flexible ⟨*whipped* the animal when it did not move fast enough to please him⟩

synonyms birch, cowhide, flagellate, flail, flog, hide, horsewhip, lash, rawhide, scourge, slash, switch, tan, thrash, whale

related words cane, club, cudgel; stripe; bang, bop, box, bust, clap, clip, clobber, clout, crack, cuff, hit, knock, lam, paste, punch, slap, slug, smack, smite, sock, spank, swat, swipe, thwack, wallop, whack; bash, batter, belt, bludgeon, buffet, bung, drub, hammer, lace, lambaste (*or* lambast), lick, mangle, maul, pelt, pound, pummel, rough, thump

2 to defeat by a large margin ⟨we *whipped* them 13-0 in the last game⟩

synonyms clobber, drub, rout, skunk, snow under, thrash, trim, trounce, wallop

related words beat, best, conquer, hurdle, lick, master, overbear, overcome, overmatch, prevail (over), subdue, surmount, throw, triumph (over), win (against), worst; crush, overpower, overthrow, subjugate, vanquish; exceed, outdo, surpass

3 to achieve a victory over — see BEAT 2

4 to change the course or direction of (something) — see TURN 2

5 to move or cause to move with a striking motion — see FLAP

6 to strike repeatedly — see BEAT 1

whip (up) *vb* to cause or encourage the development of — see INCITE 1

whipper *n* one that defeats an enemy or opponent — see VICTOR 1

whippersnapper *n* a person of no importance or influence — see NOBODY

whipping *n* failure to win a contest — see DEFEAT 1

whipping boy *n* a person or thing taking the blame for others — see SCAPEGOAT

whir *also* **whirr** *vb* to fly, turn, or move rapidly with a fluttering or vibratory sound ⟨the hummingbird *whirred* as it hovered over a flower⟩ ⟨our tires *whirred* as we traveled over the rough road⟩

synonyms buzz, drone, hum, whish, whiz (*or* whizz), zip, zoom

related words thrum; hiss, murmur, purr, rustle, sigh, whisper

whir *n* a monotonous sound like that of an insect in motion — see HUM

whirl *n* **1** a rapid turning about on an axis or central point — see SPIN 1

2 a state of mental uncertainty — see CONFUSION 1

3 a state of noisy, confused activity — see COMMOTION

whirl *vb* **1** to cause (as a liquid) to move about in a circle especially repeatedly — see STIR 1

2 to move (something) in a curved or circular path on or as if on an axis — see TURN 1

3 to move in circles around an axis or center — see SPIN 1

4 to proceed or move quickly — see HURRY 2

5 to be in a confused state as if from being twirled around — see SPIN 2

whirling *adj* having a feeling of being whirled about and in danger of falling down — see DIZZY 1

whirlpool *n* water moving rapidly in a circle with a hollow in the center ⟨in *The Odyssey*, Ulysses is trapped between the six-headed monster Scylla and Charybdis, a deadly *whirlpool* that threatens to suck his ship down⟩

synonyms maelstrom, vortex

related words eddy, swirl, whirl

whirlwind *adj* moving, proceeding, or acting with great speed — see FAST 1

whish *n* a sound similar to the speech sound \s\ stretched out — see HISS 1

whish *vb* **1** to fly, turn, or move rapidly with a fluttering or vibratory sound — see WHIRR

2 to make a sound like that of stretching out the speech sound \s\ — see HISS

whisk *vb* **1** to cause to move or proceed fast or faster — see HURRY 1

2 to move or proceed smoothly and readily — see FLOW 2

3 to proceed or move quickly — see HURRY 2

whisper *n* a rumor or report of a personal or sensational nature — see TALE 1

whisper *vb* to make (as a piece of information) the subject of common talk without any authority or confirmation of accuracy — see RUMOR

whistling *adj* having a high musical pitch or range — see SHRILL

whit *n* the smallest amount or part imaginable — see JOT

white *adj* **1** lacking an addition of color — see COLORLESS

2 not causing injury or hurt — see HARMLESS

whiten *vb* to make white or whiter by removing color ⟨years of sunlight had almost completely *whitened* the flag⟩

synonyms blanch, bleach, blench, decolorize, dull, fade, pale, wash out

related words brighten, lighten; dim, matte (*also* mat *or* matt); whitewash; frost, silver

near antonyms blacken; blotch, discolor, mottle, shade, splotch, spot, tarnish; color, dye, paint, stain, tinge, tint; burnish, polish, shine

antonyms darken, deepen

whitewash *vb* to make (something) seem less bad by offering excuses — see PALLIATE 1

whither *adv* at, in, or to what place — see WHERE

[1]**whiz** *or* **whizz** *n* **1** a sound similar to the speech sound \s\ stretched out — see HISS 1

2 a monotonous sound like that of an insect in motion — see HUM

[2]**whiz** *n* **1** a person with a high level of knowledge or skill in a field — see EXPERT

2 a very smart person — see GENIUS 1

whiz *or* **whizz** *vb* **1** to make a sound like that of stretching out the speech sound \s\ — see HISS

2 to fly, turn, or move rapidly with a fluttering or vibratory sound — see WHIRR

whole *adj* **1** not divided or scattered among several areas of interest or concern ⟨you'll need to put your *whole* effort into this project⟩
synonyms all, concentrated, entire, exclusive, focused (*also* focussed), undivided
related words absolute, complete, full, thorough, total; comprehensive, intact, integral, perfect
near antonyms deficient, fragmental, fragmentary, incomplete, partial
antonyms diffuse, divided, scattered
2 enjoying health and vigor — see HEALTHY 1
3 not lacking any part or member that properly belongs to it — see COMPLETE 1
whole *n* a complete amount of something ⟨the landlord eventually refunded the *whole* of our deposit⟩
synonyms aggregate, full, sum, summation, total, totality
related words gross; completeness, comprehensiveness, entirety; bulk, lion's share, mass
phrases the whole kit and kaboodle, the whole shebang
near antonyms net
wholehearted *adj* characterized by unqualified enthusiasm — see HEARTY 1
wholeness *n* the condition of being sound in body — see HEALTH
whole number *n* a character used to represent a mathematical value — see NUMBER
wholesome *adj* **1** enjoying health and vigor — see HEALTHY 1
2 good for the health — see HEALTHFUL
wholesomeness *n* the condition of being sound in body — see HEALTH
wholly *adv* to a full extent or degree — see FULLY 1
whoop *n* a loud vocal expression of strong emotion — see SHOUT
whopper *n* **1** a statement known by its maker to be untrue and made in order to deceive — see LIE
2 something that is unusually large and powerful — see GIANT
whopping *adj* unusually large — see HUGE
whore *n* a woman who engages in sexual activities for money — see PROSTITUTE
why *interj* how surprising, doubtful, or unbelievable — see NO
why *n* something (as a belief) that serves as the basis for another thing — see REASON 2
wicked *adj* **1** not conforming to a high moral standard; morally unacceptable — see BAD 2
2 tending to or exhibiting reckless playfulness — see MISCHIEVOUS 1
wickedly *adv* in a mean or spiteful manner — see NASTILY
wickedness *n* **1** playful, reckless behavior that is not intended to cause serious harm — see MISCHIEF 1
2 the state or quality of being utterly evil — see ENORMITY 1
wide *adj* **1** having a greater than usual measure across ⟨the river was so *wide* that it was impossible to cross it in less than a day⟩
synonyms broad, fat, thick
related words expansive, extensive; commodious, roomy, spacious
near antonyms fine, hairlike; elongated; needlelike; close, compressed, condensed, constricted, contracted, squeezed, tight, tightened
antonyms narrow, skinny, slender, slim, thin
2 having considerable extent — see EXTENSIVE
wide–awake *adj* **1** not sleeping or able to sleep — see WAKEFUL
2 paying close attention usually for the purpose of anticipating approaching danger or opportunity — see ALERT 1
wide–eyed *adj* lacking in worldly wisdom or informed judgment — see NAIVE 1
widespread *adj* having considerable extent — see EXTENSIVE
width *n* an area over which activity, capacity, or influence extends — see RANGE 2
wield *vb* to bring to bear especially forcefully or effectively — see EXERT
wife *n* the female partner in a marriage ⟨a husband and *wife* who treat each other as equals in their marriage⟩
synonyms helpmate, helpmeet, lady
related words bride; consort, mate, partner, spouse; dowager, matron; homemaker, housewife
wiggle *vb* to make jerky or restless movements — see FIDGET
wight *n* a member of the human race — see HUMAN
wild *adj* **1** living outdoors without taming or domestication by humans ⟨*wild* animals can be shy or aggressive when confronted by humans⟩
synonyms feral, savage, unbroken, undomesticated, untamed
related words uncontrolled, unsubdued; bestial, brutal, brute; barbarous, uncivilized
near antonyms controlled, subdued; housebroken, trained; civilized, socialized
antonyms broken, busted, domestic, domesticated, tame, tamed
2 existing without human habitation or cultivation ⟨that land has been completely *wild* since the owners abandoned it⟩
synonyms natural, uncultivated, untamed
related words native; uninhabited; overgrown, untended; waste; undeveloped
near antonyms inhabited; developed
antonyms cultivated, tamed
3 marked by turmoil or disturbance especially of natural elements ⟨a *wild* night, full of wind and rain⟩
synonyms stormy, tempestuous, tumultuous, turbulent
related words blustery, rough, violent; brutal, harsh, severe; unsettled
near antonyms calm, halcyon, peaceful, placid, quiet, serene, tranquil
4 conceived or made without regard for reason or reality — see FANTASTIC 1
5 different from the ordinary in a way that causes curiosity or suspicion — see ODD 2
6 marked by great and often stressful excitement or activity — see FURIOUS 1
7 not civilized — see SAVAGE 1
wild *adv* in a confused and reckless manner — see HELTER-SKELTER 1
wild *n* that part of the physical world that is removed from human habitation — see NATURE 2
wilderness *n* that part of the physical world that is removed from human habitation — see NATURE 2
wildly *adv* in a confused and reckless manner — see HELTER-SKELTER 1

wile *n* **1** a clever often underhanded means to achieve an end — see TRICK 1
2 the use of clever underhanded actions to achieve an end — see TRICKERY

wile *vb* to attract or delight as if by magic — see CHARM 1

wiliness *n* **1** skill in achieving one's ends through indirect, subtle, or underhanded means — see CUNNING 1
2 the inclination or practice of misleading others through lies or trickery — see DECEIT

will *n* **1** the power to control one's actions, impulses, or emotions ⟨she kept her face still by sheer force of *will*⟩
synonyms restraint, self-containment, self-control, self-discipline, self-government, self-possession, self-restraint, willpower
related words self-denial; moderation, temperance; determination, nerve; command, control, discipline, mastery; aplomb, assurance, composure, confidence, coolness, equanimity, poise, self-confidence; discretion
near antonyms gratification, indulgence, self-indulgence; immoderacy, intemperance, overindulgence; demerit, failing, fault, feebleness, foible, frailty, shortcoming, vice, weakness
2 the act or power of making one's own choices or decisions — see FREE WILL

will *vb* **1** to give by means of a will — see LEAVE 2
2 to see fit — see CHOOSE 2

willful *or* **wilful** *adj* **1** given to resisting authority or another's control — see DISOBEDIENT
2 given to resisting control or discipline by others — see UNCONTROLLABLE
3 having or showing a tendency to force one's will on others without any regard to fairness or necessity — see ARBITRARY 1
4 made, given, or done with full awareness of what one is doing — see INTENTIONAL
5 sticking to an opinion, purpose, or course of action in spite of reason, arguments, or persuasion — see OBSTINATE

willfully *adv* with full awareness of what one is doing — see INTENTIONALLY

willfulness *n* **1** a steadfast adherence to an opinion, purpose, or course of action — see OBSTINACY
2 refusal to obey — see DISOBEDIENCE

willies *n pl* a sense of panic or extreme nervousness — see JITTERS

willing *adj* **1** having a desire or inclination (as for a specified course of action) ⟨I'm a little confused, but perfectly *willing* to do as you ask⟩
synonyms amenable, disposed, game, glad, inclined, ready
related words predisposed; agreeable, compliant, obedient, submissive; favorable, receptive; prepared, prompt, quick, responsive, swift
near antonyms averse, loath, reluctant
antonyms disinclined, unwilling
2 having or showing the ability to respond without delay or hesitation — see QUICK 1
3 done, made, or given with one's own free will — see VOLUNTARY 1

willingly *adv* **1** by choice or preference — see RATHER 1
2 of one's own free will — see VOLUNTARILY

willingness *n* cheerful readiness to do something — see ALACRITY

williwaw *n* a sudden brief rush of wind — see GUST 1

willowy *adj* able to bend easily without breaking ⟨the rattan's stems are split into *willowy* staves that are woven together to produce exquisite baskets⟩
synonyms flexible, limber, lissome (*also* lissom), lithe, pliable, pliant, supple
related words adaptable, ductile, elastic, fluid, malleable, modifiable, plastic, variable, yielding; flaccid, floppy
near antonyms inelastic, nonmalleable, unyielding; breakable, brittle, fragile
antonyms inflexible, rigid, stiff

willpower *n* the power to control one's actions, impulses, or emotions — see WILL 1

wilt *vb* **1** to be limp from lack of water or vigor — see DROOP 1
2 to lose bodily strength or vigor — see WEAKEN 2
3 to lose liveliness, force, or freshness — see WITHER

wily *adj* clever at attaining one's ends by indirect and often deceptive means — see ARTFUL 1

wimp *n* **1** a person lacking in physical strength — see WEAKLING 1
2 a person without strength of character — see WEAKLING 2

wimpy *adj* **1** lacking bodily strength — see WEAK 1
2 lacking strength of will or character — see WEAK 2

win *n* an instance of defeating an enemy or opponent — see VICTORY

win *vb* **1** to achieve victory (as in a contest) ⟨the kind of person who always has to *win* —even if the game is just for fun⟩
synonyms conquer, prevail, triumph
related words overcome, sweep; squeak, squeeze; contend, vie; succeed
phrases carry the day
near antonyms collapse, fail, flop, fold, wash out; flounder, struggle; decline, slip, slump, wane
antonyms lose
2 to receive as return for effort — see EARN 1
3 to obtain (as a goal) through effort — see ACHIEVE 1

win (against) *vb* to achieve a victory over — see BEAT 2

win (over) *vb* to cause (someone) to agree with a belief or course of action by using arguments or earnest requests — see PERSUADE

wince *vb* to draw back in fear, pain, or disgust — see FLINCH

[1]**wind** *n* **1** noticeable movement of air in a particular direction ⟨there's a *wind* coming from underneath the front door⟩
synonyms current, draft
related words blast, blow, flurry, gale, gust, head wind, squall, tail wind, tempest, tornado, windstorm; breath, breeze, puff, waft, zephyr
2 a prevailing or general movement or inclination — see TREND 1
3 language that is impressive-sounding but not meaningful or sincere — see RHETORIC 1

[2]**wind** *n* something that curves or is curved — see BEND 1

wind *vb* to follow a circular or spiral course ⟨flowering vines *wind* around the porch's graceful columns⟩
synonyms coil, curl, entwine, spiral, twine, twist
related words arc, arch, bend, crook, curve, hook,

sweep, swerve, turn, veer, wheel; swirl, whirl; circle, encircle, loop, interlace, intertwine, lace; bow, bulge; meander, weave, zigzag
near antonyms straighten

windfall *n* something that provides happiness or does good for a person or thing — see BLESSING 2

windiness *n* the use of too many words to express an idea — see VERBIAGE

winding *adj* **1** marked by a long series of irregular curves — see CROOKED 1
2 turning around an axis like the thread of a screw — see SPIRAL

windjammer *n* a boat equipped with one or more sails — see SAILBOAT

windup *n* the last part of a process or action — see FINALE

wind up *vb* **1** to bring (an event) to a natural or appropriate stopping point — see CLOSE 3
2 to come to an end — see CEASE 1

windy *adj* **1** marked by strong wind or more wind than usual ⟨one particularly *windy* day should shake the last of the autumn leaves from the trees⟩
synonyms blowy, blustery, breezy, gusty
related words drafty; stormy, tempestuous
near antonyms breathless, calm, motionless, still
2 marked by the use of impressive-sounding but mostly meaningless words and phrases — see RHETORICAL
3 using or containing more words than necessary to express an idea — see WORDY

wing *n* a group of people acting together within a larger group — see FACTION

wing *vb* to move through the air with or as if with outstretched wings — see FLY 1

wink *n* **1** a short sleep — see [1]NAP
2 a very small space of time — see INSTANT

wink *vb* **1** to rapidly open and close one's eyes ⟨she *winked* several times to get the dust and grit out of her eyes⟩
synonyms blink
related words bat, flutter; squint
2 to shine with light at regular intervals — see BLINK 1
3 to shoot forth bursts of light — see FLASH 1
4 to secretly sympathize with or pretend ignorance of something improper or unlawful — see CONNIVE

wink (at) *vb* to overlook or dismiss as of little importance — see EXCUSE 1

winner *n* **1** a person or thing that is successful — see HIT 1
2 one that defeats an enemy or opponent — see VICTOR 1
3 the person who comes in first in a competition — see CHAMPION 1

winning *adj* **1** having qualities that tend to make one loved — see LOVABLE
2 likely to win one's affection — see INGRATIATING

winsome *adj* likely to win one's affection — see INGRATIATING

wintry *adj* **1** having a low or subnormal temperature — see COLD 1
2 lacking in friendliness or warmth of feeling — see COLD 2

wipe out *vb* to destroy all traces of — see ANNIHILATE 1

wire *n* a length of braided, flexible material that is used for tying or connecting things — see CORD

wisdom *n* **1** the ability to understand inner qualities or relationships ⟨with age and experience comes *wisdom* —hopefully⟩ ⟨neither book learning nor simple intelligence should be confused with *wisdom*⟩
synonyms discernment, insight, perception, perceptiveness, sagaciousness, sagacity, sageness, sapience
related words acuity, acumen, astuteness, penetration, perspicacity, sensitivity, understanding; appreciation, apprehension, comprehension, grasp; braininess, brain(s), brightness, brilliance, canniness, cleverness, gray matter, intellect, intelligence, judgment (*or* judgement), mentality, power, reason, sense, smartness, wit; discrimination, judiciousness, prudence, sanity; logic, rationality
near antonyms density, dullness (*or* dulness), obtuseness; brainlessness, folly, foolishness, idiocy, imbecility, mindlessness, silliness, simpleness, stupidity, witlessness; illogic, irrationality, unreasonableness, unsoundness; craziness, insanity, lunacy, madness; preposterousness, senselessness, silliness, zaniness
2 a body of facts learned by study or experience — see KNOWLEDGE 1
3 the ability to make intelligent decisions especially in everyday matters — see COMMON SENSE

wise *adj* **1** having or showing deep understanding and intelligent application of knowledge ⟨a respected and *wise* old judge famous for her sensible rulings⟩
synonyms discerning, insightful, perceptive, sagacious, sage, sapient
related words acute, perspicacious; experienced; discriminating, discriminative; brainy, brilliant, bright, clever, intelligent, keen, nimble, quick, quick-witted, smart; cerebral, erudite, knowledgeable, learned, literate, scholarly; astute, sharp, shrewd; contemplative, reflective, thoughtful
near antonyms dense, dull, obtuse; brainless, dumb, feebleminded, foolish, idiotic, imbecilic, moronic, silly, simple, slow, stupid, thoughtless, unintelligent, witless; undiscriminating
antonyms undiscerning, unperceptive, unwise
2 having inside information ⟨they fooled everyone else, but I'd heard them talking and was *wise* to their true intentions⟩
synonyms hip, knowing
related words alerted, aware, clued, forewarned, informed, prepared, ready, warned; observant, observing, sharp, sharp-eyed; alert, attentive, open-eyed, vigilant, watchful
phrases in the know
near antonyms oblivious, unaware, unconscious, uninformed, unperceiving, unseeing, unwitting; heedless, unmindful, unobservant, unobserving; unprepared, unready, unwary
antonyms unknowing
3 suitable for bringing about a desired result under the circumstances — see EXPEDIENT

wise (up) *vb* to give information to — see ENLIGHTEN 1

wiseacre *n* a person who likes to show off in a clever but annoying way — see SMART ALECK

wisecrack *n* something said or done to cause laughter — see JOKE 1

wisecrack *vb* to make jokes — see JOKE

wise guy *n* a person who likes to show off in a clever but annoying way — see SMART ALECK
wish *vb* to see fit — see CHOOSE 2
wish (for) *vb* to have an earnest wish to own or enjoy — see DESIRE
wishy–washy *adj* **1** lacking in qualities that make for spirit and character <this story is too *wishy-washy*; you need to add some verve to it>
synonyms banal, flat, insipid
related words unentertaining, unexciting, uninspiring, unrewarding, unsatisfying; bland, boring, drab, dreary, dry, dull, heavy, humdrum, jading, leaden, monotonous, pedestrian, ponderous, tedious, tiresome, tiring, uninteresting, wearisome, weary, wearying; inane; innocuous, inoffensive; mild, soft, subdued, tame, weak; common, commonplace, ordinary, stale, unexceptional
near antonyms piquant, poignant, pungent, racy, spicy; meaty, substantial; entertaining, exciting, galvanizing, inspiring, invigorating, thrilling
2 lacking strength of will or character — see WEAK 2
wit *n* **1** a person (as a writer) noted for or specializing in humor — see HUMORIST
2 the ability to make intelligent decisions especially in everyday matters — see COMMON SENSE
3 the normal or healthy condition of the mental abilities — see MIND 2
witch *n* **1** a woman believed to have often harmful supernatural powers <in the old days women were sometimes accused of being *witches* and using evil magic to make the crops fail or an animal die suddenly>
synonyms enchantress, hag, hex, sorceress
related words charmer, conjuror (*or* conjurer), enchanter, necromancer, voodoo; magician, sorcerer, warlock, wizard
2 a mean or ugly old woman — see CRONE
3 a person skilled in using supernatural forces — see MAGICIAN 1
witchcraft *n* the power to control natural forces through supernatural means — see MAGIC 1
witchery *n* **1** the power of irresistible attraction — see CHARM 2
2 the power to control natural forces through supernatural means — see MAGIC 1
with *prep* **1** as the result of — see BECAUSE OF
2 using the means or agency of — see BY 2
3 without being prevented by — see DESPITE
withal *adv* **1** in addition to what has been said — see MORE 1
2 in spite of that — see HOWEVER
withdraw *vb* **1** to move back or away (as from something difficult, dangerous, or disagreeable) — see RETREAT 1
2 to solemnly or formally reject or go back on (as something formerly adhered to) — see ABJURE
3 to take away from a place or position — see REMOVE 2
withdrawal *n* an act of moving away especially from something difficult, dangerous, or disagreeable — see RETREAT 1
wither *vb* to lose liveliness, force, or freshness <shortly after the moon landing, interest in the space program *withered*> <the old man seemed to *wither* suddenly when he turned eighty>
synonyms dry, wilt
related words mummify, shrivel, wizen; decline, fade, wane; decrease, diminish, lessen
near antonyms freshen, revive; flourish, prosper, thrive; develop, grow, increase, wax; crest, peak, surge
withhold *vb* **1** to be unwilling to grant — see DENY 2
2 to continue to have in one's possession or power — see KEEP 2
within *n* an interior or internal part — see INSIDE 1
without *prep* **1** not having <spent two days *without* food>
synonyms minus, sans, wanting
2 out of the reach or sphere of — see BEYOND 2
withstand *vb* to refuse to give in to — see RESIST
witless *adj* **1** not having or showing an ability to absorb ideas readily — see STUPID 1
2 showing or marked by a lack of good sense or judgment — see FOOLISH 1
witlessness *n* **1** lack of good sense or judgment — see FOOLISHNESS 1
2 the quality or state of lacking intelligence or quickness of mind — see STUPIDITY 1
witness *n* something presented in support of the truth or accuracy of a claim — see PROOF
witness *vb* **1** to declare (something) to be true or genuine — see CERTIFY 1
2 to make note of (something) through the use of one's eyes — see SEE 1
3 to make a solemn declaration under oath for the purpose of establishing a fact — see TESTIFY
witticism *n* something said or done to cause laughter — see JOKE 1
wittingly *adv* with full awareness of what one is doing — see INTENTIONALLY
witty *adj* given to or marked by mature intelligent humor <Susan is popular because she is so *witty* and fun-loving> <he's well-known for his *witty* retorts>
synonyms clever, facetious, humorous, jocular, smart
related words cerebral, highbrow, intellectual; bantering, frivolous, jesting, joking, joshing, teasing; antic, comic, comical, droll, farcical, funny, hysterical, laughable, ludicrous, ridiculous, riotous, risible, rollicking, screaming, side-splitting, uproarious; amusing, diverting, entertaining; mischievous, playful, prankish; jocose, jocund, jolly, jovial, laughing, merry, mirthful, sunny; scintillating, sparkling; flip, flippant, pert, smart-alecky (*or* smart-aleck); whimsical
near antonyms brainless, lowbrow, stupid, witless; corny, hackneyed, lame; humorless, uncomic, unfunny; earnest, grave, serious, sober, solemn, somber (*or* sombre); doleful, dolorous, lachrymose, plaintive, sorry, tearful, woeful
wizard *n* **1** a person skilled in using supernatural forces — see MAGICIAN 1
2 a person with a high level of knowledge or skill in a field — see EXPERT
3 a very smart person — see GENIUS 1
wizardry *n* the power to control natural forces through supernatural means — see MAGIC 1
wobble *vb* **1** to make a series of small irregular or violent movements — see SHAKE 1
2 to make a series of unsteady side-to-side motions — see ROCK 1
3 to show uncertainty about the right course of action — see HESITATE
4 to swing unsteadily back and forth or from side to side — see TEETER 1
wobbling *adj* marked by or given to small uncontrollable bodily movements — see SHAKY 1

wobbling *n* the act or an instance of pausing because of uncertainty about the right course of action — see HESITATION
wobbly *adj* marked by or given to small uncontrollable bodily movements — see SHAKY 1
woe *n* **1** a state of great suffering of body or mind — see DISTRESS 1
2 deep sadness especially for the loss of someone or something loved — see SORROW
woebegone *adj* feeling unhappiness — see SAD 1
woeful *adj* **1** expressing or suggesting mourning — see MOURNFUL 1
2 feeling unhappiness — see SAD 1
3 of a kind to cause great distress — see REGRETTABLE
woefully *adv* with feelings of bitterness or grief — see HARD 2
woman *n* an adult female human being ⟨for a while, the toddler called every *woman* "mama"⟩
synonyms female, lady
related words dame, gentlewoman; madam, madame, senora (*or* señora); beauty, belle, chick [*slang*], damsel, doll, gal, girl, ingenue (*or* ingénue), lass, lassie, mademoiselle, maid, maiden, miss, senorita (*or* señorita)
womanish *adj* **1** having or displaying qualities more suitable for women than for men — see EFFEMINATE
2 of, relating to, or marked by qualities traditionally associated with women — see FEMININE 1
womanlike *adj* **1** having or displaying qualities more suitable for women than for men — see EFFEMINATE
2 of, relating to, or marked by qualities traditionally associated with women — see FEMININE 1
womanly *adj* **1** having or displaying qualities more suitable for women than for men — see EFFEMINATE
2 of, relating to, or marked by qualities traditionally associated with women — see FEMININE 1
wonder *n* **1** something extraordinary or surprising ⟨the cunningly crafted miniature of our house is a *wonder*, perfect in every detail⟩
synonyms caution, flash, marvel, miracle, phenomenon, portent, prodigy, sensation
related words curiosity, sight, spectacle; apparition, appearance
2 the rapt attention and deep emotion caused by the sight of something extraordinary ⟨when we first saw the pyramids of Egypt, we gazed with openmouthed *wonder*⟩
synonyms admiration, amazement, astonishment, awe, wonderment
related words dread; fear; respect, reverence, veneration; curiosity, interest; shock, surprise; disbelief, incomprehension, incredulity; beguilement, bewitchment, captivation, enchantment, fascination; animation, enlightenment, enlivenment, excitement, invigoration, stimulation; absorption, engagement, engrossment, enthrallment, immersion, involvement
near antonyms apathy, disinterest, incuriosity, indifference, unconcern; boredom, doldrums, ennui, listlessness, restlessness, tedium, tiredness, weariness; cheerlessness, dispiritedness, joylessness, melancholy
wonderful *adj* **1** causing wonder or astonishment — see MARVELOUS 1
2 of the very best kind — see EXCELLENT
wondering *adj* filled with amazement or wonder — see OPENMOUTHED
wonderment *n* the rapt attention and deep emotion caused by the sight of something extraordinary — see WONDER 2
wondrous *adj* causing wonder or astonishment — see MARVELOUS 1
wont *adj* being in the habit or custom — see ACCUSTOMED
wont *n* a usual manner of behaving or doing — see HABIT
woo *vb* to act so as to make (something) more likely — see COURT 1
wood *n* tree logs as prepared for human use ⟨a huge load of *wood* outside the furniture maker's factory⟩
synonyms lumber, timber
related words beam, brace, pile, post, ridgepole, sill, splint, stake, stave, stick; bar, billet, block; cordwood, firewood
wood *n, often* **woods** *pl* a dense growth of trees and shrubs covering a large area — see FOREST
wooden *adj* lacking social grace and assurance — see AWKWARD 1
woodland *n* a dense growth of trees and shrubs covering a large area — see FOREST
wooer *n* a man who courts a woman usually with the goal of marrying her — see SUITOR 1
wool *n* the hairy covering of a mammal especially when fine, soft, and thick — see FUR 1
woolgathering *n* the state of being lost in thought — see REVERIE
woolly *also* **wooly** *adj* **1** made of or resembling hair — see HAIRY 2
2 covered with or as if with hair — see HAIRY 1
word *n* **1** a pronounceable series of letters having a distinct meaning especially in a particular field ⟨my doctor used all of these medical *words* that I didn't understand⟩
synonyms expression, term
related words linguistic form, monosyllable, morpheme; collocation, idiom, locution, phrase; archaism, coinage, colloquialism, euphemism, loan word, modernism, neologism
2 something that is said ⟨people who believe that the Bible is the literal *word* of God⟩
synonyms statement, utterance
related words communication, message; announcement, declamation, declaration, manifesto, proclamation, pronouncement
3 a report of recent events or facts not previously known — see NEWS
4 a person's solemn declaration that he or she will do or not do something — see PROMISE
5 a statement of what to do that must be obeyed by those concerned — see COMMAND 1
word *vb* to convey in appropriate or telling terms — see PHRASE
wordbook *n* a reference book giving information about the meanings, pronunciations, uses, and origins of words listed in alphabetical order — see DICTIONARY
wordiness *n* the use of too many words to express an idea — see VERBIAGE
wording *n* the way in which something is put into words ⟨it's important to get the *wording* of this law precisely correct⟩
synonyms diction, language, phraseology, phrasing
related words expression, formulation, locution;

enunciation, phrase, speech, style, utterance, voice

wordless *adj* understood although not put into words — see IMPLICIT

wordy *adj* using or containing more words than necessary to express an idea <your paper is two pages too long—it doesn't need to be so *wordy*>
synonyms circuitous, circumlocutory, diffuse, long-winded, prolix, rambling, verbose, windy
related words chatty, communicative, conversational, gabby, garrulous, loquacious, talkative, talky, voluble; redundant, repetitious, tautological; embellished, embroidered, exaggerated; bombastic, grandiloquent, highfalutin
near antonyms brief, short; aphoristic, epigrammatic, sententious; compendious, summary; abbreviated, abridged, condensed, shortened; abrupt, blunt, brusque, curt, laconic, snippy
antonyms compact, concise, crisp, pithy, succinct, terse

work *n* **1** a literary, musical, or artistic production — see COMPOSITION 1
2 something produced by physical or intellectual effort — see PRODUCT 1
3 the action for which a person or thing is specially fitted or used or for which a thing exists — see ROLE
4 the active use of energy in producing a result — see EFFORT
5 the activity by which one regularly makes a living — see OCCUPATION
6 works *pl* a building or set of buildings for the manufacturing of goods — see FACTORY

work *vb* **1** to be the cause of (a situation, action, or state of mind) — see EFFECT
2 to find an answer for through reasoning — see SOLVE
3 to have a certain purpose — see FUNCTION
4 to produce a desired effect — see ACT 2
5 to set or keep in motion — see MOVE 2
6 to control the mechanical operation of — see OPERATE 1
7 to devote serious and sustained effort — see LABOR

work (for) *vb* to be a servant for — see SERVE 1

work (in) *vb* to introduce in a gradual, secret, or clever way — see INSINUATE

workable *adj* **1** capable of being done or carried out — see POSSIBLE 1
2 capable of being put to use or account — see PRACTICAL 1

workaday *adj* **1** being of the type that is encountered in the normal course of events — see ORDINARY 1
2 having to do with the practical details of regular life — see MUNDANE 1
3 not designed for special occasions — see CASUAL 1

worker *n* **1** a person who does very hard or dull work — see SLAVE 2
2 one who works for another for wages or a salary — see EMPLOYEE

working *adj* **1** being in effective operation — see ACTIVE 1
2 capable of being put to use or account — see PRACTICAL 1
3 involved in often constant activity — see BUSY 1

workmanlike *adj* accomplished with trained ability — see SKILLFUL 1

workout *n* something done over and over in order to develop skill — see EXERCISE 2

work out *vb* **1** to find an answer for through reasoning — see SOLVE
2 to produce or bring about especially by long or repeated effort — see HAMMER (OUT)
3 to turn out as planned or desired — see SUCCEED 1
4 to determine (a value) by doing the necessary mathematical operations — see CALCULATE 1

workshop *n* a building or set of buildings for the manufacturing of goods — see FACTORY

world *n* **1** human beings in general — see PEOPLE 1
2 the celestial body on which we live — see EARTH 1
3 the whole body of things observed or assumed — see UNIVERSE

worldly *adj* **1** having a wide and refined knowledge of the world especially from personal experience — see WORLDLY-WISE
2 having to do with life on earth especially as opposed to that in heaven — see EARTHLY

worldly–wise *adj* having a wide and refined knowledge of the world especially from personal experience <having followed their father on his military assignments all over the world, the Johnson kids have become very *worldly-wise*>
synonyms cosmopolitan, smart, sophisticated, worldly
related words suave, urbane; civilized, cultivated, cultured, polished, refined; experienced, knowing, practiced, schooled, seasoned; bored, cynical, jaded, skeptical; down-to-earth, pragmatic (*also* pragmatical), realistic, sober
near antonyms callow, green, inexperienced, raw; parochial, provincial, rustic; philistine, uncivilized, uncultured, unrefined; childlike, simple, simpleminded; idealistic, impractical; uncritical, unknowing
antonyms ingenuous, innocent, naive (*or* naïve), unsophisticated, unworldly, wide-eyed

worm *vb* **1** to advance gradually beyond the usual or desirable limits — see ENCROACH
2 to introduce in a gradual, secret, or clever way — see INSINUATE
3 to move slowly with the body close to the ground — see CRAWL 1

worn *adj* depleted in strength, energy, or freshness — see WEARY 1

worn–out *adj* **1** depleted in strength, energy, or freshness — see WEARY 1
2 worn or torn into or as if into rags — see RAGGED 2

worried *adj* feeling or showing uncomfortable feelings of uncertainty — see NERVOUS 1

worrisome *adj* **1** causing worry or anxiety — see TROUBLESOME
2 marked by or causing agitation or uncomfortable feelings — see NERVOUS 2

worry *n* an uneasy state of mind usually over the possibility of an anticipated misfortune or trouble — see ANXIETY 1

worry *vb* **1** to experience concern or anxiety <they *worried* for days about the upcoming exam>
synonyms bother, fear, fret, stew, sweat, trouble
related words agonize; long, pine, yearn; chafe; despair
phrases care a hang, give a hang
near antonyms accept; abide, bear, endure, stick out, stomach, sustain, take, tolerate

2 to trouble the mind of; to make uneasy — see DISTURB 1

worsen *vb* to become worse or of less value — see DETERIORATE

worship *n* excessive admiration of or devotion to a person ⟨his *worship* of his big brother meant that he'd go to any extreme for his idol⟩
synonyms adulation, deification, idolatry, idolization, worshipping (*also* worshiping)
related words adoration, deference, glorification, reverence, veneration; idealization, romanticization; affection, fancy, favor, fondness, like, liking, love; appreciation, esteem, regard, respect; approval
near antonyms condemnation, disapproval, disfavor, dislike, dismissal, disregard, hatred, loathing, scorn

worship *vb* **1** to offer honor or respect to (someone) as a divine power ⟨the ancient Greeks *worshipped* many different gods⟩
synonyms adore, deify, glorify, revere, reverence, venerate
related words admire, honor, love, regard, respect; dignify, exalt, magnify; extol (*also* extoll), laud, praise; delight, gratify, please, satisfy
near antonyms blaspheme, desecrate, profane, violate; affront, dishonor, disrespect, insult, offend, outrage, pique, ridicule, scorn, slight; displease; defame, disparage, libel, malign, slander, slur, smear
2 to feel passion, devotion, or tenderness for — see LOVE 2
3 to love or admire too much — see IDOLIZE

worshipful *adj* reflecting great admiration or devotion ⟨a movie fan's *worshipful* stare upon finally meeting her idol⟩ ⟨a teacher surrounded by *worshipful* little children⟩
synonyms adoring, adulatory, deifying, idolizing, worshipping (*also* worshiping)
related words glorifying, reverential, venerating; affectionate, fond, loving; appreciative, deferential, respectful; approving
near antonyms condemning, contemptuous, disapproving, hateful, loathing, scornful

worshipping *also* **worshiping** *n* excessive admiration of or devotion to a person — see WORSHIP

worshipping *also* **worshiping** *adj* reflecting great admiration or devotion — see WORSHIPFUL

worst *vb* to achieve a victory over — see BEAT 2

worth *n* **1** the relative usefulness or importance of something as judged by specific qualities ⟨money alone cannot determine the true *worth* of some things⟩
synonyms account, merit, valuation, value
related words assessment, estimation, evaluation; excellence, greatness, perfection; consequence, importance, significance, weight; desirability
near antonyms emptiness, worthlessness; baseness, cheapness, inferiority, meanness, paltriness, pettiness, poorness; deficiency, inadequacy, insufficiency, unacceptability
2 the amount of money for which something will find a buyer — see VALUE 1

worthless *adj* having no usefulness ⟨that expensive toy is *worthless* now that it's broken⟩
synonyms chaffy, empty, no-good, junky, null, valueless
related words base, cheap, inferior, lousy, low-grade, second-rate; bad, defective, flawed, imperfect, substandard, unsatisfactory; deficient, inadequate, insufficient, unacceptable
near antonyms invaluable, precious, priceless; cherished, esteemed, prized, treasured; choice, exceptional, fancy, high-grade, special
antonyms useful, valuable, worthy

worthy *adj* having sufficient worth or merit to receive one's honor, esteem, or reward ⟨made charitable contributions to the American Red Cross and other *worthy* causes⟩ ⟨a *worthy* opponent in a tennis match⟩
synonyms deserving, good, meritorious
related words admirable, commendable, creditable, laudable, praiseworthy; invaluable, priceless; cherished, prized, treasured; choice, excellent, exceptional, fancy, high-grade, primary, prime, special
near antonyms base, cheap, inferior, second-rate, substandard; bad, defective, flawed, imperfect; deficient, inadequate, insufficient, unacceptable, unsatisfactory
antonyms no-good, undeserving, valueless, worthless

wound *vb* **1** to cause bodily damage to — see INJURE 1
2 to cause hurt feelings or deep resentment in — see INSULT

wraith *n* the soul of a dead person thought of especially as appearing to living people — see GHOST

wrangle *n* an often noisy or angry expression of differing opinions — see ARGUMENT 1

wrangle *vb* to express different opinions about something often angrily — see ARGUE 2

wrangler *n* a person who takes part in a dispute — see DISPUTANT

wrap *vb* **1** to encircle or bind with or as if with a belt — see GIRD 1
2 to surround or cover closely — see ENFOLD 1

wrap up *vb* **1** to bring (an event) to a natural or appropriate stopping point — see CLOSE 3
2 to make into a short statement of the main points (as of a report) — see SUMMARIZE 1

wrath *n* **1** an intense emotional state of displeasure with someone or something — see ANGER
2 suffering, loss, or hardship imposed in response to a crime or offense — see PUNISHMENT

wrathful *adj* feeling or showing anger — see ANGRY

wrathfulness *n* an intense emotional state of displeasure with someone or something — see ANGER

wreathe *vb* to scatter or set here and there among other things — see THREAD 1

wreck *n* **1** the portion or bits of something left over or behind after it has been destroyed — see REMAINS 1
2 the destruction or loss of a ship — see SHIPWRECK
3 the violent coming together of two bodies into destructive contact — see CRASH 1

wreck *vb* **1** to cause irreparable damage to (a ship) by running aground or sinking — see SHIPWRECK
2 to bring to a complete end the physical soundness, existence, or usefulness of — see DESTROY 1

wreckage *n* **1** the state or fact of being rendered nonexistent, physically unsound, or useless — see DESTRUCTION
2 the portion or bits of something left over or behind after it has been destroyed — see REMAINS 1

3 the destruction or loss of a ship — see SHIPWRECK

wrecking *n* the destruction or loss of a ship — see SHIPWRECK

wrench *n* **1** a forceful rotating or pulling motion for the purpose of dislodging something ⟨a sharp *wrench* only served to lodge the bent nail more securely into the wood⟩
synonyms twist, twisting, wrenching, wresting, wringing
related words draft, draw, extraction, pull, tug, yank; dislocation, displacement
2 the act or an instance of applying force on something so that it moves in the direction of the force — see PULL 1

wrench *vb* **1** to move by or as if by a forceful rotation ⟨with one last sharp yank, he *wrenched* the cap off the medicine bottle⟩
synonyms twist, wrest, wring
related words draw, dredge (up), extract, jerk, lug, pluck, pull, tug, tweak, yank; jimmy, lever, pry; budge, dislocate, displace, disturb, remove; shift, transfer, transpose
2 to injure by overuse, misuse, or pressure — see STRAIN 1
3 to separate or remove by forceful pulling — see TEAR 2

wrenching *n* a forceful rotating or pulling motion for the purpose of dislodging something — see WRENCH 1

wrest *vb* **1** to draw out by force or with effort — see EXTRACT 1
2 to get (as money) by the use of force or threats — see EXTORT
3 to get with great difficulty — see EKE OUT
4 to move by or as if by a forceful rotation — see WRENCH 1
5 to separate or remove by forceful pulling — see TEAR 2

wresting *n* a forceful rotating or pulling motion for the purpose of dislodging something — see WRENCH 1

wrestle *vb* to seize and attempt to unbalance one another for the purpose of achieving physical mastery ⟨the sisters *wrestled* on the floor over the last cookie⟩
synonyms grapple, scuffle, tussle
related words battle, clash (with), combat, contend, fight, war (against); duel, bash, batter, beat, buffet, hit, punch, slug, strike; box, spar; brawl, skirmish

wretch *n* a mean, evil, or unprincipled person — see VILLAIN

wretched *adj* **1** extremely unsatisfactory ⟨this paper is simply *wretched* —you'll have to rewrite it⟩
synonyms atrocious, awful, execrable, lousy, punk, rotten, terrible
related words bad, deficient, inferior, off, poor, substandard, unsatisfactory, wanting; contemptible, miserable, shameful; defective, faulty, flawed; low-grade, mediocre, reprehensible, second-rate; bum, useless, valueless, worthless; inadequate, insufficient, lacking; abominable, odious, vile
near antonyms choice, excellent, exceptional, first-class, first-rate, premium, prime, superior; adequate, sufficient; acceptable, satisfactory
antonyms great, marvelous (*or* marvellous), wonderful
2 arousing or deserving of one's loathing and disgust — see CONTEMPTIBLE 1
3 causing or marked by an atmosphere lacking in cheer — see GLOOMY 1
4 falling short of a standard — see BAD 1
5 feeling unhappiness — see SAD 1
6 not following or in accordance with standards of honor and decency — see IGNOBLE 2
7 of low quality — see CHEAP 2
8 deserving of one's pity — see PATHETIC 1

wretchedly *adv* with feelings of bitterness or grief — see HARD 2

wriggle *vb* **1** to make jerky or restless movements — see FIDGET
2 to move slowly with the body close to the ground — see CRAWL 1

wring *vb* **1** to get (as money) by the use of force or threats — see EXTORT
2 to get with great difficulty — see EKE OUT
3 to move by or as if by a forceful rotation — see WRENCH 1

wringing *n* a forceful rotating or pulling motion for the purpose of dislodging something — see WRENCH 1

wrinkle *n* **1** a small fold in a soft and otherwise smooth surface ⟨the old woman's face creased into *wrinkles* as she smiled⟩ ⟨the curtains cascaded onto the floor in ripples and *wrinkles*⟩
synonyms crease, crimp, crinkle, furrow
related words corrugation, layer, loop, plait, pleat, ply, pucker, seam, tuck; crow's-foot
2 something (as a device) created for the first time through the use of the imagination — see INVENTION 1

wrinkle *vb* **1** to develop creases or folds ⟨if you don't fold clothes promptly after drying, they'll *wrinkle*⟩
synonyms crease, crinkle, furrow, rumple
related words collapse, crumple, double, fold
2 to create (as by crushing) an irregular mass of creases in — see CRUMPLE 1

write *vb* **1** to compose and set down on paper the words of ⟨*write* a theme in which you name your choice for the most important person in human history⟩
synonyms author, pen, pencil (in), scratch (out)
related words cast, compose, craft, draft, draw (up), formulate, frame, prepare; recast, redraft, revise, rewrite; letter, print, type, typewrite; record, take down, transcribe; autograph, register, sign; couch, express, phrase, put, word
2 to engage in an exchange of written messages — see CORRESPOND 1

writer *n* a person who creates a written work — see AUTHOR 1

write off *vb* **1** to express scornfully one's low opinion of — see DECRY 1
2 to lower the price or value of — see DEPRECIATE 1

writhe *vb* to make jerky or restless movements — see FIDGET

wrong *adj* **1** falling short of a standard — see BAD 1
2 having an opinion that does not agree with truth or the facts — see INCORRECT 1
3 not appropriate for a particular occasion or situation — see INAPPROPRIATE
4 not being in agreement with what is true — see FALSE 1
5 not conforming to a high moral standard; morally unacceptable — see BAD 2

wrong *adv* off the desired or intended path or course ⟨all of our carefully laid plans went *wrong*⟩
synonyms afield, amiss, astray, awry
related words badly; faultily, improperly, inappropriately, incorrectly, mistakenly, wrongly; inadequately, insufficiently
near antonyms perfectly; auspiciously, favorably, promisingly; correctly, properly, rightly; appropriately, fittingly, suitably
antonyms aright, right, well

wrong *n* **1** that which is morally unacceptable — see EVIL
2 unfair or inadequate treatment of someone or something or an instance of this — see DISSERVICE

wrongdoer *n* a person who commits moral wrongs — see EVILDOER 1

wrongdoing *n* **1** a breaking of a moral or legal code — see OFFENSE 1
2 improper or illegal behavior — see MISCONDUCT

wrongful *adj* contrary to or forbidden by law — see ILLEGAL 1

wrongly *adv* in a mistaken or inappropriate way ⟨you have *wrongly* interpreted this passage in the Bible⟩
synonyms amiss, erroneously, faultily, improperly, inaccurately, inappropriately, inaptly, incorrectly, mistakenly, unsuitably
related words fallibly, imperfectly; extraneously, irrelevantly, meaninglessly, pointlessly, senselessly; inadequately, insufficiently; undesirably, unsatisfactorily; foolishly, unwisely
near antonyms infallibly, perfectly; meaningfully, pertinently, relevantly, sensibly; acceptably, adequately, satisfactorily, sufficiently; prudently, sagely, wisely
antonyms appropriately, aptly, correctly, fittingly, properly, right, rightly, suitably

wrongness *n* the quality or state of being unsuitable or unfitting — see INAPPROPRIATENESS 1

wroth *adj* feeling or showing anger — see ANGRY

X (out) *vb* to show (something written) to be no longer valid by drawing a cross over or a line through it ⟨*x out* the names of the people who have already left⟩
synonyms cancel, cross (out), delete, kill, scratch (out), strike (out), stroke (out)
related words blot out, efface, erase, expunge, obliterate, rub out, wipe out; cut, excise, remove

yammer *vb* to express dissatisfaction, pain, or resentment usually tiresomely — see COMPLAIN

yank *n* the act or an instance of applying force on something so that it moves in the direction of the force — see PULL 1

yank *vb* **1** to move or cause to move with a sharp quick motion — see JERK 1
2 to draw out by force or with effort — see EXTRACT
3 to separate or remove by forceful pulling — see TEAR 2

yard *n* **1** an open space wholly or partly enclosed (as by buildings or walls) — see COURT 2
2 the area around and belonging to a building — see GROUND 1

yardstick *n* something set up as an example against which others of the same type are compared — see STANDARD 1

yarn *n* **1** a brief account of something interesting that happened especially to one personally — see STORY 2
2 a work with imaginary characters and events that is shorter and usually less complex than a novel — see STORY 1

yaw *vb* to depart abruptly from a straight line or course — see SWERVE 1

yea *adv* **1** not merely this but also — see EVEN
2 used to express agreement — see YES

yeah *adv* used to express agreement — see YES

yearn (for) *vb* to have an earnest wish to own or enjoy — see DESIRE

yearning *n* a strong wish for something — see DESIRE

yeast *n* something that arouses action or activity — see IMPULSE

yell *n* a loud vocal expression of strong emotion — see SHOUT

yell *vb* **1** to cry out loudly and emotionally — see SCREAM
2 to speak so as to be heard at a distance — see CALL 1

yellow *adj* having or showing a shameful lack of courage — see COWARDLY

yellowness *n* a shameful lack of courage in the face of danger — see COWARDICE

yelp *vb* to cry out loudly and emotionally — see SCREAM

yen *n* a strong wish for something — see DESIRE

yes *adv* used to express agreement ⟨*yes*, I'll be ready for the test tomorrow⟩
synonyms all right, alright, aye (*also* ay), OK (*or* okay), yea, yeah

related words certainly, indeed, indisputably, undoubtedly, unquestionably
antonyms nay, no, no way
yesterday *n* the events or experience of former times — see PAST
yesteryear *n* the events or experience of former times — see PAST
yet *adv* **1** at a later time <we may *yet* figure it out>
synonyms eventually, finally, someday, sometime, ultimately
phrases at last, at length, at long last
near antonyms ne'er, never, nevermore
2 in addition to what has been said — see MORE 1
3 in spite of that — see HOWEVER
4 up to this or that time — see HITHERTO
yet *conj* if it were not for the fact that — see EXCEPT
yield *n* **1** an increase usually measured in money that comes from labor, business, or property — see INCOME
2 something produced by physical or intellectual effort — see PRODUCT 1
3 the total amount collected or obtained especially at one time — see HAUL 1
yield *vb* **1** to give up and cease resistance (as to a liking, temptation, or habit) <I finally *yielded* to temptation and had a bowl of ice cream>
synonyms bow, give in, submit, succumb, surrender
related words gratify, indulge, wallow; acquiesce (to), concede (to)
near antonyms battle, breast, combat, confront, counter, defy, face, meet, object, oppose, repel; thwart, withstand
antonyms hold off, resist
2 to produce as revenue <I expect that stock to *yield* at least 14% profit this year>
synonyms give, pay, return
related words bring in, produce; afford, furnish, provide, supply
3 to cease resistance (as to another's arguments, demands, or control) <after insisting that her answer was not incorrect, Mary *yielded* when her teacher threatened her with detention>
synonyms bow, budge, capitulate, concede, give in, knuckle under, quit, submit, succumb, surrender
related words acquiesce
near antonyms contend, fight
antonyms resist
4 to be the cause of (a situation, action, or state of mind) — see EFFECT
5 to fall down or in as a result of physical pressure — see COLLAPSE 1
6 to give (something) over to the control or possession of another usually under duress — see SURRENDER 1
yielding *adj* **1** receiving or enduring without offering resistance — see PASSIVE
2 not stiff in structure — see LIMP 1
yoke *n* the state of being a slave — see SLAVERY 1
yoke *vb* to put or bring together so as to form a new and longer whole — see CONNECT 1
yokel *n* an awkward or simple person especially from a small town or the country — see HICK
yon *adv* at or to a greater distance or more advanced point — see FARTHER
yonder *adv* at or to a greater distance or more advanced point — see FARTHER
yore *n* the events or experience of former times — see PAST
young *adj* being in the early stage of life, growth, or development <a *young* cat requires more food than an older one> <a *young* tree that will eventually reach 50 feet tall>
synonyms adolescent, immature, juvenile, youngish, youthful
related words minor, underage; embryonic; callow, green, inexperienced, puerile, raw; babyish, childish, childlike, infantile; undeveloped, unfinished, unfledged, unformed, unripe, unripened; blooming, blossoming, burgeoning, flourishing, flowering
near antonyms aged, aging, elderly, old; full-blown, full-fledged; golden, mellow, ripe, ripened
antonyms adult, full-grown, mature, matured
youngish *adj* being in the early stage of life, growth, or development — see YOUNG
youngster *n* a young person who is between infancy and adulthood — see CHILD 1
youth *n* **1** a male person who has not yet reached adulthood — see BOY
2 a young person who is between infancy and adulthood — see CHILD 1
3 the state or time of being a child — see CHILDHOOD
youthful *adj* being in the early stage of life, growth, or development — see YOUNG
yowl *n* a loud vocal expression of strong emotion — see SHOUT
yowl *vb* to make a long loud mournful sound — see HOWL 1
yo–yo *n* a person who lacks good sense or judgment — see FOOL 1
yuletide *n* the season celebrating Christmas <these days, as far as the stores are concerned, *yuletide* starts in September>
synonyms Christmastime, Noel
related words Advent; Christmas, nativity, Xmas, yule
yummy *adj* very pleasing to the sense of taste — see DELICIOUS 1

zaniness *n* lack of good sense or judgment — see FOOLISHNESS 1

zany *adj* showing or marked by a lack of good sense or judgment — see FOOLISH 1

zany *n* a comically dressed performer (as at a circus) who entertains with playful tricks and ridiculous behavior — see CLOWN 1

zap *vb* to deliver a blow to (someone or something) usually in a strong vigorous manner — see HIT 1

zealot *n* one who is intensely or excessively devoted to a cause ⟨some people called John a *zealot* because he was always crusading for human rights⟩
synonyms crusader, fanatic, militant, partisan
related words activist; dreamer, visionary; cultist, disciple, follower, idolizer, votary; addict, aficionado, buff, bug, devotee, enthusiast, fan, fancier, fiend, freak, lover, maniac, nut; backer, patron, promoter, supporter; booster, rooter, well-wisher; faddist
near antonyms dabbler, dilettante

zenith *n* the highest part or point — see HEIGHT 1

zephyr *n* a slight or gentle movement of air — see BREEZE 1

zero *n* **1** the numerical symbol 0 or the absence of number or quantity represented by it ⟨anything multiplied by *zero* comes out to zero⟩
synonyms aught, cipher, goose egg, naught (*also* nought), nil, nothing, oh, zilch, zip
related words blank, void
2 a person of no importance or influence — see NOBODY

zero hour *n* a time or state of affairs requiring prompt or decisive action — see EMERGENCY

zest *n* the quality or state of being stimulating to the mind or senses — see PIQUANCY

zesty *adj* sharp and pleasantly stimulating to the mind or senses — see PIQUANT

zigzag *vb* to move suddenly aside or to and fro — see DODGE 1

zilch *n* **1** a person of no importance or influence — see NOBODY
2 the numerical symbol 0 or the absence of number or quantity represented by it — see ZERO 1

zing *n* active strength of body or mind — see VIGOR 1

zip *n* **1** active strength of body or mind — see VIGOR 1
2 the numerical symbol 0 or the absence of number or quantity represented by it — see ZERO 1

zip *vb* **1** to fly, turn, or move rapidly with a fluttering or vibratory sound — see WHIRR
2 to make an irregular series of quick, sudden movements — see FLIT
3 to proceed or move quickly — see HURRY 2

zippy *adj* having much high-spirited energy and movement — see LIVELY 1

zone *n* **1** a broad geographical area — see RE-GION 2
2 a part or portion having no fixed boundaries — see REGION 1

zoom *n* a monotonous sound like that of an insect in motion — see HUM

zoom *vb* **1** to fly, turn, or move rapidly with a fluttering or vibratory sound — see WHIRR
2 to proceed or move quickly — see HURRY 2
3 to rise abruptly and rapidly — see SKYROCKET